W9-CHG-536

You are
SPECIAL!

We are God's accomplishment, created in Christ Jesus to do good things.
—Ephesians 2:10

PRESENTED TO

BY

OCCASION

DATE

Welcome to the

CEB

DEEP BLUE

Kids Bible!

We're glad you're here to dive deep with us into God's word. We'll have adventures and learn fun facts on our journey.

The Bible is more than just a big book. It's a gift to us from God! It's also a gift to us from many people. It took hundreds of years and thousands of people to bring us this gift. And like all good gifts, this Bible is meant to be opened, explored, and enjoyed. It's our hope that you will learn more about God, the Bible, Jesus, faith, and how it all fits into life today.

But before we dive in, let us introduce ourselves.

We're the Deep Blue Crew!

Hi! My name is **Asia** and I love to talk. Well, not just talk. Communicate. Report on what I see. Vlog, you name it. Friends think I might make it on TV one day, but for now I'm just happy to document all the great discoveries we'll make in the *CEB Deep Blue Kids Bible*.

Hello. I'm pleased to meet you. My name is **Edgar** and I'm always trying to figure things out. Some people say I'm too curious but I just need to understand things. One of my favorite things to do is figure out how to get somewhere and then investigate everything I find in that new place.

My name is **Kat**. What's yours? I LOVE adventure, and I bet you do too! We're going to have so much fun with the *CEB Deep Blue Kids Bible*. There's so much to discover and explore.

Acknowledgments

We'd also like to introduce some wonderful people who helped put this Bible together.

Writers

Elizabeth Caldwell, Olivia M. Cloud, Jeannie Merz-Edwards, Eric Friesen, Heather Harriss, Cathy Hoop, Kevin Johnson, Lisa Barber Kilsdonk, Paula K. Parker, Michael Stephens, Donna Upchurch, Andy Upchurch, Suzann Wade, Jenny Youngman.

Designers

Jeff Moore, design director; Emily Keafer / Every Little Thing Studio, brand logo and character art interior design; Keata Brewer / E.T. Lowe Publishing, typesetting; Dan Lynch, art design/direction; Tim Moen, character designer; Jesse Griffin, 3D artist; Julio Medina, 3D artist; Eric M. Mikula, facial rigging; Christopher Slavik, layout artist; Cory Jones, interior logo design

Editors

Lynnette Davidson, copyeditor; Robin Pippin, editor; Kimberly Shell, senior editor; Paul Franklyn, associate publisher; Neil M. Alexander, publisher

Advisors

Sonua Bohannon, Elizabeth Caldwell, Daphna Flegal, LeeDell Stickler

Now that you know who we are,

let's dive in!

How to Use the *CEB* *Deep Blue Kids Bible*

First, let's open this gift called a Bible.

- With a hand on each side of the Bible, hold it in your lap with the open edge up facing you. Place your thumbs in the middle and divide the pages in half.

- Open your Bible. Did you find the book of Psalms? If not, turn a few pages to the front or back until you find Psalms. This book is sometimes called the song-book of the Bible, and it's located in the middle.

- Now with your Bible still divided in half, hold the back half between your hands. Follow the same process and use your thumbs to divide this section in half.

- Did you find the book of Matthew? Matthew is the fortieth book of the Bible and the first book of the New Testament. The New Testament tells us about Jesus. But more on that in a bit.

Did you know the Bible isn't just one big book? It's really a library you can hold in your hands! In fact, there are thirty-nine books in the Old Testament (or the front part) and twenty-seven books in the New Testament (the back part of the Bible).

Because the Bible is really a big collection of books, the people who put the *CEB Deep Blue Kids Bible* together have given us some really great features to help us along the way. So let's dig in and check them out!

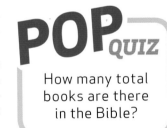

POP QUIZ

How many total books are there in the Bible?

Introduction Pages

Each book of the Bible starts with an introduction that explains the things you'll learn, the people you'll meet, the places you'll go, and the words you'll remember in each of the Bible's sixty-six books. Whenever you read something in the Bible, turn to the front of that book to find out more about it and what it tells us.

In-text Notes

Throughout the Bible there are notes that talk about what the Bible says.

- **Sailboat** notes help us grow stronger with God by pointing out positive traits we can have in our lives.

- **Umbrella** notes give us help for difficult times by explaining how unhappy emotions and traits aren't good for us.

- **Lighthouse** notes help us develop rock solid faith by discussing the basics of following God for life.

- **Life Preserver** notes give us answers to tough questions and hard-to-understand sections of the Bible.

Other Features

- **Did You Know!** call-outs point out interesting Bible trivia, customs, and practices.

- **God Thoughts / My Thoughts** devotions help us dive deeper by explaining how the Bible applies to life today.

- **Navigation Point!** memory verses mark key promises and passages to memorize.

- **Bet You Can!** reading challenges encourage us to read the Bible for ourselves.

Bible Exploration Tools

- **Discovery Central** dictionary has definitions for more than three hundred fifty words. If you don't understand a word in the Bible, look in Discovery Central for the definition.

- **I Wonder What to Do When I Feel...** verses point us to promises and actions to take when we don't know what to do.

- **In-text Notes** list helps us explore the *CEB Deep Blue Kids Bible* topic by topic.

- **Life Preserver Notes** list shows us where to find answers to difficult questions in each book of the Bible.

- **God Thoughts / My Thoughts** lists all one hundred seventy devotions in order by book of the Bible

- **Bet You Can!** reading challenge tracker helps us track our memorization progress.

Maps

Discover the part of the world events in the Bible took place with eight color maps from

NATIONAL GEOGRAPHIC

CEB

DEEP BLUE KIDS BIBLE

COMMON ENGLISH BIBLE

a translation to touch the heart and mind

Library of Congress Cataloging-in-Publication Data Available

ISBN 978-1-60926-200-6 Classic Navy DecoTone
ISBN 978-1-60926-198-6 Classic Burgundy DecoTone
ISBN 978-1-60926-211-2 Compass DecoTone
ISBN 978-1-60926-081-1 Bright Sky Paperback
ISBN 978-1-60926-135-1 Bright Sky Hardcover
ISBN 978-1-60926-031-6 Midnight Splash DecoTone

17 18 19 20 21 22 23—10 9 8 7 6 5 4 3

Printed in China

Contents

OLD TESTAMENT

continued ⟶

Contents

NEW TESTAMENT

Deep Blue Bible Exploration Tools

Alphabetical Books of the Bible

OLD TESTAMENT

continued ➞

Alphabetical Books of the Bible

NEW TESTAMENT

Bible Basics

What is the Bible?

The Bible is a very special collection of books (or scrolls) filled with stories of God's love for people. These sixty-six books tell about God, the creator of the universe who made people and wants them to follow God's ways. God loves people and sent Jesus to be the savior of the people of the whole world. The books in the Bible show us what God is like and how we can know God. The Bible comes from God, who inspired people to write down God's teaching. *Inspire* means that God's Spirit breathed through the writers who wrote the books. God also inspires us to read and understand those same teachings. Throughout history and still today the Bible changes people's lives.

Who wrote the Bible, and when was it written?

This collection of books was written by many different people. A long time ago there weren't written Bible stories. For hundreds of years, people told their children the stories from memory and those children told the same stories to their children. About 950 years before Jesus, people began writing down the stories and teachings found in the Old Testament in the Hebrew language.

The stories and teachings in the New Testament were also told for many years before they were written. Some of the letters were written about twenty-five years after Jesus died. About five years later, people started writing down in the Greek language the stories and teachings of Jesus that are called *Gospels*: the books of Matthew, Mark, Luke, and John.

Why is the Bible important to people today?

As we read our Bibles, we learn more about God's great love for all people and about how Jesus taught us to live. God inspires us to read and understand the Bible for ourselves. The Bible shows us how awesome God is and how we can know God!

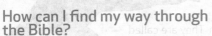

POP **QUIZ**

Is the Bible
a single book?
Why or why not?

How can I find my way through the Bible?

The Bible is like a library you can hold in your hand. Each book has its own name and place in the Bible library. Different books of the Bible library have different kinds of writings. Some give God's Instruction. Others tell stories of history. Some are songs or poems. Others contain warnings. Some tell about Jesus. Others are letters to individuals or groups of people.

The Bible has two main parts: **The Old Testament** and **The New Testament**. Each part contains a large group of books. There are thirty-nine books in the Old Testament and twenty-seven books in the New Testament.

The Old Testament covers a period of several thousand years. It tells the story of Israel, a nation in the Middle East. The Old Testament contains many stories about God's love and mighty acts. This was the Hebrew Bible Jesus learned as a child. There are five types of books in the Old Testament (see pages iii-iv to see how these books are arranged in the Bible library):

[Instruction] The first five books of the Old Testament contain the history of God's people from the creation of the world to Joseph's leadership of the Israelite people. Jewish people call these books the *Torah*. These books contain the Instruction given to Moses, which God gave the people to help them live the way God wanted them to live.

[History] These twelve books tell stories about people who often failed to follow God's Instruction so God chose leaders to help them. These books are filled with stories about good and bad leaders. They tell the history of God's people from Joshua's leadership to the return of the Israelite people from exile in Babylon.

[Songs] The book of Psalms is the largest book of the Bible. It contains poems that were used as songs in Israel's worship. The poems helped the people praise God. Some honest songs complained about things that were going wrong.

[Wisdom] The four books of wisdom contain poetry and speeches that express deep human emotions. Some are filled with wise sayings. Others are filled with words of praise to God. Some try to figure out what life really means.

[Prophets] The seventeen books named for prophets contain God's messages to God's people so they would remember God's Instruction for living.

The New Testament covers a period of about one hundred years and wasn't written until many years after Jesus lived on earth. It tells about Jesus and the people who told his story around the world.

[Gospels] The first four books of the New Testament tell the story of Jesus' life, death, and resurrection. They are called *Gospels* because they tell the good news about Jesus.

[Journeys] The fifth book Acts reports the actions and journeys of Jesus' followers and the beginning of the Christian church.

[Letters] Twenty-one books are actually letters written by early Christian leaders to help other people become faithful followers of Jesus.

[Revelation] The last book of the Bible describes how God comforts Christians, including the first Christians who suffered terribly when they began the early churches. This book is called *Revelation* because it reveals or makes known something that seems to be hidden.

How can I find a specific place in the Bible?

A Bible reference tells you where to look to find part of a book in the Bible. The first thing a Bible reference tells us is which book in the Bible to look up. On pages iii-iv are Contents pages listing all the books of the Bible in the order they appear and which page each book begins on.

The next thing a Bible reference tells us is what chapter or part of the book to look for. The beginning of each chapter in the Bible is marked with a big number.

The last thing a Bible reference tells us is what verse or small part of the chapter to look for. Each verse has been given a small number. The next verse begins when you come to a new verse number or when you reach the end of a section.

To review, each book in the Bible is divided into chapters and each chapter is divided into verses. To find a specific Bible passage you need to know what book, chapter, and verse to look for.

Let's practice!

Genesis 1:3

book   chapter   verse

To find this Bible reference, find the book of Genesis, then chapter 1 and then the small 3. Note: the number for verse 1 is not printed in most Bibles, but every chapter begins with verse 1 even though it isn't printed there.

Let's try some more.

Genesis 1:3-5

Bible references that have a hyphen between verse numbers want us to read more than one verse. In this case, find the book of Genesis, then chapter 1, and read from the beginning of verse 3 to the end of verse 5. Stop when you see the small 6.

Genesis 1:26-27, 31

Bible references that have a comma tell us something different. They're telling us to read just the verses listed. In the reference above, find the first chapter of the book of Genesis. Read verses 26 and 27. Then skip verses 28, 29, and 30, but read verse 31.

Genesis 1

Sometimes a Bible reference doesn't show any verse numbers. In this case the reference is telling us to read the entire chapter. Find Genesis and read from the beginning of the first verse until you reach the number 2 for the next chapter.

One more thing!

Sometimes you'll see small letters next to certain words or verses. These little letters tell us to look to the bottom of the Bible text on a page to learn more. At the bottom of the Bible text there is a matching letter with the extra information. This extra information is called a footnote.

Where do we get started?

The more we read our Bibles the more we learn to treasure God's word. And the more we know God's word, the smarter we get! Navigation Point! verses are a great way to start learning God's word. Page xi lists the verses we'll learn together. Start with Genesis 1:31 and memorize it. Have a friend or family member quiz you to see how you're doing. Once you have that verse down, move on to the next one. When you finish the list, you'll know more than one hundred forty-five verses of the Bible!

Navigation Point

VERSES

A Note to the Adults in Your life

Now that your child has received a personal copy of the *CEB Deep Blue Kids Bible*, we hope you'll join us on the journey and explore this treasure together. You are your child's most influential teacher and the gift of your time will build their confidence and faith in God. The *CEB Deep Blue Kids Bible* contains numerous study aids to help your child understand life in Bible times and life for today's children of God.

Below are some tips to get started,
but you'll find much more on-line at
www.deepbluekidsbible.com.

- Work with your child to read the Bet You Can! reading challenges on a regular basis (perhaps at mealtime or bedtime) and keep track of their progress.

- After your child reads a Bible story to you, challenge him or her to retell the story in his or her own words.

- Take time to have your child read in-text notes near the reading selection and talk about the information together.

- Read the introduction for the book of the Bible containing the reading selection together and discuss its overview.

With continued use of the Bible,
your child may soon be able to name:

• The book of songs

• The book of journeys

• All four Gospels

• The four books of wisdom (poetry)

• The five books of Instruction

• The twelve books of history

• The seventeen books of prophecy

• The twenty-one letters

Please visit us on-line at

www.deepbluekidsbible.com

for even more ways to make the

CEB Deep Blue Kids Bible a vital part

of your relationship with your child.

Abbreviations and Terms

Aram Aramaic
BCE Before the Common Era; traditionally BC: before Christ
CE Common Era; traditionally Anno Domini: year since the Lord's birth
cf compare
chap chapter
DSS Dead Sea Scrolls found at Qumran
  (1QIsa^a) Isaiah scroll *a* in Cave 1 of the Dead Sea Scrolls
  (1QDeut^b) Deuteronomy scroll *b* in Cave 1 of the Dead Sea Scrolls
  (4QDeut^b) Deuteronomy scroll *b* in Cave 4 of the Dead Sea Scrolls
  (4QDeut^h) Deuteronomy scroll *h* in Cave 4 of the Dead Sea Scrolls
  (4QDeut^j) Deuteronomy scroll *j* in Cave 4 of the Dead Sea Scrolls
  (4QDeut^q) Deuteronomy scroll *q* in Cave 4 of the Dead Sea Scrolls
  (4QPhyl^n) Phylactery scroll *n* in Cave 4 of the Dead Sea Scrolls
  (4QSam^a) Samuel scroll *a* in Cave 4 of the Dead Sea Scrolls
  (4QSam^b) Samuel scroll *b* in Cave 4 of the Dead Sea Scrolls
  (4QSam^c) Samuel scroll *c* in Cave 4 of the Dead Sea Scrolls
  (8QMez) Mezuza scroll in Cave 8 of the Dead Sea Scrolls
  (11QPs^a) Psalms scroll *a* in Cave 11 of the Dead Sea Scrolls
Eth Ethiopic translation of 2 Esdras in the Ge'ez language
Gk Greek
  Gk uncertain The meaning of the Greek text is uncertain.
Heb Hebrew
  Heb uncertain The meaning of the Hebrew text is uncertain.
Josephus *Ant* Works of Flavius Josephus: Antiquities of the Jews
Kethib Aramaic term meaning what is written (the written consonantal text)
Lat Latin
LXX Septuagint; Greek translation of Hebrew Bible by seventy translators
  LXX^A In Samuel, the Greek uncial Alexandrinus
  LXX^B In Samuel, the Greek uncial Vaticanus
  LXX^L In Samuel, Lucianic Greek manuscripts
  LXX^M In Samuel, the Greek uncial Coislinianus
  LXX^N In Samuel, the Greek uncials Basilianus and Vaticanus
  LXX^1 In Tobit, the Greek uncial Sinaiticus
  LXX^2 In Tobit, the Greek uncials Alexandrinus and Vaticanus
  LXX^a in Sirach the Greek uncials Sinaiticus, Alexandrinus, and Vaticanus
  LXX^b In Sirach the Origenic and Lucianic Greek manuscripts
MT Masoretic Text; the Hebrew Bible
NT New Testament
OL Old Latin; manuscripts in Latin prior to the Vulgate
OT Old Testament
pl plural
Qere Aramaic term meaning what is read aloud (the vocalized text)
Selah Musical direction of uncertain meaning found in Psalms
Sym Greek version of the Old Testament translated by Symmachus
Syr Syriac, a translation known as the Peshitta in a dialect of the Aramaic language
Tg Targum; Aramaic translation of Hebrew Bible
Vulg Vulgate; standardized Latin version of the Bible

Measures

Capacity and linear measures

ammah *length of a forearm, standardized at eighteen inches; traditionally a cubit*
bath *a liquid measure approximately equivalent to twenty quarts*
ephah *a dry measure for flour or grains, approximately twenty quarts (five gallons)*
etsbah *length of the finger or thumb; traditionally a fingerbreadth*
hin *a liquid measure for wine or water, approximately one gallon*
homer *the largest dry measure, fifty gallons, equivalent to ten ephah*
issaron *one tenth of an unknown weight; possibly an equivalent for omer*
kab *an unknown measure in 2 Kgs 6:25*
kor *a dry measure for grain, possibly equal to a homer; approximately fifty gallons as a liquid measure in Ezekiel*
litra *a Roman pound equal to approximately twelve ounces dry*
log *a liquid measure for oil in Leviticus, approximately two-thirds of a pint*
metretes *a liquid measure of approximately ten gallons*
milion *a mile; a Roman mile was 1,000 paces or approximately 4,855 feet*
omer *one tenth of an ephah or two quarts dry*
pechon *approximately eighteen inches; traditionally a cubit*
pim *two-thirds of a shekel*
qaneh *a measuring rod in Ezekiel equivalent to six ammah or nine feet*
seah *a dry measure of grain, possibly seven and a half quarts but may be smaller amount in Genesis*
shearim *an unknown dry measure of grain*
stadion *a Roman linear measurement of approximately 607 feet*
tefakh or tofakh *width of the hand at the base of the fingers; traditionally a handbreadth or a palm*
tsimdo *traditionally an acre, the area that a team can plow in a day*
zereth *distance between tip of thumb to little finger; traditionally a span*

Monetary measures

beqa *one-half shekel, typically one-fifth of an ounce; ten or twelve gerahs*
daric *a gold Persian coin named after Darius 1, weighing one-third of an ounce*
denarion, denaria (pl) *a coin equivalent in value to one day's work*
drachme, drachmen (pl) *a silver coin equivalent in value to a denarion; also possibly a daric*
gerah *one-twentieth or one twenty-fourth of a shekel*
kikkar *a unit of weight in the common shekel system; traditionally a talent*
kodrantes *a coin equivalent to two lepta*
lepto *a coin equivalent to one-one hundred twenty-eighth of a denarion*
maneh *in the Old Testament possibly fifty or sixty sanctuary shekels; in the New Testament a monetary unit equivalent to one hundred denaria*
shekel *basic measure, typically two-fifths of an ounce, for three monetary weight systems attested in the Old Testament: the royal shekel, the sanctuary shekel, and the common shekel*
talanta *a coin equivalent to six thousand denaria; traditionally a talent. In the Greek period, one talent is approximately 57 pounds of weight.*
qesitah *an unknown monetary weight*

The King James Version of the Bible was published in 1611. For two centuries the KJV competed for readership with the Geneva Bible. However, by the nineteenth century in America, the KJV would be described as the "common English Bible," because it was the most widely used translation of Christian scripture. Numerous translations have appeared since that time. However, it has proved difficult to combine concern for accuracy and accessibility in one translation that the typical reader or worshipper would be able to understand. Therefore, readers in the twenty-first century, four hundred years after the creation of the KJV, need and deserve a new translation that is suitable for personal devotion, for communal worship, and for classroom study.

The Common English Bible (CEB), completed in 2011, is a fresh translation of the Bible. Some editions include the Apocrypha that are used in Anglican, Orthodox, and Catholic congregations. The translation is sponsored by the Common English Bible Committee, which is an alliance of denominational publishers, including Presbyterian (USA), Episcopalian, United Methodist, Disciples of Christ, and United Church of Christ representatives.

One hundred twenty biblical scholars from twenty-two faith traditions worked as translators for the CEB. In addition, members of seventy-seven reading groups from congregations throughout North America reviewed and responded to early drafts of the translation. As a result, more than five hundred individuals were integrally involved in the preparation of the CEB. These individuals represent the sorts of diversity that permit this new translation to speak to people of various religious convictions and different social locations.

The translators, reviewers, and editors represent the following faith communities: African Methodist Episcopal Church, American Baptist, Anglican, Baptist, Baptist General Conference, Church of the Nazarene, Disciples of Christ, Episcopal Church, Evangelical Free Church, Evangelical Lutheran Church, Free Methodist, Mennonite, Moravian, National Baptist, Presbyterian (USA), Progressive National Baptist, Quaker, Reformed Church in America, Reform Judaism, Roman Catholic Church, Seventh-day Adventist, United Churches of Christ, and United Methodist. The CEB is truly a Bible created by churches and for the Church.

Accuracy and clarity. The CEB translators balance rigorous accuracy in the rendition of ancient texts with an equally passionate commitment to clarity of expression in the target language. Translators create sentences and choose vocabulary that will be readily understood when the biblical text is read aloud. Two examples illustrate this concern for accuracy and clarity.

First, *ben 'adam* (Hebrew) or *huios tou anthrōpou* (Greek) are best translated as "human being" (rather than "son of man") except in cases of direct address, where CEB renders "human one" (instead of "son of man" or "mortal"; e.g., Ezek 2:1). When *ho huios tou anthrōpou* is used as a title for Jesus, the CEB refers to Jesus as "the Human One." People who have grown accustomed to hearing Jesus refer to himself in the Gospels as "the Son of Man" may find this jarring. Why "Human One"? Jesus' primary language would have been Aramaic, so he would have used the Aramaic phrase *bar enosha*. This phrase has the sense of "a human" or "a human such as I." This phrase was taken over into Greek in a phrase that might be translated woodenly as "son of humanity." However, Greek usage often refers to "a son of x" in the sense of "one who has the character of x." For example, Luke 10:6 refers in Greek to "a son of peace," a phrase that has the sense of "one who shares in peace." In Acts 13:10 Paul calls a sorcerer "a son of the devil." This is not a reference to the sorcerer's actual ancestry, but it serves to identify his character. He is devilish—or more simply in English "a devil." *Human* or *human one* represents accurately the Aramaic and Greek idioms and reflects common English usage. Finally, many references to Jesus as "the Human One" refer back to Daniel 7:13, where Daniel "saw one like a human being" (Greek *huios anthropou*). By using the title Human One in the Gospels and Acts, the CEB preserves this connection to Daniel's vision.

Second, the phrase "Lord of hosts" (*Yahweh sebaoth* in Hebrew; *Kyrios sabaoth* in Greek) appears hundreds of times in older Bibles and persists as an idiom in translations that preserve King James usage. This archaic translation is no longer meaningful to most English speakers. The CEB renders *Yahweh sebaoth* and *Kyrios sabaoth* as "Lord of heavenly forces," which conveys accurately the meaning of the Hebrew and Greek phrases by using contemporary English language.

English speakers, especially when telling a story, writing a letter, or engaging in conversation, make frequent use of contractions. As a result, translators have often used contractions, particularly in direct speech, in the CEB. However, formal genres of literature typically do not include contractions. As a result, translators did not include contractions in contexts such as (a) formal trials or royal interviews (socially formal situations), (b) much divine discourse (e.g., Hos 11:9; Exod 24:12), and (c) poetic and/or liturgical discourse (several types of psalms).

Texts. Translators of the Old Testament used as their base text the Masoretic Text (MT) as found in Biblia Hebraica Stuttgartensia and the published fascicles of Biblia Hebraica Quinta. For some books the Hebrew University Bible Project was consulted. Judicious departures from the Masoretic Text, based on ancient manuscript (e.g., reading with the Dead Sea Scrolls in 1 Sam 10:27b or Deut 32:8) and versional evidence (e.g., reading with the Septuagint in Gen 4:8), were sometimes necessary. In those situations, in which one may postulate two literary editions of a biblical book, or in which there are major or lengthy differences between the Masoretic Text and other texts or versions (e.g., 1 Sam 17), the CEB translated the edition that became canon in the Masoretic Text.

Translators of the New Testament used as their base text the eclectic Greek text known as Nestle Aland, the twenty-seventh edition, which was published in 1993.

Translators of the Apocrypha faced a more complicated set of choices. Translators generally used the base text presented in the Göttingen Septuagint. For those books not yet published in the fascicles of the Göttingen Septuagint, translators used the 2006 revised edition of Rahlfs' Septuaginta, edited by Robert Hanhart. However, in those instances in which Hebrew texts have survived and offer a better reading (e.g., in Sirach and Tobit), the translator noted alternative readings to the Greek Septuagint. Second Esdras presents a special problem, explained in a footnote about the Latin text.

Footnotes. Translators decided, in certain instances, that they should explain their translations or textual decisions. However, notes are kept to a minimum and are rendered with utmost concision. Such notes when present offer: (a) evidence from ancient texts and versions (e.g., LXX; MT *men of*); (b) brief philological comment (e.g., Heb uncertain); (c) explanations of anomalies in versification (e.g., Acts 8:37: Critical editions of the Gk New Testament do not include 8:37 *Philip said to him, "If you believe with your whole heart, you can be." The eunuch answered, "I believe that Jesus Christ is God's Son."*); (d) citations of the Old Testament in the New Testament; and rarely (e) alternative translations (e.g., Or *everyone*). In those instances in which the Old Testament is cited in the New Testament the quoted text is set in italic font.

Measurements. When possible, the CEB converts linear and spatial dimensions to feet and inches. Thus archaic terms such as rods, cubits, spans, handbreadths, and fingerbreadths are replaced with feet and inches. For example, Genesis 6:15 gives the dimensions of Noah's ark in *'ammah* or "forearms." Most translations since the KJV use the archaic English cubit to translate *'ammah*: "the length of the ark three hundred cubits, its width fifty cubits, and its height thirty cubits." The CEB translatesthe dimensions of the ark as "four hundred fifty feet, its width seventy-five feet, and its height forty-five feet."

The CEB prefers to transliterate (rather than translate) measurements of capacity, both wet (e.g., bath) and dry (e.g., homer), as well as measurements of weight (e.g., kikkar). When feasible, a footnote is allowed to calculate the rough equivalent in a U.S. English measurement, such as quarts.

Monetary values are inherently relative, and prices are constantly changing. Therefore, the CEB prefers to transliterate (rather than translate) monetary weights (e.g., shekel) and coins (e.g., denarion).

Months in the biblical lunar calendar are transliterated, with a footnote to indicate the approximate month or months in the Gregorian solar calendar (e.g., Nisan is March-April).

Pronouns. In ancient Hebrew and Greek a pronoun is often bound with the verb. If the translator is too literal, the English reader loses the antecedent of the pronoun so that one cannot tell who is speaking or acting in the sentence or paragraph. This problem occurs throughout much biblical literature. The CEB addresses this issue by substituting a noun for a pronoun, but only when the antecedent is clear. Because this problem and its resolution are so common, the CEB usually does not offer footnotes to identify these substitutions. CEB translators also use gender-inclusive or neutral syntax for translating pronouns that refer to humans, unless context requires otherwise.

Consistency. Although translators often try to use the same English word for a Hebrew or Greek word, many words in any language offer a breadth of meanings that do not readily correlate with a single word in the target language. For example, the Hebrew word *torah*, which has often been translated as Law, is often better translated as Instruction. The same could be said for *Sheol* (Hebrew) or *Hades* (Greek). The CEB translates these two terms as "grave" or "death" and "underworld" or "hell" respectively, depending on context. A mechanical selection of any one term for words that involve semantic breadth would preclude a translation sensitive to the originating literary context.

The women and men who participated in the creation of the CEB hope that those who read and study it will find the translation to be an accurate, clear, and inspiring version of Christian scripture.

The Editorial Board of the Common English Bible
www.CommonEnglishBible.com

OLD
TESTAMENT

Genesis

Genesis tells us that our world began with God's wind sweeping over the waters. God spoke and then our world existed—the sun and the stars, the plants, the animals, and the people. God told the first man and woman to care for everything God made, including the beautiful garden in Eden. God created Adam and Eve to be partners, to have good relationships with God and each other.

This book tells a story of God's amazing creation but also explains the disaster of human sin. Adam and Eve didn't follow God's command. God sent a giant flood, but saved Noah in an ark that floated on the rising waters. Then God made promises to Abraham and his children as the first of God's new people. God sent this faith-filled follower on a daring journey from the distant city of Ur to Canaan, the land that is now Israel.

Genesis also tells the story of Joseph, a boastful young man who was sold as a slave by his brothers. God made Joseph a leader in Egypt, which made it possible for him to save Egypt and then his family from famine. In the end, Joseph and his brothers became friends again.

Genesis says that God created the world—and the stories show why. God wants to be connected with all people—including you! 💧

things YOU'LL DISCOVER

The book of Genesis tells us about the amazing beginning of the world. God created the earth, sky, and everything in the world. God made human beings to enjoy and take care of the world. This book also explains the beginning of God's people, the Israelites.

people YOU'LL MEET

Adam and Eve—the Bible's first man and woman (Gen 1–4)
Abraham—the father of the nation of Israel, first called Abram (Gen 11–25)
Sarah—Abraham's wife, first called Sarai (Gen 11–23)
Isaac and Rebekah, Jacob and Rachel—Abraham's son and grandson and their wives (Gen 17–49)
Joseph—a young man who became a ruler in Egypt (Gen 37–50)

places YOU'LL GO

Eden, Ur (present-day Iraq), **Canaan** (present-day Israel), **Egypt**

words YOU'LL REMEMBER

"When God began to create the heavens and the earth—the earth was without shape or form, it was dark over the deep sea, and God's wind swept over the waters—God said, 'Let there be light'. And so light appeared" (Gen 1:1-3).

World's creation in seven days

1 When God began to create[a] the heavens and the earth— [2]the earth was without shape or form, it was dark over the deep sea, and God's wind swept over the waters— [3]God said, "Let there be light." And so light appeared. [4]God saw how good the light was. God separated the light from the darkness. [5]God named the light Day and the darkness Night.

There was evening and there was morning: the first day.

[6]God said, "Let there be a dome in the middle of the waters to separate the waters from each other." [7]God made the dome and separated the waters under the dome from the waters above the dome. And it happened in that way. [8]God named the dome Sky.

There was evening and there was morning: the second day.

[9]God said, "Let the waters under the sky come together into one place so that the dry land can appear." And that's what happened. [10]God named the dry land Earth, and he named the gathered waters Seas. God saw how good it was. [11]God said, "Let the earth grow plant life: plants yielding seeds and fruit trees bearing fruit with seeds inside it, each according to its kind throughout the earth." And that's what happened. [12]The earth produced plant life: plants yielding seeds, each according to its kind, and trees bearing fruit with seeds inside it, each according to its kind. God saw how good it was.

[13]There was evening and there was morning: the third day.

[14]God said, "Let there be lights in the dome of the sky to separate the day from the night. They will mark events, sacred seasons, days, and years. [15]They will be lights in the dome of the sky to shine on the earth." And that's what happened. [16]God made the stars and two great lights: the larger light to rule over the day and the smaller light to rule over the night. [17]God put them in the dome of the sky to shine on the earth, [18]to rule over the day and over the night, and to separate the light from the darkness. God saw how good it was.

[19]There was evening and there was morning: the fourth day.

[20]God said, "Let the waters swarm with living things, and let birds fly above the earth up in the dome of the sky." [21]God created the great sea animals and all the tiny living things that swarm in the waters, each according to its kind, and all the winged birds, each according to its kind. God saw how good it was. [22]Then God blessed them: "Be fertile and multiply and fill the waters in the seas, and let the birds multiply on the earth."

[23]There was evening and there was morning: the fifth day.

[24]God said, "Let the earth produce every kind of living thing: livestock, crawling things, and wildlife." And that's what happened. [25]God made every kind of wildlife, every kind of livestock, and every kind of creature that crawls on the ground. God saw how good it was. [26]Then God said, "Let us make humanity in our image to resemble us so that they may take charge of the fish of the sea, the birds in the sky, the livestock, all the earth, and all the crawling things on earth."

[a]Or *In the beginning, God created*

27 God created humanity in God's own image,
in the divine image God created them,[b]
male and female God created them.

28 God blessed them and said to them, "Be fertile and multiply; fill the earth and master it. Take charge of the fish of the sea, the birds in the sky, and everything crawling on the ground." 29 Then God said, "I now give to you all the plants on the earth that yield seeds and all the trees whose fruit produces its seeds within it. These will be your food. 30 To all wildlife, to all the birds in the sky, and to everything crawling on the ground—to everything that breathes—I give all the green grasses for food." And that's what happened. 31 God saw everything he had made: it was supremely good.

Memorize
Gen 1:31

There was evening and there was morning: the sixth day.

2 The heavens and the earth and all who live in them were completed. 2 On the sixth[c] day God completed all the work that he had done, and on the seventh day God rested from all the work that he had done. 3 God blessed the seventh day and made it holy, because on it God rested from all the work of creation.[d] 4 This is the account of the heavens and the earth when they were created.

World's creation in the garden

On the day the Lord God made earth and sky—5 before any wild plants appeared on the earth, and before any field crops grew, because the Lord God hadn't yet sent rain on the earth and there was still no human being[e] to farm the fertile land, 6 though a stream rose from the earth and watered all of the fertile land— 7 the Lord God formed the human[f] from the topsoil of the fertile land[g] and blew life's breath into his nostrils. The human came to life. 8 The Lord God planted a garden in Eden in the east and put there the human he had formed. 9 In the fertile land, the Lord God grew every beautiful tree with edible fruit, and also he grew the tree of life in the middle of the garden and the tree of the knowledge of good and evil.

did you know? The word used for *image* in Gen 1:27 comes from the same root word used for *imagination*. So our ability to imagine and be creative is part of how we're made in the image of our creator.

10 A river flows from Eden to water the garden, and from there it divides into four headwaters. 11 The name of the first river is the Pishon. It flows around the entire land of Havilah, where there is gold. 12 That land's gold is pure, and the land also has sweet-smelling resins and gemstones.[h] 13 The name of the second river is the Gihon. It flows around the entire land of Cush. 14 The name of the third river is the Tigris, flowing east of

LIFE PRESERVER

Why are the trees in the garden of Eden important?
Genesis 2:9

In the second story of creation, we read about two trees that were planted in the garden of Eden. One tree, sometimes called the tree of life, had fruit that would make whoever ate it live forever. The fruit on the other tree, sometimes called the tree of the knowledge of good and evil, gave the person who ate it self-awareness and knowledge about life.

Although humans had work to do in the garden, they also had freedom to do as they pleased as long as they didn't eat fruit from the tree of the knowledge of good and evil. You may know what happened next. Eve and Adam did what they weren't supposed to do. They ate the fruit from the forbidden tree. Rather than being protected from the knowledge of everything good and everything evil, they gained knowledge meant only for God. They didn't have the wisdom to handle this knowledge.

This story reminds us that like Eve and Adam, we're all human. We'd all like to have the knowledge God has. But we don't have the wisdom to handle it. Like Eve and Adam, we do the wrong things and make bad choices. Even so, God forgives us, continues to love us, and stays with us as we try to live as God's faithful people. ◆

bHeb has singular *him*, referring to *humanity*. cLXX, Sam, Syr; MT *seventh* dOr *from all his work, which God created to do* eOr *man* (Heb *adam*) fHeb *adam* gHeb *adamah* hHeb uncertain

Assyria; and the name of the fourth river is the Euphrates.

¹⁵The Lord God took the human and settled him in the garden of Eden to farm it and to take care of it. ¹⁶The Lord God commanded the human, "Eat your fill from all of the garden's trees; ¹⁷but don't eat from the tree of the knowledge of good and evil, because on the day you eat from it, you will die!" ¹⁸Then the Lord God said, "It's not good that the human is alone. I will make a helper that is perfect for him." ¹⁹So the Lord God formed from the fertile land all the wild animals and all the birds in the sky and brought them to the human to see what he would name them. The human gave each living being its name. ²⁰The human named all the livestock, all the birds in the sky, and all the wild animals. But a helper perfect for him was nowhere to be found.

²¹So the Lord God put the human into a deep and heavy sleep, and took one of his ribs and closed up the flesh over it. ²²With the rib taken from the human, the Lord God fashioned a woman and brought her to the human being. ²³The human[i] said,

"This one finally is bone from my bones
    and flesh from my flesh.
She will be called a woman[j]
    because from a man[k] she was taken."

²⁴This is the reason that a man leaves his father and mother and embraces his wife, and they become one flesh. ²⁵The two of them were naked, the man and his wife, but they weren't embarrassed.

Knowledge, not eternal life

3 The snake was the most intelligent[l] of all the wild animals that the Lord God had made. He said to the woman, "Did God really say that you shouldn't eat from any tree in the garden?"

²The woman said to the snake, "We may eat the fruit of the garden's trees ³but not the fruit of the tree in the middle of the garden. God said, 'Don't eat from it, and don't touch it, or you will die.'"

⁴The snake said to the woman, "You won't die! ⁵God knows that on the day you eat from it, you will see clearly and you will be like God,

knowing good and evil." ⁶The woman saw that the tree was beautiful with delicious food and that the tree would provide wisdom, so she took some of its fruit and ate it, and also gave some to her husband, who was with her, and he ate it. ⁷Then they both saw clearly and knew that they were naked. So they sewed fig leaves together and made garments for themselves.

⁸During that day's cool evening breeze, they heard the sound of the Lord God walking in the garden; and the man and his wife hid themselves from the Lord God in the middle of the garden's trees. ⁹The Lord God called to the man and said to him, "Where are you?"

¹⁰The man[m] replied, "I heard your sound in the garden; I was afraid because I was naked, and I hid myself."

¹¹He said, "Who told you that you were naked? Did you eat from the tree, which I commanded you not to eat?"

LIFE PRESERVER

What does the snake represent?
Genesis 3:1, 4-5, 14-15

The snake in the garden asked Eve the question that she and Adam had probably been thinking about. "Did God really say that you shouldn't eat from any tree in the garden?" So Eve was tempted by the snake's offer. Who wouldn't want to see clearly and be like God? When Eve and Adam ate the fruit, they realized they were naked and needed to find some clothes. And since they were ashamed of what they did, they hid from God when God came looking for them.

The snake wasn't some strange creature that came into the garden. The snake was there all along. Think about a time in your life when you were trying to figure out what to do. Perhaps like Eve there was something whispering in your ear, telling you what to do, and part of you knew it was wrong. That's like the snake speaking to Eve. The snake represents the temptation everyone faces to make poor choices.

Like Eve and Adam, we have choices to make in life. God knows us, loves us, and supports us as we try to make right choices. ◆

---

[i]Or man (Heb adam) [j]Or wife (Heb ishshah) [k]Or husband (Heb ish) [l]Heb sounds like naked. [m]Or He

¹²The man said, "The woman you gave me, she gave me some fruitⁿ from the tree, and I ate."

¹³The Lᴏʀᴅ God said to the woman, "What have you done?!"

And the woman said, "The snake tricked me, and I ate."

¹⁴The Lᴏʀᴅ God said to the snake,

"Because you did this,
   you are the one cursed
      out of all the farm animals,
      out of all the wild animals.
   On your belly you will crawl,
      and dust you will eat
      every day of your life.
¹⁵ I will put contempt
      between you and the woman,
      between your offspring and hers.
   They will strike your head,
      but you will strike at their heels."

ⁿHeb lacks *some fruit.*

¹⁶To the woman he said,

"I will make your pregnancy very painful;
      in pain you will bear children.
   You will desire your husband,
      but he will rule over you."

¹⁷To the man he said, "Because you listened to your wife's voice and you ate from the tree that I commanded, 'Don't eat from it,'
   cursed is the fertile land because of you;
      in pain you will eat from it
      every day of your life.
¹⁸ Weeds and thistles will grow for you,
      even as you eat the field's plants;
¹⁹ by the sweat of your face
      you will eat bread—
   until you return to the fertile land,
      since from it you were taken;
   you are soil,
      to the soil you will return."

God's Special Gift   *Genesis 3:1-24*

Have you ever disobeyed? Adam and Eve did.

When God put Adam and Eve in the garden, God gave them everything they needed—food to eat, water to drink, sunlight to keep them warm, and soft grass to sleep on at night. God gave them love and visited with them every day.

God also gave Adam and Eve a special gift, something they couldn't see or feel. It was the gift of free will, which is the right to choose to obey or disobey God. God wanted Adam and Eve to show love by obeying, but their free will meant they had a choice. They chose to disobey and did not do what God had asked.

Even though their disobedience broke God's heart, God didn't stop loving Adam and Eve. God disciplined them, causing them to leave the garden and have to raise their own food, but God also cared for them, giving them clothes to wear and sending the rain and sunlight to make their crops grow.

God gave us the same gift of free will that Adam and Eve had. When we choose to obey, we show that we love God.

How can you obey God?

Name two things God has given you.

20The man named his wife Eve[o] because she is the mother of everyone who lives. 21The LORD God made the man and his wife leather clothes and dressed them. 22The LORD God said, "The human being[p] has now become like one of us, knowing good and evil." Now, so he doesn't stretch out his hand and take also from the tree of life and eat and live forever, 23the LORD God sent him out of the garden of Eden to farm the fertile land from which he was taken. 24He drove out the human. To the east of the garden of Eden, he stationed winged creatures wielding flaming swords to guard the way to the tree of life.

Cain and Abel

4 The man Adam knew his wife Eve intimately. She became pregnant and gave birth to Cain, and said, "I have given life to[q] a man with the LORD's help." 2She gave birth a second time to Cain's brother Abel. Abel cared for the flocks, and Cain farmed the fertile land.

3Some time later, Cain presented an offering to the LORD from the land's crops 4while Abel presented his flock's oldest offspring with their fat. The LORD looked favorably on Abel and his sacrifice 5but didn't look favorably on Cain and his sacrifice. Cain became very angry and looked resentful. 6The LORD said to Cain, "Why are you angry, and why do you look so resentful? 7If you do the right thing, won't you be accepted? But if you don't

did you know? Some people thought God put a sign on Cain as a punishment for murdering his brother Abel. But the Bible says God put the sign on Cain to show the world that Cain was under God's protection. Anyone who tried to harm Cain for revenge would be in trouble with God.

do the right thing, sin will be waiting at the door ready to strike! It will entice you, but you must rule over it."

8Cain said to his brother Abel, "Let's go out to the field."[T] When they were in the field, Cain attacked his brother Abel and killed him.

9The LORD said to Cain, "Where is your brother Abel?"

UMBRELLA

JEALOUSY

A Jealous Rage *Genesis 4:5-6, 8*

It is an awful truth that envy, jealousy, and shame often lead to violence and acts of anger. We can feel very upset when someone else gets the thing we want the most. When this happens, we may feel desperately angry. Cain was so filled with rage toward his younger brother Abel that he killed him. There are terrible and long-lasting consequences when we seek to solve our problems with violence. God wants us to find better ways to resolve our conflicts with each other.

Cain said, "I don't know. Am I my brother's guardian?"

10The LORD said, "What did you do? The voice of your brother's blood is crying to me from the ground. 11You are now cursed from the ground that opened its mouth to take your brother's blood from your hand. 12When you farm the fertile land, it will no longer grow anything for you, and you will become a roving nomad on the earth."

13Cain said to the LORD, "My punishment is more than I can bear. 14Now that you've driven me away from the fertile land and I am hidden from your presence, I'm about to become a roving nomad on the earth, and anyone who finds me will kill me."

15The LORD said to him, "It won't happen;[s] anyone who kills Cain will be paid back seven times. The LORD put a sign on Cain so that no one who found him would assault him. 16Cain left the LORD's presence, and he settled down in the land of Nod, east of Eden.

Cain's descendants

17Cain knew his wife intimately. She became pregnant and gave birth to Enoch. Cain built a city and named the city after his son Enoch.

18Irad was born to Enoch. Irad fathered Mehujael, Mehujael fathered Methushael, and Methushael fathered Lamech. 19Lamech

[o]Heb sounds like *live.* [p]Or *man* (Heb *adam*) [q]Or *created;* Heb sounds similar to *Cain.* [T]LXX, Syr, Vulg, Sam; MT lacks *Let's go out to the field.* [s]LXX, Syr, Vulg; MT *therefore*

took two wives, the first named Adah and the second Zillah. ²⁰Adah gave birth to Jabal; he was the ancestor of those who live in tents and own livestock. ²¹His brother's name was Jubal; he was the ancestor of those who play stringed and wind instruments. ²²Zillah also gave birth to Tubal-cain, the ancestor of^t blacksmiths and all artisans of bronze and iron. Tubal-cain's sister was Naamah.

²³Lamech said to his wives,

"Adah and Zillah, listen to my voice;
> wives of Lamech,
>   pay attention to my words:
> I killed a man for wounding me,
>   a boy for striking me;
> ²⁴ so Cain will be paid back seven times
>   and Lamech seventy-seven times."

²⁵Adam knew his wife intimately again, and she gave birth to a son. She named him Seth^u "because God has given me another child in place of Abel, whom Cain killed." ²⁶Seth also fathered a son and named him Enosh. At that time, people began to worship in the Lord's name.

did you know? Methuselah was the oldest person ever to live. He didn't become a father until he was 187 years old, and he lived until he was 969 years old. Even if people in ancient times had fewer than 365 days in their year, as some people think, that's still really old.

Adam's descendants

5 This is the record of Adam's descendants. On the day God created humanity, he made them to resemble God ²and created them male and female. He blessed them and called them humanity^v on the day they were created. ³When Adam was 130 years old, he became the father of a son in his image, resembling him, and named him Seth. ⁴After Seth's birth, Adam lived 800 years; he had other sons and daughters. ⁵In all, Adam lived 930 years, and he died.

⁶When Seth was 105 years old, he became the father of Enosh. ⁷After the birth of Enosh, Seth lived 807 years; and he had other sons and daughters. ⁸In all, Seth lived 912 years, and he died.

⁹When Enosh was 90 years old, he became the father of Kenan. ¹⁰After Kenan's birth, Enosh lived 815 years; and he had other sons and daughters. ¹¹In all, Enosh lived 905 years, and he died.

¹²When Kenan was 70 years old, he became the father of Mahalalel. ¹³After the birth of Mahalalel, Kenan lived 840 years; and he had other sons and daughters. ¹⁴In all, Kenan lived 910 years, and he died.

¹⁵When Mahalalel was 65 years old, he became the father of Jared. ¹⁶After Jared's birth, Mahalalel lived 830 years; and he had other sons and daughters. ¹⁷In all, Mahalalel lived 895 years, and he died.

¹⁸When Jared was 162 years old, he became the father of Enoch. ¹⁹After Enoch's birth, Jared lived 800 years; and he had other sons and daughters. ²⁰In all, Jared lived 962 years, and he died.

²¹When Enoch was 65 years old, he became the father of Methuselah. ²²Enoch walked with God. After Methuselah's birth, Enoch lived 300 years; and he had other sons and daughters. ²³In all, Enoch lived 365 years. ²⁴Enoch walked with God and disappeared because God took him.

²⁵When Methuselah was 187 years old, he became the father of Lamech. ²⁶After Lamech's birth, Methuselah lived 782 years; and he had other sons and daughters. ²⁷In all, Methuselah lived 969 years, and he died.

²⁸When Lamech was 182 years old, he became the father of a son ²⁹and named him Noah, saying, "This one will give us relief^w from our hard work, from the pain in our hands, because of the fertile land that the Lord cursed." ³⁰After Noah's birth, Lamech lived 595 years; and he had other sons and daughters. ³¹In all, Lamech lived 777 years, and he died.

³²When Noah was 500 years old, Noah became the father of Shem, Ham, and Japheth.

Ancient heroes

6 When the number of people started to increase throughout the fertile land, daughters were born to them. ²The divine beings

---

^tHeb lacks *the ancestor of*. ^uSounds like the Heb verb *gave* ^vHeb *adam* ^wHeb resembles the sound of Noah's name.

saw how beautiful these human women were, so they married the ones they chose. ³The LORD said, "My breath˟ will not remain in humans forever, because they are flesh. They will live one hundred twenty years." ⁴In those days, giants^y lived on the earth and also afterward, when divine beings and human daughters had sexual relations and gave birth to children. These were the ancient heroes, famous men.

Great flood

⁵The LORD saw that humanity had become thoroughly evil on the earth and that every idea their minds thought up was always completely evil. ⁶The LORD regretted making human beings on the earth, and he was heartbroken. ⁷So the LORD said, "I will wipe off of the land the human race that I've created: from human beings to livestock to the crawling things to the birds in the skies, because I regret I ever made them." ⁸But as for Noah, the LORD approved of him.

⁹These are Noah's descendants. In his generation, Noah was a moral and exemplary man; he^z walked with God. ¹⁰Noah had three sons: Shem, Ham, and Japheth. ¹¹In God's sight, the earth had become corrupt and was filled with violence. ¹²God saw that the earth was corrupt, because all creatures behaved corruptly on the earth.

¹³God said to Noah, "The end has come for all creatures, since they have filled the earth with violence. I am now about to destroy them along with the earth, ¹⁴so make a wooden ark.^a Make the ark with nesting places and cover it inside and out with tar. ¹⁵This is how you should make it: four hundred fifty feet long, seventy-five feet wide, and forty-five feet high. ¹⁶Make a roof^b for the ark and complete it one foot from the top.^c Put a door in its side. In the hold below, make the second and third decks.

¹⁷"I am now bringing the floodwaters over the earth to destroy everything under the sky that breathes. Everything on earth is about to take its last breath. ¹⁸But I will set up my covenant with you. You will go into the ark together with your sons, your wife, and your sons' wives. ¹⁹From all living things—from

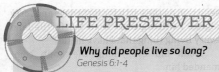

LIFE PRESERVER

Why did people live so long?
Genesis 6:1-4

In Genesis humans lived for one hundred and twenty years. That's an amazing fact, especially since a life span today may be only forty or fifty years in countries where people don't have access to medical care or healthy living conditions.

As you continue to read stories in the Old Testament, you will read about people's long life spans. We don't really know how time was counted when these books were written or if one hundred and twenty years is the same as we count it. In Psalm 90, which was written later than the book of Genesis, a normal lifetime is described as seventy to eighty years.

Another way to make sense of longer life spans is that the biblical numbers refer to a good long life for very important people. ◆

all creatures—you are to bring a pair, male and female, into the ark with you to keep them alive. ²⁰From each kind of bird, from each kind of livestock, and from each kind of everything that crawls on the ground—a pair from each will go in with you to stay alive. ²¹Take some from every kind of food and stow it as food for you and for the animals."

²²Noah did everything exactly as God commanded him.

did you know? Imagine a modern-day football stadium. The ark Noah built would take up almost the whole field, stretching from end zone to end zone and from one side of the field to the other. Plus it would be taller than a three-story building. That's a big boat!

7 The LORD said to Noah, "Go into the ark with your whole household, because among this generation I've seen that you are a moral man. ²From every clean animal, take seven pairs, a male and his mate; and from every unclean animal, take one pair, a male and his mate; ³and from the birds in the sky as well, take seven pairs, male and female, so that their offspring will survive throughout the earth. ⁴In seven days from now I will

---

˟Or spirit ^yOr the Nephilim ^zHeb Noah ^aOr ark of gopher wood, an unknown species of tree ^bOr window ^cHeb uncertain

send rain on the earth for forty days and forty nights. I will wipe off from the fertile land every living thing that I have made."

⁵Noah did everything the LORD commanded him.

⁶Noah was 600 years old when the floodwaters arrived on earth. ⁷Noah, his sons, his wife, and his sons' wives with him entered the ark to escape the floodwaters. ⁸From the clean and unclean animals, from the birds and everything crawling on the ground, ⁹two of each, male and female, went into the ark with Noah, just as God commanded Noah. ¹⁰After seven days, the floodwaters arrived on the earth. ¹¹In the six hundredth year of Noah's life, in the second month, on the seventeenth day—on that day all the springs of the deep sea erupted, and the windows in the skies opened. ¹²It rained on the earth forty days and forty nights. ¹³That same day Noah, with his sons Shem, Ham, and Japheth, Noah's wife, and his sons' three wives, went into the ark. ¹⁴They and every kind of animal—every kind of livestock, every kind that crawls on the ground, every kind of birdᵈ—¹⁵they came to Noah and entered the ark, two of every creature that breathes. ¹⁶Male and female of every creature went in, just as God had commanded him. Then the LORD closed the door behind them.ᵉ

¹⁷The flood remained on the earth for forty days. The waters rose, lifted the ark, and it rode high above the earth. ¹⁸The waters rose and spread out over the earth. The ark floated on the surface of the waters. ¹⁹The waters rose even higher over the earth; they covered all of the highest mountains under the sky. ²⁰The waters rose twenty-three feet high, covering the mountains. ²¹Every creature took its last breath:

the things crawling on the ground, birds, livestock, wild animals, everything swarming on the ground, and every human being. ²²Everything on dry land with life's breath in its nostrils died. ²³God wiped away every living thing that was on the fertile land—from human beings to livestock to crawling things to birds in the sky. They were wiped off the earth. Only Noah and those with him in the ark were left. ²⁴The waters rose over the earth for one hundred fifty days.

8 God remembered Noah, all those alive, and all the animals with him in the ark. God sent a wind over the earth so that the waters receded. ²The springs of the deep sea and the skiesᶠ closed up. The skies held back the rain. ³The waters receded gradually from the earth. After one hundred fifty days, the waters decreased; ⁴and in the seventh month, on the seventeenth day, the ark came to rest on the Ararat mountains. ⁵The waters decreased gradually until the tenth month, and on the first day of the tenth month the mountain peaks appeared.

⁶After forty days, Noah opened the window of the ark that he had made. ⁷He sent out a raven, and it flew back and forth until the waters over the entire earth had dried up. ⁸Then he sent out a dove to see if the waters on all of the fertile land had subsided, ⁹but the dove found no place to set its foot. It returned to him in the ark since waters still covered the entire earth. Noah stretched out his hand, took it, and brought it back into the ark. ¹⁰He waited seven more days and sent the dove out from the ark again. ¹¹The dove came back to him in the evening, grasping a torn olive leaf in its beak. Then Noah knew that the waters were subsiding from the earth. ¹²He waited seven more days and sent out the dove, but it didn't come back to him again. ¹³In Noah's six hundred first year, on the first day of the first month, the waters dried up from the earth. Noah removed the ark's hatch and saw that the surface of the fertile land had dried up. ¹⁴In the second month, on the twenty-seventh day, the earth was dry.

¹⁵God spoke to Noah, ¹⁶"Go out of the ark, you and your wife, your sons, and your sons' wives with you. ¹⁷Bring out with you all the

Bet you can read this in 3 minutes. Ready, set, go!

did you know? Noah's family spent more than forty days and nights in the ark while it rained. The named days listed in Genesis 7:10, 12, 17 and 8:3, 10, 12 total 293 days. Using the dates the Bible says Noah entered and exited the ark gives us a total of 377 days. That's more than a year on a boat with animals.

ᵈLXX; MT *every bird, every winged thing* ᵉHeb lacks *the door.* ᶠOr *the windows of the skies*

animals of every kind—birds, livestock, everything crawling on the ground—so that they may populate the earth, be fertile, and multiply on the earth." ¹⁸So Noah went out of the ark with his sons, his wife, and his sons' wives. ¹⁹All the animals, all the livestock,ᵍ all the birds, and everything crawling on the ground, came out of the ark by their families.

God's promise for the earth

²⁰Noah built an altar to the Lord. He took some of the clean large animals and some of the clean birds, and placed entirely burned offerings on the altar. ²¹The Lord smelled the pleasing scent, and the Lord thought to himself, I will not curse the fertile land anymore because of human beings since the ideas of the human mind are evil from their youth. I will never again destroy every living thing as I have done.

²² As long as the earth exists,
    seedtime and harvest,
    cold and hot,
    summer and autumn,
    day and night
    will not cease.

God's covenant with all life

9 God blessed Noah and his sons and said to them, "Be fertile, multiply, and fill the earth. ²All of the animals on the earth will fear you and dread you—all the birds in the skies, everything crawling on the ground, and all of the sea's fish. They are in your power. ³Everything that lives and moves will be your food. Just as I gave you the green grasses, I now give you everything. ⁴However, you must not eat meat with its life, its blood, in it.

⁵ I will surely demand your blood
    for a human life,
    from every living thing I will demand it.
    From humans, from a man for his brother,
    I will demand something
    for a human life.

⁶ Whoever sheds human blood,
    by a human his blood will be shed;
    for in the divine image
    God made human beings.

⁷As for you, be fertile and multiply. Populate the earth and multiply in it." ⁸God said to Noah and to his sons with him, ⁹"I am now setting up my covenant with you, with your descendants, ¹⁰and with every living being with you—with the birds, with the large animals, and with all the animals of the earth, leaving the ark with you.ʰ ¹¹I will set up my covenant with you so that never again will all life be cut off by floodwaters. There will never again be a flood to destroy the earth."

¹²God said, "This is the symbol of the covenant that I am drawing up between me and you and every living thing with you, on behalf of every future generation. ¹³I have placed my bow in the clouds; it will be the symbol of the covenant between me and the earth. ¹⁴When I bring clouds over the earth and the bow appears in the clouds, ¹⁵I will remember the covenant between me and you and every living being among all the creatures. Floodwaters will never again destroy all creatures. ¹⁶The bow will be in the clouds, and upon seeing it I will remember the enduring covenant between God and every living being of all the earth's creatures." ¹⁷God said to Noah, "This is the symbol of the covenant that I have set up between me and all creatures on earth."

LIFE PRESERVER

What is a covenant?
Genesis 9:8-17; 15

Have you ever made a promise to someone? Maybe you have said to a friend, or to your mom or dad, "I promise, I won't do that again," or "I promise I will…." A promise is like a covenant. The word *covenant* is used a lot in the Old Testament. After the flood, God made a covenant with Noah. You can read about it in Genesis 9. God promised Noah that God would help protect every living thing on the earth—people, plants, and animals—so they would thrive and not be destroyed.

Another example is in Genesis 15, where God made a covenant with Abraham and promised to give him land for his family. As you continue to read through the Old Testament, you will see this word a lot. Whenever God made a covenant with someone or with the Israelites, God promised to love them and expected them to be faithful and show love in return. ◆

Shem's blessing and Canaan's curse

¹⁸Noah's sons Shem, Ham, and Japheth came out of the ark. Now Ham was Canaan's father. ¹⁹These were Noah's three sons, and from them the whole earth was populated. ²⁰Noah, a farmer, made a new start and planted a vineyard. ²¹He drank some of the wine, became drunk, and took off his clothes in his tent. ²²Ham, Canaan's father, saw his father naked and told his two brothers who were outside. ²³Shem and Japheth took a robe, threw it over their shoulders, walked backward, and covered their naked father without looking at him because they turned away. ²⁴When Noah woke up from his wine, he discovered what his youngest son had done to him. ²⁵He said,

---

ⁱHeb sounds like *Japheth.*

"Cursed be Canaan:
the lowest servant
he will be for his brothers."
²⁶He also said,
"Bless the Lord,
the God of Shem;
Canaan will be his servant.
²⁷May God give spaceⁱ to Japheth;
he will live in Shem's tents,
and Canaan will be his servant."
²⁸After the flood, Noah lived 350 years.
²⁹In all, Noah lived 950 years; then he died.

Noah's descendants

10 These are the descendants of Noah's sons Shem, Ham, and Japheth, to whom children were born after the flood. ²Japheth's

---

God's THOUGHTS ▶ My THOUGHTS

Rainbows Remind Us to Trust God *Genesis 9:12-17*

If the sound of thunder exploding over your house makes you cover your ears in fear, you're not alone. Many people are afraid of storms—they can be really loud and scary! Now imagine what it would be like if it rained for more than a month.

Noah and his family had that scary experience. One day God told Noah to build a really big boat, and Noah did what God asked. Noah built an ark that he, his family, and a whole bunch of animals could live in. Then a wild and fierce rain came down. For forty days and nights it rained so hard that the earth flooded and all the humans and animals that were not in the ark died.

When they came out of the ark, God promised rain would never again flood the whole earth. As a sign of this promise, God caused a beautiful rainbow to appear in the sky. From that time, whenever a storm came, the rainbow was a reminder that Noah and his family could trust God and not be afraid.

Has someone ever broken a promise they made to you? People aren't always able to do what they say they will, but God is different. The next time you see a rainbow, remember that when God makes a promise, God will keep it.

What does a rainbow remind you of? Why?

Name two promises God made.

sons: Gomer, Magog, Madai, Javan, Tubal, Meshech, and Tiras. ³Gomer's sons: Ashkenaz, Riphath, and Togarmah. ⁴Javan's sons: Elishah, Tarshish, Kittim, and Rodanim.ʲ ⁵From these the island-nations were divided into their own countries, each according to their languages and their clans within their nations.

did you know? Genesis 10 lists seventy people who were the children, grandchildren, and great-grandchildren of Noah. In Bible times, the number seventy meant perfection. Noah's family is listed as having the perfect number of people to restart life on earth.

⁶Ham's sons: Cush, Egypt, Put, and Canaan. ⁷Cush's sons: Seba, Havilah, Sabtah, Raamah, and Sabteca. Raamah's sons: Sheba and Dedan. ⁸Cush fathered Nimrod, the first great warrior on earth. ⁹The LORD saw him as a great hunter, and so it is said, "Like Nimrod, whom the LORD saw as a great hunter." ¹⁰The most important cities in his kingdom were Babel, Erech, Accad, and Calneh in the land of Shinar. ¹¹Asshur left that land and built Nineveh, Rehoboth City, Calah, ¹²and Resen, the great city between Nineveh and Calah. ¹³Egypt fathered Ludim, Anamim, Lehabim, Naphtuhim, ¹⁴Pathrusim, Casluhim, and Caphtorim,ᵏ from which the Philistines came.

¹⁵Canaan fathered Sidon his oldest son, and Heth, ¹⁶the Jebusites, the Amorites, the Girgashites, ¹⁷the Hivites, the Arkites, the Sinites, ¹⁸the Arvadites, the Zemarites, and the Hamathites. After this the Canaanite clans were dispersed. ¹⁹The Canaanite boundary extends from Sidon by way of Gerar to Gaza and by way of Sodom, Gomorrah, Admah, and Zeboiim to Lasha. ²⁰These are Ham's sons according to their clans, their languages, their lands, and their nations.

²¹Children were also born to Shem the father of all Eber's children and Japheth's older brother.

²²Shem's sons: Elam, Asshur, Arpachshad, Lud, and Aram. ²³Aram's sons: Uz, Hul, Gether, and Mash. ²⁴Arpachshad fathered Shelah, and Shelah fathered Eber. ²⁵To Eber were born two sons: The first was named Peleg,ˡ because during his lifetime the earth was divided. His brother's name was Joktan. ²⁶Joktan fathered Almodad, Sheleph, Hazarmaveth, Jerah, ²⁷Hadoram, Uzal, Diklah, ²⁸Obal, Abimael, Sheba, ²⁹Ophir, Havilah, and Jobab. All of these were Joktan's sons. ³⁰Their settlements extended from Mesha by way of Sephar, the eastern mountains. ³¹These are Shem's sons according to their clans, their languages, their lands, and their nations.

³²These are the clans of Noah's sons according to their generations and their nations. From them the earth's nations branched out after the flood.

Origin of languages and cultures

11 All peopleᵐ on the earth had one language and the same words. ²When they traveled east,ⁿ they found a valley in the land of Shinar and settled there. ³They said to each other, "Come, let's make bricks and bake them hard." They used bricks for stones and asphalt for mortar. ⁴They said, "Come, let's build for ourselves a city and a tower with its top in the sky, and let's make a name for ourselves so that we won't be dispersed over all the earth."

⁵Then the LORD came down to see the city and the tower that the humans built. ⁶And the LORD said, "There is now one people and they all have one language. This is what they have begun to do, and now all that they plan to do will be possible for them. ⁷Come, let's go down and mix up their language there so they won't understand each other's language." ⁸Then the LORD dispersed them from there over all of the earth, and they stopped building the city. ⁹Therefore, it is named Babel, because there the LORD mixed upᵒ the language of all the earth; and from there the LORD dispersed them over all the earth.

ʲLXX, Sam, 1 Chron 1:7; MT *Dodanim* ᵏOr *Casluhim, from which the Philistines set out, and Caphtorim* ˡOr *separation*
ᵐHeb lacks *people*. ⁿOr *from the east* ᵒHeb *balal*, wordplay on Babel

LIFE PRESERVER

How did we get to be so different? *Genesis 11:1-9*

You may have heard the story about when people all spoke the same language. They liked this so much they decided to build a city and a tower so they could stay together. But God had a bigger plan. God knew it would be better if everyone on the earth could learn to live with difference—in language, culture, religion, even food. So God mixed up their language and sent the people to many places on earth. In doing this, God hoped they would learn how to listen to each other and live with people who were different from themselves.

In many Bibles this section is called "The Tower of Babel." Here it is given the title "Origin of languages and cultures," because it is the first story in the Bible that helps us understand how we got to be so different. ◆

Shem's descendants

[10] These are Shem's descendants.

When Shem was 100 years old, he became the father of Arpachshad, two years after the flood. [11] After Arpachshad was born, Shem lived 500 years; he had other sons and daughters.

[12] When Arpachshad was 35 years old, he became the father of Shelah. [13] After Shelah was born, Arpachshad lived 403 years; he had other sons and daughters.

[14] When Shelah was 30 years old, he became the father of Eber. [15] After Eber was born, Shelah lived 403 years; he had other sons and daughters.

[16] When Eber was 34 years old, he became the father of Peleg. [17] After Peleg was born, Eber lived 430 years; he had other sons and daughters.

[18] When Peleg was 30 years old, he became the father of Reu. [19] After Reu was

born, Peleg lived 209 years; he had other sons and daughters.

[20] When Reu was 32 years old, he became the father of Serug. [21] After Serug was born, Reu lived 207 years; he had other sons and daughters.

[22] When Serug was 30 years old, he became the father of Nahor. [23] After Nahor was born, Serug lived 200 years; he had other sons and daughters.

[24] When Nahor was 29 years old, he became the father of Terah. [25] After Terah was born, Nahor lived 119 years; he had other sons and daughters.

[26] When Terah was 70 years old, he became the father of Abram, Nahor, and Haran.

[27] These are Terah's descendants. Terah became the father of Abram, Nahor, and Haran. Haran became the father of Lot. [28] Haran died while with his father Terah in his native land,[p] in Ur of the Chaldeans. [29] Abram and Nahor both married; Abram's wife was Sarai, and Nahor's wife was Milcah the daughter of Haran, father of both Milcah and Iscah. [30] Sarai was unable to have children. [31] Terah took his son Abram, his grandson Lot (son of Haran), and his son Abram's wife, Sarai his daughter-in-law. They left Ur of the Chaldeans for the land of Canaan, and arriving at Haran, they settled there. [32] Terah lived 205 years, and he died in Haran.

Abram's family moves to Canaan

12 The LORD said to Abram, "Leave your land, your family, and your father's household for the land that I will show you. [2] I will make of you a great nation and will bless you. I will make your name respected, and you will be a blessing.

[3] I will bless those who bless you,
those who curse you I will curse;
all the families of the earth
will be blessed because of you."[q]

[4] Abram left just as the LORD told him, and Lot went with him. Now Abram was 75 years old when he left Haran. [5] Abram took his wife Sarai, his nephew Lot, all of their possessions, and those who became members of their household in Haran; and they set out

did you know?

Blessing is a big theme in the book of Genesis. The word *blessing* appears eighty-eight times in Genesis. To bless someone was to wish good would happen to that person.

for the land of Canaan. When they arrived in Canaan, [6]Abram traveled through the land as far as the sacred place at Shechem, at the oak of Moreh. The Canaanites lived in the land at that time. [7]The LORD appeared to Abram and said, "I give this land to your descendants," so Abram built an altar there to the LORD who appeared to him. [8]From there he traveled toward the mountains east of Bethel, and pitched his tent with Bethel on the west and Ai on the east. There he built an altar to the LORD and worshiped in the LORD's name. [9]Then Abram set out toward the arid southern plain, making and breaking camp as he went.

Abram and Sarai visit Egypt

[10]When a famine struck the land, Abram went down toward Egypt to live as an immigrant since the famine was so severe in the land. [11]Just before he arrived in Egypt, he said to his wife Sarai, "I know you are a good-looking woman. [12]When the Egyptians see you, they will say, 'This is his wife,' and they will kill me but let you live. [13]So tell them you are my sister so that they will treat me well for your sake, and I will survive because of you."

[14]When Abram entered Egypt, the Egyptians saw how beautiful his wife was. [15]When Pharaoh's princes saw her, they praised her to Pharaoh; and the woman was taken into Pharaoh's household. [16]Things went well for Abram because of her: he acquired flocks, cattle, male donkeys, men servants, women servants, female donkeys, and camels. [17]Then the LORD struck Pharaoh and his household with severe plagues because of Abram's wife Sarai. [18]So Pharaoh summoned Abram and said, "What's this you've done to me? Why didn't you tell me she was your wife? [19]Why did you say, 'She's my sister,' so that I made her my wife? Now, here's your wife. Take her and go!" [20]Pharaoh gave his men orders concerning Abram, and they expelled him with his wife and everything he had.

Abram and Lot separate

13Abram went up from Egypt toward the arid southern plain with his wife, with everything he had, and with Lot. [2]Abram was very wealthy in livestock, silver, and gold. [3]Abram traveled, making and breaking camp, from the arid southern plain to Bethel and to the sacred place there, where he had first pitched his tent between Bethel and Ai, [4]that is, to the place at which he had earlier built the altar. There he worshiped in the LORD's name. [5]Now Lot, who traveled with Abram, also had flocks, cattle, and tents. [6]They had so many possessions between them that the land couldn't support both of them. They could no longer live together. [7]Conflicts broke out between those herding Abram's livestock and those herding Lot's livestock. At that time the Canaanites and the Perizzites lived in the land.

[8]Abram said to Lot, "Let's not have disputes between me and you and between our herders since we are relatives. [9]Isn't the whole land in front of you? Let's separate. If you go north, I will go south; and if you go south, I will go north." [10]Lot looked up and saw the entire Jordan Valley. All of it was well irrigated, like the garden of the LORD, like the land of Egypt, as far as Zoar (this was before the LORD destroyed Sodom and Gomorrah). [11]So Lot chose for himself the entire Jordan Valley. Lot set out toward the east, and they separated from each other. [12]Abram settled in the land of Canaan, and Lot settled near the cities of the valley and pitched his tent close to Sodom. [13]The citizens of Sodom were very evil and sinful against the LORD.

SAILBOAT

GENEROUS

Abram Is Generous *Genesis 13:8-12*
Abram trusted God, believing God's promise to give land to him and his descendants forever. Because of this Abram responded to Lot with a generous heart and told Lot to choose the land he wanted. When we trust in God's blessings, it is easier to respond with generosity. ◊

[14]After Lot separated from him, the LORD said to Abram, "From the place where you are standing, look up and gaze to the north, south, east, and west, [15]because all the land that you see I give you and your descendants forever. [16]I will make your descendants like the dust of the earth. If someone could count

the bits of dust on the earth, then they could also count your descendants. [17]Stand up and walk around through the length and breadth of the land because I am giving it to you." [18]So Abram packed his tent and went and settled by the oaks of Mamre in Hebron. There he built an altar to the LORD.

Abram rescues Lot

14While Amraphel was king of Shinar, El-lasar's King Arioch, Elam's King Chedor-laomer, and Goiim's King Tidal [2]declared war on Sodom's King Bera, Gomorrah's King Birsha, Admah's King Shinab, Zeboiim's King Shem-eber, and the king of Bela, that is, Zoar. [3]These latter kings formed an alliance in the Siddim Valley (that is, the Dead Sea[r]). [4]For twelve years they had served Chedorlaomer, and in the thirteenth year they revolted. [5]In the four-teenth year, Chedorlaomer and the kings of his alliance came and attacked the Rephaim in Ashteroth-karnaim, the Zuzim in Ham, the Emim in Shaveh-kiriathaim, [6]and the Horites in the mountains of Seir as far as El-paran near the desert. [7]Then they turned back, came to En-mishpat (that is, Kadesh), and attacked the territory of the Amalekites, as well as the Amorites who lived in Hazazon-tamar.

[8]Then the kings of Sodom, Gomorrah, Admah, Zeboiim, and Bera (that is, Zoar) took up battle positions in the Siddim Val-ley [9]against King Chedorlaomer of Elam, King Tidal of Goiim, King Amraphel of Shi-nar, and King Arioch of Ellasar, four kings against five.

[10]Now the Siddim Valley was filled with tar pits. When the kings of Sodom and Gomor-rah retreated, they fell into them; and the rest fled to the mountains. [11]They took every-thing from Sodom and Gomorrah, including its food supplies, and left. [12]They also took Lot, Abram's nephew who lived in Sodom, and everything he owned, and took off. [13]When a survivor arrived, he told Abram the He-brew, who lived near the oaks of the Amorite Mamre, who was the brother of Eshcol and Aner, Abram's treaty partners.

[14]When Abram heard that his relative had been captured, he took all of the loyal men born in his household, three hundred

eighteen, and went after them as far as Dan. [15]During the night, he and his servants di-vided themselves up against them, attacked, and chased them to Hobah, north of Damas-cus. [16]He brought back all of the looted prop-erty, together with his relative Lot and Lot's property, wives, and people.

Abram blessed by Melchizedek

[17]After Abram returned from his attack on Chedorlaomer and the kings who were with him, the king of Sodom came out to the Shaveh Valley (that is, the King's Valley) to meet him. [18]Now Melchizedek the king of Salem and the priest of El Elyon[s] had brought bread and wine, [19]and he blessed him,

"Bless Abram by El Elyon,
      creator of heaven and earth;
[20]bless El Elyon,
      who gave you the victory
      over your enemies."

Abram gave Melchizedek one-tenth of everything. [21]Then the king of Sodom said to Abram, "Give me the people and take the property for yourself."

LIGHTHOUSE

GIVING A TENTH

Giving Back to God Genesis 14:17-21
An important part of many church services is the offering, when people give money to be used for God's service. Giving an offering is a way to express thanks and gratitude for all that God has done. In this passage, Abram gave King Melchizedek one-tenth of everything. We still follow this model today by giving to the church one-tenth of what we have. With each offering we show our thanks to God and are part of creating God's kingdom here on earth. ◆

[22]But Abram said to the king of Sodom, "I promised the LORD, El Elyon, creator of heaven and earth, [23]that I wouldn't take even a thread or a sandal strap from anything that was yours so that you couldn't say, 'I'm the one who made Abram rich.' [24]The only excep-tion is that the young men may keep what-ever they have taken to eat, and the men who

[r]Or Salt Sea [s]Or God Most High

went with me—Aner, Eshcol, and Mamre—may keep their share."

God's covenant with Abram

15 After these events, the Lord's word came to Abram in a vision, "Don't be afraid, Abram. I am your protector.[t] Your reward will be very great."

[2] But Abram said, "Lord God, what can you possibly give me, since I still have no children? The head of my household is Eliezer, a man from Damascus."[u] [3] He continued, "Since you haven't given me any children, the head of my household will be my heir."

[4] The Lord's word came immediately to him, "This man will not be your heir. Your heir will definitely be your very own biological child." [5] Then he brought Abram outside and said, "Look up at the sky and count the stars if you think you can count them." He continued, "This is how many children you will have." [6] Abram trusted the Lord, and the Lord recognized Abram's high moral character.

[7] He said to Abram, "I am the Lord, who brought you out of Ur of the Chaldeans to give you this land as your possession."

[8] But Abram said, "Lord God, how do I know that I will actually possess it?"

[9] He said, "Bring me a three-year-old female calf, a three-year-old female goat, a three-year-old ram, a dove, and a young

did you **know?** The vessel with the flame that passed between the split-open animals showed Abram that God would keep God's promise. Jeremiah 34:18-20 says when someone sealed a promise by walking between the two parts of an animal that had been killed and then split in half it meant, "May I die and be torn in two if I break this promise."

pigeon." [10] He took all of these animals, split them in half, and laid the halves facing each other, but he didn't split the birds. [11] When vultures swooped down on the carcasses, Abram waved them off. [12] After the sun set, Abram slept deeply. A terrifying and deep darkness settled over him.

[13] Then the Lord said to Abram, "Have no doubt that your descendants will live as immigrants in a land that isn't their own, where they will be oppressed slaves for four hundred years. [14] But after I punish the nation they serve, they will leave it with great wealth. [15] As for you, you will join your ancestors in peace and be buried after a good long life. [16] The fourth generation will return here since the Amorites' wrongdoing won't have reached its peak until then."

[17] After the sun had set and darkness had deepened, a smoking vessel with a fiery flame passed between the split-open animals. [18] That day the Lord cut a covenant with Abram: "To your descendants I give this land, from Egypt's river to the great Euphrates, [19] together with the Kenites, the Kenizzites, the Kadmonites, [20] the Hittites, the Perizzites, the Rephaim, [21] the Amorites, the Canaanites, the Girgashites, and the Jebusites."

Hagar and the Ishmaelites' origins

16 Sarai, Abram's wife, had not been able to have children. Since she had an Egyptian servant named Hagar, [2] Sarai said to Abram, "The Lord has kept me from giving birth, so go to my servant. Maybe she will provide me

[t] Or *shield* or *benefactor*   [u] Heb uncertain

with children." Abram did just as Sarai said. ³After Abram had lived ten years in the land of Canaan, Abram's wife Sarai took her Egyptian servant Hagar and gave her to her husband Abram as his wife. ⁴He slept with Hagar, and she became pregnant. But when she realized that she was pregnant, she no longer respected her mistress. ⁵Sarai said to Abram, "This harassment is your fault. I allowed you to embrace my servant, but when she realized she was pregnant, I lost her respect. Let the Lord decide who is right, you or me."

⁶Abram said to Sarai, "Since she's your servant, do whatever you wish to her." So Sarai treated her harshly, and she ran away from Sarai.

⁷The Lord's messenger found Hagar at a spring in the desert, the spring on the road to Shur, ⁸and said, "Hagar! Sarai's servant! Where did you come from and where are you going?"

She said, "From Sarai my mistress. I'm running away."

⁹The Lord's messenger said to her, "Go back to your mistress. Put up with her harsh treatment of you." ¹⁰The Lord's messenger also said to her,

"I will give you many children,
    so many they can't be counted!"

¹¹The Lord's messenger said to her,

"You are now pregnant
    and will give birth to a son.
You will name him Ishmaelᵛ
    because the Lord has heard about your
        harsh treatment.
¹² He will be a wild mule of a man;
    he will fight everyone,
        and they will fight him.
    He will live at odds
        with all his relatives."ʷ

¹³Hagar named the Lord who spoke to her, "You are El Roi"ˣ because she said, "Can I still see after he saw me?"ʸ ¹⁴Therefore, that well is called Beer-lahai-roi;ᶻ it's the well between Kadesh and Bered. ¹⁵Hagar gave birth to a son for Abram, and Abram named him Ishmael. ¹⁶Abram was 86 years old when Hagar gave birth to Ishmael for Abram.

UMBRELLA
JEALOUSY

Misery *Genesis 16:5*

Things were not working out as Sarai had thought they would. She longed to have a baby, but as each year passed that seemed more and more unlikely. To make matters worse, her servant Hagar became pregnant. Sarai felt angry and jealous. Hagar had what Sarai wanted more than anything else. In her anger and sadness, Sarai treated Hagar so harshly that she ran away. A poor servant, Hagar had nowhere to go. When we are filled with jealousy or anger, we are in danger of doing things we will deeply regret.

God's covenant with Abraham

17 When Abram was 99 years old, the Lord appeared to Abram and said to him, "I am El Shaddai.ᵃ Walk with me and be trustworthy. ²I will make a covenant between us and I will give you many, many descendants." ³Abram fell on his face, and God said to him, ⁴"But me, my covenant is with you; you will be the ancestor of many nations. ⁵And because I have made you the ancestor of many nations, your name will no longer be Abramᵇ but Abraham.ᶜ ⁶I will make you very fertile. I will produce nations from you, and kings will come from you. ⁷I will set up my covenant with you and your descendants after you in every generation as an enduring covenant. I will be your God and your descendants' God after you. ⁸I will give you and your descendants the land in which you are immigrants, the whole land of Canaan, as an enduring possession. And I will be their God."

⁹God said to Abraham, "As for you, you must keep my covenant, you and your descendants in every generation. ¹⁰This is my covenant that you and your descendants must keep: Circumcise every male. ¹¹You must circumcise the flesh of your foreskins, and it will be a symbol of the covenant between us. ¹²On the eighth day after birth, every male

---

ᵛOr *God hears* ʷOr *he will live at odds with all his kin; or he will reside near all his relatives* ˣOr *God who sees* or *God whom I've seen* ʸHeb uncertain; or *Have I really seen God and survived?* ᶻOr *the Well of the Living One who sees me* or *whom I've seen* ᵃOr *God Almighty* or *God of the Mountain* ᵇOr *exalted ancestor* ᶜOr *ancestor of a multitude*

in every generation must be circumcised, including those who are not your own children: those born in your household and those purchased with silver from foreigners. ¹³Be sure you circumcise those born in your household and those purchased with your silver. Your flesh will embody my covenant as an enduring covenant. ¹⁴Any uncircumcised male whose flesh of his foreskin remains uncircumcised will be cut off from his people. He has broken my covenant."

¹⁵God said to Abraham, "As for your wife Sarai, you will no longer call her Sarai. Her name will now be Sarah. ¹⁶I will bless her and even give you a son from her. I will bless her so that she will become nations, and kings of peoples will come from her."

ᵈOr he laughs

¹⁷Abraham fell on his face and laughed. He said to himself, Can a 100-year-old man become a father, or Sarah, a 90-year-old woman, have a child? ¹⁸To God Abraham said, "If only you would accept Ishmael!"

¹⁹But God said, "No, your wife Sarah will give birth to a son for you, and you will name him Isaac.ᵈ I will set up my covenant with him and with his descendants after him as an enduring covenant. ²⁰As for Ishmael, I've heard your request. I will bless him and make him fertile and give him many, many descendants. He will be the ancestor of twelve tribal leaders, and I will make a great nation of him. ²¹But I will set up my covenant with Isaac, who will be born to Sarah at this time next year." ²²When God finished speaking to him, God ascended, leaving Abraham alone.

Big Promises from a Big God *Genesis 17:1-18*

God made promises to Noah, Abraham, and many other people in the Bible. Some of those promises are also meant for us today.

One promise God made was to be with Abraham and be his God. From that time on, God took care of Abraham, just like a good parent would. Even when Abraham made mistakes or disobeyed, God helped Abraham and didn't give up on him.

Another promise God made was that Abraham's family members would be God's people. This meant God would be with Abraham's son Isaac, his grandchildren, his great-grandchildren, and so on. Just like with Abraham, God took care of Abraham's family. God provided for their needs, protected them, and corrected them when they made mistakes.

This promise didn't stop with Abraham's family. In the letter the Apostle Paul wrote to the church at Galatia, he said, "Those who believe are the children of Abraham" (Gal 3:7). If we believe in God's son Jesus, then we're part of Abraham's family and God's promise to them is true for us. God will be with us and care for us always.

This is a big promise! You're the child of a big and loving God who always keeps promises.

How does a good parent take care of a child?

Name some promises God will keep.

²³Abraham took his son Ishmael, all those born in his household, and all those purchased with his silver—that is, every male in Abraham's household—and he circumcised the flesh of their foreskins that same day, just as God had told him to do. ²⁴Abraham was 99 years old when he circumcised the flesh of his foreskin, ²⁵and his son Ishmael was 13 years old when the flesh of his foreskin was circumcised. ²⁶That same day Abraham and his son Ishmael were circumcised. ²⁷All the men of his household, those born in his household and those purchased with silver from foreigners, were circumcised with him.

Isaac's birth announced

18 The LORD appeared to Abraham at the oaks of Mamre while he sat at the entrance of his tent in the day's heat. ²He looked up and suddenly saw three men standing near him. As soon as he saw them, he ran from his tent entrance to greet them and bowed deeply. ³He said, "Sirs, if you would be so kind, don't just pass by your servant. ⁴Let a little water be brought so you may wash your feet and refresh yourselves under the tree. ⁵Let me offer you a little bread so you will feel stronger, and after that you may leave your servant and go on your way—since you have visited your servant."

They responded, "Fine. Do just as you have said."

⁶So Abraham hurried to Sarah at his tent and said, "Hurry! Knead three seahsᵉ of the finest flour and make some baked goods!" ⁷Abraham ran to the cattle, took a healthy young calf, and gave it to a young servant, who prepared it quickly. ⁸Then Abraham took butter, milk, and the calf that had been prepared, put the food in front of them, and stood under the tree near them as they ate.

⁹They said to him, "Where's your wife Sarah?"

And he said, "Right here in the tent."

¹⁰Then one of the men said, "I will definitely return to you about this time next year. Then your wife Sarah will have a son!"

Sarah was listening at the tent door behind him. ¹¹Now Abraham and Sarah were both very old. Sarah was no longer menstruating. ¹²So Sarah laughed to herself, thinking, I'm no longer able to have children and my husband's old.

¹³The LORD said to Abraham, "Why did Sarah laugh and say, 'Me give birth? At my age?' ¹⁴Is anything too difficult for the LORD? When I return to you about this time next year, Sarah will have a son."

¹⁵Sarah lied and said, "I didn't laugh," because she was frightened.

But he said, "No, you laughed."

Abraham pleads for Sodom

¹⁶The men got up from there and went over to look down on Sodom. Abraham was walking along with them to send them off ¹⁷when the LORD said, "Will I keep from Abraham what I'm about to do? ¹⁸Abraham will certainly become a great populous nation, and all the earth's nations will be blessed because of him. ¹⁹I have formed a relationship with him so that he will instruct his children and his household after him. And they will keep to the LORD's path, being moral and just so that the LORD can do for Abraham everything he said he would." ²⁰Then the LORD said, "The cries of injustice from Sodom and Gomorrah are countless, and their sin is very serious! ²¹I will go down now to examine the cries of injustice that have reached me. Have they really done all this? If not, I want to know."

²²The men turned away and walked toward Sodom, but Abraham remained standing in front of the LORD.ᶠ ²³Abraham approached and said, "Will you really sweep away the innocentᵍ with the guilty?ʰ ²⁴What if there are fifty innocent people in the city? Will you really sweep it away and not save the place for the sake of the fifty innocent people in it? ²⁵It's not like you to do this, killing the innocent with the guilty as if there were no difference. It's not like you! Will the judge of all the earth not act justly?"

ᵉOne seah is seven and a half quarts. ᶠSome ancient manuscripts read *but the LORD remained standing in front of Abraham.* ᵍOr *righteous* ʰOr *wicked*

LIFE PRESERVER

What happened to Sodom and Gomorrah?

Genesis 18:16-33

God heard cries of injustice from people in the cities of Sodom and Gomorrah and decided to destroy those cities because of the sins of the people. The people in those two cities didn't care for each other and weren't living as God wanted them to. They weren't kind or welcoming, and they acted violently toward others. When Abraham learned of God's decision, he tried to change God's mind. God listened and agreed that if there were ten faithful people, the cities would be saved. But ten faithful people could not be found, and so the cities were destroyed.

Even more than the story of Adam and Eve in the garden of Eden, this story reveals the reality of evil and punishment. It teaches about the nature of God, who is both a God of compassion and care and a God of judgment. The kind of violence that happened in Sodom and Gomorrah still happens today. God sees our lives and actions and is sad when we don't act kindly toward each other. ◆

---

²⁶The LORD said, "If I find fifty innocent people in the city of Sodom, I will save it because of them."

²⁷Abraham responded, "Since I've already decided to speak with my Lord, even though I'm just soil and ash, ²⁸what if there are five fewer innocent people than fifty? Will you destroy the whole city over just five?"

The LORD said, "If I find forty-five there, I won't destroy it."

²⁹Once again Abraham spoke, "What if forty are there?"

The LORD said, "For the sake of forty, I will do nothing."

³⁰He said, "Don't be angry with me, my Lord, but let me speak. What if thirty are there?"

The LORD said, "I won't do it if I find thirty there."

³¹Abraham said, "Since I've already decided to speak with my Lord, what if twenty are there?"

The LORD said, "I won't do it, for the sake of twenty."

³²Abraham said, "Don't be angry with me, my Lord, but let me speak just once more. What if there are ten?"

And the LORD said, "I will not destroy it

because of those ten." ³³When the LORD finished speaking with Abraham, he left; but Abraham stayed there in that place.

Lot leaves Sodom

19 The two messengers entered Sodom in the evening. Lot, who was sitting at the gate of Sodom, saw them, got up to greet them, and bowed low. ²He said, "Come to your servant's house, spend the night, and wash your feet. Then you can get up early and go on your way."

But they said, "No, we will spend the night in the town square." ³He pleaded earnestly with them, so they went with him and entered his house. He made a big meal for them, even baking unleavened bread, and they ate.

⁴Before they went to bed, the men of the city of Sodom—everyone from the youngest to the oldest—surrounded the house ⁵and called to Lot, "Where are the men who arrived tonight? Bring them out to us so that we may have sex with them."

⁶Lot went out toward the entrance, closed the door behind him, ⁷and said, "My brothers, don't do such an evil thing. ⁸I've got two daughters who are virgins. Let me bring them out to you, and you may do to them whatever you wish. But don't do anything to these men because they are now under the protection of my roof."

⁹They said, "Get out of the way!" And they continued, "Does this immigrant want to judge us? Now we will hurt you more than we will hurt them." They pushed Lot back and came close to breaking down the door. ¹⁰The men inside reached out and pulled Lot back into the house with them and slammed the door. ¹¹Then the messengers blinded the men near the entrance of the house, from the youngest to the oldest, so that they groped around trying to find the entrance.

¹²The men said to Lot, "Who's still with you here? Take away from this place your sons-in-law, your sons, your daughters, and everyone else you have in the city ¹³because we are about to destroy this place. The LORD has found the cries of injustice so serious that the LORD sent us to destroy it."

¹⁴Lot went to speak to his sons-in-law, married to his daughters, and said, "Get up and get out of this place because the LORD is

about to destroy the city." But his sons-in-law thought he was joking.

¹⁵When dawn broke, the messengers urged Lot, "Get up and take your wife and your two daughters who are here so that you are not swept away because of the evil in this city." ¹⁶He hesitated, but because the Lᴏʀᴅ intended to save him, the men grabbed him, his wife, and two daughters by the hand, took him out, and left him outside the city.

¹⁷After getting them out, the men said, "Save your lives! Don't look back! And don't stay in the valley. Escape to the mountains so that you are not swept away."

¹⁸But Lot said to them, "No, my lords, please. ¹⁹You've done me a favor and have been so kind to save my life. But I can't escape to the mountains since the catastrophe might overtake me there and I'd die. ²⁰This city here is close enough to flee to, and it's small. It's small, right? Let me escape there, and my life will be saved."

²¹He said to Lot, "I'll do this for you as well; I won't overthrow the city that you have described. ²²Hurry! Escape to it! I can't do anything until you get there." That is why the name of the city is Zoar.ⁱ

Sodom and Gomorrah destroyed

²³As the sun rose over the earth, Lot arrived in Zoar; ²⁴and the Lᴏʀᴅ rained down burning asphalt from the skies onto Sodom and Gomorrah. ²⁵The Lᴏʀᴅ destroyed these cities, the entire valley, everyone who lived in the cities, and all of the fertile land's vegetation. ²⁶When Lot's wife looked back, she turned into a pillar of salt.

²⁷Abraham set out early for the place where he had stood with the Lᴏʀᴅ, ²⁸and looked out over Sodom and Gomorrah and over all the land of the valley. He saw the smoke from the land rise like the smoke from a kiln.

Origin of Moab and Ammon

²⁹When God destroyed the cities in the valley, God remembered Abraham and sent Lot away from the disaster that overtook the cities in which Lot had lived. ³⁰Since Lot had become fearful of living in Zoar, he and his two daughters headed up from Zoar and settled in

UMBRELLA
Disobedience

A Pillar of Salt *Genesis 19:19-20, 26*
Lot, his wife, and daughters fled from everything that was familiar. Abraham told them that God would save them from destruction. However they must not look back. Lot's wife couldn't resist one last look at all that she knew, at all that she would never see again. Though she had been instructed not to look, she disobeyed. She glanced back and immediately became a pillar of salt. This story reminds us that it is important to obey directions when someone we trust tells us not to do something, even if we don't understand why. ◆

the mountains where he and his two daughters lived in a cave. ³¹The older daughter said to the younger, "Our father is old, and there are no men in the land to sleep with us as is the custom everywhere. ³²Come on, let's give our father wine to drink, lie down with him, and we'll have children from our father." ³³That night they served their father wine, and the older daughter went in and lay down with her father, without him noticing when she lay down or got up. ³⁴The next day the older daughter said to the younger, "Since I lay down with our father last night, let's serve him wine tonight too, and you go in and lie down with him so that we will both have children from our father." ³⁵They served their father wine that night also, and the younger daughter lay down with him, without him knowing when she lay down or got up. ³⁶Both of Lot's daughters became pregnant by their father. ³⁷The older daughter gave birth to a son and named him Moab. He is the ancestor of today's Moabites. ³⁸The younger daughter also gave birth to a son and named him Ben-ammi.ʲ He is the ancestor of today's Ammonites.

Abraham and Sarah visit Gerar

20 Abraham traveled from there toward the land of the arid southern plain, and he settled as an immigrant in

---

ⁱOr small ʲOr son of my people

Gerar, between Kadesh and Shur. [2]Abraham said of his wife Sarah, "She's my sister." So King Abimelech of Gerar took her into his household.

[3]But God appeared to Abimelech that night in a dream and said to him, "You are as good as dead because of this woman you have taken. She is a married woman."

[4]Now Abimelech hadn't gone near her, and he said, "Lord, will you really put an innocent nation to death? [5]Didn't he say to me, 'She's my sister,' and didn't she—even she—say, 'He's my brother'? My intentions were pure, and I acted innocently when I did this."

[6]God said to him in the dream, "I know that your intentions were pure when you did this. In fact, I kept you from sinning against me. That's why I didn't allow you to touch her. [7]Now return the man's wife. He's a prophet; he will pray for you so you may live. But if you don't return her, know that you and everyone with you will die!"

[8]Abimelech got up early in the morning and summoned all of his servants. When he told them everything that had happened, the men were terrified. [9]Then Abimelech summoned Abraham and said to him, "What have you done to us? What sin did I commit against you that you have brought this terrible sin to me and my kingdom, by doing to me something that simply isn't done?" [10]Abimelech said to Abraham, "What were you thinking when you did this thing?"

[11]Abraham said, "I thought to myself, No one reveres God here and they will kill me to get my wife. [12]She is, truthfully, my sister—my father's daughter but not my mother's daughter—and she's now my wife. [13]When God led me away from my father's household, I said to her, 'This is the loyalty I expect from you: in each place we visit, tell them, "He is my brother."'"

[14]Abimelech took flocks, cattle, male servants, and female servants, and gave them to Abraham; and Abimelech returned his wife Sarah. [15]Abimelech said, "My land is here available to you. Live wherever you wish." [16]To Sarah, he said, "I've given your brother one thousand pieces of silver. It means that neither you nor anyone with you has done anything wrong. Everything has been set right." [17]Abraham prayed to God; and God restored Abimelech, his wife, and his women servants to health, and they were able to have children. [18]Because of the incident with Abraham's wife Sarah, the LORD had kept all of the women in Abimelech's household from having children.

UMBRELLA

FEAR

Abraham Does It Again! *Genesis 20:2-12*
More than one time, Abraham put his wife Sarah in harm's way in an effort to protect himself. Even though God reminded him many times of God's blessing and promise, Abraham's fear still overcame his faith and good judgment. The story of Abraham reminds us that even though we may be afraid and make bad choices, God won't give up on us, just as God didn't give up on Abraham. ●

Isaac's birth

21 The LORD was attentive to Sarah just as he had said, and the LORD carried out just what he had promised her. [2]She became pregnant and gave birth to a son for Abraham when he was old, at the very time God had told him. [3]Abraham named his son—the one Sarah bore him—Isaac.[k] [4]Abraham circumcised his son Isaac when he was eight days old just as God had commanded him. [5]Abraham was 100 years old when his son Isaac was born. [6]Sarah said, "God has given me laughter. Everyone who hears about it will laugh with me.[l] [7]She said, "Who could have told Abraham that Sarah would nurse sons? But now I've given birth to a son when he was old!"

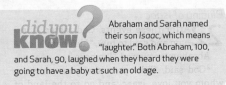

did you **know?** Abraham and Sarah named their son *Isaac*, which means "laughter." Both Abraham, 100, and Sarah, 90, laughed when they heard they were going to have a baby at such an old age.

[k]*Or he laughs* [l]*Or God has made a joke of me. Everyone who hears about it will laugh at me.*

Hagar and Ishmael evicted

[8]The boy grew and stopped nursing. On the day he stopped nursing, Abraham prepared a huge banquet. [9]Sarah saw Hagar's son laughing, the one Hagar the Egyptian had borne to Abraham. [10]So she said to Abraham, "Send this servant away with her son! This servant's son won't share the inheritance with my son Isaac."

[11]This upset Abraham terribly because the boy was his son. [12]God said to Abraham, "Don't be upset about the boy and your servant. Do everything Sarah tells you to do because your descendants will be traced through Isaac. [13]But I will make of your servant's son a great nation too, because he is also your descendant." [14]Abraham got up early in the morning, took some bread and a flask of water, and gave it to Hagar. He put the boy in her shoulder sling and sent her away.

She left and wandered through the desert near Beer-sheba. [15]Finally the water in the flask ran out, and she put the boy down under one of the desert shrubs. [16]She walked away from him about as far as a bow shot and sat down, telling herself, I can't bear to see the boy die. She sat at a distance, cried out in grief, and wept.

[17]God heard the boy's cries, and God's messenger called to Hagar from heaven and said to her, "Hagar! What's wrong? Don't be afraid. God has heard the boy's cries over there. [18]Get up, pick up the boy, and take him by the hand because I will make of him a great nation." [19]Then God opened her eyes, and she saw a well. She went over, filled the water flask, and gave the boy a drink. [20]God remained with the boy; he grew up, lived in the desert, and became an expert archer. [21]He lived in the Paran desert, and his mother found him an Egyptian wife.

Abraham's treaty with the Philistines

[22]At that time Abimelech, and Phicol commander of his forces, said to Abraham, "God is with you in everything that you do. [23]So give me your word under God that you won't cheat me, my children, or my descendants. Just as I have treated you fairly, so you must treat me and the land in which you are an immigrant."

[24]Abraham said, "I give you my word." [25]Then Abraham complained to Abimelech about a well that Abimelech's servants had seized.

[26]Abimelech said, "I don't know who has done this, and you didn't tell me. I didn't even hear about it until today." [27]Abraham took flocks and cattle, gave them to Abimelech, and the two of them drew up a treaty.[m] [28]Abraham set aside, by themselves, seven female lambs from the flock. [29]So Abimelech said to Abraham, "What are these seven lambs you've set apart?"

[30]Abraham said, "These seven lambs that you take from me will attest that I dug this well." [31]Therefore, the name of that place is Beer-sheba[n] because there they gave each other their word. [32]After they drew up a treaty[o] at Beer-sheba, Abimelech, and Phicol commander of his forces, returned to the land of the Philistines. [33]Abraham planted a tamarisk tree in Beer-sheba, and he worshipped there in the name of the LORD, El Olam.[p] [34]Abraham lived as an immigrant in the Philistines' land for a long time.

Binding of Isaac

22[1]After these events, God tested Abraham and said to him, "Abraham!"

Abraham answered, "I'm here."

[2]God said, "Take your son, your only son whom you love, Isaac, and go to the land of

UMBRELLA
HOPELESS

Never Without Hope *Genesis 21:17*
Sometimes bad things happen in our lives. This was true for people in the Bible too. Hagar and Ishmael were forced to leave their family and live in the desert. Before long they were out of water and food. Hagar lost hope and was scared that her son wouldn't survive. But the Bible tells us God showed her a well she hadn't seen before. When we feel hopeless and afraid, God comes to us and shows us a way to survive. With God we are never without hope. ◊

---

[m]Or *covenant* [n]Or *Well of seven; or Well of giving one's word* [o]Or *covenant* [p]Or *the eternal God*

LIFE PRESERVER

Why did Abraham almost kill his son Isaac? *Genesis 22:1-14*

If an adult you trust ever told you to do something you just didn't understand, you know a little how Isaac and Abraham might have felt when God told Abraham to offer Isaac as a sacrifice. In that ancient time, a few people sacrificed children to their gods, but this was never part of the culture of God's people. God's command must have seemed just as strange to Abraham as it does to us.

But even though it didn't make sense, both Abraham and Isaac chose to be completely obedient to God. Abraham risked everything, including the symbol of God's promise, and Isaac risked his life. The result of their absolute trust in God was that God provided a substitute sacrifice. Although this story is extreme, it shows how important obedience and trust are to God.

Moriah. Offer him up as an entirely burned
offering there on one of the mountains that
I will show you." 3 Abraham got up early in the
morning, harnessed his donkey, and took two
of his young men with him, together with his
son Isaac. He split the wood for the entirely
burned offering, set out, and went to the
place God had described to him.
4 On the third day, Abraham looked up and
saw the place at a distance. 5 Abraham said
to his servants, "Stay here with the donkey.
The boy and I will walk up there, worship, and
then come back to you."
6 Abraham took the wood for the entirely
burned offering and laid it on his son Isaac.
He took the fire and the knife in his hand, and
the two of them walked on together. 7 Isaac
said to his father Abraham, "My father?"

Abraham said, "I'm here, my son."

Isaac said, "Here is the fire and the wood, but where is the lamb for the entirely burned offering?"

8 Abraham said, "The lamb for the entirely
burned offering? God will see to it,[q] my son."
The two of them walked on together.
9 They arrived at the place God had described to him. Abraham built an altar there
and arranged the wood on it. He tied up his
son Isaac and laid him on the altar on top of
the wood. 10 Then Abraham stretched out his
hand and took the knife to kill his son as a
sacrifice. 11 But the LORD's messenger called
out to Abraham from heaven, "Abraham?
Abraham?"

Abraham said, "I'm here."

12 The messenger said, "Don't stretch out
your hand against the young man, and don't
do anything to him. I now know that you revere God and didn't hold back your son, your
only son, from me." 13 Abraham looked up and
saw a single ram[r] caught by its horns in the
dense underbrush. Abraham went over, took
the ram, and offered it as an entirely burned
offering instead of his son. 14 Abraham named
that place "the LORD sees."[s] That is the reason
people today say, "On this mountain the LORD
is seen."[t]
15 The LORD's messenger called out to
Abraham from heaven a second time 16 and
said, "I give my word as the LORD that because you did this and didn't hold back your
son, your only son, 17 I will bless you richly
and I will give you countless descendants, as
many as the stars in the sky and as the grains
of sand on the seashore. They will conquer
their enemies' cities. 18 All the nations of the
earth will be blessed because of your descendants, because you obeyed me." 19 After Abraham returned to the young men, they got
up and went to Beer-sheba where Abraham
lived.

Abraham's nephews in Syria

20 After these events, Abraham was told:
"Milcah has now also given birth to sons for
your brother Nahor. 21 They are Uz his oldest
son, Buz his brother, Kemuel the father of
Aram, 22 Chesed, Hazo, Pildash, Jidlaph, and
Bethuel." 23 Bethuel became the father of Rebekah. These are the eight Milcah bore for
Nahor, Abraham's brother. 24 His secondary
wife's name was Reumah, and she gave birth
to Tebah, Gaham, Tahash, and Maacah.

Sarah's death and burial site

23 Sarah lived to be 127 years old; this
was how long she lived. 2 She died in

[q]*Or God will see; or God will provide* [r]LXX, Sam, Syr, Tg; MT *a ram behind* [s]*Or the* LORD *is seen; or the* LORD *provides* [t]*Or the* LORD *sees; or on the* LORD*'s mountain, it will be provided*

UMBRELLA

MOURNING

Weeping and Remembering *Genesis 23:2*

When someone we love dies, we feel really sad. We remember all the things we did together. One thing that can help in these times is sharing stories about the person you loved so much. Abraham and Sarah probably told stories about their lives to their son Isaac. They may have told him again and again how they laughed when they found out they were going to become parents at such an old age. Isaac and his wife Rebekah probably told this story to their children, who then told it to their children. Stories about Sarah were told so many times that someone eventually wrote them down, so no one would ever forget how Sarah was part of God's family. Sharing our stories reminds us that God is still with us even when we're sad. ◆

Kiriath-arba, that is, in Hebron, in the land of Canaan; and Abraham cried out in grief and wept for Sarah. ³After he got up from embracing his deceased wife, he spoke with the Hittites: ⁴"I am an immigrant and a temporary resident with you. Give me some property for a burial plot among you so that I can bury my deceased wife near me."

⁵The Hittites responded to Abraham, ⁶"Listen to us, sir. You are an eminent man of God among us. Bury your dead in one of our own select burial sites. None of us will keep our own burial plots from you to bury your dead."

⁷Abraham rose, bowed to the local citizens the Hittites, ⁸and spoke with them: "If you yourselves allow me to bury my dead near me, listen to me and ask Ephron, Zohar's son, ⁹to give me his own cave in Machpelah at the edge of his field. Let him give it to me for the full price, to be witnessed by you, as my own burial property."

¹⁰Now Ephron was a native Hittite. So Ephron the Hittite responded to Abraham publicly in order that the Hittites and everyone at his city's gate could hear: ¹¹"No, sir. Listen, I will give you the field, and I will give you the cave in it. In front of my people's witnesses, I will give it to you. Bury your dead!"

¹²Abraham bowed before the local citizens ¹³and spoke to Ephron publicly in the presence of the local citizens: "If only you would accept my offer. I will give you the price of the field. Take it from me so that I can bury my dead there."

¹⁴Ephron responded to Abraham, ¹⁵"Sir, what is four hundred shekels of silver between me and you for the land so that you can bury your dead?" ¹⁶Abraham accepted Ephron's offer and weighed out for Ephron the silver he requested publicly before the Hittites: four hundred shekels of silver at the current rate of exchange.

¹⁷So the field of Ephron in Machpelah near Mamre—the field and the cave in it, and all the trees within the field's boundaries—was officially transferred ¹⁸to Abraham as his property in the presence of the Hittites and of everyone at his city's gate. ¹⁹After this, Abraham buried his wife Sarah in the cave in the field of Machpelah near Mamre, that is, Hebron, in the land of Canaan. ²⁰The field and the cave in it were officially transferred from the Hittites to Abraham as his burial property.

Isaac marries Rebekah

24 As the days went by and Abraham became older, the LORD blessed Abraham in every way. ²Abraham said to the oldest servant of his household, who was in charge of everything he owned, "Put your hand under my thigh. ³By the LORD, God of heaven and earth, give me your word that you won't choose a wife for my son from the Canaanite women among whom I live. ⁴Go to my land and my family and find a wife for my son Isaac there."

⁵The servant said to him, "What if the woman doesn't agree to come back with me to this land? Shouldn't I take your son back to the land you left?"

⁶Abraham said to him, "Be sure you don't take my son back there. ⁷The LORD, God of heaven—who took me from my father's household and from my family's land, who spoke with me and who gave me his word, saying, 'I will give this land to your descendants'—he will send his messenger in front of you, and you will find a wife for my son there. ⁸If the woman won't agree to come back with you, you will be free from this obligation to me. Only don't take my son back

there." ⁹So the servant put his hand under his master Abraham's thigh and gave him his word about this mission.

¹⁰The servant took ten of his master's camels and all of his master's best provisions, set out, and traveled to Nahor's city in Aram-naharaim. ¹¹He had the camels kneel down outside the city at the well in the evening, when women come out to draw water. ¹²He said, "LORD, God of my master Abraham, make something good happen for me today and be loyal to my master Abraham. ¹³I will stand here by the spring while the daughters of the men of the city come out to draw water. ¹⁴When I say to a young woman, 'Hand me your water jar so I can drink,' and she says to me, 'Drink, and I will give your camels water too,' may she be the one you've selected for your servant Isaac. In this way I will know that you've been loyal to my master." ¹⁵Even before he finished speaking, Rebekah—daughter of Bethuel the son of Milcah wife of Nahor, Abraham's brother—was coming out with a water jar on her shoulder. ¹⁶The young woman was very beautiful, old enough to be married, and hadn't known a man intimately. She went down to the spring, filled her water jar, and came back up.

¹⁷The servant ran to meet her and said, "Give me a little sip of water from your jar."

¹⁸She said, "Drink, sir." Then she quickly lowered the water jar with her hands and gave him some water to drink. ¹⁹When she finished giving him a drink, she said, "I'll draw some water for your camels too, till they've had enough to drink." ²⁰She emptied her water jar quickly into the watering trough, ran to the well again to draw water, and drew water for all of the camels. ²¹The man stood gazing at her, wondering silently if the LORD had made his trip successful or not.

²²As soon as the camels had finished drinking, the man took out a gold ring, weighing a half shekel,ᵘ and two gold bracelets for her arms, weighing ten shekels. ²³He said, "Please tell me whose daughter you are. Is there room in your father's house for us to spend the night?"

²⁴She responded, "I'm the daughter of Bethuel, who is the son of Milcah and Nahor."

²⁵She continued, "We have plenty of straw and feed for the camels, and a place to spend the night."

²⁶The man bowed down and praised the LORD: ²⁷"Bless the LORD, God of my master Abraham, who hasn't given up his loyalty and his faithfulness to my master. The LORD has shown me the way to the household of my master's brother."

²⁸The young woman ran and told her mother's household everything that had happened. ²⁹Rebekah had a brother named Laban, and Laban ran to the man outside by the spring. ³⁰When he had seen the ring and the bracelets on his sister's arms, and when he had heard his sister Rebekah say, "This is what the man said to me," he went to the man, who was still standing by the spring with his camels. ³¹Laban said, "Come in, favored one of the LORD! Why are you standing outside? I've prepared the house and a place for the camels." ³²So the man entered the house. Then Laban unbridled the camels, provided straw and feed for them and water to wash his feet and the feet of the men with him, ³³and set out a meal for him.

But the man said, "I won't eat until I've said something."

Laban replied, "Say it."

³⁴The man said, "I am Abraham's servant. ³⁵The LORD has richly blessed my master, has made him a great man, and has given him flocks, cattle, silver, gold, men servants, women servants, camels, and donkeys. ³⁶My master's wife Sarah gave birth to a son for my master in her old age, and he's given him everything he owns. ³⁷My master made me give him my word: 'Don't choose a wife for my son from the Canaanite women, in whose land I'm living. ³⁸No, instead, go to my father's household and to my relatives and choose a wife for my son.' ³⁹I said to my master, 'What if the woman won't come back with me?' ⁴⁰He said to me, 'The LORD, whom I've traveled with everywhere, will send his messenger with you and make your trip successful; and you will choose a wife for my son from my relatives and from my father's household. ⁴¹If you go to my relatives, you will be free from your obligation

ᵘHeb beqa

to me. Even if they provide no one for you, you will be free from your obligation to me.'

⁴²"Today I arrived at the spring, and I said, 'LORD, God of my master Abraham, if you wish to make the trip I'm taking successful, ⁴³when I'm standing by the spring and the young woman who comes out to draw water and to whom I say, "Please give me a little drink of water from your jar," ⁴⁴and she responds to me, "Drink, and I will draw water for your camels too," may she be the woman the LORD has selected for my master's son.' ⁴⁵Before I finished saying this to myself, Rebekah came out with her water jar on her shoulder and went down to the spring to draw water. And I said to her, 'Please give me something to drink.' ⁴⁶She immediately lowered her water jar and said, 'Drink, and I will give your camels something to drink too.' So I drank and she also gave water to the camels. ⁴⁷Then I asked her, 'Whose daughter are you?' And she said, 'The daughter of Bethuel, Nahor's son whom Milcah bore him.' I put a ring in her nose and bracelets on her arms. ⁴⁸I bowed and worshipped the LORD and blessed the LORD, the God of my master Abraham, who led me in the right direction to choose the granddaughter of my master's brother for his son. ⁴⁹Now if you're loyal and faithful to my master, tell me. If not, tell me so I will know where I stand either way."

⁵⁰Laban and Bethuel both responded, "This is all the LORD's doing. We have nothing to say about it. ⁵¹Here is Rebekah, right in front of you. Take her and go. She will be the wife of your master's son, just as the LORD said." ⁵²When Abraham's servant heard what they said, he bowed low before the LORD. ⁵³The servant brought out gold and silver jewelry and clothing and gave them to Rebekah. To her brother and to her mother he gave the finest gifts. ⁵⁴He and the men with him ate and drank and spent the night.

When they got up in the morning, the servant said, "See me off to my master."

⁵⁵Her brother and mother said, "Let the young woman stay with us not more than ten days, and after that she may go."

⁵⁶But he said to them, "Don't delay me. The LORD has made my trip successful. See me off so that I can go to my master."

⁵⁷They said, "Summon the young woman, and let's ask her opinion." ⁵⁸They called Rebekah and said to her, "Will you go with this man?"

She said, "I will go."

⁵⁹So they sent off their sister Rebekah, her nurse, Abraham's servant, and his men. ⁶⁰And they blessed Rebekah, saying to her,

"May you, our sister, become
    thousands of ten thousand;
may your children possess
    their enemies' cities."

⁶¹Rebekah and her young women got up, mounted the camels, and followed the man. So the servant took Rebekah and left.

⁶²Now Isaac had come from the region of[ᵛ] Beer-lahai-roi and had settled in the arid southern plain. ⁶³One evening, Isaac went out to inspect the pasture,[ʷ] and while staring he saw camels approaching. ⁶⁴Rebekah stared at Isaac. She got down from the camel ⁶⁵and said to the servant, "Who is this man walking through the pasture to meet us?"

The servant said, "He's my master." So she took her headscarf and covered herself. ⁶⁶The servant told Isaac everything that had happened. ⁶⁷Isaac brought Rebekah into his mother Sarah's tent. He received Rebekah as his wife and loved her. So Isaac found comfort after his mother's death.

Abraham and Keturah's children

25Abraham married another wife, named Keturah. ²The children she bore him were Zimran, Jokshan, Medan, Midian, Ishbak, and Shuah. ³Jokshan became the father of Sheba and Dedan. Dedan's sons were Asshurim, Letushim, and Leummim. ⁴Midian's sons were Ephah, Epher, Enoch, Abida, and Eldaah. All of these were Keturah's sons. ⁵Abraham gave everything he owned to Isaac. ⁶To the sons of Abraham's secondary wives, Abraham gave gifts and, while he was still living, sent them away from his son Isaac to land in the east.

Abraham's death

⁷Abraham lived to the age of 175. ⁸Abraham took his last breath and died after a good long life, a content old man, and he was placed with his ancestors. ⁹His sons Isaac and Ishmael buried him in the cave in Machpelah,

---

ᵛHeb uncertain; LXX *through the desert of* ʷHeb uncertain; possibly *to walk around in the pasture* or *to meditate in the pasture*

which is in the field of Zohar's son Ephron the Hittite, near Mamre. ¹⁰Thus Abraham and his wife Sarah were both buried in the field Abraham had purchased from the Hittites. ¹¹After Abraham's death, God blessed his son Isaac, and Isaac lived in Beer-lahai-roi.

Ishmael's descendants

¹²These are the descendants of Ishmael, Abraham's son, whom Hagar the Egyptian, Sarah's servant, bore for Abraham. ¹³These are the names of Ishmael's sons, by their names and according to their birth order: Nebaioth, Ishmael's oldest son; Kedar; Adbeel; Mibsam; ¹⁴Mishma; Dumah; Massa; ¹⁵Hadad; Tema; Jetur; Naphish; and Kedemah. ¹⁶These are Ishmael's sons. These are their names by their villages and their settlements: twelve tribal leaders according to their tribes. ¹⁷Ishmael lived to the age of 137. He took his last breath and died, and was placed with his ancestors. ¹⁸He established camps˟ from Havilah to Shur, which is near Egypt on the road to Assyria. He diedʸ among all of his brothers.

did you know? In Bible times, the oldest son received most of his father's land, animals, and wealth when his father died. This was called a *birthright*. When Esau sold his birthright to his younger brother Jacob, he gave Jacob the right to receive the larger part of their father Isaac's possessions when Isaac died.

Jacob and Esau are born

¹⁹These are the descendants of Isaac, Abraham's son. Abraham became the father of Isaac. ²⁰Isaac was 40 years old when he married Rebekah the daughter of Bethuel the Aramean and the sister of Laban the Aramean, from Paddan-aram. ²¹Isaac prayed to the Lord for his wife, since she was unable to have children. The Lord was moved by his prayer, and his wife Rebekah became pregnant. ²²But the boys pushed against each other inside of her, and she said, "If this is what it's like, why did it happen to me?"ᶻ

So she went to ask the Lord. ²³And the Lord said to her,

"Two nations are in your womb;
    two different peoples will emerge
        from your body.
One people will be stronger than the other;
    the older will serve the younger."

²⁴When she reached the end of her pregnancy, she discovered that she had twins. ²⁵The first came out red all over, clothed with hair, and she named him Esau. ²⁶Immediately afterward, his brother came out gripping Esau's heel, and she named him Jacob. Isaac was 60 years old when they were born.

Jacob acquires the oldest son's rights

²⁷When the young men grew up, Esau became an outdoorsman who knew how to hunt, and Jacob became a quiet man who stayed at home. ²⁸Isaac loved Esau because he enjoyed eating game, but Rebekah loved Jacob. ²⁹Once when Jacob was boiling stew, Esau came in from the field hungry ³⁰and said to Jacob, "I'm starving! Let me devour some of this red stuff." That's why his name is Edom.ᵃ

³¹Jacob said, "Sell me your birthrightᵇ today."

³²Esau said, "Since I'm going to die anyway, what good is my birthright to me?"

³³Jacob said, "Give me your word today." And he did. He sold his birthright to Jacob. ³⁴So Jacob gave Esau bread and lentil stew. He ate, drank, got up, and left, showing just how little he thought of his birthright.

UMBRELLA
TEMPTED

A Costly Bowl of Soup *Genesis 25:29-33*
Jacob came to Esau with a delicious bowl of soup right at mealtime. The soup smelled good, and Esau was hungry. But before Jacob gave Esau the soup, he told Esau to sell him his birthright, which Esau did. Esau gave away something very important and long-lasting for the temporary joy of a full belly. There are times when it's important to practice self-control and wait for what we want. This can be hard to do, but waiting for what matters is important. It's much better than making an impulsive decision that has no lasting value. ◗

˟LXX; MT *they established camps* ʸOr *He fell* ᶻHeb uncertain ᵃOr *red* ᵇOr *oldest son's rights*

Isaac and Rebekah visit Gerar

26 When a famine gripped the land, a different one from the first famine that occurred in Abraham's time, Isaac set out toward Gerar and toward King Abimelech of the Philistines. [2]The LORD appeared to him and said, "Don't go down to Egypt but settle temporarily in the land that I will show you. [3]Stay in this land as an immigrant, and I will be with you and bless you because I will give all of these lands to you and your descendants. I will keep my word, which I gave to your father Abraham. [4]I will give you as many descendants as the stars in the sky, and I will give your descendants all of these lands. All of the nations of the earth will be blessed because of your descendants. [5]I will do this because Abraham obeyed me and kept my orders, my commandments, my statutes, and my instructions."

[6]So Isaac lived in Gerar. [7]When the men who lived there asked about his wife, he said, "She's my sister," because he was afraid to say, "my wife," thinking, The men who live there will kill me for Rebekah because she's very beautiful. [8]After Isaac had lived there for some time, the Philistines' King Abimelech looked out his window and saw Isaac laughing together with his wife Rebekah.

[9]So Abimelech summoned Isaac and said, "She's your wife, isn't she? How could you say, 'She's my sister'?"

Isaac responded, "Because I thought that I might be killed because of her."

[10]Abimelech said, "What are you trying to do to us? Before long, one of the people would have slept with your wife; and you would have made us guilty." [11]Abimelech gave orders to all of the people, "Anyone who touches this man or his wife will be put to death!"

Isaac's treaty with the Philistines

[12]Isaac planted grain in that land and reaped one hundred shearim[c] that year because the LORD had blessed him. [13]Isaac grew richer and richer until he was extremely wealthy. [14]He had livestock, both flocks and cattle, and many servants. As a result, the Philistines envied him. [15]The Philistines closed up and filled with dirt all of the wells that his father's servants had dug during his father Abraham's lifetime. [16]Abimelech said to Isaac, "Move away from us because you have become too powerful among us."

[17]So Isaac moved away from there, camped in the valley of Gerar, and lived there. [18]Isaac dug out again the wells that were dug during the lifetime of his father Abraham. The Philistines had closed them up after Abraham's death. Isaac gave them the same names his father had given them. [19]Isaac's servants dug wells in the valley and found a well there with fresh water. [20]Isaac's shepherds argued with Gerar's shepherds, each claiming, "This is our water." So Isaac named the well Esek[d] because they quarreled with him. [21]They dug another well and argued about it too, so he named it Sitnah.[e] [22]He left there and dug another well, but they didn't argue about it, so he named it Rehoboth[f] and said, "Now the LORD has made an open space for us and has made us fertile in the land."

[23]Then he went up from Gerar to Beer-sheba. [24]The LORD appeared to him that night and said, "I am the God of your father Abraham. Don't be afraid because I am with you. I will bless you, and I will give you many children for my servant Abraham's sake." [25]So Isaac built an altar there and worshipped in the LORD's name. Isaac pitched his tent there, and his servants dug a well.

[26]But Abimelech set out toward him from Gerar, with Ahuzzath his ally and Phicol the commander of his forces. [27]Isaac said to him, "Why have you come after me? You resented me and sent me away from you."

SAILBOAT

HONEST AND TRUE

Act with Honesty *Genesis 26:9-11*
Abimelech is someone who acted with wisdom and honesty. He was observant and trusted his instincts. If something didn't seem right, he found out more about the situation. Abimelech didn't hesitate to confront Isaac and took quick action to end Isaac's lies. Because Abimelech acted with honesty and courage, he saved many people from harm.

[c]An unknown measure of grain [d]Or *quarrel* [e]Or *accusation* [f]Or *open spaces*

28They said, "We now see that the LORD was with you. We propose that there be a formal agreement between us and that we draw up a treaty8 with you: 29you must not treat us badly since we haven't harmed you and since we have treated you well at all times. Then we will send you away peacefully, for you are now blessed by the LORD." 30Isaac prepared a banquet for them, and they ate and drank. 31They got up early in the morning, and they gave each other their word. Isaac sent them off, and they left peacefully.

32That day Isaac's servants informed him about the well that they had been digging and said to him, "We found water." 33He called it Shibah;h therefore, the city's name has been Beer-shebai until today.

Esau's wives

34When Esau was 40 years old, he married Judith daughter of Beeri the Hittite, and Basemath daughter of Elon the Hittite. 35They made life very difficult for Isaac and Rebekah.

Jacob acquires his father's blessing

27When Isaac had grown old and his eyesight was failing, he summoned his older son Esau and said to him, "My son?"

And Esau said, "I'm here."

2He said, "I'm old and don't know when I will die. 3So now, take your hunting gear, your bow and quiver of arrows, go out to the field, and hunt game for me. 4Make me the delicious food that I love and bring it to me so I can eat. Then I can bless you before I die."

5Rebekah was listening when Isaac spoke to his son Esau. When Esau went out to the field to hunt game to bring back, 6Rebekah said to her son Jacob, "I just heard your father saying to your brother Esau, 7'Bring me some game and make me some delicious food so I can eat, and I will bless you in the LORD's presence before I die.' 8Now, my son, listen to me, to what I'm telling you to do. 9Go to the flock and get me two healthy young goats so I can prepare them as the delicious food your father loves. 10You can bring it to your father, he will eat, and then he will bless you before he dies."

11Jacob said to his mother Rebekah, "My brother Esau is a hairy man, but I have smooth skin. 12What if my father touches me and thinks I'm making fun of him? I will be cursed instead of blessed."

13His mother said to him, "Your curse will be on me, my son. Just listen to me: go and get them for me." 14So he went and got them and brought them to his mother, and his mother made the delicious food that his father loved. 15Rebekah took her older son Esau's favorite clothes that were in the house with her, and she put them on her younger son Jacob. 16On his arms and smooth neck she put the hide of young goats, 17and the delicious food and the bread she had made she put into her son's hands.

18Jacob went to his father and said, "My father."

And he said, "I'm here. Who are you, my son?"

19Jacob said to his father, "I'm Esau your oldest son. I've made what you asked me to. Sit up and eat some of the game so you can bless me."

20Isaac said to his son, "How could you find this so quickly, my son?"

He said, "The LORD your God led me right to it."j

21Isaac said to Jacob, "Come here and let me touch you, my son. Are you my son Esau or not?" 22So Jacob approached his father Isaac, and Isaac touched him and said, "The voice is Jacob's voice, but the arms are Esau's arms." 23Isaac didn't recognize him because his arms were hairy like Esau's arms, so he blessed him.

24Isaac said, "Are you really my son Esau?"

And he said, "I am."

25Isaac said, "Bring some food here and let me eat some of my son's game so I can bless you." Jacob put it before him and he ate, and he brought him wine and he drank. 26His father Isaac said to him, "Come here and kiss me, my son." 27So he came close and kissed him. When Isaac smelled the scent of his clothes, he blessed him,

"See, the scent of my son
    is like the scent of the field
    that the LORD has blessed.
28 May God give you
    showers from the sky,

8Or covenant hOr giving one's word or seven iOr Well of giving one's word or Well of seven jOr made something good happen for me

olive oil from the earth,
plenty of grain and new wine.
29 May the nations serve you,
may peoples bow down to you.
Be the most powerful man
among your brothers,
and may your mother's sons
bow down to you.
Those who curse you will be cursed,
and those who bless you
will be blessed."

Esau receives a secondary blessing

30 After Isaac had finished blessing Jacob, and just as Jacob left his father Isaac, his brother Esau came back from his hunt. 31He too made some delicious food, brought it to his father, and said, "Let my father sit up and eat from his son's game so that you may bless me."

k Heb *ya'acob*, a wordplay on Jacob

32 His father Isaac said to him, "Who are you?" And he said, "I'm your son, your oldest son, Esau."

33Isaac was so shocked that he trembled violently. He said, "Who was the hunter just here with game? He brought me food, and I ate all of it before you came. I blessed him, and he will stay blessed!"

34When Esau heard what his father said, he let out a loud agonizing cry and wept bitterly. He said to his father, "Bless me! Me too, my father!"

35Isaac said, "Your brother has already come deceitfully and has taken your blessing."

36Esau said, "Isn't this why he's called Jacob? He's taken me[k] twice now: he took my birthright, and now he's taken my blessing." He continued, "Haven't you saved a blessing for me?"

God's Thoughts ◆ My Thoughts

God's Way Instead of Your Way   *Genesis 27:1-46*

Before Jacob and Esau were born, God told their mother Rebekah she would have twins and that the older child would serve the younger. Rebekah told her husband Isaac—and maybe even her younger son Jacob—about what God had said. Instead of trusting God and following God's way, however, everyone tried to get their own way.

In Bible times, the oldest son inherited special rights and privileges, called a birthright. Even though Esau was the older brother, he didn't care about his birthright and gave it to his younger brother Jacob for a bowl of stew. When Isaac tried to give his son Esau a special blessing, his wife Rebekah tricked her husband by having Jacob pretend to be Esau to receive the blessing instead. Jacob went along with this plan. He wasn't concerned that they lied to his father. All he wanted was Isaac's blessing.

In the end, Jacob got the birthright and his father's blessing, but at a great cost. Esau hated Jacob and threatened to kill him. Rebekah didn't trust God to protect Jacob and talked Isaac into sending Jacob away to live with her family.

When God tells us something will happen, we don't have to worry. We can trust that God's way is always better than our way.

Have you ever tried to force your own way?

Were you happy with the results? Why or why not?

37Isaac replied to Esau, "I've already made him more powerful than you, and I've made all of his brothers his servants. I've made him strong with grain and wine. What can I do for you, my son?"

38Esau said to his father, "Do you really have only one blessing, Father? Bless me too, my father!" And Esau wept loudly.

39His father Isaac responded and said to him,

"Now, you will make a home
    far away from the olive groves
    of the earth,
    far away from the showers
    of the sky above.
40You will live by your sword;
    you will serve your brother.
But when you grow restless,[1]
    you will tear away his harness
    from your neck."

Jacob sent away for protection

41Esau was furious at Jacob because his father had blessed him, and Esau said to himself, When the period of mourning for the death of my father is over, I will kill my brother.

42Rebekah was told what her older son Esau was planning, so she summoned her younger son Jacob and said to him, "Esau your brother is planning revenge. He plans to kill you. 43So now, my son, listen to me: Get up and escape to my brother Laban in Haran. 44Live with him for a short while until your brother's rage subsides, 45until your brother's anger at you goes away and he forgets what you did to him. Then I will send for you and bring you back from there. Why should I suffer the loss of both of you on one day?"

46Rebekah then said to Isaac, "I really loathe these Hittite women. If Jacob marries one of the Hittite women, like the women of this land, why should I go on living?"

28So Isaac summoned Jacob, blessed him, and gave him these orders: "Don't marry a Canaanite woman. 2Get up and go to Paddan-aram, to the household of Bethuel, your mother's father, and once there, marry one of the daughters of Laban, your mother's

brother. 3God Almighty[m] will bless you, make you fertile, and give you many descendants so that you will become a large group of peoples. 4He will give you and your descendants Abraham's blessing so that you will own the land in which you are now immigrants, the land God gave to Abraham." 5So Isaac sent Jacob off, and he traveled to Paddan-aram, to Laban son of Bethuel the Aramean and brother of Rebekah, Jacob and Esau's mother.

6Esau understood that Isaac had blessed Jacob and sent him to Paddan-aram to marry a woman from there. He recognized that, when Isaac blessed Jacob, he had ordered him, "Don't marry a Canaanite woman," 7and that Jacob had listened to his father and mother and gone to Paddan-aram. 8Esau realized that his father Isaac considered Canaanite women unacceptable. 9So he went to Ishmael and married Mahalath daughter of Abraham's son Ishmael and sister of Nebaioth, in addition to his other wives.

Jacob's dream at Bethel

10Jacob left Beer-sheba and set out for Haran. 11He reached a certain place and spent the night there. When the sun had set, he took one of the stones at that place and put it near his head. Then he lay down there. 12He dreamed and saw a raised staircase, its foundation on earth and its top touching the sky, and God's messengers were ascending and descending on it. 13Suddenly the LORD was standing on it[n] and saying, "I am the LORD, the God of your father Abraham and the God of Isaac. I will give you and your descendants the land on which you are lying. 14Your descendants will become like the dust of the earth; you will spread out to the west, east, north, and south. Every family of earth will be blessed because of you and your descendants. 15I am with you now, I will protect you everywhere you go, and I will bring you back to this land. I will not leave you until I have done everything that I have promised you."

16When Jacob woke from his sleep, he thought to himself, The LORD is definitely in this place, but I didn't know it. 17He was terrified and thought, This sacred place is awesome. It's none other than God's house and the

[1]Heb uncertain   [m]Heb El Shaddai or God of the Mountain   [n]Or beside it or beside him

entrance to heaven. [18]After Jacob got up early in the morning, he took the stone that he had put near his head, set it up as a sacred pillar, and poured oil on the top of it. [19]He named that sacred place Bethel,° though Luz was the city's original name. [20]Jacob made a solemn promise: "If God is with me and protects me on this trip I'm taking, and gives me bread to eat and clothes to wear, [21]and I return safely to my father's household, then the Lord will be my God. [22]This stone that I've set up as a sacred pillar will be God's house, and of everything you give me I will give a tenth back to you."

LIGHTHOUSE

Respect for God

This Sacred Place Is Awesome!
Genesis 28:16-22

Jacob had an amazing experience of God. One night he woke up and realized he was in a place filled with God's presence. To mark the place and experience, he set up a stone as a sacred pillar, pouring oil on top of it. That experience gave Jacob the courage and resolve to go on his way, knowing God would be with him wherever he went. ◊

Jacob meets Rachel

29Jacob got to his feet and set out for the land of the easterners. [2]He saw a well in the field in front of him, near which three flocks of sheep were lying down. That well was their source for water because the flocks drank from that well. A huge stone covered the well's opening. [3]When all of the flocks were gathered there, the shepherds would roll the stone from the well's opening, water the sheep, and return the stone to its place at the well's opening. [4]Jacob said to them, "Where are you from, my brothers?"

They said, "We're from Haran."

[5]Then he said to them, "Do you know Laban, Nahor's grandson?"

They said, "We know him."

[6]He said to them, "Is he well?"

They said, "He's fine. In fact, this is his daughter Rachel now, coming with the flock."

[7]He said to them, "It's now only the middle of the day. It's not time yet to gather the animals. Water the flock, and then go, put them out to pasture."

[8]They said to him, "We can't until all the herds are gathered, and then we^p roll the stone away from the well's opening and water the flock."

[9]While he was still talking to them, Rachel came with her father's flock since she was its shepherd. [10]When Jacob saw Rachel the daughter of Laban his uncle, and the flock of Laban, Jacob came up, rolled the stone from the well's opening, and watered the flock of his uncle Laban. [11]Jacob kissed Rachel and wept aloud. [12]Jacob told Rachel that he was related to her father and that he was Rebekah's son. She then ran to tell her father. [13]When Laban heard about Jacob his sister's son, he ran to meet him. Laban embraced him, kissed him, and invited him into his house, where Jacob recounted to Laban everything that had happened. [14]Laban said to him, "Yes, you are my flesh and blood."

Jacob marries Leah and Rachel

After Jacob had stayed with Laban for a month, [15]Laban said to Jacob, "You shouldn't have to work for free just because you are my relative. Tell me what you would like to be paid."

[16]Now Laban had two daughters: the older was named Leah and the younger Rachel. [17]Leah had delicate eyes,^{q} but Rachel had a beautiful figure and was good-looking. [18]Jacob loved Rachel and said, "I will work for you for seven years for Rachel, your younger daughter."

[19]Laban said, "I'd rather give her to you than to another man. Stay with me."

[20]Jacob worked for Rachel for seven years, but it seemed like a few days because he loved her. [21]Jacob said to Laban, "The time has come. Give me my wife so that I may sleep with her." [22]So Laban invited all the people of that place and prepared a banquet. [23]However, in the evening, he took his daughter Leah and brought her to Jacob, and he slept with her. [24]Laban had given his servant Zilpah to his daughter Leah as her servant. [25]In the morning, there she was—Leah! Jacob said to Laban,

---

°Or *God's house* ^{p}Or *they* ^{q}Heb uncertain; perhaps *Leah had poor eyesight*

"What have you done to me? Didn't I work for you to have Rachel? Why did you betray me?"

²⁶Laban said, "Where we live, we don't give the younger woman before the oldest. ²⁷Complete the celebratory week with this woman. Then I will give[r] you this other woman too for your work, if you work for me seven more years." ²⁸So that is what Jacob did. He completed the celebratory week with this woman, and then Laban gave him his daughter Rachel as his wife. ²⁹Laban had given his servant Bilhah to his daughter Rachel as her servant. ³⁰Jacob slept with Rachel, and he loved Rachel more than Leah. He worked for Laban seven more years.

Jacob's sons are born

³¹When the Lord saw that Leah was unloved, he opened her womb; but Rachel was unable to have children. ³²Leah became pregnant and gave birth to a son. She named him Reuben[s] because she said, "The Lord saw my harsh treatment, and now my husband will love me." ³³She became pregnant again and gave birth to a son. She said, "The Lord heard that I was unloved, so he gave me this son too," and she named him Simeon.[t] ³⁴She became pregnant again and gave birth to a son. She said, "Now, this time my husband will embrace me,[u] since I have given birth to three sons for him." So she named him Levi.[v] ³⁵She became pregnant again and gave birth to a son. She said, "This time I will praise the Lord." So she named him Judah.[w] Then she stopped bearing children.

30

When Rachel realized that she could bear Jacob no children, Rachel became jealous of her sister and said to Jacob, "Give me children! If you don't, I may as well be dead."

²Jacob was angry at Rachel and said, "Do you think I'm God? God alone has kept you from giving birth!"

³She said, "Here's my servant Bilhah. Sleep with her, and she will give birth for me. Because of her, I will also have children." ⁴So Rachel gave her servant Bilhah to Jacob as his wife, and he slept with her. ⁵Bilhah became pregnant and gave birth to a son for Jacob. ⁶Rachel said, "God has judged in my favor, heard my voice, and given me a son." So she named him Dan.[x] ⁷Rachel's servant Bilhah became pregnant again and gave birth to a second son for Jacob. ⁸Rachel said, "I've competed fiercely with my sister, and now I've won." So she named him Naphtali.[y]

⁹When Leah realized that she had stopped bearing children, she took her servant Zilpah and gave her to Jacob as his wife. ¹⁰Leah's servant Zilpah gave birth to a son for Jacob, ¹¹and Leah said, "What good luck!" So she named him Gad.[z] ¹²Leah's servant Zilpah gave birth to a second son for Jacob, ¹³and Leah said, "I'm happy now because women call me happy." So she named him Asher.[a]

¹⁴During the wheat harvest, Reuben found some erotic herbs[b] in the field and brought them to his mother Leah. Rachel said to Leah, "Give me your son's erotic herbs."

¹⁵Leah replied, "Isn't it enough that you've taken my husband? Now you want to take my son's erotic herbs too?"

Rachel said, "For your son's erotic herbs, Jacob[c] may sleep with you tonight."

¹⁶When Jacob came back from the field in the evening, Leah went out to meet him and said, "You must sleep with me because I've paid for you with my son's erotic herbs." So he slept with her that night.

¹⁷God responded to Leah. She became pregnant and gave birth to a fifth son for Jacob. ¹⁸Leah said, "God gave me what I paid for, what I deserved for giving my servant to my husband." So she named him Issachar.[d] ¹⁹Leah became pregnant again and gave birth to a sixth son for Jacob, ²⁰and she said, "God has given me a wonderful gift. Now my husband will honor me since I've borne him six sons." So she named him Zebulun.[e] ²¹After this, she gave birth to a daughter and named her Dinah.

²²Then God remembered Rachel, responded to her, and let her conceive. ²³She became pregnant and gave birth to a son and said, "God has taken away my shame." ²⁴She named

---

[r]LXX, Sam, Syr, Tg, Vulg; MT *we will give* [s]Or *see, a son* [t]Sounds like the Heb verb *hear* [u]Or *be connected to me* [v]Sounds like the Heb verb *embrace,* or *connect* [w]Sounds like the Heb verb *praise* [x]Or *he judged* [y]Or *my competition* or *my wrestling* [z]Or *good fortune* [a]Or *happy* [b]Or *mandrakes* [c]Or *he* [d]Or *there is payment* [e]Or *honor*

him Joseph,[f] saying to herself, May the Lord give me another son.

God blesses Jacob and Laban

[25] After Rachel gave birth to Joseph, Jacob said to Laban, "Send me off so that I can go to my own place and my own country. [26] Give me my wives and children whom I've worked for, and I will go. You know the work I've done for you."

[27] Laban said to him, "Do me this favor. I've discovered by a divine sign that the Lord has blessed me because of you, [28] so name your price and I will pay it."

[29] Jacob said to him, "You know how I've worked for you, and how well your livestock have done with me. [30] While in my care, what little you had has multiplied a great deal. The Lord blessed you wherever I took your livestock.[g] Now, when will I be able to work for my own household too?"

[31] Laban said, "What will I pay you?"

Jacob said, "Don't pay me anything. If you will do this for me, I will take care of your flock again, and keep a portion.[h] [32] I will go through the entire flock today, taking out all of the speckled and spotted sheep, all of the black male lambs, and all of the spotted and speckled female goats. That will be my price. [33] I will be completely honest with you: when you come to check on our agreement, every female goat with me that isn't speckled or spotted and every male lamb with me that isn't black will be considered stolen."

[34] Laban said, "All right; let's do it." [35] However, on that very day Laban took out the striped and spotted male goats and all of the speckled and spotted female goats—any with some white in it—and all of the black male lambs, and gave them to his sons. [36] He put a three-day trip between himself and Jacob, while Jacob was watching the rest of Laban's flock.

[37] Then Jacob took new branches from poplar, almond, and plane trees; and he peeled white stripes on them, exposing the branches' white color. [38] He set the branches that he had peeled near the watering troughs so that they were in front of the flock when they drank,

because they often mated when they came to drink. [39] When the flock mated in front of the branches, they gave birth to striped, speckled, and spotted young. [40] Jacob sorted out the lambs, turning the flock to face the striped and black ones in Laban's flock but keeping his flock separate, setting them apart from Laban's flock. [41] Whenever the strongest of the flock mated, Jacob put the branches in front of them near the watering troughs so that they mated near the branches. [42] But he didn't put branches up for the weakest of the flock. So the weakest became Laban's and the strongest Jacob's. [43] The man Jacob became very, very rich: he owned large flocks, female and male servants, camels, and donkeys.

LIFE PRESERVER

How was Jacob able to have more than one wife?
Genesis 30

When you read about Jacob and his wives Leah, Rachel, Zilpah, and Bilhah, you may wonder why he had so many of them. Jacob met and fell in love with Rachel first, but her father made him work seven years before he could marry her. Then he tricked Jacob into marrying Leah instead. Jacob had to work seven more years before he could marry Rachel.

Being married to more than one woman might sound very strange today, because women are now equal to men. But in Jacob's time a family's survival depended on having many children to help with the work. They also didn't have medicine and doctors like we do, so not all babies lived to become adults. It was common and accepted in that culture for a man to have several wives.

When Rachel had no children, she felt a sense of failure. In that culture, one way Rachel could be respected as a woman was to allow her servant to become another one of Jacob's wives so that they could have children. Any children Rachel's servant had would be Jacob's children and hers as well.

Fortunately, Rachel's story had a happy ending. She finally had a son, whom she named Joseph. More important, all the sons born to Jacob and his wives were important to the future of the Israelites. Each of his twelve sons became an ancestor of a tribe of Israel. ◊

---

[f]Or he adds [g]Or them [h]Heb uncertain

Jacob's household leaves Laban

31 Jacob heard that Laban's sons were saying, "Jacob took everything our father owned and from it he produced all of this wealth." ²And Jacob saw that Laban no longer liked him as much as he used to.

³Then the LORD said to Jacob, "Go back to the land of your ancestors and to your relatives, and I will be with you."

⁴So Jacob sent for Rachel and Leah and summoned them into the field where his flock was. ⁵He said to them, "I am aware that your father no longer likes me as much as he used to. But my father's God has been with me. ⁶You know that I've worked for your father as hard as I could. ⁷But your father cheated me and changed my payment ten times. Yet God didn't let him harm me. ⁸If he said, 'The speckled ones will be your payment,' the whole flock gave birth to speckled young. And if he said, 'The striped ones will be your payment,' the whole flock gave birth to striped young. ⁹God took away your father's livestock and gave them to me. ¹⁰When the flocks were mating, I looked up and saw in a dream that the male goats that mounted the flock were striped, speckled, and spotted. ¹¹In the dream, God's messenger said to me, 'Jacob!' and I said, 'I'm here.' ¹²He said, 'Look up and watch all the striped, speckled, and spotted male goats mounting the flock. I've seen everything that Laban is doing to you. ¹³I am the God of Bethel, where you anointed a sacred pillar and where you made a solemn promise to me. Now, get up and leave this country and go back to the land of your relatives.'"

¹⁴Rachel and Leah answered him, "Is there any share or inheritance left for us in our father's household? ¹⁵Doesn't he think of us as foreigners since he sold us and has even used up the payment he received for us? ¹⁶All of the wealth God took from our father belongs to us and our children. Now, do everything God told you to do."

¹⁷So Jacob got up, put his sons and wives on the camels, ¹⁸and set out with all of his livestock and all of his possessions that he had acquired[i] in Paddan-aram in order to return to his father Isaac in the land of Canaan. ¹⁹Now, while Laban was out shearing his sheep, Rachel stole the household's divine images that belonged to her father. ²⁰Moreover, Jacob deceived Laban the Aramean by not sending word to him that he was leaving. ²¹So Jacob and his entire household left. He got up, crossed the river, and set out directly for the mountains of Gilead.

²²Three days later, Laban found out that Jacob had gone, ²³so Laban took his brothers with him, chased Jacob for seven days, and caught up with him in the mountains of Gilead. ²⁴That night, God appeared to Laban the Aramean in a dream and said, "Be careful and don't say anything hastily to Jacob one way or the other."

²⁵Laban reached Jacob after Jacob had pitched his tent in the mountains. So Laban and his brothers also pitched theirs in the mountains of Gilead. ²⁶Laban said to Jacob, "What have you done? You have deceived me and taken off with my daughters as if they were prisoners of war. ²⁷Why did you leave secretly, deceiving me, and not letting me know? I would've sent you off with a celebration, with songs and tambourines and harps. ²⁸You didn't even let me kiss my sons and my daughters good-bye. Now you've acted like a fool, ²⁹and I have the power to punish you. However, your father's God told me yesterday, 'Be careful and don't say anything hastily to Jacob one way or the other.' ³⁰You've rushed off now because you missed your father's household so much, but why did you steal my gods?"

³¹Jacob responded to Laban, "I was afraid and convinced myself that you would take your daughters away from me. ³²Whomever you find with your divine images won't live. Identify whatever I have that is yours, in front of your brothers, and take it." Jacob didn't know that Rachel had stolen them. ³³Laban went into Jacob's tent, Leah's tent, and her two servants' tent and didn't find them.

So he left Leah's tent and went into Rachel's. ³⁴Now Rachel had taken the divine images and put them into the camel's saddlebag and sat on them. Laban felt around in the whole tent but couldn't find them. ³⁵Rachel said to her father, "Sir, don't be angry with me because I can't get up for you; I'm having

---

ⁱLXX; MT includes *he had acquired, the livestock in his possession.*

my period." He searched but couldn't find the
divine images.
36 Jacob was angry and complained to
Laban, "What have I done wrong and what's
my crime that you've tracked me down like
this? 37 You've now felt through all of my baggage, and what have you found from your
household's belongings? Put it in front of our
relatives, and let them decide between us.
38 For these twenty years I've been with you,
your female sheep and goats haven't miscarried, and I haven't eaten your flock's rams.
39 When animals were killed, I didn't bring
them to you but took the loss myself. You demanded compensation from me for any animals poached during the day or night. 40 The
dry heat consumed me during the day, and the
frost at night; I couldn't sleep. 41 I've now spent
twenty years in your household. I worked for
fourteen years for your two daughters and
for six years for your flock, and you changed
my pay ten times. 42 If the God of my father—
the God of Abraham and the awesome one
of Isaac—hadn't been with me, you'd have no
doubt sent me away without anything. God
saw my harsh treatment and my hard work
and reprimanded you yesterday."

Jacob and Laban's treaty

43 Laban responded and told Jacob, "The
daughters are my daughters, the children
are my children, and the flocks are my flocks.
Everything you see is mine. But what can I
do now about my daughters and about their
sons? 44 Come, let's make a treaty, you and me,
and let something be our witness."[j]
45 So Jacob took a stone, set it up as a sacred pillar, 46 and said to his relatives, "Gather
stones." So they took stones, made a mound,
and ate there near the mound. 47 Laban called
it Jegar-sahadutha,[k] but Jacob called it Galeed.[l]
48 Laban said, "This mound is our witness
today," and, therefore, he too named it Galeed. 49 He also named it Mizpah,[m] because he
said, "The LORD will observe both of us when
we are separated from each other. 50 If you
treat my daughters badly and if you marry
other women, though we aren't there, know
that God observed our witness."
51 Laban said to Jacob, "Here is this mound
and here is the sacred pillar that I've set up
for us. 52 This mound and the sacred pillar
are witnesses that I won't travel beyond this
mound and that you won't travel beyond this
mound and this pillar to do harm. 53 The God
of Abraham and the God of Nahor[n] will keep
order between us." So Jacob gave his word in
the name of the awesome one of his father
Isaac. 54 Jacob offered a sacrifice on the
mountain, and invited his relatives to a meal.
They ate together and spent the night on the
mountain. 55[o] Laban got up early in the morning, kissed his sons and daughters, blessed
them, and left to go back to his own place.

Jacob prepares to meet Esau

32 Jacob went on his way, and God's messengers approached him. 2 When Jacob
saw them, he said, "This is God's camp," and he
named that sacred place Mahanaim.[p] 3 Jacob
sent messengers ahead of him to his brother
Esau, toward the land of Seir, the open country of Edom. 4 He gave them these orders: "Say
this to my master Esau. This is the message of
your servant Jacob: 'I've lived as an immigrant
with Laban, where I've stayed till now. 5 I own
cattle, donkeys, flocks, men servants, and
women servants. I'm sending this message to
my master now to ask that he[q] be kind.'"
6 The messengers returned to Jacob and said,
"We went out to your brother Esau, and he's
coming to meet you with four hundred men."
7 Jacob was terrified and felt trapped,
so he divided the people with him, and the
flocks, cattle, and camels, into two camps. 8 He
thought, If Esau meets the first camp and attacks it, at least one camp will be left to escape.
9 Jacob said, "LORD, God of my father Abraham, God of my father Isaac, who said to me, 'Go
back to your country and your relatives, and
I'll make sure things go well for you,' 10 I don't
deserve how loyal and truthful you've been to
your servant. I went away across the Jordan
with just my staff, but now I've become two
camps. 11 Save me from my brother Esau! I'm
afraid he will come and kill me, the mothers,
and their children. 12 You were the one who
told me, 'I will make sure things go well for

[j] Or *covenant* or *testimony* [k] Or *mound of witness* (Aram) [l] Or *mound of witness* [m] Or *observation* [n] LXX; MT includes *their father's God.* [o] 32:1 in Heb [p] Or *two camps* [q] Or *you*

you, and I will make your descendants like the sand of the sea, so many you won't be able to count them.'"

¹³Jacob spent that night there. From what he had acquired, he set aside a gift for his brother Esau: ¹⁴two hundred female goats and twenty male goats, two hundred ewes

and twenty rams, ¹⁵thirty nursing camels with their young, forty cows and ten bulls, and twenty female donkeys and ten male donkeys. ¹⁶He separated these herds and gave them to his servants. He said to them, "Go ahead of me and put some distance between each of the herds." ¹⁷He ordered the first group, "When my brother Esau meets you and asks you, 'Who are you with? Where are you going? And whose herds are these in front of you?' ¹⁸say, 'They are your servant Jacob's, a gift sent to my master Esau. And Jacob is actually right behind us.'" ¹⁹He also ordered the second group, the third group, and everybody following the herds, "Say exactly the same thing to Esau when you find him. ²⁰Say also, 'Your servant Jacob is right behind us.'" Jacob thought, I may be able to pacify Esau with the gift I'm sending ahead. When I meet him, perhaps he will be kind to me. ²¹So Jacob sent the gift ahead of him, but he spent that night in the camp.

Jacob wrestles with God

²²Jacob got up during the night, took his two wives, his two women servants, and his eleven sons, and crossed the Jabbok River's shallow water. ²³He took them and everything that belonged to him, and he helped them cross the river. ²⁴But Jacob stayed apart by himself, and a man wrestled with him until dawn broke. ²⁵When the man saw that he couldn't defeat Jacob, he grabbed Jacob's thigh and tore a muscle in Jacob's thigh as he wrestled with him. ²⁶The man said, "Let me go because the dawn is breaking."

But Jacob said, "I won't let you go until you bless me."

²⁷He said to Jacob, "What's your name?" and he said, "Jacob." ²⁸Then he said, "Your name won't be Jacob any longer, but Israel,^r because you struggled with God and with men and won."

²⁹Jacob also asked and said, "Tell me your name."

But he said, "Why do you ask for my name?" and he blessed Jacob there. ³⁰Jacob named the place Peniel,^s "because I've seen God face-to-face, and my life has been saved." ³¹The sun rose as Jacob passed Penuel, limping because of his thigh. ³²Therefore, Israelites don't eat the tendon attached to the thigh muscle to this day, because he grabbed Jacob's thigh muscle at the tendon.

Esau forgives Jacob

33 Jacob looked up and saw Esau approaching with four hundred men. Jacob divided the children among Leah, Rachel, and the two women servants. ²He put the servants and their children first, Leah and her children after them, and Rachel and Joseph last. ³He himself went in front of them and bowed to the ground seven times as he was approaching his brother. ⁴But Esau ran to meet him, threw his arms around his neck, kissed him, and they wept. ⁵Esau looked up and saw the women and children and said, "Who are these with you?"

Jacob said, "The children that God generously gave your servant." ⁶The women

LIFE PRESERVER

Who was Jacob wrestling?
Genesis 32:22-32

Jacob was traveling with his family to meet his brother Esau when he met a man one night and wrestled with him. Jacob was winning until the man tore one of Jacob's muscles. That's when he realized he was wrestling with God and asked for a blessing. The blessing gave Jacob was a new name, Israel. Jacob knew he hadn't been wrestling a stranger but had actually seen God face-to-face.

^rOr God struggles or one who struggles with God ^sOr face of God

servants and their children came forward and bowed down. [7]Then Leah and her servants also came forward and bowed, and afterward Joseph and Rachel came forward and bowed.

[8]Esau said, "What's the meaning of this entire group of animals that I met?"

Jacob said, "To ask for my master's kindness."

[9]Esau said, "I already have plenty, my brother. Keep what's yours."

[10]Jacob said, "No, please, do me the kindness of accepting my gift. Seeing your face is like seeing God's face, since you've accepted me so warmly. [11]Take this present that I've brought because God has been generous to me, and I have everything I need." So Jacob persuaded him, and he took it.

SAILBOAT

FORGIVENESS

Unexpected Joy *Genesis 33:4, 11*
Jacob expected to be killed for the ways in which he had wronged his brother Esau. Instead, Esau ran to meet Jacob and gave him a big hug. If you've ever expected to be punished for something you did wrong but were forgiven instead, you know how Jacob must have felt. Being welcomed with forgiveness when we expect anger or punishment is an unexpected joy. Forgiveness is an amazing gift both to offer and to receive. ◆

[12]Esau said, "Let's break camp and set out, and I'll go with you."

[13]But Jacob said to him, "My master knows that the children aren't strong and that I am responsible for the nursing flocks and cattle. If I push them hard for even one day, all of the flocks will die. [14]My master, go on ahead of your servant, but I've got to take it easy, going only as fast as the animals in front of me and the children are able to go, until I meet you in Seir."

[15]Esau said, "Let me leave some of my people with you."

But Jacob said, "Why should you do this since my master has already been so kind to me?" [16]That day Esau returned on the road to Seir, [17]but Jacob traveled to Succoth. He built

a house for himself but made temporary shelters for his animals; therefore, he named the place Succoth.[t]

Dinah and the conflict at Shechem

[18]Jacob arrived safely at the city of Shechem in the land of Canaan on his trip from Paddan-aram, and he camped in front of the city. [19]He bought the section of the field where he pitched his tent from the sons of Hamor, Shechem's father, for one hundred qesitahs.[u] [20]Then he set up an altar there and named it El Elohe Israel.[v]

34 Dinah, the daughter whom Leah had borne to Jacob, went out to meet the women of that country. [2]When Shechem the son of the Hivite Hamor and the country's prince saw her, he took her, slept with her, and humiliated her. [3]He was drawn to Dinah, Jacob's daughter. He loved the young woman and tried to win her heart. [4]Shechem said to his father Hamor, "Get this girl for me as my wife." [5]Now Jacob heard that Shechem defiled his daughter Dinah; but his sons were with the animals in the countryside, so he decided to keep quiet until they got back. [6]Meanwhile, Hamor, Shechem's father, went out to Jacob to speak with him. [7]Just then, Jacob's sons got back from the countryside. When they heard what had happened, they were deeply offended and very angry, because Shechem had disgraced Israel by sleeping with Jacob's daughter. Such things are simply not done.

[8]Hamor said to them, "My son Shechem's heart is set on your daughter. Please let him marry her. [9]Arrange marriages with us: give us your daughters and take our daughters for yourselves. [10]Live with us. The land is available to you: settle down, travel through it, and buy property in it."

[11]Shechem said to Dinah's father and brothers, "If you approve of me, tell me what you want, and I will give it to you. [12]Make the bride price and marriage gifts as large as you like, and I will pay whatever you tell me. Then let me marry the young woman."

[13]Jacob's sons responded deviously to Shechem and his father Hamor because Shechem defiled their sister Dinah. [14]They

[t]Or *temporary shelters* [u]A monetary weight [v]Or *El, God of Israel*

LIFE PRESERVER

Dinah, Jacob's daughter, is hurt *Genesis 34*

In a very violent story, Jacob's only daughter Dinah was attacked by a man who wanted to marry her. This behavior is just as hard to hear about and understand in the Bible as it is when violent acts happen to people today. It's important to understand that the same questions and emotions we have when bad things happen were also present in Bible times. And just as we would today, people close to Dinah wanted revenge. However, Jacob didn't believe violence would resolve conflict, so he didn't allow his sons, Simeon and Levi, to inherit his estate because he knew they had violently attacked the man who hurt their sister.

The world Dinah lived in was dominated by men. Fathers, brothers, or husbands were responsible for the care of wives, daughters, and sisters. All we hear in this story is a description of what happened and the response of Dinah's family. We're left to wonder what this woman thought and how she reacted to this situation. But we can be sure she experienced emotions as varied and deep as our own. ⬧

---

said to them, "We can't do this, allowing our sisters to marry uncircumcised men, because it's disgraceful to us. ¹⁵We can only agree to do this if you circumcise every male as we do. ¹⁶Then we will give our daughters to you, and we will take your daughters for ourselves. We will live with you and be one people. ¹⁷But if you don't listen to us and become circumcised, we will take our daughter and leave."

¹⁸Their idea seemed like a good one to Hamor and Hamor's son Shechem. ¹⁹The young man didn't waste any time doing this because he liked Jacob's daughter so much. He was more respected than anyone else in his father's household. ²⁰Hamor and his son Shechem went to their city's gate and spoke to the men of their city: ²¹"These men want peace with us. Let them live in the land and travel through it; there's plenty of land for them. We will marry their daughters and give them our daughters. ²²But the men will agree to live with us and become one people only if we circumcise every male just as they do. ²³Their livestock, their property, and all of their animals—won't they be ours? Let's agree with them and let them live with

us." ²⁴Everyone at the city gate agreed with Hamor and his son Shechem, so every able-bodied male in the city was circumcised.

²⁵On the third day, when they were still in pain, two of Jacob's sons and Dinah's brothers Simeon and Levi took their swords, came into the city, which suspected nothing, and killed every male. ²⁶They killed Hamor and his son Shechem with their swords, took Dinah from Shechem's household, and left. ²⁷When Jacob's other sons discovered the dead, they looted the city that had defiled their sister. ²⁸They took their flocks, their cattle, and their donkeys, whether in the city or in the fields nearby. ²⁹They carried off their property, their children, and their wives. They looted the entire place. ³⁰Jacob said to Simeon and Levi, "You've put me in danger by making me offensive to those who live here in the land, to the Canaanites and the Perizzites. I have only a few men. They may join forces, attack me, and destroy me, me and my household."

³¹They said, "But didn't he treat our sister like a prostitute?"

Jacob establishes worship at Bethel

35 God said to Jacob, "Get up, go to Bethel, and live there. Build an altar there to the God who appeared to you when you ran away from your brother Esau."

²Jacob said to his household and to everyone who was with him, "Get rid of the foreign gods you have with you. Clean yourselves and change your clothes. ³Then let's rise and go up to Bethel so that I can build an altar there to the God who answered me when I was in trouble and

SAILBOAT

OBEDIENCE

New Purpose *Genesis 35:1-7*

God told Jacob to go to Bethel, live there, and build an altar. Jacob did what God asked. With a renewed sense of purpose he did everything he could to be obedient to God, who had done so much for him. Not only did Jacob become more obedient to God, he also made sure everyone in his household did the same. In the past Jacob had been full of tricks and cheating, but in this story he was ready to live in obedience to God and follow God's commands. ⬧

who has been with me wherever I've gone." [4]So they gave Jacob all of the foreign gods they had, as well as the rings in their ears, and Jacob buried them under the terebinth at Shechem. [5]When they set out, God made all of the surrounding cities fearful so that they didn't pursue Jacob's sons. [6]Jacob and all of the people with him arrived in Luz, otherwise known as Bethel, in the land of Canaan. [7]He built an altar there and named the place El-bethel,[w] because God had revealed himself to him there when he ran away from his brother. [8]Rebekah's nurse Deborah died and was buried at Bethel under the oak, and Jacob named it Allon-bacuth.[x]

did you know? Jacob, also called Israel, had twelve sons who became the foundation of the twelve tribes of Israel. Ishmael, Jacob's uncle and Abraham's oldest son, also had twelve sons. Jesus had twelve disciples. In Bible times, the number twelve meant that something was complete.

[9]God appeared to Jacob again, while he was on his way back from Paddan-aram, and blessed him. [10]God said to him, "Your name is Jacob, but your name will be Jacob no longer. No, your name will be Israel." And he named him Israel. [11]God said to him, "I am El Shaddai.[y] Be fertile and multiply. A nation, even a large group of nations, will come from you; kings will descend from your own children. [12]The land I gave to Abraham and to Isaac, I give to you; and I will give the land to your descendants after you." [13]Then God ascended, leaving him alone in the place where he spoke to him. [14]So Jacob set up a sacred pillar, a stone pillar, at the place God spoke to him. He poured an offering of wine on it and then poured oil over it. [15]Jacob named the place Bethel where God spoke to him.

Benjamin's birth and Rachel's death

[16]They left Bethel, and when they were still some distance from Ephrath, Rachel went into hard labor. [17]During her difficult labor, the midwife said to her, "Don't be afraid. You have another son." [18]As her life faded away,

just before she died, she named him Ben-oni,[z] but his father named him Benjamin.[a] [19]Rachel died and was buried near the road to Ephrath, that is, Bethlehem. [20]Jacob set up a pillar on her grave. It's the pillar on Rachel's tomb that's still there today. [21]Israel continued his trip and pitched his tent farther on near the tower of Eder.

Jacob's family

[22]While Israel stayed in that place, Reuben went and slept with Bilhah his father's secondary wife, and Israel heard about it.

Jacob had twelve sons. [23]The sons of Leah were Reuben, Jacob's oldest son, and Simeon, Levi, Judah, Issachar, and Zebulun. [24]The sons of Rachel were Joseph and Benjamin. [25]The sons of Bilhah, Rachel's servant, were Dan and Naphtali. [26]The sons of Zilpah, Leah's servant, were Gad and Asher. These were Jacob's sons born to him in Paddan-aram.

Isaac's death

[27]Jacob came to his father Isaac at Mamre, that is, Kiriath-arba. This is Hebron, where Abraham and Isaac lived as immigrants. [28]At the age of 180 years, [29]Isaac took his last breath and died. He was buried with his ancestors after a long, satisfying life. His sons Esau and Jacob buried him.

Esau's descendants

36These are the descendants of Esau, that is, Edom. [2]Esau married Canaanite women: Adah the daughter of the Hittite Elon; Oholibamah the daughter of Anah son of the Hittite Zibeon,[b] [3]and Basemath the daughter of Ishmael and sister of Nebaioth. [4]Adah gave birth to Eliphaz for Esau, Basemath gave birth to Reuel, [5]and Oholibamah gave birth to Jeush, Jalam, and Korah. These are Esau's sons born to him in the land of Canaan.

[6]Esau took his wives, his sons, his daughters, and everyone in his household, and his livestock, all of his animals, and all of the property he had acquired in the land of Canaan; and he moved away from the land of Canaan[c] and from his brother Jacob. [7]They had so many possessions that they couldn't

[w]Or *God of Bethel* [x]Or *oak of weeping* [y]Or *God Almighty* or *God of the Mountain* [z]Or *my suffering son* [a]Or *right-hand son* or *strong son* [b]LXX, Sam, Syr; MT *daughter* [c]LXX, Sam; MT *to a land*

live together. The land where they lived as immigrants couldn't support all of their livestock. [8]So Esau, that is, Edom, lived in the mountains of Seir.

[9]These are the descendants of Esau, the ancestor of Edom, which lies in the mountains of Seir. [10]These are the names of Edom's sons: Eliphaz son of Esau's wife Adah, and Reuel son of Esau's wife Basemath. [11]Eliphaz's sons were Teman, Omar, Zepho, Gatam, and Kenaz. [12]Timna was the secondary wife of Eliphaz, Esau's son, and she gave birth to Amalek for Eliphaz. These are the sons of Esau's wife Adah. [13]These are Reuel's sons: Nahath, Zerah, Shammah, and Mizzah. These are the sons of Esau's wife Basemath. [14]These are the sons of Esau's wife Oholibamah, the daughter of Anah, Zibeon's son:[d] she gave birth to Esau, Jeush, Jalam, and Korah.

[15]These are the tribal chiefs from Esau's sons. The sons of Eliphaz, Esau's oldest son: Chief Teman, Chief Omar, Chief Zepho, Chief Kenaz, [16]Chief Korah, Chief Gatam, and Chief Amalek. These are the tribal chiefs of Eliphaz in the land of Edom; they are Adah's sons. [17]These are the sons of Reuel, Esau's son: Chief Nahath, Chief Zerah, Chief Shammah, and Chief Mizzah. These are the tribal chiefs of Reuel in the land of Edom; they are the sons of Esau's wife Basemath. [18]These are the sons of Esau's wife Oholibamah: Chief Jeush, Chief Jalam, and Chief Korah. They are the tribal chiefs of Esau's wife Oholibamah the daughter of Anah. [19]These are the sons of Esau, who is Edom, and these are their tribal chiefs.

[20]These are the sons of Seir, the Horite, who live in the land: Lotan, Shobal, Zibeon, Anah, [21]Dishon, Ezer, and Dishan. These are the Horite tribal chiefs, Seir's sons, in the land of Edom. [22]Lotan's sons are Hori and Heman, and Lotan's sister was Timna. [23]These are Shobal's sons: Alvan, Manahath, Ebal, Shepho, and Onam. [24]These are Zibeon's sons: Aiah and Anah. Anah is the one who found water[e] in the desert while pasturing his father Zibeon's donkeys. [25]These are Anah's children: Dishon and Anah's daughter Oholibamah. [26]These are Dishon's[f] sons: Hemdan, Eshban, Ithran, and Cheran. [27]These are Ezer's sons: Bilhan, Zaavan, and Akan. [28]These are Dishan's sons: Uz and Aran. [29]These are the Horite tribal chiefs: Chiefs Lotan, Shobal, Zibeon, Anah, [30]Dishon, Ezer, and Dishan. These are the Horite tribal chiefs, listed according to their chiefs in the land of Seir.

[31]These are the kings who ruled in the land of Edom before a king ruled over the Israelites. [32]Bela, Beor's son, ruled in Edom; his city's name was Dinhabah. [33]After Bela died, Jobab son of Zerah from Bozrah became king. [34]After Jobab died, Husham from the land of the Temanites became king. [35]After Husham died, Hadad, Bedad's son who defeated Midian in the countryside of Moab, became king; his city's name was Avith. [36]After Hadad died, Samlah from Masrekah became king. [37]After Samlah died, Shaul from Rehoboth on the river became king. [38]After Shaul died, Baal-hanan, Achbor's son, became king. [39]After Baal-hanan, Achbor's son, died, Hadar became king; his city's name was Pau and his wife's name was Mehetabel the daughter of Matred and granddaughter of Me-zahab.

[40]These are the names of Esau's tribal chiefs according to their families, their locations, and their names: Chief Timna, Chief Alvah, Chief Jetheth, [41]Chief Oholibamah, Chief Elah, Chief Pinon, [42]Chief Kenaz, Chief Teman, Chief Mibzar, [43]Chief Magdiel, and Chief Iram. These are Edom's tribal chiefs according to their settlements in the land they possessed. This is Esau, the ancestor of the Edomites.

Joseph dreams of power

37 Jacob lived in the land of Canaan where his father was an immigrant. [2]This is the account of Jacob's descendants. Joseph was 17 years old and tended the flock with his brothers. While he was helping the sons of Bilhah and Zilpah, his father's wives, Joseph told their father unflattering things about them. [3]Now Israel loved Joseph more

[d]LXX, Sam, Syr; MT *daughter* [e]Syr; Heb uncertain [f]Sam, Syr; MT *Dishan's*

than any of his other sons because he was born when Jacob was old. Jacob had made for him a long[g] robe. [4]When his brothers saw that their father loved him more than any of his brothers, they hated him and couldn't even talk nicely to him.

[5]Joseph had a dream and told it to his brothers, which made them hate him even more. [6]He said to them, "Listen to this dream I had. [7]When we were binding stalks of grain in the field, my stalk got up and stood upright, while your stalks gathered around it and bowed down to my stalk."

[8]His brothers said to him, "Will you really be our king and rule over us?" So they hated him even more because of the dreams he told them.

[9]Then Joseph had another dream and described it to his brothers: "I've just dreamed again, and this time the sun and the moon and eleven stars were bowing down to me."

[10]When he described it to his father and brothers, his father scolded him and said to him, "What kind of dreams have you dreamed? Am I and your mother and your brothers supposed to come and bow down to the ground in front of you?" [11]His brothers were jealous of him, but his father took careful note of the matter.

Joseph's brothers take revenge

[12]Joseph's brothers went to tend their father's flocks near Shechem. [13]Israel said to Joseph, "Aren't your brothers tending the sheep near Shechem? Come, I'll send you to them."

And he said, "I'm ready."

[14]Jacob said to him, "Go! Find out how your brothers are and how the flock is, and report back to me."

So Jacob sent him from the Hebron Valley. When he approached Shechem, [15]a man found him wandering in the field and asked him, "What are you looking for?"

[16]Joseph said, "I'm looking for my brothers. Tell me, where are they tending the sheep?"

[17]The man said, "They left here. I heard them saying, 'Let's go to Dothan.'" So Joseph went after his brothers and found them in Dothan.

[18]They saw Joseph in the distance before he got close to them, and they plotted to kill him. [19]The brothers said to each other, "Here comes the big dreamer. [20]Come on now, let's kill him and throw him into one of the cisterns, and we'll say a wild animal devoured him. Then we will see what becomes of his dreams!"

[21]When Reuben heard what they said, he saved him from them, telling them, "Let's not take his life." [22]Reuben said to them, "Don't spill his blood! Throw him into this desert cistern, but don't lay a hand on him." He intended to save Joseph from them and take him back to his father.

did you know? Dreams are a big part of Joseph's story. In Joseph's time, people believed dreams showed people truths about themselves or their world. When Joseph's brothers heard his dreams, they were jealous and angry that Joseph thought he would rule over them, so they sold him as a slave.

[23]When Joseph reached his brothers, they stripped off Joseph's long robe, [24]took him, and threw him into the cistern, an empty cistern with no water in it. [25]When they sat down to eat, they looked up and saw a caravan of Ishmaelites coming from Gilead, with camels carrying sweet resin, medicinal resin, and fragrant resin on their way down to Egypt. [26]Judah said to his brothers, "What do we gain if we kill our brother and hide his blood? [27]Come on, let's sell him to the Ishmaelites. Let's not harm him because he's our brother; he's family." His brothers agreed. [28]When some Midianite traders passed by, they pulled Joseph up out of the cistern. They sold him to the Ishmaelites for twenty pieces of silver, and they brought Joseph to Egypt.

[29]When Reuben returned to the cistern and found that Joseph wasn't in it, he tore his clothes. [30]Then he returned to his brothers and said, "The boy's gone! And I—where can I go now?"

[31]His brothers took Joseph's robe, slaughtered a male goat, and dipped the robe in the blood. [32]They took the long robe, brought it to their father, and said, "We found this. See if it's your son's robe or not."

---

[g]LXX many-colored

³³He recognized it and said, "It's my son's robe! A wild animal has devoured him. Joseph must have been torn to pieces!" ³⁴Then Jacob tore his clothes, put a simple mourning cloth around his waist, and mourned for his son for many days. ³⁵All of his sons and daughters got up to comfort him, but he refused to be comforted, telling them, "I'll go to my grave mourning for my son." And Joseph's father wept for him. ³⁶Meanwhile the Midianites had sold Joseph to the Egyptians, to Potiphar, Pharaoh's chief officer, commander of the royal guard.

Tamar's place in Judah's family

38 At that time, Judah moved away from his brothers and settled near an Adullamite named Hirah. ²There Judah saw the daughter of a Canaanite whose name was Shua, and he married her. After he slept with her, ³she became pregnant and gave birth to a son, whom sheʰ named Er. ⁴She became

pregnant again, gave birth to a son, and named him Onan. ⁵Then she gave birth to one more son and named him Shelah. She was in Chezib when she gave birth to him.

⁶Judah married his oldest son Er to a woman named Tamar. ⁷But the LORD considered Judah's oldest son Er immoral, and the LORD put him to death. ⁸Judah said to Onan, "Go to your brother's wife, do your duty as her brother-in-law, and provide children for your brother." ⁹Onan knew the children wouldn't be his so when he slept with his brother's wife, he wasted his semen on the ground, so he wouldn't give his brother children. ¹⁰The LORD considered what he did as wrong and put him to death too. ¹¹Judah said to Tamar his daughter-in-law, "Stay as a widow in your father's household until my son Shelah grows up." He thought Shelah would die like his brothers had. So Tamar went and lived in her father's household.

ʰSam, Tg; MT *he*

The Terrible Power of Jealousy *Genesis 37:1-36*

It's not always easy to get along with others. Sometimes it's even hard to get along with people who are close to us, like family or friends.

It was difficult for Joseph and his brothers. Joseph's brothers knew their father Jacob loved Joseph more than he loved them. This made the brothers feel jealous and angry. They wanted the things Joseph had. They hated Joseph so much that they wanted to kill him. In the end, they decided to sell him into slavery and tell their father that Joseph was dead. But instead of making things better at home, the brothers' jealousy tore their family apart and left their father feeling sad, believing that Joseph had died.

It's hard when other people have more talents or things than we have. The Apostle Paul wrote that it isn't wise for us to compare ourselves with others (2 Cor 10:12). It's better to be grateful for the ways we're different from everyone else than to focus on what other people have that we don't. God created each one of us to be different for God's good purpose.

Name two things that are special about you.

How can you use those special things to serve God?

LIFE PRESERVER

What happened to Tamar?
Genesis 38

Many customs described in the Bible sound strange to us because we live in a very different time and place. In the culture Judah and Tamar lived in, women had no legal rights. If a woman's husband died, she had nothing, no way to provide for herself and no way of having children. It was the duty of her husband's closest male relative to take care of her.

When his son died, Judah should have helped his daughter-in-law, Tamar, find a new husband from among his other sons, but he didn't. Tamar got tired of living without rights, so she tricked Judah into sleeping with her so she could get pregnant and have a child. Some months later people told Judah his daughter-in-law was pregnant. When he met with Tamar and heard her story, he realized her situation was his fault.

Though this story may sound strange to us, it provides a glimpse into the life of women in this culture. Tamar's desire to be taken care of, respected as a woman, and have a child were the reasons for her actions. She is recognized as part of the family tree from which David, the second king of Israel, would descend. ◆

---

¹²After a long time, Judah's wife the daughter of Shua died. Then, after a period of mourning, he and his neighbor Hirah the Adullamite went up to Timnah, to those who were shearing his sheep. ¹³Tamar was told, "Your father-in-law is now on his way up to Timnah to shear his sheep." ¹⁴So Tamar took off the clothing she wore as a widow, covered herself with a veil, put on makeup,ⁱ and sat down at the entrance to Enaim on the road to Timnah, since she realized that although Shelah had already grown up, she hadn't been given to him as a wife.

¹⁵Judah saw her and thought she was a prostitute because she had covered her face. ¹⁶He turned to her beside the road and said, "Let me sleep with you," because he didn't know she was his daughter-in-law.

She said, "What will you give me for sleeping with you?"

¹⁷He said, "I will give you a kid goat from my flock."

She said, "Only if you give me some deposit, as security to guarantee that you will send it."

¹⁸He said, "What kind of deposit should I give you?"

And she said, "Your seal, its cord, and the staff in your hand." He gave these to her, slept with her, and she became pregnant by him.

¹⁹Then she got up, left, and took off her veil, dressing once again in the clothing she wore as a widow. ²⁰Judah sent the kid goat with his neighbor Hirah the Adullamite so he could take back the deposits from the woman, but he couldn't find her. ²¹He asked the locals of that place, "Where's the consecrated workerʲ who was at Enaim on the road?"

But they said, "There's no consecrated worker here."

²²So he went back to Judah and said, "I couldn't find her. The locals even said, 'There's no holy woman here.'"

²³Judah said, "Let her keep everything so we aren't laughed at. I did send this kid goat, but you couldn't find her."

²⁴About three months later, Judah was told, "Your daughter-in-law Tamar has become a prostitute and is now pregnant because of it."

And Judah said, "Bring her out so that she may be burned."

²⁵When she was brought out, she sent this message to her father-in-law, "I'm pregnant by the man who owns these things. See if you recognize whose seal, cord, and staff these are."

²⁶Judah recognized them and said, "She's more righteous than I am, because I didn't allow her to marry my son Shelah." Judah never knew her intimately again.

²⁷When she gave birth, she discovered she had twins in her womb. ²⁸At birth, one boy put out his hand, and the midwife took it and tied a red thread on his hand, saying, "This one came out first." ²⁹As soon as he pulled his hand back, his brother came out, and she said, "You've burst out on your own." So he was named Perez.ᵏ ³⁰Afterward, his brother with the red thread on his hand came out, and he was named Zerah.ˡ

Joseph's rise and betrayal

39 When Joseph had been taken down to Egypt, Potiphar, Pharaoh's chief

---

ⁱOr *perfumed herself* or *wrapped herself up* ʲTraditionally *cultic prostitute* ᵏOr *bursting out* ˡOr *dawn*

officer, the commander of the royal guard and an Egyptian, purchased him from the Ishmaelites who had brought him down there. [2]The LORD was with Joseph, and he became a successful man and served in his Egyptian master's household. [3]His master saw that the LORD was with him and that the LORD made everything he did successful. [4]Potiphar thought highly of Joseph, and Joseph became his assistant; he appointed Joseph head of his household and put everything he had under Joseph's supervision. [5]From the time he appointed Joseph head of his household and of everything he had, the LORD blessed the Egyptian's household because of Joseph. The LORD blessed everything he had, both in the household and in the field. [6]So he handed over everything he had to Joseph and didn't pay attention to anything except the food he ate.

Now Joseph was well-built and handsome. [7]Some time later, his master's wife became attracted to Joseph and said, "Sleep with me."

[8]He refused and said to his master's wife, "With me here, my master doesn't pay attention to anything in his household; he's put everything he has under my supervision. [9]No one is greater than I am in this household, and he hasn't denied me anything except you, since you are his wife. How could I do this terrible thing and sin against God?" [10]Every single day she tried to convince him, but he wouldn't agree to sleep with her or even to be with her.

[11]One day when Joseph arrived at the house to do his work, none of the household's men were there. [12]She grabbed

his garment, saying, "Lie down with me." But he left his garment in her hands and ran outside. [13]When she realized that he had left his garment in her hands and run outside, [14]she summoned the men of her house and said to them, "Look, my husband brought us a Hebrew to ridicule us. He came to me to lie down with me, but I screamed. [15]When he heard me raise my voice and scream, he left his garment with me and ran outside." [16]She kept his garment with her until Joseph's master came home, [17]and she told him the same thing: "The Hebrew slave whom you brought to us, to ridicule me, came to me; [18]but when I raised my voice and screamed, he left his garment with me and ran outside."

[19]When Joseph's master heard the thing that his wife told him, "This is what your servant did to me," he was incensed. [20]Joseph's master took him and threw him in jail, the place where the king's prisoners were held. While he was in jail, [21]the LORD was with Joseph and remained loyal to him. He caused the jail's commander to think highly of Joseph. [22]The jail's commander put all of the prisoners in the jail under Joseph's supervision, and he was the one who determined everything that happened there. [23]The jail's commander paid no attention to anything under Joseph's supervision, because the LORD was with him and made everything he did successful.

Joseph interprets dreams in prison

40 Some time later, both the wine steward and the baker for Egypt's king offended their master, the king of Egypt. [2]Pharaoh was angry with his two officers, the chief wine steward and the chief baker, [3]and he put them under arrest with the commander of the royal guard in the same jail where Joseph was imprisoned. [4]The commander of the royal guard assigned Joseph to assist them. After they had been under arrest for some time, [5]both of them—the wine steward and the baker for Egypt's king who were imprisoned in the jail—had dreams one night, and each man's dream had its own meaning. [6]When Joseph met them in the morning, he saw that they were upset. [7]He asked the officers of Pharaoh who were under arrest with him in his master's house, "Why do you look so distressed today?"

SAILBOAT

HONEST AND TRUE

Be Responsible Genesis 39:8-12
Potiphar, Pharaoh's top officer, put great trust in Joseph. Joseph was his assistant and supervised Potiphar's entire household. This was a big responsibility and showed Potiphar trusted Joseph. When Potiphar's wife tried to get Joseph to do something wrong, Joseph refused, even though he knew his refusal would cause trouble for him. It takes integrity and a strong character to do what is right, especially if those actions are unpopular with others. ◈

[8]They answered, "We've both had dreams, but there's no one to interpret them."

Joseph said to them, "Don't interpretations belong to God? Describe your dreams to me."

[9]The chief wine steward described his dream to Joseph: "In my dream there was a vine right in front of me, [10]and on the vine were three branches. When it budded, its blossoms appeared, and its clusters ripened into grapes. [11]Pharaoh's cup was in my hand, so I took the grapes, crushed them into Pharaoh's cup, and put the cup in Pharaoh's hand."

[12]Joseph said to him, "This is the dream's interpretation: The three branches are three days. [13]After three days, Pharaoh will give you an audience and return you to your position. You will put Pharaoh's cup in his hand, just the way things were before when you were his wine steward. [14]But please, remember me when you are doing well and be loyal to me. Put in a good word for me to Pharaoh, so he sets me free from this prison. [15]I was stolen from the land of the Hebrews, and here too I've done nothing to be thrown into this dungeon."

SAILBOAT

HONEST AND TRUE

Dream On *Genesis 40:15*
Joseph's life was about to take another turn. He went from favored son, to servant, to prisoner, but no matter where he was, he did his best to follow God's ways. Joseph interpreted the dream of the chief wine steward and let him know things were going to work out for him. Even though he was in prison, Joseph didn't give up. He continued to believe God was with him and trusted things would eventually work out for him too. Because he trusted God, he continued to act with integrity even when it looked like he had been forgotten. ♦

[16]When the chief baker saw that the interpretation was favorable, he said to Joseph, "It was the same for me. In my dream, there were three baskets of white bread[m] on my head. [17]In the basket on top there were baked goods for Pharaoh's food, but birds were eating them out of the basket on my head."

[18]Joseph responded, "This is the dream's interpretation: The three baskets are three days. [19]After three days, Pharaoh will give you an audience and will hang you from a tree where birds will peck your flesh from you."

[20]The third day was Pharaoh's birthday, and he gave a party for all of his servants. Before all of his servants, he gave an audience to the chief wine steward and the chief baker. [21]He returned the chief wine steward to his position, and he placed the cup in Pharaoh's hand. [22]But the chief baker he hanged, just as Joseph had said would happen when he interpreted their dreams for them. [23]But the chief wine steward didn't remember Joseph; he forgot all about him.

Joseph interprets Pharaoh's dreams

41 Two years later, Pharaoh dreamed that he was standing near the Nile. [2]In front of him, seven healthy-looking, fattened cows climbed up out of the Nile and grazed on the reeds. [3]Just then, seven other cows, terrible-looking and scrawny, climbed up out of the Nile after them and stood beside them on the bank of the Nile. [4]The terrible-looking, scrawny cows devoured the seven healthy-looking, fattened cows. Then Pharaoh woke up. [5]He went back to sleep and had a second dream, in which seven ears of grain, full and healthy, grew on a single stalk. [6]Just then, seven ears of grain, scrawny and scorched by the east wind, sprouted after them, [7]and the scrawny ears swallowed up the full and well-formed ears. Then Pharaoh woke up and realized it was a dream. [8]In the morning, he was disturbed and summoned all of Egypt's religious experts[n] and all of its advisors. Pharaoh described his dreams[o] to them, but they couldn't interpret them for Pharaoh.

[9]Then the chief wine steward spoke to Pharaoh: "Today I've just remembered my mistake. [10]Pharaoh was angry with his servants and put me and the chief baker under arrest with the commander of the royal guard. [11]We both dreamed one night, he and I, and each of our dreams had its own interpretation. [12]A young Hebrew man, a servant of the commander of the royal guard, was with us. We described our dreams to him,

[m]Heb uncertain [n]Or *magicians* [o]Sam; MT *dream*

and he interpreted our dreams for us, giving us an interpretation for each dream. [13]His interpretations came true exactly: Pharaoh restored me to my position but hanged him."

[14]So Pharaoh summoned Joseph, and they quickly brought him from the dungeon. He shaved, changed clothes, and appeared before Pharaoh. [15]Pharaoh said to Joseph, "I had a dream, but no one could interpret it. Then I heard that when you hear a dream, you can interpret it."

[16]Joseph answered Pharaoh, "It's not me. God will give Pharaoh a favorable response."

SAILBOAT

HUMILITY

It's Not Me, It's God *Genesis 41:16*
Two years had passed since Joseph, who was in prison, had interpreted a dream of the chief wine steward. The wine steward remembered this when Pharaoh needed someone to interpret his strange dreams. Joseph was able to interpret Pharaoh's dreams correctly. Joseph could have taken credit for this ability, but he was humble and acknowledged it came from God. When we receive praise for doing something very well, we can be tempted to be proud. But all our abilities come from God. ◆

[17]So Pharaoh said to Joseph, "In my dream I was standing on the bank of the Nile. [18]In front of me, seven fattened, stout cows climbed up out of the Nile and grazed on the reeds. [19]Just then, seven other cows, weak and frail and thin, climbed up after them. I've never seen such awful cows in all the land of Egypt. [20]Then the thin, frail cows devoured the first seven, fattened cows. [21]But after they swallowed them whole, no one would have known it. They looked just as bad as they had before. Then I woke up. [22]I went to sleep again[p] and saw in my dream seven full and healthy ears of grain growing on one stalk. [23]Just then, seven hard and thin ears of grain, scorched by the east wind, sprouted after them, [24]and the thin ears swallowed up the healthy ears. I told the religious experts,[q] but they couldn't explain it to me."

[25]Joseph said to Pharaoh, "Pharaoh has actually had one dream. God has announced to Pharaoh what he is about to do. [26]The seven healthy cows are seven years, and the seven healthy ears of grain are seven years. It's actually one dream. [27]The seven thin and frail cows, climbing up after them, are seven years. The seven thin ears of grain, scorched by the east wind, are seven years of famine. [28]It's just as I told Pharaoh: God has shown Pharaoh what he is about to do. [29]Seven years of great abundance are now coming throughout the entire land of Egypt. [30]After them, seven years of famine will appear, and all of the abundance in the land of Egypt will be forgotten. The famine will devastate the land. [31]No one will remember the abundance in the land because the famine that follows will be so very severe. [32]The dream occurred to Pharaoh twice because God has determined to do it, and God will make it happen soon.

Joseph's rise to power

[33]"Now Pharaoh should find an intelligent, wise man and give him authority over the land of Egypt. [34]Then Pharaoh should appoint administrators over the land and take one-fifth of all the produce of the land of Egypt during the seven years of abundance. [35]During the good years that are coming, they should collect all such food and store the grain under Pharaoh's control, protecting the food in the cities. [36]This food will be reserved for the seven years of famine to follow in the land of Egypt so that the land won't be ravaged by the famine."

[37]This advice seemed wise to Pharaoh and all his servants, [38]and Pharaoh said to his servants, "Can we find a man with more God-given gifts[r] than this one?" [39]Then Pharaoh said to Joseph, "Since God has made all this known to you, no one is as intelligent and wise as you are. [40]You will be in charge of my kingdom,[s] and all my people will obey[t] your command. Only as the enthroned king will I be greater than you." [41]Pharaoh said to Joseph, "Know this: I've given you authority over the entire land of Egypt." [42]Pharaoh took his signet ring from his hand and put it on

---

[p]LXX, Syr, Vulg; MT lacks *I went to sleep again.* [q]Or *magicians* [r]Or *like this one, in whom is the spirit of God* [s]Or *house* [t]LXX; Heb uncertain, perhaps *submit themselves to your command*

Joseph's hand, he dressed him in linen clothes, and he put a gold necklace around his neck. ⁴³He put Joseph on the chariot of his second-in-command, and everyone in front of him cried out, "Attention!"ᵘ So Pharaoh installed him over the entire land of Egypt. ⁴⁴Pharaoh said to Joseph, "I am Pharaoh; no one will do anything or go anywhere in all the land of Egypt without your permission." ⁴⁵Pharaoh renamed Joseph, Zaphenath-paneah, and married him to Asenath, the daughter of Potiphera the priest of Heliopolis.ᵛ

Then Joseph assumed control of the land of Egypt. ⁴⁶Joseph was 30 years old when he began to serve Pharaoh, Egypt's king, when he left Pharaoh's court and traveled through the entire land of Egypt. ⁴⁷During the seven years of abundance, the land produced plentifully. ⁴⁸He collected all of the food during the seven years of abundanceʷ in the land of Egypt, and stored the food in cities. In each city, he stored the food from the fields surrounding it. ⁴⁹Joseph amassed grain like the sand of the sea. There was so much that he stopped trying to measure it because it was beyond measuring. ⁵⁰Before the years of famine arrived, Asenath the daughter of Potiphera, priest of Heliopolis,ˣ gave birth to two sons for Joseph. ⁵¹Joseph named the oldest son Manasseh,ʸ "because," he said, "God has helped me forget all of my troubles and everyone in my father's household." ⁵²He named the second Ephraim,ᶻ "because," he said, "God has given me children in the land where I've been treated harshly."

⁵³The seven years of abundance in the land of Egypt came to an end, ⁵⁴and the seven years of famine began, just as Joseph had said. The famine struck every country, but the entire land of Egypt had bread. ⁵⁵When the famine ravaged the entire land of Egypt and the people pleaded to Pharaoh for bread, Pharaoh said to all of the Egyptians, "Go to Joseph. Do whatever he tells you." ⁵⁶The famine covered every part of the land, and Joseph opened all of the granariesᵃ and sold grain to the Egyptians. In the land of Egypt, the famine became more and more severe. ⁵⁷Every country came to Egypt to buy grain from Joseph, because in

did you know? Pharaoh gave Joseph his signet ring. When Pharaoh made a law, he used this ring to make an impression in wax at the bottom of the scroll. This sign showed that the law came from Pharaoh. With Pharaoh's ring, Joseph had the power to make laws and rule the people.

every country the famine had also become more severe.

Joseph's brothers arrive in Egypt

42When Jacob learned that there was grain in Egypt, he said to his sons, "Why are you staring blankly at each other? ²I've just heard that there's grain in Egypt. Go down there and buy some for us so that we can survive and not starve to death." ³So Joseph's ten brothers went down to buy grain in Egypt. ⁴However, Jacob didn't send Joseph's brother Benjamin along with his brothers because he thought something bad might happen to him. ⁵Israel's sons came to buy grain with others who also came since the famine had spread to the land of Canaan.

⁶As for Joseph, he was the land's governor, and he was the one selling grain to all the land's people. When Joseph's brothers arrived, they bowed down to him, their faces to the ground. ⁷When Joseph saw his brothers, he recognized them, but he acted like he didn't know them. He spoke to them with a harsh tone and said, "Where have you come from?"

And they said, "From the land of Canaan to buy food."

⁸Joseph recognized his brothers, but they didn't recognize him. ⁹Joseph remembered the dreams he had dreamed about them, and said to them, "You are spies. You've come to look for the country's weaknesses."

¹⁰They said to him, "No, Master. Your servants have just come to buy food. ¹¹We are all sons of one man. We are honest men. Your servants aren't spies."

¹²He said to them, "No. You've come to look for the country's weaknesses."

¹³They said, "We, your servants, are twelve brothers, sons of one man in the land of Canaan. The youngest is now with our father, but one is gone."

ᵘAn Egyptian loanword similar to the Heb word *kneel*. ᵛHeb *On* ʷLXX; MT lacks *of abundance*. ˣHeb *On* ʸOr *making forget*
ᶻSounds like *has given me children*. ᵃLXX, Syr; MT *what was in them*

[14] Joseph said to them, "It's just as I've said to you. You are spies! [15] But here is how to prove yourselves: As Pharaoh lives, you won't leave here until your youngest brother arrives. [16] Send one of you to get your brother, but the rest of you will stay in prison. We will find out if your words are true. If not, as Pharaoh lives, you are certainly spies."

Joseph's brothers return to Canaan

[17] He put them all in prison for three days. [18] On the third day, Joseph said to them, "Do this and you will live, for I'm a God-fearing man. [19] If you are honest men, let one of your brothers stay in prison, and the rest of you, go, take grain back to those in your households who are hungry. [20] But bring your youngest brother back to me so that your words will prove true and you won't die."

So they prepared to do this. [21] The brothers said to each other, "We are clearly guilty for what we did to our brother when we saw his life in danger and when he begged us for mercy, but we didn't listen. That's why we're in this danger now."

[22] Reuben responded to them, "Didn't I tell you, 'Don't do anything wrong to the boy'? But you wouldn't listen. So now this is payback for his death." [23] They didn't know that Joseph was listening to them because they were using an interpreter. [24] He stepped away from them and wept. When he returned, he spoke with them again. Then he took Simeon from them and tied him up in front of them.

[25] Then Joseph gave orders to fill their bags with grain, to put back each man's silver into his own sack, and to give them provisions for their trip, and it was done. [26] They loaded their grain onto their donkeys, and they set out. [27] When they stopped to spend the night, one of them opened his sack to feed his donkey, and he saw his silver at the top of his

Planting and Harvesting *Genesis 42:1-25*

If you planted a green bean seed would it grow into a tomato? Of course not. God created all things—flowers, trees, birds, fish, animals, and people—to grow from their own types. A sunflower seed grows into a sunflower. A baby lion grows into an adult lion. This same idea is also true for our actions. Small acts of kindness, which we could call seeds, grow into large acts of kindness, which we could call plants.

Joseph's brothers had hatred in their hearts. Their hatred may have started small, like a seed, but it grew much, much bigger. Joseph's brothers' hatred grew so large that they sold him into slavery, which was hurtful to Joseph and also bad for their family. Years later they feared losing another brother as payback for what they had done!

Have you ever done or said something unkind to someone else? Did anything good come from those words or actions? The Apostle Paul wrote about planting and harvesting. He said that whatever we plant in selfishness—like when we're unkind to someone else—will result in a bad harvest. When we plant good things for God, we'll reap a harvest of eternal life (Gal 6:7-8).

Name two things you're planting in your heart.

What will grow from these things?

sack. 28He said to his brothers, "My silver's been returned. It's right here in my sack." Their hearts stopped. Terrified, they said to each other, "What has God done to us?"

LIGHTHOUSE

CHANGED HEART AND LIFE

Time to Change *Genesis 42:17-28*

Joseph's brothers were in a difficult situation. They didn't recognize their brother Joseph, and they were in jail so Joseph could find out more about their motives. While in prison they expressed deep regret for what they had done to Joseph. When Joseph heard their words of regret, he cried. When we realize we've done something wrong, it's important to seek forgiveness and see if there is a way to make things right. 💧

29When they got back to their father Jacob in the land of Canaan, they described to him everything that had happened to them: 30"The man, the country's governor, spoke to us with a harsh tone and accused us of being spies in the country. 31We told him, 'We're honest men, not spies. 32We are twelve brothers, all our father's sons. One of us is gone, but the youngest is right now with our father in the land of Canaan.' 33The man, the country's governor, told us, 'This is how I will know you are honest men: Leave one of your brothers with me, take grain for those in your households who are hungry, and go. 34But bring back your youngest brother to me. Then I will know that you are not spies but honest men. I will give your brother back to you, and you may travel throughout the country.'"

35When they opened their sacks, each man found a pouch of his silver in his sack. When they and their father saw their pouches of silver, they were afraid. 36Their father Jacob said to them, "You've taken my children from me. Joseph's gone. Simeon's gone. And you are taking Benjamin. All this can't really be happening to me!"

37Reuben said to his father, "You may put both of my sons to death if I don't bring him back to you. Make him my responsibility, and I will make sure he returns to you."

38But Jacob said to him, "My son won't go down with you because his brother's dead and he's been left all alone. If anything were to happen to him on the trip you are taking, you would send me—old as I am—to my grave in grief."

Joseph's brothers return with Benjamin

43 The famine was severe in the land, 2and when they had eaten all the grain that they brought from Egypt, their father said to them, "Go back and buy us a little food."

3Judah said to him, "The man was absolutely serious when he said, 'You may not see me again without your brother with you.' 4If you agree to send our brother with us, then we will go down and buy you food. 5But if you don't agree to send him, then we can't go down because the man said to us, 'You may not see me again without your brother with you.'"

6Israel said, "Why have you caused me such pain by telling the man you had another brother?"

7They said, "The man asked us pointedly about our family: 'Is your father still alive? Do you have a brother?' So we told him just what we've said. How were we to know he'd say, 'Bring your brother down here'?"

8Judah said to his father Israel, "Send the young man with me. Let's get ready to leave so that we can stay alive and not die—we, you, and our children. 9I will guarantee his safety; you can hold me responsible. If I don't bring him back to you and place him here in front of you, it will be my fault forever. 10If we hadn't waited so long, we would've returned twice by now."

11Their father Israel said to them, "If it has to be, then do this. Take in your bags some of the land's choice produce, and bring it down to the man as a gift: a little medicinal resin, a little honey, gum, resin, pistachios, and almonds. 12Take twice as much silver with you, and take back the silver returned in the top of your sacks. It might have been a mistake. 13And take your brother, get ready, and go back to the man. 14May God Almighty[b] make the man compassionate toward you so that he may send back your other brother and Benjamin with you. But me, if I'm left childless, then I'm left childless."

b Heb *El Shaddai* or *God of the Mountain*

¹⁵So the men took this gift. They took twice as much silver with them, together with Benjamin. They left, traveled down to Egypt, and received an audience with Joseph. ¹⁶When Joseph saw Benjamin with them, he said to the manager of his household, "Bring the men to the house and slaughter an animal and prepare it because the men will have dinner with me at noon." ¹⁷The man did as Joseph told him and brought the men to Joseph's house.

SAILBOAT

HONEST AND TRUE

Honesty Is the Best Policy *Genesis 43:12*

Joseph's brothers went back home unaware that the Egyptian they had met was their brother Joseph. They explained what had happened to their father, who now went by the name Israel, instead of Jacob. Israel encouraged his sons to do everything that was asked of them and more. Israel believed being honest and truthful would make this unknown man show them mercy. ◖

¹⁸When they were brought to Joseph's house, the men were frightened and said, "We've been brought here because of the silver put back in our sacks on our first trip so he can overpower us, capture us, make slaves of us, and take our donkeys." ¹⁹They approached the man who was Joseph's household manager and spoke to him at the house's entrance: ²⁰"Please, Master, we came down the first time just to buy food, ²¹but when we stopped to spend the night and opened our sacks, there was the exact amount of each man's silver at the top of his sack. We've brought it back with us, ²²and we've brought down with us additional silver to buy food. We don't know who put our silver in our sacks." ²³He said, "You are fine. Don't be afraid. Your God and your father's God must have hidden a treasure in your sacks. I received your money." Then he brought Simeon out to them. ²⁴The manager brought the men into Joseph's house and gave them water to wash their feet and feed for their donkeys. ²⁵They prepared the gift, anticipating Joseph's arrival at noon, since they had heard that they would have a meal there. ²⁶When Joseph came into the house, they presented him the gift they had brought with them into the house, and they bowed low in front of him. ²⁷He asked them how they were and said, "How is your elderly father, about whom you spoke? Is he still alive?"

²⁸They said, "Your servant our father is fine. He's still alive." And they bowed down again with deep respect.

²⁹Joseph looked up and saw his brother Benjamin, his own mother's son, and he said, "Is this your youngest brother whom you told me about? God be gracious to you, my son." ³⁰Joseph's feelings for his brother were so strong he was about to weep, so he rushed to another room and wept there. ³¹He washed his face, came back, pulled himself together, and said, "Set out the dinner." ³²So they set out his food by himself, their food by themselves, and the Egyptians' who ate with him by themselves because Egyptians don't allow themselves to eat with Hebrews; the Egyptians think it beneath their dignity. ³³They were seated in front of him from the oldest to the youngest in their exact birth order, and the men looked at each other with amazement. ³⁴Portions of food from Joseph's table were brought to them, but Benjamin's portion was five times as large as theirs. So they drank together and were at ease.

Joseph tests his brothers

44 Joseph gave commands to his household manager: "Fill the men's sacks with as much silver as they'll hold, and put each man's silver at the top of his sack. ²Put my cup, the silver cup, on top of the youngest brother's sack, together with the silver for his grain." So he did just as Joseph told him to do.

³At dawn, the men and their donkeys were sent off. ⁴They had left the city but hadn't gone far when Joseph said to his household manager, "Get ready, go after the men and catch up with them! Ask them, 'Why have you repaid hospitality with ingratitude?ᶜ ⁵Isn't this the cupᵈ my master drinks from and uses to discover God's plans?ᵉ What you've done is despicable.'"

ᶜLXX adds *Why have you stolen my silver cup?* ᵈSyr; MT lacks *cup*. ᵉOr *uses for divination*

⁶When he caught up to them, he repeated these words. ⁷They replied, "Why does my master talk to us like this? Your servants would never do such a thing. ⁸The silver that we found at the top of our sacks, we've just brought back to you from the land of Canaan. We didn't steal silver or gold from your master's house. ⁹Whoever of your servants is found with it will be put to death, and we'll be my master's slaves."

¹⁰He said, "Fine. We'll do just as you've said. Whoever is found with it will be my slave, and the rest of you will go free." ¹¹Everyone quickly lowered their sacks down to the ground and each opened his sack. ¹²He searched the oldest first and the youngest last, and the cup was found in Benjamin's sack. ¹³At this, they tore their clothing. Then everyone loaded their donkeys, and they returned to the city.

¹⁴When Judah and his brothers arrived at Joseph's house, he was still there, and they fell to the ground in front of him. ¹⁵Joseph said to them, "What's this you've done? Didn't you know someone like me can discover God's plans?"f

¹⁶Judah replied, "What can we say to my master? What words can we use? How can we prove we are innocent? God has found your servants guilty. We are now your slaves, all of us, including the one found with the cup."

¹⁷Joseph said, "I'd never do such a thing. Only the man found with the cup will be my slave. As for the rest of you, you are free to go back to your father."

Judah appeals for Benjamin

¹⁸Judah approached him and said, "Please, my master, allow your servant to say something to my master without getting angry with your servant since you are like Pharaoh himself. ¹⁹My master asked his servants, 'Do you have a father or brother?' ²⁰And we said to my master, 'Yes, we have an elderly father and a young brother, born when he was old. His brother is dead and he's his mother's only child. But his father loves him.' ²¹You told your servants, 'Bring him down to me so I can see him.' ²²And we said to my master, 'The young man can't leave his father. If he leaves, his father will die.' ²³You said to your servants,

'If your youngest brother doesn't come down with you, you'll never see my face again.'

²⁴"When we went back to my father your servant, we told him what you said. ²⁵Our father told us, 'Go back and buy for us a little food.' ²⁶But we said, 'We can't go down. We will go down only if our youngest brother is with us. We won't be able to gain an audience with the man without our youngest brother with us.' ²⁷Your servant my father said to us, 'You know that my wife gave birth to two sons for me. ²⁸One disappeared and I said, "He must have been torn up by a wild animal," and I haven't seen him since. ²⁹And if you take this one from me too, something terrible will happen to him, and you will send me—old as I am—to my grave in despair.' ³⁰When I now go back to your servant my father without the young man—whose life is so bound up with his— ³¹and when he sees that the young man isn't with us,g he will die, and your servants will have sent our father your servant—old as he is—to his grave in grief. ³²I, your servant, guaranteed the young man's safety to my father, telling him, 'If I don't bring him back to you, it will be my fault forever.' ³³Now, please let your servant stay as your slave instead of the young man so that he can go back with his brothers. ³⁴How can I go back to my father without the young man? I couldn't bear to see how badly my father would be hurt."

Joseph reveals his identity

45 Joseph could no longer control himself in front of all his attendants, so he declared, "Everyone, leave now!" So no one stayed with him when he revealed his identity to his brothers. ²He wept so loudly that the Egyptians and Pharaoh's household heard him. ³Joseph said to his brothers, "I'm Joseph! Is my father really still alive?" His brothers couldn't respond because they were terrified before him.

⁴Joseph said to his brothers, "Come closer to me," and they moved closer. He said, "I'm your brother Joseph! The one you sold to Egypt. ⁵Now, don't be upset and don't be angry with yourselves that you sold me here. Actually, God sent me before you to save lives. ⁶We've already had two years of famine in the

---

f Or *can practice divination*   g Sam, LXX; MT lacks *with us*.

land, and there are five years left without planting or harvesting. [7]God sent me before you to make sure you'd survive[h] and to rescue your lives in this amazing way. [8]You didn't send me here; it was God who made me a father to Pharaoh, master of his entire household, and ruler of the whole land of Egypt.

[9]"Hurry! Go back to your father. Tell him this is what your son Joseph says: 'God has made me master of all of Egypt. Come down to me. Don't delay. [10]You may live in the land of Goshen, so you will be near me, your children, your grandchildren, your flocks, your herds, and everyone with you. [11]I will support you there, so you, your household, and everyone with you won't starve, since the famine will still last five years.' [12]You and my brother Benjamin have seen with your own eyes that I'm speaking to you. [13]Tell my father about my power in Egypt and about everything you've seen. Hurry and bring my father down here." [14]He threw his arms around his brother Benjamin's neck and wept, and Benjamin wept on his shoulder. [15]He kissed all of his brothers and wept, embracing them. After that, his brothers were finally able to talk to him.

SAILBOAT

FORGIVENESS

At Long Last *Genesis 45:5-15*
When Joseph finally revealed himself to his brothers, he had completely forgiven them for selling him into slavery many years before. In fact, he told them that God had sent him to Egypt to save their lives. Joseph looked at the high points and the low points of his life and saw that God was with him through all of it. Because of that understanding, he was able to truly forgive his brothers. ◊

Joseph's brothers return for Jacob

[16]When Pharaoh's household heard the message "Joseph's brothers have arrived," both Pharaoh and his servants were pleased. [17]Pharaoh said to Joseph, "Give your brothers these instructions: Load your pack animals and go back to the land of Canaan. [18]Get your father and your households and come back to me. Let me provide you with good things

from the land of Egypt so that you may eat the land's best food. [19]Give them these instructions too: Take wagons from the land of Egypt for your children and wives, and pick up your father and come back. [20]Don't worry about your possessions because you will have good things from the entire land of Egypt."

[21]So Israel's sons did that. Joseph gave them wagons as Pharaoh instructed, and he gave them provisions for the road. [22]To all of them he gave a change of clothing, but to Benjamin he gave three hundred pieces of silver and five changes of clothing. [23]To his father he sent ten male donkeys carrying goods from Egypt, ten female donkeys carrying grain and bread, and rations for his father for the road. [24]He sent his brothers off; and as they were leaving, he told them, "Don't be worried about the trip."[i]

[25]So they left Egypt and returned to their father Jacob in the land of Canaan. [26]They announced to him, "Joseph's still alive! He's actually ruler of all the land of Egypt!" Jacob's heart nearly failed, and he didn't believe them.

[27]When they told him everything Joseph had said to them, and when he saw the wagons Joseph had sent to carry him, Jacob recovered. [28]Then Israel said, "This is too much! My son Joseph is still alive! Let me go and see him before I die."

Jacob's household moves to Egypt

46Israel packed up everything he owned and traveled to Beer-sheba. There he offered sacrifices to his father Isaac's God. [2]God said to Israel in a vision at night, "Jacob! Jacob!" and he said, "I'm here." [3]He said, "I am El,[j] your father's God. Don't be afraid to go down to Egypt because I will make a great nation of you there. [4]I will go down to Egypt with you, and I promise to bring you out again. Joseph will close your eyes when you die." [5]Then Jacob left Beer-sheba. Israel's sons put their father Jacob, their children, and their wives on the wagons Pharaoh had sent to carry him. [6]They took their livestock and their possessions that they had acquired in the land of Canaan, and arrived in Egypt, Jacob and all of his children with him. [7]His sons and grandsons, his daughters and his granddaughters—all

---

[h]*Or survive on earth* [i]*Or Don't quarrel during the trip.* [j]*Or God*

of his descendants he brought with him to Egypt.

8These are the names of the Israelites who went to Egypt, including Jacob and his sons. Jacob's oldest son was Reuben. 9Reuben's sons were Hanoch, Pallu, Hezron, and Carmi. 10Simeon's sons were Jemuel, Jamin, Ohad, Jachin, Zohar, and Shaul, whose mother was a Canaanite. 11Levi's sons were Gershon, Kohath, and Merari. 12Judah's sons were Er, Onan, Shelah, Perez, and Zerah. Er and Onan both died in the land of Canaan. Perez's sons were Hezron and Hamul. 13Issachar's sons were Tola, Puvah, Iob, and Shimron. 14Zebulun's sons were Sered, Elon, and Jahleel. 15These are the sons Leah bore to Jacob in Paddan-aram. Her daughter was Dinah. All of these persons, including his sons and daughters, totaled 33.

16Gad's sons were Ziphion, Haggi, Shuni, Ezbon, Eri, Arodi, and Areli. 17Asher's sons were Imnah, Ishvah, Ishvi, Beriah, and their sister Serah. Beriah's sons were Heber and Malchiel. 18These are the sons of Zilpah, whom Laban gave to his daughter Leah. She bore these to Jacob, a total of 16 persons.

19The sons of Jacob's wife Rachel were Joseph and Benjamin. 20To Joseph, in the land of Egypt, were born Manasseh and Ephraim. Asenath daughter of Potiphera, priest of Heliopolis,k bore them to him. 21Benjamin's sons were Bela, Becher, Ashbel, Gera, Naaman, Ehi, Rosh, Muppim, Huppim, and Ard. 22These are Rachel's sons who were born to Jacob, a total of 14 persons.

23Dan's sonl was Hushim. 24Naphtali's sons were Jahzeel, Guni, Jezer, and Shillem. 25These are the sons of Bilhah, whom Laban gave to his daughter Rachel. She bore these to Jacob, a total of 7 persons.

26All of the persons going to Egypt with Jacob—his own children, excluding Jacob's sons' wives—totaled 66 persons. 27Joseph's sons born to him in Egypt were 2 persons. Thus, all of the persons in Jacob's household going to Egypt totaled 70.

28Israel had sent Judah ahead to Joseph so that Joseph could explain the way to Goshen. Then they arrived in the land of Goshen. 29Joseph hitched up his chariot and went to meet his father Israel in Goshen. When he arrived, he threw his arms around his neck and wept, embracing him for a long time. 30Israel said to Joseph, "I can die now after seeing your face. You are really still alive!"

Jacob's household settles in Egypt

31Joseph said to his brothers and to his father's household, "Let me go up and inform Pharaoh and tell him, 'My brothers and my father's household who were in the land of Canaan have arrived. 32The men are shepherds, because they own livestock. They've brought with them their flocks and herds and everything they own.' 33When Pharaoh summons you and says, 'What do you do?' 34say, 'Your servants have owned livestock since we were young, both we and our ancestors,' so that you will be able to settle in the land of Goshen, since Egyptians think all shepherds are beneath their dignity."

47 Joseph went to inform Pharaoh and said, "My father and brothers with their flocks, herds, and everything they own have come from the land of Canaan and are now in the land of Goshen." 2From all of his brothers, he selected five men and presented them before Pharaoh.

3Pharaoh said to Joseph's brothers, "What do you do?"

They said to Pharaoh, "Your servants are shepherds, both we and our ancestors." 4They continued, "We've come to the land as immigrants because the famine is so severe in the land of Canaan that there are no more pastures for your servants' flocks. Please allow your servants to settle in the land of Goshen."

5Pharaoh said to Joseph, "Since your father and brothers have arrived, 6the land of Egypt

did you know? Years with little rain meant there wasn't enough water to grow food, which led to famines where people went hungry. When this happened in Canaan, Joseph's family moved to Egypt. Even though there hadn't been enough rain in Egypt, Joseph's leadership was able to provide food.

kHeb *On* lOr *sons*

is available to you. Settle your father and brothers in the land's best location. Let them live in the land of Goshen. And if you know capable men among them, put them in charge of my own livestock."

[7] Joseph brought his father Jacob and gave him an audience with Pharaoh. Jacob blessed Pharaoh, [8] and Pharaoh said to Jacob, "How old are you?"

[9] Jacob said to Pharaoh, "I've been a traveler for 130 years. My years have been few and difficult. They don't come close to the years my ancestors lived during their travels." [10] Jacob blessed Pharaoh and left Pharaoh's presence. [11] Joseph settled his father and brothers and gave them property in the land of Egypt, in the best location in the land of Rameses, just as Pharaoh had ordered. [12] Joseph provided food for his father, his brothers, and his father's entire household, in proportion to the number of children.

Joseph centralizes power in Egypt

[13] There was no food in the land because the famine was so severe. The land of Egypt and the land of Canaan dried up from the famine. [14] Joseph collected all of the silver to be found in the land of Egypt and in the land of Canaan for the grain, which people came to buy, and he deposited it in Pharaoh's treasury. [15] The silver from the land of Egypt and from the land of Canaan had been spent, and all of the Egyptians came to Joseph and said, "Give us food. Why should we die before your eyes, just because the silver is gone?"

[16] Joseph said, "Give me your livestock, and I will give you food for your livestock if the silver is gone." [17] So they brought their livestock to Joseph, and Joseph gave them food for the horses, flocks, cattle, and donkeys. He got them through that year with food in exchange for all of their livestock.

[18] When that year was over, they came to him the next year and said to him, "We can't hide from my master that the silver is spent and that we've given the livestock to my master. All that's left for my master is our corpses and our farmland. [19] Why should we die before your eyes, we and our farmland too? Buy us and our farms for food, and we and our farms

will be under Pharaoh's control. Give us seed so that we can stay alive and not die, and so that our farmland won't become unproductive." [20] So Joseph bought all of Egypt's farmland for Pharaoh because every Egyptian sold his field when the famine worsened. So the land became Pharaoh's. [21] He moved the people to the cities[m] from one end of Egypt to the other. [22] However, he didn't buy the farmland of the priests because Pharaoh allowed the priests a subsidy, and they were able to eat from the subsidy Pharaoh gave them. Therefore, they didn't have to sell their farmland.

[23] Joseph said to the people, "Since I've now purchased you and your farmland for Pharaoh, here's seed for you. Plant the seed on the land. [24] When the crop comes in, you must give one-fifth to Pharaoh. You may keep four-fifths for yourselves, for planting fields, and for feeding yourselves, those in your households, and your children."

[25] The people said, "You've saved our lives. If you wish, we will be Pharaoh's slaves." [26] So Joseph made a law that still exists today: Pharaoh receives one-fifth from Egypt's farmland. Only the priests' farmland didn't become Pharaoh's.

Jacob blesses Ephraim and Manasseh

[27] Israel lived in the land of Egypt, in the land of Goshen. They settled in it, had many children, and became numerous. [28] After Jacob had lived in the land of Egypt for seventeen years, and after he had lived a total of 147 years, [29] Israel's death approached. He summoned his son Joseph and said to him, "If you would be so kind, lay your hand under my thigh, and be loyal and true to me. Don't bury me in Egypt. [30] When I lie down with my fathers, carry me from Egypt and bury me in their grave."

Joseph said, "I will do just as you say."

[31] Israel said, "Give me your word!" and Joseph gave his word. Then Israel slumped down at the head of the bed.

48

After this happened, Joseph was told,[n] "Your father is getting weaker," so he took his two sons Manasseh and Ephraim

---

[m] Sam, LXX *he made the people slaves* [n] LXX, Syr, Tg, Vulg; MT *he told*

with him. [2]When Jacob was informed,[o] "Your son Joseph is here now," he[p] pulled himself together and sat up in bed. [3]Jacob said to Joseph, "God Almighty[q] appeared to me in Luz in the land of Canaan. He blessed me [4]and said to me, 'I am about to give you many children, to increase your numbers, and to make you a large group of peoples. I will give this land to your descendants following you as an enduring possession.' [5]Now, your two sons born to you in the land of Egypt before I arrived in Egypt are my own. Ephraim and Manasseh are just like Reuben and Simeon to me. [6]Your family who is born to you after them are yours, but their inheritance will be determined under their brothers' names. [7]When I came back from Paddan-aram,[r] Rachel died, to my sorrow, on the road in the land of Canaan, with some distance yet to go to Ephrathah, so I buried her there near the road to Ephrathah,[s] which is Bethlehem."

[8]When Israel saw Joseph's sons, he said, "Who are these?"

[9]Joseph told his father, "They're my sons, whom God gave me here."

Israel said, "Bring them to me and I will bless them." [10]Because Israel's eyesight had failed from old age and he wasn't able to see, Joseph brought them close to him, and he kissed and embraced them.

[11]Israel said to Joseph, "I didn't expect I'd see your face, but now God has shown me your children too." [12]Then Joseph took them from Israel's knees, and he bowed low with his face to the ground. [13]Joseph took both of them, Ephraim in his right hand at Israel's left hand, and Manasseh in his left hand at Israel's right hand, and brought them close to him. [14]But Israel put out his right hand and placed it on the head of Ephraim, the younger one, and his left hand on Manasseh's head, crossing his hands because Manasseh was the oldest son. [15]He blessed them[t] and said,

"May the God before whom my fathers
    Abraham and Isaac walked,
may the God who was my shepherd
    from the beginning until this day,
[16] may the divine messenger
    who protected me from all harm,
    bless the young men.

Through them may my name be kept alive
    and the names of my fathers
        Abraham and Isaac.
May they grow into a great multitude
    throughout the land."

[17]When Joseph saw that his father had placed his right hand on Ephraim's head, he was upset and grasped his father's hand to move it from Ephraim's head to Manasseh's head. [18]Joseph said to his father, "No, my father! This is the oldest son. Put your right hand on his head."

[19]But his father refused and said, "I know, my son, I know. He'll become a people too, and he'll also be great. But his younger brother will be greater than he will, and his descendants will become many nations." [20]Israel blessed them that day, saying,

"Through you, Israel will
    pronounce blessings, saying,
    'May God make you
        like Ephraim and Manasseh.'"

So Israel put Ephraim before Manasseh. [21]Then Israel said to Joseph, "I'm about to die. God will be with you and return you to the land of your fathers. [22]I'm giving you one portion more than to your brothers,[u] a portion that I took from the Amorites with my sword and my bow."

Jacob reveals his sons' destinies

49

[1]Jacob summoned his sons and said, "Gather around so that I can tell you what will happen to you in the coming days.
[2] Assemble yourselves and listen,
    sons of Jacob;
        listen to Israel your father.

[3] Reuben, you are my oldest son,
    my strength and my first contender,[v]
    superior in status and superior in might.
[4] As wild as the waters, you won't endure,
    for you went up to your father's bed,
    you went up[w] and violated my couch.

[5] Simeon and Levi are brothers,
    weapons of violence their stock in trade.
[6] May I myself never enter their council.
May my honor never be linked
    to their group;

[o]LXX; MT *he informed* [p]Heb *Israel* [q]Heb *El Shaddai* or *God of the Mountain* [r]Sam, LXX, Syr; MT lacks *aram.* [s]Sam; MT *Ephrath* [t]LXX; MT *Joseph* [u]Heb uncertain [v]Or *first of my power* [w]LXX; MT *he went up*

for when they were angry,
  they killed men,
and whenever they wished,
  they maimed oxen.
[7] Cursed be their anger; it is violent,
  their rage; it is relentless.
I'll divide them up within Jacob
  and disperse them within Israel.

[8] Judah, you are the one
  your brothers will honor;
  your hand will be
    on the neck of your enemies;
  your father's sons
    will bow down to you.
[9] Judah is a lion's cub;
  from the prey, my son, you rise up.
He lies down and crouches like a lion;
  like a lioness—
    who dares disturb him?
[10] The scepter won't depart from Judah,
  nor the ruler's staff
    from among his banners.[x]
Gifts will be brought to him;
  people will obey him.
[11] He ties his male donkey to the vine,
  the colt of his female donkey
    to the vine's branches.
He washes his clothes in wine,
  his garments in the blood of grapes.
[12] His eyes are darker than wine,
  and his teeth whiter than milk.

[13] Zebulun will live at the seashore;
  he'll live at the harbor of ships,
  his border will be at Sidon.

[14] Issachar is a sturdy donkey,
  bedding down
    beside the village hearths.[y]
[15] He saw that a resting place was good
  and that the land was pleasant.
He lowered his shoulder to haul loads
  and joined the work gangs.

[16] Dan[z] will settle disputes for his people,
  as one of Israel's tribes.
[17] Dan will be a snake on the road,
  a serpent on the path,

biting a horse's heels,
  so its rider falls backward.

[18] I long for your victory, Lord.

[19] Gad[a] will be attacked by attackers,
  but he'll attack their back.

[20] Asher[b] grows fine foods,
  and he will supply
    the king's delicacies.

[21] Naphtali is a wild doe
  that gives birth to beautiful fawns.[c]

[22] Joseph is a young bull,[d]
  a young bull by a spring,
  who strides with oxen.[e]
[23] They attacked him fiercely
  and fired arrows;
    the archers attacked him furiously.
[24] But his bow stayed strong,
  and his forearms were nimble,[f]
    by the hands of the strong one
      of Jacob,
    by the name of the shepherd,
      the rock of Israel,
[25] by God, your father,
  who supports you,
by the Almighty[g] who blesses you
  with blessings from the skies above
    and blessings from the deep sea below,
    blessings from breasts and womb.
[26] The blessings of your father exceed
  the blessings of the eternal mountains,[h]
    the wealth of the everlasting hills.
May they all rest on Joseph's head,
  on the forehead of the one
    set apart from his brothers.

[27] Benjamin is a wolf who hunts:
  in the morning he devours the prey;
  in the evening he divides the plunder."

[28] These are the twelve tribes of Israel, and this is what their father said to them. He blessed them by giving each man his own particular blessing.

---

[x]Sam; MT *his feet* [y]Or *stubbornly lying beneath its saddlebags* [z]Or *he judges,* or *settles disputes* [a]Or *he attacks* or *good fortune* [b]LXX, Syr, Vulg; MT *from Asher* [c]Or *who gives beautiful words* [d]Heb uncertain [e]Heb uncertain [f]Heb uncertain; or *flexible* [g]Heb *Shaddai* or *the Mountain One* [h]LXX; Heb uncertain

UMBRELLA
MOURNING

Joseph Weeps *Genesis 49:29–50:14*
When Joseph was finally reunited with his beloved father, he had very little time with him before his father's death. Even though that made him sad, Joseph was thankful his father lived long enough to learn he was alive and doing great things. Losing a close friend or family member, no matter their age, is always sad and calls for a time of grief. Joseph prepared a funeral that allowed him and everyone who loved Israel to grieve the loss. ◊

Jacob's death and burial

²⁹Jacob ordered them, "I am soon to join my people. Bury me with my ancestors in the cave that's in the field of Ephron the Hittite; ³⁰in the cave that's in the field of Machpelah near Mamre in the land of Canaan that Abraham bought from Ephron the Hittite as a burial property. ³¹That is where Abraham and his wife Sarah are buried, and where Isaac and his wife Rebekah are buried, and where I buried Leah. ³²It is the field and the cave in it that belonged to the Hittites." ³³After he finished giving orders to his sons, he put his feet up on the bed, took his last breath, and joined his people.

50Joseph fell across his father's body, wept over him, and kissed him. ²Joseph then ordered the physicians in his service to embalm his father, and the physicians embalmed Israel. ³They mourned for him forty days because that is the period required for embalming. Then the Egyptians mourned him for seventy days. ⁴After the period of mourning had passed, Joseph spoke to Pharaoh's household: "If you approve my request, give Pharaoh this message: ⁵My father made me promise, telling me, 'I'm about to die. You must bury me in the tomb I dug for myself in the land of Canaan.' Now, let me leave and let me bury my father, and then I will return."

⁶Pharaoh replied, "Go, bury your father as you promised."

⁷So Joseph left to bury his father. All of Pharaoh's servants went with him, together with the elder statesmen in his household and all of the elder statesmen in the land of Egypt, ⁸Joseph's entire household, his brothers, and his father's household. Only the children, flocks, and cattle remained in the land of Goshen. ⁹Even chariots and horsemen went with him; it was a huge collection of people. ¹⁰When they arrived at the threshing floor of Atad on the other side of the Jordan River, they observed a solemn, deeply sorrowful period of mourning. He grieved seven days for his father.

¹¹When the Canaanites who lived in the land saw the observance of grief on Atad's threshing floor, they said, "This is a solemn observance of grief by the Egyptians." Therefore, its name is Abel-mizraim.ⁱ It is on the other side of the Jordan River. ¹²Israel's sons did for him just as he had ordered. ¹³His sons carried him to the land of Canaan and buried him in the cave in the field of Machpelah near Mamre, which Abraham had purchased as burial property from Ephron the Hittite. ¹⁴Thenʲ Joseph returned to Egypt, he, his brothers, and everyone who left with him to bury his father.

Joseph and his brothers in Egypt

¹⁵When Joseph's brothers realized that their father was now dead, they said, "What if Joseph bears a grudge against us, and wants to pay us back seriously for all of the terrible things we did to him?" ¹⁶So they approachedᵏ Joseph and said, "Your father gave orders before he died, telling us, ¹⁷'This is what you should say to Joseph. "Please, forgive your brothers' sins and misdeeds, for they did terrible things to you. Now, please forgive the sins of the servants of your father's God."'" Joseph wept when they spoke to him.

¹⁸His brothers weptˡ too, fell down in front of him, and said, "We're here as your slaves."

¹⁹But Joseph said to them, "Don't be afraid. Am I God? ²⁰You planned something bad for me, but God produced something good from it, in order to save the lives of many people, just as

Memorize
Gen 50:20

ⁱ*Or the Egyptians' observance of grief* ʲLXX; MT includes *after he buried his father.* ᵏLXX, Syr; MT *they commanded* ˡ*Or came*

he's doing today. ²¹Now, don't be afraid. I will take care of you and your children." So he put them at ease and spoke reassuringly to them.

²²Thus Joseph lived in Egypt, he and his father's household. Joseph lived 110 years ²³and saw Ephraim's grandchildren. The children of Machir, Manasseh's son, were also born on Joseph's knees. ²⁴Joseph said to his brothers, "I'm about to die. God will certainly take care of you and bring you out of this land to the land he promised to Abraham, to Isaac, and to Jacob." ²⁵Joseph made Israel's sons promise, "When God takes care of you, you must bring up my bones out of here." ²⁶Joseph died when he was 110 years old. They embalmed him and placed him in a coffin in Egypt.

did you **know?**

Joseph promised Israel's sons they would one day return to Canaan. He made them promise to take his bones back to Canaan when he died. Exodus 13:19 says when Moses and the Israelites left Egypt they kept this promise and took Joseph's bones with them. Years later the bones were buried in Shechem (Josh 24:32).

God Used Bad for Good *Genesis 50:20*

Bad things happened to Joseph. His brothers hated him. He was sold into slavery, lied about, and thrown into prison. Joseph had every reason to be angry toward the people who did those things to him. Eventually he was in a position to get back at them, but he didn't.

Joseph realized God had taken care of him during every moment in his life. That didn't mean everything was good or easy. When Potiphar's wife lied about him, Joseph couldn't defend himself. Being thrown in to prison was harder than being a slave. But Joseph didn't give up. During all that time, Joseph remembered God loved him, and he trusted that love.

Joseph's situation looked really bad, but nothing is impossible for God. God used the things that were bad in Joseph's life as a way to bring about good. During his time in prison, Joseph's ability to interpret dreams made it possible for him to meet Pharaoh, the man who ruled Egypt at the time. Because of this, Joseph became Pharaoh's second-in-command, which allowed Joseph to save his family at a time when they had no food.

Sometimes bad things happen to our family, our friends, or us. But just like Joseph, we can remember God promised never to leave us. If we trust God, God will take those bad things and turn them into something good.

Name two times when something bad happened to you.

How did God take care of you during those times?

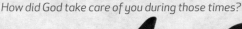

Exodus

In the book of Genesis, Jacob's family traveled to Egypt to escape starvation. Hundreds of years later, that small family had grown into a large group of people known as the Israelites. Egypt's king, Pharaoh, was so afraid the Israelites would cause him trouble that he forced them to become slaves.

Pharaoh was cruel to the Israelite slaves, but God saw their suffering. God heard their prayers for help. God sent Moses to tell Pharaoh to set the Israelites free.

The word *exodus* means "the way out," and the miraculous escape known as "the exodus" is considered one of the Bible's most important events. At first God sent diseases and plagues to force Pharaoh to free the Israelite slaves. When Pharaoh didn't obey, God told the Israelites to paint the doorframes of their homes with the blood of a lamb. This saved God's people from a deadly plague. God finally led the slaves to freedom, pushing back the waters of the Reed Sea so they could walk across on dry ground (Exod 1–15).

As the Israelites camped in the desert, God gave the Ten Commandments (Exod 20) and asked the people to obey God. They complained of thirst and hunger, but God gave them water and food. This exciting story explains how God saved a people and taught them to trust! ◊

1 These are the names of the Israelites who came to Egypt with Jacob along with their households: [2]Reuben, Simeon, Levi, and Judah, [3]Issachar, Zebulun, and Benjamin, [4]Dan and Naphtali, Gad and Asher. [5]The total number in Jacob's family was seventy. Joseph was already in Egypt. [6]Eventually, Joseph, his brothers, and everyone in his generation died. [7]But the Israelites were fertile and became populous. They multiplied and grew dramatically, filling the whole land.

Israel is oppressed

[8]Now a new king came to power in Egypt who didn't know Joseph. [9]He said to his people, "The Israelite people are now larger in number and stronger than we are. [10]Come on, let's be smart and deal with them. Otherwise, they will only grow in number. And if war breaks out, they will join our enemies, fight against us, and then escape from the land." [11]As a result, the Egyptians put foremen of forced work gangs over the Israelites to harass them with hard work. They had to build storage cities named Pithom and Rameses for Pharaoh. [12]But the more they were oppressed, the more they grew and spread, so much so that the Egyptians started to look at the Israelites with disgust and dread. [13]So the Egyptians enslaved the Israelites. [14]They made their lives miserable with hard labor, making mortar and bricks, doing field work, and by forcing them to do all kinds of other cruel work.

[15]The king of Egypt spoke to two Hebrew midwives named Shiphrah and Puah: [16]"When you are helping the Hebrew women give birth and you see the baby being born, if it's a boy, kill him. But if it's a girl, you can let her live." [17]Now the two midwives respected God so they didn't obey the Egyptian king's order. Instead, they let the baby boys live.

[18]So the king of Egypt called the two midwives and said to them, "Why are you doing this? Why are you letting the baby boys live?" [19]The two midwives said to Pharaoh, "Because Hebrew women aren't like Egyptian women. They're much stronger and give birth before any midwives can get to them." [20]So God treated the midwives well, and the people kept on multiplying and became very strong. [21]And because the midwives respected God, God gave them households of their own.

[22]Then Pharaoh gave an order to all his people: "Throw every baby boy born to the Hebrews into the Nile River, but you can let all the girls live."

Moses' birth

2 Now a man from Levi's household married a Levite woman. [2]The woman became pregnant and gave birth to a son. She saw that the baby was healthy and beautiful, so she hid him for three months. [3]When she couldn't hide him any longer, she took a reed basket and sealed it up with black tar. She put the child in the basket and set the basket among the reeds at the riverbank. [4]The baby's older sister stood watch nearby to see what would happen to him.

[5]Pharaoh's daughter came down to bathe in the river, while her women servants walked along beside the river. She saw the basket among the reeds, and she sent one of her servants to bring it to her. [6]When she opened it, she saw the child. The boy was crying, and she felt sorry for him. She said, "This must be one of the Hebrews' children."

[7]Then the baby's sister said to Pharaoh's daughter, "Would you like me to go and find one of the Hebrew women to nurse the child for you?"

[8]Pharaoh's daughter agreed, "Yes, do that." So the girl went and called the child's mother. [9]Pharaoh's daughter said to her, "Take this child and nurse it for me, and I'll pay you for your work." So the woman took the child and nursed it. [10]After the child had grown up, she brought him back to Pharaoh's daughter, who adopted him as her son. She named him Moses, "because," she said, "I pulled him out[a] of the water."

did you know? *Moses* sounds like the Hebrew word that means "to draw out." Pharaoh's daughter chose the name because she drew him out of the water. Moses was saved when his mother placed him in a basket on the river and when Pharaoh's daughter drew his basket out of the water.

[a]Heb *mashah* sounds like Moses (*moshe*).

Moses runs away to Midian

¹¹One day after Moses had become an adult, he went out among his people and he saw their forced labor. He saw an Egyptian beating a Hebrew, one of his own people. ¹²He looked around to make sure no one else was there. Then he killed the Egyptian and hid him in the sand.

¹³When Moses went out the next day, he saw two Hebrew men fighting with each other. Moses said to the one who had started the fight, "Why are you abusing your fellow Hebrew?"

¹⁴He replied, "Who made you a boss or judge over us? Are you planning to kill me like you killed the Egyptian?"

Then Moses was afraid when he realized: They obviously know what I did. ¹⁵When Pharaoh heard about it, he tried to kill Moses.

But Moses ran away from Pharaoh and settled down in the land of Midian. One day Moses was sitting by a well. ¹⁶Now there was a Midianite priest who had seven daughters. The daughters came to draw water and fill the troughs so that their father's flock could drink. ¹⁷But some shepherds came along and rudely chased them away. Moses got up, rescued the women, and gave their flock water to drink.

¹⁸When they went back home to their father Reuel,ᵇ he asked, "How were you able to come back home so soon today?"

¹⁹They replied, "An Egyptian man rescued us from a bunch of shepherds. Afterward, he even helped us draw water to let the flock drink."

²⁰Reuel said to his daughters, "So where is he? Why did you leave this man? Invite him to eat a meal with us."

²¹Moses agreed to come and live with the man, who gave his daughter Zipporah to Moses as his wife. ²²She gave birth to a son, and Moses named him Gershom, "because," he said, "I've been an immigrantᶜ living in a foreign land."

²³A long time passed, and the Egyptian king died. The Israelites were still groaning because of their hard work. They cried out, and their cry to be rescued from the hard work rose up to God. ²⁴God heard their cry of grief, and God remembered his covenant with Abraham, Isaac, and Jacob. ²⁵God looked at the Israelites, and God understood.

ᵇAlso called Jethro ᶜHeb *ger* sounds like *Gershom.*

Why Do People Suffer Before God Rescues Them?
Exodus 1:8-14

This is a difficult question, one people still struggle to answer, just like the people we read about in the Bible did. In Exodus, we read how the Israelites worked as slaves for the pharaoh in Egypt for a very long time. Their lives were difficult and filled with suffering. It's easy for us to ask *Why did God wait so long to rescue them?* Why didn't God do something sooner?

Slaves brought to America from Africa probably asked this same kind of question. How long would they suffer before they were set free? We learn from them and from this story in Exodus that God works in mysterious ways. We don't always know how or why suffering is allowed to happen. But we do know that we're in God's hands. God works through people and situations to help those who suffer.

Have you ever been through a hard time?

How did God care for you during this time?

Moses at the burning bush

3 Moses was taking care of the flock for his father-in-law Jethro,[d] Midian's priest. He led his flock out to the edge of the desert, and he came to God's mountain called Horeb. [2] The LORD's messenger appeared to him in a flame of fire in the middle of a bush. Moses saw that the bush was in flames, but it didn't burn up. [3] Then Moses said to himself, Let me check out this amazing sight and find out why the bush isn't burning up.

[4] When the LORD saw that he was coming to look, God called to him out of the bush, "Moses, Moses!"

Moses said, "I'm here."

[5] Then the LORD said, "Don't come any closer! Take off your sandals, because you are standing on holy ground." [6] He continued, "I am the God of your father, Abraham's God, Isaac's God, and Jacob's God." Moses hid his face because he was afraid to look at God.

[7] Then the LORD said, "I've clearly seen my people oppressed in Egypt. I've heard their cry of injustice because of their slave masters. I know about their pain. [8] I've come down to rescue them from the Egyptians in order to take them out of that land and bring them to a good and broad land, a land that's full of milk and honey, a place where the Canaanites, the Hittites, the Amorites, the Perizzites, the Hivites, and the Jebusites all live. [9] Now the

Memorize Exod 3:8

Israelites' cries of injustice have reached me. I've seen just how much the Egyptians have oppressed them. [10] So get going. I'm sending you to Pharaoh to bring my people, the Israelites, out of Egypt."

[11] But Moses said to God, "Who am I to go to Pharaoh and to bring the Israelites out of Egypt?"

did you know? Moses asked God for God's name. In Moses' time, people believed that knowing a god's true name meant they had that god's power. God answered by saying, "I AM WHO I AM." In short, God told Moses that God's full power was too big to capture in a name.

LIFE PRESERVER

How did Moses first hear God's voice? *Exodus 3:1-12*

Throughout the Old Testament there are stories of people who heard God speaking to them, or who met God in strange and interesting places. For example, Moses was taking care of a flock of sheep when all of a sudden the Lord's messenger appeared in a bush that was on fire. And then Moses heard God's voice calling him. It was at this place that God called Moses to lead God's people out of Egypt and made a promise to be with Moses.

God may not speak to you today in a burning bush, but God is certainly present and active in your life. Look for the ways you hear God's voice and see the work of God's hands in the world today. We hear God's voice when, like Moses, we agree to take on important tasks of leadership. We hear God's voice when we feed the hungry, help a friend, or take care of those who are sick. We hear God's voice when we visit with someone who is lonely. We hear God's voice whenever we remember to share our love and our talents with someone else. ◉

[12] God said, "I'll be with you. And this will show you that I'm the one who sent you. After you bring the people out of Egypt, you will come back here and worship God on this mountain."

God's special name

[13] But Moses said to God, "If I now come to the Israelites and say to them, 'The God of your ancestors has sent me to you,' they are going to ask me, 'What's this God's name?' What am I supposed to say to them?"

[14] God said to Moses, "I Am Who I Am.[e] So say to the Israelites, 'I Am has sent me to you.'" [15] God continued, "Say to the Israelites, 'The LORD, the God of your ancestors, Abraham's God, Isaac's God, and Jacob's God, has sent me to you.' This is my name forever; this is how all generations will remember me.

[16] "Go and get Israel's elders together and say to them, 'The LORD, the God of your ancestors, the God of Abraham, of Isaac, and of Jacob, has appeared to me. The LORD said, "I've been paying close attention to you and to what has been done to you in Egypt. [17] I've decided to take you away from the harassment in Egypt

to the land of the Canaanites, the Hittites, the Amorites, the Perizzites, the Hivites, and the Jebusites, a land full of milk and honey.'' [18]They will accept what you say to them. Then you and Israel's elders will go to Egypt's king and say to him, 'The LORD, the Hebrews' God, has met with us. So now let us go on a three-day journey into the desert so that we can offer sacrifices to the LORD our God.' [19]However, I know that Egypt's king won't let you go unless he's forced to do it. [20]So I'll use my strength and hit Egypt with dramatic displays of my power. After that, he'll let you go.

[21]"I'll make it so that when you leave Egypt, the Egyptians will be kind to you and you won't go away empty-handed. [22]Every woman will ask her neighbor along with the immigrant in her household for their silver and their gold jewelry as well as their clothing. Then you will put it on your sons and daughters, and you will rob the Egyptians."

Signs of power

4 Then Moses replied, "But what if they don't believe me or pay attention to me? They might say to me, 'The LORD didn't appear to you!'"

[2]The LORD said to him, "What's that in your hand?"

Moses replied, "A shepherd's rod."

[3]The LORD said, "Throw it down on the ground." So Moses threw it on the ground,

God Uses Unlikely People to Do Amazing Things   *Exodus 4:1-17*

Sometimes we're asked to do things we are afraid of. Some people may be scared to talk to a new student in their class at school. Others may worry about singing or talking in front of a group of people. When we're afraid, we may feel hot all over and have trouble speaking or moving. Whenever you feel frightened, it may help to remember that you're not alone. Many people, including Moses, have been afraid.

When God told Moses to go and tell Pharaoh to free the Israelites, Moses—the former prince of Egypt—tried to get out of it. Moses asked God, "What if the Israelites don't believe me?" He even told God that he had a problem speaking, as if God didn't already know.

In the end, Moses obeyed God. The Israelites were freed from their slavery, and Moses became one of the greatest leaders in history.

God uses unlikely people to do amazing things. Pharaoh had many advisors, but only Joseph the prisoner explained the king's dreams and saved the land of Egypt from drought. There were many soldiers in the army of Israel, but God used David, a young boy, to defeat Goliath. Esther was understandably terrified of being killed when she approached the king to save her people.

God doesn't use only the people who are strong, talented, or rich. God chooses people who will obey.

Think of a time when you overcame a fear.

What did you learn about being afraid?

and it turned into a snake. Moses jumped back from it. ⁴Then the Lᴏʀᴅ said to Moses, "Reach out and grab the snake by the tail." So Moses reached out and grabbed it, and it turned back into a rod in his hand. ⁵"Do this so that they will believe that the Lᴏʀᴅ, the God of their ancestors, Abraham's God, Isaac's God, and Jacob's God has in fact appeared to you."

⁶Again, the Lᴏʀᴅ said to Moses, "Put your hand inside your coat." So Moses put his hand inside his coat. When he took his hand out, his hand had a skin disease flaky like snow. ⁷Then God said, "Put your hand back inside your coat." So Moses put his hand back inside his coat. When he took it back out again, the skin of his hand had returned to normal. ⁸"If they won't believe you or pay attention to the first sign, they may believe the second sign. ⁹If they won't believe even these two signs or pay attention to you, then take some water from the Nile River and pour it out on dry ground. The water that you take from the Nile will turn into blood on the dry ground."

¹⁰But Moses said to the Lᴏʀᴅ, "My Lord, I've never been able to speak well, not yesterday, not the day before, and certainly not now since you've been talking to your servant. I have a slow mouth and a thick tongue."

¹¹Then the Lᴏʀᴅ said to him, "Who gives people the ability to speak? Who's responsible for making them unable to speak or hard of hearing, sighted or blind? Isn't it I, the Lᴏʀᴅ? ¹²Now go! I'll help you speak, and I'll teach you what you should say."

¹³But Moses said, "Please, my Lord, just send someone else."

¹⁴Then the Lᴏʀᴅ got angry at Moses and said, "What about your brother Aaron the Levite? I know he can speak very well. He's on his way out to meet you now, and he's looking forward to seeing you. ¹⁵Speak to him and tell him what he's supposed to say. I'll help both of you speak, and I'll teach both of you what to do. ¹⁶Aaron will speak for you to the people. He'll be a spokesperson for you, and you will be like God for him. ¹⁷Take this shepherd's rod with you too so that you can do the signs."

Moses goes back to Egypt

¹⁸Moses went back to his father-in-law Jethro and said to him, "Please let me go back to my family in Egypt and see whether or not they are still living."

Jethro said to Moses, "Go in peace."

¹⁹The Lᴏʀᴅ said to Moses in Midian, "Go back to Egypt because everyone there who wanted to kill you has died." ²⁰So Moses took his wife and his children, put them on a donkey, and went back to the land of Egypt. Moses also carried the shepherd's rod from God in his hand.

²¹The Lᴏʀᴅ said to Moses, "When you go back to Egypt, make sure that you appear before Pharaoh and do all the amazing acts that I've given you the power to do. But I'll make him stubborn so that he won't let the people go. ²²Then say to Pharaoh, 'This is what the Lᴏʀᴅ says: Israel is my oldest son. ²³I said to you, "Let my son go so he could worship me." But you refused to let him go. As a result, now I'm going to kill your oldest son.'"

²⁴During their journey, as they camped overnight, the Lᴏʀᴅ met Moses[f] and tried to

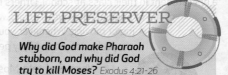

LIFE PRESERVER

Why did God make Pharaoh stubborn, and why did God try to kill Moses? *Exodus 4:21-26*

This part of the story of Moses and Pharaoh can be a bit confusing. One phrase is repeated many times, about how Pharaoh became stubborn. Pharaoh had made up his mind to keep the Israelites in slavery in Egypt. He would not let the people go. But the Bible says it was God who made Pharaoh stubborn, which might seem odd.

This story teaches that God considered Israel to be God's oldest child, and that God tried to call Moses to lead the people. This might have been an example of what was eventually going to happen after God had sent all the plagues and none of them had convinced Pharaoh to let God's people go. The only thing left was to send the final plague of the killing of the oldest male child.

God may have made Pharaoh stubborn, causing Pharaoh to resist God so that God could reveal God's power to the Israelites who were enslaved in Egypt. Sometimes God used miraculous events to convince people of God's power. ◆

///

kill him. ²⁵But Zipporah took a sharp-edged flint stone and cut off her son's foreskin. Then she touched Moses' genitals[g] with it, and she said, "You are my bridegroom because of bloodshed." ²⁶So the Lord let him alone. At that time, she announced, "A bridegroom because of bloodshed by circumcision."

²⁷The Lord said to Aaron, "Go into the desert to meet Moses." So he went, and Aaron met him at God's mountain and greeted him with a kiss. ²⁸Moses told Aaron what the Lord had said about his mission and all the signs that the Lord had told him to do. ²⁹Then Moses and Aaron called together all the Israelite elders. ³⁰Aaron told them everything that the Lord had told to Moses, and he performed the signs in front of the people. ³¹The people believed. When they heard that the Lord had paid attention to the Israelites and had seen their oppression, they bowed down and worshipped.

First meeting with Pharaoh

5 Afterward, Moses and Aaron went to Pharaoh and said, "This is what the Lord, Israel's God, says: 'Let my people go so that they can hold a festival for me in the desert.'"

Bet you can read this in 2 minutes. Ready, set, go!

²But Pharaoh said, "Who is this Lord whom I'm supposed to obey by letting Israel go? I don't know this Lord, and I certainly won't let Israel go."

³Then they said, "The Hebrews' God has appeared to us. Let us go on a three-day journey into the desert so we can offer sacrifices to the Lord our God. Otherwise, the Lord will give us a deadly disease or violence."

⁴The king of Egypt said to them, "Moses and Aaron, why are you making the people slack off from their work? Do the hard work yourselves!" ⁵Pharaoh continued, "The land's people are now numerous. Yet you want them to stop their hard work?"

⁶On the very same day Pharaoh commanded the people's slave masters and supervisors, ⁷"Don't supply the people with the straw they need to make bricks like you did before. Let them go out and gather the straw for themselves. ⁸But still make sure that they produce the same number of bricks as they made before. Don't reduce the number! They are weak and lazy, and that's why they cry, 'Let's go and offer sacrifices to our God.' ⁹Make the men's work so hard that it's all they can do, and they can't focus on these empty lies."

¹⁰So the people's slave masters and supervisors came out and spoke to the people, "This is what Pharaoh says, 'I'm not giving you straw anymore. ¹¹Go and get the straw on your own, wherever you can find it. But your work won't be reduced at all.'" ¹²So the people spread out all through the land of Egypt to gather stubble for straw. ¹³The slave masters drove them hard and said, "Make sure you make the same daily quota as when you had the straw." ¹⁴The Israelite supervisors, whom Pharaoh's slave masters had set over them, were also beaten and asked, "Why didn't you produce the same number of bricks yesterday and today as you did before?"

¹⁵Then the Israelite supervisors came and pleaded to Pharaoh, "Why do you treat your servants like this? ¹⁶No straw is supplied to your servants, yet they say to us, 'Make bricks!' Look at how your servants are being beaten! Your own people are to blame!"

¹⁷Pharaoh replied, "You are lazy bums, nothing but lazy bums. That's why you say, 'Let us go and offer sacrifices to the Lord.' ¹⁸Go and get back to work! No straw will be given to you, but you still need to make the same number of bricks."

¹⁹The Israelite supervisors saw how impossible their situation was when they were commanded, "Don't reduce your daily quota of bricks." ²⁰When they left Pharaoh, they met Moses and Aaron, who were waiting for them. ²¹The supervisors said to them, "Let the Lord see and judge what you've done! You've made us stink in the opinion of Pharaoh and his servants. You've given them a reason to kill us."

²²Then Moses turned to the Lord and said, "My Lord, why have you abused this people? Why did you send me for this? ²³Ever since I first came to Pharaoh to speak in your name, he has abused this people. And you've done absolutely nothing to rescue your people."

[g]Or *his feet*

God reassures Moses

6 The LORD replied to Moses, "Now you will see what I'll do to Pharaoh. In fact, he'll be so eager to let them go that he'll drive them out of his land by force."

²God also said to Moses: "I am the LORD. ³I appeared to Abraham, Isaac, and Jacob as God Almighty,ʰ but I didn't reveal myself to them by my name 'The LORD.' ⁴I also set up my covenant with them to give them the land of Canaan where they lived as immigrants. ⁵I've also heard the cry of grief of the Israelites, whom the Egyptians have turned into slaves, and I've remembered my covenant. ⁶Therefore, say to the Israelites, 'I am the LORD. I'll bring you out from Egyptian forced labor. I'll rescue you from your slavery to them. I'll set you free with great power and with momentous events of justice. ⁷I'll take you as my people, and I'll be your God. You will know that I, the LORD, am your God, who has freed you from Egyptian forced labor. ⁸I'll bring you into the land that I promised to give to Abraham, Isaac, and Jacob. I'll give it to you as your possession. I am the LORD.'" ⁹Moses told this to the Israelites. But they didn't listen to Moses, because of their complete exhaustion and their hard labor.

¹⁰Then the LORD said to Moses, ¹¹"Go and tell Pharaoh, Egypt's king, to let the Israelites out of his land."

¹²But Moses said to the LORD, "The Israelites haven't even listened to me. How can I expect Pharaoh to listen to me, especially since I'm not a very good speaker?" ¹³Nevertheless, the LORD spoke to Moses and Aaron about the Israelites and

Pharaoh, Egypt's king, giving them orders to let the Israelites go from the land of Egypt.

did you **know?** The Hebrew word translated "I am the LORD" is *YAHWEH*. This was the name God gave to Moses at the burning bush. The Israelites believed the name YAHWEH was so holy they would not say it out loud or write it completely.

Family line of Moses and Aaron

¹⁴These were the leaders of their households.

The descendants of Reuben, Israel's oldest son: Hanoch, Pallu, Hezron, and Carmi. These were Reuben's clans. ¹⁵The Simeonites: Jemuel, Jamin, Ohad, Jachin, Zohar, and Shaul, a Canaanite woman's son. These were Simeon's clans.

¹⁶These were the Levites' names by their generations: Gershon, Kohath, and Merari. Levi lived 137 years. ¹⁷The Gershonites: Libni and Shimei and their clans. ¹⁸The Kohathites: Amram, Izhar, Hebron, and Uzziel. Kohath lived 133 years. ¹⁹The Merarites: Mahli and Mushi. These were the Levite clans by their generations.

²⁰Amram married Jochebed, his father's sister. She gave birth to Aaron and Moses. Amram lived 137 years. ²¹The Izharites: Korah, Nepheg, and Zichri. ²²The Uzzielites: Mishael, Elzaphan, and Sithri. ²³Aaron married Elisheba, Amminadab's daughter and Nahshon's sister. She gave birth to Nadab, Abihu, Eleazar, and Ithamar. ²⁴The Korahites: Assir, Elkanah, and Abiasaph. These were the Korahite clans. ²⁵Aaron's son Eleazar married one of Putiel's daughters. She gave birth to Phinehas. These were the leaders of Levite households by their clans.

²⁶It was this same Aaron and Moses whom the LORD commanded, "Bring the Israelites out of the land of Egypt in military formation." ²⁷It was also this same Moses and Aaron who spoke to Pharaoh king of Egypt to bring the Israelites out of Egypt.

²⁸At the time the LORD spoke to Moses in the land of Egypt, ²⁹the LORD said to him, "I am the LORD. Tell Pharaoh, Egypt's king, everything that I've said to you."

LIGHTHOUSE

PRAYER

God Listens to Our Prayers *Exodus 6:5*
When we pray to God, God listens. God told Moses that God had heard the cries of the Israelite people, who were slaves in Egypt. God promised to remember the covenant God had made and to deliver the people from slavery and lead them to the promised land. God hears every one of our prayers.◊

ʰHeb *El Shaddai* or *God of the Mountain*

[30]But Moses replied to the LORD, "Look, I'm not a very good speaker. How is Pharaoh ever going to listen to me?"

7 The LORD said to Moses, "See, I've made you like God to Pharaoh, and your brother Aaron will be your prophet. [2]You will say everything that I command you, and your brother Aaron will tell Pharaoh to let the Israelites out of his land. [3]But I'll make Pharaoh stubborn, and I'll perform many of my signs and amazing acts in the land of Egypt. [4]When Pharaoh refuses to listen to you, then I'll act against Egypt and I'll bring my people the Israelites out of the land of Egypt in military formation by momentous events of justice. [5]The Egyptians will come to know that I am the LORD, when I act against Egypt and bring the Israelites out from among them." [6]Moses and Aaron did just as the LORD commanded them. [7]Moses was 80 years old and Aaron was 83 when they spoke to Pharaoh.

Turning rods into snakes

[8]The LORD said to Moses and Aaron, [9]"When Pharaoh says to you, 'Do one of your amazing acts,' then say to Aaron, 'Take your shepherd's rod and throw it down in front of Pharaoh, and it will turn into a cobra.'"[i]

[10]So Moses and Aaron went to Pharaoh and did just as the LORD commanded. Aaron threw down his shepherd's rod in front of Pharaoh and his officials, and it turned into a cobra. [11]Then Pharaoh called together his wise men and wizards, and Egypt's religious experts[j] did the same thing by using their secret knowledge. [12]Each one threw down his rod, and they turned into cobras. But then Aaron's rod swallowed up each of their rods. [13]However, Pharaoh remained stubborn. He wouldn't listen to them, just as the LORD had said.

Water into blood

[14]Then the LORD said to Moses, "Pharaoh is stubborn. He still refuses to let the people go. [15]Go to Pharaoh in the morning. As he is going out to the water, make sure you stand at the bank of the Nile River so you will run into him. Bring along the shepherd's rod that turned into a snake. [16]Say to him, The LORD, the Hebrews' God, has sent me to you with this message: Let my people go so that they can worship me in the desert. Up to now you still haven't listened. [17]This is what the LORD says: By this you will know that I am the LORD. I'm now going to hit the water of the Nile River with this rod in my hand, and it will turn into blood. [18]The fish in the Nile are going to die, the Nile will stink, and the Egyptians won't be able to drink water from the Nile." [19]The LORD said to Moses, "Say to Aaron, 'Take your shepherd's rod and stretch out your hand over Egypt's waters—over their rivers, their canals, their marshes, and all their bodies of water—so that they turn into blood. There will be blood all over the land of Egypt, even in wooden and stone containers.'"

[20]Moses and Aaron did just as the LORD commanded. He raised the shepherd's rod and hit the water in the Nile in front of Pharaoh and his officials, and all the water in the Nile turned into blood. [21]The fish in the Nile died, and the Nile began to stink so that the Egyptians couldn't drink water from the Nile. There was blood all over the land of Egypt. [22]But the Egyptian religious experts did the same thing with their secret knowledge. As a result, Pharaoh remained stubborn, and he wouldn't listen to them, just as the LORD had said. [23]Pharaoh turned and went back to his palace. He wasn't impressed even by this. [24]Meanwhile, all the Egyptians had to dig for drinking water along the banks of the Nile River, because they couldn't drink the water of the Nile itself. [25]Seven days went by after the LORD had struck the Nile River.

Invasion of frogs

8 [k]Then the LORD said to Moses, "Go to Pharaoh and tell him: This is what the LORD says: Let my people go so that they can worship me. [2]If you refuse to let them go, then I'll send a plague of frogs over your whole country. [3]The Nile will overflow with frogs. They'll get into your palace, into your bedroom and onto your bed, into your officials' houses, and among all your people, and even into your ovens and bread pans. [4]The frogs will crawl up on you, your people, and all your officials." [5]And[l] the LORD said to Moses, "Tell

[i]Or serpent [j]Or magicians [k]7:26 in Heb [l]8:1 in Heb

Aaron, 'Stretch out your hand with your shepherd's rod over the rivers, the canals, and the marshes, and make the frogs crawl up all over the land of Egypt.'" ⁶So Aaron stretched out his hand over the waters of Egypt. The frogs crawled up and covered the land of Egypt. ⁷However, the Egyptian religious experts were able to do the same thing by their secret knowledge. They too made frogs crawl up onto the land of Egypt.

⁸Then Pharaoh called for Moses and Aaron, and said, "If you pray to the Lord to get rid of the frogs from me and my people, then I'll let the people go so that they can offer sacrifices to the Lord."

⁹Moses said to Pharaoh, "Have it your way. When should I pray for you and your officials and your people to remove the frogs from your houses, courtyards, and fields? They'll stay only in the Nile."

¹⁰Pharaoh said, "Tomorrow!"

Moses said, "Just as you say! That way you will know that there is no one like the Lord our God. ¹¹The frogs will leave you,

your houses, your officials, and your people. They'll stay only in the Nile." ¹²After Moses and Aaron had left Pharaoh, Moses cried out to the Lord about the frogs that the Lord had brought on Pharaoh. ¹³The Lord did as Moses asked. The frogs died inside the houses, out in the yards, and in the fields. ¹⁴They gathered them together in big piles, and the land began to stink. ¹⁵But when Pharaoh saw that the disaster was over, he became stubborn again and wouldn't listen to them, just as the Lord had said.

Swarming lice

¹⁶Then the Lord said to Moses, "Tell Aaron, 'Stretch out your shepherd's rod and hit the land's dirt so that lice[m] appear in the whole land of Egypt.'" ¹⁷They did this. Aaron stretched out his hand with his shepherd's rod, hit the land's dirt, and lice appeared on both people and animals. All the land's dirt turned into lice throughout the whole land of Egypt.

¹⁸The religious experts[n] tried to produce lice by their secret knowledge, but they

[m]Heb uncertain [n]Or *magicians*

What Did the Plagues of Egypt Mean in Those Times? *Exodus 7–11*

During the time the Israelites were slaves in Egypt, the Egyptian people believed there were many different gods who ruled over different parts of nature, including insects, animals, water, and the sky. Many believed that Pharaoh, the ruler of Egypt, was a god called Horus. Because the Israelites had been in slavery for such a long time—over four hundred years—they had begun to forget about God.

The plagues were a way to prove to both the Egyptians and the Israelites that these many different gods were not real. God showed that even the god Pharaoh could not stand up to God or protect the people of Egypt.

By sending the plagues against the Egyptians while protecting the Israelites, God proved that God was the creator of the universe. Only God could control the forces of nature, animals, insects, darkness and light, and life and death. Only God was worthy of being worshipped.

What are some things people worship today?

What does God do today to get people's attention?

weren't able to do it. There were lice on people and animals. [19]The religious experts said to Pharaoh, "This is something only God could do!" But Pharaoh was stubborn, and he wouldn't listen to them, just as the LORD had said.

Insects fill Egypt

[20]The LORD said to Moses, "Get up early in the morning and confront Pharaoh as he goes out to the water. Say to him, This is what the LORD says: Let my people go so that they can worship me. [21]If you refuse to let my people go, I'll send swarms of insects[o] on you, your officials, your people, and your houses. All Egyptian houses will be filled with swarms of insects and also the ground that they cover. [22]But on that day I'll set apart the land of Goshen, where my people live. No swarms of insects will come there so you will know that I, the LORD, am in this land. [23]I'll put a barrier between my people and your people. This sign will happen tomorrow." [24]The LORD did this. Great swarms of insects came into the houses of Pharaoh and his officials and into the whole land of Egypt. The land was ruined by the insects.

[25]Then Pharaoh called in Moses and Aaron and said, "Go, offer sacrifices to your God within the land."

[26]Moses replied, "It wouldn't be right to do that, because the sacrifices that we offer to the LORD our God will offend Egyptians. If we openly offer sacrifices that offend Egyptians, won't they stone us to death? [27]We need to go for a three-day journey into the desert to offer sacrifices to the LORD our God as he has ordered us."

[28]So Pharaoh said, "I'll let you go to offer sacrifices to the LORD your God in the desert, provided you don't go too far away and you pray for me."

[29]Moses said, "I'll leave you now, and I'll pray to the LORD. Tomorrow the swarms of insects will leave Pharaoh, his officials, and his people. Just don't let Pharaoh lie to us again and not let the people go to offer sacrifices to the LORD."

[30]So Moses left Pharaoh and prayed to the LORD. [31]The LORD did as Moses asked and removed the swarms of insects from Pharaoh,

from his officials, and from his people. Not one insect remained. [32]But Pharaoh was stubborn once again, and he wouldn't let the people go.

Animals sick and dying

9 Then the LORD said to Moses, "Go to Pharaoh and say to him, This is what the LORD, the Hebrews' God, says: Let my people go so that they can worship me. [2]If you refuse to let them go and you continue to hold them back, [3]the LORD will send a very deadly disease on your livestock in the field: on horses, donkeys, camels, cattle, and flocks. [4]But the LORD will distinguish Israel's livestock from Egypt's livestock so that not one that belongs to the Israelites will die." [5]The LORD set a time and said, "Tomorrow the LORD will do this in the land." [6]And the next day the LORD did it. All of the Egyptian livestock died, but not one animal that belonged to the Israelites died. [7]Pharaoh asked around and found out that not one of Israel's livestock had died. But Pharaoh was stubborn, and he wouldn't let the people go.

Skin sores and blisters

[8]Then the LORD said to Moses and Aaron, "Take handfuls of ashes from a furnace and have Moses throw it up in the air in front of Pharaoh. [9]The ashes will turn to soot over the whole land of Egypt. It will cause skin sores that will break out in blisters on people and animals in the whole land of Egypt." [10]So they took ashes from the furnace, and they stood in front of Pharaoh. Moses threw the ash up in the air, and it caused skin sores and blisters to break out on people and animals. [11]The religious experts[p] couldn't stand up to Moses because of the skin sores, because there were skin sores on the religious experts as well as on all the Egyptians. [12]But the LORD made Pharaoh stubborn, and Pharaoh wouldn't listen to them, just as the LORD had said to Moses.

Hail and thunder

[13]Then the LORD said to Moses, "Get up early in the morning and confront Pharaoh. Say to him, This is what the LORD, the God of

the Hebrews, says: Let my people go so that they can worship me. [14]This time I'm going to send all my plagues on you, your officials, and your people so that you will know that there is no one like me in the whole world. [15]By now I could have used my power to strike you and your people with a deadly disease so that you would have disappeared from the earth. [16]But I've left you standing for this reason: in order to show you my power and in order to make my name known in the whole world. [17]You are still abusing your power against my people, and you refuse to let them go. [18]Tomorrow at this time I'll cause the heaviest hail to fall on Egypt that has ever fallen from the day Egypt was founded until now. [19]So bring under shelter your livestock and all that belongs to you that is out in the open. Every person or animal that is out in the open field and isn't brought inside will die when the hail rains down on them." [20]Some of Pharaoh's officials who took the LORD's word seriously rushed to bring their servants and livestock inside for shelter. [21]Others who didn't take the LORD's word to heart left their servants and livestock out in the open field.

LIGHTHOUSE

RESPECT FOR GOD

Follow God's Commandments *Exodus 9:20*
Pharaoh refused to let God's people go. So God told Pharaoh that the heaviest hail that had ever fallen on Egypt was going to fall the next day. Egypt is normally very dry, like a desert with hardly any rain! It would have been completely strange for hail to fall in this part of the world. Some of Pharaoh's officials took God's word seriously and rushed to bring their servants and livestock inside for shelter. Others did not. The ones who followed God's commandments were spared the damage of the hailstorm. ◆

[22]The LORD said to Moses, "Raise your hand toward the sky so that hail will fall on the whole land of Egypt, on people and animals and all the grain in the fields in the land of Egypt." [23]Then Moses raised his shepherd's rod toward the sky, and the LORD sent thunder and hail, and lightning struck the earth. The LORD rained hail on the land of Egypt. [24]The hail and the lightning flashing in the middle of the hail were so severe that there had been nothing like it in the entire land of Egypt since it first became a nation. [25]The hail beat down everything that was in the open field throughout the entire land of Egypt, both people and animals. The hail also beat down all the grain in the fields, and it shattered every tree out in the field. [26]The only place where hail didn't fall was in the land of Goshen where the Israelites lived.

[27]Then Pharaoh sent for Moses and Aaron and said to them, "This time I've sinned. The LORD is right, and I and my people are wrong. [28]Pray to the LORD! Enough of God's thunder and hail! I'm going to let you go. You don't need to stay here any longer."

[29]Moses said to him, "As soon as I've left the city, I'll spread out my hands to the LORD. Then the thunder and the hail will stop and won't return so that you will know that the earth belongs to the LORD. [30]But I know that you and your officials still don't take the LORD God seriously." ([31]Now the flax and the barley were destroyed, because the barley had ears of grain and the flax had buds. [32]But both durum and spelt wheat weren't ruined, because they hadn't come up.) [33]Moses left Pharaoh and the city, and spread out his hands to the LORD. Then the thunder and the hail stopped, and the rain stopped pouring down on the earth. [34]But when Pharaoh saw that the rain, hail, and thunder had stopped, he sinned again. Pharaoh and his officials became stubborn. [35]Because of his stubbornness, Pharaoh refused to let the Israelites go, just as the LORD had told Moses.

Invasion of locusts

10 Then the LORD said to Moses, "Go to Pharaoh. I've made him and his officials stubborn so that I can show them my signs [2]and so that you can tell your children and grandchildren how I overpowered the Egyptians with the signs I did among them. You will know that I am the LORD."

[3]So Moses and Aaron went to Pharaoh and said to him, "This is what the LORD, the Hebrews' God, says: How long will you refuse to respect me? Let my people go so that they can worship me. [4]Otherwise, if you refuse to let my people go, I'm going to bring locusts

into your country tomorrow. [5]They will cover the landscape so that you won't be able to see the ground. They will eat the last bit of vegetation that was left after the hail. They will eat all your trees growing in the fields. [6]The locusts will fill your houses and all your officials' houses and all the Egyptians' houses. Your parents and even your grandparents have never seen anything like it during their entire lifetimes in this fertile land." Then Moses turned and left Pharaoh.

[7]Pharaoh's officials said to him, "How long will this man trap us in a corner like this? Let the people go so that they can worship the LORD their God. Don't you get it? Egypt is being destroyed!"

[8]So Moses and Aaron were brought back to Pharaoh, and he said to them, "Go! Worship the LORD your God! But who exactly is going with you?"

[9]Moses said, "We'll go with our young and old, with our sons and daughters, and with our flocks and herds, because we all must observe the LORD's festival."

[10]Pharaoh said to them, "Yes, the LORD will be with you, all right, especially if I let your children go with you! Obviously, you are plotting some evil scheme. [11]No way! Only your men can go and worship the LORD, because that's what you asked for." Then Pharaoh had them chased out of his presence.

[12]Then the LORD said to Moses: "Stretch out your hand over the land of Egypt so that the locusts will swarm over the land of Egypt and eat all of the land's grain and everything that the hail left." [13]So Moses stretched out his shepherd's rod over the land of Egypt, and the LORD made an east wind blow over the land all that day and all that night. When morning came, the east wind had carried in the locusts. [14]The locusts swarmed over the whole land of Egypt and settled on the whole country. Such a huge swarming of locusts had never happened before and would never happen ever again. [15]They covered the whole landscape so that the land turned black with them. They ate all of the land's grain and all of the orchards' fruit that the hail had left. Nothing green was left in any orchard or in any grain field in the whole land of Egypt.

[16]Pharaoh called urgently for Moses and Aaron and said, "I've sinned against the LORD your God and against you. [17]Please forgive my sin this time. Pray to the LORD your God just to take this deathly disaster away from me."

[18]So Moses left Pharaoh and prayed to the LORD. [19]The LORD turned the wind into a very strong west wind that lifted the locusts and drove them into the Reed Sea.[q] Not a single locust was left in the whole country of Egypt. [20]But the LORD made Pharaoh stubborn so that he wouldn't let the Israelites go.

Darkness covers Egypt

[21]Then the LORD said to Moses, "Raise your hand toward the sky so that darkness spreads over the land of Egypt, a darkness that you can feel." [22]So Moses raised his hand toward the sky, and an intense darkness fell on the whole land of Egypt for three days. [23]People couldn't see each other, and they couldn't go anywhere for three days. But the Israelites all had light where they lived.

[24]Then Pharaoh called Moses and said, "Go! Worship the LORD! Only your flocks and herds need to stay behind. Even your children can go with you."

[25]But Moses said, "You need to let us have sacrifices and entirely burned offerings to present to the LORD our God. [26]So our livestock must go with us. Not one animal can be left behind. We'll need some of them for worshipping the LORD our God. We won't know which to use to worship the LORD until we get there."

[27]But the LORD made Pharaoh stubborn so that he wasn't willing to let them go. [28]Pharaoh said to him, "Get out of here! Make sure you never see my face again, because the next time you see my face you will die."

[29]Moses said, "You've said it! I'll never see your face again!"

God announces the final disaster

11 The LORD said to Moses, "I'll bring one more disaster on Pharaoh and on Egypt. After that, he'll let you go from here. In fact, when he lets you go, he'll eagerly chase you out of here. [2]Tell every man to ask his neighbor and every woman to ask her neighbor for

[q]Or *Red Sea*

all their silver and gold jewelry." ³The Lᴏʀᴅ made sure that the Egyptians were kind to the Hebrew people. In addition, Pharaoh's officials and the Egyptian people even came to honor Moses as a great and important man in the land.

⁴Moses said, "This is what the Lᴏʀᴅ says: At midnight I'll go throughout Egypt. ⁵Every oldest child in the land of Egypt will die, from the oldest child of Pharaoh who sits on his throne to the oldest child of the servant woman by the millstones, and all the first offspring of the animals. ⁶Then a terrible cry of agony will echo through the whole land of Egypt unlike any heard before or that ever will be again. ⁷But as for the Israelites, not even a dog will growl at them, at the people, or at their animals. By this, you will know that the Lᴏʀᴅ makes a distinction between Egypt and Israel. ⁸Then all your officials will come down to me, bow to me, and say, 'Get out, you and all your followers!' After that I'll leave." Then Moses, furious, left Pharaoh.

⁹The Lᴏʀᴅ said to Moses, "Pharaoh won't listen to you so that I can perform even more amazing acts in the land of Egypt." ¹⁰Now Moses and Aaron did all these amazing acts in front of Pharaoh, but the Lᴏʀᴅ made Pharaoh stubborn so that he didn't let the Israelites go from his land.

First Passover

12 The Lᴏʀᴅ said to Moses and Aaron in the land of Egypt, ²"This month will be the first month; it will be the first month of the year for you.ʳ ³Tell the whole Israelite community: On the tenth day of this month they must take a lamb for each household, a lamb per house. ⁴If a household is too small for a lamb, it should share one with a neighbor nearby. You should divide the lamb in proportion to the number of people who will be eating it. ⁵Your lamb should be a flawless year-old male. You may take it from the sheep or from the goats. ⁶You should keep close watch over it until the fourteenth day of this month. At twilight on that day, the whole assembled Israelite community should slaughter their lambs. ⁷They should take some of the blood and smear it on the two doorposts

and on the beam over the door of the houses in which they are eating. ⁸That same night they should eat the meat roasted over the fire. They should eat it along with unleavened bread and bitter herbs. ⁹Don't eat any of it raw or boiled in water, but roasted over fire with its head, legs, and internal organs. ¹⁰Don't let any of it remain until morning, and burn any of it left over in the morning. ¹¹This is how you should eat it. You should be dressed, with your sandals on your feet and your walking stick in your hand. You should eat the meal in a hurry. It is the Passover of the Lᴏʀᴅ. ¹²I'll pass through the land of Egypt that night, and I'll strike down every oldest child in the land of Egypt, both humans and animals. I'll impose judgments on all the gods of Egypt. I am the Lᴏʀᴅ. ¹³The blood will be your sign on the houses where you live. Whenever I see the blood, I'll pass overˢ you. No plague will destroy you when I strike the land of Egypt.

¹⁴"This day will be a day of remembering for you. You will observe it as a festival to the Lᴏʀᴅ. You will observe it in every generation

---

ʳMarch–April; cf Exod 13:4   ˢHeb verb of the noun *Passover*

as a regulation for all time. [15]You will eat un-leavened bread for seven days. On the first day you must remove yeast from your houses because anyone who eats leavened bread any-time during those seven days will be cut off from Israel. [16]The first day and the seventh day will be a holy occasion for you. No work at all should be done on those days, except for preparing the food that everyone is going to eat. That is the only work you may do. [17]You should observe the Festival of Unleavened Bread, because on this precise day I brought you out of the land of Egypt in military for-mation. You should observe this day in every generation as a regulation for all time. [18]In the first month, from the evening of the four-teenth day until the evening of the twenty-first day, you should eat unleavened bread. [19]For seven days no yeast should be found in your houses because whoever eats leav-ened bread will be cut off from the Israelite community, whether the person is an immi-grant or a native of the land. [20]You should not eat anything made with yeast in all your settlements. You should eat only unleavened bread."

[21]Then Moses called together all of Israel's elders and said to them, "Go pick out one of the flock for your families, and slaughter the Passover lamb. [22]Take a bunch of hyssop, dip it into the blood that is in the bowl, and touch the beam above the door and the two doorposts with the blood in the bowl. None of you should go out the door of your house until morning. [23]When the LORD comes by to strike down the Egyptians and sees the blood on the beam above the door and on the two doorposts, the LORD will pass over that door. He won't let the destroyer enter your houses to strike you down. [24]You should observe this ritual as a regulation for all time for you and

your children. [25]When you enter the land that the LORD has promised to give you, be sure that you observe this ritual. [26]And when your children ask you, 'What does this ritual mean to you?' [27]you will say, 'It is the Passover sac-rifice to the LORD, for the LORD passed over the houses of the Israelites in Egypt. When he struck down the Egyptians, he spared our houses.'" The people then bowed down and worshipped. [28]The Israelites went and did ex-actly what the LORD had commanded Moses and Aaron to do.

Death of Egypt's oldest children

[29]At midnight the LORD struck down all the first offspring in the land of Egypt, from the oldest child of Pharaoh sitting on his throne to the oldest child of the prisoner in jail, and all the first offspring of the animals. [30]When Pharaoh, all his officials, and all the Egyptians got up that night, a terrible cry of agony rang out across Egypt because every house had someone in it who had died. [31]Then Pharaoh called Moses and Aaron that night and said, "Get up! Get away from my people, both you and the Israelites! Go! Worship the LORD, as you said! [32]You can even take your flocks and herds, as you asked. Just go! And bring a blessing on me as well!"

Israel set free

[33]The Egyptians urged the people to hurry and leave the land because they thought, 'We'll all be dead. [34]So the people picked up their bread dough before the yeast made it rise, with their bread pans wrapped in their robes on their shoulders. [35]The Israelites did as Moses had told them and asked the Egyp-tians for their silver and gold jewelry as well as their clothing. [36]The LORD made sure that the Egyptians were kind to the people so that they let them have whatever they asked for. And so they robbed the Egyptians.

[37]The Israelites traveled from Rameses to Succoth. They numbered about six hun-dred thousand men on foot, besides children. [38]A diverse crowd also went up with them along with a huge number of livestock, both flocks and herds. [39]They baked unleavened cakes from the dough they had brought out of Egypt. The dough didn't rise because they were driven out of Egypt and they couldn't

did you **know?**

Talk about a massive caravan! The Bible says six hundred thousand Israelite men left Egypt. This does not include the number of women and children who also left with them. We might estimate the total number of people by adding one woman and one or two children for each man, which would add up to about two million people, plus their livestock (animals), as well as some other diverse people who joined them. What a crowd!

wait. In fact, they didn't have time to prepare any food for themselves.

⁴⁰The length of time that the Israelites had lived in Egypt was four hundred thirty years. ⁴¹At the end of four hundred thirty years, on that precise day, all the Lᴏʀᴅ's people in military formation left the land of Egypt. ⁴²For the Lᴏʀᴅ, that was a night of intent watching, to bring them out of the land of Egypt. For all Israelites in every generation, this same night is a time of intent watching to honor the Lᴏʀᴅ.

SAILBOAT

Giving Thanks

Remember to Be Thankful *Exodus 12:14, 17, 42*

God did something extreme to free the Israelites from slavery in Egypt and told them to remember the day as a festival. The Israelites were thankful for all that God had done and was still doing to save them from slavery. They were given careful instructions for how and when to offer thanks to God. A major part of thanksgiving is remembering all that God has done for us. Today, Jewish people still celebrate Passover and remember when God delivered the Israelites from Egypt. ♦

Instructions for observing Passover

⁴³The Lᴏʀᴅ said to Moses and Aaron: This is the regulation for the Passover. No foreigner may eat it. ⁴⁴However, any slave who has been bought may eat it after he's been circumcised. ⁴⁵No temporary foreign resident or day laborer may eat it. ⁴⁶It should be eaten in one house. You shouldn't take any of the meat outside the house, and you shouldn't break the bones. ⁴⁷The whole Israelite community should observe it. ⁴⁸If an immigrant who lives with you wants to observe the Passover to the Lᴏʀᴅ, then he and all his males should be circumcised. Then he may join in observing it. He should be regarded as a native of the land. But no uncircumcised person may eat it. ⁴⁹There will be one Instruction for the native and for the immigrant who lives with you.

⁵⁰All the Israelites did just as the Lᴏʀᴅ had commanded Moses and Aaron. ⁵¹On that

precise day, the Lᴏʀᴅ brought the Israelites out of the land of Egypt in military formation.

13 The Lᴏʀᴅ said to Moses: ²Dedicate to me all your oldest children. Each first offspring from any Israelite womb belongs to me, whether human or animal.

Unleavened bread

³Moses said to the people, "Remember this day which is the day that you came out of Egypt, out of the place you were slaves, because the Lᴏʀᴅ acted with power to bring you out of there. No leavened bread may be eaten. ⁴Today, in the month of Abib,ᵗ you are going to leave. ⁵The Lᴏʀᴅ will bring you to the land of the Canaanites, the Hittites, the Amorites, the Hivites, and the Jebusites. It is the land that the Lᴏʀᴅ promised your ancestors to give to you, a land full of milk and honey. You should perform this ritual in this month. ⁶You must eat unleavened bread for seven days. The seventh day is a festival to the Lᴏʀᴅ. ⁷Only unleavened bread should be eaten for seven days. No leavened bread and no yeast should be seen among you in your whole country. ⁸You should explain to your child on that day, 'It's because of what the Lᴏʀᴅ did for me when I came out of Egypt.' ⁹"It will be a sign on your hand and a reminder on your forehead so that you will often discuss the Lᴏʀᴅ's Instruction, for the Lᴏʀᴅ brought you out of Egypt with great power. ¹⁰So you should follow this regulation at its appointed time every year.

Dedication of Israel's oldest offspring

¹¹"When the Lᴏʀᴅ brings you into the land of the Canaanites and gives it to you as promised to you and your ancestors, ¹²you should set aside for the Lᴏʀᴅ whatever comes out of the womb first. All of the first males born to your animal belong to the Lᴏʀᴅ. ¹³But every first male donkey you should ransom with a sheep. If you don't ransom it, you must break its neck. You should ransom every oldest male among your children. ¹⁴When in the future your child asks you, 'What does this mean?' you should answer, 'The Lᴏʀᴅ brought us with great power out of Egypt, out of the place we were slaves. ¹⁵When Pharaoh refused to let

ᵗMarch–April, named Nisan after the exile

us go, the Lord killed all the oldest offspring in the land of Egypt, from the oldest sons to the oldest male animals. That is why I offer to the Lord as a sacrifice every male that first comes out of the womb. But I ransom my oldest sons.' [16]It will be a sign on your hand and a symbol on your forehead that the Lord brought us out of Egypt with great power."

God leads the way

[17]When Pharaoh let the people go, God didn't lead them by way of the land of the Philistines, even though that was the shorter route. God thought, If the people have to fight and face war, they will run back to Egypt. [18]So God led the people by the roundabout way of the Reed Sea[u] desert. The Israelites went up out of the land of Egypt ready for battle. [19]Moses took with him Joseph's bones just as Joseph had made Israel's sons promise when he said to them, "When God takes care of you, you must carry my bones out of here with you." [20]They set out from Succoth and camped at Etham on the edge of the desert. [21]The Lord went in front of them during the day in a column of cloud to guide them and at night in a column of lightning to give them light. This way they could travel during the day and at night. [22]The column of cloud during the day and the column of lightning at night never left its place in front of the people.

LIGHTHOUSE
RESPECT FOR GOD

A Column of Cloud *Exodus 13:17-22*
This passage shows how God tended to the Israelites. God sensed that if they had to face one more hurdle, they might give up. God chose a path for them that would avoid those who might seek to destroy them. By day God went in front of them in a column of cloud and at night in a column of lightning to guide them. ◊

Israel crossing the sea

14 Then the Lord said to Moses: [2]Tell the Israelites to turn back and set up camp in front of Pi-hahiroth, between Migdol and the sea in front of Baal-zephon. You should set up camp in front of it by the sea. [3]Pharaoh will think to himself, The Israelites are lost and confused in the land. The desert has trapped them. [4]I'll make Pharaoh stubborn, and he'll chase them. I'll gain honor at the expense of Pharaoh and all his army, and the Egyptians will know that I am the Lord. And they did exactly that.

UMBRELLA
HOPELESS

This Is Too Hard! *Exodus 14:15*
The Israelites were so tired. They thought when they left Egypt all of their problems would be over. Instead, they were hot, miserable, and moving slowly through the desert. The Egyptians were pursuing them, and the Israelites believed they would be defeated. They began to wonder if it would have been better for them to have stayed in Egypt as slaves. Hopelessness is the sense of wanting to give up, which is how the Israelites probably felt during this time. Thankfully, they had Moses to lead them. Moses knew God would be with them every step of the way. ◊

[5]When Egypt's king was told that the people had run away, Pharaoh and his officials changed their minds about the people. They said, "What have we done, letting Israel go free from their slavery to us?" [6]So he sent for his chariot and took his army with him. [7]He took six hundred elite chariots and all of Egypt's other chariots with captains on all of them. [8]The Lord made Pharaoh, Egypt's king, stubborn, and he chased the Israelites, who were leaving confidently. [9]The Egyptians, including all of Pharaoh's horse-drawn chariots, his cavalry, and his army, chased them and caught up with them as they were camped by the sea, by Pi-hahiroth in front of Baal-zephon.

[10]As Pharaoh drew closer, the Israelites looked back and saw the Egyptians marching toward them. The Israelites were terrified and cried out to the Lord. [11]They said to Moses, "Weren't there enough graves in Egypt

[u]Or Red Sea

that you took us away to die in the desert? What have you done to us by bringing us out of Egypt like this? ¹²Didn't we tell you the same thing in Egypt? 'Leave us alone! Let us work for the Egyptians!' It would have been better for us to work for the Egyptians than to die in the desert."

¹³But Moses said to the people, "Don't be afraid. Stand your ground, and watch the Lord rescue you today. The Egyptians you see today you will never ever see again. ¹⁴The Lord will fight for you. You just keep still."

¹⁵Then the Lord said to Moses, "Why do you cry out to me? Tell the Israelites to get moving. ¹⁶As for you, lift your shepherd's rod, stretch out your hand over the sea, and split it in two so that the Israelites can go into the sea on dry ground. ¹⁷But me, I'll make the Egyptians stubborn so that they will go in after them, and I'll gain honor at the expense of Pharaoh, all his army, his chariots, and his cavalry. ¹⁸The Egyptians will know that I am

the Lord, when I gain honor at the expense of Pharaoh, his chariots, and his cavalry."

¹⁹God's messenger, who had been in front of Israel's camp, moved and went behind them. The column of cloud moved from the front and took its place behind them. ²⁰It stood between Egypt's camp and Israel's camp. The cloud remained there, and when darkness fell it lit up the night. They didn't come near each other all night.

²¹Then Moses stretched out his hand over the sea. The Lord pushed the sea back by a strong east wind all night, turning the sea into dry land. The waters were split into two. ²²The Israelites walked into the sea on dry ground. The waters formed a wall for them on their right hand and on their left. ²³The Egyptians chased them and went into the sea after them, all of Pharaoh's horses, chariots, and cavalry. ²⁴As morning approached, the Lord looked down on the Egyptian camp from the column of lightning and cloud and

God's THOUGHTS ◆ My THOUGHTS

God Makes a Way When There Isn't a Way *Exodus 14:1-31*

As they were leaving Egypt, the Israelites were camping near the Reed Sea when they saw the Egyptian army coming after them. This was a large army, with soldiers, chariots, and horses.

The Israelites were afraid. Even after all the miracles they had experienced, they were scared that Pharaoh and his armies would defeat them.

It's easy for us to look at the Israelites and think they were just a bunch of cowards. We have the Bible, and we know how that story ends. But they didn't. All they knew were the weak, useless gods of Egypt. They were just getting to know God and didn't yet know about God's power.

This situation wasn't a surprise to God. God parted the waters of the Reed Sea so that the Israelites could escape from the Egyptians. Through this, God showed the Israelites that God would take care of them. When the Israelites walked away from the Reed Sea, they had a greater faith in God.

Think of a time when something that looked bad turned out to be good.

Thank God for using that time to help you grow stronger in your faith.

threw the Egyptian camp into a panic. ²⁵The LORD jammed their chariot wheels so that they wouldn't turn easily. The Egyptians said, "Let's get away from the Israelites, because the LORD is fighting for them against Egypt!"

²⁶Then the LORD said to Moses, "Stretch out your hand over the sea so that the water comes back and covers the Egyptians, their chariots, and their cavalry." ²⁷So Moses stretched out his hand over the sea. At daybreak, the sea returned to its normal depth. The Egyptians were driving toward it, and the LORD tossed the Egyptians into the sea. ²⁸The waters returned and covered the chariots and the cavalry, Pharaoh's entire army that had followed them into the sea. Not one of them remained. ²⁹The Israelites, however, walked on dry ground through the sea. The waters formed a wall for them on their right hand and on their left.

³⁰The LORD rescued Israel from the Egyptians that day. Israel saw the Egyptians dead on the seashore. ³¹Israel saw the amazing power of the LORD against the Egyptians. The people were in awe of the LORD, and they believed in the LORD and in his servant Moses.

Moses' victory song

15 Then Moses and the Israelites sang this song to the LORD:

I will sing to the LORD,
  for an overflowing victory!
  Horse and rider he threw
    into the sea!
²The LORD is my strength
  and my power;ᵛ
  he has become
    my salvation.
This is my God, whom I will praise,
  the God of my ancestors,
  whom I will acclaim.
³The LORD is a warrior;
  the LORD is his name.

⁴Pharaoh's chariots and his army
  he hurled into the sea;
  his elite captains were sunk
    in the Reed Sea.ʷ
⁵The deep sea covered them;
  they sank into the deep waters
    like a stone.

⁶Your strong hand, LORD,
  is dominant in power;
  your strong hand, LORD,
    shatters the enemy!
⁷With your great surge
  you overthrow your opponents;
  you send out your hot anger;
    it burns them up like straw.
⁸With the breath of your nostrils
  the waters swelled up,
  the floods surged up in a great wave;
  the deep waters foamed
    in the depths of the sea.
⁹The enemy said, "I'll pursue, I'll overtake,
  I'll divide the spoils of war.
  I'll be overfilled with them.
  I'll draw my sword;
    my hand will destroy them."
¹⁰You blew with your wind;
  the sea covered over them.
  They sank like lead
    in the towering waters.
¹¹Who is like you among the gods, LORD?
  Who is like you, foremost in holiness,
    worthy of highest praise,
    doing awesome deeds?
¹²You raised your strong hand;
  earth swallowed them up.
¹³With your great loyalty
  you led the people you rescued;
  with your power you guided them
    to your sanctuary.
¹⁴The peoples heard,
  they shook in terror;
  horror grabbed hold
    of Philistia's inhabitants.
¹⁵Then Edom's tribal chiefs were terrified;
  panic grabbed hold of Moab's rulers;
  all of Canaan's inhabitants
    melted in fear.
¹⁶Terror and fear came over them;
  because of your great power,
  they were as still as a stone
  until your people, LORD, passed by,
  until the people you made your own
    passed by.
¹⁷You brought them in and planted them on
  your own mountain,
  the place, LORD,
  that you made your home,

Memorize Exod 15:2

ᵛOr song ʷOr Red Sea

the sanctuary, Lord,
that your hand created.
¹⁸ The Lord will rule forever and always.

¹⁹When Pharaoh's horses, chariots, and cavalry went into the sea, the Lord brought back the waters of the sea over them. But the Israelites walked through the sea on dry ground.

Miriam's victory song

²⁰Then the prophet Miriam, Aaron's sister, took a tambourine in her hand. All the women followed her playing tambourines and dancing. ²¹Miriam sang the refrain back to them:
Sing to the Lord,
for an overflowing victory!
Horse and rider he threw into the sea!

Turning bitter water sweet

²²Then Moses had Israel leave the Reed Seaˣ and go out into the Shur desert. They traveled for three days in the desert and found no water. ²³When they came to Marah, they couldn't drink Marah's water because it

No one knows what manna was. It was described as bread that would melt away. Some people think it was like a cracker, while others think it was more like a marshmallow. Even the Israelites weren't sure what they were eating. The Hebrew word *manna* means "What is it?"

was bitter. That's why it was called Marah.ʸ ²⁴The people complained against Moses, "What will we drink?" ²⁵Moses cried out to the Lord, and the Lord pointed out a tree to him. He threw it into the water, and the water became sweet.

The Lord made a regulation and a ruling there, and there he tested them. ²⁶The Lord said, "If you are careful to obey the Lord your God, do what God thinks is right, pay attention to his commandments, and keep all of his regulations, then I won't bring on you any of the diseases that I brought on the Egyptians. I am the Lord who heals you.'"

²⁷Then they came to Elim, where there were twelve springs of water and seventy palm trees. They camped there by the water.

Wilderness food: manna and quail

16The whole Israelite community set out from Elim and came to the Sin desert, which is located between Elim and Sinai. They set out on the fifteenth day of the second monthᶻ after they had left the land of Egypt. ²The whole Israelite community complained against Moses and Aaron in the desert. ³The Israelites said to them, "Oh, how we wish that

For many years, Bible stories were told by mouth before they were written. Because Miriam's song was sung whenever this important story was told, people who study the Bible think the words written are the words Miriam used and believe they are among the oldest words in the Bible.

the Lord had just put us to death while we were still in the land of Egypt. There we could sit by the pots cooking meat and eat our fill of bread. Instead, you've brought us out into this desert to starve this whole assembly to death."

⁴Then the Lord said to Moses, "I'm going to make bread rain down from the sky for you. The people will go out each day and gather just enough for that day. In this way, I'll test them to see whether or not they follow my Instruction. ⁵On the sixth day, when they measure out what they have collected, it will be twice as much as they collected on other days." ⁶So Moses and Aaron said to all the Israelites, "This evening you will know that it was the Lord who brought you out of the land of Egypt. ⁷And in the morning you will see the Lord's glorious presence, because your complaints against the Lord have been heard. Who are we? Why blame us?" ⁸Moses continued, "The Lord will give you meat to eat in the evening and your fill of bread in the morning because the Lord heard the complaints you made against him. Who are we? Your complaints aren't against us but against the Lord."

⁹Then Moses said to Aaron, "Say to the whole Israelite community, 'Come near to the Lord, because he's heard your complaints.'" ¹⁰As Aaron spoke to the whole Israelite community, they turned to look toward the

---

ˣOr *Red Sea* ʸOr *bitter* ᶻApril–May, Iyar

desert, and just then the glorious presence of the LORD appeared in the cloud.

¹¹The LORD spoke to Moses, ¹²"I've heard the complaints of the Israelites. Tell them, 'At twilight you will eat meat. And in the morning you will have your fill of bread. Then you will know that I am the LORD your God.'"

¹³In the evening a flock of quail flew down and covered the camp. And in the morning there was a layer of dew all around the camp. ¹⁴When the layer of dew lifted, there on the desert surface were thin flakes, as thin as frost on the ground. ¹⁵When the Israelites saw it, they said to each other, "What[a] is it?" They didn't know what it was.

Moses said to them, "This is the bread that the LORD has given you to eat. ¹⁶This is what the LORD has commanded: 'Collect as much of it as each of you can eat, one omer[b] per person. You may collect for the number of people in your household.'" ¹⁷The Israelites did as Moses said, some collecting more, some less. ¹⁸But when they measured it out by the omer, the ones who had collected more had nothing left over, and the ones who had collected less had no shortage. Everyone collected just as much as they could eat. ¹⁹Moses said to them, "Don't keep any of it until morning." ²⁰But they didn't listen to Moses. Some

UMBRELLA
GREED

Always Enough *Exodus 16:19-20*
God was providing meat and bread for the Israelites every day while they moved through the desert. Moses had told them God would provide enough for each day as that day came. Still the Israelites gathered more than they could eat, trying to save it for later. Because they did not trust God, they acted greedy, taking more food than they needed. They soon discovered that following their own ways rather than God's ways wouldn't work. By the next day the food they had saved was rotten—it stank and had worms in it. Yuck! This story reminds us that even when it seems there will never be enough, God will provide what we need, just as we need it. ◖

kept part of it until morning, but it became infested with worms and stank. Moses got angry with them. ²¹Every morning they gathered it, as much as each person could eat. But when the sun grew hot, it melted away.

²²On the sixth day the people collected twice as much food as usual, two omers per person. All the chiefs of the community came and told Moses. ²³He said to them, "This is what the LORD has said, 'Tomorrow is a day of rest, a holy Sabbath to the LORD. Bake what you want to bake and boil what you want to boil. But you can set aside and keep all the leftovers until the next morning.'" ²⁴So they set the leftovers aside until morning, as Moses had commanded. They didn't stink or become infested with worms. ²⁵The next day Moses said, "Eat it today, because today is a Sabbath to the LORD. Today you won't find it out in the field. ²⁶Six days you will gather it. But on the seventh day, the Sabbath, there will be nothing to gather."

²⁷On the seventh day some of the people went out to gather bread, but they found nothing. ²⁸The LORD said to Moses, "How long will you refuse to obey my commandments and instructions? ²⁹Look! The LORD has given you the Sabbath. Therefore, on the sixth day he gives you enough food for two days. Each of you should stay where you are and not leave your place on the seventh day." ³⁰So the people rested on the seventh day.

³¹The Israelite people called it manna. It was like coriander seed, white, and tasted like honey wafers. ³²Moses said, "This is what the LORD has commanded: 'Let an omer of it be kept safe for future generations so that they can see the food that I used to feed you in the desert when I brought you out of the land of Egypt.'"

³³Moses said to Aaron, "Take a jar, and put one full omer of manna in it. Then set it in the LORD's presence, where it should be kept safe for future generations." ³⁴Aaron did as the LORD commanded Moses, and he put it in front of the covenant document for safekeeping. ³⁵The Israelites ate manna for forty years, until they came to a livable land. They ate manna until they came to the border of the land of Canaan. (³⁶An omer[c] is one-tenth of an ephah.)

[a]Heb *man* (= *What?*); cf Exod 16:31 [b]Two quarts [c]Two quarts

Water from a rock

17 The whole Israelite community broke camp and set out from the Sin desert to continue their journey, as the LORD commanded. They set up their camp at Rephidim, but there was no water for the people to drink. ²The people argued with Moses and said, "Give us water to drink."

Moses said to them, "Why are you arguing with me? Why are you testing the LORD?"

³But the people were very thirsty for water there, and they complained to Moses, "Why did you bring us out of Egypt to kill us, our children, and our livestock with thirst?"

⁴So Moses cried out to the LORD, "What should I do with this people? They are getting ready to stone me."

ᵈOr test ᵉOr argument

---

⁵The LORD said to Moses, "Go on ahead of the people, and take some of Israel's elders with you. Take in your hand the shepherd's rod that you used to strike the Nile River, and go. ⁶I'll be standing there in front of you on the rock at Horeb. Hit the rock. Water will come out of it, and the people will be able to drink." Moses did so while Israel's elders watched. ⁷He called the place Massahᵈ and Meribah,ᵉ because the Israelites argued with and tested the LORD, asking, "Is the LORD really with us or not?"

Israel defeats Amalek

⁸Amalek came and fought with Israel at Rephidim. ⁹Moses said to Joshua, "Choose some men for us and go fight with Amalek.

God Provides for Our Needs   Exodus 16:1–17:6

Newborn babies know only one way to get what they want: crying. They cry when they're hungry, tired, or need a clean diaper. At first a baby's cries are very loud and strong, as if there is an emergency. As they grow older babies begin to realize their parents will take care of them, and they don't cry as much.

The Israelites were acting like newborn babies. Even though God had done so much for them, they complained to Moses whenever things got hard. This time they complained about food. Though they had suffered for a long time as slaves in Egypt, they announced that slavery was better than freedom in the desert.

They were still getting to know God. They knew God could send death and destruction, but they had never known God to provide for their daily needs. They were about to learn.

First, God gave manna daily from the sky. Then, God sent quail and fresh, cold water to drink.

The Israelites were learning that God would provide whatever they needed. They didn't get everything they wanted, but God took care of all of their needs. Little by little, their faith in God grew stronger.

Explain the difference between something you need and something you want.

Thank God for providing for your daily needs.

Tomorrow I'll stand on top of the hill with the shepherd's rod of God in my hand." [10]So Joshua did as Moses told him. He fought with Amalek while Moses, Aaron, and Hur went up to the top of the hill. [11]Whenever Moses held up his hand, Israel would start winning the battle. Whenever Moses lowered his hand, Amalek would start winning. [12]But Moses' hands grew tired. So they took a stone and put it under Moses so he could sit down on it. Aaron and Hur held up his hands, one on each side of him so that his hands remained steady until sunset. [13]So Joshua defeated Amalek and his army with the sword.

[14]Then the Lord said to Moses, "Write this as a reminder on a scroll and read it to Joshua: I will completely wipe out the memory of Amalek under the sky."

[15]Moses built an altar there and called it, "The Lord is my banner." [16]He said, "The power of the Lord's banner![f] The Lord is at war with Amalek in every generation."

Sharing the burden of leadership

18Jethro, Midian's priest and Moses' father-in-law, heard about everything that God had done for Moses and for God's people Israel, how the Lord had brought Israel out of Egypt. [2]Moses' father-in-law Jethro took with him Zipporah, Moses' wife whom he had sent away, [3]along with her two sons. One was named Gershom because he said, "I have been an immigrant[g] living in a foreign land." [4]The other was named Eliezer[h] because he said, "The God of my ancestors was my helper who rescued me from Pharaoh's sword." [5]Jethro, Moses' father-in-law, brought Moses' sons and wife back to him in the desert where he had set up camp at God's mountain. [6]He sent word to Moses: "I, your father-in-law Jethro, am coming to you along with your wife and her two sons." [7]Moses went out to meet his father-in-law, and he bowed down and kissed him. They asked each other how they were doing, and then they went into the tent. [8]Moses then told his father-in-law everything that the Lord had done to Pharaoh and to the Egyptians on Israel's behalf, all the difficulty they had on their journey, and how the Lord had rescued them. [9]Jethro was

glad about all the good things that the Lord had done for Israel in saving them from the Egyptians' power.

[10]Jethro said, "Bless the Lord who rescued you from the Egyptians' power and from Pharaoh's power, who rescued the people from Egypt's oppressive power. [11]Now I know that the Lord is greater than all the gods, because of what happened when the Egyptians plotted against them." [12]Then Jethro, Moses' father-in-law, brought an entirely burned offering and sacrifices to God. Aaron came with all of Israel's elders to eat a meal with Moses' father-in-law in God's presence.

[13]The next day Moses sat as a judge for the people, while the people stood around Moses from morning until evening. [14]When Moses' father-in-law saw all that he was doing for the people, he said, "What's this that you are doing for the people? Why do you sit alone, while all the people are standing around you from morning until evening?"

[15]Moses said to his father-in-law, "Because the people come to me to inquire of God. [16]When a conflict arises between them, they come to me and I judge between the two of them. I also teach them God's regulations and instructions."

[17]Moses' father-in-law said to him, "What you are doing isn't good. [18]You will end up totally wearing yourself out, both you and these people who are with you. The work is too difficult for you. You can't do it alone. [19]Now listen to me and let me give you some advice. And may God be with you! Your role should be to represent the people before God. You should bring their disputes before God yourself. [20]Explain the regulations and instructions to them. Let them know the way they are supposed to go and the things they are supposed to do. [21]But you should also look among all the people for capable persons who respect God. They should be trustworthy and not corrupt. Set these persons over the people as officers of groups of thousands, hundreds, fifties, and tens. [22]Let them sit as judges for the people at all times. They should bring every major dispute to you, but they should decide all of the minor cases themselves. This will be much easier for you, and they will share your load.

---

[f]Heb uncertain [g]Heb *ger* sounds like *Gershom.* [h]Or *my God is a helper.*

23If you do this and God directs you, then you will be able to endure. And all these people will be able to go back to their homes much happier."

24Moses listened to his father-in-law's suggestions and did everything that he had said. 25Moses chose capable persons from all Israel and set them as leaders over the people, as officers over groups of thousands, hundreds, fifties, and tens. 26They acted as judges for the people at all times. They would refer the hard cases to Moses, but all of the minor cases they decided themselves. 27Then Moses said good-bye to his father-in-law, and Jethro went back to his own country.

LIGHTHOUSE

RESPECT FOR GOD

Delegate Authority *Exodus 18:17-23*
Moses' father-in-law, Jethro, had come to visit Moses. All day long Jethro watched the Israelites come to Moses, who was doing everything he could for the Israelites. Moses explained to Jethro that whenever the people were in conflict he served as the judge, teaching them God's instructions. Jethro saw that Moses was worn out after doing all of this on his own. Jethro told Moses to look for capable people who respected God so that these good people could hear and judge minor disputes. This made life much easier for Moses, who could then focus on larger issues. Jethro saw that God's people needed levels of authority and many people to take responsibility for the needs of the tribe to thrive and endure. ◊

Arrival at Mount Sinai

19 On exactly the third-month anniversary of the Israelites' leaving the land of Egypt, they came into the Sinai desert. 2They traveled from Rephidim, came into the Sinai desert, and set up camp there. Israel camped there in front of the mountain 3while Moses went up to God. The Lord called to him from the mountain, "This is what you should say to Jacob's household and declare to the Israelites: 4You saw what I did to the Egyptians, and how I lifted you up on eagles' wings and brought you to me. 5So now, if you faithfully obey me and stay true to my covenant, you will be my most precious possession out of all the peoples, since the whole earth belongs to me. 6You will be a kingdom of priests for me and a holy nation. These are the words you should say to the Israelites."

7So Moses came down, called together the people's elders, and set before them all these words that the Lord had commanded him. 8The people all responded with one voice: "Everything that the Lord has said we will do." Moses reported to the Lord what the people said.

Preparing for a divine encounter

9Then the Lord said to Moses, "I'm about to come to you in a thick cloud in order that the people will hear me talking with you so that they will always trust you."

Moses told the Lord what the people said, 10and the Lord said to Moses: "Go to the people and take today and tomorrow to make them holy. Have them wash their clothes. 11Be ready for the third day, because on the third day the Lord will come down on Mount Sinai for all the people to see. 12Set up a fence for the people all around and tell them, 'Be careful not to go up the mountain or to touch any part of it.' Anyone who even touches the mountain must be put to death. 13No one should touch anyone who has touched it, or they must be either stoned to death or shot with arrows. Whether an animal or a human being, they must not be allowed to live. Only when the ram's horn sounds may they go up on the mountain."

14So Moses went down the mountain to the people. He made sure the people were holy and that they washed their clothes. 15He told the men, "Prepare yourselves for three days. Don't go near a woman."

16When morning dawned on the third day, there was thunder, lightning, and a thick cloud on the mountain, and a very loud blast of a horn. All the people in the camp shook with fear. 17Moses brought the people out of the camp to meet God, and they took their place at the foot of the mountain. 18Mount Sinai was all in smoke because the Lord had come down on it with lightning. The smoke went up like the smoke of a hot furnace, while the whole mountain shook violently. 19The blasts of the horn grew louder and louder. Moses would speak, and God would answer him with thunder. 20The Lord came down on

Mount Sinai to the top of the mountain. The LORD called Moses to come up to the top of the mountain, and Moses went up. ²¹The LORD said to Moses, "Go down and warn the people not to break through to try to see the LORD, or many of them will fall dead. ²²Even the priests who come near to the LORD must keep themselves holy, or the LORD will break loose against them."

²³Moses said to the LORD, "The people aren't allowed to come up on Mount Sinai because you warned us and said, 'Set up a fence around the mountain to keep it holy.'"

²⁴The LORD said to him, "Go down, and bring Aaron back up with you. But the priests and the people must not break through and come up to the LORD. Otherwise, the LORD will break loose against them." ²⁵So Moses went down to the people and told them.

ⁱOr besides ^jOr to thousands

The Ten Commandments

20 Then God spoke all these words: ²I am the LORD your God who brought you out of Egypt, out of the house of slavery.

³You must have no other gods beforeⁱ me.

⁴Do not make an idol for yourself—no form whatsoever—of anything in the sky above or on the earth below or in the waters under the earth. ⁵Do not bow down to them or worship them, because I, the LORD your God, am a passionate God. I punish children for their parents' sins even to the third and fourth generations of those who hate me. ⁶But I am loyal and gracious to the thousandth generation^j of those who love me and keep my commandments.

Bet you can read this in 3 minutes. Ready, set, go!

Why Rules Are Good for Us *Exodus 20:3-17*

Many items, like video games and telephones, come with instructions to help the owner know how to properly use them. Some people read the instructions from cover to cover before using the item and then save them in case they're needed later. If these people have a problem, they know where to go for help. Others ignore the instructions and throw them away. If something goes wrong, they may struggle to find the answers they need.

The Ten Commandments that God gave to Moses were the first of many instructions to God's people. The first four commandments focused on the Israelites' relationship with God. The next six focused on their relationships with each other. They were still learning about God, who wasn't like the gods in Egypt. They had to learn what God wanted from them.

The Bible has many instructions for us, and they are all for our good. Some rules, like "Do not kill," probably seem easy to obey. Other instructions, like "Honor your father and mother," are harder to follow. But God loves us, and by obeying God's rules, we show that we love God.

Name a commandment that is easy to obey.

Name one that is hard to obey.

[7]Do not use the LORD your God's name as if it were of no significance; the LORD won't forgive anyone who uses his name that way.

[8]Remember the Sabbath day and treat it as holy. [9]Six days you may work and do all your tasks, [10]but the seventh day is a Sabbath to the LORD your God. Do not do any work on it—not you, your sons or daughters, your male or female servants, your animals, or the immigrant who is living with you. [11]Because the LORD made the heavens and the earth, the sea, and everything that is in them in six days, but rested on the seventh day. That is why the LORD blessed the Sabbath day and made it holy.

[12]Honor your father and your mother so that your life will be long on the fertile land that the LORD your God is giving you.

[13]Do not kill.[k]

[14]Do not commit adultery.

[15]Do not steal.

[16]Do not testify falsely against your neighbor.

[17]Do not desire and try to take your neighbor's house. Do not desire and try to take your neighbor's wife, male or female servant, ox, donkey, or anything else that belongs to your neighbor.

[18]When all the people witnessed the thunder and lightning, the sound of the horn, and the mountain smoking, the people shook with fear and stood at a distance. [19]They said to Moses, "You speak to us, and we'll listen. But don't let God speak to us, or we'll die."

[20]Moses said to the people, "Don't be afraid, because God has come only to test you and to make sure you are always in awe of God so that you don't sin." [21]The people stood at a distance while Moses approached the thick darkness in which God was present.

Instructions about worship

[22]The LORD said to Moses: "Say this to the Israelites: You saw for yourselves how I spoke with you from heaven. [23]Don't make alongside me gods of silver or gold for yourselves. [24]Make for me an altar from fertile soil on which to sacrifice your entirely burned offerings, your well-being sacrifices, your sheep, and your oxen. I will come to you and bless you in every place where I make sure my name is remembered. [25]But if you do make for me an altar from stones, don't build it with chiseled stone since using your chisel on the stone will make it impure. [26]Don't climb onto my altar using steps: then your genitals won't be exposed by doing so."

Instructions about slaves

21 These are the case laws that you should set before them:

[2]When you buy a male Hebrew slave, he will serve you for six years. But in the seventh year, he will go free without any payment. [3]If he came in single, he will leave single. If he came in married, then his wife will leave with him. [4]If his master gave him a wife and she bore him sons or daughters, the wife and her children will belong to her master. He will leave single. [5]However, if the slave clearly states, "I love my master, my wife, and my children, and I don't want to go free," [6]then his master will bring him before God. He will bring him to the door or the doorpost. There his master will pierce his ear with a pointed tool, and he will serve him as his slave for life.

[7]When a man sells his daughter as a slave, she shouldn't be set free in the same way as male slaves are set free. [8]If she doesn't please her master who chose her for himself, then her master must let her be bought back by her family. He has no right to sell her to a foreign people since he has treated her unfairly. [9]If he assigns her to his son, he must give her the rights of a daughter. [10]If he takes another woman for himself, he may not reduce her food, clothing, or marital rights. [11]If he doesn't do these three things for her, she will go free without any payment, for no money.

Instructions about human violence

[12]Anyone who hits and kills someone should be put to death. [13]If the killing wasn't on purpose but an accident allowed by God, then I will designate a place to which the killer can run away. [14]But if someone plots and kills another person on purpose, you should remove the killer from my altar and put him to death.

[k]Or murder

[15]Anyone who violently hits their father or mother should be put to death.

[16]Anyone who kidnaps a person, whether they have been sold or are still being held, should be put to death.

[17]Anyone who curses their father or mother should be put to death.

[18]When two people are fighting and one hits the other with a stone or with his fist so that he is in bed for a while but doesn't die— [19]if he recovers and is able to walk around outside with a cane, then the one who hit him shouldn't be punished, except to pay for the loss of time from work and to pay for his full recovery.

[20]When a slave owner hits a male or female slave with a rod and the slave dies immediately, the owner should be punished. [21]But if the slave gets up after a day or two, the slave owner shouldn't be punished because the slave is the owner's property.

[22]When people who are fighting injure a pregnant woman so that she has a miscarriage but no other injury occurs, then the guilty party will be fined what the woman's husband demands, as negotiated with the judges. [23]If there is further injury, then you will give a life for a life, [24]an eye for an eye, a tooth for a tooth, a hand for a hand, a foot for a foot, [25]a burn for a burn, a bruise for a bruise, a wound for a wound.

[26]When a slave owner hits and blinds the eye of a male or female slave, he should let the slave go free on account of the eye. [27]If he knocks out a tooth of a male or female slave, he should let the slave go free on account of the tooth.

Instructions about animals and property

[28]When an ox gores a man or a woman to death, the ox should be stoned to death, and the meat of the ox shouldn't be eaten. But the owner of the ox shouldn't be punished. [29]However, if the ox had gored people in the past and its owner had been warned but didn't watch out for it, and the ox ends up killing a man or a woman, then the ox should be stoned to death, and its owner should also be put to death. [30]If the owner has to pay compensation instead, he must pay the agreed amount to save his life. [31]If the ox gores a boy or a girl, this same case law applies to the owner. [32]If the ox gores a male or female slave, the owner will pay thirty silver shekels to the slave's owner, and the ox will be stoned to death.

[33]When someone leaves a pit open or digs a pit and doesn't cover it and an ox or a donkey falls into the pit, [34]the owner of the pit must make good on the loss. He should pay money to the ox's owner, but he may keep the dead animal.

[35]When someone's ox hurts someone else's ox and it dies, then they should sell the live ox and divide its price. They should also divide the dead animal between them. [36]But if the ox was known for goring in the past and its owner hadn't watched out for it, the owner must make good the loss, an ox for an ox, but may keep the dead animal.

22 When[1] someone steals an ox or a sheep and then slaughters or sells it, the thief must pay back five oxen for the one ox or four sheep for the one sheep.

[2m]If the thief is caught breaking in and is beaten and dies, the one who killed him won't be guilty of bloodshed. [3]However, if this happens in broad daylight, then the one who killed him is guilty of bloodshed. For his part, the thief must make good on what he stole. If

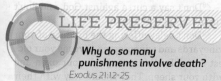

LIFE PRESERVER

Why do so many punishments involve death?

Exodus 21:12-25

Communities of people have always had rules regarding behavior, laws for living together, and punishments designed to be appropriate for those who break those laws. This was true in Bible times, just as it is true today. In our culture, for example, a person who is caught speeding in a car might receive a ticket and have to pay a fine. Some of the punishments we read about in the book of Exodus or other books of the Bible seem much stricter than the laws we follow today.

In the laws concerning violence, for example, the penalty for breaking the law was often death. It must have been very important to God that God's people learn to live together peacefully. God didn't want them to be violent toward each other, so God placed a heavy punishment on crimes of violence. ◐

[1]21:37 in Heb [m]22:1 in Heb

he has nothing, he must be sold to pay for his theft. ⁴If an animal (whether ox, donkey, or sheep) is found alive in the thief's possession, he must pay back double.

⁵When someone lets an animal loose to eat in another person's field and causes the field or vineyard to be stripped of its crop, the owner must pay them back with the best from his own field or vineyard.

⁶When someone starts a fire and it catches in thorns and then spreads to someone else's stacked grain, standing grain, or a whole field, the one who started the fire must fully repay the loss.

⁷When someone entrusts money or other items to another person to keep safe and they are stolen from the other person's house and the thief is caught, the thief must pay back double. ⁸If the thief isn't caught, the owner of the house should be brought before God to determine whether or not the owner stole the other's property.

⁹When any dispute of ownership over an ox, donkey, sheep, piece of clothing, or any other loss arises in which someone claims, "This is mine," the cases of both parties should come before God. The one whom God finds at fault must pay double to the other.

¹⁰When someone gives a donkey, ox, sheep, or any other animal to another person to keep safe, and the animal dies or is injured or taken and no one saw what happened, ¹¹the person should swear a solemn pledge before the Lord in the presence of the owner that he didn't touch the other's property. The owner must accept that, and no payment needs to be made. ¹²But if the animal was stolen, the person must make full payment to its owner. ¹³If the animal was attacked and ripped apart and its torn body is brought as evidence, no payment needs to be made.

¹⁴When someone borrows an animal from another and it is injured or dies while the owner isn't present, full payment must be made. ¹⁵If the owner was present, no payment needs to be made. If the animal was hired, only the fee for hiring the animal is due.

Instructions about social and religious matters

¹⁶When a man seduces a young woman who isn't engaged to be married yet and he sleeps with her, he must marry her and pay the bride-price for her. ¹⁷But if her father absolutely refuses to let them marry, he must still pay the same amount as the bride-price for young women.

¹⁸Don't allow a female sorcerer to live.

¹⁹Anyone who has sexual relations with an animal should be put to death.

²⁰Anyone who offers sacrifices to any god, other than the Lord alone, should be destroyed.

²¹Don't mistreat or oppress an immigrant, because you were once immigrants in the land of Egypt. ²²Don't treat any widow or orphan badly. ²³If you do treat them badly and they cry out to me, you can be sure that I'll hear their cry. ²⁴I'll be furious, and I'll kill you with the sword. Then your wives will be widows, and your children will be orphans.

²⁵If you lend money to my people who are poor among you, don't be a creditor and charge them interest. ²⁶If you take a piece of clothing from someone as a security deposit, you should return it before the sun goes down. ²⁷His clothing may well be his only blanket to cover himself. What else will that person have to sleep in? And if he cries out to me, I'll listen, because I'm compassionate.

²⁸Don't say a curse against God, and don't curse your people's chief.

²⁹Don't delay offering the produce of your vineyards and winepresses. Give me your oldest son. ³⁰Do the same with your oxen and with your sheep. They should stay with their mother for seven days. On the eighth day, you should give them to me.

³¹You are holy people to me. Don't eat any meat killed by wild animals out in the field. Throw it to the dogs instead.

23 Don't spread false rumors. Don't plot with evil people to act as a lying witness. ²Don't take sides with important people to do wrong. When you act as a witness, don't stretch the truth to favor important people. ³But don't privilege unimportant people in their lawsuits either.

⁴When you happen to come upon your enemy's ox or donkey that has wandered off, you should bring it back to them.

⁵When you see a donkey that belongs to someone who hates you and it's lying down

under its load and you are inclined not to help set it free, you must help set it free.

⁶Don't undermine the justice that your poor deserve in their lawsuits. ⁷Stay away from making a false charge. Don't put an innocent person who is in the right to death, because I will not consider innocent those who do such evil. ⁸Don't take a bribe, because a bribe blinds the clear-sighted and subverts the cause of those who are in the right.

⁹Don't oppress an immigrant. You know what it's like to be an immigrant, because you were immigrants in the land of Egypt.

Sabbaths and festivals

¹⁰For six years you should plant crops on your land and gather in its produce. ¹¹But in the seventh year you should leave it alone and undisturbed so that the poor among your people may eat. What they leave behind, the wild animals may eat. You should do the same with your vineyard and your olive trees.

¹²Do your work in six days. But on the seventh day you should rest so that your ox and donkey may rest, and even the child of your female slave and the immigrant may be refreshed.

¹³Be careful to obey everything that I have said to you. Don't call on the names of other gods. Don't even mention them.

¹⁴You should observe a festival for me three times a year. ¹⁵Observe the Festival of Unleavened Bread, as I commanded you. Eat unleavened bread for seven days at the appointed time in the month of Abib,ⁿ because it was in that month that you came out of Egypt.

No one should appear before me empty-handed. ¹⁶Observe the Harvest Festival for the early produce of your crops that you planted in the field, and the Gathering Festival at the end of the year, when you gather your crop of fruit from the field. ¹⁷All your males should appear three times a year before the Lord God.

¹⁸Don't offer the blood of my sacrifice with anything leavened. Don't let the fat of my festival offering be left over until the morning.

¹⁹Bring the best of your land's early produce to the Lord your God's temple.

Don't boil a young goat in its mother's milk.

God's promise: messenger and land

²⁰I'm about to send a messenger in front of you to guard you on your way and to bring you to the place that I've made ready. ²¹Pay attention to him and do as he says. Don't rebel against him. He won't forgive the things you do wrong because I° am with him. ²²But if you listen carefully to what he says and do all that I say, then I'll be an enemy to your enemies and fight those fighting you.

SAILBOAT

OBEDIENCE

God Is with Us Exodus 23:22

The book of Exodus tells how God guided the Israelites to the promised land. Through Moses, God explained to the Israelites that God would be with them as long as they obeyed God's commands and lived by God's rules. However, the stories here show how very hard it was for the Israelites to believe and be faithful. Exodus reminds us that God is always with us and that amazing things happen when we obey and are faithful to God. ◊

²³When my messenger goes in front of you and brings you to the Amorites, the Hittites, the Perizzites, the Canaanites, the Hivites, and the Jebusites, and I wipe them out, ²⁴don't bow down to their gods, worship them, or do what they do. Instead, you should completely destroy them and smash their sacred stone pillars to bits. ²⁵If you worship the Lord your God, the Lord will bless your bread and your water. I'll take sickness away from you, ²⁶and no woman will miscarry or be infertile in your land. I'll let you live a full, long life. ²⁷My terrifying reputation will precede you, and I'll throw all the people that you meet into a panic. I'll make all your enemies turn their backs to you. ²⁸I'll send insect swarms in front of you and drive out the Hivites, the Canaanites, and the Hittites before you. ²⁹I won't drive them out before you in a single year so the land won't be abandoned and the wild animals won't multiply around you. ³⁰I'll drive them out before you little by little, until your numbers grow and you eventually possess the land. ³¹I'll set your borders from the Reed Seaᵖ to the Philistine Sea and from the

ⁿMarch–April, named Nisan after the exile   °Or *my name*   ᵖOr *Red Sea*

desert to the River. I'll hand the inhabitants of the land over to you, and you will drive them out before you. [32]Don't make any covenants with them or their gods. [33]Don't allow them to live in your land, or else they will lead you to sin against me. If you worship their gods, it will become a dangerous trap for you.

Covenant at Sinai

24 Then the Lord said to Moses, "Come up to the Lord, you and Aaron, Nadab and Abihu, and seventy of Israel's elders, and worship from a distance. [2]Only Moses may come near to the Lord. The others shouldn't come near, while the people shouldn't come up with him at all."

[3]Moses came and told the people all the Lord's words and all the case laws. All the people answered in unison, "Everything that the Lord has said we will do." [4]Moses then wrote down all the Lord's words. He got up early in the morning and built an altar at the foot of the mountain. He set up twelve sacred stone pillars for the twelve tribes of Israel. [5]He appointed certain young Israelite men to offer entirely burned offerings and slaughter oxen as well-being sacrifices to the Lord. [6]Moses took half of the blood and put it in large bowls. The other half of the blood he threw against the altar. [7]Then he took the covenant scroll and read it out loud for the people to hear. They responded, "Everything that the Lord has said we will do, and we will obey."

[8]Moses then took the blood and threw it over the people. Moses said, "This is the blood of the covenant that the Lord now makes with you on the basis of all these words."

Covenant meal with God

[9]Then Moses and Aaron, Nadab and Abihu, and seventy elders of Israel went up, [10]and they saw Israel's God. Under God's feet there was what looked like a floor of lapis-lazuli tiles, dazzlingly pure like the sky. [11]God didn't harm the Israelite leaders, though they looked at God, and they ate and drank.

[12]The Lord said to Moses, "Come up to me on the mountain and wait there. I'll give you the stone tablets with the instructions and the commandments that I've written in order to teach them."

[13]So Moses and his assistant Joshua got up, and Moses went up God's mountain. [14]Moses had said to the elders, "Wait for us here until we come back to you. Aaron and Hur will be here with you. Whoever has a legal dispute may go to them."

[15]Then Moses went up the mountain, and the cloud covered the mountain. [16]The Lord's glorious presence settled on Mount Sinai, and the cloud covered it for six days. On the seventh day the Lord called to Moses from the cloud. [17]To the Israelites, the Lord's glorious presence looked like a blazing fire on top of the mountain. [18]Moses entered the cloud and went up the mountain. Moses stayed on the mountain for forty days and forty nights.

Gifts offered for the dwelling

25 The Lord said to Moses: [2]Tell the Israelites to collect gift offerings for me. Receive my gift offerings from everyone who freely wants to give. [3]These are the gift offerings that you should receive from them: gold, silver, and copper; [4]blue, purple, and deep red yarns; fine linen; goats' hair; [5]rams' skins

---

LIFE PRESERVER

Why does a covenant require blood? *Exodus 24:3-8*

In this story, Moses was involved in an important religious event for the Israelites. He was building an altar to mark the place where God gave the commandments to the people. Moses wanted the people to remember this moment and this covenant God made with them. The people celebrated this holy event in a ceremony that was familiar to the Israelites and often involved animal sacrifice. Because blood is a sign of life, it was used in covenant ceremonies to symbolize the deep relationship being created between those swearing loyalty to each other. Marking this important moment with God in this way ensured the people would remember God's covenant with them and the ways they were to live faithfully in response.

Today we no longer sacrifice animals. However, whenever we celebrate communion in church, we are involved in a very old practice that began in Egypt (Exod 12:1–20) and has its roots in the Passover celebration of the Israelites. We break bread together (representing Jesus' body) and drink from a cup (representing Jesus' blood) and remember God's faithfulness in sending us his son Jesus.

dyed red; beaded leather;q acacia wood; 6oil for the lamps; spices for the anointing oil and for the sweet-smelling incense; 7gemstones; and gems for setting in the priest's vestr and chest piece. 8They should make me a sanctuary so I can be present among them. 9You should follow the blueprints that I will show you for the dwelling and for all its equipment.

Instructions for building the chest containing the covenant

10Have them make an acacia-wood chest. It should be forty-five inches long, twenty-seven inches wide, and twenty-seven inches high. 11Cover it with pure gold, inside and out, and make a gold molding all around it. 12Cast four gold rings for it and put them on its four feet, two rings on one side and two rings on the other. 13Make acacia-wood poles and cover them with gold. 14Then put the poles into the rings on the chest's sides and use them to carry the chest. 15The poles should stay in the chest's rings. They shouldn't be taken out of them. 16Put the covenant document that I will give you into the chest.

17Then make a cover of pure gold, forty-five inches long and twenty-seven inches wide. 18Make two winged heavenly creatures of hammered gold, one for each end of the cover. 19Put one winged heavenly creature at one end and one winged heavenly creature at the other. Place the winged heavenly creatures at the cover's two ends. 20The heavenly creatures should have their wings spread out above, shielding the cover with their wings. The winged heavenly creatures should face each other toward the cover's center. 21Put the gold cover on top of the chest and put the covenant document that I will give you inside the chest. 22There I will meet with you. From there above the cover, from between the two winged heavenly creatures that are on top of the chest containing the covenant, I will deliver to you all that I command you concerning the Israelites.

Instructions for the table

23Make an acacia-wood table, three feet long, eighteen inches wide, and twenty-seven inches high. 24Cover it with pure gold and make a gold molding all around it. 25Make a frame around it that is four inches wide and a gold molding around the frame. 26Make four gold rings for the table. Fasten the rings to the four corners at its four legs. 27The rings that house the poles used for carrying the table should be close to the frame. 28Make the poles from acacia wood and cover them with gold. The table should be carried with these poles. 29Make its plates, dishes, jars,

did you know? God commanded the people to build a chest to carry the stone tablets on which God wrote the commandments. This special chest was known as *the chest containing the covenant*. In some Bibles it is called the ark of the covenant.

and bowls for pouring drink offerings. Make them of pure gold. 30Set the bread of the presence on the table so it is always in front of me.

Instructions for the lampstand

31Make a lampstand of pure hammered gold. The lampstand's base, branches, cups, flowers, and petals should all be attached to it. 32It should have six branches growing out from its sides, three branches on one side of the lampstand and three branches on the other side of the lampstand. 33One branch will have three cups shaped like almond blossoms, each with a flower and petals, and the next branch will also have three cups shaped like almond blossoms, each with a flower and petals. So it will be for the six branches that grow out of the lampstand. 34In addition, on the lampstand itself there will be four cups shaped like almond blossoms, each with its flower and petals. 35There will be a flower attached under the first pair of branches, a flower attached under the next pair of branches, and a flower attached under the last pair of branches. So it will be for the six branches that grow out of the lampstand. 36Their flowers and their branches will be permanently attached to it. The whole lampstand should be one piece of pure hammered gold. 37Make its seven lamps and set up its lamps so that they direct their light in front

qOr *dolphin skins* rHeb *ephod*

of the lampstand. ³⁸You should also make its tongs and fire pans out of pure gold. ³⁹All these items should be made from pure gold weighing one kikkar. ⁴⁰See to it that you make them according to the blueprint for them that you were shown on the mountain.

Instructions for building the dwelling

26Make the dwelling with ten curtains of fine twisted linen and blue, purple, and deep red yarns. Work figures of winged heavenly creatures into their design. ²Each curtain should be forty-two feet long and each curtain six feet wide. All the curtains should be the same size. ³Five curtains will be joined to each other as one set, while the other five curtains will be joined together as a second set. ⁴Make loops of blue thread on the edge of the outer curtain in the first set. Do the same on the edge of the outer curtain in the second set. ⁵Make fifty loops on the one curtain in the first set and fifty loops on the edge of the curtain that is in the second set. The loops should be opposite each other. ⁶Then make fifty gold clasps. Join the curtains to each other with the clasps so that the dwelling becomes one whole structure.

⁷You should also make curtains of goats' hair for a tent over the dwelling. Make eleven curtains. ⁸Each curtain should be forty-five feet long and each curtain six feet wide. The eleven curtains should all be the same size. ⁹Join five of the curtains together, and join the six other curtains together. Double over the sixth curtain at the front of the tent. ¹⁰Make fifty loops on the edge of the outer curtain in one set and fifty loops on the edge of the outer curtain in the second set. ¹¹Make fifty copper clasps. Put the clasps into the loops and join the tent together so that it becomes one whole structure. ¹²The extra cloth that is left over from the tent curtains, that is, the half curtain that remains, should hang over the back of the dwelling. ¹³Eighteen inches on one side and eighteen inches on the other side of the leftover length of the tent's curtains will hang over the two sides of the dwelling to cover it. ¹⁴Then for the tent, make a covering of rams' skins dyed red and an outer covering of beaded leather.§

§Or dolphin skin

¹⁵Make acacia-wood boards to stand upright as a frame for the dwelling. ¹⁶Each board will be fifteen feet long and twenty-seven inches wide. ¹⁷Put two pegs on each board for joining them to each other. Do this for all the dwelling's boards. ¹⁸Make twenty boards for the dwelling's southern side. ¹⁹Then make forty silver bases to go under the twenty boards. There will be two bases under the first board for its two pegs, two bases under the next board for its two pegs, and so on. ²⁰For the dwelling's other side on the north, make twenty boards ²¹and their forty silver bases, two bases under the first board, two bases under the next board, and so on. ²²For the back of the dwelling on the west, make six boards. ²³Make two additional boards for the dwelling's rear corners. ²⁴They should be spread out at the bottom but joined together at the top with one ring. In this way, these two boards will form the two corners. ²⁵And so there will be eight boards with their sixteen silver bases, two bases under the first board, two bases under the next board, and so on.

²⁶You should also make acacia-wood bars: five for the boards on one side of the dwelling, ²⁷five bars for the boards on the other side of the dwelling, and five bars for the boards on the back wall of the dwelling on the west. ²⁸The middle bar, halfway up the boards, should run from one end to the other. ²⁹Cover the boards with gold. Make gold rings to house the bars. Cover the bars with gold. ³⁰Then set up the dwelling according to the plan for it that you were shown on the mountain.

³¹Make a veil of blue, purple, and deep red yarns and of fine twisted linen. Work figures of winged heavenly creatures into its design. ³²Hang it on four acacia-wood posts covered in gold. They should have gold hooks and stand on four silver bases. ³³Hang the veil under the clasps, and put the chest containing the covenant there behind the veil. The veil will separate for you the holy from the holiest space. ³⁴Place the gold cover on the chest containing the covenant in the holiest space. ³⁵Place the table outside the veil, and set the lampstand opposite the table by the south wall of the dwelling. Place the table by the north wall.

³⁶Make a screen for the tent's entrance of blue, purple, and deep red yarns and of fine twisted linen, decorated with needlework. ³⁷Make five acacia-wood posts for the screen. Cover the posts with gold. Their hooks should be gold. Cast five copper bases for the posts.

Instructions for the altar

27 Make an acacia-wood altar. The altar should be square, seven and a half feet long and seven and a half feet wide. It should be four and a half feet high. ²Make horns for the altar and attach them to it, one horn on each of its four corners. Cover it with copper. ³Make pails for removing its ashes and its shovels, bowls, meat forks, and trays. Make all its equipment out of copper. ⁴Make for the altar a grate made of copper mesh. Make four copper rings for each of the four corners of the mesh. ⁵Slide the mesh underneath the bottom edge of the altar and then extend the mesh halfway up to the middle of the altar. ⁶Make acacia-wood poles for the altar and cover them with copper. ⁷Put the poles through the rings so that the poles will be on the two sides of the altar when it is carried. ⁸Make the altar with planks but hollow inside. All these should be made just as you were shown on the mountain.

Instructions for the dwelling's courtyard

⁹You should also set up the dwelling's courtyard. The courtyard's south side should have drapes of fine twisted linen stretching one hundred fifty feet on that side, ¹⁰with twenty posts, twenty copper bases, and silver hooks and bands for the posts. ¹¹Likewise along the north side the drapes should stretch one hundred fifty feet, with twenty posts, twenty copper bases, and silver hooks and bands for the posts. ¹²The courtyard's width on the west side should consist of seventy-five feet of drapes with their ten posts and their ten bases. ¹³The courtyard's width on the front, facing east, should be seventy-five feet. ¹⁴There should be twenty-two and a half feet of drapes on one side with three posts and three bases for them. ¹⁵There should be twenty-two and a half feet of drapes on the other side with three posts and three bases for them. ¹⁶For the gate into the courtyard there will be a screen thirty feet long, made

of blue, purple, and deep red yarns and of fine twisted linen, decorated with needlework. It will have four posts with their four bases. ¹⁷All the posts around the courtyard will have silver bands, silver hooks, and copper bases. ¹⁸The courtyard will be one hundred fifty feet long and seventy-five feet wide. Its walls' height will be seven and a half feet of fine twisted linen and its copper bases. ¹⁹All the dwelling's equipment for any use and all its tent pegs and all the courtyard's tent pegs will be made of copper.

Olive oil for the lampstand

²⁰You must require the Israelites to bring you pure oil of crushed olives for the light so that the lamp may be set up to burn continually. ²¹In the meeting tent, outside the veil that hangs in front of the covenant document, Aaron and his sons will tend the lamp from evening to morning in the Lord's presence. It will be a permanent regulation for the Israelites in every generation.

Instructions for the priests' clothing

28 Summon to you your brother Aaron and his sons from among the Israelites to serve me as priests—Aaron and Aaron's sons, Nadab and Abihu, and Eleazar and Ithamar. ²Make holy clothing that will give honor and dignity to your brother Aaron. ³Tell all who are skilled, to whom I have given special abilities, to make clothing for Aaron for his dedication to serve me as a priest. ⁴These are the articles of clothing that they should make: a chest pendant, a vest, a robe, a woven tunic, a turban, and a sash. When they make this holy clothing for your brother Aaron and his sons to serve me as priests, ⁵they should use gold, blue, purple, and deep red yarns and fine linen.

Priest's ornamental vest

⁶They should make the vest of gold, of blue, purple, and deep red yarns and of fine twisted linen with embroidered designs. ⁷The vest will have two shoulder pieces attached to its two edges so that they may be joined together. ⁸The vest's belt should be attached to it and made in the same way of gold, of blue, purple, and deep red yarns and fine twisted linen. ⁹Take two gemstones and engrave on

them the names of Israel's sons, [10]six names on one stone and the other six names on the other stone, in the order of their birth. [11]Like a gem cutter who engraves official seals, you will engrave the two stones with the names of Israel's sons. Mount them in gold settings. [12]Attach the two stones to the vest's shoulder pieces as stones of reminder for the Israelites. Aaron will carry into the LORD's presence their names on his two shoulders as a reminder. [13]Then make gold settings [14]along with two chains of pure gold, twisted like cords. Attach the corded chains to the gold settings.

Priest's chest pendant used for making decisions

[15]Make an embroidered chest pendant used for making decisions. Make it in the style of the vest, using gold, blue and purple and deep red yarns, and fine twisted linen. [16]It will be square and doubled, nine inches long and nine inches wide. [17]Set in it four rows of gemstone settings. The first row will be a row of carnelian, topaz, and emerald stones. [18]The second row will be a turquoise, a sapphire, and a moonstone. [19]The third row will be a jacinth, an agate, and an amethyst. [20]The fourth row will be a beryl, an onyx, and a jasper. Their settings will be made of decorative gold. [21]There will be twelve stones with names corresponding to the names of Israel's sons. They will be engraved like official seals, each with its name for the twelve tribes.

[22]Make chains of pure gold twisted like cords for the chest pendant. [23]Make two gold rings for the chest pendant and attach the two rings to the two edges of the chest pendant. [24]Attach the two gold cords to the two rings at the edges of the chest pendant. [25]Then fasten the two ends of the cords to the two settings, which you should attach to the vest's two front shoulder pieces. [26]Make two gold rings and attach them to the two ends of the chest pendant on its inside edge facing the vest. [27]Make two gold rings and fasten them on the front of the lower part of the two shoulder pieces of the vest, at its seam just above the vest's belt. [28]The chest pendant should be held in place by a blue cord binding its rings to the vest's rings so that the chest pendant rests on the vest's belt and

won't come loose from the vest. [29]In this way, Aaron will carry the names of Israel's sons on the chest pendant for making decisions over his heart when he goes into the sanctuary as a reminder before the LORD at all times. [30]Put into the chest pendant used for making decisions the Urim and the Thummim, so they will be over Aaron's heart when he goes into the LORD's presence. In this way, Aaron will carry the means to make decisions for the Israelites over his heart when in the LORD's presence at all times.

Instructions for other priestly clothing

[31]You will make the robe for the vest all of blue. [32]The opening for the head should be in the middle of it. The opening should be reinforced by a woven binding, a strong border so that it doesn't tear. [33]On its lower hem add pomegranates made of blue, purple, and deep red yarns all around the lower hem, with gold bells between the pomegranates all around it. [34]A gold bell and a pomegranate should alternate all around the lower hem of the robe. [35]Aaron will wear the robe when he ministers as a priest. Its sound will be heard when he goes into the sanctuary in the LORD's presence and when he comes out, so that he will not die.

[36]Make a flower ornament of pure gold and engrave on it like an official seal: "Holy to the LORD." [37]You should fasten it on the turban with a blue cord. It should be on the front of the turban. [38]It will be on Aaron's forehead, and Aaron will take on himself any guilt connected with the holy offerings that the Israelites give as their sacred donations. It will always be on his forehead so that the people may be remembered favorably in the LORD's presence.

[39]Weave the tunic out of fine linen. Make the turban out of fine linen. Make a sash decorated with needlework. [40]For Aaron's sons, you should also make tunics, sashes, and turbans to mark their honor and dignity. [41]Put these garments on your brother Aaron and on his sons with him. Anoint them with oil, ordain them, and make them holy to serve me as priests. [42]You should also make linen undergarments for them to cover their naked skin from their hips to their thighs. [43]Aaron and his sons should wear this clothing when they go

into the meeting tent or when they approach the altar to minister as priests in the sanctuary. Otherwise, they will bring guilt on themselves and die. This will be a permanent regulation for him and for his descendants after him.

Instructions for the priests' ordination

29 Now this is what you should do to make them holy in order to serve me as priests. Take a young bull and two flawless rams. ²Take unleavened bread, unleavened flatbread made with oil, and unleavened wafers spread with oil. Make them out of high-quality wheat flour. ³Put them all in one basket and present them in the basket along with the bull and the two rams. ⁴Present Aaron and his sons at the entrance to the meeting tent and wash them with water. ⁵Then take the priestly clothes and put them on Aaron: the tunic, the vest's robe, the vest itself, and the chest pendant. Put the vest on him with the vest's belt. ⁶Set the turban on his head and place the holy crown on the turban. ⁷Take the anointing oil and pour it on his head to anoint him. ⁸Then present his sons and put the tunics on them. ⁹Tighten the sashes on them, on both Aaron and his sons. Wrap the turbans on their heads. It will be a permanent regulation that the duties of priesthood belong to them. In this way, you will ordain Aaron and his sons.

¹⁰Present the bull at the front of the meeting tent. Aaron and his sons will lay their hands on the bull's head. ¹¹Then slaughter the bull in the LORD's presence at the meeting tent's entrance. ¹²Take some of the bull's blood and smear it on the altar's horns with your finger. Pour out the rest of the blood at the altar's base. ¹³Then take all the fat that covers the inner organs, the lobe of the liver, and the two kidneys along with the fat that is on them, and burn them up in smoke on the altar. ¹⁴Burn the rest of the meat of the bull, its hide, and the intestines with their contents with a fire outside the camp. It is a purification offering.

¹⁵Choose one of the rams, and have Aaron and his sons lay their hands on the ram's head. ¹⁶Then slaughter the ram. Take its blood and throw it against all the altar's sides. ¹⁷Cut up the ram into parts. Wash its inner organs and legs, and put them together with its parts

and its head. ¹⁸Then turn the entire ram into smoke by burning it on the altar. It is an entirely burned offering for the LORD, a soothing smell, a food gift for the LORD.

¹⁹Take the second ram, and have Aaron and his sons lay their hands on the ram's head. ²⁰Slaughter the ram. Take some of its blood and smear it on the right earlobes of Aaron and his sons, on the thumbs of their right hands, and on the big toes of their right feet. Throw the rest of the blood against all the altar's sides. ²¹Then take some of the blood on the altar and some of the anointing oil and sprinkle them on Aaron and on his clothes and on his sons and on his sons' clothes. In this way, Aaron, his sons, and all their priestly garments will be holy.

²²Take the fatty parts of the ram: the fat tail, the fat around the inner organs, the lobe of the liver, the two kidneys with the fat around them, and the right thigh (because it is a ram for ordination). ²³Add one loaf of bread, one flatbread made with oil, and one wafer from the basket of unleavened bread that was presented to the LORD. ²⁴Place all of these in the hands of Aaron and his sons, and lift them as an uplifted offering in the LORD's presence. ²⁵Then take them from their hands and turn them into smoke by burning them on the altar with the entirely burned offering as a soothing smell in the LORD's presence. It is a food gift for the LORD.

²⁶Take the breast of the ram for Aaron's ordination and lift it as an uplifted offering in the LORD's presence. It will be your portion. ²⁷Make holy the breast that was lifted for the uplifted offering and the thigh that was raised for the gift offering from the ram for the ordination. They belong to Aaron and his sons. ²⁸Those parts will be given to Aaron and his sons from the Israelites as a permanent provision, because they are a gift offering. They will be a gift offering from the Israelites, their gift offering to the LORD from their well-being sacrifices.

[29]Aaron's holy clothes should be passed on to his sons after him. His sons should be anointed in them and ordained in them. [30]The son who is priest in his place should wear them seven days when he comes into the meeting tent to minister in the sanctuary.

[31]Take the ram for the ordination and boil its meat in a holy place. [32]Aaron and his sons will eat the ram's meat and the bread that is in the basket at the meeting tent's entrance. [33]They alone should eat the food that was used to purify them, to ordain them, and to make them holy. No one else should eat it because it is holy. [34]If any meat for the ordination or any of the bread is left over until morning, then you should burn the leftovers with fire. It shouldn't be eaten because it's holy.

[35]Treat Aaron and his sons just as I have commanded you. Ordain them for seven days. [36]Every day you should offer a bull as a purification offering for reconciliation. You should remove the sin from the altar through a ritual of reconciliation, and you should anoint the altar to make it holy. [37]Seven days you should perform the ritual of reconciliation for the altar and make it holy. In this way, the altar will become most holy, and whatever touches the altar will also become holy.

Instructions for daily entirely burned offerings

[38]Now this is what you should offer on the altar: two one-year-old lambs regularly every day. [39]Offer one lamb in the morning and offer the other lamb at twilight. [40]With the first lamb, add one-tenth of a measure of the high-quality flour mixed with a quarter of a hin[t] of oil from crushed olives and a quarter of a hin of wine for a drink offering. [41]With the second lamb offered at twilight, again include a grain offering and its drink offering as in the morning as a soothing smell, a gift offering for the LORD. [42]This should be the regular entirely burned offering in every generation at the meeting tent's entrance in the LORD's presence. There I will meet with you, and there I will speak to you. [43]I will meet with the Israelites there, and it will be made holy by my glorious presence. [44]I will make the meeting tent and the altar holy. Likewise,

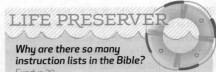

LIFE PRESERVER

Why are there so many instruction lists in the Bible?
Exodus 29

We sometimes get tired of things we should remember to do at home, at school, and at other places in our lives. Sometimes the lists get really long!

Exodus 20–32 begins with the Ten Commandments and then goes on to describe instructions that relate to almost every part of life for the Israelites, including worship in the temple, slaves, violence, religion, festivals, sabbatical years, and more.

The Israelites were becoming a people with a new identity as God's children as they left their slavery in Egypt. During this time God gave them instructions to help them learn how to live together with their new freedom. God wanted the people to learn how to live in faithfulness to God and God's plan for their lives as they made their way through the wilderness to the promised land that God would provide. ◆

I will make Aaron and his sons holy to serve me as priests. [45]I will be at home among the Israelites, and I will be their God. [46]They will know that I am the LORD their God, who brought them out of the land of Egypt so that I could make a home among them. I am the LORD their God.

Instructions for the incense altar

30Make an acacia-wood altar for burning incense. [2]The altar should be square, eighteen inches long and eighteen inches wide. It should be three feet high. Its horns should be permanently attached. [3]Cover the altar with pure gold, including its top, all its sides, and its horns. You should also make a gold molding all around it. [4]Make two gold rings and attach them under the molding on two opposite sides of the altar. They will house the poles used to carry the altar. [5]Make acacia-wood poles and cover them with gold. [6]Place the incense altar in front of the veil that hangs before the chest containing the covenant, in front of the cover that is on top of the covenant document where I will meet with you. [7]Aaron will burn sweet-smelling incense on the incense altar every morning when he takes care of the lamps. [8]And again when Aaron lights the lamps at twilight, he will burn incense. It should be a regular incense offering in the Lord's presence in every generation. [9]Don't offer the wrong incense on the altar or an entirely burned offering or a grain offering. Don't pour a drink offering on it. [10]Once a year Aaron should perform a ritual of reconciliation on its horns with the blood of the purification offering for reconciliation. Once a year in every generation he should perform a ritual of reconciliation at the altar. It is most holy to the Lord.

Census and compensation

[11]The Lord spoke to Moses: [12]When you take a census of the Israelites to count them, each of them should pay compensation for their life to the Lord when they are counted. Then no plague will descend on them when they are counted. [13]Every one who is counted should pay a half shekel according to the official shekel of the sanctuary (the shekel is twenty gerahs). The half shekel is a gift offering to the Lord. [14]Every one who is counted, from 20 years old and above, should present a gift offering to the Lord. [15]When you bring this gift offering to the Lord to pay compensation for your lives, the rich shouldn't give more and the poor shouldn't give less than the half shekel. [16]Take the compensation money from the Israelites and use it to support the service of the meeting tent. It will serve for the Israelites as a reminder in the Lord's presence of the compensation paid for your lives.

Instructions for the washbasin

[17]The Lord spoke to Moses: [18]Make a copper basin for washing along with its copper stand. Put it between the meeting tent and the altar, and put water in it. [19]Aaron and his sons will use it to wash their hands and their feet. [20]When they go into the meeting tent or approach the altar to minister and to offer a food gift to the Lord, they must wash with water so that they don't die. [21]They must wash their hands and their feet so that they don't die. This will be a permanent regulation for

them, for Aaron and his descendants in every generation.

Instructions for oil and incense

[22]The Lord spoke to Moses: [23]Now take for yourself high-quality spices: five hundred weight of solid myrrh; half as much of sweet-smelling cinnamon, that is, two hundred fifty; two hundred fifty weight of sweet-smelling cane; [24]five hundred of cassia—measured by the sanctuary shekel—and a hin[u] of olive oil. [25]Prepare a holy anointing oil, blending them like a skilled perfume maker to produce the holy anointing oil. [26]Use it to anoint the meeting tent, the chest containing the covenant, [27]the table and all its equipment, the lampstand and its equipment, the incense altar, [28]the altar for entirely burned offerings and all its equipment, and the washbasin with its stand. [29]Make them holy so that they may be perfectly holy. Whatever touches them will become holy. [30]Then anoint Aaron and his sons and make them holy to serve me as priests. [31]Say to the Israelites: This will be my holy anointing oil in every generation. [32]Don't allow anyone else to use this oil. Don't make another oil like it by using the same formula. This oil is holy, and you should regard it as holy. [33]Whoever blends an oil like it or whoever uses the oil on someone else will be cut off from the people.

[34]The Lord said to Moses: Take an equal amount of each of these spices: gum resin, onycha, galbanum, and pure frankincense. [35]Like a skilled perfume maker, carefully blend them together and make incense, seasoned with salt, pure and holy. [36]Beat some of it into a fine powder and put part of it in front of the covenant document in the meeting tent where I will meet with you. You should regard it as perfectly holy. [37]When you make incense according to this formula, you shouldn't make any of it for your own use. You should regard it as holy to the Lord. [38]Whoever makes incense with this same formula to enjoy its fragrance will be cut off from the people.

Construction leaders: Bezalel and Oholiab

31 The Lord spoke to Moses: [2]Look, I have chosen Bezalel, Uri's son and Hur's

---

[u]One hin is approximately one gallon.

grandson from the tribe of Judah. ³I have filled him with the divine spirit, with skill, ability, and knowledge for every kind of work. ⁴He will be able to create designs; do metal-work in gold, silver, and copper; ⁵cut stones for setting; carve wood; and do every kind of work. ⁶I have also appointed with him Oho-liab, Ahisamach's son from the tribe of Dan. To all who are skillful, I have given the skill to make everything that I have commanded you: ⁷the meeting tent, the chest containing the covenant, the cover that is on top of it, all the tent's furnishings, ⁸the table and its equip-ment, the pure lampstand with all its equip-ment, the incense altar, ⁹the altar for entirely burned offerings with all its equipment, the washbasin with its stand, ¹⁰the woven cloth-ing, the holy clothes for Aaron the priest and for his sons for their service as priests, ¹¹the anointing oil, and the sweet-smelling incense for the sanctuary. They will do just as I have commanded you.

Instructions for keeping the Sabbath

¹²The LORD said to Moses: ¹³Tell the Isra-elites: "Be sure to keep my sabbaths, because the Sabbath is a sign between me and you in every generation so you will know that I am the LORD who makes you holy. ¹⁴Keep the Sabbath, because it is holy for you. Everyone who violates the Sabbath will be put to death. Whoever does any work on the Sabbath, that person will be cut off from the people. ¹⁵Do your work for six days. But the seventh day is a Sabbath of complete rest that is holy to the LORD. Whoever does any work on the Sabbath day will be put to death. ¹⁶The Isra-elites should keep the Sabbath. They should observe the Sabbath in every generation as a covenant for all time. ¹⁷It is a sign forever be-tween me and the Israelites that in six days the LORD made the heavens and the earth, and on the seventh day the LORD rested and was refreshed."

¹⁸When God finished speaking with Moses

Gifted for Service   *Exodus 31:1-11*

You don't have to be a minister or missionary to serve God. During the time of Moses, the Isra-elites gathered to worship God in the meeting tent. There were specific instructions for how it was to be built and what would be in it. God chose Bezalel, Oholiab, and others who could make things out of gold, silver, wood, precious gems, and woven cloth. These people used their artis-tic ability to make beautiful things for the meeting tent.

God has given everyone special gifts. Some gifts are artistic, such as singing, painting, speak-ing, or acting. Other gifts may be relational, like teaching, encouraging, welcoming, or caring for people. Even taking care of the church building by emptying the trash or pulling weeds can be a gift of service.

You might wonder if some gifts are more important than others. But all gifts are important. We need people to cook meals for the sick or make others laugh just as much as we need ministers, missionaries, and Sunday school teachers. We should all use our own special gifts—the things we're really good at—to serve God.

Name two things you're really good at.

How can you use these special gifts to serve God?

on Mount Sinai, God gave him the two covenant tablets, the stone tablets written by God's finger.

Worshipping the gold bull calf

32 The people saw that Moses was taking a long time to come down from the mountain. They gathered around Aaron and said to him, "Come on! Make us gods[v] who can lead us. As for this man Moses who brought us up out of the land of Egypt, we don't have a clue what has happened to him."

[2] Aaron said to them, "All right, take out the gold rings from the ears of your wives, your sons, and your daughters, and bring them to me." [3] So all the people took out the gold rings from their ears and brought them to Aaron. [4] He collected them and tied them up in a cloth.[w] Then he made a metal image of a bull calf, and the people declared, "These are your gods, Israel, who brought you up out of the land of Egypt!"

[5] When Aaron saw this, he built an altar in front of the calf. Then Aaron announced, "Tomorrow will be a festival to the Lord!" [6] They got up early the next day and offered up entirely burned offerings and brought wellbeing sacrifices. The people sat down to eat and drink and then got up to celebrate.

[7] The Lord spoke to Moses: "Hurry up and go down! Your people, whom you brought up out of the land of Egypt, are ruining everything! [8] They've already abandoned the path that I commanded. They have made a metal bull calf for themselves. They've bowed down to it and offered sacrifices to it and declared, 'These are your gods, Israel, who brought you up out of the land of Egypt!'" [9] The Lord said to Moses, "I've been watching these people, and I've seen how stubborn they are. [10] Now leave me alone! Let my fury burn and devour them. Then I'll make a great nation out of you."

[11] But Moses pleaded with the Lord his God, "Lord, why does your fury burn against your own people, whom you brought out of the land of Egypt with great power and amazing force? [12] Why should the Egyptians say, 'He had an evil plan to take the people out and kill them in the mountains and so wipe them

off the earth'? Calm down your fierce anger. Change your mind about doing terrible things to your own people. [13] Remember Abraham, Isaac, and Israel, your servants, whom you yourself promised, 'I'll make your descendants as many as the stars in the sky. And I've promised to give your descendants this whole land to possess for all time.'" [14] Then the Lord changed his mind about the terrible things he said he would do to his people.

[15] Moses then turned around and came down the mountain. He carried the two covenant tablets in his hands. The tablets were written on both sides, front and back. [16] The tablets were God's own work. What was written there was God's own writing inscribed on the tablets. [17] When Joshua heard the noise of the people as they shouted, he said to Moses, "It sounds like war in the camp."

[18] But Moses said,

"It isn't the sound of a victory song.
It isn't the sound of a song of defeat.
The sound of party songs is what I hear."

[19] When he got near the camp and saw the bull calf and the dancing, Moses was furious. He hurled the tablets down and shattered them in pieces at the foot of the mountain. [20] He took the calf that they had made and burned it in a fire. Then he ground it down to crushed powder, scattered it on the water, and made the Israelites drink it.

[21] Moses said to Aaron, "What did these people do to you that you led them to commit such a terrible sin?"

[22] Aaron replied, "Don't get angry with me, sir. You know yourself that these people are out of control.[x] [23] They said to me, 'Make us gods who can lead us. As for this man Moses who brought us up out of the land of Egypt, we don't have a clue what has happened to him.' [24] So I said to them, 'Whoever has gold, take it off!' So they gave it to me, I threw it into the fire, and out came this bull calf!"

[25] Moses saw that the people were out of control because Aaron had let them get out of control, making them an easy target for their enemies. [26] So Moses stood at the camp's gate and said, "Whoever is on the Lord's side, come to me!" All the Levites gathered around him. [27] Moses said to them, "This is what the

---

[v] Or *a god* [w] Or *formed them into a mold* or *engraved them with a stylus* [x] Sam; MT *evil*

LORD, Israel's God, says: Each of you, strap on your sword! Go back and forth from one end of the camp to the other. Each of you, kill your brother, your friend, and your neighbor!" ²⁸The Levites did as Moses commanded. About three thousand people were killed that day. ²⁹Moses said, "Today you've been ordained to the LORD, each one of you at the cost of a son or a brother. Today you've gained a special blessing for yourselves."

³⁰The next day Moses said to the people, "You've committed a terrible sin. So now I will go up to the LORD. Maybe I can arrange reconciliation on account of your sin." ³¹So Moses went back to the LORD and said, "Oh, what a terrible sin these people have committed! They made for themselves gods[y] of gold. ³²But now, please forgive their sin! And if not, then wipe me out of your scroll that you've written."

³³But the LORD said to Moses, "The ones I'll wipe out of my scroll are those who sinned against me. ³⁴Now go and lead the people to the place I described to you. My messenger here will go in front of you. When the day of reckoning comes, I'll count their sin against them." ³⁵Then the LORD sent a plague on the people because of what they did with the bull calf that Aaron made.

LIGHTHOUSE

FALSE GODS

Oh No! *Exodus 32:1-35*

After everything that the Israelites had been through—all the times God had shown that God was with them—still they doubted. While Moses went up on the mountain to talk with God, the Israelites grew restless and fearful. They pleaded with Moses' brother Aaron to make them gods who would lead them. And Aaron agreed! The people gathered gold, melted it down, and formed it in the image of a calf they could worship. Despite how far they had come, the Israelites made a terrible choice. God was furious at their disobedience. But Moses pleaded with God not to give up on the Israelites. ◊

///

The LORD: "I can't go"

33 The LORD said to Moses, "Go and leave this place, you and the people whom you brought up out of the land of Egypt. Go to the land I promised to Abraham, Isaac, and Jacob when I said, 'I'll give it to your descendants.' ²I'll send a messenger before you. I'll drive out the Canaanites, the Amorites, the Hittites, the Perizzites, the Hivites, and the Jebusites. ³Go to this land full of milk and honey. But I won't go up with you because I would end up destroying you along the way since you are a stubborn people."

⁴When the people heard the bad news, they were sorry. No one put on any jewelry, ⁵because the LORD had said to Moses, "Tell the Israelites, 'You are a stubborn people. If I were to go up with you even for a single moment, I would destroy you. So now take off your jewelry, while I figure out what to do with you.'" ⁶So after leaving Mount Horeb the Israelites rid themselves of their jewelry.

Speaking with the LORD at the meeting tent

⁷Moses took the tent and pitched it outside the camp, far away from the camp. He called it the meeting tent. Everyone who wanted advice from the LORD would go out to the meeting tent outside the camp. ⁸Whenever Moses went out to the tent, all the people would rise and stand at the entrance to their tents and watch Moses until he had gone into the tent. ⁹When Moses entered the tent, the column of cloud would come down and stand at the tent's entrance while the LORD talked with Moses. ¹⁰When all the people saw the column of cloud standing at the tent's entrance, they would all rise and then bow down at the entrances to their tents. ¹¹In this way the LORD used to speak to Moses face-to-face, like two people talking to each other. Then Moses would come back to the camp. But his young assistant Joshua, Nun's son, wouldn't leave the tent.

Moses pleads with God

¹²Moses said to the LORD, "Look, you've been telling me, 'Lead these people forward.' But you haven't told me whom you will send with me. Yet you've assured me, 'I know you by name and think highly of you.' ¹³Now if you do think highly of me, show me your ways so that

---

[y] Or *a god*

I may know you and so that you may really approve of me. Remember too that this nation is your people."

¹⁴The Lord replied, "I'll go myself, and I'll help you."

¹⁵Moses replied, "If you won't go yourself, don't make us leave here. ¹⁶Because how will anyone know that we have your special approval, both I and your people, unless you go with us? Only that distinguishes us, me and your people, from every other people on the earth."

¹⁷The Lord said to Moses, "I'll do exactly what you've asked because you have my special approval, and I know you by name."

¹⁸Moses said, "Please show me your glorious presence."

¹⁹The Lord said, "I'll make all my goodness pass in front of you, and I'll proclaim before you the name, 'The Lord.' I will be kind to whomever I wish to be kind, and I will have compassion to whomever I wish to be compassionate. ²⁰But," the Lord said, "you can't see my face because no one can see me and live." ²¹The Lord said, "Here is a place near me where you will stand beside the rock. ²²As my glorious presence passes by, I'll set you in a gap in the rock, and I'll cover you with my hand until I've passed by. ²³Then I'll take away my hand, and you will see my back, but my face won't be visible."

A deeper revealing of God's character

34 The Lord said to Moses, "Cut two stone tablets like the first ones. I'll write on these tablets the words that were on the first tablets, which you broke into pieces. ²Get ready in the morning and come up to Mount Sinai. Stand there on top of the mountain in front of me. ³No one else can come up with you. Don't allow anyone even to be seen anywhere on the mountain. Don't even let sheep and cattle graze in front of the mountain." ⁴So Moses cut two stone tablets like the first ones. He got up early in the morning and climbed up Mount Sinai, just as the Lord had commanded him. He carried the two stone tablets in his hands. ⁵The Lord came down in the cloud and stood there with him, and proclaimed the name, "The Lord."

⁶The Lord passed in front of him and proclaimed:

> Memorize
> Exod 34:6

"The Lord!
    The Lord!
a God who is
    compassionate and merciful,
    very patient,
    full of great loyalty and faithfulness,
⁷ showing great loyalty
    to a thousand generations,
    forgiving every kind of sin
    and rebellion,
    yet by no means clearing the guilty,
    punishing for their parents' sins
    their children and their grandchildren,
    as well as the third
    and the fourth generation."

⁸At once Moses bowed to the ground and worshipped. ⁹He said, "If you approve of me, my Lord, please go along with us.ᶻ Although these are stubborn people, forgive our guilt and our sin and take us as your own possession."

Renewing the broken covenant

¹⁰The Lord said: I now make a covenant. In front of all your people, I'll perform dramatic displays of power that have never been done before anywhere on earth or in any nation. All the people who are around you will see what the Lord does, because I will do an awesome thing with you.

¹¹Be sure to obey what I command you today. I'm about to drive out before you the Amorites, the Canaanites, the Hittites, the Perizzites, the Hivites, and the Jebusites. ¹²Be careful that you don't make a covenant with the inhabitants of the land to which you are going, or it will become a dangerous trap for you. ¹³You must tear down their altars, smash their sacred stone pillars, and cut down their sacred poles. ¹⁴You must not bow down to another god, because the Lord is passionate: the Lord's name means "a passionate God." ¹⁵Don't make a covenant with those who live in the land. When they prostitute themselves with their gods and sacrifice to their gods, they may invite you and you may end up eating some of the sacrifice. ¹⁶Then you might go and choose their daughters as wives for your sons. And their daughters who prostitute

---

ᶻLXX; MT adds *my Lord.*

themselves with their gods might lead your sons to prostitute themselves with their gods. [17]Don't make metal gods for yourself.

[18]Observe the Festival of Unleavened Bread. You should eat unleavened bread for seven days, as I commanded you, at the set time in the month of Abib,[a] because it was in the month of Abib that you came out of Egypt.

[19]Every first offspring is mine. That includes all your male livestock, the oldest offspring of cows and sheep. [20]But a donkey's oldest offspring you may ransom with a sheep. Or if you don't ransom it, you must break its neck. You should ransom all of your oldest sons. No one should appear before me empty-handed.

[21]You should do your work for six days, but on the seventh day you should rest. Even during plowing or harvesttime you should rest. [22]You should observe the Festival of Weeks, for the early produce of the wheat harvest, and the Gathering Festival at the end of the year. [23]All your males should appear three times a year before the Lord God, Israel's God. [24]I will drive out nations before you and extend your borders. No one will desire and try to take your land if you go up and appear before the Lord your God three times a year.

[25]Don't slaughter the blood of my sacrifice with anything leavened. The sacrifice of the Passover Festival shouldn't be left over until the morning.

[26]Bring the best of the early produce of your farmland to the Lord your God's temple.

Don't boil a young goat in its mother's milk.

[27]The Lord said to Moses: "Write down these words because by these words I hereby make a covenant with you and with Israel." [28]Moses was there with the Lord forty days

[a]March–April, named Nisan after the exile

God's Character Revealed Exodus 34:6-7

People often spend a lot of time and money on how they look. They want to have the right haircut and the right clothes. The old saying *Beauty is only skin deep* is true. It doesn't matter whether you're tall, strong, thin, or attractive. What really matters is what kind of person you are on the inside.

God had spoken directly to Moses several times. Moses had seen God send horrible plagues against Egypt and part the Reed Sea so the Israelites could escape. He had seen God give manna, quail, and water to care for the Israelites' needs. God showed power that was greater than all the gods of Egypt. But Moses wanted more; he wanted to see God.

God told Moses that he wouldn't be able to see God's face. Instead, God offered to show Moses God's glory. What Moses saw wasn't what he expected. God's glory wasn't a powerful warrior or an angry judge, but God's goodness. Moses saw a God of love, mercy, loyalty, faithfulness, and forgiveness.

As God's children, we can grow closer to God and reflect God's goodness in our hearts.

How do you see God's goodness in your life?

How do you share this goodness with other people?

and forty nights. He didn't eat any bread or drink any water. He wrote on the tablets the words of the covenant, the ten words.

Moses' brightly shining face

²⁹Moses came down from Mount Sinai. As he came down from the mountain with the two covenant tablets in his hand, Moses didn't realize that the skin of his face shone brightly because he had been talking with God. ³⁰When Aaron and all the Israelites saw the skin of Moses' face shining brightly, they were afraid to come near him. ³¹But Moses called them closer. So Aaron and all the leaders of the community came back to him, and Moses spoke with them. ³²After that, all the Israelites came near as well, and Moses commanded them everything that the LORD had spoken with him on Mount Sinai. ³³When Moses finished speaking with them, he put a veil over his face. ³⁴Whenever Moses went into the LORD's presence to speak with him, Moses would take the veil off until he came out again. When Moses came out and told the Israelites what he had been commanded, ³⁵the Israelites would see that the skin of Moses' face was shining brightly. So Moses would put the veil on his face again until the next time he went in to speak with the LORD.

35 Moses gathered together the whole Israelite community and said to them: These are the things that the LORD has commanded you to do:

Instructions for the Sabbath

²Do your work for six days, but the seventh day should be holy to you, a Sabbath of complete rest for the LORD. Whoever does any work on the Sabbath will be put to death. ³Don't start a fire in any of your homes on the Sabbath day.

Preparing to build the dwelling

⁴Moses said to the whole Israelite community, This is what the LORD has commanded: ⁵Collect gift offerings for the LORD from all of you. Whoever freely wants to give should bring the LORD's gift offerings: gold, silver, and copper; ⁶blue, purple, and deep red yarns;

fine linen; goats' hair; ⁷rams' skins dyed red; beaded leather;ᵇ acacia wood; ⁸the oil for the light; spices for the anointing oil and for the sweet-smelling incense; ⁹gemstones; and gems for setting in the priest's vestᶜ and in the priest's chest pendant.

did you know? When Moses brought the people the second set of tablets from God, they were afraid because Moses glowed. Because of this, Moses started wearing a veil so people would not see his skin.

¹⁰All of you who are skilled in crafts should come forward and make everything that the LORD has commanded: ¹¹the dwelling, its tent and its covering, its clasps, its boards, its bars, its posts, and its bases, ¹²the chest with its poles and its cover, the veil for a screen, ¹³the table with its poles and all its equipment, the bread of the presence, ¹⁴the lampstand for light with its equipment and its lamps, the oil for the light, ¹⁵the incense altar with its poles, the anointing oil and the sweet-smelling incense, the entrance screen for the dwelling's entrance, ¹⁶the altar for entirely burned offerings with its copper grate, its poles, and all its equipment, the washbasin with its stand, ¹⁷the courtyard's drapes, its posts, and its bases, and the screen for the courtyard gate, ¹⁸the dwelling's tent pegs and the courtyard's tent pegs, and their cords, ¹⁹the woven clothing for ministering in the sanctuary, and the holy clothes for Aaron the priest and his sons for their service as priests.

Gifts for building the dwelling

²⁰The whole Israelite community left Moses. ²¹Everyone who was excited and eager to participate brought the LORD's gift offerings to be used for building the meeting tent and all its furnishings and for the holy clothes. ²²Both men and women came forward. Everyone who was eager to participate brought pins, earrings, rings, and necklaces, all sorts of gold objects. Everyone raised an uplifted offering of gold to the LORD. ²³And everyone who had blue or purple or deep red yarn or

ᵇOr *dolphin skins* ᶜHeb *ephod*

fine linen or goats' hair or rams' skins dyed red or beaded leather brought them. [24]Everyone who could make a gift offering of silver or copper brought it as the Lᴏʀᴅ's gift offering. Everyone who had acacia wood that could be used in any kind of building work brought it. [25]All the skilled women spun cloth with their hands, and brought what they had spun in blue and purple and deep red yarns and fine linen. [26]All the women who were eager to use their skill spun the goats' hair. [27]The chiefs brought gemstones and gems to be set in the priest's vest and the chest pendant, [28]spices and oil for light and for the anointing oil, and for the sweet-smelling incense. [29]All the Israelite men and women who were eager to contribute something for the work that the Lᴏʀᴅ had commanded Moses to do brought it as a spontaneous gift to the Lᴏʀᴅ.

Moses introduces Bezalel and Oholiab

[30]Then Moses said to the Israelites: "Look, the Lᴏʀᴅ has chosen Bezalel, Uri's son and Hur's grandson from the tribe of Judah. [31]The Lᴏʀᴅ has filled him with the divine spirit that will give him skill, ability, and knowledge for every kind of work. [32]He will be able to create designs, do metalwork in gold, silver, and copper, [33]cut stones for setting, carve wood, do every kind of creative work, [34]and have the ability to teach others. Both he and Oholiab, Ahisamach's son from the tribe of Dan, [35]have been given the skill to do every kind of work done by a gem cutter or a designer or a needleworker in blue, purple, and deep red yarns and in fine linen or a weaver or anyone else doing work or creating designs.

36 "Let Bezalel, Oholiab, and every other skilled worker whom the Lᴏʀᴅ has given skill, ability, and knowledge for the work of building the sanctuary do all that the Lᴏʀᴅ has commanded."

[2]Moses then called together Bezalel, Oholiab, and every skilled person whom the Lᴏʀᴅ had given skill and who was eager to come and do the work. [3]Moses gave them all the gift offerings that the Israelites had contributed to the work on the sanctuary. They kept bringing him spontaneous gifts, morning after morning.

[4]Finally, all the skilled workers building the sanctuary left their work that they were

doing one by one to come [5]and say to Moses, "The people are contributing way too much material for doing the work that the Lᴏʀᴅ has commanded us to do."

[6]So Moses issued a command that was proclaimed throughout the camp: "Every man and woman should stop making gift offerings for the sanctuary project." So the people stopped bringing anything more [7]because what they had already brought was more than enough to do all the work.

Construction of the dwelling

[8]All the skilled workers made the dwelling out of ten curtains of fine twisted linen and blue, purple, and deep red yarns, with figures of winged heavenly creatures worked into their design. [9]Each curtain was forty-two feet long and six feet wide. All the curtains were the same size.

[10]They joined five of the curtains to each other and joined the other five curtains to each other. [11]They made loops of blue thread on the edge of the outer curtain of the first set. They did the same on the edge of the outer curtain of the second set. [12]They made fifty loops on the one curtain and fifty loops on the outer curtain that was in the second set. The loops were opposite each other. [13]They also made fifty gold clasps, and they used the clasps to join the curtains to each other so that the dwelling was one whole structure.

[14]They also made curtains of goats' hair for a tent over the dwelling. They made eleven curtains. [15]Each curtain was forty-five feet long and each curtain six feet wide. All eleven curtains were the same size. [16]They joined five curtains together and the six other curtains together. [17]They made fifty loops on the edge of the outer curtain of the one set and fifty loops on the edge of the other set of curtains. [18]They made fifty copper clasps to join the tent together so that it would be one whole structure. [19]They also made a covering for the tent of rams' skins dyed red and an outer covering of beaded leather.

[20]Then they made acacia-wood boards to stand upright as a frame for the dwelling. [21]Each board was fifteen feet long and twenty-seven inches wide. [22]Each board had two pegs for joining them to each other. They

did this for all the dwelling's boards. 23They made twenty boards for the dwelling's southern side. 24They made forty silver bases under the twenty boards, with two bases under the first board for its two pegs, two bases under the next board for its two pegs, and so on. 25For the dwelling's other side on the north, they made twenty boards 26and forty silver bases, two bases under the first board, two bases under the next board, and so on. 27For the back of the dwelling on the west, they made six boards. 28They made two additional boards for the dwelling's rear corners. 29They were spread out at the bottom but joined together at the top with one ring. In this way, these two boards formed the two corners. 30And so there were eight boards with their sixteen silver bases, with two bases under every board.

31They also made acacia-wood bars: five for the boards on one side of the dwelling, 32five bars for the boards on the other side of the dwelling, and five bars for the boards on the back wall of the dwelling on the west. 33They made the middle bar, which was halfway up the boards, run from one end to the other. 34They covered the boards with gold. They made gold rings to house the bars and covered the bars with gold.

35They made the veil of blue, purple, and deep red yarns and fine twisted linen, with figures of winged heavenly creatures worked into its design. 36They made for it four acacia-wood posts covered in gold with gold hooks and cast four silver bases for them. 37They made a screen for the entrance to the tent of blue, purple, and deep red yarns and fine twisted linen, decorated with needlework. 38They made its five posts with hooks. They covered their tops and bands with gold, but made their five bases out of copper.

Building the chest containing the covenant document

37 Bezalel made the chest of acacia wood. It was forty-five inches long, twenty-seven inches wide, and twenty-seven inches high. 2He covered the chest with pure gold inside and out, and made a gold molding all around it. 3He cast four gold rings for it and put them on its four feet, two rings on one side and two rings on the other. 4He made

acacia-wood poles and covered them with gold. 5He put the poles into the rings on the chest's sides to use to carry the chest. 6He made a cover for the chest out of pure gold, forty-five inches long and twenty-seven inches wide. 7He made two winged heavenly creatures of hammered gold for the two ends of the cover, 8one winged heavenly creature at one end and one winged heavenly creature at the other. He placed the winged heavenly creatures at the cover's two ends. 9The winged heavenly creatures spread out their wings above, shielding the cover with their wings. The winged heavenly creatures faced each other toward the cover's center.

Constructing the table and lampstand

10He also made the table of acacia wood, three feet long, eighteen inches wide, and twenty-seven inches high. 11He covered it with pure gold and made a gold molding all around it. 12He made a frame around it that was four inches wide and gold molding around the frame. 13He made four gold rings for the table. He fastened the rings to the four corners at its four legs. 14The rings that housed the poles used for carrying the table were close to the frame. 15He made the poles used to carry the table out of acacia wood, and he covered them with gold. 16He made the containers of pure gold that were to be on the table: its plates, dishes, bowls, and jars for pouring drink offerings.

17He also made the lampstand of pure, hammered gold. The lampstand's base, branches, cups, flowers, and petals were all attached to it. 18It had six branches growing out from its sides, three branches on one side of the lampstand and three branches on the other side of the lampstand. 19One branch had three cups shaped like almond blossoms, each with a flower and petals, and the next branch also had three cups shaped like almond blossoms, each with a flower and petals. A total of six branches grew out of the lampstand. 20In addition, on the lampstand itself there were four cups shaped like almond blossoms, each with its flower and petals. 21There was a flower attached under the first pair of branches, a flower attached under the next pair of branches, and a flower attached under the last pair of branches. 22Their flowers and their branches were attached to it. The whole lampstand was one piece of pure hammered gold. ²³He made its seven lamps and its tongs and its fire pans out of pure gold. ²⁴He made the lampstand and all its equipment from pure gold weighing one kikkar.

Making the incense altar, incense, and oil

²⁵He made the incense altar out of acacia wood. The altar was square, eighteen inches long by eighteen inches wide. It was three feet high, and its horns were permanently attached. ²⁶He covered it with pure gold, including its top, all its sides, and its horns. He also made a gold molding all around it. ²⁷He made two gold rings, and he attached them under the molding on two opposite sides of the altar. They housed the poles used to carry it. ²⁸He made the poles of acacia wood, and he covered them with gold.

²⁹He also made the holy anointing oil and the pure sweet-smelling incense like a skilled perfume maker.

Making the altar for entirely burned offerings

38 He made the altar for entirely burned offerings out of acacia wood. The altar was square, seven and a half feet long and seven and a half feet wide. It was four and a half feet high. ²He made horns for it, one horn on each of its four corners. Its horns were attached to the altar, and he covered it with copper. ³He made all the altar's equipment: the pails, the shovels, the bowls, the meat forks, and the trays. He made all its equipment out of copper. ⁴He made a grate for the altar of copper mesh underneath its bottom edge and extending halfway up to the middle of the altar. ⁵He made four rings for each of the four corners of the copper grate to house the poles. ⁶He made the poles out of acacia wood, and he covered them with copper. ⁷He put the poles through the rings so that the poles were on the two sides of the altar when it was carried. He made the altar with planks but hollow inside.

⁸He made the copper washbasin with its copper stand from the copper mirrors among the ranks of women assigned to the meeting tent's entrance.

Constructing the dwelling's plaza

⁹He also set up the courtyard. The courtyard's south side had drapes of fine twisted linen stretching one hundred fifty feet ¹⁰with twenty posts, twenty copper bases, and silver hooks and bands for the posts. ¹¹Likewise the north side stretched one hundred fifty feet, with twenty posts, twenty copper bases, and silver hooks and bands for the posts. ¹²On the west side the drapes stretched seventy-five feet, with their ten posts, their ten bases, and silver hooks and bands for the posts. ¹³The front side facing east was seventy-five feet. ¹⁴There were twenty-two and a half feet of drapes on one side with three posts and three bases for them. ¹⁵Likewise, there were twenty-two and a half feet of drapes on the other side of the plaza's gate with three posts and three bases for them. ¹⁶All the drapes around the courtyard were made of fine twisted linen.

¹⁷The bases for the posts were made of copper, but the hooks for the posts and their bands were made of silver. The tops of the posts were covered with silver, and all the posts surrounding the courtyard had silver bands. ¹⁸The screen for the gate into the courtyard was made with blue, purple, and deep red yarns and fine twisted linen, decorated with needlework. It was thirty feet long and, along the width of it, seven and a half feet high, corresponding to the courtyard's drapes. ¹⁹It had four posts, their four copper bases, their silver hooks, and their tops and bands covered with silver. ²⁰All the tent pegs for the dwelling and for the courtyard all around were made of copper.

A listing of materials used

²¹These are the accounts of the dwelling, the covenant dwelling, that were recorded at Moses' instructions. They are the work of the Levites, under the direction of Ithamar, Aaron the priest's son. ²²Bezalel, Uri's son and Hur's grandson from the tribe of Judah, made everything that the LORD had commanded Moses to make. ²³Working with Bezalel was Oholiab, Ahisamach's son from the tribe of Dan, who was a gem cutter, a designer, and a needleworker in blue, purple, and deep red yarns and in fine linen. ²⁴The total amount of the gold that was

used for construction of the whole sanctuary, gold from the uplifted offerings, was twenty-nine kikkars and seven hundred thirty shekels in weight, measured by the sanctuary shekel. ²⁵The silver from the community census totaled one hundred kikkars and one thousand seven hundred seventy-five shekels in weight, measured by the sanctuary shekel. ²⁶They gave a beqa per person (that is, half a shekel, measured by the sanctuary shekel) for everyone who was counted in the census, 20 years old and above, 603,550 men. ²⁷One hundred kikkars of silver were used to cast the bases for the sanctuary and the bases for the veil, one hundred bases from one hundred kikkars of silver, one kikkar for every base. ²⁸He used one thousand seven hundred seventy-five shekels of silver^d to make the hooks for the posts, cover their tops, and make bands for them. ²⁹The amount of copper from the uplifted offering was seventy kikkars and two thousand four hundred shekels in weight. ³⁰He used it to make the bases for the meeting tent's entrance, the copper altar, its copper grate, and all the altar's equipment, ³¹the bases all around the courtyard, and the bases for the courtyard's gate, all the dwelling's tent pegs, and all the tent pegs used around the courtyard.

Making the priests' clothing

39 They used the blue, purple, and deep red yarns to make the woven clothing for those ministering as priests in the sanctuary. They made the holy clothes for Aaron as the Lord had commanded Moses.

²They made the vest^e of gold, of blue, purple, and deep red yarns, and of fine twisted linen. ³They beat out thin sheets of gold and cut them into threads to work into designs among the blue, purple, and deep red yarns and the fine linen. ⁴They made shoulder pieces for it attached to its two edges so that they could be joined together. ⁵The vest's belt was attached to it and made in the same way of gold, of blue, purple, and deep red yarns, and of fine twisted linen, just as the Lord had commanded Moses.

⁶They prepared the gemstones by mounting them in gold settings and engraving on them the names of Israel's sons, like an official seal is engraved. ⁷The stones were attached to the vest's shoulder pieces as reminder stones for the Israelites, just as the Lord had commanded Moses.

⁸They made the embroidered chest pendant in the style of the vest, using gold, blue, purple, and deep red yarns, and fine twisted linen. ⁹They made the chest pendant square and doubled, nine inches long and nine inches wide when doubled. ¹⁰They set in it four rows of gemstones. The first row was a row of carnelian, topaz, and emerald stones. ¹¹The second row was a turquoise, a sapphire, and a moonstone. ¹²The third row was a jacinth, an agate, and an amethyst. ¹³The fourth row was a beryl, an onyx, and a jasper. The settings around them were decorative gold. ¹⁴There were twelve stones with names corresponding to the names of Israel's sons. They were engraved like official seals, each with its name for the twelve tribes. ¹⁵They made chains of pure gold, twisted like cords, for the chest pendant. ¹⁶They made two gold settings and two gold rings. They attached the two rings to the two edges of the chest pendant. ¹⁷They attached the two gold cords to the two rings at the edges of the chest pendant. ¹⁸Then they fastened the two ends of the two cords to the two gold settings and attached them to the front of the vest's shoulder pieces. ¹⁹They made two gold rings, and they attached them to the two edges of the chest pendant, on its inside edge facing the vest. ²⁰They made two gold rings and fastened them on the front of the lower part of the two shoulder pieces of the vest, at its seam just above the vest's belt. ²¹The chest pendant was held in place by a blue cord binding its rings to the vest's rings so that the chest pendant rested on the vest's belt and didn't come loose from the vest, just as the Lord had commanded Moses.

²²They also made the vest's robe, woven completely in blue. ²³The opening of the robe in the middle of it was reinforced with a strong border so that it didn't tear. ²⁴On the robe's lower hem, they added pomegranates made of blue, purple, and deep red yarns and of fine twisted linen. ²⁵They also made pure gold bells and sewed the bells between the

^dHeb lacks *shekels of silver.* ^eHeb *ephod*

pomegranates, all around the robe's lower hem, ²⁶with a bell and a pomegranate alternating all around the lower hem of the robe that is used for ministering as a priest, just as the Lord had commanded Moses.

²⁷They also made the tunics woven out of fine linen for Aaron and his sons, ²⁸the turban of fine linen, the decorated turbans of fine linen, the linen undergarments of fine twisted linen, ²⁹the sashes of fine twisted linen, and of blue, purple, and crimson yarns, decorated with needlework, just as the Lord had commanded Moses.

³⁰They made the flower ornament for the holy crown out of pure gold. Like the engraving on an official seal, they engraved on it the saying "Holy to the Lord." ³¹They fastened to it a blue cord to tie it to the top of the turban, just as the Lord had commanded Moses.

Completion of dwelling construction

³²In this way all the work of the meeting tent dwelling was finished. The Israelites did everything just exactly as the Lord had commanded Moses. ³³Then they brought to Moses the dwelling, the tent, and all its equipment: its clasps, its boards, its bars, its posts, and its bases,

³⁴the covering of rams' skins dyed red, the covering of beaded leather, and the veil for a screen,

³⁵the chest containing the covenant with its poles and the cover,

³⁶the table with all its equipment and the bread of the presence,

³⁷the pure lampstand with its lamps set on it and all its equipment, and the oil for the light,

³⁸the gold altar, the anointing oil, and the sweet-smelling incense, the screen for the tent's entrance,

³⁹the copper altar and its copper grate, its poles, and all its equipment, the washbasin with its stand,

⁴⁰the courtyard's drapes, its posts, and its bases, the screen for the plaza's gate, its cords, and its tent pegs, and all the other equipment for the service of the dwelling, for the meeting tent,

⁴¹the woven clothes for ministering as priests in the sanctuary, the holy clothes for the priest Aaron and the clothes for his sons to serve as priests.

⁴²The Israelites did all of the work just as the Lord had commanded Moses. ⁴³When Moses saw that they in fact had done all the work exactly as the Lord had commanded, Moses blessed them.

SAILBOAT

OBEDIENCE

Obedience Leads to Blessing
Exodus 39:32-43

The Israelites had done an amazing thing—they had followed God's Instruction exactly. When Moses first led the Israelites out of slavery in Egypt, it was very difficult, and the people found it hard to be obedient and thankful. But Moses remained faithful to God and God's people. Moses' obedience to God not only resulted in the deliverance of the Israelites, but the people became obedient to God's ways. Through this story, we see how God is constantly growing and taking care of God's people. When we're obedient to God, amazing things happen, and God's blessing comes our way. ◊

Moses sets up the dwelling

40 The Lord spoke to Moses: ²Set up the meeting tent dwelling on the first day of the first month.ᶠ ³Place the chest containing the covenant inside the dwelling. Hide the chest from view with the veil. ⁴Bring in the table and arrange its items. Bring in the lampstand and set up its lamps. ⁵Place the gold altar for burning incense in front of the chest containing the covenant. Set up the screen at the dwelling's entrance. ⁶Put the altar for entirely burned offerings in front of the entrance to the meeting tent dwelling. ⁷Put the washbasin between the meeting tent and the altar and put water in it. ⁸Set up the courtyard all around. Hang up the screen at the courtyard gate. ⁹Then take the anointing oil and anoint the dwelling and everything in it. Make holy the dwelling and all its equipment, and it will be holy. ¹⁰Anoint the altar for entirely burned offerings and all its equipment. Make the altar holy, and the altar will be most holy. ¹¹Anoint the wash-basin with its stand and make it holy.

¹²Then bring Aaron and his sons to the meeting tent's entrance and wash them with water. ¹³Dress Aaron in the holy clothes. Anoint him and make him holy so that he may serve me as priest. ¹⁴Then bring his sons and dress them in tunics. ¹⁵Anoint them like you anointed their father so that they may serve me as priests. Their anointing is to the priesthood for all time in every generation.

¹⁶Moses did everything exactly as the Lord had commanded him. ¹⁷In the first month in the second year, on the first day of the month, the dwelling was set up. ¹⁸Moses set up the dwelling. He laid out its bases.

He set up its boards, inserted its bars, and raised up its posts. ¹⁹He spread the tent out over the dwelling, and he put the covering of the tent over it, just as the Lord had commanded Moses. ²⁰He took the covenant document and placed it inside the chest. He put the poles on the chest, and he set the cover on top of the chest. ²¹He brought the chest into the dwelling. He set up the veil as a screen to hide from view the chest containing the covenant, just as the Lord had commanded Moses. ²²He placed the table in the meeting tent, on the north side of the dwelling, outside the veil. ²³He set the bread in its proper place on the table in the Lord's presence, just as the Lord had commanded Moses. ²⁴He put the lampstand in the meeting tent, opposite the table on the south side of the dwelling. ²⁵He set up the lamps in the Lord's presence, just as the Lord had commanded Moses. ²⁶He put the gold altar in the meeting tent in front of the veil. ²⁷He burned sweet-smelling incense on it, just as the Lord had commanded Moses. ²⁸He also set up the screen

God's THOUGHTS ◆ THOUGHTS My

Meeting with Other Believers   Exodus 40:1-38

Moses set up the meeting tent in the center of the Israelites' camp. It was used as a place for them to worship and learn about God. Today, Christians are a part of a church community for the same reasons. To better understand, think of the following groups as examples:

Family. Families don't spend every minute of the day together. Parents often have jobs, and children have school. Being together doesn't make you a family, but when families are together, there is time for taking care of family business, learning, growing, and having fun together. Attending church allows Christians to grow closer as a family of believers.

School. Even if you don't always enjoy it, school is a necessary part of life. You might be able to learn to read and write on your own, but you'll learn faster and more easily with experienced teachers to help you. At church teachers and pastors help you learn more about God and the Bible.

Team. When we work with a group of people for a common goal, as a sports team would do, we learn more about ourselves and how to get along with others. Teams can also offer us support, protection, friendship, and fun. Going to church is like being a part of a team—it's a community of people who are working together to love God and show God's love to others.

What do you like about going to church?

How does going to church help you?

at the entrance to the dwelling. ²⁹He placed the altar for entirely burned offerings at the entrance to the meeting tent dwelling. He offered the entirely burned offering and the grain offering on it, just as the LORD had commanded Moses. ³⁰He put the washbasin between the meeting tent and the altar, and put water in it for washing. ³¹Moses, Aaron, and his sons used it to wash their hands and their feet. ³²Whenever they went into the meeting tent and whenever they approached the altar,

did you **know?** The people followed God's presence in a cloud like they did when they left Egypt. They stayed when God's cloud rested in God's tent. They moved when God moved. With a cloud by day and lightning at night, the people of Israel saw God was with them.

they washed themselves, just as the LORD had commanded Moses. ³³He set up the courtyard around the dwelling and the altar, and he hung up the screen at the courtyard's gate.

God's presence fills the dwelling!

When Moses had finished all the work, ³⁴the cloud covered the meeting tent and the LORD's glorious presence filled the dwelling. ³⁵Moses couldn't enter the meeting tent because the cloud had settled on it, and the LORD's glorious presence filled the dwelling. ³⁶Whenever the cloud rose from the dwelling, the Israelites would set out on their journeys. ³⁷But if the cloud didn't rise, then they didn't set out until the day it rose. ³⁸The LORD's cloud stayed over the dwelling during the day, with lightning in it at night, clearly visible to the whole household of Israel at every stage of their journey.

Leviticus

God gave the Israelites the Instruction for living so they could follow God completely. After God freed the Israelites from slavery in Egypt, God led them into the desert where they learned a way of life that was obedient to God.

The name Leviticus comes from the tribe of Levi, a family whose men served as priests. This book of the Bible reads much like passages from Exodus 25 to Numbers 10, a portion of the Bible where God told Moses to build a "dwelling," or meeting tent. At that meeting tent God promised to meet with Moses and explain God's commands, and to be present always with God's people.

The first seven chapters of Leviticus list God's instructions for sacrifices. The rest of the book offers instructions about purity, the foods people should and shouldn't eat, and special days and weeks of worship. The most important of those times of worship was the day of reconciliation that happened once a year (Lev 16).

God had high expectations for the Israelites. As God's people, they were called to be holy or "set apart" for God. The Instruction in Leviticus showed the Israelites how to be set apart and what to do when they missed that mark. Although today we may not offer the type of sacrifices listed in Leviticus, the principle of being set apart for God still applies! ◊

1 Then the LORD called to Moses and said to him from the meeting tent, ²Speak to the Israelites and say to them: When any of you present a livestock offering to the LORD, you can present it from either the herd or the flock.

The entirely burned offering

³If the offering is an entirely burned offering from the herd, you must present a flawless male, bringing it to the meeting tent's entrance for its acceptance before the LORD. ⁴You must press your hand on the head of the entirely burned offering so that it will be accepted for you, to make reconciliation for you. ⁵Then you will slaughter the bull before the LORD. Aaron's sons the priests will present the blood and toss it against every side of the altar at the meeting tent's entrance. ⁶Then the entirely burned offering will be skinned and cut up into pieces. ⁷The sons of Aaron the priest[a] will light the altar and lay wood on the fire. ⁸Then Aaron's sons the priests will arrange the pieces, the head, and the fat on the wood that is on the altar fire, ⁹but the animal's insides and lower legs must be washed with water. The priest will then completely burn all of it on the altar as an entirely burned offering, a food gift[b] of soothing smell to the LORD.

¹⁰If the offering is an entirely burned offering from the flock—whether sheep or goat—you must present a flawless male.

---

[a]Some Heb sources, Sam, LXX, Syr, and some Tg sources have *Aaron's sons, the priests,* as in 1:5, 8. [b]Or (here and throughout Leviticus) *offering by fire* (cf 3:11)

God's Rules for Life   *Leviticus 1–3*

Sometimes it can seem like life is full of rules. Clean your room. Put your backpack on the hook by the front door. Finish your homework before you watch television. Don't run inside. Raise your hand before you talk in class.

God gave Moses the Instruction for God's people to follow so they would know how to live a holy life. There were commandments about killing and stealing, requirements on what to wear and what to eat, and even what to do about skin rashes. The people were expected to follow this way of life. If they were unable to live as expected, a sacrifice of grain or an animal might be required. Some sacrifices involved killing the best animal they owned and offering it to God. People made these sacrifices so that they could restore their relationship with God.

Some sacrifices were a regular part of life as God's people offered gifts to God. For example, the people gave grain, oil, or incense to thank God for a good harvest or to celebrate the birth of a new baby.

Followers of this way of life no longer sacrifice animals to restore their relationship with God or to thank God. Jews and Christians no longer offer grain, oil, or incense as gifts, though we may offer our time, our gifts, and our money as service to God and our neighbor.

Name some gifts you can offer to God.

What kind of service can you offer God?

¹¹You must slaughter it on the north side of the altar before the Lord. Aaron's sons the priests will toss its blood against every side of the altar. ¹²Once it has been cut into pieces, including the head and the fat, the priest will arrange these out on the wood that is on the altar fire, ¹³but its insides and lower legs must be washed with water. Then the priest will present all of it and completely burn it on the altar. It is an entirely burned offering, a food gift of soothing smell to the Lord.

¹⁴If the offering for the Lord is an entirely burned offering from the birds, you can present your offering from the doves or pigeons. ¹⁵The priest will bring it to the altar. He will tear off its head and completely burn it on the altar. Its blood will be drained against the side of the altar. ¹⁶Then the priest will remove its throat along with its contents[c] and throw it by the east side of the altar, into the place for the ashes. ¹⁷He will then tear the bird open by its wings, without splitting it. The priest

did you know? Salt is a seasoning that people in Bible times used only at very special meals. When the people salted the offerings they made to God, they showed that their offerings were very special.

will completely burn it on the altar, on the wood that is on the altar fire. It is an entirely burned offering, a food gift of soothing smell to the Lord.

The grain offering

2 When anyone presents a grain offering to the Lord, the offering must be of choice flour. They must pour oil on it and put frankincense on it, ²then bring it to Aaron's sons, the priests. A priest will take a handful of its choice flour and oil, along with all of its frankincense, and will completely burn this token portion on the altar as a food gift of soothing smell to the Lord. ³The rest of the grain offering belongs to Aaron and his sons as a most holy portion from the Lord's food gifts.

⁴When you present a grain offering baked in an oven, it must be of choice flour: unleavened flatbread mixed with oil or unleavened

wafers spread with oil. ⁵If your offering is grain prepared on a griddle, it must be of choice flour mixed with oil and it must be unleavened. ⁶Crumble it into pieces and pour oil on it; it is a grain offering. ⁷If your offering is grain prepared in a pan, it must be made of choice flour with oil. ⁸You will bring the grain offering made in one of these ways to the Lord, presenting it to the priest, who will then bring it to the altar. ⁹The priest will remove from the grain offering the token portion and completely burn it on the altar as a food gift of soothing smell to the Lord. ¹⁰The rest of the grain offering belongs to Aaron and his sons as a most holy portion from the Lord's food gifts.

¹¹No grain offering that you give to the Lord can be made with yeast. You must not completely burn any yeast or honey as a food gift for the Lord. ¹²You can present those as first-choice offerings to the Lord, but they must not be entirely burned up on the altar as a soothing smell.

¹³You must season all your grain offerings with salt. Do not omit the salt of your God's covenant from your grain offering. You must offer salt with all your offerings.

¹⁴If you present a grain offering to the Lord from the first produce, you must make such an offering from the crushed heads of newly ripe grain, roasted with fire. ¹⁵You must put oil and frankincense on it; it is a grain offering. ¹⁶The priest will completely burn the token portion—some of the crushed new grain and oil along with all of the frankincense—as a food gift for the Lord.

The well-being sacrifice

3 If the offering is a communal sacrifice of well-being,[d] the one who offers the herd animal—whether it is male or female—must present a flawless specimen before the Lord. ²You must press your hand on the head of the offering and slaughter it at the meeting tent's entrance. Aaron's sons the priests will toss the blood against every side of the altar. ³Then you can offer a food gift to the Lord from the communal sacrifice of well-being: the fat that covers and surrounds the insides; ⁴the two kidneys and the fat around them

[c]Heb uncertain [d]Or *peace offering*

at the loins; and the lobe on the liver, which should be removed with the kidneys. ⁵Aaron's sons will completely burn all of this on the altar—along with the entirely burned offering on the wood that is on the altar fire—as a food gift of soothing smell to the Lord.

⁶If the offering for a communal sacrifice of well-being for the Lord is from the flock—whether it is male or female—you must present a flawless specimen. ⁷If you present a sheep as the offering, you must present it before the Lord. ⁸You must press your hand on the head of the offering and slaughter it before the meeting tent. Aaron's sons will toss the blood against every side of the altar. ⁹Then you may offer the fat from the communal sacrifice of well-being as a food gift for the Lord: the whole fat tail, which should be removed close to the tailbone; the fat that covers and surrounds the insides; ¹⁰the two kidneys and the fat around them at the loins; and the lobe on the liver, which should be removed with the kidneys. ¹¹The priest will then completely burn all of this on the altar as food—as a food gift for the Lord.

¹²If the offering is a goat, you must present it before the Lord. ¹³You must press your hand on its head and slaughter it before the meeting tent. Aaron's sons will toss its blood against every side of the altar. ¹⁴Then you may present as your offering—a food gift for the Lord—the fat that covers and surrounds the insides; ¹⁵the two kidneys and the fat around them at the loins; and the lobe on the liver, which should be removed with the kidneys. ¹⁶The priest will then completely burn all of this on the altar as food—as a food gift for a soothing smell.

All fat belongs to the Lord. ¹⁷This is a permanent rule for your future generations, wherever you live: you must not eat any fat or blood.

The purification offering

4 The Lord said to Moses, ²Say to the Israelites: Do the following whenever someone sins unintentionally against any of the Lord's commands, doing something that shouldn't be done:

³If it is the anointed priest who has sinned, making the people guilty of sin, he must

LIFE PRESERVER

Why were there so many offerings? *Leviticus 3*

When you worship in your church, you pass an offering plate and put in some of your money to help support what your church does. This is one way for people to help out, giving something from what they have. When we give something as an offering, we are giving something to God. The Hebrew word for *offering* means "something that is brought near." So offerings were a way of bringing the people closer to God.

The Israelites gave three kinds of gift offerings: entirely burned offerings, grain offerings, and sacrifices of animals. They could make these offerings to God at any time. If a person had recovered from an illness or had been saved from a dangerous situation, they would make a gift offering. Or if a person simply wanted to honor God, they could make a gift offering in the temple. The book of Leviticus has a lot of instructions about offerings, all of which were written to help the people learn how to live as God's people in a new land. ◗

present to the Lord a flawless bull from the herd as a purification offeringᵉ for the sin he has committed. ⁴He will bring the bull before the Lord at the entrance to the meeting tent and press his hand on the bull's head. Then he will slaughter the bull before the Lord. ⁵The anointed priest will take some of the bull's blood and take it into the meeting tent. ⁶The priest will dip his finger into the blood and sprinkle some of it seven times before the Lord, toward the sanctuary's inner curtain. ⁷Then the priest will put some of the blood on the horns of the altar of perfumed incense, which is in the meeting tent before the Lord. But he will pour out all the rest of the bull's blood at the base of the altar of entirely burned offerings, which is at the meeting tent's entrance. ⁸Then he will remove all the fat from the bull for the purification offering: the fat that covers and surrounds the insides; ⁹the two kidneys and the fat around them at the loins; and the lobe on the liver, which he will remove with the kidneys, ¹⁰just as this is removed from the ox for the communal sacrifice of well-being. Then the priest will completely burn these on the altar of entirely

---

ᵉOr *sin offering* (Heb *hatta't*, which recurs frequently in Leviticus)

burned offerings. [11]But the bull's hide and all of its flesh, along with its head, lower legs, entrails, and dung— [12]all that remains of the bull—will be taken to a clean location outside the camp, to the ash heap. It should be burned there at the ash heap on a wood fire.

[13]If it is the entire Israelite community that has done something wrong unintentionally and the deed escapes the assembly's notice—but they've done something that shouldn't be done in violation of the Lord's commands, becoming guilty of sin— [14]once the sin that they committed becomes known, the assembly must present a bull from the herd as a purification offering. They will bring it before the meeting tent. [15]The community elders will press their hands on the bull's head before the Lord and then slaughter it before the Lord. [16]The anointed priest will take some of the bull's blood into the meeting tent. [17]The priest will dip his finger into the blood and sprinkle it seven times before the Lord toward the inner curtain. [18]Then he will put some of the blood on the horns of the altar that is before the Lord in the meeting tent. But he will pour all the rest of the blood out at the base of the altar of entirely burned offerings that is at the meeting tent's entrance. [19]Then he will remove all the fat from it and completely burn it on the altar. [20]He will do the same with this bull as he did with the other bull for the purification offering; that is exactly what he must do. In this way, the priest will make reconciliation for them, and they will be forgiven. [21]Then the priest will take the bull outside the camp and burn it, just as the first bull was burned. It is the purification offering for the assembly.

[22]If a leader sins by unintentionally breaking any of the commands of the Lord his God, doing something that shouldn't be done, and becomes guilty of sin— [23]once the sin that he committed is made known to him—he must bring as his offering a flawless male goat. [24]He will press his hand on the goat's head. It will be slaughtered[f] at the place where an entirely burned offering would be slaughtered before the Lord. It is a purification offering. [25]The priest will take some of the blood

from the purification offering and, using his finger, will put it on the horns of the altar of entirely burned offerings. But he will pour the rest of the blood out at the base of the altar of entirely burned offerings. [26]He will completely burn all of its fat on the altar just as the fat of the communal sacrifice of well-being is burned. In this way the priest will make reconciliation for the leader to remove his sin, and he will be forgiven.

[27]If any ordinary person[g] sins unintentionally by breaking one of the Lord's commands, doing something that shouldn't be done, and becomes guilty of sin— [28]once the sin they committed is made known to them—they must bring as their offering a flawless female goat because of the sin that was committed. [29]They will press their hand on the head of the purification offering. It will be slaughtered[h] at the place for the entirely burned offerings. [30]The priest will take some of its blood and, using his finger, will put it on the horns of the altar of entirely burned offerings. But he will pour all the rest of the blood out at the base of the altar. [31]He will remove all of its fat, just as the fat from a communal sacrifice of well-being is removed. Then the priest will completely burn it on the altar as a soothing smell to the Lord. In this way, the priest will make reconciliation for them, and they will be forgiven.

[32]If you offer a sheep as a purification offering, it must be a flawless female. [33]You must press your hand on the head of the purification offering. It will be slaughtered[i] as a purification offering in the

SAILBOAT

FORGIVENESS

Making Amends *Leviticus 4*
Moses and the Israelites often made mistakes. God saw their good intentions, but God also saw their wrongdoing—some on purpose, some by accident. God gave Moses specific instructions about how the Israelites could seek forgiveness. God wanted very much to be in relationship with the people, but their wrongdoing, or sin, separated them from God. God did not like this separation, so God gave careful instructions about how they could make things right. ◢

---

[f]Or *He will slaughter it … where he would slaughter* [g]Or *one of the people of the land* [h]Or *They will slaughter it.* [i]Or *You will slaughter it.*

place where the entirely burned offering is slaughtered. [34]Then the priest will take some of the blood from the purification offering and, using his finger, will put it on the horns of the altar of entirely burned offerings. But he will pour all the rest of the blood out at the base of the altar. [35]He will remove all of its fat, just as the fat of a sheep would be removed from the communal sacrifice of well-being. Then the priest will completely burn it on the altar along with the Lord's food gifts. In this way, the priest will make reconciliation for you for the sin you committed, and you will be forgiven.

Unintentional sin

5 If you sin:
by not providing information after hearing a public solemn pledge even though you are a witness, knowing something, or having seen something so that you become liable to punishment;

[2]or by touching some unclean thing—the dead body of an unclean wild animal, unclean livestock, or unclean swarming creature—but the fact goes unknown so that you become unclean and guilty of sin;

[3]or by touching human uncleanness—any uncleanness that makes one unclean—and the fact goes unknown, but you later learn of it and become guilty of sin;

[4]or by carelessly swearing to do something, whether bad or good—whatever one might swear carelessly—and the fact goes unknown, but you later learn of it and become guilty of sin concerning one of these things—

[5]at that point, when you have become guilty of sin in one of these ways, you must confess how you have sinned [6]and bring to the Lord as compensation for the sin that was committed a female from the flock, either a sheep or goat, as a purification offering. The priest will then make reconciliation for you, to remove your sin.

Alternative offerings

[7]If you can't afford an animal from the flock, you can bring to the Lord as compensation for your sin two doves or two pigeons, one as a purification offering and the other as an entirely burned offering. [8]You will bring them to the priest, who will first present the one for the purification offering. He will pinch off its head at the back of its neck without splitting it. [9]Then he will sprinkle some of the blood of the purification offering on the side of the altar. The rest of the blood will be drained out at the base of the altar. It is a purification offering. [10]Then, with the second bird, the priest will perform an entirely burned offering according to the regulation. In this way, the priest will make reconciliation for you because of the sin you committed, and you will be forgiven.

[11]If you cannot afford two doves or two pigeons, you can bring as the offering for your sin a tenth of an ephah[j] of choice flour as a purification offering. You must not put any oil on it, nor any frankincense, because it is a purification offering. [12]You will bring it to the priest, and the priest will take a handful from it—the token portion—and will burn it completely on the altar along with the food gifts for the Lord. It is a purification offering. [13]In this way, the priest will make reconciliation for you for whichever one of the sins you committed, and you will be forgiven. The rest of the offering will belong to the priest like the grain offering.

The compensation offering

[14]The Lord said to Moses, [15]Whenever you commit wrongdoing, unintentionally sinning against any of the Lord's holy things, you must bring to the Lord as your compensation a flawless ram from the flock, its value calculated in silver shekels according to the sanctuary's shekel, as a compensation offering. [16]You will make amends for the way you have sinned against the holy thing: you will add one-fifth to its value and give it to the priest. Then the priest will make reconciliation for you with the ram for the compensation offering, and you will be forgiven.

[17]If you sin by breaking any of the Lord's commands, but without realizing it, doing

---

[j]Two quarts; one ephah is approximately twenty quarts dry.

something that shouldn't be done, and then become guilty and liable to punishment, [18]you must bring a flawless ram from the flock, at the standard value, as a compensation offering to the priest. The priest will make reconciliation for you for the unintentional fault that you committed, even though you didn't realize it, and you will be forgiven. [19]It is a compensation offering. You have definitely become guilty before the Lord.

6 [k]The Lord said to Moses, [2]If you sin:

by acting unfaithfully against the Lord;

by deceiving a fellow citizen concerning a deposit or pledged property;

by cheating a fellow citizen through robbery;

[3]or, though you've found lost property, you lie about it;

[k]5:20 in Heb

or by swearing falsely about anything that someone might do and so sin,

[4]at that point, once you have sinned and become guilty of sin, you must return the property you took by robbery or fraud, or the deposit that was left with you for safekeeping, or the lost property that you found, [5]or whatever it was that you swore falsely about. You must make amends for the principal amount and add one-fifth to it. You must give it to the owner on the day you become guilty. [6]You must bring to the priest as your compensation to the Lord a flawless ram from the flock at the standard value as a compensation offering. [7]The priest will make reconciliation for you before the Lord, and you will be forgiven for anything you may have done that made you guilty.

Unintentional Sin: Making Things Right   *Leviticus 5*

We don't sacrifice animals anymore as a way to seek forgiveness for our sins, but that doesn't mean our sins aren't important to God. Everyone makes mistakes, sometimes without meaning to do so. You might drop dirty shoes on some newly cleaned carpet in your house. You might eat cookies your mother or father made for someone else. You might accidentally hit a ball through a neighbor's window while playing in your backyard. Even if you didn't intend to do wrong, some mistakes have consequences. Part of growing up means facing those consequences.

The first thing you should do is apologize by saying, "I'm sorry." This can be hard to say when what you did was an accident, but an apology is often helpful in making things right between you and the other person. Apologizing means that you're sorry for how your actions hurt that person, even if you didn't mean to hurt them.

At times your apology may need to go a step further than just words. You could offer to vacuum the carpet or bake more cookies. You could use money from your savings, or find ways to earn money, to pay for the broken window. This part can be difficult, but offering to make up for the damage you've done is the right thing to do.

Have you accidentally done something wrong?

What will you do to make it right?

Priestly instructions

[8]The[1] LORD said to Moses: [9]Command Aaron and his sons: This is the Instruction for the entirely burned offering—the entirely burned offering that must remain on the altar hearth all night until morning, while the fire is kept burning. [10]The priest will dress in his linen robe, with linen undergarments on his body. Because the fire will have devoured the entirely burned offering on the altar, he must remove the ashes and place them beside the altar. [11]The priest will then take off his clothes, dress in a different set of clothes, and take the ashes outside the camp to a clean location. [12]The altar fire must be kept burning; it must not go out. Each morning the priest will burn wood on it, will lay out the entirely burned offering on it, and will completely burn the fat of the well-being offering on it. [13]A continuous fire must be kept burning on the altar; it must not go out.

[14]This is the Instruction for the grain offering: Aaron's sons will present it before the LORD in front of the altar. [15]The priest will remove a handful of the choice flour and oil from the grain offering, and all of the frankincense that is on it, and burn this token portion completely on the altar as a soothing smell to the LORD. [16]Aaron and his sons will eat the rest of it. It must be eaten as unleavened bread in a holy place; the priests must eat it in the meeting tent's courtyard. [17]It must not be baked with leaven. I have made it the priests' share from my food gifts. It is most holy like the purification offering and the compensation offering. [18]Only the males from Aaron's descendants can eat it as a permanent portion from the LORD's food gifts throughout your future generations. Anything that touches these food gifts will become holy.

[19]The LORD said to Moses, [20]This is the offering that Aaron and his sons must present to the LORD on the day of his anointment: one-tenth of an ephah[m] of choice flour as a regular grain offering, half in the morning and half in the evening. [21]It must be prepared on a griddle with oil. You must bring it thoroughly mixed up and must present it as a grain offering of crumbled pieces[n] as a soothing smell to the LORD. [22]The priest who is anointed from among Aaron's sons to succeed him will prepare the offering as a permanent portion for the LORD. It will be completely burned as a complete offering. [23]Every priestly grain offering must be a complete offering; it must not be eaten.

[24]The LORD said to Moses, [25]Say to Aaron and his sons: This is the Instruction for the purification offering: The purification offering must be slaughtered before the LORD at the same place the entirely burned offering is slaughtered; it is most holy. [26]The priest who offers it as a purification offering will eat it. It must be eaten in a holy place, in the meeting tent's courtyard. [27]Anything that touches the purification offering's flesh will become holy. If some of its blood splashes on a garment, you must wash the bloodied part in a holy place. [28]A pottery container in which the purification offering is cooked must be broken, but if it is cooked in a bronze container, that must be scrubbed and rinsed with water. [29]Any male priest can eat it; it is most holy. [30]But no purification offering can be eaten

LIFE PRESERVER

Why were animals sacrificed? *Leviticus 6:25*

Three thousand years ago when the Israelites were learning how to worship, the sacrifice of animals was a common practice. This might sound like a violent practice today, but in the times that the Israelites lived preparing an animal for sacrifice to God was a way that the sins of the people were wiped clean with the blood of the animal that was killed.

Leviticus contains very specific instructions for the sacrifice of animals. Animals offered in sacrifice included sheep, goats, and birds such as doves and pigeons.

We live in very different times, and we worship very differently. When we say prayers in worship or at home, we tell God the bad things we have done and ask God to forgive us and help us do better. The Israelites were doing the same thing with their sacrifices, making an offering to God as a promise to live better and to love God. Today, we promise with our hearts, hands, and voices to live as God wants us to live. ◆

---

[1]6:1 in Heb   [m]Two quarts; an ephah is approximately twenty quarts dry.   [n]Heb uncertain

if blood from it is brought into the meeting tent to make reconciliation in the holy place; it must be burned with fire.

7 This is the Instruction for the compensation offering: It is most holy. [2]The compensation offering must be slaughtered at the same place where the entirely burned offering is slaughtered, and its blood must be tossed against all sides of the altar. [3]All of its fat will be offered: the fat tail; the fat that covers the insides; [4]the two kidneys and the fat around them at the loins; and the lobe on the liver, which must be removed with the kidneys. [5]The priest must burn them completely on the altar as a food gift for the LORD; it is a compensation offering. [6]Any male priest can eat it. It must be eaten in a holy place; it is most holy.

[7]The compensation offering is like the purification offering—they share the same Instruction: It belongs to the priest who makes reconciliation with it. [8]The hide of the entirely burned offering that a priest has offered belongs to the priest who offered it. [9]Any grain offering that is baked in an oven or that is prepared in a pan or on a griddle also belongs to the priest who offered it. [10]But every other grain offering, whether mixed with oil or dry, will belong to all of Aaron's sons equally.

[11]This is the Instruction for the communal sacrifice of well-being that someone may offer to the LORD: [12]If you are offering it for thanksgiving, you must offer the following with the communal sacrifice of thanksgiving: unleavened flatbread mixed with oil, unleavened thin loaves spread with oil, and flatbread of choice flour thoroughly mixed with oil. [13]You must present this offering, plus the leavened flatbread, with the communal thanksgiving sacrifice of well-being. [14]From this you will present one of each kind of offering as a gift to the LORD. It will belong to the priest who tosses the blood of the well-being offering.

[15]The flesh of your communal thanksgiving sacrifice of well-being must be eaten on the day you offer it; you cannot save any of it until morning. [16]But if your communal sacrifice of well-being is payment for a solemn promise or if it is a spontaneous gift, it may be eaten on the day you offer it as your communal sacrifice, and whatever is left over can be eaten the next day. [17]But whatever is left over of the flesh of the communal sacrifice on the third day must be burned with fire. [18]If any of it is eaten on the third day, it will not be accepted. It will not be credited to the one who offered it. It will be considered foul, and the person who eats of it will be liable to punishment.

[19]Flesh that touches any unclean thing must not be eaten; it must be burned with fire. Any clean person may eat the flesh, [20]but anyone who eats the flesh of a communal sacrifice of well-being that belongs to the LORD while in an unclean state will be cut off from their people. [21]Whenever anyone touches any unclean thing—whether it is human uncleanness, an unclean animal, or any unclean and disgusting creature—and then eats the flesh of a communal sacrifice of well-being that belongs to the LORD, that person will be cut off from their people.

[22]The LORD said to Moses: [23]Tell the Israelites: You must not eat the fat of an ox, sheep, or goat. [24]The fat of an animal that has died naturally or the fat of an animal that was killed by another animal may be put to any use, but you must definitely not eat it. [25]If anyone eats the fat of an animal from which a food gift could be offered to the LORD, that person will be cut off from their people. [26]You must not consume any blood whatsoever—whether bird or animal blood—wherever you may live. [27]Any person who consumes any blood whatsoever will be cut off from their people.

[28]The LORD said to Moses: [29]Say to the Israelites: If you wish to offer a communal sacrifice of well-being to the LORD, you are allowed to bring your offering to the LORD as your communal sacrifice of well-being.[o] [30]Your own hands must bring the LORD's food gifts. You will bring the fat with the breast so that the breast can be lifted as an uplifted offering before the LORD. [31]The priest will completely burn the fat on the altar, but the breast will go to Aaron and his sons. [32]You will give the right thigh of your communal sacrifice of

[o]Heb uncertain

well-being to the priest as a gift. [33]The right thigh will belong to the son of Aaron who offers the blood and fat of the well-being offering. [34]I have taken the breast of the uplifted offering and the thigh that is given by the Israelites from their communal sacrifices of well-being, and have given them to Aaron the priest and to his sons as a permanent portion from the Israelites.

[35]This is what Aaron and his sons are allotted from the LORD's food gifts once they have been presented to serve the LORD as priests. [36]The LORD commanded that these things be given to the priests by the Israelites, following their anointment. It is their permanent portion throughout their future generations.

Conclusion concerning offerings

[37]This concludes the Instructions for the entirely burned offering, the grain offering, the purification offering, the compensation offering, the ordination offering, and the communal sacrifice of well-being, [38]which the LORD commanded Moses at Mount Sinai on the day when he ordered the Israelites to present their offerings to the LORD, in the Sinai desert.

The priests' ordination

8 The LORD said to Moses, [2]Take Aaron and his sons with him, the priestly clothing, the anointing oil, a bull for the purification offering, two rams, and a basket of unleavened bread, [3]and assemble the whole community at the meeting tent's entrance.

[4]Moses did as the LORD commanded him, and the community assembled at the meeting tent's entrance. [5]Moses said to the community, "This is what the LORD has commanded us to do." [6]Then Moses brought Aaron and his sons forward and washed them in water. [7]Moses put the tunic on Aaron, tied the sash around him, and dressed him in the robe. Moses then put the priestly vest on Aaron, tied the woven waistband of the vest around him, and secured the vest to him with it. [8]Then Moses placed the chest piece on Aaron and set the Urim and Thummim into the chest piece. [9]Moses placed the turban on Aaron's head and put the gold flower ornament, the holy crown, on the turban's front, just as the LORD had commanded him.

[10]Moses then took the anointing oil and anointed the dwelling[p] and everything in it, making them holy by doing so. [11]He sprinkled some of the oil on the altar seven times, and anointed the altar and all its equipment, as well as the basin and its base, to make them holy. [12]He poured some of the anointing oil on Aaron's head, thereby anointing him to make him holy. [13]Then Moses brought Aaron's sons forward, dressed them in tunics, tied sashes around them, and wrapped headbands on them, just as the LORD had commanded him.

did you know? Aaron and his sons were priests and received a part of every offering made to God. Since they were called to serve God, they were no longer considered to be part of one of the twelve tribes and were not allowed to own land or make money. God provided for them by giving them a part of every offering.

Set Apart for Service *Leviticus 8:4-13*

The Israelites held an elaborate ceremony to set Aaron and his sons apart to be priests. The community gathered, and then Moses washed Aaron and his sons with water and clothed Aaron with a tunic, a sash, a vest, a chest piece, and a turban with a gold flower ornament. Following all of these specific instructions helped the people, Aaron and Aaron's sons understood how important it was to serve God and their community.

[14]Next Moses brought forward the bull for the purification offering. Aaron and his sons pressed their hands on its head. [15]Moses slaughtered it, then took the blood and, using his finger, put it on all of the altar's horns, purifying the altar. He poured the rest of the blood out at the altar's base. Then he made the altar holy so that reconciliation could be performed on it.[q] [16]Moses removed all the fat

[p]*Or tabernacle* [q]Or *to make reconciliation for it* (i.e., the altar)

that was around the insides, the lobe of the liver, the two kidneys and their fat, and he completely burned it on the altar. [17]But the rest of the bull, including its hide, its flesh, and its dung, he burned with fire outside the camp just as the Lord had commanded him.

[18]Then Moses presented the ram for the entirely burned offering, and Aaron and his sons pressed their hands on its head. [19]Moses slaughtered it, then tossed the blood against all sides of the altar. [20]He cut up the ram into pieces, and then completely burned the head, pieces, and fat. [21]After he washed the insides and lower legs with water, Moses completely burned the whole ram on the altar. It was an entirely burned offering for a soothing smell; it was a food gift for the Lord, as the Lord had commanded Moses.

[22]Moses then presented the second ram, the ram for ordination, and Aaron and his sons pressed their hands on its head. [23]Moses slaughtered it, then took some of its blood and put it on Aaron's right earlobe, on his right thumb, and on his right big toe. [24]Then Moses brought forward Aaron's sons and put some of the blood on their right earlobes, their right thumbs, and their right big toes. Moses tossed the rest of the blood against all of the altar's sides. [25]Then he took the fat—the fat tail, all the fat that was around the insides, the lobe of the liver, the two kidneys and their fat—as well as the right thigh. [26]From the basket of unleavened bread that was before the Lord, he took one loaf of unleavened flatbread, one loaf of flatbread made with oil, and one unleavened wafer, and he placed these on the fat pieces and on the right thigh. [27]Moses set all of this in Aaron's and his sons' hands, then lifted them as an uplifted offering before the Lord. [28]Next Moses took this out of their hands and completely burned it on the altar, along with the entirely burned offering. This was an ordination offering for a soothing smell; it was a food gift for the Lord. [29]Next Moses took the breast from the ram for the ordination offering and lifted it as an uplifted offering before the Lord. It belonged to Moses as his portion, just as the Lord had commanded him. [30]Moses took some of the anointing oil and some of the blood

that was on the altar and sprinkled it on Aaron and his clothes, and on his sons and their clothes as well. In this way, Moses made holy Aaron, his clothing, and Aaron's sons and their clothing.

[31]Moses said to Aaron and his sons: "Cook the meat at the meeting tent's entrance. You may eat it there along with the bread that is in the basket of the ordination offering, just as I was commanded,[r] 'Aaron and his sons can eat it.' [32]But you must burn whatever is left over of the meat and bread with fire. [33]You must not leave the meeting tent's entrance for seven days, until the period of your ordination is completed, because your ordination takes seven days. [34]What was done today was commanded by the Lord, to make reconciliation for you. [35]You must stay at the meeting tent's entrance for seven days, day and night, observing the Lord's requirement so you don't die, because that's what I was commanded." [36]Aaron and his sons did everything the Lord commanded through Moses.

The priests' initiation

9 On the eighth day, Moses called for Aaron, Aaron's sons, and Israel's elders. [2]He said to Aaron, "Take a young bull from the herd as a purification offering and a ram as an entirely burned offering, both flawless animals, and bring them before the Lord. [3]Then tell the Israelites, 'Take a male goat as a purification offering; a young bull and a sheep—both one-year-old flawless animals—as an entirely burned offering; [4]an ox and a ram as a well-being sacrifice before the Lord; and a grain offering mixed with oil, because today the Lord will appear to you.'"

[5]They brought what Moses had commanded to the front of the meeting tent. Then the whole community came forward and stood before the Lord. [6]Moses said, "The Lord has ordered you to do this so that the Lord's glorious presence will appear to you." [7]Moses said to Aaron, "Come up to the altar and perform your purification offering and your entirely burned offering, making reconciliation for yourself and the people. Then perform the people's offering in order to make reconciliation for them, just as the Lord commanded."

[r]LXX, Syr, Tg; cf 8:35; MT *as I commanded*

[8]Aaron went to the altar and slaughtered the young bull for his purification offering. [9]Then Aaron's sons presented the blood to him, and he dipped his finger into the blood and put it on the altar's horns. He poured the rest of the blood out at the altar's base. [10]He completely burned on the altar the fat, kidneys, and lobe of the liver from the purification offering, just as the LORD commanded Moses. [11]But he burned the flesh and hide with fire outside the camp.

[12]Then Aaron slaughtered the entirely burned offering. Aaron's sons handed him the blood, and he tossed it against all sides of the altar. [13]They handed him the entirely burned offering in pieces, including the head, and he completely burned them on the altar. [14]Then he washed the insides and lower legs and completely burned them on the altar along with the rest of the entirely burned offering.

[15]Next, Aaron presented the people's offering. He took the male goat for the people's purification offering, slaughtered it, and offered it as a purification offering like the first purification offering. [16]He presented the entirely burned offering and did with it according to the regulation. [17]Then he presented the grain offering, took a handful from it, and completely burned it on the altar, in addition to the morning's entirely burned offering.

[18]Aaron then slaughtered the ox and the ram—the people's communal sacrifice of well-being. Aaron's sons handed him the blood, which he tossed against all sides of the altar,

What Does a Priest Do? *Leviticus 9:22-24*

The priests served as representatives of the Israelite people before God. Their role was to oversee the worship at the altar, burn sacrifices, and teach the Instruction to the people. If someone needed help with a decision, they would go to the priest, who would speak to God on their behalf and communicate God's requirements to them. Because of their special role, the priests were treated with honor among the Israelites.

Originally, only Aaron, his sons, and his grandsons served as priests. When God gave the Instruction to Moses, God said the Israelites would be "a kingdom of priests" and "a holy nation" (Exod 19:6). All the Israelites were expected to serve God with their obedient lives.

We have people today who lead by serving in our churches and synagogues. They preach, teach, and take care of the congregation. They pray with and for people, visit those who are sick, and help those who are having problems. We should treat these leaders with honor by listening to them, helping them, and praying for them.

Like the Israelites, we also can serve as priests by living a life that pleases God. Jesus explained that we're to love God with everything that is within us—our heart, being, strength, and mind—and that we are to love others as we love ourselves (Luke 10:26–28).

Name two ways you can show you love God.

Name two ways you can show love to others.

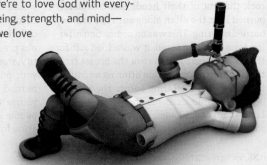

¹⁹and the fat pieces of the ox and ram—the fat tail, the covering fat, the kidneys, and the lobe of the liver. ²⁰They placed these fat pieces on the animals' breasts, and Aaron completely burned them on the altar. ²¹But Aaron lifted up the breasts and the right thigh as an uplifted offering before the Lord, just as Moses had commanded.

²²Aaron then raised his hands toward the people and blessed them. After performing the purification offering, the entirely burned offering, and the well-being sacrifice, he came down. ²³Moses and Aaron then entered the meeting tent. When they came out, they blessed the people, and the Lord's glorious presence appeared to all the people. ²⁴Fire flew out from before the Lord and devoured the entirely burned offering and the fat pieces on the altar. All the people saw it. They shouted for joy and fell facedown.

Nadab and Abihu

10 Now Nadab and Abihu, two of Aaron's sons, each took an incense pan. They put fire and incense on them and offered unauthorized fire before the Lord, which he had not commanded them. ²Then fire flew out from before the Lord and devoured them, and they died before the Lord.

³Moses said to Aaron, "When the Lord said, 'I will show that I am holy among those near me, and before all the people I will manifest my glorious presence,' this is what he meant!" But Aaron was silent.

⁴Then Moses called Mishael and Elzaphan the sons of Uzziel, Aaron's uncle, and told them, "Go carry your relatives out from the front of the sanctuary to a place outside the camp." ⁵So they went forward and carried Nadab and Abihu out by their tunics to a place outside the camp, just as Moses had ordered. ⁶Moses then said to Aaron and his sons, Eleazar and Ithamar, "Don't dishevel your hair and don't rip your clothes into pieces, or you will die and bring anger upon the whole community. Your family—all of Israel's house—will mourn the burning the Lord has done. ⁷But you must not leave the meeting tent, or you will die because the Lord's anointing oil is on you." So they did what Moses ordered.

Priestly drinking and eating

⁸The Lord said to Aaron: ⁹Both you and your sons must not drink wine or beer when you enter the meeting tent so that you don't die—this is a permanent rule throughout your future generations— ¹⁰so that you can distinguish between the holy and the common, and between the unclean and the clean, ¹¹and so that you can teach the Israelites all the rules that the Lord spoke to them through Moses.

¹²Moses then told Aaron and his remaining sons, Eleazar and Ithamar, "Take the grain offering that is left over from the Lord's food gifts and eat it unleavened next to the altar, because it is most holy. ¹³You must eat it in a holy place because it is your portion and your sons' portion from the Lord's food gifts, as I have been commanded. ¹⁴You must eat the breast for the uplifted offering and the thigh for the gift offering in a clean place—both you and your sons and daughters. These things are designated as your portion and your children's portion from the Israelites' communal sacrifices of well-being. ¹⁵The Israelites must bring the thigh for the gift and the breast for the uplifted offering along with the food gifts of the fat pieces, to be lifted up as an uplifted offering before the Lord. These will belong to both you and your children as a permanent portion, just as the Lord has commanded."

¹⁶Then Moses asked about the male goat for the purification offering, and discovered that it had already been burned. He was angry with Eleazar and Ithamar, Aaron's remaining sons, and asked, ¹⁷"Why didn't you eat the purification offering in the holy area? It's most

UMBRELLA
DISOBEDIENCE

Things Go Terribly Wrong *Leviticus 10:1-3*
Moses, Aaron, and Aaron's sons had been following God's Instruction, remembering that God is set apart. When all of the Israelites had gathered to participate in worship as a community, two of Aaron's sons, Nadab and Abihu, took an incense pan and offered unauthorized fire before God, which God had not commanded them to do. As they did this, fire flew out and devoured Nadab and Abihu, and they died as a result. There are times when not doing things the way that we know we should has horrible consequences.◈

holy, and it was assigned to you for bearing the community's punishment by making reconciliation for them before the Lord. [18]Since its blood wasn't brought into the sanctuary's interior, you were to have eaten it in the sanctuary, just as I was commanded."[s]

[19]"Look," Aaron said to Moses, "today they offered their purification offerings and their entirely burned offerings before the Lord, but these things still happened to me! Would the Lord have approved if I had eaten a purification offering today?" [20]When Moses heard that, he approved.[t]

Dietary rules

11 The Lord said to Moses and Aaron: [2]Say to the Israelites: These are the creatures that you are allowed to eat from the land animals: [3]You can eat any animal that has divided hoofs, completely split, and that rechews food. [4]But of animals that rechew food and have divided hoofs you must not eat the following: the camel—though it rechews food, it does not have divided hoofs, so it is unclean for you; [5]the rock badger—though it rechews food, it does not have divided hoofs, so it is unclean for you; [6]the hare—though it rechews food, it does not have divided hoofs, so it is unclean for you; [7]the pig—though it has completely divided hoofs, it does not rechew food, so it is unclean for you. [8]You must not eat the flesh of these animals or touch their dead bodies; they are unclean for you.

[9]You are allowed to eat the following from all water animals: You may eat anything in the water that has fins and scales, whether in sea or stream. [10]But anything in the seas or streams that does not have fins and scales—whether it be any of the swarming creatures in the water or any of the other living creatures in the water—is detestable to you [11]and must remain so. You must not eat their flesh, and you must detest their dead bodies. [12]Anything in the water that does not have fins or scales is detestable to you.

[13]Of the birds, the following are the ones you must detest—they must not be eaten; they are detestable: the eagle, the black vulture, the bearded vulture, [14]the kite, any kind of falcon, [15]any kind of raven, [16]the eagle owl, the short-eared owl, the long-eared owl, any kind of hawk, [17]the tawny owl, the fisher owl, the screech owl, [18]the white owl, the scops owl, the osprey, [19]the stork, any kind of heron, the hoopoe, and the bat.[u]

[20]Any flying insect that walks on four feet is detestable to you, [21]but you can eat four-footed flying insects that have jointed legs above their feet with which they hop on the ground. [22]Of these you can eat the following: any kind of migrating locust, any kind of bald locust, any kind of cricket, and any kind of grasshopper. [23]But every other flying insect that has four feet is detestable to you.

Unclean animals

[24]You make yourself unclean by the following animals—whoever touches their dead bodies will be unclean until evening, [25]and anyone who carries any part of their dead bodies must wash their clothes and will be unclean until evening: [26]All animals that have divided hoofs, but they are not completely split, and that do not rechew food are unclean for you—whoever touches them will be unclean. [27]Of all the animals that walk on four feet, the ones that walk on their paws are unclean for you—anyone who touches their dead bodies will be unclean until evening. [28]Anyone who carries one of their dead bodies must wash their clothes and will be unclean until evening; these animals are unclean for you.

[29]The following are unclean for you among the small creatures that move about on the

LIGHTHOUSE

SPECIAL AND SET APART

Eat This, Not That! *Leviticus 11:1-8*
God gave Moses very specific guidelines about what to eat and what not to eat. God told him that paying attention to this Instruction would keep the Israelites holy, set apart for God. God commanded the people to be set apart because God is set apart. By following these practices, the Israelites drew closer to God. ◊

[s]Syr, Tg, Vulg; MT *as I commanded*; cf 8:31 [t]Or *he was satisfied*. [u]Many of the species in 11:13–19 cannot be identified with certainty.

ground: the rat, the mouse, any kind of large lizard, ³⁰the gecko, the spotted lizard, the lizard, the skink, and the chameleon.^v ³¹Of all small moving creatures, these are unclean for you—anyone who touches them when they are dead will be unclean until evening. ³²Moreover, anything on which one of these creatures falls when it is dead will be unclean, whether it is wood, cloth, skin, or funeral clothing—any such item that can be used to do work. It must be put into water and will be unclean until evening. Then it will be clean again. ³³If any of these creatures fall

did you know? People in Bible times considered some animals to be clean and therefore okay to eat, and others to be unclean and therefore not okay to eat. Today we know that some animals called unclean can make people sick if the meat is not cooked just right or served during the right time of year.

into a pottery jar, everything inside it will be unclean; you must smash the pot. ³⁴If water from such a jar gets on any edible food, it will be unclean; any drinkable beverage in such a jar will be unclean. ³⁵Anything on which a part of these animals' dead bodies might fall will be unclean. If it is an oven or stove, it must be destroyed; they are unclean for you and must remain that way. ³⁶Now, a spring or cistern that collects water is clean, but anyone who touches one of these animals' dead bodies in it will be unclean.^w ³⁷If any part of these animals' dead bodies falls on seed that is to be planted, the seed is still clean. ³⁸But if water is poured on some seed and part of their dead bodies falls on it, it is unclean for you.

³⁹If one of the animals that you are allowed to eat dies naturally, anyone who touches its dead body will be unclean until evening. ⁴⁰Anyone who eats from the dead body must wash their clothes and will be unclean until evening. Anyone who carries such a dead body must wash their clothes and will be unclean until evening.

⁴¹Every creature that swarms on the earth is detestable; it must not be eaten. ⁴²Among all such creatures that swarm on the earth,

you must not eat anything that moves on its belly or anything that walks on four or more feet because they are detestable. ⁴³Do not make yourselves detestable by means of any swarming creatures. Do not make yourselves unclean with them or be made unclean by them. ⁴⁴I am the Lord your God. You must keep yourselves holy and be holy, because I am holy. You must not make yourselves unclean by any swarming creature that crawls on the ground. ⁴⁵I am the Lord, who brought you up from the land of Egypt to be your God. You must be holy, because I am holy.

Conclusion concerning animals and diet

⁴⁶This concludes the Instruction concerning animals, birds, all creatures that live in water, and all the creatures that swarm on the earth, ⁴⁷in order to distinguish between the unclean and the clean and between creatures that can be eaten and those that cannot.

Purification after childbirth

12 The Lord said to Moses: ²Say to the Israelites: If a woman conceives a child and gives birth to a son, she will be unclean for seven days—just as she is during her menstrual period. ³On the eighth day, the flesh of the boy's foreskin must be circumcised. ⁴For thirty-three days the mother will be in a state of blood purification. She must not touch anything holy or enter the sacred area until her time of purification is completed. ⁵But if the woman gives birth to a daughter, she will be unclean for two weeks—just as she is during her menstrual period—and will be in a state of blood purification^x for sixty-six days.

⁶When the time of purification is complete, whether for a son or a daughter, the mother must bring a one-year-old lamb as an entirely burned offering and a pigeon or turtledove as a purification offering to the priest at the meeting tent's entrance. ⁷The priest will present it before the Lord and make reconciliation for her. She will then be cleansed from her blood flow. This is the Instruction for any woman who has a child, male or female. ⁸But if the mother cannot afford a sheep, she can bring two turtledoves or two pigeons—one for the entirely burned

^vMany of the species in 11:29–30 cannot be identified with certainty. ^wHeb lacks *in it.* ^xHeb uncertain

offering and the other for the purification offering. The priest will then make reconciliation for her, and she will be clean.

Diagnosis of skin disease

13 The LORD said to Moses and Aaron, [2]When a person has a swelling, a scab, or a shiny spot on their skin, and it becomes an infection of skin disease[y] on their skin, they will be brought to the priests, either to Aaron or one of his sons. [3]The priest will examine the infection on the skin. If hair in the infected area has turned white and the infection appears to be deeper than the skin, then it is an infection of skin disease. Once the priest sees this, he will declare the person unclean. [4]But if the shiny spot on the skin is white and does not appear to be deeper than the skin and the hair has not turned white, the priest will quarantine the infected person for seven days. [5]On the seventh day the priest will again examine the infection. If he sees that it has remained the same—the infection has not spread on the skin—the priest will quarantine the person for seven more days. [6]On the seventh day the priest will examine it again. If the infection has faded and has not spread over the skin, the priest will declare the person clean; it is just a rash. The person must wash their clothes, then they will be clean again. [7]But if the rash continues to spread over the skin after they appeared before the priest for purification, they must again show themselves to the priest. [8]If the priest sees that the rash has spread over the skin, the priest will declare the person unclean; it is a case of skin disease.

[9]Whenever someone has an infection of skin disease, they will be brought to the priest. [10]If the priest sees that there is a white swelling on the skin, it has turned the hair white, and there is a patch of raw flesh in the swelling, [11]then it is a case of chronic skin disease on their skin. The priest will declare the person unclean. The priest will not quarantine such persons, because they are already unclean. [12]But if the skin disease continues to break out so that the disease covers all of the infected person's skin from head to toe, as far as the priest can tell— [13]then the priest will make an examination. If the skin disease has covered the person's whole body, the priest will declare the infected person clean. The person has turned entirely white; he is clean. [14]But as soon as raw flesh appears in the swelling, they will be unclean. [15]When the priest sees the raw flesh, he will declare the person unclean. Raw flesh is unclean; it is a case of skin disease. [16]But if the raw flesh turns white again, the person will go back to the priest. [17]The priest will examine it. If the infection has turned white, the priest will declare the infected person clean; at that point, the person is clean.

[18]Whenever someone has a boil on their skin, it heals, [19]and in place of the boil there is a white swelling or reddish-white shiny spot, it must be shown to the priest. [20]If the priest sees that it appears to be lower than the skin, and its hair has turned white, the priest will declare the person unclean. It is an infection of skin disease that has broken out in the boil. [21]But if the priest examines it and there is no white hair in it, it is not lower than the skin, and it is faded, the priest will quarantine the person seven days. [22]If it continues to spread over the skin, the priest will declare the person unclean; it is an infection. [23]But if the shiny spot remains where it was and does not spread, it is just a scar from the boil. The priest will declare the person clean.

[24]Whenever there is a burn on someone's skin, and the raw patch of the burn becomes a reddish-white or white shiny spot, [25]the priest will examine it. If the hair has turned white in the shiny spot, and it appears to be deeper than the skin, it is a case of skin disease that has broken out in the burn. The priest will declare the person unclean; it is an infection of skin disease. [26]But if the priest examines it, and there is no white hair in the shiny spot, it is not lower than the skin, and it is faded, the priest will quarantine the person seven days. [27]On the seventh day the priest will again examine it. If it has continued to spread over the skin, the priest will declare the person unclean; it is an infection of skin disease. [28]But if the shiny spot remains where it was, has not spread over the skin, and is faded, it is just swelling from the burn.

---

[y]The precise meaning is uncertain; traditionally *leprosy*—a term used for several different skin diseases.

The priest will declare the person clean, because it is just the scar from the burn.

²⁹Whenever a man or woman has an infection, whether on the head or in the beard, ³⁰the priest will examine it. If it appears to be deeper than the skin, and there is thin yellow hair in it, the priest will declare the person unclean; it is a case of scabies—a skin disease of the head or beard. ³¹When the priest examines the scabies infection, if it does not appear to be deeper than the skin, but there is no black hair in it, the priest will quarantine the person with the scabies infection for seven days. ³²On the seventh day the priest will examine the infection again. If the scabies has not spread, there is no yellow hair in it, and it does not appear to be deeper than the skin, ³³the person must shave the area, without shaving the scabies. The priest will then quarantine that person another seven days. ³⁴On the seventh day the priest will again examine the scabies. If it has not spread over the skin and does not appear to be deeper than the skin, the priest will declare the person clean. They must wash their clothes; then they will be clean again. ³⁵But if the scabies continues to spread over the skin after the person's purification, ³⁶the priest must examine it again. If the scabies has spread over the skin at all, the priest does not need to look for the yellow hair; the person is unclean. ³⁷But if the priest sees that the scabies has remained the same, and black hair has grown in it, the scabies has healed. The person is clean, and the priest will declare them to be so.

³⁸Whenever a man or woman has many white shiny spots on their skin, ³⁹if the priest sees that there are faded white shiny spots on the skin of the body, it is just a rash that has broken out on the skin; the person is clean.

⁴⁰If someone loses their hair, they are bald, but they are clean. ⁴¹If the hair is lost at the sides of the forehead, the person has a receding hairline, but they are clean. ⁴²But whenever there is a reddish-white infection in the bald spot or in the receding hairline, it is a case of skin disease breaking out there. ⁴³The priest must examine it. If the swelling of the infection is reddish white in the bald spot or receding hairline and resembles skin disease

on the body, ⁴⁴the person is afflicted with skin disease; they are unclean. The priest must declare them unclean on account of the head infection.

⁴⁵Anyone with an infection of skin disease must wear torn clothes, dishevel their hair, cover their upper lip, and shout out, "Unclean! Unclean!" ⁴⁶They will be unclean as long as they are infected. They are unclean. They must live alone outside the camp.

Articles with skin disease

⁴⁷Whenever there is an infection of skin disease on clothing—on wool or linen clothing, ⁴⁸in the weaving of the linen or wool, or on a skin or skin item— ⁴⁹and the infection is greenish or reddish on the clothing, the weaving, or the skin or skin item, it is an infection of skin disease. It must be shown to the priest. ⁵⁰The priest will examine the infection and quarantine the infected item seven days. ⁵¹On the seventh day he will examine the infection again. If the infection has spread in the clothing, the weaving, or the skin, whatever it is used for, the infection is a case of infectious skin disease; the item is unclean. ⁵²The priest will burn the clothing, the weaving of the wool or linen, or whatever skin item in which the infection was found, because it is an infectious skin disease; it must be burned with fire.

⁵³But if the priest sees that the infection has not spread in the clothing, the weaving, or on any skin item, ⁵⁴the priest will order that the infected piece be washed, and he will quarantine it for another seven days. ⁵⁵After it has been washed, if the priest sees that the infection has not changed its appearance, even though the infection has not spread, it is unclean. You must burn it with fire. It is a fungus,ᶻ whether it is on the inside or outside. ⁵⁶But if, after it is washed, the priest sees that the infection has faded, he will tear the infected part out of the cloth, the weaving, or the skin. ⁵⁷If it appears again in the cloth, the weaving, or any item of skin, it is starting to break out. You must burn the infected item with fire. ⁵⁸But if the infection disappears from the cloth, the weaving, or any item of skin that you washed, it must be washed again. Then it will be clean.

ᶻHeb uncertain

⁵⁹This concludes the Instruction about the infection of skin disease in a woolen or linen cloth, weaving, or any skin item, in order to declare whether it is clean or unclean.

Persons with skin disease

14The LORD said to Moses, ²This will be the Instruction for anyone with skin disease[a] at the time of purification: When it has been reported to the priest, ³he will go outside the camp. If the priest sees that the person afflicted with skin disease has been healed of the infection, ⁴the priest will order that two birds—wild[b] and clean—and cedarwood, crimson yarn, and hyssop be brought for the person who needs purification. ⁵The priest will order that one bird be slaughtered over fresh water in a pottery jar. ⁶He will then take the other wild bird, along with the cedarwood, crimson yarn, and hyssop, and will dip all of this into the blood of the bird that was slaughtered over the fresh water. ⁷He will sprinkle the person who needs purification from skin disease seven times and declare that they are clean. Then the priest will release the wild bird into the countryside. ⁸The person who needs purification will then wash their clothes, shave off all of their hair, and bathe in water; at that point, they will be clean. After that, they can return to the camp, but they must live outside their tent for seven days. ⁹On the seventh day, the person must shave off all their hair again: head, beard, and eyebrows—everything. They must wash their clothes and bathe in water; then they will be clean again.

¹⁰On the eighth day, that person must take two flawless male sheep, one flawless one-year-old ewe, a grain offering of three-tenths of an ephah[c] of choice flour mixed with oil, and one log[d] of oil. ¹¹The priest performing the purification will place these and the person needing purification before the LORD at the meeting tent's entrance.

¹²The priest will take one of the male sheep and present it as a compensation offering,

---

[a]The precise meaning is uncertain; traditionally *leprosy*—a term used for several different skin diseases. [b]*live or healthy*; also in 14:6–7 [c]Heb lacks *ephah*; an ephah is approximately twenty quarts dry. [d]Heb *log*; two-thirds of a pint; also in 14:12, 15, 21, 24

Clean and Unclean Leviticus 14

We're not entirely sure what is meant by the words *clean* and *unclean* in the Instruction from Moses. The meaning for the Israelites may have been different from how we understand these words today. In Bible times, for example, being clean had nothing to do with whether something was covered in mud or freshly washed. Being unclean didn't necessarily mean a person had sinned intentionally. Many times people became unclean through simple everyday acts, through illness, or by accident.

God is the only one who fully understands the teaching about what was clean and unclean. Whether the Israelites understood all of the reasons for how they should live, they knew it was important to obey the teaching. They obeyed because God loved them and they loved God. The same is true for us. We may not always know or understand what God is asking from us, but we can still follow God's ways and do what God wants us to do.

Name a time when you obeyed without knowing why.

Why was that a good thing to do?

along with the log of oil, and will lift them as an uplifted offering before the Lord. ¹³The priest will slaughter the sheep at the same place where the purification offering and the entirely burned offering are slaughtered: in the holy area. The compensation offering, like the purification offering, belongs to the priest; it is most holy. ¹⁴The priest will take some of the blood from the compensation offering and will put it on the right earlobe, the right thumb, and the right big toe of the person needing purification. ¹⁵Then the priest will take some of the log of oil and pour it into his left palm. ¹⁶The priest will then dip his right finger into the oil and sprinkle some of it with his finger seven times before the Lord. ¹⁷Then the priest will put some of the oil that is left in his hand on the right earlobe, the right thumb, and the right big toe of the person needing purification—this oil will be placed on top of the blood of the compensation offering. ¹⁸The priest will put whatever is left of the oil in his hand on the head of the person needing purification. In this way, the priest will make reconciliation for the person before the Lord.

¹⁹The priest will then perform the purification offering and make reconciliation for the person needing purification from their uncleanness. After that, the entirely burned offering will be slaughtered. ²⁰The priest will offer up the entirely burned offering and the grain offering on the altar. In this way, the priest will make reconciliation for the person, and they will be clean again.

²¹Now if the person is poor and cannot afford these things, they can bring one male sheep as a compensation offering, to be lifted up in order to make reconciliation for them; a grain offering of one-tenth of an ephah of choice flour mixed with oil; a log of oil; ²²and two turtledoves or two pigeons, whatever they can afford—one as a purification offering and the other as an entirely burned offering. ²³On the eighth day, they must bring these items for their purification to the priest at the meeting tent's entrance before the Lord.

²⁴The priest will take the male sheep for the compensation offering and the log of oil,

and will lift them as an uplifted offering before the Lord. ²⁵The priest will slaughter the sheep for the compensation offering and will take some of its blood and put it on the right earlobe, the right thumb, and the right big toe of the person needing purification. ²⁶The priest will pour some of the oil into his left palm. ²⁷Next, the priest will sprinkle some of the oil seven times before the Lord using his right finger. ²⁸The priest will then put some of the oil that is in his hand on the right earlobe, the right thumb, and the right big toe of the person needing purification—on top of the same places as the blood of the compensation offering. ²⁹The priest will put whatever is left of the oil in his hand on the head of the person needing purification, to make reconciliation for them before the Lord.

³⁰The person will then offer one of the turtledoves or pigeons, whatever they can afford—³¹one as a purification offering and the other as an entirely burned offering along with the grain offering.ᵉ In this way, the priest will make reconciliation before the Lord for the person needing purification.

³²This is the Instruction concerning those who have an infection of skin disease but who cannot afford the normal means of purification.

Houses with skin disease

³³The Lord said to Moses and Aaron: ³⁴When you enter the land of Canaan, which I am giving to you as a possession, and I put an infection of skin disease on a house in the land you possess, ³⁵the homeowner must come and tell the priest, "I think some sort of infection is in my house." ³⁶The priest will order that the house be emptied before he comes to examine it so that nothing else in the house will become unclean. After that, the priest will come to examine the house. ³⁷If he examines the infection, and the infection in the walls of the house consists of greenish or reddish depressions, which appear to be deeper than the surface of the wall, ³⁸the priest will exit the house, go to the front door, and quarantine the house for seven days. ³⁹On the seventh day, the priest will return. If he finds that the infection has spread over the walls of the house, ⁴⁰the priest will

ᵉLXX, Syr; MT repeats *whatever they can afford* at the beginning of 14:31.

order the stones in which the infection is found to be pulled out and discarded outside the city in an unclean area. [41]The inside of the house will then be scraped on all sides, and the plaster that has been scraped off must be dumped outside the city in an unclean area. [42]Then different stones will be used in place of the first ones, and new coating will be used to replaster the house.

[43]If the infection breaks out again in the house after the stones have been pulled out and the house scraped and replastered, [44]the priest will return. If he finds that the infection has spread throughout the house, it is a case of infectious skin disease in the house; the house is unclean. [45]The house must be destroyed—its stones, wood, and all the plaster in the house. All of it must be taken outside the city to an unclean area. [46]Anyone who enters the house during the entire period when it is quarantined will be unclean until evening. [47]Anyone who lies down in the house must wash their clothes. Anyone who eats in the house must also wash their clothes.

[48]But if the priest arrives and finds that the infection has not spread after the house was replastered, the priest will declare the house clean because the infection has been healed. [49]To cleanse the house, the priest will take two birds, cedarwood, crimson yarn, and hyssop. [50]He will slaughter one bird over fresh water in a pottery jar. [51]He will then take the cedarwood, hyssop, and crimson yarn, along with the wild[f] bird, and will dip all of this into the fresh water and into the blood of the bird that was slaughtered. He will then sprinkle the house seven times. [52]In this way, the priest will cleanse the house with the blood of the bird, the fresh water, the wild bird, the cedarwood, the hyssop, and the crimson yarn. [53]Then he will release the wild bird outside the city into the countryside. In this way, he will make reconciliation for the house, and it will be clean.

Conclusion concerning skin disease

[54]This concludes the Instruction concerning every infection of skin disease: for scabies, [55]for skin disease on clothing or in houses, [56]and for swelling, scabs, or shiny spots, [57]in order to determine when it is unclean or clean. This concludes the Instruction concerning skin disease.

Male genital emissions

15 The LORD said to Moses and Aaron: [2]Speak to the Israelites and say to them: Whenever a man has a genital emission, that emission is unclean. [3]This is the nature of the uncleanness brought about by his emission: regardless of whether his genital organ allows his emission to flow or blocks the flow, it is unclean to him. [4]Any bed on which someone with an emission lies will be unclean, and any object on which that person sits will be unclean. [5]Anyone who touches such a bed must wash their clothes, bathe in water, and will be unclean until evening. [6]Anyone who sits on something that the one with the emission also sat on must wash their clothes, bathe in water, and will be unclean until evening. [7]Anyone who touches the body of the one with the emission must wash their clothes, bathe in water, and will be unclean until evening. [8]If the one with the emission spits on a clean person, the clean person must wash their clothes, bathe in water, and will be unclean until evening. [9]Every saddle on which the person with the emission rode will be unclean. [10]Anyone who touches anything that has been under such a person will be unclean until evening. Anyone who carries such items must wash their clothes, bathe in water, and will be unclean until evening. [11]If the one with the emission touches someone without first rinsing his hands with water, that person must wash their clothes, bathe in water, and will be unclean until evening. [12]Any pottery jar that the one with the emission touches must be broken, and any wooden tool must be rinsed with water.

[13]When the man with the emission is cleansed of his emission, he will count off seven days for his purification. He must wash his clothes and bathe his body in running water; then he will be clean again. [14]On the eighth day he will take two turtledoves or two pigeons and come before the LORD to the meeting tent's entrance and give these to the priest. [15]The priest will offer them, one as

[f]Or *live* or *healthy*

a purification offering and the other as an entirely burned offering. In this way, the priest will make reconciliation for him before the LORD because of his emission.

[16]If it is an emission of semen, the man must bathe his whole body in water and will be unclean until evening. [17]Any clothing or skin on which there is an emission of semen must be washed in water and will be unclean until evening. [18]If a man lies with a woman and has an emission of semen, both of them must bathe in water and will be unclean until evening.

Female genital emissions

[19]Whenever a woman has a discharge of blood that is her normal bodily discharge, she will be unclean due to her menstruation for seven days. Anyone who touches her will be unclean until evening. [20]Anything on which she lies or sits during her menstruation will be unclean. [21]Anyone who touches her bed must wash their clothes, bathe in water, and will be unclean until evening. [22]Anyone who touches anything on which she has sat must wash their clothes, bathe in water, and will be unclean until evening. [23]Whenever anyone touches something—whether it was on the bed or where she has been sitting—they will be unclean until evening. [24]If a man has sexual intercourse with her and her menstruation gets on him, he will be unclean for seven days. Any bed he lies on will be unclean.

[25]Whenever a woman has a bloody discharge for a long time, which is not during her menstrual period, or whenever she has a discharge beyond her menstrual period, the duration of her unclean discharge will be like the period of her menstruation; she will be unclean. [26]Any bed she lies on during the discharge should be treated like the bed she uses during her menstruation; and any object she sits on will be unclean, as during her menstruation. [27]Anyone who touches these things will be unclean. They must wash their clothes, bathe in water, and will be unclean until evening.

[28]When the woman is cleansed of her discharge, she will count off seven days; after that, she will be clean again. [29]On the eighth day she will take two turtledoves or two pigeons and bring them to the priest at the meeting tent's entrance. [30]The priest will perform a purification offering with one and an entirely burned offering with the other. In this way, the priest will make reconciliation for her before the LORD because of her unclean discharge.

[31]You must separate the Israelites from their uncleanness so that they don't die on account of it, by making my dwelling[g] unclean, which is in their midst.

[32]This concludes the Instruction concerning those with discharges: men with emissions of semen that make them unclean, [33]women during their menstruation, men or women with discharges, and men who have had sexual intercourse with an unclean woman.

The Day of Reconciliation

16After the death of Aaron's two sons, which happened when they approached the LORD and died, the LORD spoke to Moses: [2]Tell your brother Aaron that he cannot come whenever he wants into the holy area inside the inner curtain, to the front of the cover[h] that is on the chest, or else he will die, because I am present[i] in the cloud above the cover. [3]No, but Aaron must enter the holy area as follows: with a bull from the herd as a purification offering and a ram as an entirely burned offering. [4]Aaron must dress in a holy linen tunic and wear linen undergarments on his body. He must tie a linen sash around himself and wrap a linen turban around his head. These are holy clothes—Aaron will first bathe his body in water and then put them on. [5]He will take from the Israelite community two male goats for a purification offering and one ram for an entirely burned offering.

[6]Aaron will offer the bull as a purification offering to make reconciliation for himself and his household. [7]He will take the two male goats and place them before the LORD at the meeting tent's entrance. [8]Aaron will cast lots over the two goats: one lot labeled "the LORD's" and the other lot labeled "Azazel's."[j] [9]Aaron will present the goat selected by the LORD's lot and perform a purification offering with it. [10]But the goat selected by Azazel's lot will be left standing alive before the LORD in

---

[g]Or *tabernacle* [h]Or *mercy seat* or perhaps *reconciliation cover* (Heb *kapporet*) [i]Or *I am seen* or *I appear* [j]Or *scapegoat*

did you
know

Each year, God's people painted a goat with the sins of every person and then cast that goat into the wilderness to die. The goat took away the sins of the people, making them free from sin. Today, we use the word *scapegoat* to mean someone who is blamed for the mistakes of others.

order to make reconciliation upon it[k] by sending it away into the wilderness to Azazel.

[11]Aaron will offer the bull for his purification offering to make reconciliation for himself and his household. He will slaughter the bull for his purification offering. [12]Then he will take an incense pan full of burning coals from the altar, from before the Lord, and two handfuls of finely ground perfumed incense and bring them inside the inner curtain. [13]He will put the incense on the fire before the Lord so that the cloud of incense conceals the cover that is on top of the covenant document, or else he will die. [14]He will take some of the bull's blood and sprinkle it with his finger on the cover from the east side. He will then sprinkle some of the blood with his finger seven times in front of the cover. [15]Then he will slaughter the goat for the people's purification offering, bring the blood inside the inner curtain, and do with it as he did with the bull's blood: he will sprinkle it on the cover and in front of the cover. [16]In this way, he will make reconciliation for the inner holy area because of the pollution of the Israelites and because of their rebellious sins, as well as for all their other sins.

Aaron must do the same for the meeting tent, which is with them among their pollution. [17]No one can be in the meeting tent from the time Aaron enters to make reconciliation in the inner holy area until the time he comes out. He will make reconciliation for himself, for his household, and for the whole assembly of Israel. [18]Aaron will then go to the altar that is before the Lord and make reconciliation for it: He will take some of the bull's blood and some of the goat's blood and put it on each of the altar's horns. [19]He will sprinkle some of the blood on the altar with his finger seven times. In this way, he will purify it and make it holy again from the Israelites' pollution.

[20]When Aaron has finished reconciling the inner holy area, the rest of the meeting tent, and the altar, he will bring forward the live goat. [21]Aaron will press both his hands on its head and confess over it all the Israelites' offenses and all their rebellious sins, as well as all their other sins, putting all these on the goat's head. Then he will send it away into the wilderness with someone designated for the job.[l] [22]The goat will carry on itself all their offenses to a desolate region, then the goat will be released into the wild.

[23]After this, Aaron will enter the meeting tent, take off the linen clothes he was wearing when he entered the inner holy area, and will leave them there. [24]He will bathe his body in water in a holy place and dress in his priestly clothing. Then he will go out and perform the entirely burned offerings for himself and for the people. In this way, he will make reconciliation for himself and for the people. [25]He will completely burn the fat of the purification offering on the altar. [26]The one who set the goat free for Azazel must wash their clothes and bathe their body in water; after that they can return to the camp. [27]The bull and the goat for the purification offerings, whose blood was brought in to make reconciliation in the inner holy area, will be taken outside the camp. Their hides, flesh, and dung will be burned with fire. [28]The person who burns them must wash their clothes and bathe their body in water; after that, they can return to the camp.

[29]This will be a permanent rule for you: On the tenth day of the seventh month,[m] you must deny yourselves. You must not do any work—neither the citizen nor the immigrant who lives among you. [30]On that day reconciliation will be made for you in order to cleanse you. You will be clean before the Lord from all your sins. [31]It will be a Sabbath of special rest for you, and you will deny yourselves. This is a permanent rule.

Conclusion concerning the Day of Reconciliation

[32]The priest who is anointed and ordained to serve as priest after his father will perform the reconciliation, wearing the holy linen clothes.

[k]Or *over it* or *for it* or *with it* [l]Heb uncertain [m]September–October, Tishrei

[33]He will reconcile the holiest part of the sanctuary and will do the same for the meeting tent and the altar. He will make reconciliation for the priests and for all the people of the assembly. [34]This will be a permanent rule for you, in order to make reconciliation for the Israelites from all their sins once a year.

It was done just as the LORD commanded Moses.

Sacrifice at the sanctuary

17 The LORD said to Moses, [2]Say to Aaron, to his sons, and to all the Israelites: This is what the LORD has commanded: [3]Anyone from the house of Israel who slaughters an ox, sheep, or goat inside or outside the camp [4]but does not bring it to the meeting tent's entrance to present it as an offering to the LORD in front of the LORD's dwelling[n] will be considered guilty of bloodshed; they have spilled blood. They will be cut off from their people. [5]This will make the Israelites bring the communal sacrifices, which they are sacrificing in the countryside, to the LORD, to the priest at the meeting tent's entrance, and sacrifice them as communal sacrifices of well-being to the LORD. [6]The priest will toss the blood

[n]Or *tabernacle* [o]Or *promiscuously* [p]Or *as life*

against the LORD's altar at the meeting tent's entrance and burn the fat completely as a soothing smell to the LORD. [7]The Israelites must no longer sacrifice their communal sacrifices to the goat demons that they follow so faithlessly.[o] This will be a permanent rule for them throughout their future generations. [8]You will also say to them: Anyone from Israel's house or from the immigrants who live with you who offers up an entirely burned offering or communal sacrifice [9]without bringing it to the meeting tent's entrance in order to offer it to the LORD will be cut off from their people.

Consuming blood forbidden

[10]I will oppose the person who consumes blood—whether they are from Israel's house or from the immigrants who live with you—and I will cut them off from their people. [11]A creature's life is in the blood. I have provided you the blood to make reconciliation for your lives on the altar, because the blood reconciles by means of the life.[p] [12]That is why I have told the Israelites: No one among you can consume blood, nor can the immigrant who lives with you consume blood.

The High Priest: The Go-Between *Leviticus 16:11*

Trying to talk to someone who speaks a different language is a challenge! Sometimes, in order to talk with that person, someone else has to stand between the two people to interpret. The person in-between, the interpreter, listens to what is said. The interpreter then tells the second person what was said in the second person's language. Then the interpreter repeats the process by listening to what the second person says and repeating it in the first person's language.

The high priest was the person who stood between the Israelites and God. The high priest helped the people present their sin offerings to God. Because God is holy and the high priest was an ordinary human, the high priest had to present a sin offering before he could enter God's presence. Then the high priest would present the sin offering for the people of Israel.

Learn how to say "thank you" in another language.

Thank Jesus in your new language.

13 Anyone who hunts any animal or bird that can be eaten—whether the hunter is an Israelite or an immigrant who lives with you—must drain its blood out and cover it with dirt. 14 Again: for every creature's life, its blood is its life. That is why I have told the Israelites: You must not consume any creature's blood because every creature's life is its blood. Anyone who consumes it will be cut off.

Eating meat

15 Anyone, whether citizen or immigrant, who eats an animal that has died naturally or that was killed by another animal, must wash their clothes, bathe in water, and will be unclean until evening. At that time, they will be clean again. 16 If they do not wash or bathe their body, they will be liable to punishment.

Sexual conduct

18 The Lord said to Moses, 2 Speak to the Israelites and say to them: I am the Lord your God. 3 You must not do things like they are done in the land of Egypt, where you used to live. And you must not do things like they are done in the land of Canaan, where I am bringing you. You must not follow the practices[q] of those places. 4 No, my regulations and my rules are the ones you must keep by following them: I am the Lord your God. 5 You must keep my rules and my regulations; by doing them one will live; I am the Lord.

6 No one is allowed to approach any blood relative for sexual contact:[r] I am the Lord. 7 You must not uncover your father's nakedness, which is your mother's nakedness. She is your mother; you must not have sexual contact with her. 8 You must not uncover the nakedness of your father's wife; it is your father's nakedness. 9 You must not have sexual contact with your sister—regardless of whether she is your father's daughter or your mother's daughter, whether born into the same household as you or outside it. 10 You must not have sexual contact with your son's daughter or your daughter's daughter, because their nakedness is your own nakedness.[s] 11 You must not have sexual contact with the daughter of your father's wife, who was born into your father's family; she is your sister. 12 You must not have sexual contact with your father's sister; she is your father's blood relative. 13 You must not have sexual contact with your mother's sister because she is your mother's blood relative. 14 You will not uncover the nakedness of your father's brother—that is, you will not approach his wife for sex; she is your aunt. 15 You must not have sexual contact with your daughter-in-law; she is your son's wife. You must not have sexual contact with her. 16 You will not uncover the nakedness of your brother's wife; it is your brother's nakedness.

17 You must not have sexual contact with a woman and her daughter. You will not marry her son's daughter or her daughter's daughter, thereby uncovering her nakedness. They are her blood relatives; it is shameful. 18 You must not marry your wife's sister as a rival and have sexual contact with her while her sister is alive. 19 You must not approach a woman for sexual contact during her menstrual uncleanness. 20 You must not have sexual relations with the wife of your fellow Israelite, becoming unclean by it.

21 You must not give any of your children[t] to offer them over to Molech so that you do not defile your God's name: I am the Lord. 22 You must not have sexual intercourse with a man as you would with a woman; it is a detestable

LIFE PRESERVER

Wow, they had instructions for everything! *Leviticus 18*

God gave the people of Israel teaching covering every part of life, including sexuality. This Instruction was meant to help God's people remember how they were to be set apart for God. They were to be different from the people who lived in Egypt (the land from which they had come) and Canaan (the place to which they were going). God wanted them to remember that even in the most private parts of life they were to abide by laws that would protect them.

As the Israelites moved out into places that were new to them, God wanted them to know how they were to live as God's people. God was preparing them for behaviors and practices they might see as they left Egypt and headed toward the promised land.

[q] *Or rules or customs* [r] *Or to uncover nakedness* [s] Heb uncertain [t] *Or seed*

practice. ²³You will not have sexual relations with any animal, becoming unclean by it. Nor will a woman present herself before an animal to mate with it; it is a perversion.

Warning against uncleanness and moral pollution

²⁴Do not make yourselves unclean in any of these ways because that is how the nations that I am throwing out before you became unclean. ²⁵That is also how the land became unclean, and I held it liable for punishment, and the land vomited out its inhabitants. ²⁶But all of you must keep my rules and my regulations. You must not do any of these detestable things, neither citizen nor immigrant who lives with you (²⁷because the people who had the land before you did all of these detestable things and the land became unclean), ²⁸so that the land does not vomit you out because you have made it unclean, just as it vomited out the nations that were before you. ²⁹Anyone who does any of these detestable things will be cut off from their people. ³⁰You must keep my requirement of not doing any of the detestable practicesᵘ that were done before you arrived so that you don't make yourselves unclean by them; I am the LORD your God.

Living as holy people

19 The LORD said to Moses, ²Say to the whole community of the Israelites: You must be holy, because I, the LORD your God, am holy. ³Each of you must respect your mother and father, and you must keep my sabbaths; I am the LORD your God. ⁴Do not turn to idols or make gods of cast metal for yourselves; I am the LORD your God. ⁵When you sacrifice a communal sacrifice of well-being to the LORD, offer it so that it will be accepted on your account. ⁶It must be eaten on the day of your sacrifice or the following day; whatever is left over on the third day must be burned with fire. ⁷If any of it is eaten on the third day, it is foul; it will not be accepted. ⁸Anyone who eats it will be liable to punishment, because they defiled what is holy to the LORD. That person will be cut off from their people.

> Memorize
> Lev 19:2

⁹When you harvest your land's produce, you must not harvest all the way to the edge of your field; and don't gather up every remaining bit of your harvest. ¹⁰Also do not pick your vineyard clean or gather up all the grapes that have fallen there. Leave these items for the poor and the immigrant; I am the LORD your God.

SAILBOAT

KINDNESS

Leave Some *Leviticus 19:9-10*
God is merciful to people who are poor or who move from one country to another, called *immigrants*. God told the Israelites to leave behind some food in the fields whenever they harvested the land's produce. In this way, people who couldn't afford to buy food or who didn't own land to grow food could come and get what they needed. This was a way of showing kindness—a way of making sure that all of God's children had enough.

¹¹You must not steal nor deceive nor lie to each other. ¹²You must not swear falsely by my name, desecrating your God's name in doing so; I am the LORD. ¹³You must not oppress your neighbors or rob them. Do not withhold a hired laborer's pay overnight. ¹⁴You must not insult a deaf person or put some obstacle in front of a blind person that would cause them to trip. Instead, fear your God; I am the LORD.

¹⁵You must not act unjustly in a legal case. Do not show favoritism to the poor or deference to the great; you must judge your fellow Israelites fairly. ¹⁶Do not go around slandering your people.ᵛ Do not stand by while your neighbor's blood is shed;ʷ I am the LORD. ¹⁷You must not hate your fellow Israelite in your heart. Rebuke your fellow Israelite strongly, so you don't become responsible for his sin.ˣ ¹⁸You must not take revenge nor hold a grudge against any of your people; instead, you must love your neighbor as yourself; I am the LORD.

¹⁹You must keep my rules. Do not crossbreed your livestock, do not plant your field

---

ᵘOr *rules or customs* ᵛHeb uncertain ʷHeb uncertain ˣOr *strongly, but don't become liable for punishment because of it*; Heb uncertain

with two kinds of seed, and do not wear clothes made from two kinds of material. ²⁰If a man has sexual relations with a woman who is a slave engaged to another man, who hasn't yet been released or given her freedom, there must be a punishment.^y But they will not be put to death because she had not yet been freed. ²¹The man must bring as his compensation to the Lᴏʀᴅ at the meeting tent's entrance a ram for a compensation offering. ²²The priest will use the ram for the compensation offering to make reconciliation for him before the Lᴏʀᴅ on account of the sin he committed. Then he will be forgiven of the sin that he committed.

²³When you enter the land and plant any fruit tree, you must consider its fruit off-limits.^z For three years it will be off-limits to you;^a it must not be eaten. ²⁴In the fourth year, all of the tree's fruit will be holy, a celebration for the Lᴏʀᴅ. ²⁵In the fifth year you can eat the fruit. This is so as to increase its produce for you; I am the Lᴏʀᴅ your God.

²⁶You must not eat anything with its blood. You must not participate in divination or fortune-telling. ²⁷You must not cut off the hair on your forehead or clip the ends of your beard. ²⁸Do not cut your bodies for the dead^b or put marks on^c yourselves; I am the Lᴏʀᴅ. ²⁹Do not defile your daughter by making her sexually promiscuous or else the land will become promiscuous^d and full of shame. ³⁰You must keep my sabbaths and treat my sanctuary with respect; I am the Lᴏʀᴅ. ³¹Do not resort to dead spirits or inquire of spirits of divination—you will be made unclean by them; I am the Lᴏʀᴅ your God. ³²You must rise in the presence of an old person and respect the elderly. You must fear your God; I am the Lᴏʀᴅ.

³³When immigrants live in your land with you, you must not cheat them. ³⁴Any immigrant who lives with you must be treated as if they were one of your citizens. You must love them as yourself, because you were immigrants in the land of Egypt; I am the Lᴏʀᴅ your God. ³⁵You must not act unjustly in a legal case involving measures of length, weight, or volume. ³⁶You must have accurate scales and accurate weights, an accurate ephah^e and an accurate hin.^f I am the Lᴏʀᴅ your God, who brought you out of the land of Egypt. ³⁷You must keep all my rules and all my regulations, and do them; I am the Lᴏʀᴅ.

> Memorize
> Lev 19:37

Worship of Molech forbidden

20 The Lᴏʀᴅ said to Moses, ²You will also say to the Israelites: Any Israelite or any immigrant living in Israel who gives their children to Molech must be executed. The common people will stone such a person. ³Moreover, I will set my own face against such a person, cutting them off from their people, because they gave their children to Molech, making my sanctuary unclean and degrading my holy name by doing so. ⁴But if the common people choose to look the other way when someone gives their children to Molech and do not execute such a person, ⁵I will set my own face against such a person and their extended family, cutting off from their people both the guilty party and anyone with them who faithlessly followed Molech. ⁶I will also oppose anyone who resorts to dead spirits or spirits of divination and faithlessly follows those things. I will cut such an individual off from their people.

Sexual prohibitions

⁷You must be holy and keep yourselves holy because I am the Lᴏʀᴅ your God. ⁸You will keep my rules and do them; I am the Lᴏʀᴅ, who makes you holy. ⁹If anyone curses their father or mother, they must be executed. They have cursed their own father and mother; that person's blood is on their own heads. ¹⁰If a man commits adultery with a married woman, committing adultery with a neighbor's wife, both the adulterer and the adulteress must be executed. ¹¹If a man has sexual intercourse with his father's wife, he has uncovered his father's nakedness. Both of them must be executed; their blood is on their own heads. ¹²If a man has sexual intercourse with his daughter-in-law, both of them must be executed. They have acted

^yOr *an inquiry* ^zOr *treat its fruit as a foreskin* ^aOr *uncircumcised to you* ^bOr *for the living* ^cOr *tattoo;* Heb uncertain ^dOr *making her a prostitute so that the land won't become a prostitute* ^eApproximately twenty quarts ^fApproximately one gallon of liquid

perversely; their blood is on their own heads. ¹³If a man has sexual intercourse with a man as he would with a woman, the two of them have done something detestable. They must be executed; their blood is on their own heads. ¹⁴If a man marries a woman and her mother as well, it is shameful. They will be burned with fire—the man and the two women—so that no such shameful thing will be found among you. ¹⁵If a man has sexual relations with an animal, he must be executed and you must kill the animal. ¹⁶If a woman approaches any kind of animal to mate with it, you must kill the woman and the animal. They must be executed; their blood is on their own heads. ¹⁷If a man marries his sister—his father's daughter or his mother's daughter—and they have sexual contact with each other, it is a disgrace. They will be cut off in the sight of their people. Such a man has had sexual contact with his sister; he will be liable to punishment. ¹⁸If a man sleeps with a woman during her menstrual period and has sexual contact with her, he has exposed the source of her blood flow and she has uncovered the same. Both of them will be cut off from their people. ¹⁹You must not have sexual contact with your mother's sister or your father's sister, because that exposes your own close relative; both of you will be liable to punishment. ²⁰If a man has sexual intercourse with his aunt, he has uncovered his uncle's nakedness. The man and the aunt will be liable to punishment; they will die childless. ²¹If a man marries his brother's wife, it is indecent. He has uncovered his brother's nakedness; the man and the woman will be childless.

Conclusion concerning conduct

²²You must keep all my rules and all my regulations, and do them so that the land I am bringing you to, where you will live, won't vomit you out. ²³You must not follow the practices[g] of the nations that I am throwing out before you, because they did all these things and I was disgusted with them. ²⁴But I have told you, "You will certainly possess their fertile land; I am giving it to you to possess. It is a land full of milk and honey." I am the LORD your God, who has separated you

from all other peoples. ²⁵So you must separate between clean and unclean animals, and between clean and unclean birds. Do not become detestable through some animal, bird, or anything that moves on the fertile ground that I have separated from you as unclean. ²⁶You must be holy to me, because I the LORD am holy, and I have separated you from all other peoples to be my own. ²⁷If someone, whether male or female, is a medium with the dead or a diviner,[h] they must be executed. They will be stoned; their blood is on their own head.

SAILBOAT

OBEDIENCE

God Doesn't Mess Around
Leviticus 20:22-26
God wanted the Israelites to understand how important it was for them to follow God's ways. God told them to keep all of the Instruction God had commanded so that the land wouldn't vomit them out. This was a serious consequence! God wanted God's people to be holy because that would bring them closer to God. ◆

Rules for priests

21 The LORD said to Moses, Say to the priests, Aaron's sons: None of you are allowed to make yourselves unclean by any dead person among your community ²except for your closest relatives: for your mother, father, son, daughter, brother; ³also for your unmarried sister, who is close to you because she isn't married—you may be polluted for her sake. ⁴You must not make yourself unclean for in-laws, defiling yourself by doing so. ⁵Priests must not shave bald patches on their heads or cut off the ends of their beards or make gashes in their bodies. ⁶They must be holy to their God so that they do not make their God's name impure. They must be holy because they offer the LORD's food gifts, their God's food. ⁷Priests must not marry a woman who is promiscuous and defiled, nor can they marry a woman divorced from her husband, because priests must be[i] holy to their God. ⁸You will treat the priests as holy, because

---

[g]Or rules or customs [h]Or has a spirit of the dead or a spirit of divination [i]Or are

they offer your God's food. The priests will be holy to you, because I am the holy Lord, who makes you holy. ⁹If the daughter of a priest defiles herself by being promiscuous, she defiles her father. She must be burned with fire.

¹⁰The high priest[j]—the one whose head has been anointed with the anointing oil and who is ordained to dress in the priestly clothing—must not dishevel his hair or tear his clothing. ¹¹He must not go near any dead bodies and cannot make himself unclean even for his father or mother. ¹²He must not exit the sanctuary, making his God's sanctuary impure by doing so, because his God's anointing oil, which separates,[k] is upon him; I am the Lord. ¹³The high priest must marry a woman who is a virgin. ¹⁴He cannot marry a widow, a divorced woman, or a woman defiled by promiscuity. He can only marry a virgin from his own people ¹⁵so that he doesn't make his children impure among his people, because I am the Lord, who makes him holy.

¹⁶The Lord said to Moses, ¹⁷Say to Aaron: None of your future descendants who have some kind of imperfection are allowed to offer their God's food. ¹⁸No one who has an imperfection will be allowed to make an offering: this includes anyone who is blind, crippled, disfigured, or deformed; ¹⁹anyone who has a broken foot or hand; ²⁰anyone who is a hunchback or too small; anyone who has an eye disease, a rash, scabs, or a crushed testicle.[l] ²¹No descendant of Aaron the priest who has an imperfection will be allowed to offer the Lord's food gifts; since he has an imperfection, he will not be allowed to offer his God's food. ²²He may, of course, eat of his God's most holy or holy food, ²³but since he has an imperfection, he cannot enter toward the inner curtain or officiate at the altar, making these parts of my sanctuary impure by doing so. I am the Lord, who makes them holy.

²⁴This is what Moses said to Aaron, his sons, and to all the Israelites.

Priestly uncleanness

22 The Lord said to Moses: ²Tell Aaron and his sons to be very careful how they treat the holy things that the Israelites devote to me so that they do not make my holy name impure: I am the Lord. ³Say to them: If any descendant of yours should ever come near the holy things that the Israelites have dedicated to the Lord while he is in an unclean state, he will be cut off from before me; I am the Lord. ⁴Any descendant of Aaron who is afflicted with skin disease[m] or has a discharge cannot eat of the holy things until he is clean. Anyone who touches anything made unclean by a dead body, or who has an emission of semen, ⁵or who touches any swarming creature or another person who makes him unclean—whatever the uncleanness might be—⁶the person who touches these things will be unclean until evening. He must not eat of the holy things unless he has bathed his body in water. ⁷Once the sun has set and he has become clean again, he may eat of the holy things, for that is his food. ⁸He must not eat an animal that has died naturally or that was killed by another animal, becoming unclean by doing so; I am the Lord. ⁹The priests must keep my requirement so that they don't become liable to punishment and die for having made it impure.[n] I am the Lord, who makes them holy.

Unauthorized eating

¹⁰No layperson is allowed to eat the holy offerings. No foreign guest or hired laborer of a priest can eat it. ¹¹But if a priest purchases a servant, that person can eat it, and servants born into the priest's household can also eat his food. ¹²If a priest's daughter marries a layman, she is not allowed to eat the holy offerings. ¹³But if a priest's daughter is a widow or divorced and has no children and so returns to her father's household as when she was young, she can eat her father's food. But, again, no layperson is allowed to eat it. ¹⁴If someone eats a holy offering unintentionally, they must provide the priest with an equal item, plus one-fifth. ¹⁵The Israelites must not make the holy offerings impure that they offer up to the Lord ¹⁶or make themselves liable to punishment requiring compensation by eating their own holy offerings. I am the Lord, who makes them holy.

---

[j]Or *the priest who is greater than his brothers* [k]Or *consecrates* [l]The meaning of several words in 21:18–20 is uncertain.
[m]The precise meaning is uncertain; traditionally *leprosy*—a term used for several different skin diseases. [n]Vulg; MT *and die in it*

Unacceptable animal offerings

¹⁷The Lord said to Moses: ¹⁸Tell Aaron, his sons, and all the Israelites: Whenever someone from Israel's house or from the immigrants in Israel presents their offering to the Lord as an entirely burned offering—whether it is payment for a solemn promise or a spontaneous gift—¹⁹for it to be acceptable on your behalf, it must be a flawless male from the herd, the sheep, or the goats. ²⁰You must not present anything that has an imperfection, because it will not be acceptable on your behalf. ²¹Whenever someone presents a communal sacrifice of well-being to the Lord from the herd or flock—whether it is payment for a solemn promise or a spontaneous gift—it must be flawless to be acceptable; it must not have any imperfection. ²²You must not present to the Lord anything that is blind or that has an injury, mutilation, warts, a rash, or scabs. You must not put any such animal on the altar as a food gift for the Lord. ²³You can, however, offer an ox or sheep that is deformed or stunted as a spontaneous gift, but it will not be acceptable as payment for a solemn promise. ²⁴You must not offer to the Lord anything with bruised, crushed, torn, or cut-off testicles. You must not do that in your land. ²⁵You are not allowed to offer such animals as your God's food even if they come from a foreigner. Because these animals have blemishes and imperfections in them, they will not be acceptable on your behalf.

Additional rules for sacrifice

²⁶The Lord said to Moses: ²⁷When an ox or sheep or goat is born, it must remain with its mother for seven days. From the eighth day on it will be acceptable as an offering, a food gift for the Lord. ²⁸But you will not slaughter an ox or sheep and its offspring on the same day. ²⁹When you sacrifice a communal sacrifice of thanksgiving for the Lord, you must sacrifice it so that it will be acceptable on your behalf. ³⁰It must be eaten on the same day; you must not leave any of it until morning; I am the Lord. ³¹You must keep my commands and do them; I am the Lord. ³²You must not make my holy name impure so that I will be treated as holy by the Israelites. I am

What was the purpose of animal sacrifices?
Leviticus 22:17-31

Some offerings were given to God as a solemn promise. Others were a way of giving thanks to God. And then some were a request for forgiveness for not obeying God's Instruction. The book of Leviticus talks about the requirements for animal sacrifice. All of these very specific instructions were written so that the people of that time would know how to make their offerings to God in a way that would honor God's holy name. God required these sacrifices so that the Israelites would remember God and never forget. Although we no longer offer animals as sacrifices to God, we do give other kinds of offerings to remember God. We put money in the offering plate on Sunday. We offer our hands to help others in need. When we say kind things to someone else, we offer care and support. ◊

the Lord—the one who makes you holy ³³and who is bringing you out of the land of Egypt to be your God; I am the Lord.

Sacred times

23The Lord said to Moses: ²Speak to the Israelites and say to them: These are my appointed times, the Lord's appointed times, which you will declare to be holy occasions: ³Work can be done for six days, but the seventh day is a Sabbath of special rest, a holy occasion. You must not do any work on it; wherever you live, it is a Sabbath to the Lord. ⁴These are the Lord's appointed times, holy occasions, which you will celebrate at their appointed times:

⁵The Lord's Passover is on the fourteenth day of the first month^o at twilight. ⁶The Lord's Festival of Unleavened Bread is on the fifteenth day of the same month. You must eat unleavened bread for seven days. ⁷On the first day you will hold a holy occasion and must not do any job-related work. ⁸You will offer food gifts to the Lord for seven days. The seventh day will be a holy occasion; you must not do any job-related work.

⁹The Lord said to Moses: ¹⁰Speak to the Israelites and say to them: When you enter the

land that I am giving you and harvest its produce, you must bring the first bundle of your harvest to the priest. 11The priest will lift up the bundle before the LORD so that it will be acceptable on your behalf. The priest will do this on the day after the Sabbath. 12On the day the bundle is lifted up for you, you must offer a flawless one-year-old lamb as an entirely burned offering to the LORD. 13The accompanying grain offering must be two-tenths of an ephah[p] of choice flour mixed with oil, as a food gift for the LORD, a soothing smell. The accompanying drink offering must be a quarter of a hin of wine. 14You must not eat any bread, roasted grain, or fresh grain until the exact day when you bring your God's offering. This is a permanent rule throughout your future generations, wherever you live.

15You must count off seven weeks starting with the day after the Sabbath, the day you bring the bundle for the uplifted offering; these must be complete. 16You will count off fifty days until the day after the seventh Sabbath. Then you must present a new grain offering to the LORD. 17From wherever you live, you will bring two loaves of bread as an uplifted offering. These must be made of two-tenths of an ephah of choice flour, baked with leaven, as early produce[q] to the LORD. 18Along with the bread you must present seven flawless one-year-old lambs, one bull from the herd, and two rams. These will be an entirely burned offering to the LORD, along with their grain offerings and drink offerings, as a food gift of soothing smell to the LORD. 19You must also offer one male goat as a purification offering and two one-year-old lambs as a communal sacrifice of well-being. 20The priest will lift up the two sheep, along with the bread of the early produce, as an uplifted offering before the LORD. These will be holy to the LORD and will belong to the priest. 21On that very same day you must make a proclamation; it will be a holy occasion for you. You must not do any job-related work. This is a permanent rule wherever you live throughout your future generations. 22When you harvest your land's produce, you must not harvest all the way to the edge of your field; and don't gather every remaining bit of your harvest. Leave these items for the poor and the immigrant; I am the LORD your God.

23The LORD said to Moses: 24Say to the Israelites: On the first day of the seventh month,[r] you will have a special rest, a holy occasion marked by a trumpet signal. 25You must not do any job-related work, and you must offer a food gift to the LORD.

26The LORD said to Moses: 27Note that the tenth day of this seventh month is the Day of Reconciliation. It will be a holy occasion for you. You must deny yourselves and offer a food gift to the LORD. 28You must not do any work that day because it is a Day of Reconciliation to make reconciliation for you before the LORD your God. 29Anyone who does not deny themselves on that day will be cut off from their people. 30Moreover, I will destroy from their people anyone who does any work on that day. 31You must not do any work! This is a permanent rule throughout your future generations wherever you live. 32This is a Sabbath of special rest for you, and you must deny yourselves. You will observe your Sabbath on the ninth day of the month from evening to the following evening.

33The LORD said to Moses: 34Say to the Israelites: The Festival of Booths to the LORD will start on the fifteenth day of the seventh month and will last for seven days. 35The first day is a holy occasion. You must not do any job-related work. 36For seven days you will offer food gifts to the LORD. On the eighth day you will have a holy occasion and must offer a food gift to

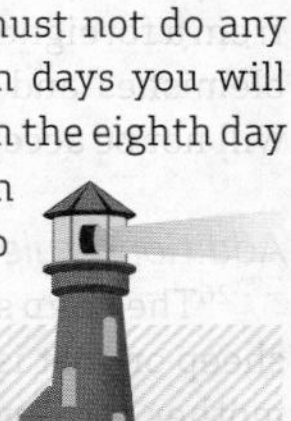

LIGHTHOUSE

SPECIAL AND SET APART

Calendar of Events Leviticus 23

The Israelites celebrated many special occasions at the same time every year. Leviticus 23 names many of these events, telling the people when and how they were to celebrate. On these occasions, the people took time to remember who God is and all that God had done for them. Today, there are people who continue to celebrate these festivals, just as God commanded.

[p]Four quarts dry; also in 23:17 [q]Or *firstfruits*; also in 23:20 [r]September–October, Tishrei; also in 23:27, 33, 39, 41

the Lord. It is a holiday: you must not do any job-related work.

[37]These are the Lord's appointed times that you will proclaim as holy occasions, offering food gifts to the Lord: entirely burned offerings, grain offerings, communal sacrifices, and drink offerings—each on its proper day. [38]This is in addition to the Lord's sabbaths and in addition to your presents, all the payments for solemn promises, and all the spontaneous gifts that you give to the Lord.

[39]Note that on the fifteenth day of the seventh month, when you have gathered the land's crops, you will celebrate the Lord's festival for seven days. The first day and the eighth day are days of special rest. [40]On the first day you must take fruit from majestic trees,[s] palm branches, branches of leafy trees,[t] and willows of the streams, and rejoice before the Lord your God for seven days. [41]You will celebrate this festival to the Lord for seven days each year; this is a permanent rule throughout your future generations. You will celebrate it in the seventh month. [42]For seven

days you must live in huts. Every citizen of Israel must live in huts [43]so that your future generations will know that I made the Israelites live in huts when I brought them out of the land of Egypt; I am the Lord your God.

[44]So Moses announced the Lord's appointed times to the Israelites.

The sanctuary's lamp and bread

24The Lord said to Moses: [2]Command the Israelites to bring pure, pressed olive oil to you for the lamp, to keep a light burning constantly. [3]Aaron will tend the lamp, which will be inside the meeting tent but outside the inner curtain of the covenant document, from evening until morning before the Lord. This is a permanent rule throughout your future generations. [4]Aaron must continually tend the lights on the pure lampstand[u] before the Lord.

[5]You will take choice flour and bake twelve loaves of flatbread, two-tenths of an ephah[v] for each loaf. [6]You must place them in two stacks, six in a stack, on the pure table[w]

---

[s]Or *hadar trees* [t]Heb uncertain [u]Perhaps *pure gold lampstand* [v]Approximately four quarts dry [w]Perhaps *pure gold table*

Hard Sayings: An Eye for an Eye *Leviticus 24:19-20*

There are parts of the Bible that are difficult for us to understand. This passage regarding "an eye for an eye" is one of them. When you read these verses for the first time, they may sound cruel, as if people were trying to get even in horrible ways when something bad happened. But this teaching was not intended for ordinary people to use as an excuse for harming someone else.

Sometimes, judges or elders gave a harsh punishment to set an example for other people. Or the judge wanted the punishment to fit the crime. So if a person's dog killed another person's cow, the victim couldn't force the first person to pay ten cows for the crime. This same principle applies today. If your brother tears up one of your trading cards, you shouldn't ask your parents to let you take ten of his cards. God wants us always to stand for justice and mercy.

Think of a time when someone hurt you.
What happened?

Think of a time when you hurt someone.
What happened?

before the Lord. ⁷Put pure frankincense on each stack, as a token portion for the bread; it is a food gift for the Lord. ⁸Aaron will always set it out before the Lord, Sabbath after Sabbath, on behalf of˟ the Israelites, as a permanent covenant. ⁹It will belong to Aaron and his sons. They must eat it in a holy place because it is the most holy part of their share of the Lord's food gifts, a permanent portion.

Assault and blasphemy

¹⁰The son of an Israelite mother and an Egyptian father came out among the Israelites. A fight broke out between this half-Israeliteʸ and another Israelite man in the camp, ¹¹during which the half-Israelite blasphemed the Lord's name and cursed. So he was brought to Moses. (His mother's name was Shelomith, Dibri's daughter from the tribe of Dan.) ¹²He was put under guard until they could determine the Lord's verdict.

¹³Then the Lord said to Moses: ¹⁴Take the one who cursed outside the camp. All who heard him will press their hands on his head. Then the whole community will stone him. ¹⁵Tell the Israelites: Anyone who curses God will be liable to punishment. ¹⁶And anyone who blasphemes the Lord's name must be executed. The whole community will stone that person. Immigrant and citizen alike: whenever someone blasphemes the Lord's name, that person will be executed.

¹⁷If anyone kills another person, they must be executed. ¹⁸Someone who kills an animal

did you **know?** Every fifty years, God's people celebrated a year of Jubilee when all debts were forgiven, land was returned to its original owner, no crops were planted, and slaves were freed. This was a way for God's people to start over with a blank slate and to ensure that no family or leader gained too much power or wealth over others.

may make amends for it: a life for a life. ¹⁹If someone injures a fellow citizen, they will suffer the same injury they inflicted: ²⁰broken bone for broken bone, an eye for an eye, a tooth for a tooth. The same injury the person

inflicted on the other will be inflicted on them. ²¹Someone who kills an animal must make amends for it, but whoever kills a human being must be executed. ²²There is but one law on this matter for you, immigrant or citizen alike, because I am the Lord your God.

²³Moses told this to the Israelites. So they took the one who had cursed outside the camp and stoned him. The Israelites did just as the Lord commanded Moses.

The sabbatical year

25 The Lord said to Moses on Mount Sinai, ²Speak to the Israelites and say to them: Once you enter the land that I am giving you, the land must celebrate a sabbath rest to the Lord. ³You will plant your fields for six years, and prune your vineyards and gather their crops for six years. ⁴But in the seventh year the land will have a special sabbath rest, a Sabbath to the Lord: You must not plant your fields or prune your vineyards. ⁵You must not harvest the secondary growth of your produce or gather the grapes of your freely growing vines. It will be a year of special rest for the land. ⁶Whatever the land produces during its sabbath will be your food—for you, for your male and female servants, and for your hired laborers and foreign guests who live with you, ⁷as well as for your livestock and for the wild animals in your land. All of the land's produce can be eaten.

The Jubilee year

⁸Count off seven weeks of years—that is, seven times seven—so that the seven weeks of years totals forty-nine years. ⁹Then have the trumpetᶻ blown on the tenth day of the seventh month.ᵃ Have the trumpet blown throughout your land on the Day of Reconciliation. ¹⁰You will make the fiftieth year holy, proclaiming freedom throughout the land to all its inhabitants. It will be a Jubilee yearᵇ for you: each of you must return to your family property and to your extended family. ¹¹The fiftieth year will be a Jubilee year for you. Do not plant, do not harvest the secondary growth, and do not gather from the freely growing vines ¹²because it is a Jubilee: it will

˟Or *from* or *as a gift of*; Heb uncertain ʸOr *Israelite woman's son*; also in 24:11 ᶻHeb *shofar* ᵃSeptember–October, Tishrei ᵇHeb *yobel*

be holy to you. You can eat only the produce directly out of the field. ¹³Each of you must return to your family property in this year of Jubilee.

¹⁴When you sell something to or buy something from your fellow citizen, you must not cheat each other. ¹⁵You will buy from your fellow citizen according to the number of years since the Jubilee; he will sell to you according to the number of years left for harvests. ¹⁶You will raise the price if there are more years, or lower the price if there are less years because it is the number of harvests that are being sold to you. ¹⁷You must not cheat each other but fear your God because I am the LORD your God. ¹⁸You will observe my rules, and you will keep my regulations and do them so that you can live securely on the land.

Food during fallow years

¹⁹The land will give its fruit so that you can eat your fill and live securely on it. ²⁰Suppose

ᶜOr *next of kin*; traditionally *redeemer*

you ask, "What will we eat in the seventh year if we don't plant or gather our crops then?" ²¹I will send my blessing on you in the sixth year so that it will make enough produce for three years. ²²You can plant again in the eighth year and eat food from the previous year's produce until the ninth year. Until its produce comes, you will eat the food from the previous year.

Buying back family property

²³The land must not be permanently sold because the land is mine. You are just immigrants and foreign guests of mine.

²⁴Throughout the whole land that you possess, you must allow for the land to be bought back. ²⁵When one of your fellow Israelites faces financial difficulty and must sell part of their family property, the closest relativeᶜ will come and buy back what their fellow Israelite has sold. ²⁶If the person doesn't have someone to buy it back, but then manages to afford buying it back, ²⁷they must calculate

Caring for God's Earth *Leviticus 25:1-7*

The idea that we need to take care of the earth isn't a recent thing. When God placed Adam and Eve in the garden, God instructed them to care for the plants and animals. That command didn't stop when they sinned and had to leave the garden. They were still expected to tend the land, but the thorns and weeds made it more difficult.

God's Instruction to the Israelites stated that one out of every seven years the people weren't to plant any crops. They could harvest and eat whatever grew naturally, but they weren't supposed to plant anything. Not only was this a reminder that they were to trust God for their food, but it was also a way to allow the soil to rest and recover.

We need to do what we can to care for the earth. This includes picking up litter, recycling and reusing, and caring for the trees, plants, and grass in our own yards. Taking care of the earth is one way we can thank God for all we have been given.

What are some things you can do to take care of the earth?

Say a prayer of thanks to God for the earth—land, water, sky, and all the creatures that share it with us.

the years since its sale and refund the balance to the person to whom they sold it. Then it will go back to the family property.[d] 28If they cannot afford to make a refund to the buyer, whatever was sold will remain in the possession of the buyer until the Jubilee year. It will be released in the Jubilee year, at which point it will return to the family property.

29When a person sells a home in a walled city, it may be bought back until a year after its sale. The period for buying it back will be one year. 30If it is not bought back before a full year has passed, the house in the walled city will belong to the buyer permanently and their descendants forever. It will not be released at the Jubilee. 31But houses in settlements that are unwalled will be considered as if they were country fields. They can be bought back, and they must be released at the Jubilee.

32Levites will always have the right to buy back homes in the levitical cities that are part of their family property. 33Levite property that can be bought back—houses sold in a city that is their family property—must be released at the Jubilee, because homes in levitical cities are the Levites' family property among the Israelites. 34But the pastureland around their cities cannot be sold, because that is their permanent family property.

Poor Israelites and slavery

35If one of your fellow Israelites faces financial difficulty and is in a shaky situation with you,[e] you must assist them as you would an immigrant or foreign guest so that they can survive among you. 36Do not take interest from them, or any kind of profit from interest, but fear your God so that your fellow Israelite can survive among you. 37Do not lend a poor Israelite money with interest or lend food at a profit. 38I am the Lord your God, who brought you out from the land of Egypt to give you Canaan's land and to be your God.

39If one of your fellow Israelites faces financial difficulty with you and sells themselves to you, you must not make him work as a slave. 40Instead, they will be like a hired laborer or foreign guest to you. They will work for you until the Jubilee year, 41at which point the poor Israelite along with their children will be released from you. They can return to their extended family and to their family property. 42You must do this because these people are my servants—I brought them out of Egypt's land. They must not be sold as slaves. 43You will not harshly rule over them but must fear your God.

44Regarding male or female slaves that you are allowed to have: You can buy a male or a female slave from the nations that are around you. 45You can also buy them from the foreign guests who live with you and from their extended families that are with you, who were born in your land. These can belong to you as property. 46You can pass them on to your children as inheritance that they can own as permanent property. You can make these people work as slaves, but you must not rule harshly over your own people, the Israelites.

47If an immigrant or foreign guest prospers financially among you, but your fellow Israelite faces financial difficulty and so sells themselves to the immigrant or foreign guest, or to a descendant of a foreigner, 48the Israelite will have the right to be bought back after they sold themselves. One of their relatives can buy them back: 49their uncle or cousin can buy them back; one of their blood relatives from their family can buy them back; or they may be able to afford their own purchase. 50The Israelite will calculate with their owner the time from the year they were sold until the Jubilee year. The price of their release will be based on the number of years they were with the owner, as in the case of a hired laborer. 51If there are many years left before the Jubilee, the Israelite will pay for their purchase in proportion to their purchase price. 52If only a few years are left, they will calculate that and pay for their purchase according to the years of service. 53Regardless, the Israelite will be to the buyer like a yearly laborer; the buyer must not harshly rule over them in your sight. 54If the Israelite is not bought back in one of these ways, they and their children must be released in the Jubilee year 55because the Israelites belong to me as servants. They are my servants—I

---

[d]Or *they will go back to their family property;* also in 25:28. [e]Heb uncertain

brought them out of Egypt's land; I am the Lord your God.

Covenant blessings

26 You must not make any idols, and do not set up any divine image or sacred pillar. You must not place any carved[f] stone in your land, bowing down to it, because I am the Lord your God. ²You must keep my sabbaths and respect my sanctuary; I am the Lord.

³If you live according to my rules, keep my commands, and do them, ⁴I will give you rain at the proper time, the land will produce its yield, and the trees of the field will produce their fruit. ⁵Your threshing season will last until the grape harvest, and the grape harvest will last until planting time. You will eat your fill of food and live securely in your land. ⁶I will grant peace in the land so that you can lie down without anyone frightening you. I will remove dangerous animals from the land, and no sword will pass through it. ⁷You will chase your enemies, and they will fall before you in battle. ⁸Five of you will chase away a hundred, and a hundred of you will chase away ten thousand, and your enemies will fall before you in battle. ⁹I will turn my face to you, will make you fruitful and numerous, and will keep my covenant with you. ¹⁰You will still be eating the previous year's harvest when the time will come to clear it out to make room for the new! ¹¹I will place my dwelling[g] among you, and I will not despise you. ¹²I will walk around among you; I will be your God, and you will be my people. ¹³I am the Lord your God, who brought you out of Egypt's land—who brought you out from being Egypt's slaves. I broke your bonds and made you stand up straight.

Covenant curses

¹⁴But if you do not obey me and do not carry out all these commands—¹⁵if you reject my rules and despise my regulations, not doing all my commands and breaking my covenant—¹⁶then I will do the following to you:

I will bring horrific things:[h] wasting diseases and fevers that make the eyes fail and drain life away.

You will plant seed for no reason because your enemies will eat the food.

¹⁷I will turn my face against you: you will be defeated by your enemies; those who hate you will rule over you; and you will run away even when no one is chasing you.

¹⁸If, despite all that, you still do not obey me, I will punish you for your sins seven more times: ¹⁹I will destroy your prideful power. I will turn your sky to iron and your land to bronze ²⁰so that your strength will be spent for no reason: your land will not produce its yield, and the trees of the land won't produce their fruit.

²¹If you continue to oppose me and are unwilling to obey me, I will strike you for your sins seven more times: ²²I will send wild animals against you, and they will kill your children and destroy your livestock. They will make you so few in number that your roads will seem deserted.

²³If, despite these things, you still do not accept my discipline and continue to oppose me, ²⁴then I will continue to oppose you. I will strike you for your sins seven more times: ²⁵I will bring the sword against you, avenging the breaking of the covenant.[i] If you retreat into your cities, I will send a plague on you, and you will be handed over to the enemy. ²⁶When I destroy your food supply, ten women will bake bread in a single oven, and they will ration out bread by weight. You will eat but will never get full.

SAILBOAT

Obedience

Covenant Blessings *Leviticus 26:1-13*

Leviticus contains many instructions that God commanded the Israelites to follow as a part of their covenant with God. This was their responsibility. But God also had a responsibility to the people. As part of the covenant, God promised that if the people lived according to God's Instruction, God would give them rain and their land would produce food they could eat. God promised that if they followed God's ways, God would dwell among you and be their God. God wanted very much to be in this close relationship with the Israelites.

Bet you can read this in 3 minutes. Ready, set, go!

---

[f]Heb uncertain [g]Or *tabernacle* [h]Precise nature of the diseases uncertain [i]Or *executing covenant vengeance*

²⁷If, despite all this, you still do not obey me and continue to oppose me, ²⁸then I will continue to oppose you—with anger! I will punish you for your sins seven more times: ²⁹You will eat the flesh of your own sons and daughters. ³⁰I will eliminate your shrines, chop down your incense altars, and pile your dead bodies on the dead bodies of your idols. I will despise you. ³¹I will turn your cities into ruins, I will devastate your sanctuaries, and I will not smell the soothing smells of your offerings. ³²I will personally devastate the land so much that your enemies who resettle it will be astonished by it. ³³I will scatter you among the nations. I will unsheathe my sword against you. Your land will be devastated and your cities will be ruins.

³⁴At that time, while it is devastated and you are in enemy territory, the land will enjoy its sabbaths. At that time, the land will rest and enjoy its sabbaths. ³⁵During the whole time it is devastated, it will have the rest it didn't have during the sabbaths you lived in it. ³⁶I will bring despair into the hearts of those of you who survive in enemy territory. Just the sound of a windblown leaf will put them to running, and they will run scared as if running from a sword! They will fall even when no one is chasing them! ³⁷They will stumble over each other as they would before a sword, even though no one is chasing them! You will have no power to stand before your enemies. ³⁸You will disappear among the nations—the land of your enemies will devour you. ³⁹Any of you who do survive will rot in enemy territory on account of their guilty deeds. And they will rot too on account of their ancestors' guilty deeds.

Covenant and restoration

⁴⁰But if they confess their and their ancestors' guilt for the wrongdoing they did to me, and for their continued opposition to me— ⁴¹which made me oppose them, so I took them into enemy territory—or if their uncircumcised hearts are humbled and they make up for their guilt, ⁴²then I will remember my covenant with Jacob. I will also remember my covenant with Isaac. And my covenant with Abraham. And I will remember the land. ⁴³The land will be absent of them and will be enjoying its sabbaths while it lies devastated, free

of them. They will be making up for their guilty deeds for no other reason than the fact that they rejected my regulations and despised my rules. ⁴⁴But despite all that, when they are in enemy territory, I will not reject them or despise them to the point of totally destroying them, breaking my covenant with them by doing so, because I am the LORD their God. ⁴⁵But for their sake I will remember the covenant with the first generation, the ones I brought out of Egypt's land in the sight of all the nations, in order to be their God; I am the LORD.

LIGHTHOUSE

CHANGED HEART AND LIFE

God Forgives *Leviticus 26:40-42*
God knew that God's people would make mistakes, turning away from God's ways. And yet God promised that if the people confessed their wrongdoing, God would remember the covenant with Jacob, Isaac, and Abraham. God provided a way for the people to make things right whenever they disobeyed. God asked the people to be honest about what they had done wrong, to ask for forgiveness, and then to live according to God's Instruction. 🔥

⁴⁶These are the rules, regulations, and instructions between the LORD and the Israelites that he gave through Moses on Mount Sinai.

Dedications

27 The LORD said to Moses, ²Speak to the Israelites and say to them: When a person makes a solemn promise to the LORD involving the value of a person, ³if it is the value for a male between 20 and 60 years old, his value is fifty silver shekels according to the sanctuary's shekel. ⁴If the person is a female, her value is thirty shekels. ⁵If the age of the person is between 5 and 20 years, the value for a male is twenty shekels, for a female ten shekels. ⁶If the age of the person is between one month and 5 years, the value for a male is five silver shekels, for a female three silver shekels. ⁷If the age of the person is 60 years or more, the value is fifteen shekels if the person is male, ten shekels for a female. ⁸But if financial difficulty prevents the promise maker from giving the full value, they must set the person before the priest. The priest will assign the person a value according to what the promise maker can afford.

⁹If a solemn promise involves livestock that can be offered to the LORD, any such animal given to the LORD will be considered holy. ¹⁰The promise maker cannot replace or substitute for it, either good for bad or bad for good. But if one should substitute one animal for another, both it and the substitute will be holy. ¹¹If the solemn promise involves any kind of unclean animal that cannot be offered to the LORD, the promise maker must set the animal before the priest. ¹²The priest will assign it a value, whether high or low.ʲ Its value will be what the priest says. ¹³If the promise maker wishes to buy it back, they must add one-fifth to its value.

¹⁴When someone dedicates their house to the LORD as holy, the priest will assign a value to it, whether high or low. The value is fixed, whatever value the priest assigns to it. ¹⁵If the one who dedicates the house wishes to buy it back, they must add one-fifth to its valued price, and it will be theirs again.

¹⁶If a person dedicates part of the land from their family property to the LORD, the value will be set according to the seed needed to plant it: fifty silver shekels per homer of barley seed. ¹⁷If the person dedicates the piece of land during the Jubilee year, its value will stay fixed. ¹⁸But if the person dedicates the piece after the Jubilee year, the priest will calculate the price according to the years that are left until the next Jubilee year, and the value will be reduced. ¹⁹If the one who dedicates the land wishes to buy it back, they must add one-fifth to its valued price, and it will be theirs again. ²⁰But if they do not buy it back or if it was sold to someone else, it is no longer able to be bought back. ²¹When the piece of land is released in the Jubilee year, it will be holy to the LORD like a piece of devoted

land; it will be the priest's property. ²²If the person dedicates land they purchased to the LORD—land that is not part of their family property—²³the priest will calculate the amount of its value until the Jubilee year. The person must pay the value on that day as a holy donation to the LORD. ²⁴In the Jubilee year the piece of land will return to the seller, to the one who is the original owner of the family property. ²⁵Every value will be according to the sanctuary's shekel. The shekel will be twenty gerahs.

²⁶But note that a person cannot dedicate any oldest offspring from livestock, which already belongs to the LORD because it is the oldest. Whether ox or sheep, it belongs to the LORD. ²⁷If it is an unclean animal, it may be bought back at its value plus twenty percent. If it is not bought back, it will be sold at its set value.

²⁸Also note that everything someone devotesᵏ to the LORD from their possessions—whether humans, animals, or pieces of land from their family property—cannot be sold or bought back. Every devoted thing is most holy to the LORD. ²⁹No human beings that have been devoted can be bought back; they must be executed.

³⁰All tenth-part giftsˡ from the land, whether of seed from the ground or fruit from the trees, belong to the LORD; they are holy to the LORD. ³¹If someone wishes to buy back part of their tenth-part gift, they must add one-fifth to it. ³²All tenth-part gifts from a herd or flock—every tenth animal that passes under the shepherd's staff—will be holy to the LORD. ³³The one bringing the tenth-part gift must not pick out the good from the bad, and cannot substitute any animal. But if one should substitute an animal, both it and the substitute will be holy and cannot be bought back.

³⁴These are the commands that the LORD gave Moses on Mount Sinai for the Israelites.

ʲOr *good or bad*; also in 27:14 ᵏOr *places under the ban* (also in 27:29), a technique of holy war, in which all is dedicated to the deity who helps in the battle; it often involved total destruction. ˡOr *tithes*

Numbers

T he book of Numbers contains a lot of numbers, lists, and detailed commands. But this book also tells of a desert adventure with God's people. It tells a sad story of the Israelites' refusal to trust God.

After God freed the Israelites from slavery, God led them into the desert between Egypt and Israel, the land God had promised to give Abraham. God planned to teach them and train them to follow God. When Moses sent spies to check out the land they had been promised, the spies discovered it was full of food and riches, just as God had said. But ten of the twelve spies who saw the land said the people living there were too big and strong to conquer. Those ten spies told the Israelites they were better off in Egypt living as slaves.

Joshua and Caleb were the only two spies who trusted God to help the people conquer the land. Although they told the people God would help, the people refused to listen. God grew so angry that God said none of the people who doubted God's power would ever enjoy the land (Num 13–14). Because of this, the Israelites spent the next forty years wandering the desert. Those who didn't trust God died in the desert, leaving the land of Canaan for their children to possess.

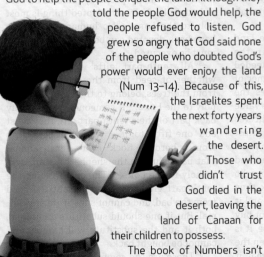

The book of Numbers isn't just about counting people. It shows that life with God is a challenging journey, often full of complaints, but we can trust God to lead us through! ◦

First census

1 The LORD spoke to Moses in the Sinai desert in the meeting tent on the first day of the second month,[a] in the second year after they left the land of Egypt: [2]Take a census of the entire Israelite community by their clans and their households, recording the name of every male, [3]20 years old and above, who is eligible for military service in Israel. These you and Aaron will enlist in their military units. [4]Take with you one man from each tribe who is the head of his household. [5]These are the names of the men who will assist you:

from Reuben, Elizur, Shedeur's son;
[6]from Simeon, Shelumiel, Zurishaddai's son;
[7]from Judah, Nahshon, Amminadab's son;
[8]from Issachar, Nethanel, Zuar's son;
[9]from Zebulun, Eliab, Helon's son;
[10]from Joseph's sons:
from Ephraim, Elishama, Ammihud's son;
from Manasseh, Gamaliel, Pedahzur's son;
[11]from Benjamin, Abidan, Gideoni's son;
[12]from Dan, Ahiezer, Ammishaddai's son;
[13]from Asher, Pagiel, Ochran's son;
[14]from Gad, Eliasaph, Deuel's son;
[15]from Naphtali, Ahira, Enan's son.

[16]These are the ones appointed from the community, chiefs of their ancestral tribes and leaders of the divisions of Israel.

[17]Moses and Aaron took these men who were selected by name [18]and they assembled the entire community on the first day of the second month. They registered them by their clans and their households, recording the name of each male 20 years old and above. [19]Moses enlisted them in the Sinai desert just as the LORD commanded him.

[20]There were the descendants of Reuben, Israel's oldest, registered by their clans and their households. Every man 20 years old and above eligible for military service was individually recorded by name. [21]Those enlisted from the tribe of Reuben were 46,500.

[22]There were the descendants of Simeon, registered by their clans and their households. Every male 20 years old and above eligible for military service was individually recorded by name. [23]Those enlisted from the tribe of Simeon were 59,300.

[24]There were the descendants of Gad, registered by their clans and their households. The men 20 years old and above eligible for military service were recorded by name. [25]Those enlisted from the tribe of Gad were 45,650.

[26]There were the descendants of Judah, registered by their clans and their households. The men 20 years old and above eligible for military service were recorded by name. [27]Those enlisted from the tribe of Judah were 74,600.

[28]There were the descendants of Issachar, registered by their clans and their households. The men 20 years old and above eligible for military service were recorded by name. [29]Those enlisted from the tribe of Issachar were 54,400.

[30]There were the descendants of Zebulun, registered by their clans and their households. The men 20 years old and above eligible for military service were recorded by name. [31]Those enlisted from the tribe of Zebulun were 57,400.

[32]From Joseph's descendants there were the descendants of Ephraim, registered by their clans and their households. The men 20 years old and above eligible for military service were recorded by name. [33]Those enlisted from the tribe of Ephraim were 40,500.

[34]There were the descendants of Manasseh, registered by their clans and their households. The men 20 years old and above eligible for military service were recorded by name. [35]Those enlisted from the tribe of Manasseh were 32,200.

[36]There were the descendants of Benjamin, registered by their clans and their households. The men 20 years old and above eligible for military service were recorded by name. [37]Those enlisted from the tribe of Benjamin were 35,400.

[38]There were the descendants of Dan, registered by their clans and their households. The men 20 years old and above eligible for military service were recorded by name. [39]Those enlisted from the tribe of Dan were 62,700.

[40]There were the descendants of Asher, registered by their clans and their

---

[a]April–May, Iyar

households. The men 20 years old and above eligible for military service were recorded by name. [41]Those enlisted from the tribe of Asher were 41,500.

[42]There were the descendants of Naphtali, registered by their clans and their households. The men 20 years old and above eligible for military service were recorded by name. [43]Those enlisted from the tribe of Naphtali were 53,400.

[44]These are the ones who were enlisted by Moses, Aaron, and the twelve chiefs of Israel, each from his own household. [45]All the Israelites 20 years old and above eligible for military service in Israel were enlisted by their households. [46]All those enlisted were 603,550. [47]But the Levites, belonging to their own ancestral tribe, weren't enlisted along with them.

The Levites' exclusion from the census

[48]The LORD spoke to Moses: [49]You must not enlist the tribe of Levi, nor should you take their census along with the Israelites. [50]Rather, assign the Levites to the covenant dwelling, to all its equipment, and to everything that belongs to it. They will carry the dwelling and all its equipment, perform its religious ceremonies, and camp around the dwelling. [51]When it's time to break camp, the Levites will take down the dwelling; and when it's time to make camp, the Levites will set up the dwelling. Any other person who approaches will be put to death. [52]The Israelites will camp each in their own place under the banner of their own military unit. [53]But the Levites will camp around the covenant dwelling so that God's anger will not strike the Israelite community. The Levites will guard the covenant dwelling.

[54]The Israelites did everything exactly as the LORD commanded Moses.

The wilderness camp's arrangement

2 The LORD spoke to Moses and Aaron: [2]The Israelites will camp each under the banner with the symbol of their household. They will camp around the meeting tent some distance from it.

The camp's east side

[3]On the east side toward the sunrise will be the banner of Judah's camp with its military units. The chief of the people of Judah is Nahshon, Amminadab's son. [4]His military unit and those enlisted in it are 74,600. [5]Those camping on one side of him are the tribe of Issachar. The chief of the people of Issachar is Nethanel, Zuar's son. [6]His military unit and those enlisted in it are 54,400. [7]On the other side, the tribe of Zebulun: the chief of the people of Zebulun is Eliab, Helon's son. [8]His military unit and those enlisted in it are 57,400. [9]All those enlisted in Judah's camp with their military units are 186,400. They will march first.

The camp's south side

[10]On the south side will be the banner of Reuben's camp with its military units. The chief of the people of Reuben is Elizur, Shedeur's son. [11]His military unit and those enlisted in it are 46,500. [12]Those camping on one side of him are the tribe of Simeon. The chief of the people of Simeon is Shelumiel, Zurishaddai's son. [13]His military unit and those enlisted in it are 59,300. [14]On the other side, the tribe of Gad: the chief of the people of Gad is Eliasaph, Reuel's son. [15]His military unit and those enlisted in it are 45,650. [16]All those enlisted in Reuben's camp with their military units are 151,450. They will march second.

The camp's center

[17]The meeting tent and the Levites' camp will march in the center of the camps. They will march in the same order as they camp: each in position under his banner.

The camp's west side

[18]On the west will be the banner of Ephraim's camp with its military units. The chief of the people of Ephraim is Elishama, Ammihud's son. [19]His military unit and those enlisted in it are 40,500. [20]On one side of him is the tribe of Manasseh. The chief of the people of Manasseh is Gamaliel, Pedahzur's son. [21]His military unit and those enlisted in it are 32,200. [22]On the other side, the tribe of Benjamin: the chief of the people of Benjamin is Abidan, Gideoni's son. [23]His military unit and those enlisted in it are 35,400. [24]All those enlisted in Ephraim's camp with their military units are 108,100. They will march third.

The camp's north side

²⁵On the north will be the banner of Dan's camp with its military units. The chief of the people of Dan is Ahiezer, Ammishaddai's son. ²⁶His military unit and those enlisted in it are 62,700. ²⁷Those camping on one side of him are the tribe of Asher. The chief of the people of Asher is Pagiel, Ochran's son. ²⁸His military unit and those enlisted in it are 41,500. ²⁹On the other side, the tribe of Naphtali: the chief of the people of Naphtali is Ahira, Enan's son. ³⁰His military unit and those enlisted in it are 53,400. ³¹All those enlisted in the camp of Dan are 157,600. They will march last under their banners.

³²These are the enlisted Israelites by their households. The total enlisted in the camps with their military units is 603,550. ³³But the Levites weren't enlisted among the Israelites, as the Lord had commanded Moses. ³⁴The Israelites did everything exactly as the Lord had commanded Moses: they camped under their banners and they marched by their clans and by their households.

Aaron's sons

3 These are the descendants of Aaron and Moses at the time when the Lord spoke with Moses on Mount Sinai. ²These are the names of Aaron's sons: Nadab the oldest, and Abihu, Eleazar, and Ithamar. ³These are the names of Aaron's sons, who are the anointed priests and ordained to the priesthood. ⁴Nadab and Abihu died before the Lord when they made an unauthorized offering to the Lord in the Sinai desert. They didn't have any sons. Eleazar and Ithamar served as priests during the lifetime of their father Aaron.

The Levites' first census

⁵The Lord spoke to Moses: ⁶Bring near the tribe of Levi and place them before Aaron the priest. They will assist him. ⁷They will perform duties for him and for the entire community before the meeting tent, doing the work of the dwelling. ⁸They will be responsible for all the equipment of the meeting tent and the duties on behalf of the Israelites when they do the work of the dwelling. ⁹You will give the Levites to Aaron and his sons. They have been assigned as a gift to him from the Israelites. ¹⁰You will appoint Aaron and his sons to be responsible for the priesthood. Any other person who approaches will be put to death.

¹¹The Lord spoke to Moses: ¹²I claim the Levites from the Israelites in place of all the oldest males who open an Israelite womb. The Levites are mine ¹³because all the oldest males are mine. When I killed all the oldest males in the land of Egypt, I reserved for myself all the oldest males in Israel, both humans and animals. They are mine; I am the Lord.

¹⁴The Lord spoke to Moses in the Sinai desert: ¹⁵Enroll the Levites by their households and their clans. You will enroll all the males over one month old. ¹⁶Moses enrolled them according to the Lord's word as he was commanded. ¹⁷These were Levi's sons by name: Gershon, Kohath, and Merari. ¹⁸These were the names of Gershon's sons by their clans: Libni and Shimei. ¹⁹Kohath's sons by their clans: Amram, Izhar, Hebron, and Uzziel. ²⁰Merari's sons by their clans: Mahli and Mushi. These were the clans of Levi by their households.

²¹To Gershon belonged the clans of Libni and Shimei. These were the clans of the Gershonites. ²²Their enrollment, according to the number of males over one month old, was 7,500. ²³The clans of the Gershonites were to camp behind the dwelling on the west side. ²⁴The chief of the household of the Gershonites was Eliasaph, Lael's son. ²⁵In the dwelling, the Gershonites were responsible for the meeting tent, the tent with its covering, the screen for the entrance of the meeting tent, ²⁶the curtains of the courtyard, the screen for the entrance of the courtyard surrounding the meeting tent and the altar, and its cords—all these structures.

²⁷To Kohath belonged the clans of the Amramites, Izharites, Hebronites, and Uzzielites. These were the clans of the Kohathites. ²⁸The number of males over one month old, who would perform duties for the sanctuary, was 8,600. ²⁹The clans of the Kohathites were to camp on the south side of the dwelling. ³⁰The chief of the household representing the clans of the Kohathites was Elizaphan, Uzziel's son. ³¹They were responsible for the chest, the table, the lampstand, the altars, the equipment of the sanctuary with which they would minister, and the screen—all these

furnishings. [32]The head chief over the chiefs of the Levites was Eleazar the son of Aaron the priest. He was supervisor over those performing the duties of the sanctuary.

[33]To Merari belonged the clans of Mahli and Mushi. These were the clans of the Merarites. [34]Their enrollment, according to the number of males over one month old, was 6,200. [35]The chief of the household representing the clans of the Merarites was Zuriel, Abihail's son. They were to camp on the north side of the dwelling. [36]The Merarites were assigned responsibility for the frames of the dwelling, its bars, pillars, bases, and all its equipment—all these items—[37]and the pillars of the courtyard all around, their bases, pegs, and cords.

[38]Those camping in front of the dwelling eastward (that is, before the meeting tent on the east side) were Moses, Aaron, and his sons, who performed the duties of the sanctuary as service for the Israelites. Anyone else who approached would be put to death. [39]The total enrollment of the Levites, all the males over one month old whom Moses and Aaron enrolled by orders from the LORD, according to their clans, was 22,000.

Levites rescue the oldest male Israelites

[40]The LORD said to Moses: Enroll all the oldest males of the Israelites over one month of age and record their names. [41]Take the Levites for me, in place of all the oldest sons of the Israelites, for I am the LORD, and the cattle of the Levites in place of all the oldest cattle of the Israelites. [42]Moses enrolled all the oldest males of the Israelites as the LORD commanded. [43]All the oldest males over one month old, recorded by name according to their enrollment, were 22,273.

[44]Then the LORD spoke to Moses: [45]Take the Levites in place of all the oldest Israelites and the cattle of the Levites in place of their cattle. The Levites are mine; I am the LORD. [46]To rescue the 273 remaining oldest Israelites over and above the number of Levites, [47]you will receive five shekels each. You will receive them according to the sanctuary shekel of twenty gerahs to the shekel. [48]You will give the money for their rescue to Aaron and his sons.

[b]Or *dolphin skin*; see also 4:8, 10–12

[49]So Moses took the money from those rescued over and above the ones rescued by the Levites. [50]He took the money from the oldest of the Israelites, 1,365 shekels, according to the sanctuary shekel. [51]Moses gave the money for those rescued to Aaron and his sons according to the LORD's word, as the LORD commanded Moses.

LIGHTHOUSE

GIVING MY BEST

Giving Our Best Numbers 3:40-51
God gave very detailed instructions to the Israelites, telling them how to organize themselves as a community. God wanted them to give their very best to God. Following these instructions was a way for them to show their faith in God with their actions. ◗

Second census and the Levites' duties

The Kohathites' duties

4 The LORD spoke to Moses and Aaron: [2]Take a census of the Kohathites from among the Levites by their clans and their households, [3]from 30 to 50 years old, all who are eligible for service to do the work of the meeting tent. [4]These are the responsibilities of the Kohathites in the meeting tent: the most holy things.

[5]When it's time to break camp, Aaron and his sons will enter and take down the screening curtain, and they will cover the chest containing the covenant with it. [6]Then they will place a covering of fine leather[b] on it. They will spread a whole cloth of blue over it, and they will set its poles in place. [7]They will spread a blue cloth on the presentation table and place on it the plates, the dishes, the bowls, and the container for the drink offering. The usual bread will be on it. [8]They will spread on them a red cloth, cover it with fine leather, and set its poles in place. [9]They will take a blue cloth and cover the lampstand used for light, its lamps, its extinguishers, its trays, and all the containers for oil that are used in its service. [10]They will place it and its equipment in a covering of fine leather, and then place it on the carrying frame. [11]They

will spread a blue cloth on the gold altar and cover it with fine leather. [12]They will take all the service equipment used in the sanctuary, place it in a blue cloth, and cover it with fine leather. Then they will place it on the carrying frame. [13]They will remove the ashes from the altar and spread a purple cloth on it. [14]They will place on it all the equipment used for servicing it, the censers, the meat fork, the shovels, the bowls, all the equipment of the altar. They will spread a covering of fine leather over it and then set its poles in place.

[15]Aaron and his sons will finish covering the sanctuary and all the equipment of the sanctuary when it is time to break camp. After that the Kohathites will enter to carry it, but they will not touch the sanctuary, lest they die. These are the objects in the dwelling that the Kohathites are to carry. [16]But Eleazar son of Aaron the priest will have oversight of the oil for lighting, the fragrant incense, the regular grain offering, and the anointing oil, as well as oversight of the entire dwelling and everything in it related to the sanctuary and its equipment.

[17]The LORD spoke to Moses and Aaron: [18]You must not let the tribe of the Kohathite clans be eliminated from the Levites. [19]This is what you must do for them so that they stay alive and don't die when they approach the most holy things. Aaron and his sons will enter and assign each of them his work and his load. [20]But they may not enter to look at the sanctuary even for a moment, lest they die.

The Gershonites' duties

[21]The LORD spoke to Moses: [22]Take a census of the Gershonites also, by their households and their clans. [23]You will enroll those from 30 to 50 years old, all who are eligible for service to do work in the dwelling. [24]This is the duty of the Gershonite clans for work and for carrying the load: [25]They will carry the fabric of the dwelling, the meeting tent with its covering, the outer covering of fine leather, the screen for the entrance of the meeting tent, [26]the curtains of the courtyard, the screen of the entrance at the gate of the courtyard that surrounds the meeting tent and the altar, their cords, and all their equipment for their work. They will do everything that needs to be done with these objects.

[27]All the duties of the Gershonites for carrying their load and for their work will be at the command of Aaron and his sons. You will assign to them the responsibility to carry their load. [28]This is the work of the Gershonite clans in the dwelling. Their responsibility will be under Ithamar son of Aaron the priest.

The Merarites' duties

[29]You will enroll the Merarites by their clans and their households. [30]You will enroll those from 30 to 50 years old, all who are eligible for service to do work in the meeting tent. [31]This is what they are responsible to carry as their work in the meeting tent: the frames of the meeting tent, its bars, pillars, and bases; [32]the pillars of the courtyard all around, with their bases, pegs, cords, and all the equipment used with them. You will list by name the objects they are required to carry. [33]This is the duty of the Merarite clans for all their work in the meeting tent under the supervision of Ithamar son of Aaron the priest.

Summary of the census

[34]So Moses, Aaron, and the chiefs of the community enrolled the Kohathites by their clans and their households, [35]those from 30 to 50 years old who were eligible for work in the meeting tent. [36]Their enrollment by their clans was 2,750. [37]These are the enrolled of the Kohathite clans, all who worked in the meeting tent and whom Moses and Aaron enrolled according to the LORD's command through Moses.

[38]The enrollment of the Gershonites by their clans and their households, [39]those 30 to 50 years old who were eligible for work in the meeting tent: [40]their enrollment by their clans and their households was 2,630. [41]These are the enrolled of the Gershonite clans, all who worked in the meeting tent, and whom Moses and Aaron enrolled according to the LORD's command.

[42]The enrollment of the Merarite clans by their clans and their households, [43]those 30 to 50 years old who were eligible for work in the meeting tent: [44]their enrollment by their clans was 3,200. [45]These are the enrolled of the Merarite clans, whom Moses and Aaron enrolled according to the LORD's command through Moses.

[46]All the enrolled Levites whom Moses, Aaron, and the chiefs of Israel enrolled by their clans and their households, [47]those 30 to 50 years old who were eligible to do the work and to carry the load of the meeting tent: [48]their enrollment was 8,580. [49]Each was enrolled by the Lord's command through Moses to work and to carry his load. Each was assigned just as the Lord had commanded Moses.

Instructions about purity in the camp

5 The Lord spoke to Moses: [2]Command the Israelites to send out from the camp anyone with a skin disease, an oozing discharge, or who has become unclean from contact with a corpse. [3]You must send out both male and female. You must send them outside the camp so that they will not make their camp, where I live among them, unclean.

[4]The Israelites did so and sent them outside the camp. The Israelites did just what the Lord said to Moses.

[5]The Lord spoke to Moses: [6]Tell the Israelites: When a man or a woman commits any sin against anyone else, thus breaking faith with the Lord, that person becomes guilty. [7]Such persons will confess the sin they have done. Each will make payment for his guilt, add one-fifth more, and give it to the injured party. [8]If the person has no close relative to whom the payment can be made, then the compensation payment will go to the Lord for the priest. This is in addition to the ram of reconciliation by which the guilty party himself is reconciled. [9]Any gift offering from all the sacred donations that the Israelites offer will be the property of the priest. [10]The sacred donations belong to each person alone; whatever anyone gives to the priest will be his.

A woman accused of adultery

[11]The Lord spoke to Moses: [12]Speak to the Israelites and say to them: A man may suspect that his wife has had an affair[c] and has broken faith with him, [13]that a man has had intercourse with her unknown to her husband and that she has defiled herself in secret—even though there are no witnesses and she isn't caught. [14]If jealousy overcomes him and he is jealous of his wife who has defiled herself, or

did you know? Whenever the people of God moved, the Gershonites, Kohathites, and Meranites carried everything from the meeting tent. It took more than 8,500 men to carry all the parts of the meeting tent from place to place when the people moved!

if jealousy overcomes him and he is jealous of his wife who hasn't defiled herself, [15]then the man will bring his wife to the priest. He will bring the offering required for her, one-tenth of an ephah[d] of barley flour. He will not pour oil on it, nor offer frankincense with it, because it is a grain offering for jealousy, a grain offering for recognition in order to recognize guilt. [16]The priest will bring her close and make her stand before the Lord. [17]The priest will take holy water in a clay jar, and taking dust from the floor of the dwelling, the priest will place it in the water. [18]The priest will make the woman stand before the Lord, let the hair of the woman hang down, and place the grain offering for recognition, that is, the grain offering for jealousy, in her hands. The water of bitterness that brings the curse will be in the hands of the priest.

[19]Then the priest will make her swear a solemn pledge, saying to the woman, "If no man has slept with you and if you haven't had an affair, becoming defiled while married to your husband, then be immune from the water of bitterness that brings these curses. [20]But if you have had an affair while married to your husband, if you have defiled yourself, and a man other than your husband has had intercourse with you"— [21]then the priest must make the woman utter the curse and say to the woman, "May the Lord make you a curse and a harmful pledge among your people, when the Lord induces a miscarriage and your womb discharges. [22]And may the water that brings these curses enter your stomach and make your womb discharge and make you miscarry."

And the woman will say, "I agree, I agree."

[23]The priest will write these curses in the scroll and wipe them off into the water of bitterness. [24]Then he will make the woman drink the water of bitterness that brings the curse. And the water that brings the curse will enter

---

[c]Or goes astray; see also 5:19–20, 29 [d]Two quarts; one ephah is approximately twenty quarts dry.

her, causing bitterness. [25]The priest will take the grain offering for jealousy from the woman's hands, elevate the grain offering before the LORD, and bring it to the altar. [26]The priest will take a handful of the grain offering as a token part of it and turn it into smoke on the altar. And afterward he will make the woman drink the water. [27]When he has made her drink the water, if she has defiled herself and has broken faith with her husband, then the water that brings the curse will enter her, causing bitterness, and her womb will discharge and she will miscarry. The woman will be a curse among her people. [28]But if the woman hasn't defiled herself and she is pure, then she will be immune and able to conceive.

[29]These are the instructions about jealousy, when a wife has an affair while married to her husband and defiles herself, [30]or when jealousy overcomes a man and he is jealous of his wife. The priest will make the woman stand before the LORD and will follow all these instructions concerning her. [31]The man will be free from guilt, but the woman will bear her guilt.

Instructions for the nazirite

6The LORD spoke to Moses: [2]Speak to the Israelites and say to them: If a man or a woman makes a binding promise to be a nazirite in order to be dedicated to the LORD, [3]that person must refrain from wine and brandy. He or she may not drink wine vinegar or brandy vinegar, nor drink any grape juice or eat grapes, whether fresh or dried. [4]While a nazirite, the person may not eat anything produced from the grapevine, not even its seeds or skin.

[5]For the term of the nazirite promise, no razor may be used on the head until the period of dedication to the LORD is fulfilled. The person is to be holy, letting his or her hair grow untrimmed. [6]The period of dedication to the LORD also requires that the person not go near a corpse, [7]whether father, mother, brother, or sister. Nazirites should not defile themselves because of the death of these people, because they bear the sign of their dedication to God on their heads.

[8]While a nazirite, the person is holy to the LORD. [9]If someone suddenly dies nearby, defiling the head of the nazirite, he or she will shave the head on the day of cleansing; they will shave it on the seventh day. [10]On the eighth day the person will bring two turtledoves or two young doves to the priest at the entrance of the meeting tent. [11]The priest will offer one for a purification offering and the other as an entirely burned offering. He will seek reconciliation for the person on account of the guilt acquired from the corpse, and he will make the head holy again on that same day. [12]The person will be rededicated to the LORD as a nazirite and bring a one-year-old male lamb for a compensation offering. The previous period will be invalid, because the nazirite promise was defiled.

[13]This is the Instruction for the nazirite. When the term as a nazirite is completed, the person will be brought to the entrance of the meeting tent [14]and offer a gift to the LORD, consisting of a flawless one-year-old male lamb as an entirely burned offering, a flawless one-year-old female lamb as a purification offering, one flawless ram as a well-being sacrifice, [15]and a basket of loaves of unleavened bread made with fine flour and mixed with oil, and unleavened wafers spread with oil, along with their grain offering and their drink offering. [16]The priest will come close to the LORD and offer the purification and entirely burned offerings. [17]The ram he will offer as a well-being sacrifice to the LORD with the basket of unleavened bread; then the priest will offer the grain offering and the drink offering. [18]The nazirite will shave his ordained head at the meeting tent's entrance, take the hair from his ordained head, and put it in the fire under the well-being sacrifice. [19]The priest will take the shoulder from the ram after it is boiled, one piece of unleavened bread from the basket, and one unleavened wafer, and place them in the hands of the nazirite after the ordained head is shaved. [20]Then the priest will raise them as an uplifted offering before the LORD; they are holy to the priest, with the breast of the uplifted offering and the thigh of the gift offering. After this the nazirite may drink wine.

[21]This is the instruction for the nazirite who takes the solemn promise. That person's offering to the LORD will be in accordance with the nazirite promise, in addition to whatever else the person may have offered.

The person must do just as they have promised, in adherence with the nazirite promise.

Priestly blessing

[22] The Lord spoke to Moses: [23] Tell Aaron and his sons: You will bless the Israelites as follows. Say to them:

[24] The Lord bless you and protect you. [25] The Lord make his face shine on you and be gracious to you.

Memorize
Num 6:24-26

[26] The Lord lift up his face to you and grant you peace.

[27] They will place my name on the Israelites, and I will bless them.

The dwelling's dedication

7 On the day when Moses finished setting up the dwelling, he anointed and made it holy. All its equipment, as well as the altar and all its equipment, he also anointed and made holy. [2] The chiefs of Israel, the leaders of their households, made their presentations. They were the tribal chiefs and those who were in charge of the enlistment. [3] They brought their offerings before the Lord: six covered wagons and twelve oxen—a wagon for every two chiefs, and an ox for every chief. They brought them near before the dwelling.

[4] The Lord said to Moses: [5] Take these from them and use them for service in the meeting tent. Give them to the Levites according to their duties.

[6] So Moses took the wagons and the oxen, and he gave them to the Levites. [7] Two wagons and four oxen he gave to the Gershonites for their duty. [8] Four wagons and eight oxen he gave to the Merarites for their duty under the supervision of Ithamar, Aaron the priest's son. [9] But to the Kohathites he gave nothing because their duty concerned the holy things that had to be carried on the shoulders. [10] The chiefs made their presentations for the dedication of the altar on the day it was anointed. The chiefs presented their offerings before the altar.

[11] The Lord said to Moses: One chief per day will present their offering for the dedication of the altar.

[12] The one presenting his offering on the first day was Nahshon, Amminadab's son, from the tribe of Judah. [13] His offering was one silver dish weighing one hundred thirty shekels, one silver basin weighing seventy shekels according to the sanctuary shekel, both of them full of fine flour mixed with oil for a grain offering; [14] one gold bowl weighing ten shekels full of incense; [15] one bull from the herd, one ram, and one year-old male lamb for an entirely burned offering; [16] one male goat for a purification offering; [17] and for the well-being sacrifice two oxen, five rams, five male goats, and five male lambs a year old. This was the offering of Nahshon, Amminadab's son.

[18] On the second day Nethanel, Zuar's son, the chief of Issachar, presented his offering. [19] He presented as his offering one silver dish weighing one hundred thirty shekels, one silver basin weighing seventy shekels according to the sanctuary shekel, both of them full of fine flour mixed with oil for a grain offering; [20] one gold bowl weighing ten shekels full of incense; [21] one bull from the herd, one ram, and one year-old male lamb for an entirely burned offering; [22] one male goat for a purification offering; [23] and for the well-being sacrifice two oxen, five rams, five male goats, and five male lambs a year old. This was the offering of Nethanel, Zuar's son.

[24] On the third day Zebulun's Chief Eliab, Helon's son: [25] his offering was one silver dish weighing one hundred thirty shekels, one silver basin weighing seventy shekels according to the sanctuary shekel, both of them full of fine flour mixed with oil for a grain offering; [26] one gold bowl weighing ten shekels full of incense; [27] one bull from the herd, one ram, and one year-old male lamb for an entirely burned offering; [28] one male goat for a purification offering; [29] and for the well-being sacrifice, two oxen, five rams, five male goats, and five male lambs a year old. This was the offering of Eliab, Helon's son.

[30] On the fourth day Reuben's Chief Elizur, Shedeur's son: [31] his offering was one silver dish weighing one hundred thirty shekels, one silver basin weighing seventy shekels according to the sanctuary shekel, both of them full of fine flour mixed with oil for a grain offering; [32] one gold bowl weighing ten shekels full of incense; [33] one bull from the herd, one ram, and one year-old male lamb for an entirely burned offering; [34] one male goat for a purification offering; [35] and for the well-being

sacrifice two oxen, five rams, five male goats, and five male lambs a year old. This was the offering of Elizur, Shedeur's son.

36On the fifth day Simeon's Chief Shelumiel, Zurishaddai's son: 37his offering was one silver dish weighing one hundred thirty shekels, one basin weighing seventy shekels according to the sanctuary shekel, both of them full of fine flour mixed with oil for a grain offering; 38one gold bowl weighing ten shekels full of incense; 39one bull from the herd, one ram, and one year-old male lamb for an entirely burned offering; 40one male goat for a purification offering; 41and for the well-being sacrifice two oxen, five rams, five male goats, and five male lambs a year old. This was the offering of Shelumiel, Zurishaddai's son.

42On the sixth day Gad's Chief Eliasaph, Deuel's son: 43his offering was one silver dish weighing one hundred thirty shekels, one silver basin weighing seventy shekels according to the sanctuary shekel, both of them full of fine flour mixed with oil for a grain offering; 44one gold bowl weighing ten shekels full of incense; 45one bull from the herd, one ram, and one year-old male lamb for an entirely burned offering; 46one male goat for a purification offering; 47and for the well-being sacrifice two oxen, five rams, five male goats, and five male lambs a year old. This was the offering of Eliasaph, Deuel's son.

48On the seventh day Ephraim's Chief Elishama, Ammihud's son: 49his offering was one silver dish weighing one hundred thirty shekels, one silver basin weighing seventy shekels according to the sanctuary shekel, both of them full of fine flour mixed with oil for a grain offering; 50one gold bowl weighing ten shekels full of incense; 51one bull from the herd, one ram, and one year-old male lamb for an entirely burned offering; 52one male goat for a purification offering; 53and for the well-being sacrifice two oxen, five rams, five male goats, and five male lambs a year old. This was the offering of Elishama, Ammihud's son.

54On the eighth day Manasseh's Chief Gamaliel, Pedahzur's son: 55his offering was one silver dish weighing one hundred thirty shekels, one silver basin weighing seventy shekels by the sanctuary scale, both of them full of fine flour mixed with oil for a grain offering; 56one gold bowl weighing ten shekels

full of incense; 57one bull from the herd, one ram, and one year-old male lamb for an entirely burned offering; 58one male goat for a purification offering; 59and for the well-being sacrifice two oxen, five rams, five male goats, and five male lambs a year old. This was the offering of Gamaliel, Pedahzur's son.

60On the ninth day Benjamin's Chief Abidan, Gideoni's son: 61his offering was one silver dish weighing one hundred thirty shekels, one silver basin weighing seventy shekels according to the sanctuary shekel, both of them full of fine flour mixed with oil for a grain offering; 62one gold bowl weighing ten shekels full of incense; 63one bull from the herd, one ram, and one year-old male lamb for an entirely burned offering; 64one male goat for a purification offering; 65and for the well-being sacrifice two oxen, five rams, five male goats, and five male lambs a year old. This was the offering of Abidan, Gideoni's son.

66On the tenth day Dan's Chief Ahiezer, Ammishaddai's son: 67his offering was one silver dish weighing one hundred thirty shekels, one silver basin weighing seventy shekels according to the sanctuary shekel, both of them full of fine flour mixed with oil for a grain offering; 68one gold bowl weighing ten shekels full of incense; 69one bull from the herd, one ram, and one year-old male lamb for an entirely burned offering; 70one male goat for a purification offering; 71and for the well-being sacrifice two oxen, five rams, five male goats, and five male lambs a year old. This was the offering of Ahiezer, Ammishaddai's son.

72On the eleventh day Asher's Chief Pagiel, Ochran's son: 73his offering was one silver dish weighing one hundred thirty shekels, one silver basin weighing seventy shekels according to the sanctuary shekel, both of them full of fine flour mixed with oil for a grain offering; 74one gold bowl weighing ten shekels full of incense; 75one bull from the herd, one ram, and one year-old male lamb for an entirely burned offering; 76one male goat for a purification offering; 77and for the well-being sacrifice two oxen, five rams, five male goats, and five male lambs a year old. This was the offering of Pagiel, Ochran's son.

78On the twelfth day Naphtali's Chief Ahira, Enan's son: 79his offering was one silver dish weighing one hundred thirty shekels, one silver basin weighing seventy shekels according to the sanctuary shekel, both of them full of fine flour mixed with oil for a grain offering; 80one gold bowl weighing ten shekels full of incense; 81one bull from the herd, one ram, one year-old male lamb for an entirely burned offering; 82one male goat for a purification offering; 83and for the well-being sacrifice two oxen, five rams, five male goats, and five male lambs a year old. This was the offering of Ahira, Enan's son.

84This is what the Israelite chiefs provided for the dedication of the altar on the day it was anointed: twelve silver dishes, twelve silver basins, and twelve gold bowls; 85each silver dish weighing one hundred thirty shekels and each basin seventy shekels—all the silver equipment weighed two thousand four hundred shekels according to the sanctuary shekel; 86the twelve gold bowls full of incense weighing ten shekels each according to the sanctuary shekel—all the gold of the bowls weighed one hundred twenty shekels; 87all the animals for the entirely burned offering were twelve bulls, twelve rams, twelve male lambs a year old, with their grain offering; twelve male goats for the purification offering; 88and all the animals for the well-being sacrifice were twenty-four bulls, sixty rams, sixty male goats, and sixty male lambs a year old. This was the dedication offering for the altar after it was anointed.

Moses in the dwelling

89When Moses entered the meeting tent to speak with the Lord,e he would hear the voice speaking to him from above the coverf that was on the chest containing the covenant, from between the two winged creatures. In this way he spoke to Moses.

The lampstand

8 The Lord spoke to Moses: 2Speak to Aaron and say to him: When you set them up, the seven lamps will give light in front of the lampstand.

3Aaron did so. He set up its lamps in front of the lampstand as the Lord commanded Moses. 4This is how the lampstand was made: it was hammered gold; from its base to its flower it was hammered. Moses made the lampstand according to the vision that the Lord had shown Moses.

Dedication of the Levites

5The Lord spoke to Moses: 6Separate the Levites from the Israelites and cleanse them. 7This is what you will do to them to cleanse them: Sprinkle water of purification on them, have them shave their bodies, wash their clothes, and cleanse themselves. 8They will take a bull from the herd, with its grain offering of fine flour mixed with oil. You will take a second bull from the herd for a purification offering. 9You will bring the Levites before the meeting tent and gather the entire Israelite community. 10Then you will bring the Levites into the Lord's presence, and the Israelites will lay their hands on the Levites. 11Aaron will present the Levites as an uplifted offering in the Lord's presence from the Israelites so that they may do the Lord's service. 12Then the Levites will lay their hands on the heads of the bulls, and Aaron will offer one as a purification offering and the other as an entirely burned offering to the Lord in order to seek reconciliation for the Levites.

13You will have the Levites stand before Aaron and his sons and you will present them as an uplifted offering to the Lord. 14You will separate the Levites from the Israelites, and the Levites will be mine. 15The Levites will enter to serve the meeting tent, after you have cleansed them and presented them as an uplifted offering. 16They are given over to me from the Israelites in place of all the newborn, the oldest of all the Israelites. I take them for myself. 17Every oldest male among the Israelites is mine, whether human or animal. When I killed all the oldest males in the land of Egypt, I dedicated them to myself. 18I have taken the Levites in place of all the oldest among the Israelites. 19I have selected the Levites from the Israelites for Aaron and his sons to perform the service of the Israelites in the meeting tent and to seek reconciliation for the Israelites so that there will not be a plague when the Israelites approach the sanctuary.

20Moses, Aaron, and the entire Israelite

---

eOr him fOr *mercy seat* or perhaps *reconciliation cover* (Heb *kapporet*) community carried out for the Levites everything the Lord had commanded Moses. That is what the Israelites did for the Levites. ²¹The Levites purified themselves and washed their clothes. Aaron presented them as an uplifted offering in the Lord's presence, and he sought reconciliation for them in order to cleanse them. ²²After this the Levites went in to perform their service in the meeting tent before Aaron and his sons. They did for the Levites just as the Lord had commanded Moses concerning them.

²³The Lord spoke to Moses: ²⁴This rule applies⁸ to the Levites: Everyone 25 years old and above will enter into service, performing the duties for the meeting tent. ²⁵At 50 years old each will retire from service. They will perform their duties no longer. ²⁶Each may assist his fellow Levites in the meeting tent with some responsibilities, but he may not perform service. This is how you should assign responsibilities to the Levites.

Passover

9 The Lord spoke to Moses in the Sinai desert in the first month⁸ of the second year after they had left the land of Egypt: ²Let the Israelites keep the Passover at its appointed time. ³On the fourteenth day of this month at twilight you will keep it at its appointed time. Keep it according to all its regulations and its customary practices.

⁴Moses instructed the Israelites to keep the Passover. ⁵At twilight on the fourteenth day of the first monthⁱ they kept the Passover in the Sinai desert. The Israelites did everything just as the Lord commanded Moses.

⁶But there were persons who were unclean from contact with a human corpse, and they were unable to keep the Passover on that day. They approached Moses and Aaron that day. ⁷These persons said to him, "Although we are unclean from contact with a human corpse, why must we be prohibited from presenting the Lord's offering at its appointed time with the rest of the Israelites?"

⁸Moses said to them, "Wait while I listen for what the Lord will command concerning you."

⁹The Lord spoke to Moses: ¹⁰Tell the Israelites: When any of you or your descendants are

unclean from contact with a corpse or are on a long trip, they may still keep the Passover to the Lord. ¹¹They will keep it at twilight on the fourteenth day of the second month.ʲ They will eat the Passover lamb with unleavened bread and bitter herbs. ¹²They must not leave any of it until morning, nor break any of its bones. They will keep the Passover according to all its regulations. ¹³But any persons who are clean and not on a trip, yet don't keep the Passover, those persons will be cut off from their people, because they didn't present the Lord's offering at its appointed time. Those persons will bear their sin. ¹⁴If an immigrant resides among you and wishes to keep the Passover to the Lord, that one also will keep it according to its regulations and its customary practices. There will be one set of regulations for both of you, for the immigrant and for the native of the land.

did you know? The people had a special meal on the first anniversary of their exodus from Egypt, when Moses led them out of slavery and they began their journey toward the promised land. This anniversary was called the Passover because the people remembered when the plague killed the oldest child of the Egyptian people but passed over their houses, sparing their children. Today, Jewish people and some Christians still celebrate the Passover each year with a special meal.

Cloud over the dwelling

¹⁵On the day the dwelling was erected, the cloud covered the dwelling, the covenant tent. At night until morning, the cloud appeared with lightning over the dwelling. ¹⁶It was always there. The cloud covered it by day,ᵏ appearing with lightning at night. ¹⁷Whenever the cloud ascended from the tent, the Israelites would march. And the Israelites would camp wherever the cloud settled. ¹⁸At the Lord's command, the Israelites would march, and at the Lord's command they would camp. As long as the cloud settled on the dwelling, they would camp. ¹⁹When the cloud lingered on the meeting tent for many days, the Israelites would observe the Lord's direction and they wouldn't march. ²⁰Sometimes the cloud

---

⁸Heb lacks *rule applies.* ʰMarch–April, Nisan ⁱMarch–April, Nisan ʲApril–May, Iyar ᵏLXX; MT lacks *by day.*

would be over the dwelling for a number of days, so they would camp at the LORD's command, marching again only at the LORD's command. ²¹Sometimes the cloud would settle only overnight, and they would march when the cloud ascended in the morning. Whether it was day or night, they would march when the cloud ascended. ²²Whether it was two days, or a month, or a long time, the Israelites would camp so long as the cloud lingered on the dwelling and settled on it. They wouldn't march. But when it ascended, they would march. ²³They camped at the LORD's command and they marched at the LORD's command. They followed the LORD's direction according to the LORD's command through Moses.

Trumpets

10 The LORD spoke to Moses: ²Make two silver trumpets and make them from hammered metalwork. Use them for summoning the community and for breaking camp. ³When both are blown, the entire community will meet you at the entrance of the meeting tent. ⁴When one is blown, the chiefs, the leaders of Israel's divisions, will meet you. ⁵When you blow a series of short blasts, the camp on the east side will march. ⁶And when you blow a second series of short blasts, the camp on the south side will march. You will blow a series of short blasts to announce their march.

⁷To gather the assembly, blow a long blast, not a series of short blasts. ⁸Aaron's sons the

How Do We Follow God Today? Numbers 9:15-23

During the day, a cloud covered the dwelling where the chest containing the covenant was kept. The dwelling was the meeting tent at the middle of the camp. At night, the cloud covering the dwelling contained lightning. When the cloud lifted and moved, the Israelites moved; when it stayed, they also stayed. The cloud was a clear sign from God telling them what to do.

We may wish we had such clear signs today. In many ways, we do. The Bible gives many clear instructions such as, "Don't lie to each other" (Col 3:9; see Exod 20:16) and "Be kind, compassionate, and forgiving to each other" (Eph 4:32). Reading the Bible is important because it teaches not only the history of our faith but also what God wants us to do.

Even if the Bible doesn't talk about every specific situation we might face, we can still use it to guide our lives today. The Bible doesn't mention cars, but speeding breaks a law, and we are told to obey the laws. The Bible doesn't teach about using drugs, but we are told that our bodies are a temple for the Holy Spirit (1 Cor 6:19).

In addition to the Bible, God has given us parents, pastors, teachers, and other wise people who love God and can help us understand how God wants us to live.

What teachings from the Bible do you follow every day? • *Who do you go to when you have questions about God?*

priests will blow the trumpets. This will be a permanent regulation for you throughout time. [9]When you go to war in your land against an enemy who is attacking you, you will blow short blasts with the trumpets so that you may be remembered by the LORD your God and be saved from your enemies.

[10]On your festival days, your appointed feasts, and at the beginning of your months, you will blow the trumpets over your entirely burned offerings and your well-being sacrifices. They will serve as a reminder of you to your God. I am the LORD your God.

Organization of the wilderness march

[11]On the twentieth day of the second month in the second year, the cloud ascended from the covenant dwelling. [12]The Israelites set out on their march from the Sinai desert, and the cloud settled in the Paran desert.

[13]They marched for the first time at the LORD's command through Moses. [14]The banner of Judah's camp marched first with its military units. Nahshon, Amminadab's son, commanded its military. [15]Nethanel, Zuar's son, commanded the military of the tribe of Issachar. [16]Eliab, Helon's son, commanded the military of the tribe of Zebulun. [17]The dwelling was taken down, and the Gershonites and the Merarites, who carried the dwelling, marched. [18]The banner of Reuben's camp marched with its military units. Elizur, Shedeur's son, commanded its military. [19]Shelumiel, Zurishaddai's son, commanded the military of the tribe of Simeon. [20]Eliasaph, Deuel's son, commanded the military of the tribe of Gad. [21]The Kohathites, who carried the holy things, marched. The dwelling would be set up before their arrival. [22]The banner of Ephraim's camp marched with its military units. Elishama, Ammihud's son, commanded its military. [23]Gamaliel, Pedahzur's son, commanded the military of the tribe of Manasseh. [24]Abidan, Gideoni's son, commanded the military of the tribe of Benjamin. [25]The banner of Dan's camp, at the rear of the whole camp, marched with its military units. Ahiezer, Ammishaddai's son, commanded its military. [26]Pagiel, Ochran's son, commanded the military of the tribe of Asher. [27]Ahira,

Enan's son, commanded the military of the tribe of Naphtali. [28]This was the order of departure of the Israelites with their military units when they set out.

The chest leads

[29]Moses said to Hobab the Midianite, Reuel's son and Moses' father-in-law, "We're marching to the place about which the LORD has said, 'I'll give it to you.' Come with us and we'll treat you well, for the LORD has promised to treat Israel well."

[30]Hobab said to him, "I won't go; I'd rather go to my land and to my folk."

[31]Moses said, "Please don't abandon us, for you know where we can camp in the desert, and you can be our eyes. [32]If you go with us, whatever good the LORD does for us, we'll do for you."

[33]They marched from the LORD's mountain for three days. The LORD's chest containing the covenant marched ahead of them for three days to look for a resting place for them. [34]Now the LORD's cloud was over them by day when they marched from the camp. [35]When the chest set out, Moses would say, "Arise, LORD, let your enemies scatter, and those who hate you flee." [36]When it rested, he would say, "Return, LORD of the ten thousand thousands of Israel."

Complaint at Taberah

11 When the people complained intensely in the LORD's hearing, the LORD heard and became angry. Then the LORD's fire burned them and consumed the edges of the camp. [2]When the people cried out to Moses, Moses prayed to the LORD, and the fire subsided. [3]The name of that place was called Taberah,[1] because the LORD's fire burned against them.

Complaint over the lack of meat

[4]The riffraff among them had a strong craving. Even the Israelites cried again and said, "Who will give us meat to eat? [5]We remember the fish we ate in Egypt for free, the cucumbers, the melons, the leeks, the onions, and the garlic. [6]Now our lives are wasting away. There is nothing but manna in front of us."

---

[1]Or *the place of burning*

⁷The manna was like coriander seed and its color was like resin. ⁸The people would roam around and collect it and grind it with millstones or pound it in a mortar. Then they would boil it in pots and make it into cakes. It tasted like cakes baked in olive oil. ⁹When the dew fell on the camp during the night, the manna would fall with it.

Moses' complaint about leadership

¹⁰Moses heard the people crying throughout their clans, each at his tent's entrance. The Lord was outraged, and Moses was upset. ¹¹Moses said to the Lord, "Why have you treated your servant so badly? And why haven't I found favor in your eyes, for you have placed the burden of all these people on me? ¹²Did I conceive all these people? Did I give birth to them, that you would say to me, 'Carry them at the breast, as a nurse carries an unweaned child,' to the fertile land that you promised their ancestors? ¹³Where am I to get meat for all these people? They are crying before me and saying, 'Give us meat, so we can eat.' ¹⁴I can't bear this people on my own. They're too heavy for me. ¹⁵If you're going to treat me like this, please kill me. If I've found favor in your eyes, then don't let me endure this wretched situation."

UMBRELLA
Stressed Out

Enough! *Numbers 11:10-15*

Moses had had it. He was angry, tired, and overwhelmed. He was doing the best he could, and the Israelites were complaining and crying for more— more food, more water, more shelter, more information, more everything. Moses was so frustrated that he told God he couldn't handle the burden of leading the people on his own. Moses was so overwhelmed he couldn't see any solution to his problems. He spoke honestly with God about his concerns, and God listened. ◆

¹⁶The Lord said to Moses, "Gather before me seventy men from Israel's elders, whom you know as elders and officers of the people. Take them to the meeting tent, and let them stand there with you. ¹⁷Then I'll descend and speak with you there. I'll take some of the spirit that is on you and place it on them. Then they will carry the burden of the people with you so that you won't bear it alone. ¹⁸To the people you will say, 'Make yourselves holy for tomorrow; then you will eat meat, for you've cried in the Lord's hearing, "Who will give us meat to eat? It was better for us in Egypt." The Lord will give you meat, and you will eat. ¹⁹You won't eat for just one day, or two days, or five days, or ten days, or twenty days, ²⁰but for a whole month until it comes out of your nostrils and nauseates you. You've rejected the Lord who's been with you and you have cried before him, saying, "Why did we leave Egypt?" ' "

²¹Moses said, "The people I'm with are six hundred thousand on foot and you're saying, 'I will give them meat, and they will eat for a month.' ²²Can flocks and herds be found and slaughtered for them? Or can all the fish in the sea be found and caught for them?"

²³The Lord said to Moses, "Is the Lord's power too weak? Now you will see whether my word will come true for you or not."

²⁴So Moses went out and told the people the Lord's words. He assembled seventy men from the people's elders and placed them around the tent. ²⁵The Lord descended in a cloud, spoke to him, and took some of the spirit that was on him and placed it on the seventy elders. When the spirit rested on them, they prophesied, but only this once. ²⁶Two men had remained in the camp, one named Eldad and the second named Medad, and the spirit rested on them. They were among those registered, but they hadn't gone out to the tent, so they prophesied in the camp. ²⁷A young man ran and told Moses, "Eldad and Medad are prophesying in the camp."

²⁸Joshua, Nun's son and Moses' assistant since his youth, responded, "My master Moses, stop them!"

²⁹Moses said to him, "Are you jealous for my sake? If only all the Lord's people were prophets with the Lord placing his spirit on them!"

Quail from the sea

³⁰Moses and Israel's elders were assembled in the camp. ³¹A wind from the Lord blew up and brought quails from the sea. It let them fall by the camp, about a day's journey

all around the camp and about three feet deep on the ground. [32]Then the people arose and gathered the quail all that day, all night, and all the next day. The least collected was ten homers,[m] and they laid them out around the camp. [33]While the meat was still between their teeth and not yet consumed, the Lord's anger blazed against the people. The Lord struck the people with a very great punishment. [34]The name of that place was called Kibroth-hattaavah,[n] because there they buried the people who had the craving.

Miriam and Aaron challenge Moses

[35]From Kibroth-hattaavah the people marched to Hazeroth.

12 When they were in Hazeroth, [1]Miriam and Aaron criticized Moses on account of the Cushite woman whom he had married—for he had married a Cushite woman. [2]They said, "Has the Lord spoken only through Moses? Hasn't he also spoken through us?" The Lord heard it. [3]Now the man Moses was humble, more so than anyone on earth.

The Lord defends Moses

[4]Immediately, the Lord said to Moses, Aaron, and Miriam, "You three go out to the meeting tent." So the three of them went out. [5]Then the Lord descended in a column of cloud, stood at the entrance of the tent, and called to Aaron and Miriam. The two of them came forward. [6]He said, "Listen to my words: If there is a prophet of the Lord among you,[o] I make myself known to him in visions. I speak to him in dreams. [7]But not with my servant Moses. He has proved to be reliable with all my household. [8]I speak with him face-to-face, visibly, not in riddles. He sees the Lord's form. So why aren't you afraid to criticize my servant Moses?" [9]The Lord's anger blazed against them, and they went back.

The Lord punishes Miriam

[10]When the cloud went away from over the tent, Miriam suddenly developed a skin disease flaky like snow. Aaron turned toward Miriam and saw her skin disease. [11]Then Aaron said to Moses, "Oh, my master, please don't punish us for the sin that we foolishly

LIFE PRESERVER

Why did God give such a strange punishment?
Numbers 12:14

Aaron and Miriam were questioning Moses' leadership. Because God had chosen Moses to lead, God was angry with Aaron and Miriam for their disobedience. God appeared to them in a cloud and reminded them of God's confidence in Moses, telling them that God spoke with Moses face-to-face. After the confrontation was over and the cloud departed, Miriam was left with a skin disease as her punishment. Aaron wasn't punished in this way, though we aren't sure why.

Moses pleaded with God on behalf of Miriam, and God allowed her to return to camp after seven days. God's presence with the Israelites was always closely connected to all of their words and actions. God came as a cloud and hovered very close, supporting the people when they followed God's ways, and judging and forgiving them when they did not.

committed. [12]Please don't let her be like the stillborn, whose flesh is half eaten as it comes out of the mother's womb."

[13]So Moses cried to the Lord, "God, please heal her!"

[14]The Lord said to Moses, "If her father had spit in her face, would she not be shamed for seven days? Let her be shut out of the camp for seven days, and afterward she will be brought back." [15]So they shut Miriam out of the camp seven days. And the people didn't march until Miriam was brought back. [16]Afterward the people marched from Hazeroth, and they camped in the Paran desert.

Leaders explore the land of Canaan

13 The Lord spoke to Moses: [2]Send out men to explore the land of Canaan, which I'm giving to the Israelites. Send one man from each ancestral tribe, each a chief among them. [3]So Moses sent them out from the Paran desert according to the Lord's command. All the men were leaders among the Israelites. [4]These are their names:

from the tribe of Reuben, Shammua, Zaccur's son;

---

[m]Five hundred gallons; one homer is two hundred quarts [n]Or graves of craving [o]Heb uncertain; LXX If there is a prophet of you for the Lord.

⁵from the tribe of Simeon, Shaphat, Hori's son;

⁶from the tribe of Judah, Caleb, Jephunneh's son;

⁷from the tribe of Issachar, Igal, Joseph's son;

⁸from the tribe of Ephraim, Hoshea, Nun's son;

⁹from the tribe of Benjamin, Palti, Raphu's son;

¹⁰from the tribe of Zebulun, Gaddiel, Sodi's son;

¹¹from the tribe of Joseph:
from the tribe of Manasseh, Gaddi, Susi's son;

¹²from the tribe of Dan, Ammiel, Gemalli's son;

¹³from the tribe of Asher, Sethur, Michael's son;

¹⁴from the tribe of Naphtali, Nahbi, Vophsi's son;

¹⁵from the tribe of Gad, Geuel, Machi's son.

¹⁶These are the names of the men whom Moses sent out to explore the land. Moses changed the name of Hoshea, Nun's son, to Joshua.

¹⁷When Moses sent them out to explore the land of Canaan, he said to them, "Go up there into the arid southern plain and into the mountains. ¹⁸You must inspect the land. What is it like? Are the people who live in it strong or weak, few or many? ¹⁹Is the land in which they live good or bad? Are the towns in which they live camps or fortresses? ²⁰Is the land rich or poor? Are there trees in it or not? Be courageous and bring back the land's fruit." It was the season of the first ripe grapes.

²¹They went up and explored the land from the Zin desert to Rehob, near Lebo-hamath. ²²They went up into the arid southern plain and entered Hebron, where Ahiman, Sheshai, and Talmai, the descendants of the Anakites, lived. (Hebron was built seven years before Tanisᵖ in Egypt.) ²³Then they entered the Clusterᵠ ravine, cut down from there a branch with one cluster of grapes, and carried it on a pole between them. They also took pomegranates and figs. ²⁴That place was called the Cluster ravine because of the cluster of grapes that the Israelites cut down from there.

Report about the land of Canaan

²⁵They returned from exploring the land after forty days. ²⁶They went directly to Moses, Aaron, and the entire Israelite community in the Paran desert at Kadesh. They brought back a report to them and to the entire community and showed them the land's fruit. ²⁷Then they gave their report: "We entered the land to which you sent us. It's actually full of milk and honey, and this is its fruit. ²⁸There are, however, powerful people who live in the land. The cities have huge fortifications. And we even saw the descendants of the Anakites there. ²⁹The Amalekites live in the land of the arid southern plain; the Hittites, Jebusites, and Amorites live in the mountains; and the Canaanites live by the sea and along the Jordan."

³⁰Now Caleb calmed the people before Moses and said, "We must go up and take possession of it, because we are more than able to do it."

³¹But the men who went up with him said, "We can't go up against the people because they are stronger than we." ³²They started a rumor about the land that they had explored, telling the Israelites, "The land that we crossed over to explore is a land that devours its residents. All the people we saw in it

UMBRELLA
FEAR

Hop! *Numbers 13:28, 31-33*
A group of scouts had gone into the land of Canaan, the land that God had promised to the Israelites, to see if it would be a good place for them to go. They came back and reported that the land was full of milk and honey, but powerful people lived in the land, and the cities had strong walls. These scouts were filled with fear at the thought of overcoming these obstacles. It looked so difficult they didn't even want to try. They saw themselves as grasshoppers facing a field of huge people. They felt small and helpless, unable to trust in all of God's promises to them. ◆

are huge men. ³³We saw there the Nephilim (the descendants of Anak come from the Nephilim). We saw ourselves as grasshoppers, and that's how we appeared to them."

The Israelites' complaint

14¹The entire community raised their voice and the people wept that night. ²All the Israelites criticized Moses and Aaron. The entire community said to them, "If only we had died in the land of Egypt or if only we had died in this desert! ³Why is the LORD bringing us to this land to fall by the sword? Our wives and our children will be taken by force. Wouldn't it be better for us to return to Egypt?" ⁴So they said to each other, "Let's pick a leader and let's go back to Egypt."

⁵Then Moses and Aaron fell on their faces before the assembled Israelite community. ⁶But Joshua, Nun's son, and Caleb, Jephunneh's son, from those who had explored the land, tore their clothes ⁷and said to the entire Israelite community, "The land we crossed through to explore is an exceptionally good land. ⁸If the LORD is pleased with us, he'll bring us into this land and give it to us. It's a land that's full of milk and honey. ⁹Only don't rebel against the LORD and don't be afraid of the people of the land. They are our prey.ʳ Their defense has deserted them, but the LORD is with us. So don't be afraid of them." ¹⁰But the entire community intended to stone them.

The LORD's anger and Moses' intercession

Then the LORD's glory appeared in the meeting tent to all the Israelites. ¹¹The LORD said to Moses, "How long will these people disrespect me? And how long will they doubt me after all the signs that I performed among them? ¹²I'll strike them down with a plague and disown them. Then I'll make you into a great nation, stronger than they."

¹³Moses said to the LORD, "The Egyptians will hear, for with your power you brought these people up from among them. ¹⁴They'll tell the inhabitants of this land. They've heard that you, LORD, are with this people. You, LORD, appear to them face-to-face. Your cloud stands over them. You go before them

in a column of cloud by day and in a column of lightning by night. ¹⁵If you kill these people, every last one of them, the nations who heard about you will say, ¹⁶'The LORD wasn't able to bring these people to the land that he solemnly promised to give them. So he slaughtered them in the desert.' ¹⁷Now let my master's power be as great as you declared when you said, ¹⁸'The LORD is very patient and absolutely loyal, forgiving wrongs and disloyalty. Yet he doesn't forgo all punishment, disciplining the grandchildren and great-grandchildren for their ancestors' wrongs.' ¹⁹Please forgive the wrongs of these people because of your absolute loyalty, just as you've forgiven these people from their time in Egypt until now."

SAILBOAT

COURAGE

Have Courage Numbers 14:6-12
Joshua and Caleb went with ten other men as scouts into the promised land of Canaan. When they returned, Joshua and Caleb heard the other scouts talk about all the ways in which the Israelites could not overcome the obstacles that were ahead of them. Joshua and Caleb tried to give the Israelites a different view. They described the land as good, and they reminded the people that God would bring them into the land and give it to them. They told the people not to be afraid—to remember that God would be with them. Joshua and Caleb were filled with courage because they trusted in God.◢

²⁰Then the LORD said, "I will forgive as you requested. ²¹But as I live and as the LORD's glory fills the entire earth, ²²none of the men who saw my glory and the signs I did in Egypt and in the desert, but tested me these ten times and haven't listened to my voice, ²³will see the land I promised to their ancestors. All who disrespected me won't see it. ²⁴But I'll bring my servant Caleb into the land that he explored, and his descendants will possess it because he has a different spirit, and he has remained true to me. ²⁵Since the Amalekites and the Canaanites live in the valley, tomorrow turn and march into the desert by the route of the Reed Sea."ˢ

ʳOr our bread ˢOr Red Sea

The Israelites' punishment

²⁶The Lᴏʀᴅ spoke to Moses and Aaron: ²⁷How long will this wicked community complain against me? I've heard the Israelites' dissent as they continue to complain against me. ²⁸Say to them, "As I live," says the Lᴏʀᴅ, "just as I've heard you say, so I'll do to you. ²⁹Your dead bodies will fall in this desert. None of you who were enlisted and were registered from 20 years old and above, who complained against me, ³⁰will enter the land in which I promised† to settle you, with the exception of Caleb, Jephunneh's son, and Joshua, Nun's son. ³¹But your children, whom you said would be taken by force, I'll bring them in and they will know the land that you rejected. ³²Your bodies, however, will fall in this desert, ³³and your children will be shepherds in the desert for forty years. They will suffer for your unfaithfulness, until the last of your bodies fall in the desert. ³⁴For as many days as you explored the land, that is, forty days, just as many years you'll bear your guilt, that is, forty years. This is how you will understand my frustration." ³⁵I the Lᴏʀᴅ have spoken. I will do this to the entire wicked community who gathered against me. They will die in this desert. There they'll meet their end.

³⁶The men whom Moses sent out to explore the land had returned and caused the entire community to complain against him by starting a rumor about the land. ³⁷These men died by a plague in the Lᴏʀᴅ's presence on account of their false rumor. ³⁸But Joshua, Nun's son, and Caleb, Jephunneh's son, survived from those men who went to explore the land.

³⁹Moses spoke these words to all the Israelites, and the people mourned bitterly. ⁴⁰They rose early in the morning and went up to the top of the mountain range, saying, "Let's go up to the place the Lᴏʀᴅ told us to, for we have sinned."

†Or raised my hand

The Cost of Doubt and Fear   Numbers 14:29-34

If you've ever disobeyed your parents or teachers, you might have felt bad later and asked for their forgiveness. Sometimes, asking for forgiveness is all you need to do. Other times, you must face consequences. This is what happened to the Israelites.

Through miracle after miracle, the Israelites saw God deliver, protect, and provide for them. They saw the army of Egypt swallowed up in the waters of the sea. They ate manna and quail that God provided, and they followed the cloud God sent to lead them. But the Israelites stood on the edge of Canaan, the land God promised to them, afraid of the people in that land.

Once again the Israelites complained. Moses prayed for them, and God forgave them. But that didn't mean everything would remain the same. God punished the people of Israel. Instead of going right into the promised land, God made them wander in the desert for forty years, until all the complainers had died.

Sin is any action that separates people from God or destroys relationships between people. Sin means we do things our own way instead of God's. When we sin, we fail to trust God's love and kindness toward us. We need to remember that the Bible says God's plans for us are good, giving us hope and a future (Jer 29:11). Trusting God means following God's ways, even when we're afraid.

Think of a time when you didn't trust God.

Ask God to forgive you for that fear and doubt.

⁴¹But Moses said, "Why do you disobey the Lord's command? It won't succeed. ⁴²Don't go up, for the Lord isn't with you. Don't be struck down before your enemies. ⁴³The Amalekites and the Canaanites will be there in front of you and you will fall by the sword because you turned away from the Lord, and the Lord is no longer with you." ⁴⁴Yet they recklessly[u] ascended toward the top of the mountains, even though Moses and the Lord's chest containing the covenant didn't depart from the camp. ⁴⁵Then the Amalekites and the Canaanites, who lived in those mountains, descended, struck them down, and beat them all the way to Hormah.

Immigrants in the land of Canaan

15 The Lord spoke to Moses: ²Speak to the Israelites and say to them: When you enter the land where you will live, which I am giving you, ³and you make a food gift[v] to the Lord as a soothing smell for the Lord from the herd or the flock—whether an entirely burned offering, or a sacrifice to fulfill a solemn promise, or a spontaneous gift, or at your sacred seasons—⁴the one presenting the offering to the Lord will bring a grain offering of one-tenth of a measure of fine flour mixed with one-fourth of a hin[w] of oil. ⁵You will also offer one-fourth of a hin of wine as a drink offering with either the entirely burned offering or the sacrifice, for each lamb. ⁶For a ram you will offer a grain offering of two-tenths of a measure of fine flour mixed with one-third of a hin of oil. ⁷You will also present one-third of a hin of wine for a drink offering as a soothing smell for the Lord. ⁸When you offer a bull for an entirely burned offering, or a sacrifice to fulfill a solemn promise, or a well-being sacrifice to the Lord, ⁹you will present[x] with the bull a grain offering of three-tenths of a measure of fine flour mixed with a half hin of oil. ¹⁰You will present a half hin of wine for a drink offering as a food gift that is a soothing smell to the Lord. ¹¹So will it be done with each ox, each ram, or for any sheep or goat. ¹²However many you offer, you will do the same for each one.

¹³Every citizen will perform these rituals in bringing a food gift that is a soothing smell to the Lord. ¹⁴If an immigrant lives with you or has settled among you for many years and would also like to offer a food gift that is a soothing smell to the Lord, that person must do just as you do. ¹⁵The assembly will have the same regulation for you and for the immigrant. The regulation will be permanent for all time. You and the immigrant will be the same in the Lord's presence. ¹⁶There will be one set of instructions and one legal norm for the immigrant and for you.

¹⁷The Lord spoke to Moses: ¹⁸Speak to the Israelites and say to them: When you enter the land to which I'm bringing you, ¹⁹whenever you eat the land's food you will present a gift offering to the Lord. ²⁰You will present a gift offering from the first bread you bake just like you present a gift offering from the threshing floor. ²¹You will give a gift offering from the first bread you bake for all time.

Offerings for accidental sin

²²If by accident you don't obey all these commands that the Lord spoke to Moses, ²³or everything that the Lord commanded you through Moses from the day of the Lord's command onward for all time, ²⁴then if it was done unintentionally without the knowledge of the community, the entire community must offer one bull from the herd as an entirely burned offering, a soothing smell to the Lord, with its grain and drink offering according to the specific instruction, and one male goat for a purification offering. ²⁵The priest will seek reconciliation for the entire Israelite community. They will be forgiven, because it was unintentional and because they brought their food gift to the Lord, along with their purification offering in the Lord's presence for their accidental error. ²⁶The entire Israelite community and the immigrant residing among them will be forgiven, because all the people acted unintentionally.

²⁷If an individual sins unintentionally, that person must present a one-year-old female goat for a purification offering. ²⁸The priest will seek reconciliation in the Lord's presence for the person who sinned unintentionally, when the sin is an accident, seeking reconciliation so that person will be forgiven.

---

[u]Heb uncertain [v]Or *offering by fire* (cf Lev 3:11) [w]One hin is approximately one gallon. [x]Or *he will present*

²⁹There will be one set of instructions for the Israelite citizen and the immigrant residing with you for anyone who commits an unintentional sin.

Punishment for intentional sin

³⁰But the person who acts deliberately,ʸ whether a citizen or an immigrant, and insults the LORD, that person will be cut off from the people ³¹for despising the LORD's word and breaking his commands. That person will be completely cut off and bear the guilt.

Instructions for Sabbath observance

³²When the Israelites were in the desert, they found a man gathering wood on the Sabbath day. ³³Those who found him gathering wood brought him to Moses, Aaron, and the entire community. ³⁴They placed him in custody, because it wasn't clear what should be done to him. ³⁵Then the LORD said to Moses: The man should be put to death. The entire community should stone him outside the camp. ³⁶The entire community took him outside the camp and stoned him. He died as the LORD had commanded Moses.

Fringes on garments

³⁷The LORD said to Moses: ³⁸Speak to the Israelites and say to them: Make fringes on the edges of your clothing for all time. Have them put blue cords on the fringe on the edges. ³⁹This will be your fringe. You will see it and remember all the LORD's commands and do them. Then you won't go exploring the lusts of your own heart or your eyes. ⁴⁰In this way you'll remember to do all my commands. Then you will be holy to your God. ⁴¹I am the LORD your God, who brought you out of the land of Egypt to be your God. I am the LORD your God.

ʸOr with a high hand

Everything Belongs to God   Numbers 15:20

Giving away the first part of their harvest or herds was not something new to the Israelites. When the seven-year drought hit Egypt, the people came to Joseph to buy grain. After they ran out of money, they sold their land to Pharaoh. They continued to live and farm the land, but from that time on they had to pay the king the first fifth (1/5) of everything they grew.

In the Instruction of God from Moses, God required the first tenth (1/10) of the first part of their crops and herds. Giving a portion from the first part of everything they grew reminded the people that all of their possessions had come from God. Although the people worked to farm the land, any crops that grew belonged to God.

You may not live on a farm, but you can still give a tenth part to God. If you are given an allowance, or if you have worked to earn money, you can offer some of that money to God, knowing that it belongs to God anyway. You can also give of your time, talents, and other resources, choosing to do things that serve and honor God.

By giving a tenth of your income to God, you are acknowledging that everything you have comes from God. This is one way to thank God for loving you, caring for you, and providing for you.

Name two things that God gave you.

How can you give a tithe to God?

A challenge to the priesthood

16 Korah—Izhar's son, Kohath's grandson, and Levi's great-grandson—with Dathan and Abiram, Eliab's sons, and On, Peleth's son, descendants of Reuben, ²rose up against Moses, along with two hundred fifty Israelite men, leaders of the community, chosen by the assembly, men of reputation. ³They assembled against Moses and Aaron and said to them, "You've gone too far, because the entire community is holy, every last one of them, and the LORD is with them. Why then do you exalt yourselves above the LORD's assembly?"

⁴When Moses heard this, he fell on his face. ⁵He spoke to Korah and all his community, "In the morning the LORD will make known who is his, who is holy, and who is able to approach him. The one he chooses for himself is the one who will be able to approach him. ⁶This is what must be done. Korah and your entire community: Take censers for yourselves. ⁷Tomorrow put fire in them and place incense on them in the LORD's presence. The man whom the LORD chooses, that one is holy. You Levites have gone too far!" ⁸Moses said to Korah, "Listen, you Levites, ⁹isn't it enough for you that Israel's God has separated you from the Israelite community to allow you to approach him, to perform the service of the LORD's dwelling, and to serve before the community by ministering for them? ¹⁰He has allowed you and all your fellow Levites with you to approach him. Yet you also seek the priesthood? ¹¹Thus you and your entire community have assembled against the LORD. But Aaron, what is he that you complain about him?"

Test of priesthood

¹²Moses sent for Dathan and Abiram, Eliab's sons. But they said, "We won't come up! ¹³Isn't it enough that you've brought us up from a land full of milk and honey to kill us in the desert so that you'd also dominate us? ¹⁴Moreover, you haven't brought us to a land full of milk and honey, nor given us the inheritance of field and vineyard. Would you also gouge out the eyes of these men? We won't come up!"

¹⁵Moses became very angry and he said to the LORD, "Pay no attention to their offering. I haven't taken a single donkey from them, nor have I wronged any one of them."

LIFE PRESERVER

What happened to Korah, Dathan, and Abiram?
Numbers 16:1-35

Revolt among the Israelites was bound to happen. Again and again they questioned the leadership of Moses and Aaron, whom God had chosen to lead the people. Korah, Dathan, and Abiram joined together with others to oppose Moses and Aaron, accusing them of being unholy. To be holy is to be set apart or totally dedicated to God. Moses dealt with these men by coming up with a way for God to reveal who was holy.

But God decided to do something much more drastic. God opened up the ground from underneath Korah, Dathan, and Abiram, and their whole households were swallowed up. When some of the people continued to complain the next day, God sent disease that killed even more. It's clear from this story that God trusted the choice of Moses and Aaron as leaders of God's people.

¹⁶Moses said to Korah, "You and your entire community should appear before the LORD tomorrow, you, they, and Aaron. ¹⁷Every person should take his censer, place incense on it, and present it before the LORD. Each person will carry his censer, two hundred fifty censers in all, including you and Aaron." ¹⁸Then every person took his censer, placed fire on it, put incense on it, and stood at the entrance of the meeting tent with Moses and Aaron. ¹⁹Korah gathered the entire community with them to the entrance of the meeting tent.

Then the LORD's glory appeared to the entire community. ²⁰The LORD spoke to Moses and Aaron, ²¹"Separate yourselves from this community so that I may consume them in a moment."

²²They fell on their faces and said, "God, the God of all living things. If one person sins, should you become angry with the entire community?"

²³The LORD said to Moses, ²⁴"Speak to the community and say, 'Withdraw from around the dwellings of Korah, Dathan, and Abiram.'" ²⁵Moses rose and went to Dathan and Abiram. Israel's elders followed him. ²⁶He spoke to the community: "Move away from the tents of these wicked men and don't touch

anything of theirs, lest you too be wiped out for all their sins." ²⁷They withdrew from around the dwellings of Korah, Dathan, and Abiram. Then Dathan and Abiram came out and stood at the entrance of their tents with their wives, children, and little ones. ²⁸Moses said, "By this you will know that the Lord sent me to do these deeds and that it wasn't my own desire. ²⁹If all these people die a natural death, or if their fate be that of all humans, then the Lord hasn't sent me. ³⁰But if the Lord performs an act of creation, and the ground opens its mouth and swallows them and everything that belongs to them, so that they descend alive to their graves, then you'll know that these men disrespected the Lord."

The rebels' punishment

³¹As soon as he finished speaking these words, the ground under them split open. ³²The earth opened its mouth and swallowed them and their households, including every human that belonged to Korah and all their possessions. ³³They along with all their possessions descended alive to their graves, and the earth closed over them. They perished in the middle of the assembly. ³⁴All the Israelites who were around them fled at their cry, for they said, "The earth may swallow us." ³⁵Then fire went out from the Lord and consumed the two hundred fifty men offering incense.

The reminder of the censers

^{36z}The Lord spoke to Moses: ³⁷Tell Eleazar, Aaron the priest's son, to raise the censers from the fire and scatter the ashes about, because they are holy. ³⁸Hammer the censers of those who sinned and lost their lives into thin plates for the altar. Since they presented them in the Lord's presence, they had become holy. They will be a sign for the Israelites. ³⁹Eleazar the priest took the bronze censers presented by those who had been consumed by fire and hammered them into a covering for the altar, ⁴⁰just as the Lord instructed him through Moses. This was a reminder for the Israelites that no outsider who isn't one of Aaron's descendants should approach to burn incense in the Lord's

presence, so as not to be like Korah and his community.

⁴¹On the next day the entire Israelite community complained to Moses and Aaron, "You killed the Lord's people." ⁴²When the community assembled against Moses and Aaron, they turned toward the meeting tent. At that moment the cloud covered it, and the Lord's glory appeared. ⁴³Moses and Aaron came to the front of the meeting tent, ⁴⁴and the Lord spoke to Moses: ⁴⁵Get away from this community, so that I may consume them in an instant.

They fell on their faces, ⁴⁶and Moses said to Aaron, "Take the censer, put fire from the altar on it, place incense on it, go quickly to the community, and seek reconciliation for them. Indeed, the Lord's anger has gone out. The plague has begun." ⁴⁷Aaron took it as Moses said and ran into the middle of the assembly, for the plague had already begun among the people. He burned incense and sought reconciliation for the people. ⁴⁸He stood between the dead and the living, and the plague stopped. ⁴⁹Those who died from the plague were fourteen thousand seven hundred, in addition to those who died because of Korah. ⁵⁰Aaron returned to Moses at the entrance of the meeting tent once the plague stopped.

Aaron's budding staff

17 ^aThe Lord spoke to Moses: ²Speak to the Israelites and take from them a staff from each household, from each of the chiefs of their households, twelve staffs. Write each person's name on his staff. ³Write Aaron's name on Levi's staff, for there will be one staff for the leader of each household. ⁴Then you will place them in the meeting tent in front of the chest containing the covenant, where I meet you. ⁵The staff of the person I choose will sprout. Then I will rid myself of the Israelites' complaints that they make against you.

⁶Moses spoke to the Israelites, and each of their chiefs gave him a staff, one staff for each chief and his household, twelve staffs, and the staff of Aaron was with their staffs. ⁷Moses placed the staffs before the Lord in the meeting tent. ⁸The next day Moses

^z17:1 in Heb ^a17:16 in Heb

LIFE PRESERVER

Did Aaron's staff really sprout? *Numbers 17:6-11*

Among the Israelites, certain tribes or families had specific roles. The Levites were the only Israelites who had been set apart as priests. Aaron was a Levite, and his job as a priest was to be in charge of the altar of the sanctuary, receiving the offerings from the people.

When the Israelites questioned Aaron's authority to do this priestly job, God told Moses to collect one staff from each of the twelve families of Israel. The next day only Aaron's staff had bloomed, producing ripe almonds. This was a sign of Aaron's leadership as a priest and a reminder to the people to remember this special role.

It must have been as amazing for the Israelites to see a stick of wood flowering with leaves and nuts as it is for us to think about today. The Bible tells many stories about impossible things happening when God takes action, including creation, seas parting, healing, and miracles. God was leading God's people out of slavery, through the wilderness into a promised land full of milk and honey. God knew that the only way the Israelites would get there would be if they remembered God and followed their leaders.◊

entered the covenant tent, and Aaron's staff of Levi's household had sprouted. It grew shoots, produced blossoms, and bore almonds. ⁹Moses brought out all the staffs from the LORD's presence to the Israelites. They saw what happened, and each person took back his staff.

¹⁰Then the LORD said to Moses, "Return Aaron's staff in front of the chest containing the covenant to serve as a sign to the rebels so that their complaints against me end and they don't die." ¹¹Moses did exactly as the LORD commanded him.

¹²The Israelites said to Moses, "We are perishing. We are being destroyed. All of us are being destroyed. ¹³Anyone who approaches the LORD's dwelling will die. Are we doomed to perish?"

The priests' and Levites' duties

18¹The LORD said to Aaron: You, your sons, and your household will bear the guilt of offenses connected with the sanctuary. You and your sons will bear the guilt of offenses connected with your priesthood.

²Bring with you your brothers from the tribe of Levi, your father's tribe, so that they can assist you and serve you and your sons before the covenant tent. ³They will perform their duties for you and the service for the entire tent. But they will not approach the holy equipment of the sanctuary or the altar, lest both they and you die. ⁴They will assist you and they will perform the duties of the meeting tent with regard to all the work of the tent. But no outsider may accompany you. ⁵You will perform the duties of the sanctuary and the altar. Then there will no longer be any anger against the Israelites. ⁶I have taken your brothers, the Levites, from the Israelites. They are a gift to you, dedicated to the LORD to perform the service of the meeting tent. ⁷You and your sons must perform the duties of your priesthood for all the matters of the altar and the area behind the curtain. I give you your priestly service as a gift. But an outsider who approaches will die.

The priests' compensation

⁸The LORD spoke to Aaron: I now place you in charge of my gifts, including all the Israelites' sacred offerings. I have given them to you and your sons as an allowance. This is a permanent regulation. ⁹This is what belongs to you from the most holy offerings, from the offerings by fire: all their offerings, including their grain offerings, their purification offerings, and their compensation offerings. The most holy offerings that they bring to me will be yours and your sons'. ¹⁰You will eat it as a most holy thing. Every male may eat it. It will be holy to you. ¹¹This will also belong to you, your sons, and your daughters: I'm giving you the gift offerings and all the Israelites' uplifted offerings. This is a permanent regulation. Anyone who is clean in your household may eat it. ¹²All the choice oil, new wine, and the grain's first harvest that they give to the LORD, I'm giving to you. ¹³The early produce of everything in their land, which they bring to the LORD, will be yours. Anyone who is clean in your household may eat it. ¹⁴Everything that is devoted to the LORD in Israel will be yours. ¹⁵Any oldest male from the womb of any living thing that is presented to the LORD, whether human or animal, will be yours. However, you will redeem the oldest

males of humans and of unclean animals.
[16]Their redemption price from one month of
age you will calculate at five shekels of silver
according to the sanctuary shekel, which is
twenty gerahs. [17]But the oldest offspring of
a cow, sheep, or goat you may not redeem.
They are holy. You must dash their blood on
the altar and turn their fat into smoke for a
soothing smell to the Lord. [18]But their meat
is yours. It will be yours just as the breast of
the uplifted offering and the right thigh are
yours. [19]All the holy gift offerings that the Israelites raise to the Lord I have given to you,
your sons, and your daughters. This is a permanent regulation. It is a covenant of salt forever in the Lord's presence, for you and your
descendants.

[20]The Lord said to Aaron: You will have no
inheritance in their land, nor will you have a
share among them. I am your share and your
inheritance among the Israelites.

The Levites' compensation

[21]I have given all the one-tenth portions in
Israel to the Levites as an inheritance. They
are a reward for performing their service in
the meeting tent. [22]The Israelites will no longer be able to approach the meeting tent, or
they will be responsible for their sin and die.
[23]The Levites will perform the service of the
meeting tent, and they will be responsible for
their own sins. This is a permanent regulation for all time. But they will not inherit land
among the Israelites [24]because I've given the
Israelites' one-tenth portion, which they have
raised to the Lord as a gift offering, as an inheritance to the Levites. Therefore, I've said
to them, "They won't inherit land among the
Israelites."

[25]The Lord spoke to Moses: [26]Speak to the
Levites and say to them: When you receive
from the Israelites the one-tenth portion that
I have given you from them as your inheritance, you also must present a gift offering to
the Lord from it, a tenth from the one-tenth
portion. [27]It will be considered your gift offering, like the grain of the threshing floor
and what fills the winepress. [28]In this way
you will also present a gift offering to the
Lord from all the one-tenth portions that
you take from the Israelites. You will provide
from it a gift offering to the Lord for Aaron

the priest. [29]You will present each gift offering to the Lord from all your gifts, from its
best portions and its holiest parts.

[30]You will say to them: When you have presented the best portion, it will be considered
for the Levites equivalent to the produce of
the grain and the produce of the winepress.
[31]You and your household may eat it anywhere, because it is payment for your service
in the meeting tent. [32]You will not bear guilt
after you have presented the best portion.
But you must not make the sacred gifts of the
Israelites impure, on penalty of death.

Instructions about the red cow and the water of purification

19 The Lord spoke to Moses and Aaron:
[2]This is the regulation in the Instruction that the Lord commanded. Tell the Israelites that they must bring you a red cow
without defect, which is flawless and on
which no yoke has been laid. [3]You will give
it to Eleazar the priest, and he will take it
outside the camp and slaughter it in front of
him. [4]Eleazar the priest will take some of its
blood with his finger and sprinkle it seven
times in front of the meeting tent. [5]Then he
will burn the cow in front of him, its skin,
flesh, and blood, with its dung. [6]The priest
will take cedarwood, hyssop, and crimson
cloth and throw them into the fire where the
cow is burning. [7]Then the priest will wash his
clothes and bathe his body in water. Afterward the priest will enter the camp, but he
will be unclean until evening. [8]The one who
burned the cow will wash his clothes in water
and bathe his body in water, but he will be
unclean until evening. [9]A person who is clean
will gather the ashes of the cow and place
them outside the camp in a clean place. They
will be kept for the water of purification for
the Israelite community as a purification offering. [10]The one who gathers the ashes of the
cow will wash his clothes but will be unclean
until evening. This will be a permanent regulation for the Israelites and for the immigrant
who lives among them.

Contact with a dead body

[11]The person who touches the dead body
of any human will be unclean for seven days.
[12]That person must be cleansed with water on

the third and seventh days to be clean. If he fails to be cleansed with water on the third and seventh days, he will not be clean. ¹³Anyone who touches the body of a human who has died and doesn't cleanse himself defiles the LORD's dwelling. Such persons must be cut off from Israel because the water of purification wasn't sprinkled on them. They remain unclean.

¹⁴This is the instruction: When anyone dies in a tent, all who go into the tent and all who are in the tent are unclean for seven days. ¹⁵Any open jar without a sealed cover on it is unclean. ¹⁶Anyone in the open field who touches a person slain by the sword, or who died naturally, or a human bone or a grave, will be unclean for seven days. ¹⁷For the unclean person, they will take some of the ashes of the purification offering and place fresh water with it in a jar. ¹⁸Then a clean person will take hyssop, dip it into the water, and sprinkle it on the tent, on all the jars, on the people who were there, and on anyone who touched bone, the slain, the dead, or the grave. ¹⁹On the third day and the seventh day the clean person will sprinkle it on the unclean, so that he will have purified him on the seventh day. He will then wash his clothes, bathe in water, and be clean at evening. ²⁰Any person who is unclean and didn't cleanse himself will be cut off from the assembly, because he has defiled the LORD's sanctuary. He didn't have the water of purification sprinkled on him. He is unclean. ²¹This will be a permanent

LIFE PRESERVER

Why did the Israelites have rules for dealing with the dead? Numbers 19:11-16

Other cultures who lived near the Israelites worshipped their ancestors. The Israelites were probably familiar with this common practice. God's Instruction commanded the Israelites not to worship death, because death does not allow a living person to be set apart for God. For the Israelites, anyone who touched a dead body was considered unclean, which meant they couldn't enter the meeting tent for worship because it was a place set apart to meet God. ◊

regulation for them. The one who sprinkles the water of purification will wash his own clothes. Anyone who touches the water of purification will be unclean until evening. ²²Whoever the unclean person touches will be unclean, and the one who touches the unclean will be unclean until evening.

Lawsuit over water and Moses' disobedience

20In the first month,ᵇ the entire Israelite community entered the Zin desert and the people stayed at Kadesh. Miriam died and was buried there. ²Now there was no water for the community, and they assembled against Moses and Aaron. ³Then the people confronted Moses and said to him, "If only we too had died when our brothers perished in the LORD's presence! ⁴Why have you brought the LORD's assembly into this desert to kill us and our animals here? ⁵Why have you led us up from Egypt to bring us to this evil place without grain, figs, vines, or pomegranates? And there's no water to drink!"

⁶Moses and Aaron went away from the assembly to the entrance of the meeting tent and they fell on their faces. Then the LORD's glory appeared to them. ⁷The LORD spoke to Moses: ⁸"You and Aaron your brother, take the staff and assemble the community. In their presence, tell the rock to provide water. You will produce water from the rock for them and allow the community and their animals to drink."

⁹Moses took the staff from the LORD's presence, as the LORD had commanded him. ¹⁰Moses and Aaron gathered the assembly before the rock. He said to them, "Listen, you rebels! Should we produce water from the rock for you?" ¹¹Then Moses raised his hand and struck the rock with his staff twice. Out flooded water so that the community and their animals could drink.

¹²The LORD said to Moses and Aaron, "Because you didn't trust me to show my holiness before the Israelites, you will not bring this assembly into the land that I am giving them." ¹³These were the waters of Meribah,ᶜ where the Israelites confronted the LORD with controversy and he showed his holiness to them.

ᵇMarch–April, Nisan ᶜOr confrontation

LIFE PRESERVER

What did Moses do wrong?
Numbers 20:1-13

The Israelites had been wandering in the wilderness for forty years. They were probably tired, and in this story they were thirsty and worried that they and their animals would die. Moses and Aaron heard their cries and met with God to ask for help.

God told them what to do, but instead of following God's instruction to command the rock to give water, Moses struck the rock and water flowed out. Because Moses didn't follow God's instruction, God didn't allow Moses to enter the promised land.

This may seem like a harsh punishment for Moses and Aaron, two men who had faithfully led God's people for so long. But in God's eyes, Moses' disobedience meant that he didn't trust God. And if he didn't trust God, then the Israelites, whom he was leading, wouldn't see God's holiness. For this reason, God didn't let Moses' sin go unpunished. ◆

The Israelites confront Edom

¹⁴Moses sent messengers from Kadesh to the king of Edom: "This is what your brother Israel says: 'You know all the adversity that has happened to us. ¹⁵How our ancestors went down to Egypt and lived in Egypt for a long time. The Egyptians oppressed us as they had our ancestors, ¹⁶and we cried out to the LORD. He heard our voice, sent a messenger, and brought us out of Egypt. Now here we are in Kadesh, a city on the edge of your border. ¹⁷Please let us cross through your land. We won't pass through any field or vineyard, or drink water from any well. We will walk on the King's Highway and not turn to the right or to the left until we have crossed your border.'"

¹⁸Edom said to him, "You won't cross through, or I will come out against you with a sword."

¹⁹The Israelites said to him, "We'll go up by the road. If we drink from your water, either we or our livestock, we'll pay for it. It's a small matter. We would only ask to cross on foot."

²⁰But he said, "You won't cross." Then Edom came out against them with a powerful army and a strong hand. ²¹Edom refused to allow Israel to cross his border. And Israel turned away from him. ²²They marched from Kadesh.

Aaron's death at Mount Hor

The entire Israelite community came to Mount Hor. ²³The LORD said to Moses and Aaron at Mount Hor on the border of the land of Edom: ²⁴Aaron will join his ancestors, for he may not enter the land that I've given to the Israelites, because you rebelled against my command at the waters of Meribah. ²⁵Take Aaron and his son Eleazar, and bring them up Mount Hor. ²⁶Strip Aaron of his clothes and put them on Eleazar his son. Then Aaron will die there.

²⁷Moses did as the LORD commanded. They went up Mount Hor in the sight of the entire community. ²⁸Moses stripped Aaron of his clothes and put them on Eleazar his son. Aaron died there at the top of the mountain. Then Moses and Eleazar descended from the mountain. ²⁹When the entire community saw that Aaron had died, the entire household of Israel wept thirty days for Aaron.

Defeat of the Canaanite king of Arad

21 When the Canaanite king of Arad, who ruled in the arid southern plain, heard that the Israelites were coming on the Atharim road, he fought against Israel and took some of them captive. ²Then Israel made a solemn promise to the LORD and said, "If you give this people into our hands, we will completely destroy their city." ³The LORD heard the voice of Israel and handed the Canaanites over. They completely destroyed them and their cities, so the name of the place is called Hormah.ᵈ

The bronze snake's healing power

⁴They marched from Mount Hor on the Reed Seaᵉ road around the land of Edom. The people became impatient on the road. ⁵The people spoke against God and Moses: "Why did you bring us up from Egypt to kill us in the desert, where there is no food or water. And we detest this miserable bread!" ⁶So the LORD sent poisonousᶠ snakes among the people and they bit the people. Many of the Israelites died.

ᵈOr destruction ᵉOr Red Sea ᶠHeb uncertain

7The people went to Moses and said, "We've sinned, for we spoke against the LORD and you. Pray to the LORD so that he will send the snakes away from us." So Moses prayed for the people.

8The LORD said to Moses, "Make a poisonous snake and place it on a pole. Whoever is bitten can look at it and live." 9Moses made a bronze snake and placed it on a pole. If a snake bit someone, that person could look at the bronze snake and live.

LIGHTHOUSE

CHANGED HEART AND LIFE

No More Complaining! *Numbers 21:4-7*
The Israelites had been traveling for a long time. They had marched from Mount Hor near the Reed Sea all the way around the land of Edom. They were growing tired of this long march, and they began to complain. They spoke against God and Moses, asking why they had been saved from Egypt only to die in the desert without food or water. God was furious and sent poisonous snakes among the people, causing many of them to die. Because of this the Israelites realized they had gone too far. They went to Moses, admitting they had done wrong, and asked Moses to pray that God would send the snakes away. God heard Moses' prayer and knew that the Israelites had changed their hearts.

March around Moab

10Then the Israelites marched and they camped at Oboth. 11They marched from Oboth and camped at Iye-abarim in the desert on the border of Moab toward the east. 12From there they marched and camped in the Zered ravine. 13From there they marched and camped across the Arnon in the desert that extends from the border of the Amorites, for the Arnon was the border of Moab, between Moab and the Amorites. 14For this reason the scroll of the LORD's wars says:

Waheb in Suphah and the ravines.
The Arnon 15and the ravines
    that extend to the settlement of Ar
    and lie along the border of Moab.

16From there they marched to Beer, the well where the LORD said to Moses, "Gather

the people, and I'll give them water." 17Then the Israelites sang this song:

"Well, flow up!
    Sing about it!
18 The well that the officials dug,
    that the officials of the people
        hollowed out
    with the ruler's scepter and their staffs."

They marched from the desert to Mattanah; 19from Mattanah to Nahaliel; from Nahaliel to Bamoth; 20from Bamoth to the valley in the Moabite countryside, to the top of Pisgah overlooking Jeshimon.8

Wars against Sihon and Og

21Then the Israelites sent messengers to Sihon the Amorite king: 22"Let us pass through your land. We won't turn aside into a field or vineyard. We won't drink water from a well. We will walk on the King's Highway until we cross your border."

23But Sihon wouldn't allow the Israelites to cross his border. Sihon gathered all his people and went out to meet the Israelites in the desert. When he came to Jahaz, he attacked the Israelites. 24The Israelites struck him down with their swords and took possession of his land from the Arnon to the Jabbok, as far as the Ammonites, for the border of the Ammonites was fortified. 25The Israelites took all these cities. Then the Israelites settled in all the cities of the Amorites, in Heshbon and all its villages.

26Now Heshbon was the city of Sihon the Amorite king who had fought against the former king of Moab. He had taken all his land from him as far as the Arnon. 27Therefore, the poets say:

"Come to Heshbon, let it be built.
    Let the city of Sihon be established.
28 Fire went out from Heshbon,
    flame from Sihon's city.
    It consumed Ar of Moab
    and swallowed up
        the shrines of the Arnon.
29 You are doomed, Moab!
    You are destroyed, people of Chemosh!
    He gave his sons as fugitives,
    and his daughters as captives
        to the Amorite king Sihon.

8Or wasteland

30 Yet we have thrown them down,
  destroying them[h]
  from Heshbon to Dibon.
We brought ruin until Nophah,
  which is by Medeba."

31 Israel settled in the land of the Amorites.
32 Moses sent spies to Jazer. They captured its villages and took possession of the Amorites who were there. 33 Then they turned and ascended the road of Bashan. Og, Bashan's king, came out at Edrei to meet them in battle, he and all his people. 34 The Lord said to Moses: Don't be afraid of him, for I have handed over all his people and his land. Do to him as you did to Sihon the Amorite king who ruled in Heshbon.

35 They slaughtered Og, his sons, and all his people until there were no survivors. Then they took possession of his land.

Balak summons Balaam to curse the Israelites

22 The Israelites marched and camped in the plains of Moab across the Jordan from Jericho. 2 Balak, Zippor's son, saw everything that the Israelites did to the Amorites. 3 The Moabites greatly feared the people, for they were so numerous. The Moabites were terrified of the Israelites. 4 The Moabites said to the elders of Midian, "Now this assembly will devour everything around us, as an ox eats up the grass in the field."

Balak, Zippor's son, was king of Moab at that time. 5 He sent messengers to Balaam, Beor's son, at Pethor, which is by the river in the land of his people,[i] to summon him: "A people has come out of Egypt, and they have now covered the land. They have settled next to me. 6 Now please come and curse this people for me because they are stronger than I am. Perhaps I'll be able to destroy them and drive them from the land, for I know that whomever you bless is blessed and whomever you curse is cursed."

7 So the elders of Moab and Midian went with the payment for divination in their hands. They came to Balaam and told him Balak's words. 8 He said to them, "Spend the night here and I'll bring back to you a word exactly as the Lord speaks to me." So the officials of Moab stayed with Balaam.

9 God came to Balaam and said, "Who are these men with you?"

10 Balaam said to God, "Moab's King Balak, Zippor's son, sent them to me with the message, 11 'A people has come out of Egypt and covered the land. Now come and curse them for me. Perhaps I'll be able to fight against them and drive them out.'"

12 God said to Balaam, "Don't go with them. Don't curse the people, because they are blessed."

13 Then Balaam arose in the morning and said to Balak's officials, "Go to your land, for the Lord has refused to allow me to go with you."

14 The officials of Moab arose, they went to Balak, and they said, "Balaam refused to come with us."

15 Balak continued to send other officials more numerous and important than these. 16 They came to Balaam and said to him, "This is what Balak, Zippor's son, says: 'Please let nothing hold you back from coming to me, 17 for I'll greatly honor you and I'll do anything you ask of me. Please come and curse this people for me.'"

18 Balaam answered and said to Balak's servants, "If Balak were to give me his house full of silver and gold, I wouldn't be able to do anything, small or great, to break the command of the Lord my God. 19 Now you also must remain the night here so that I may know what else the Lord may say to me."

20 God came to Balaam in the night and said to him, "If the men have come to summon you, arise and go with them. But you must do only what I tell you to do." 21 So Balaam arose in the morning, saddled his donkey, and went with the officials of Moab.

Balaam and the Lord's messenger

22 Then God became angry because he went. So while he was riding on his donkey accompanied by his two servants, the Lord's messenger stood in the road as his adversary. 23 The donkey saw the Lord's messenger standing in the road with his sword drawn in his hand, so the donkey turned from the road and went into the field. Balaam struck the donkey in order to turn him back onto the road. 24 Then the Lord's messenger stood in

---

[h] Heb uncertain; LXX *their posterity has perished* [i] Sam, Syr, Vulg *the Ammonites*

the narrow path between vineyards with a stone wall on each side. ²⁵When the donkey saw the LORD's messenger, it leaned against the wall and squeezed Balaam's foot against the wall, so he continued to beat it. ²⁶The LORD's messenger persisted and crossed over and stood in a narrow place, where it wasn't possible to turn either right or left. ²⁷The donkey saw the LORD's messenger and lay down underneath Balaam. Balaam became angry and beat the donkey with the rod. ²⁸Then the LORD opened the donkey's mouth and it said to Balaam, "What have I done to you that you've beaten me these three times?"

²⁹Balaam said to the donkey, "Because you've tormented me. If I had a sword in my hand, I'd kill you now."

³⁰The donkey said to Balaam, "Am I not your donkey, on whom you've often ridden to this day? Have I been in the habit of doing this to you?"

Balaam said, "No."

³¹Then the LORD uncovered Balaam's eyes, and Balaam saw the LORD's messenger standing in the road with his sword drawn in his hand. Then he bowed low and worshipped. ³²The LORD's messenger said to him, "Why have you beaten your donkey these three times? I've come out here as an adversary, because you took the road recklessly in front of me. ³³The donkey saw me and turned away from me these three times. If it hadn't turned away from me, I would just now have killed you and let it live."

³⁴Balaam said to the LORD's messenger, "I've sinned, because I didn't know that you were standing against me in the road. Now, if you think it's wrong, I'll go back."

³⁵The LORD's messenger said to Balaam, "Go with the men. But don't say anything. Say only that which I tell you." So Balaam went with Balak's officials.

Balaam and Balak meet

³⁶When Balak heard that Balaam was coming, he went out to meet him at Ir-moab, which is on the border of the Arnon at the farthest point of the border. ³⁷Balak said to Balaam, "Didn't I send urgently and summon you? Why didn't you come to me? Am I really not able to honor you?"

³⁸Balaam said to Balak, "I've now come to you. But I'm only able to speak whatever word God gives me to say. That is what I will speak."

Balaam's first blessing of the Israelites

³⁹Then Balaam went with Balak and they came to Kiriath-huzoth. ⁴⁰Balak sacrificed oxen and sheep and sent them to Balaam and the officials who were with him. ⁴¹In the morning Balak took Balaam and brought him up to Bamoth-baal, where he could see part of the people.

did you know? Balaam's donkey is the only talking mammal in the Bible. The donkey not only spoke but saved Balaam's life three times. God used this experience to get Balaam's attention and convince him to deliver God's message.

23 Balaam said to Balak, "Build me seven altars here and prepare for me seven bulls and seven rams." ²Balak did as Balaam had said. Then Balak and Balaam offered a bull and a ram on each altar. ³Balaam said to Balak, "Stay by your entirely burned offering. I will go and perhaps the LORD will grant me an appearance and speak. Whatever he shows me, I will tell you." Then he went off to a high outlook.

⁴God granted Balaam an appearance. Balaam said to him, "I have arranged seven altars and I have sacrificed a bull and a ram on each altar."

⁵The LORD gave Balaam something to say, and said to him, "Return to Balak and say this."

⁶Balaam returned to him, while he and all the officials of Moab were standing next to his entirely burned offering. ⁷Then he raised his voice and made his address:

"From Aram Balak led me,
    the king of Moab,
        from the eastern mountains.
Come, curse Jacob for me;
    come, denounce Israel.
⁸ How can I curse
    whom God hasn't cursed?
How can I denounce
    whom God hasn't denounced?
⁹ From the top of the rocks I see him;
    from the hills I gaze on him.
Here is a people living alone;

it doesn't consider itself
among the nations.
¹⁰ Who can count the dust of Jacob,
or number a fourth of Israel?
Let me die the death of those who do right,
and let my end be like his."

¹¹Then Balak said to Balaam, "What have you done to me? I took you to curse my enemy. But now you've blessed him."

¹²He answered and said, "Don't I have to take care to speak whatever the LORD gives me to say?"

Balaam's second blessing of the Israelites

¹³Then Balak said to Balaam, "Come with me, please, to another place where you'll see them. You'll see only part of them. You won't see all of them. Then curse them for me from there." ¹⁴He took him to the field of Zophim, to the top of Pisgah. He built seven altars and offered a bull and a ram on each altar.

¹⁵Then Balaam said to Balak, "Stand here by your entirely burned offering, while I seek an appearance over there."

¹⁶The LORD granted Balaam an appearance and gave him a message. He said, "Return to Balak and say this."

¹⁷Balaam approached Balak, who was standing by his entirely burned offering with the officials of Moab. Balak said to him, "What did the LORD say?"

¹⁸Then Balaam raised his voice and made his address:

"Arise, Balak, and listen;
hear me out, Zippor's son.
¹⁹ God isn't a man that
he would lie,
or a human being that he would
change his mind.
Has he ever spoken and not done it,
or promised and not fulfilled it?
²⁰ I received a blessing, and he blessed.
I can't take it back.
²¹ He hasn't envisioned misfortune for Jacob,
nor has he seen trouble for Israel.
The LORD his God is with him,
proclaimed as his king.
²² God, who brought them out of Egypt,
is like a magnificent wild bull
for him.
²³ There is no omen against Jacob,
no divination against Israel.
Instantly it is told to Jacob,
and to Israel, what God performs.
²⁴ A people now rises like a lioness,

> **Memorize**
> Num 23:19

The Basic Truth: God Cannot Lie Numbers 23:18-20

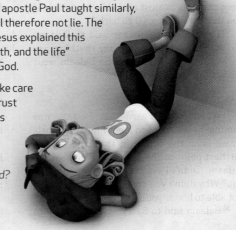

Balaam announced that God is not a human being who will lie or go back on a promise. The prophet Samuel and the apostle Paul taught similarly, each stating that God is not human and will therefore not lie. The nature of God is to tell the truth always. Jesus explained this further when he said, "I am the way, the truth, and the life" (John 14:6). If Jesus is the truth, then so is God.

When we read that God loves us and will take care of us even when things are bad, we can trust that God will do just that. God always keeps God's promises.

Name your favorite promise in the Bible.

What does this promise tell you about God?

like a lion it stands up.
It doesn't lie down until it eats the prey
and drinks the blood of the slain."

²⁵Then Balak said to Balaam, "Don't curse them or bless them."

²⁶But Balaam answered and said to Balak, "Didn't I say to you, 'I'll do whatever the Lord tells me to'?"

Balaam's third blessing of the Israelites

²⁷Balak said to Balaam, "Please come and I'll take you to another place. Perhaps God will prefer it, so that you could curse him for me from there."

²⁸So Balak took Balaam to the top of Peor, which overlooks Jeshimon.^j ²⁹Balaam said to Balak, "Build me seven altars here and prepare for me seven bulls and seven rams." ³⁰Balak did just as Balaam said. He offered a bull and a ram on each altar.

24 Balaam saw that it pleased the Lord to bless the Israelites, so he didn't go as the other times to seek omens. Instead, he turned toward the desert. ²Balaam looked up and saw Israel camping by tribes. Then God's spirit came on him. ³He raised his voice and made his address:

"The oracle of Balaam, Beor's son;
the oracle of a man whose eye is open.^k
⁴ The oracle of one
who hears God's speech,
who perceives the Almighty's^l visions,
who falls down with eyes uncovered.
⁵ How beautiful are your tents, Jacob,
your camps, Israel!
⁶ Like palm groves that stretch out,
like gardens next to a river,
like eaglewood trees
that the Lord has planted,
like cedar trees next to water.
⁷ Water will drip from his branches;
his seed will have plenty of water;
his king will be higher than Agag,
and his kingdom will be lifted up.
⁸ God, who brought him from Egypt,
is like a magnificent wild bull for him.
He will devour enemy nations
and break their bones;
he will strike with his arrows.
⁹ He crouched and lay down like a lion;
like a lioness, who can make her rise?

The one blessing you will be blessed,
and the one cursing you will be cursed."

¹⁰Balak was angry with Balaam. He pounded his fists. Balak said to Balaam, "I summoned you to curse my enemies, but now you've given a blessing these three times. ¹¹Now get out of here and go home. I told you I'd greatly honor you, but the Lord has denied you any honor."

Balaam predicts Moab's destruction

¹²Balaam said to Balak, "Didn't I tell your messengers, whom you sent to me, ¹³'If Balak would give me his house full of silver and gold, I wouldn't be able to break the Lord's command for good or ill by my own will. I'll say whatever the Lord says'? ¹⁴So now I'm going to my people. Let me advise you what this people will do to your people in the days to come." ¹⁵He raised his voice and made his address:

"The oracle of Balaam, Beor's son,
the oracle of a man whose eye is open.
¹⁶ The oracle of one who hears God's speech,
and understands
the Most High's^m knowledge,
who perceives the Almighty'sⁿ visions,
who falls down with eyes uncovered.
¹⁷ I see him, but not now;
I look at him, but not nearby.
A star comes from Jacob;
a scepter arises from Israel,
smashing Moab's forehead,
the head of all the Sethites.
¹⁸ Edom will become a possession,
Seir a possession of its enemies.
But Israel acts powerfully.
¹⁹ Someone from Jacob will rule
and destroy the survivors from Ir."

²⁰ He looked at Amalek
and raised his voice
and gave his address:
"Amalek is foremost among the nations,
but its end is to perish forever."
²¹ He looked at the Kenites
and raised his voice
and gave his address:
"Your dwelling is secure;
your nest is set in the rock.
²² Yet Kain will burn
when Asshur takes you away captive."

^jOr *wasteland* ^kHeb uncertain ^lHeb *Shaddai* or *Mountain One* ^mHeb *Elyon* ⁿHeb *Shaddai* or *Mountain One*

²³ He raised his voice
and made his address:
"How terrible!
Who will live when God does this?
²⁴ Ships from Kittim will attack Asshur;
they will attack Eber,
and even he will perish forever."
²⁵ Then Balaam arose, set out, and returned home. Balak also went on his way.

Israelites and Moabites intermarry

25 When the Israelites lived at Shittim, the people made themselves impure by having illicit sex with Moabite women. ²The Moabite women invited the people to the sacrifices for their god. So the people ate a meal, and they worshipped their god. ³Israel became attached to the Baal of Peor, and the LORD was angry at the Israelites. ⁴The LORD said to Moses: Take all the leaders of the people and kill them on behalf of the LORD in broad daylight, so that the LORD's anger turns away from Israel.

⁵Then Moses said to Israel's officials, "Each of you: kill your men who are attached to the Baal of Peor."

Israelites and Midianites intermarry

⁶An Israelite man brought a Midianite woman to his brothers in the sight of Moses and the entire Israelite community, who were weeping at the entrance of the meeting tent. ⁷When Phinehas (Eleazar's son and Aaron the priest's grandson) saw this, he arose in the middle of the community, took a spear in his hand, ⁸went after the Israelite man into the chamber, and stabbed the two of them, the Israelite man and the woman, through the stomach. Then the plague stopped spreading among the Israelites. ⁹Yet those who died by the plague numbered twenty-four thousand.

¹⁰The LORD spoke to Moses: ¹¹Phinehas (Eleazar's son and Aaron the priest's grandson) has turned back my rage toward the Israelites. Because he was jealous for me among you, I didn't consume the Israelites due to my jealousy. ¹²Therefore, say: I'm now giving him my covenant of well-being. ¹³It will be for him and his descendants a covenant of permanent priesthood, because he was jealous

for his God and sought reconciliation for the Israelites.

¹⁴The name of the slain Israelite man who was killed with the Midianite woman was Zimri the son of Salu, chief of Simeon's household. ¹⁵The name of the slain Midianite woman was Cozbi the daughter of Zur, a tribal leader of a Midianite household. ¹⁶The LORD spoke to Moses: ¹⁷Go after the Midianites and destroy them ¹⁸because they went after you by the deception they devised for you at Peor with Cozbi, the Midianite chief's daughter and their sister, who was killed on the same day as the plague during the events at Peor.

Second census of the Israelite tribes

26 ᵒAfter the plague ᴾthe LORD said to Moses and Eleazar, Aaron the priest's son: ²Take a census of the entire Israelite community, from 20 years old and above by their households, to determine everyone in Israel who is eligible for military service.

³Moses and Eleazar the priest spoke to the people on the plains of Moab by the Jordan opposite Jericho: ⁴"Take a census of those 20 years old and above as the LORD commanded Moses." The Israelites who left the land of Egypt were:

⁵Reuben, Israel's oldest son.

Reuben's descendants: from Hanoch, the Hanochite clan; from Pallu, the Palluite clan; ⁶from Hezron, the Hezronite clan; from Carmi, the Carmite clan. ⁷These are the Reubenite clans. Their enrollment was 43,730.

⁸Pallu's descendants: Eliab.

⁹Eliab's descendants: Nemuel, Dathan, and Abiram. These are the Dathan and Abiram chosen by the community who fought against Moses and Aaron with the community of Korah, when they fought against the LORD. ¹⁰The earth opened its mouth and swallowed them, along with Korah, when the community died and fire devoured 250 persons. They became a warning sign. ¹¹But Korah's descendants didn't die.

¹²Simeon's descendants according to their clans: from Nemuel, the Nemuelite clan; from Jamin, the Jaminite clan; from

ᵒ25:19 in Heb ᴾ26:1 in Heb

Jachin, the Jachinite clan; [13]from Zerah, the Zerahite clan; from Shaul, the Shaulite clan. [14]These are the Simeonite clans, 22,200.

[15]Gad's descendants according to their clans: from Zephon, the Zephonite clan; from Haggi, the Haggite clan; from Shuni, the Shunite clan; [16]from Ozni, the Oznite clan; from Eri, the Erite clan; [17]from Arod, the Arodite clan; from Areli, the Arelite clan. [18]These are the Gadite clans. Their enrollment was 40,500.

[19]Judah's descendants: Er and Onan. Er and Onan died in the land of Canaan. [20]Judah's descendants according to their clans: from Shelah, the Shelanite clan; from Perez, the Perezite clan; from Zerah, the Zerahite clan.

[21]Perez's descendants: from Hezron, the Hezronite clan; from Hamul, the Hamulite clan. [22]These are the Judahite clans. Their enrollment was 76,500.

[23]Issachar's descendants according to their clans: from Tola, the Tolaite clan; from Puvah, the Punite clan; [24]from Jashub, the Jashubite clan; from Shimron, the Shimronite clan. [25]These are the Issacharite clans. Their enrollment was 64,300.

[26]Zebulun's descendants according to their clans: from Sered, the Seredite clan; from Elon, the Elonite clan; from Jahleel, the Jahleelite clan. [27]These are the Zebulunite clans. Their enrollment was 60,500.

[28]Joseph's descendants according to their clans: Manasseh and Ephraim.

[29]Manasseh's descendants: from Machir, the Machirite clan. Machir fathered Gilead. From Gilead, the Gileadite clan. [30]These are Gilead's descendants: from Iezer, the Iezerite clan; from Helek, the Helekite clan; [31]from Asriel, the Asrielite clan; from Shechem, the Shechemite clan; [32]from Shemida, the Shemidaite clan; and from Hepher, the Hepherite clan. [33]But Zelophehad, Hepher's son, had no sons, only daughters. The names of Zelophehad's daughters were Mahlah, Noah, Hoglah, Milcah, and Tirzah. [34]These are the Manassehite clans. Their enrollment was 52,700.

[35]These are Ephraim's descendants according to their clans: from Shuthelah, the Shuthelahite clan; from Becher, the Becherite clan; from Tahan, the Tahanite clan. [36]These are Shuthelah's descendants: from Eran, the Eranite clan. [37]These are Ephraim's descendants. Their enrollment was 32,500.

These are Joseph's descendants according to their clans.

[38]Benjamin's descendants according to their clans: from Bela, the Belaite clan; from Ashbel, the Ashbelite clan; from Ahiram, the Ahiramite clan; [39]from Shupham,[q] the Shuphamite clan; from Hupham, the Huphamite clan. [40]Bela's descendants were Ard and Naaman: from Ard, the Ardite clan; from Naaman, the Naamite clan. [41]These are Benjamin's descendants according to their clans. Their enrollment was 45,600.

[42]These are Dan's descendants according to their clans: from Shuham, the Shuhamite clan. These are the Danite clans according to their clans. [43]All the Shuhamite clans according to their enrollment were 64,400.

[44]Asher's descendants according to their clans: from Imnah, the Imnite clan; from Ishvi, the Ishvite clan; from Beriah, the Beriite clan. [45]From Beriah's descendants: from Heber, the Heberite clan; from Malchiel, the Malchielite clan. [46]The name of Asher's daughter was Serah. [47]These are the clans of Asher's descendants. Their enrollment was 53,400.

[48]Naphtali's descendants according to their clans: from Jahzeel, the Jahzeelite clan; from Guni, the Gunite clan; [49]from Jezer, the Jezerite clan; from Shillem, the Shillemite clan. [50]These are Naphtali's clans according to their clans. Their enrollment was 45,400.

[51]These are the ones enrolled as Israelites: 601,730.

[52]The LORD spoke to Moses: [53]The land will be apportioned to these as an inheritance according to the number of names.

[q]LXX, Syr, Tg, Vulg; MT *Shephupham*

⁵⁴To a large clan you will give a large inheritance, and to a small clan you will give a small inheritance. Each will be given its inheritance according to the number of its enrollment. ⁵⁵The land, however, will be apportioned by lot. They will inherit according to the names of their ancestral tribes. ⁵⁶Whether they are large or small, each tribe will inherit by means of the lot.

Second census of the Levites

⁵⁷These are the ones enrolled as Levites according to their clans: from Gershon, the Gershonite clan; from Kohath, the Kohathite clan; from Merari, the Merarite clan.

⁵⁸These are the Levite clans: the Libnite clan, the Hebronite clan, the Mahlite clan, the Mushite clan, and the Korahite clan. Now Kohath fathered Amram. ⁵⁹The name of Amram's wife was Jochebed, Levi's daughter, who was born to Levi in Egypt. She gave birth for Amram to Aaron, Moses, and Miriam their sister. ⁶⁰To Aaron were born Nadab, Abihu, Eleazar, and Ithamar. ⁶¹Nadab and Abihu died when they made an unauthorized offering to the Lord. ⁶²Their enrollment was 23,000, consisting of every male one month old and above. They weren't enrolled with the Israelites because no inheritance of land was given to them among the Israelites.

Summary

⁶³These are the ones whom Moses and Eleazar the priest enrolled. They enrolled the Israelites on the plains of Moab by the Jordan opposite Jericho. ⁶⁴There wasn't one person among these from those enrolled by Moses and Aaron the priest when they enrolled the Israelites in the Sinai desert. ⁶⁵The Lord had said to them, "They will die in the desert." Not one of them remained, except Caleb, Jephunneh's son, and Joshua, Nun's son.

God's THOUGHTS ◆ My THOUGHTS

God Keeps All God's Promises   Numbers 26:63-65

Not all promises result in good things. For example, you might have been warned that if you didn't clean your room, you would be grounded. And you might have disobeyed your parents and failed to clean it, whether you forgot or just didn't care, and been grounded for one week.

God is sad when we disobey what God has asked us to do. But for us to be able to trust, God has to keep all of God's promises, even the ones that we might not like. God told the Israelites that because they didn't obey, they wouldn't enter the promised land. God said only Caleb and Joshua, who had been faithful, would enter. But first they had to face some consequences.

Wandering in the desert for forty more years might have seemed like punishment for Caleb and Joshua. After all, they believed God and tried to convince the Israelites to obey. However, sin or disobeying to do things our own way affects more than just those people who disobey; sin affects others. God kept the promise to punish the Israelites for their disobedience, which meant Caleb and Joshua had to wait forty more years to enter the promised land. But God also kept the promise that they would enter this land, which they did!

Name a time when your parents kept a promise you didn't like.

What did you learn from that time?

Zelophehad's daughters' inheritance

27 The daughters of Zelophehad, Hepher's son, Gilead's grandson, Machir's great-grandson, and Manasseh's great-great-grandson, belonging to the clan of Manasseh son of Joseph, came forward. His daughters' names were Mahlah, Noah, Hoglah, Milcah, and Tirzah. ²They stood before Moses, Eleazar the priest, the chiefs, and the entire community at the entrance of the meeting tent and said, ³"Our father died in the desert. He wasn't part of the community who gathered against the LORD with Korah's community. He died for his own sin, but he had no sons. ⁴Why should our father's name be taken away from his clan because he didn't have a son? Give us property among our father's brothers."

⁵Moses brought their case before the LORD. ⁶The LORD said to Moses: ⁷Zelophehad's daughters are right in what they are saying. By all means, give them property as an inheritance among their father's brothers. Hand over their father's inheritance to them. ⁸Speak to the Israelites and say: If a man dies and doesn't have a son, you must hand his inheritance over to his daughters. ⁹If he doesn't have a daughter, you will give his inheritance to his brothers. ¹⁰If he doesn't have any brothers, you should give his inheritance to his father's brothers. ¹¹If his father had no brothers, you should give his inheritance to his nearest relative from his clan. He will take possession of it. This will be a regulation and a case law for the Israelites, as the LORD commanded Moses.

Announcement of Moses' death

¹²The LORD said to Moses, "Go up this mountain, Abarim, and look at the land that I've given to the Israelites. ¹³You will see it and then join your ancestors just as Aaron your brother has, ¹⁴because in the Zin desert, when the community confronted you, you rebelled against my command to show them my holiness by means of the water." (These are the waters of Meribah^r of Kadesh in the Zin desert.)

¹⁵Moses spoke to the LORD: ¹⁶"Let the LORD, the God of all living things, appoint someone over the community ¹⁷who will go out before them and return before them, someone who will lead them out and bring them back, so that the LORD's community won't be like sheep without their shepherd."

¹⁸The LORD said to Moses, "Take Joshua, Nun's son, a man who has the spirit, and lay your hand on him. ¹⁹Place him before Eleazar the priest and the entire community and commission him before them. ²⁰You will give him some of your power so that the entire Israelite community may obey. ²¹He will stand before Eleazar the priest, who will determine for him the decision by lot before the LORD. At his command, he and all the Israelites with him, the entire community, will go out, and at his command they will return."

²²Moses did as the LORD commanded him. He took Joshua and placed him before Eleazar the priest and the entire community. ²³He laid his hands on him and commissioned him as the LORD had spoken through Moses.

SAILBOAT

OBEDIENCE

Moses Was Obedient *Numbers 27:12-22*
Moses had been a great leader, serving God by serving the Israelites. Even as his time of leadership was coming to an end due to his approaching death, Moses' main concern was for the people. He asked God to appoint someone as leader of the Israelite people so that they wouldn't be lost—like sheep without a shepherd. Moses stayed obedient to God until the end of his life.◆

Daily offering

28 The LORD spoke to Moses: ²Command the Israelites and say to them: Make sure to offer to me my offering, my food, my food gift as a soothing smell to me at its appointed time.

³You will say to them: This is the food gift that you must present to the LORD: two flawless one-year-old lambs as the regular entirely burned offering every day. ⁴One lamb you will offer in the morning and the second at twilight, ⁵with a tenth of an ephah^s of fine

---

^rOr *confrontation*   ^sOne ephah is approximately twenty quarts.

flour for a grain offering mixed with a fourth of a hin[t] of beaten oil. [6]It is the regular entirely burned offering begun at Mount Sinai, a food gift that is a soothing smell to the LORD. [7]Their drink offering will be a fourth of a hin for each lamb. In the sanctuary a drink offering of brandy will be poured out for the LORD. [8]The second lamb you will offer at twilight like the grain offering and the drink offering in the morning. You will offer a food gift that is a soothing smell to the LORD.

[9]On the Sabbath day: two flawless one-year-old male lambs and two-tenths of fine flour for a grain offering, mixed with oil, and its drink offering. [10]This is the entirely burned offering for every Sabbath, in addition to the regular entirely burned offering and its drink offering.

Monthly offering

[11]At the beginning of every month you will present an entirely burned offering to the LORD: two bulls from the herd, one ram, and seven one-year-old male lambs, all flawless. [12]Use three-tenths of fine flour for a grain offering mixed with oil for each bull, two-tenths of fine flour for a grain offering mixed with oil for each ram, [13]and one-tenth of fine flour for a grain offering mixed with oil for each lamb. It is an entirely burned offering with a soothing smell, a food gift to the LORD. [14]Their drink offerings will be half a hin of wine for a bull, a third hin of wine for a ram, and a fourth hin of wine for a lamb. This is the monthly entirely burned offering for every month through the months of the year. [15]There will be one male goat for a purification offering to the LORD in addition to the regular entirely burned offering and its drink offering.

Yearly offerings

Passover and unleavened bread

[16]On the fourteenth day of the first month[u] there will be a Passover offering to the LORD. [17]On the fifteenth day of this month there will be a festival. For seven days unleavened bread will be eaten. [18]The first day will be a holy occasion. You will not do any job-related work.

[19]You will bring a food gift, an entirely burned offering to the LORD: two bulls from the herd, one ram, and seven male lambs one year old. They will be flawless. [20]Their grain offering will be fine flour mixed with oil. You will offer three-tenths for the bull, two-tenths for the ram, [21]and one-tenth for each of the seven lambs, [22]along with one male goat for a purification offering to seek reconciliation for yourselves. [23]You will offer these in addition to the entirely burned offering of the morning, which is the regular entirely burned offering. [24]Like these, you will also offer each day for seven days a food gift as a soothing smell to the LORD. It will be offered in addition to the regular entirely burned offering and its drink offering. [25]The seventh day will be a holy occasion for you. You will not do any job-related work.

Festival of Weeks

[26]The day of the early produce, when you present your new grain offering to the LORD at your Festival of Weeks, will be a holy occasion for you. You will not do any job-related work. [27]You will present an entirely burned offering as a soothing smell to the LORD: two bulls from the herd, one ram, and seven male lambs one year old. [28]Their grain offering will be fine flour mixed with oil: three-tenths for each bull, two-tenths for the one ram, [29]and one-tenth for each of the seven lambs. [30]Offer one male goat to seek reconciliation for yourselves. [31]You will offer these in addition to the regular entirely burned offering, its grain offering and drink offerings. They will be flawless.

Blowing of the trumpet

29 The first day of the seventh month[v] will be a holy occasion for you. You will not do any job-related work. It will be for you a day of the trumpet's sound. [2]You will offer an entirely burned offering as a soothing smell to the LORD: one bull from the herd, one ram, and seven male lambs one year old, all flawless. [3]Their grain offering will be fine flour mixed with oil, three-tenths for the bull, two-tenths for the ram, [4]and one-tenth for each of the seven lambs. [5]There will be one

---

[t]One hin is approximately one gallon. [u]March–April, Nisan [v]September–October, Tishrei

male goat for a purification offering to seek reconciliation for yourselves. [6]This is in addition to the monthly entirely burned offering with its grain offering, and the regular entirely burned offering with its grain offering and drink offerings as prescribed. It will be a soothing smell, a food gift to the Lord.

Day of Reconciliation

[7]The tenth day of this seventh month will be a holy occasion for you. You will deny yourselves and not do any work. [8]You will present an entirely burned offering to the Lord as a soothing smell: one bull from the herd, one ram, and seven male lambs one year old. They will be flawless. [9]Their grain offering will be fine flour mixed with oil, three-tenths for the bull, two-tenths for the one ram, [10]and one-tenth for each of the seven lambs. [11]There will be one male goat for a purification offering in addition to the purification offering of reconciliation, and the regular entirely burned offering with its grain offering and drink offerings.

Festival of Booths

[12]The fifteenth day of the seventh month[w] will be a holy occasion for you. You will not do any job-related work. You will celebrate a festival to the Lord for seven days. [13]You will present an entirely burned offering, a food gift as a soothing smell to the Lord: thirteen bulls from the herd, two rams, and fourteen male lambs one year old. They will be flawless. [14]Their grain offering will be fine flour mixed with oil: three-tenths for each of the thirteen bulls, two-tenths for each of the two rams, [15]and one-tenth for each of the fourteen lambs. [16]There will be one male goat for a purification offering in addition to the regular entirely burned offering with its grain offering and its drink offering.

[17]On the second day: twelve bulls from the herd, two rams, and fourteen male lambs one year old, all flawless. [18]The grain offering and drink offerings for the bulls, rams, and lambs will be as prescribed for their number. [19]There will be one male goat for a purification offering in addition to the regular entirely burned offering with its grain offering and drink offerings.

[20]On the third day: eleven bulls, two rams, and fourteen male lambs one year old, all flawless. [21]The grain offering and drink offerings for the bulls, rams, and lambs will be as prescribed for their number. [22]There will be one male goat for a purification offering in addition to the regular entirely burned offering with its grain offering and drink offering.

[23]On the fourth day: ten bulls, two rams, and fourteen male lambs one year old, all flawless. [24]The grain offering and drink offerings for the bulls, rams, and lambs will be as prescribed for their number. [25]There will be one male goat for a purification offering in addition to the regular entirely burned offering with its grain offering and drink offering.

[26]On the fifth day: nine bulls, two rams, and fourteen male lambs one year old, all flawless. [27]The grain offering and their drink offerings for the bulls, rams, and lambs will be as prescribed for their number. [28]There will be one male goat for a purification offering in addition to the regular entirely burned offering with its grain offering and drink offering.

[29]On the sixth day: eight bulls, two rams, and fourteen male lambs one year old, all flawless. [30]The grain offering and their drink offerings for the bulls, rams, and lambs will be as prescribed for their number. [31]There will be one male goat for a purification offering in addition to the regular entirely burned offering with its grain offering and its drink offerings.

[32]On the seventh day: seven bulls, two rams, and fourteen male lambs one year old, all flawless. [33]The grain offering and their drink offering for the bulls, rams, and lambs will be as prescribed for their number. [34]There will be one male goat for a purification offering in addition to the regular entirely burned offering with its grain offering and its drink offering.

[35]On the eighth day you will have a holiday. You will not do any job-related work. [36]You will present an entirely burned offering, a food gift as a soothing smell to the Lord: one bull, one ram, and seven male lambs one year old, all without blemish. [37]The grain offering and their drink offerings for the bull,

---

[w]September–October, Tishrei

ram, and lambs will be as prescribed for their number. ³⁸There will be one male goat for a purification offering in addition to the regular entirely burned offering with its grain offering and its drink offering.

³⁹These you will offer to the LORD at your appointed times in addition to your payments for solemn promises, your spontaneous gifts, your entirely burned offerings, your grain offerings, your drink offerings, and your well-being sacrifices.

⁴⁰ˣ Moses told the Israelites everything that the LORD commanded Moses.

Solemn promises by men

30Moses spoke to the leaders of the tribes of the Israelites: This is what the LORD has commanded: ²When a man makes a solemn promise to the LORD or swears a solemn pledge of binding obligation for himself, he cannot break his word. He must do everything he said.

Solemn promises by women

³When a woman makes a solemn promise to the LORD or a binding obligation while she is young and in her father's household, ⁴and her father hears her solemn promise or her binding obligation for herself and keeps silentʸ—then all her solemn promises and any of her binding obligations for herself will stand. ⁵But if her father expresses disapproval to her on the day that he hears her, none of her solemn promises nor any of her binding obligations for herself will stand. The LORD will forgive her, because her father expressed disapproval to her.

⁶If she marries while her solemn promise is in effect or makes a statement by which she binds herself, ⁷and her

husband hears it and on the day he hears it keeps silent—her solemn promises will stand as well as her binding obligations for herself. ⁸But if on the day that her husband hears it he expresses disapproval to her, he can break her solemn promise and the statement by which she bound herself. Then the LORD will forgive her.

⁹Every solemn promise of a widow or a divorced woman who makes a binding obligation for herself will stand.

¹⁰If a woman makes a solemn promise in her husband's household or makes a binding obligation for herself with a solemn pledge, ¹¹and her husband hears, keeps silent, and doesn't express disapproval to her—then all her solemn promises will stand and all her binding obligations for herself will stand. ¹²If her husband breaks them on the day he hears them, then whatever she said with regard to her solemn promises or the binding obligations for herself will not stand. Her husband has broken them. The LORD will forgive her.

¹³Her husband may allow any solemn promise or any binding pledge of self-denial to stand or be broken. ¹⁴But if her husband keeps silent from one day to the next, he has upheld all her solemn promises, or all her binding obligations. He has upheld them because he remained silent on the day he heard them. ¹⁵If he breaks them after he has heard them, he will assume her guilt.

¹⁶These are the regulations that the LORD commanded Moses concerning a husband and his wife and between a father and his daughter while she is young and in her father's household.

War against the Midianites

31The LORD spoke to Moses: ²Take just reparations for the Israelites from the Midianites. Afterward you will join your ancestors.

³Moses spoke to the people: "Equip some of your men for battle so that they may go against Midian and execute the LORD's just punishment against Midian. ⁴You will send out for battle one thousand from each of the tribes of Israel."

⁵From the thousands of Israel, one

ˣ30:1 in Heb ʸOr *her father is deaf to her.*

thousand from each tribe were selected. Twelve thousand were equipped for battle. [6]Moses sent them to battle, one thousand from each tribe, along with Phinehas, Eleazar the priest's son, who carried the sanctuary equipment and the trumpets for sounding the alarm in his hand. [7]They battled against Midian as the LORD had commanded Moses, and they killed every male. [8]They killed the kings of Midian: Evi, Rekem, Zur, Hur, and Reba, the five kings of Midian, along with others slain. They also killed Balaam, Beor's son, with the sword. [9]The Israelites took captive the Midianite women, their little ones, all their cattle, their herds, and their possessions. [10]They burned all the cities where they lived and their encampments. [11]They took all the spoils of war and the valuable property, both human and animal, [12]and they brought the captives, the valuable property, and the spoils of war to Moses, Eleazar the priest, and the Israelite community, at the camp on the plains of Moab by the Jordan across from Jericho.

Purification from war

[13]Moses, Eleazar the priest, and the chiefs of the community went to meet them outside the camp. [14]Moses became angry with the commanders of the army, the officers of thousands and the officers of hundreds, who came back from the battle. [15]Moses said to them, "Have you let all the women live? [16]These very women, on Balaam's advice, made the Israelites break faith with the LORD in the affair at Peor, so there was a plague among the LORD's community. [17]Now kill every male child and every female who has known a man intimately by sleeping with him. [18]But all the young girls who have not known a man intimately by sleeping with him, spare for yourselves. [19]You will remain outside the camp for seven days. Everyone among you or your captives who has killed a person or touched a corpse who must purify themselves on the third and seventh days. [20]You must also purify every garment, and everything made of leather, goats' hair, or wood."

Instructions about the spoils of war

[21]Eleazar the priest said to the men of battle who had gone out to war, "This is the regulation in the Instruction that the LORD commanded Moses: [22]Gold, silver, copper, iron, tin, and lead—[23]anything that can withstand fire—you will put through the fire and it will be clean. It will also be purified with the water of purification. Anything that isn't able to withstand fire, you will immerse in water. [24]You must wash your clothes on the seventh day and you will be clean. Afterward you may enter the camp."

[25]The LORD said to Moses: [26]You, Eleazar the priest, and the leaders of the community's households must take an inventory of the valuable property and the captives, both human and animals, [27]and divide the valuable property between the warriors who went into battle and the entire community. [28]You will offer as tribute to the LORD from each warrior who went into battle one living being in five hundred, whether human, oxen, donkeys, or flocks. [29]Take it from the warriors' half and give it to Eleazar the priest as a gift offering to the LORD. [30]But from the Israelites' half you will take one out of every fifty, whether from human, oxen, donkeys, or flock—all the animals. You will give them to the Levites who carry out the duties of the LORD's dwelling.

[31]Moses and Eleazar the priest did as the LORD commanded Moses. [32]The valuable property remaining from the spoils of war that the people of the army had taken was 675,000 sheep, [33]72,000 oxen, [34]61,000 donkeys, [35]and 32,000 women who hadn't known a man intimately by sleeping with him. [36]The half-share of those who had gone out to battle numbered 337,500 sheep, [37]of which the LORD's tribute was 675. [38]The oxen were 36,000, of which the LORD's tribute was 72. [39]The donkeys were 30,500, of which the LORD's tribute was 61. [40]Humans were 16,000, of which the LORD's tribute was 32 persons. [41]Moses gave the tribute, a gift offering for the LORD, to Eleazar the priest as the LORD had commanded Moses.

[42]As for the half-share of the Israelites that Moses divided from those who had gone out to battle: [43]the community's half-share was 337,500 sheep, [44]36,000 oxen, [45]30,500 donkeys, [46]and 16,000 humans. [47]Moses took from the Israelites' half one out of every fifty, from humans and animals. He gave them to the Levites who carry out the duties of the

Lᴏʀᴅ's dwelling, just as the Lᴏʀᴅ had commanded Moses.

⁴⁸The commanders over the thousands of the army, officers over thousands and officers over hundreds, approached Moses ⁴⁹and said to Moses, "Your servants have counted the warriors in our charge and not one of us is missing. ⁵⁰We have brought the Lᴏʀᴅ's offering that each found, gold articles—anklets, bracelets, signet rings, earrings, and necklaces—to seek reconciliation for ourselves before the Lᴏʀᴅ." ⁵¹Moses and Eleazar the priest took all the gold articles from them. ⁵²All the gold for the gift offering that was presented to the Lᴏʀᴅ from the officers of thousands and the officers of hundreds was sixteen thousand seven hundred fifty shekels. ⁵³Each of the men of battle took spoils of war for himself. ⁵⁴Yet Moses and Eleazar the priest also received the gold from the officers of thousands and of hundreds, and they brought it to the meeting tent as a memorial for the Israelites before the Lᴏʀᴅ.

Reuben and Gad request land

32 The livestock owned by the Reubenites and the Gadites were unusually vast and numerous. They saw that the land of Jazer and the land of Gilead were exactly the place for livestock. ²So the Gadites and the Reubenites came and said to Moses, Eleazar the priest, and the chiefs of the community: ³"Ataroth, Dibon, Jazer, Nimrah, Heshbon, Elealeh, Sebam, Nebo, and Beon is ⁴the land that the Lᴏʀᴅ struck down before the Israelite community. It is a land for livestock, and your servants have livestock." ⁵They said, "If you approve our request, give this land to your servants as property. Don't make us cross the Jordan."

⁶Moses said to the Gadites and the Reubenites, "Should your brothers go to war, while you stay here? ⁷Why would you destroy the Israelites' resolve to cross into the land that the Lᴏʀᴅ gave them? ⁸Your ancestors did this, when I sent them from Kadesh-barnea to inspect the land. ⁹They went up to the Cluster ravine, saw the land, and destroyed the Israelites' resolve to enter the land that the Lᴏʀᴅ had given them. ¹⁰The Lᴏʀᴅ became angry on that day and promised, ¹¹'None of the persons that went up from Egypt, those 20 years old

and above, will see the fertile ground that I promised to Abraham, Isaac, and Jacob, because they didn't remain true to me, ¹²except Caleb, Jephunneh the Kennizite's son, and Joshua, Nun's son, because they remained true to the Lᴏʀᴅ.' ¹³The Lᴏʀᴅ became angry with the Israelites and made them wander in the desert for forty years until the entire generation had died, which had done evil in the Lᴏʀᴅ's eyes. ¹⁴Now you've taken the place of your ancestors, a group of sinful men, to intensify the Lᴏʀᴅ's anger against Israel. ¹⁵If you turn away from him, he will turn away again to abandon Israel in the desert. Then you will destroy this entire people."

Conditions for possession of the land

¹⁶So they approached him and said, "We will build walled enclosures here for our livestock and towns for our children. ¹⁷Then we will eagerly fight in front of the Israelites until we have brought them into their place. Our children will live in the fortified cities because of the land's inhabitants. ¹⁸And we won't return to our homes until each one of the Israelites takes possession of his property. ¹⁹We won't inherit land with them there across the Jordan, because we've received our property on the east side of the Jordan."

²⁰Moses said to them, "Do this and fight before the Lᴏʀᴅ in war. ²¹All of you who are equipped for war, cross the Jordan before the Lᴏʀᴅ until he has driven his enemies out before him ²²and the land is subdued in the Lᴏʀᴅ's presence. Then you may return innocently before the Lᴏʀᴅ and Israel, and this land will be your property before the Lᴏʀᴅ. ²³But if you don't do this, you've sinned against the Lᴏʀᴅ. Know that your sin will find you. ²⁴So build towns for your children and walled enclosures for your flocks, but do what you have promised."

²⁵The Gadites and the Reubenites said to Moses, "Your servants will do as my master has commanded. ²⁶Our children, wives, livestock, and all of our animals will remain in the cities of Gilead. ²⁷But your servants, everyone equipped for war before the Lᴏʀᴅ, will go over to do battle as my master said."

²⁸Moses made demands for them to Eleazar the priest, to Joshua, Nun's son, and to the leaders of the households of the Israelite

tribes. ²⁹Moses said to them, "If the Gadites and the Reubenites cross the Jordan with you, each equipped for battle before the LORD, and the land is subdued before you, then you will give them the land of Gilead as a possession. ³⁰If, however, they don't cross with you, equipped for war, they will take possession of property with you in the land of Canaan."

³¹The Gadites and the Reubenites answered, "We'll do just as the LORD has spoken to your servants. ³²We'll cross into the land of Canaan before the LORD, equipped for war. But the property we inherit will be across the Jordan."

Territory of Gad, Reuben, and half the tribe of Manasseh

³³So Moses gave to them—to the Gadites, the Reubenites, and half the tribe of Manasseh, Joseph's son—the kingdom of Sihon the king of the Amorites, and the kingdom of Og the king of Bashan, including the land, its cities, and the territory surrounding the land's cities. ³⁴The Gadites built Dibon, Ataroth, Aroer, ³⁵Atroth-shophan, Jazer, Jogbehah, ³⁶Beth-nimrah, and Beth-haran, fortified cities and walled enclosures for flocks. ³⁷The Reubenites built Heshbon, Elealeh, Kiriathaim, ³⁸Nebo, and Baal-meon (whose names were changed), and Sibmah. They named the cities that they built. ³⁹The descendants of Machir, Manasseh's son, went to Gilead, captured it, and drove out the Amorites who were there. ⁴⁰So Moses gave Gilead to Machir, Manasseh's son, and he lived there. ⁴¹Manasseh's son Jair went and captured their villages and named them Havvoth-jair.^z ⁴²Nobah went and captured Kenath and its surrounding villages. He renamed it Nobah after himself.

March out of Egypt and through the sea

33 These were the stages by which the Israelites marched when they left the land of Egypt, according to their military units under the leadership of Moses and Aaron. ²Moses recorded the points of departure for each stage of the march at the LORD's command. These are the stages of their march according to their points of departure. ³They marched from Rameses on the

fifteenth day of the first month.^a On the day after the Passover the Israelites went out defiantly^b in the sight of all the Egyptians, ⁴while the Egyptians were burying their oldest males, whom the LORD had killed. The LORD also executed judgments against their gods. ⁵The Israelites marched from Rameses and they camped at Succoth. ⁶They marched from Succoth and camped at Etham on the edge of the desert. ⁷They marched from Etham and turned back to Pi-hahiroth, which faces Baal-zephon, and they camped before Migdol. ⁸They marched from Pi-hahiroth and they crossed through the sea toward the desert.

March through the southern desert

Then they traveled three days in the Etham desert and they camped at Marah. ⁹They marched from Marah and arrived at Elim. At Elim there were twelve springs of water and seventy palm trees and they camped there.

¹⁰They marched from Elim and camped by the Reed Sea.^c

¹¹They marched from the Reed Sea and camped in the Sin desert.

¹²They marched from the Sin desert and camped at Dophkah.

¹³They marched from Dophkah and camped at Alush.

¹⁴They marched from Alush and camped at Rephidim, where there was no water for the people to drink.

¹⁵They marched from Rephidim and camped in the Sinai desert.

¹⁶They marched from the Sinai desert and camped at Kibroth-hattaavah.

¹⁷They marched from Kibroth-hattaavah and camped at Hazeroth.

¹⁸They marched from Hazeroth and camped at Rithmah.

¹⁹They marched from Rithmah and camped at Rimmon-perez.

²⁰They marched from Rimmon-perez and camped at Libnah.

²¹They marched from Libnah and camped at Rissah.

²²They marched from Rissah and camped at Kehelathah.

²³They marched from Kehelathah and camped at Mount Shepher.

---

^zOr the villages of Jair ^aMarch–April, Nisan ^bOr with a high hand ^cOr Red Sea

[24]They marched from Mount Shepher and camped at Haradah.

[25]They marched from Haradah and camped at Makheloth.

[26]They marched from Makheloth and camped at Tahath.

[27]They marched from Tahath and camped at Terah.

[28]They marched from Terah and camped at Mithkah.

[29]They marched from Mithkah and camped at Hashmonah.

[30]They marched from Hashmonah and camped at Moseroth.

[31]They marched from Moseroth and camped at Bene-jaakan.

[32]They marched from Bene-jaakan and camped at Hor-haggidgad.

[33]They marched from Hor-haggidgad and camped at Jotbathah.

[34]They marched from Jotbathah and camped at Abronah.

[35]They marched from Abronah and camped at Ezion-geber.

[36]They marched from Ezion-geber and camped in the Zin desert (that is, Kadesh).

March through the Transjordan region

[37]They marched from Kadesh and camped at Mount Hor, on the edge of the land of Edom. [38]Aaron the priest ascended Mount Hor at the LORD's command, and he died there in the fortieth year on the first day of the fifth month[d] after the Israelites left the land of Egypt. [39]Aaron was 123 years old when he died on Mount Hor. [40]The Canaanite king of Arad, who ruled in the arid southern plain in the land of Canaan, heard of the Israelites' coming.

[41]They marched from Mount Hor and camped at Zalmonah.

[42]They marched from Zalmonah and camped at Punon.

[43]They marched from Punon and camped at Oboth.

[44]They marched from Oboth and camped at Iye-abarim in the territory of Moab.

[45]They marched from Iyim and camped at Dibon-gad.

[46]They marched from Dibon-gad and camped at Almon-diblathaim.

[47]They marched from Almon-diblathaim and camped in the Abarim mountains in front of Nebo.

[48]They marched from the Abarim mountains and camped in the plains of Moab by the Jordan across from Jericho.

[49]They camped by the Jordan from Beth-jeshimoth to Abel-shittim in the plains of Moab.

Divine instruction about the land

[50]The LORD spoke to Moses on the plains of Moab by the Jordan across from Jericho: [51]Speak to the Israelites and say to them: When you cross the Jordan into the land of Canaan, [52]you will drive out all the inhabitants of the land before you. You will destroy all their carved figures. You will also destroy all their cast images. You will eliminate all their shrines. [53]You will take possession of the land and live in it, because I've given the land to you to possess. [54]You will divide up the land by lot according to your clans. To the large you will make its inheritance large, and to the small you will make its inheritance small. To whomever the lot falls, that place will be his. You will inherit land according

did you know? It took forty-three years from the time the Israelites crossed the Reed Sea as they left Egypt to the time they crossed the Jordan River into the promised land. In the years in between, the Israelite people camped in forty-six different places. That's a lot of moving!

to your ancestral tribes. [55]But if you don't drive out the inhabitants of the land before you, then those you allow to remain will prick your eyes and be thorns in your side. They will harass you in the land in which you are living. [56]Then what I intended to do to them, I'll do to you.

Boundaries of the land of Canaan

34 The LORD said to Moses: [2]Command the Israelites and say to them: When you enter the land of Canaan, this is the land

[d]July–August, probably Av

that will fall to you as an inheritance. The land of Canaan according to its boundaries:

³Your southern boundary extends from the Zin desert alongside Edom. Your southern border extends from the edge of the Dead Sea on the east. ⁴Your border will turn south of the ascent of Akrabbim and cross toward Zin. Its limit will be south of Kadesh-barnea. It will go out to Hazar-addar and cross toward Azmon. ⁵The border will then turn from Azmon to the Egypt ravine. Its limit will be at the Mediterranean Sea.

⁶Your western border will be the Mediterranean Sea. This will be your western border.

⁷This will be your northern border: From the Mediterranean Sea you will mark out your boundary to Mount Hor. ⁸From Mount Hor you will mark out your boundary to Lebo-hamath. The limit of the border will be Zedad. ⁹The border will go out to Ziphron. Its limit will be Hazar-enan. This will be your northern border.

¹⁰You will mark out your eastern border from Hazar-enan to Shepham. ¹¹The border will descend from Shepham to Riblah on the east side of Ain. The border will go down and meet the eastern slope of the Galilee Sea. ¹²The border will descend to the Jordan. Its limit will be the Dead Sea.

This will be your land with its borders all around.

¹³Moses commanded the Israelites: This is the land that you will inherit by lot, which the Lord has commanded to give to the nine and a half tribes, ¹⁴because the tribe of Reuben by their households and the tribe of Gad by their households, and half the tribe of Manasseh have taken their inheritance. ¹⁵The two and a half tribes have taken their inheritance across the Jordan at Jericho toward the east.

Appointment of leaders to assign the inheritance

¹⁶The Lord spoke to Moses: ¹⁷These are the names of the men who will assign the inheritance of the land: Eleazar the priest and Joshua, Nun's son. ¹⁸You will also take one chief from each tribe to apportion the land. ¹⁹These are the names of the men: from the tribe of Judah, Caleb, Jephunneh's son; ²⁰from the tribe of the Simeonites, Shemuel, Ammihud's son; ²¹from the tribe of Benjamin, Elidad, Chislon's son; ²²from the tribe of the Danites, a chief, Bukki, Jogli's son; ²³from Joseph's descendants: of the tribe of the Manassites, a chief, Hanniel, Ephod's son; ²⁴and from the tribe of the Ephraimites, a chief, Kemuel, Shiphtan's son; ²⁵from the tribe of the Zebulunites, a chief, Elizaphan, Parnach's son; ²⁶from the tribe of the Issacharites, a chief, Paltiel, Azzan's son; ²⁷from the tribe of the Asherites, a chief, Ahihud, Shelomi's son; ²⁸from the tribe of the Naphtalites, a chief, Pedahel, Ammihud's son.

²⁹These are the ones whom the Lord commanded to assign the inheritance of the Israelites in the land of Canaan.

Cities and pastures of the Levites

35 The Lord spoke to Moses in the Moab plains by the Jordan across from Jericho: ²Command the Israelites that they give cities from their inherited property to the Levites in which to live. You will also give the Levites pastures around their cities. ³The cities will be theirs in which to live. Their pastures will be for their cattle, their possessions, and all their animals. ⁴The pastures of the cities that you must give to the Levites will extend from the wall of the city outward for one thousand five hundred feet in all directions. ⁵You will measure outside the city on the east side three thousand feet, on the south side three thousand feet, on the west side three thousand feet, and on the north side three thousand feet, with the city in the middle. These will be their cities' pastures.

⁶Six of the cities that you give to the Levites will be refuge cities. You will allow the person who kills someone to flee there. In addition to these you will give them forty-two cities. ⁷All the cities that you give to the Levites will total forty-eight, along with their pastures. ⁸As for the cities that you give from the property of the Israelites, you will take more from the larger tribes and less from the smaller. Each in proportion to its inheritance will give cities to the Levites.

Refuge cities

⁹The Lord spoke to Moses: ¹⁰Speak to the Israelites and say to them: When you cross

the Jordan into the land of Canaan, [11]identify for yourselves cities to be refuge cities, where a person who kills someone by accident may flee. [12]The cities will be for you a place of refuge from the close relative of the dead. The person who killed someone may not be put to death until he stands before the community for judgment. [13]You will establish six refuge cities for yourselves. [14]You will establish three cities across the Jordan and three cities in the land of Canaan. They will be the refuge cities. [15]These six cities will be refuge for Israelites, immigrants, and temporary residents, as a place to flee for anyone who kills a person by accident.

[16]But if someone strikes a person with an iron object and he dies, he is a murderer. The murderer must definitely be put to death. [17]If someone strikes another with a stone in hand that could cause death and he dies, he is a murderer. The murderer must definitely be put to death. [18]Or if someone strikes with a wood object in hand that could cause death, he is a murderer. The murderer must definitely be put to death. [19]The close relative responsible for the blood[e] of the dead is the one who will put the murderer to death. When he meets him, he will execute him. [20]If in hatred someone hits another or throws something at him with premeditation, he will be put to death. [21]Or if in hostility someone strikes another with his hand and he dies, the one who struck is a murderer and he will be put to death. The close relative will put the murderer to death when he meets him.

[22]But if suddenly and without hostility someone hits another or throws any object at him without premeditation, [23]or accidentally

[e]Or (here and throughout Num 35) *the close relative of the blood*

Refuge Cities Numbers 35:6-28

In ancient times crimes were dealt with by the elders in the community. People convicted of crimes usually had to pay a penalty but didn't go to jail. The penalty was different when someone was killed. Often a member of the dead person's family would kill the murderer when that happened. Even if the death had been an accident, the family would still try to kill the person responsible. This practice would sometimes lead to a bitter feud, with families hating and fighting each other for generations.

Refuge cities were meant to do away with this practice. They were located in the land where the priests lived, because the priests would stand for God's Instruction and not a particular person or family.

If someone accidentally killed another person, the killer could go to a refuge city and live there safely until an investigation took place. If they were declared innocent, they would continue to live in the refuge city until the death of the high priest, when they could return to their own home.

The refuge cities showed God's concern for justice in a time when people were more concerned with revenge than with guilt or innocence. It's dangerous to ignore wrong or to unfairly assume someone is guilty. It's important to stand up for justice and listen to all sides of a story.

Think of a time when you accidentally hurt someone.

What did you say or do to apologize to that person?

drops any stone on him that could cause death and he dies—even though they weren't enemies and no evil was intended—²⁴then the community must come to a verdict between the killer and the close relative in accordance with these case laws. ²⁵The community will protect the killer from the hand of the close relative and return him to the refuge city where he fled. He will live there until the death of the high priest who was anointed with holy oil. ²⁶But if the killer ever goes outside the boundaries of the refuge city where he fled ²⁷and the close relative finds him outside the boundary of his refuge city and kills him, he will not be responsible for his blood. ²⁸The killer must live in his refuge city until the high priest's death. After the high priest's death the killer may return to the land he owns.

²⁹These will be the regulations and case laws for all time in all your settlements.

³⁰Anyone who kills another will be executed on the evidence of witnesses. But one witness alone cannot testify against a person for a death sentence. ³¹You may not accept a ransom for the life of a killer, who is guilty of a capital crime, for he must definitely be put to death. ³²You may not accept a ransom for someone who has fled to his refuge city so that he can return and live in the land before the priest's death. ³³You may not pollute the land in which you live, for the blood pollutes the land. There can be no recovery[f] for the land from the blood that is shed in it, except by the blood of the one who shed it. ³⁴You will not make the land in which you live unclean, the land in the middle of which I reside, for I the Lord reside among the Israelites.

Inheritance of Zelophehad's daughters

36 The leaders of the households of the clans of Gilead, Machir's son and Manasseh's grandson, of Joseph's clans, approached and spoke before Moses and the chiefs, who were the leaders of the Israelite households. ²They said, "The Lord commanded my master to give the land as an inheritance by lot to the Israelites. But my master was also commanded by the Lord to give the inheritance of Zelophehad our brother to his daughters. ³If they are married to someone from another Israelite tribe, their inheritance will be taken away from our household and given to another tribe into which they marry. Then it will be taken away from the lot of our inheritance. ⁴At the Israelite Jubilee, their inheritance will be added to the inheritance of the tribe into which they married. Then their inheritance will be taken away from the inheritance of our ancestral tribe."

⁵Then Moses commanded the Israelites according to the Lord's word: "The tribe of Joseph's descendants are correct in what they're saying. ⁶This is the word that the Lord commands to Zelophehad's daughters: They may marry whomever seems best to them, but they may only marry into one of the clans of their ancestral tribe, ⁷so that the inheritance of the Israelites doesn't transfer from one tribe to another. The Israelites will each retain the tribal inheritance of his ancestral tribe. ⁸Every daughter who inherits land from an Israelite tribe must marry into one of the clans of her father's tribe. In this way each Israelite will own the land of his ancestors. ⁹An inheritance of land may not be transferred from one tribe to another, for the Israelite tribes will each retain its own inheritance."

¹⁰Zelophehad's daughters did as the Lord commanded Moses. ¹¹Mahlah, Tirzah, Hoglah, Milcah, and Noah, Zelophehad's daughters, married their cousins. ¹²They married into the clan of Manasseh, Joseph's son. Their inheritance remained in the tribe of their father's clan.

Conclusion

¹³These are the commandments and the case laws that the Lord commanded the Israelites through Moses in the plains of Moab by the Jordan across from Jericho.

---

[f] Or reconciliation

Deuteronomy

things
YOU'LL DISCOVER

In Deuteronomy, Moses gave long speeches that told all the important things the Israelites needed to know before they finally moved into Canaan, the promised land.

people
YOU'LL MEET

Moses—the leader of Israel and God's spokesperson (Deut 1–34)
Joshua—Moses' helper and Israel's new leader (Deut 1; 31–34)

places
YOU'LL GO

The wilderness (present-day eastern Egypt)

words
YOU'LL REMEMBER

"Israel, listen! Our God is the Lord! Only the Lord! Love the Lord your God with all your heart, all your being, and all your strength" (Deut 6:4-5).

The book of Deuteronomy begins as the Israelites are about to cross the Jordan River and enter the land God had promised to their ancestor Abraham. After forty years of wandering in the desert between Egypt and their future home, Moses gathered the Israelites so he could tell them again everything that had happened since they escaped slavery.

Some of the Israelites hadn't even been alive when the journey began. So Moses told stories of the Israelites' time in the desert, recalling God's miracles of feeding and caring for the people. He told about the painful times when they failed to follow God's Instruction. He also reminded them that God chose them to be a special people who would always need to live by God's Instruction.

Deuteronomy means "Instruction" and is the fifth book in the Pentateuch, called *Torah* (tor-ah). This Instruction told the people everything they needed to know before they entered the land God had promised to them. The people were expected to listen to and live by these important words.

Jesus referenced the Torah when he said the greatest commandment of all is that we love God with all of our heart (Matt 22:37). Deuteronomy reminds us again and again why it's so good to listen to God! ◊

The first heading:
Introducing Deuteronomy

1 These are the words that Moses spoke to all Israel across the Jordan River, in the desert, on the plain across from Suph, between Paran and Tophel, Laban, Hazeroth, and Di-zahab. (²It is eleven days from Horeb to Kadesh-barnea along the Mount Seir route.) ³It was in the fortieth year, on the first day of the eleventh month, that Moses spoke to the Israelites precisely what the Lord had commanded him for them. (⁴This was after the defeat of Sihon, the Amorite king who ruled in Heshbon, and Og, Bashan's king, who ruled in Ashtaroth and[a] Edrei.) ⁵Beyond the Jordan, in the land of Moab, Moses began to explain this Instruction. He said the following:

Leaving Mount Horeb

⁶At Horeb, the Lord our God told us: You've been at this mountain long enough. ⁷Get going! Enter the hills of the Amorites and the surrounding areas in the desert, the highlands, the lowlands, the arid southern region, and the seacoast—the land of the Canaanites—and the Lebanon range, all the way to the great Euphrates River. ⁸Look, I have laid the land before you. Go and possess the land that I[b] promised to give to your ancestors Abraham, Isaac, and Jacob, as well as to their descendants after them.

⁹At that same time, I told you: I can't handle all of you by myself. ¹⁰The Lord your God has multiplied your number—you are now as countless as the stars in the sky. ¹¹May the Lord, your ancestors' God, continue to multiply you—a thousand times more! And may God bless you, just as he promised. ¹²But how can I handle all your troubles, burdens, and disputes by myself? ¹³Now, for each of your tribes, choose wise, discerning, and well-regarded individuals. I will appoint them as your leaders.

¹⁴You answered me: "What you have proposed is a good idea."

¹⁵So I took leading individuals from your tribes, people who were wise and well-regarded, and I set them up as your leaders. There were commanders over thousands, hundreds, fifties, and tens, as well as officials for each of your tribes.

¹⁶At that same time, I commanded your judges: Listen to your fellow tribe members and judge fairly, whether the dispute is between one fellow tribe member or between a tribe member and an immigrant. ¹⁷Don't show favoritism in a decision. Hear both sides out, whether the person is important or not. Don't be afraid of anyone because the ruling belongs to God. Any dispute that is too difficult for you to decide, bring to me and I will take care of it.

¹⁸So at that time, I commanded you concerning everything you were to do.

The spy disaster

¹⁹We left Horeb and journeyed through that vast and terrifying desert you saw, on the way to the hills of the Amorites, exactly as the Lord our God commanded us. Then we arrived at Kadesh-barnea. ²⁰I said to you: You have come to the hills of the Amorites, which the Lord our God is giving to us. ²¹Look! The Lord your God has laid out the land before you. Go up and take it, just as the Lord, your ancestors' God, has promised you. Don't be afraid! Don't be frightened!

²²Then all of you approached me, saying, "Let's send spies ahead of us—they can check out the land for us. Then they can return with word about the route we should use and bring a report about the cities that we'll be entering."

²³This idea seemed good to me, so I selected twelve men, one from each tribe. ²⁴These set out and went up into the hills, going as far as the Cluster[c] ravine. They walked all around that area. ²⁵They took some of the land's fruit and then came back down to us. They reported to us: "The land that the Lord our God is giving to us is wonderful!" ²⁶But you weren't willing to go up. You rejected the Lord your God's instruction. ²⁷You complained in your tents, saying things like, "The Lord hates us! That's why he brought us out of Egypt—to hand us over to the Amorites, to destroy us! ²⁸What are we doing? Our brothers have made our hearts sick by saying, 'People far stronger and much taller than we live there, and the cities are huge, with walls sky-high! Worse still, we saw the descendants of the Anakites there!'"

²⁹But I said to you: Don't be terrified!

---

[a]LXX, Syr, Vulg; MT lacks *and.* [b]Sam, LXX; MT *the Lord* [c]Heb *Eshcol* means *bunch, a cluster* (of grapes); cf Num 13:23–24; 32:9.

Don't be afraid of them! [30]The LORD your God is going before you. He will fight for you just as he fought for you in Egypt while you watched, [31]and as you saw him do in the desert. Throughout your entire journey, until you reached this very place, the LORD your God has carried you just as a parent carries a child.

[32]But you had no faith in the LORD your God about this matter, [33]even though he went ahead of you, scouting places where you should camp, in fire by night, so you could see the road you were taking, and in cloud during the daytime.

[34]The LORD heard what you said. He was angry and he swore: [35]Not even one of these people—this wicked generation!—will see the wonderful land that I promised to give to your ancestors. [36]The only exception is Caleb, Jephunneh's son. He will see it. I will give the land he walked on to him and his children for this reason: he was completely devoted to the LORD.

([37]The LORD was even angry with me because of what you did. "You won't enter the land either," God said. [38]"But Nun's son Joshua, your assistant, will enter it. Strengthen him because he's the one who will help Israel inherit the land.")

[39]Now as for your toddlers, those you said would be taken in war, and your young children who don't yet know right and wrong—they will enter the land. I will give it to them. They will possess it! [40]But you all must now

God's Thoughts ◆ My Thoughts

Hard Times Make Us Strong *Deuteronomy 1:1-45*

You may have noticed there are people who tend to focus on the bad rather than the good things that happen in life. From what we read in the Bible, it seems the Israelites did this a lot.

In one of his last messages to the Israelite people, Moses talked about their lack of trust in God. He reminded them how God had loved them like a parent loves their child and named some of the good things God had done for them.

Moses also told them that whenever they faced a challenge, they complained that things were horrible or that God didn't love them. Moses wanted to help the people learn to think differently.

Hard times can help us grow stronger. Think about people who lift weights. They might struggle at first to lift three-pound weights, but this becomes easier after a while. So they move on to five- and then ten-pound weights.

Life will always have good and bad times. When things are bad, consider it as a chance to grow stronger. It can also help to try to focus on the things that are good, such as God's promises of love and protection.

Name a time when something bad in your life turned into something good.

What lesson did you learn during that time?

turn around. Head back toward the wilderness along the route of the Reed Sea.[d]

⁴¹You replied to me: "We've sinned against the LORD! We will go up! We will fight, just as the LORD our God commanded." Each one of you grabbed your weapons. You thought it would be easy[e] to go up into the hills. ⁴²But the LORD told me: Tell them: Don't go up! Don't fight because I will not be with you. You will be defeated by your enemies.

⁴³I reported this to you but you wouldn't listen. You disobeyed the LORD's instruction. Hotheadedly, you went up into the hills. ⁴⁴And the Amorites who lived in those hills came out to meet you in battle. They chased you like bees give chase! They gave you a beating from Seir all the way to Hormah. ⁴⁵When you came back, you cried before the LORD, but he wouldn't respond to your tears or give you a hearing.

⁴⁶And so you stayed in Kadesh-barnea for quite some time.

Journeys in Transjordan

2 Next, we turned around and headed back toward the wilderness along the Reed Sea[f] road, exactly as the LORD instructed me. We traveled all around Mount Seir for a long time.

²Eventually the LORD said: ³You've been traveling around this mountain long enough. Head north. ⁴Command the people as follows: You are

SAILBOAT

HONEST AND TRUE

Do the Right Thing *Deuteronomy 2:4-6*
As the Israelites entered the territory of Seir, God commanded them to leave the people who lived in that land alone. God knew that those people, who were Esau's descendants, would be afraid of the Israelites. This would give the Israelites the power to take advantage, claim land, and steal food if they wanted to. But God told them not to bother Esau's descendants. This passage teaches that Israel's God is also God of all humanity. God gave clear instructions directing the Israelites to do the right thing. God told them not to use power and strength to take something that didn't belong to them.◗

about to enter into the territory of your relatives who live in Seir: Esau's descendants. They will be afraid of you, so watch yourselves most carefully. ⁵Don't fight with them because I will not give the tiniest parcel of their land to you. I have given Mount Seir to Esau's family as their property. ⁶Of course you may buy food from them with money so you can eat, and also water with money so you can drink.

⁷No doubt about it: the LORD your God has blessed you in all that you have done. He watched over your journey through that vast desert. Throughout these forty years the LORD your God has been with you. You haven't needed a thing.

⁸So we passed through the territory of our relatives who live in Seir, Esau's descendants, leaving the desert road from Elath and from Ezion-geber. Next we turned and went along the Moab wilderness route. ⁹The LORD said to me: Don't aggravate Moab. Don't fight them in battle because I won't give any part of their land to you as your own. I have given Ar to Lot's descendants as their property.

(¹⁰Now the Emim[g] had lived there before. They were big and numerous and tall—just like the Anakim. ¹¹Most people thought the Emim were Rephaim, like the Anakim were. But the Moabites called them "Emim." ¹²Additionally, the Horim[h] had lived in Seir previously, but Esau's descendants took possession of their area, eliminating them altogether and settling in their place. That is exactly what Israel did in the land it took possession of, which the LORD gave to them.)

¹³"So then, get going. Cross the Zered ravine." So we crossed the Zered ravine.

¹⁴It took us a total of thirty-eight years to go from Kadesh-barnea until we crossed the Zered ravine. It was at that point that the last of the previous generation, every one of fighting age in the camp, had died, just as the LORD had sworn about them. ¹⁵In fact, the LORD's power was against them, to rid the camp of them, until they were all gone.

¹⁶Now as soon as all those of fighting age had died, ¹⁷the LORD said to me: ¹⁸Today you are crossing through the territory of Moab and Ar ¹⁹and you will come close to the

---

[d]Or *Red Sea* [e]Heb uncertain [f]Or *Red Sea* [g]Or *Frighteners* [h]Or *Cave-dwellers* or *Hurrians*

Ammonites. Don't aggravate them. Don't fight with them because I won't give any part of the Ammonites' land to you as your own. I've given it to Lot's descendants as their property.

20Now people thought that land was Rephaim territory as well. The Rephaim had lived there previously. But the Ammonites called them "Zamzummim."[i] 21They were large, numerous, and tall, just like the Anakim. But the LORD completely destroyed the Zamzummim before the Ammonites, and they took possession of that area, settling in their place. 22That is exactly what God did for Esau's descendants, who live in Seir, when he completely destroyed the Horites in their presence, and they took possession of the Horites' area, settling in their place to this very day. 23The Avvim,[j] who had lived in settlements around Gaza, were completely destroyed by the Caphtorim, who had come from Caphtor. They replaced the Avvim there.

Victories in Transjordan

24"So get going. Cross the Arnon ravine. I have handed Sihon the Amorite king of Heshbon and his land over to you. It's time to possess the area! It's time to fight him in battle! 25Starting right now, I am making everyone everywhere afraid of you and scared of you. Once they hear news of you, they will be shaking and worrying because of you."

26I then sent messengers from the Kedemoth desert to Sihon, Heshbon's king, with words of peace: 27"Please let us[k] pass through your land. We promise to stay on the road. We won't step off it, right or left. 28Please sell us food for money so we can eat; sell us water for money so we can drink. Let us pass through on foot—29just as Esau's descendants who live in Seir and the Moabites who live in Ar did for me—until we cross the Jordan River into the land that the LORD our God is giving to us."

30But Sihon, Heshbon's king, wasn't willing to let us pass through his land because the LORD your God had made his spirit hard and his heart inflexible so that God could hand him over to you, which is exactly how it happened. 31The LORD said to me: Look! Right now I'm laying Sihon and his land before you. It's time to take possession of his land!

32Sihon and all his forces came out to meet us in battle at Jahaz. 33But the LORD our God gave him to us. We struck him down, along with his sons, and all his forces. 34At that time, we captured all of Sihon's cities, and we placed every town—men, women, and children—under the ban.[l] We left no survivors. 35The only things we kept for ourselves were the animals and the plunder from the towns we had taken. 36From Aroer, which is on the edge of the Arnon Ravine, to the town that is in the valley there,[m] even as far as Gilead, there wasn't a city that could resist us. The LORD our God laid everything out before us. 37But you didn't go near the Ammonite lands or hillside cities alongside the Jabbok River, in compliance with all[n] that the LORD our God had commanded.

3 Next we turned and went up along the road to Bashan. Og, Bashan's king, came out with all his forces to meet us in battle at Edrei. 2The LORD said to me: Don't be afraid of him! I have handed him, all his forces, and his land over to you. Do the same thing to him that you did to Sihon, the Amorite king who ruled in Heshbon.

3And so the LORD our God also handed Og, Bashan's king, along with his forces, over to us. We struck them down until no survivor was left. 4We also captured all of Og's towns at that time. There wasn't a single city that we didn't take from them—a total of sixty towns, the entire region of Argob, the whole kingdom of Og in Bashan. 5Each of these towns was fortified with high walls, double gates, and crossbars. Outside the towns there were also a great number of villages.[o] 6We placed them under the ban, just as we did with Sihon, Heshbon's king. Every town—men, women, and children—was under the ban.[p] 7The only things we kept for ourselves were the animals and the plunder from the towns.

8So at that time, we took the land that had belonged to the two Amorite kings beyond the Jordan, all the way from the Arnon Ravine to Mount Hermon (9Sidonians call Hermon

---

[i]Or *Mumblers* [j]Or *Ruiners* [k]Heb here and through 2:29a is singular *me, I.* [l]A technique of holy war that often involves total destruction, in which everything that is destroyed is dedicated to the deity who helps in the battle [m]Heb uncertain [n]LXX, Tg Jonathan; MT *and all* [o]Heb uncertain [p]See note at 2:34.

"Sirion," but the Amorites call it "Senir"), [10]including all the towns on the plateau, in the regions of Gilead and Bashan, and all the way to Salecah and Edrei—all the towns that belonged to Og's kingdom in Bashan.

([11]By the way, Bashan's King Og was the last of the Rephaim. His bed was made of iron. Isn't it still in the Ammonite town of Rabbah? By standard measurements, it was thirteen and a half feet long and six feet wide.)

[12]So this is the land we possessed at that time. I gave some of it, from Aroer, which is beside the Arnon River, up through half of the Gilead highlands, along with its cities, to the Reubenites and the Gadites. [13]The rest of the Gilead region and all of Bashan, Og's kingdom, I gave to half the tribe of Manasseh.

(Now the whole Argob area, including all of Bashan, was often called Rephaim Country. [14]Jair, from the tribe of Manasseh, took possession of the entire Argob region, as far

as the border with the Geshurites and the Maacathites. He named the Bashan area after himself, Jair's Settlement. That's what it's still called today.)

[15]I also gave Gilead to Machir. [16]To the Reubenites and the Gadites, I gave land from the Gilead, as far as the Arnon River—the middle of the river being the boundary line—to the Jabbok River, which is the boundary line with the Ammonites. [17]Also the desert plain, with the Jordan River as the boundary, from the Galilee Sea[q] down to the desert sea (the Dead Sea[r]) below the slopes of Mount Pisgah on the east.

[18]Then I commanded you: Although the LORD your God has given you this land to possess, you must now cross over before the rest of your Israelite relatives as a fighting force ready for battle! [19]However, your wives, children, and herds—I know you have lots of herds!—may remain in the towns that I have

[q]Heb *Chinnereth* [r]Or *the Salt Sea*

God's THOUGHTS ◆ My THOUGHTS

Praying for Your Leaders Deuteronomy 3

It isn't always easy to be in charge. Whenever a leader makes a decision, no matter what it is, someone might not like it. As an example, consider your family. Your father might say he is making meat loaf and mashed potatoes for supper. You might respond that you don't like meat loaf and would rather have a sandwich, or your brother might ask for macaroni and cheese instead of potatoes. Deciding what to cook for dinner is a small decision; imagine the challenge of making big decisions!

In his last message to the Israelites, after Moses talked about the journey the people had made over the last forty years, he told them that God had appointed Joshua to be their next leader. By announcing ahead of time that Joshua was going to take on this role, Moses reminded the people that God had made this choice.

There are people in your life today who are in charge of making decisions—your parents, teachers, church leaders, and government officials. It is important to pray for these leaders. Even if you don't always like their decisions, you should ask God to bless them with wisdom and the strength to lead as God wants.

Name people who are leaders in your life.

Pray for these people today.

given to you. ²⁰Once the Lord settles your relatives, as you have been settled, and they also possess the land that the Lord your God is giving them across the Jordan River, each of you can return to the property that I have given to you.

²¹It was at that same time that I commanded Joshua: You saw everything that the Lord your God did to these two kings. That is exactly what the Lord will do to all the kingdoms where you're going! ²²Don't be afraid of them because the Lord your God is the one who will be fighting for you.

Moses' prayer

²³It was also at that same time that I begged the Lord: ²⁴Please, Lord God! You have only begun to show your servant your greatness and your mighty hand. What god in heaven or on earth can act as you do or can perform your deeds and powerful acts? ²⁵Please let me cross over the Jordan River so I can see the wonderful land that lies beyond it: those beautiful highlands, even the Lebanon region.

²⁶But the Lord was angry with me because of you! He wouldn't listen to me. He said to me: That's enough from you! Don't ever ask me about this again! ²⁷Go up to the top of Mount Pisgah. Look west, north, south, and east. Have a good look, but you will not cross the Jordan River. ²⁸Instead, command Joshua, strengthen him, and encourage him because he's the one who will cross the river before this people. He's the one who will make sure they inherit the land you will see.

²⁹After that, we stayed in the valley across from Beth-peor.

The events at Mount Horeb

4 Now, Israel, in light of all that, listen to the regulations and the case laws that I am teaching you to follow, so that you may live, enter, and possess the land that the Lord, your ancestors' God, is giving to you. ²Don't add anything to the word that I am commanding you, and don't take anything away from it. Instead, keep the commands of the Lord your God that I am commanding all of you.

³You saw with your own eyes what the Lord did concerning the Baal of Peor. The Lord your God destroyed everyone who followed the Baal of Peor, ⁴but all of you who stayed true to the Lord your God are alive today. ⁵So pay attention! I am teaching all of you the regulations and the case laws exactly as the Lord my God commanded me. You must do these in the land you are entering to possess. ⁶Keep them faithfully because that will show your wisdom and insight to the nations who will hear about all these regulations. They will say, "Surely this great nation is a wise and insightful people!" ⁷After all, is there any great nation that has gods[s] as close to it as the Lord our God is close to us whenever we call to him? ⁸Or does any great nation have regulations and case laws as righteous as all this Instruction that I am setting before you today?

⁹But be on guard and watch yourselves closely so that you don't forget the things your eyes saw and so they never leave your mind as long as you live. Teach them to your children and your grandchildren. ¹⁰Remember that[t] day when you stood before the Lord your God at Horeb, when the Lord said to me: "Gather the people to me. I will declare my words to them so that they will learn to fear me every day of their lives on the fertile land, and teach their children to do the same." ¹¹Then you all came close and stood at the foot of the mountain. The mountain was blazing with fire up to the sky, with darkness, cloud, and thick smoke! ¹²The Lord spoke to you out of the very fire itself. You heard the sound of words, but you didn't see any form. There was only a voice. ¹³The Lord declared his covenant to you, which he commanded you to do—the Ten Commandments[u]—and wrote them on two stone tablets. ¹⁴At that time, the Lord commanded me to teach you all the regulations and the case laws that you must keep in the land that you are entering to possess.

¹⁵So watch your conduct closely, because you didn't see any form on the day the Lord spoke to you at Horeb out of the very fire itself. ¹⁶Don't ruin everything and make an idol for yourself: a form of any image, any likeness—male or female—¹⁷or any likeness whatsoever, whether of a land animal, a bird

---

[s]MT; LXX, Syr, Tg *a god so close* [t]Heb lacks *remember that.* [u]*Or the ten words*

that flies in the sky, [18]an insect that crawls on the earth, or a fish that lives in the sea. [19]Don't look to the skies, to the sun or the moon or the stars, all the heavenly bodies, and be led astray, worshipping and serving them. The LORD your God has granted these things to all the nations who live under heaven. [20]But the LORD took you and brought you out of that iron furnace, out of Egypt, so that you might be his own treasured people, which is what you are right now.

[21]The LORD was angry with me because of your deeds and swore that I couldn't cross the Jordan River or enter the wonderful land that the LORD your God is giving you as an inheritance. [22]I will die here in this land. I won't cross the Jordan River. But you will, and you will take possession of that wonderful land. [23]So all of you, watch yourselves! Don't forget the covenant that the LORD your God made with you by making an idol or an image of any kind or anything the LORD your God forbids, [24]because the LORD your God is an all-consuming fire. He is a passionate God.

Warnings and teachings about future disobedience

[25]Once you have had children and grandchildren and have grown old on the land, if you ruin things by making an idol, in any form whatsoever, and do what is evil in the eyes of the LORD your God and anger him, [26]I call heaven and earth as my witnesses against you today: You will definitely disappear—and quickly—from the land that you are crossing over the Jordan River to possess. You won't extend your time there but will instead be totally destroyed. [27]The LORD will scatter you among the nations. Only a very few of you will survive in the countries where the LORD will drag you. [28]There you will worship other[v] gods, made of wood and stone by human hands—gods that cannot see, listen, eat, or smell. [29]You will seek the LORD your God from there, and you will find him[w] if you seek him with all your heart and with all your being. [30]In your distress, when all these things happen to you in the future, you will return to the LORD your God and you will obey his voice, [31]because the LORD

your God is a compassionate God. He won't let you go, he won't destroy you, and he won't forget the covenant that he swore to your ancestors.

[32]Now look into it: into days long past, before your time—all the way back to the day God first created human beings on earth, from one end of heaven to the other. Has anything this amazing ever happened? Has anything like it ever been heard of before? [33]Has any people ever listened to a god's voice speaking out of fire, as each of you have, and survived? [34]Or has any god ever tried to take one nation out of another nation using tests, miracles, wonders, war, a strong hand and outstretched arm, or awesome power like all that the LORD your God did for you in Egypt while you watched? [35]You were shown these things so that you would know this: The LORD is the only God. There's no other god except him. [36]From heaven he made you hear his voice in order to discipline you. On earth he showed you his great fire. You heard his words from that very fire. [37]And because he loved your ancestors and chose their descendants after them, God brought you out of Egypt with his own presence, by his own great power, [38]in order to remove larger and stronger nations from before you and bring you into their land, giving it to you as an inheritance. That's where things stand right now. [39]Know then today and keep in mind that the LORD is the only God in heaven above or on earth below. There is no other. [40]Keep the Lord's regulations and his commandments. I'm commanding them to you today for your well-being and for the well-being of your children after you, so that you may extend your time on the fertile land that the LORD your God is giving you forever.

Cities of refuge

[41]Then Moses set aside three cities on the eastern side of the Jordan River [42]so that anyone who killed someone accidentally and without prior hatred could flee to one of these cities and be safe: [43]Bezer in the wilderness on the plateau for the Reubenites, Ramoth in Gilead for the Gadites, and Golan in Bashan for the Manassites.

[v]LXX; MT lacks *other*. [w]Heb lacks *him*.

The second heading:
Recounting the Horeb covenant

⁴⁴Now this is the Instruction that Moses set before the Israelites. ⁴⁵These are the laws and the regulations and the case laws that Moses spoke to the Israelites when they came out of Egypt. ⁴⁶This took place across the Jordan River, in the valley opposite Beth-peor, in the land of Sihon the Amorite king who ruled in Heshbon, whom Moses and the Israelites defeated when they came out of Egypt. ⁴⁷They took possession of his land and the land of Og, Bashan's king—the two Amorite kings across the Jordan River to the east— ⁴⁸from Aroer, which is on the banks of the Arnon River, all the way to Mount Sion,ˣ also known as Hermon, ⁴⁹and all the desert regions across the Jordan River, on the east, down to the Dead Sea, beneath the slopes of Mount Pisgah.

Ten Commandments

5 Moses called out to all Israel, saying to them: "Israel! Listen to the regulations and the case laws that I'm recounting in your hearing right now. Learn them and carefully do them. ²The Lord our God made a covenant with us at Mount Horeb. ³The Lord didn't make this covenant with our ancestors but with us—all of us who are here and alive right now. ⁴The Lord spoke with you face-to-face on the mountain from the very fire itself. ⁵At that time, I was standing between the Lord and you, declaring to you the Lord's word, because you were terrified of the fire and didn't go up on the mountain."

The Lord said:

⁶"I am the Lord your God, who brought you out of Egypt, out of the house of slavery.

⁷You must have no other gods beforeʸ me. ⁸Do not make an idol for yourself—no form whatsoever—of anything in the sky above or on the earth below or in the waters under the earth. ⁹Do not bow down to them or worship them because I, the Lord your God, am a passionate God. I punish children for their parents' sins—even to

---

ˣSyr *Sirion*; see 3:9. ʸOr *besides*

Rewards of Obedience Deuteronomy 4:1-40

More than likely, you will face consequences if you don't clean your room, do your chores, or finish your homework. There is a cost to disobedience.

From snakebites to defeat in battle, the Israelites knew the cost of disobeying God. But there was also reward for following God's ways. After reminding the people of their past and their disobedience, Moses turned their attention to the rewards of obedience.

Blessing for themselves was the first reward. Obeying God's commands would bring life to them and their children. God promised to watch over them and protect them, even when things looked bad.

Another reward was finally entering and living fully in the land God had promised them. For more than four hundred years, the Israelites had lived as slaves, unable to settle down. Now God was blessing them with the gift of land.

The last reward was that their obedience would show other nations how God blessed them. This would make people want to love and serve the one true God.

Name a cost of disobeying your parents.

Name a reward or blessing of obeying them.

the third and fourth generations of those who hate me. [10]But I am loyal and gracious to the thousandth generation[z] of those who love me and keep my commandments.

[11]Do not use the LORD your God's name as if it were of no significance; the LORD won't forgive anyone who uses his name that way.

[12]Keep the Sabbath day and treat it as holy, exactly as the LORD your God commanded: [13]Six days you may work and do all your tasks, [14]but the seventh day is a Sabbath to the LORD your God. Don't do any work on it—not you, your sons or daughters, your male or female servants, your oxen or donkeys or any of your animals, or the immigrant who is living among you—so that your male and female servants can rest just like you. [15]Remember that you were a slave in Egypt, but the LORD your God brought you out of there with a strong hand and an outstretched arm. That's why the LORD your God commands you to keep the Sabbath day.

[16]Honor your father and your mother, exactly as the LORD your God requires, so that your life will be long and so that things will go well for you on the fertile land that the LORD your God is giving you.

[17]Do not kill.[a]

[18]Do not commit adultery.

[19]Do not steal.

[20]Do not testify falsely against your neighbor.

[21]Do not desire and try to take your neighbor's wife.

Do not crave your neighbor's house, field, male or female servant, ox, donkey, or anything else that belongs to your neighbor.

[22]Those are the words the LORD spoke to your entire assembly with a loud voice while on the mountain, from the midst of the fire, the cloud, and the thick smoke. He added no more. God wrote them on two stone tablets, then gave them to me.

Moses' intercessory role

[23]Now once you heard the voice from the darkness while the mountain was blazing

LIFE PRESERVER

This sounds familiar. Why is it being repeated?
Deuteronomy 5

Reading the Bible would be so much easier if each book picked up where the last one left off like a chapter book. The book of Deuteronomy contains a lot of the story of Moses that you may have already read in the books that come before this one. For example, Deuteronomy 5 contains the Ten Commandments, and so does Exodus 20.

The book of Deuteronomy was written at a different time than the earlier books in the Bible were written. Moses had been leading the Israelites for forty years, and he was getting older. As the people got closer to the end of their journey to the promised land, they needed new leadership. As they looked toward this time of establishing themselves as a nation, it was important for them to remember the instruction that God had given them so they could live together in community. The repetition of story and God's Instruction helped them remember.

This may be similar to when your parents or a teacher tells you the same thing over and over again. That probably means they are telling you something important that they want you to remember. Deuteronomy contains a lot of reminders for God's people so they would remember God, who had chosen them, and the covenant God had made with them. ♦

with fire, you came to me—more specifically, all the chiefs of your tribes and your elders came—[24]and you said: "Look here! The LORD our God has shown us his glory and greatness. We've heard his voice come out of the very fire itself. We've seen firsthand that God can speak to a human being and they can survive! [25]But why should we die? Surely this massive fire will consume us! If we hear any more of the LORD our God's voice, we will die. [26]Is there anyone who has heard the living God's voice speaking out of the very fire itself, like we have, and survived? [27]You go and listen to all that the LORD our God says. Then tell us all that the LORD our God speaks to you. We'll listen and we'll do it."

[28]The LORD heard what you said, when you said this to me. The LORD then told me: I heard what the people said when they spoke with you. Everything they suggest is good.

[z]Or to thousands [a]Or murder

²⁹If only their minds were like this: always fearing me and keeping all my commandments so that things would go well for them and their children forever! ³⁰Go and tell them: You may go back to your tents. ³¹But you, Moses, must stay here with me. I will tell you all the commandments,[b] the regulations, and the case laws that you must teach the Israelites to do in the land that I am giving them to possess.

³²So you must carefully do exactly what the Lord your God commands you. Don't deviate even a bit! ³³You must walk the precise path that the Lord your God indicates for you so that you will live, and so that things will go well for you, and so you will extend your time on the land that you will possess.

The great commandment

6 Now these are the commandments, the regulations, and the case laws that the Lord your God commanded me to teach you to follow in the land you are entering to possess, ²so that you will fear the Lord your God by keeping all his regulations and his commandments that I am commanding you—both you and your sons and daughters—all the days of your life and so that you will lengthen your life. ³Listen to them, Israel! Follow them carefully so that things will go well for you and so that you will continue to multiply exactly as the Lord, your ancestors' God, promised you, in a land full of milk and honey.

⁴Israel, listen! Our God is the Lord! Only the Lord![c]

> Memorize
> Deut 6:4

⁵Love the Lord your God with all your heart, all your being, and all your strength. ⁶These words that I am commanding you today must always be on your minds. ⁷Recite them to your children. Talk about them when you are sitting around your house and when you are out and about, when you are lying down and when you are getting up. ⁸Tie them on your hand as a sign. They should be on your forehead as a symbol.[d] ⁹Write them on your house's doorframes and on your city's gates.

¹⁰Now once the Lord your God has brought you into the land that he swore to your ancestors, to Abraham, Isaac, and Jacob, to give to you—a land that will be full of large and wonderful towns that you didn't build, ¹¹houses stocked with all kinds of goods that you didn't stock, cisterns that you didn't make, vineyards and olive trees that you didn't plant—and you eat and get stuffed, ¹²watch yourself! Don't forget the Lord, who brought you out of Egypt, out of the house of slavery. ¹³Revere the Lord your God, serve him, and take your solemn pledges in his name! ¹⁴Don't follow other gods, those gods of the people around you—¹⁵because the Lord your God, who is with you and among you, is a passionate God. The Lord your God's anger will burn against you, and he will wipe you off the fertile land. ¹⁶Don't test the Lord your God the way you frustrated him at Massah. ¹⁷You must carefully follow the Lord your God's commands along with the laws and regulations he has given you. ¹⁸Do what is right and good in the Lord's sight so that things will go well for you and so you will enter and take possession of the wonderful land that the Lord swore to your ancestors, ¹⁹and so the Lord will drive out all your enemies from before you, just as he promised.

The next generation

²⁰In the future, your children will ask you, "What is the meaning of the laws,[e] the regulations, and the case laws that the Lord our God commanded you?" ²¹Tell them: We were Pharaoh's slaves in Egypt. But the Lord brought us out of Egypt with a mighty hand. ²²Before our own eyes, the Lord performed great and awesome deeds of power[f] against Egypt, Pharaoh, and his entire dynasty. ²³But the Lord

> **did you know?** Deuteronomy 6:4-8 is called the *Shema* by people who speak Hebrew. God told the Israelites to remember these words every day. They placed copies of these verses in special boxes, called *mezuzahs*, which hung by their doors. Each time they went through the door, they would touch the box and remember to love God.

---

[b]Heb is singular, *commandment* (see 6:1). [c]Or *The Lord is our God, the Lord only*; or *The Lord is our God, the Lord alone*; or *The Lord our God is one Lord*; or *The Lord our God, the Lord is one*; or *The Lord is our God, the Lord is one*. [d]Heb uncertain; cf Exod 13:16; Syr *sign or mark*; Tg *phylacteries* [e]Or *What are the laws…?* [f]Or *signs and wonders*

brought us out from there so that he could bring us in, giving us the land that he swore to our ancestors. ²⁴Then the LORD commanded us to perform all these regulations, revering the LORD our God, so that things go well for us always and so we continue to live, as we're doing right now. ²⁵What's more, we will be considered righteous if we are careful to do all this commandment before the LORD our God, just as he commanded us.

Dealing with foreign worship

7 Now once the LORD your God brings you into the land you are entering to take possession of, and he drives out numerous nations before you—the Hittites, the Girgashites, the Amorites, the Canaanites, the Perizzites, the Hivites, and the Jebusites: seven nations that are larger and stronger than you—²once the LORD your God lays them before you, you must strike them down,

placing them under the ban.⁸ Don't make any covenants with them, and don't be merciful to them. ³Don't intermarry with them. Don't give your daughter to one of their sons to marry, and don't take one of their daughters to marry your son, ⁴because they will turn your child away from following me so that they end up serving other gods. That will make the LORD's anger burn against you, and he will quickly annihilate you.

⁵Instead, this is what you must do with these nations: rip down their altars, smash their sacred stones, cut down their sacred poles,ʰ and burn their idols ⁶because you are a people holy to the LORD your God. The LORD your God chose you to be his own treasured people beyond all others on the fertile land. ⁷It was not because you were greater than all other people that the LORD loved you and chose you. In fact, you were the smallest of peoples! ⁸No, it is because the LORD

⁸See note at 2:34. ʰHeb *asherim*, perhaps objects devoted to the goddess Asherah

Don't Worship Idols Deuteronomy 7:1-8

Many people think that idol worship is something that happened a long time ago or that happens only in certain parts of the world. But idols can be anything that gets in the way of worshipping God and following God's ways.

For instance, you might flip through the television channels and come across a popular show known to have bad language. You might think that it can't hurt you, since everyone else seems to be watching it. You might decide to watch for a while. At first you might be shocked by what you hear, but later you might begin to think it isn't so bad. Before you know it, you're laughing and enjoying the show. That show has become more important than you intended it to be.

God chose the Israelites to be different from other people. They were to be living examples of how to love and serve God. God still wants this from God's people today. The choices we make—even when no one sees— reflect our love for God. God wants us to put God first in our lives, choosing to follow God's ways in everything we do.

What keeps you from obeying God completely?

What will you do to change that habit?

loved you and because he kept the solemn pledge he swore to your ancestors that the LORD brought you out with a strong hand and saved you from the house of slavery, from the power of Pharaoh, Egypt's king. ⁹Know now then that the LORD your God is the only true God! He is the faithful God, who keeps the covenant and proves loyal to everyone who loves him and keeps his commands—even to the thousandth generation! ¹⁰He is the God who personally repays anyone who hates him, ultimately destroying that kind of person. The LORD does not waste time with anyone who hates him; he repays them personally. ¹¹So make sure you carefully keep the commandment, the regulations, and the case laws that I am commanding you right now.

¹²If you listen to these case laws and follow them carefully, the LORD your God will keep the covenant and display the loyalty that he promised your ancestors. ¹³He will love you, bless you, and multiply you. He will bless the fruit of your wombs and the fruit of your fertile land—all your grain, your wine, your oil, and the offspring of your cattle and flocks—upon the very fertile land that he swore to your ancestors to give to you. ¹⁴You will be more blessed than any other group of people. No one will be sterile or infertile—not among you or your animals. ¹⁵The LORD will remove all sickness from you. As for all those dreadful Egyptian diseases you experienced, the Lord won't put them on you but will inflict them on all who hate you. ¹⁶You will destroy all the peoples that the LORD your God is handing over to you. Show them no pity. And don't serve their gods because that would be a trap for you.

Against power and lack of trust

¹⁷If you happen to think to yourself, These nations are greater than we are; how can we possibly possess their land? ¹⁸don't be afraid of them! Remember, instead, what the LORD your God did to Pharaoh and all Egypt: ¹⁹the great trials that you saw with your own eyes, the signs and wonders, and the strong hand and outstretched arm the LORD your God used to rescue you. That's what the LORD your God will do to any people you fear. ²⁰The LORD

your God will send terror[i] on them until even the survivors and those hiding from you are destroyed. ²¹Don't dread these nations because the LORD your God, the great and awesome God, is with you and among you. (²²The LORD your God will drive out these nations before you bit by bit. You won't be able to finish them off quickly; otherwise, the wild animals would become too much for you to handle.) ²³The LORD your God will lay these nations before you, throwing them into a huge panic until they are destroyed. ²⁴He will hand their kings over to you, and you will wipe their names out from under the skies. No one will be able to stand before you; you will crush them.

²⁵Burn the images of their gods. Don't desire the silver or the gold that is on them and take it for yourself, or you will be trapped by it. That is detestable to the LORD your God. ²⁶Don't bring any detestable thing into your house, or you will be placed under the ban too, just like it is! You must utterly detest these kinds of things, despising them completely, because they are under the ban.

8 You must carefully perform all of the commandment that I am commanding you right now so you can live and multiply and enter and take possession of the land that the LORD swore to your ancestors. ²Remember the long road on which the LORD your God led you during these forty years in the desert so he could humble you, testing you to find out what was in your heart: whether

UMBRELLA
HARD TIMES

God Provides *Deuteronomy 8:1-5*
Spending forty years in the desert was extremely hard for the Israelites. During this time they were afraid they would starve, be killed by attackers, or even wander around lost forever. They were in a terrible situation for a very long time. But finally things got better. They had survived. Looking back, the Israelites could see how God had provided for them every step of the way, even during the most difficult times.◊

ⁱHeb uncertain; perhaps *wasp*, *plague*, or *pestilence*

you would keep his commandments or not. [3]He humbled you by making you hungry and then feeding you the manna that neither you nor your ancestors had ever experienced, so he could teach you that people don't live on bread alone. No, they live based on whatever the LORD says.[j] [4]During these forty years, your clothes didn't wear out and your feet didn't swell up. [5]Know then in your heart that the LORD your God has been disciplining you just as a father disciplines his children. [6]Keep the commandments of the LORD your God by walking in his ways and by fearing him, [7]because the LORD your God is bringing you to a wonderful land, a land with streams of water, springs, and wells that gush up in the valleys and on the hills; [8]a land of wheat and barley, vines, fig trees, and pomegranates; a land of olive oil and honey; [9]a land where you will eat food without any shortage—you won't lack a thing there—a land where stone is hard as iron and where you will mine copper from the hills. [10]You will eat, you will be satisfied, and you will bless the LORD your God in the wonderful land that he's given you.

Against wealth and overconfidence

[11]But watch yourself! Don't forget the LORD your God by not keeping his commands or his case laws or his regulations that I am commanding you right now. [12]When you eat, get full, build nice houses, and settle down, [13]and when your herds and your flocks are growing large, your silver and gold are multiplying, and everything you have is thriving, [14]don't become arrogant, forgetting the LORD your God:

the one who rescued you from Egypt, from the house of slavery;

[15]the one who led you through this vast and terrifying desert of poisonous snakes and scorpions, of cracked ground with no water;

the one who made water flow for you out of a hard rock;

[16]the one who fed you manna in the wilderness, which your ancestors had never experienced, in order to humble and test you, but in order to do good to you in the end. [17]Don't think to yourself, My own strength and abilities have produced all this prosperity for me. [18]Remember the LORD your

God! He's the one who gives you the strength to be prosperous in order to establish the covenant he made with your ancestors—and that's how things stand right now. [19]But if you do, in fact, forget the LORD your God and follow other gods, serving and bowing down to them, I swear to you right now that you will be completely destroyed. [20]Just like the nations that the LORD is destroying before you, that's exactly how you will be destroyed—all because you didn't obey the LORD your God's voice.

Against false piety and immodesty

9Listen, Israel! Today you will cross the Jordan River to enter and take possession of nations larger and more powerful than you, along with huge cities with fortifications that reach to the sky. [2]These people are large and tall—they are the Anakim. You know and have heard what people say: "Who can stand up to the Anakim?" [3]Know right now that the LORD your God, who is crossing over before you, is an all-consuming fire! He will wipe them out! He will subdue them before you! Then you will take possession of their land, eliminating them quickly, exactly as the LORD told you.

[4]Once the LORD your God has driven them out before you, don't think to yourself, It's because I'm righteous that the LORD brought me in to possess this land. It is instead because of these nations' wickedness that the LORD is removing them before you. [5]You aren't entering and taking possession of their land because you are righteous or because your heart is especially virtuous; rather, it is because these nations are wicked—that's why the LORD your God is removing them before you, and because he wishes to establish the promise he made to your ancestors: to Abraham, Isaac, and Jacob.

Gold calf

[6]Know then that the LORD your God isn't giving you this excellent land for you to possess on account of your righteousness—because you are a stubborn people! [7]Remember—don't ever forget!—how you made the LORD your God furious in the wilderness. From the very first day you stepped out of Egypt

Bet you can read this in 3 minutes. Ready, set, go!

---

[j]Or *whatever comes out of the* LORD's *mouth*

until you arrived at this place, you have been rebels against the Lord. [8]Even at Horeb you angered the Lord! He was so enraged by you that he threatened to wipe you out. [9]When I went up on the mountain to get the stone tablets, the covenant tablets that the Lord made with you, I was up there forty days and forty nights. I ate no bread, drank no water. [10]The Lord gave me the two stone tablets, written by God's finger, and on them were all the words that the Lord had said to you on the mountain, out of the very fire itself, on the day we assembled. [11]At the end of those forty days and nights, the Lord gave me the two stone tablets—the covenant tablets. [12]Then the Lord said to me, "Get going! Get down from here quickly because your people, whom you brought out of Egypt, have ruined everything! They couldn't wait to turn from the path I commanded them! They've made themselves an idol out of cast metal."

[13]The Lord said more to me: "I have seen this people. Look! What a stubborn people they are! [14]Now stand back. I am going to wipe them out. I will erase their name from under heaven, then I will make a nation out of you—one stronger and larger than they were."

[15]So I went down the mountain while it was blazing with fire. The two covenant tablets were in my two hands. [16]It was then that I saw how you sinned against the Lord your God: you made yourselves a calf, an idol made of cast metal! You couldn't wait to turn from the path the Lord commanded you! [17]I grabbed the two tablets and threw them down with my own hands, shattering them while you watched. [18]Then I fell before the Lord as I had done the previous forty days and forty nights. I ate no bread and drank no water, all because of the sin that you had committed by doing such evil in the Lord's sight, infuriating him. [19]I was afraid of the massive anger and rage the Lord had for you—he was going to wipe you out! However, the Lord listened to me again in that moment.

[20]But the Lord was furious with Aaron—he was going to wipe him out! So I also prayed hard for Aaron at that time. [21]And as for that sinful thing you made, that calf, I took it and I burned it with fire. Then I smashed it, grinding it thoroughly until it was as fine as dust.

Then I dumped the dust into the stream that ran down the mountain.

[22]Also at Taberah, again at Massah, and then again at Kibroth-hattaavah, you have been the kind of people who make the Lord angry. [23]And then, when the Lord sent you from Kadesh-barnea, telling you: "Go up and take possession of the land that I'm giving you," you disobeyed the Lord your God's command. You didn't trust him. You didn't obey God's voice. [24]You've been rebellious toward the Lord from the day I[k] met you.

Moses' intercessory prayer

[25]But I fell on my knees in the Lord's presence forty days and forty nights, lying flat out, because the Lord planned on wiping you out. [26]But I prayed to the Lord! I said: Lord, my Lord! Don't destroy your people, your own possession, whom you saved by your own power, whom you brought out of Egypt with a strong hand! [27]Remember your servants: Abraham, Isaac, and Jacob! Don't focus on this people's stubbornness, wickedness, and sin. [28]Otherwise, that land out of which you brought us will say: The Lord wasn't strong enough to bring them into the land he'd promised them. Because he didn't care for them in the least, he brought them out to die in the desert. [29]But these are your people! Your own possession! The people you brought out by your great power and by your outstretched arm!

New tablets

10At that time the Lord told me: Carve two stone tablets, just like the first ones, and hike up the mountain to me. Construct a wooden chest as well. [2]I will write on the tablets the words that were on the first tablets—the ones you smashed—then you will place them in the chest.

[3]So I built a chest out of acacia wood and carved two stone tablets just like the first ones. Then I hiked up the mountain holding the two tablets in my hands. [4]God wrote on the new tablets what had been written on the first set: the Ten Commandments that the Lord spoke to you on the mountain, from the very fire itself, on the day we assembled there. Then the Lord gave them to me.

[5]So I came back down the mountain. I put

[k]LXX, Sam *he* (God) *met you* (so)

the tablets in the chest that I'd made, and that's where they are now, exactly as the LORD commanded me.

(⁶Now, the Israelites had set out from Beeroth-bene-jaakan[1] to Moserah. It was there that Aaron died and was buried. His son Eleazar succeeded him in the priestly role. ⁷From there the Israelites traveled to Gudgodah, then from Gudgodah to Jotbathah, which is a land with flowing streams. ⁸At that time, the LORD selected the tribe of Levi to carry the chest containing the LORD's covenant, to minister before the LORD, to serve him, and to offer blessings in his name. That's the way things are right now. ⁹That's why the Levites don't have a stake or inheritance with the rest of their relatives. The LORD is the Levites' inheritance, just as the LORD your God promised them.)

¹⁰Just as the first time, I remained on the mountain forty days and nights. And the LORD listened to me again in this instance. The LORD wasn't willing to destroy you. ¹¹Then the LORD told me: Get going. Lead the people so they can enter and take possession of the land that I promised I'd give to their ancestors.

What the LORD requires

¹²Now in light of all that, Israel, what does the LORD your God ask of you? Only this: to revere the LORD your God by walking in all his ways, by loving him, by serving the LORD your God with all your heart and being, ¹³and by keeping the LORD's commandments and his regulations that I'm commanding you right now. It's for your own good!

¹⁴Clearly, the LORD owns the sky, the highest heavens, the earth, and everything in it. ¹⁵But the LORD adored your ancestors, loving them and choosing the descendants that followed them—you!—from all other people. That's how things still stand now. ¹⁶So circumcise your hearts[m] and stop being so stubborn, ¹⁷because the LORD your God is the God of all gods and Lord of all lords, the great, mighty, and awesome God who doesn't play favorites and doesn't take bribes. ¹⁸He enacts justice for orphans and widows, and he loves immigrants, giving them food and clothing. ¹⁹That means you must also love immigrants because

you were immigrants in Egypt. ²⁰Revere the LORD your God, serve him, cling to him, swear by his name alone! ²¹He is your praise, and he is your God—the one who performed these great and awesome acts that you witnessed with your very own eyes. ²²Your ancestors went down to Egypt with a total of seventy people, but now look! The LORD your God has made you as numerous as the stars in the nighttime sky!

LIGHTHOUSE

CHANGED HEART

Be Renewed *Deuteronomy 10:12-22*
The Israelites had come a long way after their escape from slavery in Egypt and wandering in the desert on their way to the promised land. Many years before, God had spoken to Abraham, who was childless and very old, and said that he would have as many descendants as the number of stars in the sky. In this passage, Moses told the people that God had made the people as numerous as the stars in the night sky. What once seemed impossible, God had made possible.◆

11 So love the LORD your God and follow his instruction, his regulations, his case laws, and his commandments always. ²And know right now what your children haven't known or yet witnessed:[n]

The LORD your God's discipline, his power, his mighty hand and outstretched arm;

³the signs and the acts that he performed in the heart of Egyptian territory, against Egypt's King Pharaoh and all his land;

⁴what God did to the Egyptian army, to its horses and chariots—how he made the water of the Reed Sea[o] flow over their heads when they chased after you, but the LORD destroyed them, and that's how things stand right now;

⁵what the Lord did for you in the desert, until you arrived at this place;

⁶and what he did to Dathan and Abiram, the descendants of Eliab the Reubenite, when the ground opened up its mouth and swallowed them, their families, their tents, and every living thing they possessed in the presence of all Israel.

---

[1]Or *from the wells of the Jaakanites* [m]Or *the foreskin of your hearts;* cf 30:6 [n]Heb uncertain [o]Or *Red Sea*

[7]Your own eyes witnessed each of these
powerful acts the LORD performed. [8]So keep
every part of the commandment that I am
giving you today so that you stay strong to
enter and take possession of the land that
you are crossing over to possess, [9]and so that
you might prolong your life on the fertile land
that the LORD swore to your ancestors to give
to them and their descendants—a land full of
milk and honey.

[10]The land you are about to enter and possess is definitely not like the land of Egypt,
where you came from, where you sowed your
seed and irrigated it by hand[p] like a vegetable
garden. [11]No, the land you are entering to possess is a land of hills and valleys, where your
drinking water will be rain from heaven. [12]It's
a land that the LORD cares for: the LORD's eyes
are on it constantly from the first of the year
until the very end of the year.

[13]Now, if you completely obey God's[q] commandments that I am giving you right now, by
loving the LORD your God and by serving him
with all your heart and all your being, [14]then
he[r] will provide rain for your land at the
right time—early rain and late rain—so you
can stock up your grain, wine, and oil. [15]He[s]
will also make your fields lush for your livestock, and you will eat and be satisfied. [16]But
watch yourselves! Otherwise, your heart
might be led astray so you stray away, serving other gods and worshipping them. [17]Then
the LORD's anger would burn against you. He
will close the sky up tight. There won't be any
rain, and the ground won't yield any of its
crops. You will quickly disappear off the wonderful land the LORD is giving to you.

[18]Place these words I'm speaking on your
heart and in your very being. Tie them on
your hand as a sign. They should be on your

[p]Or *foot* [q]LXX *his*; MT *my* [r]Sam, LXX, DSS (8QMez); Heb, Vulg, Syr, Tg, and several DSS *I*, in which case the text shifts to direct divine discourse. [s]Sam, LXX, two DSS; Heb, four DSS, Syr, Tg *I*, in which case the text shifts to direct divine discourse.

God's THOUGHTS / My THOUGHTS

What Does "Write Them on Your Doorframes" Mean?

Deuteronomy 11:18-20

This passage teaches that we are to teach God's Instruction by talking about it. It is easy to understand what this means, but these verses also say that we are to tie God's instructions on our hands, put them on our foreheads, and write them on our doorframes. This second part may be confusing.

These actions showed that the people kept God's Instruction close to them at all times. We are to love God and God's word more than anything else.

For example, think about a new movie that is coming to the theater that you can't wait to see. You probably watch the preview over and over again. You might read about it on the Internet. You most likely talk about it with your friends and family. Now, switch out the idea of a movie with God's instructions. This helps to show what these verses mean.

Nothing should be as important to us as loving God and following God's ways.

Name two of your favorite Bible verses.

Tell someone what these verses mean to you.

forehead as a symbol.[t] [19]Teach them to your children, by talking about them when you are sitting around your house and when you are out and about, when you are lying down and when you are getting up. [20]Write them on your house's doorframes and on your city's gates. [21]Do all that so your days and your children's days on the fertile land the LORD swore to give to your ancestors are many—indeed, as many as the number of days that the sky's been over the earth!

[22]It's true: if you carefully keep all this commandment that I'm giving you, by doing it, by loving the LORD your God, by walking in all his ways, and by clinging to him, [23]then the LORD will clear out all these nations before you. You will inherit what belonged to nations that are larger and stronger than you are. [24]Every place you set foot on will be yours: your territory will run from the wilderness all the way to the Lebanon range, and from the Euphrates River all the way to the Mediterranean Sea. [25]No one will be able to stand up to you. Just as he promised, the LORD your God will make the entire land deathly afraid of you wherever you advance in it.

Ceremony on Mount Gerizim and Mount Ebal

[26]Pay attention! I am setting blessing and curse before you right now: [27]the blessing if you obey the LORD your God's commandments that I am giving you right now, [28]but the curse if you don't obey the LORD your God's commandments and stray from the path that I am giving you today by following other gods that you have not known. [29]Now when the LORD your God brings you into the land that you are entering to take possession of, put the blessing on Mount Gerizim and the curse on Mount Ebal. ([30]Aren't both of these mountains across the Jordan River, down along the western road in the region of the Canaanites who live in the desert plain, across from Gilgal, next to the Moreh Oak Grove?)

[31]So then, once you cross the Jordan River to enter and possess the land that the LORD your God is giving you, and you take possession of it, settling down in it, [32]you must

carefully follow the regulations and the case laws that I am laying out before you right now.

Regulations and the case laws:

Worship at the location the LORD selects

12These are the regulations and the case laws that you must carefully keep in the fertile land the LORD, your ancestors' God, has given to you to possess for as long as you live on that land:

[2]You must completely destroy every place where the nations that you are displacing worshipped their gods—whether on high mountains or hills or under leafy green trees. [3]Rip down their altars and shatter their sacred stones. Burn their sacred poles[u] with fire. Hack their gods' idols into pieces. Wipe out their names from that place.

[4]Don't act like they did toward the LORD your God!

[5]Instead, you must search for the location the LORD your God will select from all your tribes to put his name there, as his residence, and you must go there. [6]You must bring your entirely burned offerings, your sacrifices, your tenth-part gifts, your contributions,[v] your payments for solemn promises, your spontaneous gifts, and the oldest offspring of your herds and flocks to that place. [7]You will have a feast there, each of you and your families, in the LORD your God's presence, and you will celebrate all you have done because the LORD your God has blessed you. [8]Don't act like we've been acting here lately—everyone doing what seems right to them— [9]because up to this point you haven't yet reached the place of rest or the inheritance the LORD your God is giving you. [10]But you are about to cross the Jordan River and will settle in the land the LORD your God is giving you as your inheritance. Then he will give you rest from all your enemies on every side so that you live safely and securely. [11]At that point, you must bring all that I am commanding you, your entirely burned offerings, your sacrifices, your tenth-part gifts, your contributions, and all your best payments that you solemnly promised to the LORD, to the location the LORD your

---

[t]Heb uncertain; cf Exod 13:16; Syr *sign or mark*; Tg *phylacteries* [u]Heb *asherim*, perhaps objects devoted to the goddess Asherah [v]Or *the contribution of your hands*; also in 12:11, 17

God selects for his name to reside. [12]Then you will rejoice in the LORD your God's presence: each of you, your sons and daughters, your male and female servants, and the Levites who dwell in your cities because they have no designated inheritance.

[13]But watch yourself! Make sure you don't offer up your entirely burned offerings in just any place you see. [14]No, only at the location the LORD selects from one of your tribal areas—that's where you must offer up your entirely burned offerings and that's where you must perform everything I'm telling you. [15]However, whenever you wish, you may slaughter and eat meat, as the LORD your God sees fit to bless you with such in your cities. People who are polluted and people who are purified can join in the feast, as they would if they were eating gazelle or deer. [16]But you must not consume any of the animals' blood. Pour it out on the ground, just like water.

[17]Within your cities you are not allowed to eat any of the following: your tenth-part gifts of grain, wine, and oil; the oldest offspring of your herds and flocks; any of the payments you have solemnly promised; your spontaneous gifts or your contributions. [18]Only in the presence of the LORD your God, at the location the LORD your God selects, can you eat these things—that holds true for you, your son and daughter, your male and female servant, and the Levite who lives in your city. Then celebrate all you have done in the LORD your God's presence. [19]But watch yourself: as long as you are on the land, don't forget about the Levites.

[20]Once the LORD your God has enlarged your territory, as he promised you, and you think to yourself, I'd like to eat some meat (because you have the desire to do so), feel free to do so whenever you want. [21]But if the location that the LORD your God will choose to put his name is far away from where you live, then slaughter an animal from your herd or flock that the LORD has given you, just as I have commanded you, and eat it in your cities whenever you wish. [22]But be sure to eat it as if it were gazelle or deer. People who are polluted and people who are purified can feast on it together.

[23]Furthermore, make sure that you don't consume any of the blood, because blood is life. You must not consume the life along with the meat. [24]You must not consume any of it. Pour it out on the ground, just like water. [25]You must not consume any of it so that things go well for you and for your children later because you did what was right in the LORD's eyes.

[26]Note that you must bring your sacred offerings and your payments for solemn promises to the location the LORD selects, [27]offering up your entirely burned sacrifices—both meat and blood—on the LORD your God's altar. The blood from your sacrifices must be poured out on the LORD your God's altar, but you are allowed to eat the meat. [28]Observe and obey all these words that I am commanding you so that things always go well for you and your children later because you did what was good and right in the LORD your God's eyes.

[29]Once the LORD your God has removed from before you all the nations that you are entering and taking possession of, and you have displaced them and are living in their land, [30]then watch yourself! Don't be trapped by following their practices after they've been wiped out before you. Don't go investigating their gods, thinking, How did these nations worship their gods? I want to do the very same thing!

[31]Don't act like they did toward the LORD your God because they did things for their gods that are detestable to the LORD, which he hates. They even burned their own sons and daughters with fire for their gods!

LIGHTHOUSE

FALSE GODS

Watch Out! Deuteronomy 12:29-31
God warned the Israelite people not to act like the people from neighboring lands because they didn't follow God's ways. God told God's people to take care not to follow the other people's practices or worship their gods. God wanted God's people to remain loyal and true to God by doing everything God had commanded.◆

³²ʷEverything I'm commanding you, you must do it with utmost care! Don't add anything to it or take anything away from it.

False prophets and false gods

13 ˣNow if a prophet or a dream interpreter appears among you and performs a sign or wonder for you, ²and the sign or wonder that was spoken actually occurs; if he says: "Come on! We should follow other gods"—ones you haven't experienced—"and we should worship them," ³you must not listen to that prophet's or dream interpreter's words, because the Lord your God is testing you to see if you love the Lord your God with all your mind and all your being. ⁴You must follow the Lord your God alone! Revere him! Follow his commandments! Obey his voice! Worship him! Cling to him—no other! ⁵That prophet or dream interpreter must be executed because he encouraged you to turn away from the Lord your God who brought you out of Egypt, who redeemed you from the house of slavery; they tried to lead you away from the path the Lord your God commanded you to take. Removeʸ such evil from your community!

⁶Similarly, if one of your relatives—even one of your own siblings—or your own son or daughter or your dear spouse or best friend entices you secretly, if someone like that says: "Come on! We should follow and worship other gods"—ones that neither you nor your ancestors have experienced, ⁷gods from all the neighboring peoples, whether nearby or far away, from one end of the earth to the other—⁸don't give in to them! Don't obey them! Don't have any mercy on them! Don't have compassion on them and don't protect them! ⁹Instead, you must execute them. Your own hand must be against them from the beginning of the execution; the hand of all the people will be involved at the end. ¹⁰Stone them until they are dead because they desired to lead you away from the Lord your God, the one who brought you out of Egypt, out of the house of slavery. ¹¹All Israel will hear about this and be afraid. They won't do that sort of evil thing among you again.

¹²Or if you hear about one of your towns the Lord your God is giving you to inhabit, that ¹³certain wicked people have gone out

from your community and they've led the citizens of their town astray by saying: "Come on! We should follow and worship other gods"—ones you haven't experienced before; ¹⁴at that point you must look into this situation very carefully to see if it's true. And if it's definitely true that this detestable thing was done in your community, ¹⁵you must completely strike down the inhabitants of that city with the sword. Place it and all that is in it under the ban.ᶻ Put its animals to the sword. ¹⁶Gather all the plunder into the middle of the town's square. Then burn the city and all of its plunder as an entirely burned offering to the Lord your God. It must remain a heap of rubble forever. It must not be rebuilt. ¹⁷Don't hold on to any of the banned items—this will ensure that the Lord turns from his great anger and is compassionate to you, showing you mercy and multiplying you just like he swore to your ancestors. ¹⁸You must definitely obey the Lord your God's voice, keeping all his commandments that I am giving you right now, by doing what is right in the Lord your God's eyes!

LIFE PRESERVER

Why does God say to kill those who worship other gods? What does this mean today? *Deuteronomy 13*

To prepare the Israelites for living in the Canaanite culture, God wanted them to remember the first commandment: to keep God first in their lives. God knew they would be tempted by the worship practices of those around them. So God gave Moses strict instructions to help the people stay faithful to the God of Israel, the God who had led them out of slavery and through the wilderness to the promised land.

The instructions in this part of the Bible sound very harsh in our culture today. God told the people that if someone, even a relative, invited them to worship another god, they were to kill that person, showing no mercy or compassion.

Today we look at people of other faiths respectfully. We have different laws than in the time of the Israelites. We believe that God wants us to learn how to live together in peace. God's heart is happy when God sees us figuring out how to live together. ◊

ʷ13:1 in Heb ˣ13:2 in Heb ʸOr *burn* ᶻSee note at 2:34.

Complete devotion to the Lord

14 You are the Lord's children. Don't cut yourselves and don't shave your foreheads for the dead, ²because you are a people holy to the Lord your God. You are the ones whom the Lord selected to be his own, to be a treasured people out of all other people on earth.

Dietary laws

³Don't eat any detestable thing. ⁴Here's a list of animals you are allowed to eat: ox, sheep, goat, ⁵deer, gazelle, roebuck, wild goat, ibex, antelope, and mountain sheep. ⁶You are also allowed to eat any animal with a divided hoof—the hoof being divided into two parts—and that rechews food among the various kinds of animals. ⁷However, here's a list of animals that either rechew food or have hooves divided in two parts that you are not allowed to eat:

the camel, the hare, and the rock badger—because these rechew food but don't have divided hoofs, they are off-limits for you;

⁸and the pig—because it has a divided hoof but doesn't rechew food, it's off-limits for you.

You may not eat these animals' meat, and you must not touch their carcasses.

⁹Here's a list of the water animals you are allowed to eat: you can eat anything that has fins and scales. ¹⁰But you aren't allowed to eat anything that lacks scales or fins. These are off-limits for you.

¹¹You are allowed to eat any clean bird. ¹²Here's a list of those you are not allowed to eat: the eagle, the vulture, the osprey, ¹³the red kite, the black kite, and any kind of bird of prey, ¹⁴any kind of raven, ¹⁵the ostrich, the nighthawk, the seagull, any kind of hawk, ¹⁶the small owl and the large owl, the water hen, ¹⁷the desert owl, the carrion vulture, the cormorant, ¹⁸the stork, any kind of heron, the hoopoe, and the bat.[a]

¹⁹Also, all winged insects are off-limits for you. They are not to be eaten. ²⁰Any clean winged creature can be eaten, however.

²¹You must not eat any decayed animal flesh because you are a people holy to the Lord your God. You can give decayed animal flesh to the immigrants who live in your cities, and they can eat it; or you can sell it to foreigners.

Don't cook a lamb in its own mother's milk.

Tenth part

²²You must reserve a tenth part of whatever your fields produce each year. ²³Eat the tenth part of your grain, wine, oil, oldest offspring of your herds and flocks in the presence of the Lord your God in the location he selects for his name to reside so that you learn to fear the Lord your God at all times. ²⁴But if the trip is too long, because the location the Lord your God has selected to put his name is far away from where you live so that you can't transport the tenth part—because the Lord your God will certainly bless you—²⁵then you can convert it to money. Take the money with you and go to the location the Lord your God selects. ²⁶Then you can use the money for anything you want:

LIFE PRESERVER

Why did the Israelites have such a strict "do not eat" list?
Deuteronomy 14:3-21

The Instruction about what God's people could and could not eat was written to help the Israelites remember that all life is set apart and dedicated to God, all creation from God is good, and there is an order in creation. The Instruction fell into two categories. The first category of animals on the "do not eat list" were scavengers that ate dead animals. All of the animals that people could eat were non-meat-eating animals. A second category of animals on the "do not eat list" were animals with a mixed species. The dietary guidance was given to help God's people remember that all life should be respected.

You may know people today who follow a "do not eat" list because of their faith or beliefs. Perhaps you know someone who is Jewish who still follows these dietary teachings and doesn't eat pork or shellfish. Or you may have a friend who is a vegetarian and eats no meat at all. Even today, people sometimes follow a "do not eat" list because it helps them remember their faith in God and believe in the goodness of all God's creation.◊

[a]The species of many of the birds in 14:12–18 is uncertain.

cattle, sheep, wine, beer, or whatever else you might like. Then you should feast there and celebrate in the presence of the Lord your God, along with your entire household. ²⁷Only make sure not to neglect the Levites who are living in your cities because they don't have a designated inheritance like you do.

²⁸Every third year you must bring the tenth part of your produce from that year and leave it at your city gates. ²⁹Then the Levites, who have no designated inheritance like you do, along with the immigrants, orphans, and widows who live in your cities, will come and feast until they are full. Do this so that the Lord your God might bless you in everything you do.

Year of canceled debts

15 Every seventh year you must cancel all debts. ²This is how the cancellation is to be handled: Creditors will forgive the loans of their fellow Israelites. They won't demand repayment from their neighbors or their relatives because the Lord's year of debt cancellation has been announced. ³You are allowed to demand payment from foreigners, but whatever is owed you from your fellow Israelites you must forgive. ⁴Of course there won't be any poor persons among you because the Lord will bless you in the land that the Lord your God is giving you to possess as an inheritance, ⁵but only if you carefully obey the Lord your God's voice, by carefully doing every bit of this commandment that I'm giving you right now. ⁶Once the Lord your God has blessed you, exactly as he said he would, you will end up lending to many different peoples but won't need to borrow a thing. You will dominate many different peoples, but they won't dominate you.

⁷Now if there are some poor persons among you, say one of your fellow Israelites in one of your cities in the land that the Lord your God is giving you, don't be hard-hearted or tight-fisted toward your poor fellow Israelites. ⁸To the contrary! Open your hand wide to them. You must generously lend them whatever they need. ⁹But watch yourself! Make sure no wicked thought crosses your mind, such as, The seventh year is coming—the year of debt cancellation—so that you resent your poor fellow Israelites and don't give them anything.

If you do that, they will cry out to the Lord against you, and you will be guilty of sin. ¹⁰No, give generously to needy persons. Don't resent giving to them because it is this very thing that will lead to the Lord your God's blessing you in all you do and work at. ¹¹Poor persons will never disappear from the earth. That's why I'm giving you this command: you must open your hand generously to your fellow Israelites, to the needy among you, and to the poor who live with you in your land.

¹²If any of your fellow Hebrews, male or female, sell themselves into your service, they can work for you for six years, but in the seventh year you must set them free from your service. ¹³Furthermore, when you set them free from your service, you must not let them go empty-handed. ¹⁴Instead, provide for them fully from your flock, food, and wine. You must give to them from that with which the Lord your God has blessed you. ¹⁵Remember how each of you was a slave in Egypt and how the Lord your God saved you. That's why I am commanding you to do this right now. (¹⁶Now if your male servant says to you: "I don't want to leave your service" because he loves you and your family and because life is good for him in your service, ¹⁷then you may take a needle and pierce his ear with it into the doorframe. From that point on, he will be your permanent servant. Do the same thing for female servants.) ¹⁸Don't consider it a hardship to set these servants free from your service, because they worked for you for six years—at a value double that of a paid worker. The Lord your God will bless you in everything that you do.

¹⁹You must devote every oldest male animal from your herds or flocks to the Lord your God. Don't plow with your oldest male ox and don't shear your oldest male sheep. ²⁰Year after year, you and your family are allowed to eat these animals in the presence of the Lord your God, in the location the Lord selects. ²¹But if there is any defect in it, lameness, blindness, any flaw whatsoever, you must not sacrifice it to the Lord your God. ²²You are allowed to eat those in your own cities, whether you are polluted or purified, just as you would eat gazelle or deer. ²³Even so, don't consume any blood. Pour it out on the ground, like water.

Passover celebration

16 Wait for the month of Abib,[b] at which time you must perform the Passover for the Lord your God, because the Lord your God brought you out of Egypt at nighttime during the month of Abib. [2] Offer a Passover sacrifice from the flock or herd to the Lord your God at the location the Lord selects for his name to reside. [3] You must not eat anything containing yeast along with it.[c] Instead, for seven days you must eat unleavened bread, bread symbolizing misery, along with it because you fled Egypt in a great hurry. Do this so you remember the day you fled Egypt for as long as you live. [4] No dough with yeast should appear in any of your territory for seven days. Furthermore, none of the meat that you sacrificed on the first night should remain until morning. [5] You are not permitted to offer the Passover sacrifice in any of the cities that the Lord your God is giving you. [6] Instead, you must offer the Passover sacrifice at the location the Lord your God selects for his name to reside, at evening time, when the sun sets, which was the time you fled Egypt. [7] Cook it and eat it in the location that the Lord your God selects. The next morning you can return to your tents. [8] For six days you will eat unleavened bread. The seventh day will be a celebration for the Lord your God. Don't do any work.

Festival of Weeks

[9] Count out seven weeks, starting the count from the beginning of the grain harvest. [10] At that point, perform the Festival of Weeks for the Lord your God. Offer a spontaneous gift in precise measure with the blessing the Lord your God gives you. [11] Then celebrate in the presence of the Lord your God—you, your sons, your daughters, your male and female servants, the Levites who live in your cities, the immigrants, the orphans, and the widows who are among you—in the location the Lord your God selects for his name to reside. [12] Remember how each of you was a slave in Egypt, so follow these regulations most carefully.

Festival of Booths

[13] Once you have collected the food and drink you need, perform the Festival of Booths for seven days. [14] Celebrate your festival: you, your sons, your daughters, your male and female servants, the Levites, the immigrants, the orphans, and the widows who live in your cities. [15] Seven days you must perform the festival for the Lord your God in the location the Lord selects because the Lord your God will bless you in all you do and in all your work. You will be overjoyed.

[16] Three times a year every male among you must appear before the presence of the Lord your God in the location he will select: at the Festival of Unleavened Bread, the Festival of Weeks, and the Festival of Booths. They must not appear before the Lord's presence empty-handed. [17] Each one should have his gift in hand, in precise measure with the blessing the Lord your God gives you.

Judges and officials

[18] Appoint judges and officials for each of your tribes in every city that the Lord your God gives you. They must judge the people fairly. [19] Don't delay justice; don't show favoritism. Don't take bribes because bribery blinds the vision of the wise and twists the words of the righteous. [20] Righteousness! Pursue righteousness so that you live long and take possession of the land that the Lord your God is giving you.

SAILBOAT

HONEST AND TRUE

Do What Is Right *Deuteronomy 16:19-20*
The Israelites were faced with many difficult decisions. God commanded them not to delay doing the right thing and not to treat one person better than another because of their position. God wanted the Israelites to do what was right and treat all people fairly. God told them to pursue a right relationship with God all the days of their lives.◆

Rules for worship

[21] Don't plant any tree to serve as a sacred pole[d] next to the altar you make for the Lord your God. [22] Don't set up any sacred stone either, because the Lord your God hates such

---

[b] March–April; called Nisan in post-exilic period [c] *lt*, the Passover sacrifice [d] Heb *asherah*, perhaps an object devoted to the goddess Asherah

17 things. [1]Don't sacrifice to the Lord your God any oxen or sheep that have defects of any kind, because that is detestable to the Lord your God.

Capital punishment

[2]If someone, whether male or female, is found in your community—in one of the cities the Lord your God is giving you—who does evil in the Lord your God's eyes, by breaking God's covenant, [3]by following and serving other gods, and by bowing down to them, to the sun or the moon or any of the heavenly bodies that I haven't permitted—[4]and you hear news about it, then you must look into this situation very carefully. And if it's definitely true that this detestable thing was done in Israel, [5]then you must bring out the man or woman who has done this evil thing to the gates of the city. Stone that person until he or she is dead.

[6]Capital punishment must be decided by two or three witnesses. No one may be executed on the basis of only one testimony. [7]In the execution, the hands of the witnesses must be against the guilty person from the start; the hand of all the people will be involved at the end. Remove[e] such evil from your community!

Legal disputes

[8]If some legal dispute in your cities is too difficult for you to decide—say, between different kinds of bloodshed, different kinds of legal ruling, or different kinds of injury—then take it to the location the Lord your God selects. [9]Go to the levitical priests and to the head judge in office at that time and look into things there. They will announce to you the correct ruling. [10]You must then act according to the ruling they announced to you from that location, the one the Lord selects. You must follow very carefully everything they instruct you to do. [11]Act precisely according to the instruction they give you and the ruling they announce to you. Don't deviate even a bit from the word they announce. [12]And whoever acts rashly by not listening to the priest who is in office serving the Lord your God or to the head judge will die. Remove[f] such evil

from Israel! [13]All the people will hear about this and be afraid. They won't act arrogantly anymore.

Law of the king

[14]Once you have entered the land the Lord your God is giving you and you have taken possession of it and settled down in it, you might say: "Let's appoint a king over us, as all our neighboring nations have done." [15]You can indeed appoint over you a king that the Lord your God selects. You can appoint over you a king who is one of your fellow Israelites. You are not allowed to appoint over you a foreigner who is not one of your fellow Israelites. [16]That granted, the king must not acquire too many horses, and he must not return the people to Egypt in order to acquire more horses, because the Lord told you: "You will never go back by that road again." [17]The king must not take numerous wives so that his heart doesn't go astray. Nor can the king acquire too much silver and gold. [18]Instead, when he sits on his royal throne, he himself must write a copy of this Instruction on a scroll in the presence of the levitical priests. [19]That Instruction must remain with him, and he must read in it every day of his life so that he learns to revere the Lord his God by keeping all the words of this Instruction and these regulations, by doing them, [20]by not being overbearing toward his fellow Israelites, and by not deviating even a bit from the commandment. If the king does all that, he will ensure lasting rule in Israel for himself and for his successors.

LIGHTHOUSE

RESPECT FOR GOD

Read and Review Every Day!

Deuteronomy 17:18-20

When the Israelites entered the promised land, they would eventually be led by many kings. This passage indicates that one of the king's responsibilities was to keep a copy of God's Instruction that he could read every day of his life. The purpose was to help the king remember to follow God's Instruction and be a good leader for God's people.◆

[e]Or burn [f]Or burn

Priests and Levites

18 Neither the levitical priests nor any Levite tribe member will have a designated inheritance in Israel. They can eat the sacrifices offered to the Lord, which are the Lord's portion,[g] ²but they won't share an inheritance with their fellow Israelites. The Lord alone is the Levites' inheritance—just as God promised them.

³Now this is what the priests may keep from the people's sacrifices of oxen or sheep: They must give the priest the shoulder, the jaws, and the stomach. ⁴You must also give the priest the first portions of your grain, wine, and oil, and the first of your sheep's shearing ⁵because the Lord your God selected Levi from all of your tribes to stand and minister in the Lord's name—both him and his descendants for all time.

⁶Now if a Levite leaves one of your cities or departs from any location in Israel where he's been living and, because he wants to, comes to the location the Lord selects ⁷and ministers in the Lord his God's name, just like his relatives—the other Levites serving there in the Lord's presence—⁸he is allowed to eat equal portions, despite the finances he has from his family.[h]

Communicating with God

⁹Once you enter the land that the Lord your God is giving you, don't try to imitate the detestable things those nations do. ¹⁰There must not be anyone among you who passes his son or daughter through fire; who practices divination, is a sign reader, fortune-teller, sorcerer, ¹¹or spell caster; who converses with ghosts or spirits or communicates with the dead. ¹²All who do these things are detestable to the Lord! It is on account of these detestable practices that the Lord your God is driving these nations[i] out before you. ¹³Instead, you must be perfect before the Lord your God. ¹⁴These nations you are displacing listened to sign readers and diviners, but the Lord your God doesn't permit you to do the same! ¹⁵The Lord your God will raise up a prophet like me from your community, from your fellow Israelites. He's the one you must listen to. ¹⁶That's exactly what you requested from the Lord your God at Horeb, on the day of the assembly, when you said, "I can't listen to the Lord my God's voice anymore or look at this great fire any longer. I don't want to die!"

¹⁷The Lord said to me: What they've said is right. ¹⁸I'll raise up a prophet for them from among their fellow Israelites—one just like you. I'll put my words in his mouth, and he will tell them everything I command him. ¹⁹I myself will hold accountable anyone who doesn't listen to my words, which that prophet will speak in my name. ²⁰However, any prophet who arrogantly speaks a word in my name that I haven't commanded him to speak, or who speaks in the name of other gods—that prophet must die.

²¹Now, you might be wondering, How will we know which word God hasn't spoken? ²²Here's the answer: The prophet who speaks in the Lord's name and the thing doesn't happen or come about—that's the word the Lord hasn't spoken. That prophet spoke arrogantly. Don't be afraid of him.[j]

Cities of refuge

19 Once the Lord your God has eliminated those nations—whose land the Lord your God is giving you—and you displace them, settling into their cities and their houses, ²you must designate three cities for your use in the land the Lord your God is giving you to possess. ³Mark out the roads to them[k] and divide the regions of the land the Lord your God is apportioning to you into three parts. These cities are the places to which a person who has killed can escape. ⁴Here is the rule concerning a person who killed someone and is permitted to escape to one of these cities and live:

If it is someone who killed his neighbor accidentally, without having hated that person previously; ⁵or if someone goes into the forest with a neighbor to chop some wood, and while swinging an ax to cut down the tree, the axhead flies off its handle and hits the neighbor, who subsequently dies—these kinds of killers may escape to one of these cities and live. ⁶Otherwise, the blood avenger will chase after the killer out of rage and—especially if

---

[g]Heb uncertain [h]Heb uncertain [i]Or *them* [j]Or *bothered by it* (the prophecy) [k]Heb uncertain and lacks *to them*.

the distance to one of these cities[1] is too far—might catch and kill him, even though a death sentence was not in order because the killer didn't have prior malice toward the other. [7]This is why I am commanding you as follows: Designate three cities for your use.

[8]Now if the Lord your God enlarges your territory, as he swore to your ancestors—and he will give you all the land he swore to give to them [9]as long as you keep all this commandment that I am giving you right now by doing it, by loving the Lord your God, and by always walking in his ways—you can add three more cities for your use along with the first three. [10]Innocent blood must not be spilled in the land the Lord your God is giving to you as an inheritance, or it will be bloodshed that will be required of you.

[11]But if someone does hate a neighbor and ambushes him, rising up against him and attacking him so he dies, and then escapes to one of these cities, [12]elders from the killer's hometown will send word, and the killer will be sent back from there. They will then hand him over to the blood avenger, and he will be executed. [13]Show no mercy to such killers. Remove[m] innocent bloodshed from Israel so that things go well for you.

Property laws

[14]Now in the land the Lord your God is giving you, in your allotted property that you will receive there, you must not tamper with your neighbor's property line, which has been previously established.

Rules for testimony

[15]A solitary witness against someone in any crime, wrongdoing, or in any sort of misdeed that might be done is not sufficient. The decision must stand by two or three witnesses. [16]Now if a spiteful witness comes forward against someone, so as to testify against them falsely, [17]the two persons who have a legal suit must stand before the Lord, before the priests, and before the judges that are in office at that time. [18]The judges will look into the situation very carefully. If it turns out that the witness is a liar—that the witness has given false testimony against his fellow Israelite—[19]then you must do to him what he had planned to do to his fellow Israelite. Remove[n] such evil from your community! [20]The rest of the people will hear about this and be afraid. They won't do that sort of evil thing among you again. [21]Show no mercy on this point: life for life, eye for eye, tooth for tooth, hand for hand, foot for foot.

Rules for warfare

20 When you march out to battle your enemies and you see horses, chariots, and a fighting force larger than yours, don't be afraid of them, because the Lord your God, the one who brought you up from Egypt, is with you. [2]As you advance toward the war, the priest will come forward and will address the troops. [3]He will say to them: "Listen, Israel: Right now you are advancing to wage war against your enemies. Don't be discouraged! Don't be afraid! Don't panic! Don't shake in fear on account of them, [4]because the Lord your God is going with you to fight your enemies for you and to save you."

[5]The officials will also say to the troops: "Is there anyone here who has just built a new house but hasn't yet dedicated it? He can leave and go back to his house; otherwise, he might die in the war and someone else would dedicate the house. [6]Or is there anyone here who has planted a vineyard but hasn't yet put it to good use? He can leave and go back to his house; otherwise, he might die in the battle and someone else would use the vineyard. [7]Or is there anyone here who is engaged but not yet married? He may leave and go back to his house; otherwise, he might die in the battle and someone else would marry his fiancée."

[8]The officials will continue to address the troops, stating: "Is there anyone here who is afraid and discouraged? He can leave and go back to his house; otherwise, his comrades might lose courage just as he has." [9]Once the officials have completed their speech to the troops, the army commanders will assume leadership of the forces.

[10]When you approach a city to fight against it, you should first extend peaceful terms to it. [11]If the city responds with peaceful terms and surrenders to you, then all the

---

[1]Heb lacks *to one of these cities.* [m]Or *burn* [n]Or *burn*

people in the city will serve you as forced laborers. [12]However, if the city does not negotiate peacefully with you but makes war against you, you may attack it. [13]The Lord your God will hand it over to you; you must kill all the city's males with the sword. [14]However, you can take for yourselves the women, the children, the animals, and all that is in the city—all its plunder. You can then enjoy your enemies' plunder, which the Lord your God has given you.

[15]That's what you must do to all the cities that are located far away from you—specifically, those cities that don't belong to these nations here. [16]But in the case of any of the cities of these peoples—the ones the Lord your God is giving you as an inheritance—you must not spare any living thing. [17]Instead, you must place these under the ban:[o] Hittites, Amorites, Canaanites, Perizzites, Hivites, and Jebusites—just as the Lord your God commanded you. [18]Then they can't teach you to do all the detestable things they did for their gods, with the result that you end up sinning against the Lord your God.

[19]Now if you have been attacking a city for some time, fighting against it and trying to conquer it, don't destroy its trees by cutting them down with axes. You can eat from those trees; don't cut them down! Do you think a tree of the field is some sort of warrior to be attacked by you in battle? [20]That said, if you know that a tree is not a food-producing tree, you are allowed to destroy it, cutting it down and using it in the siege against the city that is fighting against you until it falls.

Unsolved homicides

21
If a corpse is found on the ground the Lord your God is giving you to possess, lying in a field, and the identity of the killer is unknown, [2]your elders and judges must come out and measure the distances to the cities nearest the body. [3]Once it is determined which city is closest to the dead body, its elders must take a young cow that hasn't been used or yet pulled a plow, [4]and those elders will take the cow down to a ravine with a flowing stream—one that has not been plowed or planted—and they will break the cow's neck right there in the river valley. [5]Then the priests, the descendants of Levi, will step forward because the Lord your God selected them to minister for him and to bless in the Lord's name, and because every legal dispute and case of assault is decided by them. [6]All the elders of the city closest to the corpse will wash their hands over the cow whose neck was broken in the river valley. [7]They will then solemnly state: "Our hands did not shed this blood. Our eyes did not see it happen. [8]Lord, please forgive your people Israel, whom you saved. Don't put the guilt of innocent bloodshed on your people Israel."

Then the bloodguilt will be forgiven them.

[9]But you must remove[p] innocent bloodshed from your community; do only what is right in the Lord's eyes.

Foreign wives

[10]When you wage war against your enemies and the Lord hands them over to you and you take prisoners, [11]if you see among the captives a beautiful woman, and you fall in love with her and take her as your wife, [12]bringing her into your home, she must shave her head, cut her nails, [13]remove her prisoner's clothing, and live in your house, mourning her father and her mother for one month. After that, you may consummate the marriage. You will be her husband, and she will be your wife. [14]But if you aren't pleased with her, you must send her away as she wishes. You are not allowed to sell her for money or treat her as a slave because you have humiliated her.

Right of the oldest son

[15]Now suppose a man has two wives—one of them loved and the other unloved. Both wives bear children, but the oldest male is the unloved wife's child. [16]On the day when the man decides what will go to each of his children as an inheritance, he isn't allowed to treat his loved wife's son as the oldest male rather than his unloved wife's son, who is the real oldest male. [17]Instead, he must acknowledge the unloved wife's son as the oldest male, giving to him two-thirds of everything that he owns, because that son is the earliest

[o]See note at Deut 2:34. [p]Or burn

produce of his physical power. The oldest male's rights belong to that son.

Rebellious children

[18]Now if someone has a consistently stubborn and rebellious child, who refuses to listen to their father and mother—even when the parents discipline him, he won't listen to them— [19]the father and mother will take the son before the elders of that city at its gates. [20]Then they will inform the city's elders: "This son of ours is consistently stubborn and rebellious, refusing to listen to us. What's more, he's wild and a drunkard." [21]Then all the people of that town will stone him until he dies.

Remove[q] such evil from your community! All Israel will hear about this and be afraid.

Hanging

[22]Now if someone is guilty of a capital crime, and they are executed, and you then hang them on a tree, [23]you must not leave the body hanging on the tree but must bury it the same day because God's curse is on those who are hanged.[r] Furthermore, you must not pollute the ground that the LORD your God is giving to you as an inheritance.

Rules for property and mixtures

22 Don't just watch your fellow Israelite's ox or sheep wandering around and do nothing about it. You must return the animal to its owner. [2]If the owner doesn't live nearby, or you don't know who owns the animal, then you must take care of it. It should stay with you until your fellow Israelite comes looking for it, at which point you must return it to him. [3]Do the same thing in the case of a donkey. Do the same thing in the case of a piece of clothing. Do the same thing in the case of anything that your fellow Israelite loses and you end up finding. You are not allowed to sit back and do nothing about it.

[4]Don't just watch your fellow Israelite's donkey or ox fall down in the road and do nothing about it. You must help your fellow Israelite get the animal up again.

[5]Women must not wear men's clothes, and men must not wear women's clothes. Everyone who does such things is detestable to the LORD your God.

[6]If you come across a bird's nest along your way, whether in a tree or on the ground, with baby birds or eggs, and the mother is sitting on the baby birds or eggs, do not remove the mother from her young. [7]You must let the mother go, though you may take the young for yourself so that things go well for you and so you can prolong your life.

[8]Whenever you build a new house, you must build a railing for the roof so that you don't end up with innocent blood on your hands because someone fell off of it.

[9]Don't plant your vineyards with two types of seed; otherwise, the entire crop that you have planted and the produce of the vineyard will be unusable.[s]

[10]Don't plow with an ox and a donkey together.

[11]Don't wear clothes that mix wool and linen together.

[12]Make tassels for the four corners of the coat you wear.

SAILBOAT

KINDNESS

Do Something! *Deuteronomy 22:1-4*
God told the people that if they saw their neighbor's sheep or ox wandering around, they should return it to their neighbor. And if the sheep or ox had wandered a long way from home, the people were to take care of it until the owner could come and get the animal. God said the people were not allowed to sit and do nothing but had to help each other instead. God called the Israelites to show kindness to each other.

Virgin bride

[13]Suppose a man gets married and consummates the marriage but subsequently despises his wife. [14]He then spreads false claims about her to the point that she has a bad reputation, because he said such things as, "I married this woman, but when I went to have sex with her, I couldn't find any proof that she was a virgin."

---

[q]Or *burn* [r]LXX, Vulg, Tg Neofiti *God's curse is on those who are hanged;* Syr, Tg Onqelos *those who curse God are to be hanged;* Heb uncertain [s]Or *sanctified*

¹⁵At that point, the young woman's father and mother will bring proof of her virginity to the city's elders at the city gate. ¹⁶The young woman's father will say to the elders: "I gave my daughter to this man to be his wife, but he doesn't like her anymore. ¹⁷That's why he has spread false claims about her, saying, 'I couldn't find any proof that your daughter was a virgin.' But look! Here's proof of my daughter's virginity." At that point they will spread out the blanket in front of the city's elders. ¹⁸The city's elders must then take that husband and punish him. ¹⁹They will fine him one hundred silver shekels, giving that to the young woman's father, because that husband gave one of Israel's virgin daughters a bad reputation. Moreover, she must remain his wife; he is never allowed to divorce her.

²⁰However, if the claim is true and proof of the young woman's virginity can't be produced, ²¹then the city's elders will bring the young woman to the door of her father's house. The citizens of that city must stone her until she dies because she acted so sinfully in Israel by having extramarital sex while still in her father's house.

Remove^t such evil from your community!

Inappropriate sexual behavior

²²If a man is found having sex with a woman who is married to someone else, both of them must die—the man who was having sex with the woman and the woman herself.

Remove such evil from Israel!

²³If a young woman who is a virgin is engaged to one man and another man meets up with her in a town and has sex with her, ²⁴you must bring both of them to the city gates there and stone them until they die—the young woman because she didn't call for help in the city, and the man because of the fact that he humiliated his neighbor's wife.

Remove such evil from your community!

²⁵But if the man met up with the engaged woman in a field, grabbing her and having sex with her there, only the man will die. ²⁶Don't do anything whatsoever to the young woman. She hasn't committed any capital crime—rather, this situation is exactly like the one where someone attacks his neighbor and kills him.^u ²⁷Since the man met up with her in a field, the engaged woman may well have called out for help, but there was no one to rescue her.

²⁸If a man meets up with a young woman who is a virgin and not engaged, grabs her and has sex with her, and they are caught in the act, ²⁹the man who had sex with her must give fifty silver shekels to the young woman's father. She will also become his wife because he has humiliated her. He is never allowed to divorce her.

³⁰^vA man cannot marry his father's former wife so that his father's private matters are not exposed.^w

The Lord's assembly

23 ^xNo man whose testicles are crushed or whose penis is cut off can belong to the Lord's assembly. ²No one born of an illegitimate marriage^y can belong to the Lord's assembly either. Not even the tenth generation of such children can belong to the Lord's assembly. ³Ammonites and Moabites can't belong to the Lord's assembly. Not even the tenth generation of such people can belong to the Lord's assembly, as a rule, ⁴because they didn't help you with food or water on your journey out of Egypt, and because they hired Balaam, Beor's son, from Pethor of Mesopotamia to curse you. ⁵But the Lord your God wasn't interested in listening to Balaam. The Lord your God turned that curse into a blessing because the Lord your God loves you. ⁶So don't be concerned with their health and well-being as long as you live.

⁷Don't detest Edomites, because they are your relatives. Don't detest Egyptians because you were immigrants in their land. ⁸Children born to them are permitted to belong to the Lord's assembly starting with the third generation.

Rules for the war camp

⁹When you are camped in battle against your enemies, guard yourself from every possible evil. ¹⁰If an individual in the camp becomes polluted due to a nighttime emission,

---

^tOr *burn*; so also 22:22, 24 ^uSee 19:11. ^v23:1 in Heb ^wOr *so that he doesn't uncover his father's skirt* ^x23:2 in Heb ^yHeb uncertain

he must exit the camp area and not reenter. [11]When the next evening arrives, he must wash with water; and when the sun sets, he can come back to the camp.

[12]The latrines[z] must be outside the camp. You will use them there, outside the camp. [13]Carry a shovel with the rest of your gear; once you have relieved yourself, use it to dig a hole, then refill it, covering your excrement.

[14]Do these things because the LORD your God travels with you, right in the middle of your camp, ready to save you and to hand your enemies over to you. For this reason your camp must be holy. The LORD must not see anything indecent among you, or he will turn away from you.

Escaped slaves

[15]Don't return slaves to owners if they've escaped and come to you. [16]They can stay with you: in your own community or in any place they select from one of your cities, whatever seems good to them. Don't oppress them.

Consecrated workers

[17]No Israelite daughter is allowed to be a consecrated worker.[a] Neither is any Israelite son allowed to be a consecrated worker.[b] [18]Don't bring a female prostitute's fee or a male prostitute's[c] payment to the LORD your God's temple to pay a solemn promise because both of these things are detestable to the LORD your God.

Charging interest

[19]Don't charge your fellow Israelites interest—whether on money, provisions, or anything one might loan. [20]You can charge foreigners interest, but not your fellow Israelite. Do this so that the LORD your God blesses you in all your work on the land you are entering to possess.

Solemn promise

[21]When you make a promise to the LORD your God, don't put off making good on it, because the LORD your God will certainly be expecting it from you; delaying would make you guilty. [22]Now if you simply don't make

any promises, you won't be guilty of anything. [23]But whatever you say, you should be sure to make good on, exactly according to the promise you freely made to the LORD your God because you promised it with your own mouth.

Neighbor's goods

[24]If you go into your neighbor's vineyard, you can eat as many grapes as you like, until full, but don't carry any away in a basket. [25]If you go into your neighbor's grain field, you can pluck ears by hand, but you aren't allowed to cut off any of your neighbor's grain with a sickle.

Marriage and divorce

24 Let's say a man marries a woman, but she isn't pleasing to him because he's discovered something inappropriate about her. So he writes up divorce papers, hands them to her, and sends her out of his house. [2]She leaves his house and ends up marrying someone else. [3]But this new husband also dislikes her, writes up divorce papers, hands them to her, and sends her out of his house (or suppose the second husband dies). [4]In this case, the first husband who originally divorced this woman is not allowed to take her back and marry her again after she has been polluted in this way because the LORD detests that. Don't pollute the land the LORD your God is giving to you as an inheritance.

[5]A newly married man doesn't have to march in battle. Neither should any related duties be placed on him. He is to live free of such responsibilities for one year, so he can bring joy to his new wife.

Pawning

[6]Millstones or even just the upper millstone must not be pawned, because that would be pawning someone's livelihood.

---

[z]LXX, Syr, Vulg *place of the hand* (a euphemism); MT has only *hand*.   [a]Traditionally *cultic prostitute*   [b]Traditionally *cultic prostitute*   [c]Or *a dog's*

Kidnapping

[7]If someone is caught kidnapping their fellow Israelites, intending to enslave the Israelite or sell them, that kidnapper must die. Remove[d] such evil from your community!

Skin disease

[8]Be on guard against outbreaks of skin disease[e] by being very careful about what you do. You must carefully do everything the levitical priests teach you, just as I have commanded them. [9]Remember, after all, what the Lord your God did to Miriam on your departure from Egypt!

did you know? When workers went through the fields harvesting grain and fruit, they sometimes left food on the plants or dropped food on the ground. Anything they left behind was offered to widows, orphans, the poor, and people from other countries. These people were allowed to go through the fields and take what remained.

Loans

[10]When you make any type of loan to your neighbor, don't enter their house to receive the collateral. [11]You must wait outside. The person to whom you are lending will bring the collateral to you out there. [12]Moreover, if the person is poor, you are not allowed to sleep in their pawned coat. [13]Instead, be certain to give the pawned coat back by sunset so they can sleep in their own coat. They will bless you, and you will be considered righteous before the Lord your God.

Payment for workers

[14]Don't take advantage of poor or needy workers, whether they are fellow Israelites or immigrants who live in your land or your cities. [15]Pay them their salary the same day, before the sun sets, because they are poor, and their very life depends on that pay, and so they don't cry out against you to the Lord. That would make you guilty.

Generational punishment

[16]Parents shouldn't be executed because of what their children have done; neither should children be executed because of what their parents have done. Each person should be executed for their own guilty acts.

Rights of widows, orphans, and immigrants

[17]Don't obstruct the legal rights of an immigrant or orphan. Don't take a widow's coat as pledge for a loan. [18]Remember how you were a slave in Egypt but how the Lord your God saved you from that. That's why I'm commanding you to do this thing.

[19]Whenever you are reaping the harvest of your field and you leave some grain in the field, don't go back and get it. Let it go to the immigrants, the orphans, and the widows so that the Lord your God blesses you in all that you do. [20]Similarly, when you beat the olives off your olive trees, don't go back over them twice. Let the leftovers go to the immigrants, the orphans, and the widows. [21]Again, when you pick the grapes of your vineyard, don't pick them over twice. Let the leftovers go to the immigrants, the orphans, and the widows. [22]Remember how you were a slave in Egypt. That's why I am commanding you to do this thing.

Corporal punishment

25 Now two people have a disagreement and they enter into litigation and their case is decided, with the judges declaring one person legally right and the other legally liable. [2]If the guilty party is to be beaten, the presiding judge will have that person lie down and be punished in his presence—the number of blows in measure with the guilt determined. [3]Give no more than forty blows. If more than that is given, your fellow Israelite would be completely disgraced in your eyes.

Working oxen

[4]Don't muzzle an ox while it is threshing grain.

The brother-in-law's duty

[5]If brothers live together and one of them dies without having a son, the dead man's wife must not go outside the family and marry a stranger. Instead, her brother-in-law should go to her and take her as his wife. He will then

---

[d]Or burn [e]Heb uncertain; traditionally *leprosy*—a term used for several different skin diseases

consummate the marriage according to the brother-in-law's duty. ⁶The brother-in-law will name the oldest male son that she bears after his dead brother so that his brother's legacy will not be forgotten in Israel. ⁷If the brother does not want to marry his sister-in-law, she can go to the elders at the city gate, informing them: "My brother-in-law refuses to continue his brother's legacy in Israel. He's not willing to perform the brother-in-law's duty with me." ⁸The city's elders will summon him and talk to him about this. If he doesn't budge, insisting, "I don't want to marry her," ⁹then the sister-in-law will approach him while the elders watch. She will pull the sandal off his foot and spit in his face. Then she will exclaim: "That's what's done to any man who won't build up his own brother's family!" ¹⁰Subsequently, that man's family will be known throughout Israel as "the house of the removed sandal."

Improper touching

¹¹If two men are fighting with each other— a man and his fellow Israelite—and the wife of one of them gets into the fight, trying to save her husband from his attacker and does so by reaching out and grabbing his genitals, ¹²you must cut off her hand. Show no mercy.

Honest business practices

¹³Don't have two different types of money weights in your bag, a heavy one and a light one. ¹⁴Don't have two different types of ephahs in your house, a large one and a small one. ¹⁵Instead, you must have only one weight, complete and correct, and only one ephah, also complete and correct, so that your life might be long in the fertile land the Lord your God is giving you. ¹⁶What's more, all who do such things, all who do business dishonestly, are detestable to the Lord your God. ¹⁷Remember, after all, what Amalek did

Helping People Who Suffer   *Deuteronomy 24:17-22*

In Bible times, men controlled all the property for their family members. This made things very hard for a woman if her husband died. If she didn't have any brothers or adult sons to care for her, people would sometimes take advantage of her and try to get her land or possessions. Sometimes, she would lose everything she had and would have to beg or else starve.

God was clear that it is very important to take care of widows and orphans. God reminded the Israelites that many years before, when they lived in Egypt, they were poor and defenseless. Just as God took care of them during their years in Egypt, God asked God's people to take care of widows and orphans. God's Instruction provided a way for widows to find food and protection.

God still wants us to care for those who are having a hard time. People might struggle after someone in their family dies. They might be sick from cancer or other illnesses. Sometimes people lose their jobs and have trouble paying their bills. No matter what the situation, we can try our best to help. Simple ways to help someone during a difficult time include mowing their lawn, raking their leaves, walking their dogs, washing their cars, or baking some cookies for them. Caring for others is a way to honor God.

Do you know someone who is suffering?

What can you do to help them?

to you on your departure from Egypt: [18]how he met up with you on the way, striking from behind those who were lagging back because you were weak and tired, and because he didn't fear God. [19]So once the Lord your God gives you relief from all the enemies that surround you in the land the Lord your God is giving you as an inheritance to possess, you must wipe out Amalek's memory from under the heavens. Don't forget this!

The ceremony upon entering the land

26 Once you have entered the land the Lord your God is giving you as an inheritance, and you take possession of it and are settled there, [2]take some of the early produce of the fertile ground that you have harvested from the land the Lord your God is giving you, and put it in a basket. Then go to the location the Lord your God selects for his name to reside. [3]Go to the priest who is in office at that time and say to him: "I am declaring right now before the Lord my[f] God that I have indeed arrived in the land the Lord swore to our ancestors to give us."

Bet you can read this in 7 minutes. *Ready, set, go!*

[4]The priest will then take the basket from you and place it before the Lord your God's altar. [5]Then you should solemnly state before the Lord your God:

"My father was a starving Aramean. He went down to Egypt, living as an immigrant there with few family members, but that is where he became a great nation, mighty and numerous. [6]The Egyptians treated us terribly, oppressing us and forcing hard labor on us. [7]So we cried out for help to the Lord, our ancestors' God. The Lord heard our call. God saw our misery, our trouble, and our oppression. [8]The Lord brought us out of Egypt with a strong hand and an outstretched arm, with awesome power, and with signs and wonders. [9]He brought us to this place and gave us this land—a land full of milk and honey. [10]So now I am bringing the early produce of the fertile ground that you, Lord, have given me."

Set the produce before the Lord your God, bowing down before the Lord your God. [11]Then celebrate all the good things the Lord your God has done for you and your family—each one of you along with the Levites and the immigrants who are among you.

[12]When you have finished paying the entire tenth part of your produce on the third year—that is the year for paying the tenth-part—you will give it to the Levites, the immigrants, the orphans, and the widows so they can eat in your cities until they are full. [13]Then announce before the Lord your God: "I have removed the holy portion from my[g] house, and I have given it to the Levites, the immigrants, the orphans, and the widows—in full compliance with your entire commandment that you commanded me. I haven't broken your commandments. I haven't forgotten one! [14]I haven't eaten from the holy portion while mourning, nor did I remove it while I was polluted, nor have I dedicated any of it to the dead. I've obeyed the Lord my God's voice. I've done everything just as you commanded me. [15]Please look down from your holy home, from heaven itself, and bless your people Israel and the fertile land that you have given us—a land full of milk and honey—just like you promised our ancestors."

Conclusion to the regulations and case laws

[16]This very moment the Lord your God is commanding you to keep these regulations and case laws. So keep them and do them with all your mind and with your entire being! [17]Today you have affirmed that the Lord will be your God and that you will walk in his ways and follow his regulations, his commandments, and his case laws, and that you will obey his voice. [18]Today the Lord has gotten your agreement[h] that you will be his treasured people, just like he promised—by keeping his commandments— [19]in order to set you high above all the other nations that he made in praise, fame, and honor; and so that you are a people holy to the Lord your God, just as he said you would be.

Stones of the Instruction

27 Then Moses and Israel's elders commanded the people:

---

[f]LXX; MT and most versions read *your.*   [g]LXX, Vulg; MT lacks *my.*   [h]Heb uncertain

Keep all of the commandment that I am giving you right now. ²The same day you cross the Jordan River to enter the land the LORD your God is giving you, set up large stones and cover them with plaster. ³Once you have crossed over, write on the stones all the words of this Instruction because you will have entered[i] the land the LORD your God is giving to you—a land full of milk and honey—exactly as the LORD, your ancestors' God, promised you. ⁴Once you have crossed over the Jordan River, set up these stones that I'm telling you about right now on Mount Ebal. Cover them with plaster ⁵and build an altar there for the LORD your God—an altar of stones that haven't been cut with iron tools. ⁶(You must build the LORD your God's altar with uncut stones.) Then offer up on that altar entirely burned sacrifices to the LORD your God. ⁷Offer up well-being sacrifices and eat them there, celebrating in the LORD your God's presence. ⁸Make sure to write all the words of this Instruction on the stones plainly and clearly.

⁹Then Moses and the levitical priests said to all Israel: Quiet down and listen, Israel! This very moment you have become the people of the LORD your God. ¹⁰So obey the LORD your God's voice. Do his commandments and his regulations that I'm giving you right now.

Ceremony on Mount Gerizim and Mount Ebal

¹¹That same day Moses commanded the people: ¹²Once you have crossed over the Jordan River, the following tribes will stand on Mount Gerizim to bless the people: Simeon, Levi, Judah, Issachar, Joseph, and Benjamin. ¹³And these are the tribes that will stand on Mount Ebal for the cursing: Reuben, Gad, Asher, Zebulun, Dan, and Naphtali. ¹⁴The Levites will address every individual Israelite with a loud voice:

¹⁵"Cursed is anyone who makes an idol or an image—things detestable to the LORD, made by artisans—and sets it up secretly."

All the people will reply: "We agree!"[j]

¹⁶"Cursed is anyone who belittles their father or mother."

All the people will reply: "We agree!"

¹⁷"Cursed is anyone who tampers with their neighbor's property lines."

All the people will reply: "We agree!"

¹⁸"Cursed is anyone who misleads a blind person on a road."

All the people will reply: "We agree!"

¹⁹"Cursed is anyone who obstructs the legal rights of immigrants, orphans, or widows."

All the people will reply: "We agree!"

²⁰"Cursed is anyone who has sex with his father's wife, because that exposes his father's private matters."[k]

All the people will reply: "We agree!"

²¹"Cursed is anyone who has sex with any kind of animal."

All the people will reply: "We agree!"

²²"Cursed is anyone who has sex with his sister, whether his father's daughter or his mother's daughter."

All the people will reply: "We agree!"

²³"Cursed is anyone who has sex with his mother-in-law."

All the people will reply: "We agree!"

²⁴"Cursed is anyone who kills his neighbor in secret."

All the people will reply: "We agree!"

²⁵"Cursed is anyone who accepts money to kill an innocent person."

All the people will reply: "We agree!"

²⁶"Cursed is anyone who doesn't support the words of this Instruction by carrying them out."

All the people will reply: "We agree!"

Future blessing

28 Now if you really obey the LORD your God's voice, by carefully keeping all his commandments that I am giving you right now, then the LORD your God will set you high above all nations on earth. ²All these blessings will come upon you and find you if you obey the LORD your God's voice: ³You will be blessed in the city and blessed in the field. ⁴Your own fertility, your soil's produce, and your livestock's offspring—the young of both cattle and flocks—will be blessed. ⁵Your basket and your kneading bowl will be blessed. ⁶You will be blessed when you are out and about and blessed when you come back. ⁷The

---

[i]Or *in order that you might enter;* Heb uncertain [j]Heb *Amen;* also in the following verses [k]Or *because that uncovers his father's skirt*

LORD will defeat any enemies who attack you. They will come against you from one direction but will run for their lives away from you in seven different directions. [8]The LORD will command the blessing to be with you—in your barns and on all the work you do—and he will bless you on the land the LORD your God is giving you. [9]The LORD will establish you as his own, a holy nation, just as he swore to you, if you keep the LORD your God's commandments and walk in his ways. [10]All the earth's peoples will see that you are called by the LORD's name, and they will be in awe of you. [11]The LORD will make good things abound for you—whether the fertility of your womb, your livestock's offspring, or your fertile soil's produce—on the very land that the LORD swore to your ancestors to give to you. [12]The LORD will open up for you his own well-stocked storehouse, the heavens, providing your land with rain at just the right time and blessing all your work. You will lend to many nations, but you won't have any need to borrow. [13]The LORD will make you the head of things, not the tail; you will be at the top of things, not the bottom, as long as you obey the LORD your God's commandments that I'm commanding you right now, by carefully doing them. [14]Don't deviate even a bit from any of these words that I'm commanding you right now by following other gods and serving them.

Future curses

[15]But if you don't obey the LORD your God's voice by carefully doing all his commandments and his regulations that I am commanding you right now, all these curses will come upon you and find you. [16]You will be cursed in the city and cursed in the field. [17]Your basket and kneading bowl will be cursed. [18]Your own fertility, your soil's produce, your cattle's young, and your flock's offspring will be cursed. [19]You will be cursed when you are out and about and cursed when you come back. [20]The LORD will send calamity, confusion, and frustration on you no matter what work you are doing until you are wiped out and until you disappear—it'll be quick!—because of the evil acts by which you have abandoned him.[1] [21]The LORD will make a plague stick to you until he has totally wiped you off the fertile land you are entering to possess. [22]The LORD will strike you with consumption, fever, and inflammation; with scorching heat and drought;[m] with destruction and disease for your crops.[n] These things will chase you until you are dead and gone. [23]The sky over your head will be as hard as bronze; the earth under your feet will be like iron. [24]The LORD will turn the rain on your land into dust. Only dirt will fall down on you from the sky until you are completely wiped out. [25]The LORD will hand you over defeated to your enemies. You will go out against them by one direction, but you will run for your life away from them in seven different directions. All the earth's kingdoms will be horrified by you. [26]Your corpses will be food for every bird in the sky and animal on earth; no one will frighten them off. [27]The LORD will afflict you with Egyptian inflammation, hemorrhoids,[o] rash, and itch. You will be untreatable. [28]The LORD will make you go crazy, make you blind, make your mind confused. [29]You will fumble around at high noon as blind people fumble around in darkness. Your plans won't prosper. Instead, you will be constantly oppressed and taken advantage of without any savior. [30]You might get engaged to a woman, but another man will have sex with her. You might build a house, but you won't get to live in it. You might plant a vineyard, but you won't enjoy it. [31]Your ox will be slaughtered while you watch, but you won't get to eat any of it. Your donkey will be stolen right out from under you, and it won't come back. Your flocks will be given to your enemies. No one will save you. [32]Your sons and daughters will be given to another nation while you watch; you will long for them constantly, but you won't have the power to do anything about it. [33]The produce of your land and all your hard work will be consumed by people you don't know. You will be nothing but oppressed and mistreated constantly. [34]The sights your eyes see will drive you insane. [35]The LORD will strike you with horrible inflammation in your knees and legs, from the sole of your foot to the top of your head. You will be untreatable. [36]The LORD will send you and the king that you appoint over

---

[1]Or *me*, in which case the text shifts to direct divine discourse.   [m]Heb uncertain   [n]Or *blight and mildew*   [o]Qere; Kethib *tumors*

LIFE PRESERVER

What is with all the blessing and cursing? *Deuteronomy 28*

This chapter contains a lot of blessings that would be given to the Israelite people if they followed God's Instruction. There were blessings upon their cities and fields, their children, their animals, and even their cooking! God wanted the Israelites to know that everything would be blessed if they remembered God's voice and lived as God's people.

But God also wanted them to remember the consequences of their choices. If they didn't remember God's voice, there would be curses. If the people didn't obey, God would send disaster, confusion, and frustration upon them until they were completely wiped out.

As God's people moved into a new land, God wanted them to remember the importance of living as God's faithful people. Today you are probably much more familiar with blessings than curses, and that's a good thing. At the end of a church worship service, you will often hear the minister give a blessing to the people who have gathered. "May the Lord bless you and keep you" is a common one. A blessing is a reminder that God loves you and is watching out for you. ◊

you far away to a nation that neither you nor your ancestors have known. There you will worship other gods made of wood and stone. ³⁷You will become a horror, fit only for use in proverbs and in insults by all the nations where the Lᴏʀᴅ drives you. ³⁸You might scatter a lot of seed on the field, but you will gather almost nothing because the locusts will eat it all. ³⁹You might plant lots of vineyards and work hard in them, but you won't drink any wine or harvest the grapes because worms will devour them. ⁴⁰You might have many olive trees throughout your territories, but you won't cover yourself with their oil because your olive trees will fail. ⁴¹You might have sons and daughters, but they won't be yours for long because they will be taken away as prisoners. ⁴²Crickets will take over all your trees and your soil's produce. ⁴³The immigrants who live among you will be promoted over you, higher and higher! But you will be demoted, lower and lower! ⁴⁴They will lend to you, but you will have nothing to lend

to them. They will be the head of things; you will be the tail.

⁴⁵That's how all these curses will come over you, pursuing you, reaching you until you are completely wiped out, because you didn't obey the Lᴏʀᴅ your God's voice by keeping his commandments and his regulations that he gave you. ⁴⁶These things will be a sign and a wonder on you and your descendants forever. ⁴⁷Because you didn't serve the Lᴏʀᴅ your God joyfully and gladly above all else,ᵖ ⁴⁸you will serve your enemies—the ones the Lᴏʀᴅ will send against you—during famine, drought, nakedness, and total deprivation. God will put an iron yoke on your neck until he has wiped you out. ⁴⁹The Lᴏʀᴅ will bring a distant nation—one from the far ends of the earth—against you as fast as the eagle flies: a nation that speaks a language you can't understand, ⁵⁰a stern nation that doesn't go easy on the very old or show pity to the very young. ⁵¹That nation will devour your livestock's offspring and your soil's produce until you yourselves are destroyed because you will have no grain, wine, or oil left—nor any young from your cattle or offspring from your flocks—that is, until that nation annihilates you. ⁵²That nation will attack you in all your cities until your high, reinforced walls that you thought were so safe fall down across your entire countryside. That nation will attack you in all your cities throughout the land the Lᴏʀᴅ your God has given you. ⁵³You will eat the offspring of your own womb—the flesh of your own sons and daughters, whom the Lᴏʀᴅ your God gave you—because of the desperate and dire circumstances that your enemy has brought on you.

⁵⁴Even the most gentle and refined man among you will scowl at his brother or his own dear wife, or the last of his surviving children. ⁵⁵He won't want to give them any of his children's flesh that he will be eating because he has no other food due to the desperate and dire circumstances that your enemy has brought on you in all your cities. ⁵⁶Even the most gentle and refined woman among you, who is so refined and gentle she wouldn't stomp her foot on the ground, will scowl at her own dear husband, her son, or her

ᵖHeb uncertain

daughter—[57]not wanting to give them any of the afterbirth she pushed out or the babies she bore, because she will be eating them secretly while starving due to the desperate and dire circumstances that your enemy will bring on you in your cities.

[58]If you don't carefully keep all the words of this Instruction that are written in this scroll, by fearing the awesome and glorious name of the LORD your God—[59]the LORD will overwhelm you and your descendants with severe and chronic afflictions, and with terrible and untreatable sicknesses. [60]He'll put on you all the Egyptian diseases about which you were so afraid; they will stick to you! [61]What's more, the LORD will bring on you all the other diseases and plagues that aren't written in this Instruction scroll until you are completely wiped out. [62]Once as countless as the stars in the night sky, only a few of you will be left alive—all because you didn't obey the LORD your God's voice. [63]And just as before, the LORD enjoyed doing good things for you and increasing your numbers, now the LORD will enjoy annihilating and destroying you. You will be torn off the very fertile land you are entering to possess. [64]The LORD will scatter you among every nation, from one end of the earth to the other. There you will serve other gods that neither you nor your ancestors have known—gods of wood and stone. [65]Among those nations you will have no rest and no place to call your own.[q] There the LORD will give you an agitated mind, failing eyes, and a depressed spirit. [66]Your life will seem to dangle before your very eyes. You will be afraid night and day. You won't be able to count on surviving for long. [67]In the morning you will say: "I wish it was nighttime," but at nighttime you will say, "I wish it was morning"—on account of your tortured mind, which will be terrified, and because of the horrible sights that your eyes will see. [68]Finally, the LORD will take you back to Egypt in ships, by the route I promised you would never see again. There you will try to sell yourselves as slaves—both male and female—but no one will want to buy you.

The third heading:
The new covenant at Moab

29 [r]These are the words of the covenant the LORD commanded Moses to make with the Israelites in the land of Moab in addition to the covenant he had made with them at Horeb. [2s]Moses summoned all Israel, saying to them:

You've seen with your own eyes everything the LORD did in Egypt, to Pharaoh, his servants, and all his land—[3]the great trials your eyes witnessed, those awesome signs and wonders! [4]But until this very moment, the LORD hasn't given you insight to understand, eyes to see, or ears to hear. [5]I've led you in the wilderness forty years now; neither the clothes on your back nor the sandals on your feet have worn out. [6]Neither have you eaten bread nor drunk wine or beer during this time—so that you would know that I am the LORD your God.[t] [7]When you arrived here, Sihon, Heshbon's king, and Og, Bashan's king, marched out to fight against us, but we defeated them. [8]We took possession of their land and gave it as an inheritance to the Reubenites, Gadites, and half of Manasseh's tribe. [9]So then keep the words of this covenant and do them so you can succeed in all you do.

[10]Right now, all of you are in the presence of the LORD your God—the leaders of your tribes,[u] your elders, and your officials, all the Israelite males, [11]your children, your wives, and the immigrants who live with you in your camp, the ones who chop your wood and those who draw your water—[12]ready to enter into the LORD your God's covenant and into the agreement that the LORD your God is making with you right now. [13]That means the Lord will make you his own people right now—he will be your God just as he promised you and just as he swore to our ancestors: to Abraham, Isaac, and Jacob. [14]But I'm not making this covenant and this agreement with you alone [15]but also with those standing here with us right now before the LORD our God, and also with those who aren't here with us right now.

[16]You know firsthand how we used to live in Egypt and how we passed right through the nations that you passed through. [17]You saw

[q]Or *resting place for the sole of your foot* [r]28:69 in Heb [s]29:1 in Heb [t]Or *that I, the* LORD, *am your God.* [u]LXX, Syr; MT *your leaders, your tribes*

the horrific things, the filthy idols of wood and stone, silver and gold, that they had with them. ¹⁸Make sure there isn't any one among you right now—male or female, clan or tribe—whose mind is turning from being with the Lᴏʀᴅ our God in favor of going to serve these nations' gods. Make sure there isn't any root among you that is sprouting poison and bitterness. ¹⁹When that kind of person hears the words of this agreement, they congratulate themselves, thinking: I'll be fine even though I insist on being stubborn. This would cause something wet to dry up and become like something parched.ᵛ ²⁰The Lᴏʀᴅ won't be willing to forgive that kind of person; instead, the Lᴏʀᴅ's anger and passion will smolder against that person. Every curse written in this scroll will stretch out over them, and the Lᴏʀᴅ will wipe out their name from under the

heavens. ²¹Out of all Israel's tribes, the Lᴏʀᴅ will single them out for disaster in compliance with all the covenant curses that are written in this Instruction scroll.

²²Future generations, your children after you, or foreigners from distant lands will say: Lookʷ at all that land's plagues and the sicknesses that the Lᴏʀᴅ laid on it! ²³Look at all its land burned by sulfur and salt, unsuitable for planting, unable to grow or produce any vegetation, as devastated as Sodom and Gomorrah, Admah and Zeboiim, which the Lᴏʀᴅ devastated in anger and wrath! ²⁴Indeed, all nations will ask: Why did the Lᴏʀᴅ do this to this land? What led to this terrible display of anger? ²⁵They will deduce: It was because those people abandoned the covenant of the Lᴏʀᴅ, their ancestors' God, which he made with them when he brought them out of

ᵛHeb uncertain; perhaps the agricultural imagery of 29:18 is continued here or the terms are metaphors for human states.
ʷOr *after they see*

Who's at Fault? *Deuteronomy 29:10-29*

Often during times of trouble people ask God, "Why would a loving God allow such bad things to happen?" Although God loves us, sometimes bad things happen because of choices that were made or because of accidents.

God warned the Israelites that they would be cursed if they didn't obey. God said there would be diseases and disaster on the people and their land. This may sound harsh, but God also promised they would be blessed if they obeyed God's Instruction.

Sometimes bad things happen and no one knows why. But sometimes bad things happen so people can learn from their mistakes or disobedience. For example, if you forget to practice your spelling words at home, you might get a bad grade on your spelling test and have to do makeup work while everyone else plays at recess. Whose fault would this be? Your parents' for not reminding you to study the night before? Your teacher's for giving a test in the first place? No. When your parents or teachers allow you to experience the results of your actions, it doesn't mean that they don't love you or care about you. The best response is to learn from this mistake and do better the next time around.

Think about a time when your actions caused something bad to happen.

What lesson did you learn?

Egypt. ²⁶They followed other gods, serving them and worshipping them—other gods that they hadn't experienced before and that the Lord hadn't designated for them. ²⁷Then the Lᴏʀᴅ's anger burned against that land, and he brought against it every curse written in this scroll. ²⁸The Lᴏʀᴅ ripped them off their land in anger, wrath, and great fury. He threw them into other lands, and that's how things still stand today.

²⁹The secret things belong to the Lᴏʀᴅ our God. The revealed things belong to us and to our children forever: to keep all the words of this covenant.

30 Now, once all these things happen to you, the blessing and the curse that I'm setting before you, you must call them to mind as you sit among the various nations where the Lᴏʀᴅ your God has driven you; ²and you must return to the Lᴏʀᴅ your God, obeying his voice, in line with all that I'm commanding you right now—you and your children—with all your mind and with all your being. ³Then the Lᴏʀᴅ your God will restore you as you were before and will have compassion on you, gathering you up from all the peoples where the Lᴏʀᴅ your God scattered you. ⁴Even if he has driven you to the far end of heaven, the Lᴏʀᴅ your God will gather you up from there; he will take you back from there. ⁵The Lᴏʀᴅ your God will bring you home to the land that your ancestors possessed; you will possess it again. And he will do good things for you and multiply you—making you more numerous even than your ancestors!

⁶Then the Lᴏʀᴅ your God will circumcise your hearts and the hearts of your descendants so that you love the Lᴏʀᴅ your God with all your mind and with all your being in order that you may live. ⁷The Lᴏʀᴅ your God will put all these curses on your enemies and on those who hate you and chase you. ⁸But you will change and obey the Lᴏʀᴅ's voice and do all his commandments that I'm commanding you right now. ⁹The Lᴏʀᴅ your God will help you succeed in everything you do—in your own fertility, your livestock's offspring, and your land's produce—everything will be great! Because the Lᴏʀᴅ will once again enjoy doing good things for you just as he enjoyed doing

them for your ancestors, ¹⁰and because you will be obeying the Lᴏʀᴅ your God's voice, keeping his commandments and his regulations that are written in this Instruction scroll, and because you will have returned to the Lᴏʀᴅ your God with all your heart and all your being.

¹¹This commandment that I'm giving you right now is definitely not too difficult for you. It isn't unreachable. ¹²It isn't up in heaven somewhere so that you have to ask, "Who will go up for us to heaven and get it for us that we can hear it and do it?" ¹³Nor is it across the ocean somewhere so that you have to ask, "Who will cross the ocean for us and get it for us that we can hear it and do it?" ¹⁴Not at all! The word is very close to you. It's in your mouth and in your heart, waiting for you to do it.

Memorize
Deut 30:14

Life and death

¹⁵Look here! Today I've set before you life and what's good versus death and what's wrong. ¹⁶If you obey the Lᴏʀᴅ your God's commandments thatˣ I'm commanding you right now by loving the Lᴏʀᴅ your God, by walking in his ways, and by keeping his commandments, his regulations, and his case laws, then you will live and thrive, and the Lᴏʀᴅ your God will bless you in the land you are entering to possess. ¹⁷But if your heart turns away and you refuse to listen, and so are misled, worshipping other gods and serving them, ¹⁸I'm telling you right now that you will definitely die. You will not prolong your life on the fertile land that you are crossing the Jordan River to enter and possess. ¹⁹I call heaven and earth as my witnesses against you right now: I have set life and death, blessing and curse before you. Now choose life—so that you and your descendants will live— ²⁰by loving the Lᴏʀᴅ your God, by obeying his voice, and by clinging to him. That's how you will survive and live long on the fertile land the Lᴏʀᴅ swore to give to your ancestors: to Abraham, Isaac, and Jacob.

Moses announces his death

31 Then Moses saidʸ these words to all Israel, ²telling them:

ˣLXX; MT lacks *if you obey the Lᴏʀᴅ your God's commandments.* ʸLXX, DSS (1QDeutᵇ) *When Moses had finished speaking*

I'm 120 years old today. I can't move around well anymore. Plus, the LORD told me "You won't cross the Jordan River." ³But the LORD your God, he's the one who will cross over before you! He's the one who will destroy these nations before you so you can displace them. Joshua too will cross over before you just like the LORD indicated. ⁴The LORD will do to these enemies the same thing he did to the Amorite kings Sihon and Og, and to their land, when he destroyed them. ⁵The LORD will lay them out before you, and you will do to them exactly what the command I've given you dictates. ⁶Be strong! Be fearless! Don't be afraid and don't be scared by your enemies, because the LORD your God is the one who marches with you. He won't let you down, and he won't abandon you.

⁷Then Moses called Joshua and, with all Israel watching, said to him: "Be strong and fearless because you are the one who will lead[z] this people to the land the LORD swore to their ancestors to give to them; you are the one who will divide up the land for them. ⁸But the LORD is the one who is marching before you! He is the one who will be with you! He won't let you down. He won't abandon you. So don't be afraid or scared!"

LIGHTHOUSE
HEART

Be Strong! Be Fearless!
Deuteronomy 31:5-8
Moses was 120 years old. He knew he would die before the Israelites crossed the Jordan River into the promised land. After working so hard for so long, he wouldn't be the one to help the people finish their journey. However disappointed he may have felt, his last words to the Israelites were focused on them. He told them to be strong and fearless, remembering that God would be with them at all times. Then he called to Joshua and told him in front of the whole community that he would be their new leader. Until the very end of his life, Moses was obedient to God and loyal to the Israelites. ◆

Regular reading of the Instruction

⁹Then Moses wrote this Instruction down and gave it to the priests—the Levites who carry the chest containing the LORD's covenant—and to all of the Israelite elders. ¹⁰Moses then commanded them:

At the end of seven years, at the appointed time in the year of debt cancellation, during the Festival of Booths, ¹¹when all Israel comes to appear before the LORD your God at the location he selects, you must read this Instruction aloud, in the hearing of all the people. ¹²Gather everyone—men, women, children, and the immigrants who live in your cities—in order that they hear it, learn it, and revere the LORD your God, carefully doing all the words of this Instruction, ¹³and so that their children, who don't yet know the Instruction, may hear it and learn to revere the LORD your God for as long as you live on the ground you are crossing the Jordan River to possess.

Joshua commissioned

¹⁴Then the LORD said to Moses: "It's almost time for you to die. Summon Joshua. The two of you must present yourselves at the meeting tent so I can command him." So Moses and Joshua went and presented themselves at the meeting tent. ¹⁵The LORD appeared in the tent in a pillar of cloud; the cloud pillar stood at the tent's entrance. ¹⁶The LORD then said to Moses:

"Soon you will rest with your ancestors, and the people will rise up and act unfaithfully, going after strange gods of the land they are entering. They will abandon me, breaking my covenant that I made with them. ¹⁷At that point my anger will burn against them, and I'll be the one who abandons them! I'll hide my face from them. They will become nothing but food for their enemies,[a] and all sorts of bad things and misfortunes will happen to them. Then they will say: 'Haven't these terrible things happened to us because our God is no longer with us?' ¹⁸But I will hide my face at that time because of the many wrong things they have done, because they have turned to other gods! ¹⁹So in light of all that, you must write down this poem and teach it to the Israelites. Put it in their mouths so that the poem becomes a witness for me against them. ²⁰When I bring the Israelites to the land I swore to their ancestors, which is full of milk and honey, and they eat, get full, then fat, and

---

[z] Sam, Vulg, Syr; MT, Tg *accompany*   [a] Heb lacks *for their enemies.*

then turn toward other gods, serving them and disrespecting me and breaking my covenant, [21]then, when all kinds of bad things and misfortunes happen to them, this poem will witness against them, giving its testimony, because it won't be lost from the mouths of their descendants. Yes, I know right now what they are inclined to do, even before I've brought them into the land I swore."

[22]So Moses wrote this poem down that very day, and he taught it to the Israelites.

[23]Then the Lord commissioned Joshua, Nun's son: "Be strong and fearless because you are the one who will bring the Israelites to the land I swore to them. I myself will be with you."

Life after Moses

[24]Once Moses had finished writing in their entirety all the words of this Instruction scroll, [25]he commanded the Levites who carry the chest containing the Lord's covenant as follows:

[26]"Take this Instruction scroll and put it next to the chest containing the Lord your God's covenant. It must remain there as a witness against you [27]because I know how rebellious and hardheaded you are. If you are this rebellious toward the Lord while I'm still alive, it's bound to get worse once I'm dead! [28]Assemble all of your tribes' elders and your officials in front of me, so I can speak these words in their hearing, and so I can call heaven and earth as my witnesses against them, [29]because I know that after I'm dead, you will ruin everything, departing from the path I've commanded you. Terrible things will happen to you in the future because you will do evil in the Lord's eyes, aggravating him with the things your hands have made."

The poem of Instruction

[30]Then Moses recited in their entirety the words of this poem in the hearing of the entire assembly of Israel:

32 Heaven! Pay attention
and I will speak;
    Earth! Listen to the words
of my mouth.

[2]My teaching will fall like raindrops;
    my speech will settle like dew—
        like gentle rains on grass,
        like spring showers
        on all that is green—
[3]because I proclaim the Lord's name:
    Give praise to our God!

[4]The rock: his acts are perfection!
    No doubt about it: all his ways are right!
    He's the faithful God, never deceiving;
        altogether righteous and true is he.
[5]But children who weren't his own[b]
    sinned against him with their defects;[c]
        they are a twisted
        and perverse generation.
[6]Is this how you thank the Lord,
    you stupid, senseless people?
    Isn't he your father, your creator?
    Didn't he make you and establish you?

[7]Remember the days long past;
    consider the years long gone.
    Ask your father, he will tell you about it;
    ask your elders,
        they will give you the details:
[8]When God Most High
    divided up the nations—
        when he divided up humankind—
        he decided the people's boundaries
        based on the number of the gods.[d]
[9]Surely the Lord's property was his people;
    Jacob was his part of the inheritance.

[10]God found[e] Israel in a wild land—
    in a howling desert wasteland—
        he protected him, cared for him,
        watched over him with his very own eye.
[11]Like an eagle protecting its nest,
    hovering over its young,
    God spread out his wings,
        took hold of Israel,
        carried him on his back.
[12]The Lord alone led Israel;
    no foreign god assisted.
[13]God[f] made Israel[g] glide over the highlands;
    he fed him[h] with food from the field,
        nursed him with honey from a boulder,
        with oil from a hard rock:

[b]Heb uncertain [c]LXX, Vulg; Heb uncertain [d]DSS (4QDeut[j]), LXX; MT the Israelites [e]Vulg, Syr, and others; Sam, LXX, Tg Onkelos sustained him [f]Or he [g]Or him [h]Sam, Syr, LXX, Tg; MT he ate

¹⁴ curds from the herd,
 milk from the flock,
 along with the best of lambs,
 rams from Bashan, he-goats too,
 along with the finest wheat—
 and for drink,
 wine from the juiciest grapes!

¹⁵ Jacob ate until he was stuffed;ⁱ
 Jeshurun^j got fat, then rebellious.^k

It was you who got fat, thick, stubborn!^l

Jeshurun^m gave up
 on the God who made him,
 thought the rock of his salvation
 was worthless.
¹⁶ They made Godⁿ jealous
 with strange gods,
 aggravated him with detestable things.
¹⁷ They sacrificed to demons, not to God,
 to deities of which
 they had no knowledge—
 new gods only recently on the scene,
 ones about which your ancestors
 had never heard.^o
¹⁸ You deserted^p the rock that sired you;
 you forgot the God who gave birth to you!

¹⁹ The LORD saw this and rejected
 out of aggravation
 his sons and his daughters.^q
²⁰ He said: I will hide my face from them—
 I will see what becomes of them—
 because they are a confused generation;
 they are children lacking loyalty.
²¹ They provoked me with "no-gods,"
 aggravated me with their pieces of junk.
 So I am going to provoke them
 with "No-People,"
 aggravate them with a nation of fools.
²² A fire burns in me—
 it will blaze to the depths of the grave;^r
 it will destroy the land and its crops;
 it will blacken the base of the mountains.
²³ I'll throw^s on them disaster after disaster;
 I'll destroy them with my arrows:

²⁴ devastating hunger, consuming plague,
 bitter sickness.
 I'll send animal fangs after them,
 venom from dust crawlers too.
²⁵ Outside, in the streets,
 the sword will bereave!
 Inside, in the safest room,
 there will be terror
 for young men and women,
 nursing baby and senior citizen.
²⁶ I thought about it:
 I could have struck them down,^t
 erased them from human memory,
²⁷ but their enemies' rage concerned me;
 their opponents might misunderstand.
 They might say, "Our strong hands,
 not the LORD's, did all this,"
²⁸ because they are not
 a thoughtful nation;
 they lack any insight.
²⁹ If they had any wisdom,
 they would understand this;
 they would discern
 what will become of them.
³⁰ How could one person
 chase off a thousand in battle?
 How could two people make ten thousand
 flee for their lives?
 Only because their rock sold them off,
 only because the LORD handed them over!
³¹ But, no, their rocks
 can't compare to our rock!
 Our enemies are completely stupid.^u
³² Their roots run straight from Sodom—
 from the fields of Gomorrah!
 Their grapes are pure poison;
 their grape clusters, nothing but bitter;
³³ their wine is snake poison,
 venom from a cruel cobra.
³⁴ Don't I have this stored up,
 sealed in my vaults?
³⁵ Revenge is my domain,
 so is punishment-in-kind,
 at the exact moment their step slips up,
 because the day of their destruction
 is just around the corner;
 their final destiny is speeding on its way!

ⁱDSS (4QPhylⁿ), Sam, LXX; MT lacks *Jacob ate until he was stuffed.* ^jA poetic name for Israel; see also 33:5, 26. ^kOr *kicked*
^lHeb uncertain ^mOr *he* ⁿOr *him* ^oHeb uncertain ^pLXX, Vulg; Heb uncertain ^qOr, following LXX, DSS (4QPhylⁿ), and correcting
the LORD saw this and was jealous; he spurned his sons and daughters. ^rHeb *Sheol* ^sLXX ^tHeb uncertain; LXX *scattered them*
^uLXX; Heb uncertain

36 But the LORD will acquit his people,
will have compassion
on those who serve him,
once he sees that their strength
is all gone,
that both prisoners and free people
are wiped out.[v]
37 The Lord will ask, "Where are their gods—
the rocks they trusted in—
38 who ate up the fat of their sacrifices,
who drank their sacred wine?
They should stand up and help you!
They should protect you now!
39 Now, look here: I myself, I'm the one;
there are no other gods with me.
I'm the one who deals death
and gives life;
I'm the one who wounded,
but now I will heal.
There's no escaping my hand.
40 But now I'm lifting my hand to heaven—
I swear by my own eternity:
41 when I sharpen my blazing sword
and my hand grabs hold of justice,
I'll pay my enemies back;
I'll punish in kind
everyone who hates me.
42 I'll make my arrows drink much blood,
while my sword devours flesh,
the blood of the dead and captured,
flowing from the heads
of enemy generals."[w]

43 Heavens:[x] Rejoice with God![y]
All you gods: bow down to the Lord![z]
Because he will avenge
his children's[a] blood;
he will pay back his enemies;
he will punish in kind
those who hate him;[b]
he will cleanse his people's land.[c]

44 So Moses came and recited all the words
of this poem in everyone's hearing; Joshua,[d]
Nun's son, joined him. 45 When Moses finished
speaking all these words to all Israel, 46 he
told them: Set your mind on all these words
I'm testifying against you right now, because
you must command your children to perform
carefully all the words of this Instruction.
47 This is no trivial matter for you—this is your
very life! It is by this means[e] alone that you
will prolong your life on the fertile land you
are crossing the Jordan River to possess.

Moses' death imminent

48 The LORD spoke to Moses that very same
day: 49 "Hike up the Abarim mountains, to
Mount Nebo, which is in the land of Moab opposite Jericho. Take a good look at the land of
Canaan, which I'm giving to the Israelites as
their property. 50 You will die on the mountain
you have hiked up, and you will be gathered
to your people just like your brother Aaron,
who died on Mount Hor and was gathered to
his people, 51 because the two of you were unfaithful toward me in front of the Israelites
at the waters of Meribath-kadesh, in the Zin
wilderness, because you didn't treat me with
proper respect before the Israelites. 52 You
can look at the land from the other side of the
river,[f] but you won't enter there."[g]

The fourth heading: Moses' blessing

33 This is the blessing that Moses the
man of God gave the Israelites before
he died. 2 He said:

The LORD came from Sinai:
from Seir he shone like the dawn on us,[h]
from Paran Mountain he beamed down.
Thousands of holy ones were with him;[i]
his warriors were next to him, ready.[j]
3 Yes, those who love[k] the nations—
all his holy ones—were at your command;
they followed your footsteps;
they got moving when you said so.

did you know? As the people prepared to go to the land God promised them, Moses sang a song about all that God had done for them. Songs like this made it easy for parents to teach their children the great stories about God.

[v] Heb uncertain [w] Heb uncertain [x] DSS (4QDeut[q]), LXX; MT *nations* [y] DSS (4QDeut[q]), LXX; MT *his people* [z] This line is missing in Heb; it is found in DSS (4QDeut[q]); LXX *him for the Lord* [a] DSS (4QDeut[q]), LXX; MT *his servants'* [b] DSS (4QDeut[q]), LXX; MT lacks this line. [c] Sam, DSS (4QDeut[q]), LXX, Vulg; MT *his land his people* or *his land for his people*; or, correcting, *he will wipe away his people's tears.* [d] Sam, Syr, Tg Neofiti; MT *Hoshea* [e] Or *word* [f] Heb lacks *of the river.* [g] LXX; MT, Sam, Vulg, Syr, Tg add *to the land that I am giving to the Israelites* [h] Correcting with LXX, Vulg, Syr, Tg Onkelos (see 33:4); MT and Sam *on them* [i] Correction; cf LXX, Sam, Syr, Vulg; MT *he came from Ribeboth-kodesh* [j] LXX *angels;* Heb uncertain [k] Correction; MT *lover of*

⁴ Moses gave the Instruction to us—
  it's the prized possession
    of Jacob's assembly.
⁵ A king came to rule in Jeshurun,
  when the people's leaders
    gathered together,
  when Israel's tribes were one.

⁶ "I pray that Reuben lives, doesn't die,
  though his numbers are so few."

⁷ Moses said this to Judah:
  "Lord, listen to Judah's voice!
  Bring him back to his own people,
    strengthen his hands;^l
  be his help against every enemy."

⁸ Then he told Levi:
  "Give your Thummim to Levi,^m
  your Urim to your faithful one—
    the one you tested at Massah,
    the one you challenged
      by Meribah's waters;
  ⁹ the one who said
    of his own mother and father:
    'I don't consider them as such';
    of their siblings: 'I don't recognize them';
    of their own children,
      'I don't know them'—
  but who obeyed your words
    and who guarded your covenant!
¹⁰ They teach your case laws to Jacob,
    your Instruction to Israel.
  They hold sweet incense to your nose;
    put the entirely burned offering
      on your altar.
¹¹ I pray that the Lord
    blesses Levi's strength,
    favors his hard work,
  and crushes the insides of his enemies
    so that those who hate him
      can't fight anymore."

¹² He said to Benjamin:
  "The Lord's dearest one
    rests safely on him.
  The Lord always shields him;
    he rests on God's chest."

¹³ Then he told Joseph:
  "I pray that his land is blessed by God:
    with heaven's gifts from above,ⁿ
    with the deep waters
      stretching out underneath;
  ¹⁴ with the gifts produced by the sun,
    with the gifts generated by the moon;^o
  ¹⁵ with the best fruit
      from ancient mountains,
    with the gifts of eternal hills;
  ¹⁶ with the gifts of the earth
      and all that fills it,
    and the favor of the one
      who lives on Sinai.^p
  I pray that all these rest on Joseph's head,
    on the crown of that prince
      among brothers.
¹⁷ A firstborn bull^q—that's how majestic he is!
  A wild ox's horns—those are his horns!
    With them he gores all peoples
      completely, to the far ends of the earth!
  His horns^r are Ephraim's
      tens of thousands.
    His horns are Manasseh's thousands."

¹⁸ Then he told Zebulun:
  "Zebulun: celebrate
    when you are out and about;
  Issachar: celebrate when you are
    at home in your tents!
¹⁹ They call all sorts of people
    to the mountain,
  where they offer right sacrifices.
  It's true: They're nourished
    on the sea's abundance;
  they are nourished
    on buried treasures in the sand."

²⁰ Then he told Gad:
  "May Gad's broad lands^s be blessed!
  He lives like a lion:
    he rips an arm, even a head!
²¹ He chose the best part for himself
    because there, where the commander's
      portion was,
    the leaders of the people
      gathered together.^t

---

^lOr with his hands he contended   ^mDSS (4QDeut^h, 4QTest) and LXX; MT lacks *Give to Levi.*   ⁿOr from the dew   ^oOr moons or months   ^pOr lives in a bush   ^qSam, LXX, Vulg; DSS (4QDeut^h) and Heb the oldest offspring of his bull   ^rOr they; also in the next line   ^sOr the one who makes Gad large   ^tCf LXX; MT there the commander's portion was reserved; he came at the front of the people or there was the portion of the respected commander; the people's leaders came.

Gad executed the Lᴏʀᴅ's justice
  and the Lord's judgments for Israel."ᵘ

²² Then he told Dan:
  "Dan is a lion cub.
  He jumps up from Bashan."

²³ Then he told Naphtali:
  "Naphtali—you are full of favor,
    overflowing with the Lᴏʀᴅ's blessing—
    go possess the west and the south!"

²⁴ Finally, he told Asher:
  "Asher is the most blessed of sons.
    I pray that he's his brothers' favorite—
    one who dips his foot in fine oil.
²⁵ I pray that your dead bolts
    are iron and copper,
    and that your strength
      lasts all your days.'"ᵛ

²⁶ Jeshurun! No one compares to God!
    He rides through heaven to help you,
      rides majestically through the clouds.
²⁷ The most ancient God is a place of safety;ʷ
    the eternal arms are a support.ˣ
  He drove out the enemy before you.
  He commanded: "Destroy them!"
²⁸ So Israel now lives in safety—
    Jacob's residenceʸ is secure—
    in a land full of grain and wine,
      where the heavens drip dew.

²⁹ Happy are you, Israel! Who is like you?
    You are a people saved by the Lᴏʀᴅ!
  He's the shield that helps you,
    your majestic sword!

Your enemies will come crawling
  on their knees to you,
  but you will stomp on their backs!ᶻ

Moses' death

34 Then Moses hiked up from the Moabite plains to Mount Nebo, the peak of the Pisgah slope, which faces Jericho. The Lᴏʀᴅ showed him the whole land: the Gilead region as far as Dan's territory; ²all the parts belonging to Naphtali along with the land of Ephraim and Manasseh, as well as the entirety of Judah as far as the Mediterranean Sea; ³also the arid southern plain, and the plain—including the Jericho Valley, Palm City—as far as Zoar.

⁴Then the Lᴏʀᴅ said to Moses: "This is the land that I swore to Abraham, Isaac, and Jacob when I promised: 'I will give it to your descendants.' I have shown it to you with your own eyes; however, you will not cross over into it."

⁵Then Moses, the Lᴏʀᴅ's servant, died—right there in the land of Moab, according to the Lᴏʀᴅ's command. ⁶The Lord buried him in a valley in Moabite country across from Beth-peor. Even now, no one knows where Moses' grave is.

⁷Moses was 120 years old when he died. His eyesight wasn't impaired, and his vigor hadn't diminished a bit.

⁸Back down in the Moabite plains, the Israelites mourned Moses' death for thirty days. At that point, the time for weeping and for mourning Moses was over.

⁹Joshua, Nun's son, was filled with wisdom because Moses had placed his hands on him. So the Israelites listened to Joshua, and they did exactly what the Lᴏʀᴅ commanded Moses.

¹⁰No prophet like Moses has yet emerged in Israel; Moses knew the Lᴏʀᴅ face-to-face! ¹¹That's not even to mention all those signs and wonders that the Lᴏʀᴅ sent Moses to do in Egypt—to Pharaoh, to all his servants, and to his entire land— ¹²as well as all the extraordinary power that Moses displayed before Israel's own eyes!

did you know? By the time people wrote down all the stories about Moses found in Exodus through Deuteronomy, many generations had passed. The writers wanted people to know that in all that time, no one had been a leader like Moses, who was able to talk to God face-to-face.

ᵘHeb uncertain ᵛHeb uncertain ʷOr *He humiliates the oldest gods.* ˣOr *He shatters the most ancient forces.* ʸOr *fountain*
ᶻOr *their shrines*

Joshua

Soon after God rescued the Israelites from slavery in Egypt, they came to the edge of the land God had promised to give them. When God told the people to enter the land, they were too scared to obey. God decided that the people who didn't obey would never live in this good place. God sent the people wandering in the wilderness for forty more years.

Many children were born and grew up as the Israelites wandered in the wilderness. After forty years had passed, God told the Israelites once again it was time to enter the land. God told them to be brave, promising to be with them wherever God commanded them to go.

The book of Joshua tells stories of battles for the promised land. It contains the story of the Israelite army marching around the city of Jericho for seven days before the city walls miraculously tumbled down (Josh 6). It also contains long lists telling Israelite tribes where they should live in the land (Josh 13–21).

After many years of wandering in the wilderness, God's people were finally permitted to cross the Jordan River and enter the promised land. Their story reminds us to always listen to God and be brave! ◊

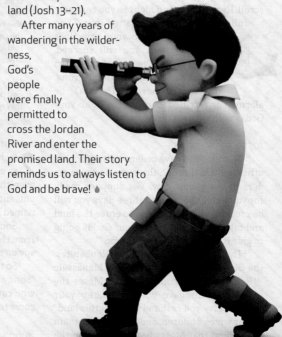

Orders from the LORD

1 After Moses the LORD's servant died, the LORD spoke to Joshua, Nun's son. He had been Moses' helper. ²"My servant Moses is dead. Now get ready to cross over the Jordan with this entire people to the land that I am going to give to the Israelites. ³I am giving you every place where you set foot, exactly as I promised Moses. ⁴Your territory will stretch from the desert and the Lebanon as far as the great Euphrates River, including all Hittite land, up to the Mediterranean Sea on the west. ⁵No one will be able to stand up against you during your lifetime. I will be with you in the same way I was with Moses. I won't desert you or leave you. ⁶Be brave and strong, because you are the one who will help this people take possession of the land, which I pledged to give to their ancestors.

⁷"Be very brave and strong as you carefully obey all of the Instruction that Moses my servant commanded you. Don't deviate even a bit from it, either to the right or left. Then you will have success wherever you go. ⁸Never stop speaking about this Instruction scroll. Recite it day and night so you can carefully obey everything written in it. Then you will accomplish your objectives and you will succeed. ⁹I've commanded you to be brave and strong, haven't I? Don't be alarmed or terrified, because the LORD your God is with you wherever you go."

Memorize
Josh 1:9

Joshua gives orders

¹⁰Then Joshua gave orders to the people's officers: ¹¹"Go through the camp and give orders to the people. Say, 'Get supplies ready for yourselves because in three days you will be crossing over the Jordan to enter the land and take it over. The LORD your God is going to give it to you as your possession.'"

¹²Then Joshua addressed the Reubenites, the Gadites, and half the tribe of Manasseh: ¹³"Remember the command that Moses the LORD's servant gave you: 'The LORD your God will give you rest and give you this land.' ¹⁴Your wives, children, and cattle may remain in the land that Moses has given you on the east side of the Jordan. But all you brave fighters, organized for war, must cross over in front of your fellow Israelites. You must help them ¹⁵until the LORD gives a rest like yours to your fellow Israelites and they too take possession of the land that the LORD your God is giving them. Then you may return and take over the land that belongs to you, which Moses the LORD's servant has given you on the east side of the Jordan."

¹⁶They answered Joshua, "We will obey everything you have commanded us and go anywhere you send us. ¹⁷We will obey you in the same way that we obeyed Moses. Just let the LORD your God be with you as he was with Moses! ¹⁸Anybody who stubbornly opposes what you declare and doesn't obey any of your commands will be put to death. Be brave and strong!"

SAILBOAT

COURAGE

Be Strong and Courageous *Joshua 1:1–9*
As the Israelite people prepared to enter the promised land, God spoke to Joshua, giving clear instructions. God said that the people would be given the land everywhere they went and no one would be able to defeat them. God promised never to leave the people but to be with them at all times. God told Joshua to follow all of God's Instruction. Three times, God told Joshua to be brave and strong. God knew there would be nothing easy about following God's Instruction and living a life God's way. But God promised to be with Joshua and the people if they were obedient.

Joshua sends spies

2 Joshua, Nun's son, secretly sent two men as spies from Shittim. He said, "Go. Look over the land, especially Jericho." They set out and entered the house of a prostitute named Rahab. They bedded down there.

²Someone told the king of Jericho, "Men from the Israelites have come here tonight to spy on the land."

³So the king of Jericho sent word to Rahab: "Send out the men who came to you, the ones who came to your house, because they have come to spy on the entire land."

Rahab takes action

⁴But the woman had taken the two men and hidden them. Then she said, "Of course

the men came to me. But I didn't know where they were from. [5]The men left when it was time to close the gate at dark, but I don't know where the men went. Hurry! Chase after them! You might catch up with them." [6]But she had taken them up to the roof and hidden them under the flax stalks that she had laid out on the roof. [7]The men from Jericho[a] chased after them in the direction of the Jordan up to the fords. As soon as those chasing them went out, the gate was shut behind them.

Rahab sets terms

[8]Before the spies bedded down, Rahab went up to them on the roof. [9]She said to the men, "I know that the LORD has given you the land. Terror over you has overwhelmed us. The entire population of the land has melted down in fear because of you. [10]We have heard how the LORD dried up the water of the Reed Sea[b] in front of you when you left Egypt. We have also heard what you did to Sihon and Og, the two kings of the Amorites on the other side of the Jordan. You utterly wiped them out. [11]We heard this and our hearts turned to water. Because of you, people can no longer work up their courage. This is because the LORD your God is God in heaven above and on earth below. [12]Now, I have been loyal to you. So pledge to me by the LORD that you in turn will deal loyally

SAILBOAT

KINDNESS

Rahab Rocks *Joshua 2:6-16*
Joshua sent two spies into Jericho to get information about conquering the land. These spies went to the house of a woman named Rahab. Jericho's king suspected something was happening, and he sent soldiers to Rahab's house to see if the spies were there. Rahab was calm under pressure and said that the scouts had already left. The king's soldiers went out to chase down the spies. Meanwhile, Rahab had hidden the men. When the soldiers were a safe distance away, Rahab lowered the men down by a rope through the window. Rahab's house was inside the wall itself. The spies made it back to Joshua to report on their successful mission due to the kindness and great courage of Rahab. ◆

with my family. Give me a sign of good faith. [13]Spare the lives of my father, mother, brothers, and sisters, along with everything they own. Rescue us from death."

[14]The men said to her, "We swear by our own lives to secure yours. If you don't reveal our mission, we will deal loyally and faithfully with you when the LORD gives us the land."

The spies escape

[15]So she lowered the spies on a rope through the window. Her house was on the outer side of the city wall, and she lived inside the wall. [16]Then she said to them, "Go toward the highlands so that those chasing you don't run into you. Hide there for three days until those chasing you return. Then you may go on your way."

[17]The men said to her, "We won't be responsible for this pledge you made us swear [18]unless, when we come into the land, you tie this red woven cord in the window through which you lowered us. Gather your father, your mother, your brothers, and your whole family into the house with you. [19]Those who go outside the doors of your house into the street will have only themselves to blame for their own deaths. We won't be responsible. If anyone lays a hand on those who are with you in the house, we will take the blame for their death. [20]But if you reveal our mission, we won't be responsible for this pledge you made us swear."

[21]She said, "These things will happen just like you said." She sent them away and they went off. Then she tied the red cord in the window.

Mission accomplished

[22]The spies went out and entered the highlands. They stayed there for three days until those chasing them came back. Those chasing them had searched all along the road but never found them. [23]Then the two men came back down from the highlands. They crossed the Jordan and came to Joshua, Nun's son. They told him everything that had happened to them. [24]They said to Joshua, "The LORD has definitely given the entire land into our power. In addition, all of the land's population has melted down in fear because of us."

---

[a]Heb lacks *from Jericho.* [b]Or *Red Sea*

Directions for crossing the Jordan

3 Joshua took down the camp early in the morning. He and all the Israelites marched out of Shittim and came to the Jordan, where they stayed overnight before crossing. ²At the end of three days the officers went through the middle of the camp. ³They commanded the people, "As soon as you see the Lord your God's chest containing the covenant and the levitical priests carrying it, you are to march out from your places and follow it. ⁴But let there be some distance between you and it, about three thousand feet. Don't come near it! You will know the way you should go, even though you've never traveled this way before."

⁵Joshua said to the people, "Make yourselves holy! Tomorrow the Lord will do wonderful things among you." ⁶Then Joshua said to the priests, "Lift up the covenant chest. Go along in front of the people." So they lifted up the covenant chest and went in front of the people.

⁷The Lord said to Joshua, "Today I will begin to make you great in the opinion of all Israel. Then they will know that I will be with you in the same way that I was with Moses. ⁸You are to command the priests who carry the covenant chest, 'As soon as you come to the bank of the Jordan, stand still in the Jordan.'"

⁹Joshua said to the Israelites, "Come close. Listen to the words of the Lord your God." ¹⁰Then Joshua said, "This is how you will know that the living God is among you and will completely remove the Canaanites, Hittites, Hivites, Perizzites, Girgashites, Amorites, and Jebusites before you. ¹¹Look! The covenant chest of the ruler of the entire earth is going to cross over in front of you in the Jordan. ¹²Now pick twelve men from the tribes of Israel, one per tribe. ¹³The soles of the priests' feet, who are carrying the chest of the Lord, ruler of the whole earth, will come to rest in the water of the Jordan. At that moment, the water of the Jordan will be cut off. The water flowing downstream will stand still in a single heap."

Marching across the Jordan

¹⁴The people marched out from their tents to cross over the Jordan. The priests carrying the covenant chest were in front of the people. ¹⁵When the priests who were carrying the

chest came to the Jordan, their feet touched the edge of the water. The Jordan had overflowed its banks completely, the way it does during the entire harvest season. ¹⁶But at that moment the water of the Jordan coming

did you know? The chest containing the covenant was used to carry the stone tablets God gave to Moses. On top of the chest was a place for God. Whenever the people moved, this sacred chest went in front of them to remind them God was going before them wherever they went.

downstream stood still. It rose up as a single heap very far off, just below Adam, which is the city next to Zarethan. The water going down to the desert sea (that is, the Dead Sea) was cut off completely. The people crossed opposite Jericho. ¹⁷So the priests carrying the Lord's covenant chest stood firmly on dry land in the middle of the Jordan. Meanwhile, all Israel crossed over on dry land, until the entire nation finished crossing over the Jordan.

LIGHTHOUSE
AWESOME GOD

God Parts Water Again! *Joshua 3:14-17*
The Israelites set out from their tents to cross over the Jordan River. In the distance, they could see the river overflowing its banks. The priests carried the chest containing the covenant and led the people forward even though crossing the river probably seemed like an impossible task. But they had faith that God would see them through. When the priests' feet touched the water, the river stopped flowing from upstream and everyone crossed over on dry ground.

Twelve stones at Gilgal

4 When the entire nation had finished crossing over the Jordan, the Lord said to Joshua, ²"Pick twelve men from the people, one man per tribe. ³Command them, 'Pick up twelve stones from right here in the middle of the Jordan, where the feet of the priests had been firmly planted. Bring them across with you and put them down in the camp where you are staying tonight.'"

Bet you can read this in 5 minutes. Ready, set, go!

[4] Joshua called for the twelve men he had appointed from the Israelites, one man per tribe. [5] Joshua said to them, "Cross over into the middle of the Jordan, up to the LORD your God's chest. Each of you, lift up a stone on his shoulder to match the number of the tribes of the Israelites. [6] This will be a symbol among you. In the future your children may ask, 'What do these stones mean to you?' [7] Then you will tell them that the water of the Jordan was cut off before the LORD's covenant chest. When it crossed over the Jordan, the water of the Jordan was cut off. These stones will be an enduring memorial for the Israelites."

[8] The Israelites did exactly what Joshua ordered. They lifted twelve stones from the middle of the Jordan, matching the number of the tribes of the Israelites, exactly as the LORD had said to Joshua. They brought them over to the camp and put them down there. [9] Joshua also set up twelve stones in the middle of the Jordan where the feet of the priests had stood while carrying the covenant chest. They are still there today.

Crossing completed

[10] Meanwhile, the priests carrying the chest were standing in the middle of the Jordan. They stood there until every command that the LORD had ordered Joshua to tell the people had been carried out. This was exactly what Moses had commanded Joshua. The people crossed over quickly. [11] As soon as all the people had finished crossing, the LORD's chest crossed over. The priests then moved to the front of the people. [12] The people of Reuben, the people of Gad, and half the tribe of Manasseh crossed over, organized for war ahead of the Israelites, exactly as Moses had told them. [13] Approximately forty thousand armed for war crossed over in the LORD's presence to the plains of Jericho, ready for battle. [14] The LORD made Joshua great in the opinion of all Israel on that day. So they revered him in the same way that they had revered Moses during all of his life.

[15] The LORD said to Joshua, [16] "Command the priests carrying the chest containing the testimony to come up out of the Jordan."

[17] So Joshua commanded the priests, "Come up from the Jordan." [18] The priests carrying the LORD's covenant chest came up from the middle of the Jordan, and the soles of their feet touched dry ground. At that moment, the water of the Jordan started flowing again. It ran as before, completely over its banks. [19] The people came up out of the Jordan on the tenth day of the first month.[c] They camped at Gilgal on the east border of Jericho.

Stones at Gilgal

[20] Joshua set up at Gilgal those twelve stones they had taken from the Jordan. [21] He said to the Israelites, "In the future your children will ask their parents, 'What about these stones?' [22] Then you will let your children know: 'Israel crossed over the Jordan here on dry ground.' [23] This was because the LORD your God dried up the water of the Jordan before you until you crossed over. This was exactly what the LORD your God did to the Reed Sea.[d] He dried it up before us until we crossed over. [24] This happened so that all the earth's peoples might know that the LORD's power is great and that you may always revere the LORD your God."

Enemy kings react

5 All the Amorite kings on the west side of the Jordan and all the Canaanite kings near the sea heard that the LORD had dried up the water of the Jordan before the Israelites until they had crossed over. Then their hearts melted. They lost all courage because of the Israelites.

Circumcision

[2] At that time the LORD said to Joshua, "Make yourself flint knives. Circumcise the Israelites for a second time." [3] So Joshua made flint knives for himself. He circumcised the Israelites at Foreskins Hill. [4] This is the reason Joshua did so: All the people who went out of Egypt, that is, all the men who were soldiers, had died in the desert on the way after they left Egypt. [5] All the people who went out were circumcised. But none of the people born in the desert on the way after they had left Egypt had been circumcised. [6] This was

[c]March–April, Nisan [d]Or Red Sea

because the Israelites journeyed forty years in the desert until the whole nation died off. These were the men old enough to fight who went out from Egypt and who hadn't obeyed the Lord. The Lord had pledged to them never to show them the land that the Lord had pledged to their ancestors to give us. It is a land full of milk and honey. ⁷Joshua circumcised their children, the ones the Lord had set in their place. They were uncircumcised because they hadn't been circumcised on the way. ⁸After the whole nation had undergone circumcision, they remained in the camp until they got well again. ⁹Then the Lord said to Joshua, "Today I have rolled away from you the disgrace of Egypt." So the place was called Gilgal,ᵉ as it is today.

Passover

¹⁰The Israelites camped in Gilgal. They celebrated Passover on the evening of the fourteenth day of the monthᶠ on the plains of Jericho. ¹¹On the very next day after Passover, they ate food produced in the land: unleavened bread and roasted grain. ¹²The manna stopped on that next day, when they ate food produced in the land. There was no longer any manna for the Israelites. So that year they ate the crops of the land of Canaan.

Commander of the Lord's heavenly force

¹³When Joshua was near Jericho, he looked up. He caught sight of a man standing in front of him with his sword drawn. Joshua went up and said to him, "Are you on our side or that of our enemies?"

¹⁴He said, "Neither! I'm the commander of the Lord's heavenly force. Now I have arrived!"

Then Joshua fell flat on his face and worshipped. Joshua said to him, "What is my master saying to his servant?"

¹⁵The commander of the Lord's heavenly force said to Joshua, "Take your sandals off your feet because the place where you are standing is holy." So Joshua did this.

Instructions about Jericho

6 Now Jericho was closed up tightly because of the Israelites. No one went out

LIFE PRESERVER

Why circumcision?
Joshua 5:2-9

Circumcision is the act of cutting off the foreskin of a baby boy. This practice is first mentioned in the Bible in the book of Genesis, at the birth of Isaac, who was Abraham and Sarah's son. For the Israelites, circumcision had a very special meaning. It was one way they remembered God's covenant with them that they would be God's faithful people.

Joshua, the leader of the Israelite people, was concerned that the male children hadn't been circumcised when they were in the wilderness. After they crossed the Jordan and entered the promised land, it was important for them to remember this important practice. Circumcising a new group of males was a way to remember and honor all the promises and blessings of God's covenant. ◊

or came in. ²The Lord said to Joshua, "Look. I have given Jericho and its king into your power, along with its mighty warriors. ³Circle the city with all the soldiers, going around the city one time. Do this for six days. ⁴Have seven priests carry seven trumpets made from rams' horns in front of the chest. On the seventh day, circle the city seven times, with the priests blowing the trumpets.

⁵"Have them blow a long blast on the ram's horn. As soon as you hear that trumpet blast, have all the people shout out a loud war cry. Then the city wall will collapse, and the people will rise up, attacking straight ahead."

Israel destroys Jericho

⁶So Joshua, Nun's son, called the priests. He said to them, "Lift up the covenant chest. Let seven priests carry seven trumpets made from rams' horns in front of the Lord's chest."

did you know? The bottoms of shoes got very dirty when the people walked on ancient roads. When they entered a holy place, they took their shoes off as a sign of respect. Even today in some places it is an insult if others can see the bottom of your shoe.

ᵉGilgal sounds like the Heb verb *galal*, "to roll away." ᶠMarch–April, Nisan

[7]He said to the people, "Go forward. Circle the city. Let the armed soldiers go in front of the Lord's chest." [8]As soon as Joshua had spoken to the people, the seven priests carrying seven ram's horn trumpets moved forward in front of the Lord. They blew the trumpets. The Lord's covenant chest followed. [9]The initial group of soldiers was going in front of the priests who were blowing the trumpets. The rear guard was coming behind the chest, with trumpets blowing continuously. [10]Joshua ordered the people, "Don't shout. Don't let your voice be heard. Don't let a word come out of your mouth until the day I tell you, 'Shout!' Then shout!"

[11]He made the Lord's chest circle the city, going around one time. They went back to the camp and stayed there overnight. [12]Joshua got up early in the morning. The priests lifted up the Lord's chest. [13]The seven priests carrying the seven trumpets made from rams'

horns were going in front of the Lord's chest, blowing trumpets continuously. The armed soldiers were going in front of them. The rear guard was coming after the Lord's chest, blowing trumpets continuously. [14]They circled the city one time on the second day. Then they went back to the camp. They did this for six days.

[15]On the seventh day, they got up at dawn. They circled the city in this way seven times. It was only on that day that they circled the city seven times. [16]The seventh time, the priests blew the trumpets. Then Joshua said to the people, "Shout, because the Lord has given you the city! [17]The city and everything in it is to be utterly wiped out as something reserved for the Lord. Only Rahab the prostitute is to stay alive, along with everyone with her in her house. This is because she hid the messengers we sent. [18]But you, keep away from the things set aside for God so that you don't desire[g] and

[g]LXX; Heb *wipe out as something reserved for God*

Obeying God Seems Strange Sometimes   *Joshua 6:1-21*

The people who lived in Jericho were terrified. They had heard how God delivered the Israelites from Egypt, divided the waters of the Reed Sea, and destroyed their enemies (Josh 2:9–11). Jericho was surrounded by a thick wall designed to protect its residents, and there were people whose job it was to stand on the wall and keep watch. The people who stood on the wall probably thought it was strange when they saw the Israelites walk around their city, blowing horns.

When this strange process was repeated several days in a row, the soldiers might have felt many emotions including amusement, frustration, anger, and fear. They were used to battles and were prepared to fight back.

On the seventh day, the Israelites walked around the city seven times, blowing horns. When they finished, they shouted loudly and the wall came down! Everyone saw that the God of the Israelites was indeed powerful.

This story reminds us through a miracle that God is the one who leads the people. Even if God asks us to do things that look strange, we can remember Jericho and know God has a purpose.

Have you ever wondered why your parents asked you to do something?

What did you feel about their request, and what did you do?

take some of the things reserved. That would turn the camp of Israel into a thing doomed to be utterly wiped out and bring calamity on it. ¹⁹All silver and gold, along with bronze and iron equipment, are holy to the LORD. They must go into the LORD's treasury." ²⁰Then the people shouted. They blew the trumpets. As soon as the people heard the trumpet blast, they shouted a loud war cry. Then the wall collapsed. The people went up against the city, attacking straight ahead. They captured the city. ²¹Without mercy, they wiped out everything in the city as something reserved for God—man and woman, young and old, cattle, sheep, and donkeys.

Consequences

²²Joshua spoke to the two men who had scouted out the land. "Go to the prostitute's house. Bring out the woman from there, along with everyone related to her, exactly as you pledged to her." ²³So the young men who had been spies went and brought Rahab out, along with her father, her mother, her brothers, and everyone related to her. They brought her whole clan out and let them stay outside Israel's camp. ²⁴They burned the city and everything in it. But they put the silver and gold, along with the bronze and iron equipment, into the treasury of the LORD's house. ²⁵Joshua let Rahab the prostitute live, her family, and everyone related to her. So her family still lives among Israel today, because she hid the spies whom Joshua had sent to scout out Jericho.

SAILBOAT

COURAGE

Rahab Lives *Joshua 6:25*

Because of Rahab's courage when the spies visited her (Josh 2:1–24), the Israelites were able to capture the city of Jericho. When the battle was finished, Joshua let Rahab and all of her family live. Her brave acts were greatly rewarded. She even became King David's great-great-grandmother (see Matt 1:5-6)! ◊

²⁶At time that time Joshua made this decree:

"Anyone who starts to rebuild this city of Jericho will be cursed before the LORD.

Laying its foundations will cost them their oldest child.

Setting up its gates will cost them their youngest child."

²⁷The LORD was with Joshua. News about him spread throughout the land.

Israel defeated at Ai

7The Israelites did a disrespectful thing concerning the items reserved for God. Achan was the son of Carmi, grandson of Zabdi, great-grandson of Zerah. He was from the tribe of Judah. He took some of the things reserved for God. So the LORD was furious with the Israelites.

²Joshua sent men from Jericho to Ai, which is near Beth-aven to the east of Bethel. He said to them, "Go up. Scout out the land."

So the men went up and scouted out Ai. ³They came back to Joshua and said to him, "There is no need for all of the people to go up. Two or three thousand men could go up and strike Ai. Don't make all of the people bother going there. There are just a few of them." ⁴So about three thousand men from the people went up in that direction. But they fled from the men of Ai. ⁵The men of Ai struck down approximately thirty-six of them. They chased them from outside the gate as far as Shebarim. They struck them down on the slope. Then the hearts of the people melted and turned to water.

Cause of Israel's defeat

⁶Joshua ripped open his clothes. He, along with the elders of Israel, lay flat on their faces before the LORD's chest until evening. They put dust on their heads. ⁷Then Joshua said, "Oh no, LORD God! Why did you ever bring this people across the Jordan? Was it to hand us over to the power of the Amorites, to destroy us? If only we had been prepared to live on the other side of the Jordan! ⁸Please forgive me, LORD. What can I say now that Israel has retreated before its enemies? ⁹The Canaanites and the whole population of the land will hear of it. They will surround us and make our name disappear from the earth. What will you do about your great name then?"

¹⁰The LORD said to Joshua, "Get up! Why do you lie flat on your face like this? ¹¹Israel has sinned. They have violated my covenant, which I commanded them to keep. They have taken some of the things reserved for me and

put them with their own things. They have stolen and kept it a secret. ¹²The Israelites can't stand up to their enemies. They retreat before their enemies because they themselves have become a doomed thing reserved for me. I will no longer be with you unless you destroy the things reserved for me that are present among you. ¹³Go and make the people holy. Say, 'Get ready for tomorrow by making yourselves holy. This is what the Lᴏʀᴅ, the God of Israel, says: "Israel! Things reserved for me are present among you. You won't be able to stand up to your enemies until you remove from your presence the things reserved for me."' ¹⁴In the morning, come forward tribe by tribe. Whichever tribe the Lᴏʀᴅ selects must come forward clan by clan. Whichever clan the Lᴏʀᴅ selects must come forward family by family. Whichever family the Lᴏʀᴅ selects will come forward by individual soldiers. ¹⁵The person selected, who has the things reserved for God, must be put to death by burning. Burn everything that belongs to him too. This is because he has violated the Lᴏʀᴅ's covenant and has committed an outrage in Israel."

Achan discovered and punished

¹⁶Joshua got up early in the morning. He made Israel come forward tribe by tribe. The tribe of Judah was selected. ¹⁷He made the clans of Judah come forward. He selected the clan of Zerah. He made the clan of Zerah come forward as individual soldiers. Zabdi was selected. ¹⁸He made each soldier of his family come forward. Achan was selected. He was a son of Carmi, grandson of Zabdi, great-grandson of Zerah, and of the tribe of Judah. ¹⁹Joshua said to Achan, "My son, give glory to the Lᴏʀᴅ the God of Israel. Tell me what you have done. Don't hide anything from me."

²⁰Achan answered Joshua, "It's true. I've sinned against the Lᴏʀᴅ, the God of Israel. This is what I have done: ²¹Among the booty I saw a single beautiful robe in the Babylonian style, two hundred shekels of silver, and a single gold bar weighing fifty shekels. I desired them and took them. Now they are hidden in the ground inside my tent, with the silver on the bottom."

²²Then Joshua sent messengers. They ran to the tent. There it was, hidden in his tent, with the silver on the bottom. ²³They took the things from inside the tent. They brought them to Joshua and to all the Israelites and emptied them out before the Lᴏʀᴅ. ²⁴Then Joshua seized Achan, Zerah's son, along with the silver, the robe, the gold bar, his sons and daughters, his cattle, donkeys, flocks, tent, and everything that belonged to him. All Israel joined Joshua. They brought them up to Achor Valley. ²⁵Joshua said, "You have brought disaster to us! May the Lᴏʀᴅ bring disaster to you today!" Then all Israel stoned him. They burned them with fire and stoned them with stones. ²⁶They raised over him a great pile of stones that is still there today. Then the Lᴏʀᴅ turned away from his fury. So he named that place Achor Valley.ʰ It is still called that today.

UMBRELLA
DISOBEDIENCE

Results of Disobedience Joshua 7:10-26
The Israelites lost an important battle and were afraid of what would happen next. Joshua didn't know why the battle turned out so badly, but God told him people were taking things that didn't belong to them. Their greed and desire for things they couldn't have distracted them from following God's Instruction. The response to their stealing was very harsh. God punished them for their disobedience. 💧

Plan to capture Ai

8 The Lᴏʀᴅ said to Joshua, "Don't be afraid or terrified. Take the entire army with you. Start to go up to Ai. Look! I have given the king of Ai, his people, his city, and his land into your power. ²Do to Ai and its king what you did to Jericho and its king. But you may take its booty and cattle as plunder. Set your ambush behind the city."

³So Joshua and the whole army got ready to go up to Ai. Joshua chose thirty thousand brave soldiers. He sent them out by night. ⁴He commanded them, "Look. You are to ambush the city from behind. Don't move too far away from the city. Be ready, all of you.

⁵I will approach the city with all the people. When they come out against us the same way as before, we will flee from them. ⁶They will come out after us until we have drawn them away from the city. They will think, They are fleeing from us as before. So we will flee from them. ⁷But you will rise up from the ambush and take over the city. The Lᴏʀᴅ your God will give it into your power. ⁸As soon as you seize the city, set it on fire. Act according to the Lᴏʀᴅ's word. Indeed, I have given you an order!"

⁹Joshua sent them off, and they went to set the ambush. They stayed between Bethel and Ai, to the west of Ai. Joshua spent that night among the people. ¹⁰Joshua got up early in the morning and mustered the people. Then he and the elders of Israel went up in front of the people to Ai. ¹¹The entire army that was with him went up. They moved in close, in front of the city. Then they camped north of Ai, with the valley between them and Ai. ¹²He took about five thousand men and positioned them as an ambush between Bethel and Ai to the west of the city. ¹³The people positioned the main camp on the north side of the city

and its rear guard on its west side. That night, Joshua went into the middle of the valley.

Israel's successful strategy

¹⁴As soon as the king of Ai saw this, he and all his troops, the men of the city, hurried out early in the morning to meet Israel in battle. They moved out to the battleground on the slopes down toward the Jordan.ⁱ He didn't know that there was an ambush set against him behind the city. ¹⁵Then Joshua and all Israel let themselves be beaten before them. They fled in the direction of the desert. ¹⁶Next, all the troops who were still in the city were called out to chase them. They chased after Joshua and so let themselves be drawn away from the city. ¹⁷No one who hadn't gone out after Israel was left in either Ai or Bethel. They left the city wide open and chased after Israel.

¹⁸The Lᴏʀᴅ said to Joshua, "Point the dagger in your hand toward Ai, because I will give it into your power." So Joshua pointed the dagger in his hand toward the city. ¹⁹The ambush quickly rose from its place. As soon as he reached out his hand, it charged. They

ⁱOr *the Arabah*

Listening and Planning   *Joshua 8:1-29*

It's usually a good idea to make a plan when you start something new. For example, if you decide to have a lemonade stand, you'll need a pitcher, lemonade mix, water, ice, and cups. You'll need to decide how much to charge and figure out how to make change for people who don't have the exact amount. Talking to someone who has had a lemonade stand before can be helpful. They can share their experience—their mistakes and successes—with you.

The king of Ai made several mistakes because Joshua had a better battle plan. If he hadn't sent all of his soldiers to chase the Israelite army in front of Ai, he wouldn't have left his city unguarded.

Taking the time to listen to God, make plans, and ask for advice is often what causes God's people to be successful. The Bible teaches that plans will fail without proper counsel or advice (Prov 15:22).

Describe an idea that you have.

Name two people who can give you advice for your idea.

entered the city and captured it. They set the city on fire at once. ²⁰Then the men of Ai turned around. They caught sight of the smoke of the city rising toward the sky. They had no chance to flee one way or the other. The troops who were fleeing toward the desert turned against the pursuit. ²¹Joshua and all Israel saw that the ambush had captured the city and that the smoke of the city was rising. So they turned and struck down the men of Ai. ²²When other Israelites came out of the city to confront them, the men of Ai were caught in the middle. Some Israelites were on one side of them and some on the other. The Israelites struck them down until there was no one left to escape. ²³But they seized the king of Ai alive and brought him to Joshua.

²⁴Israel finished killing the entire population of Ai that had chased them out into the open wasteland. All of them were finished off without mercy. Then all Israel went back to Ai and struck it down without mercy. ²⁵Twelve thousand men and women died that day, all the people of Ai. ²⁶Joshua didn't pull back the hand that was stretched out holding a dagger until he had wiped out the whole population of Ai as something reserved for God. ²⁷However, Israel did take the cattle and other booty of that city as plunder for themselves, in agreement with the command that the Lord had given Joshua. ²⁸Then Joshua burned Ai. He made it a permanently deserted mound. That is still the case today. ²⁹He hanged the king of Ai on a tree until evening. At sundown, Joshua gave an order, and they took his body down from the tree. They threw it down at the opening of the city gate. Then they raised over it a great pile of stones that is still there today.

Joshua reads the Instruction

³⁰Then Joshua built an altar on Mount Ebal to the Lord, the God of Israel. ³¹This was exactly what Moses the Lord's servant had commanded the Israelites. It is what is written in the Instruction scroll from Moses: "an altar of crude stones against which no iron tool has swung."ʲ On it they offered entirely burned offerings to the Lord and sacrificed well-being offerings. ³²There, in the presence of the Israelites, Joshua wrote on the stones a copy of the Instruction from Moses, which Moses had written earlier. ³³All Israel—with its elders, officers, and judges—were standing on either side of the chest. They were facing the levitical priests who carry the Lord's chest containing the covenant. They included both immigrants and full citizens. Half stood facing Mount Gerizim and half stood facing Mount Ebal. This was exactly what Moses the Lord's servant had initially commanded for the blessing of the Israelite people. ³⁴Afterward, Joshua read aloud all the words of the Instruction, both blessing and curse, in agreement with everything written in the Instruction scroll. ³⁵There wasn't a single word of all that Moses had commanded that Joshua failed to read aloud in the presence of the entire assembly of Israel. This assembly included the women and small children, along with the immigrants who lived among them.

The Gibeonites' trick

9 All the kings on the west side of the Jordan heard about this, including those in the highlands, the lowlands, and along the entire coast of the Mediterranean Sea toward Lebanon. They were Hittites and Amorites, Canaanites, Perizzites, Hivites, and Jebusites. ²They formed an alliance to fight Joshua and Israel. ³In contrast, when the population of Gibeon heard what Joshua had done to Jericho and Ai, ⁴they acted cleverly. They set out pretending to be messengers.ᵏ They took worn-out sacks for their donkeys and worn-out wineskins that were split and mended. ⁵They had worn-out, patched sandals on their feet and were wearing worn-out clothes. All the bread in their supplies was dry and crumbly.

⁶They went to Joshua at the camp at Gilgal. They said to him and to Israel, "We have come from a distant country. So now, make a treaty with us."

⁷Israel said to the Hivites, "Perhaps you live among us. How then could we make a treaty with you?"

⁸Then they said to Joshua, "We are your servants."

ʲDeut 27:5–6 ᵏHeb uncertain

Joshua said to them, "Who are you? Where have you come from?"

⁹They said to him, "Your servants have come from a very distant country because of the reputation of the Lord your God. We have heard a report about him and everything he did in Egypt. ¹⁰We heard about everything he did to the two kings of the Amorites on the east side of the Jordan, Heshbon's King Sihon and Bashan's King Og, who was in Ashtaroth. ¹¹Our elders and all the population of our land said to us, 'Take along supplies for the journey. Go meet them and say to them, "We are your servants. So now make a treaty with us."'¹²This is our bread. On the day we left to come to you we took it warm from our houses as supplies. But now here it is, dried up and crumbly. ¹³These wineskins were new when we filled them. But here they are, split open. These clothes and sandals of ours are worn out from the very long journey." ¹⁴The Israelites¹ took some of their supplies, but they didn't ask for any decision from the Lord. ¹⁵Joshua made peace with them. He made a treaty with them to protect their lives. The leaders of the community made a solemn pledge to them.

Israel discovers the trick

¹⁶Three days after the Israelites made a treaty with the Gibeonites, the Israelites heard that they were actually their neighbors and were living among them. ¹⁷So on the third day the Israelites marched out and came to their cities: Gibeon, Chephirah, Beeroth, and Kiriath-jearim. ¹⁸But the Israelites didn't strike at them. This was because the leaders of the community had made a solemn pledge to them by the Lord, the God of Israel. The entire community grumbled against the leaders. ¹⁹Then all the leaders said to the whole community, "We have made a solemn pledge to them by the Lord, the God of Israel. So we can't touch them now. ²⁰This is what we'll do with them. We'll let them live so that wrath won't come down on us because of the solemn pledge that we made to them." ²¹The leaders went on to say to them, "Let them live." So they became woodcutters and water haulers for the whole community, exactly as the leaders had intended for them.

²²Joshua called for the Gibeonites and spoke to them: "Why have you deceived us by saying, 'We live very far away from you,' when actually you live among us? ²³So now you are cursed. Some of you will always serve as woodcutters and water haulers for my God's house."

²⁴They answered Joshua, "Your servants had been told that the Lord your God had commanded his servant Moses to give you the entire land and to wipe out all its population on your account. So we feared for our very lives because of you and did this thing. ²⁵Now, here we are in your power. Do to us whatever seems good and proper to you." ²⁶So Joshua treated them in this way. He spared them from the power of the Israelites, and they didn't kill them. ²⁷That day Joshua assigned them as woodcutters and water haulers for the community and for the Lord's altar, located wherever Godᵐ would choose. That is still the case today.

Gibeonites under attack

10 Jerusalem's King Adoni-zedek heard that Joshua had captured Ai and had wiped it out as something reserved for God. Joshua did the same thing to Ai and its king that he had done to Jericho and its king. He also heard that the population of Gibeon had made peace with Israel and were living among them. ²Adoni-zedek and his peopleⁿ were very afraid, because Gibeon was a large city, like one of the royal cities. It was larger than Ai. All its men were soldiers. ³So Jerusalem's King Adoni-zedek sent word to Hebron's King Hoham, Jarmuth's King Piram, Lachish's King Japhia, and Eglon's King Debir: ⁴"Come up and help me. We will strike at Gibeon, because it has made peace with Joshua and with the Israelites." ⁵Then the five kings of the Amorites gathered. These were the kings of Jerusalem, Hebron, Jarmuth, Lachish, and Eglon. They went up with all their armies, camped against Gibeon, and attacked it. ⁶The people of Gibeon sent word to Joshua in the camp at Gilgal: "Don't desert your servants! Come to us quickly. Rescue us! Help us! All the Amorite kings from the highlands have assembled together against us." ⁷So Joshua went up from Gilgal with the entire army and all the bravest soldiers.

---

¹Or *men* ᵐOr *he* ⁿOr *they*

The Lord fights for Israel

8Then the Lord said to Joshua, "Don't be afraid of them. I have given them into your power. Not a single one of them can stand up against you." 9Joshua quickly attacked them, having come up overnight from Gilgal. 10Then the Lord threw them into a panic before Israel. Joshua struck a mighty blow against them at Gibeon. He chased them on the way up to Beth-horon and struck them down as far as Azekah and Makkedah. 11When they were fleeing from Israel and were on the slope of Beth-horon, the Lord threw down large stones from the sky all the way to Azekah. So they died. More died from the hailstones than the Israelites killed with the sword.

12On the day the Lord gave the Amorites into the power of Israel, Joshua spoke to the Lord in the presence of the Israelites:

> "Sun, stand still at Gibeon!
>   and Moon, at the Aijalon Valley!"
> 13The sun stood still
>   and the moon stood motionless
> until a nation took revenge
>   on its enemies.

Bet you can *read this in 2 minutes. Ready, set, go!*

Isn't this written in the Jashar scroll? So the sun stood motionless in the middle of the sky. For a whole day, it was in no hurry to go down. 14There hasn't been a day like it before or since, when the Lord responded to a human voice. The Lord fought for Israel. 15Then Joshua along with all Israel came back to the camp at Gilgal.

Israel executes five kings

16Then those five kings fled and hid in the cave at Makkedah. 17It was reported to Joshua, "The five kings have been found, hidden in the cave at Makkedah."

18Joshua said, "Roll large stones over the mouth of the cave. Station some men by it to guard them, 19but don't you stay there. Chase after your enemies and attack them from the rear. Don't let them enter their cities, because the Lord your God has given them into your power." 20Joshua and the Israelites finished dealing them a stunning blow until they were finished off. Some survivors among them escaped into the fortified cities. 21Then the whole people came back safely to Joshua in the camp at Makkedah. Not a single person threatened the Israelites.

22Joshua said, "Open up the mouth of the cave. Bring those five kings out of the cave to me." 23They did so. They brought the five kings out of the cave to him: the kings of Jerusalem, Hebron, Jarmuth, Lachish, and Eglon. 24When they brought these kings out to Joshua, Joshua called for every Israelite. He said to the military commanders who had gone out with him, "Come forward. Put your feet on the necks of these kings." So they went forward and put their feet on their necks. 25Then Joshua said to them, "Don't be afraid or terrified. Be brave and strong, because this is how the Lord will deal with all the enemies you fight." 26Next, Joshua struck them down. He put them to death and then hanged them on five trees. They were hanging on the trees until evening. 27At sundown, Joshua gave an order, and they took them down from the trees. They threw them into the cave where they had hidden themselves, and they set large stones over the mouth of the cave. The stones are still there to this very day.

Victories in the south

28On that day, Joshua captured Makkedah. With a sword, he struck it and its king without mercy. He wiped them out, treating everyone in the city as something reserved for God. He left no survivors. He did to the king of Makkedah exactly as he had done to the king of Jericho.

29Then Joshua along with all Israel moved on from Makkedah to Libnah. They attacked Libnah. 30The Lord also gave it and its king into the power of Israel. With a sword, he struck it and everyone in it without mercy. He left no survivors in it. He did to its king exactly as he had done to the king of Jericho.

31Joshua along with all Israel moved on from Libnah to Lachish. They camped near it and attacked it. 32The Lord gave Lachish into the power of Israel. Joshua captured it on the second day. With a sword, he struck it and everyone in it without mercy, just exactly as he had done to Libnah. 33Then Gezer's King Horam came up to help Lachish. But Joshua struck him and his people down, until no survivors were left.

34Joshua along with all Israel moved on from Lachish to Eglon. They camped against it and attacked it. 35They captured it on the same day and struck it down without mercy. On that day, he wiped out everyone in it as something reserved for God, just exactly as he had done to Lachish.

36 Joshua along with all Israel went up from Eglon to Hebron and attacked it. 37 They captured it and struck it down without mercy, along with its king, all its towns, and everyone in it. He left no survivors, just exactly as he had done to Eglon. He wiped out the city and everyone in it as something reserved for God.

38 Joshua along with all Israel turned back to Debir and attacked it. 39 He captured it along with its king and all its cities. They struck them down without mercy and wiped out everyone in it as something reserved for God. He left no survivors. Exactly as he had done to Hebron, so he did to Debir and its king—exactly as he had done to Libnah and its king.

40 So Joshua struck at the whole land: the highlands, the arid southern plains, the lowlands, the slopes, and all their kings. He left no survivors. He wiped out everything that breathed as something reserved for God, exactly as the Lord, the God of Israel, had commanded. 41 Joshua struck them down from Kadesh-barnea to Gaza, and the whole land of Goshen as far as Gibeon. 42 Joshua captured all these kings and their land all at the same time. This was because the Lord, the God of Israel, fought for Israel. 43 Then Joshua along with all Israel came back to the camp at Gilgal.

Victories in the north

11 King Jabin of Hazor heard about this. So he sent word to Madon's King Jobab, to the king of Shimron, and to the king of Achshaph. 2 He sent word to the kings from the north part of the highlands, in the desert plain south of Chinneroth, in the lowlands, and in Naphoth-dor on the west. 3 He sent word to the Canaanites from east and west, to the Amorites, Hittites, Perizzites, and Jebusites in the highlands, and to the Hivites at the foot of Hermon in the land of Mizpah. 4 They went out with all their battalions as a great army. They were as numerous as the grains of sand on the seashore. There were very many horses and chariots. 5 All these kings came together. They came and camped together at the waters of Merom to fight against Israel.

6 The Lord said to Joshua, "Don't be afraid of them. By this time tomorrow, I will make them all dead bodies in Israel's presence. Cripple their horses! Burn their chariots!"

7 Then Joshua along with the entire army launched a surprise attack against them at the waters of Merom. 8 The Lord gave them into Israel's power. They struck them down. They chased them as far as Great Sidon and Misrephoth-maim, then to the east as far as the Mizpeh Valley. They struck them down until no survivors were left. 9 Joshua dealt with them exactly as the Lord had told him. He crippled their horses and burned their chariots.

10 Joshua turned back at that time. He captured Hazor and struck down its king with the sword. Hazor had been the head of all those kingdoms in the past. 11 They struck down everyone there without mercy, wiping them out as something reserved for God. Nothing that breathed was left. Hazor itself he burned. 12 Joshua captured all these kings and their cities. He struck them down without mercy. He wiped them out as something reserved for God. This was exactly as Moses the Lord's servant had commanded. 13 But Israel didn't burn any of the cities that still are standing on their mounds. Joshua burned only Hazor. 14 The Israelites took all the valuable things from those cities and the cattle as plunder for themselves. But they struck down every person without mercy until they had wiped them out. They didn't let anything that breathed survive. 15 What the Lord had commanded Moses his servant, Moses had commanded Joshua, and Joshua did exactly that. He didn't deviate a bit from any command that the Lord had given Moses.

Summary of Israel's victories

16 So Joshua took this whole land: the highlands, the whole arid southern plain, the whole land of Goshen, the lowlands, the desert plain, and both the highlands and the lowlands of Israel. 17 He took land stretching from Mount Halak, which goes up toward Seir, as far as Baal-gad at the foot of Mount Hermon in the Lebanon Valley. He captured all their kings. He struck them down and killed them. 18 Joshua waged war against all these kings for a long time. 19 There wasn't one city that

made peace with the Israelites, except the Hivites who lived in Gibeon. They captured every single one in battle. ²⁰Their stubborn resistance came from the LORD and led them to wage war against Israel. Israel was then able to wipe them out as something reserved for God, without showing them any mercy. This was exactly what the LORD had commanded Moses.

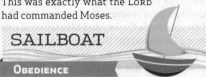

SAILBOAT

OBEDIENCE

A Purpose and a Plan *Joshua 11:15-18*
Both Moses and Joshua were obedient to God. They had important roles as leaders of the Israelite people. They set an example for the people they led by faithfully following God's instruction. Their obedience helped to carry out God's plan for all of God's people. ◆

²¹At that time, Joshua went and wiped out the Anakim from the highlands. He wiped them out from Hebron, from Debir, and from Anab, from the whole highlands of Judah, and the whole highlands of Israel. Joshua wiped them out along with their cities as something reserved for God. ²²The Anakim no longer remained in the land of the Israelites. They survived only in Gaza, Gath, and Ashdod. ²³So Joshua took the whole land, exactly as the LORD had promised Moses. Joshua gave it as a legacy to Israel according to their tribal shares. Then the land had a rest from war.

Moses defeated two kings

12 The Israelites struck down these kings of the land and took over their land on the east side of the Jordan. This ran from the Arnon Valley as far as Mount Hermon and included the whole eastern part of the desert plain. ²First there was the Amorites' King Sihon, who lived in Heshbon. He ruled from Aroer by the rim of Arnon Valley and then from the middle of the valley as far as the Jabbok Valley, the border of the Ammonites. This was half of Gilead. ³He ruled the desert plain up to the east side of the Chinneroth Sea. This ran southward in the direction of Beth-jeshimoth at the foot of the Pisgah slopes as far as

the east side of the desert plain (that is, the Dead Sea) and ⁴the territory next to it.º Then there was Bashan's King Og. He was one of the last of the Rephaim. He lived in Ashtaroth and Edrei. ⁵He ruled over Mount Hermon, Salecah, and all of Bashan as far as the border of the Geshurites and the Maacathites, and half of Gilead down to the border of Heshbon's King Sihon. ⁶Moses the LORD's servant and the Israelites struck them down. Moses the LORD's servant gave their land as property to the Reubenites, Gadites, and half the tribe of Manasseh.

Kings west of the Jordan

⁷Joshua and the Israelites struck down these kings of the land and took over their land on the west side of the Jordan. This ran from Baal-gad in the Lebanon Valley as far as Mount Halak, which goes up toward Seir. Joshua gave it to the tribes of Israel as shares of property. ⁸This was in the highlands, in the lowlands, in the desert plain, in the slopes, in the desert, and in the arid southern plain. The land belonged to Hittites, Amorites, Canaanites, Perizzites, Hivites, and Jebusites. They were:

⁹the king of Jericho	one
the king of Ai (which is near Bethel)	one
¹⁰the king of Jerusalem	one
the king of Hebron	one
¹¹the king of Jarmuth	one
the king of Lachish	one
¹²the king of Eglon	one
the king of Gezer	one
¹³the king of Debir	one
the king of Geder	one
¹⁴the king of Hormah	one
the king of Arad	one
¹⁵the king of Libnah	one
the king of Adullam	one
¹⁶the king of Makkedah	one
the king of Bethel	one
¹⁷the king of Tappuah	one
the king of Hepher	one
¹⁸the king of Aphek	one
the king of Lasharon	one
¹⁹the king of Madon	one
the king of Hazor	one
²⁰the king of Shimron-meron	one
the king of Achshaph	one

ºHeb lacks *next to it.*

²¹ the king of Taanach	one
the king of Megiddo	one
²² the king of Kedesh	one
the king of Jokneam in Carmel	one
²³ the king of Dor in Naphath-dor	one
the king of Goiim of Gilgal	one
²⁴ the king of Tirzah	one
Total of all kings:	thirty-one.

Land still unconquered

13 Now Joshua had reached old age. The LORD said to him, "You have reached old age, but much of the land remains to be taken over. ²This is the land that remains: All the districts of the Philistines and all those of the Geshurites. ³(The land stretching from the Shihor near Egypt northward as far as the Ekron territory is considered to be Canaanite. There are five rulers of the Philistines, for Gaza, Ashdod, Ashkelon, Gath, and Ekron.) The land of the Avvites ⁴in the south. The whole land of the Canaanites, along with Mearah, which belongs to the Sidonians, as far as Aphek and as far as the Amorite border. ⁵The land of the Gebalites and the whole Lebanon eastward, stretching from Baal-gad at the foot of Mount Hermon to Lebo-hamath.

⁶"I myself will remove the entire population of the highlands from Lebanon to Misrephoth-maim before the Israelites, that is, all the Sidonians. You have only to allot it to Israel as a legacy exactly as I commanded you. ⁷So now divide up this land as a legacy for the nine tribes and half the tribe of Manasseh. You will give it out from the Jordan to the Mediterranean Sea in the west. The Mediterranean Sea is the border."^p

Land east of the Jordan

⁸As for the other half of the tribe of Manasseh,^q the Reubenites and Gadites together with it had already taken their legacy that Moses had given them on the east side of the Jordan. It was exactly what Moses the LORD's servant had given them. ⁹It ran from Aroer by the rim of the Arnon Valley and the city in the middle of the valley through the whole Medeba plateau as far as Dibon. ¹⁰It included all the cities of the Amorites' King

Sihon, who ruled in Heshbon, as far as the Ammonite border. ¹¹It also included Gilead and the territory of the Geshurites and Maacathites, all Mount Hermon, and all Bashan as far as Salecah— ¹²the entire kingdom of Og in Bashan, who ruled in Ashtaroth and in Edrei. He survived as the last of the Rephaim. Moses had struck down and removed them. ¹³But the Israelites didn't remove the Geshurites or the Maacathites. So Geshur and Maacath still live among Israel today. ¹⁴It was only to the tribe of Levi that he gave no legacy. Their legacy consists of the fire offerings for the LORD, the God of Israel, exactly as he had promised them.

For Reuben

¹⁵Moses provided for the clans of the Reubenite tribe. ¹⁶Their territory ran from Aroer by the rim of the Arnon Valley and the city in the middle of the ravine, and the whole plateau as far as Medeba. ¹⁷It included Heshbon and all its cities that are on the plateau: Dibon, Bamoth-baal, Beth-baal-meon, ¹⁸Jahaz, Kedemoth, Mephaath, ¹⁹Kiriathaim, Sibmah, the Zereth-shahar highlands, ²⁰Beth-peor, the slopes of Pisgah, and Beth-jeshimoth. ²¹It included all the cities of the plateau and the whole kingdom of Sihon king of the Amorites, who ruled in Heshbon. Moses had struck him down, along with Evi, Rekem, Zur, Hur, and Reba, the leaders of Midian. They had lived in the land as princes of Sihon. ²²In addition to those others slain, the Israelites killed the fortune-teller Balaam, Beor's son, with the sword. ²³The border of the people of Reuben was the Jordan and the territory next to it. This was the legacy of the people of Reuben—for their clans, their cities, and their settlements.

For Gad

²⁴Moses provided for the clans of the Gadite tribe. ²⁵Their territory was Jazer, all the cities of Gilead, and half the land of the Ammonites as far as Aroer near Rabbah. ²⁶It also ran from Heshbon as far as Ramath-mizpeh and Betonim, and from Mahanaim as far as the territory of Lidebir. ²⁷In the valley were Beth-haram, Beth-nimrah, Succoth, and Zaphon. This was the rest of the kingdom of

---

^pLXX; MT lacks *You will give it out from the Jordan to the Mediterranean Sea in the west. The Mediterranean Sea is the border.*
^qLXX; MT lacks *As for the other half of the tribe of Manasseh.*

Sihon king of Heshbon. It included the Jordan and the territory next to it up to the tip of the Chinnereth Sea on the east side of the Jordan. ²⁸This was the legacy of the Gadites—for their clans, their cities, and their settlements.

For half of Manasseh

²⁹Moses provided for half the tribe of Manasseh. It was for the clans in half the tribe of the people of Manasseh. ³⁰Their territory ran from Mahanaim, all Bashan, the whole kingdom of Og king of Bashan, and all sixty of the tent villages of Jair that are in Bashan. ³¹Half of Gilead along with Ashtaroth and Edrei, cities of the kingdom of Og in Bashan, belonged to the people of Machir son of Manasseh. It belonged to the clans for half of the people of Machir.

³²Moses assigned these territories when he was in the Moab plains on the other side of the Jordan, east of Jericho. ³³But Moses gave no legacy to the tribe of Levi. The Lord God of Israel is their legacy, exactly as he promised them.

Dividing up Canaan

14The Israelites received these inheritances in the land of Canaan. Eleazar the priest, Joshua son of Nun, and the heads of the families of the Israelite tribes assigned them. ²Their legacy was assigned by lot, exactly as the Lord had commanded the nine and a half tribes through Moses. ³In fact, Moses had given out the legacy of the two and a half tribes on the other side of the Jordan. But he gave no legacy among them to the Levites. ⁴The people of Joseph consisted of two tribes, Manasseh and Ephraim. The Levites weren't given any portion of the land, except cities to live in and pastureland for their cattle and flocks. ⁵The Israelites divided up the land exactly as the Lord had commanded Moses.

Caleb receives Hebron

⁶In Gilgal, the people of Judah approached Joshua. Caleb son of Jephunneh the Kenizzite said to him, "You know what the Lord said to Moses, man of God, about you and me when we were in Kadesh-barnea. ⁷I was 40 years old when Moses the Lord's servant sent me

from Kadesh-barnea to scout out the land. I brought back a report to him of what I really thought. ⁸My companions who had gone up with me made the people's heart melt. But I remained loyal to the Lord my God. ⁹So Moses pledged on that day, 'The land on which you have walked will forever be a legacy for you and your children. This is because you remained loyal to the Lord my God.' ¹⁰Now look. The Lord has kept me alive, exactly as he promised. It is forty-five years since the Lord spoke about this to Moses. It was while Israel was journeying in the desert. Now look. Today I'm 85 years old. ¹¹I'm just as strong today as I was the day Moses sent me out. My strength then was as my strength is now, whether for war or for everyday activities. ¹²So now, give me this highland that the Lord promised me that day. True, the Anakim are there with large fortified cities, as you yourself heard that day. But if the Lord is with me, I should be able to remove them, exactly as the Lord promised."

¹³So Joshua blessed him. He gave Hebron to Caleb, Jephunneh's son, as a legacy. ¹⁴So Hebron still belongs to Caleb son of Jephunneh the Kenizzite as a legacy today. This was because he remained loyal to the Lord God of Israel. ¹⁵(Hebron used to be called Kiriath-arba. Arba had been the greatest of the Anakim.) Then the land rested from war.

Border of Judah

15The land determined by lot for the clans of the Judahite tribe ran southward to the border of Edom. The Zin wasteland was the southern limit. ²Their south border ran from the end of the Dead Sea, from the bay that faces south. ³It went south from the ascent of Akrabbim, passed on to Zin, and went up south of Kadesh-barnea. It passed on to Hezron, went up to Addar, and turned toward Karka. ⁴It passed on to Azmon and went by the border^r of Egypt. The border ended at the sea. This will be their south border.

⁵The east border was the Dead Sea as far as the mouth of the Jordan.

The border on the north side ran from the bay of the sea at the mouth of the Jordan. ⁶The border went up to Beth-hoglah

---

^rOr *Wadi*, traditionally Brook; LXX *their south border*; MT *your south border*

and passed north of Beth-arabah. The border went up to the Stone of Bohan (Reuben's son). [7]The border went up to Debir from the Achor Valley, turning north to Gilgal. Gilgal was opposite the ascent of Adummim, which was south of the ravine. The border passed on to the waters of En-shemesh and ended at En-rogel. [8]The border went up by the valley of Ben-Hinnom to the slope of the Jebusite city, Jerusalem, on the south. The border went up to the top of the mountain that is opposite the Hinnom Valley on the west, which is at the north end of the Rephaim Valley. [9]The border turned from the top of the mountain to the waters of Nephtoah Spring and went to the cities of Mount Ephron. The border turned toward Baalah (that is, Kiriath-jearim). [10]The border turned westward from Baalah to Mount Seir. It passed on to the slope of Mount Jearim on the north (that is, Chesalon), went

down to Beth-shemesh, and passed by Timnah. [11]The border went to the slope of Ekron on the north. The border turned toward Shikkeron, passed on to Mount Baalah, and went to Jabneel. The border ended at the sea.

[12]The west border was the Mediterranean Sea and its shoreline. This was the border surrounding the clans of the Judahites.

Caleb and Achsah

[13]In agreement with the LORD's command to him, Joshua gave a portion among the Judahites to Caleb, Jephunneh's son. It was Kiriath-arba, that is, Hebron (Arba was the father of Anak). [14]Caleb removed the three sons of Anak from there: Sheshai, Ahiman, and Talmai. They were the offspring of Anak. [15]Then he went up from there against the population of Debir. Debir used to be called Kiriath-sepher. [16]Caleb said, "I will give Achsah my

God's ⟩ My

THOUGHTS ⟩ THOUGHTS

Waiting for God's Promises Joshua 14:6-15

If you've ever had to wait a long time for something that had been promised to you, you might have wondered if it would ever really happen. You may have worried that even if it did finally happen, too much time would have passed for you to enjoy it.

Caleb was 40 years old when he and Joshua went with ten other men to check out the land promised to them by God. They were the only men who believed God would give them that land. Because of their faith, God promised Joshua and Caleb that they would enter the promised land. But they had to wander in the desert until everyone who didn't believe finally died. Caleb waited forty-five years for God's promise to be fulfilled.

When he finally entered the promised land, God gave him another blessing. Although Caleb was 85 years old when he went to claim his portion of land, Caleb was as strong and healthy as a man half his age!

Caleb waited a long time to receive what God had promised, but he chose to obey. Caleb trusted that nothing would prevent God from keeping God's promise. This is still true for us today. God always keeps God's promises.

Name two good things that come as a result of waiting.

Name two things you can do while you are waiting.

daughter in marriage to whoever strikes Kiriath-sepher and captures it." ¹⁷So Othniel son of Kenaz, Caleb's brother, captured it, and Caleb gave him Achsah his daughter in marriage.

¹⁸Now when she arrived, she prodded Othniel into asking for a field from her father. After she got down off her donkey, Caleb asked her, "What do you want?"

¹⁹She said, "Give me a blessing. Since the land you've given me is in the arid southern plain, you should also give me springs of water." So he gave her the upper springs and the lower springs.

Cities of Judah

²⁰This is the legacy for the clans of the tribe of the people of Judah. ²¹The outlying cities of the tribe of the people of Judah ran down to the border of Edom.

In the arid southern plain: Kabzeel, Eder, Jagur, ²²Kinah, Dimonah, Adadah, ²³Kedesh, Hazor, Ithnan, ²⁴Ziph, Telem, Bealoth, ²⁵Hazor-hadattah, Kerioth-hezron (that is, Hazor), ²⁶Amam, Shema, Moladah, ²⁷Hazar-gaddah, Heshmon, Beth-pelet, ²⁸Hazar-shual, Beer-sheba and its dependent cities,ˢ ²⁹Baalah, Iim, Ezem, ³⁰Eltolad, Chesil, Hormah, ³¹Ziklag, Madmannah, Sansannah, ³²Lebaoth, Shilhim, Ain, and Rimmon. In total: twenty-nine cities and their surrounding areas.

³³In the lowlands: Eshtaol, Zorah, Ashnah, ³⁴Zanoah, En-gannim, Tappuah, Enam, ³⁵Jarmuth, Adullam, Socoh, Azekah, ³⁶Shaaraim, Adithaim, Gederah, and Gederothaim. In total: fourteen cities and their surrounding areas.

³⁷Zenan, Hadashah, Migdal-gad, ³⁸Dilan, Mizpeh, Jokthe-el, ³⁹Lachish, Bozkath, Eglon, ⁴⁰Cabbon, Lahmam, Chitlish, ⁴¹Gederoth, Beth-dagon, Naamah, and Makkedah. In total: sixteen cities and their surrounding areas.

⁴²Libnah, Ether, Ashan, ⁴³Iphtah, Ashnah, Nezib, ⁴⁴Keilah, Achzib, and Mareshah. In total: nine cities and their surrounding areas.

⁴⁵Ekron, its dependent cities and surrounding areas. ⁴⁶From Ekron toward the sea, everything that was near Ashdod and its surrounding areas. ⁴⁷Ashdod, its dependent cities and surrounding areas. Gaza, its dependent cities and surrounding areas as far as

the border of Egypt and the Mediterranean Sea and its shoreline.

⁴⁸In the highlands: Shamir, Jattir, Socoh, ⁴⁹Dannah, Kiriath-sannah (that is, Debir), ⁵⁰Anab, Eshtemoh, Anim, ⁵¹Goshen, Holon, and Giloh. In total: eleven cities and their surrounding areas.

⁵²Arab, Dumah, Eshan, ⁵³Janim, Beth-tappuah, Aphekah, ⁵⁴Humtah, Kiriath-arba (that is, Hebron), and Zior. In total: nine cities and their surrounding areas.

⁵⁵Maon, Carmel, Ziph, Juttah, ⁵⁶Jezreel, Jokdeam, Zanoah, ⁵⁷Kain, Gibeah, and Timnah. In total: ten cities and their surrounding areas.

⁵⁸Halhul, Beth-zur, Gedor, ⁵⁹Maarath, Beth-anoth, and Eltekon. In total: six cities and their surrounding areas.

Tekoah, Ephrathah (that is, Bethlehem), Peor, Etam, Koulon, Tatam, Sores, Karem, Gallim, Bether, and Manahath. In total: eleven cities and their surrounding areas.ᵗ

⁶⁰Kiriath-baal (that is, Kiriath-jearim) and Rabbah. In total: two cities and their surrounding areas.

⁶¹In the desert: Beth-arabah, Middin, Secacah, ⁶²Nibshan (the Salt City), and En-gedi. In total: six cities and their surrounding areas.

⁶³But the people of Judah couldn't remove the Jebusites who lived in Jerusalem. So today the Jebusites still live along with the people of Judah in Jerusalem.

Ephraim

16 The land determined by lot for the people of Joseph went out from the Jordan near Jericho eastward to the waters of Jericho. It went up by the desert from Jericho to the Bethel highlands. ²It goes from Bethel to Luz and passes on to the border of the Archites at Ataroth. ³It goes down westward to the border of the Japhletites as far as the border of Lower Beth-horon and as far as Gezer. It ends at the sea. ⁴The people of Joseph, Manasseh and Ephraim, received their legacy.

⁵This was the territory for the clans of the people of Ephraim. The border of their legacy ran from Ataroth-adar on the east as far as Upper Beth-horon. ⁶The border goes to the sea. Michmethath is on the north. The border

---

ˢLXX and Neh 11:27; Heb *Biziothiah* ᵗLXX; MT lacks *Tekoa, Ephrathah … surrounding areas.*

LIFE PRESERVER

Why does the Bible include lists of family members and the location of a tribe's land?

Joshua 13–21

The Bible contains many different kinds of writings. Stories are full of drama and intrigue. Poetry and proverbs use beautiful language to express thoughts and emotions. The book of Joshua has many lists. As the Israelites were moving into the land where they would live, it was important that the land be divided fairly among the tribes.

This part of Joshua tells where each tribe would live. Though Joshua was the one giving the information about the land, the people believed that God was the one making the decisions about how it would be divided among the tribes of Israel. ◆

turns east of Taanath-shiloh and passes along beyond it east of Janoah. [7]It goes down from Janoah to Ataroth and to Naarah, touches Jericho, and goes to the Jordan. [8]From Tappuah the border goes westward by the Kanah Valley. It ends at the sea. This is the legacy for the clans of the Ephraimite tribe. [9]It included cities set apart for the people of Ephraim within the legacy of the people of Manasseh, all the cities and their surrounding areas. [10]But they didn't remove the Canaanites who lived in Gezer. So today the Canaanites, who were used for forced labor, still live within Ephraim.

Manasseh

17 Land was determined by lot for the tribe of Manasseh, who was actually Joseph's oldest son. Gilead and Bashan belonged to Machir, who was Manasseh's oldest son and Gilead's father. This was because he was a warrior. [2]So an allotment took place for the rest of the clans of the people of Manasseh—for the people of Abiezer, Helek, Asriel, Shechem, Hepher, and Shemida. These were the sons of Manasseh the son of Joseph, the male descendants by their clans.

[3]Zelophehad was Hepher's son, Gilead's grandson, Machir's great-grandson and Manasseh's great-great-grandson. Zelophehad had no sons, only daughters, who were named Mahlah, Noah, Hoglah, Milcah, and Tirzah. [4]The daughters approached Eleazar the priest, Joshua, Nun's son, and the leaders. They said, "The LORD commanded Moses to give us a legacy along with our male relatives." So in agreement with the LORD's command, they were given a legacy along with their uncles. [5]Manasseh had ten parcels in addition to the land of Gilead and Bashan on the other side of the Jordan. [6]This was because the daughters of Manasseh received a legacy along with his sons. The land of Gilead belonged to the rest of the people of Manasseh.

[7]The border of Manasseh ran from Asher to Michmethath, which is opposite Shechem. The border went south to the population of En-tappuah. [8]The land of Tappuah belonged to Manasseh. But Tappuah itself belonged to the people of Ephraim, even though it was on the border of Manasseh. [9]The border went down by the Kanah Valley. South of the ravine are those cities that belong to Ephraim, even though they are located among the cities of Manasseh. The border of Manasseh lay on the north side of the ravine and ended at the sea. [10]What lay south of the border belonged to Ephraim, and what lay north of it belonged to Manasseh. The sea was its border. The territory bordered Asher on the north and Issachar on the east.

[11]Belonging to Manasseh in Issachar and in Asher were Beth-shean and its dependent cities, Ibleam and its dependent cities, the population of Dor and its dependent cities, the population of En-dor and its dependent cities, the population of Taanach and its dependent cities, and the population of Megiddo and its dependent cities. (The third one is Naphath.)[u] [12]The people of Manasseh couldn't take over these cities, and the Canaanites were determined to live in this land. [13]When the Israelites grew strong, they subjected the Canaanites to hard labor but didn't remove them.

Future expansion for Joseph

[14]The tribe of Joseph spoke to Joshua: "Why have you only given us a single lot and a solitary parcel for a legacy? We are a numerous people whom the LORD has blessed so richly."

[u] Heb uncertain

¹⁵Then Joshua said, "Yes, you are a numerous people. So go up to the forest and clear ground for yourselves there in the land of the Perizzites and Rephaim, because the Ephraimite highland is too small for you."

¹⁶The people of Joseph said, "The highland isn't enough for us. But all the Canaanites who live in the valley region have iron chariots, both those in Beth-shean and its dependent cities and those in the Jezreel Valley."

¹⁷Joshua then said to the house of Joseph, to Ephraim and to Manasseh, "You are a numerous people and possess great strength. You will have more than a single lot. ¹⁸The highland will belong to you. Because it is a forest, you can clear it. Its farthest limits will be yours. You will definitely remove the Canaanites, even though they have iron chariots and are strong."

Remainder of the land

18 The whole community of the Israelites assembled at Shiloh and set up the meeting tent there. The conquered land lay before them. ²Among the Israelites, seven tribes were left that had not yet received their legacy. ³Joshua said to the Israelites, "How long will you avoid going to take over the land that the LORD, the God of your ancestors, has given you? ⁴Pick out three men for each tribe. I will send them out, and they will go up and travel throughout the land. They will write a description of it as the basis for determining their legacy. Then they will come back to me. ⁵They will divide up the land among themselves into seven portions. Judah will stay on its territory to the south. The house of Joseph will stay on their territory to the north. ⁶But you will write a report in seven parts and bring the report back here to me. Then I will cast the lot for you here, before the LORD our God. ⁷However, there won't be a portion among you for the Levites because their legacy is the priesthood of the LORD. Gad, Reuben, and half the tribe of Manasseh have already received their legacy on the east side of the Jordan. Moses the LORD's servant gave it to them."

⁸When the men had prepared to go, Joshua gave orders to those going to write a description of the land. "Go and travel around the land, write about it, and return to me. I will cast the lot for you before the LORD here in Shiloh." ⁹So the men went and passed through the land and wrote about it in a document, city by city, in seven sections. They came back to Joshua in the camp at Shiloh. ¹⁰Then Joshua cast lots for them in Shiloh before the LORD. There Joshua divided up the shares of the land for the Israelites.

Border of Benjamin

¹¹The lot for the clans of the Benjaminite tribe appeared first. The border of their allotment went out between the people of Judah and the people of Joseph. ¹²Their border on the north side ran from the Jordan. The border went up to the slope of Jericho on the north. It went up westward in the highlands and ended at the wasteland of Beth-aven. ¹³The border passed on from there to Luz, to the slope of Luz on the south (that is, Bethel). The border went down to Ataroth-adar on the mountain that is south of Lower Beth-horon. ¹⁴The border turned and came around southward on the west side, running from the mountain that is opposite Beth-horon on the south. It ended at Kiriath-baal (that is, Kiriath-jearim), a city of the people of Judah. This was its west side.

¹⁵The south side ran from the limits of Kiriath-jearim. The border went out westward. It then proceeded to the waters of Nephtoah Spring. ¹⁶The border went down to the foot of the mountain that is opposite the valley of the son of Hinnom, which is in the north part of the Rephaim Valley. It went down through the Hinnom Valley to the slope of the Jebusite city on the south. It then went down to En-rogel. ¹⁷It turned northward. Then it went to En-shemesh and then to Geliloth, which is opposite the ascent of Adummim. It went down to the Stone of Bohan (Reuben's son). ¹⁸It passed on to the slope of Beth-arabah^v on the north and went down into the desert plain. ¹⁹The border passed on to the slope of Beth-hoglah on the north. The border ended at the north bay of the Dead Sea, at the southern mouth of the Jordan. This was the southern border. ²⁰The Jordan bordered it on the east

^vLXX and Josh 15:6; MT *slope opposite the desert plain*

side. This is the legacy of the Benjaminite clans according to its borders.

Cities of Benjamin

²¹The cities of the clans of the Benjaminite tribe are Jericho, Beth-hoglah, Emek-keziz, ²²Beth-arabah, Zemaraim, Bethel, ²³Avvim, Parah, Ophrah, ²⁴Chephar-ammoni, Ophni, and Geba. In total: twelve cities and their surrounding areas.

²⁵Gibeon, Ramah, Beeroth, ²⁶Mizpeh, Chephirah, Mozah, ²⁷Rekem, Irpeel, Taralah, ²⁸Zela, Haeleph, the Jebusite city (that is, Jerusalem), Gibeath, and Kiriath. In total: fourteen cities and their surrounding areas. This is the legacy of the Benjaminite clans.

Simeon

19 The second lot fell to Simeon. The legacy of the clans of the Simeonite tribe lay inside the legacy of the people of Judah. ²They had in their legacy: Beer-sheba, Sheba, Moladah, ³Hazar-shual, Balah, Ezem, ⁴Eltolad, Bethul, Hormah, ⁵Ziklag, Beth-marcaboth, Hazar-susah, ⁶Beth-lebaoth, and Sharuhen. In total: thirteen cities and their surrounding areas. ⁷Ain, Rimmon, Ether, and Ashan. In total: four cities and their surrounding areas. ⁸In addition were all the areas that surround these cities as far as Baalath-beer and Ramah of the arid southern plain. This is the legacy of the clans of the Simeonite tribe. ⁹Some of the portion of the people of Judah belonged to the legacy of the people of Simeon. This was because the portion of the people of Judah was too large for them. So the people of Simeon received a legacy inside Judah's legacy.

Zebulun

¹⁰The lot turned up third for the clans of Zebulun. The border of their legacy ran as far as Sarid. ¹¹Their border went up westward to Maralah, touched Dabbesheth, and touched the ravine that is opposite Jokneam. ¹²It reversed from Sarid eastward toward the east to the border of Chisloth-tabor. It went to Daberath and then up to Japhia. ¹³From there it passed on the east side, running eastward to Gath-hepher and Eth-kazin. Going to

Rimmon, it bent toward Neah. ¹⁴The border turned north of Hannathon and ended at the Iphtah-el Valley. ¹⁵They also owned Kattath, Nahalal, Shimron, Idalah, and Bethlehem; in total: twelve cities and their surrounding areas. ¹⁶These cities and their surrounding areas are the legacy of Zebulun's clans.

did you know?

Once the land was conquered, it was divided into twelve parts and given to the twelve tribes who could own land. These were the tribes of Asher, Benjamin, Dan, Ephraim, Gad, Issachar, Judah, Manasseh, Naphtali, Reuben, Simeon, and Zebulun. The Levites didn't receive land of their own because they served as priests.

Issachar

¹⁷The lot went out fourth for the clans of Issachar. ¹⁸Their border ran toward Jezreel. They also owned Chesulloth, Shunem, ¹⁹Hapharaim, Shion, Anaharath, ²⁰Rabbith, Kishion, Ebez, ²¹Remeth, En-gannim, En-haddah, and Beth-pazzez. ²²The border touched Tabor, Shahazumah, and Bethshemesh. Their border ended at the Jordan; in total: sixteen cities with their surrounding areas. ²³These cities and their surrounding areas are the legacy for the clans of the Issachar tribe.

Asher

²⁴The lot went out fifth for the clans of the tribe of Asher. ²⁵Their border included Helkath, Hali, Beten, Achshaph, ²⁶Allammelech, Amad, and Mishal. It touched Carmel on the west and Shihor-libnath. ²⁷The border reversed eastward to Beth-dagon. It touched Zebulun and the Iphtah-el Valley on the north, also Beth-emek and Neiel. It went to Cabul on the north, ²⁸as far as Great Sidon. They also owned Ebron, Rehob, Hammon, and Kanah. ²⁹The border turned around to Ramah as far as the fortified city of Tyre. The border turned around to Hosah and ended at the sea. They also owned Mahalab,ʷ Achzib, ³⁰Ummah, Aphek, and Rehob; in total: twenty-two cities and their surrounding areas. ³¹These cities and their surrounding areas are the legacy for the clans of the Asher tribe.

ʷLXX; MT *Mehebel*

Naphtali

³²For the people of Naphtali, the lot went out sixth. For the clans of Naphtali ³³their border ran from Heleph, from the oak in Zaanannim and Adami-nekeb and Jabneel as far as Lakkum. It ended at the Jordan. ³⁴The border reversed westward to Aznoth-tabor. It went from there to Hukkok. It touched Zebulun on the south, Asher on the west, and Judah at the Jordan on the east. ³⁵They also owned the fortified cities Ziddim, Zer, Hammath, Rakkath, Chinnereth, ³⁶Adamah, Ramah, Hazor, ³⁷Kedesh, Edrei, En-hazor, ³⁸Iron, Migdal-el, Horem, Beth-anath, and Beth-shemesh; in total: nineteen cities and their surrounding areas. ³⁹These cities and their surrounding areas are the legacy for the clans of the Naphtali tribe.

Dan

⁴⁰The lot went out seventh for the clans of the Danite tribe. ⁴¹The territory of their legacy was Zorah, Eshtaol, Ir-shemesh, ⁴²Shaalabbin, Aijalon, Ithlah, ⁴³Elon, Timnah, Ekron, ⁴⁴Eltekeh, Gibbethon, Baalath, ⁴⁵Jehud, Bene-berak, Gath-rimmon, ⁴⁶Me-jarkon, and Rakkon, along with the territory opposite Joppa. ⁴⁷But the territory of the people of Dan was lost to them. So the people of Dan went up and attacked Leshem and captured it. They struck it down without mercy. They took it over and settled it. Then they named Leshem as Dan, after the name of Dan their ancestor. ⁴⁸These cities and their surrounding areas are the legacy for the clans of the Danite tribe.

Legacy for Joshua

⁴⁹So when they finished assigning the borders of the land, the Israelites gave to Joshua, Nun's son, a legacy among them. ⁵⁰By the Lord's command, they gave him the city that he asked for. This was Timnath-serah in the highlands of Ephraim. He built a city and lived in it. ⁵¹These are the legacies that Eleazar the priest, Joshua, Nun's son, and the heads of the families of the Israelite tribes assigned by lot at Shiloh. They did this before the Lord at the entrance of the meeting tent and finished dividing up the land.

Refuge cities

20The Lord spoke to Joshua: ²"Say to the Israelites, 'Set up refuge cities for yourselves. I spoke to you about these through Moses. ³Anyone who kills by striking down someone unintentionally or by mistake may flee there. These places will be a refuge for you from any member of the victim's family seeking revenge. ⁴The killer will flee to one of these cities, stand at the entrance of the city gate, and explain their situation to the elders of that city. The elders are to let the killer into the city and provide a place of refuge for the killer to live with them. ⁵If a member of the victim's family follows, seeking revenge, they won't hand the killer over. This is because the killer struck down the neighbor by accident and hadn't been an enemy in the past. ⁶The killer will live in that city until there can be a trial before the community orˣ until the death of the one who is high priest at that time. Then the killer may return home, back to the city from which the flight began.'"

⁷So they set apart Kedesh in Galilee in the highlands of Naphtali, Shechem in the highlands of Ephraim, and Kiriath-arba (that is, Hebron) in the highlands of Judah. ⁸On the other side of the Jordan east of Jericho, they set up Bezer in the wasteland on the plateau from the tribe of Reuben, Ramoth in Gilead from the tribe of Gad, and Golan in Bashan from the tribe of Manasseh. ⁹These cities were the ones designated for all the Israelites and for immigrants residing among them. Anyone who struck down a person by mistake could flee there and escape death at the hand of some member of the victim's family seeking revenge, until there could be a trial before the community.

Cities for the Levites

21The heads of the levitical families approached Eleazar the priest, Joshua, Nun's son, and the heads of the families of the Israelite tribes. ²They spoke to them at Shiloh in the land of Canaan: "The Lord gave a command through Moses to give us cities to live in and their pasturelands for our cattle." ³So the Israelites gave the Levites the following

ˣHeb uncertain

cities and their pasturelands out of their own legacy. This was in agreement with the LORD's command.

[4] The lot went out for the clans of the Kohathites. The descendants of Aaron the priest from among the Levites acquired thirteen cities by lot from the tribes of Judah, Simeon, and Benjamin. [5] The rest of the descendants of Kohath acquired ten cities by lot from the clans of the tribes of Ephraim, Dan, and half of Manasseh. [6] The descendants of Gershon acquired thirteen cities by lot from the clans of the tribes of Issachar, Asher, Naphtali, and the half of Manasseh located in Bashan. [7] The descendants of Merari acquired twelve cities for their clans from the tribes of Reuben, Gad, and Zebulun. [8] So the Israelites gave these cities and their pasturelands to the Levites by lot, exactly as the LORD had commanded through Moses.

[9] They gave the following cities, identified here by name, from the tribe of the Judahites and the tribe of the Simeonites. [10] The cities belonged to the descendants of Aaron, one of the Kohathite clans of the Levites, because the lot had fallen to them first. [11] They gave them Kiriath-arba (that is, Hebron) in the highlands of Judah and the pastures around it. (Arba was the father of Anak.) [12] But they had already given the fields of the city and its surrounding areas to Caleb, Jephunneh's son, as his property. [13] To the descendants of Aaron the priest they gave: Hebron, the refuge city for a killer, and its pastures; Libnah and its pastures; [14] Jattir and its pastures; Eshtemoa and its pastures; [15] Holon and its pastures; Debir and its pastures; [16] Ain and its pastures; Juttah and its pastures; and Bethshemesh and its pastures. Total from these two tribes: nine cities. [17] From the tribe of Benjamin: Gibeon and its pastures, Geba and its pastures, [18] Anathoth and its pastures, and Almon and its pastures. In total: four cities. [19] This is the total of all the cities of the priests descended from Aaron: thirteen cities with their pastures.

[20] Other clans from the levitical descendants of Kohath still remained from among the descendants of Kohath. Some of their allotted cities were from the tribe of Ephraim.

[21] They gave them: Shechem, the refuge city for a killer, and its pastures in the highlands of Ephraim; Gezer and its pastures; [22] Kibzaim and its pastures; and Beth-horon and its pastures; in total: four cities. [23] From the tribe of Dan: Elteke and its pastures, Gibbethon and its pastures, [24] Aijalon and its pastures, Gath-rimmon and its pastures; in total: four cities. [25] From half the tribe of Manasseh: Taanach and its pastures, and Gath-rimmon and its pastures; in total: two cities. [26] This is the total of all cities for the clans of the remaining descendants of Kohath: ten cities with their pastures.

[27] To the descendants of Gershon, one of the clans of the Levites, from half the tribe of Manasseh: Golan in Bashan, the refuge city for a killer, and its pastures; and Beeshterah and its pastures; in total: two cities. [28] From the tribe of Issachar: Kishion and its pastures, Daberath and its pastures, [29] Jarmuth and its pastures, En-gannim and its pastures; in total: four cities. [30] From the tribe of Asher: Mishal and its pastures, Abdon and its pastures, [31] Helkath and its pastures, and Rehob and its pastures; in total: four cities. [32] From the tribe of Naphtali: Kedesh in Galilee, the refuge city for the killer, and its pastures; Hammoth-dor and its pastures; and Kartan and its pastures; in total: three cities. [33] This is the total of all cities of the Gershonites for their clans: thirteen cities with their pastures.

[34] To the clans of the descendants of Merari, the rest of the Levites, from the tribe of Zebulun: Jokneam and its pastures, Kartah and its pastures, [35] Dimnah and its pastures, Nahalal and its pastures; in total: four cities. [36] From the tribe of Reuben: Bezer and its pastures, Jahaz and its pastures, [37] Kedemoth and its pastures, and Mephaath and its pastures; in total: four cities.[y] [38] From the tribe of Gad: Ramoth in Gilead, the refuge city for a killer, and its pastures; Mahanaim and its pastures; [39] Heshbon and its pastures; Jazer and its pastures; in total: four cities. [40] As for the cities of the descendants of Merari for their clans, the remaining clans of the Levites, their total allotment was twelve cities.

[41] This is the total of all the cities of the Levites within the property of the Israelites:

---

[y] LXX and 1 Chron 6:78–79 (Heb 6:63–64); some Heb manuscripts lack 21:36–37.

forty-eight cities with their pastures. ⁴²Each of these cities had its pastures around it. This was the case for all these cities.

Summary of the conquest

⁴³The LORD gave to Israel all the land he had pledged to give to their ancestors. They took it over and settled there. ⁴⁴The LORD gave them rest from surrounding danger, exactly as he had pledged to their ancestors. Not one of all their enemies held out against them. The LORD gave all their enemies into their power. ⁴⁵Not one of all the good things that the LORD had promised to the house of Israel failed. Every promise was fulfilled.

Bet you can read this in 1 minute. Ready, set, go!

Eastern tribes go home

22Then Joshua summoned the Reubenites, the Gadites, and half the tribe of Manasseh. ²He said to them, "You obeyed everything that Moses the LORD's servant commanded you. You have also obeyed me in everything that I have commanded you. ³During these many years, you never once deserted your fellow Israelites. You faithfully obeyed the command of the LORD your God. ⁴The LORD your God has now given rest to your fellow Israelites, exactly as he promised them. So turn around and go back home. Go to the land where you hold property, which Moses the LORD's servant gave you on the other side of the Jordan. ⁵Just be very careful to carry out the commandment and Instruction that Moses the LORD's servant commanded you. Love the LORD your God. Walk in all his ways and obey his commandments. Hold on to him and serve him with all your heart and being." ⁶Then Joshua blessed them. He sent them away, and they went home.

⁷Moses had provided for half of the tribe of Manasseh in Bashan. But Joshua provided for the other half on the west side of the Jordan along with their fellow Israelites. When he sent them back home, Joshua also blessed them. ⁸He said to them, "Return home with great wealth and many cattle, with silver, gold, bronze, and iron, and with much clothing. Divide the spoil taken from your enemies among your own people."

Disagreement about an altar

⁹So the people of Reuben, the people of Gad, and half the tribe of Manasseh went back. They left the Israelites at Shiloh, which is in the land of Canaan. They went to the land of Gilead, to the land that they owned. They had settled there at the LORD's command given by Moses. ¹⁰They came to the districts[z] of the Jordan that are in the land of Canaan. The people of Reuben, the people of Gad, and half the tribe of Manasseh built an altar there by the Jordan, an altar that appeared to be immense. ¹¹Then the Israelites heard a report: "Look. The people of Reuben, the people of Gad, and half the tribe of Manasseh have built an altar at the far edge of the land of Canaan. It lies in the districts of the Jordan on the Israelite side!" ¹²When the Israelites heard this, the entire Israelite community assembled at Shiloh to go up to war against them.

¹³Then the Israelites sent Phinehas son of Eleazar the priest to the people of Reuben, the people of Gad, and half the tribe of Manasseh in the land of Gilead. ¹⁴They sent with him ten leaders, one leader from each important family among the tribes of Israel. Each was the head of an important family among the military units of Israel. ¹⁵They came to the people of Reuben, the people of Gad, and half the tribe of Manasseh in the land of Gilead and spoke with them. ¹⁶They said, "Here is what the LORD's entire community says: 'What's this disrespectful thing that you've done to the God of Israel? Today you've turned away from following the LORD by building yourselves an altar as an act of rebellion against the LORD. ¹⁷Wasn't the offense of Peor enough for us? Even today we still haven't cleansed ourselves from that sin, when there was a plague on the LORD's community! ¹⁸Today you are turning away from following the LORD. If you rebel against the LORD today, he will be angry with the entire community of Israel tomorrow. ¹⁹If your own property is unclean land, then cross over into the land of the LORD's property and settle among us. That's where the dwelling of the LORD stands. But don't rebel against the LORD. And don't involve us in rebellion[a] by building an altar for yourselves other than the altar of

---

²Heb *Geliloth* ᵃOr *rebel against us*

the Lord our God. ²⁰Didn't Achan, Zerah's son, do such a disrespectful thing with the items reserved for God? Wrath came on the entire community of Israel. And he wasn't the only one to die for his crime.'"

²¹Then the people of Reuben, the people of Gad, and half the tribe of Manasseh answered the heads of the military units of Israel: ²²"The Lord is God of gods! The Lord is God of gods! He already knows, and now let Israel also know it! If we acted in rebellion or in disrespect against the Lord, don't spare us today. ²³If we've built ourselves an altar to turn away from following the Lord or to offer on it an entirely burned offering or gift offering, or to perform well-being sacrifices on it, let the Lord himself seek punishment. ²⁴No! The truth is we did this out of concern for what might happen. In the future your children might say to our children, 'What have you got to do with the Lord, the God of Israel? ²⁵The Lord has set the Jordan as a border between us and you people of Reuben and Gad. You have no portion in the Lord!' So your children might make our children stop worshipping the Lord. ²⁶As a result we said, 'Let's protect ourselves by building an altar. It isn't to be for an entirely burned offering or for sacrifice.' ²⁷But it is to be a witness between us and you and between our descendants after us. It witnesses that we too perform the service of the Lord in his presence through our entirely burned offerings, sacrifices, and well-being offerings. So in the future your children could never say to our children, 'You have no portion in the Lord.' ²⁸We thought, If in the future they ever say this to us or to our descendants, we could say, 'Look at this replica of the altar of the Lord that our ancestors made. It isn't for entirely burned offerings or for sacrifice but to be a witness between us and you.' ²⁹God forbid that we should rebel against the Lord and turn away today from following the Lord by building an altar for an entirely burned offering, gift offering, or sacrifice, other than the altar of the Lord our God that stands before his dwelling!"

³⁰Phinehas the priest, the leaders of the community, and the heads of the military units of Israel who were with him heard the words that the people of Reuben, Gad, and Manasseh spoke and approved them. ³¹So

LIFE PRESERVER

Why get angry about an altar? *Joshua 22*

Some of the Israelite tribes saw that other tribes were building an altar, and they were really angry. They believed the altar was disrespectful to God and meant that they were turning away from God's ways. They were concerned that God would be angry and punish the entire community, not just the people who built the altar.

Finally, everyone seemed to calm down and start listening to each other. The tribes who were building the altar explained that they did it out of faithfulness to God. Once their good intentions became clear, the Israelites were no longer angry. ◆

Phinehas the son of Eleazar the priest said to the people of Reuben, Gad, and Manasseh, "Today we know that the Lord is among us, because you haven't done a disrespectful thing against the Lord. Now you've delivered the Israelites from the power of the Lord." ³²Then Phinehas the son of Eleazar the priest and the leaders left the people of Reuben and Gad in the land of Gilead and came back to the Israelites in the land of Canaan. They brought word back to them. ³³The Israelites agreed and blessed God. They no longer spoke of going to war against them to destroy the land where the people of Reuben and Gad were living. ³⁴The people of Reuben and Gad referred to the altar in this way: "It is a witness between us that the Lord is God."

Joshua's word of warning

23 A long time passed. The Lord had given rest to Israel from all their surrounding enemies, and Joshua had grown very old. ²Joshua summoned all Israel, their elders, their heads, their judges, and their officers. He said to them, "I've grown very old. ³You've seen all that the Lord your God has done to all these nations because of you. It is

did you know? Community is the word used to describe the gathering of all the people of all the twelve tribes of Israel. Generally, all the tribes came together like this to honor or worship God.

the LORD your God who fights for you. ⁴Look. I've allotted to you these remaining nations as a legacy for your tribes, along with all the nations I have destroyed. They stretch from the Jordan to the Mediterranean Sea. ⁵The LORD your God will force them out before you and remove them from you. Then you will take over their land, exactly as the LORD your God has promised you. ⁶Be very strong. Carefully obey everything written in the Instruction scroll from Moses. Don't deviate a bit from it either to the right or to the left. ⁷Don't have anything to do with these nations that remain with you. Don't invoke the names of their gods or take oaths by them. Don't serve them or worship them. ⁸Hold on to the LORD your God instead, exactly as you've done right up to today.

⁹"The LORD has removed great and powerful nations before you. To this day, no one has stood up to you. ¹⁰A single one of you puts a thousand to flight. This is because the LORD

your God fights for you, exactly as he promised you. ¹¹For your own sake, be very careful to love the LORD your God. ¹²But if you should turn away and join the rest of these nations that remain with you, intermarry with them, and associate with each other, ¹³then know for certain that the LORD your God won't keep on removing these nations before you. Instead, they will be a snare and a trap for you. They will be a whip on your sides and thorns in your eyes, until you vanish from this fertile land that the LORD your God has given you.

¹⁴"Look. I'm now walking on the road to death that all the earth must take. You know with all your heart and being that not a single one of all the good things that the LORD your God promised about you has failed. They were all fulfilled for you. Not a single one of them has failed. ¹⁵But in the same way that every good thing that the LORD your God promised about you has been fulfilled, so the LORD could bring against you every bad thing as

Don't Give Up! *Joshua 23:6-11*

Imagine a brother and sister decided to clean their rooms as a surprise for their parents. They picked up the toys on the floor and from under their beds. They organized their games and books. They even took their dirty clothes to the laundry room! But it was seeing the pleased looks on their parents' faces and hearing their praise for doing a great job that made the effort seem worthwhile. The brother and sister might have decided to keep their rooms clean from that day forward.

At first it was easy to keep things picked up. But one day the brother was in a hurry and thought *I'll make my bed up later.* Or the sister was too tired to pick up the game she was finished playing. Little by little, the two slipped back into old habits until one day their parents asked, "What happened?"

Joshua knew that this sort of thing could happen to the Israelites. So he warned them to be strong and carefully obey God's ways. He wanted them to stay in the habit of following God, because blessings would come from their obedience. It's important for us to keep doing our best to keep following God's ways. Good things happen when we don't give up.

Name something you need to get back in the habit of doing.

What can you do to get started again?

well. He could wipe you out from this fertile land that the Lord your God has given you. [16]If you violate the covenant of the Lord your God, which he commanded you to keep, and go on to serve other gods and worship them, then the Lord will be furious with you. You will quickly vanish from the fertile land that he has given you."

What God has done

24 Joshua gathered all the tribes of Israel at Shechem. He summoned the elders of Israel, its leaders, judges, and officers. They presented themselves before God. [2]Then Joshua said to the entire people, "This is what the Lord, the God of Israel, says: Long ago your ancestors lived on the other side of the Euphrates. They served other gods. Among them was Terah the father of Abraham and Nahor. [3]I took Abraham your ancestor from the other side of the Euphrates. I led him around through the whole land of Canaan. I added to his descendants and gave him Isaac. [4]To Isaac I gave Jacob and Esau. I gave Mount Seir to Esau to take over. But Jacob and his sons went down to Egypt. [5]Then I sent Moses and Aaron.

I plagued Egypt with what I did to them. After that I brought you out. [6]I brought your ancestors out of Egypt, and you came to the sea. The Egyptians chased your ancestors with chariots and horses to the Reed Sea.[b] [7]Then they cried for help to the Lord. So he set darkness between you and the Egyptians. He brought the sea down on them, and it covered them. With your own eyes you saw what I did to the Egyptians. You lived in the desert for a long time.

[8]"Then I brought you into the land of the Amorites who lived on the other side of the Jordan. They attacked you, but I gave them into your power, and you took over their land. I wiped them out before you. [9]Then Moab's King Balak, Zippor's son, set out to attack Israel. He summoned Balaam, Beor's son, to curse you. [10]But I wasn't willing to listen to Balaam, so he actually blessed you. I rescued you from his power. [11]Then you crossed over the Jordan. You came to Jericho, and the citizens of Jericho attacked you. They were Amorites, Perizzites, Canaanites, Hittites, Girgashites, Hivites, and Jebusites. But I gave them into your power. [12]I sent the hornet[c] before you. It drove them out before you and

[b]Or *Red Sea* [c]Heb uncertain

God's THOUGHTS ◆ My THOUGHTS

Famous Last Words *Joshua 24:1-15*

Joshua spent his last days reminding the Israelites of their history, from the time of Abraham to their years as slaves in Egypt. He reminded them how God delivered them from slavery, bringing them through the Reed Sea and across the desert. He recounted how God had been with them at all times, helping them to defeat their enemies and settle in the promised land.

Then Joshua asked the Israelites to make a choice: either serve the gods of their enemies or serve the one true God. Joshua declared that he and his family would serve God. No matter what others thought or who they chose to follow, Joshua promised to obey God and follow God's ways. Joshua's famous words, "My family and I will serve the Lord" (Josh 24:15), would be something his friends and family could remember when times were hard. These are words we can still remember today. We can choose to serve God with all that we have and all that we are.

With what words would you like to be remembered?

How can you serve God in your daily life?

did the same to the two kings of the Amorites. It wasn't your sword or bow that did this. [13]I gave you land on which you hadn't toiled and cities that you hadn't built. You settled in them and are enjoying produce from vineyards and olive groves that you didn't plant.

Challenge to be faithful

[14]"So now, revere the LORD. Serve him honestly and faithfully. Put aside the gods that your ancestors served beyond the Euphrates and in Egypt and serve the LORD. [15]But if it seems wrong in your opinion to serve the LORD, then choose today whom you will serve. Choose the gods whom your ancestors served beyond the Euphrates or the gods of the Amorites in whose land you live. But my family and I will serve the LORD."

[16]Then the people answered, "God forbid that we ever leave the LORD to serve other gods! [17]The LORD is our God. He is the one who brought us and our ancestors up from the land of Egypt, from the house of bondage. He has done these mighty signs in our sight. He has protected us the whole way we've gone and in all the nations through which we've passed. [18]The LORD has driven out all the nations before us, including the Amorites who lived in the land. We too will serve the LORD, because he is our God."

[19]Then Joshua said to the people, "You can't serve the LORD, because he is a holy God. He is a jealous God. He won't forgive your rebellion and your sins. [20]If you leave the LORD and serve foreign gods, then he will turn around and do you harm and finish you off, in spite of having done you good in the past."

[21]Then the people said to Joshua, "No! The LORD is the one we will serve."

[22]So Joshua said to the people, "You are witnesses against yourselves that you have chosen to serve the LORD."

They said, "We are witnesses!"

[23]"So now put aside the foreign gods that are among you. Focus your hearts on the LORD, the God of Israel."

[24]The people said to Joshua, "We will serve the LORD our God and will obey him."

Joshua makes a covenant

[25]On that day Joshua made a covenant for the people and established just rule for them at Shechem. [26]Joshua wrote these words in God's Instruction scroll. Then he took a large stone and put it up there under the oak in the sanctuary of the LORD. [27]Joshua said to all the people, "This stone will serve here as a witness against us, because it has heard all the LORD's words that he spoke to us. It will serve as a witness against you in case you aren't true to your God." [28]Then Joshua sent the people away to each one's legacy.

Three important graves

[29]After these events, Joshua, Nun's son, the LORD's servant, died. He was 110. [30]They buried him within the border of his own legacy, in Timnath-serah in the highlands of Ephraim north of Mount Gaash. [31]Israel served the LORD all the days of Joshua and all the days of the elders who outlived Joshua. They had known every act the LORD had done for Israel.

[32]The Israelites had brought up the bones of Joseph from Egypt. They buried them at Shechem in the portion of field that Jacob had purchased for one hundred qesitahs from the descendants of Hamor the father of Shechem. They became a legacy of the descendants of Joseph.

[33]Eleazar son of Aaron died. They buried him at Gibeah, which belonged to his son Phinehas. It had been given to him in the highlands of Ephraim.

Judges

The stories in the book of Judges took place after the Israelites entered the land God promised to give to them. The people who battled to win the land had seen God's power with their own eyes. When they grew old and died, there was no one left who could remind the Israelites of God's power in this way (Judg 2:10). God's people often forgot God's promises. They struggled to remember God's Instruction and obey God's commands. They did whatever they wanted, and they began to follow their neighbors' gods.

When the Israelites disobeyed God, their enemies often defeated them in battle. Their enemies stole their food, animals, farms, and homes. But when the Israelites prayed for help, God rescued them. God sent leaders to remind people to obey God and to lead them in battle. Some leaders are well-known Bible characters—like Deborah, Gideon, and Samson. Others aren't as well known—like Othniel, Ehud, and Shamgar.

The book of Judges shows what life was like in Israel before Israel had a king. Life was difficult and

often full of pain. But God watched over God's people and took care of them. The stories in Judges remind us that God cares for us and expects us to follow instructions! ◊

The tribes and their military conflicts

1 After Joshua's death, the Israelites asked the LORD, "Who should go up first to fight for us against the Canaanites?"

2 The LORD said, "The tribe of Judah will go up. I've handed over the land to them."

3 So the tribe of Judah said to the tribe of Simeon, their brothers, "Come up with us into our territory, and let's fight against the Canaanites. Then we'll go with you into your territory too." So Simeon went with them.

4 When Judah went up, the LORD handed them the Canaanites and Perizzites. They defeated ten thousand men at Bezek. 5 There they found Adoni-bezek at Bezek, fought against him, and defeated the Canaanites and Perizzites. 6 Adoni-bezek fled, but they chased after him, captured him, and cut off his thumbs and big toes. 7 He said, "Seventy kings with severed thumbs and big toes used to pick up scraps under my table, so God has paid me back exactly for what I did." They brought him to Jerusalem, where he died. 8 The people of Judah fought against Jerusalem and captured it. They killed its people with their swords and set the city on fire.

9 Afterward, the people of Judah went down to fight against the Canaanites who lived in the highlands, the southern plain,[a] and the western foothills.[b] 10 Judah moved against the Canaanites who lived in Hebron, known before as Kiriath-arba, and they defeated Sheshai, Ahiman, and Talmai. 11 From there they moved against those who lived in Debir, known before as Kiriath-sepher. 12 Caleb said, "I'll give my daughter Achsah as a wife to the one who defeats and captures Kiriath-sepher." 13 Othniel son of Kenaz, Caleb's younger brother, captured it; so Caleb gave him his daughter Achsah as a wife. 14 When she arrived, she convinced Othniel to ask her father for a certain piece of land. As she got down from her donkey, Caleb said to her, "What do you want?"

15 Achsah said to Caleb, "Give me a gift. Since you've given me land in the southern plain, give me springs of water." So Caleb gave her the upper and lower springs.

16 The descendants of Moses' father-in-law the Kenite went up with the people of Judah from Palm City into the Judean desert, which was in the southern plain near Arad. They went and lived with the Amalekites.[c] 17 Then the Judahites went with the Simeonites, their brothers, and they defeated the Canaanites who lived in Zephath, and they completely destroyed it. So the city was called Hormah.[d] 18 Judah also captured Gaza, Ashkelon, Ekron, and all their territories. 19 Thus the LORD was with the tribe of Judah, and they took possession of the highlands. However, they didn't drive out those who lived in the plain because they had iron chariots. 20 They gave Hebron to Caleb, just as Moses had commanded, and they drove out from there the three sons of Anak. 21 But the people of Benjamin didn't drive out the Jebusites who lived in Jerusalem. So the Jebusites still live with the people of Benjamin in Jerusalem today.

22 In the same way, Joseph's household went up against Bethel, and the LORD was with them. 23 When they sent men to spy on Bethel, previously named Luz, 24 the spies saw a man coming out of the city, and they said to him, "Show us the way into the city, and we'll be loyal to you in return." 25 So he showed them the way into the city. They killed the city's people with their swords, but they let that man and all his relatives go. 26 The man went to the land of the Hittites and built a city. He named it Luz, which is still its name today.

27 The tribe of Manasseh didn't drive out the people in Beth-shean, Taanach, Dor, Ibleam, Megiddo, or any of their villages. The Canaanites were determined to live in that land. 28 When Israel became stronger they forced the Canaanites to work for them, but they didn't completely drive them out. 29 The tribe of Ephraim didn't drive out the Canaanites living in Gezer, so the Canaanites kept on living there with them.

30 The tribe of Zebulun didn't drive out the people living in Kitron or Nahalol. These Canaanites lived with them but were forced to work for them. 31 The tribe of Asher didn't drive out the people living in Acco, Sidon, Ahlab, Achzib, Helbah, Aphik, or Rehob. 32 The people of Asher settled among the Canaanites in the land because they couldn't drive them out. 33 The tribe of Naphtali didn't drive

---

[a] Heb *negeb* [b] Heb *shephelah* [c] LXX (cf 1 Sam 15:6); MT *people* [d] Or *destruction*

out the people living in Beth-shemesh or Beth-anath but settled among the Canaanites in the land. The people living in Beth-shemesh and Beth-anath were forced to work for them.

³⁴The Amorites pushed the people of Dan back into the highlands because they wouldn't allow them to come down to the plain. ³⁵The Amorites were determined to live in Har-heres, Aijalon, and Shaalbim, but Joseph's household became strong, and the Amorites were forced to work for them. ³⁶The border of the Amorites ran from the Akrabbim pass, from Sela, and upward.

UMBRELLA
HARD TIMES

No Easy Answers Judges 1:20-35
The Israelites lived among the Canaanites, Hittites, Amorites, Perizzites, Hivites, and Jebusites. They were no longer at war with each other and were trying to live in the same land. Although they might have seen each other, worked together, or even played together, they didn't worship the same God. When the Israelites began to marry people who weren't Israelites, some began to worship other gods. They began to forget all that God had done for them. Their disobedience made God very sad and angry. ♦

The LORD's messenger condemns

2 The LORD's messenger came up from Gilgal to Bochim and said, "I brought you up from Egypt and led you into the land that I had promised to your ancestors. I said, 'I will never break my covenant with you, ²and you are not to make a covenant with those who live in this land. You should break down their altars.' But you didn't obey me. What have you done? ³So now I tell you, I won't drive them out before you, but they'll be a problemᵉ for you, and their gods will be a trap for you." ⁴When the LORD's messenger spoke these words to all the Israelites, they raised their voices and cried out loud. ⁵So they named that place Bochim,ᶠ and they offered a sacrifice to the LORD there.

Death of Joshua and his generation

⁶When Joshua dismissed the people, the Israelites each went to settle on their own family property in order to take possession of the land. ⁷The people served the LORD throughout the rest of Joshua's life and throughout the next generation of elders who outlived him, those who had seen all the great things that the LORD had done for Israel. ⁸Joshua, Nun's son and the LORD's servant, died when he was 110 years old. ⁹They buried him within the boundaries of his family property in Timnath-heres in the highlands of Ephraim north of Mount Gaash. ¹⁰When that whole generation had passed away, another generation came after them who didn't know the LORD or the things that he had done for Israel.

Israel's pattern of sin and punishment

¹¹Then the Israelites did things that the LORD saw as evil: They served the Baals; ¹²and they went away from the LORD, their ancestors' God, who had brought them out of the land of Egypt. They went after other gods from among the surrounding peoples, they worshipped them, and they angered the LORD. ¹³They went away from the LORD and served Baal and the Astartes. ¹⁴So the LORD became angry with Israel, and he handed them over to raiders who plundered them. He let them be defeated by their enemies around them, so that they were no longer able to stand up to them. ¹⁵Whenever the Israelites marched out, the LORD's power worked against them, just as the LORD had warned them. And they were very distressed.

¹⁶Then the LORD raised up leadersᵍ to rescue them from the power of these raiders. ¹⁷But they wouldn't even obey their own leaders because they were unfaithful, following other gods and worshipping them. They quickly deviated from the way of their ancestors, who had obeyed the LORD's commands, and didn't follow their example. ¹⁸The LORD was moved by Israel's groaning under those who oppressed and crushed them. So the LORD would raise up leaders for them, and the LORD would be with the leader, and he would rescue Israel from the power of their enemies as long as that leader lived.

ᵉHeb uncertain ᶠOr *weepers or weeping* ᵍOr *judges*

¹⁹But then when the leader died, they would once again act in ways that weren't as good as their ancestors', going after other gods, to serve them and to worship them. They wouldn't drop their bad practices or hardheaded ways. ²⁰So the Lord became angry with Israel and said, "Because this nation has violated my covenant that I required of their ancestors and hasn't obeyed me, ²¹I in turn will no longer drive out before them any of the nations that Joshua left when he died." ²²As a test for Israel, to see whether they would carefully walk in the Lord's ways just as their ancestors had done, ²³the Lord left these nations instead of driving them out immediately or handing them over to Joshua.

Nations remaining in the land

3These are the nations that the Lord left to test all those Israelites who had no firsthand knowledge of the wars of Canaan. ²They survived only to teach war to the generations of Israelites who had no firsthand knowledge of the earlier wars: ³the five rulers of the Philistines, and all the Canaanites, Sidonians, and Hivites who lived in the highlands of Lebanon from Mount Baal-hermon to Lebo-hamath. ⁴They were to be the test for Israel, to find out whether they would obey the Lord's commands, which he had made to their ancestors through Moses. ⁵So the Israelites lived among the Canaanites, Hittites, Amorites, Perizzites, Hivites, and Jebusites.

God's THOUGHTS / My THOUGHTS

Roller-Coaster Obedience   *Judges 2:1-23*

At an amusement park, the roller coaster is the attraction that most people want to ride. With grinding, creaking jerks, the cars are pulled up the first hill. People in the cars are grinning and laughing. Suddenly everything shifts as the cars start racing downhill. This time not everyone is smiling. Some scream with delight, while others scream in fear. But when the ride is over, everyone is laughing again. Then the cars are pulled to the top once more, starting the cycle over.

Up and down. Up and down. Throughout the book of Judges, the people of Israel were like those on a roller coaster. They would obey God's Instruction for a while, and then they would disobey. Bad things would begin to happen, and they would call out to God. God would send a man or woman to lead them back to obedience. The Israelites would follow that leader, and God would defeat their enemies. Then they would disobey. It happened again and again because God's people didn't appreciate the blessings they had. They had grown used to having an easy life and forgot that God had provided for and protected them.

Are you on a roller coaster of obedience?

What can you do to be consistent in following God?

⁶But the Israelites intermarried with them and served their gods.

Othniel, the model judge

⁷The Israelites did things that the Lord saw as evil, and they forgot the Lord their God. They served the Baals and the Asherahs.ʰ ⁸The Lord became angry with Israel and gave them over to King Cushan-rishathaim of Aram-naharaim. The Israelites served Cushan-rishathaim eight years. ⁹But then they cried out to the Lord. So the Lord raised up a deliverer for the Israelites, Othniel, Kenaz's son, Caleb's younger brother, who rescued them. ¹⁰The Lord's spirit was in Othniel, and he led Israel. When he marched out for war, the Lord handed over Aram's King Cushan-rishathaim. Othniel overpowered Cushan-rishathaim, ¹¹and the land was peaceful for forty years, until Othniel, Kenaz's son, died.

Ehud

¹²The Israelites again did things that the Lord saw as evil, and the Lord put Moab's King Eglon in power over them, because they did these things that the Lord saw as evil. ¹³He convinced the Ammonites and Amalekites to join him, defeated Israel, and took possession of Palm City. ¹⁴So the Israelites served Moab's King Eglon eighteen years.

¹⁵Then the Israelites cried out to the Lord. So the Lord raised up a deliverer for them, Ehud, Gera's son, a Benjaminite, who was left-handed. The Israelites sent him to take their tribute payment to Moab's King Eglon. ¹⁶Now Ehud made for himself a double-edged sword that was about a foot and a half long, and he strapped it on his right thigh under his clothes. ¹⁷Then he presented the tribute payment to Moab's King Eglon, who was a very fat man. ¹⁸When he had finished delivering the tribute payment, Ehud sent on their way the people who had carried it. ¹⁹But he himself turned back at the carved stones near Gilgal, and he said, "I have a secret message for you, King."

So Eglon said, "Hush!" and all his attendants went out of his presence. ²⁰Ehud approached him while he was sitting alone in his cool second-story room, and he said, "I have a message from God for you." At that, Eglon got up from his throne. ²¹Ehud reached with his left hand and grabbed the sword from his right thigh. He stabbed it into Eglon's stomach, ²²and even the handle went in after the blade. Since he did not pull the sword out of his stomach, the fat closed over the blade, and his guts spilled out.ⁱ ²³Ehud slipped out to the porch, and closed and locked the doors of the second-story room behind him.

²⁴After Ehud had slipped out, the king's servants came and found that the room's doors were locked. So they thought, He must be relieving himself in the cool chamber. ²⁵They waited so long that they were embarrassed, but he never opened the doors of the room. Then they used the key to open them, and there was their master lying dead on the ground!

²⁶Ehud had gotten away while they were waiting and had passed the carved stones and escaped to Seirah. ²⁷When he arrived, he blew the ram's horn in the Ephraim highlands. So the Israelites went down from the highlands with Ehud leading them. ²⁸He told them, "Follow me, for the Lord has handed over your enemies the Moabites." So they followed him,

did you know? Ehud was a leader God raised up to help the people. He was left-handed, which meant he could surprise his enemy in battle because he pulled his sword from his right side instead of his left side like most fighters did.

and they took control of the crossing points of the Jordan in the direction of Moab, allowing no one to cross. ²⁹This time, they defeated the Moabites, about ten thousand big and strong men, and no one escaped. ³⁰Moab was brought down by the power of Israel on that day, and there was peace in the land for eighty years.

Shamgar

³¹After Ehud, Shamgar, Anath's son, struck down six hundred Philistines with an animal prod. He too rescued Israel.

ʰHeb *asherim*; perhaps objects or a pole devoted to the goddess Asherah   ⁱHeb uncertain

Deborah, Barak, and Jael

4 After Ehud had died, the Israelites again did things that the Lord saw as evil. ²So the Lord gave them over to King Jabin of Canaan, who reigned in Hazor. The commander of his army was Sisera, and he was stationed in Harosheth-ha-goiim. ³The Israelites cried out to the Lord because Sisera[j] had nine hundred iron chariots and had oppressed the Israelites cruelly for twenty years.

⁴Now Deborah, a prophet, the wife of Lappidoth,[k] was a leader of Israel at that time. ⁵She would sit under Deborah's palm tree between Ramah and Bethel in the Ephraim highlands, and the Israelites would come to her to settle disputes. ⁶She sent word to Barak, Abinoam's son, from Kedesh in Naphtali and said to him, "Hasn't the Lord, Israel's God, issued you a command? 'Go and assemble at Mount Tabor, taking ten thousand men from the

people of Naphtali and Zebulun with you. ⁷I'll lure Sisera, the commander of Jabin's army, to assemble with his chariots and troops against you at the Kishon River, and then I'll help you overpower him.'"

⁸Barak replied to her, "If you'll go with me, I'll go; but if not, I won't go."

⁹Deborah answered, "I'll definitely go with you. However, the path you're taking won't bring honor to you, because the Lord will hand over Sisera to a woman." Then Deborah got up and went with Barak to Kedesh. ¹⁰He summoned Zebulun and Naphtali to Kedesh, and ten thousand men marched out behind him. Deborah marched out with him too.

¹¹Now Heber the Kenite had moved away from the other Kenites, the descendants of Hobab, Moses' father-in-law, and had settled as far away as Elon-bezaanannim, which is near Kedesh.

[j] Or he [k] Or a woman of torches

Overcoming Limitations *Judges 4:1-8*

Sometimes we're afraid to do something because we believe we're limited. We might think we aren't smart enough or strong enough to accomplish a task. We may make excuses for why we can't do something, even if God has asked us.

Deborah didn't let anything stop her. She was a wise woman who loved and obeyed God. Deborah served as a prophet and leader of Israel in a time when men were the ones who tended to lead. Many people came to her for advice or to help settle arguments. She cared for God's people and came to be known as "a mother in Israel" (Judg 5:7).

When Sisera and his army invaded Israel, Deborah took action. She called Barak, one of the tribal leaders of Israel, and told him that God wanted him to take men from his tribe and from two other tribes and defeat Sisera. Barak said he would do this only if Deborah went with him. Barak knew Deborah was loved and respected by the Israelites. He knew that if she was with him, the men from the other tribes would follow him into battle.

The story of Deborah shows that no matter what we may believe our limitations are, God can use us! God uses those who are willing to obey.

Name some things you believe limit what you are able to do.

Ask God to use you despite these limitations.

¹²When it was reported to Sisera that Barak, Abinoam's son, had marched up to Mount Tabor, ¹³Sisera summoned all of his nine hundred iron chariots and all of the soldiers who were with him from Harosheth-ha-goiim to the Kishon River. ¹⁴Then Deborah said to Barak, "Get up! This is the day that the Lord has handed Sisera over to you. Hasn't the Lord gone out before you?" So Barak went down from Mount Tabor with ten thousand men behind him. ¹⁵The Lord threw Sisera and all the chariots and army into a panic^l before Barak; Sisera himself got down from his chariot and fled on foot. ¹⁶Barak pursued the chariots and the army all the way back to Harosheth-ha-goiim, killing Sisera's entire army with the sword. No one survived.

¹⁷Meanwhile, Sisera had fled on foot to the tent of Jael, the wife of Heber the Kenite, because there was peace between Hazor's King Jabin and the family of Heber the Kenite. ¹⁸Jael went out to meet Sisera and said to him, "Come in, sir, come in here. Don't be afraid." So he went with her into the tent, and she hid him under a blanket.

¹⁹Sisera said to her, "Please give me a little water to drink. I'm thirsty." So she opened a jug of milk, gave him a drink, and hid him again. ²⁰Then he said to her, "Stand at the entrance to the tent. That way, if someone comes and asks you, 'Is there a man here?' you can say, 'No.'"

SAILBOAT

COURAGE

Jael Kills Sisera *Judges 4:18-22*

The Israelites were under the rule of King Jabin of Canaan. The commander of his army was Sisera. Sisera and his army had oppressed the Israelites cruelly for twenty years. Deborah was a great prophet and leader who saw an opportunity to defeat Sisera. She knew that it would take tremendous courage and that a woman named Jael had this courage. Sisera, who had ruled strongly and harshly for years and had fought countless battles, didn't expect danger from Jael, who welcomed him into her tent to rest. But Jael killed Sisera while he was sleeping, which was a victory for the Israelite people. ◆

²¹But Jael, Heber's wife, picked up a tent stake and a hammer. While Sisera was sound asleep from exhaustion, she tiptoed to him. She drove the stake through his head and down into the ground, and he died. ²²Just then, Barak arrived after chasing Sisera. Jael went out to meet him and said, "Come and I'll show you the man you're after." So he went in with her, and there was Sisera, lying dead, with the stake through his head.

²³So on that day God brought down Canaan's King Jabin before the Israelites. ²⁴And the power of the Israelites grew greater and greater over Canaan's King Jabin until they defeated him completely.

Deborah's song

5At that time, Deborah and Barak, Abinoam's son, sang:

² When hair is long in Israel,
   when people willingly offer themselves—
      bless the Lord!

³ Hear, kings!
   Listen, rulers!
I, to the Lord,
   I will sing.
I will make music to the Lord,
   Israel's God.

⁴ Lord, when you set out from Seir,
   when you marched out
      from Edom's fields,
      the land shook,
   the sky poured down,
   the clouds poured down water.
⁵ The mountains quaked
   before the Lord, the one from Sinai,
   before the Lord, the God of Israel.

⁶ In the days of Shamgar, Anath's son,
   in the days of Jael, caravans ceased.
Those traveling by road
   kept to the backroads.
⁷ Villagers disappeared;
   they disappeared in Israel,
      until you,^{m} Deborah, arose,
      until you arose as a mother in Israel.
⁸ When they chose new gods,
   then war came to the city gates.^{n}

---

^{l}MT adds *before the edge of the sword.* ^{m}Or I ^{n}Heb uncertain

Yet there wasn't a shield
or spear to be seen
among forty thousand in Israel!
9 My heart is with Israel's commanders,
who willingly offered themselves
among the people—bless the LORD!

10 You who ride white donkeys,
who sit on saddle blankets,[o]
who walk along the road: tell of it.
11 To the sound of instruments[p]
at the watering places,
there they repeat the LORD's victories,
his villagers' victories in Israel.

Then the LORD's people marched
down to the city gates.
12 "Wake up, wake up, Deborah!
Wake up, wake up, sing a song!
Arise, Barak!
Capture your prisoners,
Abinoam's son!"
13 Then those who remained marched down
against royalty;
the LORD's people marched down[q]
against warriors.
14 From Ephraim they set out[r]
into the valley,[s]
after you, Benjamin, with your people!
From Machir commanders
marched down,
and from Zebulun
those carrying the official's staff.
15 The leaders of Issachar came
along with Deborah;
Issachar was attached to Barak,
and was sent into the valley behind him.
Among the clans of Reuben
there was deep soul-searching.
16 "Why did you stay back
among the sheep pens,
listening to the music for the flocks?"
For the clans of Reuben
there was deep soul-searching.
17 Gilead stayed on the other side
of the Jordan,
and Dan, why did he remain
with the ships?
Asher stayed by the seacoast,
camping at his harbors.
18 Zebulun is a people
that readily risked death;
Naphtali too in the high countryside.

19 Kings came and made war;
the kings of Canaan fought
at Taanach by Megiddo's waters,
but they captured no spoils of silver.
20 The stars fought from the sky;
from their orbits
they fought against Sisera.
21 The Kishon River swept them away;
the advancing river, the Kishon River.
March on, my life,
with might!

SAILBOAT

Joy

Deborah's Song Judges 5

After many years of being ruled and oppressed by the Canaanites, the Israelites had finally defeated them. Deborah, a prophet and leader who helped lead them to victory, reminded the people that they belonged to God. In their joyful celebration, they gave credit and glory to God, knowing that God had once again delivered them from bondage.

22 Then the horses' hooves pounded
with the galloping,
galloping of their stallions.
23 "Curse Meroz," says the LORD's messenger,
"curse its inhabitants bitterly,
because they didn't come
to the LORD's aid,
to the LORD's aid against the warriors."

24 May Jael be blessed above all women;
may the wife of Heber the Kenite
be blessed above all
tent-dwelling women.
25 He asked for water,
and she provided milk;
she presented him cream
in a majestic bowl.
26 She reached out her hand for the stake,
her strong hand
for the worker's hammer.
She struck Sisera;

[o]Heb uncertain [p]Heb uncertain [q]Heb adds *for me.* [r]Or *From Ephraim their root* [s]LXX; MT *in Amalek*

she crushed his head;
she shattered and pierced his skull.
²⁷ At her feet he sank, fell, and lay flat;
at her feet he sank, he fell;
where he sank, there he fell—dead.

²⁸ Through the window she watched,
Sisera's mother looked longingly[t]
through the lattice.
"Why is his chariot taking so long to come?
Why are the hoofbeats
of his chariot horses delayed?"
²⁹ Her wisest attendants answer;
indeed, she replies to herself:
³⁰ "Wouldn't they be finding
and dividing the loot?
A girl or two for each warrior;
loot of colored cloths for Sisera;
loot of colored, embroidered cloths;
two colored, embroidered cloths
as loot for every neck."

Gideon was a farmer, not a trained warrior. He didn't have any special training in leading troops in battle. He sent a message to the men of the other tribes of Israel, asking them to send men to fight with him against the Midianites. With three hundred men willing to carry out what God told Gideon to do, the Israelites used trumpets, torches, and trickery to defeat the huge Midianite army of thousands.

³¹ May all your enemies perish
like this, LORD!
But may your allies be like the sun,
rising in its strength.

And the land was peaceful for forty years.

Oppression by the Midianites

6 The Israelites did things that the LORD saw as evil, and the LORD handed them over to the Midianites for seven years. ²The power of the Midianites prevailed over Israel, and because of the Midianites, the Israelites used crevices and caves in the mountains as hidden strongholds. ³Whenever the Israelites planted seeds, the Midianites, Amalekites, and other easterners would invade. ⁴They would set up camp against the Israelites and destroy the land's crops as far as Gaza, leaving nothing to keep Israel alive, not even sheep, oxen, or donkeys. ⁵They would invade with their herds and tents, coming like a swarm of locusts, so that no one could count them or their camels. They came into the land to destroy it. ⁶So Israel became very weak on account of Midian, and the Israelites cried out to the LORD.

⁷This time when the Israelites cried out to the LORD because of Midian, ⁸the LORD sent them a prophet, who said to them, "The LORD, Israel's God, proclaims: I myself brought you up from Egypt, and I led you out of the house of slavery. ⁹I delivered you from the power of the Egyptians and from the power of all your oppressors. I drove them out before you and gave you their land. ¹⁰I told you, 'I am the LORD your God; you must not worship the gods of the Amorites, in whose land you are living.' But you have not obeyed me."

Gideon's commissioning

¹¹Then the LORD's messenger came and sat under the oak at Ophrah that belonged to Joash the Abiezrite. His son Gideon was threshing wheat in a winepress to hide it from the Midianites. ¹²The LORD's messenger appeared to him and said, "The LORD is with you, mighty warrior!"

¹³But Gideon replied to him, "With all due respect, my Lord, if the LORD is with us, why has all this happened to us? Where are all his amazing works that our ancestors recounted to us, saying, 'Didn't the LORD bring us up from Egypt?' But now the LORD has abandoned us and allowed Midian to overpower us."

¹⁴Then the LORD turned to him and said, "You have strength, so go and rescue Israel from the power of Midian. Am I not personally sending you?"

¹⁵But again Gideon said to him, "With all due respect, my Lord, how can I rescue Israel? My clan is the weakest in Manasseh, and I'm the youngest in my household."

¹⁶The LORD replied, "Because I'm with you, you'll defeat the Midianites as if they were just one person."[u]

¹⁷Then Gideon said to him, "If I've gained

---

[t]LXX; MT *cried* [u]Or *each and every one of them*

your approval, please show me a sign that it's really you speaking with me. [18]Don't leave here until I return, bring out my offering, and set it in front of you."

The Lord replied, "I'll stay until you return."

[19]So Gideon went and prepared a young goat and used an ephah[v] of flour for unleavened bread. He put the meat in a basket and the broth in a pot and brought them out to him under the oak and presented them. [20]Then God's messenger said to him, "Take the meat and the unleavened bread and set them on this rock, then pour out the broth." And he did so. [21]The Lord's messenger reached out the tip of the staff that was in his hand and touched the meat and the unleavened bread. Fire came up from the rock and devoured the meat and the unleavened bread; and the Lord's messenger vanished before his eyes.

[22]Then Gideon realized that it had been the Lord's messenger. Gideon exclaimed, "Oh no, Lord God! I have seen the Lord's messenger face-to-face!"

[23]But the Lord said to him, "Peace! Don't be afraid! You won't die."

[24]So Gideon built an altar there to the Lord and called it "The Lord makes peace." It still stands today in Ophrah of the Abiezrites.

[25]That night the Lord said to him, "Take your father's bull and a second bull seven years old. Break down your father's altar to Baal and cut down the Asherah[w] that is beside it. [26]Build an altar to the Lord your God in the proper way on top of this high ground. Then take the second bull and offer it as an entirely burned offering with the wood of the Asherah that you cut down." [27]So Gideon took ten of his servants and did just as the Lord

[v]An ephah is approximately twenty quarts.   [w]Heb *asherah*; perhaps an object or a pole devoted to the goddess Asherah

God Uses People Who Are Scared   *Judges 6:1-22*

If you've ever been afraid to do something for God, there's good news. God doesn't require us to be brave to do God's work. In fact, God has used many people who weren't brave at all when they were first called to serve.

The Midianites were enemies of the Israelite people. Midianite soldiers would ride through the Israelites' fields and destroy their crops. Gideon was afraid. In fact, he was hiding food from the Midianites when a messenger from God appeared. Gideon complained to this messenger about the troubles the Israelites were having. He asked why God was letting this happen instead of rescuing them from their enemies.

When God's messenger told Gideon to go and defeat the Midianites, Gideon wasn't happy. He listed all the reasons why he couldn't rescue Israel. He asked for a sign and then offered food to the messenger by setting bread on a rock. When the messenger touched the rock, fire came out and devoured the food and the messenger vanished. Suddenly Gideon realized this stranger had been sent from God. Gideon was terrified, but the messenger told him not to be afraid.

Many times, God calls people to do scary things. God knows we may be afraid, but God also wants us to trust that God will take care of us.

When have you felt afraid?

What are ways to remind yourself that God cares for you?

had told him. But because he was too afraid of his household and the townspeople to do it during the day, he did it at night.

²⁸When the townspeople got up early in the morning, there was the altar to Baal broken down, with the asherah image that had been beside it cut down, and the second bull offered on the newly built altar! ²⁹They asked each other, "Who did this?" They searched and investigated, and finally they concluded, "Gideon, Joash's son, did this!" ³⁰The townspeople said to Joash, "Bring out your son for execution because he tore down the altar to Baal and cut down the Asherah that was beside it."

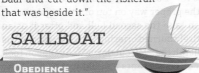

SAILBOAT

OBEDIENCE

Don't Be Afraid to Obey *Judges 6:25-28*

Gideon was afraid. The Midianites were making life hard for the Israelites. God wanted to use Gideon to save the Israelites from their enemies. But God needed to know if Gideon could be trusted to do everything God said. God decided to test Gideon. God commanded Gideon to break his father's altars—the altars to false gods—and build an altar to the one true God in their place. When Gideon learned what he had to do, he was worried. Gideon knew if he obeyed God, his father and neighbors were going to be very angry—enough to kill him. Gideon was scared, but he knew it was more important to obey God. That night, Gideon did everything God asked of him in spite of his fear. Because Gideon obeyed, God knew Gideon could be trusted. God used him to save the Israelites from the Midianites (Judg 7:19-25). ◖

³¹But Joash replied to all who were lined up against him, "Will you make Baal's complaint for him? Will you come to his rescue? Anyone who argues for him will be killed before morning. If he is a god, let him argue for himself, because it was his altar that was torn down." ³²So on that day Gideon became known as Jerubbaal, meaning, "Let Baal argue with him," because he tore down his altar.

Gideon seeks a sign

³³Some time later, all the Midianites, Amalekites, and other easterners joined together, came over, and set up camp in the Jezreel Valley. ³⁴Then the LORD's spirit came over Gideon, and he sounded the horn and summoned the Abiezrites to follow him. ³⁵He sent messengers into all of Manasseh, and they were also summoned to follow him. Then he sent messengers into Asher, Zebulun, and Naphtali too, and they marched up to meet them.

³⁶But then Gideon said to God, "To see if you really intend to rescue Israel through me as you have declared, ³⁷I'm putting a wool fleece on the threshing floor. If there is dew only on the fleece but all the ground is dry, then I'll know that you are going to rescue Israel through me, as you have declared." ³⁸And that is what happened. When he got up early the next morning and squeezed the fleece, he wrung out enough dew from the fleece to fill a bowl with water.

³⁹Then Gideon said to God, "Don't be angry with me, but let me speak just one more time. Please let me make just one more test with the fleece: now let only the fleece be dry and let dew be on all the ground." ⁴⁰And God did so that night. Only the fleece was dry, but there was dew on all the ground.

Battle with Midian

7 Then Jerubbaal, that is, Gideon, and all of the people with him rose early and set up camp beside the Harod spring; Midian's camp was north of theirs, in the valley by the Moreh hill. ²The LORD said to Gideon: "You have too many people on your side. If I were to hand Midian over to them, the Israelites might claim credit for themselves rather than for me, thinking, We saved ourselves. ³So now, announce in the people's hearing, 'Anyone who is afraid or unsteady may return home from Gideon's mountain.'ˣ At this, twenty-two thousand people went home, and ten thousand were left.

⁴The LORD said to Gideon, "There are still too many people. Take them down to the water, and I will weed them out for you there. Whenever I tell you, 'This one will go with you,' he should go with you; but whenever I tell you, 'This one won't go with you,' he should not go." ⁵So he took the people down to the water. And

the LORD said to Gideon, "Set aside those who lap the water with their tongues, as a dog laps, from those who bend down on their knees to drink." [6]The number of men who lapped was three hundred, and all the rest of the people bent down on their knees to drink water, with their hands to their mouths.[y] [7]Then the LORD said to Gideon, "With the three hundred men who lapped I will rescue you and hand over the Midianites to you. Let everyone else go home." [8]So the people gathered their supplies and trumpets,[z] and Gideon sent all the Israelites home, but kept the three hundred.

Now Midian's camp was below Gideon in the valley. [9]That night the LORD said to him, "Get up and attack the camp, because I've handed it over to you. [10]But if you're afraid to attack, go down to the camp with your servant Purah, [11]and you'll hear what they are saying. May you then get the courage to attack the camp." So he went down with his servant Purah to the outpost of the armies that were in the camp. [12]The Midianites, Amalekites, and other easterners were spread across the valley like a swarm of locusts; their camels were too many to count, like the grains of sand on the seashore.

[13]Just when Gideon arrived, there was a man telling his friend about a dream. He said, "Get this! I had a dream that a loaf of barley bread was rolling into the Midianite camp. It came to a tent and hit it, and the tent collapsed. In fact, it rolled the tent over upside down, so it fell flat."

[14]His friend replied, "Can this be anything other than the sword of the Israelite Gideon, Joash's son? God has handed over Midian and its entire camp to him!"

[15]When Gideon heard the telling of the dream and its meaning, he worshipped. Then he returned to the Israelite camp and said, "Get up! The LORD has handed over the Midianite camp to you." [16]He divided the three hundred men into three units and equipped every man with a trumpet and an empty jar, with a torch inside each jar. [17]"Now watch me," he ordered them, "and do what I do. When I get to the outpost of the camp, do just what I do. [18]When I blow the trumpet, along with all who are with me, then you blow the trumpets, all of you surrounding the whole camp. And then shout, 'For the LORD and for Gideon!'"

[19]Gideon and one hundred of his men moved to the outpost of the camp at the middle watch of the night, when they had just changed the guards. Then they blew the trumpets and smashed the jars that were in their hands. [20]So the three units blew their trumpets and broke their jars, holding the torches with their left hands and blowing trumpets in their right hands. And they called out, "A sword for the LORD and for Gideon!" [21]Each man stood fast in his position around the camp, and the entire camp took off running, shouting, and fleeing. [22]When the three hundred trumpets sounded, the LORD turned the swords of fellow soldiers against each other throughout the whole camp. The camp fled as far as Beth-shittah toward Zererah, to the border of Abel-meholah, beside Tabbath.

[23]The Israelites from Naphtali, Asher, and all of Manasseh were called out, and they chased after the Midianites. [24]Then Gideon sent messengers into all of the Ephraim highlands, saying, "Go down to meet the Midianites and take

SAILBOAT

COURAGE

Courage Comes from God *Judges 7:7-23*
Gideon had proved his courage (Judg 6:25-28). Now God asked Gideon to do something even more frightening. God made Gideon send home his great army—an army of thirty-two thousand men. Now Gideon only had three hundred men against the enemies of Israel who were compared to a swarm of locusts covering the valley (Judg 7:12)! God wanted the Israelites badly outnumbered so that all the credit for the victory would go to God. God knew that Gideon was afraid and that he needed to know God was with him. God sent Gideon into the enemy camp to give him the necessary courage. There Gideon overheard the Midianites talking about a dream of their defeat. God gave the dream. The dream gave Gideon the courage to lead his impossibly small army against the enemies of Israel and win. Gideon learned that God gives people courage to do what God asks. ◆

[y]MT places the words *with their hands to their mouths* after the word *lapped*. [z]Or *the ones who lapped took the people's supplies and trumpets for themselves.*

control of the Jordan's waters as far as Beth-barah." So all the Ephraimite men were called out, and they took control of the Jordan's waters as far as Beth-barah. [25]They also captured two Midianite officers, Oreb and Zeeb. They killed Oreb at Oreb's Rock, and killed Zeeb at Zeeb's Winepress. Then they went on chasing the Midianites, and they brought the heads of Oreb and Zeeb to Gideon on the other side of the Jordan.

Gideon's acts of vengeance

8 Then the Ephraimites said to him, "Why did you offend us this way by not calling us when you went to fight the Midianites?" And they argued with him fiercely.

[2]But he said to them, "What have I done now, compared to you? Aren't Ephraim's left-overs better than Abiezer's main harvest? [3]God handed you the Midianite officers Oreb and Zeeb. What have I been able to do compared to you?" When he said this, their anger against him passed.

[4]Then Gideon came to the Jordan. As he and the three hundred men with him crossed over, they were exhausted but still giving chase. [5]So he said to the people of Succoth, "Please give some loaves of bread to those who are on foot, because they're exhausted, but I'm chasing Zebah and Zalmunna, the kings of Midian."

[6]But the officials of Succoth replied, "Haven't you already almost gotten your hands on Zebah and Zalmunna? Why should we give food to your army now?"

[7]"Just for that," Gideon said, "when the LORD has handed over Zebah and Zalmunna to me, I'm going to beat your skin with desert thorns and briars!" [8]From there he went up to Penuel and made the same request. And the people of Penuel responded in the same way the people of Succoth had. [9]So he also told the people of Penuel, "When I return in victory,[a] I'll break down this tower!"

[10]Now Zebah and Zalmunna were in Kar-kor with their camp, about fifteen thousand men, all the ones who were left from the easterners' entire camp. One hundred twenty thousand armed men had fallen. [11]Gideon marched up the caravan road[b] east of Nobah

and Jogbehah, and attacked the camp while it was off-guard. [12]Zebah and Zalmunna fled, and he chased after them. He captured the two Midianite kings Zebah and Zalmunna and threw the entire army into panic.

[13]Then Gideon, Joash's son, returned from the battle by the Heres Pass. [14]He captured a young man from the people of Succoth and interrogated him. He listed for Gideon the seventy-seven officials and elders of Succoth. [15]So Gideon went to the people of Succoth and said, "Here are Zebah and Zalmunna! You made fun of me because of them by saying, 'Haven't you already almost gotten your hands on Zebah and Zalmunna? Why should we give food to your exhausted men now?'" [16]Then he seized the city's elders, and he beat[c] the people of Succoth with desert thorns and briars. [17]He also broke down Penuel's tower, and killed the city's people.

[18]Then he asked Zebah and Zalmunna, "What kind of men were those whom you killed at Tabor?"

They replied, "They were just like you; each one looked like a king's son."

[19]"They were my brothers," Gideon said, "my own mother's sons. As surely as the LORD lives, I promise that if you had let them live, I wouldn't kill you!" [20]So he ordered his oldest son Jether, "Stand up and kill them." But the young man didn't draw his sword because he was afraid, since he was still young.

[21]So Zebah and Zalmunna said, "You stand up and strike us yourself, because as they say, 'A man is measured by his strength!'" So Gideon stood up and killed Zebah and Zalmunna, and took the crescents that were on their camels' necks.

Gideon's request

[22]Then the Israelites said to Gideon, "Rule over us, you and then your son and then your grandson, because you've rescued us from Midian's power."

[23]Gideon replied to them, "I'm not the one who will rule over you, and my son won't rule over you either. The LORD rules over you." [24]But Gideon said to them, "May I make one request of you? Everyone give me the earrings from their loot"; the Midianites had worn gold earrings because they were Ishmaelites.

---

[a]Or *in peace*   [b]Or *the road of the tent dwellers*   [c]Cf 8:7, cf LXX; MT *he taught a lesson to*

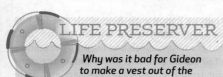

LIFE PRESERVER

Why was it bad for Gideon to make a vest out of the enemy's jewelry? Judges 8:22-28

Gideon was very faithful to God until the story in this passage. Gideon made a priestly vest out of stolen gold and set it up in his hometown, Ophrah. The problem was not that he made the vest, but that he displayed it and that the people of Israel became unfaithful to God because of it.

We don't know why Gideon made the vest, but it had an impact on the people who saw it as an object of worship. This vest caused people to turn away from God.

---

²⁵"We'll gladly give them," they replied. And they spread out a piece of cloth, and everyone pitched in the earrings from their loot. ²⁶The weight of the gold earrings that he requested was one thousand seven hundred shekels of gold, not counting the crescents, the pendants, and the purple robes worn by the Midianite kings, or the collars that were on their camels' necks. ²⁷Gideon fashioned a priestly vest[d] out of it, and put it in his hometown of Ophrah. All Israel became unfaithful there because of it, and it became a trap for Gideon and his household.

²⁸So Midian was brought down before the Israelites and no longer raised its head. The land was peaceful for forty years during Gideon's time.

Gideon's death

²⁹Jerubbaal, Joash's son, went home to live with his own household. ³⁰Gideon had seventy sons of his own because he had many wives. ³¹His secondary wife who was in Shechem also bore him a son, and he named him Abimelech. ³²Gideon, Joash's son, died at a good old age and was buried in the tomb of his father Joash in Ophrah of the Abiezrites.

³³Right after Gideon died, the Israelites once again acted unfaithfully by worshipping the Baals, setting up Baal-berith as their god. ³⁴The people of Israel didn't remember the Lord their God, who had delivered them from the power of all their enemies on every side. ³⁵Nor did they act loyally toward the household of Jerubbaal, that is, Gideon, in return for all the good that he had done on Israel's behalf.

Abimelech becomes a king

9Abimelech, Jerubbaal's son, went to his mother's brothers in Shechem. He spoke to them and to the entire clan of the household to which his mother belonged: ²"Ask all the leaders of Shechem, 'Which do you think is better to have ruling over you: seventy men—all of Jerubbaal's sons—or one man?' And remember that I'm your flesh and blood!"

³So his mother's brothers spoke all these words on his behalf to all the leaders of Shechem. They decided to follow Abimelech because they said, "He's our relative." ⁴They gave him seventy pieces of silver from the temple of Baal-berith, with which Abimelech hired worthless and reckless men, who became his posse. ⁵He went to his household in Ophrah and killed all seventy of his brothers, Jerubbaal's sons, on a single stone. Only Jotham the youngest of Jerubbaal's sons survived, because he had hidden himself. ⁶Then all the leaders of Shechem and all Beth-millo assembled and proceeded to make Abimelech king by the oak at the stone pillar[e] in Shechem.

Jotham's fable

⁷When Jotham was told about this, he went and stood on the top of Mount Gerizim. He raised his voice and called out, "Listen to me, you leaders of Shechem, so that God may listen to you!

⁸"Once the trees went out to anoint a king over themselves. So they said to the olive tree, 'Be our king!'

⁹"But the olive tree replied to them, 'Should I stop producing my oil, which is how gods and humans are honored, so that I can go to sway over the trees?'

¹⁰"So the trees said to the fig tree, 'You come and be king over us!'

¹¹"The fig tree replied to them, 'Should I stop producing my sweetness and my delicious fruit, so that I can go to sway over the trees?'

¹²"Then the trees said to the vine, 'You come and be king over us!'

---

[d]Heb *ephod* [e]Heb uncertain

¹³"But the vine replied to them, 'Should I stop providing my wine that makes gods and humans happy, so that I can go to sway over the trees?'

¹⁴"Finally, all the trees said to the thornbush, 'You come and be king over us!'

¹⁵"And the thornbush replied to the trees, 'If you're acting faithfully in anointing me king over you, come and take shelter in my shade; but if not, let fire come out of the thornbush and burn up the cedars of Lebanon.'

¹⁶"So now, if you acted faithfully and innocently when you made Abimelech king, and if you've done right by Jerubbaal and his household, and have treated him as his actions deserve—¹⁷my father fought for you and risked his life to rescue you from Midian's power, ¹⁸but today you've risen up against my father's household, killed his seventy sons on a single stone, and made Abimelech, his female servant's son, king over the leaders of Shechem, because he's your relative—¹⁹so if you've acted faithfully and innocently toward Jerubbaal and his household today,

then be happy with Abimelech and let him be happy with you. ²⁰But if not, let fire come out from Abimelech and burn up the leaders of Shechem and Beth-millo; and let fire come out from the leaders of Shechem and Beth-millo and burn up Abimelech."

²¹Then Jotham ran away. He fled to Beer and stayed there for fear of his brother Abimelech.

Abimelech's monarchy fails

²²Abimelech ruled over Israel for three years. ²³Then God stirred up ill will between Abimelech and the leaders of Shechem, and they acted like traitors toward Abimelech. ²⁴This occurred because of the violence done to Jerubbaal's seventy sons. Their blood came back on their brother Abimelech, who killed them, and on the leaders of Shechem, who supported him when he killed his brothers. ²⁵As an act against him, the leaders of Shechem set ambushes on the hilltops that robbed everyone who passed by them on the road. This was reported to Abimelech.

²⁶Then Gaal, Ebed's son, and his relatives came passing through Shechem, and the leaders of Shechem shifted their allegiance to him. ²⁷They went out into the field, cut off clusters from their vineyards, trampled them out, and had a celebration. They entered their god's temple and ate, drank, and made fun of Abimelech. ²⁸Gaal, Ebed's son, said, "Who is Abimelech, and who are we of Shechem that we ought to serve him? Didn't this son of Jerubbaal and his deputy Zebul once serve the men of Hamor, Shechem's father? Why should we of all people serve him? ²⁹If only this people were under my command! I would push Abimelech aside! Iᶠ would tell Abimelech, 'Build up your army and march out for battle.'"

³⁰When Zebul the city's ruler heard the words of Gaal, Ebed's son, he became angry. ³¹He sent messengers to Abimelech at Arumahᵍ to say, "Watch out! Gaal, Ebed's son, and his relatives have come to Shechem and are stirring up the city against you. ³²Now, you and the men who are with you: Get up tonight and set an ambush in the fields. ³³Then in the morning, at sunrise, rise early and rush

UMBRELLA
Not Grateful

Selfishness Causes Trouble *Judges 9:17-18*
Abimelech didn't want to share power with his many brothers. When his father died, Abimelech went to the relatives he didn't share with the rest of his family—the Shechemites. Abimelech told them it would be better for one man who was related to them to rule them than seventy strangers. The Shechemites thought it would be great to be related to a king, so they gave Abimelech their support. They didn't think about the rest of Gideon's children—the children of the man who saved them from the Midianites (Judg 8:28). The Shechemites thought Abimelech would give them special favors as a king. Their selfishness was greater than their gratitude toward Gideon and his family. Because the Shechemites looked after only their own concerns, a noble family was almost completely wiped out. They also brought sadness on themselves when Abimelech turned against them (Judg 9:22-49). ◖

on the city. Just as he and the men with him are marching out to face you, you can do to him whatever you wish."

³⁴So Abimelech and all the men who were with him got up that night and set an ambush around Shechem in four companies. ³⁵When Gaal, Ebed's son, came out and stood in the entrance of the city's gate, Abimelech and the men with him sprang up from the ambush. ³⁶Gaal saw the men and said to Zebul, "Look! People are coming down from the hilltops."

Zebul replied to him, "The shadows on the hills just look like persons to you."

³⁷But Gaal spoke up again, "Look! People are coming down from Tabbur-erez, and one company is coming from the direction of Elon-meonenim."ʰ

³⁸Then Zebul replied to him, "Where's all your talk now, you who said, 'Who is Abimelech that we ought to serve him?' Aren't these the men you despised? Now march out and fight them!" ³⁹So Gaal marched out at the head of the leaders of Shechem and fought with Abimelech. ⁴⁰Abimelech routed him, and he ran away. Many fell wounded, all the way up to the entrance of the gate. ⁴¹Afterward, Abimelech stayed in Arumah, and Zebul drove away Gaal and his relatives so they couldn't stay in Shechem.

⁴²The next day, the men of Shechem went out into the fields. When it was reported to Abimelech, ⁴³he took his men, divided them into three companies, and set an ambush in the fields. As soon as he saw the men coming from the city, he sprang upon them and attacked them. ⁴⁴Abimelech and his company charged forward and took a position at the entrance of the city's gate, while the other two companies charged at all those in the fields and attacked them. ⁴⁵Abimelech fought against the city that entire day. He captured the city and killed its people. Then he leveled the city and scattered salt over it.

⁴⁶When all the leaders in the Tower of Shechem heard about this, they entered the side rooms in the El-berith temple. ⁴⁷It was reported to Abimelech that all the leaders from the Tower of Shechem had gathered in one place. ⁴⁸So Abimelech and all the men who were with him went up on Mount Zalmon. He grabbed an ax, cut off a bundle of branches, and hoisted them onto his shoulder. Then he ordered the men who were with him, "Hurry up and do what you've seen me do!" ⁴⁹Each one of the men cut off a bundle as well and followed Abimelech. They piled them up against the side rooms and set fire to the side rooms above them. So all the people in the Tower of Shechem died too, about one thousand men and women.

⁵⁰Then Abimelech moved on to Thebez, set up camp against it, and captured it. ⁵¹But there was a strong tower inside the city. All the men and women and all the city's leaders had fled there, shut themselves inside, and climbed to the tower's roof. ⁵²Abimelech came to the tower to storm it. But when he approached the tower's entrance to set it on fire, ⁵³a woman dropped an upper millstone on Abimelech's head and cracked his skull. ⁵⁴He quickly cried out to the servant who carried his armor, "Draw your sword and kill me. Don't let it be said of me, 'A woman killed him.'" So his servant stabbed him, and he died. ⁵⁵When the Israelites saw that Abimelech was dead, they all went home.

⁵⁶Thus God paid back Abimelech for the evil he had done to his father by killing his seventy brothers. ⁵⁷God also paid back the people of Shechem for their evil. The curse of Jotham, Jerubbaal's son, had come upon them.

Tola and Jair

10 After Abimelech, Tola son of Puah and grandson of Dodo, a man of Issachar, arose to rescue Israel. He lived in Shamir in the Ephraim highlands. ²For twenty-three years he led Israel; then he died and was buried in Shamir.

³After Tola, Jair from Gilead arose, and he led Israel for twenty-two years. ⁴He had thirty sons who were mounted on thirty donkeys and controlled thirty towns in the land of Gilead—these are still known as Havvoth-jair today. ⁵When Jair died, he was buried in Kamon.

Israel's unfaithfulness and oppression by the Ammonites

⁶Then the Israelites again did things that the LORD saw as evil. They served the Baals

ʰ Or the Diviners' Oak

and the Astartes, as well as the gods of Aram, Sidon, Moab, the Ammonites, and the Philistines. They went away from the LORD and didn't serve him. ⁷The LORD became angry with Israel and handed them over to the Philistines and the Ammonites. ⁸Starting that year and for the next eighteen years, they beat and bullied the Israelites, especially all the Israelites who lived on the east side of Jordan in the territory of the Ammonites in Gilead. ⁹The Ammonites also crossed the Jordan to make raids into Judah, Benjamin, and the households of Ephraim. So Israel was greatly distressed.

¹⁰Then the Israelites cried out to the LORD, "We've sinned against you, for we went away from our God and served the Baals."

¹¹The LORD replied to the Israelites, "When the Egyptians, Amorites, Ammonites, Philistines, ¹²Sidonians, Amalekites, and Maonites oppressed you and you cried out to me, didn't I rescue you from their power? ¹³But you have gone away from me and served other gods, so I won't rescue you anymore! ¹⁴Go cry out to the gods you've chosen. Let them rescue you in the time of your distress."

¹⁵The Israelites responded to the LORD, "We've sinned. Do to us whatever you see as

LIGHTHOUSE

CHANGED HEART

A Changed Heart Requires a Changed Life *Judges 10:6-16*
The Israelites weren't very good at following God. Whenever the Israelites turned away from God, God sent other people—such as the Philistines and Ammonites—to make life hard for them. When the Israelites cried out to God to save them, God reminded them that this had all happened before (Judg 2:11-23). God was tired of saving the Israelites time after time, only to have them leave and serve other gods yet again. "No more!" God said. But the Israelites continued to cry out. They admitted their mistakes and recognized how much they needed God. They also took down all their false gods and served the one true God instead. They acknowledged they had done wrong and turned in the opposite direction to do good. When God saw that the Israelites' change of heart was strong enough that it changed their actions, God agreed to save them from their enemies. ◗

right, but please save us this time." ¹⁶They put away the foreign gods from among them and served the LORD. And the LORD could no longer stand to see Israel suffer.

¹⁷The Ammonites called out their army and made camp in Gilead, while the Israelites gathered and set up their camp at Mizpah. ¹⁸Gilead's rulers said to each other, "Whoever is willing to launch the attack against the Ammonites will become the leader over all those living in Gilead."

Rise of Jephthah

11 Now Jephthah the Gileadite was a mighty warrior. Gilead was his father, but he was a prostitute's son. ²Gilead's wife gave birth to other sons for him, and when his wife's sons grew up, they drove Jephthah away. They told him, "You won't get an inheritance in our father's household because you're a different woman's son." ³So Jephthah ran away from his brothers and lived in the land of Tob. Worthless men gathered around Jephthah and became his posse.

⁴Sometime afterward, the Ammonites made war against Israel. ⁵And when the Ammonites attacked Israel, Gilead's elders went to bring Jephthah back from the land of Tob. ⁶They said to him, "Come be our commander so we can fight against the Ammonites."

⁷But Jephthah replied to Gilead's elders, "Aren't you the ones who hated me and drove me away from my father's household? Why are you coming to me now when you're in trouble?"

⁸Gilead's elders answered Jephthah, "That may be, but now we're turning back to you, so come with us and fight the Ammonites. Then you'll become the leader over us and everyone who lives in Gilead."

⁹And Jephthah said to Gilead's elders, "If you bring me back to fight the Ammonites and the LORD gives them over to me, I alone will be your leader."

¹⁰Gilead's elders replied to him, "The LORD is our witness; we will surely do what you've said." ¹¹So Jephthah went with Gilead's elders, and the people made him leader and commander over them. At Mizpah before the LORD, Jephthah repeated everything he had said.

¹²Then Jephthah sent messengers to the Ammonite king, saying, "What is the problem

between us that you've come against me to make war in my land?"

¹³The Ammonite king responded to Jephthah's messengers, "When the Israelites were coming up from Egypt, they seized my land from the Arnon to the Jabbok and all the way to the Jordan. Now give it back peacefully!"

¹⁴Then Jephthah again sent messengers to the Ammonite king ¹⁵and said to him, "Jephthah states: Israel didn't seize the land of the Moabites or the land of the Ammonites. ¹⁶When they were coming up from Egypt, the Israelites went through the desert to the Reed Seaⁱ and came to Kadesh. ¹⁷Then the Israelites sent messengers to the king of Edom, saying, 'Please allow us to pass through your land'; but the Edomite king refused. They sent the same request to the king of Moab, and he was unwilling. So the Israelites stayed at Kadesh.

¹⁸"Later they journeyed into the desert but went around the lands of Edom and Moab, arriving on the east side of the land of Moab and setting up camp on the other side of the Arnon. They never entered Moabite territory, because the Arnon was the boundary of Moab. ¹⁹Then the Israelites sent messengers to Sihon king of the Amorites and king of Heshbon and said to him, 'Please allow us to pass through your land to our own place.' ²⁰Yet Sihon didn't trust the Israelites to pass through his territory. He assembled his entire army, set up camp at Jahaz, and went to war with the Israelites. ²¹The Lᴏʀᴅ, Israel's God, handed over Sihon and his entire army to the Israelites, and they defeated Sihon. So the Israelites took possession of all the land of the Amorites who were living in that area. ²²They took possession of all the Amorite territory from the Arnon to the Jabbok and from the desert to the Jordan.

²³"So now that the Lᴏʀᴅ, Israel's God, has driven out the Amorites before his people Israel, will you take possession of their land? ²⁴Shouldn't you possess what Chemosh your god has given you to possess? And shouldn't we possess everything that the Lᴏʀᴅ our God has given us to possess? ²⁵Do you now have a better case than Moab's King Balak, Zippor's son? Did he make an accusation against

the Israelites or go to war with them? ²⁶Why didn't you take back this territory while the Israelites lived in Heshbon and its villages, in Aroer and its villages, and in all the towns along the branches of the Arnon for three hundred years? ²⁷I haven't sinned against you, but you're doing me wrong by making war against me. Let the Lᴏʀᴅ, who is the judge, decide today between the Israelites and the Ammonites!"

²⁸But the Ammonite king refused to listen to the message that Jephthah sent to him.

Jephthah's promise

²⁹Then the Lᴏʀᴅ's spirit came on Jephthah. He passed through Gilead and Manasseh, then through Mizpah in Gilead, and from there he crossed over to the Ammonites. ³⁰Jephthah made a solemn promise to the Lᴏʀᴅ: "If you will decisively hand over the Ammonites to me, ³¹then whatever comes out the doors of my house to meet me when I return victorious from the Ammonites will be given over to the Lᴏʀᴅ. I will sacrifice it as an entirely burned offering." ³²Jephthah crossed over to fight the Ammonites, and the Lᴏʀᴅ handed them over to him. ³³It was an exceptionally great defeat; he defeated twenty towns from Aroer to the area of Minnith, and on as far as Abel-keramim. So the Ammonites were brought down before the Israelites.

³⁴But when Jephthah came to his house in Mizpah, it was his daughter who came out to meet him with tambourines and dancing! She was an only child; he had no other son or daughter except her. ³⁵When he saw her, he tore his clothes and said, "Oh no! My daughter! You have brought me to my knees! You are my agony! For I opened my mouth to the Lᴏʀᴅ, and I can't take it back."

³⁶But she replied to him, "My father, you've opened your mouth to the Lᴏʀᴅ, so you should do to me just what you've promised. After all, the Lᴏʀᴅ has carried out just punishment for you on your enemies the Ammonites." ³⁷Then she said to her father, "Let this one thing be done for me: hold off for two months and let me and my friends wander the hills in sadness, crying over the fact that I never had children."

ⁱOr Red Sea

LIFE PRESERVER

Did Jephthah really sacrifice his only child? Why?

Judges 11:30-40

Jephthah had an interesting family story. But his story was very sad and became tragic when Jephthah promised God that he would sacrifice whatever came out the door of his house if God would help him defeat the Ammonites.

In that culture, it would have been natural for one of the animals to come out of the courtyard. But the kitchen was also in the courtyard, so it would not have been uncommon for a woman to come out either. Women were leaders in the celebrations that followed military victories. That's what happened. Jephthah's daughter ran out, dancing with a tambourine. This is hard for us to understand. We wonder why God didn't intervene and save Jephthah's daughter like God saved Isaac, the son of Abraham (Gen 22:1-14). Before she was sacrificed, Jephthah's daughter went on a journey with her friends, which would be remembered in a journey that would be passed on to other women in Israel. She is remembered. ◆

---

³⁸"Go," he responded, and he sent her away for two months. She and her friends walked on the hills and cried because she would never have children.

³⁹When two months had passed, she returned to her father, and he did to her what he had promised. She had not known a man intimately. But she gave rise to a tradition in Israel where ⁴⁰for four days every year Israelite daughters would go away to recount the story of the Gileadite Jephthah's daughter.

Jephthah defeats the Ephraimites

12 The Ephraimites were called up for battle and crossed over to Zaphon. They said to Jephthah, "Why did you cross over to fight the Ammonites and not call us to go with you? We're going to burn down your house over you!"

²Jephthah replied to them, "My people and I were in a great conflict with the Ammonites. But when I cried out to you, you didn't rescue me from their power. ³When I saw that you weren't going to rescue me, I risked my own life and crossed over against the Ammonites, and the LORD handed them over to me. So

why have you marched against me today to fight me?"

⁴So Jephthah gathered all the men of Gilead and fought the Ephraimites. The Gileadites defeated the Ephraimites, because they had said, "You are fugitives from Ephraim! Gilead stands within Ephraim and Manasseh." ⁵The Gileadites took control of the Jordan's crossing points into Ephraim. Whenever one of the Ephraimite fugitives said, "Let me cross," the Gileadites would ask him, "Are you an Ephraimite?" If he said, "No," ⁶they would tell him, "Then say *shibboleth*." But he would say, "*sibboleth*," because he couldn't pronounce it correctly. So they would seize him and kill him at the Jordan's crossing points. Forty-two thousand of the Ephraimites fell at that time.

⁷Jephthah led Israel for six years. Then Jephthah the Gileadite died and was buried in one of the towns in Gilead.

Ibzan, Elon, and Abdon

⁸After Jephthah, Ibzan from Bethlehem led Israel. ⁹He had thirty sons and thirty daughters. He married his thirty daughters to those outside his clan, and brought in thirty young women from outside for his sons. He led Israel for seven years. ¹⁰Then Ibzan died and was buried in Bethlehem.

¹¹After Ibzan, Elon from Zebulun led Israel; he did so for ten years. ¹²Then Elon the Zebulunite died and was buried in Aijalon in the land of Zebulun.

¹³After Elon, Abdon, Hillel's son from Pirathon, led Israel. ¹⁴He had forty sons and thirty grandsons mounted on seventy donkeys. He led Israel for eight years. ¹⁵Then Abdon, Hillel's son from Pirathon, died and was buried in Pirathon in the land of Ephraim, in the Amalekite highlands.

Samson's birth

13 The Israelites again did things that the LORD saw as evil, and he handed them over to the Philistines for forty years.

²Now there was a certain man from Zorah, from the Danite clan, whose name was Manoah. His wife was unable to become pregnant and had not given birth to any children. ³The LORD's messenger appeared to the woman and said to her, "Even though you've been unable to become pregnant and haven't

given birth, you are now pregnant and will give birth to a son! [4]Now be careful not to drink wine or brandy or to eat anything that is ritually unclean, [5]because you are pregnant and will give birth to a son. Don't allow a razor to shave his head, because the boy is going to be a nazirite for God from birth. He'll be the one who begins Israel's rescue from the power of the Philistines."

[6]Then the woman went and told her husband, "A man of God came to me, and he looked like God's messenger—very scary! I didn't ask him where he was from, and he didn't tell me his name. [7]He said to me, 'You are pregnant and will give birth to a son, so don't drink wine or brandy or eat anything that is ritually unclean, because the boy is going to be a nazirite for God from birth until the day he dies.'"

[8]Manoah asked the LORD, "Please, my Lord," he said, "let the man of God whom you sent come back to us once more, so he can teach us how we should treat the boy who is to be born."

[9]God listened to Manoah, and God's messenger came once more to the woman. She was sitting in the field, but her husband Manoah wasn't with her. [10]So the woman hurriedly ran and informed her husband. She said to him, "The man who came to me the other day has just appeared to me."

[11]Manoah got up and followed his wife. He came to the man and said to him, "Are you the man who spoke to this woman?"

"I am," he replied.

[12]Manoah said, "Now when your words come true, what should be the rules for the boy and how he should act?"

[13]The LORD's messenger answered Manoah, "The woman should be careful to do everything that I told her. [14]She must not consume anything that comes from the grapevine, drink wine or brandy, or eat anything that is ritually unclean. She must be careful to do everything I have commanded her."

[15]Manoah said to the LORD's messenger, "Please let us persuade you to stay so we can prepare a young goat for you."

[16]But the LORD's messenger replied to Manoah, "If you persuaded me to stay, I wouldn't eat your food. If you prepare an entirely burned offering, offer it to the LORD."

Indeed, Manoah didn't know that he was the LORD's messenger. [17]Manoah said to the LORD's messenger, "What's your name, so that we may honor you when your words come true?"

[18]The LORD's messenger responded to him, "Why do you ask my name? You couldn't understand it."

[19]So Manoah took a young goat and a grain offering and offered them on a rock to the LORD. While Manoah and his wife were looking, an amazing thing happened: [20]as the flame from the altar went up toward the sky, the LORD's messenger went up in the altar's flame. When Manoah and his wife saw this, they fell facedown on the ground. [21]The LORD's messenger didn't reappear to Manoah or his wife, and Manoah then realized that it had been the LORD's messenger. [22]Manoah said to his wife, "We are certainly going to die, because we've seen God!"

[23]But his wife replied to him, "If the LORD wanted to kill us, he wouldn't have accepted the entirely burned offering and grain offering from our hands. He wouldn't have shown us all these things or told us all of this now."

[24]The woman gave birth to a son and named him Samson. The boy grew up, and the LORD blessed him. [25]The LORD's spirit began to move him when he was in Mahaneh-dan, between Zorah and Eshtaol.

LIFE PRESERVER

Who is the Lord's messenger? *Judges 13*

Samson's mother wasn't able to have a child. Then she was visited by a messenger from God who told her she would have a child. The messenger gave her a long list of instructions to follow during her pregnancy. Everything worked out fine, and Samson was born.

When God wanted to make a connection with someone, God would send a messenger to deliver a personal message. The messenger in Judges 13 was described as a "man of God," which means that God was seen in the form of this messenger. This story is similar to the stories of the birth of Isaac in Genesis and of Samuel in 1 Samuel.

The story of the birth of Samson was told to help the Israelites remember how closely God was involved in their lives, leading and directing them, providing them with leaders and prophets. God was not far away but was close to God's people. ◖

Samson's marriage to a Philistine woman

14 Samson traveled down to Timnah. While he was in Timnah, a Philistine woman caught his eye. ²He went back home and told his father and mother, "A Philistine woman in Timnah caught my eye; now get her for me as a wife!"

³But his father and mother replied to him, "Is there no woman among your own relatives or among all our people that you have to go get a wife from the uncircumcised Philistines?"

Yet Samson said to his father, "Get her for me, because she's the one I want!" ⁴His father and mother didn't know that the LORD was behind this. He was looking for an opening with the Philistines, because they were ruling over Israel at that time.

⁵Then Samson traveled down to Timnah with his father and mother. When he came to the vineyards in Timnah, suddenly a lone young lion came roaring to meet him. ⁶The LORD's spirit rushed over him, and he tore the lion apart with his bare hands as one might tear apart a young goat. But he didn't tell his father or mother what he had done. ⁷Then he traveled down and talked with the woman; she was the one Samson wanted.

⁸After a while, he came back again to marry her. He turned aside to look at the lion's remains, and there was a swarm of bees with honey inside the lion's skeleton. ⁹He scooped the honey into his hands, eating it as he continued along. When he got to his father and mother, he gave some to them, and they ate it too. But he didn't tell them that he had scooped the honey from the lion's skeleton.

¹⁰His father traveled down to the woman, and Samson put on a feast there, as was the custom for young men. ¹¹When the townspeople saw him, they selected thirty companions to be with him. ¹²Then Samson said to them, "Let me tell you a riddle. If you can figure it out and tell me the answer within the seven days of the feast, I'll give you thirty linen robes

God's THOUGHTS ◆ My THOUGHTS

The Price of Disobedience   Judges 14:1–16:22

God can use people for good, even when they don't always follow God's ways. Samson didn't care about the traditions of his people. He lived a wild life of partying and hanging around with the wrong people. However, Samson did keep his hair long, which was a visible part of the promise he had made to God (see Num 6:1-7).

God used Samson to deliver the Israelites from the power of the Philistines. Samson overcame thirty Philistines and took their clothes to pay a wager. He killed a thousand Philistines with the jawbone of a donkey. When the Philistines tried to trap him in Gaza, Samson ripped the doors off the city gate and carried them to the top of a hill.

You may wonder why it's important to follow God's ways if God is willing to use people who disobey. The Bible says that the good time sin brings doesn't last long. This was true for Samson, who eventually paid the price for his disobedience. He fell in love with Delilah, who plotted with the Philistine leaders to discover the secret of his amazing strength. In the end, the once strong and mighty Samson became a blind slave grinding grain.

Think of a time when you did something bad that felt good at the time.

How did you feel later when you had to pay the price for your disobedience?

and thirty sets of clothes. [13]But if you can't tell me the answer, then it's you who have to give me thirty linen robes and thirty sets of clothes."

So they replied to him, "Tell your riddle; let's hear it."

[14]He said to them,

"Out of the eater
there came something to eat.
Out of the strong
there came something sweet."

For three days they couldn't tell the answer to the riddle. [15]On the fourth[j] day they said to Samson's wife, "Seduce your husband so he'll tell us the answer to the riddle, or else we'll set fire to you and your household. Were we invited here just to become poor?"

[16]So Samson's wife cried on his shoulder and said, "You hate me! You don't love me! You told a riddle to my people but didn't tell me the answer."

He replied to her, "Look, I haven't even told the answer to my father and mother. Why should I tell it to you?" [17]But she cried on his shoulder for the rest of the seven days of the feast. Finally, on the seventh day, he told her the answer, for she had nagged him. And she told her people the answer to the riddle. [18]So on the seventh day, before the sun set, the townspeople said to him,

"What's sweeter than honey?
What's stronger than a lion?"

He replied to them,

"If you hadn't plowed with my heifer,
you wouldn't have figured out my riddle!"

[19]Then the LORD's spirit rushed over him, and he went down to Ashkelon. He killed thirty of their men, stripped them of their gear, and gave the sets of clothes to the ones who had told the answer to the riddle. In anger, he went back up to his father's household. [20]And Samson's wife married one of those who had been his companions.

Samson attacks the Philistines

15 Later on, at the time of the wheat harvest, Samson went to visit his wife, bringing along a young goat. He said, "Let me go into my wife's bedroom."

But her father wouldn't allow him to go in. [2]Her father said, "I was so sure that you had completely rejected her that I gave her in marriage to one of your companions. Don't you think her younger sister is even better? Let her be your wife instead."

[3]Samson replied, "No one can blame me now for being ready to bring down trouble on the Philistines!"

[4]Then Samson went and caught three hundred foxes. He took torches, turned the foxes tail to tail, and put a torch between each pair of tails. [5]He lit the torches and released the foxes into the Philistines' grain fields. So he burned the stacked grain, standing grain, vineyards, and olive orchards.

[6]The Philistines inquired, "Who did this?"

So it was reported, "Samson the Timnite's son-in-law did it, because his father-in-law gave his wife in marriage to one of his companions." So the Philistines went up and burned her and her father to death.

[7]Samson then responded to them, "If this is how you act, then I won't stop until I get revenge on you!" [8]He struck them hard, taking their legs right out from under them.[k] Then he traveled down and stayed in a cave in the rock at Etam.

[9]The Philistines marched up, made camp in Judah, and released their forces on Lehi. [10]The people of Judah asked, "Why have you marched up against us?"

"We've marched up to take Samson prisoner," they replied, "and to do to him just what he did to us."

[11]So three thousand people from Judah traveled down to the cave in the rock at Etam and said to Samson, "Don't you realize that the Philistines rule over us? What have you done to us?"

But he told them, "I did to them just what they did to me."

[12]Then the people of Judah said to him, "We've come down to take you prisoner so we can turn you over to the Philistines."

Samson responded to them, "Just promise that you won't attack me yourselves."

[13]"We won't," they said to him. "We'll only take you prisoner so we can turn you over to them. We won't kill you." Then they tied him up with two new ropes, and brought him up from the rock.

Bet you can read this in 3 minutes. **Ready, set, go!**

---

[j]LXX, Syr; MT *seventh* [k]Or *struck them hip and thigh*

[14]When Samson arrived at Lehi, the Philistines met him and came out shouting. The LORD's spirit rushed over him, the ropes on his arms became like burned-up linen, and the ties melted right off his hands. [15]He found a donkey's fresh jawbone, picked it up, and used it to attack one thousand men. [16]Samson said,

"With a donkey's jawbone,
    stacks on stacks!
With a donkey's jawbone,
    I've killed one thousand men."

[17]When he finished speaking, he tossed away the jawbone. So that place became known as Ramath-lehi.[1]

[18]Now Samson was very thirsty, so he called out to the LORD, "You are the one who allowed this great victory to be accomplished by your servant's hands. Am I now going to die of thirst and fall into the hands of the uncircumcised?" [19]So God split open the hollow rock in Lehi, and water flowed out of it. When Samson drank, his energy returned and he was recharged. Thus that place is still called by the name En-hakkore[m] in Lehi today.

[20]Samson led Israel for twenty years during the time of the Philistines.

Samson and the prostitute

16 One day Samson traveled to Gaza. While there, he saw a prostitute and had sex with her. [2]The word spread[n] among the people of Gaza, "Samson has come here!" So they circled around and waited in ambush for him all night at the city gate. They kept quiet all night long, thinking, We'll kill him at the first light in the morning. [3]But Samson slept only half the night. He got up in the middle of the night, grabbed the doors of the city gate and the two gateposts, and pulled them up with the bar still across them. He put them on his shoulders and carried them up to the top of the hill that is beside Hebron.

Samson and Delilah

[4]Some time after this, in the Sorek Valley, Samson fell in love with a woman whose name was Delilah. [5]The rulers of the Philistines confronted her and said to her, "Seduce him and find out what gives him such great strength and what we can do to overpower him, so that we can tie him up and make him weak. Then we'll each pay you eleven hundred pieces of silver."

[6]So Delilah said to Samson, "Please tell me what gives you such great strength and how you can be tied up and made weak."

[7]Samson replied to her, "If someone ties me up with seven fresh bowstrings that aren't dried out, I'll become weak. I'll be like any other person." [8]So the rulers of the Philistines brought her seven fresh bowstrings that weren't dried out, and she tied him up with them.

[9]While an ambush was waiting for her signal in an inner room, she called out to him, "Samson, the Philistines are on you!" And he snapped the bowstrings like a thread of fiber snaps when it touches a flame. So the secret of his strength remained unknown.

[10]Then Delilah said to Samson, "You made a fool out of me and lied to me. Now please tell me how you can really be tied up!"

[11]He replied to her, "If someone ties me up with new ropes that haven't been used for work, I'll become weak. I'll be like any other person."

[12]So Delilah took new ropes and tied him up with them. Then she called out to him, "Samson, the Philistines are on you!" Once again, an ambush was waiting in an inner room. Yet he snapped them from his arms like thread.

[13]And Delilah said to Samson, "Up to now, you've made a fool out of me and lied to me. Tell me how you can be tied up!"

He responded to her, "If you weave the seven braids of my hair into the fabric on a loom and pull it tight with a pin, then I'll become weak. I'll be like any other person."[o]

[14]So she got him to fall asleep, wove the seven braids of his hair into the fabric on a loom,[p] and pulled it tight with a pin. Then she called out to him, "Samson, the Philistines are on you!" He woke up from his sleep and pulled loose the pin, the loom, and the fabric.

[15]Delilah said to him, "How can you say, 'I love you,' when you won't trust me? Three

---

[1]Or *Jawbone Hill* [m]Or *Caller's Spring* [n]LXX; MT lacks *spread*. [o]LXX; MT lacks *and pull it… other person.* [p]LXX; MT lacks *so she got him… on a loom.*

times now you've made a fool out of me and not told me what gives you such great strength!" ¹⁶She nagged him with her words day after day and begged him until he became worn out to the point of death.

¹⁷So he told her his whole secret. He said to her, "No razor has ever touched my head, because I've been a nazirite for God from the time I was born. If my head is shaved, my strength will leave me, and I'll become weak. I'll be like every other person."

¹⁸When Delilah realized that he had told her his whole secret, she sent word to the rulers of the Philistines, "Come one more time, for he has told me his whole secret." The rulers of the Philistines came up to her and brought the silver with them.

¹⁹She got him to fall asleep with his head on her lap. Then she called a man and had him shave off the seven braids of Samson's hair. He began to weaken,^q and his strength left him. ²⁰She called out, "Samson, the Philistines are on you!"

He woke up from his sleep and thought, I'll escape just like the other times and shake myself free. But he didn't realize that the Lord had left him. ²¹So the Philistines captured him, put out his eyes, and took him down to Gaza. They bound him with bronze chains, and he worked the grinding mill in the prison.

²²But the hair on his head began to grow again right after it had been shaved.

Samson's death

²³The rulers of the Philistines gathered together to make a great sacrifice to their god Dagon and to hold a celebration. They cheered, "Our god has handed us Samson our enemy!" ²⁴When the people saw him, they praised their god, for they said, "Our god has handed us our enemy, the very one who devastated our land

UMBRELLA
PRIDE

Spiritual Strength Beats Physical
Judges 16:4-21

Samson thought he had it all under control. Samson was the strongest man alive. He tore a lion in half (Judg 14:5-6). He killed one thousand men with a donkey's jawbone (Judg 15:14-17). Samson even carried off the gates of a town (Judg 16:1-3)! Samson was physically very strong. But spiritually he was weak. Samson's enemies offered Delilah a fistful of money if she could discover the secret of Samson's strength. After several failures, Delilah finally heard Samson's secret from his own lips. Samson had forgotten that his great strength was from God. He had come to believe that his great feats were his own doing—that his long hair had nothing to do with his power. Why else would he admit his secret to someone who had already betrayed him twice? Samson's pride cost him his strength and his freedom. ♦

and killed so many of our people." ²⁵At the height of the celebration,^r they said, "Call for Samson so he can perform for us!" So they called Samson from the prison, and he performed in front of them. Then they had him stand between the pillars.

²⁶Samson said to the young man who led him by the hand, "Put me where I can feel the pillars that hold up the temple, so I can lean on them." ²⁷Now the temple was filled with men and women. All the rulers of the Philistines were there, and about three thousand more men and women were on the roof watching as Samson performed. ²⁸Then Samson called out to the Lord, "Lord God, please remember me! Make me strong just this once more, God, so I can have revenge on the Philistines, just one act of revenge for my two eyes."^s ²⁹Samson grabbed the two central pillars that held up the temple. He leaned against one with his right hand and the other with his left. ³⁰And Samson said, "Let me die with the Philistines!" He strained with all his might, and the temple collapsed on the rulers and all the people who were in it. So it turned out that he killed

did you know? The strength Samson needed to push down the columns holding up the building where he was held by his enemies would have been about the same as the force of two oxen. That's a lot of strength that God gave Samson to help him protect his people from their enemies!

^qLXX; MT *she began to torment him.* ^rOr *When their hearts were glad* ^sor *so I can have revenge on the Philistines for one of my two eyes*

more people in his death than he did during his life.

³¹His brothers and his father's entire household traveled down, carried him back up, and buried him between Zorah and Eshtaol in the tomb of his father Manoah. He had led Israel for twenty years.

Micah's sanctuary and the Levite priest

17Once there was a man named Micah who lived in the Ephraim highlands. ²He said to his mother, "The eleven hundred pieces of silver that were taken from you led you to declare a curse and even to repeat it when I could hear. I have that silver. I'm the one who took it, and now I'll give it back to you."ᵗ

His mother replied, "May the LORD bless you, my son!" ³When he gave the eleven hundred pieces of silver back to his mother, she said, "I wholeheartedly devote this silver to the LORD, to be made into a sculpted image and a molded image for my son." ⁴So he gave the silver back to his mother, and she took two hundred pieces of silver and gave them to a silversmith, who used it for a sculpted image and a molded image. And they were placed in Micah's house. ⁵This man Micah had his own sanctuary.ᵘ He made a priestly vestᵛ and divine imagesʷ and appointed one of his sons to be his personal priest. ⁶In those days there was no king in Israel; each person did what they thought to be right.

⁷Now there was a young man from Bethlehem in Judah, from the area of the Judahite clan. He was a Levite residing there as an immigrant. ⁸The man left the town of Bethlehem in Judah to settle as an immigrant wherever he could find a place. He came to Micah's house in the Ephraim highlands while he was making his way.ˣ

⁹"Where are you from?" Micah asked him.

He replied, "I'm a Levite from Bethlehem in Judah, and I'm looking to settle as an immigrant anywhere I can find a place."

¹⁰So Micah said to him, "Stay with me and be a father and a priest to me, and I'll give you ten pieces of silver a year, a set of clothes, and your basic needs."ʸ ¹¹The Levite agreed to stay with him; and the young man became like one of his own sons. ¹²Micah appointed the Levite so that the young man became his personal priest and lived in Micah's sanctuary. ¹³And Micah said to himself, Now I know that the LORD will give me good things, because a Levite has become my priest.

UMBRELLA
LYING

You Can't Fool God *Judges 17:13*

Micah was cursed by his mother. Someone had stolen her silver. She didn't know her own son was the thief. Frightened, Micah quickly returned the silver, which was good. But his mother had the silver made into images for worship, which was bad (Exod 20:4-5). Then Micah made his own sanctuary and found someone to be his own personal priest, both of which were against God's Instruction (Deut 12:1-14; Num 18:1-7). All of Micah's bad actions began with dishonesty—Micah stealing from his mother. Worst of all, Micah thought God would do all sorts of good for him despite all his bad actions. Micah was being lied to himself and God. Micah thought God would forget his failures to meet God's standards for worship. But God doesn't reward disobedience, and God didn't give Micah good things (Judg 18:14-26). ◆

Dan's search for a land

18In those days there was no king in Israel. Also in those days the tribe of Dan was searching for a territory of their own to live in, since no permanent territory had been assigned to them among the tribes of Israel up to that point. ²The Danites sent five men from their whole clan, strong men from Zorah and Eshtaol, to spy on the land and explore it. They told them, "Go explore the land." So they went into the Ephraim highland as far as Micah's house, and they spent the night there. ³When they were in the area of Micah's house, they recognized the accent of the young Levite. They turned in there and said to him, "Who brought you here? What are you doing in these parts? What is there for you here?"

ᵗThe words *and now I'll give it back to you* are relocated from the end of 17:3 in Heb. ᵘOr *god's house* ᵛHeb *ephod* ʷHeb *terafim* ˣOr *to carry on his work* ʸHeb adds *and the Levite went.*

[4]"Micah has done a lot for me," he replied to them. "He hired me to be his personal priest."

[5]They said to him, "Ask for an answer from God so we can know whether we'll be successful on this trip we've taken."

[6]The priest replied to them, "Go in peace. The Lord is watching over you on this trip you've taken."

[7]So the five men journeyed on until they reached Laish. There they saw that its people were living without worry in the same way as the Sidonians, undisturbed and secure. Nobody held back anything in the land, so no one had to hoard.[z] Yet they lived far away from the Sidonians and had no dealings with anyone else.[a]

[8]When the men came back to their relatives at Zorah and Eshtaol, they asked them, "What did you find?"

[9]"Come on," they replied, "let's march up against them! Indeed, we've seen the land, and it's very good. Right now you're doing nothing! Don't hold back from going and taking possession of the land. [10]When you arrive, you'll come upon a secure people and a wide-open land, because God has given to you a place where nothing on earth is lacking."

[11]At this, six hundred men from the Danite clan at Zorah and Eshtaol set out armed for battle. [12]They marched up and made camp at Kiriath-jearim in Judah. This is why the place west of Kiriath-jearim is still known as Dan's Camp today. [13]From there they crossed into the Ephraim highlands and came to Micah's house.

Dan acquires a levitical priest

[14]Then the five men who had gone to spy on the land around Laish reported to their relatives, "Did you know that there is a priestly vest, divine images, a sculpted image, and a molded image in these buildings? Now think about what you should do!" [15]So they turned in there and went to the young Levite's house in Micah's compound and greeted him. [16]While the six hundred Danites armed for battle stood at the entrance of the gate, [17]the five men who had gone to spy on the land moved up, went inside, and took the sculpted image, the priestly vest, the divine images, and

the molded image. The priest was standing at the entrance of the gate with the six hundred men armed for battle [18]when these five entered Micah's sanctuary and took the sculpted image, the priestly vest, the divine images, and the molded image.

The priest said to them, "What are you doing?"

[19]"Shut up!" they said to him. "Put your hand over your mouth! Come with us and be a father and a priest for us. Would you rather be a priest for one man's household or a priest for a tribe and a clan in Israel?" [20]The priest was convinced, so he took the priestly vest, the divine images, and the sculpted image and went along with the people.

[21]They headed back on their way, but they put the children, the livestock, and the prized possessions in front of them. [22]After they had gone a good distance away from Micah's house, the men who were in the houses around Micah's home were summoned for battle and caught up to the Danites. [23]They called out to the Danites, who turned around and said to Micah, "Why have you summoned men for battle?"

[24]Micah replied, "You've taken my gods that I made, and the priest, and have gone off! What do I have left? How can you ask me what is wrong?"

[25]But the Danites said to him, "Don't raise your voice with us or else hotheaded men will attack you, and you and your household will lose your lives." [26]Then the Danites went on their way. When Micah realized that they were too strong for him, he turned around and went home.

The Danites take possession of Laish

[27]The Danites took along the things that Micah had made, as well as the priest who had been with him, and came to Laish, to a people who were undisturbed and secure. They killed the people and burned down the city. [28]No one was there to rescue them because the city was far away from Sidon and had no dealings with anyone else.[b] It was in the Beth-rehob Valley.

They rebuilt the city and settled in it. [29]They renamed the city Dan, after their

[z]Heb uncertain [a]Or with Aram [b]Or with Aram

ancestor Dan who had been one of Israel's sons; but in fact, the original name of the city was Laish. ³⁰The Danites set up the sculpted image for themselves, and Jonathan son of Gershom and grandson of Moses,ᶜ and his sons became priests for the Danite tribe until the land went into exile. ³¹They kept for themselves the sculpted image that Micah had made throughout the whole time that God's sanctuary was in Shiloh.

A Levite, a woman, and her father

19In those days when there was no king in Israel, there was a certain Levite living as an immigrant in the far corners of the Ephraim highlands. He married a secondary wife from Bethlehem in Judah. ²In an act of unfaithfulness toward him, his secondary wife left him and went back to her father's household at Bethlehem in Judah. She stayed there four full months. ³Then her husband set out after her to convince her to come back. He had his servant and a couple of donkeys with him. She took him into her father's house, and when the young woman's father saw him, he was happy to welcome him. ⁴Since his father-in-law, the young woman's father, insisted, he stayed with him three days, eating, drinking, and spending the night there.

⁵On the fourth day, they got up early in the morning, and he got ready to set out. But the young woman's father said to his son-in-law, "Eat a little food to give you strength, and then you can go." ⁶So the two of them sat down and ate and drank together. The young woman's father said to the man, "Why not spend the night and enjoy yourself?" ⁷When the man got ready to set out, his father-in-law persuaded him, and he spent the night there again. ⁸On the fifth day, he got up early in the morning to set out, and the young woman's father said, "Have some food for strength." So the two of them ate, sitting around until late in the day. ⁹When the man got ready to set out with his secondary wife and servant, his father-in-law, the young woman's father, said, "Look, the day has turned to evening, so spend the night. Seriously, the day is over. Spend the night here and enjoy yourself. Then you can get up early tomorrow for your journey, and you can head home."

¹⁰But the man was unwilling to spend another night. He got up, set out, and went as far as the area of Jebus, that is, Jerusalem. He had a couple of saddled donkeys and his secondary wife with him. ¹¹When they were near Jebus, the day was totally gone. The servant said to his master, "Come on, let's turn into this Jebusite city and spend the night in it."

¹²But his master replied to him, "We won't turn into a city of foreigners who aren't Israelites. We'll travel on to Gibeah. ¹³"Come on," he said to his servant, "let's reach Gibeah or Ramah and spend the night in one of those places." ¹⁴So they traveled on, and the sun set when they were near Gibeah in Benjamin. ¹⁵They turned in to enter there, so they could spend the night in Gibeah, and he went and sat down in the city square. But no one offered to take them home to spend the night.

Rape and murder at Gibeah

¹⁶Then in the evening, an old man was coming home from his daily work in the fields. This man was from the Ephraim highlands and was an immigrant in Gibeah, the people of that place being Benjaminites. ¹⁷He looked up and saw the traveler in the city square. "Where are you heading and where have you come from?" the old man asked.

¹⁸"We're traveling from Bethlehem in Judah to the far corners of the Ephraim highlands," he replied to the old man. "That's where I'm from. I went to Bethlehem in Judah, and I'm heading to my home.ᵈ But no one has offered to take me in tonight. ¹⁹We've got our own straw and feed for our donkeys, plus food and wine to provide for me, the woman, and my servant with us. We don't need anything."

²⁰The old man answered, "You're welcome to stay with me,ᵉ but let me take care of all your needs. Just don't spend the night in the square." ²¹And he took him into his house. He mixed feed for the donkeys, and they washed their feet, ate, and drank.

²²While they were relaxing, suddenly the men of the city, a perverse bunch, surrounded the house and started pounding on the door. They said to the old man, the owner of the house, "Send out the man who came to your house, so we can have sex with him!"

ᶜOr *Manasseh* ᵈLXX; MT *to the* Lᴏʀᴅ's *house* ᵉOr *Peace be with you*

²³The owner of the house went outside and said to them, "No, my friends, please don't commit such an evil act, given that this man has come to my home as a guest. Don't do this disgraceful thing! ²⁴Here's my daughter, the young woman, and his secondary wife. Let me send them out, and you can abuse them and do whatever you want to them. But don't do such a disgraceful thing to this man!" ²⁵But the men refused to listen to him.

So the Levite grabbed his secondary wife and sent her outside to them. They raped her and abused her all night long until morning. They finally let her go as dawn was breaking. ²⁶At daybreak, the woman came and collapsed at the door of the man's house where her husband was staying, where she lay until it was daylight. ²⁷When her husband got up in the morning, he opened the doors of the house and went outside to set out on his journey. And there was his secondary wife, lying at the entrance of the house, with her hands clutching the doorframe. ²⁸"Get up," he said to her, "let's go." But there was no response. So he laid her across a donkey, and the man set out for home. ²⁹When he got home, he picked up a knife, took his secondary wife, and chopped her, limb by limb, into twelve pieces. Then he sent them into all the areas of Israel. ³⁰Everyone who saw it said, "Has such a thing ever happened or been seen since the time when the Israelites came up from the land of Egypt until today? Think about it, decide what to do, and speak out!"

Civil war between the Benjaminites and the Israelites

20 Then all the Israelites from Dan to Beer-sheba, as well as from the area of Gilead, marched out, and the group assembled as one body in the Lord's presence at Mizpah. ²The commanders of the people and of all the tribes of Israel took their place in the assembly of God's people, four hundred thousand foot soldiers armed with swords. ³And the Benjaminites got word that the Israelites had marched up to Mizpah.

The Israelites inquired, "Tell us how this evil act happened."

⁴So the Levite, the husband of the murdered woman, answered, "My secondary wife and I came to Gibeah of Benjamin to spend the night, ⁵and the leading citizens of Gibeah tried to attack me. They surrounded me in the house at night and were determined to kill me. They abused my secondary wife until she died. ⁶I took her, chopped her up, and sent her pieces into every part of Israel's territory, because they had committed a disgraceful act in Israel. ⁷All you Israelites, say what you think should be done here and now!"

⁸At this, all the people stood as one to say, "Not a single one of us is going home or returning to our house! ⁹This is what we're now going to do to Gibeah: We'll march up[f] against it as the lot determines. ¹⁰From all the tribes of Israel, we'll get ten men for every hundred, one hundred for every thousand, and one thousand for every ten thousand to take supplies for the troops who are going to pay back[g] Gibeah of Benjamin for the disgraceful act they've done in Israel." ¹¹So all the Israelites joined together and were united as one against the city.

¹²The Israelite tribes sent men throughout the whole tribe of Benjamin with this message: "What about this evil act that happened among you? ¹³Now hand over those perverse men in Gibeah so that we can execute them and remove the evil from Israel." But the Benjaminites refused to comply with the demand of their own relatives the Israelites. ¹⁴Instead, the Benjaminites from all the cities came together at Gibeah to march out for battle against the Israelites. ¹⁵On that day, the Benjaminites called up from their cities twenty-six thousand men armed with swords, not counting those living in Gibeah.[h] ¹⁶Out of this entire army, seven hundred specially chosen

---

[f] LXX; MT lacks *We'll march up.* [g] Cf LXX; Heb uncertain [h] LXX, Vulg, Syr; MT adds *seven hundred specially chosen men were called up.*

men were left-handed, and every one of them could sling a stone at a hair and not miss. [17]Not counting Benjamin, the Israelites called up four hundred thousand men armed with swords, and every one of them was a trained warrior.

[18]Then the Israelites marched up to Bethel to ask for direction from God. They inquired, "Who should go up first to fight against the Benjaminites for us?"

And the Lord said, "Let the tribe of Judah be first."

[19]So the next morning, the Israelites got up and camped near Gibeah. [20]They marched out to fight against the Benjaminites, lining up in battle formation against them at Gibeah. [21]But the Benjaminites marched out from Gibeah and cut down twenty-two thousand Israelite men that day.

[23i] So the Israelites went back up and wept before the Lord until evening. They asked the Lord, "Should we move in again to fight our relatives the Benjaminites?"

And the Lord replied, "March out against them."

[22]The Israelite troops regrouped and lined up in battle formation again in the same place they had lined up the first day. [24]The Israelites moved in against the Benjaminites the second day. [25]But the Benjaminites marched out of Gibeah to meet them on that second day and cut down another eighteen thousand Israelite men, all of whom were armed with swords.

[26]Then all the Israelite troops went back up to Bethel and wept, just sitting there in the Lord's presence. They fasted that whole day until evening. Then they offered entirely burned offerings and well-being sacrifices to the Lord. [27]Now in those days the chest containing God's covenant was there, [28]and Phinehas, Eleazar's son and Aaron's grandson, was in charge of ministering before it. The Israelites asked the Lord, "Should we march out once again to fight our relatives the Benjaminites or should we give up?"

And the Lord replied, "March up, for I'll hand them to you tomorrow."

[29]So the Israelites set ambushes around Gibeah. [30]Three days later, the Israelites marched out against the Benjaminites. They lined up for battle against Gibeah as before. [31]When the Benjaminites came out to meet them, they were drawn away from the city. They began to strike down some of the troops just like the last time, about thirty Israelites along the main roads, one of which goes up to Bethel and one to Gibeah, as well as in the open fields. [32]The Benjaminites thought, They're being wiped out before us like the first time. But the Israelites had planned, We'll retreat and draw them away from the city toward the main roads. [33]The Israelites moved from their position and reformed their battle lines at Baal-tamar. Then the Israelites who had been set in ambush charged out from their positions west of Gibeah.[j] [34]Ten thousand specially chosen men from all the Israelites came against Gibeah. The fighting was fierce, and the Benjaminites didn't realize that disaster was almost on them. [35]The Lord wiped out the Benjaminites before Israel. The Israelites slaughtered twenty-five thousand one hundred Benjaminite men that day, all of them armed with swords. [36]Then the Benjaminites saw that they had been defeated.

The Israelites had given ground to the Benjaminites because they relied on the ambush that they had set around Gibeah. [37]Indeed, those in the ambush had dashed swiftly into Gibeah and killed all the people in the city with their swords. [38]The plan between the main force of the Israelites and those in the ambush was that when they sent up a big cloud of smoke from the city, [39]the Israelites would turn around in battle. The Benjaminites had begun to defeat some of the Israelites and had killed about thirty men, thinking, They are definitely going to be wiped out before us, as in the first battle! [40]But then the column of smoke began to rise from the city. When the Benjaminites looked back, there was the entire city going up in smoke to the sky. [41]The main force of the Israelites turned around, and the Benjaminites lost heart, because they recognized that disaster had fallen on them. [42]They turned back before the Israelites in the direction of the desert, but the fighting caught up with them, and those from the

---

i20:22 and 20:23 are reversed. jHeb *Geba*

towns were slaughtering them there.^k ^43They encircled the Benjaminites, chased them from Nohah,^l and trampled them to the east of Gibeah. ^44Eighteen thousand Benjaminites fell, all of whom were strong warriors. ^45When they turned back and fled toward the desert to the rock of Rimmon, the Israelites picked off another five thousand men on the main roads. And when they caught up with them at Gidom, they struck down two thousand more.

^46All in all, the total number of Benjaminites who fell that day was twenty-five thousand men, all of whom were armed with swords and were strong warriors. ^47Six hundred men turned back and fled toward the desert to the rock of Rimmon. They stayed at the rock of Rimmon for four months. ^48But the Israelites turned their attention to the rest of the Benjaminites and massacred them entirely—the city, the people, even the animals, and everything else they found. They also burned down every city they came across.

LIFE PRESERVER

How can we understand scary stories of kidnapping, violence, and trading of people? *Judges 19–21*

Some stories in the Bible are very hard for us to understand. There are tales of kidnapping, violence against women, and trading of women like they are pieces of property. However, some women are held in high honor. They are leaders like Deborah. They took charge, and they are respected.

But by the end of the book of Judges, women had become property, traded so that the men in the tribe of Benjamin would have wives. They were stolen and abused. These chapters really show the worst behaviors people can exhibit.

Notice how the chapter ends: "In those days there was no king in Israel; each person did what they thought to be right." A great nation had become a collection of individuals who cared more about themselves than following God's ways, to love God and live in harmony with other people. ◈

Wives for the Benjaminites

21 The Israelites had made a pledge at Mizpah, declaring, "None of us will allow his daughter to marry a Benjaminite." ^2But the people came to Bethel and sat there until evening before God, raising their voices and crying bitterly. ^3"Lord, God of Israel," they said, "why has this happened among us that as of today one tribe will be missing from Israel?" ^4And the next day, the people got up early and built an altar there. They offered entirely burned offerings and well-being sacrifices.

^5Then the Israelites asked, "Were there any out of all the tribes of Israel who didn't march up to the assembly before the Lord?" Indeed, they had made a solemn pledge that anyone who didn't march up before the Lord at Mizpah would be put to death. ^6The Israelites had a change of heart concerning their relatives the Benjaminites. They said, "Today one tribe has been cut off from Israel. ^7What can we do to provide wives for the ones who are left, since we ourselves have made a pledge before the Lord not to allow our daughters to marry them?" ^8So they asked, "Is there anyone from the tribes of Israel who didn't march up before the Lord at Mizpah?" There was! No one from Jabesh-gilead had come to the assembly at the camp. ^9When the people's attendance was taken, not one of those who lived in Jabesh-gilead had been there.

^10The community dispatched twelve thousand warriors there with these orders: "Go kill all the people in Jabesh-gilead, including women and children. ^11Here's what you should do: Exterminate every man and every woman who has slept with a man." ^12Among the people of Jabesh-gilead, they found four hundred young women who had not known a man intimately or slept with one, and they brought them to the camp at Shiloh in the land of Canaan. ^13The whole community then sent word to the Benjaminites who were at the rock of Rimmon and offered them a truce.^m ^14So the Benjaminites returned at that time, and they gave them the women from Jabesh-gilead that they had allowed to live. Even so, there weren't enough for them.

^15Since the people had a change of heart concerning the Benjaminites because the Lord had caused a rupture in the tribes of

---

^k Heb uncertain ^l LXX; MT *to a resting place* ^m Or *peace*

Israel, ¹⁶the community elders said, "What can we do to provide wives for the ones who are left, seeing that the Benjaminite women have been destroyed? ¹⁷There must be a surviving line for those who remain from Benjamin," they continued, "so that a tribe won't be erased from Israel. ¹⁸But we can't allow our daughters to marry them, for we Israelites have made this pledge: 'Let anyone who provides a wife for Benjamin be cursed!' ¹⁹However," they said, "the annual festival of the Lᴏʀᴅ is under way in Shiloh, which is north of Bethel, east of the main road that goes up from Bethel to Shechem, and south of Lebonah." ²⁰So they instructed the Benjaminites, "Go and hide like an ambush in the vineyards ²¹and watch. At the moment the women of Shiloh come out to participate in the dances, rush out from the vineyards. Each one of you, capture a wife for

yourself from the women of Shiloh and go back to the land of Benjamin. ²²When their fathers or brothers come to us to object, we'll tell them, 'Do us a favor for their sake. We didn't capture enough women for every man during the battle, and this way you are not guilty because you didn't give them anything willingly.'" ²³And that is what the Benjaminites did. They took wives for their whole group from the dancers whom they abducted. They returned to their territory, rebuilt the cities, and lived in them. ²⁴Likewise, the Israelites set out from there at that time, heading home to their respective tribes and clans. They all left there for their own territories.

²⁵In those days there was no king in Israel; each person did what they thought to be right.

Memorize Judg 21:25

The Benefit of God's Instruction   *Judges 21:25*

It's easy to think that life would be wonderful if we could do what we wanted when we wanted to do it. We may dream about sleeping in as long as we want, playing as long as we want, and eating whatever we want. We may long for a time when we don't have to do what someone else tells us to do.

This might sound wonderful, but what would happen if other people only did what they wanted to do? What if someone wanted to take your bike or gaming system? What if they wanted to take your parents' car or money? What if they wanted to hurt you or someone you loved?

Parents, teachers, other leaders, and governments set up ways to live and communicate so that life is better for people as a whole. In the time of the judges, the people of Israel forgot about God's Instruction. Since there wasn't a king or other leader to create a way of life that applied to everyone in Israel, each person did what they thought was right. Instead of making life wonderful for everyone, this nearly destroyed the Israelites. It would have been better for them to follow God's Instruction.

Think of a law that makes your life better.

Pray for leaders who help to create laws.

Ruth

The book of Ruth tells us how families take care of each other. The story takes place in the days when Israel had tribal leaders, before Israel had a king. Naomi and her husband Elimelech faced famine and hunger in Israel. So they left their home and traveled to the land of Moab to find food. While they were in Moab, their two sons married women from that country.

Eventually, Elimelech died. Then his two sons died. Their three wives were left alone with no family to care for them. In those days it would have been very hard for these women to provide for themselves apart from a family.

Naomi decided to return home to Israel, and Ruth wanted to go with her. Naomi told Ruth to remain with her own people in Moab, but Ruth promised to stay with Naomi no matter what happened. Ruth vowed that Naomi's God would now be her God.

In this book we learn how God led Ruth to a kind man, Boaz, who cared for her and Naomi. At the end of this story, Boaz and Ruth get married. Her story shows us how to be loyal and loving! ◗

The family in Moab

1 During the days when the judges ruled, there was a famine in the land. A man with his wife and two sons went from Bethlehem of Judah to dwell in the territory of Moab. [2] The name of that man was Elimelech, the name of his wife was Naomi, and the names of his two sons were Mahlon and Chilion. They were Ephrathites from Bethlehem in Judah. They entered the territory of Moab and settled there.

[3] But Elimelech, Naomi's husband, died. Then only she was left, along with her two sons. [4] They took wives for themselves, Moabite women; the name of the first was Orpah and the name of the second was Ruth. And they lived there for about ten years.

[5] But both of the sons, Mahlon and Chilion, also died. Only the woman was left, without her two children and without her husband.

[6] Then she arose along with her daughters-in-law to return from the field of Moab, because while in the territory of Moab she had heard that the Lord had paid attention to his people by providing food for them. [7] She left the place where she had been, and her two daughters-in-law went with her. They went along the road to return to the land of Judah.

[8] Naomi said to her daughters-in-law, "Go, turn back, each of you to the household of your mother. May the Lord deal faithfully with you, just as you have done with the dead and with me. [9] May the Lord provide for you so that you may find security, each woman in the household of her husband." Then she kissed them, and they lifted up their voices and wept.

[10] But they replied to her, "No, instead we will return with you, to your people."

[11] Naomi replied, "Turn back, my daughters. Why would you go with me? Will there again be sons in my womb, that they would be husbands for you? [12] Turn back, my daughters. Go. I am too old for a husband. If I were to say that I have hope, even if I had a husband tonight, and even more, if I were to bear sons— [13] would you wait until they grew up? Would you refrain from having a husband? No, my daughters. This is more bitter for me than for you, since the Lord's will has come out against me."

LIFE PRESERVER

Why would Naomi talk about Orpah and Ruth marrying any new sons she had? *Ruth 1:11-13*

After her husband died, Naomi planned to travel home to Judah. She knew that her sons' wives, Orpah and Ruth, would face challenges as widows. So Naomi encouraged them to stay in Moab and go home to their families. When Naomi told them to go back to the households of their mothers, she was encouraging them to find new husbands who would take care of them.

In the culture in which they lived, the only way that a woman could expect to have a good life and have shelter and food was to be married. Naomi knew that she couldn't provide another marriage for either of her daughters-in-law. She had no more sons they could marry and wouldn't have any more children herself. Naomi wanted the best future possible for Orpah and Ruth. ◗

---

[14] Then they lifted up their voices and wept again. Orpah kissed her mother-in-law, but Ruth stayed with her. [15] Naomi said, "Look, your sister-in-law is returning to her people and to her gods. Turn back after your sister-in-law."

[16] But Ruth replied, **Memorize Ruth 1:16** "Don't urge me to abandon you, to turn back from following after you. Wherever you go, I will go; and wherever you stay, I will stay. Your people will be my people, and your God will be my God. [17] Wherever you die, I will die, and there I will be buried. May the Lord do this to me and more so if even death separates me from you." [18] When Naomi saw that Ruth was determined to go with her, she stopped speaking to her about it.

[19] So both of them went along until they arrived at Bethlehem. When they arrived at Bethlehem, the whole town was excited on account of them, and the women of the town asked, "Can this be Naomi?"

[20] She replied to them, "Don't call me Naomi,[a] but call me Mara,[b] for the Almighty[c] has made me very bitter. [21] I went away full, but the Lord has returned me empty. Why

---

[a] Naomi means *pleasant*. [b] Mara means *bitter*. [c] Heb *El Shaddai* or *God of the Mountain*

would you call me Naomi, when the Lᴏʀᴅ has testified against me, and the Almighty has deemed me guilty?"

²²Thus Naomi returned. And Ruth the Moabite, her daughter-in-law, returned with her from the territory of Moab. They arrived in Bethlehem at the beginning of the barley harvest.

Gleaning in Bethlehem

2 Now Naomi had a respected relative, a man of worth, through her husband from the family of Elimelech. His name was Boaz. ²Ruth the Moabite said to Naomi, "Let me go to the field so that I may glean among the ears of grain behind someone in whose eyes I might find favor."

Naomi replied to her, "Go, my daughter." ³So she went; she arrived and she gleaned in the field behind the harvesters. By chance, it happened to be the portion of the field that belonged to Boaz, who was from the family of Elimelech.

⁴Just then Boaz arrived from Bethlehem. He said to the harvesters, "May the Lᴏʀᴅ be with you."

And they said to him, "May the Lᴏʀᴅ bless you."

⁵Boaz said to his young man, the one who was overseeing the harvesters, "To whom does this young woman belong?"

⁶The young man who was overseeing the harvesters answered, "She's a young Moabite woman, the one who returned with Naomi from the territory of Moab. ⁷She said, 'Please let me glean so that I might gather up grain from among the bundles behind the harvesters.' She arrived and has been on her feet from the morning until now, and has sat down for only a moment."ᵈ

⁸Boaz said to Ruth, "Haven't you understood, my daughter? Don't go glean in another field; don't go anywhere else. Instead, stay here with my young women. ⁹Keep your eyes on the field that they are harvesting and go along after them. I've ordered the young men not to assault you. Whenever you are thirsty, go to the jugs and drink from what the young men have filled."

¹⁰Then she bowed down, face to the ground, and replied to him, "How is it that I've found favor in your eyes, that you notice me? I'm an immigrant." ¹¹Boaz responded to her, "Everything that you did for your mother-in-law after your husband's death has been reported fully to me: how you left behind your father, your mother, and the land of your birth, and came to a people you hadn't known beforehand. ¹²May the Lᴏʀᴅ reward youᵉ for your deed. May you receive a rich reward from the Lᴏʀᴅ, the God of Israel, under whose wings you've come to seek refuge." ¹³She said, "May I continue to find favor in your eyes, sir, because you've comforted me and because you've spoken kindly to your female servant—even though I'm not one of your female servants."

¹⁴At mealtime Boaz said to her, "Come over here, eat some of the bread, and dip your piece in the vinegar." She sat alongside the harvesters, and he served roasted grain to her. She ate, was satisfied, and had leftovers. ¹⁵Then she got up to glean.

Boaz ordered his young men, "Let her glean between the bundles, and don't humiliate her. ¹⁶Also, pull out some from the bales for her and leave them behind for her to glean. And don't scold her."

Bet you can read this in 5 minutes. Ready, set, go!

SAILBOAT

Kindness

Kindness Brings Kindness *Ruth 2:8-9*

Ruth was a kind woman. When her husband died, Ruth followed her mother-in-law, Naomi, back to Israel. Ruth did this because she loved Naomi and wanted to help her. As an immigrant—someone who moves from one country to live in another—Ruth could have been treated very badly. There are always people who will mistreat those who are viewed as outsiders. But Ruth was ready to risk this challenge to help Naomi. Boaz was a kind man. Boaz had heard of Ruth's kindness to Naomi and was impressed. When he found Ruth gathering the grain dropped by harvesters in his field, he made sure his workers treated her well. ◗

ᵈHeb uncertain ᵉLXX

¹⁷So she gleaned in the field until evening. Then she threshed what she had gleaned; it was about an ephah[f] of barley. ¹⁸She picked it up and went into town. Her mother-in-law saw what she had gleaned. She brought out what she had left over after eating her fill and gave it to her. ¹⁹Her mother-in-law said to her, "Where did you glean today? Where did you work? May the one who noticed you be blessed."

She told her mother-in-law with whom she had worked and said, "The name of the man with whom I worked today is Boaz."

²⁰Naomi replied to her daughter-in-law, "May he be blessed by the Lord, who hasn't abandoned his faithfulness with the living or with the dead." Naomi said to her, "The man is one of our close relatives; he's one of our redeemers."

²¹Ruth the Moabite replied, "Furthermore, he said to me, 'Stay with my workers until they've finished all of my harvest.'"

²²Naomi said to Ruth her daughter-in-law, "It's good, my daughter, that you go out with his young women, so that men don't assault you in another field."

²³Thus she stayed with Boaz's young women, gleaning until the completion of the barley and wheat harvests. And she lived with her mother-in-law.

Encounter at the threshing floor

3 Naomi her mother-in-law said to her, "My daughter, shouldn't I seek security for you, so that things might go well for you? ²Now isn't Boaz, whose young women you were with, our relative? Tonight he will be winnowing barley at the threshing floor. ³You should bathe, put on some perfume, wear nice clothes, and then go down to the threshing floor. Don't make yourself known to the man until he has finished eating and drinking. ⁴When he lies down, notice the place where he is lying. Then go, uncover his feet, and lie down. And he will tell you what to do."

⁵Ruth replied to her, "I'll do everything you are telling me."

⁶So she went down to the threshing floor, and she did everything just as her mother-in-law had ordered.

LIFE PRESERVER

What is a redeemer, and why is a redeemer important? Ruth 3:1-13

The words *redeem* and *redeemer* are used many times in the book of Ruth. As a widow, Ruth had no place, no rights, and no security. As a way to provide for Ruth, Naomi sent her to Boaz, who she thought could help. Boaz was a relative, or redeemer. Ruth went to Boaz, who told her that he really was a relative of hers. He also promised that he would help, or redeem, her. Boaz promised to be her husband. With that promise, Ruth's future was secure, and she didn't have to worry anymore about how she would survive. ◆

---

⁷Boaz ate and drank, and he was in a good mood. He went over to lie down by the edge of the grain pile. Then she quietly approached, uncovered his legs, and lay down. ⁸During the middle of the night, the man shuddered and turned over—and there was a woman lying at his feet. ⁹"Who are you?" he asked.

She replied, "I'm Ruth your servant. Spread out your robe[g] over your servant, because you are a redeemer."

¹⁰He said, "May you be blessed by the Lord, my daughter! You have acted even more faithfully than you did at first. You haven't gone after rich or poor young men. ¹¹And now, my daughter, don't be afraid. I'll do for you everything you are asking. Indeed, my people—all who are at the gate—know that you are a woman of worth. ¹²Now, although it's certainly true that I'm a redeemer, there's a redeemer who is a closer relative than I am. ¹³Stay the night. And in the morning, if he'll redeem you—good, let him redeem. But if he doesn't want to redeem you, then—as the Lord lives—I myself will redeem you. Lie down until the morning."

¹⁴So she lay at his feet until morning. Then she got up before one person could recognize another, for he had said, "No one should know that the woman came to the threshing floor." ¹⁵He said, "Bring the cloak that you have on and hold it out." She held it out, and he measured out six measures of barley and placed it upon her. Then she[h] went into town.

---

[f]An ephah is approximately twenty quarts of grain. [g]Or *wing*; cf 2:12; Ps 91:4 [h]MT *he*; other Heb sources, Syr, Vulg *she*

[16]She came to her mother-in-law, who said, "How are you, my daughter?"

So Ruth told her everything the man had done for her. [17]She said, "He gave me these six measures of barley, for he said to me, 'Don't go away empty-handed to your mother-in-law.'"

[18]"Sit tight, my daughter," Naomi replied, "until you know how it turns out. The man won't rest until he resolves the matter today."

A new family brings fulfillment

4 Meanwhile, Boaz went up to the gate and sat down there. Just then, the redeemer about whom Boaz had spoken was passing by. He said, "Sir, come over here and sit down." So he turned aside and sat down. [2]Then he took ten men from the town's elders and said, "Sit down here." And they sat down.

[3]Boaz said to the redeemer, "Naomi, who has returned from the field of Moab, is selling the portion of the field that belonged to our brother Elimelech. [4]I thought that I should let you know and say, 'Buy it, in the presence of those sitting here and in the presence of the elders of my people.' If you will redeem it, redeem it; but if you[i] won't redeem it, tell me so that I may know. There isn't anyone to redeem it except you, and I'm next in line after you."

He replied, "I will redeem it."

[5]Then Boaz said, "On the day when you buy the field from Naomi, you also buy[j] Ruth the Moabite, the wife of the dead man, in order to preserve the dead man's name for his inheritance."

[6]But the redeemer replied, "Then I can't redeem it for myself, without risking damage to my own inheritance. Redeem it for yourself. You can have my right of redemption, because I'm unable to act as redeemer."

[7]In Israel, in former times, this was the practice regarding redemption and exchange to confirm any such matter: a man would take off his sandal and give it to the other person.

did you know? In Bible times, when people were serious about showing that an agreement they had just made with someone was legal and binding, they took off their sandal and gave it to the other person.

[i]MT *he*; LXX, Syr *you* [j]Vulg; MT *On the day that you buy the field from Naomi and from Ruth the Moabite*

God's THOUGHTS / My THOUGHTS

Unexpected Blessings Ruth 4:1-22

Life for Ruth and Naomi wasn't easy. They had to work hard to find food and other resources. According to God's Instruction, the poor and the widows could pick up any grain that remained after the harvesters went through the field. This was how Ruth could find food for Naomi and herself. But God had unexpected blessings for Ruth.

Ruth chose a field that belonged to Boaz, a relative of Naomi's dead husband. Boaz had heard how Ruth had chosen to come to Judah with Naomi. He gave Ruth special treatment by allowing her to work with his people and offering her something to eat. Boaz spoke a blessing over Ruth, asking God to reward her for all she had done. What Boaz didn't know was that God would use him to fulfill that blessing and that he would become Ruth's husband.

Ruth came to the land of Judah prepared to live as a poor widow. What she didn't know was that God would greatly bless her with a husband, a home, a son, and a place in history.

Think of a time when you received an unexpected blessing.

Think of a time when you got to bless someone else.

This was the process of making a transaction binding in Israel. [8]Then the redeemer said to Boaz, "Buy it for yourself," and he took off his sandal.

[9]Boaz announced to the elders and all the people, "Today you are witnesses that I've bought from the hand of Naomi all that belonged to Elimelech and all that belonged to Chilion and Mahlon. [10]And also Ruth the Moabite, the wife of Mahlon, I've bought to be my wife, to preserve the dead man's name for his inheritance so that the name of the dead man might not be cut off from his brothers or from the gate of his hometown—today you are witnesses."

did you know? Boaz's mother was Rahab, the woman who helped the spies at Jericho (Matt 1:5; Josh 2:1–21, 6:21–25). Boaz and Ruth's son Obed was King David's grandfather and an ancestor of Jesus (Matt 1:16).

[11]Then all the people who were at the gate and the elders said, "We are witnesses. May the LORD grant that the woman who is coming into your household be like Rachel and like Leah, both of whom built up the house of Israel. May you be fertile in Ephrathah and may you preserve a name in Bethlehem. [12]And may your household be like the household of Perez, whom Tamar bore to Judah—through the children that the LORD will give you from this young woman."

[13]So Boaz took Ruth, and she became his wife.

He was intimate with her, the LORD let her become pregnant, and she gave birth to a son. [14]The women said to Naomi, "May the LORD be blessed, who today hasn't left you without a redeemer. May his name be proclaimed in Israel. [15]He will restore your life and sustain you in your old age. Your daughter-in-law who loves you has given birth to him. She's better for you than seven sons." [16]Naomi took the child and held him to her breast, and she became his guardian. [17]The neighborhood women gave him a name, saying, "A son has been born to Naomi." They called his name Obed.[k] He became Jesse's father and David's grandfather.

[18]These are the generations of Perez: Perez became the father of Hezron, [19]Hezron the father of Ram, Ram the father of Amminadab, [20]Amminadab the father of Nahshon, Nahshon the father of Salmon, [21]Salmon the father of Boaz, Boaz the father of Obed, [22]Obed the father of Jesse, and Jesse the father of David.

[k]Obed means *one who serves (God)*.

1 Samuel

First Samuel is named for Samuel, the main character of the first stories in this book. Before Samuel was born, his mother promised he would serve God his whole life. When he was a little boy, she brought him to the temple to learn how to serve God. One night Samuel heard God call out his name and speak to him. As Samuel grew older, he shared God's messages with God's people.

Samuel was a good leader. But the Israelites demanded that God give them a king. So God crowned Saul as Israel's first king. When Saul disobeyed God's commands, God said Saul could no longer be Israel's king.

God chose David as the next king. David was just a young shepherd when God picked him. But David was brave and believed that God was with him. When the giant Goliath made fun of Israel's army, everyone else was scared. But David fought Goliath with just a sling and small stones (1 Sam 17). He knew God would help him win the battle.

This book reminds us that God is in charge even when people demand their own king!

things YOU'LL DISCOVER

First Samuel explains the history of Israel from the time of the boy Samuel to Israel's first king. It tells exciting stories of Samuel, Saul, and David.

people YOU'LL MEET

Eli—a priest who served God in the temple (1 Sam 1–4)

Hannah—Samuel's mother (1 Sam 1–2)

Samuel—a priest and prophet who began serving God as a little boy (1 Sam 1–16; 25; 28)

Saul—Israel's first king (1 Sam 9–31)

David—Israel's second and greatest king (1 Sam 9–30)

places YOU'LL GO

Israel,
Philistia (in present-day Israel along the Mediterranean Sea)

words YOU'LL REMEMBER

"God doesn't look at things like humans do. Humans see only what is visible to the eyes, but the LORD sees into the heart" (1 Sam 16:7).

Samuel's birth

1 Now there was a certain man from Ramathaim, a Zuphite[a] from the highlands of Ephraim, whose name was Elkanah. He was from the tribe of Ephraim, and he was the son of Jeroham son of Elihu son of Tohu son of Zuph. ²Elkanah had two wives, one named Hannah and the other named Peninnah. Peninnah had children, but Hannah didn't.

³Every year this man would leave his town to worship and sacrifice to the LORD of heavenly forces in Shiloh, where Eli's two sons Hophni and Phinehas were the LORD's priests. ⁴Whenever he sacrificed, Elkanah would give parts of the sacrifice to his wife Peninnah and to all her sons and daughters. ⁵But he would give only one part of it to Hannah, though he loved her, because the LORD had kept her from conceiving.[b] ⁶And because the LORD had kept Hannah from conceiving, her rival would make fun of her mercilessly,

just to bother her. ⁷So that is what took place year after year. Whenever Hannah went to the Lord's house, Peninnah would make fun of her. Then she would cry and wouldn't eat anything.

⁸"Hannah, why are you crying?" her husband Elkanah would say to her. "Why won't you eat? Why are you[c] so sad? Aren't I worth more to you than ten sons?"

did you know? When Joshua first went into the promised land, his main camp was at Shiloh. Shiloh was where the meeting tent and the chest containing the covenant were kept. So the people went to Shiloh to worship and offer sacrifices to God.

⁹One time, after eating and drinking in Shiloh, Hannah got up and presented herself before the LORD.[d] (Now Eli the priest was sitting in the chair by the doorpost of

---

[a] LXX; MT *Ramathaim-zophim* [b] Heb uncertain; Syr *But he would give a double portion to Hannah, because he loved her, though the LORD had kept her from conceiving.* [c] Or *your heart* [d] LXX; MT lacks *presented herself before the LORD.*

God's THOUGHTS ◆ My THOUGHTS

Strength in Prayer 1 Samuel 1:1-20

It may be hard to believe, but people in the Bible faced many of the same problems we face today. Their stories can help us when we face tough times, such as when we are teased. Hannah knew what it was like to be picked on. She wanted very much to have a baby, but she was unable to become pregnant. Peninnah *could* have a baby, and so she made fun of Hannah. The Bible calls Peninnah a "rival" of Hannah's and says that she would mercilessly make fun of Hannah, "just to bother her" (1:6). You can imagine how sad Hannah must have been. She desperately wanted a child; she didn't need Peninnah rubbing it in her face.

Hannah cried and felt like she would never be happy, but she did one very important thing—she prayed. She prayed and prayed and prayed. In fact, Eli, who was the priest, thought she must be drunk because she was so deep in prayer. Her heart prayed, her body prayed, her lips prayed, her breath prayed, her whole self prayed that God would give her what she wanted most—a child. Peninnah picked on Hannah and tried to tear her down. But God lifted Hannah's spirits. And God answered her prayers, giving her a son who became a great leader.

Have you ever been bullied or picked on for something that you had no control over?

What does it mean to you to be strong in prayer?

the Lord's temple.) [10]Hannah was very upset and couldn't stop crying as she prayed to the Lord. [11]Then she made this promise: "Lord of heavenly forces, just look at your servant's pain and remember me! Don't forget your servant! Give her a boy! Then I'll give him to the Lord for his entire life. No razor will ever touch his head."

[12]As she kept praying before the Lord, Eli watched her mouth. [13]Now Hannah was praying in her heart; her lips were moving, but her voice was silent, so Eli thought she was drunk. [14]"How long will you act like a drunk? Sober up!" Eli told her.

[15]"No sir!" Hannah replied. "I'm just a very sad woman. I haven't had any wine or beer but have been pouring out my heart to the Lord. [16]Don't think your servant is some good-for-nothing woman. This whole time I've been praying out of my great worry and trouble!"

[17]Eli responded, "Then go in peace. And may the God of Israel give you what you've asked from him."

[18]"Please think well of me, your servant," Hannah said. Then the woman went on her way, ate some food, and wasn't sad any longer.[e]

[19]They got up early the next morning and worshipped the Lord. Then they went back home to Ramah. Elkanah had sex with his wife Hannah, and the Lord remembered her. [20]So in the course of time, Hannah conceived and gave birth to a son. She named him Samuel, which means "I asked the Lord for him."[f]

Samuel's dedication

[21]When Elkanah and all his household went up to make the annual sacrifice and keep his solemn promise, [22]Hannah didn't go.

"I'll bring the boy when he is weaned," she told her husband, "so he can be presented to the Lord and stay there permanently. I will offer him as a nazirite forever."[g]

[23]"Do what seems best to you," said her husband Elkanah. "Stay here until you've weaned him. But may the Lord bring to pass what you've[h] promised." So the woman stayed home and nursed her son until she had weaned him.

[24]When he had been weaned and was still very young,[i] Hannah took him, along with a three-year-old bull,[j] an ephah[k] of flour, and a jar of wine, and brought him to the Lord's house at Shiloh. [25]They slaughtered the bull, then brought the boy to Eli.

[26]"Excuse me, sir!" Hannah said. "As surely as you live, sir, I am the woman who stood here next to you, praying to the Lord. [27]I prayed for this boy, and the Lord gave me what I asked from him. [28]So now I give this boy back to the Lord. As long as he lives, he is given to the Lord."

Then they worshipped there before the Lord.[l]

Hannah's song

2 Then Hannah prayed:
My heart rejoices in the Lord.
My strength[m] rises up in the Lord!
My mouth mocks my enemies
because I rejoice in your deliverance.
[2] No one is holy like the Lord—
no, no one except you!
There is no rock like our God!

[3] Don't go on and on, talking so proudly,
spouting arrogance from your mouth,
because the Lord is the God who knows,
and he weighs every act.

[4] The bows of mighty warriors
are shattered,
but those who were stumbling
now dress themselves in power!
[5] Those who were filled full
now sell themselves for bread,
but the ones who were starving
are now fat from food!
The woman who was barren
has birthed seven children,
but the mother with many sons
has lost them all!
[6] The Lord!
He brings death, gives life,
takes down to the grave,[n]
and raises up!

---

[e]LXX; MT lacks *sad*. [f]Samuel means *God has heard* but here is connected to the Heb verb *to ask*. [g]DSS (4QSam[a]); MT lacks *I will offer … forever*. [h]LXX, DSS (4QSam[a]); MT *he* [i]Or *and the boy was a boy*; Heb uncertain [j]LXX, DSS (4QSam[a]), Syr; MT *three bulls* [k]An ephah was approximately twenty quarts. [l]Some Heb manuscripts, Syr, Vulg; MT *he (Eli?) worshipped*; DSS (4QSam[a]) *and she (Hannah) left him there and worshipped the Lord.* [m]Or *my horn*; also in 2:10 [n]Heb *Sheol*

⁷ The Lᴏʀᴅ!
  He makes poor, gives wealth,
    brings low, but also lifts up high!
⁸ God raises the poor from the dust,
    lifts up the needy from the garbage pile.
  God sits them with officials,
    gives them the seat of honor!
  The pillars of the earth belong to the Lᴏʀᴅ;
    he set the world on top of them!
⁹ God guards the feet of his faithful ones,
    but the wicked die in darkness
      because no one succeeds
        by strength alone.

¹⁰ The Lᴏʀᴅ!
  His enemies are terrified!
    God thunders against them
      from heaven!
  The Lᴏʀᴅ!
  He judges the far corners of the earth!

  May God give strength to his king
    and raise high the strength
      of his anointed one.

¹¹Then Elkanah went home to Ramah, but
the boy served the Lᴏʀᴅ under Eli the priest.

Corruption of Eli's sons

¹²Now Eli's sons were despicable men who
didn't know the Lᴏʀᴅ. ¹³This was how the
priest was supposed to act with the people:
Whenever anyone made a sacrifice, while the
meat was boiling, the priest's assistant would
come with a three-pronged fork in hand. ¹⁴He
would thrust it into the cauldron or the pot.ᵒ
Whatever the fork brought up, the priest
would take for himself. This is how it was
done for all the Israelites who came to Shiloh.

¹⁵But with Eli's sons,ᵖ even before the fat
was burned, the priest's assistant would come
and say to the person offering the sacrifice,
"Give the priest some meat to roast. He won't
accept boiled meat from you."�q ¹⁶If anyone
said, "Let the fat be burned off first, as usual,
then take whatever you like for yourself," the
assistant would reply, "No, hand it over now.
If not, I'll take it by force." ¹⁷The sin of these
priestly assistants was very serious in the
Lᴏʀᴅ's sight because they were disrespecting
the Lord's own offering.

UMBRELLA
Iᴛ's Nᴏᴛ Yᴏᴜʀs

Don't Give Greed Control *1 Samuel 2:13-17*
Eli's two sons, Hophni and Phinehas, should have
known better. They were priests who had been
dedicated to serve God and the rest of the Israelites. God's Instruction gave priests a portion of the
food from all the different offerings and sacrifices
the Israelites gave to God (Num 18:8-9). But the
priests could take the food only after the meat was
boiled and offered to God. Hophni and Phinehas
were stealing from God. They were taking the food
before it went in the boiling pot—before it was
given to God. They wanted the meat before all the
juicy parts were burned up. Hophni and Phinehas
didn't respect God. Because they could think only
with their appetites, they both died the same day
in a battle. Their father died when he heard about
their deaths. Because of the greed of Hophni and
Phinehas, their family suffered (1 Sam 2:27-36). ◊

¹⁸Now Samuel was serving the Lᴏʀᴅ. He
was a young boy, clothed in a linen priestly
vest.ʳ ¹⁹His mother would make a small robe
for him and take it to him every year when
she went up with her husband to offer the annual sacrifice. ²⁰Eli would bless Elkanah and
his wife: "May the Lᴏʀᴅ replaceˢ the child of
this woman that you gave back to the Lᴏʀᴅ."
Then they would return home. ²¹The Lᴏʀᴅ
paid attention to Hannah, and she conceived
and gave birth to three sons and two daughters. Meanwhile, the boy Samuel grew up in
the Lᴏʀᴅ's service.

²²Eli was very old, but he heard everything his sons were doing to the Israelites,
and how they had sex with the women who
served at the meeting tent's entrance. ²³Eli
said to his sons, "Why are you doing these
terrible things that I'm hearing about from
everybody? ²⁴No, my sons. Don't do this.ᵗ The
report I hear spreading among God's people
isn't good. ²⁵If someone sins against someone
else, God can intercede; but if someone sins
against the Lᴏʀᴅ, who will intercede then?"
But they wouldn't obey their father because

ᵒCf DSS (4QSamᵃ); Heb has four different words for pots. ᵖMT lacks *with Eli's sons*. qLXX; MT adds *only raw*. ʳHeb *ephod*
ˢDSS (4QSamᵃ); MT *give* ᵗLXX, DSS (4QSamᵃ); MT lacks *Don't do this*.

the Lord wanted to kill them. ²⁶Meanwhile, the boy Samuel kept growing up and was more and more liked by both the Lord and the people.

²⁷Now a man of God came to Eli and said, "This is what the Lord says: I revealed myself very clearly to your father's household when they were slaves[u] in Egypt to the house of Pharaoh. ²⁸I chose your father from all of Israel's tribes to be my priest, to go up onto my altar, to burn incense, and to wear the priestly vest[v] in my presence. I also gave all of the Israelites' food offerings to your father's household. ²⁹Why then do you kick my sacrifices and my offerings—the very ones I commanded for my dwelling place? Why do you respect your sons more than me, getting fat off the best parts of every offering from my people Israel? ³⁰Because of all that, this is what the Lord, the God of Israel, declares: I had promised that your household and your father's household would serve me forever. But now—this is what the Lord declares: I'll do no such thing! No. I honor those who honor me, and whoever despises me will be cursed. ³¹The days are coming soon when I will eliminate both your children[w] and the children of your father's household. There won't be an old person left in your family tree. ³²You'll see trouble in my dwelling place, though all will go well for Israel.[x] But there will never be an old person in your family tree. ³³One of your descendants whom I don't eliminate from serving at my altar will cry his[y] eyes out and be full of grief. Any descendants in your household will die by the sword.[z] ³⁴And what happens to your two sons Hophni and Phinehas will be a sign for you: they will both die on the same day. ³⁵Then I will establish for myself a trustworthy priest who will act in accordance with my thoughts and desires. I will build a trustworthy household for him, and he will serve before my anointed one forever. ³⁶Anyone left from your household will come and beg him for a bit of silver or a loaf of bread, saying: 'Please appoint me to some priestly duty so I can have a scrap of bread to eat.'"

Samuel's call

3 Now the boy Samuel was serving the Lord under Eli. The Lord's word was rare at that time, and visions weren't widely known. ²One day Eli, whose eyes had grown so weak he was unable to see, was lying down in his room. ³God's lamp hadn't gone out yet, and Samuel was lying down in the Lord's temple, where God's chest[a] was.

⁴The Lord called to Samuel. "I'm here," he said.

⁵Samuel hurried to Eli and said, "I'm here. You called me?"

"I didn't call you," Eli replied. "Go lie down." So he did.

⁶Again the Lord called Samuel, so Samuel got up, went to Eli, and said, "I'm here. You called me?"

"I didn't call, my son," Eli replied. "Go and lie down."

(⁷Now Samuel didn't yet know the Lord, and the Lord's word hadn't yet been revealed to him.)

⁸A third time the Lord called Samuel. He got up, went to Eli, and said, "I'm here. You called me?"

Then Eli realized that it was the Lord who was calling the boy. ⁹So Eli said to Samuel, "Go and lie down. If he calls you, say, 'Speak, Lord. Your servant is listening.'" So Samuel went and lay down where he'd been.

LIFE PRESERVER

What does "God's lamp hadn't gone out yet" mean?
1 Samuel 3:3

Reading the Bible gives us a glimpse into life in a very different culture. We learn a lot about how people thought, the ways they lived their lives, and the language they used. This verse is a good example of how they spoke about time in relation to their belief in God. The writer described time in terms of God. "God's lamp hadn't gone out yet." The lamp of God, which gave light in the night, was still lit. This poetic description of time means that it was nighttime and not daytime. It was also a way the writer marked the time so that people knew it was under God's control. ◊

---

[u]DSS (4QSamᵃ), LXX; MT lacks *slaves*. [v]Heb *ephod* [w]LXX; MT *arm or power* [x]Heb uncertain; LXX and DSS (4QSamᵃ) omit 2:31b–32a. [y]DSS (4QSamᵃ), LXX; MT *your* [z]LXX, DSS (4QSamᵃ); MT *die by men* or *die as men* [a]Traditionally *ark*

¹⁰Then the Lᴏʀᴅ came and stood there, calling just as before, "Samuel, Samuel!"

Samuel said, "Speak. Your servant is listening."

¹¹The Lᴏʀᴅ said to Samuel, "I am about to do something in Israel that will make the ears of all who hear it tingle! ¹²On that day, I will bring to pass against Eli everything I said about his household—every last bit of it!ᵇ ¹³I told him that I would punish his family forever because of the wrongdoing he knew about—how his sons were cursing God,ᶜ but he wouldn't stop them. ¹⁴Because of that I swore about Eli's household that his family's wrongdoing will never be reconciled by sacrifice or by offering."

¹⁵Samuel lay there until morning, then opened the doors of the Lᴏʀᴅ's house. Samuel was afraid to tell the vision to Eli. ¹⁶But Eli called Samuel, saying: "Samuel, my son!"

"I'm here," Samuel said.

¹⁷"What did he say to you?" Eli asked. "Don't hide anything from me. May God deal harshly with you and worse still if you hide from me a single word from everything he said to you." ¹⁸So Samuel told him everything and hid nothing from him.

"He is the Lᴏʀᴅ," Eli said. "He will do as he pleases."

¹⁹So Samuel grew up, and the Lᴏʀᴅ was with him, not allowing any of his words to fail. ²⁰All Israel from Dan to Beer-sheba knew that Samuel was trustworthy as the Lᴏʀᴅ's prophet. ²¹The Lᴏʀᴅ continued to appear at Shiloh because the Lᴏʀᴅ revealed himself to Samuel at Shiloh through the Lᴏʀᴅ's own word. ¹And Samuel's word went out to all Israel.

ᵇOr the beginning and the end   ᶜLXX; MT to themselves, one of several intentional scribal corrections to avoid the phrase cursing God

Is That You, God? 1 Samuel 3:1–4:1

Hearing God's voice can be like trying to hear the person sitting next to you at a basketball game. You can tell they are talking to you because you can see their lips moving. You can make out some of the words, but mostly you just hear the noise of the crowds, the buzzer, or the announcer on the loudspeaker. Samuel encountered God in a similar way. He heard a voice, but he couldn't make out where the voice was coming from or what the voice was saying.

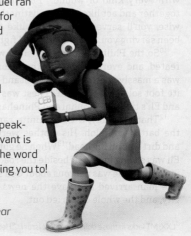

Three different times, God spoke to Samuel and Samuel ran to his teacher, Eli, thinking his teacher must have called for him. The third time, Eli figured out what was going on and instructed Samuel to say, "Speak. Your servant is listening" (3:10). Samuel was a young boy at the time. He wouldn't expect God to come down and speak to him at all. But God called Samuel to be a leader, and Samuel listened and obeyed.

When you feel a nudge in your heart that God might be speaking to you, remember Samuel and say, "Speak. Your servant is listening." And then, open your ears and your heart for the word God has for you. You never know what God might be calling you to!

Have you ever heard from God? What was it like?

List some things that get in the way of your ability to hear God's voice.

The Philistines capture God's chest

In those days the Philistines gathered for war against Israel,[d] so Israel went out to engage the Philistines in war. Israel camped at Ebenezer, while the Philistines camped at Aphek. [2]The Philistines readied themselves to fight Israel. When the battle was joined, Israel was defeated by the Philistines, who killed about four thousand men on the battlefield. [3]When the troops returned to the camp, Israel's elders said, "Why did the Lord defeat us today before the Philistines? Let's bring the chest containing the Lord's covenant from Shiloh so it can go with us and save us from our enemies' power." [4]So the people sent to Shiloh and brought from there the chest containing the covenant of the Lord of heavenly forces, who sits enthroned on the winged heavenly creatures.[e] Eli's two sons Hophni and Phinehas were there with the chest containing God's covenant.

[5]When the chest containing the Lord's covenant entered the camp, all Israel let out such a loud shout that the ground shook. [6]When the Philistines heard the sound of that shout, they asked, "What is that loud shouting in the Hebrew camp about?" When they learned that the Lord's chest had come into the camp, [7]the Philistines were afraid and said, "A god has come into that camp! We're doomed," they said, "because nothing like this has ever happened before. [8]We're doomed! Who will deliver us from the grip of these powerful deities? They are the same gods who struck the Egyptians in the desert with every kind of wound. [9]Pull yourselves together and act like men, Philistines! Otherwise, you'll serve the Hebrews like they've been serving you. Act like men and fight!"

[10]So the Philistines fought. Israel was defeated, and everyone fled to their homes. It was a massive defeat: thirty thousand Israelite foot soldiers fell, [11]God's chest was taken, and Eli's two sons Hophni and Phinehas died.

[12]That very day, a Benjaminite ran from the battle to Shiloh. His clothes were torn, and dirt was on his head. [13]When he got there, Eli was sitting in a chair beside the road, waiting because he was nervous about God's chest. The man arrived and gave the news to the city, and the whole city cried out.

LIFE PRESERVER

Why was the chest containing the covenant so important? 1 Samuel 4:4

The chest containing the covenant was an important symbol for God's people. The chest contained the tablets on which God's covenant was written. When the Israelites were in the wilderness, they carried the chest into battle at the very front of the warriors. Because God's words were written on the tablets in the chest, the people believed that God was with them when the chest was present and would make them victorious in battle.

The next time you're in your church's worship space, look around. What symbol reminds you most of God's presence? Or think about the things in your home, perhaps this Bible. Symbols can help us remember how much God loves us and how God wants us to live. ◊

[14]Eli heard the sound of the cry and said, "What's all this noise about?"

The man hurriedly went and told Eli the news. ([15]Now Eli was 98 years old, and his eyes stared straight ahead, unable to see.) [16]The man told Eli, "I'm the one who just came from the battle. I fled from the battle today."

"What's the report, my son?" Eli asked.

[17]The messenger answered, "Israel has fled from the Philistines. The army has suffered a massive defeat. Also, your own two sons Hophni and Phinehas have died, and God's chest has been taken!" [18]At the mention of God's chest, Eli fell backward off the chair beside the gate. His neck broke, and he died because he was an old man and overweight. Eli had judged Israel for forty years.

[19]Now Eli's daughter-in-law, Phinehas' wife, was pregnant and about to give birth. When she heard the news that God's chest had been captured and that her father-in-law and her husband had died, she doubled over and gave birth because her labor pains overwhelmed her. [20]As she was about to die, the women standing by helping her said, "Don't be afraid. You've given birth to a son!" But she didn't answer or pay them any attention. [21]She named the boy Ichabod,[f] saying, "The glory has left Israel," referring to the capture of God's chest

[d]LXX; MT lacks In those days ... against Israel. [e]Heb cherubim [f]Meaning Where is the glory?

and the death of her father-in-law and her husband. [22]"The glory has left Israel because God's chest has been taken," she said.

God's chest among the Philistines

5After the Philistines took God's chest, they brought it from Ebenezer to Ashdod. [2]Then the Philistines took God's chest and brought it into Dagon's temple and set it next to Dagon. [3]But when the citizens of Ashdod got up early the next morning, there was Dagon, fallen facedown on the ground before the LORD's chest! So they took Dagon and set him back up where he belonged. [4]But when they got up early the next morning, there was Dagon again, fallen facedown on the ground before the LORD's chest—and this time Dagon's head along with both his hands were cut off and lying on the doorstep! Only Dagon's body[g] was left intact. [5]That's why to this day Dagon's priests or anyone else who enters his temple in Ashdod doesn't step on the threshold.

[6]The LORD's hand was heavy on the people of Ashdod: God terrified them and struck them in Ashdod and its surroundings with tumors.[h] [7]When Ashdod's inhabitants saw what was happening, they said, "The chest of Israel's God must not stay here with us because his hand is hard against us and against our god Dagon."

[8]So they summoned all the Philistine rulers to a meeting and asked, "What should we do with the chest of Israel's God?" The people of Gath said, "Let the chest of Israel's God be moved to us." So they moved the chest of Israel's God to Gath.[i] [9]But once they moved it, the LORD's hand came against the city, causing a huge panic. God struck the city's inhabitants, both young and old, and tumors broke out on them.

[10]Then they sent God's chest to Ekron, but as soon as God's chest entered Ekron, the inhabitants cried out, "Why have you moved the chest of Israel's God to us? In order to kill us and our people?"[j]

[11]So they summoned all the Philistine

rulers to a meeting and said, "Send the chest of Israel's God away! Let it go back to its own home so it doesn't kill us and our people," because there was a deadly panic throughout the whole city. The hand of God was very heavy there. [12]The people who didn't die were struck with tumors, and the screams of the city went all the way up to heaven.

God's chest is returned

6The LORD's chest was in Philistine territory for seven months. [2]The Philistines called for the priests and the diviners. "What should we do with the LORD's chest?" they asked. "Tell us how we should send it back to its own home."

[3]They replied, "If you are returning the chest of Israel's God, don't send it back empty, but be sure to return a guilt offering to him.[k] Then you will be healed, and it will become clear to you why God's hand hasn't left you alone."

[4]"What compensation offering should we return to him?" they asked.

The priests and diviners replied: "Five gold tumors[l] and five gold mice,[m] matching the number of the Philistine rulers, because the same plague came on all of you and your rulers. [5]You must make images of your tumors and the mice that have devastated the land. Honor Israel's God. Perhaps he will lighten the weight of his hand on you, your gods, and your land. [6]Why be stubborn like the Egyptians and Pharaoh? After God had dealt harshly with them, didn't they send the Israelites on their way? [7]So get a new cart ready along with two nursing cows that have never been yoked before. Harness the cows to the cart, but take any of their calves that are following back home. [8]Next, take the LORD's chest and put it in the cart. Set the gold items that you are giving God as a compensation offering in a box next to the chest. Then send it on its way. [9]Then watch what happens: If the cart goes up the road to its own territory toward Bethshemesh, then Israel's God has brought this great disaster on us. If the cart goes another way, then we'll know that it wasn't God's hand that struck us. It happened to us randomly."

[10]The rulers[n] did just that. They took two

[g]Cf LXX [h]Kethib; Qere *hemorrhoids* (cf Deut 28:27); also in 5:9, 12 [i]LXX [j]DSS (4QSamᵃ), LXX [k]Or *be sure to return it with a compensation offering.* [l]Kethib; Qere *hemorrhoids* (cf Deut 28:27); also in 6:5; see note at 6:11. [m]LXX lacks *and five gold mice.* [n]See 6:12; MT *men*

nursing cows and harnessed them to the cart, penning their calves up at home. 11They put the LORD's chest on the cart along with the box containing the gold mice and the images of their tumors.[o] 12The cows went straight ahead, following the road to Beth-shemesh. They kept to one route, mooing as they went, without turning right or left. The Philistine rulers followed them as far as the territory of Beth-shemesh.

13Now the people of Beth-shemesh were harvesting wheat in the valley. When they looked up and saw the chest, they were overjoyed at the sight. 14The cart entered the field belonging to Joshua of Beth-shemesh and stopped right by a large stone. They chopped up the wood of the cart and offered the cows as an entirely burned offering to the LORD. 15The Levites unloaded the LORD's chest and the box that was with it that contained all the gold items, and they set them on the large stone. That very day the people of Beth-shemesh offered entirely burned offerings and made sacrifices to the LORD. 16When the five Philistine rulers witnessed this, they went straight back to Ekron.

17These are the gold tumors that the Philistines returned as a compensation offering to the LORD: one for Ashdod, one for Gaza, one for Ashkelon, one for Gath, and one for Ekron. 18The gold mice matched the number of Philistine cities belonging to the five rulers, from fortified cities to country villages. And the large stone[p] they set the LORD's chest on is a witness even now in the field that belongs to Joshua of Beth-shemesh.

19But God struck down some of the people from Beth-shemesh because they looked into the LORD's chest. God struck seventy people,[q] and the community grieved because the LORD had struck them so severely. 20The people of Beth-shemesh said, "Who can stand before the LORD, this holy God? Where can he go that is away from us here?" 21They sent messengers to the inhabitants of Kiriath-jearim. "The Philistines returned the LORD's chest!" they said. "Come down and take it back with you."

7 So the people of Kiriath-jearim came and took the LORD's chest. They brought it to Abinadab's house, which was on the hill. Then they dedicated Eleazar, Abinadab's son, to care for the LORD's chest.

Samuel leads Israel

2Now a long time passed—a total of twenty years—after the chest came to stay in Kiriath-jearim, and the whole house of Israel yearned for[r] the LORD.

3Then Samuel said to the whole house of Israel, "If you are turning to the LORD with all your heart, then get rid of all the foreign gods and the Astartes you have. Set your heart on the LORD! Worship him only! Then he will deliver you from the Philistines' power." 4So the Israelites got rid of the Baals and the Astartes and worshipped the LORD only.

5Next Samuel said, "Assemble all Israel at Mizpah. I will pray to the LORD for you."

6So they assembled at Mizpah, and they drew water and poured it out in the LORD's presence. They fasted that same day and confessed, "We have sinned against the LORD." Samuel served as judge of the Israelites at Mizpah.

7When the Philistines heard that the Israelites had assembled at Mizpah, the Philistine rulers went up to attack Israel. When the Israelites learned of this, they were afraid of the Philistines. 8The Israelites said to Samuel, "Please don't stop praying to the LORD our God for us, so God will save us from the Philistines' power!" 9So Samuel took a suckling lamb and offered it as an entirely burned offering to the LORD. Samuel cried out in prayer to the LORD for Israel, and the LORD answered him.

10While Samuel was offering the entirely burned offering, the Philistines advanced to

did you know? Before they lost the chest containing the covenant, the Israelites believed having this sacred chest meant they had God's power on their side. Their enemies believed that once they had this chest they would have God's power too. However, both groups learned God's power could not be controlled by having the chest containing the covenant in their possession.

[o]Or *hemorrhoids;* also in 6:17, the Qere form for the Hebrew written form of *tumors* used in 6:4-5 [p]LXX [q]LXX; MT adds *fifty thousand people.* [r]Heb uncertain; LXX *searched for*

attack Israel. But the LORD thundered against the Philistines with a great blast on that very day, throwing the Philistines into such a panic that they were defeated by Israel. ¹¹The Israelite soldiers came out of Mizpah and pursued the Philistines. They struck them down until they reached a place just below Beth-car. ¹²Then Samuel took a stone and set it up between Mizpah and Jeshanah.ˢ He named it Ebenezer,ᵗ explaining, "The LORD helped us to this very point."

¹³So the Philistines were defeated, and they stopped coming into Israelite territory. The LORD's hand was against the Philistines throughout Samuel's life. ¹⁴The towns the Philistines had captured from Israel, from Ekron to Gath, were returned to Israel. Israel also recovered the territory around those two cities from the Philistines. And there was peace between Israel and the Amorites.

¹⁵Samuel served as Israel's judge his whole life. ¹⁶Each year he traveled between Bethel, Gilgal, and Mizpah, serving as Israel's judge in each of those locations. ¹⁷Then he would return to Ramah because that's where his home was. In Ramah too he served as Israel's judge, and that is also where he built an altar to the LORD.

Israel demands a king

8 Now when Samuel got old, he appointed his sons to serve as Israel's judges. ²The name of his oldest son was Joel; the name of the second was Abijah. They served as judges in Beer-sheba. ³But Samuel's sons didn't follow in his footsteps. They tried to turn a profit, they accepted bribes, and they perverted justice.

⁴So all the Israelite elders got together and went to Samuel at Ramah. ⁵They said to him, "Listen. You are old now, and your sons don't follow in your footsteps. So appoint us a king to judge us like all the other nations have." ⁶It seemed very bad to Samuel when they said, "Give us a king to judge us," so he prayed to the LORD.

⁷The LORD answered Samuel, "Comply with the people's request—everything they ask of you—because they haven't rejected you. No, they've rejected me as king over them. ⁸They are doing to you only what they've been doing to meᵘ from the day I brought them out of Egypt to this very minute, abandoning me and worshipping other gods. ⁹So comply with their request, but give them a clear warning, telling them how the king will rule over them."ᵛ

¹⁰Then Samuel explained everything the LORD had said to the people who were asking for a king. ¹¹"This is how the king will rule over you," Samuel said:

"He will take your sons, and will use them for his chariots and his cavalry and as runners for his chariot. ¹²He will use them as his commanders of troops of one thousand and troops of fifty, or to do his plowing and his

did you **know?** Samuel had two jobs during his lifetime. First, he served with Eli as a priest. Then when the people demanded a king, God chose Samuel to be the prophet who anointed and advised King Saul.

harvesting, or to make his weapons or parts for his chariots. ¹³He will take your daughters to be perfumers, cooks, or bakers. ¹⁴He will take your best fields, vineyards, and olive groves and give them to his servants. ¹⁵He will give one-tenth of your grain and your vineyards to his officials and servants. ¹⁶He will take your male and female servants, along with the best of your cattleʷ and donkeys, and make them do his work. ¹⁷He will take one-tenth of your flocks, and then you yourselves will become his slaves! ¹⁸When that day comes, you will cry out because of the king you chose for yourselves, but on that day the LORD won't answer you."

¹⁹But the people refused to listen to Samuel and said, "No! There must be a king over us ²⁰so we can be like all the other nations. Our king will judge us and lead us and fight our battles."

²¹Samuel listened to everything the people said and repeated it directly to the LORD. ²²Then the LORD said to Samuel, "Comply with their request. Give them a king."

ˢLXX, Syr; MT *Ha-shen* (the tooth) ᵗMeaning *stone of help* ᵘLXX; MT lacks *to me.* ᵛOr *telling them the lawful practice of the king;* also in 8:11; cf 10:25 ʷLXX; MT *young men*

Samuel then told the Israelite people, "Go back, each of you, to your own hometown."

Saul chosen to lead Israel

9 There was a wealthy man from the tribe of Benjamin named Kish. He was the son of Abiel son of Zeror son of Becorath son of Aphiah, a Benjaminite. ²He had a son named Saul, who was a handsome young man. No one in Israel was more handsome than Saul, and he stood head and shoulders above everyone else.

³When the donkeys belonging to Saul's father Kish were lost, Kish said to his son Saul, "Take one of the servant boys with you and go look for the donkeys." ⁴So he traveled through the highlands of Ephraim and the land of Shalishah, but they didn't find anything. They traveled through the land of Shaalim, but still found nothing, so they crossed back into the land of Benjamin, but they still couldn't find the donkeys. ⁵When they came to the territory of Zuph, Saul said to the boy who was with him, "Let's go back before my father stops worrying about the donkeys and starts worrying about us."

⁶But the boy said to him, "Listen, there's a man of God in this town. He's famous—everything he says actually happens! So let's go there. Maybe he'll be able to tell us which way we should go."

⁷Saul said to his young boy, "But if we go, what should we bring to the man? The food in our bags is all gone. We don't have any gift to offer the man of God. Do we have anything?"

⁸"Here," the boy answered Saul, "I've got a quarter-shekel of silver. I'll give that to the man of God so he tells us which way to go." (⁹Earlier in Israel, someone going to consult with God would say, "Let's go to the seer,"

Bad Pride   *1 Samuel 8:1-22*

Pride is a tricky word. It can mean something good, like when we take pride in hard work or when we're proud of ourselves for making a good decision. But pride can also be a bad thing, like when we think we know all of the answers and don't need anyone to tell us what to do. In 1 Samuel 8, God's people had the bad kind of pride. They decided they didn't want God's leader anymore. God chose the leaders and spoke to the people through them. But the people decided that they wanted a king like all the other nations had instead of God's leader. They didn't think they needed God anymore and wanted to serve an earthly king who would lead them. Samuel warned them that this was a bad idea and would change everything—forever. But the people wanted to be like everyone else, and so Samuel gave them what they asked for. God's people got their king.

Have you ever thought you knew better than your parents, teachers, or even God? Sometimes we get impatient waiting for an answer, or we get frustrated because we would have solved a problem differently. We start to think that we should take matters into our own hands. That's when the bad kind of pride sneaks in and takes over. Watch out for times when you start to think that you have all the answers, and remember that God wants to be the leader of your life.

Think of a time when you got your way, but the situation didn't turn out the way you thought it would.

How can you make sure to avoid the bad kind of pride?

because the people who are called prophets today were previously called seers.)

¹⁰Saul said to the boy, "Great idea! Let's go." So they went into the town where the man of God lived. ¹¹They were going up the hill to the town when they met some young women coming out to draw water. "Is the seer here?" they asked them.

¹²"He's just ahead of you," they answered. "Hurry up! He has just come to town because there is a sacrifice today for the people at the shrine. ¹³You'll find him as soon as you enter the town, before he goes up to the shrine to eat. The people won't eat until he gets there, because he must bless the sacrifice. Only after that can the invited guests eat. Now get going because you'll find him momentarily."

¹⁴So Saul and the boy went up to the town, and as they entered it, suddenly Samuel came toward them on his way up to the shrine. ¹⁵Now the day before Saul came, the Lᴏʀᴅ had revealed the following to Samuel: ¹⁶"About this time tomorrow I will send you a man from the Benjaminite territory. You will anoint him as leader of my people Israel. He will save my people from the Philistines' power because I have seen the suffering of[x] my people, and their cry for help has reached me." ¹⁷When Samuel saw Saul, the Lᴏʀᴅ told him, "That's the man I told

you about. That's the one who will rule[y] my people."

¹⁸Saul approached Samuel in the city gate and said, "Please tell me where the seer's house is."

¹⁹"I'm the seer," Samuel told Saul. "Go on ahead of me to the shrine. You can eat with me today. In the morning I'll send you on your way, and I will tell you everything you want to know. ²⁰As for the donkeys you lost three days ago, don't be worried about them because they've been found. Who owns all of Israel's treasures, anyway? Isn't it you and your whole family?"[z]

²¹"I'm a Benjaminite," Saul responded, "from the smallest Israelite tribe, and my family is the littlest of the families in the tribe of Benjamin. Why would you say something like that to me?"

²²Then Samuel took Saul and his young servant and brought them to the banquet room. He gave them an honored place among the invited guests. There were about thirty total. ²³Samuel said to the cook, "Serve the portion I gave you—the one I told you to set aside." ²⁴So the cook took the thigh and what was on it,[a] and put it in front of Saul. Samuel said, "Look, what had been reserved is now in front of you. Eat up, because it was set apart for you for this specific occasion, ever since I invited the guests."[b] So Saul ate with Samuel that day. ²⁵When they came back from the shrine to the town, a bed was made for Saul on the roof, and he slept.[c]

²⁶Near dawn, Samuel called to Saul on the roof, "Wake up! I will send you on your way." So Saul got up, and the two of them, he and Samuel, went outside. ²⁷As they were nearing the edge of town Samuel said, "Tell the boy to go on ahead of us" (the servant did so) "but you stop for a bit so I can tell you God's word."

Samuel anoints Saul as king

10 Samuel took a small jar of oil and poured it over Saul's head and kissed him. "The Lᴏʀᴅ hereby anoints you leader of his people Israel," Samuel said. "You will rule the Lᴏʀᴅ's people and save them from the power of the

SAILBOAT

GIVING THANKS

Be Thankful Before Meals 1 Samuel 9:1-14

Saul wanted to find his father's donkeys. When his servant told him about the prophet of God who lived nearby, Saul knew he should ask him about the donkeys. The first townsperson they met knew exactly where the prophet Samuel could be found. It was mealtime. There was a sacrifice at the shrine. Samuel was on his way to bless the food. Everyone in town knew the schedule because they followed it regularly. Everyone knew to wait before eating because it was important to thank God for the food. Whether they grew it themselves or bought it—the food still came from God. ◆

enemies who surround them. And this will be the sign for you that the LORD has anointed you as leader of his very own possession:[d] [2]When you leave me today, you will meet two men near Rachel's tomb at Zelzah on the border of Benjamin. They will tell you, 'The donkeys you went looking for have been found. Now your father has stopped thinking about the donkeys and is worried about you. He's asking: What should I do about my son?' [3]Then, when you've gone on a bit farther, you will come to the oak at Tabor. Three men who are going to consult God at Bethel will meet up with you there, one carrying three young goats, one carrying three loaves of bread, and one carrying a jar of wine. [4]They will ask how you're doing and will offer you sacrificial bread,[e] which you should accept. [5]After that, you will come to Gibeath-elohim, which is a Philistine fort. When you enter the town, you will encounter a group of prophets coming down from the shrine preceded by harps, tambourines, flutes, and lyres. They will be caught up in a prophetic frenzy. [6]Then the LORD's spirit will come over you, and you will be caught up in a prophetic frenzy right along with them; it will be like you've become a completely different person. [7]Once these signs have happened to you, do whatever you would like to do, because God is with you. [8]Then go down to Gilgal ahead of me. I'll come down to meet you to offer entirely burned offerings and to make well-being sacrifices. Wait seven days until I get to you, then I'll tell you what you should do next."

[9]And just as Saul turned to leave Samuel's side, God gave him a different heart, and all these signs happened that very same day. [10]When Saul and the boy got to Gibeah, there was a group of prophets coming to meet him. God's spirit came over Saul, and he was caught up in a prophetic frenzy right along with them. [11]When all the people who had known Saul saw him prophesying with the prophets, they said to each other, "What's happened to Kish's son? Is Saul also one of the prophets?" [12]One of the locals then asked, "And who is their leader?"[f] So it became a proverb: "Is Saul also one of the prophets?" [13]When the prophetic frenzy was over, Saul went home.[g]

LIFE PRESERVER

What is a "prophetic frenzy"?
1 Samuel 10:1-16

Samuel poured oil on Saul as a symbol of Saul's leadership as king and a sign that God would be with him. In order for Saul to know that he had God's blessing, Samuel told Saul to look for certain things: men carrying bread, wine, and goats. Then when Saul got to the fort, he would meet some prophets who were playing musical instruments and so overcome by God's presence that they weren't aware of anything else around them. Samuel told Saul that God's spirit would come over him, and he would be caught up in a prophetic frenzy, as if he were a different person. This story shows that the future king should be under God's control. ◢

[14]Saul's uncle said to him and to his young servant, "Where did you go?"

"To look for the donkeys," Saul replied, "but when we couldn't find anything, we went to Samuel."

[15]"Please tell me what Samuel told you," Saul's uncle said.

[16]"He reassured us that the donkeys had been found," Saul answered. But Saul didn't tell his uncle what Samuel had said about the kingship.

Saul selected as king

[17]Samuel summoned the people to the LORD at Mizpah. [18]Then he told the Israelites: "This is what the LORD God of Israel says: I brought Israel up out of Egypt, and I delivered you from the Egyptians' power and from the power of all the kingdoms that oppressed you. [19]But today you've rejected your God who saved you from all your troubles and difficulties by saying, 'No! Appoint a king over us!' So now assemble yourselves before the LORD by your tribes and clans."

[20]Then Samuel brought all the Israelite tribes forward, and the tribe of Benjamin was selected. [21]Next Samuel brought the tribe of Benjamin forward by its families, and the family of Matri was selected. Samuel then

[d]LXX; MT lacks *of his people Israel.... And this will be the sign for you that.* [e]LXX; DSS (4QSamᵃ) *uplifted bread* (see Num 18:11); MT *two of bread* [f]Or *father* [g]Correction; MT *Saul entered the shrine.*

brought the family of Matri forward, person by person,[h] and Saul, Kish's son, was selected. But when they looked for him, he wasn't to be found. [22]So they asked another question of the Lord: "Has the man come here yet?"

The Lord said, "Yes, he's hiding among the supplies." [23]They ran and retrieved Saul from there, and when he stood up in the middle of the people, he was head and shoulders taller than anyone else.

[24]"Can you see the one the Lord has chosen?" Samuel asked all the people. "He has no equal among the people."

Then the people shouted, "Long live the king!"

[25]Samuel then explained to the people how the monarchy should operate[i] and wrote it in a scroll and placed it in the Lord's presence. Then Samuel sent every person back to their homes. [26]Saul also went back to his home in Gibeah. Along with him went courageous men whose hearts God had touched. [27]But some despicable people said, "How can this man save us?" They despised Saul and didn't bring him gifts, but Saul didn't say anything.

Saul delivers Jabesh-gilead

[j]Nahash the Ammonite king had been severely oppressing the Gadites and the Reubenites. He gouged out everyone's right eye, thereby not allowing Israel to have a deliverer. There wasn't a single Israelite left across the Jordan River who hadn't had their right eye gouged out by the Ammonite king Nahash. But seven thousand people had escaped from the Ammonites' power and fled to Jabesh-gilead.

11 About a month later,[k] Nahash the Ammonite went up and laid siege to Jabesh-gilead. All the men of Jabesh said to Nahash, "Make a treaty with us, and we'll be your servants."

[2]"I will make a treaty with you on one condition: that everyone's right eye be gouged out!" Nahash the Ammonite said to them. "That's how I bring humiliation on all Israel."

[3]The elders of Jabesh replied to him, "Leave us alone for seven days so we can send messengers throughout Israel's territory. If there's no one to save us, then we'll surrender to you."

[4]When the messengers reached Gibeah where Saul lived, they reported the news directly to the people there. Then they all wept aloud. [5]At just that moment, Saul was coming back from keeping the cattle in the fields. "What's wrong with everybody?" he asked. "Why are they crying?" Saul was then told what the men from Jabesh had said.

[6]God's spirit came over Saul when he heard those words, and he burned with anger. [7]He took two oxen, cut them into pieces, and sent them by messengers throughout Israel's territory. "This is exactly what will be done to the oxen of anyone who doesn't come to the aid of Saul and Samuel," he said. Great fear of the Lord came over the people, and they came to Saul completely unified.[l] [8]When Saul counted them at Bezek, the soldiers from Israel totaled three hundred thousand and those from Judah thirty thousand.

[9]The messengers who had come were then told, "Say this to the people of Jabesh-gilead: Tomorrow by the time the sun is hot, you will be saved." When the messengers returned and reported this to the people of Jabesh, they were overjoyed.

[10]Then the people of Jabesh told the Ammonites, "We will surrender to you tomorrow. Then you can do whatever you want to us."

[11]The next day Saul organized his troops into three formations. They attacked the Ammonite camp during the morning watch and slaughtered them until the heat of the day. The survivors were so scattered that not even two of them could be found together.

[12]Then people asked Samuel, "Who was it who said, 'Will Saul rule over us?' Give us those people; we'll kill them!"

[13]But Saul said, "No one will be executed because today the Lord has saved Israel."

[14]"Let's go to Gilgal," Samuel told the people, "and renew the monarchy there." [15]So everyone went to Gilgal, and there at Gilgal they made Saul king in the Lord's presence. They offered well-being sacrifices in the Lord's presence, and Saul and all the Israelites held a great celebration there.

---

[h]LXX; MT lacks *Samuel then brought the family of Matri forward, person by person.* [i]Or *the lawful practices of the monarchy* [j]This paragraph is found in DSS (4QSamᵃ) and is also attested in Josephus (*Ant.* 6.5.1 [68-71]), but is missing in MT. [k]DSS (4QSamᵃ), LXX; MT lacks *About a month later.* [l]MT lacks *to Saul.*

Samuel's last speech

12 Samuel said to all Israel: "Listen: I have done everything you asked of me and have placed a king over you. [2]The king will lead you now. I am old and gray, though my sons are still with you, and I've been your leader since I was young until now. [3]So I'm here: Tell the truth about me in the presence of the LORD and his anointed. Have I ever stolen someone's ox? Have I ever taken someone's donkey? Have I ever oppressed or mistreated anyone? Have I ever taken bribes from someone and looked the other way about something? Tell me the truth.[m] I will make it right."

[4]"You haven't oppressed or mistreated us, and you've never taken anything from anyone," the people answered.

[5]Samuel replied, "The LORD and his anointed one are witnesses against you today that you haven't found anything in my possession."

"Agreed," they said.

[6]Then Samuel told the people: "The witness[n] is indeed the LORD, who appointed Moses and Aaron and brought your ancestors up from the land of Egypt. [7]So now stand here, and I will judge you in the LORD's presence because of all the LORD's righteous acts that he has done for you and your ancestors:

[8]"When Jacob entered Egypt, the Egyptians oppressed them.[o] So your ancestors cried out to the LORD. The LORD then sent Moses and Aaron, who brought your ancestors out of Egypt and settled them here. [9]But your ancestors forgot the LORD their God, so he handed them over to Sisera the commander of Hazor's army, and to the Philistines, and to the Moabite king, all of whom fought against them. [10]Then your ancestors cried out to the LORD and said: 'We have sinned because we have abandoned the LORD and have worshipped the Baals and the Astartes. But now deliver us from the power of our enemies, and we will worship you.' [11]So the LORD sent Jerubbaal, Barak,[p] Jephthah, and Samson,[q] and he delivered you from the power of your enemies on every side. And you lived safe and secure. [12]But when you saw that Nahash the Ammonite king was coming against you, you said to me, 'No! There must be a king to rule over us.' But the LORD your God was already your king!

[13]"So now, here is the king you chose, the one you asked for. Yes, the LORD has put a king over you! [14]If you will fear the LORD, worship him, obey him, and not rebel against the LORD's command, and if both you and the king who rules over you follow the LORD your God—all will be well. [15]But if you don't obey the LORD and rebel against the LORD's command, then the LORD's power will go against you and your king to destroy you.[r]

[16]"So now take a stand! Look at this awesome thing the LORD is doing. [17]Isn't the wheat harvest today? I will call upon the LORD to send thunder and rain. Then you will know and will see for yourselves what great evil you've done in the LORD's eyes by asking for a king."

[18]Samuel called upon the LORD, and God sent thunder and rain on that very day. Then all the people were in awe of the LORD and Samuel.

[19]All of them said to Samuel, "Please pray for us, your servants, to the LORD your God so we don't die because we have added to our many sins the evil of asking for a king."

[20]But Samuel answered the people, "Don't be afraid. Yes, you've done all this evil; just don't turn back from following the LORD. Serve the LORD with all your heart. [21]Don't turn aside to follow useless idols that can't help you or save you. They're absolutely useless! [22]For the sake of his reputation, the LORD won't abandon his people, because the LORD has decided to make you his very own people. [23]But me? I would never sin against the LORD by failing to pray for you. I will teach you what is good and right. [24]Just fear the LORD and serve him faithfully with all your heart. Look at what great things he has done for you! [25]But if you continue to do evil, then both you and your king will be destroyed."

Samuel rejects Saul's dynasty

13 Saul was 30 years old[s] when he became king, and he ruled over Israel forty-two

[m]LXX [n]LXX; MT lacks *witness*. [o]LXX; MT lacks *the Egyptians oppressed them*. [p]LXX, Syr; MT *Bedan* [q]Syr (cf Targ), LXX[L] *Samson*; MT, LXX[AB] *Samuel* [r]LXX[L]; MT *against you and against your ancestors* [s]LXX[L]; Syr *twenty-one*; MT lacks a number; 13:1 is omitted in LXX[B].

years.[t] ²Saul selected three thousand men from Israel. Two thousand of those were with Saul at Michmash in the hills near Bethel, and one thousand were with Jonathan at Gibeah in Benjamin. He sent the remaining men home. ³Jonathan attacked the Philistine fort at Geba, and the Philistines heard about it. So Saul sounded the alarm[u] throughout the land and said, "Hebrews! Listen up!" ⁴When all Israel heard that Saul had attacked the Philistine fort and that Israel was hated by the Philistines, the troops were called to Saul's side at Gilgal. ⁵The Philistines also were gathered to fight against Israel. They brought thirty thousand chariots with them, six thousand cavalry, and as many soldiers as there is sand on the seashore to fight Israel.[v] They marched up and camped at Michmash, east of Beth-aven. ⁶When the Israelites saw that they were in trouble and that their troops were threatened, they hid in caves, in thickets, among rocks, in tunnels, and in cisterns.

⁷Some Hebrews even crossed the Jordan River, going into the land of Gad and Gilead.

Saul stayed at Gilgal, and the troops followed him anxiously. ⁸He waited seven days, the time appointed by Samuel, but Samuel didn't come to Gilgal, and his troops began to desert. ⁹So Saul ordered, "Bring me the entirely burned offering and the well-being sacrifices." Then he offered the entirely burned offering.

¹⁰The very moment Saul finished offering up the entirely burned offering, Samuel arrived. Saul went out to meet him and welcome him. ¹¹But Samuel said, "What have you done?"

"I saw that my troops were deserting," Saul replied. "You hadn't arrived by the appointed time, and the Philistines were gathering at Michmash. ¹²I thought, The Philistines are about to march against me at Gilgal and I haven't yet sought the LORD's favor. So I took control of myself[w] and offered the entirely burned offering."

[t]Part of the number is missing in MT (*. . . and two years*) and all ancient witnesses. Acts 13:21 says Saul ruled forty years, as does Josephus (*Ant.* 6.14.9 [378]), though Josephus also says Saul ruled twenty years (*Ant.* 10.8.4 [143]). [u]Heb *shofar* [v]LXX; MT lacks *They brought*, *with them*, and *to fight Israel.* [w]Or *forced myself*; Heb uncertain

Take a Stand   1 Samuel 12:13-25

Have you ever had to take a stand—to be different when everyone around you is doing something else? Maybe you had to leave a sleepover early to go to church when the rest of your friends were sleeping in. Maybe you aren't allowed to play any soccer or baseball games with your team on Sundays. Or maybe you chose not to go along with friends who were doing something they shouldn't be doing. It can be really hard to take a stand when it feels like no one else is.

Samuel called God's people to serve God only and not to be distracted by what other people were doing. The people who lived near them didn't follow God. They looked to useless things to save them. God's people had to choose whether they would try to be like everyone else or faithfully obey God. When you're tempted to go along with the crowd and you can't remember why it's important to take a stand, remember that God's blessings come to those who follow God's commands.

Make a list of all that God has done for you.

How can you use this list to help you take a stand for what's right?

[13]"How stupid of you to have broken the commands the LORD your God gave you!" Samuel told Saul. "The LORD would have established your rule over Israel forever, [14]but now your rule won't last. The LORD will search for a man following the Lord's own heart,[x] and the LORD will commission him as leader over God's people, because you didn't keep the LORD's command."

UMBRELLA

DISOBEDIENCE

Obedience Is Better than Sacrifice
1 Samuel 13:13

King Saul was running out of time. His army was badly outnumbered by the Philistines. His men were afraid and beginning to run away. God told Saul to wait for Samuel so that Samuel could offer a sacrifice and ask for God's favor before the battle. But Saul was afraid his entire army would run away if he waited any longer for the prophet to show up. So Saul offered the sacrifice himself, which disobeyed God's Instruction. Saul thought he was doing a good thing—offering a sacrifice. But it was more important for Saul to obey God exactly, instead of doing his own thing. God was so upset over Saul doing things his own way that God told Saul his crown would never pass to his children. God would give Israel another king—someone not from Saul's family. Because Saul didn't trust God enough to wait and obey God, Saul's family lost power forever. ◔

[15]Samuel got up and went on his way from Gilgal, but the rest of the people followed Saul to join the army, and they went from Gilgal[y] to Gibeah in Benjamin. Saul counted about six hundred men still with him. [16]Saul, his son Jonathan, and the people who were with him were staying at Geba in Benjamin, while the Philistines camped at Michmash. [17]Three raiding parties left the Philistine camp. One took the road to Ophrah toward the territory of Shual. [18]Another took the road to Beth-horon, and the last took the border road that overlooks the Zeboim Valley toward the desert.

Philistine ironworking

[19]No metalworker was to be found anywhere in Israelite territory because the Philistines had said, "The Hebrews must not make swords and spears." [20]So every Israelite had to go down to the Philistines to sharpen their plowshares, mattocks, axes, and sickles. [21]The cost was two-thirds of a shekel[z] for plowshares and mattocks, but one-third of a shekel for sharpening axes and for setting goads. [22]So on the day of the battle, no swords or spears were to be found in the possession of any of the troops with Saul and Jonathan, but Saul and his son Jonathan had them.

Jonathan leads Israel to victory

[23]Now a group of Philistine soldiers had marched out to the pass at Michmash. **14**One day Jonathan, Saul's son, said to his young armor-bearer, "Come on! Let's go over to the Philistine fort on the opposite side." But he didn't tell his father. [2]Saul was sitting on the outskirts of Gibeah under the pomegranate tree at Migron. He had about six hundred men with him, [3]including Ahijah, the son of Ahitub, who was Ichabod's brother and the son of Phinehas the son of Eli, who was the LORD's priest at Shiloh. He was wearing a priestly vest.[a] None of the troops knew that Jonathan had gone.

[4]There were two stone outcroppings in the pass where Jonathan planned on crossing over to the Philistine fort—one on each side. One of these was named Bozez; the other was named Seneh. [5]One outcropping was on the north side, in front of Michmash, and the other was on the south side, in front of Geba. [6]Jonathan said to his young armor-bearer, "Come on, let's go over to the fort of these uncircumcised men. Maybe the LORD will act on our behalf. After all, nothing can stop the LORD from saving, whether there are many soldiers[b] or few."

[7]"Go ahead with whatever you're planning," his armor-bearer replied. "I'm with you, whatever you decide."

[8]"All right then," Jonathan said. "We'll go over to the men and show ourselves. [9]If they say to us, 'Stay there until we get to you,' then we'll stay where we are and won't go up to them. [10]But if they say, 'Come on up,' then

Bet you can read this in 8 minutes. **Ready, set, go!**

[x]Or *a man loyal to the Lord* [y]LXX; MT lacks much of this verse. [z]Heb *pim*, which is two-thirds of a shekel [a]Heb *ephod*
[b]MT lacks *soldiers*.

we'll go up because that will be the sign that the Lord has handed them over to us."

[11]So they showed themselves to the Philistine fort, and the Philistines said, "Look, the Hebrews are coming out of the holes they've been hiding in!" [12]Then the troops in the fort yelled to Jonathan and his armor-bearer, "Come on up! We'll teach you a lesson!"

So Jonathan said to his armor-bearer, "Follow me, because the Lord has handed them over to Israel!" [13]So Jonathan scrambled up on his hands and feet with his armor-bearer right behind him. The Philistines fell before Jonathan. His armor-bearer, coming behind him, would then finish them off. [14]In the first attack, Jonathan and his armor-bearer killed about twenty men in an area of about half an acre.[c] [15]Panic broke out in the camp, in the field, and among all the troops. Even those in the fort and the raiders shook with fear. The very ground shook! It was a terror from God.

[16]Now Saul's lookouts at Gibeah in Benjamin saw the Philistine camp running all over the place.[d] [17]Saul said to the troops with him, "Take a count and see who is missing." So they counted, and Jonathan and his armor-bearer were gone. [18]Saul said to Ahijah, "Bring the priestly vest!"[e] because at that time, Ahijah wore the priestly vest in Israel's presence.[f] [19]As Saul was talking to the priest, the confusion in the Philistine camp continued to grow. Saul said to the priest, "Withdraw your hand."[g]

[20]Then Saul called all his troops together, and they went into battle. The Philistines were completely confused; every soldier's sword was turned against his fellow soldier. [21]Even those Hebrews who had earlier joined up with the Philistines and moved into their camp changed sides to be with the Israelites who were with Saul and Jonathan. [22]Similarly, when all the Israelites who had been hiding in the highlands of Ephraim heard that the Philistines were on the run, they also joined the battle in hot pursuit of the Philistines. [23]The Lord saved Israel that day, and the fighting carried on beyond Beth-aven.

[24]Now the Israelite soldiers were in a difficult situation that day because Saul had bound the troops by a solemn pledge: "Anyone who eats anything before evening when I have taken revenge on my enemies is doomed." So none of the army ate anything. [25]The troops[h] came across a honeycomb with honey on the ground. [26]But even when they came across the honeycomb with the honey still flowing, no one ate any of it because the troops were afraid of the solemn pledge. [27]But Jonathan hadn't heard his father make the people swear the pledge, so he dipped the end of the staff he was carrying into the honeycomb. When he ate some his eyes lit up. [28]Then one of the soldiers spoke up: "Your father bound the troops by a solemn pledge: 'Anyone who eats food today is doomed.' That's why the troops are exhausted."

[29]Jonathan said, "My father has brought trouble to the land. Look how my eyes lit up when I tasted just a bit of that honey! [30]It would have been even better if the troops had eaten some of their enemies' plunder today when they found it! But now the Philistine defeat isn't as thorough as it might have been."

[31]That day, after they had fought the Philistines from Michmash to Aijalon, the troops were completely exhausted. [32]So the troops tore into the plunder, taking sheep, cattle, and calves. They slaughtered them right on the ground and devoured them with the blood still in them. [33]When it was reported to Saul, "The troops are sinning against the Lord by eating meat with blood in it," Saul said, "All of you are traitors! Roll a large stone over here right now. [34]Go among the troops and say to them, 'Everyone must bring their ox or sheep, and slaughter them here with me. Don't sin against the Lord by eating meat with blood still in it.'" So everyone brought whatever they had and slaughtered it there.[i] [35]And Saul built an altar to the Lord. It was the first altar he had built to the Lord.

[36]"Let's go after the Philistines tonight and plunder them until morning," Saul said. "We won't leave them a single survivor!"

"Do whatever you think is best," the troops replied.

---

[c]Heb uncertain [d]LXX [e]LXX *ephod* [f]LXX; MT "*Bring out God's chest!*" *because at that time God's chest was with the Israelites;* cf 14:3. [g]*That is, from the priestly vest (Heb ephod) or from the Urim and Thummim contained therein* [h]MT *land* [i]LXX; MT *brought their ox and slaughtered it there that night.*

But the priest said, "Let's ask God first."

[37] So Saul questioned God: "Should I go after the Philistines? Will you hand them over to Israel?" But God did not answer him that day.

[38] Then Saul said, "All you officers in the army, come forward! Let's find out what sin was committed today. [39] As surely as the LORD lives—the one who has saved Israel—even if it's my own son Jonathan, that person will be executed." Not one of the soldiers answered him. [40] So Saul said to all Israel, "You be on one side, and my son Jonathan and I will be on the other."

"Do whatever you think is best," the troops said.

[41] Then Saul asked the LORD God of Israel, "Why haven't you answered your servant today? If the wrongdoing is mine or my son Jonathan's, respond with Urim, but if the wrongdoing belongs to your people Israel, respond with Thummim."[j] Jonathan and Saul were taken by lot, and the troops were cleared.

[42] Then Saul said, "Decide between me and my son Jonathan."[k] And Jonathan was selected.

[43] "Tell me what you've done," Saul said to Jonathan.

So Jonathan told him. "I only took a very small taste of honey on the end of my staff," he said. "And now I'm supposed to die?"

[44] "May God deal harshly with me and worse still if you don't die today!"[l] Saul swore.

[45] But the troops said to Saul, "Why should Jonathan die when he has won this great victory for Israel? No way! As surely as the LORD lives, not one hair off his head will fall to the ground, because he did this today with God's help." So the troops rescued Jonathan, and he wasn't executed.

[46] Then Saul stopped chasing the Philistines, and the Philistines went back to their own country.

Saul's wars

[47] Saul secured his kingship over Israel. He fought against his enemies on every side: against Moab, the Ammonites, Edom, the king of Zobah,[m] and the Philistines. Wherever

he turned, he was victorious.[n] [48] He acted heroically, defeating the Amalekites and rescuing Israel from the power of any who had plundered them.

[49] Saul's sons were Jonathan, Ishvi, and Malchishua. The names of his two daughters were Merab, the oldest, and Michal, the younger daughter. [50] The name of Saul's wife was Ahinoam, Ahimaaz's daughter. The name of his general was Abner, Ner's son, Saul's uncle. [51] Kish, Saul's father, and Ner, Abner's father, were Abiel's sons.

[52] There was fierce warfare against the Philistines throughout Saul's lifetime. So whenever Saul saw any strong or heroic man, he would add him to his troops.

Samuel rejects Saul's kingship

15 Samuel said to Saul, "The LORD sent me to anoint you king over his people Israel. Listen now to the LORD's words! [2] This is what the LORD of heavenly forces says: I am going to punish the Amalekites for what they did to Israel: how they attacked the Israelites as they came up from Egypt. [3] So go! Attack the Amalekites; put everything that belongs to them under the ban.[o] Spare no one. Kill men and women, children and infants, oxen and sheep, camels and donkeys."

[4] Saul called out the troops and counted them at Telaim: two hundred thousand foot soldiers and ten thousand more troops from Judah. [5] Then Saul advanced on the Amalekite city and laid an ambush in the valley. [6] Saul told the Kenites, "Get going! Leave the Amalekites immediately because you showed kindness to the Israelites when they came out of Egypt. Otherwise, I'll destroy you right along with them." So the Kenites left the Amalekites. [7] Then Saul attacked the Amalekites from Havilah all the way to Shur, which is near Egypt. [8] He captured Agag the Amalekite king alive, but Saul placed all the people under the ban, killing them with the sword. [9] Saul and the troops spared Agag along with the best sheep, cattle, fattened calves,[p] lambs, and everything of value. They weren't willing to put them under the ban; but anything

---

[j] LXX, Vulg; MT *Saul asked the Lord God of Israel, "Give the right answer."* Urim and Thummim were sacred lots carried by the priest. [k] LXX adds *Whoever the Lord selects will die. The army said to Saul, "Don't do this!"* But Saul forced them, so they decided between him and Jonathan his son. [l] LXX; MT *if you don't die, Jonathan* [m] LXX, DSS (4QSam[a]); MT *kings of Zobah* [n] LXX [o] A technique of holy war that often involves total destruction, in which everything that is destroyed is dedicated to the deity who helps in the battle; also in 15:8-9, 15, 18, 20-21. [p] LXX

that was despised or of no value[q] they placed under the ban.

¹⁰Then the Lord's word came to Samuel: ¹¹"I regret making Saul king because he has turned away from following me and hasn't done what I said." Samuel was upset at this, and he prayed to the Lord all night long.

¹²Samuel got up early in the morning to meet Saul, and was told, "Saul went to Carmel, where he is setting up a monument for himself. Then he left and went down to Gilgal."

¹³When Samuel reached Saul,[r] Saul greeted him, "The Lord bless you! I have done what the Lord said."

¹⁴"Then what," Samuel asked, "is this bleating of sheep in my ears and mooing of cattle I hear?"

¹⁵"They were taken from the Amalekites," Saul said, "because the troops spared the best sheep and cattle in order to sacrifice them to the Lord your God. The rest was placed under the ban."

¹⁶Samuel then said to Saul, "Enough! Let me tell you what the Lord said to me last night."

"Tell me," Saul replied.

¹⁷Samuel said, "Even if you think you are insignificant, aren't you the leader of Israel's tribes? The Lord anointed you king over Israel. ¹⁸The Lord sent you on a mission, instructing you, 'Go, and put the sinful Amalekites under the ban. Fight against them until you've wiped them out.' ¹⁹Why didn't you obey the Lord? You did evil in the Lord's eyes when you tore into the plunder!"

²⁰"But I did obey the Lord!" Saul protested to Samuel. "I went on the mission the Lord sent me on. I captured Agag the Amalekite king, and I put the Amalekites under the ban. ²¹Yes, the troops took sheep and cattle from the plunder—the very best items placed under the ban—but in order to sacrifice them to the Lord your God at Gilgal."

²²Then Samuel replied,

"Does the Lord want
    entirely burned offerings and sacrifices
    as much as obedience to the Lord?
Listen to this:
    obeying is better than sacrificing,
    paying attention
    is better than fat from rams,

²³because rebellion is as bad
    as the sin of divination;
    arrogance is like the evil of idolatry.[s]
Because you have rejected
    what the Lord said,
    he has rejected you as king."

²⁴Saul said to Samuel, "I have sinned because I disobeyed the Lord's command and your instructions. I was afraid of the troops and obeyed them. ²⁵But now please forgive my sin! Come back with me, so I can worship the Lord."

UMBRELLA

DISOBEDIENCE

Don't Make Excuses for Disobeying
1 Samuel 15:24

Saul hadn't learned his lesson. Earlier he went against God by offering a sacrifice without God's priest, Samuel (1 Sam 13:1-14). Now, when he was commanded to kill all the Amalekites and their animals, he spared the Amalekite king and saved the best of all the sheep and cattle. Once Samuel arrived, Saul lied and said he saved the best of the animals so they could be sacrificed to God. But God knew the truth—that Saul was afraid his own men wouldn't let him kill the best animals. Saul was more worried about what his men might do than about obeying God. Saul thought he could get away with doing as he wished, as long as he did something good—like offer a sacrifice to God—to make up for it. Saul was trying to bribe God with sacrifices. Because Saul couldn't be trusted to do what God wanted, God rejected Saul as king.

²⁶But Samuel said to Saul, "I can't[t] return with you because you have rejected what the Lord said, and the Lord has rejected you from being king over Israel."

²⁷Samuel turned to leave, but Saul grabbed at the edge of his robe, and it ripped. ²⁸Then Samuel told him, "The Lord has ripped the kingdom of Israel from you today. He will give it to a friend of yours, someone who is more worthy than you. ²⁹What's more, the enduring one of Israel

Memorize
1 Sam 15:29

doesn't take back what he says and doesn't change his mind. He is not a human being who would change his mind."

q LXX; Heb uncertain r LXX adds *he was offering entirely burned sacrifices to the Lord, the best of the plunder that he had taken from Amalek. As Samuel approached Saul.* s Sym, LXX[B]; MT *evil and idolatry* t Or *won't*

³⁰"I have sinned," Saul said, "but please honor me in front of my people's elders and before Israel, and come back with me so I can worship the Lord your God." ³¹So Samuel went back with Saul, and Saul worshipped the Lord.

³²"Bring me Agag the Amalekite king," Samuel said.

Agag came to him in chains, asking, "Would death have been as bitter as this is?"ᵘ

³³Samuel said, "Just as your sword left women without their children, now your mother will be childless among women." Then Samuel cut Agag to pieces in the Lord's presence at Gilgal.

³⁴Then Samuel went to Ramah, but Saul went up to his home in Gibeah. ³⁵Samuel never saw Saul again before he died, but he grieved over Saul. However, the Lord regretted making Saul king over Israel.

Samuel anoints David

16 The Lord said to Samuel, "How long are you going to grieve over Saul? I have rejected him as king over Israel. Fill your horn with oil and get going. I'm sending you to Jesse of Bethlehem because I have foundᵛ my next king among his sons."

²"How can I do that?" Samuel asked. "When Saul hears of it he'll kill me!"

"Take a heifer with you," the Lord replied, "and say, 'I have come to make a sacrifice to the Lord.' ³Invite Jesse to the sacrifice, and I will make clear to you what you should do. You will anoint for me the person I point out to you."

⁴Samuel did what the Lord instructed. When he came to Bethlehem, the city elders came to meet him. They were shaking with fear. "Do you come in peace?" they asked.

⁵"Yes," Samuel answered. "I've come to make a sacrifice to the Lord. Now make yourselves holy, then come with me to the sacrifice." Samuel made Jesse and his sons holy and invited them to the sacrifice as well.

⁶When they arrived, Samuel looked at Eliab and thought, That must be the Lord's anointed right in front.

Memorize 1 Sam 16:7

⁷But the Lord said to Samuel, "Have no regard for his appearance or stature, because I haven't selected him. Godʷ doesn't look at things like humans do. Humans see only what is visible to the eyes, but the Lord sees into the heart."

⁸Next Jesse called for Abinadab, who presented himself to Samuel, but he said, "The Lord hasn't chosen this one either." ⁹So Jesse presented Shammah, but Samuel said, "No, the Lord hasn't chosen this one." ¹⁰Jesse presented seven of his sons to Samuel, but Samuel said to Jesse, "The Lord hasn't picked any of these." ¹¹Then Samuel asked Jesse, "Is that all of your boys?"

"There is still the youngest one," Jesse answered, "but he's out keeping the sheep."

"Send for him," Samuel told Jesse, "because we can't proceed until he gets here."ˣ

¹²So Jesse sent and brought him in. He was reddish brown, had beautiful eyes, and was good-looking. The Lord said, "That's the one. Go anoint him." ¹³So Samuel took the horn of oil and anointed him right there in front of his brothers. The Lord's spirit came over David from that point forward.

Then Samuel left and went to Ramah.

LIGHTHOUSE

Heart

God Knows the Heart *1 Samuel 16:7-13*

David, the shepherd boy, had the heart of a king. God had sent Samuel to the family of Jesse in order to find Israel's new king. It took only one look at Jesse's son Eliab for Samuel to think he knew exactly who God wanted for king. Eliab was probably tall, with a strong body like King Saul (1 Sam 10:23-24). But God told Samuel that God looks at the heart to decide worth, not the outward appearance. God knew the shepherd boy David was the one whose heart was worthy to be a king. God knew David's heart—that David was brave and that he loved and served God. David's heart, and not his appearance, helped him to become one of Israel's greatest kings. ◊

David is introduced to Saul

¹⁴Now the Lord's spirit had departed from Saul, and an evil spirit from the Lord tormented him. ¹⁵Saul's servants said to him, "Look, an evil spirit from God is tormenting you. ¹⁶If our master just says the word, your

---

ᵘLXX; Heb uncertain ᵛOr *seen* ʷLXX; MT lacks *God.* ˣMT; LXX *we won't sit down* (that is, to eat)

servants will search for someone who knows how to play the lyre. The musician can play whenever the evil spirit from God is affecting you, and then you'll feel better."

¹⁷Saul said to his servants, "Find me a good musician and bring him to me."

¹⁸One of the servants responded, "I know that one of Jesse's sons from Bethlehem is a good musician. He's a strong man and heroic, a warrior who speaks well and is good-looking too. The Lᴏʀᴅ is with him."

¹⁹So Saul sent messengers to Jesse to say, "Send me your son David, the one who keeps the sheep."

²⁰Jesse then took a donkey and loaded it with a homer of bread,ʸ a jar of wine, and a young goat, and he sent it along with his son David to Saul. ²¹That is how David came to Saul and entered his service. Saul liked David very much,ᶻ and David became his armor-bearer. ²²Saul sent a message to Jesse: "Please allow David to remain in my service because I am pleased with him." ²³Whenever the evil spirit from God affected Saul, David would take the lyre and play it. Then Saul would relax and feel better, and the evil spirit would leave him alone.

David defeats Goliath

17 The Philistines assembled their troops for war at Socoh of Judah. They camped between Socoh and Azekah at Ephes-dammim. ²Saul and the Israelite army assembled and camped in the Elah Valley, where they got organized to fight the Philistines. ³The Philistines took positions on one hill while Israel took positions on the opposite hill. There was a valley between them.

⁴A champion named Goliath from Gath came out from the Philistine camp. He was more than nine feet tall.ᵃ ⁵He had a bronze helmet on his head and wore bronze scale-armor weighing one hundred twenty-five pounds.ᵇ ⁶He had bronze plates on his shins, and a bronze scimitar hung on his back. ⁷His spear shaftᶜ was as strong as the bar on a weaver's loom, and its iron head weighed fifteen pounds.ᵈ His shield-bearer walked in front of him.

⁸He stopped and shouted to the Israelite troops, "Why have you come and taken up battle formations? I am the Philistine champion,ᵉ and you are Saul's servants. Isn't that right? Select one of your men, and let him come down against me. ⁹If he is able to fight me and kill me, then we will become your slaves, but if I overcome him and kill him, then you will become our slaves and you will serve us. ¹⁰I insult Israel's troops today!" The Philistine continued, "Give me an opponent, and we'll fight!" ¹¹When Saul and all Israel heard what the Philistine said, they were distressed and terrified.ᶠ

¹²Now David was Jesse's son, an Ephraimite from Bethlehem in Judah who had eight sons. By Saul's time, Jesse was already quite old and far along in age.ᵍ ¹³Jesse's three oldest sons had gone with Saul to war. Their names were Eliab the oldest, Abinadab the second oldest, and Shammah the third oldest. ¹⁴(David was the youngest.) These three older sons followed Saul, ¹⁵but David went back and forth from Saul's side to shepherd his father's flock in Bethlehem.

¹⁶For forty days straight the Philistine came out and took his stand, both morning and evening. ¹⁷Jesse said to his son David, "Please take your brothers an ephahʰ of this roasted grain and these ten loaves of bread. Deliver them quickly to your brothers in the camp. ¹⁸And here, take these ten wedges of cheese to their unit commander. Find out how your brothers are doing and bring back some sign that they are okay. ¹⁹They are with Saul and all the Israelite troops fighting the Philistines in the Elah Valley."

²⁰So David got up early in the morning, left someone in charge of the flock, and loaded up and left, just as his father Jesse had instructed him. He reached the camp right when the army was taking up their battle formations and shouting the war cry. ²¹Israel and the Philistines took up their battle formations opposite each other. ²²David left his things with an attendant and ran to the front line. When he arrived, he asked how his brothers were doing. ²³Right when David was speaking with

---

ʸLXX ᶻOr David liked Saul very much. ᵃLXX over six feet tall ᵇFive thousand shekels ᶜQere, LXX, Syr (cf 2 Sam 21:19); Kethib the point of his spear ᵈSix hundred shekels ᵉMT the Philistine lacks champion. ᶠThe following verses are absent from LXXᴮ: 17:12-31, 41, 48b, 50, 55-58. ᵍLXX, Syr ʰOne ephah is approximately twenty quarts.

them, Goliath, the Philistine champion from Gath, came forward from the Philistine ranks and said the same things he had said before. David listened. [24]When the Israelites saw Goliath, every one of them ran away terrified of him. ([25]Now the Israelite soldiers had been saying to each other: "Do you see this man who keeps coming out? How he comes to insult Israel? The king will reward with great riches whoever kills that man. The king will give his own daughter to him and make his household exempt from taxes[i] in Israel.")

[26]David asked the soldiers standing by him, "What will be done for the person who kills that Philistine over there and removes this insult from Israel? Who is that uncircumcised Philistine, anyway, that he can get away with insulting the army of the living God?"

[27]Then the troops repeated to him what they had been saying. "So that's what will be done for the man who kills him," they said.

[28]When David's oldest brother Eliab heard him talking to the soldiers, he got very mad at David. "Why did you come down here?" he said. "Who is watching those few sheep for you in the wilderness? I know how arrogant you are and your devious plan: you came down just to see the battle!"

[29]"What did I do wrong this time?" David replied. "It was just a question!"

[30]So David turned to someone else and asked the same thing, and the people said the same thing in reply. [31]The things David had said were overheard and reported to Saul, who sent for him.

[32]"Don't let anyone[j] lose courage because of this Philistine!" David told Saul. "I, your servant, will go out and fight him!"

[33]"You can't go out and fight this Philistine," Saul answered David. "You are still a boy. But he's been a warrior since he was a boy!"

[34]"Your servant has kept his father's sheep," David replied to Saul, "and if ever a lion or a bear came and carried off one of the flock, [35]I would go after it, strike it, and rescue the animal from its mouth. If it turned on me, I would grab it at its jaw, strike it, and kill it. [36]Your servant has fought both lions and bears. This uncircumcised Philistine will be

just like one of them because he has insulted the army of the living God.

[37]"The LORD," David added, "who rescued me from the power of both lions and bears, will rescue me from the power of this Philistine."

"Go!" Saul replied to David. "And may the LORD be with you!"

[38]Then Saul dressed David in his own gear, putting a coat of armor on him and a bronze helmet on his head. [39]David strapped his sword on over the armor, but he couldn't walk around well because he'd never tried it before. "I can't walk in this," David told Saul, "because I've never tried it before." So he took them off. [40]He then grabbed his staff and chose five smooth stones from the streambed. He put them in the pocket of his shepherd's bag and with sling in hand went out to the Philistine.

[41]The Philistine got closer and closer to David, and his shield-bearer was in front of him. [42]When the Philistine looked David over, he sneered at David because he was just a boy; reddish brown and good-looking.

[43]The Philistine asked David, "Am I some sort of dog that you come at me with sticks?" And he cursed David by his gods. [44]"Come here," he said to David,

SAILBOAT

COURAGE

Trusting God Brings Bravery
1 Samuel 17:32-50

David the shepherd boy went alone to face a giant enemy of God. The Philistine soldier Goliath scared everyone. He was huge—almost twice as tall as an ordinary person. He'd been a warrior since he was a boy. Every day Goliath walked onto the field between the Philistine and Israelite armies and called for an Israelite to come fight him. Every day the Israelites listened to the insults Goliath called down on Israel and did nothing. This went on, day after day, until David walked onto the field. This wasn't David's first act of courage. He'd already killed lions and bears that came after his father's sheep. David killed Goliath with stones thrown from the same sling he used to kill those lions and bears. David didn't need a sword. He knew God didn't save by sword or spear. David needed only God and the courage to trust in God. ◗

"and I'll feed your flesh to the wild birds and the wild animals!"

[45]But David told the Philistine, "You are coming against me with sword, spear, and scimitar, but I come against you in the name of the Lord of heavenly forces, the God of Israel's army, the one you've insulted. [46]Today the Lord will hand you over to me. I will strike you down and cut off your head! Today I will feed your dead body and the dead bodies of the entire Philistine camp[k] to the wild birds and the wild animals. Then the whole world will know that there is a God on Israel's side. [47]And all those gathered here will know that the Lord doesn't save by means of sword and spear. The Lord owns this war, and he will hand all of you over to us."

[48]The Philistine got up and moved closer to attack David, and David ran quickly to the front line to face him. [49]David put his hand in his bag and took out a stone. He slung it, and it hit the Philistine on his forehead. The stone penetrated his forehead, and he fell facedown on the ground. [50]And that's how David triumphed over the Philistine with just a

> **did you know?**
> The robe Jonathan gave David wasn't like robes we have today that we wear over other clothes. In Bible times, robes were long-sleeved gowns that reached the ground. Men wore these robes under outer cloaks.

sling and a stone, striking the Philistine down and killing him—and David didn't even have a sword! [51]Then David ran and stood over the Philistine. He grabbed the Philistine's sword, drew it from its sheath, and finished him off. Then David cut off the Philistine's head with the sword.

When the Philistines saw that their hero was dead, they fled. [52]The soldiers from Israel and Judah jumped up with a shout and chased the Philistines all the way to Gath[l] and the gates of Ekron. The dead Philistines were littered along the Shaarim road all the way to Gath and Ekron. [53]When the Israelites came back from chasing the Philistines, they plundered their camp. [54]David took the head

of the Philistine and brought it to Jerusalem, but he put the Philistine's weapons in his own tent.

[55]Now when Saul saw David go out to meet the Philistine, he asked Abner the army general, "Abner, whose son is that boy?"

"As surely as you live, Your Majesty, I don't know," Abner answered.

[56]"Then find out whose son that young man is," the king replied.

[57]So when David came back from killing the Philistine, Abner sent for him and presented him to Saul. The Philistine's head was still in David's hand. [58]Saul said to him, "Whose son are you, my boy?"

"I'm the son of your servant Jesse from Bethlehem," David answered.

Jonathan and David

18As soon as David had finished talking with Saul, Jonathan's life[m] became bound up with David's life, and Jonathan loved David as much as himself.[n] [2]From that point forward, Saul kept David in his service[o] and wouldn't allow him to return to his father's household. [3]And Jonathan and David made a covenant together because Jonathan loved David as much as himself. [4]Jonathan took off the robe he was wearing and gave it to David, along with his armor, as well as his sword, his bow, and his belt. [5]David went out and was successful in every mission Saul sent him to do. So Saul placed him in charge of the soldiers, and this pleased all the troops as well as Saul's servants.

Saul jealous of David

[6]After David came back from killing the Philistine, and as the troops returned home, women from all of Israel's towns came out to meet King Saul[p] with singing and dancing, with tambourines, rejoicing, and musical instruments. [7]The women sang in celebration:

"Saul has killed his thousands,
but David has killed
his tens of thousands!"

[8]Saul burned with anger. This song annoyed him. "They've credited David with tens

---

[k]LXX; MT lacks *your dead body.* [l]LXX; MT *Gai* or *a valley* [m]Or *soul;* also twice more in this verse and in 18:3 [n]The following verses are absent from LXX[B]: 18:1-5, 10-11, 17-19, 29b-30. [o]MT lacks *in his service.* [p]MT; LXX *to meet David*

of thousands," he said, "but only credit me with thousands. What's next for him—the kingdom itself?" [9]So Saul kept a close eye on David from that point on.

[10]The next day an evil spirit from God came over Saul,[q] and he acted like he was in a prophetic frenzy in his house. So David played the lyre as he usually did. Saul had a spear in his hand, [11]and he threw it, thinking, I'll pin David to the wall. But David escaped from him two different times.

[12]Saul was afraid of David because the LORD was with David but no longer with Saul. [13]So Saul removed David from his service, placing him in command of a unit of one thousand men. David led the men out to war and back. [14]David was successful in everything he did because the LORD was with him. [15]Saul saw that he was very successful, and he was afraid of him. [16]Everyone in Israel and Judah loved David because he led them out in war and back again.

[17]Saul said to David, "Look, here is my oldest daughter Merab. I will give her to you in marriage on this condition: you must be my warrior and fight the LORD's battles." I won't raise my hand against him, Saul thought; let the Philistines do that!

[18]"I'm not worthy," David replied to Saul, "and neither is my family or my father's clan in Israel, to become the king's son-in-law." [19]And so when the time came for Saul's daughter Merab to be married to David, she was given to Adriel from Meholah instead.

[20]Now Saul's younger daughter Michal loved David. When this was reported to Saul, he was happy about it. [21]I'll give her to him, Saul thought; she'll cause him problems, and the Philistines will be against him.

So Saul said to David a second time, "Become my son-in-law now."

[22]Saul instructed his servants, "Tell David in private: 'Look, the king likes you, and all his servants love you. You should become the king's son-in-law.'"

[23]Saul's servants whispered these things in David's ear. But David said, "Do you think it's a simple matter to become the king's son-in-law? I don't! I'm poor and insignificant."

[24]Saul's servants reported what David said, [25]and Saul replied, "Tell David this: 'The king doesn't want any bridal gift, just a hundred Philistine foreskins as vengeance on the king's enemies.'" (Saul was hoping that David would die at the hands of the Philistines.) [26]When the servants reported this to David, he was happy to become the king's son-in-law. Even before the allotted time had expired,[r] [27]David got up and went with his soldiers and killed one hundred Philistines.[s] David brought their foreskins and counted them out for the king so he could become the king's son-in-law. Then Saul gave his daughter Michal to him in marriage.

[28]When Saul knew for certain that the LORD was with David and that his daughter Michal loved him, [29]then Saul was even more afraid of David. Saul was David's enemy for the rest of his life.[t] [30]And whenever the Philistine commanders came out for battle, David would have more success than the rest of Saul's officers, so his fame spread widely.

UMBRELLA

JEALOUSY

Jealousy Is Deadly   *1 Samuel 18:6-30*

King Saul was sick and tired of hearing about David. Many people were saying the same thing—that God was with David and made him successful at everything he tried. It was worse when some women compared Saul and David. "Saul has killed his thousands," they sang, "but David has killed his tens of thousands!" (1 Sam 18:7). Saul knew God no longer favored him. Saul knew God was going to raise someone else to replace him as king (1 Sam 15:27-28). More and more, it seemed like David would be that person. When Saul compared himself to David, Saul felt bad about himself. But instead of making good changes in his life, Saul chose the most hurtful path to rid himself of David. Saul's jealousy would lead him to kill innocent men, women, and children (1 Sam 22:6-19), and even almost kill his own son (1 Sam 20:32-33). Saul's uncontrollable jealousy proved he wasn't fit to remain king. ◆

David escapes Saul

19 Saul ordered his son Jonathan and all his servants to kill David, but Jonathan, Saul's son, liked David very much. [2]So

Jonathan warned David, "My father Saul is trying to kill you. Be on guard tomorrow morning. Stay somewhere safe and hide. ³I'll go out and stand by my father in the field where you'll be. I'll talk to my father about you, and I'll tell you whatever I find out."

⁴So Jonathan spoke highly about David to his father Saul, telling him, "The king shouldn't do anything wrong to his servant David, because he hasn't wronged you. In fact, his actions have helped you greatly. ⁵He risked his own life when he killed that Philistine, and the Lord won a great victory for all Israel. You saw it and were happy about it. Why then would you do something wrong to an innocent person by killing David for no reason?"

⁶Saul listened to Jonathan and then swore, "As surely as the Lord lives, David won't be executed." ⁷So Jonathan summoned David and told him everything they had talked about. Then Jonathan brought David back to Saul, and David served Saul as he had previously.

⁸War broke out again. When David went out to fight the Philistines, he struck them with such force that they ran from him.

⁹Then an evil spirit from the Lord came over Saul.ᵘ He was sitting in his house with his spear in hand while David was playing music. ¹⁰Saul tried to pin David to the wall with his spear, but David escaped Saul. Saul drove the spear into the wall, but David fled and got away safely. That night ¹¹Saul sent messengers to David's house to keep watch on it and kill him in the morning. David's wife Michal warned him, "If you don't escape with your life tonight, you are a dead man tomorrow." ¹²So Michal lowered David through a window. He took off and ran, and he got away. ¹³Then Michal took the household's divine image and laid it in the bed, putting some goat's hair on its head and covering it with clothes.

¹⁴Saul sent messengers to arrest David, but she said, "He's sick."

¹⁵Saul sent the messengers back to check on David for themselves. "Bring him to me on his bed," he ordered, "so he can be executed." ¹⁶When the messengers arrived, they found the idol in the bed with the goat's hair on its head. ¹⁷Saul said to Michal, "Why could you betray me like this, letting my enemy go so that now he has escaped?"

LIFE PRESERVER

Why would God put an evil spirit in Saul? *1 Samuel 19:9*

This description of an evil spirit being put in Saul is a way of describing how he was no longer fit or able to be the leader of God's people. We don't really know what the evil spirit was. Saul began to behave strangely, and some Bible teachers wonder if he had a mental illness. People in Saul's culture believed that mental problems were caused by evil spirits. And so they also believed that evil spirits were the result of God's actions. ◆

Michal said to Saul, "David told me, 'Help me get away or I'll kill you!'"

¹⁸So David fled and escaped. When he reached Samuel at Ramah, he reported to him everything Saul had done to him. Then he and Samuel went to stay in the camps.ᵛ

¹⁹When Saul was told that David was in the camps at Ramah, ²⁰he sent messengers to arrest David. They saw a group of prophets in a prophetic frenzy, with Samuel standing there as their leader. God's spirit came over Saul's messengers, and they also fell into a prophetic frenzy. ²¹This was reported to Saul, and he sent different messengers, but they also fell into a prophetic frenzy. So Saul sent a third group of messengers, and they did the very same thing.

²²At that point, Saul went to Ramah himself. He came to the well at the threshing floor that was on the bare hill thereʷ and asked, "Where are Samuel and David?"

"In the camps at Ramah," he was told. ²³So Saul went to the camps at Ramah, and God's spirit came over him too. So as he traveled, he was in a prophetic frenzy until he reached the camps at Ramah. ²⁴He even took off all his clothes and fell into a prophetic frenzy in front of Samuel. He lay naked that whole day and night. That's why people say, "Is Saul also one of the prophets?"

Jonathan and David's friendship

20 David fled from the camps at Ramah. He came to Jonathan and asked, "What have I done? What is my crime? How

---

ᵘOr *to Saul* ᵛOr *Naioth,* also in 19:19, 22-23 ʷLXX; MT *the large well at Secu*

have I wronged your father that he wants me dead?"

²Jonathan said to him, "No! You are not going to die! Listen: My father doesn't do anything big or small without telling me first. Why would my father hide this from me? It isn't true!"

³But David solemnly promised in response, "Your father knows full well that you like me. He probably said, 'Jonathan must not learn about this or he'll be upset.'ˣ But I promise you—on the Lord's life and yours!—that I am this close to death!"

⁴"What do you want me to do?" Jonathan said to David. "I'll do it."

⁵"Okay, listen," David answered Jonathan. "Tomorrow is the new moon, and I'm supposed to sit with the king at the feast. Instead, let me go and I'll hide in the field until nighttime.ʸ ⁶If your father takes note of my absence, tell him, 'David begged my permission to run down to his hometown Bethlehem, because there is an annual sacrifice there for his whole family.' ⁷If Saul says 'Fine,' then I, your servant, am safe. But if he loses his temper, then you'll know for certain that he intends to harm me. ⁸So be loyal to your servant, because you've brought your servant into a sacred covenantᶻ with you. If I'm guilty, then kill me yourself; just don't take me back to your father."

⁹"Enough!" Jonathan replied. "If I can determine for certain that my father intends to harm you, of course I'll tell you!"

¹⁰"Who will tell me if your father responds harshly?" David asked Jonathan.

¹¹"Come on," Jonathan said to David. "Let's go into the field." So both of them went out into the field. ¹²Then Jonathan told David, "I pledge by the Lord God of Israel that I will question my father by this time tomorrow or on the third day. If he seems favorable toward David, I will definitely send word and make sure you know. ¹³But if my father intends to harm you, then may the Lord deal harshly with me, Jonathan, and worse still if I don't tell you right away so that you can escape safely. May the Lord be with you as he once was with

my father. ¹⁴If I remain alive, be loyal to me.ᵃ But if I die, ¹⁵don't ever stop being loyal to my household. Once the Lord has eliminated all of David's enemies from the earth, ¹⁶if Jonathan's name is also eliminated, then the Lord will seek retribution from David!"ᵇ

¹⁷So Jonathan again made a pledge to Davidᶜ because he loved David as much as himself. ¹⁸"Tomorrow is the festival of the new moon," Jonathan told David. "You will be missed because your seat will be empty. ¹⁹The day after tomorrow, go all the way to the spot where you hid on the day of the incident, and stay close to that mound.ᵈ ²⁰On the third day I will shoot an arrow to the side of the mound as if aiming at a target.ᵉ ²¹Then I'll send the servant boy, saying, 'Go retrieve the arrow.' If I yell to the boy, 'Hey! The arrow is on this side of you. Get it!' then you can come out because it will be safe for you. There won't be any trouble—I make a pledge on the Lord's life. ²²But if I yell to the young man, 'Hey! The arrow is past you,' then run for it, because the Lord has sent you away. ²³Either way, the Lord is witnessᶠ between us forever regarding the promise we made to each other." ²⁴So David hid himself in the field.

When the new moon came, the king sat at the feast to eat. ²⁵He took his customary seat by the wall. Jonathan sat opposite himᵍ while Abner sat beside Saul. David's seat was empty. ²⁶Saul didn't say anything that day because he thought, Perhaps David became unclean somehow. That must be it. ²⁷But on the next day, the second of the new moon, David's seat was still empty. Saul said to his son Jonathan, "Why hasn't Jesse's son come to the table,ʰ either yesterday or today?"

²⁸Jonathan answered Saul, "David begged my permission to go to Bethlehem. ²⁹He said, 'Please let me go because we have a family sacrifice there in town, and my brother has ordered me to be present. Please do me a favor and let me slip away so I can see my family.' That's why David hasn't been at the king's table."

ˣLXX *or he'll tell David;* cf 20:34 ʸLXX; MT *until the third evening;* cf 20:12, 19-20 ²MT *the Lord's covenant* ᵃLXX; MT *show me the Lord's faithful love* ᵇ20:14-16 follows LXX. ᶜLXX; MT *Jonathan made David pledge.* ᵈLXX; MT *to the stone Ezel;* cf 20:41 ᵉCorrection; MT *arrows* (plural here and in 20:21-22, 36, 38 Qere) ᶠLXX; MT lacks *witness;* also in 20:42. ᵍLXX; MT *Jonathan arose* ʰLXX, DSS (4QSamᵇ); MT *to the feast*

30At that, Saul got angry at Jonathan. "You son of a stubborn, rebellious woman!" he said. "Do you think I don't know how you've allied yourself with Jesse's son? Shame on you and on the mother who birthed you!i 31As long as Jesse's son lives on this earth, neither you nor your dynasty will be secure. Now have him brought to me because he's a dead man!"

32But Jonathan answered his father Saul, "Why should David be executed? What has he done?"

33At that, Saul threwj his spear at Jonathan to strike him, and Jonathan realized that his father intended to kill David. 34Jonathan got up from the table in a rage. He didn't eat anything on the second day of the new moon because he was worried about David and because his father had humiliated him.

35In the morning, Jonathan went out to the field for the meeting with David, and a young servant boy went with him. 36He said to the boy, "Go quickly and retrieve the arrow that I shoot." So the boy ran off, and he shot an arrow beyond him. 37When the boy got to the spot where Jonathan shot the arrow, Jonathan yelled to him, "Isn't the arrow past you?" 38Jonathan yelled again to the boy, "Quick! Hurry up! Don't just stand there!" So Jonathan's servant boy gathered up the arrow and came back to his master. 39The boy had no idea what had happened; only Jonathan and David knew. 40Jonathan handed his weapons to the boy and told him, "Get going. Take these back to town."

41As soon as the boy was gone, David came out from behind the moundk and fell down, face on the ground, bowing low three times. The friends kissed each other, and cried with each other, but David cried hardest. 42Thenl Jonathan said to David, "Go in peace because

iOr *and shame on your mother's nakedness.* jMT; LXX; *pointed* kLXX; MT *beside the south* l21:1 in Heb

BFF (Best Friends Forever!) *1 Samuel 20:1-42*

Who is your best friend? Do you have just one BFF, or lots of really great friends? Usually, at least one time in our lives we find one person who really gets us, knows everything about us, and *still* wants to be our friend. That's the kind of friend who knows what we're thinking, finishes our sentences, cries with us, and laughs with us. This person is the kind of friend who would save our life if given the chance.

Jonathan and David were best friends. The Bible says they each cared about the other as much as they cared for themselves. But their friendship was put to the ultimate test. Jonathan was King Saul's son, and the king was growing very jealous of David. When Jonathan discovered his father was so jealous of David that he planned to kill David, Jonathan knew he had to do something. He quickly planned to help David escape. Before David left town, the friends hugged and promised to be friends forever. Then David got out of there!

Think about your friendships. The best ones are strong and include God, like David and Jonathan's friendship.

Write a letter to a close friend and tell her or him how you thank God for the friendship you share.

Say a prayer right now, asking God to help you make strong, godly friendships that last.

the two of us made a solemn pledge in the Lord's name when we said, 'The Lord is witness between us and between our descendants forever.'" Then David got up and left, but Jonathan went back to town.

David helped at Nob

21 [m] David came to Nob where Ahimelech was priest. Ahimelech was shaking in fear when he met David. "Why are you alone? Why is no one with you?" he asked.

[2] David answered Ahimelech the priest, "The king has given me orders, but he instructed me, 'Don't let anyone know anything about the mission I'm sending you on or about your orders.' As for my troops, I told them to meet me at an undisclosed location. [3] Now what do you have here with you? Give me five loaves of bread or whatever you can find."

[4] "I don't have any regular bread on hand," the priest answered David, "just holy bread—but only if your troops have abstained from sexual activity."

[5] "Definitely," David answered the priest. "Whenever I go out to war, women are off-limits; that's our standard operating procedure. Even on regular missions, the men's gear is[n] kept holy. That's even more true today, with the mission holy along with the gear."[o] [6] So the priest gave David holy bread, because there was no other bread except the bread of the presence, which is removed from the Lord's presence and replaced by warm bread as soon as it is taken away.

[7] Now one of Saul's servants was there that day, detained in the Lord's presence. His name was Doeg. He was an Edomite and Saul's head shepherd.

[8] David asked Ahimelech, "Do you have a spear or sword on hand? I didn't bring my sword or gear with me because the king's mission was urgent."

[9] The priest said, "The sword of Goliath, the Philistine you killed in the Elah Valley, is here wrapped in a cloth behind a priestly vest.[p] If you want it, take it, because there are no other swords here."

David said, "No sword is as good as that one! Give it to me!"

David pretends to be crazy

[10] So David got up and continued running from Saul. He went to Achish, Gath's king. [11] Achish's servants said to him, "Isn't that David, king of the land? He's the one people sing about in their dances,

'Saul has killed his thousands,
    but David has killed
        his tens of thousands!'"

[12] David took these words very seriously and became very frightened of Achish, Gath's king. [13] So he changed the way he acted with them, pretending to be insane while he was with them.[q] He scratched marks on the doors of the city gates[r] and let spit run down his chin.

[14] "Can't you see he's crazy?" Achish asked his servants. "Why bring him to me? [15] Am I short on insane people that you've brought this person to go crazy right in front of me? Do you really think I'm going to let this man enter my house?"

David gathers support

22 David left Gath and escaped to Adullam's fortress.[s] When David's siblings and all his extended family learned of this, they went to join him there. [2] Everyone who was in trouble, in debt, or in desperate circumstances gathered around David, and he became their leader. Approximately four hundred men joined him.

[3] From there David went to Mizpeh in Moab. He said to the Moabite king, "Please let my father and mother stay with you until I know what God will do to me." [4] So David left his parents with the Moabite king, and they stayed with him the whole time David was in the fortress.

[5] Then the prophet Gad told David, "Don't stay in the fortress any longer. Leave now and go to the land of Judah." So David left and went to Hereth forest.

Saul kills the priests of Nob

[6] Saul learned that David and his soldiers had been located. Saul was sitting under the tamarisk tree on the hill at Gibeah, spear in

---

[m]21:2 in Heb [n]MT; LXX *all the men are* [o]Heb uncertain [p]DSS (4QSam[b]); MT *behind the priestly vest* (Heb *ephod*) [q]Or *in their hand*; Heb uncertain [r]Or with correction *he spit on the doors of the city gate* or *he fell down at the doors of the city gate* (cf LXX). [s]Correction; cf 22:4-5; MT *cave*

hand, with all his servants waiting on him. ⁷He said to them, "Listen up, Benjaminites! Will Jesse's son give fields and vineyards to each and every one of you? Will he make each one of you commanders of units of one thousand men or commanders of units of one hundred? ⁸Is that why all of you have conspired against me? No one informed me when my son made a covenant with Jesse's son! Not one of you is concerned about me or informs me when my own son sets my servant against me in an ambush—but that's what has happened today!"

⁹Doeg the Edomite, who was standing with Saul's servants, responded, "I saw Jesse's son go to Ahimelech, Ahitub's son, at Nob. ¹⁰Ahimelech questioned the Lord for David, and gave him provisions as well as the sword of Goliath the Philistine."

¹¹The king then sent for the priest Ahimelech, Ahitub's son, and all his extended family, who were the priests at Nob. All of them came to the king.

¹²"Listen here, son of Ahitub," Saul said.

"Yes sir," he replied.

¹³Saul said to him, "Why have you conspired against me—you with Jesse's son—giving him food and a sword and questioning God for him so that he is now against me, waiting in ambush, which is what has happened today?"

¹⁴Ahimelech answered the king, "Out of all your servants, who is as trustworthy as David? He is the king's son-in-law, does whatever you ask, and is well respected in your house. ¹⁵Was that the first time I questioned God for him? Of course not! But please, the king shouldn't accuse me, his servant, or anyone in my father's household of any wrongdoing, because your servant knew nothing whatsoever about this matter."

¹⁶But the king said, "You will be executed, Ahimelech—you and all of your father's household!"

¹⁷The king ordered the guards waiting on him: "Go ahead and kill the Lord's priests because they've joined up with David too. They knew he was on the run but didn't inform me."

But the king's servants were unwilling to lift a hand to attack the Lord's priests.

¹⁸The king then ordered Doeg, "Doeg! You go attack the priests." So Doeg the Edomite went and attacked the priests, killing eighty-five men who wore the linen priestly vest[t] that day. ¹⁹He put the whole priestly city of Nob to the sword: men and women, children and infants, even oxen, donkeys, and sheep.

²⁰But one of the sons of Ahimelech, Ahitub's son, escaped. His name was Abiathar, and he fled to David. ²¹Abiathar reported to David that Saul had slaughtered the Lord's priests. ²²David told Abiathar, "That day, when Doeg the Edomite was there, I knew that he would tell Saul everything. I am to blame[u] for the deaths in your father's family. ²³Stay with me, and don't be afraid. The one who seeks my life now seeks yours too. But you'll be safe with me."

Saul chases David

23David was told, "The Philistines are now attacking Keilah and looting the threshing floors!"

²David asked the Lord, "Should I go and fight these Philistines?"

"Go!" the Lord answered. "Fight the Philistines and save Keilah!"

³But David's men said to him, "Look how frightened we are here in Judah. It'll be worse if we go to Keilah against Philistine forces!"

⁴So David asked the Lord again, and the Lord reaffirmed, "Yes, go down to Keilah, because I will hand the Philistines over to you."

⁵Then David and his soldiers went to Keilah and fought the Philistines, driving off their cattle and defeating them decisively. And that's how David saved the residents of Keilah.

⁶Now after Abiathar, Ahimelech's son, fled to David, he had accompanied David to Keilah,[v] bringing a priestly vest[w] with him. ⁷When Saul was told that David had gone to Keilah, he said, "God has handed him over[x] to me now because he has trapped himself by entering a town with gates and bars!" ⁸So Saul called up all his troops for war, to go down to Keilah and attack David and his soldiers.

⁹When David learned that Saul was planning to harm him, he told the priest Abiathar, "Bring the priestly vest now."

---

[t]Heb *ephod* [u]LXX, Vulg; Heb uncertain [v]LXX; MT lacks *he had accompanied David to.* [w]Heb *ephod* [x]LXX, Targ; MT *made a stranger of him*

¹⁰Then David said, "LORD God of Israel, I, your servant, have heard that Saul plans on coming to Keilah and will destroy the town because of me. ¹¹LORD God of Israel, will Saul come down as your servant has heard?ʸ Please tell your servant."

"Yes, he will come down," the LORD answered.

¹²Next David asked, "Will the citizens of Keilah hand me and my soldiers over to Saul?"

"Yes, they will hand you over," the LORD replied.

¹³So David and his troops—approximately six hundred men—got up and left Keilah. They kept moving, going from one place to the next. When Saul was told that David had escaped from Keilah, he didn't go there.

¹⁴David lived in the fortresses in the wilderness and in the hills of the Ziph wilderness. Saul searched for him constantly, but God did not hand David over to Saul. ¹⁵While David was at Horesh in the Ziph wilderness he learned that Saul was looking to kill him. ¹⁶Saul's son Jonathan came to David at Horesh and encouraged him with God. ¹⁷Jonathan said to him, "Don't be afraid! My father Saul's hand won't touch you. You will be king over Israel, and I will be your second in command. Even my father Saul knows this." ¹⁸Then the two of them made a covenant before the LORD. David stayed at Horesh, but Jonathan went back home.

¹⁹Some Ziphites came to Saul at Gibeah. "David is hiding among us in the fortresses at Horesh on the hill of Hachilah, south of Jeshimon," they said. ²⁰"So whenever you want to come down, Your Majesty, do it! Leave it to us to hand him over to the king."

²¹"The LORD bless you because you have shown this kindness to me!" Saul said. ²²"Go now and get everything ready. Find out everything you can: where he stays, where he goes, who has seen him. I am told he is very shrewd. ²³Find out every hiding place he uses there and come back to me when you know for certain. I will then go with you. If David is in the area, I will hunt him down among any of Judah's clans!" ²⁴So they got up and left for Ziph ahead of Saul.

Meanwhile, David and his soldiers were in the Maon wilderness in the desert plain south of Jeshimon. ²⁵When Saul and his troops went looking for him, David was told about it, so he went down to a certain rock there and stayed in the Maon wilderness. When Saul heard that, he went into the Maon wilderness after David. ²⁶Saul was going around one side of a hill there while David and his soldiers were going around the other. David was hurrying to get away from Saul while Saul and his troops were trying to surround David and his soldiers in order to capture them. ²⁷But a messenger suddenly came to Saul. "Come quick!" he said. "The Philistines have invaded the land!" ²⁸So Saul broke off his pursuit of David and went to fight the Philistines. That's why that place is called Escape Rock. ²⁹ᶻThen David went from there and lived at the En-gedi fortresses.

David spares Saul's life

24 ᵃEven as Saul returned from pursuing the Philistines, he was informed that David was in the En-gedi wilderness. ²So Saul took three thousand men selected from all Israel and went to look for David and his soldiers near the rocks of the wild goats. ³He came to the sheep pens beside the road where there was a cave. Saul went into the cave to use the restroom.ᵇ Meanwhile, David and his soldiers were sitting in the very back of the cave.

⁴David's soldiers said to him, "This is the day the LORD spoke of when he promised you, 'I will hand your enemy over to you, and you can do to him whatever you think best.'" So David snuck up and cut off a corner of Saul's robe. ⁵But immediately David felt horrible that he had cut off a corner of Saul's robe.ᶜ

⁶"The LORD forbid," he told his men, "that I should do something like that to my master, the LORD's anointed, or lift my hand against him, because he's the LORD's anointed!" ⁷So David held his soldiers in check by what he said,ᵈ and he wouldn't allow them to attack Saul. Saul then left the cave and went on his way.

⁸Then David also went out of the cave and

ʸDSS (4QSamᵇ), LXX; MT LORD *God of Israel, will the citizens of Keilah hand me over to him? Will Saul come down as your servant has heard?* Cf 23:12 ᵃ ᶻ24:1 in Heb ᵃ24:2 in Heb ᵇOr *to cover his feet* (a euphemism) ᶜLXX, Syr, Targ; MT lacks *robe.* ᵈHeb uncertain yelled after Saul, "My master the king!" Saul looked back, and David bowed low out of respect, nose to the ground.

⁹David said to Saul, "Why do you listen when people say, 'David wants to ruin you'? ¹⁰Look! Today your own eyes have seen that the LORD handed you over to me in the cave. But I refused[e] to kill you. I spared you, saying, 'I won't lift a hand against my master because he is the LORD's anointed.' ¹¹Look here, my protector! See the corner of your robe in my hand? I cut off the corner of your robe but didn't kill you. So know now that I am not guilty of wrongdoing or rebellion. I haven't wronged you, but you are hunting me down, trying to kill me. ¹²May the LORD judge between me and you! May the LORD take vengeance on you for me, but I won't lift a hand against you. ¹³As the old proverb goes, 'Evil deeds come from evildoers!' but I won't lift a hand against you. ¹⁴So who is Israel's king coming after? Who are you chasing? A dead dog? A single flea? ¹⁵May the LORD be the judge and decide between you and me. May he see what has happened, argue my case, and vindicate me against you!"

¹⁶As soon as David finished saying all this to Saul, Saul said, "David, my son, is that your voice?" Then he broke down in tears, ¹⁷telling David, "You are more righteous than I am because you have treated me generously, but I have treated you terribly. ¹⁸Today you've told me the good you have done for me—how the LORD handed me over to you, but how you didn't kill me. ¹⁹When someone finds an enemy, do they send the enemy away in peace? May the LORD repay you with good for what you have done for me today. ²⁰Now even I know that you will definitely become king, and Israel's kingdom will flourish in your hands. ²¹Because of that, make a solemn pledge to me by the LORD that you won't kill off my descendants after I'm gone and that you won't destroy my name from my family lineage."

²²David made a solemn pledge to Saul. Then Saul went back home, but David and his soldiers went up to the fortress.

Abigail saves David

25 Now Samuel died, and all Israel gathered to mourn for him. They buried him at his home in Ramah. David then left and went down to the Maon wilderness.[f]

²There was a man in Maon who did business in Carmel. He was a very important man and owned three thousand sheep and one thousand goats. At that time, he was shearing his sheep in Carmel. ³The man's name was Nabal, and his wife's name was Abigail. She was an intelligent and attractive woman, but her husband was a hard man who did evil things. He was a Calebite.

⁴While in the wilderness, David heard that Nabal was shearing his sheep. ⁵So David sent ten servants, telling them, "Go up to Carmel. When you get to Nabal, greet him for me. ⁶Say this to him: 'Peace to you,[g] your household, and all that is yours! ⁷I've heard that you are now shearing sheep. As you know, your shepherds were with us in the wilderness.[h] We didn't mistreat them. Moreover, the whole time they were at Carmel, nothing of theirs went missing. ⁸Ask your servants; they will tell you the same. So please receive these young men favorably, because we've come on a special day. Please give whatever you have on hand to your servants and to your son David.'"

⁹When David's young men arrived, they said all this to Nabal on David's behalf. Then

SAILBOAT

KINDNESS

Kindness for the Kind   *1 Samuel 24:10-13, 17*
King Saul didn't deserve kindness. He was completely unaware that David was in the very same cave he was in. Out of jealousy, Saul had done terrible things to people who helped David (1 Sam 22:6-19). It seemed like David had every reason to kill Saul. With his knife out, David crept toward Saul. David raised the blade and secretly cut off a corner of Saul's robe. David knew that if he wanted kindness from God, he needed to be kind to others. God was kind to the people of Israel again and again, despite the many times they did things their own way. David was kind to Saul again and again (1 Sam 24:10-13; 26:22-24). Sadly, David's kindness didn't change Saul, but it made David more like God. 🌢

they waited. ¹⁰But Nabal answered David's servants, "Who is David? Who is Jesse's son? There are all sorts of slaves running away from their masters these days. ¹¹Why should I take my bread, my water, and the meat I've butchered for my shearers and give it to people who came here from who knows where?" ¹²So David's young servants turned around and went back the way they came. When they arrived, they reported every word of this to David.

¹³Then David said to his soldiers, "All of you, strap on your swords!" So each of them strapped on their swords, and David did the same. Nearly four hundred men went up with David. Two hundred men remained back with the supplies.

¹⁴One of Nabal's servants told his wife Abigail, "David sent messengers from the wilderness to greet our master, but he just yelled at them. ¹⁵But the men were very good to us and didn't mistreat us. Nothing of ours went missing the whole time we were out with them in the fields. ¹⁶In fact, the whole time we were with them, watching our sheep, they were a protective wall around us both night and day. ¹⁷Think about that and see what you can do, because trouble is coming for our master and his whole household. But he's such a despicable person no one can speak to him."

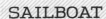

SAILBOAT

HONEST AND TRUE

Stay Honest and True in Hard Times
1 Samuel 25:15-16

King Saul was chasing David all over Israel. David was desperate. David was traveling with a large group of armed men, so he could have easily fought Saul or taken what he wanted. But David refused to act that way. When David and his men came across shepherds in the wilderness, shearing their sheep, David didn't mistreat them. David didn't take anything from the shepherds, even though those sheep would have made a tasty meal for his hungry men. Though he was living in difficult times, David knew that it was important to treat people well. David's integrity, or good character and honesty, was one of the reasons God chose David to be king. ♦

did you know?

In Bible times, people were expected to show hospitality to others. They were required to be kind to travelers and to offer food, water, and a place to sleep to anyone who came along, even enemies. Hospitality sometimes included the host offering to wash the traveler's feet. People's feet were very dirty because they walked on dusty paths and roads while wearing sandals.

¹⁸Abigail quickly took two hundred loaves of bread, two skins of wine, five sheep ready for cooking, five seahs^i of roasted grain, one hundred raisin cakes, and two hundred fig cakes. She loaded all this on donkeys ¹⁹and told her servants, "Go on ahead of me. I'll be right behind you." But she didn't tell her husband Nabal.

²⁰As she was riding her donkey, going down a trail on the hillside, David and his soldiers appeared, descending toward her, and she met up with them. ²¹David had just been saying, "What a waste of time—guarding all this man's stuff in the wilderness so that nothing of his went missing! He has repaid me evil instead of good! ²²May God deal harshly with me, David,^j and worse still if I leave alive even one single one who urinates on a wall^k belonging to him come morning!"

²³When Abigail saw David, she quickly got off her donkey and fell facedown before him, bowing low to the ground. ²⁴She fell at his feet and said, "Put the blame on me, my master! But please let me, your servant, speak to you directly. Please listen to what your servant has to say. ²⁵Please, my master, pay no attention to this despicable man Nabal. He's exactly what his name says he is! His name means fool,^l and he is foolish!^m But I myself, your servant, didn't see the young men that you, my master, sent. ²⁶I pledge, my master, as surely as the LORD lives and as you live, that the LORD has held you back from bloodshed and taking vengeance into your own hands! But now let your enemies and those who seek to harm my master be exactly like Nabal! ²⁷Here is a gift, which your servant has brought to my master. Please let it be given to the young men who follow you, my master.

---

^i One seah is approximately seven and a half quarts. ^j LXX; MT *with David's enemies* ^k Descriptive phrase meaning "a male"; also in 25:34 ^l Heb *nabal* ^m Heb *nebalah*

[28]Please forgive any offense by your servant. The Lord will definitely make an enduring dynasty for my master because my master fights the Lord's battles, and nothing evil will be found in you throughout your lifetime. [29]If someone chases after you and tries to kill you, my master, then your life will be bound up securely in the bundle of life[n] by the Lord your God, but he will fling away your enemies' lives as from the pouch of a sling. [30]When the Lord has done for my master all the good things he has promised you, and has installed you as Israel's leader, [31]don't let this be a blot or burden on my master's conscience, that you shed blood needlessly or that my master took vengeance into his own hands. When the Lord has done good things for my master, please remember your servant."

[32]David said to Abigail, "Bless the Lord God of Israel, who sent you to meet me today! [33]And bless you and your good judgment for preventing me from shedding blood and taking vengeance into my own hands today! [34]Otherwise, as surely as the Lord God of Israel lives—the one who kept me from hurting you—if you hadn't come quickly and met up with me, there wouldn't be one single one who urinates on a wall left come morning." [35]Then David accepted everything she had brought for him. "Return home in peace," he told her. "Be assured that I've heard your request and have agreed to it."

[36]When Abigail got back home to Nabal, he was throwing a party fit for a king in his house. Nabal was in a great mood and very drunk, so Abigail didn't tell him anything until daybreak. [37]In the morning, when Nabal was sober, his wife told him everything. Nabal's heart failed inside him, and he became like a stone. [38]About ten days later, the Lord struck Nabal, and he died.

[39]When David heard that Nabal was dead, he said, "Bless the Lord, who has rendered a verdict regarding Nabal's insult to me and who kept me, his servant, from doing something evil! The Lord has brought Nabal's evil down on his own head." Then David sent word to Abigail, saying that he would take her as his wife. [40]When David's servants reached Abigail at Carmel, they said to her, "David has sent us to you so you can become his wife."

[41]She bowed low to the ground and said, "I am your servant, ready to serve and wash the feet of my master's helpers." [42]Then Abigail got up quickly and rode on her donkey, with five of her young women going with her. She followed David's messengers and became his wife.

[43]David also married Ahinoam from Jezreel, so both of them were his wives. [44]But Saul had given his daughter Michal, David's wife, to Palti, Laish's son, from Gallim.

David spares Saul's life a second time

26The Ziphites came to Saul at Gibeah. "David is hiding on Hachilah's hill, which faces Jeshimon," they said. [2]So Saul got up and went down to the Ziph wilderness to look for David there. He had three thousand handpicked soldiers from Israel with him. [3]Saul camped on Hachilah's hill opposite Jeshimon beside the road, but David stayed in the wilderness. When David learned that Saul had come after him into the wilderness, [4]he sent spies and discovered that Saul had definitely arrived.

[5]So David got up and went to the place where Saul camped, and saw the place where Saul and Abner, Ner's son and Saul's general, were sleeping. Saul was sleeping inside the camp with the troops camped all around him. [6]David asked Ahimelech the Hittite and Joab's brother Abishai, Zeruiah's son, "Who will go down into the camp with me to Saul?"

"I'll go down with you," Abishai answered.

[7]So David and Abishai approached the troops at night and found Saul lying there, asleep in the camp, with his spear stuck in the ground by his head. Abner and the army were sleeping all around him.

[8]Abishai said to David, "God has handed your enemy over to you today! Let me pin him to the ground with my spear. One stroke is all I need! I won't need a second."

[9]But David said to Abishai, "Don't kill him! No one can lift a hand against the Lord's anointed and go unpunished. [10]As surely as the Lord lives," David continued, "it will be the Lord who will strike him down, or his day will come and he will die, or he'll fall in battle and be destroyed. [11]The Lord forbid that I lift

---

[n]Or *bundle of the living*; Heb uncertain; perhaps a tied-up scroll (cf Exod 32:32-33; Ps 69:28; Isa 8:16)

my hand against the Lord's anointed! But go ahead and take the spear by Saul's head and the water jug and let's go!" [12]So David took the spear and the water jug that were by Saul's head, and he and Abishai left. No one saw them, no one knew they were there, and no one woke up. All of them remained asleep because a deep sleep from the Lord had come over them.

[13]David crossed over to the other side and stood on top of a hill with considerable distance between them. [14]Then David shouted to the army and to Abner, Ner's son, "Abner! Aren't you going to answer me?"

"Who are you to shout to the king?" Abner asked.

[15]David answered Abner, "You are a man, aren't you? And you have no equal in Israel, right? Then why haven't you kept watch over your master the king? One of the soldiers came to kill your master the king. [16]What you've done is terrible! As surely as the Lord lives, all of you are dead men because you didn't keep close watch over your master, the Lord's anointed. Have a look around! Where are the king's spear and the water jug that were by his head?"

[17]Saul recognized David's voice and said, "David, my son, is that your voice?"

David said, "Yes it is, my master the king. [18]Why," David continued, "is my master chasing me, his servant? What have I done and what wrong am I guilty of? [19]My master the king, please listen to what your servant has to say. If it is the Lord who has incited you against me, then let him accept an offering! But if human beings have done it, then let them be cursed before the Lord because they have now driven me off, keeping me from sharing in the Lord's inheritance. 'Go!' they tell me. 'Worship other gods!' [20]Don't let my blood spill on the ground apart from the Lord's presence, because the king of Israel has come out looking for a single flea[o] like someone hunting a partridge[p] in the mountains."

[21]Then Saul said, "I have sinned! David, my son, come back! Because you considered my life precious today, I won't harm you again. I have acted foolishly and have made a huge mistake."

[22]"Here is the king's spear," David answered.

"Allow one of your servants to come over and get it. [23]Remember: The Lord rewards every person for their righteousness and loyalty, and I wasn't willing to lift a hand against the Lord's anointed, even though the Lord handed you over to me today. [24]And just as I considered your life valuable today, may the Lord consider my life valuable, and may he deliver me from all trouble."

[25]Then Saul said to David, "Bless you, David, my son! You will accomplish much and will certainly succeed." Then David went on his way, but Saul went back home.

SAILBOAT

HUMILITY

God Rewards Kindness and Respect
1 Samuel 26:20

For the second time, David chose to spare Saul's life. When David confronted Saul, he asked why Saul kept chasing him. Throughout their relationship, David always avoided acting high-and-mighty before the king. He acted with humility toward Saul, instead of with too much pride. David could have acted like he was someone important because he was going to be the next king. But David knew that God dislikes it when people act like they're better than other people. Instead God wants people to treat others with kindness and respect. David respected Saul's position as king. David stayed humble, knowing God would someday make him king. ◊

David serves the Philistine Achish

27David thought, One day I will be destroyed by Saul's power. The best thing for me to do is to escape to Philistine territory. Then Saul will give up looking for me in Israelite territory, and I will escape his power. [2]So David set out with his six hundred soldiers and went to Achish, Maoch's son and Gath's king. [3]David and his soldiers stayed there at Gath with Achish. Each man had his family with him, and David had his two wives, Ahinoam from Jezreel and Abigail, Nabal's widow from Carmel. [4]When Saul was told that David had fled to Gath, he didn't pursue him anymore.

[5]Then David said to Achish, "If you approve

---

[o]Cf 24:14; LXX *my life* [p]Or *a caller*, Heb sounds like verb *to shout* or *call* in 26:14.

of me, please give me a place in one of the towns in the country so I can live there. Why should I, your servant, live in the capital city with you?" [6]So Achish gave the town of Ziklag to David at that time. That's why Ziklag has belonged to the kings of Judah until now. [7]David lived in the Philistine countryside for a total of one year and four months.

[8]David and his soldiers went out on raids against the Geshurites, the Girzites, and the Amalekites. They were the people who lived in the land from Telam[q] to Shur all the way to the land of Egypt. [9]When David attacked an area, he wouldn't leave anyone alive, man or woman. He would take the sheep, the cattle, the donkeys, the camels, and the clothes and would then go back to Achish. [10]When Achish asked, "Where did you raid today?"[r] David would say, "The southern plain of Judah," or "The southern plain of the Jerahmeelites," or "The southern plain of the Kenites." [11]David never spared a man or woman so they could be brought back alive to Gath. "Otherwise," he said, "they might talk about us, and say, 'David did this or that.'" So this was David's practice during the entire time he lived in the Philistine countryside.

[12]Achish trusted David, thinking, David has alienated himself so badly from his own people in Israel that he'll serve me forever.

28 At that time, the Philistines gathered their troops for war to fight against Israel. Achish said to David, "Count on you and your soldiers marching out with me in the army."

[2]"Excellent," David answered Achish. "Now you'll see for yourself what your servant can do."

"Excellent," Achish replied. "I will make you my permanent bodyguard."

Saul and the woman of En-dor

[3]Now Samuel had died, and all Israel mourned him and buried him in Ramah, his hometown. And Saul had banned all mediums and diviners from the land.

[4]The Philistines gathered their forces and advanced to camp at Shunem. Saul gathered all Israel, and they camped at Gilboa. [5]When Saul saw the Philistine army, he was so afraid that his heart beat wildly. [6]When Saul questioned the LORD, the LORD didn't answer him—not by dreams, not by the Urim, and not by the prophets. [7]So Saul said to his servants, "Find me a woman who communicates with ghosts! I'll then go to her and ask by using her techniques."[s]

"There is such a medium in En-dor," his servants replied.

[8]So Saul disguised himself, dressing in different clothes. Then he and two men set out, going to the woman at nighttime.

"Please call up a ghost for me! Bring me the one I specify," Saul said.

[9]"Listen," the woman said to him, "you know what Saul has done, how he has banned all mediums and diviners from the land. What are you doing? Trying to get me killed?"

[10]But Saul promised to her by the LORD, "As surely as the LORD lives, you won't get into trouble for this."

[11]So the woman said, "Who do you want me to bring up for you?"

"Bring up Samuel," he said.

[12]When the woman saw Samuel, she screamed at Saul, "Why have you tricked me? You are Saul!"

[13]"Don't be afraid!" the king said to her. "What do you see?"

The woman said to Saul, "I see a god[t] coming up from the ground."

[14]"What does he look like?" Saul asked her.

"An old man is coming up," she said. "He's wrapped in a robe." Then Saul knew that it was Samuel, and he bowed low out of respect, nose to the ground.

[15]"Why have you disturbed me by bringing me up?" Samuel asked Saul.

"I'm in deep trouble!" Saul replied. "The Philistines are at war with me, and God has turned away from me and no longer answers me by prophets or by dreams. So I have called on you to tell me what I should do."

[16]"Why do you ask me," Samuel said, "since the LORD has turned away from you and has become your enemy?[u] [17]The LORD has done to you[v] exactly what he spoke through me: The LORD has ripped the kingdom out of your hands and has given it to your friend David.

[q]LXX; MT *from long ago* [r]DSS (4QSam[a]), LXX [s]Or *through her or by her* [t]Or *I see gods or I see divine figures* [u]LXX *is with your neighbor; cf 15:28; 28:17* [v]LXX; MT *The LORD himself has done just what*

¹⁸The LORD has done this very thing to you today because you didn't listen to the LORD's voice and didn't carry out his fierce anger against the Amalekites. ¹⁹The LORD will now hand over both you and Israel to the Philistines. And come tomorrow, you and your sons will be with me!ʷ The LORD will hand Israel's army over to the Philistines."

UMBRELLA
DISOBEDIENCE

Disobedience Can Become a Habit
1 Samuel 28:18

The last decision of Saul's life was a bad one. From the beginning of his reign as king, Saul made one bad choice after another. He sacrificed when he wasn't supposed to (1 Sam 13:8-14). He failed to sacrifice when he was supposed to (1 Sam 15:9-25). He killed a whole town of innocent Israelites (1 Sam 22:6-19). He tried to kill David out of jealousy (1 Sam 19:9-11). Now he was scared. The Philistine army he was supposed to face the next day was huge. Because Saul continually did things his own way instead of God's, God no longer spoke to Saul through prophets or dreams. Saul didn't know what to do. So he visited a witch, which was against God's Instruction (Deut 18:9-11). Saul had made a habit of not doing things God's way. He did this for so long it became hard not to. Saul's sad kingship began and ended with Saul not being obedient. ♦

²⁰Saul immediately fell full length on the ground, utterly terrified at what Samuel had said. He was weak because he hadn't eaten anything all day or night. ²¹The woman approached Saul, and after seeing how scared he was, she said, "Listen, your servant has obeyed you. I risked my life and did what you told me to do. ²²Now it's your turn to listen to me, your servant. Let me give you a bit of food. Eat it, then you'll have the strength to go on your way."

²³But Saul refused. "I can't eat!" he said. But his servants and the woman urged him to do so, and so he did. He got up off the ground and sat on a couch. ²⁴The woman had a fattened calf in the house, and she quickly butchered it.ˣ She took flour, kneaded it, and baked unleavened bread. ²⁵She served this to Saul and his servants, and they ate. They got up and left that very night.

David sent home from fighting Saul

29 The Philistines assembled all their forces at Aphek, and the Israelites camped by the spring in Jezreel. ²As the Philistine rulers went out marching in units of hundreds and thousands, David and his soldiers were in the rear with Achish.

³"Who are these Hebrews?" the Philistine commanders asked.

"That's David," Achish told them, "the servant of Israel's King Saul. He's been with me a year or so now. I haven't found anything wrong with him from the day he defected until now."

⁴But the Philistine commanders were angry with Achish. "Send the man home!" they told Achish. "He can go back to the place you gave him, but he won't go with us into battle. Couldn't he turn against us in the middle of the fight? How better to please his former master than by taking the heads of our soldiers? ⁵After all, this is the same David people sing about in their dances,

'Saul has killed his thousands,

but David has killed

his tens of thousands!'"

⁶So Achish summoned David and told him, "As surely as the LORD lives, you are an upstanding individual. I would very much like you to serve with me in the army because I haven't found anything wrong with you from the day you came to me until now. But the rulers don't approve of you. ⁷So go back home now, and go in peace. Don't do anything to upset the Philistine rulers."

⁸"But what have I done?" David asked Achish. "What wrong have you found in me, your servant, from the day I came to you until now? Why shouldn't I go and fight the enemies of my master the king?"

⁹"I agree," Achish answered David. "I think you're as good as one of God's own messengers. Despite that, the Philistine commanders have ordered, 'He can't go into battle with us.' ¹⁰So get up early in the morning, both you and your master's servants who came with you, and return to the place I gave you. Don't worry about this negative report, because

---

ʷLXX *you and your sons will fall in battle.* ˣOr *sacrificed it*

you've done well before me.[y] Now get up early in the morning and leave as soon as it is light."

[11]So David and his soldiers got up early in the morning to go back to Philistine territory, but the Philistines went up to Jezreel.

The Amalekite raid on Ziklag

30 Three days later, David and his soldiers reached Ziklag. The Amalekites had raided the arid southern plain and Ziklag. They had attacked Ziklag and burned it down, [2]taking the women and everyone in the city prisoner, whether young or old.[z] They hadn't killed anyone but carried them off and went on their way. [3]When David and his soldiers got to the town and found it burned down, and their wives, their sons, and their daughters taken prisoner, [4]David and the troops with him broke into tears and cried until they could cry no more. [5]David's two wives had been captured as well: Ahinoam from Jezreel and Abigail, Nabal's widow from Carmel.

[6]David was in deep trouble because the troops were talking about stoning him. Each of the soldiers was deeply distressed about their sons and daughters. But David found strength in the LORD his God. [7]David said to the priest Abiathar, Ahimelech's son, "Bring the priestly vest[a] to me." So Abiathar brought it to David.

[8]Then David asked the LORD, "Should I go after this raiding party? Will I catch them?"

"Yes, go after them!" God answered. "You will definitely catch them and will succeed in the rescue!"

[9]So David set off with six hundred men. They came to the Besor ravine, where some stayed behind. [10]David and four hundred men continued the pursuit, while two hundred men stayed there, too exhausted to cross the Besor ravine.

[11]They found an Egyptian in the countryside and brought him to David. They gave him bread, and he ate, and they gave him water to drink. [12]They also gave him a piece of fig cake and two raisin cakes. He ate and regained his strength because he hadn't eaten any food or drunk any water for three days and nights. [13]Then David asked him, "Whose slave are you? Where do you come from?"

"I'm an Egyptian servant boy," he said, "and the slave of an Amalekite. My master abandoned me when I got sick three days ago. [14]We had raided the arid southern plain belonging to the Cherethites, the territory belonging to Judah, and the southern plain of Caleb. We also burned Ziklag down."

[15]"Can you guide me to this raiding party?" David asked him.

"Make a pledge to me by God that you won't kill me or hand me over to my master," the boy said, "and I will guide you to the raiding party."

[16]So the boy led David to them, and he found them scattered all over the countryside, eating, drinking, and celebrating over the large amount of plunder they had taken from Philistine and Judean territory.

[17]David attacked them from twilight until evening of the next day. He killed them all.[b] No one escaped except four hundred young men who got on camels and fled. [18]David rescued everything that the Amalekites had taken, including his own two wives. [19]Nothing was missing from the plunder or anything that they had taken, neither old nor young, son nor daughter. David brought everything back. [20]David also captured all the sheep and cattle, which were driven in front of the other livestock. The troops said, "This is David's plunder!"

[21]David reached the two hundred men who were too exhausted to follow him and had stayed behind at the Besor ravine. They came out to greet him and the troops who were with him. When David approached them, he asked how they were doing. [22]But then all the evil and despicable individuals who had accompanied David said, "We won't share any of the plunder we rescued with them because they didn't go with us. Each of them can take his wife and children and go—but that's it."

[23]"Brothers!" David said. "Don't act that way with the things the LORD has given us. He has protected us and handed over to us the raiding party that had attacked us. [24]How could anyone agree with you on this plan? The share of those who went into battle and the share of those who stayed with the supplies will be divided equally." [25]So from that day

[y]LXX; MT lacks *and return to the place … done well before me.* [z]LXX; MT lacks *and everyone in the city.* [a]Heb *ephod* [b]LXX; MT lacks *He killed them all.*

forward, David made that a regulation and a law in Israel, which remains in place even now.

[26]When David returned to Ziklag, he sent some of the plunder to the elders of Judah and to his friends. "Here is a gift for you from the plunder of the Lord's enemies," he said. [27]It went to those in Bethel, Ramoth of the arid southern plain, Jattir, [28]Aroer,[c] Siphmoth, Eshtemoa, [29]Racal, the towns of the Jerahmeelites, the towns of the Kenites, [30]Hormah, Bor-ashan, Athach, [31]Hebron, and all the places where David and his soldiers had spent time.

Saul dies in the battle of Gilboa

31 When the Philistines attacked the Israelites, the Israelites ran away from the Philistines, and many fell dead on Mount Gilboa. [2]The Philistines overtook Saul and his sons, and they killed his sons Jonathan, Abinadab, and Malchishua. [3]The battle was fierce around Saul. When the archers located him, they wounded him badly.[d]

[4]Saul said to his armor-bearer, "Draw your sword and kill me with it! Otherwise, these uncircumcised men will come and kill me or torture me." But his armor-bearer refused because he was terrified. So Saul took the sword

and impaled himself on it. [5]When the armor-bearer saw that Saul was dead, he also impaled himself on his sword and died with Saul. [6]So Saul, his three sons, his armor-bearer, and all his soldiers died together that day.

[7]When the Israelites across the valley and across the Jordan learned that the Israelite army had fled and that Saul and his sons were dead, they abandoned their towns and fled. So the Philistines came and occupied the towns.

[8]The next day, when the Philistines came to strip the dead, they found Saul and his three sons lying dead on Mount Gilboa. [9]They cut off Saul's head and stripped off his armor, and then sent word throughout Philistine territory, carrying the good news to their gods' temples and to their people. [10]They put Saul's armor in the temple of Astarte, and hung his body on the wall of Beth-shan.

[11]But when all the people of Jabesh-gilead heard what the Philistines had done to Saul, [12]the bravest of their men set out, traveled all night long, and took the bodies of Saul and his sons off the wall of Beth-shan. Then they went back to Jabesh, where they burned them. [13]Then they took their bones and buried them under the tamarisk tree at Jabesh, and they fasted seven days.

[c]LXX *Ararah* [d]Correction; LXX *wounded in the belly*

2 Samuel

Second Samuel begins with the death of Saul, Israel's first king. When David heard Saul was killed in battle, he mourned for Saul and the people of Israel. God had said that David would be the next king, and so David was crowned king of Israel.

As Israel's new king, David made Israel a strong nation. He battled Israel's enemies. He conquered the city of Jerusalem and made it the nation's capital. He took the chest containing the covenant (the Instruction from Moses) to Jerusalem and made plans to build an incredible temple where the people would worship God.

This book reminds us that even the best leaders sometimes disobey God or have painful family problems. David did many good things for God's people. He also made some mistakes. But whenever David did something wrong, he admitted his sin and asked God to forgive him. This book shows that God forgives us when we tell God our sins! ◗

David learns of Saul's death

1 After Saul's death, when David had returned from defeating the Amalekites, he stayed in Ziklag two days. [2]On the third day, a man showed up from Saul's camp with his clothes torn and dirt on his head. When he reached David, he fell to the ground, bowing low out of respect.

[3]"Where have you come from?" David asked him.

"I've escaped from the Israelite army!" he answered.

[4]"What's the report?" David asked him. "Tell me!"

The man answered, "The troops fled from the battle! Many of the soldiers have fallen and died. What's more, Saul and his son Jonathan have also died!"

[5]"How do you know," David asked the young man who brought the news, "that Saul and his son Jonathan are dead?"

[6]The young man who brought the news replied, "I just happened to be on Mount Gilboa and Saul was there, leaning on his spear, with chariots and horsemen closing in on him. [7]He turned around and saw me, then he called to me. 'Yes, sir,' I answered. [8]'Who are you?' he asked, and I told him, 'I'm an Amalekite.' [9]He said to me, 'Please come over here and kill me, because convulsions have come over me but I'm still alive.'[a] [10]So I went over to him and killed him, because I knew he couldn't survive after being wounded like that. I took the crown that was on his head and the bracelet that was on his arm, and I've brought them here to you, my master."

[11]Then David grabbed his clothes and ripped them—and all his soldiers did the same. [12]They mourned and cried and fasted until evening for Saul, his son Jonathan, the Lord's army, and the whole house of Israel, because they had died by the sword.

[13]"Where are you from?" David asked the young man who brought him the news.

"I'm the son of an immigrant," he answered. "An Amalekite."

[14]Then David said to him, "How is it that you weren't afraid to raise your hand and destroy the Lord's anointed?" [15]Then David called for one of the young servants. "Come here!" he said. "Strike him down!" So the servant struck the Amalekite down, and he died.

[16]"Your blood is on your own head," David said to the Amalekite, "because your own mouth testified against you when you admitted, 'I killed the Lord's anointed.'"

David mourns Saul and Jonathan

[17]Then David sang this funeral song[b] for Saul and his son Jonathan. [18]David ordered everyone in Judah to learn the Song of the Bow.[c] (In fact, it is written in the scroll from Jashar.)

[19] Oh, no, Israel! Your prince[d] lies dead
    on your heights.[e]
  Look how the mighty warriors
    have fallen!
[20] Don't talk about it in Gath;
    don't bring news of it
    to Ashkelon's streets,
  or else the Philistines' daughters
    will rejoice;
  the daughters of the uncircumcised
    will celebrate.
[21] You hills of Gilboa!
  Let there be no dew or rain on you,
    and no fields yielding grain offerings.[f]
  Because it was there
    that the mighty warrior's[g] shield
    was defiled—
    the shield of Saul!—
    never again anointed with oil.
[22] Jonathan's bow never wavered
    from the blood of the slain,
    from the gore of the warriors.
    Never did Saul's sword
    return empty.

[23] Saul and Jonathan! So well loved,
    so dearly cherished!
  In their lives and in their deaths
    they were never separated.
  They were faster than eagles,
    stronger than lions!

---

[a]Syr, Tg; Heb uncertain   [b]Or *lament*   [c]Heb lacks *Song.*   [d]Or *gazelle* or *splendor* or *splendid one*   [e]Correction   [f]Heb uncertain, perhaps *bountiful fields*; alternatively, with LXX [L], *fields of death*, or with correction *and no springs from the deep*   [g]Or *warriors'* (plural)

²⁴ Daughters of Israel, weep over Saul!
He dressed you in crimson with jewels;
he decorated your clothes
with gold jewelry.
²⁵ Look how the mighty warriors
have fallen in the midst of battle!
Jonathan lies dead on your heights.
²⁶ I grieve for you, my brother Jonathan!
You were so dear to me!
Your love was more amazing to me^h
than the love of women.
²⁷ Look how the mighty warriors
have fallen!
Look how the weapons of war
have been destroyed!

did you know? Olive oil was poured on someone's head to anoint them and show they had been chosen for a great position. In this passage, the people chose David as their king. While still a boy, David already had been anointed by Samuel as God's choice to be king.

UMBRELLA
MOURNING

Some People Are Hard to Mourn
2 Samuel 1:17-27
King Saul was dead. Saul had chased David all over Israel (1 Sam 23); killed an entire town full of innocent Israelite men, women, and children (1 Sam 22:6-19); and lost the favor of God because he was more concerned with the good opinion of people (1 Sam 15:24-26). But when Israel's first king died, David sang a heartbreaking funeral song for him and ordered all of Judah to learn it. Why would David honor a person like Saul? David knew that in spite of the bad choices Saul made, he still had done good things as king of Israel. He saved the people of Jabesh-gilead (1 Sam 11:1-11) and rescued Israel from the bullying Amalekites (1 Sam 15:1-9). It was right to be sad for God's chosen king—for the good things he did as well as the good things he could have done. ◈

did you know? In Bible times, women would sound the cry to let people know it was a time for celebration, or, as it was in this case, a time for grief and sadness. The crowds would then join in with the cries of the women.

David made king in Hebron

2 Some time later, David questioned the LORD, "Should I go to one of the towns in Judah?"

"Yes, go," the LORD told him.

"Which one should I go to?" David asked.

"To Hebron," the LORD replied.

²So David went there, along with his two wives: Ahinoam from Jezreel and Abigail, Nabal's widow, from Carmel. ³David also took the soldiers who were with him, each with his family, and they lived in the towns around Hebron. ⁴Then the people of Judah came to Hebron and anointed David king over the house of Judah.

When David was informed that it was the people of Jabesh-gilead who had buried Saul, ⁵he sent messengers to the people of Jabesh-gilead. "The LORD bless you," he said to them, "for doing this loyal deed for your master Saul by burying him. ⁶May the LORD now show you loyal love and faithfulness. I myself will also reward you because you did this. ⁷So now take courage and be brave—yes, your master Saul is dead, but the house of Judah has anointed me king over them."

Israel's King Ishbosheth

⁸Meanwhile, Abner, Ner's son, the commander of Saul's army, had taken Ishbosheth,ⁱ Saul's son, and brought him over to Mahanaim. ⁹There he made him king over Gilead, the Geshurites,^j Jezreel, Ephraim, and Benjamin—over all Israel. ¹⁰Saul's son Ishbosheth was 40 years old when he became king over Israel, and he ruled for two years. The house of Judah, however, followed David. ¹¹The amount of time David ruled in Hebron over the house of Judah totaled seven and a half years.

^hOr *your love* (or *care*; cf 1 Sam 18:1, 3; 20:17) *for me was more amazing* ⁱIshbosheth means *man of shame; shame* (Heb *bosheth*) may be a deliberate alteration from *Baal* (cf Esh-baal, *man of Baal* in 1 Chron 8:33; 9:39; see also 2 Sam 4:4); one manuscript of LXX^L reads *Ishbaal*. ^jSyr, Vulg; MT *Ashurites* or *Assyrians*; cf Tg, LXX^L, Judg 1:32 *Asherites*

Conflict between Judah and Israel

[12]Abner, Ner's son, along with the soldiers of Ishbosheth, Saul's son, left Mahanaim to go to Gibeon. [13]Joab, Zeruiah's son, and David's soldiers also came out and confronted them at the pool of Gibeon. One group sat on one side of the pool; the other sat on the opposite side of the pool. [14]Abner said to Joab, "Let's have the young men fight in a contest[k] before us."

"All right," Joab said, "let's do it." [15]So the men came forward and were counted as they passed by: twelve for Benjamin and Ishbosheth, Saul's son; and twelve of David's soldiers. [16]Each man grabbed his opponent by the head and stuck[l] his sword into his opponent's side so that they both fell dead together. That's why that place is called The Field of Daggers,[m] which is located in Gibeon. [17]A fierce battle took place that day, and Abner and the Israelite troops were defeated by David's soldiers.

[18]Now Zeruiah's three sons were present at the battle: Joab, Abishai, and Asahel. Asahel was as fast as a gazelle in an open field. [19]Asahel went after Abner, staying completely focused in his pursuit of Abner.

[20]Abner looked behind him and said, "Is that you, Asahel?"

"Yes, it's me," Asahel answered.

[21]"Break off your pursuit!" Abner told him. "Fight one of the young warriors and take his gear for yourself!" But Asahel wouldn't stop chasing him.

[22]So Abner repeated himself to Asahel: "Stop chasing me. Why should I kill you? How could I look your brother Joab in the face?" [23]But Asahel wouldn't turn back, so Abner hit him in the stomach with the back end of his spear. But the spear went through Asahel's back. He fell down and died right there. Everyone who came to the place where Asahel had fallen and died just stood there, [24]but Joab and Abishai went after Abner. The sun was setting when they came to the hill of Ammah, which faces Giah on the road to the Gibeon wilderness. [25]The Benjaminites rallied behind Abner, forming a single unit. Then they took their positions on the top of a hill. [26]Abner yelled down to Joab, "Must the sword keep killing forever? Don't you realize that this will end bitterly? How long before you order the troops to stop chasing their brothers?"

[27]"As surely as God lives," Joab replied, "if you hadn't just said that, the soldiers would have continued after their brothers until morning." [28]Joab blew the trumpet,[n] and all the soldiers stopped. They didn't pursue Israel anymore, nor did they continue to fight.

[29]Abner and his men then marched all night through the wilderness, crossing the Jordan River and marching all morning[o] until they got to Mahanaim. [30]Joab, meanwhile, returned from pursuing Abner and assembled the troops. Nineteen of David's soldiers were counted missing in addition to Asahel. [31]But David's soldiers had defeated the Benjaminites, killing three hundred sixty of Abner's soldiers. [32]They took Asahel and buried him in his father's tomb in Bethlehem. Then Joab and his men marched all night. When daylight came, they were in Hebron.

3 The war between Saul's house and David's house was long and drawn out. David kept getting stronger, while Saul's house kept getting weaker.

David's family

[2]David's sons were born in Hebron. His oldest son was Amnon, by Ahinoam from Jezreel; [3]the second was Chileab, by Abigail, Nabal's widow from Carmel; the third was Absalom, by[p] Maacah, who was the daughter of Geshur's King Talmai; [4]the fourth was Adonijah, by Haggith; the fifth was Shephatiah, by Abital; [5]and the sixth was Ithream, by David's wife Eglah. These are David's sons that were born in Hebron.

Joab kills Abner

[6]Throughout the war between Saul's house and David's house, Abner was gaining power in Saul's house. [7]Now Saul had a secondary wife named Rizpah, Aiah's daughter. Ishbosheth[q] said to Abner, "Why have you had sex with my father's secondary wife?"

[8]Abner got very angry over what Ishbosheth had said.

---

[k]Or *come forward and play* or *compete* [l]Heb lacks *stuck.* [m]Heb *Helkath-hazzurim* [n]Heb *shofar* [o]Heb uncertain [p]Or *son of*; also twice in 3:4 [q]Or *he,* supplied from 3:8; see note at 2:8 on *Ishbosheth.*

"Am I some sort of dog's head?"[r] Abner asked. "I've been nothing but loyal to the house of your father Saul and to his brothers and his friends. I haven't handed you over to David, but today you accuse me of doing something wrong with this woman. [9]May God deal harshly with me, Abner, and worse still if I don't do for David exactly what the Lord swore to him—[10]removing the kingdom from Saul's house and securing David's throne over Israel and over Judah, from Dan all the way to Beer-sheba!"

[11]Ishbosheth couldn't say a single word in reply to Abner because he was afraid of him.

[12]Abner sent messengers to represent him to David and to say, "Who will own the land?[s] Make a covenant with me, then I'll help bring all Israel over to your side."

[13]"Good!" David replied. "I will make a covenant with you, but on one condition: don't show yourself in my presence unless you bring Saul's daughter Michal when you come to see me."

[14]Then David sent messengers to Saul's son Ishbosheth. "Give me my wife Michal," he demanded. "I became engaged to her at the cost of one hundred Philistine foreskins."

[15]Ishbosheth then sent for Michal and took her from her husband Paltiel, Laish's son. [16]Her husband went with her all the way to Bahurim, crying as he followed her.

"Go home!" Abner told him. So he went home.

[17]Abner then sent word to Israel's elders. "You've wanted David to be your king for some time now," he said. [18]"It's time to act because the Lord has said about David: I will rescue my people Israel from the power of the Philistines and all their enemies through my servant David."

[19]Abner also spoke directly to the Benjaminites. He then went to inform David in person at Hebron regarding everything that all Israel and the house of Benjamin were willing to do.

[20]When Abner, along with twenty others, reached David at Hebron, David threw a celebration for Abner and his men. [21]Then Abner said to David, "Please let me get going so I can assemble all Israel for my master the king.

Then they can make a covenant with you, and you will rule over everything your heart[t] desires." At that, David sent Abner off in peace.

[22]Right then, David's soldiers and Joab returned from a raid, bringing a great deal of loot with them. Abner was no longer with David in Hebron because David had sent him off in peace. [23]When Joab and all the troops with him returned, Joab was told that Abner, Ner's son, had come to the king and that David had sent him off in peace.

[24]Joab went to the king and asked, "What have you done? Abner came to you here! Why did you send him off? Now he's gotten away! [25]Don't you know the evil ways of Abner, Ner's son?[u] He came to trick you, to find out where you come and go, and to learn everything you do!"

[26]Joab left David and sent messengers after Abner. They brought him back from the well at Sirah, but David didn't know anything of this. [27]When Abner returned to Hebron, Joab took him aside next to[v] the gate to speak with him in private. But instead Joab stabbed Abner in the stomach, and he died for shedding the blood of Asahel, Joab's brother.

UMBRELLA
ANGRY

Don't Feed Anger　2 Samuel 3:24-27

Joab couldn't get over his anger. The kingdom of Israel was split. Part of the kingdom followed Saul's son Ishbosheth. The other part followed David. Ishbosheth and David were fighting over who was going to be the king to follow Saul. Although Abner twice tried to avoid a fight with Joab's brother, Abner was eventually forced to kill Joab's brother in a battle (2 Sam 2:18-23). When Abner decided to leave Ishbosheth and serve David, Joab saw his chance to have his revenge on Abner. Without David knowing, Joab tricked Abner into being alone and then killed him. David was upset that Joab had killed Abner and cursed Joab for his angry act. Joab had thought that the only way to deal with his anger was to hurt or kill Abner, but Joab's anger eventually led to his own death (1 Kgs 2:5-6, 28-34). ◗

[r]LXX; MT adds that belongs to Judah.　[s]Heb uncertain; LXX lacks Who will own the land?　[t]Or soul　[u]LXX; MT You know Abner, Ner's son　[v]LXX; MT to the middle of

²⁸When David heard about this later, he said, "I and my kingdom are forever innocent before the LORD concerning the shedding of the blood of Abner, Ner's son. ²⁹May it fall upon the head of Joab and his entire family tree! May Joab's family never be without someone with a discharge or a skin disease,ʷ someone who uses a crutch,ˣ someone who dies by the sword, or someone who is hungry!"

³⁰So that is how Joab and his brother Abishai murdered Abner, because he killed their brother Asahel in the battle at Gibeon.

³¹Then David ordered Joab and all the troops who were with him, "Tear your clothes and put on funeral clothes! Mourn for Abner!" King David himself walked behind the body. ³²They buried Abner in Hebron. The king wept loudly at Abner's grave. All the troops cried too. ³³Then the king sang this funeral songʸ for Abner:

"Should Abner have died like a fool dies?
³⁴ Your hands weren't bound,
    your feet weren't chained,
    but you have fallen
    like someone falls before the wicked."

Then the troops cried over Abner again.

³⁵Then all the soldiers came to urge David to eat something while it was still day, but David swore, "May God deal harshly with me and worse still if I eat bread or anything else before the sun goes down." ³⁶All the troops took notice of this and were pleased by it. Indeed, everything that the king did pleased them. ³⁷So on that day all the troops and all Israel knew that it wasn't the king's idea to kill Abner, Ner's son.

³⁸The king told his soldiers, "Don't you know that a prince and a great man in Israel has fallen today? ³⁹And today, though I am the anointed king, I am weak. These men, Zeruiah's sons, are too strong for me.ᶻ May the LORD repay the one who does evil according to the evil they did!"

Ishbosheth murdered

4 When Ishbosheth,ᵃ Saul's son, heard that Abner had died in Hebron, he lost his courage,ᵇ and all Israel was alarmed. ²Saul's son had two men who led the raiding parties—one was named Baanah and the other Rechab. Both were sons of Rimmon, a Benjaminite from Beeroth. (Beeroth was considered part of Benjamin. ³The people of Beeroth had fled to Gittaim and even now live there as immigrants.)

⁴Now Saul's son Jonathan had a boy whose feet were crippled. He was only 5 years old when the news about Saul and Jonathan came from Jezreel, and so his nurse snatched him up and fled. But as she hurried to get away, he fell and was injured. His name was Mephibosheth.ᶜ

⁵Rechab and Baanah, the sons of Rimmon from Beeroth, set out and reached Ishbosheth's house at the heat of the day, right when he was lying down, taking an afternoon rest. ⁶They went straight into his house, as if getting wheat,ᵈ and they stabbed him in the stomach. Then Rechab and his brother Baanah escaped. ⁷They had entered the house while Ishbosheth was lying on the bed in his bedroom. After they stabbed him and killed him, they cut off his head, took it, and traveled all night through the wilderness.

⁸They brought Ishbosheth's head to David at Hebron. "Here is the head of Ishbosheth," they told the king, "the son of Saul your enemy, who wanted you dead. Today the LORD has avenged our masterᵉ the king on Saul and his descendants."

⁹David answered Rechab and his brother Baanah, the sons of Rimmon from Beeroth, "As surely as the LORD lives, who has rescued meᶠ from all kinds of trouble," he told them, ¹⁰"when someone told me Saul was dead back in Ziklag, thinking he was bringing good news, I grabbed him and killed him. That was the reward I gave him for his news! ¹¹What do you think I'll do when evil people kill a righteous person in his own house on his own bed? Why shouldn't I demand his blood from your hands and rid the earth of you both?"

¹²So David gave the order to his servants, and they killed Rechab and Baanah, cutting

---

ʷTraditionally *leprosy*, a term used for several different skin diseases ˣOr *who holds a spindle* ʸOr *lament* ᶻOr *more ruthless than me*; DSS (4QSamᵃ) lacks this clause. ᵃHeb lacks *Ishbosheth*; LXX, DSS (4QSamᵃ) *Mephibosheth*; cf 4:4 and the note at 2 Sam 2:8. ᵇOr *his hands grew weak* ᶜCalled *Merib-baal* in 1 Chron 8:34; 9:40. See the note at 2 Sam 2:8. ᵈHeb uncertain ᵉOr *my master* ᶠOr *my life* or *my soul*

off their hands and feet and hanging them up by the pool at Hebron. But they took Ish-bosheth's head and buried it in the grave of Abner at Hebron.

David becomes king of Israel and Judah

5 All the Israelite tribes came to David at Hebron and said, "Listen: We are your very own flesh and bone. ²In the past, when Saul ruled over us, you were the one who led Israel out to war and back. What's more, the Lord told you, You will shepherd my people Israel, and you will be Israel's leader.

³So all the Israelite elders came to the king at Hebron. King David made a covenant with them at Hebron before the Lord, and they anointed David king over Israel.

⁴David was 30 years old when he became king, and he ruled for forty years. ⁵He ruled over Judah for seven and a half years in Hebron. He ruled thirty-three years over all Israel and Judah in Jerusalem.

Jerusalem is captured

⁶The king and his troops marched on Jerusalem against the Jebusites, who inhabited the territory. The Jebusites said to David, "You'll never get us in here! Even the blind and the lame will beat you back!" "David will never enter here," they said to each other.ᵍ ⁷But David did capture the fortress of Zion—which became David's City. ⁸"On that day," David said, "whoever attacks the Jebusites should strike the windpipe because David hates the lame and the blind."ʰ That is why people say, "The blind and the lame will not enter the temple."ⁱ ⁹David occupied the fortress, so it was renamed David's City. David built a city around it from the earthen terracesʲ inward.ᵏ ¹⁰David grew increasingly powerful, and the Lord of heavenly forces was with him.

¹¹Tyre's King Hiram sent messengers to David with cedar logs, bricklayers, and carpenters to build David a palace. ¹²Then David knew that the Lord had established him as king over Israel, and that his kingship was held in great honor for the sake of his people

Israel. ¹³After he left Hebron, David married more secondary wives in Jerusalem and fathered more sons and daughters. ¹⁴The names of his children in Jerusalem were as follows: Shammua, Shobab, Nathan, Solomon, ¹⁵Ibhar, Elishua, Nepheg, Japhia, ¹⁶Elishama, Eliada, and Eliphelet.

David defeats the Philistines

¹⁷When the Philistines heard that David had been anointed king over Israel, they all marched up to find him, but David heard of it and went down to the fortress. ¹⁸The Philistines arrived and spread out over the Rephaim Valley. ¹⁹David asked the Lord, "Should I attack the Philistines? Will you hand them over to me?"

"Attack them," the Lord replied, "because I will definitely hand the Philistines over to you."

²⁰So David arrived at Baal-perazim and defeated the Philistines there. He said, "The Lord has burst out against my enemies, the way water bursts out!" That is why that place is called Baal-perazim.ˡ ²¹The Philistines left their divine images behind, and David and his men carried them off.

did you know? The people of Israel conquered the city of Jerusalem from the inside out, taking it from the Jebusites, who lived in the land. By tunneling to find the underground well that supplied water to Jerusalem, the Israelites were able to sneak in through the water tunnels under the city and take the people inside the city walls by surprise.

²²Once again the Philistines came up and spread out across the Rephaim Valley. ²³When David asked the Lord, God replied, "Don't attack them directly. Circle around behind them and come at them from in front of the balsam trees. ²⁴As soon as you hear the sound of marching in the tops of the trees, then attack, for God has attacked in front of you to defeat the Philistine army." ²⁵David followed God's orders exactly, and they defeated the Philistine army from Gibeon all the way to Gezer.

ᵍOr they thought; Heb lacks to each other. ʰOr take the water shaft against the lame and the blind who hate David; Heb uncertain ⁱOr palace ʲHeb Millo ᵏDSS (4QSamᵃ); MT lacks city. ˡBaal-perazim means the lord (Heb baal) of breaking out; see note at 2 Sam 6:8.

God's chest is brought to Jerusalem

6 Once again David assembled the select warriors of Israel, thirty thousand strong. [2] David and all the troops who were with him set out for Baalah, which is Kiriath-jearim of Judah,[m] to bring God's chest up from there— the chest that is called by the name[n] of the LORD of heavenly forces, who sits enthroned on the winged creatures. [3] They loaded God's chest on a new cart and carried it from Abinadab's house, which was on the hill. Uzzah and Ahio, Abinadab's sons, were driving the new cart. [4o] Uzzah was beside God's chest while Ahio was walking in front of it. [5] Meanwhile, David and the entire house of Israel celebrated in the LORD's presence with all their strength, with songs,[p] zithers, harps, tambourines, rattles, and cymbals.

[6] When they approached Nacon's threshing floor, Uzzah reached out to God's chest and grabbed it because the oxen had stumbled.[q] [7] The LORD became angry at Uzzah, and God struck him there because of his mistake,[r] and he died there next to God's chest. [8] Then David got angry because the LORD's anger lashed out against Uzzah, and so that place is called Perez-uzzah today.[s]

[9] David was frightened by the LORD that day. "How will I ever bring the LORD's chest to me?" he asked. [10] So David didn't take the chest away with him to David's City. Instead, he had it put in the house of Obed-edom, who was from Gath. [11] The LORD's chest stayed with Obed-edom's household in Gath for three months, and the LORD blessed Obed-edom's household and all that he had.

[12] King David was told, "The LORD has blessed Obed-edom's family and everything he has because of God's chest being there."[t] So David went and brought God's chest up from Obed-edom's house to David's City with celebration. [13] Whenever those bearing the chest advanced six steps, David sacrificed an ox and a fatling calf. [14] David, dressed in a linen priestly vest,[u] danced with all his strength before the LORD. [15] This is how David and the entire house of Israel brought up the LORD's chest with shouts and trumpet blasts.

[16] As the LORD's chest entered David's City, Saul's daughter Michal was watching from a window. She saw King David jumping and dancing before the LORD, and she lost all respect for him.[v]

[17] The LORD's chest was brought in and put in its place inside the tent that David had pitched for it. Then David offered entirely burned offerings in the LORD's presence in addition to well-being sacrifices. [18] When David finished offering the entirely burned offerings and the well-being sacrifices, he blessed the people in the name of the LORD of heavenly forces. [19] He distributed food among all the people of Israel—to the whole crowd, male and female—each receiving a loaf of bread, a date cake, and a raisin cake. Then all the people went back to their homes.

[20] David went home to bless his household, but Saul's daughter Michal came out to meet him. "How did Israel's king honor himself today?" she said. "By exposing himself in plain view of the female servants of his subjects like any indecent person would!"

[21] David replied to Michal, "I was celebrating before the LORD, who chose me over your father and his entire family, and who appointed me leader over the LORD's people, over Israel—and I will celebrate before the LORD again! [22] I may humiliate myself even more, and I may be humbled in my own eyes, but I will be honored by the female servants you are talking about!"

[23] Michal, Saul's daughter, had no children to the day she died.

God's promise to David

7 When the king was settled in his palace,[w] and the LORD had given him rest from all his surrounding enemies, [2] the king said to the prophet Nathan, "Look! I'm living in a cedar palace, but God's chest is housed in a tent!"[x]

---

[m] DSS (4QSam[a]), 1 Chron 13:6; MT *from Baale-judah* [n] MT repeats *name*, but 1 Chron 13:6 omits one of these and LXX reads the first as *there*. [o] LXX, DSS (4QSam[a]), 1 Chron 13:7; MT repeats *they carried it from the house of Abinadab on the hill*; Uzzah has dropped out and must be restored. [p] LXX, DSS (4QSam[a]), 1 Chron 13:8; MT *with all sorts of pine instruments* [q] Heb uncertain [r] Heb uncertain; LXX lacks this phrase; cf Targ, Syr, 1 Chron 13:10 *because he had placed his hand on the chest.* [s] *Perez-uzzah* means *Uzzah-outbreak*; cf 2 Sam 5:20. [t] Heb lacks *being there.* [u] Heb *ephod* [v] Or *despised him for it* [w] Or *house*; the same Heb word (*beth*) appears with different nuances (*house, temple, palace, dynasty, family*) in 7:2, 5, 6, 7, 11, 13, 16, 18, 19, 25–26, 27, 29. [x] Or *among curtains*

³Nathan said to the king, "Go ahead and do whatever you are thinking, because the Lord is with you."

⁴But that very night the Lord's word came to Nathan: ⁵Go to my servant David and tell him: This is what the Lord says: You are not the one to build the temple for me to live in. ⁶In fact, I haven't lived in a temple from the day I brought Israel out of Egypt until now. Instead, I have been traveling around in a tent and in a dwelling. ⁷Throughout my traveling around with the Israelites, did I ever ask any of Israel's tribal leaders I appointed to shepherd my people: Why haven't you built me a cedar temple?

⁸So then, say this to my servant David: This is what the Lord of heavenly forces says: I took you from the pasture, from following the flock, to be leader over my people Israel. ⁹I've been with you wherever you've gone, and I've eliminated all your enemies before you. Now I will make your name great—like the name of the greatest people on earth. ¹⁰I'm going to provide a place for my people Israel, and plant them so that they may live there and no longer be disturbed. Cruel people will no longer trouble them, as they had been earlier, ¹¹when I appointed leaders over my people Israel. And I will give you rest from all your enemies.

And the Lord declares to you that the Lord will make a dynasty for you. ¹²When the time comes for you to die and you lie down with your ancestors, I will raise up your descendant—one of your very own children—to succeed you, and I will establish his kingdom. ¹³He will build a temple for my name, and I will establish his royal throne forever. ¹⁴I will be a father to him, and he will be a son to me. Whenever he does wrong, I will discipline him with a human rod, with blows from human beings. ¹⁵But I will never take my faithful love away from him like I took it away from Saul, whom I set aside in favor of you. ¹⁶Your dynasty and your kingdom will be secured

Dance Like Crazy 2 Samuel 6:16-23

When you get really excited about something or hear some great news, what is your first reaction? Do you jump and scream? Do you pump your fist and say, "Oh, yeah!"? Or are you calm and cool no matter what comes your way?

King David's response was a dance. He got to take the chest containing the covenant (which represented God's holiness and presence with the people) back into Jerusalem, and he was so excited. The Bible says that David "danced with all his strength before the Lord" (6:14).

David felt the need to worship with his whole body. His wife thought he was making a fool of himself, but he didn't care. He longed to worship; he had to. He couldn't be still. He told his wife that he might be embarrassed, but he would celebrate what God had done, no matter what people thought of him.

The next time you feel excited about what God has done in your life, or when God calls you to be a part of something really great and you just can't contain yourself—dance! Let your whole self praise God.

How do you like to worship God?

What are ways you can praise God with your whole body?

forever before me.[y] Your throne will be established forever.

[17]Nathan reported all of these words and this entire vision to David.

David's prayer

[18]Then King David went and sat in the LORD's presence. He asked:

Who am I, LORD God, and of what significance is my family that you have brought me this far? [19]But even this was too small in your eyes, LORD God! Now you have also spoken about your servant's dynasty in the future and the generation to come,[z] LORD God! [20]What more can David say to you? You know your servant, LORD God. [21]For the sake of your word and according to your own will, you have done this great thing so that your servant would know it.

Bet you can read this in 5 minutes. Ready, set, go!

Memorize 2 Sam 7:22

[22]That is why you are so great, LORD God! No one can compare to you, no god except you, just as we have always heard with our own ears.

[23]And who can compare to your people Israel? They are the one nation on earth that God redeemed as his own people, establishing his name by doing great and awesome things for them,[a] by driving out nations and their gods before your people, whom you redeemed from Egypt.[b] [24]You established your people Israel as your own people forever, and you, LORD, became their God.

[25]Now, LORD God, confirm forever the promise you have made about your servant and his dynasty. Do just as you have promised [26]so that your name will be great forever when people say, "The LORD of heavenly forces is Israel's God!" May your servant David's household be established before you, [27]because you, LORD of heavenly forces, Israel's God, have revealed to your servant that you will build a dynasty for him. That is why your servant has found the courage to pray this prayer to you.

[28]LORD God, you are truly God! Your words are trustworthy, and you have promised this good thing to your servant. [29]So now willingly bless your servant's dynasty so that it might continue forever before you, because you, LORD God, have promised. Let your servant's dynasty be blessed forever by your blessing.

David's wars

8 Some time later, David defeated the Philistines and subdued them. David captured Metheg-ammah from Philistine control.

[2]David also defeated the Moabites and made them lie on the ground, measuring them with a rope. He measured two rope lengths for those who were to be killed and one rope length for those who were to be spared. The Moabites became David's subjects and brought him tribute.

[3]Next David defeated Zobah's King Hadadezer, Rehob's son, as Hadadezer was on his way to put[c] his monument along the Euphrates River.[d] [4]David captured one thousand chariots, seven hundred charioteers,[e] and twenty thousand foot soldiers. He cut the hamstrings of all but one hundred of

[y]LXX (cf 7:26, 29); MT *you*   [z]Correction; Heb uncertain *this is the law of humankind*   [a]Or *you* (plural)   [b]LXX, 1 Chron 17:21; MT *for your land before your people whom you redeemed for yourself from Egypt, the nations and their gods*   [c]Or *to restore*   [d]DSS(4QSam[a]), 1 Chron 18:3   [e]LXX, DSS(4QSam[a]), 1 Chron 18:4; MT *seventeen hundred chariots*

the chariot horses. ⁵When the Arameans of Damascus came to help Zobah's King Hadadezer, David killed twenty-two thousand of them. ⁶David set up forts among the Arameans of Damascus. And the Arameans became David's subjects and brought him tribute. The LORD gave David victory wherever he went. ⁷David took the gold shields carried by Hadadezer's servants and brought them to Jerusalem. ⁸King David also took a large amount of bronze from Tebah[f] and Berothai, towns that belonged to Hadadezer.

⁹When Hamath's King Toi heard that David had defeated the entire army of Hadadezer, ¹⁰he sent his son Joram to King David to wish him well and congratulate him on his battle and defeat of Hadadezer, because Toi was an enemy of Hadadezer. Joram brought silver, gold, and bronze objects with him. ¹¹King David dedicated these to the LORD, along with the silver and gold he had dedicated from all the nations that he had subdued: ¹²Edom, Moab, the Ammonites, the Philistines, and Amalek, including the plunder of Zobah's King Hadadezer, Rehob's son.

¹³So David made a name for himself.[g] When he returned, he killed eighteen thousand Edomites[h] in the Salt Valley. ¹⁴He set up forts in Edom,[i] and all the Edomites became David's subjects. The LORD gave David victory wherever he went.

David's administration

¹⁵David ruled over all Israel and maintained justice and righteousness for all his people. ¹⁶Zeruiah's son Joab was in command of the army; Ahilud's son Jehoshaphat was recorder; ¹⁷Ahitub's son Zadok and Ahimelech's son[j] Abiathar were priests; Seraiah was secretary; ¹⁸Jehoiada's son Benaiah was in command of[k] the Cherethites and the Pelethites; and David's sons were priests.

David and Mephibosheth

9David asked, "Is there anyone from Saul's family still alive that I could show faithful love for Jonathan's sake?" ²There was a servant from Saul's household named Ziba, and he was summoned before David.

"Are you Ziba?" the king asked him.

"At your service!" he answered.

³The king asked, "Is there anyone left from Saul's family that I could show God's kindness to?"

"Yes," Ziba said to the king, "one of Jonathan's sons, whose feet are crippled."

⁴"Where is he?" the king asked.

"He is at the house of Ammiel's son Machir at Lo-debar," Ziba told the king.

⁵So King David had him brought from the house of Ammiel's son Machir at Lo-debar. ⁶Mephibosheth, Jonathan's son and Saul's grandson, came to David, and he fell to the ground, bowing low out of respect.

"Mephibosheth?" David said.

"Yes," he replied. "I am at your service!"

⁷"Don't be afraid," David told him, "because I will certainly show you faithful love for the sake of your father Jonathan. I will restore to you all the fields of your grandfather Saul, and you will eat at my table always."

⁸Mephibosheth bowed low out of respect and said, "Who am I, your servant, that you should care about a dead dog like me?"

⁹Then David summoned Saul's servant Ziba and said to him, "I have given your master's grandson everything

SAILBOAT

KINDNESS

Kindness Before Cruelty *2 Samuel 9:1-13*

King David could be fierce but also kind. Mephibosheth was related to David's old enemy, King Saul. In those days it was common for new kings to kill every relative of the old king. This was to make sure none of the relatives could stir up trouble or try to take the kingdom from the new king. But Mephibosheth's father, Jonathan, had been David's closest friend before he died. David had promised Jonathan that he would never be cruel to his family (1 Sam 20:12-17). Now Jonathan was dead. David could have easily broken his promise and removed a future threat to his power. But David was a man who shared God's desires (Acts 13:21-22). David restored all of Mephibosheth's property to him and invited him to eat at the king's table every day. ♦

ᶠSome LXX manuscripts and 1 Chron 18:8; MT *Betah* ᵍOr *built a monument* ʰLXX; MT *he returned from killing eighteen thousand Arameans* ⁱCf 1 Chron 18:13; MT repeats *in all Edom he set up forts.* ʲMT *Abiathar's son Ahimelech*; cf 1 Sam 22:20; 23:6; 30:7; 2 Sam 20:25 ᵏSyr, Tg, Vulg, 1 Chron 18:17; MT lacks *in command of.*

belonging to Saul and his family. [10]You will work the land for him—you, your sons, and your servants—and you will bring food into your master's house for them to eat.[1] But Mephibosheth, your master's grandson, will always be at my table." (Now Ziba had fifteen sons and twenty servants.)

[11]Then Ziba said to the king, "Your servant will do whatever my master the king commands."

So Mephibosheth ate at David's[m] table, like one of the king's own sons. [12]Mephibosheth had a young son named Mica. All who lived in Ziba's household became Mephibosheth's servants. [13]Mephibosheth lived in Jerusalem, because he always ate at the king's table. He was crippled in both feet.

War with the Ammonites and Arameans

10 Some time later, the king of the Ammonites died, and his son Hanun succeeded him as king. [2]David said, "I'll be loyal to Nahash's son Hanun, just as his father was loyal to me." So David sent his servants with condolences concerning Hanun's father.

But when David's servants arrived in Ammonite territory, [3]the Ammonite officials asked their master Hanun, "Do you really believe David is honoring your father because he has sent you condolences? Of course not! David has sent his servants to you to search the city, spy it out, and overthrow it." [4]So Hanun seized David's servants and shaved off their beards,[n] cut off half their garments, from their buttocks down, and sent them off.

[5]When this was reported to David, he sent men to meet them because they were completely ashamed. The king said, "Stay in Jericho until your beards have grown. Then you can come back."

[6]When the Ammonites realized that they had offended David, they sent for and hired the Arameans of Beth-rehob and the Arameans of Zobah, totaling twenty thousand foot soldiers; the king of Maacah with one thousand soldiers; and twelve thousand soldiers from Tob. [7]When David heard this, he sent Joab with the entire army of warriors. [8]The Ammonites marched out and formed a battle line at the entrance to the city. The Arameans of Zobah and Rehob and the soldiers from Tob and Maacah remained in the countryside.

[9]When Joab saw that the battle would be fought on two fronts, he chose some of Israel's finest warriors and deployed them to meet the Arameans. [10]The rest of the army Joab placed under the command of his brother Abishai. When they took up their positions to meet the Ammonites, Joab said, [11]"If the Arameans prove too strong for me, you must help me, and if the Ammonites prove too strong for you, I'll help you. [12]Be brave! We must be courageous for the sake of our people and the cities of our God. The LORD will do what is good in his eyes."

[13]When Joab and the troops who were with him advanced into battle against the Arameans, they fled from him. [14]When the Ammonites saw that the Arameans had fled, they also fled from Abishai and retreated to the city. Then Joab returned from fighting the Ammonites and went to Jerusalem.

[15]The Arameans saw that they had been defeated by Israel, so they regrouped. [16]Hadadezer sent for Arameans from beyond the Euphrates River. They came to Helam with Shobach leading them as commander of Hadadezer's army. [17]When this was reported to David he gathered all Israel, crossed the Jordan, and went to Helam. The Arameans formed battle lines against David and fought with him. [18]But the Arameans fled before Israel, and David destroyed seven hundred of their chariots and forty thousand horsemen. David wounded their army commander Shobach, and he died there. [19]When all the kings who served Hadadezer saw that they were defeated by Israel, they made peace with Israel and became their subjects. Never again would the Arameans come to the aid of the Ammonites.

David and Bathsheba

11 In the spring,[o] when kings[p] go off to war, David sent Joab, along with his servants and all the Israelites, and they destroyed the Ammonites, attacking the city of Rabbah. But David remained in Jerusalem.

[1]LXX[L]; MT *You will bring food for your master's son and he will eat it.* [m]LXX; MT *my* [n]LXX; MT *half their beard* [o]Or *At the turn of the year* [p]LXX, Tg, Vulg; MT *messengers*

²One evening, David got up from his couch and was pacing back and forth on the roof of the palace. From the roof he saw a woman bathing; the woman was very beautiful. ³David sent someone and inquired about the woman. The report came back: "Isn't this Eliam's daughter Bathsheba, the wife of Uriah the Hittite?" ⁴So David sent messengers to take her. When she came to him, he had sex with her. (Now she had been purifying herself after her monthly period.) Then she returned home. ⁵The woman conceived and sent word to David.

"I'm pregnant," she said.

⁶Then David sent a message to Joab: "Send me Uriah the Hittite." So Joab sent Uriah to David. ⁷When Uriah came to him, David asked about the welfare of Joab and the army and how the battle was going. ⁸Then David told Uriah, "Go down to your house and wash your feet."

Uriah left the palace, and a gift from the king was sent after him. ⁹However, Uriah slept at the palace entrance with all his master's servants. He didn't go down to his own house. ¹⁰David was told, "Uriah didn't go down to his own house," so David asked Uriah, "Haven't you just returned from a journey? Why didn't you go home?"

¹¹"The chest and Israel and Judah are all living in tents," Uriah told David. "And my master Joab and my master's troops are camping in the open field. How^q could I go home and eat, drink, and have sex with my wife? I swear on your very life,^r I will not do that!"

¹²Then David told Uriah, "Stay here one more day. Tomorrow I'll send you back." So Uriah stayed in Jerusalem that day. The next day ¹³David called for him, and he ate and drank, and David got him drunk. In the evening Uriah went out to sleep in the same place, alongside his master's servants, but he did not go down to his own home.

¹⁴The next morning David wrote a letter to Joab and sent it with Uriah. ¹⁵He wrote in the letter, "Place Uriah at the front of the fiercest battle, and then pull back from him so that he will be struck down and die."

¹⁶So as Joab was attacking the city, he

LIFE PRESERVER

David made a terrible mistake. *2 Samuel 11:2-5*

It's clear that David enjoyed God's favor. David knew that God had chosen him, and he was successful as a leader because of God's love for God's people, the Israelites. However, power can be dangerous because leaders sometimes take whatever they want.

Everything was going David's way, but in one moment of seeing something he wanted, he decided to take what wasn't his: Uriah's wife. Her name was Bathsheba. Even though he was Israel's greatest king, David sinned and disobeyed God. Even worse, he tried to cover it up. 🔹

put Uriah in the place where he knew there were strong warriors. ¹⁷When the city's soldiers came out and attacked Joab, some of the people from David's army fell. Uriah the Hittite was also killed. ¹⁸Joab sent a complete report of the battle to David.

¹⁹"When you have finished reporting all the news of the battle to the king," Joab instructed the messenger, ²⁰"if the king gets angry and asks you, 'Why did you go so close to the city to fight? didn't you know they would shoot from the wall? ²¹Who killed Jerubbaal's son Abimelech?^s didn't a woman throw an upper millstone on top of him from the wall so that he died in Thebez? Why did you go so close to the wall?' then say: 'Your servant Uriah the Hittite is dead too.'"

²²So the messenger set off, and when he arrived he reported to David everything Joab sent him to say.

²³"The men overpowered us," the messenger told David. "They came out against us in the open field, but we fought against them^t up to the entrance of the city gate. ²⁴Archers shot down on your servants from the wall. Some of the king's servants died. And your servant Uriah the Hittite is dead too."

²⁵David said to the messenger, "Say this to Joab: 'Don't be upset about this because the sword is that way: taking the life of this person or that person. Continue attacking the city and destroy it!' Encourage Joab!"

---

^q LXX^L; MT lacks *How*. ^r Or *I swear on your life and your soul's life*; cf LXX ^s LXX, Syr, Judg 7:1; MT *Jerub-besheth* ^t Or *we were upon them*

²⁶When Uriah's wife heard that her husband Uriah was dead, she mourned for her husband. ²⁷After the time of mourning was over, David sent for her and brought her back to his house. She became his wife and bore him a son.

But what David had done was evil in the LORD's eyes.

Nathan pronounces God's judgment

12 So the LORD sent Nathan to David. When Nathan arrived he said, "There were two men in the same city, one rich, one poor. ²The rich man had a lot of sheep and cattle, ³but the poor man had nothing—just one small ewe lamb that he had bought. He raised that lamb, and it grew up with him and his children. It would eat from his food and drink from his cup—even sleep in his arms! It was like a daughter to him.

⁴"Now a traveler came to visit the rich man, but he wasn't willing to take anything from his own flock or herd to prepare for the guest who had arrived. Instead, he took

Truth Can Hurt   *2 Samuel 12:1-7*

It doesn't always feel good to tell or to hear the truth—like when you have to confess that you were the one who broke your mom's favorite vase. Sometimes you might be close to getting away with something when someone comes along to tell you that they know what you did. Ouch! The truth can hurt.

King David made some pretty big mistakes early on in his kingship. He had stolen another man's wife and killed her husband because he was afraid that someone would find out. His lies grew and grew, but he thought he was close to getting away with his sins. But the prophet Nathan came to tell David the truth. At first, he told him a story of a man who had done an evil thing. When David got mad at the thought of such an evil thing, Nathan said to David, "You are that man!" (12:7).

Ouch! The truth really, really hurts sometimes. With those words, David's secret was out. He couldn't hide his sins. All he could do was seek God's forgiveness and mercy.

You can probably imagine how tangled up inside David must have felt, carrying around all of those lies. Whenever we're tangled up in lies, the best thing we can do is tell the truth. And if one of our friends is tangled up in lies, we can be like Nathan and help them come clean. The truth may hurt for a bit, but God's forgiveness makes us feel much better!

Think of some times when telling or hearing the truth has hurt.

Say a prayer of thanks for God's faithfulness and forgiveness.

the poor man's ewe lamb and prepared it for the visitor."

[5]David got very angry at the man, and he said to Nathan, "As surely as the LORD lives, the one who did this is demonic![u] [6]He must restore the ewe lamb seven times over[v] because he did this and because he had no compassion."

[7]"You are that man!" Nathan told David. "This is what the LORD God of Israel says: I anointed you king over Israel and delivered you from Saul's power. [8]I gave your master's house[w] to you, and gave his wives into your embrace. I gave you the house[x] of Israel and Judah. If that was too little, I would have given even more. [9]Why have you despised the LORD's word by doing what is evil in his eyes? You have struck down Uriah the Hittite with the sword and taken his wife as your own. You used the Ammonites to kill him. [10]Because of that, because you despised me and took the wife of Uriah the Hittite as your own, the sword will never leave your own house.

[11]"This is what the LORD says: I am making trouble come against you from inside your own family. Before your very eyes I will

LIGHTHOUSE

CHANGED HEART

Forgiveness and Consequences
2 Samuel 12:7-12

King David knew he had done something terrible. David killed one of his own soldiers to hide that David had stolen his wife. God told David that because of his evil deed, there would always be fighting in David's family. God also said that someone in David's own family would fight against him. Finally God said that the son born to David and his stolen wife would die. When David heard all this, he admitted his evil and turned back to God. But even though God forgave David, all the sad things that God said would happen to David's family still happened. David's children fought each other (2 Sam 13:1-33). David's son Absalom briefly took the kingdom away from David (2 Sam 15–18). And the son of David and Bathsheba died (2 Sam 12:15-19). Even though David was forgiven, there were still consequences from his mistakes. ◆

take your wives away and give them to your friend, and he will have sex with your wives in broad daylight. [12]You did what you did secretly, but I will do what I am doing before all Israel in the light of day."

[13]"I've sinned against the LORD!" David said to Nathan.

"The LORD has removed your sin," Nathan replied to David. "You won't die. [14]However, because you have utterly disrespected the LORD[y] by doing this, the son born to you will definitely die." [15]Then Nathan went home.

Bathsheba's child dies

The LORD struck the child that Uriah's wife had borne for David, and he became very sick. [16]David begged God for the boy. He fasted and spent the night sleeping on the ground. [17]The senior servants of his house approached[z] him to lift him up off the ground, but he refused, and he wouldn't eat with them either.

[18]On the seventh day, the child died. David's servants were afraid to tell him that the child had died. "David wouldn't listen to us when we talked to him while the child was still alive," they said. "How can we tell him the child has died? He'll do something terrible!"

[19]But when David saw his servants whispering, he realized the child had died.

"Is the child dead?" David asked his servants.

"Yes," they said, "he is dead."

[20]Then David rose from the ground, bathed, anointed himself, and changed his clothes. He entered the LORD's house and bowed down. Then he entered his own house. He requested food, which was brought to him, and he ate.

[21]"Why are you acting this way?" his servants asked. "When the child was alive, you fasted and cried and kept watch,[a] but now that the child is dead, you get up and eat food!"

[22]David replied, "While the child was alive I fasted and wept because I thought, Who knows? The LORD may have mercy on me and let the child live. [23]But he is dead now. Why should I fast? Can I bring him back again? No. I am going where he is, but he won't come back to me."

---

[u]Or *as good as dead*; MT *a son of death* [v]LXX; MT *fourfold* (cf Exod 22:1) [w]Syr *daughters* [x]Syr *daughters* [y]MT *the LORD's enemies*—a euphemism or ancient scribal correction (cf note at 1 Sam 25:22) [z]LXX[L], DSS(4QSam[a]); MT *stood over* [a]LXX[L], OL; MT lacks *kept watch*.

²⁴Then David comforted his wife Bathsheba. He went to her and had sex with her. She gave birth to a son and named him Solomon.ᵇ The LORD loved him ²⁵and sent word by the prophet Nathan to name him Jedidiahᶜ because of the LORD's grace.ᵈ

Defeat of the Ammonites

²⁶Meanwhile, Joab fought the Ammonites at Rabbah and captured the royal city. ²⁷Joab then sent messengers to David, saying, "I have fought against Rabbah and captured the city's water supply.ᵉ ²⁸So gather the rest of the troops, attack the city, and capture it. Otherwise, I will capture the city myself, and it will be named after me."

²⁹So David gathered all the troops, marched to Rabbah, fought against it, and captured it. ³⁰David took Milcom'sᶠ crown off his head. It weighed one kikkar of gold and was set with a valuable stone. It was placed on David's head. The amount of loot David took from the city was huge. ³¹He brought out the people who were in the city and put them to work making bricks. David demolished the city with saws, iron picks, and axes;ᵍ he did this to all the Ammonite cities. Then David and all the troops returned to Jerusalem.

Amnon rapes Tamar

13 Some time later, David's son Amnon fell in love with Tamar the beautiful sister of Absalom, who was also David's son. ²Amnon was so upset over his half sister that he made himself sick. She was a virgin, and it seemed impossible in Amnon's view to do anything to her. ³But Amnon had a very clever friend named Jonadab, who was David's brother Shimeah's son.

⁴"Prince," Jonadab said to him, "why are you so down, morning after morning? Tell me about it."

So Amnon told him, "I'm in love with Tamar, the sister of my brother Absalom."

⁵"Lie down on your bed and pretend to be sick," Jonadab said to him. "When your father comes to see you, tell him, 'Please let my sister Tamar come and give me some food to eat.

Let her prepare the food in my sight so I can watch and eat from her own hand.'"

⁶So Amnon lay down and pretended to be sick. The king came to see him, and Amnon told the king, "Please let my sister Tamar come and make a couple of heart-shaped cakes in front of me so I can eat from her hand."

⁷David sent word to Tamar at the palace: "Please go to your brother Amnon's house and prepare some food for him."

⁸So Tamar went to her brother Amnon's house where he was lying down. She took dough, kneaded it, made heart-shaped cakes in front of him, and then cooked them. ⁹She took the pan and served Amnon, but he refused to eat.

"Everyone leave me," Amnon said. So everyone left him. ¹⁰Then Amnon said to Tamar, "Bring the food into the bedroom so I can eat from your hand." So Tamar took the heart-shaped cakes she had made and brought them to her brother Amnon in the bedroom. ¹¹When she served him the food, he grabbed her and said, "Come have sex with me, my sister."

¹²But she said to him, "No, my brother! Don't rape me. Such a thing shouldn't be done in Israel. Don't do this horrible thing. ¹³Think about me—where could I hide my shame? And you—you would become like some fool in Israel! Please, just talk to the king! He won't keep me from marrying you."

¹⁴But Amnon refused to listen to her. He was stronger than she was, and so he raped her.

¹⁵But then Amnon felt intense hatred for her. In fact, his hatred for her was greater than the love he had felt for her. So Amnon told her, "Get out of here!"

¹⁶"No, my brother!"ʰ she said. "Sending me away would be worse than the wrong you've already done."

But Amnon wouldn't listen to her. ¹⁷He summoned his young servant and said, "Get this woman out of my presence and lock the door after her." (¹⁸She was wearing a long-sleeved robe because that was what the virgin princesses wore as garments.)ⁱ So Amnon's servant put her out and locked the door after her.

¹⁹Tamar put ashes on her head and tore the

ᵇQere; Kethib he (David) named ᶜJedidiah means Loved by the LORD. ᵈHeb uncertain; some Heb and LXX manuscripts by the LORD's word ᵉHeb uncertain ᶠLXX; MT their king's crown ᵍCf LXXᴸ, OL, Tg, 1 Chron 20:3 ʰCorrection; Heb uncertain; cf LXX, Vulg   ⁱHeb uncertain

LIFE PRESERVER

Why are violent stories in the Bible? *2 Samuel 13:1-22*

The Bible contains some stories about very violent behavior. It's difficult to understand why a brother would hurt his own sister, which is what happened when Amnon raped Tamar. It's even more difficult to understand why King David did nothing in response, other than protect his son Amnon who committed the crime.

Tamar's life was forever changed as a result of this violence. No other man would marry her, and she would never have children. She would live with this for the rest of her life, and her brother would never be punished. How sad that David's son committed a crime similar to the one he committed with Uriah's wife, Bathsheba. It would be interesting to read this story from Tamar's point of view. After this story, we never hear about her again. We don't know exactly what it was like to live as David's daughter, yet not be welcome in the culture in which she lived.

One thing this story shows is that people's lives were just as messy back then as they are today. David was a great leader, one chosen by God, but he was far from perfect. In addition to making some poor choices in his own life, David sometimes failed to protect the most defenseless people. This story shows that actions have consequences. David's family paid for its sins with much violence and suffering. Even with all of this pain, we see God at work, making things right. ◖

long-sleeved robe she was wearing. She put her hand on her head and walked away, crying as she went.

²⁰Her brother Absalom said to her, "Has your brother Amnon been with you? Keep quiet about it for now, sister; he's your brother. Don't let it bother you." So Tamar, a broken woman, lived in her brother Absalom's house.

²¹When King David heard about all this he got very angry, but he refused to punish his son Amnon because he loved him as his oldest child.[j] ²²Absalom never spoke to Amnon, good word or bad, because he hated him for raping his sister Tamar.

Absalom kills Amnon

²³Two years later, Absalom was shearing sheep at Baal-hazor near Ephraim, and he invited all the king's sons. ²⁴Absalom approached the king and said, "Your servant is shearing sheep. Would the king and his advisors please join me?"

²⁵But the king said to Absalom, "No, my son. We shouldn't all go, or we would be a burden on you." Although Absalom urged him, the king wasn't willing to go, although he gave Absalom a blessing.

²⁶Then Absalom said, "If you won't come, then let my brother Amnon go with us."

"Why should he go with you?" they asked him. ²⁷But Absalom urged him until he sent Amnon and all the other princes. Then Absalom made a banquet fit for a king.[k]

²⁸Absalom commanded his servants, "Be on the lookout! When Amnon is happy with wine and I tell you to strike Amnon down, then kill him! Don't be afraid, because I myself am giving you the order. Be brave and strong men." ²⁹So Absalom's servants did to Amnon just what he had commanded. Then all the princes got up, jumped onto their mules, and fled.

³⁰While they were on the way, the report came to David: "Absalom has killed all of the princes! Not one remains." ³¹The king got up, tore his garments, and lay on the ground. All his servants stood near him, their garments torn as well. ³²But Jonadab, the son of David's brother Shimeah, said, "My master shouldn't think that all the young princes have been killed—only Amnon is dead. This has been Absalom's plan ever since the day Amnon raped his sister Tamar. ³³So don't let this bother you, my master; don't think that all the princes are dead, because only Amnon is dead, ³⁴and Absalom has fled." Just then the young man on watch looked up and saw many people coming on the road behind him alongside the mountain. ³⁵Jonadab told the king, "Look, the princes are coming, just as I, your servant, said they would."

³⁶When Jonadab finished speaking, the princes arrived. They broke into loud crying, and the king and his servants cried hard as well.

³⁷Meanwhile, Absalom had fled and gone to Geshur's King Talmai, Ammihud's son. David mourned for his son a long time. ³⁸But

[j]LXX, DSS(4QSamª); MT lacks *but he refused . . . oldest child.* [k]LXX; MT lacks *Then Absalom . . . king.*

Absalom, after fleeing to Geshur, stayed there for three years. [39]Then the king's desire to go out after Absalom faded away because he had gotten over Amnon's death.[l]

Absalom is restored

14 Now Joab, Zeruiah's son, could see that the king's mind was on Absalom. [2]So Joab sent someone to Tekoa and brought a wise woman from there. He said to her, "Pretend to be in mourning. Dress in mourning clothes. Don't anoint yourself with oil. Act like a woman who has spent a long time mourning over someone who has died. [3]Go to the king and speak to him as follows." Then Joab told her what to say.

[4]When the woman from Tekoa came to the king, she fell facedown, bowing low out of respect. "King, help me!" she said.

[5]"What is wrong?" the king asked her.

"It's terrible!" she said. "I am a widow; my husband is dead. [6]Your servant had two sons, but the two of them fought in the field. No one could separate them, and one struck the other and killed him. [7]Now the entire clan has turned against your servant. They say, 'Hand over the one who killed his brother so we can execute him for murdering his brother, even though we would destroy the heir as well.' So they would snuff out the one ember I have left, leaving my husband without name or descendant on the earth."

[8]The king said to the woman, "Return home, and I will issue an order in your behalf."

[9]The woman of Tekoa said to the king, "My master and king, let the guilt be on me and on my father's household. The king and his throne are innocent."

[10]"If anyone speaks against you, bring him to me, and he will never trouble you again," the king replied.

[11]She said, "Please let the king remember the LORD your God so that the one seeking revenge doesn't add to the destruction and doesn't kill my son."

"As surely as the LORD lives," David said, "not one of your son's hairs will fall to the ground."

[12]Then the woman said, "May your female servant say something to my master the king?"

"Speak!" he said.

[13]The woman said, "Why have you planned the very same thing against God's people? In giving this order, the king has become guilty because the king hasn't restored his own banished son. [14]We all have to die—we're like water spilled out on the ground that can't be gathered up again. But God doesn't take life away; instead, he makes plans so those banished from him don't stay that way.[m]

[15n]"I have come to my master the king to talk about this because people have made me afraid. Your servant thought, I must speak with the king. Maybe the king will act on the request of his servant, [16]because the king will agree to deliver his servant from the power of anyone who would destroy both me and my son from the inheritance God gave. [17]Your servant thought, The word of my master the king will definitely comfort me, because my master the king is like one of God's messengers, understanding good and evil. May the LORD your God be with you!"

[18o] The king answered the woman, "I must ask you something—don't hide anything from me!"

The woman said, "Please, my master and king, speak."

[19]So the king said, "Has Joab put you up to this?"

The woman answered, "As surely as you live, my master and king, no one can deviate a bit from whatever my master and king says. Yes, it was your servant Joab who directed me, and it was Joab who told your female servant to say all these things. [20]Your servant Joab did this to change the way things look.[p] But my master's wisdom is like the wisdom of one of God's own messengers—he knows everything that takes place in the land."

[21]So the king said to Joab, "All right then. I will do it. Go and bring back my boy Absalom."

[22]Joab fell facedown, bowing low out of respect, and he blessed the king.

"Today your servant knows that you think well of me, my master and king," Joab said, "because the king has followed up on his servant's recommendation."

[23]So Joab got up, went to Geshur, and brought Absalom back to Jerusalem.

---

[l]DSS(4QSamᵃ), LXX; Heb uncertain [m]Heb uncertain [n]14:15–17 may have originally followed 14:7. [o]14:18 may have originally followed 14:14. [p]Heb uncertain

UMBRELLA

ANGRY

Don't Forget God's Love *2 Samuel 14:23-33*

Absalom hadn't seen his father, King David, in two years because of family fighting that resulted in Absalom being expelled from Jerusalem. When Absalom was allowed back, he wasn't permitted to see David's face. After two years, Absalom didn't know why he had returned home. He still hadn't seen his father. David loved his son (2 Sam 18:5, 32-33), but Absalom didn't feel loved. Feeling unloved made Absalom angry, and then he acted badly. Absalom burned Joab's fields. He stole the kingdom away from David (2 Sam 15:1-17). Instead of telling David how he felt, or accepting the love of God, Absalom let his hurt rule him until he only wanted to hurt others—his father especially. Absalom's hurt eventually killed him (2 Sam 18:9-15).

24 The king said, "He must go straight to his own house. He must not see my face." So Absalom went straight to his own house and did not see the king.

25 No man throughout Israel was as praised for his good looks as Absalom. From the soles of his feet to the crown of his head there was nothing wrong with him. 26 When he shaved his head—he had to shave his head at the end of each year because his hair was so heavy that he had to shave it—the weight of the hair from his head was two hundred shekels by the royal weight. 27 Absalom had three sons and one daughter. The daughter's name was Tamar. She was a beautiful woman.

28 Absalom lived in Jerusalem two years without ever seeing the king's face. 29 Absalom called for Joab in order to send Joab to the king, but Joab refused to come. Absalom called for Joab a second time, but he still wouldn't come. 30 So Absalom said to his servants, "Look, Joab's property is next to mine. He has barley there. Go and set it on fire." So Absalom's servants set the property on fire. Then Joab's servants went to Joab with their clothes torn. "Absalom's servants set the property on fire," they said.[q]

31 So Joab went straight to Absalom's house and said to him, "Why have your servants set my property on fire?"

32 Absalom answered Joab, "Look, I sent you a message: Come here so I can send you to the king to ask, 'Why have I returned from Geshur? I would be better off if I were still there!' Please let me see the king's face. If I'm guilty, then the king can kill me."

33 Joab went to the king and reported this to him. Then the king called for Absalom, and Absalom came to the king. He bowed low out of respect, nose to the ground before the king. Then the king kissed Absalom.

Absalom plots rebellion

15 Some time later, Absalom got a chariot and horses for his own use, along with fifty men to run ahead of him. 2 Absalom would get up early and stand by the side of the road that went through the city gate. Whenever anyone had a lawsuit to bring before the king for judgment, Absalom would call to him, "What city are you from?" When the person said, "Your servant is from one of the tribes of Israel," 3 then Absalom would say to him, "No doubt your claims are correct and valid, but the king won't listen to you. 4 If only I were made a judge in the land," Absalom would continue, "then anyone with a lawsuit could come to me, and I would give them justice."

5 Whenever anyone came near to Absalom, bowing low out of respect, he would reach his hand out, grab them, and kiss them. 6 This is how Absalom treated every Israelite who came to the king seeking justice. This is how Absalom stole the hearts of the Israelites.

7 At the end of four[r] years, Absalom said to the king, "Please let me go to Hebron so I can fulfill a promise I made to the LORD. 8 Your servant made this promise when I lived in Geshur, in Aram. I promised that if the LORD would bring me back to Jerusalem, then I would worship the LORD in Hebron."[s]

9 "Go in peace," the king said. So Absalom left and went to Hebron.

10 But Absalom sent secret agents throughout the tribes of Israel with this message: "When you hear the sound of the trumpet, then say, 'Absalom has become king in

[q]DSS (4QSam[c]), LXX; MT lacks *Then Joab's servants . . . said.* [r]LXX, Syr, Vulg, Josephus; MT *forty* [s]LXX; MT lacks *in Hebron.*

Hebron!'" [11]Two hundred invited guests went with Absalom from Jerusalem. They were innocent and knew nothing of this matter when they went. [12]While Absalom was offering the sacrifices, he summoned David's advisor Ahithophel, who was from Giloh, to come from his hometown. So the conspiracy grew stronger, and Absalom's following grew.

David flees from Jerusalem

[13]A messenger came to David, reporting, "The hearts of the Israelites have gone over to Absalom." [14]Then David told all the servants who were with him in Jerusalem, "Come on! We have to run for it, or we won't be able to escape Absalom. Hurry, or he will catch up with us in no time, destroy us,[t] and attack the city with the sword."

[15]The king's servants said to him, "Your servants are ready to do whatever our master the king decides." [16]So the king left, with his entire household following him, but he left ten secondary wives behind to take care of the palace.

[17]So the king left, with all his people following him, and they stopped at the last house. [18]All the king's servants marched past him, as did all the Cherethites, all the Pelethites, and the six hundred Gittites who had followed him from Gath. [19]The king said to Ittai the Gittite, "Why are you coming with us too? Go back! Stay with King Absalom.[u] You are a foreigner and an exile from your own country. [20]You just got here yesterday. So today should I make you wander around with us while I go wherever I have to go? No. Go back, and take

[t]Heb uncertain; LXX[L] *bring the city down on top of us*. [u]Heb lacks *Absalom*.

Feeling Defeated   *2 Samuel 15:13-31*

It is always painful when we feel like someone has turned against us. We might think everything is fine in one of our friendships, but then find out that person is upset and telling other people bad things about us.

This happened to King David. His people were secretly turned against him by his own son Absalom. Before David knew it, he ran to get away from Absalom's army. You can imagine that David probably felt a little defeated—like he lost everything.

But even in the middle of thinking the whole world was against him, David believed that God would take care of him. He trusted God no matter what the outcome—whether he died in battle or returned to his dearly loved city.

When you feel like everyone is against you, remember this point in David's story. His people turned against him. His own son turned against him. He left behind the city he loved, where the chest containing the covenant (which represented God's presence) stayed. But David continued to believe that God is good. He trusted in God's goodness, even when he felt defeated and lonely.

How can you trust and believe in God's goodness even when you feel completely alone?

Write a poem or a list of all of the blessings in your life. Read it again the next time you start to feel defeated and lonely.

your relatives with you. May the Lord show you loyal love and faithfulness."ᵛ

²¹But Ittai answered the king, "As surely as the Lord lives and as surely as my master the king lives, wherever my master the king may be, facing death or facing life, your servant will be there too."

²²"Okay then," David replied to Ittai. "Keep marching!"

So Ittai the Gittite and all of his men and all the little children with him marched past. ²³The whole countryside cried loudly as all the troops marched past. The king crossed the Kidron Valley, and all the troops passed by on the Olive roadᵂ into the wilderness.

²⁴Zadok was there too, along with all the Levites carrying the chest containing God's covenant. They set God's chest down, and Abiathar offered sacrifices until all the troops had finished marching out of the city. ²⁵Then the king said to Zadok, "Carry God's chest back into the city. If the Lord thinks well of me, then he will bring me back and let me see it and its home again. ²⁶But if God says, 'I'm not pleased with you,' then I am ready. Let him do to me whatever pleases him."

²⁷"Do you understand?" the king said to the priest Zadok. "Go back to the city in safety—you and Abiatharˣ with your two sons, your son Ahimaaz and Abiathar's son Jonathan. ²⁸I will be waiting in the desert plains until you send word telling me what to do." ²⁹So Zadok and Abiathar took God's chest back to Jerusalem and stayed there.

³⁰But David, his head covered, walked barefoot up the slope of the Mount of Olives crying. All the people who were with him covered their heads too and cried as they went up. ³¹David was told that Ahithophel was also among the conspirators with Absalom, so he prayed, "Please, Lord, make Ahithophel's advice foolish."

David and Hushai

³²When David came to the summit where people used to worship God, Hushai from Erek met him. Hushai's clothes were ripped, and dirt was on his head. ³³David said to him, "If you come with me, you will be a burden

to me. ³⁴But if you return to the city and say to Absalom, 'King, I am your servant!'ʸ Please spare my life! I was your father's servant in the past, but now I am your servant,' then you can help me by countering Ahithophel's advice. ³⁵The priests Zadok and Abiathar will be with you there. So report everything you hear in the king's palace to the priests Zadok and Abiathar. ³⁶Their two sons, Zadok's son Ahimaaz and Abiathar's son Jonathan, are also there. Use them to report to me everything you hear."

³⁷So David's friend Hushai went into Jerusalem, just as Absalom was entering the city.

David and Ziba

16 When David had passed a short distance beyond the summit, Ziba, Mephibosheth's servant, met him with a pair of saddled donkeys loaded with two hundred loaves of bread, one hundred bunches of raisins, one hundred figs,ᶻ and a jar of wine.

²"What is all this for?" the king asked Ziba.

"The donkeys are for the royal family to ride," Ziba explained. "The bread and summer fruit are for the young people to eat, and the wine is for those who get exhausted in the wilderness."

³"Where is your master's grandson?" the king asked.

"He is still in Jerusalem," Ziba answered the king, "because he thinks that the Israelites are now going to give his grandfather's kingdom back to him."

⁴"Look here," the king said to Ziba. "Everything that belonged to Mephibosheth now belongs to you."

Ziba said, "I bow out of respect! Please think well of me, my master and king."

Shimei curses David

⁵When King David came to Bahurim, a man from the same clan as Saul's family came out from there. His name was Shimei; he was Gera's son. He was cursing as he came out. ⁶He threw rocks at David and at all of King David's servants, even though the entire army and all the warriors were on either side of him.

⁷This is what Shimei said as he cursed

ᵛLXX; MT lacks *may the Lord show you.* ᵂLXXᴸ; MT lacks *Olive.* ˣCorrection; MT lacks *and Abiathar.* ʸCorrection, LXX; MT *King, I will be your servant.* ᶻOr *summer fruit*

David: "Get out of here! Get out of here! You are a murderer! You are despicable! [8]The Lord has paid you back for all the blood of Saul's family, in whose place you rule, and the Lord has handed the kingdom over to your son Absalom. You are in this trouble because you are a murderer!"

[9]Zeruiah's son Abishai said to the king, "Why should this dead dog curse my master the king? Let me go over and cut his head off!"

[10]But the king said, "My problems aren't yours, you sons of Zeruiah. If he is cursing because the Lord told him to curse David, then who is to question, 'Why are you doing this?'"

[11]Then David addressed Abishai and all his servants: "Listen! My own son, one of my very own children, wants me dead. This Benjaminite can only feel the same—only more! Leave him alone. And let him curse, because the Lord told him to. [12]Perhaps the Lord will see my distress; perhaps the Lord will repay me with good for this cursing today."

[13]So David and his men kept walking, while Shimei went along on the hillside next to him, cursing as he went, throwing rocks and dirt at him. [14]The king and all the people who were with him reached the Jordan River[a] exhausted, and he rested there.

Ahithophel's advice

[15]Now Absalom and all the Israelites entered Jerusalem, and Ahithophel was with him. [16]Then David's friend Hushai, who was from Erek, approached Absalom and said to him, "Long live the king! Long live the king!"

[17]But Absalom said to Hushai, "Is this how you show loyal love to your friend? Why didn't you go with him?"

[18]"No," Hushai replied to Absalom, "I will belong to the one chosen by the Lord, by this people, and by all Israel, and I will stay with him. [19]What's more, whom should I serve if not David's son? I served your father, and so I will serve you in the same way."

[20]Then Absalom said to Ahithophel, "Give your advice then. What should we do?"

[21]"Have sex with your father's secondary wives—the ones he left to take care of the palace," Ahithophel told Absalom. "Then all Israel will hear that you have alienated yourself from your father, and everyone who supports you will be encouraged."

[22]So they set up a tent for Absalom on the roof, and he had sex with his father's secondary wives in plain sight before all Israel. ([23]Now in those days, the advice Ahithophel gave was like asking for a word from God. That's why Ahithophel's advice was valued by both David and Absalom.)

17 Then Ahithophel said to Absalom, "Let me pick twelve thousand men, and I will go after David tonight. [2]I will attack him while he is tired and weak, and I will throw him into a panic. All the troops with him will run off. I promise to kill the king alone, [3]and I will bring all the people back to you like a bride comes back to her husband.[b] It's only one man's life you are seeking; everyone else can be at peace."

[4]This plan seemed excellent to Absalom and the Israelite elders.

Hushai's advice

[5]But Absalom said, "Call Hushai from Erek. Let's hear what he has to say as well." [6]When

UMBRELLA
Hard Times

Rise Above Hard Times *2 Samuel 16:10, 12*
David was having a very bad day. His son Absalom wanted to kill him, and now David was running away. Just when things looked like they couldn't get any worse, a man began cursing David as he passed by. David kept his servants from killing the man. David didn't blame the man for his troubles, and he didn't blame God for his hard times. David accepted the hard times. He didn't waste time and energy blaming others and feeling sorry for himself. He didn't lie down and wait for other people to make everything in his life better. Instead, David worked toward changing his situation. He prayed that his enemies would make foolish choices (2 Sam 15:31). He sent people who were loyal to him back into the city to spy for him (2 Sam 15:32-37). David relied on both God and himself to make a difference in his difficult situation, which helped him regain his kingdom. ◉

Hushai from Erek arrived, Absalom said to him, "This is what Ahithophel has advised. Should we follow it or not? What do you say?"

[7]Hushai said to Absalom, "This time, the advice Ahithophel has given isn't right. [8]You know that your father and his men are warriors," he continued, "and they are as desperate as a wild bear robbed of her cubs. Your father is a seasoned fighter. He won't spend the night with his troops. [9]Even now he has probably hidden himself in one of the caves or some other place. When some of the troops[c] fall in the first attack, whoever hears it will say, 'The soldiers who follow Absalom have been defeated!' [10]Then even the bravest soldier, whose heart is like a lion's, will melt in fear because all Israel knows that your father is a warrior and that those who are with him are brave. [11]So I would advise that all the Israelites, from Dan to Beer-sheba—a group as countless as sand on the seashore—be summoned to join you, and that you yourself go into battle. [12]When we attack him wherever he might be, we will fall on him like dew that falls on the ground. No one will survive—not him and not one of the soldiers who are with him! [13]If he retreats into a city, all Israel will bring ropes to that city, and we will drag it into a valley until not even a pebble of it will be found."

[14]Then Absalom and everyone in Israel agreed, "The advice of Hushai from Erek is better than Ahithophel's advice." This was because the Lord had decided to counter Ahithophel's good advice so that the Lord could bring disaster on Absalom.

Hushai warns David

[15]Hushai told the priests Zadok and Abiathar, "Here is what Ahithophel advised Absalom and the Israelite elders, and here is what I advised. [16]Now send word immediately to David and tell him, 'Don't spend the night in the desert plains. You must cross over immediately. Otherwise, the king and all the troops who are with him will be swallowed up whole.'"

[17]Jonathan and Ahimaaz were standing by at En-rogel. A female servant would come and report to them, and they would then travel and report to King David because they couldn't risk being seen entering the city. [18]But a boy saw them and reported it to Absalom. So the two of them left immediately and came to a man's house at Bahurim. He had a well in his courtyard, and they climbed down into it. [19]The man's wife took a covering and spread it over the well's opening, then scattered grain over it so no one would notice. [20]When Absalom's servants came to the woman at the house they demanded, "Where are Ahimaaz and Jonathan?"

The woman told them, "They crossed over the stream."[d] They looked for them but found nothing, so they returned to Jerusalem.

[21]After they had left, Jonathan and Ahimaaz climbed out of the well. They went and reported to King David, "Get up! Cross the water immediately because Ahithophel has made plans against you!" [22]So David and all the troops who were with him got up and crossed the Jordan River. By daybreak there was no one left who hadn't crossed the Jordan.

[23]Meanwhile, once Ahithophel saw that his advice hadn't been followed, he saddled his donkey and went home to his own town. He gave instructions to his household, then hanged himself and died. He was buried in his father's tomb.

[24]David had reached Mahanaim by the time Absalom and all the Israelites who were with him crossed the Jordan River. [25]Absalom had put Amasa in charge of the army instead of Joab. Amasa was the son of a man named Ithra, an Ishmaelite[e] who had married Abigail, who was Nahash's daughter and the sister of Zeruiah, Joab's mother. [26]Israel and Absalom camped in the territory of Gilead.

[27]When David arrived in Mahanaim, Nahash's son Shobi, who was from Rabbah of the Ammonites; Ammiel's son Machir, who was from Lo-debar; and Barzillai the Gileadite

did you know? One of the responsibilities of young female servants was to get water. Because these servants often went back and forth across the field to get to the well, they were the perfect people to carry messages back and forth between people who did not want to be seen.

---

[c]LXX [d]Heb uncertain [e]LXX[A] and 1 Chron 2:17; MT *an Israelite*; LXX[M] *a Jezreelite*

from Rogelim [28]brought couches, basins, and pottery, along with wheat, barley, flour, roasted grain, beans, lentils, [29]honey, curds, sheep, and cheese from the herd so that David and the troops who were with him could eat. They said, "The troops have grown hungry, tired, and thirsty in the wilderness."

Absalom's death

18 Then David gathered the troops who were with him and appointed unit commanders over thousands and hundreds. [2]David sent out the army—a third under Joab's command, a third under the command of Abishai, Zeruiah's son, and a third under the command of Ittai the Gittite. The king told the troops, "I will march out with you myself."

[3]But the troops replied, "No! You must not march out! If we flee, they won't care about us. Even if half of us die, they won't care about us. But you are worth ten thousand of us. It is much better if you support us from the city."

[4]The king said to them, "I will do whatever you think is best." So the king stood beside the gate as all the troops marched out by hundreds and thousands. [5]The king gave orders to Joab, Abishai, and Ittai: "For my sake, protect my boy Absalom." All the troops heard what the king ordered regarding Absalom to all the commanders.

[6]So the troops marched into the field to meet the Israelites. The battle was fought in the Ephraim forest. [7]The army of Israel was defeated there by David's soldiers. A great slaughter of twenty thousand men took place that day. [8]The battle spread out over the entire countryside, and the forest devoured more soldiers than the sword that day.

[9]Absalom came upon some of David's men. Absalom was riding on a mule, and the mule went under the tangled branches of a large oak tree. Absalom's head got caught in the tree. He was left hanging in midair while the mule under him kept on going. [10]One of the men saw this and reported to Joab, "I just saw Absalom hanging from an oak tree."

[11]Joab said to the man who told him, "You saw this? Why didn't you kill him on the spot? I would have given you ten pieces of silver and a belt."

[12]But the man said to Joab, "Even if I had a thousand pieces of silver in my hand, I wouldn't touch the king's son! We heard what the king commanded you, Abishai, and Ittai—'For my sake, take care of my boy Absalom.'[f] [13]If I had taken Absalom's life behind the king's back then—though nothing is hidden from the king—you would have kept your distance from me."[g]

[14]Joab said, "I won't waste time like this with you!" He took three sticks in his hand and drove them into Absalom's chest while he was still alive in the oak. [15]Then ten young armor-bearers of Joab surrounded Absalom, struck him, and killed him. [16]Then Joab sounded the trumpet, and the troops stopped chasing the Israelites, because Joab held them back.

[17]They took Absalom and threw him into a big pit in the forest. They piled over him a huge heap of stones. Meanwhile, all the Israelites fled to their homes. [18]When he was alive, Absalom had raised a large pillar for himself in the King's Valley because he said, "I have no son to carry on the memory of my name." He named the pillar after himself. It is called Absalom's Monument to this day.

David mourns for Absalom

[19]Then Zadok's son Ahimaaz said, "Please let me run and take the news to the king that the LORD has vindicated him against his enemies' power."

[20]Joab said to him, "You aren't the one to bring the news today. You can bring news on another day, but not today, because the king's son is dead." [21]Then Joab said to a Cushite, "Go tell the king what you have seen." The Cushite bowed low before Joab, then ran off.

[22]But Zadok's son Ahimaaz again said to Joab, "I don't care what happens, just let me run after the Cushite too."

"Why do you want to go, son?" Joab asked. "You'll get no reward for going."[h]

[23]"I don't care what happens, I want to go," Ahimaaz said.[i]

So Joab said to him, "Run off then!"

Ahimaaz ran off, going by way of the plain, and passed the Cushite.

[24]Now David was sitting between the two

[f]LXX, Vulg, Syr; Heb uncertain [g]Or *Otherwise, I would have been dealing recklessly with my own life, because nothing is hidden from the king and you were stationed far from me;* Heb uncertain. [h]Heb uncertain [i]LXX; MT lacks *Ahimaaz said.*

gates. The watchman on duty went up on the roof of the gate by the wall. He looked out and saw a man running alone. ²⁵The watchman called out and reported this to the king. The king said, "If he's alone, it's good news."

The man got nearer and nearer, ²⁶and the watchman saw another man running and called down to the gatekeeper, "There's another man running alone."

The king said, "That one must be bringing good news too."

²⁷The watchman said, "I can see that the first one runs like Zadok's son Ahimaaz."

"He's a good man," the king said, "and is coming with good news."

²⁸Ahimaaz called out to the king, "Peace!" then bowed low before the king, his nose to the ground. He said, "Bless the Lord your God, who has delivered up the men who raised their hands against my master the king."

²⁹The king said, "Is my boy Absalom okay?"

Ahimaaz said, "I saw a large crowd right when Joab, the king's servant, sent your servant off, but I don't know what it was about."

³⁰"Step aside and stand right here," the king said. So Ahimaaz stepped aside and waited.

³¹Then the Cushite arrived and said, "My master the king: Listen to this good news! The Lord has vindicated you this day against the power of all who rose up against you."

³²The king said to the Cushite, "Is my boy Absalom okay?"

The Cushite answered, "May the enemies of my master the king and all who rise up against you to hurt you end up like that young man."

^{33j}The king trembled. He went up to the room over the gate and cried. As he went, he said, "Oh, my son Absalom! Oh, my son! My son Absalom! If only I had died instead of you! Oh, Absalom, my son! My son!"

19 ^kJoab was told that the king was crying and mourning Absalom. ²So the victory that day was turned into mourning for all the troops because they heard that day that the king was grieving for his son. ³So that day the troops crept back into the city like soldiers creep back ashamed after they've fled from battle. ⁴The king covered his face and cried out in a loud voice, "Oh, my son Absalom! Oh, Absalom, my son! My son!"

⁵Joab came to the king inside and said, "Today you have humiliated all your servants who have saved your life today, not to mention the lives of your sons, your daughters, your wives, and your secondary wives, ⁶by loving those who hate you and hating those who love you! Today you have announced that the commanders and their soldiers are nothing to you, because I know that if Absalom were alive today and the rest of us dead, that would be perfectly fine with you! ⁷Now get up! Go out and encourage your followers! I swear to the Lord that if you don't go out there, not one man will stick with you tonight—and that will be more trouble for you than all the trouble that you've faced from your youth until now."

⁸So the king went and sat down in the city gate. All the troops were told that the king was sitting in the gate, so they came before the king.

David returns to Jerusalem

Meanwhile, the Israelites had fled to their homes. ⁹Everyone was arguing throughout Israel's tribes, saying, "The king delivered us from our enemies' power, and he rescued us from the Philistines' power, but now he has fled from the land and from controlling his own kingdom.^l ¹⁰And Absalom, the one we anointed over us, is dead in battle. So why do you say nothing about bringing the king back?"

¹¹When the things that all the Israelites were saying reached the king,^m David sent a message to the priests Zadok and Abiathar: "Say the following to the elders of Judah: 'Why should you be the last to bring the king back to his palace?'ⁿ ¹²You are my relatives! You are my flesh and bones! Why should you be the last to bring the king back?' ¹³And tell Amasa, 'Aren't you my flesh and bones too? May God deal harshly with me and worse still if you don't become commander of my army from now on instead of Joab!'"

¹⁴So he won over the hearts of everyone in Judah as though they were one person, and they sent word to the king: "Come back—you and all your servants." ¹⁵So the king came back and arrived at the Jordan River. Judah came to Gilgal to meet the king and bring him across the Jordan.

^j19:1 in Heb ^k19:2 in Heb ^lLXX; MT *from over Absalom* ^mLXX, OL; MT lacks *When . . . the king,* though a version of this clause appears in 19:12. ⁿMT adds *The things that all the Israelites were saying reached the king in his home* (or *palace*).

¹⁶Gera's son Shimei, the Benjaminite from Bahurim, hurried down with the people of Judah to meet King David. ¹⁷A thousand men from Benjamin were with him. Ziba too, the servant of Saul's house, along with his fifteen sons and twenty servants, rushed to the Jordan ahead of the king ¹⁸to do the work of ferrying^o over the king's household and to do whatever pleased him.

Gera's son Shimei fell down before the king when he crossed the Jordan. ¹⁹He said to the king, "May my master not hold me guilty or remember your servant's wrongdoing that day my master the king left Jerusalem. Please forget about it, Your Majesty,^{p 20}because your servant knows that I have sinned. But look, I am the first person from the entire family of Joseph to come down today and meet my master the king."

²¹Zeruiah's son Abishai responded, "Shouldn't Shimei be put to death for that—for cursing the LORD's anointed?"

²²But David said, "My problems aren't yours, you sons of Zeruiah. Why are you becoming my enemy today? Should anyone in Israel be put to death

SAILBOAT

FORGIVENESS

Does Forgiving Mean Forgetting?
2 Samuel 19:16-23

King David had a good memory. David remembered who sided with him when Absalom took the kingdom away. When David escaped the city, he passed a man who cursed him. Shimei was distantly related to the former king, Saul. Shimei mistakenly thought David was responsible for the ruin of Saul's family and that David's trouble with Absalom was his right punishment. When David was king again, he completely forgave Shimei. David showed mercy to Shimei like he showed mercy to his other enemies (1 Sam 24). But David did not forget what Shimei had done. Forgiving Shimei didn't mean David risked trusting him again. When David passed his kingdom to his son Solomon, David didn't want Shimei causing trouble for the new king. David advised Solomon to make sure Shimei felt the full effect of his curses years after he was forgiven (1 Kgs 2:8-9). ◆

today? Don't I know that today I am again king over Israel?"

²³Then the king told Shimei, "You will not die." And the king swore this to him.

²⁴Mephibosheth, Saul's grandson, also came down to meet the king. He hadn't taken care of his feet, trimmed his beard, or washed his clothes from the day the king left until the day he returned safely. ²⁵When he came from Jerusalem to meet the king, the king asked him, "Mephibosheth, why didn't you go with me?"

²⁶"My master and king," Mephibosheth answered, "my servant abandoned me! Because your servant is lame, I asked my servant, 'Saddle a donkey for me^q so I can ride and go to the king.' ²⁷So Ziba has slandered your servant to my master and king, but my master and king is a messenger of God. So do whatever seems best to you. ²⁸Even though all the members of my grandfather's family were nothing short of demonic^r toward my master and king, you still put your servant with those who eat at your table. So what right do I have to beg for still more from the king?"

²⁹"You don't need to talk any more about this," the king said to him. "I order you and Ziba to divide the property."

³⁰Mephibosheth said to the king, "Let him take all of it, since my master and king has come home safely."

³¹Now Barzillai the Gileadite had come down from Rogelim. He accompanied the king to the Jordan River to send him off there. ³²Barzillai was very old, 80 years of age. He had supported the king during his stay at Mahanaim because Barzillai was a very wealthy man.

³³The king said to Barzillai, "Come over the Jordan with me. I will provide for you at my side in Jerusalem."

³⁴But Barzillai said to the king, "How many years do I have left that I should go up with the king to Jerusalem? ³⁵I am now 80 years old. Do I know what is good or bad anymore? Can your servant taste what I eat or drink? Can I even hear the voices of men or women singers? Why should your servant be a burden to my master and king? ³⁶Your servant will cross a short way over the Jordan with the king, but why should the king give me

such a reward? ³⁷Let your servant return so I may die in my own town near the grave of my parents. But here is your servant Chimham. Let him cross over with my master and king, and treat him as you think best."

³⁸The king said, "Okay. Chimham will cross over with me, and I will treat him as I[s] think best. And I will do for you anything you desire from me."

³⁹So all the people crossed over the Jordan River, and the king stayed behind.[t] The king kissed Barzillai and blessed him, and then Barzillai went back to his home. ⁴⁰When the king crossed over to Gilgal, Chimham went with him. All the troops of Judah and half the troops of Israel escorted the king across.

⁴¹Then everyone in Israel came and said to the king, "Why did our relatives the people of Judah steal you away, and bring the king and his household across the Jordan River, along with all of his soldiers?"

⁴²Then all the people of Judah answered the Israelites, "Because the king is our relative! Why are you angry at us about this? Have we taken any of the king's food? Has he given us any gifts?"

⁴³But the Israelites answered the people of Judah, "We have ten shares in the monarchy! What's more, we are the oldest offspring, not you![u] So why have you disrespected us? Weren't we the first to talk about bringing back our king?"

But the words of the people of Judah were even harsher than the words of the Israelites.[v]

Sheba's rebellion

20 Now a despicable man named Sheba, Bichri's son, from Benjamin, was also there. He sounded the trumpet and said:

"We don't care about David!
We have no stake in Jesse's son!
Go back to your homes, Israel!"

²So all the Israelites left David to follow Bichri's son Sheba. But all the people of Judah stayed close to their king from the Jordan River all the way to Jerusalem.

³When David arrived at his palace in Jerusalem, the king took the ten secondary wives he had left to take care of the palace and put them in a house under guard. He provided for them, but he didn't have sex with them. They were confined until the day they died, and lived like widows.

⁴Then the king said to Amasa, "Call everyone in Judah here to me three days from now. You should be here too." ⁵So Amasa went to call Judah together, but he took longer than the allotted time.

⁶David told Abishai, "Bichri's son Sheba will cause more trouble for us than Absalom did. Take your master's servants and chase after him before he finds fortified cities and escapes from us." ⁷So Joab's men marched out after Sheba—this included the Cherethites, the Pelethites, and all the warriors. They marched out of Jerusalem to pursue Bichri's son Sheba.

⁸When they got to the great stone in Gibeon, Amasa came to meet them. Joab was dressed in his soldier's uniform. Over the tunic at his waist he wore a sword in its sheath. As Joab went forward it slipped out.

⁹"How are you, my brother?" Joab asked Amasa, and with his right hand he took hold of Amasa's beard as if to kiss him. ¹⁰But Amasa didn't notice the sword in Joab's hand. Joab struck him in the stomach with it so that Amasa's intestines spilled out on the ground.

UMBRELLA
LYING

Nobody Trusts a Liar
2 Samuel 20:6-10

Joab was very good at being deceitful. Joab commanded all of King David's armies until David gave the job to Amasa. Joab didn't like that at all. Joab welcomed Amasa back from a mission he was carrying out for the king. But when Amasa got close, Joab stabbed him. Joab did the same thing to Abner when David showed him favor. Joab pretended he had something private to tell Abner, got him alone, and killed him (2 Sam 3:20-27). In fact, Joab told David that Abner was full of trickery before Joab tricked Abner to his death! Though Joab served David well in most ways, David remembered Joab's deceit. David made sure his son Solomon, the next king, never trusted Joab (1 Kgs 2:5-6). ◊

He died without Joab striking him a second time. Then Joab and his brother Abishai pursued Sheba, Bichri's son.

[11]One of Joab's men stood by Amasa and said, "Whoever favors Joab, and whoever is for David, follow Joab!" [12]Amasa was writhing in blood in the middle of the road, and the man saw that everyone was stopping. When he saw this, he dragged Amasa from the road into a field and threw a robe over him. [13]Once Amasa was moved out of the road, everyone who followed Joab marched past in pursuit of Bichri's son Sheba.

[14]Sheba went through all the Israelite tribes up to Abel of Beth-maacah. All the Bichrites[w] assembled and followed Sheba in. [15]Then Joab's men arrived and attacked Sheba at Abel of Beth-maacah. They piled up a ramp against the city, and it stood against the outer wall.[x] All of Joab's troops were hammering the wall, trying to bring it down.

[16]Then a wise woman called from the city, "Listen! Listen! Tell Joab to come over here, so I can talk to him."

[17]So Joab approached her, and the woman said, "Are you Joab?"

"I am," he answered.

"Pay close attention to the words of your female servant," she said.

"I'm listening," Joab replied.

[18]She said, "People used to say long ago: 'Ask your question at Abel,' and that settled the matter. [19]I am one of the peaceful and faithful in Israel, but you are trying to kill a city that is one of Israel's mothers! Why would you annihilate the LORD's inheritance?"

[20]Joab answered, "I would never, ever annihilate or destroy such a thing! [21]That's not the issue. A man named Sheba, Bichri's son, who is from the Ephraim highlands, has rebelled against King David. Just hand him over, and I'll leave the city alone."

The woman said to Joab, "His head will be thrown over the wall to you!"

[22]When the woman went to everyone with her wise counsel, they cut off the head of Sheba, Bichri's son, and threw it out to Joab. Then Joab sounded the trumpet, and his troops left the city, returning to their homes. But Joab returned to the king in Jerusalem.

David's officials

[23]Now Joab was in command of Israel's army; Jehoiada's son Benaiah commanded the Cherethites and the Pelethites; [24]Adoram was in charge of the forced labor; Ahilud's son Jehoshaphat was the recorder; [25]Sheva was secretary; Zadok and Abiathar were priests; [26]and Ira from Jair was also a priest for David.

Avenging the Gibeonites

21 There was a famine for three years in a row during David's rule. David asked the LORD about this, and the LORD said, "It is caused by Saul and his household, who are guilty of bloodshed because he killed the people of Gibeon." [2]So the king called for the Gibeonites and spoke to them.

(Now the Gibeonites weren't Israelites but were survivors of the Amorites. The Israelites had sworn a solemn pledge to spare them, but Saul tried to eliminate them in his enthusiasm for the people of Israel and Judah.)

[3]David said to the Gibeonites, "What can I do for you? How can I fix matters so you can benefit from the LORD's inheritance?"

[4]The Gibeonites said to him, "We don't want any silver or gold from Saul or his family, and it isn't our right to have anyone in Israel killed."

"What do you want?"[y] David asked. "I'll do it for you."

[5]"Okay then," they said to the king. "That man who opposed and oppressed[z] us, who planned to destroy us, keeping us from having a place to live anywhere in Israel— [6]hand over seven of his sons to us, and we will hang them before the LORD at Gibeon[a] on the LORD's mountain."

"I will hand them over," the king said.

[7]But the king spared Mephibosheth, Jonathan's son and Saul's grandson, because of the LORD's solemn pledge that was between them—between David and Saul's son Jonathan. [8]So the king took the two sons of Aiah's daughter Rizpah, Armoni and Mephibosheth, whom she had birthed for Saul; and the five sons of Saul's daughter Merab,[b] whom she birthed for Adriel, Barzillai's son, who was from Meholah, [9]and he handed them over

---

[w]Cf LXX, Vulg; MT *Berites* [x]Heb uncertain [y]LXX[L], OL; MT *What are you saying?* [z]LXX[B]; MT *annihilated us* [a]Correction; cf LXX and 21:9; MT *at Gibeah of Saul, the LORD's chosen one* [b]LXX[LN]; MT *Michal* (but cf 2 Sam 6:23)

to the Gibeonites. They hanged them on the mountain before the Lord. The seven of them died at the same time. They were executed in the first days of the harvest, at the beginning of the barley harvest.

¹⁰Aiah's daughter Rizpah took funeral clothing and spread it out by herself on a rock. She stayed there from the beginning of the harvest until the rains poured down on the bodies from the sky, and she wouldn't let any birds of prey land on the bodies during the day or let wild animals come at nighttime. ¹¹When David was told what Aiah's daughter Rizpah, Saul's secondary wife, had done, ¹²he went and retrieved the bones of Saul and his son Jonathan from the citizens of Jabesh-gilead, who had stolen the bones from the public square in Beth-shan, where the Philistines had hanged them on the day the Philistines killed Saul at Gilboa. ¹³David brought the bones of Saul and his son Jonathan from there and collected the bones of the men who had been hanged by the Gibeonites. ¹⁴The bones of Saul and his son Jonathan were then buried in Zela, in Benjaminite territory, in the tomb of Saul's father Kish. Once everything the king had commanded was done, God responded to prayers for the land.

War with the Philistines

¹⁵Once again war broke out between the Philistines and Israel. David and the soldiers who were with him went down and fought the Philistines. When David grew tired, ¹⁶Ishbi-benob, a descendant of the Raphah,ᶜ planned on killing David.ᵈ The weight of his spear was three hundred shekels of bronze, and he was wearing new armor. ¹⁷But Zeruiah's son Abishai came to David's aid, striking the Philistine down and killing him. Then David's men swore a solemn pledge to him: "You will never march out to battle with us again! You must not snuff out Israel's lamp!"

¹⁸Some time later, another battle with the Philistines took place at Gob. Then Sibbecai from Hushah killed Saph, a descendant of Raphah. ¹⁹There was yet another battle with the Philistines at Gob; and Elhanan, Jair's

sonᵉ from Bethlehem, killed Goliath from Gath, whose spear shaft was as strong as the bar on a weaver's loom. ²⁰In another battle at Gath, there was a hugeᶠ man who had six fingers on his hands and six toes on his feet, twenty-four in all. He too was descended from the Raphah. ²¹When he insulted Israel, Jonathan, who was the son of David's brother Shimei, killed him. ²²These four Philistines were descended from the Raphah in Gath, and they fell by the hands of David and his servants.

David's thanksgiving psalm

22 ⁸ David spoke the words of this song to the Lord after the Lord delivered him from the power of all his enemies and from Saul.

² He said:

> The Lord is my solid rock,
> my fortress, my rescuer.
> ³ My God is my rock—
> I take refuge in him!—
> he's my shield and
> my salvation's strength,
> my place of safety and my shelter.
> My savior! Save me from violence!
> ⁴ Because he is praiseworthy,ʰ
> I cried out to the Lord,
> and I was saved from my enemies.
> ⁵ Death's waves were all around me;
> rivers of wickedness terrified me.

LIFE PRESERVER

Is this psalm like one in the book of Psalms?
2 Samuel 22:2-51

The words of David's song in this chapter may sound familiar to you. David is named as the author of many of the psalms contained in the book of Psalms. Look up Psalm 18 and compare it with this one, and you'll see that they are almost identical.

This psalm was probably sung after a military victory as a song of thanksgiving. The words give us a glimpse into understanding David—what he thought about his life and his relationship with God. ◊

ᶜOr *giants*; also in 21:18, 20, 22 ᵈLXX *Joash's son Dodo, a descendant of the Raphah* (see previous note), *captured David.*
ᵉSee 1 Chron 20:5, LXX ᴸ ᴹ ᴺ (cf 2 Sam 23:24); Heb *Jaare-oregim* ᶠSee 1 Chron 20:6; MT *a Midianite* or *a combative man*
ᵍThis poem also occurs in Psalm 18 with some variations. ʰHeb uncertain

⁶ The cords of the grave[i] surrounded me;
  death's traps held me tight.
⁷ In my distress I cried out to the Lord;
  I cried out to my God.
 God heard my voice from his temple;
  my cry for help reached his ears.

⁸ The earth rocked and shook;
  the sky's foundations trembled
  and reeled because of God's anger.
⁹ Smoke went up from God's nostrils;
  out of his mouth came a devouring fire;
  flaming coals blazed out in front of him!
¹⁰ God parted the skies and came down;
  thick darkness was beneath his feet.
¹¹ God mounted the heavenly creatures
  and flew;
  he was seen on the wind's wings.
¹² God made darkness his covering;
  water gathered in dense clouds!
¹³ Coals of fire blazed
  out of the brightness before him.
¹⁴ The Lord thundered from heaven;
  the Most High made his voice heard.
¹⁵ God shot arrows, scattering the enemy;
  he sent the lightning
  and whipped them into confusion.
¹⁶ The seabeds were exposed;
  the earth's foundations were laid bare
  at the Lord's rebuke,
  at the angry blast of air
  coming from his nostrils.

¹⁷ From on high God reached down
  and grabbed me;
  he took me out of deep waters.
¹⁸ God saved me from my powerful enemy,
  saved me from my foes,
  who were too much for me.
¹⁹ They came at me
  on the very day of my distress,
  but the Lord was my support.
²⁰ He brought me out to wide-open spaces;
  he pulled me out
  because he is pleased with me.
²¹ The Lord rewarded me
  for my righteousness;
  he restored me
  because my hands are clean,
²² because I have kept the Lord's ways.
  I haven't acted wickedly against my God.

²³ All his rules are right in front of me;
  I haven't turned away
  from any of his laws.
²⁴ I have lived with integrity before him;
  I've kept myself from wrongdoing.
²⁵ And so the Lord restored me
  for my righteousness,
  because I am clean in his eyes.

²⁶ You deal faithfully with the faithful;
  you show integrity toward the one
  who has integrity.
²⁷ You are pure toward the pure,
  but toward the crooked, you are tricky.
²⁸ You are the one
  who saves people who suffer,
  but your eyes are against the proud.
  You bring them down!
²⁹ You are my lamp, Lord;
  the Lord illumines my darkness.
³⁰ With you I can charge into battle;
  with my God
  I can leap over a wall.
³¹ God! His way
  is perfect;
  the Lord's word is tried and true.
  He is a shield for all who take refuge
  in him.

**Memorize
2 Sam 22:31**

³² Now really, who is divine except the
  Lord?
  And who is a rock except our God?
³³ Only God! My mighty fortress,
  who makes my way[j] perfect,
³⁴ who makes my step[k] as sure as the deer's,
  who lets me stand securely
  on the heights,
³⁵ who trains my hands for war
  so my arms can bend a bronze bow.
³⁶ You've given me
  the shield of your salvation;
  your help has made me great.
³⁷ You've let me walk fast and safe,
  without even twisting an ankle.
³⁸ I chased my enemies and destroyed them!
  I didn't come home until I finished
  them off.
³⁹ I ate them up! I struck them down!
  They couldn't get up;
  they fell under my feet.
⁴⁰ You equipped me with strength for war;

[i] Heb *Sheol* [j] Qere; Kethib *his way* [k] Qere; Kethib *his step*

you brought my adversaries
down underneath me.
⁴¹ You made my enemies turn tail from me;
I destroyed my foes.
⁴² They looked around,
but there was no one to save them.
They looked to the Lᴏʀᴅ,
but he wouldn't answer them.
⁴³ I crushed them like dust on the ground;
I stomped on them,
trampled them like mud
dumped in the streets.
⁴⁴ You delivered me from struggles
with many people;
you appointed me the leader
of many nations.
Strangers come to serve me.
⁴⁵ Foreigners grovel before me;
after hearing about me, they obey me.
⁴⁶ Foreigners lose their nerve;

they come trembling
out of their fortresses.[1]
⁴⁷ The Lᴏʀᴅ lives! Bless God, my rock!
Let my God, the rock of my salvation,
be lifted high!
⁴⁸ This is the God who avenges
on my behalf,
who subdues peoples before me,
⁴⁹ who rescues me from my enemies.
You lifted me high above my adversaries;
you delivered me from violent people.
⁵⁰ That's why I thank you, Lᴏʀᴅ,
in the presence of the nations.
That's why I sing praises to your name.
⁵¹ You are the one who gives
great victories to your king,
who shows faithful love
to your anointed one—
to David and to his descendants forever.

[1] Or *prisons*

Safe Place *2 Samuel 22:1-51*

A safe place is the spot you go to when storms rush in. If you live in the midwest or the south, you probably practice tornado drills where everyone goes to a safe place and covers their heads. If you live where there are earthquakes, you know how to find the nearest doorframe to stand in to protect you from falling items. If you live near the ocean, you probably know where to go when a hurricane blows in. Safe places are meant to protect and shield us from the strong winds and destructive forces.

God wants to be our spiritual safe place. When life comes at us like a hurricane and we need to get away quick, we can run to God.

David ran to God when he felt like the world was against him. He trusted God to be his rock, his shield, and his shelter. When his enemies were defeated and he was finally home again, David cried out in thanksgiving to God. We can read his prayer in 2 Samuel 22.
Look at the verses, and see how almost every line tells of God's greatness.

God is our rock, our safe place on good days and bad days. When we hold on tight to our rock, we find that God will still be there holding on to us when the storm blows over.

What words do you use to describe God?

When have you held on tight to God and felt like God was holding on tight to you as well?

David's last words

23

These are David's last words:
This is the declaration
of Jesse's son David,
the declaration of a man raised high,
a man anointed by the God of Jacob,
a man favored
by the strong one of Israel.[m]

2 The LORD's spirit speaks through me;
his word is on my tongue.
3 Israel's God has spoken,
Israel's rock said to me:
"Whoever rules rightly over people,
whoever rules in the fear of God,
4 is like the light of sunrise
on a morning with no clouds,
like the bright gleam after the rain
that brings grass from the ground."
5 Yes, my house is this way with God![n]
He has made an eternal covenant
with me,
laid out and secure in every detail.
Yes, he provides every one of my victories
and brings my every desire to pass.
6 But despicable people are like thorns,
all of them good for nothing,
because they can't be carried by hand.
7 No one can touch them,
except with iron bar or the shaft
of a spear.
They must be burned up with fire
right on the spot!

David's warriors

8 These are the names of David's warriors: Jeshbaal[o] from Hachmon[p] was chief of the Three.[q] He raised his spear[r] against eight hundred, killing them on a single occasion.

9 Next in command was Eleazar, Dodo's son and Ahohi's grandson. He was among the three warriors with David when they insulted the Philistines who had gathered there for battle. The Israelites retreated, 10 but he stood his ground and fought the Philistines until his hand was weary and stuck to the sword. But the LORD accomplished a great victory that day. The troops then returned to Eleazar, but only to plunder the dead.

11 Next in command was Agee's son Shammah, who was from Harar. The Philistines had gathered at Lehi, where there was a plot of land full of lentils. The troops fled from the Philistines, 12 but Shammah took a position in the middle of the plot, defended it, and struck down the Philistines. The LORD accomplished a great victory.

13 At harvesttime, three of the thirty chiefs went down and joined David at the fortress[s] of Adullam, while a force of Philistines were camped in the Rephaim Valley. 14 At that time, David was in the fortress, and a Philistine fort was in Bethlehem. 15 David had a craving and said, "If only someone could give me a drink of water from the well by the gate in Bethlehem." 16 So the three warriors broke through the Philistine camp and drew water from the well by the gate in Bethlehem and brought it back to David. But he refused to drink it and poured it out to the LORD.

17 "The LORD forbid that I should do that," he said. "Isn't this the blood of men who risked their lives?" So he refused to drink it.

These were the kinds of things the three warriors did.

18 Now Zeruiah's son Abishai, the brother of Joab, was chief of the Thirty.[t] He raised his spear against three hundred men, killed them, and made a name for himself along with the Three. 19 He was the most famous of the Thirty.[u] He became their commander, but he wasn't among the Three.

20 Jehoiada's son Benaiah was a hero from Kabzeel who performed great deeds. He killed the two sons[v] of Ariel from Moab. He once went down into a pit and killed a lion on a snowy day. 21 He also killed a giant[w] Egyptian who had a spear in his hand. Benaiah went against him armed with a staff. He grabbed the spear out of the Egyptian's hand and killed him with his own spear. 22 These were the kinds of things Jehoiada's son Benaiah did. He made a name for himself along with the three warriors. 23 He was famous among the Thirty, but he didn't become one of the Three. David placed him in command of his own bodyguard.

---

[m]Or *Israel's favorite singer* or *the favorite of Israel's songs* [n]Or *Yes, my house is surely with God!* [o]LXX[L], OL; MT *Josheb-basheheth*; cf 1 Chron 11:11 [p]See 1 Chron 11:11. [q]LXX[L], Vulg; cf 1 Chron 11:11; MT *chief of the officers* [r]Cf 1 Chron 11:11; Heb uncertain [s]Or *cave*; cf 2 Sam 23:14 [t]Some Heb manuscripts, Syr; MT *third* or *three* [u]Syr; cf 1 Chron 11:25; MT *Wasn't he the most famous of the Three?* [v]LXX; MT lacks *sons*. [w]MT *handsome*; cf 1 Chron 11:23

²⁴Among the Thirty were:

Asahel, Joab's brother;

Elhanan, Dodo's son from Bethlehem;

²⁵Shammah from Harod;

Elika from Harod;

²⁶Helez from Pelet;

Ira, Ikkesh's son from Tekoa;

²⁷Abiezer from Anathoth;

Mebunnai the Hushathite;

²⁸Zalmon from Ahoh;

Maharai from Netophah;

²⁹Heleb, Baanah's son from Netophah;

Ittai, Ribai's son from Gibeah in Benjamin;

³⁰Benaiah from Pirathon;

Hiddai from the Gaash ravines;

³¹Abi-albon from the desert plain;

Azmaveth from Bahurim;

³²Eliahba from Shaalbon;

Jashen the Gizonite;^x

Jonathan, ³³Shammah's son^y from Harar;

Ahiam, Sharar's son from Harar;

³⁴Eliphelet, Ahasbai's son from Maacah;

Eliam, Ahithophel's son from Giloh;

³⁵Hezro from Carmel;

Paarai from Erab;

³⁶Igal, Nathan's son from Zobah;

Bani the Gadite;

³⁷Zelek the Ammonite;

Naharai from Beeroth, and the armor-bearer for Zeruiah's son Joab;

³⁸Ira from Ither;

Gaeb from Ither;

³⁹and Uriah the Hittite—

thirty-seven in all.

David's census

24 The Lord burned with anger against Israel again, and he incited David against them: Go and count the people of Israel and Judah.

²So the king said to Joab and the military commanders^z who were with him, "Go throughout all the tribes of Israel, from Dan to Beer-sheba, and take a census of the people so I know how many people there are."

³Joab said to the king, "May the Lord your God increase the number of people a hundred times while the eyes of my master the king can still see it! But why does my master the king want to do this?"

⁴But the king's word overruled Joab and the military commanders. So Joab and the commanders left the king's presence to take a census of the Israelites. ⁵They crossed the Jordan River and began from Aroer and from^a the town that is in the middle of the valley of Gad, then on to Jazer. ⁶They continued to Gilead and on to Kadesh in Hittite territory.^b They came to Dan^c and went around to Sidon. ⁷They went to the fortress of Tyre and to all the towns of the Hivites and the Canaanites. They went out to Beer-sheba in the arid southern plain of Judah. ⁸At the end of nine months and twenty days, after going through the entire country, they came back to Jerusalem. ⁹Joab reported to the king the number of the people who had been counted: in Israel there were eight hundred thousand strong men who could handle a sword; in Judah the total was five hundred thousand men.

¹⁰But after this David felt terrible that he had counted the people. David said to the Lord, "I have sinned greatly in what I have done. Now, Lord, please take away the guilt of your servant because I have done something very foolish."

¹¹When David got up the next morning, the Lord's word came to the prophet Gad, David's seer: ¹²Go and tell David, This is what the Lord says: I'm offering you three punishments. Choose one of them, and that is what I will do to you.

¹³So Gad went to David and said to him, "Will three^d years of famine come on your land? Or will you run from your enemies for three months while they chase you? Or will there be three days of plague in your land? Decide now what answer I should take back to the one who sent me."

¹⁴"I'm in deep trouble," David said to Gad. "Let's fall into the Lord's hands because his mercy is great, but don't let me fall into human hands."

¹⁵So the Lord sent a plague on Israel from that very morning until the allotted time. Seventy thousand people died, from Dan to

^xCf 1 Chron 11:34; MT *Jashen's sons* ^yLXX; MT lacks *son.* ^zLXX and 2 Sam 24:4; MT *commander* ^aLXX; MT *camped in Aroer south of the city* ^bHebrew uncertain; correction *on to the area beneath Hermon* ^cLXX^L; MT *Dan-jaan* ^dLXX, 1 Chron 21:12; MT *seven*

UMBRELLA

PRIDE

Pride in the Wrong Things Is Costly

2 Samuel 24:10, 17

David wanted to count all the men of Israel. This was like David saying, "Let's see how strong my kingdom really is, so I can feel high-and-mighty about it." But God didn't want David to feel high-and-mighty because of Israel's huge army. God wanted David to feel high-and-mighty because of Israel's God. So God punished David with a deadly sickness that spread throughout the nation. When David admitted he was wrong, God told him to build an altar and offer a sacrifice at a specific spot to stop the sickness. The owner of the spot wanted to give David everything for the sacrifice for free. But David refused. David knew being sorry for what he'd done wrong and changing his heart had to cost him something personally, otherwise it would be worthless. David paid full price—money for the sacrifice and seventy thousand lives—before God stopped the sickness. 💧

Beer-sheba. ¹⁶But when the divine messenger stretched out his hand to destroy Jerusalem, the Lord regretted doing this disaster and said to the messenger who was destroying the people, "That's enough! Withdraw your hand." At that time the Lord's messenger was by the threshing floor of Araunah from Jebus. ¹⁷When David saw the messenger who was striking down the people, he said, "I'm the one who sinned! I'm the one who has done wrong. But these sheep—what have they done wrong? Turn your hand against me and my household."

¹⁸That same day Gad came to David and told him, "Go up and build an altar to the Lord on the threshing floor of Araunah from Jebus." ¹⁹So David went up, following Gad's instructions, just as the Lord had commanded.

²⁰Araunah looked up and saw the king and his servants approaching him. Araunah rushed out and bowed low before the king, his nose to the ground. ²¹Araunah said, "Why has my master and king come to his servant?"

David said, "To buy this threshing floor from you to build an altar to the Lord, so the plague among the people may come to an end."

²²Then Araunah said to David, "Take it for yourself, and may my master the king do what he thinks is best. Here are oxen for the entirely burned offering, and here are threshing boards and oxen yokes for wood. ²³All this, Your Majesty, Araunah gives to the king." Then he added, "May the Lord your God respond favorably to you!"

²⁴"No," the king said to Araunah. "I will buy them from you at a fair price. I won't offer up to the Lord my God entirely burned offerings that cost me nothing." So David bought the threshing floor and the oxen for fifty shekels of silver. ²⁵David built an altar there for the Lord and offered entirely burned offerings and well-being sacrifices. The Lord responded to the prayers for the land, and the plague against Israel came to an end.

1 Kings

After King David died, his son Solomon became Israel's king. One day God offered to give Solomon anything he asked. Solomon asked to be able to tell the difference between good and evil. This is called discernment, or wisdom. God was happy that Solomon asked for this. So God gave Solomon not only wisdom but also wealth and fame (1 Kgs 3).

First Kings tells the stories of Solomon and the kings who ruled after him. Solomon didn't always obey God. Because of this, the kingdom of Israel split into two kingdoms: Judah in the south and Israel in the north.

Each kingdom had a different king. Some kings ruled for many years, but some ruled only for a few days or months. Some kings loved God, but most kings disobeyed. They worshipped idols, which are statues of gods that aren't real. These kings' actions caused many people whom they ruled to worship false gods too.

First Kings tells a thrilling story about when the prophet Elijah confronted King Ahab and the prophets of a false god called Baal. When Elijah prayed for fire from heaven, God answered him and sent fire (1 Kgs 18). This book shows us that following God is the best way to live! 💧

things YOU'LL DISCOVER

First Kings continues the long story started in 1 and 2 Samuel. It tells Israel's history from King Solomon to King Ahab. It also explains how the nation of Israel divided into two kingdoms, Judah and Israel.

people YOU'LL MEET

Solomon—King David's son and Israel's third king (1 Kgs 1–11)
Jeroboam and Rehoboam—the first kings of the divided kingdom of Israel and Judah (1 Kgs 12–14)
Elijah—a prophet who spoke for God and confronted King Ahab (1 Kgs 17–21)
Ahab— one of Israel's kings who did evil in God's eyes (1 Kgs 17–22)

places YOU'LL GO

Israel (the northern kingdom), **Judah** (the southern kingdom)

words YOU'LL REMEMBER

"The LORD said to him, 'I have heard your prayer and your cry to me. I have set apart this temple that you built, to put my name there forever. My eyes and my heart will always be there'" (1 Kgs 9:3).

David and Abishag

1 King David had become very old. His servants covered him with blankets, but he couldn't stay warm. ²They said to him, "Allow us to find a young woman for our master the king. She will serve the king and take care of him by lying beside our master the king and keeping him warm." ³So they looked in every corner of Israel until they found Abishag from Shunem. They brought her to the king. ⁴She was very beautiful. She cared for the king and served him, but the king didn't have sex with her.

Adonijah's rebellion

⁵Adonijah, Haggith's son, bragged about himself and said, "I'll rule as king myself." He got his own chariot and horses with fifty runners to go in front. ⁶Now Adonijah's father had never given him direction; he never questioned why Adonijah did what he did. He was very handsome and was born after Absalom. ⁷He took advice from Joab, Zeruiah's son, and from the priest Abiathar. They assisted Adonijah. ⁸But Zadok the priest, Jehoiada's son Benaiah, the prophet Nathan, Shimei and his friends, and David's veterans didn't join Adonijah. ⁹So Adonijah prepared lamb, oxen, and fattened cattle at the Stone of Zoheleth, next to En-rogel. He invited his brothers (the royal princes) and all the citizens of Judah who were the royal servants to come. ¹⁰But he didn't invite the prophet Nathan, Benaiah, David's veterans, or his brother Solomon.

¹¹Nathan said to Bathsheba, Solomon's mother, "Did you hear that Adonijah, Haggith's son, has become king, but our master David doesn't know about it? ¹²Let me give you some advice on how you and your son Solomon can survive this. ¹³Go to King David and say, 'Didn't my master the king swear to your servant, "Your son Solomon will certainly rule after me. He will sit on my throne"? Why then has Adonijah become king?' ¹⁴While you are speaking there with the king, I'll come along and support your words."

¹⁵So Bathsheba went to the king in his bedroom. The king was very old, and Abishag from Shunem was serving the king. ¹⁶Bathsheba bowed down on her face before the king.

The king asked, "What do you want?"

¹⁷She said to him, "Your Majesty, you swore by the LORD your God to your servant, 'Your son Solomon will certainly rule after me. He will sit on my throne.' ¹⁸But now, look, Adonijah has become king, and my master the king doesn't know about it. ¹⁹He has prepared large quantities of oxen, fattened cattle, and lamb. He has invited all the royal princes as well as Abiathar the priest and Joab the general. However, he didn't invite your servant Solomon. ²⁰As for you, my master the king, the eyes of all Israel are upon you to tell them who will follow you on the throne of my master the king. ²¹When my master the king lies down with his ancestors, then I and my son Solomon will become outlaws."

²²While she was still speaking with the king, the prophet Nathan arrived. ²³The king was informed, "The prophet Nathan is here." Then Nathan came in before the king and bowed his face to the ground. ²⁴He said, "My master the king, you must have said, 'Adonijah will become king after me and will sit on my throne.' ²⁵Indeed, today he went down and prepared oxen, fattened cattle, and lamb in large numbers. He invited all the royal princes, the generals, and Abiathar the priest. They are eating and drinking with him, and they said, 'Long live King Adonijah!' ²⁶Adonijah didn't invite me, your servant, Zadok the priest, Jehoiada's son Benaiah, or your servant Solomon. ²⁷If this message was from my master the king, you didn't make it known to your servant. Who should follow you on the throne of my master the king?"

²⁸King David answered, "Bring me Bathsheba." She came and stood before the king. ²⁹The king made a solemn pledge and said, "As surely as the LORD lives, who rescued me from every trouble, ³⁰regarding what I swore to you by the LORD, Israel's God, 'Your son Solomon will certainly succeed me; he will sit on the throne after me'—I'll see that it happens today."

³¹Bathsheba bowed down with her face to the ground. She honored the king and said, "May my master King David live forever!"

³²King David said, "Bring me Zadok the priest, the prophet Nathan, and Benaiah, Jehoiada's son." They came to the king, ³³who said to them, "Take with you the servants of your masters. Put my son Solomon on my mule and bring him down to Gihon. ³⁴There

Zadok the priest and the prophet Nathan will anoint him king over Israel. Blow the ram's horn and say, 'Long live King Solomon!' ³⁵You will follow him. He will enter and sit on my throne, and so he will succeed me as king. I have appointed him to become ruler over Israel and Judah."

³⁶Benaiah, Jehoiada's son, responded to the king, "Yes, may it happen as the Lord, the God of my king, says. ³⁷Just as the Lord was with my master the king, so may he be with Solomon. May his throne be even greater than the throne of my master King David." ³⁸Zadok the priest, the prophet Nathan, Jehoiada's son Benaiah, and the Cherethites and the Pelethites went down and put Solomon on King David's mule. They led him to Gihon. ³⁹Zadok the priest took the horn of oil from the tent and anointed Solomon. They blew the ram's horn, and all the people said, "Long live King Solomon!" ⁴⁰All the people followed him playing flutes and celebrating. The ground shook at their noise.

⁴¹Adonijah and all his invited guests heard this when they had finished eating. When Joab heard the sound of the ram's horn, he said, "What's that noise coming from the city?" ⁴²While he was still speaking, Jonathan, Abiathar the priest's son, arrived.

Adonijah said, "Come on in! You are an honest man and will bring a good report."

⁴³Jonathan replied to Adonijah, "No! Our master King David has made Solomon king! ⁴⁴To support him, the king sent along Zadok the priest; the prophet Nathan; Benaiah, Jehoiada's son; and the Cherethites and the Pelethites. They've put Solomon on the royal mule. ⁴⁵Zadok the priest and the prophet Nathan have anointed him king at Gihon. They went up from there celebrating so that the city was thrown into a commotion. That is the sound you heard. ⁴⁶There's more: Solomon has taken over the throne of the kingdom. ⁴⁷The royal attendants blessed our master King David: 'May your God make Solomon's name better than your name. May God elevate his throne above your throne.'"

The king then worshipped on his bed ⁴⁸and said, "Bless Israel's God, the Lord, who today has set my son[a] on my throne, and has allowed my eyes to see it."

⁴⁹Trembling with fear, all of Adonijah's guests got up and fled, each going a different way. ⁵⁰Adonijah was afraid of Solomon, so he got up and went to grab hold of the horns of the altar. ⁵¹Solomon was told, "Look! Adonijah is afraid of King Solomon and has grabbed the horns of the altar. He's saying, 'King Solomon must swear to me first that he won't execute his servant with the sword.'"

⁵²Solomon said, "If he shows himself to be an honorable person, then not a hair of his head will be harmed. But if any evil is found in him, he will die." ⁵³King Solomon sent word and had him brought down from the altar. He came and bowed down to King Solomon. Solomon said to him, "Go home!"

SAILBOAT

FORGIVENESS

Forgiveness Is Learned *1 Kings 1:53*
Solomon nearly lost his kingdom. Solomon's father, King David, had declared that Solomon was the son he wanted to take the throne of Israel once he was gone. David's son Adonijah had other plans. Adonijah, who wanted the kingdom for himself, threw a great party and invited the most important people in Israel to come so they would give him their support as king. Nathan the prophet knew David wanted Solomon to become king, so Nathan helped Solomon's mother tell David how Adonijah was acting. Once David found out what Adonijah was doing, David quickly had Solomon officially crowned king. When Adonijah heard that Solomon was king, he was afraid. He was afraid Solomon would kill him for trying to take his crown away. But Solomon forgave Adonijah. Like his father, Solomon had learned how to forgive his enemies (1 Sam 24:1-15).

David's last words

2 David's time was coming to an end. So he commanded Solomon his son, ²"I'm following the path that the whole earth takes. Be strong and be a man. ³Guard what is owed to the Lord your God, walking in his ways and observing his laws, his commands, his judgments, and his testimonies, just as it is written in the Instruction from Moses. In this way you will succeed in whatever you do and

---

[a]Heb lacks *my son*; other versions have it or something similar

wherever you go. ⁴So also the LORD will confirm the word he spoke to me: 'If your children will take care to walk before me faithfully, with all their heart and all their being, then one of your own children will never fail to be on the throne of Israel.' ⁵You should know what Joab, Zeruiah's son, has done to me and what he did to the two generals of Israel, Abner, Ner's son, and Amasa, Jether's son. He murdered them, spilling blood at peacetime and putting the blood of war on the belt around his waist and on the sandals on his feet. ⁶So act wisely: Don't allow him to die a peaceful death. ⁷As for Barzillai's sons from Gilead, show them kindness. Let them eat with you. When I was running away from your brother Absalom, they came to me. ⁸Now as for this Shimei, Gera's son—a Benjaminite from Bahurim—who is with you, he cursed me viciously when I went to Mahanaim. When he came down to meet me at the Jordan, I swore to him by the LORD, 'Surely I won't execute you with the sword.' ⁹But you don't need to

excuse him. You are wise and know what to do to him. Give him a violent death."

¹⁰Then David lay down with his ancestors and was buried in David's City. ¹¹He ruled over Israel forty years—seven years in Hebron and thirty-three years in Jerusalem.

Solomon secures his throne

¹²Solomon sat on the throne of his father David, and his royal power was well established. ¹³Adonijah, Haggith's son, went to Bathsheba, Solomon's mother. She said, "Are you coming in peace?"

He said, "Yes. ¹⁴I have something to say to you."

She said, "Say it."

¹⁵He said, "You know how the kingdom was mine. All Israel had appointed me as their king. Then suddenly the kingdom went to my brother as the LORD willed. ¹⁶Now I have just one request of you. Don't refuse me!"

She said to him, "Go on."

¹⁷Adonijah continued, "Ask King Solomon

Advice from Parents   1 Kings 2:1-3

Parents often like to give advice to help their children grow and do well in life. Most of the time, their advice is good, helping their children learn more about who they are and who God is.

When King David was dying, he made his son Solomon the new king. Like most parents, he had lots of advice for Solomon. He told Solomon to be a strong man, to follow God's Instruction. This is very good advice for anyone—not just someone about to become a king.

David knew that being king would be hard and lonely sometimes. He knew it would be easy for Solomon to think that he held all the power and didn't need God anymore. David knew that the best way to keep God first would be to remember all the good things God had done and to stay close to God.

When your parents give you advice, listen carefully. They are speaking as people who have probably been through the same things you are going through. They have walked the road you are walking and have some wisdom to share with you.

What is the best piece of advice a parent has ever given you?

How do you remember all that God has done for you? How can that help you stay close to God every day?

to let me marry Abishag from Shunem—he won't refuse you."

¹⁸Bathsheba said, "Okay; I'll speak to the king for you."

¹⁹So Bathsheba went to King Solomon to talk with him about Adonijah. The king stood up to meet her and bowed low to her. Then he returned to his throne and had a throne set up for the queen mother. She sat to his right. ²⁰She said, "I have just one small request for you. Don't refuse me."

The king said to her, "Mother, ask me. I won't refuse you."

²¹"Let Abishag from Shunem be married to your brother Adonijah," she said.

²²King Solomon replied to his mother, "Why ask only for Abishag from Shunem for Adonijah? Why not ask for the entire kingdom for him? After all, he is my older brother and has the support of Abiathar the priest and Joab, Zeruiah's son." ²³King Solomon swore by the LORD, "May God do to me as he sees fit! Adonijah has made this request at the cost of his life! ²⁴Now, as surely as the LORD lives—the one who supported me, put me on the throne of my father David, and provided a royal house for me exactly as he promised—Adonijah will be executed today." ²⁵So King Solomon sent Benaiah, Jehoiada's son. He attacked Adonijah, and Adonijah died.

²⁶The king said to the priest Abiathar, "Go to your fields at Anathoth, because you are a condemned man. However, I won't kill you today because you carried the LORD's chest in front of my father David and because you shared in all my father's sufferings." ²⁷So Solomon expelled Abiathar from the LORD's priesthood in order to fulfill the LORD's word that was spoken against Eli's family at Shiloh.

²⁸Now the news reached Joab because he had supported Adonijah, though he hadn't supported Absalom. Joab ran to the LORD's tent and grabbed the horns of the altar. ²⁹King Solomon was told that Joab had fled to the LORD's tent and was now beside the altar. So Solomon sent Benaiah, Jehoiada's son, instructing him, "Go. Attack Joab!"

³⁰Benaiah came to the LORD's tent and said to Joab, "The king says, 'Come out!'"

Joab said, "No! I'd rather die here."

Benaiah sent a report back to the king: "This is what Joab said and how he answered me."

³¹The king said to him, "Do as he said. Attack him and then bury him. In doing this, you will remove from me and from my father's royal house the guilt over the innocent blood that Joab shed. ³²May the LORD return that bloodguilt back on his own head for attacking the two men who were better and more righteous than he was. He murdered those two with the sword: Abner, Ner's son and Israel's general, and Amasa, Jether's son and Judah's general. But my father David didn't know about it. ³³May the bloodguilt for their deaths return on Joab's head and on the head of his family line forever. But may the LORD's peace be on David, his family, and his royal house forever." ³⁴So Benaiah, Jehoiada's son, went and attacked Joab and killed him.

Joab was buried at his home in the wilderness. ³⁵In his place, the king gave leadership of the army to Benaiah, Jehoiada's son. The king put the priest Zadok in Abiathar's position. ³⁶Then he sent for Shimei and said, "Build a house for yourself in Jerusalem and stay in the city. Don't leave to go anywhere else. ³⁷If you try to leave, be advised that on the day you cross the Kidron Valley you will most certainly die. Your bloodguilt will be on your own head."

³⁸Shimei said to the king, "This is a good idea. Your servant will do just what my master the king said." So Shimei stayed in Jerusalem for a long time.

³⁹After three years, two of Shimei's servants fled to the king of Gath, Achish, Maacah's son. Shimei was informed, "Your servants are now in Gath." ⁴⁰Shimei saddled his donkey and went to Achish in Gath to look for his servants. Shimei then brought his servants back from Gath. ⁴¹Solomon was told that Shimei had left Jerusalem for Gath and then returned.

⁴²The king sent for Shimei and asked him, "Didn't I make you swear a solemn pledge by the LORD? And didn't I swear to you, 'If you try to leave and go anywhere, be advised that on that very day you will most certainly die'? You said to me, 'This is a good idea. I agree to it.' ⁴³Why didn't you keep your solemn promise to the LORD and the command that I gave you?" ⁴⁴The king said further, "You know quite well all the evil that you did to my father David. May the LORD return your evil on your

own head. ⁴⁵However, may King Solomon be blessed and David's throne be secure before the Lord forever." ⁴⁶Then the king commanded Benaiah, Jehoiada's son, who went and attacked Shimei, and he died.

In these ways royal power was handed over to Solomon.

Solomon first meets God

3 Solomon became the son-in-law of Pharaoh, Egypt's king, when he married Pharaoh's daughter. He brought her to David's City until he finished building his royal palace, the Lord's temple, and the wall around Jerusalem. ²Unfortunately, the people were sacrificing at the shrines because a temple hadn't yet been built for the Lord's name in those days. ³Now Solomon loved the Lord by

walking in the laws of his father David, with the exception that he also sacrificed and burned incense at the shrines.

⁴The king went to the great shrine at Gibeon in order to sacrifice there. He used to offer a thousand entirely burned offerings on that altar. ⁵The Lord appeared to Solomon at Gibeon in a dream at night. God said, "Ask whatever you wish, and I'll give it to you."

⁶Solomon responded, "You showed so much kindness to your servant my father David when he walked before you in truth, righteousness, and with a heart true to you. You've kept this great loyalty and kindness for him and have now given him a son to sit on his throne. ⁷And now, Lord my God, you have made me, your servant, king in my father David's place. But I'm young and inexperienced.

But I Don't Know Anything   1 Kings 3:1-15

When Solomon met God for the first time, he told God he was young and didn't know anything. Solomon was worried he would fail at being king because he didn't know how to do the job. But he did one thing that was exactly what God wanted him to do—he was humble.

Solomon was standing before God, and God asked him what he wanted. Solomon could have said he wanted to be the most famous king ever. He could have asked to be the richest king in history. He could have asked God to make people everywhere loyal to him alone. But he didn't. He didn't ask for any of these things. Instead, he asked for wisdom.

There are different kinds of wisdom. One kind of wisdom comes from experience. When someone goes through something, they know better how to handle it the next time. Another kind of wisdom comes from seeking God. That's what Solomon wanted. He wanted God to help him do the right things and be a wise king.

Do you ever feel like you are too young or like you don't know enough to be a leader? Ask God for wisdom. God's wisdom helps us to know the difference between good choices and bad ones. God's wisdom helps us understand hard situations. God's wisdom helps us know how to lead others out of trouble and back to God.

When you start to feel like you are too young to make a difference, seek God's wisdom. Ask God to help you make good decisions and to walk in God's ways.

What kinds of things have you asked from God?

Say a prayer to God, asking God to give you wisdom.

I know next to nothing. [8]But I'm here, your servant, in the middle of the people you have chosen, a large population that can't be numbered or counted due to its vast size. [9]Please give your servant a discerning mind in order to govern your people and to distinguish good from evil, because no one is able to govern this important people of yours without your help."

[10]It pleased the Lord that Solomon had made this request. [11]God said to him, "Because you have asked for this instead of requesting long life, wealth, or victory over your enemies—asking for discernment so as to acquire good judgment—[12]I will now do just what you said. Look, I hereby give you a wise and understanding mind. There has been no one like you before now, nor will there be anyone like you afterward. [13]I now also give you what you didn't ask for: wealth and fame. There won't be a king like you as long as you live. [14]And if you walk in my ways and obey my laws and commands, just as your father David did, then I will give you a very long life."

[15]Solomon awoke and realized it was a dream. He went to Jerusalem and stood before the chest containing the Lord's covenant. Then he offered entirely burned offerings and well-being sacrifices, and held a celebration for all his servants.

Solomon and the prostitutes

[16]Sometime later, two prostitutes came and stood before the king. [17]One of them said, "Please, Your Majesty, listen: This woman and I have been living in the same house. I gave birth while she was there. [18]This woman gave birth three days after I did. We stayed together. Apart from the two of us, there was no one else in the house. [19]This woman's son died one night when she rolled over him. [20]She got up in the middle of the night and took my son from my side while I was asleep. She laid him on her chest and laid her dead son on mine. [21]When I got up in the morning to nurse my son, he was dead! But when I looked more closely in the daylight, it turned out that it wasn't my son—not the baby I had birthed."

[22]The other woman said, "No! My son is alive! Your son is the dead one."

But the first woman objected, "No! Your son is dead! My son is alive!" In this way they argued back and forth in front of the king.

[23]The king said, "This one says, 'My son is alive and your son is dead.' The other one says, 'No! Your son is dead and my son is alive.' [24]Get me a sword!" They brought a sword to the king. [25]Then the king said, "Cut the living child in two! Give half to one woman and half to the other woman."

[26]Then the woman whose son was still alive said to the king, "Please, Your Majesty, give her the living child; please don't kill him," for she had great love for her son.

But the other woman said, "If I can't have him, neither will you. Cut the child in half."

[27]Then the king answered, "Give the first woman the living newborn. Don't kill him. She is his mother."

[28]All Israel heard about the judgment that the king made. Their respect for the king grew because they saw that God's wisdom was in him so he could execute justice.

Solomon's administration

4 King Solomon became king of all Israel. [2]These were his officials: the priest Azariah, Zadok's son; [3]the scribes Elihoreph and Ahijah, the sons of Shisha; Jehoshaphat, the recorder, Ahilud's son; [4]the general Benaiah, Jehoiada's son; the priests Zadok and Abiathar; [5]Azariah, Nathan's son, who was in charge of the officials; Zabud, Nathan's son, a priest and royal friend; [6]Ahishar, who was in charge of the palace; and Adoniram, Abda's son, who was supervisor of the work gangs.

[7]Solomon had twelve officers over all Israel. They supplied the king and his palace with food. Each would provide the supplies for one month per year. [8]Here are their names:

Ben-hur in the highlands of Ephraim;

[9]Ben-deker in Makaz, Shaalbim, Beth-shemesh, and Elon-bethhanan;

[10]Ben-hesed in Arubboth, who had Socoh and all the land of Hepher;

[11]Ben-abinadab in all of Naphath-dor (Taphath, Solomon's daughter, was his wife);

[12]Baana, Ahilud's son, in Taanach, Megiddo, and all Beth-shean beside Zarethan and below Jezreel, from Beth-shean to Abel-meholah and over to the region opposite Jokmeam;

[13]Ben-geber in Ramoth-gilead, who controlled the villages of Jair, Manasseh's son, which were in Gilead, and who had the

Argob region that was in Bashan—sixty large walled cities with bronze bars;

[14]Ahinadab, Iddo's son, in Mahanaim;

[15]Ahimaaz in Naphtali, who also took Solomon's daughter Basemath as his wife;

[16]Baana, Hushai's son, in Asher and Bealoth;

[17]Jehoshaphat, Paruah's son, in Issachar;

[18]Shimei, Ela's son, in Benjamin;

[19]Geber, Uri's son, in the land of Gilead, the land of the Amorite king Sihon and of King Og of Bashan;

and there was a single officer who was in the land of Judah.[b]

[20]Judah and Israel grew numerous like the sand alongside the sea. They ate, drank, and celebrated.

[21c] Solomon ruled over all the states from the Euphrates River through the Philistines' land and as far as the border of Egypt. These areas brought tribute to Solomon and served him all the days of his life. [22]Solomon's food requirements for a single day included thirty kors[d] of refined flour; sixty kors of flour; [23]ten head of grain-fattened cattle; twenty head of pastured cattle; one hundred sheep; as well as deer, gazelles, roebucks, and the best of fowl. [24]He ruled over all the lands west of the Euphrates River, from Tiphsah to Gaza, and over all the kings west of the Euphrates. He had peace on all sides. [25]The people of Judah and Israel from Dan all the way to Beer-sheba lived securely under their vines and fig trees throughout the days of Solomon.

[26]Solomon had forty thousand horse stalls for his chariots and twelve thousand additional horses. [27]The officials provided King Solomon and all who joined him at the royal table with monthly food rations. They left out nothing. [28]Each brought their share of barley and straw for the horses and for the chariot horses, bringing it to its proper place. [29]And God gave Solomon wisdom and very great understanding—insight as long as the sea-shore itself. [30]Solomon's wisdom was greater than all the famous Easterners, greater even than all the wisdom of Egypt. [31]He was wiser than anyone, more wise than Ethan the Ezrahite or Mahol's sons: Heman, Calcol, and Darda. His reputation was known throughout the region. [32]Solomon spoke three thousand proverbs and one thousand five songs. [33]He described the botany of trees, whether the cedar in Lebanon or the hyssop that grows out of the wall. He also described cattle, birds, anything that crawls on the ground, and fish. [34]People came from everywhere to listen to Solomon's wisdom; even the earth's kings who had heard about his wisdom came!

SAILBOAT

OBEDIENCE

God Blesses Obedience *1 Kings 4:20-34*

Solomon and the people of Israel were living the good life. Solomon was the wisest man in the world. His kingdom stretched all the way from Egypt to the Euphrates River. The people of Israel had secure and happy lives while Solomon was their king. Solomon and Israel were very blessed by God, in part because Solomon's father David had obeyed God (1 Chron 17:7-14). The other part of that blessing came from God's promise to Solomon if he continued to obey (1 Kgs 3:4-14). Solomon and Israel benefited from God's blessing. But that blessing didn't last because later in his life Solomon stopped following God's Instruction. Very few of the Israelite kings after Solomon obeyed God. Israel would never again be as prosperous as it was under Solomon's reign. ◊

Wood and stone for the temple

5[e] Because King Hiram[f] of Tyre was loyal to David throughout his rule, Hiram sent his servants to Solomon when he heard that Solomon had become king after his father. [2]Solomon sent the following message to Hiram: [3]"You know that my father David wasn't able to build a temple for the name of the Lord my God. This was because of the enemies that fought him on all sides until the Lord put them under the soles of his feet. [4]Now the Lord my God has given me peace on every side, without enemies or misfortune. [5]So I'm planning to build a temple for the name of the Lord my God, just as the Lord indicated to my father David, 'I will give you a son to

---

[b]LXX; MT lacks *of Judah.* [c]5:1 in Heb [d]One kor is possibly equal to fifty gallons. [e]5:15 in Heb [f]Chronicles spells the king's name *Huram,* for example, 2 Chron 2:3, 11–12; but cf 1 Chron 14:1 Kethib.

follow you on your throne. He will build the temple for my name.' [6]Now give the order and have the cedars of Lebanon cut down for me. My servants will work with your servants. I'll pay your servants whatever price you set, because you know we have no one here who is skilled in cutting wood like the Sidonians."

[7]Hiram was thrilled when he heard Solomon's message. He said, "Today the Lord is blessed because he has given David a wise son who is in charge of this great people." [8]Hiram sent word back to Solomon: "I have heard your message to me. I will do as you wish with the cedar and pinewood. [9]My servants will bring the wood down the Lebanon Mountains to the sea. I'll make rafts out of them and float them on the sea to the place you specify. There I'll dismantle them, and you can carry them away. Now, as for what you must do for me in return, I ask you to provide for my royal house."

[10]So Hiram gave Solomon all the cedar and pinewood that he wanted. [11]In return, Solomon gave an annual gift to Hiram of twenty thousand kors[g] of wheat to eat, and twenty thousand kors of pure oil for his palace use. [12]Now the Lord made Solomon wise, just as he had promised. Solomon and Hiram made a covenant and had peace.

[13]King Solomon called up a work gang of thirty thousand workers from all over Israel. [14]He sent ten thousand to work in Lebanon each month. Then they would spend two months at home. Adoniram was in charge of the work gang. [15]Solomon had 70,000 laborers and 80,000 stonecutters in the highlands. [16]This doesn't include Solomon's 3,300 supervisors in charge of the work, who had oversight over the laborers. [17]At the king's command, they quarried huge stones of the finest quality in order to lay the temple's foundation with carefully cut stone. [18]The craftsmen of Solomon and Hiram, along with those of Byblos, prepared the timber and the stones for the construction of the temple.

Solomon builds the temple

6 In the four hundred eightieth year after the Israelites left Egypt, in the month of Ziv, the second month,[h] in the fourth year of Solomon's rule over Israel, he built the Lord's temple. [2]The temple that King Solomon built for the Lord was ninety feet long, thirty feet wide, and forty-five feet high. [3]The porch in front of the temple's main hall was thirty feet long. It ran across the whole width of the temple and extended fifteen feet in front of the temple. [4]He made recessed and latticed windows[i] for the temple [5]and built side rooms against the temple walls around both the main hall and the most holy place. [6]The lower walls were seven and a half feet wide. At the second floor the walls were nine feet wide, and at the third floor they were ten and a half feet wide. He made niches around the outside of the temple so the beams wouldn't be inserted into the temple walls.[j] [7]When the temple was built, they did all the stonecutting

did you know? In Bible times, instead of buying things with money, people would sometimes trade things they had for things they needed. Today we call this *bartering*. To get the wood to build the temple, King Solomon traded Hiram thousands of bushels of wheat and thousands of gallons of pure olive oil every year.

at the quarry. No hammers, axes, or any iron tools were heard in the temple during its construction. [8]The door to the stairs was at the south side of the temple. Winding stairs went up to the second floor and from there to the third floor. [9]He completed the temple with a roof of cedar beams and cross-planks.[k] [10]Then he built the side rooms all around the temple. They were seven and a half feet high. He attached them to the temple with cedarwood.

[11]The Lord's word came to Solomon, [12]Regarding this temple that you are building: If you follow my laws, enact my regulations, and keep all my commands faithfully, then I will fulfill for you my promise that I made to your father David. [13]I will live among the Israelites. I won't abandon my people Israel.

[14]So Solomon constructed the temple and

---

[g]One kor is possibly equal to fifty gallons. [h]April–May, Iyar; Ziv is a month from a Canaanite calendar. [i]Heb architectural and decorative terminology in 6:4–6 and elsewhere in chaps 6–7 is often uncertain. [j]Heb uncertain; Heb lacks *the beams*. [k]Heb uncertain

completed it. [15]He built the walls within the temple with cedar planks, paneled from the floor to the ceiling. He overlaid the floor of the temple with pine planks. [16]At the back of the temple he built thirty feet of cedar panels from the floor to the ceiling. Solomon built the inner sanctuary, the most holy place. [17]In front of this, the main hall was sixty feet. [18]The cedar inside the temple was carved with gourds and blossoming flowers. The whole thing was cedar. No stone was seen. [19]He set up the inner sanctuary inside the temple so that he could put the chest containing the LORD's covenant there. [20]The inner sanctuary was thirty feet in length, width, and height. Solomon overlaid it with pure gold and covered the altar with cedar.[1] [21]Solomon covered the temple's interior with pure gold. He placed gold chains in front of the inner sanctuary and covered it with gold. [22]He overlaid the whole temple inside with gold until the temple was completely covered. He covered the whole altar that was in the inner sanctuary with gold. [23]He made two winged creatures of olive wood for the inner sanctuary, each fifteen feet high. [24]The wings of the first winged creature were each seven and a half feet long. It was fifteen feet from the end of one wing to the end of the other. [25]The second winged creature also measured fifteen feet. Both winged creatures had identical measurements and form. [26]The height of both winged creatures was fifteen feet. [27]Solomon placed the winged creatures inside the temple. Their wings spread out so that the wing of the one touched one wall and the wing of the other touched the other wall. In the middle of the temple, the wings of the two winged creatures touched each other. [28]He covered the winged creatures with gold.

[29]Solomon carved all the walls of the temple—inner and outer rooms—with engravings of winged creatures, palm trees, and blossoming flowers. [30]He also covered the floor of the temple with gold, in both the inner and the outer rooms. [31]He made the doors of the inner sanctuary from olive wood and carved the doorframes with five recesses.[m] [32]He overlaid the two olive-wood doors with

LIFE PRESERVER

Why did the temple need to be so big and fancy? 1 Kings 6

God's people were finally settled in one place. As they became more settled, it became important for them to build a temple as a place where they could worship God. The temple was at the heart of their religious life. The people believed that God would be present in the temple and would therefore bless them and be near to them.

After waiting so long to build a temple, Solomon wanted it to be the finest and most beautiful place where God's people could worship. Everything was made of the nicest materials. Solomon planned for everything, from the wood used in construction to the pots, lampstands, and basins used in worship. Everything was to be made ready so that the chest containing the covenant, which was the symbol for God's presence, could be brought into the temple when it was dedicated. ◆

gold-plated carvings of winged creatures, palm trees, and blossoming flowers. [33]He made the door of the main hall with doorframes of olive wood with four recesses.[n] [34]The two doors of pinewood each pivoted on a socket. [35]Solomon carved winged creatures, palm trees, and blossoming flowers, and covered them with gold. [36]He built the inner courtyard with three rows of cut stone followed by one row of trimmed cedar.

[37]Solomon laid the foundation of the LORD's temple in the fourth year in the month of Ziv.[o] [38]He finished the temple in all its details and measurements in the eleventh year during the eighth month, the month of Bul.[p] He built it in seven years.

Solomon builds palaces

7 Now as for Solomon's palace, it took thirteen years for him to complete its construction. [2]He built the Forest of Lebanon Palace one hundred fifty feet in length, seventy-five feet in width, and forty-five feet in height. It had four rows of cedar columns with cedar engravings above the columns. [3]The palace's cedar roof stood above forty-five beams resting on the columns, fifteen beams to each row. [4]Three sets of window

[1]Heb uncertain [m]Heb uncertain [n]Heb uncertain [o]April–May, Iyar; Ziv is a month in the Canaanite calendar. [p]October–November, Heshvan; Bul is a month in the Canaanite calendar.

frames faced each other. [5]All the doorframes were rectangular, facing each other in three sets. [6]He made a porch with columns that was seventy-five feet long and forty-five feet wide. Another porch was in front of these with roofed columns in front of them.[q] [7]He made the throne room the Hall of Justice, where he would judge. It was covered with cedar from the lower to the upper levels. [8]The royal residence where Solomon lived was behind this hall. It had a similar design. Solomon also made a similar palace for his wife, Pharaoh's daughter. [9]He built all these with the best stones cut to size, sawed with saws, back and front, from the foundation to the highest points and from the outer boundary to the great courtyard. [10]The foundation was laid with large stones of high quality, some of fifteen feet and some of twelve feet. [11]Above them were high-quality stones cut to measure, as well as cedar. [12]The surrounding great courtyard had three rows of cut stones and a row of trimmed cedar just like the inner courtyard of the Lord's temple and its porch.

Solomon's temple equipment

[13]Then King Solomon sent a message and brought Hiram from Tyre. [14]Hiram's mother was a widow from the tribe of Naphtali. His father was a Tyrian skilled in bronze work. He was amazingly skillful in the techniques and knowledge for doing all kinds of work in bronze. He came to King Solomon and did all his work.

[15]He[r] cast two bronze pillars. Each one was twenty-seven feet high and required a cord of eighteen feet to reach around it.[s] [16]He made two capitals of cast bronze for the tops of the columns. They were each seven and a half feet high. [17]He made an intricate network of chains for the capitals on top of the columns, seven for each capital. [18]He made the pillars and two rows of pomegranates for each network to adorn each of the capitals. [19]The capitals on top of the columns in the porch were made like lilies, each six feet high. [20]Above the round-shaped part and next to the network were two hundred pomegranates. These were placed in rows around both of the

capitals on top of the columns. [21]He set up the columns at the temple's porch. He named the south column Jachin. The north column he named Boaz. [22]After putting the lily shapes on top of the columns, he was finished with the columns.

[23]He also made a tank of cast metal called the Sea. It was circular in shape, fifteen feet from rim to rim, seven and a half feet high, forty-five feet in circumference. [24]Under the rim were two rows of gourds completely encircling it, ten every eighteen inches, each cast in its mold. [25]The Sea rested on twelve oxen with their backs toward the center, three facing north, three facing west, three facing south, and three facing east. [26]The Sea was as thick as the width of a hand. Its rim was shaped like a cup or an open lily blossom. It could hold two thousand baths.[t]

[27]He also made ten bronze stands. Each was six feet long, six feet wide, and four and a half feet high. [28]This is how each stand was made: There were panels connected between the legs. [29]Lions, bulls, and winged otherworldly creatures appeared on the panels between the legs. On the legs above and below the lions and bulls were wreaths on panels hanging off the stands. [30]There were four bronze wheels with bronze axles for each stand. There were four feet and supports cast for each basin with wreaths on their sides.[u] [31]Inside the bowl was an opening eighteen inches deep. The opening was round, measuring twenty-seven inches, with engravings. The panels of the stands were square rather than round. [32]There were four wheels beneath the panels. The axles of the wheels were attached to the stand. Each wheel was twenty-seven inches in height. [33]The construction of the wheels resembled chariot wheels. The axles, rims, spokes, and hubs were all made of cast metal. [34]There was a handle on each of the four corners of every stand, projecting from the side of the stand. [35]The top of the stand had a band running around the perimeter that was nine inches deep. The stand had its own supports and panels. [36]On the surfaces of the supports and panels he carved winged otherworldly creatures, lions, and palm trees with wreaths

---

[q]Heb uncertain [r]Either Solomon or Hiram; this ambiguity continues in the following verses, but cf 1 Kgs 7:1, 8, 13; 1 Kgs 7:40. [s]Or *the second*; cf Jer 52:21 [t]One bath is approximately twenty quarts or five gallons. [u]Heb uncertain

everywhere.ᵛ ³⁷In this manner he made ten stands, each one cast in a single mold of the same size and shape.

³⁸He made ten bronze washbasins, each able to hold forty baths.ʷ Every washbasin was six feet across, and there was one for each of the ten stands. ³⁹He placed five stands on the south of the temple and five on the north of the temple. He placed the Sea at the southeast corner of the temple.

⁴⁰Hiram made the basins, shovels, and bowls.

And so Hiram finished his work on the LORD's temple for King Solomon:

⁴¹two columns;

two circular capitals on top of the columns;

two networks, adorning the two circular capitals on top of the columns;

⁴²four hundred pomegranates for the two networks, with two rows of pomegranates for each network that adorned the two circular capitals on top of the columns;

⁴³ten stands with ten basins on them;

⁴⁴one Sea;

twelve oxen beneath the Sea;

⁴⁵and the pots, shovels, and bowls.

All the equipment that Hiram made for King Solomon for the LORD's temple was made from polished bronze. ⁴⁶The king cast it in clay molds in the Jordan Valley between Succoth and Zarethan. ⁴⁷Due to the very large number of objects, Solomon didn't even try to weigh the bronze.

⁴⁸Solomon also made all the equipment for the LORD's temple: the gold altar; the gold table for the bread of the presence; ⁴⁹the lampstands of pure gold, five on the right and five on the left in front of the inner sanctuary; the flowers, the lamps, and the tongs of gold; ⁵⁰the cups, wick trimmers, bowls, ladles, and censers of pure gold; and the gold sockets for the doors to the most holy place and for the doors to the main hall. ⁵¹When all King Solomon's work on the LORD's temple was finished, he brought the silver, gold, and all the objects his father David had dedicated and put them in the treasuries of the LORD's temple.

ᵛHeb uncertain ʷOne bath is approximately twenty quarts or five gallons.

God's THOUGHTS ◆ My THOUGHTS

Your Artistic Side 1 Kings 5–7

Think about how many people it takes to build a house. First, someone must clear the ground and make it smooth. Then workers have to lay a foundation, build a structure of wood or stone, make a roof, put up walls, lay down floors, paint walls, run electrical cords, and install pipes. There are also designers who help choose furniture and other decor. So many different skills and gifts go into building just one house!

When King Solomon decided to build the temple to serve God and honor his father, he called on people who cut down the very best kinds of wood. Then there were woodworkers who carved the wood into stairs, walls, lattices, winged creatures, palm trees, and doors. Then the wood was covered with gold. Some workers cut stone, while others worked with bronze and metal. Finally, creative people had to bring in the decorations. Many people used their gifts to make something beautiful for God.

What gifts do you have?

How can you use your gifts to make beautiful things for God?

Solomon dedicates the temple

8 Then Solomon assembled Israel's elders, all the tribal leaders, and the chiefs of Israel's clans at Jerusalem to bring up the chest containing the LORD's covenant from David's City Zion. ²Everyone in Israel assembled before King Solomon in the seventh month, the month of Ethanim,ˣ during the festival. ³When all of Israel's elders had arrived, the priests picked up the chest. ⁴They brought the LORD's chest, the meeting tent, and all the holy equipment that was in the tent. The priests and the Levites brought them up, ⁵while King Solomon and the entire Israelite assembly that had joined him before the chest sacrificed countless sheep and oxen. ⁶The priests brought the chest containing the LORD's covenant to its designated spot beneath the wings of the winged creatures in the inner sanctuary of the temple, the most holy place. ⁷The winged creatures spread their wings over the place where the chest rested, covering the chest and its carrying poles. ⁸The carrying poles were so long that their tips could be seen from the holy place in front of the inner sanctuary, though they weren't visible from outside. They are still there today. ⁹Nothing was in the chest except the two stone tablets Moses had placed there while at Horeb, where the LORD made a covenant with the Israelites after they left Egypt. ¹⁰When the priests left the holy place, the cloud filled the LORD's temple, ¹¹and the priests were unable to carry out their duties due to the cloud because the LORD's glory filled the LORD's temple.

¹²Then Solomon said, "The LORD said that he would live in a dark cloud, ¹³but I have indeed built you a lofty temple as a place where you can live forever." ¹⁴The king turned around, and while the entire assembly of Israel was standing there, he blessed them, ¹⁵saying, "Bless Israel's God, the LORD, who spoke directly to my father David and now has kept his promise: ¹⁶'From the day I brought my people Israel out of Egypt I haven't selected a city from any Israelite tribe as a site for the building of a temple for my name. But now I have chosen David to be over my people

Israel.' ¹⁷My father David wanted to build a temple for the name of the LORD, Israel's God.

¹⁸"But the LORD said to my father David, 'It is very good that you thought to build a temple for my name. ¹⁹Nevertheless, you yourself won't build that temple. Instead, your very own son will build the temple for my name.' ²⁰The LORD has kept his promise—I have succeeded my father David on Israel's throne just as the LORD said, and I have built the temple for the name of the LORD, Israel's God. ²¹There I've placed the chest that contains the covenant that the LORD made with our ancestors when he brought them out of Egypt."

²²Solomon stood before the LORD's altar in front of the entire Israelite assembly and, spreading out his hands toward the sky, ²³he said:

LORD God of Israel, there's no god like you in heaven above or on earth below. You keep the covenant and show loyalty to your servants who walk before you with all their heart. ²⁴This is the covenant you kept with your servant David, my father, which you promised him. Today, you have fulfilled what you promised. ²⁵So now, LORD, Israel's God, keep what you promised my father David, your servant, when you said to him, "You will never fail to have a successor sitting on Israel's throne as long as your descendants carefully walk before me just as you walked before me." ²⁶So now, God of Israel, may your promise to your servant David, my father, come true.

²⁷But how could God possibly live on earth? If heaven, even the highest heaven, can't contain you, how can this temple that I've built contain you? ²⁸LORD my God, listen to your servant's prayer and request, and hear the cry and prayer that your servant prays to you today. ²⁹Constantly watch over this temple, the place about which you said, "My name will be there," and listen to the prayer that your servant is praying towardʸ this place. ³⁰Listen to the request of your servant and your people Israel when they pray toward this place. Listen from your heavenly dwelling place, and when you hear, forgive!

ˣSeptember–October, Tishrei; Ethanim is a month from a Canaanite calendar. ʸOr *for, regarding*; also used in several verses that follow

³¹If someone wrongs another and must make a solemn pledge asserting innocence before your altar in this temple,ᶻ ³²then listen from heaven, act, and decide which of your servants is right. Condemn the guilty party, repaying them for their conduct, but justify the innocent person, repaying them for their righteousness.

³³If your people Israel are defeated by an enemy because they have sinned against you, but then they change their hearts and lives, give thanks to your name, and ask for mercy before you at this temple, ³⁴then listen from heaven and forgive the sin of your people Israel. Return them to the land you gave their ancestors.

³⁵When the sky holds back its rain because Israel has sinned against you, but they then pray toward this place, give thanks to your name, and turn away from their sin because you have punished them for it,ᵃ ³⁶then listen from heaven and forgive the sin of your servants, your people Israel. Teach them the best way for them to follow, and send rain on your land that you gave to your people as an inheritance.

³⁷Whenever there is a famine or plague in the land; or whenever there is blight, mildew, locust, or grasshopper; or whenever someone's enemy attacks them in their cities;ᵇ or any plague or illness comes; ³⁸whatever prayer or petition is made by any individual or by all of your people Israel—because people will recognize their own pain and spread out their hands toward this temple—³⁹then listen from heaven where you live. Forgive, act, and repay each person according to all their conduct, because you know their hearts. You alone know the human heart. ⁴⁰Do this so that they may revere you all the days they live on the land that you gave to our ancestors.

⁴¹Listen also to the immigrant who isn't from your people Israel but who comes from a distant country because of your reputation—⁴²because they will hear of your great reputation, your great power, and your outstretched arm. When the immigrant comes and prays toward this temple, ⁴³then listen from heaven, where you live, and do everything the immigrant asks. Do this so that all the people of the earth may know your reputation and revere you, as your people Israel do, and recognize that this temple I have built bears your name.

⁴⁴When your people go to war against their enemies, wherever you may send them, and they pray to the LORD toward the city you have chosen and toward this temple that I have built for your name, ⁴⁵then listen from heaven to their prayer and request and do what is right for them.

⁴⁶When they sin against you (for there is no one who doesn't sin) and you become angry with them and hand them over to an enemy who takes them away as prisoners to enemy territory, whether distant or nearby, ⁴⁷if they change their heart in whatever land they are held captive, changing their lives and begging for your mercy,ᶜ saying, "We have sinned, we have done wrong, we have acted wickedly!" ⁴⁸and if they return to you with all their heart and all their being in the enemy territory where they've been taken captive, and pray to you, toward their land, which you gave their ancestors, toward the city you have

LIGHTHOUSE
HEAVEN

A Temple—Not a Living Space
1 Kings 8:30, 39, 43, 49

After seven years of backbreaking work, God's temple was complete. King Solomon knew the new temple wasn't where God lived. God's presence is larger than that. A simple building couldn't hold the God who created all things (1 Kgs 8:27)—the God who was everywhere. The temple was where God could be specially honored. It was the place where all the sacrifices could be made. It replaced the dwelling that was built during the time of Moses (Exod 25:8) as the place where the chest containing the covenant would sit. God said it was the place where God would put God's name forever if Israel obeyed (1 Kgs 9:2-4). Even though it was all those things, the temple was still only a building. ◆

ᶻHeb uncertain ᵃOr answered them ᵇLXX one of; MT in the land of their gates ᶜHeb adds in the land they are held captive.

chosen, and toward the temple I have built for your name, [49]then listen to their prayer and request from your heavenly dwelling place. Do what is right for them, [50]and forgive your people who have sinned against you. Forgive all their wrong that they have done against you. See to it that those who captured them show them mercy. [51]These are your people and your inheritance. You brought them out of Egypt, from the iron furnace.

[52]Open your eyes to your servant's request and to the request of your people Israel. Hear them whenever they cry out to you. [53]You set them apart from all the earth's peoples as your own inheritance, Lord, just as you promised through your servant Moses when you brought our ancestors out of Egypt.

[54]As soon as Solomon finished praying and making these requests to the Lord, he got up from before the Lord's altar, where he had been kneeling with his hands spread out to heaven. [55]He stood up and blessed the whole Israelite assembly in a loud voice: [56]"May the Lord be blessed! He has given rest to his people Israel just as he promised. He hasn't neglected any part of the good promise he made through his servant Moses. [57]May the Lord our God be with us, just as he was with our ancestors. May he never leave us or abandon us. [58]May he draw our hearts to him to walk in all his ways and observe his commands, his laws, and his judgments that he gave our ancestors. [59]And may these words of mine that I have cried out before the Lord remain near to the Lord our God day and night so that he may do right by his servant and his people Israel for each day's need, [60]and so that all the earth's peoples may know that the Lord is God. There is no other God! [61]Now may you be committed to the Lord our God with all your heart by following his laws and observing his commands, just as you are doing right now."

[62]Then the king and all Israel with him sacrificed to the Lord. [63]Solomon offered well-being sacrifices to the Lord: twenty-two thousand oxen and one hundred twenty thousand sheep when the king and all Israel dedicated the Lord's temple. [64]On that day the king made holy the middle of the courtyard in front of the Lord's temple. He had to offer the entirely burned offerings, grain offerings, and the fat of well-being sacrifices there, because the bronze altar that was in the Lord's presence was too small to contain the entirely burned offerings, the grain offerings, and the fat of well-being sacrifices. [65]At that time Solomon, together with all Israel, held a celebration. It was a large assembly from Lebo-hamath to the border of Egypt. They celebrated for seven days and then for another seven days in the presence of the Lord our God: fourteen days in all. [66]On the eighth day,[d] Solomon dismissed the people. They blessed the king and went back to their tents happy and pleased about all the good that the Lord had done for his servant David and for his people Israel.

Solomon again meets God

9 Now once Solomon finished building the Lord's temple, the royal palace, and everything else he wanted to accomplish, [2]the Lord appeared to him a second time in the same way he had appeared to him at Gibeon. [3]The Lord said to him, "I have heard your prayer and your cry to me. I have set apart this temple that you built, to put my name there forever. My eyes and my heart will always be there. [4]As for you, if you walk before me just as your father David did, with complete dedication and honesty, and if you do all that I have commanded, and keep my regulations and case laws, [5]then I will establish your royal throne over Israel forever, just as I promised your father David, 'You will never fail to have a successor on the throne of Israel.' [6]However, if you or your sons turn away from following me and don't observe the commands and regulations that I gave you, and go to serve other gods, and worship them, [7]then I will remove Israel from the land I gave them and I will reject the temple that I dedicated for my name. Israel will become a joke, insulted by everyone. [8]Everyone who passes by this temple, so lofty now,[e] will be shocked and will whistle, wondering, Why

Memorize
1 Kgs 9:3

---

[d]The second seven-day celebration (see 2 Chron 7:8–9); but contrast LXX.   [e]Or *will become high*; OL, Syr, Tg *will become a ruin*

has the LORD done such a thing to this land and this temple? [9]The answer will come: Because they deserted the LORD their God, who brought their ancestors out of Egypt's land. They embraced other gods, worshipping and serving them. That is why the LORD brought all this disaster on them.'"

Solomon's buildings and prosperity

[10]It took twenty years for Solomon to build the two structures, the LORD's temple and the royal palace. [11]King Hiram of Tyre gave Solomon all the cedar, pinewood, and gold that he wanted. Then King Solomon gave Hiram twenty towns in the region of Galilee. [12]Hiram went from Tyre to inspect the towns Solomon had given him. They didn't seem adequate in his view. [13]So Hiram remarked, "My brother, are these towns you've given me good for anything?" The cities are thus called the land of Cabul to this very day. [14]But Hiram sent the king one hundred twenty gold kikkars, nevertheless.

[15]This is the story of the labor gang that King Solomon put together to build the LORD's temple and his own palace, as well as the stepped structure, the wall of Jerusalem, Hazor, Megiddo, and Gezer: ([16]Pharaoh, Egypt's king, had attacked and captured

Gezer, setting it on fire. He killed the Canaanites who lived in the city and gave it as a dowry to his daughter, Solomon's wife.) [17]Solomon built Gezer, Lower Beth-horon, [18]Baalath, and Tamar in the wilderness (within the land), [19]along with all the storage cities that belonged to Solomon, as well as the cities used for storing chariots and cavalry and whatever he wanted to build in Jerusalem, Lebanon, and throughout his kingdom. [20]Any non-Israelite people who remained of the Amorites, Hittites, Perizzites, Hivites,

and Jebusites—[21]that is, the descendants of such people who were still in the land because the Israelites weren't able to wipe them out—Solomon forced into the labor gangs that are still in existence today. [22]However, Solomon didn't force the Israelites to work as slaves; instead, they became warriors, his servants, his leaders, his officers, and those in charge of his chariots and cavalry.

[23]These were the chief officers over Solomon's work: five hundred fifty had charge of the people who did the work. [24]When Pharaoh's daughter went up from David's City to the palace he had built for her, Solomon built the stepped structure. [25]Three times a year Solomon would offer entirely burned offerings and well-being sacrifices on the altar that he had built for the LORD. Along with this he would burn incense to the LORD. In this way, he completed the temple.[f] [26]King Solomon built a fleet near Eloth in Ezion-geber, on the coast of the Reed Sea[g] in the land of Edom. [27]Hiram sent his expert sailors on the fleet along with Solomon's workers. [28]They went to Ophir for four hundred twenty kikkars of gold, which they brought back to King Solomon.

Queen of Sheba

10 When the queen of Sheba heard reports about Solomon, due to the LORD's name,[h] she came to test him with riddles. [2]Accompanying her to Jerusalem was a huge entourage with camels carrying spices, a large amount of gold, and precious stones. After she arrived, she told Solomon everything that was on her mind. [3]Solomon answered all her questions; nothing was too difficult for him to answer. [4]When the queen of Sheba saw how wise Solomon was, the palace he had built, [5]the food on his table, the servants' quarters, the function and dress of his attendants, his cupbearers, and the entirely burned offerings that he offered at the LORD's temple, it took her breath away.

[6]"The report I heard about your deeds and wisdom when I was still at home is true," she said to the king. [7]"I didn't believe it until I came and saw it with my own eyes. In fact, the half of it wasn't even told to me! You have

[f]Heb uncertain [g]Traditionally *Red Sea* [h]Heb uncertain

far more wisdom and wealth than I was told. ⁸Your people and these servants who continually serve you and get to listen to your wisdom are truly happy! ⁹Bless the LORD your God because he was pleased to place you on Israel's throne. Because the LORD loved Israel with an eternal love, the LORD made you king to uphold justice and righteousness."

¹⁰The queen gave the king one hundred twenty kikkars of gold, a great quantity of spice, and precious stones. Never again has so much spice come to Israel as when the queen of Sheba gave this gift to King Solomon. ¹¹Hiram's fleet went to Ophir and brought back gold, much almug wood, and precious stones. ¹²The king used the almug wood to make parapets for the LORD's temple and for the royal palace as well as lyres and harps for the musicians. To this day, that much almug wood hasn't come into or been seen in Israel. ¹³King Solomon gave the queen of Sheba everything she wanted and all that she had asked for, in addition to what he had already given her from his own personal funds. Then she and her servants returned to her homeland.

Solomon's wealth

¹⁴Solomon received an annual income of six hundred sixty-six kikkars of gold, ¹⁵not including income from the traders, the merchants and their profits, all the Arabian kings, and the officials of the land. ¹⁶King Solomon made two hundred body-sized shields of hammered gold, using fifteen pounds[i] of gold in each shield, ¹⁷and three hundred small shields of hammered gold, using sixty ounces[j] of gold in each shield. The king placed these in the Forest of Lebanon Palace.

¹⁸The king also made a large ivory throne and covered it with pure gold. ¹⁹Six steps led up to the throne, and the back of the throne was rounded at the top. Two lions stood beside the armrests on both sides of the throne. ²⁰Another twelve lions stood on both sides of the six steps. No other kingdom had anything like this. ²¹All of King Solomon's drinking cups were made of gold, and all the items in the Forest of Lebanon Palace were made of pure gold, not silver, since even silver wasn't considered good enough in Solomon's time!

²²The royal fleet of Tarshish-style ships was at sea with Hiram's fleet, returning once every three years with gold, silver, ivory, monkeys, and peacocks.[k]

²³King Solomon far exceeded all the earth's kings in wealth and wisdom, ²⁴and so the whole earth wanted an audience with Solomon in order to hear his God-given wisdom. ²⁵Year after year they came with tribute: objects of silver and gold, clothing, weapons, spices, horses, and mules.

²⁶Solomon acquired more and more chariots and horses until he had fourteen hundred chariots and twelve thousand horses that he kept in chariot cities and with the king in Jerusalem. ²⁷In Jerusalem, the king made silver as common as stones and cedar as plentiful as sycamore trees that grow in the foothills. ²⁸Solomon's horses were imported from Egypt and Kue, purchased from Kue by the king's agents at the going price. ²⁹They would import a chariot from Egypt for six hundred pieces of silver and a horse for one hundred fifty, and then export them to all the Hittite and Aramean kings.

Solomon meets God a third time

11 In addition to Pharaoh's daughter, King Solomon loved many foreign women, including Moabites, Ammonites, Edomites, Sidonians, and Hittites. ²These came from the nations that the LORD had commanded the Israelites about: "Don't intermarry with them. They will definitely turn your heart toward their gods." Solomon clung to these women in love. ³He had seven hundred royal wives and three hundred secondary wives. They turned his heart. ⁴As Solomon grew old, his wives turned his heart after other gods. He wasn't committed to the LORD his God with all his heart as was his father David. ⁵Solomon followed Astarte the goddess of the Sidonians, and Milcom the detestable god of the Ammonites. ⁶Solomon did what was evil in the LORD's eyes and wasn't completely devoted to the LORD like his father David. ⁷On the hill east of Jerusalem, Solomon built a shrine to Chemosh the detestable god of Moab, and to Molech the detestable god of the Ammonites. ⁸He did the same for all his foreign wives, who

---

[i]Or six hundred (shekels) [j]three manehs [k]Heb uncertain

burned incense and sacrificed to their gods. [9]The LORD grew angry with Solomon, because his heart had turned away from being with the LORD, the God of Israel, who had appeared to him twice. [10]The LORD had commanded Solomon about this very thing, that he shouldn't follow other gods. But Solomon didn't do what the LORD commanded.

UMBRELLA
DISOBEDIENCE

Disobedience Begins in the Heart
1 Kings 11:7-10

At first, Solomon did many things right. He honored God with sacrifices. He asked for wisdom from God and used it well when he received it. He built God's temple. God greatly blessed Solomon and all of Israel for Solomon's obedience. But Solomon made a fatal mistake. He married women who weren't Israelites. God knew the Israelites would have trouble following God's ways if they married people from other nations. God knew they would start following the gods of whomever they married. That's why it was part of God's Instruction not to marry anyone outside of Israel (1 Kgs 11:1-2). By marrying women from other countries, Solomon broke God's Instruction again and again. And sure enough, Solomon began building altars to other gods. All of Solomon's earlier obedience didn't earn him the right to disobey later. Solomon's disobedience cost his son half the kingdom (1 Kgs 11:11-13). ◆

///

[11]The LORD said to Solomon, "Because you have done all this instead of keeping my covenant and my laws that I commanded you, I will most certainly tear the kingdom from you and give it to your servant. [12]Even so, on account of your father David, I won't do it during your lifetime. I will tear the kingdom out of your son's hands. [13]Moreover, I won't tear away the entire kingdom. I will give one tribe to your son on account of my servant David and on account of Jerusalem, which I have chosen."

Solomon and Hadad

[14]So the LORD raised up an opponent for Solomon: Hadad the Edomite from the royal line of Edom. [15]When David was fighting against Edom, Joab the general had gone up to bury the Israelite dead, and he had killed

every male in Edom. [16]Joab and all the Israelites stayed there six months, until he had finished off every male in Edom. [17]While still a youth, Hadad escaped to Egypt along with his father's Edomite officials. [18]They set out from Midian and went to Paran. They took men with them from Paran and came to Egypt and to Pharaoh its king. Pharaoh assigned him a home, food, and land. [19]Pharaoh was so delighted with Hadad that he gave him one of his wife's sisters for marriage, a sister of Queen Tahpenes. [20]This sister of Tahpenes bore Hadad a son, Genubath. Tahpenes weaned him in Pharaoh's house. So it was that Genubath was raised in Pharaoh's house, among Pharaoh's children. [21]While in Egypt, Hadad heard that David had lain down with his ancestors and that Joab the general was also dead. Hadad said to Pharaoh, "Let me go to my homeland."

[22]Pharaoh said to him, "What do you lack here with me that would make you want to go back to your homeland?"

Hadad said, "Nothing, but please let me go!"

Solomon and Rezon

[23]God raised up another opponent for Solomon: Rezon, Eliada's son, who had escaped from Zobah's King Hadadezer. [24]Rezon recruited men and became leader of a band when David was killing them. They went to Damascus, stayed there, and ruled it. [25]Throughout Solomon's lifetime, Rezon was Israel's opponent and added to the problems caused by Hadad. Rezon hated Israel while he ruled as king of Aram.

Solomon and Jeroboam

[26]Now Nebat's son Jeroboam was an Ephraimite from Zeredah. His mother's name was Zeruah; she was a widow. Although he was one of Solomon's own officials, Jeroboam fought against the king. [27]This is the story of why Jeroboam fought against the king:

Solomon had built the stepped structure and repaired the broken wall in his father David's City. [28]Now Jeroboam was a strong and honorable man. Solomon saw how well this youth did his work. So he appointed him over all the work gang of Joseph's house.

[29]At that time, when Jeroboam left Jerusalem, Ahijah the prophet of Shiloh met him

along the way. Ahijah was wearing a new garment. The two of them were alone in the country. ³⁰Ahijah tore his new garment into twelve pieces. ³¹He said to Jeroboam, "Take ten pieces, because Israel's God, the LORD, has said, 'Look, I am about to tear the kingdom from Solomon's hand. I will give you ten tribes. ³²But I will leave him one tribe on account of my servant David and on account of Jerusalem, the city I have chosen from all the tribes of Israel. ³³I am doing this because they have abandoned me¹ and worshipped the Sidonian goddess Astarte, the Moabite god Chemosh, and the Ammonite god Milcom. They haven't walked in my ways by doing what is right in my eyes—keeping my laws and judgments—as Solomon's father David did. ³⁴But I won't take the whole kingdom from his hand. I will keep him as ruler throughout his lifetime on account of my servant David, who did keep my commands and my laws. ³⁵I will take the kingdom from the hand of Solomon's son, and I will give you ten tribes. ³⁶I will give his son a single tribe so that my servant David will always have a lamp before me in Jerusalem, the city that I chose for myself to place my name. ³⁷But I will accept you, and you will rule over all that you could desire. You will be king of Israel. ³⁸If you listen to all that I command and walk in my ways, if you do what is right in my eyes, keeping my laws and my commands just as my servant David did, then I will be with you and I will build you a lasting dynasty just as I did for David. I will give you Israel. ³⁹I will humble David's descendants by means of all this, though not forever.'"

⁴⁰Then Solomon tried to kill Jeroboam. But Jeroboam fled to Egypt and its king Shishak. Jeroboam remained in Egypt until Solomon died.

Solomon's remaining days

⁴¹The rest of Solomon's deeds, including all that he did and all his wisdom, aren't they written in the official records of Solomon? ⁴²The amount of time Solomon ruled over all Israel in Jerusalem was forty years. ⁴³Then Solomon lay down with his ancestors. He was buried in his father David's City, and Rehoboam his son succeeded him as king.

How Rehoboam lost the kingdom

12Rehoboam went to Shechem where all Israel had come to make him king. ²When Jeroboam, Nebat's son, heard the news, he returned from Egypt where he had fled from King Solomon. ³The people sent and called for Jeroboam, who along with the entire Israelite assembly went and said to Rehoboam, ⁴"Your father made our workloadᵐ very hard for us. If you will lessen the demands your father made of us and lighten the heavy workload he demanded from us, then we will serve you."

⁵He answered them, "Come back in three days." So the people left.

⁶King Rehoboam consulted the elders who had served his father Solomon when he was alive. "What do you advise?" Rehoboam asked. "How should I respond to these people?"

⁷"If you will be a servant to this people by answering them and speaking good words today," they replied, "then they will be your servants forever."

⁸But Rehoboam ignored the advice the elders gave him and instead sought the counsel of the young advisors who had grown up with him and now served him. ⁹"What do you advise?" he asked them. "How should we respond to these people who have said to me, 'Lighten the workload your father demanded of us'?"

¹⁰The young people who had grown up with him said to him, "This people said to you, 'Your father made our workload heavy; lighten it for us!' Now this is what you should say to them: 'My baby fingerⁿ is thicker than my father's entire waist! ¹¹So if my father made your workload heavy, I'll make it even heavier! If my father disciplined you with whips, I'll do it with scorpions!'"

¹²Jeroboam and all the people returned to Rehoboam on the third day, just as the king had specified when he said, "Come back to me in three days." ¹³The king then answered the people harshly. He ignored the elders' advice ¹⁴and instead followed the young people's advice. He said, "My father made your workload heavy, but I'll make it even heavier! My father disciplined you with whips, but I'll do it with scorpions!"

---

¹LXX, Syr, Vulg *he has abandoned me* ᵐOr *our yoke*; also in the verses that follow ⁿOr *pinky finger*, perhaps a euphemism

¹⁵The king didn't listen to the people because this turn of events came from the Lord so that he might keep the promise he delivered through Ahijah from Shiloh concerning Jeroboam, Nebat's son. ¹⁶When all Israel saw that the king wouldn't listen to them, the people answered the king:

"Why should we care about David?
We have no stake in Jesse's son!
Go back to your homes, Israel!
You better look
    after your own house now, David!"

Then the Israelites went back to their homes, ¹⁷and Rehoboam ruled over only the Israelites who lived in the cities of Judah.

UMBRELLA
PRIDE

The Greatest Are Servants *1 Kings 12:6-17*
Rehoboam had to choose between some really good and some really bad advice. His father, Solomon, was dead, and now Rehoboam was king. The people of Israel asked him not to work them as hard as his father did. Rehoboam brought the request to his advisors. His older, more experienced advisors suggested he treat the Israelites kindly and act like a servant to the people. But Rehoboam didn't like that advice. He thought he was too important to be anyone's servant. Rehoboam liked his friends' advice better: treat people harshly. They thought being in a powerful position made it okay for Rehoboam to take advantage of other people. Rehoboam wanted everyone to know that he was a king who ruled over everyone. He spoke to Israel with an attitude of pride, and he lost half his kingdom for it. ◊

¹⁸When King Rehoboam sent Adoram to them (he was the leader of the work gang), all Israel stoned him to death. King Rehoboam quickly got into his chariot and fled to Jerusalem. ¹⁹Israel has been in rebellion against the house of David to this day. ²⁰When all Israel heard that Jeroboam had returned, they sent for him. They called him to the assembly and crowned him king of all Israel.

Nothing was left to the house of David except the tribe of Judah. ²¹When Rehoboam arrived at Jerusalem, he assembled the whole house of Judah and the tribe of Benjamin—one hundred eighty thousand select warriors—to fight against the house of Israel and restore the kingdom for Rehoboam, Solomon's son. ²²But God's word came to Shemaiah the man of God, ²³"Tell Judah's King Rehoboam, Solomon's son, and all the house of Judah and Benjamin, and the rest of the people, ²⁴'This is what the Lord says: Don't make war against your relatives the Israelites. Go home, every one of you, because this is my plan.'" When they heard the Lord's words, they went back home, just as the Lord had said.

Jeroboam I and the shrines

²⁵Jeroboam fortified Shechem at Mount Ephraim and lived there. From there he also fortified Penuel. ²⁶Jeroboam thought to himself, The kingdom is in danger of reverting to the house of David. ²⁷If these people continue to sacrifice at the Lord's temple in Jerusalem, they will again become loyal to their master Rehoboam, Judah's king, and they will kill me so they can return to Judah's King Rehoboam. ²⁸So the king asked for advice and then made two gold calves. He said to the people, "It's too far for you to go all the way up to Jerusalem. Look, Israel! Here are your gods who brought you out from the land of Egypt." ²⁹He put one calf in Bethel, and the other he placed in Dan. ³⁰This act was sinful. The people went to worship before the one calf at Bethel and before the other one as far as Dan.^o ³¹Jeroboam made shrines on the high places and appointed priests from all sorts of people, but none were Levites. ³²Jeroboam set a date for a celebration on the fifteenth day of the eighth month.^p It was just like the celebration in Judah. He sacrificed on the altar. At Bethel he sacrificed to the calves he had made. There also he installed the priests for the shrines he had made. ³³On the fifteenth day of the eighth month—the time he alone had decided—Jeroboam went up^q to the altar he had built in Bethel. He made a celebration for the Israelites and offered sacrifices on the altar by burning them up.^r

---

^oCf LXX; MT lacks *before the one at Bethel.* ^pOctober–November ^qOr *offered sacrifices* ^rOr *went up on the altar to burn incense*

LIFE PRESERVER

Why were the gold calves sinful? *1 Kings 12: 25-30*

Jeroboam didn't want his people to travel to Jerusalem to worship in the temple there. Instead, he had two gold calves made so that the people could make their sacrifices right where they were. Using gold calves in worship was a common worship practice among the Canaanites, who were neighbors and enemies of God's people.

By setting up a separate altar and priests, Jeroboam was making a substitute for worship in the temple in Jerusalem. This was not a good thing. Jeroboam's actions disobeyed God's Instruction and showed disrespect for God. ◆

///

Jeroboam I and the man of God

13 A man of God came from Judah by God's command to Bethel. Jeroboam was standing at the altar burning incense. ²By the LORD's word, the man of God cried out to the altar: "Altar! Altar! The LORD says this: Look! A son will be born to the house of David. His name will be Josiah. He will sacrifice on you, Altar, the very priests of the shrines who offer incense on you. They will burn human bones on you." ³At that time the man of God gave a sign: "This is the sign that the LORD mentioned: 'Look! The altar will be broken apart, and its ashes will spill out.'"

⁴When the king heard the word of the man of God and how he cried out to the altar at Bethel, Jeroboam stretched his hand from the altar and said, "Seize him!" But the hand that Jeroboam stretched out against the man of God grew stiff. Jeroboam wasn't able to bend it back to himself. ⁵The altar broke apart, and the ashes spilled out from the altar, just like the sign that the man of God gave by the LORD's word. ⁶The king said to the man of God, "Plead before the LORD your God and pray for me so that I can bend my hand back again." So the man of God pleaded before the LORD, and the king's hand returned to normal and was like it used to be. ⁷The king spoke to the man of God: "Come with me to the palace and refresh yourself. Let me give you a gift."

⁸The man of God said to the king, "Even if you gave me half your palace, I wouldn't go with me, nor would I eat food or drink water

in this place. ⁹This is what God commanded me by the LORD's word: Don't eat food! Don't drink water! Don't return by the way you came!"

¹⁰So the man of God went by a different way. He didn't return by the way he came to Bethel. ¹¹Now there was an old prophet living in Bethel. His sons came and told him everything that the man of God had done that day at Bethel. They also told their father the words that he spoke to the king. ¹²"Which way did he go?" their father asked them. His sons had seen the way the man of God went when he came from Judah. ¹³The old prophet said to his sons, "Saddle my donkey." So they saddled his donkey, and he got on it. ¹⁴He went after the man of God and found him sitting underneath a terebinth tree. He said to him, "Are you the man of God who came from Judah?"

"I am," he replied.

¹⁵The old prophet then said to him, "Come home with me and eat some food."

¹⁶But the man of God answered, "I can't return or go with you, and I can't eat food or drink water with you in this place ¹⁷because of the message that came to me from the LORD's word: Don't eat food! Don't drink water! Don't return by the way you came!"

¹⁸The old prophet said to the man of God, "I'm also a prophet like you. A messenger spoke to me with the LORD's word, 'Bring him back with you to your house so that he may eat food and drink water.'"

But the old prophet was lying to him. ¹⁹So the man of God went back with the old prophet. He ate food in his home and drank water. ²⁰Then as they were sitting at the table, the LORD's word came to the prophet who had brought him back. ²¹He cried out to the man of God who had come from Judah:

"The LORD says this:
You rebelled against the LORD's word!
  You didn't keep the command
    that the LORD your God gave you!
²² You came back and ate food
    and drank water in this place.

"But he had commanded you: 'Don't eat food! Don't drink water!' Now your body won't go to the grave of your ancestors."

²³After he ate food and drank, the old prophet saddled the donkey for the prophet he had brought back. ²⁴The man of God departed, and a lion found him on the road and

killed him. His body was thrown down on the road. The donkey stood beside it, and the lion also stood beside the body. ²⁵Some people were traveling nearby, and they discovered the body thrown down on the road and the lion standing beside it. They entered the town where the old prophet lived and were talking about it. ²⁶The prophet who brought the man of God back from the road overheard. He thought: That's the man of God who rebelled against the LORD's command. The LORD has given him to that lion that tore him apart, killing him in agreement with the LORD's word that was spoken to him.

²⁷The old prophet told his sons, "Saddle the donkey." They did so, ²⁸and he went and found the body thrown down on the road. The donkey and the lion were still standing beside the body. The lion hadn't eaten the body, nor had it torn the donkey apart. ²⁹The prophet lifted the body of the man of God and put it on the donkey. He brought it back, arriving in the old prophet's town to mourn and bury the man of God. ³⁰He placed the body in his own grave, and they mourned over him, "Oh, my brother!" ³¹After the old prophet buried him, he said to his sons, "When I die, bury me in the grave where the man of God is. Put my bones beside his bones. ³²The message he gave by the LORD's word concerning the altar of Bethel and all the shrines in the towns of Samaria will most certainly come true."

³³Even after this happened, Jeroboam didn't change his evil ways. Instead, he continued to appoint all sorts of people as priests of the shrines. Anyone who wanted to be a priest Jeroboam made a priest for the shrines. ³⁴In this way the house of Jeroboam acted sinfully, leading to its downfall and elimination from the earth.

Not for a Million Dollars! *1 Kings 13:8-9*

Remember the story of the Three Little Pigs? The big, bad wolf came to get the pigs, but they wouldn't let him in—not by the hair on his chinny-chin-chin! They knew opening that door was a matter of life and death, so there was nothing the wolf could do to get them to open the door!

Sometimes we must be strong when other people try to lead us away from God's Instruction. A man of God in 1 Kings 13 was tempted to ignore what God had told him to do. A king asked him to go back to his palace so he could give the man a gift. But God told the man not to go there. So the man of God told the king, "Even if you gave me half your palace, I wouldn't go with you." That's like saying, "I wouldn't go with you for anything—not even for a million dollars!" The man had to stay strong and not change his mind just because he could have been comfortable and wealthy.

If someone offered you something you really enjoy and asked you to disobey God, how could you stay strong?

Write a prayer asking God to help you be strong when you're tempted to disobey.

Abijah's illness

14 At that time, Jeroboam's son Abijah became sick. ²Jeroboam said to his wife, "Please go with a disguise so no one will recognize you as Jeroboam's wife. Go to Shiloh where the prophet Ahijah is. He told me I would be king of this people. ³Take ten loaves of bread, cakes, and a bottle of honey with you. Go to him. He will tell you what will happen to the boy." ⁴Jeroboam's wife did precisely this. She left and went to Shiloh and came to Ahijah's house. Now Ahijah had become blind in his old age.

⁵The Lord said to Ahijah, "Look! Jeroboam's wife has come seeking a word from you about her son. He is sick. Say this and that to her. When she comes, she will be disguised."

⁶When Ahijah heard the sound of her feet coming through the doorway, he said, "Come in, Jeroboam's wife! Why have you disguised yourself? I have hard news for you. ⁷Tell Jeroboam: This is what the Lord, Israel's God, says: When I lifted you up from among the people, I appointed you as a leader over my people Israel. ⁸I tore the kingdom from David's house and gave it to you. But you haven't been like my servant David, who kept my commands and followed me with all his heart by doing only what is right in my eyes. ⁹Instead, you have done more evil than any who were before you. You have made other gods and metal images to anger me. You have turned your back on me. ¹⁰Therefore, I'm going to bring disaster on Jeroboam's house! Because of Jeroboam, I will eliminate everyone who urinates on a wall, whether slave or free. Then I will set fire to the house of Jeroboam, as one burns dung until it is gone. ¹¹Dogs will eat any of Jeroboam's family who die in town. Birds will eat those who die in the field. The Lord has spoken!

¹²"As for you, get up and go back home. When your feet enter the town, the boy will die. ¹³All Israel will mourn for him and will bury him. Out of the whole line of Jeroboam, he alone will have a tomb, because only in him did Israel's God, the Lord, find something good. ¹⁴For this reason the Lord will raise up a king over Israel who will eliminate the house of Jeroboam. This begins today. What's that?

Even now!ˢ ¹⁵The Lord will strike Israel so that it shakes like a reed in water. He will uproot Israel from this fertile land that he gave to their ancestors and their offspring, and he will scatter them across the Euphrates River, because they made the Lord angry by making their sacred poles.ᵗ ¹⁶Because of the sins Jeroboam committed, and because he made Israel sin too, God will give Israel up."

¹⁷Then Jeroboam's wife left and went to Tirzah. When she stepped across the threshold of the house, the boy died. ¹⁸All Israel buried him and mourned him in agreement with the Lord's word spoken through his servant the prophet Ahijah. ¹⁹The rest of Jeroboam's deeds—how he fought and how he ruled—are written in the official records of Israel's kings. ²⁰Jeroboam ruled twenty-two years and he lay down with his ancestors. His son Nadab succeeded him as king.

LIGHTHOUSE

FALSE GODS

Don't Make the Same Mistake Twice
1 Kings 14:1-17

Jeroboam could have had it all. Because Solomon had stopped following God's Instruction, God tore half the kingdom of Israel from his son and gave it to a servant named Jeroboam (1 Kgs 11:26-39). God told Jeroboam that if he obeyed God's law in all ways, then God would set up a kingdom for him forever. But Jeroboam didn't trust God enough to obey completely. Once Jeroboam had his kingdom, Jeroboam was afraid he would lose control of what he had if his people had to travel into Judah to worship God and offer sacrifices at God's temple. So Jeroboam made two gold calves and told his people to worship them as the gods that brought them out of Egypt (1 Kgs 12:25-33). Jeroboam hadn't learned from the mistake of the first gold calf in the desert (Exod 32). Jeroboam's distrust of God cost him his new kingdom and the life of a son.◆

Rehoboam rules Judah

²¹Rehoboam, Solomon's son, ruled over Judah. Rehoboam was 41 years old when he became king. He ruled for seventeen years in Jerusalem, the city the Lord chose from among all the tribes of Israel to set his name.

ˢHeb uncertain ᵗHeb *asherim*, perhaps objects devoted to the goddess Asherah

Rehoboam's mother's name was Naamah from Ammon. [22]Judah did evil in the LORD's eyes. The sins they committed made the LORD angrier than anything their ancestors had done. [23]They also built shrines, standing stones, and sacred poles[u] on top of every high hill and under every green tree. [24]Moreover, the consecrated workers[v] in the land did detestable things, just like those nations that the LORD had removed among the Israelites.

[25]During King Rehoboam's fifth year, King Shishak of Egypt attacked Jerusalem. [26]He seized the treasures of the LORD's temple and the royal palace. He took everything, even all the gold shields that Solomon had made. [27]King Rehoboam replaced them with bronze shields and assigned them to the officers of the guard who protected the entrance to the royal palace. [28]Whenever the king entered the LORD's temple, the guards would carry the shields and then return them to the guardroom. [29]The rest of Rehoboam's deeds and all that he accomplished, aren't they written in the official records of Judah's kings? [30]There was continual warfare between Rehoboam and Jeroboam. [31]When Rehoboam died, he was buried with his ancestors in David's City. His mother's name was Naamah from Ammon. His son Abijam[w] succeeded him as king.

Abijam rules Judah

15Abijam[x] became king of Judah in the eighteenth year of King Jeroboam, Nebat's son. [2]He ruled for three years in Jerusalem. His mother's name was Maacah, and she was Abishalom's daughter. [3]Abijam followed all the sinful ways of his father before him. He didn't follow the LORD his God with all his heart like his ancestor David. [4]Even so, on account of David, the LORD his God gave Abijam a lamp in Jerusalem by supporting his son who succeeded him and by preserving Jerusalem. [5]This was because David did the right thing in the LORD's eyes. David didn't deviate from anything the LORD commanded him throughout his life—except in the matter of Uriah the Hittite. [6]There was war between Rehoboam and Jeroboam as long as Abijam lived. [7]The rest of Abijam's deeds and all that he did, aren't they written in the official records of Judah's kings? There was war between Abijam and Jeroboam. [8]Abijam lay down with his ancestors; he was buried in David's City. His son Asa succeeded him as king.

Asa rules Judah

[9]In the twentieth year of Israel's King Jeroboam, Asa became king of Judah. [10]He ruled in Jerusalem for forty-one years. His grandmother's[y] name was Maacah; she was Abishalom's daughter. [11]Asa did the right things in the LORD's eyes, just like his father David. [12]He removed the consecrated workers[z] from the land, and he did away with all the worthless idols that his predecessors had made. [13]He even removed his grandmother Maacah from the position of queen mother because she had made an image of Asherah. Asa cut down her image and burned it in the Kidron Valley. [14]Though the shrines weren't eliminated, nevertheless Asa remained committed with all his heart to the LORD throughout his life. [15]He brought into the LORD's temple the silver and

SAILBOAT

OBEDIENCE

Obedience Has Lasting Results
1 Kings 15:5

David was so obedient to God that God called David "a man who shares my desires" (Acts 13:21-22). Because of this, God promised David that someone from David's family would always sit on the throne of Israel (2 Sam 7:8-16). After David died, it didn't take long before the kings of Israel began to disobey God. Kings like Rehoboam, Baasha, and Ahab treated people cruelly and led Israel into following false gods. There were good kings too, such as Asa, Jehoshaphat, and Josiah. But there were more bad kings. No matter how wickedly the Israelite kings acted, God never forgot his promise to David. Even during the worst of times, God never let Israel be completely wiped out. Many years later, one of David's descendants was Jesus, who fulfilled God's promise to David by living and ruling forever (Acts 13:34). ♦

---

[u]Heb *asherim*, perhaps objects devoted to the goddess Asherah   [v]Traditionally *cultic prostitutes*   [w]Spelled *Abijah* in 2 Chron 12:16; LXX, Syr, Targ *Abijah* in 1 Kgs   [x]Spelled *Abijah* in 2 Chron 12   [y]Or *mother*; also in 15:13; cf 2 Chron 13:2   [z]Traditionally *cultic prostitutes*

gold equipment that he and his father had dedicated. [16]There was war between Asa and Israel's King Baasha throughout their lifetimes. [17]Israel's King Baasha attacked Judah and fortified Ramah to prevent Judah's King Asa from moving into that area.

[18]Asa took all the silver and gold that remained in the treasuries of the LORD's temple and the royal palace, and he gave them to his officials. Then King Asa sent them with the following message to Aram's King Ben-hadad, Tabrimmon's son and Hezion's grandson, who ruled from Damascus: [19]"Let's make a covenant similar to the one between our fathers. Since I have already sent you a gift of silver and gold, break your covenant with Israel's King Baasha so that he will leave me alone." [20]Ben-hadad agreed with King Asa and sent his army commanders against the cities of Israel, attacking Ijon, Dan, Abel-beth-maacah, and all Chinneroth, along with all the land of Naphtali. [21]As soon as Baasha learned this, he stopped building Ramah and stayed in Tirzah. [22]King Asa issued an order to every Judean without exception: all the people carried away the stone and timber that Baasha was using to build Ramah, and King Asa used it to build Geba of Benjamin and Mizpah. [23]The rest of Asa's deeds, his strength, and all that he did, as well as the towns that he built, aren't they written in the official records of Judah's kings? When he was old, Asa developed a severe foot disease. [24]He died and was buried with his ancestors in David's City.[a] His son Jehoshaphat succeeded him as king.

Nadab rules Israel

[25]Jeroboam's son Nadab became king of Israel in the second year of Judah's King Asa. He ruled over Israel for two years. [26]He did evil in the LORD's eyes by walking in the way of his father Jeroboam and the sin Jeroboam had caused Israel to commit. [27]Baasha, Ahijah's son from the house of Issachar, plotted against him and attacked him at Gibbethon, which belonged to the Philistines. Nadab and all Israel were laying siege against Gibbethon. [28]Baasha killed Nadab in the third year of Judah's King Asa and ruled in Nadab's place.

[29]When he became king, Baasha attacked the entire house of Jeroboam. He didn't allow any living person to survive in Jeroboam's family; he wiped them out according to the LORD's word spoken by the LORD's servant Ahijah of Shiloh. [30]This happened because of Jeroboam's sins that he committed and that he caused Israel to commit, and because he angered the LORD, Israel's God. [31]The rest of Nadab's deeds and all that he did, aren't they written in the official records of Israel's kings? [32]There was war between Asa and Israel's King Baasha throughout their lifetimes.

Baasha rules Israel

[33]In the third year of Judah's King Asa, Baasha, Ahijah's son, became king over all Israel. He ruled in Tirzah for twenty-four years. [34]He did evil in the LORD's eyes by walking in Jeroboam's ways and the sin he had caused Israel to commit.

16 The LORD's word came to Jehu, Hanani's son, against Baasha: [2]I raised you up from the dust and made you a leader over my people Israel, but you walked in Jeroboam's ways, making my people Israel sin, making me angry with their sins. [3]So look, I am about to set fire to Baasha and his household, and I will make your house like the house of Jeroboam, Nebat's son. [4]Dogs will eat any of Baasha's family who die in town. Birds will eat any who die in the country.

[5]Now the rest of Baasha's deeds, what he did, and his powerful acts, aren't they written in the official records of Israel's kings? [6]Baasha lay down with his ancestors and was buried in Tirzah. His son Elah succeeded him as king.

[7]But the LORD's word came through the prophet Jehu, Hanani's son, concerning Baasha and his house. It concerned everything evil in the LORD's eyes that Baasha had done, angering the Lord by his actions so that he would end up just like the house of Jeroboam. The message was also about how the Lord attacked Baasha.[b]

Elah rules Israel

[8]In the twenty-sixth year of Judah's King Asa, Elah, Baasha's son, became king over

---

[a]Heb adds *his father.* [b]Or *also about how he attacked him* or *and because Baasha had attacked Jeroboam*

Israel. He ruled in Tirzah for two years. [9]Zimri, his officer who led half the chariots, plotted against him. Elah was at Tirzah, getting drunk at the house of Arza, who had charge over the palace at Tirzah. [10]Zimri came, attacked, and killed Elah in the twenty-seventh year of Judah's King Asa. Zimri succeeded him as king.

[11]Once Zimri became king and sat on the throne, he attacked all of Baasha's house. He didn't spare anyone who urinates on a wall, whether relative or friend. [12]Zimri destroyed the entire house of Baasha in agreement with the Lord's word that had been spoken by the prophet Jehu to Baasha. [13]This happened because of all Baasha's sins, as well as the sins of his son Elah and because they caused Israel to sin. They angered Israel's God, the Lord, with their insignificant idols. [14]The rest of Elah's deeds and all that he did, aren't they written in the official records of Israel's kings?

Zimri rules Israel

[15]In the twenty-seventh year of Judah's King Asa, Zimri became king. He ruled in Tirzah for seven days. The army was camped at Gibbethon in Philistia. [16]They heard the news: "Zimri has plotted against the king and killed him." Right then, in the camp, the whole Israelite army made their general Omri king of Israel. [17]Omri and the entire army then went up from Gibbethon and laid siege to Tirzah. [18]When Zimri saw that the city was captured, he went into the fort of the royal palace and burned it down on top of himself. So he died. [19]This happened because of the sins Zimri had committed by doing evil in the Lord's eyes and by walking in Jeroboam's ways and the sin he had done by causing Israel to sin. [20]The rest of Zimri's deeds and the plot he carried out, aren't they written in the official records of Israel's kings?

Omri rules Israel

[21]At this time the people of Israel were split in two. One half of the people followed Tibni, Ginath's son, making him king; the other half followed Omri. [22]Omri's side was stronger than those who followed Tibni, Ginath's son. So Tibni died and Omri became king. [23]In the thirty-first year of Judah's King Asa, Omri became king of Israel. He ruled for twelve years,

six of which were in Tirzah. [24]He bought the hill of Samaria from Shemer for two kikkars of silver. He fortified the hill and named the town that he built there after Shemer, the previous owner of the hill of Samaria. [25]Omri did evil in the Lord's eyes, more evil than anyone who preceded him. [26]He walked in all the ways and sins of Jeroboam, Nebat's son, because he caused Israel to sin. They angered Israel's God, the Lord, with their worthless idols. [27]The rest of Omri's deeds and his powerful acts, aren't they written in the official records of Israel's kings? [28]Omri lay down with his ancestors and was buried in Samaria. His son Ahab succeeded him as king.

Ahab rules Israel

[29]In the thirty-eighth year of Judah's King Asa, Ahab, Omri's son, became king of Israel. He ruled over Israel in Samaria for twenty-two years [30]and did evil in the Lord's eyes, more than anyone who preceded him. [31]Ahab found it easy to walk in the sins of Jeroboam, Nebat's son. He married Jezebel the daughter of Ethbaal, who was the king of the Sidonians. He served and worshipped Baal. [32]He made an altar for Baal in the Baal temple he had constructed in Samaria. [33]Ahab also made a sacred pole[c] and did more to anger the Lord,

LIFE PRESERVER

What was Baal?
1 Kings 16:31-33; 18:15-18

Baal was a god worshipped by the Canaanites. The Canaanites prayed that Baal would bless them and provide them with food and water. Israel's King Ahab built not only an altar for Baal but also a place of worship outside of the temple.

God sent Elijah to Ahab with the words God wanted Ahab to hear. God considered Baal to be a false god. Elijah was sent to remind the people of God's covenant with them and the commandments God had given them.

Today we don't build gold calves to worship. But we do worship other things that are just as troublesome, like money and fame. In some ways we are really not too different from the people who were living in the time of Elijah. We sometimes put things in the way of living the way God would like for us to live. ◢

[c]Heb *asherah*, perhaps an object devoted to the goddess Asherah

the God of Israel, than any of Israel's kings who preceded him. ³⁴During Ahab's time, Hiel from Bethel rebuilt Jericho. He set up its foundations at the cost of his oldest son Abiram. He hung its gates at the cost of his youngest son Segub. This fulfilled the Lord's word spoken through Joshua, Nun's son.

Elijah and the ravens

17 Elijah from Tishbe, who was one of the settlers in Gilead, said to Ahab, "As surely as the Lord lives, Israel's God, the one I serve, there will be neither dew nor rain these years unless I say so."

²Then the Lord's word came to Elijah: ³Go from here and turn east. Hide by the Cherith Brook that faces the Jordan River. ⁴You can drink from the brook. I have also ordered the ravens to provide for you there. ⁵Elijah went and did just what the Lord said. He stayed by the Cherith Brook that faced the Jordan River. ⁶The ravens brought bread and meat in the mornings and evenings. He drank from the Cherith Brook. ⁷After a while the brook dried up because there was no rain in the land.

Elijah and the widow from Zarephath

⁸The Lord's word came to Elijah: ⁹Get up and go to Zarephath near Sidon and stay there. I have ordered a widow there to take care of you. ¹⁰Elijah left and went to Zarephath. As he came to the town gate, he saw a widow collecting sticks. He called out to her, "Please get a little water for me in this cup so I can drink." ¹¹She went to get some water. He then said to her, "Please get me a piece of bread."

¹²"As surely as the Lord your God lives," she replied, "I don't have any food; only a handful of flour in a jar and a bit of oil in a bottle. Look at me. I'm collecting two sticks so that I can make some food for myself and my son. We'll eat the last of the food and then die."

¹³Elijah said to her, "Don't be afraid! Go and do what you said. Only make a little loaf of bread for me first. Then bring it to me. You can make something for yourself and your son after that. ¹⁴This is what Israel's God, the Lord, says: The jar of flour won't decrease and the bottle of oil won't run out until the

Bet you can *read this in 5 minutes. Ready, set, go!*

day the Lord sends rain on the earth." ¹⁵The widow went and did what Elijah said. So the widow, Elijah, and the widow's household ate for many days. ¹⁶The jar of flour didn't decrease nor did the bottle of oil run out, just as the Lord spoke through Elijah.

did you know? The name *Elijah* means "Yahweh is my God." Through the miracles he performed, Elijah showed again and again that God was his God. Elijah brought the dead son of the widow of Zarephath back to life.

¹⁷After these things, the son of the widow, who was the matriarch of the household, became ill. His sickness got steadily worse until he wasn't breathing anymore. ¹⁸She said to Elijah, "What's gone wrong between us, man of God? Have you come to me to call attention to my sin and kill my son?"

¹⁹Elijah replied, "Give your son to me." He took her son from her and carried him to the upper room where he was staying. Elijah laid him on his bed. ²⁰Elijah cried out to the Lord, "Lord my God, why is it that you have brought such evil upon the widow that I am staying with by killing her son?" ²¹Then he stretched himself over the boy three times and cried out to the Lord, "Lord my God, please give this boy's life back to him." ²²The Lord listened to Elijah's voice and gave the boy his life back. And he lived. ²³Elijah brought the boy down from the upper room of the house and gave him to his mother. Elijah said, "Look, your son is alive!"

²⁴"Now I know that you really are a man of God," the woman said to Elijah, "and that the Lord's word is truly in your mouth."

Elijah versus Baal's prophets

18 After many days, the Lord's word came to Elijah (it was the third year of the drought): Go! Appear before Ahab. I will then send rain on the earth. ²So Elijah went to appear before Ahab.

Now the famine had become especially bad in Samaria. ³Ahab had called Obadiah, who was in charge of the palace affairs. (Obadiah greatly feared the Lord. ⁴When Jezebel killed the Lord's prophets, Obadiah took one hundred of them and hid them, fifty each in two caves. He supplied them with food and water.) [5]Ahab said to Obadiah, "Go throughout the land and check every spring of water and every brook. Perhaps we can find some grass to keep our horses and mules alive so we don't have to kill any of them." [6]To search, they divided the land between themselves. Ahab went one way by himself, while Obadiah went a different way by himself.

LIGHTHOUSE

RESPECT FOR GOD

Respect God First　*1 Kings 18:3-4*

Israel's King Ahab acted so bad that he did more to anger God than any other king before him (1 Kgs 16:33). Queen Jezebel was even worse. She wanted to make sure that all of Israel followed the false god Baal. Jezebel did this by killing every prophet of the true God that she could find. Obadiah was a man in Ahab's service who still respected God. Obadiah respected the people who ruled over him, which is why he was allowed to take care of all the palace business, but he respected God even more. When the laws of the people didn't match up with God's Instruction, Obadiah knew he needed to obey God's Instruction. That's why he saved one hundred of God's prophets. Obadiah's respect for God helped others keep following God during a hard time in their history (1 Kgs 18:4).

[7]While Obadiah was out searching, suddenly Elijah met up with him. When Obadiah saw him, he fell on his face. "My master!" he said. "Are you Elijah?"

[8]Elijah replied, "I am. Go and say to your master, 'Elijah is here!'"

[9]Then Obadiah said, "How have I sinned that you are handing me, your servant, over to Ahab so he can kill me? [10]As surely as the Lord your God lives, there's no nation or kingdom where my master Ahab hasn't looked for you. They would insist, 'He's not here,' but Ahab would make them swear that they couldn't find you. [11]And now you are commanding me: 'Go and say to your master, "Elijah is here"'? [12]But here's what will happen: As soon as I leave you, the Lord's spirit will carry you off somewhere—I don't know

where—then I'll report to Ahab, but he won't be able to find you. Then he will kill me! But your servant has feared the Lord from my youth. [13]Wasn't my master told what I did when Jezebel killed the Lord's prophets? I hid one hundred of the Lord's prophets, fifty each in two caves. I also supplied them with food and water. [14]But even after all that, you tell me, 'Say to your master, "Elijah is here"'! Ahab will kill me!"

[15]Elijah said, "As surely as the Lord of heavenly forces lives, the one I serve, I will appear before Ahab today."

[16]So Obadiah went to meet Ahab. He told him what had happened. Then Ahab went to meet Elijah. [17]When Ahab saw Elijah, Ahab said to him, "Is that you, the one who troubles Israel?"

[18]Elijah answered, "I haven't troubled Israel; you and your father's house have! You did as much when you deserted the Lord's commands and followed the Baals. [19]Now send a message and gather all Israel to me at Mount Carmel. Gather the four hundred fifty prophets of Baal and the four hundred prophets of Asherah who eat at Jezebel's table."

[20]Ahab sent the message to all the Israelites. He gathered the prophets at Mount Carmel. [21]Elijah approached all the people and said, "How long will you hobble back and forth between two opinions? If the Lord[d] is God, follow God. If Baal is God, follow Baal." The people gave no answer.

[22]Elijah said to the people, "I am the last of the Lord's prophets, but Baal's prophets number four hundred fifty. [23]Give us two bulls. Let Baal's prophets choose one. Let them cut it apart and set it on the wood, but don't add fire. I'll prepare the other bull, put it on the wood, but won't add fire. [24]Then all of you will call on the name of your god, and I will call on the name of the Lord. The god who answers with fire—that's the real God!"

All the people answered, "That's an excellent idea."

[25]So Elijah said to the prophets of Baal, "Choose one of these bulls. Prepare it first since there are so many of you. Call on the name of your god, but don't add fire."

[26]So they took one of the bulls that had

---

[d]The contrast between the Lord's divine name (*YHWH*) and Baal's name is crucial throughout this passage.

been brought to them. They prepared it and called on Baal's name from morning to mid-day. They said, "Great Baal, answer us!" But there was no sound or answer. They performed a hopping dance around the altar that had been set up.

²⁷Around noon, Elijah started making fun of them: "Shout louder! Certainly he's a god! Perhaps he is lost in thought or wandering or traveling somewhere.ᵉ Or maybe he is asleep and must wake up!"

²⁸So the prophets of Baal cried with a louder voice and cut themselves with swords and knives as was their custom. Their blood flowed all over them. ²⁹As noon passed they went crazy with their ritual until it was time for the evening offering. Still there was no sound or answer, no response whatsoever.

³⁰Then Elijah said to all the people, "Come here!" All the people closed in, and he repaired the LORD's altar that had been damaged. ³¹Elijah took twelve stones, according to the number of the tribes of the sons of Jacob—to whom the LORD's word came: "Your name will be Israel." ³²He built the stones into an altar in the LORD's name, and he dug a trench around the altar big enough to hold two seahsᶠ of dry grain. ³³He put the wood in order, butchered the bull, and placed the bull on the wood. "Fill four jars with water and pour it on the sacrifice and on the wood," he commanded. ³⁴"Do it a second time!" he said. So they did it a second time. "Do it a third time!" And so they did it a third time. ³⁵The water flowed around the altar, and even the trench filled with water. ³⁶At the time of the evening offering, the prophet Elijah drew near and prayed: "LORD, the God of Abraham, Isaac, and Israel, let it be known today that you are God in Israel and that I am your servant. I have done all these things at your instructions. ³⁷Answer me, LORD! Answer me so that this people will know that you, LORD, are the real God and that you can change their hearts."ᵍ ³⁸Then the

---

ᵉHeb uncertain ᶠOne seah is approximately seven and a half quarts. ᵍHeb uncertain

It's a Miracle! *1 Kings 17:8-16*

Baking a loaf of bread takes a lot of flour. Usually, the recipe requires a few cups just to make the dough. Extra is needed for the baker's hands, the rolling pin, and the counter—to keep the dough from sticking to everything. Without flour, you can't make bread.

During a famine in Israel a widow was almost out of flour. She only had enough flour for a few more loaves, and that would be all the food she had to eat. She decided that she and her son would eat their last meal and then die.

Right about that time, Elijah the prophet came to visit and asked her to bake him some bread. She was nervous at first because it was the last of her food. But Elijah promised that her flour and oil wouldn't run out—for a long, long time. She believed that God was with him, so she did what he asked and her flour and oil never ran out. It was a miracle!

Ask your parents if you can bake bread together this week. Feel the flour in your hands and remember the widow who had faith that God's word is trustworthy.

Make a list of ways that God has provided for you.

LORD's fire fell; it consumed the sacrifice, the wood, the stones, and the dust. It even licked up the water in the trench!

³⁹All the people saw this and fell on their faces. "The LORD is the real God! The LORD is the real God!" they exclaimed.

⁴⁰Elijah said to them, "Seize Baal's prophets! Don't let any escape!" The people seized the prophets, and Elijah brought them to the Kishon Brook and killed them there. ⁴¹Elijah then said to Ahab, "Get up! Celebrate with food and drink because I hear the sound of a rainstorm coming." ⁴²So Ahab got up to celebrate with food and drink. But Elijah went up to the top of Mount Carmel. He bowed down to the ground and put his face between his knees. ⁴³He said to his assistant, "Please get up and look toward the sea."

So the assistant did so. He said, "I don't see anything."

Seven times Elijah said, "Do it again."

⁴⁴The seventh time the assistant said, "I see a small cloud the size of a human hand coming up from the sea."

Elijah said, "Go and tell Ahab, 'Pull yourself together, go down the mountain, and don't let the rain hold you back.'" ⁴⁵After a little while, the sky became dark with clouds, and a wind came up with a huge rainstorm. Ahab was already riding on his way to Jezreel, ⁴⁶but the LORD's power strengthened Elijah. He gathered up his clothes and ran in front of Ahab until he came to Jezreel.

Elijah runs to Mount Horeb

19Ahab told Jezebel all that Elijah had done, how he had killed all Baal's prophets with the sword. ²Jezebel sent a messenger to Elijah with this message: "May the gods do whatever they want to me if by this time tomorrow I haven't made your life like the life of one of them."

³Elijah was terrified. He got up and ran for his life. He arrived at Beer-sheba in Judah and left his assistant there. ⁴He himself went farther on into the desert a day's journey. He finally sat down under a solitary broom bush. He longed for his own death: "It's more than enough, LORD! Take my life because I'm no better than my ancestors." ⁵He lay down and slept under the solitary broom bush.

Then suddenly a messenger tapped him

UMBRELLA
DEPRESSED

God Helps with Sad Feelings *1 Kings 19:4*
Elijah had just won a great victory, but he was still sad. Elijah had proved to Israel that God was the true God and Baal didn't exist at all. God also used Elijah to bring rain after three years of drought. But Queen Jezebel ordered Elijah's death when she heard how all the prophets of Baal had been killed. So Elijah ran. He ran all the way to Mount Horeb, collapsed in a cave, and prayed that he would die. Elijah felt like he was all alone. He thought that his victory hadn't made any difference. But God told Elijah that he wasn't alone. There were still seven thousand Israelites who followed God's ways. God gave Elijah a new purpose—finding God's next servant. God helped Elijah rise up ready to live and serve again. ◊

and said to him, "Get up! Eat something!" ⁶Elijah opened his eyes and saw flatbread baked on glowing coals and a jar of water right by his head. He ate and drank, and then went back to sleep. ⁷The LORD's messenger returned a second time and tapped him. "Get up!" the messenger said. "Eat something, because you have a difficult road ahead of you." ⁸Elijah got up, ate and drank, and went refreshed by that food for forty days and nights until he arrived at Horeb, God's mountain. ⁹There he went into a cave and spent the night.

The LORD's word came to him and said, "Why are you here, Elijah?"

¹⁰Elijah replied, "I've been very passionate for the LORD God of heavenly forces because the Israelites have abandoned your covenant. They have torn down your altars, and they have murdered your prophets with the sword. I'm the only one left, and now they want to take my life too!"

¹¹The LORD said, "Go out and stand at the mountain before the LORD. The LORD is passing by." A very strong wind tore through the mountains and broke apart the stones before the LORD. But the LORD wasn't in the wind. After the wind, there was an earthquake. But the LORD wasn't in the earthquake. ¹²After the earthquake, there was a fire. But the LORD wasn't in the fire. After the fire, there

was a sound. Thin. Quiet. ¹³When Elijah heard it, he wrapped his face in his coat. He went out and stood at the cave's entrance. A voice came to him and said, "Why are you here, Elijah?"

¹⁴He said, "I've been very passionate for the LORD God of heavenly forces because the Israelites have abandoned your covenant. They have torn down your altars, and they have murdered your prophets with the sword. I'm the only one left, and now they want to take my life too."

¹⁵The LORD said to him, "Go back through the desert to Damascus and anoint Hazael as king of Aram. ¹⁶Also anoint Jehu, Nimshi's son, as king of Israel; and anoint Elisha from Abel-meholah, Shaphat's son, to succeed you as prophet. ¹⁷Whoever escapes from the sword of Hazael, Jehu will kill. Whoever escapes from the sword of Jehu, Elisha will kill. ¹⁸But I have preserved those who remain in Israel, totaling seven thousand—all those whose knees haven't bowed down to Baal and whose mouths haven't kissed him."

¹⁹So Elijah departed from there and found Elisha, Shaphat's son. He was plowing with twelve yoke of oxen before him. Elisha was with the twelfth yoke. Elijah met up with him and threw his coat on him. ²⁰Elisha immediately left the oxen and ran after Elijah. "Let me kiss my father and my mother," Elisha said, "then I will follow you."

Elijah replied, "Go! I'm not holding you back!" ²¹Elisha turned back from following Elijah, took the pair of oxen, and slaughtered them. Then with equipment from the oxen, Elisha boiled the meat, gave it to the people, and they ate it. Then he got up, followed Elijah, and served him.

Ben-hadad's wars with Ahab

20King Ben-hadad of Aram brought together all his army along with thirty-two kings plus horses and chariots. He went up, surrounded Samaria, and made war against it. ²He sent messengers to Ahab, Israel's king, inside Samaria. ³The message said, "This is what Ben-hadad says: 'Your silver and your gold are mine. Your good-looking wives and children are mine.'"

⁴Israel's king answered, "Whatever you say, my master, great king. I am yours and so is everything I have."

⁵The messengers came back again: "This is what Ben-hadad says: 'I sent you the message: Give me your silver and gold, your wives and your sons. ⁶However, at this time tomorrow I will send my officers to you, and they will search your palace and the houses of your officers. Everything that you find valuable they will seize and take away.'"

⁷Then Israel's king called all the elders of the land and he said, "Please know and understand the evil this man wants to do! He demanded from me my wives and sons, and my silver and gold; and I didn't refuse him."

⁸All of the elders and the people said to him, "Don't obey and don't give in!"

⁹So the king said to Ben-hadad's messengers, "Say to my master the king: 'Everything that you first ordered your servant, I will do. But I can't comply with this new command.'"

The messengers took this response to Ben-hadad, ¹⁰who sent back this reply: "May the gods do whatever they want to me if there is even a handful of dust left in Samaria for the armies under me!"

¹¹Then Israel's king replied, "The one who prepares for battle shouldn't brag like one returning from battle."

¹²When Ben-hadad heard this message, he and the other kings were drinking in their tents. Ben-hadad said to his officers, "Take your positions!" So they took up their positions against the city.

¹³Suddenly a prophet approached Israel's King Ahab. He said, "This is what the LORD says: Do you see that great army? Today I am handing it over to you. Then you will know that I am the LORD."

¹⁴Ahab said, "Who will do it?"

The prophet answered, "This is what the LORD says: The servants of the district officials will do it."

"Who should start the battle?" Ahab asked.

"You should," the prophet replied.

¹⁵So Ahab assembled the servants of the district officials. There were two hundred

thirty-two of them. Next he assembled the entire Israelite army, seven thousand total. [16]At noon they marched for battle. Meanwhile, Ben-hadad and the thirty-two kings allied with him were getting drunk in their tents. [17]The servants of the district officials were at the head of the march. Ben-hadad sent for information and was told, "Some men have marched out of Samaria."

[18]He said, "If they have come out in peace, take them alive; if they have come out for war, take them alive as well." [19]So the servants of the district governors with the army behind them marched out from the city. [20]Each one struck down his opponent, so that the Arameans fled. Israel chased after them. Ben-hadad, Aram's king, escaped with some horses and chariots. [21]Israel's king went out and attacked the horses and chariots. He attacked the Arameans with a fierce assault.

[22]The prophet came to Israel's king and said to him, "Maintain your strength! Know and understand that at the turn of the coming year, Aram's king will attack you again."

[23]The officers of Aram's king said to him, "Israel's god is a god of the mountains. That's why they were stronger than us. But if we fight them on the plains, we will certainly be stronger than they are. [24]This is what you need to do: Remove the kings from their military posts and appoint officials in their place. [25]Then raise another army like the one that was destroyed, with horses like those horses and chariots like those chariots. Then we will fight them on the plains, and we will certainly be stronger than they are." The king took their advice and followed it.

[26]So in the spring of the year, Ben-hadad assembled the Arameans and marched up to Aphek to fight with Israel. [27]Now the Israelites had already been assembled and provisioned, so they went to engage the Arameans. The Israelites camped before them like two small flocks of goats, but the Arameans filled the land.

[28]Then the man of God came forward and said to Israel's king, "This is what the LORD says: Because the Arameans said that the LORD is a god of the mountains but not a god of the valleys, I am handing this whole great

army over to you. Then you will know that I am the LORD."

[29]The two armies camped opposite each other for seven days. On the seventh day, the battle began. The Israelites attacked and destroyed one hundred thousand Aramean foot soldiers in a single day. [30]Those who were left fled to Aphek, into the city where a wall fell on twenty-seven thousand more of them. But Ben-hadad escaped and hid in an inner room within the city.

[31]Ben-hadad's officers said to him, "Listen, we have heard that the kings of Israel are merciful kings. Allow us to put mourning clothes on our bodies and cords around our heads. We will then go to Israel's king. Perhaps he will let you live." [32]So they put mourning clothes on their bodies and cords around their heads. They went to Israel's king and said, "Ben-hadad is your slave. He begs, 'Please let me live!'"

Israel's king said, "Is he still alive? He is my brother."

[33]Taking this as a good sign, Ben-hadad's men quickly accepted this statement.[h] "Yes, Ben-hadad is your brother!" they said.

"Go and get him," the king ordered. So Ben-hadad came to him, and the king received him into his chariot.

[34]Ben-hadad said to the king, "I will return the towns that my father took from your father. Furthermore, you can set up markets for yourself in Damascus just as my father did in Samaria."

The king replied,[i] "On the basis of this covenant, I will let you go." So he made a covenant with Ben-hadad and set him free.

[35]At the LORD's command a certain man who belonged to a prophetic group said to his friend: "Please strike me." But his friend refused to hit him. [36]So he said to his friend, "Because you didn't obey the LORD's voice, a lion will attack you as soon as you leave me." And as the friend left the prophet, a lion found him and attacked him. [37]Then the prophet found another man and said, "Please strike me." He hit the prophet, and the attack left a wound. [38]The prophet went and stood before the king by the road. He disguised himself by putting a bandage over his eyes. [39]When

---

[h]Heb uncertain [i]Heb lacks *The king replied.*

the king passed by, the prophet called out to the king, "Your servant was in the middle of the battle when someone brought a prisoner. 'Guard this man,' he said. 'If he escapes it will be your life for his—that, or you will owe me a kikkar of silver.' ⁴⁰Your servant got busy doing this and that, and the prisoner disappeared."

Israel's king replied, "It appears you have decided your own fate."

⁴¹The prophet quickly tore the bandage from over his eyes, and Israel's king recognized him as one of the prophets. ⁴²Then the prophet said to the king, "This is what the LORD says: Because you freed a man I condemned to die, it will be your life for his life, and your people for his people."

⁴³So Israel's king went to his palace at Samaria, irritated and upset.

Naboth's vineyard

21 Now it happened sometime later that Naboth from Jezreel had a vineyard in Jezreel that was next to the palace of King Ahab of Samaria. ²Ahab ordered Naboth, "Give me your vineyard so it can become my vegetable garden, because it is right next to my palace. In exchange for it, I'll give you an even better vineyard. Or if you prefer, I'll pay you the price in silver."

³Naboth responded to Ahab, "LORD forbid that I give you my family inheritance!"

⁴So Ahab went to his palace, irritated and upset at what Naboth[j] had said to him—because Naboth had said, "I won't give you my family inheritance!" Ahab lay down on his bed and turned his face away. He wouldn't eat anything.

⁵His wife Jezebel came to him. "Why are you upset and not eating any food?" she asked.

⁶He answered her, "I was talking to Naboth. I said, 'Sell me your vineyard. Or if you prefer, I'll give you another vineyard for it.' But he said, 'I won't give you my vineyard!'"

⁷Then his wife Jezebel said to him, "Aren't you the one who rules Israel? Get up! Eat some food and cheer up. I'll get Naboth's vineyard for you myself." ⁸So she wrote letters in Ahab's name, putting his seal on them. She sent them to the elders and officials who lived in the

same town as Naboth. ⁹This is what she wrote in the letters: "Announce a fast and place Naboth at the head of the people. ¹⁰Then bring in two liars in front of him and have them testify as follows: 'You cursed God and king!' Then take Naboth outside and stone him so he dies."

¹¹The elders and the officials who lived in Naboth's town did exactly as Jezebel specified in the letters that she had sent. ¹²They announced a fast and placed Naboth at the head of the people. ¹³Then the two liars came and sat in front of him. They testified against Naboth in front of the people, "Naboth cursed God and king!" So the people took Naboth outside the town and stoned him so that he died.

¹⁴It was then reported to Jezebel, "Naboth was stoned. He's dead." ¹⁵As soon as Jezebel heard that Naboth had been stoned to death, she said to Ahab, "Get up and take ownership of the vineyard of Naboth, which he had refused to sell to you. Naboth is no longer alive; he's dead." ¹⁶When Ahab heard that Naboth had died, he got up and went down to Naboth's vineyard to take ownership of it.

UMBRELLA
LYING

God's Truth Always Comes Out
1 Kings 21:2-16

Ahab wanted a vineyard that belonged to Naboth. Ahab first tried to buy or trade for the vineyard. But the vineyard had belonged to Naboth's family for a long time. It was worth more than just money to Naboth. He couldn't sell it. Ahab went home and pouted. When Ahab's queen, Jezebel, heard why he was upset, she decided to take action. Jezebel had people lie about Naboth, saying that he would curse God and the king. When the people killed Naboth because of this lie, Ahab took over the vineyard. Jezebel had so little respect for God that she thought she could get away with her dishonesty. The truth wasn't important to Jezebel and Ahab so long as they got what they wanted—even if it cost someone else their life. But this wasn't the end of the story. Jezebel and Ahab died violent deaths for their actions (1 Kgs 22:35-38 and 2 Kgs 9:30-37). ◈

¹⁷The LORD's word came to Elijah from Tishbe: ¹⁸Get up and go down to meet Israel's King Ahab in Samaria. He is in Naboth's vineyard. He has gone down to take ownership of it. ¹⁹Say the following to him: This is what the LORD says: So, you've murdered and are now taking ownership, are you? Then tell him: This is what the LORD says: In the same place where the dogs licked up Naboth's blood, they will lick up your own blood.

²⁰Ahab said to Elijah, "So you've found me, my old enemy!"

"I found you," Elijah said, "because you've enslaved yourself by doing evil in the LORD's eyes. ²¹So I am now bringing evil on you! I will burn until you are consumed, and I will eliminate everyone who urinates on a wall that belongs to Ahab, whether slave or free. ²²I will make your household like that of Jeroboam, Nebat's son, and like the household of Baasha, Ahijah's son, because of the way you've angered me and because you've made Israel sin. ²³As for Jezebel, the LORD says this: Dogs will devour Jezebel in the area of Jezreel. ²⁴Dogs will eat anyone of Ahab's family who dies in town, and birds will eat anyone who dies in the country."

(²⁵Truly there has never been anyone like Ahab who sold out by doing evil in the LORD's eyes—evil that his wife Jezebel led him to do. ²⁶Ahab's actions were deplorable. He followed after the worthless idols exactly like the Amorites had done—the very ones the LORD had removed before the Israelites.)

²⁷When Ahab heard these words, he tore his clothes and put mourning clothes on his body. He fasted, even slept in mourning clothes, and walked around depressed. ²⁸The LORD's word then came to Elijah from Tishbe: ²⁹Have you seen how Ahab has humbled himself before me? Because he has done so, I won't bring the evil during his lifetime. Instead, I will bring the evil on his household in the days of his son.

Jehoshaphat and Ahab

22 For three years there was no war between Aram and the Israelites. ²In the third year, Judah's King Jehoshaphat visited Israel's king. ³Israel's king said to his servants, "You know, don't you, that Ramoth-gilead is ours? But we aren't doing anything to take it back from the king of Aram." ⁴He said to Jehoshaphat, "Will you go with me into battle at Ramoth-gilead?"

Jehoshaphat said to Israel's king, "I am with you, and my troops and my horses are united with yours. ⁵But," Jehoshaphat said to Israel's king, "first let's see what the LORD has to say."

⁶So Israel's king gathered about four hundred prophets, and he asked them, "Should I go to war with Ramoth-gilead or not?"

"Attack!" the prophets answered. "The LORD will hand it over to the king."

⁷But Jehoshaphat said, "Isn't there any other prophet of the LORD whom we could ask?"

⁸"There is one other man who could ask the LORD for us," Israel's king told Jehoshaphat, "but I hate him because he never prophesies anything good about me, only bad. His name is Micaiah, Imlah's son."

"The king shouldn't speak like that!" Jehoshaphat said.

⁹So Israel's king called an officer and ordered, "Bring Micaiah, Imlah's son, right away."

¹⁰Now Israel's king and Judah's King Jehoshaphat were sitting on their thrones, dressed in their royal robes at the threshing floor beside the entrance to the gate of Samaria. All the prophets were prophesying in front of them. ¹¹Zedekiah, Chenaanah's son, made iron horns for himself and said, "This is what the LORD says: With these horns you will gore the Arameans until there's nothing left of them!"

¹²All the other prophets agreed: "Attack Ramoth-gilead and win! The LORD will hand it over to the king!"

¹³Meanwhile, the messenger who had gone to summon Micaiah said to him, "Listen, the prophets all agree that the king will succeed. You should say the same thing they say and prophesy success."

¹⁴But Micaiah answered, "As surely as the LORD lives, I will say only what the LORD tells me to say."

¹⁵When Micaiah arrived, the king asked him, "Micaiah, should we go to war with Ramoth-gilead or not?"

"Attack and win!" Micaiah answered. "The LORD will hand it over to the king!"

¹⁶But the king said, "How many times must I demand that you tell me the truth when you speak in the name of the LORD?"

[17]Then Micaiah replied, "I saw all Israel scattered on the hills like sheep without a shepherd! And then the Lord said: They have no master. Let them return safely to their own homes."

[18]Then Israel's king said to Jehoshaphat, "Didn't I tell you? He never prophesies anything good about me, only bad."

[19]Then Micaiah said, "Listen now to the Lord's word: I saw the Lord enthroned with all the heavenly forces stationed beside him, at his right and at his left. [20]The Lord said, 'Who will persuade Ahab so that he attacks Ramoth-gilead and dies there?' There were many suggestions [21]until one particular spirit approached the Lord and said, 'I'll persuade him.' 'How?' the Lord asked. [22]'I will be a lying spirit in the mouth of all his prophets,' he said. The Lord agreed, 'You will succeed in persuading him! Go ahead!' [23]So now, since the Lord has placed a lying spirit in the mouths of every one of these prophets of yours, it is the Lord who has pronounced disaster against you!"

[24]Zedekiah, Chenaanah's son, approached Micaiah and slapped him on the cheek. "Just how did the Lord's spirit leave me to speak to you?" he asked.

SAILBOAT

HONEST AND TRUE

Honesty Beats the Odds   *1 Kings 22:1-28*
Ahab was looking for a fight. He wanted King Jehoshaphat's help in attacking a shared enemy. But Jehoshaphat respected God and refused to attack without God's command. So Ahab called in four hundred prophets of God to ask whether or not to go to battle. "Go for it!" they all cried. "God is with you!" But Jehoshaphat didn't believe them. He asked for a true prophet to advise them. Ahab didn't want a true prophet. He wanted people who would tell him what he wanted—people like the four hundred. Micaiah was a true prophet. Micaiah wouldn't say anything but God's truth no matter how much trouble it brought him. And when he told Ahab the battle would be a disaster, this brought him trouble indeed. It got him slapped and thrown into prison. But Micaiah stood firm against a king and four hundred other false prophets. And he was proved right (1 Kgs 22:29-38). ◆

[25]Micaiah answered, "You will find out on the day you try to hide in an inner room."

[26]"Arrest him," ordered Israel's king, "and turn him over to Amon the city official and to Joash the king's son. [27]Tell them, 'The king says: Put this man in prison and feed him minimum rations of bread and water until I return safely.'"

[28]"If you ever return safely," Micaiah replied, "then the Lord wasn't speaking through me." Then he added, "Pay attention, every last one of you!"

[29]So Israel's king and Judah's King Jehoshaphat attacked Ramoth-gilead. [30]Israel's king said to Jehoshaphat, "I will disguise myself when we go into battle,[k] but you should wear your royal attire." When Israel's king had disguised himself, they entered the battle.

[31]Meanwhile, Aram's king had commanded his thirty-two chariot officers, "Don't bother with anyone big or small. Fight only with Israel's king."

[32]As soon as the chariot officers saw Jehoshaphat, they assumed that he must be Israel's king, so they turned to attack him. But Jehoshaphat cried out for help. [33]When the chariot officers realized that he wasn't Israel's king, they stopped chasing him. [34]But someone randomly shot an arrow that struck Israel's king between the joints in his armor.[l]

"Turn around and get me out of the battle," the king told his chariot driver. "I've been hit!"

[35]While the battle raged all that day, the king stood propped up in the chariot facing the Arameans. But that evening he died after his blood had poured from his wound into the chariot. [36]When the sun set, a shout spread throughout the camp: "Retreat to your towns! Retreat to your land!" [37]Once the king died, people came from Samaria and buried the king there. [38]They cleaned the chariot at the pool of Samaria. The dogs licked up the king's blood and the prostitutes bathed in it, just as the Lord had spoken.

Ahab's last days

[39]The rest of Ahab's deeds and all that he did—including the ivory palace he built and all the towns he constructed—aren't they written in the official records of Israel's

---

[k]LXX, Tg; MT *Disguise yourself and go*   [l]Heb uncertain

kings? ⁴⁰Ahab lay down with his ancestors. His son Ahaziah succeeded him as king.

Jehoshaphat rules Judah

⁴¹Jehoshaphat, Asa's son, became king over Judah in the fourth year of Israel's King Ahab. ⁴²Jehoshaphat was 35 years old when he became king, and he ruled for twenty-five years in Jerusalem. His mother's name was Azubah; she was Shilhi's daughter. ⁴³Jehoshapat walked in all the ways of his father Asa, not deviating from it. He did the right things in the LORD's eyes, with the exception that he didn't remove the shrines. The people continued to sacrifice and offer incense at them. ⁴⁴Jehoshaphat made peace with Israel's king. ⁴⁵The rest of Jehoshaphat's deeds, the great acts he did, and how he fought in battle, aren't they written in the official records of Judah's kings? ⁴⁶Additionally, Jehoshaphat purged the land of the consecrated workers^m who remained from the days of Asa.

⁴⁷Now Edom had no king; only a deputy was ruler. ⁴⁸Jehoshaphat built Tarshish-styled ships to go to Ophir for gold. But the fleet didn't go because it was wrecked at Eziongeber. ⁴⁹Then Ahaziah, Ahab's son, said to Jehoshaphat, "Let my sailors go with your sailors on the ships." But Jehoshaphat didn't agree to this. ⁵⁰Jehoshaphat died and was buried with his ancestors in his ancestor David's City. His son Jehoram succeeded him as king.

Ahaziah rules Israel

⁵¹In the seventeenth year of Judah's King Jehoshaphat, Ahaziah, Ahab's son, became king over Israel in Samaria. He ruled over Israel for two years. ⁵²He did evil in the LORD's eyes. He walked in his father's ways and his mother's ways—that is, in the ways of Jeroboam, Nebat's son, who had caused Israel to sin. ⁵³Ahaziah served Baal and worshipped him. He angered the LORD, Israel's God, by doing all the same things his father had done.

---

^m Traditionally *cultic prostitutes*

2 Kings

God crowned Saul as Israel's first king. Under the next kings, David and Solomon, God's people enjoyed peace and wealth. But then the nation broke into two parts: the northern kingdom of Israel and the southern kingdom of Judah.

First Kings tells the story of these two kingdoms in their earliest days. Second Kings tells the rest of the story. It describes miracles God performed through the prophet Elisha, including healing a man named Naaman who washed in the muddy Jordan River (2 Kgs 5).

Second Kings shows that God's people often weren't loyal to God. They disobeyed God's Instruction and worshipped other gods. In the end, Israel and Judah were both defeated in war. The citizens of Israel were taken as prisoners to Assyria (2 Kgs 17). The people of Judah were taken to Babylon (2 Kgs 25).

That part of the story is sad. But there were times when God's people followed the Lord. One of those times was when Josiah, an amazing 8-year-old, became king and led his people back to God (2 Kgs 22–23). Second Kings teaches that God never stops inviting people to follow God's ways! ◊

things YOU'LL DISCOVER

Second Kings finishes the story that began in 1 Kings. It tells of Israel's northern and southern kingdoms, Israel and Judah. Each kingdom was defeated in war and their citizens taken as prisoners to distant lands.

people YOU'LL MEET

Elijah—a prophet who was swept up to heaven in a fiery chariot (2 Kgs 1–2)

Elisha—Elijah's assistant and a prophet to Israel (2 Kgs 2–9; 13)

Naaman—a general from Aram (2 Kgs 5)

Hezekiah—a king of Judah who did what was right in God's eyes (2 Kgs 18–20)

Josiah—a boy who became king of Judah at age 8 and led people back to God (2 Kgs 22–23)

places YOU'LL GO

Israel (the northern kingdom), **Judah** (the southern kingdom), **Aram** (present-day Syria), **Assyria** (present-day northern Iraq), **Babylon** (present-day southern Iraq)

words YOU'LL REMEMBER

"He did what was right in the Lord's eyes, and walked in the ways of his ancestor David—not deviating from it even a bit to the right or left" (2 Kgs 22:2).

Ahaziah's death

1 After Ahab died, Moab rebelled against Israel.

²Ahaziah fell out the window of his second-story room in Samaria and was hurt. He sent messengers, telling them, "Go to Ekron's god Baal-zebub, and ask if I will recover from this injury."

³But the LORD's messenger said to Elijah from Tishbe, "Go, intercept the messengers of Samaria's king, and ask them, 'Is it because there's no God in Israel that you are going to question Ekron's god Baal-zebub? ⁴This is what the LORD says: You will never get out of the bed you are lying in; you will die for sure!'" So Elijah set off.

⁵The messengers returned to Ahaziah. He said to them, "Why have you come back?"

⁶They said to him, "A man met us and said, 'Go back to the king who sent you. Say to him, This is what the LORD says: Is it because there's no God in Israel that you've come to question Ekron's god Baal-zebub? Because of this, you will never get out of the bed you are lying in; you will die for sure!'"

⁷Ahaziah said to them, "Describe the man who met you and said these things."

⁸They said to him, "He wore clothes made of hair[a] with a leather belt around his waist."

Ahaziah said, "That was Elijah from Tishbe."

⁹So Ahaziah sent out a commander with fifty soldiers. The commander met up with Elijah while he was sitting on a hilltop. The commander said, "Man of God, the king says, 'Come down!'"

¹⁰Elijah replied to the commander of the fifty soldiers, "If I really am a man of God, may fire come down from the sky and burn up you and your fifty soldiers." Then fire came down from the sky and burned up the commander and his fifty soldiers.

¹¹Ahaziah then sent another commander with fifty soldiers. The commander said to Elijah, "Man of God, this is what the king says: 'Hurry and come down!'"

¹²Elijah said to them, "If I really am a man of God, may fire come down from the sky and burn up you and your fifty soldiers." Then God's fire came down from the sky and burned up the commander and his fifty soldiers.

¹³For a third time Ahaziah sent a commander with fifty soldiers. So the third commander arrived. He kneeled before Elijah and begged him, "Man of God! Please have some regard for my life and the lives of these fifty soldiers who are your servants. ¹⁴Look, fire came from the sky and burned up the two earlier commanders and their troops of fifty soldiers. Please have regard for my life."

¹⁵Then the LORD's messenger said to Elijah, "Go down with him. Don't be afraid of him." So Elijah set out to go with him to the king.

¹⁶Elijah said to the king: "This is what the LORD says: Why did you send messengers to question Ekron's god Baal-zebub? Is there no God in Israel whose word you could seek? Because of this, you won't ever get out of the bed you are lying in; you'll die for sure!" ¹⁷So Ahaziah died in agreement with the LORD's word that Elijah had spoken.

LIGHTHOUSE

RESPECT FOR GOD

Be Respectful of God's Servants
2 Kings 1:2-17

When King Ahaziah hurt himself, he sent messengers to a false god in another country to ask if he would recover. God was angry at being treated without respect. Elijah went with God's own message for Ahaziah—"For dishonoring me, you're going to die for sure!" The people working for the king shared his careless attitude toward God. Ahaziah sent soldiers to bring Elijah to the palace. The first two soldiers came to Elijah and spoke to him as though he were a servant to the king and not a prophet of God. They died for their disrespect of God. Only the third soldier lived, because he asked humbly for Elijah to come. The soldier had learned that treating God's servants poorly was like treating God poorly. ◆

Because Ahaziah had no son, Joram[b] became king after him in the second year of Judah's King Jehoram, who was Jehoshaphat's son. ¹⁸The rest of Ahaziah's deeds, aren't they written in the official records of Israel's kings?

Elijah goes to heaven

2 Now the LORD was going to take Elijah up to heaven in a windstorm, and Elijah and

---

[a] Or *He was a hairy man.* [b] Heb *Jehoram*; the king's name is variously spelled in either long *Jehoram* or short *Joram* form.

Elisha were leaving Gilgal. ²Elijah said to Elisha, "Stay here, because the Lord has sent me to Bethel."

But Elisha said, "As the Lord lives and as you live, I won't leave you." So they went down to Bethel.

³The group of prophets from Bethel came out to Elisha. These prophets said to Elisha, "Do you know that the Lord is going to take your master away from you today?"

Elisha said, "Yes, I know. Don't talk about it!"

⁴Elijah said, "Elisha, stay here, because the Lord has sent me to Jericho."

But Elisha said, "As the Lord lives and as you live, I won't leave you." So they went to Jericho.

⁵The group of prophets from Jericho approached Elisha and said to him, "Do you know that the Lord is going to take your master away from you today?"

He said, "Yes, I know. Don't talk about it!"

⁶Elijah said to Elisha, "Stay here, because the Lord has sent me to the Jordan."

But Elisha said, "As the Lord lives and as you live, I won't leave you." So both of them went on together. ⁷Fifty members from the group of prophets also went along, but they stood at a distance. Both Elijah and Elisha stood beside the Jordan River. ⁸Elijah then took his coat, rolled it up, and hit the water. Then the water was divided in two! Both of them crossed over on dry ground. ⁹When they had crossed, Elijah said to Elisha, "What do you want me to do for you before I'm taken away from you?"

Elisha said, "Let me have twice your spirit."

¹⁰Elijah said, "You've made a difficult request. If you can see me when I'm taken from you, then it will be yours. If you don't see me, it won't happen."

¹¹They were walking along, talking, when suddenly a fiery chariot and fiery horses appeared and separated the two of them. Then Elijah went to heaven in a windstorm.

¹²Elisha was watching, and he cried out, "Oh, my father, my father! Israel's chariots and its riders!" When he could no longer see him, Elisha took hold of his clothes and ripped them in two.

LIGHTHOUSE

HEAVEN

Servants of God Who Didn't Die
2 Kings 2:11-12

Elijah was a special servant of God. Elijah faced four hundred fifty false prophets in a dramatic showdown that proved the God of Israel is the one true God (1 Kgs 18:22-39). God used Elijah to keep rain from falling in Israel for three years (1 Kgs 17:1; 18:41-46). Elijah saved a widow and her son from starving (1 Kgs 17:8-16), and when that widow's son died from illness, God used Elijah to bring him back to life (1 Kgs 17:17-24). When the time came for Elijah to die, God brought Elijah straight into heaven instead of letting him die naturally. This also happened to another of God's servants, Enoch, who walked so closely with God that God simply took him away (Gen 5:24). ◊

Elisha succeeds Elijah

¹³Then Elisha picked up the coat that had fallen from Elijah. He went back and stood beside the banks of the Jordan River. ¹⁴He took the coat that had fallen from Elijah and hit the water. He said, "Where is the Lord, Elijah's God?" And when he hit the water, it divided in two! Then Elisha crossed over.

¹⁵The group of prophets from Jericho saw him from a distance. They said, "Elijah's spirit has settled on Elisha!" So they came out to meet him, bowing down before him. ¹⁶"Look," they told him, "there are fifty strong men among us, your servants. Please let them go and search for your master. Perhaps the Lord's spirit has picked him up and put him down on some mountain or in some valley."

Elisha said, "Don't send them." ¹⁷They insisted until he became embarrassed and said, "Okay, send them." So they sent fifty men who searched for three days. But they couldn't find Elijah. ¹⁸When these men returned to Elisha, who was staying in Jericho, he said to them, "Didn't I tell you not to go?"

¹⁹The citizens said to Elisha, "As you can see, sir, this city is in a good location, but the water is bad, and the land causes miscarriages."

²⁰He said, "Bring me a new bowl, and put some salt in it." They did so. ²¹Elisha then went out and threw salt into the spring. He said, "This is what the LORD has said: I have purified this water. It will no longer cause death and miscarriage." ²²The water has stayed pure right up to this very day, in agreement with the word that Elisha spoke.

Elisha and the bears

²³Elisha went up from there to Bethel. As he was going up the road, some young people came out of the city. They mocked him: "Get going, Baldy! Get going, Baldy!" ²⁴Turning around, Elisha looked at them and cursed them in the LORD's name. Then two bears came out of the woods and mangled forty-two of the youths. ²⁵From there Elisha went to Mount Carmel and then back to Samaria.

Moab's rebellion

3 Joram,ᶜ Ahab's son, became king of Israel in Samaria in the eighteenth year of Jehoshaphat, Judah's king. He ruled for twelve years. ²He did what was evil in the LORD's eyes, but he wasn't as bad as his father and mother. He removed the sacred pillar of Baal that his father had made. ³But he nevertheless clung to the sins that Jeroboam, Nebat's son, had caused Israel to commit. He didn't deviate from them.

did you know? Elisha insisted on having someone play a harp while he sang to Joram and told him the prophecy God had for him. People often played instruments during worship or times when they wanted to focus on God.

⁴Now Moab's King Mesha kept sheep. He would pay Israel's king one hundred thousand lambs and the wool from one hundred thousand rams. ⁵But when Ahab died, Moab's king rebelled against Israel's king. ⁶So King Joram set out from Samaria at once. He prepared all Israel for war. ⁷He sent word to Judah's King Jehoshaphat, "Moab's king has rebelled against me. Will you go with me to fight against Moab?"

Jehoshaphat responded, "Yes, I'll go. We'll fight as one: you and I, our troops and our horses."

⁸"Which road should we take?" Joram asked.

Jehoshaphat responded, "The road that goes through the Edomite wilderness."

⁹So Israel's and Judah's kings set out with the king of Edom. They marched around for seven days until there was no water left for the army or for the animals with them. ¹⁰Israel's king said, "This is terrible! Has the LORD brought us three kings together only to hand us over to Moab?"

¹¹Jehoshaphat said, "Isn't there any prophet of the LORD around, so we could question the LORD through him?"

One of the servants of Israel's king answered, "Elisha, Shaphat's son, is here. He used to pour water on Elijah's hands."

¹²Jehoshaphat said, "He has the LORD's word!" So Israel's king and Jehoshaphat and Edom's king went down to see Elisha.

¹³Elisha said to Israel's king, "What do we have to do with each other? Go to your father's or mother's prophets."

Then Israel's king said to him, "Don't say that, because it is the LORD who has brought us three kings together—but only to hand us over to Moab!"

¹⁴Elisha said, "I swear by the life of the LORD of heavenly forces, the one I stand before and serve, if I didn't care about Judah's King Jehoshaphat, I wouldn't notice you or even look at you! ¹⁵Now bring me a musician." While the musician played, the LORD's power came over Elisha. ¹⁶He said, "This is what the LORD says: This valley will be filled with pools.ᵈ ¹⁷This is what the LORD says: You won't see any wind or rain, but that valley will be full of water. Then you'll be able to drink—you, your cattle, and your animals. ¹⁸This is easy for the LORD to do. He will also hand Moab over to you. ¹⁹You will then attack every fort and every grand city, cutting down all the good trees, stopping up all the springs, and ruining the good fields with stones."

ᶜHeb *Jehoram* (also in 3:6); the king's name is variously spelled in either long *Jehoram* or short *Joram* form. ᵈLXX, Vulg *Fill this valley with ditches.*

²⁰The next morning, at the time to offer the grain offering, water came flowing from the direction of Edom. The land filled up with water.

²¹Now all the Moabites had heard how these kings had come to fight against them. So all who were able to fight were summoned, and they took up positions along the border. ²²They got up early in the morning as the sun's rays shone on the water. The Moabites saw the water from a distance. It looked as red as blood. ²³They said, "It's blood! The kings must have fought each other and killed themselves! Now get the plunder, Moab!"

²⁴But when they entered Israel's camp, the Israelites rose up and attacked the Moabites. The Moabites fled from them. Israel moved forward, striking the Moabites down as they went.ᵉ ²⁵Then the Israelites destroyed the Moabite cities. Each Israelite threw a stone on every piece of good land until it was covered. They stopped up every spring and cut down every good tree. Only Kir-hareseth remained with its stone wall intact,ᶠ but then stone throwersᵍ surrounded it and attacked it.

²⁶Moab's king saw that he was losing the battle. So he took seven hundred soldiers with him, each with sword in hand, to break through to Edom's king. But they failed. ²⁷Then he took his oldest son, who was to succeed him as king, and he offered him on the wall as an entirely burned offering. As a result, outrage was expressed by Israel. So they pulled back from Moab's king and returned to their own country.

A poor widow

4 Now there was a woman who had been married to a member of a group of prophets. She appealed to Elisha, saying, "My husband, your servant, is dead. You know how he feared the LORD. But now someone he owed money to has come to take my two children away as slaves."

²Elisha said to her, "What can I do for you? Tell me what you still have left in the house."

She said, "Your servant has nothing at all in the house except a small jar of oil."

³He said, "Go out and borrow containers from all your neighbors. Get as many empty containers as possible. ⁴Then go in and close the door behind you and your sons. Pour oil into all those containers. Set each one aside when it's full."

⁵She left Elisha and closed the door behind her and her sons. They brought her containers as she kept on pouring. ⁶When she had filled the containers, she said to her son, "Bring me another container."

He said to her, "There aren't any more." Then the oil stopped flowing, ⁷and she reported this to the man of God.

He said, "Go! Sell the oil and pay your debts. You and your sons can live on what remains."

A rich woman

⁸One day Elisha went to Shunem. A rich woman lived there. She urged him to eat something, so whenever he passed by, he would stop in to eat some food. ⁹She said to her husband, "Look, I know that he is a holy man of God and he passes by regularly. ¹⁰Let's make a small room on the roof. We'll set up a bed, a table, a chair, and a lamp for him there. Then when he comes to us, he can stay there."

¹¹So one day Elisha came there, headed to the room on the roof, and lay down. ¹²He said to his servant Gehazi, "Call this Shunammite woman." Gehazi called her, and she stood before him. ¹³Elisha then said to Gehazi, "Say to her, 'Look, you've gone to all this trouble for us. What can I do for you? Is there anything I can say on your behalf to the king or to the commander of the army?'"

She said, "I'm content to live at home with my own people."

¹⁴Elisha asked, "So what can be done for her?"

Gehazi said, "Well, she doesn't have a son, and her husband is old."

¹⁵Elisha said, "Call her." So Gehazi called her, and she stood at the door. ¹⁶Elisha said, "About this time next year, you will be holding a son in your arms."

But she said, "No, man of God, sir; don't lie to your servant."

¹⁷But the woman conceived and gave birth to a son at about the same time the next year. This was what Elisha had promised her.

¹⁸The child grew up. One day he ran to his father, who was with the harvest workers. ¹⁹He said to his father, "Oh, my head! My head!"

ᵉHeb uncertain ᶠHeb uncertain ᵍHeb uncertain

The father said to a young man, "Carry him to his mother." [20]So he picked up the boy and brought him to his mother.

The boy sat on her lap until noon. Then he died. [21]She went up and laid him down on the bed for the man of God. Then she went out and closed the door. [22]She called her husband and said, "Send me one of the young men and one of the donkeys so that I can hurry to the man of God and come back."

[23]Her husband said, "Why are you going to him today? It's not a new moon or sabbath."

She said, "Don't worry about it." [24]She saddled the donkey, then said to her young servant, "Drive the donkey hard. Don't let me slow down unless I tell you." [25]So she went off and came to the man of God at Mount Carmel.

As soon as the man of God saw her from a distance, he said to Gehazi his servant, "Look, it's the Shunammite woman! [26]Run out to meet her and ask her, 'Are things okay with you, your husband, and your child?'"

She said, "Things are okay."

[27]When she got to the man of God at the mountain, she grabbed his feet. Gehazi came up to push her away, but the man of God said, "Leave her alone! She is distraught, but the LORD has hidden the reason from me and hasn't told me why."

[28]She said, "Did I ask you for a son, sir? Didn't I say, 'Don't raise my hopes'?"

[29]Elisha said to Gehazi, "Get ready, take my staff, and go! If you encounter anyone, don't stop to greet them. If anyone greets you, don't reply. Put my staff on the boy's face."

[30]But the boy's mother said, "I swear by your life and by the LORD's life, I won't leave you!" So Elisha got up and followed her.

[31]Gehazi went on ahead of them. He set the staff on the young boy's face, but there was no

God Fills Us Up 2 Kings 4:1-7

Elisha was a prophet who did great things with God. He even brought some miracles. One time, a woman came to him and said that her husband had died. She owed a lot of money to different people who were threatening to take her children. In those days, if someone couldn't pay back what they borrowed, their children might be taken to work off the debt as slaves.

This woman was sad about losing her husband, but she was also scared about owing money and possibly losing her children. She didn't know what to do, so she went to Elisha. She knew that if anyone could tell her what to do, it would be the man of God. After she told Elisha her story, he told the woman to gather as many empty jars as she could find. Then she and her sons were to take the little bit of oil they had in the cupboard and begin to fill the jars. The oil kept on pouring out into all of the jars they had gathered right up to the top of the very last jar! Their little bit of oil was multiplied to fill many jars full. Elisha told the woman to sell the jars of oil and pay off her debts. It was a miracle!

We can trust God when we have a need, when we're afraid, or when we feel empty. We can also go to people like our pastors, our Sunday school teachers, or our parents for advice and instruction. When you have a need or are afraid, be like the woman in this story and seek out advice. Then have faith that God can do great things.

Who could you talk to about your fears and needs?

How can you have faith that God will meet your needs?

sound or response. So he went back to meet Elisha and told him, "The boy didn't wake up."

³²Elisha came into the house and saw the boy lying dead on his bed. ³³He went in and closed the door behind the two of them. Then he prayed to the Lord. ³⁴He got up on the bed and lay down on top of the child, putting his mouth on the boy's mouth, his eyes on the boy's eyes, his hands on the boy's hands. And as he bent over him, the child's skin grew warm. ³⁵Then Elisha got down and paced back and forth in the house. Once again he got up on the bed and bent over the boy, at which point the boy sneezed[h] seven times and opened his eyes. ³⁶Elisha called for Gehazi and said, "Call the Shunammite woman." Gehazi called her, and she came to Elisha. He told her, "Pick up your son." ³⁷She came and fell at his feet, facedown on the ground. Then she picked up her son and left.

Miracles with food

³⁸When Elisha returned to Gilgal, there was a famine in the land. A group of prophets was sitting before him. He said to his servant, "Put on the big pot and cook some stew for the prophets." ³⁹So one of them went out to

LIGHTHOUSE

GIVING MY BEST

God Can Use Our Best in Hard Times

2 Kings 4:42

It was hard to find food in Gilgal. Despite this, a man brought fresh bread and grain for Elisha the prophet from God. The man did this in obedience to God's commandment, which said that the Israelites should give a small portion of the best of everything they owned to God (Lev 27:30-33). This portion was supposed to go to God's servants (Num 18:21). Giving the best of their crops and herds to God was a way for the people to show that everything they owned came from God. They proved in a real way that they would follow God with every part of their lives. Giving the best of what they owned also made sure God's servants were taken care of. Though times were hard, this man still brought food—food he could have used himself—to Elisha. God used this man's gift and made it grow into something even more. ◆

the field to gather plants; he found a wild vine and gathered wild gourds from it, filling his garment. He came and cut them up into the pot of stew, but no one knew what they were.

⁴⁰The stew was served to the men, but as they started to eat it, they cried out and said, "There is death in that pot, man of God!" They couldn't eat it.

⁴¹Elisha said, "Get some flour." He threw it into the pot and said, "Serve the people so they can eat." At that point, there was nothing bad left in the pot.

⁴²A man came from Baal-shalishah, bringing the man of God some bread from the early produce—twenty loaves of barley bread and fresh grain from his bag.[i] Elisha said, "Give it to the people so they can eat."

⁴³His servant said, "How can I feed one hundred men with this?"

Elisha said, "Give it to the people so they can eat! This is what the Lord says: 'Eat and there will be leftovers.'" ⁴⁴So the servant gave the food to them. They ate and had leftovers, in agreement with the Lord's word.

Naaman is healed

5 Naaman, a general for the king of Aram, was a great man and highly regarded by his master, because through him the Lord had given victory to Aram. This man was a mighty warrior, but he had a skin disease.[j] ²Now Aramean raiding parties had gone out and captured a young girl from the land of Israel. She served Naaman's wife.

³She said to her mistress, "I wish that my master could come before the prophet who lives in Samaria. He would cure him of his skin disease." ⁴So Naaman went and told his master what the young girl from the land of Israel had said.

⁵Then Aram's king said, "Go ahead. I will send a letter to Israel's king."

So Naaman left. He took along ten kikkars of silver, six thousand shekels of gold, and ten changes of clothing. ⁶He brought the letter to Israel's king. It read, "Along with this letter I'm sending you my servant Naaman so you can cure him of his skin disease."

⁷When the king of Israel read the letter, he ripped his clothes. He said, "What? Am I

---

[h]Or *gasped*; Heb uncertain [i]Or *still on its stem* [j]Traditionally *leprosy*, a kind of scale skin disease

God to hand out death and life? But this king writes me, asking me to cure someone of his skin disease! You must realize that he wants to start a fight with me."

[8]When Elisha the man of God heard that Israel's king had ripped his clothes, he sent word to the king: "Why did you rip your clothes? Let the man come to me. Then he'll know that there's a prophet in Israel."

[9]Naaman arrived with his horses and chariots. He stopped at the door of Elisha's house. [10]Elisha sent out a messenger who said, "Go and wash seven times in the Jordan River. Then your skin will be restored and become clean."

[11]But Naaman went away in anger. He said,

"I thought for sure that he'd come out, stand and call on the name of the LORD his God, wave his hand over the bad spot, and cure the skin disease. [12]Aren't the rivers in Damascus, the Abana[k] and the Pharpar, better than all Israel's waters? Couldn't I wash in them and get clean?" So he turned away and proceeded to leave in anger.

[13]Naaman's servants came up to him and spoke to him: "Our father, if the prophet had told you to do something difficult, wouldn't you have done it? All he said to you was, 'Wash and become clean.'" [14]So Naaman went down and bathed in the Jordan seven times, just as the man of God had said. His skin was

[k]Or Amana

Speak Up! 2 Kings 5:1-14

Sometimes grown-ups forget that young people can have good ideas. This Bible story tells us about Naaman, who was the leader of a large army. Although he was a great and dearly loved leader, he was very sick. He had spots all over his skin, and he was miserable. Naaman didn't know what to do. But a young servant girl in his house knew exactly what he needed. She told Naaman to go see the prophet Elisha in Israel. She knew the prophet would know how to cure Naaman of his disease. Thankfully, instead of ignoring the young girl, Naaman went to see Elisha.

Elisha told Naaman to wash in the river seven times. Even though Naaman thought it was crazy advice, he did it anyway and was healed. His spots were gone, and he was washed clean! Because of this miracle, he came to love and trust God.

The little servant girl is mentioned in one sentence out of the story, but we remember her courage. When people around you wonder what to do and you know the answer is to seek God, find the courage to speak up. You could be part of an amazing miracle!

How do you find strength and courage when you are afraid?

Do you have an idea right now that could lead someone to God?

restored like that of a young boy, and he became clean.

[15] He returned to the man of God with all his attendants. He came and stood before Elisha, saying, "Now I know for certain that there's no God anywhere on earth except in Israel. Please accept a gift from your servant."

[16] But Elisha said, "I swear by the life of the LORD I serve that I won't accept anything."

Naaman urged Elisha to accept something, but he still refused. [17] Then Naaman said, "If not, then let me, your servant, have two mule loads of earth. Your servant will never again offer entirely burned offerings or sacrifices to any other gods except the LORD. [18] But may the LORD forgive your servant for this one thing: When my master comes into Rimmon's temple to bow down there and is leaning on my arm, I must also bow down in Rimmon's temple. When I bow down in Rimmon's temple, may the LORD forgive your servant for doing that."

[19] Elisha said to him, "Go in peace."

But when Naaman had gone some distance from Elisha, [20] Gehazi (who was the servant of Elisha the man of God) thought, My master let this Aramean Naaman off the hook by not accepting the gift he brought! As surely as the LORD lives, I'll go after him and accept something from him. [21] So Gehazi pursued Naaman.

Naaman saw him running after him, so he got down off his chariot to meet him. He said, "Is everything okay?"

[22] Gehazi answered, "Yes, but my master sent me to say, 'Two young men who are members of a group of prophets have just now come to me from the hills of Ephraim. Give them a kikkar of silver and two changes of clothing.'"

[23] Naaman said, "By all means, take two kikkars!" He encouraged Gehazi to accept them. He tied two kikkars of silver up in two bags, along with two changes of clothes. Naaman gave them to two of his servants, and they carried them in front of Gehazi. [24] When Gehazi arrived at the elevated fortress,[l] he took the items from them and stored them in his house. Then he sent the servants away, and they left. [25] Gehazi then went and stood before his master.

Elisha said to Gehazi, "Where did you come from, Gehazi?"

"Your servant didn't go anywhere," Gehazi replied.

[26] Elisha said to him, "Wasn't my heart going along with you[m] when the man got off his chariot to meet you? Is this the time to accept silver, clothes, olive trees, vineyards, sheep, cattle, or male and female servants? [27] Naaman's skin disease will now cling to you and to your descendants forever!" And Gehazi left Elisha's presence, flaky like snow with skin disease.

An ax head floats

6 The members of the group of prophets said to Elisha, "Look, the place where we now live under your authority is too small for us. [2] Let's go to the Jordan River and each get a log from there. Then we can make a place to live there."

Elisha said, "Do it!"

[3] One of them said, "Please come with us, your servants."

Elisha said, "Okay, I'll go." [4] So he went with them. They came to the Jordan River and began cutting down trees. [5] One of them was cutting down a tree when his ax head fell into the water. He cried out, "Oh, no! Master, it was a borrowed ax!"

[6] The man of God said, "Where did it fall?" He showed Elisha the place. Elisha then cut a piece of wood, threw it into the river there, and the ax head floated up. [7] "Lift it out," Elisha said. So the man then reached out and grabbed it.

Aramean attacks are stopped

[8] Aram's king was fighting against Israel. He took counsel with his officers, saying, "I'll camp at such-and-such a place."

[9] The man of God sent word to Israel's king: "Beware of passing by this place because the Arameans are going down there." [10] Then Israel's king sent word to the place the man of God had mentioned to him. Time after time, Elisha warned the king, and the king stayed on the alert.

[11] Aram's king was extremely upset about this. He called his officers and said to them,

Bet you can read this in 1 minute. Ready, set, go!

---

[l] Or *hillside;* Heb uncertain [m] LXX; MT lacks *along with you.*

"Tell me! Who among us is siding with Israel's
king?"
12 One of his officers said, "No one, Your
Majesty! It's Elisha the Israelite prophet who
tells Israel's king the words that you speak in
the privacy of your bedroom."
13 He said, "Go and find out where he is.
Then I will send men to capture him."
They told him, "He is in Dothan." 14 So the
king sent horses and chariots there with a
strong army. They came at night and surrounded the city.
15 Elisha's servant got up early and went
out. He saw an army with horses and chariots
surrounding the city. His servant said to Elisha, "Oh, no! Master, what will we do?"
16 "Don't be afraid," Elisha said, "because
there are more of us than there are of them."
17 Then Elisha prayed, "LORD, please open his
eyes that he may see." Then the LORD opened
the servant's eyes, and he saw that the mountain was full of horses and fiery chariots
surrounding Elisha. 18 The Arameans came
toward him, so Elisha prayed to the LORD,
"Strike this nation with blindness." And the
LORD struck them blind, just as Elisha asked.
19 Elisha said to them, "This isn't the right road
or the right city. Follow me, and I'll lead you
to the man you are looking for." But he took
them to Samaria!
20 When they arrived in Samaria, Elisha
said, "LORD, open the eyes of these men so
they can see." The LORD opened their eyes,
and they saw that they were right in the
middle of Samaria! 21 When he saw them, Israel's king said to Elisha, "Should I kill them,
my father? Should I?"
22 He said, "No, don't kill them. Did you capture them with your own sword or bow? Do you
have the right to kill them?[n] Put food and water
in front of them so they can eat and drink and
return to their master." 23 So the king gave
them a great feast, and they ate and drank.
Then the king let them go, and they returned
to their master. After that, Aramean raiding
parties didn't come into Israel anymore.

Ben-hadad attacks Samaria

24 Now it happened later that Aram's King
Ben-hadad gathered all his forces and went
up to attack Samaria. 25 The siege lasted so
long that there was a great famine in Samaria. A donkey's head sold for eighty shekels of silver and a quarter kab of doves' dung[o]
for five shekels. 26 Israel's king was passing
by on the city wall when a woman appealed to
him, "Help me, Your Majesty!"
27 The king said, "No! May the LORD help
you! Where can I find help for you? From the
threshing floor or the winepress?" 28 But then
the king asked her, "What's troubling you?"
She answered, "A woman said to me, 'Give
up your son so we can eat him today; we'll eat
my son tomorrow.' 29 So we cooked and ate my
son. The next day I said to her, 'Hand over your
son so we can eat him.' But she had hidden her
son."
30 When the king heard the woman's story,
he ripped his clothes. And as he passed by
along the wall, the people could see that he
was wearing mourning clothes underneath.
31 He said, "So may God do to me, and more, if
the head of Elisha, Shaphat's son, remains on
his shoulders today!"
32 Elisha was sitting in his house, and the
elders were sitting with him. The king sent a
messenger on ahead, but before the man arrived, Elisha said to the elders, "Do you see
that this murderer has sent someone to cut
off my head? Watch for when the messenger
comes, then close the door and hold it
shut against him. The sound of his
master's feet is right behind him,
isn't it?"
33 While Elisha was still speaking with them, the messenger[p]
arrived and said, "Look, this
disaster is the LORD's doing.
Why should I trust the LORD
any longer?"

7 Elisha said, "Hear the LORD's word!
This is what the LORD says: At this
time tomorrow a seah[q] of wheat flour will
sell for a shekel at Samaria's gate, and
two seahs of barley will sell for a shekel."
2 Then the officer, the one the king
leaned on for support, spoke to the man
of God: "Come on! Even if the LORD should
make windows in the sky, how could that
happen?"

[n] Heb uncertain [o] Or *wild onions* or *carob pods* [p] Or perhaps *the king*; cf 7:2 [q] One seah is approximately seven and a half quarts.

Elisha said, "You will see it with your own eyes, but you won't eat from it."

The siege is broken

³Now there were four men with skin disease[r] at the entrance to the city. They said to each other, "What are we doing sitting here until we die? ⁴If we decide, 'Let's go into the city,' the famine is there, and we'll die in the city. But if we stay here, we'll die just the same. So let's go and surrender to the Aramean camp. If they let us live, we'll live. If they kill us, we'll die." ⁵So they set out in the evening to the Aramean camp, and they came to the edge of the camp. But there was no one there because ⁶the Lord had made the Aramean camp hear the sound of chariots, horses, and a strong army. They had said to each other, "Listen! Israel's king has hired the Hittite and Egyptian kings to come against us!" ⁷So they had got up and fled in the evening, leaving their tents, horses, and donkeys. They left the camp exactly as it was and ran for their lives.

⁸So these men with skin disease came to the edge of the camp. They entered a tent where they ate and drank. They carried off some silver, gold, and garments, and they hid them. Then they returned and went into another tent. They took more things from there, went away, and hid them. ⁹But then they said to each other, "What we're doing isn't right. Today is a day of good news, but we're keeping quiet about it. If we wait until dawn, something bad will happen to us. Come on! Let's go and tell the palace." ¹⁰So they went and called out to the gatekeepers, telling them, "We went to the Aramean camp, and listen to this: No one was there, not even the sound of anyone! The only things there were tied-up horses and donkeys, and the tents left just as they were." ¹¹The gatekeepers shouted out the news, and it was reported within the palace.

¹²The king got up in the night. He said to his servants, "Let me tell you what the Arameans are doing to us. They know we are starving, so they've left the camp to hide in the

---

[r]Traditionally *leprosy*, a term used for several different skin diseases

Doing the Right Thing Is Hard Sometimes   2 Kings 7:1-15

Four friends were sick and not allowed inside the city, but they did a great thing for the people anyway. Everyone in town was worried because their food and money were running out. When the four friends found an empty campsite full of food and money, they started to gather as much as they could for themselves. But they got a sad feeling in their stomachs because they knew they were being greedy. The friends knew they weren't doing the right thing. So they told the king about what they had found. The king sent a team to look at the campsite, and what the four friends had said was true. Because these friends did the right thing, they saved their country.

It would have been easy for the friends to just take what they wanted. No one would have ever known. But they showed good character— they did the right thing even when no one was watching.

What would you have done if you were one of the friends in this story?

Pray that God will give you courage and wisdom as you seek the right thing in every situation.

LIFE PRESERVER

Why are women usually not named in these stories?

2 Kings 8:1-6

The people in the Bible lived in a culture organized and controlled by men. Power and authority were passed through men, and men were most often the recognized leaders. Women were considered to be less important than men. Men were most likely the authors of these books. In the story about Elisha and the rich woman, the important character is male, so his name is mentioned.

As you read the Bible, including the New Testament, you will read very interesting stories about women, many of whom are never called by name. But all their stories are important in the history of God's work with God's people, just as the stories of modern women are important to know and remember in our world. ◊

fields. They are thinking, The Israelites will come out from the city, and then we'll capture them alive and invade the city."

[13]But one of his servants answered, "Please let some men take five of the horses that are left, and let's send them out to see what happens. They are in the same situation as the large number of Israelites who are left here; they are no better off than the large number of Israelites who've already perished."[s] [14]So they chose two chariots with their horses.

The king sent them after the Aramean army, saying, "Go and see!" [15]So they went after the Arameans as far as the Jordan River. The road was filled the whole way with garments and equipment that the Arameans had thrown away in their rush. The messengers returned and reported this to the king.

[16]Then the people went out and looted the Aramean camp. And so it happened that a seah of wheat flour did sell for a shekel, and two seahs of barley sold for a shekel, in agreement with the LORD's word. [17]But the king had put the officer whom he leaned on for support in charge of the city gate. The people trampled the officer at the gate, and he died. This was just what the man of God said when the king had come down to him. [18]Because when the man of God said to the king, "At this

time tomorrow two seahs of barley will sell for a shekel at Samaria's gate, and one seah of wheat flour will sell for a shekel," [19]the officer had answered the man of God, "Come on! Even if the LORD should make windows in the sky, how could that happen?" Then Elisha had said, "You will see it with your own eyes, but you won't eat from it." [20]That's exactly what happened to him. The people trampled him at the city gate, and he died.

The woman from Shunem

8Elisha spoke to the woman whose son he had brought back to life: "You and your household must go away and live wherever you can, because the LORD has called for a famine. It is coming to the land and will last seven years."

[2]So the woman went and did what the man of God asked. She and her household moved away, living in Philistia seven years. [3]When seven years had passed, the woman returned from Philistia. She went to appeal to the king for her house and her farmland. [4]The king was speaking to Gehazi, the man of God's servant, asking him, "Tell me about all the great things Elisha has done." [5]So Gehazi was telling the king how Elisha had brought the dead to life. At that very moment, the woman whose son he

SAILBOAT

KINDNESS

Kindness Repays Kindness *2 Kings 8:1*

When the prophet Elisha first came by Shunem, a rich woman who knew who he was insisted that he stop and eat at her house whenever he passed by. Elisha came by often enough that the woman of Shunem soon convinced her husband to make up a room for Elisha to stay in when he visited. (2 Kgs 4:8-10). Because the woman had been so kind to Elisha, he wanted to do something kind for her in return. God gave the woman a son for her kindness to God's servant and then restored her son to life when he unexpectedly died (2 Kgs 4:11-37). Later, Elisha warned the woman and her son to leave Israel before it became hard to find food. The woman discovered how God rewards kindness shown to people who serve God. ◊

had brought back to life began to appeal to the king for her house and her farmland.

Gehazi said, "Your Majesty, this is the woman herself! And this is her son, the one Elisha brought to life!"

⁶The king questioned the woman, and she told him her story. Then the king appointed an official to help her, saying, "Return everything that belongs to her, as well as everything that the farmland has produced, starting from the day she left the country until right now."

Hazael becomes king

⁷Now Elisha had gone to Damascus when Aram's King Ben-hadad became sick. The king was told, "The man of God has come all this way."

⁸So the king said to Hazael, "Take a gift with you and go to meet the man of God. Question the LORD through him: 'Will I recover from this sickness?'"

⁹So Hazael went out to meet Elisha. He took along forty camel-loads of Damascus' finest goods as a gift. He came and stood before Elisha and said, "Your son Ben-hadad, the king of Aram, sent me to you to ask, 'Will I recover from this sickness?'"

¹⁰Elisha said to him, "Go and tell him, 'You will definitely recover,' but actually the LORD has shown me that he will die." ¹¹Elisha stared straight at Hazael until he felt uneasy.^t Then the man of God began to cry.

¹²Hazael said, "Master, why are you crying?"

"Because I know what violence you will do to the Israelites," Elisha said. "You will drive them from their forts with fire. You will kill their young men with the sword. You will smash their children and rip open their pregnant women."

¹³Hazael replied, "How could your servant, who is nothing but a dog, do such mighty things?"

Elisha said, "The LORD has shown me that you will be king over Aram." ¹⁴Then Hazael left Elisha and returned to his master.

"What did Elisha say to you?" Ben-hadad asked.

"He told me that you will certainly live," Hazael replied. ¹⁵But the next day he took a blanket, soaked it in water, and put it over Ben-hadad's face until he died. Hazael succeeded him as king.

Jehoram rules Judah

¹⁶In the fifth year of Israel's King Joram, Ahab's son, Jehoram, the son of Judah's King Jehoshaphat, became king.^u ¹⁷He was 32 years old when he became king, and he ruled for eight years in Jerusalem. ¹⁸He walked in the ways of Israel's kings, just as Ahab's dynasty had done, because he married Ahab's daughter. He did what was evil in the LORD's eyes. ¹⁹Nevertheless, because of his servant David, the LORD wasn't willing to destroy Judah. The LORD had promised to preserve a lamp for David and his sons forever. ²⁰During Jehoram's rule Edom rebelled against Judah's power and appointed their own king. ²¹Jehoram^v along with all his chariots crossed over to Zair. He got up at night to attack the Edomites who had surrounded him and his chariot commanders,^w but his army fled back home. ²²So Edom has been independent of Judah to this day. Libnah rebelled at the same time. ²³The rest of Jehoram's deeds and all that he accomplished, aren't they written in the official records of Judah's kings? ²⁴Jehoram died and was buried with his ancestors in David's City. His son Ahaziah succeeded him as king.

Ahaziah rules Judah

²⁵Ahaziah, the son of Judah's king Jehoram, became king in the twelfth year of Israel's King Joram,^x Ahab's son. ²⁶Ahaziah was 22 years old when he became king, and he ruled for one year in Jerusalem. His mother's name was Athaliah; she was the granddaughter of Israel's King Omri. ²⁷He walked in the ways of Ahab's dynasty, doing what was evil in the LORD's eyes, just as Ahab's dynasty had done, because he had married into Ahab's family. ²⁸Ahaziah went with Joram, Ahab's son, to fight against Aram's King Hazael at Ramoth-gilead, where the Arameans wounded Joram.

---

^tHeb uncertain ^uLXX, Syr; MT includes *Jehoshaphat had been Judah's king.* ^vHeb *Joram* (also in 8:23-24); the king's name is usually spelled in its long form *Jehoram* (cf 2 Chron 21:9). ^wHeb uncertain ^xHeb *Jehoram* (also in 8:29); the king's name is variously spelled in either long *Jehoram* or short *Joram* form.

²⁹King Joram returned to Jezreel to recover from the wounds the Arameans had given him at Ramah in his battle with Aram's King Hazael. Then Judah's King Ahaziah, the son of Jehoram, went down to visit Joram, Ahab's son, at Jezreel because he had been wounded.

Jehu rules Israel

9 The prophet Elisha called to a member of the group of prophets, "Get ready, take this jug of oil with you, and go to Ramoth-gilead. ²When you arrive there, look for Jehu, Jehoshaphat's son and Nimshi's grandson. Go to him, then pull him away from his associates, taking him to a private room. ³Take the jug of oil and pour it on his head. Then say, 'This is what the LORD has said: I anoint you king of Israel.' Then open the door, and run out of there without stopping."

⁴So the young prophet went to Ramoth-gilead. ⁵He came in, and the military commanders were sitting right there. He said, "Commander, I have a word for you."

"For which one of us?" Jehu asked.

The young prophet said, "For you, Commander."

⁶So Jehu got up and went inside. The prophet then poured oil on his head and said to him, "This is what the LORD, Israel's God, says: I anoint you king over the LORD's people, over Israel. ⁷You will strike down your master Ahab's family. In this way I will take revenge for the violence done by Jezebel to my servants the prophets and to all the LORD's servants. ⁸Ahab's whole family will die. I will eliminate from Ahab everyone who urinates on a wall, whether slave or free, in Israel. ⁹I will make Ahab's dynasty like the dynasty of Jeroboam, Nebat's son, and like the dynasty of Baasha, Ahijah's son. ¹⁰And as for Jezebel: The dogs will devour her in the area of Jezreel. No one will bury her." Then the young prophet opened the door and ran.

¹¹Jehu went out to his master's officers. They said to him, "Is everything okay? Why did this fanatic come to you?"

Jehu said to them, "You know the man and the nonsense he talks."

¹²"That's a lie!" they said. "Come on, tell us!"

Jehu replied, "This is what he said to me: 'This is what the LORD says: I anoint you king of Israel.'"

¹³Then each man quickly took his cloak and put it beneath Jehu on the paved steps.ʸ They blew a trumpet and said, "Jehu has become king!"

Jehu kills his enemies

¹⁴Then Jehu, Jehoshaphat's son and Nimshi's grandson, plotted against Joram. Now Joram along with all of Israel had been guarding Ramoth-gilead against Aram's King Hazael, ¹⁵but King Joramᶻ had gone back to Jezreel to recover from wounds that the Arameans had given him when he fought Hazael. So Jehu said, "If this is the way you feel, then don't let anyone escape from the city to talk about it in Jezreel." ¹⁶Then Jehu got on a chariot and drove to Jezreel because Joram was resting there. Judah's King Ahaziah had also come to visit Joram.

¹⁷The guard standing on the tower at Jezreel saw a crowd of people coming with Jehu. He said, "I see a crowd of people."

Joram said, "Take a chariot driver. Send him out to meet them to ask, 'Do you come in peace?'"

¹⁸So the driver went to meet him and said, "The king asks, 'Do you come in peace?'"

Jehu replied, "What do you care about peace? Come around and follow me."

Meanwhile, the tower guard reported, "The messenger met them, but he isn't returning."

¹⁹The king sent a second driver. He came to them and said, "The king asks, 'Do you come in peace?'"

Jehu said, "What do you care about peace? Come around and follow me."

²⁰The tower guard reported, "The messenger met them, but he isn't returning. And the style of chariot driving is like Jehu, Nimshi's son. Jehu drives like a madman."

²¹Joram said, "Hitch up the chariot!" So they hitched up his chariot. Then Israel's King Joram and Judah's King Ahaziah—each in his own chariot—went out to meet Jehu. They happened to meet him at the plot of ground that belonged to Naboth the Jezreelite. ²²When Joram saw Jehu, he said, "Do you come in peace, Jehu?"

ʸHeb uncertain ᶻHeb *Jehoram* (also in 9:17, 21-24); the king's name is variously spelled in either long *Jehoram* or short *Joram* form.

He said, "How can there be peace as long as the immoralities of your mother Jezebel and her many acts of sorcery continue?"

²³Then Joram turned his chariot around and fled. He shouted to Ahaziah, "It's a trap, Ahaziah!"

²⁴Jehu took his bow and shot Joram in the back. The arrow went through his heart, and he fell down in his chariot. ²⁵Jehu said to Bidkar his chariot officer, "Pick him up, and throw him on the plot of ground belonging to Naboth the Jezreelite. Remember how you and I were driving chariot teams behind his father Ahab when the LORD spoke this prophecy about him: ²⁶Yesterday I saw Naboth's blood and his sons' blood, declares the LORD. I swear that I will pay you back on this very plot of ground, declares the LORD. Now pick him up, and throw him on that plot of ground, in agreement with the LORD's word."

²⁷Judah's King Ahaziah saw this and fled on the road to Beth-haggan. Jehu chased after him. "Do the same to him!" he commanded. They shot him[a] in his chariot on the way up to Gur, near Ibleam. Ahaziah fled to Megiddo and died there. ²⁸His servants carried him back in a chariot to Jerusalem. He was buried in his tomb with his ancestors in David's City. ²⁹Ahaziah had become Judah's king in the eleventh year of Ahab's son Joram.

³⁰Jehu then went to Jezreel. When Jezebel heard of it, she put on her eye shadow and arranged her hair. She looked down out of the window. ³¹When Jehu came through the gate, she said, "Do you come in peace, Zimri, you master murderer?"

³²Jehu looked up to the window and said, "Who's on my side? Anyone?" Two or three high officials looked down at him. ³³Then he said, "Throw her out!" So they threw her out of the window. Some of her blood splattered against the wall and on the horses, and they trampled her. ³⁴Jehu then went in to eat and drink. He said, "Deal with this cursed woman and bury her. She was, after all, a king's daughter." ³⁵They went to bury her, but they couldn't find her body. Only her skull was left, along with her hands and feet. ³⁶They went back and reported this to Jehu. He said, "This is the LORD's word spoken through his servant Elijah from Tishbe: Dogs will devour Jezebel's flesh in the area of Jezreel. ³⁷Jezebel's corpse will be like dung spread out in a field in that plot of land in Jezreel, so no one will be able to say, This was Jezebel."

Jehu kills Ahab's family

10 Now Ahab had seventy sons in Samaria. So Jehu wrote letters and sent them to Samaria, to the senior officers of the city,[b] the elders, and the guardians of Ahab's sons.[c] ²The letters said: "Your master's sons are in your possession, along with horses and chariots, a fortified city, and weapons. Now when this letter reaches you, ³look for the best and most capable of your master's sons. Place him on his father's throne. Then fight for your master's family."

⁴But they were frozen with fear. They said, "Not even two kings could resist him! How can we?" ⁵So the palace administrator, the mayor, the elders, and the guardians sent a letter back to Jehu that read, "We are your servants. We will do whatever you tell us. We won't make anyone king. Do whatever seems right to you."

⁶Jehu wrote them a second letter: "If you are loyal to me and ready to obey me, take the heads of your master's sons and bring them to me at Jezreel at this time tomorrow."

Now the king's seventy sons were with the city leaders who were raising them. ⁷So when the letter came to them, they took the king's sons and slaughtered all seventy of them. They placed their heads in baskets and sent them to Jehu at Jezreel.

⁸A messenger came and told Jehu, "They have brought the heads of the king's sons."

He responded, "Pile them in two stacks at the entrance of the gate where they will stay until morning." ⁹In the morning he went out and stood there to address all the people. "You are innocent. I'm the one who plotted against my master and killed him, but who killed all these people? ¹⁰Know this: Nothing that the LORD has said against Ahab's dynasty will fail to come true. The LORD has done what he said he would do, speaking through his servant Elijah." ¹¹Then Jehu struck down all those belonging to Ahab's family who were left in

---

[a]LXX, Vulg; MT lacks *They shot him.* [b]Vulg, LXX; MT *Jezreel.* [c]LXX; MT lacks *sons.*

Jezreel, so that not one of his leaders, close acquaintances, or priests remained. ¹²Next Jehu set out for Samaria. Beth-eked of the Shepherds was on his way. ¹³There Jehu met up with the brothers of Judah's King Ahaziah. "Who are you?" he asked.

"We're Ahaziah's relatives," they replied. "We've come down for a visit with the king's sons and the queen mother's sons."

¹⁴Jehu then commanded, "Take them alive!" His soldiers took them alive, then slaughtered them at the well of Beth-eked. There were forty-two of them, but not one was left.

Jehu kills Baal worshippers

¹⁵Jehu departed from there and encountered Rechab's son Jehonadab. Jehu greeted him, and asked, "Are you as committed to me as I am to you?"

Jehonadab responded, "Yes, I am."

"If so," said Jehu, "then give me your hand." So Jehonadab put out his hand, and Jehu pulled him up into the chariot. ¹⁶Jehu said, "Come with me and see my zeal for the LORD." So Jehu had Jehonadab ride with him in his chariot. ¹⁷When Jehu arrived in Samaria, he killed all those belonging to Ahab who were left in Samaria until they were completely wiped out, in agreement with the LORD's word that was spoken to Elijah.

¹⁸Then Jehu gathered all the people, saying to them, "Ahab served Baal a little. Jehu will serve him a great deal! ¹⁹So invite all of Baal's prophets, all his worshippers, and all his priests to come to me. Don't leave anyone out, because I have a great sacrifice planned for Baal. Anyone who doesn't show up won't survive." But Jehu was lying so that he could wipe out Baal's worshippers. ²⁰Jehu called for a holy assembly for Baal, and it was done. ²¹Jehu then sent word throughout Israel. All Baal's worshippers came. No one stayed away. They entered Baal's temple until it was packed from one end to the other. ²²Then Jehu said to the person in charge of the vestments, "Bring out the special clothes for all Baal's worshippers." So he brought out robes for them. ²³Then Jehu and Jehonadab, Rechab's son, entered Baal's temple. They said to Baal's worshippers, "Make sure there are no worshippers of the LORD here with you. There should be only Baal worshippers." ²⁴Then they went in to offer sacrifices and entirely burned offerings. But Jehu had stationed eighty soldiers outside and told them, "I'm handing these people over to you. Whoever lets even one of them escape will pay for it with his life." ²⁵So when Jehu finished offering the entirely burned offering, he said to the guards and the officers, "Go in and kill everyone! Don't let anyone escape!" They killed the Baal worshippers without mercy. The guards and the officers then disposed of the bodies and entered the inner part of Baal's temple. ²⁶They brought the sacred pillarᵈ out of Baal's temple and burned it. ²⁷They tore down Baal's sacred pillar and destroyed Baal's temple, turning it into a public restroom, which is what it still is today.

²⁸This is how Jehu eliminated Baal from Israel. ²⁹However, Jehu didn't deviate from the sins that Jeroboam, Nebat's son, had caused Israel to commit—specifically, the gold calves that were in Bethel and Dan.

Jehu rules Israel

³⁰The LORD said to Jehu: Because you've done well by doing what is right in my eyes, treating Ahab's family as I wished, your descendants will sit on Israel's throne for four generations. ³¹But Jehu wasn't careful to keep the LORD God of Israel's Instruction with all his heart. He didn't deviate from the sins that Jeroboam had caused Israel to commit.

³²In those days the LORD began to reduce Israel's size. Hazael struck them down in every region of Israel: ³³from the Jordan River eastward, throughout the land of Gilead (Gad, Reuben, and Manasseh), and from Aroer by the Arnon Valley (that is, Gilead) and Bashan. ³⁴The rest of Jehu's deeds, all that he accomplished, and all his powerful acts, aren't they written in the official records of Israel's kings? ³⁵Jehu lay down with his ancestors. He was buried in Samaria. His son Jehoahaz succeeded him as king. ³⁶Jehu

ᵈLXX, Syr, Vulg; MT *pillars*

had ruled over Israel for twenty-eight years in Samaria.

Queen Athaliah rules Judah

11 When Athaliah, Ahaziah's mother, learned of her son's death, she immediately destroyed the entire royal family. ²But Jehosheba, King Jehoram's[e] daughter and Ahaziah's sister, secretly took Ahaziah's son Jehoash[f] from the rest of the royal children who were about to be murdered and hid[g] him in a bedroom along with his nurse. In this way Jehoash was hidden from Athaliah and wasn't murdered. ³He remained hidden with his nurse in the Lord's temple for six years while Athaliah ruled the country.

⁴But in the seventh year Jehoiada sent for the commanders of the Carites and of the guards and had them come to him at the Lord's temple. He made a covenant with them, and made them swear a solemn pledge in the Lord's temple. Then he showed them the king's son. ⁵He commanded them, "This is what you must do: A third of you coming on sabbath duty will guard the palace, ⁶a second third will be at the Sur Gate, and the final third will be at the gate behind the guards. You will take turns guarding the temple.[h] ⁷You who are in the first two groups that usually go off duty on the Sabbath should also guard the Lord's temple to protect the king. ⁸Surround the king completely, each of you with your weapons drawn. Whoever comes near your ranks must be killed. Stay near the king wherever he goes."

⁹The unit commanders did everything that Jehoiada the priest ordered. They each took charge of those men reporting for duty on the Sabbath as well as those going off duty on the Sabbath. They came to the priest Jehoiada. ¹⁰Then the priest gave the unit commanders King David's spears and shields, which were kept in the Lord's temple. ¹¹The guards, each with their weapons drawn, then took up positions near the temple and the altar, stretching from the south side of the temple to the north side to protect the king. Everyone was

holding his weapons, surrounding the king. ¹²Jehoiada then brought out the king's son, crowned him, gave him the royal law,[i] and made him king and anointed him, as everyone applauded and cried out, "Long live the king!"

¹³When Athaliah heard the noise made by the guard and the people, she went to the people at the Lord's temple ¹⁴and saw the king standing by the royal pillar, as was the custom, with the commanders and trumpeters beside the king. All the people of the land were rejoicing and blowing trumpets. Athaliah ripped her clothes and screamed, "Treason! Treason!"

¹⁵Then the priest Jehoiada ordered the unit commanders who were in charge of the army: "Take her out under guard,"[j] he told them, "and kill anyone who follows her." This was because the priest had said, "She must not be executed in the Lord's temple." ¹⁶They arrested her when she reached the entrance of the Horse Gate at the royal palace. She was executed there.

¹⁷Jehoiada then made a covenant between the Lord, the king, and the people, that the people would belong to the Lord. The king and the people also made a covenant. ¹⁸Then all the people of the land went to Baal's temple and tore it down, smashing its altars and images into pieces. They executed Mattan, Baal's priest, in front of the altars. The priest Jehoiada posted guards at the Lord's temple. ¹⁹Then he took the unit commanders, the Carites, the guards, and all the people of the land, and they led the king down from the Lord's temple, processing through the Guards' Gate to the palace, where the king sat upon the royal throne. ²⁰All the people of the land rejoiced, and the city was at peace now that Athaliah had been executed at the palace.

Jehoash rules Judah

²¹[k]Jehoash was 7 years old when he became king. ¹He[l] became king in Jehu's seventh year, and he ruled for forty years in Jerusalem. His mother's name was Zibiah; she was from Beer-sheba. ²Jehoash

---

[e]Heb *Joram*; the king's name is usually spelled in its long form *Jehoram* (cf 2 Chron 22:11). [f]Heb *Joash*; the king's name is variously spelled in either long *Jehoash* or short *Joash* form. The latter is the form used in 2 Chron. [g]See 2 Chron 22:11; Heb lacks *hid*. [h]Heb uncertain [i]Heb lacks *royal*. [j]Heb uncertain [k]12:1 in Heb [l]12:2 in Heb

always did what was right in the Lord's eyes, because the priest Jehoiada was his teacher. [3]However, the shrines were not removed. People kept sacrificing and burning incense at them. [4]Jehoash said to the priests, "Collect all the currently available money relating to holy things that is brought to the temple— some is money people pay to redeem persons according to their assessed value. Collect all the money brought to the Lord's temple that people offer voluntarily.[m] [5]The priests should take the money from their donors and use it to repair the temple wherever such a need for repair is discovered."

[6]But by the twenty-third year of King Jehoash, the priests still hadn't repaired the temple. [7]So King Jehoash summoned Jehoiada the priest and the other priests together. "Why haven't you repaired the temple?" he asked them. "Stop taking money from your donors; instead, give it directly for temple repairs." [8]The priests agreed that they wouldn't take any more money from the

people nor be responsible for temple repairs. [9]Then the priest Jehoiada took a box, made a hole in its lid, and placed it beside the altar, to the right as one enters the Lord's temple. The priests who stood watch at the door put all the money brought to the Lord's temple in the box. [10]As soon as they saw that a large amount of money was in the box, the royal scribe and the high priest would come, count the money that was in the temple, and put it in a bag. [11]They would then hand over the money that had been counted[n] to those who supervised the work on the temple. These supervisors then paid money to those who worked on the Lord's temple: carpenters, builders, [12]masons, and stonecutters. The money was used to purchase wood and quarried stone to repair the Lord's temple and for every other cost involved in repairing it. [13]But the money that was brought to the Lord's temple was not used to make silver basins, wick trimmers, sprinkling bowls, trumpets, or any gold or silver object for the Lord's temple.

[m]Heb uncertain [n]Heb uncertain

A 7-Year-Old King 2 Kings 12:1-12

It may seem like a kid could never be in charge of an entire country, but that's exactly what happened in this story. Jehoash was only 7 when he became the king in Jerusalem! Even though he was young, Jehoash stayed close to God so he would know how to lead. The Bible says he did all the things God wanted him to do and followed God his whole life.

In this story, Jehoash got serious about cleaning up God's temple. The priests who were responsible for collecting money to repair God's temple weren't using the money wisely, and nothing was being done to clean it up. Jehoash told the priests to stop wasting the money set aside for this project and to get busy making repairs. Finally, the temple was fixed up, clean, and ready for people to come and worship God.

Jehoash was young, but God used him to do big things. God set him apart to be a leader and do great work. Today, even though we may not be able to lead a country at such a young age, God can still call us to do great things!

How can you make sure your church is clean and fixed up, ready for people to worship God?

How is God calling you to be a leader right where you are?

[14]Instead, it was given directly to those who did the repair work; they used it to repair the LORD's temple. [15]There was no need to check on those who received the money and paid the workers, because they acted honestly. [16]Now as for the money for compensation and purification offerings, it wasn't brought to the LORD's temple. It belonged to the priests.

[17]About this same time, Aram's King Hazael came up, attacked Gath, and captured it. Next Hazael decided to march against Jerusalem. [18]Judah's King Jehoash took all the holy objects that had been dedicated by his ancestors—Judah's kings Jehoshaphat, Jehoram, and Ahaziah—along with the holy objects he himself had dedicated, as well as all the gold in the treasure rooms of the LORD's temple and the palace, and he sent them to Aram's King Hazael. Hazael then pulled back from Jerusalem.

[19]The rest of Jehoash's[o] deeds and all that he accomplished, aren't they written in the official records of Judah's kings? [20]Jehoash's officials plotted a conspiracy and killed him at Beth-millo on the road that goes down to Silla. [21]It was Jozacar son of Shimeath and Jehozabad son of Shomer, his officials, who struck him so that he died. He was buried with his ancestors in David's City. His son Amaziah succeeded him as king.

Jehoahaz rules Israel

13 Jehoahaz, Jehu's son, became king of Israel in Samaria in the twenty-third year of Judah's King Jehoash,[p] who was Ahaziah's son. He ruled for seventeen years. [2]He did what was evil in the LORD's eyes. He walked in the sins that Jeroboam, Nebat's son, had caused Israel to commit. He didn't deviate from them. [3]So the LORD was angry at Israel. Time after time God handed them over to Aram's king Hazael, and to Hazael's son Ben-hadad.

[4]But Jehoahaz sought the LORD's presence, and the LORD listened to him because he saw how badly Aram's king was oppressing Israel. [5]The LORD sent Israel a savior, and they escaped from Aram's power. Then the Israelites lived peacefully at home, just as they had in the past. [6]But they didn't deviate from the sins that Jeroboam's dynasty had caused Israel to commit; they walked in them! Moreover, a sacred pole[q] stood in Samaria. [7]No, nothing was left of Jehoahaz's army except fifty chariot riders, ten chariots, and ten thousand foot soldiers, because Aram's king had decimated them, trampling them as if they were dirt. [8]The rest of Jehoahaz's deeds, all that he accomplished, and all his powerful acts, aren't they written in the official records of Israel's kings? [9]Jehoahaz lay down with his ancestors. He was buried in Samaria. His son Joash succeeded him as king.

LIGHTHOUSE

CHANGED HEART AND LIFE

A Change in Actions Follows a Change of Heart *2 Kings 13:4*

Jehoahaz was the latest in a long line of disobedient kings. None of the kings of the northern kingdom of Israel had served God like King David had. They stuck to the evil ways of the first king of northern Israel, Jeroboam (1 Kgs 12:25-33). Sometimes they did even worse things. To punish the northern kingdom, God let Israel's enemies run all over them again and again. Finally, Jehoahaz grew tired of defeat and began following God's Instruction. Because God loved Israel, God quickly rescued the kingdom. But even though Jehoahaz started obeying God, he didn't stick with it. He didn't take down the altars built to worship false gods. Jehoahaz wanted a quick fix to his problem so that he could keep living the same wrong way. Because Jehoahaz didn't follow God by changing his actions, Israel remained a weak nation throughout his lifetime. ♦

Joash rules Israel

[10]Joash,[r] Jehoahaz's son, became king of Israel in Samaria in the thirty-seventh year of Judah's King Jehoash. He ruled for sixteen years. [11]He did what was evil in the LORD's

---

[o]Heb *Joash* (also in 12:20); the king's name is variously spelled in either long *Jehoash* or short *Joash* form. The latter is the form used in 2 Chron. [p]Heb *Joash* (also in 13:10); the king's name is variously spelled in either long *Jehoash* or short *Joash* form. The latter is the form used in 2 Chron. [q]Heb *asherah*, perhaps an object devoted to the goddess Asherah [r]Heb *Jehoash* (also in 13:25); the king's name is variously spelled in either long *Jehoash* or short *Joash* form. The latter is the form used in 2 Chron.

eyes. He didn't deviate from all the sins that Jeroboam, Nebat's son, had caused Israel to commit, but he walked in them! [12]The rest of Joash's deeds, all that he accomplished, and his powerful acts—how he fought against Judah's King Amaziah—aren't they written in the official records of Israel's kings? [13]Joash lay down with his ancestors, and Jeroboam followed him on the throne. Joash was buried in Samaria with the kings of Israel.

Elisha's last days

[14]Now Elisha became sick with the illness that would kill him. So Israel's King Joash went down to see him. Joash cried over Elisha, saying, "Oh, my father, my father! Israel's chariots and its riders!"

[15]Elisha told Joash, "Get a bow and some arrows." So he brought Elisha a bow and some arrows. [16]Elisha then said to Israel's king, "Put your hand on the bow." So Joash put his hand on the bow. Elisha then put his hands over the king's hands [17]and said, "Open the window to the east." The king did so. "Now shoot!" Elisha told him. Joash shot, then Elisha announced, "That's the LORD's rescue arrow! The rescue arrow against the Arameans! You will finish the Arameans off at Aphek." [18]Then Elisha said, "Take the arrows!" so Joash took them. Elisha then said to Israel's king, "Hit the ground with them!" Joash hit the ground three times and stopped. [19]The man of God became angry with him. He said, "If only you had struck five or six times, you would have finished the Arameans off. As it is, you will defeat them only three times."

[20]So Elisha died, and he was buried.

Sometimes Moabite raiding parties used to come into the land each spring. [21]Now it happened once that while a man was being buried, the people at the funeral suddenly saw a raiding party. They threw the body into Elisha's tomb and ran off. When the body touched Elisha's bones, the man came to life and stood up on his feet!

[22]Aram's King Hazael had oppressed Israel throughout Jehoahaz's rule. [23]But the LORD was gracious to Israel and had compassion on them, turning back to them because of his covenant with Abraham, Isaac, and Jacob; he didn't want to destroy them or throw them out of his presence until now. [24]Aram's King Hazael died. His son Ben-hadad succeeded him as king. [25]Then Jehoahaz's son Joash recaptured from Hazael's son Ben-hadad those cities that Hazael had won in battle from Joash's father Jehoahaz. Joash attacked Ben-hadad three times and took back these Israelite cities.

Amaziah rules Judah

14Amaziah, the son of Judah's King Jehoash,[s] became king in the second year of Israel's King Joash, who was Jehoahaz's son. [2]Amaziah was 25 years old when he became king, and he ruled for twenty-nine years in Jerusalem. His mother's name was Jehoaddin; she was from Jerusalem. [3]He did what was right in the LORD's eyes, but not as well as his ancestor King David. He did everything his father Jehoash did. [4]However, the shrines weren't removed. People kept sacrificing and burning incense at them. [5]Once he had secured control over his kingdom, he executed the officials who had assassinated his father the king. [6]However, he didn't kill the children of the murderers, because of what is written in the Instruction scroll from Moses, where the LORD commanded, *Parents shouldn't be executed because of what their children have done; neither should children be executed because of what their parents have done. Each person should be executed for their own guilty acts.[t]*

[7]Next Amaziah struck down ten thousand Edomites in the Salt Valley and captured Sela in battle. He renamed it Jokthe-el, which is what it is still called today. [8]Then Amaziah sent messengers to Israel's King Joash[u] son of Jehoahaz son of Israel's King Jehu, saying, "Come on! Let's go head-to-head."

[9]But Israel's King Joash responded to Judah's King Amaziah, "Once upon a time, a thistle in Lebanon sent a message to a cedar, 'Give your daughter to my son as a wife.' But then a wild beast in Lebanon came along and

[s]Heb *Joash* (also in 14:3, 17, 23); the king's name is variously spelled in either long *Jehoash* or short *Joash* form. The latter is the form used in 2 Chron. [t]Deut 24:16 [u]Heb *Jehoash* (also in 14:9, 11, 13, 15, 16-17); the king's name is variously spelled in either long *Jehoash* or short *Joash* form. The latter is the form used in 2 Chron.

trampled the thistle. [10]You have definitely defeated Edom and have now become conceited. Enjoy the honor, but stay home. Why invite disaster when both you and Judah will fall?"

[11]But Amaziah wouldn't listen, so Israel's King Joash moved against him, and he and Judah's King Amaziah went head-to-head in battle at Beth-shemesh in Judah. [12]Judah was defeated by Israel, and everyone ran home. [13]At Beth-shemesh, Israel's King Joash captured Judah's King Amaziah, Jehoash's son and Ahaziah's grandson. Joash then marched to Jerusalem and broke down six hundred feet of the Jerusalem wall from the Ephraim Gate to the Corner Gate. [14]Joash took all the gold and silver, and all the objects he could find in the LORD's temple and the treasuries of the palace, along with some hostages and returned to Samaria. [15]The rest of Joash's deeds and his powerful acts—how he fought against Judah's King Amaziah—aren't they written in the official records of Israel's kings? [16]Joash lay down with his ancestors. He was buried in Samaria with the kings of Israel. His son Jeroboam succeeded him as king.

[17]Judah's King Amaziah, Jehoash's son, lived fifteen years after the death of Israel's King Joash, Jehoahaz's son. [18]The rest of Amaziah's deeds, aren't they written in the official records of Judah's kings? [19]Some people in Jerusalem plotted against him. When Amaziah fled to Lachish, they sent men after him to Lachish, and they murdered him there. [20]They carried him back on horses, and he was buried in Jerusalem with his ancestors in David's City.

[21]Then all the people of Judah took Azariah and made him king after his father Amaziah. He was 16 years old. [22]He rebuilt Elath, restoring it to Judah after King Amaziah had lain down with his ancestors.

Jeroboam II rules Israel

[23]Jeroboam, the son of Israel's King Joash, became king in Samaria in the fifteenth year of Judah's King Amaziah, Jehoash's son. He ruled for forty-one years. [24]He did what was evil in the LORD's eyes. He didn't deviate from all the sins that Jeroboam, Nebat's son, had caused Israel to commit. [25]He reestablished Israel's border from Lebo-hamath to the Dead Sea. This was in agreement with the word that the LORD, the God of Israel, spoke through his servant the prophet Jonah, Amittai's son, who was from Gath-hepher. [26]The LORD saw how brutally Israel suffered, whether slave or free, with no one to help Israel. [27]But the LORD hadn't said he would erase Israel's name from under heaven, so he saved them through Jeroboam, Joash's son. [28]The rest of Jeroboam's deeds, all that he accomplished, and his powerful acts—how he fought and how he restored Damascus and Hamath to Judah in Israel[v]—aren't they written in the official records of Israel's kings? [29]Jeroboam lay down with his ancestors the kings of Israel. His son Zechariah succeeded him as king.

Azariah rules Judah

15 Azariah, Amaziah's son, became king of Judah in the twenty-seventh year of Israel's King Jeroboam. [2]He was 16 years old when he became king, and he ruled for fifty-two years in Jerusalem. His mother's name was Jecoliah; she was from Jerusalem. [3]He did what was right in the LORD's eyes, just as his father Amaziah had done. [4]However, the shrines weren't removed. People kept sacrificing and burning incense at them. [5]Now the LORD afflicted the king with a skin disease that he had until his dying day, so he lived in a separate house.[w] The king's son Jotham supervised the palace administration and governed the people of the land. [6]The rest of Azariah's deeds and all he accomplished, aren't they written in the official records of Judah's kings? [7]Azariah died and was buried with his ancestors in David's City. His son Jotham succeeded him as king.

Zechariah rules Israel

[8]Zechariah, Jeroboam's son, became king of Israel in Samaria in the thirty-eighth year of Judah's King Azariah. He ruled for six months. [9]He did what was evil in the LORD's eyes, just as his ancestors had done. He didn't deviate from the sins that Jeroboam, Nebat's son, had caused Israel to commit. [10]Shallum, Jabesh's son, plotted against Zechariah. He struck him down in public,[x] murdering him.

---

[v]Heb uncertain [w]Heb uncertain [x]LXX *in Keblaam*; Heb uncertain

Shallum then succeeded him as king. ¹¹The rest of Zechariah's deeds are written in the official records of Israel's kings. ¹²This was exactly what the LORD spoke to Jehu: Your descendants will sit on Israel's throne for four generations. And that's exactly what happened.

Shallum rules Israel

¹³Shallum, Jabesh's son, became king in the thirty-ninth year of Judah's King Uzziah. He ruled for one month in Samaria. ¹⁴Menahem, Gadi's son, went up from Tirzah and came to Samaria. He struck down Jabesh's son Shallum in Samaria, murdering him. Menahem then succeeded him as king. ¹⁵The rest of Shallum's deeds and the conspiracy he plotted are written in the official records of Israel's kings.

Menahem rules Israel

¹⁶Menahem then moved from Tirzah and attacked Tiphsah, all its citizens, and its neighboring areas. Because they wouldn't surrender, he attacked and ripped open all its pregnant women. ¹⁷Menahem, Gadi's son, became king of Israel in the thirty-ninth year of Judah's King Azariah. He ruled for ten years in Samaria. ¹⁸He did what was evil in the LORD's eyes. Throughout his life, he didn't deviate from the sins that Jeroboam, Nebat's son, had caused Israel to commit. ¹⁹When Assyria's King Tiglath-pileser[y] marched against the land, Menahem gave Tiglath-pileser one thousand silver kikkars in order to become his ally and to strengthen his hold on the kingdom. ²⁰Menahem taxed Israel for this money. All the wealthy people had to give fifty silver shekels each to Assyria's king. So Assyria's king went home and didn't stay there in the land. ²¹The rest of Menahem's deeds and all that he accomplished, aren't they written in the official records of Israel's kings? ²²Menahem lay down with his ancestors. His son Pekahiah succeeded him as king.

Pekahiah rules Israel

²³Pekahiah, Menahem's son, became king of Israel in the fiftieth year of Judah's King Azariah. He ruled for two years in Samaria.

²⁴He did what was evil in the LORD's eyes. He didn't deviate from the sins that Jeroboam, Nebat's son, had caused Israel to commit. ²⁵Pekah, Remaliah's son and Pekahiah's officer, plotted against him. Pekah struck Pekahiah in Samaria at the palace fortress, along with Argob and Arieh.[z] Pekah had fifty Gileadites with him. He murdered Pekahiah and succeeded him as king. ²⁶The rest of Pekahiah's deeds and all that he accomplished are written in the official records of Israel's kings.

Pekah rules Israel

²⁷Pekah, Remaliah's son, became king of Israel in the fifty-second year of Judah's King Azariah. Pekah ruled for twenty years in Samaria. ²⁸He did what was evil in the LORD's eyes. He didn't deviate from the sins that Jeroboam, Nebat's son, had caused Israel to commit. ²⁹In the days of Israel's King Pekah, Assyria's King Tiglath-pileser came and captured Ijon, Abel-beth-maacah, Janoah, Kedesh, and Hazor. He also captured Gilead, Galilee, and all the land of Naphtali. He sent the people into exile to Assyria. ³⁰Then Hoshea, Elah's son, plotted against Pekah, Remaliah's son. He struck Pekah down, murdering him. Hoshea became king after Pekah in the twentieth year of Uzziah's son Jotham. ³¹The rest of Pekah's kingship and all that he accomplished are written in the official records of Israel's kings.

Jotham rules Judah

³²Jotham, Uzziah's son, became king of Judah in the second year of Israel's King Pekah, Remaliah's son. ³³Jotham was 25 years old when he became king, and he ruled for sixteen years in Jerusalem. His mother's name was Jerusha; she was Zadok's daughter. ³⁴Jotham did what was right in the LORD's eyes, just as his father Uzziah had done. ³⁵However, he didn't remove the shrines. The people continued to sacrifice and burn incense at them. Jotham rebuilt the Upper Gate of the LORD's temple. ³⁶The rest of Jotham's deeds, aren't they written in the official records of Judah's kings? ³⁷It was in those days that the LORD began to send Aram's King Rezin and Pekah, Remaliah's son, against Judah. ³⁸Jotham died

and was buried with his ancestors in David's City.[a] His son Ahaz succeeded him as king.

Ahaz rules Judah

16 Ahaz, Jotham's son, became king of Judah in the seventeenth year of Pekah, Remaliah's son. [2]Ahaz was 20 years old when he became king, and he ruled for sixteen years in Jerusalem. He didn't do what was right in the LORD's eyes, unlike his ancestor David. [3]Instead, he walked in the ways of Israel's kings. He even burned his own son alive, imitating the detestable practices of the nations that the LORD had driven out before the Israelites. [4]He also sacrificed and burned incense at the shrines on every hill and beneath every shady tree. [5]Then Aram's King Rezin and Israel's King Pekah, Remaliah's son, came up to Jerusalem to fight. They surrounded Ahaz, but they weren't able to defeat him. [6]At that time Aram's King Rezin recovered Elath for the Arameans, driving the Judeans out of Elath. The Edomites[b] came to Elath and settled there, and that's still the case now.

[7]Ahaz sent messengers to Assyria's King Tiglath-pileser, saying, "I'm your servant and your son. Come up and save me from the power of the kings of Aram and Israel. Both of them are attacking me!" [8]And Ahaz took the silver and the gold that was in the LORD's temple and in the palace treasuries, and sent a gift to Assyria's king. [9]The Assyrian king heard the request and marched against Damascus. He captured it and sent its citizens into exile to Kir. He also killed Rezin.

[10]Then King Ahaz went to Damascus to meet up with Assyria's King Tiglath-pileser. King Ahaz noticed the altar that was in Damascus, and he sent the altar's plan and details for its construction to the priest Uriah. [11]Uriah built the altar, following the plans that King Ahaz had sent from Damascus; he had it finished before King Ahaz returned from Damascus.

[12]When the king arrived from Damascus, he inspected the altar. He came close to it, then went up on it, [13]burning his entirely burned offering and grain offering, pouring out his drink offering, and sprinkling the blood of his well-being sacrifices on the altar. [14]As for

UMBRELLA
FEAR

Trust God During Fearful Times
2 Kings 16:7-8

King Ahaz had a lot of enemies. Ahaz was afraid he would lose his kingdom if he didn't quickly find someone stronger to help him. Whenever Ahaz's ancestor King David had been afraid, David called out to God (Ps 27:1-3) But Ahaz didn't think about God when he was afraid. Instead, Ahaz thought of a man—the king of the powerful nation of Assyria. Ahaz had wandered so far away from following God's Instruction that he took all the special equipment out of God's temple and sent it to the Assyrian king as a payment. The king of Assyria saved Ahaz, but he wasn't worthy of Ahaz's trust. Assyria later went to war with northern Israel and defeated it forever (2 Kgs 17:5-6). In his time of fear, Ahaz should have trusted that God could rescue him like God had rescued others (Exod 14:10-31). ◆

the bronze altar that used to stand before the LORD, Ahaz moved it away from the front of the temple where it had stood between the main altar and the LORD's temple. He put it on the north side of the new altar. [15]Then King Ahaz ordered the priest Uriah, saying, "Burn the following sacrifices on the main altar:

in the morning, the entirely burned offering;

in the evening, the grain offering;

the king's entirely burned offering and his grain offering;

the entirely burned offering for all the people of the land, their grain offering, and their drink offerings.

"Sprinkle all the blood of the entirely burned offerings and all the blood of the sacrifices on it. I will use the bronze altar for seeking guidance."[c] [16]Uriah the priest did everything that King Ahaz commanded. [17]King Ahaz cut off the side panels from the stands and removed the basins from them. He took the Sea down from the bronze bulls that were under it and put it on a stone pavement. [18]He also took away the sabbath canopy that had been built in the temple. He removed

---

[a]Heb adds *his ancestor.*   [b]Qere; Kethib *Arameans*   [c]Heb uncertain

the royal entrance outside the LORD's temple. This was done because of the Assyrian king.

¹⁹The rest of Ahaz's deeds, aren't they written in the official records of Judah's kings? ²⁰Ahaz died and was buried with his ancestors in David's City. His son Hezekiah succeeded him as king.

Hoshea rules Israel

17 Hoshea, Elah's son, became king in Samaria in the twelfth year of Judah's king Ahaz. He ruled over Israel for nine years. ²He did what was evil in the LORD's eyes, but he wasn't as bad as the Israelite kings who preceded him. ³Assyria's King Shalmaneser marched against Hoshea, and Hoshea became Shalmaneser's servant, paying him tribute. ⁴But the Assyrian king discovered that Hoshea was a traitor, because Hoshea sent messengers to Egypt's King So. Hoshea stopped paying tribute to the Assyrian king as he had in previous years, so the Assyrian king arrested him and put him in prison. ⁵Then the Assyrian king invaded the whole country. He marched against Samaria and attacked it for three years. ⁶In Hoshea's ninth year, the Assyrian king captured Samaria. He sent Israel into exile to Assyria, resettling them in Halah, in Gozan on the Habor River, and in the cities of the Medes.

The northern kingdom falls

⁷All this happened because the Israelites sinned against the LORD their God, who brought them up from the land of Egypt, out from under the power of Pharaoh, Egypt's king. They worshipped other gods. ⁸They followed the practices of the nations that the LORD had removed before the Israelites, as well as the practices that the Israelite kings had done.ᵈ ⁹The Israelites secretly did things against the LORD their God that weren't right. They built shrines in all their towns, from watchtowers to fortified cities. ¹⁰They set up sacred pillars and sacred polesᵉ on every high hill and beneath every green tree. ¹¹At every shrine they burned incense, just as the nations did that the LORD sent into exile before them. They did evil things that made

the LORD angry. ¹²They worshipped images about which the LORD had said, Don't do such things! ¹³The LORD warned Israel and Judah through all the prophets and seers, telling them, Turn from your evil ways. Keep my commandments and my regulations in agreement with the entire Instruction that I commanded your ancestors and sent through my servants the prophets.

¹⁴But they wouldn't listen. They were stubborn like their ancestors who didn't trust the LORD their God. ¹⁵They rejected his regulations and the covenant he had made with their ancestors, along with the warnings he had given them. They followed worthless images so that they too became worthless. And they imitated the neighboring nations that the LORD had forbidden them to imitate. ¹⁶They deserted all the commandments of the LORD their God. They made themselves two metal idols cast in the shape of calves and made a sacred pole.ᶠ They bowed down to all the heavenly bodies. They served Baal. ¹⁷They burned their sons and daughters alive. They practiced divination and sought omens. They gave themselves over to doing what was evil in the LORD's eyes and made him angry.

LIFE PRESERVER

Why do the people of Israel keep making the same mistakes? *2 Kings 17:7-23*

Some things never change. Every generation seems to make the same mistakes. This history of God's people in 1 and 2 Kings reminds us that the people tried to follow God's Instruction and remember God's covenant with them.

Their real failure was that they refused to listen to God's prophet, admit their sins, and change their hearts and lives. The people always seemed to think they could do things better on their own, rather than by following God.

Today, we often do the same thing. We make a lot of mistakes. We may not worship gold calves or other idols, but we do other things that aren't pleasing to God. This is part of being human. But we also know God hears, forgives, and loves us with an everlasting love. ◆

ᵈHeb uncertain ᵉHeb *asherim*, perhaps objects devoted to the goddess Asherah ᶠHeb *asherah*, perhaps an object devoted to the goddess Asherah

[18]So the LORD was very angry at Israel. He removed them from his presence. Only the tribe of Judah was spared. [19]But Judah didn't keep the commands of the LORD their God either. They followed the practices of Israel. [20]So the LORD rejected all of Israel's descendants. He punished them, and he handed them over to enemies who plundered them until he finally threw them out of his sight.

[21]When Israel broke away[g] from David's dynasty, they made Nebat's son Jeroboam the king. Jeroboam drove Israel away from the LORD. He caused them to commit great sin. [22]And the Israelites continued walking in all the sins that Jeroboam did. They didn't deviate from them, [23]and the LORD finally removed Israel from his presence. That was exactly what he had warned through all his servants the prophets. So Israel was exiled from its land to Assyria. And that's still how it is today.

New settlers in Samaria

[24]The Assyrian king brought people from Babylon, Cuth, Avva, Hamath, and Sepharvaim, resettling them in the cities of Samaria in place of the Israelites. These people took control of Samaria and settled in its cities. [25]But when they began to live there, they didn't worship the LORD, so the LORD sent lions against them, and the lions began to kill them. [26]Assyria's king was told about this: "The nations you sent into exile and resettled in the cities of Samaria don't know the religious practices of the local god. He's sent lions against them, and the lions are killing them because none of them know the religious practices of the local god."

[27]So Assyria's king commanded, "Return one of the priests that you exiled from there. He[h] should go back and live there. He should teach them the religious practices of the local god." [28]So one of the priests who had been exiled from Samaria went back. He lived in Bethel and taught the people how to worship the LORD.

[29]But each nationality still made its own gods. They set them up in the houses that the people of Samaria had made at the shrines. Each nationality did this in whichever cities they lived. [30]The Babylonian people made the god Succoth-benoth, the Cuthean people made Nergal, and the people from Hamath made Ashima. [31]The Avvites made Nibhaz and Tartak. The Sepharvites burned their children alive as a sacrifice to Adrammelech and Anammelech, the Sepharvite gods. [32]They also worshipped the LORD, but they appointed priests for the shrines from their whole population. These priests worked in the houses at the shrines. [33]So they worshipped the LORD, but they also served their own gods according to the religious practices of the nations from which they had been exiled.

[34]They are still following their former religious practices to this very day. They don't really worship the LORD. Nor do they follow the regulations, the case laws, the Instruction, or the commandment that the LORD commanded the children of Jacob, whom he renamed Israel. [35]The LORD had made a covenant with them, commanding them, Don't worship other gods. Don't bow down to them or serve them. Don't sacrifice to them. [36]Instead, worship only the LORD. He's the one who brought you up from the land of Egypt with great strength and an outstretched arm. Bow down to him! Sacrifice to him! [37]You must carefully keep the regulations and case laws, the Instruction, and the commandment that he wrote for you. Don't worship other gods. [38]Don't forget the covenant that I made with you. Don't worship other gods. [39]Instead, worship only the LORD your God. He will rescue you from your enemies' power.

[40]But they wouldn't listen. Instead, they continued doing their former religious practices. [41]So these nations worship the LORD, but they also serve their idols. The children and the grandchildren are doing the very same thing their parents did. And that's how things still are today.

Hezekiah rules Judah

18 Hezekiah, Ahaz's son, became king of Judah in the third year of Israel's King Hoshea, Elah's son. [2]He was 25 years old when he became king, and he ruled twenty-nine years in Jerusalem. His mother's name was Abi;[i] she was Zechariah's daughter. [3]Hezekiah

[g]Or *When he (God) tore Israel away* [h]LXX, Vulg, Syr; MT *They* [i]Cf 2 Chron 29:1 *Abijah*

did what was right in the LORD's eyes, just as his ancestor David had done. ⁴He removed the shrines. He smashed the sacred pillars and cut down the sacred pole.ʲ He crushed the bronze snake that Moses made, because up to that point the Israelites had been burning incense to it. (The snake was named Nehushtan.)

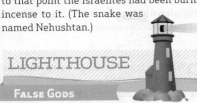

LIGHTHOUSE

FALSE GODS

Idols Can Take Many Forms 2 Kings 18:4

When Hezekiah took over the southern kingdom of Israel, called Judah, he wanted to make sure his people were serving God. He got rid of all the altars and idols to false gods. Hezekiah also rid Israel of idols that had been around for a long time. The bronze snake Hezekiah crushed existed before Israel was even a nation. This snake didn't begin as an idol—at first it was meant for good (Num 21:4-9). While wandering the wilderness, the Israelites began complaining about the food God had given to them. God was angry and sent poisonous snakes that killed many people. When the people admitted their mistakes, God had Moses make a bronze snake so that anyone who was bitten could look at it and live. Later, the snake became an object of worship instead of reminding the Israelites to worship God. Idols can take all sorts of forms. This idol deserved to be destroyed. ◆

⁵Hezekiah trusted in the LORD, Israel's God. There was no one like him among all of Judah's kings—not before him and not after him. ⁶He clung to the LORD and never deviated from him. He kept the commandments that the LORD had commanded Moses. ⁷The LORD was with Hezekiah; he succeeded at everything he tried. He rebelled against Assyria's king and wouldn't serve him. ⁸He struck down the Philistines as far as Gaza and its territories, from watchtower to fortified city.

⁹Assyria's King Shalmaneser marched against Samaria and attacked it in the fourth year of King Hezekiah, which was the seventh year of Israel's King Hoshea, Elah's son. ¹⁰After three years the Assyrians captured the city. Samaria was captured in Hezekiah's sixth year, which was Hoshea's ninth year. ¹¹Assyria's king sent Israel into exile to Assyria. He settled them in Halah, in Gozan on the Habor River, and in the cities of the Medes. ¹²All this happened because they wouldn't listen to the LORD their God. They broke his covenant—all that the LORD's servant Moses had commanded them. They didn't listen, and they didn't do it.

¹³Assyria's King Sennacherib marched against all of Judah's fortified cities and captured them in the fourteenth year of King Hezekiah. ¹⁴Judah's King Hezekiah sent a message to the Assyrian king at Lachish, saying, "I admit wrongdoing. Please withdraw from me, and I'll agree to whatever you demand from me." Assyria's king required Judah's King Hezekiah to pay him three hundred kikkars of silver and thirty kikkars of gold. ¹⁵So Hezekiah gave him all the silver that was in the LORD's temple and in the palace treasuries. ¹⁶At that time King Hezekiah had to strip down the doors and doorposts of the LORD's temple, which he had covered with gold. He gave all of it to the Assyrian king.

¹⁷Assyria's king sent his general, his chief officer, and his field commander from Lachish, together with a large army, to King Hezekiah at Jerusalem. They went up and arrived at Jerusalem. They stood at the water channel of the Upper Pool, which is on the road to the field where clothes are washed. ¹⁸Then they called for the king. Hilkiah's son Eliakim, who was the palace administrator, Shebna the secretary, and Asaph's son Joah the recorder went out to them.

¹⁹Then the field commander said to them, "Say to Hezekiah: This is what Assyria's Great King says: Why do you feel so confident? ²⁰Do you think that empty words are the same as good strategy and the strength to fight? Who are you trusting in that you now rebel against me? ²¹It appears that you are trusting in a staff—Egypt—that's nothing but a broken reed! It will stab the hand of anyone who leans on it! That's all that Pharaoh, Egypt's king, is to anyone who trusts in him. ²²Now suppose you say to me, 'We trust in the LORD our God.' Isn't he the one whose shrines and altars Hezekiah removed, telling Judah and

ʲHeb *asherah*, perhaps an object devoted to the goddess Asherah

Jerusalem, 'You must worship before this altar in Jerusalem'?

²³"So now make a wager with my master, Assyria's king. I'll give you two thousand horses if you can supply the riders! ²⁴How will you drive back even the least important official among my master's servants when you are relying on Egypt for chariots and riders? ²⁵What's more, do you think I've marched against this place to destroy it without the LORD's support? It was the LORD who told me, March against this land and destroy it!"

²⁶Hilkiah's son Eliakim, Shebna, and Joah said to the field commander, "Please speak to your servants in Aramaic because we understand it. Don't speak with us in Hebrew, because the people on the wall will hear it."

²⁷The field commander said to them, "Did my master send me to speak these words just to you and your master and not also to the men on the wall? They are the ones who will have to eat their dung and drink their urine along with you." ²⁸Then the field commander stood up and shouted in Hebrew at the top of his voice, saying, "Listen to the message of the great king, Assyria's king. ²⁹This is what the king says: Don't let Hezekiah lie to you. He won't be able to rescue you from the power of Assyria's king. ³⁰Don't let Hezekiah persuade you to trust the LORD by saying, 'The LORD will certainly rescue us. This city won't be handed over to Assyria's king.'

³¹"Don't listen to Hezekiah, because this is what Assyria's king says: Surrender to me and come out. Then each of you will eat from your own vine and fig tree, and drink water from your own well ³²until I come to take you to a land just like your land. It will be a land of grain and new wine, a land of bread and vineyards, a land of olive oil and honey. Then you will live and not die! Don't listen to Hezekiah, because he will mislead you by saying, 'The LORD will rescue us.' ³³Were any of the gods of the other nations able to rescue their lands from the power of Assyria's king? ³⁴Where are the gods of Hamath and Arpad? Where are the gods of Sepharvaim, Hena, and Ivvah? Have they rescued Samaria from my power? ³⁵Which one of any of the gods of those lands has rescued their country from my power? Why should the LORD rescue Jerusalem from my power?"

³⁶But the people kept quiet and didn't answer him with a single word, because King Hezekiah's command was, "Don't answer him!" ³⁷Hilkiah's son Eliakim, who was the palace administrator, Shebna the secretary, and Asaph's son Joah the recorder, came to Hezekiah with ripped clothes. They told him what the field commander had said.

Hezekiah and Isaiah

19 When King Hezekiah heard this, he ripped his clothes, covered himself with mourning clothes, and went to the LORD's temple. ²He sent Eliakim the palace administrator, Shebna the secretary, and the senior priests to the prophet Isaiah, Amoz's son. They were all wearing mourning clothes. ³They said to him, "This is what Hezekiah says: Today is a day of distress, punishment, and humiliation. It's as if children are ready to be born, but there's no strength to see it through. ⁴Perhaps the LORD your God has heard all the words of the field commander who was sent by his master, Assyria's king—how he insulted the living God—perhaps God will punish him for the words the LORD your God heard. Send up a prayer for those few people who still survive."

⁵When King Hezekiah's servants got to Isaiah, ⁶Isaiah said to them, "Say this to your master: 'This is what the LORD says: Don't be afraid at the words you heard, which the officers of Assyria's king have used to insult me. ⁷I'm about to put a spirit in him, so when he hears a rumor, he'll go back to his own country. Then I'll have him cut down by the sword in his own land.'"

⁸The field commander heard that the Assyrian king had left Lachish. So he went back to the king and found him attacking Libnah. ⁹Then the Assyrian king learned that Cush's King Tirhakah was on his way to fight against him. So he sent messengers to Hezekiah again, saying, ¹⁰"Say this to Judah's King Hezekiah: Don't let the God you trust in persuade you by saying, 'Jerusalem won't be handed over to the Assyrian king.' ¹¹You yourself have heard what Assyrian kings do to other countries, wiping them out. Is it likely that you will be saved? ¹²Did the gods of the nations destroyed by my fathers—Gozan, Haran, Rezeph, or the people of Eden in Telassar—save

them? ¹³Where now is Hamath's king, Arpad's king, or the kings of Lair, Sepharvaim, Hena, or Ivvah?"ᵏ

Hezekiah's prayer

¹⁴Hezekiah took the letters from the messengers and read them. Then he went to the temple and spread them out before the LORD. ¹⁵Hezekiah prayed to the LORD, saying, "LORD God of Israel, you sit enthroned on the winged creatures. You alone are God over all the earth's kingdoms. You made both heaven and earth. ¹⁶LORD, turn your ear this way and hear! LORD, open your eyes and see! Listen to Sennacherib's words. He sent them to insult the living God! ¹⁷It's true, LORD, that the Assyrian kings have destroyed many nations and their lands. ¹⁸The Assyrians burned the gods of those nations with fire because they aren't real gods. They are only man-made

creations of wood and stone. That's how the Assyrians could destroy them. ¹⁹So now, LORD our God, please save us from Sennacherib's power! Then all the earth's kingdoms will know that you, LORD, are the only true God."

²⁰Then Isaiah, Amoz's son, sent a message to Hezekiah: "This is what the LORD, Israel's God, says: I have heard your prayer about Assyria's King Sennacherib. ²¹This is the message that the LORD has spoken against him:

The young woman, Daughter Zion,
    despises you and mocks you;
    Daughter Jerusalem shakes her head
    behind your back.
²² Whom did you insult and ridicule?
    Against whom did you raise your voice
    and pridefully lift your eyes?
    It was against the holy one of Israel!
²³ You've insulted the Lord
    with your messengers;

ᵏOr *the king of the city of Sepharvaim* or *the king of the city of Sepharvaim, Hena, and Ivvah*

Embarrassed but Victorious   *2 Kings 18:17–19:36*

After Jehoash, there were some kings who didn't follow God's Instruction and led the people to ignore and forget God. They made a mess of many things. Thankfully, Hezekiah came next. He became the king of Judah when he was 25 years old, and he was one of the greatest kings God's people ever had. The Bible says that Hezekiah trusted God no matter what came his way.

One day, another king made fun of Hezekiah in front of his entire army! This king went so far as to send his servants to Hezekiah's place to make fun of his leadership, his ability, and his faith in God. They even threatened to take over his kingdom. All of Hezekiah's people listened to these men make fun of their king and threaten their lives. For a short while, Hezekiah was very embarrassed and stressed out. But he remembered that God had promised to be with him, so he didn't need to be afraid. Hezekiah remembered that he should pray and trust God, and that's just what he did. He encouraged his people to do the same.

When someone makes fun of you, or when you feel very embarrassed, remember that you can trust God and ask for help with your hurt feelings.

Have you ever been made fun of for believing in God?

Write a prayer asking God for courage to trust God no matter what.

you said, 'I, with my many chariots,
    have gone up to the highest mountains,
    to the farthest reaches of Lebanon.
I have cut down its tallest cedars,
    the best of its pine trees.
I have reached its most
    remote lodging place,
    its best forest.
24 I have dug wells,
    have drunk waters in foreign lands.[1]
With my own feet, I dried up
    all of Egypt's streams.'
25 Haven't you heard?
I set this up long ago;
    I planned it in the distant past!
Now I have made it happen,
    making fortified cities
    collapse into piles of rubble.
26 Their citizens have lost their power.
    They are frightened and ashamed.
They've become like plants in a field,
    tender green shoots,
    the grass on rooftops,
    burned up before it matures.
27 I know where you live,
    how you go out and come in,
    and how you rage against me.
28 And because you rage against me
    and because your pride
    has reached my ears,

did you know? Sometimes the Bible describes God's messengers as mighty warriors. In this verse, a single messenger defeated an army of 185,000 Assyrian soldiers. No wonder the Lord's messengers would say, "Don't be afraid," when they appeared to God's people!

I will put my hook in your nose,
    and my bit in your mouth.
I will make you go back
    the same way you came.

29"Now this will be the sign for you, Hezekiah: This year you will eat what grows by itself. Next year you will eat what grows from that. But in the third year, sow seed and harvest it; plant vineyards and eat their fruit. 30The survivors of the house of Judah who have escaped will take root below and bear

LIFE PRESERVER

What does Isaiah's prophecy mean? 2 Kings 19:29-34

When the prophet Isaiah said, "Now this will be the sign for you," he meant the people were to pay attention, because the sign would be a communication from God. This particular sign told them they would have to eat what was left from the land. The Assyrians took the crops and ruined the land, so God told them to eat what was left for two years. In the third year, they would be able to reclaim the land and plant seeds and vineyards.

The new seeds and vines would take hold in the land and produce food for them to eat, which was a sign that the people would also be planted and rooted in this place. Like the newly planted seeds, they would thrive, grow, and produce. This was God's sign and promise to them. ◆

fruit above. 31Those who remain will go out from Jerusalem, and those who survive will go out from Mount Zion. The zeal of the Lord of heavenly forces[m] will do this.

32"Therefore, this is what the Lord says about Assyria's king: He won't enter this city. He won't shoot a single arrow there. He won't come near the city with a shield. He won't build a ramp to besiege it. 33He will go back by the same way he came. He won't enter this city, declares the Lord. 34I will defend this city and save it for my sake and for the sake of my servant David."

35That night the Lord's messenger went out and struck down one hundred eighty-five thousand soldiers in the Assyrian camp. When people got up the next morning, there were dead bodies everywhere. 36So Assyria's King Sennacherib departed, returning to Nineveh, where he stayed. 37Later, while he was worshipping in the temple of his god Nisroch, his sons Adrammelech and Sharezer killed him with a sword. They then escaped to the land of Ararat. His son Esarhaddon succeeded him as king.

Hezekiah's illness

20 Around that same time, Hezekiah became deathly ill. The prophet Isaiah, Amoz's son, came to him and said, "This is

[1]Heb uncertain [m]Qere, some Heb sources, and the parallel in Isa 32; Kethib lacks *of heavenly forces*.

what the Lord says: Put your affairs in order because you are about to die. You won't survive this."

²Hezekiah turned his face to the wall and prayed to the Lord, saying, ³"Please, Lord, remember how I have walked before you in truth and sincerity. I have done what is right in your eyes." Then Hezekiah cried and cried.

⁴Isaiah hadn't even left the middle courtyard of the palace when the Lord's word came to him: ⁵Turn around. Say to Hezekiah, my people's leader: This is what the Lord, the God of your ancestor David, says: I have heard your prayer and have seen your tears. So now I'm going to heal you. Three days from now you will be able to go up to the Lord's temple. ⁶I will add fifteen years to your life. I will rescue you and this city from the power of the Assyian king. I will defend this city for my sake and for the sake of my servant David.

⁷Then Isaiah said, "Prepare a bandage made of figs." They did so and put it on the swelling, at which point Hezekiah started getting better.

⁸Hezekiah said to Isaiah, "What is the sign that the Lord will heal me and that I'll be able to go up to the Lord's temple in three days?"

did you know?
King Hezekiah ordered one of the largest, most important building projects in Bible times, but the work wasn't visible to most people. Hezekiah had workers dig 582 yards of tunnels under the city to make sure the people would have access to enough water to last through any attack.

⁹Isaiah said, "This will be your sign from the Lord that he will make his promise come true: Should the shadow go forward ten steps or back ten steps?"

¹⁰"It's easy for the shadow to go forward ten steps," Hezekiah said, "but not for the shadow to go back ten steps." ¹¹So the prophet Isaiah called on the Lord, who made the shadow go back ten steps, down the flight of stairs built by Ahaz.ⁿ

¹²At that time Merodach-baladan, son of Babylon's King Baladan, sent messengers to Hezekiah with letters and a gift. This was because he had heard that Hezekiah was sick. ¹³Hezekiah granted them an audience and showed them everything in his treasury—the silver, the gold, the spices, and the fine oil. He also showed them his stock of weaponry and everything in his storehouses. There wasn't a single thing in his palace or his whole kingdom that Hezekiah didn't show them. ¹⁴Then the prophet Isaiah came to King Hezekiah and said to him, "What did these men say? Where have they come from?"

Hezekiah said, "They came from a distant country: Babylon."

¹⁵"What have they seen in your palace?" Isaiah asked.

"They have seen everything in my palace," Hezekiah answered. "There's not a single thing in my storehouses that I haven't shown them."

¹⁶Then Isaiah said to Hezekiah, "Listen to the Lord's word: ¹⁷The days are nearly here when everything in your palace and all that your ancestors collected up to now will be carried off to Babylon. Not a single thing will be left, says the Lord. ¹⁸Some of your children, your very own offspring, will be taken away. They will become eunuchs in the palace of Babylon's king."

¹⁹Hezekiah said to Isaiah, "The Lord's word that you've spoken is good," because he thought: There will be peace and security in my lifetime.

²⁰The rest of Hezekiah's deeds and all his powerful acts—how he made the pool and the channel and brought water inside the city—aren't they written in the official records of Judah's kings? ²¹Hezekiah lay down with his ancestors. His son Manasseh succeeded him as king.

Manasseh rules Judah

21 Manasseh was 12 years old when he became king, and he ruled for fifty-five years in Jerusalem. His mother's name was Hephzibah. ²He did what was evil in the Lord's eyes, imitating the detestable practices of the nations that the Lord had driven out before the Israelites. ³He rebuilt the shrines that his father Hezekiah had destroyed, set up altars for Baal, and made a sacred pole,ᵒ just as

ⁿHeb uncertain ᵒHeb *asherah*, perhaps a pole devoted to the goddess Asherah

Israel's King Ahab had done. He bowed down to all the stars in the sky and worshipped them. [4]He even built altars in the two court-yards of the Lord's temple—the very place the Lord was speaking of when he said: "I will put my name in Jerusalem." [5]Manasseh built altars for all the stars in the sky in both courtyards of the Lord's temple. [6]He burned his own son alive, consulted sign readers and fortune-tellers, and used mediums and divin-ers. He did much evil in the Lord's eyes and made him angry.

[7]Manasseh set up the carved Asherah image he had made in the temple—the very temple the Lord had spoken about to David and his son Solomon, saying, In this temple and in Jerusalem, which I have chosen out of all Israel's tribes, I will put my name forever. [8]I will never again remove Israel from the land I gave to their ancestors, provided they carefully do everything I have commanded them—keeping all the Instruction my servant Moses commanded them. [9]But they wouldn't listen. Manasseh led them into doing even more evil than the nations the Lord had wiped out before the Israelites.

[10]The Lord spoke through his servants the prophets: [11]Judah's King Manasseh has done detestable things, things more evil than the Amorites had done before his time. He has caused Judah to sin with his images. [12]Because of this, the Lord, Israel's God, has said: I'm about to bring on Jerusalem and Judah such a great disaster that the ears of anyone who hears about it will ring. [13]I will stretch out over Jerusalem the same line that I used to measure Samaria and the same ma-son's level that I used on Ahab's family. I will wipe Jerusalem clean the same way someone wipes a plate clean, wiping it clean then turn-ing it facedown. [14]Whatever survives of my inheritance, I'll leave behind, handing them over to their enemies. They will be nothing but plunder and loot for every one of their enemies. [15]This will happen because they have done what is evil in my eyes, making me angry from the day their ancestors left Egypt until this very moment.

[16]Manasseh spilled so much innocent blood that he filled up every corner of Jerusa-lem with it. And this doesn't include the sins he caused Judah to commit so that they did what was evil in the Lord's eyes. [17]The rest of Manasseh's deeds, all that he accomplished, and the sin he committed, aren't they writ-ten in the official records of Judah's kings? [18]Manasseh lay down with his ancestors. He was buried in his palace garden, the Uzza Gar-den. His son Amon succeeded him as king.

Amon rules Judah

[19]Amon was 22 years old when he became king, and he ruled for two years in Jerusalem. His mother's name was Meshullemeth; she was Haruz's daughter and was from Jotbah. [20]He did what was evil in the Lord's eyes, just as his father Manasseh had done. [21]He walked in all the ways his father had walked. He wor-shipped the same worthless idols his father had worshipped, bowing down to them. [22]He deserted his ancestors' God, the Lord—he didn't walk in the Lord's way.

[23]Amon's officials plotted against him and assassinated the king in his palace. [24]The people of the land then executed all those who had plotted against King Amon and made his son Josiah the next king. [25]The rest of Amon's deeds, aren't they written in the offi-cial records of Judah's kings? [26]He was buried in his tomb in the Uzza Garden. His son Josiah succeeded him as king.

Josiah rules Judah

22 Josiah was 8 years old when he be-came king, and he ruled for thirty-one years in Jerusalem. His mother's name was Jedidah; she was Adaiah's daughter and was from Bozkath. [2]He did what was right in the Lord's eyes, and | Memorize 2 Kgs 22:2 | walked in the ways of his ancestor David—not deviating from it even a bit to the right or left.

[3]In the eighteenth year of King Josiah's rule, he sent the secretary Shaphan, Azaliah's son and Meshullam's grandson, to the Lord's

did you know? Like King Jehoash (2 Kgs 11:21), King Josiah was very young when he became king: 8 years old! Both of these young kings of Judah followed God's Instruction. They were good leaders even though they became kings when kids today are in second or third grade.

temple with the following orders: ⁴"Go to the high priest Hilkiah. Have him carefully count[p] the money that has been brought to the Lord's temple and that has been collected from the people by the doorkeepers. ⁵It should be given to the supervisors in charge of the Lord's temple, who in turn should pay it to those who are in the Lord's temple, repairing the temple—⁶the carpenters, the builders, and the masons. It should be used to pay for lumber and quarried stone to repair the temple. ⁷But there's no need to check on them regarding the money they receive, because they are honest workers."

⁸The high priest Hilkiah told Shaphan the secretary: "I have found the Instruction scroll in the Lord's temple." Then Hilkiah turned the scroll over to Shaphan, who read it.

⁹Shaphan the secretary then went to the king and reported this to him: "Your officials have released the money that was found in the temple and have handed it over to those who supervise the work in the Lord's temple." ¹⁰Then Shaphan the secretary told the king, "Hilkiah the priest has given me a scroll," and he read it out loud before the king.

¹¹As soon as the king heard what the Instruction scroll said, he ripped his clothes. ¹²The king ordered the priest Hilkiah, Shaphan's son Ahikam, Micaiah's son Achbor, Shaphan the secretary, and Asaiah the royal officer as follows: ¹³"Go and ask the Lord on my behalf, and on behalf of the people, and on behalf of all Judah concerning the contents of this scroll that has been found. The Lord must be furious with us because our ancestors failed to obey the words of this scroll and do everything written in it about us."

¹⁴So Hilkiah the priest, Ahikam, Achbor, Shaphan, and Asaiah went to the prophetess Huldah. She was married to Shallum, Tikvah's son and Harhas' grandson, who was in charge of the wardrobe. She lived in Jerusalem in the second district. When they spoke to her, ¹⁵she replied, "This is what the Lord, Israel's God, says: Tell this to the man who sent you to me: ¹⁶This is what the Lord says: I am about to bring disaster on this place and its citizens—all the words in the scroll that Judah's king has read! ¹⁷My anger burns against this place, never to be quenched, because

they've deserted me and have burned incense to other gods, angering me by everything they have done.[q] ¹⁸But also say this to the king of Judah, who sent you to question the Lord: This is what the Lord, Israel's God, says about the message you've just heard: ¹⁹Because your heart was broken and you submitted before the Lord when you heard what I said about this place and its citizens—that they will become a horror and a curse—and because you ripped your clothes and cried before me, I have listened to you, declares the Lord. ²⁰That's why I will gather you to your ancestors, and you will go to your grave in peace. You won't experience the disaster I am about to bring on this place."

LIGHTHOUSE

Heart

A Tender Heart Obeys God *2 Kings 22:19*
God's temple wasn't in good shape, so King Josiah had it repaired. While it was being fixed, workers found a scroll containing God's Instruction. It had been so long since anyone in Israel had truly followed God's Instruction that most people had forgotten about it. When Josiah read God's Instruction, his tender heart broke. Josiah knew that Israel had broken God's Instruction over and over again. Josiah respected God and was upset by how much Israel had disobeyed. He wanted Israel to start following God's Instruction. Josiah's heart wasn't like the heart of Egypt's pharaoh, who refused to obey (Exod 8:1-15). Josiah's heart was tender enough to hear what God was saying, understand it, and obey (2 Kgs 23:1-25). ◗

Josiah's reform

When they reported Huldah's words to the king, ¹the king sent a message, and all of Judah's and Jerusalem's elders gathered before him. ²Then the king went up to the Lord's temple, together with all the people of Judah and all the citizens of Jerusalem, the priests and the prophets, and all the people, young and old alike. There the king read out loud all the words of the covenant scroll that had been found in the Lord's temple. ³The king stood beside the pillar and made a covenant with the Lord that he would follow the Lord by keeping his commandments, his laws, and his regulations with all his heart and all his being in order to fulfill the words of this covenant that were written in this scroll. All of the people accepted the covenant.

⁴The king then commanded the high priest Hilkiah, the second-order priests, and the doorkeepers to remove from the Lᴏʀᴅ's temple all the religious objects made for Baal, Asherah, and all the heavenly bodies. The king burned them outside Jerusalem in the Kidron fields and took the ashes to Bethel. ⁵He got rid of the pagan priests that the Judean kings had appointed to burn incense at the shrines in Judah's cities and the areas around Jerusalem. He did the same to those who burned incense to Baal, to the sun, to the moon, to the constellations, and to all the heavenly bodies. ⁶He removed the Asherah image[r] from the Lᴏʀᴅ's temple, taking it to the Kidron Valley outside Jerusalem. There he burned it, ground it to dust, and threw the dust on the public graveyard. ⁷The king tore down the shrines for the consecrated workers[s] that were in the Lᴏʀᴅ's temple, where women made woven coverings[t] for Asherah.

⁸Then Josiah brought all the priests out of Judah's cities. From Geba to Beer-sheba, he defiled the shrines where the priests had been burning incense. He also tore down the shrines at the gates at the entrance to the gate of Joshua the city's governor, which were on the left as one entered the city gate. ⁹Although the priests of these shrines didn't go up on the Lᴏʀᴅ's altar in Jerusalem, they did eat unleavened bread with their fellow priests.

¹⁰Josiah defiled the Topheth in the Ben-hinnom Valley so no one could burn their child alive in honor of the god Molech. ¹¹He did away with the horses that Judah's kings had dedicated to the sun. They were kept at the entrance to the Lᴏʀᴅ's temple near a room in the annex[u] that belonged to an official named Nathan-melech. Josiah set fire to the chariots that were dedicated to the sun. ¹²The king also tore down the altars that were on the roof of Ahaz's upper story, which had been made by the Judean kings, and he did the same with the altars that Manasseh had built in the two courtyards of the Lᴏʀᴅ's temple. He broke

them up there[v] and threw their dust into the Kidron Valley. ¹³The king then defiled the shrines facing Jerusalem, south of the Mountain of Destruction. Solomon the king of Israel had built these for Ashtoreth, the monstrous Sidonian god, for Chemosh, the monstrous Moabite god, and for Milcom, the detestable Ammonite god. ¹⁴He smashed the sacred pillars and cut down the sacred poles,[w] filling the places where they had been with human bones.

¹⁵Josiah also tore down the altar that was in Bethel. That was the shrine made by Jeroboam, Nebat's son, who caused Israel to sin. Josiah tore down that altar and its shrine. He burned the shrine, grinding it into dust. Then he burned its sacred pole.[x] ¹⁶When Josiah turned around, he noticed tombs up on the hillside. So he ordered the bones to be taken out of the tombs. He then burned them on the altar, desecrating it. (This was in agreement with the word that the Lᴏʀᴅ announced by the man of God when Jeroboam stood by the altar at the festival.) Josiah then turned and saw the tomb of the man of God[y] who had predicted these things. ¹⁷"What's this gravestone I see?" Josiah asked.

The people of the city replied, "That tomb belongs to the man of God who came from Judah and announced what you would do to the altar of Bethel."

¹⁸"Let it be," Josiah said. "No one should disturb his bones." So they left his bones untouched, along with the bones of the prophet who came from Samaria.

¹⁹Moreover, Josiah removed all the shrines on the high hills that the Israelite kings had constructed throughout the cities of Samaria. These had made the Lᴏʀᴅ angry. Josiah did to them just what he did at Bethel. ²⁰He actually slaughtered on those altars all the priests of the shrines who were there, and he burned human bones on them. Then Josiah returned to Jerusalem.

²¹The king commanded all the people, "Celebrate a Passover to the Lᴏʀᴅ your God following what is instructed in this scroll containing the covenant." ²²A Passover like this hadn't been celebrated since the days when the judges judged Israel; neither had it been

---

[r]Heb lacks *image*; perhaps a pole dedicated to the goddess [s]Traditionally *cultic prostitutes* [t]Heb uncertain [u]Heb uncertain [v]Correction; MT *removed them quickly* or *ran from there* [w]Heb *asherim*, perhaps objects devoted to the goddess Asherah [x]Heb *asherah*, perhaps an object devoted to the goddess Asherah [y]LXX; MT lacks *when Jeroboam stood by the altar at the festival. Josiah then turned and saw the tomb of the man of God.*

celebrated during all the days of the Israelite and Judean kings. ²³But in the eighteenth year of King Josiah's rule, this Passover was celebrated to the Lord in Jerusalem.

²⁴Josiah burned those who consulted dead spirits and the mediums, the household gods and the worthless idols—all the monstrous things that were seen in the land of Judah and in Jerusalem. In this way Josiah fulfilled the words of the Instruction written in the scroll that the priest Hilkiah found in the Lord's temple. ²⁵There's never been a king like Josiah, whether before or after him, who turned to the Lord with all his heart, all his being, and all his strength, in agreement with everything in the Instruction from Moses.

SAILBOAT

Obedience

Complete Obedience Is Best
2 Kings 23:24-25

King Josiah obeyed God like no other king of Israel. When Josiah heard about God's Instruction—the teaching that the people of Israel had forgotten about—Josiah turned to God with all his heart. First, Josiah made sure Israel celebrated Passover, which is the special meal celebrating the time when God rescued the Israelites from Egypt. Even though this is an important meal and God told Israel always to remember it, no one had celebrated Passover since the time before the Israelite kings (2 Kgs 23:21-23). Josiah also got rid of every false god in Israel. Some Israelite kings who honored God had removed most of the false gods, but no one got rid of every last one like Josiah did. The people of Israel had done so many evil things that God was still mad, even after Josiah's obedience. But because Josiah obeyed with all his heart, God promised Josiah he wouldn't feel God's anger (2 Kgs 22:15-20). ◆

²⁶Even so, the Lord didn't turn away from the great rage that burned against Judah on account of all that Manasseh had done to make him angry. ²⁷The Lord said, "I will remove Judah from my presence just as I removed Israel. I will reject this city, Jerusalem, which I chose, and this temple where I promised my name would reside."

²⁸The rest of Josiah's deeds and all that he accomplished, aren't they written in the official records of Judah's kings? ²⁹In his days, the Egyptian king Pharaoh Neco marched

against the Assyrian king at the Euphrates River. King Josiah marched out to intercept him. But when Neco encountered Josiah in Megiddo, he killed the king. ³⁰Josiah's servants took his body from Megiddo in a chariot. They brought him to Jerusalem and buried him in his own tomb. The people of the land took Jehoahaz, Josiah's son, anointed him, and made him king after his father.

Jehoahaz rules Judah

³¹Jehoahaz was 23 years old when he became king, and he ruled for three months in Jerusalem. His mother's name was Hamutal; she was Jeremiah's daughter and was from Libnah. ³²He did what was evil in the Lord's eyes, just as all his ancestors had done. ³³Pharaoh Neco made Jehoahaz a prisoner at Riblah in the land of Hamath, ending his rule in Jerusalem. Pharaoh Neco imposed a fine on the land totaling one hundred kikkars of silver and one kikkar of gold.

Jehoiakim rules Judah

³⁴Pharaoh Neco made Eliakim, Josiah's son, king after his father Josiah. Neco changed Eliakim's name to Jehoiakim. Neco took Jehoahaz away; he later died in Egypt. ³⁵Jehoiakim gave Pharaoh the silver and gold, but he taxed the land in order to meet Pharaoh's financial demands. Each person was taxed appropriately. Jehoiakim exacted silver and the gold from the land's people in order to give it to Pharaoh Neco. ³⁶Jehoiakim was 25 years old when he became king, and he ruled for eleven years in Jerusalem. His mother's name was Zebidah; she was Pedaiah's daughter and was from Rumah. ³⁷He did what was evil in the Lord's eyes, just as all his ancestors had done.

24 In Jehoiakim's days, King Nebuchadnezzar of Babylon attacked. Jehoiakim had submitted to him for three years, but then Jehoiakim changed his mind and rebelled against him. ²The Lord sent Chaldean, Aramean, Moabite, and Ammonite raiding parties against Jehoiakim, sending them against Judah in order to destroy it. This was in agreement with the word that the Lord had spoken through his servants the prophets. ³Indeed, this happened to Judah because the Lord commanded them to be removed from his presence on account of all the sins that Manasseh had committed ⁴and because of the innocent blood that he had spilled. Manasseh had filled Jerusalem with innocent blood, and the LORD didn't want to forgive that.

⁵The rest of Jehoiakim's deeds and all that he accomplished, aren't they written in the official records of Judah's kings? ⁶Jehoiakim lay down with his ancestors. His son Jehoiachin succeeded him as king.

⁷The Egyptian king never left his country again because the Babylonian king had taken over all the territory that had previously belonged to him—from the border of Egypt to the Euphrates River.

Jehoiachin rules Judah

⁸Jehoiachin was 18 years old when he became king, and he ruled for three months in Jerusalem. His mother's name was Nehushta; she was Elnathan's daughter and was from Jerusalem. ⁹He did what was evil in the LORD's eyes, just as all his ancestors had done. ¹⁰At that time, the officers of Babylon's King Nebuchadnezzar attacked Jerusalem and laid siege to the city. ¹¹Babylon's King Nebuchadnezzar himself arrived at the city while his officers were blockading it. ¹²Judah's King Jehoiachin, along with his mother, his servants, his officers, and his officials, came out to surrender to the Babylonian king. The Babylonian king took Jehoiachin prisoner in the eighth year of Jehoiachin's rule.

¹³Nebuchadnezzar also took away all the treasures of the LORD's temple and of the royal palace. He cut into pieces all the gold objects that Israel's King Solomon had made for the LORD's temple, which is exactly what the LORD said would happen. ¹⁴Then Nebuchadnezzar exiled all of Jerusalem: all the officials, all the military leaders—ten thousand exiles—as well as all the skilled workers and metalworkers. No one was left behind except the poorest of the land's people. ¹⁵Nebuchadnezzar exiled Jehoiachin to Babylon; he also exiled the queen mother, the king's wives, the officials, and the land's elite leaders from Jerusalem to Babylon. ¹⁶The Babylonian king also exiled seven thousand warriors—each one a hero trained for battle—as well as a thousand skilled workers and metalworkers to Babylon. ¹⁷Then the Babylonian king made Mattaniah, Jehoiachin's uncle, succeed

Jehoiachin as king. Nebuchadnezzar changed Mattaniah's name to Zedekiah.

Zedekiah rules Judah

¹⁸Zedekiah was 21 years old when he became king, and he ruled for eleven years in Jerusalem. His mother's name was Hamutal; she was Jeremiah's daughter and was from Libnah. ¹⁹He did what was evil in the LORD's eyes, just as Jehoiakim had done. ²⁰It was precisely because the LORD was angry with Jerusalem and Judah that he thrust them out of his presence.

The southern kingdom falls

Now Zedekiah rebelled against the Babylonian king. ¹So in the ninth year of **25** Zedekiah's rule, on the tenth day of the tenth month, Babylon's King Nebuchadnezzar attacked Jerusalem with his entire army. He camped beside the city and built a siege wall all around it. ²The city was under attack until King Zedekiah's eleventh year. ³On the ninth day of the month, the famine in the city got so bad that no food remained for the common people. ⁴Then the enemy broke into the city. All the soldiers fledᶻ by night using the gate between the two walls near the King's Garden. The Chaldeans were surrounding the city, so the soldiers ran toward the desert plain. ⁵But the Chaldean army chased King Zedekiah and caught up with him in the Jericho plains. His entire army deserted him. ⁶So the Chaldeans captured the king and brought him back to the Babylonian king, who was at Riblah. There his punishment was determined. ⁷Zedekiah's sons were slaughtered right before his eyes. Then he was blinded, put in bronze chains, and taken off to Babylon.

⁸On the seventh day of the fifth month in the nineteenth year of Babylon's King Nebuchadnezzar, Nebuzaradan arrived at Jerusalem. He was the commander of the guard and an official of the Babylonian king. ⁹He burned down the LORD's temple, the royal palace, and all of Jerusalem's houses. He burned down every important building. ¹⁰The whole Chaldean army under the commander of the guard tore down the walls surrounding Jerusalem. ¹¹Then Nebuzaradan the commander of the guard exiled the people who were left in the

---

ᶻLXX, cf Jer 52:7; MT lacks *fled.*

city, those who had already surrendered to Babylon's king, and the rest of the population. [12]The commander of the guard left some of the land's poor people behind to work the vineyards and be farmers. [13]The Chaldeans shattered the bronze columns, the stands, and the bronze Sea that were in the Lord's temple. They carried the bronze off to Babylon. [14]They also took the pots, the shovels, the wick trimmers, the dishes, and all the bronze items that had been used in the temple. [15]The commander of the guard took the fire pans and the sprinkling bowls, which were made of pure gold and pure silver. [16]The bronze in all these objects—the two pillars, the Sea, and the stands that Solomon had made for the Lord's temple—was too heavy to weigh. [17]Each pillar was twenty-seven feet high. The bronze capital on top of the first pillar was four and a half feet high. Decorative lattices and pomegranates, all made from bronze, were around the capital. And the second pillar was decorated with lattices just like the first.

[18]The commander of the guard also took away Seraiah the chief priest, Zephaniah the priest next in rank, and the three doorkeepers. [19]Of those still left in the city, Nebuzaradan took away an officer who was in charge of the army and five royal advisors who were discovered in the city. He also took away the secretary of the officer responsible for drafting the land's people to fight, as well as sixty people who were discovered in the city. [20]Nebuzaradan the commander of the guard took all of these people and brought them to the Babylonian king at Riblah. [21]The king of Babylon struck them down, killing them in Riblah in the land of Hamath.

So Judah was exiled from its land.

Gedaliah governs Judah

[22]Babylon's King Nebuchadnezzar put Gedaliah, Ahikam's son and Shaphan's grandson, in charge of the people he had left behind in the land of Judah. [23]All the army officers and their soldiers heard that the Babylonian king had appointed Gedaliah as governor, so they came with their men to Gedaliah at Mizpah. The officers were Ishmael, Nethaniah's son; Johanan, Kareah's son; Seraiah, Tanhumeth's son who was a Netophathite; and Jaazaniah, Maacathite's son. [24]Gedaliah made a solemn pledge to them and their soldiers, telling them, "Don't be afraid of the Chaldean officials. Stay in the land and serve the Babylonian king, and things will go well for you."

[25]But in the seventh month, Ishmael, Nethaniah's son and Elishama's grandson, who was from the royal family, came with ten soldiers, and they struck Gedaliah, and he died. They also killed the Judeans and the Chaldeans who were with him at Mizpah. [26]Then all the people, young and old, along with the army officers, departed for Egypt because they were afraid of the Chaldeans.

Jehoiachin in Babylon

[27]In the year that Awil-merodach[a] became king of Babylon, he released Judah's King Jehoiachin from prison. This happened in the thirty-seventh year of the exile of King Jehoiachin, on the twenty-seventh day of the twelfth month. [28]Awil-merodach spoke kindly to Jehoiachin and seated him above the other kings who were with him in Babylon. [29]So Jehoiachin took off his prisoner clothes and ate regularly in the king's presence for the rest of his life. [30]At the king's command, a regular food allowance was given to him every day for the rest of his life.

SAILBOAT

Kindness

Kindness Can Show Up Unexpectedly

2 Kings 25:28-30

The nation of Babylon had completely destroyed Judah just like God had warned (2 Kgs 24:1-4). But before wiping out Judah, Babylon captured King Jehoiachin and threw him into prison for rebelling (2 Kgs 24:8-12). After Jehoiachin sat in prison for thirty-seven years, the new king of Babylon, Awil-merodach, released him. This king of Babylon didn't just release his enemy, he spoke kindly to Jehoiachin and gave him a place to eat in his presence—a place above the other captured kings in Babylon. Even though Awil-merodach didn't follow God, his kindness was like the kindness King David showed the grandson of his greatest enemy (2 Sam 9). Because people are all made in the image of God (Gen 1:27), the kindness of God can show up in anyone, whether they follow God or not. ◈

---

[a]*Awil-merodach* means Man of Marduk in Akkadian.

1 Chronicles

Sometimes a story is so good you want to hear it twice! Much of the history told in 1 and 2 Samuel and 1 and 2 Kings is retold in 1 and 2 Chronicles. At the end of those books, the people of Judah were taken as prisoners to Babylon. But many years later, some of them went home. Their history, including how the people worshipped God, is recorded in 1 and 2 Chronicles.

First Chronicles begins with long lists of names. These names are the people who were a part of the families of Israel (1 Chron 1–9). Keeping a record of these names reminded the people of God's promise to be with them.

The rest of this book tells about King David. It tells how he brought the chest containing the covenant to Jerusalem and how he worshipped God (1 Chron 13–16). This book also records all the ways David prepared for his son Solomon to build a beautiful temple for God. David called for skilled workers and expensive materials. He organized priests and musicians to serve in the temple (1 Chron 22–29). David wanted the whole world to know that God is great. First Chronicles shows how important it is to worship God! ◊

Adam to Israel

1 Adam, Seth, Enosh; [2]Kenan, Mahalalel, Jared; [3]Enoch, Methuselah, Lamech; [4]Noah; Noah's family:[a] Shem, Ham, and Japheth.

[5]Japheth's family: Gomer, Magog, Madai, Javan, Tubal, Meshech, and Tiras.

[6]Gomer's family: Ashkenaz, Riphath,[b] and Togarmah.

[7]Javan's family: Elishah, Tarshish, Kittim, and Rodanim.

[8]Ham's family: Cush, Egypt, Put, and Canaan.

[9]Cush's family: Seba, Havilah, Sabta, Raama, and Sabteca.

Raamah's family: Sheba and Dedan.

[10]Cush was the father of Nimrod, the first warrior in the land.

[11]Egypt was the father of Ludim, Anamim, Lehabim, Naphtuhim, [12]Pathrusim, Casluhim, from whom the Philistines came, and Caphtorim.

[13]Canaan was the father of Sidon his oldest son, Heth, [14]the Jebusites, the Amorites, the Girgashites, [15]the Hivites, the Arkites, the Sinites, [16]the Arvadites, the Zemarites, and the Hamathites.

[17]Shem's family: Elam, Asshur, Arpachshad, Lud, and Aram.

Aram's family:[c] Uz, Hul, Gether, and Meshech.

[18]Arpachshad was Shelah's father, and Shelah was Eber's father. [19]Two sons were born to Eber: one was named Peleg,[d] because in his days the land was divided; and his brother's name was Joktan.

[20]Joktan was the father of Almodad, Sheleph, Hazarmaveth, Jerah, [21]Hadoram, Uzal, Diklah, [22]Ebal, Abimael, Sheba, [23]Ophir, Havilah, and Jobab. All these were Joktan's family.

[24]Shem, Arpachshad, Shelah; [25]Eber, Peleg, Reu; [26]Serug, Nahor, Terah; [27]and Abram, that is, Abraham.

[28]Abraham's family: Isaac and Ishmael. [29]These were their descendants. Ishmael's oldest son was Nebaioth, then Kedar, Adbeel, Mibsam, [30]Mishma, Dumah, Massa, Hadad, Tema, [31]Jetur, Naphish, and Kedemah. This was Ishmael's family.

[32]Abraham's secondary wife Keturah's family: she gave birth to Zimran, Jokshan, Medan, Midian, Ishbak, and Shuah.

Jokshan's family: Sheba and Dedan.

[33]Midian's family: Ephah, Epher, Hanoch, Abida, and Eldaah. All these were members of Keturah's family.

[34]Abraham was Isaac's father. Isaac's family: Esau and Israel.

[35]Esau's family: Eliphaz, Reuel, Jeush, Jalam, and Korah.

[36]Eliphaz's family: Teman, Omar, Zephi, Gatam, Kenaz, Timna, and Amalek.

[37]Reuel's family: Nahath, Zerah, Shammah, and Mizzah.

[38]Seir's family: Lotan, Shobal, Zibeon, Anah, Dishon, Ezer, and Dishan.

[39]Lotan's family: Hori and Homam; Lotan's sister was Timna.

[40]Shobal's family: Alian, Manahath, Ebal, Shephi, and Onam.

Zibeon's family: Aiah and Anah.

[41]Anah's family: Dishon.

Dishon's family: Hamran, Eshban, Ithran, and Cheran.

[42]Ezer's family: Bilhan, Zaavan, and Jaakan.

Dishan's family:[e] Uz and Aran.

[43]These were the kings who ruled in the land of Edom before any king ruled over the Israelites: Bela, Beor's son, whose city was called Dinhabah. [44]When Bela died, Jobab, Zerah's son from Bozrah, succeeded him. [45]When Jobab died, Husham from the land of the Temanites succeeded him. [46]When Husham died, Hadad, Bedad's son who defeated Midian in the Moabite countryside, succeeded him; his city was called Avith. [47]When Hadad died, Samlah from Masrekah succeeded him. [48]When Samlah died, Shaul from Rehoboth on the river succeeded him. [49]When Shaul died, Baal-hanan, Achbor's son, succeeded him. [50]When Baal-hanan died, Hadad succeeded him; his city was called Pai. His wife's name was Mehetabel, Matred's daughter and Me-zahab's granddaughter. [51]When Hadad died, Edom's tribal chiefs were: Chief Timna, Chief Aliah, Chief Jetheth, [52]Chief Oholibamah, Chief Elah, Chief Pinon, [53]Chief Kenaz, Chief Teman, Chief Mibzar,

---

[a]LXX; MT lacks *Noah's family*. [b]LXX; MT *Diphath* [c]LXX; MT lacks *Aram's family*. [d]Or *division* [e]Cf 1:38; or *Dishon's family*

⁵⁴Chief Magdiel, and Chief Iram. These were Edom's tribal chiefs.

2 This was Israel's family: Reuben, Simeon, Levi, Judah, Issachar, Zebulun, ²Dan, Joseph, Benjamin, Naphtali, Gad, and Asher.

Judah's line

³Judah's family: Er, Onan, and Shelah. These three were born to him with Bath-shua the Canaanite. Although Er was Judah's oldest, the Lord considered him wicked and put him to death. ⁴His daughter-in-law Tamar bore him Perez and Zerah. Judah had five sons in all.

⁵Perez's family: Hezron and Hamul.

⁶Zerah's family: Zimri, Ethan, Heman, Calcol, and Darda^f—five in all.

⁷Carmi's family: Achar, who made trouble for Israel by disobeying the law dedicating war spoils to God.

⁸Ethan's family: Azariah.

⁹Hezron's family, who were born to him: Jerahmeel, Ram, and Chelubai. ¹⁰Ram was the father of Amminadab, and Amminadab was the father of Nahshon, tribal chief of the Judeans. ¹¹Nahshon was the father of Salma, Salma was the father of Boaz, ¹²Boaz was the father of Obed, and Obed was the father of Jesse. ¹³Jesse was the father of Eliab his oldest son, Abinadab his second, Shimea his third, ¹⁴Nethanel his fourth, Raddai his fifth, ¹⁵Ozem his sixth, and David his seventh. ¹⁶Their sisters were Zeruiah and Abigail.

Zeruiah's family: Abishai, Joab, and Asahel—three in all. ¹⁷Abigail gave birth to Amasa, whose father was Jether the Ishmaelite.

¹⁸Caleb, Hezron's son, had children with his wife Azubah, and with Jerioth. These were her sons: Jesher, Shobab, and Ardon. ¹⁹After Azubah died, Caleb married Ephrath, who gave birth to Hur for him. ²⁰Hur was the father of Uri, and Uri was the father of Bezalel. ²¹Later, Hezron had sexual relations with the daughter of Machir, Gilead's father, whom he married when he was 60 years old, and she gave birth to Segub for him. ²²Segub was the

father of Jair, who owned twenty-three towns in the land of Gilead, ²³but Geshur and Aram took Havvoth-jair from them, as well as Kenath and its villages, sixty towns.

All these were descendants of Machir, Gilead's father. ²⁴After Hezron's death, Caleb went to Ephrath.^g Abijah, Hezron's wife, bore him Ashhur, Tekoa's father.

²⁵The family of Jerahmeel, Hezron's oldest son: Ram his oldest, Bunah, Oren, Ozem, and Ahijah. ²⁶Jerahmeel had another wife named Atarah; she was the mother of Onam.

²⁷The family of Ram, Jerahmeel's oldest son: Maaz, Jamin, and Eker.

²⁸Onam's family: Shammai and Jada.

Shammai's family: Nadab and Abishur. ²⁹Abishur's wife's name was Abihail, and she gave birth to Ahban and Molid for him.

³⁰Nadab's family: Seled and Appaim, but Seled died without children.

³¹Appaim's family: Ishi.

Ishi's family: Sheshan.

Sheshan's family: Ahlai.

³²The family of Jada, Shammai's brother: Jether and Jonathan, but Jether died without children.

³³Jonathan's family: Peleth and Zaza. These were Jerahmeel's descendants.

did you know? King David's ancestors are listed to show how David came from a line of important people who had done great things for God.

³⁴Sheshan had no sons, only daughters; but Sheshan had an Egyptian servant whose name was Jarha. ³⁵Sheshan gave his daughter in marriage to Jarha his servant, and she gave birth to Attai for him.

³⁶Attai was the father of Nathan, Nathan was the father of Zabad, ³⁷Zabad was the father of Ephlal, Ephlal was the father of Obed, ³⁸Obed was the father of Jehu, Jehu was the father of Azariah, ³⁹Azariah was the father of Helez, Helez was the father of Eleasah, ⁴⁰Eleasah was the father of Sismai, Sismai was the father of Shallum, ⁴¹Shallum was the father of

---

^f LXX, Syr; MT *Dara* ^g LXX, Vulg; MT *in Caleb-ephrathah*

Jekamiah, and Jekamiah was the father of Elishama.

⁴²The family of Caleb, Jerahmeel's brother: Mesha his oldest son and Ziph's father; and his second son[h] Mareshah, Hebron's father.

⁴³Hebron's family: Korah, Tappuah, Rekem, and Shema. ⁴⁴Shema was the father of Raham, Jorkeam's father; and Rekem was the father of Shammai.

⁴⁵Shammai's son: Maon; Maon was Beth-zur's father. ⁴⁶Ephah, Caleb's secondary wife, gave birth to Haran, Moza, and Gazez. Haran was the father of Gazez.

⁴⁷Jahdai's family: Regem, Jotham, Geshan, Pelet, Ephah, and Shaaph. ⁴⁸Maacah, Caleb's secondary wife, gave birth to Sheber and Tirhanah. ⁴⁹She also gave birth to Shaaph, Madmannah's father; and to Sheva, Machbenah and Gibea's father. Caleb's daughter was Achsah. ⁵⁰These were Caleb's descendants.

The family of Hur, Ephrathah's oldest son: Shobal, Kiriath-jearim's father; ⁵¹Salma, Bethlehem's father; and Hareph, Beth-gader's father.

⁵²Shobal, Kiriath-jearim's father, had a family: Haroeh, and the ancestor of half of the Menuhoth.[i] ⁵³Kiriath-jearim's clans: the Ithrites, the Puthites, the Shumathites, and the Mishraites. From these came the Zorathites and the Eshtaolites.

⁵⁴The family of Salma, Bethlehem's father:[j] the Netophathites, Atroth-beth-joab, half of the Manahathites, and the Zorites.

⁵⁵The clans of the scribes who lived at Jabez: the Tirathites, the Shimeathites, and the Sucathites. They were Kenites who descended from Hammath, Beth-rechab's father.

David's line

3 This is David's family born to him in Hebron: the oldest Amnon, with Ahinoam the Jezreelite; the second Daniel, with Abigail the Carmelite; ²the third Absalom son of Maacah, the daughter of Geshur's King Talmai; the fourth Adonijah, Haggith's son; ³the fifth Shephatiah

with Abital; the sixth Ithream, with his wife Eglah. ⁴Six were born to him in Hebron, where he reigned for seven and a half years. He also reigned in Jerusalem for thirty-three years. ⁵These were born to him in Jerusalem: Shimea, Shobab, Nathan, and Solomon—four from Bath-shua, Ammiel's daughter; ⁶Ibhar, Elishama, Eliphelet, ⁷Nogah, Nepheg, Japhia, ⁸Elishama, Eliada, and Eliphelet—nine in all. ⁹This was all of David's family, except for his secondary wives' children. Tamar was their sister.

¹⁰The descendants[k] of Solomon: Rehoboam, his son Abijah, his son Asa, his son Jehoshaphat, ¹¹his son Joram, his son Ahaziah, his son Joash, ¹²his son Amaziah, his son Azariah, his son Jotham, ¹³his son Ahaz, his son Hezekiah, his son Manasseh, ¹⁴his son Amon, and his son Josiah.

¹⁵Josiah's family: the oldest Johanan, the second Jehoiakim, the third Zedekiah, and the fourth Shallum.

¹⁶Jehoiakim's family: his son Jeconiah and his son Zedekiah.

¹⁷The family of Jeconiah the prisoner: Shealtiel his son; ¹⁸Malchiram, Pedaiah, Shenazzar, Jekamiah, Hoshama, and Nedabiah.

¹⁹Pedaiah's family: Zerubbabel and Shimei.

Zerubbabel's family:[l] Meshullam, Hananiah, and their sister Shelomith; ²⁰Hashubah, Ohel, Berechiah, Hasadiah, and Jushab-hesed—these five also.

²¹Hananiah's family:[m] Pelatiah, Jeshaiah, Rephaiah's family, Arnan's family, Obadiah's family, and Shecaniah's family.

²²Shecaniah's family: Shemaiah and his family, Hattush, Igal, Bariah, Neariah, and Shaphat—six in all.

²³Neariah's family: Elioenai, Hizkiah, and Azrikam—three in all.

²⁴Elioenai's family: Hodaviah, Eliashib, Pelaiah, Akkub, Johanan, Delaiah, and Anani—seven in all.

Judah's line

4 Judah's family: Perez, Hezron, Caleb,[n] Hur, and Shobal.

---

[h]Or the family of [i]Heb lacks the ancestor of. [j]Cf 2:51; Heb lacks father. [k]LXX, Syr; MT son [l]LXX, Syr; MT son [m]LXX, Syr, Tg; MT son [n]Cf 1 Chron 2:19; MT Carmi

[2]Shobal's son Reaiah was Jahath's father, and Jahath was the father of Ahumai and Lahad. These were the Zorathite clans.

[3]This was Etam's family:[o] Jezreel, Ishma, and Idbash. Their sister's name was Hazzelelponi. [4]Penuel was Gedor's father, and Ezer was Hushah's father.

This was the family of Hur the oldest son of Ephrathah, Bethlehem's father: [5]Ashhur, Tekoa's father, had two wives, Helah and Naarah. [6]Naarah gave birth to Ahuzzam, Hepher, Temeni, and Haahashtari for him. This was Naarah's family.

[7]Helah's family: Zereth, Zohar,[p] and Ethnan. [8]Koz was the father of Anub, Hazzobebah, and the clans of Aharhel, Harum's son.

[9]Jabez was more honored than his brothers. His mother had named him Jabez, saying, "I bore him in pain."[q] [10]Jabez called on Israel's God: "If only you would greatly bless me and increase my terri-

did you know? Sometimes the Bible lists names of people in families. These lists contain the names of people going back hundreds or even thousands of years. These lists may be hard to read, but people in Bible times believed it was important to know who was in their family and where they were from. Today information like this is called a *genealogy* or family tree.

tory. May your power go with me to keep me from trouble, so as not to cause me pain." And God granted his request.

[11]Chelub, Shuhah's brother, was the father of Mehir, who was Eshton's father. [12]Eshton was the father of Beth-rapha, Paseah, and Tehinnah, Ir-nahash's father. These are the men of Recah.

[13]Kenaz's family: Othniel and Seraiah. Othniel's family: Hathath and Meonothai.[r] [14]Meonothai was the father of Ophrah. Seraiah was the father of Joab the father of Ge-harashim,[s] so-called because they were skilled workers. [15]The family of Caleb, Jephunneh's son: Iru, Elah, and Naam. This was Kenaz's family.[t]

[16]Jehallelel's family: Ziph, Ziphah, Tiria, and Asarel.

[17]Ezrah's family:[u] Jether, Mered, Epher, and Jalon. Jether was the father of[v] Miriam, Shammai, and Ishbah, Eshtemoa's father. [18]His Judean wife gave birth to Jered, Gedor's father; Heber, Soco's father; and Jekuthiel, Zanoah's father.

This is the family of Bithiah, Pharaoh's daughter, whom Mered married. [19]The family of his Judean wife,[w] the sister of Naham, Keilah's father the Garmite and Eshtemoa the Maacathite.

[20]Shimon's family: Amnon, Rinnah, Ben-hanan, and Tilon.

Ishi's family: Zoheth and Ben-zoheth.

[21]The family of Shelah, Judah's son: Er, Lecah's father; Laadah, Mareshah's father; the clans of the linen workers at Bethashbea; [22]Jokim; the men of Cozeba; Joash; and Saraph, who married into[x] Moab but returned to Bethlehem[y] (the records are ancient). [23]They were the potters who lived in Netaim and Gederah; they lived there with the king in his service.

Simeon's line

[24]Simeon's family: Nemuel, Jamin, Jarib, Zerah, Shaul, [25]his son Shallum, his son Mibsam, and his son Mishma. [26]Mishma's family: his son Hammuel, his son Zaccur, and his son Shimei. [27]Shimei had sixteen sons and six daughters; but his brothers didn't have many children, and none of their clans became as numerous as the Judeans.

[28]They lived in Beer-sheba, Moladah, Hazar-shual, [29]Bilhah, Ezem, Tolad, [30]Bethuel, Hormah, Ziklag, [31]Beth-marcaboth, Hazar-susim, Beth-biri, and Shaaraim. These were their towns until David became king. [32]Their villages were Etam, Ain, Rimmon, Tochen, and Ashan—five towns—[33]as well as all their villages around these towns as far as Baal. These were their settlements, and they kept their own family records:

[34]Meshobab, Jamlech, Joshah son of Amaziah, [35]Joel, Jehu son of Joshibiah son

[o]LXX; MT *father* [p]Qere, LXX; Kethib *Izhar* [q]Heb sounds like *Jabez.* [r]LXX, Vulg; MT lacks *Meonothai.* [s]Or *the valley of skilled workers* [t]Cf 4:13; MT *the family of Elah and Kenaz* [u]LXX, Vulg; MT *son* [v]LXX; MT *and she conceived* [w]LXX; MT *the wife of Hodiah* [x]Or *ruled over* [y]Cf Tg, Vulg; MT *Lehem returned*

of Seraiah son of Asiel, [36]Elioenai, Jaakobah, Jeshohaiah, Asaiah, Adiel, Jesimiel, Benaiah, [37]and Ziza son of Shiphi son of Allon son of Jedaiah son of Shimri son of Shemaiah. [38]These mentioned by name were leaders in their clans, and their households increased greatly.

[39]They went to the entrance of Gedor, as far as the east side of the valley, to find pasture for their flocks. [40]They found fertile pasture, and the land was spacious, quiet, and peaceful; the people of Ham used to live there. [41]These whose names were recorded, however, came in the days of Judah's King Hezekiah, attacked their tents and the Meunim[z] found there, and completely destroyed them, as can be seen today. They settled in their place, because there was pasture there for their flocks. [42]Some of them, five hundred Simeonites, went to Mount Seir, led by Pelatiah, Neariah, Rephaiah, and Uzziel, Ishi's sons. [43]They struck down those who were left of the Amalekites and have lived there ever since.

Lines of Reuben, Gad, and East Manasseh

5 The family of Reuben, Israel's oldest son: he was actually the oldest, but when he dishonored his father's bed his birthright[a] was given to the family of Joseph, Israel's son, so Reuben isn't listed as the oldest in the records. [2]Although Judah became the strongest among his brothers and a leader came from him, the birthright belonged to Joseph.

[3]The family of Reuben, Israel's oldest son: Hanoch, Pallu, Hezron, and Carmi.

[4]Joel's family: his son Shemaiah, his son Gog, his son Shimei, [5]his son Micah, his son Reaiah, his son Baal, [6]and his son Beerah, whom Assyria's King Tilgath-pilneser carried away into exile. He was a chief of the Reubenites. [7]His relatives, by their[b] clans when their genealogy was listed in the records, were: Jeiel the first; Zechariah; [8]and Bela, Azaz's son, Shema's grandson, and Joel's great-grandson.

They lived in Aroer, as far as Nebo and Baal-meon. [9]They also settled in the east as far as the edge of the desert that stretches to the Euphrates River, because their livestock

had increased in the land of Gilead. [10]In Saul's days they waged war on the Hagrites, whom they defeated. So they lived in their tents throughout the entire region east of Gilead.

[11]Gad's family lived opposite them in the land of Bashan as far as Salecah: [12]Joel was the first, Shapham the second, and Janai governed[c] Bashan.

[13]Their relatives according to their households: Michael, Meshullam, Sheba, Jorai, Jacan, Zia, and Eber—seven in all.

[14]This was the family of Abihail son of Huri son of Jaroah son of Gilead son of Michael son of Jeshishai son of Jahdo son of Buz. [15]Ahi, Abdiel's son and Guni's grandson, was the head of their household.

[16]They lived in Gilead, in Bashan and in its towns, and as far as the boundaries of all the open lands of Sharon. [17]They were all listed in the records in the days of Judah's King Jotham and Israel's King Jeroboam. [18]The Reubenites, the Gadites, and half the tribe of Manasseh were warriors who carried shield and sword, drew the bow, and were trained for war—44,760 ready for military service. [19]When they waged war on the Hagrites (the Jeturites, the Naphishites, and the Nodabites), [20]they received help against them. The Hagrites and all who were with them were handed over to them, because they cried out to God in battle. God granted their prayer because they trusted in him. [21]They seized their livestock: 50,000 of their camels, 250,000 sheep and goats, 2,000 donkeys, and 100,000 captives. [22]Many died, because God fought the battle. They lived there in place of the inhabitants until the exile.

[23]The members of half the tribe of Manasseh lived in the land from Bashan to Baal-hermon, Senir, and Mount Hermon. They were very numerous.

[24]These were the heads of their households:

Epher, Ishi, Eliel, Azriel, Jeremiah, Hodaviah, and Jahdiel—mighty warriors, famous men, heads of their households.

[25]But they were unfaithful to the God of their ancestors and faithlessly followed the gods of the peoples of the land, whom God had destroyed before them. [26]As a result,

---

[z] Qere; Kethib *Meinim* [a] Or *oldest son's rights* [b] LXX[L], Syr; MT *his* [c] LXX, Tg; MT *Shaphat in*

Israel's God stirred up the spirit of Assyria's King Pul, otherwise known as Assyria's King Tilgath-pilneser, who led the Reubenites, the Gadites, and half the tribe of Manasseh into exile, and brought them to Halah, Habor, Hara, and the Gozan River, where they remain to this day.

High priests

6[d] Levi's family: Gershom, Kohath, and Merari.

²Kohath's family: Amram, Izhar, Hebron, and Uzziel.

³Amram's family: Aaron, Moses, and Miriam.

Aaron's family: Nadab, Abihu, Eleazar, and Ithamar.

⁴Eleazar was the father of Phinehas, Phinehas of Abishua, ⁵Abishua of Bukki, Bukki of Uzzi, ⁶Uzzi of Zerahiah, Zerahiah of Meraioth, ⁷Meraioth of Amariah, Amariah of Ahitub, ⁸Ahitub of Zadok, Zadok of Ahimaaz, ⁹Ahimaaz of Azariah, Azariah of Johanan, ¹⁰and Johanan of Azariah. He was the one who served as priest in the temple that Solomon built in Jerusalem.

¹¹Azariah was the father of Amariah, Amariah of Ahitub, ¹²Ahitub of Zadok, Zadok of Shallum, ¹³Shallum of Hilkiah, Hilkiah of Azariah, ¹⁴Azariah of Seraiah, and Seraiah of Jehozadak. ¹⁵Jehozadak went away when the Lord caused Judah and Jerusalem to be exiled by Nebuchadnezzar.

Levites

¹⁶ᵉLevi's family: Gershom, Kohath, and Merari.

¹⁷These are the names of Gershom's family: Libni and Shimei.

¹⁸Kohath's family: Amram, Izhar, Hebron, and Uzziel.

¹⁹Merari's family: Mahli and Mushi.

These are the Levites' clans according to their fathers:

²⁰Of Gershom: his son Libni, his son Jahath, his son Zimmah, ²¹his son Joah, his son Iddo, his son Zerah, and his son Jeatherai.

²²Kohath's family: his son Amminadab, his son Korah, his son Assir, ²³his son Elkanah, his son Ebiasaph, his son Assir,

²⁴his son Tahath, his son Uriel, his son Uzziah, and his son Shaul.

²⁵Elkanah's family: Amasai and Ahimoth, ²⁶his son Elkanah,[f] his son Zophai, his son Nahath, ²⁷his son Eliab, his son Jeroham, and his son Elkanah.

²⁸Samuel's family: the oldest Joel,[g] and the second Abijah.

²⁹Merari's family: Mahli, his son Libni, his son Shimei, his son Uzzah, ³⁰his son Shimea, his son Haggiah, and his son Asaiah.

Levitical singers

³¹David put the following in charge of the music in the Lord's house after the chest was placed there. ³²They ministered with song before the dwelling of the meeting tent, until Solomon built the Lord's temple in Jerusalem. They carried out their usual duties. ³³Those who served and their families were:

Kohath's family: Heman the singer, son of Joel son of Samuel ³⁴son of Elkanah son of Jeroham son of Eliel son of Toah ³⁵son of Zuph son of Elkanah son of Mahath son of Amasai ³⁶son of Elkanah son of Joel son of Azariah son of Zephaniah ³⁷son of Tahath son of Assir son of Ebiasaph son of Korah ³⁸son of Izhar son of Kohath son of Levi son of Israel. ³⁹His relative was Asaph, who stood on his right, that is, Asaph son of Berechiah son of Shimea ⁴⁰son of Michael son of Baaseiah son of Malchijah ⁴¹son of Ethni son of Zerah son of Adaiah ⁴²son of Ethan son of Zimmah son of Shimei ⁴³son of Jahath son of Gershom son of Levi.

⁴⁴On the left were their relatives, Merari's family: Ethan son of Kishi son of Abdi son of Malluch ⁴⁵son of Hashabiah son of Amaziah son of Hilkiah ⁴⁶son of Amzi son of Bani son of Shemer ⁴⁷son of Mahli son of Mushi son of Merari son of Levi. ⁴⁸Their relatives the Levites were dedicated to all the services of the dwelling for God's house.

Priests from Aaron's line

⁴⁹Aaron and his sons sacrificed on the altar for entirely burned offerings and on the altar for incense, doing all the work of the holiest place, to make reconciliation for Israel, just as Moses, God's servant, had commanded.

ᵈ5:27 in Heb ᵉ6:1 in Heb ᶠLXX; MT repeats *Elkanah*. ᵍLXX, Syr; MT lacks *Joel*.

⁵⁰This was Aaron's family: his son Eleazar, his son Phinehas, his son Abishua, ⁵¹his son Bukki, his son Uzzi, his son Zerahiah, ⁵²his son Meraioth, his son Amariah, his son Ahitub, ⁵³his son Zadok, and his son Ahimaaz.

Levitical cities

⁵⁴These are the places they lived by their camps within their territory. To Aaron's family from the Kohathite clan, as chosen by lot, ⁵⁵they gave Hebron in the land of Judah with its surrounding pasturelands. ⁵⁶But the city's fields and its settlements they gave to Caleb, Jephunneh's son. ⁵⁷To Aaron's family they gave the refuge cities: Hebron, Libnah with its pasturelands, Jattir, Eshtemoa with its pasturelands, ⁵⁸Hilenʰ with its pasturelands, Debir with its pasturelands, ⁵⁹Ashan with its pasturelands, Juttah with its pasturelands,ⁱ and Beth-shemesh with its pasturelands. ⁶⁰From Benjamin's tribe: Gibeon with its pasturelands,ʲ Geba with its pasturelands, Alemeth with its pasturelands, and Anathoth with its pasturelands. They had thirteen towns within their clan.

⁶¹The remaining Kohathites were given ten towns by lot from the clan of half the tribe of Manasseh. ⁶²The Gershomites received by lot according to their clans thirteen towns from the tribes of Issachar, Asher, Naphtali, and Manasseh in Bashan. ⁶³The Merarites received by lot according to their clans twelve towns from the tribes of Reuben, Gad, and Zebulun. ⁶⁴In this way the Israelites gave the Levites the towns with their pasturelands. ⁶⁵They gave these towns, which they designated by name, by lot from the tribes of Judah, Simeon, and Benjamin.

⁶⁶Some of the Kohathite clans had towns of their territory from the tribe of Ephraim. ⁶⁷They gave them refuge cities: Shechem with its pasturelands in the Ephraimite highlands, Gezer with its pasturelands, ⁶⁸Jokmeam with its pasturelands, Beth-horon with its pasturelands, ⁶⁹Aijalon with its pasturelands, Gath-rimmon with its pasturelands; ⁷⁰and from half the tribe of Manasseh, Taanachᵏ with its pasturelands, and Bileam with its pasturelands, for the Kohathite clans who remained.

⁷¹To the Gershomites from the clan of half the tribe of Manasseh: Golan in Bashan with its pasturelands and Ashtaroth with its

---

ʰLXX, cf Josh 15:51; MT *Hilez*   ⁱLXX, Syr, cf Josh 21:16; MT lacks *Juttah.*   ʲCf Josh 21:17; MT lacks *Gibeon.*   ᵏCf Josh 21:25; MT *Aner*

If You Sing, Sing!   *1 Chronicles 6:31-32*

When David brought the chest containing the covenant back into God's temple, he appointed some people to be in charge of the singing. Their music was a way to worship God and to minister to others with their voices. People have always used music as one way to worship God. In many churches today, some people have the job to plan the singing and help people learn to sing to God.

Music helps us think about God and talk to God in a special way. It helps us feel God's love and spirit in us. Throughout the Bible are songs that praise God and tell the world what God has done. Singing songs together in church about who God is and what God has done helps us grow closer to God and closer as God's people.

How does music help you feel close to God?

How can you use your voice to sing for God?

pasturelands; [72] from the tribe of Issachar: Kedesh with its pasturelands and Daberath with its pasturelands,[73] Ramoth with its pasturelands and Anem with its pasturelands; [74] from the tribe of Asher: Mashal with its pasturelands, Abdon with its pasturelands, and [75] Helkath[l] with its pasturelands and Rehob with its pasturelands; [76] and from the tribe of Naphtali: Kedesh in Galilee with its pasturelands, Hammon with its pasturelands, and Kiriathaim with its pasturelands. [77] To the remaining Merarites from the tribe of Zebulun: Jokneam with its pasturelands,[m] Rimmon[n] with its pasturelands, Tabor with its pasturelands, and Nahalal with its pasturelands;[o] [78] on the other side of the Jordan at Jericho, on the east side of the Jordan, from the tribe of Reuben: Bezer in the desert with its pasturelands, Jahzah with its pasturelands, [79] Kedemoth with its pasturelands, and Mephaath with its pasturelands; [80] and from the tribe of Gad: Ramoth in Gilead with its pasturelands, Mahanaim with its pasturelands, [81] Heshbon with its pasturelands, and Jazer with its pasturelands.

Issachar's line

7 Issachar's family: Tola, Puah, Jashub, and Shimron—four in all. [2] Tola's family: Uzzi, Rephaiah, Jeriel, Jahmai, Ibsam, and Shemuel—the heads of their households in Tola's line, mighty warriors of their generations. In David's time they numbered 22,600. [3] Uzzi's family: Izrahiah; and Izrahiah's family—Michael, Obadiah, Joel, and Isshiah—five in all, and all of them leaders. [4] According to the family records of their households, they had 36,000 troops in the units of their fighting force, since they had many wives and children. [5] Their relatives from all of Issachar's clans were 87,000 mighty warriors, all listed in the family records.

Lines of Benjamin and Naphtali

[6] Benjamin's family:[p] Bela, Becher, and Jediael—three in all. [7] Bela's family: Ezbon, Uzzi, Uzziel,

Jerimoth, and Iri—five heads of households, mighty warriors; 22,034 were listed in their family records. [8] Becher's family: Zemirah, Joash, Eliezer, Elioenai, Omri, Jeremoth, Abijah, Anathoth, and Alemeth. These were all Becher's family. [9] As listed in their family records by generation, as heads of their households, mighty warriors, there were 22,200. [10] Jediael's family: Bilhan.

Bilhan's family: Jeush, Benjamin, Ehud, Chenaanah, Zethan, Tarshish, and Ahishahar. [11] All these were Jediael's family, heads of their households, and mighty warriors. There were 17,200 ready for battle. [12] The Shuppites and Huppites were Ir's family, and the Hushites were Aher's family.

[13] Naphtali's family: Jahziel, Guni, Jezer, and Shallum. These were Bilhah's family.

Manasseh's line

[14] Manasseh's family: Asriel, to whom his Aramean secondary wife gave birth. She gave birth to Machir, Gilead's father. [15] Machir married Huppite and Shuppite women. His sister's name was Maacah. The second descendant's name was Zelophehad, who had only daughters. [16] Machir's wife Maacah gave birth to a son and named him Peresh. His brother's name was Sheresh, and his sons were Ulam and Rekem.

[17] Ulam's family: Bedan.

This was the family of Gilead, Machir's son and Manasseh's grandson. [18] His sister Hammolecheth gave birth to Ishhod, Abiezer, Mahlah, and Shemida.[q] [19] The members of Shemida's family were Ahian, Shechem, Likhi, and Aniam.

Ephraim's line

[20] Ephraim's family: Shuthelah, his son Bered, his son Tahath, his son Eleadah, his son Tahath, [21] his son Zabad, his son Shuthelah, and Ezer and Elead. The men of Gath, who were born in the land, killed them when they came down to take their cattle. [22] Ephraim their father mourned many days, and his brothers came to comfort him.

---

[l] Cf Josh 21:31; MT *Hukkok* [m] Cf Josh 21:34; MT lacks *Jokneam*. [n] LXX; MT *Rimmono* [o] Cf Josh 21:35; MT lacks *Nahalal*. [p] LXX; MT lacks *family*. [q] Cf 7:19, Josh 17:2; MT lacks *and Shemida*.

²³Ephraim had sex with his wife, and she conceived and gave birth to a son. He named him Beriah, because misfortune had come to his house. ²⁴His daughter was Sheerah. She built both Lower and Upper Beth-horon and Uzzen-sheerah. ²⁵His son was Rephah, his son[r] Resheph, his son Telah, his son Tahan, ²⁶his son Ladan, his son Ammihud, his son Elishama, ²⁷his son Nun, and his son Joshua. ²⁸Their possessions and settlements were Bethel and its towns, to the east Naaran, and to the west Gezer and its towns, and Shechem and its towns as far as Ayyah and its towns. ²⁹Beth-shean and its towns, Taanach and its towns, Megiddo and its towns, and Dor and its towns were under Manassite authority. The family of Joseph, Israel's son, lived in them.

Asher's line

³⁰Asher's family: Imnah, Ishvah, Ishvi, Beriah, and their sister Serah. ³¹Beriah's family: Heber and Malchiel, who was Birzaith's father. ³²Heber was the father of Japhlet, Shomer, Hotham, and their sister Shua. ³³Japhlet's family: Pasach, Bimhal, and Ashvath. This is Japhlet's family. ³⁴Shemer's family: Ahi, Rohgah, Jehubbah, and Aram. ³⁵His brother Helem's family: Zophah, Imna, Shelesh, and Amal. ³⁶Zophah's family: Suah, Harnepher, Shual, Beri, Imrah, ³⁷Bezer, Hod, Shamma, Shilshah, Ithran, and Beera. ³⁸Jether's family: Jephunneh, Pispa, and Ara. ³⁹Ulla's family: Arah, Hanniel, and Rizia. ⁴⁰All these were Asher's family, heads of households, select mighty warriors, the heads of the princes. Those ready for battle listed in the records numbered 26,000.

Benjamin's line

8Benjamin was the father of Bela his oldest son, Ashbel his second son, Aharah the third, ²Nohah the fourth, and Rapha the fifth.

³Bela had a family: Addar, Gera, Abihud, ⁴Abishua, Naaman, Ahoah, ⁵Gera, Shephuphan, and Huram.

⁶This was Ehud's family. They were heads of households of the inhabitants of Geba, who were sent into exile to Manahath. ⁷Gera[s] sent them into exile and was the father of Uzza and Ahihud.

⁸Shaharaim had children in the country of Moab after he divorced his wives Hushim and Baara. ⁹He had children with his wife Hodesh: Jobab, Zibia, Mesha, Malcam, ¹⁰Jeuz, Sachia, and Mirmah. These were his sons, heads of households. ¹¹He also had children with Hushim: Abitub and Elpaal.

¹²Elpaal's family: Eber, Misham, Shemed, who built Ono and Lod with its towns, ¹³Beriah, and Shema. They were heads of households of the inhabitants of Aijalon, who drove out the inhabitants of Gath. ¹⁴Their brothers[t] were Shashak and Jeremoth.

¹⁵Beriah's family: Zebadiah, Arad, Eder, ¹⁶Michael, Ishpah, and Joha.

¹⁷Elpaal's family: Zebadiah, Meshullam, Hizki, Heber, ¹⁸Ishmerai, Izliah, and Jobab.

¹⁹Shimei's family: Jakim, Zichri, Zabdi, ²⁰Elienai, Zillethai, Eliel, ²¹Adaiah, Beraiah, and Shimrath.

²²Shashak's family: Ishpan, Eber, Eliel, ²³Abdon, Zichri, Hanan, ²⁴Hananiah, Omri,[u] Elam, Anthothijah, ²⁵Iphdeiah, and Penuel.

²⁶Jeroham's family: Shamsherai, Shehariah, Athaliah, ²⁷Jaareshiah, Elijah, and Zichri.

²⁸These were the heads of households, in their generations. They were leaders who lived in Jerusalem. ²⁹Jeiel,[v] Gibeon's father, lived in Gibeon. His wife's name was Maacah; ³⁰his oldest son was Abdon, then Zur, Kish, Baal, Ner,[w] Nadab, ³¹Gedor, Ahio, Zecher, and Mikloth.

³²Mikloth was the father of Shimeah. These also lived near their relatives in Jerusalem.[x]

³³Ner was the father of Kish, Kish was the father of Saul, and Saul was the father

---

[r]MT lacks *his son.* [s]MT *Naaman, Ahijah, and Gera* [t]LXX; MT *Ahio* [u]LXX; MT lacks *Omri.* [v]LXX; MT lacks *Jeiel.* [w]LXX; MT lacks *Ner.* [x]Syr; MT adds *with their relatives.*

of Jonathan, Malchishua, Abinadab, and Esh-baal.

³⁴Jonathan's son was Merib-baal, and Merib-baal was Micah's father.

³⁵Micah's family: Pithon, Melech, Tarea, and Ahaz.

³⁶Ahaz was the father of Jehoaddah; Jehoaddah was the father of Alemeth, Azmaveth, and Zimri; and Zimri was the father of Moza. ³⁷Moza was the father of Binea; his son was Raphah, his son El-easah, and his son Azel. ³⁸Azel had six sons, named Azrikam, his oldest,ʸ Ishmael, Sheariah, Azariah,ᶻ Obadiah, and Hanan. All these were in Azel's family.

³⁹His brother Eshek's family: Ulam his oldest, Jeush the second, and Eliphelet the third. ⁴⁰Ulam's family were mighty warriors and archers, having many children and grandchildren—150 in all and all were Benjaminites.

9 So all Israel was listed in the official records of Israel's kings.

Restored Jerusalem community

Judah was carried into exile in Babylon because of their unfaithfulness. ²The first to resettle their property in their towns were the Israelite people, the priests, the Levites, and the temple servants. ³Those settling in Jerusalem included some from Judah, some from Benjamin, and some from Ephraim and Manasseh:

Judah and Benjamin

⁴Uthai son of Ammihud son of Omri son of Imri son of Bani from the family of Perez, Judah's son.

⁵From the Shilonites: Asaiah the oldest son and his family.

⁶From Zerah's family: Jeuel and their relatives—690 in all.

⁷From Benjamin's family: Sallu son of Meshullam son of Hodaviah son of Senaah;ᵃ ⁸Ibneiah, Jeroham's son; Elah son of Uzzi son of Michri; Meshullam son of Shephatiah son of Reuel son of Ibnijah; ⁹and their relatives in their line of descent—956 in all. All of these were heads of their households.

Priests and Levites

¹⁰From the priests: Jedaiah, Jehoiarib, Jachin, ¹¹and Azariah son of Hilkiah son of Meshullam son of Zadok son of Meraioth son of Ahitub the leader of God's house; ¹²Adaiah son of Jeroham son of Pashhur son of Malchijah; Maasai son of Adiel son of Jahzerah son of Meshullam son of Meshillemith son of Immer; ¹³and their relatives, heads of their households, 1,760 capable men for the religious work of God's house.

¹⁴From the Levites: Shemaiah son of Hasshub son of Azrikam son of Hashabiah, from Merari's family; ¹⁵Bakbakkar, Heresh, Galal, and Mattaniah son of Mica son of Zichri son of Asaph; ¹⁶Obadiah son of Shemaiah son of Galal son of Jeduthun; and Berechiah son of Asa son of El-kanah, who lived in the settlements of the Netophathites.

Gatekeepers

¹⁷The gatekeepers: Shallum, Akkub, Talmon, and Ahiman. Their brother Shallum was the leader, ¹⁸stationed until now in the King's Gate on the east side. These were the gatekeepers belonging to the Levites' camp.

¹⁹Shallum, Kore's son, Ebiasaph's grandson, and Korah's great-grandson, and his relatives belonging to his household, the Korahites, served as gatekeepers at the tent's entrances, as their ancestors had been gatekeepers at the entrance to the LORD's camp.

²⁰Phinehas, Eleazar's son, the LORD be with him, was their leader in former times.

²¹Zechariah, Meshelemiah's son, was gatekeeper at the meeting tent's entrance.

²²All those selected as gatekeepers at the entrances were two hundred twelve. They were listed in the family records by their settlements. David and Samuel the seer assigned them to their trusted position. ²³So they and their descendants were the gatekeepers guarding the LORD's house, that is, the tent.ᵇ ²⁴The gatekeepers were on the four sides: east, west, north, and south. ²⁵Their relatives came in from their settlements, from time

---

ʸLXX,Tg; MT *Bocheru* ᶻLXX; MT lacks *Azariah*. ᵃLXX; MT *Hassenuah* ᵇOr *house of the tent*

to time, to assist them for a period of seven days. ²⁶Due to their trustworthiness, the four master gatekeepers, who were Levites, were in charge of the rooms and the treasuries of God's house. ²⁷They would spend the night patrolling God's house since they had guard duty and were responsible for unlocking it every morning. ²⁸Some of them were responsible for the worship objects; they counted them when they were brought in and taken out. ²⁹Others were appointed over the furniture, the holy equipment, the flour, wine, oil, incense, and spices. ³⁰Some of the priests blended the ointment for the spices; ³¹and Mattithiah, one of the Levites, the oldest son of Shallum the Korahite, was entrusted with baking the flat cakes. ³²Also some of their Kohathite relatives were responsible for preparing the stacks of bread for each Sabbath. ³³The singers were the heads of the households of the Levites. They lived in temple rooms and were free from other service because they were on duty day and night. ³⁴These were the heads of the households of the Levites, according to descent. They lived in Jerusalem.

Saul's family

³⁵Jeiel, Gibeon's father, lived in Gibeon. His wife's name was Maacah. ³⁶His oldest son was Abdon, followed by Zur, Kish, Baal, Ner, Nadab, ³⁷Gedor, Ahio, Zechariah, and Mikloth. ³⁸Mikloth was the father of Shimeam. They too lived near their relatives in Jerusalem.ᶜ ³⁹Ner was the father of Kish, Kish of Saul, Saul of Jonathan, Malchishua, Abinadab, and Esh-baal. ⁴⁰Jonathan's son was Merib-baal, and Merib-baal was the father of Micah. ⁴¹Micah's family were Pithon, Melech, Tahrea, and Ahaz.ᵈ ⁴²Ahaz was the father of Jarah; and Jarah of Alemeth, Azmaveth, and Zimri. Zimri was the father of Moza. ⁴³Moza was the father of Binea; Rephaiah was his son, Eleasah was his son, and Azel was his son. ⁴⁴Azel had six sons whose names were Azrikam, Bocheru, Ishmael, Sheariah, Obadiah, and Hanan. This was Azel's family.

Saul's death

10When the Philistines attacked the Israelites, the Israelites ran away from the Philistines, and many fell dead on Mount Gilboa. ²The Philistines overtook Saul and his sons, and they killed his sons Jonathan, Abinadab, and Malchishua. ³The battle was fierce around Saul, and when the archers located him, he trembled in fear. ⁴Saul said to his armor-bearer, "Draw your sword and kill me with it! Otherwise, these uncircumcised men will come and kill me or torture me." But his armor-bearer refused because he was terrified. So Saul took the sword and impaled himself on it. ⁵When the armor-bearer saw that Saul was dead, he also impaled himself on his sword and died with Saul. ⁶So Saul and his three sons died; his whole household died together. ⁷When all the Israelites who were in the valley saw that the army had run away and that Saul and his sons were dead, they abandoned their towns and fled. So the Philistines came to live in them.

⁸The next day when the Philistines came to strip the dead, they found Saul and his sons lying dead on Mount Gilboa. ⁹They stripped him, carried off his head and armor, and sent messengers throughout the land of the Philistines to spread the news to their idols and to the people. ¹⁰They placed his armor in their god's temple and displayed his skull on a pole in the temple of Dagon.

¹¹When all the people of Jabesh-gilead heard all that the Philistines had done to Saul, ¹²all their warriors arose and recovered the corpses of Saul and his sons. They brought them back to Jabesh, buried their bones under the oak in Jabesh, and fasted for seven days.

¹³Saul died because he was unfaithful to the LORD and hadn't followed the LORD's word. He even consulted a medium for guidance. ¹⁴He didn't consult the LORD, so the LORD killed him and gave the kingdom to David, Jesse's son.

All Israel makes David king

11All the Israelites gathered around David at Hebron. "We're your own flesh and blood," they said. ²"In the past, even when

---

ᶜHeb adds *with their relatives.* ᵈCf 8:35; MT lacks *Ahaz.*

Saul ruled over us, you were the one who led Israel. The LORD your God told you, 'You will shepherd my people Israel, and you will become a leader over my people Israel.'" ³So all of Israel's elders came to the king at Hebron, and David made a covenant with them before the LORD. They anointed David to make him king over Israel, just as the LORD had promised through Samuel.

David captures Jerusalem

⁴Then David and all Israel marched to Jerusalem, that is, Jebus, where the Jebusites lived. ⁵The people who lived in Jebus told David, "You'll never get in here!"

But David captured the mountain fortress of Zion, which became David's City. ⁶David had said, "The first one to kill a Jebusite will become commander in chief!" Joab, Zeruiah's son, was the first to attack and so became

LIFE PRESERVER

Didn't David die before the exile? 1 Chronicles 11:3

The author of Chronicles repeated a lot of information about the reign of David and his leadership of God's people. The purpose of retelling these stories was to help the people remember their exile in Babylon and their safe return. The author wanted them to understand that God had provided for them every step of the way. Remembering their history as God's people was important. ⬦

commander in chief. ⁷David occupied the fortress, so it was renamed David's City. ⁸He also built up the city on all sides, including its own foundations and the surrounding areas, while Joab restored the rest of the city. ⁹David grew increasingly powerful, and the LORD of heavenly forces was with him.

Following Directions   1 Chronicles 10:13

The game "Simon Says" is fun to play. Sometimes "Simon" calls out instructions so quickly that we have to listen extra closely to know if it was a true "Simon Says" or just a regular suggestion.

We should listen for instructions from God with the same focus. We should be really careful to hear the full instructions so we can obey without straying from our directions or adding to what was asked of us.

King Saul knew what his instructions from God were. He was supposed to lead an army to defeat the Amalekites, and he did. But his troops wanted to steal some of the farm animals from the defeated nation and give them to God. King Saul might have thought his heart was in the right place when he agreed to their suggestion, but he got into trouble because he did more than what God told him to do.

Samuel told King Saul, "Obeying is better than sacrificing, paying attention is better than fat from rams" (1 Sam 15:22). To *sacrifice* means to give something up for God or another person. Back then, God's people worshipped by sacrificing, or giving up their animals to God. Although worship is important, God wanted Saul to follow directions and not add to them. Obedience is even more important than worship.

How can you pay careful attention to God's directions?

How can you obey without straying or adding to what God asks?

David and his warriors

¹⁰These are the commanders of David's warriors who continued to support him while he was king. Together with all Israel, they made him king, as the LORD had promised Israel. ¹¹This is the list of David's warriors:

Jashobeam, a Hacmonite, was commander of the Thirty. He raised his spear against eight hundred, killing them on a single occasion.

¹²Next in command came Eleazar, Dodo's son the Ahohite, who was one of the three warriors. ¹³He was with David at Pas-dammim. The Philistines were gathered there for battle, where part of a field was full of barley. When the people ran away from the Philistines, ¹⁴he and David stood in the middle of the field, held their ground, and defeated the Philistines. So the LORD achieved a great victory.

¹⁵Three of the thirty commanders went down from the rock to David at the fortress*e* of Adullam, while the army of the Philistines camped in the Rephaim Valley. ¹⁶At that time David was in the fortress, and a Philistine fort was in Bethlehem. ¹⁷David had a craving and said, "If only someone could give me a drink of water from the well by the gate in Bethlehem." ¹⁸So the three warriors broke through the Philistine camp and drew water from the well by the gate in Bethlehem and brought it back to David. But he refused to drink it and poured it out to the LORD.

¹⁹"God forbid that I should do that," he said. "Isn't this the blood of men who risked their lives?" So he refused to drink it. Since they had brought it at the risk of their lives, David refused to drink it.

These were the kinds of things the three warriors did.

²⁰Abishai, Joab's brother, was chief of the Thirty.*f* He raised his spear against the three hundred men he had slain, but he wasn't considered one of the Three. ²¹He was the most famous of the Thirty. He became their commander, but he wasn't among the Three.

²²Benaiah, Jehoiada's son from Kabzeel, was a hero who performed great deeds. He killed two of Moab's leaders,*g* and on a snowy day went down into a pit where he killed a lion. ²³He also killed an Egyptian seven and a half feet tall, who was holding a spear like a weaver's beam. Benaiah went down to him with a club, grabbed the spear from the Egyptian's hand, and killed him with it. ²⁴These were the exploits of Benaiah, Jehoiada's son; he wasn't considered one of the three warriors. ²⁵He was famous among the Thirty, but didn't become one of the Three. David placed him in command of his own bodyguard.

²⁶The mighty warriors:

Asahel, Joab's brother;
Elhanan, Dodo's son from Bethlehem;
²⁷Shammoth from Haror;
Helez from Pelon;
²⁸Ira, Ikkesh's son from Tekoa;
Abiezer from Anathoth;
²⁹Sibbecai the Hushathite;
Ilai from Ahoh;
³⁰Maharai from Netophah;
Heled, Baanah's son from Netophah;
³¹Ithai, Ribai's son from Gibeah
of the Benjaminites;
Benaiah from Pirathon;
³²Hurai from the Gaash ravines;
Abiel the Arbathite;
³³Azmaveth from Baharum;
Eliahba from Shaalbon;
³⁴Hashem*h* the Gizonite;
Jonathan, Shagee's son from Harar;

SAILBOAT

COURAGE

Loyalty Brings Courage *1 Chronicles 11:15-19*
Because David was brave, other brave men followed him. One time David was thirsty between battles and really wanted the sweet water from a particular well next to a Philistine fort. Three of David's famous commanders overheard him talking about his wish. These three men then risked going to get the water for David. They were brave men, but they had seen and heard David do even braver things like kill Goliath (1 Sam 17) and lead men into victory, battle after battle (1 Sam 18:12-16). They loved and respected their commander so much that they were willing to do anything for him. The three men broke through the enemy camp and brought back a drink for David. David was honored, but he dedicated the water to God and poured it out. He knew only God deserved the kind of loyalty that made people risk their lives. ◊

---

*e*Or *cave;* cf 2 Sam 23:14   *f*Syr; MT *three*   *g*Heb *Ariel*   *h*MT *the family of Hashem*

³⁵Ahiam, Sachar's son from Harar;
Eliphal, Ur's son;
³⁶Hepher the Mecherathite;
Ahijah the Pelonite;
³⁷Hezro from Carmel;
Naarai, Ezbai's son;
³⁸Joel, Nathan's brother;
Mibhar, Hagri's son;
³⁹Zelek the Ammonite;
Naharai from Beeroth, Zeruiah's son
and the armor-bearer for Joab;
⁴⁰Ira from Ither;
Gareb from Ither;
⁴¹Uriah the Hittite;
Zabad, Ahlai's son;
⁴²Adina son of Shiza the Reubenite,
a leader of the Reubenites,
and thirty with him;
⁴³Hanan, Maacah's son;
Joshaphat the Mithnite;
⁴⁴Uzzia the Ashterathite;
Shama and Jeiel the sons of Hotham
the Aroerite;
⁴⁵Jediael, Shimri's son, and his brother
Joha the Tizite;
⁴⁶Eliel the Mahavite;
Jeribai and Joshaviah, Elnaam's sons;
Ithmah the Moabite;
⁴⁷Eliel, Obed, and Jaasiel the Mezobaite.

David's desert army

12 The following persons came to David at Ziklag while he was banished from the presence of Saul, Kish's son. They were some of the warriors who helped him in battle, ²armed with bows, and they could use either hand to shoot arrows or sling stones. They were Saul's relatives from Benjamin:

³Ahiezer was the leader, then Joash, both Shemaah's sons from Gibeah; Jeziel and Pelet, Azmaveth's sons; Beracah; Jehu of Anathoth; ⁴Ishmaiah from Gibeon, a warrior in the Thirty and a leader over the Thirty;ⁱ Jeremiah; Jahaziel; Johanan; Jozabad from Gederah; ⁵ʲEluzai; Jerimoth; Bealiah; Shemariah; Shephatiah the Haruphite; ⁶Elkanah, Isshiah, Azarel, Joezer, and Jashobeam the Korahites; ⁷Joelah; and Zebadiah, Jeroham's son from Gedor.

⁸Some left Gad to join David at the desert fortress, brave warriors trained for battle,

armed with shield and spear, who looked like lions and who were swift as gazelles on the mountains: ⁹Ezer the leader, Obadiah second, Eliab third, ¹⁰Mishmannah fourth, Jeremiah fifth, ¹¹Attai sixth, Eliel seventh, ¹²Johanan eighth, Elzabad ninth, ¹³Jeremiah tenth, Machbannai eleventh.

¹⁴These Gadites were military officers, the least of them ready to fight a hundred and the greatest a thousand. ¹⁵These are the ones who crossed the Jordan in the first month, when it was overflowing all its banks, and chased away everyone living in the valleys to the east and the west.

¹⁶Some Benjaminites and Judahites also came to David at the fortress. ¹⁷David went out to meet them and said to them, "If you've come to me with good intentions in order to help me, then we will join forces. But if you've come to betray me to my enemies, though I've done no wrong, then may our ancestors' God see it and punish you."

¹⁸Then a spirit took hold of Amasai, the leader of the Thirty:

David, we are yours;
and on your side, Jesse's son!
May it go very well for you,
and may it go well for whoever
helps you!
Yes, your God has helped you.

Then David received them, and put them at the head of his troops.

¹⁹Some of the Manassites also joined David when he came with the Philistines for the battle against Saul. But heᵏ didn't help them, because after considering the matter, the Philistine rulers sent him away. "He'll rejoin his master Saul," they said, "and it will cost us our heads." ²⁰When he went to Ziklag some joined him from Manasseh: Adnah, Jozabad, Jediael, Michael, Jozabad, Elihu, and Zillethai, leaders of units of a thousand in Manasseh. ²¹They helped David against the raiding bands because they were all warriors and officers in the army. ²²Reinforcements came to David daily until there was an army as mighty as God's army.

²³These are the numbers of the commanders of those armed for battle who came to

Bet you can
read this in 1 minute. Ready, set, go!

ⁱ12:5 in Heb ʲ12:6 in Heb ᵏLXX; MT *they*

David in Hebron to make sure he took over Saul's kingdom, according to the Lord's word: 24from Judah, carrying shield and spear, 6,800 troops armed for battle; 25from Simeon, mighty warriors, 7,100; 26from Levi, 4,600; 27also Jehoiada, leader of Aaron's line, and with him 3,700; 28and Zadok, a young man, a mighty warrior, and 22 officers from his household; 29from Benjamin, Saul's relatives, 3,000, most of whom had been loyal to Saul's household; 30from Ephraim, 20,800, mighty warriors, famous in their households; 31from half the tribe of Manasseh, 18,000, designated by name to come and make David king; 32from Issachar, those who understood the times and what Israel should do, 200 chiefs, with all their relatives under their command; 33from Zebulun, 50,000 experienced troops, armed for battle with all the weapons of war, to help with undivided loyalty; 34from Naphtali, 1,000 officers, as well as 37,000 armed with shield and spear; 35from Dan, 28,600 armed for battle; 36from Asher, 40,000 experienced troops armed for battle; 37from the other side of the Jordan, the Reubenites, Gadites, and the other half of the tribe of Manasseh, 120,000 armed with all the weapons of war.

38All these men of war, armed[l] for battle, came to Hebron determined to make David king over all Israel, and all the rest of Israel were fully agreed to make David king. 39They were there with David for three days, eating and drinking, while their relatives provided food for them. 40Even their neighbors from as far away as Issachar, Zebulun, and Naphtali were bringing food by donkeys, camels, mules, and oxen. There was an abundance of flour, fig cakes, clusters of raisins, wine, oil, oxen, and sheep, because Israel was joyful.

David's first attempt to move the chest

13After consulting with the captains of the units of a thousand and a hundred, in fact with every leader, 2David said to the entire Israelite assembly: "If you approve, and if the Lord our God agrees, let's spread the word to the rest of our relatives in all the regions of Israel, including the priests and Levites in their cities with pasturelands. Let's ask them to join us 3so that we may bring the chest of our God back to us, because we didn't look for it in Saul's days." 4The whole assembly agreed to do so, because all the people thought it was the right thing to do.

5So David assembled all Israel, from the border[m] of Egypt to Lebo-hamath in order to bring up God's chest from Kiriath-jearim. 6Then David and all Israel went up toward Baalah, to Kiriath-jearim, which belongs to Judah, to bring up from there the chest of God, the Lord, who sits enthroned on the winged creatures, where he is called by name.[n] 7They moved God's chest on a new cart from Abinadab's house. Uzzah and Ahio were guiding the cart, 8while David and all Israel celebrated in

LIGHTHOUSE
Special and Set Apart

Being Special and Set Apart Comes with a Cost *1 Chronicles 13:6-14*
A great day ended badly. David wanted the chest containing the covenant to be moved to Jerusalem. During the trip, Uzzah touched the chest to keep it from falling. God struck Uzzah for touching the chest, and Uzzah died. Despite his good heart, David didn't treat the chest like God wanted. The Israelites were moving the chest of God on a wagon, but it was supposed to be held by special poles (Exod 25:13-15) and carried only by special people (Deut 10:8). God made specific rules about the chest because it represented God's presence. God wanted Israel to know that God is completely set apart from the normal (Lev 11:44-45). This means God needs to be treated in a special way, and everything representing God is supposed to be treated in a special way. David paid the price for forgetting God is special and set apart. ◊

lLXX; MT *helpers* mHeb *Shikhor, river*; cf Josh 15:4; 1 Kgs 8:65; 2 Chron 7:8 nHeb uncertain

God's presence with all their strength, accompanied by songs, zithers, harps, tambourines, cymbals, and trumpets. ⁹When they came to Chidon's threshing floor, Uzzah reached out to the chest and grabbed it because the oxen had stumbled. ¹⁰But the LORD became angry with Uzzah and struck him because he had placed his hand on the chest. He died right there before God. ¹¹David was angry that the LORD lashed out at Uzzah; and so that place is still called Perez-uzzah today. ¹²David was frightened by God that day. "How will I ever bring God's chest home to me?" he asked. ¹³So David didn't take the chest away with him to David's City. Instead, he had it put in the house of Obed-edom the Gittite. ¹⁴God's chest stayed with Obed-edom's household for three months, and the LORD blessed Obed-edom's household and all that he had.

David's kingship established in Jerusalem

14Tyre's King Hiram sent messengers to David with cedar logs, bricklayers, and carpenters to build David a palace. ²Then David knew that the LORD had established him as king over Israel, and that his kingship was held in great honor for the sake of his people Israel. ³David married more secondary wives in Jerusalem and fathered more sons and daughters. ⁴The names of his children in Jerusalem were as follows: Shammua, Shobab, Nathan, Solomon, ⁵Ibhar, Elishua, Elpelet, ⁶Nogah, Nepheg, Japhia, ⁷Elishama, Beeliada, and Eliphelet.

David defeats the Philistines

⁸When the Philistines heard that David had been anointed king over all Israel, they all marched up to find him. David heard this and went out to confront them. ⁹The Philistines had invaded and were plundering the Rephaim Valley. ¹⁰David asked God for advice: "Should I attack the Philistines, and will you hand them over to me?"

The LORD answered, "Attack them, and I'll definitely hand them over to you."

¹¹So they marched up to Baal-perazim, and David defeated them there. "By my strength," David exclaimed, "God has burst out against my enemies, the way water bursts out." That's

why the place is called Baal-perazim.º ¹²The Philistines left their divine images behind, and David ordered them burned.

¹³When the Philistines plundered the valley a second time, ¹⁴David again asked God's advice, but God answered, "Don't attack them directly. Circle around behind them and come at them from in front of the balsam trees. ¹⁵As soon as you hear the sound of marching in the tops of the trees, then attack, for God has attacked in front of you to defeat the Philistine army." ¹⁶David followed God's orders exactly, and they defeated the Philistine army from Gibeon all the way to Gezer. ¹⁷David's fame spread throughout all lands, and the LORD made all the nations fear him.

LIGHTHOUSE

PRAYER

Pray for Wisdom *1 Chronicles 14:8-17*
When the Philistines invaded Israel shortly after David became king, David asked God whether or not he should attack them. God told him to attack and promised to help David defeat his enemies. Events happened just as God said. When the Philistines attacked again, David asked God once more what he should do. God gave David specific directions on how to win the battle over the Philistines. David obeyed God and sent his enemies running. One of the reasons David became famous was because he trusted God (1 Chron 14:16-17). Whenever he had an important decision to make, David trusted in God's wisdom to guide him to the right decision. God rewarded David's trust by giving him wisdom. ◉

David prepares to bring the chest to Jerusalem

15After he had built houses for himself in David's City, David prepared a place for God's chest and pitched a tent for it. ²David said, "Only the Levites may carry God's chest, because the LORD has chosen them to carry the LORD's chest and to minister to him forever."

³David assembled all Israel in Jerusalem to bring the LORD's chest to the place he had prepared for it. ⁴David also gathered Aaron's family and the Levites:

ºOr *master of outbursts*

5Uriel, the leader of Kohath's family,
and 120 of his relatives;
6Asaiah, the leader of Merari's family,
and 220 of his relatives;
7Joel, the leader of Gershom's family,
and 130 of his relatives;
8Shemaiah, the leader of Elizaphan's
family, and 200 of his relatives;
9Eliel, the leader of Hebron's family,
and 80 of his relatives;
10and Amminadab, the leader of Uzziel's family, and 112 of his relatives.

11David called for the priests Zadok and
Abiathar, and the Levites Uriel, Asaiah, Joel,
Shemaiah, Eliel, and Amminadab. 12He said
to them, "You are the household heads of
the Levites. Make yourselves holy, you and
your brothers, and then bring the chest of
the LORD, Israel's God, to the place I've prepared for it. 13When you weren't with us the
first time, the LORD our God burst out against
us because we didn't ask his advice properly." 14So the priests and the Levites made
themselves holy to bring up the chest of the
LORD, Israel's God. 15The Levites carried God's
chest with poles on their shoulders, just as
Moses had commanded according to the
LORD's word.

16Then David told the leaders of the Levites to appoint some of their relatives as
singers to raise their voices joyfully, accompanied by musical instruments, including
harps, lyres, and cymbals.

17So the Levites appointed Heman, Joel's
son; and from his relatives, Asaph, Berechiah's son; and from their Merarite relatives,
Ethan, Kushaiah's son; 18and second in rank
with them their relatives: Zechariah, Jaaziel,[p]
Shemiramoth, Jehiel, Unni, Eliab, Benaiah,
Maaseiah, Mattithiah, Eliphelehu, Mikneiah,
and Obed-edom and Jeiel the gatekeepers.

19The singers Heman, Asaph, and Ethan
were to make music with bronze cymbals.
20Zechariah, Aziel, Shemiramoth, Jehiel, Unni, Eliab, Maaseiah, and Benaiah
were to play harps tuned to the Alamoth.
21Mattithiah, Eliphelehu, Mikneiah,
Obed-edom, Jeiel, and Azaziah were to
lead with lyres tuned to the Sheminith.
22Chenaniah was leader of the Levites
who provided transportation,[q] because he
was skilled at it.
23Berechiah and Elkanah were gatekeepers for the chest.
24The priests Shebaniah, Joshaphat,
Nethanel, Amasai, Zechariah, Benaiah,
and Eliezer were to blow the trumpets
before God's chest. Obed-edom and Jehiah
also were to be gatekeepers for the chest.

David brings the chest to Jerusalem

25Then David, along with Israel's elders
and the captains of the thousands, went
with rejoicing to bring up the chest containing the LORD's covenant from Obed-edom's
house. 26Since God had helped the Levites
who were carrying the chest containing the
LORD's covenant, they sacrificed seven bulls
and seven rams. 27David wore a fine-linen
robe, as did the singers, all the Levites who
were carrying the chest, and Chenaniah, the
leader of transportation.[r] David also wore
a linen priestly vest.[s] 28So all Israel brought
up the chest containing the LORD's covenant
with shouts of joy, accompanied by the blast
of the ram's horn, by trumpets and cymbals,
and playing on harps and lyres. 29As the chest
containing the LORD's covenant entered David's City, Michal, Saul's daughter, looked
out the window. When she saw King David
leaping and dancing, she lost all
respect for him.

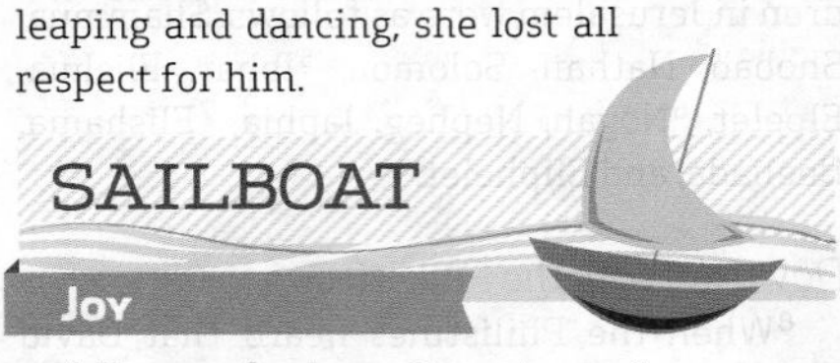

A Reason for Joy 1 Chronicles 15:28

The chest containing the covenant was coming to Jerusalem. It had been gone for a long time. First it was taken by the Philistines (1 Sam 4:10-11). Then when God punished the Philistines, they sent the chest back to Israel where it stayed in an out-of-the-way place (1 Sam 6:1–7:1). While Saul was king, he didn't care if the chest was close to him or not. But when David became king, he wanted the chest of God nearby. The Israelites rejoiced when David brought the chest into Jerusalem. They were joyful because they had a king who wanted God to be at the center of things. Putting God first was something to be happy about.

[p]LXX; MT *Jaaziel's son* [q]Heb uncertain [r]MT adds *the singers.* [s]Heb *ephod*

16

They brought in God's chest and placed it inside the tent David had pitched for it. Then they brought entirely burned offerings and well-being sacrifices before God. ²When David had finished offering the entirely burned offerings and the well-being sacrifices, he blessed the people in the LORD's name ³and distributed a loaf of bread, a piece of meat,ᵗ and a raisin cake to every Israelite man and woman.

LIGHTHOUSE

PRAISE GOD

A Name to Be Praised *1 Chronicles 16:1-7*

King David gave God the praise and glory God deserved. The chest containing the covenant had been brought into Jerusalem. The chest had been forgotten for a long time. But now that David was king, he was going to honor God by setting Levites around the chest to constantly remember, give thanks, and praise God. David himself sang praise to God on that first day. David's song remembered the promises God made to the Israelites—how God protected them and brought them into their own land. Then David praised God for simply being God. Even if God had never done anything for the Israelites, David knew God was so big and powerful that God deserved praise and honor just for existing. ♦

David establishes worship

⁴David appointed some of the Levites to serve before the LORD's chest in order to remember, to give thanks, and to praise the LORD, Israel's God: ⁵Asaph was the leader, and Zechariah his assistant; also Jeiel, Shemiramoth, Jehiel, Mattithiah, Eliab, Benaiah, Obed-edom, and Jeiel with harps and lyres; Asaph sounding the cymbals; ⁶and the priests Benaiah and Jahaziel blowing trumpets regularly before the chest containing God's covenant. ⁷On the same day, for the first time, David ordered Asaph and his relatives to give thanks to the LORD.

David's song of praise

⁸ Give thanks to the LORD,
  call on his name;
  make his deeds known to all people!
⁹ Sing to God, sing praises to him;
  dwell on all his wondrous works!
¹⁰ Give praise to God's holy name!
  Let the hearts of all those
    seeking the LORD rejoice!
¹¹ Pursue the LORD and his strength;
  seek his face always!
¹² Remember the wondrous works
    he has done,
  all his marvelous works,
    and the justice he declared—
¹³ you who are the offspring of Israel,
    his servant,
  and the children of Jacob,
    his chosen ones.
¹⁴ The LORD—he is our God.
  His justice is everywhere
    throughout the whole world.
¹⁵ God remembersᵘ his covenant forever,
  the word he commanded
    to a thousand generations,
¹⁶ which he made with Abraham,
    the solemn pledge he swore to Isaac.
¹⁷ God set it up as binding law for Jacob,
  as an eternal covenant for Israel,
¹⁸ promising, "I hereby give you
    the land of Canaan
  as your allotted inheritance."
¹⁹ When theyᵛ were few in number—
  insignificant, just immigrants—
²⁰ wandering from nation to nation,
  from one kingdom to the next,
²¹ God didn't let anyone oppress them.
  God punished kings for their sake:
²² "Don't touch my anointed ones;
  don't harm my prophets!"
²³ Sing to the LORD, all the earth!
  Share the news of his saving work
    every single day!
²⁴ Declare God's glory among the nations;
  declare his wondrous works
    among all people
²⁵ because the LORD is great
    and so worthy of praise.
He is awesome beyond all other gods
²⁶ because all the gods of the nations
    are just idols,
  but it is the LORD who created heaven!
²⁷ Greatness and grandeur
  are in front of him;
  strength and joy are in his place.

ᵗCf LXX, Syr, Vulg; Heb uncertain   ᵘLXX; MT *Remember*   ᵛLXX, Vulg; MT *when you were*

²⁸ Give to the Lᴏʀᴅ,
  all families of the nations—
  give to the Lᴏʀᴅ glory and power!
²⁹ Give to the Lᴏʀᴅ the glory due his name!
  Bring gifts! Enter his presence!
  Bow down to the Lᴏʀᴅ
  in his holy splendor!
³⁰ Tremble before him, all the earth!
  Yes, he set the world firmly in place;ʷ
  it won't be shaken.
³¹ Let heaven celebrate!
  Let the earth rejoice!
  Let the nations say, "The Lᴏʀᴅ rules!"
³² Let the sea and everything in it roar!
  Let the countryside and
  everything in it celebrate!
³³ Then the trees of the forest
  will shout out joyfully
  before the Lᴏʀᴅ, because he is coming
  to establish justice on earth!
³⁴ Give thanks to the Lᴏʀᴅ
  because he is good,
  because his faithful love endures forever.
³⁵ Say: "Save us, God, our savior!
  Gather us! Deliver us from among
    the nations
  so we can give thanks to your holy name
  and rejoice in your praise."
³⁶ Bless the Lᴏʀᴅ, Israel's God,
  from forever in the past to forever always.

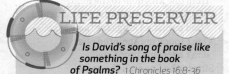

LIFE PRESERVER

Is David's song of praise like something in the book of Psalms? *1 Chronicles 16:8-36*

David's psalm of praise recorded here in 1 Chronicles is similar to songs found in the book of Psalms. It's actually quoted from Psalms 47–48; 96; 105; and 106. You can look up those psalms and compare them with what is here.

After the chest containing the covenant was brought into the tent, the people were able to worship God together. As the Israelites returned from exile, the chest containing the covenant symbolized God's presence among them, helping them remember God's promises and faithfulness to them. As they started rebuilding their life and community, they praised God with this song. ◆

And let all the people say, "Amen!"
  Praise the Lᴏʀᴅ!

³⁷ Then David placed Asaph and his relatives, together with Obed-edom and sixty-eight of his relatives, to minister there continually before the chest containing the Lᴏʀᴅ's covenant, following the routines required on each day. ³⁸ Obed-edom, Jeduthun's son, and Hosah served as gatekeepers. ³⁹ David also placed the priest Zadok and his other priestly relatives at the Lᴏʀᴅ's dwelling at the shrine in Gibeon. ⁴⁰ They were to offer continually, both morning and evening, entirely burned offerings to the Lᴏʀᴅ on the altar for entirely burned offerings, following the written requirements in the Lᴏʀᴅ's Instruction, which he had given Israel. ⁴¹ With them were Heman and Jeduthun and the rest of those chosen by name to give thanks to the Lᴏʀᴅ, because his faithful love lasts forever. ⁴² With them were alsoˣ the trumpets and the cymbals for the musicians and the instruments for God's songs. Jeduthun's family was at the gate. ⁴³ Then all of the people left for their homes. And David returned to bless his household.

God's promise to David

17 When David was settled into his palace,ʸ he said to the prophet Nathan, "I'm living in a cedar palace while the chest containing the Lᴏʀᴅ's covenant is under curtains."

² Nathan replied, "Go ahead and do whatever you are thinking, because God is with you."

³ But that very night God's word came to Nathan: ⁴ Go to my servant David and tell him, This is what the Lᴏʀᴅ says: You are not the one to build the templeᶻ for me to live in. ⁵ In fact, I haven't lived in a temple from the day I brought Israel out until this very day. I've been traveling from tent to tent and from dwelling to dwelling.ᵃ ⁶ Throughout my traveling with the Israelites, did I ever ask one of Israel's tribal leaders, whom I appointed to shepherd my people, Why haven't you built me a cedar temple?

⁷ So then, say this to my servant David: This is what the Lᴏʀᴅ of heavenly forces says: I myself took you from the pasture,

---

ʷLXX; MT *the world is firmly established* ˣLXX; MT adds *Heman and Jeduthun.* ʸOr, here and elsewhere in this chapter, *house*
ᶻOr, here and elsewhere in this chapter, *house* ᵃMT lacks *to dwelling.*

from following the flock, to be leader over my people Israel. [8]I've been with you wherever you've gone. I've eliminated all your enemies before you. Now I will make your name great—like the name of the greatest people on earth. [9]I'm going to provide a place for my people Israel, and plant them so that they may live there and no longer be disturbed. Cruel people will no longer trouble them as they did earlier, [10]when I appointed judges over my people Israel. I'll subdue all your enemies and make you great. As for a dynasty,[b] the LORD will build one for you! [11]When the time comes for you to die, I will raise up a descendant of yours after you, one of your own sons, to succeed you, and I will establish his kingship. [12]He is the one who will build me a temple, and I will establish his throne forever. [13]I will become his father and he will become my son, and I'll never withdraw my faithful love from him as I did from the one before you. [14]I'll install him in my house and in my kingdom forever, and his throne will be established forever.

[15]Nathan faithfully reported all that he had seen and heard to David.

David's prayer

[16]Then King David went and sat in the LORD's presence. He asked:

Who am I, LORD God, and of what significance is my family that you have brought me this far? [17]But even this was too small in your eyes, God. You have spoken about the future of your servant's dynasty and have chosen me as an important person, LORD God.

[18]What more can I say to you for honoring your servant? You yourself know your servant. [19]LORD, for your servant's sake and according to your will, you have done this great thing in order to make all these great things known. [20]LORD, no one can compare to you, no God except you, just as we have heard with our own ears.

> Memorize
> 1 Chron 17:20

[21]Who is like your people Israel, a unique nation on the earth, that God redeemed as his own people, establishing a name for yourself by doing great and awesome things, by driving out nations before your people whom you saved from Egypt? [22]You established your people Israel as your own people forever, and you, LORD, became their God.

[23]Now, LORD, confirm forever the promise you have made about your servant and his dynasty. Do as you have promised [24]so that it may be established and so that your name may be made great forever when people say, "The LORD of heavenly forces, the God of Israel, is Israel's God." May your servant David's household be established before you. [25]You, my God, have revealed to your servant that you will build him a dynasty. That is why your servant has found the courage to pray this prayer to you. [26]LORD, you are truly God, and you promised this good thing to your servant. [27]So now willingly bless your servant's dynasty so that it might continue forever before you, because you, LORD God, have promised. Let your servant's dynasty be blessed forever by your blessing.

David's wars

18Some time later, David defeated the Philistines, subdued them, and took Gath and its villages from Philistine control. [2]He also defeated Moab, enslaving them and requiring payment. [3]David defeated Zobah's King Hadadezer at Hamath, as he continued to establish his control along the Euphrates River. [4]David captured one thousand chariots from him, seven thousand cavalry, and twenty thousand foot soldiers. Then David cut the hamstrings of all but one hundred of the chariot horses. [5]When the Arameans of Damascus came to help Zobah's King Hadadezer, David killed twenty-two thousand of the Arameans. [6]David stationed soldiers[c] in Aram of Damascus, enslaved them, and required payment. The LORD gave David victory wherever he went.

[7]David took the gold shields carried by Hadadezer's servants and brought them to Jerusalem. [8]From Tibhath and Cun, Hadadezer's cities, David took large amounts of bronze, with which Solomon made the bronze basin,[d] the pillars, and the bronze equipment.

---

[b]Or, here and elsewhere in this chapter, *house*   [c]Cf 2 Sam 8:6; Heb lacks *soldiers*.   [d]Or *sea*

⁹When Hamath's King Tou heard that David had defeated the entire army of Zobah's King Hadadezer, ¹⁰he sent his son Hadoram to King David to wish him well and to congratulate him over his battle and defeat of Hadadezer, because Tou was an enemy of Hadadezer. Hadoram brought with him all kinds of gold, silver, and bronze objects. ¹¹King David dedicated these to the LORD along with the silver and the gold he had taken from all these nations: Edom, Moab, the Ammonites, the Philistines, and Amalek. ¹²Abishai, Zeruiah's son, struck down eighteen thousand Edomites in the Salt Valley. ¹³He stationed soldiers in Edom, and all the Edomites became David's slaves. The LORD gave David victory wherever he went.

David's administration

¹⁴David ruled over all Israel and maintained justice and righteousness for all his people. ¹⁵Zeruiah's son Joab was in command of the army; Ahilud's son Jehoshaphat was recorder; ¹⁶Ahitub's son Zadok and Abiathar's son Ahimelechᵉ were priests; Shavsha was secretary; ¹⁷Jehoiada's son Benaiah was in command of the Cherethites and the Pelethites; and David's sons were the king's chief personal advisors.

War with the Ammonites and Arameans

19 Some time later, the Ammonite King Nahash died, and his son succeeded him as king. ²"I'll be loyal to Nahash's son Hanun," David said, "because his father was loyal to me." So David sent messengers with condolences about his father's death.

But when David's servants arrived in the Ammonite territory to express his sympathy to Hanun, ³the Ammonite leaders asked Hanun, "Do you really believe David is honoring your father because he has sent you condolences? Of course not! His servants have come to search the city, spy it out, and overthrow it!" ⁴So Hanun took David's servants, shaved them, cut off half their garments from their buttocks down, and sent them off.

⁵When this was reported to David, he sent messengers to the men because they were completely ashamed. The king said, "Stay in

Jericho until your beards have grown. Then you can come back."

⁶When the Ammonites realized that they had offended David, Hanun and the Ammonites sent one thousand kikkars of silver to hire chariots and cavalry for themselves from Aram-naharaim, Aram-maacah, and Zobah. ⁷They hired thirty-two thousand chariots, as well as King Maacah and his army, who came and camped in front of Medeba, while the Ammonites left their cities and came together ready for battle. ⁸When David heard this, he sent Joab and the entire army of warriors. ⁹The Ammonites marched out and formed a battle line at the entrance to the city, while the kings who had come remained in the countryside.

UMBRELLA
PRIDE

Pride Won't Admit Mistakes
1 Chronicles 19:1-7
The Ammonite king Hanun made a terrible mistake and acted on some bad advice. King David sent men to give Hanun messages of friendship. But Hanun thought they were spies and treated them like they were enemies. Hanun embarrassed David and his messengers by shaving off their beards and cutting their clothes in half. Soon after this, Hanun realized he'd made a mistake. But instead of admitting his wrong and trying to apologize to David, Hanun began to prepare for war with Israel. David was known for showing mercy (1 Sam 24:1-15). If Hanun had been willing to stop acting high-and-mighty and humble himself before David, everything might have worked out. But Hanun was too stubborn. He wasn't going to lower himself to anyone. Because of Hanun's foolishness, the Ammonites suffered a big defeat from the armies of Israel (1 Chron 19:15). ☂

¹⁰When Joab saw that the battle would be fought on two fronts, he chose some of Israel's finest warriors and deployed them to meet the Arameans. ¹¹The rest of the army Joab placed under the command of his brother Abishai. When they took up their positions to meet the Arameans, ¹²Joab said, "If

ᵉLXX, Syr; MT *Abimelech*

the Arameans prove too strong for me, you must help me, and if the Ammonites prove too strong for you, I'll help you. ¹³Be brave! We must be courageous for the sake of our people and the cities of our God. The LORD will do what is good in his eyes."

¹⁴When Joab and the troops who were with him advanced into battle against the Arameans, they fled from him. ¹⁵When the Ammonites saw that the Arameans had fled, they also fled from his brother Abishai and retreated into the city. So Joab returned to Jerusalem.

¹⁶The Arameans saw that they had been defeated by Israel. They sent out messengers to bring Aramean reinforcements from the other side of the river, with Shophach the commander of Hadadezer's army at their head. ¹⁷Upon hearing this, David gathered all Israel and crossed the Jordan. David advanced and took up positions against the Arameans to meet them in battle. After initiating the battle, ¹⁸the Arameans fled before Israel, and David killed seven thousand Aramean chariot drivers and forty thousand foot soldiers. Shophach the commander of their army was killed too. ¹⁹When the servants of Hadadezer saw that they had been defeated by Israel, they made peace with David and served him. Never again would the Arameans come to the aid of the Ammonites.

Defeat of the Ammonites

20 In the spring, the time when kings go to war, Joab marched out with the army, destroyed the land of the Ammonites, and besieged Rabbah. David stayed in Jerusalem while Joab attacked Rabbah and overthrew it. ²David took Milcom's[f] crown from his head. He found that it weighed one kikkar of gold and was set with a valuable stone. It was placed on David's head. The amount of loot David took from the city was huge. ³After removing the people who were in the city, David demolished the city with saws, iron picks, and axes,[g] as he did to all the Ammonite cities. Then David and all his troops returned to Jerusalem.

War with the Philistines

⁴Once again war broke out at Gezer with the Philistines. At that time Sibbecai the

Hushathite killed Sippai, one of the descendants of the Rephah,[h] and the Philistines were subdued. ⁵In another war with the Philistines, Jair's son Elhanan killed Lahmi the brother of Goliath the Gittite. The shaft of his spear was like a weaver's beam. ⁶At another war in Gath there was a huge man with six fingers on each hand and six toes on each foot, twenty-four in all, who was also descended from Raphah. ⁷When he taunted Israel, Jonathan the son of David's brother Shimea killed him. ⁸These were descended from the Raphah in Gath, and they fell by the hands of David and his servants.

David's census

21 A heavenly Adversary[i] arose against Israel and incited David to count Israel. ²So David told Joab and the leaders of the people, "Go throughout all the tribes of Israel, from Dan to Beer-sheba, and take a census of the people so I know how many people there are."

³But Joab replied, "May the LORD increase his people a hundred times! Sir, aren't you the king, and aren't they all your servants? Why do you want to do this? Why bring guilt on Israel?"

⁴But the king overruled Joab, who left and traveled throughout all Israel. When he returned to Jerusalem, ⁵he reported to David the total number: there were 1,100,000 men available for military service in all Israel, while Judah alone had 470,000. ⁶He didn't include Levi and Benjamin among them, because Joab disagreed with the king's order.

⁷God was offended by this census and punished Israel. ⁸Then David said to God, "I have sinned greatly in what I have done! Now please take away the guilt of your servant because I have done something very foolish."

⁹The LORD told Gad, David's seer: ¹⁰Go and tell David, This is what the LORD says: I'm offering you three punishments. Choose one of them, and that is what I will do to you.

¹¹When Gad came to David, he said to him, "This is what the LORD says: Take your choice: ¹²three years of famine, three months of fleeing[j] from your enemies while your enemies' sword overtakes you, or three days of the

---

[f]LXX, Vulg; MT *their king* [g]Cf 2 Sam 12:31; MT *saws* [h]Or *giants*; also in 20:6–7 [i]Heb *satan* [j]LXX, cf 2 Sam 24:13; MT *being swept away*

LORD's sword, that is, plague in the land and the LORD's messenger bringing disaster in every part of Israel. Decide now what answer I should take back to the one who sent me."

¹³"I'm in deep trouble," David said to Gad. "I'd rather fall into the hands of the LORD, who is very merciful; don't let me fall into human hands." ¹⁴So the LORD sent a plague throughout Israel, and seventy thousand Israelites fell dead.

¹⁵Then God sent a messenger to Jerusalem to destroy it. But just as the messenger was about to destroy it, the LORD looked and changed his mind about the destruction. He said to the messenger who was destroying it, "That's enough! Withdraw your hand!" At that time the LORD's messenger was standing near the threshing floor of Ornan the Jebusite.

¹⁶When David looked up, he saw the LORD's messenger stationed between the earth and the sky with a drawn sword in his hand stretched out against Jerusalem. Then David and the elders, dressed in mourning clothes, fell on their faces; ¹⁷and David said to God, "Wasn't it I who ordered the numbering of the people? I'm the sinner, the one responsible for this evil. But these sheep—what have they done? LORD, my God, turn your hand against me and my household, but spare your people from the plague."

¹⁸The LORD's messenger ordered Gad to tell David that he should go up to the threshing floor of Ornan the Jebusite in order to set up an altar for the LORD. ¹⁹So David went up, following the instructions Gad had delivered in the LORD's name.

²⁰Ornan turned around and saw the king.ᵏ His four sons who were with him hid themselves, but Ornan continued threshing wheat. ²¹When David approached Ornan, Ornan looked up, recognized David, left the threshing floor, and bowed to David with his face to the ground. ²²David said to Ornan, "Give me the site of the threshing floor, charging me full price, so that I may build an altar to the LORD, and the plague among the people may come to an end."

²³Ornan replied to David, "Take it for yourself, and may my master the king do

Bet you can read this in 3 minutes. Ready, set, go!

what he thinks is best. I'll even provide the oxen for the entirely burned offerings, the threshing boards for wood, and the wheat for the grain offering—I'll provide everything!"

²⁴But King David said to Ornan, "No, I will buy them from you at a fair price. I won't offer to the LORD what belongs to you nor offer an entirely burned offering that costs me nothing." ²⁵Then David gave Ornan six hundred shekels of gold by weight for the site. ²⁶David built an altar there for the LORD and offered entirely burned offerings and well-being sacrifices. He called on the LORD, who answered him with fire from heaven on the altar of the entirely burned offering, consuming the entirely burned offering.ˡ ²⁷Then the LORD commanded the messenger to return his sword to its sheath.

Location of the future temple

²⁸At that time, after David saw that the LORD had answered him at the threshing floor of Ornan the Jebusite, he offered sacrifices there. ²⁹The LORD's dwelling that Moses had made in the desert and the altar for entirely burned offerings were then at the shrine in Gibeon, ³⁰but David couldn't go there to seek God because he feared the sword of the LORD's messenger.

22 Then David said, "This is where the LORD God's temple will be, along with Israel's altar for entirely burned offerings."

David prepares to build the temple

²David gave orders to gather the immigrants living in the land of Israel, and he appointed masons who would cut stones for building God's temple. ³David also provided a huge amount of iron for nails for the doors of the gates and for the braces, so much bronze that it couldn't be weighed, ⁴and innumerable cedar logs from the Sidonians and the Tyrians, who gave them to David. ⁵David thought, My son Solomon is too inexperienced to build the LORD's temple. It must be great beyond compare in order to win fame and glory throughout all lands, so I myself will prepare things for him. So David made extensive preparations before his death.

ᵏLXX, cf 2 Sam 24:20; MT *messenger* ˡLXX; MT lacks *consuming the entirely burned offering.*

Instructions to Solomon

[6]David sent for his son Solomon and instructed him to build a temple for the LORD, the God of Israel. [7]David said to Solomon, "My son,[m] I had intended to build a temple for the name of the LORD my God. [8]But the LORD told me: You've shed much blood and waged great wars. You won't build a temple for my name because you've spilled so much blood on the ground before me. [9]A son has just been born to you. He'll be a man of peace, and I'll give him peace with all his surrounding enemies. In fact, his name will be Solomon,[n] and I'll give Israel peace and quiet during his reign. [10]He will be the one to build a temple for my name. He'll become my son, and I'll become his father, and I'll establish his royal throne over Israel forever.

[11]"Now, my son, may the LORD be with you so that you may successfully build the temple of the LORD your God, as he promised you. [12]May the LORD be sure to give you insight and understanding so that when he appoints you over Israel, you will observe the Instruction from the LORD your God.[o] [13]Then, if you carefully follow the regulations and case laws that the LORD commanded Moses concerning Israel, you'll prosper. Be strong and brave. Don't be afraid or lose heart! [14]With great effort I've now provided for the LORD's temple one hundred thousand kikkars of gold, one million kikkars of silver, and so much bronze and iron that it can't be weighed, as well as wood and stone, though you may add to these. [15]You also have innumerable people to do the work: stonecutters, masons, and carpenters with every skill required for any task, [16]whether in gold, silver, bronze, or iron. So get to work, and may the LORD be with you."

Instructions to Israel's leaders

[17]Then David ordered all of Israel's leaders to help his son Solomon: [18]"The LORD your God is with you! He's given you peace on every side. He's placed under my power the land's people, so that the land is under the control of the LORD and his people. [19]Now then, dedicate yourselves to seeking the LORD your God. Get to work and build the sanctuary of the LORD God, so that the chest containing the LORD's covenant together with God's holy equipment may be brought into the temple built for the LORD's name."

David appoints the Levites

23 When David had grown old after a long life, he made his son Solomon king over Israel. [2]He then gathered together all Israel's leaders along with the priests and the Levites. [3]When the Levites were counted, the head count of every male 30 and older totaled 38,000. [4]Of these, there were 24,000 to supervise the work on the LORD's temple, 6,000 officers and judges, [5]4,000 gatekeepers, and 4,000 praising the LORD with instruments made[p] for offering praise. [6]Then David divided them into three groups named after Levi's family members: Gershon, Kohath, and Merari.

Gershonites

[7]The Gershonites included Ladan and Shimei.

[8]Ladan's family: Jehiel the first, Zetham, and Joel—three in all. [9]Jehiel's[q] family: Shelomith, Haziel, and Haran—three in all. These were the heads of the households of Ladan.

LIGHTHOUSE

GIVING MY BEST

Work Is a Service to God *1 Chronicles 22:1*
David wanted to build a temple for God, but God said David's son Solomon would build the temple instead. David knew how important the temple would be. He wanted Solomon to have everything he needed for such an important project. So David decided where the temple was going to be located. Then David prepared all the supplies that would be needed. He organized all the right people to work, telling them to dedicate themselves to God before they got started. David wanted everyone and everything to be just right for this project. He knew that as much as the temple would honor God when it was finished, the actual work of building the temple could honor God. David knew that all work—if done with the right attitude—can be service for God (Col 3:23-24). ◈

[m]LXX, DSS; MT *his son* [n]*Solomon* sounds like *peace* in Heb. [o]Heb uncertain [p]LXX, Vulg; MT *I made* [q]Cf 23:8, 10; MT *Shimei's*

¹⁰Shimei's family: Jahath, Ziza,ʳ Jeush, and Beriah. These four were Shimei's family: ¹¹Jahath was the first, and Ziza the second; since Jeush and Beriah didn't have many children, they became a single household.

Kohathites

¹²Kohath's family: Amram, Izhar, Hebron, and Uzziel—four in all.

¹³Amram's family: Aaron and Moses. Aaron, together with his sons, was set apart to make the holiest objects holy, to make offerings before the LORD, to serve him, and to give blessings in his name forever.

¹⁴As for Moses the man of God, his sons were considered to be Levites. ¹⁵Moses' family: Gershom and Eliezer.

¹⁶Gershom's family: Shebuel the first.

¹⁷Eliezer's family: Rehabiah the first; Eliezer had no other sons, but Rehabiah had many children.

¹⁸Izhar's family: Shelomothˢ the first.

¹⁹Hebron's family: Jeriah the first, Amariah the second, Jahaziel the third, and Jekameam the fourth.

²⁰Uzziel's family: Micah the first and Isshiah the second.

Merarites

²¹Merari's family: Mahli and Mushi. Mahli's family: Eleazar and Kish.

²²Eleazar died without sons, but he did have daughters who married their relatives from Kish's family.

²³Mushi's family: Mahli, Eder, and Jeremoth—three in all.

²⁴These were the members of Levi's family according to their households. The household heads were registered, along with a listing of the names of each person 20 years old and above who carried out assigned tasks in the LORD's temple.

Levites' duties

²⁵David said, "Since the LORD, Israel's God, has given his people peace and has made his home in Jerusalem forever, ²⁶the Levites need no longer carry the dwelling or any of the equipment used in its service." ²⁷David's

last instructions were to count the Levites 20 years old and above. ²⁸Their assignment was to be at the side of the Aaronites to serve in the LORD's temple, maintaining the courtyards and side rooms and cleansing all of the holy objects and doing whatever was needed in the service of God's temple. ²⁹They were responsible for the stacks of bread, the fine flour for grain offerings, the wafers of unleavened bread, the cakes made on the griddle, the offering mixed with oil, as well as all the measuring. ³⁰They were to be present every morning to thank and praise the LORD, and to do the same every evening. ³¹Whenever entirely burned offerings were offered to the LORD for the sabbaths, the new moons, and festivals, a designated number were to serve in the LORD's presence continuously. ³²In this way they were to observe the instructions for the meeting tent, the instructions for the sanctuary, and the instructions for Aaron's family and relatives about serving in the LORD's temple.

SAILBOAT

GIVING THANKS

Giving Thanks Helps Us Remember
1 Chronicles 23:30

David was determined to honor God. Before his son Solomon built the temple, David organized the Levites—God's special servants—so they'd know their responsibilities when the temple was ready. One of their most important jobs was to thank and praise God every morning and evening. David knew giving thanks was important because it helped the Israelites remember what God had done for them. Giving thanks to God twice a day, every day, made sure the Israelites wouldn't forget God and start getting into trouble. Much later, the Israelites deserted God's temple. Without the reminder to give thanks, they worshipped false gods (2 Chron 24:17-19). Eventually, the Israelites forgot God so completely that God let both the temple and the nation of Israel be destroyed (2 Kgs 25:1-21). ◊

Divisions of the priests

24 The divisions of the Aaronites: Aaron's family: Nadab, Abihu, Eleazar, and Ithamar.

²Nadab and Abihu died before their father did, without having sons, and so Eleazar

and Ithamar served as priests. ³David, with the help of Zadok from Eleazar's family and Ahimelech from Ithamar's family, divided them according to their appointed duties. ⁴Since Eleazar's family was found to have more male heads than Ithamar's family, they divided them so that Eleazar's family had sixteen household heads and Ithamar's family had eight. ⁵They divided both groups by lots because there were holy leaders, even outstanding leaders, among both Eleazar's and Ithamar's descendants. ⁶Shemaiah, Nethanel's son, the levitical scribe, recorded their names in the presence of the king; the leaders; Zadok the priest; Ahimelech, Abiathar's son; and the household heads of the priests and Levites. One household was taken from Eleazar followed by one from Ithamar.

⁷The first lot fell to Jehoiarib,
     the second to Jedaiah,
⁸the third to Harim, the fourth to Seorim,
⁹the fifth to Malchijah,
     the sixth to Mijamin,
¹⁰the seventh to Hakkoz,
     the eighth to Abijah,
¹¹the ninth to Jeshua,
     the tenth to Shecaniah,
¹²the eleventh to Eliashib,
     the twelfth to Jakim,
¹³the thirteenth to Huppah,
     the fourteenth to Jeshebeab,
¹⁴the fifteenth to Bilgah,
     the sixteenth to Immer,
¹⁵the seventeenth to Hezir,
     the eighteenth to Happizzez,
¹⁶the nineteenth to Pethahiah,
     the twentieth to Jehezkel,
¹⁷the twenty-first to Jachin,
     the twenty-second to Gamul,
¹⁸the twenty-third to Delaiah,
     and the twenty-fourth to Maaziah.

¹⁹These were to enter the LORD's temple according to their appointed duty and by the procedure established for them by their ancestor Aaron, just as the LORD God of Israel had instructed him.

Rest of the Levites

²⁰The rest of the Levites included:
from Amram's family: Shubael;

from Shubael's family: Jehdeiah;
²¹from Rehabiah and his family: Isshiah the first;
²²from the Izharites: Shelomoth;
     from Shelomoth's family: Jahath;
²³Hebron's family:ᵗ Jeriah the first,ᵘ Amariah the second, Jahaziel the third, Jekameam the fourth;
²⁴Uzziel's family: Micah;
     from Micah's family: Shamir;
²⁵Micah's brother Isshiah;
     from Isshiah's family: Zechariah;
²⁶Merari's family: Mahli, Mushi and his son Jaaziah's family;
²⁷Merari's family by his son Jaaziah: Shoham, Zaccur, and Ibri;
²⁸from Mahli: Eleazar, who had no sons;
²⁹from Kish and his family: Jerahmeel;
³⁰and Mushi's family: Mahli, Eder, and Jerimoth.

These were the Levites according to their households. ³¹Both the household head and his youngest brother cast lots, just as their relatives, Aaron's descendants, had done in the presence of King David, Zadok, Ahimelech, and the heads of the priestly and levitical households.

Temple musicians

25 David and the army officersᵛ set apart Asaph's family, Heman and Jeduthun, for service to prophesyʷ accompanied by lyres, harps, and cymbals.

This is the list of those who performed this special service:

²From Asaph's family: Zaccur, Joseph, Nethaniah, and Asarelah. Asaph's family was under Asaph's direction and prophesied by order of the king.

³From Jeduthun and his family: Gedaliah, Izri,ˣ Jeshaiah, Shimei,ʸ Hashabiah, and Mattithiah—six in all. They were under their father Jeduthun's direction, prophesying with the lyre and giving thanks and praise to the LORD.

⁴From Heman and his family: Bukkiah, Mattaniah, Uzziel, Shebuel, Jerimoth, Hananiah, Hanani, Eliathah, Giddalti, Romamti-ezer, Joshbekashah, Mallothi, Hothir, and Mahazioth.

⁵All these were the family of Heman the king's seer, according to God's promise to honor him. God gave Heman fourteen sons and three daughters. ⁶They were all under their father's direction when singing in the LORD's temple with cymbals, harps, and lyres to provide service in God's temple, by order of the king.

As for Asaph, Jeduthun, and Heman, ⁷the number of themselves and their relatives, who were trained in singing to the LORD and who were all skillful, was 288. ⁸They cast lots for their assigned duties, small as well as great, teacher and pupil alike. ⁹The first lot fell for Asaph to Joseph; the second to Gedaliah, his relatives, and his family, 12; ¹⁰the third to Zaccur, his family, and his relatives, 12; ¹¹the fourth to Izri, his family, and his relatives, 12; ¹²the fifth to Nethaniah, his family, and his relatives, 12; ¹³the sixth to Bukkiah, his family, and his relatives, 12; ¹⁴the seventh to Jesarelah, his family, and his relatives, 12; ¹⁵the eighth to Jeshaiah, his family, and his relatives, 12; ¹⁶the ninth to Mattaniah, his family, and his relatives, 12; ¹⁷the tenth to Shimei, his family, and his relatives, 12; ¹⁸the eleventh to Uzziel,ᶻ his family, and his relatives, 12; ¹⁹the twelfth to Hashabiah, his family, and his relatives, 12; ²⁰the thirteenth to Shubael, his family, and his relatives, 12; ²¹the fourteenth to Mattithiah, his family, and his relatives, 12; ²²the fifteenth to Jerimoth,ᵃ his family, and his relatives, 12; ²³the sixteenth to Hananiah, his family, and his relatives, 12; ²⁴the seventeenth to Joshbekashah, his family, and his relatives, 12; ²⁵the eighteenth to Hanani, his family, and his relatives, 12; ²⁶the nineteenth to Mallothi, his family, and his relatives, 12;

²⁷the twentieth to Eliathah, his family, and his relatives, 12; ²⁸the twenty-first to Hothir, his family, and his relatives, 12; ²⁹the twenty-second to Giddalti, his family, and his relatives, 12; ³⁰the twenty-third to Mahazioth, his family, and his relatives, 12; ³¹and the twenty-fourth to Romamti-ezer, his family, and his relatives, 12.

did you know? As part of their duties in leading worship, the Levite priests chose which psalms best fit with each festival or celebration and which instruments best fit with each song.

Gatekeepers

26 The divisions of the gatekeepers: from the Korahites: Meshelemiah, Kore's son, one of Ebiasaph'sᵇ family.

²Meshelemiah's family: Zechariah the oldest, Jediael the second, Zebadiah the third, Jathniel the fourth, ³Elam the fifth, Jehohanan the sixth, and Eliehoenai the seventh.

⁴Obed-edom's family: Shemaiah the oldest, Jehozabad the second, Joah the third, Sachar the fourth, Nethanel the fifth, ⁵Ammiel the sixth, Issachar the seventh, and Peullethai the eighth. God truly blessed him. ⁶To his son Shemaiah were born sons who ruled over their household, because they were valiant men. ⁷Shemaiah's family: Othni, Rephael, Obed, Elzabad, and his relatives, Elihu and Semachiah, who were valiant men. ⁸All these were members of Obed-edom's family, they, their sons, and their relatives. They were valiant and strong in their service, 62 men belonging to Obed-edom. ⁹Meshelemiah's family and relatives, valiant men, numbered 18.

¹⁰Hosah, one of Merari's family, also had a family: Shimri the first (though he wasn't the oldest, his father gave him that status), ¹¹Hilkiah the second, Tebaliah the third, and Zechariah the fourth. All of Hosah's family and relatives numbered 13.

ᶻLXX, Syr; MT *Azrael* ᵃCf 25:4; MT *Jeremoth* ᵇLXX; MT *Asaph*

¹²These were the divisions of the gate-keepers with their leaders, who were responsible to minister in the Lord's temple, along with their relatives. ¹³They cast lots for each gate in the same way, whether their household was small or large. ¹⁴The lot for the East Gate fell to Shelemiah. They then cast lots for his son Zechariah, a wise counselor, and his lot indicated the North Gate. ¹⁵Obed-edom was assigned the South Gate, and his sons were assigned the storehouses. ¹⁶Hosah^c was assigned the West Gate, that is, the chamber^d gate on the upper road.

The guards had the same task: ¹⁷each day^e the East had six, the North four, and the South four, with two at each of the storehouses. ¹⁸At the courtyard on the West, there were four at the road and two at the courtyard. ¹⁹These were the divisions of the gatekeepers from Korah's family and Merari's family.

²⁰Their fellow^f Levites were in charge of the treasuries of God's temple and the treasuries of the dedicated gifts: ²¹from Ladan's family, the family of the Gershonites belonging to Ladan, and the heads of the households belonging to Ladan the Gershonite: Jehieli. ²²Jehieli's family: Zetham and Joel his brother were in charge of the treasuries of the Lord's temple. ²³From the Amramites, Izharites, Hebronites, and Uzzielites: ²⁴Shebuel, a descendant of Gershom, Moses' son, was the chief officer in charge of the treasuries. ²⁵His relatives through Eliezer included his son Rehabiah, his son Jeshaiah, his son Joram, his son Zichri, and his son Shelomoth. ²⁶This Shelomoth and his relatives were in charge of all the treasuries of the gifts dedicated by King David, by the household leaders, by the commanders^g of the units of a thousand and a hundred, and by the army officers. ²⁷They had dedicated some of the valuable objects won in battle to repair the Lord's temple. ²⁸Everything that was dedicated by Samuel the seer, as well as by Saul, Kish's son; Abner, Ner's son; and Joab, Zeruiah's son—in fact, anything that had been dedicated—was under the supervision of Shelomoth^h and his relatives. ²⁹From the Izharites: Chenaniah and his family had responsibilities over Israel outside

the temple as officials and judges. ³⁰From the Hebronites: Hashabiah and his relatives, 1,700 capable men, were put in charge of Israel west of the Jordan concerning all of the Lord's affairs and the king's service. ³¹From the Hebronites: Jerijah was the head of the Hebronites according to the family records of their households. In the fortieth year of David's rule, a search was made and capable men were found among them in Jazer in Gilead. ³²Jerijah's relatives, capable men, were 2,700 heads of households. King David put them in charge of Reuben, Gad, and half the tribe of Manasseh concerning all of God's and the king's affairs.

Divisions of the military

27This is the list of the Israelites, the heads of households, the commanders of units of a thousand and a hundred, and their officers. They served the king in every way their divisions required, and they were on duty for a month at a time through all the months of the year. Each division numbered 24,000.

²In charge of the first division for the first month was Jashobeam, Zabdiel's son. His division numbered 24,000. ³He was a Perezite and the head of all the army officers for the first month.

⁴In charge of the division for the second month was Dodai the Ahohite.^i His division numbered 24,000.

⁵The third army commander for the third month was Benaiah the chief priest Jehoiada's son. His division numbered 24,000. ⁶This Benaiah was a warrior of the Thirty and in command of the Thirty. In command of his division was his son Ammizabad.

⁷The fourth for the fourth month was Asahel, Joab's brother, and after him his son Zebadiah. His division numbered 24,000.

⁸The fifth for the fifth month was the commander Shammoth the Zerahite.^j His division numbered 24,000.

⁹The sixth for the sixth month was Ira the Tekoite Ikkesh's son. His division numbered 24,000.

¹⁰The seventh for the seventh month was Helez the Pelonite from Ephraim's family. His division numbered 24,000.

¹¹The eighth for the eighth month was Sibbecai the Hushathite from the Zerahites. His division numbered 24,000.

¹²The ninth for the ninth month was Abiezer of Annathoth from the Benjaminites. His division numbered 24,000.

¹³The tenth for the tenth month was Maharai the Netophathite from the Zerahites. His division numbered 24,000.

¹⁴The eleventh for the eleventh month was Benaiah the Pirathonite from Ephraim's family. His division numbered 24,000.

¹⁵The twelfth for the twelfth month was Heldai the Netophathite from Othniel. His division numbered 24,000.

Tribal leaders

¹⁶In charge of the tribes of Israel:

for the Reubenites—the leader was Eliezer, Zichri's son;

for the Simeonites—Shephatiah, Maacah's son;

¹⁷for the Levites—Hashabiah, Kemuel's son;

for Aaron—Zadok;

¹⁸for Judah—Eliab,ᵏ one of David's relatives;

for Issachar—Omri, Michael's son;

¹⁹for Zebulun—Ishmaiah, Obadiah's son;

for Naphtali—Jerimoth, Azriel's son;

²⁰for the Ephraimites—Hoshea, Azaziah's son;

for half the tribe of Manasseh—Joel, Pedaiah's son;

²¹for half the tribeˡ of Manasseh in Gilead—Iddo, Zechariah's son;

for Benjamin—Jaasiel, Abner's son;

²²for Dan—Azarel, Jeroham's son.

These were the leaders of the tribes of Israel. ²³But David didn't count those younger than 20 years of age, because the LORD had promised to make Israel as numerous as the stars in the sky. ²⁴Joab, Zeruiah's son, began to count them, but he never finished. Since Israel experienced wrath because of this, the number wasn't entered into the official records of King David.

Civil servants

²⁵In charge of the king's treasuries—Azmaveth, Adiel's son;

in charge of the treasuries in the country, cities, villages, and towers—Jonathan, Uzziah's son;

²⁶in charge of agricultural workers cultivating the fertile land—Ezri, Chelub's son;

²⁷in charge of the vineyards—Shimei the Ramathite;

in charge of the vineyard's produce for the wine cellars—Zabdi the Shiphmite;

²⁸in charge of the olive and sycamore trees in the western foothills—Baal-hanan the Gederite;

in charge of the stores of oil—Joash;

²⁹in charge of the cattle that grazed in Sharon—Shitrai the Sharonite;

in charge of the cattle in the valleys—Shaphat, Adlai's son;

³⁰in charge of the camels—Obil the Ishmaelite;

in charge of the female donkeys—Jehdeiah the Meronothite;

³¹in charge of the flocks of sheep and goats—Jaziz the Hagrite.

All these were stewards of King David's property.

Royal advisors

³²Jonathan, David's uncle, was a counselor, a man of understanding, and a scribe. Jehiel, Hachmoni's son, took care of the king's sons. ³³Ahithophel was the king's counselor, and Hushai the Archite was the king's political advisor.ᵐ ³⁴After Ahithophel came Benaiah's son Jehoiada, and Abiathar. Joab was commander of the king's army.

David addresses Israel's leaders

28David assembled all of Israel's leaders in Jerusalem, the leaders of the tribes, the leaders of the divisions that served the king, the commanders of units of a thousand and a hundred, the officials in charge of all the property and livestock of the king and his sons, as well as the officers, warriors, and all the valiant men. ²Then King David stood up and said:

Listen to me, my relatives and my people. I wanted to build a temple as the

---

ᵏLXX; MT *Elihu* ˡLXX, Vulg; MT lacks *for half the tribe*. ᵐOr *friend*

permanent home for the chest containing
the LORD's covenant, our God's footrest.
But when I prepared to build it, 3God said
to me, You must not build a temple for my
name, because you are a military man and
you've shed blood. 4The LORD, the God of Israel, chose me from my whole household to
become king over Israel forever. He chose
Judah as leader, and within Judah's family,
my household, and among my father's
family he was pleased with me, making
me king over all Israel. 5And from all the
many sons the LORD has given me, he has
chosen my son Solomon to sit on the throne
of the LORD's kingdom over Israel. 6He
said to me: Your son Solomon will build my
temple and my courtyards, for I've chosen
him to become my son even as I myself will
become his father. 7I'll establish his kingdom forever if he remains committed to
keeping my commands and case laws as he
does now.

8So now, in the presence of all the
LORD's assembly[n] and with God as our witness, carefully observe all the commands
of the LORD your God, so that you may hold
on to this good land and pass it on to your
children forever. 9As for you, Solomon, my
son, acknowledge your father's God and
serve him with enthusiastic devotion, because the LORD searches every mind and
understands the motive behind every
thought. If you seek him, he will be found
by you; but if you abandon him, he will
reject you forever. 10Now then, since the
LORD has chosen you to build a temple for
him[o] as the sanctuary, work hard.

11Then David gave his son Solomon the plan
for the entrance hall, its buildings, treasuries,
upper and inner rooms, and the room for the
cover.[p] 12He provided all of the plans he had in
mind: for the courtyards of the LORD's temple,
and for all its surrounding rooms where the
treasures of God's temple and the dedicated
gifts would be stored; 13for the divisions of
the priests and Levites, for all their responsibilities within the LORD's temple, and for
all the equipment used in its service; 14for
the weight of all the gold equipment used
for every kind of service, and the weight of
all the silver equipment used for every kind
of service; 15for the weight of the gold lampstands and their gold lamps—the weight of
gold for each lampstand with its lamps—and
for the weight of each silver lampstand and
its lamps depending on how each would be
used; 16for the weight of gold for each table
with the stacks of bread, and the silver for the
silver tables; 17for the forks, bowls, and cups
of pure gold; for the weight of each gold dish
and the weight of each silver dish; 18for the
weight of the incense altar made of refined
gold; and for the construction of the chariot—
with the gold winged creatures spreading
their wings and covering the chest containing the LORD's covenant. 19All of this the LORD
made clear to David[q] directly in a document,
including the plan for all of the work.

20"Be strong and courageous," David said
to his son Solomon. "Get to work. Don't be
afraid or discouraged, because the LORD God,
my God, is with you. He'll neither let you down
nor leave you before all the work for the service of the LORD's temple is done. 21Here are
the divisions of the priests and the Levites
who will perform all the service of God's temple. For all this work you will have willing and
able workers with you to do it. The officials
and all the people are ready to
follow your instructions."

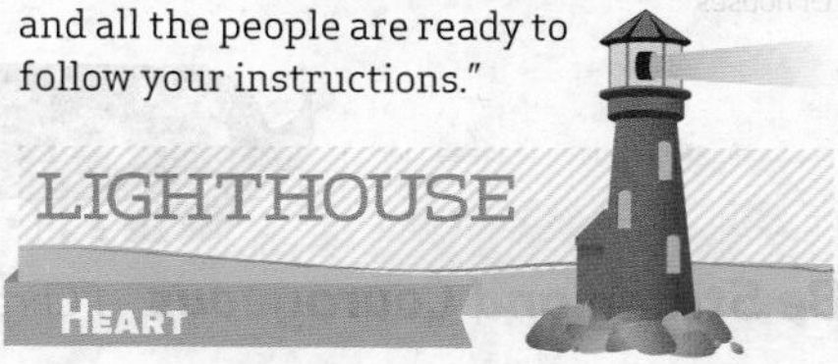

Keep Your Heart True *1 Chronicles 28:9*

Before David died, he told Solomon always to remember God and to keep his heart right. At first, Solomon took these words seriously. After Solomon took the throne, God told him in a dream he could have whatever he asked. Because Solomon's heart was right, he asked for wisdom to govern God's people (1 Kgs 3:4-14). God knew Solomon's heart was true, and God was pleased to make Solomon the wisest man in the world. But Solomon didn't stay true forever. He loved many women from other countries who worshipped other gods. This caused Solomon to worship those other gods as well. When God knew Solomon no longer followed God's ways, God punished him by taking half of Israel away from his son (1 Kgs 11:1-13).

[n]LXX; MT *all Israel, the assembly of the* LORD [o]LXX; MT lacks *for him.* [p]Or *mercy seat* or perhaps *reconciliation cover* (Heb kapporet) [q]LXX; MT *to me*

Offerings for building the temple

29 Then King David said to the whole assembly:

My son Solomon, the one whom God chose, is too inexperienced for this great task, since this temple won't be for humans but for the LORD God. ²Using every resource at my disposal, I've provided everything for my God's temple: gold for gold objects, silver for silver objects, bronze for bronze objects, iron for iron objects, lumber for wooden objects, carnelian stones for settings, antimony, colorful stones, every kind of precious stone, and a large amount of marble. ³What's more, because of my delight in my God's temple, I have dedicated my own private treasure of gold and silver to my God's temple, in addition to all that I've provided for the holy temple: ⁴three thousand kikkars of gold from the gold of Ophir, seven thousand kikkars of refined silver for covering the walls of the rooms,ʳ ⁵gold for gold objects, and silver for silver objects, to be used for everything the skilled workers will make. Who else, then, will

ʳOr *houses*

volunteer, dedicating themselves to the LORD today? ⁶Then the leaders of the households, the leaders of the tribes of Israel, and the commanders of the units of a thousand and a hundred, and the supervisors of the king's work volunteered ⁷to give five thousand kikkars and ten thousand darics of gold, ten thousand kikkars of silver, eighteen thousand kikkars of bronze, and one hundred thousand kikkars of iron for the work on God's temple. ⁸Anyone who had precious stones donated them to the treasury of the LORD's temple under the care of Jehiel the Gershonite. ⁹The people rejoiced at this response, because they had presented their offerings to the LORD so willingly and wholeheartedly. King David also rejoiced greatly.

¹⁰Then David blessed the LORD before the whole assembly:

Blessed are you, LORD,
God of our ancestor Israel,
forever and always.
¹¹ To you, LORD,
belong greatness
and power,

Memorize
1 Chron 29:11

God's ◀ My
THOUGHTS ▶ THOUGHTS

Be Strong and Courageous *1 Chronicles 28:9-20*

What is the best advice you have ever been given? This section of 1 Chronicles shows King David passing on wisdom to his son Solomon. David told Solomon to serve God with "enthusiastic devotion" (1 Chron 28:9). That means to serve God with excitement and commitment. David told Solomon that God knows our every thought and that when we seek God we will find God. But here is the best part of David's advice: David told Solomon to be "strong and courageous" because God is always with us (1 Chron 28:20).

To be strong and courageous means to expect that God will be with you and will show you the way. God will never let us down or leave us alone. Even when friends let us down or when we are treated unfairly, we can be sure that God is with us and will give us strength to serve God with enthusiastic devotion.

When have you felt strong and courageous for God?

How does it feel to know that God will never leave you or let you down?

honor, splendor, and majesty,
because everything in heaven
and on earth belongs to you.
Yours, Lord, is the kingship,
and you are honored as head of all.
¹² You are the source of wealth and honor,
and you rule over all.
In your hand are strength and might,
and it is in your power to magnify
and strengthen all.
¹³ And now, our God, we thank you
and praise your glorious name.
¹⁴ Who am I,
and who are my people,
that we should be able to offer
so willingly?
Since everything comes from you,
we have given you
that which comes from your own hand.
¹⁵ To be sure, we are like all our ancestors,
immigrants without permanent homes.
Our days are like a shadow on the ground,
and there's no hope.

¹⁶Lord, our God, all this abundance that we have provided to build you a temple for your holy name comes from your hand and belongs to you. ¹⁷Since I know, my God, that you examine the mind and take

LIGHTHOUSE

RESPECT FOR GOD

Respect God with Giving
1 Chronicles 29:3-17

David was very happy. He had announced to all the leaders of Israel that he was giving his private store of treasure to the building of God's temple. In response, the leaders of Israel generously and wholeheartedly gave up their own jewels, gold, and silver for the temple. They gave so much because God was important to them. They respected all that God had given them. In his blessing to God, David recognized that everything he and the Israelites owned came from God. The Israelites didn't act as though they had earned their wealth only through their hard work. Because of their respect for God, they returned a portion of everything they owned to God. This pleased God, who blessed the Israelites throughout Solomon's reign. ◗

delight in honesty, I have freely given all these things with the highest of motives. And now I've been delighted to see your people here offering so willingly to you.

¹⁸Lord, God of our ancestors Abraham, Isaac, and Israel, keep these thoughts in the mind of your people forever, and direct their hearts toward you. ¹⁹As for Solomon my son, give him the wholehearted devotion to keep your commands, laws, and regulations—observing all of them—and to build the temple that I have prepared.

²⁰Then David said to the whole assembly, "Bless the Lord your God," and the whole assembly blessed the Lord, the God of their ancestors, bowed down, and worshipped before the Lord and the king. ²¹On the very next day they offered sacrifices and entirely burned offerings to the Lord—a thousand bulls, a thousand rams, and a thousand lambs, along with their drink offerings—and many other sacrifices for all Israel's sake. ²²They ate and drank with great joy before the Lord that day and made David's son Solomon the king.ˢ They anointed himᵗ in the Lord's presence as prince, and Zadok as priest. ²³Thus Solomon sat on the Lord's throne as king, succeeding his father David, and he prospered. All Israel obeyed him, ²⁴and all the commanders and warriors, as well as all of King David's sons, submitted to King Solomon's authority. ²⁵Moreover, the Lord magnified Solomon before all Israel, giving him such royal majesty as no king before himᵘ had enjoyed.

Summary of David's reign

²⁶David, Jesse's son, was king over all Israel. ²⁷He reigned over Israel for forty years: seven years in Hebron and thirty-three in Jerusalem. ²⁸He died at a good old age, having enjoyed a full life, wealth, and honor; and his son Solomon followed him as king. ²⁹The account of King David from beginning to end is written in the records of Samuel the seer, Nathan the prophet, and Gad the visionary, ³⁰including everything concerning his powerful rule, and what happened to him, to Israel, and to all the kingdoms in other lands.

ˢLXX, Syr; MT adds *for the second time.* ᵗLXX; MT lacks *him.* ᵘLXX; MT adds *in Israel.*

2 Chronicles

Much of the history explained in 1 and 2 Samuel and 1 and 2 Kings is retold in 1 and 2 Chronicles. At the end of those books, the people of Judah were taken as prisoners to Babylon. But many years later, some of them went home. Their history is recorded in 1 and 2 Chronicles.

This book begins with stories of King Solomon. When God offered to give Solomon whatever he wanted, Solomon asked for wisdom and knowledge to lead the people. God was pleased with this request and gave Solomon not only wisdom but also wealth and fame. When Solomon was king, God's people spread across the land and grew powerful.

Second Chronicles then tells how the nation of Israel broke into two kingdoms, Israel and Judah. After that division, 2 Chronicles mostly tells the story of Judah and its kings. Many kings failed to follow God. But there were also kings like Jehoshaphat, Hezekiah, and Josiah who did what was right and helped people follow God.

The story ends with a decree by King Cyrus of Persia, who let the people go free after they were prisoners in Babylon. King Cyrus said that God's people should build a temple for God. Second Chronicles shows that God always has a plan to help people worship God! ◊

things YOU'LL DISCOVER

Second Chronicles continues to retell the history of God's people. It explains how Israel split into two kingdoms—the northern kingdom of Israel and the southern kingdom of Judah. It tells the story of the people of Judah from the time of King Solomon until they were taken as prisoners to Babylon.

people YOU'LL MEET

Solomon—King David's son and Israel's third king (2 Chron 1–9)
Jehoshaphat—a king of Judah who was faithful to God (2 Chron 17–21)
Hezekiah—a king of Judah who did what was right in God's eyes (2 Chron 29–32)
Josiah—a boy who became king of Judah at age 8 and led people back to God (2 Chron 34–35)

places YOU'LL GO

Israel (the northern kingdom), **Judah** (the southern kingdom), **Babylon** (present-day southern Iraq), **Persia** (present-day Iran)

words YOU'LL REMEMBER

"If my people who belong to me will humbly pray, seek my face, and turn from their wicked ways, then I will hear from heaven, forgive their sin, and heal their land" (2 Chron 7:14).

Solomon first meets God

1 Solomon, David's son, was securely established over his kingdom because the Lord his God was with him and made him very great. ²Solomon summoned all Israel, including the officers of the army,ᵃ the judges, and every Israelite leader who was the head of a family. ³Then Solomon, accompanied by the whole assembly, went to the shrine at Gibeon because that is where God's meeting tent was, the tent that the Lord's servant Moses had made in the wilderness. ⁴Now David had already brought God's chest from Kiriath-jearim to the place he had prepared for it because he had pitched a tent for the chest in Jerusalem. ⁵But the bronze altar that Bezalel, Uri's son and Hur's grandson, had made was there in front of the Lord's dwelling, so that is where Solomon and the assembly worshipped. ⁶Solomon went there to the bronze altar in the Lord's presence at the meeting tent and offered a thousand entirely burned offerings upon it.

⁷That night God appeared to Solomon and said, "Ask whatever you wish, and I will give it to you."

⁸"You showed so much kindness to my father David," Solomon replied to God, "and you have made me king in his place. ⁹Now, Lord God, let your promise to my father David be fulfilled because you have made me king over a people as numerous as the earth's dust. ¹⁰Give me wisdom and knowledge so I can lead this people, because no one can govern this great people of yours without your help."

¹¹God said to Solomon, "Since this is what you wish, and because you've asked for wisdom and knowledge to govern my people over whom I've made you king—rather than asking for wealth, riches, fame, victory over those who hate you, or even a long life—¹²your request for wisdom and knowledge is granted. But I will also give you wealth, riches, and

fame beyond that of any king before you or after you." ¹³Then Solomon went fromᵇ the shrine in Gibeon, from the meeting tent to Jerusalem where he ruled over Israel.

LIGHTHOUSE

PRAYER

God Gives Wisdom 2 Chronicles 1:10-12

Solomon was Israel's king. He wanted to make a good start as king, so he made a special sacrifice to God. God came to Solomon in a dream and told him he could have anything he wanted. Solomon knew that more than anything else he needed wisdom to rule over God's people. Because Solomon asked for such a selfless gift, God gave Solomon wisdom as well as other things he didn't ask for: health, wealth, and power. Solomon knew God gave wisdom, because his father David frequently asked for and received wisdom from God (1 Sam 23:10-13; 1 Chron 14:8-16). Nearly one thousand years later in the New Testament, James wrote a letter that says, "Anyone who needs wisdom should ask God, whose very nature is to give to everyone without a second thought, without keeping score" (James 1:5). Both Solomon and David were rewarded for seeking wisdom from God and not merely relying on themselves. ◊

Solomon's wealth

¹⁴Solomon acquired more and more chariots and horses until he had fourteen hundred chariots and twelve thousand horses, which he stationed in chariot cities and with the king in Jerusalem. ¹⁵In Jerusalem, the king made silver and gold as common as stones, and cedar as plentiful as sycamore trees that grow in the foothills. ¹⁶Solomon's horses were imported from Egypt and Kue, purchased from Kue by the king's agents at the going price. ¹⁷They would import a chariot from Egypt for six hundred pieces of silver and a horse for one hundred fifty, and then export them to all the Hittite and Aramean kings.

Solomon prepares to build the temple

2ᶜ Solomon gave orders to build a temple for the Lord's name and to build a royal palace for himself. ²ᵈTo work in the highlands, Solomon drafted 70,000 laborers,

did you know? Solomon wanted a special building where the chest containing the covenant could be kept and people could come to worship God. So Solomon began building a great temple and a palace for himself next to it. More than 150,000 men worked on the construction of the temple.

ᵃOr *officers over thousands and hundreds* ᵇLXX, Vulg; MT *to* ᶜ1:18 in Heb ᵈ2:1 in Heb

80,000 stonecutters, and 3,600 supervisors. [3]Solomon sent the following message to King Huram[e] of Tyre:

When my father David was building his palace, you sent him cedar logs. [4]Now as his son[f] I am about to build a temple in the name of the LORD my God. I will dedicate it to him to burn fragrant incense before him, to set out the bread that is regularly displayed, and to offer entirely burned offerings every morning and evening, on the sabbaths, the first of every month, and the festivals of the LORD our God, as Israel has been commanded to do forever. [5]The temple I am about to build must be magnificent, because our God is greater than all other gods. [6]But who is able to build such a temple when even the highest heaven can't contain God? And who am I that I should build this temple for God, except as a place to burn incense in his presence? [7]So now send me a craftsman skilled in gold, silver, bronze, and iron, as well as in purple, crimson, and violet yarn—someone also experienced as an engraver. He will work with my craftsmen in Judah and Jerusalem who were provided by my father David. [8]Also send me cedar, cypress, and sandalwood logs from Lebanon. I know your servants know how to cut Lebanese timber, so my servants will work with your servants [9]to prepare plenty of timber for me, because the temple that I am about to build will be magnificent and amazing. [10]I will pay the woodcutters twenty thousand kors[g] of crushed wheat, twenty thousand kors of barley, twenty thousand baths[h] of wine, and twenty thousand baths of olive oil.

[11]Tyre's King Huram replied in a letter that he sent to Solomon:

The LORD must love his people Israel because he has made you their king! [12]Bless the LORD, Israel's God, who made heaven and earth. He gave King David a wise son who possesses the knowledge and understanding to build a temple for the LORD and a royal palace for himself. [13]I'm sending you a skilled and experienced craftsman, Huram-abi, [14]whose mother is from the tribe of Dan and whose father is from Tyre. He's skilled in working with gold, silver, bronze, iron, stone, and wood, as well as purple, violet, and crimson yarn, and fine linen. He can do any kind of engraving and make any design given to him with the assistance of your craftsmen and the craftsmen of my master, your father David. [15]So once my master sends the wheat, barley, olive oil, and wine he has promised, [16]we will cut as much timber as you need from Lebanon and bring it by raft on the sea to you at Joppa, where you can take it up to Jerusalem.

[17]Then Solomon counted all the immigrants in the land of Israel, as his father David had done, and the total was 153,600. [18]He made 70,000 of these immigrants laborers, 80,000 of them stonecutters in the highlands, and 3,600 of them supervisors to keep the people working.

Solomon builds the temple

3 Solomon began to build the LORD's temple in Jerusalem on Mount Moriah, where the LORD[i] had appeared to his father David, on the place David had prepared at the threshing floor of Ornan the Jebusite. [2]He began building in the second month[j] of the fourth year of his rule. [3]Solomon laid the foundations[k] for these structures in order to build the temple of God. The length according to the old standard of measurement was ninety feet and the width thirty feet. [4]Across the front of the temple[l] was a porch as long as the temple was and thirty feet wide, and thirty feet[m] high. He covered the inside walls with pure gold. [5]He paneled the walls of the main room with pine, covered them with fine gold, and decorated them with palm trees and chains. [6]He studded the room with precious stones for beauty; the gold was from Parvaim. [7]He covered the room, its beams, doorframes, walls, and doors with gold, and carved images of winged creatures on the walls. [8]Then he made the most holy place. It was as long as the temple was

---

[e]1 Kings spells the king's name as Hiram. [f]LXX; MT lacks *his son.* [g]One kor is equivalent to a homer and is possibly equal to fifty gallons of grain. [h]One bath is approximately twenty quarts or five gallons. [i]LXX; MT lacks *the LORD.* [j]LXX; MT adds *on the second (day).* [k]Syr *the measurements* [l]LXX; cf 1 Kgs 6:3 [m]LXX, Syr; MT *one hundred eighty feet*

wide, thirty feet long and thirty feet wide. He covered it with six hundred kikkars of fine gold. [9]The gold nails weighed fifty shekels.[n] He also covered the upper rooms with gold.

[10]In the most holy place he formed two statues of winged creatures and covered them with gold. [11]Together the wingspan of these creatures was thirty feet. One of the first creature's wings was seven and a half feet long and touched the temple wall, while the other wing was seven and a half feet long, touching the wing of the other creature. [12]Similarly, one wing of the other creature was seven and a half feet long and touched the temple wall, while the other wing was seven and a half feet long and touched the other creature. [13]The wings of these creatures extended thirty feet. They stood on their feet facing the main room.

[14]Then he made the curtain out of fine linen and violet, purple, and crimson yarn, weaving winged creatures into it. [15]Then he made two columns in front of the temple, fifty-two and a half feet high, with a seven and a half foot cap on top of each. [16]Then he made chains like a necklace[o] and placed them on the tops of the columns. He made a hundred pomegranates and placed them into the chains. [17]Then he set up the pillars in front of the sanctuary, one on the south, the other on the north. The one on the south he named Jachin, and the one on the north he named Boaz.

Solomon's temple equipment

4 He[p] also made a bronze altar thirty feet long, thirty feet wide, and fifteen feet high. [2]Then he made a tank of cast metal called the Sea. It was circular in shape, fifteen feet from rim to rim, seven and a half feet high, and forty-five feet in circumference. [3]Under the rim were two rows of oxlike figures completely encircling it, ten every eighteen inches, each cast in its mold. [4]The Sea rested on twelve oxen with their backs toward the center, three facing north, three facing west, three facing south, and three facing east. [5]The Sea was as thick as

did you know? The most holy place was the most inner room of the temple where the chest containing the covenant was kept. Two giant statues of winged creatures with wings fifteen feet long were placed outside it to show that no one other than the high priest was allowed to enter there.

the width of a hand. Its rim was shaped like a cup or an open lily blossom. It could hold three thousand baths.[q] [6]He also made ten washbasins and put five on the south and five on the north. The items used for the entirely burned offerings were rinsed in these. The priests washed in the Sea. [7]He made ten gold lampstands as prescribed and put them in the sanctuary, five on the south and five on the north. [8]He also made ten tables and put them in the sanctuary, five on the south and five on the north, as well as a hundred gold bowls. [9]He made the courtyard of the priests and the great courtyard, with doors covered with bronze for the courtyard. [10]He placed the Sea at the southeast corner.

[11]Huram made the pots, the shovels, and the bowls. So Huram finished all his work on God's temple for King Solomon:

[12]two columns;

two circular capitals on top of the columns;

two networks adorning the two circular capitals on top of the columns;

[13]four hundred pomegranates for the two networks, with two rows of pomegranates for each network that adorned the two circular capitals on top of the columns;

[14]ten[r] stands with ten[s] basins on them;

[15]one Sea;

twelve oxen beneath the Sea;

[16]and the pots, the shovels, and the meat forks.

All the things that Huram-abi made for King Solomon for the LORD's temple were made of polished bronze. [17]The king cast them in clay molds in the Jordan Valley between Succoth and Zarethan.[t] [18]Due to the

---

[n]Or approximately thirty ounces [o]Heb adds *in the inner room.* [p]*Solomon* or *Huram*; this ambiguity with the pronoun continues in the following verses, but compare 2 Chron 3:1, 3; 4:11. If Huram is meant, this is a worker whose name is spelled Hiram in 1 Kgs 7:13-14. [q]One bath is approximately twenty quarts or five gallons. [r]LXX and 1 Kgs 7:43; MT *he made* [s]1 Kgs 7:43; MT *he made* [t]With 1 Kgs 7:46; Heb *Zeredah*

very large number of objects, Solomon didn't even try to weigh the bronze. ¹⁹Solomon also made all the equipment for God's temple: the gold altar; the tables for the bread of the presence; ²⁰the lampstands with their lamps, all of pure gold, to burn before the inner sanctuary as prescribed; ²¹the flowers, the lamps, and the tongs of pure gold; ²²and the wick trimmers, bowls, ladles, and censers of pure gold. As for the temple entrance, the inner doors to the most holy place as well as the doors to the main hall were made of gold.

5 When all of Solomon's work on the LORD's temple was finished, he brought the silver, gold, and all the objects his father David had dedicated and put them in the treasuries of God's temple.

Solomon dedicates the temple

²Then Solomon assembled Israel's elders, all the tribal leaders, and the clan chieftains of Israel at Jerusalem to bring up the chest containing the LORD's covenant from Zion, David's City. ³Everyone in Israel assembled before the king in the seventh month,ᵘ during the festival. ⁴When all Israel's elders had arrived, the Levites picked up the chest. ⁵They brought the chest, the meeting tent, and all the holy objects that were in the tent. The priests andᵛ the Levites brought them up, ⁶while King Solomon and the entire Israelite assembly that had joined him before the chest sacrificed countless sheep and oxen. ⁷The priests brought the chest containing the LORD's covenant to its designated spot beneath the wings of the winged creatures in the inner sanctuary of the temple, the most holy place. ⁸The winged creatures spread their wings over the place where the chest rested, covering the chest and its carrying poles. ⁹The carrying poles were so long that their tips could be seen from the holy placeʷ in front of the inner sanctuary, though they weren't visible from outside. They are still there today. ¹⁰Nothing was in the chest except the two stone tablets Moses placed there while at Horeb, where the LORD made a covenant with the Israelites after they left Egypt.

Bet you can read this in 5 minutes. Ready, set, go!

¹¹Then the priests left the holy place. All the priests who were present had sanctified themselves, regardless of their divisions. ¹²All the levitical musicians—Asaph, Heman, Jeduthun, and their families and relatives—were dressed in fine linen and stood east of the altar with cymbals, harps, and zithers, along with one hundred twenty priests blowing trumpets. ¹³The trumpeters and singers joined together to praise and thank the LORD as one. Accompanied by trumpets, cymbals, and other musical instruments, they began to sing, praising the LORD:

Yes, God is good!

Yes, God's faithful love lasts forever!

Then a cloud filled the LORD's temple.ˣ ¹⁴The priests were unable to carry out their duties on account of the cloud because the LORD's glory filled God's temple.

6 Then Solomon said, "The LORD said that he would live in a dark cloud; ²but God, I have built you a lofty temple—a place where you can live forever."

³The king turned around, and while the entire assembly of Israel was standing there, he blessed them, ⁴saying:

Bless the LORD, the God of Israel, who spoke directly to my father David and now has kept his promise: ⁵"From the day I brought my people out of the land of Egypt, I haven't selected a city from any Israelite tribe as a site for the building of a temple for my name. Neither have I chosen anyone as prince over my people Israel. ⁶But now I have chosen Jerusalem as a place for my name, and David as prince over my people Israel."

⁷My father David wanted to build a temple for the name of the LORD, Israel's God. ⁸But the LORD said to my father David: "It is very good that you thought to build a temple for my name. Nevertheless, ⁹you yourself won't build that temple. Instead, your very own son will build the temple for my name." ¹⁰The LORD has kept his promise—I have succeeded my father David on Israel's throne, just as the LORD said, and I have built the temple for the name of the LORD, Israel's God. ¹¹There I've placed the chest that contains the covenant that the LORD made with the Israelites.

ᵘSeptember-October, Tishrei ᵛLXX; MT *the levitical priests* ʷLXX; MT *the chest* ˣCf LXX; MT *the temple, the LORD's temple*

¹²Solomon stood before the Lᴏʀᴅ's altar in front of the entire Israelite assembly and spread out his hands. ¹³Now Solomon had made a bronze platform seven and a half feet long, seven and a half feet wide, and four and a half feet high, and he set it in the middle of the enclosure. He stood on it. Then, kneeling before the whole assembly of Israel and spreading his hands toward the sky, ¹⁴he said:

> Memorize
> 2 Chron 6:14

Lᴏʀᴅ God of Israel, there is no god like you in heaven or on the earth. You keep the covenant and show loyalty to your servants who walk before you with all their heart. ¹⁵This is the covenant you kept with your servant David my father, which you promised him. Today you have fulfilled what you promised.

¹⁶So now, Lᴏʀᴅ God of Israel, keep what you promised my father David your servant when you said to him, "You will never fail to have a successor sitting on Israel's throne as long as your descendants carefully walk according to my Instruction, just as you have walked before me." ¹⁷So now, Lᴏʀᴅ God of Israel, may your promise to your servant David come true.

¹⁸But how could God possibly live on earth with people? If heaven, even the highest heaven, can't contain you, how can this temple that I have built contain you? ¹⁹Lᴏʀᴅ, my God, listen to your servant's prayer and request, and hear the cry and prayer that I your servant pray to you. ²⁰Constantly watch over this temple, the place where you promised to put your name, and listen to the prayer your servant is praying concerning this place. ²¹Listen to the request of your servant and your people Israel when they pray concerning this place. Listen from your heavenly dwelling place, and when you hear, forgive!

²²If someone wrongs another and must take a solemn pledge asserting his innocence before your altar in this temple, ²³then listen from heaven, act, and decide which of your servants is right. Condemn the guilty party, repaying them for their conduct, but justify the innocent person, repaying them for their righteousness.

²⁴If your people Israel are defeated by an enemy because they have sinned against you, but then they change their hearts, give thanks to your name, and ask for mercy in your presence at this temple, ²⁵then listen from heaven and forgive the sin of your people Israel. Return them to the land you gave to them and their ancestors.

²⁶When the sky holds back its rain because Israel has sinned against you, but they then pray concerning this place, give thanks to your name, and turn away from their sin because you have punished them for it,ʸ ²⁷then listen from heaven and forgive the sin of your servants, your people Israel. Teach them the best way for them to follow, and send rain on your land that you gave to your people as an inheritance.

²⁸Whenever there is a famine or plague in the land, or whenever there is blight, mildew, locusts, or grasshoppers, or whenever someone's enemies attack them in their cities, or any plague or illness comes, ²⁹whatever prayer or petition is made

UMBRELLA
Hard Times

Hard Times Draw People to God
2 Chronicles 6:28-30

After seven years, King Solomon had completed building God's temple. Solomon threw a huge celebration to dedicate the temple for God. During the dedication, Solomon prayed a long prayer. He asked God to accept the temple as God's own. Solomon also asked God to remember Israel if the people should ever stop following God. Solomon asked God to be quick to forgive the nation when it turned away from sin. He asked God to listen for Israel's prayers during times when sickness or natural disasters came. Solomon knew that hard times help people quickly turn to God. Hard times remind people how much they need God. Sometimes hard times are a result of people's sin, and sometimes they just happen. No matter how hard times come about, God wants people to rely on God's love and care. ◖

by any individual or by all of your people Israel—because people will recognize their own pain and suffering and spread out their hands toward this temple— [30]then listen from heaven where you live. Forgive, act, and repay each person according to all their conduct because you know their hearts. You alone know the human heart! [31]Do this that they may revere you by following your ways all the days they live on the fertile land that you gave to our ancestors.

[32]Listen also to the foreigner who isn't from your people Israel, but who comes from a distant country because of your great reputation, your great power, and your outstretched arm. When they come and pray toward this temple, [33]then listen from heaven where you live, and do everything the foreigner asks. Do this so that all the people of the earth may know your reputation and revere you, as your people Israel do, and recognize that this temple I have built bears your name.

[34]When your people go to war against their enemies, wherever you may send them, and they pray to you toward this city that you have chosen and concerning this temple that I have built for your name, [35]then listen from heaven to their prayer and request and do what is right for them.

[36]When they sin against you, for there is no one who doesn't sin, and you become angry with them and hand them over to an enemy who takes them away as prisoners to enemy territory, whether distant or nearby, [37]if they change their heart in whatever land they are held captive, turning back and begging for your mercy,[z] saying, "We have sinned, we have done wrong, and we have acted wickedly!" [38]and if they return to you with all their heart and all their being in the enemy territory where they've been taken captive, and pray concerning their land, which you gave to their ancestors, concerning the city you have chosen, and concerning this temple I have built for your name, [39]then

listen to their prayer and request from your heavenly dwelling place. Do what is right for them, and forgive your people who have sinned against you.

[40]Now, my God, may your eyes be open and your ears attentive to the prayers of this place. [41]And now go, Lord God, to your resting place, you and your mighty chest. May your priests, Lord God, be clothed with salvation; may those loyal to you rejoice in what is good. [42]Lord God, don't reject your anointed one.[a] Remember your faithful loyalty to your servant David.

7 As soon as Solomon finished praying, fire came down from heaven and consumed the entirely burned offering and the sacrifices, while the Lord's glory filled the temple. [2]The priests were unable to enter the Lord's temple because the Lord's glory had filled the Lord's temple. [3]All the Israelites were watching when the fire fell. As the Lord's glory filled the temple, they knelt down on the pavement with their faces to the ground, worshipping and giving thanks to the Lord, saying, "Yes, God is good! Yes, God's faithful love lasts forever!"

[4]Then the king and all the people sacrificed to the Lord. [5]King Solomon sacrificed twenty-two thousand oxen and one hundred twenty thousand sheep when the king and all the people dedicated God's temple. [6]The priests stood at their posts, as did the Levites with the Lord's musical instruments, which King David had made for giving thanks to the Lord, saying, "Yes, God's faithful love lasts forever!" and which David had used when he gave praise. Across from them, the priests were blowing trumpets while all Israel was standing.

[7]Solomon also dedicated the middle of the courtyard in front of the Lord's temple. He had to offer the entirely burned offerings and the fat of the well-being sacrifices there because the bronze altar Solomon had made was too small to contain the entirely burned offerings, the grain offerings, and the pieces of fat.

[8]At that time Solomon, together with all Israel, celebrated the festival for seven days.

---

[z]MT adds *in the land they are held captive.* [a]LXX; MT *anointed ones*

It was a very large assembly that came from Lebo-hamath to the border[b] of Egypt. [9]On the eighth day there was a gathering. They had dedicated the altar for seven days and celebrated the festival for another seven days. [10]On the twenty-third day of the seventh month,[c] Solomon dismissed the people to their tents, happy and content because of the goodness the LORD had shown to David, to Solomon, and to his people Israel. [11]In this way, Solomon finished the LORD's temple and the royal palace. He successfully accomplished everything he intended for the LORD's temple and his own palace.

Solomon again meets God

[12]Then the LORD appeared to Solomon at night and said to him: I have heard your prayer and have chosen this place as my house of sacrifice. [13]When I close the sky so that there is no rain or I order the locusts to consume the land or I send a plague against

my people, [14]if my people who belong to me will humbly pray, seek my face, and turn from their wicked ways, then I will hear from heaven, forgive their sin, and heal their land. [15]From now on my eyes will be open and my ears will pay attention to the prayers offered in this place, [16]because I have chosen this temple and declared it holy so that my name may be there forever. My eyes and my heart will always be there. [17]As for you, if you will walk before me just as your father David did, doing all that I have commanded you and keeping my regulations and case laws, [18]then I will establish your royal throne, just as I promised your father David: You will never fail to have a successor ruling in Israel. [19]But if any of you ever turn away from and abandon the regulations and commands that I have given you, and go to serve other gods and worship them, [20]then I will uproot you[d] from my land that I

> Memorize
> 2 Chron 7:14

[b]Or *Wadi*, traditionally *Brook*   [c]September-October, Tishrei   [d]Or *Israel* (or *them*)

Seeking God   *2 Chronicles 7:12-16*

Sometimes we pray for our hearts and eyes to be open to God. When they are open, we see God moving in our lives and we let God's love fill us up. But Solomon prayed for God's heart and eyes to be open toward us. When God is open to us, we are in God's care—God sees us, knows us, loves us, and protects us.

King Solomon built the temple and dedicated it to God. He asked God to remember God's covenant with the people and to show kindness, mercy, justice, and love. God heard his prayer and promised to open God's heart and eyes toward God's people. God said to Solomon, "If my people who belong to me will humbly pray, seek my face, and turn from their wicked ways, then I will hear from heaven, forgive their sin, and heal their land" (7:14).

This is a promise for us today as well. To be humble means to put God first in our lives. When we pray to God and ask God to take away all of the bad things in our lives and in our world, God promises to hear us, forgive us, and heal us. This is quite a promise!

How can you "humbly pray" and "seek God's face"?

How can you turn from any "wicked ways"?

gave you, and I will reject this temple that I made holy for my name. I will make it a joke, insulted by everyone. ²¹Everyone who passes by this temple—so lofty now—will be shocked and will wonder, Why has the LORD done such a thing to this land and temple? ²²The answer will come, Because they abandoned the LORD, the God of their ancestors, who brought them out of Egypt. They embraced other gods, worshipping and serving them. This is why God brought all this disaster on them.

Solomon's buildings and prosperity

8After twenty years of building the LORD's temple and his royal palace, ²Solomon next rebuilt the cities Huram had given him, and he settled Israelites there.

³Solomon went to Hamath-zobah and seized it. ⁴He fortified Tadmor in the wilderness, along with all the storage cities he had built in Hamath. ⁵Solomon also built Upper Beth-horon and Lower Beth-horon as fortress cities with walls, gates, and crossbars; ⁶Baalath; all the cities he used for storage; and all the cities used for chariots and cavalry—along with everything else he wanted to build in Jerusalem, Lebanon, and throughout his kingdom.

⁷Any non-Israelite people who remained of the Hittites, Amorites, Perizzites, Hivites, and Jebusites—⁸that is, the descendants of such people who were still in the land because the Israelites weren't able to destroy them—Solomon forced into the labor gangs that are still in existence today. ⁹However, Solomon didn't force the Israelites to work as slaves; instead, they became warriors, chief officers, and the commanders of his chariots and cavalry. ¹⁰And Solomon had two hundred fifty chief officers^e who were in charge of the people.

¹¹Solomon brought Pharaoh's daughter from David's City to a palace he had built for her, because he said, "My wife mustn't live in the palace of Israel's King David, because the places where the LORD's chest has been are holy."

¹²Then Solomon offered entirely burned offerings to the LORD on the LORD's altar that Solomon had built in front of the porch,

¹³as each day required, according to the commandment of Moses for sabbaths, new moon festivals, and the three annual festivals—Unleavened Bread, Weeks, and Booths. ¹⁴Just as his father David had ordered, Solomon set up the divisions of the priests for their services and the Levites to their posts for offering praise and ministering in front of the priests, doing what needed to be done each day; as well as the gatekeepers in their divisions at each gate, because this was what David the man of God had commanded. ¹⁵They didn't deviate in any way from the king's commands concerning the priests, the Levites, or the treasuries. ¹⁶All Solomon's work was carried out from the day the foundation of the LORD's temple was laid until its completion. Then the LORD's temple was completely finished.

¹⁷Then Solomon went to Ezion-geber and Eloth on the coast in the land of Edom. ¹⁸Huram had his servants bring ships to Solomon, along with crews of expert sailors. They went with Solomon's servants to Ophir and imported four hundred fifty kikkars of gold, which they brought back to King Solomon.

Queen of Sheba

9When the queen of Sheba heard reports about Solomon, she came to Jerusalem to test Solomon with riddles. Accompanying her was a huge entourage, with camels carrying spices, large amounts of gold, and precious stones. After she arrived, she told Solomon everything that was on her mind. ²Solomon answered all her questions; nothing was too difficult for him to answer. ³When the queen of Sheba saw how wise Solomon was, the palace he had built, ⁴the food on his table, his servants' quarters, the function and dress of his attendants, his cupbearers and their dress, and the entirely burned offerings he offered at the LORD's temple,^f it took her breath away.

⁵"The report I heard about your deeds and wisdom when I was still at home is true," she said to the king. ⁶"I didn't believe it until I came and saw it with my own eyes. In fact, the half of it wasn't told to me! You have far more than I was told. ⁷Your people and these servants who continually serve you and get to listen to your wisdom are truly happy! ⁸Bless

---

^eQere; Kethib *officers of the troops*   ^fLXX, Syr, Vulg, 1 Kgs 10:5; MT *how he processed* (or *went up*) *to the* LORD's *temple.*

the LORD your God because he was pleased to put you on the throne as king for the LORD your God. Because your God loved Israel and wanted to establish them forever, he has made you their king to uphold justice and righteousness."

⁹Then she gave the king one hundred twenty kikkars of gold, a great quantity of spices, and precious stones. Never again has such a quantity of spice come to Israel as when the queen of Sheba gave this gift to King Solomon.

¹⁰In addition, Huram's servants and the servants of Solomon, who had brought gold back from Ophir, also brought algum wood and precious stones. ¹¹The king made steps⁸ for the LORD's temple and for the royal palace with the algum wood, as well as lyres and harps for the musicians. Never before had anything like them been seen in the land of Judah. ¹²King Solomon gave the queen of Sheba everything she wanted, even more than she had brought the king. Then she and her servants returned to her homeland.

Solomon's wealth

¹³Solomon received an annual income of six hundred sixty-six kikkars of gold, ¹⁴not including income from the traders and merchants. All the Arabian kings and the governors of the land also brought Solomon gold and silver. ¹⁵King Solomon made two hundred body-sized shields of hammered gold, using fifteen poundsʰ of hammered gold in each shield; ¹⁶and three hundred small shields of hammered gold, using seven and a half poundsⁱ of hammered gold in each shield. The king placed these in the Forest of Lebanon Palace.

¹⁷The king also made a large ivory throne and covered it with pure gold. ¹⁸Six steps led up to the throne, which had a gold footrest attached. Two lions stood beside the armrests on both sides of the throne. ¹⁹Another twelve lions stood on both sides of the six steps. No other kingdom had anything like this.

²⁰All King Solomon's drinking cups were made of gold, and all the items in the Forest of Lebanon Palace were made of pure gold, not silver, since even silver wasn't considered

good enough in Solomon's time! ²¹The royal fleet sailed to Tarshish with the servants of Huram, returning once every three years with gold, silver, ivory, monkeys, and peacocks.ʲ

²²King Solomon far exceeded all the earth's kings in wealth and wisdom, ²³and kings of every nation wanted an audience with Solomon in order to hear his God-given wisdom. ²⁴Year after year they came with tribute: objects of silver and gold, clothing, weapons, spices, horses, and mules.

²⁵Solomon also had four thousand stalls for horses and chariots, together with twelve thousand horsemen that he kept in the chariot cities and with the king in Jerusalem. ²⁶He ruled all the kings from the Euphratesᵏ to the Philistines' land and the border of Egypt. ²⁷In Jerusalem, the king made silver as common as stones and cedar as common as sycamore trees that grow in the foothills. ²⁸Solomon's horses were imported from Egypt and every land.

Solomon's remaining days

²⁹The rest of Solomon's deeds, from beginning to end, aren't they written in the records of the prophet Nathan, the prophecies of Ahijah from Shiloh, and the visions of the seer Iddo concerning Jeroboam, Nebat's son? ³⁰Solomon ruled over all Israel in Jerusalem for forty years. ³¹Solomon lay down with his ancestors and was buried in David's City with his father. His son Rehoboam succeeded him as king.

How Rehoboam lost the kingdom

10Rehoboam went to Shechem, where all Israel had come to make him king. ²When Jeroboam, Nebat's son, heard the news, he returned from Egypt where he had fled from King Solomon. ³The people sent and called for Jeroboam, who along with all Israel came and said to Rehoboam, ⁴"Your father made our workloadˡ very heavy; if you will lessen the demands your father made of us and lighten the heavy workload he demanded from us, then we will serve you."

⁵He answered them, "Come back in three days." So the people left.

---

⁸LXX, Vulg; Heb uncertain ʰOr *six hundred shekels* ⁱOr *three hundred shekels* ʲOr possibly *apes*; Heb uncertain ᵏOr *the river* ˡOr *our yoke*

⁶King Rehoboam consulted the elders who had served his father Solomon when he was alive. "What do you advise?" Rehoboam asked. "How should I respond to these people?"

⁷"If you are kind to these people and try to please them by speaking gently with them," they replied, "they will be your servants forever."

⁸But Rehoboam ignored the advice the elders gave him and instead sought the counsel of the young advisors who had grown up with him and now served him. ⁹"What do you advise?" he asked them. "How should we respond to these people who said to me, 'Lighten the workload your father demanded from us'?"

¹⁰The young people who had grown up with Rehoboam said to him, "This people said to you, 'Your father made our workload heavy. Lighten it for us!' Now this is what you should

ᵐOr pinky; perhaps a euphemism

say to them, 'My babyᵐ finger is thicker than my father's waist!' ¹¹So if my father made your workload heavy, I'll make it even heavier! If my father disciplined you with whips, I'll do it with scorpions!'"

¹²Jeroboam and all the people returned to Rehoboam on the third day, just as the king had specified when he said, "Come back in three days." ¹³The king then answered the people harshly. He ignored the elders' advice, ¹⁴and instead followed the young people's advice. He said, "My father made your workload heavy, but I'll make it even heavier; my father disciplined you with whips, but I'll do it with scorpions!"

¹⁵The king didn't listen to the people because this turn of events came from God so that the LORD might keep his promise concerning Jeroboam, Nebat's son, which God delivered through Ahijah from Shiloh. ¹⁶When

God's THOUGHTS ◊ My THOUGHTS

Wrong Answer   *2 Chronicles 10*

Sometimes people give us really bad advice. This might have happened to you before. Maybe you knew the answer to a problem, but you went with someone's wrong advice instead of trusting yourself. Or maybe your parents had given you some ideas about a problem, but you listened to a friend's advice instead.

That's what Rehoboam did. He became king after Solomon died, and he didn't follow God. In fact, Rehoboam made some terrible decisions. The people told Rehoboam that they needed a break. They had worked so hard for Solomon that they wanted Rehoboam to go easy on them. The older people around Rehoboam told him to listen to them and to give the people some rest from their hard work. But Rehoboam decided to ask his younger friends. He and his friends decided to be even harder on the people and demand even more from them. Rehoboam was not a king who served God. He didn't set his heart on God. He did whatever he wanted to do instead.

The next time you need advice about something, remember to choose someone wise to help you think it through. You may not get the answer you want to hear, but you will be better off following wise advice.

What good advice have you gotten from older people in your life?

Make a list of all the wise people in your life who you can trust to help you when you need good advice.

all Israel saw[n] that the king wouldn't listen to them, the people answered the king,

"Why should we care about David?
We have no stake in Jesse's son!
Go back to your homes, Israel!
You better look after
    your own house now, David!"

Then all Israel went back to their homes, [17] and Rehoboam ruled over only the Israelites who lived in the cities of Judah.

[18] When King Rehoboam sent Hadoram to them (he was the leader of the work gang), the Israelites stoned him to death. King Rehoboam quickly got into his chariot and fled to Jerusalem. [19] And so Israel has been in rebellion against David's dynasty to this day.

11 When Rehoboam arrived at Jerusalem, he assembled the house of Judah and Benjamin, one hundred eighty thousand select warriors, to fight against Israel and to restore the kingdom to Rehoboam. [2] But the LORD's word came to Shemaiah the man of God: [3] Tell Judah's King Rehoboam, Solomon's son, and all Israel in Judah and Benjamin, [4] This is what the LORD says: Don't make war against your relatives. Go home, every one of you, because this is my plan. When they heard the LORD's words, they abandoned their attack against Jeroboam.

[5] Rehoboam lived in Jerusalem, but he built cities for Judah's defense [6] in Bethlehem, Etam, Tekoa, [7] Beth-zur, Soco, Adullam, [8] Gath, Mareshah, Ziph, [9] Adoraim, Lachish, Azekah, [10] Zorah, Aijalon, and Hebron. These were the fortified cities in Judah and Benjamin. [11] He made the fortifications stronger, placed commanders in them, and supplied them with food, oil, and wine. [12] He also stored shields and spears in each of the cities, making them very strong. This is how Judah and Benjamin remained under his control.

[13] The priests and the Levites from every region throughout all Israel sided with Rehoboam. [14] The Levites left their pastures and property to come to Judah and Jerusalem because Jeroboam and his sons had refused to let them serve as the LORD's priests, [15] having appointed his own priests for the shrines and the goat and calf idols he had made. [16] People from every tribe of Israel who had made up their minds to seek the LORD, Israel's God, came to Jerusalem to sacrifice to the LORD, the God of their ancestors. [17] They strengthened the kingdom of Judah and supported Rehoboam, Solomon's son, for three years by following the way of David and Solomon those three years.

[18] Rehoboam married Mahalath daughter of Jerimoth, David's son, and Abihail daughter of Eliab, Jesse's son. [19] The sons she bore him were Jeush, Shemariah, and Zaham. [20] Later he married Maacah, Absalom's daughter, who bore him Abijah, Attai, Ziza, and Shelomith. [21] Rehoboam loved Absalom's daughter Maacah more than all his wives and secondary wives. In all, he had eighteen wives and sixty secondary wives, twenty-eight sons, and sixty daughters. [22] Rehoboam named Abijah, Maacah's son, as his successor in order to make him king. [23] He wisely placed some of his sons in every region of Judah and Benjamin, in every fortified city, and gave them plenty of food and sought many wives for them.

12 But as soon as Rehoboam had secured his royal power, he, along with all Israel, abandoned the LORD's Instruction.

Rehoboam rules

[2] Egypt's King Shishak attacked Jerusalem in the fifth year of King Rehoboam because Israel had been unfaithful to the LORD. [3] Accompanying Shishak from Egypt were twelve hundred chariots, sixty thousand horses, and countless Libyan, Sukkite, and Cushite warriors. [4] He captured the fortified cities of Judah and came toward Jerusalem. [5] Then the prophet Shemaiah went to Rehoboam and the leaders of Judah who had gathered at Jerusalem because of Shishak, and told them, This is what the LORD says: Since you have abandoned me, now I am abandoning you to Shishak's power.

[6] Then the leaders of Israel and the king submitted. "The LORD is right," they said.

[7] When the LORD saw that they had submitted, the LORD's word came to Shemaiah: Since they have submitted, I won't destroy them. I will deliver them in a little while, and I won't use Shishak to pour out my anger against Jerusalem. [8] Nevertheless, they will be subject

to him so that they learn the difference between serving me and serving other nations.
9Egypt's King Shishak attacked Jerusalem and seized the treasures of the LORD's
temple and the royal palace. He took everything, even the gold shields Solomon had
made. 10King Rehoboam replaced them with
bronze shields and assigned them to the officers of the guard who protected the entrance
to the royal palace. (11Whenever the king entered the LORD's temple, the guards would
carry the shields and then return them to the
guardroom.) 12When Rehoboam submitted,
the LORD was no longer angry with him, and
total destruction was avoided. There were,
after all, some good things still in Judah.
13So King Rehoboam was securely established in Jerusalem. Rehoboam was 41 years
old when he became king, and he ruled seventeen years in Jerusalem, the city the LORD had
chosen from all the tribes of Israel to put his
name. His mother's name was Naamah from
Ammon. 14But Rehoboam did what was evil
because he didn't set his heart on seeking the
LORD. 15The deeds of Rehoboam, from beginning to end, aren't they written in the records
of the prophet Shemaiah and the seer Iddo,
including the genealogical records? There
was continual warfare between Rehoboam
and Jeroboam. 16Rehoboam lay down with his
ancestors and was buried in David's City. His
son Abijah[o] succeeded him as king.

Abijah rules Judah

13 Abijah[p] became king over Judah in the
eighteenth year of King Jeroboam.
2He ruled for three years in Jerusalem. His
mother's name was Micaiah; she was Uriel's
daughter from Gibeah. When war broke out
between Abijah and Jeroboam, 3Abijah went
to fight with an army of four hundred thousand select troops against Jeroboam's select
forces numbering eight hundred thousand,
who were arrayed in battle formation.
4Abijah stood on the heights of Mount
Zemaraim in Ephraim's highlands and said:
"Listen to me, Jeroboam and all Israel!
5Surely you know that the LORD, Israel's
God, made an unbreakable covenant[q] with
David and his descendants that they would
rule Israel forever. 6It was Jeroboam, Nebat's son, the servant of Solomon, David's
son, who rebelled against his master.
7When some useless, worthless people
joined his cause, they overpowered Rehoboam, Solomon's son, who was too young
and timid to resist them. 8And now do you
intend to challenge the LORD's royal rule,
entrusted to David's descendants? You may
have a numerical advantage, as well as the
gold calves Jeroboam made for you as gods.
9But you've banished the LORD's priests,
Aaron's sons, along with the Levites, so
that you could appoint your own priests as
other countries do. Now anyone who shows
up with a young bull and seven rams can become a priest of these phony gods!
10"But us? The LORD is our God, and we
haven't abandoned him. Aaron's descendants serve as the LORD's priests, assisted

did you know? The temple had been finished for only thirty-five years when it was attacked. King Shishak of Egypt stole all of the gold and treasures from inside when he took control of Jerusalem.

UMBRELLA
DISOBEDIENCE

God Rewards Obedience

2 Chronicles 13:4-21

Israel's King Jeroboam had everything going for him. God had given Jeroboam half of Israel because King Solomon had stopped following God (1 Kgs 11:27-39). But like Solomon, Jeroboam disobeyed. Instead of completely following God, he made gold calves for his people to worship. Jeroboam threw out God's special priests, the Levites, so that he could choose his own priests and control them. Now Jeroboam was going to attack the southern kingdom of Judah. It looked like he was going to win—he outnumbered King Abijah's army and had it completely surrounded. But Abijah obeyed God and made sure his people followed God too. God honored Abijah's obedience and punished Jeroboam's disobedience.

[o]Spelled Abijam in 1 Kgs 14:31 [p]Spelled Abijam in 1 Kgs 15:1, 7-8 [q]Or *a covenant of salt*

in the work by the Levites. [11]Every morning and every evening they offer entirely burned offerings and fragrant incense to the Lord, and set out bread in stacks upon a clean table. At night they light the lamps on the gold lampstand. Yes, while you are abandoning the Lord our God, we are doing what he requires. [12]Listen! God is on our side, at our head, along with his priests, who are ready to sound the battle trumpets against you. So, Israelites, don't fight against the Lord, the God of your ancestors, for you won't succeed!"

[13]Meanwhile, Jeroboam had sent troops around behind them for an ambush so that the main force was in front of Judah while the ambush was behind. [14]When Judah looked around and suddenly realized that they were surrounded, they cried out to the Lord while the priests sounded the trumpets [15]and raised the battle cry. When they raised the battle cry, God defeated Jeroboam and all Israel before Abijah and Judah. [16]So the Israelites fled before Judah, and God gave Judah the victory. [17]Abijah and his people struck them severely: five hundred thousand select warriors were killed. [18]Israel was subdued on that occasion, and Judah succeeded because they relied on the Lord, the God of their ancestors. [19]Abijah pursued Jeroboam and took these cities away from him: Bethel, Jeshanah, and Ephron,ʳ along with their villages. [20]Jeroboam failed to regain power during the time of Abijah. The Lord finally struck him down, and he died. [21]Abijah, however, grew strong. He married fourteen wives; he had twenty-two sons and sixteen daughters. [22]The rest of Abijah's deeds, what he did and what he said, are written in the account of the prophet Iddo.

14 Abijah lay down with his ancestors and was buried in David's City. His son Asa succeeded him as king.

Asa rules Judah

[s] In Asa's time, the land had peace for ten years. [2t]Asa did what was right and good in the Lord his God's eyes. [3]He removed the foreign altars and shrines, smashed the sacred pillars, cut down the sacred poles,ᵘ [4]and urged Judah to seek the Lord, the God of their ancestors, by doing what the Instruction and the commandments required. [5]He also removed the shrines and incense altars from all the cities of Judah so that the kingdom was

ʳQere, LXX; Kethib *Ephrain* ˢ13:23 in Heb ᵗ14:1 in Heb ᵘHeb *asherim*, perhaps objects devoted to the goddess Asherah; cf 1 Kgs 15:13

God's THOUGHTS ◆ My THOUGHTS

God Helps the Weak   2 Chronicles 14:11-15

There are many stories in the Bible about God helping the weak against the powerful. Some of these include David and Goliath, Daniel in the lion's den, and Shadrach, Meshach, and Abednego in the fiery furnace. God has proved over and over again that no matter how big an enemy we face, we can trust God.

Asa was a faithful leader who ruled Judah and looked to God for guidance and strength. When a large army came against his people, he prayed to God and trusted God to help the weak against the powerful. God was faithful and gave Asa victory over this huge enemy. His trust in God was his greatest tool.

What are the problems in your life that seem too big for you to handle?

How can trust in God be your greatest tool in handling these problems?

at peace under him. ⁶When the land was at peace, he built fortified cities in Judah; there was no war in those years because the LORD had given him rest.

⁷"Let's build up these cities," Asa told Judah. "We'll surround them with walls, towers, gates, and crossbars while the land is still ours, because we sought the LORD our God and he sought us^v and surrounded us with rest." As a result, the people successfully completed their building projects.

Judah defeats Cush

⁸Asa had an army of three hundred thousand Judeans armed with body-sized shields and spears and another two hundred eighty thousand from Benjamin armed with small shields and bows. All were brave warriors. ⁹Zerah the Cushite marched against him with an army of one million men and three hundred chariots. When he got as far as Mareshah, ¹⁰Asa marched against him, setting up for battle in a valley north^w of Mareshah.

¹¹Then Asa cried out to the LORD his God, "LORD, only you can help the weak against the powerful.^x Help us, LORD our God, because we rely on you and we have marched against this multitude in your name. You are the LORD our God. Don't let a mere human stand against you!"

¹²So the LORD struck the Cushites before Asa and Judah, and the Cushites fled. ¹³Asa and his troops chased them as far as Gerar. The Cushites fell until there were no survivors. They were completely crushed by the LORD and his army, who carried off a huge amount of loot, ¹⁴and attacked all the cities surrounding Gerar who were terrified of the LORD. They plundered all these cities as well because there was a great amount of loot in them. ¹⁵They also attacked the herdsmen's camps, taking many sheep and camels before returning to Jerusalem.

15 When God's spirit came upon Azariah, Oded's son, ²he confronted Asa: "Listen to me, Asa and all Judah and Benjamin," he said. "The LORD is with you as long as you are with him. If you seek him, he will be found by you; but if you abandon him, he will abandon you. ³For a long time Israel was without

the true God, without a priest to teach them, and without the Instruction. ⁴But in their time of trouble they turned to the LORD, Israel's God. They sought him and found him! ⁵At that time, it wasn't safe to travel because great turmoil affected all the inhabitants of the area. ⁶Nation was crushed by nation and city by city, as God troubled them with every kind of problem. ⁷But as for you, be brave and don't lose heart, because your work will be rewarded!"

Asa's reforms

⁸As soon as Asa heard these words and the prophecy of Azariah, Oded's son,^y he felt brave and removed the detestable idols from all of Judah and Benjamin, as well as from the cities he had captured in Ephraim's highlands, and he repaired the LORD's altar that stood before the LORD's entrance hall. ⁹Then Asa gathered all Judah and Benjamin, along with those who were living among them as immigrants from Ephraim, Manasseh, and Simeon, because many people from Israel had joined up with him when they saw that the LORD his God was with him. ¹⁰They gathered in Jerusalem in the third month of the fifteenth year of Asa's

SAILBOAT

COURAGE

God Gives the Courage to Obey

2 Chronicles 15:1-16

Israel's king Asa heard just what he needed. God told Asa that God would be with him as long as he obeyed and that God would reward his obedience. Those words from God were enough to make Asa bold. Asa had the courage to follow God even when following God might have been dangerous or risky to him. Asa took down all the idols in the kingdom. Destroying those idols probably made many people angry enough to rebel against the king. But Asa wouldn't let someone else's anger stop him from obeying God. Asa even removed his own grandmother from power because she had made an image of a false god. Asa was brave enough to risk the wrath of his own family in order to serve God. God rewarded Asa's bravery with long-lasting peace for his kingdom. ◆

^vLXX; MT lacks *and* and repeats *we sought.* ^wLXX; MT an otherwise unknown *Zephathah Valley* ^xHeb uncertain; or *it is not with you to help between the many and the powerless.* ^yCf Syr, Vulg; MT *and the prophecy of the prophet Oded*

rule. ¹¹On that day they sacrificed to the Lᴏʀᴅ part of the loot they had taken: seven hundred oxen and seven thousand sheep. ¹²They made a covenant to seek the Lᴏʀᴅ, the God of their ancestors, with all their heart and all their being. ¹³They agreed that anyone who refused to seek the Lᴏʀᴅ, Israel's God, would be put to death, whether young or old, male or female. ¹⁴They swore this to the Lᴏʀᴅ with a loud voice, shouts of joy, and blasts from trumpets and horns. ¹⁵All Judah was delighted with the solemn pledge because they had sworn it with all their hearts. When they enthusiastically sought God, he was found by them, and the Lᴏʀᴅ gave them peace on every side. ¹⁶Asa the king even removed his grandmother Maacah from the position of queen mother because she had made an image of Asherah. Asa cut down her image, pulverized it, and burned it in the Kidron Valley. ¹⁷Although the shrines weren't removed from Israel, Asa nevertheless remained committed with all his heart throughout his life. ¹⁸He brought into God's temple the various silver and gold objects that he and his father had dedicated. ¹⁹There was no war until the thirty-fifth year of Asa's rule.

Aram invades Judah

16 In the thirty-sixth year of Asa's rule, Israel's King Baasha attacked Judah and fortified Ramah to prevent Judah's King Asa from moving into that area. ²Asa took silver and gold from the treasuries of the Lᴏʀᴅ's temple and the royal palace and sent them to Aram's King Ben-hadad, who ruled in Damascus, with the following message: ³"Let's make a covenant similar to the one between our fathers. Since I have already sent you silver and gold, break your covenant with Israel's King Baasha so that he will leave me alone." ⁴Ben-hadad agreed with King Asa and sent his army commanders against the cities of Israel, attacking Ijon, Dan, Abel-maim, and all the store-cities of Naphtali. ⁵As soon as Baasha learned of this, he stopped building Ramah and abandoned his work. ⁶Then King Asa had all Judah carry away the stone and timber that Baasha was using to build Ramah, and King Asa used it to build Geba and Mizpah. ⁷At that time Hanani the seer came to Judah's King Asa and said to him, "Because

you relied on Aram's king and not on the Lᴏʀᴅ your God, the army of Aram's king has slipped out of your grasp. ⁸Weren't the Cushites and the Libyans a vast army with chariots and horsemen to spare? Still, when you relied on the Lᴏʀᴅ, he delivered them into your power, ⁹because the Lᴏʀᴅ's eyes scan the whole world to strengthen those who are committed to him with all their hearts. Your foolishness means that you will have war on your hands from now on." ¹⁰Asa was angry with the seer. Asa was so mad he threw Hanani in jail and took his anger out on some of the people.

Asa's disease and death

¹¹The rest of Asa's deeds, from beginning to end, are written in the official records of Israel's and Judah's kings. ¹²In the thirty-ninth year of his rule, Asa developed a severe foot disease. But even in his illness he refused to seek the Lᴏʀᴅ and consulted doctors instead. ¹³In the forty-first year of his rule, Asa lay down with his ancestors. ¹⁴He was buried in the tomb he had prepared for himself in David's City, and was laid on a bed filled with sweet spices and various kinds of perfume, with a huge fire made in his honor.

UMBRELLA

ᴀɴɢʀʏ

Don't Get Angry at Discipline
2 Chronicles 16:1-12

Asa made a mistake. When his kingdom was under attack, he chose to rely on a person to save him instead of God. This was unusual because Asa had trusted God for most of his life (2 Chron 15:17). Now God had some harsh words for Asa. God told Asa that he would face constant war because of his mistake. God punished Asa because he wanted Asa to learn from his mistakes. God disciplines a king because God loves him (Prov 3:11-12). But Asa didn't see it this way. He grew so angry at God that he mistreated people around him who had nothing to do with his punishment. Asa let his anger take control. He never got over it. Later, when Asa fell ill with a foot disease, he stubbornly refused to ask God to help him. Asa's anger turned a good king into a poor one. ◖

Jehoshaphat rules Judah

17 Asa's son Jehoshaphat succeeded him as king. Jehoshaphat strengthened his position against Israel ²by stationing troops in the fortified cities of Judah and placing soldiers throughout the land of Judah and in the cities of Ephraim that his father Asa had captured. ³The LORD was with Jehoshaphat because he followed the earlier ways of his father² by not seeking Baal. ⁴Instead, he sought the God of his father, and unlike Israel, he followed God's commandments. ⁵The LORD gave him firm control over the kingdom, and all Judah brought Jehoshaphat tribute, so that he had abundant riches and honor. ⁶Jehoshaphat took pride in the LORD's ways and again removed the shrines and the sacred polesª from Judah.

⁷In the third year of his rule, Jehoshaphat sent his officials Ben-hail, Obadiah, Zechariah, Nethanel, and Micaiah to teach in the cities of Judah. ⁸They were accompanied by the Levites Shemaiah, Nethaniah, Zebadiah, Asahel, Shemiramoth, Jehonathan, Adonijah, Tobijah, and Tob-adonijah, and by the priests Elishama and Jehoram. ⁹They taught throughout Judah. They brought with them the LORD's Instruction scroll as they made their rounds to all the cities of Judah, teaching the people.

SAILBOAT

OBEDIENCE

Don't Forget the Details of Obedience
2 Chronicles 17:3-9

Jehoshaphat knew how to follow God. The king of Judah was careful to follow God's Instruction. Obeying God was so important to the king that even the smallest details of God's Instruction never escaped his attention. Jehoshaphat sent priests throughout the cities of Judah, teaching the people from God's Instruction scroll so that they could also follow God. It would have been easy for Jehoshaphat to disobey God. His kingdom was surrounded by nations that didn't follow God's Instruction. Those nations would trip up many Israelite kings (2 Chron 21:1-6; 28:1-4). His own father had turned away from God later in his life (2 Chron 16:1-12). But Jehoshaphat stayed true to God. And God rewarded him for his obedience, keeping Israel safe and powerful throughout his life.◆

¹⁰All the kingdoms surrounding Judah were afraid of the LORD and didn't wage war against Jehoshaphat. ¹¹Some of the Philistines brought a load of silver as tribute to Jehoshaphat. The Arabians also brought flocks to Jehoshaphat: seventy-seven hundred rams and seventy-seven hundred goats. ¹²As Jehoshaphat grew increasingly powerful, he built fortresses and storage cities in Judah ¹³and had many supplies in the cities of Judah. He also had an army of mighty warriors in Jerusalem, ¹⁴registered by their clans as follows: Judah's officers over units of a thousand included Commander Adnah with three hundred thousand soldiers; ¹⁵next to him was Commander Jehohanan with two hundred eighty thousand soldiers; ¹⁶at his side was Amasiah, Zichri's son, who volunteered for the LORD with two hundred thousand soldiers. ¹⁷From Benjamin came a valiant warrior: Eliada, together with two hundred thousand armed with bow and shield; ¹⁸next to him was Jehozabad, together with one hundred eighty thousand soldiers. ¹⁹These were the individuals who served the king in addition to those the king placed in the fortified cities throughout Judah.

Jehoshaphat and Ahab

18 Even though Jehoshaphat already had great wealth and honor, he allied himself with Ahab through marriage. ²A few years later, while Jehoshaphat was visiting Ahab in Samaria, Ahab slaughtered many sheep and oxen for Jehoshaphat and those who were with him in order to persuade him to attack Ramoth-gilead. ³"Will you go with me to Ramoth-gilead?" Israel's King Ahab asked Judah's King Jehoshaphat.

Jehoshaphat replied, "I and my people will be united with you and your people in battle. ⁴But," Jehoshaphat said to Israel's king, "first, let's see what the LORD has to say." ⁵So Israel's king gathered four hundred prophets and asked them, "Should we go to war with Ramoth-gilead or not?"

"Attack!" the prophets answered. "God will hand it over to the king."

⁶But Jehoshaphat said, "Isn't there any other prophet of the LORD around whom we could ask?"

---

²LXX; MT *in the ways of his father David* ªHeb *asherim*, perhaps objects devoted to the goddess Asherah

⁷"There's one other man who could ask the Lord for us," Israel's king told Jehoshaphat, "but I hate him because he never prophesies anything good about me, only bad. His name is Micaiah, Imlah's son."

"The king shouldn't speak like that!" Jehoshaphat said.

⁸So Israel's king called an officer and ordered, "Bring Micaiah, Imlah's son, right away."

⁹Now Israel's king and Judah's King Jehoshaphat were sitting on their thrones dressed in their royal robes at the threshing floor beside the entrance to the gate of Samaria. All the prophets were prophesying in front of them. ¹⁰Zedekiah, Chenaanah's son, made iron horns for himself and said, "This is what the Lord says: With these horns you will gore the Arameans until there's nothing left of them!"

¹¹The other prophets agreed: "Attack Ramoth-gilead and win! The Lord will hand it over to the king!"

¹²Meanwhile, the messenger who had gone to summon Micaiah said to him, "Listen, the prophets all agree that the king will succeed. You should say the same thing they say and prophesy success."

¹³But Micaiah answered, "As surely as the Lord lives, I will say only what God tells me to say."ᵇ

¹⁴When Micaiah arrived, the king asked him, "Micaiah, should we go to war with Ramoth-gilead or not?"

"Attack and win!" Micaiah answered. "The Lord will hand it over to the king."

ᵇLXX, 1 Kgs 22:14; MT omits *me*.

See What God Says *2 Chronicles 18:1-13*

Making decisions is a part of life. Maybe you've had to choose between spring soccer and baseball. Sometimes there are even bigger decisions that you might get to be a part of—like standing up for a friend or choosing kindness when it would be easier to get back at someone. We can ask God to help us know the way we should go in all our decisions.

Judah's King Jehoshaphat foolishly promised to help Israel's King Ahab if Ahab ever asked. Ahab wanted Jehoshaphat to join him in battle against another country. Jehoshaphat didn't really care about the battle, but he was committed to his promise. First though, Jehoshaphat told Ahab they needed to see what God had to say about it. Jehoshaphat wanted to do what God wanted him to do.

Ahab agreed to listen to the advice of all of the prophets except for Micaiah. Ahab didn't like Micaiah's words because they usually weren't what he wanted to hear. Jehoshaphat decided that he *did* want to hear what Micaiah had to say, and sure enough, Ahab didn't like the prophet's words.

This story teaches that we should remember to seek God in our decisions and not go to people who will tell us what we want to hear. Sometimes it's hard to hear harsh words, but it's better to hear the truth and learn to trust in God.

How can you remember to seek God when you have big decisions to make?

Who are the people you turn to for advice?

¹⁵But the king said, "How many times must I demand that you tell me the truth when you speak in the LORD's name?"

¹⁶Then Micaiah replied, "I saw all Israel scattered on the hills like sheep without a shepherd! And then the LORD said: 'They have no master. Let them return safely to their own homes.'"

¹⁷Then Israel's king said to Jehoshaphat, "Didn't I tell you? He never prophesies anything good about me, only bad."

¹⁸Then Micaiah said, "Listen now to the LORD's word: I saw the LORD enthroned with all the heavenly forces stationed at his right and at his left. ¹⁹The LORD said, 'Who will persuade Israel's King Ahab so that he attacks Ramoth-gilead and dies there?' There were several suggestions, ²⁰until one particular spirit approached the LORD and said, 'I will persuade him.' 'How?' the LORD asked. ²¹'I will be a lying spirit in the mouths of all his prophets,' he said. The LORD agreed: 'You will succeed in persuading him! Go ahead!' ²²So now, since the LORD placed a lying spirit in the mouths of these prophets of yours, it is the LORD who has pronounced disaster against you!"

²³Zedekiah, Chenaanah's son, approached Micaiah and slapped him on the cheek. "Just how did the LORD's spirit leave me to speak to you?" he asked.

²⁴Micaiah answered, "You will find out on the day you try to hide in an inner room."

²⁵"Arrest him," ordered Israel's king, "and turn him over to Amon the city governor and to Joash the king's son. ²⁶Tell them, 'The king says: Put this man in prison and feed him minimum rations of bread and water until I return safely.'"

²⁷"If you ever return safely," Micaiah replied, "then the LORD wasn't speaking through me." Then he added, "Mark my words, every last one of you!"

²⁸So Israel's king and Judah's King Jehoshaphat attacked Ramoth-gilead. ²⁹Israel's king said to Jehoshaphat, "I will disguise myself when we go into battle, but you should wear your royal attire." When the king of Israel had disguised himself, they entered the battle.

³⁰Meanwhile, Aram's king had commanded his chariot officers, "Don't bother with anyone big or small. Fight only with Israel's king."

³¹When the chariot officers saw Jehoshaphat, they assumed that he must be Israel's king, so they turned to attack him. But when Jehoshaphat cried out, the LORD helped him, and God lured them away from him. ³²When the chariot officers realized that he wasn't Israel's king, they stopped chasing him.

³³Someone, however, randomly shot an arrow that struck Israel's king between the joints in his armor. "Turn around and get me out of the battle," the king told his chariot driver. "I've been hit!" ³⁴While the battle raged all that day, Israel's king stood propped up in his chariot facing the Arameans. But that evening he died, just as the sun was going down.

19 Upon the safe arrival of Judah's King Jehoshaphat to his palace in Jerusalem, ²Jehu son of Hanani the seer came out to meet him and said, "Why did you help the wicked? Why have you loved those who hate the LORD? This is why the LORD is angry with you. ³Nevertheless, there is some good to be found in you, in that you have removed the sacred poles^c from the land and set your mind to seek God."

LIGHTHOUSE

HEART

God's Discipline Can Renew the Heart

2 Chronicles 19:1-3

Jehoshaphat made a poor choice for a friend. King Ahab was one of the worst kings of Israel (1 Kgs 16:33). Jehoshaphat followed God with all his heart, but he joined with Ahab for a fight. A prophet of God tried to warn them away from their plans, but they didn't listen (2 Chron 18:1-34). The battle ended in disaster. God spoke harshly to Jehoshaphat when he got home. God knew Jehoshaphat had already obeyed God in many ways (2 Chron 17:3-9). But after the bad influence of Ahab, God knew Jehoshaphat needed to recommit to following God. Jehoshaphat didn't get angry at God's harsh words like his father Asa did (2 Chron 16:1-12). Jehoshaphat knew the truth of God's words. The king changed his heart and determined to follow God better than ever (2 Chron 19:4-11). ◊

Jehoshaphat's reforms

⁴Though Jehoshaphat lived in Jerusalem, he regularly went out among the people

---

^cHeb *asherot*, perhaps objects devoted to the goddess Asherah

between Beer-sheba and Ephraim's highlands, and encouraged them to return to the Lord, the God of their ancestors. ⁵He appointed judges throughout the land in each of the fortified cities of Judah, ⁶instructing them, "Be careful when you pass judgment. You aren't dispensing justice by merely human standards but for the Lord, who is with you. ⁷Therefore, respect the Lord and act accordingly, because there can be no injustice, playing favorites, or taking bribes when it comes to the Lord our God."

⁸Jehoshaphat also appointed judges in Jerusalem from among the Levites, the priests, and the family heads of Israel to administer the Lord's Instruction and to settle disputes among those living[d] in Jerusalem. ⁹He instructed them, "You must respect the Lord at all times, in truth, and with complete integrity. ¹⁰In any case that comes before you from a fellow citizen in an outlying town, whether it involves bloodshed or is an issue

of instruction, commandment, regulations, or case laws, you must warn them not to sin against the Lord, consequently making him angry with both you and your fellow citizen. Do this, and you won't sin. ¹¹Amariah the chief priest will be in charge of all religious matters, and Zebadiah, Ishmael's son, the leader of Judah's house, will be in charge of all civil matters. The Levites will serve as your officers of the court. Carry out your duties with confidence, and may the Lord be with those who do good."

Jehoshaphat's victory

20 Some time later, the Moabites and the Ammonites, along with some of the Meunites,[e] attacked Jehoshaphat. ²Jehoshaphat was told, "A large army from beyond the sea, from Edom,[f] is coming to attack you. They are already at Hazazon-tamar!" (that is, En-gedi). ³Frightened, Jehoshaphat decided to seek the Lord's help

[d]LXX, Vulg; MT *they returned to Jerusalem* [e]LXX; MT *Ammonites* [f]OL; MT *Aram*

Don't Worry, Just Worship *2 Chronicles 20:1-18*

Worry is one of the worst feelings in the world. When we're worried, we feel stuck in a bad place with no way forward, backward, or to the side. Worry keeps us from being happy and trusting God. Worry is not what God wants for us.

Jehoshaphat was worried. He was about to be attacked by an enemy army, and feared for his life and the lives of his people. So Jehoshaphat prayed. He gathered all of the people together in front of the temple and prayed out loud to God. He declared that God was the only one who could save them. He declared that no matter what might happen, they would stand in front of that temple and before God.

Instead of giving in to worry and fear, Jehoshaphat worshipped God. He made sure that God was first in his heart above his fears, his position as king, and even his life. God heard his prayer and defeated Jehoshaphat's enemy. You can probably imagine what Jehoshaphat did when he heard God's answer to prayer. He prayed and worshipped some more!

What kinds of things do you worry about?

How can worship help you work through your worries?

and proclaimed a fast for all Judah. ⁴People from all of Judah's cities came to ask the Lᴏʀᴅ for help. ⁵Then Jehoshaphat stood up in the congregation of Judah and Jerusalem in the Lᴏʀᴅ's temple in front of the new courtyard. ⁶"Lᴏʀᴅ, the God of our ancestors, you alone are God in heaven. You rule all the kingdoms of the nations. You are so powerful that no one can oppose you. ⁷You, our God, drove out the inhabitants of this land before your people Israel and gave this land to the descendants of your friend Abraham forever. ⁸They have lived in it and have built a sanctuary in honor of your name in it, saying, ⁹'If calamity, sword, flood,ᵍ plague, or famine comes upon us, we will stand before this temple, before you, because your name is in this temple. We will cry out to you in our distress, and you will hear us and save us.' ¹⁰So look here! The Ammonites, the Moabites, and those from Mount Seir—the people you wouldn't let Israel invade when they came out of Egypt's land, so Israel avoided them and didn't destroy them— ¹¹here they are, returning the favor by coming to drive us out of your possession that you gave to us! ¹²Our God, won't you punish them? We are powerless against this mighty army that is about to attack us. We don't know what to do, and so we are looking to you for help."

¹³All Judah was standing before the Lᴏʀᴅ, even their little ones, wives, and children. ¹⁴Then the Lᴏʀᴅ's spirit came upon Jahaziel son of Zechariah son of Benaiah son of Jeiel son of Mattaniah, a Levite of the line of Asaph, as he stood in the middle of the assembly.

¹⁵"Pay attention, all of Judah, every inhabitant of Jerusalem, and King Jehoshaphat," Jahaziel said. "This is what the Lᴏʀᴅ says to you: Don't be afraid or discouraged by this great army because the battle isn't yours. It belongs to God! ¹⁶March out against them tomorrow. Since they will be coming through the Ziz pass, meet them at the end of the valley that opens into the Jeruel wilderness. ¹⁷You don't need to fight this battle. Just take your places, stand ready, and watch how the Lᴏʀᴅ, who is with you, will deliver you, Judah and Jerusalem. Don't be afraid or discouraged! Go out tomorrow and face them. The Lᴏʀᴅ will be with you."

¹⁸Then Jehoshaphat bowed down with his face to the ground, and all Judah and the inhabitants of Jerusalem fell before the Lᴏʀᴅ in worship. ¹⁹Levites from the lines of Kohath and Korah stood up to loudly praise the Lᴏʀᴅ, the God of Israel.

²⁰Early the next morning they went into the Tekoa wilderness. When they were about to go out, Jehoshaphat stood and said, "Listen to me, Judah and every inhabitant of Jerusalem! Trust the Lᴏʀᴅ your God, and you will stand firm; trust his prophets and succeed!"

²¹After consulting with the people, Jehoshaphat appointed musicians to play for the Lᴏʀᴅ, praising his majestic holiness. They were to march out before the warriors, saying, "Give thanks to the Lᴏʀᴅ because his faithful love lasts forever!" ²²As they broke into joyful song and praise, the Lᴏʀᴅ launched a surprise attack against the Ammonites, the Moabites, and those from Mount Seir who were invading Judah, so that they were defeated. ²³The Ammonites and the Moabites turned on those from Mount Seir, completely destroying them. Once they had finished off the inhabitants of Seir, they helped to destroy each other!

²⁴When Judah arrived at the point overlooking the wilderness, all they could see were corpses lying all over the ground. There were no survivors. ²⁵When Jehoshaphat and his army came to take the loot, they found a great amount of cattle,ʰ goods, clothing,ⁱ and other valuables—much more than they could carry. In fact, there was so much it took three days to haul it away. ²⁶On the fourth day they assembled in Blessing Valley, where they blessed the Lᴏʀᴅ. That's why it is called Blessing Valley to this day. ²⁷Then everyone from Judah and Jerusalem, with Jehoshaphat at their head, joyfully returned home to Jerusalem because the Lᴏʀᴅ had given them reason to rejoice over their enemies. ²⁸They entered Jerusalem accompanied by harps, lutes, and trumpets, and they went to the Lᴏʀᴅ's temple.

²⁹The fear of God came on all the surrounding kingdoms when they heard how the Lᴏʀᴅ had fought against Israel's enemies. ³⁰As a result, Jehoshaphat's rule was peaceful because his God gave him rest on all sides.

ᵍLXX; MT *judgment* ʰLXX; MT *among them* ⁱVulg; MT *corpses*

Jehoshaphat's last days

³¹Jehoshaphat ruled over Judah. He was 35 years old when he became king, and he ruled for twenty-five years in Jerusalem. His mother's name was Azubah; she was Shilhi's daughter. ³²Jehoshaphat walked in the way of his father Asa and didn't turn aside from it, doing what was right in the LORD's eyes, ³³with the exception that he didn't remove the shrines. The people were still not committed with all their hearts to the God of their ancestors. ³⁴The rest of Jehoshaphat's deeds, from beginning to end, are written in the records of Jehu, Hanani's son, which are included in the records of Israel's kings.

³⁵Sometime later, Judah's King Jehoshaphat formed an alliance with Israel's King Ahaziah, which caused him to sin. ³⁶They agreed to build a fleet of Tarshish-styled ships, and they built them in Ezion-geber. ³⁷Eliezer, Dodavahu's son from Mareshah, prophesied against Jehoshaphat: "Because you have formed an alliance with Ahaziah, the LORD will destroy what you have made." The ships were wrecked and couldn't sail to Tarshish.

21 Jehoshaphat died and was buried with his ancestors in David's City. His son Jehoram succeeded him as king.

Jehoram rules

²Jehoram's brothers, the other sons of Jehoshaphat, were Azariah, Jehiel, Zechariah, Azariah, Michael, and Shephatiah. All of these were the sons of Israel's King Jehoshaphat. ³Their father had given them many gifts of silver, gold, and other valuables, along with fortified cities in Judah, but he gave the kingdom to Jehoram because he was the oldest son.

⁴When Jehoram had taken control of his father's kingdom, he established his rule by killing all his brothers, along with some other leaders of Israel. ⁵Jehoram was 32 years old when he became king, and he ruled for eight years in Jerusalem. ⁶He walked in the ways of Israel's kings, just as Ahab's dynasty had done, because he married Ahab's daughter. He did what was evil in the LORD's eyes. ⁷Nevertheless, because of the covenant he had made with David, the LORD wasn't willing to destroy David's dynasty. He had promised to preserve a lamp for David and his sons forever. ⁸During Jehoram's rule, Edom rebelled against Judah's power and appointed its own king. ⁹Jehoram, along with all his chariots, crossed over to Zair.ʲ The Edomites, who had surrounded him, attacked at night, defeating himᵏ and his chariot officers. ¹⁰So Edom has been independent of Judah to this day. Libnah rebelled against Jehoram's rule at the same time because he had abandoned the LORD, the God of his ancestors. ¹¹As if that wasn't enough, Jehoram constructed shrines throughout Judah's highlands, encouraged Jerusalem's citizens to be unfaithful, and led Judah astray.

¹²A letter from the prophet Elijah came to Jehoram that read, "This is what the LORD, the God of your ancestor David, says: Because you haven't walked in the ways of your father Jehoshaphat or the ways of Judah's King Asa, ¹³but have walked in the ways of Israel's kings and have encouraged Judah and Jerusalem's citizens to be unfaithful, just as the house of Ahab did, and because you have even murdered your own brothers, your father's family, who were better than you, ¹⁴the LORD will now strike your family, your

LIGHTHOUSE

RESPECT FOR GOD

No Respect for Disrespect
2 Chronicles 21:4-20

King Jehoram was completely unlike his father Jehoshaphat who greatly respected God. Jehoshaphat turned to God in times of danger (2 Chron 17–20) and encouraged the Israelites to follow God's ways (2 Chron 17:3-6; 19:4). Jehoram did none of those things. Even though he grew up with a father who respected God, Jehoram had no respect for God. He killed all his brothers. He built new shrines to false gods and encouraged the Israelites to worship them instead of God. Because Jehoram wouldn't respect God, God showed Jehoram no respect. God raised enemies against Jehoram who took away his wealth and his family. Then he got sick with a terrible disease that killed him slowly, without dignity. By the time Jehoram died, no one in Israel respected him. ◗

ʲCorrection with 2 Kgs 8:21; MT *with his officers* ᵏOr *he defeated Edom*

children, your wives, and all your possessions with a heavy blow. [15]You yourself will become deathly ill with a chronic disease that will cause your intestines to fall out."

[16]Then the LORD made the Philistines and the Arabs, who lived near the Cushites, angry with Jehoram. [17]They attacked Judah, broke down its defenses, and hauled off all the goods that were found in the royal palace, along with the king's children and wives. Only Jehoahaz, Jehoram's youngest son, was spared. [18]After all this, the LORD struck Jehoram with an incurable intestinal disease. [19]For almost two years he grew steadily worse, until two days before his death, when his intestines fell out, causing him to die in horrible pain. His people didn't make a fire in his honor as they had done for his ancestors. [20]He was 32 years old when he became king, and he ruled for eight years in Jerusalem. No one was sorry he died. He was buried in David's City but not in the royal cemetery.

22The inhabitants of Jerusalem made his youngest son Ahaziah succeed him as king because the raiding party that had invaded the camp with the Arabs had killed all the older sons. So Ahaziah, Jehoram's son, became king of Judah.

Ahaziah rules

[2]Ahaziah was 22 years old[1] when he became king, and he ruled for one year in Jerusalem. His mother's name was Athaliah; she was the granddaughter of Omri. [3]Ahaziah walked in the ways of Ahab's dynasty, encouraged in this wickedness by his mother. [4]He did what was evil in the LORD's eyes, just as Ahab's dynasty had done, because after his father's death they gave him advice that led to his downfall. [5]Ahaziah was following their advice when he went with Israel's King Joram,[m] Ahab's son, to fight against Aram's King Hazael at Ramoth-gilead, where the Arameans wounded Joram. [6]Joram returned to Jezreel to recover from the wounds he suffered at Ramah in his battle with Aram's King Hazael. Then Judah's King Ahaziah,[n] Jehoram's son, went down to visit Joram,

Ahab's son, at Jezreel because he had been wounded. [7]But God used this visit to Joram to bring about Ahaziah's downfall. After his arrival, Ahaziah went with Joram to meet Jehu, Nimshi's son, whom the LORD had anointed to destroy Ahab's dynasty. [8]While Jehu was executing judgment on Ahab's dynasty, he discovered the princes of Judah, Ahaziah's nephews, serving Ahaziah, and Jehu killed them. [9]Jehu went looking for Ahaziah, who was captured while hiding in Samaria. He was then brought to Jehu and executed. He was given a decent burial, however, because people said, "He was the grandson of Jehoshaphat, who sought the LORD with all his heart."

There were now no members of Ahaziah's dynasty strong enough to rule the kingdom.

Queen Athaliah rules Judah

[10]When Athaliah, Ahaziah's mother, learned of her son's death, she immediately destroyed the entire royal family of Judah's dynasty. [11]But Jehoshabeath the king's daughter secretly took Ahaziah's son Jehoash[o] from the rest of the royal children who were about to be murdered, and

SAILBOAT

KINDNESS

Kindness Can Be Risky
2 Chronicles 22:10-12

Athaliah wanted power. Once she heard that her son King Ahaziah had been killed, Athaliah knew what she wanted to do. Her son had no older male children who could take over Israel, so now was her chance to become the first queen of Israel. But Athaliah knew she'd have to give up power once the dead king's sons became old enough to take the crown. Athaliah wanted to be in power for as long as she could, so she killed all her own grandchildren. Fortunately, Athaliah missed killing one son. Athaliah's daughter, Jehoshabeath, knew her mother was doing an evil thing so she had pity on the royal children. Knowing she could save only one, she risked her own life and hid Jehoash from his grandmother. Because of Jehoshabeath's kindness, the royal line of David—the same line that Jesus would be born from—was kept safe. ◗

[1]LXX, Syr, 2 Kgs 8:26; MT *42* [m]Or *Jehoram* (also in 22:6-7); the king's name is variously spelled in either long *Jehoram* or short *Joram* form. [n]LXX, Syr, Vulg; MT *Azariah* [o]Or *Joash*; the king's name is variously spelled in either long *Jehoash* or short *Joash* form in 2 Kgs.

hid him in a bedroom, along with his nurse. In this way Jehoshabeath, the daughter of King Jehoram, the wife of the priest Jehoiada and the sister of Ahaziah, hid Jehoash from Athaliah so she couldn't murder him. ¹²He remained hidden with them in God's temple for six years while Athaliah ruled the country.

23 But in the seventh year Jehoiada boldly formed a conspiracy with the following unit commanders: Jeroham's son Azariah, Jehohanan's son Ishmael, Obed's son Azariah, Adaiah's son Maaseiah, and Zichri's son Elishaphat. ²They went throughout Judah recruiting the Levites from all the cities of Judah, as well as the family heads of Israel, who then came to Jerusalem. ³The entire assembly made a covenant with the king in God's temple. Jehoiada said, "Look! Here is the king's son. He must be king, just as the LORD promised about David's descendants. ⁴This is what you must do: A third of you priests and Levites coming on sabbath duty will guard the gates, ⁵another third will be at the royal palace, and another third will be at the Foundation Gate. Meanwhile, all the people will be in the courtyards of the LORD's temple. ⁶Don't enter the LORD's temple, because only the priests or Levites on duty can do that. They are allowed to enter because they are holy, but the rest of the people must follow the LORD's requirements. ⁷The Levites must surround the king, each with his weapons drawn. Whoever comes near your ranks must be killed; stay near the king wherever he goes."

⁸The Levites and all Judah did everything that the priest Jehoiada ordered. They each took charge of those men reporting for duty on the Sabbath, as well as those going off duty, since Jehoiada hadn't released any divisions from duty. ⁹Then the priest Jehoiada gave the unit commanders King David's spears and large and small shields that were kept in God's temple. ¹⁰He positioned all the people, each with their weapons drawn, near the altar and the temple, stretching from the south side of the temple to the north side, so as to protect the king. ¹¹Then they brought out the king's son, crowned him, gave him the royal law,ᵖ and made him king. Jehoiada and his sons anointed him as everyone cried out, "Long live the king!"

¹²When Athaliah heard the noise made by the people running and cheering the king, she went to the people at the LORD's temple ¹³and saw the king standing by the royal pillar at the entrance, with the commanders and trumpeters beside the king. All the people of the land were rejoicing and blowing trumpets, and singers accompanied by musical instruments were leading the praise. Athaliah ripped her clothes and screamed, "Treason! Treason!"

¹⁴Then the priest Jehoiada brought out the unit commanders who were in charge of the army. "Take her out under guard,"�q he told them, "and kill anyone who follows her." This was because the priest had said, "She must not be executed in the LORD's temple." ¹⁵They arrested her when she reached the entrance of the Horse Gate at the royal palace. She was executed there.

¹⁶Jehoiada then made a covenant between himself, all the people, and the king, that they would be the LORD's people. ¹⁷Then all the people went to Baal's temple and tore it down, smashing its altars and images into pieces. They executed Baal's priest Mattan in front of the altars. ¹⁸Jehoiada appointed the priests andʳ Levites in

SAILBOAT

Joy

Good Leaders Are a Joy
2 Chronicles 23:16-21

Israel had reason to be joyful. After several years of wicked rulers, the kingdom had a king who followed God. Jehoshaphat was the last Israelite king to be obedient to God. While he lived, Israel enjoyed wealth and peace (2 Chron 17:3-5; 20:29-30). The next king, Jehoram, did evil things in God's eyes (2 Chron 21:12-15). Jehoram's son Ahaziah also disobeyed God (2 Chron 22:2-4). Finally, wicked Athaliah took over Israel as the kingdom's only queen. The king after Athaliah was young, but his protector was a faithful priest of God. The good priest Jehoiada got rid of the wicked queen and tore down her altars to false gods. There had been no peace in all the years that Israel disobeyed God. When Israel finally had leaders who helped the people follow God, peace returned. That was something to be joyful over. ◗

ᵖOr *testimony*; MT lacks *royal*. �q Heb uncertain ʳLXX; MT *levitical priests*

charge of the Lord's temple, and then appointed the divisions of the priests and Levites[s] that David had assigned to the Lord's temple to offer entirely burned sacrifices to the Lord, as written in the Instruction from Moses, with rejoicing and singing, just as David had ordered. [19]He posted guards at the gates of the Lord's temple so that no one who was unclean in any way could enter. [20]Then he took the unit commanders, the officials, the rulers of the people, and all the people of the land, and they led the king down from the Lord's temple, processing through the Upper Gate to the palace, where the king sat upon the royal throne. [21]All the people of the land rejoiced, and the city was at peace now that Athaliah had been executed at the palace.

Jehoash rules

24 Jehoash[t] was 7 years old when he became king, and he ruled for forty years in Jerusalem. His mother's name was Zibiah; she was from Beer-sheba. [2]Jehoash did what was right in the Lord's eyes as long as Jehoiada the priest was alive. [3]Jehoiada had him marry two wives, and Jehoash fathered sons and daughters.

[4]Sometime later, Jehoash wanted to renovate the Lord's temple. [5]He gathered the priests and the Levites and said, "Go to the cities of Judah and collect the annual tax of silver due from all Israel for the upkeep of God's temple. Do it right away."

But the Levites procrastinated. [6]So the king summoned the chief priest Jehoiada and asked him, "Why haven't you required the Levites to bring in from Judah and Jerusalem the tax imposed by the Lord's servant Moses and the Israelite assembly for the covenant tent?" ([7]Now wicked Athaliah and her followers had broken into God's temple and used all the holy objects of the Lord's temple in their worship of the Baals.) [8]So at the king's command a box was made and placed outside the gate of the Lord's temple. [9]Then a proclamation was issued throughout Judah and Jerusalem requiring the people to bring to the Lord the tax that God's servant Moses had imposed

on Israel in the wilderness. [10]This so pleased all the leaders and all the people that they gladly dropped their money in the box until it was full. [11]Whenever the box was brought by the Levites to the royal accountants, as soon as they saw that a large amount of money was in the box, the royal scribe and the representative of the high priest would come, empty the box, and return it to its place. This took place day after day, and a large amount of money was collected. [12]The king and Jehoiada would give it to those in charge of the work on the Lord's temple who in turn hired masons and carpenters to renovate the Lord's temple, as well as metalworkers for the iron and bronze to repair the Lord's temple. [13]The workers labored hard, and the restoration progressed smoothly under their control until they had brought God's temple back to its original state and reinforced it. [14]As soon as they finished, they brought the remaining money to the king and Jehoiada. They used it to make equipment for the Lord's temple, including what was used for the service and the entirely burned offerings, pans, and other objects made of gold and silver. As long as Jehoiada lived, the entirely burned offerings were regularly offered in the Lord's temple.

[15]Jehoiada grew old, and when he reached the age of 130, he died. [16]He was buried among the kings in David's City because of his exemplary service to Israel, God, and God's temple.

[17]After Jehoiada's death, however, the leaders of Judah came and bowed before the king, and the king listened to them. [18]They abandoned the temple of the Lord, their ancestors' God, and worshipped sacred poles[u] and idols. Anger came upon Judah and Jerusalem as a consequence of their sin, [19]and though God sent prophets to them to bring them back to the Lord and to warn them, they refused to listen. [20]Then the spirit of God enwrapped Zechariah the son of the priest Jehoiada. Standing before the people, he told them, "This is what God says: Why do you defy the Lord's commands and keep yourselves from prospering? Because you

---

[s]LXX; MT lacks *and then appointed the divisions of the priests and the Levites* [t]Heb *Joash* (see 24:2, 4, 22, 24); the king's name is variously spelled in either long *Jehoash* or short *Joash* form in 2 Kgs. [u]Heb *asherim*, perhaps objects devoted to the goddess Asherah

have abandoned the Lord, he has abandoned you!" ²¹But the people plotted against Zechariah, and at the king's command stoned him to death in the courtyard of the Lord's temple. ²²King Jehoash failed to remember the loyalty that Jehoiada, Zechariah's father, had shown him and murdered Jehoiada's son, who cried out as he lay dying, "May the Lord see and seek vengeance!"

UMBRELLA
Not Grateful

Be Grateful for the Kindness of Others
2 Chronicles 24:22

King Jehoash owed the priest Jehoiada his life and throne. When Jehoash's grandmother Athaliah took over as queen, she killed all her grandchildren except for Jehoash, who was hidden away by an aunt and given to the priest Jehoiada for safekeeping (2 Chron 22:10-12). Jehoiada kept Jehoash safely hidden from his grandmother for six years. At great risk to his life, Jehoiada made plans to overthrow the wicked Athaliah and put Jehoash on the throne of Israel (2 Chron 23). While Jehoiada was alive, King Jehoash listened to his advice and followed God. But when the priest died, Jehoash listened to evil people and turned away from God. Jehoiada's son Zechariah warned Jehoash against doing evil. But Jehoash had Zechariah killed. Jehoash was too selfish to care whose son Zechariah was. Because he forgot the kindness of Jehoiada's family, Jehoash lost an easy battle and was killed by his own officials (2 Chron 24:23-25). ◆

²³That spring the Aramean army marched against Jehoash. They attacked Judah and Jerusalem, destroyed all the people's leaders, and sent all the loot to the king of Damascus. ²⁴Although the Aramean forces were relatively small, the Lord handed over to them a very large army, because the people of Judah had abandoned the Lord, their ancestors' God. Jehoash was justly punished. ²⁵The Arameans left him badly wounded, but his own officials plotted against him for murdering the son^v of the priest Jehoiada. So they killed him in his bed. He died and was buried in David's City but not in the royal cemetery. ²⁶Those

who plotted against him were the Ammonite Zabad, Shimeath's son, and the Moabite Jehozabad, Shimrith's son. ²⁷The list of Jehoash's sons, the many prophecies against him, and the account of his restoration of God's temple are written in the comments on the records of the kings. His son Amaziah succeeded him as king.

Amaziah rules

25 Amaziah was 25 years old when he became king, and he ruled for twenty-nine years in Jerusalem. His mother's name was Jehoaddan; she was from Jerusalem. ²He did what was right in the Lord's eyes but not with all his heart. ³Once he had secured control over his kingdom, he executed the officials who had assassinated his father the king. ⁴However, he didn't kill their children because of what is written in the Instruction scroll from Moses, where the Lord commanded, *Parents shouldn't be executed because of what their children have done; neither should children be executed because of what their parents have done. Each person should be executed for their own guilty acts.*^w

⁵Amaziah gathered the people of Judah, organizing them into family units under captains of thousands and hundreds for all Judah and Benjamin. He summoned everyone 20 years old and older and found that there were three hundred thousand select troops, ready for service and able to handle spears and body-sized shields. ⁶He also hired one hundred thousand warriors from Israel for one hundred kikkars of silver.

⁷But a man of God confronted him. "King," he said, "the troops from Israel must not go with you, because the Lord isn't on the side of Israel or any Ephraimite. ⁸Should you go with them anyway, even if you fight fiercely, God will make you stumble before the enemy, because God has the ability to either help or make someone stumble."

⁹Amaziah asked the man of God, "What about the hundred kikkars I paid for the Israelite troops?"

"God can give you much more than that," the man of God replied.

¹⁰Amaziah released the Ephraimite troops

who had joined him so they could go home, but this only infuriated them against Judah, and they left in a rage. ¹¹Amaziah courageously led his people to the Salt Valley, where they killed ten thousand people from Seir. ¹²The Judean forces captured another ten thousand alive, brought them to the top of a cliff, and threw them off so that all were dashed to pieces. ¹³Meanwhile, the troops Amaziah had released from fighting alongside him raided cities in Judah from Samaria to Beth-horon, killing three thousand people and carrying off a large amount of loot. ¹⁴When Amaziah returned after defeating the Edomites, he brought the gods of the people of Seir. He set them up as his own gods, bowed down before them, and burned incense to them. ¹⁵As a result, the Lᴏʀᴅ was angry with Amaziah and sent a prophet to him.

"Why do you seek the gods of this people?" the prophet asked. "They couldn't even deliver their own people from you!"

¹⁶"Since when do you give me advice?" Amaziah interrupted. "You better quit before you end up dead!"

So the prophet stopped, but not until he said, "I know God plans to destroy you because you've done this and because you've refused to listen to my advice."

¹⁷After Judah's King Amaziah consulted with his advisors, he sent a challenge to Israel's King Joash, Jehoahaz's son and Jehu's grandson. "Come on," he said, "let's go head-to-head!"

¹⁸Israel's King Joash sent the following reply to Judah's King Amaziah: "Once upon a time, a thistle in Lebanon sent a message to a cedar: 'Give your daughter to my son as a wife.' But then a wild beast in Lebanon came along and trampled the thistle. ¹⁹Do you think that because you've defeated Edom, you can arrogantly seek even more? Stay home! Why invite disaster when both you and Judah will fall?" ²⁰But Amaziah wouldn't listen, because God intended to use this to destroy them since they had sought Edom's gods. ²¹So Israel's King Joash moved against Judah's King Amaziah and went head-to-head in battle at Beth-shemesh in Judah. ²²Judah was defeated by Israel, and everyone ran home. ²³At Beth-shemesh, Israel's King Joash captured

Judah's King Amaziah, Jehoash's[x] son and Ahaziah's[y] grandson. Joash brought him to Jerusalem and broke down six hundred feet of the Jerusalem wall from the Ephraim Gate to the Corner Gate. ²⁴Joash took[z] all the gold and silver, and all the objects he could find in God's temple in the care of Obed-edom, and in the treasuries of the palace, along with some hostages. Then he returned to Samaria.

UMBRELLA
Pride

Don't Take God's Credit for Yourself
2 Chronicles 25:5-24

King Amaziah didn't know good advice when he heard it. God helped Amaziah defeat his enemies. But Amaziah disrespected God by taking his defeated enemies' false gods and worshipping them. When God's prophet told Amaziah to stop his wickedness, Amaziah threatened to kill the prophet. Amaziah felt too proud to give God any credit for defeating his enemies. Amaziah thought he would defeat them himself and believed he was tougher than he really was. Amaziah thought he was so tough he could win against King Joash. So Amaziah tried to start a fight with Joash. King Joash warned Amaziah against acting bigger than he was but Amaziah didn't listen. Joash defeated Amaziah's army and broke down the walls of his city. Later, Amaziah's own men killed him. 💧

²⁵Judah's King Amaziah, Jehoash's son, lived fifteen years after the death of Israel's King Joash, Jehoahaz's son. ²⁶The rest of Amaziah's deeds, from beginning to end, aren't they written in the official records of Israel's and Judah's kings? ²⁷From the time Amaziah turned away from the Lᴏʀᴅ, some people conspired against him in Jerusalem. When Amaziah fled to Lachish, they sent men after him, and they murdered him in Lachish. ²⁸They carried him back on horses and he was buried with his ancestors in David's City.[a]

Uzziah rules Judah

26 Then all the people of Judah took Uzziah,[b] who was 16 years old, and

---

[x] Or *Joash* (see also 25:25); the king's name is variously spelled in either long *Jehoash* or short *Joash* form in 2 Kgs. [y] See 2 Kgs 14:13; MT *Jehoahaz* [z] See 2 Kgs 14:14; Heb omits *took*. [a] LXX; MT *Judah* [b] Uzziah is usually named Azariah in 2 Kgs 14:21; 15:1, 6-7.

made him king after his father Amaziah. ²He rebuilt Eloth, restoring it to Judah after King Amaziah had lain down with his ancestors.

³Uzziah was 16 years old when he became king, and he ruled for fifty-two years in Jerusalem. His mother's name was Jecoliah; she was from Jerusalem. ⁴He did what was right in the LORD's eyes, just as his father Amaziah had done. ⁵He sought God as long as Zechariah, who instructed him in the fearᶜ of God, was alive. And as long as he sought the LORD, God gave him success. ⁶He marched against the Philistines and broke down the walls of Gath, Jabneh, and Ashdod. Then he rebuilt towns near Ashdod and elsewhere among the Philistines. ⁷God helped him against the Philistines, the Arabs who inhabited Gur,ᵈ and the Meunites. ⁸The Meunitesᵉ paid taxes to Uzziah, whose fame spread even to Egypt because he had grown so powerful. ⁹He built towers in Jerusalem, at the Corner Gate, the Valley Gate, and at the Angle, and reinforced them. ¹⁰He also built towers in the wilderness and dug many wells for his large herds in the lowlands and the plain. He had many workers who tended his farms and vineyards, because he loved the soil. ¹¹Uzziah had a standing army equipped for combat whose units went to war according to the number determined by the scribe Jeiel and Maaseiah, an officer under

ᶜLXX; MT *visions* ᵈTg; MT *Gur-baal* ᵉLXX; MT *Ammonites*

Don't Be So Full of Yourself *2 Chronicles 26*

What are you really good at doing? Maybe you play a sport or an instrument and get compliments from other people. Maybe you're really good at math or spelling and get straight A's. Or maybe you're a great leader who can bring people together to solve a problem. We're all good at different things. But we all have to be careful that we don't become full of ourselves. God is the one who made us to be the way we are. We should use our talents and abilities for God's work in the world, not to make ourselves powerful or popular.

King Uzziah grew to be a great king. He began his reign when he was 16 years old and had great success until he got a little too full of himself. He decided that he didn't need God as much as he used to because he was so good at being king. One day he decided to light the incense—a fragrance offering to God that made the temple smell good—which was a job only for the priests. The priests told Uzziah not to do it, but he didn't listen. Immediately, he became sick with spots on his skin and had a skin disease for the rest of his life.

It's important to stay humble before God and give your talents back in worship. Let God use your talents and abilities to bless others.

How can you use your talents and abilities for God?

Who can help you remember not to become too full of yourself and forget God?

the authority of Hananiah, one of the king's officials. ¹²The grand total of family heads in charge of these courageous warriors was twenty-six hundred. ¹³They commanded an army of three hundred seven thousand five hundred. They formed a powerful force that could support the king against the enemy. ¹⁴Uzziah supplied the entire force with shields, spears, helmets, armor, bows, and sling stones. ¹⁵He set up clever devices in Jerusalem on the towers and corners of the wall designed to shoot arrows and large stones. And so Uzziah's fame spread far and wide, because he had received wonderful help until he became powerful.

¹⁶But as soon as he became powerful, he grew so arrogant that he acted corruptly. He was unfaithful to the LORD his God by entering the LORD's sanctuary to burn incense upon the incense altar. ¹⁷The priest Azariah, accompanied by eighty other of the LORD's courageous priests, went in after him ¹⁸and confronted King Uzziah.

"You have no right, Uzziah," he said, "to burn incense to the LORD! That privilege belongs to the priests, Aaron's descendants, who have been ordained to burn incense. Get out of this holy place because you have been unfaithful! The LORD God won't honor you for this."

¹⁹Then Uzziah, who already had a censer in his hand ready to burn the incense, became angry. While he was fuming at the priests, skin disease[f] erupted on his forehead in the presence of the priests before the incense altar in the LORD's temple. ²⁰When Azariah the chief priest and all the other priests turned and saw the skin disease on his forehead, they rushed him out of there. Uzziah also was anxious to leave because the LORD had afflicted him. ²¹King Uzziah had skin disease until the day he died. He lived in a separate house,[g] diseased in his skin, because he was barred from the LORD's temple. His son Jotham supervised the palace administration and governed the people of the land. ²²The rest of Uzziah's deeds, from beginning to end, were written down by the prophet Isaiah, Amoz's son. ²³Uzziah died and was buried with his ancestors in a field belonging to the kings, because people said, "He had skin disease." His son Jotham succeeded him as king.

Jotham rules

27Jotham was 25 years old when he became king, and he ruled for sixteen years in Jerusalem. His mother's name was Jerushah; she was Zadok's daughter. ²Jotham did what was right in the LORD's eyes, just as his father Uzziah had done. Unlike Uzziah, Jotham didn't enter the LORD's temple. But the people continued their crooked practices. ³Jotham rebuilt the Upper Gate of the LORD's temple and did extensive work on the wall of the elevated fortress.[h] ⁴He built towns in Judah's highlands and fortresses and towers in the wooded areas. ⁵He fought against the king of the Ammonites and defeated the Ammonites. They paid him one hundred kikkars of silver, ten thousand kors[i] of wheat, and ten thousand kors of barley that year and for the next two years. ⁶Jotham was securely established because he maintained a faithful life before the LORD his God. ⁷The rest of Jotham's deeds, including all his wars and accomplishments, are written in the official records of Israel's and Judah's kings. ⁸He was 25 years old when he became king, and he ruled for sixteen years in Jerusalem. ⁹Jotham lay down with his ancestors and was buried in David's City. His son Ahaz succeeded him as king.

Ahaz rules

28Ahaz was 20 years old when he became king, and he ruled for sixteen years in Jerusalem. He didn't do what was right in the LORD's eyes, unlike his ancestor David. ²Instead, he walked in the ways of Israel's kings, making images of the Baals ³and burning incense in the Ben-hinnom Valley. He even burned his own sons alive, imitating the detestable practices of the nations the LORD had driven out before the Israelites. ⁴He also sacrificed and burned incense at the shrines on every hill and beneath every shady tree. ⁵So the LORD his God handed him over to Aram's king, who defeated him and carried off many prisoners, bringing them

---

[f]The precise meaning is uncertain; traditionally *leprosy*—a term used for several different skin diseases. Also in 26:21-20, 23.
[g]Heb uncertain [h]Or *hillside*; Heb uncertain [i]One kor is equivalent to a homer and is possibly equal to fifty gallons of grain.

to Damascus. Ahaz was also handed over to Israel's king, who defeated him with a severe beating. ⁶In Judah, Pekah, Remaliah's son, killed one hundred twenty thousand warriors in the course of a single day because they had abandoned the LORD, God of their ancestors. ⁷An Ephraimite warrior named Zichri killed the king's son Maaseiah, the palace administrator Azrikam, and Elkanah, the king's second in command. ⁸The Israelites took captive two hundred thousand women, boys, and girls from their Judean relatives and seized enormous amounts of plunder, which they took back to Samaria.

⁹One of the LORD's prophets named Oded lived in Samaria. When the army arrived there, he went to meet them and said, "Don't you see that the LORD God of your ancestors was angry with Judah and let you defeat them? But look what you've done! Your merciless slaughter of them stinks to high heaven! ¹⁰And now you think you can enslave the men and women of Judah and Jerusalem? What about your own guilt before the LORD your God? ¹¹Listen to me! Send back the captives you took from your relatives, because the LORD is furious with you."

¹²At this, some of the Ephraimite leaders—Johanan's son Azariah, Meshillemoth's son Berechiah, Shallum's son Jehizkiah, and Hadlai's son Amasa—confronted those returning from battle. ¹³"Don't bring the captives here," they told them. "Your plan will only add to our sin and guilt before the LORD. We're already guilty enough, and great anger is already directed at Israel." ¹⁴So the warriors released the captives and brought the loot before the officers and the whole assembly. ¹⁵Then people named for this task took charge of the captives and dressed everyone who was naked with items taken from the loot. They gave them clothing, sandals, food and drink, and bandaged their wounds. Everyone who couldn't walk they placed on donkeys, and they brought them to Jericho, Palm City, near their Judean relatives. Then they returned to Samaria.

¹⁶At that time King Ahaz sent for help from the king[j] of Assyria. ¹⁷Once again, the Edomites had invaded Judah, defeating Judah

and carrying off captives. ¹⁸The Philistines had raided the towns in the lowlands and the arid southern plain of Judah, capturing Beth-shemesh, Aijalon, and Gederoth, along with Soco and its surrounding villages, Timnah and its surrounding villages, and Gimzo and its surrounding villages, and occupying all of these cities. ¹⁹The LORD was humiliating Judah on account of Israel's King Ahaz, because he had exercised no restraint in Judah and had been utterly unfaithful to the LORD. ²⁰Assyria's King Tiglath-pileser[k] came to Ahaz, but he brought trouble, not support. ²¹Even though Ahaz took items from the LORD's temple, the royal palace, and the officials to buy off the king of Assyria, it was of no help.

²²It was during this troubled time that King Ahaz became even more unfaithful to the LORD ²³by sacrificing to the gods of Damascus, who had defeated him.

"Since the gods of Aram's kings are helping them," he said, "I'll sacrifice to them too, so that they will help me."

But they became the ruin of both him and all Israel. ²⁴Ahaz gathered the objects from God's temple, cut them up, shut the doors of the

LIGHTHOUSE

FALSE GODS

Trust in God, Not in Idols *2 Chronicles 28:23*
King Ahaz put his faith in the wrong things. He thought a stronger king, rather than God, could save him from his problems (2 Chron 28:16-21). When that didn't work, Ahaz decided that his enemies were winning because they had stronger gods. He wrongly believed that these false gods were stronger than Israel's God. Ahaz locked the doors to God's temple. He made altars on every corner in Jerusalem and in all the towns in his kingdom so that the people could worship false gods. But that didn't solve his problems either. Ahaz didn't realize that there really weren't any gods helping his enemies. The kings of Aram, Edom, and Philistia were always defeating Ahaz because God was using them to punish Ahaz for turning away from God (2 Chron 28:19). Ahaz's problems started and then got worse because he trusted in something other than God. ◊

LORD's temple, and made himself altars on every corner in Jerusalem. [25] He made shrines in all the towns of Judah for burning incense to other gods. This made the LORD, the God of his ancestors, very angry.

[26] The rest of Ahaz's deeds, from beginning to end, are written in the official records of Israel's and Judah's kings. [27] Ahaz lay down with his ancestors and was buried in the city, in Jerusalem, but not in the royal cemetery of Israel's kings. His son Hezekiah succeeded him as king.

Hezekiah rules

29 Hezekiah became king when he was 25 years old, and he ruled for twenty-nine years in Jerusalem. His mother's name was Abijah; she was Zechariah's daughter. [2] He did what was right in the LORD's eyes, just as his ancestor David had done. [3] In the very first year of his rule, during the first month, Hezekiah reopened the doors of the LORD's temple, having repaired them. [4] Then he brought in the priests and Levites and assembled them in the eastern square.

[5] "Listen to me, you Levites!" he said. "Make yourselves holy so you can make holy the temple of the LORD God of your ancestors by removing from the sanctuary any impure thing. [6] Our ancestors were unfaithful and did what was evil in the LORD our God's eyes. They abandoned him, they ignored the LORD's dwelling, and they defied him. [7] They even closed the doors of the entrance hall, snuffed out the lamps, and stopped burning incense and offering entirely burned offerings in the sanctuary of the God of Israel. [8] This angered the LORD so much that he made Judah and Jerusalem an object of terror and horror, something people hiss at, as you can see with your own eyes. [9] That's why our ancestors died violent deaths, while our sons, daughters, and wives were taken captive. [10] But now I intend to make a covenant with the LORD, Israel's God, so God will no longer be angry with us. [11] Don't be careless, my sons! The LORD has chosen you to stand in his presence to serve him, so that you can be his servants and burn incense to him."

[12] Then the following Levites got up:

from the descendants of the Kohathites: Mahath, Amasai's son, and Joel, Azariah's son;

from the descendants of Merari: Kish, Abdi's son, and Azariah, Jehallelel's son;

from the Gershonites: Joah, Zimmah's son, and Eden, Joah's son;

[13] from the descendants of Elizaphan: Shimri and Jeuel;

from the descendants of Asaph: Zechariah and Mattaniah;

[14] from the descendants of Heman: Jehuel and Shimei;

and from the descendants of Jeduthun: Shemaiah and Uzziel.

did you know? In 2 Kings, King Hezekiah was praised for rebuilding the kingdom's strength and might. The writer of Chronicles, who focused more on the priests and the temple, praised Hezekiah for restoring the temple. Because of Hezekiah, the temple was reopened and people could once again gather and worship God.

[15] These men gathered their relatives, made themselves holy, and went in to purify the LORD's temple by obeying the king's command as the LORD had told him. [16] The priests went in to purify the inner portion of the LORD's temple. They brought out to the courtyard of the LORD's temple all the impurities they discovered inside. Then the Levites took them out to the Kidron Valley. [17] They began to make things holy on the first day of the first month.[1] On the eighth day of the month they reached the LORD's entrance hall. They made holy the LORD's temple for eight days, finishing on the sixteenth day of the first month.

[18] Then they went before King Hezekiah. "We have purified the LORD's entire temple," they said, "and the altar for the entirely burned offering together with all its equipment, and the table for the stacks of bread together with all its equipment. [19] We have also restored and made holy all the items King Ahaz threw out during his rule in his unfaithfulness. They are now before the LORD's altar."

[1] March-April, Nisan

Hezekiah rededicates the temple

²⁰Early the next morning Hezekiah gathered the city leaders and went to the LORD's temple. ²¹They brought seven bulls, seven rams, and seven lambs, along with seven male goats, for a purification offering on behalf of the kingdom, the sanctuary, and Judah. Hezekiah ordered the priests, Aaron's sons, to offer them up on the LORD's altar. ²²When they slaughtered the bulls, the priests took the blood and splashed it against the altar. Next they slaughtered the rams and splashed their blood against the altar, and also slaughtered the lambs, splashing their blood against the altar as well. ²³Finally, they brought the goats for the purification offering before the king and the assembly. After laying their hands on them, ²⁴the priests slaughtered them and smeared the blood on the altar as a purification offering to take away the sin of all Israel, because the king had specifically ordered that the entirely burned sacrifice and the purification offering should be on behalf of all Israel. ²⁵Hezekiah had the Levites stand in the LORD's temple with cymbals, harps, and zithers, just as the LORD had ordered through David, the king's seer Gad, and the prophet Nathan. ²⁶While the Levites took their places holding David's instruments, and the priests their trumpets, ²⁷Hezekiah ordered the entirely burned offering to be offered up on the altar. As they began to offer the entirely burned offering, the LORD's song also began, accompanied by the trumpets and the other instruments of Israel's King David. ²⁸The whole congregation worshipped with singing choirs and blaring trumpets until the end of the entirely burned offering. ²⁹After the entirely burned offering was complete, the king and all who were with him bowed down in worship. ³⁰Then King Hezekiah and the leaders ordered the Levites to praise the LORD by using the words of David and the seer Asaph. They did so joyously; then they bowed down in worship too.

³¹"Now that you have dedicated yourselves to the LORD," King Hezekiah told them, "bring sacrificial thank offerings to the LORD's temple." So the assembly brought sacrificial thank offerings, with some people volunteering to provide entirely burned offerings. ³²All in all, the congregation brought seventy bulls, a hundred rams, and two hundred lambs as entirely burned offerings for the LORD, ³³as well as six hundred bulls and three thousand sheep as holy offerings. ³⁴Unfortunately, there weren't enough priests to skin all these entirely burned offerings. So their relatives the Levites (who had been more conscientious about preparing themselves than the priests) stepped in and helped them until the work was done or additional priests had made themselves holy. ³⁵In addition to the wealth of entirely burned offerings, there was the fat of the well-being sacrifices and drink offerings accompanying the entirely burned offerings. In this way, the service of the LORD's temple was restored, ³⁶and Hezekiah and all the people rejoiced at what God had done for them, since it had happened so quickly.

Hezekiah's Passover

30Then Hezekiah sent word to all Israel and Judah, and wrote letters to Ephraim and Manasseh as well, inviting them to the LORD's temple in Jerusalem to celebrate the Passover of the LORD God of Israel. ²The king, his officials, and the entire Jerusalem congregation had decided to celebrate Passover in the second month.ᵐ ³They had been unable to celebrate it at the usual time because the priests had failed to make themselves holy in sufficient numbers, and the people hadn't gathered at Jerusalem. ⁴Since the plan seemed good to the king and the entire congregation, ⁵they made arrangements to circulate an announcement throughout all Israel, from Beer-sheba to Dan, to come to Jerusalem to celebrate the Passover of the LORD God of Israel, because they hadn't often kept it as written. ⁶Under the authority of the king, runners took letters from the king and his officials throughout all Israel and Judah, which read:

People of Israel! Return to the LORD, the God of Abraham, Isaac, and Israel, so that he may return to those of you who remain, who have escaped capture by the Assyrian kings. ⁷Don't be like your ancestors

ᵐApril-May, Iyar

and relatives, who were unfaithful to the LORD, the God of their ancestors, so that he made them an object of horror as you can see for yourselves. [8]So don't be stubborn like your ancestors. Surrender to the LORD! Come to God's sanctuary, which he has made holy forever, and serve the LORD your God so that he won't be angry with you any longer. [9]When you return to the LORD, your relatives and your children will receive mercy from their captors and be allowed to return to this land. The LORD your God is merciful and compassionate. He won't withdraw his presence from you if you return to him.

[10]So the runners went from town to town in Ephraim and Manasseh, all the way to Zebulun. But they were laughed at and made fun of. [11]Even so, some people from Asher, Manasseh, and Zebulun were submissive and came to Jerusalem. [12]Moreover, God's power was at work in Judah, unifying them to do what the king and his officials had ordered by the LORD's command.

[13]A huge crowd gathered in Jerusalem to celebrate the Festival of Unleavened Bread in the second month. A very large congregation gathered. [14]First, they removed the altars in Jerusalem, and hauled off the incense altars and dumped them in the Kidron Valley. [15]They slaughtered the Passover lambs on the fourteenth day of the second month. Ashamed of themselves, the priests and the Levites made themselves holy and brought entirely burned offerings to the LORD's temple. [16]They now took their places as laid out in the Instruction from Moses the man of God, and the priests splashed the blood they received from the Levites against the altar. [17]Since many in the congregation hadn't made themselves holy, the Levites slaughtered the Passover lambs, making them holy to the LORD for all who weren't ceremonially clean. [18]This included most of those who had come from Ephraim, Manasseh, Issachar, and Zebulun—people who hadn't purified themselves and so hadn't eaten the Passover meal in the prescribed way. But Hezekiah prayed for them: "May the good LORD forgive [19]everyone who has decided to seek the true God, the LORD, the God of their ancestors, even though they aren't ceremonially clean by sanctuary

standards." [20]The LORD heard Hezekiah and healed the people. [21]So the Israelites in Jerusalem joyfully celebrated the Festival of Unleavened Bread for seven days, with the Levites and the priests praising the LORD every day, accompanied by the LORD's mighty instruments. [22]Hezekiah congratulated all the Levites who had performed so skillfully for the LORD. They feasted throughout the seven days of the festival, sacrificing well-being offerings and praising the LORD, the God of their ancestors.

[23]Then the whole congregation agreed to celebrate another seven days, which they joyfully did. [24]Judah's King Hezekiah contributed one thousand bulls and seven thousand sheep for the congregation, while the officials provided another thousand bulls and ten thousand sheep, and great numbers of priests made themselves holy. [25]Then the whole congregation of Judah rejoiced, as did the priests and the Levites, the whole congregation from Israel, the immigrants who had come from the land of Israel, and those who lived in Judah. [26]There was great joy in Jerusalem. Nothing like this had taken place in Jerusalem since the days of Israel's King Solomon, David's son. [27]Then the levitical priests blessed the people, and their voice was heard when their prayer reached God's holy dwelling in heaven.

LIGHTHOUSE

GOOD NEWS

Why Passover Was Important
2 Chronicles 30

King Hezekiah knew how important the Passover celebration was for Israel. For many years the Israelites hadn't cared about celebrating Passover regularly. But now Hezekiah made preparations across the kingdom to celebrate this special feast. Passover marked the time when God set God's people free from slavery in Egypt. During that time, God had commanded every Hebrew family to kill an unspotted lamb and spread its blood over the doorways of their houses. When God sent a heavenly messenger of death to punish the Egyptians, the messenger "passed over" the houses with blood on the doorways (Exod 12:1-30). Hezekiah knew it was important to remember what God had done for the Israelites. 🌢

31 When all of these things were finished, all of the Israelites who were present went out to the cities of Judah, smashed the sacred pillars, cut down the sacred poles,[n] and completely destroyed the shrines and altars throughout Judah as well as Benjamin, Ephraim, and Manasseh. Then all the Israelites returned to their individual homes in their own cities.

Hezekiah's reform

[2] Hezekiah reappointed the priests and the Levites, each to their divisions and their tasks, to make entirely burned offerings and well-being sacrifices, to serve, to give thanks, and to offer praise in the gates of the Lord's camp. [3] As his portion, the king personally contributed the entirely burned offerings for the morning and evening sacrifices, as well as the entirely burned offerings for the Sabbaths, new moons, and festivals, as written in the Lord's Instruction. [4] He ordered the people living in Jerusalem to provide the required portion for the priests and the Levites so they could devote themselves to the Lord's Instruction. [5] As soon as the order was issued, the Israelites generously gave the best of their grain, new wine, oil, honey, and all their crops—a tenth of everything, a huge amount. [6] The people of Israel and Judah, living in the cities of Judah, also brought in a tenth of their herds and flocks and a tenth of the items that had been dedicated to the Lord their God, stacking it up in piles. [7] They began stacking up the piles in the third month[o] and finished them in the seventh.[p] [8] When Hezekiah and the officials saw the piles, they blessed the Lord and his people Israel.

[9] When Hezekiah asked the priests and Levites about the piles, [10] the chief priest Azariah, who was from Zadok's family, answered, "Ever since the people started bringing contributions to the Lord's temple we've had enough to eat with plenty to spare. The Lord has definitely blessed his people! There's a lot left over."

[11] So Hezekiah ordered them to prepare storerooms in the Lord's temple. When they finished preparing them, [12] the priests

LIFE PRESERVER

Why did the Israelites give a tenth of what they had?
2 Chronicles 31:4-8

Throughout the Bible, there are stories about God's people giving God a tenth of what they had. Under Hezekiah's reform, the religious leaders were busy organizing the temple. Offerings from the first harvest of grain, wine, oil, honey, and other crops were needed to feed the priests and Levites so that they would be free to study God's Instruction and prepare for worship. The people's tenth made sure God's servants could give their best to God's work. Giving a tenth of everything they owned was a way for the Israelites to show God what was important to them. When everyone obeyed, there was plenty for all, and God's work was done.

We still share what we have today. We are encouraged to give a tenth of our income or our time to help out with God's work. When everyone shares, there is always a lot left over. ⬧

conscientiously brought in the contributions, the tenth-part gifts, and the dedicated things. Conaniah, a Levite, was put in charge, assisted by his brother Shimei, [13] while Jehiel, Azaziah, Nahath, Asahel, Jerimoth, Jozabad, Eliel, Ismachiah, Mahath, and Benaiah served as supervisors under them, as appointed by King Hezekiah and Azariah the official in charge of God's temple. [14] The Levite Kore, Imnah's son, who was keeper of the east gate, was in charge of the spontaneous gifts to God. He was responsible for distributing the contribution reserved for the Lord and the dedicated gifts. [15] Eden, Miniamin, Jeshua, Shemaiah, Amariah, and Shecaniah faithfully assisted him regarding[q] the priests by distributing the portions to their relatives, old and young alike, by divisions. [16] Additionally, they also distributed daily rations to those males, registered by genealogy, three years old and older, all who entered the Lord's temple to carry out their daily duties as their divisions required. [17] They also distributed to those priests registered by their families, and to Levites 20 years of age and older according to their divisional responsibilities.

[n] Heb *asherim*, perhaps objects devoted to the goddess Asherah [o] May–June, Sivan [p] September–October, Tishrei [q] Or *with the assistance of*, cf LXX; MT *in the cities of*

¹⁸The official genealogy included all their small children, their wives, their sons, and their daughters—the entire congregation—for they had faithfully made themselves holy. ¹⁹As for Aaron's descendants, the priests who lived in the outskirts of the cities, men were assigned to distribute portions to every male among the priests and to every Levite listed in the genealogical records. ²⁰This is what Hezekiah did throughout all Judah, doing what the LORD his God considered good, right, and true. ²¹Everything that Hezekiah began to do for the service of God's temple, whether by the Instruction or the commands, in order to seek his God, he did successfully and with all his heart.

Sennacherib's invasion

32 After these things and these faithful acts, Assyria's King Sennacherib invaded Judah and attacked its fortified cities, intending to capture them. ²When Hezekiah realized that Sennacherib also planned on fighting Jerusalem, ³he consulted with his officials and soldiers about stopping up the springs outside the city, and they supported him. ⁴A large force gathered to stop up all the springs and the streams that flowed through the land. "Why should the kings of Assyria come and find plenty of water?" they asked. ⁵Hezekiah vigorously rebuilt all the broken sections of the wall, erected towers, constructed another wall outside the first, reinforced the terrace of David's City, and made a large supply of weapons and shields. ⁶He appointed military officers over the troops, assembled them in the square of the city gate, and spoke these words of encouragement: ⁷"Be brave and be strong! Don't let the king of Assyria and all those warriors he brings with him scare you or cause you dismay, because our forces are greater than his.^r ⁸All he has is human strength, but we have the LORD our God, who will help us fight our battles!"

The troops trusted Judah's King Hezekiah.

⁹After this Assyria's King Sennacherib, who was attacking Lachish with all his forces, sent his servants to Jerusalem with the following message for Judah's King Hezekiah and all the people of Judah who were in Jerusalem:

¹⁰This is what Assyria's King Sennacherib says: What makes you so confident that you stay put in Jerusalem while it is being attacked? ¹¹Obviously, Hezekiah has fooled you into surrendering yourselves to death by hunger and thirst when he says, "The LORD our God will rescue us from Assyria's king." ¹²Isn't this the same Hezekiah who got rid of his shrines and altars, and then demanded of Judah and Jerusalem, "You must worship and burn incense before only one altar"? ¹³Don't you know what I and my predecessors have done to the people of other nations? Were any of the gods of these other nations able to rescue their lands from my power? ¹⁴Which one of any of the gods of these nations that my predecessors destroyed was able to rescue them from my power? So why should your god be able to rescue you from my power? ¹⁵Don't let Hezekiah seduce you like fools. Don't believe him! No god of any other nation or kingdom has been able to rescue their people from me or from my predecessors. No, your gods won't rescue you from my power.

¹⁶The Assyrian king's servants continued to make fun of the LORD God and his servant Hezekiah. ¹⁷He wrote other letters insulting the LORD God of Israel, defying him by saying, "Just as the gods of the nations in other countries couldn't rescue their people from my power, Hezekiah's god won't be able to rescue his people from my power." ¹⁸Then they shouted loudly in Hebrew^s at the people of Jerusalem gathered on the wall, in an attempt to frighten and demoralize them, in order to capture the city. ¹⁹They spoke about the God of Jerusalem as though he were the work of human hands, like the gods of the other peoples of the earth. ²⁰King Hezekiah and the prophet Isaiah, Amoz's son, prayed about this, crying out to heaven. ²¹Then the LORD sent a messenger who destroyed every warrior, leader, and officer in the camp of the Assyrian king. When Sennacherib went home in disgrace, he entered the temple of his god, and his own sons killed him with a sword. ²²This is how the LORD rescued Hezekiah and the citizens of Jerusalem from the power of Assyria's

---

^r*Or there is greater power with us than with him* ^s*Or the language of Judah*

King Sennacherib, and all others, giving them rest[t] on all sides. ²³Many people brought offerings to the LORD in Jerusalem and costly gifts to Judah's King Hezekiah, who was highly regarded by all the nations from then on.

Hezekiah's illness

²⁴Around that same time, Hezekiah became deathly ill and prayed to the LORD, who answered him with a miraculous sign. ²⁵But Hezekiah was too proud to respond appropriately to the kindness he had received, and he, along with Judah and Jerusalem, experienced anger. ²⁶However, Hezekiah and the citizens of Jerusalem humbled themselves in their pride, and so they didn't experience the LORD's anger for the rest of Hezekiah's reign.

²⁷Hezekiah became very wealthy and greatly respected. He made storehouses for his silver, gold, precious stones, spices, shields, and other valuables. ²⁸He made barns to store the harvest of grain, wine, and olive oil; stalls for all kinds of cattle; and pens for flocks. ²⁹He acquired towns for himself and many flocks and herds because God had given him great wealth. ³⁰Hezekiah was the one who blocked the upper outlet of the waters of the Gihon Spring, channeling them down to the west side of David's City. Hezekiah succeeded in all that he did, ³¹even in the matter of the ambassadors sent from Babylonian officials to find out about the miraculous sign that occurred in the land, when God had abandoned him in order to test him and to discover what was in his heart.

³²The rest of Hezekiah's deeds, including his faithfulness, are written in the vision of the prophet Isaiah, Amoz's son, in the records of Israel's and Judah's kings. ³³Hezekiah lay down with his ancestors and was buried in the upper area of the tombs of David's sons. All Judah and the inhabitants of Jerusalem honored him at his death. His son Manasseh succeeded him as king.

Manasseh rules

33 Manasseh was 12 years old when he became king, and he ruled for

fifty-five years in Jerusalem. ²He did what was evil in the LORD's eyes, imitating the detestable practices of the nations that the LORD had driven out before the Israelites. ³He rebuilt the shrines that his father Hezekiah had destroyed, set up altars for the Baals, and made sacred poles.[u] He bowed down to all the stars in the sky and worshipped them. ⁴He even built altars in the LORD's temple, the very place the LORD was speaking about when he said, "My name will remain in Jerusalem forever." ⁵Manasseh built altars for all the stars in the sky in both courtyards of the LORD's temple. ⁶He burned his own sons alive in the Ben-hinnom Valley, consulted sign readers, fortune-tellers, and sorcerers, and used mediums and diviners. He did much evil in the LORD's eyes and made him angry.

⁷Manasseh set up the carved image he had made in God's temple, the very temple God had spoken about to David and his son Solomon, saying: In this temple and in Jerusalem, which I have selected out of all Israel's tribes, I will put my name forever. ⁸I will never again remove Israel from the fertile land I gave to your ancestors, provided they carefully do everything I have commanded them—keeping all the Instruction, the regulations, and the case laws given through Moses. ⁹In this way Manasseh led Judah and the residents of Jerusalem into doing even more evil than the nations that the LORD had wiped out before the Israelites.

¹⁰The LORD spoke to Manasseh and his people, but they wouldn't listen. ¹¹So the LORD brought the army commanders of Assyria's king against them. They captured Manasseh with hooks, bound him with bronze chains, and carried him off to Babylon. ¹²During his distress, Manasseh made peace with the LORD his God, truly submitting himself to the God of his ancestors. ¹³He prayed, and God was moved by his request. God listened to Manasseh's prayer and restored him to his rule in Jerusalem. Then Manasseh knew that the LORD was the true God.

¹⁴After this, Manasseh rebuilt the outer wall of David's City, west of the Gihon Spring in the valley, extending as far as the entrance of the Fish Gate, enclosing the elevated fortress[v]

Bet you can read this in 3 minutes. Ready, set, go!

---

[t]LXX; MT *he led them* [u]Heb *asherot*, perhaps objects devoted to the goddess Asherah [v]Or *hillside*; Heb uncertain

and greatly increasing its height. He also installed military commanders in all the fortified cities of Judah. ¹⁵He removed the foreign gods and the idol from the Lᴏʀᴅ's temple, as well as all the altars he had built on the hill of the Lᴏʀᴅ's temple and in Jerusalem, dumping them outside the city. ¹⁶He restored the Lᴏʀᴅ's altar, offered well-being sacrifices and thank offerings on it, and ordered the people of Judah to worship the Lᴏʀᴅ, Israel's God. ¹⁷The people, however, still sacrificed at the shrines, but only to the Lᴏʀᴅ their God. ¹⁸The rest of Manasseh's deeds, including his prayer to God and what the seers told him in the name of the Lᴏʀᴅ, Israel's God, are found in the records of Israel's kings. ¹⁹Manasseh's prayer and its answer, all his sin and unfaithfulness, and the locations of the shrines, sacred poles,ʷ and idols he set up before he submitted are written in the records of Hozai.ˣ ²⁰Manasseh lay down with his ancestors and was buried in his palace. His son Amon succeeded him as king.

Amon rules

²¹Amon was 22 years old when he became king, and he ruled for two years in Jerusalem.

²²He did what was evil in the Lᴏʀᴅ's eyes, just as his father Manasseh had done. He sacrificed to all the idols his father had made and worshipped them. ²³But unlike his father Manasseh, Amon didn't submit before the Lᴏʀᴅ; instead, Amon increased his guilt. ²⁴His own officials plotted against him and killed him in his palace. ²⁵The people of the land then executed all those who had plotted against King Amon and made his son Josiah the next king.

Josiah rules

34 Josiah was 8 years old when he became king, and he ruled for thirty-one years in Jerusalem. ²He did what was right in the Lᴏʀᴅ's eyes and walked in the ways of his ancestor David, not deviating from it even a bit to the right or left. ³In the eighth year of his rule, while he was just a boy, he began to seek the God of his ancestor David, and in the twelfth year he began purifying Judah and Jerusalem of the shrines, the sacred poles,ʸ idols, and images. ⁴Under his supervision, the altars for the Baals were torn down, and the incense altars that were above them were smashed. He broke up the sacred poles, idols,

---

ʷHeb *asherim*, perhaps objects devoted to the goddess Asherah   ˣLXX *the seers*   ʸHeb *asherim*, perhaps objects devoted to the goddess Asherah; also in 34:4, 7

God's ❯ My
THOUGHTS ❯ THOUGHTS

Committed to God   2 Chronicles 34:1-7

Some kings are great, and their people remember them as amazing leaders. Other kings are disasters, known for their pride and disloyalty. Josiah was known for loving God. He worked hard to turn the people back to God, even though the people had fallen away. He wanted to lead the people the way his ancestor David had led. He wanted to seek God first and to keep all other gods out of his kingdom. In fact, when some of his servants found scrolls containing God's Instruction in the temple, Josiah read them and knew he had to lead his people back to God's way.

God's people were sometimes led by very bad kings, but Josiah was great because he helped the people return to God. Remember that God wants to be number one in your life. God wants your heart, your mind, and your strength. God wants to work in you and through you to lead others to know and love God.

What kind of leader are you?

How can you make sure that you seek God first in everything you do?

and images, grinding them to dust and scattering them over the graves of those who had sacrificed to them. [5]He burned the bones of the priests on their altars, purifying Judah and Jerusalem. [6]In the cities of Manasseh, Ephraim, and Simeon, all the way up to Naphtali, he removed their temples,[z] [7]tore down the altars and sacred poles, ground the idols to dust, and smashed all the incense altars throughout the land of Israel. Then Josiah returned to Jerusalem.

Josiah repairs the temple

[8]In the eighteenth year of his rule, after he had purified the land and the temple, Josiah sent Azaliah's son Shaphan, Maaseiah the mayor of the city, and Joahaz's son Joah the secretary to repair the LORD his God's temple. [9]When they came to the high priest Hilkiah, they delivered the money that had been collected in God's temple by the levitical gatekeepers from Manasseh, Ephraim, and the rest of Israel, as well as from Judah, Benjamin, and the residents of Jerusalem. [10]They handed it over to the supervisors[a] in charge of the LORD's temple, who in turn paid it to those working on, repairing, and restoring the LORD's temple. [11]They then gave it to the carpenters and the builders to pay for quarried stone and lumber for rafters and beams in the buildings the kings of Judah had neglected. [12]The men worked conscientiously under the supervision of Jahath and Obadiah, who were Levites descended from Merari, and Zechariah and Meshullam from the Kohathites. The Levites, all of whom were accomplished musicians, [13]were also in charge of the laborers and all the workers, no matter what their jobs, while some of the Levites served as scribes, officials, and guards.

The Instruction scroll

[14]While they were bringing out the money that had been brought into the LORD's temple, Hilkiah the priest found the Instruction scroll that the LORD had given through Moses. [15]Hilkiah told the secretary Shaphan, "I have found the Instruction scroll in the LORD's temple."

Then Hilkiah turned the scroll over to Shaphan, [16]who brought it to the king with this report: "Your servants are doing everything you've asked them to do. [17]They have released the money that was found in the LORD's temple and have handed it over to the supervisors and the workers." [18]Then the secretary Shaphan told the king, "The priest Hilkiah has given me a scroll," and he read it out loud before the king.

[19]As soon as the king heard what the Instruction scroll said, he ripped his clothes. [20]The king ordered Hilkiah, Shaphan's son Ahikam, Micah's son Abdon, the secretary Shaphan, and the royal officer Asaiah as follows: [21]"Go and ask the LORD on my behalf, and on behalf of those who still remain in Israel and Judah, concerning the contents of this scroll that has been found. The LORD must be furious with us because our ancestors failed to obey the LORD's word and do everything written in this scroll."

[22]So Hilkiah and the royal officials went to the prophetess Huldah. She was married to Shallum, Tokhath's son and Hasrah's grandson, who was in charge of the wardrobe. She lived in Jerusalem in the second district. When they spoke to her, [23]she replied, "This is what the LORD, Israel's God, says: Tell this to the man who sent you to me: [24]This is what the LORD says: I am about to bring disaster on this place and its citizens—all the curses written in the scroll that they have read to Judah's king. [25]My anger burns against this place, never to be quenched, because they've deserted me and have burned incense to other gods, angering me by everything they have done.[b] [26]But also say this to the king of Judah, who sent you to question the LORD: This is what the LORD, Israel's God, says about the message you've just heard: [27]Because your heart was broken and you submitted before the LORD when you heard what he said against this place and its citizens,[c] and because you ripped your clothes and cried before me, I have listened to you, declares the LORD. [28]I will gather you to your ancestors, and you will go to your grave in peace. You won't experience the disaster I am about to bring on this place and its citizens."

[z]Heb uncertain [a]LXX, Vulg; MT *supervisor* [b]Or *made*; perhaps a reference to idols [c]MT repeats *and because you humbled yourself before me.*

When they reported Huldah's words to the king, ²⁹the king sent a message and gathered together all the elders of Judah and Jerusalem. ³⁰Then the king went up to the Lord's temple, together with all the people of Judah and all the citizens of Jerusalem, the priests and the Levites, and all the people, young and old alike. There the king read out loud all the words of the covenant scroll that had been found in the Lord's temple. ³¹The king stood in his place and made a covenant with the Lord that he would follow the Lord by keeping his commandments, his instructions, and his regulations with all his heart and all his being, in order to fulfill the words of the covenant that were written in this scroll. ³²Then he made everyone found in Jerusalem and Benjamin join in a similar promise. The citizens of Jerusalem lived according to the covenant made with God, the God of their ancestors. ³³Josiah got rid of all the detestable idols from all the regions that belonged to the Israelites, and he made everyone who lived in Israel serve the Lord their God. As long as Josiah lived, they didn't turn away from following the Lord God of their ancestors.

Josiah's Passover

35Then Josiah celebrated the Lord's Passover in Jerusalem. They slaughtered the Passover lambs on the fourteenth day of the first month.ᵈ ²He assigned the priests to their posts, encouraging them to fulfill their responsibilities in the Lord's temple. ³Next Josiah ordered the Levites, who were holy to the Lord and who instructed all Israel: "Put the holy chest in the temple built by Israel's King Solomon, David's son. You don't need to carry it around on your shoulders anymore. Now serve the Lord your God and his people Israel. ⁴Organize yourselves by families according to your divisions, as directed by Israel's King David and his son Solomon. ⁵Stand in the sanctuary, according to the family divisions of your relatives the laypeople, so that there can be Levites for each family division.ᵉ ⁶Slaughter the Passover lambs and prepare the holy sacrificesᶠ for your relatives in order to celebrate according to the Lord's word through Moses."

⁷On behalf of the laypeople, Josiah donated from his personal holdings thirty thousand lambs and young goats, and three thousand bulls, all for the Passover offerings. ⁸His officials also provided spontaneous gift offerings for the people, the priests, and the Levites. Hilkiah, Zechariah, and Jehiel, the ones in charge of God's temple, gave two thousand six hundred Passover lambs and three hundred bulls for the priests. ⁹Conaniah and his brothers Shemaiah and Nethanel, along with Hashabiah, Jeiel, and Jozabad, the leaders of the Levites, provided the Levites with five thousand lambs and five hundred bulls as Passover sacrifices. ¹⁰When everything was ready, the priests and the Levites took their places as the king had ordered. ¹¹Then they slaughtered the Passover lambs, and the priests splashed the bloodᵍ while the Levites skinned the animals. ¹²Next they divided the entirely burned offerings among the laypeople by their families to sacrifice to the Lord as written in the scroll from Moses, and they did the same with the bulls. ¹³They roasted the Passover lambs in the fire as instructed, cooked the holy offerings in pots, kettles, and pans, and brought them quickly to all the laypeople. ¹⁴Next they prepared food for themselves and for the priests. Since the priests, Aaron's descendants, were busy offering up the entirely burned offerings and fat pieces until nighttime, the Levites prepared food for themselves and for the priests, Aaron's descendants. ¹⁵The Asaphite singers also remained at their stations as ordered by David, Asaph, Heman, and the king's seer Jeduthun, as did the guards at the various gates. They didn't need to leave their tasks because their fellow Levites prepared food for them. ¹⁶So on that day all of the Lord's service was prepared for celebrating Passover and offering up entirely burned offerings on the Lord's altar, just as King Josiah had ordered. ¹⁷The Israelites who were present celebrated the Passover at that time, and observed the Festival of Unleavened Bread for seven days. ¹⁸Not since the days of the prophet Samuel had such a Passover been celebrated in Israel. And no other king of Israel had celebrated a Passover like the one Josiah celebrated with the

---

ᵈMarch-April, Nisan ᵉHeb uncertain ᶠCorrection; cf 1 Esdr 1:6; MT *and sanctify yourselves* ᵍLXX; MT *from their hand*

priests, the Levites, all the people of Judah and Israel who were present, and the residents of Jerusalem. ¹⁹This Passover was celebrated in the eighteenth year of Josiah's rule.

Josiah's death

²⁰After all of these things, when Josiah had finished restoring the temple, Egypt's King Neco marched against Carchemish by the Euphrates, and Josiah marched out against him. ²¹But Neco sent messengers to Josiah. "What do you want with me, king of Judah?" he asked. "I haven't come to attack you today. I'm after the dynasty that wars with me. God told me to hurry, and he is on my side. Get out of God's way, or he will destroy you."

²²But Josiah wouldn't turn back. Instead, he camouflaged himself in preparation for battle, refusing to listen to Neco's words from God's own mouth, and went to fight Neco on the plain of Megiddo. ²³When archers shot King Josiah, he said to his servants, "Take me away; I'm badly wounded!" ²⁴So his servants took him out of his chariot, placed him in another one, and brought him to Jerusalem, where he died and was buried in the tombs of his ancestors. All Judah and Jerusalem mourned for Josiah. ²⁵Jeremiah composed a funeral songʰ for Josiah, and to this day every singer, man or woman, continues to remember Josiah in their funeral songs. They are now traditional in Israel and are written down among the funeral songs.

²⁶The rest of Josiah's deeds, including his faithfulness in acting according to what is written in the LORD's Instruction, ²⁷and everything else he did, from beginning to end, are written in the official records of Israel's and Judah's kings.

Jehoahaz rules

36The people of the land took Jehoahaz, Josiah's son, and made him the next king in Jerusalem. ²Jehoahaz was 23 years old when he became king, and he ruled for three months in Jerusalem. ³The king of Egypt removed him from office in Jerusalem. The Egyptian king imposed a fine on the land totaling one hundred kikkars of silver and one kikkar of gold. ⁴Then the king of Egypt made Jehoahaz's brother Eliakim king of Judah and Jerusalem, and changed his name to Jehoiakim. Neco took his brother Jehoahaz prisoner and carried him off to Egypt.

UMBRELLA
MOURNING

Good Leaders Deserve Honor in Death
2 Chronicles 35:25

When King Josiah died, all Israel mourned him. Israel benefited from Josiah's obedience to God (2 Chron 34:26-28). As a result, his people greatly mourned him after his death. Jeremiah didn't want to forget the good things Josiah did for God and for Israel. So Jeremiah honored the memory of Josiah with a song that became well-known among all the Israelite singers. Whenever a king of Israel like Josiah followed God faithfully, God kept the kingdom safe and prosperous (2 Chron 20:27-30). Whenever a wicked king ruled, foreign armies usually defeated Israel (2 Chron 33:10-11). Often when wicked kings died, no one mourned them (2 Chron 21:18-20). Some, like King Jehoash and King Ahaz, weren't even buried in the royal cemetery where kings were traditionally buried (2 Chron 24:23-25; 28:27). Others, like King Amaziah, were so bad that their own people rebelled and killed them (2 Chron 25:27-28). ⬥

Jehoiakim rules

⁵Jehoiakim was 25 years old when he became king, and he ruled for eleven years in Jerusalem. He did what was evil in the LORD's eyes. ⁶Babylon's King Nebuchadnezzar attacked him, bound him with bronze chains, and took him to Babylon. ⁷Nebuchadnezzar also took some equipment from the LORD's temple to Babylon and placed them in his own temple there. ⁸The rest of Jehoiakim's deeds, including his detestable practices and all that was charged against him, are written in the official records of Israel's and Judah's kings. His son Jehoiachin succeeded him as king.

Jehoiachin rules

⁹Jehoiachin was 18ⁱ years old when he became king, and he ruled for three monthsʲ in

---

ʰOr *lament*, twice more in this verse   ⁱLXX, 2 Kgs 24:8; MT *eight* ʲ2 Kgs 24:8; MT adds *and ten days.*

Jerusalem. He did what was evil in the LORD's eyes. [10]In the springtime, King Nebuchadnezzar sent for him to be brought to Babylon, along with valuable equipment from the LORD's temple. Then he made Zedekiah his uncle the next king of Judah and Jerusalem.

Zedekiah rules

[11]Zedekiah was 21 years old when he became king, and he ruled for eleven years in Jerusalem. [12]He did what was evil in the LORD his God's eyes and didn't submit before the prophet Jeremiah, who spoke for the LORD. [13]Moreover, he rebelled against King Nebuchadnezzar, despite the solemn pledge Nebuchadnezzar had forced him to swear in God's name. He became stubborn and refused to turn back to the LORD, Israel's God. [14]All the leaders of the priests and the people also grew increasingly unfaithful, following all the detestable practices of the nations. They polluted the LORD's temple that God had dedicated in Jerusalem. [15]Time and time again, the LORD, the God of their ancestors, sent word to them through his messengers because he had compassion on his people and his dwelling. [16]But they made fun of God's messengers, treating God's words with contempt and ridiculing God's prophets to such an extent that there was no hope of warding off the LORD's rising anger against his people.

Jerusalem destroyed

[17]So God brought the Babylonian[k] king against them. The king killed their young

[k]Heb *Chaldean*

men with the sword in their temple's sanctuary, and showed no pity for young men or for virgins, for the old or for the feeble. God handed all of them over to him. [18]Then the king hauled everything off to Babylon, every item from God's temple, both large and small, including the treasures of the LORD's temple and those of the king and his officials. [19]Next the Babylonians burned God's temple down, demolished the walls of Jerusalem, and set fire to all its palaces, destroying everything of value. [20]Finally, he exiled to Babylon anyone who survived the killing so that they could be his slaves and the slaves of his children until Persia came to power. [21]This is how the LORD's word spoken by Jeremiah was carried out. The land finally enjoyed its sabbath rest. For as long as it lay empty, it rested, until seventy years were completed.

Cyrus' decree

[22]In the first year of Persia's King Cyrus, to carry out the LORD's promise spoken through Jeremiah, the LORD moved Persia's King Cyrus to issue the following proclamation throughout his kingdom, along with a written decree:

[23]This is what Persia's King Cyrus says: The LORD, the God of heaven, has given me all the earth's kingdoms and has instructed me to build a temple for him at Jerusalem in Judah. Whoever among you belong to God's people, let them go up, and may the LORD their God be with them!

Ezra

God's people knew what it was like to be homesick. Many years before, they had been taken as prisoners from their homeland of Judah to Babylon, a place that was far away. While they were in Babylon, the Persians battled and defeated the Babylonians. Then Persia's King Cyrus did a surprising thing. He said that the people of Judah could return home to Jerusalem and build a new temple for God. He even sent them home with treasures that the Babylonians had stolen from the old temple.

The book of Ezra is named for a priest who taught the people God's Instruction. The book begins with a list of the exiles who returned from Babylon (Ezra 1–2). It tells how Zerubbabel the priest built an altar for God and rebuilt the temple even when enemies tried to stop the work (Ezra 3–6). After the temple was finished, Ezra the priest returned to Jerusalem. He taught God's people to follow God's commands (Ezra 7–10).

In Ezra you will see how happy God's people felt when they went back to their homes, started a new life, and worshipped God. Ezra shows that God helps people start over! ♦

Permission to return to Jerusalem

1 In the first year of King Cyrus of Persia's rule, to fulfill the LORD's word spoken by Jeremiah, the LORD stirred up the spirit of Persia's King Cyrus. The king issued a proclamation throughout his kingdom (it was also in writing) that stated:

² Persia's King Cyrus says: The LORD, the God of heaven, has given me all the kingdoms of the earth. He has commanded me to build him a house at Jerusalem in Judah. ³ If there are any of you who are from his people, may their God be with them! They may go up to Jerusalem in Judah and build the house of the LORD, the God of Israel— he is the God who is in Jerusalem. ⁴ And as for all those who remain in the various places where they are living, let the people of those places supply them with silver and gold, and with goods and livestock, together with spontaneous gifts for God's house in Jerusalem.ª

ª Heb uncertain

Preparing to return

⁵ Then the heads of the families of Judah and Benjamin, and the priests and the Levites—everyone whose spirit God had stirred up—got ready to go up and build God's house in Jerusalem. ⁶ All their neighbors assisted them with silver equipment, with gold, with goods, livestock, and valuable gifts, in addition to all that was freely offered. ⁷ King Cyrus brought out the equipment of the LORD's house—those items that Nebuchadnezzar brought from Jerusalem and placed in the house of his gods. ⁸ Persia's King Cyrus handed them over to Mithredath the treasurer, who counted

did you know? God's people were held captive for seventy years in Babylon. King Cyrus ordered that they be freed and allowed to return home. Because it had been so long, most of the people who journeyed back to rebuild the temple had never even seen Jerusalem before.

God Stirs Our Hearts Ezra 1:1-4

God is always working, moving, and stirring in the hearts of God's people. Sometimes God whispers ideas to us. Sometimes we hear something and know God is speaking to us. Sometimes we feel something deep in our hearts and know God is calling us. God is always leading and guiding us.

King Cyrus was called to action by God stirring in his heart. In Cyrus' first year as king, God told him to rebuild the temple and send God's people back to Jerusalem. God's people had been scattered and the temple destroyed. The kings before Cyrus had turned away from God and didn't care about God's Instruction. But God moved King Cyrus' heart and used him to begin bringing God's people back to Jerusalem—the place they loved and where they would eventually rebuild a house for God. God used Cyrus to begin a *restoration*, which means to put together again something that is broken.

Although you may not be in a powerful position right now, God can use you to do God's work in the world. There are lots of broken places where God can use you to make a difference. When God stirs your heart, be sure to pay attention. You just might become part of a great work for God.

How have you felt God stirring in your heart?

What did God ask you to do?

them out to Sheshbazzar the prince of Judah. ⁹This was the count: thirty gold dishes, one thousand silver dishes, twenty-nine knives,ᵇ ¹⁰thirty gold bowls, four hundred ten largerᶜ silver bowls, and one thousand other objects. ¹¹The total of the gold and silver objects numbered five thousand four hundred. Sheshbazzar brought up all of these when the exiles went up from Babylonia to Jerusalem.

List of the returnees

2 These were the people of the province who went up from there—from among those captive exiles whom Babylon's King Nebuchadnezzar had deported to Babylonia. They returned to Jerusalem and Judah, all to their own towns. ²They came with Zerubbabel, Jeshua, Nehemiah, Seraiah, Reelaiah, Mordecai, Bilshan, Mispar, Bigvai, Rehum, and Baanah.

The number of the people of Israel

³ The family of Parosh	2,172
⁴ of Shephatiah	372
⁵ of Arah	775
⁶ of Pahath-moab, namely the family of Jeshua and Joab	2,812
⁷ of Elam	1,254
⁸ of Zattu	945
⁹ of Zaccai	760
¹⁰ of Bani	642
¹¹ of Bebai	623
¹² of Azgad	1,222
¹³ of Adonikam	666
¹⁴ of Bigvai	2,056
¹⁵ of Adin	454
¹⁶ of Ater, namely of Hezekiah	98
¹⁷ of Bezai	323
¹⁸ of Jorah	112
¹⁹ of Hashum	223
²⁰ of Gibbar	95
²¹ of Bethlehem	123
²² The people of Netophah	56
²³ of Anathoth	128
²⁴ The family of Azmaveth	42
²⁵ of Kiriatharim, Chephirah, and Beeroth	743
²⁶ of Ramah and Geba	621
²⁷ The people of Michmash	122
²⁸ of Bethel and Ai	223

²⁹ The family of Nebo	52
³⁰ of Magbish	156
³¹ of the other Elam	1,254
³² of Harim	320
³³ of Lod, Hadid, and Ono	725
³⁴ of Jericho	345
³⁵ of Senaah	3,630

³⁶ The priests

The family of Jedaiah, namely the house of Jeshua	973
³⁷ of Immer	1,052
³⁸ of Pashhur	1,247
³⁹ of Harim	1,017
⁴⁰ The Levites: the family of Jeshua and Kadmiel— the family of Hodaviah	74

⁴¹ The singers

The family of Asaph	128

⁴² The family of the gatekeepers

of Shallum, Ater, Talmon, Akkub, Hatita, and Shobai	139 in all

⁴³ The temple servants

The family of Ziha, Hasupha, Tabbaoth, ⁴⁴Keros, Siaha, Padon, ⁴⁵Lebanah, Hagabah, Akkub, ⁴⁶Hagab, Shamlai, Hanan, ⁴⁷Giddel, Gahar, Reaiah, ⁴⁸Rezin, Nekoda, Gazzam, ⁴⁹Uzza, Paseah, Besai, ⁵⁰Asnah, Meunim, Nephisim, ⁵¹Bakbuk, Hakupha, Harhur, ⁵²Bazluth, Mehida, Harsha, ⁵³Barkos, Sisera, Temah, ⁵⁴Neziah, and Hatipha

⁵⁵ The family of Solomon's servants

Sotai, Hassophereth, Peruda, ⁵⁶Jaalah, Darkon, Giddel, ⁵⁷Shephatiah, Hattil, Pocherethhazzebaim, and Ami.

⁵⁸ All of the temple servants and the family of Solomon's servants	392

Exclusions

⁵⁹The following came up from Tel-melah, Tel-harsha, Cherub, Addan, and Immer, but

ᵇVulg; Heb uncertain ᶜHeb double

they were unable to demonstrate that their family or their descent was from Israel:

⁶⁰ the family of Delaiah, Tobiah, and
Nekoda,   652
⁶¹ and of the family of the priests:
the family of Habaiah, Hakkoz,
and Barzillai (who had married
one of the daughters of Barzillai
the Gileadite and was called by
their name).

⁶²They looked for their entries in the genealogical records, but they were not found there, so they were excluded from the priesthood as unclean. ⁶³The governor ordered them not to eat of the most holy food until a priest arose who could consult Urim and Thummim.

Total

⁶⁴The whole assembly together totaled 42,360, ⁶⁵not including their 7,337 male and female servants; they also had 200 male and female singers, ⁶⁶736 horses, 245 mules, ⁶⁷435 camels, and 6,720 donkeys.

Arrival in Jerusalem

⁶⁸When they arrived at the Lord's house in Jerusalem, some of the heads of the families brought spontaneous gifts for the rebuilding of God's house on its site. ⁶⁹According to their means, they gave to the building fund 61,000 drachmen of gold, 5,000 manehs of silver, and 100 priestly robes.

⁷⁰The priests, the Levites, some of the people, the singers, the gatekeepers, and the temple servants settled in their own towns, and all Israel in their towns.

Rebuilding the altar

3 When the seventh month[d] came and the Israelites were in their towns, the people gathered together as one in Jerusalem. ²Then Jeshua, Jozadak's son along with his fellow priests, and Zerubbabel, Shealtiel's son along with his kin, started to rebuild the altar of Israel's God so that they might offer entirely burned offerings upon it as prescribed in the Instruction from Moses the man of God. ³They set up the altar on its foundations,[e] because they were afraid of the neighboring peoples,[f] and they offered entirely burned offerings upon it to the Lord, both the morning and the evening offerings.

⁴They celebrated the Festival of Booths, as prescribed. Every day they presented the number of entirely burned offerings required by ordinance for that day. ⁵After this, they presented the continual burned offerings, the offerings at the new moons, and at all the sacred feasts of the Lord, and the offerings of everyone who brought a spontaneous gift to the Lord. ⁶From the first day of the seventh month, they began to present entirely burned offerings to the Lord.

However, the foundation of the Lord's temple had not yet been laid. ⁷So they gave money to the masons and carpenters; and food, drink, and oil to the Sidonians and the Tyrians to bring cedarwood by sea from Lebanon to Joppa, according to the authorization given them by Persia's King Cyrus.

Laying the foundations of God's house

⁸In the second month of the second year after their arrival at God's house in Jerusalem, Zerubbabel, Shealtiel's son, and Jeshua, Jozadak's son, and the rest of their kin—the priests and the Levites and all who had come from the captivity to Jerusalem—made a beginning. They appointed Levites 20 years old and above to oversee the work on the Lord's house. ⁹Then Jeshua with his sons and his kin, Kadmiel and his sons, Binnui and his sons, the sons of Judah, along with the sons of Henadad, the Levites, and their sons and kin, collaborated to supervise the workers in God's house.

¹⁰When the builders laid the foundation of the Lord's temple, the priests clothed in their

---

[d]September–October, Tishrei   [e]A technical word meaning *pedestals*   [f]Or *peoples of the lands*

vests and carrying their trumpets, and the Levites the sons of Asaph with cymbals, arose to praise the Lord according to the directions of Israel's King David. [11] They praised and gave thanks to the Lord, singing responsively, "He is good, his graciousness for Israel lasts forever."

All of the people shouted with praise to the Lord because the foundation of the Lord's house had been laid. [12] But many of the older priests and Levites and heads of families, who had seen the first house, wept aloud when they saw the foundation of this house, although many others shouted loudly with joy. [13] No one could distinguish the sound of the joyful shout from the sound of the people's weeping, because the people rejoiced very loudly. The sound was heard at a great distance.

SAILBOAT

Joy

The Joy of a New Start Ezra 3:11-13
The newly returned Israelites were building a new temple for God in the same place the old one had stood before it was torn down seventy years earlier. The Israelites were joyful when they finished laying the foundation for the second temple. For them, the new temple was like a new beginning. The Israelites knew they had paid for their earlier mistake of forgetting God and were committed to serving God again. The temple they were building represented that commitment. Their new start was a reason to celebrate—a reason to be joyful. ♦

Facing opposition

4 When the enemies of Judah and Benjamin heard that the returned exiles were building a temple for the Lord, the God of Israel, [2] they came to Zerubbabel and the heads of the families and said to them, "Let's build with you, for we worship your God as you do, and we've been sacrificing to him ever since the days of Assyria's King Esarhaddon, who brought us here."

[3] But Zerubbabel, Jeshua, and the rest of the heads of the families in Israel replied,

"You'll have no part with us in building a house for our God. We alone will build because the Lord, the God of Israel, and Persia's King Cyrus commanded us."

[4] The neighboring peoples[g] discouraged the people of Judah, made them afraid to build, [5] and bribed officials to frustrate their plan. They did this throughout the rule of Persia's King Cyrus until the rule of Persia's King Darius.

Writing to King Artaxerxes

[6] In the rule of Ahasuerus, at the beginning of his rule, they composed an indictment against those who lived in Judah and Jerusalem. [7] In the days of Artaxerxes, Bishlam, Mithredath, Tabeel, and the rest of their associates wrote to Persia's King Artaxerxes. The letter was written in Aramaic and translated.[h] [8] Rehum the royal deputy and Shimshai the scribe wrote a letter concerning Jerusalem to King Artaxerxes as follows:

[9] From Rehum the royal deputy and Shimshai the scribe and the rest of their colleagues, the judges, the administrators, the officials, the Persians, the people of Erech, the Babylonians, the people of Susa (that is, the Elamites), [10] and the rest of the nations whom the great and famous Osnappar deported and settled in the cities of Samaria and in the rest of the province Beyond the River.

([11] This is a copy of the letter they sent to him.)

To King Artaxerxes from your servants, the people of the province Beyond the River. [12] May it be known to the king that the Jews who left you and came to us have arrived in Jerusalem. They are rebuilding the rebellious and wicked city; they are completing the walls and repairing the foundations. [13] May it be known to the king that if this city is rebuilt and the walls completed, they will not pay tribute or tax or dues, and the royal revenue will be reduced.

[14] Since we receive our salary from the palace,[i] and since it is not fitting for us to witness the king's dishonor, we now send

[g] Or peoples of the lands [h] Heb adds in Aramaic, reporting that 4:8–6:18 is written in Aramaic. [i] Or since we have salted the salt of the palace

this letter[j] and inform the king. [15]so that you may search the records of your ancestors. You will discover in the records that this is a rebellious city, harmful to kings and provinces, and that it has been in revolt over a long period of time. As a result, this city was laid waste. [16]We tell the king that if this city is rebuilt and its walls completed, you will then have no possession in the province Beyond the River.

Artaxerxes responds

[17]The king sent this answer:

Greetings to Rehum the royal deputy and Shimshai the scribe and the rest of their colleagues who live in Samaria and elsewhere in the province Beyond the River. [18]The entire letter that you sent to us has been read in translation for me. [19]I issued an order; they searched and discovered that this city has revolted against kings over a long period of time. There has been much rebellion and revolt there. [20]However, there have been mighty kings over Jerusalem who also ruled over the whole province Beyond the River. Tribute and taxes and dues were paid to them. [21]Therefore, issue an order to stop these people: this city is not to be rebuilt until I make a decree. [22]Be sure to carry out this order! Why should danger grow and threaten the king?

[23]When the copy of King Artaxerxes' letter was read before Rehum and Shimshai the

[j]Heb lacks this letter.

God's THOUGHTS ◆ My THOUGHTS

Frustrated Plans   Ezra 4

There were many people who didn't want God's people to return to Jerusalem or build a place to worship God. They were worried God's people would have too much power and not give any of their money to the city. They didn't care about God and didn't want any part of God's Instruction.

These people decided they would try to stop God's people from rebuilding the temple. They tried to bribe and discourage God's people. When God's people didn't give up, their enemies sent word to the new King Artaxerxes, who didn't really care about the work of God's people. Artaxerxes ordered God's people to stop building, and nothing was done to the temple for several more years until a king named Darius came to power.

Even though God stirred King Cyrus' heart and Cyrus was obedient (Ezra 1:1), there were still challenges. Sometimes God asks us just to get started, and then other people finish the task. Other times, God asks us to finish a task someone else has started. No matter what, we can be sure our plans may be frustrated. Not everyone will understand why we do what we do. We might be made fun of or put down because we obey God. But God will always be faithful and give us what we need for whatever God calls us to do. When God stirs our hearts, we can act boldly because we know God is making us a part of God's forever story.

When have you felt frustrated when you obeyed God?

When have you felt comfort from God?

scribe and their colleagues, they hurried to Jerusalem to oppose the Jews and made them stop by force of arms.[k] [24]At that time the work on God's house in Jerusalem stopped and was suspended until the second year of the rule of Persia's King Darius.

Work on God's house continues

5 Then the prophet Haggai and the prophet Zechariah, Iddo's son, prophesied to the Jews who were in Judah and Jerusalem in the name of Israel's God who was over them. [2]Subsequently, Zerubbabel, Shealtiel's son, and Jeshua, Jozadak's son, began to rebuild God's house in Jerusalem. God's prophets were with them, helping them.

[3]At the same time, Tattenai, the governor of the province Beyond the River, and Shethar-bozenai and their colleagues came to them and spoke to them, asking, "Who authorized you to build this house and finish preparing[l] this building material?"[m] [4]They[n] also asked them, "What are the names of the people who are building this building?" [5]But their God looked after the elders of the Jews, and they didn't stop them until a report reached Darius and a letter with his response had arrived.

Writing to King Darius

[6]This is a copy of the letter that Tattenai, the governor of the province Beyond the River, and Shethar-bozenai and his colleagues the officials who were in the province Beyond the River sent to King Darius. [7]In the message they sent him, the following was written:

To King Darius, all peace! [8]Let the king know that we went to the province of Judah, to the house of the great God. It is being built with dressed stone and with timber set into the walls. This work makes good progress and prospers in their hands. [9]We asked those elders, "Who authorized you to build this house and to complete the preparation of this material?" [10]We also asked them their names so that we could write down the names of the leaders for your information.

[11]This was their reply to us: "We are the servants of the God of heaven and earth. We are rebuilding the house that

was built many years ago, which a great king of Israel built and completed. [12]But because our ancestors angered the God of heaven, he gave them over into the power of Babylon's King Nebuchadnezzar, the Chaldean, who destroyed this house and deported the people to Babylonia. [13]However, in the first year of his rule, Babylon's King Cyrus issued a decree to rebuild this house of God. [14]King Cyrus also took the gold and silver equipment from God's house out of the temple in Babylon (the ones that Nebuchadnezzar took from the temple in Jerusalem and placed in the temple in Babylon) and gave them to a man named Sheshbazzar, whom he had appointed governor. [15]Cyrus said to him, 'Take this equipment and go and put it in Jerusalem's temple, and let God's house be rebuilt on its original site.' [16]Then Sheshbazzar came and laid the foundations of God's house in Jerusalem. From then until now the rebuilding work has continued but is not yet complete."

[17]And now, if it seems good to the king, may a search be made in the royal archives in Babylon to see if King Cyrus had issued a decree to rebuild this house of God in Jerusalem. Then may the king be pleased to send us his decision about this matter.

SAILBOAT

COURAGE

Take Courage in Doing Right Ezra 5:11-17
Years passed after King Cyrus sent God's people back to Jerusalem to rebuild the temple. An official of the new King Darius wanted to know who told the people they could do this work. The official could have gotten them in big trouble. But God's people knew the truth was on their side. They knew there was no need to be afraid for doing the right thing. They told the official to check the records for the original command. Because God's people were bold enough to speak up for themselves, Darius let them keep building. He also told his official to help the people and pay for it out of the royal treasury. One king tore down God's temple (2 Kings 25:8-9), but God used another king to build it back up! ◊

Darius responds

6 Then King Darius made a decree, and they searched the archives where the documents were stored in Babylon. ²But a scroll was found in Ecbatana, the capital of the province of Media, on which was written the following:

Bet you can read this in 5 minutes. Ready, set, go!

A memorandum— ³In the first year of his rule, King Cyrus made a decree: Concerning God's house in Jerusalem: Let the house at the place where they offered sacrifices be rebuilt and let its foundations be retained. Its height will be ninety feet and its width ninety feet, ⁴with three layers of dressed stones and one° layer of timber. The cost will be paid from the royal treasury. ⁵In addition, the gold and silver equipment from God's house, which Nebuchadnezzar took out of the temple in Jerusalem and brought to Babylon, is to be restored, that is, brought back to Jerusalem and put in their proper place in God's house.

⁶Now you, Tattenai, governor of the province Beyond the River, Shethar-bozenai, and you, their colleagues, the officials in the province Beyond the River, keep away! ⁷Leave the work on this house of God alone. Let the governor of the Jews and the elders of the Jews rebuild this house of God on its original site.

⁸I also issue a decree about what you should do to help these elders of the Jews as they rebuild this house of God: The total cost is to be paid to these people, and without delay, from the royal revenue that is made up of the tribute of the province Beyond the River. ⁹And whatever is needed— young bulls, rams, or sheep for entirely burned offerings to the God of heaven, wheat, salt, wine, or oil, as requested by the priests in Jerusalem—let that be given to them day by day without fail ¹⁰so that they may offer pleasing sacrifices to the God of heaven and pray for the lives of the king and his sons.

¹¹I also decree that if anyone disobeys this edict, a beam is to be pulled out of the house of the guilty party, and the guilty party will then be impaled upon it. The house will be turned into a trash heap.

¹²May the God who has established his name there overthrow any king or people who try to change this order or to destroy God's house in Jerusalem. I, Darius, have decreed it; let it be done with all diligence.

God's house is completed and dedicated

¹³Then Tattenai, the governor of the province Beyond the River, Shethar-bozenai, and their colleagues carried out the order of King Darius with all diligence. ¹⁴So the elders of the Jews built and prospered because of the prophesying of the prophet Haggai and Zechariah, Iddo's son. They finished building by the command of Israel's God and of Cyrus, Darius, and King Artaxerxes of Persia. ¹⁵This house was completed on the third day of the month of Adar,ᵖ in the sixth year of the rule of King Darius.

¹⁶Then the Israelites, the priests and the Levites, and the rest of the returned exiles joyfully celebrated the dedication of this house of God. ¹⁷At the dedication of this house of God, they offered one hundred bulls, two hundred rams, four hundred lambs, and as a purification offering for all Israel, twelve male goats, according to the number of the tribes of Israel. ¹⁸They set the priests in their divisions and the Levites in their sections for the service of God in Jerusalem, as it is written in the scroll from Moses.

¹⁹ᑫOn the fourteenth day of the first month,ʳ the returned exiles celebrated the Passover. ²⁰All of the priests and the Levites had purified themselves; all of them were clean. They slaughtered the Passover animals for all the returned exiles, their fellow priests, and themselves. ²¹The Israelites who had returned from exile, together with all those who had joined them by separating themselves from the pollutions of the nations of the land to worship the LORD, the God of Israel, ate the Passover meal.ˢ

²²They also joyfully celebrated the Festival of Unleavened Bread for seven days, because the LORD had made them joyful by changing the attitude of the king of Assyria toward them so that he assisted them in the work on the house of God, the God of Israel.

°LXX; Heb *new* ᵖFebruary–March ᑫHeb resumes with this verse. ʳMarch–April, Nisan ˢHeb lacks *Passover meal.*

Introduction to Ezra

7 After this, in the rule of Persia's King Artaxerxes, Ezra son of Seraiah son of Azariah son of Hilkiah [2]son of Shallum son of Zadok son of Ahitub [3]son of Amariah son of Azariah son of Meraioth [4]son of Zerahiah son of Uzzi son of Bukki [5]son of Abishua son of Phinehas son of Eleazar son of Aaron the chief priest— [6]this Ezra came up from Babylon. He was a scribe skilled in the Instruction from Moses, which the Lord, the God of Israel, had given. Moreover, the king gave him everything he requested because the Lord his God's power was with him.

[7]Some of the Israelites and some of the priests and the Levites, the singers and gatekeepers and the temple servants also came up to Jerusalem in the seventh year of King Artaxerxes. [8]They reached Jerusalem in the fifth month, in the seventh year of the king. [9]The journey from Babylon began on the first day of the first month, and they came to Jerusalem on the first day of the fifth month, for the gracious hand of his God was upon him. [10]Ezra had determined to study and perform the Lord's Instruction, and to teach law and justice in Israel.

Letter from Artaxerxes

[11]This is a copy of the letter that Artaxerxes gave to Ezra the priest and scribe, a scholar of the text of the Lord's commandments and his requirements for Israel:

[12]t Artaxerxes, king of kings,

to Ezra the priest, the scribe of the Instruction from the God of heaven.

Peace![u]

And now [13]I decree that any of the people of Israel or their priests or Levites in my kingdom who volunteer to go to Jerusalem with you may go. [14]You are sent by the king and his seven counselors to investigate Judah and Jerusalem according to the Instruction from your God, which is in your hand. [15]You should bring the silver and gold that the king and his counselors have freely offered to the God of Israel, whose dwelling is in Jerusalem, [16]together with any of the silver and gold that you find

in the entire province of Babylonia. You should also bring the spontaneous gifts of the people and the priests, given freely for God's house in Jerusalem. [17]With this money you will be careful to buy bulls, rams, and lambs, as well as their grain offerings and their drink offerings. And you will offer them on the altar of God's house in Jerusalem. [18]As long as it is God's will, you and your colleagues may do what you think best with the rest of the silver and gold. [19]You will deliver the equipment that has been given to you for the service of God's house to the God of Jerusalem. [20]If anything else is required for God's house that you are responsible to provide, you may provide it from the royal treasury.

[21]I, King Artaxerxes, decree to all of the treasurers in the province Beyond the River: Whatever Ezra the priest and scribe of the Instruction from the God of heaven requires of you, it must be provided precisely, [22]even up to one hundred kikkars of silver, one hundred kors of wheat, one

did you know? Ezra had never been to Israel. He was born in Babylon, the country where his people were taken as prisoners. But Ezra had two jobs that helped him lead God's people. He was a priest whose family traced back to Aaron, the first priest. As a priest, he was an expert in God's Instruction. Ezra was also a trusted messenger for King Artaxerxes, who controlled the Persian empire, including Jerusalem.

hundred baths[v] of wine, one hundred baths of oil, and unlimited salt. [23]Whatever the God of heaven commands will be done carefully for the house of the God of heaven, or wrath will come upon the realm of the king and his heirs. [24]You must also know that it is illegal for you to charge tribute, custom, or dues on any of the priests and Levites, the singers, the doorkeepers, the temple servants, or other servants of this house of God.

[25]And you, Ezra, based on the divine wisdom that you have, appoint supervisors

and judges to adjudicate among all the people in the province Beyond the River who know the laws of your God. You will also teach those who do not know them. [26]Let judgment be strictly carried out upon anyone who does not obey the Instruction from your God and the law of your king, including death, banishment, confiscation of property, or imprisonment.

Ezra prepares to leave

[27]Bless the Lord, the God of our ancestors, who has moved the king to glorify the Lord's house in Jerusalem, [28]and who has demonstrated his graciousness for me before the king and his counselors and all the king's mighty officers. I took courage because the Lord my God's power was with me. I gathered leaders from Israel to go up with me.

8 These are the heads of the families, and this is the genealogy of those who went up with me during the rule of King Artaxerxes:

[2]of the family of Phinehas, Gershom; of Ithamar, Daniel; of David, Hattush, [3]Shecaniah's son;[w] of Parosh, Zechariah and with him were registered 150 men;

[4]of Pahath-moab, Eliehoenai, Zerahiah's son and with him 200 men;

[5]of Zattu,[x] Shecaniah, Jahaziel's son and with him 300 men;

[6]of Adin, Ebed, Jonathan's son and with him 50 men;

[7]of Elam, Jeshaiah, Athaliah's son and with him 70 men;

[8]of Shephatiah, Zebadiah, Michael's son and with him 80 men;

[9]of Joab, Obadiah, Jehiel's son and with him 218 men;

[10]of Bani,[y] Shelomith, Josiphiah's son and with him 160 men;

[11]of Bebai, Zechariah, Bebai's son and with him 28 men;

[12]of Azgad, Johanan, Hakkatan's son and with him 110 men;

[13]of the last of Adonikam, namely Eliphelet, Jeuel, and Shemaiah and with them 60 men;

[14]of Bigvai, Uthai and Zaccur and with them were 70 men.

Voyage to Jerusalem

[15]I gathered them by the river that runs to Ahava, and there we camped for three days. As I reviewed the people and the priests, I found no Levites there. [16]So I called for Eliezer, Ariel, Shemaiah, Elnathan, Jarib, Elnathan, Nathan, Zechariah, and Meshullam, all leaders, together with Joiarib and Elnathan, who were wise. [17]I sent them[z] to Iddo, the leader at the place named Casiphia, telling them what to say to Iddo and his colleagues the temple servants at Casiphia, namely, to send us ministers for God's house. [18]Because we were favored by God, they brought us Sherebiah, a skillful man of the family of Mahli, Levi's son and Israel's grandson, together with his sons and relatives so that there were eighteen in total. [19]They also brought us Hashabiah and with him Jeshaiah of the family of Merari, together with his relatives and their sons so that there were twenty in total. [20]In addition, there were two hundred twenty temple servants whom David and the princes had appointed to serve the Levites. These were all recorded by name.

[21]Then I called for a fast there at the Ahava River so that we might submit before our God and ask of him a safe journey for ourselves, our children, and all our possessions. [22]I had been ashamed to ask the king for a group of soldiers and cavalry to help us in facing enemies on the way, because we had told the king, "The power of God favors all who seek him, but his fierce wrath is against all who abandon him." [23]So we fasted and prayed to our God for this, and he responded to us.

[24]Then I selected twelve of the leading priests, Sherebiah and Hashabiah and ten of their relatives with them. [25]I weighed out to them the silver and the gold and the equipment, the offering for the house of our God that the king, his counselors, his officials, and all Israel present there had offered. [26]I weighed out into their keeping six hundred fifty kikkars of silver, one hundred silver containers weighing a certain number of kikkars, one hundred kikkars of gold, [27]twenty gold bowls worth one thousand darics, and two containers of highly polished copper,

[w]LXX and 1 Esdr 8:29; Heb *of the descendants of Shecaniah* [x]LXX and 1 Esdr 8:32; Heb lacks *of Zattu*. [y]LXX and 1 Esdr 8:36; Heb lacks *of Bani*. [z]Kethib *I ordered them*

which were as precious as gold. ²⁸I said to them, "You are holy to the LORD, and the equipment is holy; the silver and the gold are a spontaneous gift to the LORD, the God of your ancestors. ²⁹Guard them carefully until you weigh them out in Jerusalem before the officials of the priests, the Levites, and the heads of the families of Israel, within the rooms of the LORD's house." ³⁰So the priests and the Levites received the silver and the gold and the utensils as they were weighed out, in order to bring them to Jerusalem, to our God's house.

SAILBOAT

HONEST AND TRUE

Honesty Earns Trust and Responsibility
Ezra 8:24-30

Ezra and a group of priests and their families were carrying treasure to Israel. The Persian king sent Ezra to Israel to teach the people God's Instruction (Ezra 7:12-14), and he also sent silver and gold for God's use. Israelites who remained in the Persian empire also sent along valuable gifts for God's newly rebuilt temple (Ezra 7:15-20). Ezra chose twelve priests to guard the treasure they were bringing. He told them they would weigh everything once they arrived in Jerusalem. He trusted that every drop of gold and silver that began the journey would end the journey safely in Jerusalem. ◐

³¹Then we left the Ahava River on the twelfth day of the first month[a] to go to Jerusalem. The power of our God was with us; he saved us from the power of the enemy and ambushes along the way.

Finishing the journey

³²After arriving in Jerusalem, we rested there three days. ³³On the fourth day, the silver and the gold and the equipment were weighed out in our God's house into the care of the priest named Meremoth, Uriah's son, together with Eleazar, Phinehas' son; and the Levites, Jozabad, Jeshua's son, and Noadiah, Binnui's son. ³⁴Everything was counted and weighed, and the total weight was recorded.

³⁵At that time, those who had come from the captivity, the returned exiles, offered as entirely burned offerings to the God of Israel twelve bulls for all Israel, ninety-six rams, seventy-seven lambs, and twelve male goats as a purification offering. All this was an entirely burned offering to the LORD. ³⁶They also delivered the king's orders to the royal chief administrators and governors of the province Beyond the River, who supported the people and God's house.

Facing a communal problem

9 When these tasks were finished, the officials approached me and said, "The people of Israel, the priests, and the Levites haven't kept themselves separate from the peoples of the neighboring lands with their detestable practices; namely, the Canaanites, the Hittites, the Perizzites, the Jebusites, the Ammonites, the Moabites, the Egyptians, and the Amorites. ²They've taken some of their daughters as wives for themselves and their sons, and the holy descendants have become mixed with the neighboring peoples.[b] Moreover, the officials and leaders have led the way in this unfaithfulness."

³When I heard this, I tore my clothes and cloak, pulled out hair from my head and beard, and sat down in shock. ⁴Then all those who trembled at the words of the God of Israel gathered around me on account of the transgression of the returned exiles while I remained sitting in shock until the evening sacrifice.

Ezra prays

⁵At the time of the evening sacrifice, I ended my penitential acts. While still wearing[c] my torn clothes and cloak, I fell upon my knees, spread out my hands to the LORD my God, ⁶and said,

"My God, I'm too ashamed to lift up my face to you. Our iniquities have risen higher than our heads, and our guilt has grown to the heavens.

⁷"From the days of our ancestors to this day, we've been deep in guilt. On account of our iniquities we, our kings, and our priests have been handed over to the kings of the lands, to the sword, to captivity, to

---

[a]March–April, Nisan [b]Or *peoples of the lands* [c]Heb uncertain

LIFE PRESERVER

Why was it important for the Israelites to be separated from people of other nations?

Ezra 9:1-15

While God's people were in exile, they were exposed to many different cultural and religious practices of other nations. After they returned, Ezra instructed God's people to become a separate community—in Jerusalem—rebuilding their homes, their lives, and their temple so they wouldn't forget God again. ◖

plundering, and to utter shame, as is now the case.

⁸"But now, for a brief while the Lord our God has shown favor in leaving us survivors and in giving us a stake in his holy place. Our God cheered us[d] and revived us for a little while in our slavery. ⁹Even though we are slaves, our God hasn't abandoned us in our slavery. Instead, he's shown us his graciousness before Persia's kings by reviving us to set up our God's house, to repair its ruins, and to give us a wall in Judea and Jerusalem.

¹⁰"And now, our God, what will we say after this? We have abandoned your commandments, ¹¹which you commanded through your servants the prophets, saying: 'The land which you are about to enter to possess is a land polluted by the impurity of the neighboring peoples.[e] Their detestable practices have filled it with uncleanness from end to end. ¹²So now, do not give your daughters to their sons in marriage, do not take their sons for your daughters to marry, and never seek their peace or prosperity. This is so you may be strong, and eat the good of the land, and leave it for an inheritance to your children forever.'

¹³"After all that has happened to us because of our evil deeds and our great guilt—although you, our God, have punished us less than our iniquities deserve and have allowed us to survive as we do—¹⁴will we once again break your commandments and intermarry with the peoples who practice these detestable things? Would you not be so angry with us that you leave us without remnant or survivor? ¹⁵Lord, God of Israel, you are righteous, for we have survived and a few remain until now. Here we are before you in our guilt, though no one can face you because of this guilt."[f]

The community responds

10 While Ezra was praying and confessing, weeping and bowing down before God's house, a very large crowd of men, women, and children of Israel gathered around him. The people also wept in distress. ²Then Shecaniah, Jehiel's son, from the family of Elam, spoke up and said to Ezra, "We've been unfaithful to our God by marrying foreign women from the neighboring peoples.[g] But even now, there is hope for Israel in spite of this. ³Let's now make a covenant with our God to send away all these wives and their children, according to the advice of my master and of those who tremble at the commandment of our God. Let it be done according to the Instruction. ⁴Get up, for it is your duty to deal with this matter; we will support you. Be strong and act." ⁵So Ezra got up and made the leading priests, the Levites, and all Israel take a solemn pledge that they would do as had been said. So they took a solemn pledge.

LIGHTHOUSE

PRAYER

Prayers Can Be Emotional *Ezra 10:1*

Ezra was upset. The Israelites were making the same mistakes their ancestors had made that led to their ancestors being taken as prisoners to another nation seventy years earlier (2 Kgs 22:16-17). Ezra had a reason for being upset, and his frustration and grief came out in a prayer filled with tears. ◖

The assembly decides

⁶Then Ezra got up from the area in front of God's house and went to the room of Jehohanan, Eliashib's son, where he spent[h] the

[d]Or *brightened our eyes* [e]Or *peoples of the lands* [f]Heb lacks *guilt.* [g]Or *peoples of the lands* [h]LXX, 1 Esdr 9:2; Heb *where he went*

night. He didn't eat food or drink water, for he was mourning because of the unfaithfulness of the exiles.

[7] An order was then circulated throughout Judah and Jerusalem that all the returned exiles should gather in Jerusalem. [8] All those who failed to appear within three days, as mandated by the officials and elders, would have all their property taken away. They would be separated from the congregation of the exiles. [9] So within three days, all the people of Judah and Benjamin gathered in Jerusalem. It was the twentieth day of the ninth month.[i] All of the people sat in the area in front of God's house, trembling because of this order and because of the heavy rain.

[10] Then Ezra the priest stood up and said to them, "You have been unfaithful by marrying foreign women and adding to Israel's guilt. [11] But now, make a confession to the LORD God of your ancestors and do his will. Separate yourselves from the neighboring peoples[j] and from the foreign wives."

[12] The whole assembly shouted in reply, "Yes. We must do as you have said. [13] But there are many people, and it's the rainy season; we can't continue to stand outside. Nor can this task be completed in a day or two because many of us have sinned in this matter. [14] Let our leaders represent the entire assembly. Let all in our towns who have taken foreign wives come at appointed times, along with the elders and judges of every town, until God's great anger at us on account of this matter be averted." [15] Only Jonathan, Asahel's son, and Jahzeiah, Tikvah's son, opposed this; Meshullam and Shabbethai the Levites supported them.

Resolving the issue

[16] Then the returned exiles did so. Ezra the priest chose[k] certain men, heads of families, each representing their family houses. Each of them was designated by name. On the first day of the tenth month[l] they sat down to examine the matter. [17] By the first day of the first month,[m] they had come to the end of all the men who had married foreign women.

LIFE PRESERVER

Were the Israelites unfaithful to God when they married people from other nations? *Ezra 10:1-15*

The Israelites returned from years in exile where they lived among the nations who conquered them. When they returned home to Jerusalem, the priest Ezra wanted them to know the importance of marrying only people within their community.

Maybe someone in your school has a mother or father from another country. In our time, we don't consider it a sin to marry someone who is from a different country. We live in a very different world, where difference and diversity within families can be appreciated. ♦

[18] Of the family of priests, there were found the following who had married foreign women—of the family of Jeshua, Jozadak's son and his brothers: Maaseiah, Eliezer, Jarib, and Gedaliah. [19] They promised to send their wives away, and their compensation offering was a ram of the flock for their guilt.

[20] Of the family of Immer: Hanani and Zebadiah.

[21] Of the family of Harim: Maaseiah, Elijah, Shemaiah, Jehiel, and Uzziah.

[22] Of the family of Pashhur: Elioenai, Maaseiah, Ishmael, Nethanel, Jozabad, and Elasah.

[23] Of the Levites: Jozabad, Shimei, Kelaiah (that is, Kelita), Pethahiah, Judah, and Eliezer.

[24] Of the singers: Eliashib. Of the gatekeepers: Shallum, Telem, and Uri.

[25] Of Israel: of the family of Parosh: Ramiah, Izziah, Malchijah, Mijamin, Eleazar, Hashabiah,[n] and Benaiah.

[26] Of the family of Elam: Mattaniah, Zechariah, Jehiel, Abdi, Jeremoth, and Elijah.

[27] Of the family of Zattu: Elioenai, Eliashib, Mattaniah, Jeremoth, Zabad, and Aziza.

[28] Of the family of Bebai: Jehohanan, Hananiah, Zabbai, and Athlai.

---

[i] November–December, Kislev [j] Or *peoples of the lands* [k] 1 Esdr 9:16; Syr; Heb *And there were separated* [l] December–January, Tevet [m] March–April, Nisan [n] 1 Esdr 9:26; LXX; Heb *Malchijah*

[29]Of the family of Bani: Meshullam, Malluch, Adaiah, Jashub, Sheal, and Jeremoth.
[30]Of the family of Pahath-moab: Adna, Chelal, Benaiah, Maaseiah, Mattaniah, Bezalel, Binnui, and Manasseh.
[31]Of the family of Harim: Eliezer, Isshijah, Malchijah, Shemaiah, Shimeon,
[32]Benjamin, Malluch, and Shemariah.
[33]Of the family of Hashum: Mattenai, Mattattah, Zabad, Eliphelet, Jeremai, Manasseh, and Shimei.
[34]Of the family of Bani: Maadai, Amram, Uel, [35]Benaiah, Bedeiah, Cheluhi,
[36]Vaniah, Meremoth, Eliashib, [37]Mattaniah, Mattenai, and Jaasu.
[38]Of the family of Binnui:[o] Shimei,
[39]Shelemiah, Nathan, Adaiah, [40]Machnadebai, Shashai, Sharai, [41]Azarel, Shelemiah, Shemariah, [42]Shallum, Amariah, and Joseph.
[43]Of the family of Nebu: Jeiel, Mattithiah, Zabad, Zebina, Jaddai, Joel, and Benaiah.
[44]All these men[p] had married foreign women, some of whom had borne children.[q]

[o]LXX; Heb *Bani, Binnui* [p]Heb lacks *men*. [q]Heb uncertain; 1 Esdr 9:36 *they sent them away with their children.*

Nehemiah

Nehemiah is an amazing story. Nehemiah was an Israelite man who was a servant of Persia's King Artaxerxes. Part of his job was to taste everything the king wanted to drink, to make sure nothing had been poisoned by the king's enemies.

One day the king noticed that Nehemiah was sad. Nehemiah told the king that his home city of Jerusalem was in ruins. The wall around the city, once strong and secure, had been destroyed. Without this wall, Jerusalem could easily be attacked and defeated.

This book tells how the king gladly sent Nehemiah back to Jerusalem to rebuild the wall. One night Nehemiah made a daring horseback ride around Jerusalem to see the damaged wall. Then he called the people together and helped them work hard to rebuild the wall. Enemies harassed them and tried to stop the work, but Nehemiah and the people kept building until the job was done.

When the wall was finished, the people praised God for helping them complete a difficult task. Nehemiah shows how to make a plan and work hard for God! ◈

Loss of Jerusalem

1 These are the words of Nehemiah, Hacaliah's son.

In the month of Kislev,[a] in the twentieth year,[b] while I was in the fortress city of Susa, [2]Hanani, one of my brothers, came with some other men from Judah. I asked them about the Jews who had escaped and survived the captivity, and about Jerusalem.

[3]They told me, "Those in the province who survived the captivity are in great trouble and shame! The wall around Jerusalem is broken down, and its gates have been destroyed by fire!"

Confession

[4]When I heard this news, I sat down and wept. I mourned for days, fasting and praying before the God of heaven. [5]I said:

"LORD God of heaven, great and awesome God, you are the one who keeps covenant and is truly faithful to those who love you and keep your commandments. [6]Let your ear be attentive and your eyes open to hear the prayer of your servant, which I now pray before you night and day for your servants, the people of Israel.

"I confess the sins of the people of Israel, which we have committed against you. Both I and my family have sinned. [7]We have wronged you greatly. We haven't kept the commandments, the statutes, and the ordinances that you commanded your servant Moses.

[8]"Remember the word that you gave to your servant Moses when you said, 'If you are unfaithful, I will scatter you among the peoples. [9]But if you return to me and keep my commandments by really doing them, then, even though your outcasts live[c] under distant skies, I will gather them from there and bring them to the

---

[a]November–December [b]Of Artaxerxes [c]Heb lacks *live.*

Nehemiah Prays *Nehemiah 1:1-11*

Nehemiah sat down and wept when he found out that God's great city of Jerusalem had been destroyed. He cried for days, giving up food and praying for the city. His prayer, recorded in the book named after him, teaches us how to pray in really hard times. Before Nehemiah said anything else, he praised God. His prayer begins with words that tell God just how awesome God is. Then Nehemiah told the truth about the actions of the people. He confessed that neither he nor the people had loved God very well. He asked God to help the Israelites and the city of Jerusalem to remember the covenant God made with the people.

We can pray like Nehemiah did. We can praise, confess, and ask. Sometimes we get this order turned around and come to God with long lists of things to ask for—almost like a wish list. Instead of reciting a list of things we want, we should remember that it's good to praise God and confess our sins before we ask for anything. By praying in that order, our hearts will be ready to ask for the things we really need and to be humble and patient as we wait for an answer to our prayers.

What do you typically do first when you pray?

Make a prayer journal and write at the top of every page, "Praise, Confess, Ask." Write down your prayers each day.

place that I have chosen as a dwelling for my name.' [10]They are your servants and your people. They are the ones whom you have redeemed by your great power and your strong hand.

[11]LORD, let your ear be attentive to the prayer of your servant and to the prayer of your servants who delight in honoring your name. Please give success to your servant today and grant him favor in the presence of this man!"

Cupbearer's plea

At that time, I was a cupbearer to the king. **2** In the month of Nisan,[d] in the twentieth year of King Artaxerxes, the king was about to be served wine. I took the wine and gave it to the king. Since I had never seemed sad in his presence, [2]the king asked me, "Why do you seem sad? Since you aren't sick, you must have a broken heart!"

I was very afraid [3]and replied, "May the king live forever! Why shouldn't I seem sad when the city, the place of my family's graves, is in ruins and its gates destroyed by fire?"

[4]The king asked, "What is it that you need?"

I prayed to the God of heaven [5]and replied, "If it pleases the king, and if your servant has found favor with you, please send me to Judah, to the city of my family's graves so that I may rebuild it."

[6]With the queen sitting beside him, the king asked me, "How long will you be away and when will you return?" So it pleased the king to send me, and I told him how long I would be gone.

[7]I also said to him, "If it pleases the king, may letters be given me addressed to the governors of the province Beyond the River to allow me to travel to Judah. [8]May the king also issue a letter to Asaph the keeper of the king's forest, directing him to supply me with timber for the beams of the temple fortress gates, for the city wall, and for the house in which I will live."

The king gave me what I asked, for the gracious power of my God was with me.

Inspecting Jerusalem

[9]So I went to the governors of the province[e] Beyond the River and gave them the king's letters. The king had sent officers of the army and cavalry with me.

[10]When Sanballat the Horonite and Tobiah the Ammonite official heard this, they were very angry that someone had come to seek the welfare of the people of Israel.

[11]When I reached Jerusalem and had been there for three days, [12]I set out at night, taking only a few people with me. I didn't tell anyone what my God was prompting me to do for Jerusalem, and the only animal I took was the one I rode. [13]I went out by night through the Valley Gate past the Dragon's Spring to the Dung Gate so that I could inspect the walls of Jerusalem that had been broken down, as well as its gates, which had been destroyed by fire. [14]Then I went on to the Spring Gate and to the King's Pool. Since there was no room for the animal on which I was riding to pass, [15]I went up by way of the valley by night and inspected the wall. Then I turned back and returned by entering through the Valley Gate.

Let's rebuild

[16]The officials didn't know where I had gone or what I was doing. I hadn't yet told the Jews, the priests, the officials, the officers, or the rest who were to do the work. [17]So I said to them, "You see the trouble that we're in: Jerusalem is in ruins, and its gates are destroyed by fire! Come, let's rebuild the wall of Jerusalem so that we won't continue to be in disgrace." [18]I told them that my God had taken care of me, and also told them what the king had said to me.

"Let's start rebuilding!" they said, and they eagerly began the work.[f]

[19]But when Sanballat the Horonite, Tobiah the Ammonite official, and Geshem the Arab heard about it, they mocked and made fun of

did you know? Nehemiah was the governor of Judah who worked for the Persian king to keep Jerusalem safe. Nehemiah gathered men from every tribe of Israel. Together they rebuilt the walls of Jerusalem in fifty-two days, a job that normally would have taken much longer to complete.

---

[d]March–April [e]Heb lacks *of the province.* [f]Or *they strengthened their hands for the good.*

us. "What are you doing?" they asked. "Are you rebelling against the king?"

20"The God of heaven will give us success!" I replied. "As God's servants, we will start building. But you will have no share, right, or claim in Jerusalem."

Rebuilding the gates and walls

3 Then Eliashib the high priest set to work with his fellow priests and built[8] the Sheep Gate. They dedicated it and set up its doors, then dedicated it as far as the Tower of the Hundred and as far as the Tower of Hananel. 2The people of Jericho built next to them, and Zaccur, Imri's son, built next to them. 3The children of Hassenaah built the Fish Gate; they laid its beams and set up its doors, bolts, and bars. 4Next to them Meremoth, Uriah's son and Hakkoz's grandson, made repairs. Meshullam, Berechiah's son and Meshezabel's grandson, made repairs next to them, and Zadok, Baana's son, made repairs next to them. 5Next to them the people from Tekoa made repairs, but their officials wouldn't help with the work[h] of their supervisors.[i]

6Joiada, Paseah's son, and Meshullam, Besodeiah's son, repaired the Mishneh Gate;[j] they laid its beams and set up its doors, bolts, and bars. 7Next to them repairs were made by Melatiah the Gibeonite, Jadon the Meronothite, and[k] the people of Gibeon and of Mizpah, who were ruled by the governor of the province Beyond the River.

8Uzziel, Harhaiah's son, one of the goldsmiths, made repairs next to them; and Hananiah, one of the perfumers, made repairs next to him. They restored Jerusalem as far as the Broad Wall. 9Next to them Rephaiah, Hur's son, ruler of half the district of Jerusalem, made repairs. 10Next to them Jedaiah, Harumaph's son, made repairs opposite his house, and Hattush, Hashabneiah's son, made repairs next to him.

11Malchijah, Harim's son, and Hasshub, Pahath-moab's son, repaired another section and the Tower of the Ovens. 12Next to them Shallum, Hallohesh's son, ruler of half the district of Jerusalem, made repairs, along with his daughters.

Bet you can read this in 1 minute. **Ready, set, go!**

13Hanun and the people of Zanoah repaired the Valley Gate; they built it and set up its doors, bolts, and bars. They also repaired fifteen hundred feet of the wall, as far as the Dung Gate.

14Malchiah, Rechab's son, ruler of the district of Beth-haccherem, repaired the Dung Gate. He rebuilt it and set up its doors, bolts, and bars.

15And Shallum, Col-hozeh's son, ruler of the Mizpah district, repaired the Spring Gate. He rebuilt and covered it, and set up its doors, bolts, and bars. He also built the wall of the Pool of Shelah of the King's Garden, as far as the stairs that go down from David's City.

16After him, Nehemiah, Azbuk's son, ruler of half the Beth-zur district, repaired from the point opposite David's tombs as far as the artificial pool and the Warriors' House. 17After him, the Levites made repairs: Rehum, Bani's son, and next to him Hashabiah, ruler of half the district of Keilah, made repairs for his district. 18After him, their relatives made repairs: Binnui,[l] Henadad's son, ruler of half the district of Keilah.

19Next to him, Ezer, Jeshua's son, ruler of Mizpah, repaired another section opposite the ascent to the armory at the Angle. 20After him, Baruch, Zabbai's son, thoroughly repaired another section from the Angle to the door of the house of the high priest Eliashib. 21After him, Meremoth, Uriah's son and Hakkoz's grandson, repaired another section from the door to the back of Eliashib's house.

22After him, the priests from the surrounding area made repairs. 23After them, Benjamin and Hasshub made repairs opposite their house. After them, Azariah, Maaseiah's son and Ananiah's grandson, repaired beside his house. 24After him, Binnui, Henadad's son, repaired another section from the house of Azariah to the Angle and to the corner. 25Palal, Uzai's son, repaired[m] from the point opposite the Angle and the tower projecting from the upper house of the king at the court of the guard. After him, Pedaiah, Parosh's son, 26and the temple servants living on Ophel made repairs[n] up to the point opposite the Water Gate to the east and the projecting tower. 27After

8Or rebuilt hOr didn't bring their neck into the service of iOr lords jOr Old Gate kSyr; Heb lacks and. lLXX, Syr; Heb Bvvai
mHeb lacks repaired. nHeb lacks made repairs.

them, the people of Tekoa repaired another
section opposite the great projecting tower
as far as the wall of Ophel. 28 From the Horse
Gate, the priests made repairs, each one opposite his own house.
29 After them, Zadok, Immer's son, made
repairs opposite his own house. After him,
Shemaiah, Shecaniah's son, the keeper of the
East Gate, made repairs. 30 After him, Hananiah, Shelemiah's son, and Hanun, Zalaph's
sixth son, repaired another section. After
them, Meshullam, Berechiah's son, made repairs opposite his own room.
31 After him, Malchiah, one of the goldsmiths, made repairs as far as the house of
the temple servants and the merchants, opposite the Parade Gate,[o] and as far as the
upper room at the corner. 32 And between the
upper room of the corner and the Sheep Gate,
the goldsmiths and the merchants made
repairs.

Opposition mounts

4 [p]When Sanballat heard that we were
building the wall, he became angry and
raged. He mocked the Jews, 2 saying in the
presence of his associates and the army of
Samaria: "What are those feeble Jews doing?
Will they restore things themselves? Will
they offer sacrifices? Will they finish it in
a day? Will they revive the stones from the
piles of rubble, even though they are burned?"
3 Tobiah the Ammonite, who was beside
him, added: "If even a fox climbs on whatever
they build, their wall of stones will crumble."
4 Listen, God; we are despised! Turn their
insults to us[q] back on their heads and
make them like plunder in a captive
land. 5 Don't forgive their iniquity or blot
out their sins from your sight. They have
thrown insults at the builders!

did you know? While rebuilding the walls of Jerusalem, the workers faced frequent attacks from their enemies, so workers took turns standing guard. In addition, each worker learned to lay bricks with one hand so his other hand would be free to grab his weapon and fight off an attacker if needed.

6 We continued to build the wall. All of it
was joined together, and it reached half of
its intended height because the people were
eager to work. 7 [r] But when Sanballat, Tobiah,
the Arabs, the Ammonites, and the people of
Ashdod heard that the work on the walls was
progressing and the gaps were being closed,
they were very angry. 8 They plotted together
to come and fight against Jerusalem and to
create a disturbance in it.
9 So we prayed to our God and set a guard as
protection against them day and night.
10 But in Judah it was said,

"The carrier's strength is failing,
for there is too much rubble.
We are unable to rebuild the wall!"

11 Meanwhile, our enemies were saying:
"Before they know or see anything, we can be
in their midst and start to kill them. We'll stop
the work!"
12 Now the Jews who were living near them
came and said to us again and again,[s] "You
must return to us!"[t]

Armed guards protect the builders

13 So I took up a position in the lowest parts
of the space behind the wall in an open area.[u]
Then I stationed the people by families, and
they had their swords, spears, and bows.
14 After reviewing this, I stood up and said to
the officials, the officers, and the rest of the
people, "Don't be afraid of them! Remember
that the LORD is great and awesome! Fight for
your families, your sons, your daughters, your
wives, and your houses!"
15 Then our enemies heard that we had
found out and that God had spoiled their plans.
So we all returned to doing our own work on
the wall. 16 But from that day on, only half of
my workers continued in the construction,
while the other half held the spears, shields,
bows, and body armor. Meanwhile, the leaders positioned themselves[v] behind the whole
house of Judah, 17 who were building the wall.
The carriers did their work with a load in one
hand and a weapon in the other. 18 The builders built with swords fastened in their belts,
and the trumpeter stayed by my side.

[o] Or *Hammiphkad Gate* [p] 3:33 in Heb [q] Heb lacks *to us.* [r] 4:1 in Heb [s] Or *ten times from all sides* [t] Heb uncertain [u] Heb uncertain [v] Heb lacks *positioned themselves.*

¹⁹Then I said to the officials, the officers, and the rest of the people, "The work is very spread out, and we are far apart from each other along the wall. ²⁰When you hear the trumpet sound, come and gather where we are. Our God will fight for us!" ²¹So we continued the work, with half of them holding spears from dawn until dusk.

²²I also said to the people at that time, "Let every man and his servant spend the night in Jerusalem so that we can guard during the night and work during the day." ²³Neither I nor my relatives, nor my servants, nor my bodyguards took off our clothes, even when they sent for water.ʷ

Internal unrest

5 Then there was a great protest of the people and their wives against their fellow Jews. ²Some said, "With our sons and daughters we are many, and we all need grain to eat and stay alive."

³Others said, "We have to mortgage our fields, our vineyards, and our houses in order to get grain during the famine."

⁴Still others said, "We have had to borrow money against our fields and vineyards in order to pay the king's tax."

⁵"We are of the same flesh and blood as our kin, and our children are the same as theirs. Yet we are just about to force our sons and daughters into slavery, and some of our daughters are already slaves! There is nothing we can do since our fields and vineyards now belong to others."

⁶I was very angry when I heard their protest and these complaints. ⁷After thinking it over, I brought charges against the officials and the officers. I told them, "You are all taking interest from your own people!" I also

ʷHeb uncertain

Work to Do Nehemiah 4

God asks us to work together to rebuild broken places in the world. Sometimes people go on mission trips to faraway places to rebuild homes that have been damaged, help in broken-down hospitals, build wells that bring clean water, and do whatever people need. Sometimes, there are places right where we live that need big and small repairs. Part of living for God is being ready to do the work God asks us to do.

Nehemiah got all of God's people together in family groups to begin rebuilding Jerusalem. The city had been destroyed by fire, and the walls around the city had crumbled. The people gathered all the way around the city and began. Each family was assigned their own section of the wall or a gate to rebuild, and they went about the work of putting it back together.

Imagine your whole family—grandparents, aunts, uncles, cousins, brothers, sisters, parents—working together to rebuild a broken place. What do you think your favorite job would be? Laying stones? Getting water? Babysitting the little ones? There is always work for God's people to do in the world. Pray now about how you can be a part of rebuilding something that got broken. God can use you and your family to put something back together or do something new to bring hope and healing to people who need it.

What is your favorite kind of thing to build?

How would you like to work with your family to do God's work in the world?

called for a large assembly in order to deal with them. [8]"To the best of our ability," I said to them, "we have bought back our Jewish kin who had been sold to other nations. But now you are selling your own kin, who must then be bought back by us!" At this they were silent, unable to offer a response.

[9]So I continued, "What you are doing isn't good! Why don't you walk in the fear of our God? This will prevent the taunts of the nations that are our enemies! [10]I myself, along with my family and my servants, am lending them money and grain. But let's stop charging this interest! [11]Give it back to them, right now. Return their fields, their vineyards, their olive orchards, and their houses. And give back the interest on money, grain, wine, and oil that you are charging them."

UMBRELLA It's Not Yours

People Come Before Money
Nehemiah 5:1-11

The Israelites weren't treating each other fairly. Food was hard to find, so it cost a lot of money. Many Israelites had to borrow money to buy food. Until they could pay with money, the borrowers gave their fields and vineyards to the lenders. But the people lending money were charging a lot of interest, which is an extra charge on top of borrowed money that grows bigger and bigger until the money is paid back. The lenders charged so much interest that the original debt grew too large for people to pay back what they owed. Charging interest like this was breaking God's Instruction (Deut 23:19-20). The people who did were focused too much on money. They didn't care how the borrowers were affected or that large debt might force a family to sell their children into slavery. The lenders' love for money caused widespread sadness until Nehemiah made them return what they took unfairly. ◊

[12]They replied, "We'll return everything, and we won't charge anything else.[x] We'll do what you've asked."

So I called the priests and made them swear to do what they had promised. [13]I also shook out the fold of my robe, saying, "So may God shake out everyone from their house and property if they don't keep this promise. So may they be shaken out and emptied!"

The whole assembly said, "Amen," and praised the LORD. And the people did as they had promised.

Generous Governor Nehemiah

[14]In addition, from the time that I was appointed to be their governor in the land of Judah (that is, from the twentieth to the thirty-second year of King Artaxerxes for a total of twelve years), neither I nor my family ate from the governor's food allowance. [15]The earlier governors who had come before me laid heavy burdens on the people. They took food and wine from them as well as[y] forty shekels of silver. Even their servants oppressed the people. But because I was God-fearing, I didn't behave in this way.

[16]Instead, I devoted myself to the work on this wall. We acquired no land, and all my servants were gathered there for the work. [17]One hundred fifty Jews and officials, along with those who came to us from the surrounding nations, gathered around my table. [18]One ox, six choice sheep, and birds were prepared each day. Every ten days there was a large amount of wine. Yet even with this I didn't ask for the governor's food allowance because of the heavy burden the people had to carry.

[19]Remember in my favor, my God, all that I've done for this people!

Nehemiah avoids his enemies

6 Now when Sanballat, Tobiah, Geshem the Arab, and the rest of our enemies heard that I had rebuilt the wall and that there were no gaps left in it (although I hadn't yet hung the doors in the gates), [2]Sanballat and Geshem sent me this message: "Come, let's meet together in one of the villages[z] in the plain of Ono."

But they wanted to harm me, [3]so I sent messengers to tell them, "I'm doing important work, so I can't come down. Why should the work stop while I leave it to come down to you?"

[4]They sent me a message like this four times, and every time I gave them a similar

[x]Heb lacks *everything . . . anything else.*   [y]Heb uncertain   [z]LXX, Vulg; MT *at Hakkephirim*

reply. [5]But the fifth time, Sanballat sent his servant to me in the same way, except that now he carried an open letter. [6]It stated:

It is reported among the nations and confirmed by Geshem[a] that you and the Jews intend to rebel. This is why you are rebuilding the wall. According to these reports, you intend to become their king. [7]You have also appointed prophets to make this announcement about you in Jerusalem: There is a king in Judah! Now, the king will hear of these reports, so come; let's talk together.

[8]So I sent him this reply: "Nothing that you say has happened. You are simply inventing this."

[9]All of them were trying to make us afraid, saying, "They will be discouraged, and the work won't get finished." But now, God, strengthen me!

[10]Later I went to see Shemaiah, Delaiah's son and Mehetabel's grandson, who was confined to his house, and he said:

"Let's meet together in God's house,
    inside the temple itself.

SAILBOAT

COURAGE

Consistent Courage Pays Off

Nehemiah 6:10-13

Many of the Israelites' neighbors didn't want to see Israel become strong. They tried to lie about the Israelites' intentions in rebuilding the walls to get them into trouble with the Persian king (Ezra 4:4-16; Neh 6:5-7). When that didn't work, they threatened to come and fight the workers who were rebuilding Jerusalem's walls (Neh 4). They even went so far as to get some important Jews to make threats and frighten the other people and their leaders into leaving. Nehemiah showed bravery in every instance. Nehemiah countered the lies of the enemies of Israel with truth (Neh 6:8). Nehemiah kept Jerusalem's enemies away by praying for God's help and giving weapons to the workers rebuilding the walls (Neh 4:11-23). When Nehemiah was told to hide from his enemies in God's temple, Nehemiah refused. Because of Nehemiah's constant courage standing up to Israel's enemies, the walls of Jerusalem were finally completed. ◆

Let's shut the doors of the temple,
    for they are coming to kill you;
        they are coming to kill you tonight!"

[11]But I replied, "Should someone like me run away? Who like me would go into the temple to save his life? I won't go in!" [12]Then I realized that God hadn't sent him at all but that he spoke this prophecy against me because Tobiah and Sanballat had hired him. [13]He was hired to frighten me and to make me sin by acting in this way. Then they could give me a bad name and discredit me. [14]My God, remember these deeds of Tobiah and Sanballat! Also remember Noadiah the prophetess and the rest of the prophets who have been trying to frighten me.

[15]So the wall was finished on the twenty-fifth day of the month of Elul.[b] It took fifty-two days. [16]When our enemies heard about this, all of the nations around us were afraid and their confidence was greatly shaken. They knew that this work was completed with the help of our God.

[17]In addition, in those days the officials of Judah sent many letters to Tobiah, and Tobiah's letters were coming to them. [18]Many in Judah were bound to him by solemn pledge because he was the son-in-law of Shecaniah, Arah's son, and his son Jehohanan had married the daughter of Meshullam, Berechiah's son. [19]They also kept talking about his good deeds in my presence and then reported back to him what I said. In addition, Tobiah sent letters to intimidate me.

The wall is complete

7When the wall had been built and I had hung the doors, the gatekeepers, singers, and Levites were appointed. [2]Then I put my brother Hanani and Hananiah the commander of the fortress in charge of Jerusalem. Hananiah was a faithful man who revered God more than many.

[3]I[c] said to them, "The gates of Jerusalem aren't to be opened during the hottest time of the day. While the gatekeepers[d] are still on duty, have them shut and bar the doors. Also, appoint guards from among those who live in Jerusalem. Station some at their watch posts and some in front of their own houses."

[a]Or *Gashmu* [b]August–September [c]Or *He* [d]Or *while they*

Nehemiah registers the families

⁴Now although the city was wide and large, only a few people were living within it, and noᵉ houses had been rebuilt. ⁵My God then prompted me to assemble the officials, the officers, and the people so that they could be registered by families. I found the record of the families who were the first to return, and I found the following written in it:

⁶These are the people of the province who returned from the captivity of those exiles whom Babylon's King Nebuchadnezzar had taken into exile. They all returned to Jerusalem and Judah, everyone to their own town.

⁷They came with Zerubbabel, Jeshua, Nehemiah, Azariah, Raamiah, Nahamani, Mordecai, Bilshan, Mispereth, Bigvai, Nehum, and Baanah.

The number of the people of Israel:

⁸ The family of Parosh	2,172
⁹ of Shephatiah	372
¹⁰ of Arah	652
¹¹ of Pahath-moab, that is, of the descendants of Jeshua and Joab	2,818
¹² of Elam	1,254
¹³ of Zattu	845
¹⁴ of Zaccai	760
¹⁵ of Binnui	648
¹⁶ of Bebai	628
¹⁷ of Azgad	2,322
¹⁸ of Adonikam	667
¹⁹ of Bigvai	2,067
²⁰ of Adin	655
²¹ of Ater, that is, of the descendants of Hezekiah	98
²² of Hashum	328
²³ of Bezai	324
²⁴ of Hariph	112
²⁵ of Gibeon	95
²⁶ The people of Bethlehem and Netophah	188
²⁷ of Anathoth	128
²⁸ of Beth-azmaveth	42
²⁹ of Kiriath-jearim, Chephirah, and Beeroth	743
³⁰ of Ramah and Geba	621
³¹ of Michmas	122
³² of Bethel and Ai	123
³³ of the other Nebo	52
³⁴ the inhabitants of the other Elam	1,254
³⁵ of Harim	320
³⁶ of Jericho	345
³⁷ of Lod, Hadid, and Ono	721
³⁸ of Senaah	3,930
³⁹ The priests: the descendants of Jedaiah, that is, of the house of Jeshua	973
⁴⁰ of Immer	1,052
⁴¹ of Pashhur	1,247
⁴² of Harim	1,017
⁴³ The Levites: the descendants of Jeshua, that is, of Kadmiel, of the descendants of Hodaviah	74
⁴⁴ The singers: the descendants of Asaph	148
⁴⁵ The descendants of gatekeepers: of Shallum, Ater, Talmon, Akkub, Hatita, and Shobai	138

⁴⁶The temple servants: the descendants of Ziha, Hasupha, Tabbaoth,
⁴⁷ Keros, Sia, Padon,
⁴⁸ Lebanah, Hagabah, Shalmai,
⁴⁹ Hanan, Giddel, Gahar,

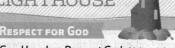

LIGHTHOUSE

RESPECT FOR GOD

Good Leaders Respect God *Nehemiah 7:2*
Nehemiah was looking for the best people to run Jerusalem. Even though Nehemiah had taken charge of rebuilding the walls of Jerusalem, he promised the Persian king that he would return to Persia when the work was complete (Neh 2:6). But who would do the best job of leading Jerusalem when Nehemiah left? The person in charge needed to be trustworthy and smart. But most of all, the new leader needed to respect God. Nehemiah knew that God would bless Israel when the people trusted and respected God (2 Chron 20:27-30; 34:26-28). Leaders who encouraged the people to respect God made sure there was justice (2 Chron 19:4-11) and helped the people to obey (2 Chron 34:30-33). Nehemiah knew that Hananiah respected God, which made him a good choice for leading Jerusalem. ◊

ᵉOr *not enough*

⁵⁰Reaiah, Rezin, Nekoda,

⁵¹Gazzam, Uzza, Paseah,

⁵²Besai, Meunim, Nephushesim,

⁵³Bakbuk, Hakupha, Harhur,

⁵⁴Bazlith, Mehida, Harsha,

⁵⁵Barkos, Sisera, Temah,

⁵⁶Neziah, and Hatipha.

⁵⁷The descendants of Solomon's servants: Sotai, Sophereth, Perida, ⁵⁸Jaala, Darkon, Giddel, ⁵⁹Shephatiah, Hattil, Pochereth-hazzebaim, and Amon.

⁶⁰All of the temple servants and the descendants of Solomon's servants totaled 392.

⁶¹The following came up from Tel-Melah, Tel-harsha, Cherub, Addon, and Immer, but were unable to prove that their family or their descent was from Israel: ⁶²the descendants of Delaiah, Tobiah, and Nekoda, 642.

⁶³And of the priests: the descendants of Hobaiah, Hakkoz, and Barzillai (who had married one of the daughters of Barzillai the Gileadite and was called by his^f name) ⁶⁴looked for their entries in the genealogical records, but they weren't found there, so they were excluded from the priesthood as unclean.

⁶⁵The governor ordered that they shouldn't eat of the most holy food until a priest arose who could consult Urim and Thummim.

⁶⁶The whole assembly together totaled 42,360. ⁶⁷This number doesn't include their 7,337 male and female servants; they also had 245 male and female singers, ⁶⁸736 horses, 245 mules,^g ⁶⁹^h 435 camels, and 6,720 donkeys.

⁷⁰^i Some of the heads of families made a donation for the work. The governor gave to the treasury 1,000 darics of gold, 50 bowls, and 530 priestly robes. ⁷¹Some of the heads of families gave 20,000 darics of gold and 2,200 manehs of silver to the treasury for the work. ⁷²The rest of the people gave 20,000 darics of gold, 2,000 manehs of silver, and 67 priestly robes.

⁷³So the priests, the Levites, the gatekeepers, the singers, some of the people, the temple servants, and all Israel settled in their towns.

Ezra reads the Instruction aloud

When the seventh month^j came and the people of Israel were settled in their towns, **8** all the people gathered together in the area in front of the Water Gate. They asked Ezra the scribe to bring out the Instruction^k scroll from Moses, according to which the LORD had instructed Israel.

²So on the first day of the seventh month, Ezra the priest brought the Instruction before the assembly. This assembly was made up of both men and women and anyone who could understand what they heard. ³Facing the area in front of the Water Gate, he read it aloud, from early morning until the middle of the day. He read it in the presence of the men and the women and those who could understand, and everyone listened attentively to the Instruction scroll.

⁴Ezra the scribe stood on a wooden platform that had been made for this purpose. And standing beside him were Mattithiah, Shema, Anaiah, Uriah, Hilkiah, and Maaseiah on his righthand side; while Pedaiah, Mishael, Malchijah, Hashum, Hash-baddanah, Zechariah, and Meshullam stood on his lefthand side.

⁵Standing above all of the people, Ezra the scribe opened the scroll in the sight of all of the people. And as he opened it, all of the people stood up. ⁶Then Ezra blessed the LORD, the great God, and all of the people answered, "Amen! Amen!" while raising their hands. Then they bowed down and worshipped the LORD with their faces to the ground.

⁷The Levites—Jeshua, Bani, Sherebiah, Jamin, Akkub, Shabbethai, Hodiah, Maaseiah, Kelita, Azariah, Jozabad, Hanan, and Pelaiah^l—helped the people to understand the Instruction while the people remained in their places. ⁸They read aloud from the scroll, the Instruction from God, explaining and interpreting it so the people could understand what they heard.

⁹Then Nehemiah the governor, Ezra the priest and scribe, and the Levites who taught the people said to all of the people, "This day

---

^f Or *their* ^g Ezra 2:66; MT lacks *they also … mules.* ^h 7:68 in Heb ^i 7:69 in Heb ^j September–October, Tishrei ^k Heb *Torah* ^l Vulg 1 Esdr 9:48; MT *and the Levites*

LIFE PRESERVER

What was the Festival of Booths? *Nehemiah 8:13-18*

The Festival of Booths was an important celebration for the Israelites. They lived in shelters, called booths, which reminded them of the way they had lived when they were in exile, living away from Jerusalem.

Many Jews today still celebrate the Festival of Booths in either late September or early October, building booths with branches and leaves at the synagogue. Children and families enjoy this festival, which is an important way to retell the story of exodus, exile, and homecoming. ◆

is holy to the LORD your God. Don't mourn or weep." They said this[m] because all the people wept when they heard the words of the Instruction.

¹⁰"Go, eat rich food, and drink something sweet," he said to them, "and send portions of this to any who have nothing ready! This day is holy to our LORD. Don't be sad, because the joy from the LORD is your strength!"

¹¹The Levites also calmed all of the people, saying, "Be quiet, for this day is holy. Don't be sad!" ¹²Then all of the people went to eat and to drink, to send portions, and to have a great celebration, because they understood what had been said to them.

The people celebrate the Festival of Booths

¹³On the second day, the heads of the families of all the people, along with the priests and the Levites, gathered together around Ezra the scribe in order to study the words of the Instruction. ¹⁴And they found written in the Instruction that the LORD had commanded through Moses that the Israelites should live in booths during the festival of the seventh month.[n]

¹⁵They also found that they should make the following proclamation and announce it throughout their towns and in Jerusalem: "Go out to the hills and bring branches of olive, wild olive, myrtle, palm, and other leafy trees to make booths, as it is written."

¹⁶So the people went out and brought them, and made booths for themselves, each on the roofs of their houses or[o] their courtyards, in the courtyards of God's house, in the area by the Water Gate, or in the area by the Gate of Ephraim.

¹⁷The whole assembly of those who had returned from captivity made booths and lived in them. This was something that the people of Israel hadn't done since the days of Joshua,[p] Nun's son, and there was very great rejoicing.

¹⁸He read from God's Instruction scroll every day, from the first until the last day of the festival.[q] They kept the festival for seven days and held a solemn assembly on the eighth day, just as the Instruction required.

Remembering the LORD's mighty deeds

9On the twenty-fourth day of this month, the people of Israel were assembled. They fasted, wore funeral clothing,[r] and had dirt on their heads.[s] ²After the Israelites separated themselves from all of the foreigners, they stood to confess their sins and the terrible behavior of their ancestors. ³They stood in their place and read the Instruction scroll from the LORD their God for a quarter of the day. For another

SAILBOAT

KINDNESS

God Is Always Kind *Nehemiah 9:1-37*

God is a kind God. Throughout their history, the Israelites constantly tested God's patience. When they were slaves in Egypt, God performed many wonders to set them free. God told them exactly how to obey. But the Israelites soon disobeyed God and made a gold calf to worship. Even though God was angry, God chose not to destroy the Israelites. Instead, God led them into Canaan and gave them the land for their kingdom. God blessed them and made them rich and happy. But the people turned away from God. So God let the Israelites' enemies have power over them. Whenever the people turned back to God, God was kind and rescued them. Even when all the Israelites were scattered, God was compassionate and took care of them. ◆

---

[m]Heb lacks *They said this.* [n]September–October, Tishrei [o]Or *and* [p]Heb *Jeshua* [q]Heb lacks *of the festival.* [r]Or *sackcloth* [s]Or *on them*

quarter of the day, they confessed and worshipped the LORD their God.

⁴On the stairs of the Levites stood Jeshua, Bani, Kadmiel, Shebaniah, Bunni, Sherebiah, Bani, and Chenani. They cried out with a loud voice to the LORD their God. ⁵Then the Levites—Jeshua, Kadmiel, Bani, Hashabneiah, Sherebiah, Hodiah, Shebaniah, and Pethahiah—said:

Stand up and bless the LORD your God.
From everlasting to everlasting
  bless your glorious name,
  which is high above
  all blessing and praise.
⁶ You alone are the LORD.
  You alone made heaven,
  even the heaven of heavens,
  with all their forces.
  You made the earth and all that is on it,
  and the seas and all that is in them.
  You preserve them all,
  and the heavenly forces
  worship you.
⁷ LORD God, you are the one
  who chose Abram.
  You brought him out
  of Ur of the Chaldeans
  and gave him the name Abraham.
⁸ You found him to be faithful before you,
  and you made a covenant with him.
You promised to give to his descendants
  the land of the Canaanites, the Hittites,
  the Amorites, the Perizzites,
  the Jebusites, and the Girgashites.
And you have kept your promise
  because you are righteous.

⁹ You saw the affliction
  of our ancestors in Egypt
  and heard their cry at the Reed Sea.^t
¹⁰ You performed signs and wonders
  against Pharaoh,
  all his servants,
  and the people of his land.
  You knew that they had acted
  arrogantly against our ancestors.
  You made a name for yourself,
  a name that is famous even today.
¹¹ You divided the sea before them so that
  they went through it on dry land.

But you cast their pursuers
  into the depths,
  as a stone into the mighty waters.
¹² With a pillar of cloud you led them by day
  and with a column of lightning by night;
  they lit the way
  in which the people should go.
¹³ You came down upon Mount Sinai
  and spoke with them from heaven.
  You gave them proper judgments
  and true Instruction,
  good statutes and commandments.
¹⁴ You made known to them
  your holy Sabbath,
  and gave them commandments,
  statutes, and Instruction
  through your servant Moses.
¹⁵ When they were hungry,
  you gave them bread from heaven;
  when they were thirsty, you brought
  water out of the rock for them.
You told them to go in to possess
  the land that you had sworn
  to give them.

¹⁶ But our ancestors acted arrogantly.
  They were stubborn and wouldn't obey
  your commandments.
¹⁷ They refused to obey,
  and didn't remember the wonders
  that you accomplished
  in their midst.
  They acted arrogantly and decided
  to return to their slavery in Egypt.
But you are a God ready to forgive,
  merciful and compassionate,
  very patient, and truly faithful.
  You didn't forsake them.
¹⁸ Even when they had cast
  an image of a calf for themselves,
  saying, "This is your God
  who brought you up out of Egypt,"
  and holding you in great contempt,
¹⁹ you, in your great mercy, didn't abandon
  them in the wilderness.
  The column of cloud continued
  to guide them on their journey
  during the day,
  and the column of lightning
  lit their path during the night.

^tOr *Red Sea*

²⁰ You gave your good spirit to teach them.
 You didn't withhold your manna
  from them,
 and you gave them water
  for their thirst.
²¹ You kept them alive for forty years—
 they lacked nothing in the wilderness!
 Their clothes didn't wear out,
  and their feet didn't swell.

²² You gave them kingdoms and peoples,
 and assigned to them every side.ᵘ
 They took possession of the land
  of King Sihon of Heshbon
 and the land of King Og of Bashan.
²³ You multiplied their descendants
  as the stars of heaven.
 You brought them into the land
  that you had told their ancestors
  to enter and possess.
²⁴ So the descendants went in
 and possessed the land.
 Before them, you subdued the
  Canaanites who inhabited the land.
 You also handed over to them their
  kings and the neighboring peoples,
  to do with as they wished.
²⁵ They captured fortified cities
 and productive land,
  and took possession of houses filled
   with all kinds of good things,
  excavated cisterns, vineyards,
   olive orchards,
  and a great many fruit trees.
 They ate until they were satisfied
  and grew fat,
 and delighted themselves
  in your great goodness.

²⁶ But they were disobedient,
 rebelled against you,
 and turned their back
  on your Instruction.
 They killed your prophets
  who had warned them
  so that they might return to you.
 They held you in great contempt.
²⁷ Therefore, you handed them over
  to the power of their enemies
  who made them suffer.

LIFE PRESERVER

Why is the history of God's people included here?
Nehemiah 9:4-37

This chapter briefly tells the story of God's people from their slavery in Egypt through their return from exile in Babylon. This story is included here as a prayer, a way for the people to remember all of the great things God had done for them.

Storytelling is a way of remembering important events and passing down information from one generation to the next. Families often have stories they like to tell about each other and things that have happened. The Israelites frequently told the story of God's faithfulness and provision throughout their history, reminding themselves and their children of God's love and forgiveness. ◖

 But when they cried out to you
  in their suffering,
  you heard them from heaven.
 Because you are merciful,
  you gave them saviors who saved them
   from the power of their enemies.
²⁸ But after they had rest from this, they
  again started doing evil against you.
 So you gave them over
  to the power of their enemies
  who ruled over them.
 Yet when they turned and cried to you,
  you heard from heaven
  and rescued them many times
  because of your great mercy.
²⁹ You also warned them
  to return to your Instruction,
 but they acted arrogantly
 and didn't obey your commands.
  They sinned against your judgments,
   even though life comes
   by keeping them.ᵛ
  They turned a stubborn shoulder,
   became headstrong, and wouldn't obey.
³⁰ You were patient with them
  for many years
 and warned them by your spirit
  through the prophets.
 But they wouldn't listen,
  so you handed them over
  to the neighboring peoples.

ᵘHeb uncertain ᵛ*Them* refers to judgments.

³¹ In your great mercy, however,
   you didn't make an end of them.
   Neither did you forsake them,
   because you are a merciful
   and compassionate God.

³² Now, our God,
   great and mighty and awesome God,
   you are the one who faithfully
   keeps the covenant.
   Don't treat lightly all of the hardship
   that has come upon us,
   upon our kings, our officials,
   our priests, our prophets,
   our ancestors, and all your people,
   from the time of the kings of Assyria
   until today.
³³ You have been just in all
   that has happened to us;
   you have acted faithfully,
   and we have done wrong.
³⁴ Our kings, our officials, our priests,
   and our ancestors
   haven't kept your Instruction.
   They haven't heeded your
   commandments and the warnings
   that you gave them.
³⁵ Even in their own kingdom,
   surrounded by the great goodness
   that you gave to them,
   even in the wide and rich land
   that you gave them,
   they didn't serve you or turn
   from their wicked works.
³⁶ So now today we are slaves,
   slaves in the land
   that you gave to our ancestors
   to enjoy its fruit and its good gifts.
³⁷ Its produce profits the kings whom you
   have placed over us because of our sins.
   They have power over our bodies and
   do as they please with our livestock.
   We are in great distress.

Commitment to follow the Instruction

³⁸ ʷBecause of all this,ˣ we are making a firm agreement in writing, with the names of our officials, our Levites, and our priests on the seal. **10** ʸUpon the seals are the names of Governor Nehemiah, Hacaliah's son, and Zedekiah;

²Seraiah, Azariah, Jeremiah,
³Pashhur, Amariah, Malchijah,
⁴Hattush, Shebaniah, Malluch,
⁵Harim, Meremoth, Obadiah,
⁶Daniel, Ginnethon, Baruch,
⁷Meshullam, Abijah, Mijamin,
⁸Maaziah, Bilgai, Shemaiah; these are the priests.

⁹The Levites: Jeshua, Azaniah's son; Binnui of the descendants of Henadad; Kadmiel; ¹⁰and their associates:
   Shebaniah, Hodiah, Kelita,
   Pelaiah, Hanan,
¹¹Mica, Rehob, Hashabiah,
¹²Zaccur, Sherebiah, Shebaniah,
¹³Hodiah, Bani, Beninu.

¹⁴The leaders of the people: Parosh, Pahath-moab, Elam, Zattu, Bani,
¹⁵Bunni, Azgad, Bebai,
¹⁶Adonijah, Bigvai, Adin,
¹⁷Ater, Hezekiah, Azzur,
¹⁸Hodiah, Hashum, Bezai,
¹⁹Hariph, Anathoth, Nebai,
²⁰Magpiash, Meshullam, Hezir,
²¹Meshezabel, Zadok, Jaddua,
²²Pelatiah, Hanan, Anaiah,
²³Hoshea, Hananiah, Hasshub,
²⁴Hallohesh, Pilha, Shobek,
²⁵Rehum, Hashabnah, Maaseiah,
²⁶Ahiah, Hanan, Anan,
²⁷Malluch, Harim, Baanah.

²⁸The rest of the people, the priests, the Levites, the gatekeepers, the singers, the temple servants, and all who have separated themselves from the neighboring peoples to follow the Instruction from God, together with their wives, their sons, their daughters, and all who have knowledge and understanding. ²⁹They join with their officials and relatives, and make a solemn pledge to live by God's Instruction, which was given by Moses, God's servant, and to observe faithfully all the commandments, judgments, and statutes of our Lord God.

³⁰We won't give our daughters in marriage to the neighboring peoples, nor take their daughters in marriage for our sons. ³¹If the neighboring peoples bring merchandise or any grain to sell on the

ʷ10:1 in Heb ˣ*This refers to* great distress *in 9:37.* ʸ10:2 in Heb

Sabbath, we won't buy it from them on the Sabbath or on any holy day.

Every seventh year we won't plant crops, and we will return anything held in debt.

³²We pledge ourselves to keep the commandment and pay one-third of a shekel each year for the service of our God's house, ³³for the stacks of bread and the regular grain offering and the regular entirely burned offering, for the sabbaths and the new moons and the appointed festivals, for the holy offerings and the purification offerings to make reconciliation for Israel, and for all the work of our God's house.

³⁴We have also cast lots among the priests, the Levites, and the people so that we bring the wood offering into our God's house by families at the appointed times every year, to burn on the altar of the LORD our God, as it is written in the Instruction.

³⁵We will also bring the early produce of our soil and the early fruit from all trees every year to the LORD's house.

³⁶We will also bring the oldest offspring of our children and our cattle, as it is written in the Instruction, and the oldest males of our herds and flocks to our God's house, to the priests who serve in our God's house.

³⁷We will also bring the first of our dough, our contributions, the fruit of every

LIGHTHOUSE

GIVING A TENTH

Why Give? *Nehemiah 10: 37-39*

There were specific reasons why God's Instruction commanded the Israelites to give God one tenth of everything they owned (Lev 27:30-33). When the Israelites gave God the best of what they owned, they showed respect and honor for God. Giving one tenth was a way for the people to show that they depended on God for everything. The tenth was given to the priests and Levites (Num 18:21) so that these servants could completely focus on doing God's work in the temple. God didn't want them constantly worrying about where they were going to get their next meal. God wanted them to focus on the work they had been given to do. The tenth-part gifts were also used to keep God's temple in good shape. Without these gifts God's work wasn't done and the temple fell apart (Neh 13:10-11). ◆

tree, the wine, and the oil to the priests at the storerooms of our God's house. We will also bring one-tenth of the produce of our soil to the Levites, for it is the Levites who collect the tenth-part gifts in all the towns where we work.

³⁸A priest from the family of Aaron must be with the Levites when they collect the tenth-part gifts. Then the Levites must bring up one-tenth of the tenth-part gifts to our God's house, to the storerooms of the treasury. ³⁹The Israelites and the Levites must bring the contribution of grain, wine, and oil to the storerooms where the sanctuary equipment is kept, and where the priests on duty, the gatekeepers, and the singers reside. We won't neglect our God's house!

Inhabitants of Jerusalem

11 The leaders of the people lived in Jerusalem. The rest of the people cast lots to bring one out of ten to live in the holy city of Jerusalem, while the remaining nine stayed in the other towns. ²The people blessed those who agreed to live in Jerusalem.

³These are the leaders of the province who lived in Jerusalem; while the Israelites, the priests, the Levites, the temple servants, and the descendants of Solomon's servants lived in the towns of Judah on their own property in their towns. ⁴Some of the descendants of Judah and Benjamin settled in Jerusalem.

From the family of Judah: Athaiah son of Uzziah son of Zechariah son of Amariah son of Shephatiah son of Mahalalel of the family of Perez; ⁵and Maaseiah son of Baruch son of Col-hozeh son of Hazaiah son of Adaiah son of Joiarib son of Zechariah son of the Shilonite. ⁶All of the family of Perez who lived in Jerusalem totaled 468 courageous people.

⁷From the family of Benjamin: Sallu son of Meshullam son of Joed son of Pedaiah son of Kolaiah son of Maaseiah son of Ithiel son of Jeshaiah. ⁸And after him were Gabbai and Sallai: 928. ⁹Joel son of Zichri was their supervisor, and Judah son of Hassenuah was second in charge of the city.

¹⁰Of the priests: Jedaiah son of Joiarib, Jachin, ¹¹Seraiah son of Hilkiah son of Meshullam son of Zadok son of Meraioth son of Ahitub the officer of God's house, ¹²and their associates who carried out the work in the

temple:[z] 822. There was also Adaiah son of Jeroham son of Pelaliah son of Amzi son of Zechariah son of Pashhur son of Malchijah, [13]and his associates, heads of families: 242. There was also Amashsai son of Azarel son of Ahzai son of Meshillemoth son of Immer [14]and their associates, for a total of 128 courageous people. Their supervisor was Zabdiel, Haggedolim's son.

[15]Of the Levites: Shemaiah son of Hasshub son of Azrikam son of Hashabiah son of Bunni; [16]as well as Shabbethai and Jozabad, who were some of the leaders of the Levites in charge of the outside work on God's house; [17]also Mattaniah son of Mica son of Zabdi son of Asaph the leader who began the thanksgiving with prayer, and Bakbukiah, who was the second among his associates; and Abda son of Shammua son of Galal son of Jeduthun. [18]All the Levites in the holy city totaled 284. [19]The gatekeepers: Akkub, Talmon, and their associates who guarded the gates totaled 172. [20]The rest of Israel, the priests, and the Levites were in all the towns of Judah, each of them in their own property. [21]But the temple servants lived in Ophel, with Ziha and Gishpa in charge of them. [22]The supervisor of the Levites in Jerusalem was Uzzi son of Bani son of Hashabiah son of Mattaniah son of Mica, from the family of Asaph, who

SAILBOAT

GIVING THANKS

Prayer and Giving Thanks Go Together
Nehemiah 11:17

Mattaniah had an important job. As one of the Levites who lived in the newly rebuilt city of Jerusalem, Mattaniah was one of God's special servants whose work involved God's temple. Part of the duties of priests and Levites was to offer praise and thanksgiving in the temple (Neh 12:46). Mattaniah's specific job was to say the prayer that went along with giving thanks. The Israelites knew it was important to have a thankful heart. They knew it was important to be grateful to God for all God has done before asking God to do new things. It's still important. Giving thanks and prayer go hand in hand.◆

were the singers in charge of the work of God's house.

[23]There was a command from the king setting out the daily requirements of the singers.

[24]Advising the king in all matters concerning the people was Pethahiah, Meshezabel's son, from the family of Zerah, Judah's son.

[25]As for the villages with their fields, some of the people of Judah lived in Kiriath-arba and its villages, in Dibon and its villages, in Jekabzeel and its villages, [26]in Jeshua, in Moladah and Beth-pelet, [27]in Hazar-shual, in Beer-sheba and its villages, [28]in Ziklag, in Meconah and its villages, [29]in En-rimmon, Zorah, Jarmuth, [30]Zanoah, Adullam, and their villages, Lachish and its fields, and Azekah and its villages. So they settled from Beer-sheba to the Hinnom Valley.

[31]The people of Benjamin also lived from beyond Geba, at Michmash, Aija, Bethel and its villages, [32]Anathoth, Nob, Ananiah, [33]Hazor, Ramah, Gittaim, [34]Hadid, Zeboim, Neballat, [35]Lod, and Ono, the valley of artisans. [36]Some divisions of the Levites in Judah were joined to Benjamin.

12These are the priests and the Levites who came up with Zerubbabel son of Shealtiel and Jeshua: Seraiah, Jeremiah, Ezra, [2]Amariah, Malluch, Hattush, [3]Shecaniah, Rehum, Meremoth, [4]Iddo, Ginnethon,[a] Abijah, [5]Mijamin, Maadiah, Bilgah, [6]Shemaiah, Joiarib, Jedaiah, [7]Sallu, Amok, Hilkiah, Jedaiah.

These were the leaders of the priests and of their associates in the days of Jeshua. [8]The Levites: Jeshua, Binnui, Kadmiel, Sherebiah, Judah, and also Mattaniah, who was in charge of the thanksgiving songs along with his associates. [9]Bakbukiah and Unn and their associates stood opposite them in the service.

[10]Jeshua was the father of Joiakim, Joiakim the father of Eliashib, Eliashib the father of Joiada, [11]Joiada the father of Jonathan, and Jonathan the father of Jaddua.

[12]These were the heads of the priestly families in the days of Joiakim: of Seraiah, Meraiah; of Jeremiah, Hananiah; [13]of Ezra, Meshullam; of Amariah, Jehohanan; [14]of Malluch,[b] Jonathan; of Shebaniah, Joseph; [15]of Harim, Adna; of Meraioth, Helkai; [16]of Iddo, Zechariah; of Ginnethon, Meshullam;

---

[z]Or house   [a]Heb Ginnethoi   [b]LXX; MT Malluchi

¹⁷of Abijah, Zichri; of Miniamin, of Moadiah, Piltai; ¹⁸of Bilgah, Shammua; of Shemaiah, Jehonathan; ¹⁹of Joiarib, Mattenai; of Jedaiah, Uzzi; ²⁰of Sallai, Kallai; of Amok, Eber; ²¹of Hilkiah, Hashabiah; of Jedaiah, Nethanel.

²²In the days of Eliashib, Joiada, Johanan, and Jaddua, the Levites and the priests were recorded as heads of families in the rule of[c] Darius the Persian.

²³The Levites who were heads of families were recorded in the official records until the time of Johanan, Eliashib's son. ²⁴These were the leaders of the Levites: Hashabiah, Sherebiah, and Jeshua, Kadmiel's son, and their associates who stood opposite them to praise and give thanks in turn according to the commandment of David, the man of God, namely, ²⁵Mattaniah, Bakbukiah, and Obadiah.

Meshullam, Talmon, and Akkub were gatekeepers standing guard by the storerooms of the gates. ²⁶These served in the days of Joiakim, Jeshua's son and Jozadak's grandson, and in the days of Governor Nehemiah and of Ezra the priest and scribe.

Dedication of the wall

²⁷When it was time for the dedication of Jerusalem's wall, they sought out the Levites in all the places where they lived in order to bring them to Jerusalem to celebrate the dedication with joy, with thanks and singing, and with cymbals, harps, and lyres.

²⁸The singers also gathered together both from the region around Jerusalem and from the villages of the Netophathites, ²⁹also from Beth-hagilgal and from the region of Geba and Azmaveth, because the singers had built themselves villages around Jerusalem. ³⁰After the priests and the Levites purified themselves, they purified the people, the gates, and the wall.

³¹Then I[d] brought the leaders of Judah up onto the wall and organized two large groups to give thanks. The first group went in procession on the wall toward the right, in the direction of the Dung Gate. ³²Following them went Hoshaiah and half the officials of Judah, ³³along with Azariah, Ezra, Meshullam, ³⁴Judah, Benjamin, Shemaiah, and Jeremiah. ³⁵There were also some young priests with trumpets—Zechariah son of Jonathan son of

Shemaiah son of Mattaniah son of Micaiah son of Zaccur son of Asaph— ³⁶along with his associates Shemaiah, Azarel, Milalai, Gilalai, Maai, Nethanel, Judah, and Hanani. They brought[e] the musical instruments of David the man of God. Ezra the scribe went in front of them.

³⁷When they reached the Fountain Gate they went straight up by the stairs of David's City, on the ascent to the wall, past the house of David to the Water Gate on the east. ³⁸The second group went in procession to the left.[f] I followed them with half of the people along the wall past the Tower of the Ovens to the Broad Wall, ³⁹past the Gate of Ephraim and over the Mishneh Gate,[g] the Fish Gate, the Tower of Hananel, and the Tower of the Hundred as far as the Sheep Gate. They came to a stop at the Gate of the Guard.

In God's house

⁴⁰Then both groups of those who gave thanks stood in God's house. I was there too along with the half of the officials who were with me. ⁴¹Also there were the priests Eliakim, Maaseiah, Miniamin, Micaiah, Elioenai, Zechariah, and Hananiah with trumpets. ⁴²Also there were Maaseiah, Shemaiah, Eleazar, Uzzi, Jehohanan, Malchijah, Elam, and Ezer. The singers sang with Jezrahiah as their leader.

⁴³They offered great sacrifices on that day and rejoiced, for God had made them rejoice with great joy. The women and

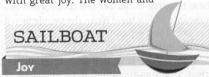

SAILBOAT

Joy

Walls of Joy *Nehemiah 12:43*
The Israelites had a reason to be happy. Years after the walls of Jerusalem had been broken down by Babylon (2 Chron 36:17-19), they had finally been rebuilt. Jerusalem was the most important city of Israel. It was called David's City (2 Sam 5:6-10). It was the city where God's temple had been built and the city where God promised to put God's name forever (2 Kgs 21:7-8). In those times, it was important for major cities to have thick walls. Without walls, enemies could walk right in and easily take over. Now that Jerusalem had walls again, it was like God had given the Israelites back their kingdom. This was a new start and a reason for joy. ◗

///

---

[c]LXX, Vulg; MT *upon*   [d]Or *I, Nehemiah*   [e]Heb lacks *they brought.*   [f]Or *opposite*   [g]Or *Old Gate*

children also rejoiced, and the sound of the joy in Jerusalem could be heard from far away.

⁴⁴On that day, people were appointed over the rooms for the things to be stored, the contributions, the early produce, and the tenth-part gifts. They were to gather into them the portions required by the Instruction for the priests and for the Levites from the fields belonging to the towns, for the people of Judah were delighted with the ministry of the priests and the Levites.

⁴⁵They performed the service of their God and the service of purification, as did the singers and the gatekeepers, according to the command of David and his son Solomon.

⁴⁶Long ago, in the days of David and Asaph, there was a leader of the singers, and there were songs of praise and thanks to God.

⁴⁷In the days of Zerubbabel and of Nehemiah all Israel gave the daily portions for the singers and the gatekeepers. They also set aside the portion for the Levites, and the Levites set aside the portion for the Aaronites.

Restoring the temple

13 On that day, when the scroll from Moses was being read to the people, they found written in it that no Ammonite or Moabite should ever enter God's assembly. ²This is because they hadn't met the Israelites with food and water but instead hired Balaam against them to curse them. Yet our God turned the curse into a blessing. ³When the people heard this law, they separated out from Israel all those of mixed descent.

⁴Now before this, however, Eliashib the priest, who was appointed to be in charge of the storerooms of our God's house and who was related to Tobiah, ⁵prepared a large room for Tobiah to use. This was the room where they had previously kept the grain offering, the incense, and the equipment, together with the tenth-part gifts of grain, wine, and oil. These items were for the Levites, singers, and gatekeepers as well as the portions for the priests.

⁶I wasn't in Jerusalem while this was happening because I had gone to Babylon's King Artaxerxes in the thirty-second year of the king. After some time, I asked the king's permission ⁷and returned to Jerusalem. That was when I saw the wrong that Eliashib had done

on behalf of Tobiah by preparing him a room in the courtyards of God's house. ⁸I was very angry and threw all of Tobiah's household furniture out of the room. ⁹Then I gave orders that the rooms be purified, and I put back the temple equipment, along with the grain offering and the incense.

¹⁰I also found out that the Levites hadn't been given their portions, so they and the singers who did the work had gone back to their fields. ¹¹So I scolded the officials, asking, "Why is God's house being neglected?" I gathered them together and set them in their stations.

¹²Then all Judah brought the tenth-part gifts of the grain, wine, and oil into the storehouses. ¹³I appointed the priest Shelemiah, the scribe Zadok, and Pedaiah of the Levites to be in charge over the storehouses. I also appointed Hanan, Zaccur's son and Mattaniah's grandson, as their assistant. These men were considered trustworthy, and their task was to hand out shares to their colleagues.

SAILBOAT

HONEST AND TRUE

People with an Honest and True Character Are Important *Nehemiah 13:13*
Shelemiah and Pedaiah were considered trustworthy. These men and their assistant were responsible for receiving the tenth-part gifts—the small portion of belongings that the Israelites gave to God (Lev 27:30-33). Being honest and truthful was probably a big concern for many people because Shelemiah and Pedaiah replaced a man who had been dishonest. The priest Eliashib took a large storeroom for his relative's personal use (Neh 13:4-9). These rooms were part of God's temple meant to house temple equipment and store the tenth-part gifts from the people. It was selfish and disrespectful for Eliashib to use the storeroom this way. Shelemiah and Pedaiah had the good character that Eliashib lacked. ◆

¹⁴Remember me, my God, concerning this. Don't erase my good deeds that I have done for my God's house and for its services.

Keeping the Sabbath

¹⁵In those days I saw people in Judah using the winepresses on the Sabbath. They were

also collecting piles of grain and loading them on donkeys, as well as wine, grapes, figs, and every kind of load, and then bringing them to Jerusalem on the Sabbath. I warned them at that time against selling food.

[16]In addition, people from Tyre who lived in the city were bringing in fish and all kinds of merchandise and selling them to the people of Judah on the Sabbath. This happened in Jerusalem itself!

[17]So I scolded the officials of Judah: "What is this evil thing that you are doing?" I asked. "You are making the Sabbath impure! [18]This is just what your ancestors did, and God brought all this evil upon us and upon this city. And now you are bringing more wrath upon Israel by making the Sabbath impure!"

[19]So when it began to grow dark at the gates of Jerusalem before the Sabbath, I gave orders that the doors should be shut. I also ordered that they shouldn't be reopened until after the Sabbath. To make sure that no load would come into the city[h] on the Sabbath, I stationed some of my own men at the gates. [20]Once or twice the traders and sellers of all kinds of merchandise spent the night outside Jerusalem. [21]But I warned them: "Why are you spending the night by the wall? If you do that again, I will lay hands on you!" At that point, they stopped coming on the Sabbath. [22]I also commanded the Levites to purify themselves and to come and guard the gates in order to keep the Sabbath day holy.

Remember this also in my favor, my God, and spare me according to the greatness of your mercy.

[h]Heb lacks *the city*.

Marrying foreign women

[23]Also in those days I saw Jews who had married women of Ashdod, Ammon, and Moab. [24]Half of their children spoke the language of Ashdod or the language of various peoples; they couldn't speak the language of Judah.

[25]So I scolded them and cursed them, and beat some of them, and pulled out their hair. I also made them swear a solemn pledge in the name of God, saying, "You won't give your daughters to their sons in marriage, or take their daughters in marriage for your sons or yourselves. [26]Didn't Israel's King Solomon sin on account of such women? Among the many nations there was no king like him. He was well loved by his God, and God made him king over all Israel. Yet foreign wives led even him into sin! [27]Should we then listen to you and do all this great evil, acting unfaithfully toward our God by marrying foreign women?"

[28]Now one of the sons of Joiada son of the high priest Eliashib was a son-in-law of Sanballat the Horonite. So I chased him away from me.

[29]Remember them, my God, because they have defiled the priesthood and the covenant of the priests and the Levites!

[30]So I purified them of everything foreign and established the services of the priests and Levites with specific duties for each person. [31]I also provided for the wood offering at appointed times as well as for the early produce.

Remember me, my God, for good.

Esther

Esther is one of the Bible's most dramatic stories. At the beginning of the book, Persia's King Ahasuerus looks for a new queen. A young Jewish woman named Esther was one of many women taken to the king's palace as candidates for the position. The king loved Esther more than the others and chose her to be queen.

Becoming queen was a surprise for Esther, an orphan who was raised by her older cousin Mordecai in the land of Persia. Esther chose not to tell anyone that she was one of God's people. She didn't know if people would like a Jewish queen.

Then an official named Haman made an evil plan to kill all of the Jews. Mordecai told Esther to beg the king to stop Haman. But even though Esther was the queen, she couldn't talk to the king without an invitation from him to enter his presence.

This book tells how Esther made a brave choice to tell the king that she was a Jew—and to ask him to save her people from death. Esther reminds us to stand up and do the right thing, even when we're afraid! ◆

Queen Vashti

1 This is what happened back when Ahasuerus lived, the very Ahasuerus who ruled from India to Cush—one hundred twenty-seven provinces in all. ²At that time, Ahasuerus ruled the kingdom from his royal throne in the fortified part of Susa. ³In the third year of his rule he hosted a feast for all his officials and courtiers. The leaders of Persia and Media attended, along with his provincial officials and officers. ⁴He showed off the awesome riches of his kingdom and beautiful treasures as mirrors of how very great he was. The event lasted a long time—six whole months, to be exact! ⁵After that the king held a seven-day feast for everyone in the fortified part of Susa. Whether they were important people in the town or not, they all met in the walled garden of the royal palace. ⁶White linen curtains and purple hangings were held up by shining white and red-purple ropes tied to silver rings and marble posts. Gold and silver couches sat on a mosaic floor made of gleaming purple crystal, marble, and mother-of-pearl. ⁷They served the drinks in cups made of gold, and each cup was different. The king made sure there was plenty of royal wine. ⁸The rule about the drinks was "No limits!" The king had ordered everyone serving wine in the palace to offer as much as each guest wanted. ⁹At the same time, Queen Vashti held a feast for women in King Ahasuerus' palace.

¹⁰On the seventh day, when wine had put the king in high spirits, he gave an order to Mehuman, Biztha, Harbona, Bigtha, Abagtha, Zethar, and Carcas, the seven eunuchs who served King Ahasuerus personally. ¹¹They were to bring Queen Vashti before him wearing the royal crown. She was gorgeous, and he wanted to show off her beauty both to the general public and to his important guests. ¹²But Queen Vashti refused to come as the king had ordered through the eunuchs. The king was furious, his anger boiling inside. ¹³Now, when a need arose, the king would often talk with certain very smart people about the best way to handle it. They were people who knew both the kingdom's written laws and what judges had decided about cases in the past. ¹⁴The ones he talked with most often were Carshena, Shethar, Admatha,

Tarshish, Meres, Marsena, and Memucan. They were seven very important people in Persia and Media who, as the kingdom's highest leaders, were in the king's inner circle. So the king said to them, ¹⁵"According to the law, what should I do with Queen Vashti since she didn't do what King Ahasuerus ordered her through the eunuchs?"

¹⁶Then Memucan spoke up in front of the king and the officials. "Queen Vashti," he said, "has done something wrong not just to the king himself. She has also done wrong to all the officials and the peoples in all the provinces of King Ahasuerus. ¹⁷This is the reason: News of what the queen did will reach all women, making them look down on their husbands. They will say, 'King Ahasuerus ordered servants to bring Queen Vashti before him, but she refused to come.' ¹⁸This very day, the important women of Persia and Media who hear about the queen will tell the royal officials the same thing. There will be no end of put-downs and arguments. ¹⁹Now, if the king wishes, let him send out a royal order and have it written into the laws of Persia and Media, laws no one can ever change. It should say that Vashti will never again come before King Ahasuerus. It should also say that the king will give her royal place to someone

LIFE PRESERVER

Why did the king get rid of Queen Vashti? *Esther 1*

King Ahasuerus was having a lot of parties. In fact, the parties had been going on for six months. He was very proud to show off all of his riches. During the last seven-day feast, the king and others at the party were drinking a lot of alcohol.

Queen Vashti was entertaining the women when she received the order that she was to come to the feast the king was hosting, wearing her royal crown. Possibly the king wanted to show off her beauty and display her before the men.

We don't know why Queen Vashti refused to come to the feast. Maybe she knew what would happen and didn't want to be displayed as a woman before a group of men who had been drinking too much. She resisted the king's authority and refused to go. The king was so angry that he passed a law that all wives must obey their husbands, and he declared that Vashti could not see him again. ◆

better than she. ²⁰When the order becomes public through the whole empire, vast as it is, all women will treat their husbands properly. The rule should touch everyone, whether from an important family or not."

²¹The king liked the plan, as did the other men, and he did just what Memucan said. ²²He sent written orders to all the king's provinces. Each province received it written in its own alphabet and each people received it in its own language. It said that each husband should rule over his own house.

Finding a new queen

2 Sometime later when King Ahasuerus was less angry, he remembered Vashti, what she had done, and what he had decided about her. ²So his young male servants said, "Let the king have a search made for beautiful young women who haven't yet married. ³And let the king choose certain people in all the royal provinces to lead the search. Have them bring all the beautiful young women together to the fortified part of Susa, to the women's house, to the care of Hegai the king's eunuch in charge of the women so that he might provide beauty treatments for them. ⁴Let the young woman who pleases you the most take Vashti's place as queen." The king liked the plan and implemented it.

⁵Now there was a Jew in the fortified part of Susa whose name was Mordecai, Jair's son. He came from the family line of Shimei and Kish; he was a Benjaminite. (⁶Benjaminites had been taken into exile away from Jerusalem along with the group, which included Judah's King Jeconiah, whom Babylon's King Nebuchadnezzar exiled to Babylon.) ⁷Mordecai had been a father to Hadassah (that is, Esther), though she was really his cousin, because she had neither father nor mother. The girl had a beautiful figure and was lovely to look at. When her parents died, Mordecai had taken her to be his daughter. ⁸When the king's order and his new law became public, many young women were gathered into the fortified part of Susa under the care of Hegai. Esther was also taken to the palace to the care of Hegai, the one in charge of the women. ⁹The young woman pleased him and won his kindness. He quickly began her beauty treatments and gave her carefully chosen foods.

He also gave her seven servants selected from among the palace servants and moved her and her servants into the nicest rooms in the women's house. (¹⁰Esther hadn't told anyone her race and family background because Mordecai had ordered her not to.) ¹¹Each day found Mordecai

SAILBOAT

KINDNESS

A Saving Kindness *Esther 2:7*

Mordecai was a kind man in a time when it was hard to be one of God's people. The land of Israel had been invaded and destroyed, which God had promised to do if Israel served false gods (1 Kgs 9:6-9). Mordecai's family was one of those taken from Israel many years before. He was living in a country not his own when Esther came into his life. Esther was his cousin, but both her father and her mother had died. Mordecai decided to take care of her. Many people would have thought that caring for someone else's child would be a burden. But Mordecai didn't think that way. He raised Esther as his own daughter. Later, Esther grew up to become a queen whose actions would protect the Israelites. The kindness of Mordecai helped to save an entire people (Esth 8). ◈

pacing back and forth along the wall in front of the women's house to learn how Esther was doing and what they were doing with her. ¹²According to the rules for women, the moment for each young woman to go to King Ahasuerus came at the end of twelve months. (She had six months of treatment with pleasant-smelling creams and six months

did you know? Esther's Hebrew name was *Hadassah*, which meant "myrtle." The myrtle plant was a symbol for renewal. *Esther* was her Persian name, which meant "star." In Esther's story, you read how as queen she became a star who renewed the status of her people.

with fragrant oils and other treatments for women.) ¹³So this is how the young woman would go to the king: They gave her anything that she asked to take with her from the women's house to the palace. ¹⁴In the evening she would go in, and the next morning she would return to the second women's house under the care of Shaashgaz. He was the king's eunuch in charge of the secondary wives. She would never go to the king again unless he was so pleased that he called for her by name. [15]Soon the moment came for Esther daughter of Mordecai's uncle Abihail, whom Mordecai had taken as his own daughter, to go to the king. But she asked for nothing except what Hegai the king's eunuch in charge of the women told her. (Esther kept winning the favor of everyone who saw her.)

[16]Esther was taken to King Ahasuerus, to his own palace, in the tenth month (that is, the month of Tevet)[a] in the seventh year of his rule. [17]The king loved Esther more than all the other women; she had won his love and his favor more than all the others. He placed the royal crown on her head and made her ruler

did you know? Haman planned awful things for God's people. Even now, each year at the Jewish Festival of Purim when Esther's story is read, people boo, hiss, and play loud instruments whenever Haman's name is said. This is a way they remember how evil he was.

in place of Vashti. [18]The king held a magnificent, lavish feast, "the feast of Esther," for all his officials and courtiers. He declared a public holiday[b] for the provinces and gave out gifts with royal generosity. [19]When they gathered the young women to the second women's house,[c] Mordecai was working for the king at the King's Gate. [20]Esther still wasn't telling anyone her family background and race, just as Mordecai had ordered her. She continued to do what Mordecai said, just as she did when she was in his care.

Mordecai saves the king

[21]At that time, as Mordecai continued to work at the King's Gate, two royal eunuchs, Bigthan and Teresh, became angry with King Ahasuerus. They were among the guards protecting the doorway to the king, but they secretly planned to kill him. [22]When Mordecai got wind of it, he reported it to Queen Esther. She spoke to the king about it, saying the information came from Mordecai. [23]The matter

was investigated and found to be true, so the two men were impaled on pointed poles.[d] A report about the event was written in the royal record with the king present.

Haman plans to destroy Mordecai

3 Sometime later, King Ahasuerus promoted Haman, Hammedatha the Agagite's son,[e] by promoting him above all the officials who worked with him. [2]All the royal workers at the King's Gate would kneel and bow facedown to Haman because the king had so ordered. But Mordecai didn't kneel or bow down. [3]So the royal workers at the King's Gate said to Mordecai, "Why don't you obey the king's order?" [4]Day after day they questioned him, but he paid no attention to them. So they let Haman know about it just to see whether or not Mordecai's words would hold true.[f] (He had told them that he was a Jew.) [5]When Haman himself saw that Mordecai didn't kneel or bow down to him, he became very angry. [6]But he decided not to kill only Mordecai, for people had told him Mordecai's race. Instead, he planned to wipe out all the Jews, Mordecai's people, throughout the whole kingdom of Ahasuerus. [7]In the first month (that is, the month of Nisan)[g] in the twelfth year of the rule of King Ahasuerus, servants threw pur, namely, dice, in front of Haman to find the best day for his plan. They tried every day and every month, and the dice chose the thirteenth[h] day of the twelfth month (that is, the month of Adar).

[8]Then Haman said to King Ahasuerus, "A certain group of people exist in pockets among the other peoples in all the provinces of your kingdom. Their laws are different from those of everyone else, and they refuse to obey the king's laws. There's no good reason for the king to put up with them any longer. [9]If the king wishes, let a written order be sent out to destroy them, and I will hand over ten thousand kikkars of silver[i] to those in charge of the king's business. The silver can go into the king's treasuries."

[10]The king removed his royal ring from his finger and handed it to Haman, Hammedatha the Agagite's son, enemy of the Jews. [11]The

---

king said to Haman, "Both the money and the people are under your power. Do as you like with them." [12]So in the first month, on the thirteenth day, royal scribes were summoned to write down everything that Haman ordered. The orders were for the king's rulers and the governors in charge of each province, as well as for the officials of each people. They wrote in the alphabet of each province and in the language of each people. They wrote in the name of King Ahasuerus and sealed the order with the king's royal ring. [13]Fast runners were to take the order to all the provinces of the king. The order commanded people to wipe out, kill, and destroy all the Jews, both young and old, even women and little children. This was to happen on a single day—the thirteenth day of the twelfth month (that is, the month of Adar).[j] They were also to seize their property. [14]A copy of the order was to become law in each province and to be posted in public for all peoples to read. The people were to be ready for this day to do as the order commanded. [15]Driven by the king's order, the runners left Susa just as the law became public in the fortified part of Susa. While the king and Haman sat down to have a drink, the city of Susa was in total shock.

A crisis for the Jews

4 When Mordecai learned what had been done, he tore his clothes, dressed in mourning clothes, and put ashes on his head. Then he went out into the heart of the city and cried out loudly and bitterly. [2]He went only as far as the King's Gate because it was against the law for anyone to pass through it wearing mourning clothes. [3]At the same time, in every province and place where the king's order and his new law arrived, a very great sadness came over the Jews. They gave up eating and spent whole days weeping and crying out loudly in pain. Many Jews lay on the ground in mourning clothes and ashes. [4]When Esther's female servants and eunuchs came and told her about Mordecai, the queen's whole body showed how upset she was. She sent everyday clothes for Mordecai to wear instead of mourning clothes, but he rejected them.

[5]Esther then sent for Hathach, one of the royal eunuchs whose job it was to wait on her. She ordered him to go to Mordecai and find out what was going on and why he was acting this way. [6]Hathach went out to Mordecai, to the city square in front of the King's Gate. [7]Mordecai told him everything that had happened to him. He spelled out the exact amount of silver that Haman promised to pay into the royal treasury. It was in exchange for the destruction of the Jews. [8]He also gave Hathach a copy of the law made public in Susa concerning the Jews' destruction so that Hathach could show it to Esther and report it to her. Through him Mordecai ordered her to go to the king to seek his kindness and his help for her people. [9]Hathach came back and told Esther what Mordecai had said.

[10]In reply Esther ordered Hathach to tell Mordecai: [11]"All the king's officials and the people in his provinces know that there's a single law in a case like this. Any man or woman who comes to the king in the inner courtyard without being called is to be put to death. Only the person to whom the king holds out the gold scepter may live. In my case, I haven't been called to come to the king for the past thirty days."

[12]When they told Mordecai Esther's words, [13]he had them respond to Esther: "Don't think for one minute that, unlike all the other Jews, you'll come out of this alive simply because you are in the

SAILBOAT

COURAGE

Being Selfless Is Brave Esther 4:1-16

It took a lot of courage to go see the king. The punishment for showing up in front of the king without an invitation was death. The only way to be saved was if the king stretched out his royal scepter. Esther had a good reason to see the king. She needed to tell him about Haman's plan to wipe out her people. But the king hadn't asked to see her for almost a month. And if she just showed up to see him, she could be killed even though she was the queen. Esther could have decided it was too big of a risk. But Esther was brave. She thought of the risk to her people before the risk to herself. Esther's bravery saved her people (Esth 8:7-17). ◆

[j]February–March

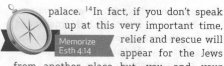

palace. ¹⁴In fact, if you don't speak up at this very important time, relief and rescue will appear for the Jews from another place, but you and your family will die. But who knows? Maybe it was for a moment like this that you came to be part of the royal family."

¹⁵Esther sent back this word to Mordecai: ¹⁶"Go, gather all the Jews who are in Susa and tell them to give up eating to help me be brave. They aren't to eat or drink anything for three whole days, and I myself will do the same, along with my female servants. Then, even though it's against the law, I will go to the king; and if I am to die, then die I will."¹⁷So Mordecai left where he was and did exactly what Esther had ordered him.

Esther acts

5 Three days later, Esther put on royal clothes and stood in the inner courtyard of the palace, facing the palace itself. At that moment the king was inside sitting on his royal throne and facing the palace doorway. ²When the king noticed Queen Esther standing in the entry court, he was pleased. The king held out to Esther the gold scepter in his hand, and she came forward and touched the scepter's tip.

³Then the king said to her, "What is it, Queen Esther? What do you want? I'll give you anything—even half the kingdom."

⁴Esther answered, "If the king wishes, please come today with Haman for the feast that I have prepared for him."

⁵"Hurry, get Haman," the king ordered, "so we can do what Esther says." So the king and Haman came to the feast that Esther had prepared. ⁶As they sipped wine, the king asked, "Now what is it you wish? I'll give it to you. What do you want? I'll do anything—even give you half the kingdom."

⁷Esther answered, "This is my wish and this is what I want: ⁸If I please the king, and if the king wishes to grant my wish and my desire, I'd like the king and Haman to come to another feast that I will prepare for them. Tomorrow I will answer the king's questions."

Haman boasts, complains, and acts

⁹That day Haman left Esther's place happy, his spirits high, but then he saw Mordecai in the King's Gate. Mordecai neither stood up nor seemed the least bit nervous around him, so Haman suddenly felt great rage toward Mordecai. ¹⁰But Haman held himself back and went on home. He sent word that his friends and his wife Zeresh should join him there. ¹¹Haman boasted to them about his great wealth and his many sons. He told all about how the king had honored him by promoting him over the officials and high royal workers. ¹²"Best of all," Haman said, "Queen Esther has invited no one else but me to join the king for food and drinks that she has prepared. In fact, I've been called to join the king at her place tomorrow! ¹³But all this loses its meaning every time I see Mordecai the Jew sitting at the King's Gate."

¹⁴So his wife Zeresh and all his friends told him: "Have people prepare a pointed pole seventy-five feet high. In the morning, tell the king to have Mordecai impaled on it. Then you can go with the king to the feast in a happy mood." Haman liked the idea and had the pole prepared.

Honor for Mordecai

6 That same night, the king simply couldn't sleep. He had the official royal records brought in, and his young male servants began reading them to the king. ²They came to the report about Mordecai informing on Bigthan and Teresh. (They were the two royal eunuchs among the guards protecting the king's doorway, who secretly planned to kill King Ahasuerus.) ³"What was done to honor and reward Mordecai for this?" the king asked.

His young male servants replied, "Nothing was done for him, sir."

⁴"Who is that out in the courtyard?" the king asked. (Haman had just entered the outer courtyard of the palace. He had come to tell the king to impale Mordecai on the pole that he had set up for him.)

⁵The king's servants answered, "That's Haman standing out in the courtyard, sir." So the king said, "Have him come in."

⁶When Haman entered, the king asked him, "What should be done for the man whom the king really wants to honor?"

Haman thought to himself, Whom would the king really want to honor more than me? [7]So Haman said to the king, "Here's what should be done for the man the king really wants to honor. [8]Have servants bring out a royal robe that the king himself has worn and a horse on which the king himself has ridden. It should have a royal crest on its head. [9]Then hand over the robe and the horse to another man, one of the king's officials. Have him personally robe[k] the man whom the king really wants to honor and lead him on the horse through the city square. As he goes, have him shout, 'This is what the king does for the man he really wants to honor!'"

[10]Then the king said to Haman, "Hurry, take the robe and the horse just as you've said and do exactly that for Mordecai the Jew, who works at the King's Gate. Don't leave out a single thing you've said!"

[11]So Haman took the robe and the horse and put the robe on Mordecai. He led him on horseback through the city square, shouting as he went, "This is what the king does for the man he really wants to honor!" [12]Afterward, Mordecai returned to the King's Gate, while Haman hurried home feeling great shame, his head covered.

[13]Haman told his wife Zeresh and all his friends everything that had happened to him. Both his friends[l] and his wife said to him, "You've already begun to lose out to Mordecai. If he is of Jewish birth, you'll not be able to win against him. You are surely going to lose out to him."

Haman's demise

[14]They were still discussing this with him when several royal eunuchs arrived. They quickly hurried Haman off to the feast that Esther had prepared. [1]When the king and Haman came in for the banquet with Queen Esther, [2]the king said to her, "This is the second day we've met for wine. What is your wish, Queen Esther? I'll give it to you. And what do you want? I'll do anything—even give you half the kingdom."

[3]Queen Esther answered, "If I please the king, and if the king wishes, give me my life—that's my wish—and the lives of my people too. That's my desire. [4]We have been sold—I and my people—to be wiped out, killed, and destroyed. If we simply had been sold as male and female slaves, I would have said nothing. But no enemy can compensate the king for this kind of damage."

[5]King Ahasuerus said to Queen Esther, "Who is this person, and where is he? Who would dare do such a thing?"

[6]Esther replied, "A man who hates, an enemy—this wicked Haman!" Haman was overcome with terror in the presence of the king and queen. [7]Furious, the king got up and left the banquet for the palace garden. But Haman stood up to beg Queen Esther for his life. He saw clearly that the king's mood meant a bad end for him.

[8]The king returned from the palace garden to the banquet room just as Haman was kneeling on the couch where Esther was reclining. "Will you even molest the queen while I am in the house?" the king said. The words had barely left the king's mouth before covering Haman's face with dread.[m]

[9]Harbona, one of the eunuchs serving

UMBRELLA
PRIDE

Pride Is a Deadly Path *Esther 6:6-12*
Haman really liked it when people recognized how great he was. Haman thought he was better than everyone else because the king himself had promoted Haman above all the other officials of the empire. He thought he could treat everybody else like dirt because he had a lot of sons and all sorts of expensive things (Esth 5:11). But Mordecai wasn't going to bow to Haman no matter how great he was. Mordecai would bow only before God. That's why Haman hated him (Esth 3:1-6). When the king wanted to honor someone, Haman automatically thought the king wanted to honor him. Haman's idea of honor was being paraded around while someone told the crowds how great Haman was. When Mordecai refused to bow, Haman wanted to punish not only Mordecai but all of Mordecai's people—the entire Israelite race. Haman's pride led him onto a path to his own destruction (Esth 7). ◊

the king, said, "Sir, look! There's the stake that Haman made for Mordecai, the man who spoke up and did something good for the king. It's standing at Haman's house—seventy-five feet high."

"Impale him on it!" the king ordered. [10]So they impaled Haman on the very pole that he had set up for Mordecai, and the king's anger went away.

Esther acts again

8That same day King Ahasuerus gave Queen Esther what Haman the enemy of the Jews owned. Mordecai himself came before the king because Esther had told the king that he was family to her. [2]The king took off his royal ring, the one he had removed from Haman, and gave it to Mordecai. Esther put Mordecai in charge of what Haman had owned.

[3]Esther again spoke before the king. She bowed at his feet, wept, and begged him to treat her kindly. She wanted him to overturn the evil plot of Haman the Agagite—his secret plan directed against the Jews. [4]The king held out the gold scepter to Esther, and she got up and stood before him. [5]She said, "If the king wishes, and if I please him—that is, if the idea seems right to the king, and if he still sees me as a good person—then have people write something to call back the order—the order that put into effect the plan of Haman, Hammedatha the Agagite's son, that he wrote to destroy the Jews in all the royal provinces. [6]How can I bear to watch the terrible evil about to sweep over my people? And how can I bear to watch others destroy my own family?"

Mordecai writes a new law

[7]King Ahasuerus said to Queen Esther and to Mordecai the Jew, "Look, I've given Esther everything Haman owned. And Haman himself my servants have impaled on the pole because he planned to attack the Jews. [8]So you yourselves write to the Jews whatever you like in the name of the king and seal the letters with the king's royal ring. Anything written in the name of the king and sealed with the king's royal ring can't be called back." [9]So that was when the royal scribes were

Important Times Esther 8:5

Sometimes people use the phrase "Timing is everything" to suggest that *when* something happens is very important. Imagine that you are set up to make the winning shot in a soccer game, but the referee blows a whistle to end the game just before you kick the ball. Or imagine you find out a secret about a friend and want to ask her about it. Instead of talking to her in front of other people and ruining the secret, you wait until you are alone with her to ask. That is timing.

Queen Esther knew the importance of timing. Before she knew what had happened, a man named Haman had tricked the king into agreeing to kill all of the Jews. Her cousin Mordecai and all of their people would be killed. Esther had to do something—and fast! Mordecai reminded her how she had become queen, and that something like this was the very reason he had helped her along that path. He said to her, "Maybe it was for a moment like this that you came to be part of the royal family" (Esth 4:14). Maybe, just maybe, she had become queen just in time to save God's people from being destroyed.

When have you acted bravely at just the right time?

How is God using you right where you are?

summoned—on the twenty-third day of the third month (that is, the month of Sivan).[n] They wrote exactly what Mordecai ordered to the Jews, rulers, governors, and officials of the provinces from India to Cush—one hundred twenty-seven in all. They wrote in the alphabet of each province and in the language of each people. [10]They wrote in the name of King Ahasuerus and sealed the order with the king's royal ring. He sent letters with riders mounted on royal horses bred from mares known to run fast.[o] [11]The order allowed Jews in each town to join together and defend their lives. The Jews were free to wipe out, kill, and destroy every army of any people and province that attacked them, along with their women and children. They could also take and keep anything their attackers owned. [12]The one day in all the provinces of King Ahasuerus on which they could do so was the thirteenth day of the twelfth month (that is, the month of Adar). [13]A copy of the writing was to become law in each province and be on public display for all its peoples to read. The Jews were to be ready on this day to get back at their enemies. [14]The riders mounted on royal horses left Susa, spurred on by the king's order, and the law also became public in the fortified part of Susa.

[15]Mordecai went out from the king's presence in a blue and white royal robe wearing a large gold crown

---

SAILBOAT

Joy

Joyful at Evil's End *Esther 8:15-16*

God's people were saved! Not only did the king write a law so the Jews could protect themselves, he punished Haman, a high official for the king, for his bad actions. The king used the same punishment for Haman that Haman had intended for the man he hated, Mordecai. No wonder the Jews were joyful—they had been safely pulled from the very edge of destruction. Haman's death wasn't something to be joyful over. No one should be happy because a person is dead. But the end of evil is something to smile about. The Jews were celebrating the fact that Haman's evil could never hurt them again. ♦

---

and a white and red-purple coat. The city of Susa greeted him with shouts of joy. [16]For the Jews it was a day of light, happiness, joy, and honor. [17]In every province and in every town—wherever the king's order and his law arrived—for the Jews it was a day of happiness and joy. For them it meant feasts and a holiday. Many people in the land became Jews themselves, out of fear of the Jews.

The fateful day

9 It was on the thirteenth day of the twelfth month (that is, the month of Adar)[p] that the king's order and his law were to be enforced. On the very day that the enemies of the Jews hoped to overpower them, the tables were turned against them. The Jews overpowered their enemies instead. [2]The Jews joined together in their towns in all the provinces of King Ahasuerus to defend themselves against those who tried to harm them. No one was able to stand in their way because everyone was afraid of the Jews. [3]All the leaders of the provinces, rulers, governors, and those in charge of the king's business helped the Jews because they were afraid of Mordecai. [4]Because Mordecai was very important in the palace, news about him was sweeping through the provinces. Indeed, Mordecai was becoming more and more important every day. [5]The Jews put down all their enemies with sword blows, killing, and destruction. They did whatever they wanted with those who hated them. [6]In the fortified part of Susa, the Jews killed five hundred people. [7]They also killed Parshandatha, Dalphon, Aspatha, [8]Poratha, Adalia, Aridatha, [9]Parmashta, Arisai, Aridai, and Vaizatha. [10]These were the ten sons of Haman, Hammedatha's son, the enemy of the Jews. But the Jews didn't lay a hand on anything their enemies owned. [11]That same day, a report concerning the number killed in the fortified part of Susa reached the king.

[12]So the king said to Queen Esther in the fortified part of Susa, "The Jews have killed five hundred people as well as the ten sons of Haman. What have they done in the rest of the royal provinces? What do you wish now?

---

[n]May–June [o]Heb uncertain [p]February–March

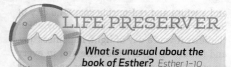

LIFE PRESERVER

What is unusual about the book of Esther? *Esther 1–10*

God is never mentioned in the book of Esther. Although Esther's story has similarities to the stories of Deborah and Ruth, other strong women who saved people by their brave actions, nobody mentions God's name. This is different from most other stories in the Bible, where it's clear that God has been actively helping those whom God has chosen to lead and save God's people.

In trying to do what is right, Esther was helped by the wise advice of her cousin Mordecai. The king had given an order that all Jews should be killed. As Esther was trying to decide whether or not to speak up, she listened to Mordecai, who told her she should do so. Esther spoke on behalf of her people, and the Jews were saved. Though God is not named in this book, God's voice is heard through the right actions of Esther, who spoke up at just the right moment.

I'll give it to you. What is your desire? I'll do it this time too."

13 Esther answered, "If the king wishes, let the Jews who are in Susa also have tomorrow to do what the law allows for today. And let them also impale the ten sons of Haman on pointed poles." 14 The king ordered that this be done, and the law became public in Susa. They impaled the ten sons of Haman just as she said. 15 The Jews in Susa joined together again, this time on the fourteenth day of the month of Adar. In Susa, they killed three hundred people, but they didn't lay a hand on anything the people owned.

16 The Jews out in the royal provinces also joined together to defend their lives. They put to rest the troubles with their enemies and killed those who hated them. The total was seventy-five thousand dead, but the Jews didn't lay a hand on anything their enemies owned. 17 They acted on the thirteenth day of the month of Adar. Then on the fourteenth day they rested, making it a day of feasts and rejoicing. (18 The Jews in Susa joined together for self-defense on the thirteenth and fourteenth days of the month. But they rested on the fifteenth day of the month and made it a day of feasts and joyous events.) 19 That is why Jews who live in villages make the fourteenth day of the month of Adar a day of rejoicing and feasts, a holiday. It is a day on which they send gifts of food to each other.

The new holiday of Purim

20 Mordecai wrote these things down and sent letters to all the Jews in all the provinces, both near and far, of King Ahasuerus. 21 He made it a rule that Jews keep the fourteenth and fifteenth days of the month of Adar as special days each and every year. 22 They are the days on which the Jews finally put to rest the troubles with their enemies. The month is the one when everything turned around for them from sadness to joy, and from sad, loud crying to a holiday. They are to make them days of feasts and joyous events, days to send food gifts to each other and money gifts to the poor. 23 The Jews agreed to continue what they had already begun to do—just what Mordecai had written to them. 24 Indeed, Haman, Hammedatha the Agagite's son, the enemy of all the Jews, had planned to destroy the Jews. He had servants throw pur (that is, the dice) to find the best month and day to trouble greatly and destroy them. 25 But when Esther came before the king, his written order said: The wicked plan that Haman made against the Jews should turn back on him instead. So they impaled him and his sons on pointed poles. 26 That is why people call these days Purim, by using the ancient word *pur*. It all fit with what this letter said, with what they saw happen, and with what they themselves went through. 27 The Jews agreed that they, their children, grandchildren, and great-grandchildren, as well as all non-Jews who become Jews, should always keep these two days. They agreed to follow the written rules—and at the proper time too—every year. 28 So forever every family, province, and town remembers to keep these days. These days of Purim won't die out among the Jews. They will remember to keep them forever. 29 Queen Esther daughter of Abihail, along with Mordecai the Jew, wrote with her full royal power to show that this second letter about Purim was correct.[q] 30 Letters conveying good wishes and

[q]*Or wrote a second time to show that this letter*

words of friendship were sent to all the Jews throughout the one hundred twenty-seven provinces in the kingdom of Ahasuerus. ³¹Their aim was to make sure that the Jews kept these days of Purim at the proper time, following the rule that Mordecai the Jew and Queen Esther had made. The rule fit well with what they themselves had agreed to do forever and with other things they did—like fasting and lamenting. ³²Esther's order made these features of Purim part of the law, so it was written down.

The fame of Mordecai

10 King Ahasuerus taxed the entire kingdom, including the islands of the Mediterranean. ²Now some may want to know about all the king's mighty, great deeds. They may also want a full report about how

did you know? In the end King Xerxes gave Esther the authority to save her people. By her power, her story was ordered to be remembered every year. She became one of two women to have a book in the Bible named for her. The other book named for a woman is Ruth.

important Mordecai became after the king honored him. Are they not written in the official records of the kings of Media and Persia? ³Certainly, Mordecai the Jew was second only to King Ahasuerus in importance. The Jews also admired him greatly, and his many brothers and sisters were proud of him. He always wanted to do good things for his Jewish people and to speak up for all his family whenever they needed help.

Speak Up for Other People   Esther 10

Some schools hold awards ceremonies at the end of every year. They celebrate students who got straight A's, worked hard, showed the most improvement, and had perfect attendance. Sometimes they give out a citizenship award. This award recognizes those who practice showing kindness, compassion, hard work, and good manners. Students who win the citizenship award put others first and look for ways to do good things.

Mordecai would have won the citizenship award. The Bible says he always wanted to do good things, and his family was always proud of him. He helped Esther become queen, encouraged her to save their people, and then became a friend to the king and worked to help his people every day.

Mordecai wasn't afraid to speak up for people who needed help. He had promised to work for his people and remember what God had done for them. This helps to remind us that we can do the same. We can try our best to follow God and to use our place in life to do good things and speak up for people who can't speak for themselves.

Make a list of the good things you can do at school, home, or in your neighborhood.

Who could you speak up for?

Job

Job begins with a scene in heaven. The Adversary came before God and complained that Job loved God and avoided evil only because God blessed Job with a great family and lots of possessions. The Adversary said that pain would make Job stop trusting God. God disagreed but allowed Job to experience suffering. Soon Job faced every kind of awful suffering. He lost all his wealth. His children were all killed in a storm. Sores broke out all over his body. Job wondered why his life was so full of pain.

This book asks big questions like *Will we still love God if bad things happen to us? Why do bad things happen? Why do good people suffer? Why doesn't God fix our problems?*

The book doesn't give all the answers. There are many speeches where Job and his friends try to understand suffering. At the end of the story, God responds to all these questions by telling Job that God is the only one who understands everything. ◊

Job's piety and life of bliss

1 A man in the land of Uz was named Job. That man was honest, a person of absolute integrity; he feared God and avoided evil. ²He had seven sons and three daughters, ³and owned seven thousand sheep, three thousand camels, five hundred pairs of oxen, five hundred female donkeys, and a vast number of servants, so that he was greater than all the people of the east. ⁴Each of his sons hosted a feast in his own house on his birthday. They invited their three sisters to eat and drink with them. ⁵When the days of the feast had been completed, Job would send word[a] and purify his children.[b] Getting up early in the morning, he prepared entirely burned offerings for each one of them, for Job thought, Perhaps my children have sinned and then cursed[c] God in their hearts. Job did this regularly.

Job's motives questioned

⁶One day the divine beings[d] came to present themselves before the Lord, and the Adversary[e] also came among them. ⁷The Lord said to the Adversary, "Where did you come from?"

The Adversary answered the Lord, "From wandering throughout the earth."

⁸The Lord said to the Adversary, "Have you thought about my servant Job; surely there is no one like him on earth, a man who is honest, who is of absolute integrity, who reveres God and avoids evil?"

⁹The Adversary answered the Lord, "Does Job revere God for nothing? ¹⁰Haven't you fenced him in—his house and all he has—and blessed the work of his hands so that his possessions extend throughout the earth? ¹¹But stretch out your hand and strike all he has. He will certainly curse you to your face."

¹²The Lord said to the Adversary, "Look, all he has is within your power; only don't stretch out your hand against him." So the Adversary left the Lord's presence.

Job passes the test

¹³One day Job's sons and daughters were eating and drinking wine in their oldest brother's house. ¹⁴A messenger came to Job and said: "The oxen were plowing, and the donkeys were grazing nearby ¹⁵when the Sabeans took them and killed the young men with swords. I alone escaped to tell you."

¹⁶While this messenger was speaking, another arrived and said: "A raging fire fell from the sky and burned up the sheep and devoured the young men. I alone escaped to tell you."

¹⁷While this messenger was speaking, another arrived and said: "Chaldeans set up three companies, raided the camels and took them, killing the young men with swords. I alone escaped to tell you."

¹⁸While this messenger was speaking, another arrived and said: "Your sons and your daughters were eating and drinking wine in their oldest brother's house, ¹⁹when a strong wind came from the desert and struck the four corners of the house. It fell upon the young people, and they died. I alone escaped to tell you."

²⁰Job arose, tore his clothes, shaved his head, fell to the ground, and worshipped. ²¹He said: "Naked I came from my mother's womb; naked I will return there. The Lord has given; the Lord has taken; bless

LIFE PRESERVER

Why did God test Job?
Job 1:13-22

The book of Job is described as wisdom literature. In it we read the story of a good, honest man who followed God's ways. The Adversary challenged God, saying that Job followed God only because he had been blessed with family, property, and health. The Adversary believed that Job would stop following God if all of these things were taken away.

God decided to test Job to see why this good, honest man followed God. The test took away everything Job had, including his family, property, and health. Sometimes when people face tragedies such as sickness, death, or loss of any kind, they turn their backs on God. Other people choose to struggle through the loss, stay close to God, and seek God's help. There is always a choice in how to respond to hard times. Ultimately, Job chose to follow God. ◊

Memorize
Job 1:21

---

[a]Heb lacks *word*. [b]Or *them* [c]Or *blessed*. The verb for *bless* is a euphemism for *curse* in 1:11; 2:5, 9; whereas in 1:10, 21 and 42:12 it has its usual meaning. [d]Or *children of God* [e]Heb *hassatan*

the LORD's name." ²²In all this, Job didn't sin or blame God.

Job's Adversary refuses to give up

2 One day the divine beings came to present themselves before the LORD. The Adversary also came among them to present himself before the LORD. ²The LORD said to the Adversary, "Where have you come from?"

The Adversary answered the LORD, "From wandering throughout the earth."

³The LORD said to the Adversary, "Have you thought about my servant Job, for there is no one like him on earth, a man who is honest, who is of absolute integrity, who reveres God and avoids evil? He still holds on to his integrity, even though you incited me to ruin him for no reason."

⁴The Adversary responded to the LORD, "Skin for skin—people will give up everything they have in exchange for their lives. ⁵But stretch out your hand and strike his bones and flesh. Then he will definitely curse^f you to your face."

⁶The LORD answered the Adversary, "There he is—within your power; only preserve his life."

The test intensifies

⁷The Adversary departed from the LORD's presence and struck Job with severe sores from the sole of his foot to the top of his head. ⁸Job took a piece of broken pottery to scratch himself and sat down on a mound of ashes. ⁹Job's wife said to him, "Are you still clinging to your integrity? Curse^g God, and die."

¹⁰Job said to her, "You're talking like a foolish woman. Will we receive good from God but not also receive bad?" In all this, Job didn't sin with his lips.

Job's three friends come to comfort him

¹¹When Job's three friends heard about all this disaster that had happened to him, they came, each one from his home—Eliphaz from Teman, Bildad from Shuah, and Zophar from Naamah. They agreed to come so they could console and comfort him. ¹²When they looked up from a distance and didn't recognize him, they wept loudly. Each one tore his garment

and scattered dust above his head toward the sky. ¹³They sat with Job on the ground seven days and seven nights, not speaking a word to him, for they saw that he was in excruciating pain.

Job responds differently

3 Afterward, Job spoke up and cursed the day he was born.

² Job said:
³ Perish the day I was born,
 the night someone said,
 "A boy has been conceived."
⁴ That day—let it be darkness;
 may God above ignore it,
 and light not shine on it.
⁵ May deepest darkness claim it
 and a cloud linger over it;
 may all that darkens the day terrify it.
⁶ May gloom seize that night;
 may it not be counted
  in the days of a year;
 may it not appear in the months.
⁷ May that night be childless;
 may no happy singing come in it.
⁸ May those who curse the day curse it,
 those with enough skill
  to awaken Leviathan.
⁹ May its evening stars stay dark;
 may it wait in vain for light;
 may it not see dawn's gleam,

An ash heap is a pile of ashes that remain after a fire. In Bible times, when people were sad about something, they would sit in ashes or rub ashes on their bodies.

¹⁰ because it didn't close
 the doors of my mother's womb,^h
 didn't hide trouble from my eyes.

Job laments his misfortune

¹¹ Why didn't I die at birth,
 come forth from the womb and die?
¹² Why did knees receive me
 and breasts let me nurse?
¹³ For now I would be lying down quietly;
 I'd sleep; rest would be mine
¹⁴ with kings and earth's advisors,
 who rebuild ruins for themselves,

---

^f Or *bless* ^g Or *bless* ^h Heb lacks *mother's*.

¹⁵ or with princes who have gold,
who fill their houses with silver.
¹⁶ Or why wasn't I
like a buried miscarried infant,
like babies who never see light?
¹⁷ There the wicked rage no more;
there the weak rest.
¹⁸ Prisoners are entirely at ease;
they don't hear a boss's voice.
¹⁹ Both small and great are there;
a servant is free from his masters.
²⁰ Why is light given to the hard worker,
life to those bitter of soul,
²¹ those waiting in vain for death,
who search for it
more than for treasure,
²² who rejoice excitedly,
who are thrilled
when they find a grave?
²³ Why is light given[i] to the person
whose way is hidden,
whom God has fenced in?

[i] Heb lacks *is light given*.

²⁴ My groans become my bread;
my roars pour out like water.
²⁵ Because I was afraid of something awful,
and it arrived;
what I dreaded came to me.
²⁶ I had no ease, quiet, or rest,
and trembling came.

Eliphaz tries to comfort Job

4 Then Eliphaz, a native of Teman,
responded:
² If one tries to answer you,
will you be annoyed?
But who can hold words back?
³ Look, you've instructed many
and given strength to drooping hands.
⁴ Your words have raised up the falling;
you've steadied failing knees.
⁵ But now it comes to you,
and you are dismayed;
it has struck you,
and you are frightened.

It's Not Fair   Job 1–3

Nearly everyone has said at some point, "But it's not fair!" Maybe your brother got to stay up late, but you had to go to bed at your regular bedtime. Or your mom took your sister's side in a recent argument. Sometimes life just isn't fair.

Job knew all too well about life being unfair sometimes. Job was a good and honorable man who loved and respected God. He loved his family and had made a good life for them. He was "a person of absolute integrity" (Job 1:1), which means he was a person of complete honesty and truth. That's why it's hard to believe such terrible things happened to Job. He lost everything—his farms, his children, his health. God allowed the Adversary to take away everything from Job because the Adversary didn't believe Job would still love God without all of the blessings in his life. The Adversary figured Job would curse God if he lost everything.

Although Job faced enormous hardships and life seemed terribly unfair, he never lost his love for God. He knew that whether God showered him with blessing or took away everything he had, he would still bless God. When you face a situation that feels unfair, remember Job.

How can you be a person of absolute honesty and truth?

How can you love God no matter what comes your way—no matter what is given or taken away?

UMBRELLA

HARD TIMES

Design of Hard Times *Job 4:5*
Job was going through some of the hardest times he had ever faced. He lived a good life, obeying and serving God to the best of his ability. Yet he lost everything he owned, and all his children died. Job couldn't figure out why these hard times happened. What Job didn't realize was that sometimes God allows difficult things to happen for reasons that have nothing to do with our actions. In this situation, Job was part of a much larger story. God used the events in Job's life to prove that God knows everything and we do not. ♦

//

⁶ Isn't your religion
   the source of[j] your confidence;
   the integrity of your conduct,
      the source of your hope?

Sinners don't live long

⁷ Think! What innocent person
   has ever perished?
   When have those who do the right thing
      been destroyed?
⁸ As I've observed, those who plow sin
   and sow trouble will harvest it.
⁹ When God breathes deeply, they perish;
   by a breath of his nostril
      they are annihilated.
¹⁰ The roar of a lion and snarl
   of the king of beasts—
   yet the teeth of lions are shattered;
¹¹ the lion perishes without prey,
   and its cubs are scattered.

A frightening dream

¹² But a word sneaked up on me;
   my ears caught a hint of it.
¹³ In profound thoughts, visions of night,
   when deep sleep falls on people,
¹⁴ fear and dread struck me;
   all of my bones shook.
¹⁵ A breeze swept by my face;
   the hair of my skin bristled.

¹⁶ It stopped. I didn't recognize
   its visible form,
   although a figure was in front of my eyes.
   Silence! Then I heard a voice:
¹⁷ "Can a human be more righteous than God,
   a person purer than their maker?"

Its interpretation

¹⁸ If he doesn't trust his servants
   and levels a charge
      against his messengers,
¹⁹ how much less those who dwell
   in houses of clay,
   whose foundations are in dust,
   and who are crushed like a moth?
²⁰ They are smashed
   between morning and evening;
   they perish forever
      without anyone knowing.
²¹ Isn't their tent cord pulled up?
   They die without wisdom.[k]

Life's problems

5 Call out. Will anyone answer you?
   To which holy one will you turn?
² Surely anger can kill the foolish;
   fury can kill the simple.
³ I've seen the foolish take root
   and promptly curse their house.
⁴ Their children are far[l] from safety,
   crushed in the gate without a deliverer.
⁵ The hungry devour[m] their crops;
   it's taken even from the thorns,[n]
   and the thirsty pant after their yield.
⁶ Surely trouble doesn't come from dust,
   nor does distress sprout
      from the ground.
⁷ Surely humans are born to distress,
   just as sparks rise up.

The answer is God

⁸ But I would seek God,
   put my case to God,
⁹ who does great things
   beyond comprehension,
   wonderful things without number;
¹⁰ who provides rain over the earth's surface,
   sends water to the open country,
¹¹ exalts the lowly,
   raises mourners to victory;

---

[j]Heb lacks *the source.* [k]Some interpreters end the quotation here rather than 4:17. [l]Or *May their children be far from safety.*
[m]or *May the hungry devour their crops.* [n]Heb uncertain

¹² who frustrates the schemes of the clever
    so that their hands achieve no success,
¹³ trapping the wise in their cleverness
    so that the plans of the devious
       don't succeed.
¹⁴ They encounter darkness during the day,
    and at noon they fumble about as at night.
¹⁵ Yet he rescues the orphanº
    from the sword of their mouth,
    the needy from the grip of the strong;
¹⁶ so the poor have hope
    and violence shuts its mouth.

Divine favor
¹⁷ Look, happy is the person
    whom God corrects;
    so don't reject
      the Almighty's instruction.

º Heb lacks *orphan*.

¹⁸ He injures, but he binds up;
    he strikes, but his hands heal.
¹⁹ From six adversities he will deliver you;
    from seven harm won't touch you.
²⁰ In famine he will ransom you from death;
    in war, from the power of the sword.
²¹ You will be hidden from the tongue's sting,
    and you won't fear destruction
      when it comes.
²² You will laugh at destruction and hunger;
    you won't be afraid of wild beasts;
²³ for you will make an agreement with
      the stones of the field;
    and the beasts of the field
      will be at peace with you.
²⁴ You will know that your tent is secure.
    You will examine your home
      and miss nothing.

God's THOUGHTS / My THOUGHTS

The Importance of Friends   *Job 2:11-13; 5:17-27*

Good friends are one of the most important parts of life. Sometimes we need to make new friends, like when we start at a new school or go to a new church. It is a good feeling to have one or two great friends who know us, love us, and help us grow closer to God.

Job had three friends who were there for him when he lost everything. They came and sat with him to share his sorrow (Job 2:11-13). When it was time to talk, they reminded Job that God is good and that there must be some reason for his loss. Some of the reasons they suggested were not helpful—and Job said so in his replies. For example, one friend thought Job did something wrong to deserve his pain. Job's loss and suffering weren't caused by his sin. The middle section of the book shares conversations Job and his friends had about why such terrible things were happening.

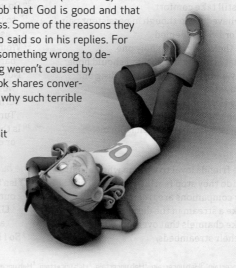

Sometimes we need friends who will sit quietly with us. Other times we need friends who will tell us what they think and give us advice.

How do your friends help you love God more?

List three ways you can be a good friend to someone you know who is hurting.

²⁵ You will know that you'll have
  many children.
  Your offspring will be
  like the grass of the earth.
²⁶ You will come to your grave in old age
  as bundles of grain stacked up
  at harvesttime.
²⁷ Look, we've searched this out, and so it is;
  listen and find out for yourself.

Job defends his anger

6 Job responded:
  ² Oh, that my grief were actually weighed,
  all of it were lifted up in scales;
³ for now it's heavier
  than the sands of the sea;
  therefore, my words are rash.^p
⁴ The Almighty's arrows are in me;
  my spirit drinks their poison,
  and God's terrors are arrayed against me.
⁵ Does a donkey bray over grass
  or an ox bellow over its fodder?
⁶ Is tasteless food eaten without salt,
  or does egg white^q have taste?
⁷ I refuse to touch them;
  they resemble food for the sick.

He wishes to die

⁸ Oh, that what I've requested would come
  and God grant my hope;
  ⁹ that God be willing to crush me,
  release his hand and cut me off.
¹⁰ I'd still take comfort,
  relieved^r even though in persistent pain;
  for I've not denied
  the words of the holy one.
¹¹ What is my strength, that I should hope;
  my end, that my life should drag on?
¹² Is my strength that of rocks,
  my flesh bronze?
¹³ I don't have a helper for myself;
  success has been taken from me.

He accuses his friends

¹⁴ Are friends loyal to the one who despairs,^s
  or do they stop fearing the Almighty?
¹⁵ My companions are treacherous
  like a stream in the desert,
  like channels that overrun
  their streambeds,

¹⁶ like those darkened by thawing ice,
  in which snow is obscured
¹⁷ but that stop flowing in dry times
  and vanish from their channels in heat.
¹⁸ Caravans turn aside from their paths;
  they go up into untamed areas
  and perish.
¹⁹ Caravans from Tema look;
  merchants from Sheba hope for it.

did you know? The story of Job was written as a poem (after chapter 2) and is the first of several books of poetry in the Bible. The poetry books teach people about God in a different way from the books of history.

²⁰ They are ashamed that they trusted;
  they arrive and are dismayed.
²¹ That's what you are like;^t
  you see something awful and are afraid.

He appeals to his friends

²² Have I said, "Give me something?
  Offer a bribe from your wealth for me?
²³ Rescue me from the hand of my enemy?
  Ransom me from the grip of the ruthless?"
²⁴ Instruct me and I'll be quiet;
  inform me how I've erred.
²⁵ How painful are truthful words,
  but what do your condemnations
  accomplish?
²⁶ Do you intend to correct my words,
  to treat the words of a hopeless man
  as wind?
²⁷ Would you even gamble over an orphan,
  barter away your friend?
²⁸ Now look at me—
  would I lie to your face?
²⁹ Turn! Don't be faithless.
  Turn now! I am righteous.
³⁰ Is there wrong on my tongue,
  or can my mouth not recognize disaster?

The human condition

7 Isn't slavery everyone's condition on earth,
  our days like those of a hired worker?
  ² Like a slave we pant for a shadow,
  await our task like a hired worker.
³ So I have inherited months of emptiness;

^pHeb uncertain ^qHeb uncertain ^rHeb uncertain ^sHeb uncertain ^tHeb uncertain

nights of toil have been measured out
for me.
⁴ If I lie down and think—
When will I get up?—
night drags on,ᵘ and restless thoughts
fill me until dawn.
⁵ My flesh is covered with worms
and crusted earth;
my skin hardens and oozes.
⁶ My days are swifter
than a weaver's shuttle;
they reach their end without hope.ᵛ
⁷ Remember that my life is wind;
my eyes won't see pleasure again.
⁸ The eye that sees me now
will no longer look on me;
your eyes will be on me, and I won't exist.
⁹ A cloud breaks apart and moves on—
like the one who descends to the graveʷ
and won't rise,
¹⁰ won't return home again,
won't be recognized in town anymore.

Job wants to be left alone

¹¹ But I won't keep quiet;
I will speak in the adversity of my spirit,
groan in the bitterness of my life.
¹² Am I Seaˣ or the Sea Monsterʸ
that you place me under guard?
¹³ If I say, "My couch will comfort me,"
my bed will diminish my murmuring.
¹⁴ You scare me with dreams,
frighten me with visions.
¹⁵ I would choose strangling
and death instead of my bones.
¹⁶ I reject life;ᶻ I don't want to live long;
leave me alone, for my days are empty.

A parody of Psalm 8

¹⁷ What are human beings,
that you exalt them,
that you take note of them,
¹⁸ visit them each morning,
test them every moment?
¹⁹ Why not look away from me;
let me alone until I swallow my spit?
²⁰ If I sinned, what did I do to you,
guardian of people?
Why have you made me your target
so that I'm a burden to myself?

²¹ Why not forgive my sin,
overlook my iniquity?
Then I would lie down in the dust;
you would search hard for me,
and I would not exist.

Bildad defends God

8 Bildad from Shuah responded:
² How long will you mouth such things
such that your utterances
become a strong wind?
³ Does God pervert justice,
or does the Almighty distort
what is right?
⁴ If your children sinned against him,
then he delivered them
into the power of their rebellion.
⁵ If you will search eagerly for God,
plead with the Almighty.
⁶ If you are pure and do the right thing,
then surely he will become
active on your behalf
and reward your innocent dwelling.
⁷ Although your former state was ordinary,
your future will be extraordinary.

Tradition

⁸ Ask a previous generation
and verify the findings
of your ancestors,
⁹ for we are only recently here
and don't know
because our days on earth are a shadow.
¹⁰ Won't they instruct you and tell you;
will words notᵃ proceed
from their hearts?

Examples from nature

¹¹ Does papyrus grow apart from a marsh?
Does a reed flourish without water?
¹² While still tender, uncut,
it will wither before every other grass.
¹³ So are the paths of all who forget God.
Hope perishes for the godless,
¹⁴ whose confidence is a fragile thing,ᵇ
their trust, a spider's web.
¹⁵ He leans on its web, and it doesn't stand;
grasps it, and it can't remain in place.
¹⁶ It's like a well-watered plant in the sun;
its runners spread over its gardens.

ᵘHeb uncertain ᵛOr *thread* ʷHeb *Sheol* ˣHeb *Yam*, a sea god ʸHeb *Tannin*, a sea dragon ᶻHeb lacks *life*. ᵃHeb lacks *not*.
ᵇHeb uncertain

¹⁷ Its roots are entwined over a pile of rocks,
  for it sees a home among stones.
¹⁸ If it's uprooted from its place,
  it lies, saying, "I can't see you."
¹⁹ Surely its way is a joy,
  for from the dust other plants[c] sprout.

God's faithfulness

²⁰ Surely God won't reject integrity,
  won't strengthen the hand of the wicked.
²¹ He will still fill your mouth with joy,
  your lips with a victorious
    shout.

SAILBOAT

Joy

Joy Is Our Strength *Job 8:21*

We don't need strength to do easy things. We need strength to do hard things. But most things don't start out easy. Running is easy for an athlete, but not a baby. A baby learns to take one step and then another. As walking gets easier, the child learns to run. In a similar way, learning to face hard times and work through them makes us stronger. When we believe in God and know God is with us, we have joy. That joy makes us strong enough to face the hardest times. ◊

²² Those who hate you
  will be clothed with shame,
  and the tent of the wicked will vanish.

Hymnic praise

9 Job responded:
² I know for certain that this is so;
  and how can anyone be innocent
    before God?
³ If one wants to contend with him,
  he won't answer one in a thousand.
⁴ He is wise[d] and powerful;
  who can resist him and prosper?
⁵ Who removes mountains,
  and they are unaware;
  who overthrows them in anger?
⁶ Who shakes the earth from its place,
  and its pillars shudder?
⁷ Who commands the sun,
  and it does not rise,
  even seals up the stars;

⁸ stretched out the heavens alone
  and trod on the waves of the Sea;[e]
⁹ made the Bear and Orion, Pleiades
  and the southern constellations;
¹⁰ does great and unsearchable things,
  wonders beyond number?

A mismatch

¹¹ If God goes by me, I can't see him;
  he glides past, and I can't perceive him.
¹² If he seizes, who can bring back?
  Who can say to him,
    "What are you doing?"
¹³ God won't retract his anger;
  the helpers of Rahab bow beneath him.
¹⁴ Yet I myself will answer him;
  I'll choose my words
    in a contest[f] with him.
¹⁵ Even if I'm innocent, I can't answer;
  I must plead for justice.
¹⁶ If I were to call and he answered me,
  I couldn't believe that he heard my voice.
¹⁷ Who bruises me with a tempest
  and multiplies my wounds for no reason?
¹⁸ He doesn't let me catch my breath,
  for he fills me with bitterness.
¹⁹ If the issue is strength—behold power!
  If justice—who calls God to meet me?

There is no justice

²⁰ If I'm innocent, my mouth condemns me;
  I have integrity;
  but God declares me perverse.
²¹ I'm blameless, yet don't know myself;
  I reject my life.
²² It's all the same;
  therefore, I say God destroys
    the blameless and the sinners.
²³ If calamity suddenly kills,
  he mocks at the slaying[g] of innocents.
²⁴ The earth is handed over to the wicked;
  he covers the faces of its judges.
  If not God, then who does?

Job wants an arbitrator

²⁵ My days are swifter than a runner;
  they flee and don't experience good.
²⁶ They sweep by like ships made of reeds,
  as an eagle swoops on prey.
²⁷ If I say, "I'll forget my lament,
  put on a different face so I can smile,"

---

[c]Heb lacks *plants*. [d]Or *wise in heart*; cf 37:24 [e]Heb *Yam*, a sea god [f]Heb lacks *in a contest*. [g]Heb uncertain

²⁸ I'm still afraid of all my suffering;
 I know that you
  won't declare me innocent.
²⁹ I myself am thought guilty;
 why have I tried so hard in vain?
³⁰ If I wash myself with snow,
 purify my hands with soap,
³¹ then you'll hurl me into a slimy pit
 so that my clothes detest me.
³² God is not a man like me—
 someone I could answer—
  so that we could come together in court.
³³ Oh, that^h there were a mediator
 between us;
  he would lay his hand on both of us,
³⁴ remove his rod from me,
 so his fury wouldn't frighten me.
³⁵ Then I would speak—unafraid—
 for I'm not that way.

Complaint to God

10 I loathe my life; I will let loose
 my complaint;
  I will speak out of my own bitterness.
² I will say to God, Don't declare me guilty;
 tell me what you are accusing me
  of doing.
³ Does it seem good to you
 that you oppress me,
  that you reject the work of your hands
  and cause the purpose of sinners
   to shine?
⁴ Do you have physical eyes;
 do you see like a human?
⁵ Are your days like those of a human,
 your years like years of a human,
  ⁶ that you search for my wrongdoing
  and seek my sin?
⁷ You know that I'm not guilty,
 yet no one delivers me from your power.

Creator

⁸ Your hands fashioned and made me;
 yet you want to destroy me utterly.
⁹ Remember that you made me fromⁱ clay,
 and you will return me to dust.
¹⁰ Didn't you pour me out like milk,
 curdle me like cheese?
¹¹ You clothed me with skin and flesh,
 wove me from bones and sinews.

¹² Life and kindness you gave me,
 and you oversaw and preserved
  my breath.

UMBRELLA
HARD TIMES

Why Do Bad Things Happen? *Job 10:8-12—*
Job realized God created every part of him—
bones, muscles, internal organs, and skin. God not
only gave Job life but a home, a wife, and a family.
Losing his family and belongings was terrible, and
Job demanded to know why from God. When bad
things happen to us, it's okay to ask God why they
happened. ◖

No hiding place
¹³ These things you hid in your heart;
 I know this is the case with you.
¹⁴ If I sin and you observe me,
 you won't consider me innocent
  of wrongdoing.
¹⁵ If I were guilty, doom to me;
 I'm innocent, but can't lift my head,
  full of shame and facing my misery.
¹⁶ I could boast like a lion,
 and you would hunt me;
  you would do awesome things
   to me again.
¹⁷ You continue to send your witnesses
 against me
  and increase your anger toward me,
  a swift army against me.^j

Death wish
¹⁸ Why did you let me emerge
 from the womb?
  I wish I had died
  without any eye seeing me.
¹⁹ Then I would be just as if I hadn't existed,
 taken from the belly to the grave.
²⁰ Aren't my few days coming to an end?
 Look away from me
  so I can brighten up a little
²¹ before I go and don't return
 to a land of deepest darkness,
²² a land whose light is like gloom,
 utter darkness and confusion,
  such that light shines like gloom.

^hOr *There is no* ⁱOr *like* ^jHeb uncertain

Zophar's rebuke

11 Zophar from Naamah responded:
² Should all these words go unanswered
or a wordy man be justified?
³ Will your idle talk silence everyone;
will you mock and not be put to shame?
⁴ You've said, "My teaching is pure,
and I'm clean in God's[k] eyes."

Divine secrecy

⁵ But oh, that God would speak,
open his lips against you
⁶ and tell you secrets of wisdom;
for sound insight has two sides.
Know that God lets some of your sin
be forgotten.
⁷ Can you find the secret of God
or find the extent of the Almighty?
⁸ They are higher than the heavens—
what can you do?
Deeper than the underworld[l]—
what can you know?
⁹ Its measurement is longer than the earth
and broader than the sea.
¹⁰ If God passes by, imprisons someone,
and calls a trial,
who can stop him?
¹¹ He knows worthless people,
sees sin, and certainly[m] takes note.
¹² A stupid person becomes intelligent
when a wild ass of a person is born tame.[n]

did you know? Job told his friends that God's greatness could be seen all around them. People can learn a lot about God by studying God's creation. Observing how the universe works or how animals survive shows how much God has always cared for the world.

Abiding hope

¹³ If you make your mind resolute
and spread your palms to him,
¹⁴ if you throw out the sin
in your hands
and don't let injustice
dwell in your tents,
¹⁵ then you will lift up your face
without blemish;

Bet you can read this in 1 minute. Ready, set, go!

¹⁶ You will forget trouble;
you will remember it
as water that flows past.
¹⁷ A life span will rise brighter than noon;
darkness will be like morning.
¹⁸ You will be secure, for there is hope;
you will look around and rest safely.
¹⁹ You will lie down
without anyone to scare you;
many will beg for your favor.
²⁰ The eyes of the wicked will grow faint;
flight has vanished from them;
their hope is a dying gasp.

A living joke

12 Job responded:
² Surely you are the people,
and wisdom will die with you.
³ I am also intelligent;
I'm not inferior to you.
Who isn't like these people?[o]
⁴ I'm a joke to friends
who called to God and he answered;
the innocent and blameless one is a joke,
⁵ a torch[p] of contempt to one who is idle,
a fixed point for slipping feet.

Proverbial wisdom

⁶ Raiders' tents are prosperous
and God's provokers secure,
who carry God in their hands.[q]
⁷ But ask Behemoth, and he will teach you,
the birds in the sky, and they will tell you;
⁸ or talk to earth, and it will teach you;
the fish of the sea will recount it for you.
⁹ Among all these, who hasn't known
that the LORD's hand did this?
¹⁰ In whose grasp is the life of every thing,
the breath of every person?
¹¹ Doesn't the ear test words
and the palate taste food?
¹² "In old age is wisdom;
understanding in a long life."

God's majesty

¹³ With him are wisdom and power;
counsel and understanding are his.
¹⁴ If he tears down, it can't be rebuilt;
if he ties a person up, he can't be set free.

---

[k] Or *your* [l] Heb *Sheol* [m] Or *does not* [n] Or a wild ass's colt can be born a man [o] Heb lacks *people.* [p] Heb uncertain [q] Heb uncertain

¹⁵ If he restricts water, they have drought;
 if he lets it loose, it overturns the land.
¹⁶ With him are might and success;
 the deceiver and the deceived are his.
¹⁷ He leads advisors away barefoot;
 makes madmen of judges;
¹⁸ unties the belt of kings,
 binds a garment around their loins;
¹⁹ leads priests away barefoot;
 overthrows the well-established;
²⁰ silences the talk of trusted people;
 takes away elders' discernment;
²¹ pours contempt on royalty;
 loosens the belt of the strong;
²² discloses deep secrets of darkness,
 makes utter darkness enter the light;
²³ makes nations prominent
 and destroys them,
 expands nations and leads them astray;
²⁴ takes away the power to think
 from earth's leaders,
 making them wander
 in untraveled wastelands.
²⁵ They feel their way in the dark
 without light;
 he makes them stumble like drunks.

Self-defense

13 Look, my eye has seen it all;
 my ear has heard and understood it.
² Just as you know, I also know;
 I'm not inferior to you.
³ But I want to speak to the Almighty;
 I would gladly present my case to God.

Friends attacked

⁴ You, however, are plasterers of lies;
 ineffective healers, all of you.
⁵ Would that you were completely quiet;
 that would be your wisdom.
⁶ Hear my teaching
 and pay attention to the arguments
 of my lips.
⁷ Will you speak injustice for God,
 speak deceit on his behalf?
⁸ Will you be partial
 or contend for God?
⁹ Will it go well when he searches you,
 or can you fool him as you fool people?
¹⁰ He will certainly correct you

if you've been secretly partial.
¹¹ Wouldn't his majesty scare you
 and dread of him fall on you?
¹² Your old sayings are proverbs
 made of ashes,
 your sayings defenses made of clay.

Job will speak out

¹³ Be quiet and I will speak,
 come what may.
¹⁴ For what reason will I take my flesh
 in my teeth,
 put my life in jeopardy?
¹⁵ He will slay me; I'm without hope;ʳ
 I will surely prove my way to his face.

UMBRELLA
HARD TIMES

Giving Up in Hard Times *Job 13:15*
Sometimes we can't see how hard times will ever
end. When that happens, some people just give up
hope and quit trying, no matter what others say to
encourage them. But just because people express
hopelessness doesn't mean they no longer trust
God. Being honest about what we're facing and
about our feelings is never wrong. The Bible shows
us that it's important to question God and to look
for answers. ◊

¹⁶ Also this will be my vindication,
 that a godless person
 won't come before him.
¹⁷ Listen closely to my words
 so that my remarks will be in your ears.

Against God

¹⁸ Look, I have laid out my case;
 I know that I'm innocent.
¹⁹ Who would dare contend with me,
 for then I would be quiet and die.
²⁰ Only don't do two things to me,
 then I won't hide from your face.
²¹ Remove your hand far from me
 and don't terrify me with your anger.
²² Then call and I'll answer,
 or I'll speak and you can reply.

ʳOr *Though he slay me, yet I will trust him.*

²³ How many are my offenses and sins?
　Inform me about my rebellions and sins.
²⁴ Why hide your face from me
　and consider me your enemy?
²⁵ Will you cause a wind-tossed
　leaf to tremble,
　or will you pursue dry straw?
²⁶ You even write bitter things about me,
　make me inherit
　　my youthful indiscretions.
²⁷ You tie up my feet and restrict all actions;
　you stamp marks on the bottom of my feet.

Human destiny

²⁸ Surely a person wastes away like refuse,
　like clothing that a moth eats.

14 All of us[s] are born of women,
　have few days, and are full of turmoil.
² Like a flower, we[t] bloom, then wither,
　flee like a shadow, and don't last.
(³ Yes, you open your eyes on this one;
　you bring me into trial against you.)
⁴ Who can make pure from impure?
　Nobody.
⁵ If our days are fixed,
　the number of our months with you,
　you set a statute and we can't exceed it.
⁶ Look away from us that we may rest,
　until we are satisfied
　　like a worker at day's end.

Trees versus humans

⁷ Indeed there is hope for a tree.
　If it's cut down and still sprouting
　and its shoots don't fail,
⁸ if its roots age in the ground
　and its stump dies in the dust,
⁹ at the scent of water, it will bud
　and produce sprouts like a plant.
¹⁰ But a human dies and lies there;
　a person expires, and where is he?
¹¹ Water vanishes from the sea;
　a river dries up completely.
¹² But a human lies down and doesn't rise
　until the heavens cease;
　they don't get up and awaken from sleep.

Momentary hope

¹³ I wish you would hide me
　in the underworld,[u]

conceal me until your anger passes,
　set a time for me, and remember me.
¹⁴ If people die, will they live again?
　All the days of my service I would wait
　until my restoration took place.
¹⁵ You would call, and I would answer you;
　you would long for your handiwork.
¹⁶ Though you now number my steps,
　you would not keep a record of my sin.
¹⁷ My rebellion is sealed in a bag;
　you would cover my sin.

God crushes hope

¹⁸ But an eroding mountain breaks up,
　and rock is displaced.
¹⁹ Water wears away boulders;
　floods carry away soil;
　you destroy a people's hope.
²⁰ You overpower them relentlessly,
　and they die;
　you change their appearance
　and send them away.
²¹ Their children achieve honor,
　and they don't know it;
　their children become insignificant,
　and they don't see it.
²² They only feel the pain of their body,
　and they mourn for themselves.

Job's intelligence questioned

15 Eliphaz answered:
² Will the wise respond
　with windy knowledge
　and fill their belly with the east wind?
³ Will they argue with a word
　that has no benefit
　and with unprofitable words?
⁴ You are truly making religion ineffective
　and restraining meditation before God.
⁵ Your mouth multiplies your sins
　a thousand times;
　you opt for a clever tongue.
⁶ Your mouth condemns you, not I;
　your lips argue against you.
⁷ Were you born the first Adam,
　brought forth before the hills?
⁸ Did you listen in God's council;
　is wisdom limited to you?
⁹ What do you know that we don't know;
　what do you understand
　　that isn't among us?

[s]Heb *adam*　[t]Or *he*; also *he* in 14:5-6　[u]Heb *Sheol*

¹⁰ Both the graybeard and the aged
are with us;
those much older than your father.
¹¹ Are God's comforts not enough for you,
a word spoken gently with you?
¹² Why has your mind seized you,
why have your eyes flashed,
¹³ so that you return your breath to God
and utter such words from your mouth?
¹⁴ What are humans that they might be pure,
and those born of woman
that they might be innocent?
¹⁵ If he doesn't trust his holy ones
and the heavens aren't pure in his eyes,
¹⁶ how much less those who are
abominable and corrupt,
for they drink sin like water.

The wicked's downfall

¹⁷ Listen to me; I will argue with you;
what I've seen, I will declare to you;
¹⁸ what the wise have told and have not
concealed from their family,
¹⁹ to whom alone the earth was given
and no stranger passed in their midst.
²⁰ All the days of the wicked are painful;
the number of years reserved
for the hateful;
²¹ a sound of terror pierces[v] their ears;
when safe, raiders overtake them.
²² They can't count on turning away
from darkness;
they are destined for a sword.
²³ They wander about for bread.
"Where is it?"
They know that their day of darkness
is fixed.
²⁴ Adversity and stress scare them,
master them like a king ready to strike;
²⁵ for they raise a fist against God
and try to overpower the Almighty.
²⁶ They run toward him aggressively,
with a massive and strong shield.
²⁷ They cover their face with grease
and make their loins gross.
²⁸ They lived in ruined cities,
unoccupied houses that turn to rubble.
²⁹ They won't get rich;
their wealth won't last;
their property won't extend
over the earth.

³⁰ They can't turn away from darkness;
a flame will dry out their shoots,
and they will be taken away
by the wind from his mouth.
³¹ They shouldn't trust in what has no worth,
for their reward will be worthless.
³² Before their branch is formed,
before it is green,
³³ like the vine, they will drop early grapes
and cast off their blossoms
like the olive.
³⁴ The ruthless gang is barren,
and fire consumes the tents of bribers.
³⁵ They conceive toil
and give birth to sorrow;
their belly establishes deceit.

Job's response

16 Then Job answered:
² I've heard many things like these.
All of you are sorry comforters.
³ Will windy talk ever cease;
what bothers you that you must argue?
⁴ In your situation I could speak like you;
I could put words together to oppose you,
shake my head over you.
⁵ I could heap up words,
strengthen you with my speech;
my trembling lips would be held in check.
⁶ If I speak, my pain is not eased;
if I hold back, what have I lost?

The innocent are God's targets

⁷ Now God has surely worn me out.
You have destroyed my entire group,
⁸ seized me, which became grounds
for an accusation.[w]
My leanness rises to bear witness
against me.
⁹ His anger tears me and afflicts me;
he slashes at me with his teeth.
My enemy pierces me with his eyes.
¹⁰ They open their mouths at me
and strike my cheek in a taunt;
they gang up on me.
¹¹ God delivers me to a criminal
and forces me into the hands
of the wicked.
¹² I was at rest, but he shattered me,
seized me by the back of my neck,

ᵛHeb lacks *pierces.* ʷHeb uncertain

dashed me into pieces;
he raised me up for his target.
¹³ His archers surround me;
he cuts my kidneys open without pity
and doesn't care,
pours my gall on the ground,
¹⁴ bursts me open over and over,
runs against me like a strong man.
¹⁵ I've sewed rough cloth over my skin
and buried my dignity in the dust.
¹⁶ My face is red from crying,
and dark gloom hangs on my eyelids.
¹⁷ But there is no violence in my hands,
and my prayer is pure.

Lingering hope

¹⁸Earth, don't cover my blood;
let my outcry never cease.
¹⁹Surely now my witness
stands in heaven;
my advocate
is on high;

²⁰ my go-between, my friend.ˣ
While my eyes drip tears to God,
²¹ let him plead with God for a human being,
like a person pleads for a friend.
²² A number of years will surely pass,
and then I'll walk a path
that I won't return.

Another lament

17My spirit is broken,
my days extinguished,
the grave,ʸ mine.
² Surely mockers are with me,
and my eye looks on their rebellion.
³ Take my guarantee.
Who else is willing
to make an agreement?
⁴ You've closed their mind to insight;
therefore, you won't be exalted.
⁵ He denounces his friends for gain,
and his children's eyes fail.
⁶ He makes me a popular proverb;
I'm like spit in people's faces.
⁷ My eye is weak from grief;
my limbs like a shadow—all of them.
⁸ Those who do the right thing
are amazed at this;
the guiltless become troubled
about the godless.

⁹ The innocent clings to his way;
the one whose hands are clean
grows stronger.
¹⁰ But you can bring all of them again,
and I won't find a wise one among you.
¹¹ My days have passed;
my goals are destroyed,
my heart's desires.
¹² They turn night into day;
light is near because of the darkness.
¹³ If I hope for the underworldᶻ
as my dwelling,
lay out my bed in darkness,
¹⁴ I've called corruption "my father,"
the worm, "my mother and sister."
¹⁵ Where then is my hope?
My hope—who can see it?
¹⁶ Will they go down with me
to the underworld;ᵃ
will we descend together to the dust?

Attack from a friend

18Bildad from Shuah answered:
²How long? Would you all stop talking.
Try to understand and then we can speak.
³ Why are we considered beasts,
ignorant in your sight?
⁴ To you who tear yourself in rage—
will earth be forsaken for your sake,
a rock be dislodged from its place?

Evil people's fate

⁵ To be sure, the light of the wicked
goes out;
the blaze of their fire doesn't shine.
⁶ The light in their tent becomes dark,
and their lamp above doesn't shine.
⁷ Their strong strides slow down;
their plans trip themselves.
⁸ They are caught by their feet in a net;
they walk on mesh.
⁹ A trap grabs them by the heel;
a snare tightens on them.
¹⁰ A rope is hidden on the ground for them,
a trap for them along the path.
¹¹ Terrors round about scare them;
they follow their steps.
¹² Their offspring hunger;
calamity is ready for their spouses.
¹³ It eats some of their skin.
Death's firstborn consumes their limbs.

ˣ*Go-between* and *friend* are plural in Heb. ʸOr *graves* ᶻHeb *Sheol* ᵃHeb *Sheol*

¹⁴ They are snatched from the safety
　　of their tent;
　　it parades them
　　　before the king of terrors.
¹⁵ Nothing they own remains in their tent;
　　sulfur is scattered over their home.
¹⁶ Their roots dry out below;
　　their branches wither above.
¹⁷ The memory of them will perish
　　from the earth;
　　they will achieve no recognition abroad.
¹⁸ They are thrust from light into darkness,
　　banished from the world.
¹⁹ They have no offspring or descendants
　　among their people,
　　no survivor in their dwelling place.
²⁰ Their successors are appalled
　　at what happens to them;
　　their predecessors pull their hair.
²¹ These are surely the dwelling places
　　of the evil;
　　this is the place of the one
　　　who doesn't know God.

LIGHTHOUSE

RESPECT FOR GOD

Result of Evil *Job 18:3-21*
Sometimes it seems like good things happen to
people who continually do bad things. They have
lots of money and nice things, and they never seem
to have problems. Sometimes we see this and think
God isn't fair. But one day, everyone will have to answer for his or her actions. Even when people do
evil things and live this life in luxury, they will still
answer to God. ◊

Failed friendship

19 Then Job responded:
　² How long will you harass me
　　and crush me with words?
³ These ten times you've humiliated me;
　　shamelessly you insult me.
⁴ Have I really gone astray?
　　If so, my error remains hidden
　　　inside me.
⁵ If you look down on me
　　and use my disgrace to criticize me,
　⁶ know then that God has wronged me
　　and enclosed his net over me.

God's treatment of Job

⁷ If I cry "Violence!" I'm not answered;
　　I shout—but there is no justice.
⁸ He walled up my path so I can't pass
　　and put darkness on my trail,
　⁹ stripped my honor from me,
　　removed the crown from my head,
¹⁰ tore me down completely so that I'll die,
　　and uprooted my hope like a tree.
¹¹ His anger burns against me;
　　he considers me his enemy.
¹² His troops come as one
　　and construct their siege ramp^b against me;
　　they camp around my tent.

Social ostracism

¹³ He has distanced my family from me;
　　my acquaintances are also alienated
　　　from me.
¹⁴ My visitors have ceased;
　　those who know me have forgotten me.
¹⁵ My guests and female servants
　　think me a stranger;
　　I'm a foreigner in their sight.
¹⁶ I call my servant, and he doesn't answer;
　　I myself must beg him.
¹⁷ My breath stinks to my wife;
　　I am odious to my children.
¹⁸ Even the young despise me;
　　I get up, and they rail against me.
¹⁹ All my closest friends despise me;
　　the ones I have loved turn against me.

Misery

²⁰ My bones cling to my skin and flesh;
　　I have escaped by the skin of my teeth.
²¹ Pity me. Pity me. You're my friends.
　　God's hand has truly struck me.
²² Why do you pursue me like God does,
　　always hungry for my flesh?

Brief hope

²³ Oh, that my words were written down,
　　inscribed on a scroll
²⁴ with an iron instrument and lead,
　　forever engraved on stone.
²⁵ But I know that my
　　redeemer^c is alive
　　and afterward
　　he'll rise upon the dust.

Memorize
Job 19:25

^b Or *their road* ^c Or *avenger*

26 After my skin has been torn apart
  this way—
  then from my flesh[d] I'll see God,
  27 whom I'll see myself—
  my eyes see,[e] and not a stranger's.
  I am utterly dejected.

Warning

28 You say, "How will we pursue him
  so that the root of the matter can be
  found in him?"[f]
29 You ought to fear the sword yourselves,
  for wrath brings punishment
  by the sword.
  You should know that there is judgment.

Traditional belief

20 Zophar from Naamah said:
  2 Therefore, my troubled thoughts
  make me turn back—
  because of my inner turmoil.
  3 I hear teaching that insults me,
  but I am forced to answer based
  on my own understanding.[g]
  4 Do you know this from long ago—

from when humans were placed
  on earth—
5 that the rejoicing of the wicked is short,
  the joy of the godless, brief?
6 Though their height reaches heaven
  and their heads touch the clouds,
7 they will perish forever like their dung;
  those who saw them will say,
  "Where are they?"
8 They will disappear like a dream,
  and none will find them,
  carried away like a nighttime vision.
9 The eye that saw them will do so no more;
  they won't be seen again at home.
10 Their children will repay the poor;
  their hands will give back their wealth.
11 Vigor filled their bones
  and now sleeps with them in the dust.
12 Though wickedness is sweet
  in their mouths,
  they hide it under their tongues;
13 they like it, won't let it go;
  they hold it in their cheeks.
14 Food turns their stomachs,
  becoming a cobra's poison inside.

[d]Or without my flesh or in my flesh [e]Or have seen [f]Heb manuscripts; MT in me [g]Heb uncertain

Job Has Hope   Job 19

When everything in life seems to go wrong, those who believe in God can still have hope. When we don't have anything else in this life, we can have hope because God has promised it to us. Hope is a feeling that things will get better, a belief that we can trust God no matter what happens.

Even through all the craziness that happened to Job, he still had hope. He believed deep down that things would be okay. His words tell the roller coaster of emotions he experienced—at times he wished he had never been born, but he also had hope that he would see God and things would be right again: "I know that my redeemer is alive" (Job 19:25). When we don't know anything else, when everything we thought turns out to be wrong, we can know for sure that God is alive and working in our lives. We can trust that we're safely in God's loving care.

What does hope mean to you?

How can hope help you get through tough times?

¹⁵ They swallow wealth and vomit it;
  God dislodges it from their belly.
¹⁶ They suck cobra's poison;
  a viper's tongue kills them.
¹⁷ They won't experience streams,
  rivers of honey, and brooks of cream.
¹⁸ They won't receive the reward
  for their labor;
  they won't enjoy the wealth
  from their business.
¹⁹ They crushed and abandoned the poor;
  stole a house they didn't build;
²⁰ didn't know contentment in their belly;
  couldn't escape with their treasure.
²¹ Nothing remained of their food,
  so their riches will not endure.
²² Even in their plenty,
  they are hard-pressed;
  all sorts of trouble come on them.
²³ Let God^h fill their belly,
  unleash his burning anger on them,
  rain punishing blows on them.
²⁴ If they flee an iron weapon,
  a bronze bow pierces them.
²⁵ They pull it out,
  but it sticks out from their backs;
  its shaft in their liver brings terror.
²⁶ Complete darkness waits for their
  treasured possessions;
  fire that no one stoked consumes them;
  what's left in their tent is ruined.
²⁷ Heaven exposes their guilt;
  earth opposes them.
²⁸ Their household wealth will be carried off
  by rushing streams on the day
  of his anger.
²⁹ This is a wicked person's lot from God,
  their heritage decreed by God.

Grant me a hearing

21 Then Job answered:
² Listen carefully to my remarks
  and let that comfort you.
³ Bear with me so I can speak, I myself;
  and after my reply you can mock.
⁴ Are my complaints against
  another human?
  why is my patience short?
⁵ Turn to me and be appalled;
  lay your hand over your mouth.

⁶ If I recall it, I'm scared;
  shaking seizes my body.

The success of the wicked

⁷ Why do the wicked live,
  grow old, and even become strong?
⁸ Their children are always with them,
  their offspring in their sight,
⁹ their houses safe from dread,
  God's punishing stick not upon them.
¹⁰ Their bull always breeds successfully;
  their cows give birth and never miscarry.
¹¹ They send forth their little ones
  like sheep;
  their infants bounce around.
¹² They raise drum and lyre,
  rejoice at the sound of a flute.
¹³ They spend their days contentedly,
  go down to the graveⁱ peacefully.
¹⁴ They say to God, "Turn away from us;
  we take no pleasure in
  knowing your ways;
¹⁵ who is the Almighty^j
  that we should serve him,
  and what can we gain if we meet him?"
¹⁶ Look, isn't their well-being the work
  of their own hands?
  A sinner's logic is beyond me.

Desired vindication

¹⁷ How often does the lamp
  of the wicked flicker
  or disaster come upon them,
  with its fury inflicting pain on them?
¹⁸ Let them be like straw in the wind,
  like dry grass stolen by a storm.
¹⁹ God stores up his punishment
  for his children.
  Let him destroy them so they know.
²⁰ Let their own eyes witness their doom.
  Let them drink
  from the Almighty's wrath.
²¹ What do they care about their household
  after they die,
  when their numbered days are cut off?

A common fate

²² Will they instruct God—
  he who judges the most powerful?
²³ Someone dies in wonderful health,
  completely comfortable and well,

^hOr him ⁱHeb Sheol ^jHeb Shaddai or Mountain One

²⁴ their buckets full of milk,
their bones marrow-filled and sound.
²⁵ Another dies in bitter spirit,
never having tasted the good things.
²⁶ They lie together in the dust
and worms cover them.

Further disagreement

²⁷ Look, I know your thoughts;
your plans harm me.
²⁸ You say, "Where is the official's house?
Where is the tent,
the dwelling of the wicked?"
²⁹ Haven't you asked travelers
or paid attention to their reports?
³⁰ On the day of disaster
the wicked are spared;
on the day of fury they are rescued.
³¹ Who can criticize their behavior
to their faces;
they act, and who can avenge them?
³² They are carried to their graves;
someone keeps guard over their tombs.
³³ The soil near the desert streambed
is sweet to them;
everyone marches after them—
those before them, beyond counting.
³⁴ How empty is your comfort to me;
only deceit remains in your responses.

Job's sins

22 Then Eliphaz from Teman answered:
²Can a human being be useful to God?
Can an intelligent person bring profit?
³ Does the Almighty delight
in your innocence?
Does he gain
when you perfect your ways?
⁴ Does he rebuke you for your piety,
bring you in for judgment?
⁵ Isn't your wickedness massive,
your iniquity endless?
⁶ You have taken payments
from your family for no reason;
stripped the naked, leaving no clothes;
⁷ denied water to the thirsty,
withheld bread from the starving.
(⁸ The powerful own land;
the favored live in it.)
⁹ You have sent widows away empty;
crushed orphans' resources.
¹⁰ For this reason, snares surround you;
sudden dread brings panic to you

¹¹ or a darkness that you can't see;
rushing water will cover you.

God's activity

¹² Isn't God in the heights of heaven;
see how high the topmost stars are?
¹³ You say: "What does God know?
Can he judge through thick clouds?
¹⁴ Clouds conceal him so he can't see
while he walks on heaven's rim."
¹⁵ Will you keep the ancient way
traveled by sinful persons,
¹⁶ who were snatched prematurely
when a river flooded their foundations,
¹⁷ who say to God, "Turn away from us;
what can the Almighty do to us?"
¹⁸ Yet he filled their houses
with good things;
a sinner's logic is beyond me.
¹⁹ The righteous see and rejoice;
the innocent mock them:
²⁰ our enemies are certainly cut off;
fire will devour what's left of them.

Turn to God

²¹ Get along well with God and be at peace;
from this something good
will come to you.
²² Receive instruction from his mouth;
put his words
in your mind.

LIGHTHOUSE

WISDOM

Wrong Assumptions About God

Job 22:4-5

You might look at the things that Eliphaz, Bildad, and Zophar said to Job and be surprised they were his friends. They were so upset at his pain that they didn't speak for seven days (Job 2:11-13). These three friends viewed Job's situation based on wrong ideas about God. Like the Adversary in chapter 1, they thought that if Job obeyed God he would always be blessed, but if he was suffering then God was punishing Job. Job's friends saw all the bad things that happened to him and assumed he had made God angry. They thought if they could get Job to admit his wrong actions and ask forgiveness, God would stop punishing him. The book of Job shows that suffering people should not be blamed for their pain. ◊

²³ If you return to the Almighty,ᵏ
  you will be restored;
  if you keep wrongdoing out of your tent.
²⁴ Lay your prized possession in the dust,
  your gold from Ophir on a rock
    in a desert streambed.
²⁵ The Almighty will be your
    prized possession,
  silver piled up for you.
²⁶ Then you will take pleasure
    in the Almighty;
  lift up your face to God.
²⁷ You will pray to him, and he will hear you;
  you will fulfill your solemn promises.
²⁸ If you decree something, it will stand;
  light will shine on your ways.
²⁹ When they're humbled, you will say:
  "Cheer up;
  God will rescue the lowly.
³⁰ He will deliver the guilty;
  they will be saved by your pure hands."

Grant me a trial

23 Job answered:
² Today my complaint is again bitter;ˡ
  my strength is weighed down
    because of my groaning.
³ Oh, that I could know how to find him—
  come to his dwelling place;
⁴ I would lay out my case before him,
  fill my mouth with arguments,
⁵ know the words
  with which he would answer,
  understand what he would say to me.
⁶ Would he contend with me
    through brute force?
  No, he would surely listen to me.
⁷ There those who do the right thing can
    argue with him;
  I could escape from my judge forever.

God's hiddenness

⁸ Look, I go east; he's not there,
  west, and don't discover him;
⁹ north in his activity,
  and I don't grasp him;
  he turns south, and I don't see.
¹⁰ Surely he knows my way;
  when he tests me,
  I will emerge as gold.

¹¹ My feet have stayed right in his tracks.
  I have kept his way and not left it,
¹² kept the commandments from his lips
    and not departed,
  valued the words from his mouth
    more than my food.

Dread

¹³ He is of one mind; who can reverse it?
  What he desires, he does.
¹⁴ He carries out what is decreed for me
  and can do many similar things with me.
¹⁵ Therefore, I am scared by his presence;
  I think and become afraid of him.
¹⁶ God has weakened my mind;
  the Almighty has frightened me.
¹⁷ Still I'm not annihilated by darkness;
  he has hidden deep darkness from me.

Absence of justice

24 Why doesn't the Almighty establish
  times for punishment?ᵐ
  Why can't those who know him
    see his days?
² People move boundary stones,
  herd flocks they've stolen,
³ drive off an orphan's donkey,
  take a widow's ox as collateral,
⁴ thrust the poor out of the way,
  make the land's needy hide together.
⁵ They are like the wild donkeys
    in the desert;
  they go forth at dawn searching for prey;
  the wasteland is food for their young.

UMBRELLA
LYING

Stealing from Widows and Orphans
Job 24:2-3
In ancient times, women couldn't get a job and earn money. They had to depend on their family and husbands to provide for them. Without family to care for them, widows and orphans were easy targets for people who wanted to harm them. Stealing from a widow or orphan was considered the worst type of theft. ◆

ᵏHeb *Shaddai* or *Mountain One*; also in 22:25 and 24:1 ˡVulg, Syr, Tg; MT *my complaint is rebellious.* ᵐHeb lacks *for punishment.*

⁶ They gather their food in the field,
glean in unproductive vineyards,
⁷ spend the night naked, unclothed,
in the cold without a cover,
⁸ wet from mountain rains,
with no refuge,
huddled against a rock.
⁹ The orphan is stolen from the breast;
the infant[n] of the poor
is taken as collateral.
¹⁰ The poor go around naked,
without clothes,
carry bundles of grain while hungry,
¹¹ crush olives between millstones,[o]
tread winepresses, but remain thirsty.
¹² From the city, the dying cry out;
the throat of the mortally wounded
screams, but God assigns no blame.

Sinners' conduct

¹³ They rebel against light,
don't acknowledge its direction,
don't dwell in its paths.
¹⁴ The murderer rises at twilight,
kills the poor and needy;
at night, they are like a thief.
¹⁵ The adulterer's eye watches for twilight,
thinking, No eye can see me,
and puts a mask over his face.
¹⁶ In the dark they break into houses;
they shut themselves in by day;
they don't know the light.
¹⁷ Deep darkness is morning to them
because they recognize the horror
of darkness.
¹⁸ They are scum on the water's surface;
their portion of the land is cursed;
no one walks down a path
in the vineyards.
¹⁹ Drought and heat steal melted snow,
just as the underworld[p] steals sinners.
²⁰ The womb forgets them;
the worm consumes them;
they aren't remembered,
and so wickedness is shattered
like a tree.
²¹ They prey on the barren, the childless,
do nothing good for the widow.
²² They drag away the strong by force;

they may get up
but without guarantee of survival.
²³ They make themselves secure;
they are at ease.
His[q] eyes are on their ways.
²⁴ They are exalted for a short time,
but no longer.
They are humbled then gathered in
like everyone else;
cut off like heads of grain.
²⁵ If this isn't so, who can prove me a liar
and make my words disappear?

Inferior humans

25 Bildad from Shuah replied:
² Supreme power and awe
belong to God;
he establishes peace on his heights.
³ Can his troops be counted?
On whom does his light not rise?
⁴ How can a person be innocent before God;
one born of a woman be pure?
⁵ If even the moon is not bright
and the stars not pure in his eyes,
⁶ how much less a human, a worm,
a person's child, a grub.

Sarcasm

26 Then Job said:
² How well you have helped the weak,
saved those with frail arms,
³ advised one lacking wisdom,
informed many with insight!
⁴ With whom have you spoken;[r]
whose breath was expelled from you?

Truth about God

⁵ The dead writhe,
the inhabitants beneath the waters
as well.
⁶ The grave[s] is naked before God;
the underworld[t] lacks covering.
⁷ He stretched the North[u] over chaos,
hung earth over nothing;
⁸ wrapped up water in his clouds,
yet they didn't burst out below;
⁹ hid the face of the full moon,[v]
spreading his cloud over it;
¹⁰ traced a circle on the water's surface,
at the limit of light and darkness.

[n]Reading Heb *we'ul* (infant) for *we'al* (against) [o]Heb uncertain [p]Heb Sheol [q]Or God's [r]Or told words [s]Heb Sheol
[t]Heb Abaddon [u]Heb Zaphon [v]Or throne; Heb uncertain

¹¹ Heaven's pillars shook,
  terrified by his blast.
¹² By his power he stilled the Sea;
  split Rahab with his cleverness.
¹³ Due to his wind, heaven became clear;
  his hand split the fleeing serpent.
¹⁴ Look, these are only the outer fringe
  of his ways;
  we hear only a whispered word
  about him.
  Who can understand
  his thunderous power?

Job rejects Bildad's argument

27 Then Job took up his topic again:
² As God lives,
  who rejected my legal claim,
  the Almighty, who made me bitter,
    ³ as long as breath
      is in me

Memorize Job 27:3-4

and God's breath is in my nostrils—
⁴ my lips will utter no wickedness;
  my tongue will mumble no deceit.
⁵ I will not agree that you are right.
  Until my dying day,
  I won't give up my integrity.
⁶ I will insist on my innocence,
  never surrendering it;
  my conscience will never blame me
  for what I have done.ʷ

Job curses his enemies

⁷ Let my enemy be like the wicked,
  my opposition like the vicious.
⁸ For what hope has the godless
  when God cuts them off,
  when he takes them away.
⁹ Will God hear their cries
  when distress comes to them;
¹⁰ will they delight in the Almighty,
  call God at any time?

Job's view of his enemies' fate

¹¹ I will teach you God's power,
  not hide what pertains to the Almighty.
¹² Look, those of you who recognize this—
  why then this empty talk?
¹³ This is the wicked's portion with God,
  the inheritance that the ruthless
  receive from the Almighty.

¹⁴ If their children increase,
  they belong to the sword;
  their offspring won't have enough bread.
¹⁵ Their survivors will be buried
  with the dead;
  their widows won't weep.
¹⁶ If they store up silver like dust,
  amass clothing like clay,
  ¹⁷ they may amass,
    but the righteous will wear it;
    the innocent will divide the silver.
¹⁸ They built their houses like nests,
  like a hut made by a watchman.
¹⁹ They lie down rich, but no longer;
  open their eyes, but it's missing.
²⁰ Terrors overtake them like waters;
  a tempest snatches them by night;
²¹ an east wind lifts them,
  and they are gone,
  removes them from their places,
²² throws itself on them without mercy;
  they flee desperately from its force.
²³ It claps its hands over them,
  hisses at them from their place.

Expertise in mining

28 There is a sure source of silver,
  a place where gold is refined.
² Iron is taken from the earth;
  rock is smelted into copper.
³ Humansˣ put an end to darkness,
  dig for ore to the farthest depths,
  into stone in utter darkness,
⁴ open a shaft away from any inhabitant,
  places forgotten by those on foot,
  apart from any human
  they hang and sway.
⁵ Earth—from it comes food—
  is turned over below ground as by fire.ʸ
⁶ Its rocks are the source for lapis lazuli;
  there is gold dust in it.
⁷ A path—
  no bird of prey knows it;
  a hawk's eye hasn't seen it;
⁸ proud beasts haven't trodden on it;
  a lion hasn't crossed over it.
⁹ Humans thrust their hands into flint,
  pull up mountains from their roots,
¹⁰ cut channels into rocks;
  their eyes see everything precious.

ʷOr *for my days* ˣOr *they* ʸHeb uncertain

¹¹ They dam up the sources of rivers;
   hidden things come to light.

Wisdom's value

¹² But wisdom, where can it be found;
   where is the place of understanding?
¹³ Humankind doesn't know its value;
   it isn't found in the land of the living.
¹⁴ The Deep^z says, "It's not with me";
   the Sea^a says, "Not alongside me!"
¹⁵ It can't be bought with gold;
   its price can't be measured in silver,
¹⁶ can't be weighed against gold from Ophir,
   with precious onyx or lapis lazuli.
¹⁷ Neither gold nor glass
   can compare with it;
   she can't be acquired with gold jewelry.
¹⁸ Coral and jasper shouldn't be mentioned;
   the price of wisdom is more than rubies.
¹⁹ Cushite topaz won't compare with her;
   she can't be set alongside pure gold.
²⁰ But wisdom, where does she come from?
   Where is the place of understanding?
²¹ She's hidden from the eyes of all the living,
   concealed from birds of the sky.
²² Destruction^b and Death have said,
   "We've heard a report of her."
²³ God understands her way;
   he knows her place;
²⁴ for he looks to the ends of the earth
   and surveys everything
      beneath the heavens.
²⁵ In order to weigh the wind,
   to prepare a measure for waters,
²⁶ when he made a decree
   for the rain,
   a path for thunderbolts,

LIGHTHOUSE
WISDOM

Wisdom Comes from God Job 28:28
Job knew what it was like to be rich. He had owned seven thousand sheep, three thousand camels, five hundred pairs of oxen, and five hundred female donkeys. He was considered the greatest man in the land. But Job realized wisdom was more important than riches. Job told his friends that true wisdom comes from respecting God. ◊

²⁷ then he observed it, spoke of it,
   established it, searched it out,
²⁸ and said to humankind: "Look,
   the fear of the LORD is wisdom;
   turning from evil is understanding."

Job's previous blessing

29 Job took up his subject again:
   ² Oh, that life was like it used to be,
   like days when God watched over me;
³ when his lamp shone on my head,
   I walked by his light in the dark;
⁴ when I was in my prime;
   when God's counsel was in my tent;
⁵ when the Almighty was with me,
   my children around me;
⁶ when my steps were washed with cream
   and a rock poured out
      pools of oil for me.

Previous honor

⁷ When I went out to the city gate,
   took my seat in the square,
⁸ the young saw me and drew back;
   the old rose and stood;
⁹ princes restrained speech,
   put their hand on their mouth;
¹⁰ the voices of officials were hushed,
   their tongue stuck to their palate.

Job's implementation of justice

¹¹ Indeed, the ear that heard blessed me;
   the eye that looked commended me,
¹² because I rescued the weak
   who cried out,
   the orphans who lacked help.
¹³ The blessing of the perishing reached me;
   I made the widow's heart sing;
¹⁴ I put on justice, and it clothed me,
   righteousness as my coat and turban;
¹⁵ I was eyes to the blind,
   feet to the lame.
¹⁶ I was a father to the needy;
   the case I didn't know, I examined.
¹⁷ I shattered the fangs of the wicked,
   rescued prey from their teeth.

Job's expected blessing

¹⁸ I thought, I'll die in my nest,
   multiply days like sand,^{c}

---

^{z} Heb *Tehom*, a reference to a divine being in the grave or underworld ^{a} Heb *Yam*, a sea god ^{b} Heb *Abaddon* ^{c} Heb uncertain

¹⁹ my roots opening to water,
  dew lingering on my branches,
²⁰ my honor newly with me,
  my bow ever successful in my hand.

Previous honor

²¹ People listened to me and waited,
  were silent for my advice.
²² After my speech, they didn't respond.
  My words fell gently on them;
²³ they waited for me as for rain,
  opened their mouth as for spring rain.
²⁴ I smiled[d] on them; they couldn't believe it.
  They never showed me disfavor.
²⁵ I decided their path, sat as chief.
  I lived like a king with his troops,
  like one who comforts mourners.

Mockers

30 But now those younger than I mock me,
  whose fathers I refused to put beside
  my sheepdogs.
² Their strength, what's it to me,
  their energy having perished?
³ Stiff from want and hunger,
  those who gnaw dry ground,
  yesterday's desolate waste,
⁴ who pluck off the leaves on a bush,
  the root of the broom—
  a shrub is their food.
⁵ People banish them from society,
  shout at them as if to a thief;
⁶ so they live in scary ravines,
  holes in the ground and rocks.
⁷ Among shrubs, they make sounds
  like donkeys;
  they are huddled together under a bush,
⁸ children of fools and the nameless,
  whipped out of the land.

Specific mocking behavior

⁹ And now I'm their song;
  I'm their cliché!
¹⁰ They detest me, keep their distance,
  don't withhold spit from my face.
¹¹ Because he loosened my bowstring
  and afflicted me,
  they throw off restraint in my presence.
¹² On the right, upstarts[e] rise
  and target my feet,

build their siege ramps against me,
¹³ destroy my road, profit from my fall,
  with no help.
¹⁴ They advance as if through
  a destroyed wall;[f]
  they roll along beneath the ruin.
¹⁵ Terrors crash upon me;
  they sweep away my honor like wind;
  my safety disappears like a cloud.

Accusation against God

¹⁶ Now my life is poured out on me;
  days of misery have seized me.
¹⁷ At night he bores my bones;
  my gnawing pain won't rest.
¹⁸ With great force he grasps[g] my clothing;[h]
  it binds me like the neck of my shirt.
¹⁹ He hurls me into mud;
  I'm a cliché, like dust and ashes.
²⁰ I cry to you, and you don't answer;
  I stand up, but you just look at me.
²¹ You are cruel to me,
  attack me with the strength of your hand.
²² You lift me to the wind and make me ride;
  you melt me in its roar.
²³ I know you will return me to death,
  the house appointed for all the living.

Job's agony

²⁴ Surely he won't strike someone in ruins
  if in distress he cries out to him,
²⁵ if I didn't weep for those
  who have a difficult day
  or my soul grieve for the needy;
²⁶ for I awaited good, but evil came;
  I expected light, but gloom arrived.
²⁷ My insides, churning, are never quiet;
  days of affliction confront me.
²⁸ I walk in the dark, lacking sunshine;
  I rise in the assembly and cry out.
²⁹ I have become a brother to jackals,
  a companion to young ostriches.
³⁰ My skin is charred;
  my bones are scorched by the heat.
³¹ My lyre is for mourning,
  my flute, a weeping sound.

Lust

31 I've made a covenant with my eyes;
  how could I look at a virgin?

---

[d]Or *laughed at* [e]Heb uncertain [f]*Or a wide opening* [g]LXX [h]Heb uncertain

² What is God's portion for me[i]
from above,
the Almighty's inheritance
from on high?
³ Isn't it disaster for the wicked,
destruction for workers of iniquity?
⁴ Doesn't he see my ways,
count all my steps?

Deceit

⁵ If I have walked with frauds
or my feet have hurried to deceit,
⁶ let him weigh me on accurate scales;
let God know my integrity.
⁷ If my step has turned from the way,
if my heart has followed my eyes
or a blemish has clung to my hands,
⁸ then let me sow and another reap;
let my offspring be uprooted.

Adultery

⁹ If my heart has been drawn
to a woman
and I have lurked
at my neighbor's door,
¹⁰ then may my wife grind for another
and others kneel over her;
¹¹ for that's a crime;
it's a punishable offense;
¹² indeed, it's a fire that consumes
to the underworld,[j]
uprooting all my harvest.

Slaves

¹³ If I've rejected the just cause
of my male or female servant
when they contended with me,
¹⁴ what could I do when God rises;
when he requires an account,
what could I answer?
¹⁵ Didn't the one who made me in the belly
make them;
didn't the same one fashion us
in the womb?

The defenseless

¹⁶ If I have denied what the poor wanted,
made a widow's eyes tired,
¹⁷ eaten my morsel alone,
and not shared any with an orphan

(¹⁸ for from my youth
I raised the orphan as a father,
and from my mother's womb
I led the widow);[k]
¹⁹ if I ever saw someone dying without
clothes, the needy naked;
²⁰ if they haven't blessed me fervently,[l]
or if they weren't warmed
by the wool from my sheep;
²¹ if I have lifted my hand
against the orphans,
when I saw that I had help
in the city gate—
²² may my arm fall from my shoulder,
my forearm be broken at the elbow—
²³ for God's calamity is terror to me;
I couldn't endure his splendor.

False worship

²⁴ If I've made gold my trust,
said to fine gold: "My security!"
²⁵ if I've rejoiced because
my wealth was great,
when my hand found plenty;
²⁶ if I've looked at the sun when it shone,
the moon, splendid as it moved;
²⁷ and my mind has been secretly enticed,
and threw a kiss with my hand,
²⁸ that also is a punishable offense,
because I would then be disloyal
to God above.

Others' misfortune

²⁹ If I have rejoiced over my foes' ruin
or was excited when evil found them,
³⁰ I didn't let my mouth sin
by asking for their life with a curse.
³¹ Surely those in my tent never said:
"Who has been filled by Job's food?"
³² A stranger didn't spend the night
in the street;
I opened my doors to the road.

Concealing sin

³³ If I have hidden my transgressions
like Adam,[m]
concealing my offenses inside me
³⁴ because I feared the large crowd;
the clan's contempt frightened me;
I was quiet and didn't venture outside.

---

[i]Heb lacks *for me.* [j]Heb *Abaddon* [k]Heb lacks *orphan…widow.* [l]Or *his loins* [m]Or *like a human*

Sealing the solemn pledge

³⁵ Oh, that I had someone to hear me!
  Here's my signature;ⁿ
  let the Almighty respond,
  and let my accuser write an indictment.
³⁶ Surely I would bear it on my shoulder,
  tie it around me like a wreath.
³⁷ I would give him an account of my steps,
  approach him like a prince.

Abuse of the land

³⁸ If my land has cried out against me,
  its rows wept together;
³⁹ if I have eaten its yield without payment
  and caused its owners grief,
⁴⁰ may briars grow instead of wheat,
  poisonous weeds instead of barley.

Job's words are complete.

Introduction of Elihu

32 These three men stopped answering Job because he thought he was righteous.ᵒ ²Elihu son of Barachel the Buzite from the clan of Ram was angry, angry with Job because he considered himself more righteous than God. ³He was also angry with his three friends because they hadn't found an answer but nevertheless thought Job wicked. ⁴Elihu had waited while Job spoke, for they were older than he. ⁵When Elihu saw that there had been no response in the speeches of the three men, he became very angry.

SAILBOAT

GENEROUS

Hospitality Job 31:32

In Job's time, traveling was different than it is today. Some people had camels, horses, or donkeys to ride, but most people walked wherever they were going. There weren't big hotels with comfortable beds and restaurants with large menus. When arriving in a village, a traveler would go to the well where everyone came at some point during the day. If a villager saw a traveler at the well, the villager would invite the traveler to spend the night at his or her home. The host would feed the traveler, tend to any animals the traveler had brought, and provide a comfortable place for the traveler to sleep. It was considered a terrible thing to not invite a traveler to your house for the night. ◆

Elihu's justification for speaking

⁶ Elihu son of Barachel the Buzite said:
  I'm young and you're old,
  so I held back, afraid to express
  my opinion to you.
⁷ I thought, Let days speak;
  let multiple years make wisdom known.
⁸ But the spirit in a person,
  the Almighty's breath,
  gives understanding.
⁹ The advanced in days aren't wise;
  the old don't understand what's right.
¹⁰ Therefore, I say: "Listen to me;
  I'll state my view, even I."
¹¹ Look, I waited while you spoke,
  listened while you reasoned,
  while you searched for words.
¹² I was attentive to you,
  but you offered no rebuke to Job,
  no answer from you for his words.
¹³ Be careful you don't say,
  "We've found wisdom;
  God, not a person, will defeat him."

¹⁴ Now Jobᵖ hasn't addressed me,
  and I won't quote you to him.
¹⁵ They are troubled, no longer answer;
  words now escape them.
¹⁶ I waited, but they didn't speak,
  for they stood but answered no more.
¹⁷ I will answer. Indeed, I will stateq my piece;
  I too will declare my view,
¹⁸ for I'm full of words.
  The spirit in my belly compels me.
¹⁹ Look, my belly is like unopened wine;
  like new wineskins it will burst.
²⁰ I will speak and get relief;
  I will open my lips and respond.
²¹ I won't be partial to anyone,
  won't flatter a person;
²² for I don't know flattery;
  otherwise my maker would quickly
  whisk me away.

Elihu's appeal to be heard

33 But now, listen to me, Job;
pay attention to all my words.
² Notice that I am opening my mouth;
  my tongue is speaking in my mouth.ʳ
³ My words come from a virtuous heart;
  my lips speak knowledge clearly.

ⁿHeb *tau*, the last letter of the Hebrew alphabet ᵒOr *was righteous in his own eyes* ᵖOr *he* qHeb lacks *will state*. ʳOr *palate*

⁴ God's spirit made me;
  the Almighty's breath enlivens me.
⁵ If you are able, answer me;
  lay out your case⁵ before me
  and take a stand.
⁶ Notice that I'm just like you to God;
  I also was pinched from clay.
⁷ Surely fear of me shouldn't scare you;
  my pressure on you shouldn't be heavy.

The argument

⁸ You certainly said in my hearing;
  I heard the sound of your words:
⁹ "I'm pure, without sin;
  I'm innocent, without offense.
¹⁰ Notice that he invents arguments
  against me;
  he considers me his enemy,
¹¹ ties up my feet,
  watches all my paths."
¹² Now you're wrong about this;
  I'll answer you,
  for God is greater than anybody.
¹³ Why do you contend with him,
  saying that he doesn't answer
  all your words?ᵗ
¹⁴ God speaks in one way,
  in two ways, but no one perceives it.
¹⁵ In the dream, a vision of the night,
  when deep sleep falls upon humans,
  during their slumber on a bed,
¹⁶ then he opens people's ears,
  scares them with warnings,
¹⁷ to turn them from a deed
  and to smother human pride.
¹⁸ He keeps one from the pit,
  a life from perishing by the sword.
¹⁹ Or a person may be disciplined by pain
  while in bed, bones ever aching
²⁰ until a person loathes food,
  an appetite rejects a delicacy;
²¹ the flesh wastes away, no longer visible;
  the bones, once hidden, protrude.
²² A life approaches the pit;
  its very being draws near
  the death dealers.
²³ Surely there's a messenger for this person,
  a mediator, one out of a thousand
  to declare one's integrity to another
²⁴ so that God has compassion
  on that person and says,

"Rescue this one from going down
  to the pit;
  I have found a ransom."
²⁵ That person's flesh is renewed
  like a child's;
  they regain their youth.
²⁶ They pray to God,
  and God is pleased with them;
  they behold God's presence
  with a joyful shout.
God rewards a person's righteousness.
²⁷ They sing before people and say:
  "I have sinned, perverted justice,
  but didn't experience the consequences.
²⁸ He ransomed me
  from crossing into the pit;
  my life beholds light."
²⁹ Look, God does all this,
  twice, three times with persons
³⁰ to bring them back from the pit,
  to shine with life's light.
³¹ Listen, Job; hear me;
  be quiet, and I will speak.
³² If you have words, answer me;
  speak, for I want to be innocent.
³³ If not, you must hear me;
  be quiet, and I will teach you wisdom.

34 Elihu continued:

² Hear my words, wise ones;
  knowledgeable ones, listen to me,
³ for the ear tests words
  like the palate tastes food.
⁴ Let's choose for us what's right;
  let's determine among ourselves
  what's good;
⁵ for Job has said, "I'm innocent;
  God has denied my just cause;
⁶ because of my cause I'm thought a liar;
  my wound from an arrow is incurable,
  even though I didn't rebel."
⁷ Who is a man like Job?
  He drinks mockery like water
⁸ and travels a path with wrongdoers,
  walking with evil persons.
⁹ Indeed he said, "No one is rewarded
  for delighting in God."
¹⁰ Therefore, intelligent ones, hear me;
  far be it from God to do evil
  and the Almighty to sin,

ˢHeb lacks *your case*. ᵗOr *his words*

¹¹ for he repays people
  based on what they do,
  paying back everyone
    according to their ways.
¹² Surely God doesn't act wickedly;
  the Almighty doesn't distort justice.
¹³ Who placed earth in his care,
  and who gave him dominion
    over the entire world?
¹⁴ If he were to decide to do it—
  to gather his spirit and breath
    back to himself—
    ¹⁵ all flesh would die together,
    and humans would return to dust.

¹⁶ But if you have understanding, hear this;
  pay attention to the sound of my words.
¹⁷ Will one who hates justice rule;
  will you condemn
    the most righteous one?
¹⁸ Will you say to a king, "Worthless!"
  to royalty, "Evil!"
¹⁹ Who shows no favor to princes
  nor regards the rich over the poor,
    for they are all the work of God's hands?
²⁰ In the middle of the night
  they suddenly die;
    people are shaken and pass away.
    The mighty are removed,
    not by a human hand.
²¹ God's eyes are on human ways,
  and he sees all their steps.
²² There's no darkness, no deep darkness,
  where evildoers can hide themselves;
²³ surely no time is set for a person
  to appear before God in judgment.
²⁴ He shatters the mighty
  without examining them;
    makes others take their place.
²⁵ Thus he regards their deeds,
  overturns them at night,
    and they are crushed.
²⁶ He strikes them
  because of their wickedness
    at a place where people can see it.
²⁷ Because they turned from following him
  and didn't value all his ways,
    ²⁸ causing the cry of the poor to reach him,
    he hears the cry of the afflicted.
²⁹ Still, if he remains quiet,
  who can condemn;
    if he hides his face, who can see him?

³⁰ He prevents a lawless person from ruling,
  from capturing people.
³¹ Has Job said to God,
  "I have borne punishment;
    I won't sin again?
³² You teach me what I can't see;
  if I've sinned, I won't do it again."
³³ Will he repay you because you reject sin,
  for you must choose, not I;
    declare what you know.
³⁴ Smart people say to me,
  the wise who hear me,
    ³⁵ "Job speaks without knowledge;
    his words aren't astute."
³⁶ I wish Job would be tested to the limit
  because he responds like evil people.
³⁷ He adds rebellion to his sin;
  mocks us openly
    and adds to his words against God.

Sin's impact

35 Elihu continued:
  ² Do you think it right?
    You say, "I'm more just than God."
³ Yet you ask, "What does it benefit you?
  What have I gained by avoiding sin?"
⁴ I'll answer you,
  and your friends along with you.
⁵ Look at the heavens and see;
  scan the clouds high over you.
⁶ If you've sinned,
  how have you affected God?
    Your offenses have multiplied;
    what have you done to him?
⁷ If you are righteous,
  what do you give to him?
    Or what does he receive from your hand?
⁸ Your evil affects others like you,
  and your righteousness affects
    fellow human beings.
⁹ People cry out
  because of heavy oppression;
    shout under the power of the mighty.
¹⁰ But no one says,
  ""Where is God my maker;
    who gives songs in the night;
    ¹¹ who teaches us more than
    the beasts of the earth,
    makes us wiser than the birds in the sky?"
¹² Then they cry out; but he doesn't answer,
  because of the pride of the wicked.

¹³ God certainly doesn't respond
   to a deceitful cry;
   the Almighty doesn't pay attention to it.
¹⁴ Although you say that you don't see him,
   the case is before him;
   so wait anxiously for him.
¹⁵ Even though his anger is now held back,
   a person doesn't know it's only delayed.ᵘ
¹⁶ So Job mouths emptiness;
   he piles up ignorant words.

Reason for continuing

36 Continuing, Elihu said,
² Wait a little while
   so I can demonstrate for you
   that there is still something more
   to say about God.
³ I will draw from my broad knowledge,
   attribute justice to my maker.
⁴ My words are certainly truthful;
   one with total knowledge
   is present with you.

Divine discipline

⁵ Look, God is mighty
   and doesn't reject anyone;
   he is mighty in strength and mind.
⁶ He doesn't let the wicked live,
   but grants justice to the poor.
⁷ He doesn't avert his eyes
   from the righteous;
   he seats kings on thrones forever,
   and they are lifted up.
⁸ If they are tied with ropes,
   caught in cords of affliction,
⁹ he informs them about their offenses
   and their grave sins.
¹⁰ He opens their ears with discipline
   and commands them to turn from wrong.
¹¹ If they listen and serve,
   they spend their days in plenty,
   their years contentedly.
¹² But if they don't listen,
   they perish by the sword,
   breathe their last without understanding.
¹³ Those with impious hearts become furious;
   they don't cry out
   even though he binds them.
¹⁴ They die young;
   they are among the holy ones.

ᵘHeb uncertain

---

¹⁵ He saves the weak in their affliction,
   opens their ears through oppression.
¹⁶ Surely he draws you up
   from the brink of trouble
   to a wide place without distress;
   your table is set with rich food.
¹⁷ You are overly concerned
   about the case of the wicked;
   justice will be upheld in it.
¹⁸ Don't let them lure you with wealth;
   don't let a huge bribe mislead you.
¹⁹ Will he arrange your rescue from distress
   or from all your exertions of strength?
²⁰ Don't wish for the night
   when people vanish from their place.
²¹ Take care; don't turn to evil
   because you've chosen it over affliction.
²² Look, God is inaccessible due to his power;
   who is a teacher like him?
²³ Who has repaid him for his action,
   and who would ever say,
   "You've done wrong"?
²⁴ Remember to praise his work
   that all of us have seen.
²⁵ Every person has seen him;
   people can observe at great distance.

God's control of the storm

²⁶ Look, God is exalted and unknowable;
   the number of his years
   is beyond counting.
²⁷ He draws up drops of water
   that distill rain from his flood;
²⁸ the clouds pour moisture
   and drip continually on humans.

²⁹ Even if one perceives a spreading cloud
  and the thunder of his pavilion,ᵛ
³⁰ look how he spreads lightning across it
  and covers the seabed;
³¹ for by waterʷ he judges peoples
  and gives food in abundance.
³² He conceals lightning in his palms
  and orders it to its target.
³³ His thunder announces it;
  even cattle proclaim its rising.

37 Oh, my mind is disturbed by this
  and is more troubled than usual.
² Listen closely to the rumble
  of his voice,
  the roar issuing from his mouth.
³ He looses it under the whole sky,
  his lightning on earth's edges.
⁴ After it, a voice roars;
  he thunders with a mighty voice,
  and no one can stop it
  when his voice is heard.
⁵ God roars with his wondrous voice;
  he does great things we can't know.
⁶ He says to the snow, "Fall to earth,"
  and to the downpour of rain,
  "Be a mighty shower."
⁷ He stamps the hand of every person
  so all can know his work.ˣ
⁸ The wild beast enters its lair,
  lies down in its den.
⁹ The storm comes
  from its chamber,

the cold from the north wind.
¹⁰ By God's breath ice forms;
  water's expanse becomes solid.
¹¹ He also fills clouds with moisture;
  his lightning scatters clouds.
¹² He overturns the circling clouds;ʸ
  by his guidance they doᶻ their work,
  doing everything he commands
  over the entire earth.
¹³ Whether for punishment, for his world,
  or for kindness,
  God makes it all happen.

¹⁴ Hear this, Job;
  stop and ponder God's mighty deeds.
¹⁵ Do you realize
  that when God commands them,
  his clouds produce lightning?
¹⁶ Do you understand the positioning
  of the clouds,
  the amazing deeds of one
  with perfect knowledge,
¹⁷ you whose clothes are hot
  when earth is calmed
  by the south wind?
¹⁸ Can you form the sky with him,
  hard like a mirror made of metal?
¹⁹ Tell us what we should say to him;
  we can't present our case
  due to darkness.
²⁰ Should someone inform him
  that I wish to speak,
  or would anyone say he wants
  to be devoured?

Divine splendor

²¹ For now, no one can look at the sun;
  it is bright in the sky;
  the wind has passed and cleared away
  the clouds.
²² From the north comes golden light,
  the awesome splendor of God.
²³ As for the Almighty,
  we can't find him—
  he is powerful and just,
  abundantly righteous—
  he won't respond.
²⁴ Therefore, people fear him;
  none of the wiseᵃ can see him.

LIGHTHOUSE

AWESOME GOD

God Controls Weather *Job 36:26–37:6*
Although Elihu was the youngest of Job's friends, he recognized the power of God. He explained that God is eternal and mere humans cannot truly understand God. With poetry, Elihu described how God draws moisture into clouds and sends it as rain for the earth. He noted how rain nourishes the land and causes crops to grow, providing food for people and animals. God causes storms with roaring thunder to spread across the sky and is so mighty that lightning is hidden within God's hand. In winter, God tells the snow to fall upon the earth. If God is so great, Elihu reasons, who are humans to question God? ◊

ᵛOr *canopy* ʷOr *them* ˣOr *that everyone he has made can know it* ʸHeb uncertain ᶻHeb lacks *they do.* ᵃOr *wise in heart*; cf 9:4

The Lord answers from a whirlwind

38
Then the Lord answered Job from the whirlwind:

Bet you can read this in 5 minutes. **Ready, set, go!**

² Who is this darkening counsel
     with words lacking knowledge?
³ Prepare yourself like a man;
     I will interrogate you,
     and you will respond to me.

The establishing of order

⁴ Where were you
     when I laid the earth's foundations?
     Tell me if you know.
⁵ Who set its measurements?
     Surely you know.
     Who stretched a measuring tape on it?
⁶ On what were its footings sunk;
     who laid its cornerstone,
⁷ while the morning stars sang in unison
     and all the divine beings shouted?
⁸ Who enclosed the Sea[b] behind doors
     when it burst forth from the womb,
⁹ when I made the clouds its garment,
     the dense clouds its wrap,
¹⁰ when I imposed[c] my limit for it,
     put on a bar and doors
¹¹ and said, "You may come this far,
     no farther;
     here your proud waves stop"?

¹² In your lifetime have you
     commanded the morning,
     informed the dawn of its place
¹³ so it would take hold of earth by its edges
     and shake the wicked out of it?
¹⁴ Do you turn it over like clay for a seal,
     so it stands out like a colorful garment?
¹⁵ Light is withheld from the wicked,
     the uplifted arm broken.

The vast beyond

¹⁶ Have you gone to the sea's sources,
     walked in the chamber of the deep?
¹⁷ Have death's gates been revealed to you;
     can you see the gates of deep darkness?
¹⁸ Have you surveyed earth's expanses?
     Tell me if you know everything about it.
¹⁹ Where's the road to the place
     where light dwells;
     darkness, where's it located?

²⁰ Can you take it to its territory;
     do you know the paths to its house?
²¹ You know, for you were born then;
     you have lived such a long time![d]
²² Have you gone to snow's storehouses,
     seen the storehouses of hail
²³ that I have reserved
     for a time of distress,
     for a day of battle and war?
²⁴ What is the way to the place
     where light is divided up;
     the east wind scattered over earth?

Meteorological facts

²⁵ Who cut a channel for the downpours
     and a way for blasts of thunder
²⁶ to bring water to uninhabited land,
     a desert with no human
²⁷ to saturate dry wasteland
     and make grass sprout?
²⁸ Has the rain a father
     who brought forth drops of dew?
²⁹ From whose belly does ice come;
     who gave birth to heaven's frost?
³⁰ Water hardens like stone;
     the surface of the deep thickens.
³¹ Can you bind Pleiades' chains
     or loosen the reins of Orion?
³² Can you guide the stars
     at their proper times,
     lead the Bear with her cubs?
³³ Do you know heaven's laws,
     or can you impose its rule on earth?
³⁴ Can you issue an order to the clouds
     so their abundant waters cover you?
³⁵ Can you send lightning so that it goes
     and then says to you, "I'm here"?
³⁶ Who put wisdom in remote places,
     or who gave understanding to a rooster?[e]
³⁷ Who is wise enough to count the clouds,
     and who can tilt heaven's
     water containers
³⁸ so that dust becomes mud
     and clods of dirt adhere?

Lion and raven

³⁹ Can you hunt prey for the lion
     or fill the cravings of lion cubs?
⁴⁰ They lie in their den,
     lie in ambush in their lair.

---

[b] Heb Yam, a sea god   [c] Heb uncertain   [d] Or the number of your days is many   [e] Heb uncertain

⁴¹ Who provides food for the raven
   when its young cry to God,
   move about without food?

Mountain goat and doe

39 Do you know when mountain goats give birth;
   do you observe the birthing of does?
² Can you count
   the months of pregnancy;
   do you know when they give birth?
³ They crouch, split open for their young,
   send forth their offspring.
⁴ Their young are healthy;
   they grow up in the open country,
   leave and never return.

Wild donkey

⁵ Who freed the wild donkey,
   loosed the ropes of the onager
⁶ to whom I gave the desert as home,
   his dwelling place in the salt flats?
⁷ He laughs at the clamor of the town,
   doesn't hear the driver's shout,
⁸ searches the hills for food
   and seeks any green sprout.

Wild ox

⁹ Will the wild ox agree to be your slave,
   or will it spend the night in your crib?
¹⁰ Can you bind it with a rope
   to a plowed row;
   will it plow the valley behind you?
¹¹ Will you trust it
   because its strength is great
   so that you can leave your work to it?
¹² Can you rely on it to bring back your grain
   to gather into your threshing floor?

Ostrich

¹³ The ostrich's wings flap joyously,
   but her wings and plumage
   are like a stork.
¹⁴ She leaves her eggs on the earth,
   lets them warm in the dust,
¹⁵ then forgets that a foot may crush them
   or a wild animal trample them.
¹⁶ She treats her young harshly
   as if they were not hers,
   without worrying that her labor
   might be in vain;
¹⁷ God didn't endow her with sense,
   didn't give her some good sense.

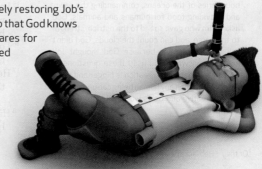

God's Thoughts ◇ My Thoughts

God Knows Everything   Job 38

Sometimes we don't like what happens to us and we blame God for it. Job argued with God because he didn't understand why terrible things were happening to him. His friends started out comforting him, but then they decided that Job must have done something wrong and started blaming him. Job argued with God because he hadn't done anything wrong even though his friends believed he had sinned greatly. He argued with God because he felt like God had abandoned him.

Finally, God spoke. Instead of immediately restoring Job's belongings and health, God reminded Job that God knows everything and that God created and cares for every single thing on the earth. Job argued with God, but God reminded Job that Job was never out of God's sight. Job was never alone.

When have you argued with God?

What does it mean to you that God knows everything?

¹⁸ When she flaps her wings high,
    she laughs at horse and rider.

Horse

¹⁹ Did you give strength to the horse,
    clothe his neck with a mane,
²⁰ cause him to leap like a locust,
    his majestic snorting, a fright?
²¹ Heᶠ paws in the valley, prances proudly,
    charges at battle weapons,
²² laughs at fear, unafraid.
  He doesn't turn away from the sword;
²³ a quiver of arrows flies by him,
    flashing spear and dagger.
²⁴ Excitedly, trembling,
    he swallows the ground;
    can't stand still at a trumpet's blast.
²⁵ At a trumpet's sound, he says, "Aha!"
    smells the battle from afar,
    hearsᵍ officers' shouting
      and the battle cry.

Hawk and eagle

²⁶ Is it due to your understanding
    that the hawk flies,
    spreading its wings to the south?
²⁷ Or at your command does the eagle soar,
    the vulture build a nest
      on high?

LIGHTHOUSE

AWESOME GOD

God Is God *Job 38:1–39:30*

When God finally answered Job, God didn't sympathize with him or even explain why the Adversary was allowed to harm him. God told Job to listen. God asked Job if he was present when the earth was created or if he witnessed the beauty of the stars' creation. God asked him about setting the boundaries of the oceans, commanding the dawn, and providing food for humans and animals. God asked him who gave speed to the ostrich, strength to the horse, and can count the clouds. God didn't ask these questions because God thought Job knew the answers. God used these questions to remind Job that God's creation is bigger and more complicated than any human being can understand. God is creative and God's world is bigger than we can imagine. ◐

²⁸ They dwell on an outcropping of rock,
    their fortress on rock's edge.
²⁹ From there they search for food;
    their eyes notice it from afar,
    ³⁰ and their young lap up blood;
      where carcasses lie, there they are.

The LORD speaks and Job answers

40 The LORD continued to respond to Job:
²Will the one who disputes with the Almighty correct him?
    God's instructor must answer him.
³ Job responded to the LORD:
⁴ Look, I'm of little worth.
    What can I answer you?
    I'll put my hand over my mouth.
⁵ I have spoken once, I won't answer;
    twice, I won't do it again.

A challenge from the LORD

⁶ The LORD answered Job
    from the whirlwind:
⁷ Prepare yourself like a man;
    I will interrogate you,
      and you will respond to me.
⁸ Would you question my justice,
    deem me guilty so you can be innocent?
⁹ Or do you have an arm like God;
    can you thunder with a voice like him?
¹⁰ Adorn yourself with splendor and majesty;
    clothe yourself with honor and esteem.
¹¹ Unleash your raging anger;
    look on all the proud and humble them.
¹² Look on all the proud and debase them;
    trample the wicked in their place.
¹³ Hide them together in the dust;
    bind their faces in a hidden place.
¹⁴ Then I, even I, will praise you,
    for your strong hand has delivered you.

Behemoth

¹⁵ Look at Behemoth,
    whom I made along with you;
    he eats grass like cattle.
¹⁶ Look, his strength is in his thighs,
    his power in stomach muscles.
¹⁷ He stiffens his tail like a cedar;
    the tendons in his thighs
      are tightly woven.
¹⁸ His bones are like bronze tubes,
    his limbs like iron bars.

ᶠOr *they* ᵍHeb lacks *hears.*

¹⁹ He is the first of God's acts;
only his maker can come near him
with a sword.
²⁰ Indeed, the hills bring him tribute,
places where all the wild animals play.
²¹ He lies under the lotuses,
under the cover of reed and marsh.
²² The lotuses screen him with shade;
poplars of the stream surround him.
²³ If the river surges, he doesn't hurry;
he is confident even though the Jordan
gushes into his mouth.
²⁴ Can he be seized by his eyes?
Can anyone pierce his nose by hooks?

Leviathan

41 ^hCan you draw out Leviathan with a hook,
restrain his tongue with a rope?
² Can you put a cord through his nose,
pierce his jaw with a barb?
³ Will he beg you at length
or speak gentle words to you?
⁴ Will he make a pact with you
so that you will take him as a
permanent slave?
⁵ Can you play with him like a bird,
put a leash on him for your girls?
⁶ Will merchants sell him;
will they divide him among traders?
⁷ Can you fill his hide with darts,
his head with a fishing spear?
⁸ Should you lay your hand on him,
you would never remember the battle.
⁹ Such hopesⁱ would be delusional;
surely the sight of him
makes one stumble.
¹⁰ Nobody is fierce enough to rouse him;
who then can stand before me?
¹¹ Who opposes me that I must repay?
Everything under heaven is mine.
¹² I'm not awed by his limbs,
his strength, and impressive form.
¹³ Who can remove his outer garment;
who can come with a bridle for him?
¹⁴ Who can open the doors of his mouth,
surrounded by frightening teeth?
¹⁵ His matching scales are his pride,
closely locked and sealed.
¹⁶ One touches another;
even air can't come between them.

did you know? Some people who study the Bible think the animal in Job 40:15-24 was a hippopotamus. These animals are so protective of the river and lake areas where they live that they kill more people each year than any other animal.

¹⁷ Each clings to its pair;
joined, they can't be separated.
¹⁸ His sneezes emit flashes of light;
his eyes are like dawn's rays.
¹⁹ Shafts of fire shoot from his mouth;
like fiery sparks they fly out.
²⁰ Smoke pours from his nostrils
like a boiling pot over reeds.
²¹ His breath lights coals;
a flame shoots from his mouth.
²² Power resides in his neck;
violence dances before him.
²³ The folds of his flesh stick together;
on him they are tough and unyielding.
²⁴ His heart is solid like a rock,
hard like a lower millstone.

LIFE PRESERVER

Why do good people suffer?
Job 38–41

The question of why good people suffer
is one that comes to mind as we read this book. Job
questioned God, and God responded to Job, beginning with this question: "Where were you when I laid
the earth's foundations? Tell me if you know" (Job
38:4). Then Job confessed that he knew God was
greater than a human being. Job admitted to talking
about things he didn't understand (Job 42:2-4).

Job was a good man who suffered unimaginable
loss. Like Job, we would love to know the answer to
tough questions. *Why did my friend get leukemia?
Why does my brother's friend suffer with seizures
that are so painful? I have a good friend whose
father lost his job. He's a good man. Why did that
need to happen to him?*

Suffering is part of living, growing, and dying.
It doesn't mean we're bad people. We don't live in
a perfect world. But we know that God is present
with us in the big mysterious world. God surrounds
us with loving people who are there to help us when
we suffer, when we have really big questions, and
when we're looking for answers. ◕

^h40:25 in Heb ⁱOr *his hopes*

²⁵ The divine beings dread his rising;
  they withdraw before his thrashing.
²⁶ The sword that touches him won't prevail;
  neither will the dart, spear, nor javelin.
²⁷ He treats iron as straw,
  bronze as rotten wood.
²⁸ Arrows can't make him flee;
  slingstones he turns to straw.
²⁹ He treats a club like straw;
  he laughs at the lance's rattle.
³⁰ His abdomen is like jagged pottery shards;
  its sharp edges leave a trail in the mud.
³¹ He causes the depths
  to churn like a boiling pot,
  stirs up the sea like a pot of scented oils,
³² leaves a bright wake behind him;
  the frothy deep seems white-haired.
³³ None on earth can compare to him;
  he is made to be without fear.
³⁴ He looks on all the proud;
  he is king over all proud beasts.

Job's second response

42 Job answered the LORD:
²I know you can do anything;
  no plan of yours
  can be opposed successfully.
³ You said,ʲ "Who is this darkening counsel
  without knowledge?"
  I have indeed spoken about
  things I didn't understand,
  wonders beyond my comprehension.
⁴ You said,ᵏ "Listen and I will speak;
  I will question you
  and you will inform me."
⁵ My ears had heard about you,
  but now my eyes have seen you.
⁶ Therefore, I relentˡ and find comfort
  on dust and ashes.

Epilogue

⁷After the LORD had spoken these words to Job, he said to Eliphaz from Teman, "I'm angry at you and your two friends because you haven't spoken about me correctly as did my servant Job. ⁸So now, take seven bulls and seven rams, go to my servant Job, and prepare an entirely burned offering for yourselves. Job my servant will pray for you, and I will

LIFE PRESERVER

Why doesn't God fix our problems like God fixed Job's problems? Job 42:10

At the end of Job's story, everything that Job had lost was restored. In fact, the Bible says his fortune was doubled. You may have a list of things you would like God to fix in your life or in the lives of people you know. The important thing to remember from Job's story is that God was present in his life and the lives of his friends. God is present in our lives today as well. We can't always know and see how God is working things out when bad things happen or we want a problem fixed. Sometimes we have to wait awhile. We might have to ask for help. At times we don't get the fairy-tale ending we want. But no matter what the outcome, God is always with us. We have the promise of God's love and presence no matter what problems we face. ◊

act favorably by not making fools of you because you didn't speak correctly, as did my servant Job."

⁹Eliphaz from Teman, Bildad from Shuah, and Zophar from Naamah did what the LORD told them; and the LORD acted favorably toward Job. ¹⁰Then the LORD changed Job's fortune when he prayed for his friends, and the LORD doubled all Job's earlier possessions. ¹¹All his brothers, sisters, and acquaintances came to him and ate food with him in his house. They comforted and consoled him concerning all the disaster the LORD had brought on him, and each one gave him a qesitahᵐ and a gold ring. ¹²Then the LORD blessed Job's latter days more than his former ones. He had fourteen thousand sheep, six thousand camels, one thousand yoke of oxen, and one thousand female donkeys. ¹³He also had seven sons and three daughters. ¹⁴He named one Jemimah,ⁿ a second Keziah,ᵒ and the third Keren-happuch.ᵖ ¹⁵No women in all the land were as beautiful as Job's daughters; and their father gave an inheritance to them along with their brothers. ¹⁶After this, Job lived 140 years and saw four generations of his children. ¹⁷Then Job died, old and satisfied.

ʲHeb lacks *You said.* ᵏHeb lacks *You said.* ˡThe verse is capable of several translations: *I despise* or *relent*, no direct object; *repent of* or *concerning dust and ashes.* ᵐA monetary unit ⁿ*Dove* ᵒ*Cinnamon* ᵖ*Jar for Dark Cosmetic*

Psalms

Psalms is a collection of songs used to worship God. Even though they were written thousands of years ago, they still inspire God's people to sing and pray today.

Words at the top of many psalms name the person said to have written or inspired that song. King David was named as the speaker for many of these lyrics. So was a worship leader named Asaph. A family known as "the Sons of Korah" was said to have composed others.

Some psalms contain prayers asking God for help. Other songs offer words of praise and thanks. Some songs express sadness about something that is wrong. Some songs were written for groups. Others were for individuals. The themes of these songs touch on almost everything that happens in our lives. They tell of all kinds of human emotions—happiness, sadness, peace, anger, fear, and confidence.

Some songs give musical details, such as "stringed instruments" (Ps 4) and "flutes" (Ps 5). You will sometimes see the word *Selah* after a sentence, but we don't know what that word means. We don't know the tunes used to sing these songs in ancient times, but the songs are filled with so many emotions that it seems likely they must have been sung to a wide variety of music. All are written as Hebrew poetry, which seldom rhymes words.

God's people all over the world and throughout history have read the Psalms to learn to sing and pray. This book helps us worship God with songs and words of praise! ◈

things YOU'LL DISCOVER

Psalms contains 150 songs and hymns written by many different people. Some are songs of praise and thanks. Others are songs asking for help or forgiveness. Psalms helps people talk with and worship God.

people YOU'LL MEET

David—Israel's second king and the named author of many psalms (Pss 3–41; 51–70; and more)

Asaph—a worship leader named as the author of many psalms (Pss 50; 73–81)

Sons of Korah—a priestly family named as the author of some psalms (Pss 42; 44–49; 84–85)

places YOU'LL GO

Israel, Jerusalem, Zion (a name for Jerusalem or Israel)

words YOU'LL REMEMBER

"The LORD is my shepherd. I lack nothing. He lets me rest in grassy meadows; he leads me to restful waters; he keeps me alive. He guides me in proper paths for the sake of his good name" (Ps 23:1-3).

BOOK I
(Psalms 1–41)

Psalm 1

¹ The truly happy person
   doesn't follow wicked advice,
   doesn't stand on the road of sinners,
   and doesn't sit with the disrespectful.
² Instead of doing those things,
   these persons
   love the Lᴏʀᴅ's Instruction,
   and they recite God's Instruction
   day and night!
³ They are like a tree
   replanted by streams of water,
   which bears fruit at just the right time
   and whose leaves don't fade.
   Whatever they do succeeds.

⁴ That's not true for the wicked!
   They are like dust
   that the wind blows away.
⁵ And that's why the wicked

will have no standing
   in the court of justice—
   neither will sinners
   in the assembly of the righteous.
⁶ The Lᴏʀᴅ is intimately acquainted
   with the way of the righteous,
   but the way of the wicked is destroyed.

did you **know?** Psalms contains material written by different writers over hundreds of years.

Psalm 2

¹ Why do the nations rant?
   Why do the peoples rave uselessly?
² The earth's rulers take their stand;
   the leaders scheme together
   against the Lᴏʀᴅ and
   against his anointed one.
³ "Come!" they say.
   "We will tear off their ropes
   and throw off their chains!"
⁴ The one who rules in heaven laughs;
   my Lord makes fun of them.

God's THOUGHTS ◆ My THOUGHTS

Happiness *Psalm 1*

Life is full of instructions. Some are instructions we live by at home and at school. Others help protect us and teach us how to make good choices. Sometimes we don't follow instructions and bad things happen. We might get hurt, hurt someone else, or experience negative results. Sometimes following instructions isn't fun or easy. It can be hard to say no when friends tell us to do the wrong thing and pressure us to go along with something we know isn't right.

Psalm 1 tells us that doing things God's way helps us to be truly happy. We have to remind ourselves every day that obeying God's Instruction is the best way to live. If you've ever had to remember something important—like words for a spelling test or your phone number— you might have repeated it over and over again so you wouldn't forget. That's what this psalm tells us to do with God's Instruction, so we can remember it and know how to live.

What are some instructions at home or at school that you think are really important?

How do you think God feels when we break God's Instruction?

⁵ But then God speaks to them angrily;
   then he terrifies them with his fury:
⁶ "I hereby appoint my king on Zion,
   my holy mountain!"

⁷ I will announce the Lᴏʀᴅ's decision:
   He said to me, "You are my son,
     today I have become your father.
⁸ Just ask me,
   and I will make the nations
     your possession;
   the far corners of the earth
     will be your property.
⁹ You will smash them with an iron rod;
   you will shatter them
     like a pottery jar."

¹⁰ So kings, wise up!
   Be warned, you rulers of the earth!
¹¹ Serve the Lᴏʀᴅ reverently—
   trembling, ¹²kiss his feetᵃ
   or else he will become angry,
   and your way will be destroyed
   because his anger ignites in an instant.

But all who take refuge in the Lᴏʀᴅ
   are truly happy!

Psalm 3
A psalm of David,
when he fled from his son Absalom.

¹ Lᴏʀᴅ, I have so many enemies!
   So many are standing against me.
² So many are talking about me:
   "Even God won't help him."   *Selah*ᵇ
³ But you, Lᴏʀᴅ, are my shield!
   You are my glory!
   You are the one who restores me.
⁴ I cry out loud to the Lᴏʀᴅ,
   and he answers me
     from his holy mountain.   *Selah*
⁵ I lie down, sleep, and wake up
   because the Lᴏʀᴅ helps me.
⁶ I won't be afraid of thousands of people
   surrounding me on all sides.

⁷ Stand up, Lᴏʀᴅ!
   Save me, my God!

did you know? When a new king was chosen as the leader of Israel, oil was poured over his head in front of the people. Some psalms about the king, including Psalm 2, were read during a ceremony to show the people and their enemies that God was on the king's side.

In fact, hit all my enemies on the jaw;
   shatter the teeth of the wicked!
⁸ Rescue comes from the Lᴏʀᴅ!
   May your blessing be on your people!
     Selah

Psalm 4
For the music leader. With stringed
instruments. A psalm of David.

¹ Answer me when I cry out,
   my righteous God!
   Set me free from my troubles!
   Have mercy on me!
   Listen to my prayer!

² How long, you people,
   will my reputation be insulted?
How long will you continue
   to love what is worthless
   and go after lies?   *Selah*
³ Know this: the Lᴏʀᴅ takes
   personal care of the faithful.
The Lᴏʀᴅ will hear me
   when I cry out to him.
⁴ So be afraid, and don't sin!
   Think hard about it in your bed
   and weep over it!   *Selah*
⁵ Bring righteous offerings,
   and trust the Lᴏʀᴅ!

⁶ Many people say,
   "We can't find goodness anywhere.
   The light of your face has left us, Lᴏʀᴅ!"ᶜ
⁷ But you have filled my heart with more joy
   than when their wheat and wine
     are everywhere!
⁸ I will lie down and fall asleep in peace
   because you alone, Lᴏʀᴅ,
     let me live in safety.

ᵃCorrection; Heb uncertain; MT *rejoice with trembling, kiss the son* (but with *son* in Aram, not Heb) ᵇHeb uncertain; probably a musical term ᶜCorrection; MT *Shine the light of your face on us,* Lᴏʀᴅ!

Psalm 5

For the music leader. For the flutes.
A psalm of David.

¹ Hear my words, Lord!
  Consider my groans!
² Pay attention to the sound of my cries,
    my king and my God,
    because I am praying to you!
³ Lord, in the morning you hear my voice.
  In the morning
    I lay it all out before you.
  Then I wait expectantly.
⁴ Because you aren't a God
  who enjoys wickedness;
    evil doesn't live with you.
⁵ Arrogant people won't last long
  in your sight;
    you hate all evildoers;
⁶ you destroy liars.
  The Lord despises people
  who are violent and dishonest.

⁷ But me? I will enter your house
    because of your abundant, faithful love;
  I will bow down
    at your holy temple,
    honoring you.

LIGHTHOUSE

PRAISE

Prayer, Praise, and Worship *Psalm 5:2-7*
Israel's king often had many possessions: a large
kingdom, a palace, wealth, weapons, horses, and
chariots. The king also had many responsibilities.
He had to make decisions that affected the lives of
everyone who lived in Israel. Wisdom doesn't come
easily, and the king knew he couldn't rule the kingdom alone. He had advisors, but he knew they only
had human wisdom. The king turned to God instead.
He began his days with prayer, praise, and worship
to God. The king knew God was his real source of
strength and wisdom. ◊

⁸ Lord, because of many enemies,
    please lead me in your righteousness.
  Make your way clear,
    right in front of me.
⁹ Because there's no truth
  in my enemies' mouths,
    all they have inside them is destruction.

Their throats are open graves;
    their tongues slick with talk.
¹⁰ Condemn them, God!
  Let them fail by their own plans.
  Throw them out for their many sins
    because they've rebelled against you.
¹¹ But let all who take refuge
  in you celebrate.
  Let them sing out loud forever!
Protect them
  so that all who love your name
  can rejoice in you.
¹² Because you, Lord, bless the righteous.
  You cover them with favor like a shield.

Psalm 6

For the music leader. On stringed
instruments. According to the eighth.[d]
A psalm of David.

¹ Please, Lord,
    don't punish me when you are angry;
    don't discipline me when you are furious.
² Have mercy on me, Lord,
    because I'm frail.
  Heal me, Lord,
    because my bones
    are shaking in terror!
³ My whole body[e] is completely terrified!
    But you, Lord! How long will this last?
⁴ Come back to me, Lord! Deliver me!
    Save me for the sake of your faithful love!
⁵ No one is going to praise you
    when they are dead.
  Who gives you thanks
    from the grave?[f]

⁶ I'm worn out from groaning.
    Every night, I drench my bed with tears;
    I soak my couch all the way through.
⁷ My vision fails because of my grief;
    it's weak because of all my distress.
⁸ Get away from me, all you evildoers,
    because the Lord has heard me crying!
⁹ The Lord has listened to my request.
  The Lord accepts my prayer.
¹⁰ All my enemies will be ashamed
    and completely terrified;
  they will be defeated
    and ashamed instantly.

---

[d] Perhaps a reference to an eight-string instrument; also in Ps 12 [e] Or *soul*; also in 6:4 [f] Heb *Sheol*

Psalm 7

A shiggayon[g] *of David, which he sang
to the* Lord *about Cush, a Benjaminite.*

[1] I take refuge in you, Lord, my God.
Save me from all who chase me!
Rescue me!

[2] Otherwise, they will rip me apart,
dragging me off
with no chance of rescue.

[3] Lord, my God, if I have done this—
if my hands have done
anything wrong,

[4] if I have repaid a friend with evil
or oppressed a foe for no reason—

[5] then let my enemy
not only chase but catch me,
trampling my life into the ground,
laying my reputation in the dirt.   *Selah*

[6] Get up, Lord; get angry!
Stand up against the fury of my foes!
Wake up, my God;[h]
you command that justice be done!

[7] Let the assembled peoples
surround you.
Rule them from on high![i]

[8] The Lord will judge the peoples.
Establish justice for me, Lord,
according to my righteousness
and according to my integrity.

[9] Please let the evil of the wicked
be over,
but set the righteous firmly in place
because you, the righteous God,
are the one who examines
hearts and minds.

[10] God is my shield;
he saves those whose heart is right.

[11] God is a righteous judge,
a God who is angry at evil[j]
every single day.

[12] If someone doesn't change their ways,
God will sharpen his sword,
will bend his bow,
will string an arrow.

[13] God has deadly weapons in store
for those who won't change;
he gets his flaming arrows ready!

[14] But look how the wicked hatch evil,
conceive trouble, give birth to lies!

[15] They make a pit, dig it all out,
and then fall right into the hole
that they've made!

[16] The trouble they cause
will come back on their own heads;
the violence they commit
will come down on their own skulls.

[17] But I will thank the Lord
for his righteousness;
I will sing praises
to the name of the Lord Most High.

Psalm 8

*For the music leader.
According to the Gittith.*[k] *A psalm of David.*

[1] Lord, our Lord, how majestic
is your name throughout the earth!
You made your glory
higher than heaven![l]

[2] From the mouths of nursing babies
you have laid a strong foundation
because of your foes,
in order to stop vengeful enemies.

[3] When I look up at your skies,
at what your fingers made—
the moon and the stars
that you set firmly in place—

[4] what are human beings
that you think about them;
what are human beings
that you pay attention to them?

[5] You've made them only slightly
less than divine,
crowning them with glory and grandeur.

[6] You've let them rule
over your handiwork,
putting everything under their feet—

[7] all sheep and all cattle,
the wild animals too,

[8] the birds in the sky,
the fish of the ocean,
everything that travels
the pathways of the sea.

[9] Lord, our Lord, how majestic
is your name throughout the earth!

---

[g]Perhaps *lament* [h]Or *for my sake* [i]Correction; MT *Come back to be exalted over them.* [j]Heb lacks *at evil.* [k]Perhaps the name of an instrument (Tg) or melody. LXX *About the winepresses;* or *About the Gittite;* also in Pss 81 and 84 [l]Correction; Heb uncertain

Psalm 9[m]

For the music leader. According to Muth-labben.[n] A psalm of David.

א ¹ I will thank you, Lord, with all my heart;
   I will talk about all your wonderful acts.
   ² I will celebrate and rejoice in you;
   I will sing praises to your name,
      Most High.

ב ³ When my enemies turn and retreat,
   they fall down and die
      right in front of you
   ⁴ because you have established justice
      for me and my claim,
   because you rule from the throne,
      establishing justice rightly.

ג ⁵ You've denounced the nations,
      destroyed the wicked.
   You've erased their names for all time.
   ⁶ Every enemy is wiped out,
      like something ruined forever.
   You've torn down their cities—
      even the memory of them is dead.

ה ⁷ But the Lord rules forever!
   He assumes his throne
      for the sake of justice.
   ⁸ He will establish justice
      in the world rightly;
   he will judge all people fairly.

ו ⁹ The Lord is a safe place
      for the oppressed—
   a safe place in difficult times.
   ¹⁰ Those who know your name trust you
   because you have not abandoned
      any who seek you, Lord.

ז ¹¹ Sing praises to the Lord,
      who lives in Zion!
   Proclaim his mighty acts
      among all people!
   ¹² Because the one who avenges bloodshed
      remembers those who suffer;
   the Lord hasn't forgotten
      their cries for help.

ח ¹³ Have mercy on me, Lord!
   Just look how I suffer
      because of those who hate me.
   But you are the one who brings me back
      from the very gates of death
   ¹⁴ so I can declare all your praises,
   so I can rejoice in your salvation
      in the gates of Daughter Zion.

ט ¹⁵ The nations have fallen
      into the hole they themselves made!
   Their feet are caught
      in the very net they themselves hid!
   ¹⁶ The Lord is famous for
      the justice he has done;
   it's his own doing that the wicked
      are trapped.
         Higgayon.[o] Selah

LIGHTHOUSE
AWESOME GOD

God Is Just *Psalm 9:16*

Justice is a word that many people associate with laws and courts. But it is similar in meaning to *fair*. People often use the word *fair* incorrectly. They say, "That's not fair!" when what they really mean is, "I didn't get what I wanted." But *fairness* or *justice* tells us what is right.

Psalm 9 says that God is famous for the justice God has done. God's justice includes actions that might appear harsh, such as the flood in which only Noah and his family were spared, the drowning of Pharaoh's army in the Reed Sea, and the destruction of the city of Jericho. But God's justice also provides for widows and orphans, people who are often overlooked or mistreated by other people. ◆

י ¹⁷ Let the wicked go straight to the grave,[p]
      the same for every nation
         that forgets God.

כ ¹⁸ Because the poor
      won't be forgotten forever,
   the hope of those who suffer
      won't be lost for all time.

---

[m]Ps 9 is an alphabetic acrostic poem (cf Ps 119) in Heb, with successive letters of the alphabet beginning every few lines, with only a few exceptions. Only ten letters are found in Ps 9; the sequence may be continued in Ps 10, suggesting that Pss 9–10 are a single poem. [n]Or *Almuth labben*; Heb uncertain; perhaps a reference to the melody; cf Pss 46:1; 48:14 [o]Heb uncertain; or *recitation* (see Pss 1:2; 19:14) or *melody* (see Ps 92:3) [p]Heb *Sheol*

19 Get up, LORD! Don't let people prevail!
Let the nations be judged before you.
20 Strike them with fear, LORD.
Let the nations know
they are only human. *Selah*

Psalm 10[q]

ל 1 Why do you stand so far away, LORD,
hiding yourself in troubling times?
2 Meanwhile, the wicked are proudly
in hot pursuit of those who suffer.
Let them get caught
in the very same schemes
they've thought up!

3 The wicked brag
about their body's[r] cravings;
the greedy reject the LORD, cursing.
4 At the peak of their wrath,
the wicked don't seek God:
There's no God—
that's what they are always thinking.
5 Their ways are always twisted.
Your rules are too lofty for them.
They snort at all their foes.
6 They think to themselves,
We'll never stumble.
We'll never encounter any resistance.
פ 7 Their mouths are filled
with curses, dishonesty, violence.
Under their tongues lie
troublemaking and wrongdoing.
8 They wait in a place perfect for ambush;[s]
from their hiding places
they kill innocent people;
ע their eyes spot those who are helpless.
9 They lie in ambush
in secret places,
like a lion in its lair.
They lie in ambush
so they can seize those who suffer!
They seize the poor, all right,
dragging them off in their nets.
10 Their helpless victims are crushed;
they collapse, falling prey
to the strength of the wicked.
11 The wicked think to themselves:
God has forgotten.
God has hidden his face.
God never sees anything!

ק 12 Get up, LORD!
Get your fist ready, God!
Don't forget the ones who suffer!
13 Why do the wicked reject God?
Why do they think to themselves
that you won't find out?
ר 14 But you do see!
You do see troublemaking and grief,
and you do something about it!
The helpless leave it all to you.
You are the orphan's helper.
ש 15 Break the arms of those
who are wicked and evil.
Seek out their wickedness
until there's no more to find.
16 The LORD rules forever and always!
The nations will vanish from his land.
ת 17 LORD, you listen to the desires
of those who suffer.
You steady their hearts;
you listen closely to them,
18 to establish justice
for the orphan and the oppressed,
so that people of the land
will never again be terrified.

Psalm 11

For the music leader. Of David.

1 I have taken refuge in the LORD.
So how can you say to me,[t]
"Flee to the hills like a bird
2 because the wicked
have already bent their bows;
they've already strung their arrows;
they are ready to secretly shoot
those whose heart is right"?
3 When the very bottom of things falls out,
what can a righteous person
possibly accomplish?

4 But the LORD is in his holy temple.
The LORD! His throne is in heaven.
His eyes see—
his vision examines all of humanity.

[q]Pss 9 and 10 contain part of an acrostic poem and might originally be one poem in Heb. [r]Or *soul's* [s]Heb uncertain [t]Or *my soul*

⁵ The Lᴏʀᴅ examines
both the righteous and the wicked;
his very being[u] hates
anyone who loves violence.
⁶ God will rain fiery coals and sulfur
on the wicked;
their cups will be filled
with nothing but a scorching hot wind
⁷ because the Lᴏʀᴅ is righteous!
He loves righteous deeds.
Those whose heart is right
will see God's face.[v]

Psalm 12

*For the music leader. According to the
Sheminith.[w] A psalm of David.*

¹ Help, Lᴏʀᴅ, because the godly are all gone;
the faithful have completely disappeared
from the human race!
² Everyone tells lies to everyone else;
they talk with slick speech
and divided hearts.
³ Let the Lᴏʀᴅ cut off all slick-talking lips
and every tongue that brags and brags,
⁴ that says, "We're unbeatable
with our tongues!
Who could get the best of us
with lips like ours?"

⁵ But the Lᴏʀᴅ says,
"Because the poor are oppressed,
because of the groans of the needy,
I'm now standing up.
I will provide the help
they are gasping for."[x]
⁶ The Lᴏʀᴅ's promises are pure,
like silver that's been refined in an oven,
purified seven times over!

⁷ You, Lᴏʀᴅ, will keep us,[y]
protecting us
from this generation forever.
⁸ The wicked roam all over the place,
while depravity is praised
by human beings.

Psalm 13

For the music leader. A song of David.

¹ How long will you forget me, Lᴏʀᴅ?
Forever?

How long will you hide your face
from me?
² How long will I be left to my own wits,
agony filling my heart? Daily?
How long will my enemy keep
defeating me?

³ Look at me!
Answer me, Lᴏʀᴅ my God!
Restore sight to my eyes!
Otherwise, I'll sleep the sleep of death,
⁴ and my enemy will say, "I won!"
My foes will rejoice over my downfall.

⁵ But I have trusted in your faithful love.
My heart will rejoice in your salvation.
⁶ Yes, I will sing to the Lᴏʀᴅ
because he has been good to me.

Many psalms are prayers asking God for help. Through these psalms, the people of God learn they can turn to God for help with anything.

Psalm 14

For the music leader. Of David.

¹ Fools say in their hearts, There is no God.
They are corrupt and do evil things;
not one of them does anything good.

² The Lᴏʀᴅ looks down
from heaven on humans
to see if anyone is wise,
to see if anyone seeks God,
³ but all of them have turned bad.
Everyone is corrupt.
No one does good—
not even one person!

⁴ Are they dumb, all these evildoers,
devouring my people
like they are eating bread
but never calling on the Lᴏʀᴅ?

⁵ Count on it:[z] they will be in utter panic
because God is with
the righteous generation.
⁶ You evildoers may humiliate
the plans of those who suffer,
but the Lᴏʀᴅ is their refuge.

---

[u]Or *soul* [v]Heb lacks *heart*, but see 11:2 and Pss 7:10; 32:11; 36:10. [w]Perhaps a reference to an eight-string instrument; also in Ps 6
[x]Heb uncertain [y]LXX; MT *keep them* [z]Or *There they will be*; cf 53:5

⁷ Let Israel's salvation come out of Zion!
  When the Lᴏʀᴅ changes
    his people's circumstances
      for the better,
  Jacob will rejoice;
  Israel will celebrate!

Psalm 15
A psalm of David.

¹ Who can live in your tent, Lᴏʀᴅ?
  Who can dwell on your holy mountain?
² The person who
    lives free of blame,
    does what is right,
    and speaks the truth sincerely;
³ who does no damage with their talk,
    does no harm to a friend,
    doesn't insult a neighbor;
⁴ someone who despises
    those who act wickedly,
    but who honors those
    who honor the Lᴏʀᴅ;
  someone who keeps their promise
    even when it hurts;
⁵ someone who doesn't lend money
    with interest,

who won't accept a bribe
  against any innocent person.
Whoever does these things
  will never stumble.

Psalm 16
*A miktam*ᵃ *of David.*

¹ Protect me, God,
  because I take refuge in you.
² I say to the Lᴏʀᴅ, "You are my Lord.
  Apart from you, I have nothing good."
³ Now as for the "holy ones" in the land,
    the "magnificent ones"
    that I was so happy about;
⁴ let their suffering increase because
    they hurried after a different god.ᵇ
  I won't participate in their blood offerings;
  I won't let their names cross my lips.
⁵ You, Lᴏʀᴅ, are my portion, my cup;
  you control my destiny.
⁶ The property lines have fallen
    beautifully for me;
  yes, I have a lovely home.

⁷ I will bless the Lᴏʀᴅ who advises me;
  even at night I am instructed

ᵃPerhaps *inscription* ᵇHeb uncertain in 16:3-4; Heb lacks *because* and *god* in 16:4.

Do What Is Right Psalm 15:1-4

You've probably heard the phrase "Do the right thing." When we're tempted to break the rules or disobey our parents or teachers, it can help to ask this question: "Am I doing what is right?"

Psalm 15:1 asks what kind of person is able to dwell or live with God. The answer is people who are free of blame, which means people who make good choices and do what is right. They tell the truth and don't hurt others with their words. They respect other people, keep their promises, and treat people fairly. The best way to live is to follow God's ways by living blamelessly, being truthful, and speaking kindly. This isn't always easy, but God will give us wisdom and help us do what is right.

Think of one kind thing you can say to a friend or family member and then tell them today.

How can you remember to do what is right?

in the depths of my mind.
⁸ I always put the Lord in front of me;
I will not stumble
because he is on my right side.
⁹ That's why my heart celebrates
and my mood is joyous;
yes, my whole body will rest in safety
¹⁰ because you won't abandon my life[c]
to the grave;[d]
you won't let your faithful follower
see the pit.

¹¹ You teach me the way of life.
In your presence is total celebration.
Beautiful things are always
in your right hand.

Psalm 17
A prayer of David.

¹ Listen to what's right, Lord;
pay attention to my cry!
Listen closely to my prayer;
it's spoken by lips that don't lie!
² My justice comes from you;
let your eyes see what is right!
³ You have examined my heart,
testing me at night.
You've looked me over closely,
but haven't found anything wrong.
My mouth doesn't sin.
⁴ But these other people's deeds?
I have avoided such violent ways
by the command from your lips.
⁵ My steps are set firmly on your paths;
my feet haven't slipped.

⁶ I cry out to you because you answer me.
So tilt your ears toward me now—
listen to what I'm saying!
⁷ Manifest your faithful love
in amazing ways
because you are the one
who saves those who take refuge in you,

saving them from their attackers
by your strong hand.
⁸ Watch me with the very pupil of your eye!
Hide me in the protection of your wings,
⁹ away from the wicked
who are out to get me,
away from my deadly enemies
who are all around me!
¹⁰ They have no pity;[e]
their mouths speak arrogantly.
¹¹ They track me down—
suddenly, they surround me!
They make their plans
to put me in the dirt.
¹² They are like a lion eager to rip its prey;
they are like a strong young lion
lying in wait.

¹³ Get up, Lord!
Confront them!
Bring them down!
Rescue my life from the wicked—
use your sword!
¹⁴ Rescue me from these people—
use your own hands, Lord!
Rescue me from these people
whose only possession
is their fleeting life.[f]
But fill the stomachs
of your cherished ones;
let their children be filled full
so that they have leftovers
enough for their babies.

¹⁵ But me? I will see your face
in righteousness;
when I awake, I will be filled full by
seeing your image.

Psalm 18[g]
For the music leader. Of David the Lord's servant, who spoke the words of this song to the Lord after the Lord delivered him from the power of all his enemies and from Saul.

¹ He said: I love you, Lord, my strength.
² The Lord is my solid rock,
my fortress, my rescuer.
My God is my rock—

did you know?
God is a solid rock, which means God gives protection. When enemies were chasing after someone, large rocks in the hills created good places to hide.

[c]Or *my soul* [d]Heb *Sheol* [e]Heb uncertain [f]Heb uncertain [g]This poem also occurs in 2 Sam 22 with some variations.

I take refuge in him!—
   he's my shield,
   my salvation's strength,
   my place of safety.
³ Because he is praiseworthy,[h]
   I cried out to the Lord,
   and I was saved from my enemies.
⁴ Death's cords were wrapped
   around me;
   rivers of wickedness terrified me.
⁵ The cords of the grave[i] surrounded me;
   death's traps held me tight.
⁶ In my distress I cried out to the Lord;
   I called to my God for help.
  God heard my voice from his temple;
   I called to him for help,
   and my call reached his ears.

⁷ The earth rocked and shook;
   the bases of the mountains
    trembled and reeled
   because of God's anger.
⁸ Smoke went up from God's nostrils;
   out of his mouth came
    a devouring fire;
   flaming coals blazed out
   in front of him!
⁹ God parted the skies and came down;
   thick darkness was beneath his feet.
¹⁰ God mounted the heavenly creatures
   and flew;
   he soared on the wings of the wind.
¹¹ God made darkness cloak him;
   his covering was dark water
   and dense cloud.
¹² God's clouds went ahead
   of the brightness before him;
   hail and coals of fire went too.
¹³ The Lord thundered in heaven;
   the Most High made his voice heard
   with hail and coals of fire.
¹⁴ God shot his arrows,
   scattering the enemy;
   he sent the lightning and threw them
   into confusion.
¹⁵ The seabeds were exposed;
   the earth's foundations were laid bare
   at your rebuke, Lord,
   at the angry blast of air coming
   from your nostrils.

¹⁶ From on high God reached down
   and grabbed me;
   he took me out of all that water.
¹⁷ God saved me
   from my powerful enemy,
   saved me from my foes,
   who were too much for me.
¹⁸ They came at me on the very day
   of my distress,
   but the Lord was my support.
¹⁹ He brought me out to wide-open spaces;
   he pulled me out safe
   because he is pleased with me.
²⁰ The Lord rewarded me
   for my righteousness;
   he restored me
   because my hands are clean,
²¹ because I have kept the Lord's ways.
   I haven't acted wickedly
   against my God.
²² All his rules are right in front of me;
   I haven't turned away from
   any of his laws.
²³ I have lived with integrity before him;
   I've kept myself from wrongdoing.
²⁴ And so the Lord restored me
   for my righteousness
   because my hands are clean in his eyes.

²⁵ You deal faithfully with the faithful;
   you show integrity
   toward the one who has integrity.
²⁶ You are pure toward the pure,
   but toward the crooked, you are tricky.
²⁷ You are the one who saves
   people who suffer
   and brings down those with proud eyes.
²⁸ You are the one who lights my lamp—
   the Lord my God illumines my darkness.
²⁹ With you I can charge into battle;
   with my God I can leap over a wall.
³⁰ God! His way is perfect;
   the Lord's word is tried and true.
  He is a shield
   for all who take refuge in him.

³¹ Now really, who is divine except the Lord?
   And who is a rock but our God?
³² Only God! The God
   who equips me with strength

Bet you can read this in 2 minutes. **Ready, set, go!**

---

and makes my way perfect,
³³ who makes my step as sure as the deer's,
who lets me stand securely
on the heights,
³⁴ who trains my hands for war
so my arms can bend a bronze bow.
³⁵ You've given me the shield
of your salvation;
your strong hand has supported me;
your help has made me great.
³⁶ You've let me walk fast and safe,
without even twisting an ankle.
³⁷ I chased my enemies and caught them!
I didn't come home
until I finished them off.
³⁸ I struck them down;
they couldn't get up again;
they fell under my feet.
³⁹ You equipped me with strength for war;
you brought my adversaries down
underneath me.
⁴⁰ You made my enemies turn tail from me;
I destroyed my foes.
⁴¹ They cried for help,
but there was no one to save them.
They cried for help to the Lord,
but he wouldn't answer them.
⁴² I crushed them
like dust blown away by the wind;
I threw them out
like mud dumped in the streets.
⁴³ You delivered me from struggles
with many people;
you appointed me the leader
of many nations.
Strangers come to serve me.
⁴⁴ After hearing about me, they obey me;
foreigners grovel before me.
⁴⁵ Foreigners lose their nerve;
they come trembling
out of their fortresses.^j
⁴⁶ The Lord lives! Bless God, my rock!
Let the God of my salvation be lifted high!
⁴⁷ This is the God who avenges on my behalf,
who subdues people before me,
⁴⁸ who delivers me from my enemies.
Yes, you lifted me high
above my adversaries;
you delivered me from violent people.

⁴⁹ That's why I thank you, Lord,
in the presence of the nations.
That's why I sing praises to your name.
⁵⁰ You are the one who gives great victories
to your king,
who shows faithful love
to your anointed one—
to David and to his descendants forever.

Psalm 19

For the music leader. A psalm of David.
¹ Heaven is declaring God's glory;
the sky is proclaiming his handiwork.
² One day gushes the news to the next,
and one night informs another
what needs to be known.
³ Of course, there's no speech, no words—
their voices can't be heard—
⁴ but their sound^k extends
throughout the world;
their words reach the ends of the earth.

God has made a tent in heaven for the sun.
⁵ The sun is like a groom
coming out of his honeymoon suite;
like a warrior,
it thrills at running its course.
⁶ It rises in one end of the sky;
its circuit is complete at the other.
Nothing escapes its heat.

⁷ The Lord's Instruction is perfect,
reviving one's very being.^l
The Lord's laws are faithful,
making naive people wise.
⁸ The Lord's regulations are right,
gladdening the heart.
The Lord's commands are pure,
giving light to the eyes.
⁹ Honoring the Lord is correct,
lasting forever.
The Lord's judgments are true.
All of these are righteous!
¹⁰ They are more desirable than gold—
than tons of pure gold!
They are sweeter than honey—
even dripping off the honeycomb!
¹¹ No doubt about it:
your servant is enlightened by them;

^jOr *prisons* ^kLXX, Vulg, Sym; MT *line or string* ^lOr *soul*

there is great reward in keeping them.
¹² But can anyone know
what they've accidentally done wrong?
Clear me of any unknown sin
¹³ and save your servant from willful sins.
Don't let them rule me.
Then I'll be completely blameless;
I'll be innocent of great wrongdoing.

Memorize
Ps 19:14
¹⁴ Let the words
of my mouth
and the meditations of my heart
be pleasing to you,
Lord, my rock and my redeemer.

Psalm 20

For the music leader. A psalm of David.

¹ I pray that the Lord answers you
whenever you are in trouble.
Let the name of Jacob's God protect you.
² Let God send help to you
from the sanctuary

and support you from Zion.
³ Let God recall your many grain offerings;
let him savor your
entirely burned offerings. *Selah*
⁴ Let God grant what is in your heart
and fulfill all your plans.
⁵ Then we will rejoice
that you've been helped.
We will fly our flags
in the name of our God.
Let the Lord fulfill all your requests!

⁶ Now I know that the Lord saves
his anointed one;
God answers his anointed one
from his heavenly sanctuary,
answering with mighty acts of salvation
achieved by his strong hand.
⁷ Some people trust in chariots,
others in horses;
but we praise the Lord's name.
⁸ They will collapse and fall,
but we will stand up straight and strong.

God's THOUGHTS ◆ My THOUGHTS

God Made Everything   *Psalm 19:1-6*

There are many passages in the Bible that tell about God's creation. God made everything there is, including us. Think about how beautiful the sky can be—with colorful sunsets, fast-moving clouds, arching rainbows, and shooting stars. The world is an amazing place. Each day has its own unique moments for us to marvel at God's beautiful work.

Look at the creation story in Genesis 1. Think of the ways God's creation gives praise back to God. How does the rising and setting of the sun make you feel? When you hear the wind blowing through the trees, do you hear songs of praise? When you see yourself in the mirror, do you think about how you are wonderfully made? Even if your body doesn't quite look or work like somebody else's, you are special to God in every way. You are unique. You are God's creation.

Find time every day to thank God for all that God has made, including you!

What is your favorite part of creation?

Write a thank-you note to God, giving thanks for creating you just as you are.

⁹ Lord, save the king!
   Let him answer us when we cry out!

Psalm 21

For the music leader. A psalm of David.

¹ The king celebrates your strength, Lord;
   look how happy he is
      about your saving help!
² You've given him what his heart desires;
   you haven't denied
      what his lips requested.   *Selah*
³ You bring rich blessings right to him;
   you put a crown of pure gold
      on his head.
⁴ He asked you for life,
   and you gave it to him, all right—
      long days, forever and always!
⁵ The king's reputation is great
   because of your saving help;
   you've conferred on him
      glory and grandeur.
⁶ You grant him blessings forever;
   you make him happy
      with the joy of your presence.
⁷ Because the king trusts the Lord,
   and because of the Most High's
      faithful love,
      he will not stumble.

⁸ Your hand will catch all your enemies;
   your strong hand will catch
      all who hate you.
⁹ When you appear, Lord,
   you will light them up
      like an oven on fire.
   God will eat them whole in his anger;
      fire will devour them.
¹⁰ You will destroy their offspring
   from the land;
   destroy their descendants
      from the human race.
¹¹ Because they sought to do you harm,
   they devised a wicked plan—
      but they will fail!
¹² Because you will make them
   turn and run
   when you aim your bow
      straight at their faces!

¹³ Be exalted, Lord, in your strength!
   We will sing and praise your power!

Psalm 22

For the music leader. According to the
"Doe of Dawn." A psalm of David.

¹ My God! My God,
   why have you left me all alone?
   Why are you so far from saving me—
      so far from my anguished groans?
² My God, I cry out during the day,
   but you don't answer;
   even at nighttime I don't stop.
³ You are the holy one, enthroned.
   You are Israel's praise.
⁴ Our ancestors trusted you—
   they trusted you and you rescued them;
   ⁵ they cried out to you
      and they were saved;
   they trusted you
      and they weren't ashamed.

⁶ But I'm just a worm, less than human;
   insulted by one person,
      despised by another.
⁷ All who see me make fun of me—
   they gape, shaking their heads:
   ⁸ "He committed himself to the Lord,
      so let God rescue him;
   let God deliver him
      because God likes him so much."
⁹ But you are the one who pulled me
   from the womb,
   placing me safely at my mother's breasts.
¹⁰ I was thrown on you from birth;
   you've been my God
   since I was in my mother's womb.
¹¹ Please don't be far from me,
   because trouble is near
      and there's no one to help.

¹² Many bulls surround me;
   mighty bulls from Bashan encircle me.
¹³ They open their mouths at me
   like a lion ripping and roaring!
¹⁴ I'm poured out like water.
   All my bones have fallen apart.
      My heart is like wax;
      it melts inside me.
¹⁵ My strength is dried up
   like a piece of broken pottery.
   My tongue sticks
      to the roof of my mouth;
   you've set me down
      in the dirt of death.

¹⁶ Dogs surround me;
    a pack of evil people
      circle me like a lion—
    oh, my poor hands and feet!
¹⁷ I can count all my bones!
    Meanwhile, they just stare at me,
      watching me.
¹⁸ They divvy up my garments
    among themselves;
    they cast lots for my clothes.

¹⁹ But you, Lᴏʀᴅ! Don't be far away!
    You are my strength!
    Come quick and help me!
²⁰ Deliver me[m] from the sword.
    Deliver my life from the power of the dog.
²¹ Save me from the mouth of the lion.
    From the horns of the wild oxen
    you have answered me!

²² I will declare your name
    to my brothers and sisters;
    I will praise you in the very center
      of the congregation!
²³ All of you who revere the Lᴏʀᴅ—praise him!
    All of you who are Jacob's descendants—
      honor him!
    All of you who are all Israel's offspring—
      stand in awe of him!
²⁴ Because he didn't despise or detest
    the suffering of the one who suffered—
    he didn't hide his face from me.
    No, he listened when I cried out to him
      for help.

²⁵ I offer praise in the great congregation
    because of you;
    I will fulfill my promises
    in the presence of those who honor God.
²⁶ Let all those who are suffering
    eat and be full!
    Let all who seek the Lᴏʀᴅ praise him!
    I pray your hearts live forever!
²⁷ Every part of the earth
    will remember and come back to the Lᴏʀᴅ;
    every family among all the nations
    will worship you.
²⁸ Because the right to rule
    belongs to the Lᴏʀᴅ,
    he rules all nations.

²⁹ Indeed, all the earth's powerful
    will worship him;[n]
    all who are descending to the dust
    will kneel before him;
    my being also lives for him.[o]
³⁰ Future descendants will serve him;
    generations to come will be told
      about my Lord.
³¹ They will proclaim God's righteousness
    to those not yet born,
    telling them what God has done.

Psalm 23

A psalm of David.

¹ The Lᴏʀᴅ is my shepherd.
    I lack nothing.
² He lets me rest in grassy meadows;
    he leads me to restful waters;
      ³ he keeps me [p] alive.
He guides me in proper paths
    for the sake of his good name.

⁴ Even when I walk
    through the darkest valley,
    I fear no danger because you are with me.
Your rod and your staff—
    they protect me.

⁵ You set a table for me
    right in front of my enemies.
You bathe my head in oil;
    my cup is so full it spills over!
⁶ Yes, goodness and faithful love

LIFE PRESERVER

Why is Psalm 23 so popular?
Psalm 23

Of all the psalms, Psalm 23 is probably the most familiar. Many people have memorized the words. This psalm is often read for people who are experiencing hard things.

    People like Psalm 23 because it's simple and comforting. It reminds us that God leads us, keeps us alive, and guides us like a shepherd. Even when we face dark or scary times or believe enemies are close by, Psalm 23 reminds us that God is with us and will protect us. ◆

---

[m]Or *my soul*; also in 22:29   [n]Correction; MT *All the earth's powerful have eaten and will worship.*   [o]Correction with LXX; Heb uncertain   [p]Or *my soul*

will pursue me all the days of my life,
and I will live[q] in the Lord's house
as long as I live.

Psalm 24
A psalm of David.

[1] The earth is the Lord's and everything in it,
the world and its inhabitants too.
[2] Because God is the one
who established it on the seas;
God set it firmly on the waters.

[3] Who can ascend the Lord's mountain?
Who can stand in his holy sanctuary?
[4] Only the one with clean hands
and a pure heart;
the one who hasn't made false promises,
the one who hasn't sworn dishonestly.
[5] That kind of person receives blessings
from the Lord
and righteousness from the God who saves.
[6] And that's how things are
with the generation that seeks him—
that seeks the face of Jacob's God.[r] *Selah*

[7] Mighty gates: lift up your heads!
Ancient doors: rise up high!
So the glorious king can enter!
[8] Who is this glorious king?
The Lord—strong and powerful!
The Lord—powerful in battle!
[9] Mighty gates: lift up your heads!
Ancient doors: rise up high!
So the glorious king can enter!
[10] Who is this glorious king?
The Lord of heavenly forces—
he is the glorious king! *Selah*

Psalm 25[s]
Of David.

א [1] I offer my life[t] to you, Lord.
ב [2] My God, I trust you.
Please don't let me be put to shame!
Don't let my enemies rejoice over me!
ג [3] For that matter,
don't let anyone who hopes in you
be put to shame;

instead, let those who are treacherous
without excuse be put to shame.

ד [4] Make your ways known to me, Lord;
teach me your paths.
ה [5] Lead me in your truth—teach it to me—
because you are the God who saves me.
ו I put my hope in you all day long.
ז [6] Lord, remember your compassion
and faithful love—
they are forever!
ח [7] But don't remember the sins
of my youth or my wrongdoing.
Remember me only
according to your faithful love
for the sake of your goodness, Lord.

ט [8] The Lord is good and does the right thing;
he teaches sinners which way
they should go.
י [9] God guides the weak to justice,
teaching them his way.
כ [10] All the Lord's paths are loving and faithful
for those who keep his covenant and laws.
ל [11] Please, for the sake of your good name,
Lord, forgive my sins, which are many!

מ [12] Where are the ones who honor the Lord?
God will teach them which path to take.
נ [13] They will live a good life,
and their descendants
will possess the land.
ס [14] The Lord counsels those who honor him;
he makes his covenant known to them.
ע [15] My eyes are always looking to the Lord
because he will free my feet from the net.

פ [16] Turn to me, God, and have mercy on me
because I'm alone and suffering.
צ [17] My heart's troubles keep getting bigger—
set me free from my distress!
[18] Look at my suffering and trouble—
forgive all my sins!
ר [19] Look at how many enemies I have
and how violently they hate me!
ש [20] Please protect my life! Deliver me!
Don't let me be put to shame
because I take refuge in you.
[21] Let integrity and virtue guard me
because I hope in you.

𝄇 ²² Please, God, save Israel
from all its troubles!

Psalm 26
Of David.

¹ Establish justice for me, Lord,
because I have walked with integrity.
I've trusted the Lord without wavering.
² Examine me, Lord; put me to the test!
Purify^u my mind^v and my heart.
³ Because your faithful love
is right in front of me—
I walk in your truth!
⁴ I don't spend time with people up to no good;
I don't keep company with liars.
⁵ I detest the company of evildoers,
and I don't sit with wicked people.
⁶ I wash my hands—they are innocent!
I walk all around your altar, Lord,
⁷ proclaiming out loud my thanks,
declaring all your wonderful deeds!
⁸ I love the beauty^w of your house, Lord;
I love the place where your glory resides.

⁹ Don't gather me^x up with the sinners,
taking my life along with violent people
¹⁰ in whose hands are evil schemes,
whose strong hands are full of bribes.
¹¹ But me? I walk with integrity.
Save me! Have mercy on me!

¹² My feet now stand on level ground.
I will bless the Lord
in the great congregation.

Psalm 27
Of David.

¹ The Lord is my light and my salvation.
Should I fear anyone?
The Lord is a fortress protecting my life.
Should I be frightened of anything?
² When evildoers come at me
trying to eat me up—
it's they, my foes and my enemies,
who stumble and fall!
³ If an army camps against me,
my heart won't be afraid.
If war comes up against me,
I will continue to trust in this:

⁴ I have asked one thing from the Lord—
it's all I seek:
to live in the Lord's house
all the days of my life,
seeing the Lord's beauty
and constantly adoring his temple.
⁵ Because he will shelter me
in his own dwelling
during troubling times;
he will hide me in a secret place
in his own tent;
he will set me up high, safe on a rock.

⁶ Now my head is higher
than the enemies surrounding me,
and I will offer sacrifices in God's tent—
sacrifices with shouts of joy!
I will sing and praise the Lord.
⁷ Lord, listen to my voice when I cry out—
have mercy on me and answer me!
⁸ Come, my heart says, seek God's face.^y
Lord, I do seek your face!
⁹ Please don't hide it from me!
Don't push your servant aside angrily—
you have been my help!
God who saves me,
don't neglect me!
Don't leave me all alone!
¹⁰ Even if my father and mother
left me all alone,
the Lord would take me in.

SAILBOAT

I'm Safe

God Is Our Fortress *Psalm 27:1-3*

In ancient times, cities were often completely surrounded by a tall, thick wall to protect the people inside. Sometimes this wall had guard towers at the corners, where soldiers would watch for enemy attacks. Some citizens actually lived on farms outside the walls. When soldiers saw an enemy approaching, they would send out a warning so the farmers would know to come inside the city walls. Anyone attacking the city had to climb over the walls to get inside. This put anyone attacking the city in a dangerous position because they were in clear sight of the soldiers' arrows. Just like the walls that surrounded ancient cities, God is our fortress, surrounding us with love and care, and defending us against evil. ◆

---

^uLXX or *investigate* ^vOr *kidneys* ^wLXX; MT *the dwelling of your house* ^xOr *my soul* ^yCorrection; MT *My heart says to/ of you . . . see my face!*

¹¹ LORD, teach me your way;
  because of my opponents,
    lead me on a good path.
¹² Don't give me over
  to the desires of my enemies,
    because false witnesses
      and violent accusers
    have taken their stand against me.
¹³ But I have sure faith
    that I will experience
      the LORD's goodness
    in the land of the living!

¹⁴ Hope in the LORD!
  Be strong! Let your heart take courage!
    Hope in the LORD!

Psalm 28
Of David.

¹ I cry out to you, LORD.
  You are my rock; don't refuse to hear me.
    If you won't talk to me,

  I'll be just like those
    going down to the pit.
² Listen to my request for mercy
  when I cry out to you,
    when I lift up my hands
      to your holy inner sanctuary.
³ Don't drag me off with the wicked
    and those who do evil;
  the type who talk nice to their friends
    while evil thoughts are in their hearts!
⁴ Pay them back for what they've done!
  Pay them back for their evil deeds!
  Pay them back for their handiwork!
  Give back to them
    exactly what they deserve!
⁵ Because they have no regard
    for what the LORD has done,
  no regard for his handiwork,
    God will tear them down and never rebuild!

⁶ Bless the LORD
    because he has listened
      to my request for mercy!

God Hears Our Prayers *Psalm 28:6-9*

God hears us every time we pray. God hears our words and knows what's in our hearts. God knows what we want and what we need. Prayer sometimes sounds like a conversation between us and God. We talk, and God listens. We can also listen for God to speak to us.

We can pray about anything and everything. We can ask for health, strength, wisdom, and courage. We can tell God how we feel no matter what our feelings may be. We can praise God for all God has done for us and in the world. We can give thanks for the blessings in our lives.

We don't need to use big, fancy words when we pray. God wants to hear from us in our own unique ways. So we can pray however we like with whatever words we know. One way to pray is to write down our prayers in a notebook. We can go back later and read earlier prayers to see how things may have changed or to know how to continue praying. No matter how we pray or what we pray about, God hears our every word!

What are some things you often pray about?

Write a prayer to God in your own words telling God whatever you would like to say.

⁷ The Lᴏʀᴅ is my strength and my shield.
  My heart trusts him.
    I was helped, my heart rejoiced,
    and I thank him with my song.
⁸ The Lᴏʀᴅ is his people's strength;
  he is a fortress of protection
    for his anointed one.
⁹ Save your people, God!
  Bless your possession!
    Shepherd them
    and carry them for all time!

Psalm 29
A psalm of David.

¹ You, divine beings! Give to the Lᴏʀᴅ—
  give to the Lᴏʀᴅ glory and power!
² Give to the Lᴏʀᴅ the glory due his name!
  Bow down to the Lᴏʀᴅ in holy splendor!

³ The Lᴏʀᴅ's voice is over the waters;
  the glorious God thunders;
    the Lᴏʀᴅ is over the mighty waters.
⁴ The Lᴏʀᴅ's voice is strong;
  the Lᴏʀᴅ's voice is majestic.
⁵ The Lᴏʀᴅ's voice breaks cedar trees—
  yes, the Lᴏʀᴅ shatters
    the cedars of Lebanon.
⁶ He makes Lebanon jump around
  like a young bull,
    makes Sirion jump around
    like a young wild ox.
⁷ The Lᴏʀᴅ's voice unleashes fiery flames;
⁸ the Lᴏʀᴅ's voice shakes the wilderness—
  yes, the Lᴏʀᴅ shakes
    the wilderness of Kadesh.
⁹ The Lᴏʀᴅ's voice convulses the oaks,
  strips the forests bare,
    but in his temple everyone shouts, "Glory!"
¹⁰ The Lᴏʀᴅ sits enthroned
  over the floodwaters;
    the Lᴏʀᴅ sits enthroned—king forever!

¹¹ Let the Lᴏʀᴅ give strength to his people!
  Let the Lᴏʀᴅ bless his people with peace!

Psalm 30
A psalm. A song for the temple dedication. Of David.

¹ I exalt you, Lᴏʀᴅ,
  because you pulled me up;

---

  you didn't let my enemies
    celebrate over me.
² Lᴏʀᴅ, my God, I cried out to you for help,
  and you healed me.
³ Lᴏʀᴅ, you brought meᶻ up from the grave,ᵃ
  brought me back to life from among
    those going down to the pit.

⁴ You who are faithful to the Lᴏʀᴅ,
  sing praises to him;
    give thanks to his holy name!
⁵ His anger lasts for only a second,
  but his favor lasts a lifetime.
  Weeping may stay all night,
    but by morning, joy!

⁶ When I was comfortable, I said,
  "I will never stumble."
⁷ Because it pleased you, Lᴏʀᴅ,
  you made me a strong mountain.
  But then you hid your presence.
  I was terrified.
⁸ I cried out to you, Lᴏʀᴅ.
  I begged my Lord for mercy:
⁹ "What is to be gained by my spilled blood,
  by my going down into the pit?
  Does dust thank you?
  Does it proclaim your faithfulness?
¹⁰ Lᴏʀᴅ, listen and have mercy on me!
  Lᴏʀᴅ, be my helper!"

¹¹ You changed my mourning into dancing.
  You took off my funeral clothes
    and dressed me up in joy
¹² so that my whole being
  might sing praises to you and never stop.
  Lᴏʀᴅ, my God,
  I will give thanks to you forever.

did you know? The people of ancient Israel believed water was underneath all the land. They believed there was a shield above the sky that protected them from the heavens filled with water. As king of the flood, God protected them from the waters that surrounded them.

Psalm 31
For the music leader. A psalm of David.

¹ I take refuge in you, Lᴏʀᴅ.
  Please never let me be put to shame.

ᶻOr *my soul* ᵃHeb *Sheol*

Rescue me by your righteousness!
² Listen closely to me!
Deliver me quickly;
be a rock that protects me;
be a strong fortress that saves me!
³ You are definitely my rock and my fortress.
Guide me and lead me
for the sake of your good name!
⁴ Get me out of this net that's been set for me
because you are my protective fortress.
⁵ I entrust my spirit into your hands;
you, Lord, God of faithfulness—
you have saved me.
⁶ I hate those who embrace
what is completely worthless.
I myself trust the Lord.
⁷ I rejoice and celebrate in your faithful love
because you saw my suffering—
you were intimately acquainted
with my deep distress.
⁸ You didn't hand me over to the enemy,
but set my feet in wide-open spaces.

⁹ Have mercy on me, Lord,
because I'm depressed.
My vision fails because of my grief,
as do my spirit and my body.
¹⁰ My life is consumed with sadness;
my years are consumed with groaning.

Strength fails me
because of my suffering;[b]
my bones dry up.
¹¹ I'm a joke to all my enemies,
still worse to my neighbors.
I scare my friends,
and whoever sees me in the street
runs away!
¹² I am forgotten, like I'm dead,
completely out of mind;
I am like a piece of pottery, destroyed.
¹³ Yes, I've heard all the gossiping,
terror all around;
so many gang up together against me,
they plan to take my life!

¹⁴ But me? I trust you, Lord!
I affirm, "You are my God."
¹⁵ My future is in your hands.
Don't hand me over to my enemies,
to all who are out to get me!
¹⁶ Shine your face on your servant;
save me by your faithful love!
¹⁷ Lord, don't let me be put to shame
because I have cried out to you.
Let the wicked be put to shame;
let them be silenced in death's domain![c]
¹⁸ Let their lying lips be shut up
whenever they speak arrogantly
against the righteous
with pride and contempt!
¹⁹ How great is the goodness
that you've reserved
for those who honor you,
that you commit to those
who take refuge in you—
in the sight of everyone!
²⁰ You hide them
in the shelter of your wings,[d]
safe from human scheming.
You conceal them in a shelter,
safe from accusing tongues.

²¹ Bless the Lord,
because he has wondrously revealed
his faithful love to me
when I was like a city under siege!
²² When I was panicked, I said,
"I'm cut off from your eyes!"
But you heard my request for mercy
when I cried out to you for help.

UMBRELLA
GRIEF

Depression *Psalm 31:9, 24*
Depression is more than feeling sad for a few days. A depressed person feels like they have a heavy weight on their heart. They're exhausted but have trouble sleeping. They may lose their energy or their appetite. They may cry over things that seem small and spend a lot of time alone. Depression can last for weeks, months, and sometimes years.

The person praying in Psalm 31:9 experienced depression. Stressful events can lead to depression. Ancient people didn't have access to counseling or the medicine we have today that can help with depression. But with or without those things, we can trust in God. 💧

---

b LXX, Syr; MT *my sin*   c Heb *Sheol*   d Correction; see Ps 61:5; MT *in the hiding place of your face*

23 All you who are faithful, love the Lord!
  The Lord protects those who are loyal,
    but he pays the proud back
      to the fullest degree.
24 All you who wait for the Lord,
  be strong and let your heart take courage.

Psalm 32

A maskil[e] of David.

1 The one whose wrongdoing is forgiven,
  whose sin is covered over, is truly happy!
2 The one the Lord doesn't consider guilty—
  in whose spirit there is no dishonesty—
    that one is truly happy!

3 When I kept quiet, my bones wore out;
  I was groaning all day long—
    every day, every night!—
4 because your hand was heavy upon me.
  My energy was sapped as if in a
    summer drought.   *Selah*
5 So I admitted my sin to you;
  I didn't conceal my guilt.
    "I'll confess my sins to the Lord,"
      is what I said.
  Then you removed the guilt of my sin.
                                    Selah
6 That's why all the faithful should pray
  to you during troubled times,[f]
    so that a great flood of water
      won't reach them.
7 You are my secret hideout!
  You protect me from trouble.
    You surround me with songs of rescue!
                                    Selah

8 I will instruct you and teach you
  about the direction you should go.
    I'll advise you and keep my eye on you.
9 Don't be like some senseless
  horse or mule,
    whose movement must be controlled
      with a bit and a bridle.[g]
    Don't be anything like that![h]
10 The pain of the wicked is severe,
  but faithful love surrounds
    the one who trusts the Lord.
11 You who are righteous,
  rejoice in the Lord and be glad!

All you whose hearts are right,
  sing out in joy!

Psalm 33

1 All you who are righteous,
  shout joyfully to the Lord!
    It's right for those who do right
      to praise God.
2 Give thanks to the Lord with the lyre!
  Sing praises to him
    with the ten-stringed harp!
3 Sing to him a new song!
  Play your best with joyful shouts!
4 Because the Lord's word is right,
  his every act is done in good faith.
5 He loves righteousness and justice;
  the Lord's faithful love
    fills the whole earth.
6 The skies were made by the Lord's word,
  all their starry multitude
    by the breath of his mouth.
7 He gathered the ocean waters into a heap;
  he put the deep seas into storerooms.
8 All the earth honors the Lord;
  all the earth's inhabitants
    stand in awe of him.
9 Because when he spoke, it happened!
  When he commanded, there it was!

10 The Lord overrules what the nations plan;
  he frustrates
    what the peoples intend to do.
11 But the Lord's plan
  stands forever;
    what he intends
      to do lasts from one generation
        to the next.
12 The nation whose God is the Lord,
  the people whom God has chosen
    as his possession,
      is truly happy!
13 The Lord looks down from heaven;
  he sees every human being.
14 From his dwelling place God observes
  all who live on earth.
15 God is the one who made
  all their hearts,
    the one who knows
      everything they do.

Memorize
Ps 33:11

¹⁶ Kings aren't saved by the strength
  of their armies;
  warriors aren't rescued
    by how much power they have.
¹⁷ A warhorse is a bad bet for victory;
  it can't save despite its great strength.
¹⁸ But look here: the LORD's eyes watch
  all who honor him,
  all who wait for his faithful love,
  ¹⁹ to deliver their lives^i from death
    and keep them alive during a famine.

²⁰ We put our hope in the LORD.
  He is our help and our shield.
²¹ Our heart rejoices in God
  because we trust his holy name.
²² LORD, let your faithful love surround us
  because we wait for you.

Psalm 34

Of David, when he pretended
to be crazy before Abimelech,
who banished him so that he left.

א ¹ I will bless the LORD at all times;
  his praise will always be in my mouth.

ב ² I^k praise the LORD—
  let the suffering listen and rejoice.
ג ³ Magnify the LORD with me!
  Together let us lift his name up high!

ד ⁴ I sought the LORD and he answered me.
  He delivered me from all my fears.
ה ⁵ Those who look to God will shine;
  their faces are never ashamed.
ז ⁶ This suffering person cried out:
  the LORD listened and saved him
    from every trouble.
ח ⁷ On every side, the LORD's messenger
  protects those who honor God;
  and he delivers them.
ט ⁸ Taste and see how good the LORD is!
  The one who takes refuge in him
    is truly happy!
י ⁹ You who are the LORD's holy ones,
  honor him,
  because those who honor him
  don't lack a thing.
כ ¹⁰ Even strong young lions
  go without and get hungry,
  but those who seek the LORD
  lack no good thing.

^i Or *souls*; also in 33:20   ^j Ps 34 is an alphabetic acrostic poem; see the note at Pss 9–10.   ^k Or *my soul*; also in 34:22

God's ◆ My
THOUGHTS THOUGHTS

God Is Our Supply   *Psalm 34:8-10*

We might read Psalm 34 and think it's talking about food or material possessions. God wants us to remember that all good things in life come from God. People who trust in God are able to be truly happy because they know God will take care of all their needs.

Being without God is like going without food. Just like food feeds our bodies and gives us strength to grow, following God's ways feeds our whole being and helps us grow spiritually. We feed our spiritual lives by learning God's Instruction, joining others in worship, and spending time with friends and family who also follow God. It's hard to grow in a relationship with God without doing these things. When we grow spiritually, we come to see more and more how God provides for us. God wants us to focus on loving God and loving others.

What good things do you have in your life?

In what ways do you feed your spiritual life?

ל ¹¹ Come, children, listen to me.
 Let me teach you how to honor the Lord:
מ ¹² Do you love life;
 do you relish the chance
  to enjoy good things?
נ ¹³ Then you must keep your tongue
 from evil
  and keep your lips from speaking lies!
ס ¹⁴ Turn away from evil! Do good!
 Seek peace and go after it!

ע ¹⁵ The Lord's eyes watch the righteous,
 his ears listen to their cries for help.
פ ¹⁶ But the Lord's face is set against
 those who do evil,
  to eliminate even the memory of them
   from the earth.
צ ¹⁷ When the righteous cry out,
 the Lord listens;
  he delivers them from all their troubles.
ק ¹⁸ The Lord is close to the brokenhearted;
 he saves those whose spirits are crushed.

ר ¹⁹ The righteous have many problems,
 but the Lord delivers them
  from every one.
ש ²⁰ He protects all their bones;
 not even one will be broken.
ת ²¹ But just one problem will kill the wicked,
 and those who hate the righteous
  will be held responsible.
²² The Lord saves his servants' lives;
 all those who take refuge in him
  won't be held responsible for anything.

Psalm 35
Of David.

¹ Lord, argue with those who argue with me;
 fight with those who fight against me!
² Grab a shield and armor;
 stand up and help me!
³ Use your spear and ax[l]
 against those who are out to get me!
 Say to me:[m] "I'm your salvation!"
⁴ Let those who want me dead
 be humiliated and put to shame.
 Let those who intend to hurt me
  be thoroughly frustrated and disgraced.
⁵ Let them be like dust on the wind—

and let the Lord's messenger
 be the one who does the blowing!
⁶ Let their path be dark and slippery—
 and let the Lord's messenger
  be the one who does the chasing!
⁷ Because they hid their net for me
 for no reason,
 they dug a pit for me for no reason.
⁸ Let disaster come to them
 when they don't suspect it.
 Let the net they hid catch them instead!
  Let them fall into it— to their disaster!

⁹ But I will rejoice in the Lord;
 I will celebrate his salvation.
¹⁰ All my bones will say, "Lord, who could
 compare to you?
 You rescue the weak
  from those who overpower them;
 you rescue the weak and the needy
  from those who plunder them."

¹¹ Violent witnesses stand up.
 They question me about things
  I know nothing about.
¹² They pay me back evil for good,
 leaving me stricken with grief.
¹³ But when they were sick,
 I wore clothes for grieving,
 and I kept a strict fast.
 When my prayer came back unanswered,[n]
¹⁴ I would wander around
 like I was grieving a friend or a brother.
 I was weighed down, sad,
  like I was a mother in mourning.
¹⁵ But when I stumbled,
 they celebrated and gathered together—
 they gathered together against me!
 Strangers[o] I didn't know tore me
  to pieces and wouldn't quit.
¹⁶ They ridiculed me over and over again,
 like godless people would do,
  grinding their teeth at me.

¹⁷ How long, my Lord,
 will you watch this happen?
 Rescue me from their attacks;
 rescue my precious life
  from these predatory lions!
¹⁸ Then I will thank you
 in the great assembly;

---

[l]Correction [m]Or *my soul*; also in 35:4, 7, 9, 12, 13, 17, 24 [n]Heb uncertain [o]Correction

I will praise you
   in a huge crowd of people.
¹⁹ Don't let those who are my enemies
   without cause celebrate over me;
   don't let those who hate me
      for no reason
   wink at my demise.
²⁰ They don't speak the truth;
   instead, they plot false accusations
   against innocent people in the land.
²¹ They speak out against me,
   saying, "Yes! Oh, yes! We've seen it
      with our own eyes!"

²² But you've seen it too, Lord.
   Don't keep quiet about it.
   Please don't be far from me, my Lord.
²³ Wake up! Get up and do justice for me;
   argue my case, my Lord and my God!
²⁴ Establish justice for me
   according to your righteousness,
      Lord, my God.
   Don't let them celebrate over me.
²⁵ Don't let them say to themselves,
   Yes! Exactly what we wanted!
   Don't let them say, "We ate him up!"
²⁶ Let all those who celebrate my misfortune
   be disgraced and put to shame!
   Let those who exalt themselves over me
   be dressed up in shame and dishonor!
²⁷ But let those who want things
   to be set right for me
      shout for joy and celebrate!
   Let them constantly say,
   "The Lord is great—
      God wants his servant to be at peace."
²⁸ Then my tongue will talk
   all about your righteousness;
   it will talk
      about your praise all day long.

Psalm 36
For the music leader.
Of the Lord's servant David.

¹ I know the sinful utterance of the wicked:ᴾ
   No fear of God confronts their own eyes,
² because in their own eyes
   they are slick with talk
   about their guilt ever being
      found out and despised. q

³ The words of their mouths
   are evil and dishonest.
   They have stopped being wise
   and stopped doing good.
⁴ They plot evil even while resting in bed!
   They commit themselves
   to a path that is no good.
   They don't reject what is evil.

⁵ But your loyal love, Lord,
   extends to the skies;
   your faithfulness reaches the clouds.
⁶ Your righteousness is
   like the strongest mountains;
   your justice is like the deepest sea.
      Lord, you save both humans
      and animals.
⁷ Your faithful love is priceless, God!
   Humanity finds refuge
   in the shadow of your wings.
⁸ They feast on the bounty of your house;
   you let them drink
   from your river of pure joy.
⁹ Within you is the spring of life.
   In your light, we see light.

¹⁰ Extend your faithful love
   to those who know you;
   extend your righteousness
   to those whose heart is right.
¹¹ Don't let the feet of arrogant people
   walk all over me;
   don't let the hands of the wicked
      drive me off.
¹² Look—right there is where
   the evildoers have fallen,
   pushed down, unable to get up!

Psalm 37ʳ
Of David.

א ¹ Don't get upset over evildoers;
   don't be jealous of those who do wrong,
   ² because they will fade fast, like grass;
   they will wither like green vegetables.
ב ³ Trust the Lord and do good;
   live in the land, and farm faithfully.
   ⁴ Enjoy the Lord,
   and he will give what your heart asks.
ג ⁵ Commit your way to the Lord!
   Trust him! He will act

ᴾHeb uncertain ᑫHeb uncertain ʳPs 37 is an alphabetic acrostic poem; see the note at Pss 9–10.

⁶ and will make your righteousness
  shine like the dawn,
  your justice like high noon.

ר ⁷ Be still before the Lord,
  and wait[s] for him.
  Don't get upset when
    someone gets ahead—
    someone who invents evil schemes.

ח ⁸ Let go of anger and leave rage behind!
  Don't get upset—it will only lead to evil.
⁹ Because evildoers will be eliminated,
  but those who hope in the Lord—
  they will possess the land.

ו ¹⁰ In just a little while the wicked won't exist!
  If you go looking around their place,
    they won't be there.
¹¹ But the weak will inherit the land;
  they will enjoy a surplus of peace.

ז ¹² The wicked plot against the righteous,
  grinding their teeth at them.
¹³ But my Lord just laughs at them
  because he knows
    that their day is coming.

ח ¹⁴ The wicked draw their swords
  and bend their bows

to bring down the weak and the needy,
  to slaughter those whose way is right.
¹⁵ But the sword of the wicked
  will enter their own hearts!
  Their bows will be broken!

ט ¹⁶ Better is the little that the righteous have
  than the overabundant wealth
    of the wicked.[t]
¹⁷ The arms of the wicked will be broken,
  but the Lord supports the righteous.

י ¹⁸ The Lord is intimately acquainted
  with the lives of the blameless;
  their heritage will last forever.
¹⁹ They won't be ashamed in troubling times,
  and in a period of famine
    they will eat their fill.

כ ²⁰ But the wicked will die,
  the Lord's enemies will disappear—
  disappear like the beauty of a meadow—
    in smoke.

ל ²¹ The wicked borrow and don't pay it back,
  but the righteous are generous
    and giving.
²² Those blessed by God will possess the land,
  but those cursed by God will be cut off.

[s]Correction with LXX, Vulg [t]LXX, Vulg, Syr; MT *abundant wealth of many wicked*

Wait on the Lord Psalm 37

Being patient isn't easy. Waiting for something we really want can seem to take a long time. You may have felt this before a birthday or a holiday. Thinking about all the fun things that might happen can keep you awake at night.

Psalm 37 tells us to wait for God, but waiting is hard. We may wonder at times why God doesn't seem to answer our prayers or give us what we think we need. God's timing isn't the same as ours. God wants us to be faithful in prayer while we wait for God to act.

Waiting on God gives us time to listen. God speaks to us through the Bible, through creation, through things we experience in life, and through other people. God has many things to tell us. We should keep listening no matter what. God doesn't always answer in the way we might expect, but we can always trust in God.

What are some things you've had to wait for?

How can you listen for God while you wait?

ב 23 A person's steps are made secure
  by the LORD
    when they delight in his way.
24 Though they trip up,
  they won't be thrown down,
    because the LORD holds their hand.
ן 25 I was young and now I'm old,
  but I have never seen
    the righteous left all alone,
  have never seen their children
    begging for bread.
26 They are always gracious and generous.
  Their children are a blessing.

ס 27 Turn away from evil! Do good!
  Then you will live in the land forever.
28 The LORD loves justice.
  He will never leave his faithful all alone.
ע They are guarded forever,
  but the children of the wicked
    are eliminated.
29 The righteous will possess the land;
  they will live on it forever.

פ 30 The mouths of the righteous
  recite wisdom;
    their tongues discuss justice.
31 The Instruction of their God
  is in their hearts;
    they don't miss a step.
צ 32 The wicked, on the other hand,
  target the righteous,
    seeking to kill them.
33 But the LORD won't leave the righteous
  to the power of the wicked,
    and won't let the righteous
  be found guilty when they are judged.

ק 34 Hope in the LORD and keep his way!
  He will lift you up
    so you can possess the land.
  When the wicked are eliminated,
    you will see it for yourself!
ר 35 I myself have seen
  wicked powerful people,
    exalting themselves
  like a stately cedar.[u]
36 But when I[v] came back, they were gone!
  I looked all over for them,
    but they couldn't be found!

ש 37 Observe those who have integrity
  and watch those whose heart is right
    because the future belongs
  to persons of peace.
38 But wrongdoers will be destroyed
  all together;
    the future of the wicked
  will be cut short.
ת 39 The salvation of the righteous
  comes from the LORD;
    he is their refuge in times of trouble.
40 The LORD will help them and rescue them—
  rescue them from the wicked—
    and he will save them
  because they have taken refuge in him.

Psalm 38

A psalm of David.
For the memorial offering.

1 Please, LORD, don't punish me
  when you are mad;
    don't discipline me when you are furious.
2 Your arrows have pierced me;
  your fist has come down hard on me.
3 There's nothing in my body
  that isn't broken
    because of your rage;
  there's no health in my bones
    because of my sin.
4 My wrongdoings are
  stacked higher than my head;
    they are a weight
  that's way too heavy for me.
5 My wounds reek; they are all infected
  because of my stupidity.
6 I am hunched over, completely down;
  I wander around all day long, sad.
7 My insides are burning up;
  there's nothing in my body
    that isn't broken.
8 I'm worn out, completely crushed;
  I groan because of my miserable heart.

9 Everything I long for
  is laid out before you, my Lord;
    my sighs aren't hidden from you.
10 My heart pounds;
  my strength abandons me.
    Even the light of my eyes is gone.

u LXX v LXX, Syr, Vulg

¹¹ My loved ones and friends
    keep their distance
        from me in my sickness;
    those who were near me
        now stay far away.
¹² Those who want me dead lay traps;
    those who want me harmed utter threats,
        muttering lies all day long.
¹³ But I'm like someone who is deaf,
    who can't hear;
    like someone who can't speak,
        whose mouth won't open.
¹⁴ I've become like a person
    who doesn't hear what is being said,
        whose mouth has no good comeback.
¹⁵ But I wait for you, Lord!
    You will answer, my Lord, my God!
¹⁶ Because I prayed:
    "Don't let them celebrate over me
    or exalt themselves over me
        when my foot slips,"
¹⁷ because I'm very close to falling,
    and my pain is always with me.
¹⁸ Yes, I confess my wrongdoing;
    I'm worried about my sin.
¹⁹ But my mortal enemies are so strong;
    those who hate me for no reason
        seem countless.
²⁰ Those who give, repay good with evil;
    they oppose me for pursuing good.

²¹ Don't leave me all alone, Lord!
    Please, my God, don't be far from me!
²² Come quickly and help me,
    my Lord, my salvation!

Psalm 39
*For the music leader. To Jeduthun.
A psalm of David.*

¹ I promised I would watch my steps
    so as not to sin with my tongue;
    promised to keep my mouth shut
        as long as the wicked were
            in my presence.
² So I was completely quiet, silent.
    I kept my peace, but it did no good.
        My pain got worse.
³ My heart got hot inside me;
    while stewing over it, the fire burned.
    Then I spoke out with my tongue:
⁴ "Let me know my end, Lord.

How many days do I have left?
    I want to know how brief my time is."
⁵ You've made my days so short;
    my lifetime is like nothing in your eyes.
    Yes, a human life
        is nothing but a puff of air!   *Selah*

⁶ Yes, people wander around like shadows;
    yes, they hustle and bustle,
        but pointlessly;
    they don't even know who will get
        the wealth they've amassed.
⁷ So now, Lord, what should I be waiting for?
    My hope is set on you.
⁸ Deliver me from all my sins;
    don't make me
        some foolish person's joke.
⁹ I am completely silent;
    I won't open my mouth
        because you have acted.
¹⁰ Get this plague of yours off me!
    I'm being destroyed by the blows
        from your fist.
¹¹ You discipline people for their sin,
    punishing them;
    like a moth,
        you ruin what they treasure.
    Yes, a human life is just a puff of air!
                                              Selah

¹² Hear my prayer, Lord!
    Listen closely to my cry for help!
    Please don't ignore my tears!
    I'm just a foreigner—
        an immigrant staying with you,
        just like all my ancestors were.
¹³ Look away from me
    so I can be happy again
    before I pass away and am gone.

Psalm 40
For the music leader. Of David. A psalm.

¹ I put all my hope in the Lord.
    He leaned down to me;
    he listened to my cry for help.
² He lifted me out of the pit
        of death,
    out of the mud and filth,
    and set my feet on solid rock.
        He steadied my legs.
³ He put a new song in my mouth,

**Bet
you
can**
read
this in 1
minute.
**Ready,
set, go!**

a song of praise for our God.
Many people will learn of this
  and be amazed;
  they will trust the LORD.
⁴ Those who put their trust in the LORD,
  who pay no attention to the proud
  or to those who follow lies,
  are truly happy!

⁵ You, LORD my God!
  You've done so many things—
  your wonderful deeds
    and your plans for us—
  no one can compare with you!
  If I were to proclaim
    and talk about all of them,
    they would be too numerous to count!
⁶ You don't relish sacrifices or offerings;
  you don't require
    entirely burned offerings
    or compensation offerings—
    but you have given me ears!
⁷ So I said, "Here I come!
  I'm inscribed in the written scroll.
⁸ I want to do your will, my God.
  Your Instruction is deep within me."
⁹ I've told the good news
  of your righteousness
  in the great assembly.
  I didn't hold anything back—
    as you well know, LORD!
¹⁰ I didn't keep your righteousness
  only to myself.
  I declared your faithfulness
    and your salvation.
  I didn't hide your loyal love
  and trustworthiness
  from the great assembly.

¹¹ So now you, LORD—
  don't hold back
  any of your compassion from me.
  Let your loyal love and faithfulness
  always protect me,
¹² because countless evils surround me.
  My wrongdoings have caught up with me—
  I can't see a thing!
  There's more of them
  than hairs on my head—
  my courage leaves me.

¹³ Favor me, LORD, and deliver me!
  LORD, come quickly and help me!
¹⁴ Let those who seek my life,
  who want me dead,
  be disgraced and put to shame.
  Let those who want to do me harm
  be thoroughly frustrated and humiliated.
¹⁵ Let those who say to me, "Yes! Oh, yes!"ʷ
  be destroyed by their shame.
¹⁶ But let all who seek you
  celebrate and rejoice in you.
  Let those who love your salvation
  always say,
  "The LORD is great!"
¹⁷ But me? I'm weak and needy.
  Let my Lord think of me.
  You are my help and my rescuer.
  My God, don't wait any longer!

Psalm 41

For the music leader. A psalm of David.

¹ Those who pay close attention
  to the poor are truly happy!
  The LORD rescues them
  during troubling times.
² The LORD protects them
  and keeps them alive;
  they are widely regarded throughout
    the land as happy people.
  Youˣ won't hand them over to the will
  of their enemies.
³ The LORD will strengthen them when
  they are lying in bed, sick.
  You will completely transform the place
  where they lie ill.

⁴ But me? I said, "LORD, have mercy on me!
  Heal me because I have sinned
    against you."
⁵ My enemies speak maliciously about me:
  "When will he die
  and his name disappear?
⁶ Whenever they come to visit,
  they say nothing of value.
  Their hearts collect evil gossip;
  once they leave, they tell it to everybody.
⁷ All of those who hate me talk about me,
  whispering to each other,
  plotting evil against me:

ʷSee Ps 35:21, 25. ˣLXX, Syr; Vulg *God won't*

8 "Some horrible thing
    has been poured into him;
    the next time he lies down,
    he won't get up."
9 Even my good friend,
    the one I trusted,
    who shared my food,
    has kicked me with his heel—
    a betrayer!
10 But you, Lord, please have mercy on me
    and lift me up
    so I can pay them back!
11 Then I'll know you are pleased with me
    because my enemy won't be shouting
    in triumph over me.
12 You support me in my integrity;
    you put me in your presence forever.

13 Bless the Lord, the God of Israel,
    from forever to forever!
    Amen and Amen!

BOOK II
(Psalms 42–72)

Psalm 42[y]
For the music leader.
A maskil[z] of the Korahites.
1 Just like a deer that craves
        streams of water,
        my whole being[a]
        craves you, God.

Memorize
Ps 42:1

2 My whole being thirsts for God,
    for the living God.
    When will I come
    and see God's face?[b]
3 My tears have been my food
    both day and night,
    as people constantly questioned me,
    "Where's your God now?"

4 But I remember these things
    as I bare my soul:
    how I made my way
    to the mighty one's abode,[c]
    to God's own house,

with joyous shouts
    and thanksgiving songs—
    a huge crowd celebrating the festival!
5 Why, I ask myself, are you so depressed?
    Why are you so upset inside?
    Hope in God!
        Because I will again give him thanks,
        my saving presence and my God.

6 My whole being is depressed.
    That's why I remember you
    from the land of Jordan and Hermon,
    from Mount Mizar.
7 Deep called to deep
    at the noise of your waterfalls;
    all your massive waves surged over me.
8 By day the Lord commands
    his faithful love;
    by night his song is with me—
    a prayer to the God of my life.

9 I will say to God, my solid rock,
    "Why have you forgotten me?
    Why do I have to walk around,
    sad, oppressed by enemies?"
10 With my bones crushed,
    my foes make fun of me,
    constantly questioning me:
    "Where's your God now?"

11 Why, I ask myself,
    are you so depressed?
    Why are you so upset inside?
    Hope in God!
        Because I will again give him thanks,
        my saving presence and my God.

Psalm 43
1 Establish justice for me, God!
    Argue my case against ungodly people!
    Rescue me from the dishonest
    and unjust!
2 Because you are my God,
    my protective fortress!
    Why have you rejected me?
    Why do I have to walk around,
    sad, oppressed by enemies?

---

[y]Pss 42–43 form one single poem; cf the note at Pss 9–10. [z]Perhaps *instruction* [a]Or *soul*; also in 42:2, 4, 5, 6, 11; 43:5 [b]Syr, Tg;
MT *and appear before God?* [c]Heb uncertain

3 Send your light and truth—
   those will guide me!
   Let them bring me to your holy mountain,
   to your dwelling place.
4 Let me come to God's altar—
   let me come to God, my joy, my delight—
   then I will give you thanks with the lyre,
   God, my God!

5 Why, I ask myself, are you so depressed?
   Why are you so upset inside?
   Hope in God!
   Because I will again give him thanks,
   my saving presence and my God.

did you know? The dwelling place referred to in Psalm 43:3 is the temple, which was built on a hill. Outside the temple was an altar where people made sacrifices to God. This songwriter wanted to worship God at the temple.

Psalm 44

For the music leader.
A maskil[d] of the Korahites.

1 We have heard it, God,
   with our own ears;
   our ancestors told us about it:
   about the deeds you did in their days,
   in days long past.
2 You, by your own hand,
   removed all the nations,
   but you planted our ancestors.
   You crushed all the peoples,
   but you set our ancestors free.
3 No, not by their own swords
   did they take possession of the land—
   their own arms didn't save them.
   No, it was your strong hand, your arm,
   and the light of your face
   because you were pleased with them.
4 It's you, God! You who are my king,
   the one who orders salvation for Jacob.
5 We've pushed our foes away
   by your help;
   we've trampled our enemies
   by your name.
6 No, I won't trust in my bow;
   my sword won't save me
7 because it's you who saved us
   from our foes,
   you who put those who hate us
   to shame.
8 So we glory in God at all times
   and give thanks to your name forever.

Selah

9 But now you've rejected
   and humiliated us.
   You no longer accompany our armies.
10 You make us retreat from the enemy;
   our adversaries plunder us.
11 You've handed us over
   like sheep for butchering;
   you've scattered us among the nations.
12 You've sold your people for nothing,
   not even bothering to set a decent price.
13 You've made us a joke
   to all our neighbors;
   we're mocked and ridiculed
   by everyone around us.
14 You've made us a bad joke to the nations,
   something to be laughed at
   by all peoples.
15 All day long my disgrace confronts me,
   and shame covers my face
16 because of the voices of those
   who make fun of me and bad-mouth me,
   because of the enemy who is out
   for revenge.

17 All this has come upon us,
   but we haven't forgotten you
   or broken your covenant.
18 Our hearts haven't turned away,
   neither have our steps
   strayed from your way.
19 But you've crushed us in the place
   where jackals[e] live,
   covering us with deepest darkness.
20 If we had forgotten the name of our God
   or spread out our hands
   to some strange deity,
21 wouldn't God have discovered it?
   After all, God knows every secret
   of the heart.
22 No, God, it's because of you
   that we are getting killed every day—
   it's because of you that we are considered
   sheep ready for slaughter.

d Perhaps *instruction* e Or *the sea monster(s)*

²³ Wake up! Why are you sleeping, Lord?
Get up! Don't reject us forever!
²⁴ Why are you hiding your face,
forgetting our suffering and oppression?
²⁵ Look: we're going down to the dust;
our stomachs are flat on the ground!
²⁶ Stand up! Help us!
Save us for the sake of your faithful love.

Psalm 45

*For the music leader. According to
"The Lilies." Of the Korahites. A maskil.ᶠ
A love song.*

¹ A marvelous word has stirred my heart
as I mention my works to the king.
My tongue is the pen
of a skillful scribe.

SAILBOAT

HONEST AND TRUE

A Good King and Queen *Psalm 45:1*
Writers use picture words to describe scenes that
people can imagine in their minds. Instead of saying,
"That man is really big," a writer using picture words
might say, "He's a mountain of a man." Many writers
in the Bible use picture words that paint scenes we
can imagine as we read or hear the words.
Psalm 45 paints a picture of Israel's king, not
any king but the kind of king who does the right
thing. He has a sword and rides out to defend truth.
The queen, also called the royal princess, is described with picture words too. She has gold robes,
with many jewels and pearls, and she brings great
honor to the kingdom. ◆

² You are the most handsome of men;
grace has been poured out on your lips.
No wonder God has blessed you forever!
³ Strap on your sword, great warrior,
with your glory and grandeur.
⁴ Go and succeed in your grandeur!
Ride out on behalf of truth, humility,
and righteousness!
Let your strong hand perform
awesome deeds.ᵍ
⁵ Let the peoples fall beneath you.
May your sharp arrows pierce
the hearts of the king's enemies.

⁶ Your divine throne is eternal
and everlasting.
Your royal scepter
is a scepter of justice.
⁷ You love righteousness
and hate wickedness.
No wonder God, your God,
has anointed you
with the oil of joy
more than all your companions!
⁸ All your clothes have the pleasing scent
of myrrh, aloes, and cinnamon.
The music of stringed instruments
coming from ivory palaces
entertains you.
⁹ The royal princess is standing
in your precious jewels;ʰ
the queen stands at your right,
dressed in the gold of Ophir.

¹⁰ Listen, daughter; pay attention,
and listen closely!
Forget your people
and your father's house.
¹¹ Let the king desire your beauty.
Because he is your master,
bow down to him now.
¹² The city of Tyre, the wealthiest of all,
will seek your favor with gifts,
¹³with riches of every sort
for the royal princess, dressed in pearls,ⁱ
her robe embroidered with gold.
¹⁴ In robes of many colors,
she is led to the king.
Her attendants,
the young women servants
following her,
are presented to you as well.
¹⁵ As they enter the king's palace,
they are led in with celebration and joy.

¹⁶ Your sons, great king,
will succeed your fathers;ʲ
you will appoint them as princes
throughout the land.
¹⁷ I will perpetuate your name
from one generation to the next
so the peoples will praise you
forever and always.

ᶠPerhaps *instruction* ᵍHeb uncertain ʰSyr; MT *royal princess is among your precious ones* ⁱCorrection; Heb lacks *for*; Heb uncertain in 45:12-13. ʲHeb lacks *great king.*

Psalm 46

For the music leader. Of the Korahites.
According to Alamoth.[k] A song.

[1] God is our refuge and strength,
    a help always near
        in times of great trouble.
[2] That's why we won't be afraid
    when the world falls apart,
    when the mountains crumble
        into the center of the sea,
[3] when its waters roar and rage,
    when the mountains shake
        because of its surging waves.   *Selah*

[4] There is a river whose streams
    gladden God's city,
    the holiest dwelling of the Most High.
[5] God is in that city. It will never crumble.
    God will help it when morning dawns.
[6] Nations roar; kingdoms crumble.
    God utters his voice; the earth melts.
[7] The LORD of heavenly forces is with us!
    The God of Jacob is our place of safety.
                                    Selah

[8] Come, see the LORD's deeds,
    what devastation he has imposed
        on the earth—
[9] bringing wars to an end
    in every corner of the world,
    breaking the bow
        and shattering the spear,
        burning chariots with fire.
[10] "That's enough!
    Now know that I am God!
    I am exalted among all nations;
        I am exalted throughout the world!"

[11] The LORD of heavenly forces is with us!
    The God of Jacob is our place of safety.
                                    Selah

Psalm 47

For the music leader.
A psalm of the Korahites.

[1] Clap your hands, all you people!
    Shout joyfully to God with a joyous shout!

LIFE PRESERVER

Why should I read Psalm 46 when I'm scared? *Psalm 46:1-3*

Psalm 46 uses the image of mountains crumbling into a roaring sea, which can seem very frightening, as if the world is falling apart. We live in a world where we very quickly learn about natural disasters, such as earthquakes, fires, tsunamis, and tornadoes. We hear about the force of nature that can destroy, and we can feel really scared. But Psalm 46 reminds us that God is always with us. Even when we feel the most afraid, we can read this psalm and remember God holds us very close.

[2] Because the LORD Most High is awesome,
    he is the great king of the whole world.
[3] He subdues the nations under us,
    subdues all people beneath our feet.
[4] He chooses our inheritance for us:
    the heights of Jacob, which he loves.
                                    Selah

[5] God has gone up with a joyous shout—
    the LORD with the blast of the ram's horn.
[6] Sing praises to God! Sing praises!
    Sing praises to our king! Sing praises
[7] because God is king of the whole world!
    Sing praises with a song of instruction![l]

[8] God is king over the nations.
    God sits on his holy throne.
[9] The leaders of all people are gathered
    with the people of Abraham's God
    because the earth's guardians
        belong to God;
        God is exalted beyond all.

Psalm 48

A song. A psalm of the Korahites.

[1] In the city belonging to our God,
    the LORD is great and so worthy of praise!
His holy mountain [2] is a beautiful summit,
    the joy of the whole world.
    Mount Zion, in the far north,
    is the city of the great king.
[3] God is in its fortifications,
    revealing himself as a place of safety.

[k]Heb uncertain; see note at Pss 9–10. [l]Or *Sing praises with understanding* or *wisely* (cf LXX, Vulg); Heb *maskil*; see the note at Ps 32.

⁴ Look: the kings assembled themselves,
    advancing all together—
  ⁵ when they saw it, they were stunned;
    they panicked and ran away frightened.
  ⁶ Trembling took hold of them right there—
    like a woman giving birth,
  ⁷ or like the east wind when it smashes
    the ships of Tarshish.
  ⁸ Just like we had heard,
    now we've seen it for ourselves
    in the city of the Lᴏʀᴅ of heavenly forces,
    in the city of our God.
       May God make it secure forever!   *Selah*

  ⁹ We dwell on your faithful love, God,
    in your temple.
  ¹⁰ Your praise, God, just like your reputation,
    extends to the far corners of the earth.
       Your strong hand is filled
       with righteousness.
  ¹¹ Let Mount Zion be glad;

let the towns of Judah rejoice
    because of your acts of justice!

  ¹² Walk around Zion;
    go all the way around it;
    count its towers.
  ¹³ Examine its defenses closely;
    tour its fortifications
    so that you may tell future generations:
  ¹⁴ "This is God,
    our God, forever and always!
    He is the one who will lead us
    even to the very end."ᵐ

Psalm 49

For the music leader.
A psalm of the Korahites.

¹ Listen to this, all you people!
    Listen closely,
    all you citizens of the world—

ᵐLXX; Heb uncertain; Heb *al muth* (*unto death* or *against death*), but see the notes at Pss 9–10, 46—the words might belong in the heading of Ps 49

Praise *Psalm 47*

What do you think about when you hear the word *worship*? Some people think of meeting to-gether with their church community, singing songs to God, or giving offerings of money. Psalm 47 talks about singing, clapping hands, and shouting.

There are many ways to worship, give thanks, and express honest emotions to God. Some people use instruments or sing. Others use dance or art. Some speak or write words that bring us closer to God. To worship something is to place worth or value on that thing. When we wor-ship God, we express how much we value God no matter what form our worship takes.

When we have something that's worth a lot to us, we often want to talk about it with everyone we know. God wants us to worship by telling others what God has done for us. We can praise God by expressing love and thanks in everyday moments of life as well as during worship services. We can worship with our whole selves in every area of life. Find ways to express how grateful you are about the life God has given you.

What are some ways you can worship God?

Write down some words that express how you feel about God.

2 people of every kind,
   rich and poor alike!
3 My mouth speaks wisdom;
   my heart's meditation is full of insight.
4 I will pay close attention to a proverb;
   I will explain my riddle on the lyre.

5 Why should I be afraid in times of trouble,
   when the wrongdoing of my bullies
     engulfs me—
    6 those people who trust in their fortunes
    and boast of their fantastic wealth?
7 Wealth? It can't save a single person!
   It can't pay a life's ransom-price to God.
8 The price to save someone's life
   is too high—
   wealth will never be enough—
    9 no one can live forever
    without experiencing the pit.

10 Everyone knows that the wise die too,
   just like foolish and stupid people do,
   all of them leaving their fortunes
    to others.
11 Their graves[n] are their eternal homes,
   the place they live for all generations,
   even if they had counties
    named after them!

did you know?

Psalm 50 and several others mention Asaph. According to 1 Chronicles 16:4-5, Asaph was a Levite from the tribe of the priests. King David chose Asaph to lead worship. He played the cymbals and led the singing.

12 People won't live any longer
   because of wealth;
   they're just like the animals
    that pass away.

13 That's how it goes
   for those who are foolish,
   as well as for those who follow their
    lead, pleased with their talk.   *Selah*
14 Like sheep, they're headed
   straight for the grave.[o]
   Death will be their shepherd—
   but those who do right in their hearts
    will rule over them come morning!—

their forms wasting away in the grave
   rather than having
    some dignified residence.[p]
15 But God will save my life
   from the power of the grave,
   because he will take me.   *Selah*

16 Don't be overly impressed
   when someone becomes rich,
   their house swelling
    to fantastic proportions,
17 because when they die,
   they won't take any of it with them.
   Their fantastic things
    won't accompany them down under.
18 Though they consider themselves
   blessed during their lives,
   and even thank you
    when you deal well with them,[q]
19 they too will join the ancestors
   who've gone ahead;
   they too will never see the light again.
20 Wealthy people?
   They just don't understand;
   they're just like the animals
    that pass away.

Psalm 50

A psalm of Asaph.

1 From the rising of the sun to where it sets,
   God, the Lord God, speaks,
   calling out to the earth.
2 From Zion, perfect in beauty,
   God shines brightly.
3 Our God is coming;
   he won't keep quiet.
   A devouring fire is before him;
   a storm rages all around him.
4 God calls out to the skies above
   and to the earth
   in order to judge his people:
5 "Bring my faithful to me,
   those who made a covenant with me
   by sacrifice."
6 The skies proclaim his righteousness
   because God himself is the judge.   *Selah*

7 "Listen, my people, I will now speak;
   Israel, I will now testify against you.
   I am God—your God!

---

[n]Correction with LXX [o]Heb *Sheol; also again in 49:7, 15* [p]Heb uncertain in 49:13-14 [q]LXX, Syr

⁸ I'm not punishing you
   for your sacrifices
   or for your entirely burned offerings,
   which are always before me.
⁹ I won't accept bulls from your house
   or goats from your corrals
¹⁰ because every forest animal
   already belongs to me,
   as do the cattle on a thousand hills.
¹¹ I know every mountain bird;
   even the insects in the fields are mine.
¹² Even if I were hungry,
   I wouldn't tell you
   because the whole world and
   everything in it already belong to me.
¹³ Do I eat bulls' meat?
   Do I drink goats' blood?
¹⁴ Offer God a sacrifice of thanksgiving!
   Fulfill the promises
   you made to the Most High!
¹⁵ Cry out to me
   whenever you are in trouble;
   I will deliver you,
   then you will honor me."

¹⁶ But to the wicked God says,
   "Why do you talk about my laws?
   Why do you even mention
   my covenant?
¹⁷ You hate discipline, and
   you toss my words behind your back.
¹⁸ You make friends with thieves whenever
   you see one;
   you spend your time with adulterers.
¹⁹ You set your mouth free to do evil,
   then harness your tongue to tell lies.
²⁰ You sit around,
   talking about your own siblings;
   you find fault with the children
   of your very own mother.
²¹ You've done these things
   and I've kept quiet.
   You thought I was just like you!
   But now I'm punishing you;
   I'm laying it all out,
   right in front of your face.
²² So consider this carefully,
   all you who forget God,
   or I'll rip you to pieces
   with no one to deliver you:

²³ The one who offers
   a sacrifice of thanksgiving
   is the one who honors me.
   And it is to the one who charts
   the correct path that I will show
   divine salvation."

Psalm 51

*For the music leader. A psalm of David,
when the prophet Nathan came to him
just after he had been with Bathsheba.*

¹ Have mercy on me, God,
   according to your faithful love!
   Wipe away my wrongdoings
   according to your great compassion!
² Wash me completely clean of my guilt;
   purify me from my sin!
³ Because I know my wrongdoings,
   my sin is always right in front of me.
⁴ I've sinned against you—you alone.
   I've committed evil in your sight.
   That's why you are justified
   when you render your verdict,
   completely correct
   when you issue your judgment.
⁵ Yes, I was born in guilt, in sin,
   from the moment my mother
   conceived me.
⁶ And yes, you want truth
   in the most hidden places;
   you teach me wisdom
   in the most secret space.ʳ

⁷ Purify me with hyssop
   and I will be clean;
   wash me
   and I will be whiter than snow.
⁸ Let me hear joy and celebration again;
   let the bones you crushed
   rejoice once more.
⁹ Hide your face from my sins;
   wipe away all my guilty deeds!
¹⁰ Create a clean heart for me, God;
   put a new, faithful spirit
   deep inside me!
¹¹ Please don't throw me
   out of your presence;
   please don't take your holy spirit
   away from me.

ʳHeb uncertain

¹² Return the joy of your salvation to me
and sustain me with a willing spirit.
¹³ Then I will teach wrongdoers your ways,
and sinners will come back to you.

¹⁴ Deliver me from violence, God,
God of my salvation,
so that my tongue can sing
of your righteousness.
¹⁵ Lord, open my lips,
and my mouth will proclaim your praise.
¹⁶ You don't want sacrifices.
If I gave an entirely burned offering,
you wouldn't be pleased.
¹⁷ A broken spirit is my sacrifice, God.ˢ
You won't despise a heart, God,
that is broken and crushed.
¹⁸ Do good things for Zion by your favor.
Rebuild Jerusalem's walls.
¹⁹ Then you will again want
sacrifices of righteousness—

ˢCorrection ᵗPerhaps *instruction*

entirely burned offerings
and complete offerings.
Then bulls will again be sacrificed
on your altar.

Psalm 52

*For the music leader. A maskil*ᵗ *of David,
when Doeg the Edomite came and told Saul,
"David has gone to Ahimelech's house."*

¹ Hey, powerful person!
Why do you brag about evil?
God's faithful love lasts all day long.
² Your tongue devises destruction:
it's like a sharpened razor,
causing deception.
³ You love evil more than good;
you love lying more than speaking
what is right.   *Selah*
⁴ You love all destructive words;
you love the deceiving tongue.

God's THOUGHTS ◆ My THOUGHTS

Forgiveness Psalm 51:10-12

Most of us have hurt someone, even if we didn't mean to do so. And most of us have been hurt by someone else. Whenever this happens, it's good for us to ask for forgiveness and to offer forgiveness to others. We should give and seek forgiveness to other people because God has forgiven us. It can be hard to forgive people who hurt us, but God asks us to forgive them even when we don't feel like it.

God sees when we do wrong and when others wrong us. God knows our sins. But God also forgives us when we ask (1 John 1:9). The amazing thing about God's forgiveness is that God forgets what we've done as if it never happened. Only God is able to forget completely.

After we ask for forgiveness, it's important to ask God to help us make better choices and do the right thing. Thankfully, God doesn't keep a list of our sins. God cleans us off and gives us a second chance.

Think of a time when you had to ask for forgiveness for something you did wrong?

How do you think God feels when you forgive someone?

⁵ But God will take you down permanently;
    he will snatch you up,
    tear you out of your tent,
    and uproot you from the land
        of the living!   *Selah*
⁶ The righteous will see and be in awe;
    they will laugh at those people:
⁷ "Look at them! They didn't make God
        their refuge.
    Instead they trusted in
        their own great wealth.
    They sought refuge in it—
        to their own destruction!"

⁸ But I am like a green olive tree
    in God's house;
    I trust in God's faithful love
        forever and always.
⁹ I will give thanks to you, God, forever,
    because you have acted.
    In the presence of your faithful people,
        I will hope in your name
        because it's so good.

Psalm 53

*For the music leader, according to the
    mahalath. A maskil[u] of David.*
¹ Fools say in their hearts, There's no God.
    They are corrupt and do horrible deeds;
        not one of them does anything good.

² God looks down from heaven
    on humans
    to see if anyone is wise,
    to see if anyone seeks God.
³ But all have turned away.
    Everyone is corrupt.
    No one does good—
        not even one person!

⁴ Are they dumb—these evildoers—
    devouring my people
        like they are eating bread
    but never calling on God?

⁵ There, where there was nothing to fear,
    they will be in utter panic
    because God will scatter the bones
        of those who attacked you.

You will put them to shame
    because God has rejected them.

⁶ Let Israel's salvation come out of Zion!
    When God changes
    his people's circumstances
        for the better,
    Jacob will rejoice;
    Israel will celebrate!

Psalm 54

*For the music leader. With stringed
instruments. A maskil[v] of David, when the
    Ziphites came and said to Saul,
    "Isn't David hiding among us?"*
¹ God! Save me by your name;
    defend me by your might!
² God! Hear my prayer;
    listen to the words of my mouth!

³ The proud have come up against me;
    violent people want me dead.
    They pay no attention to God.   *Selah*

⁴ But look here: God is my helper;
    my Lord sustains my life.
⁵ He will bring disaster on my opponents.
    By your faithfulness, God, destroy them!

⁶ I will sacrifice to you freely;
    I will give thanks to your name, Lord,
        because it's so good,
⁷ and because God has delivered me
    from every distress.
    My eyes have seen my enemies' defeat.[w]

Psalm 55

*For the music leader. With stringed
    instruments. A maskil[x] of David.*
¹ God, listen to my prayer;
    don't avoid my request!
² Pay attention! Answer me!
    I can't sit still while complaining.
    I'm beside myself
³ over the enemy's noise,
    at the wicked person's racket,
    because they bring disaster on me
    and harass me furiously.

---

[u]Perhaps *instruction* [v]Perhaps *instruction* [w]Heb lacks *defeat.* [x]Perhaps *instruction*

4 My heart pounds in my chest
because death's terrors have reached me.
5 Fear and trembling have come upon me;
I'm shaking all over.
6 I say to myself,
I wish I had wings like a dove!
I'd fly away and rest.
7 I'd run so far away!
I'd live in the desert. *Selah*
8 I'd hurry to my hideout,
far from the rushing wind and storm.

9 Baffle them, my Lord!
Confuse their language
because I see violence and conflict
in the city.
10 Day and night they make their rounds
on its walls,
and evil and misery live inside it.
11 Disaster lives inside it;
oppression and fraud
never leave the town square.

12 It's not an enemy that is insulting me—
I could handle that.
It's not someone who hates me
who is exalted over me—
I could hide from them.
13 No. It's you, my equal,
my close companion, my good friend!
14 It was so pleasant when
together we entered God's house
with the crowd.

15 Let death devastate my enemies;
let them go to the grave[y] alive
because evil lives with them—
even inside them!
16 But I call out to God,
and the Lord will rescue me.
17 At evening, morning, and midday
I complain and moan
so that God will hear my voice.
18 He saves me,[z] unharmed,
from my struggle,
though there are many
who are out to get me.
19 God, who is enthroned
from ancient days,
will hear and humble them *Selah*

because they don't change
and they don't worship God.
20 My friend attacked his allies,
breaking his covenant.
21 Though his talk is smoother than butter,
war is in his heart;
though his words are more silky than oil,
they are really drawn swords:
22 "Cast your burden on the Lord—
he will support you!
God will never let the righteous
be shaken!"

23 But you, God, bring the wicked
down to the deepest pit.
Let bloodthirsty and treacherous people
not live out even half their days.
But me? I trust in you!

Psalm 56

*For the music leader. According to
"The Silent Dove of Distant Places."
A miktam[a] of David, when the Philistines
seized him in Gath.*

1 God, have mercy on me
because I'm being trampled.
All day long the enemy oppresses me.
2 My attackers trample me all day long
because I have so many enemies.
Exalted one, 3whenever I'm afraid,
I put my trust in you—
4 in God, whose word I praise.
I trust in God; I won't be afraid.
What can mere flesh do to me?

5 All day long they frustrate my pursuits;
all their thoughts are evil against me.
6 They get together and set an ambush—
they are watching my steps,
hoping for my death.
7 Don't rescue them for any reason!
In wrath bring down the people, God!

8 You yourself have kept track of my misery.
Put my tears into your bottle—
aren't they on your scroll already?
9 Then my enemies will retreat
when I cry out.

---

[y] Heb *Sheol* [z] Or *my life* or *soul* [a] Perhaps *inscription*

I know this because God is mine.
¹⁰ God: whose word I praise.
    The LORD: whose word I praise.
¹¹ I trust in God; I won't be afraid.
    What can anyone do to me?

¹² I will fulfill my promises to you, God.
    I will present thanksgiving offerings
        to you
¹³ because you have saved my life
        from death,
    saved my feet from stumbling
    so that I can walk before God
        in the light of life.

Psalm 57

For the music leader. Do not destroy.
*A miktam*ᵇ *of David, when he fled*
    from Saul into the cave.

¹ Have mercy on me, God;
    have mercy on me
    because Iᶜ have taken refuge in you.
    I take refuge
    in the shadow of your wings
        until destruction passes by.

ᵇPerhaps *inscription* ᶜOr *my soul*

² I call out to God Most High—
    to God, who comes through for me.
³ He sends orders from heaven
    and saves me,
        rebukes the one who tramples me. *Selah*
    God sends his loyal love
        and faithfulness.

⁴ My life is in the middle of a pack of lions.
    I lie down
        among those who devour humans.
        Their teeth are spears and arrows;
        their tongues are sharpened swords.
⁵ Exalt yourself, God, higher than heaven!
    Let your glory be over all the earth!
⁶ They laid a net for my feet
    to bring me down;
    they dug a pit for me,
    but they fell into it instead! *Selah*

⁷ My heart is unwavering, God—
    my heart is unwavering.
    I will sing and make music.
⁸ Wake up, my glory!
    Wake up, harp and lyre!
    I will wake the dawn itself!

God's THOUGHTS ◆ My THOUGHTS

God Is Our Hiding Place *Psalm 55–57*

Where do you go to feel safe? Who do you talk to when you feel scared? Everybody feels afraid sometimes. It's part of life. These psalms talk about a heart pounding from fear (Ps 55:4) or feeling like you are in the middle of a pack of lions (Ps 57:4). Now that's a scary thought! But these psalms teach that God is present in very dangerous places.

What we do when we're afraid is important. God wants us to call on God in these times, trusting that God will provide for our needs. We can also pray when we're scared. We can read our Bible. We can talk to family or friends who follow God. God is love and God's love is loyal, which means God is present.

We can ask God to help us trust this promise when things are tough.

What do you do when you feel afraid?

What verse or story from the Bible helps you when you feel afraid?

⁹ I will give thanks to you, my Lord,
  among all the peoples;
 I will make music to you
  among the nations
¹⁰ because your faithful love
  is as high as heaven;
  your faithfulness reaches the clouds.
¹¹ Exalt yourself, God, higher than heaven!
  Let your glory be over all the earth!

Psalm 58

For the music leader. Do not destroy.
*A psalm of David, a miktam.*ᵈ

¹ Do you really speak what is right,
  you gods?
 Do you really judge humans fairly?
² No: in your hearts you plan injustice;
  your hands do violence on the earth.

³ The wicked backslide from the womb;
  liars go astray from birth.
⁴ Their venom is like a snake's venom—
  like a deaf cobra's—
  one that shuts its ears
  ⁵ so it can't hear
  the snake charmer's voice
  or the spells of a skillful enchanter.

⁶ God, break their teeth out of their mouths!
  Tear out the lions' jawbones, Lᴏʀᴅ!
⁷ Let them dissolve
  like water flowing away.
  When they bend the bow,
  let their arrows be like headless shafts.ᵉ
⁸ Like the snail that dissolves into slime,
  like a woman's stillborn child,
  let them never see the sun.
⁹ Before your pots feel the thorns,
  whether green or burned up,
  God will sweep them away!ᶠ

¹⁰ But the righteous will rejoice
  when they see vengeance done,
  when they wash their feet
  in the blood of the wicked.
¹¹ Then it will be said:
 "Yes, there is a reward for the righteous!
 Yes, there is a God who judges people
  on the earth."

Psalm 59

For the music leader. Do not destroy.
*A miktam*ᵍ *of David, when Saul sent men*
to watch the house in order to kill him.

¹ Oh, my God, deliver me from my enemies;
  put me out of reach from those
  who rise up against me.
² Deliver me from evildoers;
  save me from the bloodthirsty.
³ Look at how they lie in ambush for my life!
  Powerful people are attacking me, Lᴏʀᴅ—
  but not because of any error
  or sin of mine.
⁴ They run and take their stand—
  but not because of any fault of mine.

 Get up when I cry out to you!
  Look at what's happening!
⁵ You are the Lᴏʀᴅ God of heavenly forces,
  the God of Israel!
 Wake up and punish all the nations!
  Grant no mercy to any wicked traitor!
                                   Selah

⁶ They come back every evening,
  growling like dogs,
  prowling around the city.
⁷ See what they belch out
  with their mouths:
  swords are between their lips!
  Who can listen to them?ʰ
⁸ But you, Lᴏʀᴅ, laugh at them.
  You mock all the nations.
⁹ I keep looking for you, my strength,
  because God is my stronghold.
¹⁰ My loving God will come to meet me.
  God will allow me to look down
  on my enemies.

¹¹ Don't kill them,
  or my people might forget;
  instead, by your power
  shake them up and bring them down,
  you who are our shield and my Lord.
¹² For the sin of their mouths,
  the words that they speak,
  let them be captured in their pride.
 For the curses and lies they repeat,
  ¹³ finish them off in anger;
  finish them off until they are gone!

ᵈPerhaps *inscription* ᵉHeb uncertain ᶠHeb uncertain ᵍPerhaps *inscription* ʰHeb uncertain

Then let it be known
to the ends of the earth
that God rules over Jacob. *Selah*

14 They come back every evening,
growling like dogs,
prowling around the city.
15 They roam about for food,
and if they don't get their fill,
they stay all night.
16 But me? I will sing of your strength!
In the morning I will shout out loud
about your faithful love
because you have been my stronghold,
my shelter when I was distraught.
17 I will sing praises to you, my strength,
because God is my stronghold,
my loving God.

Psalm 60

For the music leader. According to "Lily."
A testimony. A miktam[i] of David.
For instruction, when he went to war with
Aram-naharaim and Aram-sobah,
and when Joab returned and defeated Edom,
killing twelve thousand in the Salt Valley.

1 God, you have rejected us—
shattered us.
You've been so angry.
Now restore us!

Many psalms were sung at
different times of worship.
Psalm 61 includes directions
about which instruments were to be played when
the psalm was sung. According to the directions,
this psalm was to be accompanied by stringed
instruments.

2 You've made the ground quake,
splitting it open.
Now repair its cracks
because it's shaking apart!
3 You've made your people suffer hardship;
you've given us wine and we stagger.
4 Give a flag to those who honor you,
so they can rally around it,
safe from attack.[j] *Selah*
5 Save us by your power and answer us

so that the people you love
might be rescued.

6 God has spoken in his sanctuary:
"I will celebrate as I divide up Shechem
and portion out the Succoth Valley.
7 Gilead is mine;
Manasseh is mine;
Ephraim is my helmet;
Judah is my scepter.
8 But Moab is my washbowl;
I'll throw my shoe at Edom.
I shout in triumph over Philistia![k]
9 I wish someone would bring me
to a fortified city!
I wish someone would lead me to Edom!"

10 But you have rejected us, God, haven't you?
God, you no longer accompany
our armies.

Some psalms refer to tunes
from other songs people
already knew. Psalm 60 was
sung to a familiar tune named "Lily."

11 Give us help against the enemy;
human help is worthless.
12 With God we will triumph;
he's the one who will trample
our adversaries.

Psalm 61

For the music leader,
with stringed instruments. Of David.

1 God, listen to my cry;
pay attention to my prayer!
2 When my heart is weak,
I cry out to you
from the very ends of the earth.
Lead me to the rock
that is higher than I am
3 because you have been my refuge,
a tower of strength
in the face of the enemy.
4 Please let me live in your tent forever!
Please let me take refuge
in the shelter of your wings! *Selah*

---

[i]Perhaps *inscription* [j]Or *the bow*; Heb uncertain [k]Syr, Ps 108:9; MT *Celebrate over me, Philistia!*

5 Because you, God,
  have heard my promises;
  you've given me[l] the same possession
    as those who honor your name.

6 Add days to the king's life!
  Let his years extend
    for many generations!
7 Let him be enthroned forever before God!
  Make it so love and faithfulness
    watch over him!
8 Then I will sing praises
  to your name forever,
  and I will do what I promised
    every single day.

Psalm 62

*For the music leader. According to Jeduthun.
A psalm of David.*

1 Only in God do I[m] find rest;
  my salvation comes from him.
2 Only God is my rock and my salvation—
  my stronghold!—
  I won't be shaken anymore.

3 How long will all of you attack others;
  how long will you tear them down[n]
  as if they were leaning walls
    or broken-down fences?
4 The only desire of this people
  is to bring others down low;
  they delight in deception.
  With their mouths they bless,
    but inside they are cursing.   *Selah*

5 Oh, I[o] must find rest in God only,
  because my hope comes from him!
6 Only God is my rock and my salvation—
  my stronghold!—I will not be shaken.
7 My deliverance and glory depend on God.
  God is my strong rock.
  My refuge is in God.
8 All you people: Trust in him at all times!
  Pour out your hearts before him!
  God is our refuge!   *Selah*

9 Human beings are nothing but a breath.
  Human beings are nothing but lies.
  They don't even register on a scale;

taken all together
  they are lighter than a breath!
10 Don't trust in violence;
  don't set false hopes in robbery.
  When wealth bears fruit,
    don't set your heart on it.
11 God has spoken one thing—
  make it two things—
  that I myself have heard:
  that strength belongs to God,
12 and faithful love comes from you,
    my Lord—
  and that you will repay
    everyone according to their deeds.

Psalm 63

*A psalm of David,
when he was in the Judean desert.*

1 God! My God! It's you—
  I search for you!
  My whole being[p] thirsts for you!
  My body desires you
    in a dry and tired land,
    no water anywhere.
2 Yes, I've seen you in the sanctuary;
  I've seen your power and glory.
3 My lips praise you
  because your faithful love
    is better than life itself!
4 So I will bless you as long as I'm alive;
  I will lift up my hands in your name.

5 I'm fully satisfied—
  as with a rich dinner.
  My mouth speaks praise
    with joy on my lips—
6 whenever I ponder you on my bed,
  whenever I meditate on you
    in the middle of the night—
7 because you've been a help to me
  and I shout for joy in the protection
    of your wings.
8 My whole being clings to you;
  your strong hand upholds me.

9 But what about those people
  who want to destroy me?
  Let them go into the bowels of the earth!
10 Let their blood flow by the sword!
  Let them be food for wild jackals!

[l]Heb lacks *me*. [m]Or *my soul* [n]Correction; MT *kill them* [o]Or *my soul* [p]Or *my soul; also in 63:5, 8*

[11] But the king should rejoice in God;
everyone who swears by God
should give praise
when the mouths of liars
are shut for good.

Psalm 64

For the music leader. A psalm of David.

[1] Listen to me when I complain, God!
Protect my life from the enemy's terror!
[2] Hide me from the secret plots
of wicked people;
hide me from the schemes of evildoers
[3] who sharpen their tongues like swords.
They aim their arrow—a cruel word—
[4] from their hiding places
so as to shoot an innocent person.
They shoot without warning
and without fear.
[5] They encourage themselves
with evil words.
They plan on laying traps in secret.
"Who will be able to see them?" they ask.
[6] "Let someone try to expose our crimes!
We've devised a perfect plot!
It's deep within
the human mind and heart."[q]

[7] But God will shoot them with an arrow!
Without warning, they will be wounded!
[8] The Lord will make them trip
over their own tongues;
everyone who sees them
will just shake their heads.
[9] Then all people will honor God,
will announce the act of God,
will understand it was God's work.
[10] Let the righteous rejoice in the Lord;
let them take refuge in him;
let everyone whose heart is
in the right place give praise!

Psalm 65

For the music leader. A psalm of David.
A song.

[1] God of Zion, to you even silence is praise.
Promises made to you are kept—
[2] you listen to prayer—
and all living things come to you.

[3] When wrongdoings become
too much for me,
you forgive our sins.
[4] How happy is the one you choose
to bring close,
the one who lives in your courtyards!
We are filled full
by the goodness of your house,
by the holiness of your temple.

[5] In righteousness you answer us,
by your awesome deeds,
God of our salvation—
you, who are the security
of all the far edges of the earth,
even the distant seas.
[6] You establish the mountains
by your strength;
you are dressed in raw power.
[7] You calm the roaring seas;
calm the roaring waves,
calm the noise of the nations.
[8] Those who dwell on the far edges
stand in awe of your acts.
You make the gateways
of morning and evening sing for joy.
[9] You visit the earth and make it abundant,
enriching it greatly
by God's stream, full of water.
You provide people with grain
because that is what you've decided.
[10] Drenching the earth's furrows,
leveling its ridges,
you soften it with rain showers;
you bless its growth.
[11] You crown the year with your goodness;
your paths overflow with rich food.
[12] Even the desert pastures drip with it,
and the hills are dressed in pure joy.
[13] The meadowlands are covered with flocks,
the valleys decked out in grain—
they shout for joy;
they break out in song!

Psalm 66

For the music leader. A song. A psalm.

[1] Shout joyfully to God, all the earth!
[2] Sing praises to the glory of God's name!
Make glorious his praise!

---

[q]Heb uncertain

³ Say to God:
"How awesome are your works!
   Because of your great strength,
      your enemies cringe before you.
⁴ All the earth worships you,
   sings praises to you,
      sings praises to your name!"   *Selah*

⁵ Come and see God's deeds;
   his works for human beings
      are awesome:
⁶ He turned the sea into dry land
   so they could cross the river on foot.
      Right there we rejoiced in him!
⁷ God rules with power forever;
   keeps a good eye on the nations.
      So don't let the rebellious
         exalt themselves.   *Selah*

⁸ All you nations, bless our God!
   Let the sound of his praise be heard!
⁹ God preserved us among the living;
   he didn't let our feet slip a bit.

¹⁰ But you, God, have tested us—
   you've refined us like silver,
¹¹ trapped us in a net,
   laid burdens on our backs,
¹² let other people run
   right over our heads—
      we've been through fire and water.

But you brought us out to freedom!
¹³ So I'll enter your house
   with entirely burned offerings.
      I'll keep the promises I made to you,
¹⁴ the ones my lips uttered,
   the ones my mouth spoke
      when I was in deep trouble.
¹⁵ I will offer the best burned offerings
   to you
      along with the smoke
         of sacrificed rams.
      I will offer both bulls and goats.   *Selah*

¹⁶ Come close and listen,
   all you who honor God;
      I will tell you what God has done for me:
¹⁷ My mouth cried out to him
   with praise on my tongue.
¹⁸ If I had cherished evil in my heart,
   my Lord would not have listened.

¹⁹ But God definitely listened.
   He heard the sound of my prayer.
²⁰ Bless God! He didn't reject my prayer;
   he didn't withhold
      his faithful love from me.

Psalm 67

*For the music leader, with stringed
instruments. A psalm. A song.*

¹ Let God grant us grace and bless us;
   let God make his face shine
      on us,   *Selah*
² so that your way
   becomes known on earth,
   so that your salvation becomes known
      among all the nations.

³ Let the people thank you, God!
   Let all the people thank you!
⁴ Let the people celebrate
   and shout with joy
   because you judge the nations fairly
      and guide all nations on the earth.
      Selah

⁵ Let the people thank you, God!
   Let all the people thank you!

⁶ The earth has yielded its harvest.
   God blesses us—
      our God blesses us!

LIGHTHOUSE

Good News

Telling Others About God *Psalm 66:16*
Ever since the creation of the world people have
been telling stories, passing history and wisdom
from one person to another. In Bible times, this
was especially important because they didn't have
the kind of written information we have today, and
most people didn't learn how to read. Parents told
stories about their ancestors to their children.
Friends shared stories with other friends. In cities
and villages people would spread news by standing
on street corners announcing the latest events.

   Because they knew how important it was for everyone to remember what happened, storytellers
repeated the stories so much that listeners could
recite the stories word-for-word with them. The
author of Psalm 66 told listeners to gather in close
and listen to all the good and wonderful things God
had done. ◆

⁷ Let God continue to bless us;
let the far ends of the earth honor him.

Psalm 68

*For the music leader. Of David.
A psalm. A song.*

¹ Let God rise up;
let his enemies scatter;
let those who hate him
run scared before him!
² Like smoke is driven away,
drive them away!
Like wax melting before fire,
let the wicked perish before God!
³ But let the righteous be glad
and celebrate before God.
Let them rejoice with
gladness!

LIGHTHOUSE

AWESOME GOD

God Cares and Provides   Psalm 68:1-3

A good father solves problems, provides for his children, is strong enough to protect his children and tender enough to love them.

Some children don't have a father. This psalm describes God as the father of orphans and defender of widows, one who settles the lonely and sets prisoners free (Ps 68:5-6). God knows what God's children need and provides and cares for them like a loving father. ◉

⁴ Sing to God! Sing praises to his name!
Exalt the one who rides the clouds!
The Lᴏʀᴅ is his name.
Celebrate before him!

⁵ Father of orphans
and defender of widows
is God in his holy habitation.
⁶ God settles the lonely in their homes;
he sets prisoners free with happiness,ʳ
but the rebellious dwell
in a parched land.

⁷ When you went forth
before your people, God,

when you marched
through the wasteland,   *Selah*
⁸ the earth shook!
Yes, heaven poured down
before God, the one from Sinai—
before God, the God of Israel!
⁹ You showered down abundant rain, God;
when your inheritance grew weary,
you restored it yourself,
¹⁰ and your creatures settled in it.
In your goodness, God,
you provided for the poor.

¹¹ My Lord gives the command—
many messengers are
bringing good news:
¹² "The kings of armies are on the run!
The women back home divide the spoil.
¹³ Even if you lie down
among the sheepfolds,
there are wings of a dove
covered with silver;
its pinions covered in precious gold."ˢ
¹⁴ When the Almightyᵗ
scattered the kings there,
snow fell on Mount Zalmon.

¹⁵ Mighty mountain, Mount Bashan;
many-peaked mountain, Mount Bashan!
¹⁶ You many-peaked mountain:
Why do you look with envy
at the mountain
God desired for his dwelling,
the mountain
where the Lᴏʀᴅ dwells forever?

¹⁷ God's chariots are twice ten thousand—
countless thousands!
My Lord came from Sinaiᵘ
into the sanctuary.
¹⁸ You ascended the heights,
leading away your captives,
receiving tribute from people,
even from those who rebel
against the Lᴏʀᴅ God's dwelling there.
¹⁹ Bless the Lord!
The God of our salvation
supports us day after day!   *Selah*
²⁰ Our God is the God of salvation,

ʳOr *skillfully;* LXX, Vulg *with strength;* Heb uncertain ˢHeb uncertain ᵗHeb *Shaddai* ᵘCorrection; MT *My Lord was among them, the one from Sinai, in holiness.*

and escape from certain death
  comes through God my Lord.

²¹ Yes, God will shatter
  the heads of his enemies—
  the very skulls of those who walk in guilt.
²² My Lord has spoken:
  "From Bashan I will bring
    those people back.
  I will bring them back
    from the ocean's depths
²³ so that you can wash your feet
    in their blood,
  so that your dogs' tongues
    can lap up their share of your enemies."

²⁴ They saw your procession, God—
  the procession of my God,
  my king, into the sanctuary.
²⁵ First came the singers,
  then the musicians;
  between them the young women
    were playing hand drums:
²⁶ "Bless God in the great congregation;
  bless the Lord from Israel's fountain!"
²⁷ There's Benjamin leading them,
  though he's little;
  then the princes of Judah,
  their speaker;
  then the princes of Zebulun
  and the princes of Naphtali.

²⁸ Summon your strength, God!
  Show how strong you are, God,
  just as you've done for us before,
²⁹ from your temple above Jerusalem,
  where kings bring you gifts.
³⁰ Rebuke the wild animals
  of the marshland,
  the herd of bulls
    among the calves of the peoples.
  Trample those who delight in money;
  scatter the peoples
    who take pleasure in battles.
³¹ Let ambassadors come from Egypt;
  let Cush stretch out its hands to God.

³² Sing to God, all kingdoms of the earth!
  Sing praises to my Lord.   *Selah*
³³ Sing to the one who rides through heaven,
  the most ancient heaven.
  Look! God sends forth his voice,
  his mighty voice.

³⁴ Recognize how strong God is!
  His majesty extends over Israel;
  his strength is in the clouds.
³⁵ You are awesome, God,
  in your sanctuaries—
  the God of Israel who gives strength
  and power to his people!

Bless God!

Psalm 69

For the music leader.
According to "The Lilies." Of David.

¹ Save me, God,
  because the waters
    have reached my neck!
² I have sunk into deep mud.
  My feet can't touch the bottom!
  I have entered deep water;
    the flood has swept me up.
³ I am tired of crying.
  My throat is hoarse.
  My eyes are exhausted
    with waiting for my God.

⁴ More numerous than the hairs
  on my head
  are those who hate me for no reason.
  My treacherous enemies,
  those who would destroy me,
    are countless.
  Must I now give back
    what I didn't steal in the first place?
⁵ God, you know my foolishness;
  my wrongdoings aren't hidden from you.

⁶ Lord God of heavenly forces!—
  don't let those who hope in you
    be put to shame because of me.
  God of Israel!—
  don't let those who seek you
    be disgraced because of me.
⁷ I am insulted because of you.
  Shame covers my face.
⁸ I have become a stranger
  to my own brothers,
  an immigrant to my mother's children.
⁹ Because passion for your house
  has consumed me,
  the insults of those who insult you
    have fallen on me!

¹⁰ I wept while I fasted—
  even for that I was insulted.
¹¹ When I wore funeral clothes,
  people made fun of me.
¹² Those who sit at the city gate
  muttered things about me;
  drunkards made up rude songs.

¹³ But me? My prayer reaches you, Lord,
  at just the right time.
 God, in your great and faithful love,
  answer me with your certain salvation!
¹⁴ Save me from the mud!
  Don't let me drown!
 Let me be saved from those who hate me
  and from these watery depths!
¹⁵ Don't let me be swept away
  by the floodwaters!
 Don't let the abyss swallow me up!
 Don't let the pit close its mouth over me!
¹⁶ Answer me, Lord,
  for your faithful love is good!
 Turn to me in your great compassion!
¹⁷ Don't hide your face from me, your servant,
  because I'm in deep trouble.
 Answer me quickly!
¹⁸ Come close to me!
  Redeem me!
 Save me because of my enemies!

¹⁹ You know full well the insults I've received;
  you know my shame and my disgrace.
 All my adversaries are right there
  in front of you.
²⁰ Insults have broken my heart.
  I'm sick about it.
 I hoped for sympathy,
  but there wasn't any;
 I hoped for comforters,
  but couldn't find any.
²¹ They gave me poison for food.
  To quench my thirst
  they gave me vinegar to drink.

²² Let the table before them become a trap,
  their offerings a snare.

²³ Let their eyes grow too dim to see;
  make their insides tremble constantly.
²⁴ Pour out your anger on them—
  let your burning fury catch them.
²⁵ Let their camp be devastated;
  let no one dwell in their tents.
²⁶ Because they go after those
  you've already struck;
 they talk about the pain
  of those you've already pierced.
²⁷ Pile guilt on top of their guilt!
  Don't let them come
  into your righteousness!
²⁸ Let them be wiped out of the scroll of life!
 Let them not be recorded
  along with the righteous!
²⁹ And me? I'm afflicted.
 I'm full of pain.
 Let your salvation keep me safe, God!

³⁰ I will praise God's name with song;
 I will magnify him with thanks
³¹ because that is more pleasing
  to the Lord than an ox,
 more pleasing than a young bull
  with full horns and hooves.
³² Let the afflicted see it and be glad!
 You who seek God—
  let your hearts beat strong again
³³ because the Lord listens to the needy
  and doesn't despise his captives.

³⁴ Let heaven and earth praise God,
  the oceans too, and all that moves
  within them!
³⁵ God will most certainly save Zion
  and will rebuild Judah's cities
 so that God's servants can live there
  and possess it.
³⁶ The offspring of God's servants
  will inherit Zion,
 and those who love God's name
  will dwell there.

Psalm 70
For the music leader. Of David.
For the memorial offering.

¹ Hurry, God, to deliver me;
 hurry, Lord, to help me!
² Let those who seek my life
 be ashamed and humiliated!

did you know? Different psalms were sung at different times in the worship gathering. Psalm 70 was sung when an offering was made to God.

Let them fall back and be disgraced—
those people who delight
in my downfall!
³ Let those who say, "Aha! Aha!"
stop because of their shameful behavior.
⁴ But let all who seek you
rejoice and be glad in you,
and let those who love your saving help
say again and again:
"God is great!"
⁵ But me? I'm poor and needy.
Hurry to me, God!
You are my helper and my deliverer.
Oh, Lord, don't delay!

Psalm 71

¹ I've taken refuge in you, Lord.
Don't let me ever be put to shame!
² Deliver me and rescue me
by your righteousness!
Bend your ear toward me and save me!
³ Be my rock of refuge
where I can always escape.
You commanded that my life be saved
because you are my rock and my fortress.

⁴ My God, rescue me
from the power of the wicked;
rescue me from the grip of the
wrongdoer and the oppressor
⁵ because you are my hope, Lord.
You, Lord, are the one I've trusted
since childhood.
⁶ I've depended on you from birth—
you cut the cord when I came
from my mother's womb.
My praise is always about you.
⁷ I've become an example to many people
because you are my strong refuge.
⁸ My mouth is filled with your praise,
glorifying you all day long.
⁹ Don't cast me off in old age.
Don't abandon me when my strength
is used up!

¹⁰ Yes, my enemies have been
talking about me;
those who stalk me plot together:
¹¹ "God has abandoned him!
Pursue him!

Grab him because no one will deliver him!"
¹² Don't be far from me, God!
My God, hurry to help me!
¹³ Let my accusers be put to shame,
completely finished off!
Let those who seek my downfall
be dressed in insults and disgrace!

¹⁴ But me? I will hope. Always.
I will add to all your praise.
¹⁵ My mouth will repeat your righteous acts
and your saving deeds all day long.
I don't even know
how many of those there are!
¹⁶ I will dwell on your mighty acts, my Lord.
Lord, I will help others remember
nothing but your righteous deeds.
¹⁷ You've taught me since my youth, God,
and I'm still proclaiming
your wondrous deeds!
¹⁸ So, even in my old age with gray hair,
don't abandon me, God!
Not until I tell generations
about your mighty arm,
tell all who are yet to come
about your strength,
¹⁹ and about your ultimate
righteousness, God,
because you've done awesome things!
Who can compare to you, God?
²⁰ You, who have shown me
many troubles and calamities,
will revive me once more.^v
From the depths of the earth,
you will raise me up one more time.
²¹ Please increase my honor
and comfort me all around.
²² Then I'll give you thanks with a harp—
I will thank you for your faithfulness,
my God.
I will make music for you with the lyre,
holy one of Israel.
²³ My lips will rejoice aloud
when I make music for you;
my whole being,^w which you saved,
will do the same.
²⁴ My tongue, also, will tell of your
righteousness all day long,
because those who seek my downfall
have been put to shame and disgraced.

^v Qere; Kethib *who have shown us … will revive us* ^w Or *soul*

Psalm 72
Of Solomon.

¹ God, give your judgments to the king.
  Give your righteousness to the king's son.
² Let him judge your people
  with righteousness
  and your poor ones with justice.
³ Let the mountains bring peace
  to the people;
  let the hills bring righteousness.
⁴ Let the king bring justice
  to people who are poor;
  let him save the children
    of those who are needy,
  but let him crush oppressors!
⁵ Let the king liveˣ as long as the sun,
  as long as the moon,
  generation to generation.
⁶ Let him fall like rain upon fresh-cut grass,
  like showers that water the earth.
⁷ Let the righteous flourish
  throughout their lives,
  and let peace prosper
    until the moon is no more.
⁸ Let the king rule from sea to sea,
  from the river to the ends of the earth.
⁹ Let the desert dwellers
  bow low before him;
  let his enemies lick the dust.
¹⁰ Let the kings of Tarshish
  and the islands bring tribute;
  let the kings of Sheba and Seba
  present gifts.
¹¹ Let all the kings bow down before him;
  let all the nations serve him.

¹² Let it be so, because he delivers
  the needy who cry out,
  the poor, and those who have no helper.
¹³ He has compassion on the weak
  and the needy;
  he saves the lives of those
    who are in need.
¹⁴ He redeems their lives from oppression
  and violence;
  their blood is precious in his eyes.

¹⁵ Let the king live long!
  Let Sheba's gold be given to him!
  Let him be prayed for always!

Let him be blessed all day long!
¹⁶ Let there be abundant grain in the land.
  Let it wave on the mountaintops.
  Let its fruit flourish like Lebanon.
  Let it thrive like grass on the land.
¹⁷ Let the king's name last forever.
  Let his name endure as long as the sun.
  Let all the nations be blessed
    through him and call him happy.

¹⁸ Bless the Lᴏʀᴅ God, the God of Israel—
  the only one who does wondrous things!
¹⁹ Bless God's glorious name forever;
  let his glory fill all the earth!
  Amen and Amen!

²⁰ The prayers of David, Jesse's son,
  are ended.

BOOK III
(Psalms 73–89)

Psalm 73
A psalm of Asaph.

¹ Truly God is good to Israel,
  to those who have a pure heart.
² But me? My feet had almost stumbled;
  my steps had nearly slipped
³ because I envied the arrogant;
  I observed how the wicked are well off:
⁴ They suffer no pain;
  their bodies are fit and strong.
⁵ They are never in trouble;
  they aren't weighed down
    like other people.
⁶ That's why they wear arrogance
  like a necklace,
  why violence covers them like clothes.
⁷ Their eyes bulge out from eating so well;
  their hearts overflow with delusions.
⁸ They scoff and talk so cruel;
  from their privileged positions
  they plan oppression.
⁹ Their mouths dare to speak
  against heaven!
  Their tongues roam the earth!
¹⁰ That's why people keep going back
  to them,
  keep approving what they say.ʸ

ˣLXX; MT *May they fear you.* ʸHeb uncertain

¹¹ And what they say is this:
  "How could God possibly know!
  Does the Most High know anything at all!"
¹² Look at these wicked ones,
  always relaxed, piling up the wealth!

¹³ Meanwhile, I've kept my heart pure
  for no good reason;
  I've washed my hands
  to stay innocent for nothing.
¹⁴ I'm weighed down all day long.
  I'm punished every morning.
¹⁵ If I said, "I will talk about all this,"
  I would have been unfaithful
  to your children.
¹⁶ But when I tried to understand
  these things,
  it just seemed like hard work
¹⁷ until I entered God's sanctuary
  and understood what would happen
  to the wicked.
¹⁸ You will definitely put them
  on a slippery path;
  you will make them fall into ruin!
¹⁹ How quickly they are devastated,
  utterly destroyed by terrors!
²⁰ As quickly as a dream departs
  from someone waking up, my Lord,
  when you are stirred up,
  you make them disappear.^z

²¹ When my heart was bitter,
  when I was all cut up inside,
²² I was stupid and ignorant.
  I acted like nothing but an animal
  toward you.
²³ But I was still always with you!
  You held my strong hand!
²⁴ You have guided me with your advice;
  later you will receive me with glory.
²⁵ Do I have anyone else in heaven?
  There's nothing on earth I desire
  except you.
²⁶ My body and my heart fail,
  but God is my heart's rock
  and my share forever.
²⁷ Look! Those far from you die;
  you annihilate all those
  who are unfaithful to you.

UMBRELLA
STRESSED OUT

Tired, Weak, and Stressed Psalm 73:26
Asaph was a priest who oversaw the music and
choirs in the temple during the reign of three of
Israel's kings: David, Solomon, and Rehoboam. He
inspired or sang twelve psalms. During his lifetime
Asaph saw Israel become a powerful kingdom and
then be split in two.
   In Psalm 73 he cried out in pain and grief saying
that evil people were in good health and had lots of
money, but good people had nothing. But in the middle
of this prayer, Asaph remembered God's goodness
and declared that God is the rock of his life. ☂

²⁸ But me? It's good for me to be near God.
  I have taken my refuge in you,
    my LORD God,
  so I can talk all about your works!

Psalm 74
A maskil^a *of Asaph.*

¹ God, why have you abandoned us forever?
  Why does your anger smolder
  at the sheep of your own pasture?
² Remember your congregation
  that you took as your own long ago,
  that you redeemed to be the tribe
  of your own possession—
  remember Mount Zion,
  where you dwell.
³ March to the unending ruins,
  to all that the enemy destroyed
  in the sanctuary.

⁴ Your enemies roared
  in your own meeting place;
  they set up their own signs there!
⁵ It looked like axes raised
  against a thicket of trees.^b
⁶ And then all its carvings
  they hacked down with hatchet and pick.
⁷ They set fire to your sanctuary,
  burned it to the ground;
  they defiled the dwelling place
  of your name.

^zHeb uncertain ^aPerhaps *instruction* ^bHeb uncertain

8 They said in their hearts,
  We'll kill all of them together!
  They burned all of God's meeting places
    in the land.
9 We don't see our own signs anymore.
  No prophet is left.
    And none of us know
      how long it will last.

10 How long, God, will foes insult you?
  Are enemies going to abuse
    your name forever?
11 Why do you pull your hand back?
  Why do you hold your strong hand
    close to your chest?

12 Yet God has been my king
  from ancient days—
  God, who makes salvation happen
    in the heart of the earth!
13 You split the sea with your power.
  You shattered the heads
    of the sea monsters on the water.
14 You crushed Leviathan's heads.
  You gave it to the desert dwellers
    for food!
15 You split open springs and streams;
  you made strong-flowing rivers
    dry right up.

16 The day belongs to you! The night too!
  You established both the moon
    and the sun.
17 You set all the boundaries of the earth
    in place.
  Summer and winter?
    You made them!

18 So remember this, LORD:
  how enemies have insulted you,
  how unbelieving fools
    have abused your name.
19 Don't deliver the life of your dove
  to wild animals!
  Don't forget the lives
    of your afflicted people forever!
20 Consider the covenant!
  Because the land's dark places
    are full of violence.
21 Don't let the oppressed live in shame.
  No, let the poor and needy
    praise your name!

22 God, rise up! Make your case!
  Remember how unbelieving fools
    insult you all day long.
23 Don't forget the voices of your enemies,
  the racket of your adversaries
    that never quits.

God's THOUGHTS ▸ ◂ My THOUGHTS

In Need *Psalm 74:2*

Psalm 74 was a cry for help. Israel's place of worship was destroyed by an invader. The temple was in ruins. The people were running for their lives. The writer wanted to know if God had forgotten about God's people.

At your school you might have classmates who are from other parts of the world that need help. Wars and mean leaders often cause people to run for their lives to a new place. Sometimes their parents were starving and needed to find a new place to provide food for them. Psalm 74 can give voice to people who lose everything and help us pray, "Don't forget us, God. We need your help."

Do you know someone whose parents lost their jobs and home and had to move away? How did that make you feel?

What would you say if you cried out to God for help?

Psalm 75

For the music leader. Do not destroy.
A psalm of Asaph. A song.

¹ We give thanks to you, God.
  Yes, we give thanks!
  Your name is near.
  Your marvelous deeds are declared.

² God says,ᶜ
  "When I decide the time is right,
  I will establish justice just so.
³ The earth and all its inhabitants will melt,
  but I will keep its pillars steady." *Selah*

⁴ I said to the arrogant,
  "Don't be arrogant!"
  To the wicked I said,
  "Don't exalt your strength!
⁵ Don't exalt your strength so highly.
  Don't speak so arrogantly
  against the rock."ᵈ
⁶ Because what exalts someone
  doesn't come from the east or west;
  it's not from the south either.
⁷ Rather it is God who is the judge.
  He brings this person down,
  but that person he lifts up.
⁸ Indeed, there's a cup in the Lᴏʀᴅ's hand
  full of foaming wine, mixed with spice.
  He will pour it out,
  and all of the earth's wicked people
  must drink it;
  they must drink every last drop!

⁹ But I will rejoiceᵉ always;
  I will sing praises to Jacob's God!
¹⁰ God says:ᶠ
  "I will demolish every bit
  of the wicked's power,
  but the strength of the righteous
  will be lifted up."

Psalm 76

For the music leader. With stringed
instruments. A psalm of Asaph. A song.

¹ God is known in Judah;
  his name is great in Israel.
² His dwelling place became Salem;

his habitation was Zion.
³ It was there that he broke
  the fiery shafts of the bow,
  the shield, the sword—
  even the battle itself! *Selah*

⁴ You are ablaze with light,
  mightier than the mountains
  that give food.
⁵ The bravehearted lie plundered.
  They sank into deep lethargy.
  All the strong troops
  couldn't even lift their hands!
⁶ At your rebuke, Jacob's God,
  both chariot and horse
  were stopped dead-still.

⁷ You! You are awesome!
  Who can stand before you
  when you are angry?
⁸ You have announced judgment
  from heaven.
  The earth grew afraid and fell silent
⁹ when God rose up to establish justice,
  when God rose up to save
  all of the earth's poor. *Selah*

¹⁰ Even human rage will turn to your praise
  when you dress yourself
  with whatever remains of your wrath.ᵍ
¹¹ Make promises to the Lᴏʀᴅ your God
  and keep them!
  Let all around him bring gifts
  to the awesome one.
¹² He breaks the spirit of princes.
  He is terrifying to all the kings
  of the earth.

Psalm 77

For the music leader. According to Jeduthun.
Of Asaph. A psalm.

¹ I cry out loud to God—
  out loud to God so that he can hear me!
² During the day when I'm in trouble
  I look for my Lord.
  At night my hands are still
  outstretched and don't grow numb;
  my whole beingʰ refuses to be comforted.

ᶜHeb lacks *God says*. ᵈLXX *against God*; MT *speak with an arrogant neck* ᵉLXX; MT *I will declare* ᶠHeb lacks *God says*.
ᵍHeb uncertain ʰOr *soul*

³ I remember God and I moan.
    I complain, and my spirit grows tired.
                    Selah

⁴ You've kept my eyelids from closing.
    I'm so upset I can't even speak.
⁵ I think about days long past;
    I remember years that seem an eternity
      in the past.
⁶ I meditate with my heart at night;ⁱ
    I complain, and my spirit
      keeps searching:
⁷ "Will my Lord reject me forever?
    Will he never be pleased again?
⁸ Has his faithful love
    come to a complete end?
    Is his promise over
      for future generations?
⁹ Has God forgotten how to be gracious?
    Has he angrily stopped up
      his compassion?"   *Selah*
¹⁰ It's my misfortune, I thought,
    that the strong hand of the Most High
      is different now.

¹¹ But I will remember the LORD's deeds;
        yes, I will remember your wondrous
          acts from times long past.
¹² I will meditate on all your works;
      I will ponder your deeds.
¹³ God, your way is holiness!
      Who is as great a god as you, God?
¹⁴ You are the God who works wonders;
    you have demonstrated your strength
      among all peoples.
¹⁵ With your mighty arm
    you redeemed your people;
    redeemed the children
      of Jacob and Joseph.   *Selah*

¹⁶ The waters saw you, God—
    the waters saw you and reeled!
      Even the deep depths shook!
¹⁷ The clouds poured water,
    the skies cracked thunder;
      your arrows were flying all around!
¹⁸ The crash of your thunder
    was in the swirling storm;
    lightning lit up the whole world;
      the earth shook and quaked.

Bet you can read this in 2 minutes. **Ready, set, go!**

¹⁹ Your way went straight through the sea;
    your pathways went right through the
      mighty waters.
    But your footprints left no trace!
²⁰ You led your people like sheep
    under the care of Moses and Aaron.

Psalm 78
A maskilʲ of Asaph.

¹ Listen, my people, to my teaching;
    tilt your ears toward
      the words of my mouth.
² I will open my mouth with a proverb.
    I'll declare riddles from days long gone—
³ ones that we've heard
    and learned about,
    ones that our ancestors told us.
⁴ We won't hide them
    from their descendants;
    we'll tell the next generation
    all about the praise due the LORD
      and his strength—
    the wondrous works God has done.
⁵ He established a law for Jacob
    and set up Instruction for Israel,
    ordering our ancestors
    to teach them to their children.
⁶ This is so that the next generation
    and children not yet born
    will know these things,
    and so they can rise up
    and tell their children
⁷ to put their hope in God—
    never forgetting God's deeds,
    but keeping God's commandments—
⁸ and so that they won't become like
    their ancestors:
    a rebellious, stubborn generation,
    a generation whose heart wasn't set firm
    and whose spirit wasn't faithful to God.

⁹ The children of Ephraim,
    armed with bows,
    retreated on the day of battle.
¹⁰ They didn't keep God's covenant;
    they refused to walk in his Instruction.
¹¹ They forgot God's deeds
    as well as the wondrous works
    he showed them.

ⁱLXX; MT *I remember my song in the night.* ʲPerhaps *instruction*

¹² But God performed wonders
in their ancestors' presence—
in the land of Egypt, in the field of Zoan.
¹³ God split the sea and led them through,
making the waters stand up like a wall.
¹⁴ God led them with the cloud by day;
by the lightning all through the night.
¹⁵ God split rocks open in the wilderness,
gave them plenty to drink—
as if from the deep itself!
¹⁶ God made streams flow from the rock,
made water run like rivers.

¹⁷ But they continued to sin against God,
rebelling against the Most High
in the desert.
¹⁸ They tested God in their hearts,
demanded food for their stomachs.
¹⁹ They spoke against God!
"Can God set a dinner table
in the wilderness?" they asked.
²⁰ "True, God struck the rock
and water gushed and streams flowed,
but can he give bread too?
Can he provide meat for his people?"
²¹ When the Lᴏʀᴅ heard this,
he became furious.
A fire was ignited against Jacob;
wrath also burned against Israel
²² because they had no faith in God,
because they didn't trust
his saving power.
²³ God gave orders to the skies above,
opened heaven's doors,
²⁴ and rained manna on them
so they could eat.
He gave them the very grain of heaven!
²⁵ Each person ate the bread
of the powerful ones;ᵏ
God sent provisions to satisfy them.
²⁶ God set the east wind moving
across the skies
and drove the south wind by his strength.
²⁷ He rained meat on them
as if it were dust in the air;
he rained as many birds
as the sand on the seashore!
²⁸ God brought the birds down
in the center of their camp,
all around their dwellings.

²⁹ So they ate and were completely satisfied;
God gave them exactly
what they had craved.
³⁰ But they didn't stop craving—
even with the food still in their mouths!
³¹ So God's anger came up against them:
he killed the most hearty of them;
he cut down Israel's youth in their prime.
³² But in spite of all that, they kept sinning
and had no faith
in God's wondrous works.
³³ So God brought their days to an end,
like a puff of air,
and their years in total ruin.
³⁴ But whenever God killed them,
they went after him!
They would turn
and earnestly search for God.
³⁵ They would remember that God
was their rock,
that the Most High was their redeemer.
³⁶ But they were just flattering him
with lip service.
They were lying to him
with their tongues.
³⁷ Their hearts weren't firmly set on him;
they weren't faithful to his covenant.

UMBRELLA
Lʏɪɴɢ

Living a Lie *Psalm 78:36-37*
Giving lip service means more than simply lying. It is a colorful phrase that describes continually living a lie. A person gives lip service when he or she says they'll do something but has no intention of doing it. Lip service is pretending to be something you're not.

In Psalm 78 unfaithful people claimed to be followers of God and then disobeyed God's Instruction or twisted it to fit what they wanted to do. People said that God would provide for them but refused to share from their possessions with people in need. People said that God is the only true god and then worshipped false gods. All of these people gave God lip service. Their lives held truth as well as a cup with holes in it holds water. They lived a lie. ♦

ᵏ*Or everyone ate the bread from heaven; Heb uncertain*

³⁸ But God, being compassionate,
    kept forgiving their sins,
    kept avoiding destruction;
    he took back his anger so many times,
    wouldn't stir up all his wrath!
³⁹ God kept remembering
    that they were just flesh,
    just breath that passes
        and doesn't come back.

⁴⁰ How often they rebelled
    against God in the wilderness
    and distressed him in the desert!
⁴¹ Time and time again they tested God,
    provoking the holy one of Israel.
⁴² They didn't remember God's power—
    the day when he saved them
        from the enemy;
    ⁴³ how God performed his signs in Egypt,
        his marvelous works
        in the field of Zoan.
⁴⁴ God turned their rivers into blood;
    they couldn't drink
        from their own streams.
⁴⁵ God sent swarms against them
    to eat them up,
    frogs to destroy them.
⁴⁶ God handed over their crops
    to caterpillars,
    their land's produce to locusts.
⁴⁷ God killed their vines with hail,
    their sycamore trees with frost.
⁴⁸ God delivered their cattle
    over to disease,¹
    their herds to plagues.
⁴⁹ God unleashed his burning anger
    against them—
    fury, indignation, distress,
    a troop of evil messengers.
⁵⁰ God blazed a path for his wrath.
    He didn't save them from death,
    but delivered their lives
        over to disease.
⁵¹ God struck down
    all of Egypt's oldest males;
    in Ham's tents,
    he struck their pride and joy.
⁵² God led his own people out like sheep,
    guiding them like a flock
        in the wilderness.

⁵³ God led them in safety—
    they were not afraid!
    But the sea engulfed their enemies!
⁵⁴ God brought them to his holy territory,
    to the mountain that his own
        strong hand had acquired.
⁵⁵ God drove out the nations before them
    and apportioned property for them;
    he settled Israel's tribes in their tents.

⁵⁶ But they tested and defied
    the Most High God;
    they didn't pay attention
        to his warnings.
⁵⁷ They turned away, became faithless
    just like their ancestors;
    they twisted away
        like a defective bow.
⁵⁸ They angered God
    with their many shrines;
    they angered him with their idols.
⁵⁹ God heard and became enraged;
    he rejected Israel utterly.
⁶⁰ God abandoned the sanctuary at Shiloh,
    the tent where he had lived
        with humans.
    ⁶¹ God let his power be held captive,
        let his glory go to the enemy's hand.
⁶² God delivered his people up to the sword;
    he was enraged at his own possession.
⁶³ Fire devoured his young men,
    and his young women
        had no wedding songs.
⁶⁴ God's priests were killed by the sword,
    and his widows couldn't even cry.
⁶⁵ But then my Lord woke up—
    as if he'd been sleeping!
    Like a warrior shaking off wine,
    ⁶⁶ God beat back his foes;
        he made them an everlasting disgrace.

⁶⁷ God rejected the tent of Joseph
    and didn't choose the tribe of Ephraim.
⁶⁸ Instead, he chose the tribe of Judah,
    the mountain of Zion, which he loves.
⁶⁹ God built his sanctuary
    like the highest heaven
    and like the earth,
        which he established forever.

¹Correction; MT *to hailstones*

70 And God chose David, his servant,
taking him from the sheepfolds.
71 God brought him from shepherding
nursing ewes
to shepherd his people Jacob,
to shepherd his inheritance, Israel.
72 David shepherded them
with a heart of integrity;
he led them with the skill of his hands.

Psalm 79
A psalm of Asaph.

1 The nations have come
into your inheritance, God!
They've defiled your holy temple.
They've made Jerusalem
a bunch of ruins.
2 They've left your servants' bodies
as food for the birds;
they've left the flesh of your faithful
to the wild animals of the earth.
3 They've poured out the blood
of the faithful
like water all around Jerusalem,
and there's no one left to bury them.
4 We've become a joke to our neighbors,
nothing but objects of ridicule
and disapproval to those around us.

5 How long will you rage, LORD? Forever?
How long will your anger burn like fire?
6 Pour out your wrath on the nations
who don't know you,
on the kingdoms
that haven't called on your name.
7 They've devoured Jacob
and demolished his pasture.
8 Don't remember the iniquities
of past generations;
let your compassion hurry to meet us
because we've been brought so low.
9 God of our salvation, help us
for the glory of your name!
Deliver us and cover our sins
for the sake of your name!
10 Why should the nations say,
"Where's their God now?"
Let vengeance for the spilled blood
of your servants
be known among the nations
before our very eyes!

11 Let the prisoners' groaning reach you.
With your powerful arm
spare those who are destined to die.
12 Pay back our neighbors seven times over,
right where it hurts,
for the insults they used on you, Lord.
13 We are, after all, your people
and the sheep of your very own pasture.
We will give you thanks forever;
we will proclaim your praises
from one generation to the next.

Psalm 80
For the music leader.
According to "Lotus Blossoms."
A testimony of Asaph. A psalm.

1 Shepherd of Israel, listen!
You, the one who leads Joseph
as if he were a sheep.
You, who are enthroned
upon the winged heavenly creatures.
Show yourself 2before Ephraim,
Benjamin, and Manasseh!
Wake up your power!
Come to save us!
3 Restore us, God!
Make your face shine
so that we can be saved!

4 LORD God of heavenly forces,
how long will you fume
against your people's prayer?
5 You've fed them bread made of tears;
you've given them tears
to drink three times over!
6 You've put us at odds
with our neighbors;
our enemies make fun of us.
7 Restore us, God of heavenly forces!
Make your face shine
so that we can be saved!

8 You brought a vine out of Egypt.
You drove out the nations and planted it.
9 You cleared the ground for it;
then it planted its roots deep,
filling the land.
10 The mountains were covered by its shade;
the mighty cedars were covered
by its branches.

¹¹ It sent its branches all the way to the sea;
 its shoots went
  all the way to the
  Euphrates River.ᵐ

LIGHTHOUSE

**SPECIAL AND
SET APART**

God Chose the Vine *Psalm 80:8-11*

Sometimes a plant suffers because it's in the wrong soil, or the sunlight it needs to survive is blocked by taller plants. In some cases the plant will die if it isn't moved to a new, better location.

Before moving the plant, the gardener selects the new location and prepares the soil. Then the gardener carefully digs up the plant and places it in its new spot. Finally, the gardener soaks the ground around the plant with water. The water settles the soil around the roots to prevent any pockets of air that might dry out the roots and cause the plant to die.

Asaph described Israel as a vine that God brought out of Egypt and placed in a land God had prepared. Like a vine moved to a better place, Israel grew into a powerful kingdom and reached all the way to the sea. ◊

––––––––––––––––––––––––––––––––––––

¹² So why have you now torn down its walls
 so that all who come along
  can pluck its fruit,
¹³ so that any boar from the forest
  can tear it up,
 so that the bugs can feed on it?

¹⁴ Please come back, God of heavenly forces!
 Look down from heaven and perceive it!
 Attend to this vine,
¹⁵ this root that you planted
  with your strong hand,
 this son whom you secured
  as your very own.
¹⁶ It is burned with fire. It is chopped down.
 They die at the rebuke coming from you.
¹⁷ Let your hand be
 with the one on your right side—
 with the one whom you secured
  as your own—
¹⁸ then we will not turn away from you!
 Revive us so that we can call
  on your name.

––––––––––––––––––––

ᵐOr *the Great River*

¹⁹ Restore us, Lord God of heavenly forces!
 Make your face shine
  so that we can be saved!

Psalm 81
For the music leader.
According to the Gittith. Of Asaph.

¹ Rejoice out loud to God, our strength!
 Shout for joy to Jacob's God!
² Take up a song and strike the drum!
 Sweet lyre along with harp!
³ Blow the horn on the new moon,
 at the full moon,
  for our day of celebration!
⁴ Because this is the law for Israel;
 this is a rule of Jacob's God.
⁵ He made it a decree for Joseph
 when he went out
  against the land of Egypt,
 when I heard a language
  I did not yet know:

⁶ "I lifted the burden off your shoulders;
 your hands are free of the brick basket!
⁷ In distress you cried out, so I rescued you.
 I answered you in the secret of thunder.
 I tested you at the waters
  of Meribah.   *Selah*
⁸ Listen, my people, I'm warning you!
 If only you would listen to me, Israel.
⁹ There must be no foreign god among you.
 You must not bow down
  to any strange deity.
¹⁰ I am the Lord your God,
 who brought you up from Egypt's land.
 Open your mouth wide—I will fill it up!

¹¹ "But my people wouldn't listen to my voice.
 Israel simply wasn't agreeable toward me.
¹² So I sent them off
 to follow their willful hearts;
 they followed their own advice.
¹³ How I wish my people would listen to me!
 How I wish Israel would walk in my ways!
¹⁴ Then I would subdue their enemies
  in a second;
 I would turn my hand against their foes.
¹⁵ Those who hate the Lord
 would grovel before me,

and their doom would last forever!
¹⁶ But I would feed you with the finest wheat.
I would satisfy you with honey
from the rock."

UMBRELLA
DISOBEDIENCE

Disobedient Children *Psalm 81:11-13*
Wear sunscreen when you're outside. Finish your homework before you play. Don't leave your bicycle in the front yard. Parents often give instructions intended to protect their kids from harm. But sometimes kids don't listen. They may even think their parents don't know what they are talking about. When kids choose to disobey instructions, they often experience consequences and learn the hard way why their parents gave the instructions in the first place. They may come home with a painful sunburn, get a bad grade in school, or have their bike stolen.

God didn't give Israel the Instruction to take away fun or make things difficult. Instead, God gave the Instruction as a loving parent who wanted to protect and bless God's children. But the people didn't listen, and God had to let them experience the consequences of their bad decisions. ♦

Psalm 82
A psalm of Asaph.

¹ God takes his stand in the divine council;
he gives judgment among the gods:
² "How long will you judge unjustly
by granting favor to the wicked?   *Selah*
³ Give justice to the lowly and the orphan;
maintain the right of the poor
and the destitute!
⁴ Rescue the lowly and the needy.
Deliver them
from the power of the wicked!

⁵ They don't know; they don't understand;
they wander around in the dark.
All the earth's foundations shake.

⁶ I hereby declare, "You are gods,
children of the Most High—all of you!
⁷ But you will die like mortals;
you will fall down like any prince."

⁸ Rise up, God! Judge the earth
because you hold all nations
in your possession!

Psalm 83
A song. A psalm of Asaph.

¹ God, don't be silent!
Don't be quiet or sit still, God,
² because—look!—
your enemies are growling;
those who hate you are acting arrogantly.
³ They concoct crafty plans
against your own people;
they plot against the people you favor.
⁴ "Come on," they say,
"let's wipe them out as a nation!
Let the name Israel
be remembered no more!"
⁵ They plot with a single-minded heart;
they make a covenant against you.
⁶ They are the clans
of Edom and the Ishmaelites,
Moab and the Hagrites,
⁷ Gebal, Ammon, Amalek,
Philistia along with the citizens of Tyre.
⁸ Assyria too has joined them—
they are the strong arm
for Lot's children.   *Selah*

⁹ Do to them what you did to Midian,
to Sisera, and to Jabin at the Kishon River.
¹⁰ They were destroyed at Endor;
they became fertilizer for the ground.
¹¹ Make their officials like Oreb and Zeeb,
all their princes
like Zebah and Zalmunna—
¹² those who said, "Let's take God's
pastures for ourselves."
¹³ My God, make them like tumbleweeds,
like chaff blown by wind.
¹⁴ Just like a fire consumes a forest,
just like flames set mountains ablaze,
¹⁵ pursue them with your storm,
terrify them with your hurricane.
¹⁶ Cover their faces with shame,
LORD, so that they might seek your name.
¹⁷ Let them be shamed and terrified forever.
Let them die in disgrace.
¹⁸ Let them know that you—
your name is the LORD!—
you alone are Most High
over all the earth.

Psalm 84

For the music leader. According to the
Gittith. Of the Korahites. A psalm.

¹ How lovely is your dwelling place,
  Lᴏʀᴅ of heavenly forces!
² My very being[n] longs, even yearns,
  for the Lᴏʀᴅ's courtyards.
  My heart and my body
    will rejoice out loud
    to the living God!

LIGHTHOUSE

Awesome God

Celebrate in God's Presence *Psalm 84:1-2*
It is good to be in the presence of God when we
worship. Psalm 84 teaches that worship affects
our hearts, which means we have great joy when
we worship. Being in God's presence feels like a
celebration (Ps 16:11). God's people can celebrate
when they know God is with them. One day in God's
worship house is better than one thousand days
anywhere else. When you pray, praise God for the
promise of presence. ◗

³ Yes, the sparrow too
  has found a home there;
  the swallow has found herself a nest
  where she can lay her young
    beside your altars,
  Lᴏʀᴅ of heavenly forces,
    my king, my God!
⁴ Those who live in your house
  are truly happy;
  they praise you constantly.   *Selah*

⁵ Those who put their strength in you
  are truly happy;
  pilgrimage is in their hearts.
⁶ As they pass through the Baca Valley,[o]
  they make it a spring of water.
  Yes, the early rain covers it
    with blessings.
⁷ They go from strength to strength,
  until they see the supreme God in Zion.[p]
⁸ Lᴏʀᴅ God of heavenly forces,
  hear my prayer;
  listen closely, Jacob's God!   *Selah*
⁹ Look at our shield, God;
  pay close attention
    to the face of your anointed one!

¹⁰ Better is a single day in your courtyards
  than a thousand days anywhere else!
  I would prefer to stand outside
    the entrance of my God's house
  than live comfortably
    in the tents of the wicked!
¹¹ The Lᴏʀᴅ is a sun and shield;
  God is favor and glory.
  The Lᴏʀᴅ gives—doesn't withhold!—
    good things
    to those who walk with integrity.
¹² Lᴏʀᴅ of heavenly forces,
  those who trust in you are truly happy!

Psalm 85

For the music leader. Of the Korahites.
A psalm.

¹ Lᴏʀᴅ, you've been kind to your land;
  you've changed Jacob's circumstances
    for the better.
² You've forgiven
  your people's wrongdoing;
  you've covered all their sins.   *Selah*
³ You've stopped being furious;
  you've turned away
    from your burning anger.
⁴ You, the God who can save us, restore us!
  Stop being angry with us!
⁵ Will you be mad at us forever?
  Will you prolong your anger
    from one generation to the next?
⁶ Won't you bring us back to life again
  so that your people can rejoice in you?
⁷ Show us your faithful love, Lᴏʀᴅ!
  Give us your salvation!

⁸ Let me hear what the Lᴏʀᴅ God says,
  because he speaks peace to his people
    and to his faithful ones.
  Don't let them return to foolish ways.
⁹ God's salvation is very close
  to those who honor him
    so that his glory can live in our land.
¹⁰ Faithful love and truth have met;
  righteousness and peace have kissed.
¹¹ Truth springs up from the ground;
  righteousness gazes down from heaven.
¹² Yes, the Lᴏʀᴅ gives what is good,
  and our land yields its produce.

---

[n]Or *soul* [o]LXX; Vulg *Valley of Tears* [p]Correction; MT *the God of gods will be seen in Zion*

¹³ Righteousness walks before God,
    making a road for his steps.

Psalm 86
A prayer of David.

¹ Lᴏʀᴅ, listen closely to me and answer me,
    because I am poor and in need.

² Guard my life because I am faithful.
    Save your servant
    who trusts in you—you! My God!

³ Have mercy on me, Lord,
    because I cry out to you all day long.

⁴ Make your servant's life^q happy again
    because, my Lord, I offer my life to you,

⁵ because, my Lord,
    you are good and forgiving,
    full of faithful love
    for all those who cry out to you.

⁶ Listen closely to my prayer, Lᴏʀᴅ;
    pay close attention to the sound
    of my requests for mercy.

⁷ Whenever I am in trouble, I cry out to you,
    because you will answer me.

did you **know?** *Zion* was the name of the hill on which the temple was built. When the writer referred to the *city of Zion*, he was referring to the city of Jerusalem.

⁸ My Lord! There is no one like you
    among the gods!
    There is nothing that can compare
    to your works!

⁹ All the nations that you've made will come
    and bow down before you, Lord;
    they will glorify your name,

¹⁰ because you are awesome
    and a wonder-worker.
    You are God. Just you.

¹¹ Teach me your way, Lᴏʀᴅ,
    so that I can walk in your truth.
    Make my heart focused
    only on honoring your name.

¹² I give thanks to you, my Lord, my God,
    with all my heart,
    and I will glorify your name forever,

¹³ because your faithful love toward me
    is awesome

and because you've rescued my life
    from the lowest part of hell.^r

¹⁴ The arrogant rise up against me, God.
    A gang of violent people want me dead.
    They don't give a thought for you.

¹⁵ But you, my Lord,
    are a God of compassion and mercy;
    you are very patient
    and full of faithful love.

¹⁶ Come back to me! Have mercy on me!
    Give your servant your strength;
    save this child of your servant!

¹⁷ Show me a sign of your goodness
    so that those who hate me
    will see it and be put to shame—
    show a sign that you, Lᴏʀᴅ,
    have helped me and comforted me.

Psalm 87
A psalm of the Korahites. A song.

¹ God's foundation is set
    on the holy mountains.

² The Lᴏʀᴅ loves Zion's gates
    more than all of Jacob's houses combined.

³ Glorious things are said about you,
    the city of God!   *Selah*

⁴ I count Rahab and Babel
    among those who know me;
    also Philistia and Tyre, along with Cush—
    each of these was born there.

⁵ And of Zion it is said:
    "Each person was born in it,
    but the one who will establish it
    is the Most High."

⁶ The Lᴏʀᴅ makes a record
    as he registers the peoples:
    "Each one was born there."   *Selah*

⁷ And while they dance, people sing:
    "The source of my life comes from you."

Psalm 88
A song. A psalm of the Korahites.
For the music leader.
According to "Mahalath Leannoth."^s
A maskil^t of Heman the Ezrahite.

¹ Lᴏʀᴅ, God of my salvation,
    by day I cry out,
    even at night, before you—

---

^qOr *soul*; also in 86:4 *b*, 13   ^rHeb *Sheol*   ^sHeb uncertain   ^tPerhaps *instruction*

² let my prayer reach you!
Turn your ear to my outcry
³ because my whole being[u]
   is filled with distress;
   my life is at the very brink of hell.[v]

⁴ I am considered as one of those
   plummeting into the pit.
   I am like those who are beyond help,
⁵ drifting among the dead,
   lying in the grave, like dead bodies—
   those you don't remember anymore,
   those who are cut off from your power.
⁶ You placed me down in the deepest pit,
   in places dark and deep.
⁷ Your anger smothers me;
   you subdue me with it,
     wave after wave.   *Selah*
⁸ You've made my friends distant.
   You've made me disgusting to them.
   I can't escape. I'm trapped!
⁹ My eyes are tired of looking
   at my suffering.
   I've been calling out
   to you every day, Lord—
   I've had my hands outstretched to you!

¹⁰ Do you work wonders for the dead?
   Do ghosts rise up and give you thanks?
             Selah
¹¹ Is your faithful love
   proclaimed in the grave,
   your faithfulness in the underworld?[w]
¹² Are your wonders known
   in the land of darkness,
   your righteousness
   in the land of oblivion?

¹³ But I cry out to you, Lord!
   My prayer meets you
   first thing in the morning!
¹⁴ Why do you reject my very being, Lord?
   Why do you hide your face from me?
¹⁵ Since I was young I've been afflicted,
   I've been dying.
   I've endured your terrors. I'm lifeless.
¹⁶ Your fiery anger has overwhelmed me;
   your terrors have destroyed me.
¹⁷ They surround me all day long like water;
   they engulf me completely.
¹⁸ You've made my loved ones
   and companions distant.
   My only friend is darkness.

Psalm 89
A maskil[x] of Ethan the Ezrahite.

¹ I will sing of the Lord's loyal love forever.
   I will proclaim your faithfulness
   with my own mouth
   from one generation to the next.
² That's why I say,
   "Your[y] loyal love is rightly built—forever!
   You establish your faithfulness
   in heaven."
³ You said,[z] "I made a covenant
   with my chosen one;
   I promised my servant David:
⁴ 'I will establish your offspring forever;
   I will build up your throne from one
     generation to the next.'"   *Selah*

⁵ Heaven thanks you
   for your wondrous acts, Lord—
   for your faithfulness too—
   in the assembly of the holy ones.
⁶ Is there any in the sky
   who could compare to the Lord?
   Who among the gods
   is equal to the Lord?
⁷ God is respected in the council
   of the holy ones;
   God is awesome and
   revered more than
   all those around him.

LIGHTHOUSE
PRAYER

Prayer *Psalm 88:13*
Nothing in the Bible says that one time of day is better for praying than another time. Many psalms talk about praying first thing in the morning. King David mentioned waking in the middle of the night to pray. The prophet Daniel prayed three times each day. Whenever we pray, we can use the time to focus our hearts and minds on God's direction for our lives. ◆

---

[u]Or *soul*, also in 88:14   [v]Heb *Sheol*   [w]Heb *Abaddon*   [x]Perhaps *instruction*   [y]Heb lacks *Your.*   [z]Heb lacks *You said.*

⁸ Who is like you,
　Lord God of heavenly forces?
　Mighty Lord, your faithfulness
　　surrounds you!
⁹ You rule over the surging sea:
　When its waves rise up,
　it's you who makes them still.
¹⁰ It's you who crushed Rahab
　like a dead body;
　you scattered your enemies
　　with your strong arm.
¹¹ Heaven is yours! The earth too!
　The world and all that fills it—
　you made all of it! North and south—you
　　created them!
¹² The mountains Tabor and Hermon
　shout praises to your name.
¹³ You have a powerful arm;
　your hand is strong;
　your strong hand is raised high!
¹⁴ Your throne is built
　on righteousness and justice;
　loyal love and faithfulness
　　stand in front of you.

¹⁵ The people who know the celebratory
　shout are truly happy!
　They walk in the light of your presence,
　　Lord!
¹⁶ They rejoice in your name all day long
　and are uplifted by your righteousness
¹⁷ because you are the splendor
　of their strength.
　By your favor you make us strong
¹⁸ because our shield is the Lord's own;
　our king belongs to the holy one of Israel!

¹⁹ Once you spoke in a vision
　to your faithful servants:
　I placed a crown on a strong man.
　I raised up someone specially chosen
　　from the people.
²⁰ I discovered my servant David.
　I anointed him with my holy oil.
²¹ My hand will sustain him—
　yes, my arm will strengthen him!
²² No enemy will oppress him;
　no wicked person will make him suffer.
²³ I will crush all his foes in front of him.
　I will strike down all those who hate him.
²⁴ My faithfulness and my loyal love
　will be with him.

He will be strengthened by my name.
²⁵ I will set his hand on the sea.
　I will set his strong hand on the rivers.
²⁶ He will cry out to me:
　"You are my father,
　my God, the rock of my salvation."
²⁷ Yes, I'll make him the one born first—
　I'll make him the high king
　of all earth's kings.
²⁸ I will always guard my loyal love
　toward him.
　My covenant with him will last forever.
²⁹ I will establish his dynasty for all time.
　His throne will last
　　as long as heaven does.
³⁰ But if his children ever
　abandon my Instruction,
　stop following my rules—
³¹ if they treat my statutes like dirt,
　stop keeping my commandments—
³² then I will punish their sin with a stick,
　and I will punish their wrongdoing
　　with a severe beating.
³³ But even then I won't withdraw
　my loyal love from him.
　I won't betray my faithfulness.
³⁴ I won't break my covenant.
　I won't renege on what crossed my lips.
³⁵ By my own holiness I've sworn one thing:
　I will not lie to David.
³⁶ His dynasty will last forever.
　His throne will be like the sun,
　　always before me.
³⁷ It will be securely established forever;
　like the moon, a faithful witness
　　in the sky.　　　　　　　　*Selah*

³⁸ But you, God, have rejected
　and despised him.
　You've become infuriated
　　with your anointed one.
³⁹ You've canceled the covenant
　with your servant.
　You've thrown his crown in the dirt.
⁴⁰ You've broken through all his walls.
　You've made his strongholds
　　a pile of ruins.
⁴¹ All those who pass by plunder him.
　He's nothing but a joke to his neighbors.
⁴² You lifted high his foes' strong hand.
　You gave all his enemies
　　reason to celebrate.

⁴³ Yes, you dulled the edge of his sword
and didn't support him in battle.
⁴⁴ You've put an end to his splendor.
You've thrown his throne to the ground.
⁴⁵ You've shortened the prime of his life.
You've wrapped him up in shame.   *Selah*

⁴⁶ How long will it last, LORD?
Will you hide yourself forever?
How long will your wrath burn like fire?
⁴⁷ Remember how short my life is!
Have you created humans
for no good reason?
⁴⁸ Who lives their life without seeing death?
Who is ever rescued
from the grip of the grave?ᵃ   *Selah*
⁴⁹ Where now are your loving acts
from long ago, my Lord—
the same ones you promised to David
by your own faithfulness?
⁵⁰ Remember your servant's abuse, my Lord!
Remember how I bear in my heart
all the insults of the nations,ᵇ
⁵¹ the ones your enemies, LORD, use—
the ones they use to abuse
every step your anointed one takes.

⁵² Bless the LORD forever!
Amen and Amen!

BOOK IV
(Psalms 90–106)

Psalm 90
A prayer of Moses, the man of God.

¹ Lord, you have been our help,
generation after generation.
² Before the mountains were born,
before you birthed the earth
and the inhabited world—
from forever in the past
to forever in the future, you are God.

³ You return people to dust,
saying, "Go back, humans,"
⁴ because in your perspective
a thousand years
are like yesterday past,

like a short period
during the night watch.
⁵ You sweep humans away like a dream,
like grass that is renewed in the morning.
⁶ True, in the morning it thrives, renewed,
but come evening it
withers, all dried up.

LIGHTHOUSE

FOREVER

Forever and Ever *Psalm 90:2*
Psalm 90 says that God has been around forever. God existed before the creation of the world, and God will exist when the world is no more. Consider a single grain of sand from the beach. Now imagine that grain of sand represents all the time in which the world has existed. Imagine the rest of the sand on the beach as forever. That single grain of sand seems like nothing compared to all the rest. Think what it would be like to count all the grains of sand on all the beaches of the world! That's what forever is like. But forever can't be measured, because it has no beginning and no end. Forever is where God dwells. ◊

⁷ Yes, we are wasting away
because of your wrath;
we are paralyzed with fear
on account of your rage.
⁸ You put our sins right in front of you,
set our hidden faults
in the light from your face.

did you know? People who study the Bible say that Psalm 90, which remembers the story of Moses, is the oldest psalm.

⁹ Yes, all our days slip away
because of your fury;
we finish up our years with a whimper.
¹⁰ We live at best to be seventy years old,
maybe eighty, if we're strong.
But their duration brings
hard work and trouble
because they go by so quickly.
And then we fly off.
¹¹ Who can comprehend
the power of your anger?

ᵃHeb *Sheol* ᵇCorrection; MT *all of many peoples*

The honor that is due you
corresponds to your wrath.
¹² Teach us to number our days
so we can have a wise heart.

¹³ Come back to us, Lᴏʀᴅ!
Please, quick!
Have some compassion for your servants!
¹⁴ Fill us full every morning
with your faithful love
so we can rejoice and celebrate
our whole life long.
¹⁵ Make us happy for the same amount of
time that you afflicted us—
for the same number of years that we
saw only trouble.
¹⁶ Let your acts be seen by your servants;
let your glory be seen by their children.
¹⁷ Let the kindness of the Lord our God
be over us.
Make the work of our hands last.
Make the work of our hands last!

Psalm 91

¹ Living in the Most High's shelter,
camping in the Almighty's[c] shade,
² I say to the Lᴏʀᴅ, "You are my refuge,
my stronghold!
You are my God—the one I trust!"

³ God will save you from the hunter's trap
and from deadly sickness.

SAILBOAT

I'ᴍ Sᴀꜰᴇ

Trust in God's Protection *Psalm 91:1-2, 4*
A stronghold is a place that is secure and safe. In
Bible times, cities had high, thick walls that protected all the people who lived inside. Psalm 91
speaks of another kind of stronghold—a mother
bird. When storms approach, mother birds lift
their wings and snuggle their babies near their
bodies. Mother birds shelter their babies from
the storm in this way. Whatever God's people may
face—whether evil attacks or stormy trials—
they can trust God. God shelters and protects
God's children. ◆

⁴ God will protect you with his pinions;
you'll find refuge under his wings.
His faithfulness is a protective shield.
⁵ Don't be afraid of terrors at night,
arrows that fly in daylight,
⁶ or sickness that prowls in the dark,
destruction that ravages at noontime.
⁷ Even if one thousand people
fall dead next to you,
ten thousand right beside you—
it won't happen to you.
⁸ Just look with your eyes,
and you will see the wicked punished.
⁹ Because you've made the Lᴏʀᴅ my refuge,
the Most High, your place of residence—
¹⁰ no evil will happen to you;
no disease will come close to your tent.
¹¹ Because he will order his messengers
to help you,
to protect you wherever you go.
¹² They will carry you with their own hands
so you don't bruise your foot on a stone.
¹³ You'll march on top of lions and vipers;
you'll trample young lions
and serpents underfoot.

¹⁴ God says,[d] "Because you are devoted to me,
I'll rescue you.
I'll protect you
because you know my name.
¹⁵ Whenever you cry out to me, I'll answer.
I'll be with you in troubling times.
I'll save you and glorify you.
¹⁶ I'll fill you full with old age.
I'll show you my salvation."

Psalm 92

A psalm. A song for the Sabbath day.

¹ It is good to give thanks to the Lᴏʀᴅ,
to sing praises to your name, Most High;
² to proclaim your loyal love
in the morning,
your faithfulness at nighttime
³ with the ten-stringed harp,
with the melody of the lyre
⁴ because you've made me happy, Lᴏʀᴅ,
by your acts.
I sing with joy
because of your handiwork.

[c]Heb *Shaddai* [d]Heb lacks *God says*.

⁵ How awesome are your works, Lᴏʀᴅ!
  Your thoughts are so deep!
⁶ Ignorant people don't know—
  fools don't understand this:
  ⁷ though the wicked spring up like grass
  and all evildoers seem to blossom,
  they do so only to be destroyed forever.
⁸ But you, Lᴏʀᴅ, are exalted forever!

⁹ Look at your enemies, Lᴏʀᴅ!
  Look at how your enemies die,
  how all evildoers are scattered abroad!
¹⁰ But you've made me as strong
  as a wild ox.
  I'm soaked in precious ointment.
¹¹ My eyes have seen my enemies' defeat;
  my ears have heard
  the downfall of my evil foes.

¹² The righteous will spring up
  like a palm tree.
  They will grow strong
  like a cedar of Lebanon.
¹³ Those who have been replanted
  in the Lᴏʀᴅ's house
  will spring up
  in the courtyards of our God.
¹⁴ They will bear fruit
  even when old and gray;
  they will remain lush and fresh
    ¹⁵in order to proclaim:
  "The Lᴏʀᴅ is righteous.
  He's my rock.
  There's nothing unrighteous in him."

Psalm 93

¹ The Lᴏʀᴅ rules!
  He is robed in majesty—
  the Lᴏʀᴅ is robed,
  clothed with strength.
  Yes, he set the world firmly in place;ᵉ
  it won't be shaken.
² Your throne is set firm
  for a very long time.
  You are eternal!

³ Lᴏʀᴅ, the floods have raised up—
  the floods have raised up their voices;
  the floods raise up a roar!

⁴ But mightier than the sound
  of much water,
  mightier than the sea's waves,
  mighty on high is the Lᴏʀᴅ!
⁵ Your laws are so faithful.
  Holiness decorates your house, Lᴏʀᴅ,
  for all time.

Psalm 94

¹ Lᴏʀᴅ, avenging God—
  avenging God, show yourself!
² Rise up, judge of the earth!
  Pay back the arrogant
  exactly what they deserve!
³ How long will the wicked—oh, Lᴏʀᴅ!—
  how long will the wicked win?
⁴ They spew arrogant words;
  all the evildoers are bragging.
⁵ They crush your own people, Lᴏʀᴅ!
  They abuse your very own possession.
⁶ They kill widows and immigrants;
  they murder orphans,
  ⁷ saying all the while,
  "The Lᴏʀᴅ can't see it;
  Jacob's God doesn't know
    what's going on!"

⁸ You ignorant people
  better learn quickly.
  You fools—when will you get some sense?
⁹ The one who made the ear,
  can't he hear?
  The one who formed the eye,
  can't he see?
¹⁰ The one who disciplines nations,
  can't he punish?
  The one who teaches humans,
  doesn't he know?ᶠ
¹¹ The Lᴏʀᴅ does indeed
  know human thoughts,
  knows that they are nothing
  but a puff of air.

¹² The people you discipline, Lᴏʀᴅ,
  are truly happy—
  the ones you teach
  from your Instruction—
¹³ giving them relief from troubling times
  until a pit is dug for the wicked.

ᵉLXX, Vulg; MT *the world is set firmly in place;* cf Ps 96:10   ᶠCorrection; MT *the one who teaches humans knowledge*

¹⁴ The Lᴏʀᴅ will not reject his people;
   he will not abandon
      his very own possession.
¹⁵ No, but justice will once again
   meet up with righteousness,
   and all whose heart is right
      will follow after.

¹⁶ Who will stand up for me
   against the wicked?
   Who will help me against evildoers?
¹⁷ If the Lᴏʀᴅ hadn't helped me,
   Iᵍ would live instantly in total silence.
¹⁸ Whenever I feel my foot slipping,
   your faithful love steadies me, Lᴏʀᴅ.
¹⁹ When my anxieties multiply,
   your comforting calms me down.

²⁰ Can a wicked ruler be your ally;
   one who wreaks havoc
      by means of the law?
²¹ The wicked gang up
   against the lives of the righteous.
   They condemn innocent blood.

ᵍOr *soul*; also in 94:19, 21

²² But the Lᴏʀᴅ is my fortress;
   my God is my rock of refuge.
²³ He will repay them
   for their wickedness,
   completely destroy them
      because of their evil.
   Yes, the Lᴏʀᴅ our God
      will completely destroy them.

Psalm 95

¹ Come, let's sing out loud to the Lᴏʀᴅ!
   Let's raise a joyful shout
      to the rock of our salvation!
² Let's come before him with thanks!
   Let's shout songs of joy to him!
³ The Lᴏʀᴅ is a great God,
   the great king over all other gods.
⁴ The earth's depths are in his hands;
   the mountain heights belong to him;
⁵ the sea, which he made, is his
   along with the dry ground,
   which his own hands formed.

God's Discipline   *Psalm 94:12*

Discipline might sound like something bad, such as a time-out or being grounded. But *discipline* is an activity, exercise, or plan that develops or improves a skill. God's discipline is training that teaches us how best to live our lives. Sometimes learning God's ways can be difficult and painful. But God's discipline is good for us and results in living better lives.

No one knows how to ride a bike the first time they try. Even after several tries, it's still difficult. We have to concentrate and stay alert the whole time so we don't wreck. It's the same way with our lives. When we first become a follower of God, we don't know how to live a God-centered life. Even after years of study we might know only the basics. Once we learn to balance and steer our lives in God's direction, God will help us learn more challenging things. We must still stay focused. But it's okay if we fall. God will help us. God loves to watch us grow and learn.

Think of a time when you were disciplined. What did you learn?

Why is it important to live by instructions?

6 Come, let's worship and bow down!
  Let's kneel before the Lord,
    our maker!
7 He is our God,
    and we are the people of his pasture,
    the sheep in his hands.

If only you would listen to his voice
  right now!

SAILBOAT

I'm Safe

God Is Our Shepherd *Psalm 95:7*

Some psalms refer to sheep and shepherding. Although sheep are soft and fluffy to touch, they aren't very smart. When they are eating, they get so focused on finding another patch of grass that they don't look where they are going. If the shepherd isn't watching over them, they will wander off and get lost. When the shepherd leads them, they don't know where they are going. They just follow the sheep in front of them. Sheep can't protect themselves from wolves, lions, or bears. They can't treat their wounds. When sheep lie down, they sometimes roll onto their backs and get stuck. When that happens all they can do is lie there bleating. A shepherd uses a long stick with a curved top called a *staff* to drive wild animals away, keep the sheep from wandering off, and pull them up when they are stuck.

Psalm 95 describes God as a good shepherd and God's children as sheep. God leads God's children to good places, protects them from evil, and finds people who have wandered from their faith in God. ◆

8 "Don't harden your hearts
  like you did at Meribah,
  like you did when you were at Massah,
    in the wilderness,
9 when your ancestors tested me
    and scrutinized me,
    even though they had already seen
    my acts.
10 For forty years
    I despised that generation;
    I said, 'These people have twisted hearts.
    They don't know my ways.'
11 So in anger I swore:
    'They will never enter my place of rest!'"

Psalm 96

1 Sing to the Lord a new song!
  Sing to the Lord, all the earth!
2 Sing to the Lord! Bless his name!
  Share the news of his saving work
    every single day!
3 Declare God's glory among the nations;
    declare his wondrous works
    among all people
4 because the Lord is great
    and so worthy of praise.
He is awesome beyond all other gods
5 because all the gods of the nations
    are just idols,
    but it is the Lord who created heaven!
6 Greatness and grandeur
    are in front of him;
    strength and beauty
    are in his sanctuary.

7 Give to the Lord,
    all families of the nations—
    give to the Lord glory and power!
8 Give to the Lord the glory due his name!
  Bring gifts!
  Enter his courtyards!
9 Bow down to the Lord in his holy splendor!
  Tremble before him, all the earth!

10 Tell the nations, "The Lord rules!
  Yes, he set the world firmly in place;[h]
  it won't be shaken.
  He will judge all people fairly."
11 Let heaven celebrate! Let the earth rejoice!
  Let the sea and everything in it roar!
12 Let the countryside
    and everything in it celebrate!
  Then all the trees of the forest too
    will shout out joyfully
13 before the Lord because he is coming!
He is coming to establish justice
    on the earth!
  He will establish justice
    in the world rightly.
  He will establish justice
    among all people fairly.

Psalm 97

1 The Lord rules! Let the earth rejoice!
  Let all the islands celebrate!

[h]LXX, Vulg; MT *the world is firmly established*; cf Ps 93:1

2 Clouds and thick darkness surround God.
His throne is built
on righteousness and justice.
3 Fire proceeds before him,
burning up his enemies on every side.
4 His lightning lights up the world;
the earth sees it and trembles!
5 The mountains melt like wax
before the Lord,
before the Lord of the whole world!

6 Heaven has proclaimed
God's righteousness,
and all nations have seen his glory.
7 All those who worship images,
those who are proud of idols,
are put to shame.
All gods bow down to the Lord!
8 Zion has heard and celebrates,
the towns[i] of Judah rejoice,
because of your acts of justice, Lord,
9 because you, Lord, are the Most High
over all the earth,
because you are so superior
to all other gods.

10 Those of you who love the Lord, hate evil!
God guards the lives of his faithful ones,
delivering them from
the power of the wicked.
11 Light is planted like seed
for the righteous person;
joy too for those whose heart is right.
12 Rejoice in the Lord, righteous ones!
Give thanks to his holy name!

Psalm 98
A psalm.

1 Sing to the Lord a new song
because he has done wonderful things!
His own strong hand and his own holy arm
have won the victory!
2 The Lord has made his salvation
widely known;
he has revealed his righteousness
in the eyes of all the nations.
3 God has remembered his loyal love
and faithfulness to the house of Israel;
every corner of the earth has seen
our God's salvation.

4 Shout triumphantly to the Lord,
all the earth!
Be happy!
Rejoice out loud!
Sing your praises!
5 Sing your praises to the Lord
with the lyre—
with the lyre and the sound of music.
6 With trumpets and a horn blast,
shout triumphantly before the Lord,
the king!
7 Let the sea and everything in it roar;
the world and all its inhabitants too.
8 Let all the rivers clap their hands;
let the mountains rejoice out loud
altogether 9before the Lord
because he is coming to establish
justice on the earth!
He will establish justice
in the world rightly;
he will establish justice
among all people fairly.

Psalm 99

1 The Lord rules—
the nations shake!
He sits enthroned on the winged
heavenly creatures—
the earth quakes!
2 The Lord is great in Zion;
he is exalted over all the nations.
3 Let them thank your great
and awesome name.
He is holy!

4 Strong king[j] who loves justice,
you are the one
who established what is fair.
You worked justice and righteousness
in Jacob.
5 Magnify the Lord, our God!
Bow low at his footstool!
He is holy!
6 Moses and Aaron were among his priests,
Samuel too among those
who called on his name.
They cried out to the Lord,
and he himself answered them—
7 he spoke to them from a pillar of cloud.

[i]Or *daughters* [j]Correction; MT *A king's strength*

They kept the laws and the rules
God gave to them.
[8] Lord our God, you answered them.
To them you were a God who forgives
but also the one who avenged
their wrong deeds.
[9] Magnify the Lord our God!
Bow low at his holy mountain
because the Lord our God is holy!

Psalm 100

A psalm of thanks.

[1] Shout triumphantly to the Lord,
all the earth!
[2] Serve the Lord with celebration!
Come before him
with shouts of joy!

Bet you can
read this in 30 seconds. Ready, set, go!

[3] Know that the Lord is God—
he made us; we belong to him.[k]
We are his people,
the sheep of his own pasture.
[4] Enter his gates with thanks;
enter his courtyards with praise!
Thank him! Bless his name!
[5] Because the Lord is good,
his loyal love lasts forever;
his faithfulness lasts
generation after generation.

Psalm 101

Of David. A psalm.

[1] Oh, let me sing
about faithful love and justice!
I want to sing my praises to you, Lord!
[2] I want to study the way of integrity—
how long before it gets here?
I will walk with a heart of integrity
in my own house.
[3] I won't set my eyes on anything worthless.
I hate wrongdoing;
none of that will stick to me.
[4] A corrupt heart will be far from me.
I won't be familiar with evil.
[5] I will destroy anyone
who secretly tells lies about a neighbor.
I can't stomach anyone
who has proud eyes or an arrogant heart.
[6] My eyes focus on those

who are faithful in the land,
to have them close to me.
The person who walks without blame
will work for me.
[7] But the person who acts deceitfully
won't stay in my house.
The person who tells lies
won't last for long before me.
[8] Every morning I will destroy
all those who are wicked in the land
in order to eliminate all evildoers
from the Lord's city.

Psalm 102

*A prayer of an oppressed person,
when weak and pouring out grief
to the Lord.*

[1] Lord, hear my prayer!
Let my cry reach you!
[2] Don't hide your face from me
in my time of trouble!
Listen to me!
Answer me quickly as I cry out!
[3] Because my days disappear like smoke,
my bones are burned up as if in an oven;
[4] my heart is smashed like dried-up grass.
I even forget to eat my food
[5] because of my intense groans.
My bones are protruding from my skin.
[6] I'm like some wild owl—
like some screech owl in the desert.
[7] I lie awake all night.
I'm all alone like a bird on a roof.
[8] All day long my enemies make fun of me;
those who mock me
curse using my name!
[9] I've been eating ashes instead of bread.
I've been mixing tears into my drinks
[10] because of your anger and wrath,
because you picked me up
and threw me away.
[11] My days are like a shadow soon gone.
I'm dried up like dead grass.

[12] But you, Lord, rule forever!
Your fame lasts
from one generation to the next!
[13] You will stand up—
you'll have compassion on Zion

---

[k] Qere; Kethib *and not we ourselves*

LIFE PRESERVER

Why are there so many psalms about feelings?
Psalm 102

One of the great things about the psalms is that even though they were written a long time ago, they talk about things that still happen to people today. For example, there are many times when we feel really sad, angry, or abandoned. Psalm 102 lets us know these emotions are part of being human. The poet wrote about being so upset that he forgot to eat! The next time you have a really terrible day when things aren't going well, read this psalm and remember it's natural to tell God what you're feeling. ◊

because it is time to have mercy on her—
    the time set for that has now come!
¹⁴ Your servants cherish Zion's stones;
    they show mercy even to her dirt.
¹⁵ The nations will honor the LORD's name;
    all the earth's rulers
        will honor your glory
¹⁶ because the LORD will rebuild Zion;
    he will be seen there in his glory.
¹⁷ God will turn
    to the prayer of the impoverished;
    he won't despise their prayers.

¹⁸ Let this be written down
    for the next generation
    so that people not yet created
        will praise the LORD:
¹⁹ The LORD looked down
    from his holy summit,
    surveyed the earth from heaven,
²⁰ to hear the prisoners' groans,
    to set free those condemned to death,
²¹ that the LORD's name
    may be declared in Zion
    and his praise declared in Jerusalem,
²² when all people are gathered together—
    all kingdoms—to serve the LORD.

²³ God broke my strength in midstride,
    cutting my days short.
²⁴ I said, "My God, don't take me away
    in the prime of life—
    your years go on
        from one generation to the next!

²⁵ You laid the earth's foundations long ago;
    the skies are your handiwork.
²⁶ These things will pass away,
    but you will last.
    All of these things will wear out
        like clothing;
    you change them like clothes,
        and they pass on.
²⁷ But you are the one!
    Your years never end!
²⁸ Let your servants' children live safe;
    let your servants' descendants live
        secure in your presence."

Psalm 103
Of David.

¹ Let my whole being¹ bless the LORD!
    Let everything inside me
        bless his holy name!
² Let my whole being bless the LORD
    and never forget all his good deeds:
³ how God forgives all your sins,
    heals all your sickness,
⁴ saves your life from the pit,
    crowns you with faithful love
        and compassion,
⁵ and satisfies you
    with plenty of good things
    so that your youth
        is made fresh like an eagle's.

⁶ The LORD works righteousness;
    does justice for all who are oppressed.
⁷ God made his ways known to Moses;
    made his deeds known to the Israelites.
⁸ The LORD is compassionate and merciful,
    very patient, and full of faithful love.
⁹ God won't always play the judge;
    he won't be angry forever.
¹⁰ He doesn't deal with us according to our sin
    or repay us according
        to our wrongdoing,
¹¹ because as high
    as heaven
    is above the earth,
    that's how large God's faithful love
    is for those who honor him.
¹² As far as east is from west—
    that's how far God has removed
        our sin from us.

Memorize
Ps 103:11-12

---

¹Or *soul*; also in 103:2, 22

¹³ Like a parent feels compassion
for their children—
that's how the Lᴏʀᴅ feels compassion
for those who honor him.
¹⁴ Because God knows how we're made,
God remembers we're just dust.

¹⁵ The days of a human life are like grass:
they bloom like a wildflower;
¹⁶ but when the wind blows through it,
it's gone;
even the ground where it stood
doesn't remember it.
¹⁷ But the Lᴏʀᴅ's faithful love is from
forever ago to forever from now
for those who honor him.
And God's righteousness reaches
to the grandchildren
¹⁸ of those who keep his covenant
and remember to keep his commands.
¹⁹ The Lᴏʀᴅ has established his throne
in heaven,
and his kingdom rules over all.

²⁰ You divine messengers,
bless the Lᴏʀᴅ!
You who are mighty in power
and keep his word,
who obey everything he says,
bless him!
²¹ All you heavenly forces,
bless the Lᴏʀᴅ!
All you who serve him and do his will,
bless him!
²² All God's creatures,
bless the Lᴏʀᴅ!
Everywhere, throughout his kingdom,
let my whole being
bless the Lᴏʀᴅ!

Psalm 104

¹ Let my whole being^m bless the Lᴏʀᴅ!
Lᴏʀᴅ my God, how fantastic you are!
You are clothed in glory and grandeur!
² You wear light like a robe;
you open the skies like a curtain.
³ You build your lofty house on the waters;
you make the clouds your chariot,
going around on the wings of the wind.

⁴ You make the winds your messengers;
you make fire and flame
your ministers.
⁵ You established the earth
on its foundations
so that it will never ever fall.
⁶ You covered it with the watery deep
like a piece of clothing;
the waters were higher
than the mountains!
⁷ But at your rebuke they ran away;
they fled in fear
at the sound of your thunder.
⁸ They flowed over the mountains,
streaming down the valleys
to the place you established for them.
⁹ You set a boundary they cannot cross
so they'll never again cover the earth.

¹⁰ You put gushing springs
into dry riverbeds.
They flow between the mountains,
¹¹ providing water for every wild animal—
the wild donkeys quench their thirst.
¹² Overhead, the birds in the sky
make their home,
chirping loudly in the trees.
¹³ From your lofty house,
you water the mountains.
The earth is filled full
by the fruit of what you've done.
¹⁴ You make grass grow for cattle;
you make plants for human farming
in order to get food from the ground,
¹⁵ and wine, which cheers people's hearts,
along with oil,
which makes the face shine,
and bread,
which sustains the human heart.
¹⁶ The Lᴏʀᴅ's trees are well watered—
the cedars of Lebanon,
which God planted,
¹⁷ where the birds make their nests,
where the stork has a home
in the cypresses.
¹⁸ The high mountains
belong to the mountain goats;
the ridges are the refuge of badgers.
¹⁹ God made the moon for the seasons,

---

^m Or *soul*; also in 104:35

and the sun too,
which knows when to set.

²⁰ You bring on the darkness and it is night,
when every forest animal prowls.

²¹ The young lions roar for their prey,
seeking their food from God.

²² When the sun rises, they gather together
and lie down in their dens.

²³ Then people go off to their work,
to do their work until evening.

²⁴ Lord, you have done so many things!
You made them all so wisely!
The earth is full of your creations!

²⁵ And then there's the sea, wide and deep,
with its countless creatures—
living things both small and large.

²⁶ There go the ships on it,
and Leviathan, which you made,
plays in it!

²⁷ All your creations wait for you
to give them their food on time.

²⁸ When you give it to them,
they gather it up;
when you open your hand,
they are filled completely full!

²⁹ But when you hide your face,
they are terrified;
when you take away their breath,
they die and return to dust.

³⁰ When you let loose your breath,
they are created,
and you make the surface of the ground
brand-new again.

³¹ Let the Lord's glory last forever!
Let the Lord rejoice in all he has made!

³² He has only to look at the earth,
and it shakes.
God just touches the mountains,
and they erupt in smoke.

³³ I will sing to the Lord as long as I live;
I will sing praises to my God
while I'm still alive.

³⁴ Let my praise be pleasing to him;
I'm rejoicing in the Lord!

³⁵ Let sinners be wiped clean
from the earth;
let the wicked be no more.
But let my whole being bless the Lord!
Praise the Lord!

Psalm 105

¹ Give thanks to the Lord;
call upon his name;
make his deeds known to all people!

² Sing to God;
sing praises to the Lord;
dwell on all his wondrous works!

³ Give praise to God's holy name!
Let the hearts rejoice of all those
seeking the Lord!

⁴ Pursue the Lord and his strength;
seek his face always!

⁵ Remember the wondrous works
he has done,
all his marvelous works,
and the justice he declared—

⁶ you who are the offspring of Abraham,
his servant,
and the children of Jacob,
his chosen ones.

⁷ The Lord—he is our God.
His justice is everywhere
throughout the whole world.

⁸ God remembers his covenant forever,
the word he commanded
to a thousand generations,

⁹ which he made with Abraham,
the solemn pledge
he swore to Isaac.

LIGHTHOUSE

Awesome God

God Keeps God's Promises *Psalm 105:8*

If someone asked you to list all the promises you've ever made—every time you said, "I will," or "I won't"—it's unlikely you would be able to do so. You might be able to remember the promises you made yesterday, or maybe even last week, but probably not those you made last year.

God remembers everything God ever said, including all the promises God made to all people throughout history. God remembers putting the rainbow in the sky and telling Noah that God wouldn't flood the earth again. God remembers telling Moses from the burning bush that God would use him to deliver the Israelites from slavery in Egypt. God remembers telling Joshua that God would destroy the city of Jericho. God remembers leading the Israelites into the promised land. God remembers every promise to everyone. God keeps promises. ◆

¹⁰ God set it up as binding law for Jacob,
    as an eternal covenant for Israel,
¹¹ promising, "I hereby give you
    the land of Canaan
    as your allotted inheritance."

¹² When they were few in number—
    insignificant, just immigrants—
    ¹³ wandering from nation to nation,
    from one kingdom to the next,
¹⁴ God didn't let anyone oppress them.
    God punished kings for their sake:
¹⁵ "Don't touch my anointed ones;
    don't harm my prophets!"

¹⁶ When God called for a famine in the land,
    destroying every source of food,
    ¹⁷ he sent a man ahead of them,
    who was sold as a slave: it was Joseph.
¹⁸ Joseph's feet hurt in his shackles;
    his neck was in an iron collar,
    ¹⁹ until what he predicted
    actually happened,
    until what the Lord had said
    proved him true.[n]
²⁰ The king sent for Joseph
    and set him free;
    the ruler of many people released him.
²¹ The king made Joseph master of his house
    and ruler over everything he owned,
    ²² to make sure his princes acted
    according to his will,
    and to teach wisdom to his advisors.
²³ That's how Israel came to Egypt,
    how Jacob became an immigrant
    in the land of Ham.

²⁴ God made his people very fruitful,
    more powerful than their enemies,
    ²⁵ whose hearts God changed
    so they hated his people
    and dealt shrewdly with his servants.
²⁶ God sent Moses his servant
    and the one he chose, Aaron.
²⁷ They put God's signs on Egypt,[o]
    his marvelous works
    on the land of Ham.
²⁸ God sent darkness, and it became dark,
    but the Egyptians rejected his word.

²⁹ God turned their waters into blood
    and killed their fish.
³⁰ God made their land swarm with frogs[p]—
    even in the bedrooms of their king!
³¹ God spoke, and the insects came—
    gnats throughout their whole country!
³² God turned their rain into hail
    along with lightning flashes
    throughout their land.
³³ God destroyed their vines
    and their fig trees;
    shattered the trees of their countryside.
³⁴ God spoke, and the locusts came—
    countless grasshoppers came!
³⁵ They devoured all the plants
    in their land;
    they devoured the fruit of their soil.
³⁶ God struck down all the oldest sons
    throughout their land;
    struck down their very pride and joy.
³⁷ Then God brought Israel out,
    filled with silver and gold;
    not one of its tribes stumbled.
³⁸ Egypt celebrated when they left,
    because the dread of Israel
    had come upon them.

³⁹ God spread out clouds as a covering;
    gave lightning to provide light at night.
⁴⁰ The people asked, and God brought quail;
    God filled them full
    with food from heaven.
⁴¹ God opened the rock
    and out gushed water—
    flowing like a river through the desert!
⁴² Because God remembered
    his holy promise
    to Abraham his servant,
⁴³ God brought his people
    out with rejoicing,
    his chosen ones with songs of joy.
⁴⁴ God gave them the lands
    of other nations;
    they inherited the wealth
    of many peoples—
    ⁴⁵ all so that they would keep his laws
    and observe his instructions.

Praise the Lord!

---

[n]Heb uncertain [o]Correction; MT *they put on them the words of God's signs* [p]Correction; DSS (11QPsᵃ) *their land swarmed with frogs*

Psalm 106

1 Praise the LORD!
   Give thanks to the LORD
   because he is good,
   because his faithful love endures forever.
2 Who could possibly repeat
   all of the LORD's mighty acts
   or publicly recount all his praise?

3 The people who uphold justice,
            who always do
            what is right,
            are truly happy!
4 Remember me, LORD, with the favor
   you show your people.
   Visit me with your saving help
      5 so I can experience the good things
         your chosen ones experience,
      so I can rejoice in the joy of your nation,
      so I can praise along
         with your possession.

6 We have sinned—
   right along with our ancestors.
   We've done what is wrong.
   We've acted wickedly.
7 Our ancestors in Egypt didn't understand
   your wondrous works.
   They didn't remember how much
      faithful love you have.
   So they rebelled by the sea—
      at the Reed Sea.q
8 But God saved them
   for the sake of his good name,
   to make known his mighty power.
9 God scolded the Reed Sea,
   and it dried right up;
   he led them through the deeps
      like they were a dry desert.
10 God saved them from hostile powers;
    he redeemed them
       from the power of the enemy.
11 But the waters covered over their foes—
    not one of them survived!
12 So our ancestors trusted God's words;
    they sang God's praise.

13 But how quickly they forgot
    what he had done!
    They wouldn't wait for his advice.

14 They were overcome with craving
    in the desert;
    they tested God in the wastelands.
15 God gave them what they asked for;
    he sent foodr to satisfy their appetites.

16 But then they were jealous of Moses
    in the camp,
    jealous too of Aaron,
       the LORD's holy one.
17 So the earth opened up,
    swallowing Dathan,
    and covering over Abiram's crowd.
18 Fire blazed throughout
    that whole group;
    flames burned up the wicked.

19 They made a calf at Horeb,
    bowing down to a metal idol.
20 They traded their glorious Gods
    for an image of a bull that eats grass.
21 They forgot the God who saved them—
    the one who had done
       great things in Egypt,
      22 wondrous works in the land of Ham,
    awesome deeds at the Reed Sea.
23 So God determined that he would
    destroy them—
    except for the fact that Moses,
       his chosen one,
    stood in the way, right in front of him,
    and turned God's destructive anger away.

24 But then they rejected the land
    that was so desirable.
    They didn't trust God's promise.
25 They muttered in their tents
    and wouldn't listen to the LORD's voice.
26 So God raised his hand against them,
    making them fall in the desert,
      27 scattering their offspring
         among the nations,
    casting them across many lands.

28 They joined themselves to Baal-peor
    and ate sacrifices offered to the dead.
29 They made God angry by what they did,
    so a plague broke out against them.
30 Then Phinehas stood up and prayed,
    and the plague was contained.

q Or *Red Sea*; also in 106:9, 22   r LXX   s Or *their Glory*

³¹ That's why Phinehas
    is considered righteous,
    generation after generation, forever.

³² But they angered God at Meribah's waters,
    and things went badly for Moses
        because of them,
³³ because they made him bitter
    so that he spoke rashly with his lips.

³⁴ They didn't destroy the nations
    as the Lᴏʀᴅ had ordered them to do.
³⁵ Instead, they got mixed up
    with the nations,
    learning what they did
³⁶ and serving those false gods,
    which became a trap for them.
³⁷ They sacrificed their own sons and
    daughters to demons!
³⁸ They shed innocent blood,
    the blood of their own
        sons and daughters—
    the ones they sacrificed
        to Canaan's false gods—
    so the land was defiled
        by the bloodshed.
³⁹ They made themselves unclean
    by what they did;
    they prostituted themselves
        by their actions.

⁴⁰ So the Lᴏʀᴅ's anger burned
    against his people;
    he despised his own possession.
⁴¹ God handed them over to the nations;
    people who hated them ruled over them.
⁴² Their enemies oppressed them,
    and they were humbled
        under their power.
⁴³ God delivered them numerous times,
    but they were determined to rebel,
    and so they were brought down
        by their own sin.
⁴⁴ But God saw their distress
    when he heard their loud cries.
⁴⁵ God remembered his covenant
    for their sake,
    and because of how much
        faithful love he has,
    God changed his mind.
⁴⁶ God allowed them to receive compassion
    from all their captors.

⁴⁷ Lᴏʀᴅ our God, save us!
    Gather us back together
        from among all the nations
    so we can give thanks to your holy name
        and rejoice in your praise!

⁴⁸ Bless the Lᴏʀᴅ, the God of Israel,
    from forever ago to forever from now!
    And let all the people say, "Amen!"

Praise the Lᴏʀᴅ!

BOOK V
(Psalms 107–150)

Psalm 107

¹ "Give thanks to the Lᴏʀᴅ
    because he is good,
    because his faithful love lasts forever!"
² That's what those who are redeemed
    by the Lᴏʀᴅ say,
    the ones God redeemed
        from the power of their enemies,
³ the ones God gathered
    from various countries,
    from east and west, north and south.

⁴ Some of the redeemed had wandered
    into the desert, into the wasteland.
    They couldn't find their way
        to a city or town.
⁵ They were hungry and thirsty;
    their lives were slipping away.
⁶ So they cried out to the Lᴏʀᴅ
    in their distress,
    and God delivered them
        from their desperate circumstances.
⁷ God led them straight
    to human habitation.
⁸ Let them thank the Lᴏʀᴅ
    for his faithful love
    and his wondrous works for all people,
⁹ because God satisfied the one
    who was parched with thirst,
    and he filled up the hungry
        with good things!

¹⁰ Some of the redeemed had been sitting
    in darkness and deep gloom;
    they were prisoners suffering in chains

¹¹ because they had disobeyed
  God's instructions
  and rejected the Most High's plans.
¹² So God humbled them with hard work.
  They stumbled, and there was no one
    to help them.
¹³ So they cried out to the Lord
  in their distress,
  and God saved them
    from their desperate circumstances.
¹⁴ God brought them out
  from the darkness and deep gloom;
  he shattered their chains.
¹⁵ Let them thank the Lord
  for his faithful love
  and his wondrous works for all people,
¹⁶ because God has shattered
  bronze doors
  and split iron bars in two!

¹⁷ Some of the redeemed were fools
  because of their sinful ways.
  They suffered because of
    their wickedness.
¹⁸ They had absolutely no appetite
  for food;
  they had arrived at death's gates.
¹⁹ So they cried out to the Lord
  in their distress,
  and God saved them
    from their desperate circumstances.
²⁰ God gave the order and healed them;
  he rescued them from their pit.
²¹ Let them thank the Lord
  for his faithful love
  and his wondrous works for all people.
²² Let them offer thanksgiving sacrifices
  and declare what God has done
    in songs of joy!

²³ Some of the redeemed had gone out
  on the ocean in ships,
  making their living on the high seas.
²⁴ They saw what the Lord had made;
  they saw his wondrous works
    in the depths of the sea.
²⁵ God spoke and stirred up a storm
  that brought the waves up high.
²⁶ The waves went as high as the sky;
  they crashed down to the depths.
  The sailors' courage melted
    at this terrible situation.

²⁷ They staggered and stumbled around
  like they were drunk.
  None of their skill was of any help.
²⁸ So they cried out to the Lord
  in their distress,
  and God brought them out safe
    from their desperate circumstances.
²⁹ God quieted the storm to a whisper;
  the sea's waves were hushed.
³⁰ So they rejoiced because the waves
  had calmed down;
  then God led them to the harbor
    they were hoping for.
³¹ Let them thank the Lord
  for his faithful love
  and his wondrous works for all people.
³² Let them exalt God
  in the congregation of the people
  and praise God
    in the assembly of the elders.

³³ God turns rivers into desert,
  watery springs into thirsty ground,
³⁴ fruitful land into unproductive dirt,
  when its inhabitants
    are wicked.
³⁵ But God can also turn the desert
  into watery pools,
  thirsty ground into
    watery springs,
³⁶ where he settles the hungry.
  They even build a city and live there!
³⁷ They plant fields and vineyards
  and obtain a fruitful harvest.
³⁸ God blesses them,
  and they become many.
  God won't even let
    their cattle diminish.
³⁹ But when they do diminish—
  when they're brought down
    by oppression, trouble, and grief—
⁴⁰ God pours contempt on their leaders,
  making them wander aimlessly
    in the wastelands.
⁴¹ But God raises the needy
  from their suffering;
  he makes their families
    as numerous as sheep!

⁴² Those who do right see it and celebrate,
  but every wicked person
    shuts their mouth.

**Bet
you
can**
read
this in 2
minutes.
**Ready,
set, go!**

⁴³ Whoever is wise will pay attention
to these things,
carefully considering
the LORD's faithful love.

Psalm 108†
A song. A psalm of David.

¹ My heart is unwavering, God.
I will sing and make music—
yes, with my whole being!
² Wake up, harp and lyre!
I will wake the dawn itself!
³ I will give thanks to you, LORD,
among all the peoples;
I will make music to you
among the nations,
⁴ because your faithful love
is higher than heaven;
your faithfulness reaches
the clouds.

LIGHTHOUSE

PRAISE

Praise *Psalm 108:1-4*
Artists are inspired by many things, including nature, love, and real-life events. Inspiration helps
artists write songs, stories, plays, books, or scripts
for movies and television shows. Psalm 108 celebrates God's faithful love as God helped the
Israelite tribes find their place in a promised land. ◖

⁵ Exalt yourself, God,
higher than heaven!
Let your glory be over all the earth!
⁶ Save me by your power and answer me
so that the people you love
might be rescued.

⁷ God has spoken in his sanctuary:
"I will celebrate as I divide up Shechem
and portion out the Succoth Valley.
⁸ Gilead is mine, Manasseh is mine;
Ephraim is my helmet,
Judah is my scepter.
⁹ But Moab is my washbowl;
I'll throw my shoe at Edom.
I shout in triumph over Philistia!

†Ps 108:1-5 parallels Ps 57:7-11; Ps 108:6-13 parallels Ps 60:5-12.

¹⁰ I wish someone would bring me
to a fortified city!
I wish someone would lead me to Edom!"

¹¹ But you have rejected us, God,
haven't you?
You, God, no longer accompany
our armies.
¹² Give us help against the enemy—
human help is worthless.
¹³ With God we will triumph:
God is the one who will trample
our adversaries.

Psalm 109
To the leader. Of David. A psalm.

¹ God of my praise, don't keep quiet,
² because the mouths of wicked liars
have opened up against me,
talking about me with lying tongues.
³ Hateful words surround me;
they attack me for no reason.
⁴ Instead of returning my love,
they accuse me—
but I am at prayer.
⁵ They repay me evil for good,
hatred in return for my love.

⁶ "Appoint a wicked person to be
against this person," they say,
"an accuser to stand right next to him.
⁷ When the sentence is passed,
let him be found guilty—
let his prayer be found sinful!
⁸ Let his days be few;
let someone else assume his position.
⁹ Let his children become orphans;
let his wife turn into a widow.
¹⁰ Let his children wander aimlessly,
begging,
driven out of their ruined homes.
¹¹ Let a creditor seize everything he owns;
let strangers plunder his wealth.

did you know? In Jewish and Arab cultures
it is a severe insult to throw
a shoe at someone. This was
also true in ancient times.

¹² Let no one extend faithful love
    to him;
    let no one have mercy
        on his orphans.
¹³ Let his descendants be eliminated;
    let their names be wiped out
        in just one generation!
¹⁴ Let his father's wrongdoing
    be remembered before the Lord;
    let his mother's sin
        never be wiped out.
¹⁵ Let them be before the Lord always,
    and let God eliminate the very memory
        of them from the land.
¹⁶ All because this person didn't remember
    to demonstrate faithful love,
    but chased after the poor and needy—
    even the brokenhearted—
        with deadly intent!
¹⁷ Since he loved to curse,
    let it come back on him!
    Since he didn't care much for blessing,
    let it be far away from him!
¹⁸ Since he wore curses like a coat,
    let them seep inside him like water,
        seep into his bones like oil!
¹⁹ Let them be like the clothes he wears,
    like a belt that is always around him."

²⁰ But let all that be the reward my accusers
    get from the Lord,
    the reward for those
        who speak evil against me!
²¹ But you, Lord, my Lord!—
    act on my behalf
        for the sake of your name;
    deliver me
        because your faithful love is so good;
²² because I am poor and needy,
    and my heart is broken.
²³ Like a lengthening shadow,
    I'm passing away;
    I'm shaken off, like some locust.
²⁴ My legs are weak from fasting;
    my body is skin and bones.
²⁵ I've become a joke to my accusers;
    when they see me,
    they just shake their heads.

²⁶ Help me, Lord my God!
    Save me according
        to your faithful love!
²⁷ And let them know
    that this is by your hand—
    that you have done it, Lord!
²⁸ Let them curse—but you, bless me!
    If they rise up, let them be disgraced,
    but let your servant celebrate!
²⁹ Let my accusers be dressed in shame;
    let them wear their disgrace like a coat.
³⁰ But I will give great thanks to the Lord
    with my mouth;
    among a great crowd I will praise God!
³¹ Because God stands
    right next to the needy,
    to save them from any
        who would condemn them.

Psalm 110
Of David. A psalm.

¹ What the Lord says to my master:
    "Sit right beside me
    until I make your enemies
        a footstool for your feet!"

² May the Lord make your mighty scepter
    reach far from Zion!
    Rule over your enemies!
³ Your people stand ready
    on your day of battle.
    "In holy grandeur,
    from the dawn's womb, fight!ᵘ
    Your youthful strength
    is like the dew itself."
⁴ The Lord has sworn a solemn pledge
    and won't change his mind:
    "You are a priest forever
    in line with Melchizedek."ᵛ
⁵ My master, by your strong hand,
    God has crushed kings
    on his day of wrath.ʷ

⁶ God brings the nations to justice,
    piling the dead bodies,
    crushing heads throughout the earth.
⁷ God drinks from a stream along the way,
    then holds his head up high.ˣ

ᵘCorrection; or Go!; MT *to you* ᵛOr *a rightful king by my decree* ʷOr *My Lord (God), because of your (the king's) strong hand, has crushed* or *The Lord is above your strong hand, crushing kings* ˣHeb uncertain

Psalm 111[y]

¹ Praise the Lord!

א   I thank the Lord with all my heart

ב   in the company of those who do right,
     in the congregation.

ג   ² The works of the Lord are magnificent;

ד   they are treasured
     by all who desire them.

ה   ³ God's deeds are majestic and glorious.

ו   God's righteousness stands forever.

ז   ⁴ God is famous for his wondrous works.

ח   The Lord is
     full of mercy and compassion.

ט   ⁵ God gives food to those who honor him.

י   God remembers his covenant forever.

כ   ⁶ God proclaimed his powerful deeds
     to his people

ל   and gave them what had belonged
     to other nations.

מ   ⁷ God's handiwork is honesty and justice;

נ   all God's rules are trustworthy—

ס   ⁸ they are established

ע   always and forever:
     they are fulfilled
      with truth and right doing.

פ   ⁹ God sent redemption for his people;

צ   God commanded
     that his covenant last forever.

ק   Holy and awesome is God's name!

ר   ¹⁰ Fear of the Lord is where wisdom begins;

ש   sure knowledge
     is for all who keep God's laws.

ת   God's praise lasts forever!

Psalm 112[z]

א   ¹ Praise the Lord!

     Those who honor the Lord,

ב   who adore God's commandments,
     are truly happy!

ג   ² Their descendants will be strong
     throughout the land.

ד   The offspring of those who do right
     will be blessed;

ה   ³ wealth and riches will be in their houses.

ו   Their righteousness stands forever.

ז   ⁴ They shine in the dark
     for others who do right.

ח   They are merciful, compassionate,
     and righteous.

ט   ⁵ Those who lend generously
     are good people—

י   as are those who conduct
     their affairs with justice.

כ   ⁶ Yes, these sorts of people
     will never be shaken;

ל   the righteous
     will be remembered forever!

מ   ⁷ They won't be frightened at bad news.

נ   Their hearts are steady,
     trusting in the Lord.

ס   ⁸ Their hearts are firm; they aren't afraid.

ע   In the end, they will witness
     their enemies' defeat.

פ   ⁹ They give freely to those in need.

צ   Their righteousness stands forever.

ק   Their strength increases gloriously.

ר   ¹⁰ The wicked see all this and fume;

ש   they grind their teeth,
     but disappear to nothing.

ת   What the wicked want to see happen
     comes to nothing!

Psalm 113

¹ Praise the Lord!
   You who serve the Lord—praise!
   Praise the Lord's name!

² Let the Lord's name be blessed
   from now until forever from now!

³ From sunrise to sunset,
   let the Lord's name be praised!

⁴ The Lord is high over all the nations;
   God's glory is higher than the skies!

⁵ Who could possibly
   compare to the Lord our God?
   God rules from on high;

⁶ he has to come down
   to even see heaven and earth!

⁷ God lifts up the poor from the dirt
   and raises up the needy
   from the garbage pile

⁸ to seat them with leaders—
   with the leaders of his own people!

⁹ God nests the once barren woman
   at home—
   now a joyful mother with children!

Praise the Lord!

---

[y] Ps 111 is an alphabetic acrostic poem; see the note at Pss 9–10.   [z] Ps 112 is an alphabetic acrostic poem; see the note at Pss 9–10.

Psalm 114

¹ When Israel came out of Egypt—
  when the house of Jacob came out
  from a people who spoke
  a different language—
² Judah was God's sanctuary;
  Israel was God's territory.

³ The sea saw it happen and ran away;
  the Jordan River retreated!
⁴ The mountains leaped away like rams;
  the hills leaped away like lambs!
⁵ Sea, why did you run away?
  Jordan, why did you retreat?
⁶ Mountains, why did you leap away
  like rams?
  Hills, why did you leap away like lambs?

⁷ Earth: Tremble before the Lord!
  Tremble before the God of Jacob,
⁸ the one who turned
  that rock into a pool of water,
  that flint stone into a spring of water!

Psalm 115

¹ Not to us, LORD, not to us—
  no, but to your own name give glory
  because of your loyal love
  and faithfulness!

² Why do the nations say,
  "Where's their God now?"
³ Our God is in heaven—
  he can do whatever he wants!
⁴ Their idols are just silver and gold—
  things made by human hands.
⁵ They have mouths, but they can't speak.
  They have eyes, but they can't see.
⁶ They have ears, but they can't hear.
  They have noses, but they can't smell.
⁷ They have hands, but they can't feel.
  They have feet, but they can't walk.
  They can't even make a noise
  in their throats!
⁸ Let the people who made these idols
  and all who trust in them
  become just like them!

God's THOUGHTS ◆ My THOUGHTS

No Comparison   *Psalm 113:5*

Throughout the Bible there are stories of people who made idols and statues to worship. Even today people treat things—friends, money, television, toys, and games—as if those things are more important than God. They may take a person's focus away from God even if he or she doesn't worship those things.

God wants our full attention and devotion. This can be difficult. Things we own may seem to own us. As we get older we own bigger, more expensive things that require more of our attention. It becomes easier to give less time to God. It's important to keep God as our first priority instead of the things we own. When we want something, we should ask God if we really need it.

Nothing can compare to God. There is nothing that we can buy or substitute for God. God's gifts are free and given generously to God's children. When something starts to compete for our attention, we should put it away for a while or maybe even get rid of it. Nothing is more important than God.

List three things that you value the most.

Is there anything on that list that gets more attention than God? If so, what can you do to change this?

9 But you, Israel, trust in the LORD!
  God is their help and shield.
10 Trust in the LORD, house of Aaron!
  God is their help and shield.
11 You who honor the LORD, trust in the LORD!
  God is their help and shield.
12 The LORD remembers us and will bless us:
  God will bless the house of Israel;
  God will bless the house of Aaron;
13 God will bless those who honor the LORD—
  from the smallest to the greatest.

14 May the LORD add to your numbers—
  both you and your children.
15 May you be blessed by the LORD,
  the maker of heaven and earth!
16 The highest heaven belongs to the LORD,
  but he gave the earth to all people.
17 The dead don't praise the LORD,
  nor do those who go down to silence.
18 But us? We will bless the LORD
  from now until forever from now!

  Praise the LORD!

Psalm 116

1 I love the LORD because he hears
  my requests for mercy.
2 I'll call out to him as long as I live,
  because he listens closely to me.
3 Death's ropes bound me;
  the distress of the grave[a] found me—
  I came face-to-face with trouble and grief.
4 So I called on the LORD's name:
  "LORD, please save me!"[b]

5 The LORD is merciful and righteous;
  our God is compassionate.
6 The LORD protects simple folk;
  he saves me whenever I am brought down.
7 I tell myself, You can be at peace again,
  because the LORD has been good to you.
8 You, God, have delivered me from death,
  my eyes from tears,
  and my foot from stumbling,
9 so I'll walk before the LORD
  in the land of the living.

10 I have remained faithful, even when I said,
  "I am suffering so badly!"
11 even when I said, out of fear,
  "Everyone is a liar!"

12 What can I give back to the LORD
  for all the good things
    he has done for me?
13 I'll lift up the cup of salvation.
  I'll call on the LORD's name.
14 I'll keep the promises I made to the LORD
  in the presence of all God's people.
15 The death of the LORD's faithful
  is a costly loss in his eyes.

16 Oh yes, LORD, I am definitely your servant!
  I am your servant and the son
    of your female servant—
  you've freed me from my chains.
17 So I'll offer a sacrifice of thanksgiving to you,
  and I'll call on
    the LORD's name.

SAILBOAT

GIVING THANKS

A Sacrifice of Thanks *Psalm 116:17*
Sacrificing something isn't easy. It means giving up something we love or treasure. So when Psalm 116 talks about offering a sacrifice of thanks to God, it means giving God our time, energy, and talents to show we are thankful. We can be grateful for all God has done for us and through us. When we go through hard times, we can declare that we trust God no matter what happens in our lives.

18 I'll keep the promises I made to the LORD
  in the presence of all God's people,
19 in the courtyards of the LORD's house,
  which is in the center of Jerusalem.

  Praise the LORD!

Psalm 117

1 Praise the LORD, all you nations!
  Worship him, all you peoples!
2 Because God's faithful love toward us
    is strong,
  the LORD's faithfulness lasts forever!
  Praise the LORD!

did you **know**? Psalm 117 is the shortest chapter in the Bible. It has only two verses.

---

a Heb *Sheol* b Or *my soul*; also in 116:7-8

Psalm 118

¹ Give thanks to the L<small>ORD</small>
because he is good,
because his faithful love lasts forever.
² Let Israel say it:
"God's faithful love lasts forever!"
³ Let the house of Aaron say it:
"God's faithful love lasts forever!"
⁴ Let those who honor the L<small>ORD</small> say it:
"God's faithful love lasts forever!"

⁵ In tight circumstances,
I cried out to the L<small>ORD</small>.
The L<small>ORD</small> answered me
with wide-open spaces.
⁶ The L<small>ORD</small> is for me[c]—I won't be afraid.
What can anyone do to me?
⁷ The L<small>ORD</small> is for me—as my helper.
I look in victory on those who hate me.
⁸ It's far better to take refuge in the L<small>ORD</small>
than to trust any human.
⁹ It's far better to take refuge in the L<small>ORD</small>
than to trust any human leader.
¹⁰ All the nations surrounded me,
but I cut them down[d]
in the L<small>ORD</small>'s name.
¹¹ Yes, they surrounded me
on every single side,
but I cut them down in the L<small>ORD</small>'s name.
¹² They surrounded me like bees,
but they were extinguished
like burning thorns.
I cut them down in the L<small>ORD</small>'s name!
¹³ I was pushed so hard[e] I nearly died,
but the L<small>ORD</small> helped me.
¹⁴ The L<small>ORD</small> was my strength
and protection;
he was my saving help!
¹⁵ The sounds of joyful songs and deliverance
are heard in the tents of the righteous:
"The L<small>ORD</small>'s strong hand is victorious!
¹⁶ The L<small>ORD</small>'s strong hand is ready to strike!
The L<small>ORD</small>'s strong hand is victorious!"

¹⁷ I won't die—no, I will live
and declare what the L<small>ORD</small> has done.
¹⁸ Yes, the L<small>ORD</small> definitely disciplined me,
but he didn't hand me over to death.

There are 1,189 chapters in the Bible. There are 594 chapters before Psalm 118, and 594 chapters after it. Psalm 118 is chapter 595, the middle chapter of the Bible.

¹⁹ Open the gates of righteousness for me
so I can come in
and give thanks to the L<small>ORD</small>!
²⁰ This is the L<small>ORD</small>'s gate;
those who are righteous enter through it.

²¹ I thank you because you answered me,
because you were my saving help.
²² The stone rejected by the builders
is now the main foundation stone!
²³ This has happened because of the L<small>ORD</small>;
it is astounding in our sight!
²⁴ This is the day the L<small>ORD</small> acted;
we will rejoice and celebrate in it!

²⁵ L<small>ORD</small>, please save us!
L<small>ORD</small>, please let us succeed!

²⁶ The one who enters in the L<small>ORD</small>'s name
is blessed;
we bless all of you
from the L<small>ORD</small>'s house.
²⁷ The L<small>ORD</small> is God!
He has shined a light on us!
So lead the festival offering with ropes
all the way to the horns of the altar.[f]
²⁸ You are my God—I will give thanks to you!
You are my God—I will lift you up high!
²⁹ Give thanks to the L<small>ORD</small>
because he is good,
because his faithful love lasts forever.

Psalm 119[g]

ℵ ALEF

¹ Those whose way is blameless—
who walk in the L<small>ORD</small>'s Instruction—
are truly happy!
² Those who guard God's laws
are truly happy!
They seek God with all their hearts.

---

[c]LXX *with me* or *mine*; also in 118:7 [d]Heb uncertain; LXX,Vulg *drove* or *warded off*; also in 118:11-12 [e]LXX, Vulg, Syr; MT *you pushed me* [f]Heb uncertain [g]Ps 119 is an alphabetic acrostic poem (cf Pss 9–10) in Heb, with each line of Heb within the marked sections beginning with the same letter of the alphabet.

³ They don't even do anything wrong!
  They walk in God's ways.
⁴ God, you have ordered that your decrees
  should be kept most carefully.
⁵ How I wish my ways were strong
  when it comes to keeping your statutes!
⁶ Then I wouldn't be ashamed
  when I examine all your commandments.
⁷ I will give thanks to you
  with a heart that does right
  as I learn your righteous rules.
⁸ I will keep your statutes.
  Please don't leave me
  all alone!

SAILBOAT

Joy

Joy of Following God *Psalm 119:1-2*
We might assume from the first two verses of
Psalm 119 that no one can be happy because no
one is truly blameless. Many people throughout
the Bible were described as blameless. This word
doesn't mean perfect. Instead, *blameless* describes
people who use God's Instruction as their basis for
living. People who have good character are happy.
By following God's Instruction and seeking God
with their whole being, they trust God to lead them,
protect them, and provide for their needs. ◈

ב BET

⁹ How can young people
  keep their paths pure?
  By guarding them
  according to what you've said.^h
¹⁰ I have sought you with all my heart.
  Don't let me stray
  from any of your commandments!
¹¹ I keep your word close, in my heart,
  so that I won't sin against you.
¹² You, Lord, are to be blessed!
  Teach me your statutes.
¹³ I will declare out loud
  all the rules you have spoken.
¹⁴ I rejoice in the content of your laws
  as if I were rejoicing over great wealth.
¹⁵ I will think about your precepts
  and examine all your paths.
¹⁶ I will delight in your statutes;
  I will not forget what you have said.

ג GIMEL

¹⁷ Be good to your servant
  so I can go on living
  and keeping your word.
¹⁸ Open my eyes so I can examine
  the wonders of your Instruction!
¹⁹ I'm an immigrant in the land.
  Don't hide your commandments from me!
²⁰ I'm worn out by longing
  every minute for your rules!
²¹ You rebuke the arrogant, accursed people
  who stray from your commandments.
²² Take all their insults and contempt
  away from me
  because I've kept your laws!
²³ Even if rulers gather and scheme
  against me,
  your servant will contemplate
  your statutes!
²⁴ Yes, your laws are my joy—
  they are my most trusted advisors!

ד DALET

²⁵ My life is stuck in the dirt.
  Now make me live again
  according to your promise!
²⁶ I confessed my ways
  and you answered me.
  Now teach me your statutes!
²⁷ Help me understand
  what your precepts are about
  so I can contemplate
  your wondrous works!
²⁸ My spirit sags because of grief.
  Now raise me up
  according to your promise!
²⁹ Remove all false ways from me;
  show mercy to me
  by means of your Instruction.
³⁰ I've chosen the way of faithfulness;
  I'm set on your rules.
³¹ I'm holding tight to your laws, Lord.
  Please don't let me be put to shame.
³² I run the same path
  as your commandments
  because you give my heart insight.

ה HE

³³ Lord, teach me what your statutes
  are about,
  and I will guard every part of them.

34 Help me understand
  so I can guard your Instruction
  and keep it with all my heart.
35 Lead me on the trail
  of your commandments
  because that is what I want.
36 Turn my heart to your laws,
  not to greedy gain.
37 Turn my eyes away from looking
  at worthless things.
  Make me live by your way.
38 Confirm your promise to your servant—
  the promise that is
  for all those who honor you.
39 Remove the insults that I dread
  because your rules are good.
40 Look how I desire your precepts!
  Make me live by your righteousness.

ו WAW

41 Lord, let your faithful love come to me—
  let your salvation come to me according
  to your promise—
42 so I can have a response
  for those who mock me
  because I have trusted in your word!
43 Please don't take your true word
  out of my mouth,
  because I have waited for your rules.
44 I will always keep your Instruction,
  always and forever!
45 I will walk around in wide-open spaces,
  because I have pursued your precepts.
46 I will talk about your laws
  before rulers with no shame whatsoever.
47 I will rejoice in your commandments
  because I love them.
48 I will lift up my hands
  to your commandments
  because I love them,
  and I will contemplate all your statutes.

ז ZAYIN

49 Remember your promise to your servant,
  for which you made me wait.
50 My comfort during my suffering is this:
  your word gives me new life.
51 The arrogant make fun of me to no end,
  but I haven't deviated
  from your Instruction.
52 When I remember your ancient rules,
  I'm comforted, Lord.

53 But I'm seized with anger
  because of the wicked—
  because of those who abandon
  your Instruction.
54 Your statutes have been
  my songs of praise
  wherever I lived as an immigrant.
55 Lord, I remember your name at nighttime,
  and I keep your Instruction.
56 This has been my practice
  because I guard your precepts.

ח KHET

57 The Lord is my possession.
  I promise to do what you have said.
58 I've sought your favor with all my heart;
  have mercy on me
  according to your word.
59 I've considered my ways and turned
  my feet back to your laws.
60 I hurry to keep your commandments—
  I never put it off!
61 Though the wicked have surrounded me
  with their ropes,
  I haven't forgotten your Instruction.
62 I get up in the middle of the night
  to give thanks to you
  because of your righteous rules.
63 I'm a friend to everyone who honors you
  and to all who keep your precepts.
64 Lord, the world is full
  of your faithful love!
  Teach me your statutes!

ט TET

65 You have treated your servant well,
  Lord, according to your promise.
66 Teach me knowledge and good judgment
  because I've put my trust
  in your commandments.
67 Before I suffered, I took the wrong way,
  but now I do what you say.
68 You are good and you do good.
  Teach me your statutes!
69 The arrogant cover me with their lies,
  but I guard your precepts
  with all my heart.
70 Their hearts are unfeeling, like blubber,
  but I rejoice in your Instruction.
71 My suffering was good for me,
  because through it
  I learned your statutes.

⁷² The Instruction you've given to me
is better
than thousands of pieces
of gold and silver!

ʾ YOD

⁷³ Your hands have made me
and set me in place.
Help me understand
so I can learn your commandments.
⁷⁴ Then those who honor you
will see me and be glad
because I have waited for your promise.
⁷⁵ Lord, I know that your rules are right
and that you rightly made me suffer.
⁷⁶ Please let your faithful love comfort me,
according to what you've said
to your servant.
⁷⁷ Let your compassion come to me
so I can live again,
because your Instruction is my joy!
⁷⁸ But let the arrogant be ashamed
because they oppressed me with lies—
meanwhile, I will be contemplating
your precepts!
⁷⁹ Let the people who honor you
come back to me;
let those who know your precepts
return to me.
⁸⁰ Let my heart be blameless in your statutes
so that I am not put to shame.

כ KAF

⁸¹ My whole being yearns
for your saving help!
I wait for your promise.
⁸² My eyes are worn out
looking for your word.
"When will you comfort me?" I ask,
⁸³ because I've become like a bottle
dried up by smoke,
though I haven't forgotten your statutes.
⁸⁴ How much more time
does your servant have?
When will you bring my oppressors
to justice?
⁸⁵ The arrogant have dug pits for me—
those people who act
against your Instruction.
⁸⁶ All your commandments are true,

but people harass me for no reason.
Help me!
⁸⁷ They've almost wiped me
off the face of the earth!
Meanwhile, I haven't abandoned
your precepts!
⁸⁸ Make me live again
according to your faithful love
so I can keep the law you've given!

ל LAMED

⁸⁹ Your word, Lord,
stands firm in heaven forever!
⁹⁰ Your faithfulness extends
from one generation to the next!
You set the earth firmly in place,
and it is still there.
⁹¹ Your rules endure to this day
because everything serves you.
⁹² If your Instruction
hadn't been my delight,
I would have died
because of my suffering.
⁹³ I will never forget your precepts
because through them
you gave me life again.
⁹⁴ I'm yours—save me
because I've pursued your precepts!
⁹⁵ The wicked wait for me,
wanting to kill me,
but I'm studying your laws.
⁹⁶ I've seen that everything,
no matter how perfect, has a limit,[i]
but your commandment is boundless.

מ MEM

⁹⁷ I love your Instruction!
I think about it constantly.
⁹⁸ Your commandment makes me wiser
than my enemies
because it is always with me.
⁹⁹ I have greater insight than all my teachers
because I contemplate your laws.
¹⁰⁰ I have more understanding than the elders
because I guard your precepts.
¹⁰¹ I haven't set my feet on any evil path
so I can make sure to keep your word.
¹⁰² I haven't deviated from any of your rules
because you are the one
who has taught me.

Bet you can read this in 1 minute. **Ready, set, go!**

[i]Heb uncertain

¹⁰³ Your word is so pleasing to my taste buds—
it's sweeter than honey in my mouth!
¹⁰⁴ I'm studying your precepts—
that's why I hate every false path.

נ NUN

¹⁰⁵ Your word is a lamp before my feet
and a light
for my journey.

Memorize
Ps 119:105

¹⁰⁶ I have sworn, and I fully mean it:
I will keep your righteous rules.
¹⁰⁷ I have been suffering so much—
LORD, make me live again
according to your promise.
¹⁰⁸ Please, LORD, accept my
spontaneous gifts of praise.
Teach me your rules!
¹⁰⁹ Though my life is constantly in danger,
I won't forget your Instruction.
¹¹⁰ Though the wicked
have set a trap for me,
I won't stray from your precepts.
¹¹¹ Your laws are my possession forever
because they are my heart's joy.
¹¹² I have decided to keep your statutes
forever, every last one.

ס SAMEK

¹¹³ I hate fickle people,
but I love your Instruction.
¹¹⁴ You are my shelter and my shield—
I wait for your promise.
¹¹⁵ Get away from me, you evildoers;
I want to guard
my God's commandments!
¹¹⁶ Sustain me according to your word
so I can live!
Don't let me be put to shame
because of hope.
¹¹⁷ Support me so I can be saved
and so I can focus constantly
on your statutes.
¹¹⁸ You discard everyone who strays
from your statutes
because they are dishonest and false.
¹¹⁹ You dispose of all the wicked people on
earth like waste—
that's why I love your laws.
¹²⁰ My body shudders because I fear you;
I'm in awe of your rules.

ע AYIN

¹²¹ I've done what is just and right.
Don't just hand me over
to my oppressors.
¹²² Guarantee good things for your servant.
Please don't let the arrogant oppress me.
¹²³ My eyes are worn out
looking for your saving help—
looking for your word
that will set things right.
¹²⁴ Act toward your servant
according to your faithful love.
Teach me your statutes!
¹²⁵ I'm your servant!
Help me understand
so I can know your laws.
¹²⁶ It is time for the LORD to do something!
Your Instruction has been broken.
¹²⁷ But I love your commandments
more than gold,
even more than pure gold.
¹²⁸ That's why I walk straight by
every single one of your precepts.
That's why I hate every false path.

פ PE

¹²⁹ Your laws are wonderful!
That's why I guard them.
¹³⁰ Access to your words^j gives light,
giving simple folk understanding.
¹³¹ I open my mouth up wide, panting,
because I long for your commandments.
¹³² Come back to me and have mercy on me;
that's only right
for those who love your name.
¹³³ Keep my steps steady by your word;
don't let any sin rule me.
¹³⁴ Redeem me from the people
who oppress me
so I can keep your precepts.
¹³⁵ Shine your face on your servant,
and teach me your statutes.
¹³⁶ Rivers of tears stream from my eyes
because your Instruction isn't being kept.

צ TSADE

¹³⁷ LORD, you are righteous,
and your rules are right.
¹³⁸ The laws you commanded are righteous,
completely trustworthy.

^j Vulg, Sym

139 Anger consumes me
   because my enemies have forgotten
      what you've said.
140 Your word has been tried and tested;
   your servant loves your word!
141 I'm insignificant and unpopular,
   but I don't forget your precepts.
142 Your righteousness lasts forever!
   Your Instruction is true!
143 Stress and strain have caught up with me,
   but your commandments are my joy!
144 Your laws are righteous forever.
   Help me understand so I can live!

ק QOF

145 I cry out with all my heart:
   "LORD, answer me
      so I can guard your statutes!"
146 I cry out to you, "Save me
      so I can keep your laws!"
147 I meet the predawn light and cry for help.
   I wait for your promise.
148 My eyes encounter each hour of the night
   as I think about your word.
149 Listen to my voice,
   according to your faithful love.
   LORD, make me live again,
      according to your justice.
150 The people who love to plot wicked
      schemes are nearby,
   but they are so far from your Instruction!
151 But you, LORD, are nearby too,
   and all your commandments are true.
152 Long ago I learned from your laws
   that you had established them forever.

ר RESH

153 Look at my suffering and deliver me
   because I haven't forgotten
      your Instruction.
154 Argue my case and redeem me.
   Make me live again by your word.
155 Salvation is far from the wicked
   because they haven't pursued
      your statutes.
156 You have so much compassion, LORD—
   make me live again,
      according to your rules.
157 My oppressors and enemies are many,
   but I haven't turned away from your laws.
158 I look on the faithless, and I am disgusted
   because they haven't kept your word.

159 Look at how much I love your precepts.
   Make me live again, LORD,
      according to your faithful love!
160 The first thing to know about your word
      is that it is true
   and that all your righteous rules
      last forever.

ש SIN AND ש SHIN

161 Rulers oppress me without cause,
   but my heart honors what you've said.
162 I'm overjoyed at your word,
   like someone who finds great treasure.
163 I hate, I absolutely despise, what is false,
   but I'm in love with your Instruction.
164 I praise you seven times a day
   for your righteous rules.
165 The people who love your Instruction
      enjoy peace—and lots of it.
   There's no stumbling
      for them!

SAILBOAT

PEACE

God's Word Brings Peace *Psalm 119:165*
Each of our actions—whether good or bad—has
consequences. If we finish our homework on time,
we'll get better grades than if we turn it in late. If
we touch a hot stove, we'll burn our hands. Even if
our actions are unintentional, there are still consequences. If we accidentally step on an ant bed, for
example, we'll still get bitten.
   Psalm 119 states an obvious consequence:
people who love God's Instruction will enjoy lots
of peace and won't stumble on the path of life. This
doesn't mean they won't have troubles. The Bible is
filled with stories of good people who faced hard
times. But people who love God's Instruction know
that God will be there to help them in hard times.
That knowledge gives them peace. ♦

166 LORD, I wait for your saving help.
   I do what you've commanded.
167 I keep your laws;
   I love them so much!
168 I keep your precepts and your laws
   because all my ways are seen by you.

ת TAV

169 Let my cry reach you, LORD;
   help me understand
      according to what you've said.

¹⁷⁰ Let my request for grace come before you;
  deliver me according to your promise!
¹⁷¹ Let my lips overflow with praise
  because you've taught me your statutes.
¹⁷²Let my tongue declare your word,
  because all your commandments
  are righteous.
¹⁷³ Let your power help me
  because I have chosen your precepts.
¹⁷⁴Lord, I long for your saving help!
  Your Instruction is my joy!
¹⁷⁵ Let me live again so I can praise you!
  Let your rules help me!
¹⁷⁶ I've wandered off like a sheep, lost.
  Find your servant
    because I haven't forgotten
    your commandments!

Psalm 120
A pilgrimage song.^k

¹ I cried out to the Lord
  when I was in trouble
  (and he answered me):
² "Lord, deliver me^l from lying lips
  and a dishonest tongue!"
³ What more will be given to you,
  what more will be done to you,
  you dishonest tongue?
⁴ Just this:^m a warrior's sharpened arrows,
  coupled with burning coals
    from a woodⁿ fire!

⁵ Oh, I'm doomed
  because I have been an immigrant
    in Meshech,
  because I've made my home
    among Kedar's tents.
⁶ I've lived far too long
  with people who hate peace.
⁷ I'm for peace,
  but when I speak, they are for war.

Psalm 121
A pilgrimage song.

¹ I raise my eyes toward the mountains.
  Where will my help come from?
² My help comes from the Lord,
  the maker of heaven and earth.

³ God won't let your foot slip.
  Your protector won't fall asleep on the job.
⁴ No! Israel's protector
  never sleeps or rests!
⁵ The Lord is your protector;
  the Lord is your shade right beside you.
⁶ The sun won't strike you during the day;
  neither will the moon at night.
⁷ The Lord will protect you from all evil;
  God will protect your very life.^o
⁸ The Lord will protect you
  on your journeys—
    whether going or coming—
  from now until forever from now.

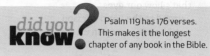

did you **know?** Psalm 119 has 176 verses. This makes it the longest chapter of any book in the Bible.

Psalm 122
A pilgrimage song. Of David.

¹ I rejoiced with those who said to me,
  "Let's go to the Lord's house!"
² Now our feet are standing
  in your gates, Jerusalem!

³ Jerusalem is built like a city
  joined together in unity.
⁴ That is where the tribes go up—
  the Lord's tribes!
  It is the law for Israel
  to give thanks there to the Lord's name,
⁵ because the thrones of justice are there—
  the thrones of the house of David!

⁶ Pray that Jerusalem has peace:
  "Let those who love you have rest.
⁷ Let there be peace on your walls;
  let there be rest on your fortifications."

did you **know?** Psalms 120–134 were sung as people traveled to Jerusalem for festivals or worship. Jerusalem was built on a series of hills including Mount Zion where God's temple was built. By looking to the hills for help, the people were looking to Jerusalem and the temple where God's presence dwelled.

^kOr *song of ascents* or *song of going up* (that is, to Jerusalem); cf Ps 122:4. The heading is found in every psalm from Ps 120 to Ps 134. ^lOr *my soul*; also in 120:6 ^mHeb lacks *this*. ⁿOr *the gorse* or *broom tree* ^oOr *your soul*

8 For the sake of my family and friends,
I say, "Peace be with you, Jerusalem."
9 For the sake of the LORD our God's house
I will pray for your good.

Psalm 123

A pilgrimage song.

1 I raise my eyes to you—
you who rule heaven.
2 Just as the eyes of servants attend
to their masters' hand,
just as the eyes of a female servant
attend to her mistress' hand—
that's how our eyes
attend to the LORD our God
until he has mercy on us.

3 Have mercy on us, LORD! Have mercy
because we've had
more than enough shame.
4 We've had more than enough mockery
from the self-confident,
more than enough shame from the proud.

Psalm 124

A pilgrimage song. Of David.

1 If the LORD hadn't been for us—
let Israel now repeat!—
2 if the LORD hadn't been for us,
when those people attacked us
3 then they would have swallowed
us up whole
with their rage burning against us!
4 Then the waters would have drowned us;
the torrent
would have come over our necks;[p]
5 then the raging waters
would have come over our necks!

6 Bless the LORD
because he didn't hand us over
like food for our enemies' teeth!
7 We escaped like a bird
from the hunters' trap;
the trap was broken so we escaped!

8 Our help is in the name of the LORD,
the maker of heaven and earth.

Psalm 125

A pilgrimage song.

1 The people who trust in the LORD
are like Mount Zion:
never shaken, lasting forever.
2 Mountains surround Jerusalem.
That's how the LORD surrounds his people
from now until forever
from now!

SAILBOAT

I'M SAFE

God Cares for Us *Psalm 125:2*

Psalm 125 uses the image of mountains to show how God protects the people God loves. God's love surrounds us like the mountains that surrounded the city of Jerusalem. That love shields us from harm. God protects us when we face trials and challenges. And God's love for us will never end.

3 The wicked rod won't remain
in the land given to the righteous
so that they don't use their hands
to do anything wrong.[q]
4 LORD, do good to people who are good,
to people whose hearts are right.
5 But as for those people
who turn to their own twisted ways—
may the LORD march them off
with other evildoers!

Peace be on Israel!

Psalm 126

A pilgrimage song.

1 When the LORD changed Zion's
circumstances for the better,
it was like we had been dreaming.
2 Our mouths were suddenly filled
with laughter;
our tongues were filled
with joyful shouts.
It was even said, at that time,
among the nations,
"The LORD has done great things
for them!"
3 Yes, the LORD has done great things for us,
and we are overjoyed.

[p]Or *soul*; also in 124:5,7 [q]Heb uncertain

⁴ Lord, change our circumstances
for the better,
like dry streams in the desert waste!
⁵ Let those who plant with tears
reap the harvest with joyful shouts.
⁶ Let those who go out,
crying and carrying their seed,
come home with joyful shouts,
carrying bales of grain!

Psalm 127

A pilgrimage song. Of Solomon.

¹ Unless it is the Lord who builds the house,
the builders' work is pointless.
Unless it is the Lord who protects the city,
the guard on duty is pointless.
² It is pointless that you get up early
and stay up late,
eating the bread of hard labor
because God gives sleep to those he loves.

³ No doubt about it:
children are a gift from the Lord;
the fruit of the womb is a divine reward.
⁴ The children born when one is young
are like arrows in the hand of a warrior.
⁵ The person who fills a quiver
full with them is truly happy!
They won't be ashamed
when arguing with their enemies
in the gate.

Psalm 128

A pilgrimage song.

¹ Everyone who honors the Lord,
who walks in God's ways, is truly happy!

² You will definitely enjoy
what you've worked hard for—
you'll be happy;
and things will go well for you.
³ In your house,
your wife will be like a vine full of fruit.
All around your table, your children will
be like olive trees, freshly planted.
⁴ That's how it goes for anyone
who honors the Lord:
they will be blessed!

⁵ May the Lord bless you from Zion.
May you experience Jerusalem's
goodness your whole life long.
⁶ And may you see your grandchildren.

Peace be on Israel!

Psalm 129

A pilgrimage song.

¹ From youth, people have constantly
attacked me—
let Israel now repeat!—
² from youth people have constantly
attacked me—
but they haven't beaten me!
³ They plowed my back like farmers;
they made their furrows deep.
⁴ But the Lord is righteous—
God cut me free
from the ropes of the wicked!

⁵ Let everyone who hates Zion be ashamed,
thoroughly frustrated.
⁶ Let them be like grass on a roof
that dies before it can be pulled up,
⁷ which won't fill the reaper's hand
or fill the harvester's arms.
⁸ Let no one who passes by say to them:
"May the Lord's blessing be on you!
We bless you in the Lord's name!"

Psalm 130

A pilgrimage song.

¹ I cry out to you from the depths, Lord—
² my Lord, listen to my voice!
Let your ears pay close attention
to my request for mercy!
³ If you kept track of sins, Lord—
my Lord, who would stand a chance?
⁴ But forgiveness is with you—
that's why you are honored.

⁵ I hope, Lord.
My whole being[r] hopes,
and I wait for God's promise.
⁶ My whole being waits for my Lord—
more than the night watch
waits for morning;

---

[r] Or *soul*; also in 132:6

yes, more than the night watch
    waits for morning!

[7] Israel, wait for the Lord!
    Because faithful love is with the Lord;
    because great redemption
        is with our God!
[8] He is the one who will redeem Israel
    from all its sin.

Psalm 131

A pilgrimage song. Of David.

[1] Lord, my heart isn't proud;
        my eyes aren't conceited.
    I don't get involved with things
    too great or wonderful for me.
[2] No. But I have calmed
        and quieted myself[s]
    like a weaned child on its mother;
    I'm like the weaned child
        that is with me.

Bet you can read this in 30 seconds. Ready, set, go!

[3] Israel, wait for the Lord—
    from now until forever from now!

Psalm 132

A pilgrimage song.

[1] Lord, remember David—
    all the ways he suffered
[2] and how he swore to the Lord,
    how he promised the strong one of Jacob:
[3] "I won't enter my house,
    won't get into my bed.
[4] I won't let my eyes close,
    won't let my eyelids sleep,
[5] until I find a place for the Lord,
    a dwelling place
        for the strong one of Jacob."

[6] Yes, we heard about it in Ephrathah;
    we found it[t] in the fields of Jaar.
[7] Let's enter God's dwelling place;
    let's worship at the place
        God rests his feet!
[8] Get up, Lord, go to your residence—
    you and your powerful covenant chest!
[9] Let your priests be dressed
    in righteousness;
    let your faithful shout out with joy!

[10] And for the sake of your servant David,
    do not reject your anointed one.

[11] The Lord swore to David
    a true promise that God
        won't take back:
    "I will put one of your own children
        on your throne.
[12] And if your children keep my covenant
    and the laws that I will teach them,
    then their children too
        will rule on your throne forever."

[13] Because the Lord chose Zion;
    he wanted it for his home.
[14] "This is my residence forever.
    I will live here
        because I wanted it for myself.[u]
[15] I will most certainly
    bless its food supply;
    I will fill its needy full of food!
[16] I will dress its priests in salvation,
    and its faithful
        will shout out loud with joy!
[17] It is there that I will make David's
    strength thrive.[v]
    I will prepare a lamp
        for my anointed one there.
[18] I will dress his enemies in shame,
    but the crown he wears
        will shine."

SAILBOAT

FAMILY AND FRIENDS

Loving Families *Psalm 133:1-2*
When God gave the Instruction to Moses, God commanded him to make fragrant anointing oil from olive oil and the finest spices. The priests used this oil for special purposes, including anointing people who entered the priesthood or became king. An older priest would pour the oil on top of the head of the other person. It would run down that person's face and drip onto his clothes. The oil's fragrance would fill the room and linger on the anointed priest for days afterward. This oil showed everyone that this person was special and set apart for service to God. Psalm 133 says that when families love each other and get along, it's as if they are anointed with oil—special and blessed by God. ◆

---

[s]Or *my soul* [t]*It may refer to the covenant chest (132:8b).* [u]Heb lacks *for myself.* [v]Or *make a horn sprout*

Psalm 133
A pilgrimage song. Of David.

¹ Look at how good and pleasing it is
  when families[w] live together as one!
² It is like expensive oil poured over the head,
  running down onto the beard—
    Aaron's beard!—
  which extended over the collar of his robes.
³ It is like the dew on Mount Hermon
  streaming down
    onto the mountains of Zion,
  because it is there that the Lord
  has commanded the blessing:
    everlasting life.

Psalm 134
A pilgrimage song.

¹ All you who serve the Lord:
  bless the Lord right now!
  All you who minister in the Lord's
    house at night: bless God!
² Lift up your hands to the sanctuary
  and bless the Lord!
³ May the Lord,
  the maker of heaven and earth,
  bless you from Zion.

Psalm 135

¹ Praise the Lord!
  Praise the Lord's name!
  All you who serve the Lord, praise God!
² All you who stand in the Lord's house—
  who stand in the courtyards
    of our God's temple—
³ praise the Lord,
  because the Lord is good!
  Sing praises to God's name
  because it is beautiful!
⁴ Because the Lord chose Jacob as his own,
  God chose Israel
  as his treasured possession.

⁵ Yes, I know for certain
  that the Lord is great—
  I know our Lord is greater
  than all other gods.
⁶ The Lord can do whatever he wants
  in heaven or on earth,
  in the seas and in every ocean depth.

⁷ God forms clouds at the far corners
  of the earth.
  God makes lightning for the rain.
  God releases the wind
  from its storeroom.
⁸ God struck down
  the Egyptians' oldest offspring—
  both human and animal!
⁹ God sent signs and wonders
  into the very center of Egypt—
  against Pharaoh and all his servants.
¹⁰ God struck down many nations
  and killed mighty kings:
¹¹ Sihon the Amorite king,
  Og the king of Bashan,
  and all the Canaanite kings.
¹² Then God handed their land
  over as an inheritance—
  as an inheritance to Israel,
  his own people.

¹³ Lord, your name is forever!
  Lord, your fame extends
  from one generation to the next!
¹⁴ The Lord gives justice to his people
  and has compassion
  on those who serve him.

¹⁵ The nations' idols are just silver and gold—
  things made by human hands.
¹⁶ They have mouths, but they can't speak.
  They have eyes,
  but they can't see.

LIGHTHOUSE

False Gods

Worshipping False Gods *Psalm 135:15-18*
During ancient times, many people believed in more than one god. They believed there were many gods who looked like humans, animals, trees, and rocks. They believed these gods behaved like humans with supernatural powers. They believed these gods would do terrible things if they got angry. In order to keep these gods happy, people made statues out of wood, precious metals, and expensive gems. Then they bowed to and worshipped these statues. But there is only one God, and statues of false gods had no power at all. Statues can't see, speak, or listen. Only the one true God has power. ◗

---

[w] Or *brothers (and sisters)*; the term often encompasses extended family relationships.

¹⁷ They have ears, but they can't listen.
No, there's no breath in their lungs!
¹⁸ Let the people who made these idols
and all who trust in them
become just like them!

¹⁹ House of Israel, bless the Lord!
House of Aaron, bless the Lord!
²⁰ House of Levi, bless the Lord!
You who honor the Lord, bless the Lord!
²¹ Bless the Lord from Zion—
bless the one who lives in Jerusalem!

Praise the Lord!

Psalm 136

¹ Give thanks to the Lord
because he is good.
God's faithful love lasts forever!

² Give thanks to the God of all gods—
God's faithful love lasts forever.
³ Give thanks to the Lord of all lords—
God's faithful love lasts forever.
⁴ Give thanks to the only one
who makes great wonders—
God's faithful love lasts forever.
⁵ Give thanks to the one
who made the skies with skill—
God's faithful love lasts forever.
⁶ Give thanks to the one
who shaped the earth on the water—
God's faithful love lasts forever.
⁷ Give thanks to the one
who made the great lights—
God's faithful love lasts forever.
⁸ The sun to rule the day—
God's faithful love lasts forever.
⁹ The moon and the stars to rule the night—
God's faithful love lasts forever!

¹⁰ Give thanks to the one who struck down
the Egyptians' oldest offspring—
God's faithful love lasts forever.
¹¹ Give thanks to the one
who brought Israel out of there—
God's faithful love lasts forever.
¹² With a strong hand
and outstretched arm—
God's faithful love lasts forever!

¹³ Give thanks to the one
who split the Reed Sea^x in two—
God's faithful love lasts forever.
¹⁴ Give thanks to the one
who brought Israel through—
God's faithful love lasts forever.
¹⁵ And tossed Pharaoh and his army
into the Reed Sea—
God's faithful love lasts forever!
¹⁶ Give thanks to the one
who led his people through the desert—
God's faithful love lasts forever.
¹⁷ Give thanks to the one
who struck down great kings—
God's faithful love lasts forever.

did you know? Psalm 136 switches
between two speakers. The
first half of each verse was
sung by a worship leader. The second half of every
verse was sung by the people in response.

¹⁸ And killed powerful kings—
God's faithful love lasts forever.
¹⁹ Sihon, the Amorite king—
God's faithful love lasts forever.
²⁰ Og, king of Bashan—
God's faithful love lasts forever.
²¹ Handing their land over as an inheritance—
God's faithful love lasts forever.
²² As an inheritance to Israel, his servant—
God's faithful love lasts forever!

²³ God remembered us
when we were humiliated—
God's faithful love lasts forever.
²⁴ God rescued us from our enemies—
God's faithful love lasts forever.
²⁵ God is the one who provides
food for all living things—
God's faithful love lasts forever!

²⁶ Give thanks to the God of heaven—
God's faithful love lasts forever!

Psalm 137

¹ Alongside Babylon's streams,
there we sat down,
crying because we remembered Zion.

^xOr *Red Sea*; also in 136:15

² We hung our lyres up
    in the trees there
  ³ because that's where
      our captors asked us to sing;
    our tormentors requested songs of joy:
    "Sing us a song about Zion!" they said.
⁴ But how could we possibly sing
    the Lord's song on foreign soil?

⁵ Jerusalem! If I forget you,
    let my strong hand wither!
⁶ Let my tongue stick
    to the roof of my mouth
    if I don't remember you,
    if I don't make Jerusalem
      my greatest joy.

⁷ Lord, remember what the Edomites did
    on Jerusalem's dark day:
    "Rip it down, rip it down!
    All the way to its foundations!"
      they yelled.
⁸ Daughter Babylon, you destroyer,ʸ
    a blessing on the one
      who pays you back
    the very deed you did to us!
  ⁹ A blessing on the one
    who seizes your children
    and smashes them against the rock!

UMBRELLA
Grief

Homesick *Psalm 137:1-6*
The Israelites considered Jerusalem to be a holy city. Jerusalem was where the temple of God was built. The temple was the home for the sacred chest containing the covenant, which symbolized God's presence. Each year, the Israelites went to Jerusalem to give offerings to God and worship in the temple. When the Israelites were taken as prisoners to Babylon, they grieved for the loss of their homeland and their temple. Psalm 137 shares that grief. Their sadness was so deep the people didn't want to sing, play their instruments, or do anything joyful. The writer of this psalm wondered how anyone could find the strength to sing when they weren't able to worship in God's temple. ◊

did you know? Psalm 137 is probably one of the last psalms written. It was written when God's people from Israel were held captive in Babylon.

Psalm 138
Of David.

¹ I give thanks to you
    with all my heart, Lord.ᶻ
    I sing your praise before all other gods.
² I bow toward your holy temple
    and thank your name
    for your loyal love and faithfulness
      because you have made
      your name and word
      greater than everything else.ᵃ
³ On the day I cried out, you answered me.
    You encouraged me with inner strength.ᵇ

⁴ Let all the earth's rulers
    give thanks to you, Lord,
    when they hear what you say.
⁵ Let them sing about the Lord's ways
    because the Lord's glory is so great!
⁶ Even though the Lord is high,
    he can still see the lowly,
    but God keeps his distance
      from the arrogant.

⁷ Whenever I am in deep trouble,
    you make me live again;
    you send your power
      against my enemies' wrath;
    you save me with your strong hand.
⁸ The Lord will do all this for my sake.

Your faithful love lasts forever, Lord!
    Don't let go of what your hands
      have made.

Psalm 139
For the music leader. Of David. A song.

¹ Lord, you have examined me.
    You know me.
² You know when I sit down
    and when I stand up.
    Even from far away,
    you comprehend my plans.

Bet you can *read this in 5 minutes. Ready, set, go!*

ʸSym, Tg, Syr; MT *the devastated* ᶻLXX, Syr, Tg, DSS (11QPsᵃ); MT lacks *Lord.* ᵃCorrection; Heb uncertain ᵇHeb uncertain

3 You study my traveling and resting.
  You are thoroughly familiar
    with all my ways.
4 There isn't a word on my tongue, Lord,
  that you don't already know completely.
5 You surround me—front and back.
  You put your hand on me.
6 That kind of knowledge
  is too much for me;
  it's so high above me
    that I can't reach it.

7 Where could I go to get away
  from your spirit?
  Where could I go to escape
    your presence?
8 If I went up to heaven,
  you would be there.
  If I went down to the grave,[c]
  you would be there too!
9 If I could fly on the wings of dawn,
  stopping to rest only
    on the far side of the ocean—
10 even there your hand would guide me;
  even there your strong hand
    would hold me tight!
11 If I said,
  "The darkness will definitely hide me;
  the light will become night around me,"
12 even then the darkness
  isn't too dark for you!
  Nighttime would shine bright as day,
  because darkness is the same
    as light to you!

Memorize
Ps 139:13-14

13 You are the one
  who created
    my innermost parts;
  you knit me together
  while I was still in my mother's womb.
14 I give thanks to you
  that I was marvelously set apart.
  Your works are wonderful—
  I know that very well.
15 My bones weren't hidden from you
  when I was being put together
    in a secret place,
  when I was being woven together
    in the deep parts of the earth.

16 Your eyes saw my embryo,
  and on your scroll every day was
    written that was being formed for me,[d]
  before any one of them
    had yet happened.[e]
17 God, your plans are incomprehensible
  to me!
  Their total number is countless!
18 If I tried to count them—
  they outnumber grains of sand!
  If I came to the very end—
    I'd still be with you.[f]

19 If only, God, you would kill the wicked!
  If only murderers
    would get away from me—
20 the people who talk about you,
  but only for wicked schemes;
  the people who are your enemies,
  who use your name as if
    it were of no significance.[g]
21 Don't I hate everyone who hates you?
  Don't I despise those who attack you?
22 Yes, I hate them—through and through!
  They've become my enemies too.

23 Examine me, God! Look at my heart!
  Put me to the test!
  Know my anxious thoughts!
24 Look to see if there is any idolatrous
  way[h] in me,
  then lead me on the eternal path!

Psalm 140

For the music leader. A psalm of David.

1 Rescue me from evil people, Lord!
  Guard me from violent people
2 who plot evil things in their hearts,
  who pick fights every single day!
3 They sharpen their tongues
  like a snake's;
  spider poison[i] is on their lips.   *Selah*

4 Protect me from the power
  of the wicked, Lord!
  Guard me from violent people
  who plot to trip me up!
5 Arrogant people have laid a trap
  for me with ropes.

---

[c] Heb *Sheol* [d] Correction; Heb lacks *for me.* [e] Heb uncertain [f] Correction [g] Heb lacks *your name.* [h] Correction; cf Tg; LXX, Syr, Vulg *painful* or *wicked* or *hurtful way* [i] LXX *snake poison*

They've spread out a net
  alongside the road.
They've set snares for me.   *Selah*

⁶ I tell the Lord, "You are my God!
  Listen to my request for mercy, Lord!"
⁷ My Lord God, my strong saving help—
  you've protected my head
    on the day of battle.
⁸ Lord, don't give the wicked
  what they want!
  Don't allow their plans to succeed,
    or they'll exalt themselves even more!ʲ
                       Selah

⁹ Let the heads of the people
  surrounding me

be covered with the trouble
  their own lips caused!ᵏ
¹⁰ Let burning coals fall on them!
  Let them fall into deep pits
    and never get out again!
¹¹ Let no slanderer be safe in the land.
  Let calamity hunt down violent people—
    and quickly!ˡ

¹² I know that the Lord
  will take up the case of the poor
    and will do what is right
    for the needy.
¹³ Yes, the righteous will give thanks
    to your name,
  and those who do right
    will live in your presence.

ʲHeb uncertain   ᵏHeb uncertain   ˡHeb uncertain

God's Thoughts ◆ My Thoughts

God Knows Us   *Psalm 139:1-6*

God knows everything about us, including the number of hairs on our heads. God knew us before we were made. God knows what we are thinking every minute. When we think about how God knows us so perfectly, it can help us remember to follow God's Instruction. When we're tempted to sin, we can remember that God is with us at that very moment watching what we're doing or saying.

Even though God knows everything about us, God doesn't live life for us. God created us to live for God, but we aren't puppets on a string. We have choices. We get to make decisions in life. The best decision we can make is to choose to follow and obey God. But even when we mess up, God surrounds us with love. God wants only the best for us.

Just as God knows us, we can know God. One way we can know God is by reading the Bible and praying. The Bible helps us know how to live and shows us God's character. Let God live through you and show you who God is.

What are two things you would like to know about God?

How do you know God is with you?

Psalm 141
A psalm of David.

¹ I cry out to you, LORD:
  Come to me—quickly!
  Listen to my voice when I cry out to you!
² Let my prayer stand before you
    like incense;
  let my uplifted hands be
    like the evening offering.

LIGHTHOUSE
PRAYER

Prayers Go Up Like Incense   *Psalm 141:2*
In the late afternoon priests in the temple would burn incense just as God had commanded in the Instruction given to Moses. Smoke from the incense would rise in the air and fill the temple with its sweet smell. Psalm 141 compares David's prayers to the aroma from the burning incense rising in the air. David wanted his prayers of worship and praise to be a sweet fragrance, a sign of surrender and honor to God. ◊

³ Set a guard over my mouth, LORD;
  keep close watch over the door
    that is my lips.
⁴ Don't let my heart turn aside to evil things
    so that I don't do wicked things
      with evildoers,
    so I don't taste their delicacies.

⁵ Instead, let the righteous discipline me;
    let the faithful correct me!
  Let my head never reject
    that kind of fine oil,
    because my prayers are always
      against the deeds of the wicked.ᵐ
⁶ Their leaders will fall from jagged cliffs,
    but my words will be heard
    because they are pleasing.ⁿ
⁷ Our bonesᵒ have been scattered
    at the mouth of the grave,ᵖ
    just like when the ground
      is broken up and plowed.۹

⁸ But my eyes are on you, my LORD God.
  I take refuge in you; don't let me die!

⁹ Protect me from the trap they've set for me;
  protect me from the snares
    of the evildoers.
¹⁰ Let the wicked fall into their own nets—
    all together!—
  but let me make it through safely.

Psalm 142
A maskilʳ of David, when he was in the cave. A prayer.

¹ I cry out loud for help from the LORD.
  I beg out loud for mercy from the LORD.
² I pour out my concerns before God;
  I announce my distress to him.
³ When my spirit is weak inside me,
  you still know my way.
  But they've hidden a trap for me
    in the path I'm taking.
⁴ Look right beside me: See?
  No one pays attention to me.
  There's no escape for me.
  No one cares about my life.

⁵ I cry to you, LORD, for help.
  "You are my refuge," I say.
  "You are all I have
    in the land of the living."
⁶ Pay close attention to my shouting,
    because I've been brought down so low!
  Deliver me from my oppressors
    because they're stronger than me.
⁷ Get me out of this prison
    so I can give thanks to your name.
  Then the righteous
    will gather all around me
    because of your good deeds to me.

Psalm 143
A psalm of David.

¹ Listen to my prayer, LORD!
  Because of your faithfulness,
    hear my requests for mercy!
  Because of your righteousness,
    answer me!
² Please don't bring your servant
    to judgment,
  because no living thing is righteous
    before you.

ᵐHeb uncertain   ⁿHeb uncertain ᵒLXX manuscripts, Syr *their bones;* DSS (11QPsᵃ) *my bones* ᵖHeb *Sheol* ۹Heb uncertain ʳPerhaps *instruction*

³ The enemy is chasing me,ˢ
    crushing my life in the dirt,
      forcing me to live in the dark
      like those who've been dead forever.
⁴ My spirit is weak inside me—
    inside, my mind is numb.

⁵ I remember the days long past;
    I meditate on all your deeds;
    I contemplate your handiwork.
⁶ I stretch out my hands to you;
    my whole being is like dry dirt,
      thirsting for you.ᵗ
                    Selah

⁷ Answer me, Lord—and quickly!
    My breath is fading.
    Don't hide your face from me
      or I'll be like those going down
      to the pit!
⁸ Tell me all about your faithful love
    come morning time,
      because I trust you.
    Show me the way I should go,
      because I offer my life up to you.
⁹ Deliver me from my enemies, Lord!
    I seek protection from you.ᵘ
¹⁰ Teach me to do what pleases you,
    because you are my God.
    Guide me by your good spirit
      into good land.
¹¹ Make me live again, Lord,
    for your name's sake.
    Bring me out of distress
      because of your righteousness.
¹² Wipe out my enemies
    because of your faithful love.
    Destroy everyone who attacks me,
      because I am your servant.

Psalm 144
Of David.

¹ Bless the Lord, my rock,
    who taught my hands how to fight,
    who taught my fingers how to do battle!
² God is my loyal one, my fortress,
    my place of safety, my rescuer,
    my shield, in whom I take refuge,
    and the one who subdues
      people before me.

did you know? The author of Psalm 143 viewed light as a place where God was. When the writer wrote that he was in total darkness, he meant that he felt completely separated from God.

³ What are human beings, Lord,
    that you know them at all?
    What are human beings
      that you even consider them?
⁴ Humans are like a puff of air;
    their days go by like a shadow.

⁵ Lord, part your skies and come down!
    Touch the mountains so they smoke!
⁶ Flash lightning and scatter the enemy!
    Shoot your arrows and defeat them!
⁷ Stretch out your hand from above!
    Rescue me and deliver me
      from deep water,
    from the power of strangers,
      whose mouths speak lies,
⁸ and whose strong hand is
    a strong hand of deception!

⁹ I will sing a new song to you, God.
    I will sing praises to you
      on a ten-stringed harp,
¹⁰ to you—the one
      who gives saving help to rulers,
    and who rescues his servant David
      from the evil sword.
¹¹ Rescue me and deliver me
    from the power of strangers,
      whose mouths speak lies,
    and whose strong hand
      is a strong hand of deception,
¹² so thatᵛ our sons can grow up fully,
    in their youth, like plants;
    so that our daughters can be like pillars
      carved to decorate a palace;
¹³ so that our barns can be full,
    providing all kinds of food;
    so that our flocks can be
      in the thousands—
    even tens of thousands—in our fields;
¹⁴ so that our cattle can be loaded
    with calves;
    so that there won't be any breach
      in the walls,
    no exile, no outcries in our streets!

ˢOr *my soul*; also in 143:6, 8, 11–12   ᵗHeb lacks *thirsting*.   ᵘHeb uncertain; MT *to you I have hidden*   ᵛHeb uncertain

¹⁵ The people who have it like this
    are truly happy!
  The people whose God is the Lᴏʀᴅ
    are truly happy!

Psalm 145ᵂ
Praise. Of David.

א ¹ I will lift you up high, my God, the true king.
    I will bless your name forever and always.

ב ² I will bless you every day.
    I will praise your name
      forever and always.

ג ³ The Lᴏʀᴅ is great and so worthy of praise!
    God's greatness can't be grasped.

ד ⁴ One generation will praise
    your works to the next one,
      proclaiming your mighty acts.

ה ⁵ They will talk all aboutˣ the glorious
    splendor of your majesty;
  I will contemplate your wondrous works.

ו ⁶ They will speak of the power
    of your awesome deeds;
  I will declare your great accomplishments.

ז ⁷ They will rave in celebration
    of your abundant goodness;
  they will shout joyfully
    about your righteousness:

SAILBOAT

FAMILY AND FRIENDS

A Family Legacy *Psalm 145:3-7*
The Israelites passed down stories about their history and faith from person to person. In this way kids learned about their grandparents, great-grandparents, great-great-grandparents, and other relatives, all the way back to Adam and Eve. Through the stories of their relatives, kids learned which ancestor fought alongside Gideon. They knew who had been there when God delivered the Israelites from the Egyptians. They knew which of Abraham and Sarah's children they were related to. They heard personal stories of how God answered prayers and touched their family's life throughout history. These stories strengthened their faith. When they grew up, they would teach their own kids the same stories. In this way, every generation knew about God by learning their family history. ◆

ח ⁸ "The Lᴏʀᴅ is merciful
    and compassionate,
  very patient, and full of faithful love.

ט ⁹ The Lᴏʀᴅ is good to everyone
    and everything;
  God's compassion extends
    to all his handiwork!"

י ¹⁰ All that you have made
    gives thanks to you, Lᴏʀᴅ;
  all your faithful ones bless you!

כ ¹¹ They speak of the glory of your kingdom;
    they talk all about your power,

ל ¹² to inform all human beings
    about God's power
  and the majestic glory of God's kingdom.

מ ¹³ Your kingdom is a kingship
    that lasts forever;
  your rule endures for all generations.

נ The Lᴏʀᴅ is trustworthy in all that he says,
    faithful in all that he does.ʸ

ס ¹⁴ The Lᴏʀᴅ supports all who fall down,
    straightens up all who are bent low.

ע ¹⁵ All eyes look to you, hoping,
    and you give them their food
      right on time,

פ ¹⁶ opening your hand
    and satisfying the desire
      of every living thing.

צ ¹⁷ The Lᴏʀᴅ is righteous in all his ways,
    faithful in all his deeds.

ק ¹⁸ The Lᴏʀᴅ is close to everyone
    who calls out to him,
  to all who call out to him sincerely.

ר ¹⁹ God shows favor to those who honor him,
    listening to their cries for help
      and saving them.

ש ²⁰ The Lᴏʀᴅ protects all who love him,
    but he destroys every wicked person.

ת ²¹ My mouth will proclaim the Lᴏʀᴅ's praise,
    and every living thing
      will bless God's holy name
        forever and always.

Psalm 146

¹ Praise the Lᴏʀᴅ!

  Let my whole beingᶻ praise the Lᴏʀᴅ!
² I will praise the Lᴏʀᴅ with all my life;

ᵂPs 145 is an alphabetic acrostic poem; see the note at Pss 9–10. ˣLXX, Syr, DSS (11QPsᵃ); MT *and words of* ʸLXX, DSS (11QPsᵃ), Syr; MT lacks these lines, but they correspond to the *nun* line in the alphabetic acrostic poem. ᶻOr *soul*

I will sing praises to my God
  as long as I live.

3 Don't trust leaders;
  don't trust any human beings—
  there's no saving help with them!
4 Their breath leaves them,
  then they go back to the ground.
  On that very same day,
    their plans die too.

5 The person whose help
  is the God of Jacob—
  the person whose hope
    rests on the LORD their God—
  is truly happy!
6 God: the maker of heaven and earth,
  the sea, and all that is in them,
  God: who is faithful forever,
   7 who gives justice to people
    who are oppressed,
  who gives bread to people
    who are starving!
The LORD: who frees prisoners.
8 The LORD: who makes the blind see.
The LORD: who straightens up
  those who are bent low.
The LORD: who loves the righteous.
9 The LORD: who protects immigrants,
  who helps orphans and widows,
  but who makes the way of the wicked
    twist and turn!

10 The LORD will rule forever!
  Zion, your God will rule
  from one generation to the next!

Praise the LORD!

Psalm 147

Bet you can read this in 1 minute. Ready, set, go!

1 Praise the LORD!
  Because it is good to sing praise
    to our God!
  Because it is a pleasure
    to make beautiful praise!
2 The LORD rebuilds Jerusalem,
  gathering up Israel's exiles.
3 God heals the brokenhearted
  and bandages their wounds.

4 God counts the stars by number,
  giving each one a name.
5 Our Lord is great and so strong!
  God's knowledge can't be grasped!
6 The LORD helps the poor,
  but throws the wicked down on the dirt!

7 Sing to the LORD with thanks;
  sing praises to our God with a lyre!
8 God covers the skies with clouds;
  God makes rain for the earth;
  God makes the mountains
    sprout green grass.
9 God gives food to the animals—
  even to the baby ravens when they cry out.
10 God doesn't prize the strength of a horse;
  God doesn't treasure the legs of a runner.
11 No. The LORD treasures
  the people who honor him,
  the people who
  wait for his
  faithful love.

Memorize Ps 147:11

12 Worship the LORD, Jerusalem!
  Praise your God, Zion!
13 Because God secures the bars
  on your gates,
  God blesses the children you have there.
14 God establishes your borders peacefully.
  God fills you full with the very best wheat.

15 God issues his command to the earth—
  God's word speeds off fast!
16 God spreads snow like it was wool;
  God scatters frost like it was ashes;
17 God throws his hail down like crumbs—
  who can endure God's freezing cold?
18 Then God issues his word
  and melts it all away!
  God makes his winds blow;
  the water flows again.

19 God proclaims his word to Jacob;
  his statutes and rules to Israel.
20 God hasn't done that
  with any other nation;
  those nations have no knowledge
    of God's rules.[a]

Praise the LORD!

---

[a] LXX, Tg, DSS (11QPsª) *God hasn't let those nations know his rules.*

Psalm 148

¹ Praise the LORD!

Praise the LORD from heaven!
 Praise God on the heights!
² Praise God, all of you
 who are his messengers!
 Praise God, all of you
 who comprise his heavenly forces!
³ Sun and moon, praise God!
 All of you bright stars, praise God!
⁴ You highest heaven, praise God!
 Do the same, you waters
 that are above the sky!
⁵ Let all of these praise the LORD's name
 because God gave the command
 and they were created!
⁶ God set them in place always and forever.
 God made a law that will not be broken.

⁷ Praise the LORD from the earth,
 you sea monsters and all you ocean depths!

⁸ Do the same, fire and hail,
 snow and smoke,
 stormy wind that does what God says!
⁹ Do the same, you mountains,
 every single hill,
 fruit trees, and every single cedar!
¹⁰ Do the same, you animals— wild or tame—
 you creatures that creep along
 and you birds that fly!
¹¹ Do the same, you kings of the earth
 and every single person,
 you princes and every single ruler
 on earth!
¹² Do the same, you young men—
 young women too!—
 you who are old together
 with you who are young!

¹³ Let all of these praise the LORD's name
 because only God's name is high over all.
 Only God's majesty
 is over earth and heaven.

Praise the Lord *Psalm 150*

Look at all the different ways to praise God! We can praise God with instruments and our voices. We can praise in our homes, on the school bus, on the playground, or anywhere we are. Praise isn't just for church. And praise isn't just about singing. We can praise God with dance, athletic ability, words, our ability to make friends, or whatever talents we may have.

We praise God because God is the only one worthy of our worship. We can praise God for helping us when we accomplish something big. When we get up in the morning, we can praise God for a new day. There are so many reasons to praise God.

Praise comes from a heart of thanks. But it's important to speak our praise out loud. God wants to hear it from our lips, and sometimes we need to hear it out loud too! We can make up the words right on the spot. We might say, "God, you're so good to me! I love you for making me just the way I am!" The more we learn about God's love and goodness, the more we'll want to offer God our praise. Praise the Lord!

Write a prayer of praise to God.

What are some gifts you have that you can praise God with?

¹⁴ God raised the strength[b] of his people,
  the praise of all his faithful ones—
  that's the Israelites,
  the people who are close to him.

Praise the Lord!

Psalm 149

¹ Praise the Lord!

Sing to the Lord a new song;
  sing God's praise
  in the assembly of the faithful!
² Let Israel celebrate its maker;
  let Zion's children rejoice in their king!
³ Let them praise God's name with dance;
  let them sing God's praise
  with the drum and lyre!
⁴ Because the Lord is pleased
  with his people,
  God will beautify the poor
  with saving help.

⁵ Let the faithful celebrate with glory;
  let them shout for joy on their beds.[c]
⁶ Let the high praises of God
  be in their mouths

and a double-edged sword
  in their hands,
⁷ to get revenge against the nations
  and punishment on the peoples,
⁸ binding their rulers in chains
  and their officials in iron shackles,
⁹ achieving the justice
  written against them.
That will be an honor
  for all God's faithful people.

Praise the Lord!

Psalm 150

¹ Praise the Lord!

Praise God in his sanctuary!
  Praise God in his fortress, the sky!
² Praise God in his mighty acts!
  Praise God as suits
  his incredible greatness!
³ Praise God with the blast
  of the ram's horn!
  Praise God with lute and lyre!
⁴ Praise God with drum and dance!
  Praise God with strings and pipe!
⁵ Praise God with loud cymbals!
  Praise God with clashing cymbals!
⁶ Let every living thing praise the Lord!

Praise the Lord!

 did you know? With a total of 2,461 verses, Psalms has more verses than any other book of the Bible.

[b]Or *horn* [c]Heb uncertain

Proverbs

The Bible says that Solomon was the wisest man ever (1 Kgs 4:29-34). His insight was a gift from God. It was God's answer to Solomon's prayer that he be able to tell the difference between good and evil (1 Kgs 3:9). Much of the book of Proverbs (1–22; 25–29) is said to be a collection of Solomon's wise sayings. Shorter sections are said to have been written by other people, including two men who weren't Israelites, Agur and King Lemuel.

Wisdom is said to "speak" to us like a living person. Wisdom commands us to listen and learn—to think and act differently (Prov 1–9). Then the book goes on to list hundreds of short sayings. These proverbs aren't in any obvious order. But they offer wisdom for people who live in cities, farms, ordinary homes, and royal palaces; and for families, neighbors, friends, and enemies.

Having wisdom helps us make good choices and do what is right. It helps us enjoy life and avoid harm. The book of Proverbs reminds us that we gain wisdom when we follow God's ways. ◊

Purpose of Proverbs

1 The proverbs of Solomon, King David's son,
  from Israel:

² Their purpose is to teach wisdom
    and discipline,
  to help one understand wise sayings.
³ They provide insightful instruction,
    which is righteous, just,
      and full of integrity.
⁴ They make the naive mature,
    the young knowledgeable and discreet.
⁵ The wise hear them and grow in wisdom;
    those with understanding gain guidance.
⁶ They help one understand
    proverbs and difficult sayings,
      the words of the wise,
        and their puzzles.

Memorize Prov 1:7

⁷ Wisdom begins with
    the fear of the Lᴏʀᴅ,
  but fools despise wisdom and instruction.

Avoid evil associations

⁸ Listen, my son, to your father's instruction;
  don't neglect your mother's teaching;

⁹ for they are a graceful wreath
    on your head,
  and beads for your neck.
¹⁰ My son, don't let sinners entice you.
  Don't go ¹¹ when they say:
    "Come with us.
    Let's set up a deadly ambush.
    Let's secretly wait for the innocent
      just for fun.
¹² Let's swallow up the living
    like the grave[a]—
  whole, like those who go down
    into the pit.
¹³ We'll find all sorts of precious wealth;
  we'll fill our houses with plunder.
¹⁴ Throw in your lot with us;
  we'll share our money."
¹⁵ My son, don't go on the path with them;
  keep your feet from their way,
¹⁶ because their feet run to evil;
    they hurry to spill blood.
¹⁷ It's useless to cast a net
    in the sight of a bird.

ᵃ Heb *Sheol*

Godly Wisdom   *Proverbs 1:1-7*

The book of Proverbs contains many poetic sayings that speak about wisdom. Proverbs 1:1-7 teaches that wisdom begins with the fear of God. Fearing God isn't like being afraid of the dark. It means having respect and reverence—treating God as the most important part of our lives.

One way to gain wisdom and to fear God, is to listen. This passage teaches that wise people hear God's instructions and grow in understanding. Once we listen, then we can act on what we know is wise. James 1:22 says we need to do God's word, not just hear it. If we only listen to good teaching but don't put what we have learned into action, then we haven't done all that God asks us to do.

Following God's ways allows us to grow our faith and live like God wants us to live. Allow God's wisdom to shape your life. Find ways to put the things you learn into practice.

What are some ways you can show your respect for God?

What are some ways you can put the things you learn into practice?

¹⁸ But these sinners set up a deadly ambush;
  they lie in wait for their own lives.
¹⁹ These are the ways of all
  who seek unjust gain;
  it costs them their lives.

Listen to "Woman Wisdom"

²⁰ Wisdom shouts in the street;
  in the public square she raises her voice.
²¹ Above the noisy crowd, she calls out.
  At the entrances of the city gates,
  she has her say:
²² "How long will you clueless people
  love your naïveté,
  mockers hold their mocking dear,
  and fools hate knowledge?
²³ You should respond when I correct you.
  Look, I'll pour out my spirit on you.
  I'll reveal my words to you.
²⁴ I invited you, but you rejected me;
  I stretched out my hand to you,
  but you paid no attention.
²⁵ You ignored all my advice,
  and you didn't want me to correct you.
²⁶ So I'll laugh at your disaster;
  I'll make fun of you
  when dread comes over you,
²⁷ when terror hits you like a hurricane,
  and your disaster comes in
  like a tornado,
  when distress and oppression
  overcome you.
²⁸ Then they will call me, but I won't answer;
  they will seek me, but won't find me
²⁹ because they hated knowledge
  and didn't choose the fear of the LORD.
³⁰ They didn't want my advice;
  they rejected all my corrections.
³¹ They will eat from the fruit of their way,
  and they'll be full of their own schemes.
³² The immature will die
  because they turn away;
  smugness will destroy fools.
³³ Those who obey me will dwell securely,
  untroubled by the dread of harm."

Benefits of wisdom

2 My son, accept my words
  and store up my commands.
² Turn your ear toward wisdom,
  and stretch your mind
  toward understanding.

LIFE PRESERVER

Why is wisdom referred to as a woman? *Proverbs 1:20-33*

Proverbs is unique in two ways. It doesn't talk about the great events or people in the history of Israel, as do many of the other books that come before it in the Bible. And when Wisdom speaks in this book, it is the voice of woman. The Bible teaches that wisdom is a skill that people have, or information, or a way to describe God. It is interesting that in a culture where men were the authority, Wisdom was viewed as a woman.

We don't really know why. Some who study the Bible have thought that wisdom in the voice of a woman would appeal to the young men who read these proverbs. They were encouraged to seek wisdom and to find her.

For those of us reading this ancient book of wisdom from another time and place, it's nice to hear a female voice speaking about the wisdom from God. 💧

---

³ Call out for insight,
  and cry aloud for understanding.
⁴ Seek it like silver;
  search for it like hidden treasure.
⁵ Then you will understand
  the fear of the LORD,
  and discover the knowledge of God.
⁶ The LORD gives wisdom;
  from his mouth come knowledge
  and understanding.
⁷ He reserves ability for those
  with integrity.
  He is a shield for those
  who live a blameless life.
⁸ He protects the paths of justice
  and guards the way of those
  who are loyal to him.
⁹ Then you will understand righteousness
  and justice,
  as well as integrity, every good course.
¹⁰ Wisdom will enter your mind,
  and knowledge will fill you with delight.
¹¹ Discretion will guard you;
  understanding will protect you.
¹² Wisdom will rescue you from the evil path,
  from people who twist their words.
¹³ They forsake the way of integrity
  and go on obscure paths.
¹⁴ They enjoy doing evil,
  rejoicing in their twisted evil.

¹⁵ Their paths are confused;
  they get lost on their way.
¹⁶ Wisdom will rescue you
  from the mysterious woman,
  from the foreign woman
    with her slick words.
¹⁷ She leaves behind the partner
  of her youth;
  she even forgets her covenant with God.
¹⁸ Her house sinks down to death,
  and her paths go down
    to the shadowy dead.
¹⁹ All those who go to her will never return;
  they will never again
    reach the ways of the living.
²⁰ So you should stay on the path
  of good people,
  guarding the road of the righteous.
²¹ Those who have integrity
  will dwell in the land;
  the innocent will remain in it.
²² But the wicked will be cut off
  from the land,
  and the treacherous will be ripped up.

Trust in the Lord

3 My son, don't forget my instruction.
  Let your heart guard my commands,
² because they will help you live
    a long time
  and provide you with well-being.
³ Don't let loyalty and faithfulness
    leave you.
  Bind them on your neck;
  write them on the tablet of your heart.
⁴ Then you will find favor and approval
  in the eyes of God and humanity.
⁵ Trust in the Lord with all your heart;
  don't rely on your own intelligence.
⁶ Know him in all your paths,
  and he will keep your ways straight.
⁷ Don't consider yourself wise.
  Fear the Lord and turn away from evil.
⁸ Then your body[b] will be healthy
  and your bones strengthened.
⁹ Honor the Lord with your wealth
  and with the first of all your crops.
¹⁰ Then your barns will be filled with plenty,
  and your vats will burst with wine.

[b]Heb *navel*

¹¹ Don't reject the instruction of the Lord,
  my son;
  don't despise his correction.
¹² The Lord loves those he corrects,
  just like a father who treats his son
    with favor.

Value of wisdom

¹³ Happy are those who find wisdom
  and those who gain understanding.
¹⁴ Her profit is better than silver,
  and her gain better than gold.
¹⁵ Her value exceeds pearls;
  all you desire can't
    compare with her.

LIGHTHOUSE

Wisdom

The Wise Are Happy *Proverbs 3:13-15*
Born a royal prince and raised in a palace, Solomon was part of a wealthy family. We can assume all his needs were taken care of and he had many things he wanted. After he became king, God made him the richest king in the history of Israel and gave him great power. Even so, Solomon realized that while money can buy things, it can't buy true happiness and peace. Solomon knew from experience that wisdom was more valuable than all the riches in the world.

¹⁶ In her right hand is a long life;
  in her left are wealth and honor.
¹⁷ Her ways are pleasant;
  all her paths are peaceful.
¹⁸ She is a tree of life
  to those who embrace her;
  those who hold her tight are happy.
¹⁹ The Lord laid the foundations
  of the earth with wisdom,
  establishing the heavens
    with understanding.
²⁰ With his knowledge,
  the watery depths burst open,
  and the skies drop dew.

Integrity of wisdom

²¹ My son, don't let them slip from your eyes;
  hold on to sound judgment
    and discretion.

²² They will be life for your whole being,
and an ornament for your neck.
²³ Then you will walk safely on your path,
and your foot won't stumble.
²⁴ If you lie down, you won't be terrified.
When you lie down,
your sleep will be pleasant.
²⁵ Don't fear sudden terror
or the ruin that comes to the wicked.
²⁶ The Lord will be your confidence;
he will guard your feet
from being snared.
²⁷ Don't withhold good
from someone who deserves it,
when it is in your power to do so.
²⁸ Don't say to your neighbor,
"Go and come back;
I'll give it to you tomorrow,"
when you have it.
²⁹ Don't plan to harm your neighbor
who trusts and lives near you.
³⁰ Don't accuse anyone without reason,
when they haven't harmed you.
³¹ Don't envy violent people
or choose any of their ways.
³² Devious people are detestable to the Lord,
but the virtuous are his close friends.
³³ The Lord's curse is on
the house of the wicked,
but he blesses the home of the righteous.
³⁴ He mocks mockers,
but he shows favor to the humble.
³⁵ The wise gain respect,
but fools receive shame.

did you know? In ancient times, people who were with God were said to be in the light. People who were separated from or had turned away from God were said to be in the dark.

Love wisdom

4 Hear, children, fatherly instruction;
pay attention to gain understanding.
² I'll teach you well.
Don't abandon my instruction.
³ When I was a son to my father,
tender and my mother's favorite,
⁴ he taught me and said to me:
"Let your heart hold on to my words:
Keep my commands and live.
⁵ Get wisdom; get understanding.

Don't forget and don't turn away
from my words.
⁶ Don't abandon her, and she will guard you.
Love her, and she will protect you.
⁷ The beginning of wisdom:
Get wisdom!
Get understanding before anything else.
⁸ Highly esteem her, and she will exalt you.
She will honor you if you embrace her.
⁹ She will place a graceful wreath
on your head;
she will give you a glorious crown."

Stay on the path of wisdom

¹⁰ Listen, my son, and take in my speech,
then the years of your life will be many.
¹¹ I teach you the path of wisdom.
I lead you in straight courses.
¹² When you walk, you won't be hindered;
when you run, you won't stumble.
¹³ Hold on to instruction; don't slack off;
protect it, for it is your life.
¹⁴ Don't go on the way of the wicked;
don't walk on the path of evil people.
¹⁵ Avoid it! Don't turn onto it;
stay off of it and keep going!
¹⁶ They don't sleep unless they do evil;
they are robbed of sleep unless
they make someone stumble.
¹⁷ They eat the bread of evil,
and they drink the wine of violence.
¹⁸ The way of the righteous
is like morning light
that gets brighter and
brighter till it is full day.
¹⁹ The path of the wicked
is like deep darkness;
they don't know where they will stumble.

Be careful about what you say

²⁰ My son, pay attention to my words.
Bend your ear to my speech.
²¹ Don't let them slip from your sight.
Guard them in your mind.
²² They are life to those who find them,
and healing for their entire body.
²³ More than anything you guard,
protect your mind, for life flows from it.
²⁴ Have nothing to do with a corrupt mouth;
keep devious lips far from you.
²⁵ Focus your eyes straight ahead;
keep your gaze on what is in front of you.

26 Watch your feet on the way,
   and all your paths will be secure.
27 Don't deviate a bit to the right
   or the left;
   turn your feet away from evil.

Avoid the mysterious woman

5 My son, pay attention to my wisdom.
   Bend your ear to what I know,
   2 so you might remain discreet,
      and your lips might guard knowledge.
3 The lips of a mysterious woman drip honey,
   and her tongue is smoother than oil,
4 but in the end she is bitter as gall,
   sharp as a double-edged sword.
5 Her feet go down to death;
   her steps lead to the grave.c
6 She doesn't stay on the way of life.

   Her paths wander,
      but she doesn't know it.
7 Now sons, listen to me,
   and don't deviate
      from the words of my mouth.
8 Stay on a path that is far from her;
   don't approach the entrance
      to her house.
9 Otherwise, you will give
   your strength to others,
      your years to a cruel person.
10 Otherwise, strangers
    will sap your strength,
       and your hard work will end up
          in a foreigner's house.
11 You will groan at the end
    when your body and flesh are exhausted,

cHeb *Sheol*

God's THOUGHTS / My THOUGHTS

Godly Words   Proverbs 4:20-27

You may have heard before that you should think before you speak. You may also have heard the saying "If you can't say something nice, don't say anything at all." Blurting out whatever comes to mind isn't usually a good idea. Once words leave our mouths, we can never take them back, although we can apologize if we need to. Sometimes the words we say get in the way of what we really mean. We can hurt people with our words even when we don't intend to.

Words can build people up or tear them down. If we use words that lie, cheat, or deceive, then we are not following God's ways or showing God's love to those around us. But if we choose positive words that encourage and support the people we speak with, we can bring life to those who hear.

What we say and how we say it is a direct result of what we put into our minds. If we constantly think negative thoughts or look down on people, our words come out as negative and mean. But we can be careful to protect our minds by turning away from things that do not honor God and thinking about positive things. The results will come out in our words, which have the potential to encourage those who really need it.

How can you protect your mind from things that do not honor God?

What are some words that could encourage someone?

¹² and you say, "How I hated instruction!
How my heart despised correction!
¹³ I didn't listen to the voice of my instructor.
I didn't obey my teacher.
¹⁴ I'm on the brink of utter ruin
in the assembled community."

¹⁵ Drink water from your own cistern,
gushing water from your own well.
¹⁶ Should your fountains flood outside,
streams of water in the public squares?
¹⁷ They are yours alone,
not for you as well as strangers.
¹⁸ May your spring be blessed.
Rejoice in the wife of your youth.
¹⁹ She is a lovely deer, a graceful doe.
Let her breasts intoxicate you all the time;
always be drunk on her love.

²⁰ Why, my son, should you lose
your senses with a mysterious woman
and embrace the breasts
of a foreign female?

²¹ The LORD's eyes watch
over every person's path,
observing all their ways.
²² The wicked will be caught
by their own evil acts,
grabbed by the ropes of their own sin.
²³ Those without instruction will die,
misled by their own stupidity.

Wise advice

6 My son, if you guarantee a loan
for your neighbor
or shake hands in agreement
with a stranger,
² you will be trapped by your words;
you will be caught by your words.
³ Do this, my son, to get out of it,
for you have come under the control
of your neighbor.
So go, humble yourself,[d]
and pester your neighbor.
⁴ Don't give sleep to your eyes
or slumber to your eyelids.
⁵ Get yourself free like a gazelle
from a hunter,
like a bird from the hand of a fowler.

⁶ Go to the ant, you lazy person;
observe its ways and grow wise.
⁷ The ant has no commander, officer,
or ruler.
⁸ Even so, it gets its food in summer;
gathers its provisions at harvest.
⁹ How long, lazy person, will you lie down?
When will you rise from your sleep?
¹⁰ A little sleep, a little slumber,
a little folding of the arms
to lie down—
¹¹ and poverty will come on you
like a prowler,
destitution like a warrior.

LIGHTHOUSE

WISDOM

Lessons on Laziness   *Proverbs 6:6-11*
Scripture often uses examples from nature to teach us lessons about life. Solomon encouraged people to study ants to grow wise. Without anyone telling them what to do, ants gather food throughout the spring and summer in order to have food during the winter.

Solomon said that lazy people spend most of their day doing nothing even though they are strong and healthy. Instead of mending his roof, a lazy person takes a nap. A lazy person rests under a shade tree instead of tending her garden. Lazy people find excuses to put off taking care of their responsibilities. By continuing on this path, they run the risk of finding themselves with a leaky roof and nothing to eat. ◆

¹² Worthless people and guilty people
go around with crooked talk.
¹³ They wink their eyes,
gesture with their feet,
and point with their fingers.
¹⁴ Their hearts are corrupt
and determined to do evil;
they create controversies all the time.
¹⁵ Therefore, sudden disaster
will come upon them;
they will be quickly broken
beyond healing.
¹⁶ There are six things that the LORD hates,
seven things detestable to him:

---

[d]Heb uncertain

¹⁷ snobbish eyes,
   a lying tongue,
   hands that spill innocent blood,
¹⁸ a heart set on wicked plans,
   feet that run quickly to evil,
¹⁹ a false witness who breathes lies,
   and one who causes conflicts
    among relatives.

Danger of adultery

²⁰ My son, keep your father's command;
   don't abandon your mother's instruction.
²¹ Bind them on your heart for all time;
   fasten them around your neck.
²² When you walk around, they will lead you;
   when you lie down, they will protect you;
   when you awake,
    they will occupy your attention.
²³ The commandment is a lamp
   and instruction a light;
   corrective teaching is the path of life.
²⁴ They guard you from the evil woman,
   from the flattering tongue
    of the foreign woman.
²⁵ Don't desire her beauty in secret;
   don't let her take you in
    with her eyelashes,
²⁶ for a prostitute costs a loaf of bread,ᵉ
   but a married woman
    hunts for a man's very life.
²⁷ Can a man scoop fire into his lap
   and his clothes not get burned?
²⁸ If a man walks on hot coals,
   don't his feet get burned?
²⁹ So is the man who approaches
   his neighbor's wife;
   anyone who touches her will be punished.
³⁰ People don't despise a thief if he steals
   to fill his starving stomach.
³¹ But if he is caught, he must pay sevenfold;
   he must give all the riches of his house.
³² He who commits adultery is senseless.
   Doing so, he destroys himself.
³³ He is wounded and disgraced.
   His shame will never be wiped away.
³⁴ Jealousy makes a man rage;
   he'll show no mercy on his day
    of revenge.
³⁵ He won't accept compensation;
   he'll refuse even a large bribe.

Avoid loose women

7 My son, keep my words;
   store up my commands within you.
² Keep my commands and live,
   and my instruction
    like the pupil of your eye.
³ Bind them on your fingers;
   write them on the tablet of your heart.
⁴ Say to wisdom, "You are my sister";
   call understanding "friend,"
⁵ so she might guard you
   against the mysterious woman,
   from the foreign woman
    who flatters you.
⁶ When from the window of my house,
   from behind the screen, I gazed down,
⁷ I looked among the naive young men
   and noticed among the youth,
    one who had no sense.
⁸ He was crossing the street at her corner
   and walked down the path to her house
⁹ in the early evening,
   at the onset of night and darkness.
¹⁰ All of a sudden a woman approaches him,
   dressed like a prostitute
    and with a cunning mind.
¹¹ She is noisy and defiant;
   her feet don't stay long
    in her own house.
¹² She has one foot in the street,
   one foot in the public square.
   She lies in wait at every corner.
¹³ She grabs him and kisses him.
   Her face is brazen as she speaks to him:
¹⁴ "I've made a sacrifice of well-being;
   today I fulfilled my solemn promises.
¹⁵ So I've come out to meet you,
   seeking you, and I have found you.
¹⁶ I've spread my bed with luxurious covers,
   with colored linens from Egypt.
¹⁷ I've sprinkled my bed with myrrh,
   aloes, and cinnamon.
¹⁸ Come, let's drink deep of love
   until morning;
   let's savor our lovemaking.
¹⁹ For my husband isn't home;
   he's gone far away.
²⁰ He took a pouch of money with him;
   he won't come home till full moon."
²¹ She seduces him with all her talk.
   She entices him with her flattery.

ᵉHeb uncertain

²² He goes headlong after her,
    like an ox to the slaughter,
    like a deer leaping into a trap,^f
 ²³ until an arrow pierces his liver,
    like a bird hurrying to the snare,
     not aware that it will cost him his life.

²⁴ Now children, listen to me,
    and pay attention to my speech.
²⁵ Don't turn your heart to her ways;
    don't wander down her paths.
²⁶ She has caused many corpses to fall;
    she has killed many people.
²⁷ Her house is a path to the grave,^g
    going down to the chambers of death.

Wisdom's autobiography

8 Doesn't Wisdom cry out
        and Understanding shout?
  ² Atop the heights along the path,
    at the crossroads
        she takes her stand.
  ³ By the gate before the city,
        at the entrances she shouts:

Bet you can read this in 6 minutes. **Ready, set, go!**

⁴ I cry out to you, people;
    my voice goes out to all of humanity.
⁵ Understand skill, you who are naive.
    Take this to heart, you fools.
⁶ "Listen, for I speak things that are correct;
    from my lips comes what is right.
⁷ My mouth utters the truth;
    my lips despise wickedness."
⁸ All the words of my mouth are righteous;
    nothing in them is twisted or crooked.
⁹ All of them are straightforward
    to those who understand,
    and upright for the knowledgeable.
¹⁰ Take my instruction rather than silver,
    knowledge rather than choice gold.
¹¹ Wisdom is better than pearls;
    nothing is more delightful than she.

¹² I, Wisdom, dwell with prudence;
    I have found knowledge and discretion.
¹³ To fear the LORD is to hate evil.
    I hate pride and arrogance,
        the path of evil and corrupt speech.
¹⁴ I have advice and ability,
    as well as understanding and strength.

¹⁵ By me kings rule,
    and princes issue righteous decrees.
¹⁶ By me rulers govern,
    and officials judge righteously.^h
¹⁷ I love those who love me;
    those who seek me will find me.
¹⁸ Riches and honor are with me,
    as well as enduring wealth
        and righteousness.
¹⁹ My fruit is better than gold, even fine gold;
    my crops are better than choice silver.
²⁰ I walk on the way of righteousness,
    on the paths of justice,
 ²¹ to provide for those who love me
    and to fill up their treasuries.

²² The LORD created me
    at the beginning of his way,
    before his deeds long in the past.
²³ I was formed in ancient times,
    at the beginning, before the earth was.
²⁴ When there were no watery depths,
    I was brought forth,
    when there were no springs
        flowing with water.
²⁵ Before the mountains were settled,
    before the hills, I was brought forth;
 ²⁶ before Godⁱ made the earth and the fields
    or the first of the dry land.
²⁷ I was there when he established
    the heavens,
    when he marked out the horizon
        on the deep sea,
²⁸ when he thickened the clouds above,
    when he secured the fountains
        of the deep,
²⁹ when he set a limit for the sea,
    so the water couldn't go beyond
        his command,
    when he marked out
        the earth's foundations.
³⁰ I was beside him as a master of crafts.^j
    I was having fun,
    smiling before him all the time,
³¹ frolicking with his inhabited earth
    and delighting in the human race.

³² Now, children, listen to me:
    Happy are those who keep to my ways!
³³ Listen to instruction, and be wise;
    don't avoid it.

^fHeb uncertain ^gHeb *Sheol* ^hHeb uncertain ⁱHeb lacks *God.* ^jHeb uncertain

³⁴ Happy are those who listen to me,
  watching daily at my doors,
  waiting at my doorposts.
³⁵ Those who find me find life;
  they gain favor from the LORD.
³⁶ Those who offend me injure themselves;
  all those who hate me love death.

"Woman Wisdom's" invitation

9 Wisdom built her house;
  she has carved out her seven pillars.
² She slaughtered her animals,
  mixed her wine,
  and set her table.
³ She sends out her female servants;
  she issues an invitation
  from the top of the city heights:
⁴ "Whoever is naive turn aside here,"
  she says to those who lack sense.
⁵ "Come, eat my food,
  and drink the wine I have mixed.
⁶ Abandon your simplistic ways and live;
  walk in the way of understanding."

Wise advice

⁷ Whoever instructs the cynic gets insulted;
  whoever corrects the wicked gets hurt.
⁸ Don't correct the impudent,
  or they will hate you;
  correct the wise, and they will love you.
⁹ Teach the wise,
  and they will become wiser;
  inform the righteous,
  and their learning will increase.
¹⁰ The beginning of wisdom
  is the fear of the LORD;
  the knowledge of the holy one
  is understanding.
¹¹ Through me your days will be many;
  years will be added to your life.
¹² If you are wise, it is to your benefit;
  if you are cynical,
  you will bear it all alone.

"Woman Folly's" invitation

¹³ Woman Folly is noisy;
  she's stupid and doesn't even know it.
¹⁴ She sits at the doorway of her house,
  on a seat at the city heights.
¹⁵ She invites those who pass by on the path,

those going straight on their way.
¹⁶ "Whoever is naive, come in here,"
  she says to those who lack sense.
¹⁷ "Stolen water is sweet;
  food eaten in secret is pleasant."
¹⁸ But they don't know that the dead
  are there;
  her guests are in the depths of the grave.ᵏ

Proverbs of Solomon

10 The proverbs of Solomon:
  A wise child makes a father glad,
  but a foolish child
  brings sorrow to his mother.
² The treasure of the wicked
  won't profit them,
  but righteousness rescues people
  from death.
³ The LORD doesn't let the righteous starve,
  but he rejects the desires of the wicked.
⁴ Laziness brings poverty;
  hard work makes one rich.
⁵ A wise son harvests in the summer;
  a disgraceful son
  sleeps right through the harvest.
⁶ Blessings cover the head of the righteous,
  but the mouth of the wicked
  conceals violence.
⁷ The memory of the righteous is a blessing,
  but the name of the wicked rots.
⁸ The skilled mind accepts commands,
  but a foolish talker is ruined.
⁹ Those who walk in innocence
  walk with confidence,
  but those on crooked paths
  will be found out.
¹⁰ Those who wink an eye bring trouble;
  those who speak foolishly are ruined.
¹¹ The mouth of the righteous
  is a fountain of life,
  but the mouth of the wicked
  conceals violence.
¹² Hate stirs up conflict,
  but love covers all offenses.
¹³ Wisdom is found on the lips
  of those who have understanding,
  but there is a rod for the back
  of those with no sense.
¹⁴ The wise store up knowledge,
  but the mouth of a fool brings on ruin.

ᵏ Heb *Sheol*

¹⁵ The riches of the wealthy
    are their strong city;
    the ruin of the poor is their poverty.
¹⁶ The wages of the righteous lead to life;
    the earnings of the wicked lead to sin.
¹⁷ Those who heed instruction
    are on the way to life,
    but those who ignore correction
      lose their way.
¹⁸ Lying lips conceal hate,
    and those who spread slander are fools.
¹⁹ With lots of words comes wrongdoing,
    but the wise restrain their lips.
²⁰ The tongue of the righteous
    is choice silver,
    but the heart of the wicked lacks value.
²¹ The lips of the righteous
    nourish many people,
    but fools who lack sense will die.
²² The Lord's blessing makes a person rich,
    and no trouble is added to it.
²³ Fools enjoy vile deeds,
    but those with understanding
      take pleasure in wisdom.
²⁴ What the wicked dread will come on them,
    but what the righteous desire
      will be given to them.
²⁵ After a whirlwind passes by,
    the wicked are no more,
    but the righteous stand firm forever.

²⁶ Like vinegar to the teeth
    and smoke to the eyes,
    so are lazy people
      to those who authorize them.
²⁷ The fear of the Lord increases one's life,
    but the years of the wicked
      will be cut short.
²⁸ The expectations of the righteous
    result in joy,
    but the hopes of the
      wicked will perish.

LIGHTHOUSE

SPECIAL AND SET APART

Blessing and Wealth *Proverbs 10:22*
At first glance people might think this proverb means that if a person is righteous, then God will give them lots of money. This might lead people to think that if a person is rich, he or she must be right with God or *righteous*. Obviously, neither thought is necessarily true. The Bible talks of many wealthy people, including Abraham and Job. While the Bible states that Abraham and Job were righteous, many other rich people were not. There were also many righteous people in the Bible who weren't wealthy, such as the poor widow who gave her last coins as an offering (Luke 21:1-4). ◗

God's THOUGHTS ◆ My THOUGHTS

Hard Work *Proverbs 10:4*

Hard work is required to do something well. Athletes train their bodies so they can play their sport to the best of their ability. Musicians practice so they can play or sing well. Christians study and pray so they can know how best to follow God.

When we study the Bible, we are like an athlete or musician in training. Learning the basics in the beginning is very important. No athlete starts out running a marathon. No musician starts out playing a symphony. Everything takes time.

What does it mean to study the Bible?

What do you think might happen if you don't "train" spiritually?

29 The path of the Lᴏʀᴅ is a refuge
   for the innocent
   and ruin for those who do evil.
30 The righteous will never be shaken,
   but the wicked won't dwell in the land.
31 The mouth of the righteous
   flows with wisdom,
   but the twisted tongue will be cut off.
32 The lips of the wise
   know what is acceptable,
   but the mouth of the wicked knows
    only what is perverse.

11 The Lᴏʀᴅ detests dishonest scales,
   but delights in an accurate weight.
2 When pride comes, so does shame,
   but wisdom brings humility.
3 Integrity guides the virtuous,
   but dishonesty ruins the treacherous.
4 Riches don't help in the day of wrath,
   but righteousness rescues from death.
5 The righteousness of the innocent
   makes their path straight,
   but the wicked fall in their wickedness.
6 Those who do right
   are saved by their righteousness,
   but the untrustworthy
    are caught by their own desires.
7 When the wicked die, their hope perishes.
   Yes, any hope based on money perishes.
8 The righteous are saved from distress,
   and the wicked take their place.
9 The godless destroy their neighbors
   by their words,
   but the righteous are saved
    by their knowledge.
10 When the righteous succeed,
   a city rejoices;
   when the wicked perish,
    there are shouts of joy.
11 A city is honored
   by the blessing of the virtuous;
   it is destroyed
    by the words of the wicked.
12 Whoever despises their neighbor
   lacks sense;
   a sensible person keeps quiet.
13 A slanderer walks around
   revealing secrets,
   but a trustworthy person
   keeps a confidence.

14 Without guidance, a people will fall,
   but there is victory with many counselors.
15 Guaranteeing the debt of a stranger
   brings big trouble,
   but the one who refuses to shake hands
    will be secure.
16 A gracious woman gains honor;
   violent men gain only wealth.
17 Kind persons benefit themselves,
   but cruel people harm themselves.
18 The wicked earn false wages,
   but those who sow righteousness
   receive a true reward.
19 The righteous are headed toward life,
   but those who pursue evil, toward death.
20 The Lᴏʀᴅ detests a crooked heart,
   but he favors those
    whose path is innocent.
21 The evil person will surely not
   go unpunished,
   but the children of the righteous
    will escape.
22 Like a gold ring in a pig's nose
   is a beautiful woman
    who lacks discretion.
23 The desires of the righteous end up well,
   but the expectations of the wicked
   bring wrath.
24 Those who give generously receive more,
   but those who are stingy with
    what is appropriate will grow needy.
25 Generous persons will prosper;
   those who refresh others
    will themselves be refreshed.
26 People curse those who hoard grain,
   but they bless those[l] who sell it.
27 Those who look for good find favor,
   but those who seek evil—
    it will come to them.
28 Those who trust in their wealth
   will wither,
   but the righteous will thrive
    like leafy trees.
29 Those who trouble their family
   will inherit the wind.
   The fool will be servant to the wise.
30 The fruit of the righteous is a tree of life,
   and the wise gather lives.[m]
31 If the righteous receive their due on earth,
   how much more the wicked and sinners?

---

[l]Or *the heads of those* [m]Or LXX, Syr *violence takes lives away*

12

Those who love discipline
love knowledge,
  and those who hate correction are stupid.
[2] The LORD favors good people,
  but he condemns schemers.
[3] No one is established by wicked acts,
  but the roots of the righteous
  can't be disturbed.
[4] A strong woman is a crown to her husband,
  but a disgraceful woman
  is like rot in his bones.
[5] The plans of the righteous are just,
  but the guidance of the wicked
  is deceptive.
[6] The words of the wicked are a deathtrap,
  but the speech of those who do right
  rescues them.
[7] The wicked are destroyed
  and are no more,
  but the family of the righteous
  will endure.
[8] A person is praised for his insight,
  but a warped mind leads to contempt.
[9] Better to be held in low regard
  and have a servant
  than to be conceited and lack food.
[10] The righteous care about
  their livestock's needs,
  but even the compassion of the wicked
  is cruel.
[11] Those who work their land
  will have plenty to eat,

LIGHTHOUSE

WISDOM

Everyday Wisdom *Proverbs 12:11*

This proverb talks about common sense. *Common sense* is good judgment and wisdom in everyday decisions. Common sense isn't taught in school. It's learned through experience.

Some people without common sense put off doing their work in favor of playing or sleeping. They use their money to buy things they do not need. They spend time with people who do things that could harm them. They know that the people they spend time with will affect their own habits.

People with common sense don't wait until the last minute to do chores or study for a test. They pay their bills and save money before spending it. ◆

but those who engage
in empty pursuits have no sense.
[12] Desiring evil is a trap for the wicked,
  but the root of the righteous endures.[n]
[13] The wicked are trapped
  by the transgressions of their lips,
  but the righteous escape from distress.
[14] From the fruit of their speech,
  people are well satisfied;
  their work results in reward.
[15] Fools see their own way as right,
  but the wise listen to advice.
[16] Fools reveal their anger right away,
  but the shrewd hide their contempt.
[17] Those who state the truth speak justly,
  but a false witness deceives.
[18] Some chatter on like a stabbing sword,
  but a wise tongue heals.
[19] Truthful lips endure forever,
  but a lying tongue
  lasts only for a moment.
[20] Deceit is in the heart
  of those who plan evil,
  but there is joy
  for those who advise peace.
[21] No harm happens to the righteous,
  but the wicked receive
  their fill of trouble.
[22] The LORD detests false lips;
  he favors those who do what is true.
[23] The shrewd conceal their knowledge,
  but the heart of fools
  proclaims their stupidity.
[24] A hard worker is in charge,
  while a lazy one will be sentenced
  to hard labor.
[25] Anxiety leads to depression,
  but a good word encourages.
[26] The righteous offer guidance
  to their neighbors,[o]
  but the path of the wicked
  makes them wander.
[27] The lazy don't roast[p] their prey,
  but hard workers receive precious riches.
[28] The way of the righteous leads to life,
  but the detestable[q] path leads to death.

13

A wise son listens to[r]
the discipline of his father,
  but a mocker doesn't listen to correction.

---

[n]Or *gives* [o]Heb uncertain [p]Heb uncertain [q]LXX; MT *the path of the trail* [r]Heb lacks *listens to.*

² People eat well from the fruit
of their words,
but the treacherous have an appetite
only for violence.
³ People who watch their mouths
guard their lives,
but those who open their lips are ruined.
⁴ The lazy have strong desires
but receive nothing;
the appetite of the diligent is satisfied.
⁵ The righteous hate false words,
but the wicked create disgust and scorn.
⁶ Righteousness guards the innocent
on the path,
but wickedness misleads sinners.
⁷ Some pretend to be rich but have nothing,
while others pretend to be poor,
but have great riches.
⁸ Wealth can ransom a person's life,
but the poor don't even receive threats.
⁹ The light of the righteous rejoices,
but the lamp of the wicked goes out.
¹⁰ The empty-headed cause conflict
out of pride;
those who take advice are wise.
¹¹ Riches gotten quickly[s] will dwindle,
but those who acquire them
gradually become wealthy.
¹² Hope delayed makes the heart sick;
longing fulfilled is a tree of life.
¹³ Trouble will come on those
who despise a word,
but those who respect
the commandment will be rewarded.
¹⁴ The teaching of the wise
is a fountain of life,
turning a person away from deathtraps.
¹⁵ Good insight brings favor,
but the way of the faithless is their ruin.[t]
¹⁶ The prudent all act intelligently,
but fools display their stupidity.
¹⁷ Wicked messengers fall into trouble,
but a reliable one brings healing.
¹⁸ Poverty and shame come to those
who don't care about instruction;
honor belongs to those
who heed correction.
¹⁹ A desire fulfilled is pleasant,
but fools find deviating
from evil disgusting.

²⁰ Walk with wise people and become wise;
befriend fools and get in trouble.
²¹ Trouble pursues sinners,
but good things reward the righteous.
²² Good people leave their grandchildren
an inheritance,
but the wealth of sinners
is stored up for the righteous.
²³ A poor person's land
might produce much food,
but it is unjustly swept away.
²⁴ Those who withhold the rod
hate their children,
but the one who loves them
applies discipline.
²⁵ The righteous eat their fill,
but the wicked have empty stomachs.

14 A wise woman builds her house,
while a foolish woman tears hers
down with her own hands.
² Those who walk with integrity
fear the LORD,
but those who take a crooked path
despise him.
³ Pride sprouts in the mouth of a fool,[u]
but the lips of the wise protect them.
⁴ When there are no oxen, the stall is clean,
but when there is a strong bull,
there is abundant produce.
⁵ A truthful witness doesn't lie,
but a false witness spews lies.
⁶ A mocker searches for wisdom
and gets none,
but knowledge comes quickly
to the intelligent.
⁷ Stay away from fools,
for you won't learn wise speech there.
⁸ By their wisdom the prudent
understand their way,
but the stupidity of fools deceives them.
⁹ Fools mock a compensation offering,
but favor is with those who do right.
¹⁰ The heart knows its own distress;
another person can't share its joy.
¹¹ The house of the wicked is destroyed,
but the tent flourishes
for those who do right.
¹² There is a path that may seem straight
to someone,
but in the end it is a path to death.

[s]LXX; MT *from meaninglessness* [t]LXX, Syr, Vulg; MT *endures* [u]Heb uncertain

¹³ The heart feels pain even in laughter,
and in the end, joy turns to sorrow.
¹⁴ Rebellious hearts receive satisfaction
from their ways;
the good receive the due reward
for their deeds.
¹⁵ The naive believe anything,
but the prudent give thought
to their steps.
¹⁶ The wise are careful and avoid evil,
but fools become excited
and overconfident.
¹⁷ Short-tempered people
make stupid mistakes,
and schemers are hated.
¹⁸ Stupidity is the lot of the naive,
but the prudent are crowned
with knowledge.
¹⁹ Evil people will bow down before the good;
wicked people are at the gates
of the righteous.
²⁰ Even their neighbors hate the poor,
but many love the wealthy.
²¹ Those who despise their neighbors
are sinners,
but happy are those
who are kind to the needy.
²² Don't those who plan evil go astray?
Those who plan good
receive loyalty and faithfulness.
²³ There is profit in hard work,
but mere talk leads to poverty.
²⁴ Wealth is the crown of the wise,
and the folly of fools is folly.
²⁵ A truthful witness saves lives,
but a deceiver proclaims lies.
²⁶ In the fear of the Lord
is strong confidence
and refuge for one's children.
²⁷ The fear of the Lord is a fountain of life,
turning people away from deathtraps.
²⁸ A king's glory is a large population,
but a dwindling people is a ruler's ruin.
²⁹ Patience leads to abundant understanding,
but impatience leads to stupid mistakes.
³⁰ A peaceful mind gives life to the body,
but jealousy rots the bones.
³¹ Those who exploit the powerless
anger their maker,
while those who are kind to the poor
honor God.

³² The wicked are thrown down
by their own evil,
but the righteous find refuge
even in death.
³³ Wisdom resides
in an understanding heart,
but it's notᵛ known in fools.
³⁴ Righteousness dignifies a nation,
but sin disgraces a people.
³⁵ The king favors an insightful servant,
but is furious at a shameful one.

15 A sensitive answer turns back wrath,
but an offensive word stirs up anger.
² The tongue of the wise
enhances knowledge,
but the mouth of a fool
gushes with stupidity.
³ The Lord's eyes are everywhere,
keeping watch on evil and good people.
⁴ Wholesome speech is a tree of life,
but dishonest talk breaks the spirit.
⁵ A fool doesn't like a father's instruction,
but those who heed correction
are mature.
⁶ Great treasure is in the house
of the righteous,
but the gain of the wicked brings trouble.
⁷ The lips of the wise spread knowledge,
but the hearts of fools have none.
⁸ The Lord detests the sacrifices
of the wicked,
but favors the prayers
of those who do right.

SAILBOAT

I'm Safe

Respect for God *Proverbs 14:26-27*

The phrase *fear of the Lord* is used throughout the Bible. This kind of fear is not dread, like being scared of something that might hurt us. It means having respect for God who is almighty. It means trusting God, knowing that God loves us, takes care of us, and corrects us when we disobey.

Children are secure when their earthly parents set limits and make rules, knowing it is for their own good. In the same way, God's people are secure when God gives rules for living, because those rules are for their own good. ◖

ᵛLXX; MT lacks *not*.

⁹ The LORD detests the path of the wicked,
  but loves those
    who pursue righteousness.
¹⁰ Discipline is severe for those
  who abandon the way;
    those who hate correction will die.
¹¹ The grave^w and the underworld^x lie open
  before the LORD;
    how much more the hearts
      of human beings!
¹² Mockers don't like those
  who correct them.
    They won't go to the wise.
¹³ A joyful heart brightens one's face,
  but a troubled heart breaks the spirit.
¹⁴ An understanding heart
  seeks knowledge;
    but fools feed on folly.
¹⁵ All the days of the needy are hard,
  but a happy heart has a continual feast.
¹⁶ Better a little with fear of the LORD
  than a great treasure with turmoil.
¹⁷ Better a meal of greens with love
  than a plump calf with hate.
¹⁸ Hotheads stir up conflict,
  but patient people calm down strife.
¹⁹ The path of the lazy
  is like a hedge of thorns,
    but the way of those who do right
      is a clear road.
²⁰ A wise child brings joy to a father,
  but fools despise their mothers.
²¹ Folly is joy to those who lack sense,
  but those with understanding
    walk straight ahead.
²² Plans fail with no counsel,
  but with many counselors they succeed.
²³ To give an appropriate answer is a joy;
  how good is a word at the right time!
²⁴ For those with insight,
  life is an upward path,
    avoiding the grave ^y below.
²⁵ The LORD snatches away
  the arrogant one's house,
    but he preserves the widow's boundaries.
²⁶ The LORD detests evil plans,
  but gracious words are pure.
²⁷ Those who acquire things unjustly
  gain trouble for their house,
    but those who hate bribes will live.

²⁸ The righteous heart reflects
  before answering,
    but the wicked mouth blurts out evil.
²⁹ The LORD is far from the wicked,
  but he listens to the prayers
    of the righteous.
³⁰ Bright eyes give joy to the heart;
  good news strengthens the bones.
³¹ The ear that listens
  to life-giving correction
    dwells among the wise.
³² Those who refuse discipline
  despise themselves,
    but those who listen to correction
      gain understanding.
³³ The fear of the LORD is wise instruction,
  and humility comes before respect.

16 To people belong the plans of the heart,
  but the answer of the tongue
    comes from the LORD.
² All the ways of people
  are pure in their eyes,
    but the LORD tests the motives.
³ Commit your work to the LORD,
  and your plans will succeed.
⁴ The LORD made everything for a purpose,
  even the wicked for an evil day.
⁵ The LORD detests all who are arrogant;
  they surely won't go unpunished.
⁶ Love and faithfulness reconcile guilt;
  the fear of the LORD turns away evil.
⁷ When people draw favor
  from the LORD,
    even their enemies are at peace
      with them.
⁸ Better a little with righteousness
  than great profits without justice.
⁹ People plan their path,
  but the LORD secures their steps.
¹⁰ A king's speech is like an oracle;
  in a judgment,
    one can't go against his words.
¹¹ Honest balances and scales are the LORD's;
  all the weights in the bag are his doing.
¹² Kings detest wicked deeds,
  for their thrones are founded
    on righteousness.
¹³ Kings favor those with righteous lips;
  they love words of integrity.
¹⁴ The king's anger is a messenger of death;
  the wise will calm him.

^w Heb *Sheol* ^x Heb *Abaddon* ^y Heb *Sheol*

¹⁵ There's life in the light of the king's face.
His favor is like a cloud
that brings spring rain.
¹⁶ Acquiring wisdom is much better
than gold,
and acquiring understanding
is better than silver.
¹⁷ The road of those who do right
turns away from evil;
those who protect their path
guard their lives.
¹⁸ Pride comes before disaster,
and arrogance before a fall.
¹⁹ Better to be humble with the needy
than to divide plunder with the proud.
²⁰ Those with insight find prosperity;
those who trust the Lord are blessed.
²¹ The skilled mind is called discerning,
and pleasant speech enhances teaching.
²² One who has insight is a fountain of life,
but the instruction of the foolish is folly.
²³ The mind of the wise
makes their speech insightful
and enhances the teaching of their lips.
²⁴ Pleasant words are flowing honey,
sweet to the taste
and healing to the bones.
²⁵ There is a path that may seem straight
to someone,
but in the end it is the path of death.
²⁶ The appetite of workers labors for them,
for their hunger presses them on.
²⁷ Worthless people dig up trouble;
their lips are like a scorching fire.
²⁸ Destructive people produce conflict;
gossips alienate close friends.
²⁹ Violent people entice their neighbors
and walk them down a path
that isn't good.
³⁰ Those who wink their eye
plot destruction;
those who purse their lips plan evil.
³¹ Gray hair is a crown of glory;
it is found on the path of righteousness.
³² Better to be patient than a warrior,
and better to have self-control
than to capture a city.
³³ The dice are cast into the lap;
all decisions are from the Lord.

17 Better a dry crust with quiet
than a house full of feasting
with quarrels.

² An insightful servant rules
over a disgraceful son
and will divide an inheritance
with the brothers.
³ A crucible is for silver
and a furnace for gold,
but the Lord tests the heart.
⁴ An evildoer pays attention to guilty lips;
a liar listens to a destructive tongue.
⁵ Those who mock the poor
insult their maker;
those who rejoice in disaster
won't go unpunished.
⁶ Grandchildren are the crown
of the elderly,
and the glory of children is their parents.
⁷ Too much talking isn't right for a fool;
even less so false speech
for an honorable person.
⁸ A bribe seems magical in the eyes
of those who give it,
granting success to all who use it.
⁹ One who seeks love conceals an offense,
but one who repeats it divides friends.
¹⁰ A rebuke goes deeper
to an understanding person
than a hundred lashes to a fool.
¹¹ Evil people seek only rebellion;
a cruel messenger
will be sent against them.
¹² Safer to meet a bear robbed of her cubs
than fools in their folly.
¹³ Evil will never depart from the house
of those who return evil for good.
¹⁴ The start of a quarrel is like
letting out water,
so drop the dispute before it breaks out.
¹⁵ Judging the righteous wicked
and the wicked righteous—
the Lord detests both of these.
¹⁶ Why should a fool have money
to pay for wisdom? He has no mind.
¹⁷ Friends love all the time,
and kinsfolk are born
for times of trouble.

did you know? Throwing dice was a way people made decisions in Bible times. They threw dice on the ground and made decisions based on how the dice fell. This is similar to how we sometimes flip a coin to make a decision today.

¹⁸ One with no sense shakes hands on a deal,
   securing a loan for a friend.
¹⁹ Those who love an offense love a quarrel;
   those who build a high doorway
      invite a collapse.
²⁰ Those with crooked hearts won't prosper,
   and those with twisted tongues
      will fall into trouble.
²¹ Having a fool for a son brings grief;
   there's no joy for a scoundrel's father.
²² A joyful heart helps healing,
   but a broken spirit dries up the bones.
²³ The wicked take secret bribes
   to twist the way of justice.
²⁴ Wisdom is right in front of those
   with understanding,
      but the eyes of fools
      are off to the edges of the earth.
²⁵ A foolish son is irritating to his father
   and bitter to her who gave birth to him.
²⁶ It isn't good to punish the righteous,
   to strike the honorable for their integrity.
²⁷ Wise are those who restrain their talking;
   people with understanding
      are coolheaded.
²⁸ Fools who keep quiet are deemed wise;
   those who shut their lips are smart.

18 Unfriendly people look out
   for themselves;
   they bicker with sensible people.
² Fools find no pleasure in understanding,
   but only in expressing their opinion.
³ When the wicked arrive, so does contempt;
   with shame comes insult.

SAILBOAT

FAMILY AND FRIENDS

A Real Friend *Proverbs 17:17*

A real friend loves us whether we're fun to be around or not. When we're feeling sad, a real friend prays for us and listens to us, or just sits with us when we don't feel like talking. A real friend helps us when we're going through bad times. A real friend will share whatever they have with us. A real friend stands up for us and will not gossip about us or allow other people to say bad things about us. A real friend is honest with us and tells us when we're making bad decisions. If we hurt a real friend, they will not give up on us and will forgive us when we ask. ♦

⁴ The words of a person's mouth
   are deep waters,
   a bubbling stream, a fountain of wisdom.
⁵ Favoring the wicked isn't good;
   it denies justice to the righteous.
⁶ The lips of fools make accusations;
   their mouths elicit beatings.
⁷ The mouth of fools is their ruin;
   their lips are a trap for their lives.
⁸ The words of gossips are like choice snacks;
   they go down to the inmost parts.
⁹ Those who are lazy in their work
   are brothers to thugs.
¹⁰ The Lᴏʀᴅ's name
   is a strong tower;
   the righteous run to it and find refuge.

> **Memorize**
> Prov 18:10

¹¹ The riches of the wealthy are a strong city
   and like a high wall in their imagination.
¹² Pride comes before a disaster,
   but humility comes before respect.
¹³ Those who answer before they listen
   are foolish and disgraceful.
¹⁴ The human spirit sustains a sick person,
   but who can bear a broken spirit?
¹⁵ An understanding mind gains knowledge;
   the ear of the wise seeks knowledge.
¹⁶ A gift opens the way
   for access to important people.
¹⁷ The first person to testify seems innocent,
   until the other comes
      and cross-examines him.
¹⁸ The dice settle conflicts
   and keep strong opponents apart.
¹⁹ An offended ally
   is more formidable than a city;
   such quarreling
      is like the bars of a castle.
²⁰ The stomach is satisfied
   by the fruit of the mouth;
   one's lips can earn a satisfying income.
²¹ Death and life
   are in the power of the tongue;
   those who love it will eat its fruit.
²² He who finds a wife finds what is good,
   gaining favor from the Lᴏʀᴅ.
²³ The poor plead for help,
   but the wealthy answer harshly.
²⁴ There are persons for companionship,
   but then there are friends
      who are more loyal than family.

19 Better to be poor and walk in innocence
   than to have dishonest lips and be a fool.

² Ignorant desire isn't good;
   rushing feet make mistakes.
³ People's own folly corrupts their way,
   but their hearts rage against the Lord.
⁴ Riches increase one's friends,
   but the poor lose their friends.
⁵ A false witness won't go unpunished,
   and a liar won't escape.
⁶ Many seek favor from rulers;
   everyone befriends a gift giver.
⁷ All the relatives of the poor hate them;
   even more, their friends
      stay far from them.
   When they pursue them with words,
      they aren't there.
⁸ Those who acquire good sense
   love themselves;
   those who keep understanding
   find success.
⁹ False witnesses won't go unpunished,
   and liars will perish.
¹⁰ Luxury isn't fitting for a fool;
   even less so for a servant
      to rule over princes.
¹¹ Insightful people restrain their anger;
   their glory is to ignore an offense.
¹² A raging king roars like a lion;
   his favor is like the dew on the grass.
¹³ A foolish son is a disaster to his father;
   a contentious wife
      is like constant dripping.
¹⁴ House and riches are an inheritance
   from one's ancestors,
   but an insightful wife is from the Lord.
¹⁵ Laziness brings on deep sleep;
   a slacker goes hungry.
¹⁶ Those who keep the commandment
   preserve their lives;
   those who disregard their ways will die.
¹⁷ Those who are gracious to the poor
   lend to the Lord,
   and the Lord will fully repay them.
¹⁸ Discipline your children while there
   is hope,
   but don't plan to kill them.
¹⁹ Angry people must pay the penalty;
   if you rescue them,
   then you will have to do it again.
²⁰ Listen to advice and accept instruction,
   so you might grow wise in the future.
²¹ Many plans are in a person's mind,
   but the Lord's purpose will succeed.

²² People long for trustworthiness;
   it is better to be poor than a liar.
²³ The fear of the Lord leads to life;
   then one rests content,
   untouched by harm.
²⁴ Lazy people bury their hand in the bowl;
   they won't even put it to their mouth.
²⁵ Strike someone who scoffs,
   and a naive person will become clever;
   correct someone with understanding,
   and they will gain knowledge.
²⁶ Those who assault their father
   and drive out their mother
   are disgraceful children,
   worthy of reproach.
²⁷ If, my child, you stop listening
   to discipline,
   you will wander away from words
   of knowledge.
²⁸ A worthless witness mocks justice;
   the wicked mouth gulps down trouble.
²⁹ Punishments were made for mockers,
   and blows for the backs of fools.

20 Wine is a mocker; beer a carouser.
   Those it leads astray
   won't become wise.
² A king is as terrifying as a lion's growl.
   Those who anger him may lose their life.
³ It is honorable to back off from a fight,
   but fools jump right in.
⁴ The lazy don't plow during winter;
   at harvest they look but find nothing.
⁵ Advice comes from the deep waters
   of the heart;
   those with understanding
   can draw it out.
⁶ Many people will say that they are loyal,
   but who can find a reliable person?
⁷ The righteous live with integrity;
   happy are their children
   who come after them.
⁸ A king who sits on his judgment throne
   sifts out all evil with his eyes.
⁹ Who can say, "I'm innocent to the core;
   I'm cleansed from my sin"?
¹⁰ False weights and measures—
   the Lord detests them both.
¹¹ Even young people are known
   by their actions,
   whether their conduct is pure
   and upright.
¹² Ears to hear and eyes to see—
   the Lord made them both.

¹³ Don't love sleep or you will be poor;
    stay alert and you will have plenty to eat.
¹⁴ The buyer says, "Bad, bad,"
    but then goes away and brags.
¹⁵ Much gold and many pearls exist,
    but wise speech
      is the most precious jewel.
¹⁶ Take the garment of the person
    who secures a loan for a stranger;
    take his pledge for a foreigner.
¹⁷ Stolen bread is sweet,
    but afterward the mouth is full
      of gravel.
¹⁸ Plans are firmed up by advice;
    wage wars with
      good guidance.

LIGHTHOUSE

WISDOM

Good Advice *Proverbs 20:18*
Solomon knew it is wise to seek the advice of other people. He had seen his father David talk to his advisors, and so Solomon did the same. Getting advice from others is important because they might see a situation differently than we do. They might see a problem to avoid or a solution we didn't think about. It is wise to slow down and listen to other people before we act. But we need to be careful whom we ask. We ought to ask someone who loves and obeys God, someone who is older and has experience in life, like a parent, pastor, or teacher. ◊

¹⁹ Gossips reveal secrets;
    don't associate with those
      who talk too much.
²⁰ Those who curse their father or mother—
    their lamp will be snuffed out
      when it becomes dark.
²¹ Inheritance gained quickly at first
    won't bless later on.
²² Don't say, "I'll repay the evildoer!"
    Wait for the LORD, and he will save you.
²³ The LORD detests false weights;
    deceptive scales aren't right.
²⁴ A person's steps are from the LORD;
    how then can people understand
      their path?
²⁵ It is a snare to say rashly, "It is holy,"
    and only reflect after making
      the promise.
²⁶ A wise king sifts out the wicked,
    and runs them over with a wheel.

²⁷ The breath of a person
    is the lamp of the LORD,
    searching all the inmost parts.
²⁸ Kindness and faithfulness
    protect the king;
    he supports his throne by kindness.
²⁹ Strength is the glory of young men;
    gray hair is the splendor of old age.
³⁰ Blows and bruises remove evil;
    beatings cleanse the inner parts.

21 The king's heart is like channels of water in the hand of the LORD;
    he directs it wherever he wants.
² Everyone's path is straight
    in their own eyes,
    but the LORD weighs the heart.
³ Acting with righteousness
    and justice
    is more valued by the LORD
      than sacrifice.

Bet you can read this in 4 minutes. Ready, set, go!

⁴ Prideful eyes, an arrogant heart, and
    the lamp of the wicked are all sinful.
⁵ The plans of the diligent
    end up in profit,
    but those who hurry end up with loss.
⁶ Those who gain treasure with lies
    are like a drifting fog, leading to death.
⁷ The violence of the wicked
    will sweep them away,
    for they refuse to act with justice.
⁸ The ways of some people
    are twisted and strange,
    but the behavior of those who do right
      is pure.
⁹ Better to live on the edge of a roof
    than with a contentious woman
      in a large house.
¹⁰ Wicked people desire evil;
    their neighbors receive
      no mercy from them.
¹¹ When a mocker is punished,
    the naive person gains wisdom;
    when insight comes to the wise,
      knowledge increases.
¹² The righteous one observes
    the house of the wicked,
    turning the wicked toward trouble.
¹³ Those who close their ears
    to the cries of the poor
    will themselves call out
      but receive no answer.
¹⁴ A secret gift calms anger,

and a hidden bribe
removes[z] furious wrath.

¹⁵ Acting justly is a joy to the righteous,
but dreaded by those who do evil.

¹⁶ People who wander
from the path of insight
will rest in the company of the dead.

¹⁷ Those who love pleasure end up poor;
lovers of wine and oil won't get rich.

¹⁸ The wicked are a ransom for the righteous;
the treacherous will be punished[a]
in the place of the virtuous.

¹⁹ Better to live in a wilderness
than in a house
with a contentious and angry woman.

²⁰ Precious treasure and oil
stay in the home of the wise,
but fools swallow them up.

²¹ Those who pursue righteousness
and kindness
will find life, righteousness, and honor.

²² A wise person fought a city of warriors
and brought down the stronghold
in which they felt safe.

²³ Those who guard their mouths
and their tongues
guard themselves from trouble.

²⁴ Incredibly proud—
mockers are their name!
Their conduct involves excessive pride.

²⁵ The desires of the lazy will kill them,
because their hands refuse
to do anything.

²⁶ The lazy desire things constantly,
but the righteous give
without holding back.

²⁷ The Lord detests
the sacrifices of the wicked,
especially when brought
with devious motives.

²⁸ A lying witness will perish,
but one who listens
will testify successfully.

²⁹ The wicked person appears brash,
but the virtuous
think about the path ahead.

³⁰ No wisdom, understanding,
or advice can stand up against the Lord.

³¹ A horse is made ready
for the day of battle,
but victory belongs to the Lord.

22 A good reputation
is better than much wealth;
high esteem is better than silver and gold.

² The rich and the poor have this in common:
the Lord made them both.

³ Prudent people see trouble and hide,
while the simpleminded
go right to it and get punished.

⁴ The reward of humility
and the fear of the Lord
is wealth, honor, and life.

⁵ Thorns and nets are in the path
of the crooked;
those who guard their lives
keep their distance.

⁶ Train children in the way they should go;
when they grow old,
they won't depart from it.

⁷ The wealthy rule over the poor;
a borrower is a slave to a lender.

⁸ Those who sow injustice will harvest evil;
the rod of their fury will come to an end.

⁹ Happy are generous people,
because they give some of their food
to the poor.

¹⁰ Remove the mocker
and conflict disappears;
judgment and shame also stop.

¹¹ Those who love a pure heart—
their speech is gracious,
and the king is their friend.

¹² The Lord's eyes protect knowledge,
but he frustrates the words
of the treacherous.

¹³ A lazy person says,
"There's a lion in the street!
I'll be killed in the town square!"

¹⁴ The mouth of a mysterious woman
is a deep pit;
those under the Lord's wrath
will fall in it.

¹⁵ Folly is bound up in a child's heart;
the rod of discipline removes it.

¹⁶ Oppressing the poor to get rich
and giving to the wealthy
lead only to poverty.

Thirty sayings of the wise

¹⁷ Turn your ear
and hear the words of the wise;
focus your mind on my knowledge.

---

[z] Heb lacks *removes*. [a] Heb lacks *will be punished*.

¹⁸ It will be pleasant
  if you keep the words in you,
  if you have them ready on your lips.
¹⁹ So that your trust will be in the Lord,
  I'm teaching you today—yes, you.
²⁰ Haven't I written for you thirty[b] sayings
  full of advice and knowledge?
²¹ Their purpose is to teach you true,
  reliable words,
  so you can report back reliably
  to those who sent you.

²² Don't steal from the poor,
  because they are poor.
  Don't oppress the needy in the gate.
²³ The Lord will take up their case
  and press the life out of those
  who oppress them.[c]

²⁴ Don't befriend people controlled by anger;
  don't associate with hot-tempered people;

UMBRELLA
ANGRY

Avoid People Controlled by Anger
Proverbs 22:24

At one time or another, everyone gets angry. Sometimes our anger is justified—someone stole something from us or hurt someone we love. But sometimes we get mad for the wrong reasons—like when someone else got something we wanted. The Bible teaches us to resolve problems quickly and not to go to bed angry. ◗

²⁵ otherwise, you will learn their ways
  and become trapped.

²⁶ Don't shake hands to guarantee a loan.
²⁷ If you can't repay,
  why should they be able
  to take your bed from you?
²⁸ Don't remove an ancient boundary marker
  that your ancestors established.

²⁹ Do you see people who work skillfully?
  They will work for kings
  but not work for lowly people.

23 When you sit down
  to dine with a ruler,
  carefully consider what is in front of you.
² Place a knife at your throat
  to control your appetite.
³ Don't long for the ruler's delicacies;
  the food misleads.

⁴ Don't wear yourself out trying to get rich;
  be smart enough to stop.
⁵ When your eyes fly to wealth
  it is gone; it grows wings
  like an eagle and flies heavenward.

⁶ Don't eat food with stingy people;
  don't long for their delicacies,
⁷ because they are like a hair
  in the throat.[d]
  They say to you, "Eat and drink!"
  but they don't mean it.
⁸ You will eat scraps and vomit them out.
  You will waste your pleasant words.
⁹ Don't speak in the ears of fools,
  for they will scorn your insightful words.

¹⁰ Don't remove an ancient
  boundary marker;
  don't invade the fields of orphans,
¹¹ for their redeemer is strong.
  He will bring charges against you.

¹² Bring your mind to instruction,
  your ear to knowledgeable sayings.

¹³ Don't withhold instruction from children;
  if you strike them with a rod,
  they won't die.
¹⁴ Strike them with a rod,
  and you will save their lives
  from the grave.[e]

¹⁵ My child, if your heart is wise,
  then my heart too will be happy.
¹⁶ My inner being will rejoice
  when your lips speak with integrity.

¹⁷ Don't let your heart envy sinners,
  but fear the Lord constantly;
¹⁸ then you will have a future,
  and your hope won't be cut off.

[b]Heb uncertain [c]Heb uncertain [d]LXX; Heb uncertain [e]Heb *Sheol*

¹⁹ Listen, my child, and be wise!
　Keep your mind straight on the path.
²⁰ Don't hang out with those
　who get drunk on wine
　or those who eat too much meat,
²¹ because drunks and gluttons
　will be impoverished;
　their stupor will clothe them in rags.

²² Listen to your father, who gave you life;
　don't despise your elderly mother.
²³ Buy truth and don't sell it;
　buy wisdom, instruction,
　and understanding.
²⁴ The father of the righteous
　will be very happy;
　the one who gives life to the wise
　will rejoice.
²⁵ Your father and your mother
　will rejoice;
　she who gave you birth will be happy.

²⁶ My child, give your mind to me
　and let your eyes keep to my path.
²⁷ A prostitute is a deep pit,
　and a foreign woman is a narrow well.
²⁸ Indeed, she ambushes like a robber

^f*Or in the heart of the sea*

　and increases the number
　of the faithless.

²⁹ Who is suffering?
　Who is uneasy?
　Who has arguments?
　Who has complaints?
　Who has unnecessary wounds?
　Who has glazed eyes?—
³⁰ those who linger over wine;
　those who go looking for mixed wine.
³¹ Don't look at wine when it is red,
　when it sparkles in the cup,
　going down smoothly.
³² In the end, it bites like a snake
　and poisons like a viper.
³³ Your eyes will see strange things,
　and your heart will speak
　distorted words.
³⁴ You will be like one who lies down
　while out on the sea^f
　or one who lies on top of a mast.
³⁵ "Though hit, I feel no pain;
　though beaten up,
　I don't know anything about it.
　When I wake up,
　I'll look for wine again!"

God's THOUGHTS ◆ My THOUGHTS

True Riches Proverbs 23:4-5

Earning money for doing a job well is rewarding. There are many examples of people using their wealth to honor God. But money is not the most important thing in life. We can have all the money in the world and never be satisfied. The Bible teaches that loving money can lead to evil (1 Tim 6:10) and that true riches are not found in what we own.

This passage in Proverbs tells us that we should not wear ourselves out trying to get rich and that wealth can disappear in an instant. While we should be thankful for all we have been given, we should also remember that there are things much more important than money. God is concerned with how we live our lives—how we show love to God and to people.

How do you think that loving money might lead to evil?

How can you use the things you have been given to serve God?

24

Don't envy evil people,
and don't long to be with them.

² Their hearts are focused on violence,
and their lips speak of trouble.

³ By wisdom a house is built;
by understanding it is established.

⁴ By knowledge rooms are filled
with all precious and pleasant wealth.

⁵ A wise person is mightier
than a strong one;⁸
a knowledgeable person
than a powerful one.

⁶ You should make war with guidance;
victory comes with many counselors.

⁷ Wisdom is beyond foolish people.
They don't open their mouths
in the gate.

⁸ Those who plot evil
will be called master schemers.

⁹ The scheming of fools is sin;
people detest mockers.

¹⁰ If you show yourself weak
on a day of distress,
your strength is too small.

¹¹ Rescue those being taken off to death;
and from those staggering
to the slaughter, don't hold back.

¹² If you say,
"Look, we didn't know about it,"
the one who weighs hearts—
doesn't he understand?
The one who protects your life—
he knows.
He makes people pay
for their actions.

did you know? People have always worried about whether other people like them. Sometimes people lie about things to try to make friends. Proverbs 24:26 teaches that being honest with people is the best way to be a good friend.

¹³ My child, eat honey, for it is good.
The honeycomb is sweet in your mouth.

¹⁴ Know that wisdom is like that
for your whole being.

If you find it, there is a future.
Your hope won't be cut off.

¹⁵ Wicked one, don't wait secretly
at the home of the righteous.
Don't destroy their dwelling.

¹⁶ The righteous may fall seven times
but still get up,
but the wicked will stumble into trouble.

¹⁷ When your enemies fall, don't rejoice.
When they stumble,
don't let your heart be glad,

¹⁸ or the LORD will see it and be displeased,
and he will turn his anger from them.

¹⁹ Don't get fighting mad at evil people;
don't be envious of the wicked.

²⁰ Indeed, there is no future for the evil;
the lamp of the wicked will be put out.

²¹ Fear the LORD, my child,
as well as the king.
Don't associate with those
who are rebellious.

²² Disaster comes suddenly from them.
Who can know the ruin
that both can bring?

More sayings of the wise

²³ These are also the sayings of the wise:

Partiality in judgment isn't good.

²⁴ Those who say to the guilty,
"You are innocent"—
the people will curse them.
Nations will condemn them.

²⁵ But it will go well for those
who rebuke them.
A rich blessing will come to them.

²⁶ Those who speak honestly
are like those who kiss on the lips.

²⁷ Get your outside work done;
make preparations in the field;
then you can build your house.

²⁸ Don't be a witness against your neighbor
without reason;
don't deceive with your lips.

---

⁸LXX; MT *A wise man is strong.*

²⁹ Don't say, "I'll do to them what they did to me.
    I'll pay them back for their actions."

³⁰ I happened upon the field of a lazy person,
    by the vineyard of one with no sense.
³¹ Thorns grew all over it;
    weeds covered the ground,
    and the stone wall was falling down.
³² I observed this and took it to heart;
    I saw it and learned a lesson.
³³ "A little sleep, a little slumber,
    a little lying down with folded arms"—
    ³⁴ and poverty will come on you
    like a prowler,
    deprivation like a man with a shield.

More proverbs of Solomon

25 These are also proverbs of Solomon,
copied by the men of Hezekiah, king
of Judah:

² It is the glory of God to hide something
    and the glory of kings
        to discover something.
³ Like the high heavens
    and the depths of the earth,
    so the mind of a king is unsearchable.

⁴ Remove the dross from the silver,
    and a vessel will come out for the refiner.
⁵ Remove the wicked
    from the king's presence,
    and his throne will be established
        in righteousness.

⁶ Don't exalt yourself
    in the presence of the king,
    or stand in the place of important people,
    ⁷ because it is better that he say to you,
    "Come up here,"
    than to be demoted before a ruler.

What your eyes see,
    ⁸don't be quick to quarrel over;
    what will you do in the future
        when your neighbor shames you?
⁹ Argue it out with your neighbor,
    and don't give away someone's secret.
¹⁰ Otherwise, the one who hears it
    will vilify you;
    the slander against you will never stop.

¹¹ Words spoken at the right time
    are like gold apples in a silver setting.
¹² Wise correction to an ear that listens
    is like a gold earring
    or jewelry of fine gold.

¹³ Like the coolness of snow on a harvest day
    are reliable messengers to those
        who send them;
    they restore the life of their master.
¹⁴ People who brag about a gift never given
    are like clouds and wind
        that produce no rain.
¹⁵ A commander can be persuaded
    with patience,
    and a tender tongue can break a bone.
¹⁶ If you find honey,
    eat just the right amount;
    otherwise, you'll get full and vomit it up.
¹⁷ Don't spend too much time
    in your neighbor's house.
    Otherwise, they'll get fed up with you
        and hate you.
¹⁸ People who testify falsely
    against their neighbors
    are like a club, sword,
        and sharpened arrow.
¹⁹ Trusting a treacherous person
    at a difficult time
    is like having a bad tooth
        or a wobbly foot.
²⁰ Singing a song to a troubled heart
    is like taking off a garment on a cold day
    or putting vinegar on a wound.ʰ
²¹ If your enemies are starving,
    feed them some bread;
    if they are thirsty,
        give them water to drink.
²² By doing this, you will heap
    burning coals on their heads,
    and the LORD will reward you.
²³ The north wind stirs up rain,
    and a person who plots quietly
        provokes angry faces.
²⁴ Better to live on the edge of a roof
    than to share a house
        with a contentious woman.
²⁵ Good news from a distant land
    is like cold water for a weary person.
²⁶ A righteous person giving in to the wicked

ʰLXX; MT *vinegar on natron* (a detergent)

is like a contaminated spring
　or a polluted fountain.
²⁷ Eating too much honey isn't good,
　nor is it appropriate to seek honor.
²⁸ A person without self-control
　is like a breached city, one with no walls.

26

Like snow in the summer
or rain at harvest,
　so honor isn't appropriate for a fool.
² Like a darting sparrow,
　like a flying swallow,
　　so an undeserved curse never arrives.
³ A whip for a horse, a bridle for a donkey,
　and a rod for the back of fools.
⁴ Don't answer fools according to their folly,
　or you will become like them yourself.
⁵ Answer fools according to their folly,
　or they will deem themselves wise.
⁶ Sending messages with a fool
　is like cutting off one's feet
　　or drinking down violence.
⁷ As legs dangle from a disabled person,
　so does a proverb in the mouth of fools.
⁸ Like tying a stone in a sling,
　so is giving respect to a fool.
⁹ Like a thorny bush in the hand of a drunk,
　so is a proverb in the mouth of fools.
¹⁰ Like an archer who wounds
　someone randomly,
　　so is one who hires a fool or a passerby.
¹¹ Like a dog that returns to its vomit,
　so a fool repeats foolish mistakes.
¹² Do you see people
　who consider themselves wise?
　There is more hope for a fool
　　than for them.
¹³ A lazy person says,
　"There's a lion in the path!
　A lion in the plazas!"
¹⁴ As a door turns on its hinge,
　so do lazy people in their beds.
¹⁵ Lazy people bury their hand into the bowl,
　too tired to return it to their mouth.
¹⁶ Lazy people think they are wiser
　than seven people who answer sensibly.

¹⁷ Like yanking the ears of a dog,
　so is one who passes by and gets
　　involved in another person's fight.

¹⁸ Like a crazy person shooting deadly
　flaming arrows
¹⁹ are those who deceive their neighbor
　and say, "Hey, I was only joking!"
²⁰ Without wood a fire goes out;
　without gossips, conflict calms down.
²¹ Like adding charcoal to embers
　or wood to fire,
　　quarrelsome people kindle strife.
²² The words of gossips
　are like choice snacks;
　　they go down to the inmost parts.
²³ Smooth[i] lips and an evil heart
　are like silver coating on clay.
²⁴ Hateful people mislead with their lips,
　keeping their deception within.
²⁵ Though they speak graciously,
　don't believe them,
　for seven horrible things
　　are in their heart.
²⁶ They may cover their hatred with trickery,
　but their evil will be revealed in public.
²⁷ Those who dig a pit will fall in it;
　those who roll a stone
　　will have it turn back on them.
²⁸ A lying tongue hates those it crushes;
　a flattering mouth causes destruction.

27

Don't brag about tomorrow,
for you don't know
　what a day will bring.
² Let another person praise you,
　and not your own mouth;

UMBRELLA
PRIDE

Let Someone Else Praise You *Proverbs 27:2*
Braggarts are people who talk about themselves all
the time, trying to show everyone else that they're
the best. Braggarts can't stand for the attention to
be on anyone but themselves. If someone is talking
about another person, braggarts will interrupt with
stories about themselves. "Let another person
praise you," says this proverb. This doesn't mean we
shouldn't be pleased with our accomplishments. It
means we shouldn't brag and make ourselves the
center of attention all the time. ♦

ⁱLXX; Heb uncertain

a stranger, and not your own lips.
³ A stone is heavy and sand weighs much,
but the nuisance of fools
is heavier than both.
⁴ Wrath is cruel and anger is a flood,
but who can withstand jealousy?
⁵ A public correction
is better than hidden love.
⁶ Trustworthy are the bruises of a friend;
excessive are the kisses of an enemy.
⁷ Someone who is full refuses honey,
but anything bitter
tastes sweet to a hungry person.
⁸ Like a bird wandering from its nest,
so is one who wanders from home.
⁹ Oil and incense make the heart glad,
and the sweetness of friends
comes from their advice.ʲ
¹⁰ Don't desert your friend
or a friend of your family;
don't go to your relative's house
when disaster strikes.
Better a neighbor nearby
than a relative far away.
¹¹ Be wise, my child, and make my heart glad,
so I can answer those who insult me.
¹² Prudent people see evil and hide;
the simpleminded go right to it
and get punished.
¹³ Take the garment of the person
who secures a loan for a stranger;
take his pledge for a foreigner.
¹⁴ Greeting a neighbor with a loud voice
early in the morning
will be viewed as a curse.
¹⁵ The constant dripping on a rainy day
and a contentious woman are alike;
¹⁶ anyone who can control her
can control the wind
or pick up oil in his hand.
¹⁷ As iron sharpens iron,
so one person sharpens a friend.
¹⁸ Those who tend a fig tree will eat its fruit,
and those who look after their master
will be honored.
¹⁹ As water reflects the face,
so the heart reflects
one person to another.
²⁰ The graveᵏ and the underworldˡ
are never satisfied;
and people's eyes are never satisfied.

²¹ A crucible is for silver
and a furnace for gold;
so are people in the presence
of someone who praises them.
²² Even if you grind fools in a mortar,
even grinding them along with the grain,
their folly won't be driven from them.
²³ Know your flock well;
pay attention to your herds,
²⁴ for no treasure lasts forever,
nor a crown generation after generation.
²⁵ When the grass goes away,
new growth appears,
and the plants of the hills are gathered,
²⁶ then the lambs will provide your clothes,
and the goats
will be the price of your fields.
²⁷ There will be enough goat's milk
for your food,
for the food of your house,
and to nourish your young women.

28

The wicked run away even though
no one pursues them,
but the righteous
are as confident as a lion.
² When a land rebels, there are many leaders;
but a person with understanding
brings order.
³ Poor people who oppress the needy
are rain that washes away food.
⁴ Those who abandon Instruction
praise the wicked,
but those who follow Instruction
battle them.
⁵ Evil people don't understand justice,
but those who seek the Lord
understand everything.

did you know? When people in ancient times needed to sharpen their iron swords, they used a coarse piece of iron. Rubbing the blade of the sword against the piece of iron would sharpen the edge of the blade.

⁶ Better to be poor and walk in innocence
than to be on crooked paths and wealthy.
⁷ Intelligent children follow Instruction,
but those who befriend gluttons
shame their parents.

ʲHeb uncertain ᵏHeb *Sheol* ˡHeb *Abaddon*

⁸ Those who become rich
through high interest rates
gather money for those
who are generous to the poor.
⁹ Those who turn their ears
from hearing Instruction—
even their prayers will be detested.
¹⁰ Whoever misleads those who do right
onto an evil path
will fall into their own pit,
but the blameless
will inherit good things.
¹¹ Rich people think they are wise,
but an insightful poor person
sees through them.
¹² When the righteous rejoice,
there is great respect,
but people hide when the wicked prosper.
¹³ Those who hide their sins won't succeed,
but those who confess
and give them up will receive mercy.
¹⁴ Happy are those
who are continually fearful,
but those whose hearts are hard
fall into trouble.
¹⁵ A wicked ruler over the poor
is like a growling lion or a prowling bear.
¹⁶ A prince without understanding
is a cruel oppressor,
but one who hates unjust gain
will live long.
¹⁷ If someone feels guilty about murder,
don't hold them back
from fleeing to the pit.
¹⁸ Those who walk in innocence
will be saved,
but those who go on twisted paths
will fall into the grave.
¹⁹ Those who work the land
will have plenty to eat,
but those with worthless pursuits
will have plenty of poverty.
²⁰ Reliable people
will have abundant blessings,
but those with get-rich-quick schemes
won't go unpunished.
²¹ Those who show favoritism aren't good;
people do wrong for a crust of bread.
²² The stingy try to get rich fast,
unaware that loss will come to them.

²³ Those who correct someone will,
in the end, find more favor
than those with flattering tongues.
²⁴ Those who steal from their father
and mother,
and say, "It's not a crime,"
are friends of vandals.
²⁵ Greedy people stir up conflict,
but those who trust the LORD
become prosperous.
²⁶ Those who trust in their own reasoning
are fools,
but those who walk in wisdom
will be kept safe.
²⁷ Those who give to the poor
will lack nothing,
but those who turn a blind eye
will be greatly cursed.
²⁸ When the wicked rise up, people hide,
but when they are destroyed,
the righteous multiply.

29 One who stays stubborn
after many corrections
will be suddenly broken, beyond healing.
² When the righteous become numerous,
the people rejoice,
but when the wicked dominate,
the people moan.
³ A man who loves wisdom
makes his father rejoice,
but one who spends time
with prostitutes destroys riches.
⁴ A king gives stability to the land by justice,
but one who imposes heavy taxes
tears it down.
⁵ People who flatter their friends
spread out a net for their feet.
⁶ The wicked are snared by their own sin;ᵐ
the righteous sing and rejoice.
⁷ The righteous know the rights of the poor,
but the wicked don't understand.
⁸ Mockers set a city on fire,
but the wise turn back anger.
⁹ When the wise make a legal charge
against the foolish,
the fools shout, they laugh—
there is no calm.
¹⁰ Murderous people hate the innocent,
and they seek the lives of the virtuous.

ᵐTg, Syr; MT *In the sin of an evil man is a snare*

¹¹ Fools show all their anger,
  but the wise hold it back.
¹² If a ruler listens to lies,
  those who serve him will be wicked.
¹³ The poor and their oppressors
  have a common bond—
  the LORD gives light to the eyes of both.
¹⁴ If a king judges the poor honestly,
  his throne will be established forever.
¹⁵ The rod and correction lead to wisdom,
  but children out of control
    shame their mothers.
¹⁶ When the wicked become numerous,
  so do crimes;
  the righteous will see their downfall.
¹⁷ Instruct your children;
  they will give you peace of mind
  and bring delight into your life.
¹⁸ When there's no vision,
  the people get out of control,
  but whoever obeys
    instruction is happy.

SAILBOAT

OBEDIENCE

Obey Instructions *Proverbs 29:18*

Have you ever tried to learn a game when people kept changing the rules? One person told you to play one way, and then another person said, "No! That's not the way to play." Soon there was an argument over whose rules to play by, and all the fun of the game was gone. There is a reason for instructions. When we know how to do something the right way, we get more enjoyment out of it. The people who follow God's instructions for life are happy. ◆

---

¹⁹ Servants aren't disciplined by words;
  they might understand,
    but they don't respond.
²⁰ Do you see people who are quick to speak?
  There is more hope for fools than for them.
²¹ Pamper servants from a young age,
  and later on there will be trouble.
²² Angry people stir up conflict;
  hotheads cause much offense.
²³ Pride lays people low,
  but those of humble spirit gain honor.
²⁴ Those who share plunder with thieves
  hate themselves;
  even under oath, they don't testify.
²⁵ People are trapped by their fear of others;
  those who trust the LORD are secure.

²⁶ Many seek access to the ruler,
  but justice comes from the LORD.
²⁷ The unjust person is disgusting
  to the righteous;
  the straight path is disgusting
    to the wicked.

Words of Agur

30 The words of Agur, Jakeh's son, from Massa.

  The man declares: I'm tired, God;
  I'm tired, God, and I'm exhausted.
² Actually, I'm too stupid to be human,
  a man without understanding.
³ I haven't learned wisdom,
  nor do I have knowledge of the holy one.

⁴ Who has gone up to heaven
  and come down?
  Who has gathered the wind
  by the handful?
  Who has bound up the waters
  in a garment?
  Who has established all the ends
  of the earth?
  What is this person's name
  and the name of this person's child—
    if you know it?

⁵ All God's words are tried and true;
  a shield for those who take refuge in him.
⁶ Don't add to his words,
  or he will correct you
  and show you to be a liar.

⁷ Two things I ask of you;
  don't keep them from me before I die:
⁸ Fraud and lies—
  keep far from me!
  Don't give me either poverty or wealth;
  give me just the food I need.
⁹ Or I'll be full and deny you,
  and say, "Who is the LORD?"
  Or I'll be poor and steal,
  and dishonor my God's name.

More sayings of the wise

¹⁰ Don't slander a servant to his master;
  otherwise, the servant will curse you,
  and you will be guilty.

¹¹ There are those who curse their father
  and don't bless their mother.

¹² There are those who think they are clean,
   but haven't washed off
      their own excrement.
¹³ There are those—
   how arrogant are their eyes;
   how their eyebrows are raised!
¹⁴ There are those whose teeth are swords;
   their jaw is a butcher's knife,
   ready to devour the needy from the earth,
   and the poor from humanity.

¹⁵ The leech has two daughters: "Give, give!"
   There are three things
      that are never satisfied,
   four that never say, "Enough!":
¹⁶ the grave[n] and a barren womb,
   a land never filled with water,
   and fire that doesn't say, "Enough!"

¹⁷ An eye that mocks a father
   and rejects obedience to a mother,
   may the ravens of the river valley
      peck it out,
   and the eagle's young eat it.
¹⁸ Three things are too wonderful for me,
   four that I can't figure out:
¹⁹ the way of an eagle in the sky,
   the way of a snake on the rock,

[n]Heb *Sheol*

the way of a ship out on the open sea,
   and the way of a man
      with a young woman.

²⁰ This is the way of an adulterous woman:
   she eats and wipes her mouth,
   and she says, "I've done nothing wrong!"

²¹ At three things the earth trembles,
   at four it can't bear up:
²² at a servant when he becomes king
   and fools when they are full of food;
²³ at a detested woman
   when she gets married
   and a female servant
      when she replaces her mistress.

²⁴ Four things are among
   the smallest on earth,
   but they are extremely wise:
²⁵ Ants as creatures aren't strong,
   but they store away their food
      in the summer.
²⁶ Badgers as creatures aren't powerful,
   but they make their homes
      in the rocks.
²⁷ Locusts don't have a king,
   but they march together in ranks.

God's Thoughts / My Thoughts

God's Words Are True *Proverbs 30:5-6*

When we rely on God, we can be ready for anything that comes our way. Trusting in God's words is like being safe in the strongest of fortresses, where no enemy can stand. This passage teaches that God's words are "tried and true" (Prov 30:5), which means we can stand firmly in them. God's words can bring healing, comfort, and peace to those who face difficult times. They can bring challenge and correction to those who have wandered from God's ways. They can bring encouragement to those who are doing their best to love and serve God. God's words are a shield of protection from the troubles of this world.

There have often been times when people have tried to twist God's words, adding some meaning that was never intended. For this reason, we should be careful to listen to those whom we know and trust, praying that God will keep our eyes open to the truth.

What are some of God's words you know to be true?

Pray that God will help you to grow in your knowledge and understanding of God's words.

did you know? Women were not valued in many ancient cultures. Among the Israelites, women were viewed as wise. They could be shop owners. They could even buy and sell property, which was unheard of in other cultures.

[28] You can catch lizards in your hand,
but they are in kings' palaces.

[29] There are three things
that are excellent in their stride,
four that are excellent as they walk:
[30] a lion, a warrior among beasts,
which doesn't back down at anything;
[31] the strut of a rooster or a male goat;
and a king with his army.

[32] If you've been foolish and arrogant,
if you've been scheming,
put your hand to your mouth,
[33] because churning milk makes curds,
squeezing the nose brings blood,
and stirring up anger produces strife.

Words of King Lemuel

31 The words of King Lemuel of Massa,
which his mother taught him:
[2] No, my son!
No, son of my womb!
No, son of my solemn promises!
[3] Don't give your strength to women,
your ways to those who wipe out kings.
[4] It isn't for kings, Lemuel,
it isn't for kings to drink wine,
for rulers to crave[o] strong drink.
[5] Otherwise, they will drink
and forget the law,
and violate the rights of the needy.
[6] Give strong drink
to those who are perishing
and wine to those whose hearts are bitter.
[7] Let them drink and forget their poverty
and no longer remember their toil.
[8] Speak out on behalf of the voiceless,
and for the rights of all
who are vulnerable.[p]
[9] Speak out in order to judge
with righteousness
and to defend the needy and the poor.

The competent wife

[10] A competent wife, how does one find her?
Her value is far above pearls.
[11] Her husband entrusts his heart to her,
and with her he will have all he needs.
[12] She brings him good and not trouble
all the days of her life.
[13] She seeks out wool and flax;
she works joyfully with her hands.
[14] She is like a fleet of merchant ships,
bringing food from a distance.
[15] She gets up while it is still night,
providing food for her household,
even some for her female servants.
[16] She surveys a field and acquires it;
from her own resources,
she plants a vineyard.
[17] She works energetically;
her arms are powerful.
[18] She realizes that her trading is successful;
she doesn't put out her lamp at night.
[19] She puts her hands to the spindle;
her palms grasp the whorl.
[20] She reaches out to the needy;
she stretches out her hands to the poor.
[21] She doesn't fear for her household
when it snows,
because they are all dressed
in warm[q] clothes.
[22] She makes bedspreads for herself;
fine linen and purple are her clothing.
[23] Her husband is known in the city gates
when he sits with the elders of the land.
[24] She makes garments and sells them;
she supplies sashes to traders.
[25] Strength and honor are her clothing;
she is confident about the future.
[26] Her mouth is full of wisdom;
kindly teaching is on her tongue.
[27] She is vigilant over the activities
of her household;
she doesn't eat the food of laziness.
[28] Her children bless her;
her husband praises her:
[29] "Many women act competently,
but you surpass them all!"
[30] Charm is deceptive and beauty fleeting,
but a woman who fears the Lord
is to be praised.
[31] Let her share in the results of her work;
let her deeds praise her in the city gates.

[o]*Or where or or* [p]*Or all children who are passing away* [q]LXX; MT *red*

Ecclesiastes

Ecclesiastes is said to have been written by Solomon, "David's son, king in Jerusalem," who is also called "the Teacher" (Eccl 1:1). Ecclesiastes challenges us to think hard about life's most important things.

The Teacher doesn't sound very happy at the beginning of the book. "Perfectly pointless, says the Teacher, perfectly pointless. Everything is pointless" (Eccl 1:2). The Teacher says that he tried everything in life and found that nothing is as great as people say.

The Teacher tried to find happiness in hard work, but ended up disappointed. He tried studying nature, enjoying pleasure, and making a lot of money, but all of those things felt pointless. The Teacher says it was like trying to chase the wind.

The Teacher had a chance to experience all the good things of life because he was wise, rich, and famous. He had everything a person could ever want. But in the end, the Teacher concluded that the best thing in life is to worship God and keep God's commandments. Ecclesiastes teaches us to follow God and all God's ways. 💧

things YOU'LL DISCOVER

The book of Ecclesiastes raises the question of what matters most in life. It begins by saying that everything is pointless. But it ends by declaring that the best thing is obeying God and keeping God's commands.

people YOU'LL MEET

Teacher—the named author of this book (Eccl 1–12)

places YOU'LL GO

Israel, Jerusalem

words YOU'LL REMEMBER

"So this is the end of the matter; all has been heard. Worship God and keep God's commandments because this is what everyone must do" (Eccl 12:13).

Opening motto

1 The words of the Teacher of the Assembly,[a] David's son, king in Jerusalem:

² Perfectly pointless,[b]
    says the Teacher,
    perfectly pointless.
    Everything is pointless.

Some things are inevitable

³ What do people gain
    from all the hard work
    that they work so hard at
        under the sun?
⁴ A generation goes,
    and a generation comes,
    but the earth remains as it always has.
⁵ The sun rises, the sun sets;
    it returns panting to the place
        where it dawns.
⁶ The wind blows to the south,
    goes around to the north;
    around and around blows the wind;
    the wind returns to its rounds again.

⁷ All streams flow to the sea,
    but the sea is never full;
    to the place where the rivers flow,
        there they continue to flow.
⁸ All words[c] are tiring;
    no one is able to speak.
    The eye isn't satisfied with seeing,
    neither is the ear filled up by hearing.
⁹ Whatever has happened—
    that's what will happen again;
    whatever has occurred—
        that's what will occur again.

There's nothing new under the sun. ¹⁰People may say about something: "Look at this! It's new!" But it was already around for ages before us. ¹¹There's no remembrance of things in the past, nor of things to come in the future. Neither will there be any remembrance among those who come along in the future.

The Teacher's quest

¹²I am the Teacher. I was king over Israel in Jerusalem.

---

[a]Or *Gatherer* or *Convener* or *Assembler* (Heb *Qoheleth*); see also 1:2, 12; 7:27; 12:8, 9, 10.   [b]Or *meaningless* or *vapor* or *puff of air* (Heb *hebel*, which often occurs in the book)   [c]Or *things*

Nothing New   Ecclesiastes 1:9-10

Solomon was a wise king who had many of the things this world has to offer. He was wealthy, powerful, and educated, but he couldn't find happiness in any of these things. Instead, they made him feel hopeless. He ultimately concluded that the most important thing is to worship God and keep God's commandments.

Having money, power, friends, and possessions isn't necessarily bad. But unless we use those things to please and honor God, they have no real meaning. Ecclesiastes teaches that it's a waste of time to try anything and everything under the sun, searching for something new that will bring meaning to life. Having the latest toy, getting the most money, or hanging out with the most popular people isn't what really brings us satisfaction. God asks us to spend our days following God's ways—using who we are and what we have to love and serve God.

What have you been blessed with that you can give back to God?

What brings you true happiness?

¹³I applied my mind to investigate and to explore by wisdom all that happens under heaven. It's an unhappy obsession that God has given to human beings.

¹⁴When I observed all that happens under the sun, I realized that everything is pointless, a chasing after wind.

¹⁵ What's crooked can't be straightened;
　what isn't there can't be counted.

¹⁶I said to myself, Look here, I have grown much wiser than any who ruled over Jerusalem before me. My mind has absorbed great wisdom and knowledge. ¹⁷But when I set my mind to understand wisdom, and also to understand madness and folly, I realized that this too was just wind chasing.

¹⁸ Remember:

In much wisdom is much aggravation;
　the more knowledge, the more pain.

2　I said to myself,ᵈ Come, I will make youᵉ experience pleasure; enjoy what is good! But this too was pointless! ²Merriment, I thought, is madness; pleasure, of no use at all. ³I tried cheering myself with wine and by embracing folly—with wisdom still guiding me—until I might see what is really worth doing in the few days that human beings have under heaven.

⁴I took on great projects: I built houses for myself, planted vineyards for myself. ⁵I made gardens and parks for myself, planting every kind of fruit tree in them. ⁶I made reservoirs for myself to water my lush groves. ⁷I acquired male servants and female servants; I even had slaves born in my house. I also had great herds of cattle and sheep, more than any who preceded me in Jerusalem. ⁸I amassed silver and gold for myself, the treasures of kings and provinces. I acquired male and female singers for myself, along with every human luxury, treasure chests galore!ᶠ ⁹So I became far greater than all who preceded me in Jerusalem. Moreover, my wisdom stood by me. ¹⁰I refrained from nothing that my eyes desired. I refused my heart no pleasure. Indeed, my heart found pleasure from the results of my hard work; that was the reward from all my hard work. ¹¹But when I surveyed all that my hands had done, and

what I had worked so hard to achieve, I realized that it was pointless—a chasing after wind. Nothing is to be gained under the sun.

¹²My reflections then turned to wisdom, madness, and folly. What can the king's heir do but what has already been done? ¹³I saw that wisdom is more beneficial than folly, as light is more beneficial than darkness.

¹⁴ The wise have eyes in their head,
　but fools walk around in darkness.

But I also realized that the same fate happens to both of them. ¹⁵So I thought to myself, What happens to the fool will also happen to me. So why have I been so very wise? I said to myself, This too is pointless. ¹⁶There is no eternal memory of the wise any more than the foolish,ᵍ because everyone is forgotten before long. How can the wise die just like the fool? ¹⁷So I hated life, because the things that

LIFE PRESERVER

Why did the Teacher think everything was pointless?
Ecclesiastes 2:1-11

There's a saying in life that some people see a glass of water and say it's half empty while others see the same glass and say it's half full. These are two ways of looking at life—one that is negative and one that is positive. The Teacher in the book of Ecclesiastes would be in the first group.

The Teacher was on a quest to figure out what was really worth doing in life. But through all his experiences he never found satisfaction. He concluded that everything is pointless, because humans aren't truly able to appreciate God's work as creator in the world.

As you read through this book of wisdom, look for positive as well as negative observations. The Teacher's thoughts that are written in this book are full of doubt and questions. If you've ever felt that way, Ecclesiastes shows that you're not alone. ◆

ᵈOr *in my heart; mind* ᵉOr *the self (or heart; mind)* ᶠOr *many secondary wives* ᵍOr *The wise and the foolish alike are never remembered*.

happen under the sun were troublesome to me. Definitely, everything is pointless—just wind chasing.

[18]I hated the things I worked so hard for here under the sun, because I will have to leave them to someone who comes after me. [19]And who knows whether that one will be wise or foolish? Either way, that person will have control over the results of all my hard work and wisdom here under the sun. That too is pointless. [20]I then gave myself up to despair, as I thought about all my laborious hard work under the sun, [21]because sometimes those who have worked hard with wisdom, knowledge, and skill must leave the results of their hard work as a possession to those who haven't worked hard for it. This too is pointless—it's a terrible wrong. [22]I mean, What do people get for all their hard work and struggles under the sun? [23]All their days are pain, and their work is aggravation; even at night, their hearts don't find rest. This too is pointless.

[24]There's nothing better for human beings than to eat, drink, and experience pleasure in their hard work. I also saw that this is from God's hand—[25]Who can eat and find enjoyment otherwise?—[26]because God gives wisdom, knowledge, and joy to those who please God. But to those who are offensive,[h] God gives the task of hoarding and accumulating, but only so as to give it all to those who do please God. This too is pointless and a chasing after wind.

A season for everything

3 There's a season for everything
and a time for every matter

Bet you can
read this in 1 minute. Ready, set, go!

under the heavens:
[2] a time for giving birth
    and a time for dying,
a time for planting and a time for
    uprooting what was planted,
[3] a time for killing
    and a time for healing,
a time for tearing down
    and a time for building up,
[4] a time for crying
    and a time for laughing,
a time for mourning
    and a time for dancing,

[5] a time for throwing stones
    and a time for gathering stones,
a time for embracing
    and a time for avoiding embraces,
[6] a time for searching
    and a time for losing,
a time for keeping
    and a time for throwing away,
[7] a time for tearing
    and a time for repairing,
a time for keeping silent
    and a time for speaking,
[8] a time for loving and a time for hating,
a time for war
    and a time for peace.

SAILBOAT

PEACE

There's a Season for Everything
Ecclesiastes 3:1-8
The Teacher wrote a beautiful poem that encourages readers with the comforting idea that there is a season, or time, for everything. The Teacher included major events in these seasons: a time to be born and a time to die, a time to plant and a time to harvest crops, a time for war and a time for peace. All of these things are part of life. By listing both the good and the bad, the Teacher reminded readers not to trust in things—no matter how good—and to realize that bad times will eventually end. ◊

Hard work

[9]What do workers gain from all their hard work? [10]I have observed the task that God has given human beings. [11]God has made everything fitting in its time, but has also placed eternity in their hearts, without enabling them to discover what God has done from beginning to end.

[12]I know that there's nothing better for them but to enjoy themselves and do what's good while they live. [13]Moreover, this is the gift of God: that all people should eat, drink, and enjoy the results of their hard work. [14]I know that whatever God does will last forever; it's impossible to add to it or take away from it. God has done this so that people are reverent before him.[i] [15]Whatever happens has already happened, and whatever will

---

[h]Or *to those who sin* [i]Or *to inspire awe before the divine*

happen has already happened before. And God looks after what is driven away.[j]

Enjoy what you do now

[16]I saw something else under the sun: in the place of justice, there was wickedness; and in the place of what was right, there was wickedness again! [17]I thought to myself, God will judge both righteous and wicked people, because there's a time for every matter and every deed. [18]I also thought, Where human beings are concerned, God tests them to show them that they are but animals [19]because human beings and animals share the same fate. One dies just like the other—both have the same life-breath. Humans are no better off than animals because everything is pointless. [20]All go to the same place:

all are from the dust;
all return to the dust.

[21]Who knows if a human being's life-breath rises upward while an animal's life-breath descends into the earth? [22]So I perceived that there was nothing better for human beings but to enjoy what they do because that's what they're allotted in life. Who, really, is able to see what will happen in the future?

Death is better than oppression

4 When I next observed all the oppressions that take place under the sun, I saw the tears of the oppressed—and they have no one to comfort them. Their oppressors wield power—but they have no one to comfort them. [2]So I declare that the dead, who have already died, are more fortunate than the living, who are still alive. [3]But happier than both are those who have never existed, who haven't witnessed the terrible things that happen under the sun.

Envy and loneliness

[4]I also observed that people work hard and become good at what they do only out of mutual envy. This too is pointless, just wind chasing.

[5] Fools fold their hands
    and eat their own flesh.

[6] But better is resting with one handful

than working hard for two fistfuls
    and chasing after wind.

[7]Next, I saw under the sun something else that was pointless: [8]There are people who are utterly alone, with no companions, not even a child or a sibling. Yet they work hard without end, never satisfied with their wealth. So for whom am I working so hard and depriving myself of enjoyment? This too is pointless and a terrible obsession.

[9]Two are better than one because they have a good return for their hard work. [10]If either should fall, one can pick up the other. But how miserable are those who fall and don't have a companion to help them up! [11]Also, if two lie down together, they can stay warm. But how can anyone stay warm alone? [12]Also, one can be overpowered, but two together can put up resistance. A three-ply cord doesn't easily snap.

SAILBOAT

FAMILY AND FRIENDS

Benefits of Family and Friends
Ecclesiastes 4:8-12

Two things the Teacher claimed were good things in life were family and friends. He studied people who didn't have family or friends and saw that even though they worked hard, they didn't have anyone to enjoy life with. When bad things happened to them, they didn't have anyone to help. The Teacher then examined people who had family and friends. These people worked together, making the job enjoyable and getting more for their effort. They shared what they had with each other, especially when times got hard. They took care of each other, even sharing their body warmth during cold weather. They protected each other from those who would harm them. Family and friends are important for us today too. ◆

[13]A poor but wise youth is better than an old and foolish king, who no longer listens to advice. [14]He emerged from prison to become king, even though during his rule a poor child[k] is born. [15]I saw all who live and walk under the sun following the next youth who would rise to take his place. [16]There was no

---

[j]Or *God seeks out what is pursued*, or *God seeks what has gone by*, or *God seeks the pursued*; Heb uncertain [k]Possibly the youth of 4:13; or *He emerged from prison to become king, even though he was born poor in the kingdom.*

counting the number of people he ruled, but those who came later aren't happy with him. This too is pointless and a chasing after wind.

Listen and speak carefully

5 Watch[1] your steps when you go to God's house. It's more acceptable to listen than to offer the fools' sacrifice—they have no idea that they're acting wrongly. [2]Don't[m] be quick with your mouth or say anything hastily before God, because God is in heaven, but you are on earth. Therefore, let your words be few.

[3] Remember:

Dreams come with many cares,
    and the voice of fools with many words.

[4]When you make a promise to God, fulfill it without delay because God has no pleasure in fools. Fulfill what you promise. [5]Better not to make a promise than to make a promise without fulfilling it. [6]Don't let your mouth make a sinner of you, and don't say to the messenger: "It was a mistake!" Otherwise, God may become angry at such talk and destroy what you have accomplished.

[7] Remember:

When dreams multiply,
    so do pointless thoughts
    and excessive speech.
Therefore, fear God.

Hoarding wealth

[8]If you witness the poor being oppressed or the violation of what is just and right in some territory, don't be surprised because a high official watches over another, and yet others stand over them. [9]But the land's yield should be for everyone if the field is cultivated.[n] [10]The money lover isn't satisfied with money; neither is the lover of wealth satisfied with income. This too is pointless. [11]When good things flow, so do those who consume them. But what do owners benefit from such goods, except to feast their eyes on them? [12]Sweet is the worker's sleep, whether there's a lot or little to eat; but the excess of the wealthy won't let them sleep.

[13]I have seen a sickening tragedy under the sun: people hoard their wealth to their own detriment. [14]Then that wealth is lost in a

[1] 4:17 in Heb   [m] 5:1 in Heb   [n] Correction; Heb uncertain; or *The land's advantage in everything is this: a king for a plowed field.*

Keep Your Promises   Ecclesiastes 5:4-7

It's easy to make a promise but not always easy to keep it. Many times, people make promises they don't keep. Even when someone has a good reason for breaking a promise, it still hurts the person to whom the promise was made.

When we promise someone something, we should do our best to follow through. It is better to say, "I will try" than to make a promise we can't keep. That way if something comes up, we won't have to go back on our word. Breaking a promise can cause other people to feel like we have lied to them or have cheated them in some way. The same is true when we make promises to God. When we promise to love and honor God, we ought to follow through. God has made promises to us and always keeps them. Best of all, God has promised never to leave us or forget us.

What are some promises God made to people in the Bible?

What are some promises God has made to you?

bad business venture so that when they have children, they are left with nothing. [15]Just as they came from their mother's womb naked, naked they'll return, ending up just like they started. All their hard work produces nothing—nothing they can take with them. [16]This too is a sickening tragedy: they must pass on just as they arrived. What then do they gain from working so hard for wind? [17]What's more, they constantly eat in darkness, with much aggravation, grief, and anger.

[18]This is the one good thing I've seen: it's appropriate for people to eat, drink, and find enjoyment in all their hard work under the sun during the brief lifetime that God gives them because that's their lot in life. [19]Also, whenever God gives people wealth and riches and enables them to enjoy it, to accept their place in the world[o] and to find pleasure in their hard work—all this is God's gift. [20]Indeed, people shouldn't brood too much over the days of their lives because God gives an answer in their hearts' joy.

Controlled appetite

6I saw a tragedy under the sun, and it weighs heavily upon humanity. [2]God may give some people plenty of wealth, riches, and glory so that they lack nothing they desire. But God doesn't enable them to enjoy it; instead, a stranger enjoys it. This is pointless and a sickening tragedy. [3]Some people may have one hundred children and live a long life. But no matter how long they live, if they aren't content with life's good things, I say that even a stillborn child with no grave is better off than they are.[p] [4]Because that child arrives pointlessly, then passes away in darkness. Darkness covers its name. [5]It hasn't seen the sun or experienced anything. But it has more peace than those [6]who live a thousand years twice over but don't enjoy life's good things. Isn't everyone heading to the same destination? [7]All the hard work of humans is for the mouth, but the appetite is never full. [8]What advantage do the wise have over the foolish? Or what do the poor gain by knowing how to conduct themselves before the living? [9]It's better to enjoy what's at hand

than to have an insatiable appetite. This too is pointless, just wind chasing.

[10]Whatever happens has already been designated, and human beings are fully known. They can't contend with the one who is stronger than they are. [11]Because the more words increase, the more everything is pointless. What do people gain by it? [12]Because who knows what's good for human beings during life, during their brief pointless life, which will pass away like a shadow? Who can say what the future holds for people under the sun?

Wisdom is better than wealth

7A good name is better than fine oil,
    and the day of death
        better than the birthday.
[2] It is better to go to a house in mourning
    than to a house party,
    because that is everyone's destiny;
        and the living should take it to heart.
[3] Aggravation is better than merriment
    because a sad face may lead to a glad heart.
[4] The wise heart is in the house that mourns,
    but the foolish heart
        is in the house that rejoices.
[5] It is better to obey the reprimand
    of the wise
        than to listen to the song of fools,
    [6] because the fool's merriment
    is like nettles crackling under a kettle.
        That too is pointless.
[7] Oppression turns the wise into fools;
    a bribe corrupts the heart.
[8] The end of something
    is better than its beginning.
        Patience is better than arrogance.
[9] Don't be too quick to get angry
    because anger lives in the fool's heart.
[10] Don't ask, "How is it that the former days
    were better than these?"
        because it isn't wise to ask this.
[11] Wisdom is as good as[q] an inheritance—
    an advantage for those who see the sun.
[12] Wisdom's protection is
    like the protection of money;
        the advantage of knowledge is that
    wisdom preserves the lives
        of its possessors.

---

[o]Or *portion in life*, as in 5:18 [p]Correction; Heb puts the lack of burial site with those who do not enjoy life's good things.
[q]Or *Wisdom is good with*

Good times and bad

¹³Consider God's work! Who can straighten what God has made crooked? ¹⁴When times are good, enjoy the good; when times are bad, consider: God has made the former as well as the latter so that people can't discover anything that will come to be after them.

¹⁵I have seen everything in my pointless lifetime: the righteous person may die in spite of their righteousness; then again, the wicked may live long in spite of their wickedness. ¹⁶Don't be too righteous or too wise, or you may be dumbfounded.ʳ ¹⁷Don't be too wicked and don't be a fool, or you may die before your time. ¹⁸It's good that you take hold of one of these without letting go of the other because the one who fears God will go forth with both.

¹⁹Wisdom makes a wise person stronger than ten rulers who are in a city. ²⁰Remember: there's no one on earth so righteous as to do good only and never make a mistake.ˢ ²¹Don't worry about all the things people say, so you don't hear your servant cursing you. ²²After all, you know that you've often cursed others yourself!

Life is complicated

²³I tested all of this by wisdom. I thought, I will be wise, but it eluded me.

²⁴All that happens is elusive and utterly unfathomable. Who can grasp it? ²⁵I turned my mind to know, to investigate, and to seek wisdom, along with an account of things, to know that wickedness is foolishness and folly is madness.

²⁶I found one woman more bitter than death: she who is a trap, her heart a snare, her hands shackles. Anyone who pleases God escapes her, but a sinner is trapped by her. ²⁷See, this is what I found, says the Teacher, examining one matter after another to account for things. ²⁸But there's something that I constantly searched for but couldn't find: I found one man among a thousand, but I couldn't find a woman among any of these.ᵗ

²⁹See, this alone I found: God made human beings straightforward, but they search for many complications.

8 Who is wise? And who knows the meaning of anything?

> A person's wisdom
> brightens the expression;
> it changes the hardness
> of someone's face.

Watch out for power

² Keepᵘ the king's command
as you would keep a solemn pledge.
³ Don't be dismayed; leave his presence.
Don't linger in a harmful situation
because he can do whatever he wants!
⁴ Because the king's word has authority,
no one can say to him,
"What are you doing?"

⁵Whoever keeps a command will meet no harm, and the wise heart knows the right time and the right way ⁶because there's a right time and right way for every matter. But human misfortunes are overwhelming ⁷because no one knows what will happen, and no one can say when something might happen. ⁸No one has control over the life-breath,ᵛ to retain it, and there's no control over the day of death. There's no release from war, and wickedness won't deliver those who practice it.

⁹I observed all of this as I paid attention to all that happens under the sun. Sometimes people exercise power over each other to their detriment. ¹⁰Then I saw the wicked brought to their graves, with people processing from a holy place,ʷ while those who had lived honestly were neglected in the city. This too is pointless.

¹¹The condemnation for wicked acts isn't carried out quickly; that's why people dare to do evil. ¹²Wrongdoers may commit a hundred crimes but still live long lives. But I also know

UMBRELLA

ANGRY

Slow to Anger Ecclesiastes 7:9
There are many times in life when we get hurt and feel angry. The Teacher encouraged readers not to get angry quickly. By slowing down and thinking about each situation, we have a chance to see things from a different point of view. 🌢

ʳOr destroyed ˢOr and never sin ᵗHeb uncertain ᵘCorrection; Heb I (say?) keep ᵛOr wind ʷOr temple

that it will go well for those who fear God, for those who are reverent before God. [13]But it will not go well for the wicked; they won't live long at all because they aren't reverent before God. [14]Here's another thing that happens on earth that is pointless: the righteous get what the wicked deserve, and the wicked get what the righteous deserve. I say that this too is pointless.

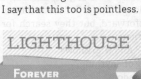

LIGHTHOUSE

FOREVER

Enjoying God's Blessings
Ecclesiastes 8:12-13

The Teacher spent time studying people who obeyed God and the law as well as people who disobeyed God and committed crimes. He noticed there were people who disobeyed their whole life and never seem to have to face the consequences for their actions. They lived a long time and had many things. However, the Teacher pointed out that "it will not go well" for those who disobey God. The Teacher compared them to the people who obey God. They may not have a long life or a lot things, but they enjoyed God's blessing in this life and in the life to come. ◢

Enjoy life

[15]So I commend enjoyment because there's nothing better for people to do under the sun but to eat, drink, and be glad. This is what will accompany them in their hard work, during the lifetime that God gives under the sun.

[16]Then I set my mind to know wisdom and to observe the business that happens on earth, even going without sleep day and night [17]I observed all the work of God—that no one can grasp what happens under the sun. Those who strive to know can't grasp it. Even the wise who are set on knowing are unable to grasp it.

Everyone faces the same fate

9 So I considered all of this carefully, examining all of it: The righteous and the wise and their deeds are in God's hand, along with both love and hate. People don't know anything that's ahead of them. [2]Everything is the same for everyone. The same fate awaits the righteous and the wicked, the good and the bad,[x] the pure and the impure, those who sacrifice and those who don't sacrifice. The good person is like the wrongdoer; the same holds for those who make solemn pledges and those who are afraid to swear. [3]This is the sad thing about all that happens under the sun: the same fate awaits everyone. Moreover, the human heart is full of evil; people's minds are full of madness while they are alive, and afterward they die. [4]Whoever is among the living can be certain about this. A living dog is definitely better off than a dead lion, [5]because the living know that they will die. But the dead know nothing at all. There is no more reward for them; even the memory of them is lost. [6]Their love and their hate, as well as their zeal, are already long gone. They will never again have a stake in all that happens under the sun.

[7]Go, eat your food joyfully and drink your wine happily because God has already accepted what you do. [8]Let your garments always be white; don't run short of oil for your head. [9]Enjoy life with your dearly loved spouse all the days of your pointless life that God[y] gives you under the sun—all the days of your pointless life![z]—because that's your part to play[a] in this life and in your hard work under the sun. [10]Whatever you are capable of doing, do with all your might because there's no work, thought, knowledge, or wisdom in the grave,[b] which is where you are headed.

Listen to common wisdom, not fools

[11]I also observed under the sun that the race doesn't always go to the swift, nor the battle to the mighty, nor food to the wise, nor wealth to the intelligent, nor favor to the knowledgeable, because accidents can happen to anyone. [12]People most definitely don't know when their time will come. Like fish tragically caught in a net or like birds trapped in a snare, so are human beings caught in a time of tragedy that suddenly falls to them.

[13]I also observed the following example of wisdom under the sun—it impressed me greatly: [14]There was a small town with only

a few residents. A mighty king came against it, surrounded it, and waged a terrible war against it. ¹⁵Now there lived in that town a poor but wise man who saved everyone by his wisdom. But no one remembered that poor man. ¹⁶So I thought, Wisdom is better than might, but the wisdom of commoners is despised and their words aren't heeded.

¹⁷The calm words of the wise are better heeded than the racket caused by a ruler among fools.

¹⁸Wisdom is better than weapons of war, but one incompetent person destroys much good.

10 As dead flies spoil the perfumer's oil,
so a little folly outweighs
wisdom and honor.

²The mind of the wise
tends toward the right,
but the mind of the fool toward the left.

³Fools lack all sense
even when they walk down the street;
they show everyone that they are fools.
⁴If a ruler's temper rises against you,
don't leave your post, because calmness
alleviates great offenses.

⁵There's an evil that I have seen under the sun: the kind of mistake that comes from people in power. ⁶Fools are appointed to high posts, while the rich sit in lowly positions. ⁷I have seen slaves on horseback, while princes walk on foot like slaves.

⁸Whoever digs a pit may fall into it,
and whoever breaks through a wall
may be bitten by a snake.
⁹Whoever quarries stones
may be injured by them;
whoever splits logs
may be endangered by them.

Listen to Wise People — Ecclesiastes 9:11-18

Sometimes it's difficult to tell the difference between wise and foolish teaching. There are many people who claim to be wise. They compete for our attention and try to get us to follow them. Being around people like that can cause us to act in ways that aren't very smart. We should be careful not to listen to people who would lead us to disobey God. Instead, we should listen to people who truly help us to follow God.

Wisdom comes from being around wise people and teaching that lines up with what God says. If we listen to what people say and then study what the Bible teaches about the subject, we can more easily decide if what they are saying is wise or foolish. As we study a Bible verse or passage, we might ask a pastor, teacher, or parent to help us figure out what it means. We can also look for other verses in the Bible that are similar so we can compare what different writers have to say about the subject. We can always trust God's word to be wise.

Who in your life do you consider to be wise?

Ask God to help you grow in wisdom.

[10] If an ax is dull
>and one doesn't sharpen it first,
>then one must exert more force.
>It's profitable to be skillful and wise.

[11] If a snake bites before it's charmed,
>then there's no profit
>for the snake charmer.

[12] Words from a wise person's mouth are beneficial, but fools are devoured by their own lips.

[13] Fools start out talking foolishness and end up speaking awful nonsense.

[14] Fools talk too much! No one knows what will happen; no one can say what will happen in the future.

[15] The hard work of fools tires them out because they don't even know the way to town!

[16] Too bad for you, land,
>whose king is a boy
>and whose princes feast in the morning.

[17] Happy is the land
>whose king is dignified
>and whose princes feast
>at the right time for energy,
>not for drunkenness.

[18] Through laziness, the roof sags;
>through idle hands, the house leaks.

[19] Feasts are made for laughter,
>wine cheers the living,
>and money answers everything.[c]

[20] Don't curse a king even in private; don't curse the rich in your bedroom, because a bird could carry your voice; some winged creature could report what you said!

Take risks; life is short

11 Send your bread out on the water because, in the course of time, you may find it again. [2] Give a portion to seven people, even to eight: you don't know what disaster may come upon the land. [3] If clouds fill up, they will empty out rain on the earth. If a tree falls, whether to the south or to the north, wherever it falls, there it will lie. [4] Those who watch the wind blow will never sow, and those who observe the clouds will never reap. [5] Just as you don't understand what the life-breath does in the fetus[d] inside a pregnant woman's womb, so you can't understand the work of God, who makes everything happen. [6] Scatter your seed in the morning, and in the evening don't be idle because you don't know which will succeed, this one or that, or whether both will be equally good.

[7] Sweet is the light, and it's pleasant for the eyes to see the sun. [8] Even those who live many years should take pleasure in them all. But they should be mindful that there will also be many dark days. Everything that happens is pointless.

[9] Rejoice, young person, while you are young! Your heart should make you happy in your prime. Follow your heart's inclinations and whatever your eyes see, but know this: God will call you to account for all of these things. [10] Remove anxiety from your heart, banish pain from your body, because youth and the dawn of life are pointless too.

Troubling days to come

12 Remember your creator
>in your prime,
>before the days of trouble arrive,
>and those years, about which you'll say,
>"I take no pleasure in these"—
[2] before the sun and the light grow dark,
>the moon and the stars too,
>before the clouds return after the rain;
[3] on the day when the housekeepers
>tremble and the strong men stoop;
>when the women who grind
>stop working because they're so few,
>and those who look
>through the windows grow dim;
[4] when the doors to the street are shut,
>when the sound of the mill fades,
>the sound of the bird rises,

---

[c] Or *money is everyone's answer.* [d] Correction with Tg; MT *like the bones*

and all the singers come down low;
[5] when people are afraid of things above
and of terrors along the way;
when the almond tree blanches,
the locust droops,
and the caper-berry comes to nothing;[e]
when the human goes
to the eternal abode,
with mourners all around in the street;
[6] before the silver cord snaps
and the gold bowl shatters;
the jar is broken at the spring
and the wheel is crushed at the pit;
[7] before dust returns to the earth
as it was before
and the life-breath returns to God
who gave it.

Motto and conclusion

[8] Perfectly pointless, says the Teacher, everything is pointless.

[9] Additionally: Because the Teacher was wise, he constantly taught the people knowledge. He listened and investigated. He composed many proverbs. [10] The Teacher searched for pleasing words, and he wrote truthful words honestly.

[11] The words of the wise
are like iron-tipped prods;

[e] Heb uncertain [f] Or fixed by one shepherd

the collected sayings of the masters
are like nails fixed firmly
by a shepherd.[f]
[12] Be careful, my child,
of anything beyond them!

There's no end to the excessive production of scrolls. Studying too much wearies the body. [13] So this is the end of the matter; all has been heard. Worship God and keep God's commandments because this is what everyone must do. [14] God will definitely bring every deed to judgment, including every hidden thing, whether good or bad.

Memorize
Eccl 12:13

LIGHTHOUSE

PRAISE GOD

The End of the Matter Ecclesiastes 12:13
After looking at all of life—both good and bad times—the Teacher summed up his studies. He stated that no matter if you are wealthy or poor, powerful or weak, there are only two things to do. We should worship God and keep God's commandments. If we love God, we will do these things. Our relationship with God influences what we do in life and how we treat others. ◖

Song of Songs

The Song of Songs is one of the world's best-known poems about love. The beginning of this book says the story is "for Solomon" (Song 1:1), but many people do not think the man in the story is King Solomon. Whoever the man and woman are, they are deeply in love.

The woman and man tell all sorts of things they like about each other. The man tells the woman her hair "is like a flock of goats as they stream down Mount Gilead" (Song 4:1). Her teeth "are like newly shorn ewes as they come up from the washing pool" (4:2). The woman tells the man his "very name is perfume" (1:3). Their descriptions of beauty might sound strange or funny to us, but this is one way they expressed their love to each other.

Many people also see in this book a picture of God's love for God's people. Some say it shows the love between Christ and the church. But there's nothing in the Song of Songs that says this. Song of Songs celebrates human love and shows us one picture of a couple who love each other! ◊

1

The Song of Songs, which is for Solomon.

Mutual admiration

[Woman][a]

² If only he would give me
some of his kisses . . .

Oh, your loving is sweeter than wine!
³ Your fragrance is sweet;
your very name is perfume.
That's why the young women love you.
⁴ Take me along with you; let's run!

My king has brought me
into his chambers, saying,
"Let's exult and rejoice in you.
Let's savor your loving more than wine!
No wonder they all love you!"

⁵ Dark am I, and lovely,
daughters of Jerusalem—
like the black tents of the Kedar nomads,
like the curtains of Solomon's palace.
⁶ Don't stare at me because I'm darkened
by the sun's gaze.
My own brothers were angry with me.
They made me a caretaker
of the vineyards—
but I couldn't care
for my own vineyard.

⁷ Tell me, you whom I love
with all my heart—
where do you pasture your flock,
where do you rest them at noon?—
so I don't wander around with the flocks
of your companions.

[Man]

⁸ If you don't know your way,
most beautiful of women,
then follow the tracks of the herds
and graze your little goats
by the tents of the shepherds.

⁹ I picture you, my dearest,
as a mare among Pharaoh's chariots!
¹⁰ Lovely are your cheeks,
adorned with ear hoops;
your neck, with beads.

¹¹ Let's make hoops of gold
beaded with silver for you!

[Woman]

¹² With my king close by,
my perfume filled the air.
¹³ A sachet of myrrh is my love to me,
lying all night between my breasts.
¹⁴ A cluster of henna flowers
is my love to me
in the desert gardens of En-gedi.

[Man]

¹⁵ Look at you—so beautiful, my dearest!
Look at you—so beautiful!
Your eyes are doves!

[Woman]

¹⁶ Look at you—so beautiful, my love!
Yes, delightful!
Yes, our bed is lush and green!
¹⁷ The ceilings of our chambers are cedars;
our rafters, cypresses.

Love in bloom

[Woman]

2

I'm a rose of the Sharon plain,
a lily of the valleys.

LIFE PRESERVER

**Why is this book
in the Bible?** *Song of Songs 1–8*

Song of Songs is a book that is unlike any
other in the Bible. It is a collection of love songs
between a man and a woman who express strong
feelings toward each other. They celebrate their
love and commitment to each other.

The book reads more like a play script with
the woman then the man speaking and different
friends commenting on what the couple says to
each other. If you have read this book, you may
have wondered why it is even in the Bible. People
who study the Bible have tried many different
ways to understand this book. Some believe it is
meant to reflect the love between God and God's
people, or between God and the church. But most
have finally agreed that it is an expression of love
between two people, which is a great example of
how all of God's creation is good. ◖

---

[a]Identification of speakers here and throughout the Song is hypothetical and in several cases uncertain.

[Man]

² Like a lily among thornbushes,
so is my dearest
among the young women.

[Woman]

³ Like an apple tree among the wild trees,
so is my lover among the young men.
In his shade I take pleasure in sitting,
and his fruit is sweet to my taste.
⁴ He has brought me to the house of wine;
his banner raised over me is love.

⁵ Sustain me with raisin cakes,
strengthen me with apples,
for I'm weak with love!

⁶ His left arm is beneath my head,
his right embraces me.

⁷ Make a solemn pledge,
daughters of Jerusalem,
by the gazelles or the wild deer:
Don't rouse, don't arouse love
until it desires.

⁸ Listen! It's my lover: here he comes now,
leaping upon the mountains,
bounding over the hills.
⁹ My lover is like a gazelle
or a young stag.
Here he stands now,
outside our wall,
peering through the windows,
peeking through the lattices.

¹⁰ My lover spoke and said to me,
"Rise up, my dearest,
my fairest, and go.
¹¹ Here, the winter is past;
the rains have come and gone.
¹² Blossoms have appeared in the land;
the season of singing^b has arrived,
and the sound of the turtledove
is heard in our land.
¹³ The green fruit is on the fig tree,
and the grapevines in bloom
are fragrant.
Rise up,^c my dearest,

my fairest, and go.
¹⁴ My dove—in the rock crevices,
hidden in the cliff face—
let me catch sight of you;
let me hear your voice!
The sound of your voice is sweet,
and the sight of you is lovely."

¹⁵ Catch foxes for us—
those little foxes
that spoil vineyards,
now that our vineyards are in bloom!

¹⁶ I belong to my lover
and he belongs to me—
the one grazing among the lilies.
¹⁷ Before the day breeze blows
and the shadows flee,
turn about, my love; be like a gazelle
or a young stag
upon the jagged mountains.^d

The search

[Woman]

3 Upon my bed, night after night,
I looked for the one whom I love
with all my heart.
I looked for him
but couldn't find him.^e
² "I will rise now
and go all around the city,
through the streets
and the squares.
I will look for the one whom I love
with all my heart."
I looked for him
but couldn't find him.
³ The guards found me,
those who make their rounds
in the city.
"The one whom I love
with all my heart—
have you seen him?"

did you **know?** This poem about a great love shared between two people shows that even romantic love is a gift from God.

---

^bOr *pruning* ^cLXX and Kethib add *go*; but Qere, DSS, Vulg, Syr, and Tg lack the verb; cf 2:10. ^dOr *upon the mountains of Bether*; cf 8:14 *mountains of spice* ^eLXX adds *I called him, but he didn't answer me*; cf 5:6.

4 No sooner did I depart from them
   than I found the one whom I love
   with all my heart.
I held on to him
   and now I won't let him go,
   until I've brought him
   to my mother's house,
   to the chamber of the one
   who conceived me.
5 I place you under oath,
   daughters of Jerusalem,
   by the gazelles or the wild deer:
   don't rouse, don't arouse love
   until it desires.

Visions of grandeur

6 Who is this,
   coming up from the wilderness,
   like pillars of smoke?
She is perfumed
   with myrrh and frankincense,
   selected from all
      the spice merchant's powders.

7 Picture Solomon's bed—
   sixty heroic men round about it,
   all from the heroes of Israel,
8 all of them skilled with the sword,
   expert in warfare,
   each with his sword ready at his thigh
   against terrors that come by night.
9 King Solomon made a canopied couch
   for himself
   from the trees of Lebanon.
10 Its pillars he made of silver,
   its covering, cloth of gold,
   its cushions, royal purple;
   its interior inlaid with love.
Daughters of Jerusalem, 11go forth!
Look, daughters of Zion—
   on King Solomon wearing the crown
   with which his mother crowned him
   on the day of his wedding,
   on the day of his heart's joy.

In praise of her

[Man]

4 Look at you—so beautiful, my dearest!
   Look at you—so beautiful!
   Your eyes are doves
   behind the veil of your hair!
   Your hair is like a flock of goats

   as they stream down Mount Gilead.
2 Your teeth are like newly shorn ewes
   as they come up
   from the washing pool—
   all of them perfectly matched,
   not one of them lacks its twin.
3 Like a crimson ribbon are your lips;
   when you smile, it is lovely.
Like a slice of pomegranate
   is the curve of your face
   behind the veil
   of your hair.

LIGHTHOUSE

PRAISE

Picture Language *Song of Songs 4:1-3*
Eyes like doves. Hair like a flock of goats. This
book is filled with what appear to be strange ways
for people to describe each other. In Bible times,
however, these phrases were understood as pictures. Comparing her eyes to doves meant that the
woman's gaze was soft when she looked at other
people. Doves are considered peaceful creatures,
and so the man was praising her for being gentle
and innocent. Comparing her teeth to a flock of
goats may sound odd. However, when seen from
a long way off, the sun shining on a flock of goats
on the mountain reflects a beautiful brightness.

4 Like David's tower is your neck,
   splendidly built!
A thousand shields are hung upon it—
   all the weapons of the warriors.
5 Your two breasts are like two fawns,
   twins of a gazelle doe,
   that graze among the lilies.
6 Before the day breeze blows
   and the shadows flee,
   I will be off to the mountain
      of myrrh,
   to the hill of frankincense.
7 You are utterly beautiful,
   my dearest;
   there's not a single flaw in you.

Garden of delight

[Man]

8 Come down with me from Lebanon,
   my bride—
   if only you would come down
   with me from Lebanon.

Descend from the peak of Amana,
  from the peaks of Senir and Hermon,
  from the lions' dens,
  from the mountain lairs of leopards.
⁹ You have captured my heart,
  my sister,[f] my bride!
  You have captured my heart
    with one glance from your eyes,
    with one strand of your necklace.
¹⁰ How beautiful is your loving,
  my sister, my bride!
  Your loving is so much better
    than wine,
  and your fragrance better
    than any perfume!
¹¹ Sweetness drops from your lips,
  my bride;
  honey and milk are
    under your tongue,
  and the fragrance of your garments
    is like the fragrance of Lebanon.
¹² An enclosed garden is my sister,
  my bride;
  an enclosed pool, a sealed spring.
¹³ Your limbs are
  an orchard of pomegranates
    with all kinds of luscious fruit,
    henna, and spices:
  ¹⁴ nard and saffron,
    sweet cane and cinnamon,
    with all scented woods,
    myrrh, and aloes,
    with the very choicest perfumes!
¹⁵ You are a garden spring,
  a well of fresh water,
  streams from Lebanon.
¹⁶ Stir, north wind, and come, south wind!
  Blow upon my garden;
    let its perfumes flow!

  [Woman]

Let my love come to his garden;
  let him eat its luscious fruit!

  [Man]

5 I have come to my garden, my sister,
  my bride!
  I have gathered my myrrh and my spices.
  I have eaten my honeycomb
    with my honey;
  I have drunk my wine and my milk.

Eat, dear friends!
Drink and get drunk on love!

A missed encounter

  [Woman]

² I was sleeping, but my heart was awake.
  A sound! My love is knocking:

  [Man]

"Open for me, my sister, my dearest,
  my dove, my perfect one!
  My head is soaked with dew,
  my hair, with the night mists."

  [Woman]

³ "I have taken off my tunic—
  why should I put it on again?
  I have bathed my feet—
  why should I get them dirty?"
⁴ My love put his hand in
  through the latch hole,
  and my body ached for him.
⁵ I rose; I went to open for my love,
  and my hands dripped myrrh,
  my fingers, liquid myrrh,
  over the handles of the lock.
⁶ I went and opened for my love,
  but my love had turned, gone away.
  I nearly died when he turned away.
  I looked for him but couldn't find him.
  I called out to him,
    but he didn't answer me.
⁷ They found me—the guards
  who make their rounds in the city.
  They struck me, bruised me.
  They took my shawl away from me,
    those guards of the city walls!
⁸ I place you under oath,
  daughters of Jerusalem:
  If you find my love,
  what should you tell him?
  That I'm weak with love!

  [Daughters of Jerusalem]

⁹ How is your lover different
  from any other lover,
  you who are the most beautiful
    of women?
  How is your lover different
  from any other lover,
  that you make us swear
    a solemn pledge?

---

[f] *Sister* here and below is a common term in ancient love poetry; it doesn't imply blood relation.

In praise of him

[Woman]

¹⁰ My lover is radiant and ruddy;
    he stands out among ten thousand!
¹¹ His head is finest gold;
    his wavy hair, black as a raven.

In Bible times, sheep and goats were prized livestock with very valuable hair and wool. So for a woman's hair to be compared to the hair of a goat or the coat of a sheep was very good.

¹² His eyes are like doves
    by channels of water.
  They are bathing in milk,
    sitting by brimming pools.
¹³ His cheeks are like fragrant plantings,
    towers of spices.
  His lips are lilies
    dripping liquid myrrh.
¹⁴ His arms are gold cylinders
    studded with jewels.
  His belly is smooth ivory
    encrusted with sapphires.
¹⁵ His thighs are pillars of whitest stone
    set on pedestals of gold.
  His appearance—like Lebanon,
    stately, like the cedars.
¹⁶ His mouth is everything sweet,
    every bit of him desirable.

  This is my love, this my dearest,
    daughters of Jerusalem!

[Daughters of Jerusalem]

6 Which way did your lover go,
    you who are the most beautiful
      of women?
  Which way did your lover turn,
    that we may look for him
      along with you?

[Woman]

² My lover has gone down to his garden,
    to the fragrant plantings,
  to graze in the gardens,
    to gather the lilies.
³ I belong to my lover
    and my lover belongs to me—
      the one grazing among the lilies.

An overwhelming sight

[Man]

⁴ You are as beautiful, my dearest, as Tirzah,
    as lovely as Jerusalem,
    formidable as those lofty sights.
⁵ Turn your eyes away from me,
    for they overwhelm me!

  Your hair is like a flock of goats
    as they stream down from Gilead.
⁶ Your teeth are like a flock of ewes
    as they come up
      from the washing pool—
    all of them perfectly matched,
    not one of them lacks its twin.
⁷ Like a slice of pomegranate
    is the curve of your face
      behind the veil of your hair.
⁸ There may be sixty queens
    and eighty secondary wives,
    young women beyond counting,
⁹ but my dove, my perfect one,
    is one of a kind.
  To her mother she's the only one,
    radiant to the one who bore her.
  Young women see her
    and declare her fortunate;
    queens and secondary wives praise her.

¹⁰ Who is this, gazing down
    like the morning star,
    beautiful as the full moon,
    radiant as the sun,
    formidable as those lofty sights?

Transported

[Man]

¹¹ To the nut grove I went down
    to look upon the fresh growth
      in the valley,
    to see whether the vine was in flower,
    whether the pomegranates
      had bloomed.
¹² I hardly knew myself;
    she had set me in an official's chariot!ᵍ

Graceful dancer

[Man]

¹³ ʰCome back, come back, Shulammite!ⁱ
    Come back, come back,
    so we may admire you.

ᵍOr *I hardly knew what happened; my passion set me in an official's chariot!* LXX, Vulg *Aminadab's chariots;* Heb uncertain
ʰ7:1 in Heb   ⁱA name or title for the woman

How you all admire the Shulammite
   as she whirls between
     two circles of dancers!

7 How graceful are your sandaled feet,
   willing woman!
The smooth curves of your thighs—
   like fine jewelry,
     the work of an artist's hands!
[2] Your navel, cupped like the full moon—
   may it never lack spiced wine!
Your belly is a mound of winnowed wheat
   edged with lilies.
[3] Your two breasts are like two fawns,
   twins of a gazelle doe;
[4] your neck, like a tower of ivory;
   your eyes, pools in Heshbon,
     by the gate of that lordly city.[j]
Your profile is like the tower of Lebanon,
   looking out toward Damascus.
[5] Your head crowns you like Mount Carmel,
   and your hair, braided in royal purple—
     a king is bound by the tresses!
[6] You are so beautiful, so lovely—
   my love, delightful one![k]
[7] Your stately form resembles a date palm,
   and your breasts
     are like clustered fruit.
[8] I say, "I will climb the palm tree;
   I will hold its fruit!"
May your breasts be now
   like grape clusters,
and the scent of your breath like apples!
  [9] Your palate is like excellent wine . . .

[Woman]

. . . flowing smoothly for my love,
   gliding through the lips and teeth.[l]
[10] I belong to my lover,
   and his longing is only for me.

The ripeness of love
[Woman]

[11] Come, my love:
   Let's go out to the field
   and rest all night
     among the flowering henna.
[12] Let's set out early for the vineyards.
   We will see if the vines have budded
   and the blossoms opened,

see if the pomegranates have bloomed.
There I'll give my loving to you.

[13] The mandrakes give off their scent,
   and at our doorways is every delicacy—
     fresh or ripened—
my love, I have kept them
   hidden for you.

Wishing
[Woman]

8 If only you were as my brother—
   the one who nursed
     at my mother's breast.
I would find you in the street and kiss you,
   and no one would shame me for it.
[2] I would lead you, I would bring you
   to my mother's house;
     she would teach me what to do.[m]
I would give you spiced wine to drink,
   some of my fresh pomegranate juice.

[3] His left arm is beneath my head,
   and his right embraces me!

[4] Make a solemn pledge,
   daughters of Jerusalem,
   never to rouse, never to arouse love
   until it desires.

Love, strong and invaluable
[Daughters of Jerusalem]

[5] Who is this coming up from the wilderness
   leaning against her lover?

[Woman]

Under the apple tree I aroused you—
   there, where your mother
   labored with you,
     there where, laboring, she bore you.
[6] Set me as a seal over your heart,
   as a seal upon your arm,
for love is as strong as death,
   passionate love unrelenting
     as the grave.[n]
Its darts are darts of fire—
divine flame!

7 Rushing waters
can't quench love;
rivers can't
wash it away.
If someone gave
all his estate in exchange for love,
he would be laughed
to utter shame.

Memorize Song 8:7

SAILBOAT

Love

Power of Love *Song of Songs 8:6-7*
These verses sum up the Song of Songs by explaining the power of love. The woman stated that love is as powerful as death, which cannot be overcome. Love's passion is as strong as a blazing fire—and not just any fire, but the fire of God. All the waters from all the powerful rivers in the world cannot put out the fire of love. And there is no amount of money or anything else that can be exchanged for love. Love must be given; true love ultimately comes as a gift from God.

[The Woman's Brothers]

8 Our sister is small;
she has no breasts.
What will we do for our sister
on the day that she is spoken for?
9 If she is a city wall,
then we will build a turret of silver
on her.[o]
And if she is a door,
then we will barricade her[p]
with a panel of cedar.

[Woman]

10 I'm a city wall,
and my breasts are the towers.
So now I'm in his eyes
as one who brings peace.

[Man]

11 Solomon had a vineyard
in Baal-hamon.
He gave charge of the vineyard to keepers;
one would bring in exchange for its fruit
a thousand pieces of silver.
12 My vineyard, my very own, is before me.
You can have the thousand, Solomon[q]—
with two hundred for those
who tend the fruit!

13 You who sit in the gardens,
my companions are listening
for your voice.
Let me hear it!

[Woman]

14 "Take flight, my love,
and be like a gazelle
or a young stag
on the mountains of spice!"

[o]Or *on it (the city wall)* [p]Or *it (the door)* [q]Cf 1 Kgs 11:3

Isaiah

This book is named for the prophet Isaiah, who spoke for God to the southern kingdom of Judah. Isaiah is sometimes called a *major prophet* because of the length of this book. His message isn't more important than others', but he spoke longer messages than those who are sometimes called *minor* prophets.

Isaiah saw trouble coming for the people of Judah because they were not following God's ways. He asked the people to seek forgiveness for their sins—to do good and seek justice. Isaiah's messages were both hopeful and gloomy. He told the people to obey God or face punishment.

This book has three parts. Chapters 1–39 talk about serious problems with worship and government—and how rich people were mistreating poor people. Chapters 40–55 address people who lived around two hundred years after the prophet Isaiah. They promise that God will bring God's people back to their homeland in Israel. Chapters 56–66 encourage and warn a generation of people who have returned to Israel.

This book often refers to "God's servant" (Isa 42–57). *Servant* is a name for God's people. The New Testament book of Matthew says that God's servant is Jesus (Matt 12:15-21). Isaiah shows us that God cares for God's people in good times and bad! ◦

things
YOU'LL DISCOVER

The book of Isaiah tells the story of God sending a man named Isaiah to remind God's people to follow God. The prophet Isaiah spoke God's messages to people who were enjoying their wealth and forgetting God.

people
YOU'LL MEET

Isaiah—a prophet who spoke for God (Isa 1–39)
Uzziah, Jotham, Ahaz, and Hezekiah—kings who ruled during the years Isaiah preached (Isa 1–39)
God's servant—a name for God's people (Isa 42–57)

places
YOU'LL GO

Judah (the southern kingdom), *Israel* (the northern kingdom), *Babylon* (present-day Iraq)

words
YOU'LL REMEMBER

"Holy, holy, holy is the Lord of heavenly forces! All the earth is filled with God's glory!" (Isa 6:3).

1 The vision about Judah and Jerusalem that Isaiah, Amoz's son, saw in the days of Judah's kings Uzziah, Jotham, Ahaz, and Hezekiah.

Rebels condemned

2 Hear you heavens, and listen earth,
   for the Lord has spoken:
I reared children; I raised them,
   and they turned against me!
3 An ox knows its owner,
   and a donkey its master's feeding trough.
But Israel doesn't know;
   my people don't behave intelligently.

4 Doom! Sinful nation,
   people weighed down with crimes,
   evildoing offspring, corrupt children!
They have abandoned the Lord,
   despised the holy one of Israel;
   they turned their backs on God.

5 Why do you invite further beatings?
   Why continue to rebel?
Everyone's head throbs,
   and everyone's heart fails.
6 From head to toe, none are well—
   only bruises, cuts, and raw wounds,
   not treated, not bandaged,
   not soothed with oil.

7 Your country is deserted,
   your cities burned with fire;
your land—strangers are devouring it
   in plain sight.
It's a wasteland, as when foreigners raid.
8 Daughter Zion is left
   like a small shelter in a vineyard,
   like a hut in a cucumber field,
   like a city besieged.[a]
9 If the Lord of heavenly forces
   had not spared a few of us,
we would be like Sodom;
   we would resemble Gomorrah.

Hands filled with bloodshed

10 Hear the Lord's word, you leaders of Sodom.
   Listen to our God's teaching,
   people of Gomorrah!
11 What should I think
   about all your sacrifices?
   says the Lord.
I'm fed up with
   entirely burned offerings of rams
   and the fat of well-fed beasts.

did you know? The children referred to in this verse were the Israelites. Throughout the Bible, the Israelites were called *the children of God*.

I don't want the blood of bulls,
   lambs, and goats.
12 When you come to appear before me,
   who asked this from you,
   this trampling of my temple's courts?
13 Stop bringing worthless offerings.
   Your incense repulses me.
New moon, sabbath,
   and the calling of an assembly—
I can't stand wickedness with celebration!
14 I hate your new moons and your festivals.
   They've become a burden
   that I'm tired of bearing.
15 When you extend your hands,
   I'll hide my eyes from you.
Even when you pray for a long time,
   I won't listen.
Your hands are stained with blood.
16 Wash! Be clean!
Remove your ugly deeds from my sight.
   Put an end to such evil;
17 learn to do good.
Seek justice:
   help the oppressed;[b]
   defend the orphan;
   plead for the widow.

18 Come now, and let's settle this,
   says the Lord.
Though your sins
   are like scarlet,

LIGHTHOUSE

Good News

Making Better Choices Isaiah 1:18-20
God chose the prophet Isaiah to speak to God's people and tell them that their lives would be so much better ("eat the best food") if they changed their ways, obeyed God, and stopped doing bad things. ◆

---

[a]LXX, Vulg; MT *spared*   [b]LXX, Vulg; MT *lead the oppressor*

they will be white as snow.
If they are red as crimson,
they will become like wool.
[19] If you agree and obey,
you will eat the best food of the land.
[20] But if you refuse and rebel,
you will be devoured by the sword.
The LORD has said this.

Zion will be redeemed

[21] This faithful town
has become a prostitute!
She was full of justice;
righteousness lived in her—
but now murderers.
[22] Your silver has become impure;
your beer is diluted with water.
[23] Your princes are rebels,
companions of thieves.
Everyone loves a bribe
and pursues gifts.
They don't defend the orphan,
and the widow's cause
never reaches them.
[24] Therefore, says the
LORD God of heavenly forces,
the mighty one of Israel:
Doom! I will vent my anger
against my foes;
I will take it out on my enemies,
[25] and I will turn my hand against you.
I will refine your impurities as with lye,
and remove all your cinders.
[26] Then I will restore your judges
as in earlier times,
and your counselors as at the beginning.
After this you will be called
Righteous City, Faithful Town.

[27] Zion will be redeemed by justice,
and those who change their lives
by righteousness.
[28] But God will shatter
rebels and sinners alike;
those who abandon the LORD
will be finished.

[29] You will be ashamed
of the oaks you once desired,
and embarrassed
by the gardens you once chose.

[30] You will be like an oak
with withering leaves,
like a garden without water.
[31] The strong will be like dry twigs,
their deeds like sparks;
the two will burn together,
with no one to extinguish them.

The LORD's mountain

2 This is what Isaiah, Amoz's son, saw concerning Judah and Jerusalem.
[2] In the days to come
the mountain of the LORD's house
will be the highest of the mountains.
It will be lifted above the hills;
peoples will stream to it.
[3] Many nations will go and say,
"Come, let's go up to the LORD's mountain,
to the house of Jacob's God
so that he may teach us his ways
and we may walk in God's paths."
Instruction will come from Zion;
the LORD's word from Jerusalem.
[4] God will judge between the nations,
and settle disputes of mighty nations.
Then they will beat
their swords into iron plows
and their spears into pruning tools.
Nation will not take up sword
against nation;
they will no longer learn
how to make war.

[5] Come, house of Jacob,
let's walk by the LORD's light.

Everyone is brought low

[6] You have abandoned your people,
house of Jacob.
They are full of sorcerers
from the east and fortune-tellers
like the Philistines;
they hold hands
with foreigners' children.[c]
[7] Their land is full of silver and gold;
they have countless treasures.
Their land is filled with horses;
they have countless chariots.
[8] Their land is filled with idols;
they worship their handiwork,
what their own fingers have made.

[c]Heb uncertain

⁹ Humanity will be brought down;
 each person laid low—don't lift them up!ᵈ
¹⁰ Go into the rocks,
 and hide yourself in the dust
 from the terror of the Lᴏʀᴅ,
 from the splendor of God's majesty!
¹¹ People's proud gazing will be stopped
 and humanity's arrogance brought down;
 the Lᴏʀᴅ alone will be exalted
 on that day.

¹² The Lᴏʀᴅ of heavenly forces
 has planned a day:
 against all that is prideful and haughty;
 against all that is lofty,
 and it will be laid low;ᵉ
¹³ against all the cedars of Lebanon,
 high and lofty;
 against all the oaks of Bashan;
¹⁴ against all the high mountains;
 against all the lofty hills;
¹⁵ against every tall tower;
 against every fortified wall;
¹⁶ against all the ships of Tarshish;
 against all the wonderful boats.ᶠ
¹⁷ People's pride will be brought down
 and human arrogance humiliated.
 The Lᴏʀᴅ alone will be exalted
 on that day;
¹⁸ the idols will completely
 pass away.

¹⁹ Go into caves in the rocks
 and holes in the dust
 before the terror of the Lᴏʀᴅ
 and the splendor of God's majesty,
 when he arises to terrify the earth.
²⁰ On that day, people will toss
 to the rodentsᵍ and to the bats
 their idols of silver and idols of gold,
 which they made for themselves
 to worship.
²¹ They will hide in fissures of rocks
 and in crevices of cliffs
 before the terror of the Lᴏʀᴅ
 and the splendor of God's majesty
 when he arises to terrify the earth.

²² Quit admiring the human race,
 who breathe through their nostrils.
 Why should they be admired?

Your leaders mislead you

3 Now the Lᴏʀᴅ God of heavenly forces is removing from Jerusalem and from Judah every form of support:
 all rations of food and water;
 ² soldier and warrior;
 judge and prophet;
 fortune-teller and elder;
 ³ commander and celebrity;
 counselor, clever craftsman,
 and cunning charmer.
⁴ I will make youths their commanders;
 mischief makers will rule over them.
⁵ The people will oppress each other,
 each one against the other,
 neighbor against neighbor.
 The young will bully the old,
 the rogue, and the respectable.

⁶ Someone will seize a family member,
 saying, "You have clothing!
 You be our leader!
 This mess will be your responsibility!"
⁷ Someone else will cry out on that day,
 "I'm no healer!
 I have neither food nor clothing
 in my house!
 Don't make me the leader of the people!"

⁸ Yes, Jerusalem has stumbled
 and Judah has fallen,

LIGHTHOUSE

FALSE GODS

Say No to Idols *Isaiah 2:17-20*

God should be the most important thing in our lives. Anything that human beings care about more than God is an idol. The people of Israel worshipped beautiful idols they made out of silver and gold to look like their gods. Their wealth and success became more important to them than God.

People still have idols—things like money, fame, cars, people, or even the Internet. These things aren't wrong in themselves, but they should never take priority over God. Nothing made by human hands can ever be more important or powerful than God. We should enjoy all of the blessings God gives us, but we should never make God's gifts more important than God. 🌢

ᵈOr *don't forgive them* ᵉLXX *and high* ᶠHeb uncertain ᵍHeb uncertain

because the way they talk and act
in word and deed insults the Lord,
defying his brilliant glory.

⁹ Their bias in judgment gives them away;
like Sodom,
they display their sins in public.
Doom to them,
for they have done themselves in!

¹⁰ Tell the righteous how blessed they are;
they will eat the fruit of their labors.

¹¹ Doom to the wicked; they are evil.
What they have done
will be done to them.

¹² As for my people—oppressors strip them
and swindlersʰ rule them.
My people—your leaders mislead you
and confuse your paths.

¹³ The Lord arises to accuse;
he stands to judge the peoples.

¹⁴ The Lord will enter into judgment
with the elders and princes
of his people:
You yourselves have devoured
the vineyard;
the goods stolen from the poor
are in your houses.

¹⁵ How dare you crush my people
and grind the faces of the poor?
says the Lord God of heavenly forces.

¹⁶ The Lord says:
Because Zion's daughters
applaud themselves,
walking with their chins in the air,
flirting with their eyes,
tiptoeing as they walk, feet jingling—

¹⁷ the Lord will shave the heads
of Zion's daughters,
and will expose their scalps.

¹⁸ On that day, the Lord will remove:
the splendid ankle chains; headbands
and moon-shaped pendants;

¹⁹ the earrings, bracelets, and veils;

²⁰ the hats, bangles, and sashes;
the amulets and charms;

²¹ the signet rings and nose rings;

²² the robes and capes;
the shawls and handbags;

²³ the mirrors and linen garments;
the turbans and the veils.

²⁴ Instead of perfume
there will be a disgusting odor;
instead of a sash, a rope;
instead of styled hair, shaved heads;
instead of expensive clothes,
rags as mourning clothes;
instead of beauty, shame.ⁱ

²⁵ Your men will fall by the sword,
your warriors in battle!

²⁶ Her gates will lament and mourn;
desolate, she will sit on the ground.

UMBRELLA
MOURNING

Sitting on the Ground *Isaiah 3:26*

The people of Israel thought they could do anything they wanted. They thought they didn't need God. But Isaiah told them God would judge them for going their own way. When this judgment came, the entire city of Jerusalem would be in mourning.

Everyone has times when they feel sad and low. When someone mourns, their heart feels broken. People mourn when they experience a great loss. But they can also mourn when they realize they've done something wrong that is not God's way. When we mourn, God can touch our hearts to lift us up on the inside. God can make us strong so our hearts leap with joy. ◆

Seven women will grab one man on that day, saying, "We will eat our own bread and wear our own clothes—only let us take your name; take away our disgrace."

Zion's glorious future

²On that day, the Lord's branch will become beautiful and glorious. The earth's fruit will be the pride and splendor of Israel's survivors. ³Whoever remains in Zion and is left in Jerusalem will be called holy, everyone who is on the list of those living in Jerusalem. ⁴When the Lord washes the filth from Zion's daughters, and cleanses Jerusalem's bloodguilt from within it by means of a wind

ʰLXX; MT *women* ⁱDSS (1QIsaª); MT lacks *shame.*

of judgment and a searing wind, ⁵then the LORD will create over the whole site of Mount Zion and over its assembly a cloud by day and smoke and the light of a blazing fire by night. Over all the glory there will be a canopy, ⁶which will be a booth by day for shade from the heat and a hiding place and shelter from a stormy downpour.

Song of the vineyard

5 Let me sing for my loved one
a love song for his vineyard.
My loved one had a vineyard
on a fertile hillside.
² He dug it,
cleared away its stones,
planted it with excellent vines,
built a tower inside it,
and dug out a wine vat in it.
He expected it to grow good grapes—
but it grew rotten grapes.
³ So now, you who live in Jerusalem,
you people of Judah,
judge between me and my vineyard:
⁴ What more was there to do
for my vineyard
that I haven't done for it?
When I expected it to grow good grapes,
why did it grow rotten grapes?
⁵ Now let me tell you
what I'm doing to my vineyard.
I'm removing its hedge,
so it will be destroyed.
I'm breaking down its walls,
so it will be trampled.
⁶ I'll turn it into a ruin;
it won't be pruned or hoed,
and thorns and thistles will grow up.
I will command the clouds not to rain on it.
⁷ The vineyard of
the LORD of heavenly forces
is the house of Israel,
and the people of Judah
are the plantings
in which God delighted.
God expected justice,
but there was bloodshed;
righteousness,
but there was a cry of distress!

The light of the Lord was a name for God's Instruction. Just as a light can show the right way to go in the dark, God's teaching helps people know the correct choices to make in a dark world.

Sayings of doom

⁸ Doom to those who acquire
house after house,
who annex field to field
until there is no more space left
and only you live alone in the land.
⁹ I heard the LORD of heavenly forces
say this:ʲ
Many houses will become total ruins,
large, fine houses,
with no one living in them.
¹⁰ Ten acres of vineyard
will produce just one bath,ᵏ
and a homer of seed
will produce only an ephah.

¹¹ Doom to those who wake up
early in the morning to run after beer,
to those who stay up late, lit up by wine.
¹² They party with lyre and harp,
tambourine, flute, and wine;
but they ignore the LORD's work;
they can't see what God is doing.

¹³ Therefore, my people go into exile
since they didn't understand—
their officials are dying of hunger;
so many of them are dried up with thirst.
¹⁴ Therefore, the graveˡ opens wide its jaws,
opens its mouth beyond all bounds,
and the splendid multitudes will go down,
with all their uproar and cheering.
¹⁵ Humanity will be humiliated;
each person laid low,
the eyes of the exalted laid low.
¹⁶ But the LORD of heavenly forces
will be exalted in justice,
and the holy God will show himself
holy in righteousness.
¹⁷ Lambs will graze as if in their pasture;
young goatsᵐ will feed
among the ruins of the rich.ⁿ

ʲHeb lacks *say this.* ᵏOne bath is approximately twenty quarts, the same as an ephah; one homer contains ten ephahs (or baths) of grain. ˡHeb *Sheol* ᵐOr *strangers* ⁿOr *Calves and young goats will feed on the ruins*; Heb uncertain

¹⁸ Doom to those who drag guilt
  along with cords of fraud,
  and haul sin as if with cart ropes,
¹⁹ who say, "God should hurry
  and work faster so we can see;
  let the plan of Israel's holy one come
  quickly, so we can understand it."

²⁰ Doom to those who call evil good
  and good evil,
  who present darkness as light
  and light as darkness,
  who make bitterness sweet
  and sweetness bitter.

²¹ Doom to those
  who consider themselves wise,
  who think of themselves as clever.

²² Doom to the wine-swigging warriors,
  mighty at mixing drinks,
²³ who spare the guilty for bribes,
  and rob the innocent of their rights.

did you know? The Hebrew word for *messengers* in Isaiah 6 means "burning ones." Isaiah said the shouts of these burning ones were so loud that they shook the temple.

²⁴ Therefore, as a tongue of fire
  devours stubble,
  and as hay shrivels in a flame,
  so their roots will rot,
  and their blossoms turn to dust,
  for they have rejected the teaching of
  the Lᴏʀᴅ of heavenly forces,
  and have despised the word
  of Israel's holy one.

God's powerful hand

²⁵ This is why the Lᴏʀᴅ's anger
  burned against the people:
  he extended his hand to strike them,
  the mountains trembled,
  and their corpses lay in the middle
  of the streets like dung.
  Even then God's anger didn't turn away;
  God's hand was still extended.

²⁶ God will raise a signal
  to a nation from far away
  and whistle to them
  from the end of the earth—
  now look—hurrying, swiftly they come!
²⁷ Not one is tired; not one stumbles;
  they don't rest or sleep;
  no belt is loose; no sandal broken;
²⁸ their arrows are sharp;
  all their bows drawn;
  their horses' hooves are like flint;
  their wheels like the whirlwind.
²⁹ Their roaring is like the lion;
  they roar like young lions;
  they growl, seize their prey,
  and carry it off, with no one to rescue.
³⁰ On that day, they will roar over it
  like the roaring of the sea.
  And if one looks toward the land,
  there's darkness.
  Tyre and the Nile
  will be darkened by the clouds.º

The divine throne room

6 In the year of King Uzziah's death, I saw the Lord sitting on a high and exalted throne, the edges of his robe filling the temple. ²Winged creatures were stationed around him. Each had six wings: with two they veiled their faces, with two their feet, and with two they flew about. ³They shouted to each other, saying:

Memorize
Isa 6:3

  "Holy, holy, holy
  is the Lᴏʀᴅ of heavenly forces!
  All the earth is filled with God's glory!"

⁴The doorframe shook at the sound of their shouting, and the house was filled with smoke.

⁵I said, "Mourn for me; I'm ruined! I'm a man with unclean lips, and I live among a people with unclean lips. Yet I've seen the king, the Lᴏʀᴅ of heavenly forces!"

⁶Then one of the winged creatures flew to me, holding a glowing coal that he had taken from the altar with tongs. ⁷He touched my mouth and said, "See, this has touched your lips. Your guilt has departed, and your sin is removed."

⁸Then I heard the Lord's voice saying, "Whom should I send, and who will go for us?"

ºHeb uncertain

LIFE PRESERVER

What did God call Isaiah to do? *Isaiah 6:1-10*

The Bible has many interesting stories of God calling a person to do something. Here Isaiah described a very colorful image of God speaking to him. First, Isaiah said, "I'm a man with unclean lips" (Isa 6:5), meaning he didn't think he was worthy to do what God asked. But God removed Isaiah's sin, making him ready to serve.

Once again, God called a prophet to speak to God's people. Isaiah's task was difficult. He was to deliver a message that the people would not want to hear: God was going to punish them. This would not be an easy assignment. ♦

I said, "I'm here; send me."

⁹God said, "Go and say to this people:
Listen intently, but don't understand;
    look carefully, but don't comprehend.
¹⁰ Make the minds of this people dull.
    Make their ears deaf
        and their eyes blind,
    so they can't see with their eyes
        or hear with their ears,
    or understand with their minds,
    and turn, and be healed."

¹¹I said, "How long, Lord?"

And God said, "Until cities lie ruined with no one living in them, until there are houses without people and the land is left devastated." ¹²The Lᴏʀᴅ will send the people far away, and the land will be completely abandoned. ¹³Even if one-tenth remain there, they will be burned again, like a terebinth or an oak, which when it is cut down leaves a stump. Its stump is a holy seed.

Reassurance to King Ahaz

7In the days of Ahaz (Jotham's son and grandson of Judah's King Uzziah), Aram's King Rezin and Israel's King Pekah (Remaliah's son) came up to attack Jerusalem, but they couldn't overpower it.

²When the house of David was told that Aram had become allies with Ephraim, their hearts and the hearts of their people shook as the trees of a forest shake when there is a wind. ³But the Lᴏʀᴅ said to Isaiah, "Go out to meet Ahaz, you and your son Shear-jashub,ᵖ at the end of the channel of the Upper Pool, by the road to the field where laundry is washed, ⁴and say to him, 'Be careful and stay calm. Don't fear, and don't lose heart over these two pieces of smoking torches, over the burning anger of Rezin, Aram, and Remaliah's son. ⁵Aram has planned evil against you with Ephraim and Remaliah's son, saying, ⁶"Let's march up against Judah, tear it apart, capture it for ourselves, and install Tabeel's son as its king." ⁷But the Lᴏʀᴅ God says: It won't happen; it won't take place. ⁸The chief of Aram is Damascus; the chief of Damascus is Rezin (in sixty-five more years Ephraim will be shattered as a nation); ⁹the chief of Ephraim is Samaria; and the chief of Samaria is the son of Remaliah. If you don't believe this, you can't be trusted.'"

The sign of Immanuel

¹⁰Again the Lᴏʀᴅ spoke to Ahaz: ¹¹"Ask a sign from the Lᴏʀᴅ your God. Make it as deep as the grave�q or as high as heaven."

¹²But Ahaz said, "I won't ask; I won't test the Lᴏʀᴅ."

¹³Then Isaiah said, "Listen, house of David! Isn't it enough for you to be tiresome for people that you are also tiresome before my God? ¹⁴Therefore, the Lord will give you a sign. The young woman is pregnant and is about

LIFE PRESERVER

What does "Immanuel" mean? *Isaiah 7:13-14*

The name *Immanuel* (also spelled *Emmanuel*) means "God is with us." God gave Ahaz a sign that God would be with Judah and Jerusalem. With this promise, God hoped Ahaz would realize there was no need for him to put his trust in the nation of Assyria. God promised to be with God's people and wanted them to remember.

This name and verse are quoted in Matthew 1:23. The child that would be born to Mary and Joseph, which was Jesus, would also be called Immanuel. God wanted them to remember that Immanuel would be a living presence of God with them. "God is with us" when we remember how God wants us to live and act. ♦

ᴾOr *the remaining few will return* qHeb *Sheol*

to give birth to a son, and she will name him Immanuel.ʳ ¹⁵He will eat butter and honey, and learn to reject evil and choose good. ¹⁶Before the boy learns to reject evil and choose good, the land of the two kings you dread will be abandoned. ¹⁷The Lᴏʀᴅ will bring upon you, upon your people, and upon your families days unlike any that have come since the day Ephraim broke away from Judah—the king of Assyria."

The devastated land

¹⁸On that day, the Lᴏʀᴅ will whistle for the flies from the remotest streams of Egypt and for the bees that are in the land of Assyria. ¹⁹They will come and settle in the steep ravines, in the cracks of the cliffs, in all the thornbushes, and in all the watering holes.

²⁰On that day, the Lord will shave with a razor hired from beyond the Euphrates—with the king of Assyria—the head and the pubic hair, and will cut off the beard as well.

²¹On that day, one will raise a young cow and two sheep ²²and will eat butter because of the abundance of milk, for all who remain in the land will eat butter and honey.

²³On that day, there will be thorns and thistles in every place where a thousand vines worth a thousand silver shekels once grew. ²⁴Only those with bows and arrows will go there, because the entire land will become thorns and thistles. ²⁵As for the hills that were once farmed with hoes, you won't go there for fear of the thorns and thistles. They will become places where cattle are turned loose and sheep wander.

Isaiah's testimonies

8 The Lᴏʀᴅ said to me, "Take a large tablet, and write on it in ordinary letters,ˢ For Maher-shalal-hash-baz.ᵗ ²Summon trusted people, Uriah the priest and Zechariah, Jeberechiah's son, to witness it."

³I then had sex with the prophetess, and she became pregnant and gave birth to a son. Then the Lᴏʀᴅ said to me, "Name him Maher-shalal-hash-baz. ⁴Before the boy knows how to say 'my father' and 'my mother,' the wealth of Damascus and the spoil of Samaria will be carried away before the king of Assyria."

⁵The Lᴏʀᴅ spoke again to me: ⁶Since this people has rejected the waters of Shiloah that flow gently, and instead rejoices overᵘ Rezin and Remaliah's son—⁷therefore, look, the Lord is raising up against them the powerful floodwaters of the Euphrates, the king of Assyria and all his glory. It will rise up over all its channels, overflowing all its banks, ⁸and sweep into Judah, flooding, overflowing, and reaching up to the neck. But God is with us;ᵛ the span of his wings will cover the width of the land.

⁹ Uniteʷ yourselves, peoples,
　and be shattered!
　Listen, all distant places of the earth!
　Prepare to be shattered!
　Prepare to be shattered!
¹⁰ Create a plan, but be frustrated!
　Speak a word, but it won't stand,
　　for God is with us.ˣ

¹¹The Lᴏʀᴅ spoke to me, taking hold of me and warning me not to walk in the way of this people: ¹²Don't call conspiracy all that this people calls conspiracy. Don't fear what they fear, and don't be terrified. ¹³It is the Lᴏʀᴅ of heavenly forces whom you should hold sacred, whom you should fear, and whom you should hold in awe.

¹⁴ God will become a sanctuary—
　but he will be a stone to trip over
　　and a rock to stumble on
　for the two houses of Israel;
　a trap and a snare
　　for those living in Jerusalem.
¹⁵ Many of them will stumble and fall,
　and be broken, snared, and captured.
¹⁶Bind up the testimony; seal up the teach-

ing among my disciples. ¹⁷I will wait for the Lᴏʀᴅ, who has hidden his face from the house of Jacob, and I will hope in God. ¹⁸Look! I and the children the Lᴏʀᴅ gave me are signs and wonders in Israel from the Lᴏʀᴅ of heavenly forces, who lives on Mount Zion.

ʳOr *God is with us*　ˢHeb uncertain　ᵗOr *spoil hastens, plunder hurries*　ᵘOr *melts before*　ᵛHeb *Immanuel*　ʷHeb uncertain
ˣHeb *Immanuel*

¹⁹ If they say to you: "Consult the ghosts and the spirits that chirp and mutter. (Shouldn't a people consult its gods?) Consult the dead on behalf of the living ²⁰ for instruction and for testimony"—they will surely say such things, but they will never see the dawn.ʸ

²¹ They will pass through the land,ᶻ dejected and hungry, and when they are hungry, they will be enraged and will curse their king and God. They will turn toward heaven ²²and look to the earth, but they will see only distress and darkness, random movement, and the anguish and doom of banishment.ᵃ

A great light

9ᵇ Nonetheless, those who were in distress won't be exhausted. At an earlier time, God cursed the land of Zebulun and the land of Naphtali, but later he glorified the way of the sea, the far side of the Jordan, and the Galilee of the nations.ᶜ

² ᵈ The people walking in darkness
have seen a great light.
On those living in a pitch-dark land,
light has dawned.

³ You have made the nation great;
you have increased its joy.
They rejoiced before you
as with joy at the harvest,
as those who divide plunder rejoice.

⁴ As on the day of Midian,
you've shattered the yoke
that burdened them,
the staff on their shoulders,
and the rod of their oppressor.

⁵ Because every boot
of the thundering warriors,
and every garment rolled in blood
will be burned, fuel for the fire.

⁶ A child is born to us, a son is given to us,
and authority will be on his shoulders.
He will be named
Wonderful Counselor, Mighty God,
Eternal Father, Prince of Peace.

⁷ There will be vast authority
and endless peace
for David's throne and for his kingdom,
establishing and sustaining it
with justice and righteousness
now and forever.

The zeal of the LORD of heavenly forces will do this.

God's hand still stretched out

⁸ The Lord sent a word against Jacob;
it fell upon Israel;

⁹ the people all knew it—
Ephraim and the one
who rules in Samaria.
But with a proud and arrogant heart
they said,

¹⁰ "Bricks have fallen,
but let's rebuild with stones.
Sycamores were cut down,
but let's replace them with cedars."

did you know? The Great Coastal Highway, was known as *the way of the sea*. It was an important road in Bible times. It ran more than 850 miles from Egypt to Babylon. Many people from all over the world traveled the road trading goods.

¹¹ So the LORD raised up their foes
against them,ᵉ
and stirred up their enemies—

¹² Aram from the east and the Philistines
from the west—
and they devoured Israel
with an open mouth.
Even then God's anger didn't turn away;
God's hand was still extended.

LIFE PRESERVER

Who is the child described in Isaiah 9:6-7? *Isaiah 9:6-7*

These verses are often read during the season of Advent because Christians interpret this passage to refer to the coming of Christ, who was Jesus. This is one way to read this passage, to see it in light of what we know from the story of Jesus in the Gospels in the New Testament.

However, these verses were actually written to celebrate the coronation of a king during Isaiah's time. "Wonderful Counselor, Mighty God, Eternal Father, Prince of Peace" (9:6) are words used to describe this king. This would help the people understand that the king's rule was divine and approved by God. ◊

ʸHeb uncertain for 8:19–20 ᶻOr *it* ᵃHeb uncertain for 8:21–22 ᵇ8:23 in Heb ᶜHeb uncertain ᵈ9:1 in Heb ᵉOr *the enemies of Rezin*

¹³ But the people didn't turn
to the one who struck them.
They didn't seek
the Lord of heavenly forces.
¹⁴ So the Lord cut off head and tail,
palm branch and reed
from Israel in one day.
¹⁵ (Elders and celebrities are the head;
prophets who teach lies are the tail.)
¹⁶ But this people's leaders were misleading,
and those being led were confused.
¹⁷ So the Lord showed their youth no pity,
and showed their orphans and widows
no mercy;
for everyone was godless and evil;
every mouth spoke nonsense.
Even then God's anger didn't turn away;
God's hand was still extended.

¹⁸ Wickedness burned like fire,
devouring thorn and thistle.
It kindled the thickets of the forest;
they swirled in rising smoke.
¹⁹ The land was scorched by the rage of
the Lord of heavenly forces;
the people were like fuel for the fire.
Not one person pitied another:
²⁰ they consumed on the right,
but remained hungry;
devoured on the left, and weren't satisfied.
They devoured the flesh
of their own children.ᶠ
²¹ Manasseh devoured Ephraim
and Ephraim Manasseh;
together they turned against Judah.
Even then God's anger didn't turn away;
God's hand was still extended.

Wicked laws

10 Doom to those
who pronounce wicked decrees,
and keep writing harmful laws,
² to deprive the needy of their rights
and to rob the poor among my people
of justice;
to make widows their loot;
to steal from orphans!
³ What will you do on the day of punishment
when disaster comes from far away?
To whom will you flee for help;

where will you stash your wealth?
⁴ How will you avoid
crouching among the prisoners
and falling among the slain?
Even so, God's anger hasn't turned away;
God's hand is still extended.

Assyria as God's punishing weapon

⁵ Doom to Assyria, rod of my anger,
in whose hand is the staff of my fury!
⁶ Against a godless nation I send him;
against an infuriating people
I direct him to seize spoil, to steal plunder,
and to trample them
like mud in the streets.
⁷ But he has other plans;
he schemes in secret;
destruction is on his mind,
extermination of nation after nation.
⁸ He says: Aren't my commanders all kings?
⁹ Isn't Calno like Carchemish?
Isn't Hamath like Arpad?
Isn't Samaria like Damascus?
¹⁰ Just as I took control
of idolatrous kingdoms
with more images
than Jerusalem and Samaria,
¹¹ just as I did to Samaria
and her false gods,
won't I also do this to Jerusalem
and her idols?
¹²But when the Lord has finished all this
work on Mount Zion and in Jerusalem, he will
punishᵍ the Assyrian king's arrogant actions
and the boasting of his haughty eyes.
¹³ He said, "By my own strength
I have achieved it,
and by my wisdom, since I'm so clever.
I disregarded national boundaries;
I raided their treasures;
I knocked down their rulers like a bull.
¹⁴ My hand found the wealth of the peoples
as if it were in a nest.
Just as one gathers abandoned eggs,
I have gathered the entire earth;
no creature fluttered a wing
or opened a mouth to chirp."

¹⁵ Will the ax glorify itself
over the one who chops with it?

ᶠOr *arm* ᵍOr *I will punish*

Or will the saw magnify itself
over its user?
As if a rod could wave the one who lifts it!
As if a staff could lift up
the one not made of wood!
¹⁶ Therefore, the LORD God of heavenly forces
will make the well-fed people waste away;
and among his officials,
a blaze will burn like scorching fire.
¹⁷ The light of Israel will become a fire,
its holy one a flame,
which will burn and devour
its thorns and thistles
in a single day.
¹⁸ Its abundant forest and farmland
will be finished completely,[h]
as when a sick person wastes away;
¹⁹ its forest's remaining trees
will be no more than a child can count.

A few will return

²⁰On that day, what's left of Israel and the survivors of the house of Jacob will no longer depend on the one who beat them. Instead, they will faithfully depend on the LORD, the holy one of Israel. ²¹A few will return, what's left of Jacob, to the mighty God. ²²Although your people, Israel, were like the sand of the sea, only a few survivors will return. The end is announced, overflowing with justice. ²³Yes, destruction has been announced; the LORD God of heavenly forces will carry it out against the entire land.

²⁴Therefore, the LORD God of heavenly forces says: My people who live in Zion, don't fear Assyria, which strikes you with the rod and raises its staff against you as Egypt did. ²⁵In a very short time my fury will end, and my anger at the world will be finished.[i]

²⁶ Therefore, the LORD of heavenly forces
will crack a whip against Assyria,
as when he struck Midian
at the rock of Oreb.
He will raise a rod over the sea,
as he did in Egypt.
²⁷ On that day, God will remove
the burden from your shoulder
and destroy the yoke on your neck.[j]

The exalted laid low

He has gone up from Samaria,
²⁸ come against Aiath,
passed to Migron.
At Michmash he stored his equipment.
²⁹ They crossed at the pass:
"We'll camp at Geba!"
Ramah trembles; Gibeah of Saul has fled.
³⁰ Cry aloud, Daughter Gallim!
Listen, Laishah! Answer her, Anathoth!
³¹ Madmenah has flown.
Gebim's inhabitants sought refuge.
³² This very day he will stand at Nob
and shake his fist[k]
at Daughter Zion's mountain,
the hill of Jerusalem!
³³ Look! The LORD God of heavenly forces
is chopping off the branches
with terrible power.
The loftiest ones are about to be cut down
and the exalted laid low.
³⁴ He will strike down the forest thickets
with an ax,
and mighty Lebanon will fall.

A shoot from Jesse's stump

11 A shoot will grow up
from the stump of Jesse;
a branch will sprout[l] from his roots.
² The LORD's spirit will rest upon him,
a spirit of wisdom and understanding,

UMBRELLA
HARD TIMES

Disobedience Leads to Hard Times
Isaiah 10:25
The Israelites knew what it felt like to be slaves. It was a bad way to live. They were suffering for their disobedience to God. Instead of trusting in God, they had trusted the Assyrians (a neighboring nation) to help them. Now the Assyrians were their worst enemy. We can learn a lot from what happened to the Israelites. If we go against God, our hard times will only last longer. Yet even in hard times, God always does what's best for us and is willing to show mercy when we follow God's ways. ☂

---

^hSyr, Vulg *body and soul* (that is, *completely*); MT *he will finish* ⁱHeb uncertain ^jOr *and his yoke from your neck, and a yoke will be destroyed because of fatness* ^kOr *wave his hand* ^lLXX, Vulg; MT *bear fruit*

a spirit of planning and strength,
a spirit of knowledge and fear of the Lord.
³ He will delight in fearing the Lord.
He won't judge by appearances,
nor decide by hearsay.
⁴ He will judge the needy
with righteousness,
and decide with equity
for those who suffer in the land.
He will strike the violent[m]
with the rod of his mouth;
by the breath of his lips
he will kill the wicked.
⁵ Righteousness will be
the belt around his hips,
and faithfulness
the belt around his waist.
⁶ The wolf will live with the lamb,
and the leopard will lie down
with the young goat;
the calf and the young lion
will feed[n] together,
and a little child will lead them.
⁷ The cow and the bear will graze.
Their young will lie down together,
and a lion will eat straw like an ox.
⁸ A nursing child
will play over the snake's hole;
toddlers will reach
right over the serpent's den.
⁹ They won't harm or destroy
anywhere on my holy mountain.
The earth will surely be filled
with the knowledge of the Lord,
just as the water covers the sea.

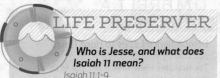

LIFE PRESERVER

Who is Jesse, and what does Isaiah 11 mean?
Isaiah 11:1-9

Jesse was David's father. This passage says the ideal king for God's people will be a descendant of Jesse. And it says that this king will bring about a peaceable kingdom, where all of creation lives together in harmony. Even more than that, everyone will know God.

Some of these verses are read during the season of Advent as we prepare to remember the birth of Jesus, another descendant of Jesse. ◈

did you know?

The Israelites believed God would one day send a king who was a descendant from David's family to reunite the twelve tribes of Israel in peace. This promised king was sometimes referred to as the *Messiah* who would come to save them.

A signal to the peoples

¹⁰ On that day, the root of Jesse will stand as a signal to the peoples. The nations will seek him out, and his dwelling will be glorious. ¹¹ On that day, the Lord will extend his hand a second time to reclaim the survivors of God's people who are left from Assyria and from Egypt, from Pathros, Cush, Elam, Shinar, Hamath, and from the coastlands[o] of the sea.
¹² God will raise a signal for the nations
and gather the outcast men of Israel.
God will collect
the dispersed women of Judah
from the four corners of the earth.
¹³ Ephraim's jealousy will cease,
and Judah's harassment
will be eliminated.
Ephraim won't be jealous of Judah,
and Judah won't harass Ephraim.
¹⁴ But they will swoop down
on the slopes of Philistia to the west;
together they will plunder
the people to the east.
Edom and Moab will be under their power,
and the Ammonites will be their subjects.
¹⁵ The Lord will split the tongue of the Egyptian sea. God will wave a hand over the Euphrates with a powerful[p] wind and break it into seven streams so that it can be crossed in sandals. ¹⁶ Then there will be a highway from Assyria for the survivors of God's people who are left from Assyria, just as there was for Israel on the day they went up from the land of Egypt.

Hymn of trust

12 You will say on that day:
"I thank you, Lord.
Though you were angry with me,
your anger turned away
and you comforted me.
² God is indeed my salvation;
I will trust and won't be afraid.

ᵐOr *land* ⁿCorrection; MT *and the calf* ᵒOr *islands* ᵖHeb uncertain

Yah, the Lord, is my strength
and my shield;
he has become my salvation."

³ You will draw water with joy
from the springs of salvation.
⁴ And you will say on that day:
"Thank the Lord; call on God's name;
proclaim God's deeds among the peoples;
declare that God's name is exalted.
⁵ Sing to the Lord,
who has done glorious things;
proclaim this throughout all the earth."
⁶ Shout and sing for joy, city of Zion,
because the holy one of Israel
is great among you.

SAILBOAT

Joy

Joy in God's Goodness *Isaiah 12:1-6*
Isaiah said that one day God's people would realize
that God had shown them love, even though they had
sinned against God. Their joy over God's goodness
would cause them to give thanks and trust God. They
would have so much joy that they would cry aloud
and shout because they knew God was with them.

We can rejoice over God's love and goodness
by praising God for the great things that God has
done for us too. Having joy doesn't mean everything is perfect or always goes our way. Joy comes
from our hearts when we know we serve a God who
always does what is best for us. ◖

Babylon falls

13 An oracle about Babylon, which Isaiah,
Amoz's son, saw.
² On a bare mountain raise a signal;
cry aloud to them;
wave a hand;
let them enter the officials' gates.
³ I have commanded my holy ones;
I have called my warriors,
my proud, jubilant ones,
to execute my wrath.
⁴ Listen!ᵍ A roar on the mountains
like that of a great crowd.
Listen! An uproar of kingdoms,
of nations coming together.
The Lord of heavenly forces
is mustering an army for battle.

⁵ They are coming from a distant land,
from the faraway heavens,
the Lord and the instruments of his fury,
to destroy the whole land.

⁶ Wail, for the day of the Lord is near.
Like destruction from the Almightyʳ
it will come.
⁷ Then all hands will fall limp;
every human heart will melt,
⁸ and they will be terrified.
Like a woman writhing in labor,
they will be seized by spasms and agony.
They will look at each other aghast,
their faces blazing.

⁹ Look, the day of the Lord is coming
with cruel rage and burning anger,
making the earth a ruin,
and wiping out its sinners.
¹⁰ Heaven's stars and constellations
won't show their light.
The sun will be dark when it rises;
the moon will no longer shine.
¹¹ I will bring disaster
upon the world for its evil,
and bring their own sin upon the wicked.
I will end the pride of the insolent,
and the conceit of tyrants I will lay low.
¹² I will make humans scarcer than fine gold;
people rarer than the gold of Ophir.
¹³ I will rattle the heavens;
the earth will shake loose
from its place—because of the rage
of the Lord of heavenly forces
on the day his anger burns.
¹⁴ They will be like hunted gazelles,
like sheep without a shepherd;
all will turn to their own people
and flee to their own lands.
¹⁵ Whoever is found will be stabbed;
whoever is caught will fall by the sword.
¹⁶ Their infants will be crushed
before their eyes;

ᵍHeb lacks *Listen!* ʳHeb *Shaddai* or *Mountain One*

their houses plundered,
their women raped.

¹⁷ Look! I'm rousing the Medes against them;
the Medes pay no mind to silver,
no desire for gold.
¹⁸ Their bows will smash youths;
they will be merciless to newborns,
pitiless to children.
¹⁹ So Babylon, a jewel among kingdoms,
the Chaldeans' splendor and pride,
will be like Sodom and Gomorrah,
destroyed by God.
²⁰ No one will ever resettle
or live there for generations.
No Arab will camp there;
no shepherds will rest flocks there.
²¹ Wildcats will rest there;
houses will be filled with owls.
Ostriches will live there,
and goat demons will dance there.
²² Hyenas will howl in its strongholds,
and jackals in its luxurious palaces.
Babylon's[s] time is coming soon;
its days won't drag on.

Compassion for Jacob

14 The LORD will have compassion on Jacob,
will again choose Israel, and will give
them rest in their own land. Immigrants will
join them, and attach themselves to the house
of Jacob. ²The peoples will take them and will
bring them to their own place. The house of
Israel will possess them as male and female
slaves in the LORD's land, making captives of
their captors and ruling their oppressors.

Mockery of a tyrant

³When the LORD has given you rest from
pain and trouble and from the hard labor
that you perform, ⁴you will take up this taunt
against the king of Babylon:
How the oppressor[t] has ceased!
How the flood[u] has receded!
⁵ The LORD has broken
the staff of the wicked,
the rod of tyrants
⁶that struck peoples in rage
with ceaseless blows,
that ruled nations with anger,
with relentless aggression.

⁷ All the earth rests quietly,
then it breaks into song.
⁸ Even the cypresses rejoice over you,
the cedars of Lebanon:
"Since you were laid low,
no logger comes up against us!"

⁹ The underworld[v] beneath
becomes restless to greet your arrival.
It awakens the ghosts,
all the leaders of earth;
it makes the kings of the nations
rise from their thrones.
¹⁰ All of them speak and say to you:
"Even you've become weak like we are!
You are the same as us!"
¹¹ Your majesty has been brought down
to the underworld,[w]
along with the sound of your harps.
Under you is a bed of maggots,
and worms are your blanket.

¹² How you've fallen from heaven,
morning star, son of dawn!
You are cut down to earth,
helpless on your back!
¹³ You said to yourself,
I will climb up to heaven;
above God's stars, I will raise my throne.
I'll sit on the mount of assembly,
on the heights of Zaphon.
¹⁴ I'll go up to the cloud tops;
I'll be like the Most High!
¹⁵ But down to the underworld[x]
you are brought,
to the depths of the pit.

¹⁶ Those who see you will stare at you;
they will examine you closely:
"Is this the man who rattled the earth,
who shook kingdoms,
¹⁷ who made the world a wasteland
and tore down its cities,
and wouldn't let his prisoners go home?"
¹⁸ All the kings of the nations
lie down honored,
all of them, each in his own tomb.
¹⁹ But you are cast away
from your own grave
like a rejected branch,

---

^sHeb *Its* ^tHeb uncertain ^uDSS (1QIsa^a), LXX, Syr, Tg; MT *fury* ^vHeb *Sheol* ^wHeb *Sheol* ^xHeb *Sheol*

covered by the dead
and those pierced by the sword—
who go down to the stony pit—
like a trampled corpse.
²⁰ You won't join them in burial,
for you destroyed your own land;
you killed your own people.
Such evil offspring
will never be mentioned again!
²¹Prepare a place to slaughter his sons for the guilt of their father. Don't let them arise to take over the earth or fill the world with cities.

²²I will arise against them, says the LORD of heavenly forces. I will cut off Babylon's renown and remnant, offshoot and offspring. ²³I will make it the home of herons, a swampland. I will sweep it away with the broom of destruction, says the LORD of heavenly forces.

Promise for oppressed Judah

²⁴ The LORD of heavenly forces has promised:
As I intended, so it will be;
and as I have planned, so it will happen:
²⁵ I will break Assyria in my land;
on my mountains I will trample it
and remove its yoke from my people;ʸ
his burden will be taken
from their shoulders.
²⁶ This is the plan that has been made
for all the earth;
this is the hand
extended over all the nations.
²⁷ The LORD of heavenly forces
has created a plan;
who can stop it?
God's hand is extended;
who will stop it?

An oracle concerning the Philistines

²⁸This oracle came in the year of King Ahaz's death:
²⁹ Don't rejoice, all you Philistines,
that the rod that struck you is broken,
because from the snake's root
a viper will grow,
and it will produce a winged creature.
³⁰ The oldest offspring of the poor will graze;
their needy will lie down secure.
But he will starve your offspring to death,
and murder all who remain.

³¹ Wail, gate! Cry out, city!
Melt in terror, all you Philistines!
Smoke is coming from the north;
there is no straggler in its ranks.ᶻ
³² What will one say
to that nation's messengers?
The LORD has founded Zion;
the oppressed among God's people
will find refuge there.

Concerning Moab

15 An oracle about Moab.
Ar was devastated in a night;
Moab is ruined!
Kir was devastated in a night;
Moab is ruined!
² Dibon has gone up to the temple,
to the shrines to weep.ᵃ
Moab wails over Nebo and over Medeba.
Every head is shaved,
every beard cut off.
³ In its streets they wear mourning clothes;
on its rooftops and in its plazas,
everyone wails and falls down weeping.
⁴ Heshbon and Elealeh cry out;
as far as Jahaz their voice is heard.
The armed men of Moab shout,
spirits trembling.
⁵ My heart cries out for Moab.
Its fugitives flee to Zoar,
to Eglath-shelishiyah.ᵇ
At the ascent of Luhith,
each will go up with weeping.
On the road to Horonaim,
they will raise a piercing cry.
⁶ The waters of Nimrim are used up.
Grass has withered;
vegetation is dead;
greenery is gone.
⁷ Therefore, they carry
what they had stored up,
all their provisions
to the Valley of the Willows.
⁸ An outcry sounds
within the borders of Moab,
as far as Eglaim, a cry of distress,
as far as Beer-elim, a cry of distress.
⁹ The waters of Dibon are full of blood.
But I will bring still more upon Dibon:
a lion for Moab's survivors,
for the remaining few in the land.

ʸOr *them* ᶻHeb uncertain ᵃHeb uncertain ᵇHeb uncertain

16 Send lambs to the ruler of the land,[c]
from Sela through the desert
to the mountain of Daughter Zion.
² The daughters of Moab
at the fords of the Arnon
are like orphaned birds
pushed from the nest.
³ Consider carefully, act justly;
at high noon
provide your shade like night.
Hide the outcasts;
keep the fugitives hidden.
⁴ Let the outcasts of Moab live among you.
Be a hiding place for them
from the destroyer.
When the oppressor is no more,
when destruction has ceased,
when the trampler has vanished
from the land,
⁵ a throne will be established
based on goodness,
and someone will sit faithfully on it
in David's dwelling[d]—
a judge who seeks justice
and timely righteousness.

⁶ We have heard of Moab's pride,
his great pride,
his outrageous pride and arrogance,
his empty boasting.
⁷ Therefore, let Moab wail;
let everyone wail for Moab.
Let them moan, utterly stricken,
for the raisin cakes of Kir-hareseth.
⁸ The fields of Heshbon languish.
The vines of Sibmah,
whose honored grapes
overpowered masters of nations,
had reached as far as Jazer
and strayed to the desert.
Their tendrils spread out
and crossed the sea.
⁹ Therefore,
I will weep with Jazer's weeping
for the vines of Sibmah.
I will drench you with my tears,
Heshbon and Elealeh.
Cheers have fallen silent
concerning your summer fruit
and your grain harvest.

¹⁰ Joy and happiness
have been harvested
from the farmland,
and in the vineyards no one sings,
no one shouts.
No treader crushes grapes
in the wine vats;
I have brought the cheers to an end.
¹¹ Therefore, my heart plays sadly
like a harp for Moab,
my inner being for Kir-heres.
¹² Even if Moab presents himself,
and Moab wears himself out
going to the shrine,
and comes to his sanctuary to pray,
he won't prevail.

¹³ This is the word that the Lord had spoken concerning Moab long ago. ¹⁴But now the Lord has said: In three years, like the years of a hired worker, the glory of Moab, with all its great multitude, will dwindle. The small remnant will be few and feeble.

Concerning Damascus and Ephraim

17 An oracle about Damascus.
Look! Damascus is finished as a city;
it will become a fallen ruin.
² The villages of Aroer
are abandoned forever.[e]
They will be pastures for flocks,[f]
which will lie down undisturbed.
³ Ephraim's security will cease,
as will Damascus' rule.
What's left of Aram will resemble
the glory of the Israelites,
says the Lord of heavenly forces.

⁴ On that day, Jacob's glory will dwindle;
his sleek body will waste away.
⁵ It will be as when harvesters gather grain.
God will harvest armfuls at a time,
like one who gathers grain
in the Rephaim Valley.
⁶ Only remaining bits are left,
like an olive tree that has been shaken:
two or three olives on the highest branch;
four or five on a fruitful twig,
says the Lord God of Israel.

⁷ On that day, people will have regard
for their maker,

---

[c]Heb uncertain [d]Or *tent* [e]Cf LXX; MT *The cities of Aroer are abandoned* [f]Or *For flocks they will be*

and their eyes will look
  to the holy one of Israel.
[8] They will have no regard for altars,
  the work of their hands,
  or look to what their fingers made:
  sacred poles[g] and incense stands.

[9] On that day, their strong cities will be like those abandoned by the Hivites and the Amorites;[h] abandoned because of the Israelites. They will be a wasteland,

[10] because you forgot the God
  who saves you,
  and didn't remember the rock
  who shelters you.
Therefore, plant your pleasant plants,
  and set out exotic sprouts;
[11] make them grow the day you plant them,
  and make them bloom
  the morning you start them.
But the harvest will disappear
  on a day of sickness and
  incurable pain.

LIGHTHOUSE

FORGETTING GOD

Unwanted Harvest *Isaiah 17:10-11*

When God delivered the people of Israel from slavery, God told them the most important thing to remember was what God had done for them. They were to teach their children and grandchildren so they wouldn't forget either. But the people did forget. They began to worship other gods.

It's important for us to pray and thank God every day. This helps us to remember the blessings God gives us. Israel was punished because the people kept forgetting about God. They had worshipped idols to help them grow food. God said they would no longer have great harvests from their fields. The harvest we get from forgetting God will always be grief and pain. ◆

[12] Doom to the raging of many peoples;
  like the thundering seas they thunder.
  Doom to the roar of nations,
  like the roaring of mighty waters.
[13] Nations roar
  like the roaring of rushing waters.
But God will rebuke them,
  and they will flee far away,

pursued like chaff
  by wind in the mountains,
  like tumbleweeds before a storm.
[14] In the evening, there is terror;
  but before morning it is gone.
This is the fate of those who loot us,
  the destiny of those who rob us.

Concerning Cush

18 Doom to the land of winged ships,
  beyond the rivers of Cush
[2] that sends messengers by sea,
  reed vessels on the water.
Go, swift messengers,
  to a nation tall and clean-shaven,
  to a people feared near and far,
  a nation barbaric and oppressive,
  whose land the rivers divide.

[3] All you who inhabit the world,
  who live on earth,
  when a signal is raised
  on the mountains, you will see!
  When the trumpet blasts, you will hear!
[4] The Lord said to me:
  I will quietly watch from my own place,
  like the shimmering heat of sunshine,
  like a cloud's shade in the harvest heat.
[5] Before the harvest,
  when the bloom is finished,
  when the blossom is becoming
  a ripening fruit,
  God will cut the shoots
  with a pruning knife,
  and lop off the spreading branches.
[6] They will all be left
  to the mountain birds
  and to the beasts of the land.
  The birds will eat them in summer,
  all the beasts of the land in winter.

[7] At that time, gifts will be brought
  to the Lord of heavenly forces
  from a tall and clean-shaven people
  and from a people feared near and far,
  a nation barbaric and oppressive,
  whose land the rivers divide,
  to the place of the name of
  the Lord of heavenly forces,
  to Mount Zion.

---

[g]Heb *asherim*, possibly objects devoted to the goddess Asherah [h]LXX; MT *like the abandonment of the forest and the bough*

Concerning Egypt

19 An oracle about Egypt.
Look! The Lord is riding
upon a swift cloud,
and is coming to Egypt.
Egypt's idols will tremble before God;
the Egyptians' hearts will melt
within them.

2 I will stir up Egyptian against Egyptian,
and they will fight,
one against another,
neighbor against neighbor,
city against city,
kingdom against kingdom.

3 Egypt's spirit will fail from within;
I will frustrate their plans.
They will consult the idols and spirits
and ghosts and fortune-tellers.

4 I will hand Egypt over to a harsh master;
a strong king will rule them,
says the Lord God of heavenly forces.

5 The waters of the sea will dry up;
the river will be parched and bare.

6 The rivers will stink;
the streams will shrink and dry;
reeds and rushes will decay.

7 Grass around the Nile,
the grass at the mouth of the Nile,
and all the sown land of the Nile
will dry up, blow away, and be no more.

8 Those who fish will lament;
all who cast fishhooks in the Nile
will mourn,
and those who spread nets
on the water will pine away.

9 Workers with flax will be dismayed;
carders and weavers will grow pale.[i]

10 Makers of cloth will be crushed;
all who earn money
will become distressed.

11 The officials of Tanis are fools;
the wisest of Pharaoh's counselors
give stupid advice.
How can you say to Pharaoh,
"I'm a wise person,
one of the ancient kings"?

12 Where now are your wise ones?
Let them tell you,

let them inform you what
the Lord of heavenly forces
has planned concerning Egypt.

13 The officials of Tanis have become fools;
the princes of Memphis are deluded;
the tribal chiefs have led Egypt astray.

14 The Lord has poured into them
a spirit of confusion.
They will make Egypt stumble
in everything it does,
just as a drunk stumbles in his vomit.

15 Neither head nor tail,
palm branch nor reed
will be able to do anything for Egypt.

Bless God's people

16 On that day, the Egyptians will be like women and will tremble with terror before the hand that the Lord of heavenly forces will raise against them. 17 Judah's land will become what the Egyptians dread; whenever anyone mentions it, they will be terrified because of the plans that the Lord of heavenly forces is making against them.

18 On that day, there will be five cities in the land of Egypt that speak the language of Canaan and swear loyalty to the Lord of heavenly forces. One of them will be called "the city of the sun."[j]

19 On that day, there will be an altar to the Lord within the land of Egypt, and a standing stone for the Lord at its border. 20 It will be a sign and a witness to the Lord of heavenly forces in the land of Egypt. When they cry out to the Lord because of oppressors, God will send them a savior and defender to rescue them. 21 The Lord will make himself known to the Egyptians; the Egyptians will know the Lord on that day. They will worship with sacrifices and offerings, making solemn promises to the Lord and fulfilling them. 22 The Lord will strike Egypt; striking and then healing. They will return to the Lord, who will hear their pleas and heal them.

did you know? When God led the people out of Egypt during the time of Moses, God appeared before them as a towering cloud in the day. Here God promised to return to Egypt in a cloud once again to cause the Egyptians to fear the God of the Israelites.

---

[i]DSS (1QIsaᵃ) [j]DSS (1QIsaᵃ), Tg, Vulg; Heb uncertain

²³On that day, there will be a highway from Egypt to Assyria. The Assyrians will come to Egypt, and the Egyptians to Assyria; and the Egyptians will worship with the Assyrians.

²⁴On that day, Israel will be the third along with Egypt and Assyria, a blessing at the center of the world. ²⁵The Lord of heavenly forces will pronounce this blessing: Bless Egypt my people, and Assyria my handiwork, and Israel my inheritance.

The land next to the Persian Gulf that was eastern Babylon was very flat and dry. In Bible times it was known as *the land beside the sea* or *the desert beside the sea.*

Isaiah naked and barefoot

20 In the year that Assyria's King Sargon sent his general to Ashdod, he fought against Ashdod and captured it. ²At that time the Lord had spoken through Isaiah, Amoz's son, "Go, take off the mourning clothes from your waist, and remove the shoes from your feet." And Isaiah did this, walking naked and barefoot.

UMBRELLA
MOURNING

Walking Barefoot *Isaiah 20:2*
Being a prophet for God could be a tough job. Sometimes God told prophets to do strange things to get people's attention. The prophet Isaiah walked barefoot and naked to show that he was mourning for the people of Israel. They had rebelled against God, and terrible things would follow.

When we mourn, many things we once cared about seem less important. In these times, we may not care what we wear, or even if we put shoes on. We may sometimes think God doesn't care what happens to us. But as sad as we may feel, God (Immanuel) is always with us. ◐

³The Lord said, "Just as my servant Isaiah has walked naked and barefoot three years, as a sign and omen against Egypt and Cush, ⁴so will the king of Assyria lead the captives of Egypt and the exiles of Cush, both young and old, naked and barefoot, with buttocks bared, humiliating Egypt. ⁵They will be shattered and shamed because of Cush their hope, and because of Egypt their glory.

⁶"On that day, those who live on this coast will say, 'Look at those in whom we had hoped, to whom we fled for help and rescue from the king of Assyria. How then will we escape?'"

Fallen, fallen is Babylon

21 An oracle about the wilderness near the sea.

Like whirlwinds sweeping
  through the arid southern plain,
  it comes from the desert,
  from a fearsome land.
² A harsh vision was proclaimed to me:
  The betrayer betrays,
   and the destroyer destroys.
  Go up, Elam! Lay siege, Media!
  Put an end to all her groaning.
³ Therefore, I'm shaken to my core
   in anguish.
  Pains have seized me
   like the pains of a woman in labor.
  I'm too bent over to hear,
   too dismayed to see.
⁴ My heart pounds;
   convulsions overpower me.
  He has turned my evening of pleasure
   into dread—
⁵ setting the table, spreading the cloth,
   eating, drinking.
  "Arise, captains!
   Polish the shields."

⁶ The Lord said this to me:
  "Go, post a lookout to report what he sees.
⁷ When he sees chariots, pairs of horsemen,
   donkey riders, camel riders,
  he should listen carefully,
   carefully, very carefully."

⁸ Then the seer^k called out:
  "Upon a watchtower, Lord,
   I'm standing all day;
  and upon my observation post
   I'm stationed throughout the night.
⁹ Here they come:
   charioteers, pairs of horsemen!"

^k DSS (1QIsaᵃ), Syr; MT *a lion*

One spoke up and said,
"Fallen, fallen is Babylon,
   and all the images of her gods
   are shattered on the ground!"
¹⁰ Oh, my downtrodden people,
   threshed on my threshing floor,
   what I heard from
      the Lord of heavenly forces,
   the God of Israel, I reported to you.

A mysterious dialogue

¹¹ An oracle about Dumah.¹
Someone is calling to me from Seir:
   "Guard, how long is the night?
   Guard, how long is the night?"
¹² The guard said,
   "Morning has come, but it is still night.
   If you must inquire, inquire;
      come back again."

¹³ An oracle about the desert.
In the woods,
   in the desert where you camp,
   caravans of the Dedanites
      ¹⁴ meet the thirsty with water;
   inhabitants of the land of Tema
   greet the refugees with bread.
¹⁵ They have fled from swords,
   from the drawn sword,
   from the bent bow
   and from the intensity of battle.
¹⁶ So the Lord said to me: Within a year, according to the number of years for which a laborer is hired, all the glory of Kedar will end; ¹⁷ there will be few Kedarite archers remaining. The Lord God of Israel has spoken.

Jerusalemites rebuked

22 An oracle about the Valley of Vision.
What is wrong with you,
   that you have all gone up to the rooftops,
   ² you who are filled with noise,
   you roaring city, you party town?
Your dead weren't slaughtered
      by the sword;
   they didn't die in battle.
³ All your leaders escaped together
   but were captured
      without a single bow shot.
   All your escapees were bound together,
   even though they fled far away.ᵐ

⁴ Therefore, I said, "Don't look at me;
   let me weep bitterly.
Don't try to comfort me
   about the destruction
   of my dearly loved people."
⁵ The Lord God of heavenly forces
   has a day of tumult and trampling
   and turmoil in the Valley of Vision,
   a breaking down of walls,
   a cry for help to the mountains.
⁶ Elam carried the quiver
   with chariots and horsemen,
   and Kir uncovered the shield.
⁷ Your finest valleys
   were filled with chariots,
   and horsemen doggedly guarded
      the gate.
⁸ Judah's covering has been stripped away.

On that day, you trusted the weapons
   in the Forest House.
⁹ You observed the many broken defenses
   in David's City,
   and you collected the waters
   of the lower pool.
¹⁰ You counted Jerusalem's houses,
   and you tore down houses
      to fortify the wall.
¹¹ You made a reservoir between the walls
   for the water of the earlier pool.
But you didn't trust its maker;
   you didn't consider the one
      who planned it long ago.

¹² The Lord God of heavenly forces
   called on that day
   for weeping and mourning,
   and shaven heads,
   and wearing of mourning clothes.
¹³ But instead there was
   fun and frivolity,
   killing of cattle
   and slaughtering of sheep,
   eating of meat and drinking of wine:
   "Eat and drink! Tomorrow we will die!"
¹⁴ But the Lord of heavenly forces
   has revealed in my hearing:
   This iniquity won't
   be forgiven you until you die,
   says the Lord God of heavenly forces.

¹LXX *Edom* ᵐHeb uncertain

An administrator rebuked

¹⁵ The LORD God of heavenly forces says,
Go now to this official, to Shebna,
who is in charge of the house,
and say to him:
¹⁶ What do you have here—
and whom do you have here—
that you have hewed out a tomb
for yourself,
you who cuts his grave on high and
carves himself a home in the cliff?
¹⁷ The LORD is about to hurl you down,
mighty man!

He is surely going to cover you
with darkness;
¹⁸ he will indeed unroll your head wrapping,
rolling it like a ball
into the open country.
There you will die,
with your glorious chariots,
you disgrace to the house
of your master!
¹⁹ I will thrust you from your monument;
you will be pulled down
from your platform.
²⁰ On that day, I will call my servant
Eliakim, Hilkiah's son.
²¹ I will give him your robe
and wrap him in your sash,
and I will hand over to him
your authority.
He will be a father
to the inhabitants of Jerusalem
and to the house of Judah.
²² I will place the key to David's house
on his shoulder;
what he opens no one will close,
and what he closes no one will open.
²³ I will fasten him securely like a tent peg,
and he will be a throne of honor
for his ancestors' house.
²⁴ All the honor of his household will hang
on him, the offspring and the offshoots, every
little dish, every bowl, every jar.
²⁵ On that day, says the LORD of heavenly
forces, the peg that is fastened securely will
give way; it will be cut down, and it will fall,
and all the load hanging on it will be lost. The
LORD has spoken.

Concerning Tyre

23 An oracle about Tyre.
Wail, ships of Tarshish,
because your port is destroyed!ⁿ
When returning from Cyprus,
they heard about it.
² Be still, inhabitants of the coast,
traders of Sidon,
whose messengers crossed over the sea,^o
³ over the mighty waters.
The grain of Shihor, the Nile's harvest,
was her income;
she was the marketplace of nations.
⁴ Be ashamed, Sidon,
because the sea has spoken;
the fortress of the sea has said,
"I haven't been in labor; I didn't give birth;
I never raised young men
or brought up young women."
⁵ When the Egyptians hear,
they will be in anguish
at the news about Tyre.
⁶ Cross over to Tarshish;
wail, inhabitants of the coast.
⁷ Is this your triumphant town,
whose origin is from ancient times,
whose feet carried her to settle far away?
⁸ Who planned this concerning Tyre,
the one who gives crowns,
whose merchants were princes,
whose traders were the honored
of the earth?
⁹ The LORD of heavenly forces planned it,
to defile the pride of all beauty,
to shame all the honored of the earth.

¹⁰ Go through your own land,
Daughter Tarshish,
for the harbor^p is gone.
¹¹ God's hand is extended over the sea,
shaking nations.
The LORD gave the command
to destroy Phoenicia's fortresses,
¹² saying, You will no longer celebrate,
violated virgin Daughter Sidon.
Get up and head to Cyprus;
even there you will find no rest.
¹³ Look at the land of the Chaldeans,
the people who are no more.
Assyria destined it for wild animals:

ⁿHeb uncertain ^oCorrection; MT *one crossing over the sea filled you* ^pHeb uncertain

they raised up their siege towers,
stripped its palaces,
and made it a ruin.
¹⁴ Wail, ships of Tarshish,
for your fortress is destroyed!

¹⁵On that day, Tyre will be forgotten seventy years, the lifetime of one king. At the end of seventy years, Tyre will become like the prostitute in the song:

did you know?

Musicians played and sang at times of worship and times of harvest. Since the crops were so bad, there was no harvest or singing for the harvest. Since the people had lost faith in God, there was no worship or singing for the times of worship.

¹⁶ Take a harp, go around the city,
forgotten prostitute.
Play well, sing many songs,
so they'll remember you.

¹⁷At the end of seventy years, the Lord will visit Tyre. She will return to her trade and will prostitute herself with all the kingdoms on the earth. ¹⁸Her profits and wages will be sacred to the Lord. They won't be stored or saved. Her profits will go to those living before the Lord, for plentiful food and elegant clothes.

City of chaos falls

24 Look! The Lord will devastate
the earth and destroy it,
will twist its face
and scatter its inhabitants.
² It will be the same for the people
and for the priest;
for the slave and for his master;
for the female servant
and for her mistress;
for the buyer and for the seller;
for the lender and for the borrower;
for the creditor and for the debtor.
³ The earth will be devastated,
totally devastated;
it will be destroyed,
completely destroyed
because the Lord has said it would be so.

⁴ The earth dries up and wilts;
the world withers and wilts;
the heavens wither away with the earth.

⁵ The earth lies polluted
under its inhabitants,
for they have disobeyed instruction,
swept aside law,
and broken the ancient covenant.
⁶ Therefore, a curse devours the earth;
its inhabitants suffer for their guilt.
Therefore, the earth's inhabitants
dwindle; very few are left.

⁷ The wine dries up;
the vine withers;
all the merry-hearted groan.
⁸ The joyous tambourines have ceased;
the roar of partiers has stopped;
the joyous harp has ceased.
⁹ No one drinks wine or sings;
beer is bitter to its drinkers.
¹⁰ The town is in chaos, broken;
every house is shut, without entrance.
¹¹ There is a cry for wine in the streets.
All joy has reached its dusk;
happiness is exiled from the earth.
¹² Ruin remains in the city,
and the gate is battered to wreckage.
¹³ It will be like this
in the central part of the land
and among the peoples,
like an olive tree that has been shaken,
like remains from the grape harvest.

¹⁴ They raise their voice;
they sing with joy;
from the west
they will shout about
the Lord's majesty.

LIGHTHOUSE

PRAISE GOD

Patient Praise *Isaiah 24:14-15*
In the middle of a terrible time, God gave the people of Israel something to be thankful for. Isaiah told them to rejoice over what God had done. They could shout praises because God is all-powerful, no matter what things look like on the outside.

Isaiah wanted people to look at God's goodness and not at the troubles around them. Praise to God shouldn't depend on how we feel or what we're doing. We should praise God because we trust God to work things out when we have trouble. We should praise God at all times, in all places. ◆

¹⁵ Therefore, in the east honor the LORD;
    in the islands of the sea,
    the name of the LORD God of Israel!
¹⁶ From the ends of the earth
    we have heard songs:
    "Glory to the righteous one!"
    But I say, "I waste away; I waste away;
    I'm doomed!
    Betrayers betray;
    treacherously betrayers betray."

¹⁷ Terror, trench, and trap are upon you,
    ruler of the earth!
¹⁸ Whoever flees from the sound of
    terror will fall into the trench;
    whoever climbs from the trench
    will be caught in the trap.

Heaven's windows will open,
    and the earth's foundations will quake.
¹⁹ The earth is shattering, shattering;
    the earth is shaking, shaking;
    the earth is teetering, tottering.
²⁰ The earth trembles like a drunk
    and shudders like a hut;
    its rebellion weighs heavy upon it;
    it will fall, no more to rise.

²¹ On that day, the LORD will punish the forces of heaven in heaven, and the kings of the earth on earth. ²² They will be gathered together like prisoners in a pit, shut into a prison, and punished after many days. ²³ The moon will be diminished, and the sun will fade, since the LORD of heavenly forces will rule on Mount Zion and in Jerusalem, glorious before his elders.

Rejoicing in God's salvation

25 LORD, you are my God.
    I will exalt you;
    I will praise your name,
    for you have done wonderful things,
    planned long ago, faithful and sure.
² You have turned the city into rubble,
    the fortified town into a ruin,
    the fortress of foreigners
    into a city no more,
    never to be rebuilt.
³ Therefore, strong people will glorify you;
    the towns of tyrant nations will fear you.

⁴ You have been a refuge
    for the poor,
    a refuge for the needy in distress,
    a hiding place from the storm,
    a shade from the heat.
When the breath of tyrants
    is like a winter^q storm,
⁵ or like heat in the desert,
    you subdue the roar of foreigners.
Like heat shaded by a cloud,
    the tyrants' song falls silent.

⁶ On this mountain,
    the LORD of heavenly forces
    will prepare for all peoples
    a rich feast, a feast of choice wines,
    of select foods rich in flavor,
    of choice wines well refined.
⁷ He will swallow up on this mountain
    the veil that is veiling all peoples,
    the shroud enshrouding
    all nations.

LIGHTHOUSE

GOOD NEWS

Light of God's Love *Isaiah 25:7*

Sometimes it's scary to be in the dark, especially if we are alone. We may imagine something is there that can harm us. But when we turn on the light, we can see there was nothing there after all.

Isaiah said God would comfort people so they wouldn't be afraid in the spiritual darkness caused by sin and death. God would send light to the world to show people the way to truth. ◆

⁸ He will swallow up death^r forever.
The LORD God will wipe tears
    from every face;
    he will remove his people's disgrace
    from off the whole earth,
    for the LORD has spoken.
⁹ They will say on that day,
    "Look! This is our God,
    for whom we have waited—
    and he has saved us!
This is the LORD,
    for whom we have waited;
    let's be glad and rejoice in his salvation!"

^q Or *wall* ^r Heb *Maveth*

¹⁰ The Lᴏʀᴅ's hand will indeed rest
    on this mountain.

Moab will be trampled down
    as straw is trampled into manure.
¹¹ When in it they spread out their hands
    as swimmers spread out
      their hands to swim,
    God will lay low their pride,
    even by the efforts of their hands.
¹² The fortified towers of their[s] walls
    will be thrown down, will be leveled,
    will be brought down to the earth,
      to the dust.

Trusting in God forever

26

**Bet
you
can**

read
this in 5
minutes.
**Ready,
set, go!**

On that day, this song
will be sung in the land of Judah:
Ours is a strong city!
    God makes salvation
      its walls and ramparts.
² Open the gates
    and let a righteous nation enter,
    a nation that keeps faith.
³ Those with sound thoughts
    you will keep in peace,
    in peace because they trust in you.
⁴ Trust in the Lᴏʀᴅ forever,
    for the Lᴏʀᴅ is a rock for all ages.
⁵ He has thrown down those living on high,
    and he will level the lofty town,
    leveling it down to the earth;
    he will bring it down to dust.
⁶ The feet trample it,
    the feet of the poor,
    the steps of the needy.

⁷ The way of the righteous is level;
    you clear a path for the righteous.
⁸ In the path of your justice, Lᴏʀᴅ,
    we wait for you;
    with all our being, we long
    for your name and your acclaim.
⁹ At night I long for you
    with my whole being;
    my spirit within me watches for you.
When your judgments
    are at work in the earth,
    those living in the world
    learn righteousness.

¹⁰ When the wicked are favored,
    they don't learn righteousness;
    even among those who do right
    they do wrong,
    and they fail to see the Lᴏʀᴅ's majesty.
¹¹ Lᴏʀᴅ, your hand is lifted up,
    but they don't see.
Let them see and shrink back
    because of your zeal for your people;
    your burning anger
    that consumes your enemies.
¹² Lᴏʀᴅ, grant us peace,
    because all that we have done
    has been your doing.
¹³ Lᴏʀᴅ our God, other masters
    besides you have ruled us,
    but we will profess your name alone.
¹⁴ The dead don't live; ghosts don't rise.
    Indeed, you have punished
      and destroyed them,
    and abolished all memory of them.
¹⁵ You've enlarged the nation, Lᴏʀᴅ.
    You've enlarged the nation;
    you are glorified.
You've expanded
    all the land's boundaries.
¹⁶ Lᴏʀᴅ, in distress they sought you out;
    they poured out prayers to you
    when you disciplined them.
¹⁷ As a pregnant woman close to
    childbirth is in labor pains,
    crying out in her pangs,
    so were we because of you, Lᴏʀᴅ.
¹⁸ We were pregnant, we writhed,
    but we gave birth to wind.
We have achieved no victories on earth;
    the inhabitants of the earth never fall.

¹⁹ Your dead will live, their[t] corpses will rise,
    and those who dwell in the dust
    will shout for joy.
Your shadow is a shadow of light,
    but you will bring down
    the ghosts into the underworld.
²⁰ Go, my people, enter your rooms
    and shut your doors behind you.
Take cover, for in a little while
    the fury will be over.
²¹ Look! The Lᴏʀᴅ is going out from his place

[s] Or *your* [t] Or *my*

to bring the iniquity of the ruler
 of the earth down upon him.
The earth will uncover its blood
 and will conceal its slain no longer.

Scattered people return

27 On that day, the Lᴏʀᴅ will take a great
sword, harsh and mighty, and will punish Leviathan the fleeing serpent, Leviathan
the writhing serpent, and will kill the dragon
that is in the sea. ²On that day:
 Sing about a delightful vineyard!
³ I, the Lᴏʀᴅ, am its guardian.
 Every moment I water it;
 night and day I guard it from attack.
⁴ I'm not angry,
 but if it yields thorns and thistles for me,
 I will march to battle against it;
 I will torch it completely.
⁵ Or let them[u] cling to me for refuge;
 let them make peace with me;
 let them make peace with me.
⁶ In coming days,[v]
 Jacob will take root;
 Israel will blossom and sprout
 and fill the whole world with produce.

⁷ Did God strike Israel
 as he struck those who struck him?
 Was Israel killed
 as his killers were killed?[w]

⁸ By frightening Jerusalem,
 by sending her away,[x]
 you contended with her,
 expelling with a fierce blast
 on the day of the east wind.
⁹ By this Jacob's guilt is reconciled,
 and this was how his sins
 were finally removed:
 he made all the altar stones
 like shattered chalk,
 sacred poles[y] and incense altars
 that couldn't stand.

¹⁰ The fortified city lies alone,
 a hut forsaken,
 abandoned like the desert.
 Calves graze there;
 they lie down there
 and feed on its boughs.
¹¹ When its branches are dry,
 they are broken.
 Women come and set fire to it.
 These people have no understanding;
 therefore, their maker
 won't have compassion;
 the one who formed them
 won't be gracious.

¹²On that day, the Lᴏʀᴅ will beat grain
from the channel of the Euphrates up to the
Valley of Egypt. You will be collected, Israelites, one by one. ¹³On that day, a great trumpet

---

[u]Or it [v]Or those coming [w]Heb uncertain [x]Heb uncertain [y]Heb *asherim*, perhaps objects devoted to the goddess Asherah

Trust in God Forever *Isaiah 26:4*

Life is full of challenges and tough times. Even if your life has been easy
so far, you will most certainly come across times when you have to make
hard decisions. Trusting God is difficult at times. But God wants people
to do just that—trust God and follow God's ways. God is
"a rock for all ages." We can completely trust God with
all that we have and all that we are. When we give our
lives to God, we belong to God forever, and nothing can
take that away. God saves us completely and blesses us more than we can
ever imagine. Trust God with everything—big and small. God cares for us.

What challenges have you faced in your life?
How can you trust God with all you have and all you are?

will be played. Those who were lost in the land of Assyria and those who were scattered in the land of Egypt will come. They will bow to the LORD at his holy mountain in Jerusalem.

Judgment on Ephraim and Judah

28 Oh, the majestic garland of
Ephraim's drunks
and the fading flower
of its splendid beauty
on the head that flows with perfume[z]
of those hammered with wine.
2 Look! The Lord has someone
who is powerful and strong;
like a hailstorm, a disastrous tempest,
like a downpour of mighty,
overflowing waters,
he can level them to the ground
with his hand.
3 The majestic garland of Ephraim's drunks
will be trampled underfoot.
4 The withered flower,
which is a thing of beauty[a]
as it sits on the head
of those bloated with fat,[b]
will be like an early fig
before the summer harvest:
whoever sees it
swallows it as soon as it is in hand.

5 On that day, the LORD of heavenly forces will be a splendid garland and a beautiful wreath for the people who survive, 6and a spirit of justice for the one who sits in judgment, and a strength for those who repel the assault at the gate.

7 These also stagger from wine
and stumble from beer:
priest and prophet stagger from beer;
they are confused by wine;
they stray on account of beer;
they err when receiving visions;
they stumble when making judgments.
8 All the tables are covered with vomit;
filth overruns the place.

9 To whom will God teach knowledge?
To whom will he explain the message?
To those just weaned from milk?
To those who have hardly
outgrown the breast?

10 It is "tsav letsav, tsav letsav;
qav leqav, qav leqav,"[c]
a little of this, a little of that.
11 With derisive speech
and a foreign tongue,
he will speak to this people.
12 He has said to them,
"This is the place of rest;
give rest to the weary;
this is the place of repose";
but they refused to listen.
13 So the LORD's word will be for them:
"tsav letsav, tsav letsav;
qav leqav, qav leqav,"
a little of this, a little of that.
So that they will go and stagger backward,
they will be broken,
snared, and captured.

The covenant with death overturned

14 Therefore, hear the LORD's word,
you scoffers who rule this people
in Jerusalem.
15 You said, "We've cut a deal with death;[d]
with the underworld[e] we made a pact.
When the overflowing flood
passes through, it won't reach us;
for we have made lies our hiding place,
and in falsehood we take shelter."
16 Therefore, the LORD God says:
Look! I'm laying in Zion a stone,
a tested stone, a valuable cornerstone,
a sure foundation:
the one who trusts won't tremble.

17 I will make justice the measuring line
and righteousness the plumb line.
But hail will sweep away
the hiding place of lies,
and water will overflow the shelter.
18 Your deal with death[f] will be dissolved,
and your pact with the grave[g]
won't stand.
The rushing flood: when it passes through,
you will be annihilated by it.
19 Every time it passes through
it will take you,
for morning by morning it will pass,
by day and by night.

---

[z]DSS (1QIsa[a]) [a]Heb uncertain [b]Or *at the head of the fat valley* [c]A Hebrew version of baby talk or gibberish [d]Heb *Maveth*
[e]Heb *Sheol* [f]Heb *Maveth* [g]Heb *Sheol*

It will be nothing but terror
  to understand the message.
20 The bed is too short to stretch out,
  and the shroud is too narrow
    to cover oneself.

21 Just as on Mount Perazim,
  the LORD will rise up;
as in the Gibeon Valley he will rage
  to do his deed—strange is his deed!—
  And to work his work—foreign is his work!
22 So now stop your scoffing,
  or your chains will be tightened,
because destruction has been ordered—
  I have heard it!—
by the LORD God of heavenly forces
  against the whole land.

Plowing and threshing

23 Listen and hear my voice;
  pay attention and hear my word:
24 Does the plowman plow
  without stopping for planting,
  opening and harrowing their ground?
25 When he has smoothed its surface,
  doesn't he scatter fennel,[h]
    and sow cumin,
  and plant wheat and barley in their places,
    and spelt as a border?
26 They are properly ordered;
  their God directs them.[i]
27 Fennel[j] isn't threshed
  with a threshing sledge,
nor is a cart wheel rolled over cumin,
  but fennel[k] is beaten with a staff,
    and cumin with a rod.
28 Bread grain is crushed,
  but the thresher[l]
    doesn't thresh it forever.
He drives the cart wheel over it;
  he spreads it out but doesn't crush it.
29 This also comes from
  the LORD of heavenly forces,
who gives wondrous counsel
  and increases wisdom.

Ariel besieged but spared

29 Oh, Ariel, Ariel,
  town where David encamped!
Year by year,
  let the festivals come around—

2 but I will oppress Ariel.
There will be mourning and lamentation;
  she will be like an Ariel to me.
3 I will surround you like a wall,
  and I will lay a siege against you
    with assault towers,
  and I will raise up siegeworks
    against you.
4 You will be brought down;
  from the ground you will speak;
  from low in the dust
    your speech will come.
Your voice will be
  like a ghost's from the earth;
  from the dust your words will whisper.
5 But your many enemies
  will be like fine dust,
  the terrible horde like passing chaff.
Suddenly, in an instant,
  6 the LORD of heavenly forces
will come to you with thunder,
  earthquake, and a mighty voice,
with whirlwind, tempest,
  and flames of devouring fire.
7 The horde of nations
  fighting against Ariel,
and all who make war on her
  and her fortress and besiege her,
will be like a dream, a vision of the night.
8 It will be like when
  a hungry person dreams of eating
  but wakes up and the mouth is empty.
Or when a thirsty person
  dreams of drinking
  but wakes up and has a dry throat.
So will it be for all the horde of nations
  who fight against Mount Zion.

9 Be shocked and stunned;
  blind yourselves; be blind!
Be drunk, but not on wine;
  stagger, but not on account of beer!
10 The LORD has poured on you
  a spirit of deep sleep,
and has shut your eyes, you prophets,
  and covered your heads, you seers.
11 This entire vision has become for you like
the words of a sealed scroll. When they give
it to one who can read, saying, "Read this,"
that one will say, "I can't, because it's sealed."

---

h Or black cumin i Or waters them j Or black cumin k Or black cumin l DSS (1QIsaᵃ)

¹²And when the scroll is given to one who can't read, saying, "Read this," that one will say, "I can't read."

The wisdom of their wise

¹³ The Lord says:
Since these people turn toward me
with their mouths,
and honor me with lip service
while their heart is distant from me,
and their fear of me is just a human
command that has been memorized,
¹⁴ I will go on doing amazing things
to these people,
shocking and startling things.
The wisdom of their wise will perish,
and the discernment of their
discerning will be hidden.
¹⁵ Doom to those who hide
their plan deep, away from the Lord,
whose deeds are in the dark,
who say, "Who sees us? Who knows us?"
¹⁶ You have everything backward!
Should the potter be thought of as clay?
Should what is made say of its maker,
"He didn't make me"?
Should what is shaped
say of the one who shaped it,
"He doesn't understand"?

¹⁷ In just a little while won't Lebanon
become farmland once again,
and the farmland be considered a forest?
¹⁸ On that day:
The deaf will hear
the words of a scroll and,

LIGHTHOUSE

Good News

Patient Faith *Isaiah 29:18*
Sometimes it's hard to wait for good things to happen. God had promised the people of Israel many wonderful things, but the people were tired of waiting for something good to happen. God promised a wonderful day would come when the good news would be heard by people who never knew about it. What God promises always comes true. God wants us to have faith and believe, even when what we hope for doesn't happen right away. ◊

freed from dimness and darkness,
the eyes of the blind will see.
¹⁹ The poor will again find joy in the Lord,
and the neediest of people
will rejoice in the holy one of Israel.
²⁰ The tyrant will be no more,
the mocker will perish,
and all who plot evil will be eliminated:
²¹ all who incriminate others wrongly,
who entrap the judge in the gate,
and pointlessly postpone justice
for the innocent.

²² Therefore, proclaims the Lord,
the God of^m the house of Jacob,
who redeemed Abraham:
Jacob won't be ashamed now,
and his face won't grow pale now.
²³ When he sees his children among them,
the work of my hands,
proclaiming my name holy,
they will make holy
the holy one of Jacob,
and stand in awe of Israel's God.
²⁴ Those who wander in spirit
will have understanding,
and those who grumble will gain insight.

Help from Egypt is futile

30Doom to you, rebellious children,
says the Lord,
who make a plan, which is not mine;
who weave a plot,^n but not by my spirit,
piling up sin on sin;
² setting out to go down to Egypt
without consulting me,
taking refuge in Pharaoh's refuge
and hiding in Egypt's shadow.
³ Pharaoh's refuge will become your shame,
hiding in Egypt's shadow your disgrace.
⁴ Though their officials are in Zoan,
and their messengers reach Hanes,
⁵ all will become shamed
because of a people
who can't assist them.
They are no help; they are no profit;
rather, shame and disgrace.

⁶An oracle about the beasts in the arid southern plain.

---

^mOr *to* ^nHeb uncertain

Through a land of distress and danger,
lioness and roaring[o] lion,
viper and flying serpent,
they will carry their wealth
on donkeys' shoulders
and their treasures on camels' humps
to a people who won't profit,
7 for Egypt's help is utterly worthless.
Therefore, I call her Rahab Who Sits Still.[p]

8 Now go, write it before them on a tablet,
inscribe it on a scroll,
so in the future
it will endure as a witness.
9 These are rebellious people,
lying children,
children unwilling
to hear the LORD's teaching,
10 who say to the seers, "Don't foresee,"
and to the visionaries,
"Don't report truthful visions;
tell us flattering things;
envision deceptions;
11 get out of the way;
step off the path;
let's have no more 'holy one of Israel.'"

12 Therefore, the holy one of Israel says:
Because you reject this word
and trust in oppression and cunning
and rely on them,
13 your sin will be like a crack in a high wall;
it bulges, about to fall:
suddenly, in an instant, it breaks!
14 Its breaking is like
the breaking of a storage jar
that is totally shattered.
No piece from among its fragments
will be large enough
to take fire from a hearth,
or to dip water from a cistern.

15 Therefore, the LORD God,
the holy one of Israel, says:
In return and rest you will be saved;
quietness and trust
will be your strength—
but you refused.
16 You said,
"No! We'll flee on horses"—
therefore, you will indeed flee—
"and we'll ride off;
on swift steeds we will ride"—
therefore, your pursuers will be swift.
17 One thousand will flee at the threat of one,
and at the threat of five you will flee,
until you are left like a flagstaff
on a mountaintop,
like a flag on a hill.
18 Nonetheless, the LORD is waiting
to be merciful to you,
and will rise up to show you compassion.
The LORD is a God of justice;
happy are all who wait for him.

This is the way

19 People in Zion, who live in Jerusalem, you
will weep no longer. God will certainly be merciful to you. Hearing the sound of your outcry,
God will answer you. 20 Though the Lord gives
you the bread of distress and the water of
oppression, your teacher will no longer hide,
but you will see your teacher. 21 If you stray to
the right or the left, you will hear a word that
comes from behind you: "This is the way; walk
in it." 22 You will defile your silver-plated idols
and your gold-covered priestly vest,[q] and you
will scatter them like menstrual rags. "Get
out," you will say to them.

23 God will provide rain for the seed you
sow in the ground, and the food the ground
produces will be rich and abundant. On that
day, your cattle will graze in large pastures.
24 The oxen and donkeys that are working the
ground will eat tasty feed spread for them
with shovel and fork.

25 On every lofty mountain, and on every
high hill, streams will run with water on the
day of the great massacre, when the towers fall. 26 The light of the moon will be like
the light of the sun, and the light of the sun
will be seven times brighter—like the light
of seven days—on the day that the LORD bandages the people's brokenness and heals the
wounds inflicted by his blows.

Assyria punished

27 Look there!
The LORD is coming from far away;
his anger blazing, his smoke-cloud thick.

[o] Or *from them* [p] Or *Rahab the silent* [q] Correction; Heb *ephod*

His lips are full of fury;
  his tongue is like a devouring fire.
²⁸ His breath is like a raging river
  that reaches up to the neck,
  to shake the nations
    with a sieve of destruction,
  and to put a misleading rein
    on the people's jaws.
²⁹ There will be singing for you
  as on the night
    that people celebrate a festival.
  The heart will be joyful as it is
    when one goes with a flute
  to the Lord's mountain,
    to the rock of Israel.

SAILBOAT

Joy

Praise Brings Joy *Isaiah 30:29*
The Jewish festivals always include singing, especially during the Festival of Passover. At church and at home we also sing songs that praise God to celebrate the things God has done. Praise songs remind us of God's goodness and power. We feel good when we sing songs that praise God for the blessings we have received. ♦

³⁰ The Lord will unleash his majestic voice
  and display his crushing arm
    in furious anger,
    with a flame of consuming fire,
  in stormy rain and hail.
³¹ The Lord's voice will terrify Assyria;
  with a rod he will smite it.
³² And every crack that is made
  in the foundation wall,
  which the Lord will bring down
    upon him,
  will be accompanied
    by timbrels and lyres.
  The Lord will raise his arm
  and fight against Assyria in battle.
³³ His place for burning[r]
  was arranged long ago;
  it is indeed made ready for a king.
  God has made its wood pile wide and deep,
  fire and wood in abundance.
  The breath of the Lord, like a stream
  of brimstone, ignites it.

Doom to those going to Egypt

31 Doom to those going down
  to Egypt for help!
  They rely on horses,
    trust in chariots because they are many,
  and on riders
    because they are very strong.
  But they don't look
    to the holy one of Israel;
  they don't seek the Lord.
² But God also knows how to bring disaster;
  he has not taken back his words.
  God will rise up
    against the house of evildoers
  and against the help
    of those who do wrong.
³ Egypt is human and not divine;
  their horses are flesh and not spirit.
  The Lord will extend his hand;
  the helper will stumble,
    those helped will fall,
  and they will all die together.

⁴ The Lord has said to me:
  When the lion growls,
    the young lion, over its prey,
  though a band of shepherds
    is summoned against it,
  isn't scared off by their noise
    or frightened by their roar.
  So the Lord of heavenly forces
    will go down
  to fight on Mount Zion and on her hill.
⁵ Like birds flying aloft,
  so the Lord of heavenly forces
    will shield Jerusalem:
  shielding and saving,
    sparing and rescuing.
⁶ People of Israel, return to the one whom you have deeply betrayed! ⁷ On that day, you will each reject the idols of silver and the idols of gold, which you have sinfully made for yourselves.

⁸ Assyria will fall,
  but not by a human sword—
  a sword not made by humans
    will devour them.
  They will flee before the sword;
  their young men
    will become forced laborers.

ʳHeb *Topheth*

[9] In horror they will flee
  from their stronghold;
  their officers will be terrified
    at the signal,
  says the LORD, whose fire is in Zion
  and whose oven is in Jerusalem.

Righteous rule

32 See here: A king rules
  to promote righteousness;
  rulers govern to promote justice,
[2] each like a shelter from the wind
  and a refuge from a storm,
  like streams of water in a wasteland,
  like the shade of a massive cliff
    in a worn-out land.
[3] Then the eyes of those who can see
  will no longer be blind,
  the ears of those who can hear will listen,
[4] the minds of the rash
    will know and comprehend,
  and the tongues of those who stammer
    will speak fluently and plainly.
[5] Then a fool will no longer
  be called honorable,
  nor a villain considered respectable.
[6] Fools speak folly;
  their minds devise wickedness,
  acting irreverently,
  speaking falsely of the LORD,
  leaving the hungry empty,
  and depriving the thirsty of drink.
[7] As for the villain, his villainies are evil.
  He plans schemes
    to destroy the poor with lying words,
  even when the needy speak justly.
[8] But an honorable person
  plans honorable things
  and stands up for what is honorable.

Warnings to the carefree

[9] Women of leisure, stand up!
  Hear my voice!
  Carefree daughters, listen to my word!
[10] In a little over a year,
  the carefree will shudder,
  because the grape harvest will fail;
  the vintage won't arrive.
[11] Tremble, all of you who are at ease;
  shudder, all of you who are secure!

Strip yourselves, bare your skin,
  and tie mourning clothes
    around your waist,
[12] beating your breasts
  for the pleasant fields,
  for the fruitful vine,
[13] for my people's soil
  growing barbs and thorns,
  for all the joyous houses
  in the jubilant town.
[14] The palace will be deserted,
  the crowded city abandoned.
  Stronghold and watchtower
  will become empty fields forever,
  suited for the pleasure
    of wild donkeys,
  and a pasture for flocks—
[15] until a spirit from on high
  is poured out on us,
  and the desert turns into farmland,
  and the farmland
    is considered a forest.
[16] Then justice will reside in wild lands,
  and righteousness
    will abide in farmlands.
[17] The fruit of righteousness will be peace,
  and the outcome of righteousness,
  calm and security forever.
[18] Then my people will live
  in a peaceful dwelling,
  in secure homes,
    in carefree resting places.
[19] Even if the forest falls[s]
  and the humbled city is laid low,
[20] those who sow beside any stream
  will be happy,
  sending out ox and donkey to graze.

LIFE PRESERVER

Who are "the carefree"?
Isaiah 32:9

The prophet Isaiah was talking to the women of Judah, warning them about what would happen because they were not being faithful to God. Because of their failure to remember God, they were described as carefree, women of leisure. Isaiah noted how they failed to focus on the things that mattered. ◆

[s] Or it will hail when the forest falls

Judgment and hope for the righteous

33 Doom to the destroyer
left undestroyed,
you traitor whom none have betrayed:
when you have finished destroying,
you will be destroyed;
and when you have stopped betraying,
they will betray you.

² Lord, show us favor;
we hope in you.
Be our strength every morning,
our salvation in times
of distress.

LIGHTHOUSE

PRAYER

Daily Prayer *Isaiah 33:2*

When the Israelites knew they were in serious trouble, they started praying to God. They knew their idols couldn't help them fight their powerful enemy. Sometimes we face things we can't defeat alone. At those times we can pray and ask God to help and deliver us. But prayer isn't just for when we're in trouble. We can pray to God every day. The more often we pray, the stronger our relationship with God grows. And as we grow closer to God, our trust grows too. When we pray to God in the morning, we start our day in close contact with our source of protection and strength. ♦

³ At the noise, peoples fled;
on account of your roar,
nations scattered.

⁴ They gathered spoil like insects;
they rushed upon it
like a swarm of locusts.ᵗ

⁵ The Lord is exalted; he lives on high,
filling Zion with
justice and righteousness.

⁶ He will provide security during a lifetime:ᵘ
a source of salvation,
wisdom, and knowledge—
fear of the Lord will be Zion's treasure.ᵛ

⁷ But then those in Arielʷ
cried out in the streets;
messengers of peace wept bitterly.

⁸ The highways were deserted;

travelers left the road.
The covenant was broken;
solemn pledgesˣ were rejected;
no one cared for humanity.

⁹ The land mourned; it wasted away;
Lebanon was ashamed; it withered.
Sharon became like the desert,
and Bashan and Carmel
were dropping their leaves.

¹⁰ Now I will arise, says the Lord.
Now I will exalt myself;
now I will stand tall.

¹¹ You conceive straw, give birth to stubble;
your breath is a fire that devours you.

¹² Peoples will be burned to lime,
thorns cut up and set ablaze.

¹³ You who are far away,
hear what I have done;
and you who are near,
know my strength!

¹⁴ Sinners became terrified in Zion;
trembling seized the godless:
"Who among us can live
with the devouring fire?
Who among us can live
with the everlasting blaze?"

¹⁵ The one who walks righteously
and speaks truthfully,
who rejects profit from extortion,
who waves away a bribe
instead of grabbing it,
who won't listen to bloody plots,
and who won't contemplate
doing something evil.

¹⁶ He will live on the heights;
fortresses in the cliffs will be his refuge.
His food will be provided,
his water guaranteed.

¹⁷ When you gaze upon a king
in his glamour
and look at the surrounding land,

¹⁸ in dismay you will think:
Where is the one who counts?
Where is the one who weighs?
Where is the one who counts towers?

¹⁹ You will no longer see the defiant people,
the people of speech
too obscure to understand,

ᵗHeb uncertain ᵘOr *your times* ᵛOr *his treasure* ʷOr *the valiant;* Heb uncertain ˣCorrection; or *cities;* DSS (1QIsaᵃ) *witnesses*

who stammer
in an incomprehensible language.
²⁰ Gaze upon Zion, our festival town.
Your eyes will see Jerusalem,
a carefree dwelling,
a tent that is not packed up,
whose stakes are never pulled up,
whose ropes won't snap.
²¹ The Lord's majesty will be there for us:
as a place of rivers, broad streams
where no boat will go,
no majestic ship will cross.
²² The Lord is our judge;
the Lord is our leader;
the Lord is our king—
he will deliver us.
²³ Your ropes are loosened;
they can't hold the mast firmly;
they can't spread the sail.
Then abundant spoil will be divided;
even the lame will seize spoil.
²⁴ And no inhabitant will say, "I'm sick."
The people living there
will be forgiven their sin.

Vengeance against Edom

34 Draw near, you nations, to hear;
and listen, you peoples.
Hear, earth and all who fill it,
world and all its offspring.
² The Lord rages against all the nations,
and is angry with all their armies.
God is about to wipe them out
and has prepared them for slaughter.
³ Their dead will be cast out,
the stench of their corpses will rise,
and the mountains
will melt from their blood.
⁴ All the stars of heaven will dissolve,
the skies will roll up like a scroll,
and all the stars will fall,
like a leaf withering from a vine,
like fruit from a fig tree.

⁵ When my sword has drunk its fill
in the heavens,
it will descend upon Edom for judgment,
upon a people
I have doomed for destruction.
⁶ The Lord has a sword covered with blood;
it is soaked with fat

from the blood of lambs and goats,
from the kidney fat of rams,
for the Lord has a sacrifice in Bozrah,
a great slaughter in the land of Edom.
⁷ Wild oxen will fall with them,
steers with mighty bulls,
and their land will be drenched with blood;
its soil soaked with fat.
⁸ The Lord has a day of vengeance,
a year of payback for Zion's cause.

⁹ Edom's streams will be turned into pitch,
its dust into sulfur,
and its land will become burning pitch.
¹⁰ Night and day won't be extinguished;
its smoke will go up forever.
From generation to generation
it will lie waste;
no one will ever pass through it again.
¹¹ Screech owls and crows will possess it;
owls and ravens will live there.^y
God will stretch over it
the measuring line of chaos
and the plummet stone of emptiness
over its officials.
¹² No Kingdom There, they will call it,
and all its princes will disappear.
¹³ Thorns will grow up in its palaces,
weeds and brambles in its fortresses.
It will be a dwelling for jackals,
a home for ostriches.
¹⁴ Wildcats will meet hyenas,
the goat demon will call to his friends,
and there Lilith^z will lurk
and find her resting place.
¹⁵ There the snake will nest and lay eggs
and brood and hatch in its shadow.
There too vultures will gather,
each with its mate.^a
¹⁶ Consult the Lord's scroll and read:
Not one of these will be missing;
none will lack its mate.
God's own mouth has commanded;
God's own spirit has gathered them.
¹⁷ God has cast the lot for them;
God's hand allotted it to them
with the measuring line.
They will possess it forever;
they will live in it
from generation to generation.

---

^ySpecies uncertain ^zName of a demon ^aSpecies uncertain

Fertile wilderness

35 The desert and the dry land
will be glad;
the wilderness will rejoice
and blossom like the crocus.
² They will burst into bloom,
and rejoice with joy and singing.
They will receive the glory of Lebanon,
the splendor of Carmel and Sharon.
They will see the Lord's glory,
the splendor of our God.

³ Strengthen the weak hands,
and support the unsteady knees.
⁴ Say to those who are panicking:
"Be strong! Don't fear!
Here's your God,
coming with vengeance;
with divine retribution
God will come to save you."

⁵ Then the eyes of the blind
will be opened,
and the ears of the deaf will be cleared.
⁶ Then the lame will leap like the deer,
and the tongue of the speechless
will sing.
Waters will spring up in the desert,
and streams in the wilderness.
⁷ The burning sand will become a pool,
and the thirsty ground,
fountains of water.
The jackals' habitat, a pasture;ᵇ
grass will become reeds and rushes.
⁸ A highway will be there.
It will be called The Holy Way.
The unclean won't travel on it,
but it will be for those walking
on that way.ᶜ
Even fools won't get lost on it;
⁹ no lion will be there,
and no predator will go up on it.
None of these will be there;
only the redeemed will walk on it.
¹⁰ The Lord's ransomed ones
will return and enter Zion
with singing,
with everlasting joy upon their heads.
Happiness and joy will overwhelm them;
grief and groaning will flee away.

Sennacherib's message

36 Assyria's King Sennacherib marched
against all of Judah's fortified cities
and captured them in the fourteenth year of
King Hezekiah. ²Assyria's king sent his field
commander from Lachish, together with a
large army, to King Hezekiah at Jerusalem.
He stood at the water channel of the Upper
Pool, which is on the road to the field where
clothes are washed. ³Hilkiah's son Eliakim,
who was the palace administrator, Shebna
the secretary, and Asaph's son Joah the recorder went out to them.

⁴Then the field commander said to them,
"Say to Hezekiah: Assyria's Great King says
this: Why do you feel so confident? ⁵Do you
think that empty words are the same as good
strategy and the strength to fight? Who are
you trusting that you now rebel against me?
⁶It appears that you are trusting in a staff—
Egypt—that's nothing but a broken reed! It
will stab the hand of anyone who leans on
it! That's all that Pharaoh, Egypt's king, is to
anyone who trusts in him. ⁷Now suppose you
say to me, 'We trust in the Lord our God.' Isn't
he the one whose shrines and altars Hezekiah
removed, telling Judah and Jerusalem, 'You
must worship only at this altar'?

⁸"So now, make a wager with my master,
Assyria's king. I'll give you two thousand
horses if you can supply the riders! ⁹How will
you drive back even the least important official among my master's servants when you
are relying on Egypt for chariots and riders?
¹⁰What's more, do you think I've marched
against this place to destroy it without the
Lord's support? It was the Lord who told me,
'March against this land and destroy it!'"

¹¹Eliakim, Shebna, and Joah said to the
field commander, "Please speak to your servants in Aramaic, because we understand it.
Don't speak with us in Hebrew,ᵈ because the
people on the wall will hear it."

¹²The field commander said to them, "Did
my master send me to speak these words just
to you and your master and not also to the
men on the wall? They are the ones who will
have to eat their dung and drink their urine
along with you." ¹³Then the field commander
stood up and shouted in Hebrew at the top of

ᵇHeb uncertain ᶜHeb uncertain ᵈMT *Judean,* so also 36:13

his voice: "Listen to the message of the great king, Assyria's king. [14]The king says this: Don't let Hezekiah lie to you. He won't be able to rescue you. [15]Don't let Hezekiah persuade you to trust the LORD by saying, 'The LORD will certainly rescue us. This city won't be handed over to Assyria's king.'

[16]"Don't listen to Hezekiah, because this is what Assyria's king says: Surrender to me and come out. Then each of you will eat from your own vine and fig tree and drink water from your own well [17]until I come to take you to a land just like your land. It will be a land of grain and new wine, a land of bread and vineyards. [18]Don't let Hezekiah fool you by saying, 'The LORD will rescue us.' Did any of the other gods of the nations save their lands from the power of Assyria's king? [19]Where are the gods of Hamath and Arpad? Where are the gods of Sepharvaim? Did they rescue Samaria from my power? [20]Which one of the gods from those countries has rescued their land from my power? Will the LORD save Jerusalem from my power?"

[21]But they kept quiet and didn't answer him with a single word, because King Hezekiah's command was, "Don't answer him!" [22]Hilkiah's son Eliakim, who was the palace administrator, Shebna the secretary, and Asaph's son Joah the recorder came to Hezekiah with ripped clothes. They told him what the field commander had said.

Hezekiah and Isaiah

37 When King Hezekiah heard this, he ripped his clothes, covered himself with mourning clothes, and went to the LORD's temple. [2]He sent Eliakim the palace administrator, Shebna the secretary, and the senior priests to the prophet Isaiah, Amoz's son. They were all wearing mourning clothes. [3]They said to him, "Hezekiah says this: Today is a day of distress, punishment, and humiliation. It's as if children are ready to be born, but there's no strength to see it through. [4]Perhaps the LORD your God heard all the words of the field commander who was sent by his master, Assyria's king. He insulted the living God! Perhaps he will punish him for the words that the LORD your God has heard. Offer up a prayer for those few people who still survive."

[5]When King Hezekiah's servants got to Isaiah, [6]Isaiah said to them, "Say this to your master: The LORD says this: Don't be afraid at the words you heard, which the officers of Assyria's king have used to insult me. [7]I'm about to mislead him, so when he hears a rumor, he'll go back to his own country. Then I'll have him cut down by the sword in his own land."

[8]The field commander heard that the Assyrian king had left Lachish. So he went back to the king and found him attacking Libnah. [9]Then the Assyrian king learned that Cush's King Tirhakah was on his way to fight against him. So he sent messengers to Hezekiah again: [10]"Say this to Judah's King Hezekiah: Don't let the God you trust deceive you by saying, 'Jerusalem won't fall to the Assyrian king.' [11]You yourself have heard what Assyrian kings do to other countries, wiping them out. Is it likely that you will be saved? [12]Did the gods of the nations that my ancestors destroyed save them, the gods of Gozan, Haran, Rezeph, or the people of Eden in Telassar? [13]Where now is Hamath's king, Arpad's king, or the kings of Lair, Sepharvaim, Hena, or Ivvah?"[e]

Hezekiah prays

[14]Hezekiah took the letters from the messengers and read them. Then he went to the temple and spread them out before the LORD. [15]Hezekiah prayed to the LORD:

[16]"LORD of heavenly forces, God of Israel: you sit enthroned on the winged creatures. You alone are God over all the earth's kingdoms. You made both heaven and earth. [17]LORD, turn your ear this way and hear! LORD, open your eyes and see! Listen to Sennacherib's words. He sent them to insult the living God! [18]It's true, LORD, that the Assyrian kings have destroyed all the nations and their lands. [19]The Assyrians burned the gods of those nations with fire because they aren't real gods. They are only man-made creations of wood and stone. That's how the Assyrians could destroy them. [20]So now, LORD our God, please save us from Sennacherib's power! Then all the earth's kingdoms will know that you alone are LORD."

Bet you can read this in 5 minutes. **Ready, set, go!**

---

[e]Or the king of the city of Sepharvaim; or the king of the city of Sepharvaim, Hena, and Ivvah

²¹Then Isaiah, Amoz's son, sent a message to Hezekiah: The Lord God of Israel says this: Since you prayed to me about Assyria's King Sennacherib, ²²this is the message that the Lord has spoken against him:

The young woman, Daughter Zion,
   despises you and mocks you;
   Daughter Jerusalem shakes her head
      behind your back.
²³ Whom did you insult and ridicule?
   Against whom did you raise your voice
      and look on with disdain?
   It was against the holy one of Israel!
²⁴ With your servants,
   you've insulted the Lord;
   you said, "I, with my many chariots,
      have gone up to
         the highest mountains,
      to the farthest reaches of Lebanon.
   I have cut down its tallest cedars,
      the best of its pine trees.
   I have reached
      its most remote lodging place,
      its best forest.
²⁵ I have dug wells,
      have drunk water in foreign lands.ᶠ
   With my own feet,
      I dried up all of Egypt's streams."
²⁶ Haven't you heard?
   I set this up long ago;
      I planned it in the distant past!
   Now I have made it happen,
      making fortified cities
         collapse into piles of rubble.
²⁷ Their citizens have lost their power;
      they are frightened and dismayed.
   They've become like plants in a field,
      tender green shoots,
      the grass on rooftops,
         blasted by the east wind.
²⁸ I know where you are,
      how you go out and come in,
      and how you rage against me.
²⁹ Because you rage against me
      and because your pride
         has reached my ears,
   I will put my hook in your nose
      and my bit in your mouth.
   I will make you go back
      the same way you came.

³⁰Now this will be the sign for you, Hezekiah: This year you will eat what grows by itself. Next year you will eat what grows from that. But in the third year, plant seed and harvest it; plant vineyards and eat their fruit. ³¹The survivors of Judah's family who have escaped will put down roots and bear fruit above. ³²Those who remain will go out from Jerusalem, and those who survive will go out from Mount Zion. The zeal of the Lord of heavenly forces will do this.

³³Therefore, the Lord says this about Assyria's king: He won't enter this city. He won't shoot a single arrow here. He won't come near the city with a shield. He won't build a ramp to besiege it. ³⁴He'll go back by the same way he came. He won't enter this city, declares the Lord. ³⁵I will defend this city and save it for my sake and for the sake of my servant David.

³⁶The Lord's messenger went out and struck down one hundred eighty-five thousand soldiers in the Assyrian camp. When people got up the next morning, there were dead bodies everywhere. ³⁷So Assyria's King Sennacherib left and went back to Nineveh, where he stayed. ³⁸Later, while he was worshipping in the temple of his god Nisroch, his sons Adrammelech and Sharezer killed him with a sword. Then they escaped to the land of Ararat. His son Esarhaddon ruled after him.

Hezekiah's illness

38At about that time Hezekiah became deathly sick. The prophet Isaiah, Amoz's son, came to him and said: "The Lord God says this: Put your affairs in order because you are about to die. You won't survive this."

²Hezekiah turned his face to the wall and prayed to the Lord: ³"Please, Lord, remember how I've walked before you in truth and sincerity. I've done what you consider to be good." Then Hezekiah cried and cried.

⁴Then the Lord's word came to Isaiah: ⁵"Go and say to Hezekiah: The Lord, the God of your ancestor David, says this: I have heard your prayer and have seen your tears. I will add fifteen years to your life. ⁶I will rescue you and this city from the power of the Assyrian king. I will defend this city. ⁷This will be your sign from the Lord that he will do what he promised: ⁸once the shadow cast by the sun

---

ᶠ Heb uncertain; DSS (1QIsaᵃ) *in foreign lands*

descends on the steps of Ahaz, I will make it back up ten steps." And the sun went back ten of the steps that it had already descended.

[9]A composition by Judah's King Hezekiah when he was sick and then recovered from his sickness:

[10] I thought, I must depart
  in the prime of my life;
  I have been relegated to the gates
    of the underworld[g]
    for the rest of my life.
[11] I thought, I won't see the LORD.
  The LORD is in the land of the living.
  I won't look upon humans again
    or be with the inhabitants of the world.
[12] My lifetime is plucked up
    and taken from me like a shepherd's tent.
  My life is shriveled like woven cloth;
    God cuts me off from the loom.
  Between daybreak and nightfall
    you carry out your verdict against me.
[13] I cried out[h] until morning:
    "Like a lion God crushes all my bones.
  Between daybreak and nightfall
    you carry out your verdict against me.
[14] Like a swallow[i] I chirp;
    I moan like a dove.
  My eyes have grown weary
    looking to heaven.
  Lord, I'm overwhelmed; support me!"

[15] What can I say?
  God has spoken to me;

he himself has acted.
  I will wander[j] my whole life
    with a bitter spirit.
[16] The LORD Most High is
  the one who gives life to every heart,
    who gives life to the spirit![k]
[17] Look, he indeed exchanged my
    bitterness for wholeness.[l]

You yourself have spared[m] my whole being
    from the pit of destruction,
  because you have cast all my sins
    behind your back.
[18] The underworld[n] can't thank you,
    nor can death[o] praise you;
  those who go down to the pit
    can't hope for your faithfulness.
[19] The living, the living can thank you,
    as I do today.
  Parents will tell children
    about your faithfulness.
[20] The LORD has truly saved me,
    and we will make music[p]
  at the LORD's house
    all the days of our lives.

[21]Then Isaiah said, "Prepare a salve made from figs, put it on the swelling, and he'll get better."

[22]Hezekiah said to Isaiah, "What's the sign that I'll be able to go up to the LORD's temple?"

The Babylonian king's messengers

39 At that time, Babylon's King Merodach-baladan, Baladan's son, sent letters and a gift to Hezekiah, for he heard that he had been ill and had recovered. [2]Hezekiah was pleased, and he showed them his treasury—the silver and the gold, the spices and fine oil—and everything in his armory, all that was found in his storerooms. There wasn't a thing in his house or in all his realm that Hezekiah didn't show them.

[3]Then Isaiah the prophet came to King Hezekiah and said to him, "What did these men say? Where did they come from?"

Hezekiah replied, "They came to me from a distant land, from Babylon."

[4]So Isaiah said, "What did they see in your house?"

SAILBOAT

OBEDIENCE

Trouble-free? *Isaiah 38:3*

When King Hezekiah heard that he would soon die, he became afraid and cried. But then he did the best thing he could do. He prayed, telling God he had always been a faithful and obedient king. People sometimes think that if they obey God, they should never have any problems. But sometimes trouble comes even when we've been obedient. No matter what happens to us, we should remember God is always near. We can talk to God about any problem that we have. God hears us when we pray and will help us. ◆

---

[g]Heb Sheol [h]Or I lay down [i]Heb uncertain [j]Heb uncertain [k]Heb uncertain [l]Heb uncertain [m]Cf LXX, Vulg; MT loved [n]Heb Sheol [o]Heb Maveth [p]Or my stringed instruments

Hezekiah said, "They saw everything in my house. There was nothing in my storerooms that I didn't show them."

⁵Isaiah said to Hezekiah, "Hear the word of the Lᴏʀᴅ of heavenly forces: ⁶Days are coming when all that is in your house, which your ancestors have stored up until this day, will be carried to Babylon. Nothing will be left, says the Lᴏʀᴅ. ⁷Some of your sons, your own descendants whom you fathered, will be taken to become eunuchs in the king of Babylon's palace."

⁸Hezekiah said to Isaiah, "The Lᴏʀᴅ's word that you delivered is good," since he thought, That means there will be peace and security in my lifetime.

Comfort for God's people

40 Comfort, comfort my people! says your God.
² Speak compassionately to Jerusalem,
   and proclaim to her that her
      compulsory service has ended,
   that her penalty has been paid,
   that she has received from the Lᴏʀᴅ's
      hand double for all her sins!

³ A voice is crying out:
"Clear the Lᴏʀᴅ's way in the desert!
   Make a level highway in the wilderness
      for our God!
⁴ Every valley will be raised up,
   and every mountain and hill
      will be flattened.
   Uneven ground will become level,
   and rough terrain a valley plain.
⁵ The Lᴏʀᴅ's glory will appear,
   and all humanity will see it together;
   the Lᴏʀᴅ's mouth has commanded it."

⁶ A voice was saying:
   "Call out!"
And another[q] said,
   "What should I call out?"
   All flesh is grass;
   all its loyalty is
      like the flowers of the field.
⁷ The grass dries up
   and the flower withers
      when the Lᴏʀᴅ's breath blows on it.

Surely the people are grass.
⁸ The grass dries up;
   the flower withers,
   but our God's word will exist forever.

⁹ Go up on a high mountain,
   messenger Zion!
Raise your voice and shout,
   messenger Jerusalem!
Raise it; don't be afraid;
   say to the cities of Judah,
   "Here is your God!"
¹⁰ Here is the Lᴏʀᴅ God,
   coming with strength,
   with a triumphant arm,
   bringing his reward with him
   and his payment before him.
¹¹ Like a shepherd, God will tend the flock;
   he will gather lambs in his arms
   and lift them onto his lap.
   He will gently guide the nursing ewes.

The incomparable God

¹² Who has measured the waters
   in the palm of a hand
   or gauged the heavens with a ruler
   or scooped the earth's dust up
      in a measuring cup
   or weighed the mountains on a scale
   and the hills in a balance?
¹³ Who directed the Lᴏʀᴅ's spirit
   and acted as God's advisor?
¹⁴ Whom did he consult
   for enlightenment?
   Who taught him the path of justice
      and knowledge
   and explained to him
      the way of understanding?
¹⁵ Look, the nations are like a drop
   in a bucket,
   and valued as dust on a scale.
   Look, God weighs the islands
   like fine dust.
¹⁶ Lebanon doesn't have enough fuel;
   its animals aren't enough
   for an entirely burned offering.
¹⁷ All the nations
   are like nothing before God.
   They are viewed as
      less than nothing and emptiness.

---

[q]MT; DSS (1QIsaᵃ), LXX *I*

¹⁸ So to whom will you equate God;
  to what likeness will you compare him?
¹⁹ An idol? A craftsman pours it,
  a metalworker covers it with gold,
  and fashions silver chains.
²⁰ The one who sets up an image
  chooses wood that won't rot[r]
  and then seeks a skilled artisan
  to set up an idol that won't move.
²¹ Don't you know? Haven't you heard?
  Wasn't it announced to you
    from the beginning?

Haven't you understood
  since the earth was founded?
²² God inhabits the earth's horizon—
  its inhabitants are like locusts—
  stretches out the skies like a curtain
  and spreads it out like a tent for dwelling.
²³ God makes dignitaries useless
  and the earth's judges into nothing.
²⁴ Scarcely are they planted, scarcely sown,
  scarcely is their shoot rooted in the earth
  when God breathes on them,
    and they dry up;
  the windstorm carries them off like straw.
²⁵ So to whom will you compare me,
  and who is my equal? says the holy one.

Power for the weary
²⁶ Look up at the sky and consider:
  Who created these?
  The one who brings out
    their attendants one by one,

did you know? In Bible times, some cultures worshipped the stars as if they were gods. Isaiah proclaimed God is bigger than the stars. God is the creator of the stars who always makes sure each one is in its right place.

[r] Heb uncertain

God's Thoughts ◆ My Thoughts

Incomparable Isaiah 40:12

If you've ever tried to hold water in the palm of your hand, then you know it's very hard to do. You might be able to scoop up a few sips, but not much more. Imagine if God had palms, says the writer of this verse. God would be able to scoop up all the waters of the world! If God had a ruler, it would be big enough to measure the sky. God's scale would be so gigantic it could weigh the mountains. God isn't some sort of invisible giant, but these images remind us that there is nothing else in the world like God. No one can do the things that God has done. One word for this is *incomparable*.

We can't hold the waters of the oceans in our palms or measure the sky with our rulers. We aren't incomparable like God. But we are incomparable in God's eyes, because God made us and loves us just the way we are.

What would happen if we stopped comparing ourselves to other people? Instead, we might say, "I don't have to be the fastest runner, or the best guitar player, or the smartest, or the _____ (fill in the blank). I like the way God made me!" When God looks at us, God says, "You are incomparable!"

Name one trait you have that you think is special. Why?

How does knowing God sees you as incomparable change your thoughts about yourself?

summoning each of them by name.
Because of God's great strength
and mighty power, not one is missing.
²⁷ Why do you say, Jacob,
and declare, Israel,
"My way is hidden from the LORD,
my God ignores my predicament"?
²⁸ Don't you know? Haven't you heard?
The LORD is the everlasting God,
the creator of the ends of the earth.
He doesn't grow tired or weary.
His understanding is beyond human reach,
²⁹ giving power to the tired
and reviving the exhausted.
³⁰ Youths will become tired and weary,
young men will certainly stumble;
³¹ but those who hope in the LORD
will renew their strength;
they will fly up on wings like eagles;
they will run and not be tired;
they will walk and not be weary.

Victor from the east

41 Be quiet before me, coastlands.
Let the nations renew their strength.
Let them approach and speak.
Let's draw near for a judgment.
² Who has awakened one from the east
and has authority to summon him
to serve—
giving him nations,
conquering kings,
making them like dust with his sword,
like scattered straw with his bow?
³ He pursues them and passes untouched,
needing no path for his feet.
⁴ Who has acted and who has done this,
calling upon generation after generation
since the beginning?
I, the LORD, was first,
and I will be the last!

⁵ The coastlands see and fear;
the ends of the earth tremble;
they draw near and arrive.
⁶ Each helps the other,
each saying to the other, "Take courage!"
⁷ The craftsman encourages the metalworker;
the one who smoothes with the hammer
encourages the one who strikes the anvil,
saying of the welding, "That's good,"
and strengthening it with nails
so it won't move.

Israel as God's servant

⁸ But you, Israel my servant,
Jacob, whom I have chosen,
offspring of Abraham, whom I love,
⁹ you whom I took
from the ends of the earth
and called from its farthest corners,
saying to you, "You are my servant;
I chose you and didn't reject you":
¹⁰ Don't fear, because I am with you;
don't be afraid, for I am your God.
I will strengthen you,
I will surely help you;
I will hold you
with my righteous strong hand.
¹¹ All who rage against you
will be shamed and disgraced.
Those who contend with you
will be as nothing and will perish.
¹² You will look for your opponents,
and won't find them.
Those who fight you
will be of no account and will die.
¹³ I am the LORD your God,
who grasps your strong hand,
who says to you,
Don't fear; I will help you.
¹⁴ Don't fear, worm of Jacob,
people of Israel!
I will help you, says the LORD.
The holy one of Israel is your redeemer.
¹⁵ Look, I've made you
into a new threshing tool
with sharp teeth.
You will thresh mountains
and pulverize them;
you will reduce hills to straw.
¹⁶ When you winnow them,
the wind will carry them off;
the tempest will scatter them.
You will rejoice in the LORD
and take pride in the holy one of Israel.
¹⁷ The poor and the needy
seek water, and there is none;
their tongues are parched with thirst.
I, the LORD, will respond to them;
I, the God of Israel, won't abandon them.
¹⁸ I will open streams on treeless hilltops
and springs in valleys.
I will make the desert into ponds
and dry land into cascades of water.

19 I will plant in the desert cedar, acacia,
  myrtle, and olive trees;
  I will put in the wilderness cypress,
    elm, and pine as well,
20 so that they will see and know
  and observe and comprehend
  that the LORD's hand has done this,
  and the holy one of Israel has created it.

Other gods challenged

21 Present your case, says the LORD.
  Bring forward your evidence,
  says Jacob's king.
22 Let the idols[s] approach
  and tell us what will happen.
  The prior things—what are they?
  Announce them,
    and we'll think about them
  and know their significance.
  Or proclaim to us what is to come!
23 Report things that will happen
  in the future,
  then we'll know that you are gods.
  Do good! Or do bad!
  Then we will all be afraid and fearful.
24 Look! You are nobody,
  and your deeds are nothing.
  Whoever chooses you is disgusting.
25 I woke up one from the north and he came;
  from the east, one who calls my name.
  He tramples governors like mud,
  as a potter treads clay.
26 Who announced this from the start
    so that we would know;
    from an earlier time

SAILBOAT

Joy

A Separation Process Isaiah 41:16
When the Israelites harvested their crops, they used different methods to separate the grain (the usable part) from the chaff (the part that was waste). People would throw the stalks into the air. The heavier grain would fall to the ground, while the lightweight chaff would be blown away by the wind. God promised to blow Israel's enemies away and scatter them about like the chaff from the grain. Then the people would have great joy. ◆

  so we would say, "That's right"?
Truly, no one announced it,
  no one proclaimed it,
  and no one heard your words.
27 I first said it to Zion, "Look, here they are";
  to Jerusalem I now send a herald.
28 But I look, and there's no one
  among them, no counselor;
  and when I ask,
  no one can answer.
29 Look, all of them are frauds;
  their deeds amount to nothing;
  their images are a total delusion.

God's servant described

42 But here is my servant,
    the one I uphold;
  my chosen, who brings me delight.
  I've put my spirit upon him;
  he will bring justice to the nations.
2 He won't cry out or shout aloud
  or make his voice heard in public.
3 He won't break a bruised reed;
  he won't extinguish a faint wick,
  but he will surely bring justice.
4 He won't be extinguished or broken
  until he has established justice
    in the land.
  The coastlands await his teaching.

5 God the LORD says—
  the one who created the heavens,
  the one who stretched them out,
  the one who spread out the earth
    and its offspring,
  the one who gave breath to its people
  and life to those who walk on it—
6 I, the LORD, have called you
  for a good reason.
  I will grasp your hand and guard you,
  and give you as a covenant to the people,
  as a light to the nations,
7 to open blind eyes,
    to lead the prisoners from prison,
  and those who sit in darkness
    from the dungeon.
8 I am the LORD;
  that is my name;
  I don't hand out my glory to others
  or my praise to idols.

---

[s]Or them

⁹ The things announced in the past—
  look—they've already happened,
  but I'm declaring new things.
  Before they even appear,
  I tell you about them.

Warrior and mother

¹⁰ Sing to the LORD a new song!
  Sing his praise
    from the ends of the earth!
  You who sail the sea and all that fills it,
    the coastlands and their residents.
¹¹ Let the desert and its towns shout aloud,
    the villages that Kedar inhabits.
  Let the cliff dwellers sing;
    from the top of the mountains
    let them shout.
¹² Let them give the LORD glory
    and declare God's praise
    in the coastlands.
¹³ The LORD will go out like a soldier;
    like a warrior God will stir up rage.
  God will shout, will roar;
    over enemies he will prevail.
¹⁴ I've kept still for a very long time.
    I've been silent and restrained myself.
  Like a woman in labor I will moan;
    I will pant, I will gasp.
¹⁵ I will wither mountains and valleys,
    and I will dry up all their vegetation.
  I will turn rivers into deserts,[t]
    and I will dry up pools.
¹⁶ I will make the blind walk a road
    they don't know,
  and I will guide them
    in paths they don't know.
  But I will make darkness before them
    into light
  and rough places into level ground.
  These things I will do;
    I won't abandon them.

Blindness and deafness

¹⁷ Turned backward, utterly shamed
    are those who trust in idols,
  who say to a cast image,
    "You are our god!"
¹⁸ Hear, deaf ones,
    and blind ones, look and see!
¹⁹ Who is blind if not my servant

and deaf like my messenger
    whom I send?
  Who is blind like the restored one,[u]
    blind like the servant of the LORD?
²⁰ You have seen many things,
    but don't keep watch.
  With ears open, you don't hear.[v]
²¹ The LORD desired
    for the sake of his righteousness
    to expand and glorify the Instruction.
²² But this is a people plundered and looted,
    everyone trapped in holes
    and hidden in dungeons.
  They have become plunder
    with no one to rescue,
  loot with no one to say, "Give it back."

²³ Which of you will listen to this,
    will pay attention and respond
    from now on?
²⁴ Who gave Jacob to the looter,
    and Israel to the plunderers?
  Wasn't it the LORD,
    the one we sinned against?
  They were not willing to walk
    in God's ways,
  and wouldn't listen to his teaching.
²⁵ So God poured out on Jacob
    the heat of his anger
    and the fury of battle.
  It scorched him, and he didn't know it;
    it burned him,
    but he didn't give it much thought.

Don't fear

43

But now, says the LORD—
  the one who created you, Jacob,
  the one who formed you, Israel:
Don't fear, for I have redeemed you;
  I have called you by name;
  you are mine.
² When you pass through the waters,
  I will be with you;
  when through the rivers,
    they won't sweep over you.
When you walk
  through the fire,
  you won't
  be scorched
  and flame won't burn you.

Bet you can!
read this in 4 minutes. Ready, set, go!

Memorize
Isa 43:2

---

[t] Or *islands* [u] Heb *Meshullam*, possibly a proper name [v] Or *he does not hear*

³I am the Lord your God,
　the holy one of Israel, your savior.
I have given Egypt as your ransom,
　Cush and Seba in your place.
⁴Because you are precious in my eyes,
　you are honored, and I love you.
I give people in your place,
　and nations in exchange for your life.
⁵Don't fear,
　I am with you.
From the east I'll bring your children;
　from the west I'll gather you.
⁶I'll say to the north, "Give them back!"
　and to the south, "Don't detain them."
Bring my sons from far away,
　and my daughters
　　from the end of the earth,
⁷everyone who is called by my name
　and whom I created for my glory,
　whom I have formed and made.

⁸Bring out the blind people who have eyes,
　the deaf ones who have ears.
⁹All the nations are gathered together;
　the peoples are assembled.
Which of them announced this?
　Who predicted to us the past events?
Let them bring their witnesses
　as a defense;
let them hear and say, "It's true!"
¹⁰You are my witnesses, says the Lord,
　my servant, whom I chose,
so that you would know and believe me
　and understand that I am the one.
Before me no god was formed;
　after me there has been no other.
¹¹I, I am the Lord,
　and there is no savior besides me.
¹²I announced, I saved, I proclaimed,
　not some stranger among you.
You are my witnesses, says the Lord,
　and I am God.
¹³From the dawn of time, I am the one.
　No one can escape my power.
　I act, and who can undo it?

Don't remember
¹⁴The Lord your redeemer,
　the holy one of Israel, says,
For your sake,
　I have sent an army^w to Babylon,
and brought down all the bars,
　turning the Chaldeans' singing
　　into a lament.^x
¹⁵I am the Lord, your holy one,
　Israel's creator, your king!
¹⁶The Lord says—
　who makes a way in the sea
　and a path in the mighty waters,
¹⁷who brings out chariot and horse,
　army and battalion;
they will lie down together
　and will not rise;
they will be extinguished,
　extinguished like a wick.
¹⁸Don't remember the prior things;
　don't ponder ancient history.
¹⁹Look! I'm doing a new thing;
　now it sprouts up; don't you recognize it?
I'm making a way in the desert,
　paths^y in the wilderness.
²⁰The beasts of the field,
　the jackals and ostriches, will honor me,
because I have put water in the desert
　and streams in the wilderness
to give water to my people,
　my chosen ones,
²¹this people whom I formed for myself,
　who will recount my praise.

²²But you didn't call out to me, Jacob;
　you were tired of me, Israel.
²³You didn't bring me lambs
　for your entirely burned offering;
　you didn't honor me with your sacrifices.
I didn't make you worship with offerings;
　I didn't weary you with frankincense.
²⁴You didn't buy spices for me
　with your money,
　or satisfy me with
　　the fat of your sacrifices.
Instead, you have burdened me
　with your sins
and wearied me with your evil actions.
²⁵I, I am the one who wipes out
　your rebellious behavior for my sake.
I won't remember your sin.
²⁶Summon me, and let's go to trial together;
　you tell your story
　so that you may be vindicated!
²⁷Your first ancestor sinned,
　and your officials rebelled against me.

---

^w Heb lacks *an army.* ^x Heb uncertain ^y DSS (1QIsaᵃ); MT *streams*

²⁸ So I made the holy officials impure,
  handed over Jacob to destruction
  and Israel to abuse.

You are my witnesses

44 But now hear this, Jacob my servant,
  and Israel, whom I have chosen.
² The Lord your maker,
  who formed you in the womb
  and will help you, says:
  Don't fear, my servant Jacob,
  Jeshurun, whom I have chosen.
³ I will pour out water upon thirsty ground
  and streams upon dry land.
  I will pour out my spirit
  upon your descendants
  and my blessing upon your offspring.
⁴ They will spring up from among the reeds
  like willows by flowing streams.
⁵ This one will say, "I am the Lord's,"
  and that one will be named after Jacob.
  Another will write on his hand,
  "The Lord's"
  and will take the name Israel.

⁶ The Lord, Israel's king and redeemer,
  the Lord of heavenly forces, says:
  I am the first, and I am the last,
  and besides me there are no gods.
⁷ Who is like me?
  Let them speak up, explain it,
  and lay it out for me.
  Who announced long ago what is to be?ᶻ
  Let them tell usᵃ what is to come.
⁸ Don't tremble; have no fear!
  Didn't I proclaim it?
  Didn't I inform you long ago?
  You are my witnesses!
  Is there a God besides me?
  There is no other rock; I know of none.

Idol-makers mocked

⁹ Idol-makers are all as nothing;
  their playthings do no good.
  Their promoters
  neither see nor know anything,
  so they ought to be ashamed.
¹⁰ Who would form a god or cast an idol
  that does no good?
¹¹ All its worshippers will be ashamed,

and its artisans, who are only human.
  They will all gather and stand,
  tremble and be ashamed together.

¹² A blacksmith with his tools
  works it over coals,
  and shapes it with hammers,
  and works it with his strong arm.
  He even becomes hungry and weak.
  If he didn't drink water, he'd pass out.
¹³ A carpenter stretches out a string,
  marks it out with a stylus,
  fashions it with carving tools,
  and marks it with a compass.
  He makes it into a human form,
  like a splendid human,
  to live in a temple.
¹⁴ He cuts down cedars for himself,
  or chooses a cypressᵇ or oak,
  selecting from all the trees of the forest.
  He plants a pine,ᶜ
  and the rain makes it grow.
¹⁵ It becomes suitable to burn for humans,
  so he takes some of the wood
  and warms himself.
  He kindles fire and bakes bread.
  He fashions a god and worships it;
  he makes an idol and bows down to it.
¹⁶ Half of it he burns in the fire;
  on that half he roasts
  and eats meat, and he is satisfied.
  He warms himself and says,
  "Ah, I'm warm, watching the fire!"
¹⁷ And the rest of it he makes into a god,
  into his idol,
  and he bows down, worships,
  and prays to it, saying,
  "Save me, for you are my god!"
¹⁸ They don't know or comprehend,
  for their eyes can't see
  and their minds can't comprehend.
¹⁹ He doesn't think,

ᶻOr *Since I placed an ancient people and coming things* ᵃOr *them* ᵇSpecies uncertain ᶜSpecies uncertain

and has no knowledge
  or understanding to think:
Half of it I burned in the fire,
  and I baked bread on its coals,
  and roasted meat and ate.
Should I make the rest
  into something detestable?
Should I bow down to a block of wood?
²⁰ He's feeding on ashes;
  his deluded mind has led him astray.
He can't save himself and say,
  "Isn't this thing in my hand a lie?"

Promises to Jacob and Jerusalem

²¹ Remember these things, Jacob;
  Israel, for you are my servant.
I formed you; you are my servant!
  I won't forget you, Israel.
²² I swept away your rebellions like a cloud,
  and your sins like fog.
Return to me,
  because I have redeemed you.

²³ Sing, heavens, for the LORD has acted;
  shout, depths of the earth!
Burst out with a ringing cry,
  you mountains, forest,
  and every tree in it.
The LORD has redeemed Jacob,
  and will glorify himself
    through Israel.

SAILBOAT

Joy

Celebration Time *Isaiah 44:23*
Isaiah told the people, "It's time to celebrate!"
Everyone in heaven and on earth would praise God
for the wonderful things God would do. God would
send a deliverer to free Israel from their captors
in Babylon. ◆

²⁴ The LORD your redeemer
  who formed you in the womb says:
I am the LORD, the maker of all,
  who alone stretched out the heavens,
  who spread out the earth by myself,
²⁵ who frustrates the omens of diviners
  and makes a mockery of magicians,

who turns back the wise
  and turns their knowledge into folly.
²⁶ But who confirms the word
  of my[d] servant,
  and fulfills the predictions
    of my messengers;
who says about Jerusalem,
  "It will be resettled";
  and who says about the cities of Judah,
  "They will be rebuilt,
  and I will restore their ruins";
²⁷ who says to the ocean depths,
  "Dry up; I will dry your streams";
²⁸ who says about Cyrus, "My shepherd—
  he will do all that I want";
who says about Jerusalem,
  "She will be rebuilt";
  and who says about the temple,
  "You will be founded once again."

Cyrus as God's anointed

45 The LORD says to his anointed,
  to Cyrus,
  whom I have grasped by the strong hand,
  to conquer nations before him,
  disarming kings,
  and opening doors before him,
  so no gates will be shut:
² I myself will go before you,
  and I will level mountains.
I will shatter bronze doors;
  I will cut through iron bars.
³ I will give you hidden treasures
  of secret riches,
  so you will know that I am the LORD,
  the God of Israel, who calls you by name.
⁴ For the sake of my servant Jacob
  and Israel my chosen,
I called you by name.
  I gave you an honored title,
  though you didn't know me.
⁵ I am the LORD, and there is no other;
  besides me there is no God.
I strengthen you—
  though you don't know me—
⁶ so all will know, from the rising
  of the sun to its setting,
  that there is nothing apart from me.
I am the LORD; there's no other.
⁷ I form light and create darkness,

---

d Or *his*; also in next line

make prosperity and create doom;
  I am the Lord, who does all these things.

8 Pour down, you heavens above,
    and let the clouds flow
      with righteousness.
  Let the earth open for salvation
    to bear fruit;
    let righteousness sprout as well.
  I, the Lord, have created these things.

Potter and clay

9 Doom to the one
    who argues with the potter,[e]
    as if he were just another clay pot!
  Does the clay say to the potter,
    "What are you making?"
    or "Your work has no handles"?
10 Doom to one who says to a father,
    "What have you fathered?"
    and to a woman,
    "With what are you in labor?"
11 The Lord, the holy one of Israel
    and its maker,[f] says:
  Are you questioning me[g]
    about my own children?
  Are you telling me what to do
    with the work of my hands?
12 I myself made the earth,
    and created humans upon it.
  My own hands stretched out the heavens.
    I commanded all their forces.
13 I have a right to awaken Cyrus;
    I will smooth all his paths.
  He will build my city
    and set my exiles free,
    not for a price and not for a bribe,
    says the Lord of heavenly forces.

14 The Lord says:
  Egypt will grow weary, Cush will be sold,[h]
    and the tall Sabeans
    will cross over to you.
  They will be yours,
    and after you they will go.
  In chains they will come;
    to you they will bow down.
  They will plead with you:
  "Truly God is with you;
    there's no other, no other God."

15 Surely you are a god who hides himself,
    Israel's God and savior.

Idols contrasted with God

16 They will all be shamed and disgraced;
    the makers of idols
    will end up disgraced together.
17 Israel has been saved by the Lord
    of everlasting salvation.
  You won't be shamed,
    and you won't be disgraced
    forever and always.
18 For this is what the Lord said,
    who created the heavens,
    who is God,
    who formed the earth and made it,
    who established it,
    who didn't create it a wasteland
      but formed it as a habitation:
    I, the Lord, and none other!
19 I didn't speak in secret
    or in some land of darkness;
  I didn't say to the offspring of Jacob,
    "Seek me in chaos."
  I am the Lord, the one who speaks truth,
    who announces what is correct.
20 Gather and come,
    draw near together,
    fugitives of the nations!
  Those who carry their wooden idols
    don't know;
    those who pray to a god who won't save.
21 Announce! Approach! Confer together!
  Who proclaimed this from the beginning,
    announced it from long ago?
  Wasn't it I, the Lord?
    There's no other God except me,
    a righteous God and a savior;
    there's none besides me!
22 Turn to me and be saved,
    all you ends of the earth,
    for I am God, and there's no other.
23 I have sworn a solemn pledge;
    a word has left my mouth;
    it is reliable and won't fail.
  Surely every knee will bow
    and every tongue will confess;
24 they will say, "Righteousness and
    strength come only from the Lord.
  All who are angry with him
    will come to shame.

---

[e]Or *maker* [f]Or *potter* [g]Or *about future things ask me* [h]Heb uncertain

²⁵ All the Israelites
will be victorious and rejoice."

Babylon's idols can't compare

46 Bel crouches down; Nebo cowers.
Their idols sit on animals, on beasts.
The objects you once carried about
are now borne as burdens
by the weary animals.
² They crouch down and cower together.
They aren't able to rescue the burden,
but they themselves go into captivity.
³ Listen to me, house of Jacob,
all that remains from the house of Israel
who have been borne by me
since pregnancy,
whom I carried from the womb
⁴ until you grow old. I am the one,
and until you turn gray I will support you.
I have done it,
and I will continue to bear it;
I will support and I will rescue.
⁵ To whom will you liken me
and count me equal
and compare me so that we are alike?
⁶ Those who pour out gold from a bag
and weigh silver with a balance
hire a metalworker;
then he makes a god.
They bow down; they worship;
⁷ they carry the idolⁱ on their
shoulders and support it;
they set it down, and it stands still,
unable to move from its place.
If one cries out to it, it doesn't answer.
It can't save people from their distress.

Remember past events

⁸ Remember this and take courage;
take it to heart, you rebels.
⁹ Remember the prior things—
from long ago;
I am God, and there's no other.
I am God! There's none like me,
¹⁰ who tells the end at the beginning,
from ancient times things not yet done,
saying, "My plan will stand;
all that I decide I will do,"
¹¹ I call a bird of prey from the east,
a man from a distant land for my plan.

As surely as I have spoken,
I'll make it happen;
I have planned, and yes, I'll do it.
¹² Listen to me, you bullheaded people
who are far from victory:
¹³ I'm bringing my victory near—it isn't far,
and my salvation—it won't delay.
I will establish salvation in Zion
and grant my splendor to Israel.

Daughter Babylon dethroned

47 Go down and sit in the dust,
virgin Daughter Babylon!
Sit on the ground without a throne,
Daughter Chaldea,
because they will no longer call you
tender and pampered.
² Take the millstones and grind flour!
Remove your veil, strip off your robe,
expose your thighs,
wade through the rivers!
³ Your nakedness will be exposed,
and your disgrace will be seen.
I will take vengeance;
no one will intervene.ʲ
⁴ Our redeemer has spoken;
the LORD of heavenly forces is his name,
the holy one of Israel.

⁵ Sit silent and go into darkness,
Daughter Chaldea,
because they will no longer
call you Queen of Kingdoms.

ⁱOr it ʲSyr, cf Vulg; MT *I won't meet a man*

⁶ I was enraged with my people;
   I made my inheritance impure
   and put them under your power.
You took no pity on them.
   You made your yoke heavy
   even on the elderly.
⁷ You said, "I'm forever;
   I'm the eternal mistress."
You didn't stop and think;
   you didn't consider the outcome.
⁸ So listen to this,
luxuriant one who sits secure,
   who says in her heart, I'm utterly unique;
I'll never sit as a widow;
   I'll never know childlessness:
⁹ Both of these will happen to you at once,
   on a single day:
   childlessness and widowhood
   will envelop you in full measure,
   despite your many sorceries,
   despite your very powerful spells.
¹⁰ You felt secure in your evil;
   you said, "No one sees me."
Your wisdom and knowledge
   spun you around.
   You thought to yourself, I and no one else.
¹¹ Now evil will come against you,
   something you won't anticipate.
A curse will fall upon you,
   something you won't be able to dispel.
Destruction will come upon you suddenly,
   something you won't foresee.

¹² Continue with your enchantments,
   and with your many spells,
   which you have practiced
   since childhood.
Maybe you will be able to succeed.
   Maybe you will inspire terror.
¹³ You are weary from all your consultations;
   let the astrologers stand up and save you,
   those who gaze at the stars,
   and predict what will happen to you
   at each new moon.
¹⁴ They are just like stubble;
   the fire burns them.
They won't save themselves
   from the powerful flames.
This is no warming ember
   or fire to sit beside.

¹⁵ Those with whom you have
   wearied yourself are like this,
   those with whom you were
   in business from your youth:
each has wandered off on their own way;
   none will save you.

New things from now on

48 Listen to this, house of Jacob,
   who are known by the name of Israel,
   descendants of Judah,ᵏ
who swear by the LORD's name
   and invoke Israel's God dishonestly and
   unrighteously.

² They are known
   as residents of the holy city,
   those who depend
   upon the God of Israel—
   the LORD of heavenly forces is his name.
³ Past things I announced long ago;
   from my mouth I proclaimed them.
I acted suddenly, and they came about.
⁴ Because I know that you are stubborn,
   your neck is made of iron,
   and your forehead is bronze,
⁵ I informed you long ago;
   before they came about
   I proclaimed them to you
so you wouldn't say, "My idol did them;
   my wood statue and metal god
   commanded them."
⁶ You've heard and seen all this—
   won't you admit it?
From now on I'll tell you new things,
   guarded secrets that you don't know.
⁷ They are created now, not long ago;
   before today you hadn't heard of them,
   so you won't say, "I already knew them."
⁸ You haven't heard, nor have you known;
   as in ages past your ears are closed,
   because I knew what a traitor you were;
   you were known as a rebel from birth.
⁹ For the sake of my reputation
   I control my anger;
   for your sake
   I restrain my powerful radiance
   so as to not destroy you.
¹⁰ See, I have refined you, but not like silver;
   I have tested youˡ
   in the furnace of misery.

ᵏ*Or came out from the waters of Judah* ˡ*Or I have chosen*

¹¹ For the sake of my reputation,
  for my own sake, I will act,
  for why will my name
    be made impure?
  I won't give my glory to another.

¹² Listen to me, Jacob;
  Israel, whom I called:
  I am the one;
  I am the first and I am the last.
¹³ My hand founded the earth;
  my strong hand
    spread out the heavens.
  When I call to them,
    they all stand up.
¹⁴ Gather yourselves, all of you,
    and listen.
  Who among you
    announced these things?
  "The LORD loves him.
  He will do
    what God wants with Babylon
  and with the descendants^m
    of Chaldea."
¹⁵ I, I have spoken and told him
  the things that will happen to him;
  I will make him succeed.
¹⁶ Come close to me; listen to this:

^mLXX; MT *his arm*

Since the very beginning
  I haven't spoken in secret.
  Whenever anything happens,
    I am there.
  (And now the LORD God
    has sent me with his spirit.)

¹⁷ The LORD your redeemer,
  the holy one of Israel, proclaims:
  I am the LORD your God
    who teaches you for your own good,
    who leads you in the way you should go.
¹⁸ If you would pay attention
    to my commands,
  your well-being would be like a river,
    and your righteousness
    like the waves of the sea.
¹⁹ Your offspring would be like the sand,
    and your descendants like its grains.
  Their name would never be eliminated,
    never wiped out from before me.

²⁰ Go out from Babylon;
  flee from the Chaldeans!
  Report this with a loud shout, proclaim it;
  broadcast it out to the end of the earth.
  Say, "The LORD has redeemed
    his servant Jacob!"

God's Thoughts / My Thoughts

God Is Our Leader   *Isaiah 48:17*

Every team has a captain or coach. Every band has a conductor. Without a good leader, it would be difficult for a group of people to know what to do and how to work together. Sometimes God tells us how to live. Other times God tells us how *not* to live. When we sin, God reminds us to stop. When we don't go the right way, God puts us back on track. When we don't know what to say, God gives us God's words to use. The Bible gives plenty of instructions. Read it. Study it. Know it.

And trust your leader. God will never leave us in our time of need. God loves us, and we are special to God. God protects us when we are in danger and comforts us when we are hurting. Thank God today for everything God has done for you.

How has God led you in the past?

Where do you think God is leading you now?

²¹ They weren't thirsty when he led
them through the deserts.
God made water flow
from the rock for them;
split the rock, and water flowed out.
²² There is no well-being,
says the Lᴏʀᴅ, for the wicked.

did you know? The reference to water from a rock reminded the people how God had led them out of Egypt and had provided them with water in the desert. Isaiah wanted the people to know God would do the same thing for them as they left Babylon.

The servant speaks up

49 Listen to me, coastlands;
pay attention, peoples far away.
The Lᴏʀᴅ called me before my birth,
called my name when
I was in my mother's womb.
² He made my mouth like a sharp sword,
and hid me in the shadow
of God's own hand.
He made me a sharpened arrow,
and concealed me in God's quiver,
³ saying to me, "You are my servant,
Israel, in whom I show my glory."
⁴ But I said, "I have wearied myself in vain.
I have used up my strength for nothing."
Nevertheless, the Lᴏʀᴅ
will grant me justice;
my reward is with my God.
⁵ And now the Lᴏʀᴅ has decided—
the one who formed me
from the womb as his servant—
to restore Jacob to God,
so that Israel might return to him.
Moreover, I'm honored in the Lᴏʀᴅ's eyes;
my God has become my strength.
⁶ He said: It is not enough,
since you are my servant,
to raise up the tribes of Jacob
and to bring back the survivors of Israel.
Hence, I will also appoint you
as light to the nations
so that my salvation may reach
to the end of the earth.

⁷ The Lᴏʀᴅ, redeemer of Israel
and its holy one,
says to one despised,
rejected by nations,
to the slave of rulers:
Kings will see and stand up;
commanders will bow down
on account of the Lᴏʀᴅ, who is faithful,

the holy one of Israel,
who has chosen you.
⁸ The Lᴏʀᴅ said:
At the right time, I answered you;
on a day of salvation, I helped you.
I have guarded you,
and given you as a covenant
to the people, to restore the land,
and to reassign deserted properties,
⁹ saying to the prisoners, "Come out,"
and to those in darkness,
"Show yourselves."
Along the roads animalsⁿ will graze;
their pasture will be
on every treeless hilltop.
¹⁰ They won't hunger or thirst;
the burning heat and sun
won't strike them,
because one who has compassion
for them will lead them
and will guide them by springs of water.
¹¹ I will turn all my mountains into roads;
my highways will be built up.
¹² Look! These will come from far away.
Look! These from the north and west,
and these from the southland.ᵒ

¹³ Sing, heavens! Rejoice, earth!
Break out, mountains, with a song.
The Lᴏʀᴅ has comforted his people,
and taken pity on those who suffer.

Compassion for Zion

¹⁴ But Zion says,
"The Lᴏʀᴅ has abandoned me;
my Lord has forgotten me."
¹⁵ Can a woman forget her nursing child,
fail to pity the child of her womb?
Even these may forget,
but I won't forget you.
¹⁶ Look, on my palms I've inscribed you;
your walls are before me continually.
¹⁷ Your buildersᵖ come quickly;

ⁿHeb lacks *animals.* ᵒHeb *Sinim* ᵖOr *children*

those who destroy and demolish you
  will depart from you.

¹⁸ Look up all around and see:
  they are all gathered;
  they come to you.
  As surely as I live, says the Lᴏʀᴅ,
  you will put them all on like ornaments,
  bind them on like a bride.

¹⁹ As for your ruins and desolate places
  and destroyed land—
  you will soon be crowded with settlers,
  and those who swallowed you
    will be far away.

²⁰ You will again hear the children
  who were born bereaved say,
  "The place is too crowded for me;
  make room for me to settle."

²¹ And you will think to yourself,
  Who bore me these?
  I was bereaved and desolate,
    exiled and sent off.
  So who raised these?
  I was left behind, I was alone;
  where were these?

²² The Lᴏʀᴅ God says:
  Look, I will raise my hand to the nations,
  and to the peoples I will lift up my signal.
  They will bring your sons in their arms,
  and will carry your daughters
    on their shoulders.

²³ Kings will be your attendants,
  and their queens your nursemaids.

With faces to the ground
  they will bow down to you;
  they will lick the dust from your feet.
  You will know that I am the Lᴏʀᴅ;
  the one who hopes in me
    won't be ashamed.

²⁴ Can loot be taken from warriors?
  Can a tyrant's captives escape?

²⁵ The Lᴏʀᴅ says:
  Even the captives of warriors
    will be taken,
  and the tyrant's loot will escape.
  I myself will oppose those who oppose you,
  and I myself will save your children.

²⁶ I will make your oppressors
    eat their own flesh;
  and as with wine, with their own
    blood they will be drunk,
  so that all flesh will know that
    I, the Lᴏʀᴅ, am your savior,
  and the mighty one of Jacob
    is your redeemer.

50

The Lᴏʀᴅ says:
  Where's your mother's divorce decree,
  with which I sent her away?
  Or to which lender did I sell you?
  On account of your sins you were sold;
  on account of your transgressions
  your mother was sent away.

² Why did I come and find no one?
  Why did I call when no one answered?
  Is my hand too small to redeem you? q
  Don't I have enough power to save?
  With my rebuke I dry up the sea
  and make the rivers into wilderness.
  Their fish stink from lack of water;
    they die of thirst.

³ I clothe the heavens with darkness
  and cover them with funeral clothing.

God's faithful servant

⁴ The Lᴏʀᴅ God gave me an educated tongue
  to know how to respond to the weary
  with a word that will awaken them
    in the morning.r
  God awakens my ear
  in the morning to listen,
  as educated people do.

⁵ The Lᴏʀᴅ God opened my ear;
  I didn't rebel; I didn't turn my back.

UMBRELLA
Depressed

Never Forgotten *Isaiah 49:13-15, 23*
The people of Israel thought God had forgotten
them. But God said this wasn't true. In fact, God
said the people were written on God's palms. The
people of Israel were God's children. God couldn't
forget them any more than a mother could forget
her child. They had known many troubles, but God
never left them. Like the Israelites, God doesn't
forget about us. ◗

 q Heb lacks *you*. r Heb uncertain

LIFE PRESERVER

What is an "educated tongue"? Isaiah 50:4

An *educated tongue* (50:4) refers to the work of the prophet, or servant, who had been given special gifts to help him with his assignment. With an educated tongue, he knew how to speak to the Israelites, especially those who were far from God. He was to speak to them and remind them of God's love for them. Through his speaking he would help those who were weary or in exile, comforting them with his words. ◗

⁶ Instead, I gave my body to attackers,
and my cheeks to beard pluckers.
I didn't hide my face
from insults and spitting.
⁷ The Lord God will help me;
therefore, I haven't been insulted.
Therefore, I set my face like flint,
and knew I wouldn't be ashamed.
⁸ The one who will declare me innocent
is near.
Who will argue with me?
Let's stand up together.
Who will bring judgment against me?
Let him approach me.
⁹ Look! The Lord God will help me.
Who will condemn me?
Look, they will wear out like clothing;
the moth will eat them.

¹⁰ Who among you fears the Lord?
Who listens to the voice of his servant,
who walks in darkness
and has no light?
They will trust in the Lord's name,
and rely upon their God.
¹¹ Look! All of you are kindling fire,
igniting torches.
Walk by the light of your fire,
by the torches you have ignited.
This is what will happen
to you by my hand:
you will lie down in grief.

Look to Abraham and Sarah

51 Listen to me,
you who look for righteousness,
you who seek the Lord:
Look to the rock from which you were cut
and to the quarry where you were dug.
² Look to Abraham your ancestor,
and to Sarah, who gave you birth.
They were alone when I called them,
but I blessed them and made them many.
³ The Lord will comfort Zion;
he will comfort all her ruins.
He will make her desert like Eden
and her wilderness
like the Lord's garden.
Happiness and joy will be found in her—
thanks and the sound of singing.

Salvation endures forever

⁴ Pay attention to me, my people;
listen to me, my nation,
for teaching will go out from me,
my justice, as a light to the nations.
⁵ I will quickly bring my victory.
My salvation is on its way,
and my arm will judge the peoples.
The coastlands hope for me;
they wait for my judgment.ˢ
⁶ Look up to the heavens,
and gaze at the earth beneath.
The heavens will disappear like smoke,
the earth will wear out like clothing,
and its inhabitants will die like gnats.
But my salvation will endure forever,
and my righteousness will be unbroken.
⁷ Listen to me, you who know
what is right,

LIGHTHOUSE

Forever

God's Word Lasts Forever Isaiah 51:6

Some things in life are only temporary, like an ice-cream cone or even a favorite toy. We get to enjoy them for a while, but then they're gone. Israel had seen a lot of things come and go. The life they once knew was gone. They wondered if anything would last. Isaiah told the people to look at the skies. The beautiful blue sky and white clouds were always there. And yet God's promises are even more stable than that. Even if the heavenly skies disappear, Isaiah said, God's word will still be standing. ◗

ˢOr for my arm

people who carry my teaching
  in your heart:
Don't fear human scorn,
  and don't be upset when they abuse you.
⁸ The moth will eat them
  as if they were clothing,
  and the worm will eat them like wool,
but my righteousness is forever,
  and my salvation for all generations.

Awake, arm of the LORD

⁹ Awake, awake, put on strength,
  arm of the LORD.
Awake as in times past,
  generations long ago.
Aren't you the one who crushed Rahab,
  who pierced the dragon?
¹⁰ Didn't you dry up the sea,
  the waters of the great deep?
And didn't you make
  the redeemed a road to cross
through the depths of the sea,
  a road for the redeemed to pass?
¹¹ Then let those
  ransomed by the LORD return
and come to Zion with singing
  and with everlasting joy
    upon their heads.
Let happiness and joy overwhelm them;
  let grief and groaning flee.

¹² I, I am the one who comforts you.
  Why should you fear humans who will die,
  mortals who are treated like grass?
¹³ You forgot the LORD your maker,
  the one who stretched out the heavens
  and founded the earth.
You were continually afraid, all day long,
  on account of the oppressor's wrath—
a fear by which they intend
  to destroy you.
Where now is the oppressor's wrath?
¹⁴ The imprisoned ones will soon be released;
  they won't die in the pit
  or even lack bread.
¹⁵ I am the LORD your God,
  who stirs up the sea
    so that its waves roar—
  the LORD of heavenly forces is his name.
¹⁶ I put my words in your mouth

and hid you in the shadow of my hand,
  stretching out[t] the heavens,
    founding the earth,
  and saying to Zion, "You are my people."

Wake yourself, Jerusalem

¹⁷ Wake yourself, wake yourself!
  Rise up, Jerusalem,
  who drank the cup of wrath
    from the LORD's hand.
You drank;
  you drained the goblet of reeling.
¹⁸ There's no one to guide her
  among all the children she bore;
there's no one to take her
  by the hand among all the children
    she raised.
¹⁹ These two things have happened to you—
  Who will be sorry for you?[u]—
    destruction and devastation,
    famine and sword—
  who will comfort you?[v]
²⁰ Your children passed out;
  they lay at the head of every street
    like antelope in a net,
  filled with the LORD's wrath,
  with the rebuke of your God.

²¹ Therefore, hear this, suffering one,
  who is drunk, but not from wine.
²² The LORD, your Lord and your God,
  who contends for his people, says:
Look, I have taken the cup of reeling,
  the goblet of my wrath, from your hand.
You will no longer drink from it.
²³ I will put it in the hand of your tormentors,
  who said to you,
"Lie down so that we can walk on you.
  Make your back like the ground,
  like a street for those walking on it."

Awake, holy Zion

52 Awake, awake,
  put on your strength, Zion!
Put on your splendid clothing,
Jerusalem, you holy city;
  for the uncircumcised and unclean
  will no longer come into you.
² Shake the dust off yourself;
  rise up; sit enthroned, Jerusalem.

---

[t]Or *planting* [u]DSS (1QIsaᵃ), LXX, Vulg; MT *How will I* [v]Or *how will I comfort you?*

Loose the bonds from your neck,
captive Daughter Zion!

3 The LORD proclaims:
You were sold for nothing,
and you will be redeemed without money.
4 The LORD God proclaims:
Long ago my people went down
to reside in Egypt.
Moreover, Assyria
has oppressed them without cause.
5 And now what have I here? says the LORD.
My people are taken away for nothing.
Their rulers wail, says the LORD,
and continually all day long
my name is despised.
6 Therefore, my people
will know my name on that day;
I'm the one who promises it; I'm here.

Your God rules

7 How beautiful upon the mountains
are the feet of a messenger
who proclaims peace,
who brings good news,
who proclaims salvation,
who says to Zion, "Your God rules!"
8 Listen! Your lookouts lift their voice;
they sing out together!
Right before their eyes they see
the LORD returning to Zion.

9 Break into song together,
you ruins of Jerusalem!
The LORD has comforted his people
and has redeemed Jerusalem.
10 The LORD has bared his holy arm
in view of all the nations;
all the ends of the earth have seen
our God's victory.

11 Depart! Depart! Go out from there!
Unclean! Don't touch!
Get out of that place; purify yourselves,
carriers of the LORD's equipment!
12 You won't go out in a rush,
nor will you run away,
because the one going before you
is the LORD;
your rear guard is the God of Israel.

God's THOUGHTS ◆ My THOUGHTS

Beautiful Feet   Isaiah 52:7

Whether you think feet look terrific or just plain awful, feet are amazing. Each human foot contains 26 bones, 33 joints, 107 ligaments, 19 muscles, and 19 tendons.

The book of Isaiah says that those who carry God's message of peace and hope have awesome, beautiful feet. Not that these messengers would have won prizes in a "pretty feet" contest. In fact, people in Bible times who traveled to spread God's word probably had feet that were dirty and calloused from walking many miles. They may even have had cuts and bruises from climbing over rocks and briars. Beautiful feet bring the message of peace, hope, and salvation.

It's not too hard to have terrific-looking feet. Simply carry the good news of God's love with you wherever you go.

How are you carrying God's message of peace and hope?

Who do you know that has the kind of beautiful feet the book of Isaiah describes? Why do they fit this description?

Suffering servant

13 Look, my servant will succeed.
   He will be exalted and lifted very high.
14 Just as many were appalled by you,
   he too appeared disfigured, inhuman,
   his appearance unlike that of mortals.
15 But he will astonish[w] many nations.
   Kings will be silenced because of him,
   because they will see
    what they haven't seen before;
   what they haven't heard before,
    they will ponder.

53 Who can believe
what we have heard,
and for whose sake has
   the Lord's arm[x] been revealed?
2 He grew up like a young plant before us,[y]
   like a root from dry ground.
   He possessed no splendid form
   for us to see,
    no desirable appearance.
3 He was despised and avoided by others;
   a man who suffered,
    who knew sickness well.
   Like someone
   from whom people hid their faces,
   he was despised,
    and we didn't think about him.

4 It was certainly our sickness
   that he carried,
   and our sufferings that he bore,
   but we thought him afflicted,
   struck down by God and tormented.
5 He was pierced because of our rebellions
   and crushed because of our crimes.
   He bore the punishment
    that made us whole;
   by his wounds we are healed.
6 Like sheep we had all wandered away,
   each going its own way,
   but the Lord let fall on him
    all our crimes.

7 He was oppressed and tormented,
   but didn't open his mouth.
   Like a lamb being brought to slaughter,
   like a ewe silent before her shearers,
   he didn't open his mouth.

8 Due to an unjust ruling
   he was taken away,
   and his fate—who will think about it?
   He was eliminated
   from the land of the living,
   struck dead
    because of my people's rebellion.
9 His grave was among the wicked,
   his tomb with evildoers,[z]
   though he had done no violence,
    and had spoken nothing false.

10 But the Lord wanted to crush him
   and to make him suffer.
   If his life is offered[a] as restitution,
   he will see his offspring;
    he will enjoy long life.
   The Lord's plans will come
    to fruition through him.
11 After his deep anguish he will see light,[b]
   and he will be satisfied.
   Through his knowledge,
   the righteous one, my servant,
   will make many righteous,
    and will bear their guilt.
12 Therefore, I will give him a share
   with the great,
   and he will divide the spoil
    with the strong,
   in return for exposing his life to death
   and being numbered with rebels,
   though he carried the sin of many
   and pleaded on behalf
    of those who rebelled.

LIFE PRESERVER

Who was described in this servant song? *Isaiah 53:1-12*

This song describes what happened to the nation of Israel. The people endured great suffering while they were in exile. They thought God had rejected them. But finally they realized that like sheep who wandered off, they had forgotten God. They expressed sorrow for their sins, and God forgave them.

Christians find many similarities between the description of the person here and what happened to Jesus when he was crucified. ◆

---

[w]Or *sprinkle*   [x]Or *power*   [y]Or *him*   [z]Cf Tg; MT *and with a rich one in his deaths*   [a]Or *if you place his life*   [b]DSS (1QIsaᵃ); MT lacks *light*.

Sing, barren woman

54 Sing, barren woman
who has borne no child;
break forth into singing and cry out,
you who were never in labor,
for the children of the wife
who has been deserted
will be more numerous than the
children of the married,
says the Lord.
² Enlarge the site of your tent,
and stretch out the drapes
of your dwellings;
don't hold back.
Lengthen your tent ropes
and strengthen your stakes.

did you know? God promised that the new Jerusalem the people would build would be even more beautiful than the one that had been destroyed. God said expensive gems and stones would be used to build the new city walls.

³ To the right and to the left
you will burst out,
and your children will possess
the nations' land
and settle their desolate cities.

⁴ Don't fear,
because you won't be ashamed;
don't be dismayed,
because you won't be disgraced.
You will forget the shame of your youth;
you'll no longer remember
the disgrace of your widowhood.
⁵ The one marrying you
is the one who made you—
the Lord of heavenly forces is his name.
The one redeeming you
is the holy one of Israel,
the one called the God of all the earth.
⁶ As an abandoned
and dejected woman
the Lord has summoned you;
as a young wife when she is rejected,
says your God.
⁷ For a brief moment I abandoned you,
but with great mercy
I will bring you back.

⁸ In an outburst of rage,
I hid my face from you for a moment,
but with everlasting love
I have consoled you,
says your redeemer, the Lord.

⁹ These are like the days^c of Noah for me,
when I promised that Noah's waters
would never again cover the earth.
Likewise I promise not to rage
against you or rebuke you.
¹⁰ The mountains may shift,
and the hills may be shaken,
but my faithful love won't shift from you,
and my covenant of peace
won't be shaken,
says the Lord, the one who pities you.

¹¹ Suffering one, storm-tossed, uncomforted,
look, I am setting your gemstones
in silvery metal
and your foundations with sapphires.
¹² I will make your towers of rubies,
and your gates of beryl,
and all your walls of precious jewels.
¹³ All your children will be disciples
of the Lord—
I will make peace abound
for your children.
¹⁴ You will be firmly founded
in righteousness.
You will stay far from oppression
because you won't fear,
far from terror
because it won't come near you.
¹⁵ If anyone attacks you,
it's none of my doing.
Whoever attacks you
will fall because of you.
¹⁶ Look, I myself created the metalworker
who blows the fire of coal
and who produces a tool for his work.
And I myself created the looter
to destroy.
¹⁷ No weapon fashioned against
you will succeed,
and you may condemn every tongue
that disputes with you.
This is the heritage of the Lord's servants,
whose righteousness
comes from me, says the Lord.

^c Or *for the waters*

Invitation to the feast

55 All of you who are thirsty,
come to the water!
Whoever has no money,
come, buy food and eat!
Without money, at no cost,
buy wine and milk!
2 Why spend money for what isn't food,
and your earnings
for what doesn't satisfy?
Listen carefully to me
and eat what is good;
enjoy the richest of feasts.
3 Listen and come to me;
listen, and you will live.
I will make
an everlasting covenant with you,
my faithful loyalty to David.
4 Look, I made him a witness
to the peoples,
a prince and commander of peoples.
5 Look, you will call a nation
you don't know,
a nation you don't know
will run to you
because of the LORD your God,
the holy one of Israel,
who has glorified you.

6 Seek the LORD
when he can still be found;
call him while he is yet near.
7 Let the wicked abandon their ways
and the sinful their schemes.
Let them return to the LORD
so that he may have mercy on them,
to our God, because he is generous
with forgiveness.
8 My plans aren't your plans,
nor are your ways my ways,
says the LORD.
9 Just as the heavens
are higher than the earth,
so are my ways higher than your ways,
and my plans than your plans.
10 Just as the rain and the snow
come down from the sky
and don't return there
without watering the earth,
making it conceive and yield plants
and providing seed to the sower
and food to the eater,

11 so is my word
that comes from my mouth;
it does not return to me empty.
Instead, it does what I want,
and accomplishes what I intend.

12 Yes, you will go out with celebration,
and you will be brought back in peace.
Even the mountains and the hills
will burst into song before you;
all the trees of the field
will clap their hands.
13 In place of the thorn
the cypress will grow;
in place of the nettle
the myrtle will grow.
This will attest to the LORD's stature,
an enduring reminder
that won't be removed.

LIFE PRESERVER

Why doesn't this sound like a story? *Isaiah 55:1-13*

Four parts of Isaiah are called "servant songs," and this is the fourth one. Some people who study the Bible think that the servant referred to in these songs was the nation of Israel. God called Israel to tell other nations about God's covenant. God asked the people to listen and remember God's covenant with them. Then God asked them to seek God. God wanted them to remember that God is both generous and forgiving.

Notice verse 12. This song says the people were going to celebrate, joining in with the mountains and trees to remember God's love for them. ◊

SAILBOAT

Joy

A Taste of Home *Isaiah 55:12*

The Israelites who were forced out of their homeland would be glad to return home. Have you ever been glad to come home after a long day or a long trip? It feels good to sleep in your own bed, sit in your own chair, and eat at your own table. The people of Israel had been away from their homeland for years. This part of Isaiah told the people that someday they would return to their land. There would be a great celebration. There would be such joy that even the trees would seem to be singing in the mountains. ◊

Keepers of God's Sabbath

56 The Lord says:
Act justly and do what is righteous,
   because my salvation is coming soon,
   and my righteousness will be revealed.
² Happy is the one who does this,
   the person who holds it fast,
   who keeps the Sabbath,
      not making it impure,
   and avoids doing any evil.

³ Don't let the immigrant
   who has joined with the Lord say,
   "The Lord will exclude me
      from the people."
   And don't let the eunuch say,
   "I'm just a dry tree."
⁴ The Lord says:
   To the eunuchs who keep my sabbaths,
   choose what I desire,
   and remain loyal to my covenant.
⁵ In my temple and courts, I will give them
   a monument and a name
      better than sons and daughters.
   I will give to them an enduring name
   that won't be removed.
⁶ The immigrants who have joined me,ᵈ
   serving me and loving my name,ᵉ
      becoming my servants,ᶠ
   everyone who keeps the Sabbath
      without making it impure,
   and those who hold fast to my covenant:
⁷ I will bring them to my holy mountain,
   and bring them joy in my house of prayer.
   I will accept their entirely burned
      offerings and sacrifices on my altar.
   My house will be known as a house
      of prayer for all peoples,
⁸ says the Lord God,
   who gathers Israel's outcasts.
   I will gather still others
   to those I have already gathered.

Neglectful leaders

⁹ All you beasts of the field,
   come and eat, all you beasts of the forest!
¹⁰ The lookouts are blind;
   they all lack sense.
   They are all mute dogs that can't bark,
   dreamers, loungers, loving to sleep.

¹¹ But the dogs have monstrous appetites.
   They never have enough.
   They are shepherds
      who don't understand.
   All of them have turned to their own ways,
   every last one greedy for profit.
¹² "Come! I'll get some wine!
   Let's drink beer!
   Tomorrow will be like today,
   or even much better."

57 The righteous person perishes,
   and no one takes it to heart.
   Loyal people are gathered together,
   and no one understands
      that because of evil
   the righteous one passed away.
² They will find peace;
   those who walk in straight paths
   will find rest on their burial beds.

Accusations against idolators

³ Come here, you children of sorcery,
   offspring of adultery and prostitution!
⁴ Whom are you mocking?
   Against whom do you
      open your mouth wide
   and stick out your tongue?
   Aren't you children of rebellion,
   offspring of lies,
⁵ who console yourselves with idols
      under every green tree,
   who slaughter children in the valleys,
      under the rocky cliffs?
⁶ You belong with the smooth talkersᵍ
      in the valley;
   they, they are your lot.
   For them you poured out a drink offering,
   and presented a grain offering.
   Should I condone these things?
⁷ On a very high mountain
      you made your bed.
   You went up there to offer a sacrifice.
⁸ Behind the door and the doorpost
      you placed your symbols.
   You abandoned me and lay down,
   making room in your bed
   and making deals for yourself
      with them.ʰ
   You loved their bed;
   you saw their nakedness.

ᵈOr to the Lord ᵉOr serving him and loving the Lord's name ᶠOr becoming his servants ᵍOr smooth things ʰHeb uncertain

⁹ You went down to Molech[i] with oil,
 and you slathered on your ointments;
 you sent your messengers far away,
 sent them down to the underworld.[j]

¹⁰ Worn out by all your efforts,
 yet you wouldn't say, "This is useless."
 You found new strength;
 therefore, you weren't tired.

¹¹ Whom did you dread and fear
 so that you lied,
 didn't remember me
 or give me a thought?
 Isn't it because I was silent
 and closed my eyes
 that you stopped fearing me?

¹² I will bring evidence about your
 righteousness and your actions;
 they won't help you.

¹³ When you cry out,
 let those things you've gathered save you!
 The wind will lift them all;
 one breath will take them away.
 But those taking refuge in me
 will inherit the land
 and possess my holy mountain.

Peace for the remorseful

¹⁴ It will be said:
 "Survey, survey; build a road!
 Remove barriers from my people's road!"

¹⁵ The one who is high and lifted up,
 who lives forever,
 whose name is holy, says:
 I live on high, in holiness,

and also with the crushed[k] and the lowly,
 reviving the spirit of the lowly,
 reviving the heart of those
 who have been crushed.[l]

¹⁶ I won't always accuse,
 nor will I be enraged forever.
 It is my own doing
 that their spirit is exhausted—
 I gave them breath!

¹⁷ I was enraged about their illegal profits;
 I struck them;
 in rage I withdrew from them.
 Yet they went on wandering
 wherever they wanted.

¹⁸ I have seen their ways,
 but I will heal them.
 I will guide them,
 and reward them with comfort.
 And for those who mourn,

¹⁹ I will create reason for praise:[m]
 utter prosperity to those far and near,
 and I will heal them, says the Lord.

²⁰ But the wicked are like the churning sea
 that can't keep still.
 They churn up from their waters
 muck and mud.

²¹ There is no peace, says my God,
 for the wicked.

Fasting from injustice

58 Shout loudly; don't hold back;
 raise your voice like a trumpet!
 Announce to my people their crime,
 to the house of Jacob their sins.

² They seek me day after day,
 desiring knowledge of my ways
 like a nation that acted righteously,
 that didn't abandon their God.
 They ask me for righteous judgments,
 wanting to be close to God.

³ "Why do we fast and you don't see;
 why afflict ourselves
 and you don't notice?"
 Yet on your fast day
 you do whatever you want,
 and oppress all your workers.

⁴ You quarrel and brawl, and then you fast;
 you hit each other violently
 with your fists.
 You shouldn't fast as you are doing today

LIGHTHOUSE

FOREVER

Forever God *Isaiah 57:15*

Everything on earth has a beginning and an end. Creatures, including humans, are born and eventually die. An apple tree grows from a single seed but doesn't last forever. The wooden furniture in your home was once a tree. Even days have a beginning time when the sun rises and an end time when the sun sets.

Unlike things on earth, God has no beginning and no end. No one knows where God came from. God has always been and will always be. God is forever. ◗

[i]Or *the king* [j]Heb *Sheol* [k]Or *contrite* [l]Or *contrite* [m]Heb uncertain

if you want to make
　　your voice heard on high.
⁵ Is this the kind of fast I choose,
　　a day of self-affliction,
　　of bending one's head like a reed
　　and of lying down
　　　in mourning clothing and ashes?
　　Is this what you call a fast,
　　　a day acceptable to the Lord?

⁶ Isn't this the fast I choose:
　　releasing wicked restraints,
　　　untying the ropes of a yoke,
　　setting free the mistreated,
　　and breaking every yoke?
⁷ Isn't it sharing your bread
　　with the hungry
　　and bringing the homeless poor
　　　into your house,
　　covering the naked
　　　when you see them,
　　and not hiding from your own family?
⁸ Then your light
　　will break out like the dawn,
　　and you will be healed quickly.
　　Your own righteousness
　　will walk before you,
　　and the Lord's glory
　　　will be your rear guard.
⁹ Then you will call,
　　and the Lord will answer;
　　you will cry for help, and God will say,
　　　"I'm here."
　　If you remove the yoke from among you,
　　the finger-pointing, the wicked speech;
¹⁰ if you open your heart to the hungry,
　　and provide abundantly
　　　for those who are afflicted,
　　your light will shine in the darkness,
　　and your gloom will be like the noon.
¹¹ The Lord will guide you continually
　　and provide for you,
　　　even in parched places.
　　He will rescue your bones.
　　You will be like a watered garden,
　　like a spring of water that won't run dry.
¹² They will rebuild ancient ruins
　　on your account;
　　the foundations of generations past
　　　you will restore.
　　You will be called Mender of Broken Walls,
　　　Restorer of Livable Streets.

LIFE PRESERVER

What is a fast? *Isaiah 58:5-12*

Fasting is going without food for some period of time as a way to focus on God and remember what God wants. God wanted the people to remember that fasting that causes fighting is not what God wants. God also didn't want them to mourn. God wanted the people to remember who God is and what God had done, and to show this in the way they acted toward others.

God wanted the people to make sure everyone was treated with justice and that those who were oppressed were freed. God wanted them to remember to share their bread with those who were hungry, their homes with those who were homeless, and their clothes with those who were in need. Evidently this idea was so important that Jesus repeated it, as recorded in Luke 4:18-19. This kind of behavior is also mentioned in Matthew 25:31-46.

¹³ If you stop trampling the Sabbath,
　　stop doing whatever you want
　　　on my holy day,
　　and consider the Sabbath a delight,
　　sacred to the Lord, honored,
　　and honor it
　　　instead of doing things your way,
　　seeking what you want
　　　and doing business as usual,
¹⁴ then you will take delight in the Lord.
　　I will let you ride on the heights
　　　of the earth;
　　I will sustain you with the heritage
　　　of your ancestor Jacob.
　　The mouth of the Lord has spoken.

Alienation from God

59 Look! The Lord does not lack
　　the power to save,
　　nor are his ears too dull to hear,
² but your misdeeds have
　　　separated you from your God.
　　Your sins have hidden his face
　　　from you
　　so that you aren't heard.
³ Your hands are stained with blood,
　　and your fingers with guilt.
　　Your lips speak lies;
　　　your tongues mutter malice.
⁴ No one sues honestly;

Bet you can *read this in 6 minutes. Ready, set, go!*

no one pleads truthfully.
By trusting in emptiness
    and speaking deceit,
    they conceive harm
    and give birth to malice.
⁵ They hatch adders' eggs,
    and weave spiderwebs.
Whoever eats their eggs will die.
    Moreover, the crushed egg
    hatches a viper.
⁶ Their webs can't serve as clothing;
    they can't cover themselves
    with their deeds.
Their deeds are deeds of malice,
    and the work of violence
    is in their hands.
⁷ Their feet run to evil;
    they rush to shed innocent blood.
Their thoughts are thoughts of malice;
    desolation and destruction
    litter their highways.
⁸ They don't know the way of peace;
    there's no justice in their paths.
They make their roads crooked;
    no one who walks in them knows peace.

Injustice obscures vision

⁹ Because of all this, justice is far from us,
    and righteousness beyond our reach.
We expect light, and there is darkness;
    we await a gleam of light,
    but walk about in gloom.
¹⁰ We grope along the wall like the blind;
    like those without eyes we grope.
We stumble at noonday
    as if it were twilight,
    and among the strong
    as if we were dying.
¹¹ All of us growl like bears,
    and like doves we moan.
We expect justice, but there is none;
    we await salvation, but it is far from us.
¹² Our rebellions are numerous
    in your presence;
    our sins testify against us.
Our rebellions are with us;
    we're aware of our guilt:
¹³ defying and denying the LORD,
    turning away from our God,
    planning oppression and revolt,
    muttering lying words
    conceived in our minds.

¹⁴ Justice is pushed aside;
    righteousness stands far off,
    because truth has stumbled
    in the public square,
    and honesty can't enter.
¹⁵ Truth is missing;
    anyone turning from evil is plundered.

God will intervene

The LORD looked and was upset
    at the absence of justice.
¹⁶ Seeing that there was no one,
    and astonished that
    no one would intervene,
God's arm brought victory,
    upheld by righteousness,
¹⁷ putting on righteousness as armor
    and a helmet of salvation on his head,
    putting on garments of vengeance,
    and wrapping himself in a cloak of zeal.
¹⁸ God will repay according to their actions:
    wrath to his foes,
    retribution to enemies,
    retribution to the coastlands,
¹⁹ so those in the west
    will fear the LORD's name,
    and those in the east
    will fear God's glory.
It will come like a rushing river
    that the LORD's wind drives on.
²⁰ A redeemer will come to Zion
    and to those in Jacob who stop rebelling,
    says the LORD.

²¹ As for me, this is my covenant with them,
    says the LORD.
My spirit, which is upon you,
    and my words, which I have placed
    in your mouth
    won't depart from your mouth,
    nor from the mouths
    of your descendants,
    nor from the mouths
    of your descendants' children,
    says the LORD,
    forever and always.

Jerusalem's coming radiance

60 Arise! Shine! Your light has come;
    the LORD's glory has shone upon you.
² Though darkness covers the earth
    and gloom the nations,

the LORD will shine upon you;
God's glory will appear over you.
[3] Nations will come to your light
and kings to your dawning radiance.

[4] Lift up your eyes and look all around:
they are all gathered;
they have come to you.
Your sons will come from far away,
and your daughters
on caregivers' hips.
[5] Then you will see and be radiant;
your heart will tremble
and open wide,
because the sea's abundance
will be turned over to you;
the nations' wealth will come to you.
[6] Countless camels will cover your land,
young camels from Midian and Ephah.
They will all come from Sheba,
carrying gold and incense,
proclaiming the LORD's praises.
[7] All Kedar's sheep
will be gathered for you;
rams from Nebaioth
will be your offerings;
they will be accepted on my altar,
and I will glorify my splendid house.

[8] Who are these who fly like a cloud,
like doves to their shelters?
[9] I'm the hope of the coastlands.
Ships from Tarshish are in the lead
to bring your children from afar,
their silver and gold with them
for the name of the LORD your God
and for the holy one of Israel,
who has glorified you.
[10] Foreigners will rebuild your walls,
and their kings will serve you.
Though in my rage I struck you down,
in my favor I have consoled you.
[11] Your gates will be open continually;
day and night they won't close,
to bring to you the wealth of nations,
and their kings led in procession.
[12] The nation and the dynasty
that won't serve you will perish;
such nations will be devastated.
[13] Lebanon's glory will come upon you,
cypress, elm, and pine,

to glorify the site of my sanctuary,
and I will honor my royal footstool.
[14] The children of your tormenters
will come bending low to you;
all who despised you
will bow down at your feet.
They will call you The LORD's City,
Zion, of the holy one of Israel.
[15] Instead of being abandoned,
hated, and forbidden,
I will make you
majestic forever,
a joy for all generations.

LIGHTHOUSE

PRAISE GOD

Blessings Lead to God's Glory *Isaiah 60:21*
God was leading Israel back to what they should
have been doing all along. Everything God had done
was designed to bless them and give God glory.
Israel had done things that made God angry and
sad. Now God would bless them again so everyone
would know they were God's people. Those who
thought Israel was a weak nation would see that
their God had made them strong and mighty. The
people of Israel would no longer give credit to idols
but would give God glory again. ◆

[16] You will suck the milk of nations,
and nurse at royal breasts.
You will know that I am the LORD,
your savior
and your redeemer,
the mighty one of Jacob.
[17] Instead of bronze I will bring gold;
instead of iron I will bring silver;
instead of wood, bronze;
and instead of stones, iron.
I will make peace your governor
and righteousness your taskmaster.
[18] Violence will no longer resound
throughout your land,
nor devastation or destruction
within your borders.
You will call your walls Salvation,
and your gates Praise.
[19] The sun will no longer
be your light by day,
nor will the moon shine
for illumination by night.[n]

[n] Cf DSS (1QIsa[a]), LXX; MT lacks *by night*.

The Lord will be your everlasting light;
your God will be your glory.
20 Your sun will no longer set;
your moon will no longer wane.
The Lord will be
an everlasting light for you,
and your days of mourning
will be ended.
21 Your people will all be righteous;
they will possess the land forever.
They are the shoot that I planted,
the work of my hands, to glorify myself.
22 The least will become a thousand,
and the smallest a powerful people.
I am the Lord; at the right moment,
I will hurry it along.

Joyful proclamations

61 The Lord God's spirit is upon me,
because the Lord has anointed me.
He has sent me
to bring good news to the poor,
to bind up the
brokenhearted,
to proclaim release for captives,
and liberation for prisoners,
2 to proclaim the year of the Lord's favor
and a day of vindication for our God,
to comfort all who mourn,
3 to provide for Zion's mourners,
to give them a crown in place of ashes,
oil of joy in place of mourning,
a mantle of praise
in place of discouragement.
They will be called Oaks of Righteousness,
planted by the Lord to glorify himself.
4 They will rebuild the ancient ruins;
they will restore
formerly deserted places;
they will renew ruined cities,
places deserted in generations past.

Memorize
Isa 61:1

5 Foreigners will stay
and shepherd your sheep,
and strangers will be
your farmers and vinedressers.
6 You will be called
The Priests of the Lord;
Ministers of Our God,
they will say about you.
You will feed on the wealth of nations,
and fatten[o] yourself on their riches.
7 Instead of shame,
their[p] portion will be double;
instead of disgrace,
they will rejoice over their share.
They will possess a double portion
in their land;
everlasting joy will be theirs.
8 I, the Lord, love justice;
I hate robbery and dishonesty.[q]
I will faithfully give them their wage,
and make with them
an enduring covenant.
9 Their offspring will be known
among the nations,
and their descendants
among the peoples.
All who see them will recognize
that they are a people
blessed by the Lord.

10 I surely rejoice in the Lord;
my heart is joyful because of my God,
because he has clothed me
with clothes of victory,
wrapped me in a robe of righteousness
like a bridegroom in a priestly crown,
and like a bride adorned in jewelry.
11 As the earth puts out its growth,
and as a garden grows its seeds,
so the Lord God will grow righteousness
and praise before all the nations.

Jerusalem redeemed

62 For Zion's sake I won't keep silent,
and for Jerusalem's sake
I won't sit still
until her righteousness
shines out like a light,
and her salvation blazes like a torch.
2 Nations will see your righteousness,
all kings your glory.
You will be called by a new name,
which the Lord's own mouth
will determine.
3 You will be a splendid garland
in the Lord's hand,
a royal turban in the palm of God's hand.
4 You will no longer be called Abandoned,
and your land will no longer
be called Deserted.

[o]Heb uncertain [p]Or *your* [q]Heb manuscripts, LXX, Syr, Tg; MT *robbery with an entirely burned offering*

Instead, you will be called
  My Delight Is in Her,
  and your land, Married.
  Because the Lord delights in you,
  your land will be cared for once again.
5 As a young man marries a young woman,
  so your sons will marry you.
  With the joy of a bridegroom
    because of his bride,
  so your God will rejoice because of you.

6 Upon your walls, Jerusalem,
  I have appointed sentinels.
  Continually, all day and all night,
  they won't keep silent.
  You who call on the Lord, don't rest,
7 and don't allow God to rest
  until he establishes Jerusalem,
  and makes it the praise of the earth.
8 The Lord has promised
  with raised hand and strong arm:
  I will never again give your grain
  as food for your enemies.
  Foreigners won't drink your wine
  for which you labored.
9 Those who harvest will eat it
  and will praise the Lord;
  those who gather will drink it
  in my holy courtyards.

10 Pass through, pass through the gates;
  prepare the way for the people!
  Build, build the road;
  clear away the stones!
  Raise up a signal for the peoples.
11 This is what the Lord announced
  to the earth's distant regions:
  Say to Daughter Zion,
  "Look! Your deliverer arrives,
  bringing reward and payment!"
12 They will be called The Holy People,
  Redeemed By the Lord.
  And you will be called Sought After—
  A City That Is Not Abandoned.

Vengeance against the nations

63 Who is this coming from Edom,
  from Bozrah in bright red garments,
  this splendidly dressed one,
  striding[r] with great power?

It is I, proclaiming righteousness,
  powerful to save!
2 Why is your clothing red,
  and your garments like those
  of one who stomps on grapes?
3 I have pressed out in the vat by myself—
  from the peoples, no one was with me.
  I stomped on them in my anger,
  trampled them in my wrath.
  Their blood splashed on my garments,
  and stained all my clothing,
4 because I intended a day of vengeance;
  the year of my deliverance had arrived.
5 I looked and found no helper;
  I was astonished to find no supporter.
  But my arm brought victory for me;
  my wrath helped me.
6 I trampled down nations in my anger
  and made them drunk on my wrath;
  I spilled their blood on the ground.

Prayer of yearning

7 I will recount the Lord's faithful acts;
  I will sing the Lord's praises,
  because of all the Lord did for us,
  for God's great favor
    toward the house of Israel.
  God treated them compassionately
  and with deep affection.
8 God said, "Truly, they are my people,
  children who won't do what is wrong."
  God became their savior.
9 During all their distress,
  God also was distressed,
  so a messenger who served him
    saved them.
  In love and mercy God redeemed them,
  lifting and carrying them
    throughout earlier times.
10 But they rebelled,
  and made God's holy spirit terribly sad,
  so that he turned into their enemy—
  he fought against them!

11 Then they remembered earlier times,
  when he rescued his people.[s]
  Where was the one
  who drew them up from the sea,
  the shepherd[t] of the flock?
  Where was the one
  who put within them his holy spirit;

---

[r]Or stooping [s]Or Moses, his people [t]LXX, Tg; MT shepherds

¹² the one who guided Moses' strong hand
  with his glorious arm;
  who split the water for them
  to create an enduring reputation
    for himself,
¹³ and who guided them through the depths?
  Like a horse in the desert,
    they didn't stumble.
¹⁴ Like cattle descending to the valley,
    the Lᴏʀᴅ's spirit brought them to rest.
  In this way you led your people
  and made for yourself
    a glorious reputation.

¹⁵ Look down from heaven and see,
    from your holy and glorious perch.
  Where are your energy and your might,
    your concern and your pity?
  Don't hold back!ᵘ
¹⁶ You are surely our father,
    even though Abraham doesn't know us,
    and Israel doesn't recognize us.
  You, Lᴏʀᴅ, are our father;
    your reputation since long ago
    is that of our redeemer.
¹⁷ Why do you lead us astray, Lᴏʀᴅ,
    from your ways?
  Why do you harden our heart
    so we don't fear you?
  Return for the sake of your servants
    the tribes that are your heritage!
¹⁸ Why did the wicked
    bring down your holy place?ᵛ
  Why did our enemies
    trample your sanctuary?
¹⁹ For too long we have been
    like those you don't rule,
    like those not known by your name.

64 ʷIf only you would tear open
    the heavens and come down!
  Mountains would quake before you
² like fire igniting brushwood
    or making water boil.
  ˣIf you would make your name known
    to your enemies,
    the nations would tremble
    in your presence.

³ When you accomplished wonders
    beyond all our expectations;

when you came down,
    mountains quaked before you.
⁴ From ancient times,
    no one has heard,
    no ear has perceived,
    no eye has seen any god but you
    who acts on behalf of
    those who wait for him!ʸ
⁵ You look after those who gladly do right;
    they will praise you for your ways.ᶻ
  But you were angry when we sinned;
    you hid yourself when we did wrong.ᵃ
⁶ We have all become like the unclean;
    all our righteous deeds
    are like a menstrual rag.
  All of us wither like a leaf;
    our sins, like the wind, carry us away.
⁷ No one calls on your name;
    no one bothers to hold on to you,
    for you have hidden yourself from us,
    and have handed us overᵇ to our sin.

⁸ But now, Lᴏʀᴅ, you are our father.
  We are the clay, and you are our potter.
  All of us are the work of your hand.
⁹ Don't rage so fiercely, Lᴏʀᴅ;
    don't hold our sins against us forever,
    but gaze now on your people, all of us:
¹⁰ Your holy cities have become a wilderness;
    Zion has become a wilderness,
    Jerusalem a wasteland.
¹¹ Our holy, glorious house,
    where our ancestors praised you,
    has gone up in flames;
    all that we treasured has become a ruin.
¹² After all this, will you hold back, Lᴏʀᴅ?
    Will you keep silent
    and torment us so terribly?

Judgment for idolators

65 I was ready to respond
    to those who didn't ask.
  I was ready to be found
    by those who didn't look for me.
  I said, "I'm here! I'm here!" to a nation
    that didn't call on my name.
² I extended my hands all day
    to a rebellious people
    walking in a way that isn't good,
    following their own plans;

ᵘHeb uncertain ᵛCf LXX, Vulg; Heb uncertain ʷ63:19b in Heb ˣ64:1 in Heb ʸHeb uncertain ᶻHeb uncertain ᵃHeb uncertain
ᵇLXX, cf Syr, Tg, Vulg; MT *melted*

³ people who provoke me
  to my face continually,
  sacrificing in gardens
    and burning incense on bricks,
⁴ who sit in tombs
  and spend the night among rocks;ᶜ
who eat swine's flesh
  with broth of unclean meat in their bowls;
⁵ who say, "Keep to yourself!
Keep away from me! I'm too holy for you."
These people ignite my anger
  like a fire that burns all day.
⁶ Look, this stands written before me.
  I won't be silent, but I will repay;
  I will repay in full measure
⁷ your sins and the sins
  of your ancestors as well,
  says the Lord.
Since they burned incense
  on the mountains,
  and mocked me in the hills,
I will count out to them
  full payment for their actions.

⁸ The Lord proclaims:
As new wine is found in the grape cluster,
  and someone says, "Don't destroy it,
    for there is a blessing in it,"
so I will do for the sake of my servants
  and not destroy everything:
⁹ I will bring out offspring from Jacob,
  and from Judah, heirs to my mountains.
My chosen ones will take possession;
  my servants will dwell there.
¹⁰ Sharon will become a pasture for sheep,
  and the Achor Valley
    a resting place for cattle,
  for my people who seek me.
¹¹ But you who abandon the Lord,
  who forget my holy mountain,
  who set a table for a god of good fortune,
  and fill cups of mixed wine
    for a god of fate:
¹² I will offer you to the sword.
  You will all bow down for slaughter,
because I called and you didn't answer;
  I spoke and you wouldn't hear.
You did what I considered evil,
  and chose what I didn't want.
¹³ Therefore, the Lord God says:

Look, my servants will eat,
  but you will hunger.
My servants will drink, but you will thirst.
My servants will rejoice,
  but you will be ashamed.
¹⁴ My servants will sing
  with contented hearts,
but you will cry out from heartache;
  with broken spirits you will wail.
¹⁵ You will leave your name behind
  for my chosen ones to curse:
  "May the Lord God kill you!
May he call his servants
  by a different name!"
¹⁶ Those who pronounce
  a blessing in the land
will do so by the God called Amen;
  those who make a solemn pledge
  in the land will do so
  by the God called Amen.ᵈ
Past troubles will be forgotten
  and hidden from my sight.

New creation and new Jerusalem

¹⁷ Look! I'm creating
  a new heaven and a new earth:
  past events won't be remembered;
  they won't come to mind.
¹⁸ Be glad and rejoice forever
  in what I'm creating,
because I'm creating Jerusalem as a joy
  and her people as a source of gladness.
¹⁹ I will rejoice in Jerusalem
  and be glad about my people.
No one will ever hear the sound
  of weeping or crying in it again.
²⁰ No more will babies live only a few days,
  or the old fail to live out their days.
The one who dies at a hundred
  will be like a young person,
and the one falling short of a hundred
  will seem cursed.
²¹ They will build houses and live in them;
  they will plant vineyards
  and eat their fruit.
²² They won't build for others to live in,
  nor plant for others to eat.
Like the days of a tree
  will be the days of my people;
  my chosen will make full use
  of their handiwork.

ᶜOr *in guarded places* ᵈOr *so be it*

²³ They won't labor in vain,
  nor bear children to a world of horrors,
  because they will be people
    blessed by the Lord,
  they along with their descendants.
²⁴ Before they call, I will answer;
  while they are still speaking,
    I will hear.
²⁵ Wolf and lamb will graze together,
  and the lion will eat straw like the ox,
  but the snake—its food will be dust.
  They won't hurt or destroy
  at any place on my holy mountain,
  says the Lord.

Where God may be found

66 The Lord says:
  Heaven is my throne,
  and earth is my footstool.

So where could you build a house for me,
  and where could my resting place be?
² My hand made all these things
  and brought them into being,
    says the Lord.
  But here is where I will look:
  to the humble and contrite in spirit,
  who tremble at my word.

³ The one who slaughters an ox kills a person;
  the one who sacrifices a sheep
    breaks a dog's neck;
  the one who makes a grain offering
    offers swine's blood;
  the one who burns incense blesses an idol.
  All these have chosen their own ways,
  and prefer their detestable things.
⁴ So I too will choose to punish them,
  to bring horrors upon them,

No Enemies   *Isaiah 65:17-25*

Can you imagine a world in which there aren't any enemies? People would live together peacefully. Even the animals would get along because the meat-eating animals would eat plants. In the story of creation from the book of Genesis, we hear about a world like this. In the first garden, animals lived together peacefully.

But that world didn't last. Countries go to war. People become enemies with each other. Wolves eat sheep. We can't do anything about some of these things. We can't convince a wolf or lion to eat fruits and vegetables. But we can work for peace.

Living in peace doesn't mean we always agree with everyone. The world would be boring if we all thought exactly the same things. Living in peace means respecting other people's opinions. It means trying to understand their points of view. Living in peace means apologizing for the things we do wrong, and then trying to make them right. It also means saying, "I forgive you," when someone does wrong to us.

These are things that all of us can do, but we can't do them on our own. Remember that God's love is inside us, giving us the strength we need to help create God's dream of a peaceful world.

What does it mean to respect someone else's opinion when you disagree with them?

Name two things you can do today to live in peace with your family.

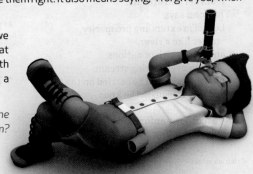

since I called and no one answered.
I spoke and no one heard,
but they did evil in my eyes.
What I didn't want, they chose.

⁵ Listen to the LORD's word,
you who tremble at his word:
Your family members,
those who hate and exclude you
because of my name,
have said, "Let the LORD be glorified;
let's see your joy."
But they will be ashamed.
⁶ The sound of an uproar from the city!
A sound from the temple!
The sound of the LORD repaying his
enemies what they have earned.

Mother Zion

⁷ Before she was in labor, she gave birth.
Before her pangs came upon her,
she delivered a boy.
⁸ Whoever heard of such a thing?
Whoever saw such things as these?
Can a land come to birth in one day?
Can a nation be born all at once?
Yet as soon as birth pangs came,
Zion bore her children.
⁹ Will I open the womb and not bring to birth?
says the LORD.
Will I, who create life, close the womb?
says your God.
¹⁰ Celebrate with Jerusalem;
be happy with her,
all you who love her!
Rejoice with her in joy,
all you who mourn over her,
¹¹ so that you may nurse and be satisfied
from her comforting breasts,
that you may drink and be refreshed
from her full breasts.
¹² The LORD says:
Look, I'm extending prosperity
to her like a river,
and the wealth of nations
like an overflowing stream.
You will nurse and be carried on the hip
and bounced upon the knee.

¹³ As a mother comforts her child,
so I will comfort you;

in Jerusalem you will be comforted.
¹⁴ When you see this, your heart will rejoice;
your entire being will flourish like grass.
The LORD's power will be known
among his servants,
but his fury among his enemies.
¹⁵ The LORD will come with fire,
God's chariots like a windstorm,
to repay in hot anger,
to rebuke with fiery flames.
¹⁶ With fire and with sword
the LORD will judge all humanity;
many will be slain by the LORD.
¹⁷ Those who became holy and purify themselves, following their leader into the gardens,ᵉ
who eat pork, detestable animals, and mice,
will meet their end together, says the LORD.

Worshippers gathered from the nations

¹⁸ Because of their actions and thoughts,
I'm coming to gather all nations and cultures.
They will come to see my glory. ¹⁹ I will put
a sign on them, by sending out some of the
survivors to the nations, to Tarshish, Libya,
and Lydia, and to the archers of Cilicia and
Greece—distant coastlands that haven't heard
of my fame or seen my glory. They will declare
my glory among the nations. ²⁰ They will bring
your family members from all nations as an
offering to the LORD—on horses, in chariots,
in wagons, on mules, and on camels—to my
holy mountain Jerusalem, says the LORD, like
Israelites bringing an offering in purified
containers to the LORD's house. ²¹ I will select
some of them as priests and Levites, says
the LORD.
²² As the new heavens
and the new earth that I'm making
will endure before me, says the LORD,
so your descendants
and your name will endure.
²³ From month to month
and from Sabbath to Sabbath,
all humanity will come
to worship me, says the LORD.
²⁴ They will go out and see the corpses
of the people who rebelled against me,
where their worm never dies,
where their fire is never extinguished.
They will be a horror to everyone.

ᵉHeb uncertain

Jeremiah

The book of Jeremiah begins with God sending Jeremiah to speak to the kingdom of Judah. When Jeremiah said he was too young and didn't know how to speak, God made an astonishing promise to make Jeremiah bold and give him the words to say (Jer 1:1-10).

Jeremiah cried because people dishonored God. He cried because people got hurt when they disobeyed God. Jeremiah felt so sad about God's people that he became known as "the weeping prophet." He said, "If only my head were a spring of water and my eyes a fountain of tears, I would weep day and night for the wounds of my people" (Jer 9:1).

Jeremiah spoke messages that were probably difficult for the people to hear. But he also declared that God would change the hearts of God's people. God would bring them back to their homeland. And one day the people would love and obey God (Jer 30–31).

As you read this book and others in the Old Testament, you will discover that *Israel* isn't always the name of a country. It's often used as a name for God's people. The book of Jeremiah teaches us that God helps us follow God's ways! ♦

things YOU'LL DISCOVER

The book of Jeremiah is named for a prophet who looked around and saw the people of Judah disobeying God. He felt sad that God's people were not living the way God wanted them to live. But he also announced that God wanted to change people's hearts so they could gladly obey and follow God's ways.

people YOU'LL MEET

Jeremiah—a prophet who spoke for God (Jer 1–51)
Josiah—a king of Judah who helped people follow God (Jer 1–3)
Zedekiah—a king of Judah who disobeyed God (Jer 21–52)
Israel—a name for God's people (Jer 1–51)

places YOU'LL GO

Judah (the southern kingdom), **Israel** (the northern kingdom), **Babylon** (present-day Iraq)

words YOU'LL REMEMBER

"This is the covenant that I will make with the people of Israel after that time, declares the LORD. I will put my Instructions within them and engrave them on their hearts. I will be their God, and they will be my people" (Jer 31:33).

Introduction

1 These are the words of Jeremiah, Hilkiah's son, who was one of the priests from Anathoth in the land of Benjamin. ²The LORD's word came to Jeremiah in the thirteenth year of Judah's King Josiah, Amon's son, ³and throughout the rule of Judah's King Jehoiakim, Josiah's son, until the fifth month of the eleventh year of King Zedekiah, Josiah's son, when the people of Jerusalem were taken into exile.

Call of Jeremiah

⁴The LORD's word came to me:

⁵ "Before I created you in the womb
  I knew you;
  before you were born I set you apart;
  I made you a prophet to the nations."

⁶ "Ah, LORD God," I said,
  "I don't know how to speak
  because I'm only a child."
⁷ The LORD responded,
  "Don't say,
  'I'm only a child.'
  Where I send you, you must go;
  what I tell you, you must say.
⁸ Don't be afraid of them,
  because I'm with you
    to rescue you,"
    declares the LORD.
⁹ Then the LORD stretched out his hand,
  touched my mouth, and said to me,
  "I'm putting my words in your mouth.
¹⁰ This very day I appoint you
  over nations and empires,
  to dig up and pull down,

Memorize Jer 1:7

What Job Will You Do? *Jeremiah 1:4-10*

What job will you do when you grow up? Maybe you imagine yourself as a musician in an orchestra, a surgeon in a hospital, or an athlete on a professional sports team. There are so many possibilities. It can be very difficult to decide! You can learn a lot about jobs by talking with the adults you know. Family members, teachers, or coaches can share with you their stories about their lives and their work. They might also have ideas about how you can use your talents one day. Some people grow up and join their family's business. That's what happened to Jeremiah.

Jeremiah was the son of a priest. Today, that would be like being the son or daughter of a rabbi or minister. When God told Jeremiah that God wanted him to be a prophet, Jeremiah wasn't so sure he wanted to do this. He wondered if God was making a mistake.

But God told Jeremiah that God knew him before he was born! Jeremiah was probably afraid, so he thought of a good excuse. He told God he was too young and wouldn't know what to say to God's people. But God promised to be with Jeremiah wherever he went and to tell him what he would need to say. Jeremiah decided to follow God, and he became an amazing prophet.

God knows you inside and out, just as God knew Jeremiah. Just as God needed Jeremiah, God needs you. You are an important part of God's creation. The world would not be the same without you!

What job do you want to do when you grow up?

How can you follow God in what you are doing today?

Jeremiah's mission confirmed

[11]The LORD asked me, "What do you see, Jeremiah?"

I said, "A branch of an almond[a] tree."

[12]The LORD then said, "You are right, for I'm watching over[b] my word until it is fulfilled." [13]The LORD asked me again, "What do you see?"

I said, "A pot boiling over from the north."

[14]The LORD said to me, "Trouble will erupt from the north against the people of this land.

[15]I'm calling for all the tribes of great nations from the north, says the LORD, and they will set up their rulers by the entrances of Jerusalem, on its walls, and in every city of Judah. [16]I will declare my judgment against them for doing evil: for abandoning me, worshipping other gods, and trusting in the works of their hands. [17]But you must prepare for battle and be ready to utter every word I command you. Don't be frightened before them, or I will frighten you before them. [18]Today I have made you an armed city, an iron pillar, and a bronze wall against the entire land—the kings of Judah, its princes, its priests, and all its people. [19]They will attack you, but they won't defeat you, because I am with you and will rescue you, declares the LORD.

God's people abandon their God

2The LORD's word came to me: [2]Go and proclaim
to the people of Jerusalem,
The LORD proclaims:
I remember your first love,[c]
  your devotion as a young bride,
  how you followed me in the wilderness,
  in an unplanted land.
[3] Israel was devoted to the LORD,
  the early produce of the harvest.
Whoever ate from it became guilty;
  disaster overtook them,
  declares the LORD.
[4] Listen to the LORD's word,
  people of Judah,
  all you families of the Israelite household.
[5]This is what the LORD says:
What wrong did your ancestors find in me
  that made them wander so far?

did you **know?** There is only one letter different between the Hebrew word for *almond* and the Hebrew word for *watchful*. In Bible times, the almond tree was used to remind people of God's watchfulness over the people.

They pursued what was worthless
  and became worthless.
[6] They didn't ask,
  "Where's the LORD who brought us up
    from the land of Egypt,
  who led us through the wilderness,
  in a land of deserts and ravines,
  in a land of drought and darkness,
  in a land of no return,
    where no one survives?"
[7] I brought you into a land of plenty,
  to enjoy its gifts and goodness,
  but you ruined my land;
  you disgraced my heritage.
[8] The priests didn't ask,
  "Where's the LORD?"
Those responsible for the Instruction
  didn't know me;
  the leaders rebelled against me;
  the prophets spoke in the name of Baal,
  going after what has no value.
[9] That is why I will take you to court
  and charge even your descendants,
  declares the LORD.
[10] Look to the west
  as far as the shores of Cyprus
  and to the east
  as far as the land of Kedar.
Ask anyone there:
  Has anything this odd ever taken place?
[11] Has a nation switched gods,
  though they aren't really gods at all?
Yet my people have exchanged
  their glory
  for what has no value.
[12] Be stunned at such a thing, you heavens;
  shudder and quake,
  declares the LORD.
[13] My people have committed two crimes:
  They have forsaken me,
  the spring of living water.
And they have dug wells,
  broken wells that can't hold water.

[a]Heb *shaqed* [b]Heb *shoqed* [c]Or *the love of your youth*

LIFE PRESERVER

What crimes did Judah and Israel commit? *Jeremiah 2:13*

The first chapters of Jeremiah retell the history of Israel and Judah. The author says they committed the crime of forgetting God and God's covenant relationship with them. They committed a second crime as well. Not only had they forgotten God, "the spring of living water," but they also dug wells that were broken and wouldn't hold water. This is a symbolic way of saying that they had substituted false gods, like Baal, in place of God, the one who led them out of Egypt in the exodus to the promised land. ◊

¹⁴ Is Israel a slave,
  a servant by birth?
  If not, why then has he become prey?
¹⁵ Lions roar at him; they growl.
  They destroy his land
    and make his towns desolate
    until nothing is left.
¹⁶ As well, the people
  of Memphis and Tahpanhes
  lay open your scalp.
¹⁷ Haven't you brought this on yourself
  by abandoning the LORD your God,
    who has directed your paths?
¹⁸ So why take the path to Egypt
  to drink water from the Nile?
  Why travel the path to Assyria
  to drink water from the Euphrates?
¹⁹ Your wrongdoing will punish you.
  Your acts of unfaithfulness
    will find you out.
  Don't you understand how terribly bitter
  it is to abandon the LORD your God
    and not fear me?
    declares the LORD of heavenly forces.
²⁰ Long ago I broke your yoke;
  I shattered your chains.
  But even then you said,
    "I won't serve you."
  On every high hill
  and under every lush tree,
    you have acted like a prostitute.
²¹ Yet it was I who planted you,
  a precious vine of fine quality;
  how could you turn into a wild vine
    and become good for nothing?

²² Even though you scrub yourself
  with soap or strong powder,
    the stain of your sin is still before me,
    declares the LORD God.
²³ How can you say,
  "I'm not dirty;
  I haven't gone after Baals."
  Look what you have done in the valley;
  consider what you have done there.
  You are like a frenzied young camel,
    racing around,
²⁴ a wild donkey in the wilderness,
  lustfully sniffing the wind.
  Who can restrain such passion?
    Those who desire her need not give up;
    with little effort
    they will find her in heat.
²⁵ Don't run about
  until your feet are blistered
  and your throat is parched.
  But you say, "What's the use?
  I have fallen in love with foreign gods,
    and I must pursue them."
²⁶ As a thief is ashamed
  when caught in his tracks,
    so the people of Israel are ashamed—
    their kings, officials,
    priests, and prophets—
²⁷ when they say to a piece of wood,
  "You are my father,"
    and to a stone, "You gave me birth."
  They have turned their backs to me
    and not their faces.
  Yet in their time of trouble they say,
    "Arise and save us!"
²⁸ Where are the gods
  you have made for yourselves?
  Let's see if they will come through
    for you in your time of trouble.
  You have as many gods, Judah,
    as you have towns.
²⁹ Why would you bring charges against me?
  You have all rebelled against me,
    declares the LORD.
³⁰ I have disciplined your children in vain;
  they have rejected my correction.
  You have devoured your prophets
    like a hungry lion.
³¹ People of this generation,
  listen closely to the LORD's word:
  Have I been a wasteland to Israel
  or a land of dense darkness?

Why then do my people say,
  "We have wandered far away;
  we'll come to you no longer"?
³² Does a young woman forget her jewelry
  or a bride her wedding dress?
  Yet you have forgotten me
  days without end!
³³ So skilled are you at pursuing lovers[d]
  that you instruct
  even the most wicked.[e]
³⁴ Your garments are stained
  with the blood of the innocent poor,
  even though you didn't catch them
  breaking and entering.
  Yet, despite all this,[f] ³⁵you still insist,
  "I'm innocent;
  as a result he will turn his anger
  away from me."
Because you claim not to have sinned,
  I will pass judgment against you.
³⁶ You change sides so casually!
  But Egypt will shame you
  no less than Assyria.
³⁷ From there you will go out
  with your hands on your heads,
  because the Lord has rejected
  those you rely on;
  they won't help you.

UMBRELLA
MOURNING

Hands on Their Heads *Jeremiah 2:37*
The people of Judah, like the people of Israel, had trusted in the wrong people to help them in times of trouble. Now they would suffer in the same way. Many of them would be forced to leave their land and go into captivity at the hands of the Babylonians.

They would leave with their hands on their heads, which was a sign of mourning. They would live with the results of their choices. They chose to follow powerful nations and their idol gods. They refused to put their trust in the one true God.

God wanted them to know that no earthly power could match God's power. Judah's only hope was God, whom Judah stubbornly refused to seek. ◑

Jeremiah's summons to change

3 If a man divorces his wife,
  and after she leaves him marries another,
  can he return to her again?
  Wouldn't such an act
  completely corrupt the land?
  Yet you have prostituted yourself
  with many lovers.
  Would you return to me?
  declares the Lord.
² Look to the well-traveled paths[g] and see!
  Where haven't you committed adultery?
  On the roadsides you sit in wait for lovers,
  like a nomad in the wilderness.
  You have corrupted the land
  with your cheap and reckless behavior.
³ That's why the showers have failed
  and the spring rains have ceased.
  Still you act like a brazen prostitute[h]
  who refuses to blush.
⁴ At the same time you say to me,
  "My father, my friend since youth,
  ⁵ will you stay angry forever?
  Will you continue to be furious?"
  This is what you say
  while you do as much evil
  as you possibly can.

⁶During the rule of King Josiah, the Lord said to me: Have you noticed what unfaithful Israel has done? She's gone about looking for lovers on top of every high hill and under every lush tree. ⁷I thought that after she had done all this she would return to me, but she didn't. Her disloyal sister Judah saw this. ⁸She[i] also saw that I sent unfaithful Israel away with divorce papers because of all her acts of unfaithfulness; yet disloyal sister Judah was not afraid but kept on playing the prostitute. ⁹She didn't think twice about corrupting the land and committing adultery with stone and tree. ¹⁰Yet even after all this, disloyal sister Judah didn't return to me with all her heart but only insincerely, declares the Lord. ¹¹Then the Lord said to me: Unfaithful Israel is less guilty[j] than disloyal Judah.

¹²Go proclaim these words to the north and say:

  Return, unfaithful Israel,
    declares the Lord.
  I won't reject you,

---

[d]Or *love* [e]Or *you have taught your ways to wicked women.* [f]Heb uncertain [g]Or *bare heights* [h]Or *You have a prostitute's forehead.* [i]LXX, Syr; MT *I* [j]Or *more righteous*

for I'm faithful,
declares the Lord;
I won't stay angry forever.
¹³ Only acknowledge your wrongdoing:
how you have rebelled
against the Lord your God,
and given yourself to strangers
under every lush tree
and haven't obeyed me,
declares the Lord.
¹⁴ Return, rebellious children,
declares the Lord,
for I'm your husband.
I'll gather you—
one from a city and two from a tribe—
and bring you back to Zion.

¹⁵ I will appoint shepherds with whom I'm pleased, and they will lead you with knowledge and understanding. ¹⁶ And in those days, when your numbers have greatly increased in the land, declares the Lord, people will no longer talk about the Lord's covenant chest; they won't recall or remember it; they won't even miss it or try to build another one. ¹⁷ At that time, they will call Jerusalem the Lord's throne, and all nations will gather there to honor the Lord's name. No longer will they follow their own willful and evil hearts. ¹⁸ In those days the people of Judah and Israel will leave the north together for the land that I gave their ancestors as an inheritance.

¹⁹ I thought to myself,
How wonderful it would be
to treat you like children
and give you a beautiful land,
an inheritance unrivaled
among the nations.
And I thought, You will call me father,
and you won't turn away from me.
²⁰ But as a woman betrays her lover,
so you, people of Israel,
have betrayed me,
declares the Lord.
²¹ A voice is heard on the well-traveled paths;ᵏ
it's the crying and pleading
of the people of Israel,
who have lost their way
and forgotten the Lord their God.
²² Return, rebellious children,
and I will heal your rebellion.

"Here we are; we come to you,
for you are the Lord our God.
²³ Surely what happens on the hillsˡ
is a waste,
as is the uproar on the mountains.
Only in the Lord our God
is the salvation of Israel.
²⁴ From our youth, shameᵐ has devoured
the fruit of our parents' labor—
their flocks and herds,
as well as their sons and daughters.
²⁵ Let's lie down in our shame.
Let our dishonor cover us,
for we have sinned
against the Lord our God,
both we and our ancestors,
from our youth to this very day.
We have disobeyed
the voice of the Lord our God."

4 If you return, Israel, return to me,
declares the Lord.
If you get rid of your disgusting idols
from my presence
and wander no more,
² and if you swear by the living God
in truth, justice, and righteousness,
then the nations
will enjoy God's blessings;ⁿ
they will boast about him.
³ This is what the Lord says to the people of Judah and to the residents of Jerusalem:
Break up your hard rocky soil;
don't plant among the thorns.
⁴ Dedicateᵒ yourselves to the Lord;
don't be thick-skinned,ᵖ
people of Judah
and residents of Jerusalem,
or else my anger will spread like a wildfire.
It will burn, with no one to put it out,
because of your evil deeds.

Disaster approaches
⁵ Announce in Judah,
in Jerusalem proclaim,
sound the alarm throughout the land,
cry out and say,
"Gather together!
Let's flee to the fortified towns!"
⁶ Set up a flag to Zion;

ᵏOr *bare heights* ˡLXX, Syr, Vulg; MT *from the hills* ᵐOr *the shame* ⁿOr *bless themselves in him* or *be blessed by him* or *will bless themselves* ᵒOr *circumcise* ᵖOr *remove the foreskins of your hearts*

take cover, don't just stand there!
I'm bringing disaster from the north,
massive devastation.

⁷ A lion bursts out of the thicket;
a destroyer of nations advances.
He's gone forth from his place
to ravage your land,
to wipe out your towns,
until no one is left.

⁸ So put on funeral clothing.
Weep and wail,
for the Lᴏʀᴅ's fierce anger
hasn't turned away from us.

⁹ On that day, declares the Lᴏʀᴅ,
the courage of the king and his princes
will fail,
the priests will be stunned,
and the prophets will be shocked.

¹⁰ Then I said, "Lᴏʀᴅ God, no!
You have utterly deceived this people
and Jerusalem
by promising them peace
even though the sword is at their throats."

¹¹ At that time, this people and Jerusalem
will be told:
A blistering wind from the bare heights;
it rages in the desert toward my people,
not merely to winnow or cleanse.

¹² This wind is too devastating for that.
Now I, even I, will pronounce
my sentence against them.

¹³ Look! He approaches like the clouds;
his chariots advance like a tempest,
his horses swifter than eagles.
How horrible! We're doomed!

¹⁴ Cleanse your heart of evil, Jerusalem,
that you may be saved.
How long will you entertain
your destructive ideas?

¹⁵ A voice declares from Dan;
someone proclaims disaster
from the highlands of Ephraim.

¹⁶ Warn the nations,
proclaim it to Jerusalem!
Armies are approaching
from a far-away country,

raising their war cries
against the towns of Judah.

¹⁷ They hem her in
like those guarding a field,
because she has rebelled against me,
declares the Lᴏʀᴅ.

¹⁸ Your own conduct, your own deeds
have done this to you.
This is your payment and how bitter it is,
piercing into the depths of your heart.

Anguish over looming disaster

¹⁹ Oh, my suffering, my suffering!
My pain is unbearable;
my heart is in turmoil;
it throbs nonstop.
I can't be silent, because I hear the blast
of the trumpet
and the roar
of the battle cry!

LIGHTHOUSE

CHANGED HEART

God Is Our Help *Jeremiah 4:19*
Jeremiah was hurting because of his people. They disobeyed God and trusted in powerful nations rather than God. Jeremiah told the people that those powerful nations couldn't help them. Only God had the power to save them. Jeremiah's heart was hurting because of what was happening to the people. He didn't want them to suffer.

Sometimes the best thing that can happen is for us to discover that God is the only one who can help us. It's tough to watch people suffer, even when they are in trouble because of their own problems. When people are in trouble, we should pray for them and try to help them in any way we can. ◊

²⁰ Disaster follows disaster;
the whole land is ruined.
Suddenly, my tents are destroyed,
my shelter in a moment.

²¹ How long must I see the battle flags
and hear the blast of the trumpet?

²² My people are foolish.
They don't even know me!
They are thoughtless children
without understanding;
they are skilled at doing wrong,
inept at doing right.

²³ I looked at the earth,
and it was without shape or form;

did you know? In his vision, Jeremiah saw a future so bad that the acts God did in creation were reversed. All sources of light disappeared, leaving only darkness.

at the heavens
and there was no light.
²⁴ I looked at the mountains
and they were quaking;
all the hills were rocking
back and forth.
²⁵ I looked and there was no one left;
every bird in the sky had taken flight.
²⁶ I looked and the fertile land
was a desert;
all its towns were in ruins
before the Lord,
before his fury.
²⁷ The Lord proclaims:
The whole earth
will become a desolation,
but I will not destroy it completely.
²⁸ Therefore, the earth will grieve
and the heavens grow dark
because I have declared my plan
and will neither change my mind
nor cancel the plan.
²⁹ As the horsemen and archers approach,
the people take flight.
They hide in the bushes
and escape to the cliffs.
Every city is deserted;
no one remains.
³⁰ And you, devastated one,
why dress up in scarlet,
deck yourself in gold jewelry,
and color your eyes with paint?
In vain you get all decked out;
your lovers have rejected you
and now seek your life.
³¹ I hear the cry of a woman in labor,
the distress of one delivering
her first child.
It is the cry of Daughter Zion,
gasping for breath,
her arms stretched out,
and moaning,
"I'm about to fall
into the hands of murderers!"

Futile search for a good person

5 Search every street in Jerusalem,
comb the squares,
look far and wide
for one person,
even one who acts justly
and seeks truth that I may pardon her!

² Even when making a pledge—
"As the Lord lives"—
they swear falsely.
³ Lord, don't you look for integrity?
You have struck them down,
but they didn't even cringe.
You have crushed them,
but they have ignored your discipline.
They make their faces harder than rock
and refuse to return.
⁴ Then I thought to myself,
These are the poor
who don't know better!
They don't understand the Lord's way
or the justice of their God.
⁵ Let me go and speak
to the powerful people,
for they will surely know the Lord's way
and the justice of their God.
But they too have broken their yoke
and shattered the chains.
⁶ Therefore, a lion from the forest
will attack them;
a wolf from the desert
will destroy them;
a leopard prowling around their towns
will tear to pieces
anyone venturing out—
because of their many crimes
and countless acts of unfaithfulness.
⁷ How can I pardon you?
Your children have forsaken me
and swear by gods that are not gods.
Although I could have satisfied them,
they committed adultery,
dashing off to the prostitution house.
⁸ They are lusty stallions roving about,
snorting for another's wife.
⁹ The Lord declares:
Shouldn't I confront these acts?
Shouldn't I take revenge
on such a nation?

Contempt for God

¹⁰ Climb through her vineyards
and ravage them,
although not completely.
Prune back her branches,
because they aren't the Lord's.
¹¹ The people of Israel and Judah
have been utterly faithless to me,
declares the Lord.

¹²They have lied about the Lord
and said, "He'll do nothing!ᑫ
Disaster won't come upon us;
we won't see war or famine."
¹³The prophets are so much wind;
the word isn't in them.
Thus and so may it be done to them.
¹⁴Therefore, the Lord God of heavenly forces proclaims:
Because you have spoken this way,
I will put my words
in your mouth as a fire;
it will consume the people,
who are but kindling.
¹⁵I am about to bring a distant nation
against you,
people of Israel,
declares the Lord.
It is an established nation,
an ancient nation,
a nation whose language
you don't know,
whose speech you won't understand.
¹⁶Its weapons are deadly;ʳ
its warriors are many.
¹⁷It will devour your harvest and food;
it will devour your sons and daughters;
it will devour your flocks and herds;
it will devour your vines and fig trees;
it will shatter your fortified towns
in which you trust—
with the sword!

¹⁸Yet even in those days, declares the Lord, I won't completely destroy you. ¹⁹And when they ask, "Why has the Lord our God done all these things to us?" you must reply, "Just as you have abandoned me and served foreign gods in your land, so you will serve strangers in a land not your own."

Shouldn't you fear me?

²⁰Declare this to the people of Jacob,
announce it in Judah:
²¹Listen, you foolish and senseless people,
who have eyes but don't see
and ears but don't hear.
²²Shouldn't you fear me,
declares the Lord,
and tremble before me,
the one who set the shoreline
for the sea,

an ancient boundary that it can't pass?
Though its waves may rise and roar,
they can't pass the limits I have set.
²³And yet the people have stubborn
and rebellious hearts;
they turn and go their own way.
²⁴They don't say in their hearts,
Let's fear the Lord our God,
who provides rain in autumn and spring
and who assures us of a harvest
in its season.
²⁵Your wrongdoing has turned
these blessingsˢ away.
Your sin has robbed you of good.
²⁶Criminals are found among my people;
they set traps to catch people,
like hunters lying in wait.ᵗ
²⁷Like a cage full of birds,
so their houses are full of loot.
No wonder they are rich and powerful
²⁸and have grown fat and sleek!
To be sure, their evil deeds
exceed all limits,
and yet they prosper.
They are indifferent
to the plight of the orphan,
reluctant to defend
the rights of the poor.
²⁹Shouldn't I punish such acts?
declares the Lord.
Shouldn't I repay that nation
for its deeds?
³⁰An awful, a terrible thing
has happened in the land:
³¹The prophets prophesy falsely,
the priests rule at their sides,ᵘ
and my people love it this way!
But what will you do when the end comes?

Prepare for war

6Escape, people of Benjamin,
get out of Jerusalem!
Blow the trumpet in Tekoa,
sound the alarm in Beth-haccherem;
for disaster looms from the north,
massive devastation.
²You are like a lovely pasture,
Daughter Zion.ᵛ
³Shepherds come to her with their flocks.
They pitch their tents around her
and graze in their place.

ᑫOr *not he* ʳOr *Its quiver is like an open grave* ˢHeb lacks *blessings.* ᵗHeb uncertain ᵘOr *by their hands* ᵛHeb uncertain

⁴ "Prepare for battle against her;
    get ready; let's attack by noon!
Oh, no! Daylight is fading,
    and the evening shadows lengthen.
⁵ Get ready, let's attack by night
    and destroy her fortresses!"
⁶ The LORD of heavenly forces proclaims:
Cut down her trees,
    and build siege ramps against Jerusalem.
This city must be held accountable,ʷ
    for there's nothing but oppression
    in her midst.
⁷ As a well brings forth fresh water,
    she brings forth evil.
Violence and destruction
    are heard within her;
    injury and wounds are ever before me.
⁸ Hear me out,ˣ Jerusalem,
    or else I'll turn away from you
    and reduce you to ruins,
    a land unfit to live in.

Unresponsive people

⁹ This is what the LORD of heavenly forces
    says:
From top to bottom, let them harvest
    the remaining few in Israel.
    Pick clean every
    last grape on the vine!
¹⁰ To whom can I speak and warn?
    How can I get someone's attention?
    Their ears are shut tight,ʸ
    so they won't hear.
They are ashamed of the LORD's word
    and take no pleasure in it.
¹¹ But I'm filled with the LORD's rage
    and am tired of holding it in.

Pour it out on the children in the streets
    and on the youths gathered together;
husband with wife will be trapped,
    as will those old and gray.
¹² Their homes will be turned over to others,
    their fields and wives as well.
I will stretch out my hand
    against the people of this land,
    declares the LORD.
¹³ From the least to the greatest,
    each is eager to profit;
    from prophet to priest,

each trades in dishonesty.
¹⁴ They treat the wound of my people
    as if it were nothing:
"All is well, all is well," they insist,
    when in fact nothing is well.
¹⁵ They should be ashamed
    of their detestable practices,
but they have no shame;
    they don't even blush!
Therefore, they will fall among the fallen
    and stumble when I bring disaster,
    declares the LORD.
¹⁶ The LORD proclaims:
Stop at the crossroads and look around;
    ask for the ancient paths.
Where is the good way?
Then walk in it
    and find a resting place for yourselves.
    But youᶻ said, "We won't go!"
¹⁷ Still, I have appointed watchmen
    to warn you.
    But youᵃ said, "We won't listen!"
¹⁸ Therefore, pay attention, nations;
    take notice, assembly,
    what is ahead of them.ᵇ
¹⁹ Pay attention, earth:
I'm bringing disaster upon my people,
    the fruit of their own devices,
because they have ignored my words
    and they have rejected my teaching.
²⁰ What use to me is incense from Sheba
    or sweet cane from a faraway land?
Your entirely burned offerings
    won't buy your pardon;
    your sacrifices won't appease me.
²¹ Therefore, the LORD proclaims:
I'm putting obstacles before this people,
    and both parents and children
    will stumble over them;
neighbor and friend alike will perish.

Panic-stricken Zion

²² The LORD proclaims:
An army is on the move
    from the northern regions;
a great nation is roused
    from the ends of the earth.
²³ Equipped with bow and spear,
    they are cruel;
    they show no mercy.

ʷHeb uncertain ˣOr *Accept correction* ʸOr *uncircumcised* ᶻOr *they* ᵃOr *they* ᵇHeb uncertain

Their horsemen sound
  like the roaring sea,
    arrayed in battle formation
      against you, Daughter Zion.

24 We have heard reports of them
  and are panic-stricken;
    distress overwhelms us,
      pain like that of a woman in labor.

25 Don't go out into the field!
  Don't walk on the road!
    The enemies' sword
      terrorizes at every turn.

26 My people,
  put on funeral clothes and roll in ashes;
    weep and wail as for an only child,
      because the destroyer
        will suddenly descend upon us.

Prophet as tester

27 I have made you a tester of metals,
  to examine my people[c]
    to know and prove their ways.

28 They are tin[d] and iron;
  they are headstrong and rebellious.
    They live to slander.
      They act corruptly—every last one!

29 The bellows roar;
  the lead is consumed.[e]
    Yet the refining fails;
      the impurities[f] remain.

30 They are called "rejected silver,"
  for the Lord has rejected them.

The Lord's temple

7 Jeremiah received the Lord's word: ²Stand near the gate of the Lord's temple and proclaim this message: Listen to the Lord's word, all you of Judah who enter these gates to worship the Lord. ³This is what the Lord of heavenly forces, the God of Israel, says: Improve your conduct and your actions, and I will dwell with you[g] in this place. ⁴Don't trust in lies: "This is the Lord's temple! The Lord's temple! The Lord's temple!" ⁵No, if you truly reform your ways and your actions; if you treat each other justly; ⁶if you stop taking advantage of the immigrant, orphan, or widow; if you don't shed the blood of the innocent in this place, or go after other gods to your own ruin, ⁷only then will I dwell with

you[h] in this place, in the land that I gave long ago to your ancestors for all time.

⁸And yet you trust in lies that will only hurt you. ⁹Will you steal and murder, commit adultery and perjury, sacrifice to Baal and go after other gods that you don't know, ¹⁰and then come and stand before me in this temple that bears my name, and say, "We are safe," only to keep on doing all these detestable things? ¹¹Do you regard this temple, which bears my name, as a hiding place for criminals? I can see what's going on here, declares the Lord. ¹²Just go to my sanctuary[i] in Shiloh, where I let my name dwell at first, and see what I did to it because of the evil of my people Israel. ¹³And now, because you have done all these things, declares the Lord, because you haven't listened when I spoke to you again and again or responded when I called you, ¹⁴I will do to this temple that bears my name and on which you rely, the place that I gave to you and your ancestors, just as I did to Shiloh. ¹⁵I will cast you out of my sight, just as I cast out the rest of your family, all the people of Ephraim.

¹⁶As for you, don't pray for these people, don't cry out or plead for them, and don't intercede with me,

LIGHTHOUSE

CHANGED HEART AND LIFE

Obey God *Jeremiah 7:3, 5-7*

A prophet's main job was to warn God's people and then urge them to turn from their disobedience. God had a message for Jeremiah to deliver to the people. God wanted them to stop doing bad things and start doing what God wanted. They abused and disrespected God's temple. They forgot it was a holy place. Some of the people pretended to be holy, but they were not. Jeremiah told them to turn from wickedness and obey God. It was the only way for them to avoid judgment and punishment.

Today God is still using prophets, ministers, and pastors as messengers to speak to us. They encourage us to do what is right, but they also warn us against the dangers of doing wrong. God wants us to worship with pure and honest hearts. ◊

---

[c]Heb uncertain [d]Or bronze [e]Heb uncertain [f]Or wicked [g]Or I will let you dwell [h]Or I will let you dwell [i]Or place

for I won't listen to you. ¹⁷Can't you see what they are doing in the towns of Judah and in the streets of Jerusalem? ¹⁸The children gather wood, the fathers light the fire, and the women knead dough to make sacrificial cakes for the queen of heaven. And to offend me all the more, they pour out drink offerings to foreign gods. ¹⁹But am I the one they are really offending? declares the Lord. Aren't they in fact humiliating themselves? ²⁰Therefore, this is what the Lord God says: I'm going to pour out my fierce anger on this place, on humans and beasts, on the trees of the field and the crops of the fertile land. It will burn and not go out.

²¹This is what the Lord of heavenly forces, the God of Israel, says: Add your entirely burned offerings to your sacrifices and eat them yourselves! ²²On the day I brought your ancestors out of the land of Egypt, I didn't say a thing—I gave no instructions—about entirely burned offerings or sacrifices. ²³Rather, this is what I required of them: Obey me so that I may become your God and you may become my people. Follow the path I mark out for you so that it may go well with you. ²⁴But they didn't listen or pay attention. They followed their willful and evil hearts and went backward rather than forward. ²⁵From the moment your ancestors left the land of Egypt to this day, I have sent you all my servants the prophets—day after day. ²⁶But they didn't listen to me or pay attention; they were stubborn and did more harm than their ancestors. ²⁷When you tell them all this, they won't listen to you. When you call to them, they won't respond. ²⁸Therefore, say to them: This nation neither obeys the Lord its God nor accepts correction; truth has disappeared; it has vanished from their lips.

²⁹ Cut off your hair and cast it away;
   grieve on the well-traveled paths.
   The Lord has rejected you
   and has cast off a generation
      that provokes his anger.

³⁰The people of Judah have done what displeases me, declares the Lord. They have corrupted the temple that bears my name by setting up their disgusting idols. ³¹They have built shrines at Topheth in the Ben-hinnom

Valley to burn their sons and daughters in the fire, although I never commanded such a thing, nor did it ever cross my mind. ³²So now the time is coming, declares the Lord, when people will no longer speak of Topheth or the Ben-hinnom Valley, but the Carnage Valley. They will bury in Topheth until no space is left. ³³The corpses of this people will be food for birds and wild animals, with no one to drive them off. ³⁴I will silence the sound of joy and delight as well as the voice of bride and bridegroom in the towns of Judah and in the streets of Jerusalem, for the country

8 will be reduced to a wasteland. ¹At that time, declares the Lord, the bones of the kings of Judah and its officers, the bones of the priests and the prophets, and the bones of the people of Jerusalem will be taken from their graves ²and exposed to the sun, the moon, and the whole heavenly forces, which they have loved and served and which they have followed, consulted, and worshipped. Their bones won't be gathered for reburial but will become like refuse lying on the ground. ³The survivors of this evil nation will prefer death to life, wherever I have scattered them, declares the Lord of heavenly forces.

Bet you can
read this in 8 minutes.
Ready, set, go!

Depth of Judah's wrongdoing

⁴ Say to them, The Lord proclaims:
   When people fall down, don't they get up?
      When they turn aside,
         don't they turn back?
⁵ Why then does this people,
      rebellious Jerusalem,
         persistently turn away from me?
   They cling to deceit
      and refuse to return.
⁶ I have listened carefully
      but haven't heard a word of truth
         from them.
   No one regrets their wrongdoing;
      no one says, "What have I done?"
   Everyone turns to their own course,
      like a stallion dashing
         into the thick of battle.
⁷ Even the stork in the sky
      knows the seasons,
   and the dove, swallow,ʲ and craneᵏ

ʲHeb uncertain ᵏHeb uncertain

return in due time.
But my people
don't know the LORD's ways.
8 How can you say, "We are wise;
we possess the LORD's Instruction,"
when the lying pen of the scribes
has surely distorted it?
9 The wise will be shamed and shocked
when they are caught.
Look, they have rejected the LORD's word;
what kind of wisdom is that?
10 Therefore, I will give their wives to others
and their fields to their captors.
From the least to the greatest,
all are eager to profit.
From prophet to priest,
all trade in falsehood.
11 They treat the wound of my people
as if it were nothing:
"All is well, all is well," they insist,
when in fact nothing is well.
12 They should be ashamed
of their detestable practices,
but they have no shame;
they don't even blush!
Therefore, they will fall among the fallen
and stumble when disaster arrives,
declares the LORD.
13 I will put an end to them,[l]
declares the LORD;
there are no grapes on the vine,
no figs on the tree,
only withered leaves.
They have squandered
what I have given them![m]

A lament for God's people

14 Why are we sitting here?
Come, let's go to the fortified towns
and meet our doom there.
The LORD our God has doomed us
by giving us poisoned water to drink,
because we have sinned
against the LORD!
15 We longed for relief,
but received none;
for a time of healing,
but found only terror.
16 The snorting of their horses
can be heard as far as Dan;
the neighing of their stallions
makes the whole land tremble.
They come to devour the land
and everything in it,
towns and people alike.
17 See, I'm sending serpents against you,
vipers that you can't charm,
and they will bite you,
declares the LORD.
18 No healing,
only grief;
my heart is broken.[n]
19 Listen to the weeping of my people
all across the land:
"Isn't the LORD in Zion?
Is her king no longer there?"
Why then did they anger me
with their images,
with pointless foreign gods?
20 "The harvest is past,
the summer has ended,
yet we aren't saved."
21 Because my people are crushed,
I am crushed;
darkness and despair overwhelm me.

What to do with God's people

22 Is there no balm in Gilead?
Is there no physician there?
Why then have my people
not been restored to health?

9 [o] If only my head were a spring of water
and my eyes a fountain of tears,
I would weep day and night
for the wounds of my people.
2 [p] If only I could flee for shelter
in the desert,
to leave my people
and forget them—
for they are all adulterers,
a bunch of crooks.
3 They bend their tongues like bows
to spew out lies;
they are renowned in the land,
but not for truth.
They go from bad to worse.
They don't know me!
declares the LORD.
4 Be wary of your friends!
Don't trust your sibling![q]

[l] Heb uncertain [m] Heb uncertain [n] Heb uncertain [o] 8:23 in Heb [p] 9:1 in Heb [q] Or *brother*

Every sibling is a cheater,
and every friend traffics in slander.
⁵ One cheats the other;
no one tells the truth;
they train themselves to lie;
they wear themselves out
by doing wrong.
⁶ You live in a world of deceit,
and in their deceit
they refuse to know me,ʳ
declares the Lᴏʀᴅ.
⁷ Therefore, the Lᴏʀᴅ of heavenly forces
proclaims:
I'm going to refine and test them,
for what else can I do with my people?
⁸ Their tongue is a lethal arrow;
their words are deceitful.
They wish their neighbors well,
but in their hearts plot their ruin.
⁹ Shouldn't I punish them for this?
declares the Lᴏʀᴅ;
shouldn't I avenge such a nation?

UMBRELLA
LYING

Lying Blocks Knowledge of God
Jeremiah 9:5-9
God wanted to know what terrible things the people
of Judah had done. They could not be trusted. They
lied and cheated. They acted so badly that there
seemed to be little hope they could change. The
people lived this way for so long that they probably
didn't know how to live any other way. Because of
their dishonest ways, they were blocked from having true knowledge of God. They refused to worship
God the way God wanted them to. ◗

¹⁰ I will weep and wail for the mountains,
and lament for the grazing lands
in the wilderness.
They are dried up and deserted;
no sound of the flocks is heard;
no sign of birds or animals is seen;
all have vanished.
¹¹ I will reduce Jerusalem to ruins,
a den for wild dogs.
I will make the towns of Judah a
wasteland, without inhabitant.

¹² Who is wise enough to understand this?
Who has been taught by the Lᴏʀᴅ
and can therefore explain it?
Why has the land been reduced to rubble
and laid waste like a desert,
with no one passing through?
¹³ The Lᴏʀᴅ says: It is because they have
abandoned my Instruction that I gave them,

did you know? When the people purified
gold, they placed it in a very
hot fire and it melted. Then
they poured the liquid through a strainer to remove
any impurities.

and haven't obeyed or followed it. ¹⁴Instead,
they have followed their own willful hearts
and have gone after the Baals, as their ancestors taught them. ¹⁵Therefore, this is what
the Lᴏʀᴅ of heavenly forces, the God of Israel,
says: I'm going to feed this people bitter food
and give them poison to drink. ¹⁶I will scatter
them among nations about whom neither they
nor their ancestors have ever heard. I will pursue them with the sword until all are gone.
¹⁷ The Lᴏʀᴅ of heavenly forces proclaims:
Pay attention!
Summon the women who mourn,
let them come;
send for those best trained,
let them come.
¹⁸ Hurry!
Let them weep for us
so that our eyes fill up with tears
and water streams down.
¹⁹ The sound of sobbing
is heard from Zion:
"We're devastated!
We're so ashamed!
We have to leave the land
and abandon our homes!"
²⁰ Women, hear the Lᴏʀᴅ's word.
Listen closely to the word
from his mouth:
teach your daughters to mourn;
teach each other to grieve.
²¹ Death has climbed through our windows;
it has entered our fortresses
to eliminate children from the streets,
the youth from the squares.

ʳHeb uncertain

²² Declare what the Lord says:
 Dead bodies will lie
  like dung on the fields,
  like bundles of grain after the harvest,
  with no one to pick them up.
²³ The Lord proclaims:
 the learned should not boast
  of their knowledge,
  nor warriors boast of their might,
  nor the rich boast of their wealth.
²⁴ No, those who boast should boast in this:
 that they understand and know me.
 I am the Lord who acts with kindness,
  justice, and righteousness in the world,
 and I delight in these things,
  declares the Lord.
 ²⁵ The time is coming, declares the Lord, when I will deal with everyone who is physically circumcised: ²⁶ whether they are Egyptians or Judeans, Edomites or Ammonites, Moabites or the desert dwellers who cut the hair on their foreheads. All these nations are really uncircumcised; even the people of Israel are uncircumcised in heart.

Living God or human handiwork

10 Listen to the word that the Lord has spoken to you, people of Israel!
 ² The Lord proclaims:
 Don't follow the ways of the nations
  or be troubled by signs in the sky,
  even though the nations
   are troubled by them.
³ The rituals of the nations are hollow:
 a tree from the forest is chopped down
  and shaped by the craftsman's tools.
⁴ It's overlaid with silver and gold,
 and fastened securely
  with hammer and nails
  so it won't fall over.
⁵ They are no different than a scarecrow
 in a cucumber patch:
 they can't speak;
 they must be carried
  because they can't walk.
 Don't be afraid of them,
  because they can't do harm or good.
⁶ Lord, no one is like you!
 You are great,
 and great is your mighty name.

⁷ Who wouldn't fear you,
 king of the nations?
 That is your due;
  among all the wise of the nations
  and in all their countries,
   there is no one like you!
⁸ But they are both foolish and silly;
 they offer nothing
  because they are mere wood.
⁹ Covered with silver from Tarshish
 and gold from Uphaz,
 they are the work of a craftsman
  and the hands of a goldsmith.
 Clothed in blue and purple,
  all of them nothing more than the
   work of artisans.
¹⁰ But the Lord is the true God!
 He's the living God
  and the everlasting king!
 When he's angry, the earth quakes;
  the nations can't endure his rage.
¹¹ Tell them this: The gods who didn't make the heavens and the earth will perish from the earth and from under the heavens.^s
¹² But God made the earth by his might;
 he shaped the world by his wisdom,
  crafted the skies by his knowledge.
¹³ At the sound of his voice,
 the heavenly waters roar.
 He raises the clouds
  from the ends of the earth.
 He sends the lightning with the rain,
  the wind from his treasuries.
¹⁴ Everyone is too foolish to understand;
 every goldsmith is dishonored by his idols,
 for their images are shams;
  they aren't alive.
¹⁵ They are a delusion, a charade;
 at the appointed time they will vanish!
¹⁶ Jacob's portion is utterly different
 because God has formed all things,
  including Israel, his very own people—
  the Lord of heavenly forces is his name!

Get ready for exile!

¹⁷ Pack your bags and get ready to leave,
 you who live under siege.^t
¹⁸ The Lord proclaims:
 I'm going to eject those who live
  in the land at this time;
 I will badger them until they leave.^u

---

^s10:11 is written in Aramaic. ^tHeb uncertain ^uOr *find it*

^{19} How terrible for me, due to my injury;
　　my wound is terrible.
　　Yet I said to myself:
　　　This is my sickness,
　　　and I must bear it.
^{20} But now my tent is destroyed;
　　all its ropes are cut,
　　　and my children are gone for good.
　　There's no one left
　　　to set up my tent frame
　　　and to attach the fabric.
^{21} The shepherd kings have lost their senses
　　and don't seek answers from the LORD.
　　That is why they have failed
　　　and their flock is scattered.
^{22} Listen! The sound is getting louder,
　　a mighty uproar
　　　from the land of the north;
　　it will reduce the towns of Judah to ruins,
　　　a den for wild dogs.
^{23} I know, LORD, that our lives
　　are not our own,
　　　that we're not able to direct our paths.
^{24} So correct me, LORD, but with justice,
　　not in your anger,
　　　or else you will reduce me to nothing.
^{25} Pour out your wrath on the nations
　　that ignore you
　　and on the people
　　　who don't call on you,
　　since they have devoured Jacob;
　　　they have devoured him completely
　　　and ruined his country.

Judah's broken covenant with God

11 Jeremiah received the LORD's word: ^{2} Listen to the terms of this covenant and proclaim them to the people of Judah and the citizens of Jerusalem. ^{3} Say to them: This is what the LORD, the God of Israel, says: Cursed are those who don't heed the terms of this covenant ^{4} that I commanded your ancestors when I bought them out of the land of Egypt, that iron crucible, saying, Obey me and observe all that I instruct you. Then you will be my people and I, even I, will be your God. ^{5} I will fulfill my solemn pledge that I made to your ancestors to give them a land full of milk and honey, as is the case today.

And I replied, "As you say, LORD!"

^{6} The LORD said to me: Announce all these words in the towns of Judah and on the streets of Jerusalem: Obey the terms of this covenant and perform them. ^{7} I repeatedly and tirelessly warned your ancestors when I brought them out of the land of Egypt to this very day, saying, Obey me. ^{8} But they didn't listen or pay attention; they followed their own willful ambitions. So I brought upon them all the punishments I prescribed for violating this covenant—for refusing to obey.

^{9} The LORD said to me: A conspiracy is taking place among the people of Judah and residents of Jerusalem. ^{10} They have returned to the sins of their ancestors who refused to obey my words. They too are following other gods and serving them. The people of Israel and the people of Judah have broken my covenant that I made with their ancestors.

^{11} Therefore, the LORD proclaims: I will bring upon them a disaster from which they won't be able to escape. They will cry out to me, but I won't listen to them. ^{12} Then the people of Judah and those living in Jerusalem will call upon the gods they worship,^{v} but they won't save them when disaster strikes. ^{13} You have as many gods as you have towns, Judah, and you have as many shameful altars for worshipping Baal as you have streets in Jerusalem.

^{14} As for you, don't pray for these people, don't cry out or plead for them, for I won't listen when they cry out to me on account of their distress.

^{15} What are my loved ones doing
　　in my temple
　　while working out
　　　their many evil schemes?
　　Can sacred offerings cancel your sin
　　　so that you revel in your evil deeds?^{w}
^{16} The LORD named you,
　　"A blossoming olive tree,
　　　fair and fruitful";
　　　but with the blast of a powerful storm
　　　he will set it ablaze,
　　　until its branches
　　　are completely consumed.^{x}
^{17} The LORD of heavenly forces who planted you has announced disaster for you, because the people of Israel and Judah have done evil and made me angry by worshipping Baal.

---

^{v} Or *to whom they burn incense* ^{w} Heb uncertain ^{x} Vulg; MT *broken*

Jeremiah's lament

¹⁸ The Lᴏʀᴅ informed me and I knew.
Then he helped me see
what they were up to.

¹⁹ I was like a young lamb
led to the slaughter;
I didn't realize that they were planning
their schemes against me:
"Let's destroy the tree with its fruit;
let's cut him off from the land
of the living
so that even any knowledge of him
will be wiped out."

²⁰ Lᴏʀᴅ of heavenly forces, righteous judge,
who tests the heart and mind,
let me see your revenge upon them,
because I have committed
my case to you.

²¹ This is what the Lᴏʀᴅ says concerning the men from Anathoth who seek your life and say, "Don't prophesy in the Lᴏʀᴅ's name or else you will die at our hands." ²² Therefore, the Lᴏʀᴅ of heavenly forces proclaims, I'm going to punish them. Their young men will die in war, and their sons and daughters will die by famine. ²³ No one will be left because I will bring disaster upon the men of Anathoth when their time comes.

12 If I took you to court, Lᴏʀᴅ,
you would win.
But I still have questions
about your justice.
Why do guilty persons enjoy success?
Why are evildoers so happy?

² You plant them, and they take root;
they flourish and bear fruit.
You are always on their lips
but far from their hearts.

³ Yet you, Lᴏʀᴅ, you know me.
You see me.
You can tell that I love you.ʸ
So drag them away
and butcher them like sheep.
Prepare them for the slaughterhouse.

⁴ How long will the land mourn
and the grass in the fields dry up?
The animals and birds are swept away
due to the evil of those in the land.
The people say,
"God doesn't see what we're up to!"

⁵ If you have raced with people
and are worn out,
how will you compete with horses?
If you fall down in an open field,ᶻ
how will you survive in the forest
along the Jordan?

⁶ Even your relatives, your very family,
are planning to trap you.
They are out to get you.
So don't trust them,
even if they appear to be on your side.

God's lament over Judah's destruction

⁷ I have abandoned my house;
I have deserted my inheritance.
I have given the one I love
into the power of her enemies.

⁸ My inheritance has turned against me
like a lion in the forest;
she growls at me;
therefore, I have rejected her.

⁹ My inheritance has become
like a bird of prey,
surrounded and attacked.ᵃ
Go, gather all the wild animals
for the feast.

¹⁰ Many shepherds have
destroyed my vineyard;

LIGHTHOUSE

Aᴡᴇsᴏᴍᴇ Gᴏᴅ

Why Are People Who Do Evil so Happy?

Jeremiah 12:1

It's easy to believe that good things happen to people who do good things and bad things happen to people who do bad things. But what about when good things keep happening to people who do bad things? We don't understand when people who obey God are unhappy while people who do wicked things seem happy.

Jeremiah wondered about the people who seemed happy but were fake worshippers of God. They had health and wealth, but their hearts were not sincere. He knew God was a just God but didn't understand why the wicked had not been punished.

We must trust God to deal justly with people who do bad things, even if it is not according to our schedule. In the same way, we can trust that God is with those who are faithful and obedient, even during difficult times. ◊

ʸOr *You test my heart.* ᶻOr *If you are at ease only when in a peaceful land* ᵃHeb uncertain

they have trampled down my field;
they have reduced my treasured field
to a desolate wilderness.
[11] They have devastated her;
desolate, she cries out to me in distress:
"The whole land is desolate,
and no one seems to care."
[12] Over all the desert roads
destroyers march;
for the sword of the Lord devours
from one end of the land to the other;
no one is safe.
[13] They have sown wheat and reaped weeds;
they have worn themselves out
for nothing.
They will be ashamed of their[b] harvest
on account of the Lord's fierce anger.

[14] The Lord proclaims: The evil nations have seized the land[c] that I gave my people Israel. I'm going to dig them up from their own lands, and I will dig up the people of Judah from among them. [15] And after I have dug them up, I will again have compassion on them and restore their inheritance and their land. [16] And then, if they will learn the ways of my people, to make a solemn pledge in my name, "As the Lord lives," just as they once taught my people to swear to Baal, then they will be built up in the midst of my people. [17] But if they don't listen, I will dig up that nation; yes, I will dig up and destroy, declares the Lord.

Jeremiah's symbolic acts

13 The Lord proclaimed to me: Go and buy a linen undergarment. Wear it for a while without washing it. [2] So I bought a linen undergarment, as the Lord told me, and I put it on. [3] The Lord spoke to me again: [4] Take the undergarment that you are wearing and go at once to the Euphrates and put it under a rock. [5] So I went and buried it at the Euphrates,[d] as the Lord instructed. [6] After a long time, the Lord said to me: Return to the Euphrates and dig up the undergarment that I commanded you to bury there. [7] So I went to the Euphrates and I dug up the linen undergarment from the place I had buried it. But it was ruined and good for nothing.

[8] Then the Lord's word came to me: [9] The

Lord proclaims: In the same way I will ruin the brazen pride of Judah and Jerusalem! [10] Instead of listening to me, this wicked people follow their own willful hearts and pursue other gods, worshipping and serving them. They will become like this linen garment—good for nothing! [11] Just as a linen undergarment clings to the body, so I created the people of Israel and Judah to cling to me, declares the Lord, to be my people for my honor, praise, and grandeur. But they wouldn't obey.

[12] So deliver this word to them: The Lord the God of Israel proclaims: Every wine jug should be filled with wine. And they will

> ## did you know?
> God told Jeremiah that the promises God made to the Israelite people are promises that can be claimed by anyone who chooses to worship God. When the Israelites heard that even their enemies could claim God's promises, they were mad and didn't like Jeremiah.

answer you, "Don't we already know that? Obviously every wine jug should be filled with wine!" [13] Then you should say to them: The Lord proclaims: I'm going to fill everyone who lives in this country with wine that makes them drunk, including the kings on David's throne, the priests, the prophets, and all those living in Jerusalem. [14] And I will shatter every one of them, even parents and children, declares the Lord. I won't take pity; I won't have compassion; I will show no mercy when I destroy them.

[15] Listen closely, don't be arrogant,
for the Lord has spoken.
[16] Honor the Lord your God,
before it's too late,
before you stumble
on the mountain paths
in the evening shadows.
Then you will hope for light,
only to find darkness and gloom.
[17] If you are too proud to listen,
I will go off alone
and cry my eyes out.
I will weep uncontrollably
because the Lord's flock
will be dragged off into exile.
[18] Tell the king and the queen mother:

[b]Or *your* [c]Or *inheritance* [d]Heb *Perath*

Come down from your lofty place,
    because your glorious crowns
        will soon be removed from your heads.
¹⁹ The towns of the arid southern plain
    will be surrounded;
    no one will get in or out;
    all Judah will be taken into exile;
        everyone will be led away.

²⁰ Lift up your eyes
    and see who is approaching
        from the north.
Where is the flock entrusted to you,
    your beautiful flock?
²¹ What will you say when he appoints
        someone as head over you:
    your defenders, your trusted allies?ᵉ
Won't pain grip you
    like that of a woman in labor?
²² And when you ask yourself,
    Why have all these things
        happened to me?
        it is because of your many sins
    that you have been stripped
        and violated.
²³ Can a Cushite change his skin
    or a leopard its spots?
Neither can you do good
    when doing evil comes so naturally.
²⁴ So I will scatter youᶠ like straw
    that is blown away by the desert winds.
²⁵ This is the future
    that I have prepared for you,
        declares the Lord,
    because you have forgotten me
        and trusted in lies.
²⁶ I myself will pull up your skirt
    over your face
    and expose your shame.
²⁷ I have seen your adultery and lust,
    your disgusting idols and shameless
        prostitution
    on the hills and in the fields.
How terrible for you, Jerusalem!
    How long will you remain dirty?

Destruction on the horizon

14 The Lord's word to Jeremiah concerning the droughts:
² Judah mourns;
    her gates wither away.

The people fall to the ground in sorrow,
    as sobs of Jerusalem ascend.
³ The rich send their servants for water,
    but the wells run dry.
They return with empty jars,
    ashamed, bewildered, and in despair.
⁴ Because the ground is cracked
    due to lack of rain,
    the farmers too are ashamed;
    they cover their heads.
⁵ Even the doe in the field
    abandons her newborn,
    for there's no grass.
⁶ The wild donkeys stand
    on the well-traveled paths,
    panting like thirsty dogs;
        they go blind
    since there's nothing to eat.

⁷ Even though our sins testify against us,
    help us, Lord, for your name's sake.
We have turned away from you
    and sinned against you time and again.
⁸ You are the hope of Israel,
    its savior in times of trouble.
Why are you like a stranger in the land,
    like a tourist spending only the night?
⁹ Why are you like one taken by surprise,
    like a warrior unable to act?
Yet you are in our midst, Lord;
    we are called by your name.
    Don't give up on us.

¹⁰ This is what the Lord proclaims about
    this people:
    Since they have loved to wander off
    and haven't restrained themselves,
        Iᵍ won't accept them.
    Now I will recall their wrongdoing
    and punish their sin.

¹¹ The Lord said to me: Don't pray for the
safety of these people. ¹² When they fast, I
won't pay attention to their pleas, and when
they offer entirely burned offerings and grain
offerings, I won't accept them. Instead, I will
devour them with war, famine, and disease.
¹³ I replied, "Lord God, the prophets are
telling them: 'You won't see war or famine, for
I will give you lasting peace in this place.'"
¹⁴ Then the Lord said to me: The prophets

are telling lies in my name. I haven't sent them. I haven't commanded them. I haven't spoken to them. They are prophesying to you false visions, worthless predictions, and deceit they have made up on their own. [15]Therefore, this is what the LORD proclaims concerning the prophets who are speaking in my name when I didn't send them, and who are telling you that war or famine will never come to this land: Those very prophets will die in war and by famine! [16]And the people they are prophesying to will be thrown into the streets of Jerusalem, victims of famine and war. There will be no one to bury them or their wives and children. I will pour out on them their own wickedness.

[17] So deliver this word to them:

My eyes well up with tears;
   I can't stop weeping—day and night,
because my virgin daughter, my people,
   has suffered a crushing blow
   and is mortally wounded.
[18] If I go into the fields,
   I see only the slain in battle.
If I enter the city,
   I see only those suffering from famine.
Even both prophet and priest
   wander about aimlessly in ignorance.
[19] Have you completely rejected Judah?
   Do you hate Zion?
   Why then have you
      mortally wounded us?
We look for peace,
   but nothing good comes of it;
   for a time of healing,
      only to be terrorized.
[20] We acknowledge our sin, LORD,
   the wrongdoing of our ancestors,
   because we have sinned against you.
[21] For your name's sake, don't reject us,
   don't scorn your glorious throne.
Remember your covenant with us;
   don't break it.
[22] Can any of the false gods of the nations
      make it rain?
   Can the sky by itself bring showers?
Aren't you the LORD, our God?
   You are our hope,
      since only you can do such things.

Lamenting Jerusalem's dire circumstances

15 The LORD said to me: Even if Moses and Samuel stood before me, I wouldn't change my mind about these people. Send them away from me. Let them go! [2]And if they say, "Go where?" tell them, This is what the LORD proclaims:

Those marked for death—to death,
   those marked for war—to war,
   those marked for famine—to famine, and
   those marked for exile—to exile.

[3]I will appoint over them four agents[h] of death, declares the LORD: soldiers to kill, dogs to drag off, and vultures and wild animals to devour and destroy. [4]Because of what Judah's King Manasseh, Hezekiah's son, has done in Jerusalem, I will make them an object of horror to all nations on earth.

[5] Who will pity you, Jerusalem?
   Who will shed tears over you?
   Who will stop and ask how you're doing?
[6] You have deserted me,
   declares the LORD.
You have turned your back on me.
   So I will turn my hand against you
   and destroy you.
I'm tired of holding back.
[7] I will winnow them
   with a winnowing fork
   at the gates of their country.
I will bereave and destroy my people
   because they haven't changed their ways.
[8] Their widows will outnumber
   the sand on the shore.
I will bring a destroyer in broad daylight
   against the mothers of young men.[i]
Suddenly I will bring distress
   and terror upon them.
[9] The mother of seven
   will grow weak and gasp for air;
   her sun will set while it is yet day;
   she will be ashamed and disgraced.
I will deliver the survivors to the sword,
   to the power of their enemies,
   declares the LORD.

[10]I wish I had never been born! I have become a source of conflict and dissension in my own country. Even though I haven't lent or borrowed, still everyone curses me.

[h]Or *families* [i]Heb uncertain

¹¹ The Lord said:
Haven't I taken care of you?
Haven't I helped you with your enemies
in time of trouble and distress?ʲ
¹² Can a person shatter iron,
iron from the north, or bronze?
¹³ Your wealth and belongings
I will deliver as plunder,
without a fee,
because of all your sins
throughout your territory.
¹⁴ I will make you serve your enemies
in a land you don't know,
for my anger blazes like a fire
that won't go out.

¹⁵ You understand, Lord!
Remember me and act on my behalf.
Bring judgment on those who torment me.
In your mercy, spare my life.ᵏ
Consider how I'm insulted
on your account.
¹⁶ When your words turned up,
I feasted on them;
and they became my joy,
the delight of my heart,
because I belong to you,
Lord God of heavenly forces.

SAILBOAT

Joy

God's Word Is Our Joy *Jeremiah 15:16*
Jeremiah had seen many sorrows. He had seen the wickedness of his people. He had been mistreated for preaching God's word. But despite how he had been treated, he still found joy. Other people were upset by the truth of God's word, but it gave Jeremiah joy.

Joy doesn't come from having lots of things, or from having things always go our way. Still we can have joy, even in difficult times. Joy comes from the fact that we serve a God who loves us and whom we can trust. We can always find joy in God's true, unchanging word. ◖

¹⁷ I didn't join the festive occasions;
I took no delight in them.
I sat alone
because your hand was upon me
and you had filled me with curses.

¹⁸ Why am I always in pain?
Why is my wound incurable,
so far beyond healing?
You have become for me as unreliable
as a spring gone dry!

¹⁹ Therefore, the Lord proclaims:
If you return to me, I will take you back
and let you stand before me.
If you utter what is worthwhile,
not what is worthless,
you will be my spokesman.
They will turn to you,
not you to them!
²⁰ I will make you a sturdy bronze wall
against these people.
They will attack you,
but they won't triumph,
because I am with you
to protect and rescue you,
declares the Lord.
²¹ I will rescue you
from the hand of the wicked;
I will redeem you
from the grasp of the violent.

Loss of hope

16 The Lord's word came to me: ²Don't marry or have children in this place. ³This is what the Lord proclaims concerning children who are born in this place and their mothers and fathers who give birth to them in this place:
⁴ They will die of horrible diseases.
No one will mourn for them or bury them.
They will be like refuse
lying on the ground.
They will die from the sword
and by famine,
and their corpses will be food
for birds and wild animals.
⁵ This is what the Lord says:
Don't enter a house
where there is mourning;
don't grieve or lament for them,
for I have taken away my blessing,
kindness, and mercy from this people,
declares the Lord.
⁶ From the least to the greatest,
all will die in this land,

ʲHeb uncertain ᵏHeb uncertain

and there will be no funerals
    or time of mourning.
No one will gash themselves in grief
    or shave their heads in sorrow.
[7] No one will bring food[l] for the mourner
    as comfort for the dead.
No one will offer a cup of consolation
    for the loss of father or mother.

[8]Don't enter a house where there is feasting and sit down to eat and drink. [9]This is what the Lord of heavenly forces, the God of Israel, proclaims:

Before your very eyes and in your own lifetime, I will silence in this place the sounds of joy and gladness and the voices of the bridegroom and the bride.

[10]When you proclaim all these things to the people, and they ask you, "Why has the Lord pronounced such massive devastation against us? What have we done wrong? How have we sinned against the Lord our God?" [11]then you should tell them: It's because your ancestors have deserted me and followed other gods, declares the Lord. They have served and worshipped them, while abandoning me and refusing to keep my Instruction. [12]And you, you have acted worse than your ancestors, each of you following your own willful, evil hearts and paying no attention to me. [13]So I will banish you from this land to a place that neither you nor your ancestors have known, and there you will serve other gods day and night, for I will show you no mercy.

[14]But the time is coming, declares the Lord, when no one will say, "As the Lord lives who brought up the Israelites from the land of Egypt"; [15]instead, they will say, "As the Lord lives who brought up the Israelites from the land of the north and from all the lands where he has banished them." I will bring them back to the land that I gave to their ancestors.

[16]I'm going to send hordes of fishermen to catch them, declares the Lord. Afterward I will send a party of hunters to hunt them down on every mountain, hill, and cave. [17]I am watching their every move; not one is hidden from me. Nor is their sin concealed from my sight. [18]I will initially pay them back double for their evil and sin, because they have corrupted my land with their disgusting, lifeless idols and have filled my inheritance with their detestable practices.

[19] Lord, you are my strength
    and my stronghold;
    you are my refuge in time of trouble.
The nations will flock to you
    from the ends of the earth,
    and they will say:
    "Our ancestors have inherited utter lies,
      things that are hollow and useless."
[20] Can humans make their own gods?
    If so, they are not gods at all!
[21] Therefore, I will teach them;
    this time I will teach them
    my power and my might.
They will understand that I am the Lord.

17 Judah's sin is engraved
    with an iron pen.
It's etched with a diamond point
    on the tablets of their hearts
    and on the horns of their altars.
[2] Their children remember their altars
    and sacred poles[m]
    by the lush trees and high hills.

[3] Because you have committed such sins
    throughout your country,
I will give to your enemies
    my mountain in the land,
    as well as your wealth
    and all that you treasure.[n]
[4] You will lose the inheritance
    that I gave you.
I will make you slaves of your enemies
    in a land you don't know,
    for my anger blazes like a fire
    that won't go out.

[5] The Lord proclaims:
Cursed are those who trust
    in mere humans,
who depend on human strength
    and turn their hearts from the Lord.
[6] They will be like a desert shrub
    that doesn't know when relief comes.
They will live in the parched places
    of the wilderness,
    in a barren land where no one survives.
[7] Happy are those who trust in the Lord,
    who rely on the Lord.

[l]LXX; Heb *break for them* [m]Heb *asherim*; perhaps objects devoted to the worship of Asherah [n]Heb uncertain

⁸ They will be like trees
    planted by the streams,
    whose roots reach down
        to the water.
They won't fear drought when it comes;
    their leaves will remain green.
They won't be stressed
    in the time of drought
    or fail to bear fruit.

⁹ The most cunning heart—
    it's beyond help.
    Who can figure it out?
¹⁰ I, the Lᴏʀᴅ, probe the heart
    and discern hidden motives,
    to give everyone what they deserve,
    the consequences of their deeds.

ᵒOr *me* ᴾHeb uncertain

¹¹ Like a partridge gathering a brood
    that is not its own,
    so are those who acquire
        their wealth corruptly.
    By midlife it will be gone;
    afterward they will look like fools.

¹² Splendid and exalted throne,
    the place of our sanctuary
        from the beginning!
¹³ Lᴏʀᴅ, the hope of Israel,
    all who forsake you will suffer disgrace;
    those who turn away from youᵒ
        in the land
    will be written off,ᴾ
    for they have abandoned the Lᴏʀᴅ,
        the fountain of living water.

Like a Tree   *Jeremiah 17:7-8*

Even in a long, hot, dry summer, a grown tree can usually survive. Other flowers and plants might die, but trees typically do not. What makes it possible for them to live? Trees send their roots down deep into the earth. The part of the tree we can't see (the root system) is bigger than the parts of the tree we can see! Those underground roots spread out into smaller and smaller roots that act like straws, drinking up the water and nutrition from the soil.

Jeremiah observed trees planted near a stream. He paid attention. He noticed that these trees blossomed and made fruit, even in the dry season. Their roots drank the water they found deep in the earth.

Jeremiah thought that some people were like these trees, and some were not. Some people did not know what to do when life was hard. They complained or blamed God for the hard times. He saw others who didn't complain or blame God. This second group of people were like the trees. Even in hard times, they knew God was with them and trusted that God loved them. They had deep roots.

There are many things we can do to grow deep roots. We can be a part of a church community. We can talk with people about God. We can read the Bible and ask questions about what we read. We can talk with God in prayer. All of these things will help our roots to grow so that we can blossom, even in the hard times.

How can you remember to trust God, even in the hard times?

What are some ways you can have deep roots?

14 Heal me, Lord, and I'll be healed.
Save me and I'll be saved,
for you are my heart's desire.
15 See how they harass me:
"Where's the Lord's word?
Let it come now!"
16 Yet I didn't urge you to bring disaster;[q]
I didn't want the calamity to happen.
You know what comes out of my mouth;
it's always before you.
17 Don't terrorize me;
you are my refuge in time of disaster.
18 Let my tormentors be disgraced,
but not me;
let them be terrorized, but not me.
Bring on them the time of disaster,
as they deserve; destroy them repeatedly.
19 The Lord proclaimed to me: Go and stand
by the People's Gate where Judah's kings go
in and out, and then by all the gates of Jerusalem, 20 and say to them: Listen to the Lord's
word, you kings of Judah, all you people of
Judah, and anyone living in Jerusalem who
passes through these gates. 21 The Lord says:
Be on guard not to carry a load on the Sabbath day or conduct business at the gates of
Jerusalem. 22 Don't carry a load from your
houses or do any kind of work on the Sabbath
day. Rather, keep the Sabbath day holy as I
commanded your ancestors, 23 although they
didn't listen or pay attention. They were stubborn and wouldn't obey or accept correction.
24 If you are careful to obey me, declares the
Lord, and don't conduct business at the gates
of this city on the Sabbath day, if you keep
the Sabbath day holy by not working, 25 then
through the gates of this city will come kings
who occupy the throne of David and their officers, all riding on chariots and horses. They
will be accompanied by the people of Judah
and those living in Jerusalem. And this city
will always be inhabited. 26 Others will come
from the towns of Judah and Benjamin, from
all around Jerusalem, and from the western
foothills, the highlands, and the arid southern plain—they will come bringing entirely
burned offerings, sacrifices, grain offerings,
incense, and thanksgiving offerings to the
Lord's temple. 27 But if you don't obey me by
keeping the Sabbath day holy, if you carry
your loads and conduct your business at the
gates of Jerusalem as usual, then I will set fire
to those gates that will completely engulf the
fortresses of Jerusalem; it will not be put out.

God the potter

18 Jeremiah received the Lord's word:
2 Go down to the potter's house, and I'll
give you instructions about what to do there.
3 So I went down to the potter's house; he was
working on the potter's wheel. 4 But the piece
he was making was flawed while still in his
hands, so the potter started on another, as
seemed best to him. 5 Then the Lord's word
came to me: 6 House of Israel, can't I deal with
you like this potter, declares the Lord? Like
clay in the potter's hand, so are you in mine,
house of Israel! 7 At any time I may announce
that I will dig up, pull down, and destroy a nation or kingdom; 8 but if that nation I warned
turns from its evil, then I'll relent and not
carry out the harm I intended for it. 9 At the
same time, I may announce that I will build
and plant a nation or kingdom; 10 but if that
nation displeases and disobeys me, then I'll
relent and not carry out the good I intended
for it. 11 Now say to the people of Judah and
those living in Jerusalem: This is what the
Lord says: I am a potter preparing a disaster
for you; I'm working out a plan against you.
So each one of you, turn from your evil ways;
reform your ways and your actions. 12 But they
said, "What's the use! We will follow our own
plans and act according to our own willful,
evil hearts."
13 Therefore, the Lord proclaims:
Ask among the nations:
Have you ever heard anything like this?
Virgin Israel has done
the most horrible thing.
14 Does the snow on the mountains of
Lebanon ever melt entirely
off their rocky cliffs?
Do the cool mountain streams
ever dry up?[r]
15 Yet my people have forgotten me;
they have offered sacrifices to a lie.
And so they have stumbled along the way,
even along the ancient paths.
They have taken side roads,
not the main roads.[s]

[q] LXX; Heb uncertain [r] Heb uncertain; or *be dug up* [s] Heb uncertain

¹⁶ They have ruined their country
and brought utter shame on it.
All who pass by are shocked
and shake their heads.
¹⁷ Like a strong east wind,
I will scatter them before their enemy.
When disaster strikes them,
I will show them my back,
not my face.
¹⁸ Then they said, "Come, let's unite against Jeremiah, for the priest's instruction won't fail, nor will the sage's counsel, nor the prophet's word. Come, let's silence him and pay no attention to his words."
¹⁹ Pay attention to me, Lord;
listen to what my enemies are saying.
²⁰ Should evil be returned for good?
Yet they have set traps for me.
Remember that I stood before you,
begging you to be merciful
and not to punish them.

UMBRELLA
Not Grateful

Jeremiah's Enemies *Jeremiah 18:18-20*
Jeremiah pleaded with God not to allow the good that Jeremiah had done for the people to be repaid with evil. Jeremiah was forced to deal with people who were satisfied with the wicked leaders who had served them. They trusted the false prophets and priests, but they mistreated Jeremiah and accused him of bad things. They welcomed false leaders but tried to drive away God's true leaders. Jeremiah didn't tell the people what they wanted to hear, so they attacked him. Jeremiah was doing God's work, but it didn't matter to his enemies. We should be grateful to God's servants who tell us the truth. ◈

///

²¹ Enough! Let their children starve;
let them die by the sword.
Let their wives be barren widows;
let their men be slaughtered
and their youth struck down in battle.
²² Let screams be heard from their homes
when you suddenly bring armies
against them.
They have dug a pit to capture me,
set traps for my feet.

LIFE PRESERVER

What do the verses about pottery mean? *Jeremiah 18–19*

There are several stories about pottery in the book of Jeremiah. In chapter 18, we read that God sent Jeremiah to the potter's house. There he learned that just like clay is reshaped in the hand of the potter and is made into something else, the same reshaping would happen with the nations.

Chapter 19 describes a pot as broken beyond repair, so much so that it can never be put back together. This broken pot represents the relationship between God and people who reject God. ◈

///

²³ But you, Lord, you know
all their sinister plots to kill me.
Don't overlook their wrongdoing;
don't cleanse their sin from before you.
May they stumble before you;
when you become angry,
do something about them.

Broken beyond repair

19 The Lord proclaims: Go buy a clay jar from a potter in the presence of the elders of the people and the priests. ²Then go out to the Ben-hinnom Valley at the entrance of the gate called Broken Pots and proclaim there the words I will tell you. ³Listen to the Lord's word, you kings of Judah and those of you living in Jerusalem: This is what the Lord of heavenly forces, the God of Israel, says: I'm going to bring such disaster upon this place that it will shock all who hear of it. ⁴They have deserted me and degraded this place into a shrine for other gods, which neither they nor their ancestors nor Judah's kings have ever known. And they have filled this place with the blood of the innocent. ⁵Yes, they have built shrines to Baal, to burn their sons and daughters in the fire, although I never commanded or ordered such a thing, nor did it ever cross my mind.

⁶So now the time is coming, declares the Lord, when people will no longer call this place Topheth or Ben-hinnom Valley but Carnage Valley. ⁷I will foil the plans of Judah and Jerusalem in this place and will have them fall in battle before their enemies, before those who seek their lives. I will give their corpses as food to the birds and the wild animals. ⁸I

will make this city something that sounds horrible; all who pass by it will be shocked at its pain. ⁹And when their enemies lay siege to the city, seeking their lives, they will resort in desperation to eating the flesh of their sons and daughters, and to devouring the flesh of their neighbors.

¹⁰Then you should shatter the clay jar in the sight of the people who are with you, ¹¹and you should say to them: This is what the Lord of heavenly forces says: Just as one smashes the potter's piece beyond repair, so I will smash this people and this city. And they will bury the dead in Topheth until there's no room left. ¹²That is what I will do to this place and its residents, declares the Lord: I will make this city like Topheth. ¹³The houses of Jerusalem and those of Judah's kings will become as foul as Topheth—all the houses on whose roofs they made offerings to the heavenly force and poured out drink offerings to other gods.

did you **know?** Jeremiah's poem of sadness shows that being a prophet for God is not easy. Speaking the truth and telling people how they need to change their lives to follow God's Instructions tend to make people angry, which is what happened in Jeremiah's case.

¹⁴When Jeremiah returned from Topheth where the Lord had sent him to prophesy, he stood in the court of the Lord's temple and said to all the people: ¹⁵The Lord of heavenly forces, the God of Israel, proclaims: I am about to bring upon this city and its surrounding towns every disaster that I have pronounced against them, because they have been stubborn and wouldn't obey my words.

20 When the priest Pashhur, Immer's son, the officer in charge of the Lord's temple, heard Jeremiah prophesying these words, ²he beat the prophet and detained him in confinement at the upper Benjamin Gate in the Lord's temple. ³The next day, when Pashhur released Jeremiah from confinement, Jeremiah said to him, "The Lord has changed your name from Pashhur to Panic Lurks Everywhere. ⁴The Lord proclaims: I'm going to strike panic into your heart and into the hearts of your friends. You will watch as they fall in battle to their enemies. I will hand

over all Judah to the king of Babylon, who will exile some to Babylon and slaughter others. ⁵I will hand over all the wealth of this city, all its goods and valuables, including the treasures of the kings of Judah, to their enemies, who will ransack and pillage and carry it all off to Babylon. ⁶And you, Pashhur, and all those in your household, will go into captivity. You will be deported to Babylon where you will die. There you will be buried with all your friends to whom you prophesied falsely."

Total despair

⁷ Lord, you enticed me, and I was taken in.
　　You were too strong for me,
　　　　and you prevailed.
　Now I'm laughed at all the time;
　　everyone mocks me.
⁸ Every time I open my mouth, I cry out
　　and say, "Violence and destruction!"
　The Lord's word has brought me
　　nothing but insult and injury, constantly.
⁹ I thought, I'll forget him;
　　I'll no longer speak in his name.
　But there's an intense fire in my heart,
　　trapped in my bones.
　I'm drained trying to contain it;
　　I'm unable to do it.
¹⁰ I hear many whispering—
　　"Panic Lurks Everywhere!—
　　proclaim, yes, let's proclaim it ourselves!"
　All my friends are waiting
　　for me to stumble:
　"Perhaps he can be enticed.
　　Then we'll prevail against him
　　　　and get our revenge on him!"
¹¹ But the Lord is with me
　　like a strong defender.
　Therefore, my oppressors
　　will stumble and not prevail.
　They will be disgraced
　　by their own failures.
　Their dishonor will never be forgotten.
¹² The Lord of heavenly forces
　　tests the righteous
　　and discerns the heart and the mind.
　Let me see your retribution upon them,
　　for I have committed my case to you.
¹³ Sing to the Lord,
　　praise the Lord,
　　　for he has rescued the needy
　　　　from the clutches of evildoers.

¹⁴ Cursed be the day that I was born.
   May the day my mother
      gave birth to me not be blessed.
¹⁵ Cursed be the one
   who delivered the news to my father,
      "You have a son!"—
   filling him with joy.
¹⁶ May the bearer of that news
      be like the cities
   that the Lord destroyed without mercy.
   May he hear screams in the morning,
      and the battle cries at noon,
¹⁷ because he didn't kill me in the womb
   and let my mother become my grave,
      her womb pregnant forever.
¹⁸ Why was I ever born
   when all I see is suffering and misery,
   and my days are filled with shame?

Verdict against king and city

21 Jeremiah received the Lord's word when King Zedekiah sent Pashhur, Malchiah's son, and the priest Zephaniah, Maaseiah's son, to him with an appeal: ²"Speak to the Lord on our behalf because Babylon's King Nebuchadnezzar^t is attacking us. Perhaps the Lord will perform one of his mighty deeds and force him to withdraw from us."

³Jeremiah answered them: This is what you should tell Zedekiah: ⁴The Lord, the God of Israel, says: I'm going to turn your own weapons against you, yes, the weapons you are using to fight the king of Babylon and the Babylonians^u who have surrounded you! I will round them up in the center of the city. ⁵Then I myself will fight against you with an outstretched hand and strong arm in fierce anger and rage. ⁶I will strike down those within this city—both people and animals—and they will die of a terrible plague. ⁷Afterward, declares the Lord, I will deliver Judah's King Zedekiah, his servants, and those in this city who have survived plague, war, and famine to Babylon's King Nebuchadnezzar^v and to their enemies who seek to do them harm. He will put them to the sword without pity, mercy, or compassion.

⁸This is what you should tell this people: The Lord says: I'm setting before you the way of life and the way of death. ⁹Whoever stays in the city will die by the sword, famine, and disease. But whoever leaves the city and surrenders to the Babylonians^w will live; yes, their lives will be spared. ¹⁰I have set my face against this city for harm and not for good, declares the Lord; it will be delivered to the king of Babylon, who will set it on fire.

Judah: Hear the Lord's word

¹¹ House of Judah!
   This is what the Lord says:
¹² House of David! The Lord proclaims:
   Begin each morning
      by administering justice,
   rescue from their oppressor
      those who have been robbed,
   or else my anger
      will spread like a wildfire,
   with no one to put it out,
      because of your evil deeds.
¹³ I am against you,
   you who live in the valley,^x
      like a rock of the plain,
      declares the Lord,
   and who say,
      "Who will come down to attack us?
      Who will breach our fortresses?"
¹⁴ I will punish you
      based on what you have done,
      declares the Lord.
   I will set your^y forests on fire;
      the flames will engulf
      everything around you.^z

Oracles against the kings

22 The Lord proclaims: Go down to the palace of the king of Judah and declare this message: ²Listen to the Lord's word, king of Judah, you who sit on David's throne—you and your attendants, and all those who go through these gates. ³The Lord proclaims: Do what is just and right; rescue the oppressed from the power of the oppressor. Don't exploit or mistreat the refugee, the orphan, and the widow. Don't spill the blood of the innocent in this place. ⁴If you obey this command, then through the gates of this palace will come kings who occupy the throne of David, riding on chariots and horses along with their entourage and subjects. ⁵But if you

---

^tHeb *Nebuchadrezzar* ^uHeb *Chaldeans* ^vHeb *Nebuchadrezzar* ^wHeb *Chaldeans* ^xHeb uncertain ^yOr *its* ^zOr *it*

ignore these words, I swear by myself, declares the Lord, that this palace will become a ruin. ⁶The Lord proclaims concerning the palace of the king of Judah:

> Though you are like Gilead to me,
>   like the summit of Lebanon,
>   I will turn you into a desert—
>   uninhabited cities.
> ⁷ I will summon destroyers against you,
>   who will use their weapons
>   to cut down your finest cedars
>   and hurl them into the fire.

⁸People from many nations will pass by this city and ask each other: "Why has the Lord treated that great city like this?" ⁹And the answer will be, "Because they abandoned the covenant with the Lord their God and worshipped and served other gods."

¹⁰ Don't weep or lament for the dead king.ᵃ
>   Weep instead for the one
>   who has gone away,
>   for he will never return
>   to see his native soil.

¹¹This is what the Lord says about Shallum son of Judah's King Josiah, who succeeded his father Josiah as king but who is now gone from this place: He will never return! ¹²He will die where he's been exiled and never see this land again.

¹³ How terrible for Jehoiakim,
>   who builds his house with corruption
>   and his upper chambers with injustice,
>   working his countrymen for nothing,
>   refusing to give them their wages.
> ¹⁴ He says, "I'll build myself a grand palace,
>   with huge upper chambers,
>   ornate windows,
>   cedar paneling,
>   and rich red decor."
> ¹⁵ Is this what makes you a king,
>   having more cedar than anyone else?
> Didn't your father eat and drink
>   and still do what was just and right?
> Then it went well for him!
> ¹⁶ He defended the rights
>   of the poor and needy;
>   then it went well.
> Isn't that what it means to know me?
>   declares the Lord.
> ¹⁷ But you set your eyes and heart
>   on nothing but unjust gain;

> you spill the blood of the innocent;
>   you practice cruelty;
>   you oppress your subjects.

¹⁸Therefore, this is what the Lord says to Jehoiakim son of Judah's King Josiah:

> They won't grieve for him, saying,
>   "My brother, my sister!"
> They won't grieve for him, saying,
>   "My master, my majesty!"
> ¹⁹ They will give him a donkey's burial,
>   dragging him outside
>   the gates of Jerusalem
>   and dumping him there.

²⁰ Go up to Lebanon and cry out,
>   lift up your voice in Bashan,
>   cry out from Abarim,
>   because all your lovers
>   have been ravished.
> ²¹ I spoke to you
>   when you felt safe and secure,
>   but you said, "I won't listen."
> You have been that way since your youth:
>   not listening to a word I say.
> ²² Your shepherds will be tossed to the wind,
>   your lovers taken off to exile.
> Then you will be embarrassed
>   and humiliated
>   by all your wickedness.

UMBRELLA
It's Not Yours

Wanting What Others Have *Jeremiah 22:17*
God had harsh words for Judah's king. He had not been a good king. He had not obeyed God. All he wanted was to satisfy his own needs. He didn't care what God wanted. He had been cruel to people, even killing them in order to take over their possessions.

God sent a warning through Jeremiah about the dangers of wanting what other people have. When we want something that belongs to someone else bad enough to hurt something or someone for it, we're in serious trouble. Instead of wanting what others have, we should trust God to provide for all of our needs. Nothing is too hard for God, so we should not act out of jealousy or envy. Those negative feelings can cause us to do bad things to get what we want. ◌

ᵃHeb lacks *king.*

²³ You who live in Lebanon,
  nestled in cedar,
  who will pity you[b]
  when you are overcome in pain,
  like that of childbirth?
²⁴ As surely as I live, declares the Lord, even if Coniah,[c] King Jehoiakim's son from Judah were a signet ring on my right hand, I would still remove you from there. ²⁵ I would hand you over to those who seek to kill you, those you dread, even Babylon's King Nebuchadnezzar and his army.[d] ²⁶ I will banish you and your mother who bore you to a land far from your native soil, and there the two of you will die. ²⁷ You[e] will never return to the land you[f] long to go back to.
²⁸ Is this man Coniah
  merely a defiled and broken pottery jar
    that no one wants?
  Why then have he and his children
  been hurled out
  and cast into an unfamiliar land?
²⁹ Land, land, land,
  hear the Lord's word:
³⁰ The Lord proclaims:
  Mark this man as childless;
  he will not prosper during his lifetime.
    None of his children
    will sit on David's throne
    and rule again in Judah.

Promise of restoration

23 Watch out, you shepherds who destroy and scatter the sheep of my pasture, declares the Lord. ² This is what the Lord, the God of Israel, proclaims about the shepherds who "tend to" my people: You are the ones who have scattered my flock and driven them away. You haven't attended to their needs, so I will take revenge on you for the terrible things you have done to them, declares the Lord. ³ I myself will gather the few remaining sheep from all the countries where I have driven them. I will bring them back to their pasture, and they will be fruitful and multiply. ⁴ I will place over them shepherds who care for them. Then they will no longer be afraid or dread harm, nor will any be missing, declares the Lord.

Promise of a righteous and just king

⁵ The time is coming, declares the Lord, when I will raise up a righteous descendant[g] from David's line, and he will rule as a wise king. He will do what is just and right in the land. ⁶ During his lifetime, Judah will be saved and Israel will live in safety. And his name will be The Lord Is Our Righteousness.[h]

⁷ So the time is coming, declares the Lord, when no one will say, "As the Lord lives who brought up the Israelites from the land of Egypt." ⁸ Instead, they will say, "As the Lord lives who brought up the descendants of the people of Israel from the land of the north and from all the lands where he[i] has banished them so that they can live in their own land."

Oracles against the prophets

⁹ As for the prophets:
  My heart inside me is broken;
  my body aches.[j]
  I stagger like a drunk
  who has had too much wine to drink,
    because of the Lord
    and because of God's holy words.
¹⁰ Because the country teems
  with adulterers,
  because of them,[k]
    yes, because their might isn't right
    and their way is evil,
    the land dries up,
    and the grazing areas
    in the wilderness wither.[l]
¹¹ Both prophet and priest are godless;
  I even find their evil in my temple,
    declares the Lord.
¹² Therefore, they will find themselves
  on slippery ground
  and will be thrust into darkness,
  where they will collapse.
  I will bring disaster upon them,
    when their time comes,
    declares the Lord.
¹³ In the prophets of Samaria
  I saw something shocking:
  They prophesied by Baal
    and led astray my people Israel.
¹⁴ In the prophets of Jerusalem
  I saw something horrible:

[b] Heb uncertain [c] Cf *Jeconiah* in Jer 24:1 [d] Or *the Babylonians* [e] Or *They* [f] Or *they* [g] Or *branch* [h] Or *of Our Righteousness*, possibly a play on the name *Zedekiah* [i] Or *I* [j] Heb uncertain; or *my bones shake* [k] LXX; MT *a curse* [l] Heb uncertain

They commit adultery and tell lies.
They encourage evildoers
  so that no one turns
    from their wickedness.
In my eyes, they are no better than Sodom;
  its people are like Gomorrah.

¹⁵Therefore, this is what the LORD of heavenly forces proclaims concerning the prophets:
  I'm going to feed them bitter food
    and give them poison to drink.
  Wickedness has spread
    from the prophets of Jerusalem
      throughout the land.

¹⁶The LORD proclaims:
  Don't listen to the prophets
    who are speaking to you;
      they are deceiving you.
  Their visions come
    from their own hearts,
      not from the LORD's mouth.
¹⁷They keep saying to those
    who scorn God's message,
  "All will go well for you,"
    and to those who follow
      their own willful hearts,
  "Nothing bad will happen to you."
¹⁸But who has stood in the LORD's council
    to listen to God's word?
  Who has paid attention
    to his word and announced it?
¹⁹Look! The LORD's angry storm breaks out;
  it whirls around the heads of the wicked.
²⁰The LORD's fierce anger
  won't turn back
    until it accomplishes
      all that he has planned.
  In the days to come,
    you will understand what this means.

²¹I didn't send the prophets,
  yet they ran anyway.
  I didn't speak to them,
    yet they prophesied anyway.
²²If they had stood in my council,
  they would have proclaimed
    my words to my people;
  they would have turned them
    from their evil ways and deeds.
²³The LORD declares, Am I a God
  who is only nearby and not far off?

²⁴Can people hide themselves
  in secret places
    so I might not see them?
  Don't I fill heaven and earth?
²⁵I have heard the prophets prophesying lies in my name. They claim, "I've had a dream; I've had a dream!" ²⁶How long will deceitful prophecies dominate the minds of the prophets? Those prophets are treacherous. ²⁷They scheme to make my people forget me by their dreams that people tell each other, just as their ancestors forgot me because of Baal. ²⁸Let the prophet who has a dream declare it, but let the one who has my word proclaim it faithfully.

UMBRELLA
LYING

Speaking the Truth *Jeremiah 23:26*
When we are trying to do right while others keep doing wrong, it can make us want to cry out, "No fair!" Jeremiah was frustrated. He was doing what was right. He spoke only the truth to God's people. But there were other prophets who were lying to the people. They were willing to tell people anything just to make them feel good. Jeremiah wondered how long this could go on. The false prophets were enemies of God because their only purpose was to lure people into forgetting God's name.

There are many false preachers today, just as there were in Jeremiah's time. A true prophet or preacher always preaches the true word of God, even when it's difficult to hear or unpopular. A true preacher gives messages to help us grow closer to God. ◊

What a difference
  between straw and wheat!
    declares the LORD.
²⁹Isn't my word like fire
  and like a hammer that shatters rock?
    declares the LORD.
³⁰Therefore, I'm against the prophets
  who steal my words from each other,
    declares the LORD.
³¹I'm against the prophets
  who carelessly deliver oracles,ᵐ
    declares the LORD.
³²I'm against the prophets
  who dream up lies

ᵐHeb uncertain

and then proclaim them,
  declares the Lord.
With their reckless lies,
  they lead my people astray.
I didn't send them;
  I didn't commission them.
They are completely useless
  to these people,
  declares the Lord.

³³When these people or a prophet or a priest asks you, "What is the Lord's message?"[n] say to them, "What message? I will cast you off, declares the Lord." ³⁴I will punish anyone, including prophet or priest, who says, "This is the Lord's message." ³⁵This is what you should ask each other: "What has the Lord said?" "What has the Lord declared?" ³⁶But you are no longer to mention the Lord's message, because everyone thinks they have received a message from the Lord. You destroy the very word of the living God, the Lord of heavenly forces, our God. ³⁷So this is what you should say to the prophet: "What has the Lord said to you?" "What has the Lord declared?" ³⁸But if you insist on saying, "This is the Lord's message," the Lord says to you: Because you have made this claim—this is the Lord's message—when I told you not to proclaim the Lord's message, ³⁹I will lift you up[o] and cast you out of my presence, together with the city that I gave to your ancestors. ⁴⁰I will make you an object of disgrace and enduring shame that no one will ever forget.

Good and bad figs

24 After Babylon's King Nebuchadnezzar had deported Judah's King Jeconiah, King Jehoiakim's son, and the Judean officials, as well as the craftsmen and metalworkers from Jerusalem to Babylon, the Lord showed me two baskets of figs set in front of the Lord's temple. ²One basket was filled with fresh and ripe figs; the other basket was filled with rotten figs—too rotten to eat. ³And the Lord asked me: "What do you see, Jeremiah?"

I replied: "Figs! Some good ones and others very bad—so bad that they can't be eaten."

⁴Then the Lord said to me: ⁵The Lord, the God of Israel, proclaims: Just as with these good figs, I will treat kindly the Judean exiles that I have sent from this place to Babylon. ⁶I regard them as good, and I will bring them back to this land. I will build them up and not pull them down; I will plant them and not dig them up. ⁷I will give them a heart to know me, for I am the Lord. They will be my people, and I will be their God, for they will return to me with all their heart. ⁸And just like the rotten figs that are so bad that they can't be eaten, the Lord says, I will do to Judah's King Zedekiah and his officials, as well as the remaining few in Jerusalem and those who are living in Egypt. ⁹I will make them an object of horror and evil to all the kingdoms of the earth. Wherever I scatter them, they will be disgraced and insulted, mocked and cursed. ¹⁰I will send the sword, famine, and disease against them until they vanish from the fertile land that I gave to their ancestors.

UMBRELLA
HARD TIMES

God Promises to Restore *Jeremiah 24:5-7*
God wants to build us up to make us better. Even when we experience pain, God uses that pain to strengthen us. The people of Judah had been through a lot of painful times, but God did not cut them off completely. Most of the people had done bad things and separated themselves from God, but God wanted to be close to them again. God promised to deliver them out of their troubles and bring them back into their own land to live a normal life.

God sees everything. When we are stuck in a painful situation, God sees and does not forget us. ◆

A summary of Jeremiah's message

25 Jeremiah received the Lord's word concerning all the people of Judah in the fourth year of Judah's King Jehoiakim, Josiah's son. This was the first year of Babylon's King Nebuchadnezzar. ²The prophet Jeremiah addressed all the people of Judah and all those living in Jerusalem. ³From the thirteenth year of Judah's King Josiah, Amon's son, to this very day—twenty-three years—the Lord's word has come to me. I have

ⁿOr *burden* ^oLXX, Syr, Vulg; MT *forget you*

delivered it to you repeatedly, although you wouldn't listen. 4In fact, the LORD has tirelessly sent you all his servants, the prophets, but you wouldn't listen or pay attention. 5They said, "Each one of you, turn from your evil ways and deeds and live in the fertile land that the LORD gave you and your ancestors for all time. 6Don't follow or worship other gods and don't anger me by what you make with your hands. Then I won't bring disaster upon you." 7But you wouldn't listen to me, making me angry by what you do and bringing disaster upon yourselves, declares the LORD.

8Therefore, this is what the LORD of heavenly forces says: Because you haven't listened to my words, 9I am going to muster all the tribes of the north and my servant King Nebuchadnezzar of Babylon, declares the LORD, and I will bring them against this country and its residents as well as against all the surrounding nations. I will completely destroy them and will make them an object of horror, shock, and ruins for all time. 10I will silence the sounds of joy and laughter and the voices of the bride and the bridegroom. Yes, I will silence the millstones and snuff out the lamplight. 11This whole country will be reduced to a wasteland, and these nations will serve the king of Babylon for seventy years. 12When the seventy years are over, I will punish the king of Babylon and his nation for their wrongdoing, declares the LORD. I will reduce the land of the Babylonians to a wasteland for all time. 13I will unleash upon that land everything I decreed, all that is written in this scroll, which Jeremiah prophesied against all the nations. 14Yes, many great nations and powerful kings will enslave them, and I will pay them back in full for what they have done and made with their hands.

15This is what the LORD, God of Israel, said to me: Take this seething cup of wine from my hand and make all the nations gulp it down where I'm sending you. 16They will drink and stagger about half-crazed because of the sword that I am sending against them.

17So I took the cup from the LORD's hand, and I made all the nations drink from it where the LORD had sent me: 18Jerusalem and the towns of Judah, its kings and officials. This was to make them a wasteland, an object of horror, shock, and cursing, as it is today; 19Pharaoh, Egypt's king, his attendants and officials, and all his people, 20including the foreigners[p] living there; all the kings of the land of Uz; all the kings of the land of the Philistines—Ashkelon, Gaza, Ekron, and what's left of Ashdod; 21Edom, Moab, and the Ammonites; 22all the kings of Tyre and Sidon, and the kings of the coastlands across the sea; 23Dedan, Tema, Buz, and all those who cut the hair of their foreheads;[q] 24all the kings of Arabia and the nomadic tribes,[r] 25all the kings of Zimri,[s] Elam, and Media; 26all the kings of the north, those nearby and those faraway, one after another, all the empires on the earth will drink from this cup.[t] And after them the king of Sheshach[u] will drink from it.

27Then say to them: The LORD of heavenly forces, the God of Israel, proclaims: Drink this seething cup of wine and get drunk. Vomit and collapse and don't get up again because of the sword that I'm thrusting into you. 28If they refuse to take the cup in your hand and drink from it, tell them: This is what the LORD of heavenly forces says: You must drink! 29Look! I'm bringing disaster upon the city that bears my name; how then will you escape unpunished? You will not! I'm summoning the sword against everyone on earth, declares the LORD of heavenly forces.

30 Now prophesy all these things
  and say to them:
The LORD roars on high;
  from his holy place he thunders.
He roars fiercely against his flock,
  like the shouting of those
    who tread on grapes,
    against everyone on earth.
31 The uproar is heard far and wide,
  because the LORD is bringing
    a lawsuit against the nations.
  He's entering into judgment
    with all people,
    sentencing the guilty to death,
      declares the LORD.
32 The LORD of heavenly forces proclaims:
  Look! Disaster travels
  from nation to nation.

[p]Heb uncertain [q]Heb uncertain [r]Heb uncertain [s]Heb uncertain [t]Heb lacks *will drink from this cup.* [u]*Sheshak* is a name for Babylon.

A terrible storm comes
from the far ends of the earth.

³³At that time, those struck down by the Lord will fill the earth. And no one will mourn for them or prepare their bodies for burial. They will become like refuse lying on the ground.

³⁴Wail, you shepherds, cry out.
Roll in the dust, you masters of the flock!
The day of your slaughter has arrived.
You will fall and shatter like a fragile vase.

³⁵The shepherds have no place to hide;
the masters of the flock can't escape.

³⁶Hear the cry of the shepherds
and the sobbing of the masters
of the flock,
because the Lord
is ravaging their pasture.

³⁷There's an eerie silence
in the peaceful meadows,
because of the Lord's fierce anger.

³⁸The lion is on the prowl,
and the land is reduced to nothing,
because of the fierce sword,ᵛ
because of his fierce anger.

Jeremiah arrested and sentenced to death

26 Early in the rule of Judah's King Jehoiakim, Josiah's son, this word came from the Lord: ²The Lord proclaims: Stand in the temple courtyard and speak to all the people of the towns of Judah who have come to the temple to worship. Tell them everything I command you; leave nothing out. ³Perhaps they will listen and each will turn from their evil ways. If they do, I will relent and not carry out the harm I have in mind for them because of the wrong they have done. ⁴So tell them, The Lord proclaims: If you don't listen to me or follow the Instruction I have set before you—⁵if you don't listen to the words of the prophets that I have sent to you time and again, though you haven't listened, ⁶then I will make this temple a ruin like Shiloh, and this city I will make a curse before all nations on earth.

⁷The priests, the prophets, and all the people heard Jeremiah declare these words in the Lord's temple. ⁸And when Jeremiah finished saying everything the Lord told

him to say, the priests and the prophets and all the people seized him and said, "You must die! ⁹Why do you prophesy in the Lord's name that 'this temple will become a ruin like Shiloh, and this city will be destroyed and left without inhabitant'?" Then all the people joined ranks against Jeremiah in the Lord's temple.

¹⁰When the officials of Judah heard these things, they went up from the royal palace to the Lord's temple and took their places at the entrance of the New Gate of the Lord's temple. ¹¹The priests and the prophets said to the officials and all the people: "This man deserves to die for prophesying against this city as you have all heard firsthand."

¹²Jeremiah said to all the officials and to all the people, "The Lord sent me to prophesy to this temple and this city everything you have heard. ¹³So now transform your ways and actions. Obey the Lord your God, and the Lord may relent and not carry out the harm that he's pronounced against you. ¹⁴But me? I'm in your hands. Do whatever you would like to me. ¹⁵Only know for certain that if you sentence me to death, you and the people of this city will be guilty of killing an innocent man. The Lord has in fact sent me to speak everything I have said to you."

¹⁶Then the officials and all the people said to the priests and the prophets, "This man doesn't deserve to die, for he has spoken to us in the name of the Lord our God."

¹⁷A few of the community elders got up and addressed the whole crowd: ¹⁸"Micah of Moresheth, who prophesied during the rule of Judah's Hezekiah, said to all the people of Judah, 'The Lord of heavenly forces proclaims:

Zion will be plowed down like a field,
Jerusalem will become piles of rubble,
and the temple mount will become
an overgrown mound.'

¹⁹"Did King Hezekiah or anyone else in Judah execute him? Didn't he instead fear the Lord and plead for his mercy? Then the Lord relented of the harm that he had pronounced against them. We are about to commit a huge mistake that will cost us our lives."

²⁰There was another man who prophesied in the Lord's name: Uriah, Shemaiah's son

from Kiriath-jearim. He prophesied the same things that Jeremiah did about this city and against this land. ²¹When King Jehoiakim and all his warriors and officials heard his words, the king sought to kill him. Uriah heard of this and fled in fear to Egypt. ²²But King Jehoiakim dispatched Elnathan, Achbor's son, and others to Egypt. ²³They brought Uriah back from Egypt to the king who had him killed, and his body was thrown into the common burial ground.

²⁴But Ahikam, Shaphan's son, protected Jeremiah and wouldn't let the people execute him.

Submit to the king of Babylon and live

27 Early in the rule of Judah's King Zedekiah,ʷ Josiah's son, this word came to Jeremiah from the LORD: ²This is what the LORD said to me: Make a yoke of straps and bars and wear it on your neck. ³Then send wordˣ to the kings of Edom, Moab, Ammon, Tyre, and Sidon through their representatives who have come to Jerusalem to Judah's King Zedekiah. ⁴Tell them to say to their masters: The LORD of heavenly forces, the God of Israel, proclaims: Say this to your masters:

⁵By my great power and outstretched arm, I have made the earth and the people and animals that are on it. I can give it to anyone I please. ⁶Now I hand over all these countries to my servant King Nebuchadnezzar of Babylon. I even give him the wild animals as subjects. ⁷All nations will serve him, his son and grandson, until the time for his land arrives; then many nations and great kings will conquer him.

LIGHTHOUSE

PRAYER

God Answers Prayer *Jeremiah 26:19*
Jeremiah was reminded that God answers prayer and that God can and will turn things around. When King Hezekiah faced trouble, he prayed and asked God to take away the evil that threatened him and his people. God heard the king's prayer and took away the threat of harm.

When we face threats of any kind, we can pray and ask God to take care of our situation and to protect us from evil. ✦

⁸As for the nation or country that won't serve Babylon's King Nebuchadnezzar and won't put its neck under his yoke, I will punish it with sword, famine, and disease until I have destroyed it by his hand, declares the LORD. ⁹As for you, don't listen to your prophets, diviners, dreamers,ʸ mediums, or your sorcerers who say to you, "Don't serve the king of Babylon." ¹⁰They are lying to you, and their lies will lead to banishment from your land. I will drive you out, and you will perish. ¹¹But any nation that puts its neck under the yoke of the king of Babylon and serves him, I will let stay in its land to till it and live on it, declares the LORD.

¹²I delivered the same message to Judah's King Zedekiah: If you want to live, put your necks under the yoke of the king of Babylon and serve him and his people. ¹³Why should you and your people die by sword, famine, and disease, as the LORD pronounced against any nation that won't serve the king of Babylon? ¹⁴Pay no attention to the words of the prophets who encourage you not to serve the king of Babylon, for they are lying to you. ¹⁵I haven't sent these prophets, declares the LORD; they are prophesying falsely in my name. If you listen to them, I will drive you out, and you will perish, both you and your prophets!

¹⁶Then I spoke to the priests and all this people: This is what the LORD says: Don't listen to the words of the prophets who are prophesying to you, "In a short while, the temple equipment will be brought back from Babylon." They are prophesying a lie to you. ¹⁷Don't listen to them; serve the king of Babylon and live. Otherwise, this city will be reduced to ruin. ¹⁸If they are really prophets and have the LORD's word, let them intercede with the LORD of heavenly forces not to let the equipment left in the LORD's temple and in the royal palace of Judah and Jerusalem be carted off to Babylon.

¹⁹This is what the LORD of heavenly forces proclaims about the pillars, the Sea, the stands, and the rest of the equipment left in this city, ²⁰which Babylon's King Nebuchadnezzar didn't plunder when he deported

ʷHeb manuscripts, Syr; MT *Jehoiakim*   ˣOr *them* (the yokes)   ʸOr *dreams*

Jeconiah the son of Judah's King Jehoiakim from Jerusalem to Babylon, along with all the officials of Judah and Jerusalem. ²¹Yes, this is what the Lord of heavenly forces, the God of Israel, proclaims about the equipment that is left in the Lord's temple and in the royal palace in Judah, and in Jerusalem: ²²They will be carted off to Babylon where they will remain until the day I come looking for them, declares the Lord; then I will bring them back and restore them to this place.

Prophet against prophet

28That same year, early in the rule of Judah's King Zedekiah, in the fifth month of his fourth year, the prophet Hananiah, Azzur's son from Gibeon, spoke to me in the Lord's temple before the priests and all the people. ²He said: "The Lord of heavenly forces, the God of Israel, proclaims: I have broken the yoke of the king of Babylon. ³In two years I will restore to this place all of the temple equipment that Babylon's King Nebuchadnezzar carted off to Babylon. ⁴I will also restore to this place Judah's King Jeconiah, Jehoiakim's son, along with all the exiles from Judah who were deported to Babylon, for I will break the yoke of the king of Babylon, declares the Lord."

⁵Then the prophet Jeremiah responded to Hananiah in the presence of the priests and all the people who were standing in the Lord's temple. ⁶The prophet Jeremiah said: "Indeed. May the Lord do just as you have said! May the Lord fulfill the words that you have prophesied and bring back from Babylon the equipment of the Lord's temple and all the exiles to this place. ⁷However, listen closely to what I have to say to you and all the people: ⁸The prophets who came before you and me long ago prophesied war, disaster, and disease against many lands and great kingdoms. ⁹So the prophet who prophesies peace is recognized as one who is actually sent by the Lord only when that prophet's message is fulfilled."

¹⁰Then the prophet Hananiah took hold of the yoke that was on the prophet Jeremiah's neck and broke it. ¹¹He said before all the people, "This is what the Lord says: Just as this yoke has been broken, I will break the yoke of Babylon's King Nebuchadnezzar from the neck of all the nations within two years." Then the prophet Jeremiah walked away.

¹²Sometime after Hananiah had broken the yoke that was on Jeremiah's neck, the Lord told him: ¹³Go, say to Hananiah, The Lord proclaims: You have broken a wooden yoke,ᶻ but Iᵃ will replace it with an iron one. ¹⁴The Lord of heavenly forces, the God of Israel, proclaims: I will put iron yokes on the necks of all these nations, and they will serve Babylon's King Nebuchadnezzar; even the wild animals will be subject to him!

¹⁵Then the prophet Jeremiah said to the prophet Hananiah: "Listen, Hananiah! The Lord hasn't sent you. All you are doing is persuading these people to believe a lie. ¹⁶Therefore, the Lord proclaims: I'm going to send you somewhere—right off the face of the earth! Before the year ends, you will die since you have incited rebellion against the Lord." ¹⁷The prophet Hananiah died in the seventh monthᵇ of that year.

Disturbing hope: Settle down in Babylon

29The prophet Jeremiah sent a letter from Jerusalem to the few surviving elders among the exiles, to the priests and the prophets, and to all the people Nebuchadnezzar had taken to Babylon from Jerusalem. ²The letter was sent after King Jeconiah, the queen mother, the court officials, the government leaders of Judah and Jerusalem, and the craftsmen and smiths had left Jerusalem. ³It was delivered to Babylon by Elasah, Shaphan's son, and Gemariah, Hilkiah's son—two men dispatched to Babylon's King Nebuchadnezzar by King Zedekiah.

⁴The Lord of heavenly forces, the God of Israel, proclaims to all the exiles I have carried off from Jerusalem to Babylon: ⁵Build houses and settle down; cultivate gardens and eat what they produce. ⁶Get married and have children; then help your sons find wives and your daughters find husbands in order that they too may have children. Increase in number there so that you don't dwindle away.

ᶻOr *yokes* ᵃHeb uncertain ᵇSeptember–October, Tishrei

⁷Promote the welfare of the city where I have sent you into exile. Pray to the Lord for it, because your future depends on its welfare.

⁸The Lord of heavenly forces, the God of Israel, proclaims: Don't let the prophets and diviners in your midst mislead you. Don't pay attention to your dreams. ⁹They are prophesying lies to you in my name. I didn't send them, declares the Lord.

¹⁰The Lord proclaims: When Babylon's seventy years are up, I will come and fulfill my gracious promise to bring you back to this place. ¹¹I know the plans I have in mind for you, declares the Lord; they are plans for peace, not disaster, to give you a future filled with hope. ¹²When you call me and come and pray to me, I will listen to you. ¹³When you search for me, yes, search for me with all your heart, you will find me. ¹⁴I will be present for you, declares the Lord, and I will

Memorize
Jer 29:11

end your captivity. I will gather you from all the nations and places where I have scattered you, and I will bring you home after your long exile,ᶜ declares the Lord.

¹⁵Yet you say, The Lord has raised up prophets for us in Babylon:

¹⁶This is what the Lord proclaims concerning the king sitting on David's throne and all the people who live in this city, that is, those among you who didn't go into exile: ¹⁷The Lord of heavenly forces proclaims: I'm going to send the sword, famine, and disease

did you know? It may seem weird that Jeremiah would have told those being held prisoner by the Babylonians to pray for the success of Babylon. However, Jeremiah knew if Babylon was attacked or had hard times, life would be harder for the Israelite prisoners. Babylon's success meant a better life for the prisoners.

ᶜOr *I will restore you to the place from which I exiled you.*

God's THOUGHTS ◆ My THOUGHTS

God's Good Plans   *Jeremiah 29:11-14*

We all make mistakes. Some are easy to fix. Others are much more difficult to make right. For example, if we don't finish our homework because we spend too much time watching television, this can result in a big mess. Our teacher may be upset. Our parents may be upset. We may be upset too! And we will probably have to face some consequences. We might lose television privileges. We might have to spend time making up the work when we would rather be doing something else. We might receive a lower grade on that work. Sometimes we are given consequences in order to help us learn from our mistakes. Good parents give consequences out of love.

Long ago, God's people lost the homeland that God had given them. They were far from home, but they were never far from God. They had made mistakes, and they were facing hard consequences. But even when they messed up, God never stopped loving them. God knew this was a sad time for them. But God told them not to lose hope, and said God had good plans for them. God was never far away. God promised then, just as God promises now, to listen to anyone who calls out to God.

What have you learned from some consequences you have faced?

Say a prayer to God, thanking God for the promise of God's love and presence at all times.

against them. I will make them like rotten figs that are too spoiled to eat. [18]I will pursue them with the sword, famine, and disease; and I will make them an object of horror to all nations on earth and an object of cursing, scorn, shock, and disgrace among all the countries where I have scattered them, [19]because they wouldn't listen to my words, declares the Lord, which I sent them time and again through my servants the prophets. They[d] wouldn't listen, declares the Lord.

[20]But now, all you exiles I deported from Jerusalem to Babylon, listen to the Lord's word. [21]This is what the Lord of heavenly forces, the God of Israel, proclaims concerning Ahab, Kolaiah's son, and Zedekiah, Maaseiah's son, who are prophesying lies to you in my name: I will hand them over to Babylon's King Nebuchadnezzar, and he will slay them before your very eyes. [22]Because of them, all the Judean exiles in Babylon will use this curse: "The Lord make you like Zedekiah and Ahab, who were burned alive by the king of Babylon." [23]They committed a horrible scandal in Israel—adultery with their neighbors' wives and deceit spoken in my name, with which I had nothing to do. Yet I'm still aware of it and am witness to it, declares the Lord.

[24]Tell Shemaiah the Nehelamite, [25]This is what the Lord of heavenly forces, the God of Israel, proclaims:[e] You sent letters on your own accord to all the people in Jerusalem, to the priest Zephaniah, Maaseiah's son, and to the rest of the priests. [26]You said to Zephaniah:[f] The Lord has appointed you priest in charge of the Lord's temple instead of Jehoiada. You are responsible for putting every madman who prophesies into stocks and neck irons. [27]So why haven't you threatened Jeremiah of Anathoth, who pretends to be a prophet among you? [28]He has sent a letter telling those of us in Babylon: "You are going to be there a long time, so build houses and settle down, plant gardens and eat what they produce."

[29]The priest Zephaniah read this letter to the prophet Jeremiah. [30]Then the Lord's word came to Jeremiah: [31]Send word to all the exiles: The Lord proclaims concerning Shemaiah the Nehelamite: Because Shemaiah prophesied to you when I didn't send him, and

because he convinced you to believe a lie, [32]I will punish Shemaiah the Nehelamite and his descendants, declares the Lord. Not one member of this people will be around to see the good that I have in store for my people, declares the Lord, for he incited rebellion against me.

THE SCROLL OF COMFORT

Healing and restoration for my people

30 Jeremiah received the Lord's word: [2]The Lord, the God of Israel, proclaims: Write down in a scroll all the words I have spoken to you. [3]The time is coming, declares the Lord, when I will bring back my people Israel and Judah from captivity,[g] says the Lord. I will bring them home to the land that I gave to their ancestors, and they will possess it. [4]Here are the words that the Lord spoke concerning Israel and Judah:

[5] The Lord proclaims:
I[h] hear screams of panic and terror;
no one is safe.
[6] Ask and see:
Can men bear children?
Then why do I see every man
bent over in pain,[i] as if he's in labor?
Why have all turned pale?
[7] That day is awful, beyond words.
A time of unspeakable pain
for my people Jacob.
But they will be delivered from it.

[8]At that time, I will break the yoke off their[j] necks and remove their[k] shackles. Foreigners will no longer enslave them, declares the Lord of heavenly forces. [9]They will serve the Lord their God and the king whom I will raise up for them from David's family.

[10] So don't be afraid, my servant Jacob,
declares the Lord,
Don't lose hope, Israel.
I will deliver you from faraway places
and your children
from the land of their exile.
My people Jacob
will again be safe and sound,
with no one harassing them.
[11] I am with you and will rescue you,
declares the Lord.

[d]Syr; MT *you* [e]Or *because you sent* [f]Heb lacks *You said to Zephaniah.* [g]Or *restore the fortunes* [h]Or *We* [i]Or *with his hands on his groin* [j]Or *your* [k]Or *your*

I will put an end to all the nations
    where I have scattered you.
But I won't put an end to you.
    I won't let you remain unpunished:
      I will discipline you as you deserve.

¹² This is what the LORD says:
    Your injury is incurable;
    your illness is grave.
¹³ No one comes to your aid;
    no one attends to your wound;
    your disease is incurable.
¹⁴ All your lovers disregard you;
    they write you off as a lost cause,
    because I have dealt harshly with you
      as an enemy would,
    because your guilt is great
      and your sins are many.
¹⁵ Why cry out for relief from your pain?
    Your wound is incurable.
I have done these things to you,
    because your guilt is great
      and your sins are many.

¹⁶ Yet all who ravage you will be ravaged;
    all who oppress you will go into exile.
Those who rob you will be robbed,
    and all who plunder you will be plundered.
¹⁷ I will restore your health,
    and I will heal your wounds,
      declares the LORD,
    because you were labeled an outcast,
    "Zion, the lost cause."

¹⁸ The LORD proclaims:
    I will restore Jacob's tents
    and have pity on their birthplace.
Their city will be rebuilt on its ruins
    and the palace in its rightful place.
¹⁹ There will be laughter
    and songs of thanks.
I will add to their numbers
    so they don't dwindle away.

did you know? God reminded the people of the story of the exodus from Egypt. God promised to rescue and help those who were slaves in Babylon just as God had helped the twelve tribes of Israel escape Egypt thousands of years before.

LIFE PRESERVER

What is the "scroll of comfort"? *Jeremiah 30*

This part of the book of Jeremiah contains some poetry (chapters 30–31) and some prose (chapters 32–33) that are called *the scroll of comfort*. The content in this section is different from that in the earlier part of this book. Here God told his prophet Jeremiah to give God's people a new vision full of healing, hope, and a new day when their relationship with God would be restored.

Within a book that is filled with the account of the sin and suffering of God's people, there are words of comfort. Once again, God used a prophet to offer a word of hope and forgiveness to God's people. ◈

I will honor them
    so they aren't humiliated.
²⁰ Their children will thrive
    as they did long ago,
    and their community will be
      established before me.
    I will punish their oppressors.
²¹ They will have their own leader;
    their ruler will come from among them.
I will let him approach me,
    and he will draw near.
Who would dare approach me
    unless I let them come?
      declares the LORD.
²² You will be my people,
    and I will be your God.

²³ Look! The LORD's anger breaks out
    like a violent storm,
    a fierce wind that strikes
      the heads of the wicked.
²⁴ The LORD's fierce anger won't turn back
    until God's¹ purposes
    are entirely accomplished.
In the days to come,
    you will understand what this means.

31 At that time, declares the LORD,
I will be the God
    of all the families of Israel,
    and they will be my people.

² The LORD proclaims:
The people who survived the sword
    found grace in the wilderness.
As Israel searched for a place of rest,

¹Or *his* or *its*

³ the Lord appeared to them^m
  from a distance:^n
I have loved you with a love
  that lasts forever.
And so with unfailing love,
  I have drawn you to myself.°
⁴ Again, I will build you up,
  and you will be rebuilt, virgin Israel.
Again, you will play your tambourines
  and dance with joy.
⁵ Again, you will plant vineyards
  on the hills of Samaria;
farmers will plant
  and then enjoy the harvests.
⁶ The time will come when
  the watchmen shout from
  the highlands of Ephraim:
"Get ready! We're going up to Zion
  to the Lord our God!"
⁷ The Lord proclaims:
Sing joyfully for the people of Jacob;
  shout for the leading nation.
Raise your voices with praise and call out:
  "The Lord has saved his people,^p
  the remaining few in Israel!"

⁸ I'm going to bring them back
  from the north;
I will gather them
  from the ends of the earth.
Among them will be
  the blind and the disabled,
  expectant mothers and those in labor;
  a great throng will return here.
⁹ With tears of joy they will come;
  while they pray, I will bring them back.
I will lead them by quiet streams
  and on smooth paths
  so they don't stumble.
I will be Israel's father,
  Ephraim will be my oldest child.

¹⁰ Listen to the Lord's word, you nations,
  and announce it to the distant islands:
The one who scattered Israel
  will gather them
  and keep them safe,
  as a shepherd his flock.
¹¹ The Lord will rescue the people of Jacob
  and deliver them from the power
  of those stronger than they are.

¹² They will come shouting for joy
  on the hills of Zion,
  jubilant over the Lord's gifts:
  grain, wine, oil, flocks, and herds.
Their lives will be like a lush garden;
  they will grieve no more.
¹³ Then the young women will dance for joy;
  the young and old men will join in.
I will turn their mourning into laughter
  and their sadness into joy;
  I will comfort them.
¹⁴ I will lavish the priests with abundance
  and shower my people with my gifts,
  declares the Lord.

¹⁵ The Lord proclaims:
A voice is heard in Ramah,
  weeping and wailing.
It's Rachel crying for her children;
  she refuses to be consoled,
  because her children are no more.
¹⁶ The Lord proclaims:
Keep your voice from crying
  and your eyes from weeping,
  because your endurance
  will be rewarded,
  declares the Lord.
They will return
  from the land of their enemy!
¹⁷ There's hope for your future,
  declares the Lord.
  Your children will return home!

¹⁸ I hear, yes, I hear Ephraim lamenting:
  "You disciplined me,
  and I learned my lesson,
  even though I was as stubborn as a mule.
Bring me back, let me return,
  because you are the Lord my God.
¹⁹ After I turned away from you,
  I regretted it;
  I realized what I had done,
  and I have hit myself^q—
  I was humiliated and disgraced,
  and I have carried this disgrace
  since I was young."

²⁰ Isn't Ephraim my much-loved child?
  Don't I utterly adore him?
Even when I scold him,
  I still hold him dear.

---

^m Or *to me* ^n Or *a long time ago* ^o Heb lacks *myself.* ^p LXX; MT *Save your people,* Lord ^q Or *struck my thigh*

I yearn for him and love him deeply,
 declares the Lord.

²¹ Set up markers,
 put up signs;
  think about the road you have traveled,
   the path you have taken.
 Return, virgin Israel;
  return to these towns of yours.
²² How long will you hem and haw,
 my rebellious daughter?
 The Lord has created
  something new on earth:
 Virgin Israel will once again
  embrace her God!^r

²³The Lord of heavenly forces, the God of Israel, proclaims: When I bring my people^s back from captivity, they will once again utter these words in the land and towns of Judah:

 The Lord bless you,
  righteous dwelling place,
  holy mountain.

²⁴Those who live in Judah and its towns will dwell together with farmers and shepherds. ²⁵I will strengthen the weary and renew those who are weak.

²⁶Then I woke up and looked around. What a pleasant sleep I had!

²⁷The time is coming, declares the Lord, when I will plant seeds in Israel and Judah, and both people and animals will spring up. ²⁸Just as I watched over them to dig up and pull down, to overthrow, destroy, and bring harm, so I will watch over them to build and plant, declares the Lord. ²⁹In those days, people will no longer say:

 Sour grapes eaten by parents
  leave a bitter taste
   in the mouths of their children.
³⁰ Because everyone will die
 for their own sins:
 whoever eats sour grapes
  will have a bitter taste
   in their own mouths.

³¹The time is coming, declares the Lord, when I will make a new covenant with the people of Israel and Judah. ³²It won't be like the covenant I made with their ancestors when I took them by the hand to lead them out of the land of Egypt. They broke that covenant with me even though I was

their husband, declares the Lord. ³³No, this is the covenant that I will make with the people of Israel after that time, declares the Lord. I will put my Instructions within them and engrave them on their hearts. I will be their God, and they will be my people. ³⁴They will no longer need to teach each other to say, "Know the Lord!" because they will all know me, from the least of them to the greatest, declares the Lord; for I will forgive their wrongdoing and never again remember their sins.

³⁵ The Lord proclaims:
 The one who established the sun
  to light up the day
  and ordered^t the moon and stars
   to light up the night,
 who stirs up the sea into crashing waves,
  whose name is
   the Lord of heavenly forces:
³⁶ If the created order should vanish
 from my sight,
  declares the Lord,
 only then would Israel's descendants
  ever stop being a nation
 before me.
³⁷ The Lord proclaims:
 If the heavens above could be measured
  and the foundation of the earth below
   could be fathomed,
 only then would I reject
  Israel's descendants

Memorize
Jer 31:33

LIFE PRESERVER

What was the "new covenant"? *Jeremiah 31:31-34*

As a part of God's new words to the prophet Jeremiah in the scroll of comfort (Jer 30–33), God decided to make a new covenant with the people that would be different from the one that was given to them after the exodus. This time, God said the covenant would be written on their hearts so that they would always remember God. Isn't that an incredible promise? "They will no longer need to teach each other to say, 'Know the Lord!' because they will all know me" (Jer 31:34). God never gave up on the people and always hoped they would remember God's love for them. ◆

^rOr *a woman surrounds a man* ^sOr *them* ^tOr *orders of*

for what they have done,
    declares the LORD.

³⁸The time is coming, declares the LORD, when the city will be rebuilt for the LORD from the Tower of Hananel to the Corner Gate. ³⁹Its boundaries will extend to the Gareb Hill and around to Goah. ⁴⁰The entire valley defiled by corpses and ashes, and all the fields as far as the Kidron Valley and the Horse Gate on the east, all this will be set apart for the LORD. And the city will never again be dug up or overthrown.

Nothing is too hard for the LORD

32 Jeremiah received the LORD's word in the tenth year of Judah's King Zedekiah, which was the eighteenth year of Nebuchadnezzar's rule. ²At that time, the army of the Babylonian king had surrounded Jerusalem, and the prophet Jeremiah was confined to the prison quarters in the palace of Judah's king. ³Judah's King Zedekiah had Jeremiah sent there after questioning him: "Why do you prophesy, 'This is what the LORD says: I'm handing this city over to the king of Babylon, and he will occupy it; ⁴and Judah's King Zedekiah will be captured and handed over to the king of Babylon; he will speak to the king of Babylon personally and see him with his very own eyes. ⁵And Zedekiah will be carried off to Babylon to live out his days until I punish him, declares the LORD. If you make war against the Babylonians, you will fail.'"

⁶Jeremiah said, The LORD's word came to me: ⁷Your cousin Hanamel, Shallum's son, is on his way to see you; and when he arrives, he will tell you: "Buy my field in Anathoth, for by law you are next in line to purchase it." ⁸And just as the LORD had said, my cousin Hanamel showed up at the prison quarters and told me, "Buy my field in Anathoth in the land of Benjamin, for you are next in line and have a family obligation to purchase it." Then I was sure this was the LORD's doing.

⁹So I bought the field in Anathoth from my cousin Hanamel, and weighed out for him seventeen shekels of silver. ¹⁰I signed the deed, sealed it, had it witnessed, and weighed out the silver on the scales. ¹¹Then I took the deed of purchase—the sealed copy, with its terms and conditions, and the unsealed copy—¹²and gave it to Baruch, Neriah's son and Mahseiah's grandson, before my cousin Hanamel and the witnesses named in the deed, as well as before all the Judeans who were present in the prison quarters. ¹³I charged Baruch before all of them: ¹⁴"The LORD of heavenly forces, the God of Israel, proclaims: Take these documents—this sealed deed of purchase along with the unsealed one—and put them into a clay container so they will last a long time. ¹⁵The LORD of heavenly forces, the God of Israel, proclaims: Houses, fields, and vineyards will again be bought in this land."

¹⁶After I had given the documents to Baruch, Neriah's son, I prayed to the LORD: ¹⁷LORD God, you created heaven and earth by your great power and outstretched arm; nothing is too hard for you! ¹⁸You act with mercy toward thousands upon thousands, but you also bring the consequences of the fathers' sins on their children after them. Great and mighty God, whose name is the LORD of heavenly forces, ¹⁹marvelous are your purposes, and mighty are your deeds. You are aware of all the ways of humanity, and you reward us for how we live and what we do even now. ²⁰You have performed signs and wonders in the land of Egypt as you do to this very day in Israel and everywhere else. That's why you are so renowned. ²¹With a strong hand, an outstretched arm, and with awesome power, yes, with signs and wonders, you brought your people Israel out of the land of Egypt. ²²You gave them this land that you promised to their ancestors, a land full of milk and honey. ²³They entered and took possession of it, but they didn't obey you or follow your Instruction. In fact, they didn't do anything you commanded them. So you brought upon them this disaster. ²⁴Now the siege ramps are in place to take the city. And the Babylonians are about to capture it by war, famine, and disease. What you have pronounced is now happening, as you can see. ²⁵So why tell me, LORD God, Buy the field for money and make sure there are witnesses, when the city is under Babylonian control?

²⁶Then the LORD's word came to Jeremiah: ²⁷I am the LORD, the God of all living things! Is anything too hard for me? ²⁸Therefore, the LORD proclaims: I'm handing this city over to the Babylonians and King Nebuchadnezzar, who will capture it. ²⁹They will enter the city,

set it on fire, and burn it down—including the houses on whose roofs offerings have been made to Baal and drink offerings to other gods, which made me especially angry. ³⁰The people of Israel and Judah have done nothing but evil in my eyes since their youth; the people of Israel and Judah have done nothing but anger me by the work of their hands, declares the Lord. ³¹This city has enraged me from the day it was built to this very day, and so it must be removed from my sight—³²because of all the evil done by the people of Israel and Judah to make me angry—they, their kings and officials, their priests and prophets, the men of Judah, and those who live in Jerusalem. ³³They turned their backs to me and not their faces; and though I taught them over and over, they wouldn't accept my correction. ³⁴They set up their disgusting idols in the temple that bears my name and violated it; ³⁵and they built shrines to Baal in the Ben-hinnon Valley, where they sacrifice their sons and daughters to Molech, though I never commanded them—nor did it even cross my mind—that they should do such detestable things, leading Judah to sin.

³⁶You have been saying, "This city will be handed over to the king of Babylon through sword, famine, and disease." But this is what the Lord, the God of Israel, says: ³⁷I will gather them from all the countries where I have scattered them in my fierce anger and rage. I will bring them back to this place to live securely. ³⁸They will be my people, and I will be their God. ³⁹I will give them one heart and one mind so that they may worship me all the days of their lives, for their own good and for the good of their children after them. ⁴⁰I will make an everlasting covenant with them, never to stop treating them graciously. I will put into their hearts a sense of awe for me so that they won't turn away from me. ⁴¹I will rejoice in treating them graciously, and I will plant them in this land faithfully and with all my heart and being.

⁴²The Lord proclaims: Just as I brought this great disaster on this people, so I will bring on them all the good I promised them. ⁴³Fields will be bought in this land, a land you have said is bleak and uninhabited and in the

possession of the Babylonians. ⁴⁴Fields will be bought, and deeds will be signed, sealed, and witnessed in the land of Benjamin and in the outlying areas of Jerusalem, in the towns of Judah and in the highlands, in the towns of the western foothills and the arid southern plain; for I will bring them back from their captivity, declares the Lord.

Restoration of Judah and Israel

33
While he was still confined to the prison quarters, the Lord's word came to Jeremiah a second time: ²The Lord proclaims, the Lord who made the earth,^u who formed and established it, whose name is the Lord: ³Call to me and I will answer and reveal to you wondrous secrets that you haven't known.

⁴This is what the Lord, the God of Israel, proclaims about the houses of this city and the palaces of the kings of Judah that were torn down to defend against the siege ramps and weapons ⁵of the invading Babylonians.^v They will be filled with the corpses of those slain in my fierce anger. I hid my face from the people of this city because of all their evil deeds, ⁶but now I will heal and mend them. I will make them whole and bless them^w with an abundance of peace and security. ⁷I will bring back the captives of Judah and Israel, and I will rebuild them as they were at first. ⁸I will cleanse them of all the wrongdoing they committed against me, and I will forgive them for all of their guilt and rebellion. ⁹Then this city^x will bring me great joy, praise, and renown before all nations on earth, when they hear of all the good I provide for them. They will be in total awe at all the good and prosperity I provide for them.

¹⁰The Lord proclaims: You have said about this place, "It is a wasteland, without humans or animals." Yet in the ravaged and uninhabited towns of Judah and the streets of Jerusalem, ¹¹the sounds of joy and laughter and the voices of the bride and the bridegroom will again be heard. So will the voices of those who say, as thank offerings are brought to the Lord's temple, "Give thanks to the Lord of heavenly forces, for the Lord is good and his kindness lasts forever." I will bring back

---

^uLXX *the earth;* MT *it* ^vHeb uncertain ^wHeb uncertain ^xOr *it*

the captives of this land as they were before, says the LORD.

¹²The LORD of heavenly forces proclaims: This wasteland, without humans or animals—and all its towns—will again become pastures for shepherds to care for their flocks. ¹³Shepherds will again count their flocks in the towns of the highlands, the western foothills and the arid southern plain, in the land of Benjamin, as well as in the outlying areas of Jerusalem and the towns of Judah, says the LORD.

¹⁴The time is coming, declares the LORD, when I will fulfill my gracious promise with the people of Israel and Judah. ¹⁵In those days and at that time, I will raise up a righteous branch from David's line, who will do what is just and right in the land. ¹⁶In those days, Judah will be saved and Jerusalem will live in safety. And this is what he will be called: The LORD Is Our Righteousness. ¹⁷The LORD proclaims: David will always have one of his descendants sit on the throne of the house of Israel. ¹⁸And the levitical priests will always have someone in my presence to make entirely burned offerings and grain offerings, and to present sacrifices.

¹⁹Then the LORD's word came to Jeremiah: ²⁰This is what the LORD says: If one could break my covenant with the day and my covenant with the night so that they wouldn't come at their proper time, ²¹only then could my covenant with my servant David and my covenant with the levitical priests who minister before me be broken; only then would David no longer have a descendant to rule on his throne. ²²And just as the stars in the sky can't be numbered and the sand on the shore can't be counted, so I will increase the descendants of my servant David and the Levites who minister before me.

²³Then the LORD's word came to Jeremiah: ²⁴Aren't you aware of what people are saying: "The LORD has rejected the two families that he had chosen"? They are insulting my people as if they no longer belong to me.ʸ ²⁵The LORD proclaims: I would no sooner break my covenant with day and night or the laws of heaven and earth ²⁶than I would reject the descendants of Jacob and my servant David and his descendants as rulers for the children of Abraham, Isaac, and Jacob. I will restore the captives and have compassion on them.

Lessons on obedience and disobedience

34 Jeremiah received the LORD's word when Babylon's King Nebuchadnezzar and his army, and all the countries and people he ruled, were attacking Jerusalem and all its towns. ²The LORD, the God of Israel, proclaims, Go and speak to Judah's King Zedekiah and say to him: The LORD proclaims, I'm handing this city over to the king of Babylon, and he will burn it down. ³You won't escape but will be captured and handed over to him. You will see the king of Babylon with your very own eyes and speak to him personally, and you will be taken to Babylon. ⁴Even so, hear the LORD's word, King Zedekiah of Judah: This is what the LORD proclaims about you: You won't die in battle; ⁵you will die a peaceful death. As burial incense was burned to honor your ancestors, the kings who came before you, so it will be burned to honor you as people mourn, "Oh, master!" I myself promise this, declares the LORD.

⁶The prophet Jeremiah delivered this message to Judah's King Zedekiah in Jerusalem ⁷when the army of the king of Babylon was attacking Jerusalem and all the remaining Judean towns, Lachish and Azekah—the only fortified towns still standing in Judah.

⁸Jeremiah received the LORD's word after King Zedekiah had made a covenant with all the people in Jerusalem to proclaim liberty for their slaves: ⁹everyone was to free their male and female Hebrew slaves and no longer hold a Judean brother or sister in bondage. ¹⁰So all the officials and people who entered into this covenant agreed to free their male and female slaves and no longer hold them in bondage; they obeyed the king's commandᶻ and let them go. ¹¹But afterward they broke their promise, took back the men and women they had freed, and enslaved them again.

¹²Then the LORD's word came to Jeremiah: ¹³The LORD, the God of Israel, proclaims: I made a covenant with your ancestors when

Bet you can read this in 8 minutes. **Ready, set, go!**

ʸHeb uncertain   ᶻHeb lacks *the king's command*.

I brought them out of the land of Egypt, out of the house of slavery. [14]I said that every seventh year each of you must free any Hebrews who have been sold to you. After they have served you for six years, you must set them free. But your ancestors didn't obey or pay any attention to me. [15]Recently you turned about and did what was right in my sight; each of you proclaimed liberty for the other and made a covenant before me in the temple that bears my name. [16]But then you went back on your word and made my name impure; each of you reclaimed the men and women you had set free and forced them to be your slaves again.

[17]Therefore, the Lord proclaims: Since you have defied me by not setting your fellow citizens free, I'm setting you free, declares the Lord, free to die by the sword, disease, and famine! And I will make you an object of horror for all nations on earth. [18]I will make those who disregarded my covenant, violating its terms that they agreed to in my presence, like the calf they cut in two and then walked between the halves of its carcass. [19]The officials of Judah and Jerusalem, the eunuchs and priests, and all the people who passed through the pieces of the calf [20]I will hand over to their enemies who seek to kill them. And their corpses will become food for birds and wild animals. [21]I will hand over Judah's King Zedekiah and his officials to their enemies who seek to kill them: namely, the army of Babylon's king, which has just withdrawn from you. [22]I'm about to issue orders, declares the Lord, that the army of Babylon return to this city. They will wage war against it, capture it, and burn it down along with other Judean cities. I will make Judah a wasteland, without inhabitants.

35 Jeremiah received the Lord's word during the rule of Judah's King Jehoiakim, Josiah's son: [2]Go to the Rechabite family and invite them to come to one of the rooms of the Lord's temple. When they arrive, offer them some wine to drink. [3]So I took Jaazaniah, Jeremiah's son and Habazziniah's grandson, and his brothers and all his sons, and the whole Rechabite family. [4]I brought them to the room in the Lord's temple assigned to the sons of Hanan, Igdaliah's son, the man of God. The room was next to the one used by the chief officers and right above the room of Maaseiah, Shallum's son, the temple doorkeeper.[a] [5]Then I set bowls full of wine before the Rechabites, along with several cups, and I said to them, "Have some."

[6]But they refused: "We don't drink wine because our ancestor Jonadab, Rechab's son, commanded us, 'You and your children are never to drink wine; [7]nor are you to build or own houses or plant gardens and vineyards; rather, you are always to dwell in tents so you may live a long time in the fertile land you pass through.' [8]We have obeyed everything our ancestor Jonadab, Rechab's son, commanded us. No one in our household, including our wives and children, has ever had wine. [9]And we haven't built houses to live in or had vineyards, fields, or crops. [10]We have lived in tents and done everything our ancestor Jonadab commanded us. [11]But when Babylon's King Nebuchadnezzar invaded the country, we said, 'We better go to Jerusalem to escape the Babylonian and Aramean armies.' That's why we're here in Jerusalem."

[12]Then the Lord's word came to Jeremiah: [13]The Lord of heavenly forces, the God of Israel, proclaims: Go and tell the people of Judah and those who live in Jerusalem: Can't you learn a lesson about what it means to obey me? declares the Lord. [14]Jonadab, Rechab's son, commanded his descendants not to drink wine, and to this very day they have not drunk wine,

SAILBOAT

HONEST AND TRUE

Faithfulness *Jeremiah 35:12-17*
Jeremiah compared the faithfulness of the Rechabites with the unfaithfulness of the people of Judah. The Rechabites lived faithfully, but the Judahites could not follow God.

No one had preached to the Rechabites, but they were faithful anyway. God sent many prophets to Judah to urge them to change their lives, but they did not. Jeremiah wanted the Judahites to be faithful to God like the Rechabites were faithful. ♦

---

[a]Or *keeper of the threshold*

obeying their ancestor's instruction. But I have spoken to you again and again, and you haven't listened to me. [15]I have sent you all my servants, the prophets, time and again, saying, "Each of you, turn from your evil ways and reform your actions; don't worship or serve other gods. Then you may live in the fertile land I gave to you and your ancestors." But you haven't paid attention or listened to me. [16]The descendants of Jonadab, Rechab's son, have thoroughly obeyed their ancestor, but this people have not listened to me. [17]Therefore, this is what the Lord of heavenly forces, the God of Israel, says: I'm going to bring upon the people of Judah and all those who live in Jerusalem the disaster I pronounced against them, because they wouldn't listen to me or respond when I called.

[18]Then Jeremiah said to the Rechabite family: The Lord of heavenly forces, the God of Israel, proclaims: Because you have obeyed all Jonadab's instructions and you have done everything he commanded you, [19]the Lord of heavenly forces, the God of Israel proclaims: Jonadab, Rechab's son, will always have a descendant that stands before me.

Enduring word of God

36In the fourth year of Judah's King Jehoiakim, Josiah's son, this word came to Jeremiah from the Lord: [2]Take a scroll and write in it all the words I have spoken to you concerning Israel, Judah, and all the nations from the time of Josiah until today. [3]Perhaps when the people of Judah hear about every disaster I intend to bring upon them, they will turn from their evil ways, and I will forgive their wrongdoing and sins. [4]So Jeremiah sent for Baruch, Neriah's son. As Jeremiah dictated all the words that the Lord had spoken to him, Baruch wrote them in the scroll. [5]Then Jeremiah told Baruch, "I'm confined here and can't go to the Lord's temple. [6]So you go to the temple on the next day of fasting, and read the Lord's words from the scroll that I have dictated to you. Read them so that all the people in the temple can hear them, as well as all the Judeans who have come from their towns. [7]If they turn from their evil ways, perhaps the Lord will hear their prayers. The Lord has threatened them

with fierce anger." [8]Baruch, Neriah's son, did everything the prophet Jeremiah instructed him: he read all the Lord's words from the scroll in the temple.

[9]In the ninth month of the fifth year of Judah's King Jehoiakim, Josiah's son, all the people in Jerusalem and all those who had come from Judean towns observed a fast for the Lord in Jerusalem. [10]Then Baruch read Jeremiah's words from the scroll to all the people in the Lord's temple; he read them in the chamber of Gemariah, Shaphan the scribe's son, in the upper courtyard near the entrance of the New Gate of the Lord's temple. [11]When Micaiah, Gemariah's son and Shaphan's grandson, heard all the Lord's words from the scroll, [12]he went down to the scribes' chamber in the royal palace. There he found all the officials meeting together: Elishama the scribe; Delaiah, Shemaiah's son; Elnathan, Achbor's son; Gemariah, Shaphan's son; Zedekiah, Hananiah's son, and all the other officials. [13]Micaiah told them all the words he heard Baruch read from the scroll before the people.

[14]Then all the officials sent Jehudi, Nethaniah's son and Shelemiah's grandson, and Cushi's great-grandson, to Baruch: "Take the scroll you read to the people and come with me." So Baruch, Neriah's son, took the scroll and went to the officials. [15]They said to him, "Sit down and read it to us." So Baruch read it to them. [16]When they heard all its words, they were alarmed and said to Baruch: "We must at once report all this to the king!" [17]Then they asked Baruch, "Tell us, how did you write all these words? Did they come from Jeremiah?" [18]Baruch replied, "He dictated all the words to me, and I wrote them with ink in the scroll." [19]The officials then said to Baruch, "You and Jeremiah had better go and hide. And don't let anyone know where you are."

[20]After leaving the scroll in the room of Elishama the scribe, they went to the king's court and told him everything. [21]The king sent Jehudi to take the scroll, and he retrieved it from the room of Elishama the scribe. Then Jehudi read it to the king and all his royal officials who were standing next to the king. [22]Now it was the ninth month,[b] and the king was staying in the winterized

[b]November–December, Kislev

part of the palace with the firepot burning near him. ²³And whenever Jehudi read three or four columns of the scroll, the king would cut them off with a scribe's knife and throw them into the firepot until the whole scroll was burned up. ²⁴Neither the king nor any of his attendants who heard all these words were alarmed or tore their clothes. ²⁵Elnathan, Delaiah, and Gemariah begged the king not to burn the scroll, but he wouldn't listen to them.

²⁶The king commanded Jerahmeel, the king's son, along with Seraiah, Azriel's son, and Shelemiah, Abdeel's son, to arrest the scribe Baruch and the prophet Jeremiah. But the LORD hid them.

²⁷The LORD's word came to Jeremiah after the king had burned the scroll containing the words written by Baruch at Jeremiah's dictation: ²⁸Get another scroll and write in it all the words that were in the first scroll that Judah's King Jehoiakim burned. ²⁹Then say to Judah's King Jehoiakim: The LORD proclaims: You burned that scroll because it declared that the king of Babylon will come and destroy this land and eliminate every sign of life from it. ³⁰Therefore, this is what the LORD proclaims about Judah's King Jehoiakim: He won't have any heirs to occupy the throne of David, and his dead body will be cast out and exposed to the heat of the day and the frost of the night. ³¹I will punish him and his family and his attendants for their wrongdoing. I will bring upon them, as well as the residents of Jerusalem and the people of Judah, every disaster I pronounced against them. But they wouldn't listen.

³²So Jeremiah took another scroll and gave it to the scribe Baruch, Neriah's son, who wrote at Jeremiah's dictation all the words in the scroll burned in the fire by Judah's King Jehoiakim. Many similar words were added to them.

Jeremiah falsely accused and imprisoned

37 Babylon's King Nebuchadnezzar appointed Zedekiah, Josiah's son, to succeed Coniah, Jehoiakim's son, as king of Judah. ²Neither Zedekiah, his attendants, nor the people of the land listened to the LORD's words spoken by the prophet Jeremiah.

³Nevertheless, King Zedekiah sent Jehucal, Shelemiah's son, and the priest Zephaniah, Maaseiah's son, to Jeremiah the prophet with this plea: "Please pray for us to the LORD our God." (⁴Now Jeremiah hadn't been imprisoned yet, so he was free to come and go among the people. ⁵Pharaoh's army had recentlyᶜ set out from Egypt; when the Babylonians who were attacking Jerusalem learned of the Egyptian advance, they withdrew from Jerusalem.)

⁶Then the LORD's word came to Jeremiah the prophet: ⁷The LORD, the God of Israel, proclaims: Tell the king of Judah who sent his emissaries to seek advice from me: "Pharaoh's army that came to assist you is heading back to Egypt. ⁸The Babylonians will return and attack this city. They will capture it and burn it down."

⁹The LORD proclaims: Don't let yourself be deceived into thinking that the Babylonians will withdraw for good.ᵈ They won't! ¹⁰Even if you were to crush the entire Babylonian army that's attacking you and only the wounded in their tents remained, they would rise up and burn this city down.

¹¹Now when the Babylonian army had withdrawn from Jerusalem due to Pharaoh's advance, ¹²Jeremiah set out for the land of Benjamin to secure his share of the family property.ᵉ ¹³He got as far as the Benjamin Gate in Jerusalem when the guard there named Irijah, Shelemiah's son and Hananiah's grandson, arrested the prophet Jeremiah, saying, "You are deserting to the Babylonians."

¹⁴"That's a lie," Jeremiah replied. "I'm not deserting to the Babylonians." But Irijah wouldn't listen to him. He arrested Jeremiah and brought him to the officials, ¹⁵who were furious with him. They beat him and threw him into the house of the scribe Jonathan, which had been turned into a prison. ¹⁶So Jeremiah was put in a cistern, which was like a dungeon, where he remained a long time.

¹⁷Later King Zedekiah sent for him and questioned Jeremiah secretly in the palace: "Is there a word from the LORD?"

"There is," Jeremiah replied. "You are going to be handed over to the king of Babylon." ¹⁸Then Jeremiah asked King Zedekiah, "What

---

ᶜHeb lacks *recently*. ᵈHeb lacks *for good*. ᵉHeb uncertain have I done wrong to you or your attendants or this people that you should throw me into prison? ¹⁹Where are your prophets now who prophesied that the king of Babylon wouldn't attack you and this land? ²⁰Now, my master and king, I beg you, don't send me back to the house of Jonathan the scribe, or I'll die there." ²¹So King Zedekiah gave orders that Jeremiah be held in the prison quarters and that he receive a loaf of bread daily from the street vendors[f]—until all the bread in the city was gone. So Jeremiah remained in the prison quarters.

38Shephatiah, Mattan's son; Gedaliah, Pashhur's son; Jucal, Shelemiah's son; and Pashhur, Malchiah's son heard what Jeremiah had been telling the people: ²The Lord proclaims: Whoever stays in this city will die by the sword, famine, and disease. But whoever surrenders to the Babylonians will live; yes, their lives will be spared. ³The Lord proclaims: This city will certainly be handed over to the army of Babylon's king, who will capture it.

⁴Then the officials said to the king: "This man must be put to death! By saying such things, he is discouraging the few remaining troops left in the city, as well as all the people. This man doesn't seek their welfare but their ruin!"

⁵"He's in your hands," King Zedekiah said, "for the king can do nothing to stop you." ⁶So they seized Jeremiah, threw him into the cistern of the royal prince Malchiah, within the prison quarters, and lowered him down by ropes. Now there wasn't any water in the cistern, only mud, and Jeremiah began to sink into the mud.

⁷Ebed-melech the Cushite, a court official in the royal palace, got word that they had thrown Jeremiah into the cistern. Since the king was sitting at the Benjamin Gate, ⁸Ebed-melech left the palace and said to the king: ⁹"My master the king, these men have made a terrible mistake in treating the prophet Jeremiah the way they have; they have thrown him into the cistern where he will die of starvation, for there's no bread left in the city."

¹⁰Then the king commanded Ebed-melech the Cushite, "Take thirty men from here and take Jeremiah the prophet out of the cistern before he dies." ¹¹So Ebed-melech took the men and returned to the palace, to an underground supply room, where he found some old rags and scraps of clothing.

Ebed-melech lowered them down the cistern by the ropes ¹²and called to Jeremiah, "Put these old rags and scraps of clothing under your arms and hold on to the ropes." When Jeremiah did this, ¹³they pulled him up by the ropes and got him out of the cistern. After that Jeremiah remained in the prison quarters.

¹⁴King Zedekiah ordered that the prophet Jeremiah be brought to him at the third entrance of the Lord's temple, where the king said to Jeremiah, "I want to ask you something, and don't hide anything from me."

¹⁵Jeremiah replied, "If I do, you'll kill me! And if I tell you what to do, you won't listen to me!"

¹⁶So King Zedekiah swore to Jeremiah behind closed doors, "As the Lord lives, who has given us this life, I won't put you to death and I won't hand you over to those who seek to kill you."

¹⁷So Jeremiah said to Zedekiah: "The Lord of heavenly forces, the God of Israel, proclaims: If you surrender to the officers of the king of Babylon, you and your family will live, and this city will not be burned down. ¹⁸If you don't surrender to the officers of the king of Babylon, the city will be handed over to the Babylonians, who will burn it down, and you won't escape from them."

¹⁹King Zedekiah said to Jeremiah, "I'm afraid that I will fall into the hands of the Judeans who have defected to the Babylonians, and they will torture me."

²⁰"That won't happen," Jeremiah replied, "if you obey the Lord, whose message I bring. You will survive, and all will go well for you. ²¹But if you refuse to surrender, this is what the Lord has shown me: ²²All the women left in the palace of the king of Judah will be led out to the officers of the king of Babylon. And they will say:

'Your trusted friends have betrayed you;
    they have deceived you;
now that your feet are stuck in the mud,
    they are nowhere to be found.'

[f]Or *from the street of the bakers*

²³"All your wives and children will be led out to the Babylonians, and you yourself won't escape from them. The king of Babylon will capture you, and this city will be burned down."

²⁴Zedekiah said to Jeremiah, "No one is to know about these matters or else you will die. ²⁵If the officials find out that we met, and they come and say to you, 'Tell us what you said to the king. Don't hide anything from us; otherwise, we'll kill you. So what did the king say to you?' ²⁶you should say to them, 'I was begging the king not to send me back to the house of Jonathan to die there.'"

²⁷Then all the officials approached Jeremiah to question him. And he responded exactly as the king had instructed him. So they stopped interrogating him because the conversation between the king and Jeremiah⁸ hadn't been overheard. ²⁸Jeremiah remained in the prison quarters until Jerusalem was captured.

Fall of Jerusalem

39 In the ninth year and the tenth month of Judah's King Zedekiah, Babylon's King Nebuchadnezzar and his entire army came against Jerusalem and surrounded it. ²In the eleventh year of Zedekiah, on the ninth day of the fourth month, they broke through the city walls. ³Then all the commanding officers of the king of Babylon—Nergal-sharezer, Samgar-nebo,ʰ Sarsechim the chief officer, Nergal-sharezer the field commander—entered it and took their places at the middle gate with the rest of the officials of the king of Babylon.

⁴When Judah's King Zedekiah and his troops saw them, they tried to escape at night through the royal gardens and the gate between the two walls, toward the desert plain. ⁵But the Babylonianⁱ army chased them down and caught Zedekiah in the plains of Jericho. They arrested him and brought him before Babylon's King Nebuchadnezzar at Riblah in the land of Hamath. There the king put him on trial. ⁶The king of Babylon slaughtered Zedekiah's children at Riblah before his very own eyes, and the king of Babylon slaughtered all the officials of Judah. ⁷Then

he gouged out Zedekiah's eyes, bound him in chains, and dragged him off to Babylon.

⁸The Babylonians burned down the royal palace and the houses of the people, and they destroyed the Jerusalem walls. ⁹Nebuzaradan the captain of the special guard rounded up the rest of the people who were left in the city, including those who had defected to the Babylonians, and deported them to Babylon. ¹⁰But Nebuzaradan the captain of the special guard left some of the poorest people in the land of Judah. He gave them vineyards and fields at that time.

¹¹Babylon's King Nebuchadnezzar gave orders concerning Jeremiah to Nebuzaradan the captain of the special guard: ¹²"Find Jeremiah and look after him; don't harm him but do whatever he asks from you." ¹³So Nebuzaradan the captain of the special guard, Nebushazban the chief officer, Nergal-sharezer the field commander, and all the commanders of the king of Babylon ¹⁴sent ordersʲ to release Jeremiah from the prison quarters. They entrusted him to Gedaliah, Ahikam's son and Shaphan's grandson, so that Jeremiah could move about freelyᵏ among the people.

SAILBOAT

KINDNESS

Nebuchadnezzar's Kindness to Jeremiah
Jeremiah 39:11-12
Sometimes people can really surprise us by being kind when we expect them to be mean. King Nebuchadnezzar had taken over the city of Jerusalem, and many of the people had been forced out, just as Jeremiah said would happen. But what would happen to the prophet? Jeremiah preached harsh words of truth against nations like Babylon. Yet God moved the king's heart to be good to Jeremiah, who was doing God's work. ◆

¹⁵The LORD's word came to Jeremiah when he was still confined to the prison quarters: ¹⁶Go and say to Ebed-melech the Cushite that the LORD of heavenly forces, the God of Israel, proclaims: I'm about to fulfill my words concerning this city, for harm and not for good.

---

⁸Heb lacks *between the king and Jeremiah.* ʰOr *Nergal-sharezer the Simmagir* ⁱHeb *Chaldean* and hereafter through Jeremiah ʲHeb lacks *orders.* ᵏHeb uncertain

You will witness it for yourself on that day. ¹⁷But on that day, declares the LORD:

I will rescue you;
  you won't be handed over
  to those you dread.
¹⁸ I will defend you;
  you won't die in battle.
You will escape with your life,
  because you have trusted in me,
  declares the LORD.

Jeremiah's release

40 Jeremiah received the LORD's word after Nebuzaradan the captain of the special guard had released him from Ramah. He had been bound in chains there along with all the other detainees from Jerusalem and Judah who were being sent off to Babylon. ²The captain of the special guard located Jeremiah and said to him, "The LORD your God declared that a great disaster would overtake this place. ³Now the LORD has made it happen. He has done just as he warned because all of you have sinned against the LORD and haven't obeyed him. That's why this has happened to you. ⁴But I'm setting you free from the chains on your hands. If you would like, come with me to Babylon, and I'll take care of you. If you would rather not come with me, that's fine too. Now, the whole land lies before you; go wherever you want. ⁵If you decide to remain here,¹ stay with Gedaliah, Ahikam's son and Shaphan's grandson—the Babylonian appointee in charge of the cities of Judah. Stay with him and the people he rules or go wherever you want." Then the captain of the special guard gave him ample provisions and let him go. ⁶Jeremiah went to Gedaliah, Ahikam's son at Mizpah, and he stayed with him and the people who remained in the land.

Gedaliah's provisional government

⁷Some of the army officers and their troops were still hiding out in the countryside when they heard that the king of Babylon had appointed Gedaliah, Ahikam's son, over the region, responsible for the men, women, and children who were the poorest in the land and who hadn't been deported to Babylon. ⁸So they went out to meet Gedaliah

at Mizpah: Ishmael, Nethaniah's son; Johanan and Jonathan, Kareah's sons; Seraiah son of Tanhumeth; the sons of Ephai the Netophathite; Jezaniah son of the Maacathite; and their troops. ⁹Gedaliah, Ahikam's son and Shaphan's grandson, firmly assured them all: "Don't be afraid of serving the Babylonians. Remain in the land, serve the king of Babylon, and all will go well for you. ¹⁰But me? I will stay at Mizpah so I can speak on your behalf when the Babylonians arrive. But you? Settle down in the towns you have taken; harvest the grapes, the summer fruits and figs, and then store them in your containers."

¹¹In the same way, all the Judeans living in Moab, Ammon, Edom, and in other countries heard that the king of Babylon had left a few people in the land and that he had put Gedaliah, Ahikam's son and Shaphan's grandson, in charge of them. ¹²So they left the places where they had been scattered and returned to the land, to Gedaliah at Mizpah. There they gathered large amounts of grapes and summer fruits.

¹³Johanan, Kareah's son, and all the army officers in the countryside approached Gedaliah at Mizpah ¹⁴and said to him, "Are you aware that King Baalis of Ammon has sent Ishmael, Nethaniah's son, to kill you?" But Gedaliah, Ahikam's son, wouldn't believe them. ¹⁵Still Johanan, Kareah's son, met with Gedaliah secretly at Mizpah and said to him, "Let me go and kill Ishmael, Nethaniah's son; no one needs to knows about this matter. Otherwise, he'll kill you, and all the Judeans who have gathered around you will be scattered, and the few who are left will perish."

¹⁶But Gedaliah son of Ahikam told Johanan, Kareah's son, "Don't do such a thing, for what you are saying about Ishmael is wrong."

Mutiny and murder

41 In the seventh month,ᵐ Ishmael, Nethaniah's son and Elishama's grandson, who was from a royal family and who was one of the chief officers of the king, came with ten men to Gedaliah, Ahikam's son, at Mizpah. While they were eating a meal together, ²Ishmael, Nethaniah's son, and the ten men got up and struck down Gedaliah, Ahikam's

¹Heb uncertain ᵐSeptember–October, Tishrei

son and Shaphan's grandson, with the sword. They murdered him because he had been appointed over the region by the king of Babylon. ³Ishmael also murdered all the Judeans who had rallied around Gedaliah at Mizpah as well as the Babylonian soldiers who were posted there.

⁴The day after Gedaliah was killed, before anyone knew of it, ⁵eighty men with shaved beards, torn clothes, and gashed bodies arrived from Shechem, Shiloh, and Samaria. They were bringing grain offerings and incense to present at the Lord's temple. ⁶Ishmael, Nethaniah's son, left Mizpah to meet them, weeping as he went. When he reached them, he said, "Come to Gedaliah, Ahikam's son!" ⁷When they arrived in the middle of the town, Ishmael, Nethaniah's son, and the men with him slaughtered them and threw their bodiesⁿ into a cistern.

⁸But there were ten men among them who begged Ishmael, "Don't kill us; we have wheat, barley, oil, and honey hidden in a field." So he stopped and didn't kill them along with the rest.

(⁹Now the cistern that Ishmael used to discard the bodies of the men he had killed because of their association with Gedaliahᵒ was the one that King Asa had made to defend against Israel's King Baasha. Ishmael, Nethaniah's son, filled it with the dead.)

¹⁰Ishmael captured the rest of the people who were at Mizpah, including the daughters of the king and all those assigned to Gedaliah, Ahikam's son, at Mizpah by Nebuzaradan the captain of the special guard. Then Ishmael, Nethaniah's son, set out to cross over to the Ammonites with the hostages.

¹¹Johanan, Kareah's son, and all the army officers at his side heard of the terrible acts committed by Ishmael, Nethaniah's son. ¹²So they mustered all their forces and went to fight him. They found Ishmael, Nethaniah's son, at the great pool in Gibeon. ¹³When all those taken by Ishmael at Mizpah saw Johanan, Kareah's son, and all his army officers with him, they were delighted. ¹⁴They rallied around Johanan, Kareah's son, and returned home with him. ¹⁵But Ishmael, Nethaniah's

son, and eight of his men eluded Johanan and went to the Ammonites.

¹⁶Then Johanan, Kareah's son, and all the army officers with him took the small group they had rescued in Gibeon, including the soldiers, women, children, and commanding officers that Ishmael, Nethaniah's son, had captured at Mizpah after killing Gedaliah, Ahikam's son. ¹⁷They set out for Egypt, stopping on the way at Geruth Chimham near Bethlehem, ¹⁸because they were afraid of what the Babylonians would do when they found out that Ishmael, Nethaniah's son, had killed Gedaliah, Ahikam's son, whom the king of Babylon had appointed over the region.

Don't go to Egypt!

42 Then all the army officers, including Johanan, Kareah's son, and Jezaniah, Hoshaiah's son, and the rest of the people, from the least to the greatest, approached ²Jeremiah the prophet and said to him, "We have something to ask you: Please pray to the Lord your God for us, this small group, for as you can see we were once many but now are very few. ³May the Lord your God show us where we should go and what we should do."

⁴The prophet Jeremiah replied, "Yes, I'll pray to the Lord your God as you have asked. And I'll tell you whatever the Lord says; I won't hide anything from you."

⁵Then they said to Jeremiah, "May the Lord be a true and faithful witness against us if we fail to do everything that the Lord your God tells us through you. ⁶Whether we like it or not, we will obey all that the Lord our God says. We will obey the Lord our God, to whom we're sending you, so it may go well for us."

⁷Ten days later Jeremiah received the Lord's word. ⁸So he called Johanan, Kareah's son, and all the army officers with him and the rest of the people, from the least to the greatest, ⁹and he said to them: You have sent me to present your plea to the Lord, and this is what the Lord, the God of Israel, says: ¹⁰If you live in this land, I will build you up and not pull you down. I will plant you and not dig you up because I grieve over the disaster I have brought upon you. ¹¹You don't have to be afraid of the king of Babylon, whom you

---

ⁿHeb lacks *and threw their bodies;* cf 41:9. ᵒOr *by the hand of Gedaliah*

now fear. You don't have to be afraid of him anymore, declares the Lord, for I will be with you to save you and rescue you from his hand. [12]I will be merciful to you, and he will be merciful and return you to your land.

LIGHTHOUSE

PRAYER

Waiting for an Answer *Jeremiah 42:7*

When we're waiting on something good to happen, it can seem to take forever. We may watch the clock or the calendar, counting away the hours, minutes, or days. Sometimes we may get anxious as we wait for God to answer our prayers. We may even start to feel like God is saying no. But God always waits until just the right time before giving an answer.

Jeremiah was used to getting quick answers from God, but this time took a lot longer. While he waited, Jeremiah and the people must have wondered what was taking so long. Perhaps God waited awhile so that the people would take time to pray and wait to hear from God.

Sometimes God needs to prepare us for the answer God wants to give. So while we're waiting for God to answer, we can keep praying and thanking God that the answer will come in time. ◊

[13]But if you say, "We won't live in this land," you will disobey the Lord your God. [14]And if you insist, "No, we're going to live in Egypt, where there's no war, battle alarms, or hunger, and there we will stay," [15]then listen to the Lord's word, you remaining Judeans. The Lord of heavenly forces, the God of Israel, proclaims: If you are determined to go to Egypt and you then go and live there, [16]then the war you fear will seize you in the land of Egypt; and the famine you dread will hunt you down in Egypt, and there you will die. [17]Every one of you who is determined to go and live in Egypt will die by the sword, famine, and disease. No one will escape the disaster that I will bring upon them there.

[18]The Lord of heavenly forces, the God of Israel, proclaims: Just as my fierce anger was poured out on the people of Jerusalem, so it will be poured out on you if you go to Egypt. You will become an object of cursing, scorn, shock, and disgrace. And you will

never see this place again. [19]You who survive from Judah, the Lord has told you: Don't go to Egypt. Know without a doubt that I have warned you this day. [20]You are putting your lives at risk[p] by sending me to the Lord your God, saying, "Pray for us to the Lord our God; tell us everything the Lord our God says, and we'll do it." [21]Today I have told you, but you still haven't obeyed all that the Lord your God has sent me to tell you. [22]So know without a doubt that you will die by war, famine, and disease in the place you yearn to go and live.

Off to Egypt with Jeremiah and Baruch

43When Jeremiah finished telling the people all the words of the Lord their God—he didn't omit anything the Lord sent him to convey—[2]Azariah, Hoshaiah's son, and Johanan, Kareah's son, and all the arrogant men said to Jeremiah, "You're lying to us! The Lord our God didn't send you to tell us not to go to Egypt to live. [3]It's Baruch, Neriah's son, who put you up to it so that we end up in the hands of the Babylonians, who will either kill us or deport us to Babylon."

[4]So Johanan, Kareah's son, and all the army officers and the rest of the people disobeyed the Lord's command to stay in the land of Judah. [5]Johanan, Kareah's son, and all the army officers took the remaining Judeans who had returned to the land of Judah after being scattered among the nations—[6]men, women, children, the king's daughters, everyone Nebuzaradan the captain of the special guard had left with Gedaliah, Ahikam's son and Shaphan's grandson, including Jeremiah the prophet and Baruch, Neriah's son. [7]They went to the land of Egypt, as far as Tahpanhes, for they wouldn't obey the Lord.

[8]The Lord's word came to Jeremiah in Tahpanhes: [9]Take some large stones and set them in the clay pavement[q] in front of Pharaoh's palace in Tahpanhes while the people of Judah are watching. [10]After that, say to the people: The Lord of heavenly forces, the God of Israel, proclaims: I'm sending for my servant King Nebuchadnezzar of Babylon, who[r] will set his throne over these stones and will spread his canopy over them. [11]He will come and ravage the land of Egypt:

[p]Or *to do evil* [q]Heb uncertain [r]LXX; MT *I*

those marked for disaster, to disaster,
   and those marked for exile, to exile.
   and those marked for war, to war.

[12]He will set on fire[s] the temples of the Egyptian gods. He will burn them down and carry off their gods. He will wrap the land of Egypt around himself, just as a shepherd wraps[t] his garment around himself, and he will move on unharmed.[u] [13]He will shatter the sacred pillars in the temple of the sun in Egypt and burn down the temples of the Egyptian gods.

Jeremiah's final words to Judeans in Egypt

44 Jeremiah received the LORD's word for the Judeans living in the land of Egypt, those living in Migdol, Tahpanhes, and Memphis and in the land of Pathros. [2]The LORD of heavenly forces, the God of Israel, proclaims: You have seen the disaster I brought on Jerusalem and the towns of Judah. They are now a wasteland with no one left [3]because of their evil ways. They have angered me by making offerings and worshipping other gods that neither they nor you nor your ancestors knew. [4]Yet time and again I sent you all my servants the prophets, saying, "Don't do these detestable things that I hate." [5]But they wouldn't listen or pay attention or turn from their evil ways. They continued making offerings to other gods. [6]So my fierce anger poured out and blazed against the towns of Judah and the streets of Jerusalem. And they were reduced to an utter wasteland, as they are today.

[7]Now the LORD of heavenly forces, the God of Israel, proclaims: Why are you committing this huge mistake that will cost you your lives? Every man, woman, child, and infant will be eliminated from the midst of Judah, and no one will be left. [8]Why do you anger me by what you do: by burning incense to other gods in the land of Egypt where you have come to live? You will be eliminated and become an object of cursing and disgrace among all the nations of the earth. [9]Have you forgotten the sins of your ancestors and the sins of the kings of Judah and their wives?[v] Have you forgotten the sins that you and your wives committed in the land of Judah and in

the streets of Jerusalem? [10]To this day you[w] haven't shown any sorrow for what you have done. And you haven't revered me or followed my Instruction and my laws that I set before you and your ancestors.

[11]Therefore, the LORD of heavenly forces, the God of Israel, proclaims: I'm determined to bring disaster on you, to eliminate all of Judah. [12]I will take the few remaining Judeans who were determined to go to the land of Egypt to live. They will all perish there. They will fall by the sword and perish due to famine. The least to the greatest will die by the sword and by famine. They will become an object of cursing, scorn, contempt, and disgrace. [13]I will punish those who live in the land of Egypt, just as I punished Jerusalem with war, famine, and disease. [14]From the few remaining in Judah, no fugitive or survivor who came to live here in the land of Egypt will be able to return to the land of Judah. Even though they want to return and live there, they won't be able to return, except for some fugitives.

[15]Then all the men who knew that their wives had made offerings to other gods, along with the great crowd of women who were present, as well as the people living in Pathros in the land of Egypt, all answered Jeremiah: [16]"We're not going to listen to a word you have said to us in the LORD's name! [17]No, we're going to do exactly what we want: We're going to burn incense to the queen of heaven and pour out drink offerings to her, as we and our ancestors, our kings and our officials, have done in the towns of Judah and in the streets of Jerusalem. Then we had plenty to eat and we were thriving; we didn't have any troubles. [18]But ever since we stopped burning incense to the queen of heaven and pouring drink offerings to her, we have been destroyed by the sword and by famine."

[19]And the women added,[x] "Do you think that we burn incense to the queen of heaven and pour drink offerings to her without our husbands' support when we make cakes in her image and pour drink offerings to her?"

[20]Jeremiah said to all the people, men and women alike, in fact everyone who had spoken this way: [21]"Do you really think the LORD was unaware of what you were up to in

---

[s]LXX, Syr; MT *I will set on fire*   [t]Or *picks clean*   [u]Heb uncertain   [v]Heb *his wives*   [w]Or *they*   [x]Syr; MT lacks *and the women added*.

the towns of Judah and the streets of Jerusalem? Don't you think the Lord knew that you and your ancestors were making offerings to other gods^y—along with your kings and officials, and the people of the land? ²²It got so bad that the Lord could no longer bear your evil and shameless acts; it was at that point that your land was reduced to an utter wasteland and a curse, as it is today. ²³The current dire situation occurred because you made offerings to other gods^z and sinned against the Lord—because you wouldn't obey the Lord or follow the Lord's instruction, laws, or warnings."

²⁴Then Jeremiah said to all the people, including the women: Listen to the Lord's word, all you Judeans in the land of Egypt. ²⁵The Lord of heavenly forces, the God of Israel, proclaims: You and your wives have done exactly what you said you would do. You said, "We will definitely fulfill our promise to burn incense to the queen of heaven and pour out drink offerings to her." Go ahead and keep your promises! ²⁶But listen to the Lord's word, all you Judeans who live in the land of Egypt. I swear by my great name, says the Lord, that no one from Judah living in Egypt will utter my name again, even in the solemn pledge: "As surely as the Lord God lives." ²⁷I'm watching over them for harm and not for good. Everyone from Judah who is living in the land of Egypt will die by the sword and by famine, until all are gone. ²⁸Those who actually survive war and return from Egypt to the land of Judah will be very few. Then the few remaining Judeans living in Egypt will know for certain whose word is true—mine or theirs! ²⁹And this will be a sign for you, declares the Lord: I will punish you here so that you know my threats against you will surely be fulfilled. ³⁰The Lord proclaims: I will hand Pharaoh Hophra, Egypt's king, over to his enemies who seek to kill him, just as I delivered Judah's King Zedekiah over to his enemy King Nebuchadnezzar of Babylon, who sought to kill him.

A final word for Baruch

45 In the fourth year of Judah's King Jehoiakim, Josiah's son, Baruch was writing in a scroll the words that Jeremiah was dictating to him. Jeremiah the prophet told Baruch, Neriah's son: ²This is what the Lord the God of Israel proclaims about you, Baruch: ³You have said, "I can't take it anymore! The Lord has added sorrow to my pain. I'm worn out from groaning and can find no rest." ⁴This is what you should say to him: "The Lord proclaims: I'm breaking down everything I have built up. I'm digging up that which I have planted—the entire land. ⁵You seek great things for yourself, but don't bother. I'm bringing disaster on all humanity, declares the Lord, but wherever you go I will let you escape with your life."

ORACLES CONCERNING THE NATIONS

46 This is what the Lord told the prophet Jeremiah concerning the nations.

Prophecy against Egypt

²About Egypt! A message for the army of Pharaoh Neco, Egypt's king, which was defeated by Babylon's Nebuchadnezzar at Carchemish near the Euphrates River in the fourth year of Judah's King Jehoiakim, Josiah's son:

³ Grab your shields
  and prepare for war!
⁴ Saddle the horses;
  mount the stallions!
 Take your positions
  with helmets on!
 Polish your spears;
  put on your armor!
⁵ Why do I see them terrified,
  retreating in haste?
 Their soldiers are crushed,
  running for cover,
  and they don't turn back.
 Panic lurks at every turn,
  declares the Lord.
⁶ The swift can't flee;
  the mighty can't escape.
 Up north by the Euphrates River,
  they stagger and fall.

⁷ Who is this that rises like the Nile,
  whose banks overflow?^a

---

^y Heb lacks *to other gods*. ^z Heb lacks *to other gods*. ^a Or *like rivers whose waters roar*

⁸ It's Egypt that rises like the Nile,
   whose banks overflow,ᵇ
   who declares, "I will arise
   and cover the earth
   and destroy cities and inhabitants."
⁹ Charge, you horses;
   advance, you chariots!
   Attack, you soldiers
   with your shield in hand,
   you people of Cush and Putᶜ
   with your bow drawn,
   you archers from Lud.

¹⁰ But that day belongs to the
   Lord God of heavenly forces;
   it's a day of reckoning,
   settling scores with enemies.
   The sword will devour
   until it has had its fill of blood.
   The Lord God of heavenly forces
   is preparing a sacrifice in the north
   by the Euphrates River.
¹¹ Go up to Gilead and seek balm,
   virgin Daughter Egypt.
   You search out remedies in vain,
   for your disease is incurable.
¹² Nations hear of your shame;
   the earth is filled with your sobs.
   Soldier stumbles over soldier;
   together they go down.

¹³This is the word that the Lord spoke to the prophet Jeremiah about the military offensive of Babylon's King Nebuchadnezzar against the land of Egypt:
¹⁴ Tell Egypt, warn Migdol,
   alert Memphis and Tahpanhes!
   Say: "Brace yourselves for what's coming.
   War is breaking out from every side!"
¹⁵ Why have your mighty fallen?
   Why haven't they stood their ground?
   Because the Lord
   has struck them down.
¹⁶ He's tripped them up;
   they fall over each other and say,
   "Let's get out of here
   and go home to our people,
   where we were born,
   far away from the oppressor's sword."ᵈ
¹⁷ There they call Pharaoh, Egypt's king,
   Loudmouth—Nothing But Hot Air!

¹⁸ As I live, declares the king,
   whose name is
   the Lord of heavenly forces,
   one is coming
   just as surely as Tabor is in the mountains
   and Carmel is by the sea.ᵉ
¹⁹ Get what you need for deportation,
   you inhabitants of Egypt.ᶠ
   Memphis will be reduced to a wasteland,
   a ruin with no one left.
²⁰ Egypt is a beautiful, yes, beautiful heifer,
   but a horsefly from the north
   is coming to bite her.ᵍ
²¹ Even her mercenaries
   are like well-fed calves;
   they too will retreat and run for cover;
   they won't survive.
   The day of disaster
   has come to haunt them,
   the time of their punishment.
²² Like the sound of a snake hissing
   as it slithers away
   is Egyptʰ as armies approach in force;
   they come against her with axes,
   like woodcutters.
²³ They destroy her dense forest,
   though it is vast,
   because they outnumber locusts
   and can't be counted,
   declares the Lord.
²⁴ Daughter Egypt will be humiliated,
   handed over to people from the north.
²⁵This is what the Lord of heavenly forces, the God of Israel, proclaims: I'm going to punish Amon of Thebes, Egypt and its gods and kings, as well as Pharaoh and all who rely on him. ²⁶I will hand them over to those who seek to kill them, namely Babylon's King Nebuchadnezzar and his servants. But afterward Egypt will dwell like it did a long time ago, declares the Lord.
²⁷ But don't be afraid, my servant Judah;
   don't lose heart, Israel.
   I will deliver you from a faraway place
   and your children
   from the land of their exile.
   My people Jacob will again
   be safe and sound,
   with no one harassing them.

ᵇOr *like rivers whose waters roar* ᶜTraditionally *Ethiopia and Libya* ᵈHeb uncertain ᵉHeb uncertain ᶠOr *inhabitant, Daughter Egypt* ᵍHeb uncertain ʰHeb lacks *is Egypt*.

28 So don't be afraid, my servant Jacob,
    declares the Lord.
I'm with you;
I will put an end to all the nations
    where I have scattered you.
But I won't put an end to you.
I won't let you avoid punishment;
I will discipline you as you deserve.

UMBRELLA
Hard Times

God Promises to Deliver *Jeremiah 46:28*
God told the people of Judah not to be afraid because nothing could stop God's plans for them. They felt hopeless and were afraid God's promises wouldn't come true. They worried their hard times would never end. They would need to suffer for a while because of their wicked ways, but God would step in because of the promise God made to Abraham.

We all experience feelings of hopelessness sometimes. We may go through difficult times, but when we suffer God wants to help us. God will come to our rescue when we are in trouble. God will not allow our troubles to become greater than we can handle with God's help. Our hard times don't last forever. ◊

Prophecy against Philistia

47 The Lord's word to the prophet Jeremiah concerning the Philistines before Pharaoh conquered Gaza.

2 The Lord proclaims:
Waters are rising from the north
    and turning into a raging flood.
They will engulf the land
    and everything in it,
the towns and those living in them.
The people cry out;
    all who live there scream.
3 At the pounding of the stallions' hooves,
    at the deafening roar
    of the chariots' wheels,
    parents abandon children,
    so paralyzed are they with fear.
4 Because the time is coming
    for the Philistines' destruction,
    for cutting off from Tyre and Sidon

anyone who might try to save Gaza,[i]
    because the Lord will destroy
    the Philistines,
    the few left from the island of Caphtor.
5 Mourning[j] will come upon Gaza;
    silence will cover Ashkelon,
    the few left in their valley.
How long will you gash yourselves
    in grief?[k]
6 You sword of the Lord,
    how long until you are silent?
Return to your sheath;
    rest and be still!
7 How can you be silent
    when the Lord has directed you[l]
    to attack Ashkelon and the coast line?

Prophecy against Moab

48 Concerning Moab:
The Lord of heavenly forces,
    the God of Israel, proclaims:
How awful for Nebo;
    it lies in ruins.
Kiriathaim is captured and shamed;
    the fortress is disgraced,
    reduced to rubble.
2 No one sings Moab's praise any longer!
In Heshbon they are hatching
    a plot against her:
"Come, let's bring down the nation!"
You too, Madmen, will be silenced;
    the sword will pursue you.
3 Listen to the cries for help
    from Horonaim:
"Destruction and massive devastation!"
4 Moab is shattered;
    its young cry for help.
5 On the way up to Luhith,
    there is uncontrollable weeping.
On the way down to Horonaim,
    they hear sobs of anguish.
6 Run for your lives!
    Be like Aroer[m] in the desert.
7 Because you have relied
    on your own strength and treasures,
    you also will be captured.
Chemosh will go into exile,
    together with his priests and officials.
8 The destroyer will sweep
    through every town;
    no town will escape.

[i]or a helper [j]Or baldness [k]Heb lacks in grief. [l]Or it [m]Heb uncertain

The valleys will be ravaged;
    the plateaus will be destroyed,
        because the Lord has declared it so.
9 Give wings to Moab,
    and it would fly away[n]
        because its towns lie in ruins,
            with no one left in them.

10 Cursed is the one who is halfhearted
    in doing the Lord's work.
Cursed is the one who restrains
    the sword from bloodshed.
11 From early on Moab has been at ease,
    like wine[o] left to settle on its sediment.
It hasn't been poured into jars;
    nor has Moab been taken into exile.
Therefore, its taste is still pleasant,
    and its aroma is the same.

12 But the time is coming, declares the Lord, when I will send to him someone to spill it—to pour out his wine and to smash his jars. 13 And Moab will be put to shame on account of Chemosh, just as the people of Israel were put to shame on account of Bethel, in which they trusted.[p]

14 How can you claim,
    "We're soldiers; we're war heroes"?
15 Moab is doomed;
    its towns will surrender;[q]
        its elite forces will go down in defeat,
            declares the king whose name
                is the Lord of heavenly forces.
16 Moab's destruction is near;
    its downfall approaches rapidly.
17 Grieve for this nation,
    you neighbors of Moab,
        all you who know his name.
Proclaim how its mighty scepter
    and magnificent staff are shattered!

18 Come down from your lofty place
    and sit in the dust,[r]
        you inhabitants of Daughter Dibon;[s]
            because Moab's destroyer
                has arrived to level your fortresses.
19 Stand by the roads and watch,
    you inhabitants of Aroer.
Ask the men who flee
    and the women who run off,
        "What's happened?"

20 Moab is shamed and shocked;
    weep and wail!
Tell it by the Arnon River:
    Moab's been destroyed!

21 Judgment has come
    to the towns of the plateau—
        to Holon, Jahzah, and Mephaath,
22 to Dibon, Nebo, and Beth-diblathaim,
23 to Kiriathaim, Beth-gamul,
    and Beth-meon,
24 to Kerioth and Bozrah,
    to all the towns of Moab, far and near.

25 Moab's horn is cut off;
    its arm is broken,
        declares the Lord.
26 Get Moab drunk,
    because it has exalted itself
        above the Lord.
Moab will collapse in its vomit
    and become the butt of every joke.
27 Wasn't Israel the butt of your jokes?
    Didn't you shake your head
        as if they were thieves
            caught in the act?
28 Leave your towns, head for the cliffs,
    you people of Moab.
Hide like a dove
    that nests in the mouth of a cave.

29 We have heard of Moab's pride:
    arrogant, puffed up, exalted,
        high and mighty, boastful!
30 I myself know about its arrogance,
    declares the Lord,
        the idle talk, the empty deeds.
31 But I'll still wail for Moab;
    I'll cry out for all Moab;
        I'll[t] sob for the people of Kir-heres.
32 I'll weep for you, vine of Sibmah,
    more than I would for Jazer.
Though your branches extended to the sea
    and reached the coast of Jazer,
        now the destroyer has come
            to harvest your grapes
                and summer fruits.
33 Joy and gladness have been taken
    from the orchards and farms of Moab.

---

[n]Heb uncertain [o]Heb lacks *like wine.* [p]Or *And Moab will be ashamed of Chemosh just as the people of Israel were ashamed of Bethel, in which they trusted.* [q]Heb uncertain [r]Or *thirst* [s]Heb uncertain, or *residing Daughter Dibon* [t]Or *He*

I have stopped making wine
in the presses.
No one shouts with joy
while treading the grapes.
Though there are shouts,
they are not shouts of joy!ᵘ
³⁴ Screams are heard from Heshbon
to Elealeh and Jahaz;
their cries resound from Zoar
to Horonaim and Eglath-shelishiyah.
Even the waters of Nimrim are dried up.
³⁵ I'll put an end to Moab,
declares the Lᴏʀᴅ,
for making offerings on the shrines,
and worshipping their gods.

³⁶ Therefore, my heart wails for Moab
like a mournfulᵛ flute
that plays the dirge;
my heart wails for the people
of Kir-heres,
like a mournful flute.
Their abundance is now gone.
³⁷ Every head is shaved,
every beard is cut off,
every hand is slashed,
and everyone wears mourning clothes.
³⁸ On every housetop of Moab
and in all its streets,
there's nothing but mourning.
I have shattered Moab
like a pottery vessel no one wants,
declares the Lᴏʀᴅ.
³⁹ How it's shattered! Go wail!
How Moab turns away!
What shame!
Moab has become the butt of every joke,
horrific to all its neighbors.

⁴⁰ The Lᴏʀᴅ proclaims:
Look! One who soars like an eagle
and spreads its wings over Moab.
⁴¹ The towns will be captured;
the strongholds will be seized.
On that day,
the heart of every soldier from Moab
will be like that of a woman
in the throes of labor.
⁴² Moab will be destroyed once and for all

because it has exalted itself
above the Lᴏʀᴅ.
⁴³ Terror, traps, and trackersʷ
are upon you, people of Moab,
declares the Lᴏʀᴅ.
⁴⁴ Those who flee from terror
will fall into a pit;
those who escape the pit
will be captured by the trap.
I will bring upon Moab
the year of its punishment,
declares the Lᴏʀᴅ.
⁴⁵ In Heshbon tired refugees seek shelter.
But fire is raging in Heshbon,
flames from the houseˣ of Sihon.
It has burned up part of Moab,
including the leader
of this rebellious nation.ʸ
⁴⁶ How terrible for you, Moab;
the people of Chemosh have perished.
Your sons have been carried off;
your daughters have been taken captive.
⁴⁷ But in the days to come
I'll bring back Moab from captivity,
declares the Lᴏʀᴅ.
Such is the judgment on Moab.

Prophecy against the Ammonites

49 Concerning the Ammonites, the Lᴏʀᴅ proclaims:
Doesn't Israel have children?
Aren't there heirs to his land?
Why then has Milcom taken over Gad?
Why have his people settled in its towns?
² Therefore, the time is coming,
declares the Lᴏʀᴅ,
when I will sound the battle alarm
against Rabbah,
the capital city of the Ammonites.
The city will be demolished,
and its neighboring villages
will be burned to the ground.
Then Israel will repossess
the land seized by its captors,
says the Lᴏʀᴅ.
³ Weep, you people of Heshbon;
Ai has been destroyed.
Wail, you daughters of Rabbah;
put on funeral clothing,

ᵘHeb uncertain.　ᵛHeb lacks *mournful*.　ʷOr *terror, pit, and trap*.　ˣHeb manuscripts; MT *from among*.　ʸHeb uncertain

cry your eyes out,
run for shelter.[z]
Milcom will surely go into exile,
together with his priests and ministers.

4 Why do you brag about your strength?
Your strength is exhausted,[a]
you rebellious daughter.
You trust in your treasures,
never imagining who would attack you.
5 I'm the one who will terrify you
from every side,
declares the Lord of heavenly forces.
Every one of you will be scattered about;
no one will gather those who fled.
6 Afterward, though, I will bring back
the Ammonites from captivity,
declares the Lord.

Prophecy against Edom

7 Concerning Edom,
the Lord of heavenly forces proclaims:
Is wisdom no longer in Teman?
Has good sense vanished
from the perceptive?
Are they no longer wise?
8 Turn, flee, and run for cover,
you inhabitants of Dedan.
I'm bringing disaster on Esau:
its day of reckoning.
9 If workers would come to you
to pick grapes,
they would at least leave
a few on the vine.
If thieves would come in the night,
they would take only what they needed.
10 But me? I will strip Esau bare.
I will expose his hiding places,
and he will find no place to take cover.
His offspring, family, and acquaintances
will perish,
and there will be no one left to say,[b]
11 "Leave me your orphans,
and I'll look after them;
trust your widows into my care."
12 The Lord proclaims: If the innocent must
drink the cup, why do you expect to escape
punishment? You won't! You will drink it! 13 I
myself swear, declares the Lord, that Bozrah

will become an object of horror and scorn, a
wasteland and a curse. And all of its towns
will lie in ruins forever.
14 I have heard a report from the Lord
that a messenger is sent
among the nations:
Join forces and come against her;
prepare for war!
15 I'm about to cut you down to size
before the nations;
you will be scorned by everyone.
16 The terror you have inflicted on others
has deceived you,
as has your own pride.
Though you live in a fortress
and occupy the high ground,
though you nest on high like the eagles,
I will bring you down,
declares the Lord.
17 Then Edom will become a wasteland.
All who pass by will be shocked
by its injuries.
18 It will be like the destruction
of Sodom and Gomorrah
and their surrounding towns,
says the Lord.
No one will live there;
no human will dwell in it.
19 Like a lion coming up
from the jungle of the Jordan
to a well-watered meadow,[c]
so I will suddenly chase down Edom
and single out its choicest of rams.[d]
Who is like me?
Who can direct me?
What shepherd can withstand me?
20 Therefore, listen to the counsel
that the Lord has for Edom
and the plans he's devised
against the people of Teman:
The little ones of the flock
will be dragged off,
as their pasture watches
in utter disbelief.[e]
21 The earth quakes
as the Edomites go down;
their screams echo
as far as the Reed Sea.[f]
22 Look! One who mounts up
and soars like an eagle,

---

[z]Heb uncertain; or *run back and forth in the sheepfolds* [a]Heb uncertain [b]LXX; MT *and there will (or he will) be no more* [c]Heb uncertain [d]Heb uncertain [e]Heb uncertain [f]Or *Red Sea*

who swoops down and spreads
his wings over Bozrah.
On that day, the heart
of every soldier from Edom
will be like that of a woman
in the throes of labor.

Prophecy against Damascus

²³ Concerning Damascus:
Hamath and Arpad lose heart
when they hear the bad news.
They are trembling with fear,
like the raging sea,
which can't become quiet.
²⁴ Damascus staggers about;
she tries to flee,
but panic overwhelms her.
She's gripped by anguish and pain,
like a woman in labor.
²⁵ Forsaken^g is the renowned city,
city of my delight.
²⁶ Yes, her young men will fall in the streets,
and her soldiers will be silent on that day,
declares the Lord of heavenly forces.
²⁷ I will set fire to the walls of Damascus;
it will burn up the fortresses
of Ben-hadad.

Prophecy against Kedar and Hazor

²⁸ Concerning Kedar and the kingdoms of
Hazor, which Babylon's King Nebuchadnezzar defeated, the Lord proclaims:
Get ready to attack Kedar;
destroy the people from the east!
²⁹ Seize^h their tents and their flocks,
their belongings and all their goods.
Take off with their camels
and shout as you go:
"Panic Lurks Everywhere!"
³⁰ Run away; take cover,
you people of Hazor,
declares the Lord.
Babylon's King Nebuchadnezzar
has taken counsel and devised a plan
against you.
³¹ Get ready to attack a nation
that feels safe and secure,
declares the Lord,
one without barred gates
that lives by itself.

³² Their camels will become plunder;
their many cattle will be pillaged.
I will scatter to the winds those
who are clean-shaven,^i
and I will bring disaster on them
from every side,
declares the Lord.
³³ Hazor will become a den for wild dogs,
a wilderness forever.
No one will live there;
no human will dwell in it.

Prophecy against Elam

³⁴ This is what the Lord told the prophet
Jeremiah concerning Elam at the beginning
of the rule of Judah's King Zedekiah. ³⁵ The
Lord of heavenly forces proclaims:
I'm going to break the bow of Elam,
the backbone of its military might.
³⁶ I will bring against Elam four winds
from the four corners of heaven,
and I will scatter them to the winds.
Those banished from Elam
will migrate to every nation.
³⁷ I will terrify Elam before their enemies,
before those who seek to kill them.
I will bring disaster upon them,
my fierce anger,
declares the Lord.
I will send the sword to attack them
until I have destroyed them all.
³⁸ I will establish my rule in Elam
and dispose of its king and officials,
declares the Lord.
³⁹ But in the days to come
I will bring back the captives of Elam,
declares the Lord.

Prophecy against Babylon

50 This is what the Lord said concerning
Babylon and the land of the Babylonians through the prophet Jeremiah:
² Tell the nations;
proclaim it far and wide!
Set up a flag;
proclaim it far and wide!
Hold nothing back;
just shout it:
"Babylon is captured;
Bel is shamed;

---

^g Vulg; MT *Not forsaken*   ^h Or *They will seize … they will take off*   ^i Or *those who have temples that are shaved*

Marduk is panic-stricken.
  Her images are shamed;
    her idols are panic-stricken."
³ A nation from the north
  has risen up against her.
It will decimate her land,
  and no one will live in it.
    Every living thing will flee.

⁴ In those days and at that time,
  declares the LORD,
    the people of Israel and Judah
    will come out of Babylon[j] together;
  with weeping they will leave
    as they seek the LORD their God.
⁵ They will search for Zion,
  turning their faces toward it.
They will come[k] and
  unite with the LORD,
in an everlasting covenant
  that will never be forgotten.
⁶ My people were lost sheep;
  their shepherds led them astray;
they deserted them on the mountains,
  where they wandered off among
    the hills;
      forgetting their resting place.
⁷ All who found them devoured them;
  and their attackers said,
    "It's not our fault,
  because they have sinned against
    the LORD,
      the true pasture,[l]
      the hope of their ancestors—
        the LORD."
⁸ Now wander far from Babylon.
  Get out of that country.
Like rams of the flock,
  lead the way home.
⁹ I'm stirring up against Babylon
  a coalition of mighty nations.
It will mobilize in the north,
  and from there she will be captured.
Their arrows are like
  those of an expert archer
  who does not return empty-handed.
¹⁰ Babylon will be defeated;
  its attackers will carry off
    all that they want,
  declares the LORD.

¹¹ Sure, you gloat and rejoice,
  you plunderers of my possession.
Sure, you dance around like a calf
  and neigh like a stallion.
¹² But Mother Babylon[m] will be humiliated;
  the one who bore you will be disgraced.
She will become the least of the nations:
  a wilderness, a desert, and parched land.
¹³ Because of the LORD's anger,
  no one will live there;
    she will be reduced to total ruin.
All who pass by Babylon will be shocked;
  they will gasp at all her injuries.
¹⁴ Take up your positions around Babylon,
  all you archers;
    now shoot at her;
  save none of your arrows,
    because she's sinned against the LORD.
¹⁵ Raise a victory shout
  against her on every side!
She's surrendered;
  her towers have collapsed;
  her walls are destroyed.
This is the LORD's retribution;
  now pay her back:
    do to her what she's done to others!
¹⁶ Cut Babylon off from those who plant
  and those who harvest the crops,
    because of its ruthless sword.[n]
Now return, all of you,
  to your people;
    flee to your homeland!

¹⁷ Israelites are
    scattered sheep,
    driven away by lions.
First the king of Assyria
    devoured them,
    and now Babylon's
    King Nebuchadnezzar
    has ravaged them.[o]
¹⁸ Therefore, the LORD of heavenly forces,
  the God of Israel, proclaims:
    I'm going to punish the king of Babylon
      and his land,
    just as I punished the king of Assyria.
¹⁹ But I will restore Israel to their pasture;
    they will graze on Carmel and Bashan;
    they will eat their fill
    in the highlands
      of Ephraim and Gilead.

---

[j]Heb lacks *of Babylon.* [k]Heb uncertain [l]Or *righteous dwelling place* [m]Or *your mother* [n]Heb uncertain [o]Or *gnawed their bones*

20 In those days and at that time,
declares the Lord,
if one searches for the sin of Israel,
they will find nothing;
if one seeks out the wrongdoing of Judah,
they will look in vain.
I will forgive those I have spared.
21 Attack the land of Merathaim;[p]
crush those living in Pekod.
Ruin and destroy them,
declares the Lord;
do all I have commanded you.
22 There's the sound of war in the land
and enormous devastation.
23 How the hammer of the whole earth
has been broken and shattered
into pieces!
How Babylon has become a wasteland
among the nations!
24 You set a trap for others, Babylon,[q]
but you yourself were caught
in it unaware;
you have been found and captured
because you have defied the Lord.
25 The Lord has opened his arsenal
and brought out his brutal weapons.
The Lord God of heavenly forces
has a job to do
in the land of the Babylonians.
26 Come against her from every side;
throw open her granaries;
pile her up like stalks of grain;
totally destroy her;
leave nothing intact.
27 Destroy all her bulls;
prepare them for slaughter.
How terrible for them!
Their time has come,
the day of reckoning.
28 A voice of fugitives and refugees,
from the land of Babylon,
declaring in Zion
the retribution of the Lord our God
because of what has been done
to his temple.
29 Send the archers against Babylon,
all who draw the bow!
Surround her
and let no one escape.
Pay her back for her deeds;
do to her what she's done to others.
She has acted arrogantly toward the Lord,
the holy one of Israel!
30 Therefore, her soldiers will fall
in the streets;
all her warriors will be silenced
on that day,
declares the Lord.
31 I'm against you, you arrogant one!
declares the Lord God
of heavenly forces.
Your day has come,
your time of reckoning.
32 The arrogant one will stumble and fall,
and no one will help her up.
I'll set your cities on fire,
and it will consume all that's around her.
33 The Lord of heavenly forces proclaims:
The people of Israel were oppressed,
together with the people of Judah.
Their captors held them
and refused to let them go.
34 Yet their redeemer is strong;
the Lord of heavenly forces is his name.
He will surely defend their cause
and give them rest in the land.
But he will unsettle the people of Babylon.

35 A sword against Babylon and its people,
declares the Lord,
along with its officials and sages.
36 A sword against its diviners
so that they become fools.
A sword against its warriors
so that they are terrified.
37 A sword against its horses and chariots,
and the mercenaries[r] in its midst
so that they lose courage.[s]
A sword against its treasures
so that they are looted.
38 A sword[t] against the water supplies
so that they dry up.
It is truly the land of idols,
idols about which they have gone
utterly mad!
39 Therefore, Babylon
will become a ghost town,

[p]Or *Double rebellion* [q]Or *I set a trap for you, Babylon, and you were* [r]Or *foreigners* [s]Or *become like women* [t]Or *A drought*

a place for desert animals,
  hyenas, and ravenous birds.[u]
No one will live there again;
  no one will make it their home.

The Hebrew word used here for Babylon is *Leb-Qamai*, which is not the word typically used for Babylon. It was a code word. That way if the scrolls were captured, the Babylonians wouldn't know the Israelites were talking about the coming destruction of Babylon.

⁴⁰ Just as God destroyed Sodom
  and Gomorrah and their neighbors,
    declares the LORD,
  so no one will live in Babylon
    or settle there again.

⁴¹ Look! An army is on the move
    from the northern regions.
  A powerful nation
    and many kings are coming
    from the ends of the earth.
⁴² Equipped with bow and spear,
    they are cruel
    and show no mercy.
  Their horsemen sound
    like the roaring sea,
  arrayed in battle formation against you,
    Daughter Babylon.
⁴³ The king of Babylon has heard
    reports of them
    and is panic-stricken;
  distress overwhelms him,
    pain like that of a woman in labor.

⁴⁴ Like a lion coming up from
    the jungle of the Jordan
    to a well-watered meadow,[v]
  so I will suddenly chase down Babylon
    and single out its choicest of rams.
  Who is like me?
  Who can direct me?
  What shepherd can withstand me?
⁴⁵ Therefore, listen to the counsel
    that the LORD has for Babylon
    and the plans he's devised
    against the land of Babylon:
  The little ones of the flock

will be dragged off,
  as their pasture watches
    in utter disbelief.[w]
⁴⁶ The earth quakes
    at the sound of Babylon's capture;
  its screams echo throughout the world.

51 The LORD proclaims:
  I'm stirring up a violent wind
    against Babylon
  and those who live in Leb-qamai.[x]
² I will send mercenaries[y] to Babylon
    who will sift her and clear out her land.
  They will surround her
    on the day of disaster.
³ Let the archers draw their bows;
    let them prepare their armor.
  Show no mercy to her young men;
    wipe out her entire company!
⁴ They will fall wounded
    in the land of Babylon,
    struck down in her streets.
⁵ God, the LORD of heavenly forces,
    hasn't abandoned Israel and Judah,
  even though they live
    in a land filled with guilt
    before the holy one of Israel.
⁶ Escape from Babylon;
    each of you run for your lives!
  Don't perish because of her guilt,
    because this is the time
    for the LORD's retribution,
  a day of reckoning
    for all that Babylon[z] has done.

⁷ Babylon was a gold cup in the LORD's hand;
    it made the whole earth drunk.
  The nations drank her wine
    and went mad.
⁸ But suddenly Babylon fell
    and shattered into pieces.
  Wail for her!
    Bring medicine for her pain;
    perhaps she will recover.
⁹ We tried to cure Babylon,
    but she was beyond help.
  Let's depart from her
    and return to your own country,
    each of you.

ᵘHeb uncertain ᵛHeb uncertain ʷHeb uncertain ˣOr *the inhabitants of Leb qamai*, a reference to Chaldea (Babylonia); or *those who rise up against me* ʸOr *foreigners* ᶻOr *she* or *it*

Her punishment reaches to heaven
and extends to the clouds.
¹⁰ The Lord has come to our defense,
so let's declare in Zion
what the Lord our God has done!

¹¹ Sharpen your arrows;
prepare your shields.
The Lord is stirring up
the spirit of kings from Media.
He intends to destroy Babylon;
this is the Lord's retribution,
a day of reckoning for his temple.
¹² Set up a flag on the walls of Babylon,
fortify the guards,
post watchmen,
prepare an ambush,
because the Lord has a plan
against the inhabitants of Babylon.
He will accomplish it,
just as he said he would.
¹³ You live beside a great river,
and you are rich in treasures.
But your time has come;
your cruelty has caught up with you.ᵃ
¹⁴ The Lord of heavenly forces
has sworn by his own name:
I'm going to fill your citiesᵇ
with soldiers like a swarm of locusts;
they will celebrate their victory over you.

¹⁵ God made the earth by his might,
shaped the world by his wisdom,
and crafted the skies by his knowledge.
¹⁶ At the sound of God's voice,
the heavenly waters roar.
God raises the clouds
from the ends of the earth.
He makes lightning for the rain
and sends the wind from his treasuries.
¹⁷ Everyone is too foolish to understand;
every smith is shamed by his idols,
for his images are shams;
they aren't alive.
¹⁸ They are a delusion, a charade;
at the appointed time they will be ruined!
¹⁹ But the portion of Jacob
is utterly different,
for he has formed all things,
including his very own tribe;
the Lord of heavenly forces is his name!

²⁰ You are my hammer,
my weapon of war.
With you I will crush the nations.
With you I will destroy kingdoms.
²¹ With you I will crush horse and rider.
With you I will crush chariot and driver.
²² With you I will crush men and women.
With you I will crush old and young.
With you I will crush
young men and young women.
²³ With you I will crush
shepherds and flocks.
With you I will crush farmers and oxen.
With you I will crush
governors and officials.

²⁴ I will repay Babylon and all its inhabitants
for the terrible things
they have done to Zion in your sight,
declares the Lord.
²⁵ I'm against you,
you mountain of destruction,
declares the Lord,
you destroyer of the whole earth!
I will reach out against you;
I will topple you from your heights;
I will turn you into a rubbish heap.
²⁶ They will never remove a cornerstone
or a foundation stone from you.
You will be a wasteland forever,
declares the Lord.

²⁷ Set up a flag in the land;
sound the alarm among the nations!
Prepare them for war against her;
summon kingdoms against her—
Ararat, Minni, and Ashkenaz.
Appoint a commander against her;
call up the troops,
like swarms of locusts!
²⁸ Prepare the nations for war against her,
the kings of Media,
its governors, all its officials,
and all the countries they rule.

²⁹ The earth quakes and trembles
because the Lord's plans
against Babylon are fulfilled:
to reduce Babylon to a wasteland,
with no one left in it.

ᵃHeb uncertain ᵇHeb lacks *cities.*

³⁰ Babylon's warriors quit fighting;
  they hide in their fortifications.
  Their strength is worn out;
    their courage is gone!
  Babylon's houses are burned down,
    and its gates are smashed.
³¹ Courier joins courier,
    messenger joins messenger
      to relate the news
        to the king of Babylon
        that his entire city has fallen.
³² The river crossings are blocked;
    the marshes are on fire;
    the soldiers are terrified.
³³ The Lord of heavenly forces, the God of
Israel, proclaims:
  Daughter Babylon is like a threshing floor
    ready to be trampled down.
    In a little while her harvest will come.

³⁴ Babylon's King Nebuchadnezzar
    has eaten us alive;
    he's drained us of strength;
    he's left us for dead.^c
  He's gobbled us up
    like a great sea monster;
    he's filled his belly with our treasures;
    and he's spit us out.
³⁵ May Babylon be violated
    as our bodies were,
    say the inhabitants of Zion.
  May our blood be on the Babylonians,
    say those from Jerusalem.
³⁶ Therefore, the Lord proclaims:
  I'm going to defend your cause;
  I'll turn the tables on your attacker.
  I'll dry up her sea;
  I'll shut up her springs.
³⁷ Babylon will become a heap of ruins,
    a den of wild dogs, a wasteland
    with no one left in it.

³⁸ Like lions they will roar together;
    they will growl like lions' cubs.
³⁹ They are ready to devour,
    so I'll prepare the feast
    and mix the drinks!
  But after their noisy drunkenness,
    they will fall fast asleep.
    They will sleep forever,

never to get up,
  declares the Lord.
⁴⁰ I'll lead them off
    like lambs for slaughter,
    like rams and goats.

⁴¹ How Sheshach^d has been defeated,
    the pride of the whole earth
      taken captive!
  How Babylon has become a wasteland
    among the nations!
⁴² The sea has risen over Babylon;
    its pounding waves overwhelm her.
⁴³ Her towns are devastated;
    her land is scorched and barren,
    a place where no one lives
    or dares to pass through.
⁴⁴ I will punish Bel in Babylon;
    I will force him to vomit
    what he's consumed.
  Then nations will no longer stream to him,
    and Babylon's walls will collapse!

⁴⁵ Get out of Babylon, my people!
    Run for your lives
      from the Lord's fierce anger.
⁴⁶ Don't be distracted or frightened
    by the rumors you hear in the land.
    Sometimes you hear one thing
    and another time something else:
    rumors of violence and uprisings.
⁴⁷ The time is coming
    when I will deal with Babylon's idols;
    the whole land will be disgraced,
    and her wounded will fall in her midst.
⁴⁸ Then all creation will rejoice over Babylon,
    because out of the north
    destroying armies will come
      to attack her,
      declares the Lord.
⁴⁹ Babylon must fall
    for the dead in Israel,
    as the dead of all the earth
    have fallen to Babylon.

⁵⁰ You survivors of war,
    leave now; don't delay!
  Remember the Lord,
    from a faraway land.
  Keep Jerusalem alive in your hearts.

^cOr *He's made us an empty container.* ^d*Sheshach* is a name for Babylon.

51 We're humiliated by their taunts;
  we're disgraced that strangers
  have violated the sacred places
  of the Lord's temple.

52 The time is coming,
  declares the Lord,
  when I will deal with her idols,
  and the wounded in her land will groan.

53 Even if Babylon scales the heavens
  and strengthens its towering defenses,
  the destroying armies will still come
  against her, at my command,
  declares the Lord.

did you know? This verse contains a note saying Jeremiah's writing ends here. It was added by an editor who lived long after Jeremiah to let people know Jeremiah did not write chapter 52. This last chapter was added years later to help people understand what was happening in the time that Jeremiah wrote.

54 Listen to the cries for help from Babylon,
  signs of massive devastation in the land,
  declares the Lord.
55 The Lord is destroying Babylon
  and silencing her outcry,
  whose roar is like the crushing waves,
  a deafening crash.
56 He certainly comes against her;
  the destroyer comes against Babylon.
  Her warriors are captured;
  their bows are broken.
  The Lord is an exacting God
  who repays in full.
57 I'll make her leaders and sages drunk,
  her governors, officials,
  and warriors as well.
  They will sleep forever, never to get up,
  declares the king,
  whose name is
  the Lord of heavenly forces.
58 The Lord of heavenly forces proclaims:
  Babylon's massive walls will come down,
  down to the ground;
  and its high gates will be burned
  to the ground.

  People labor in vain;
  nations toil for nothing but ashes!

59 This is what the prophet Jeremiah instructed the staff officer[e] Seraiah, Neriah's son and Mahseiah's grandson, when Seraiah went to Babylon with Judah's King Zedekiah in the fourth year of his rule. 60 Jeremiah wrote down in a single scroll all the disasters that would happen to Babylon—all these things concerning Babylon. 61 Jeremiah said to Seraiah: When you get to Babylon, see to it that you read all these words. 62 Then say, "Lord, you declared that this place will be destroyed and nothing will remain in it—neither human nor animal; that it will forever be a wasteland!" 63 When you finish reading the scroll, tie a stone to it and throw it into the Euphrates River. 64 Then say, "In the same way, Babylon will sink and never rise again because of the disaster I'm bringing against it."

Jeremiah's words end here.

Rule of Zedekiah and the fall of Jerusalem

52 Zedekiah was 21 years old when he became king, and he ruled for eleven years in Jerusalem. His mother's name was Hamutal; she was a daughter of Jeremiah from Libnah. 2 He did evil in the Lord's eyes just as Jehoiachin had done. 3 It was because the Lord was angry against Jerusalem and Judah that he thrust them out of his presence. Zedekiah rebelled against the king of Babylon.

4 In the ninth year, the tenth month, and the tenth day of the month, Babylon's King Nebuchadnezzar attacked Jerusalem with all of his army. He camped beside the city and built a siege wall around it. 5 The city was under siege until the eleventh year of King Zedekiah. 6 On the ninth day of the fourth month, the famine in the city reached a point that no food remained for the people. 7 The enemy entered the city, and all the soldiers fled by night along the gate between the two walls by the royal gardens. So the Babylonians surrounded the city while the soldiers fled toward the desert plain. 8 However, the Babylonian army chased down Zedekiah and caught him in the plains of Jericho. (His entire army had fled from him.) 9 They arrested the king and brought him before the king of Babylon at Riblah in the land of Hamath. And

[e] Or *officer of rest*, often translated as *quartermaster*

he pronounced sentence on him. [10]The king of Babylon slaughtered Zedekiah's children before his very own eyes, and he slaughtered all Judah's officers at Riblah. [11]Then he gouged out Zedekiah's eyes and bound him in chains. The king of Babylon dragged him off to Babylon and put him in prison, where he remained until he died.

[12]In the tenth day of the fifth month, which was the nineteenth year of Babylon's King Nebuchadnezzar, Nebuzaradan commander of the guard came to Jerusalem on behalf of his king. [13]He burned down the Lord's temple, the royal palace, all the houses of Jerusalem, and all the important buildings. [14]The entire Babylonian army and the commander of the guard destroyed the walls surrounding Jerusalem. [15]Nebuzaradan commander of the guard deported some of the poorest people, the rest of the people left in the city, a few skilled workers, and those who had joined the king of Babylon. [16]But Nebuzaradan commander of the guard left some of the poor to tend the vineyards and till the land.

[17]The Babylonians broke apart the bronze columns, the stands, and the bronze Sea in the Lord's temple. They carried the bronze to Babylon. [18]They took the pots, the shovels, the wick trimmers, the sprinkling bowls, the incense dishes, and all the bronze equipment used for the temple services. [19]The commander of the guard took whatever gold or silver he could find as well: the small bowls, the fire pans, the sprinkling bowls, the pots, the lampstands, the basins, and the offering bowls. [20]There was too much bronze to be weighed: two columns, the bronze Sea and the twelve bronze bulls that held it up, and the stands, all of which Solomon had made for the Lord's temple. [21]Each column was about twenty-seven feet high and eighteen feet around. They were hollow, but the bronze was about three inches thick. [22]Each

had a capital of bronze above it that towered seven and a half feet high, and each had an ornate design of bronze pomegranates around it. The second column was the same, also with pomegranates. [23]There were ninety-six pomegranates on the sides, a total of one hundred pomegranates around the ornate design.

[24]The commander of the guard also took Seraiah the high priest, Zephaniah the deputy priest, and the three doorkeepers. [25]From the city, he took a eunuch who was appointed over the army and the seven royal advisors who remained in the city. He also took the scribe of the commander of the army in charge of military conscription and sixty military personnel[f] who were found in the city. [26]Nebuzaradan the commander of the guard took them and brought them to the king of Babylon at Riblah. [27]The king of Babylon struck them and put them to death at Riblah in the land of Hamath. And Judah went away from its land into exile.

[28]This is the number of people whom Nebuchadnezzar deported: In the seventh year, 3,023 Judeans. [29]In the eighteenth year of Nebuchadnezzar, he took 832 people from Jerusalem. [30]In the twenty-third year of Nebuchadnezzar, he dispatched Nebuzaradan commander of the guard, who deported 745 Judeans. Altogether, 4,600 were taken captive.

[31]Judah's King Jehoiachin had been in exile for thirty-seven years when Awil-merodach[g] became king in Babylon. He took note of Jehoiachin's plight and released him from prison on the twenty-fifth day of the twelfth month[h] of that very year. [32]Awil-merodach treated Jehoiachin kindly and gave him a throne higher than those of the other kings with him in Babylon. [33]So Jehoiachin discarded his prison clothes and ate his meals at the king's table for the rest of his life. [34]The Babylonian king provided him daily provisions for the rest of his life, right up until he died.

[f]Or *from the people of the land* [g]Or Evil-merodach [h]February–March, Adar

Lamentations

The prophet Jeremiah warned that Judah would be defeated in war because of its sin. If the people didn't stop following false gods, disaster would strike. Those terrible warnings came true when Judah was defeated and God's people were taken as prisoners to Babylon. You can read their story in 2 Kings 24–25 and Jeremiah 25.

The songs in Lamentations express deep sadness. God's people cried because their dearly loved city and country were destroyed. They cried because they were taken from their homes. They cried because they were living in a strange, distant land.

Some people believe Lamentations was written by Jeremiah, the weeping prophet, but the book doesn't mention him. The first four chapters are "acrostic" poems. Each line begins with a letter of the Hebrew alphabet, in order, from beginning to end.

Even when God's people were sad, they remembered that God loved them. They declared that God's love never ends (Lam 3:22). Lamentations teaches us that God loves us always! ♦

Jerusalem's suffering

1 ^a"Oh, no!
She sits alone,
    the city that was once full of people.
Once great among nations,
    she has become like a widow.
Once a queen over provinces,
    she has become a slave.

² She weeps bitterly in the night,
    her tears on her cheek.
None of her lovers comfort her.
All her friends lied to her;
    they have become her enemies.

³ Judah was exiled after suffering
    and hard service.
She lives among the nations;
    she finds no rest.
All who were chasing her caught her—
    right in the middle of her distress.

⁴ Zion's roads are in mourning;
    no one comes to the festivals.
All her gates are deserted.
    Her priests are groaning,
her young women grieving. She is bitter.

⁵ Her adversaries have become rulers;
    her enemies relax.
Certainly the Lord caused her grief
    because of her many wrong acts.
Her children have gone away,
    captive before the enemy.

⁶ Daughter Zion lost all her glory.
Her officials are like deer
    that can't find pasture.
They have gone away, frail,
    before the hunter.

⁷ While suffering and homeless,
    Jerusalem remembers all her treasures
    from days long past.
When her people fell by the enemy's hand,
    there was no one to help her.
Enemies saw her, laughed at her defeat.

LIFE PRESERVER

Who is actually speaking in these poems of lament?
Lamentations 1–4

Four different voices speak in these poems of lament. One voice is that of a poet who *laments* or cries out about what has happened to the city. Another voice is that of a woman who is a widow. She is named Daughter Zion, or Zion. A third voice is that of a man who is not named. The fourth voice is that of the community. All of these voices express sadness at the fall of Jerusalem.

Even today, we may wonder if God has forgotten us when we feel lonely, sad, and even hopeless. When we feel this way, we can pray to God and express our feelings and concerns. And when we worship together at church, we can offer prayers of lament for things that are going wrong in our world. We know that God hears our cries and is always with us.

---

⁸ Jerusalem has sinned greatly;
    therefore, she's become a joke.^b
All who honored her now detest her,
    for they've seen her naked.
Even she groans and turns away.

⁹ Her uncleanness shows on her clothing;
    she didn't consider
    what would happen to her.
She's gone down shockingly;
    she has no comforter.
"Lord, look at my suffering—
    the enemy has definitely triumphed!"

¹⁰ The enemy grabbed all her treasures.
She watched nations
    enter her sanctuary—
nations that you, God,^c commanded:
    They must not enter your assembly.

¹¹ All her people are groaning, seeking bread.
They give up their most precious things
    for food to survive.
"Lord, look and take notice: I am most
    certainly despised."

---

^aFour of the five chaps of Lamentations are alphabetically structured (acrostic) poems. Each verse in chaps 1, 2, and 4 begins with a consecutive letter of the Hebrew alphabet. Chap 3 is a triple acrostic: three verses in a row use the same letter before moving to the next letter. The acrostic form is not used in chap 5, though it does contain twenty-two verses, the same number as chaps 1, 2, and 4. ^bOr *she's become unclean.* ^cHeb lacks *God.*

ל ¹² Is this nothing to all you who pass by?[d]
　　Look around: Is there any suffering like
　　　the suffering inflicted on me,
　　the grief that the Lord caused
　　　on the day of his fierce anger?

מ ¹³ From above he sent fire into my bones;
　　　he trampled them.
　　He spread a net for my feet;
　　　he forced me backward.
　　He left me devastated, constantly sick.

נ ¹⁴ My steps[e] are being watched;[f]
　　　by his hand they are tripped up.
　　His yoke is on my neck;
　　　he makes my strength fail.
　　My Lord has handed me over
　　　to people I can't resist.

ס ¹⁵ My Lord has despised my mighty warriors.
　　He called a feast for me—
　　　in order to crush my young men!
　　My Lord has stomped on the winepress
　　　of the young woman Daughter Judah.

ע ¹⁶ Because of all these things I'm crying.
　　My eyes, my own eyes pour water
　　because a comforter who might
　　　encourage me is nowhere near.
　　My children are destroyed because the
　　　enemy was so strong.

פ ¹⁷ Zion spreads out her hands;
　　　she has no comforter.
　　The Lord commanded Jacob's enemies
　　　to surround him.
　　Jerusalem is just a piece of garbage
　　　to them.

צ ¹⁸ The Lord is right,
　　　because I disobeyed his word.
　　Listen, all you people;
　　　look at my suffering.
　　My young women and young men
　　　have gone away as prisoners.

ק ¹⁹ I called to my lovers, but they deceived me.
　　My priests and my elders
　　　have perished in the city;
　　they were looking for food to survive.

ר ²⁰ Pay attention, Lord, for I am in trouble.
　　My stomach is churning;
　　my heart is pounding inside me
　　　because I am so bitter.
　　In the streets the sword kills;
　　　in the house it is like death.

ש ²¹ People heard that I was groaning,
　　　that I had no comforter.
　　All my enemies heard about my distress;
　　　they were thrilled
　　　that you had done this.
　　Bring the day you have announced
　　　so they become like me!

ת ²² Let all their evil come before you.
　　Then injure them like you've injured me
　　　because of all my wrong acts;
　　my groans are many;
　　　my heart is sick.

God's anger toward Jerusalem

2 Oh, no!
א 　In anger, my Lord put Daughter Zion
　　under a cloud;[g]
　　he threw Israel's glory from heaven
　　　down to earth.
　　On that day of wrath,
　　　he didn't consider his own footstool.

ב ² Showing no compassion, my Lord
　　　devoured each of Jacob's meadows;
　　in his wrath he tore down the walled cities
　　　of Daughter Judah.
　　The kingdom and its officials,
　　　he forced to the ground, shamed.

ג ³ In his burning rage,
　　　he cut off each of Israel's horns;
　　right in front of the enemy,
　　　he withdrew his strong hand;
　　he burned against Jacob like a flaming fire
　　　that ate up everything nearby.

ד ⁴ He bent his bow as an enemy would;
　　　his strong hand was poised
　　　like an adversary.
　　He killed every precious thing in sight;
　　he poured out his wrath
　　　like fire on Daughter Zion's tent.

---

[d]Heb uncertain　[e]Correction; or *my wrong acts*　[f]Or *a yoke is bound to my wrong acts*; Heb uncertain　[g]Heb uncertain

ה ⁵ My Lord has become like an enemy.
   He devoured Israel;
he devoured all her palaces;
   he made ruins of her city walls.
In Daughter Judah he multiplied mourning
   along with more mourning!

ו ⁶ He wrecked his booth like a garden;
   he destroyed his place for festivals.
The Lᴏʀᴅ made Zion forget
   both festival and sabbath;
in his fierce rage, he scorned
   both monarch and priest.

ז ⁷ My Lord rejected his altar,
   he abandoned his sanctuary;
he handed Zion's palace walls
   over to enemies.
They shouted in the Lᴏʀᴅ's own house
   as if it were a festival day.

ח ⁸ The Lᴏʀᴅ planned to destroy
   Daughter Zion's wall.
He stretched out a measuring line,
   didn't stop himself from devouring.
He made barricades and walls wither—
   together they wasted away.

ט ⁹ Zion's gates sank into the ground;
   he broke and shattered her bars;
her king and her officials are now
   among the nations.
There is no Instruction!ʰ
Even her prophets couldn't find
   a vision from the Lᴏʀᴅ.

י ¹⁰ Daughter Zion's elders
   sit on the ground and mourn.
They throw dust on their heads;
   they put on mourning clothes.
Jerusalem's young women bow
   their heads all the way to the ground.

כ ¹¹ My eyes are worn out from weeping;
   my stomach is churning.
My insides are poured on the ground
   because the daughter of my people
      is shattered,
because children and babies
   are fainting in the city streets.

LIFE PRESERVER

What are the letters beside the verses? *Lamentations 1–4*

The letters beside the verses in chapters 1–4 are letters from the Hebrew alphabet. These chapters are acrostic poems, written so that the verses in each chapter begin with a letter of the alphabet, starting with the first letter, *alef*, and then following on through the alphabet to *taw*, the last letter.

   Chapter 5 is not an acrostic but is written like an ending to the poems in chapters 1–3. Although it does not follow the Hebrew alphabet, chapter 5 is written in 22 lines, which is the exact number of letters in the Hebrew alphabet. ⬥

ל ¹² They say to their mothers,
   "Where are grain and wine?"
while fainting like the wounded
   in the city streets,
while their lives are draining away
   at their own mothers' breasts.

מ ¹³ What can I testify about you,
   Daughter Jerusalem?ⁱ
To what could I compare you?
   With what could I equate you?
How can I comfort you,
   young woman Daughter Zion?
Your hurt is as vast as the sea.
   Who can heal you?

נ ¹⁴ Your prophets gave you worthless
   and empty visions.
They didn't reveal your sin
   so as to prevent your captivity.
Instead, they showed you
   worthless and incorrect prophecies.

ס ¹⁵ All who pass by on the road
   clap their hands about you;
they whistle, shaking their heads
   at Daughter Jerusalem:
"Could this be the city called Perfect
   Beauty, the Joy of All the Earth?"

פ ¹⁶ All your enemies open wide their mouths
   against you;
they whistle, grinding their teeth.
   They say, "We have devoured!

ʰHeb *Torah* ⁱOr *How can I warn you?* or *To what could I liken you?*; Heb uncertain

This is definitely the day
  we've been waiting for.
  We've seen it come to pass."

ע ¹⁷ The Lᴏʀᴅ did what he had planned.
  He accomplished the word
that he had commanded long ago.
  He ripped down,
  showing no compassion.
  He made the enemy rejoice over you;
  he raised up your adversaries' horn.

צ ¹⁸ Cry out to my Lord from the heart,[j]
  you wall of Daughter Zion;
make your[k] tears run down like a flood
  all day and night.
Don't relax at all;
  don't rest your eyes a moment.

ק ¹⁹ Get up and cry out at nighttime,
  at the start of the night shift;

pour out your heart
  before my Lord like water.
Lift your hands up to him
  for the life of your children—
the ones who are fainting from hunger
  on every street corner.

ר ²⁰ Lᴏʀᴅ, look and see to whom
  you have done this!
Should women eat their own offspring,
  their own beautiful babies?
Should priest and prophet be killed
  in my Lord's own sanctuary?

ש ²¹ Young and old alike
  lie on the ground in the streets;
my young women and young men
  fall dead by the sword.
On the day of your anger, you killed;
  you slaughtered,
  showing no compassion.

[j]Correction; or *their heart cried out to my Lord* [k]Heb lacks *your*.

God's THOUGHTS ◆ My THOUGHTS

God's Home   *Lamentations 3:22-25*

Can you imagine how it would feel to lose your home? Sometimes disasters such as fires, floods, tornadoes, and wars destroy homes. Sometimes when parents divorce, their children must move to a new home. Sometimes a parent takes a job in a new city, and the family must move and start over.

Long ago God's people lost their land in a war. They lost their homes, and they also lost the temple where they gathered to worship God. The temple had taken many years to build, and the people were very sad when it was gone. The temple was where the people went to feel close to God. They even thought of it as God's home.

A *lamentation* is a sad song, and that's what this book of the Bible contains: sad songs. But look at what is right in the middle of this sad song: happy words! God's love is new every morning. God's compassion is new every morning. The sunrise marks a new day and a fresh start. Even though they were far from home and sad because of what was lost, the people could look at the sunrise and remember God's love.

Have you ever lost something that was important to you?

When you feel like home is far away, look at the sunrise and remember God's love!

ח ²² You invited—as if to a festival!—
terrors[l] from every side.
On the day of the LORD's anger,
no one escaped, not one survived.
The children that I nurtured,
that I raised myself,
my enemy finished them off.

An individual's complaint

3 I am someone[m] who saw the suffering
caused by God's[n] angry rod.

א ² He drove me away, forced me to walk
in darkness, not light.
³ He turned his hand even against me,
over and over again, all day long.

ב ⁴ He wore out my flesh and my skin;
he broke my bones.
⁵ He besieged me, surrounding me
with bitterness and weariness.
⁶ He made me live in dark places like those
who've been dead a long time.

ג ⁷ He walled me in so I couldn't escape;
he made my chains heavy.
⁸ Even though I call out and cry for help,
he silences my prayer.
⁹ He walled in my paths with stonework;
he made my routes crooked.

ד ¹⁰ He is a bear lurking for me,
a lion in hiding.
¹¹ He took me from my path[o]
and tore me apart;
he made me desolate.
¹² He drew back his bow,
made me a shooting target for arrows.

ה ¹³ He shot the arrows of his quiver
into my inside parts.
¹⁴ I have become a joke to all my people,
the object of their song of ridicule
all day long.
¹⁵ He saturated me with grief,
made me choke on bitterness.

ו ¹⁶ He crushed my teeth into the gravel;
he pressed me down into the ashes.

¹⁷ I've[p] rejected peace;
I've forgotten what is good.
¹⁸ I thought: My future is gone,
as well as my hope from the LORD.

ז ¹⁹ The memory of my suffering and
homelessness is bitterness and poison.
²⁰ I[q] can't help but remember
and am depressed.
²¹ I call all this to mind—therefore, I will wait.

ח ²² Certainly the faithful love
of the LORD
hasn't ended;[r]
certainly God's compassion isn't through!
²³ They are renewed every morning.
Great is your faithfulness.
²⁴ I think:[s] The LORD is my portion!
Therefore, I'll wait for him.

> **Memorize**
> **Lam 3:22-23**

ט ²⁵ The LORD is good to those who hope in him,
to the person[t] who seeks him.
²⁶ It's good to wait in silence
for the LORD's deliverance.
²⁷ It's good for a man to carry a yoke
in his youth.
י ²⁸ He should sit alone and be silent
when God lays it on him.
²⁹ He should put his mouth in the dirt—
perhaps there is hope.
³⁰ He should offer his cheek for a blow;
he should be filled with shame.

UMBRELLA

DEPRESSED

Discouraged and Harassed
Lamentations 3:19-33
This writer shared his feelings about suffering and
pain. He had been through a lot of bad experiences,
but he was determined to hang on to his faith. He
would wait on God and believe that things would
get better. When we feel discouraged, we can wait
on God, knowing that God has promised to be with
us no matter what. ◊

---

[l]Correction; or *my attackers*   [m]Or *the man*; also in 3:27, 35, 39   [n]Or *his*   [o]Heb uncertain   [p]Or *my spirit*; also in 3:20, 24, 25, 51, 58   [q]Or *My spirit can't help but remember and is depressed*   [r]Tg, Syr, and other ancient sources; MT *we aren't finished.*   [s]Or *My spirit thinks*   [t]Or *spirit*

 כ ³¹ My Lord definitely[u] won't reject forever.
³² Although he has caused grief,
he will show compassion in measure
with his covenant loyalty.
³³ He definitely doesn't enjoy affliction,[v]
making humans suffer.

ל ³⁴ Now crushing underfoot
all the earth's prisoners,
³⁵ denying someone justice
before the Most High,
³⁶ subverting a person's lawsuit—
doesn't my Lord see all this?

מ ³⁷ Who ever spoke and it happened if my
Lord hadn't commanded the same?
³⁸ From the mouth of the Most High
evil things don't come, but rather good!
³⁹ Why then does any living person complain;
why should anyone complain
about their sins?

נ ⁴⁰ We must search and examine our ways;
we must return to the LORD.
⁴¹ We should lift up our hearts and hands
to God in heaven.
⁴² We are the ones who did wrong;
we rebelled.
But you, God, have not forgiven.

ס ⁴³ You wrapped yourself up in wrath
and hunted us;
you killed, showing no compassion.
⁴⁴ You wrapped yourself up in a cloud;
prayers can't make it through!
⁴⁵ You made us trash and garbage
in front of all other people.

פ ⁴⁶ All our enemies have opened
their mouths against us.
⁴⁷ Terror and trap have come upon us,
catastrophe and collapse!
⁴⁸ Streams of water pour from my eyes
because of the destruction of the
daughter of my people.

ע ⁴⁹ My eyes flow and don't stop.
There is no relief
⁵⁰ until the LORD looks down
from the heavens and notices.

⁵¹ My eyes hurt me[w] because
of what's happened to
my city's daughters.

LIGHTHOUSE

HEART

Compassionate *Lamentations 3:51*
It hurts to see people suffer, especially when we
can't do anything to help them. The prophet was
sad because he had seen all the ways in which his
people were suffering. They lost their homes, their
temple, and their land. They felt far from God. The
prophet saw his people struggling, and this caused
him to feel pain. ♦

צ ⁵² My enemies hunted me down like a bird,
relentlessly, for no reason.
⁵³ They caught me alive in a pit
and threw stones at me;
⁵⁴ water flowed over my head.
I thought: I'm finished.

ק ⁵⁵ I call on your name, LORD,
from the depths of the pit.
⁵⁶ Hear my voice. Don't close your ear[x]
to my need for relief,
to my cry for help.[y]
⁵⁷ Come near to me on the day I call to you.
Say to me, "Don't be afraid."

ר ⁵⁸ My Lord! Plead my desperate case;[z]
redeem my life.
⁵⁹ LORD, look at my mistreatment;
judge my cause.
⁶⁰ Look at all of my enemies' vengeance,
all of their scheming against me.

ש ⁶¹ Hear their jeering, LORD,
all of their scheming against me,
⁶² the speech of those
who rise up against me,
their incessant gossiping about me.
⁶³ Whether sitting or standing,
look at how I am the object
of their song of ridicule.

ת ⁶⁴ Pay them back fully, LORD,
according to what they have done.

^uOr *Because my Lord won't reject forever* ^vHeb *He does not afflict from his heart.* ^wOr *my spirit* ^xOr *You didn't close your ear.*
^yOr *You have heard my voice.* ^zOr *my spirit's case* or *my spirit's grievance*

65 Give them a tortured mind—
  put your curse on them!
66 Angrily hunt them down; wipe them out
  from under the LORD's heaven.

The people's suffering

4 Oh, no!
  Gold is tarnished;[a]
  even the purest gold is changed.
  Sacred jewels are scattered
  on every street corner.

ב 2 Zion's precious children,
  once valued as pure gold—
  oh no!—now they are worth no more
  than clay pots made by a potter.

ג 3 Even jackals offer the breast;
  they nurse their young.
  But the daughter of my people
  has become cruel, like desert ostriches.

ד 4 The baby's tongue sticks to the roof
  of its mouth, thirsty.
  Children ask for bread, beg for it—
  but there is no bread.

ה 5 Those who once ate gourmet food
  now tremble in the streets.
  Those who wore the finest purple clothes
  now cling to piles of garbage.

ו 6 Greater was the punishment[b]
  of the daughter of my people
  than Sodom's penalty,[c]
  which was quickly overthrown
  without any hand-wringing.[d]

ז 7 Her nazirites were purer than snow;
  they were more dazzling than milk.
  Their limbs were redder than coral;
  their bodies were sapphire.

ח 8 But their appearance grew darker than soot;
  they weren't recognized in the streets.
  Their skin shriveled on their bones;
  it became dry like wood.

ט 9 Things were better for those stabbed
  by the sword
  than for those stabbed by famine—

those who bled away, pierced,
  lacking food from the field.

י 10 The hands of loving women
  boiled their own children
  to become their food during
  the destruction of the daughter
  of my people.

כ 11 The LORD let loose his fury;
  he poured out his fierce anger.
  He started a fire in Zion;
  it licked up its foundations.

ל 12 The earth's rulers didn't believe it—
  neither did any who inhabit the world—
  that either enemy or adversary
  could enter Jerusalem's gates.

מ 13 It was because of her prophets' sins,
  her priests' iniquities,
  those who shed righteous blood
  in the middle of the city.

נ 14 People wandered blindly in the streets,
  polluted with blood.
  No one would even touch their clothing.

ס 15 "Go away! Unclean!" was shouted at them,
  "Go away! Away! Don't touch!"
  So they fled and wandered around.
  The nations said,
  "They can't stay here anymore."

פ 16 It was the LORD's presence
  that scattered them;[e]
  he no longer notices them.
  They didn't honor the priests' presence;
  they didn't favor the elders.

ע 17 Our eyes continually failed,
  looking for some help, but for nothing.
  From our watchtower we watched
  for a nation that doesn't save.

צ 18 Our steps were tracked;
  we could no longer walk in our streets.
  Our end had drawn near;
  our days were done—
  our end had definitely come.

---

[a]Heb uncertain [b]Or *iniquity* [c]Or *sin* [d]Heb uncertain [e]Heb uncertain

ק ¹⁹ Our hunters were faster
    than airborne eagles.
    They chased us up the mountains;
    they ambushed us in the wilderness.

ר ²⁰ The Lᴏʀᴅ's chosen one,
    the very breath in our lungs,
    was caught in their traps—
    the one we used to talk about, saying,
    "Under his protection we will live
    among the nations."

ש ²¹ Rejoice and be happy, Daughter Edom,
    you who live in the land of Uz.
    But this cup will pass over to you too.
    You will get drunk on it.
    You will be stripped naked.

ת ²² Your punishmentᶠ is over, Daughter Zion;
    God won't expose you anymore.
    But he will attend to your punishment,
    Daughter Edom; he will expose your sins.

The people's complaint

5 Lᴏʀᴅ, consider what has become of us;
    take notice of our disgrace. Look at it!
² Our property has been turned
    over to strangers;
    our houses belong to foreigners.
³ We have become orphans, having no father;
    our mothers are like widows.
⁴ We drink our own water—but for a price;
    we gather our own wood—but pay for it.
⁵ Our hunters have been at our necks;ᵍ
    we are worn out, but have no rest.
⁶ We held out a hand to Egypt
    and to Assyria, to get sufficient food.
⁷ Our fathers have sinned and are gone,
    but we are burdened with their iniquities.
⁸ Slaves rule over us;
    there is no one to rescue us
    from their power.
⁹ We get our bread at the risk of our lives
    because of the desert heat.ʰ
¹⁰ Our skin is as hot as an oven
    because of the burning heat of famine.
¹¹ Women have been raped in Zion,
    young women in Judah's cities.
¹² Officials have been hung up by their hands;
    elders have been shown no respect.

¹³ Young men have carried grinding stones;
    boys have stumbled
    under loads of wood.
¹⁴ Elders have left the city gate;
    young people stop their music.
¹⁵ Joy has left our heart;
    our dancing has changed
    into lamentation.
¹⁶ The crown has fallen off our head.
    We are doomed
    because we have sinned.
¹⁷ Because of all this our heart is sick;
    because of these things
    our glance is dark.
¹⁸ Mount Zion, now deserted—
    only jackals walk on it now!
¹⁹ But you, Lᴏʀᴅ, will rule forever;
    your throne lasts from one generation
    to the next.
²⁰ Why do you forget us continually;
    why do you abandon us
    for such a long time?
²¹ Return us, Lᴏʀᴅ, to yourself.
    Please let us return!ⁱ
    Give us new days, like those long ago—
²² unless you have completely rejected us,
    or have become too angry with us.ʲ

LIFE PRESERVER

Why were the people so sad?
Lamentations 5:15

This book of sad poems or *lamentations*
makes clear all the things that the people had done
wrong and the result of those bad decisions. In the
last chapter, God's people made their complaints
to God even clearer. Each example builds on the
one before, ending with these words: "Joy has left
our heart; our dancing has changed into lamentation" (Lam 5:15).

The writer of this poem went on to say that the
people's hearts were sick. They thought God had
forgotten them and would reject them forever. This
book ends on a very sad note. But what we know
from other books in the Bible is that God had not
forgotten God's people. God knew their sin. God
heard their laments. And God forgave. God does
the same for us—God remembers us, hears us, and
forgives us. ◆

ᶠOr iniquity ᵍHeb uncertain ʰOr sword; Heb uncertain ⁱOr and we will return or so that we can return ʲOr But instead you have
completely rejected us, become too angry with us, or Because if you have completely rejected us, have become too angry with us.

Ezekiel

things
YOU'LL DISCOVER

The book of Ezekiel reports the visions of the prophet Ezekiel, who preached during the years when God's people lived as prisoners in Babylon. Ezekiel taught that God's people would experience God's love in a new way, and one day they would eagerly obey God.

people
YOU'LL MEET

Ezekiel—a prophet who spoke for God (Ezek 1–48)
Israel—a name for God's people (Ezek 2–48)

places
YOU'LL GO

Chebar River (present-day Iraq),
Babylon (present-day Iraq),
Judah (the southern kingdom),
Jerusalem

words
YOU'LL REMEMBER

"The LORD God proclaims to these bones: I am about to put breath in you, and you will live again…. When I put breath in you, and you come to life, you will know that I am the LORD" (Ezek 37:5-6).

The book of Ezekiel contains language and images that can be hard for us to understand. At the start, God spoke to the prophet Ezekiel. When God's power came over Ezekiel, he saw clouds and flashes of lightning. He looked into heaven and saw creatures floating alongside wheels within wheels. He saw a bright light shining around everything.

Ezekiel's visions are not easy to interpret, so people sometimes come up with different ideas of what they might mean. In addition to the visions, the book of Ezekiel also tells how Ezekiel used symbols and surprising actions to catch people's attention and get them to listen to God's words.

The book of Ezekiel has an important message. God's people were living as prisoners in a distant land, but God still loved them very much. God promised to wash away their guilt and give them new hearts so they would gladly obey God. God would bring them back to their homes (Ezek 36:23-28). And God's glory would once again fill the temple (Ezek 43:4-5).

Ezekiel said God's people were like a valley full of dead bones, but God would bring them to life (Ezek 37). The people were broken, but God would make them whole again. God brings life even when it seems all hope is lost! ◊

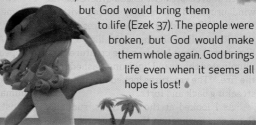

First vision

1 In the thirtieth year, on the fifth day of the fourth month, I was with the exiles at the Chebar River when the heavens opened and I saw visions of God. [2](It happened on the fifth day of the month, in the fifth year after King Jehoiachin's deportation. [3]The LORD's word burst in on the priest Ezekiel, Buzi's son, in the land of Babylon at the Chebar River. There the LORD's power overcame him.)

[4]As I watched, suddenly a driving storm came out of the north, a great cloud flashing fire, with brightness all around. At its center, in the middle of the fire, there was something like gleaming amber. [5]And inside that were forms of four living creatures. This was what they looked like: Each had the form of a human being, [6]though each had four faces and four wings. [7]Their feet looked like proper feet, but the soles of their feet were like calves' hooves, and they shone like burnished bronze. [8]Human hands were under their wings on all four sides. All four creatures had faces and wings, and [9]their wings touched each other's wings. When they moved, they each went straight ahead without turning. [10]As for the form of their faces: each of the four had a human face, with a lion's face on the right and a bull's face on the left, and also an eagle's face. [11]The pairs of wings[a] that stretched out overhead touched each other, while the other pairs covered their bodies. [12]Each moved straight ahead wherever the wind propelled them; they moved without turning. [13]Regarding the creatures' forms: they looked like blazing coals, like torches. Fire darted about between the creatures and illuminated them, and lightning flashed from the fire. [14]The creatures looked like lightning streaking back and forth.

[15]As I looked at the creatures, suddenly there was a wheel on the earth corresponding to all four faces of the creatures. [16]The appearance and composition of the wheels were like sparkling topaz. There was one shape for all four of them, as if one wheel were inside another. [17]When they moved in any of the four directions, they moved without swerving. [18]Their rims were tall and terrifying, because all four of them were filled with eyes all around. [19]When the creatures moved, the wheels moved next to them. Whenever the creatures rose above the earth, the wheels also rose up. [20]Wherever the wind would appear to go, the wind would make them go there too. The wheels rose up beside them, because the

did you **know?** Lightning and fiery clouds were both signs God was present. Moses saw a burning bush. A cloud of lightning led the people out of Egypt. Lightning clouds surrounded the top of Mount Sinai. Here Ezekiel sees God amid clouds of lightning and fire.

spirit[b] of the creatures was in the wheels. [21]When they moved, the wheels[c] moved; when they stood still, the wheels stood still; and when they rose above the earth, the wheels rose up along with them, because the spirit[d] of the creatures was in the wheels.

[22]The shape above the heads of the creatures[e] was a dome; it was like glittering ice stretched out over their heads. [23]Just below the dome, their outstretched wings touched each other. They each also had two wings to cover their bodies. [24]Then I heard the sound of their wings when they moved forward. It was like the sound of mighty waters, like the sound of the Almighty,[f] like the sound of tumult or the sound of an army camp. When they stood still, their wings came to rest. [25]Then there was a sound from above the dome over their heads. They stood still, and their wings came to rest.

[26]Above the dome over their heads, there appeared something like lapis lazuli in the form of a throne. Above the form of the throne there was a form that looked like a human being. [27]Above what looked like his waist, I saw something like gleaming amber, something like fire enclosing it all around. Below what looked like his waist, I saw something that appeared to be fire. Its brightness shone all around. [28]Just as a rainbow lights up a cloud on a rainy day, so its brightness shone all around. This was how the form of the LORD's glory appeared. When I saw it, I fell on my face. I heard the sound of someone speaking.

---

[a]LXX; MT adds *and their faces.* [b]Or *wind* [c]Or *they* [d]Or *wind* [e]LXX; MT *creature* [f]Heb *Shaddai* or *Mountain One*

Ezekiel's commissioning

2 The voice said to me: Human one, stand on your feet, and I'll speak to you. [2] As he spoke to me, a wind[g] came to me and stood me on my feet, and I heard someone addressing me. [3] He said to me: Human one, I'm sending you to the Israelites, a traitorous and rebellious people. They and their ancestors have

did you know? Ezekiel said the scroll containing God's word was sweeter than honey. From this, a habit grew that continued through Jesus' time and even today. Before scripture was read or heard, people would sometimes take a taste of honey to remind them of the sweet gift they were about to receive.

been rebelling against me to this very day. [4] I'm sending you to their hardheaded and hard-hearted descendants, and you will say to them: The Lord God proclaims. [5] Whether they listen or whether they refuse, since they are a household of rebels, they will know that a prophet has been among them.

[6] And as for you, human one, don't be afraid of them or their words. Don't be afraid! You possess thistles and thorns that subdue scorpions.[h] Don't be afraid of their words or shrink from their presence, because they are a household of rebels. [7] You'll speak my words to them whether they listen or whether they refuse. They are just a household[i] of rebels!

SAILBOAT

COURAGE

Delivering God's Message *Ezekiel 2:6*

Having courage means doing what must be done despite being afraid. That's what the prophet Ezekiel had to do. God had a lot of work for Ezekiel, but some of the people around him didn't want him doing God's work. Some of these people did not want to hear God's word. The messenger from God told Ezekiel not to be afraid. God already had given him what he needed to do God's work. Ezekiel had courage and delivered God's message as he had been called to do. ◆

[8] As for you, human one, listen to what I say to you. Don't become rebellious like that household of rebels. Open your mouth and eat what I give you. [9] Then I looked, and there in a hand stretched out to me was a scroll. [10] He spread it open in front of me, and it was filled with writing on both sides, songs of mourning, lamentation, and doom.

3 Then he said to me: Human one, eat this thing that you've found. Eat this scroll and go, speak to the house of Israel. [2] So I opened my mouth, and he fed me the scroll. [3] He said to me: Human one, feed your belly and fill your stomach with this scroll that I give you. So I ate it, and in my mouth it became as sweet as honey.

Memorize Ezek 3:3

[4] Then he said to me: Human one, go! Go to the house of Israel and speak my words to them. [5] You aren't being sent to a people whose language and speech are difficult and obscure but to the house of Israel. [6] No, not to many peoples who speak difficult and obscure languages, whose words you wouldn't understand. If I did send you to them, they would listen to you. [7] But the house of Israel—they will refuse to listen to you because they refuse to listen to me. The whole house of Israel is hardheaded and hard-hearted too. [8] I've now hardened your face so that you can meet them head-on. [9] I've made your forehead like a diamond, harder than stone. Don't be afraid of them or shrink away from them, because they are a household of rebels.

[10] He said to me: Human one, listen closely, and take to heart every word I say to you. [11] Then go to the exiles, to your people's children. Whether they listen or not, speak to them and say: The Lord God proclaims!

[12] Then a wind lifted me up, and I heard behind me a great quaking sound from his place. Blessed is the Lord's glory! [13] The sound was the creatures' wings beating against each other and the sound of the wheels beside them; it was a great rumbling noise. [14] Then the wind picked me up and took me away. With the Lord's power pressing down against me I went away, bitter and deeply angry, [15] and I came to the exiles who lived beside the Chebar River at Tel-abib. I stayed there among them for seven desolate days.

[g] Or *spirit* [h] Or *thistles and thorns are with you, and you sit on scorpions.* [i] LXX, Syr, Tg; MT lacks *household.*

¹⁶At the end of the seven days, the Lord's word came to me: ¹⁷Human one, I've made you a lookout for the house of Israel. When you hear a word from me, deliver my warning. ¹⁸If I declare that the wicked will die but you don't warn them, if you say nothing to warn them from their wicked ways so that they might live, they will die because of their guilt, but I will hold you accountable for their deaths. ¹⁹If you do warn the wicked and they don't turn from their wickedness or their wicked ways, they will die because of their guilt, but you will save your life.

²⁰Or suppose righteous people turn away from doing the right thing. If they act dishonestly, and I make them stumble because of it, they will die because you didn't warn them of their sin. Their righteous deeds won't be remembered, and I will hold you accountable for their deaths. ²¹But if you do warn the righteous not to sin, and they don't sin, they will be declared righteous. Their lives will be preserved because they heeded the warning, and you will save your life.

²²The Lord's power overcame me, and he said to me: Get up! Go out to the valley, and I'll speak to you there. ²³So I got up and went out to the valley. Suddenly, the Lord's glory stood there, like the glory that I had seen at the Chebar River, and I fell on my face. ²⁴When a wind came to me and stood me on my feet, he spoke to me and said: Go, shut yourself up inside your house. ²⁵Look at you, human one! They've now put cords on you and bound you up so that you can't go out among them. ²⁶I'll make your tongue stick to the roof of your mouth and take away your ability to speak. You won't be able to correct them, because they are a household of rebels. ²⁷But whenever I speak to you, I'll open your mouth, and you will say to them: The Lord God proclaims. Those who hear will understand, but those

Sweet as Honey *Ezekiel 3*

Dreams can be funny, silly, sad, strange, or even scary. Sometimes the questions we wonder about in the daytime appear in our dreams at night in crazy ways. Things that are impossible in real life are possible in dreams. Long ago people took dreams much more seriously than most people do today. They believed that God spoke to them through special dreams called *visions*.

The prophet Ezekiel wrote about his visions, which are not easy for us to understand. Ezekiel had a vision of God giving him a scroll. The funny thing is, God didn't want Ezekiel to read this scroll but to eat it. What would you say if someone told you to take a page out of the Bible and eat it? You wouldn't expect it to taste very good! But Ezekiel obeyed God, and ate the scroll. He said it tasted as sweet as honey.

God's words tasted good to Ezekiel because they were full of God's love and truth. The words on the scroll contained God's strength and power. They were good words of hope and faith.

When you read the Bible, imagine how some of the words might "taste." Imagine eating these words: *love, peace, hope.* These words might just be as sweet as honey.

What is your favorite sweet food?

How could "eating" God's word be sweet to your soul?

who refuse will not. They are just a household of rebels.

Jerusalem's siege

4 You, human one, take a brick. Put it in front of you and draw the city of Jerusalem on it. [2]Prepare the siege: Build a wall, construct ramps, set up army camps, and place battering rams all around. [3]Take an iron plate and set it up as an iron wall between you and the city. Face it directly. When it is under siege like this, press hard against it. This is a sign for the house of Israel.

[4]Now, lie on your left side, and set the guilt of the house of Israel on it. For the length of time that you lie on your side, you will bear their punishment. [5]I appoint to you three hundred ninety days, one day for each year of their guilt. So you will bear the punishment of the house of Israel. [6]When you have completed these days, lie on your right side to bear the guilt of the house of Judah. I appoint forty days to you, one day for each year. [7]With your arm stretched out, face the siege of Jerusalem directly and prophesy against it. [8]I've now bound you with cords so that you can't turn from one side to the other until you have completed the days of your siege.

[9]You, gather some wheat and barley, beans and lentils, and millet and spelt. Put them in a bowl and make your bread from them. Eat it during the three hundred ninety days that you lie on your side. [10]At fixed times you will eat your food by weight, fourteen ounces a day.[j] [11]You will also ration your water by measure, drinking a sixth of a hin[k] at fixed times each day. [12]Eat it like barley bread, and bake it on human excrement while they watch. [13]The Lord says: In this same way the Israelites will eat their unclean bread among the nations where I am scattering them.

[14]And I said: "Ah, Lord God! I've never been unclean! From my childhood until now I've never eaten anything that wasn't properly slaughtered,[l] and no unclean meat has ever entered my mouth!"

[15]He answered me: "Then I'll let you use cow dung instead of human excrement. You can make your bread over that."

[16]Then he said to me: Human one, I'm destroying the food supply in Jerusalem. They will anxiously ration and eat their food, and in dismay they will dole out and drink their water. [17]When their food and water dwindles away, everyone will be horrified, and they will waste away because of their guilt.

5 You, human one, take a sharp sword. Use it like a razor and shave your head and beard. Then use scales to divide the hair. [2]At the end of the siege, burn one-third of it in the city. Strike another third with the sword left and right. Then scatter one-third to the wind and let loose[m] the sword after it. [3]From that third, take a few strands and hide them in your garment. [4]From that hair, take yet another batch and throw it into the fire and burn it up. From there, fire will spread to the whole house of Israel.

did you know? Unlike other prophets who were called to go and simply speak about the coming destruction of Jerusalem, Ezekiel was called by God to do something more. Ezekiel actually acted out what was going to happen when Jerusalem was attacked.

[5]The Lord God proclaims: This is Jerusalem! I have set her in the middle of the nations and surrounding countries. [6]But she rebelled against my case laws and my regulations with greater treachery than these nations and surrounding countries, who also rejected my case laws and didn't follow my regulations. [7]Therefore, the Lord God proclaims: You have become more turbulent than these nations around you because you haven't obeyed my regulations or followed my case laws. You haven't even followed the case laws of the nations around you! [8]So now the Lord God proclaims: I myself am now against you! I will impose the case law penalties on you in the sight of the nations. [9]Because of you, I will do what I've never done before and will never do again—all because of your detestable practices. [10]Therefore, parents among you will eat their children, and children will eat their parents. I will impose penalties from case laws on you and scatter all that is left of you to the winds. [11]Therefore, as surely as I live, this is what the Lord God says: Because you made

---

[j]Or *twenty shekels* [k]A hin is approximately one gallon. [l]Or *what died of itself* or *was torn by wild beasts* [m]Or *I will let loose*

my sanctuary unclean with all your disgusting practices and detestable things, I myself will shave you. I will not shed a tear. You will have no compassion, even from me. ¹²One-third of you will die of plague and waste away by famine among you. One-third will fall by the sword all around you. And one-third I will scatter to all the winds, letting loose a sword to pursue them. ¹³My anger will be complete. I will exhaust my wrath against them and take my revenge. Then they will know that I, the Lord, have spoken against them in my zeal and consumed them in my wrath. ¹⁴I will turn you into a desolation to the ridicule of the nations all around you, in the sight of all who pass by. ¹⁵You will become an object of ridicule, a mockery, and a horrifying lesson to the nations all around you, when I impose penalties from case laws against you in anger, wrath, and overflowing fury. I, the Lord, have spoken. ¹⁶When I launch my deadly arrows of famine against you, I have released them for your destruction! I will add to your famine and completely cut off your food supply. ¹⁷I will send famine and wild animals against you, and they will leave you childless. Plague and bloodshed will come to you, and I will bring the sword against you. I, the Lord, have spoken.

Against the mountains of Israel

6 The Lord's word came to me: ²Human one, face Israel's mountains, and prophesy to them. ³Say:

Hear the Lord God's word,
  mountains of Israel!
The Lord God proclaims
  to the mountains and hills,
  to the valleys and their deepest ravines:
I'm about to bring a sword against you
  and destroy your shrines.
⁴ Your altars will be destroyed,
  your incense altars broken.
And I'll make your slain
  fall in front of your idols.
⁵ I'll throw the Israelites' corpses
  in front of their idols,
  and I'll scatter your bones
  all around your altars.
⁶ Wherever you live,
  cities will be in ruins,
  shrines made desolate,
  turned into utter ruin.

Your altars will be punished
  and then broken down.
Your idols will be demolished,
  your incense altars shattered,
  and all your works wiped out.
⁷ The slain will fall among you,
  and you will know that I am the Lord.

⁸ But I will spare a few.
  Some of you will escape
  the nations' swords
  when you are scattered
  throughout the lands.
⁹ Your fugitives will remember me
  in the nations
  to which they've been banished,
  how I was crushed
  when their roving hearts
  turned away from me,
  and their roving eyes
  went after their idols.
They will loathe themselves
  for their treacherous acts
  and detestable practices,
¹⁰ and they will know that I am the Lord.
Not in vain have I threatened
  to bring this evil against them.

¹¹The Lord God proclaims: Clap your hands, stamp your feet, and cry "Horror" over all the detestable practices of the house of Israel. They will fall by the sword, famine, and plague. ¹²Whoever is far off will die of plague, whoever is nearby will fall to the sword, and whoever finds refuge will die of famine. I'll satisfy my wrath against them! ¹³They will

LIFE PRESERVER

Why was God so mad at Israel? *Ezekiel 6*

Again and again, we read the same story in the Bible: The people in Jerusalem forgot they belonged to God. They forgot God's covenant with them. They took on the habits and practices of other nations that did not know God. So God's punishment awaited them.

Here in this chapter we read about this punishment, which was very severe. And again, this is a familiar story. God punished the people for their sins, but in the end God forgave the people and welcomed them back. So keep reading this book until you get to that part! ◗

know that I am the Lord when their slain appear among their idols and around their altars, wherever they offered up pleasing aromas for all their idols, on every high hill and mountaintop, and under every lofty tree and leafy oak. ¹⁴Wherever they live, I will direct my power against them. I will turn the land into a greater wasteland than the Riblah desert. Then they will know that I am the Lord.

The end

7 The Lord's word came to me: ²You, human one, this is what the Lord God proclaims to the land of Israel:

An end! The end has come
to the four corners of the earth!
³ Even now the end is upon you!
I'll send my anger against you,
I'll judge you according to your ways,
and I'll turn all your detestable practices
against you.
⁴ I won't shed a tear for you
or show any pity.
Instead, I'll turn your ways against you,
and your detestable practices
will stay with you.
Then you will know that I am the Lord.

⁵The Lord God proclaims:
Disaster! A singular disaster!
Look, it comes!
⁶ The end has come!
Oh, yes, it has come!
It has come to you! Look, it's here!
⁷ You who live on the earth,
you are finally caught in your own trap!
The time has come; the day draws near.
On the hills panic, not glory.
⁸ And now it's near!
Against you I will pour out my wrath,
and my anger will be satisfied.
I'll judge you according to your ways,
and turn all your detestable practices
against you.
⁹ I won't shed a tear or show any pity
when I turn your ways against you,
and your detestable practices
stay with you.
Then you will know that I, the Lord,
am the one who strikes you!

¹⁰ Look, the day! Look, it comes!
Doom has arrived!
The staff blossoms,
and pride springs up!
¹¹ Violence rises up as a wicked master.[n]
It isn't from others
or their armies or their violence.
It hasn't loomed up because of them.
¹² The time is coming! The day draws near!
No buyer should rejoice,
and no seller should mourn,
because wrath overcomes
the whole crowd.
¹³ The seller will never get back
what was sold,
even if both of them survive.
The vision concerns the whole crowd.
It won't be revoked.
And the guilty ones—
they won't even be able
to hang on to their lives.
¹⁴ They have blown the horn,
and everything is ready,
but no one goes to battle,
because my wrath
overcomes the whole crowd.
¹⁵ Outside, the sword!
Inside, plague and famine!
Whoever is out in the field
will die by the sword.
Whoever is in the city,
plague and famine will consume them.
¹⁶ And those who flee?
They will turn up on the hills
like valley doves,
all of them moaning, those guilty ones.
¹⁷ Every hand will hang limp;
urine will run down every leg.
¹⁸ They will put on mourning clothes,
and horror will cover them.
On every face, shame;
on all their heads, baldness.
¹⁹ They will hurl their silver into the street,
and their gold will seem unclean.
Their silver and their gold
won't deliver them
on the day of the Lord's anger.
They won't satisfy their appetites
or fill their bellies.
Their guilt will bring them down.

[n]Or *wicked staff*

20 From their beautiful ornament,
  in which they took pride,
  they have made horrible
  and detestable images!
  Therefore, I've declared it
  an unclean thing for them.
21 I'll hand it over to foreigners
  as loot taken in war,
  to the earth's wicked ones as plunder—
  they will defile it!
22 When I hide my face from my people,
  foreigners will defile my treasured place.
  Violent intruders will invade it;
  they will defile it!

23 Make a chain!
  The earth is full of perverted justice,
  the city full of violence.
24 I'll bring up the cruelest nations,
  and they will seize their houses.
  I'll break their proud strength,
  and their sanctuaries will be defiled.

25 Disaster! It has come!
  They seek peace, but there is none.
26 One disaster comes after another,
  and rumor follows rumor.

  They seek a vision from the prophet.
  Instruction disappears from the priest,
  and counsel from the elders.
27 The king will go into mourning,
  the prince will clothe himself
  in despair,
  and the hands of the land's people
  will tremble.

LIFE PRESERVER

What happens when God hides God's face? Ezekiel 7:22

Occasionally we see references in the Old Testament to God's face. These are not as frequent as references to God's voice, which was more common, particularly when God spoke through the prophets like Ezekiel.

When God's face is hidden, it means that God's presence is absent. So when Ezekiel said God's face would be hidden, he was warning that violence would happen. God's people and the places where they lived, worked, and worshipped would no longer be protected. ◉

When I do to them as they have done
and judge them by their own justice,
  they will know that I am the LORD.

Temple vision

8 In the sixth year, on the fifth day of the sixth month, I was sitting in my house, and Judah's elders were sitting with me, when the LORD God's power overcame me. 2I looked, and there was a form that looked like fire. Below what looked like his waist was fire, but above his waist it looked like gold, like gleaming amber. 3He stretched out the form of a hand and picked me up by the hair of my head. A wind lifted me up between earth and heaven, and in a divine vision it brought me to Jerusalem, to the north-facing entrance of the gate to the inner court. That was where the pedestal was for the outrageous image that incites outrage. 4There I saw the glory of Israel's God, exactly like what I had seen in the valley. 5He said to me: Human one, look toward the north. So I looked north, and there, north of the altar gate, was this outrageous image in the entrance. 6He said to me: Human one, do you see what they are doing, the terribly detestable practices that the house of Israel is doing here that drive me far from my sanctuary? Yet you will see even more detestable practices than these.

7Then he brought me to the court entrance. When I looked, I saw a hole in the wall. 8He said to me: Human one, dig through the wall. So I dug through the wall, and I discovered a doorway. 9And he said to me: Go in and see what wicked and detestable things they are doing in there. 10So I went in and looked, and I saw every form of loathsome beasts and creeping things and all the idols of the house of Israel engraved on the walls all around. 11The seventy elders of the house of Israel were standing in front of them, and all of them were holding censers in their hands. Jaazaniah, Shaphan's son, was standing right there with them, and the scent of the incense cloud rose up. 12He said to me: Human one, do you see what the elders of the house of Israel are doing in the dark, every one of them in their rooms full of sculptured images? They say, "The LORD doesn't see us; the LORD has abandoned the land." 13He said to me: You will see them performing even more detestable practices.

14He brought me to the entrance of the north
gate of the temple, where women were sitting
and performing the Tammuz lament.
15He said to me: Human one, do you see?
Yet you will see even more detestable practices than these. 16He brought me to the inner
court of the LORD's temple. There, at the entrance to the LORD's temple, between the
porch and the altar, were twenty-five men
facing toward the east with their backs to
the LORD's temple. They were bowing to the
sun in the east. 17He said to me: Do you see,
human one? Isn't it enough that the house
of Judah has observed here all these detestable things? They have filled the land with
violence, and they continue to provoke my
fury. Look at them! They even put the branch
to their noses! 18I will certainly respond with
wrath. I won't spare or pity anyone. Even
though they call out loudly to
me in my hearing, I won't listen to them.

LIGHTHOUSE

FALSE GODS

Pictures on Walls *Ezekiel 8:10*

The new generation of Israelites did not respect God or God's temple. They put images of false gods on the walls of God's holy temple. When the prophet Ezekiel saw this, he knew the people no longer believed the temple belonged to God. God's house belongs to God, not people. And nothing made by human hands can ever be more important than God. Only God is worthy of worship.

9 Then in my hearing he called out loudly:
Draw near, you guardians of the city, and
bring your weapons of destruction! 2Sud-
denly, six men came from the Upper Gate
that faces north. All of them were holding
weapons of destruction. Among them was another man who was dressed in linen and had
a writing case at his side. When they came in
and stood beside the bronze altar, 3the glory
of Israel's God rose from above the winged
creatures[o] where he had been and moved toward the temple's threshold. The LORD called
to the man who was dressed in linen with
the writing case at his side: 4Go through the
city, through Jerusalem, and mark the foreheads of those who sigh and groan because
of all the detestable practices that have been
conducted in it. 5To the others he said in my
hearing: Go through the city after him, and
attack. Spare no one! Be merciless! 6Kill them
all, old men, young men and women, babies
and mothers. Only don't touch anyone who
has the mark. Begin at my sanctuary. So they
began with the men, the elders in front of the
temple. 7He said to them: Make the temple
unclean! Fill the courts with the slain! Go! And
they went out and attacked the city.
8While they were attacking, I was left alone.
I fell on my face, and I cried out, "Oh, LORD God!
When you pour out your wrath on Jerusalem,
will you destroy all that is left of Israel?"
9He said to me: "Judah and the house of
Israel are very, very guilty. The land is filled
with blood, and the city is full of injustice.
They have said, 'The LORD has forsaken the
land; the LORD sees nothing.' 10I most definitely won't spare or pity anyone! I will hold
them accountable for their ways."
11Just then the man who was dressed in
linen with the writing case at his side returned
and said, "I've done just as you commanded."

10 At that moment I saw a form of a
throne in the dome above the heads
of the winged creatures. It appeared above
them, and it looked like lapis lazuli. 2He said
to the man clothed in linen: Go in between
the wheels under the winged creatures.[p] Fill
your hands with fiery coals from between
the winged creatures, and scatter them over
the city. As I watched, he went in. 3Now the
winged creatures were standing to the right
of the temple when the man went in, and
the cloud filled the inner courtyard. 4Then
the LORD's glory rose from above the winged
creatures[q] and moved toward the temple's
threshold. The temple was filled with the
cloud, and the courtyard was filled with the
brightness of the LORD's glory. 5The sound of
the winged creatures' wings could be heard
as far as the outer courtyard. It was like the
sound of God Almighty[r] when he speaks.
6When he instructed the man clothed in
linen to take fire from between the winged
creatures and their wheels, the man went

[o]LXX; MT *creature* [p]LXX; MT *creature* [q]LXX; MT *creature* [r]Heb *El Shaddai* or *God of the Mountain*

and stood next to the wheel. ⁷Then one of the winged creatures stretched a hand between the winged creatures into the fire that was between them, and he drew out some of it and set it in the palm of the one clothed in linen. He took it and went out. ⁸It appeared that the winged creatures had the form of a human hand under their wings.

⁹Suddenly, I saw four wheels next to the winged creatures. There was a wheel next to each winged creature, and the appearance of the wheels was like sparkling topaz. ¹⁰It appeared that there was one shape for all four of them, as if one wheel were inside another. ¹¹When they moved in any of the four directions, they moved without swerving. Whichever way the leading one faced, they moved in that direction without swerving. ¹²Their whole body—backs, hands, and wings—as well as their wheels, all four of them, were covered with eyes all around. ¹³It was these wheels that were called "the wheels" in my hearing. ¹⁴Each winged creature had four faces. The first face was that of a winged creature, the second face was that of a human being, the third that of a lion, and the fourth that of an eagle. ¹⁵The winged creatures rose up, the same creatures that I had seen at the Chebar River. ¹⁶When the winged creatures moved, the wheels moved beside them. When the winged creatures lifted their wings to ascend above the earth, the wheels remained beside them without swerving. ¹⁷When they stood still, the wheels stood still; when they rose up, they rose up with them, because the spiritˢ of the living creatures was in them. ¹⁸Then the Lord's glory went out from above the temple's threshold and it stood over the winged creatures. ¹⁹While I watched, the winged creatures raised their wings and rose from the ground to leave, with their wheels beside them. They stopped at the entrance to the east gate of the temple, and the glory of Israel's God was up above them. ²⁰These were the same living creatures that I saw underneath Israel's God at the Chebar River, and I realized that they were winged creatures. ²¹Each had four faces and four wings, with the form of a human hand under their wings. ²²The forms of their faces were the same faces that I saw at the Chebar River. Their appearance was also the same. All four of them moved straight ahead.

11A wind lifted me up and brought me to the east gate of the Lord's temple. There at the entrance to the gate were twenty-five men, and I saw that two officials of the people, Jaazaniah, Azzur's son, and Pelatiah, Benaiah's son, were with them.

²He said to me: Human one, these men devise evil plans and give wicked advice in this city. ³They are the ones who say, "The nearest relatives aren't building houses.ᵗ The city is the cooking pot, and we are the meat." ⁴Therefore, prophesy against them, human one, prophesy! ⁵The Lord's spirit took hold of me, and he said to me: Say, This is what the Lord God proclaims: So you have said, house of Israel! But I know what you really mean. ⁶You continue to commit murder in this city, and you fill its streets with the slain.

⁷Therefore, the Lord God proclaims: The city is the cooking pot, and the ones you have slain in it are the meat. But you will be taken out of it. ⁸You fear the sword, so I will bring the sword against you. This is what the Lord God says! ⁹I will lead you out of the city, hand you over to foreigners, and execute judgments against you. ¹⁰You will fall by the sword! At Israel's borders I will judge you, and you will know that I am the Lord. ¹¹The city won't be your cooking pot, and you won't be the meat in it. At Israel's borders, I will judge you. ¹²You will know that I am the Lord, whose regulations you didn't observe and whose case laws you didn't follow. Instead, you followed the case laws of the nations around you.

¹³While I was prophesying, Benaiah's son Pelatiah dropped dead. I fell on my face, and I wailed and said, "Oh, Lord God! Are you finishing off even the Israelites who are left?"

¹⁴The Lord's word came to me: ¹⁵Human one, when the people living in Jerusalem said, "They've gone far from the Lord, and we've been given the land as an inheritance," they were talking about your family, your nearest relatives, the whole house of Israel, all of it.

¹⁶Therefore, say, The Lord God proclaims: Even though I made them go far away among the nations and caused them to scatter

---

ˢOr wind ᵗOr it is not time to build houses

throughout the earth, I've provided some sanctuary for them in the countries to which they've gone.

¹⁷Therefore, say, The Lord God proclaims: I will gather you from the nations, assemble you from the countries where you were scattered, and I will give you Israel's fertile land. ¹⁸They will enter the land, and they will remove from it all its disgusting and detestable things. ¹⁹I will give them a single heart, and I will put a new spirit in them. I will remove the stony hearts from their bodies and give them hearts of flesh ²⁰so that they may follow my regulations and carefully observe my case laws. They will be my people, and I will be their God. ²¹As for those whose hearts continue to go after their disgusting and detestable things, I will hold them accountable for their ways. This is what the Lord God says!

²²Then the winged creatures raised their wings. The wheels were next to them, and the glory of Israel's God was above them. ²³The Lord's glory ascended from the middle of the city, and it stopped at the mountain east of the city. ²⁴And a wind lifted me up and brought me to the exiles in Chaldea, through a vision with a divine wind.^u When the vision I had seen left me, ²⁵I spoke to the exiles about everything the Lord had shown to me.

Baggage for exile

12 The Lord's word came to me: ²Human one, you live in a household of rebels. They have eyes to see but they don't see, ears to hear but they don't hear, because they are a household of rebels. ³But you, human one, prepare a backpack for going into exile. In the daytime while they watch, go into exile; while they watch, go out from your place to another. Even though they are a household of rebels, perhaps they will understand. ⁴In the daytime while they watch, carry your backpack as if for exile. At twilight while they watch, go out like those who are led out to exile. ⁵While they watch, dig a hole through the wall and take your backpack out through it. ⁶While they watch, shoulder your backpack and carry it out in the dark. Cover your face so that you can't

Bet you can
read this in 8 minutes.
Ready, set, go!

see the land, because I'm making you a sign for the house of Israel. ⁷So I did as I was commanded. I carried out my backpack like an exile's backpack in the daytime. At night I dug a hole through the wall with my hands. In the darkness, I shouldered my backpack and carried it out while they watched.

⁸In the morning, the Lord's word came to me: ⁹Human one, has the house of Israel, that household of rebels, asked you, "What are you doing?" ¹⁰Say to them, The Lord God proclaims: This concerns the prince in Jerusalem, along with the entire house of Israel in it.^v ¹¹Say: I'm your sign. Just as I have done, so it will be done to them. They will go into captivity in exile. ¹²Their prince will shoulder his backpack at night and go out. They will dig through the wall to lead him out through it, and he will cover his face so that his eyes won't see the land. ¹³But I will spread my net over him, catch him in my trap, and bring him to Babylon, to the land of the Chaldeans. He won't see it, but he will die there. ¹⁴As for all those who are in league with him, I will scatter his helpers and all his troops to the winds and let the sword loose after them. ¹⁵They will know that I am the Lord when I disperse them among the nations and scatter them throughout the lands. ¹⁶But I will preserve a few of their number from the sword, famine, and plague, so that they may confess all their detestable practices among the nations where they go. Then they will know that I am the Lord.

¹⁷The Lord's word came to me: ¹⁸Human one, eat your bread in trembling, and drink your water in anxious agitation. ¹⁹Say to the land's people, The Lord God proclaims to those living in Jerusalem regarding Israel's fertile land: As they anxiously eat up their bread and drink up their water in dismay, the land will be emptied of everything in it because of the violence of all who live there. ²⁰The inhabited cities will be laid waste, the land left desolate, and you will know that I am the Lord.

Fulfillment of prophecy

²¹The Lord's word came to me: ²²Human one, what is this proverb of your people

^uOr *spirit* ^vOr *them*

concerning Israel's fertile land? They say, "The days go by, and every vision vanishes." 23Therefore, say to them, The Lord God proclaims: I'll put an end to this proverb! It will never again be uttered in Israel. Tell them instead: The days are coming soon for the fulfillment of every vision. 24Never again will there be any worthless vision or deceptive divination in the house of Israel. 25I am the Lord! The word that I speak is the word that I will speak! It will happen and be delayed no longer. In your own days, household of rebels, I speak a word and make it happen. This is what the Lord God says!

26The Lord's word came to me: 27Human one, the house of Israel is now saying, "The vision that he sees is for distant days; he prophesies about future times." 28Therefore, say to them, The Lord God proclaims: It will be delayed no longer. Every word of mine that I've spoken is certain, and it will happen. This is what the Lord God says.

Against the prophets

13 The Lord's word came to me: 2Human one, prophesy to Israel's prophets who prophesy from their own imaginations. Say, Hear the Lord's word! 3The Lord God proclaims: Doom to the foolish prophets who follow their own whims but see nothing. 4Israel, your prophets have been like jackals among ruins. 5You haven't gone up into the breach or reinforced the wall of the house of Israel, so that it might withstand the battle on the day of the Lord. 6They saw worthless visions and performed deceptive divinations. Even though the Lord didn't send them, they said, "This is what the Lord says" and expected their word to stand. 7Didn't you see worthless visions? And didn't you report deceptive divinations and say, "This is what the Lord says," even though I didn't speak?

8Therefore, the Lord God proclaims: Because you spoke worthless things and had false visions, I'm against you. This is what the Lord God says! 9I'll wield my power against the prophets, those seers of nothingness and diviners of lies. They won't be included in my people's council, or recorded in the house of Israel's official records, or enter Israel's fertile land. Then you will know that I am the Lord.

10Without a doubt, they led my people astray, saying "Peace" when there was no peace, and "He is building a wall" when they were the ones who laid on the plaster. 11Say to those who laid on the plaster that it will fall. When the flooding rains appear and I send hailstones, it will collapse, and the storm winds will break it apart. 12The wall will certainly fall. Won't it be said about you, "Where is your plaster now?"

13Therefore, the Lord God proclaims: In my fury I will make a storm wind break out, and in my anger there will be flooding rains and hailstones in consuming wrath. 14I will tear down the wall on which you laid plaster. I will raze it to the ground and expose its foundation. When it falls, you will be destroyed with it, and you will know that I am the Lord. 15I will exhaust my fury on the wall and on those who laid plaster on it. Then I will say to you, "Where is the wall?"w and "Where are those who plastered it, 16those prophets of Israel who prophesied to Jerusalem and envisioned peace when there was no peace?" This is what the Lord God says!

17You, human one, face the daughters of your people, those women who prophesy from their imaginations. Prophesy against them 18and say, The Lord God proclaims: Doom to the women who sew bands on every wrist and make veils for heads of all sizes to entrap human lives. Will you ensnare my people's lives but preserve your own? 19When you degrade me to my people for handfuls of barley and bread crumbs, you mislead my gullible people, and you bring about the death of those who shouldn't die and keep alive those who shouldn't live.

20Therefore, the Lord God proclaims: I'm against the bands that you use to trap human lives.x I will tear them from your arms, and I will set free the lives that you've trapped like birds. 21I will tear off your veils and snatch my people out of your clutches. They will be prey in your clutches no longer. Then you will know that I am the Lord. 22You hurt the righteous with slander—I didn't wound them!—and you strengthened the hands of the wicked so that they survived without changing their evil ways! 23Therefore, you will no longer see empty visions or perform divinations. I will rescue my people from your clutches, and you will know that I am the Lord.

False devotion

14 When some of the elders of the house of Israel came to sit in my presence, [2]the Lord's word came to me: [3]Human one, these men decide on their own to set up their idols, so the cause of their downfall is right in front of them. Why should I allow them to ask me anything? [4]Therefore, speak to them and tell them, The Lord God proclaims: If anyone from the house of Israel decides on his own to set up his idols and puts the cause of his downfall right in front of him, but then comes to the prophet, I, the Lord, will require an answer from him through his many idols. [5]So I'll seize the hearts of the house of Israel, whose idols have made them all strangers to me.

[6]Therefore, say to the house of Israel, The Lord God proclaims: Come back! Turn away from your idols and from all your detestable practices. Turn away! [7]Or anyone of the house of Israel or any immigrant in Israel who becomes estranged from me by deciding on their own to set up their idols and puts the cause of their downfall right in front of them, but then comes to the prophet to ask me something through him, I, the Lord, will require an answer. [8]I will confront that one. I will set them up as a sign and an object lesson, and I will cut them off from my people. Then you will know that I am the Lord.

[9]As for the prophet who was seduced into speaking a word, even though it was I, the Lord, who seduced that prophet, I will use my power against him and cut him off completely from my people Israel. [10]The prophet and the inquirer alike will bear their guilt, [11]so that the house of Israel won't stray away from me again or make themselves impure with any of their sins. They will be my people, and I will be their God. This is what the Lord God says!

Failed request

[12]The Lord's word came to me: [13]Human one, suppose a land sins against me by acting faithlessly, so that I use my power against it, break off its food supply, let famine run rampant, and eliminate both humans and animals. [14]If these three men, Noah, Daniel,

and Job, lived there, their lives alone would be saved because they were righteous. This is what the Lord God says. [15]Or suppose I allow wild animals to roam through the land, and it becomes so wild that no one can live there or even travel through it on account of the wild animals. [16]If these three men lived there, as surely as I live, proclaims the Lord God, they wouldn't be able to rescue even their sons or daughters. They alone would be rescued, but the land would become a ruin. [17]Or suppose I bring a sword against that land and command the sword to pass through and eliminate both humans and animals. [18]If these three men lived there, as surely as I live, proclaims the Lord God, they wouldn't be able to rescue even their sons or daughters. They alone would be rescued. [19]Or suppose I send a plague against that land and pour out my fury on it. With great bloodshed I would eliminate both humans and animals. [20]If Noah, Daniel, and Job lived there, as surely as I live, proclaims the Lord God, they wouldn't be able to rescue either sons or daughters. But they would save their lives because they were righteous.

[21]The Lord God proclaims: How much more if I send all four of these terrible acts of judgment—sword, famine, wild animals, and plague—against Jerusalem, to eliminate both humans and animals? [22]Yet a few survivors will be left. Sons and daughters will be brought out to you. When you see their ways and their deeds, you will be consoled for the evil that I inflicted on Jerusalem, for all that I brought against it. [23]Seeing their ways and their deeds will bring you some consolation, because then you will understand what I've done, and that I didn't do any of these things without cause. This is what the Lord God says.

The vine's wood

15 The Lord's word came to me: [2]Human one, how is the vine's wood better than the wood of all the trees in the forest? ³Can you make anything useful from its wood? Can you make a peg from it and hang objects on it? ⁴If not, can it be used as firewood? Fire would consume its two ends, but its middle part would only get charred. So is it useful for anything? ⁵Look, even when it was whole, it was worthless. Now that the fire has consumed it, and it is charred, it's even more useless.

⁶Therefore, the Lord God proclaims: Of all the trees in the forest, I have decreed that the vine's wood is destined to be consumed by fire. So also have I decreed for those who live in Jerusalem, ⁷and I have confronted them. They may try to go out from the fire, but the fire will consume them. You will know that I am the Lord, because I confronted them. ⁸I will turn the land into a ruin because they acted faithlessly, proclaims the Lord God.

Jerusalem's unfaithfulness

16 The Lord's word came to me: ²Human one, show Jerusalem her detestable practices. ³Say, The Lord God proclaims to Jerusalem: By origin and birth you are from the land of Canaan. Your father was an Amorite, your mother a Hittite. ⁴This is how you were treated on the day you were born: Your umbilical cord wasn't cut, you weren't washed clean with water or rubbed with salt, and you weren't wrapped in blankets. ⁵No one took pity or cared enough to do any of these things for you. You were despised on the day of your birth and thrown out on the open field. ⁶When I happened to come by, I saw you flailing about in your blood. I said to you while you were still bloody, "Live!" ⁷I helped you to flourish like a young plant in the field, and you grew tall and became wonderfully endowed. Your breasts were firm, your hair beautifully thick. And you were completely naked.

⁸When I passed by you, I realized that you were ready for love. So I spread my cloak over you and covered your nakedness. I made a solemn promise and entered into a covenant with you, and you became mine. This is what the Lord God says. ⁹Then I washed you with water, rinsed off your blood, and poured oil on you. ¹⁰I clothed you with colorful garments, put fine sandals on you, wrapped your head in linen, and covered you with jewels. ¹¹I adorned you with fine jewelry, and put bracelets on

your wrists and a necklace around your neck. ¹²I put a ring in your nose, earrings in your ears, and a beautiful crown on your head. ¹³I adorned you with gold and silver, and your garments were made of the finest linen and brocade. You ate the finest flour, honey, and oil. You became very beautiful, fit for royalty. ¹⁴Among the nations you were famous for your beauty. It was perfect because of the splendor that I had given you. This is what the Lord God says.

¹⁵But you trusted in your beauty and traded on your fame. At every opportunity, you seduced all who came by. ¹⁶You took some of your clothing to make colorful shrines and prostituted yourself in them. ¹⁷You took the beautiful gold and silver jewelry that I had given to you, and you made male images for yourself and prostituted yourself with them. ¹⁸You took your fine garments and clothed them. You set my oil and incense before them. ¹⁹You set my food that I had given you to eat—fine wheat, oil, and honey—before them as a pleasing aroma. This is what the Lord God says. ²⁰You took your sons and daughters, which you had borne to me, and you sacrificed these to them so they could consume them. Was this promiscuity of yours a small thing? ²¹You slaughtered my sons and placed them in the fire for them! ²²In all your detestable practices and promiscuities, you didn't remember the days of your infancy when you lay completely naked, flailing about in your blood.

²³After all your wickedness—doom, doom to you, proclaims the Lord God—²⁴you built a pavilion for yourself and set up platforms in every square. ²⁵At every crossroad you built your platform and degraded your beauty by spreading your legs to all comers. And so you encouraged even more promiscuity. ²⁶You prostituted yourself with the Egyptians, your neighbors with the large sexual organs, and as you added to your seductions, you provoked me to anger. ²⁷So I used my power against you, cut off your allowance, and gave you up to the passions of the Philistine women who had been confounded by your infamous ways and had rejected you. ²⁸Still not satisfied, you prostituted yourself to the Assyrians, but they weren't enough for you either. ²⁹So you prostituted yourself with the Babylonians, the land of traders, but

again you weren't satisfied. ³⁰How sick was your heart—the Lord God proclaims—that you could do all these things, the deeds of a hardened prostitute. ³¹But you weren't like an ordinary prostitute! When you built your pavilion at the head of every street and made your platform in every square, you refused to be paid. ³²You are like an adulterous wife: you take in strangers instead of your husband. ³³Ordinary prostitutes are given gifts, but you gave your gifts to all your lovers. From every direction you even bribed them to come to you for your sexual favors. ³⁴As a prostitute, you were more perverse than other women. No one approached you for sexual favors, but you yourself gave gifts instead of receiving them. You are perversion itself! ³⁵Therefore, you prostitute, hear the Lord's word!

³⁶The Lord God proclaims: You were in a constant state of arousal[y] and exposed yourself when you acted like a prostitute with your lovers and with the idols to which you gave your children's blood. ³⁷Therefore, I will now gather all of your lovers whom you pleased, the ones you loved and the ones you rejected. I will gather them against you from all around, and I will expose you to them. They will see it all. ³⁸I will convict you of adultery and murder, and I will hand you over in bloody fury and zeal. ³⁹I will hand you over to them, and they will tear down your pavilion and destroy your platforms. They will strip you of your garments, take your beautiful jewels, and they will leave you completely naked. ⁴⁰They will bring an army against you, pelt you with stones, and slaughter you with their swords. ⁴¹They will burn down your houses and execute judgments against you in the sight of many women. I will bring an end to your prostitution; indeed, you will never again give payment. ⁴²When I've satisfied my anger, and my rage has turned away from you, I will be calm and no longer angry. ⁴³Because you didn't remember your youthful days, and infuriated me with all these things, I will hold you accountable for what you've done. This is what the Lord God says.

Have you not added bad reputation to all your detestable acts? ⁴⁴Now everyone who speaks in proverbs will say this about you:

"Like mother, like daughter." ⁴⁵You are your mother's daughter! She loathed her husband and also her children. You are just like your sisters too! They also loathed their husbands and children. Your mother was a Hittite, and your father was an Amorite. ⁴⁶Your older sister is Samaria, who lives with her daughters in the north. Your younger sister is Sodom, who lives with her daughters in the south. ⁴⁷You didn't follow in their ways or engage in their detestable practices in any small way. You were far more destructive. ⁴⁸As surely as I live, says the Lord God, not even your sister Sodom and her daughters did what you and your daughters have done! ⁴⁹This is the sin of your sister Sodom: She and her daughters were proud, had plenty to eat, and enjoyed peace and prosperity; but she didn't help the poor and the needy. ⁵⁰They became haughty and did detestable things in front of me, and I turned away from them as soon as I saw it.

⁵¹Samaria didn't sin even half as much as you did. You've so outstripped her in multiplying your detestable practices, with all the detestable things you've done, that you've even made your sisters seem innocent. ⁵²Bear your disgrace, which has actually improved your sisters' position. Because your sins and detestable acts were greater than theirs, they are now more righteous than you. Be ashamed, and bear the disgrace of making your sisters righteous! ⁵³I will improve the circumstances of Sodom and her daughters and the circumstances of Samaria and her daughters. And what's left of your fortune will go to them, ⁵⁴so that you will bear your disgrace and be humiliated by all that you've done to make them feel better. ⁵⁵Then your sister Sodom and her daughters will return to their former state, and your sister Samaria and her daughters will return to their former state. You and your daughters will return to your former state, ⁵⁶but you will no longer talk about your sister Sodom as in your haughty days ⁵⁷before your wickedness was exposed. You are now the reproach of all the daughters of Edom[z] and all those around her, including the daughters of the Philistines. They mock you on every side. ⁵⁸You alone must bear your bad reputation and your detestable ways. This is what the Lord says.

ʸHeb uncertain ᶻSyr; MT *Aram*

⁵⁹The Lord God proclaims: I will do to you just as you have done, despising solemn pledges and breaking covenants. ⁶⁰Nevertheless, I will remember my covenant with you when you were young, and I will establish an everlasting covenant with you. ⁶¹And you will remember your ways and be ashamed, when in spite of your covenant Iᵃ take your big sisters and little sisters from you and give them back to you as daughters. ⁶²I myself will establish my covenant with you, and you will know that I am the Lord. ⁶³Then you will remember and be ashamed, and you won't even open your mouth because of your shame, after I've forgiven you for all that you've done. This is what the Lord God says.

Transplanted cedar

17 The Lord's word came to me: ²Human one, compose a riddle and a parable about the house of Israel. ³Say, The Lord God proclaims: The great eagle with great wings, long feathers, and full, colorful plumage came to Lebanon and took the top branch of the cedar. ⁴He plucked a twig from the cedar's crown, brought it to the land of traders, and set it down in a city of merchants. ⁵He took a native seed and planted it in a prepared field, placing it like a willow beside plentiful water. ⁶It grew and became a low-spreading vine. Its foliage turned toward him, and its roots developed under him. And so it became a vine, and it produced branches and sent out its shoots.

⁷Now there was another great eagle with great wings and much plumage. This vine bent its roots and turned its branches toward him so that it might draw more water from him than from its own bed, ⁸a good field with plentiful water where it was planted to grow branches, bear fruit, and become a splendid vine. ⁹Say, The Lord God proclaims: Will it thrive? Won't he tear out its roots, strip its fruit, and cause all the leaves of its branches to wither? It will dry up, and no one will need a strong arm or a mighty army to uproot it. ¹⁰Though it is planted, will it thrive? When the east wind touches it, won't it completely wither? On the bed in which it was planted, it will wither away.

¹¹The Lord's word came to me: ¹²Say now to the rebellious household: Don't you know what these things mean? Say: The king of Babylon came to Jerusalem and carried its king and its officers away with him to Babylon. ¹³Then he took a prince from the royal line, made an agreement with him, and made him take a solemn pledge of loyalty. He also took away the land's officials. ¹⁴Thus it would be a lowly kingdom, not asserting its own interests but observing the agreement so that it would survive. ¹⁵But the prince rebelled against him and sent messengers to Egypt to supply him with horses and a great army. Can such a person succeed? Can one who does these things escape? Can he overturn the agreement and escape capture? ¹⁶As surely as I live, says the Lord God, he will die in Babylon, in the place of the king who gave him the authority to rule, whose solemn pledge he scorned and whose agreement he overturned. ¹⁷Pharaoh won't help him. There will be no strong force or mighty army in battle when siege ramps are set up and towers are built to eliminate many lives. ¹⁸He scorned the solemn pledge and overturned the agreement! Even though he made a promise, he did all these things, and he won't escape capture. ¹⁹So now the Lord God proclaims: As surely as I live, it was my solemn pledge that he scorned and my agreement that he overturned, and I will hold him accountable. ²⁰I will spread my net over him, and he will be caught in my trap. I will bring him to Babylon, and I myself will enter into judgment with him there for rebelling against me. ²¹All his elite fightersᵇ along with all his troops will fall by the sword, and those who are left will be scattered to the winds. Then you will know that I, the Lord, have spoken.

²²The Lord God proclaims: I myself will take one of the top branches from the tall cedar. I will pluck a tender shoot from its crown, and I myself will plant it on a very high and lofty mountain. ²³On Israel's mountainous highlands I will plant it, and it will send out branches and bear fruit. It will grow into a mighty cedar. Birds of every kind will nest in it and find shelter in the shade of its boughs. ²⁴Then all the trees in the countryside will

---

ᵃLXX; MT *you* ᵇLXX, Syr, Tg; MT *his fugitives*

know that I, the Lord, bring down the tall tree and raise up the lowly tree, and make the green tree wither and the dry tree bloom. I, the Lord, have spoken, and I will do it.

Sins of parents and children

18 The Lord's word came to me: [2]What do you mean by this proverb of yours about the land of Israel: "When parents eat unripe grapes, the children's teeth suffer"? [3]As surely as I live, says the Lord God, no longer will you use this proverb in Israel! [4]All lives are mine; the life of the parent and the life of the child belong to me. Only the one who sins will die.

[5]People are declared innocent when they act justly and responsibly. [6]They don't eat on the hills or give their attention to the idols of the house of Israel. They don't defile the wives of their neighbors or approach menstruating women. [7]They don't cheat anyone, but fulfill their obligations. They don't rob others, but give food to the hungry and clothes to the naked. [8]They don't impose interest or take profit. They refrain from evil and settle cases between people fairly. [9]They follow my regulations, keep my case laws, and act faithfully. Such people are innocent, and they will live, proclaims the Lord God.

[10]But suppose one of them has a violent child who sheds blood or does any one of these things, [11]even though his parents didn't do any of them. He eats on the mountains, defiles his neighbor's wife, [12]oppresses the poor and needy, robs others and doesn't fulfill his obligations, pays attention to the idols and does detestable things, [13]and takes interest and profit. Should he live? He should not. He engaged in all these detestable practices. He will surely die, and his blood will be on him.

[14]But suppose he has a child who sees all the sins that his father committed. He becomes alarmed and doesn't do them. [15]He doesn't eat on the mountains or pay attention to the idols of the house of Israel. He doesn't defile his neighbor's wife. [16]He doesn't cheat anyone, either by seizing collateral for loans or committing robbery. He gives his food to the hungry and clothes to the naked. [17]He refrains from oppressing the poor by taking neither interest nor profit. He observes my case laws and follows my regulations. He

won't die because of his father's guilt. He will surely live. [18]As for his father: If he exploited the weak or committed robbery, or did anything else that wasn't good for the people, he will die because of his own guilt.

LIGHTHOUSE
False Gods

Annual Feasts *Ezekiel 18:6, 11-12, 15*

God told the prophet Ezekiel that all people who didn't take part in idol worship activities would be declared innocent. God told him how to identify those who were righteous. The first way to identify the righteous person was to see who respected the Instruction from Moses. That Instruction included obeying the teaching regarding food as a part of their worship. Those who ate on the mountains where idol worship took place were eating food that wasn't prepared according to God's Instruction. People offered animal sacrifices on these mountains and then had feasts to honor false gods. At these feasts, they ate meat that had been sacrificed to idols. Those who were righteous didn't participate in these activities.

[19]You will say, "Why doesn't the child bear his parent's guilt?" The child has acted justly and responsibly. The child kept all my regulations and observed them. The child will surely live. [20]Only the one who sins will die. A child won't bear a parent's guilt, and a parent won't bear a child's guilt. Those who do right will be declared innocent, and the wicked will be declared guilty.

[21]But if the wicked turn away from all the sins that they have committed, keep all my regulations, and act justly and responsibly, they will surely live and not die. [22]None of the sins that they committed will be held against them, but they will live because they do the right things. [23]Do I take pleasure in the death of the wicked? says the Lord God. Certainly not! If they change their ways, they will live.

[24]If those who do the right thing turn from righteousness and engage in the same detestable practices that the wicked committed, can they do these things and live? None of their righteous deeds will be remembered. They will die because of their treacheries and sins. [25]But you say, "My Lord's way doesn't measure up." Listen, house of Israel, is it my ways

that don't measure up? Isn't it your ways that don't measure up? ²⁶When those who do the right thing turn from their responsible ways and act maliciously, they will die because of it. For their malicious acts they will die. ²⁷And when the wicked turn from their wicked deeds and act justly and responsibly, they will preserve their lives. ²⁸When they become alarmed and turn away from all their sins, they will surely live; they won't die. ²⁹Yet the house of Israel says, "My Lord's way doesn't measure up." Is it my ways that don't measure up? Isn't it your ways that don't measure up, house of Israel? ³⁰Therefore, I will judge each of you according to your ways, house of Israel. This is what the Lord God says. Turn, turn away from all your sins. Don't let them be sinful obstacles for you. ³¹Abandon all of your repeated sins. Make yourselves a new heart and a new spirit. Why should you die, house of Israel? ³²I most certainly don't want anyone to die! This is what the Lord God says. Change your ways, and live!

A mother's sons

19 You, raise a lament for Israel's princes. ²Say:

What a lioness among lionesses
was your mother!
She bedded down among the strong
young lions and reared her cubs.
³ She singled out one of her cubs
and he became a strong young lion;
he learned to tear flesh
and devour humans.
⁴ When the nations heard about him,
they caught him in their trap
and carried him with hooks
to the land of Egypt.
⁵ When she realized that she waited in vain,
her hope faded.
So she took another of her cubs
and set him up as a strong young lion.
⁶ He went on the prowl with the other lions
and became a strong young lion.
He learned to tear flesh
and devour humans;
⁷ he ravaged^c their widows
and laid waste to their cities.
When the earth and everything in it

became horrified by the sound
of his raging,
⁸ the nations from the surrounding regions
allied against him.
They cast their nets over him
and caught him in their trap.
⁹ They put a collar on him
and brought him with hooks.
They brought him with nets
to the king of Babylon
so that his voice would no longer be
heard on the mountains of Israel.

The proud mother

¹⁰ Your mother was like a vine in a vineyard^d
planted beside the waters;
she bore lush fruit and foliage
because of the plentiful water,
¹¹ and she produced mighty branches,
fit for rulers' scepters.
She grew tall, and her crown went up
between the clouds.
Because of her height and thick growth,
she became conspicuous.
¹² So she was struck down in anger,
thrown down to the ground.
The east wind dried her out
and destroyed her fruit;
it sapped the branch of its strength,
and fire consumed it.
¹³ So now she is planted in the desert,
in a parched and thirsty land,
¹⁴ and fire has gone out from her branch
and consumed her foliage and fruit,
leaving her no strong branch
or ruler's scepter.
This is a lamentation, and it will serve as a lamentation.

History of rebellion

20 In the seventh year, on the tenth day of the fifth month, some of Israel's elders came to inquire of the Lord. As they were sitting with me, ²the Lord's word came to me: ³Human one, speak to Israel's elders and say to them, The Lord God proclaims: Have you come to petition me? As surely as I live, I reject your petitions. This is what the Lord God says! ⁴Will you judge them, human one, will you judge them? Then expose to

^cOr knew ^dOr in your blood

them the detestable practices of their ancestors. [5]Say to them, The Lord God proclaims: On the day I chose Israel, I swore a solemn pledge to the descendants of Jacob's household. When I made myself known to them in the land of Egypt, I swore a solemn pledge: I am the Lord your God. [6]On that day I swore that I would lead them out of the land of Egypt to a land that I would show them, a land full of milk and honey, the most splendid of all lands. [7]And I said to them, Every one of you must cast away your disgusting things. Don't let yourselves be defiled by Egypt's idols. I am the Lord your God. [8]But they rebelled against me and refused to listen to me. No one cast off their disgusting things or abandoned their Egyptian idols. So I declared that I would pour out my wrath on them and satisfy my anger against them in the land of Egypt. [9]But I acted for my name's sake, so that it wouldn't be degraded in the sight of the nations among whom they lived, and in whose sight I made it known that I would lead them out of the land of Egypt.

[10]So I led them out of the land of Egypt and brought them into the desert. [11]I gave them my regulations and made known to them my case laws, which bring life to all who observe them. [12]I also gave them my sabbaths as a sign between us that I, the Lord, have set them apart for my purpose.[e] [13]But the house of Israel rebelled against me in the desert. They didn't follow my regulations and rejected my case laws, which bring life to all who observe them. They completely degraded my sabbaths. So I declared that I would pour out my anger against them and destroy them in the desert. [14]But instead, I acted for the sake of my name so that it wouldn't be degraded in the sight of the nations who saw me lead them out of Egypt. [15]So in the desert I swore another solemn pledge, that I wouldn't bring them to the land that I had given to them, a land full of milk and honey, a land more splendid than any other, [16]because they rejected my case laws, didn't follow my regulations, and degraded my sabbaths. They had their hearts set on their idols. [17]But I had too much compassion to

destroy them, so I didn't put an end to them in the desert.

[18]In the desert, I said to their children, Don't follow your parents' regulations or observe their case laws or become defiled by their idols. [19]I am the Lord your God! Follow my regulations! Observe my case laws and do them! [20]Make my sabbaths holy, and let them be a sign between us that I am the Lord your God. [21]But the children rebelled against me. They didn't follow my regulations or observe my case laws, which bring life to all who observe them. They also degraded my sabbaths. So I declared that I would pour out my wrath on them and satisfy my anger against them in the desert. [22]But I restrained myself and acted for the sake of my name so that it wouldn't be diminished in the sight of the nations who saw me lead them out of Egypt. [23]And I swore yet another solemn pledge in the desert, that I would disperse them among the nations and scatter them throughout the earth, [24]because they didn't observe my case laws, they rejected my regulations, and they degraded my sabbaths while they kept looking to their parents' idols. [25]I also issued regulations that were not good and case laws by which they could not live. [26]I defiled them with their very gifts when they offered up all their oldest children. They were supposed to be so horrified that they would acknowledge that I am the Lord.

[27]Therefore, human one, speak to the house of Israel and say to them, The Lord God proclaims: Yet again your ancestors defamed me by rebelling against me! [28]I brought them into the land that I swore to give to them. But when they saw all the high hills and lofty trees, there they made their sacrifices: irksome offerings here, pleasing aromas there, and drink offerings elsewhere! [29]I said to them, What shrine are you going to now? So it's called Shrine[f] to this very day.

[30]So now say to the house of Israel, The Lord God proclaims: Will you defile yourselves as your ancestors did, and will you prostitute yourself after their disgusting things? [31]When you offer up your gifts and make your children pass through the fire, you defile yourselves with all your idols to this

[e]Or to make them holy [f]Heb sounds like *Where are you going?*

very day. Should I let you seek me out, house of Israel? This is what the Lord God says: As surely as I live, I won't let you seek me. ³²What is in your minds will never happen! You've been saying, "Let's be like the nations and the clans of the lands in the service of wood and stone." ³³This is what the Lord God says: As surely as I live, with a strong hand, an outstretched arm, and with wrath poured out, I will be your king! ³⁴I will lead you out from the peoples and gather you from the countries where you've been scattered—yes, with a strong hand and an outstretched arm and with wrath poured out! ³⁵I will march you out to the wilderness nations, and there I will judge you face-to-face. ³⁶Just as I judged your ancestors in the desert of the land of Egypt, so will I judge you. This is what the Lord God says. ³⁷I will make you walk under the rod, and I will bring you into the covenant bond. ³⁸I will remove from among you those who rebel and transgress against me. I will lead them out from the land where they lived as immigrants, but they won't enter Israel's fertile land. Then you will know that I am the Lord.

³⁹But to you, house of Israel, the Lord God proclaims: Go ahead and serve your idols, all of you! But afterward, if any of you are left to listen to me,ᵍ you will no longer make my holy name impure with your gifts or your idols! ⁴⁰On my holy mountain, on the high mountain in Israel, the whole house of Israel will serve me there—every one of them in the land! This is what the Lord God says. There I will accept them, and there I will ask for their offerings, their finest gifts, and all their holy things. ⁴¹When I bring you out from the nations and gather you from the countries where you are scattered, I will accept you as a pleasing aroma. Through you I will be made holy in the sight of the nations. ⁴²Then you will know that I am the Lord, when I bring you to Israel's fertile land, to the land that I swore to give to your ancestors. ⁴³There you will remember how your ways and all your wicked deeds defiled you, and you will loathe yourselves for all the wicked things that you've done. ⁴⁴Then, house of Israel, you will know that I am the Lord, when I deal with you for the sake of my name and not according to

your wicked ways and ruinous deeds. This is what the Lord God says.

Fire in the southern plain

⁴⁵ʰThe Lord's word came to me: ⁴⁶Human one, face Teman, preach against the south, and prophesy against the thicket in the arid southern plain. ⁴⁷Say to the thicket in the arid southern plain: Hear the Lord God's word. This is what the Lord God says: I'm about to set a fire in you, and it will consume every green and every dry tree in you. Its blazing flame won't be put out, and everything from south to north will be scorched. ⁴⁸Everyone will see that I, the Lord, have set it on fire. It won't be quenched. ⁴⁹Then I said, "Oh, Lord God! They say about me, 'Isn't he one for making metaphors?'"

The sword

21 Theⁱ Lord's word came to me: ²Human one, face Jerusalem, preach against their sanctuary, and prophesy against Israel's fertile land. ³Say to Israel's fertile land, The Lord proclaims: I'm now against you! I will draw my sword from its sheath and cut off both the righteous and the wicked from you. ⁴In order to cut off the righteous and wicked from you, my sword will go out from its sheath against everyone from south to north. ⁵And everyone will know that I, the Lord, have taken my sword out of its sheath. It won't be put away again.

⁶You, human one, groan in their sight; groan bitterly with trembling knees. ⁷If they ask you why you're groaning, say to them, "Because of the news." When it comes, every heart will despair, every hand will hang lifeless, every spirit will be listless, and urine will run down every leg. It's coming! It will happen! This is what the Lord God says.

The sword dance

⁸The Lord's word came to me: ⁹Human one, prophesy! Say, The Lord proclaims! Say:
A sword! A sharp and polished sword!
¹⁰ For utter slaughter it is sharpened,
polished to flash like lightning.
Let's not rejoice,
because no one will escape the purge.ʲ

ᵍHeb uncertain ʰ21:1 in Heb ⁱ21:6 in Heb ʲHeb uncertain

¹¹ He appoints it for polishing,
  to seize in the hand.
  The sword is sharpened,
    it is polished;
    it is ready for the destroyer's hand.
¹² Human one, cry aloud, and wail,
  for it comes against my people,
  against all of Israel's princes,
    handed over to the sword
      along with my people.
  Therefore, strike your thigh.
    ¹³ He's testing.
  When even the rod rejects,
    will it not certainly happen?^k
  This is what the Lord God says.

¹⁴ And you, human one, prophesy!
  Strike hand to hand.
    Let the sword strike twice,
      three times!
  It's a deadly sword,
    a great deadly sword.
  It whirls around them
¹⁵ to make hearts shudder,
    to make many stumble and fall.
  I've set the slaughtering sword
    against all their gates.
  Oh! It's crafted to flash like
    lightning,
    polished for slaughter!
¹⁶ Stab again and again!
    Plunge right,
    plunge left,
    wherever
    your edge goes.
¹⁷ It is I who strike hand to hand!
    I'll satisfy my wrath!
    I, the Lord, have spoken.

Guilt remembered

¹⁸ The Lord's word came to me: ¹⁹ You, human one, mark two roads for the coming of the sword of the king of Babylon. They should diverge from a single country. Where the road to the city begins, set up a sign, ²⁰ and point out the way for the sword to come: "To Rabbah of the Ammonites" or "To Judah in its stronghold Jerusalem." ²¹ The king of Babylon stands at the fork in the road where the two roads begin and performs his divinations. He shakes the arrows, consults the divine images, and inspects the liver. ²² On his right side appeared the omen for Jerusalem: to put battering rams in place, to proclaim war and raise the alarm, to place battering rams against the gates, and to set up siege ramps and build towers. ²³ It seems to them like a lying divination, because solemn pledges had been sworn to them. But he will remind them of their guilt, and they will be captured.

²⁴ So the Lord God proclaims: Now that you have remembered your guilt and your treacheries are exposed, your sins can be seen in everything you do. Because you have brought your guilt to light, you will be captured! ²⁵ But you vile, wicked prince of Israel whose day has come, the time of final punishment, ²⁶ this is what the Lord God says: Remove the turban, take off the crown! Nothing will be as it was. Bring down the exalted, and exalt the lowly. ²⁷ A ruin, ruin, ruin, I'll make it! Such a thing has never happened! Even before the rightful judge comes, I've handed it over to him.

Avenging Ammon's disgrace

²⁸ You, human one, prophesy and say, The Lord God proclaims to the Ammonites concerning their disgrace. Say, Sword! Sword unsheathed for slaughter, burnished, battle-ready,^l flashing like lightning: ²⁹ False visions and lying divinations set you against the necks of vile, wicked men whose day had come, the time of final punishment. ³⁰ Return it to its sheath. In the place where you were created, in the land of your origin, I will judge you. ³¹ I will pour out my wrath against you. With a raging fire I will blow against you, and I will

^kHeb uncertain ^lOr *to take in the hand*

hand you over to those who burn and forge destruction. ³²Fire will consume you, your blood will sink into the earth, and you will no longer be remembered. I, the LORD, have spoken.

Bloody city

22The LORD's word came to me: ²You, human one, will you judge? Will you judge the bloody city? Then explain all her detestable practices to her. ³Say, The LORD God proclaims: City, self-destructive blood-letter, self-defiling idol maker: ⁴All the blood that you've shed is your punishment, and all the idols that you've made are your defilement. This is how you've shortened your days and hastened the end[m] of your years! For this reason I've given you over to the ridicule of nations and the derision of every land. ⁵Those from near and far will mock your infamous name and great chaos. ⁶Look, Israel's princes, every one of them, have joined forces to shed blood in you. ⁷In you they treat father and mother with contempt. In you they oppress immigrants and deny the rights of orphans and widows. ⁸You despise my holy things and degrade my sabbaths. ⁹In you slanderers show up to shed blood. In you they eat on the mountains. In you they do obscene things. ¹⁰In you a father's nakedness is uncovered. In you menstruating women are violated. ¹¹Every man engages in detestable practices with his neighbor's wife, every man defiles his daughter-in-law with obscene acts, and every man violates his sister, his own father's daughter. ¹²In you they take bribes to shed blood. You collect interest and fees, you profit by extorting your neighbor, and you neglect even me! This is what the LORD God says.

¹³I now strike my hands over your ill-gotten gain and blood that's been shed in you. ¹⁴Will your strength and courage endure when I deal with you? I am the LORD: I speak, and I act! ¹⁵I will scatter you among the nations and disperse you throughout the lands, and so I will remove your uncleanness from you. ¹⁶When you are degraded[n] like this in the sight of the nations, then you will know that I am the LORD.

¹⁷The LORD's word came to me: ¹⁸Human one, the house of Israel has become a waste product for me. They are all copper, tin, iron, and lead. In the furnace, they've become the waste product of silver. ¹⁹So this is what the LORD God says: Because you've all become a waste product, I'm now gathering you into the middle of Jerusalem. ²⁰Just as silver, copper, iron, lead, and tin are collected and placed in a furnace to fan the flames under them and melt them down, so in my anger and rage I will collect you, put you in, and melt you down. ²¹I will gather you, fan the flames of my wrath under you, and melt you down in the middle of it. ²²As silver is melted in a furnace, so you will be melted in it. You will know that I, the LORD, have poured out my rage on you.

²³The LORD's word came to me: ²⁴Human one, say to her, You are an unclean land without rain on the day of reckoning. ²⁵The conspiracy of princes[o] in her is like a roaring lion ripping up prey. They've piled up wealth and precious goods and made many widows in her. ²⁶Her priests have done violence to my instructions and made my holy things impure. They have not clearly separated the holy from the ordinary, and they have not taught the difference between unclean and clean things. They've disregarded my sabbaths. So I've been degraded among them. ²⁷The officials in her are like wolves ripping up prey. They shed blood and destroy lives for unjust riches. ²⁸Her prophets have whitewashed everything for them, seeing false visions and making wrong predictions for them, saying, "This is what the LORD God says," when the LORD hasn't spoken. ²⁹The important people of the land have practiced extortion and have committed robbery. They've oppressed the poor and mistreated the immigrant. They've oppressed and denied justice. ³⁰I looked for anyone to repair the wall and stand in the gap for me on behalf of the land, so I wouldn't have to destroy it. But I couldn't find anyone. ³¹So I've poured out my anger on them. With my furious fire I've finished them off. I've held them accountable. This is what the LORD God proclaims.

Two sisters

23The LORD's word came to me: ²Human one, there were two women, daughters of one woman. ³When they were girls in Egypt, they began to prostitute themselves

---

[m]LXX, Syr; Vulg *time*; MT *until*   [n]MT adds *in you*.   [o]LXX; MT *prophets*

by allowing their young and nubile breasts to be touched and fondled. ⁴The older sister was named Oholah, and the younger sister was named Oholibah. They became mine and gave birth to sons and daughters. Now Oholah is Samaria, and Oholibah is Jerusalem. ⁵But Oholah became unfaithful to me and lusted after her lovers the Assyrians: ⁶warriors dressed in fine blue cloth, governors and officers, charioteers and horsemen, all of them the most handsome of men. ⁷She sought them out to seduce them, all of them men of the highest rank of Assyria. She defiled herself by everyone she lusted after and also by all their idols. ⁸But she never gave up her promiscuities with the Egyptians, who had slept with her in her girlhood and fondled her nubile breasts, and who continued to seduce her. ⁹Therefore, I handed her over to her lovers, to the Assyrians for whom she lusted. ¹⁰They stripped her naked, took her sons and daughters, and killed her with the sword. And she became notorious among women for the punishments they enacted against her.

¹¹Her sister Oholibah saw it, and she proceeded to outdo her sister in her lust and in her seductions. ¹²She lusted after the Assyrians, governors and officers, warriors richly clothed, charioteers and horsemen, all of them the most handsome of men. ¹³I saw that she too defiled herself. Both had the same tendencies, ¹⁴but she was even more promiscuous. She saw men carved in wall reliefs, images of Chaldeans outlined in vermilion, ¹⁵wearing only loincloths around their hips and flowing headbands on their heads. All of them had the appearance of warriors of the third rank, the likeness of Babylonians whose native land is Chaldea. ¹⁶Aroused just by looking at them, she sent messengers to them in Chaldea. ¹⁷The Babylonians came to her to lie down and make love with her, defiling her with their seductions. But once she had defiled herself with them, she recoiled from them in disgust. ¹⁸When her seductions became known and her nakedness exposed, I recoiled from her just as I had recoiled from her sister. ¹⁹But she added to her promiscuities, bringing to mind her youthful days when she was a prostitute in the land of Egypt.

²⁰She lusted after their male consorts, whose sexual organs were like those of donkeys, and whose ejaculation was like that of horses. ²¹She relived the wicked days of her youth, when the Egyptians touched and fondled her young and nubile breasts.

²²So Oholibah, the LORD God proclaims: I'm now inciting your lovers against you, all those from whom you recoiled, and I will bring them against you from all around—²³Babylonians and all the Chaldeans, Pekod and Shoa and Koa, all the Assyrians with them, the most handsome young men, all of them governors and officers, career officers and conscripts, all of them on horseback. ²⁴They will come against you with weapons,ᵖ chariots, and wagons, and with a great army, with shield, buckler, and helmet; and they will surround you. I will hand your punishment over to them, and they will judge you according to their laws. ²⁵I will direct my passion against you, and they will deal with you in wrath. They will cut off your nose and ears, and those who are left will fall by the sword. They will seize your sons and daughters, and those who are left will be burned with fire. ²⁶They will strip your clothing from you and remove your beautiful crown. ²⁷That's how I will put an end to your lewdness and your Egyptian-styled promiscuity. Never again will you stare at them, and you won't remember Egypt anymore. ²⁸The LORD God proclaims: I'm now handing you over to those whom you hate and from whom you recoil. ²⁹They will deal hatefully with you: They will seize your pay and leave you completely naked. Your promiscuity, betrayal, and seductions will be exposed. ³⁰This will be done to you because you sold yourself to the nations and became defiled by their idols. ³¹You followed in your sister's path, so I have put her cup into your hand.

³²The LORD God proclaims:
Deep and wide is your sister's cup. Drink!
    Appointed for abuse and scorn,
        it overflows.
³³ You will be filled with drunken sadness.
    A cup of devastation and dismay
        is the cup of your sister Samaria.
³⁴ Drink it, drain it dry, break it into pieces,
    and tear off your breasts, for I have spoken.
    This is what the LORD God says.

ᵖHeb uncertain

35So now the LORD God proclaims: Because you forgot me and turned your back on me, you alone will bear the consequences of your betrayal and promiscuities.

36Then the LORD said to me, Human one, judge Oholah and Oholibah, and make known their detestable practices to them. 37They committed adultery, so now blood is on their hands. They committed adultery with their idols, and they even took their children whom they had borne to me and offered them up to be consumed for them. 38They also did this to me: On the same day, they made my sanctuary unclean and made my sabbaths impure. 39When they slaughtered their children for their idols, they came into my sanctuary and made it impure on that very same day. They actually did this inside my temple. 40They even sent for men who came from a great distance. No sooner than a messenger was sent, they arrived! For these men you bathed, you painted your eyes, and you put on your jewelry. 41You took your place on a splendid couch with a richly set table in front of it, and you set my incense and my oil on it. 42The sound of a noisy crowd was around her. Men from the common multitude, drinkers of wine, were brought from the desert. They put bracelets on their wrists and beautiful crowns on their heads. 43Then I thought, For a foolish woman they become adulterers! Incited by her seduction, they prostitute themselves—for her![q] 44They come as if coming to a prostitute, first to Oholah, and then to Oholibah, those traitorous women. 45But men who do the right thing will judge them, and they will be punished as adulterers and murderers, because they are in fact adulterers, and blood is on their hands.

46The LORD God proclaims: Bring up an assembly against them, and decree terror and plunder for them. 47Let the assembly stone them! Let them carve them up with their swords, slay their sons and daughters, and burn their houses with fire! 48So I will put an end to betrayal in the land. Taking warning, no woman will betray as you have done. 49You will be held accountable for your betrayals, and you will bear the sins of your idols. Then you will know that I am the LORD God.

The useless pot

24 In the ninth year, on the tenth day of the tenth month, the LORD's word came to me: 2Human one, write down today's date, because today the king of Babylon has set up camp at Jerusalem—today! 3Compose a parable for the rebels' household and say to them, The LORD God proclaims:

Put on the pot, set it on,
  and fill it with water.
4Add meat to it,
  every good piece.
  With shoulder and thigh,
  the meatiest bones, fill it up.
5Take the flock's best animal;
  arrange the wood[r] beneath it.
Bring it to a rolling boil,
  and cook its bones in it.

6The LORD God proclaims: Horror! You bloody city, you corroded pot; pot whose corrosion can't be removed! Empty it piece by piece. She is rejected[s] 7because her blood is still with her. She didn't pour it out on the ground so that it could be covered with dirt, but she spread it out on a bare rock. 8In order to arouse wrath, to guarantee vengeance, I will spread her blood on a bare rock, never to be covered.

9So now the LORD God proclaims:
Horror! You bloody city!
  I myself will add fuel to the fire!
10Pile on the wood, light the fire,
  and cook the meat.
  Season it well and let the bones be charred.
11Let the pot stand empty on its coals
  until it's so hot that its copper glows,
  its impurities melt in it,
  and its corrosion is consumed.
12It's a worthless task.
  Even by fire its great corrosion
    isn't removed.

13How your betrayals defile you! I cleansed you, but you didn't come clean from your impurities. You won't be clean again until I have exhausted my anger against you. 14I, the LORD, have spoken! It's coming, and I'll do it. I won't relent or have any pity or compassion. Your punishments will fit your ways and your deeds! This is what the LORD God says.

[q]Heb uncertain [r]Or *bones* [s]Or *the lot did not fall to her*

Ezekiel's wife dies

¹⁵The Lord's word came to me: ¹⁶Human one, I am about to take the delight of your eyes away from you in a single stroke. Don't mourn or weep. Don't even let your tears well up. ¹⁷Sigh inwardly; be deathly still. Don't perform mourning rites, but bind on your turban and put your shoes on your feet. And don't cover your upper lip or eat in human company.

¹⁸I spoke with the people in the morning, and by evening my wife was dead. The next morning I did as I was commanded. ¹⁹The people asked, "Won't you tell us what your actions mean for us?"

²⁰So I said to them, The Lord's word came to me: ²¹Say to the house of Israel, the Lord God proclaims: I'm about to make my sanctuary impure, the pride of your strength, the delight of your eyes. Your heart's desire, the sons and daughters you left behind, will fall by the sword. ²²You will do as I have done. You will neither cover your upper lip nor eat in human company. ²³Your turbans will be on your heads, your sandals on your feet. You won't mourn or weep. You will waste away in your guilt, all of you groaning to each other. ²⁴Ezekiel is your sign. You will do everything that he has done. When this happens, you will know that I am the Lord God.

²⁵And you, human one: On the day that I take from them their proud stronghold—their crowning joy, the delight of their eyes—and their sons and daughters, whose fate weighs on them, ²⁶on that day, a refugee will come to you so that you yourself will hear the news. ²⁷On that day your mouth will be opened to the refugee, and you will speak and no longer be silent. You will be their sign, and they will know that I am the Lord.

Against the neighboring nations

25 The Lord's word came to me: ²Human one, face the Ammonites and prophesy against them. ³Say to the Ammonites: Hear the Lord God's word! The Lord God proclaims:

You laughed when my sanctuary was degraded, when Israel's fertile land was laid waste, and when the house of Judah went into exile; ⁴therefore, I'm handing you over to people in the east for them to take possession. They will set up their encampments against you, establish residence, devour your fruit, and drink your milk. ⁵I'll make Rabbah into pastureland for camels and Ammon a resting place for flocks. Then you will know that I am the Lord.

⁶The Lord God proclaims: Because you clapped your hands and stamped your feet when you rejoiced with utter contempt for Israel's fertile land, ⁷I'm about to overpower you. Nations will plunder you. I will cut you off from the peoples, remove you from the lands, and utterly destroy you. Then you will know that I am the Lord.

⁸The Lord God proclaims: Because Moab and Seir say, "Aha! The house of Judah has become like all the nations," ⁹I'll open up the flank of Moab from the cities at its border, the land's splendid cities, Beth-jeshimoth, Baal-meon, and Kiriathaim. ¹⁰I'll hand it over, along with the Ammonites, to people in the east for them to take possession. And so Ammon will no longer be remembered among the nations. ¹¹I'll execute judgments in Moab, and they will know that I am the Lord.

¹²The Lord God proclaims: Edom acted with excessive force against the house of Judah. The Judeans were guilty, but Edom's vengeance was excessive. ¹³So the Lord God now proclaims: I'll overpower Edom, eliminate all living creatures, and make it a wasteland from Teman to Dedan. They will fall by the sword. ¹⁴I will execute my vengeance in Edom through my people Israel's power. They will act in Edom according to my anger and fury, and they will know my vengeance. This is what the Lord God says.

¹⁵The Lord God proclaims: When the Philistines set out to right the wrongs done to them, they enacted revenge with utter contempt and old hatreds. ¹⁶So now the Lord God proclaims: I will overpower the Philistines, eliminate the Cherethites, and obliterate all who are left along the coastline. ¹⁷I will act

against them with great vengeance and with wrathful punishments. When I execute my vengeance against them, they will know that I am the Lord.

Against Tyre

26 In the eleventh year, on the first day of the month, the Lord's word came to me:

² Human one,
  because Tyre laughed at Jerusalem:
"The gate of the peoples is broken,
  she lies open before me,
  she is destroyed, but I will succeed!"

³The Lord God now proclaims:
Tyre, I'm now against you!
Just as the sea hurls up its waves,
  I will bring many nations up against you.
⁴ When they destroy the walls of Tyre
  and throw down its towers,
I will scrape off all its dirt
  and make it into a bare rock,
⁵ a place for drying nets
  in the middle of the sea.
I have spoken!
This is what the Lord God says.
It will become prey for the nations,
⁶ and its towns around it
  will be put to the sword.
    Then they will know that I am the Lord.

⁷ The Lord God proclaims:
I'm bringing Nebuchadrezzar against Tyre,
  the king of Babylon from the north,
  the greatest of all kings,
  with horses, chariots, and charioteers,
  an assembly, a great army.
⁸ The towns around you
  he will destroy with the sword.
  Then he will build towers against you,
  erect siege ramps against you,
    and set up shields.
⁹ He will pound his battering ram
  against your walls;
  with crowbars he will tear down
    your towers.
¹⁰ The dust from all his horses will cover you
  when he enters your gates
  as one who enters a breached city.

Your walls will quake
  at the thundering of the charioteers
    and chariot wheels.
¹¹ His horses' hooves will trample
  all your courtyards;
  he will cut down your people
    with the sword,
  and the monuments to your strength
    he will bring down† to the ground.
¹² They will destroy your wealth,
  plunder your goods,
  tear down your walls,
    and raze your fine houses.
  Your stone, lumber, and rubble
    they will dump into the sea.

¹³ I will bring an end
  to your cacophonous songs;
  the sound of your lyres
    will never be heard again.
¹⁴ I will make you into a bare rock,
  a place for drying nets,
    and you will never be rebuilt.
  I, the Lord, have spoken.
    This is what the Lord God says.

A lament for Tyre

¹⁵The Lord God proclaims to Tyre: Won't the coastlands quake at the news of your downfall, when the wounded groan, and when the slaughter in your midst goes on and on? ¹⁶All the princes of the sea will come down from their thrones, remove their royal robes, and strip off their fine garments. They will be clothed only in terror as they sit on the ground. They will be so terrified, they won't stop shuddering because of you. ¹⁷They will sing a lament for you, and they will say:

How you have perished, queen of the sea,
  city once praised,
  who once dominated the sea,
  she and her rulers,
  who spread their terror abroad,
    every one of them.
¹⁸ Now the wastelands tremble
  on the day of your fall.
  Your expulsion horrifies
    the islands of the sea.
¹⁹The Lord God proclaims: When I turn you into ruins like uninhabitable cities, when

† LXX; MT *it will fall*

the deep sea washes over you and the raging seas cover you, ²⁰I will lead you down into the pit, to the everlasting people. I will install you in the world below,ᵘ in the everlasting ruins, with those who go down to the pit. And so you will neither rule nor radiate splendor in the land of the living. ²¹I will terrify you, and you will disappear. You will be sought but never found again. This is what the LORD God says.

Tyre, the ship of state

27 The LORD's word came to me: ²You, human one, sing a lament for Tyre. ³Say this about Tyre, who sits enthroned at the entrance to the sea, the people's agent for trade throughout the coastlands. The LORD God proclaims:

Tyre, you say,
"I'm perfectly beautiful!"
⁴ But your territory is
in the depths of the sea,
and it's your builders
who made you beautiful.
⁵ For you they made your deck
of cypress from Senir.
To make your mast,
they took cedar from Lebanon.
⁶ For your oars,
they used the oaks of Bashan.
They made your hull, inlaid with ivory,
of boxwood from the coasts of Cyprus.
⁷ Fine embroidered linen from Egypt
was your sail;
it became your emblem.
Your awning was made of blue and
purple cloth from the coasts of Elishah.

⁸The princes of Sidon and Arvad were your oarsmen. Your own wise men were in you as your helmsmen. ⁹The elders and wise men of Gebal were in you, patching up your leaks. Every seagoing ship and its sailors came to do business with you. ¹⁰Paras, Lud, and Put were the warriors in your army. By hanging their shields and helmets on you, they made you radiant. ¹¹The men of Arvad and Helech were stationed on your walls all around; the men of Gamad were in your towers. They hung their weapons on your walls all around. They were the ones who completed your beauty.

¹²Tarshish was your procurer of great wealth. For your wares, they exchanged silver, iron, tin, and lead. ¹³Javan, Tubal, and Meshech were your agents in human trafficking. They gave you bronze vessels for these wares of yours. ¹⁴Beth-togarmah traded horses, warhorses, and mules for your wares. ¹⁵Islanders from Rhodesᵛ were your agents. By contract they procured ebony and ivory

did you know? Tyre was one of the wealthiest, most successful cities of the ancient world. It was a port city with lots of trade. People went there from all over Europe, Africa, and Asia to buy and sell things, including metals, animals, spices, clothing, rugs, and jewels.

for you from many coastlands. ¹⁶Aram was your agent for many products. They traded turquoise, purple cloth, colorful brocades, linen, coral, and rubies for your wares. ¹⁷Judah and the land of Israel were your agents, trading the finest wheat,ʷ millet,ˣ honey, oil, and balm for your wares. ¹⁸For many of your finished products, Damascus traded out of its great wealth the wine of Helbon and white wool. ¹⁹Vedan and Javan from the region of Uzal traded with you. They exchanged wrought iron, cinnamon, and spices for your wares. ²⁰Dedan was your agent for saddle blankets. ²¹Arabia and all the princes of Kedar traded for you. They procured lambs, rams, and goats for you. ²²They were your agents in Sheba and Raamah. For your wares they exchanged the finest spices, every kind of precious stone, and gold. ²³Haran, Canneh, and Eden were your agents,ʸ and also Assyria and Chilmad. ²⁴They procured fine finished goods for you, garments of purple and brocade, and plush carpets rolled up and securely tied with ropes, among your acquisitions. ²⁵The ships of Tarshish carried your goods.

You were filled to capacity
and heavily laden
in the middle of the sea.
²⁶ Your oarsmen brought you out
onto the high seas;
an east wind sank you
into the sea's depths.

ᵘOr the land of the lowest places ᵛHeb Dedan ʷOr wheat from Minnith ˣHeb uncertain ʸLXX; MT adds Sheba.

27 Your goods, your wares, your wealth,
   your sailors, your helmsmen,
     those patching your leaks,
   your merchants, all your warriors in you,
   and all the company that is with you—
     they also sank into the sea's depth
       on the day of your demise.
28 At your helmsmen's cries for help,
   the troubled waters seethe.
29 Those entrusted with the oars
   desert their posts.
   All sailors and helmsmen
     seek footing on the shore.
30 Loudly they cry,
   bitterly they wail,
   and they put dust on their heads
   and cover themselves with ashes.

UMBRELLA
MOURNING

Covered with Ashes   Ezekiel 27:30

In ancient times, people often used ashes to show mourning, sorrow, and that they were fasting. When they were grieving or suffering, they placed ashes on their heads or they sat in ashes.

The Israelites lost many things. Most important, they lost their relationship with God. Though they had already lost everything that was important to them, they would see even more destruction. Ezekiel warned they would mourn because one of the greatest cities known to them would fall. They needed to put their trust in God. ⬥

31 They cut off all their hair
   and put on mourning clothes.
   In despair they weep for you,
     and bitterly perform the mourning rites.
32 In their lamentation
     they raise a lament for you;
     they sing lamentions over you:
     "Who was like Tyre,
       silenced in the middle of the sea?"
33 When your wares came out from the seas,
   you satisfied many people.
   Your abundant wealth and merchandise
     enriched the kings of the earth.
34 Now you are shattered by the seas;
   your cargoes,
     as well as everyone in your company,

are sunk into the water's depths.
35 Now the inhabitants of the coastlands
   shudder on account of you.
   And as for their kings,
     their hair stands on end;
     their faces betray their horror.
36 The merchants for the peoples
   hiss because of you.
   You have become a terror;
     from now on you are nothing.

Prince of Tyre

28 The LORD's word came to me: 2Human one, say to the prince of Tyre, The LORD God proclaims: In your arrogance, you say, "I am God, and as God I rule the seas!" Though you claim to have the mind of a god, you are mortal, not divine. 3You are certainly wiser than Daniel; no secrets are hidden from you. 4By your wisdom and discernment, you made yourself rich, and you filled your storehouses with silver and gold. 5Through your shrewd trading you multiplied your riches. But then you became proud of your riches.

6So now the LORD God proclaims: Because you claim to have the mind of a god, 7I'll bring foreigners, the most ruthless nations, against you. They will let loose their swords against your fine wisdom, and they will degrade your splendor. 8They will hurl you to destruction, and you will die, murdered, on the high seas. 9When you face your murderers, will you still say, "I'm God"? In your killers' hands, you are mortal, not divine. 10You will die as the uncircumcised do, at the hands of foreigners. I have spoken. This is what the LORD God has said.

11The LORD's word came to me: 12Human one, sing a lament for the king of Tyre. Say to him, The LORD God proclaims: You were full of wisdom and beauty, the image of perfection. 13You were in Eden, God's garden. You were covered with gold and every precious stone: carnelian, topaz, and moonstone; beryl, onyx, and jasper; lapis lazuli, turquoise, and emerald. On the day that you were created, finely crafted pendants and engravings were prepared. 14You, a winged creature, were installed as a guardian. I placed you in God's holy mountain where you walked among the stones of fire. 15From the day you were created until injustice was found in you, your ways were assured. 16But because of your trade, your oppressive business practices piled up, and you became impure. So I expelled you from God's mountain. I removed you, winged creature, guardian, from among the stones of fire. [17]You exalted yourself because of your beauty and corrupted your wisdom for the sake of your splendor. I will cast you down to the earth in the sight of kings, and I will make a spectacle of you. [18]Because of your corrupt trade, which surpassed your many other sins, you made your sanctuaries impure. Therefore, I will bring fire from your midst. When it has consumed you, I will turn you into dust on the earth in the sight of all who see you. [19]Everyone among the peoples who knows you will be appalled because of you. You will become a terror. From that time on, you will be nothing.

Against Sidon

[20]The Lord's word came to me: [21]Human one, face Sidon, prophesy against it, [22]and say, The Lord God proclaims: I'm against you, Sidon, and I will manifest my glory in you. When I've executed judgment against it and through it have manifested my holiness, they will know that I am the Lord. [23]I will hurl plague against it, and blood will run in its streets. When the sword comes against it from all sides, the slain will fall within it. Then they will know that I am the Lord. [24]The house of Israel will no longer suffer from the pricking thorn or painful briar of any of its neighbors who hold it in contempt. And they will know that I am the Lord God.

[25]The Lord God proclaims: When I gather the house of Israel from the peoples among whom they've scattered, and I demonstrate my holiness through them in the sight of the nations, they will live on their fertile land, which I gave to my servant Jacob. [26]They will live on it in safety. They will build houses, plant vineyards, and live in safety. When I execute judgments against all who hold them in contempt on every side, they will know that I, the Lord, am their God.

Against Egypt

29 In the tenth year, on the twelfth day of the tenth month, the Lord's word came to me: [2]Human one, face Pharaoh, Egypt's king, and prophesy against him and against all of Egypt. [3]Speak and say, The Lord God proclaims:

I'm against you, Pharaoh, Egypt's king,
  great crocodile lurking
  in the Nile's canals,
    who says, "The Nile is all mine;
    I made it for myself!"
[4] I will set hooks in your jaws;
  I will make the fish
    from the Nile's canals
    cling to your scales.
  I will drag you out of the Nile's canals,
    and also all the fish
    from the Nile's canals
    clinging to your scales.
    [5] I will fling you out into the desert,
    and also all the fish
      from the Nile's canals.
  You will fall on the open ground,
    and won't be gathered or retrieved.

I've given you to the beasts of the earth
  and the birds in the sky for food.
[6] Everyone living in Egypt
  will know that I am the Lord.

Because they were a flimsy crutch for the house of Israel—[7]when they took you in hand, you would splinter and make their shoulders sore; when they leaned on you, you would break, bringing them to their knees—[8]now the Lord God proclaims: I'm bringing a sword against you, and I will cut off from you human and beast. [9]The land of Egypt will be turned into a wasteland and ruins. Then they will know that I am the Lord.

Because you[z] said, "The Nile is mine; I made it," [10]I'm against you and against the Nile's canals. I will make the land of Egypt into an utter ruin, a wasteland, from Migdol to Syene and as far as its boundary with Cush. [11]No foot, animal or human, will walk across it, and it won't be inhabited for forty years. [12]I will make the land of Egypt the most desolate of wastelands and its cities the most devastated of ruined cities. It will be a wasteland for forty years, and the Egyptians will be scattered among the nations and dispersed throughout the lands.

[13]The Lord God proclaims: At the end of

[z]Or he

forty years, I will gather the Egyptians from among the nations where they are scattered. [14] I will improve their circumstances and bring them back to the land of Pathros, the land of their origin. Egypt will be a lowly kingdom there. [15] Out of all the kingdoms, it will be the lowliest. It will never again exalt itself over the nations, and I will make it small to keep it from ruling the nations. [16] The house of Israel will never again bring guilt on itself by faithlessly turning to Egypt for help, for they will know that I am the Lord God.

[17] In the twenty-seventh year, on the first day of the first month, the Lord's word came to me: [18] Human one, Babylon's King Nebuchadrezzar made his army labor very hard against Tyre. Every head was scraped bald, and every shoulder was rubbed raw, yet he got nothing from Tyre for himself or for his army for any of his efforts against it. [19] So now the Lord God proclaims: I'm going to give the land of Egypt to Babylon's King Nebuchadrezzar. He will carry off its wealth, he will plunder and loot it, and it will be the wages for his army. [20] I will give him the land of Egypt as payment for his laboring for me. This is what the Lord God says.

[21] On that day I will give new strength[a] to the house of Israel, and I will open your mouth among them. Then they will know that I am the Lord.

30

The Lord's word came to me: [2] Human one, prophesy and say, The Lord God proclaims:

Howl! Horror for the day!
[3] The day is coming,
    the day of the Lord comes,
    a day of clouds;
        the nations' time has come.
[4] A sword will come into Egypt,
    and trembling will overcome Cush,
    when the slain fall in Egypt,
    its wealth carried away,
    and its foundations razed.
[5] Cush, Put, and Lud,
    all Arabia and Cub,
    and the people from
        the allied country[b] with them
    will fall by the sword.

[6] The Lord proclaims:
    When Egypt's helpers fall,
    its proud strength will decline.
    From Migdol to Syene
    they will fall by the sword.
    This is what the Lord God says.

[7] Of all the lands laid waste, it will be the most desolate; of all cities, the most ruined. [8] They will know that I am the Lord. On the day that I set fire to Egypt and all its helpers are broken, [9] messengers in ships will go out from me to startle the complacent Cushites. Anguish will overcome them on Egypt's day. It's certainly coming.

[10] The Lord God proclaims:
    I will bring an end to the hordes of Egypt
        through the power
        of Babylon's King Nebuchadrezzar.
[11] He and his people with him,
        the most terrible of the nations,
    will be brought in to destroy the land.
    They will draw their swords
        against Egypt
    and fill the land with the slain.
[12] I will dry up the Nile canals;
    I will sell the land to evildoers.
    With the help of foreigners
    I will lay waste to the land
    and everything in it.
    I, the Lord, have spoken.

[13] The Lord God proclaims:
    I will destroy the idols
        and bring an end to the images
        in Memphis.
    Never again will there be
        a prince from the land of Egypt;
    so I will kindle fear in the land of Egypt.
[14] I will turn Pathros into a desolation,
    set fire to Zoan,
        and execute judgments in Thebes.
[15] I will pour out my anger on Pelusium,
    the stronghold of Egypt,
    and I will cut down pompous Thebes.
[16] I will set Egypt on fire;
    Pelusium will writhe in travail,
    Thebes will be split open,
    Memphis assaulted in broad daylight.
[17] The elite troops of On and Pi-beseth
    will fall by the sword,

---

[a] Or *make a horn sprout* [b] Or *land of the covenant*

and the cities themselves
will go into captivity.

¹⁸At Tehaphnehes the day will go dark when I break Egypt's yoke and bring an end to its proud strength. A cloud will cover it, and the towns around it will go into captivity. ¹⁹I will execute judgments in Egypt, and they will know that I am the Lord.

²⁰In the eleventh year, on the seventh day of the first month, the Lord's word came to me: ²¹Human one, I've broken the arm of Pharaoh, Egypt's king, and it hasn't been set so that it might heal, nor has it been braced or wrapped up so that it might be strong enough to grasp a sword.

²²So now the Lord God proclaims: I'm against Pharaoh, and I will break his arms, both the sound one and the broken one, and I'll make the sword fall out of his hand. ²³I will scatter the Egyptians among the nations and disperse them throughout the earth. ²⁴I will strengthen the arms of the king of Babylon, and I will put my sword into his hand. When I break the arms of Pharaoh, he will groan like a dying man in his presence. ²⁵I will strengthen the arms of the king of Babylon, but the arms of Pharaoh will fall. They will know that I am the Lord, when I put my sword into the hand of the king of Babylon and he uses it against the land of Egypt. ²⁶When I scatter the Egyptians among the nations and disperse them throughout the earth, they will know that I am the Lord.

Egypt is not Assyria

31 In the eleventh year, on the first day of the third month, the Lord's word came to me: ²Human one, say to Pharaoh, Egypt's king, and his troops:

With whom do you compare
in your greatness?
³ Consider Assyria, a cedar of Lebanon:
beautiful branches, dense shade,
towering height;
indeed, its top went up
between the clouds.
⁴ Waters nourished it; the deep raised it up,
because its streams flowed around
the place where it was planted.
From there, water trickled down
to all the other trees of the field.

⁵ And so it became higher than
all the trees of the field.
Its branches became abundant;
its boughs grew long.
Because of the plentiful water,
it grew freely.
⁶ All the birds in the sky
made nests in its branches;
all the beasts of the field
gave birth under its boughs,
and in its shade, every great nation lived.
⁷ It became beautiful in its greatness
and in its lush foliage,
because it took root in plentiful water.
⁸ No cedar was its equal in God's garden.
The fir trees didn't have anything
like its branches,
and the plane trees had nothing
like its boughs.
None of the trees in God's garden
could compare to it in its beauty.
⁹ As for its beauty—I made it so,
with its abundant foliage.
All the trees of Eden envied it,
all that were in God's garden.

¹⁰So now the Lord God proclaims:
Consider the fate of those who tower high!
When it allowed its branches to reach up
among the clouds,
it became arrogant.
¹¹ So I handed it over
to the most powerful nation,
who continually
acted treacherously against it.
I banished it!
¹² Foreigners, the worst of the nations,
cut it down
and left it to lie among the hills.
All its branches fell among the valleys,
and its boughs were broken off
in the earth's deep ravines.
All the earth's peoples departed
from its shade and abandoned it.
¹³ On its trunk roost all the birds in the sky,
and on its boughs lie
all the beasts of the field.

¹⁴All this has happened so that no other well-watered tree would tower high or allow its branches to reach among the clouds. Nor would their leaders achieve the towering stature of such well-watered trees. Certainly,

all of them are consigned to death, to the world below,[c] among human beings who go down to the pit.

[15] The Lord God proclaims: On the day that it went down to the underworld,[d] I caused mourning. I blocked off the deep sea against it. I dried up its rivers and restrained the mighty waters. I made Lebanon go into mourning for it, and all the trees of the field languished on its account. [16] When it was felled, the nations quaked at the sound. When I cast it down into the underworld, with those who go down to the pit, all the trees of Eden were comforted in the world below, the choicest and the best of Lebanon, all the trees that depended on water. [17] His allies,[e] those among the nations who lived under his shade, these also went down with him to the underworld, to those who are slain by the sword.

[18] Are you like any of these in glory or greatness among Eden's trees? Then you too will go down with Eden's trees to the world below. You will lie among the uncircumcised, with those who are slain by the sword. This is Pharaoh and his entire horde. This is what the Lord God says.

Egypt the crocodile

32 In the twelfth year, on the first day of the twelfth month, the Lord's word came to me: [2] Human one, sing a lament for Pharaoh, Egypt's king. Say to him:

You consider yourself a young lion
  among the nations,
  but you are like the sea monster!
You thrash about in your rivers,
  you roil the waters with your feet,
  and you muddy your[f] rivers.
[3] The Lord God proclaims:
In the company of many peoples
  I will spread my net over you,
  and I will haul you up in my dragnet.
[4] I will cast you out on the earth
  and throw you on the open ground.
I will cause all the birds in the sky
  to settle on you,
  and all the beasts of the earth
  to devour you.
[5] Your flesh I will set upon the mountains,

and I will fill the valleys with your gore.
[6] With your blood I will soak
  your irrigated land,[g]
  and the streambeds
  will be filled with you.
[7] When you are snuffed out,
  I will cover the sky,
  and I will darken the stars.
I will cover the sun with a cloud,
  and the moon won't radiate its light.
[8] As for the shining lights of the heavens,
  I will make them dark over you,
  and set darkness over your land.
  This is what the Lord God says.

[9] I will trouble the hearts of many peoples
  when I bring about your destruction
  with nations from lands you didn't know.
[10] I will make many peoples appalled
  because of you.
  Their kings will shudder violently
  on your account
  when I brandish my sword before them.
They will tremble for their lives
  again and again
  on the day of your downfall.
[11] The Lord God proclaims: The sword of the king of Babylon is coming against you! [12] I will make your hordes fall by the swords of mighty men, the most terrifying of the nations, all of them. They will bring an end to Egypt's pride, and all of its hordes will be destroyed. [13] I will remove all its livestock from beside the plentiful waters so that neither human foot nor livestock's hoof will trouble it again. [14] At that time, I will allow the waters to run clear, and make its rivers flow like oil. This is what the Lord God says. [15] When I turn the land of Egypt into a wasteland and the land is deprived of all that fills it, and when I strike down those who live there, then they will know that I am the Lord. [16] This is a lament, and it will be sung as a lament. The daughters of the nations will lament for Egypt, and they will also lament for Egypt's hordes. This is what the Lord God says.

[17] In the twelfth year, on the fifteenth day of the first month,[h] the Lord's word came to me: [18] Human one, mourn for Egypt's hordes.

[c] Or the land of the lowest places [d] Heb Sheol [e] Or his arms [f] LXX; MT their [g] MT adds to the mountains. [h] LXX; MT lacks the first month.

Send Egypt down
with the mighty nations subject[i] to it,
to the world below,[j]
among those who go down to the pit.
[19] Whom do you surpass in beauty?
Go down and take your bed
with the uncircumcised,
[20] among those who fall slain by the sword.
A sword is appointed, and all his hordes
will carry him off. [21]The mighty chieftains,
those who once came to his aid, will speak to
him from the middle of the underworld,[k] for
the uncircumcised have gone down and have
lain down, slain by the sword.

Vanished glory

[22] Assyria is there, and all its assembly
round about his grave,
all of them slain, fallen by the sword,
[23] who were assigned graves
in the deepest region of the pit.
His assembly surrounded his grave,
all of them slain, fallen by the sword,
who caused terror
in the land of the living.

[24] Elam is there, her entire horde
round about her grave,
all of them slain, fallen by the sword,
who went down uncircumcised
to the world below,[l]
who caused terror
in the land of the living.
They bore their shame
like those who go down to the pit.
[25] Among the slain they made a bed for her,
with all her hordes round about her grave,
all of them uncircumcised,
slain by the sword,
for they caused terror
in the land of the living.
They bore their shame
like those who go down to the pit;
in the midst of the slain she[m] was placed.

[26] Meshech and Tubal are there,
and all their hordes around their graves,
all of them uncircumcised,
slain by the sword,
for they caused terror
in the land of the living.

[27] They don't lie with the mighty men fallen
among the uncircumcised. When they went
down to the underworld[n] with their weapons of war, they put their swords under their
heads and their shields[o] over their bones.
The terror of the mighty men is in the land of
the living.
[28] But you, you will be broken among the
uncircumcised, and you will lie with those
who are slain by the sword.
[29] Edom is there, its kings and all its princes,
who, though strong,
were put with those slain
by the sword.
They lie with the uncircumcised,
like those who go down to the pit.

[30] All the princes of the north are there,
and all the Sidonians
who went down with the slain;
in spite of the terror of their strength,
they were disgraced.
They lie uncircumcised with
those slain by the sword.
They bore their shame
like those who go down to the pit.

[31] When Pharaoh sees them,
he will be sorry for all his hordes
who are slain by the sword—
Pharaoh and all his army.
This is what the LORD God says,
[32] Though it was I who put his terror
in the land of the living,
he will be laid out
among the uncircumcised,
with those slain by the sword,
Pharaoh and all his horde.
This is what the LORD God says.

The lookout

33 The LORD's word came to me: [2]Human
one, speak to your people and say to
them: Suppose I bring a sword against a country, and the people of the land take a certain
person from their assembly and make him
their lookout. [3]When he sees the sword coming against the land, he blows the trumpet
and warns the people. [4]If they hear the sound
of the trumpet but don't heed the warning,

---

[i]Or daughter nations [j]Or the land of the lowest places [k]Heb Sheol [l]Or the land of the lowest places [m]Or he [n]Heb Sheol [o]Or sin

when the sword comes and they are taken away, they are responsible for their blood. [5]They heard the sound of the trumpet but didn't heed the warning, so their blood is on them. If they had paid attention to the warning, they would have saved their lives. [6]If the lookout sees the sword coming but doesn't blow the trumpet to warn the people, when the sword comes and takes away any of them, they are taken away in their sin, but I'll hold the lookout responsible for their blood.

[7]You, human one, I've made you a lookout for the house of Israel. Whenever you hear me speaking, you must give them warning from me. [8]If I pronounce a death sentence on wicked people, and you don't warn them to turn from their way, they will die in their guilt, but I will hold you responsible for their blood. [9]But suppose you do warn the wicked of their ways so that they might turn from them. If they don't turn from their ways, they will die in their guilt, but you will save your life.

[10]You, human one, say to the house of Israel: This is what all of you are saying: "How our transgressions and our sins weigh on us! We waste away because of them. How can we live?" [11]Say to them, This is what the Lord God says: As surely as I live, do I take pleasure in the death of the wicked? If the wicked turn from their ways, they will live. Turn, completely turn from your wicked ways! Why should you die, house of Israel?

[12]You, human one, say to your people: The righteousness of the righteous doesn't rescue them when they begin to sin. Nor does the wickedness of the wicked make them stumble if they turn from their wickedness. If the righteous sin, their righteousness won't protect them. [13]Even if I've told the righteous they will live, none of their righteous deeds will be remembered if they trust in their righteousness and do wrong. They will die because of their evil deeds. [14]And even if I have pronounced a death sentence on the wicked, if they turn from sin and do what is just and right—[15]if they return pledges, make restitution for robbery, and walk in life-giving regulations in order not to sin—they will live and not die. [16]None of the sins they've committed

will be remembered against them. They've done what is just and right, and they will live.

[17]Yet your people say, "My Lord's way doesn't measure up." Isn't it their ways that don't measure up? [18]When the righteous turn from their righteousness to do wrong, they will die because of it. [19]And when the wicked turn from their wickedness to do what is just and right, it is for that reason they will live. [20]Yet you say, "My Lord's way doesn't measure up." I judge each one of you according to your ways, house of Israel!

News from Jerusalem

[21]In the twelfth year, on the fifth day of the tenth month of our exile, a survivor from Jerusalem came to me and reported, "The city has fallen!" [22]The Lord's power was with me in the evening before the survivor arrived, and just before he arrived in the morning, God opened my mouth. So my mouth was opened, and I was no longer speechless.

Some of the Israelites were saying that God took pleasure in killing wicked people, or the enemies of the Israelites. This passage makes clear that God never takes pleasure in death. Instead, God's hope is always that people stop sinning and turn to God.

[23]The Lord's word came to me: [24]Human one, those who live among those ruins in Israel's fertile land are saying, "Abraham was just one man, and he inherited the land. We are many, so certainly the land has been given to us as an inheritance."

[25]So say to them, The Lord God proclaims: You eat with the blood, you lift your eyes to the idols, and you shed blood. Should you inherit the land? [26]You live by the sword, you observe detestable practices, and every one of you commits adultery.[p] Should you inherit the land?

[27]Say to them, The Lord God proclaims: As surely as I live, those in the ruins will fall by the sword, those in the countryside I will give to the wild beasts to consume, and those in the strongholds and caves will die of plague. [28]I will make the land an uninhabitable waste.

[p]Or *defiles his neighbor's wife*

Its proud strength will come to an end, and Israel's highlands will become so deserted that no one will cross through them. [29]They will know that I am the LORD when I make the land an uninhabitable waste because of all their detestable practices.

A fickle audience

[30]As for you, human one, your people talk about you beside the walls and in their doorways. One by one, they say to each other, "Let's go hear what sort of message has come from the LORD." [31]So they come to you as people do, and they sit before you as my people. They listen to your words, but they refuse to do them. Though they speak of their longing[q] for me, they act out of their own interests and opinions. [32]To them you are like a singer of love songs with a lovely voice and skilled technique. They listen to your words, but no one does them. [33]When this comes—and it is certainly coming—they will know that a prophet has been among them.

The good shepherd

34 The LORD's word came to me: [2]Human one, prophesy against Israel's shepherds. Prophesy and say to them, The LORD God proclaims to the shepherds: Doom to Israel's shepherds who tended themselves! Shouldn't shepherds tend the flock? [3]You drink the milk, you wear the wool, and you slaughter the fat animals, but you don't tend the flock. [4]You don't strengthen the weak, heal the sick, bind up the injured, bring back the strays, or seek out the lost; but instead you use force to rule them with injustice. [5]Without a shepherd, my flock was scattered; and when it was scattered, it became food for all the wild animals. [6]My flock strayed on all the mountains and on every high hill throughout all the earth. My flock was scattered, and there was no one to look for them or find them. [7]So now shepherds, hear the LORD's word! [8]This is what the LORD God says: As surely as I live, without a shepherd, my flock became prey. My flock became food for all the wild animals. My shepherds didn't seek out my flock. They tended themselves, but they didn't tend my flock.

[9]So, shepherds, hear the LORD's word! [10]The LORD God proclaims: I'm against the shepherds! I will hold them accountable for my flock, and I will put an end to their tending the flock. The shepherds will no longer tend them, because I will rescue my flock from their mouths, and they will no longer be their food.

[11]The LORD God proclaims: I myself will search for my flock and seek them out. [12]As a shepherd seeks out the flock when some in the flock have been scattered, so will I seek out my flock. I will rescue them from all the places where they were scattered during the time of clouds and thick darkness. [13]I will gather and lead them out from the countries and peoples, and I will bring them to their own fertile land. I will feed them on Israel's highlands, along the riverbeds, and in all the inhabited places. [14]I will feed them in good pasture, and their sheepfold will be there, on Israel's lofty highlands. On Israel's highlands, they will lie down in a secure fold and feed on green pastures. [15]I myself will feed my flock and make them lie down. This is what the LORD God says. [16]I will seek out the lost, bring back the strays, bind up the wounded, and strengthen the weak. But the fat and the strong I will destroy, because I will tend my sheep[r] with justice.

[17]As for you, my flock, the LORD God proclaims: I will judge between the rams and the bucks among the sheep and the goats. [18]Is feeding in good pasture or drinking clear water such a trivial thing that you should trample and muddy what is left with your

LIFE PRESERVER

Where else do we read about God as a shepherd?
Ezekiel 34:11-16

This passage reminds us of Psalm 23 because of the language about sheep and the shepherd. It also reminds us of the Gospel of John, where Jesus is described as the good shepherd (John 10:1-18). Here Ezekiel contrasted God, the good shepherd, with false shepherds. He made clear that God, the good shepherd, is always concerned for all the sheep. ◆

---

[q]Or love songs [r]Or them

feet? ¹⁹But now my flock must feed on what your feet have trampled and drink water that your feet have muddied.

²⁰So the Lord God proclaims to them: I will judge between the fat and the lean sheep. ²¹You shove with shoulder and flank, and with your horns you ram all the weak sheep until you've scattered them outside. ²²But I will rescue my flock so that they will never again be prey. I will even judge between the sheep! ²³I will appoint for them a single shepherd, and he will feed them. My servant David will feed them. He will be their shepherd. ²⁴I, the Lord, will be their God, and my servant David will be their prince. I, the Lord, have spoken. ²⁵I will make a covenant of peace for them, and I will banish the wild animals from the land. Then they will safely live in the desert and sleep in the forest. ²⁶I will give them and those around my hill a blessing by sending the rain in its season. They will be rains of blessing. ²⁷The trees in the field will bear fruit, and the earth will yield its harvest. They will be safe on their fertile land, and they will know that I am the Lord when I break the bars of their yoke and deliver them from those who enslaved them. ²⁸The nations will no longer prey on them, and wild animals will no longer devour them. They will live in safety, with no one to trouble them. ²⁹I will establish for them a place famous for what it grows. No longer will they experience famine in the land, nor will they bear the disgrace of the nations. ³⁰They will know that I, the Lord their God, am with them, and they, the house of Israel, are my people. This is what the Lord God says. ³¹You are my flock, the flock of my pasture. You are human, and I am your God. This is what the Lord God says.

Against Edom

35The Lord's word came to me: ²Human one, face Mount Seir, and prophesy against it. ³Say to it, The Lord God proclaims:

I'm against you, Mount Seir!
   I will use my power against you.
I will make you into a desolate wasteland,
⁴ I will turn your cities into ruins,
   and you will become a desolation.
Then you will know that I am the Lord.

⁵Because you nursed an ancient grudge, you handed the Israelites over to the sword

in the time of their distress, during their final punishment. ⁶So now the Lord God proclaims: As surely as I live, I will prepare you for blood, and blood will pursue you. Because you don't hate bloodshed, bloodshed will pursue you. ⁷I will turn Mount Seir into a desolate wasteland, when I cut off from it both passerby and homecomer. ⁸I will fill its highlands—your hills and your valleys, and all your ravines—with its slain. Those who are slain by the sword will fall on them. ⁹I will turn you into an eternal desolation. Your cities won't be inhabited, and you will know that I am the Lord.

¹⁰You said, "These two nations and these two territories are mine. We will take possession of them even if the Lord is there." ¹¹Therefore, the Lord God proclaims: As surely as I live, I will act according to the anger and zeal you displayed when you dealt with them so hatefully. When I judge you, I will make myself known to them, ¹²and you will know that I am the Lord. I've heard the lies and libels that you uttered against Israel's highlands when you said, "They are laid waste. They've been given to us to consume." ¹³With your mouths you exalted yourselves against me and spoke your words against me. I myself heard it!

¹⁴The Lord God proclaims: As the whole world rejoices, I will turn you into a desolation. ¹⁵Just as you rejoiced over the house of Israel's inheritance because it became desolate, so I will deal with you. Mount Seir, you will become a desolation, with all of Edom, all of it. Then they will know that I am the Lord.

Mountains of Israel

36You, human one, prophesy to Israel's mountains and say, Hear the Lord's word, mountains of Israel! ²The Lord God proclaims: The enemy mocked you and said, "The ancient heights belong to us." ³Therefore, prophesy and say, The Lord God proclaims: When the surviving nations pressed in and ravaged you from all around to lay claim to you, you became an object of the people's slander and derision. ⁴Hear the Lord God's word, mountains of Israel! The Lord God proclaims to the mountains and the hills, the watercourses and the valleys, the desolate ruins and the abandoned cities that were contemptuously looted by the surviving nations all around you.

⁵So now, says the Lᴏʀᴅ God, I will speak in my fiery passion against the surviving nations and against Edom, all those who gleefully and spitefully took my land for themselves as a possession only for plunder.ˢ ⁶Prophesy concerning Israel's fertile land, and say to the mountains and to the hills, to the ravines and to the valleys, The Lᴏʀᴅ God proclaims: Because you endured the ridicule of the nations, my passion and fury lead me to speak. ⁷So now the Lᴏʀᴅ God proclaims: I myself swear that the nations round about you will themselves suffer ridicule. ⁸But you, mountains of Israel, will extend your branches and bear your fruit for my people Israel, because they will come home very soon. ⁹Look, I'm here for you, and I will turn toward you, and you will be farmed and sown. ¹⁰I will populate you with human beings, the whole house of Israel, all of them. The cities will be inhabited, the ruins rebuilt. ¹¹When I make people and animals increase on you, they will multiply and be fruitful. I will cause you to be inhabited as you were before. I will do more good for you than in the beginning, and you will know that I am the Lᴏʀᴅ. ¹²I will let people walk through you, my people Israel! They will lay claim to you, you will be their inheritance, and you will no longer deprive them of anything.

¹³The Lᴏʀᴅ God proclaims: Because people say, "You are a devourer of human beings" and "You are depriving your nation," ¹⁴therefore, you will no longer devour human beings or deprive your nation of anything. This is what the Lᴏʀᴅ God says. ¹⁵You won't have to listen anymore to the taunts of the nations or endure the scorn of the peoples. And you will no longer deprive your nation of anything. This is what the Lᴏʀᴅ God says.

A new heart

¹⁶The Lᴏʀᴅ's word came to me: ¹⁷Human one, when the house of Israel lived on their fertile land, they polluted it with their ways and deeds. Their ways before me were polluted like the blood of menstruation, ¹⁸and so I poured out my fury on them for all the blood they had poured out on the land and for all the defilement of their idols. ¹⁹When I scattered them to the nations and dispersed them into other lands, I judged them according to their ways and deeds. ²⁰But then when they entered the other nations, they degraded my holy name because it was said of them, "These are the Lᴏʀᴅ's people, yet they had to leave his land." ²¹So I had compassion on my holy name, which the house of Israel degraded among the nations where they had gone.

²²Therefore, say to the house of Israel, The Lᴏʀᴅ God proclaims: House of Israel, I'm not acting for your sake but for the sake of my holy name, which you degraded among the nations where you have gone. ²³I will make my great name holy, which was degraded among the nations when you dishonored it among them. Then the nations will know that I am the Lᴏʀᴅ. This is what the Lᴏʀᴅ God says.

When I make myself holy among you in their sight, ²⁴I will take you from the nations, I will gather you from all the countries, and I will bring you to your own fertile land. ²⁵I will sprinkle clean water on you, and you will be cleansed of all your pollution. I will cleanse you of all your idols. ²⁶I will give you a new heart and put a new spirit in you. I will remove your stony heart from your body and replace it with a living one, ²⁷and I will give you my spirit so that you may walk according to my regulations and carefully observe my case laws. ²⁸Then you will live in the land that I gave to your ancestors, you will be my people, and I will be your God. ²⁹I will save you from all your uncleanness, and I will summon the grain and make it grow abundantly so that you won't endure famine. ³⁰I will make abundant the orchards' fruit and the fields' produce so that you will never again endure the shame of famine among the nations. ³¹Then you will remember your evil ways and no-good deeds, and you will feel disgust for yourselves because of your sinful and detestable practices. ³²Not for your sake do I act. This is what the Lᴏʀᴅ God proclaims. Let that be known to you! Be ashamed and be humiliated because of all your ways, house of Israel.

³³The Lᴏʀᴅ God proclaims: On the day that I cleanse you of all your guilt, I will cause the cities to be inhabited, and the ruins will be rebuilt. ³⁴The desolate land will be farmed,

---

ˢMT adds *to drive it out.*

and it won't be like it was when it seemed a wasteland to all who passed by. ³⁵They will say, "This land, which was a desolation, has become like the garden of Eden." And the cities that were ruined, ravaged, and razed are now fortified and inhabited. ³⁶The surviving nations around you will know that I, the LORD, have rebuilt what was torn down and have planted what was made desolate. I, the LORD, have spoken, and I will do it.

³⁷The LORD God proclaims: I will also allow the house of Israel to ask me to do this for them: that I increase them like a human flock. ³⁸Like the holy flock, like the flock of Jerusalem at its festivals, the ruined cities will be filled with a human flock. Then they will know that I am the LORD.

Valley of dry bones

37 The LORD's power overcame me, and while I was in the LORD's spirit, he led me out and set me down in the middle of a certain valley. It was full of bones. ²He led me through them all around, and I saw that there were a great many of them on the valley floor, and they were very dry. ³He asked me, "Human one, can these bones live again?"

I said, "LORD God, only you know."

⁴He said to me, "Prophesy over these bones, and say to them, Dry bones, hear the LORD's word! ⁵The LORD God proclaims to these bones: I am about to put breath in you, and you will live again. ⁶I will put sinews on you, place flesh on you, and cover you with skin. When I put breath in you, and you come to life, you will know that I am the LORD."

Memorize Ezek 37:5-6

⁷I prophesied just as I was commanded. There was a great noise as I was prophesying, then a great quaking, and the bones came together, bone by bone. ⁸When I looked, suddenly there were sinews on them. The flesh appeared, and then they were covered over with skin. But there was still no breath in them. ⁹He said to me, "Prophesy to the breath; prophesy, human one! Say to the breath, The LORD God proclaims: Come from the four winds, breath! Breathe into these dead bodies and let them live."

¹⁰I prophesied just as he commanded me. When the breath entered them, they came to life and stood on their feet, an extraordinarily large company.

¹¹He said to me, "Human one, these bones are the entire house of Israel. They say, 'Our bones are dried up, and our hope has perished. We are completely finished.' ¹²So now, prophesy and say to them, The LORD God proclaims: I'm opening your graves! I will raise you up from your graves, my people, and I will bring you to Israel's fertile land. ¹³You will know that I am the LORD, when I open your graves and raise you up from your graves, my people. ¹⁴I will put my breath^t in you, and you will live. I will plant you on your fertile land, and you will know that I am the LORD. I've spoken, and I will do it. This is what the LORD says."

Divided kingdom united

¹⁵The LORD's word came to me: ¹⁶You, human one, take a stick, and write on it, "Belonging to Judah and to the Israelites associated with him." Take another stick and write on it, "Stick of Ephraim belonging to Joseph and everyone of the house of Israel associated with him." ¹⁷Join them to each other to make a single stick so that they become one stick in your hand. ¹⁸When your people ask you, "Why won't you tell us what these sticks mean to you?" ¹⁹say to them, The LORD God proclaims: I'm taking Joseph's stick, which

The Hebrew word *ruach* used throughout Isaiah 37 means "wind, breath, or spirit." *Ruach* is used in Genesis to describe how God's wind moved to bring creation to life.

has been in Ephraim's hand, and the tribes of Israel associated with him, and I'm putting it with Judah's stick, and I'm making them into a single stick so that they will be one stick in my hand. ²⁰When the two sticks that you've written on are in your hand in their sight, ²¹speak to them, This is what the LORD God says: I will take the Israelites from among the nations where they've gone, I will gather them from all around, and I will bring them to their fertile land. ²²I will make them into a

^tOr *spirit*

single nation in the land on Israel's highlands. There will be just one king for all of them. They will no longer be two nations, and they will no longer be divided into two kingdoms. ²³They will no longer defile themselves with their idols or their worthless things or with any of their rebellions. I will deliver them from all the places where they sinned, and I will cleanse them. They will be my people, and I will be their God. ²⁴My servant David will be king over them. There will be just one shepherd for all of them. They will follow my case laws and carefully observe my regulations. ²⁵They will live on the land that I gave to my servant Jacob, where their ancestors lived. They will live on it, they and their children and their grandchildren, forever. My servant David will be their prince forever. ²⁶I will make a covenant of peace for them. It will be their covenant forever. I will grant it to

them and allow them to increase. I will set my sanctuary among them forever. ²⁷My dwelling will be with them, and I will be their God, and they will be my people. ²⁸The nations will know that I, the Lᴏʀᴅ, make Israel holy, when my sanctuary is among them forever.

Attack of Gog

38 The Lᴏʀᴅ's word came to me: ²Human one, face Gog in the land of Magog, chief prince of Meshech and Tubal. Prophesy concerning him ³and say, The Lᴏʀᴅ God proclaims: I challenge you, Gog, chief prince of Meshech and Tubal! ⁴I will turn you about, set hooks in your jaws, and lead you out, you and all your army, horses and riders, handsomely dressed, all of them, a great assembly, with buckler and shield, all of them wielding swords. ⁵Persia, Cush, and Put are with you,ᵘ all of them equipped with shield and helmet.

ᵘCf 38:6; MT *them*

God's
THOUGHTS   THOUGHTS   My

Dry Bones and New Homes   *Ezekiel 37*

This book is full of Ezekiel's visions or dreams from God. This chapter contains Ezekiel's vision where God took him to a valley filled with bones of people who had died. When God asked Ezekiel if the bones could live again, Ezekiel had a very good answer. He told God that God was the only one who knew. Then God told Ezekiel to preach to the bones!

Ezekiel did what God said, and while he was preaching, the bones became people again. They had muscles and skin. But there was one problem: they weren't breathing. So God told Ezekiel to command the winds to fill them. Then they started breathing and stood up.

This all sounds a bit strange. But it helps to remember that God's love is what made these bones live again. These people weren't coming back to life to frighten everyone, like in a scary movie. Instead, they were a symbol of what God can do.

God's people were far from home. They felt sad and lost, as if they were no longer alive. God gave them a symbol of bones coming back to life so they would understand that they could come back to life too. When you feel sad, try reading this story. Imagine those bones standing up and coming to life. Nothing is too hard for God.

What was the last strange dream you had that you can remember?

Say a prayer of thanks to God for God's power and love.

⁶Gomer and all his troops, Beth-togarmah from the far north and all his troops; many peoples are with you. ⁷Stand ready and be prepared, you and all your assembly. You will watch out for those who gather against you.

⁸After many days you will be called out. In future years you will enter a country that has been freed from the sword, a gathering from many peoples on the mountains of Israel, which had become a perpetual ruin. This country was brought out from the peoples, and all of them live securely. ⁹You will invade like a sudden storm. You and all your troops, and the many peoples with you, will be like clouds covering the earth.

¹⁰The Lord God proclaims: On that day, thoughts will come into your mind, and you will devise an evil plan. ¹¹You will say, "I will go up against the open country and come against a quiet people who all live securely without walls, bars, or doors ¹²to take plunder and seize loot, to use myᵛ power against the resettled waste places, against a people gathered from the nations, who are acquiring goods and cattle, and who live at the centerʷ of the earth." ¹³Sheba and Dedan and the merchants and officials of Tarshish will say to you, "Have you come to take plunder and seize loot? Have you assembled your army to take silver and gold, to take goods and cattle, to engage in great looting?"

¹⁴So now, prophesy, human one, and say to Gog, The Lord God proclaims: Isn't that what you will decide to doˣ on that day, when my people Israel live securely? ¹⁵You will come up from your place from the far north, you and many peoples with you, all of them riding horses, a great assembly, a mighty army. ¹⁶You will go up against my people Israel like a cloud covering the earth. But when this happens in future days, I will be the one who brings you up against my land, so that the nations may know me, Gog, when through you I show my holiness in their sight!

¹⁷The Lord God proclaims: Are you the one about whom I spoke in former times through my servants, Israel's prophets, the ones who prophesied for years in those days to bring you against them? ¹⁸On that day, the day when Gog comes against Israel's fertile land, my wrath will be aroused. This is what the Lord God says. ¹⁹In my jealousy and blazing anger I declare: On that day, a great quaking will come over Israel's fertile land. ²⁰The fish of the sea, the birds in the sky, the beasts of the field, all the creatures crawling on the ground, and every living human being will quake in my presence. Mountains will be thrown down and cliffs will crumble; every wall will fall to the ground. ²¹I will summon a sword against Gog on all my mountains. This is what the Lord God says! The swords of the warriors will be against each other, ²²and I will enter into judgment with him, with plague and blood. I will pour out flooding rain, hailstones, fire, and sulfur on him, on all his troops, and on the many peoples with him. ²³So I will display my greatness, show my holiness, and make myself known in the sight of many nations. And they will know that I am the Lord.

39 You, human one, prophesy about Gog and say, The Lord God proclaims: I challenge you, Gog, chief prince of Meshech and Tubal! ²I will turn you about, drag you out, and bring you out of the far north, and I will bring you to Israel's mountains. ³I will strike your bow from your left hand, and make your arrows fall from your right. ⁴You will fall on Israel's mountains, you, all your troops, and the peoples who are with you. I will give you to the birds of prey, to every kind of bird and wild animal as food. ⁵You will fall on the open field, for I have spoken! This is what the Lord God says! ⁶I will send fire on Magog and on those who live securely in the coastlands, and they will know that I am the Lord. ⁷I will make known my holy name among my people Israel. They will never again degrade my holy name, and the nations will know that I, the Lord, am holy in Israel. ⁸Look, it has come! It has happened! This is what the Lord God says. This is the day that I spoke about.

⁹Those who live in Israel's cities will go out and kindle a fire with the weapons—shield and buckler, bow and arrow, spear and lance. They will burn them with fire for seven years. ¹⁰They won't gather wood from the field or chop down trees from the forest, because they will be able to keep the fire burning with

the weapons. So they will take plunder and seize loot. This is what the LORD says.

[11]On that day, I will assign Gog a place for burial in Israel in the Travelers' Valley east of the sea. It will block the travelers' way, because Gog and all of his horde will be buried there. It will be called Hamon-gog[y] Valley. [12]For seven months, the house of Israel will bury them in order to cleanse the land. [13]All the people of the land will take part in the burial, so they will make a name for themselves on the day that I glorify myself. This is what the LORD God says. [14]They will appoint people who will continually cross through the land and bury[z] the human remains that are left on the surface of the ground in order to purify it. They will begin their search at the end of seven months. [15]As the travelers cross through the land, when they see a human bone, they will set up a marker next to it until the gravediggers bury it in Hamon-gog Valley [16](the name of the city is Hamonah). So they will purify the land.

[17]And you, human one, the LORD God proclaims: Say to the birds of prey, to every kind of bird and every wild animal: Assemble and come! Come together from all around for the sacrifice that I make for you, a great sacrifice on Israel's mountains! You will eat flesh and drink blood. [18]You will eat the flesh of warriors and drink the blood of the princes of the earth: rams, lambs, goats, bulls, all fattened animals from Bashan. [19]Gorge yourselves on their fat, and get drunk on their blood, from the sacrifice that I have made for you. [20]Satisfy yourselves at my table with horses and riders, mighty men and every warrior. This is what the LORD God says! [21]When I glorify myself among the nations, all the nations will understand the judgments that I executed and the power that I used among them. [22]And the house of Israel will know that I, the LORD, am their God, from that day on. [23]The nations will know that the house of Israel went into exile because of their guilt. Because they rebelled against me, I hid my face from them.

When I handed them over to their enemies, all of them fell by the sword. [24]I dealt with them according to their uncleanness and their transgressions and hid my face from them.

[25]So the LORD God proclaims: Now I will bring back the captives of Jacob. I will have compassion on the whole house of Israel and defend my holy name. [26]They will forget their humiliation and all their rebellions against me when they live securely on their fertile land with no one to frighten them. [27]When I bring them back from the peoples and gather them from the lands of their enemies, I will be made holy through them in the sight of the many nations. [28]They will know that I am the LORD their God when, after I made them go into exile among the nations, I gathered them to their land. I won't leave any of them behind. [29]When I pour my Spirit upon the house of Israel, I won't hide my face from them again. This is what the LORD God says.

Vision of restoration

40In the beginning of the twenty-fifth year of our exile, on the tenth day of the month, exactly fourteen years after the city was struck down, on that very day, the LORD's power was on me, and he took me there. [2]In God's visions, he brought me to the land of Israel and set me down on a very high mountain, where there was a city structure to the south. [3]When he brought me there, I saw a man standing in the gate. He appeared to be bronze, and he had a linen cord and a measuring rod in his hand. [4]The man spoke to me, "Human one, look and listen well, and take seriously everything I show you, because you were brought here so that these things could be revealed to you. Describe everything you see to the house of Israel."

Temple compound

[5]Now there was an outer wall that went all the way around the temple compound. The measuring rod in the man's hand was ten and a half feet[a] (based on a standard eighteen inches[b] plus three inches[c]). When he

---

[y]Or *horde of Gog* [z]LXX; MT adds *the travelers.* [a]Heb *shesh ammoth ba'ammah* traditionally *six long cubits,* which is defined as six times a standard *ammah* of eighteen inches plus a *topha* (traditionally *handbreadth*) of three inches. So the measuring rod has six segments of twenty-one inches each, which equals ten and a half feet. It is unclear whether the measurements with the rod continue past 40:8, when standard *ammah* appear, though the longer *ammah* do continue briefly in 43:13-17 for the altar.
[b]Or *a standard cubit* [c]Or *a handbreadth*

measured the wall's height and width it was ten and a half feet high and ten and a half feet wide. ⁶He entered the gate facing east. He went up its steps, and he measured the plaza^d at the gate. It was ten and a half feet wide: the plaza was ten and a half feet wide. ⁷The rooms were ten and a half feet long and ten and a half feet wide, with a space of seven and a half feet between them. The plaza next to the porch at the gate opposite the temple was ten and a half feet. ⁸He measured the porch of the gate opposite the temple: it was ten and a half feet. ⁹Then he measured the porch of the gate: it was twelve feet,^e and its arches were three feet. The porch of the gate was opposite the temple. ¹⁰Inside the east gate, there were three rooms on each side. Each was the same size, and the arches on each side were the same size also. ¹¹Then he measured the width of the gate opening, which was fifteen feet, and the gate's length, which was nineteen and a half feet. ¹²A border running along the front of the rooms on each side was eighteen inches wide, and each of the rooms was nine feet square. ¹³He measured the gate through the room openings that faced each other. From the outer ceiling edge of one room to the outer ceiling edge of the other, the gate was thirty-seven and a half feet wide. ¹⁴Next he made out the perimeter of the hallway, defined by the arches inside the gate: it was ninety feet. ¹⁵It was seventy-five feet from the front of the outer gate to the front of the inner porch of the gate. ¹⁶Inside the gate, all of the rooms and their arches had closed windows; there were also niches inside the porch all the way around. The arches were decorated with palm trees.

¹⁷Then he brought me to the outer courtyard, which consisted of chambers and a pavement all the way around. Thirty chambers came up to the pavement, ¹⁸and the pavement came up to the facades of the gates along their entire length. That was the lower pavement. ¹⁹When he measured the width from the inside of the lower gate to the outer edge of the inner courtyard, it was one hundred fifty feet.

After he measured the east gate, he measured the north gate, ²⁰the one facing north at the outer courtyard. He measured its length and width, ²¹its three inner rooms on each side, its arches, and its porch. Its measurements were the same as the first gate: seventy-five feet long and thirty-seven and a half feet wide. ²²The windows, porch, and palm decorations had the same measurements as those of the east gate. Seven steps led up to the entrance, and the porch was at the other end. ²³There were also gates to the inner courtyard opposite the north and east gates. When he measured from gate to gate, it was one hundred fifty feet.

²⁴Then he had me walk toward the south, where there was a gate facing south. He measured its arches and porch using the same measurements. ²⁵Its windows and its porch all around were like the others, and the gate also was seventy-five feet long and thirty-seven and a half feet wide. ²⁶Its stairway had seven steps, and its porch was at the other end. On its arches, one on either side, were palm decorations. ²⁷There was a gate to the inner courtyard on the south. When he measured from gate to gate on the south side, it was one hundred fifty feet.

²⁸When he brought me to the inner courtyard by way of the south gate, he took the same measurements of the south gate. ²⁹Its rooms, arches, and porch, as well as its windows and porch all the way around, measured the same as the others. It was seventy-five feet long and thirty-seven and a half feet wide. ³⁰There were porches all around, thirty-seven and a half feet long and seven and a half feet wide. ³¹Its porch faced the outer courtyard. Palms decorated its arches, and its stairway had eight steps.

³²Then he brought me to the inner courtyard on the east side, and again he took the same measurements of the gate. ³³Its rooms, arches, and porch measured the same as the others, as well as its windows and porch all the way around. It was seventy-five feet long and thirty-seven and a half feet wide. ³⁴Its porch faced the outer courtyard. Palm trees decorated its arches on both sides, and its stairway had eight steps. ³⁵Then he brought me to the north gate and took the same measurements of the ³⁶rooms, arches, and

^dOr *threshold*; Heb architectural and decorative terminology in Ezek 40–48 is often uncertain. ^eOr *eight cubits*

porch, and also its windows all around. It was seventy-five feet long and thirty-seven and a half feet wide. [37]Its porch[f] faced the outer courtyard. Palm trees decorated its arches on both sides, and its stairway had eight steps.

[38]At that gate, there was a room with an entrance in the arches for washing the entirely burned offering, [39]and inside the porch on each side of the gate were two tables where the entirely burned offerings, the purification offerings, and the compensation offerings were slaughtered. [40]Outside, two pairs of tables flanked the entrance of the north gate at both ends, at the steps on one end and the porch on the other. [41]There were four tables on each side of the gate, eight tables in all, for preparing the animal offerings. [42]The four tables that were used for the entirely burned offering as well as for the communal sacrifices were made of hewn stone. Each was twenty-seven inches square and eighteen inches high. Equipment used in the ritual slaughter was set on them. [43]Hooks,[g] three inches wide, were securely fixed all the way around. The tables were for the flesh of the offerings.

[44]Outside the inner gate there were two[h] chambers in the inner courtyard. The one beside the north gate faced south, and the one beside the east gate faced north. [45]He spoke to me: "The chamber facing south is for the priests who keep watch over the temple, [46]and the chamber facing north is for the priests who keep watch over the altar. Of all the Levites, only the Zadokites may draw near to serve the LORD." [47]Then he measured the courtyard. It was square, one hundred fifty feet long and one hundred fifty feet wide. The altar was in front of the temple.

The temple

[48]Then he brought me to the porch of the temple and measured its arches. They were seven and a half feet on each side, and the width of the gate was four and a half feet on each side. [49]The porch was thirty feet long and eighteen feet wide. Steps led up into the porch, and there were columns for the arches, one on each side.

41 He brought me to the main hall, and he measured the arches. They were nine feet deep on both sides, so that was also the depth of the tent. [2]The entrance was fifteen feet wide, and the facades on either side of the entrance were seven and a half feet. When he measured its length, it was sixty feet, and its width was thirty feet. [3]Then he went into the inner room, and he measured the arches on both sides of the entrance; they were each three feet. The entrance was nine feet wide, and its depth was ten and a half feet. [4]When he measured the length of the inner room, it was thirty feet, and the width of the side adjoining the main hall was also thirty feet. He said to me, "This is the most holy place."

[5]When he measured the wall of the temple, it was nine feet, and the side chambers that went all the way around the temple were six feet. [6]Now these side chambers adjoined each other, thirty chambers in three stories. The side chambers had a ledge in the temple wall all the way around to serve as supports, but these supports were not inserted into the temple wall itself. [7]A wide ramp ascended stage by stage to the side chambers all the way around the temple. In this way, the ascent stage by stage all around the temple added to the temple's width. One ascended from the foundation to the top by way of the middle story. [8]Then I looked at the temple: Its roof all around rested on the side chambers. Each raised section was ten and a half feet, and the indentations between them were nine feet.[i] [9]The width of the outer wall of the side chambers was seven and a half feet. The space left free between the temple's side chambers and [10]the other chambers was thirty feet wide all the way around the temple. [11]There were two entrances from the side chambers to the free space, one facing north, the other facing south. And the width of the

did you know? God gave Ezekiel a vision of a completely rebuilt Jerusalem, including very specific measurements and details of a new temple. For the people of God, their greatest hope was that the temple would be rebuilt one day.

[f]LXX; MT *arches* [g]Heb uncertain [h]LXX; MT *singing* [i]Heb uncertain

place that was left free was seven and a half feet all the way around. ¹²The structure facing the yard on the west was one hundred five feet wide. The structure's wall was seven and a half feet wide all the way around, and its length was one hundred thirty-five feet.

¹³Then he measured the temple. It was one hundred fifty feet long. The yard, the structure, and its walls were also one hundred fifty feet. ¹⁴The area in front of the house and the yard to the east was one hundred fifty feet also. ¹⁵Then he measured the length of the structure along the side of the yard, including its promenades on both sides: one hundred fifty feet.

Now the interior of the main hall as well as the porches in the courtyard ¹⁶were paneled all around, including the ceilings,ʲ closed windows, and its three courses of promenades that adjoined the ceiling. From the ground up to the windows was covered. ¹⁷Above the entrance, from the interior to the exterior of the temple, and on every interior and exterior wall, ¹⁸there were carved winged creatures and palm trees. The palm trees were positioned between the winged creatures, and each winged creature had two faces. ¹⁹A human face turned toward one palm tree, and the face of a lion turned toward another. They were carved on the temple all the way around. ²⁰From the ground to above the entrance, the walls of the main hall were carved with winged creatures and palm trees. ²¹In the main hall itself, there were square doorposts in front of the holy place, where there was the appearance of ²²the altar. It was four and a half feet high and three feet wide. It was made of wood, and its corners, base, and sides were also wood. He said to me, "This is the table that stands before the Lord."

²³The main hall and the holy place each had two doors, ²⁴and each door had two turning panels, two for one door and two for the other. ²⁵Like the walls, the doors of the main hall were carved with winged creatures and palm trees. A single luxuriantᵏ tree stood outside, in front of the porch, ²⁶while closed windows and palm trees decorated both sides of the facade of the porch, the temple's side chambers, and the beams.

Chambers and promenades

42Then he led me north to the outer courtyard and brought me into the set of chambers opposite the yard and the structure to the north. ²The length of the facade at the north entrance was one hundred fifty feet, its depth seventy-five feet. ³It was next to the twenty chambers that belonged to the inner courtyard and next to the pavement of the outer courtyard, and it had three courses of promenades. ⁴In front of the chambers there was a passage fifteen feet wide, and to the inside, a passage eighteen inches wide. The entrance to the chambers was on the north. ⁵The upper chambers were smaller, because the promenades took up more space from them than from the first and second stories. ⁶This was because the promenades were arranged in three levels, but they didn't have columns like those in the courtyards. For this reason, the top story was narrower than the first and second stories. ⁷A stone wall ran parallel to the chambers facing the outer courtyard. It was seventy-five feet long, ⁸the same length, seventy-five feet, as the chambers facing the outer courtyard. Those facing the temple were one hundred fifty feet. ⁹⁻¹⁰These chambers were entered from the outer courtyard at the end of the courtyard wall, because the entrance was at the end of the chambers at the east. South of the yard and the building, there were more chambers with a passage ¹¹in front of them. The design of the chambers resembled the ones to the north in length and width, as well as in all their exits. The arrangement of the entrances ¹²to the chambers on the south side was identical as well. One entered from the east at the beginning of the corresponding wall.

¹³Then he said to me, "The north and south chambers that face the building and the yard are the holy chambers where the priests eat the offerings that have been brought to the Lord. They are most holy. Here they will place the most holy things, the grain offering, the purification offering, and the compensation offering. The place is holy. ¹⁴When the priests enter, they won't go out of the sanctuary to the outer courtyard. There they will place the priestly vests that they wore when they were

ministering, because these garments are also holy. They will put on other garments when they go out to the people's area."

¹⁵When he finished making the interior measurements of the temple, he led me out toward the east gate, and he measured all the way around. ¹⁶He used the same measuring rod on all four sides. He measured the east side, seven hundred fifty feet; ¹⁷the north side, seven hundred fifty feet; and ¹⁸the south side, seven hundred fifty feet. ¹⁹He turned to the west side, seven hundred fifty feet. ²⁰On all four sides he measured the wall all the way around. Its length was seven hundred fifty feet, and its width seven hundred fifty feet. So he made a division between the holy and the ordinary.

Return of the divine glory

43 Then he led me to the east gate, ²where the glory of Israel's God was coming in from the east. Its sound was like the sound of a mighty flood, and the earth was lit up with his glory. ³What appeared when I looked was like what I had seen when he¹ came to destroy the city, and also like what I saw at the Chebar River, and I fell on my face. ⁴Then the LORD's glory came into the temple by way of the east gate. ⁵A wind picked me up and brought me to the inner courtyard, and there the LORD's glory filled the temple. ⁶A man was standing next to me, but the voice that I heard came from inside the temple. ⁷He said to me, Human one, this is the place for my throne and the place for the soles of my feet, where I will dwell among the Israelites forever. The house of Israel will never again defile my holy name, neither they nor their kings, with their disloyalties^m and with their kings' corpses at the shrines. ⁸When they set their plazas^n with mine and their doorposts next to mine, the wall was between us. They defiled my holy name with their detestable practices, so I consumed them in my anger. ⁹Now let them remove their disloyalties and their kings' corpses from me, and I will dwell among them forever.

Bet you can read this in 8 minutes. Ready, set, go!

¹⁰You, human one, describe the temple to the house of Israel. Let them be humiliated because of their guilt when they think about its design. ¹¹When they feel humiliated by all that they have done, make known to them the shape of the temple and its adornment, its exits and its entrances, its entire plan and all of its regulations.^o Write them down in their sight so that they may observe all of its entire plan and all its regulations and perform them.

¹²These are the instructions for the temple: the top of the mountain, as well as its boundaries all around, are most holy. These are the instructions for the temple.

The altar

¹³These are the dimensions of the altar, according to a twenty-one-inch unit of measure.^P The base is twenty-one inches high and twenty-one inches wide, with an outer curb measuring one and a half inches all around. This is the altar's height. ¹⁴From the base at ground level to the lower ledge is forty-two inches; the lower ledge is twenty-one inches wide. The distance from the lower to the upper ledge is seven feet; the upper ledge is twenty-one inches wide. ¹⁵The hearth is seven feet high, with four horns projecting upward from the hearth. ¹⁶The hearth is twenty-one feet square; each side is equal to the others. ¹⁷The ledge around the hearth is twenty-four and a half feet long by twenty-four and a half feet wide, a square. Its outer rim is ten and a half inches, and its base all around is twenty-one inches. Its ramp faces east.

Purification of the altar

¹⁸He said to me, Human one, the LORD God proclaims: These are the regulations established for the altar on the day when it is prepared for making entirely burned offerings and dashing blood on it. ¹⁹You will provide a young bull as a purification offering to the levitical priests who are descendants of Zadok, the ones who may draw near to minster to me. This is what the LORD God says. ²⁰You will take some of its blood and

---

¹Vulg; MT *I* ^mOr *prostitution* ^nOr *thresholds* ^oLXX; MT adds *and all of its structures and all of its instructions.* ^PHeb *ammah ammah*, traditionally *a long cubit*

set it on the four horns of the altar and on the four sides of the ledge and on the curb all around. So you will purify it and purge it. 21 Then you will take the bull selected as the purification offering, and the priests will burn it in a designated place of the temple outside of the sanctuary. 22 On the second day, you will present a flawless male goat as a purification offering. The priests will purify the altar just as they purified the altar with the bull. 23 When you have completed the purification, you will present a flawless bull from the herd and a flawless ram from the flock. 24 You will present them to the LORD. The priests will throw salt on them and offer them as entirely burned offerings to the LORD. 25 Daily, for seven days, you will present a male goat for a purification offering. You will also present a bull from the herd and a ram from the flock, both flawless. 26 For seven days the priests will purge the altar in order to purify it and to dedicate it. 27 When the seven days are completed, the priests will offer your entirely burned offerings and your well-being sacrifices on the altar from the eighth day on, and I will accept you with pleasure. This is what the LORD God says.

The closed gate

44 He brought me back to the outer sanctuary gate that faces east. It was closed. 2 The LORD said to me, This gate remains closed. It shouldn't be opened. No one should come in through it because the LORD, Israel's God, has entered through it. It will remain closed. 3 As for the prince, he may sit in it to eat bread in the LORD's presence. He may come in and go out by way of the gate's porch.

Foreigners, Levites, Zadokites

4 Then he brought me by way of the north gate to the front of the temple. I looked, and suddenly the LORD's glory filled the LORD's temple, and I fell on my face. 5 Then the LORD said to me: Human one, pay close attention! Use your eyes and ears and listen to all that I say to you concerning the regulations of the LORD's temple and all its instructions. Pay close attention to the access to the temple through all the sanctuary portals.[q] 6 Speak to the rebels, to the house of Israel, The LORD God proclaims: Enough of your detestable practices, house of Israel! 7 You made my temple unclean because you brought into my sanctuary foreigners who were physically and spiritually uncircumcised. When you offered my food of fat and blood to me, you[r] broke my covenant with all your detestable practices. 8 You didn't keep charge of my holy things. On the contrary, you appointed them[s] to keep charge in my sanctuary for you.

9 The LORD God proclaims: Foreigners who are spiritually and physically uncircumcised must not enter my sanctuary; that is, all foreigners among the Israelites. 10 But the Levites, who went far from me when Israel went astray, who went astray from me after their idols, will bear their guilt. 11 They will keep charge in my sanctuary, and they will oversee the temple gates and keep charge of the temple. They will slaughter the entirely burned offerings and the sacrifices for the people, and they will stand before them to minister to them. 12 Because they ministered to them before their idols, they brought about the downfall of the house of Israel. For that reason I made a solemn pledge against them—this is what the LORD God says—and they will bear their guilt. 13 They won't approach me to officiate for me as priests or approach any of my holy things or the most holy place. Though they will bear their humiliation and the consequences of their detestable practices, 14 I will appoint them to keep charge of the temple, all its work, and all that is done in it.

15 As for the priests of the levitical family of Zadok who did keep charge of my sanctuary when the Israelites strayed away from me, they will draw near to me to serve me. They will stand in my presence to present fat and blood to me. This is what the LORD God says. 16 They will come into my sanctuary, and they will approach my table to minister to me. They will keep my charge. 17 When they come through the gates to the inner courtyard, they will wear linen garments. They won't wear

[q] Or *exits* [r] LXX, Syr, Vulg; MT *they* [s] Heb lacks *them*.

any wool when they minister at the gates of the inner courtyard or in the temple. [18]They will have linen turbans on their heads and linen undergarments around their waists. They won't wear anything that makes them sweat. [19]When they go out to the outer courtyard to the people, they will remove the garments in which they were ministering. They will lay them aside in the holy chambers and wear other clothing. They must not transfer holiness to the people through their clothing. [20]They must neither shave their heads nor let their hair grow long, but they will trim the hair on their heads. [21]None of the priests should drink wine when they come into the inner courtyard. [22]They must not marry widows or divorced women, but only Israelite virgins. Priests may, however, marry the widows of other priests. [23]They must teach my people the difference between the holy and the ordinary, and show them the difference between clean and unclean. [24]They must execute judgments according to my case laws in cases of civil conflict. They must observe my instructions and my regulations regarding all my festivals. They must keep my sabbaths holy. [25]In order to avoid uncleanness, they must not approach the dead. They may, however, become unclean for their father or mother, son or daughter, brother or unmarried sister. [26]Once the priest is clean again, he must count off seven days. [27]On the day that he comes into the holy place, the inner courtyard, to minister in the holy place, he will present his purification offering. This is what the Lord God says. [28]As for their inheritance, I am their inheritance. They won't be given family property in Israel; I am their family property. [29]They will eat the grain offerings, the purification offerings, and the compensation offerings. Every dedicated thing in Israel belongs to them. [30]The best of the early produce of every kind, and every contribution, all of them, belong to the priests. You will give the best of your bread dough to the priest so that a blessing may come to rest on your household. [31]The priests must not eat any bird or animal that dies naturally or is torn apart by prey.

The holy portion

45 When you distribute the land as an inheritance, you will set aside a holy portion of land for the Lord. It will be 7.1 miles long and 5.68 miles[t] wide. It will be holy throughout the entire area. [2]Out of this portion, an area seven hundred fifty feet by seven hundred fifty feet square will be for the sanctuary. All around it will be an open space seventy-five feet wide. [3]Beginning with this measurement, you will measure out an area 7.1 miles long and 2.84 miles wide. The sanctuary, the most holy place, will lie on it. [4]It is holy, set apart from the land, and it belongs to the priests who draw near to minister in the Lord's sanctuary. It will be a place for their houses, and a holy place for the sanctuary. [5]The area 7.1 miles long and 2.84 miles wide will be for the Levites who minister in the temple. Twenty chambers are theirs as their property. [6]As the property for the city, you will set aside an area 1.42 miles wide and 7.1 miles long next to the holy portion. It will be for the whole house of Israel. [7]The territory for the prince will be on both sides of the holy portion and the city property, alongside the holy portion and alongside the city property, from their western boundaries westward and from their eastern boundaries eastward. Its length will equal one tribal portion, from the western border to the eastern border. [8]The land will be his property in Israel, and my princes will no longer oppress my people. They will give the land to the house of Israel according to their tribes.

LIGHTHOUSE

GIVING MY BEST

An Offering to God Ezekiel 44:30
The Israelites were to give God an offering from the first and best produce from the harvest. They were also to give offerings to the priests so that the priests could be free to pray to God and minister to the people. The priests were not allowed to own property. Their only job was to minister to the people. The priests would bless the homes of those who gave to take care of them. ⬥

---

[t]LXX *twenty thousand* (*pechon*, standard cubit); MT *ten thousand* (*ammah*); see note at Ezek 40:5.

9The Lord God proclaims: Enough, princes of Israel! Turn aside from violence and oppression. Establish justice and righteousness. Cease your evictions of my people! This is what the Lord God says: 10You must use fair scales, a fair ephah,u and a fair bath.v 11The ephah and the bath must be the same size. Both should be calibrated to the homer: each will contain one-tenth of a homer. 12The shekel must weigh twenty gerahs. Twenty shekels, twenty-five shekels, and fifteen shekels will equal one maneh for you.

Sacrificial offerings and gifts

13These are your prescribed contributions: one-sixth of an ephah for each homer of wheat, and one-sixth of an ephah for each homer of barley; 14a regular amount of oil,w one-tenth of a bath for each korx (each kory contains ten baths); 15and one sheep from the flock for every two hundred from Israel's pastureland, for grain offerings, for entirely burned offerings, and for well-being sacrifices to make reconciliation for them. This is what the Lord God says. 16All the people will make this contribution on behalf of the prince in Israel. 17The prince will be responsible for the entirely burned offerings, grain offerings, and drink offerings for the festivals, new moons, and sabbaths, all the appointed festivals of the house of Israel. He will offer the purification offering, the grain offering, the entirely burned offering, and the well-being sacrifice to make reconciliation on behalf of the house of Israel.

Festivals

18The Lord God proclaims: On the first day of the first month,z you will take a flawless young bull from the herd, and you will purify the sanctuary. 19The priest will take some of the blood from the purification offering, and he will set it on the doorposts of the temple and on the four corners of the ledge of the altar and on the doorposts of the gate to the inner courtyard. 20You will do the same on the seventh day of the month for anyone who sins through inadvertence or ignorance. So

you will purge the temple. 21Your Passover will be on the fourteenth day of the first month. Unleavened bread will be eaten during the seven days of the festival. 22On that day, the prince will provide a young bull as the purification offering for himself and for the people of the land. 23For the seven days of the festival, he will provide seven flawless bulls and seven flawless rams, one for each day of the festival, as the entirely burned offering for the Lord, and, for the purification offering, one male goat for each day. 24He will also provide the grain offerings, one ephaha for each bull, and one ephah for each ram, with one hinb of oil for each ephah. 25For the festival that begins on the fifteenth day of the seventh month,c he will make the same provisions for the purification offerings, entirely burned offerings, grain offerings, and oil, for all seven days of the festival.

Sabbaths and gift offerings

46 The Lord God proclaims: The east-facing gate of the inner courtyard will remain closed for the six days of the workweek. But on the Sabbath and on the day of the new moon it will be opened, 2and the prince will come in from outside by way of the porch of the gate and stand at the gate's doorposts. The priests will present the prince's entirely burned offerings and well-being sacrifices, and then he will bow down on the threshold of the gate and go out. The gate won't be closed until evening 3so that the people of the land may bow in the presence of the Lord on sabbaths and new moons at the opening of that gate. 4On the Sabbath day, the prince will offer to the Lord an entirely burned offering of six flawless lambs and a flawless ram, 5a grain offering of one ephah for the ram, and a grain offering at his discretion for the lambs, with one hin of oil for each ephah. 6For the day of the new moon, the offering will be a flawless young bull from the herd, six lambs, and a flawless ram, 7and he will provide a grain offering of one ephah each for the bull and the ram, and for the lambs

---

uOne ephah is approximately twenty quarts of grain. vOne bath is approximately twenty quarts of liquid. wSyr, Tg; MT adds *a bath of oil.* xMT adds *each homer contains ten baths.* yVulg; MT *homer* zMarch-April, Nisan aOne ephah is approximately twenty quarts of grain. bOne hin is approximately equal to one gallon. cSeptember-October, Tishrei

as much as he likes, with one hin of oil for each ephah.

⁸When the prince enters, he comes in by way of the porch of the gate and goes out in the same direction. ⁹When the people of the land come into the LORD's presence for the festivals, those who enter through the north gate to worship should go out through the south, and those who come in through the south gate should go out through the north gate. They shouldn't turn around and go out the same way they came in. Instead, they should go out the opposite gate. ¹⁰The prince should accompany them: when they come in, he comes in, and when they go out, he goes out. ¹¹At the festivals and appointed gatherings, the grain offering is one ephah for each bull, one ephah for each ram, and whatever one is able to give for each lamb, with one hin of oil for each ephah.

¹²Whenever the prince makes a spontaneous gift to the LORD, whether it is an entirely burned offering or a well-being sacrifice, the gate facing east will be opened for him, and he will present his entirely burned offering and well-being sacrifices, just as he does on the Sabbath day. When he leaves, the gate will be closed after he has gone out.

Daily offerings

¹³As a daily entirely burned offering for the LORD, you will provide a flawless year-old lamb. You will make the offering every morning. ¹⁴You will provide a grain offering along with it every morning, one-sixth of an ephah along with one-third of a hin of oil to moisten the choice flour. This is a permanent and perpetual regulation for the grain offering to the LORD. ¹⁵So the lamb, the grain offering, and the oil are provided every morning as a perpetual entirely burned offering.

Royal land grants

¹⁶The LORD God proclaims: When the prince gives a gift to each of his sons, it becomes their inheritance. It becomes their family property as an inheritance. ¹⁷And if he gives one of his servants a gift from his inheritance, it will belong to the servant only until the year of release, and then it will revert to the prince. It is his children's inheritance; it belongs to them. ¹⁸The prince won't take the people's inheritance by evicting them from their family property. He will bequeath only his own property to his sons, lest any of my people be deprived of their rightful property.

Kitchens

¹⁹Then he brought me through the passage beside the gate next to the priests' quarters, the holy chambers facing north. There was a place hidden away on the western side. ²⁰He said to me, "Rather than taking these offerings out into the outer courtyard and transferring holiness to the people, this is the place where the priests will boil the compensation offerings and the purification offerings, and where they will bake the grain offerings."

²¹Then he took me to the outer courtyard, and he had me pass through its four corners, and I saw that there were additional courtyards in each of the corners. ²²In all four corners of the courtyard, these courtyards were constructed to handle smoke. All four were the same size, sixty feet long by forty-five feet wide. ²³All four had stone masonry all the way around, and hearths were built under this masonry all the way around. ²⁴He said to me, "These are the kitchens where those who minister in the temple cook the people's sacrifices."

The river

47When he brought me back to the temple's entrance, I noticed that water was flowing toward the east from under the temple's threshold (the temple faced east). The water was going out from under the temple's facade toward the south, south of the altar. ²He led me out through the north gate and around the outside to the outer east gate, where the water flowed out under the facade on the south side. ³With the line in his hand, the man went out toward the east. When he measured off fifteen hundred feet, he made me cross the water; it was ankle-deep. ⁴He measured off another fifteen hundred feet and made me cross the water; it was knee-deep. He measured off another fifteen hundred feet and made me cross the water, and it was waist-high. ⁵When he measured off another fifteen hundred feet, it had become a river that I couldn't cross. The water was high, deep enough for swimming but too high to cross. [6]He said to me, "Human one, do you see?" Then he led me back to the edge of the river. [7]When I went back, I saw very many trees on both banks of the river. [8]He said to me, "These waters go out to the eastern region, flow down the steep slopes,[d] and go into the Dead Sea.[e] When the flowing waters enter the sea, its water becomes fresh. [9]Wherever the river flows, every living thing that moves will thrive. There will be great schools of fish, because when these waters enter the sea, it will be fresh. Wherever the river flows, everything will live. [10]People will stand fishing beside it, from En-gedi to En-eglayim, and it will become a place for spreading nets. It will be like the Mediterranean Sea,[f] having all kinds of fish in it. [11]Its marshes and swamps won't be made fresh (they are left for salt), [12]but on both banks of the river will grow up all kinds of fruit-bearing trees. Their leaves won't wither, and their fruitfulness won't wane. They will produce fruit in every month, because their water comes from the sanctuary. Their fruit will be for eating, their leaves for healing."

[13]The LORD God proclaims: These[g] are the boundaries of the portions of land that will be distributed as an inheritance to the twelve tribes of Israel. Joseph will receive two portions. [14]What I swore to give to your ancestors, you will distribute as an inheritance equally. This land is given to you as an inheritance. [15]This is the boundary of the land. The northern limit begins at the Mediterranean Sea and goes in the direction of Hethlon toward Lebo-hamath, Zedad,[h] [16]Berothah, Sibraim (which is between the boundary of Damascus and the boundary of Hamath), and Hazar-hatticon (that is on the boundary of Hauran). [17]So the boundary from the Mediterranean Sea[i] to Hazar-enon will run north of the boundary of Damascus, with the boundary of Hamath to the north. This is the northern limit. [18]For the eastern limit, you will measure continuously between Hauran and Damascus and between Gilead and the land of Israel, along the Jordan River as far as the Dead Sea.[j] This is the eastern limit. [19]The southern limit runs from

Tamar to the waters of Meribath-kadesh and from there along the border[k] of Egypt to the Mediterranean Sea. This is the southern limit. [20]For the western limit, the Mediterranean Sea is the boundary up to Lebo-hamath. This is the western limit. [21]You will apportion this land among yourselves according to the tribes of Israel. [22]When you distribute the land as an inheritance, the immigrants who reside with you and raise families among you are considered full citizens along with the Israelites. They will receive an inheritance along with you among the tribes of Israel. [23]You will assign the immigrants' inheritance with the tribe with whom they reside. This is what the LORD God says.

48 These are the tribes' names: Beginning at the north, along the Hethlon road from Lebo-hamath to Hazar-enon, the boundary of Damascus with Hamath to the north, from the eastern border to the western border: Dan, one portion. [2]Along the boundary of Dan from the eastern border to the western border: Asher, one portion. [3]Along the boundary of Asher from the eastern border to the western border: Naphtali, one portion. [4]Along the boundary of Naphtali from the eastern border to the western border: Manasseh, one portion. [5]Along the boundary of Manasseh from the eastern border to the western border: Ephraim, one portion. [6]Along the boundary of Ephraim from the eastern border to the western border: Reuben, one portion. [7]Along the boundary of Reuben from the eastern border to the western border: Judah, one portion.

[8]Along the boundary of Judah from the eastern border to the western border will be the portion that you will set aside, 7.1 miles wide and the length of a tribal portion from the eastern border to the western border. The sanctuary is in its center. [9]The portion that you will set aside for the LORD will be 7.1

miles long and 5.68 miles[l] wide. [10]These measurements define the holy portion for the priests: along the north, a length of 7.1 miles; along the west, a width of 2.84 miles; along the east, a width of 2.84 miles; and along the south, a length of 7.1 miles. The LORD's sanctuary is in its center. [11]This holy area is for the Zadokite priests who kept my charge and didn't stray as the Levites did when the house of Israel strayed away from me. [12]It belongs to them as a most special portion of the land, a most holy place, up to the border of the Levites. [13]The Levites' allotment is next to the boundary of the priests, a length of 7.1 miles and a width of 2.84 miles. The entire length is 7.1 miles and the width 2.84 miles. [14]None of it will be sold, exchanged, or transferred. It is the choicest land, because it is holy to the LORD. [15]The remaining area, 1.42 miles wide and 7.1 miles long, is for ordinary use for the city, for residences, and for pastures. The city will be in the middle of it. [16]It measures 1.28 miles on its northern border, 1.28 miles on its southern border, 1.28 miles on its eastern border, and 1.28 miles on its western border. [17]There will be pastures for the city, three hundred seventy-five feet on the north side, three hundred seventy-five feet on the south side, three hundred seventy-five feet on the east side, and three hundred seventy-five feet on the west side. [18]The remaining area alongside the holy portion is 2.84 miles on the east and 2.84 miles on the west. These areas that adjoin the holy portion will produce the food for the city's workers. [19]The city's workers from every tribe of Israel will farm it. [20]The entire portion that you will set aside is 7.1 miles by 7.1 miles, a square; it includes the holy portion in addition to the city property. [21]What is left on both sides of the holy portion and the city property belongs to the prince. The land from the edge of the portion of 7.1 miles, to the eastern boundary, and on the western edge of the 7.1 miles to the western boundary, belongs to the prince. It corresponds to one tribal portion. The holy portion and the temple sanctuary are in the middle of it, [22]but what belongs to the prince is separate from both the levitical property and the city property. The prince's territory will be between the boundary of Judah and the boundary of Benjamin.

[23]Now for the rest of the tribes: From the eastern border to the western border: Benjamin, one portion. [24]Along the boundary of Benjamin from the eastern border to the western border: Simeon, one portion. [25]Along the boundary of Simeon from the eastern border to the western border: Issachar, one portion. [26]Along the boundary of Issachar from the eastern border to the western border: Zebulun, one portion. [27]Along the boundary of Zebulun from the eastern border to the western border: Gad, one portion. [28]Along the boundary of Gad to the southern border, the boundary will run from Tamar to the waters of Meribath-kadesh and from there to the border of Egypt[m] and to the Mediterranean Sea.[n] [29]This is the land that you will distribute as an inheritance for the tribes of Israel. These are their portions. This is what the LORD God says.

[30]These are the city exits. The north side is measured at 1.28 miles. [31]The gates of the city go by the names of the tribes of Israel. There are three gates on the north side: one gate for Reuben, one gate for Judah, and one gate for Levi. [32]There are three gates on the east side along its 1.28 miles: one gate for Joseph, one gate for Benjamin, and one gate for Dan. [33]There are three gates on the south side measuring 1.28 miles: one gate for Simeon, one gate for Issachar, and one gate for Zebulun. [34]There are three gates on the west side along its 1.28 miles: one gate for Gad, one gate for Asher, and one gate for Naphtali. [35]The circumference of the city is 5.1 miles. As of today, the name of the city is The LORD Is There.

---

[l] Cf LXX and Ezek 45:1; MT *ten thousand ammah* equals 2.84 miles. [m] Or *Wadi*; traditionally *Brook*, MT lacks *of Egypt*.
[n] Or *Great Sea*

Daniel

At the start of this book, Daniel and his friends Shadrach, Meshach, and Abednego were training to serve babylon's King Nebuchadnezzar. These four young men wanted to obey God in everything they did. So when the king ordered them to eat foods that broke God's Instructions, they refused to do so. Even though they chose a simple diet of vegetables and water, they grew stronger (Dan 1:3-21). When the king commanded everyone to bow to a giant statue of himself, Shadrach, Meshach, and Abednego bravely stood up straight. The king threw them into a blazing furnace, but God rescued them (Dan 3:1-30). When Daniel broke the law by praying to God, he was tossed into a pit of lions. But God saved him by shutting the lions' mouths (Dan 6:1-22).

The book's first half (Dan 1–6) tells these famous stories. The book's second half (Dan 7–12) contains visions from a period of history much later than the stories from the beginning of the book. There is also a well-known prayer where Daniel confesses his own sins and the sins of God's people (Dan 9:1-19).

Daniel and his friends had many enemies who wanted to punish them for worshipping the one real God. But they chose to follow God anyway. This book shows us how to be courageous even when people dislike our faith in God. It reminds us that we can trust God in all things. ◆

Jerusalem taken by the Babylonians

1 In the third year of the rule of Judah's King Jehoiakim, Babylon's King Nebuchadnezzar came to Jerusalem and attacked it. ²The Lord handed Judah's King Jehoiakim over to Nebuchadnezzar, along with some of the equipment from God's house. Nebuchadnezzar took these to Shinar, to his own god's temple, putting them in his god's treasury.

Training for royal service

³Nebuchadnezzar instructed his highest official Ashpenaz to choose royal descendants and members of the ruling class from the Israelites—⁴good-looking young men without defects, skilled in all wisdom, possessing knowledge, conversant with learning, and capable of serving in the king's palace. Ashpenaz was to teach them the Chaldean language and its literature. ⁵The king assigned these young men daily allotments from his own food and from the royal wine. Ashpenaz was to teach them for three years so that at the end of that time they could serve before the king. ⁶Among these young men from the Judeans were Daniel, Hananiah, Mishael, and Azariah. ⁷But the chief official gave them new names. He named Daniel "Belteshazzar," Hananiah "Shadrach," Mishael "Meshach," and Azariah "Abednego."

Test

⁸Daniel decided that he wouldn't pollute himself with the king's rations or the royal wine, and he appealed to the chief official in hopes that he wouldn't have to do so. ⁹Now God had established faithful loyalty between Daniel and the chief official; ¹⁰but the chief official said to Daniel, "I'm afraid of my master, the king, who has mandated what you are to eat and drink. What will happen if he sees your faces looking thinner than the other young men in your group? The king will have my head because of you!"

¹¹So Daniel spoke to the guard whom the chief official had appointed over Daniel, Hananiah, Mishael, and Azariah: ¹²"Why not test your servants for ten days? You could give us a diet of vegetables to eat and water to drink. ¹³Then compare our appearance to the appearance of the young men who eat the king's food. Then deal with your servants according to what you see."

¹⁴The guard decided to go along with their plan and tested them for ten days. ¹⁵At the end of ten days they looked better and healthier than all the young men who were eating the king's food. ¹⁶So the guard kept taking away their rations and the wine they were supposed to drink and gave them vegetables instead. ¹⁷And God gave knowledge, mastery of all literature, and wisdom to these four men. Daniel himself gained understanding of every type of vision and dream.

Result of the training

¹⁸When the time came to review the young men as the king had ordered, the chief official brought them before Nebuchadnezzar. ¹⁹When the king spoke with them, he found no one as good as Daniel, Hananiah, Mishael, and Azariah. So they took their place in the king's service. ²⁰Whenever the king consulted them about any aspect of wisdom and understanding, he found them head and shoulders above all the dream interpreters and enchanters in his entire kingdom. ²¹And Daniel stayed in the king's service until the first year of King Cyrus.

An impossible challenge

2 In the second year of Nebuchadnezzar's rule, he had many dreams. The dreams made him anxious, but he kept sleeping. ²The king summoned the dream interpreters, enchanters, diviners, and Chaldeans to explain his dreams to him. They came and stood before the king.

³Then the king said to them: "I had a dream, and I'm anxious to know its meaning."

⁴The Chaldeans answered the king in Aramaic:ᵃ "Long live the king! Tell your servants the dream, and we will explain its meaning."

did you **know?** To honor God, Daniel and his friends ate only fruits and vegetables. After ten days, they were so healthy they were allowed to keep their diet. After three years, they were so strong they were given special jobs in the king's court.

ᵃThe book switches into Aramaic at this point, returning to Hebrew in 8:1

⁵The king answered the Chaldeans: "My decision is final: If you can't tell me the dream and its meaning, you will be torn limb from limb, and your houses will be turned into trash dumps. ⁶But if you do explain the dream and its meaning, you'll receive generous gifts and glorious honor from me. So explain to me the dream as well as its meaning."

⁷They answered him again: "The king must tell his servants the dream. We will then explain the meaning."

⁸The king replied: "Now I definitely know you are stalling for time, because you see that my decision is final ⁹and that if you can't tell me the dream, your fate is certain. You've conspired to make false and lying speeches before me until the situation changes. Tell me the dream now! Then I'll know you can explain its meaning to me."

¹⁰The Chaldeans answered the king: "No one on earth can do what the king is asking! No king or ruler, no matter how great, has ever asked such a thing of any dream interpreter, enchanter, or Chaldean. ¹¹What the king is asking is impossible! No one could declare the dream to the king but the gods, who don't live among mere humans."

¹²At this, the king exploded in a furious rage and ordered that all Babylon's sages be wiped out. ¹³So the command went out: The sages were to be killed. Daniel and his friends too were hunted down; they were to be killed as well.

God reveals the mystery

¹⁴Then Daniel, with wisdom and sound judgment, responded to Arioch the king's chief executioner, who had gone out to kill Babylon's sages. ¹⁵He said to Arioch the king's royal officer, "Why is the king's command so unreasonable?" After Arioch explained the situation to Daniel, ¹⁶Daniel went and asked the king to give him some time so he could explain the dream's meaning to him. ¹⁷Then Daniel went to his house and explained the situation to his friends Hananiah, Mishael, and Azariah ¹⁸so that they would ask the God of heaven for help about this mystery, in hopes that Daniel and his friends wouldn't die with the rest of Babylon's sages. ¹⁹Then, in a

God's Thoughts ◆ My Thoughts

Eating Habits *Daniel 1:8-21*

Daniel knew a trap when he saw one. After defeating Israel, the Babylonians took Daniel back to their capital city. The Babylonian king kept servants from defeated nations so those countries wouldn't try to fight him again. Part of Daniel's training to serve the king was to eat the food of the new country. But Daniel knew that this kind of food was another way to make him forget about Israel and God. God's Instruction had already told him the best kind of food to eat. Because Daniel and his friends stayed away from Nebuchadnezzar's food, God gave them health and wisdom greater than the other king's servants.

It's hard to be different from other people around you. It's also hard to avoid doing dangerous things that your friends want to do. But no matter what hard things you face, God can give you courage to do the right thing.

Are you careful about what you eat? Is your food healthy?

What would you say to a leader who wants you to be just like everyone else?

vision by night, the mystery was revealed to Daniel! Daniel praised the God of heaven:

²⁰ God's name be praised
from age to eternal age!
Wisdom and might are his!
²¹ God is the one who changes
times and eras,
who dethrones one king,
only to establish another,
who grants wisdom to the wise and
knowledge to those with insight.
²² God is the one who uncovers
what lies deeply hidden;
he knows what hides in darkness,
light lives with him!
²³ I acknowledge and praise you,
my fathers' God!
You've given me wisdom and might,
and now you've made known to me
what we asked of you:
you've made known to us
the king's demand.

Daniel recounts the dream

²⁴ So Daniel went to Arioch, the man the king had appointed to wipe out Babylon's sages. Daniel said to him, "Don't wipe out the sages of Babylon! Bring me before the king, and I will explain the dream's meaning to him." ²⁵ Wasting no time, Arioch brought Daniel before the king, telling him, "I have found someone from the Judean exiles who will tell the dream's meaning to the king."

²⁶ In reply the king said to Daniel (whose name was Belteshazzar), "Can you really tell me the dream that I saw, as well as its meaning?"

²⁷ Daniel answered the king, "Sages, enchanters, dream interpreters, and diviners can't explain to the king the mystery he seeks. ²⁸ But there is a God in heaven, a revealer of mysteries, who has shown King Nebuchadnezzar what will happen in the days to come! Now this was your dream—this was the vision in your head as you lay in your bed:

²⁹ "As you lay in bed, Your Majesty, your thoughts turned to what will happen in the future. The revealer of mysteries has revealed to you what will happen. ³⁰ Now this mystery was revealed to me, not because I have more wisdom than any other living person but so that the dream's meaning might be made known to the king, and so that you might know the thoughts of your own mind.

³¹ "Your Majesty, you were looking, and there, rising before you, was a single, massive statue. This statue was huge, shining with dazzling light, and was awesome to see. ³² The statue's head was made of pure gold; its chest and arms were made from silver; its abdomen and hips were made of bronze. ³³ Its legs were of iron, and its feet were a mixture of iron and clay. ³⁴ You observed this until a stone was cut, but not by hands; and it smashed the statue's feet of iron and clay and shattered them. ³⁵ Then all the parts shattered simultaneously—iron, clay, bronze, silver, and gold. They became like chaff, left on summer threshing floors. The wind lifted them away until no trace of them remained. But the stone that smashed the statue became a mighty mountain, and it filled the entire earth.

The dream's meaning: four future rulers

³⁶ "This was the dream. Now we will tell the king its meaning: ³⁷ You, Your Majesty, are the king of kings. The God of heaven has given kingship, power, might, and glory to you! ³⁸ God has delivered into your care human beings, wild creatures, and birds in the sky—wherever they live—and has made you ruler of all of them. You are the gold head. ³⁹ But in your place, another kingdom will arise, one inferior to yours, and then a third, bronze kingdom will rule over all the earth. ⁴⁰ Then will come a fourth kingdom, mighty like iron. Just as iron shatters and crushes everything; so like an iron that smashes, it will shatter and crush all these others. ⁴¹ As for the feet and toes that you saw, which were a mixture of potter's clay and iron, that signifies a divided kingdom; but it will possess some of the unyielding strength of iron. Even so, you saw the iron mixed with earthy clay ⁴² so that the toes were made from a mixture of iron and clay. Part of the kingdom will be mighty, but part of it will be fragile. ⁴³ Just as you saw the iron mixed with earthy clay, they will join together by intermarrying, but they will not bond to each other, just as iron does not fuse with clay.

⁴⁴ "But in the days of those kings, the God of heaven will raise up an everlasting kingdom that will be indestructible. Its rule will never pass to another people. It will shatter

other kingdoms. It will put an end to all of them. It will stand firm forever, ⁴⁵just like you saw when the stone, which was cut from the mountain, but not by hands, shattered the iron, bronze, clay, silver, and gold. A great God has revealed to the king what will happen in the future. The dream is certain. Its meaning can be trusted."

Nebuchadnezzar honors Daniel

⁴⁶Then King Nebuchadnezzar bowed low and honored Daniel. The king ordered that grain and incense offerings be made to Daniel. ⁴⁷The king declared to Daniel, "No doubt about it: your God is God of gods, Lord of kings, and a revealer of mysteries because you were able to reveal this mystery!" ⁴⁸Then the king exalted Daniel and lavished gifts on him, making him ruler over all the province of Babylon and chief minister over all Babylon's sages. ⁴⁹At Daniel's urging, the king appointed Shadrach, Meshach, and Abednego to administer the province of Babylon, but Daniel himself remained at the royal court.

SAILBOAT

GIVING THANKS

Don't Wait to Give Thanks *Daniel 2:23-47*
God gave Daniel the key to saving his life. Babylon's King Nebuchadnezzar was going to kill all of his wise men if none of them could tell him what his dream was and what that dream meant. Daniel didn't know what the king's dream was or what it meant, but he knew God did. When God gave Daniel the king's dream and the meaning, Daniel knew it was important to pause and be thankful to God. He knew that in the excitement of getting exactly what we want it's easy to forget to say thanks. That's why Daniel didn't rush out to see the king as soon as God gave him the answer. He wanted to make sure God received all the credit God was due. Daniel's readiness to give thanks and credit to God led Nebuchadnezzar to praise God above his own gods. ◖

Gold statue

3 King Nebuchadnezzar made a gold statue. It was ninety feet high and nine feet wide. He set it up in the Dura Valley in the province of Babylon. ²King Nebuchadnezzar then ordered the chief administrators, ministers, governors, counselors, treasurers, judges, magistrates, and all the provincial officials to assemble and come for the dedication of the statue that he had set up. ³So the chief administrators, ministers, governors, counselors, treasurers, judges, magistrates, and all the provincial officials assembled for the dedication of the statue that King Nebuchadnezzar had set up. They stood in front of the statue the king had set up. ⁴The herald proclaimed loudly: "Peoples, nations, and languages! This is what you must do: ⁵When you hear the sound of the horn, pipe, zither, lyre, harp, flute, and every kind of instrument, you must bow down and worship the gold statue that King Nebuchadnezzar has set up. ⁶Anyone who will not bow down and worship will be immediately thrown into a furnace of flaming fire." ⁷So because of this order as soon as they heard the sound of the horn, pipe, zither, lyre, harp, flute,^b and every kind of instrument, all the peoples, nations, and languages bowed down and worshipped the gold statue that King Nebuchadnezzar had set up.

Plot against Shadrach, Meshach, and Abednego

⁸At that moment some Chaldeans came forward, seizing a chance to attack the Jews. ⁹They said to King Nebuchadnezzar:

"Long live the king! ¹⁰Your Majesty, you gave a command that everyone who hears the sound of the horn, pipe, zither, lyre, harp, flute, and every kind of instrument should bow down and worship the gold statue. ¹¹Anyone who wouldn't bow and worship would be thrown into a furnace of flaming fire. ¹²Now there are some Jews, ones you appointed to administer the province of Babylon—specifically, Shadrach, Meshach, and Abednego—who have ignored your command. They don't serve your gods, and they don't worship the gold statue you've set up."

¹³In a violent rage Nebuchadnezzar ordered them to bring Shadrach, Meshach, and Abednego. They were brought before the king.

¹⁴Nebuchadnezzar said to them: "Shadrach, Meshach, and Abednego: Is it true that you don't serve my gods or worship the gold

---

^bIdentification of the instruments is not certain; several of the Aramaic terms are Greek loanwords.

statue I've set up? [15]If you are now ready to do so, bow down and worship the gold statue I've made when you hear the sound of horn, pipe, zither, lyre, harp, flute, and every kind of instrument. But if you won't worship it, you will be thrown straight into the furnace of flaming fire. Then what god will rescue you from my power?"

[16]Shadrach, Meshach, and Abednego answered King Nebuchadnezzar: "We don't need to answer your question. [17]If our God—the one we serve—is able to rescue us from the furnace of flaming fire and from your power, Your Majesty, then let him rescue us.[c] [18]But if he doesn't, know this for certain, Your Majesty: we will never serve your gods or worship the gold statue you've set up."

Memorize
Dan 3:17-18

Inside the furnace

[19]Nebuchadnezzar was filled with rage, and his face twisted beyond recognition because of Shadrach, Meshach, and Abednego. In response he commanded that the furnace be heated to seven times its normal heat. [20]He told some of the strongest men in his army to bind Shadrach, Meshach, and Abednego and throw them into the furnace of flaming fire. [21]So Shadrach, Meshach, and Abednego were bound, still dressed in all their clothes, and thrown into the furnace of flaming fire. ([22]Now the king's command had been rash, and the furnace was heated to such an extreme that the fire's flame killed the very men who carried Shadrach, Meshach, and Abednego to it.) [23]So these three men, Shadrach, Meshach, and Abednego, fell, bound, into the furnace of flaming fire.

[24]Then King Nebuchadnezzar jumped up in shock and said to his associates, "Didn't we throw three men, bound, into the fire?"

They answered the king, "Certainly, Your Majesty."

[25]He replied, "Look! I see four men, unbound, walking around inside the fire, and they aren't hurt! And the fourth one looks like one of the gods." [26]Nebuchadnezzar went near the opening of the furnace of flaming fire and said, "Shadrach, Meshach, and Abednego, servants of the Most High God, come

LIFE PRESERVER

Who was the fourth person in the furnace? *Daniel 3:8-27*

King Nebuchadnezzar was really mad because Shadrach, Meshach, and Abednego wouldn't worship the gold statue. So he threw them into a furnace. The men didn't seem to be worried, though. They believed that God would save them.

In some ways, this is a miracle story. The men survived the fire. And the king's officials reported that they had seen four men walking around in the furnace, not three. It seems clear that God was present with them, perhaps sending a representative or messenger to be with them. So King Nebuchadnezzar changed his heart and decided to trust the God who had saved these men. ◆

out! Come here!" Then Shadrach, Meshach, and Abednego came out of the fire. [27]The chief administrators, ministers, governors, and the king's associates crowded around to look at them. The fire hadn't done anything to them: their hair wasn't singed; their garments looked the same as before; they didn't even smell like fire!

Nebuchadnezzar praises God

[28]Nebuchadnezzar declared: "May the God of Shadrach, Meshach, and Abednego be praised! He sent his messenger[d] to rescue his servants who trusted him. They ignored the king's order, sacrificing their bodies, because they wouldn't serve or worship any god but their God. [29]I now issue a decree to every people, nation, and language: whoever speaks disrespectfully about Shadrach, Meshach, and Abednego's God will be torn limb from limb and their house made a trash heap, because there is no other god who can rescue like this."

[30]Then the king made Shadrach, Meshach, and Abednego prosperous in the province of Babylon.

Nebuchadnezzar's testimony

4 [e]King Nebuchadnezzar's message to all the peoples, nations, and languages inhabiting the entire earth: "I wish you much peace. [2]I'm delighted to share the signs and miracles that the Most High God has worked in my life.

[c]Or *he will deliver us* [d]Or *angel* [e]3:31 in Aram

³ His signs are superb!
His miracles so powerful!
His kingdom is everlasting.
His rule is for all time.

⁴ᶠ"While I, Nebuchadnezzar, was safe in my house, content in my palace, ⁵I had a terrifying dream. My thoughts while I was lying in bed and the vision in my mind overwhelmed me. ⁶I ordered all Babylon's sages to come before me, so they might tell me the dream's meaning. ⁷So the dream interpreters, enchanters, Chaldeans, and diviners came. I told them the dream, but they couldn't interpret it for me. ⁸Daniel, who is called Belteshazzar after the name of my god, was the last to come before me. In him is the breathᵍ of the holy gods! I told Daniel the dream:

Nebuchadnezzar's dream

⁹"Belteshazzar, chief of the dream interpreters, I know the breath of the holy gods is in you, and no mystery is too difficult for you.

ᶠ 4:1 in Aram ᵍOr *spirit*; also in 4:9, 18

Tell me the meaning of the visions I had in my dream. ¹⁰In my mind, as I lay in bed, I saw a vision:

At the center of the earth
was a towering tree.
¹¹The tree grew in size and strength;
it was as high as the sky;
it could be seen
from every corner of the earth.
¹²Its leaves were beautiful,
its fruit abundant;
it had enough food for everyone.
Wild animals took shade under it;
birds nested in its branches.
All living things lived off that tree.

¹³"In my mind, as I lay in bed, I saw another vision: A holy watcher came down from heaven. ¹⁴He proclaimed loudly:

'Cut down the tree
and shear off its branches!
Strip its leaves and scatter its fruit!
The creatures should flee from its shelter;

Standing Up for Your Faith *Daniel 3:8-30*

Shadrach, Meshach, and Abednego obeyed God, no matter what. The problem began when Babylon's King Nebuchadnezzar built a huge gold statue. Nebuchadnezzar wanted everyone in the empire to bow down and worship the statue. But his loyal servants Shadrach, Meshach, and Abednego wouldn't do that. They knew that one of God's first commandments was to never bow before or worship an idol (Exod 20:3-6). When the time came and everyone around them bent toward the gleaming statue, Shadrach, Meshach, and Abednego stayed standing—even though they would likely be killed for not doing what the king commanded. But God saved them because of their obedience to God. And when Nebuchadnezzar saw God's power, he ordered that no one was to speak disrespectfully about God again.

We may never be asked to bow down to an idol made of gold. But other things can be idols in our lives. Some people worship money. Other people worship sports stars or music stars. Those idols keep us from living a life in which we care more about God and about helping others.

Do you have a favorite sports star or music star?

Is that person more important to you than God?

the birds should take flight
    from its branches.
¹⁵ But leave its deepest root in the earth,
    bound with iron and bronze
    in the field grass.
Dew from heaven is to wash it,
    and it must live with the animals
    in the earth's vegetation.
¹⁶ Its[h] human mind is to be changed:
    it will be given the mind of an animal.
    Seven periods of time will pass over it.
¹⁷ This sentence is by the watchers' decree;
    this decision is the holy ones' word
    so that all who live might know
    that the Most High
        dominates human kingship.
The Most High gives kingship
    to anyone he wants
    and sets over it the lowest of people.'

¹⁸"This is the dream that I, King Nebuchadnezzar, had. So now Belteshazzar, tell me the meaning because all the sages in my kingdom were unable to interpret it for me. But you are able to do it because the breath of the holy gods is in you."

Daniel interprets the visions

¹⁹Daniel, who was called Belteshazzar, was shocked for a bit. What he thought about frightened him.

The king declared, "Don't let the dream and its meaning scare you, Belteshazzar."

Then Belteshazzar answered, "Sir, I wish the dream to be for those who hate you and its meaning to be for your enemies! ²⁰The tree you saw that grew in size and strength, that was as high as the sky, that could be seen from every corner of the earth, ²¹with its beautiful leaves and its abundant fruit, and that had enough food for everyone, with wild animals living under it and birds nesting in its branches—²²Your Majesty, that tree is you! You have grown large and become powerful. Your greatness is as high as the sky; your rule extends to the edge of the earth!

²³"Your Majesty, the holy watcher you saw coming down from heaven, who said, 'Cut down the tree and destroy it, but leave its deepest root in the earth, bound with iron and bronze in the field grass, dew from heaven is to wash it, and it must live with the wild animals until seven periods of time pass over it'—²⁴Your Majesty, this is the dream's meaning: It is the sentence of the Most High, delivered to my master the king. ²⁵You will be driven away from other humans and will live with the wild animals. You will eat grass like cattle and will be washed by dew from heaven. Seven periods of time will pass over you, until you acknowledge that the Most High dominates human kingship, giving it to anyone he wants. ²⁶And when he said to leave the deepest root of the tree—that means your kingship will again be yours, once you acknowledge that heaven rules all. ²⁷Therefore, Your Majesty, please accept my advice: remove your sins by doing what is right; remove your wrongdoing by showing mercy to the poor. Then your safety will be long lasting."

Visions come true

²⁸All this happened to King Nebuchadnezzar. ²⁹Twelve months later, he was walking on the roof of the royal palace in Babylon. ³⁰The king declared, "Isn't this Babylon, the magnificent city that I built as the royal house by my own mighty strength and for my own majestic glory?"

³¹These words hadn't even left the king's mouth when a voice came from heaven: "You, King Nebuchadnezzar, are now informed: Kingship is taken away from you. ³²You will be driven away from other humans and will live with the wild animals. You will eat grass like cattle, and seven periods of time will pass over you until you acknowledge that the Most High dominates human kingship, giving it to anyone he wants."

³³Nebuchadnezzar's sentence was immediately carried out. He was driven away from other humans and ate grass like cattle. Dew from heaven washed his body until he grew hair like eagles' feathers and claws like a bird.

Nebuchadnezzar is restored

³⁴"At the end of that time, I, Nebuchadnezzar, raised my eyes to heaven. My reason returned to me, and I praised the Most High. I worshipped and glorified the one who lives forever because his rule is everlasting; his

---

[h]Throughout 4:15–16 and later in this chap, *it* and *its* could also be translated *he* and *his*.

kingdom is for all time. ³⁵All of earth's inhabitants are nothing in comparison. The Most High does whatever he wants with heaven's forces and with earth's inhabitants. No one can contain his power or say to him, 'What do you think you are doing?' ³⁶So at that moment my reason returned to me. My honor and splendor came back to me for the glory of my kingdom. My associates and my princes wanted to be with me again. Not only was I reinstated over my kingdom, I received more power than ever before.

³⁷"Now I, Nebuchadnezzar, worship, magnify, and glorify the king of heaven. All his works are truth, all his paths are justice, and he is able to humble all who walk in pride."

UMBRELLA
PRIDE

Don't Take All the Credit *Daniel 4:28-37*

It's hard to be humble when you're in a position of power. God gave two dreams to Babylon's King Nebuchadnezzar. In the first dream, the king saw himself as the gold head of a great statue (Dan 2:36-38). After this dream, he built a gold statue for people to worship (Dan 3:1-7). In the second dream, Nebuchadnezzar saw himself as a glorious tree that was cut down. Daniel told the king exactly what the dream meant and the warning it represented, but Nebuchadnezzar heard only the first part—the part about how important he was. Nebuchadnezzar wasn't concerned about his pride. He forgot that acting high and mighty brings all sorts of trouble. He lacked humility, and he faced harsh consequences as a result. But when Nebuchadnezzar returned to thinking about God, praising God for God's greatness, God restored him and gave him more than he ever had before. 💧

Belshazzar's party

5 King Belshazzar threw a huge party for a thousand of his princes, and he drank a lot of wine in front of them. ²While he was under the wine's influence, Belshazzar commanded that the gold and silver equipment that his father Nebuchadnezzar had taken from Jerusalem's temple be brought to the party so that the king, his princes, his consorts, and

his secondary wives could drink wine out of them. ³So the goldⁱ equipment that had been carried out of the temple, God's house in Jerusalem, was brought in; and the king, his princes, his consorts, and his secondary wives drank out of it. ⁴They drank a lot of wine; and they praised the gods of gold, silver, bronze, iron, wood, and stone.

Writing on the wall

⁵Right then the fingers of a human hand appeared and wrote on the plaster of the king's palace wall in the light of the lamp. The king saw the hand that wrote. ⁶The king's mood changed immediately, and he was deeply disturbed. He felt weak, and his knees were shaking. ⁷The king yelled, calling for the enchanters, the Chaldeans, and the diviners.

The king told these sages of Babylon: "Anyone who can read this writing and tell me its meaning will wear royal robes, will have a gold chain around his neck, and will rule the kingdom as third in command."

⁸Then all the king's sages arrived, but they couldn't read the writing or interpret it for the king. ⁹At that point King Belshazzar was really frightened. All the color drained from his face, and his princes were also very worried.

¹⁰Upon hearing the commotion coming from the king and his princes, the queen entered the banqueting hall and declared, "Long live the king! Don't be so disturbed. Don't be so frightened. ¹¹There is a man in your kingdom who has the breath^j of holy gods in him! When your father was alive, this man was shown to possess illumination, insight, and wisdom like the very wisdom of the gods.^k Your father King Nebuchadnezzar appointed this man as chief over the dream interpreters, enchanters, Chaldeans, and diviners. Yes, your father did this ¹²because this man—Daniel, the one the king named Belteshazzar—possesses an extraordinary spirit, knowledge, and insight into the meaning of dreams. He can explain ambiguities and resolve mysteries. Now in light of all that, summon Daniel! He will explain the meaning of this thing."

¹³So Daniel was brought before the king. The king said to him, "So you are Daniel, the

Daniel from the exiles that my father the king brought from Judah? [14] I have heard that the breath of the gods is in you and that you possess illumination, insight, and extraordinary wisdom. [15] Now, the sages and the dream interpreters were brought before me to read this writing and interpret it for me, but they couldn't explain its meaning. [16] But I've heard that you can explain meanings and solve mysteries. So if you can read this writing and interpret it for me, you will wear royal robes, have a gold chain around your neck, and will rule the kingdom as third in command."

Daniel interprets the writing

[17] Daniel answered the king: "Keep your gifts. Give the rewards to someone else. But I will still read the writing to the king and interpret it for him. [18] Listen, Your Majesty: The Most High God gave kingship, power, glory, and majesty to your father Nebuchadnezzar. [19] Because of the power God gave Nebuchadnezzar, all peoples, nations, and languages were terrified of him. He did whatever he wanted, whenever he wanted: killing or

LIGHTHOUSE

RESPECT FOR GOD

God Expects Respect *Daniel 5:5-30*

The writing was on the wall for everyone to see— the king didn't respect God. King Belshazzar used the special equipment from God's temple as ordinary drinking cups, all while praising false gods! He was bragging about how much better he was than Israel's God. Daniel reminded the king that Belshazzar's own father, King Nebuchadnezzar, learned the hard way to respect God. Belshazzar knew exactly what had happened to his father—how Nebuchadnezzar grew so proud of his wealth and power that he claimed it all came from his own doing. Daniel reminded Belshazzar how God took away his father's reason and made him like a wild animal until Nebuchadnezzar turned away from his pride and gave God the credit God deserved (Dan 4:28-37). It was too late for Belshazzar to learn his father's lesson. He already had plenty of time to respect God. He lost his kingdom and his life that very night. ◊

sparing, exalting or humbling. [20] But when he became arrogant, acting in stubborn pride, he was pulled off his royal throne and the glory was taken from him. [21] He was driven away from other humans, and his mind became like an animal's. He lived with wild donkeys, he ate grass like cattle, and dew from heaven washed his body until he realized that the Most High God dominates human kingship and sets over it anyone he wants.

[22] "But you who are his son, Belshazzar, you haven't submitted, even though you've known all this. [23] Instead, you've set yourself up against the Lord of heaven! The equipment of God's house was brought to you; and you, your princes, your consorts, and your secondary wives drank wine out of it, all the while praising the gods of silver, gold, bronze, iron, wood, and stone—gods who can't see, hear, or know anything. But you didn't glorify the true God who holds your very breath in his hand and who owns every road you take.

[24] "That's why this hand was sent from God and why this message was written down. [25] This is what was written down:

MENE, MENE, TEKEL, and PARSIN.[l]

[26] "This is the meaning of the word MENE: God has numbered[m] the days of your rule. It's over! [27] TEKEL means that you've been weighed[n] on the scales, and you don't measure up. [28] PERES[o] means your kingship is divided[p] and given to the Medes and the Persians."[q]

[29] Then Belshazzar commanded that Daniel be dressed in a purple robe, have a gold chain around his neck, and be officially appointed as third in command in the kingdom.

[30] That very same night, Belshazzar the Chaldean king was killed. [31] Darius the Mede received the kingdom at the age of 62.

Plot against Daniel

6 Darius decided to appoint one hundred twenty chief administrators throughout the kingdom, [2] and to set over them three main officers to whom they would report so that the king wouldn't have to be bothered with too much.[r] One of these main officers was Daniel. [3] Because of his extraordinary

---

[l] Aram *Upharsin* [m] Aram *menah*, which is a wordplay with *Mene* [n] Aram *teqal*, which is a wordplay with *Tekel* [o] The singular form of the plural *Parsin* in 5:25 [p] Aram *peras*, which is a wordplay with *Parsin* [q] Aram *Paras*, another wordplay with *Parsin* [r] Aram uncertain

spirit, Daniel soon surpassed the other officers and the chief administrators—so much so that the king had plans to set him over the entire kingdom. ⁴As a result, the other officers and the chief administrators tried to find some problem with Daniel's work for the kingdom. But they couldn't find any problem or corruption at all because Daniel was trustworthy. He wasn't guilty of any negligence or corruption.

⁵So these men said, "We won't find any fault in Daniel, unless we can find something to use against him from his religious practice."ˢ

⁶So these officers and chief administrators ganged together and went to the king. They said to him, "Long live King Darius! ⁷All the officers of the kingdom, the ministers, the chief administrators, the royal associates, and the governors advise the king to issue an edict and enforce a law, that for thirty days anyone who says prayers to any god or human being except you, Your Majesty, will be thrown into a pit of lions. ⁸Now, Your Majesty, issue the law and sign the document so that it cannot be changed, as per the law of Media and Persia, which cannot be annulled." ⁹Because of this, King Darius signed the document containing the law.

Daniel prays

¹⁰When Daniel learned that the document had been signed, he went to his house. Now his upper room had open windows that faced Jerusalem. Daniel knelt down, prayed, and praised his God three times that day, just like he always did. ¹¹Just then these men, all ganged together, came upon Daniel praying and seeking mercy from his God. ¹²They then went and talked to the king about the law: "Your Majesty! Didn't you sign a law, that for thirty days any person who prays to any god or human being besides you, Your Majesty, would be thrown into a pit of lions?"

The king replied, "The decision is absolutely firm in accordance with the law of Media and Persia, which cannot be annulled."

¹³So they said to the king, "One of the Judean exiles, Daniel, has ignored you, Your Majesty, as well as the law you signed. He says his prayers three times a day!"

¹⁴When the king heard this report, he was very unhappy. He decided to rescue Daniel and did everything he could do to save Daniel before the sun went down. ¹⁵But these men, all ganged together, came and said to the king, "You must realize, Your Majesty, that the law of Media and Persia, including every law and edict the king has issued, cannot be changed."

Daniel in the lions' pit

¹⁶So the king gave the order, and they brought Daniel and hurled him into the pit of lions.

The king said to Daniel: "Your God—the one you serve so consistently—will rescue you."ᵗ

¹⁷A single stone was brought and placed over the entrance to the pit. The king sealed it with his own ring and with those of his princes so that Daniel's situation couldn't be changed. ¹⁸The king then went home to his palace and fasted through the night. No pleasuresᵘ were brought to him, and he couldn't sleep. ¹⁹At dawn, at the first sign of light, the king rose and rushed to the lions' pit.

²⁰As he approached it, he called out to Daniel, worried: "Daniel, servant of the living God! Was your God—the one you serve so consistently—able to rescue you from the lions?"

did you know? The name *Daniel* means "God is my judge." In this story and throughout his life, Daniel lived up to his name. Daniel never seemed to care what anyone except God thought about what he did or how he lived.

²¹Then Daniel answered the king: "Long live the king! ²²My God sent his messenger, who shut the lions' mouths. They haven't touched me because I was judged innocent before my God. I haven't done anything wrong to you either, Your Majesty."

²³The king was thrilled. He commanded that Daniel be brought up out of the pit, and Daniel was lifted out. Not a scratch was found on him, because he trusted in his God. ²⁴The king then ordered that the men who had accused Daniel be brought and thrown into the lions' pit—including their wives and children. They hadn't even reached the bottom of the

---

ˢOr *in the Instruction of his God* ᵗOr *May your God—the one you serve so consistently—rescue you.* ᵘAram uncertain

pit before the lions overpowered them, crushing all their bones.

New decree

25Then King Darius wrote the following decree:

To all the peoples, nations, and languages inhabiting the entire earth: I wish you much peace. 26I now issue this command: In every region of my kingdom, all people must fear and revere Daniel's God because:

He is the living God.

God stands firm forever.

His kingship is indestructible.

God's rule will last until the end of time.

27 He is rescuer and savior;

God performs signs and miracles

in heaven and on earth.

Here's the proof:

He rescued Daniel from the lions' power.

28And so Daniel was made prosperous during the rule of Darius and during the rule of Cyrus the Persian.

LIGHTHOUSE

PRAYER

Keep Praying! *Daniel 6:1-28*

Nothing was going to distract Daniel from praying to God. Thanks to the favor of God and his own hard work, Daniel rose quickly to high positions in the kingdom of Babylon, no matter who was in charge. But others were jealous of Daniel's success. When the king's other officers discovered the king planned to place Daniel over the entire kingdom, they decide to ruin him. Daniel prayed three times to God every day, so the officers came up with a new law that said anyone who prayed to anyone other than the king would be put to death. When Daniel heard about this law, he didn't stop praying. He didn't even try to hide his prayers. He kept his windows open toward Jerusalem and prayed as he always did. Daniel would have rather died than lose his way of talking with God. His relationship with God was more important than his own life. Because Daniel was faithful in prayer, God saved him from death, and the king wrote a new law saying that everyone should respect God. ♦

Daniel's vision: four beasts

7In the first year of Babylon's King Belshazzar, Daniel had a dream—a vision in his head as he lay on his bed. He wrote the dream down. Here is the beginning of the account:

2I am Daniel. In the vision I had during the night I saw the four winds of heaven churning the great sea. 3Four giant beasts emerged from the sea, each different from the others. 4The first was like a lion with eagle's wings. I observed it until its wings were pulled off, and it was lifted up from the ground. It was then set on two feet, like a human being, and it received a human mind. 5Then I saw another beast, a second one, like a bear. It was raised on one side. It had three ribs in its mouth between its teeth. It was told: "Get up! Devour much flesh!" 6I kept watching, and suddenly there was another beast, this one like a leopard. On its back it had four wings like bird wings. This beast had four heads. Authority was given to it.

7After this, as I continued to watch this night vision, I saw a fourth beast, terrifying and hideous, with extraordinary power and with massive iron teeth. As it ate and crushed, its feet smashed whatever was left over. It was different from all the other beasts before it, and it had ten horns. 8I was staring at the horns when, suddenly, another small horn came up between them. Three of the earlier horns were ripped out to make room for it. On this new horn were eyes like human eyes and a mouth that bragged and bragged.

Throne of fire and the human figure

9As I was watching,

thrones were raised up.

The ancient one took his seat.

His clothes were white like snow;

his hair was like a lamb's wool.

His throne was made of flame;

its wheels were blazing fire.

10 A river of fire flowed out

from his presence;

thousands upon thousands served him;

ten thousand times ten thousand

stood ready to serve him!

The court sat in session;

the scrolls were opened.

11I kept watching. I watched from the moment the horn started bragging until the beast was killed and its body was destroyed, handed over to be burned with fire. 12Then the authority of the remaining beasts was brought to an end, but they were given an extension among the living for a set time and season.

¹³As I continued to watch this night vision of mine, I suddenly saw

> one like a human being[v]
>> coming with the heavenly clouds.
> He came to the ancient one
>> and was presented before him.

¹⁴Rule, glory, and kingship
>> were given to him;
> all peoples, nations, and languages
>> will serve him.
> His rule is an everlasting one—
>> it will never pass away!—
> his kingship is indestructible.

Beasts interpreted

¹⁵Now this caused me, Daniel, to worry.[w] My visions disturbed me greatly. ¹⁶So I went to one of the servants who was standing ready nearby. I asked him for the truth about all this.

He spoke to me and explained to me the meaning of these things. ¹⁷"These four giant beasts are four kings that will rise up from the earth, ¹⁸but the holy ones of the Most High will receive the kingship. They will hold the kingship securely forever and always."

UMBRELLA
Fear

Don't Be Afraid of the Future *Daniel 7:1-28*
Daniel was used to dreams. After all, he was the chief of dreamers and interpreted dreams for the king himself (Dan 5:11-12). A little nightmare probably wouldn't have bothered Daniel. But God gave Daniel a dream that was far from ordinary—a dream about future events, like those in Nebuchadnezzar's dreams that Daniel had explained (Dan 2:24-45; 4:19-27). Just as in those dreams, Daniel's dreams had pictures or symbols that represented events that were going to take place some day. Instead of seeing armies and powerful rulers, Daniel saw terrible beasts and talking horns. This was scary! The dream stuck with Daniel long after he woke up. God didn't send the visions to Daniel to upset him. God wanted Daniel and those who heard about the dreams to be prepared. ◆

¹⁹Next I wanted greater clarity about the fourth beast, the one that was different from all the others and utterly terrifying with its iron teeth and bronze claws. As it ate and crushed, its feet smashed whatever was left over. ²⁰I wanted greater clarity about the ten horns on its head, and the other horn that came up, along with the three that fell out to make room for it—but especially about the horn that had eyes and a mouth that bragged, and that seemed more important than the others. ²¹As I watched, this same horn waged war against the holy ones and defeated them, ²²until the Ancient One came. Then judgment was given in favor of the holy ones of the Most High. The set time arrived, and the holy ones held the kingship securely.

did you know? The word *El* is an ancient word for God. It is usually paired with another word that describes something about God. For example, *El Elyon* means "God Most High."

²³This is what he said:
"The fourth beast means
> that there will be a fourth kingship
>> on the earth.
It will be different
> from all the other kingships.
It will devour the entire earth,
> trample it, crush it.
²⁴The ten horns mean
> that from this kingship will rise ten kings,
>> and after them will rise yet another.
He will be different
> from the previous ones.
He will defeat three kings.
²⁵He will say things against the Most High
> and will exhaust the holy ones
>> of the Most High.
He will try to change times set by law.
And for a period of time,
> periods of time,
>> and half a period of time,
>> they will be delivered into his power.
²⁶Then the court will sit in session.
> His rule will be taken away—
>> ruined and wiped out for all time.

---

[v]Aram *kebar enash* (*like a son of man*) is an idiom that means *like a human being*; cf also 8:17; 10:16, 18 for Heb approximations.
[w]Or *my spirit was distressed in its sheath*; Aram uncertain

²⁷ The kingship, authority, and power
     of all kingdoms under heaven
     will be given to the people,
     the holy ones of the Most High.
   Their kingship is an everlasting one;
     every authority will serve them
     and obey."

²⁸The account ends here.

Now as for how I, Daniel, felt about this:
My thoughts disturbed me greatly. My mood
darkened considerably, and I kept thinking
about this matter.

Vision of a ram and a goat

8 In the third year of King Belshazzar's
rule, a vision came to me, Daniel, some
time after the earlier vision I had. ²I saw this
vision, and as I experienced it I was in the
walled city of Susa in the province of Elam,ˣ
by the Ulai canal. ³When I lifted my eyes, I
suddenly saw a ram with two horns standing
in front of the canal. Both horns were high,
but one was higher than the other. The higher
one came up after the other one. ⁴I saw the
ram goring west, north, and south. No animal
could resist the ram, and no one could stop it,
rescuing others from its power. The ram did
whatever it pleased. It became powerful.

⁵I was trying to understand this when suddenly a he-goat came from the west, crossing
the entire earth but not touching the ground.
Between this goat's eyes was a horn that was
a sight to see. ⁶The he-goat came to the ram
that had two horns, the one I'd seen standing
in front of the canal. The he-goat charged the
ram in powerful anger. ⁷I saw the he-goat approach the ram. It was enraged at the ram and
attacked it, shattering the ram's two horns.
The ram couldn't resist the he-goat. The he-
goat threw the ram on the ground and trampled on it. No one could rescue the ram from
the he-goat's power.

⁸The he-goat became even greater, but
at the height of its power, its large horn
snapped. In its place, four horns, each a
sight to see, came up toward the four winds
of heaven. ⁹A single, very small horn came
out of one of the four horns. It grew bigger
and bigger, stretching toward the south, the

east, and the beautiful country. ¹⁰It grew as
high as the heavenly forces, until it finally
threw some of them and some of the stars
down to the earth. Then it trampled on them.
¹¹It grew as high as the very leader of those
forces, taking the daily sacrifice away from
himʸ and overturning his holy place. ¹²In an
act of rebellion, another force will take control of the daily sacrifice. It will throw truth
to the ground and will succeed in everything
it does.ᶻ

How long?

¹³I then heard a certain holy one speaking.
A second holy one said to the first one: "How
long will this vision last—the one concerning
the daily sacrifice, the desolating rebellion,
and the handing over of the sanctuary and its
forces to be trampled?"

¹⁴He said to me, "For two thousand three
hundred evenings and mornings. Then the
sanctuary will be restored."

Vision interpreted

¹⁵Now I, Daniel, needed help understanding the vision I saw. Suddenly standing in
front of me was someone who looked like a
man. ¹⁶I then heard a human voice coming out
of the center of the Ulai canal. It called out:
"Gabriel, help this person understand what he
has seen."

¹⁷Gabriel approached me, and I was terrified when he came. I fell with my face to the
ground. Gabriel said to me, "Know this, human
one: the vision is for the end time." ¹⁸As soon
as he said this to me, I fell into a trance. My
face was still on the ground. Then Gabriel
touched me and set me up on my feet.

¹⁹He said, "Now, I am going to tell you what
will happen during the time of doom that is
coming, because at the appointed time there
will be an end. ²⁰The two-horned ram you saw
represents the kings of Media and Persia.
²¹The long-haired he-goat is the king of Greece,
and the big horn between its eyes is the first
king. ²²The horn that snapped so that four
came up in its place means that four kingdoms will come from one nation, but these
four won't have the strength of the first one.

ˣSome LXX sources; MT repeats *I had this vision before I was by the Ulai canal.*   ʸOr *the daily sacrifice was taken away from him.*
ᶻHeb uncertain

²³ When their kingship nears its end
  and their sins[a] are almost complete,
  a king will step forward.
He will be stern and a master of deception.
  ²⁴ At the height of his power,[b]
  he will wreak unbelievable destructions.
He will succeed in all he does.
  He will destroy both the mighty
  and the people of the holy ones.
²⁵ Along with his cunning,
  he will succeed by using deceit.
In his own mind, he will be great.
  In a time of peace,
  he will bring destruction on many,
  opposing even the supreme leader.
But he will be broken—
  and not by a human hand.
²⁶ Now this vision of evening and morning, which has been announced, is true. But you must seal it up, because it is for days far in the future."

²⁷ Then I, Daniel, was overwhelmed and felt sick for days. When I finally got up and went about the king's business, I remained troubled by the vision and couldn't understand it.

Daniel's prayer

9 In the first year of Darius' rule—Darius, who was Ahasuerus' son, a Median by birth and who ruled the Chaldean kingdom— ²I, Daniel, pondered the scrolls, specifically the number of years that it would take to complete Jerusalem's desolation according to the LORD's word to the prophet Jeremiah. It was seventy years. ³I then turned my face to my Lord God, asking for an answer with prayer and pleading, and with fasting, mourning clothes, and ashes. ⁴As I prayed to the LORD my God, I made this confession:

Please, my Lord—you are the great and awesome God, the one who keeps the covenant, and truly faithful to all who love him and keep his commands: ⁵We have sinned and done wrong. We have brought guilt on ourselves and rebelled, ignoring your commands and your laws. ⁶We haven't listened to your servants, the prophets, who spoke in your name to our kings, our leaders, our parents, and to all the land's people. ⁷Righteousness belongs to you, my Lord! But we are ashamed this day—we, the people of Judah, the inhabitants of Jerusalem, all Israel whether near or far, in whatever country where you've driven them because of their unfaithfulness when they broke faith with you. ⁸LORD, we are ashamed—we, our kings, our leaders, and our parents who sinned against you. ⁹Compassion and deep forgiveness belong to my Lord, our God, because we rebelled against him. ¹⁰We didn't listen to the voice of the LORD our God by following the teachings he gave us through his servants, the prophets. ¹¹All Israel broke your Instruction and turned away, ignoring your voice. Then the curse that was sworn long ago—the one written in the Instruction from Moses, God's servant—swept over us because we sinned against God. ¹²God confirmed the words he spoke against us and against our rulers, bringing great trouble on us. What happened in Jerusalem hasn't happened anywhere else in the entire world! ¹³All this trouble came upon us, exactly as it was written in the Instruction of Moses, but we didn't try to reconcile with the LORD our God by turning from our wrongdoing or by finding wisdom in your faithfulness. ¹⁴So the LORD oversaw the great trouble and brought it on us, because the LORD our God has been right in every move he's made, but we haven't listened to his voice.

¹⁵"But now, my Lord, our God—you who brought your people out of Egypt with a strong hand, making a name for yourself even to this day: We have sinned and done the wrong thing." ¹⁶My Lord, please! In line with your many righteous acts, please turn your raging anger from Jerusalem, which is your city, your own holy mountain. Because of our sins and the wrongdoing of our parents, both Jerusalem and your people have become a disgrace to all our neighbors.

¹⁷"But now, our God, listen to your servant's prayer and pleas for help. Shine your face on your ruined sanctuary, for your own sake, my Lord. ¹⁸Open your ears, my God, and listen! Open your eyes and

---

[a]LXX; MT *rebels*   [b]LXX sources; MT *His power will grow strong, but not by his own power,* perhaps influenced by 8:22.

look at our devastation. Look at the city called by your name! We pray our prayers for help to you, not because of any righteous acts of ours but because of your great compassion. ¹⁹My Lord, listen! My Lord, forgive! My Lord, pay attention and act! Don't delay! My God, do all this for your own sake, because your city and your people are called by your name.

LIGHTHOUSE

CHANGED HEART AND LIFE

A Prayer Asking Forgiveness *Daniel 9:4-19*

Daniel was in Babylon because of Israel's sin. God let the nation of Babylon defeat Israel and take away all of its people. When God first chose Israel, God told the Israelites not to forget God's Instruction and not to make false idols to worship (Deut 4:23). God promised to bless the Israelites with good things if they obeyed, but he warned they would be destroyed if they disobeyed (Deut 30:15-18). Again and again Israel forgot God, until God finally had enough and took away their land. Daniel knew God would forgive if the Israelites turned away from their mistakes. They needed to admit to God what they had done wrong. Daniel prayed and asked forgiveness for all of Israel's sin along with his own. Daniel's prayer was a reminder to himself that God would forgive. And God did forgive Israel, allowing the Israelites to return some day to their land (Ezra 1:2-4). 🔥

Seventy weeks

²⁰While I was still speaking, praying, and confessing my sin and the sins of my people Israel—while I was still praying my prayer for help to the LORD my God about my God's holy mountain—²¹while I was still speaking this prayer, the man Gabriel approached me at the time of the evening offering. This was the same Gabriel I had seen in my earlier vision. He was weary with exhaustion.ᶜ

²²He explained as he spoke with me: "Daniel, here's why I've come: to give you insight and understanding. ²³When you began making your requests, a word went out, and I've come to tell it to you because you are

greatly treasured. So now understand this word and grasp the meaning of this vision! ²⁴Seventy weeks are appointed for your people and for your holy city to complete the rebellion, to end sins, to cover over wrongdoing, to bring eternal righteousness, to seal up prophetic vision, and to anoint the most holy place.

²⁵"So you must know and gain wisdom about this: There will be seven weeks from the moment the word went out to restore and rebuild Jerusalem until a leader is anointed. And for sixty-two weeks the city will be rebuilt with a courtyard and a moat. But in difficult times, ²⁶after the sixty-two weeks, an anointed one will be eliminated. No one will support him.ᵈ The army of a future leader will destroy the city and the sanctuary. Hisᵉ end will come in a flood, but devastations will be decreed until the end of the war.ᶠ ²⁷For one week, he will make a strong covenant with many people. For a half-week, he will stop both sacrifices and offerings. In their placeᵍ will be the desolating monstrosities until the decreed destruction sweeps over the devastator."

Vision of a man

10 In the third year of Persia's King Cyrus, a message was revealed to Daniel, who was called Belteshazzar. The message was true: there would be a great conflict. Daniel understood the message, having discerned the meaning of the vision.

²During that time, I, Daniel, had been mourning for three weeks. ³I didn't eat any rich foods. Neither meat nor wine passed my lips, and I didn't clean up at all until the three weeks were up. ⁴Then, on the twenty-fourth day of the first month, as I was on the bank of the great Tigris River, ⁵I looked up and suddenly saw a man clothed in linen in front of me. He had a brilliant gold belt around his waist, ⁶and his body was like topaz. His face was like a flash of lightning, and his eyes were like burning torches. His arms and feet looked like polished bronze. When he spoke, it sounded like the roar of a crowd. ⁷Only I, Daniel, saw this vision. The other people who

---

ᶜOr *approached me in swift flight at the time of the evening offering;* Heb uncertain ᵈOr *and will have nothing* or *and will disappear;* Heb uncertain ᵉOr *Its* (the army's) ᶠHeb uncertain ᵍCorrection *on the wing;* Heb uncertain

were with me didn't see it. Despite that, they were terrified and ran away to hide.

⁸So I was left alone to see this great vision all by myself. All my strength left me. My energy was sapped, and I couldn't stay strong. ⁹Then I heard the sound of the man's words. When I heard it, I fell into a trance with my face on the ground. ¹⁰But then a hand touched me, lifting me up to my hands and knees.

¹¹The man said to me, "Daniel, you are greatly treasured. Now grasp the meaning of what I'm saying to you. And stand up, because I've been sent to you."

As he said this to me, I stood up, shaking.

¹²Then the man said to me, "Don't be afraid, Daniel, because from the day you first set your mind to understand things and to humble yourself before your God, your words were heard. I've come because of your words! ¹³For twenty-one days the leader of the Persian kingdom blocked my way. But then Michael, one of the highest leaders, came to help me. I left Michael there with the leader of the Persian kingdom.ʰ ¹⁴But I've come to help you understand what will happen to your people in the future, because there is another vision concerning that time."

¹⁵While he said this to me, I turned my face to the ground and kept quiet. ¹⁶But then someone who looked like a human beingⁱ touched my lips. Then I opened my mouth and spoke, saying to the person standing in front of me: "My lord, the vision bothered me deeply, and I couldn't stay strong during it. ¹⁷So how can I, my lord's servant, speak with you, my lord? Even now there's no strength in me, and I can barely breathe."

¹⁸The one who looked like a human being touched me again and gave me strength. ¹⁹He said, "Don't be afraid. You are greatly treasured. All will be well with you. Be strong!"

As he spoke to me, I suddenly felt strong. Then I said: "My lord can go on, because you've made me strong."

²⁰Then he said: "Do you know why I have come to you? Now I must go back to fight the leader of Persia. As I leave, the leader of Greece will come! ²¹But I will tell you what is written in the Scroll of Truth. No one stands

UMBRELLA
STRESSED OUT

God Can Overcome Our Weakness
Daniel 10:2-19

Daniel was getting an eyeful of the future, and it was wearing him out. A messenger from God frightened everyone when he showed up with his face flashing like lightning. Daniel couldn't even keep standing when the messenger first spoke. Daniel's earlier visions had come in the form of terrifying pictures of beasts that fought or devoured everything and everyone in their path (Dan 7:28; 8:1-12). Now God's messenger filled Daniel's mind with details about the messy future of several important kings. Faced with this powerful being, Daniel felt weak. His body was already frail from eating lightly for three weeks of mourning. But God gave him strength. With one touch, Daniel was strong enough to receive God's visions and write them down to encourage and prepare those who would hear them later. ◆

strong with me against these leaders except your leader Michael.

A vast empire divided

11 "In the first year of Darius the Mede's rule, I took my stand to strengthen and protect him." ²I will now tell you the truth. Persia will have three more kings, but the fourth will be richer than all of them. Once he has become strong through his great riches, he will disturb everyone, including the Greek kingdom. ³Then a warrior-king will come forward, ruling over a vast empire and doing whatever he wants. ⁴But even as he takes control, his kingdom will be broken, divided to the four winds of heaven. It won't pass to his descendants. No one will rule like he did because his kingdom will be uprooted. It will belong to others, not to these.

South and north

⁵"Then the southern king will gain power, but one of his princes will overpower him, ruling in his place. His empire will be vast. ⁶After some years, they will make an agreement

---

ʰLXX; Heb *after I was detained there with the kings of Persia* ⁱHeb *bene adam* (*a son of a man*) is an idiom that means *human being*; cf 7:13.

together. The southern king's daughter will go to the northern king to finalize the agreement, but she won't retain her great power. Neither will his power remain in place. In those times she will be handed over, along with her escort, the one who fathered her, and the one who strengthened her.[j]

⁷"A branch from her roots will rise up in his place. Attacking the army, he will enter the walled fortress of the northern king. He will fight with them, and he will conquer. ⁸He will even carry off their gods to Egypt, along with their statues and their silver and gold equipment. For years he will avoid the northern king. ⁹Then the northern king will attack the kingdom of the southern king, but will return to his own land. ¹⁰His sons will get ready for war, gathering massive forces. Their attack will be like an overwhelming flood. And they will attack again, taking the battle as far as his walled fortress.

¹¹"The southern king, in a bitter rage, will come out to battle the northern king. He will muster a huge army, but the army will be handed over to his enemy. ¹²When the army is carried off, he will become confident. He will kill tens of thousands, but he will not stand strong. ¹³The northern king will then muster another army—this one bigger than the first. After some years have passed, he will attack with a large and well-equipped army. ¹⁴In those times, many will oppose the southern king. Violent persons from among your people also will rise up to support the vision, but they will fail.

¹⁵"When the northern king attacks, he will throw up a siege ramp and occupy a walled city. The southern forces will not be able to resist—not even its elite forces. No one will be strong enough to resist. ¹⁶The one who comes to attack will do whatever he wants; no one will be able to oppose him. He will take his place in the beautiful country, and he will hand out destruction. ¹⁷He will decide to occupy his entire kingdom by force. He will make an agreement with him and will give him a wife, intending to destroy him,[k] but it won't succeed and it won't happen.[l] ¹⁸He will turn his face to the coastlands, capturing many people. A commander

will put an end to his disgrace,[m] even though he won't repay that disgrace. ¹⁹Then he will turn his attention to the walled fortresses of his own country but will stumble, fall, and disappear.

²⁰"In his place one will arise who will send his agent to exact a kingdom's glory, but in a few days he will be broken, though not by anger and not by war. ²¹A worthless person will arise in his place. Royal majesty will not have been given to him, but he will come in a time of security and seize the kingdom by deceitful means. ²²Forces will be completely swept away and broken before him. The same is true for the leader of the covenant. ²³From the moment they make an agreement with him, he will act deceitfully. He will gain power at the expense of a small nation. ²⁴He will come into a province's richest places untroubled and will do what his fathers and grandfathers never could. He will hand out plunder, spoil, and wealth to them. He will make plans against fortresses, but only for a time.

²⁵"Then with a large army he will gather his strength and courage against the southern king. The southern king, with a large and super powerful army, will prepare for war, but he won't endure because they will make plans against him. ²⁶Those who eat the king's provisions will destroy him. His army will be overrun. Many will die.

²⁷"These two kings, with their minds set on evil, will sit at one table, telling lies, but with no success because the end will come at the set time. ²⁸He will return to his country with great wealth and set his mind against a holy covenant. He will do what he wants and then return to his country. ²⁹At the set time he will again battle against the south, but the second time will be different from the first. ³⁰Kittim ships will fight against him, and he will retreat in fear. He will rage against a holy covenant and will do what he wants. Then he will pay special attention to those who violate a holy covenant. ³¹His forces will come and make the sanctuary fortress impure. They will stop the daily sacrifice and set up a desolating monstrosity. ³²By deceitful means he will corrupt those who violate a covenant, but

---

[j]Heb uncertain [k]DSS; MT *her* or *it* (the kingdom) [l]Heb adds *for him.* [m]Heb adds *for him.*

the people who acknowledge their God will stand strong and will act.

[33]"The people's teachers will help many understand, but for a time they will fall by sword and by flame, by captivity and by plunder. [34]When they fall, they will receive a little help, but many will join them with deceitful plans. [35]Some of the teachers too will fall in order that they might be refined, purified, and cleansed—until an end time, because it is still not yet the set time.

An end to the arrogant king

[36]"The king will do whatever he wants. He will exalt himself, making himself greater than any god. He will say unbelievable things against the God of gods. He will succeed until the doom is completed, because what is decreed must take place. [37]He will give no thought to the gods of his fathers, nor to the god cherished by women. He will give no thought to any god, because he will make himself greater than all of them. [38]In their place, he will worship a god of walled fortresses. With gold and silver, rare stones and precious things, he will worship a god his fathers did not acknowledge. [39]He will deal with walled fortresses with the help of a foreign god. He will heap rewards on those who support him, making them rule over many and dividing up the land for a price. [40]At the end time, the southern king will attack him. The northern king will storm against him with chariots and horses and many ships. He will invade countries, sweeping over them like a flood. [41]He will invade the beautiful country, and tens of thousands will die. But Edom, Moab, and the best of the Ammonites will escape from his hand. [42]He will extend his power into other countries. Even Egypt won't escape. [43]He will take control of Egypt's hidden treasures of gold, silver, and all its precious things. Libyans and Cushites will follow at his feet. [44]But reports from the east and north will alarm him, and in a great rage he will set off to devastate and destroy many. [45]He will pitch his royal tents between the sea and the beautiful holy mountain. But he will come to his end, and no one will help him.

Eternal life or eternal disgrace

12 "At that time, Michael the great leader who guards your people will take his stand. It will be a difficult time—nothing like it has ever happened since nations first appeared. But at that time every one of your people who is found written in the scroll will be rescued. [2]Many of those who sleep in the dusty land[n] will wake up—some to eternal life, others to shame and eternal disgrace. [3]Those skilled in wisdom[o] will shine like the sky. Those who lead many to righteousness will shine like the stars forever and always. [4]But you, Daniel, must keep these words secret! Seal the scroll until the end time! Many will stray far, but knowledge will increase."

Bet you can read this in 2 minutes. Ready, set, go!

Waiting for the end time

[5]I, Daniel, looked and suddenly saw two other figures—one standing on each side of the stream. [6]One said to the man clothed in white linen, who was farther upstream: "When will these astonishing things be over?"

[7]I heard the man clothed in white linen, who was farther upstream, swear by the one who lives forever as he raised both hands to heaven: "For one set time, two set times, and half a set time. When the breaking of the holy people's power is over, all these things will be over."

[8]I heard it, but I didn't understand it. "My lord," I said, "what will happen after all this?"

[9]He said, "Get going now, Daniel, because these words must remain secret and sealed up until the end time. [10]Many will purify, cleanse, and refine themselves, but the wicked will act wickedly. None of the wicked will understand, but those skilled in wisdom will understand. [11]There will be one thousand two hundred ninety days from the time the daily sacrifice is stopped to the setting up of the desolating monstrosity. [12]Happy is the one who waits and reaches one thousand three hundred thirty-five days. [13]Now as for you, go on to the end. You will rest and will stand to receive your reward at the end of days.

---

[n]*Or earthy soil or dust of the earth*   [o]*See 1:4; or The teachers; see 11:33, 35; also in 12:10.*

Hosea

This book contains the teachings of Hosea, a prophet who spoke to the northern kingdom of Israel.

Long before Hosea began to speak, God taught God's people that their most important duty was to worship God. Serving other gods would bring terrible pain. God said, "If you do, in fact, forget the LORD your God and follow other gods, serving and bowing down to them, I swear to you right now that you will be completely destroyed" (Deut 8:19).

God's people didn't listen to that warning. They stopped loving God. They prayed to other gods— Asherah, Baal, Ashtoreth, Molech. The people were unfaithful. But God still loved them and had compassion for them.

The prophet Hosea continued to love his wife Gomer even after she left him. Even though people quit caring about God, God never quit caring about people. Hosea shows that God loves us even when we don't love God! ◆

things YOU'LL DISCOVER

This book tells a story of how God's people stopped loving God even though God loved them very much. The people acted like a married person who is unfaithful to their spouse.

people YOU'LL MEET

Hosea—a prophet who spoke for God (Hos 1–14)
Gomer—Hosea's wife (Hos 1)
Jezreel, No Compassion, Not My People—Hosea and Gomer's children (Hos 1–2)

places YOU'LL GO

Israel (the northern kingdom), **Judah** (the southern kingdom), **Ephraim** (the central and important part of God's land)

words YOU'LL REMEMBER

"I led them with bands of human kindness, with cords of love. I treated them like those who lift infants to their cheeks; I bent down to them and fed them" (Hos 11:4).

1

The LORD's word that came to Hosea, Beeri's son, in the days of Judah's Kings Uzziah, Jotham, Ahaz, and Hezekiah, and in the days of Israel's King Jeroboam, Joash's son.

God commands Hosea to marry

2 When the LORD first spoke through Hosea, the LORD said to him, "Go, marry a prostitute and have children of prostitution, for the people of the land commit great prostitution by deserting the LORD." 3 So Hosea went and took Gomer, Diblaim's daughter, and she became pregnant and bore him a son. 4 The LORD said to him, "Name him Jezreel; for in a little while I will punish the house of Jehu for the blood of Jezreel, and I will destroy the kingdom of the house of Israel. 5 On that day I will break the bow of Israel in the Jezreel Valley." 6 Gomer became pregnant again and gave birth to a daughter. Then the LORD said to Hosea, "Name her No Compassion, because I will no longer have compassion on the house of Israel or forgive them. 7 But I will have compassion on the house of Judah. I, the LORD their God, will save them; I will not save them by bow, or by sword, or by war, or by horses, or by horsemen." 8 When Gomer finished nursing No Compassion, she became pregnant and gave birth to a son. 9 Then the LORD said, "Name him Not My People because you are not my people, and I am not your God."[a]

Hope for the future

10b Yet the number of the people of Israel will be like the sand of the sea, which can be neither measured nor numbered; and in the place where it was said to them, "You are not my people," it will be said to them, "Children of the living God." 11 The people of Judah and the people of Israel will be gathered together, and they will choose one head. They will become fruitful in the land.[c] The day will be a wonderful one for Jezreel.

Proclamation of wrongdoing

2

[d] Say to your brother, My People, and to your sister, Compassion:

2 Level a charge against your mother;
 plead with her!
 She is not my wife,

 and I am not her husband.
 Let her remove prostitution
 from her presence,
 and adultery from between her breasts,
3 or else I will strip her naked
 and expose her
 as on the day she was born.
 I will make her like a desert,
 and turn her into a dry land,
 and make her die of thirst.
4 I will also have no compassion
 on her children
 because they are
 children of prostitution.
5 Their mother has played the prostitute;
 she who conceived them
 has behaved shamefully.
 She said, "I will seek out my lovers;
 they give me my bread and my water,
 my wool and my linen cloth,
 my oil and my drink."

Divine correction

6 Therefore, I will line her path with thorns;
 and I will build a wall against her,
 so that she can't find her paths.
7 She will go after her lovers,
 but she won't catch up with them;
 she will seek them,
 but she won't find them.
 Then she will say,
 "I will return to my first husband,
 for I had it better then than now."

---

[a] Or *I am not yours.* [b] 1:10–11=Heb 2:1-2 [c] Or *They will go up from the land.* [d] 2:1–23=Heb 2:3–25

⁸ She didn't know that I gave her
    the corn, the new wine,
      and the fresh oil,
    and that I gave her much silver,
      and gold that they used for Baal.
⁹ So now I will take back
    my corn in its time,
    and my wine in its season;
    and I will take away my wool
    and my linen cloth,
    which were to cover her nakedness.
¹⁰ Now I will uncover her nakedness
    in plain view of her lovers,
    and no one will rescue her from me.
¹¹ I will end all her religious celebrations,
    her festivals, her new moons,
      her Sabbath days,
    and all her sacred seasons.
¹² I will destroy her vines and her fig trees,
    of which she said,
    "These are my pay,
    which my lovers have given to me."
    I will change them into a forest,
    and the wild animals will eat them.
¹³ I will punish her for the days
    dedicated to the Baals,
    when she offered sweet-smelling
      sacrifices to them
    and dressed herself up
      with rings and jewelry,
    and went after her lovers,
    and forgot me, says the LORD.

Promises: restoration and covenant love

¹⁴ Therefore, I will charm her,
    and bring her into the desert,
    and speak tenderly to her heart.
¹⁵ From there I will give her vineyards,
    and make the Achor Valley
      a door of hope.
    There she will respond to me
    as in the days of her youth,
    like the time when she came out of
      the land of Egypt.

¹⁶ On that day, says the LORD, you will call me, "My husband," and no longer will you call me, "My Lord." ¹⁷ I will take away the names of the Baals from her mouth, and they will not be mentioned by name anymore. ¹⁸ On that day, I will make a covenant for them with the wild animals, the birds in the sky, and the creeping creatures of the fertile ground. I will do away with the bow, the sword, and war from the land; I will make you lie down in safety.

¹⁹ I will take you for my wife forever;
    I will take you for my wife in
      righteousness and in justice,
    in devoted love, and in mercy.
²⁰ I will take you for my wife in faithfulness;
    and you will know the LORD.

²¹ On that day I will answer, says the LORD.
    I will answer the heavens
    and they will answer the earth.
²² The earth will answer the corn,
    the new wine, and the fresh oil,
    and they will answer Jezreel;
²³ I will sow him for myself in the land;
    and I will have compassion on
      No Compassion,
    and I will say to Not My People,
      "You are my people";
    and he will say, "You are my God."

The lesson of infidelity

3 Then the LORD said to me again, "Go, make love to a woman who has a lover and is involved in adultery, just as the LORD loves the people of Israel, though they turn to other gods and love raisin cakes." ² So I bought her for fifteen pieces of silver, a large amount of barley, and a portion of wine.ᵉ ³ I said to her, "You must stay with me for many days; you won't act like a prostitute; you won't have sex with a man, nor I with you." ⁴ Similarly, the Israelites will remain many days without king or prince, without sacrifice or sacred standing stone, without a priestly vest or household divine images. ⁵ Afterward the Israelites will return and seek the LORD their God and David their king; they will come trembling to the LORD and to the LORD's goodness in the latter days.

Israel's sins and coming punishment

4 Hear the LORD's word,
    people of Israel;
    for the LORD has a dispute
    with the inhabitants of the land.

There's no faithful love or loyalty,
and no knowledge of God in the land.
2 Swearing, lying, murder,
together with stealing and adultery
are common;
bloody crime followed by bloody crime.
3 Therefore, the earth itself becomes sick,
and all who live on it grow weak;
together with the wild animals
and the birds in the sky,
even the fish of the sea are dying.
4 Yet let no one protest,
and let no one complain.

Listen, priest,
I am angry with your people.[f]
5 You will stumble by day;
and at nighttime so will your prophet,
and I will destroy your mother.
6 My people are destroyed
from lack of knowledge.
Since you have rejected knowledge,
so I will reject you
from serving me as a priest.
Since you have forgotten the
Instruction of your God,
so also I will forget
your children.

LIGHTHOUSE

FORGETTING GOD

Rejection and Destruction *Hosea 4:6*

When God said the people had been destroyed because they lacked knowledge, this didn't refer to the kind of knowledge they would gain in school. God was speaking to the religious teachers whose job was to teach people the truth about God's Instruction and wisdom. The priests weren't doing a good job teaching people about God's ways, though, and some harsh consequences resulted. But the people of Israel and Judah were God's special people, chosen to have a close friendship with God. God refused to forget them. ◆

7 The more they increased,
the more they sinned against me;
they exchanged their glory for shame.
8 They feed on the sin of my people;
they set their hearts on evil things.

9 The priest will be just like the people;
I will punish them for their ways,
and judge them for their deeds.
10 They will eat but not be satisfied;
they will have sex like prostitutes,
but they will not have children,
because they have rejected the LORD
to devote themselves
to [11]false religious practices.

Description of Israel's idolatry

Wine and new wine
destroy understanding.
12 My people take advice
from a piece of wood,
and their divining rod
gives them predictions.
A spirit of prostitution
has led them astray;
they have left God
to follow other gods.
13 They offer sacrifices on mountaintops,
and make entirely burned offerings
on hills;
they offer sacrifices
under various green trees,
because their shade is pleasant.
Therefore, your daughters
act like prostitutes,
and your daughters-in-law
commit adultery.
14 I will not punish your daughters
because they act like prostitutes,
nor your daughters-in-law
because they commit adultery;
for the men themselves visit prostitutes,
and offer sacrifices
with consecrated workers at temples;
so now the people without sense
must come to ruin.
15 Israel, even though you act
like a prostitute,
don't let Judah become guilty.
Don't enter into Gilgal,
or go up to Beth-aven,
and don't swear, "As the LORD lives."
16 Like a stubborn cow Israel is stubborn.
Now the LORD will tend them,[g]
as the LORD tends a lamb in a pasture.
17 Ephraim is associated with idols—
let him alone!

[f]Heb uncertain [g]Or *her*

LIFE PRESERVER

What's going on with Hosea's family? Hosea 1-5

The first chapters in the book of Hosea are hard to read. They tell about Hosea and his wife Gomer, their children, and Hosea's accusation that Gomer had not been faithful to him and their marriage. But we never hear Gomer's voice.

It may be helpful to remember that Hosea was using his family as a comparison for what was going on with Israel and its relationship with God. Israel had been unfaithful to God—seeking other gods and forgetting God's Instruction and promises. Hosea said there was no faithful love or loyalty, no knowledge of God in the land (Hos 4:1). That was a major problem! ♦

18 Though they have stopped drinking,
    they continue to behave
        like prostitutes;
    indeed, they "love"; shame is their pride.
19 The wind has wrapped her in its wings;
    they will be ashamed of their sacrifices.

Judgment on Israel and Judah

5 Hear this, priests!
    Pay attention, house of Israel!
    Listen, house of the king!
        The judgment concerns you because
            you have been a trap at Mizpah,
            and a net spread out upon Tabor.
2 In their wicked condition,
    they have sunk deep into corruption;
        I will correct them through judgment.
3 I know Ephraim;
    Israel doesn't escape my eye;
    for now Ephraim
        you have acted like a prostitute;
    Israel is defiled.
4 Their deeds don't allow them
        to return to their God,
    because the spirit of prostitution
        is within them,
    and they don't know the LORD.
5 Israel's pride is a witness against him;
    both Israel and Ephraim stagger
        because of their guilt;
    Judah staggers with them.
6 With their sheep and their cattle
    they will go

to seek the LORD,
    but they will not find him;
    he has withdrawn from them.
7 They have acted faithlessly
    against the LORD;
    for their children have produced
        illegitimate children.
    Now the new moon will devour them[h]
        along with their fields.

8 Blow a horn in Gibeah;
    blow a trumpet in Ramah.
    Sound the warning at Beth-aven:
        "Look behind you, Benjamin!"
9 Ephraim will become a horrible place
        on the Judgment Day.
    Against the tribes of Israel
        I will certainly announce
            what is to take place.
10 The princes of Judah act like raiders
        who steal the land;
    I will pour out my anger
        like water upon them.
11 Ephraim is under pressure
        from its enemies;
    Ephraim's rights aren't protected.
    This is because Ephraim chose to
        pursue worthless things.
12 Therefore, I am like a moth to Ephraim,
        and like decay to the house of Judah.
13 When Ephraim saw his sickness,
        and Judah his wound,
    then Ephraim went to Assyria,
        and Ephraim sent for the great king.
    But he could not heal them;
        nor could he cure their wound.
14 I am like a lion to Ephraim,
        like a young lion to the house of Judah.
    I am the one who tears the prey
        and goes forth;
    no one can snatch it from me.
15 I will leave so that I can return
        to my place
    until they pay for their deeds,
        until they seek me.
    In their distress,
        they will beg for my favor:
6 "Come, let's return to the LORD;
    for it is he who has injured us
        and will heal us;

[h]Heb uncertain

he has struck us down,
  but he will bind us up.
² After two days he will revive us;
  on the third day he will raise us up,
    so that we may live before him.
³ Let's know, let's press on
  to know the LORD;
    whose appearing
    is as certain as the dawn;
  who will come to us like the showers,
  like the spring rains
    that give drink to the earth."

Infidelity and divine retribution
⁴ Ephraim, what will I do with you?
  Judah, what will I do with you?
  Your love is like a morning cloud,
    like the dew that vanishes quickly.
⁵ Therefore, I have attacked them
  by the prophets,
    I have killed them
    by the words of my mouth,
    and my judgment goes forth
    like a light.
⁶ I desire faithful love and not sacrifice,
  the knowledge of God
    instead of entirely burned offerings.
⁷ But like Adamⁱ they broke the covenant;

then they acted in bad faith
    against me.
⁸ Gilead is a city of wicked people,
  tracked with blood.
⁹ As robbers lie in wait for someone,
  so the priests are in league
    with each other;
    they murder on the road to Shechem;
    they have done evil things.
¹⁰ In the house of Israel I have seen
  something horrible;
    Ephraim acts like a prostitute;
    Israel is defiled.
¹¹ For you also, Judah,
  a harvest is appointed,
    when I would improve
    the circumstances of my people.

7 When I would heal Israel,
    the evil acts of Ephraim are exposed,
    and the wicked deeds of Samaria;
    for they deceive and steal,
    a thief breaks in;
    a group of bandits raid outside.
² But they don't consider
  within their hearts
    that I remember all their wickedness.
  Now their deeds show who they are,
    right in front of my face.

ⁱ*Or at Adam*

Head and Heart   Hosea 6:6-7

Hosea was a prophet who knew a lot about how to worship God. He was very concerned about leaders who knew many things about God but who didn't love God with all their hearts. God did not care so much about the things people did out of fear or guilt (such as sacrificing animals). Instead, God cared more about the loyal love that people showed to God and to others.

We can be just like the people in Israel. Sometimes we know a lot of things about God, but we forget how to love God and love others. We forget that love is more important than knowledge.

Name one thing you know about God in your head.

Name one thing that shows you love God with all your heart.

3 By their wickedness
they make the king glad,
and give joy to the officials
with their lies.

4 They all act like adulterers;
they are like a heated oven,
whose baker doesn't need
to stoke the fire,
from the kneading of the dough
until it is leavened.

5 On the day of our king,
the officials became sick with the
heat of wine;
he stretched out his hand to those
who mocked him.

6 They approach like a hot oven,
their hearts burning.
Throughout the night,
their anger smolders;
in the morning, it continues
to burn like a flaming fire.

7 All of them are hot as an oven;
they devour their rulers.
All their kings have fallen;
none of them call upon me.

8 Ephraim mixes himself
among the people;
Ephraim is like flatbread that is
cooked on only one side.

9 Strangers have eaten up his strength,
yet he doesn't know it;
gray hairs are sprinkled
here and there upon him,
yet he doesn't know it.

10 Israel's pride is a witness against him;
yet they don't return
to the LORD their God,
or seek him because of all this.

Foolishness and God's wrath

11 Ephraim has become like a dove,
silly and without common sense;
they call upon Egypt; they go to Assyria.

12 As they go, I will spread my net over them;
like birds in the sky,
I will bring them down;
I will judge them according to the
report made to their assembly.

13 Doom to them,
for they have strayed from me;
destruction will be their lot
because they have rebelled
against me.
I would redeem them,
but they speak lies against me.

14 They don't cry to me from the heart,
but they sob upon their beds;
they fight[j] over grain and wine;
they resist me.

15 It was I who gave them their strength,
yet they plot evil against me.

16 They return, but not to the Most High;[k]
they have become like a worthless bow;
their officials will fall by the sword
because of the rage of their tongues;
in Egypt they will make fun of them.[l]

Divine proclamation about Israel's idolatry

8 Put a trumpet to your lips!
It's as if a bird of prey has flown over
the LORD's house,
because they have broken my covenant,
and have not kept my Instruction.

2 Israel cries to me,
"My God, we know you!"

3 Israel has turned away from the good;
the enemy will pursue him.

4 They set up kings, but not through me;
they chose princes,
but without my knowledge.
With silver and gold they crafted idols
for their own destruction.

LIFE PRESERVER

**How was Ephraim like an
oven or bread?** *Hosea 7:1-10*

Like other prophets writing in this time,
Hosea's purpose was to remind the people of
God's covenant with them. A covenant is an agreement between God and the people. God desired
faithful love rather than sacrifice, and knowledge
of God rather than entirely burned offerings (Hos
6:6). Hosea 7 uses many different picture words to
describe the unfaithfulness of God's people. One is
bread. Hosea said that the people were like a loaf
that is cooked only halfway through, so it crumbles
when the baker turns it over. Because the people
didn't remember God, their nation wasn't strong
and was easily defeated by their enemies. ◖

⁵ Your calf is rejected, Samaria.
My anger burns against them.
How long will they remain guilty?
⁶ The calf is from Israel,
a person made it;
it is not God.
The calf of Samaria will be smashed.
⁷ Because they sow the wind,
they will get the whirlwind.
Standing grain, but no fresh growth;
it will yield no meal;
if it were to yield,
strangers would devour it.

Bargains, apostasy, and coming punishment

⁸ Israel is swallowed up;
among the nations,
they are now
like a useless jar.
⁹ They have gone up to Assyria,
a wild ass wandering alone;
Ephraim has hired lovers.
¹⁰ Though they have bargained
with the nations,
I will now gather them up.
They will soon be diminished
due to the burden of kings and princes.
¹¹ When Ephraim added more altars
to take away sin,
they became altars to him for sinning.
¹² Even though I write out for him
a large number of my instructions,
they are regarded as strange.
¹³ Though they offer choice sacrifices,ᵐ
though they eat flesh,
the Lord doesn't accept them.
Now he will remember their wickedness
and punish their sins;
they will return to Egypt.
¹⁴ Israel has forgotten his maker,
and built palaces;
and Judah has multiplied walled cities;
but I will send a fire upon his cities,
and it will devour his fortresses.

Arrival of divine judgment

9 Don't rejoice, Israel!
Don't celebrate as other nations do;
for as whores you have gone away
from your God.

You have loved a prostitute's pay
on all threshing floors of grain.
² Threshing floor and wine vat
won't feed them;
the new wine will fail them.
³ They won't remain in the land of the Lord;
but Ephraim will return to Egypt,
and in Assyria
they will eat unclean food.
⁴ They won't pour wine
as an offering to the Lord;
their sacrifices won't please him.
Such sacrifices will be like food
for those who touch the dead;
all who eat of it will be unclean;
their bread will be
for their hunger alone;
it will not come to the Lord's house.
⁵ What will you do
on the day of appointed festival,
on the day of the Lord's festival?
⁶ Even if they escape destruction,
Egypt will gather them,
Memphis will bury them.
Briars will possess
their precious things of silver;ⁿ
thorns will be in their tents.
⁷ The days of punishment have come;
the days of judgment have arrived;
Israel cries,
"The prophet is a fool,
the spiritual man is mad!"
Because of your great wickedness,
your rejection of me is great.

Tragic consequences

⁸ The prophet is God's watchman
looking over Ephraim,
yet a hunter's trap is set,
covering all his ways,
and rejection is in his God's house.
⁹ They have corrupted themselves terribly
as in the days of Gibeah;
he will remember their wickedness;
he will punish their sins.

¹⁰ Like grapes in the wilderness,
I found Israel.
In its first season,
like the first fruit on the fig tree,

ᵐCorrection; Heb uncertain ⁿOr *the proud glory pertaining to their silver*; Heb uncertain

I saw your ancestors.
But they came to Baal-peor,
and worshipped a thing of shame;
they became detestable
like the thing they loved.°

¹¹ Ephraim's glory will fly away like a bird—
no birth, no pregnancy, no conception!

¹² Though they bring up children,
I will make them childless
until no one is left.
Doom to them indeed when I leave them!

¹³ When I looked toward Tyre,
Ephraim was planted in a lovely meadow;
but now Ephraim must lead out his
children for slaughter.

¹⁴ Give them, Lord—
what will you give them?
Give them a womb that miscarries
and breasts that are dried up.

¹⁵ Every wickedness of theirs
began at Gilgal;
there I came to hate them.
Because of the wickedness of their deeds
I will drive them out of my house.
I will love them no more;
all their officials are rebels.

¹⁶ Ephraim is sick,
their root is dried up,
they will bear no fruit.
Even though they give birth,
I will put to death
their much-loved little ones.

¹⁷ Because they haven't listened to him,
my God will reject them;
they will wander among the nations.

The folly of Israel's idolatry

10 Israel is a growing vine
that yields its fruit.
The more his fruit increased,
the more altars he built;
the richer his land became,
the more he set up
sacred standing stones.

² Their heart is false;
now they must bear their guilt.
The Lord will break down their altars
and destroy their standing stones.

³ For now they will say:
"We have no king,

because we don't love the Lord.
What then could a king do for us?"

⁴ They have spoken empty words,
swearing falsely
when making covenants;
so judgment springs up
like poisonous weeds
in the furrows of the field.

⁵ The inhabitants of Samaria shake
because of the calf of Beth-aven.
Its people will mourn over it,
just as its idolatrous priests
who rejoiced over its glory
that is now gone.

Shame and punishment

⁶ To Assyria it will be carried
as a gift for the great king.
Ephraim will be put to shame;
Israel will be ashamed of his own idol.

⁷ Samaria will be cut off;
her king is like a chip of wood
on the surface of the water.

⁸ The sin of Israel, the shrines of Aven
will be torn down.
Thorn and thistle will sprout up
on their altars.
They will say to the mountains,
"Cover us,"
to the hills, "Fall on us."

⁹ Since the days of Gibeah,
you have sinned, Israel;
there they have continued.
Will not war overtake them in Gibeah?

¹⁰ I will come and punish them;
nations will be gathered against them
when they are punished
for their double crime.

¹¹ Ephraim was a trained cow
that loved to pull a plow;
I spared her fair neck;
but I will make Ephraim
break through the ground;
Judah will plow;
Jacob will turn the soil for himself.

¹² Sow for yourselves righteousness;
reap faithful love;
break up your unplanted ground,
for it is time to seek the Lord,
that he may come
and rain righteousness upon you.

°Heb uncertain

¹³ You have plowed wickedness,
  you have reaped depravity,
  you have eaten the fruit of lies,
  because you have trusted in your way
    and in your many warriors.
¹⁴ Therefore, the noise of war
  will rise against your people;
  all your fortresses will be destroyed,
  as Shalman destroyed Beth-arbel
    on the day of battle,
  when mothers were dashed
    into pieces with their children.
¹⁵ It will indeed happen to you, Bethel,
  because of your great wickedness.
  At dawn, the king of Israel
    will be cut off completely.

Divine love

11 When Israel was a child, I loved him,
    and out of Egypt I called my son.
² The more I called them,
    the further they went from me;
  they kept sacrificing to the Baals,
    and they burned incense to idols.
³ Yet it was I who taught Ephraim
    to walk;
  I took them up in my arms,
    but they did not know
      that I healed them.

> Memorize
> Hos 11:4

⁴ I led them
    with bands
  of human kindness,
  with cords of love.
  I treated them like those
  who lift infants to their cheeks;
  I bent down to them and fed them.

Divine frustration

⁵ They will return to the land of Egypt,
    and Assyria will be their king,
  because they have refused
    to return to me.
⁶ The sword will strike wildly
    in their cities;
  it will consume the bars of their gates
  and will take everything
    because of their schemes.
⁷ My people are bent on turning
    away from me;

and though they cry out
  to the Most High,^p
  he will not raise them up.

Divine compassion

⁸ How can I give you up, Ephraim?
  How can I hand you over, Israel?
  How can I make you like Admah?
  How can I treat you like Zeboiim?
  My heart winces within me;
    my compassion grows warm and tender.

Israel's and Judah's responses

⁹ I won't act on the heat of my anger;
  I won't return to destroy Ephraim;
  for I am God and not a human being,
    the holy one in your midst;
  I won't come in harsh judgment.
¹⁰ They will walk after the Lord,
    who roars like a lion.
  When he roars,
    his children will come trembling
      from the west.
¹¹ They will come trembling like a bird,
    and like a dove from the land of Assyria;
  and I will return them to their homes,
    says the Lord.
¹² ^qEphraim has surrounded me with lies,
    the house of Israel with faithless acts;
  but Judah still walks with God,
    and is faithful to the holy one.

SAILBOAT

Honest and True

Can't Fool God *Hosea 11:12*
Schoolteachers sometimes see three types of student: those who follow the rules, those who don't follow them, and those who follow only when the teacher is watching. Sooner or later, the last type of students reveal the type of person they are, even if the teacher is fooled at first. God is never fooled, even for a moment. God knew the people of Judah loved and worshipped God. God also knew the people of Israel sometimes pretended to follow God's Instruction but didn't really mean it. God knows the difference between true worshippers and religious pretenders. ◆

God's charge against Judah

12 ¹ᵃEphraim herds the wind,
and pursues the east wind all day long;
they multiply lies and violence;
they make a treaty with Assyria,
and oil is carried to Egypt.

² The Lᴏʀᴅ has a charge against Judah,
and will punish Jacob
according to his ways,
and respond to him according to his deeds.

³ From the womb he tried to be
the oldest of twin brothers;
as an adult he struggled with God.

⁴ He struggled with the messenger
and survived;
he wept and sought his favor;
he met him at Bethel,
and there he spoke with him.

⁵ The Lᴏʀᴅ God of heavenly forces,
the Lᴏʀᴅ is his name!

⁶ But you! Return to your God
with faithful love and justice,
and wait continually for your God.

⁷ He is a merchant;
the means to cheat are in his hands;
he loves to take advantage of others.

⁸ Ephraim has said,
"I'm rich,
I've gained wealth for myself;
in all of my gain
no offense has been found in me
that would be sin."

⁹ I am the Lᴏʀᴅ your God
from the land of Egypt;
I will make you live in tents again,
as in former days.

¹⁰ I spoke to the prophets;
and I multiplied visions,
and through them I uttered parables.

¹¹ In Gilead there is wickedness;
they will surely come to nothing.
In Gilgal they sacrifice bulls,
so their altars will be like piles of stones
on the rows of the field.

¹² Jacob fled to the land of Aram;
there Israel served for a wife,
and for a wife he kept watch
over livestock.

¹³ By a prophet the Lᴏʀᴅ
brought Israel up from Egypt,

and by a prophet he was guarded.

¹⁴ Ephraim has given bitter offense;
so the Lᴏʀᴅ will bring his crimes
down on him
and pay him back for his wrongdoing.

Infidelity despite divine goodness

13 ¹When Ephraim spoke,
there was excitement;
he was praised in Israel;
but he became guilty through Baal
and died.

² And now they keep on sinning;
they have made metal images,
idols of silver,
as a result of their skill,
all of them the work of craftsmen.
"Sacrifice to these," they say.
People are kissing calves!

³ Therefore, they will be
like the morning mist,
like the dew that passes away early,
like husks that swirl
from the threshing floor,
or like smoke from a window.

⁴ Yet I have been the Lᴏʀᴅ your God
ever since the land of Egypt;
and you will know no other gods but me;
there is no savior besides me.

⁵ I knew you in the wilderness,
in the land of no rain.

⁶ When I fed them,
they were satisfied;

LIGHTHOUSE

Forgetting God

Forgotten in the Good Times *Hosea 13:6*
It may sound odd, but it's common for people to forget God when things are good. People often remember to pray when someone gets sick or a family member in the military is sent to war. They turn to God when there is a flood, tornado, earthquake, or fire. But sometimes people get so caught up in all the good things in their lives that they forget God is the one who made all of the good possible. We should always remember that the God who rescues us from bad things is the same God who blesses us with good things. ◆

and their hearts became proud;
   therefore, they forgot me.

Consequences of infidelity
⁷ So I will become like a lion to them;
   like a leopard I will lurk beside the road.
⁸ I will fall upon them
   like a bear robbed of her cubs,
   and I will tear open
      the covering of their hearts.
   I will devour them like a lion,
   as a wild animal would eat them.
⁹ I will destroy you, Israel;
   for you didn't realize
      that I could help you.
¹⁰ Where is your king now,
   so that he can save you?
   Where in all your cities are your judges,
   of whom you said,
   "Give me a king and rulers"?
¹¹ I gave you a king in my anger,
   and I took him away in my wrath.
¹² Ephraim's wickedness is bound up;
   his sin is kept in store.
¹³ The pangs of a woman in childbirth
   come for him,

but he is not aware
   of the time to be born;
for at the proper time
   he doesn't present himself
   at the mouth of the womb.
¹⁴ Will I ransom them
   from the power of the grave?ˢ
   Will I redeem them from death's hold?
   Death, where are your diseases?
   Grave,ᵗ where is your destruction?
   Compassion is hidden from my eyes.
¹⁵ Although he may flourish among rushes,
   the east wind will come—
   the breath of God
   rising from the wilderness;
   and his spring will dry up;
   his fountain will be dried up.
   It will strip his household
   of every cherished possession.
¹⁶ ᵘSamaria will be desolate,
   because she has rebelled
      against her God;
   by the sword they will fall—
   their babies will be dashed,
   and their pregnant women
   ripped open.

ˢHeb *Sheol* ᵗHeb *Sheol* ᵘ14:1 in Heb

God Loves Us   *Hosea 14*

Hosea tells us that God was upset with the people of Israel who did bad things and failed to do what was right. Sometimes the people worshipped other gods or idols. Sometimes they made traps to hurt other people. God got angry with Israel because of how they behaved.

But God doesn't stay angry. The people of Israel knew who God is and why God ruled their lives. They could return to God because God promised to heal them from doing the wrong thing. God said, "I will love them freely" (Hos 14:4).

We can be like the people of Israel too. Sometimes we know all about God or even know the right thing to do, but we don't know how to love God. Hosea teaches us about God's faithful love so that we can learn how to love God and care for others.

How can you show that you love God?

When you're angry with someone, what can you do to show them love?

A plea: Return to God

14 ᵛReturn, Israel, to the Lᴏʀᴅ your God;
you have stumbled
because of your wickedness.
² Prepare to speak
and return to the Lᴏʀᴅ;
say to the Lᴏʀᴅ,
"Forgive all wickedness;
and receive the good.
Instead of bulls,
let us offer what we can say:
³ Assyria won't save us;
we won't ride upon horses;
we will no longer say, 'Our God,'
to the work of our hands.
In you the orphan
finds compassion."

LIGHTHOUSE

CHANGED HEART AND LIFE

Real Change   *Hosea 14:1-3*
Saying "I'm sorry" and then showing that with actions means change has really happened. God asked the people of Israel to come back to God. God told them they needed to ask for forgiveness for the bad things they had done and to use their words to praise God. This would show a real change of heart. They also were to stop worshipping gods they had made themselves and to realize their need for God. The promise was that when they returned to God, they would find love, kindness, help, and hope. ◊

Divine promise of healing

⁴ I will heal their faithlessness;
I will love them freely,
for my anger has turned from them.
⁵ I will be like the dew to Israel;
he will blossom like the lily;
he will cast out his roots
like the forests of Lebanon.ʷ
⁶ His branches will spread out;
his beauty will be like the olive tree,
and his fragrance like that of Lebanon.

LIFE PRESERVER

What did God promise?
Hosea 14

There are many stories in the Bible of God's people turning from God and failing to follow God's commands. And yet many of these stories end in the same way—with God forgiving the people when they confess their sins and try to live as God had asked. After describing the sins of the people and all the ways they had forgotten God and God's covenant with them, the prophet Hosea reminded the people of God's forever love and forgiveness.

God's anger was gone, and God promised to "love them freely." Hosea has a beautiful image of God who is like the dew, bringing water to all the trees and plants. Once again, God hoped that the nation of Israel would bloom, thrive, and flourish with God's watering love. ◊

⁷ They will again live beneath my shadow,
they will flourish like a garden;
they will blossom like the vine,
their fragrance will be
like the wine of Lebanon.
⁸ Ephraim, what do idols
have to do with me?
It is I who answer and look after you.
I am like a green cypress tree;
your fruit comes from me.

Be careful

⁹ Whoever is wise understands these things.
Whoever observes carefully knows them.
Truly, the Lᴏʀᴅ's ways are right,
and the righteous will walk in them,
but evildoers will stumble in them.

did you know?   Being compared to an olive tree or a cedar tree was a good thing. Olives from the olive trees of Israel were eaten as food and juiced for their oil that was sold throughout the ancient world. The cedar trees of the Lebanon forest made the best wood and gave off a very pleasant smell.

Joel

things
YOU'LL DISCOVER

The book of Joel starts with the gloomy report of a natural disaster, the destruction of Israel's crops by flying insects. But the book also gives good news that God will comfort God's people and give God's spirit to them.

people
YOU'LL MEET

Joel—a prophet who spoke for God (Joel 1–3)
Israel—a name for God's people (Joel 2–3)

places
YOU'LL GO

Zion (a name for Jerusalem or Israel),
Judah (the southern kingdom),
Jerusalem

words
YOU'LL REMEMBER

"I will pour out my spirit upon everyone; your sons and your daughters will prophesy, your old men will dream dreams, and your young men will see visions" (Joel 2:28).

The book of Joel begins with terrible news. The land has been attacked by locusts (flying insects similar to grasshoppers). A swarm of locusts could easily eat an entire field of crops in a few minutes. God's people could do nothing to stop countless swarms that covered the land of Israel and devoured their harvest. With no food left to eat, the people soon faced terrible hunger.

The prophet Joel said that the locust attack was a sign that the people hadn't followed God. The people were surprised by the disaster, but Joel told them that they should ask God for help. He said, "Return to the LORD your God, for he is merciful and compassionate, very patient, full of faithful love, and ready to forgive" (Joel 2:13).

As you read this book, you will come across important words later quoted in the New Testament. In Romans 10:13 Paul repeated Joel 2:32: "Everyone who calls on the LORD's name will be saved." And in Acts 2 Peter talked about Joel 2:28, God's promise to pour out God's spirit. The book of Joel shows that God is full of compassion and always ready to forgive! ◊

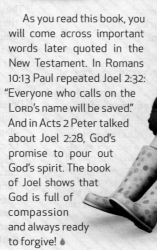

Song of lament

1 The Lord's word that came to Joel, Pethuel's son:

2 Hear this, elders;
   pay attention, everyone in the land!
Has anything like this ever happened
   in your days,
   or in the days of your ancestors?[a]
3 Tell it to your children,
   and have your children
      tell their children,
   and their children tell their children.
4 What the cutting locust left,
   the swarming locust has eaten.
What the swarming locust left,
   the hopping locust has eaten.
And what the hopping locust left,
   the devouring locust has eaten.[b]
5 Wake up, you who drink too much,
   and weep.
Scream over the sweet wine,
   all you wine drinkers,
   because it is snatched from your mouth;
6 because a nation,
   powerful and beyond number,
   has invaded my land.

Its teeth are like lions' teeth;
   its fangs are like those of a lioness.
7 It has destroyed my vines,
   splintered my fig trees,
   stripped off their bark
      and thrown it down;

their branches have turned white.
8 Lament like a woman
   dressed in funeral clothing,
   one who has lost
      the husband of her youth.
9 The grain offering and the drink offering
   are gone from the Lord's temple.
The priests
   and the Lord's ministers mourn.

---

did you know? Locusts in Africa travel by the millions in swarms and eat every living plant until nothing is green. This disaster is hard for us to imagine, but many kids can imagine cicadas, which are not locusts. Every thirteen or seventeen years some cicadas (which means "tree cricket") come out of the ground in the springtime. They fly overhead or swarm around trees, covering the ground and the tree trunks. And they make a lot of noise! The sound can be deafening.

---

10 The fields are devastated,
   the ground mourns;
   for the grain is destroyed,
   the new wine dries up,
   the olive oil fails.
11 Be shocked, you farmers;
   howl, you vinedressers,
   over the wheat and the barley,
   for the crops of the field are destroyed.
12 The grapevine is dried up;
   the fig tree withers.
Pomegranate, palm, and apple—
   all the trees of the field are dried up.
Joy fades away from the people.[c]

Call to mourn

13 Dress for a funeral and grieve,
   you priests;
   lament, ministers of the altar.
Come, spend the night in funeral
   clothing, servants of my God,
because the grain offering
   and the drink offering
   have gone from the temple of your God.
14 Demand a fast,
   request a special assembly.
Gather the elders
   and all the land's people

LIFE PRESERVER

What is the meaning of the locusts? Joel 1:1-4

Because God's people had been unfaithful, they were devastated by a swarm of locusts that moved across their land and destroyed all of their grain and plants. The prophet Joel compared this invasion of locusts to the arrival of an enemy army because the effects were just as bad. The loss of so much food was terrifying. Joel said the locusts were God's punishment for their sin. He asked the people to seek God's forgiveness and return to following God's ways. ◆

---

[a]Or your fathers [b]The Heb uses several different words for *locust*; none of the meanings are identical. [c]Or *from the sons of men*; cf 2:1 Heb *the people of the land*

to the temple of the Lord your God,
and cry out to the Lord.

Time of suffering

15 What a terrible day!
The day of the Lord is near;
it comes like chaos from the Almighty.[d]
16 Isn't the food cut off
right before our eyes?
Aren't joy and gladness
also gone from our God's house?
17 The grain shrivels under the shovels;[e]
the barns are empty.
The granaries are in ruin
because the grain has dried up.
18 How the animals groan!
Herds of cattle are in distress
because there is no pasture for them;
even the flocks of sheep pant.

The prophet's prayer

19 To you, Lord, I cry,
for fire has completely destroyed
the pastures of the wilderness;
and flames have burned
all the trees of the field.
20 Even the field's wild animals cry to you
because the streams have dried up;
the fire has completely destroyed
the meadows of the wilderness.

Announcement of alarm and peril

2 Blow the horn in Zion;
give a shout on my holy mountain!
Let all the people of the land tremble,
for the day of the Lord is coming.
It is near—
2 a day of darkness and no light,
a day of clouds and thick darkness!
Like blackness spread out
upon the mountains,
a great and powerful army[f] comes,
unlike any that has ever come
before them,
or will come after them
in centuries ahead.
3 In front of them a fire consumes;
and behind them a flame burns.
Land ahead of them is like Eden's garden,
but they leave behind them
a barren wasteland;

nothing escapes them.
4 They resemble horses,
and like warhorses they charge,
5 like the rumbling of chariots.
They leap on the mountaintops—
like the crackling of a fire's flame,
devouring the stubble;
like a powerful army
ready for battle.
6 In their presence, peoples shake with fear;
all faces turn red with worry.
7 Like warriors they charge;
like soldiers they climb the wall.
Each keeps to their own path;
they didn't change their course.
8 They don't crowd each other;
each keeps to their own path.
Even if they fall among the weapons,
they won't stop.
9 They rush upon the city;
they run upon the walls.
They climb into the houses;
they enter through the windows
like thieves.
10 The earth quakes before them;
the heavens shake.
The sun and the moon are darkened;
the stars have stopped shining,
11 because the Lord utters his voice
at the head of his army.
How numerous are his troops!
Mighty are those who obey his word.
The day of the Lord is great;
it stirs up great fear—who can endure it?

Change your hearts

12 Yet even now, says the Lord,
return to me with all your hearts,
with fasting, with weeping,
and with sorrow;
13 tear your hearts
and not your clothing.
Return to the Lord your God,
for he is merciful and compassionate,
very patient, full of faithful love,
and ready to forgive.
14 Who knows whether he will have
a change of heart
and leave a blessing behind him,
a grain offering and a drink offering
for the Lord your God?

---

d Heb *Shaddai* e Heb uncertain f Or *a great and strong people*

¹⁵ Blow the horn in Zion;
    demand a fast;
    request a special assembly.
¹⁶ Gather the people;
    prepare a holy meeting;
    assemble the elders;
    gather the children,
        even nursing infants.
Let the groom leave his room
    and the bride her chamber.
¹⁷ Between the porch and the altar
    let the priests,
    the LORD's ministers, weep.
Let them say, "Have mercy, LORD,
    on your people,
    and don't make your inheritance
        a disgrace,
    an example of failure
        among the nations.
Why should they say among the peoples,
    'Where is their God?'"

Words of compassion and promise

¹⁸Then the LORD became passionate about
this land,ᵍ and had pity on his people.
¹⁹ The LORD responded to the people:
See, I am sending you
    the corn, new wine, and fresh oil,
    and you will be fully satisfied by it;
    and I will no longer make you
        a disgrace among the nations.
²⁰ I will remove the northern army
    far from you
    and drive it into a dried-up
        and desolate land,
    its front into the eastern sea,
    and its rear into the western sea.
Its stench will rise up;
    its stink will come to the surface.
The LORD is about to do great things!
²¹ Don't fear, fertile land;
    rejoice and be glad,
    for the LORD is about to do great things!
²² Don't be afraid, animals of the field,
    for the meadows of the wilderness
        will turn green;
    the tree will bear its fruit;
    the fig tree and grapevine
        will give their full yield.
²³ Children of Zion,
    rejoice and be glad in the LORD your God,

because he will give you the early rain
    as a sign of righteousness;
he will pour down abundant rain
    for you,
    the early and the late rain,
    as before.ʰ

SAILBOAT

Joy

A Good Relationship with God Brings Joy
Joel 2:23
Joy is a natural outcome of having a good relationship with God. Joel told the people of Israel that if they were truly sorry for their sins, then God would forgive them. Joel also said that God would end the drought and send the rain the people needed to grow the crops, water the animals, and replenish the grasslands. God didn't tell Israel to be joyful because of the blessings, but because God was their God. Now that's a reason for joy! ◆

²⁴ The threshing floors will be full of grain;
    the vats will overflow with new wine
        and fresh oil.
²⁵ I will repay you for the years
    that the cutting locust,
    the swarming locust, the hopping locust,
    and the devouring locust have eaten—
        my great army, which I sent against you.
²⁶ You will eat abundantly and be satisfied,
    and you will praise the name
        of the LORD your God,
    who has done wonders for you;
    and my people will never again
        be put to shame.
²⁷ You will know
    that I am in the midst of Israel,
    and that I am the LORD your God—
        no other exists;
    never again will my people
        be put to shame.
²⁸After that I will
    pour out my spirit
    upon everyone;
    your sons and your daughters
        will prophesy,
    your old men will dream dreams,
    and your young men will see visions.
²⁹ In those days, I will also pour out my
    spirit on the male and female slaves.

Memorize
Joel 2:28

ᵍOr *then the LORD became jealous for his land* ʰOr *at the first*

³⁰I will give signs in the heavens and on the earth—blood and fire and columns of smoke. ³¹The sun will be turned to darkness, and the moon to blood before the great and dreadful day of the Lord comes. ³²But everyone who calls on the Lord's name will be saved; for on Mount Zion and in Jerusalem there will be security, as the Lord has promised; and in Jerusalem, the Lord will summon those who survive.

Judgment on the nations

3 Truly, in those days and in that time, I will bring back to Judah and Jerusalem those who were sent away. ²I will gather all the nations, and I will bring them to the Jehoshaphat Valley. There I will enter into judgment with them in support of my people and my possession, Israel, which they have scattered among the nations. They have divided my land, ³and have cast lots for my people. They have traded boys for prostitutes, and sold girls for wine, which they drank down. ⁴What are you to me, Tyre and Sidon, and all the regions of Philistia? Are you paying me back for something? If you are paying me back, then in a flash I will turn your deeds back upon your own heads. ⁵You have taken my silver and my gold, and have carried my rich treasures into your temples. ⁶You have sold the people of Judah and Jerusalem to the Greeks, removing them far from their own border. ⁷But now I am calling them from the places where you have sold them, and I will repay you for your deeds. ⁸I will sell your sons and your daughters as a possession of the people of Judah, and they will sell them to the Sabeans, to a nation far away; for the Lord has spoken.

Declaration of war

⁹ Announce this among the nations:
Prepare a holy war,
wake up the warriors;
let all the soldiers draw near,
let them come up!
¹⁰ Beat the iron tips of your plows
into swords
and your pruning tools into spears;
let the weakling say, "I am mighty."
¹¹ Come quickly,
all you surrounding nations;
gather yourselves there;

bring your mighty ones, Lord.
¹² Let the nations prepare themselves,
and come up to the Jehoshaphat Valley;
for there I will sit to judge
all the surrounding nations.
¹³ Cut with the sickle,
for the harvest is ripe.
Go and crush grapes,
for the winepress is full.
The jars overflow with wine,
for their wickedness is great.
¹⁴ Crowd after crowd
fills the valley of judgment,
for the day of the Lord is near
in the valley of judgment.
¹⁵ The sun and the moon are darkened;
the stars have ceased shining.

Salvation for God's people

¹⁶ The Lord roars from Zion,
and utters his voice from Jerusalem;
the heavens and the earth quake.
But the Lord is a refuge for his people,
a shelter for the people of Israel.
¹⁷ So you will know
that I am the Lord your God,
settle down in Zion, my holy mountain.
Jerusalem will be holy,
and never again
will strangers pass through it.
¹⁸ In that day
the mountains will drip sweet wine,
the hills will flow with milk,
and all the streambeds of Judah
will flow with water;
a spring will come forth
from the Lord's house
and water the Shittim Valley.
¹⁹ Egypt will become desolate
and Edom a desolate wilderness.
This is because of the violence
done to the people of Judah,
in whose land they have shed
innocent blood.
²⁰ But Judah will be inhabited forever,
and Jerusalem for all generations.
²¹ I will forgive their bloodguilt,
which I had not forgiven.
I will act on their account;
I will not pardon the guilty.

The Lord dwells in Zion.

Amos

The prophet Amos watched God's people grow more and more wealthy. But Amos saw that some people were getting rich by taking advantage of the poor. They cheated people who had very little and didn't act to stop their suffering.

Amos challenged religious and political leaders. He said, "Let justice roll down like waters, and righteousness like an ever-flowing stream" (Amos 5:24). The leaders were angry when they heard his words.

The prophet Amos preached to the southern kingdom of Judah and to many neighboring nations. But he spoke his toughest words to citizens of the northern kingdom, Israel. Amos shared five visions of the nation's punishment.

The end of this book looks ahead to a time when God will one day rebuild God's people (Amos 9:11-15). But the main message of Amos is that God pays attention to how we treat people who don't have money or food or a place to live. God cares about the needy no matter where they live. Showing true kindness to people who suffer is more important than any religious activity we might do. The book of Amos reminds us to seek justice and to care for others. ◔

things YOU'LL DISCOVER

The book of Amos describes a time when life was good for God's people and yet they forgot God's commands. The prophet Amos, who was a shepherd and farmer, spoke to the people about their sins.

people YOU'LL MEET

Amos—a prophet who spoke for God (Amos 1–9)

places YOU'LL GO

Judah (the southern kingdom);
Israel (the northern kingdom);
Damascus, Gaza, Tyre, Edom, Ammon, Moab (kingdoms close to Israel)

words YOU'LL REMEMBER

"But let justice roll down like waters, and righteousness like an ever-flowing stream" (Amos 5:24).

Introduction

1 These are the words of Amos, one of the shepherds of Tekoa. He perceived these things concerning Israel two years before the earthquake, in the days of Judah's King Uzziah and in the days of Israel's King Jeroboam, Joash's son.

Proclamation of divine judgment

² He said:

The LORD roars from Zion.
  He shouts from Jerusalem;
  the pastures of the shepherds wither,
  and the top of Carmel dries up.

A word to Damascus

³ The LORD proclaims:

For three crimes of Damascus,
  and for four,
  I won't hold back the punishment,
  because they have harvested Gilead
  with sharp iron tools.
⁴ I will send down fire
  on the house of Hazael;
  it will devour the palaces of Ben-hadad.
⁵ I will break the fortified
  gates of Damascus,
  and eliminate the people
  from the Aven Valley,
  including the one who rules
  from Beth-eden;
  the people of Aram will be forced
  to live in Kir,
        says the LORD.

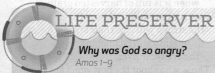

LIFE PRESERVER

Why was God so angry?
Amos 1–9

God was angry because God grew tired of watching the bad things the Israelites were doing. Through the prophet Amos, God reminded them of all the ways they were not following God's commands. God had tried to help them remember what was expected of them, but either they didn't want to listen or they chose to forget.

In this book, we see God being very angry! God was tired of their bad choices and wanted them to do better. God wanted them to live differently, like they promised. God told the people not to give offerings or make music but to "let justice roll down like waters, and righteousness like an ever-flowing stream" (5:24). ◊

A word to Gaza and Ashdod

⁶ The LORD proclaims:

For three crimes of Gaza,
  and for four,
  I won't hold back the punishment,
  because they rounded up
  entire communities,
  to hand them over to Edom.
⁷ I will send down a fire
  on the wall of Gaza;
  it will devour Gaza's palaces.
⁸ I will eliminate the people
  from Ashdod,
  the one who rules from Ashkelon.
  I will turn my hand against Ekron,
  and the Philistines who remain
  will perish,
        says the LORD God.

A word to Tyre

⁹ The LORD proclaims:

For three crimes of Tyre,
  and for four,
  I won't hold back the punishment,
  because they have delivered up
  entire communities over to Edom,
  and neglected
  their covenantal obligations.
¹⁰ So I will send a fire on the wall of Tyre;
  it will devour their palaces.

A word to Edom

¹¹ The LORD proclaims:

For three crimes of Edom,
  and for four,
  I won't hold back the punishment,
  because he chased after his brother
  with the sword,
  denied all compassion,
  kept his anger alive,
  and fueled his wrath forever.
¹² So I will send a fire on Teman;
  it will devour the fortresses
  of Bozrah.

A word to Ammon

13 The LORD proclaims:
     For three crimes of the Ammonites,
        and for four,
          I won't hold back the punishment,
     because they have ripped open
        pregnant women in Gilead
        in order to possess more land.
14 So I will start a fire at the wall of Rabbah;
     the fire will devour its palaces,
        with a war cry on the day of battle,
        with strong wind on the day of the storm.
15 Then their king will be taken away,
     he and his officials together,
                              says the LORD.

A word to Moab

2 The LORD proclaims:
     For three crimes of Moab,
        and for four,
          I won't hold back the punishment,
     because he burned to lime
        the bones of the king of Edom.
2 So I will send down a fire on Moab;
     it will devour the palaces of Kerioth.
     Moab will die in a great uproar,
        with a war cry,
          with the sound of the ram's horn.
3 I will remove their judge from them
     and slay all their officials with him,
                              says the LORD.

A word to Judah

4 The LORD proclaims:
     For three crimes of Judah,
        and for four,
          I won't hold back the punishment,
     because they have rejected the
        Instruction of the LORD,
        and haven't kept his laws.
     They have been led off the right path by
        the same lies
        after which their ancestors walked.
5 So I will send a fire on Judah,
     and it will devour the palaces
        of Jerusalem.

A word to Israel

6 The LORD proclaims:
     For three crimes of Israel,
        and for four,
          I won't hold back the punishment,

     because they have sold the innocent
        for silver,
          and those in need for a pair of sandals.
7 They crush the head of the poor
     into the dust of the earth,
        and push the afflicted out of the way.
     Father and son have intercourse
        with the same young woman,
        degrading my holy name.
8 They stretch out beside every altar
     on garments taken in loan;
     in the house of their god they drink
        wine bought with fines they imposed.
9 Yet I destroyed the Amorite before them,
     whose height was as tall as cedar trees,
        and whose strength
          was as strong as oak trees.
     I destroyed his fruit above
        and his roots below.
10 Also I brought you up
     out of the land of Egypt,
        and led you forty years in the wilderness,
        to lay claim to the land of the Amorite.
11 I raised up some of your children
     to be prophets
        and some of your youth to be nazirites.
     Isn't this so, people of Israel?
                              says the LORD.

12 But you made the nazirites drink wine,
     and commanded the prophets,
        saying, "You won't prophesy."
13 So now I will oppress you,
     just like a cart is weighed down[a]
        when it is full of harvested grain.
14 Fast runners will find no refuge;
     the strong will lose their strength;
     the mighty will be unable
        to save their lives.
15 Those who shoot the bow won't survive.
     Fast runners won't escape;
     those who ride horses
        won't save themselves.
16 The bravest warrior
     will flee away naked in that day,
                              says the LORD.

Words of doom for Israel

3 Hear this word that the LORD has spoken
against you, people of Israel, against the
whole family that I brought out of the land
of Egypt:

---

a Heb uncertain

2 You only have I loved so deeply
    of all the families of the earth.
  Therefore, I will punish you
    for all your wrongdoing.
3 Will two people walk together
    unless they have agreed to do so?[b]
4 Does a lion roar in the forest
    when it has no prey?
  Does a young lion cry out from its den
    if it has caught nothing?
5 Will a bird fall into a trap on the ground
    when there is no bait for it?
  Will a trap spring up from the ground
    when it has taken nothing?
6 If a ram's horn is blown in a city,
    won't people tremble?
  If disaster falls on a city,
    is it the Lord who has done it?
7 Surely the Lord God does nothing
    without revealing his secret
    to his servants the prophets.

8 A lion has roared;
    who will not fear?
  The Lord God has spoken;
    who can but prophesy?
9 Proclaim it to the palaces of Ashdod
    and to the palaces in the land of Egypt.
  Say, "Gather yourselves
    on Mount Samaria,
    and see the great turmoil in the city,
    and what violent deeds are inside it."
10 They don't know how to do right,
                    says the Lord—
    those who store up violence and
      robbery in their palaces.
11 Therefore, the Lord my God proclaims:
    An enemy will surround the land;
  he will bring you down
    from your protected places,
    and your palaces will be robbed.

12 The Lord proclaims:
  Just as the shepherd rescues two legs or
the piece of an ear from the mouth of the lion,
so will the people of Israel be rescued. Those
who live in Samaria will escape with the corner of a bed, and those in Damascus with a
piece of a couch.[c]
13 Hear this and speak
    against the house of Jacob,

  says the Lord God,
    the God of heavenly forces:
14 On the day I punish the crimes of Israel,
    I will also visit the altars of Bethel;
  the horns of the altar will be cut off
    and will fall to the ground.
15 I will tear down the winter house
    as well as the summer house;
  the houses of ivory will perish;
    the great houses will be swept away,
                    says the Lord.

Judgment on Israel's elite

4 Hear this word, you cows of Bashan,
    who are on Mount Samaria,
  who cheat the weak,
    who crush the needy,
  who say to their husbands,
    "Bring drinks,
    so we can get drunk!"
2 The Lord God
    has solemnly promised
    by his holiness:
  The days are surely coming upon you,
    when they will take you away
      with hooks,
    even the last one of you
      with fishhooks.
3 You will go out through the broken wall,
    each one after another;
    and you will be flung out into Harmon,
                    says the Lord.

Bet you can *read this in 4 minutes. Ready, set, go!*

A divine taunt

4 Come to Bethel—and commit a crime;
    multiply crimes at Gilgal.
  Bring your sacrifices every morning,
    your tenth-part gifts every three days.
5 Offer a thanksgiving sacrifice
    of leavened bread,
    and publicize your gifts to the Lord;
  for so you love to do, people of Israel!
                    says the Lord God.

Israel's stubbornness

6 I have sent a famine in all your cities,
    and not provided enough bread
    in all your places,
  yet you didn't return to me,
                    says the Lord.

[b]Or Will two walk together unless they have agreed? [c]Heb uncertain

⁷ I also withheld rain from you
  when there were still three months
  to the harvest.
  I allowed rain to fall on one city,
  no rain to fall on another city.
  One field was rained on,
  and the field dried up
  where it didn't rain.
⁸ So two or three thirsty towns went to
  one city to drink water,
  and weren't satisfied;
  yet you didn't return to me,
                says the LORD.

⁹ I struck you with disease and mildew.
  I destroyed your gardens
  and your vineyards.
  The locust devoured your fig trees
  and your olive trees;
  yet you didn't return to me,
                says the LORD.

¹⁰ I sent a plague against you
  like the one in Egypt.
  I killed your young men with the sword.
  I carried away your horses.
  I made the stink of your camp
  go up into your nostrils;
  yet you didn't return to me,
                says the LORD.

¹¹ I destroyed some of you,
  as when God destroyed
  Sodom and Gomorrah.
  You were like a burning coal
  plucked out of the fire;
  yet you didn't return to me,
                says the LORD.
¹² Truly, Israel,
  I will act in this way toward you;
  therefore, I will do this to you.
  Prepare to meet your God, Israel!

¹³ The one who forms the mountains,
  creates the wind,
  makes known his thoughts
  to humankind,
  makes the morning darkness,
  and moves over the heights
  of the earth—
  the LORD, the God of heavenly forces
  is his name!

A song of lament

5 Hear this word—a funeral song—that I am
lifting up against you, house of Israel:
² Fallen, no more to rise,
  is virgin Israel,
  deserted on her land,
  with no one to raise her up.
³ The LORD God proclaims:
  The city that marched out
  one thousand people
  will have one hundred left,
  and the city that marched out
  one hundred will have ten left
  in the house of Israel.

Words of encouragement

⁴ The LORD proclaims
  to the house of Israel:
  Seek me and live.
⁵ But don't seek Bethel,
  don't enter into Gilgal,
  or cross over to Beer-sheba;
  for Gilgal will go into exile,
  and Bethel will come to nothing.
⁶ Seek the LORD and live,
  or else God might rush like a fire
  against the house of Joseph.
  The fire will burn up Bethel,
  with no one to put it out.

Words of doom

⁷ Doom to you who turn justice into poison,
  and throw righteousness
  to the ground!

LIGHTHOUSE

CHANGED HEART AND LIFE

Seeking God Brings Hope *Amos 5:6*
Often God told prophets to deliver messages about
how hard life would be for people who didn't follow
God. Just like the other prophets, Amos delivered
the message he was given. Almost all of the words
in Amos are about God's punishment. But in one
place God wanted the people of Israel to know
that if they changed their hearts and chose to seek
God instead of following the false religions of the
people around them, they would experience life
the way God wanted it to be. God offers hope for
those who turn toward God. 🔥

8 The one who made
　the Pleiades and Orion,
　and turns deep darkness
　　into the morning,
　and darkens the day into night;
　who summons the waters of the sea,
　and pours them out
　　on the surface of the earth—
　this one's name is the Lord—
9 who causes destruction to flash out
　against the strong,
　so that destruction comes
　　upon the fortress.

10 They hate the one who judges
　at the city gate,
　and they reject the one
　　who speaks the truth.
11 Truly, because you crush the weak,
　and because you tax their grain,
　you have built houses of carved stone,
　but you won't live in them;
　you have planted pleasant vineyards,
　but you won't drink their wine.
12 I know how many are your crimes,
　and how numerous are your sins—

afflicting the righteous,
　taking money on the side,
　turning away the poor who seek help.
13 Therefore, the one who is wise
　will keep silent in that time;
　it is an evil time.

Words of inspiration

14 Seek good and not evil,
　that you may live;
　and so the Lord,
　the God of heavenly forces,
　will be with you just as you have said.
15 Hate evil, love good,
　and establish justice at the city gate.
　Perhaps the Lord God of heavenly forces
　will be gracious to what is left of Joseph.

Divine wrath anticipated

16 Truly, the Lord proclaims,
　the God of heavenly forces, the Lord:
　Crying will be heard in all the squares.
　In all the streets they will say,
　"Oh no! Oh no!"
　They will call upon the farmers to wail,
　and those skilled in mourning to lament.

When You Disagree, Seek Good *Amos 5:14-15*

It's important for us to have our own opinions and beliefs; this is part of growing up. Having our own thoughts also means we won't always agree with someone else's ideas. Sometimes we might get in a really strong argument with another person. When this happens, it may seem that there's no way to work out the disagreement; but God wants us to get along with each other.

Instead of hurting each other, we could choose to go to a wise person who can listen to each side and help make things fair. That's what the people in Israel did. When two people disagreed with each other, they went to the elders, or wise people, who sat at the city gate to hear complaints. These wise people knew what kind of behavior was good and what was evil. The wise elders then decided the best way to make things fair. God wants each of us to seek good and not evil.

Who are some wise people in your life who can help when you have a bad disagreement?

Do you sense that God is near when you're doing good things? Why or why not?

¹⁷ In all the vineyards
there will be bitter crying because
I will pass through your midst,
says the Lord.

A statement of divine disgust

¹⁸ Doom to those who desire
the day of the Lord!
Why do you want the day of the Lord?
It is darkness, not light;
¹⁹ as if someone fled from a lion,
and was met by a bear;
or sought refuge in a house,
rested a hand against the wall,
and was bitten by a snake.
²⁰ Isn't the day of the Lord darkness,
not light,
all dark with no brightness in it?

²¹ I hate, I reject your festivals;
I don't enjoy your joyous assemblies.
²² If you bring me your entirely burned
offerings and gifts of food—
I won't be pleased;
I won't even look at your offerings
of well-fed animals.
²³ Take away the noise of your songs;
I won't listen to the melody
of your harps.

**Memorize
Amos 5:24**

²⁴ But let justice roll
down like waters,
and righteousness
like an ever-flowing stream.

²⁵ Did you bring me sacrifices and offerings
during the forty years in the wilderness,
house of Israel?
²⁶ You will take up Sakkuth your king,
and Kaiwan your star-god,
your images,
which you made for yourselves.
²⁷ Therefore, I will take you away
beyond Damascus, says the Lord,
whose name is
the God of heavenly forces.

Warnings to the self-satisfied

6 Doom to those resting
comfortably in Zion
and those trusting in Mount Samaria,
the chiefs of the nations,
to whom the house of Israel comes!
² Cross over to Calneh and see;

from there go to Hamath the great;
then go down to Gath of the Philistines.
Are you better than these kingdoms?
Or is your territory greater
than their territory?

³ Doom to those who ignore the evil day
and make violent rule draw near:
⁴ who lie on beds of ivory,
stretch out on their couches,
eat lambs from the flock,
and bull calves from the stall;
⁵ who sing idle songs
to the sound of the harp,
and, like David, compose tunes
on musical instruments;

⁶ who drink bowls of wine,
put the best of oils on themselves,
but who aren't grieved
over the ruin of Joseph!
⁷ Therefore, they will now
be the first to be taken away,
and the feast of those who lounged
at the table will pass away.

⁸ The Lord God has solemnly sworn,
says the Lord,
the God of heavenly forces:
I reject the pride of Jacob.
I hate his fortresses.
I will hand over the city
and all that is in it.
⁹ If ten people remain in one house,
then they will die.
¹⁰ If a relative, someone who burns the dead,
picks up the body to bring it out
of the house,
and says to someone inside the house,
"Is anyone else with you?"
the answer will be, "No."
Then the relative will say,
"Hush! We mustn't mention
the name of the Lord."
¹¹ Look, the Lord is giving an order;
he will shatter the great house into bits

and the little house into pieces.
¹² Do horses run on rocks?
  Does one plow the sea with oxen?
  But you have turned justice
    into poison
  and the fruit of righteousness
    into bitterness—
¹³ you who rejoice in Lo-debar,
  who say, "Haven't we by our own strength
    taken Karnaim for ourselves?"
¹⁴ Indeed, I will raise up against you a nation,
  house of Israel,
  says the Lord God of heavenly forces,
  and they will oppress you from
    Lebo-hamath to the desert ravine.

A vision of locusts

7 This is what the Lord God showed me: The Lord God was forming locusts at the time the late grass began to sprout. (It was the late grass after the king's harvest.) ²When they had finished eating the green plants of the land, I said,
  "Lord God, please forgive!
  How can Jacob survive?
  He is so small!"
³ The Lord relented concerning this:
  "It won't take place,"
                            says the Lord.

A vision of fire

⁴This is what the Lord God showed me: The Lord God was calling for judgment with fire, and it devoured the great deep and was eating up part of the land. ⁵Then I said,
  "Lord God, I beg you, stop!
  How can Jacob survive?
  He is so small!"
⁶ The Lord relented concerning this:
  "This also won't take place,"
                        says the Lord God.

A vision of a plumb line

⁷This is what the Lord showed me: The Lord was standing by a wall, with a plumb line in his hand. ⁸The Lord said to me, "Amos, what do you see?"
  "A plumb line," I said.
  Then the Lord said,
  "See, I am setting a plumb line
    in the middle of my people Israel.

I will never again forgive them.
⁹ The shrines of Isaac
  will be made desolate,
  and the holy places of Israel
    will be laid waste,
  and I will rise against the house of
    Jeroboam with the sword."

Exchange between Amaziah, Jeroboam, and Amos

¹⁰Then Amaziah, the priest of Bethel, reported to Israel's King Jeroboam, "Amos has plotted against you within the house of Israel. The land isn't able to cope with everything that he is saying. ¹¹Amos has said, 'Jeroboam will die by the sword, and Israel will be forced out of its land.'"

¹²Amaziah said to Amos, "You who see things, go, run away to the land of Judah, eat your bread there, and prophesy there; ¹³but never again prophesy at Bethel, for it is the king's holy place and his royal house."

¹⁴Amos answered Amaziah, "I am^d not a prophet, nor am I a prophet's son; but I am a shepherd, and a trimmer of sycamore trees. ¹⁵But the Lord took me from shepherding the flock, and the Lord said to me, 'Go, prophesy to my people Israel.'
¹⁶ "Now then hear the Lord's word.
  You say, 'Don't prophesy against Israel,
  and don't preach
    against the house of Isaac.'

LIFE PRESERVER

What is a "plumb line"?
Amos 7:7

Amos tried to get God's people to see that the ways they were living were evil. Earlier he encouraged them to change. Here he used the example of a plumb line. A plumb line is a tool that a builder or carpenter uses to measure a wall to make sure it is straight.

If God used a plumb line to measure Israel and their acts as a nation, the tool would show that the nation was crooked. In God's measurement, they were found to be leaning toward wrong or evil things. God used Amos to send this message to Israel. ⬥

---

^dOr *was*; the verb is implied.

¹⁷ "Therefore, the Lord proclaims:
'Your wife will become a prostitute
in the city,
and your sons and your daughters
will fall by the sword,
and your land will be measured
and divided up;
you yourself will die in an unclean land,
and Israel will surely be taken away
from its land.'"

A vision of summer fruit

8 This is what the Lord God showed me: a basket of summer fruit. ²He said, "Amos, what do you see?"

I said, "A basket of summer fruit."

Then the Lord said to me,
"The end has come upon my people Israel;
I will never again forgive them.
³ On that day, the people
will wail the temple songs,"
says the Lord God;
"there will be many corpses,
thrown about everywhere.ᵉ
Silence."

Judgment on oppressors and hypocrites

⁴ Hear this, you who trample
on the needy and destroy
the poor of the land, ⁵saying,
"When will the new moon
be over so that we may sell grain,
and the Sabbath
so that we may offer wheat for sale,
make the ephah smaller,
enlarge the shekel,
and deceive with false balances,
⁶ in order to buy the needy for silver
and the helpless for sandals,
and sell garbage as grain?"

⁷ The Lord has sworn by the pride of Jacob:
Surely I will never forget
what they have done.
⁸ Will not the land tremble on this account,
and all who live in it mourn,
as it rises and overflows like the Nile,
and then falls again,
like the River of Egypt?ᶠ

LIFE PRESERVER

What is a "basket of summer fruit"? Amos 8:1-2

The Hebrew words for *summer fruit* and for *end* are very close in spelling. Amos was playing with these two words to indicate that God had given up on God's people. Amos had a very sad word of prophecy to give to the people: "The end has come upon my people Israel; I will never again forgive them" (Amos 8:2). If you keep reading this chapter, you will hear about all the terrible things Amos warned the people about. But if you read to the end of the book, you'll see that God promised to forgive the people—to restore their land and fortunes and begin again with them.

---

⁹ On that day, says the Lord God,
I will make the sun go down at noon,
and I will darken the earth
in broad daylight.
¹⁰ I will turn your feasts into sad affairs
and all your singing
into a funeral song;
I will make people
wear mourning clothes
and shave their heads;
I will make it like the loss
of an only child,
and the end of it like a bitter day.
¹¹ The days are surely coming,
says the Lord God,
when I will send hunger and thirst
on the land;
neither a hunger for bread,
nor a thirst for water,
but of hearing the Lord 's words.
¹² They will wander from sea to sea,
and from north to east;
they will roam all around,
seeking the Lord's word,
but they won't find it.
¹³ On that day the beautiful young women
and the young men
will faint with thirst.
¹⁴ Those who swear by the guilt of Samaria,
and say, "As your god lives, Dan,"
and, "As the way of Beer-sheba lives"—
even they will fall
and never rise again.

ᵉHeb uncertain ᶠHeb uncertain

Description of Israel's fate

9 I saw the Lord standing beside the altar,
    and the Lord said:
    Strike the pillars
      until the foundations shake,
    shatter them on the heads
      of all the people.
    With the sword,
      I will kill the last of them;
    not one of them will flee,
    not one of them will escape.
² If they dig through into the underworld,ᵍ
    from there my hand will take them.
  If they climb up to the heavens,
    from there I will bring them down.
³ If they hide themselves
    on the top of Carmel,
  I will search for them there
    and remove them.
  If they hide from my sight
    at the bottom of the sea,
  I will give an order to the sea serpent,
    and it will bite them.
⁴ If they are forced from their homes
    before their enemies,
  there I will give an order to the sword,
    and it will kill them.
  I will fix my eyes on them
    for harm and not for good.

A divine confession

⁵ The Lord, God of heavenly forces,
    touches the earth and it melts,
    and all who live in it are sick to death.
  All of itʰ rises up like the Nile
    and sinks again, like the Nile of Egypt.
⁶ It is the Lord who builds
    his upper rooms in the heavens
    and establishes his residence
      upon the earth;
  who summons the waters of the sea,
    and pours them out
      upon the face of the earth—
      the Lord is his name.

Divine address to the Israelites

⁷ Aren't you like the Cushites to me,
    people of Israel?
                              says the Lord.

  Haven't I brought Israel up
    from the land of Egypt,

and the Philistines from Caphtor
    and the Arameans from Kir?
⁸ Look, the Lord God is eyeing
    the sinful kingdom,
    and I will destroy it
      from the face of the earth.
  However, I won't destroy fully
    the house of Jacob,
                              says the Lord.

Warning to the house of Israel

⁹ Look, I am giving orders,
    and I will shake the house of Israel
    among all the nations
    as one sifts dirt with a screen,
    but no pebble will fall to the ground.
¹⁰ All the sinners of my people
    will die by the sword,
    those who say,
    "Evil won't overtake or meet us."

Divine promise of restoration

¹¹ On that day I will raise up
    the meeting tent of David that has fallen,
    and repair its broken places.
  I will raise up its ruins,
    and I will rebuild it like a long time ago;
¹² so that they may possess
    what is left of Edom,
    as well as all the nations
    who are called by my name,
                              says the Lord who will do this.
¹³ The days are surely coming, says the Lord,
    when the one who plows
    will overtake the one who gathers,
    when the one who crushes grapes
    will overtake the one who sows the seed.
  The mountains will drip wine,
    and all the hills will flow with it.
¹⁴ I will improve the circumstances
    of my people Israel;
    they will rebuild the ruined cities
    and inhabit them.
  They will plant vineyards
    and drink their wine;
  and they will make gardens
    and eat their fruit.
¹⁵ I will plant them upon their land,
    and they will never again be plucked up
  out of the land that I have given them,
                              says the Lord your God.

ᵍHeb *Sheol* ʰOr *the earth*

Obadiah

Obadiah is the shortest of all the Old Testament books, with only twenty-one verses from start to finish. Because this book is only one chapter long, you won't find any chapter numbers—only a number for each verse.

This small book is about a family fight that grew into a feud between nations that lasted hundreds of years. Genesis 25–28 tells the story of the birth of twin brothers, Jacob and Esau. The younger brother, Jacob, cheated the older brother, Esau. He first stole Esau's rights as older brother to a larger share of the family's wealth. He then tricked his father into giving him the important blessing that belonged to his older brother. The two brothers became bitter enemies. Even though they made up with each other later (Gen 33:1-17), their children remembered their battles.

Jacob's family grew into the nation of Israel, and Esau's family became Edom. Over the centuries, Edom often bullied Israel. The people of Edom were glad when other nations attacked Israel and carried off its wealth. They took advantage of these battles to steal whatever they could from Israel.

Obadiah made this short speech to say that Edom would face punishment for its actions. This book shows us that God cares how families and nations get along! ◊

things
YOU'LL DISCOVER

In this book the prophet Obadiah speaks to the nation of Edom, a land to the south and southeast of the Dead Sea. Obadiah condemns Edom for centuries of treating Israel badly.

people
YOU'LL MEET

Obadiah—a prophet who spoke for God (Obad 1-21)
Jacob—a name for God's people (Obad 10)
Edom—the name of a people descended from Esau, and their country

places
YOU'LL GO

Edom (a kingdom south of the Dead Sea),
Judah (the southern kingdom),
Jerusalem

words
YOU'LL REMEMBER

"But you should have taken no pleasure over your brother on the day of his misery; you shouldn't have rejoiced over the people of Judah on the day of their devastation; you shouldn't have bragged on their day of hardship" (Obad 12).

Edom falls

¹ The vision of Obadiah.
 The LORD God proclaims
  concerning Edom:

did you know? People who harvested grapes always left some grapes on the vines in the field. This provided a way for people who were poor and couldn't afford food to get grapes to eat from the field.

We have heard a message
 from the LORD—
  a messenger has been sent
   among the nations:
"Rise up! Let us rise against her
 for battle!"
² Look now, I will make you of little
 importance among the nations;
  you will be totally despised.
³ Your proud heart has tricked you—
 you who live in the cracks
  of the rock,
   whose dwelling is high above.
 You who say in your heart,
  "Who will bring me
   down to the ground?"
⁴ Though you soar like the eagle,

UMBRELLA
PRIDE

They Thought Wrong *Obadiah 3-7*
Jacob and Esau were twins who did not get along. (You can read their story in Genesis 25.) Jacob's descendants became the nations of Israel and Judah, but Esau's descendants became the nation of Edom. All three nations should have been each other's allies in battle, but that was not the case. Edom let Judah be defeated and have its people and wealth carried away. Edom was located on a rocky cliff, and so the people believed their city could not be taken in battle. They thought they were untouchable, but they were wrong. Because of their pride, the people of Edom deceived themselves. God sent Obadiah a message about the defeat that was coming their way. ♦

though your nest is set among the stars,
 I will bring you down from there,
           says the LORD.

Edom is robbed

⁵ If thieves approach you,
 if robbers by night—
  how you've been devastated!—
   wouldn't they steal
    only what they wanted?
 If those who gather grapes came to you,
  wouldn't they leave some grapes?
⁶ How Esau has been looted,
 his treasures taken away!
⁷ All those who were your allies
 have driven you to the border.
  Those who were on your side
   tricked you
    and triumphed over you.
 They are setting your own bread
  as a trap under you,ᵃ
   but you don't see it coming.
⁸ Won't I on that day, says the LORD,
 destroy the wise from Edom
  and understanding from Mount Esau?
⁹ Your warriors will be shattered, Teman,
 and everyone from Mount Esau
  will be eliminated.

Edom's misdeeds

¹⁰ Because of the slaughter and violence
 done to your brother Jacob,
  shame will cover you,
   and you will be destroyed forever.
¹¹ You stood nearby,
 strangers carried off his wealth,
  and foreigners entered his gates
   and cast lots for Jerusalem;
    you too were like one of them.
¹² But you should have
 taken no pleasure
  over your brother
   on the day of his misery;
    you shouldn't have rejoiced
     over the people of Judah
      on the day of their devastation;
       you shouldn't have bragged
        on their day of hardship.
¹³ You shouldn't have entered
 the gate of my people

Memorize
Obad 12

ᵃHeb uncertain

on the day of their defeat;
you shouldn't have even looked
on his suffering
on the day of his disaster;
you shouldn't have stolen
his possessions
on the day of his distress.
¹⁴ You shouldn't have waited on the roads
to destroy his escapees;
you shouldn't have handed over
his survivors
on the day of defeat.
¹⁵ The day of the Lᴏʀᴅ is near
against all the nations.
As you have done,
so it will be done to you;
your actions will make you suffer!
¹⁶ Just as you have drunk
on my holy mountain,
so will all the nations
around you drink;
they will drink and swallow quickly,
and they will be like they've never
been before.

Edom's punishers

¹⁷ But on Mount Zion
there will be those who escape,
and it will be holy;
and the house of Jacob will drive out
those who drove them out.
¹⁸ The house of Jacob will be a fire,
the house of Joseph a flame,
and the house of Esau straw;
they will burn them up completely,

and there will be no one left
of the house of Esau,
for the Lᴏʀᴅ has spoken.
¹⁹ Those of the arid southern plain
will possess Mount Esau,
and those of the western foothills,
the land of the Philistines;
they will possess the land of Ephraim
and the land of Samaria,
and Benjamin will possess Gilead.
²⁰ Those who remain of the Israelites
will possess the land of the
Canaanites as far as Zarephath;
and those left from Jerusalem
and who are now living in Sepharad
will possess the cities
of the arid southern plain.
²¹ The deliverers will go up to Mount Zion
to rule Mount Esau,
and the kingdom will be the Lᴏʀᴅ's.

Jonah

things YOU'LL DISCOVER

The book of Jonah tells the story of a prophet who didn't want to obey God's command to preach to an enemy nation. When the prophet Jonah tried to escape God's order by taking a boat to a distant place, a great fish swallowed Jonah.

people YOU'LL MEET

Jonah—a prophet who spoke for God (Jonah 1–4)

places YOU'LL GO

Nineveh (capital of Assyria, present-day northern Iraq), **Tarshish** (a distant place), **Jaffa** (modern Tel Aviv, Israel)

words YOU'LL REMEMBER

"I know that you are a merciful and compassionate God, very patient, full of faithful love, and willing not to destroy" (Jonah 4:2).

God told the prophet Jonah to go and preach a warning to the people of Nineveh. But that was a job Jonah didn't want to do. Nineveh was the capital of Assyria, one of Israel's most frightening enemies. Jonah didn't want God to give the people of Nineveh the chance to stop sinning. Because Nineveh was east of Israel, Jonah fled as far west as he could.

Jonah boarded a boat in Jaffa, a city on the Mediterranean coast. He headed to Tarshish, which might have been in Spain. While we don't know the exact location of Tarshish, we know it was "away from the LORD" (Jonah 1:3). Jonah was trying to get as far from God as possible.

When God started a storm, sailors on the boat tossed Jonah into the sea. A great fish swallowed the prophet, and he stayed in the belly of the fish until he prayed and told God he would go preach in Nineveh. When Jonah preached, the people of that city heard God's word and believed in God. They were sad for their sins and quit their evil behavior. God was glad the people turned back to God, but Jonah was angry that God hadn't punished them.

Jonah discovered that God is "a merciful and compassionate God, very patient, full of faithful love, and willing not to destroy" (Jonah 4:2). This book shows us that God is eager to forgive. God wants people everywhere to believe in God and stop doing wrong! ◆

Commissioning of a reluctant prophet

1 The LORD's word came to Jonah, Amittai's son: ²"Get up and go to Nineveh, that great city, and cry out against it, for their evil has come to my attention."

³So Jonah got up—to flee to Tarshish from the LORD! He went down to Joppa and found a ship headed for Tarshish. He paid the fare and went aboard to go with them to Tarshish, away from the LORD. ⁴But the LORD hurled a great wind upon the sea, so that there was a great storm on the sea; the ship looked like it might be broken to pieces. ⁵The sailors were terrified, and each one cried out to his god. They hurled the cargo that was in the ship into the sea to make it lighter.

Now Jonah had gone down into the hold of the vessel to lie down and was deep in sleep. ⁶The ship's officer came and said to him, "How can you possibly be sleeping so deeply? Get up! Call on your god! Perhaps the god will give some thought to us so that we won't perish."

⁷Meanwhile, the sailors said to each other, "Come on, let's cast lots so that we might learn who is to blame for this evil that's happening to us." They cast lots, and the lot fell on Jonah. ⁸So they said to him, "Tell us, since you're the cause of this evil happening to us: What do you do and where are you from? What's your country and of what people are you?"

⁹He said to them, "I'm a Hebrew. I worship the LORD, the God of heaven—who made the sea and the dry land."

¹⁰Then the men were terrified and said to him, "What have you done?" (The men knew that

LIFE PRESERVER

Was Jonah really inside a big fish? *Jonah 1–2*

Many people who study the Bible think the book of Jonah is a parable, which is a short story that teaches an important lesson, like some stories that Jesus taught in the New Testament.

Whether or not the book is a parable, we see what the story is trying to teach us. Jonah didn't want to be a prophet. The good news, however, was that he finally gave God's word to the people of Nineveh, who listened and turned from their sins. Jonah was successful in delivering his message, but he had a hard time with God's forgiveness. He seemed to resent what God had done. Is the fish the main focus of Jonah and its meaning? Probably not. The book is really a story about how God can work through humans, even ones who don't always agree with the way God works. ◊

Jonah was fleeing from the LORD, because he had told them.)

¹¹They said to him, "What will we do about you so that the sea will become calm around us?" (The sea was continuing to rage.)

¹²He said to them, "Pick me up and hurl me into the sea! Then the sea will become calm around you. I know it's my fault that this great storm has come upon you."

¹³The men rowed to reach dry land, but they couldn't manage it because the sea continued to rage against them. ¹⁴So they called on the LORD, saying, "Please, LORD, don't let us perish on account of this man's life, and don't blame us for innocent blood! You are the LORD: whatever you want, you can do." ¹⁵Then they picked up Jonah and hurled him into the sea, and the sea ceased its raging. ¹⁶The men worshipped the LORD with a profound reverence; they offered a sacrifice to the LORD and made solemn promises.

LIGHTHOUSE

RESPECT FOR GOD

Worthy of Respect *Jonah 1:9*

Even though Jonah disobeyed God by sailing away from where God had asked him to go, Jonah told the sailors about his religion. First he told them he was a Hebrew, and then he told them whom he worshipped. Jonah said he worshipped the LORD who rules heaven, the creator of both the land and the sea. Jonah showed respect for God by telling the truth about who God is: creator and ruler. ◊

No escape for the prophet

¹⁷ᵃMeanwhile, the LORD provided a great fish to swallow Jonah. Jonah was in the belly of the fish for three days and three nights.

2 Jonah prayed to the LORD his God from the belly of the fish:

²"I called out to the LORD in my distress,
  and he answered me.

ᵃ2:1 in Heb

From the belly of the underworld[b]
  I cried out for help;
  you have heard my voice.
³ You had cast me into the depths
  in the heart of the seas,
  and the flood surrounds me.
  All your strong waves and rushing
    water passed over me.
⁴ So I said, 'I have been driven
  away from your sight.
  Will I ever again look
    on your holy temple?
⁵ Waters have grasped me
  to the point of death;
  the deep surrounds me.
  Seaweed is wrapped around my head
    ⁶ at the base of the undersea[c] mountains.

I have sunk down to the underworld;
  its bars held me with no end in sight.
  But you brought me out of the pit.'
⁷ When my endurance[d] was weakening,
  I remembered the Lord,
  and my prayer came to you,
    to your holy temple.
⁸ Those deceived by worthless things lose
  their chance for mercy.[e]
⁹ But me, I will offer a sacrifice to you
  with a voice of thanks.
  That which I have promised, I will pay.
    Deliverance belongs to the Lord!"
¹⁰Then the Lord spoke to the fish, and it
vomited Jonah onto the dry land.

Nineveh hears God's word

3 The Lord's word came to Jonah a second
time: ²"Get up and go to Nineveh, that
great city, and declare against it the proclamation that I am commanding you." ³And
Jonah got up and went to Nineveh, according
to the Lord's word. (Now Nineveh was indeed
an enormous city, a three days' walk across.)

---

did you know? In Bible times, cities were surrounded by walls for protection. The walls around the city of Nineveh were so thick that six chariots could ride side by side on the top of the wall. That's a really wide wall!

---

[b]Heb *Sheol* [c]Heb lacks *undersea*. [d]*Endurance* here renders the same Heb word as *life* in 1:14 and *death* in 2:5. [e]Heb uncertain

God's THOUGHTS ◆ My THOUGHTS

God Gives Jonah a Do-Over *Jonah 2*

Sometimes in life we ask for a do-over. For example, when we play games with others, we sometimes want to better our chances of winning. So we ask to try again when we realize we've made
a mistake. Sometimes we mess up bigger things in life and
wish we could have a second chance to do something right.
That happened to a prophet named Jonah.

God told Jonah to go to a faraway city, Nineveh, to tell
other people about God. Nineveh was located in a place
that today we call Iraq. Jonah ran away in the opposite
direction and got on a boat, but he was swallowed by a fish
during a storm. So Jonah asked God to forgive him for choosing
to do the wrong thing. God had mercy on Jonah. God gave him
another chance to tell the people of Nineveh about God.

*How would you feel if God asked you to go tell others about God in a
place you didn't want to go?*

*When you disobey God by doing the opposite of what you should do,
how can you get a second chance?*

⁴Jonah started into the city, walking one day, and he cried out, "Just forty days more and Nineveh will be overthrown!" ⁵And the people of Nineveh believed God. They proclaimed a fast and put on mourning clothes, from the greatest of them to the least significant.

⁶When word of it reached the king of Nineveh, he got up from his throne, stripped himself of his robe, covered himself with mourning clothes, and sat in ashes. ⁷Then he announced, "In Nineveh, by decree of the king and his officials: Neither human nor animal, cattle nor flock, will taste anything! No grazing and no drinking water! ⁸Let humans and animals alike put on mourning clothes, and let them call upon God forcefully! And let all persons stop their evil behavior and the violence that's under their control!" ⁹He thought, Who knows? God may see this and turn from his wrath, so that we might not perish.ᶠ

¹⁰God saw what they were doing—that they had ceased their evil behavior. So God stopped planning to destroy them, and he didn't do it.

Jonah balks at God's mercy

4 But Jonah thought this was utterly wrong, and he became angry. ²He prayed to the LORD, "Come on, LORD! Wasn't this precisely my point when I was back in my own land? This is why I fled to Tarshish earlier! I know that you are a merciful and compassionate God, very patient, full of faithful love, and willing not to destroy. ³At this point, LORD, you may as well take my life from me, because it would be better for me to die than to live."

Memorize Jonah 4:2

⁴The LORD responded, "Is your anger a good thing?" ⁵But Jonah went out from the city and sat down east of the city. There he

UMBRELLA
Sad

Focus on Others *Jonah 4:3-11*
Jonah delivered God's message, and the people of Nineveh changed their hearts. This sounds like the perfect ending, but Jonah's story isn't over yet. Jonah was so upset that God chose to be merciful to Nineveh that he figured he was better off dead. Later Jonah got angry about a bush that died and left him without shade, and again he said he would be better off dead. Jonah was discouraged. God pointed out to Jonah that he had more concern for a bush than for a whole city of people. God wanted Jonah to focus on others. ◖

made himself a hut and sat under it, in the shade, to see what would happen to the city.

⁶Then the LORD God provided a shrub,ᵍ and it grew up over Jonah, providing shade for his head and saving him from his misery. Jonah was very happy about the shrub. ⁷But God provided a worm the next day at dawn, and it attacked the shrub so that it died. ⁸Then as the sun rose God provided a dry east wind, and the sun beat down on Jonah's head so that he became faint. He begged that he might die, saying, "It's better for me to die than to live."

⁹God said to Jonah, "Is your anger about the shrub a good thing?"

Jonah said, "Yes, my anger is good—even to the point of death!"

¹⁰But the LORD said, "You 'pitied' the shrub, for which you didn't work and which you didn't raise; it grew in a night and perished in a night. ¹¹Yet for my part, can't I pity Nineveh, that great city, in which there are more than one hundred twenty thousand people who can't tell their right hand from their left, and also many animals?"

ᶠHeb lacks *He thought.* ᵍBotanists disagree about whether Heb *qiqayon* refers to a climbing gourd plant, a castor bean plant, or some other shrub.

Micah

The prophet Micah saw trouble coming. The nation of Assyria attacked the northern kingdom of Israel and took away its people as prisoners. Micah said the southern kingdom of Judah now faced similar danger. But the people of Judah thought they were safe.

Micah spoke for God during a time when some of God's people were becoming wealthy. But the wealthy were using religion and politics to gain power rather than helping people in need. Rich landowners were taking advantage of the poor people who farmed the land.

Micah told these people they were doing wrong and explained how God's people should live. God's people should "do justice, embrace faithful love, and walk humbly with your God" (Mic 6:8). These simple actions are far more important than doing religious things. The book of Micah tells us that treating others the right way is a part of what it means to follow God.

Micah said that a ruler of Israel would be born in Bethlehem (Mic 5:2), the small town where Jesus was born hundreds of years later (Matt 2:1). That king would unite God's people and bring peace and justice to the land. ◊

"He has told you, human one, what is good and what the LORD requires from you: to do justice, embrace faithful love, and walk humbly with your God."

Micah 6:8

The LORD is coming!

1 The LORD's word that came to Micah of Moresheth in the days of Judah's Kings Jotham, Ahaz, and Hezekiah, which he saw concerning Samaria and Jerusalem:

² Listen, all you peoples!
    Pay attention, earth, and all that fills it!
May the LORD God
    be a witness against you,
        the Lord from his holy temple.
³ Look! The LORD is coming out
    from his place;
he will go down and tread
    on the shrines of the earth.
⁴ Then the mountains will melt under him;
    the valleys will split apart,
    like wax yielding to the fire,
    like waters poured down a slope.
⁵ All this is for the crime of Jacob
    and the sins of the house of Israel.
Who is responsible
    for the crime of Jacob?ᵃ
        Isn't it Samaria?
Who is responsible
    forᵇ the shrines of Judah?
        Isn't it Jerusalem?
⁶ So I will make Samaria
    a pile of rubble in the open field,
    a place for planting vineyards.
I will pour her stones into the valley;
    her foundations I will lay bare.
⁷ All her images will be beaten to pieces;
    all her wages will be burned;
I will make all her idols worthless.
    Since she gathered them
        from the wages of a prostitute,
    they will again become
        wages of a prostitute.
⁸ On account of this, I will cry out and howl;
    I will go about barefoot and stripped.
I will cry out like the jackals,
    and mourn like the ostriches.

Destruction looms

⁹ Indeed, Zion has been weakened
    by her wounds!
        It has come as far as Judah;
    he has struck as far as the gate
        of my people,
            as far as Jerusalem.

¹⁰ In Gath tell it not;
    no need to weep there!ᶜ
In Beth-le-aphrah,
    roll yourself in the dust!
¹¹ Pass by (for your sake),ᵈ
    inhabitants of Shaphir!
In nakedness and shame
    she will not go out,
        inhabitants of Zaanan.
The cry of Beth-ezel
    will take away from youᵉ
    any place to stand.
¹² How she longs for good,
    inhabitants of Maroth!
        Calamity has come down from the LORD
            to the gate of Jerusalem.
¹³ Harness the horses to the chariot,
    inhabitants of Lachish!
It was the beginning of sin
    for Daughter Zion;
        the crimes of Israel
            have been found in you.
¹⁴ Therefore, you will give good-bye gifts
    to Moresheth-gath;
        the houses of Achzib have become
            a deception for the kings of Israel.
¹⁵ Again I will bring to you
    the one who conquers,
        inhabitants of Mareshah;
            the glory of Israel
                will come as far as Adullam.
¹⁶ Make yourself bald and cut off your hair
    because of your cherished children!
        Make yourself as bald as the vulture,
            for they have gone from you
                into exile.

Oppressors will themselves be ruined

2 Doom to those who devise wickedness,
    to those who plan evil
        when they are in bed.
By the light of morning they do it,
    for they are very powerful.
² They covet fields and seize them,
    houses and take them away.

ᵃHeb lacks *responsible for.* ᵇHeb lacks *responsible for.* ᶜHeb lacks *there.* ᵈ*You* (plural) ᵉ*You* (feminine singular)

They oppress a householder
and those in his house,
a man and his estate.

³ Therefore, the Lᴏʀᴅ proclaims:
I myself am devising an evil
against this family
from which you will not be able
to remove your necks!
You will no longer be able
to go about arrogantly,
for it will be an evil time.

⁴ On that day, a taunt will be raised
against you;
someone will wail bitterly:
"We are utterly destroyed!
He exchanges the portion of my people;
he removes what belongs to me;
he gives away our fields to a rebel."

⁵ Therefore, you will have no one
to set boundary lines
by lot in the Lᴏʀᴅ's assembly.

Leaders unwilling to hear God's word

⁶ "They mustn't preach!" so they preach.
"They mustn't preach of such things!
Disgrace won't overtake us."
⁷ (Should this be said, house of Jacob?)
"Is the Lᴏʀᴅ's patience cut short?
Are these his deeds?"
Don't my words help
the one who behaves righteously?
⁸ But yesterday, my people,
the Lᴏʀᴅ rose up as an enemy.ᶠ
You strip off the glorious clothesᵍ
from trusting passersby,
those who reject war.
⁹ You drive out the women of my people,
each from her cherished house;
from their young children
you take away my splendor forever.
¹⁰ Rise up and go!
This can't be the resting place;
because of its uncleanness,
it destroys and the destruction
is horrific.
¹¹ If someone were to go about inspired
and say deceitfully:
"I will preach to you for wine and liquor,"
such a one would be
the preacher for this people!

*The false prophet's "peace"
will be destruction*

¹² I'll surely gather Jacob—all of you!
I'll surely assemble you,
those who are left of Israel!
I'll put them together
like sheep in Bozrah,ʰ
like a flock in its pen,
noisy with people.
¹³ The one who breaks out
will go before them;
they will break out
and pass through the gate;
they will leave by it.
They will pass on,
their king before them,
the Lᴏʀᴅ at their head.

Micah justifies the coming destruction

3 But I said:
Hear, leaders of Jacob,
rulers of the house of Israel!
Isn't it your job to know justice?—
² you who hate good and love evil,
who tear the skin off them,
and the flesh off their bones,
³ who devour the flesh of my people,
tear off their skin,
break their bones in pieces,
and spread them out as if in a pot,
like meat in a kettle.
⁴ Then they will cry out to the Lᴏʀᴅ,
but he won't answer them.
He will hide his face from them
at that time,
because of their evil deeds.
⁵ The Lᴏʀᴅ proclaims
concerning the prophets,
those who lead my people astray,
those who chew with their teeth
and then proclaim "Peace!"
but stir up war against the one
who puts nothing in their mouths:
⁶ Therefore, it will become night for you,
without vision, only darkness
without divination!
The sun will set on the prophets;
the day will be dark upon them.
⁷ Those seeing visions will be ashamed,
and the diviners disgraced;

ᶠHeb lacks *the* Lᴏʀᴅ. ᵍHeb uncertain ʰSee Isa 34:6; 63:1.

they will all cover their upper lips,[i]
for there will be no answer from God.
[8] But me! I am filled with power,
with the spirit of the LORD,
with justice and might,
to declare to Jacob his wrongdoing
and to Israel his sin!
[9] Hear this, leaders of the house of Jacob,
rulers of the house of Israel,
you who reject justice
and make crooked all that is straight,
[10] who build Zion with bloodshed
and Jerusalem with injustice!
[11] Her officials give justice for a bribe,
and her priests teach for hire.
Her prophets offer divination for silver,
yet they rely on the LORD, saying,
"Isn't the LORD in our midst?
Evil won't come upon us!"
[12] Therefore, because of you,
Zion will be plowed like a field,
Jerusalem will become piles of rubble,
and the temple mount will become
an overgrown mound.

A peaceable world

4 But in the days to come,
the mountain of the LORD's house
will be the highest of the mountains;
it will be lifted above the hills;
peoples will stream to it.
[2] Many nations will go and say:
"Come, let's go up
to the mountain of the LORD,
to the house of Jacob's God,
so that he may teach us his ways
and we may walk in God's paths!"
Instruction will come from Zion
and the LORD's word from Jerusalem.
[3] God will judge between the nations
and settle disputes of mighty nations,
which are far away.
They will beat their swords into iron plows
and their spears into pruning tools.
Nation will not take up sword
against nation;
they will no longer learn
how to make war.
[4] All will sit underneath
their own grapevines,

Bet you can
read this in 2 minutes.
Ready, set, go!

under their own fig trees.
There will be no one to terrify them;
for the mouth of the LORD of heavenly
forces has spoken.

An assertion of enduring loyalty

[5] Each of the peoples walks
in the name of their own god;
but as for us, we will walk
in the name of the LORD our God
forever and always.

Dominion in Zion

[6] On that day, says the LORD,
I will gather the lame;
I will assemble those
who were driven away
and those whom I have harmed.
[7] I will make the lame into survivors,
those driven away
into a mighty nation.
The LORD will rule over them
on Mount Zion
from now on and forever.
[8] As for you, Tower of Eder,[j]
hill of Daughter Zion,
as for you it will come,
the former dominion will come,
the royal power
belonging to Daughter Zion.

God is in control

[9] Now why do you cry out so loudly?
Isn't the king in you?
Or has your counselor perished,
so that pain has seized you
like that of a woman in labor?
[10] Writhe and scream, Daughter Zion,
like a woman in labor!
Now you will leave the city
and dwell in the open field;
you will go to Babylon.
There you will be rescued;
there the LORD will redeem you
from the power of your enemies.
[11] Now many nations
may gather against you;
they say, "Let her be defiled,"
or "Let our eyes look with desire
at Zion."
[12] But they don't know the plans of the LORD;

[i] Or *mustache* or *beard* [j] Or *tower of the flock*

they can't understand his scheme,
namely, that he will bring them
like grain to the threshing floor!
[13] Arise and thresh, Daughter Zion,
for I will make your horn out of iron;
your hooves I will make out of bronze.
You will crush many peoples;
you will dedicate their ill-gotten gains
to the LORD,
their wealth to the LORD
of all the earth.

Call to arms; the future is secure

5 [k]Now muster your troops,
Daughter Troop![l]
They have laid siege against us;
with a rod they will strike the cheek
of the judge of Israel.
[2] As for you, Bethlehem of Ephrathah,
though you are the least significant
of Judah's forces,
one who is to be a ruler in Israel
on my behalf will come out from you.
His origin is
from remote times,
from ancient days.

LIGHTHOUSE

FOREVER

Bigger Than Time *Micah 5:2*
Most gravestones show the year someone was
born and the year they died. Being born and dying
are part of being human. God is not human. God
doesn't have a beginning or an end. When Micah
tried to explain this concept to the people of Samaria and Jerusalem, he used terms like "remote
times" and "ancient days." God is eternal. That
means God existed before time started. It also
means God will be around after time runs out—
forever. No one invented God, and no one can end
God's existence. God is bigger than time. ◊

[3] Therefore, he will give them up
until the time when
she who is in labor gives birth.
The rest of his kin will return
to the people of Israel.
[4] He will stand and shepherd his flock[m]
in the strength of the LORD,

in the majesty of the name
of the LORD his God.
They will dwell secure,
because he will surely become great
throughout the earth;
[5] he will become one of peace.[n]
When Assyria invades our land
and treads down our fortresses,
then we will raise up against him
seven shepherds and
eight human princes.
[6] They will shepherd the land of Assyria
with the sword,
the land of Nimrod
with the drawn sword.
He will rescue us from Assyria
when he invades our land
and treads within our territory.
[7] Then the few remaining in Jacob
will be amid many peoples
like dew from the LORD,
like spring showers upon the grass,
which does not hope for humans
or wait for human ones.
[8] Then the few remaining in Jacob
will be among the nations,
amid many peoples,
like a lion among the creatures
of the forest,
like a young lion among flocks
of sheep, which when it passes by,
tramples and tears to pieces
with no one to deliver.
[9] Your hand will be lifted over your foes;
all your enemies will be cut off.

Doom for Israel's enemies

[10] On that day—says the LORD—
I will cut down your horses
in your midst;
I will destroy your chariots!
[11] I will cut down the cities of your land;
I will tear down your defenses!
[12] I will demolish
the sorceries you perform;
you will have no more diviners!
[13] I will cut down your images
and your sacred pillars in your midst.
You will no longer bow down
to the works of your hands!

[k]4:14 in Heb [l]Heb uncertain [m]Heb lacks *his flock.* [n]Or *this will ensure peace.*

14 I will tear down your sacred poles[o]
  in your midst;
    I will destroy your cities!
15 I will exact vengeance in anger
    and in wrath
      on the nations that don't obey!

God's dispute with Israel

6 Hear what the Lord is saying:
  Arise, lay out the lawsuit
    before the mountains;
      let the hills hear your voice!
2 Hear, mountains, the lawsuit of the Lord!
    Hear, eternal foundations of the earth!
  The Lord has a lawsuit against his people;
    with Israel he will argue.
3 "My people, what did I ever do to you?
    How have I wearied you? Answer me!
4 I brought you up out of the land of Egypt;
    I redeemed you
      from the house of slavery.
    I sent Moses, Aaron, and Miriam
      before you.
5 My people, remember what
    Moab's King Balak had planned,
    and how Balaam, Beor's son,
      answered him!
    Remember everything[p]
      from Shittim to Gilgal,
    that you might learn to recognize
      the righteous acts of the Lord!"

What does the Lord require?

6 With what should I approach the Lord
    and bow down before God on high?
  Should I come before him
    with entirely burned offerings,
    with year-old calves?
7 Will the Lord be pleased
    with thousands of rams,
    with many torrents of oil?
  Should I give my oldest child for my crime;
    the fruit of my body
      for the sin of my spirit?
8 He has told you,
      human one,
  what is good and
  what the Lord requires from you:
    to do justice, embrace faithful love,
    and walk humbly with your God.

Memorize Mic 6:8

What is the "lawsuit of the Lord"? *Micah 6:1-3*

God spoke through the prophet Micah about a familiar problem: God's people had forgotten their promises to God. They had promised to love God and to follow God's commandments. In this passage, Micah said God was setting up a court and had filed a lawsuit against the people. God was both judge and prosecutor. God demanded that Israel defend itself against the charges. And God called the mountains and hills as witnesses.

Following the style of a courtroom, God asked specific questions of the accused, which was the nation of Israel. Acting as a prosecuting attorney, God asked the people to show evidence of God's unfaithful actions. Then God presented evidence of God's faithfulness, reminding the people how God saved them with the exodus from Egypt. ◊

Punishment is near

9 The voice of the Lord calls out to the city;
    wisdom appears
      when one fears your name.[q]
    Hear, tribe, and who appointed her![r]
10 Are the treasures of wickedness
    still in the house of wickedness,
      while the shorted basket[s]
      is denounced?[t]
11 Can I approve wicked scales
    and a bag of false weights
12 in a city[u] whose wealthy
    are full of violence
    and whose inhabitants speak falsehood
      with lying tongues in their mouths?
13 So I have made you sick by striking you!
    I have struck you because of your sins.
14 You devour, but you aren't satisfied;
    a gnawing emptiness is within you.
  You put something aside,
    but you don't keep it safe.
  That which you do try to keep safe,
    I will give to the sword.
15 You sow, but you don't gather.
  You tread down olives,
    but you don't anoint with oil;
    you tread grapes, but don't drink wine.
16 Yet you[v] have kept the policies of Omri,

---

[o]Heb *asherim*. [p]Heb lacks *everything*. [q]Heb uncertain [r]Heb uncertain [s]Or *ephah*, approximately twenty quarts of grain [t]Heb uncertain [u]Heb lacks *in a city*. [v]Or *he*

all the practices of the house of Ahab;
   you have followed their counsels.
Therefore, I will make you
   a sign of destruction,
   your[w] inhabitants an object of hissing!
You must bear the reproach of my people.

The prophet laments

7 I'm doomed!
   I've become like one who,
      even after the summer fruit
      has been gathered,
      after the ripened fruits
      have been collected,
      has no cluster of grapes to eat,
      no ripe fig that I might desire.
2 Faithful ones have perished from the land;
   there is no righteous one
      among humanity.
   All of them lie in wait for bloodshed;
      they hunt each other with nets.
3 Their hands are skilled at doing evil.
   Official and judge alike ask for a bribe;
      the powerful speak however they like;
      this is how they conspire.
4 The good among them are like a briar;
   those who do the right thing are
      like a thorny thicket.
      (A day for your lookouts![x]
      Your punishment has arrived.
      The confusion of the wicked[y]
      is nearby.)
5 Don't rely on a friend;
   put no trust in a companion;
   guard the doors of your mouth
      from she who lies in your embrace.
6 Son disrespects father;
   a daughter rises up against her mother,
   a daughter-in-law against
      her mother-in-law;
   the enemies of a man
      are those of his own household.
7 But me! I will keep watch for the LORD;
   I will wait for the God of my salvation;
      my God will hear me.

Zion speaks

8 Do not rejoice[z] over me, my enemy,
   because when I fall, I will rise;
      if I sit in darkness, the LORD is my light.

9 I must bear the raging of the LORD,
   for I have sinned against him,
      until he decides my case
      and provides justice for me.
   He will bring me out into the light;
      I will see by means of his righteousness.
10 Then my enemy will see;
   shame will cover her who said to me:
      "Where is the LORD your God?"
   My eyes will see her ruin;[a]
      now she will become something
      to be trampled,
      like mud in the streets.

Micah responds to Zion

11 A day for the building of your walls!
   On that day, the boundary
      will be distant.
12 On that day, they will come to you
      from Assyria and the cities of Egypt,
      from Egypt to the River,
      from sea to sea,
      and from mountain to mountain.
13 And the earth will become desolate
   because of her inhabitants,
      because of the fruit of their actions.

Micah intercedes for the people

14 Shepherd your people with your staff,
   the sheep of your inheritance,
      those dwelling alone in a forest
      in the midst of Carmel.
   Let them graze in Bashan and Gilead,
      as a long time ago.

God agrees

15 As in the days when you came
   out of the land of Egypt,
      I will show Israel wonderful things.

The prophet continues

16 Nations will see and be ashamed
   of all their strength;
      they will cover their mouths;
      their ears will be deaf.
17 They will lick dust like the snake,
   like things that crawl on the ground.
   They will come trembling from their
      strongholds to the LORD our God;
      they will dread and fear you!

---

[w]Or *her* [x]Heb uncertain [y]Heb lacks *the wicked.* [z]*Rejoice* (feminine singular) [a]Heb lacks *ruin.*

¹⁸ Who is a God like you,
    pardoning iniquity,
        overlooking the sin of the few
            remaining for his inheritance?
    He doesn't hold on to his anger forever;
        he delights in faithful love.
¹⁹ He will once again
        have compassion on us;
    he will tread down our iniquities.
    You will hurl all our sins
        into the depths of the sea.
²⁰ You will provide faithfulness to Jacob,
        faithful love to Abraham,
    as you swore to our ancestors
        a long time ago.

LIFE PRESERVER

What was Micah's purpose in ending this book this way?
Micah 7:18-20

The last chapter starts out with great hopelessness and ends on a very hopeful note. Micah searched and couldn't find one faithful person left in the land. The prophet reminded the people to trust in God and asked God to continue to take care of the people as a good shepherd would take care of sheep. Perhaps Micah knew how important it was to encourage the people and reminded them that God loved them, would forgive them, and wanted them to live faithfully. ◊

Nahum

The prophet Jonah once took God's word to the people of Nineveh. The people of that large city heard God's word and believed in God. They were sorry for their sins and stopped their evil behavior. God was glad the people turned back to God (Jonah 3:1-10).

A hundred years later, the prophet Nahum began to speak for God. He said, "The LORD is very patient but great in power" (Nah 1:3). Nahum said that God was angry with the people of Nineveh because they had gone back to doing wrong. God was tired of their evil deeds and decided to destroy Nineveh, capital of the Assyrian Empire. Nahum, whose name means "comfort," said that God would bring destruction like "a rushing flood" (Nah 1:8).

Assyria had long been an enemy of Israel and Judah. The nation had become famous for its cruelty to other nations. Assyria conquered the northern kingdom of Israel and took its people away as prisoners. Its armies also attacked and almost defeated Judah and Jerusalem (2 Kgs 19:35-37). While God had forgiven Nineveh's sins during the days of Jonah, God would now allow other nations to attack the city.

Nahum's words can be hard to read, but this book reminds us that God expects people everywhere to do good. ◆

1 An oracle about Nineveh: the scroll containing the vision of Nahum the Elkoshite.

Power of the creator

² The Lord is a jealous and vengeful God;
  the Lord is vengeful
    and strong in wrath.
The Lord is vengeful against his foes;
  he rages against his enemies.
³ The Lord is very patient
  but great in power;
    the Lord punishes.
His way is in whirlwind and storm;
  clouds are the dust of his feet.
⁴ He can blast the sea and make it dry up;
  he can dry up all the rivers.
Bashan and Carmel wither;
  the bud of Lebanon withers.
⁵ The mountains quake because of him;
  the hills melt away.
The earth heaves before him—
  the world and all who dwell in it.
⁶ Who can stand before his indignation?
  Who can confront the heat of his fury?
His wrath pours out like fire;
  the rocks are shattered
    because of him.

Memorize
Nah 1:7

⁷ The Lord is good,
  a haven in a day
    of distress.
He acknowledges those
  who take refuge in him.
⁸ With a rushing flood,
  he will utterly destroy her[a] place
    and pursue his enemies into darkness.

A challenge to God's enemies

⁹ What are you plotting against the Lord?
  He is one who can annihilate!
  Distress will not arise twice.
¹⁰ They are tangled up like thorns,
  like drunkards in their cups.
They are consumed like stubble
  that is entirely dried up.
¹¹ From you[b] goes out
  one who plots evil against the Lord—
    a worthless counselor!

Reassurance for God's people

¹² The Lord proclaims:
Though once they were a healthy
  and numerous force,

they have been cut off
  and have disappeared.
I have afflicted you;
  I won't afflict you further, Zion.[c]
¹³ Now I will break off his yoke from you
  and tear off your chains.

Assyrian king's future doom

¹⁴ The Lord has commanded concerning you:
  You will have no children
    to carry on your name.
I will remove carved idol and cast
  image from the house of your gods;
I will make your grave,
  for you are worthless.
¹⁵ [d] Look, on the mountains: the feet of a
  messenger who announces peace!

---

[a] *her*; likely Nineveh [b] *you* (feminine singular); likely Nineveh [c] Heb lacks *Zion* [d] 2:1 in Heb

Celebrate your festivals, Judah!
Fulfill your solemn promises!
The worthless one
will never again invade you;
he has been completely cut off.

A city under attack

2 A scatterer has come up against you.
Guard the ramparts, watch the road,
protect your groin,
save your[e] strength!
2 The LORD will restore the pride of Jacob,
indeed, the pride of Israel,
because ravagers have destroyed
them and spoiled their branches.
3 The shields of his warriors are red;
his soldiers are dressed in crimson.
The ironwork of the chariots
flashes like fire
on the day he has prepared;
the horses quiver.
4 The chariots race wildly
through the streets;
they rush back and forth
through the squares.
They look like flaming torches;
they dart like bolts of lightning.
5 He musters his officers;
they stumble as they press forward.
They hurry to the city wall,
and the portable shield is set up.
6 The gates of the rivers are opened;
the palace melts.
7 It is decreed:[f]
She is sent into exile, carried away,
while her female servants moan
like doves, beating their breasts.
8 Nineveh has been like a pool of water.
Such are its waters,[g]
and others are fleeing.
"Stop, stop!"—but no one
can turn them back.
9 Plunder silver! Plunder gold!
There is no end to the supplies,
an abundance of precious objects!
10 Destruction and devastation;
the city is laid waste!
The heart grows faint and knees buckle;
there is anguish in every groin;
all the faces grow pale.

Cruel Nineveh will be destroyed

11 Where is the lions' den,
the meadow of the young lions,
where lion, lioness, even lion cub go
about with no one to terrify them?
12 The lion has torn enough prey
for his cubs and strangled enough
for his lionesses;
he has filled his lairs with prey,
his dens with torn flesh.
13 Look! I am against you, proclaims
the LORD of heavenly forces.
I will burn your[h] chariots in smoke;
the sword will devour your young lions;
I will cut off your prey from the earth,
the voice of your messengers
will never again be heard!

3 Doom, city of bloodshed—all deceit,
full of plunder: prey cannot get away.
2 Cracking whip and rumbling wheel,
galloping horse and careening chariot!
3 Charging cavalry, flashing sword,
and glittering spear;
countless slain, masses of corpses,
endless dead bodies—they stumble
over their dead bodies!
4 Because of the many whorings
of the whore,
the lovely graces
of the mistress of sorceries,
the one who sells nations
by means of her whorings
and peoples by means of her sorceries:
5 Look! I am against you, proclaims
the LORD of heavenly forces.
I will lift your skirts over your face;
I will show nations your nakedness
and kingdoms your dishonor.
6 I will throw disgusting things at you;
I will treat you with contempt
and make you a spectacle.
7 Then all who look at you
will recoil from you and say,
"Nineveh has been devastated!
Who will lament for her?"
Where could I possibly
seek comforters for you?
8 Are you better than Thebes,
situated by the Nile,
waters surrounding her,

[e]Heb lacks your. [f]Heb uncertain [g]Heb uncertain [h]Or her

whose fortress is sea
and whose city wall is waters?
⁹ Cush[i] and Egypt constituted
her strength, without limit;
Put and the Libyans were her[j] help.
¹⁰ Yet even she was destined for exile;
she went into captivity.
Indeed, her infants were dashed
to pieces at the head of every street.
They cast lots for her officials;
all of her powerful citizens
were bound in chains.
¹¹ Yes, even you will become drunk;
you will have to hide!
Even you will have to seek refuge
from the enemy!
¹² All your fortifications
are fig trees with ripe fruit;
when the trees are shaken, the fruit
falls into the mouth of the eater.
¹³ Look, your people are women
in your midst.
The gates of your land have been flung
wide open to your enemies.
Fire consumes the bars of your gates.

LIFE PRESERVER

What is the "injury" and the "wound"? *Nahum 3:19*

When the prophet Nahum spoke about an *injury* and a *wound*, he was describing Assyria, one of the enemies of God's people, and what would happen to this nation. Assyria would face serious consequences. Nahum said that in the end, the Assyrians would all be scattered. Their injury wouldn't get better because their wound would cause their death. They were cruel to God's people and would now suffer because of it. ◆

[i]Traditionally *Ethiopia*   [j]LXX; MT *your*

¹⁴ Draw water for yourself
to prepare for siege!
Strengthen your fortifications!
Tread the clay, trample the mortar,
grab the brick mold!
¹⁵ Fire will consume you there;
the sword will cut you down;
like the locust it will consume you.
Multiply like the locust;
multiply like the grasshopper!
¹⁶ You boasted more traders
than the heavens have stars.
The locust sheds its skin and flies away.

did you know?

When figs were ripe, a person simply shook the trunk of the fig tree and all the figs fell to the ground. Nahum said Nineveh had become so weak that the bricks of its mighty walls would shake away as easily as ripe figs if the city were attacked.

¹⁷ Your guards are like grasshoppers,
your marshals like swarms of cicadas
that encamp on stone fences
on a chilly day;
when the sun rises, they take flight;
no one knows where they have gone.
¹⁸ Your shepherds have fallen asleep,
king of Assyria!
Your officials are lying down.
Your people are scattered
across the mountains;
there is no one to gather them.
¹⁹ There is no remedy for your injury;
your wound is grievous.
All who hear the news about you
clap their hands over you.
Who has not suffered
from your continual cruelty?

Habakkuk

Habakkuk **followed God's ways.** He obeyed God's commands as well as he could. But wherever the prophet looked, he saw people doing evil and getting away with it.

The book of Habakkuk is full of questions. Habakkuk wondered how long God would put up with violence. He asked, "How long will I call for help and you not listen?" (Hab 1:2). But God was about to do something astonishing. God was about to bring to power the dreaded Chaldeans, a violent people who would take many captives.

Then Habakkuk asked how God could "keep silent when the wicked swallows one who is more righteous" (Hab 1:13). He wanted to know how a holy God could use such an evil nation to punish others. But God promised that at the right time God would also punish the Chaldeans.

Habakkuk trusted God and accepted these answers. He knew that God is powerful. He understood that God saves God's people. So the prophet would wait and watch God work. Habakkuk didn't expect life to get any safer or easier. But he knew that he could trust God no matter what. This book reminds us that we can be joyful about our trust in God even when bad things happen. ◆

1

The oracle that Habakkuk the prophet saw.

The prophet complains

² LORD, how long will I call for help
and you not listen?
I cry out to you,
"Violence!"
but you don't deliver us.

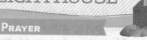

LIGHTHOUSE

PRAYER

Waiting for God to Answer *Habakkuk 1:2*
Some people complain a lot to anyone who will listen. Even the prophet Habakkuk complained! But
Habakkuk wisely brought his complaints to the one
who has the answers: God. Believe it or not, even
complaining to God can be a kind of prayer. Habakkuk wanted to know how long his prayers would
go unanswered. God had been listening the whole
time. God had a plan and an answer for Habakkuk,
and God has a plan and an answer for you too. ◊

³ Why do you show me injustice
and look at anguish
so that devastation and violence
are before me?
There is strife, and conflict abounds.
⁴ The Instruction is ineffective.
Justice does not endure
because the wicked
surround the righteous.
Justice becomes warped.

The LORD responds

⁵ Look among the nations and watch!
Be astonished and stare
because something is happening
in your days
that you wouldn't believe even if told.
⁶ I am about to rouse the Chaldeans,
that bitter and impetuous nation,
which travels throughout the earth
to possess dwelling places
it does not own.
⁷ The Chaldean is dreadful and fearful.
He makes his own justice and dignity.ᵃ
⁸ His horses are faster than leopards;
they are quicker than
wolves of the evening.

His horsemen charge forward;
his horsemen come from far away.
They fly in to devour, swiftly,
like an eagle.ᵇ
⁹ They come for violence,
the horde with all their faces
set toward the desert.ᶜ
He takes captives like sand.
¹⁰ He makes fun of kings;
rulers are ridiculous to him.
He laughs at every fortress,
then he piles up dirt and takes it.
¹¹ He passes through like the wind
and invades;
but he will be held guilty,
the one whose strength is his god.

The prophet questions the LORD

¹² LORD, aren't you ancient,
my God, my holy one?
Don't let us die.ᵈ
LORD, you put the Chaldean here
for judgment.
Rock, you established him as a rebuke.
¹³ Your eyes are too pure to look on evil;
you are unable to look at disaster.
Why would you look at the treacherous
or keep silent when the wicked
swallows one who is more righteous?
¹⁴ You made humans like the fish of the sea,
like creeping things
with no one to rule over them.
¹⁵ The Chaldean brings all of them up
with a fishhook.
He drags them away with a net;
he collects them in his fishing net,
then he rejoices and celebrates.
¹⁶ Therefore, he sacrifices to his net;
he burns incense to his fishing nets,
because due to them
his portion grows fat
and his food becomes luxurious.
¹⁷ Should he continue to empty his net
and continue to slay nations
without sparing them?

2

I will take my post;
I will position myself on the fortress.
I will keep watch to see
what the Lord says to me
and how heᵉ will respond
to my complaint.

ᵃOr *his justice and dignity come from him* ᵇOr *vulture* ᶜHeb uncertain ᵈHeb uncertain ᵉSyr *he*; MT *I*

The LORD responds

²Then the LORD answered me and said,
Write a vision,
 and make it plain upon a tablet
 so that a runner can read it.[f]
³ There is still a vision
 for the appointed time;
 it testifies to the end;
 it does not deceive.[g]
If it delays, wait for it;
 for it is surely coming;
 it will not be late.
⁴ Some people's desires
 are truly audacious;[h]
 they don't do the right thing.
 But the righteous person
 will live honestly.
⁵ Moreover, wine betrays
 an arrogant man.
 He doesn't rest.

He opens his jaws[i] like the grave;[j]
 like death, he is never satisfied.
He gathers all nations to himself
 and collects all peoples for himself.
⁶ Won't everyone tell parables about him
 or mocking poems concerning him?
They will say:
Doom to the one who multiplies
 what doesn't belong to him
 and who increases his own burden.
How long?
⁷ Won't they suddenly rise up to bite you?
 Those who frighten you will awaken;
 you will become plunder for them.
⁸ Since you yourself
 have plundered many nations,
 all the rest of the peoples
 will plunder you
 because of the human bloodshed
 and the violence done to the earth,

---

[f] Or *a reader can run with it*   [g] Heb uncertain; antecedents to pronouns in 2:3–6 are uncertain.   [h] Heb uncertain   [i] Or *throat*   [j] Heb *Sheol*

Demanding Help from God   *Habakkuk 1:1-4*

The world can be a scary place. God wants all of us to feel safe from violence. God doesn't want us to hurt each other when we disagree. But sometimes adults and countries get so mad at each other that they fail to work through their disagreements and instead start wars. They create armies and kill each other by the thousands.

In Bible times, when Habakkuk was a prophet, the winners of a war carried the losers to a new land and made them live in a strange place, eat strange food, and do work they didn't like. The world was especially scary for Habakkuk. Powerful nations around him were at war. Habakkuk knew it was just a matter of time before the people of his small nation were taken away to a foreign land. Imagine what you would say to God if someone suddenly came to your home or school and said, "Grab anything you can carry. You're coming with me and never going home again." Habakkuk did the best thing. He called out to God and was honest with his feelings.

When was the last time you felt scared about something that was happening around you? What did you do?

What would you say to God if someone took you away from your home and made you live in a faraway place?

⁹ Doom to the one making evil gain
for his own house,
for putting his own nest up high,
for delivering himself
from the grasp of calamity.
¹⁰ You plan shame for your own house,
cutting off many peoples
and sinning against your own life.
¹¹ A stone will cry out from a village wall,
and a tree branch will respond.
¹² Pity the one building a city with bloodshed
and founding a village with injustice.
¹³ Look, isn't this from the LORD of
heavenly forces?
Peoples grow weary from making just
enough fire;
nations become tired for nothing.ᵏ
¹⁴ But the land will be full of the knowledge
of the LORD's glory,
just as water covers the sea.

¹⁵ Doom to the one
who makes his companions drunk,
pouring out your wrath
in order to see them naked.ˡ
¹⁶ You have drunk your fill of dishonor
rather than glory.
So drink and stagger.ᵐ
The cup of the LORD's strong hand
will come around to you;
disgrace will engulf you.
¹⁷ Because of the violence done to Lebanon,
he will overwhelm you;
the destruction of animals
will terrify you,
as will human bloodshed and violence
throughout the land, the villages,
and all their inhabitants.ⁿ

¹⁸ Of what value is an idol,
when its potter carves it,
or a cast image that has been shaped?
It is a teacher of lies,
for the potter trusts the pottery,
though it is incapable of speaking.
¹⁹ Doom to the one saying to the tree,
"Wake up!"

or "Get up" to the silent stone.
Does it teach?
Look, it is overlaid with gold and silver,
but there is no breath within it.
²⁰ But the LORD is in his holy temple.
Let all the earth be silent before him.

The LORD's victory

3 The prayer of Habakkuk the prophet,
according to Shigionoth:
² LORD, I have heard your reputation.
I have seen your work.
Over time, revive it.
Over time, make it known.
Though angry, remember compassion.
³ God comes from Teman
and the holy one
from the mountain of Paran.   *Selah*
His majesty covers the heavens
and his praise fills the earth.
⁴ His radiance is like the sunlight,
with rays flashing from his hand.
That is the hiding place of his power.
⁵ Pestilence walks in front of him.
Plague marches at his feet.
⁶ He stops and measures the earth.
He looks and sets out
against the nations.
The everlasting mountains collapse;
the eternal hills bow down;
the eternal paths belong to him.
⁷ I saw the tents of Cushan under duress.
The curtains of the land of Midian
were quaking.

⁸ Was the LORD raging against the rivers?
Or was your anger directed
against the rivers?
Or was your fury directed
against the sea
when you rode on your horses
or rode your chariots to victory?
⁹ You raise up your empty bow,
uttering curses for the arrows.ᵒ   *Selah*
With rivers you split open the earth.
¹⁰ The mountains see you and writhe.
A flood of water rushes through.
The deep utters its voice;
it raises its hands aloft.ᵖ
¹¹ Sun and moon stand still high above.

ᵏHeb uncertain ˡHeb uncertain ᵐDSS, LXX; MT *uncircumcised* ⁿHeb uncertain ᵒHeb uncertain ᵖHeb uncertain

With the light, your arrows shoot,
  your spear at the flash of lightning.
[12] In fury, you stride the earth;
  in anger you tread the nations.
[13] You go out to save your people.
  For the salvation of your anointed
  you smashed the head
    of the house of wickedness,
  laying bare the foundation
    up to the neck. *Selah*

[14] You pierce the head of his warrior
    with his own spear.
  His warriors are driven off,
    those who take delight
      in oppressing us,[q]
    those who take pleasure
      in secretly devouring the poor.
[15] You make your horses tread on the sea;
    turbulent waters foam.

The prophet responds

[16] I hear and my insides tremble.
  My lips quiver at the sound.
  Rottenness enters my bones.
  I tremble while I stand,[r]
    while I wait for the day of distress

[q]Or *me* [r]Or *I tremble beneath me.* [s]Or *my heights*

to come against the people
  who attack us.
[17] Though the fig tree
    doesn't bloom,
  and there's no
    produce on the vine;
  though the olive crop withers,
    and the fields don't provide food;
  though the sheep are cut off
    from the pen,
  and there are no cattle in the stalls;
[18] I will rejoice in the LORD.
  I will rejoice in the God
    of my deliverance.
[19] The LORD God is my strength.
  He will set my feet like the deer.
  He will let me walk upon the heights.[s]

To the director,
with stringed instruments

SAILBOAT

JOY

No Matter What *Habakkuk 3:18-19*
Habakkuk learned some things from his conversations with God. He talked to God, and God answered him. Habakkuk understood that no matter what happened, his only source of true joy was God. God would rescue him, give him strength, watch over him, and keep him safe—even in dangerous situations—no matter what. ◆

Zephaniah

Many years before Zephaniah began to speak for God, a king named Hezekiah ruled Judah. Hezekiah was a good leader remembered for teaching people to obey God (2 Kgs 18–20). The prophet Zephaniah was the great-great-grandson of King Hezekiah. Like his famous ancestor, Zephaniah worked hard to bring Judah back to God.

Zephaniah saw God's people worshipping other gods like Baal and Milcom. He noticed people who thought they could get away with evil. Zephaniah believed the southern kingdom of Judah would soon be conquered by other nations. So he told people how they should come back to God. He said, "Seek the LORD, all you humble of the land who practice his justice; seek righteousness; seek humility" (Zeph 2:3). Zephaniah called the people to pray to God and quit being proud, to treat others fairly and do right.

With the help of his partner King Josiah, Zephaniah helped people worship the one true God. The nation got rid of its idols (2 Kgs 21:23–23:30). The book of Zephaniah ends with hope, looking forward to a time when God's people would obey God completely (Zeph 3:8-20). This book reminds us that we can always turn back to God when we do wrong. ♦

things YOU'LL DISCOVER

The book of Zephaniah gets its name from the prophet Zephaniah, who helped the nation of Judah follow God during the days of King Josiah.

people YOU'LL MEET

Zephaniah—a prophet who spoke for God (Zeph 1–3)
Daughter Zion—a name for the city of Jerusalem (Zeph 2)

places YOU'LL GO

Judah (the southern kingdom); **Philistia, Moab, Ammon, Cush** (nations surrounding Judah); **Assyria** (present-day northern Iraq); **Nineveh** (capital of Assyria)

words YOU'LL REMEMBER

"The LORD your God is in your midst…. He will create calm with his love; he will rejoice over you with singing" (Zeph 3:17).

1 The Lord's word that came to Zephaniah, Cushi's son, Gedaliah's grandson, Amariah's great-grandson, and Hezekiah's great-great-grandson in the days of Judah's King Josiah, Amon's son.

Judgment on the world and Judah

² I will wipe out everything
from the earth, says the Lord.
³ I will destroy humanity and the beasts;
I will destroy the birds in the sky
and the fish in the sea.
I will make the wicked
into a heap of ruins;
I will eliminate humanity
from the earth, says the Lord.

⁴ I will stretch out my hand against Judah
and against all the inhabitants
of Jerusalem.
I will eliminate what's left of Baal
from this place
and the names of the priests
of foreign gods,ᵃ
⁵ those bowing down to the
forces of heaven on the rooftops,
those swearing by the Lord along
with those swearing by Milcom,
⁶ those turning away from the Lord,
those who don't seek the Lord
and don't pursue him.

The day of the Lord

⁷ Hush before the Lord God,
for the day of the Lord is near!
The Lord has established a sacrifice;
he has made holy those
he has summoned.
⁸ On the day of the Lord's sacrifice,
I will punish the princes, the king's sons,
and all those wearing foreign clothes.
⁹ I will punish the one leaping
on the threshold on that day,
those filling the house of their master
with violence and deceit.
¹⁰ On that day—says the Lord—
an outcry will resound
from the Fish Gate,
wailing from the second quarter,
a loud crash from the hills.

¹¹ The ones who grind the grainᵇ will wail;
all the merchants will be silenced.
I will eliminate all those
weighing out silver.
¹² At that time,
I will search Jerusalem with lamps;
I will punish the men growing fat
on the sediment in their wine,
those saying to themselves,
The Lord won't do good or evil.
¹³ Their wealth will be looted
and their houses destroyed.
They will rebuild houses,
but not live in them;
they will plant vineyards,
but not drink the wine.
¹⁴ The great day of the Lord is near;
it is near and coming very quickly.
The sound of the day of the Lord is bitter.
A warrior screams there.
¹⁵ That day is a day of fury,
a day of distress and anxiety,
a day of desolation and devastation,
a day of darkness and gloominess,
a day of clouds and deep darkness,

LIFE PRESERVER

Why would God punish the people? *Zephaniah 1:2-18*

God asked the prophet Zephaniah to give a message to the people living in Judah who were not following God's ways. Zephaniah did so, telling about punishment from God with the hope that the people would change their hearts, say they were sorry, and remember God's Instruction.

Zephaniah warned that God would punish those who were satisfied with the way things were, the rich who didn't share with the poor, and those who didn't believe God could do anything. In the midst of all of these threats of punishment, the prophet also reminded the people that God would be present with them (Zeph 3:14-20). ♦

ᵃOr *the name of the priests of foreign gods along with the priests* ᵇOr *keeper of the mortar*

¹⁶ a day for blowing the trumpet
and alarm
against their invincible cities
and against their high towers.
¹⁷ I will make humanity suffer;
they will walk like the blind
because they sinned against the LORD.
Their blood will be poured out like dust
and their intestines like manure.
¹⁸ Moreover, their silver and their gold
won't be able to deliver them
on the day of the LORD's fury.
His jealousy will devour
the entire land with fire;
he will make an end,
a truly horrible one,
for all the inhabitants of the land.

2 Gather together and assemble
yourselves, shameless nation,
² before the decision is made—
the day vanishes like chaff^c—
before the burning anger
of the LORD comes against you,
before the day of the LORD's anger
comes against you.
³ Seek the LORD, all you humble
of the land who practice his justice;
seek righteousness;
seek humility.
Maybe you will be hidden
on the day of the LORD's anger.

Oracles against foreign nations

⁴ Gaza will certainly be abandoned;
and Ashkelon destroyed.
Ashdod will be driven out at noon;
Ekron will be uprooted.
⁵ Doom, inhabitants of the seacoast,
nation of Cretans.
The LORD's word is against you,
Canaan, land of the Philistines.
I will exterminate you,
leaving no inhabitant.
⁶ The seacoast will become pastureland,
with wells for shepherds
and pens for the flocks.
⁷ The coast will belong to the
survivors from the house of Judah;
they will pasture beside the sea;^d
in the houses of Ashkelon
they will lie down in the evening.

The LORD their God will visit them
and restore their possessions.

⁸ I have heard the taunting of Moab
and the defamation of the Ammonites;
they taunted my people
and enlarged their borders.
⁹ Therefore, as I live—
says the LORD of heavenly forces,
the God of Israel—
Moab will become like Sodom
and the Ammonites like Gomorrah:
a plot of weeds, salt pits,
and devastation forever.
The few remaining from my people
will plunder them;
the rest of my nation will possess them.
¹⁰ This will happen on account of their pride,
because they taunted and boasted
over the people
of the LORD of heavenly forces.
¹¹ The LORD will terrify them;
he will make all the gods
of the earth disappear.
All the coastlands of the nations
will bow down to the LORD,
each one in its own place.

¹² Moreover, you too, Cushites,
will be pierced by my sword.
¹³ He will stretch out his hand
against the north
and will cause Assyria to perish.
Let him make Nineveh a desolation,
a desolate place like the wilderness.
¹⁴ Flocks will lie down in its midst,
every living thing of the nation.
Moreover, the owl and the porcupine
will spend the night on its columns.
A bird's call will resound from the window.
Desolation will be on the sill,
for the cedar will be stripped bare.
¹⁵ This is the jubilant city,
the one dwelling securely,
the one saying in her heart,
I, and no one else, will endure forever.
How she has become a desolation,
a resting place for the wild animals.
All those who pass through her
hiss and shake their fist.

---

^cHeb uncertain ^dOr *they will pasture by them.*

Judgment against Jerusalem

3 Doom, obstinate one,
the defiled one,
the violent city.

[2] She listened to no voice;
she accepted no discipline.
She didn't trust in the LORD,
nor did she draw near to her God.

[3] The princes in her midst
are roaring lions.
Her judges are wolves of the evening;
they leave nothing for the morning.

[4] Her prophets are reckless,
men of treachery.
Her priests pollute that which is holy;
they do violence to the Instruction.

[5] The LORD is righteous in her midst.
He does nothing unjust.
Morning by morning
he renders justice,
but the unrighteous one
knows no shame.

[6] I will cut off nations;
their towers will be destroyed;
I will devastate their streets.
No one will pass through.
Their cities will be laid waste.
There will be no person,
no inhabitant left.

[7] I said, "Surely, she will fear me;
she will take instruction
so that her habitation won't be cut off[e]
because of everything I did to her."
However, they rose early
to corrupt their deeds.

[8] Therefore, wait for me, says the LORD,
wait for the day
when I rise up as a witness,[f]
when I decide to gather nations,
to collect kingdoms,
to pour out my indignation upon them,
all the heat of my anger.
In the fire of my jealousy,
all the earth will be devoured.

Restoration of the nations and Jerusalem

[9] Then I will change the speech
of the peoples into pure speech,
that all of them will call on
the name of the LORD
and will serve him as one.[g]

[10] From beyond the rivers of Cush,
my daughter, my dispersed ones,
will bring me offerings.

[11] On that day, you won't be ashamed
of all your deeds
with which you sinned against me;
then I will remove from your midst
those boasting with pride.
No longer will you be haughty
on my holy mountain,

[12] but I will cause a humble and powerless
people to remain in your midst;
they will seek refuge
in the name of the LORD.

[13] The few remaining from Israel
won't commit injustice;
they won't tell lies;
a deceitful tongue
won't be found on their lips.
They will graze and lie down;
no one will make them afraid.

[14] Rejoice, Daughter Zion! Shout, Israel!
Rejoice and exult with all your heart,
Daughter Jerusalem.

[15] The LORD has removed your judgment;
he has turned away your enemy.
The LORD, the king of Israel,
is in your midst;
you will no longer
fear evil.

SAILBOAT

Joy

Something to Shout About
Zephaniah 3:14-15
Sometimes, people get so excited that they jump up and down and shout. Maybe you've done this when you got a present you really wanted for Christmas or when your parents surprised you with a vacation to a really cool amusement park. God told God's people to get excited and express their joy. Their enemy had been defeated. There would be no judgment. And better yet, God was with them. Now that's something to shout about! ⬦

[16] On that day,
it will be said to Jerusalem:
Don't fear, Zion.
Don't let your hands fall.

---

[e]Heb uncertain [f]LXX; MT *it* [g]Or *with one shoulder*

¹⁷The Lᴏʀᴅ your God is in your midst—
a warrior bringing victory.
He will create calm
with his love;
he will rejoice over you
with singing.

¹⁸ I will remove from you those worried
about the appointed feasts.ʰ
They have been a burden for her,
a reproach.
¹⁹ Watch what I am about to do
to all your oppressors at that time.

ʰHeb uncertain ⁱOr *before your eyes*

I will deliver the lame;
I will gather the outcast.
I will change their shame
into praise and fame
throughout the earth.
²⁰ At that time,
I will bring all of you back,
at the time when I gather you.
I will give you fame and praise
among all the neighboring peoples
when I restore your possessions
and you can see themⁱ—
says the Lᴏʀᴅ.

Haggai

God's people came home. The people spent many years as prisoners in a distant country, but King Cyrus of Persia declared they could finally return to their homeland. He also gave them permission to rebuild God's temple that was destroyed when their nation was invaded (2 Chron 36:23).

The people were happy to be home, but they came back to a land that was destroyed. They found much work to do. They needed to build homes, plant crops, and make a living. The people were so busy with these tasks that they forgot about rebuilding the temple. The people had nowhere to gather for worship. They hadn't done their most important job.

This book says that the prophet Haggai began to preach during the reign of Persia's King Darius. Haggai pointed out that the people built themselves houses with beautiful wood walls. He asked if it was right for God's people to live in fine houses while God's house, the temple, remained in ruins.

With Haggai's help, the people soon got to work. Enemies tried to stop their rebuilding, but they finally got the job done (Ezra 6:15-18). This book shows us that it's never too late to serve God! ◊

The challenge to rebuild

1 The LORD's word came through Haggai the prophet in the second year of King Darius, in the sixth month on the first day of the month, to Judah's governor Zerubbabel, Shealtiel's son, and to the high priest Joshua, Jehozadak's son:

² This is what the LORD
　of heavenly forces says:
　These people say, "The time hasn't come,
　　the time to rebuild the LORD's house."
³ Then the LORD's word came through
　　Haggai the prophet:

> Memorize
> Hag 1:4

⁴ Is it time for you
　　　to dwell in
your own paneled houses
　while this house lies in ruins?
⁵ So now, this is what
　the LORD of heavenly forces says:
　Take your ways to heart.
⁶ You have sown much,
　but it has brought little.

You eat, but there's not enough to satisfy.
You drink, but not enough to get drunk.
There is clothing, but not enough
　to keep warm.
Anyone earning wages puts those
　wages into a bag with holes.

⁷ This is what the LORD
　of heavenly forces says:
　Take your ways to heart.
⁸ Go up to the highlands
　and bring back wood.
　Rebuild the temple
　so that I may enjoy it
　and that I may be honored,
　　says the LORD.
⁹ You expect a surplus,
　but look how it shrinks.
You bring it home, and I blow it away,
　says the LORD of heavenly forces,
　because my house lies in ruins.
But all of you hurry to your own houses.

God's Thoughts ◆ My Thoughts

Helping Others and Not Just Ourselves　Haggai 1:1-10

After hundreds of years in a strange and frustrating land, God's people were starting to return home to Israel. Their great-grandparents were taken against their will from their homes during a war and forced to live far away. A new king in the enemy land was letting them return to build new homes and rebuild the temple, where they could worship God again.

Haggai noticed that the returning families built houses and spent money on themselves, but they weren't building a place where they could worship God together. So God told Haggai to convince the people that praising God for rescuing them from their enemy was just as important as taking care of their own physical needs.

We appreciate this story about the need for the temple, and so we build a place to worship and thank God for God's mercy and loyal love. By setting aside part of our money to give to God, we're able to meet together and take care of people who need our help.

When you get an allowance or earn some money, do you spend it all on yourself? Why or why not?

Are you part of a worship community where you can meet with others to thank God and help others who have needs?

UMBRELLA
It's Not Yours

More, More, More! *Haggai 1:4-9*
When these verses talk about people eating but not being satisfied, they aren't referring to a lack of food. God was pointing out to the people that they were trying to fill the emptiness of their hearts with stuff, instead of with God's love. But the people seemed to want something more. They wanted things they couldn't or shouldn't have; they desired what other people had. Almost one thousand years earlier, God put together a list of ten important Instructions for God's people to follow. Not desiring what other people had was on the list (Exod 20:17). God still wants God's people to want more of God, not just more stuff. 🌢

---

¹⁰ Therefore, the skies above you
   have withheld the dew,
   and the earth has withheld
      its produce because of you.
¹¹ I have called for drought
   on the earth,
      on the mountains, on the grain,
      on the wine, on the olive oil,
      on that which comes forth
         from the fertile ground,
      on humanity, on beasts,
      and upon everything that
         handles produce.

¹²Zerubbabel, Shealtiel's son, and the high priest Joshua, Jehozadak's son, along with all who remained among the people, listened to the voice of the Lord God and to the words of Haggai the prophet because the Lord their God sent him. Then the people feared the Lord.

¹³Then Haggai, the Lord's messenger, gave the Lord's message to the people:
   I am with you, says the Lord.

¹⁴The Lord moved the spirit of Judah's governor Zerubbabel, Shealtiel's son, and the spirit of the high priest Joshua, Jehozadak's son, and the spirit of all the rest of the people. Then they came and did work on the house of the Lord of heavenly forces, their God, ¹⁵on the twenty-fourth day of the sixth month in the second year of Darius the king.

Encouraging the people

2¹On the twenty-first day of the seventh month, the Lord's word came through Haggai the prophet: ²Say to Judah's governor Zerubbabel, Shealtiel's son, and to the chief priest Joshua, Jehozadak's son, and to the rest of the people:

³ Who among you is left who saw
   this house in its former glory?
 How does it look to you now?
   Doesn't it appear as nothing to you?
⁴ So now, be strong, Zerubbabel,
   says the Lord.
 Be strong, High Priest Joshua,
   Jehozadak's son,
      and be strong, all you people
         of the land, says the Lord.
 Work, for I am with you,
   says the Lord of heavenly forces.
⁵ As with our agreement
   when you came out of Egypt,
      my spirit stands in your midst.
 Don't fear.
⁶ This is what the Lord
   of heavenly forces says:
 In just a little while,
   I will make the heavens, the earth,
      the sea, and the dry land quake.
⁷ I will make all the nations quake.
   The wealth of all the nations
      will come.
 I will fill this house with glory,
   says the Lord of heavenly forces.
⁸ The silver and the gold belong to me,
   says the Lord of heavenly forces.
⁹ This house will be more glorious
   than its predecessor,
   says the Lord of heavenly forces.
   I will provide prosperity in this place,
      says the Lord of heavenly forces.

Cleansing the work

¹⁰On the twenty-fourth day of the ninth month in the second year of Darius, the Lord's word came to Haggai the prophet:
¹¹ This is what the Lord
   of heavenly forces says:
 Go ahead and ask the priests
   for a ruling:
¹² "If someone lifts holy meat
   into the hem of one's garment

LIFE PRESERVER

What does "my spirit stands in your midst" mean?

Haggai 2:5

Haggai was a prophet who spoke to God's people. The people listened to his words and obeyed what he said. This didn't always happen to prophets. Haggai encouraged the people to be strong and remember God's presence with them. Notice how he reminded them of an event from many years before in their history: the exodus from Egypt when God gave them a covenant, which is a promise. When God told the people, "My spirit stands in your midst," God was saying, "I will always be with you, wherever you are." God promised to be present with God's people at all times. ♦

//

and that hem touches bread,
   stew, wine, oil, or any kind of food,
   will it be made holy?"
And the priests responded, "No."
¹³ Haggai said,
   "If an unclean person touches
   any of these things,
   will it become unclean?"
And the priests responded,
   "It will be unclean."
¹⁴ Then Haggai responded:
   Thus has this people and this nation
   become to me, says the LORD,
   and everything that they do
   with their hands.
   Whatever they offer is unclean.
¹⁵ So now, take it to heart
   from this day forward.
   Before stone was placed on stone
   in the LORD's temple,
¹⁶ when one came to the granary
   for twenty measures,
   there were only ten;

and when one came to the wine vat
   for fifty measures,
   there were only twenty.
¹⁷ I struck you—
   everything you do with your hands—
   with blight and mildew and hail;
   but you didn't return to me.ᵃ
¹⁸ So take it to heart from this day forward,
   from the twenty-fourth day
   of the ninth month.
   Take it to heart from the day when
   the foundation for the LORD's
   temple was laid.
¹⁹ Is the seed yet in the granary—
   or the vine, the fig tree,
   or the pomegranate—
   or has the olive tree not borne fruit?
   From this day forward, I will bless you.

Royal expectations

²⁰ And the LORD's word came to Haggai a second time on the twenty-fourth of the month, saying:
²¹ Speak to Judah's governor Zerubbabel:
   I am about to make the heavens
   and the earth quake.
²² I will overthrow the thrones
   of the kingdoms;
   I will destroy the strength
   of the nations.ᵇ
   I will overthrow chariot and rider;
   horses and riders will fall.
   Each one will fall
   by the sword of his companion.
²³ On that day,
   says the LORD of heavenly forces:
   I will take you, Zerubbabel, Shealtiel's son,
   my servant, says the LORD;
   I will make you like a signet ring
   because I have chosen you,
   says the LORD of heavenly forces.

ᵃOr *but you weren't with me.*   ᵇOr *of the kingdoms of the nations*

Zechariah

The prophet Zechariah was probably a priest, and this book calls him a "young man" (Zech 2:4). Like the prophet Haggai, Zechariah challenged God's people to rebuild the temple. Although Zechariah began preaching just two months after Haggai spoke his message from God, this book doesn't mention Haggai.

This book has two main parts. Zechariah 1–8 contains seven visions of a future temple. The words encouraged God's people to work hard at their task, to be different from their ancestors, and to stop doing evil. Building the temple would bring God close to the people. Zechariah 9–14 tells the people to rebuild the temple to prepare for the arrival of a new king, a savior God would send to help the people. This section speaks of a future "day of the Lord" when God will be king over the whole land.

New Testament writers looked to this book for details about this king. Zechariah 9:9 says a king would ride into Jerusalem "on a colt, the offspring of a donkey." Matthew refers to this verse when he writes about Jesus' victorious entry into Jerusalem on the day we call Palm Sunday (Matt 21:1-11).

The book of Zechariah says God's work can only be done with God's help (Zech 4:6). This teaching reminds us to count on God when life gets tough! ◊

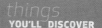

things
YOU'LL DISCOVER

The book of Zechariah was named for the prophet Zechariah, who encouraged God's people to rebuild the temple that had been destroyed when their land was invaded.

people
YOU'LL MEET

Zechariah—a temple official who spoke for God (Zech 1–14)
Darius—king of Persia (Zech 1; 7)
Daughter Zion—a loving name for Jerusalem (Zech 9)

places
YOU'LL GO

Judah (the southern kingdom),
Israel (the northern kingdom),
Ephraim (the central and important part of God's land),
Jerusalem

words
YOU'LL REMEMBER

"This is the LORD's word to Zerubbabel: Neither by power, nor by strength, but by my spirit, says the LORD of heavenly forces" (Zech 4:6).

The people change

1 In the eighth month in the second year of Darius, the Lord's word came to Zechariah the prophet, Berechiah's son and Iddo's grandson:

² The Lord was terribly angry
    with your ancestors.
³ But you must say to the people,
    The Lord of heavenly forces proclaims:
    Return to me,
    says the Lord of heavenly forces,
    and I will return to you,
        says the Lord of heavenly forces.
⁴ Don't be like your ancestors to whom
    the former prophets preached:
    The Lord of heavenly forces proclaims:
    Turn from your evil ways
    and your evil deeds.
    But they didn't listen;
        they didn't draw near to me.
⁵ So where are your ancestors?
    Do the prophets live forever?
⁶ In fact, didn't my words and laws,
    which I gave to my servants,
        the prophets,
        pursue your ancestors?
    And then the people changed their hearts,
    and they said,
    The Lord of heavenly forces
    has treated us according to
    what we have done,ᵃ
    exactly as he planned.

First night vision

⁷ On the twenty-fourth day of the eleventh month (the month of Shebatᵇ) in the second year of Darius, the Lord's word came to Zechariah the prophet, Berechiah's son and Iddo's grandson:

⁸ Tonight I looked and saw a man
    riding on a red horse,
        which was standing
    among the myrtle trees in the valley;
    and behind him were red, sorrel,
    and white horses.
⁹ I said, "What are these, sir?"
    The messenger speaking with me said,
    "I will show you what they are."
¹⁰ The man standing
    among the myrtles responded,

did you know? The name *Zechariah* means "the Lord remembers." Like other prophets, Zechariah encouraged the Israelite people to remember God by rebuilding the temple when they returned to Jerusalem.

"These are the ones the Lord sent
    to patrol the earth."
¹¹ Then they responded
    to the Lord's messenger,
    who was standing among the myrtles,
    "We have patrolled the earth.
    The whole earth is peaceful and quiet."
¹² Then the Lord's messenger,
    who was speaking with me, said:
    "Lord of heavenly forces,
    how long will you withhold
        compassion from Jerusalem
        and the cities of Judah,
        with whom you have been angry
        these seventy years?"
¹³ The Lord responded to the messenger
    who was speaking with me
    with kind and compassionate words.
¹⁴ The messenger speaking with me
    called out,
    "This is what
    the Lord of heavenly forces says:
    I care passionately
        about Jerusalem and Zion.
¹⁵ And I am exceedingly angry
    with those carefree nations.
    Though I was somewhat angry,
        they added to the violence."
¹⁶ Therefore, this is what the Lord says:
    I have returned to Jerusalem
    with compassion.
    My house will be built in it,
    says the Lord of heavenly forces.
    Let a measuring line
    be stretched over Jerusalem.
¹⁷ "Call out again,
    The Lord of heavenly forces proclaims:
    My cities will again
        overflow with prosperity.
    The Lord will again
        show compassion to Zion
        and will again choose Jerusalem."

ᵃOr *our ways and our actions* ᵇJanuary–February

Second night vision

18 cThen I looked up and saw four horns.

19 I said to the messenger speaking with me,

"What are these?"

He said to me,

"These are the horns that scattered
Judah, Israel, and Jerusalem."

20 Then the Lord showed me
four metalworkers.

21 I said,

"What are they coming to do?"

And he said,

"These are the horns that scattered
Judah so that no one could raise
his head.

The metalworkers have come to terrify
them and to destroy the horns of the
nations, those who were attacking
the land of Judah withd their horns
to scatter it."

Third night vision

2 eThen I looked up and saw a man.
In his hand was a measuring line.

2 I said, "Where are you going?"

He said to me,

"To measure Jerusalem to see how
wide and long it will be."

3 As I watched, the messenger speaking
with me went ahead and another
messenger came to meet him.

4 He said to him,

"Run! Say to this young man:

Jerusalem will be inhabited
like open fields
because of the throngs
of people and cattle inside it.

5 But I will be a wall of fire around it,
says the Lord,
and I will be glorious inside it.

6 Look out; look out!

Flee from the land of the north,
says the Lord,
for I will scatter you like the four
winds of heaven, says the Lord.

7 Look out, Zion.

Flee, you who dwell
with Daughter Babylon!

8 The Lord of heavenly forces proclaims
(after his glory sent me)f

concerning the nations plundering you:

Those who strike you
strike the pupil of my eye.

9 But look, I am about to raise my hand
against them;
they will become prey
to their own slaves,
so you will know that the Lord of
heavenly forces sent me.

10 Rejoice and be glad, Daughter Zion,
because I am about to come
and dwell among you,
says the Lord.

SAILBOAT

Joy

Rescued *Zechariah 2:10*

God had big plans. God gathered the people who
were scattered far from their homeland and
brought them together to rebuild the city of Jerusalem. But God's people had enemies who didn't
want this to happen. One name for God's special
people is *Daughter Zion* (Zech 2:10). A good father
would never stand by and let someone bully his
daughter. He would arrive and rescue them from
the threats of their enemies. God told God's people
to rejoice—the rescuer was on the way! ◗

11 Many nations will be joined
to the Lord on that day.

They will become my people,
and I will dwell among you
so you will know that
the Lord of heavenly forces
sent me to you."

12 The Lord will possess Judah as his
inheritance upon the holy land;
he will again choose Jerusalem.

13 Be silent, everyone, in the Lord's
presence, because he has moved
from his holy habitation!

Fourth night vision

3 Then the Lord showed me the high
priest Joshua, standing before the
messenger from the Lord,
and the Adversaryg was standing by
his right side to accuse him.

2 And the Lord said to the Adversary:

---

c2:1 in Heb dOr *those lifting their horns toward Judah* e2:5 in Heb fHeb uncertain gHeb *hassatan*; cf Job 1:6

"The LORD rebukes you, Adversary.
The LORD, the one choosing Jerusalem,
rebukes you.
Is this one not a log
snatched from the fire?"

³ Joshua was wearing filthy clothes
and standing before the messenger.
⁴ He responded
to those standing before him,
"Take off his filthy clothes."
And he said to Joshua,
"Look, I have removed your guilt
from you.
Put on priestly robes."

⁵ He^h said, "Put a clean turban
upon his head."
So they put the clean turban
upon his head,
and they dressed him in garments
while the LORD's messenger stood by.

⁶ Then the LORD's messenger
admonished Joshua:
⁷ "The LORD of heavenly forces proclaims:
If you will walk in my paths,
if you will keep my charge,
then you will lead my house
and guard my courts,
and I will allow you to walk among
those standing here.

⁸ Now listen, High Priest Joshua,
you and your companions
sitting before you—
for these men are a sign—
look, I am about to bring
my servant, Branch.
⁹ See this stone
that I have put before Joshua.
Upon one stone,
there are seven facets.
I am about to engrave
an inscription on it,
says the LORD of heavenly forces.
I will remove the guilt of that land
in one day.
¹⁰ On that day,
says the LORD of heavenly forces,
everyone will invite their neighbors
to sit beneath their vines
and the fig trees."

Fifth night vision

4 The messenger speaking with me returned and woke me like one who awakens someone who is asleep.
² Then he said to me, "What do you see?"
I said, "I see a lampstand
made entirely of gold.
It has a bowl on top.
The bowl has seven lamps on top
and seven metal pipes
for those lamps.
³ It has two olive trees beside the
lampstand,
one to the right of its bowl
and one to the left."
⁴ I responded to the messenger speaking
with me,
"What are these, sir?"
⁵ The messenger responded to me:
"Don't you know what these are?"
I said, "No, sir. I don't."
⁶ He answered me:
"This is the LORD's
word to Zerubbabel:
Neither by power, nor by strength,
but by my spirit,
says the LORD of heavenly forces."

Memorize Zech 4:6

⁷ Who are you, great mountain?
Before Zerubbabel
you will become a plain.
He will present the capstone
to shouts of great gratitude.

⁸ The LORD's word came to me:
⁹ The hands of Zerubbabel laid the
foundation of this house,
and his hands will finish it
so that you will know
that the LORD of heavenly forces
has sent me to you.
¹⁰ Those who despise a time
of little things will rejoice
when they see the plumb lineⁱ
in Zerubbabel's hand.
These are the seven eyes of the LORD,
surveying the entire earth.
¹¹ I responded to him,
"What are these two olive trees
on the right and left sides
of the lampstand?"

---

^hOr I ⁱOr stone, tin

¹² Then I responded a second time,
"What are these two olive branches
that empty out golden oil
through the two gold pipes?"
¹³ He said to me,
"Don't you know what these are?"
I said, "No, sir."
¹⁴ He said,
"These are the two anointed ones[j]
standing beside the Lord
of all the earth."

Sixth night vision

5 I looked up again and saw a flying scroll. ² And he said to me, "What do you see?"
I said, "I see a flying scroll, thirty feet long and fifteen feet wide."

³ He said to me,
"This is the curse
going out across all the land.
Anyone stealing will be purged
according to what's on one side
of the scroll,[k]

did you know?

In Bible times, one of the places people believed God lived was beyond the mountains. When the chariots came from an opening between two mountains in Zechariah's vision, the people understood this to mean that the chariots came from heaven where God lived.

and anyone swearing lies[l]
will be purged according to
what's on the other side.
⁴ I sent it out,
says the Lord of heavenly forces.
It will come to the house of the thief
and the one swearing lies in my name.
It will lodge in their house and
destroy the wood and stones
of that house."

Seventh night vision

⁵ Then the messenger speaking with me came forward and said,
"Look up and see what's approaching."
⁶ I said, "What's this?"
He said, "This is the basket[m]
that is going out.

This is how it appears[n]
throughout the entire land."[o]
⁷ Then a lead cover was lifted,
showing a woman sitting
in the middle of the basket.
⁸ He said, "This is wickedness."
He shoved her back into the basket,
and he put the lead stone
over its opening.
⁹ I looked up again and saw two women
going out.
There was a wind in their wings;
their wings were like
the wings of a stork.
They carried the basket
between the earth and the sky.
¹⁰ I said to the messenger speaking with me,
"Where are they taking the basket?"
¹¹ He said to me,
"To build a house for it
in the land of Shinar.
It will be firmly placed there
on its base."

Eighth night vision

6 I looked up again
and saw four chariots coming out
from between two mountains;
the mountains were made of bronze.
² The first chariot had red horses,
and the second chariot had black horses.
³ The third chariot had white horses,
and the fourth chariot
had horses that were heavily spotted.
⁴ I responded and said to the messenger
speaking with me,
"What are these, sir?"
⁵ The messenger answered and said to me,
"These are the four winds of heaven
that are going out
after presenting themselves
to the Lord of all the earth.
⁶ The one with the black horses
is going to the north country;
the white ones are going to the west;[p]
and the spotted ones are going south."
⁷ Then the powerful ones approached,
intent on going to patrol the earth.
He said, "Go! Patrol the earth!"
So they patrolled the earth.

---

[j]Or *sons of oil* [k]Heb lacks *of the scroll.* [l]Heb lacks *lies.* [m]Heb *ephah,* a basket measuring approximately twenty quarts [n]Or *their eye* [o]Heb uncertain [p]Or *after them*

8 Then he called out and said to me,
"Look, the ones going north
have provided rest for my spirit
in the north."

9 The Lord's word came to me:
10 Take silver and gold[q] from the exiles
who came from Babylon,
from Heldai, from Tobijah,
and from Jedaiah.
As for you, go that same day to the
house of Josiah son of Zephaniah.
11 Take silver and gold
and make a crown.[r]
Place it on the head of the
high priest Joshua,
Jehozadak's son.
12 Say to him,
"The Lord of heavenly forces proclaims:
Here is a man.
His name is Branch, and he will
branch out from his place;
he will build the Lord's temple.
13 He will build the Lord's temple.
He will be majestic;
he will sit and rule on his throne.
There will be a priest on his throne,
and the two of them
will share a peaceable plan.
14 The crown will be a memorial
in the Lord's temple
for Helem, Tobijah, Jedaiah,
and for Hen, Zephaniah's son.
15 People from far away will come
and build the Lord's temple
so you might know that
the Lord of heavenly forces
has sent me to you.
It will happen if you truly obey
the voice of the Lord your God."

[q]Heb lacks *silver and gold*; cf 6:11. [r]LXX; Heb *crowns*, so also 6:14

God's THOUGHTS My THOUGHTS

Paying Attention to God *Zechariah 7*

Zechariah had many visions with amazing images that came to him during the night. Zechariah saw visions of horsemen, horns and blacksmiths, a man with a measuring line, Joshua and the Adversary, a lampstand and olive trees, a flying scroll, a woman in a basket, and four chariots. What a variety of visions!

Each vision contributes to the story of Israel's exile in foreign countries, along with their hope to return to Jerusalem. The visions also speak of God's forgiveness and presence with the people. Zechariah reminded them of what God expected from them: "Make just and faithful decisions; show kindness and compassion to each other! Don't oppress the widow, the orphan, the stranger, and the poor; don't plan evil against each other!" (Zech 7:9-10). Sadly, this book tells us that the people refused to pay attention; they stopped listening to God and following God's ways.

Today, we face some of the same things as people in Zechariah's time: people who are hungry, children who need love and care from families, the challenge to be honest and fair in business and in the ways we live with each other. Perhaps we can remember to pay attention, to listen to God, and to follow God's ways.

When you dream, do you sometimes talk to people in your dream or imagine unusual things like flying scrolls?

Draw a picture of one of Zechariah's night visions in chapters 1–7.

Answering the Bethel delegation

7 In the fourth year of Darius the king, the Lord's word came to Zechariah on the fourth day of the ninth month, Kislev.[s] [2]The people of[t] Bethel sent Sharezer and Regem-Melech,[u] along with his men, to seek the Lord's favor, [3]saying to the priests who were in the house of the Lord of heavenly forces and to the prophets: "Should I weep in the fifth month and abstain as I have done for a number of years?"

did you know? In Bible times, children often played games together in the street. During wars, the streets were not safe, and children could not play there. When Zechariah spoke of children playing in the streets, he was promising that a time of peace was coming.

[4]Then the word of the Lord of heavenly forces came to me: [5]Say to all the land's people and to the priests: When you fasted and lamented in the fifth month and the seventh month for these past seventy years, did you fast for me? [6]When you ate and drank, weren't you the ones eating and drinking? [7]Weren't these the words that the Lord proclaimed through the former prophets when Jerusalem was dwelling quietly along with the surrounding cities, and when the arid southern plain and the western foothills were inhabited?

[8] The Lord's word came to Zechariah:

[9] The Lord of heavenly forces proclaims:

Make just and faithful decisions; show kindness and compassion to each other! [10]Don't oppress the widow, the orphan, the stranger, and the poor; don't plan evil against each other! [11]But they refused to pay attention. They turned a cold shoulder and stopped listening.

[12]They steeled their hearts against hearing the Instruction and the words that the Lord of heavenly forces sent by his spirit through the earlier prophets. As a result, the Lord of heavenly forces became enraged.

[13]So just as he called and they didn't listen, when they called, I didn't listen, says the Lord of heavenly forces. [14]I scattered them throughout the nations whom they didn't know. The land was devastated behind them, with no one leaving or returning. They turned a delightful land into a wasteland.

8 The word from the Lord of heavenly forces came to me:[v]

[2] The Lord of heavenly forces proclaims:

I care passionately about Zion; I burn with passion for her. [3]The Lord proclaims: I have returned to Zion; I will settle in Jerusalem. Jerusalem will be called the city of truth; the mountain of the Lord of heavenly forces will be the holy mountain.

[4] The Lord of heavenly forces proclaims:

Old men and old women will again dwell in the plazas of Jerusalem. Each of them will have a staff in their hand because of their great age. [5]The city will be full of boys and girls playing in its plazas.

[6] The Lord of heavenly forces proclaims:

Even though it may seem to be a miracle for the few remaining among this people in these days, should it seem to be a miracle for me? says the Lord of heavenly forces.

[7] The Lord of heavenly forces proclaims:

I'm about to deliver my people from the land of the east and the land of the west. [8]I'll bring them back so they will dwell in Jerusalem. They will be my people, and I will be their God—in truth and in righteousness.

[9] The Lord of heavenly forces proclaims:

Be strong, you who are now hearing these words from the mouths of the prophets spoken on the day when the foundations for the house of the Lord of heavenly forces were laid. [10]Before this time, there were no wages for people or animals; there was no relief from distress about going out or coming in, because I set everyone against their own neighbor. [11]But now, unlike those earlier days, I'll be with the few remaining among this people, says the Lord of heavenly forces.

[12] The seed is healthy:
   the vine will give its fruit.
The land will give its produce;
   the heavens will give its dew.
I will give the remnant of
   this people all these things.
[13] Just as you were a curse

among the nations,
house of Judah and house of Israel,
so now I will deliver you;
you will be a blessing.
Don't fear, but be strong.

14 The Lord of heavenly forces proclaims:

Just as I planned evil against you when your ancestors angered me, says the Lord of heavenly forces, and did not relent, 15so now I have changed course and again plan to do good to Jerusalem and the house of Judah. Don't be afraid.

16These are the things you should do: Speak the truth to each other; make truthful, just, and peaceable decisions within your gates. 17Don't plan evil for each other. Don't adore swearing falsely, for all of these are things that I hate, says the Lord.

18 The word of the Lord of heavenly forces came to me:

19 The Lord of heavenly forces proclaims:

The fasts of the fourth, fifth, seventh, and tenth months will become times of joy and gladness, pleasant feasts for the house of Judah. Love truth and peace!

LIFE PRESERVER

Can God change God's mind?
Zechariah 8:14-19

As God's people prepared to rededicate the second temple, God's words through the prophet Zechariah reminded them of the consequences of not listening to God's commands. But the prophet also reminded the people about God's promises. God had promised that the Israelites would be God's people and God would be their God.

It may seem then that God's mind was changed when God said that God had "changed course" and planned to "do good to Jerusalem and the house of Judah" (Zech 8:15). We may wonder why God didn't punish the people, as they had been warned. One way to look at this change is to remember that God's love is very big and God's heart is very forgiving. God reminded the people how they should live with each other, loving truth and peace.

Isn't it amazing that in spite of all the bad choices they made and all the evil things they did, God always forgave and loved them? Wouldn't it be nice if we could love and forgive like this—and if we too could love truth and peace? ◖

20 The Lord of heavenly forces proclaims:

Peoples will still come, the inhabitants of many cities. 21The inhabitants of one city will go to another saying, "Let's go and seek the favor of the Lord, and look for the Lord of heavenly forces. I'm going too." 22Many peoples and mighty nations will come to seek the Lord of heavenly forces in Jerusalem and to seek the favor of the Lord.

23 The Lord of heavenly forces proclaims:

In those days ten men from nations with entirely different languages will grab hold of a Judean's clothes and say, "Let's go with you, for we have heard that God is with you."

Fate of the nations

9 A pronouncement. The Lord's word is
against the land of Hadrach,
and Damascus is its resting place,
for the city of Aram^W and all the tribes
of Israel belong to the Lord.
2 Hamath also borders on it.
Tyre and Sidon, indeed,
each is exceedingly wise.
3 Tyre built a fortress for herself.
She piled up silver like dust
and gold like mud in the streets,
4 but the Lord will take
her possessions away
and knock her wealth into the sea.
She will be devoured with fire.

5 Ashkelon will look and be afraid.
Gaza will writhe in agony,
and also Ekron,
because her hope has dried up.
The king will perish from Gaza;
Ashkelon won't be inhabited.
6 An illegitimate child will dwell in Ashdod;
I will eliminate
the pride of the Philistines.
7 I will remove bloody food from his mouth
and pieces of unclean food
from between his teeth.
He will be a survivor
who belongs to our God.
He will be like a chieftain in Judah;
Ekron will be like a Jebusite.
8 I will encamp before my house as a guard
against anyone departing or returning.

A slave driver will no longer
pass through against them,
for I have seen you[x] with my eyes.

Joy and protection for Judah and Ephraim

9 Rejoice greatly, Daughter Zion.
Sing aloud, Daughter Jerusalem.
Look, your king will come to you.
He is righteous and victorious.
He is humble and riding on an ass,
on a colt, the offspring
of a donkey.

SAILBOAT

Joy

The King Is Coming *Zechariah 9:9*

In Bible times, the people could tell a lot about a king's plans by how he came into their city. Zechariah told them their king would come riding on a colt whose mother is a donkey. This display was meant to show that the king was coming to bring peace. About five hundred years later, Jesus rode into Jerusalem exactly in this manner. You can read this story in Matt 21:1-9 or John 12:12-16. ◆

10 He[y] will cut off the chariot from Ephraim
and the warhorse from Jerusalem.
The bow used in battle will be cut off;
he will speak peace to the nations.
His rule will stretch from sea to sea,
and from the river
to the ends of the earth.
11 Moreover,[z] by the blood of your covenant,
I will release your prisoners
from the waterless pit.
12 Return to the stronghold,
prisoners of hope.
Moreover, declare today
that I will return double to you.
13 Indeed, I myself will bend Judah as a bow;
I will fill it with Ephraim.
Zion, I will rouse your sons
against your sons.
Greece, I will make you
like a warrior's sword.
14 The Lord will appear above them;
his arrow will go forth like lightning.
The Lord God will blow the horn;

he will march forth on the stormy
winds of the south.
15 The Lord of heavenly forces
will protect them.
They will devour and subdue
like sling stones.[a]
They will drink,
mumbling like one having wine.
They will be filled like a bowl,
like the corners of the altar.
16 The Lord their God will deliver them
on that day as the flock of his people;
they will be the jewels
in a crown dotting his land.
17 What is his goodness,
and what is his beauty?
Grain will make his young men flourish;
so too wine his young women.

Fate of Judah and Ephraim

10 Ask the Lord for rain when it is time
for the spring rain.
The Lord is the one
who makes the thunderstorms.
He gives them rain showers.
He gives vegetation in the field
to each of them.[b]
2 The household divine images
speak idolatry, and diviners see lies.
They interpret dreams falsely
and provide empty comfort.
Therefore, they wander like sheep,
but they are oppressed
because there is no shepherd.
3 My anger burns hot
against the shepherds;
I will punish the goats.
The Lord of heavenly forces
will take care of his splendor,
the house of Judah.
He will make them
like his majestic horse in battle.
4 The cornerstone, the tent peg,
and the bow used in battle
will come from Judah.
Every oppressor
will leave Judah simultaneously.
5 Judah will be like warriors,
trampling through the muddy streets
during battle.

[x]Heb lacks *you*. [y]LXX; MT *I* [z]Heb uncertain [a]Heb uncertain [b]Heb lacks *of them*.

They will do battle
because the Lᴏʀᴅ is with them.
All the cavalry will be ashamed.
⁶ I will strengthen the house of Judah
and deliver the house of Joseph.
I will bring them back^c because I have
compassion on them.
They will be as though
I hadn't rejected them,
for I am the Lᴏʀᴅ their God;
I will respond to them.

⁷ Ephraim will be like a warrior.
They will be as glad
as if they were drinking wine.
Their children will watch and be glad.
Their hearts will rejoice in the Lᴏʀᴅ.
⁸ I will whistle for them and gather them,
because I have ransomed them.
They will be as numerous
as they were previously.
⁹ Though I sowed them among the peoples,
they will remember me
in the distant places
where they are living with
their children until they return.
¹⁰ I will bring them back
from the land of Egypt;
I will collect them from Assyria.
I will bring them to the land
of Gilead and Lebanon
until there is no more room for them.
¹¹ They^d will pass through the sea of distress
and strike the sea with waves.^e
All the depths of the river will dry up.
The pride of Assyria
will be brought down;
the scepter of Egypt will turn away.
¹² I will strengthen them in the Lᴏʀᴅ,
and they will walk in his name,
says the Lᴏʀᴅ.

11 Open your doors, Lebanon,
so that fire will devour your cedars.
² Scream, cypress, for the cedar has fallen;
those majestic ones
have been devastated.
Scream, oaks of Bashan,
for the deep forest has fallen.
³ The sound of screaming
appears among the shepherds

because their majesty
has been devastated.
The sound of roaring can be heard
among the young lions
because the pride of the Jordan
has been devastated.

The shepherd's two staffs

⁴ This is what the Lᴏʀᴅ my God says:
Shepherd the flock
intended for slaughter.
⁵ Those who buy them will kill them,
but they will go unpunished.
Those who sell them will say,
"Blessed is the Lᴏʀᴅ,
for I have become rich."
And their own shepherds
won't spare them.
⁶ In fact, I will no longer spare
the inhabitants of the land,
says the Lᴏʀᴅ.
But look what I am about to bring
upon humanity,
upon each of them by their neighbor's
hand and by the hand of their king:
They will beat the land to pieces,
but I won't rescue anyone
from their hand.
⁷ So I shepherded the flock
intended for slaughter,
the afflicted of the flock.^f
I took two staffs for myself.
I named one Delight;
the other I named Harmony.
I shepherded the flock.
⁸ I removed three shepherds in one month
when I grew impatient with them.
Moreover, they detested me.
⁹ Then I said, "I won't shepherd you.
Let the dying die,
and let what is to be removed
be removed.
Let those who are left
devour the flesh of their neighbor."

¹⁰ Then I took the staff Delight,
and I chopped it up
in order to break my covenant
that I had made with all the peoples.
¹¹ It was broken on that day.

---

^cOr *I will restore them* ^dLXX; MT *he* ^eHeb uncertain ^fHeb uncertain

As a result, the afflicted[g] of the flock
knew that it was the LORD's word.
[12] And I said to them,
"If it appears good to you,
give me my wages;
but if not, then stop."
So they weighed out my wages,
thirty shekels of silver.
[13] The LORD said to me,
"Put it in the treasury.[h]
They value me
at too magnificent a price."
So I took the thirty shekels[i] of silver
and put them in the treasury
of the LORD's house.

[14] Then I chopped up
my second staff Harmony,
to break the alliance
between Judah and Israel.
[15] Then the LORD said to me,
"Take for yourself again the equipment
of a foolish shepherd,
[16] because I am about to appoint
a shepherd in the land.
He won't tend to those
who have been removed.
He won't seek the young
or heal the broken.
He won't sustain the one standing.
Instead, he will devour the flesh
of the fat ones,
even tearing off their hooves.
[17] Doom, foolish shepherd
who forsakes the flock.
A sword will strike[j] his arm
and his right eye.
His arm will wither completely;
his right eye will become blind."

Jerusalem on that day

12 A pronouncement.
The LORD's word against Israel,
an utterance of the LORD
who stretches out the heavens,
who establishes the earth,
and who fashions the spirit
of humanity within it:
[2] I am about to make Jerusalem a cup
that will stagger
all the surrounding nations.

There will be a siege against Judah
and against Jerusalem.
[3] On that day I will make Jerusalem
into a heavy stone[k] for all the peoples.
All who carry it will hurt themselves;
nevertheless, the nations of the earth
will conspire against it.

[4] On that day, says the LORD, I will strike
every horse with confusion
and its rider with madness.
I will keep my eyes open
for the house of Judah;
I will strike blind
every horse of the peoples.
[5] The chieftains of Judah will say to
themselves, We are strong;
the inhabitants of Jerusalem will say,
The LORD their God of heavenly
forces is strong.[l]

[6] On that day I will place
the chieftains of Judah like a pot
on a wood fire and like a burning torch
among the bundles of grain.
They will devour all the surrounding
nations to the right and the left.
Jerusalem will dwell again in its place,
in Jerusalem.
[7] The LORD will first deliver
the tents of Judah
so that the splendor of David's house
and the splendor
of Jerusalem's inhabitants
won't overshadow Judah.

[8] On that day the LORD will protect
the inhabitants of Jerusalem.
Anyone among them who stumbles
on that day will become like David,
and David's house will become like God,
like the LORD's messenger
in front of them.

[9] On that day I intend to destroy all the
nations who come against Jerusalem,
[10] but I will pour out a spirit of grace
and mercy on David's house
and on the inhabitants of Jerusalem.

---

[g]Cf Zech 11:7 [h]Syr; MT *to the potter* [i]Heb lacks *shekels*. [j]Heb lacks *will strike*. [k]Heb uncertain [l]Heb uncertain

They will look to me concerning
  the one whom they pierced;
  they will mourn over him
    like the mourning for an only child.
  They will mourn bitterly over him
    like the bitter mourning
    over the death of[m] an oldest child.

11 On that day, the mourning in Jerusalem
  will be as great
    as the mourning of Hadad-Rimmon
    in the Megiddo Valley.
12 The land will mourn,
  each of the clans by itself:
    the clan of David's house by themselves,
    and their women by themselves;
      the clan of Nathan's house
      by themselves,
      and their women by themselves;

UMBRELLA
Mourning

Sad Together *Zechariah 12:12-14*
All people are sad sometimes. Some people cry
when they are sad. Others talk about why they
are sad. Still others just sit silently. In Bible times,
men and women showed their sadness in different ways. The women often cried loudly, while the
men sat quietly, hardly speaking at all. Both were
sad, and God knew how they felt. So the women
got together to cry with each other, and the men
mourned separately. ◊

13 the clan of Levi's house by themselves,
  and their women by themselves;
  and the Shimeites' clan by themselves,
  and their women by themselves;
14 and all the remaining clans,
  each clan by itself,
  and their women by themselves.

13 On that day, a fountain will open
  to cleanse[n] the sin and impurity
  of David's house
  and the inhabitants of Jerusalem.

2 On that day,
  says the Lord of heavenly forces,
  I will eliminate the names of the idols
  from the land;
  they will no longer be remembered.
  Moreover, I will remove the prophets
  and the sinful spirit from the land.
3 If anyone again prophesies,
  then that person's
  birth father and mother will say,
  "You won't live, for you have told a lie
  in the name of the Lord."
  That person's own birth father and
  mother will stab him
  when he prophesies.

4 On that day each of the prophets
  will be ashamed of his vision
  when he prophesies
  and won't put on a shaggy coat
  in order to deceive.
5 Each will say, "I'm not a prophet.
  I'm a man who works the ground,
  for the soil has been my occupation
  since I was young."
6 Someone will say to him,
  "What are these wounds
  between your hands?"
  And he will say, "These happened
  when I was hit in my friends' home."

7 Sword, arise against my shepherd,
  against the man responsible for[o]
  my community,
  says the Lord of heavenly forces!
  Strike the shepherd
  in order to scatter the flock!
  I will turn my hand
  against the little ones.
8 Throughout all the land, says the Lord,
  two-thirds will be cut off and die;
  but one-third will be left in it.
9 I will put the third part into the fire.
  I will refine them like one refines silver;
  I will test them like one tests gold.
  They will call on my name,
  and I will respond to them.
  I will say, "They are my people."
  And they will say,
  "The Lord is our God."

---

[m]Heb lacks *the death of.* [n]Heb lacks *to cleanse.* [o]Heb lacks *responsible for.*

The day of the Lord

14 A day is coming
that belongs to the Lord,
when that which has been plundered
from you will be divided among you.
2 I will gather all the nations to Jerusalem
for the battle,
the city will be captured,
the houses will be plundered,
and the women will be raped.
Half of the city will go forth into exile,
but what is left of the people
won't be eliminated from the city.
3 The Lord will go out and fight
against those nations
as when he fights on a day of battle.
4 On that day he will stand upon
the Mount of Olives,
to the east of Jerusalem.
The Mount of Olives will be split
in half by a very large valley
running from east to west.
Half of the mountain will move north,
and the other half will move south.
5 You will flee
through the valley of my mountain,
because the valley of the mountains
will reach to Azal.
You will flee just as you fled
from the earthquake in the days
of Judah's King Uzziah.
The Lord my God will come,
and all the holy ones with him.[p]
6 On that day, there will be no light.
Splendid things will disappear.[q]
7 On one day known to the Lord,
there will be neither day nor night,
but at evening time there will be light.
8 On that day, running water will flow
out from Jerusalem,
half of it to the Dead Sea[r]
and half of it to the Mediterranean;[s]
this will happen
during the summer and the fall.
9 The Lord will become king
over all the land.
On that day the Lord will be one,
and the Lord's name will be one.
10 The entire land will become
like the desert[t]
from Geba to Rimmon,
south of Jerusalem.
Jerusalem will be high up
and firmly in place
from the Benjamin Gate
to the place of the former gate,
to the Corner Gate,
and from the Hananel Tower
to the king's wine vats.
11 People will dwell in it;
it will never again be destroyed.
Jerusalem will dwell securely.
12 This will be the plague
with which the Lord
will strike all the peoples
who swarmed against Jerusalem:
their flesh will rot,
even while standing on their feet;
their eyes will rot in their sockets;
and their tongues will rot
in their mouths.
13 On that day, a great panic brought on
by the Lord will fall upon them;
they will all grasp at the hand
of their neighbors;
neighbors will attack each other.
14 Even Judah will fight in Jerusalem.
The wealth of all the surrounding
nations will be collected:
gold, silver, and a great abundance
of garments.
15 This[u] plague will also affect the horses,
mules, camels, donkeys, and any cattle
in those camps during this plague.

16 All those left from all the nations who
attacked Jerusalem will go up annually to
pay homage to the king, the Lord of heavenly forces, and to celebrate the Festival
of Booths.

17 Whoever among the families of the earth
doesn't go up to Jerusalem to pay homage to
the king, the Lord of heavenly forces, upon
them no rain will fall.

18 And if the family of Egypt doesn't go up
and doesn't present itself, then no rain[v] will
fall on them. There will[w] be a plague like the

[p] Or *you* [q] Heb uncertain [r] Or *eastern sea* [s] Or *western sea* [t] Heb *Arabah* [u] Heb lacks *this*; cf 14:12. [v] Heb lacks *rain*.
[w] Or *will not*.

one with which the Lord struck the nations that didn't go up to celebrate the Festival of Booths.

¹⁹This would be the sin of Egypt and the sin of all the nations who don't go up to celebrate the Festival of Booths.

²⁰ On that day, *Holy to the Lord*
  will be inscribed[x] on the bells
    of the horses,
      and the pots in the Lord's house
  will be holy[y] like the bowls
    before the altar.

²¹ Every pot in Jerusalem and in Judah
  will be holy to the Lord
    of heavenly forces.

  All those who sacrifice will come.
  They will take some of the pots
    and cook with them.

  There will no longer
    be any merchants[z] in the house
      of the Lord of heavenly forces
        on that day.

---

[x]Heb lacks *inscribed.* [y]Heb lacks *holy.* [z]Heb *Canaanite*

LIFE PRESERVER

What's the meaning of the "bells" and the "pots"?
Zechariah 14:16-21

At the end of Zechariah, which is the next to the last book in the Hebrew Bible, is an interesting vision of what would happen to God's people. The text says that all people, including Jews and Gentiles, would celebrate the Festival of Booths, one of the main festivals for pilgrims. It's surprising that Gentiles were included in this Jewish festival.

Zechariah went on to say that God would make sure the land would be holy for all people. It would be marked on the bells worn by the horses and all the pots used for everyday cooking as well as for sacrifice in the temple. Everything used in daily life would be as holy as the things that were used in the temple on the Sabbath. Everything and everyone would be seen by God to be holy.

In God's plan and vision for the world, everyone is welcome and included. What an incredible vision, then and today! ◈

Malachi

After many years as prisoners in a distant country, God's people returned to their land. They constructed homes, planted crops, and began to earn a living. They even rebuilt the temple destroyed by the army that conquered their nation. Now they looked around and felt disappointed. Why wasn't life as good as they hoped?

The first words of this book point to the problem. God said to God's people, "I have loved you." But the people didn't believe God. They asked, "How have you loved us?" (Mal 1:2).

The prophet Malachi explained what was wrong. The people didn't love God and didn't love each other. The nation's priests ignored God's rules for worship. People made no effort to obey God's commands. They turned away from God and worshipped other gods. It was no surprise that they felt far away from God.

God promised to send a messenger to prepare the people for God's arrival (Mal 3:1; 4:5). Not everyone would like the messenger. He would purify the people to remove their sin, like metal is heated in a fire to remove its impurities. This would be painful. But the messenger would bring people closer to God.

Malachi told God's people not to give up hope. They should expect God to act. This book tells us to look forward to God's arrival! ◊

things YOU'LL DISCOVER

Malachi is the last book of the Old Testament. Named for the prophet Malachi, it describes the time about a hundred years after the temple was rebuilt in Jerusalem. Even though people had a place to worship together, they still felt far away from God.

people YOU'LL MEET

Malachi—a prophet who spoke for God (Mal 1–4)
Jacob—an early follower of God (Mal 1) and a name for God's people (Mal 3)

places YOU'LL GO

Judah (the southern kingdom), **Jerusalem**

words YOU'LL REMEMBER

"But the sun of righteousness will rise on those revering my name; healing will be in its wings so that you will go forth and jump about like calves in the stall" (Mal 4:2).

1 A pronouncement. The Lord's word to Israel through Malachi.[a]

Love of Jacob

2 I have loved you, says the Lord;
  but you say, "How have you loved us?"
Wasn't Esau Jacob's brother?
            says the Lord.
  I loved Jacob, 3 but I rejected Esau.
I turned Esau's mountains into desolation,
  his inheritance into a wilderness
    for jackals.
4 Edom may say, "We are beaten down,
  but we will rebuild the ruins";
but the Lord of heavenly forces
  proclaims:
They may build,
  but I will tear them down.
They will call themselves
  a wicked territory,
    the people against whom
    the Lord rages forever.
5 Your eyes will see it and you will say,
  "May the Lord be great
  beyond the borders of Israel."

Honoring the Lord

6 A son honors a father,
  and a servant honors his master.
But if I'm a father,
  where is my honor?
Or if I'm a master,
  where is my respect?
            says the Lord of heavenly forces
  to you priests who despise my name.
So you say,
  "How have we despised your name?"
7 By approaching my altar
  with polluted food.
But you say, "How have we polluted it[b]?"
  When you say,
    "The table of the Lord can be despised."
8 If you bring a blind animal to sacrifice,
  isn't that evil?
If you bring a lame or sick one,
  isn't that evil?
Would you bring it to your governor?
Would he be pleased with it
  or accept you?
            says the Lord of heavenly forces.

9 So now ask God
  to be gracious to us.
After what you have done,
  will he accept you?
            says the Lord of heavenly forces.
10 Who among you will shut
  the doors of the temple[c]
    so that you don't burn something
    on my altar in vain?
  I take no delight in you,
            says the Lord of heavenly forces.
I won't accept a grain offering
  from your hand.

11 Nevertheless, from sunrise to sunset,
  my name will be great
    among the nations.
Incense and a pure grain offering will be
  offered everywhere in my name,
    because my name is great
      among the nations,
            says the Lord of heavenly forces.
12 But you make my name impure
  when you say,
    "The table of the Lord is polluted.
    Its fruit, its food, is despised."
13 But you say,
    "How tedious!"
  and you groan about it,
            says the Lord of heavenly forces.
You permit what is stolen, lame,
  or sick to be brought for a sacrifice,[d]
  and you bring the grain offering.
Should I accept such from your hands?
            says the Lord.
14 I will curse the cheater
  who has a healthy[e] male in his flock,
  but who promises and sacrifices
    to the Lord that which is corrupt.
  I am truly a great king,
            says the Lord of heavenly forces,
  and my name is feared
    among the nations.

2 But now, this command is for you,
  priests:
2 If you don't listen,
  or don't intend to glorify my name,
            says the Lord of heavenly forces,
  then I will send a curse among you.

---

[a]Or *my messenger* [b]Gk; Heb *you* [c]Heb lacks *of the temple.* [d]Heb lacks *for a sacrifice.* [e]Heb lacks *healthy*

I will curse your blessings,
and I mean really curse them,
because none of you
intend to do it.

SAILBOAT

HONEST AND TRUE

No Cheating *Malachi 2:2*
Having integrity means living out your beliefs all
the time—even if no one is watching. The people
in the time of Malachi were pretending to honor
God. They were sacrificing less-healthy animals
and keeping the best ones for themselves. Those
people forgot something very important. God is
always watching. God knows when our actions
truly honor God. God also knows when we are just
trying to get by. God is not honored by those kinds
of choices. ◆

3 I am about to denounce your offspring;
   I will scatter feces on your faces,
   the feces of your festivals.
Then I will lift you up to me,[f]
4 and you will know that I have sent
   this command to you
   so that my covenant with Levi
   can continue to exist,
      says the Lord of heavenly forces.
5 My covenant with him involved
   life and peace, which I gave him,
   and also fear so that he honored me.
   He was in awe of my name.
6 True Instruction was in his mouth;
   injustice wasn't found on his lips.
He walked with me in peace
   and did the right thing;
   he made many turn from iniquity.
7 The lips of the priest
   should guard knowledge;
   everyone[g] should seek Instruction
      from his mouth,
   for he is the messenger from
      the Lord of heavenly forces.
8 But you have turned from the path.
   You have caused many to stumble
      by your instruction.
   You have corrupted
      the covenant of Levi,
         says the Lord of heavenly forces.

9 Moreover, I have made you despised
   and humiliated in the view
      of all the people,
   since none of you keep my ways
      or show respect for Instruction.

Judah's dishonesty
10 Isn't there one father for all of us,
   one God who created us?
Why does everyone cheat each other
   to make the covenant
      of our ancestors impure?
11 Judah cheated—
   a detestable thing was done
      in Israel and Jerusalem.
   Judah made the Lord's
      holy place impure, which God loved,
   and married the daughter
      of a foreign god.
12 May the Lord eliminate anyone
   who does so from the tents of Jacob,
   anyone awaking, testifying,[h]
   and making an offering
      to the Lord of heavenly forces.
13 You should do this as well:
   cover the altar of the Lord
      with tears, weeping, and groaning
   because there is still no divine favor
      for your offering
   or favorable regard
      for anything from your hand.
14 But you say, "Why?"
   Because the Lord testifies about you
   and the wife of your youth
      against whom you cheated.
   She is your partner,
      the wife of your covenant.
15 Didn't he make her[i] the one[j] and the
   remnant of his spirit?[k]
What is the one?
   The one seeking godly offspring.
You should guard your own spirit.
   Don't cheat on the wife of your youth
      16because he hates divorce,
         says the Lord God of Israel,
   and he also hates the one covering
      his garment with violence,[l]
         says the Lord of heavenly forces.
   Guard your own life, and don't cheat.

[f]Heb uncertain; MT *He will carry you to it.* [g]Or *they* [h]Heb uncertain [i]Heb lacks *her.* [j]Heb uncertain; *her* refers to the *wife* in Mal 2:14. [k]Heb uncertain [l]Heb uncertain

Purifying judgment

¹⁷ You have made the Lᴏʀᴅ tired
  with your words.
You say, "How have we made him tired?"
When you say:
    "Anyone doing evil is good in the
      Lᴏʀᴅ's eyes,"
    or "He delights in those doing evil,"ᵐ
    or "Where is the God of justice?"

3 Look, I am sending my messenger
  who will clear the path before me;
  suddenly the Lᴏʀᴅ whom you are
    seeking will come to his temple.
The messenger of the covenant
  in whom you take delight is coming,
    says the Lᴏʀᴅ of heavenly forces.

did you know?

In Bible times, people believed there was a dome above the sky that kept the waters of heaven from flooding the earth. They believed rain fell whenever God opened the windows in the ceiling of the dome and let in some of the water.

² Who can endure the day of his coming?
  Who can withstand his appearance?
He is like the refiner's fire
  or the cleaner's soap.
³ He will sit as a refiner
  and a purifier of silver.
  He will purify the Levites
    and refine them like gold and silver.
  They will belong to the Lᴏʀᴅ,
    presenting a righteous offering.
⁴ The offering of Judah and Jerusalem
  will be pleasing to the Lᴏʀᴅ
    as in ancient days and in former years.
⁵ I will draw near to you for judgment.
I will be quick to testify
  against the sorcerers,
  the adulterers, those swearing falsely,
  against those who cheat
    the day laborers out of their wages
  as well as oppress the widow
    and the orphan,
  and against those who brush aside
    the foreigner and do not revere me,
      says the Lᴏʀᴅ of heavenly forces.
⁶ I am the Lᴏʀᴅ, and I do not change;
  and you, children of Jacob,
    have not perished.

Return to the Lᴏʀᴅ

⁷ Ever since the time of your ancestors,
  you have deviated from my laws
    and have not kept them.
Return to me and I will return to you,
    says the Lᴏʀᴅ of heavenly forces.
But you say,
  "How should we return?"
⁸ Should a person deceive God?
  Yet you deceive me.
But you say,
  "How have we deceived you?"
With your tenth-part gifts and offerings.
⁹ You are being cursed with a curse,
  and you, the entire nation,
    are robbing me.
¹⁰ Bring the whole tenth-part
  to the storage house so there
    might be food in my house.
  Please test me in this,
      says the Lᴏʀᴅ of heavenly forces.
See whether I do not open all the
  windows of the heavens for you
  and empty out a blessing
    until there is enough.ⁿ
¹¹ I will threaten the one
  who wants to devour you
  so that it doesn't spoil the fruit
    of your fertile land,
  and so that the vine doesn't abort
    its fruit in your field,
      says the Lᴏʀᴅ of heavenly forces.
¹² All the nations will
  consider you fortunate,

LIGHTHOUSE

GIVING A TENTH

Learning to Give *Malachi 3*
God told the prophet Malachi to tell the people they were robbing God by not giving in the way God had told them to. Everything we have is God's. To help us not get too focused on money and the things we own, God asks us to give one-tenth, or ten percent, back to God. Some people call this a *tithe*, and it's given to the church we attend. Tithes and offerings (additional money given above the tenth-part gift) allow churches to support their ministries and help people in need. ◗

ᵐOr them ⁿOr Until what is required is lacking.

for you will be a desirable land,
　　says the Lord of heavenly forces.

¹³ You have spoken harshly about me,
　　　　says the Lord;
but you say,
　　"What have we spoken about you?"
¹⁴ You said,
　　"Serving God is useless.
　　What do we gain
　　by keeping his obligation
　　or by walking around as mourners
　　before the Lord of heavenly forces?
¹⁵ So now we consider the arrogant
　　fortunate.
　　Moreover, those doing evil are built up;
　　they test God and escape."

The scroll of remembrance
¹⁶ Then those revering the Lord,
　　each and every one,
　　spoke among themselves.

^o3:19 in Heb

The Lord paid attention
　　and listened to them.
Then a scroll of remembrance
　　was written before the Lord
　　about those revering the Lord,
　　the ones meditating on his name.
¹⁷ On the day that I am preparing,
　　　　says the Lord of heavenly forces,
　　they will be my special possession.
　　I will spare them just as parents
　　spare a child who serves them.
¹⁸ You will again distinguish
　　between the righteous and the wicked,
　　between those serving God
　　and those not serving him.

The day of the Lord
4 ^oLook, the day is coming,
　　burning like an oven.
All the arrogant ones and
　　all those doing evil
　　will become straw.

Do the Right Thing   *Malachi 4:1-6*

Not everyone grows up in a loving family. Some children are abused and harmed by their parents or other caregivers who are supposed to look out for them. This terrible and frightening behavior can get worse and spread because some parents were treated badly when they were children.

But it isn't always the parent who behaves poorly toward a child. Sometimes, children become selfish and abuse their parents. With so many persons in families not caring for each other, it's time to ask God for help.

God wants wicked and selfish behavior to stop. God wants people to do the right thing and will do whatever is necessary to get people to show love toward each other. The prophet Malachi said there would be terrible consequences if people failed to do the right thing and family members continued to treat each other badly.

Imagine God as a loving parent. How would a loving parent treat a child?

When you are selfish or don't remember to do the right thing, what is God's response to your behavior?

The coming day will burn them,
  says the Lord of heavenly forces,
 leaving them neither
  root nor branch.
   ² But the sun of righteousness will rise
    on those revering my name;

       healing will be
       in its wings
 so that you will go forth and jump
  about like calves in the stall.
³ You will crush the wicked;
 they will be like dust
  beneath the soles of your feet
  on the day that I am preparing,
   says the Lord of heavenly forces.
⁴ Remember the Instruction from Moses,
 my servant,
  to whom I gave Instruction
  and rules for all Israel at Horeb.
⁵ Look, I am sending
 Elijah the prophet to you,
  before the great and terrifying
  day of the Lord arrives.
⁶ Turn the hearts of the parents
 to the children
 and the hearts of the children
  to their parents.
   Otherwise, I will come and
   strike the land with a curse.

Memorize Mal 4:2

LIFE PRESERVER

How does the Old Testament end? *Malachi 4*

The last chapter in the last book in the Hebrew Bible, or Old Testament, looks both forward and backward. The writing looks forward to a time in the future when the battle between evil and good will be over and good will have won.

It also looks backward and recalls two of the most important people in the Old Testament. The first is Moses, who led God's people out of slavery and into freedom. And the second is the prophet Elijah.

The chapter, book, and Old Testament ends with a warning. God wanted God's people to turn their hearts to God. This was God's plea and God's hope. And it is still God's greatest hope this day. God wants our hearts to be turned to God's love, justice, mercy, and kindness. 💧

did you know? The last words of the Hebrew scriptures are a promise that before God comes to earth, Elijah will come to prepare the way. Each year at Passover, the people place a cup on the table for Elijah in case he comes to tell the people God is coming. Some people still follow this practice today during Passover.

NEW TESTAMENT

Matthew

The first four books of the New Testament—Matthew, Mark, Luke, and John—each tell exciting stories about Jesus. These books are called *Gospels* because they tell good news about Jesus. Matthew is like a bridge between the Old Testament and the New Testament. This book describes Jesus as the king promised in the Old Testament. It shows how Jesus' teachings compare to the Instruction God gave in the Old Testament.

Matthew tells a lot about Jesus. Men from other countries called magi, searched for him after his birth (Matt 2:1-12). Jesus taught crowds about God (Matt 5–7). He did miraculous acts (Matt 8–9). He predicted his return to earth (Matt 24–25). Jesus died on a cross and rose from the dead (Matt 26:1–28:15). Then he sent his followers to tell the world about him (Matt 28:16-20).

In this book Jesus often calls himself the Human One. He also calls himself God's Son (Matt 27:43). He came so people could experience God's kingdom. When Jesus was about to begin preaching, his cousin John the Baptist shouted, "Here comes the kingdom of heaven!" (Matt 3:2). ◈

things YOU'LL DISCOVER

Matthew tells the story of the arrival of Jesus the king. This book tells all about Jesus, starting with his family history and birth and ending with his death and resurrection.

people YOU'LL MEET

Jesus—the Human One (Matt 1–28)

Mary and Joseph—the mother and father of Jesus (Matt 1–2)

John the Baptist—a prophet who prepared people to meet Jesus (Matt 3; 11; 14)

The Twelve—Jesus' closest disciples, including Peter, James, and John (Matt 4–28)

Pharisees—Jewish religious leaders (Matt 3–27)

places YOU'LL GO

Nazareth (a town in northern Israel), **Jordan River,**
Galilee (a lake and region in northern Israel),
Jerusalem,
Skull Place (the site outside Jerusalem where Jesus was crucified)

words YOU'LL REMEMBER

"You must love the Lord your God with all your heart, with all your being, and with all your mind. This is the first and greatest commandment. And the second is like it: You must love your neighbor as you love yourself" (Matt 22:37-39).

Matthew 1:25

Genealogy of Jesus

1 A record of the ancestors of Jesus Christ, son of David, son of Abraham:

²Abraham was the father of Isaac.

Isaac was the father of Jacob.

Jacob was the father of Judah and his brothers.

³Judah was the father of Perez and Zerah, whose mother was Tamar.

Perez was the father of Hezron.

Hezron was the father of Aram.

⁴Aram was the father of Amminadab.

Amminadab was the father of Nahshon.

Nahshon was the father of Salmon.

⁵Salmon was the father of Boaz, whose mother was Rahab.

Boaz was the father of Obed, whose mother was Ruth.

Obed was the father of Jesse.

⁶Jesse was the father of David the king.

David was the father of Solomon, whose mother had been the wife of Uriah.

⁷Solomon was the father of Rehoboam.

Rehoboam was the father of Abijah.

Abijah was the father of Asaph.

⁸Asaph was the father of Jehoshaphat.

Jehoshaphat was the father of Joram.

Joram was the father of Uzziah.

⁹Uzziah was the father of Jotham.

Jotham was the father of Ahaz.

Ahaz was the father of Hezekiah.

¹⁰Hezekiah was the father of Manasseh.

Manasseh was the father of Amos.

Amos was the father of Josiah.

¹¹Josiah was the father of Jechoniah and his brothers.

This was at the time of the exile to Babylon.

¹²After the exile to Babylon: Jechoniah was the father of Shealtiel.

Shealtiel was the father of Zerubbabel.

¹³Zerubbabel was the father of Abiud.

Abiud was the father of Eliakim.

Eliakim was the father of Azor.

¹⁴Azor was the father of Zadok.

Zadok was the father of Achim.

Achim was the father of Eliud.

¹⁵Eliud was the father of Eleazar.

Eleazar was the father of Matthan.

Matthan was the father of Jacob.

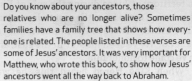

LIFE PRESERVER

Who are all these people?
Matthew 1:1-17

Do you know about your ancestors, those relatives who are no longer alive? Sometimes families have a family tree that shows how everyone is related. The people listed in these verses are some of Jesus' ancestors. It was very important for Matthew, who wrote this book, to show how Jesus' ancestors went all the way back to Abraham.

Look at the names. You might recognize some of them. You might also notice that a few women are named in this family tree. That is interesting because usually only men's names were included in these lists of ancestors. ♦

¹⁶Jacob was the father of Joseph, the husband of Mary—of whom Jesus was born, who is called the Christ.

¹⁷So there were fourteen generations from Abraham to David, fourteen generations from David to the exile to Babylon, and fourteen generations from the exile to Babylon to the Christ.

Birth of Jesus

¹⁸This is how the birth of Jesus Christ took place. When Mary his mother was engaged to Joseph, before they were married, she became pregnant by the Holy Spirit. ¹⁹Joseph her husband was a righteous man. Because he didn't want to humiliate her, he decided to call off their engagement quietly. ²⁰As he was thinking about this, an angel from the Lord appeared to him in a dream and said, "Joseph son of David, don't be afraid to take Mary as your wife, because the child she carries was conceived by the Holy Spirit. ²¹She will give birth to a son, and you will call him Jesus, because he will save his people from their sins." ²²Now all of this took place so that what the Lord had spoken through the prophet would be fulfilled:

²³ *Look! A virgin will become pregnant and give birth to a son,*
And they will call him, Emmanuel.ᵃ
(*Emmanuel* means "God with us.")

²⁴When Joseph woke up, he did just as an angel from God commanded and took Mary as his wife. ²⁵But he didn't have sexual relations

ᵃIsa 7:14

with her until she gave birth to a son. Joseph called him Jesus.

Coming of the magi

2 After Jesus was born in Bethlehem in the territory of Judea during the rule of King Herod, magi came from the east to Jerusalem. ²They asked, "Where is the newborn king of the Jews? We've seen his star in the east, and we've come to honor him."

³When King Herod heard this, he was troubled, and everyone in Jerusalem was troubled with him. ⁴He gathered all the chief priests and the legal experts and asked them where the Christ was to be born. ⁵They said, "In Bethlehem of Judea, for this is what the prophet wrote:

⁶ You, Bethlehem, land of Judah,
   by no means are you least
      among the rulers of Judah,
   because from you will come
      one who governs,
   who will shepherd my people Israel."ᵇ

⁷Then Herod secretly called for the magi and found out from them the time when the star had first appeared. ⁸He sent them to Bethlehem, saying, "Go and search carefully for the child. When you've found him, report to me so that I too may go and honor him." ⁹When they heard the king, they went; and look, the star they had seen in the east went ahead of them until it stood over the place where the child was. ¹⁰When they saw the star, they were filled with joy. ¹¹They entered the house and saw the child with Mary his mother. Falling to their knees, they honored him. Then they opened their treasure chests and presented him with gifts of gold, frankincense, and myrrh. ¹²Because they were warned in a dream not to return to Herod, they went back to their own country by another route.

Escape to Egypt

¹³When the magi had departed, an angel from the Lord appeared to Joseph in a dream and said, "Get up. Take the child and his mother and escape to Egypt. Stay there until I tell you, for Herod will soon search for the child in order to kill him." ¹⁴Joseph got up and, during the night, took the child and

his mother to Egypt. ¹⁵He stayed there until Herod died. This fulfilled what the Lord had spoken through the prophet: *I have called my son out of Egypt.*ᶜ

did you know? We don't know how many magi there were, but this book lists three gifts they brought. For this reason, people typically say there were three magi who came to see Jesus.

Murder of the Bethlehem children

¹⁶When Herod knew the magi had fooled him, he grew very angry. He sent soldiers to kill all the children in Bethlehem and in all the surrounding territory who were two years old and younger, according to the time that he had learned from the magi. ¹⁷This fulfilled the word spoken through Jeremiah the prophet:

¹⁸ A voice was heard in Ramah,
   weeping and much grieving.
   Rachel weeping for her children,
      and she did not want to be comforted,
      because they were no more.ᵈ

Return from Egypt

¹⁹After King Herod died, an angel from the Lord appeared in a dream to Joseph in Egypt. ²⁰"Get up," the angel said, "and take the child and his mother and go to the land of Israel. Those who

SAILBOAT
Joy

Joy of the Magi *Matthew 2:10-12*
The magi first spotted a special star in the night sky where they lived. The magi were most likely scholars who studied stars, along with the religious writings of the day. This would explain how they knew the unusual star symbolized the birth of a king. Because a Jewish king might be born in Jerusalem, the magi went to the palace and spoke to King Herod. It was an obvious location, but there was no newborn king. King Herod's priests and experts knew where this king was to be born: in Bethlehem, just four and a half miles away. So the magi set out again, and there was the same special star they had first seen where they lived, guiding them to Jesus. ◊

were trying to kill the child are dead." ²¹Joseph got up, took the child and his mother, and went to the land of Israel. ²²But when he heard that Archelaus ruled over Judea in place of his father Herod, Joseph was afraid to go there. Having been warned in a dream, he went to the area of Galilee. ²³He settled in a city called Nazareth so that what was spoken through the prophets might be fulfilled: He will be called a Nazarene.

Ministry of John the Baptist

3 In those days John the Baptist appeared in the desert of Judea announcing, ²"Change your hearts and lives! Here comes the kingdom of heaven!" ³He was the one of whom Isaiah the prophet spoke when he said:

The voice of one shouting
in the wilderness,
"Prepare the way for the Lord;
make his paths straight."ᵉ

ᵉIsa 40:3

⁴John wore clothes made of camel's hair, with a leather belt around his waist. He ate locusts and wild honey.

⁵People from Jerusalem, throughout Judea, and all around the Jordan River came to him. ⁶As they confessed their sins, he baptized them in the Jordan River. ⁷Many Pharisees and Sadducees came to be baptized by John. He said to them, "You children of snakes! Who warned you to escape from the angry judgment that is coming soon? ⁸Produce fruit that shows you have changed your hearts and lives. ⁹And don't even think about saying to yourselves, Abraham is our father. I tell you that God is able to raise up Abraham's children from these stones. ¹⁰The ax is already at the root of the trees. Therefore, every tree that doesn't produce good fruit will be chopped down and tossed into the fire. ¹¹I baptize with water those of you who have changed your hearts and lives. The one who

Jesus' Baptism Matthew 3:13-17

When Jesus had grown up and was ready to begin his ministry, he went to the Jordan River to see John the Baptist. John had been baptizing people. When Jesus asked John to baptize him, John tried to stop him! John must have felt confused. He probably thought that Jesus should be baptizing John and everyone else there. He might have wondered why Jesus needed to be baptized.

From this first scene of Jesus' ministry, Jesus showed that his way would be different from what people might expect. Instead of riding into town on a royal horse, he came quietly to the river and asked John to wash him. As he came out of the water, the heavens opened and God spoke: "This is my Son whom I dearly love; I find happiness in him" (Matt 3:17). When children or adults are baptized today, God finds happiness in them too.

Draw a picture of Jesus being baptized in the Jordan River. Imagine that you were there and heard God speak from heaven.

If you are baptized, thank God for bringing you into God's family. If you have not been baptized, talk to a trusted adult about when you might be ready to take that step.

is coming after me is stronger than I am. I'm not worthy to carry his sandals. He will baptize you with the Holy Spirit and with fire. [12]The shovel he uses to sift the wheat from the husks is in his hands. He will clean out his threshing area and bring the wheat into his barn. But he will burn the husks with a fire that can't be put out."

Baptism of Jesus

[13]At that time Jesus came from Galilee to the Jordan River so that John would baptize him. [14]John tried to stop him and said, "I need to be baptized by you, yet you come to me?"

[15]Jesus answered, "Allow me to be baptized now. This is necessary to fulfill all righteousness."

So John agreed to baptize Jesus. [16]When Jesus was baptized, he immediately came up out of the water. Heaven was opened to him, and he saw the Spirit of God coming down like a dove and resting on him. [17]A voice from heaven said, "This is my Son whom I dearly love; I find happiness in him."

Temptation of Jesus

4 Then the Spirit led Jesus up into the wilderness so that the devil might tempt him. [2]After Jesus had fasted for forty days and forty nights, he was starving. [3]The tempter came to him and said, "Since you are God's Son, command these stones to become bread."

[4]Jesus replied, "It's written, *People won't live only by bread, but by every word spoken by God.*"[f]

[5]After that the devil brought him into the holy city and stood him at the highest point of the temple. He said to him, [6]"Since you are God's Son, throw yourself down; for it is written, *I will command my angels concerning you, and they will take you up in their hands so that you won't hit your foot on a stone.*"[g]

[7]Jesus replied, "Again it's written, *Don't test the Lord your God.*"[h]

[8]Then the devil brought him to a very high mountain and showed him all the kingdoms of the world and their glory. [9]He said, "I'll give you all these if you bow down and worship me."

[10]Jesus responded, "Go away, Satan, because it's written, *You will worship the Lord*

your God and serve only him."[i] [11]The devil left him, and angels came and took care of him.

Move to Galilee

[12]Now when Jesus heard that John was arrested, he went to Galilee. [13]He left Nazareth and settled in Capernaum, which lies alongside the sea in the area of Zebulun and Naphtali. [14]This fulfilled what Isaiah the prophet said:

[15] *Land of Zebulun and land of Naphtali,*
alongside the sea, across the Jordan,
Galilee of the Gentiles,
[16] *the people who lived in the dark*
have seen a great light,
and a light has come upon those
who lived in the region
and in shadow of death.[j]

[17]From that time Jesus began to announce, "Change your hearts and lives! Here comes the kingdom of heaven!"

Calling of the first disciples

[18]As Jesus walked alongside the Galilee Sea, he saw two brothers, Simon, who is called Peter, and Andrew, throwing fishing nets into the sea, because they were fishermen. [19]"Come, follow me," he said, "and I'll show you how to fish for people." [20]Right away, they left their nets and followed him. [21]Continuing on, he saw another set of brothers, James the son of Zebedee and his brother John. They were in a boat with Zebedee their father repairing

[f]Deut 8:3 [g]Ps 91:11-12 [h]Deut 6:16 [i]Deut 6:13 [j]Isa 9:1-2

their nets. Jesus called them and ²²immediately they left the boat and their father and followed him.

Ministry to the crowds

²³Jesus traveled throughout Galilee, teaching in their synagogues. He announced the good news of the kingdom and healed every disease and sickness among the people. ²⁴News about him spread throughout Syria. People brought to him all those who had various kinds of diseases, those in pain, those possessed by demons, those with epilepsy, and those who were paralyzed, and he healed them. ²⁵Large crowds followed him from Galilee, the Decapolis, Jerusalem, Judea, and from the areas beyond the Jordan River. ¹Now when Jesus saw the crowds, he went up a mountain. He sat down and his disciples came to him. ²He taught them, saying:

Happy people

³"Happy are people who are hopeless, because the kingdom of heaven is theirs.
⁴"Happy are people who grieve, because they will be made glad.

⁵"Happy are people who are humble, because they will inherit the earth.
⁶"Happy are people who are hungry and thirsty for righteousness, because they will be fed until they are full.
⁷"Happy are people who show mercy, because they will receive mercy.
⁸"Happy are people who have pure hearts, because they will see God.
⁹"Happy are people who make peace, because they will be called God's children.
¹⁰"Happy are people whose lives are harassed because they are righteous, because the kingdom of heaven is theirs.
¹¹"Happy are you when people insult you and harass you and speak all kinds of bad and false things about you, all because of me. ¹²Be full of joy and be glad, because you have a great reward in heaven. In the same way, people harassed the prophets who came before you.

Salt and light

¹³"You are the salt of the earth. But if salt loses its saltiness, how will it become salty

Happiness Is a Choice   *Matthew 5:3-12*

Sometimes you feel tired or upset. You may even feel like nobody understands you. Jesus said that you can still be happy in those moments because that is when you know how much Jesus loves you.

Jesus spoke to a huge crowd on the side of a mountain and preached his most famous sermon, which is sometimes called the Sermon on the Mount. To begin his sermon, he spoke twelve statements that encouraged a crowd who was hungry for good news. When we're hopeless, grieving, humble, and hungry to do the right thing, God plants happiness within us. We don't let negative feelings get to us or ruin our lives, and we try to do the right thing (such as making peace or being humble) because we know Jesus is with us in those very moments.

How can these verses help you find true happiness?

How could you have a happy attitude this week?

again? It's good for nothing except to be thrown away and trampled under people's feet. [14]You are the light of the world. A city on top of a hill can't be hidden. [15]Neither do people light a lamp and put it under a basket. Instead, they put it on top of a lampstand, and it shines on all who are in the house. [16]In the same way, let your light shine before people, so they can see the good things you do and praise your Father who is in heaven.

Jesus and the Law

[17]"Don't even begin to think that I have come to do away with the Law and the Prophets. I haven't come to do away with them but to fulfill them. [18]I say to you very seriously that as long as heaven and earth exist, neither the smallest letter nor even the smallest stroke of a pen will be erased from the Law until everything there becomes a reality. [19]Therefore, whoever ignores one of the least of these commands and teaches others to do the same will be called the lowest in the kingdom of heaven. But whoever keeps these commands and teaches people to keep them will be called great in the kingdom of heaven. [20]I say to you that unless your righteousness is greater than the righteousness of the legal experts and the Pharisees, you will never enter the kingdom of heaven.

Law of murder

[21]"You have heard that it was said to those who lived long ago, Don't commit murder,[k] and all who commit murder will be in danger of judgment. [22]But I say to you that everyone who is angry with their brother or sister will be in danger of judgment. If they say to their brother or sister, 'You idiot,' they will be in danger of being condemned by the governing council. And if they say, 'You fool,' they will be in danger of fiery hell. [23]Therefore, if you bring your gift to the altar and there remember that your brother or sister has something against you, [24]leave your gift at the altar and go. First make things right with your brother or sister and then come back and offer your gift. [25]Be sure to make friends quickly with your opponents while you are with them on the way to court. Otherwise, they will haul you before the judge, the judge will turn you over to the officer of the court, and you will be thrown into prison. [26]I say to you in all seriousness that you won't get out of there until you've paid the very last penny.

Law of adultery

[27]"You have heard that it was said, Don't commit adultery.[l] [28]But I say to you that every man who looks at a woman lustfully has already committed adultery in his heart. [29]And if your right eye causes you to fall into sin, tear it out and throw it away. It's better that you lose a part of your body than that your whole body be thrown into hell. [30]And if your right hand causes you to fall into sin, chop it off and throw it away. It's better that you lose a part of your body than that your whole body go into hell.

Law of divorce

[31]"It was said, 'Whoever divorces his wife must give her a divorce certificate.'[m] [32]But I say to you that whoever divorces his wife except for sexual unfaithfulness forces her to commit adultery. And whoever marries a divorced woman commits adultery.

Making solemn pledges

[33]"Again you have heard that it was said to those who lived long ago: Don't make a false solemn pledge, but you should follow through on what you have pledged to the Lord.[n] [34]But I say to you that you must not pledge at all. You must not pledge by heaven, because it's God's throne. [35]You must not pledge by the earth, because it's God's footstool. You must not pledge by Jerusalem, because it's the city of the great king. [36]And you must not pledge by your head, because you can't turn one hair white or black. [37]Let your yes mean yes, and your no mean no. Anything more than this comes from the evil one.

Law of retaliation

[38]"You have heard that it was said, An eye for an eye and a tooth for a tooth.[o] [39]But I say to you that you must not oppose those who

[k]Exod 20:13 [l]Exod 20:14; Deut 5:18 [m]Deut 24:1 [n]Lev 19:12; Num 30:2; Deut 23:21 [o]Exod 21:24; Lev 24:20; Deut 19:21

want to hurt you. If people slap you on your right cheek, you must turn the left cheek to them as well. ⁴⁰When they wish to haul you to court and take your shirt, let them have your coat too. ⁴¹When they force you to go one mile, go with them two. ⁴²Give to those who ask, and don't refuse those who wish to borrow from you.

Law of love

⁴³"You have heard that it was said, *You must love your neighbor*ᴾ and hate your enemy. ⁴⁴But I say to you, love your enemies and pray for those who harass you ⁴⁵so that you will be acting as children of your Father who is in heaven. He makes the sun rise on both the evil and the good and sends rain on both the righteous and the unrighteous. ⁴⁶If you love only those who love you, what reward do you have? Don't even the tax collectors do the same? ⁴⁷And if you greet only your brothers and sisters, what more are you doing? Don't even the Gentiles do the same? ⁴⁸Therefore, just as your heavenly Father is complete in showing love to everyone, so also you must be complete.

Showy religion

6 "Be careful that you don't practice your religion in front of people to draw their attention. If you do, you will have no reward from your Father who is in heaven.

²"Whenever you give to the poor, don't blow your trumpet as the hypocrites do in the synagogues and in the streets so that they may get praise from people. I assure you, that's the only reward they'll get. ³But when you give to the poor, don't let your left hand know what your right hand is doing ⁴so that you may give to the poor in secret. Your Father who sees what you do in secret will reward you.

Showy prayer

⁵"When you pray, don't be like hypocrites. They love to pray standing in the synagogues and on the street corners so that people will see them. I assure you, that's the only reward they'll get. ⁶But when you pray, go to your

room, shut the door, and pray to your Father who is present in that secret place. Your Father who sees what you do in secret will reward you.

Proper prayer

⁷"When you pray, don't pour out a flood of empty words, as the Gentiles do. They think that by saying many words they'll be heard. ⁸Don't be like them, because your Father knows what you need before you ask. ⁹Pray like this:

Our Father who is in heaven,
> uphold the holiness of your name.
¹⁰Bring in your kingdom
> so that your will is done on earth as
> it's done in heaven.
¹¹Give us the bread we need for today.
¹²Forgive us for the ways
> we have wronged you,
> just as we also forgive those
> who have wronged us.
¹³And don't lead us into temptation,
> but rescue us from the evil one.

¹⁴"If you forgive others their sins, your heavenly Father will also forgive you. ¹⁵But if you don't forgive others, neither will your Father forgive your sins.

LIGHTHOUSE

PRAYER

Prayer: Heart to Heart *Matthew 6:6-7*
Prayer isn't a speech we give for others to listen to while we pretend to speak to God. Long prayers in front of lots of people don't impress God. If you're tempted to pray just for show, don't bother. God would rather hear from us in private because God prefers a good heart-to-heart talk over a performance with an audience. ◆

ᴾLev 19:18

Showy fasting

¹⁶"And when you fast, don't put on a sad face like the hypocrites. They distort their faces so people will know they are fasting. I assure you that they have their reward. ¹⁷When you fast, brush your hair and wash your face. ¹⁸Then you won't look like you are fasting to people, but only to your Father who is present in that secret place. Your Father who sees in secret will reward you.

Earthly and heavenly treasures

¹⁹"Stop collecting treasures for your own benefit on earth, where moth and rust eat them and where thieves break in and steal them. ²⁰Instead, collect treasures for yourselves in heaven, where moth and rust don't eat them and where thieves don't break in and steal them. ²¹Where your treasure is, there your heart will be also.

Seeing and serving

²²"The eye is the lamp of the body. Therefore, if your eye is healthy, your whole body will be full of light. ²³But if your eye is bad, your whole body will be full of darkness. If then the light in you is darkness, how terrible that darkness will be! ²⁴No one can serve two masters. Either you will hate the one and love the other, or you will be loyal to the one and have contempt for the other. You cannot serve God and wealth.

Worry about necessities

²⁵"Therefore, I say to you, don't worry about your life, what you'll eat or what you'll drink, or about your body, what you'll wear. Isn't life more than food and the body more than clothes? ²⁶Look at the birds in the sky. They don't sow seed or harvest grain or gather crops into barns. Yet your heavenly Father feeds them. Aren't you worth much more than they are? ²⁷Who among you by worrying can add a single moment to your life? ²⁸And why do you worry about clothes? Notice how the lilies in the field grow. They don't wear themselves out with work, and they don't spin cloth. ²⁹But I say to you that even Solomon in all of his splendor wasn't dressed like one of these. ³⁰If God dresses

LIFE PRESERVER

Why was fasting an important practice?
Matthew 6:16

Fasting, or going without food for a period of time, helped people remember their relationship with God. Fasting also included activities of prayer and acts of kindness and mercy for others. Jesus reminded the people that fasting wasn't something to do to show off in front of others. He wanted them to know that fasting should be private and personal.

Today people of faith, including Jews and Muslims, have times of fasting related to holy days. Some Christians fast during Lent by not eating meat. Fasting is a spiritual practice that helps people feel closer to God. ◊

grass in the field so beautifully, even though it's alive today and tomorrow it's thrown into the furnace, won't God do much more for you, you people of weak faith? ³¹Therefore, don't worry and say, 'What are we going to eat?' or 'What are we going to drink?' or 'What are we going to wear?' ³²Gentiles long for all these things. Your heavenly Father knows that you need them. ³³Instead, desire first and foremost God's kingdom and God's righteousness, and all these things will be given to you as well. ³⁴Therefore, stop worrying about tomorrow, because tomorrow will worry about itself. Each day has enough trouble of its own.

Judging

7"Don't judge, so that you won't be judged. ²You'll receive the same judgment you give. Whatever you deal out will be dealt out to you. ³Why do you see the splinter that's in your brother's or sister's eye, but don't notice the log in your own eye? ⁴How can you say to your brother or sister, 'Let me take the splinter out of your eye,' when there's a log in your eye? ⁵You deceive yourself! First take the log out of your eye, and then you'll see clearly to take the splinter out of your brother's or sister's eye. ⁶Don't give holy things to dogs, and don't throw your pearls in front of pigs. They will stomp on the pearls, then turn around and attack you.

Asking, seeking, knocking

7"Ask, and you will receive. Search, and you will find. Knock, and the door will be opened to you. 8For everyone who asks, receives. Whoever seeks, finds. And to everyone who knocks, the door is opened. 9Who among you will give your children a stone when they ask for bread? 10Or give them a snake when they ask for fish? 11If you who are evil know how to give good gifts to your children, how much more will your heavenly Father give good things to those who ask him. 12Therefore, you should treat people in the same way that you want people to treat you; this is the Law and the Prophets.

Bet you can *read this in 1 minute. Ready, set, go!*

Memorize Matt 7:12

Narrow gate

13"Go in through the narrow gate. The gate that leads to destruction is broad and the road wide, so many people enter through it. 14But the gate that leads to life is narrow and the road difficult, so few people find it.

Tree and fruit

15"Watch out for false prophets. They come to you dressed like sheep, but inside they are vicious wolves. 16You will know them by their fruit. Do people get bunches of grapes from thorny weeds, or do they get figs from thistles? 17In the same way, every good tree produces good fruit, and every rotten tree produces bad fruit. 18A good tree can't produce bad fruit. And a rotten tree can't produce good fruit. 19Every tree that doesn't produce good fruit is chopped down and thrown into the fire. 20Therefore, you will know them by their fruit.

Entrance requirements

21"Not everybody who says to me, 'Lord, Lord,' will get into the kingdom of heaven. Only those who do the will of my Father who is in heaven will enter. 22On the Judgment Day, many people will say to me, 'Lord, Lord, didn't we prophesy in your name and expel demons in your name and do lots of miracles in your name?' 23Then I'll tell them, 'I've never known you. Get away from me, you people who do wrong.'

Two foundations

24"Everybody who hears these words of mine and puts them into practice is like a wise builder who built a house on bedrock. 25The rain fell, the floods came, and the wind blew and beat against that house. It didn't fall because it was firmly set on bedrock. 26But everybody who hears these words of mine and doesn't put them into practice will be like a fool who built a house on sand. 27The rain fell, the floods came, and the wind blew and beat against that house. It fell and was completely destroyed."

Crowd's response

28When Jesus finished these words, the crowds were amazed at his teaching 29because he was teaching them like someone with authority and not like their legal experts.

A man with a skin disease

8 Now when Jesus had come down from the mountain, large crowds followed him. 2A man with a skin disease came, kneeled before him, and said, "Lord, if you want, you can make me clean."

3Jesus reached out his hand and touched him, saying, "I do want to. Become clean." Instantly his skin disease was cleansed. 4Jesus said to him, "Don't say anything to anyone. Instead, go and show yourself to the priest and offer the gift that Moses commanded. This will be a testimony to them."

Healing of the centurion's servant

5When Jesus went to Capernaum, a centurion approached, 6pleading with him, "Lord, my servant is flat on his back at home, paralyzed, and his suffering is awful."

7Jesus responded, "I'll come and heal him."

8But the centurion replied, "Lord, I don't deserve to have you come under my roof. Just say the word and my servant will be healed. 9I'm a man under authority, with soldiers under me. I say to one, 'Go,' and he goes, and to another, 'Come,' and he comes. I say to my servant, 'Do this,' and the servant does it."

10When Jesus heard this, he was impressed and said to the people following him, "I say to you with all seriousness that even in Israel I haven't found faith like this. 11I say to you that there are many who will come from east and west and sit down to eat with Abraham and Isaac and Jacob in the kingdom of heaven. [12]But the children of the kingdom will be thrown outside into the darkness. People there will be weeping and grinding their teeth." [13]Jesus said to the centurion, "Go; it will be done for you just as you have believed." And his servant was healed that very moment.

Healing of many people

[14]Jesus went home with Peter and saw Peter's mother-in-law lying in bed with a fever. [15]He touched her hand, and the fever left her. Then she got up and served them. [16]That evening people brought to Jesus many who were demon-possessed. He threw the spirits out with just a word. He healed everyone who was sick. [17]This happened so that what Isaiah the prophet said would be fulfilled: *He is the one who took our illnesses and carried away our diseases.*[q]

Discussions about following

[18]Now when Jesus saw the crowd, he ordered his disciples to go over to the other side of the lake. [19]A legal expert came and said to him, "Teacher, I'll follow you wherever you go." [20]Jesus replied, "Foxes have dens, and the birds in the sky have nests, but the Human One[r] has no place to lay his head." [21]Another man, one of his disciples, said to him, "Lord, first let me go and bury my father." [22]But Jesus said to him, "Follow me, and let the dead bury their own dead."

Calming a storm

[23]When Jesus got into a boat, his disciples followed him. [24]A huge storm arose on the

[q]Isa 53:4 [r]Or *Son of Man*

God's ◆ My
THOUGHTS ◆ THOUGHTS

Jesus Calms the Storm Matthew 8:23-27

In a miraculous display of power, Jesus lifted up his hands to a storm and waved off the wind and the rain bringing a "great calm" to a lake in the middle of a storm. Just minutes before, Jesus' friends were afraid for their lives. The rain was coming down. The waves were blowing their little boat all over the place. As they were worried about staying alive, Jesus was sleeping! His friends went to wake Jesus up and begged him to rescue them. They had seen Jesus do miraculous things before and knew he was their only hope.

So Jesus woke up and did exactly what they thought he would do. He rescued them. But before he told the wind and the waves to calm down, he told his friends to calm down. Instead of having faith in him, they panicked. Jesus reminded them to have faith when they got scared.

Sometimes we get really scared about something and forget to trust Jesus with our fears. Just like Jesus' friends in the boat, we can have faith that Jesus will calm the storms in our lives. Whether it is a fight with friends, family troubles, school struggles, or something else, Jesus can make us calm even when it feels like life has turned into one giant storm. He will calm our fears if we remember to turn to him.

What fears do you have that you can trust Jesus with?

How can you remember to ask Jesus to make you calm when you get stressed out?

they saw him, they pleaded with him to leave their region.

Healing of a man who was paralyzed

9 Boarding a boat, Jesus crossed to the other side of the lake and went to his own city. ²People brought to him a man who was paralyzed, lying on a cot. When Jesus saw their faith, he said to the man who was paralyzed, "Be encouraged, my child, your sins are forgiven."

³Some legal experts said among themselves, "This man is insulting God."

⁴But Jesus knew what they were thinking and said, "Why do you fill your minds with evil things? ⁵Which is easier—to say, 'Your sins are forgiven,' or to say, 'Get up and walk'? ⁶But so you will know that the Human One^s has authority on the earth to forgive sins"— he said to the man who was paralyzed—"Get up, take your cot, and go home." ⁷The man got up and went home. ⁸When the crowds saw what had happened, they were afraid and praised God, who had given such authority to human beings.

Calling of Matthew

⁹As Jesus continued on from there, he saw a man named Matthew sitting at a kiosk for collecting taxes. He said to him, "Follow me," and he got up and followed him. ¹⁰As Jesus sat down to eat in Matthew's house, many tax collectors

---

LIFE PRESERVER

Why are there so many healing stories? *Matthew 8–9*

Matthew 8–9 contain stories of Jesus healing a man with a skin disease, a servant, Peter's mother-in-law, a man possessed by demons, a paralyzed man, a ruler's daughter, a sick woman, and two blind men. That's a lot of healing and a lot of miracles! This kind of ability to heal was expected of a religious prophet like Jesus. By healing people, Jesus was restoring their mental or physical health so they were able to have life again.

Jesus told his disciples and anyone who would listen that he came to help people like this— people who others don't want to see. Jesus taught that everyone is welcome in God's world, including the people no one wants or cares about. ◆

---

lake so that waves were sloshing over the boat. But Jesus was asleep. ²⁵They came and woke him, saying, "Lord, rescue us! We're going to drown!"

²⁶He said to them, "Why are you afraid, you people of weak faith?" Then he got up and gave orders to the winds and the lake, and there was a great calm.

²⁷The people were amazed and said, "What kind of person is this? Even the winds and the lake obey him!"

Jesus frees demon-possessed men

²⁸When Jesus arrived on the other side of the lake in the country of the Gadarenes, two men who were demon-possessed came from among the tombs to meet him. They were so violent that nobody could travel on that road. ²⁹They cried out, "What are you going to do with us, Son of God? Have you come to torture us before the time of judgment?" ³⁰Far off in the distance a large herd of pigs was feeding. ³¹The demons pleaded with him, "If you throw us out, send us into the herd of pigs."

³²Then he said to the demons, "Go away," and they came out and went into the pigs. The whole herd rushed down the cliff into the lake and drowned. ³³Those who tended the pigs ran into the city and told everything that had happened to the demon-possessed men. ³⁴Then the whole city came out and met Jesus. When

SAILBOAT

OBEDIENCE

Tax Man Matthew *Matthew 9:9*

Matthew was a tax collector. Tax collectors were disliked in the Jewish culture at that time. They collected taxes to support the Roman Empire, which controlled their country against the will of the people. Jews considered other Jews who were tax collectors to be traitors. Most tax collectors overcharged citizens and kept the extra money for themselves. They grew wealthy by making others poor. It was hard for the people to understand why Jesus would want someone like Matthew around. They didn't understand that God's love and forgiveness are for everyone. ◆

and sinners joined Jesus and his disciples at the table.

¹¹But when the Pharisees saw this, they said to his disciples, "Why does your teacher eat with tax collectors and sinners?"

¹²When Jesus heard it, he said, "Healthy people don't need a doctor, but sick people do. ¹³Go and learn what this means: *I want mercy and not sacrifice.*ᵗ I didn't come to call righteous people, but sinners."

Question about fasting

¹⁴At that time John's disciples came and asked Jesus, "Why do we and the Pharisees frequently fast, but your disciples never fast?"

¹⁵Jesus responded, "The wedding guests can't mourn while the groom is still with them, can they? But the days will come when the groom will be taken away from them, and then they'll fast.

¹⁶"No one sews a piece of new, unshrunk cloth on old clothes because the patch tears away the cloth and makes a worse tear. ¹⁷No one pours new wine into old wineskins. If they did, the wineskins would burst, the wine would spill, and the wineskins would be ruined. Instead, people pour new wine into new wineskins so that both are kept safe."

A ruler's daughter and the woman who touched Jesus' clothes

¹⁸While Jesus was speaking to them, a ruler came and knelt in front of him, saying, "My daughter has just died. But come and place your hand on her, and she'll live." ¹⁹So Jesus and his disciples got up and went with him. ²⁰Then a woman who had been bleeding for twelve years came up behind Jesus and touched the hem of his clothes. ²¹She thought, If I only touch his robe I'll be healed.

²²When Jesus turned and saw her, he said, "Be encouraged, daughter. Your faith has healed you." And the woman was healed from that time on.

²³When Jesus went into the ruler's house, he saw the flute players and the distressed crowd. ²⁴He said, "Go away, because the little girl isn't dead but is asleep"; but they laughed at him. ²⁵After he had sent the crowd away, Jesus went in and touched her hand, and the

UMBRELLA
MOURNING

Mourning to Joy! *Matthew 9:23-24*
The flute players and most of the crowd in this story were professional mourners. When someone died, this group showed up, cried, and played music. Then they were paid. When Jesus informed the crowd of professional mourners that the girl wasn't dead but asleep, they didn't respond with joy or even quiet hope. They laughed at Jesus, but soon they were the ones spreading the news that he had brought a girl back to life. ◈

little girl rose up. ²⁶News about this spread throughout that whole region.

Healing of two blind men

²⁷As Jesus departed, two blind men followed him, crying out, "Show us mercy, Son of David."

²⁸When he came into the house, the blind men approached him. Jesus said to them, "Do you believe I can do this?"

"Yes, Lord," they replied.

²⁹Then Jesus touched their eyes and said, "It will happen for you just as you have believed." ³⁰Their eyes were opened. Then Jesus sternly warned them, "Make sure nobody knows about this." ³¹But they went out and spread the word about him throughout that whole region.

Healing of a man unable to speak

³²As they were leaving, people brought to him a man who was demon-possessed and unable to speak. ³³When Jesus had thrown out the demon, the man who couldn't speak began to talk. The crowds were amazed and said, "Nothing like this has ever been seen in Israel."

³⁴But the Pharisees said, "He throws out demons with the authority of the ruler of demons."

Compassion

³⁵Jesus traveled among all the cities and villages, teaching in their synagogues, announcing the good news of the kingdom, and

ᵗHos 6:6

healing every disease and every sickness. [36]Now when Jesus saw the crowds, he had compassion for them because they were troubled and helpless, like sheep without a shepherd. [37]Then he said to his disciples, "The size of the harvest is bigger than you can imagine, but there are few workers. [38]Therefore, plead with the Lord of the harvest to send out workers for his harvest."

Mission of the Twelve

10 He called his twelve disciples and gave them authority over unclean spirits to throw them out and to heal every disease and every sickness. [2]Here are the names of the twelve apostles: first, Simon, who is called Peter; and Andrew his brother; James the son of Zebedee; and John his brother; [3]Philip; and Bartholomew; Thomas; and Matthew the tax collector; James the son of Alphaeus; and Thaddaeus; [4]Simon the Cananaean;[u] and Judas, who betrayed Jesus.

Commissioning of the Twelve

[5]Jesus sent these twelve out and commanded them, "Don't go among the Gentiles or into a Samaritan city. [6]Go instead to the lost sheep, the people of Israel. [7]As you go, make this announcement: 'The kingdom of heaven has come near.' [8]Heal the sick, raise the dead, cleanse those with skin diseases, and throw out demons. You received without having to pay. Therefore, give without demanding payment. [9]Workers deserve to be fed, so don't gather gold or silver or copper coins for your money belts to take on your trips. [10]Don't take a backpack for the road or two shirts or sandals or a walking stick. [11]Whatever city or village you go into, find somebody in it who is worthy and stay there until you go on your way. [12]When you go into a house, say, 'Peace!' [13]If the house is worthy, give it your blessing of peace. But if the house isn't worthy, take back your blessing. [14]If anyone refuses to welcome you or listen to your words, shake the dust off your feet as you leave that house or city. [15]I assure you that it will be more bearable for the land of Sodom and Gomorrah on Judgment Day than it will be for that city.

Response to harassment

[16]"Look, I'm sending you as sheep among wolves. Therefore, be wise as snakes and innocent as doves. [17]Watch out for people—because they will hand you over to councils and they will beat you in their synagogues. [18]They will haul you in front of governors and even kings because of me so that you may give

Twelve is an important number in the Bible. Before Jesus' time, the Israelites were divided into twelve tribes. Jesus also chose twelve disciples to help spread the good news about his life, death, and resurrection.

your testimony to them and to the Gentiles. [19]Whenever they hand you over, don't worry about how to speak or what you will say, because what you can say will be given to you at that moment. [20]You aren't doing the talking, but the Spirit of my Father is doing the talking through you. [21]Brothers and sisters will hand each other over to be executed. A father will turn his child in. Children will defy their parents and have them executed. [22]Everyone will hate you on account of my name. But whoever stands firm until the end will be saved. [23]Whenever they harass you in one city, escape to the next, because I assure you that you will not go through all the cities of Israel before the Human One[v] comes.

[24]"Disciples aren't greater than their teacher, and slaves aren't greater than their master. [25]It's enough for disciples to be like their teacher and slaves like their master. If they have called the head of the house Beelzebul, it's certain that they will call the members of his household by even worse names.

Whom to fear

[26]"Therefore, don't be afraid of those people because nothing is hidden that won't be revealed, and nothing secret that won't be brought out into the open. [27]What I say to you in the darkness, tell in the light; and what you hear whispered, announce from the rooftops. [28]Don't be afraid of those who kill the body but can't kill the soul. Instead, be afraid of the one who can destroy both body and soul in hell. [29]Aren't two sparrows sold for a small

[u]Or zealot [v]Or Son of Man

coin? But not one of them will fall to the ground without your Father knowing about it already. ³⁰Even the hairs of your head are all counted. ³¹Don't be afraid. You are worth more than many sparrows.

Confessing Christ to people

³²"Therefore, everyone who acknowledges me before people, I also will acknowledge before my Father who is in heaven. ³³But everyone who denies me before people, I also will deny before my Father who is in heaven.

Trouble in the family

³⁴"Don't think that I've come to bring peace to the earth. I haven't come to bring peace but a sword. ³⁵I've come to turn a man *against his father, a daughter against her mother, and a daughter-in-law against her mother-in-law.* ³⁶*People's enemies are members of their own households.*ʷ

³⁷"Those who love father or mother more than me aren't worthy of me. Those who love son or daughter more than me aren't worthy of me. ³⁸Those who don't pick up their crosses and follow me aren't worthy of me. ³⁹Those who find their lives will lose them, and those who lose their lives because of me will find them.

Rewards

⁴⁰"Those who receive you are also receiving me, and those who receive me are receiving the one who sent me. ⁴¹Those who receive a prophet as a prophet will receive a prophet's reward. Those who receive a righteous person as a righteous person will receive a righteous person's reward. ⁴²I assure you that everybody who gives even a cup of cold water to these little ones because they are my disciples will certainly be rewarded."

Ministry to the people

11 When Jesus finished teaching his twelve disciples, he went on from there to teach and preach in their cities.

Question from John the Baptist

²Now when John heard in prison about the things the Christ was doing, he sent word by his disciples to Jesus, asking, ³"Are you the one who is to come, or should we look for another?"

⁴Jesus responded, "Go, report to John what you hear and see. ⁵*Those who were blind are able to see.* Those who were crippled are walking. People with skin diseases are cleansed. Those *who were deaf now hear. Those who were dead are raised up. The poor have good news proclaimed to them.*ˣ ⁶Happy are those who don't stumble and fall because of me."

Appeal of John's ministry

⁷When John's disciples had gone, Jesus spoke to the crowds about John: "What did you go out to the wilderness to see? A stalk blowing in the wind? ⁸What did you go out to see? A man dressed up in refined clothes? Look, those who wear refined clothes are in royal palaces. ⁹What did you go out to see? A prophet? Yes, I tell you, and more than a prophet. ¹⁰He is the one of whom it is written: *Look, I'm sending my messenger before you, who will prepare your way before you.*ʸ

Significance of John's ministry

¹¹"I assure you that no one who has ever been born is greater than John the Baptist. Yet whoever is least in the kingdom of heaven is greater than he. ¹²From the days of John the Baptist until now the kingdom of heaven is violently attacked as violent people seize it. ¹³All the Prophets and the Law prophesied until John came. ¹⁴If you are willing to accept it, he is Elijah who is to come. ¹⁵Let the person who has ears, hear.

This generation

¹⁶"To what will I compare this generation? It is like a child sitting in the marketplaces calling out to others, ¹⁷'We played the flute for you and you didn't dance. We sang a funeral song and you didn't mourn.' ¹⁸For John came neither eating nor drinking, and they say, 'He has a demon.' ¹⁹Yet the Human Oneᶻ came eating and drinking, and they say, 'Look, a glutton and a drunk, a friend of tax collectors and sinners.' But wisdom is proved to be right by her works."

ʷMic 7:6 ˣIsa 35:5-6; 61:1 ʸMal 3:1 ᶻOr *Son of Man*

Condemnation of Bethsaida and Capernaum

²⁰Then he began to scold the cities where he had done his greatest miracles because they didn't change their hearts and lives. ²¹"How terrible it will be for you, Chorazin! How terrible it will be for you, Bethsaida! For if the miracles done among you had been done in Tyre and Sidon, they would have changed their hearts and lives and put on funeral clothes and ashes a long time ago. ²²But I say to you that Tyre and Sidon will be better off on Judgment Day than you. ²³And you, Capernaum, will you be honored by being raised up to heaven? No, you will be thrown down to the place of the dead. After all, if the miracles that were done among you had been done in Sodom, it would still be here today. ²⁴But I say to you that it will be better for the land of Sodom on the Judgment Day than it will be for you."

The Father and the Son

²⁵At that time Jesus said, "I praise you, Father, Lord of heaven and earth, because you've hidden these things from the wise and intelligent and have shown them to babies. ²⁶Indeed, Father, this brings you happiness.

²⁷"My Father has handed all things over to me. No one knows the Son except the Father. And nobody knows the Father except the Son and anyone to whom the Son wants to reveal him.

²⁸"Come to me, all you who are struggling hard and carrying heavy loads, and I will give you rest. ²⁹Put on my yoke, and learn from me. I'm gentle and humble. And you will find rest for yourselves. ³⁰My yoke is easy to bear, and my burden is light."

Working on the Sabbath

12 At that time Jesus went through the wheat fields on the Sabbath. His disciples were hungry so they were picking heads of wheat and eating them. ²When the Pharisees saw this, they said to him, "Look, your disciples are breaking the Sabbath law."

³But he said to them, "Haven't you read what David did when he and those with him were hungry? ⁴He went into God's house and broke the law by eating the bread of the presence, which only the priests were allowed to eat. ⁵Or haven't you read in the Law that on the Sabbath the priests in the temple treat the Sabbath as any other day and are still innocent? ⁶But I tell you that something greater than the temple is here. ⁷If you had known what this means, *I want mercy and not sacrifice,*ᵃ you wouldn't have condemned the innocent. ⁸The Human Oneᵇ is Lord of the Sabbath."

Healing on the Sabbath

⁹Jesus left that place and went into their synagogue. ¹⁰A man with a withered hand was there. Wanting to bring charges against Jesus, they asked, "Does the Law allow a person to heal on the Sabbath?"

¹¹Jesus replied, "Who among you has a sheep that falls into a pit on the Sabbath and will not take hold of it and pull it out? ¹²How much more valuable is a person than a sheep!

UMBRELLA
Sad

Willing and Waiting *Matthew 11:28-30*
"Come here! I'll help you. You look exhausted. Let me carry that while you rest for a bit." Who wouldn't like to get an offer of help like that? Sometimes life gets hard, and we get discouraged. We may feel stressed, worried, or depressed. Especially in those times, we need someone dependable to help. God is willing and waiting to step into our lives to provide that help. In fact, Jesus compares it to being harnessed together with God to share the load. ☂

So the Law allows a person to do what is good on the Sabbath." ¹³Then Jesus said to the man, "Stretch out your hand." So he did and it was made healthy, just like the other one. ¹⁴The Pharisees went out and met in order to find a way to destroy Jesus.

Healing the crowd

¹⁵Jesus knew what they intended to do, so he went away from there. Large crowds followed him, and he healed them all. ¹⁶But he

---

ᵃHos 6:6 ᵇOr *Son of Man*

ordered them not to spread the word about him, ¹⁷so that what was spoken through Isaiah the prophet might be fulfilled:

¹⁸ *Look, my Servant whom I chose,*
the one I love,
in whom I find great pleasure.
I'll put my Spirit upon him,
and he'll announce judgment
to the Gentiles.
¹⁹ *He won't argue or shout,*
and nobody will hear his voice
in the streets.
²⁰ *He won't break a bent stalk,*
and he won't snuff out a smoldering wick,
until he makes justice win.
²¹ *And the Gentiles will put their hope*
*in his name.*ᶜ

²²They brought to Jesus a demon-possessed man who was blind and unable to speak. Jesus healed him so that he could both speak and see. ²³All the crowds were amazed and said, "This man couldn't be the Son of David, could he?"

²⁴When the Pharisees heard, they said, "This man throws out demons only by the authority of Beelzebul, the ruler of the demons."

²⁵Because Jesus knew what they were thinking, he replied, "Every kingdom involved in civil war becomes a wasteland. Every city or house torn apart by divisions will collapse. ²⁶If Satan throws out Satan, he is at war with himself. How then can his kingdom endure? ²⁷And if I throw out demons by the authority of Beelzebul, then by whose authority do your followers throw them out? Therefore, they will be your judges. ²⁸But if I throw out demons by the power of God's Spirit, then God's kingdom has already overtaken you. ²⁹Can people go into a house that belongs to a strong man and steal his possessions, unless they first tie up the strong man? Then they can rob his house. ³⁰Whoever isn't with me is against me, and whoever doesn't gather with me scatters.

Insulting the Holy Spirit

³¹"Therefore, I tell you that people will be forgiven for every sin and insult to God. But insulting the Holy Spirit won't be forgiven. ³²And whoever speaks a word against the Human One ᵈ will be forgiven. But whoever speaks against the Holy Spirit won't be forgiven, not in this age or in the age that is coming.

Trees and fruits

³³"Either consider the tree good and its fruit good, or consider the tree rotten and its fruit rotten. A tree is known by its fruit. ³⁴Children of snakes! How can you speak good things while you are evil? What fills the heart comes out of the mouth. ³⁵Good people bring out good things from their good treasure. But evil people bring out evil things from their evil treasure. ³⁶I tell you that people will have to answer on Judgment Day for every useless word they speak. ³⁷By your words you will be either judged innocent or condemned as guilty."

LIGHTHOUSE

Heart

Inside to the Outside   *Matthew 12:34*
Almost anyone can pretend to be nice for a while. But eventually, who you are on the inside—your thoughts, feelings, emotions, and opinions—shows on the outside. If you hear mean words coming out of someone's mouth or see somebody treating somebody else cruelly, you've seen a glimpse of what that person's heart is like. An evil heart leads to evil actions. Only the power of God's love and forgiveness can change hearts. ◊

Request for a sign

³⁸At that time some of the legal experts and the Pharisees requested of Jesus, "Teacher, we would like to see a sign from you."

³⁹But he replied, "An evil and unfaithful generation searches for a sign, but it won't receive any sign except Jonah's sign. ⁴⁰Just as *Jonah was in the whale's belly for three days and three nights,*ᵉ so the Human Oneᶠ will be in the heart of the earth for three days and three nights. ⁴¹The citizens of Nineveh will stand up at the judgment with this generation and condemn it as guilty, because they changed their hearts and lives in response to Jonah's preaching. And look, someone greater than Jonah is here. ⁴²The queen of the South

---

ᶜIsa 42:1-4 ᵈOr *Son of Man* ᵉJonah 1:17 ᶠOr *Son of Man*

will be raised up by God at the judgment with this generation and condemn it because she came from a distant land to hear Solomon's wisdom. And look, someone greater than Solomon is here.

Unclean spirit seeking a home

⁴³"When an unclean spirit leaves a person, it wanders through dry places looking for a place to rest. But it doesn't find any. ⁴⁴Then it says, 'I'll go back to the house I left.' When it arrives, it finds the place vacant, cleaned up, and decorated. ⁴⁵Then it goes and brings with it seven other spirits more evil than itself. They go in and make their home there. That person is worse off at the end than at the beginning. This is the way it will be also for this evil generation."

Jesus' family

⁴⁶While Jesus was speaking to the crowds, his mother and brothers stood outside trying to speak with him. ⁴⁷Someone said to him, "Look, your mother and brothers are outside wanting to speak with you."

⁴⁸Jesus replied, "Who is my mother? Who are my brothers?" ⁴⁹He stretched out his hand toward his disciples and said, "Look, here are my mother and my brothers. ⁵⁰Whoever does the will of my Father who is in heaven is my brother, sister, and mother."

Setting for the parables

13 That day Jesus went out of the house and sat down beside the lake. ²Such large crowds gathered around him that he climbed into a boat and sat down. The whole crowd was standing on the shore.

Parable of the soils

³He said many things to them in parables: "A farmer went out to scatter seed. ⁴As he was scattering seed, some fell on the path, and birds came and ate it. ⁵Other seed fell on rocky ground where the soil was shallow. They sprouted immediately because the soil wasn't deep. ⁶But when the sun came up, it scorched the plants, and they dried up because they had no roots. ⁷Other seed fell among thorny plants. The thorny plants grew

and choked them. ⁸Other seed fell on good soil and bore fruit, in one case a yield of one hundred to one, in another case a yield of sixty to one, and in another case a yield of thirty to one. ⁹Everyone who has ears should pay attention."

Why Jesus speaks in parables

¹⁰Jesus' disciples came and said to him, "Why do you use parables when you speak to the crowds?"

¹¹Jesus replied, "Because they haven't received the secrets of the kingdom of heaven, but you have. ¹²For those who have will receive more and they will have more than enough. But as for those who don't have, even the little they have will be taken away from them. ¹³This is why I speak to the crowds in parables: although they see, they don't really see; and although they hear, they don't really hear or understand. ¹⁴What Isaiah prophesied has become completely true for them:

> *You will hear, to be sure,*
>   *but never understand;*
>   *and you will certainly see*
>   *but never recognize*
>   *what you are seeing.*
> ¹⁵ *For this people's senses*
>   *have become calloused,*
>   *and they've become hard of hearing,*
>   *and they've shut their eyes*
>   *so that they won't see with their eyes*
>   *or hear with their ears*
>   *or understand with their minds,*
>   *and change their hearts and lives*
>   *that I may heal them.*^g

¹⁶"Happy are your eyes because they see. Happy are your ears because they hear. ¹⁷I assure you that many prophets and righteous people wanted to see what you see and hear what you hear, but they didn't.

Explanation of the parable of the farmer

¹⁸"Consider then the parable of the farmer. ¹⁹Whenever people hear the word about the kingdom and don't understand it, the evil one comes and carries off what was planted in their hearts. This is the seed that was sown on the path. ²⁰As for the seed that was spread on rocky ground, this refers to people who hear the word and immediately receive it joyfully.

^gIsa 6:9-10

²¹Because they have no roots, they last for only a little while. When they experience distress or abuse because of the word, they immediately fall away. ²²As for the seed that was spread among thorny plants, this refers to those who hear the word, but the worries of this life and the false appeal of wealth choke the word, and it bears no fruit. ²³As for what was planted on good soil, this refers to those who hear and understand, and bear fruit and produce—in one case a yield of one hundred to one, in another case a yield of sixty to one, and in another case a yield of thirty to one."

Parable of the weeds

²⁴Jesus told them another parable: "The kingdom of heaven is like someone who planted good seed in his field. ²⁵While people were sleeping, an enemy came and planted weeds among the wheat and went away. ²⁶When the stalks sprouted and bore grain, then the weeds also appeared.

²⁷"The servants of the landowner came and said to him, 'Master, didn't you plant good seed in your field? Then how is it that it has weeds?'

²⁸"'An enemy has done this,' he answered.

"The servants said to him, 'Do you want us to go and gather them?'

²⁹"But the landowner said, 'No, because if you gather the weeds, you'll pull up the wheat along with them. ³⁰Let both grow side by side until the harvest. And at harvesttime I'll say to the harvesters, "First gather the weeds and tie them together in bundles to be burned. But bring the wheat into my barn."'"

Parable of the mustard seed

³¹He told another parable to them: "The kingdom of heaven is like a mustard seed that someone took and planted in his field. ³²It's the smallest of all seeds. But when it's grown, it's the largest of all vegetable plants. It becomes a tree so that the birds in the sky come and nest in its branches."

Parable of the yeast

³³He told them another parable: "The kingdom of heaven is like yeast, which a woman took and hid in a bushel of wheat flour until the yeast had worked its way through all the dough."

LIFE PRESERVER

What was the purpose of telling all these parables?
Matthew 13:1-53

Parables are short stories with a hidden meaning. Jesus told seven parables to help people understand the difference between God's kingdom and the world in which they lived. Jesus used stories about everyday things like seeds, weeds, yeast, and treasures to help the people think in new ways about their lives. Jesus used common things and asked the people to think about them in new ways.

The parable in Matthew 13:33 tells about yeast. Bakers use yeast when they make bread. When yeast mixes with warm water, it starts to grow. Added to flour, this yeast and water mixture helps the bread rise into a loaf while it bakes. Just as yeast works quietly in the dough helping to make bread, God's kingdom is growing too. ◆

Purpose of parables to the crowds

³⁴Jesus said all these things to the crowds in parables, and he spoke to them only in parables. ³⁵This was to fulfill what the prophet spoke:

I'll speak in parables;
I'll declare what has been hidden
*since the beginning of the world.*ʰ

Explanation of the parable of the weeds

³⁶Jesus left the crowds and went into the house. His disciples came to him and said, "Explain to us the parable of the weeds in the field."

³⁷Jesus replied, "The one who plants the good seed is the Human One.ⁱ ³⁸The field is the world. And the good seeds are the followers of the kingdom. But the weeds are the followers of the evil one. ³⁹The enemy who planted them is the devil. The harvest is the end of the present age. The harvesters are the angels. ⁴⁰Just as people gather weeds and burn them in the fire, so it will be at the end of the present age. ⁴¹The Human Oneʲ will send his angels, and they will gather out of his kingdom all things that cause people to fall away and all people who sin. ⁴²He will throw them into a burning furnace. People there will be weeping and grinding their teeth.

⁴³Then the righteous will shine like the sun in their Father's kingdom. Those who have ears should hear."

Parable of the treasure

⁴⁴"The kingdom of heaven is like a treasure that somebody hid in a field, which someone else found and covered up. Full of joy, the finder sold everything and bought that field.

Parable of the merchant

⁴⁵"Again, the kingdom of heaven is like a merchant in search of fine pearls. ⁴⁶When he found one very precious pearl, he went and sold all that he owned and bought it.

LIGHTHOUSE

GOD'S KINGDOM

One Precious Pearl *Matthew 13:45*

A pearl is one of nature's most beautiful jewels. Unlike gemstones that have to be cut and polished, a pearl needs no enhancing. A pearl merely has to be discovered to be valued and enjoyed. Like pearls, there are many things in life that are important and valuable, but none more precious than establishing God's kingdom in your own heart and life. That one precious pearl is worth any cost. ◊

Parable of the net

⁴⁷"Again, the kingdom of heaven is like a net that people threw into the lake and gathered all kinds of fish. ⁴⁸When it was full, they pulled it to the shore, where they sat down and put the good fish together into containers. But the bad fish they threw away. ⁴⁹That's the way it will be at the end of the present age. The angels will go out and separate the evil people from the righteous people, ⁵⁰and will throw the evil ones into a burning furnace. People there will be weeping and grinding their teeth.

Treasures new and old

⁵¹"Have you understood all these things?" Jesus asked.

They said to him, "Yes."

⁵²Then he said to them, "Therefore, every

legal expert who has been trained as a disciple for the kingdom of heaven is like the head of a household who brings old and new things out of their treasure chest."

Jesus in his hometown

⁵³When Jesus finished these parables, he departed. ⁵⁴When he came to his hometown, he taught the people in their synagogue. They were surprised and said, "Where did he get this wisdom? Where did he get the power to work miracles? ⁵⁵Isn't he the carpenter's son? Isn't his mother named Mary? Aren't James, Joseph, Simon, and Judas his brothers? ⁵⁶And his sisters, aren't they here with us? Where did this man get all this?" ⁵⁷They were repulsed by him and fell into sin.

But Jesus said to them, "Prophets are honored everywhere except in their own hometowns and in their own households." ⁵⁸He was unable to do many miracles there because of their disbelief.

Death of John the Baptist

14 At that time Herod the ruler[k] heard the news about Jesus. ²He said to his servants, "This is John the Baptist. He's been raised from the dead. This is why these miraculous powers are at work through him." ³Herod had arrested John, bound him, and put him in prison because of Herodias, the wife of Herod's brother Philip.

⁴That's because John told Herod, "It's against the law for you to marry her."

⁵Although Herod wanted to kill him, he feared the crowd because they thought John was a prophet. ⁶But at Herod's birthday party Herodias' daughter danced in front of the guests and thrilled Herod. ⁷Then he swore to give her anything she asked.

⁸At her mother's urging, the girl said, "Give me the head of John the Baptist here on a plate." ⁹Although the king was upset, because of his solemn pledge and his guests he commanded that they give it to her. ¹⁰Then he had John beheaded in prison. ¹¹They brought his head on a plate and gave it to the young woman, and she brought it to her mother. ¹²But John's disciples came and took his body and buried it. Then they went and told Jesus what had happened.

[k]Or *tetrarch*, which refers to a prince over a small region

Feeding the five thousand

¹³When Jesus heard about John, he withdrew in a boat to a deserted place by himself. When the crowds learned this, they followed him on foot from the cities. ¹⁴When Jesus arrived and saw a large crowd, he had compassion for them and healed those who were sick. ¹⁵That evening his disciples came and said to him, "This is an isolated place and it's getting late. Send the crowds away so they can go into the villages and buy food for themselves."

¹⁶But Jesus said to them, "There's no need to send them away. You give them something to eat."

¹⁷They replied, "We have nothing here except five loaves of bread and two fish."

¹⁸He said, "Bring them here to me." ¹⁹He ordered the crowds to sit down on the grass. He took the five loaves of bread and the two fish, looked up to heaven, blessed them and broke the loaves apart and gave them to his disciples. Then the disciples gave them to the crowds. ²⁰Everyone ate until they were full, and they filled twelve baskets with the leftovers. ²¹About five thousand men plus women and children had eaten.

Walking on the water

²²Right then, Jesus made the disciples get into the boat and go ahead to the other side of the lake while he dismissed the crowds. ²³When he sent them away, he went up onto a mountain by himself to pray. Evening came and he was alone. ²⁴Meanwhile, the boat, fighting a strong headwind, was being battered by the waves and was already far away from land. ²⁵Very early in the morning he came to his disciples, walking on the lake. ²⁶When the disciples saw him walking on the lake, they were terrified and said, "It's a ghost!" They were so frightened they screamed.

²⁷Just then Jesus spoke to them, "Be encouraged! It's me. Don't be afraid."

²⁸Peter replied, "Lord, if it's you, order me to come to you on the water."

²⁹And Jesus said, "Come."

Then Peter got out of the boat and was walking on the water toward Jesus. ³⁰But

Bet you can *read this in 3 minutes. Ready, set, go!*

when Peter saw the strong wind, he became frightened. As he began to sink, he shouted, "Lord, rescue me!"

³¹Jesus immediately reached out and grabbed him, saying, "You man of weak faith! Why did you begin to have doubts?" ³²When they got into the boat, the wind settled down.

³³Then those in the boat worshipped Jesus and said, "You must be God's Son!"

Healing the sick

³⁴When they had crossed the lake, they landed at Gennesaret. ³⁵When the people who lived in that place recognized him, they sent word throughout that whole region, and they brought to him everyone who was sick. ³⁶Then they begged him that they might just touch the edge of his clothes. Everyone who touched him was cured.

Rules from the elders

15 Then Pharisees and legal experts came to Jesus from Jerusalem and said, ²"Why are your disciples breaking the elders' rules handed down to us? They don't ritually purify their hands by washing before they eat."

³Jesus replied, "Why do you break the command of God by keeping the rules handed down to you? ⁴For God said, *Honor your father and your mother,*[1] and *The person who speaks against father or mother will certainly be put to death.*[m] ⁵But you say, 'If you tell your father or mother, "Everything I'm expected to contribute to you I'm giving to God as a gift,"

LIGHTHOUSE

PRAYER

Time with God *Matthew 14:21-23*
Jesus' relationship with God was important. After teaching and feeding a huge crowd of people, Jesus sent his friends on to their next stop and then headed up a mountain to spend time with God. His time alone with God helped Jesus find the strength and direction to continue his ministry on earth. Being alone with God is just as important for our relationship with God. ◈

[1]Exod 20:12; Deut 5:16 [m]Exod 21:17; Lev 20:9

then you don't have to honor your father.' [6]So you do away with God's Law for the sake of the rules that have been handed down to you. [7]Hypocrites! Isaiah really knew what he was talking about when he prophesied about you, [8]*This people honors me with their lips, but their hearts are far away from me.* [9]*Their worship of me is empty since they teach instructions that are human rules.*["n]

[10]Jesus called the crowd near and said to them, "Listen and understand. [11]It's not what goes into the mouth that contaminates a person in God's sight. It's what comes out of the mouth that contaminates the person."

[12]Then the disciples came and said to him, "Do you know that the Pharisees were offended by what you just said?"

[13]Jesus replied, "Every plant that my heavenly Father didn't plant will be pulled up. [14]Leave the Pharisees alone. They are blind people who are guides to blind people. But if a blind person leads another blind person, they will both fall into a ditch."

[15]Then Peter spoke up, "Explain this riddle to us."

[16]Jesus said, "Don't you understand yet? [17]Don't you know that everything that goes into the mouth enters the stomach and goes out into the sewer? [18]But what goes out of the mouth comes from the heart. And that's what contaminates a person in God's sight. [19]Out of the heart come evil thoughts, murders, adultery, sexual sins, thefts, false testimonies, and insults. [20]These contaminate a person in God's sight. But eating without washing hands doesn't contaminate in God's sight."

Canaanite woman

[21]From there, Jesus went to the regions of Tyre and Sidon. [22]A Canaanite woman from those territories came out and shouted, "Show me mercy, Son of David. My daughter is suffering terribly from demon possession." [23]But he didn't respond to her at all.

His disciples came and urged him, "Send her away; she keeps shouting out after us."

[24]Jesus replied, "I've been sent only to the lost sheep, the people of Israel."

[25]But she knelt before him and said, "Lord, help me."

[26]He replied, "It is not good to take the children's bread and toss it to dogs."

[27]She said, "Yes, Lord. But even the dogs eat the crumbs that fall off their masters' table."

[28]Jesus answered, "Woman, you have great faith. It will be just as you wish." And right then her daughter was healed.

Healing of many people

[29]Jesus moved on from there along the shore of the Galilee Sea. He went up a mountain and sat down. [30]Large crowds came to him, including those who were paralyzed, blind, injured, and unable to speak, and many others. They laid them at his feet, and he healed them. [31]So the crowd was amazed when they saw those who had been unable to speak talking, and the paralyzed cured, and the injured walking, and the blind seeing. And they praised the God of Israel.

Feeding the four thousand

[32]Now Jesus called his disciples and said, "I feel sorry for the crowd because they have been with me for three days and have nothing to eat. I don't want to send them away hungry for fear they won't have enough strength to travel."

[33]His disciples replied, "Where are we going to get enough food in this wilderness to satisfy such a big crowd?"

[34]Jesus said, "How much bread do you have?"

They responded, "Seven loaves and a few fish."

[35]He told the crowd to sit on the ground. [36]He took the seven loaves of bread and the fish. After he gave thanks, he broke them into pieces and gave them to the disciples, and the disciples gave them to the crowds. [37]Everyone ate until they were full. The disciples collected seven baskets full of leftovers. [38]Four thousand men ate, plus women and children. [39]After dismissing the crowds, Jesus got into the boat and came to the region of Magadan.

Demand for a sign

16 The Pharisees and Sadducees came to Jesus. In order to test him they asked him to show them a sign from heaven. [2]But he replied, "At evening you say, 'It will

---

[n]Isa 29:13

be nice weather because the sky is bright red.' ³And in the morning you say, 'There will be bad weather today because the sky is cloudy.' You know how to make sense of the sky's appearance. But you are unable to recognize the signs that point to what the time is. ⁴An evil and unfaithful generation searches for a sign. But it won't receive any sign except Jonah's sign." Then he left them and went away.

Yeast of the Pharisees and Sadducees

⁵When the disciples arrived on the other side of the lake, they had forgotten to bring bread. ⁶Jesus said to them, "Watch out and be on your guard for the yeast of the Pharisees and Sadducees."

⁷They discussed this among themselves and said, "We didn't bring any bread."

⁸Jesus knew what they were discussing and said, "You people of weak faith! Why are you discussing among yourselves the fact that you don't have any bread? ⁹Don't you

did you know? Peter called Jesus God's Son when they were in Caesarea Philippi. There was a cliff in Caesarea Philippi with statues of dozens of different gods tucked into notches in the rocks. Unlike these statues, Peter said Jesus was the God who was alive.

understand yet? Don't you remember the five loaves that fed the five thousand and how many baskets of leftovers you gathered? ¹⁰And the seven loaves that fed the four thousand and how many large baskets of leftovers you gathered? ¹¹Don't you know that I wasn't talking about bread? But be on your guard for the yeast of the Pharisees and Sadducees." ¹²Then they understood that he wasn't telling them to be on their guard for yeast used in making bread. No, he was telling them to watch out for the teaching of the Pharisees and Sadducees.

Peter's declaration about Jesus

¹³Now when Jesus came to the area of Caesarea Philippi, he asked his disciples, "Who do people say the Human One° is?"

¹⁴They replied, "Some say John the Baptist,

others Elijah, and still others Jeremiah or one of the other prophets."

¹⁵He said, "And what about you? Who do you say that I am?"

¹⁶Simon Peter said, "You are the Christ, the Son of the living God."

¹⁷Then Jesus replied, "Happy are you, Simon son of Jonah, because no human has shown this to you. Rather my Father who is in heaven has shown you. ¹⁸I tell you that you are Peter.ᴾ And I'll build my church on this rock. The gates of the underworld won't be able to stand against it. ¹⁹I'll give you the keys of the kingdom of heaven. Anything you fasten on earth will be fastened in heaven. Anything you loosen on earth will be loosened in heaven." ²⁰Then he ordered the disciples not to tell anybody that he was the Christ.

First prediction of Jesus' death and resurrection

²¹From that time Jesus began to show his disciples that he had to go to Jerusalem and suffer many things from the elders, chief priests, and legal experts, and that he had to be killed and raised on the third day. ²²Then Peter took hold of Jesus and, scolding him, began to correct him: "God forbid, Lord!

°Or Son of Man ᴾPeter means rock.

This won't happen to you." ²³But he turned to Peter and said, "Get behind me, Satan. You are a stone that could make me stumble, for you are not thinking God's thoughts but human thoughts."

Saving and losing life

²⁴Then Jesus said to his disciples, "All who want to come after me must say no to themselves, take up their cross, and follow me. ²⁵All who want to save their lives will lose them. But all who lose their lives because of me will find them. ²⁶Why would people gain the whole world but lose their lives? What will people give in exchange for their lives? ²⁷For the Human One[q] is about to come with the majesty of his Father with his angels. And then he will repay each one for what that person has done. ²⁸I assure you that some standing here won't die before they see the Human One[r] coming in his kingdom."

Jesus' transformation

17 Six days later Jesus took Peter, James, and John his brother, and brought them to the top of a very high mountain. ²He was transformed in front of them. His face shone like the sun, and his clothes became as white as light.

³Moses and Elijah appeared to them, talking with Jesus. ⁴Peter reacted to all of this by saying to Jesus, "Lord, it's good that we're here. If you want, I'll make three shrines: one for you, one for Moses, and one for Elijah."

⁵While he was still speaking, look, a bright cloud overshadowed them. A voice from the cloud said, "This is my Son whom I dearly love. I am very pleased with him. Listen to him!" ⁶Hearing this, the disciples fell on their faces, filled with awe.

⁷But Jesus came and touched them. "Get up," he said. "Don't be afraid." ⁸When they looked up, they saw no one except Jesus.

⁹As they were coming down the mountain, Jesus commanded them, "Don't tell anybody about the vision until the Human One[s] is raised from the dead."

¹⁰The disciples asked, "Then why do the legal experts say that Elijah must first come?"

¹¹Jesus responded, "Elijah does come first and will restore all things. ¹²In fact, I tell you that Elijah has already come, and they didn't know him. But they did to him whatever they wanted. In the same way the Human One[t] is also going to suffer at their hands." ¹³Then the disciples realized he was telling them about John the Baptist.

Healing of a boy who was demon-possessed

¹⁴When they came to the crowd, a man met Jesus. He knelt before him, ¹⁵saying, "Lord, show mercy to my son. He is epileptic and suffers terribly, for he often falls into the fire or the water. ¹⁶I brought him to your disciples, but they couldn't heal him."

¹⁷Jesus answered, "You faithless and crooked generation, how long will I be with you? How long will I put up with you? Bring the boy here to me." ¹⁸Then Jesus spoke harshly to the demon. And it came out of the child, who was healed from that time on.

¹⁹Then the disciples came to Jesus in private and said, "Why couldn't we throw the demon out?"

²⁰"Because you have little faith," he said. "I assure you that if you have faith the size of a mustard seed, you could say to this mountain, 'Go from here to there,' and it will go. There will be nothing that you can't do."[u]

Second prediction of Jesus' death and resurrection

²²When the disciples came together in Galilee, Jesus said to them, "The Human One[v] is about to be delivered over into human hands. ²³They will kill him. But he will be raised on the third day." And they were heartbroken.

Paying the temple tax

²⁴When they came to Capernaum, the people who collected the half-shekel temple tax came to Peter and said, "Doesn't your teacher pay the temple tax?"

²⁵"Yes," he said.

But when they came into the house, Jesus spoke to Peter first. "What do you think, Simon? From whom do earthly kings collect taxes, from their children or from strangers?"

²⁶"From strangers," he said.

Jesus said to him, "Then the children don't have to pay. ²⁷But just so we don't offend them, go to the lake, throw out a fishing line and hook, and take the first fish you catch. When you open its mouth, you will find a shekel coin. Take it and pay the tax for both of us."

Greatest in the kingdom

18At that time the disciples came to Jesus and asked, "Who is the greatest in the kingdom of heaven?"

²Then he called a little child over to sit among the disciples, ³and said, "I assure you that if you don't turn your lives around and become like this little child, you will definitely not enter the kingdom of heaven. ⁴Those who humble themselves like this little child will be the greatest in the kingdom of heaven. ⁵Whoever welcomes one such child in my name welcomes me.

Falling into sin

⁶"As for whoever causes these little ones who believe in me to trip and fall into sin, it would be better for them to have a huge stone hung around their necks and be drowned in the bottom of the lake. ⁷How terrible it is for the world because of the things that cause people to trip and fall into sin! Such things have to happen, but how terrible it is for the person who causes those things to happen! ⁸If your hand or your foot causes you to fall into sin, chop it off and throw it away. It's better to enter into life crippled or lame than to be thrown into the eternal fire with two hands or two feet. ⁹If your eye causes you to fall into sin, tear it out and throw it away. It's better to enter into life with one eye than to be cast into a burning hell with two eyes.

Parable of the lost sheep

¹⁰"Be careful that you don't look down on one of these little ones. I say to you that their angels in heaven are always looking into the face of my Father who is in heaven.ʷ ¹²What do you think? If someone had one hundred sheep and one of them wandered off, wouldn't he leave the ninety-nine on the hillsides and go in search for the one that wandered off? ¹³If he finds it, I assure you that he is happier about having that one sheep than about the ninety-nine who didn't wander off. ¹⁴In the same way, my Father who is in heaven doesn't want to lose one of these little ones.

Sinning brother or sister

¹⁵"If your brother or sister sins against you, go and correct them when you are alone together. If they listen to you, then you've won over your brother or sister. ¹⁶But if they won't listen, take with you one or two others so that *every word may be established by the mouth of two or three witnesses.*ˣ ¹⁷But if they still won't pay attention, report it to the church. If they won't pay attention even to the church, treat them as you would a Gentile and tax collector. ¹⁸I assure you that whatever you fasten on earth will be fastened in heaven. And whatever you loosen on earth will be loosened in heaven. ¹⁹Again I assure you that if two of you agree on earth about anything you ask, then my Father who is in heaven will do it for you. ²⁰For where two or three are gathered in my name, I'm there with them."

Parable of the unforgiving servant

²¹Then Peter said to Jesus, "Lord, how many times should I forgive my brother or sister who sins against me? Should I forgive as many as seven times?"

²²Jesus said, "Not just seven times, but rather as many as seventy-seven times.ʸ ²³Therefore, the kingdom of heaven is like a king who wanted to settle accounts with his servants. ²⁴When he began to settle accounts, they brought to him a servant who owed him ten thousand bags of gold.ᶻ ²⁵Because the servant didn't have enough to pay it back, the master ordered that he should be sold, along with his wife and children and everything he had, and that the proceeds should be used as payment. ²⁶But the servant fell down, kneeled before him, and said, 'Please, be patient with me, and I'll pay you back.' ²⁷The master had compassion on that servant, released him, and forgave the loan.

Bet you can

read this in 4 minutes. Ready, set, go!

ʷ18:11 is omitted in most critical editions of the Gk New Testament *For the Human One has come to save the lost.* ˣDeut 19:15 ʸOr *seventy times seven* ᶻOr *ten thousand talanta,* an amount equal to the wages for sixty million days

[28]"When that servant went out, he found one of his fellow servants who owed him one hundred coins.[a] He grabbed him around the throat and said, 'Pay me back what you owe me.'

[29]"Then his fellow servant fell down and begged him, 'Be patient with me, and I'll pay you back.' [30]But he refused. Instead, he threw him into prison until he paid back his debt.

[31]"When his fellow servants saw what happened, they were deeply offended. They came and told their master all that happened. [32]His master called the first servant and said, 'You wicked servant! I forgave you all that debt because you appealed to me. [33]Shouldn't you also have mercy on your fellow servant, just as I had mercy on you?' [34]His master was furious and handed him over to the guard responsible for punishing prisoners, until he had paid the whole debt.

[35]"My heavenly Father will also do the same to you if you don't forgive your brother or sister from your heart."

Teaching about divorce

19 When Jesus finished saying these things, he left Galilee and came to the area of Judea on the east side of the Jordan. [2]Large crowds followed him, and he healed them. [3]Some Pharisees came to him. In order to test him, they said, "Does the Law allow a man to divorce his wife for just any reason?"

[4]Jesus answered, "Haven't you read that at the beginning the creator *made them male and female*?[b] [5]And God said, '*Because of this a man should leave his father and mother and be joined together with his wife, and the two will be one flesh.*'[c] [6]So they are no longer two but one flesh. Therefore, humans must not pull apart what God has put together."

[7]The Pharisees said to him, "Then why did Moses command us to *give a divorce certificate and divorce her*?"[d]

[8]Jesus replied, "Moses allowed you to divorce your wives because your hearts are unyielding. But it wasn't that way from the beginning. [9]I say to you that whoever divorces his wife, except for sexual unfaithfulness, and marries another woman commits adultery."

[10]His disciples said to him, "If that's the way things are between a man and his wife, then it's better not to marry."

[11]He replied, "Not everybody can accept this teaching, but only those who have received the ability to accept it. [12]For there are eunuchs who have been eunuchs from birth. And there are eunuchs who have been made eunuchs by other people. And there are eunuchs who have made themselves eunuchs because of the kingdom of heaven. Those who can accept it should accept it."

Jesus blesses children

[13]Some people brought children to Jesus so that he would place his hands on them and pray. But the disciples scolded them. [14]"Allow the children to come to me," Jesus said. "Don't forbid them, because the kingdom of heaven belongs to people like these children." [15]Then he blessed the children and went away from there.

A rich man's question

[16]A man approached him and said, "Teacher, what good thing must I do to have eternal life?"

[17]Jesus said, "Why do you ask me about what is good? There's only one who is good. If you want to enter eternal life, keep the commandments."

[18]The man said, "Which ones?"

Then Jesus said, "*Don't commit murder. Don't commit adultery. Don't steal. Don't give false testimony. [19]Honor your father and mother,*[e] and *love your neighbor as you love yourself.*"[f]

SAILBOAT

OBEDIENCE

Complete Obedience *Matthew 19:16-22*
God wants us to be completely obedient. That means not only doing the right actions on the outside, but also having the right attitude on the inside. We can't reach this level of obedience on our own. We need help. When Jesus asked the young man to come and follow him, he was offering help. ◐

---

[a]Or *one hundred denaria*, an amount equal to the wages for one hundred days   [b]Gen 1:27; 5:2   [c]Gen 2:24   [d]Deut 24:1   [e]Exod 20:12-16; Deut 5:16-20   [f]Lev 19:18

²⁰The young man replied, "I've kept all these. What am I still missing?"

²¹Jesus said, "If you want to be complete, go, sell what you own, and give the money to the poor. Then you will have treasure in heaven. And come follow me."

²²But when the young man heard this, he went away saddened, because he had many possessions.

Teaching about giving up things

²³Then Jesus said to his disciples, "I assure you that it will be very hard for a rich person to enter the kingdom of heaven. ²⁴In fact, it's easier for a camel to squeeze through the eye of a needle than for a rich person to enter God's kingdom."

²⁵When his disciples heard this, they were stunned. "Then who can be saved?" they asked.

²⁶Jesus looked at them carefully and said, "It's impossible for human beings. But all things are possible for God."

²⁷Then Peter replied, "Look, we've left everything and followed you. What will we have?"

²⁸Jesus said to them, "I assure you who have followed me that, when everything is made new, when the Human One⁸ sits on his magnificent throne, you also will sit on twelve thrones overseeing the twelve tribes of Israel. ²⁹And all who have left houses, brothers, sisters, father, mother, children, or farms because of my name will receive one hundred times more and will inherit eternal life. ³⁰But many who are first will be last. And many who are last will be first.

Memorize Matt 19:30

Workers in the vineyard

20 "The kingdom of heaven is like a landowner who went out early in the morning to hire workers for his vineyard. ²After he agreed with the workers to pay them a denarion,ʰ he sent them into his vineyard.

³"Then he went out around nine in the morning and saw others standing around the marketplace doing nothing. ⁴He said to them, 'You also go into the vineyard, and I'll pay you whatever is right.' ⁵And they went.

UMBRELLA
JEALOUSY

Not Fair? *Matthew 20:1-16*

There are many times in life when it seems as though things are not fair. When you read about this landowner paying the people who worked all day the same amount as the people who worked only a little while, you think something was wrong. However, when the landowner hired the first group of men, he promised to pay them a day's wages, and he did. He simply chose to be generous with the remaining workers. The first group hired assumed they would get more than those hired later. They were wrong, but they weren't treated unfairly. They were tangled up in the comparison trap. Comparing ourselves to others can make us jealous and frustrated. ◊

"Again around noon and then at three in the afternoon, he did the same thing. ⁶Around five in the afternoon he went and found others standing around, and he said to them, 'Why are you just standing around here doing nothing all day long?'

⁷"'Because nobody has hired us,' they replied.

"He responded, 'You also go into the vineyard.'

⁸"When evening came, the owner of the vineyard said to his manager, 'Call the workers and give them their wages, beginning with the last ones hired and moving on finally to the first.' ⁹When those who were hired at five in the afternoon came, each one received a denarion. ¹⁰Now when those hired first came, they thought they would receive more. But each of them also received a denarion. ¹¹When they received it, they grumbled against the landowner, ¹²These who were hired last worked one hour, and they received the same pay as we did even though we had to work the whole day in the hot sun.'

¹³"But he replied to one of them, 'Friend, I did you no wrong. Didn't I agree to pay you a denarion? ¹⁴Take what belongs to you and go. I want to give to this one who was hired last the same as I give to you. ¹⁵Don't I have the

---

⁸Or *Son of Man*   ʰA denarion was a typical day's wage.

right to do what I want with what belongs to me? Or are you resentful because I'm generous?' ¹⁶So those who are last will be first. And those who are first will be last."

Jesus predicts his death and resurrection

¹⁷As Jesus was going up to Jerusalem, he took the Twelve aside by themselves on the road. He told them, ¹⁸"Look, we are going up to Jerusalem. The Human One[i] will be handed over to the chief priests and legal experts. They will condemn him to death. ¹⁹They will hand him over to the Gentiles to be ridiculed, tortured, and crucified. But he will be raised on the third day."

Request from James and John's mother

²⁰Then the mother of Zebedee's sons came to Jesus along with her sons. Bowing before him, she asked a favor of him.

²¹"What do you want?" he asked.

She responded, "Say that these two sons of mine will sit, one on your right hand and one on your left, in your kingdom."

²²Jesus replied, "You don't know what you're asking! Can you drink from the cup that I'm about to drink from?"

They said to him, "We can."

²³He said to them, "You will drink from my cup, but to sit at my right or left hand isn't mine to give. It belongs to those for whom my Father prepared it."

did you know? When a king entered a city, he rode either on a white horse to show he came to conquer the city, or on a donkey to show he came in peace. Zechariah 9:9 promised the new king of Jerusalem would enter Jerusalem on a donkey's colt.

²⁴Now when the other ten disciples heard about this, they became angry with the two brothers. ²⁵But Jesus called them over and said, "You know that those who rule the Gentiles show off their authority over them and their high-ranking officials order them around. ²⁶But that's not the way it will be with you. Whoever wants to be great among you will be your servant. ²⁷Whoever wants to

be first among you will be your slave—²⁸just as the Human One[j] didn't come to be served but rather to serve and to give his life to liberate many people."

Healing of two blind men

²⁹As Jesus and his disciples were going out of Jericho a large crowd followed him. ³⁰When two blind men sitting along the road heard that Jesus was passing by, they shouted, "Show us mercy, Lord, Son of David!"

³¹Now the crowd scolded them and told them to be quiet. But they shouted even louder, "Show us mercy, Lord, Son of David!"

³²Jesus stopped in his tracks and called to them. "What do you want me to do for you?" he asked.

³³"Lord, we want to see," they replied.

³⁴Jesus had compassion on them and touched their eyes. Immediately they were able to see, and they followed him.

Entry into Jerusalem

21 When they approached Jerusalem and came to Bethphage on the Mount of Olives, Jesus gave two disciples a task. ²He said to them, "Go into the village over there. As soon as you enter, you will find a donkey tied up and a colt with it. Untie them and bring them to me. ³If anyone says anything to you, say that their master needs them." He sent them off right away. ⁴Now this happened to fulfill what the prophet said, ⁵*Say to Daughter Zion, "Look, your king is coming to you, humble and riding on a donkey, and on a colt the donkey's offspring."*[k] ⁶The disciples went and did just as Jesus had ordered them. ⁷They brought the donkey and the colt and laid their clothes on them. Then he sat on them.

⁸Now a large crowd spread their clothes on the road. Others cut palm branches off the trees and spread them on the road. ⁹The crowds in front of him and behind him shouted, "*Hosanna* to the Son of David! *Blessings on the one who comes in the name of the Lord!*[l] *Hosanna* in the highest!" ¹⁰And when Jesus entered Jerusalem, the whole city was stirred up. "Who is this?" they asked. ¹¹The crowds answered, "It's the prophet Jesus from Nazareth in Galilee."

---

[i]Or *Son of Man* [j]Or *Son of Man* [k]Isa 62:11; Zech 9:9 [l]Ps 118:26

Cleansing the temple

Bet you can *read this in 1 minute. Ready, set, go!*

¹²Then Jesus went into the temple and threw out all those who were selling and buying there. He pushed over the tables used for currency exchange and the chairs of those who sold doves. ¹³He said to them, "It's written, *My house will be called a house of prayer.*ᵐ But you've made it a hideout for crooks."

¹⁴People who were blind and lame came to Jesus in the temple, and he healed them. ¹⁵But when the chief priests and legal experts saw the amazing things he was doing and the children shouting in the temple, "*Hosanna* to the Son of David!" they were angry. ¹⁶They said to Jesus, "Do you hear what these children are saying?"

"Yes," he answered. "Haven't you ever read, *From the mouths of babies and infants you've arranged praise for yourself?*ⁿ ¹⁷Then he left them and went out of the city to Bethany and spent the night there.

Cursing the fig tree

¹⁸Early in the morning as Jesus was returning to the city, he was hungry. ¹⁹He saw a fig tree along the road, but when he came to it, he found nothing except leaves. Then he said to it, "You'll never again bear fruit!" The fig tree dried up at once.

²⁰When the disciples saw it, they were amazed. "How did the fig tree dry up so fast?" they asked.

²¹Jesus responded, "I assure you that if you have faith and don't doubt, you will not only do what was done to the fig tree. You will even say to this mountain, 'Be lifted up and thrown into the lake.' And it will happen. ²²If you have faith, you will receive whatever you pray for."

Jesus' authority questioned

²³When Jesus entered the temple, the chief priests and elders of the people came to him as he was teaching. They asked, "What kind of authority do you have for doing these things? Who gave you this authority?"

²⁴Jesus replied, "I have a question for you. If you tell me the answer, I'll tell you what kind of authority I have to do these things. ²⁵Where did John get his authority to baptize? Did he get it from heaven or from humans?"

They argued among themselves, "If we say 'from heaven,' he'll say to us, 'Then why didn't you believe him?' ²⁶But we can't say 'from humans' because we're afraid of the crowd, since everyone thinks John was a prophet." ²⁷Then they replied, "We don't know."

Jesus also said to them, "Neither will I tell you what kind of authority I have to do these things.

Parable of two sons

²⁸"What do you think? A man had two sons. Now he came to the first and said, 'Son, go and work in the vineyard today.'

²⁹'No, I don't want to,' he replied. But later he changed his mind and went.

³⁰"The father said the same thing to the other son, who replied, 'Yes, sir.' But he didn't go.

³¹"Which one of these two did his father's will?"

They said, "The first one."

Jesus said to them, "I assure you that tax collectors and prostitutes are entering God's kingdom ahead of you. ³²For John came to you on the righteous road, and you didn't believe him. But tax collectors and prostitutes believed him. Yet even after you saw this, you didn't change your hearts and lives and you didn't believe him.

Parable of the tenant farmers

³³"Listen to another parable. There was a landowner who planted a vineyard. He put a fence around it, dug a winepress in it, and built a tower. Then he rented it to tenant farmers and took a trip. ³⁴When it was time for harvest, he sent his servants to the tenant farmers to collect his fruit. ³⁵But the tenant farmers grabbed his servants. They beat some of them, and some of them they killed. Some of them they stoned to death.

³⁶"Again he sent other servants, more than the first group. They treated them in the same way. ³⁷Finally he sent his son to them. 'They will respect my son,' he said.

³⁸"But when the tenant farmers saw the son, they said to each other, 'This is the heir. Come on, let's kill him and we'll have his

inheritance.' ³⁹They grabbed him, threw him out of the vineyard, and killed him.

⁴⁰"When the owner of the vineyard comes, what will he do to those tenant farmers?"

⁴¹They said, "He will totally destroy those wicked farmers and rent the vineyard to other tenant farmers who will give him the fruit when it's ready."

⁴²Jesus said to them, "Haven't you ever read in the scriptures, *The stone that the builders rejected has become the cornerstone. The Lord has done this, and it's amazing in our eyes?*^o ⁴³Therefore, I tell you that God's kingdom will be taken away from you and will be given to a people who produce its fruit. ⁴⁴Whoever falls on this stone will be crushed. And the stone will crush the person it falls on."

⁴⁵Now when the chief priests and the Pharisees heard the parable, they knew Jesus was talking about them. ⁴⁶They were trying to arrest him, but they feared the crowds, who thought he was a prophet.

Parable of the wedding party

22 Jesus responded by speaking again in parables: ²"The kingdom of heaven is like a king who prepared a wedding party for his son. ³He sent his servants to call those invited to the wedding party. But they didn't want to come. ⁴Again he sent other servants and said to them, 'Tell those who have been invited, "Look, the meal is all prepared. I've butchered the oxen and the fattened cattle. Now everything's ready. Come to the wedding party!"' ⁵But they paid no attention and went away—some to their fields, others to their businesses. ⁶The rest of them grabbed his servants, abused them, and killed them.

⁷"The king was angry. He sent his soldiers to destroy those murderers and set their city on fire. ⁸Then he said to his servants, 'The wedding party is prepared, but those who were invited weren't worthy. ⁹Therefore, go to the roads on the edge of town and invite everyone you find to the wedding party.' ¹⁰"Then those servants went to the roads and gathered everyone they found, both evil and good. The wedding party was full of guests. ¹¹Now when the king came in and saw the guests, he spotted a man who wasn't wearing wedding clothes. ¹²He said to him, 'Friend, how did you get in here without wedding clothes?' But he was speechless. ¹³Then the king said to his servants, 'Tie his hands and feet and throw him out into the farthest darkness. People there will be weeping and grinding their teeth.'

¹⁴"Many people are invited, but few people are chosen."

Question about taxes

¹⁵Then the Pharisees met together to find a way to trap Jesus in his words. ¹⁶They sent their disciples, along with the supporters of Herod, to him. "Teacher," they said, "we know that you are genuine and that you teach God's way as it really is. We know that you are not swayed by people's opinions, because you don't show favoritism. ¹⁷So tell us what you think: Does the Law allow people to pay taxes to Caesar or not?"

¹⁸Knowing their evil motives, Jesus replied, "Why do you test me, you hypocrites? ¹⁹Show me the coin used to pay the tax." And they brought him a denarion. ²⁰"Whose image and inscription is this?" he asked.

²¹"Caesar's," they replied.

Then he said, "Give to Caesar what belongs to Caesar and to God what belongs to God." ²²When they heard this they were astonished, and they departed.

Question about resurrection

²³That same day Sadducees, who deny that there is a resurrection, came to Jesus. ²⁴They asked, "Teacher, Moses said, *If a man who doesn't have children dies, his brother must marry his wife and produce children for his brother.*^p ²⁵Now there were seven brothers among us. The first one married, then died. Because he had no children he left his widow to his brother. ²⁶The same thing happened with the second brother and the third, and in fact with all seven brothers. ²⁷Finally, the woman died. ²⁸At the resurrection, which of the seven brothers will be her husband? They were all married to her."

²⁹Jesus responded, "You are wrong because you don't know either the scriptures or God's

^oPs 118:22-23 ^pDeut 25:5

power. 30At the resurrection people won't
marry nor will they be given in marriage. Instead, they will be like angels from God. 31As
for the resurrection of the dead, haven't you
read what God told you, 32*I'm the God of Abraham, the God of Isaac, and the God of Jacob?*[q]
He isn't the God of the dead but of the living."
33Now when the crowd heard this, they were
astonished at his teaching.

Great commandment

34When the Pharisees heard that Jesus
had left the Sadducees speechless, they met
together. 35One of them, a legal expert, tested
him. 36"Teacher, what is the greatest commandment in the Law?"

37He replied, *"You must love the Lord your
God with all your heart, with all your being,*[r]
and with all your mind. 38This is the first and
greatest commandment. 39And the second is
like it: *You must love your neighbor as you
love yourself.*[s] 40All the Law and the Prophets
depend on these two commands."

Question about David's son

41Now as the Pharisees were gathering,
Jesus asked them, 42"What do you think about
the Christ? Whose son is he?"

"David's son," they replied.

43He said, "Then how is it that David, inspired by the Holy Spirit, called him Lord
when he said, 44*The Lord said to my lord, 'Sit
at my right side until I turn your enemies into
your footstool'?*[t] 45If David calls him Lord,
how can he be David's son?" 46Nobody was
able to answer him. And from that day forward nobody dared to ask him anything.

Ways of the legal experts and the Pharisees

23 Then Jesus spoke to the crowds and
his disciples, 2"The legal experts and
the Pharisees sit on Moses' seat. 3Therefore,
you must take care to do everything they
say. But don't do what they do. 4For they tie
together heavy packs that are impossible to
carry. They put them on the shoulders of others, but are unwilling to lift a finger to move

LIFE PRESERVER

Why is the great commandment important?

Matthew 22:34-40

The religious leaders tested Jesus repeatedly. They thought they could catch him making a mistake. In this story they asked him a legal question. The Pharisees and the Sadducees were proud that they knew religious law.

To answer them, Jesus quoted Deuteronomy 6:5, which says we should love God with all our heart, being, and mind. But then Jesus surprised them by adding a second commandment about loving our neighbor. When you think about everything Jesus was trying to teach his followers, it's really all about these two commandments—love God and love your neighbor. Together we call these the great commandment.

them. 5Everything they do, they do to be noticed by others. They make extra-wide prayer
bands for their arms and long tassels for their
clothes. 6They love to sit in places of honor at
banquets and in the synagogues. 7They love
to be greeted with honor in the markets and
to be addressed as 'Rabbi.'

8"But you shouldn't be called *Rabbi*, because you have one teacher, and all of you
are brothers and sisters. 9Don't call anybody
on earth your father, because you have one
Father, who is heavenly. 10Don't be
called *teacher*, because Christ is
your one teacher. 11But
the one who is great-
est among you will be your servant. 12All who
lift themselves up will be brought low. But all
who make themselves low will be lifted up.

Memorize Matt 23:11-12

Condemnation of the legal experts and the Pharisees

13"How terrible it will be for you legal experts and Pharisees! Hypocrites! You shut
people out of the kingdom of heaven. You
don't enter yourselves, and you won't allow
those who want to enter to do so.[u]

15"How terrible it will be for you, legal experts and Pharisees! Hypocrites! You travel

[q]Exod 3:6, 15-16 [r]Deut 6:5 [s]Lev 19:18 [t]Ps 110:1 [u]Most critical editions of the Gk New Testament omit 23:14 *How terrible it will be for you legal experts and Pharisees! Hypocrites! You eat up widows' houses and make a show of praying long prayers. Therefore, you will receive greater judgment.*

over sea and land to make one convert. But when they've been converted, they become twice the child of hell you are.

[16]"How terrible it will be for you blind guides who say, 'If people swear by the temple, it's nothing. But if people swear by the gold in the temple, they are obligated to do what they swore.' [17]You foolish and blind people! Which is greater, the gold or the temple that makes the gold holy? [18]You say, 'If people swear by the altar, it's nothing. But if they swear by the gift on the altar, they are obligated to do what they swore.' [19]You blind people! Which is greater, the gift or the altar that makes the gift holy? [20]Therefore, those who swear by the altar swear by it and by everything that's on it. [21]Those who swear by the temple swear by it and by everything that's part of it. [22]Those who swear by heaven swear by God's throne and by the one who sits on it.

[23]"How terrible it will be for you legal experts and Pharisees! Hypocrites! You give to God a tenth of mint, dill, and cumin, but you forget about the more important matters of the Law: justice, peace, and faith. You ought to give a tenth but without forgetting about those more important matters. [24]You blind guides! You filter out an ant but swallow a camel.

[25]"How terrible it will be for you legal experts and Pharisees! Hypocrites! You clean the outside of the cup and plate, but inside they are full of violence and pleasure seeking. [26]Blind Pharisee! First clean the inside of the cup so that the outside of the cup will be clean too.

[27]"How terrible it will be for you legal experts and Pharisees! Hypocrites! You are like whitewashed tombs. They look beautiful on the outside. But inside they are full of dead bones and all kinds of filth. [28]In the same way you look righteous to people. But inside you are full of pretense and rebellion.

[29]"How terrible it will be for you legal experts and Pharisees! Hypocrites! You build tombs for the prophets and decorate the graves of the righteous. [30]You say, 'If we had lived in our ancestors' days, we wouldn't have joined them in killing the prophets.' [31]You testify against yourselves that you are children of those who murdered the prophets.

[32]Go ahead, complete what your ancestors did. [33]You snakes! You children of snakes! How will you be able to escape the judgment of hell? [34]Therefore, look, I'm sending you prophets, wise people, and legal experts. Some of them you will kill and crucify. And some you will beat in your synagogues and chase from city to city. [35]Therefore, upon you will come all the righteous blood that has been poured out on the earth, from the blood of that righteous man Abel to the blood of Zechariah the son of Barachiah, whom you killed between the temple and the altar. [36]I assure you that all these things will come upon this generation.

Crying over Jerusalem

[37]"Jerusalem, Jerusalem! You who kill the prophets and stone those who were sent to you. How often I wanted to gather your people together, just as a hen gathers her chicks under her wings. But you didn't want that. [38]Look, your house is left to you deserted. [39]I tell you, you won't see me until you say, *Blessings on the one who comes in the Lord's name.*"[v]

The temple's fate

24 Now Jesus left the temple and was going away. His disciples came to point out to him the temple buildings. [2]He responded, "Do you see all these things? I assure that no stone will be left on another. Everything will be demolished."

Beginning of troubles

[3]Now while Jesus was sitting on the Mount of Olives, the disciples came to him privately and said, "Tell us, when will these things happen? What will be the sign of your coming and the end of the age?"

[4]Jesus replied, "Watch out that no one deceives you. [5]Many will come in my name, saying, 'I'm the Christ.' They will deceive many people. [6]You will hear about wars and reports of wars. Don't be alarmed. These things must happen, but this isn't the end yet. [7]Nations and kingdoms will fight against each other, and there will be famines and earthquakes in all sorts of places. [8]But all these things are just

the beginning of the sufferings associated with the end. [9]They will arrest you, abuse you, and they will kill you. All nations will hate you on account of my name. [10]At that time many will fall away. They will betray each other and hate each other. [11]Many false prophets will appear and deceive many people. [12]Because disobedience will expand, the love of many will grow cold. [13]But the one who endures to the end will be delivered. [14]This gospel of the kingdom will be proclaimed throughout the world as a testimony to all the nations. Then the end will come.

The great suffering

[15]"When you see the disgusting and destructive thing that Daniel talked about standing in the holy place (the reader should understand this), [16]then those in Judea must escape to the mountains. [17]Those on the roof shouldn't come down to grab things from their houses. [18]Those in the field shouldn't come back to grab their clothes. [19]How terrible it will be at that time for women who are pregnant and for women who are nursing their children. [20]Pray that it doesn't happen in winter or on the Sabbath day. [21]There will be great suffering such as the world has never before seen and will never again see. [22]If that time weren't shortened, nobody would be rescued. But for the sake of the ones whom God chose, that time will be cut short.

[23]"Then if somebody says to you, 'Look, here's the Christ,' or 'He's over here,' don't believe it. [24]False christs and false prophets will appear, and they will offer great signs and wonders in order to deceive, if possible, even those whom God has chosen. [25]Look, I've told you ahead of time. [26]So if they say to you, 'Look, he's in the desert,' don't go out. And if they say, 'Look, he's in the rooms deep inside the house,' don't believe it. [27]Just as the lightning flashes from the east to the west, so it will be with the coming of the Human One.[w] [28]The vultures gather wherever there's a dead body.

Coming of the Human One

[29]"Now immediately after the suffering of that time the sun will become dark, and the moon won't give its light. The stars will fall from the sky and the planets and other heavenly bodies will be shaken. [30]Then the sign of the Human One[x] will appear in the sky. At that time all the tribes of the earth will be full of sadness, and they will see *the Human One[y] coming in the heavenly clouds*[z] with power and great splendor. [31]He will send his angels with the sound of a great trumpet, and they will gather his chosen ones from the four corners of the earth, from one end of the sky to the other.

A lesson from the fig tree

[32]"Learn this parable from the fig tree. After its branch becomes tender and it sprouts new leaves, you know that summer is near. [33]In the same way, when you see all these things, you know that the Human One[a] is near, at the door. [34]I assure you that this generation won't pass away until all these things happen. [35]Heaven and earth will pass away, but my words will certainly not pass away.

Day and hour

[36]"But nobody knows when that day or hour will come, not the heavenly angels and not the Son. Only the Father knows. [37]As it was in the time of Noah, so it will be at the coming of the Human One.[b] [38]In those days before the flood, people were eating and drinking, marrying and giving in marriage, until the day Noah entered the ark. [39]They didn't know what was happening until the flood came and swept them all away. The coming of the Human One[c] will be like that. [40]At that time there will be two men in the field. One will be taken and the other left. [41]Two women will be grinding at the mill. One will be taken and the other left. [42]Therefore, stay alert! You don't know what day the Lord is coming. [43]But you understand that if the head of the house knew at what time the thief would come, he would keep alert and wouldn't allow the thief to break into his house. [44]Therefore, you also should be prepared, because the Human One[d] will come at a time you don't know.

---

[w]Or Son of Man [x]Or Son of Man [y]Or Son of Man [z]Dan 7:13 *I suddenly saw one like a human being* (Aram *kebar enash*) *coming with the heavenly clouds.* [a]Or Son of Man [b]Or Son of Man [c]Or Son of Man [d]Or Son of Man

Faithful and unfaithful servants

⁴⁵"Who then are the faithful and wise servants whom their master puts in charge of giving food at the right time to those who live in his house? ⁴⁶Happy are those servants whom the master finds fulfilling their responsibilities when he comes. ⁴⁷I assure you that he will put them in charge of all his possessions. ⁴⁸But suppose those bad servants should say to themselves, My master won't come until later. ⁴⁹And suppose they began to beat their fellow servants and to eat and drink with the drunks? ⁵⁰The master of those servants will come on a day when they are not expecting him, at a time they couldn't predict. ⁵¹He will cut them in pieces and put them in a place with the hypocrites. People there will be weeping and grinding their teeth.

Parable of the ten young bridesmaids

25 "At that time the kingdom of heaven will be like ten young bridesmaids who took their lamps and went out to meet the groom. ²Now five of them were wise, and the other five were foolish. ³The foolish ones took their lamps but didn't bring oil for them. ⁴But the wise ones took their lamps and also brought containers of oil.

⁵"When the groom was late in coming, they all became drowsy and went to sleep. ⁶But at midnight there was a cry, 'Look, the groom! Come out to meet him.'

⁷"Then all those bridesmaids got up and prepared their lamps. ⁸But the foolish bridesmaids said to the wise ones, 'Give us some of your oil, because our lamps have gone out.'

⁹"But the wise bridesmaids replied, 'No, because if we share with you, there won't be enough for our lamps and yours. We have a better idea. You go to those who sell oil and buy some for yourselves.' ¹⁰But while they were gone to buy oil, the groom came. Those who were ready went with him into the wedding. Then the door was shut.

¹¹"Later the other bridesmaids came and said, 'Lord, lord, open the door for us.'

¹²"But he replied, 'I tell you the truth, I don't know you.'

¹³"Therefore, keep alert, because you don't know the day or the hour.

Parable of the valuable coins

¹⁴"The kingdom of heaven is like a man who was leaving on a trip. He called his servants and handed his possessions over to them. ¹⁵To one he gave five valuable coins,ᵉ and to another he gave two, and to another he gave one. He gave to each servant according to that servant's ability. Then he left on his journey.

¹⁶"After the man left, the servant who had five valuable coins took them and went to work doing business with them. He gained five more. ¹⁷In the same way, the one who had two valuable coins gained two more. ¹⁸But the servant who had received the one valuable coin dug a hole in the ground and buried his master's money.

¹⁹"Now after a long time the master of those servants returned and settled accounts with them. ²⁰The one who had received five valuable coins came forward with five additional coins. He said, 'Master, you gave me five valuable coins. Look, I've gained five more.'

²¹"His master replied, 'Excellent! You are a good and faithful servant! You've been faithful over a little. I'll put you in charge of much. Come, celebrate with me.'

²²"The second servant also came forward and said, 'Master, you gave me two valuable coins. Look, I've gained two more.'

UMBRELLA
FEAR

Fear Not! *Matthew 25:14-30*

Taking risks is a normal, healthy part of living for God. Although God doesn't tell us exactly how things are going to turn out, God asks us to trust. In this parable, the first two servants took risks and received the same words of appreciation from the master even though their results were different from each other. The third servant, who had less to lose, played it safe. He thought he would be praised for losing nothing. Instead, he got in trouble for not taking a risk. He made a bad choice because he was afraid. Fear can paralyze us, leaving us too scared to try something new. ◆

ᵉOr *talantas* (talents)

²³"His master replied, 'Well done! You are a good and faithful servant. You've been faithful over a little. I'll put you in charge of much. Come, celebrate with me.'

²⁴"Now the one who had received one valuable coin came and said, 'Master, I knew that you are a hard man. You harvest grain where you haven't sown. You gather crops where you haven't spread seed. ²⁵So I was afraid. And I hid my valuable coin in the ground. Here, you have what's yours.'

²⁶"His master replied, 'You evil and lazy servant! You knew that I harvest grain where I haven't sown and that I gather crops where I haven't spread seed? ²⁷In that case, you should have turned my money over to the bankers so that when I returned, you could give me what belonged to me with interest. ²⁸Therefore, take from him the valuable coin and give it to the one who has ten coins. ²⁹Those who have much will receive more, and they will have more than they need. But as for those who don't have much, even the little bit they have will be taken away from them. ³⁰Now take the worthless servant and throw him outside into the darkness.'

"People there will be weeping and grinding their teeth.

Judgment of the nations

³¹"Now when the Human One^f comes in his majesty and all his angels are with him, he will sit on his majestic throne. ³²All the nations will be gathered in front of him. He will separate them from each other, just as a shepherd separates the sheep from the goats. ³³He will put the sheep on his right side. But the goats he will put on his left.

³⁴"Then the king will say to those on his right, 'Come, you who will receive good things from my Father. Inherit the kingdom that was prepared for you before the world began. ³⁵I was hungry and you gave me food to eat. I was thirsty and you gave me a drink. I was a stranger and you welcomed me. ³⁶I was naked and you gave me clothes to wear. I was sick and you took care of me. I was in prison and you visited me.'

³⁷"Then those who are righteous will reply to him, 'Lord, when did we see you hungry and feed you, or thirsty and give you a drink? ³⁸When did we see you as a stranger and welcome you, or naked and give you clothes to wear? ³⁹When did we see you sick or in prison and visit you?'

⁴⁰"Then the king will reply to them, 'I assure you that when you have done it for one of the least of these brothers and sisters of mine, you have done it for me.'

⁴¹"Then he will say to those on his left, 'Get away from me, you who will receive terrible things. Go into the unending fire that has been prepared for the devil and his angels. ⁴²I was hungry and you didn't give me food to eat. I was thirsty and you didn't give me anything to drink. ⁴³I was a stranger and you didn't welcome me. I was naked and you didn't give me clothes to wear. I was sick and in prison, and you didn't visit me.'

⁴⁴"Then they will reply, 'Lord, when did we see you hungry or thirsty or a stranger or naked or sick or in prison and didn't do anything to help you?' ⁴⁵Then he will answer, 'I assure you that when you haven't done it for one of the least of these, you haven't done it for me.' ⁴⁶And they will go away into eternal punishment. But the righteous ones will go into eternal life."

Plot to kill Jesus

26 When Jesus finished speaking all these words, he said to his disciples, ²"You know that the Passover is two days from now. And the Human One^g will be handed over to be crucified."

³Then the chief priests and elders of the people gathered in the courtyard of Caiaphas the high priest. ⁴They were plotting to arrest Jesus by cunning tricks and to kill him. ⁵But they agreed that it shouldn't happen during the feast so there wouldn't be an uproar among the people.

A woman pouring perfume on Jesus

⁶When Jesus was at Bethany visiting the house of Simon, who had a skin disease, ⁷a woman came to him with a vase made of alabaster containing very expensive perfume. She poured it on Jesus' head while he was sitting at dinner. ⁸Now when the disciples saw it

---

^f Or *Son of Man* ^g Or *Son of Man*

they were angry and said, "Why this waste? ⁹This perfume could have been sold for a lot of money and given to the poor."

¹⁰But Jesus knew what they were thinking. He said, "Why do you make trouble for the woman? She's done a good thing for me. ¹¹You always have the poor with you, but you won't always have me. ¹²By pouring this perfume over my body she's prepared me to be buried. ¹³I tell you the truth that wherever in the whole world this good news is announced, what she's done will also be told in memory of her."

Judas betrays Jesus

¹⁴Then one of the Twelve, who was called Judas Iscariot, went to the chief priests ¹⁵and said, "What will you give me if I turn Jesus over to you?" They paid him thirty pieces of silver. ¹⁶From that time on he was looking for an opportunity to turn him in.

Passover with the disciples

¹⁷On the first day of the Festival of Unleavened Bread, the disciples came to Jesus and said, "Where do you want us to prepare for you to eat the Passover meal?"

¹⁸He replied, "Go into the city, to a certain man, and say, 'The teacher says, "My time is near. I'm going to celebrate the Passover with my disciples at your house." '" ¹⁹The disciples did just as Jesus instructed them. They prepared the Passover.

²⁰That evening he took his place at the table with the twelve disciples. ²¹As they were eating he said, "I assure you that one of you will betray me."

²²Deeply saddened, each one said to him, "I'm not the one, am I, Lord?"

²³He replied, "The one who will betray me is the one who dips his hand with me into this bowl. ²⁴The Human One[h] goes to his death just as it is written about him. But how terrible it is for that person who betrays the Human One![i] It would have been better for him if he had never been born."

²⁵Now Judas, who would betray him, replied, "It's not me, is it, Rabbi?"

Jesus answered, "You said it."

LIFE PRESERVER

What is Passover?
Matthew 26:17-19

Passover is a Jewish holy day that has been celebrated by faithful Jews since Bible times. On Passover, the people remember how God saved them when they were in slavery in Egypt, passing over their houses in the final plague. During Passover, people retell the story of their exodus from Egypt. At a Passover meal the people eat *matzah*, which is bread that has no yeast in it. Sometimes this is also called *unleavened* bread. It is part of the Passover meal because bread didn't have time to rise when the Israelites left Egypt quickly. Also on the table is a small bowl of bitter herbs to represent when the Israelites were slaves in Egypt.

Jesus gathered with the disciples to celebrate Passover. Then he added something to this meal. He wanted them to remember the story of his presence with them. Jesus told his disciples that when they broke bread together they should remember his body, and when they drank wine together they should remember the life that he gave for them. ◆

Last supper

²⁶While they were eating, Jesus took bread, blessed it, broke it, and gave it to the disciples and said, "Take and eat. This is my body." ²⁷He took a cup, gave thanks, and gave it to them, saying, "Drink from this, all of you. ²⁸This is my blood of the covenant, which is poured out for many so that their sins may be forgiven. ²⁹I tell you, I won't drink wine again until that day when I drink it in a new way with you in my Father's kingdom." ³⁰Then, after singing songs of praise, they went to the Mount of Olives.

Predictions about disciples leaving Jesus

³¹Then Jesus said to his disciples, "Tonight you will all fall away because of me. This is because it is written, *I will hit the shepherd, and the sheep of the flock will go off in all directions.*[j] ³²But after I'm raised up, I'll go before you to Galilee."

³³Peter replied, "If everyone else stumbles because of you, I'll never stumble."

³⁴Jesus said to him, "I assure you that, before the rooster crows tonight, you will deny me three times."

---

[h]Or *Son of Man* [i]Or *Son of Man* [j]Zech 13:7

[35]Peter said, "Even if I must die alongside you, I won't deny you." All the disciples said the same thing.

Jesus in prayer

[36]Then Jesus went with his disciples to a place called Gethsemane. He said to the disciples, "Stay here while I go and pray over there." [37]When he took Peter and Zebedee's two sons, he began to feel sad and anxious. [38]Then he said to them, "I'm very sad. It's as if I'm dying. Stay here and keep alert with me." [39]Then he went a short distance farther and fell on his face and prayed, "My Father, if it's possible, take this cup of suffering away from me. However—not what I want but what you want."

[40]He came back to the disciples and found them sleeping. He said to Peter, "Couldn't you stay alert one hour with me? [41]Stay alert and pray so that you won't give in to temptation. The spirit is eager, but the flesh is weak." [42]A second time he went away and prayed, "My Father, if it's not possible that this cup be taken away unless I drink it, then let it be what you want."

UMBRELLA
TEMPTED

Alert and Praying Matthew 26:41
We can all use the advice Jesus gave to Peter. We may not be facing death, but we all face the temptation to take the easy way. Jesus told Peter to be alert in addition to being awake. All we need to do to show we're awake is to keep our eyes open. But being alert means something more. When we're alert, we look around and listen. We're aware of our surroundings. When we're alert, we also know what things to pray about. Jesus knew Peter would give in to the temptation coming his way, but that didn't stop Jesus from offering Peter the help he needed. ◖

[43]Again he came and found them sleeping. Their eyes were heavy with sleep. [44]But he left them and again went and prayed the same words for the third time. [45]Then he

came to his disciples and said to them, "Will you sleep and rest all night? Look, the time has come for the Human One[k] to be betrayed into the hands of sinners. [46]Get up. Let's go. Look, here comes my betrayer."

Arrest

[47]While Jesus was still speaking, Judas, one of the Twelve, came. With him was a large crowd carrying swords and clubs. They had been sent by the chief priests and elders of the people. [48]His betrayer had given them a sign: "Arrest the man I kiss." [49]Just then he came to Jesus and said, "Hello, Rabbi." Then he kissed him.

[50]But Jesus said to him, "Friend, do what you came to do." Then they came and grabbed Jesus and arrested him.

[51]One of those with Jesus reached for his sword. Striking the high priest's slave, he cut off his ear. [52]Then Jesus said to him, "Put the sword back into its place. All those who use the sword will die by the sword. [53]Or do you think that I'm not able to ask my Father and he will send to me more than twelve battle groups[l] of angels right away? [54]But if I did that, how would the scriptures be fulfilled that say this must happen?" [55]Then Jesus said to the crowds, "Have you come with swords and clubs to arrest me, like a thief? Day after day, I sat in the temple teaching, but you didn't arrest me. [56]But all this has happened so that what the prophets said in the scriptures might be fulfilled." Then all the disciples left Jesus and ran away.

Jesus before the council

[57]Those who arrested Jesus led him to Caiaphas the high priest. The legal experts and the elders had gathered there. [58]Peter followed him from a distance until he came to the high priest's courtyard. He entered that area and sat outside with the officers to see how it would turn out.

[59]The chief priests and the whole council were looking for false testimony against Jesus so that they could put him to death. [60]They didn't find anything they could use from the many false witnesses who were willing to come forward. But finally they found

[k]Or Son of Man [l]Or legions (of the Roman army, about five thousand soldiers each)

two ⁶¹who said, "This man said, 'I can destroy God's temple and rebuild it in three days.'"

⁶²Then the high priest stood and said to Jesus, "Aren't you going to respond to the testimony these people have brought against you?"

⁶³But Jesus was silent.

The high priest said, "By the living God, I demand that you tell us whether you are the Christ, God's Son."

⁶⁴"You said it," Jesus replied. "But I say to you that from now on you'll see *the Human One*ᵐ *sitting on the right side of the Almighty*ⁿ *and coming on the heavenly clouds.*"ᵒ

⁶⁵Then the high priest tore his clothes and said, "He's insulting God! Why do we need any more witnesses? Look, you've heard his insult against God. ⁶⁶What do you think?"

And they answered, "He deserves to die!" ⁶⁷Then they spit in his face and beat him. They hit him ⁶⁸and said, "Prophesy for us, Christ! Who hit you?"

Peter's denial

⁶⁹Meanwhile, Peter was sitting outside in the courtyard. A servant woman came and said to him, "You were also with Jesus the Galilean."

⁷⁰But he denied it in front of all of them, saying, "I don't know what you are talking about."

⁷¹When he went over to the gate, another woman saw him and said to those who were there, "This man was with Jesus, the man from Nazareth."

⁷²With a solemn pledge, he denied it again, saying, "I don't know the man."

⁷³A short time later those standing there came and said to Peter, "You must be one of them. The way you talk gives you away."

⁷⁴Then he cursed and swore, "I don't know the man!" At that very moment the rooster crowed. ⁷⁵Peter remembered Jesus' words, "Before the rooster crows you will deny me three times." And Peter went out and cried uncontrollably.

Jesus before Pilate

27Early in the morning all the chief priests and the elders of the people reached the decision to have Jesus put to death. ²They bound him, led him away, and turned him over to Pilate the governor.

Judas' death

³When Judas, who betrayed Jesus, saw that Jesus was condemned to die, he felt deep regret. He returned the thirty pieces of silver to the chief priests and elders, and ⁴said, "I did wrong because I betrayed an innocent man."

But they said, "What is that to us? That's your problem." ⁵Judas threw the silver pieces into the temple and left. Then he went and hanged himself.

LIGHTHOUSE

CHANGED HEART

Regret vs. Changed Life *Matthew 27:3-5*
There is a difference between regretting something we did and truly changing our hearts and lives because of it. Judas regretted his actions. His betrayal of Jesus obviously didn't bring about the result he wanted. Judas even returned the money to the chief priests. When people change their hearts and lives, they focus on making things right—not just with the person they wronged but with God. Judas' next action leads us to think his focus still wasn't on God and forgiveness but on his sin. Regret and focusing on the wrong things we've done lead us to forget about God's forgiveness and love. When we focus on changing our hearts and lives, we learn from our mistakes and leave regret behind. 🔥

⁶The chief priests picked up the silver pieces and said, "According to the Law it's not right to put this money in the treasury. Since it was used to pay for someone's life, it's unclean." ⁷So they decided to use it to buy the potter's field where strangers could be buried. ⁸That's why that field is called "Field of Blood" to this very day. ⁹This fulfilled the words of Jeremiah the prophet: *And I took the thirty pieces of silver, the price for the one whose price had been set by some of the Israelites,* ¹⁰*and I gave them for the potter's field, as the Lord commanded me.*ᵖ

Questioned by Pilate

¹¹Jesus was brought before the governor. The governor said, "Are you the king of the Jews?"

Jesus replied, "That's what you say." ¹²But he

ᵐOr *Son of Man* ⁿOr *the Power* ᵒDan 7:13 ᵖZech 11:12-13; Jer 32:6-9 didn't answer when the chief priests and elders accused him.

¹³Then Pilate said, "Don't you hear the testimony they bring against you?" ¹⁴But he didn't answer, not even a single word. So the governor was greatly amazed.

Death sentence

¹⁵It was customary during the festival for the governor to release to the crowd one prisoner, whomever they might choose. ¹⁶At that time there was a well-known prisoner named Jesus Barabbas. ¹⁷When the crowd had come together, Pilate asked them, "Whom would you like me to release to you, Jesus Barabbas or Jesus who is called Christ?" ¹⁸He knew that the leaders of the people had handed him over because of jealousy.

did you **know?** *Golgotha* means "Skull Place." It was located outside Jerusalem near a large rock that looked like a human skull. This was the place in Jerusalem where the Romans crucified people, including Jesus.

¹⁹While he was serving as judge, his wife sent this message to him, "Leave that righteous man alone. I've suffered much today in a dream because of him."

²⁰But the chief priests and the elders persuaded the crowds to ask for Barabbas and kill Jesus. ²¹The governor said, "Which of the two do you want me to release to you?"

"Barabbas," they replied.

²²Pilate said, "Then what should I do with Jesus who is called Christ?"

They all said, "Crucify him!"

²³But he said, "Why? What wrong has he done?"

They shouted even louder, "Crucify him!"

²⁴Pilate saw that he was getting nowhere and that a riot was starting. So he took water and washed his hands in front of the crowd. "I'm innocent of this man's blood," he said. "It's your problem."

²⁵All the people replied, "Let his blood be on us and on our children." ²⁶Then he released Barabbas to them. He had Jesus whipped, then handed him over to be crucified.

Soldiers mocking Jesus

²⁷The governor's soldiers took Jesus into the governor's house, and they gathered the whole company*q* of soldiers around him. ²⁸They stripped him and put a red military coat on him. ²⁹They twisted together a crown of thorns and put it on his head. They put a stick in his right hand. Then they bowed down in front of him and mocked him, saying, "Hey! King of the Jews!" ³⁰After they spit on him, they took the stick and struck his head again and again. ³¹When they finished mocking him, they stripped him of the military coat and put his own clothes back on him. They led him away to crucify him.

Crucifixion

³²As they were going out, they found Simon, a man from Cyrene. They forced him to carry his cross. ³³When they came to a place called Golgotha, which means Skull Place, ³⁴they gave Jesus wine mixed with vinegar to drink. But after tasting it, he didn't want to drink it. ³⁵After they crucified him, they divided up his clothes among them by drawing lots. ³⁶They sat there, guarding him. ³⁷They placed above his head the charge against him. It read, "This is Jesus, the king of the Jews." ³⁸They crucified with him two outlaws, one on his right side and one on his left.

³⁹Those who were walking by insulted Jesus, shaking their heads ⁴⁰and saying, "So you were going to destroy the temple and rebuild it in three days, were you? Save yourself! If you are God's Son, come down from the cross."

did you **know?** *Crucifixion* was an extreme method of carrying out a death penalty for a person's crime. In the Roman Empire, people who caused political or religious trouble and people without civil rights were typically punished in this way. Crucifixion was ended by Constantine I in 337 CE after his conversion to Christianity.

⁴¹In the same way, the chief priests, along with the legal experts and the elders, were making fun of him, saying, ⁴²"He saved others, but he can't save himself. He's the king

*q*Or *cohort* (approximately six hundred soldiers)

of Israel, so let him come down from the cross now. Then we'll believe in him. ⁴³He trusts in God, so let God deliver him now if he wants to. He said, 'I'm God's Son.'" ⁴⁴The outlaws who were crucified with him insulted him in the same way.

Death

⁴⁵From noon until three in the afternoon the whole earth was dark. ⁴⁶At about three Jesus cried out with a loud shout, "*Eli, Eli, lama sabachthani*," which means, "My God, my God, why have you left me?"ʳ

⁴⁷After hearing him, some standing there said, "He's calling Elijah." ⁴⁸One of them ran over, took a sponge full of vinegar, and put it on a pole. He offered it to Jesus to drink.

⁴⁹But the rest of them said, "Let's see if Elijah will come and save him."

⁵⁰Again Jesus cried out with a loud shout. Then he died.

⁵¹Look, the curtain of the sanctuary was torn in two from top to bottom. The earth shook, the rocks split, ⁵²and the bodies of many holy people who had died were raised. ⁵³After Jesus' resurrection they came out of their graves and went into the holy city where they appeared to many people. ⁵⁴When the centurion and those with him who were guarding Jesus saw the earthquake and what had just happened, they were filled with awe and said, "This was certainly God's Son."

⁵⁵Many women were watching from a distance. They had followed Jesus from Galilee to serve him. ⁵⁶Among them were Mary Magdalene, Mary the mother of James and Joseph, and the mother of Zebedee's sons.

Burial

⁵⁷That evening a man named Joseph came. He was a rich man from Arimathea who had become a disciple of Jesus. ⁵⁸He came to Pilate and asked for Jesus' body. Pilate gave him permission to take it. ⁵⁹Joseph took the body, wrapped it in a clean linen cloth, ⁶⁰and laid it in his own new tomb, which he had carved out of the rock. After he rolled a large stone at the door of the tomb, he went away. ⁶¹Mary Magdalene and the other Mary were there, sitting in front of the tomb.

Guard at the tomb

⁶²The next day, which was the day after Preparation Day, the chief priests and the Pharisees gathered before Pilate. ⁶³They said, "Sir, we remember that while that deceiver was still alive he said, 'After three days I will arise.' ⁶⁴Therefore, order the grave to be sealed until the third day. Otherwise, his disciples may come and steal the body and tell the people, 'He's been raised from the dead.' This last deception will be worse than the first."

⁶⁵Pilate replied, "You have soldiers for guard duty. Go and make it as secure as you know how." ⁶⁶Then they went and secured the tomb by sealing the stone and posting the guard.

did you know? The temple curtain was an extremely large, heavy drape that separated the people from the inner sanctuary, the most holy place where the symbols of God's presence were kept in the temple.

Resurrection

28 After the Sabbath, at dawn on the first day of the week, Mary Magdalene and the other Mary came to look at the tomb. ²Look, there was a great earthquake, for an angel from the Lord came down from heaven. Coming to the stone, he rolled it away and sat on it. ³Now his face was like lightning and his clothes as white as snow. ⁴The guards were so terrified of him that they shook with fear and became like dead men. ⁵But the angel said to the women, "Don't be afraid. I know that you are looking for Jesus who was crucified. ⁶He isn't here, because he's been raised from the dead, just as he said. Come, see the place where they laid him. ⁷Now hurry, go and tell his disciples, 'He's been raised from the dead. He's going on ahead of you to Galilee. You will see him there.' I've given the message to you."

⁸With great fear and excitement, they hurried away from the tomb and ran to tell his disciples. ⁹But Jesus met them and greeted them. They came and grabbed his feet and

worshipped him. ¹⁰Then Jesus said to them, "Don't be afraid. Go and tell my brothers that I am going into Galilee. They will see me there."

Guards' report

¹¹Now as the women were on their way, some of the guards came into the city and told the chief priests everything that had happened. ¹²They met with the elders and decided to give a large sum of money to the soldiers. ¹³They told them, "Say that Jesus' disciples came at night and stole his body while you were sleeping. ¹⁴And if the governor hears about this, we will take care of it with him so you will have nothing to worry about." ¹⁵So the soldiers took the money and did as they were told. And this report has spread throughout all Judea to this very day.

Commissioning of the disciples

¹⁶Now the eleven disciples went to Galilee, to the mountain where Jesus told them to go. ¹⁷When they saw him, they worshipped him, but some doubted. ¹⁸Jesus came near and spoke to them, "I've received all authority in heaven and on earth. ¹⁹Therefore, go and make disciples of all nations, baptizing them in the name of the Father and of the Son and of the Holy Spirit, ²⁰teaching them to obey everything that I've commanded you. Look, I myself will be with you every day until the end of this present age."

did you know? This is the first place in the Bible where God the Father, God the Son, and God the Holy Spirit are mentioned together. The understanding of God relating to people in these three ways is known as *the Trinity*.

God's THOUGHTS ◆ My THOUGHTS

The Great Commission   Matthew 28:16-20

One of the best things about following Jesus is that he passed on his work to his followers. Jesus did amazing things on earth. He healed people, fed people, and made it possible for us to know God. When his time on earth was over, he passed that work on to the people who followed him—including us! We're called to continue Jesus' work in this world.

A calling is an instruction given by God, a mission to carry out. The calling of people who follow Jesus is called *the Great Commission*. Jesus called his disciples to tell the whole world about God's love for them. That's our mission too. No matter where we are or where we go, our mission is to tell other people about God's love for them.

You may not feel ready to carry out this mission, but there is a promise that goes along with it. Jesus promised that he would be with us until time ends. When we feel like we don't have what it takes to tell people about Jesus or when we get scared or confused, we can remember that Jesus promised to be with us, help us, work in us, and work through us. We can trust him to guide us as we carry out our mission.

How does it feel to know that Jesus has passed on his mission to you?

How can you tell others about Jesus?

Mark

things
YOU'LL DISCOVER

The book of Mark is an action-packed summary of the things Jesus said and did, beginning with Jesus' baptism by John the Baptist and ending with Jesus' resurrection. This book helps people learn important truths about Jesus.

people
YOU'LL MEET

Jesus—the Human One and God's Son (Mark 1–16)

John the Baptist—Jesus' cousin and a prophet who prepared people to meet Jesus (Mark 1; 6)

The Twelve—Jesus' closest disciples, including Peter, James, and John (Mark 1–16)

places
YOU'LL GO

Bethlehem (a town south of Jerusalem),
Nazareth (a town in northern Israel),
Jordan River,
Galilee (a lake and region in northern Israel),
Jerusalem,
Skull Place
(the site outside Jerusalem where Jesus was crucified)

words
YOU'LL REMEMBER

"He said to them, 'Don't be alarmed! You are looking for Jesus of Nazareth, who was crucified. He has been raised. He isn't here. Look, here's the place where they laid him'" (Mark 16:6).

Mark doesn't say anything about the birth of Jesus. Instead, it jumps right into the main action of Jesus' life, starting with the messenger promised in the Old Testament. John the Baptist was that messenger. He prepared people to meet Jesus (Mark 1:1-11).

Mark shows that Jesus wanted all people to listen to his words and obey his teachings. His first followers fished for a living. He told them, "Come, follow me…and I'll show you how to fish for people" (Mark 1:17). Those early disciples left their boats and their nets to travel and learn with Jesus.

This book is the shortest of the four Gospels (Matthew, Mark, Luke, and John). Each Gospel gives a slightly different view of Jesus' life. Mark's Gospel doesn't tell as much as other books about what Jesus taught. Instead, it highlights what he did, especially his bold actions like healings and other miracles. This book often uses the terms *right then* or *suddenly* to make stories seem as though they move quickly.

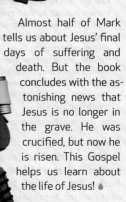

Almost half of Mark tells us about Jesus' final days of suffering and death. But the book concludes with the astonishing news that Jesus is no longer in the grave. He was crucified, but now he is risen. This Gospel helps us learn about the life of Jesus! ◊

Beginning of good news

1 The beginning of the good news about Jesus Christ, God's Son, [2] happened just as it was written about in the prophecy of Isaiah:

> Look, I am sending my messenger
> before you.
>
> He will prepare your way,
> [3] a voice shouting in the wilderness:
> "Prepare the way for the Lord;
> make his paths straight."[a]

John's preaching

[4] John the Baptist was in the wilderness calling for people to be baptized to show that they were changing their hearts and lives and wanted God to forgive their sins. [5] Everyone in Judea and all the people of Jerusalem went out to the Jordan River and were being baptized by John as they confessed their sins. [6] John wore clothes made of camel's hair, with a leather belt around his waist. He ate locusts and wild honey. [7] He announced, "One stronger than I am is coming after me. I'm not even worthy to bend over and loosen the strap of his sandals. [8] I baptize you with water, but he will baptize you with the Holy Spirit."

SAILBOAT

HUMILITY

Humility *Mark 1:7*
Sometimes when people become famous they focus on staying famous. John the Baptist did the opposite. People came from all around to see and hear him, but he wasn't interested in staying well known. Instead, he told everyone that someone even greater was coming. John said that the one who was coming was so incredible that John wasn't even good enough to help him take his shoes off. Helping people remove their shoes when they entered a house was the job of the lowest-ranking servants in the house. It was a job nobody wanted. John knew what job God had given him, and he did it with humility. ◊

Jesus is baptized and tempted

[9] About that time, Jesus came from Nazareth of Galilee, and John baptized him in the Jordan River. [10] While he was coming up out of the water, Jesus saw heaven splitting open and the Spirit, like a dove, coming down on him. [11] And there was a voice from heaven: "You are my Son, whom I dearly love; in you I find happiness."

[12] At once the Spirit forced Jesus out into the wilderness. [13] He was in the wilderness for forty days, tempted by Satan. He was among the wild animals, and the angels took care of him.

Jesus' message

[14] After John was arrested, Jesus came into Galilee announcing God's good news, [15] saying, "Now is the time! Here comes God's kingdom! Change your hearts and lives, and trust this good news!"

Jesus calls disciples

[16] As Jesus passed alongside the Galilee Sea, he saw two brothers, Simon and Andrew, throwing fishing nets into the sea, for they were fishermen. [17] "Come, follow me," he said, "and I'll show you how to fish for people." [18] Right away, they left their nets and followed him. [19] After going a little farther, he saw James and John, Zebedee's sons, in their boat repairing the fishing nets. [20] At that very moment he called them. They followed him, leaving their father Zebedee in the boat with the hired workers.

Jesus throws a demon out

[21] Jesus and his followers went into Capernaum. Immediately on the Sabbath Jesus entered the synagogue and started teaching. [22] The people were amazed by his teaching, for he was teaching them with authority, not like the legal experts. [23] Suddenly, there in the synagogue, a person with an evil spirit screamed, [24] "What have you to do with us, Jesus of Nazareth? Have you come to destroy us? I know who you are. You are the holy one from God."

[25] "Silence!" Jesus said, speaking harshly

did you know? When Jesus was baptized, Mark said the Holy Spirit came down like a dove to where Jesus was. This is why the dove is a symbol of the Holy Spirit in the church.

[a] Isa 40:3; Mal 3:1; Exod 23:20

to the demon. "Come out of him!" [26]The unclean spirit shook him and screamed, then it came out.

[27]Everyone was shaken and questioned among themselves, "What's this? A new teaching with authority! He even commands unclean spirits and they obey him!" [28]Right away the news about him spread throughout the entire region of Galilee.

Jesus heals Simon's mother-in-law

[29]After leaving the synagogue, Jesus, James, and John went home with Simon and Andrew. [30]Simon's mother-in-law was in bed, sick with a fever, and they told Jesus about her at once. [31]He went to her, took her by the hand, and raised her up. The fever left her, and she served them.

Jesus' ministry spreads

[32]That evening, at sunset, people brought to Jesus those who were sick or demon-possessed. [33]The whole town gathered near the door. [34]He healed many who were sick with all kinds of diseases, and he threw out many demons. But he didn't let the demons speak, because they recognized him.

[35]Early in the morning, well before sunrise, Jesus rose and went to a deserted place where he could be alone in prayer. [36]Simon and those with him tracked him down. [37]When they found him, they told him, "Everyone's looking for you!"

[38]He replied, "Let's head in the other direction, to the nearby villages, so that I can preach there too. That's why I've come." [39]He traveled throughout Galilee, preaching in their synagogues and throwing out demons.

A man with a skin disease

[40]A man with a skin disease approached Jesus, fell to his knees, and begged, "If you want, you can make me clean."

[41]Incensed,[b] Jesus reached out his hand, touched him, and said, "I do want to. Be clean." [42]Instantly, the skin disease left him, and he was clean. [43]Sternly, Jesus sent him away, [44]saying, "Don't say anything to anyone. Instead, go and show yourself to the priest and offer the sacrifice for your cleansing that Moses commanded. This will be a testimony

to them." [45]Instead, he went out and started talking freely and spreading the news so that Jesus wasn't able to enter a town openly. He remained outside in deserted places, but people came to him from everywhere.

Healing and forgiveness

2 After a few days, Jesus went back to Capernaum, and people heard that he was at home. [2]So many gathered that there was no longer space, not even near the door. Jesus was speaking the word to them. [3]Some people arrived, and four of them were bringing to him a man who was paralyzed. [4]They couldn't carry him through the crowd, so they tore off part of the roof above where Jesus was. When they had made an opening, they lowered the mat on which the paralyzed man was lying. [5]When Jesus saw their faith, he said to the paralytic, "Child, your sins are forgiven!"

[6]Some legal experts were sitting there, muttering among themselves, [7]"Why does he speak this way? He's insulting God. Only the one God can forgive sins."

[8]Jesus immediately recognized what they were discussing, and he said to them, "Why do you fill your minds with these questions? [9]Which is easier—to say to a paralyzed person, 'Your sins are forgiven,' or to say, 'Get up, take up your bed, and walk'? [10]But so you will know that the Human One[c] has authority on the earth to forgive sins"— he said to the man who was paralyzed, [11]"Get up, take your mat, and go home."

[12]Jesus raised him up, and right away he picked up his mat and walked out in front of everybody. They were all amazed and praised God, saying, "We've never seen anything like this!"

Eating with sinners

[13]Jesus went out beside the lake again. The whole crowd came to him, and he began to teach them. [14]As he continued along, he saw Levi, Alphaeus' son, sitting at a kiosk for collecting taxes. Jesus said to him, "Follow me." Levi got up and followed him.

[15]Jesus sat down to eat at Levi's house.

Bet you can read this in 3 minutes. Ready, set, go!

---

[b]Most critical editions of the Gk New Testament read *filled with compassion.* [c]Or *Son of Man*

Many tax collectors and sinners were eating with Jesus and his disciples. Indeed, many of them had become his followers. ¹⁶When some of the legal experts from among the Pharisees saw that he was eating with sinners and tax collectors, they asked his disciples, "Why is he eating with sinners and tax collectors?"

¹⁷When Jesus heard it, he said to them, "Healthy people don't need a doctor, but sick people do. I didn't come to call righteous people, but sinners."

When to fast

¹⁸John's disciples and the Pharisees had a habit of fasting. Some people asked Jesus, "Why do John's disciples and the Pharisees' disciples fast, but yours don't?"

¹⁹Jesus said, "The wedding guests can't fast while the groom is with them, can they? As long as they have the groom with them, they can't fast. ²⁰But the days will come when the groom will be taken away from them, and then they will fast.

²¹"No one sews a piece of new, unshrunk cloth on old clothes; otherwise, the patch tears away from it, the new from the old, and makes a worse tear. ²²No one pours new wine into old leather wineskins; otherwise, the wine would burst the wineskins and the wine would be lost and the wineskins destroyed. But new wine is for new wineskins."

Scripture and the Sabbath

²³Jesus went through the wheat fields on the Sabbath. As the disciples made their way, they were picking the heads of wheat. ²⁴The Pharisees said to Jesus, "Look! Why are they breaking the Sabbath law?"

²⁵He said to them, "Haven't you ever read what David did when he was in need, when he and those with him were hungry? ²⁶During the time when Abiathar was high priest, David went into God's house and ate the bread of the presence, which only the priests were allowed to eat. He also gave bread to those who were with him." ²⁷Then he said, "The Sabbath was created for humans; humans weren't created for the Sabbath. ²⁸This is why the Human One[d] is Lord even over the Sabbath."

Healing on the Sabbath

3 Jesus returned to the synagogue. A man with a withered hand was there. ²Wanting to bring charges against Jesus, they were watching Jesus closely to see if he would heal on the Sabbath. ³He said to the man with the withered hand, "Step up where people can see you." ⁴Then he said to them, "Is it legal on the Sabbath to do good or to do evil, to save life or to kill?" But they said nothing. ⁵Looking around at them with anger, deeply grieved at their unyielding hearts, he said to the man, "Stretch out your hand." So he did, and his hand was made healthy. ⁶At that, the Pharisees got together with the supporters of Herod to plan how to destroy Jesus.

Healing and throwing demons out

⁷Jesus left with his disciples and went to the lake. A large crowd followed him because they had heard what he was doing. They were from Galilee, ⁸Judea, Jerusalem, Idumea, beyond the Jordan, and the area surrounding Tyre and Sidon. ⁹Jesus told his disciples to get a small boat ready for him so the crowd wouldn't crush him. ¹⁰He had healed so many people that everyone who was sick pushed forward so that they could touch him. ¹¹Whenever the evil spirits saw him, they fell down at his feet and shouted, "You are God's Son!" ¹²But he strictly ordered them not to reveal who he was.

Jesus appoints twelve apostles

¹³Jesus went up on a mountain and called those he wanted, and they came to him. ¹⁴He appointed twelve and called them apostles. He appointed them to be with him, to be sent out to preach, ¹⁵and to have authority to throw out demons. ¹⁶He appointed twelve: Peter, a name he gave Simon; ¹⁷James and John, Zebedee's sons, whom he nicknamed Boanerges, which means "sons of Thunder"; ¹⁸and Andrew; Philip; Bartholomew; Matthew; Thomas; James, Alphaeus' son; Thaddaeus; Simon the Cananaean;[e] ¹⁹and Judas Iscariot, who betrayed Jesus.

Misunderstandings about Jesus

²⁰Jesus entered a house. A crowd gathered again so that it was impossible for him and

[d]Or Son of Man [e]Or zealot

his followers even to eat. ²¹When his family heard what was happening, they came to take control of him. They were saying, "He's out of his mind!"

²²The legal experts came down from Jerusalem. Over and over they charged, "He's possessed by Beelzebul. He throws out demons with the authority of the ruler of demons."

²³When Jesus called them together he spoke to them in a parable: "How can Satan throw Satan out? ²⁴A kingdom involved in civil war will collapse. ²⁵And a house torn apart by divisions will collapse. ²⁶If Satan rebels against himself and is divided, then he can't endure. He's done for. ²⁷No one gets into the house of a strong person and steals anything without first tying up the strong person. Only then can the house be burglarized. ²⁸I assure you that human beings will be forgiven for everything, for all sins and insults of every kind. ²⁹But whoever insults the Holy Spirit will never be forgiven. That

person is guilty of a sin with consequences that last forever." ³⁰He said this because the legal experts were saying, "He's possessed by an evil spirit."

³¹His mother and brothers arrived. They stood outside and sent word to him, calling for him. ³²A crowd was seated around him, and those sent to him said, "Look, your mother, brothers, and sisters are outside looking for you."

³³He replied, "Who is my mother? Who are my brothers?" ³⁴Looking around at those seated around him in a circle, he said, "Look, here are my mother and my brothers. ³⁵Whoever does God's will is my brother, sister, and mother."

Parable of the soils

4 Jesus began to teach beside the lake again. Such a large crowd gathered that he climbed into a boat there on the lake. He sat in the boat while the whole crowd was

Jesus Called His Disciples . . . and Us Mark 3:13-19

People on soccer, basketball, dance, and swim teams work together toward a goal. Team members cheer for and support each other. Being on a team can help individual members bump up to a higher level in skill or task, which helps the team as a whole. Teams do best when members stay focused on a common goal.

Jesus put together a team of people to help him carry out his work on earth. His team wasn't in a competition trying to beat out another team. Instead, his team joined together to do God's work. Jesus taught them everything they needed to know about preaching, healing, and loving people in need so the team could do everything he did.

Jesus' team of disciples included Peter, James, John, Andrew, Philip, Bartholomew, Matthew, Thomas, James (Alphaeus' son), Thaddaeus, Simon, and Judas. These disciples were Jesus' closest friends. They were like his family. But this wasn't a limited group. We can be Jesus' friends as well. When we choose to follow Jesus, we join his team of disciples doing God's work in the world.

What is your favorite team?

What does it feel like to be chosen to be on Jesus' team?

LIFE PRESERVER

Why did people misunderstand Jesus?

Mark 3:20-35

Leaders are often misunderstood. Think about the president of a country. There is no way everyone will like the president's decisions all of the time. There will always be someone who disagrees or doesn't understand a particular action. This was true for Jesus as well. He challenged religious authorities. He healed people and performed miracles. Jesus attracted a lot of followers and gained more wherever he went.

Jesus' popularity with the common people upset the religious leaders. Perhaps the religious leaders thought they could make people stop following him if they said he was evil, but it didn't work. Their false claim didn't keep Jesus from teaching and helping people understand about God's love either. ◆

nearby on the shore. ²He said many things to them in parables. While teaching them, he said, ³"Listen to this! A farmer went out to scatter seed. ⁴As he was scattering seed, some fell on the path; and the birds came and ate it. ⁵Other seed fell on rocky ground where the soil was shallow. They sprouted immediately because the soil wasn't deep. ⁶When the sun came up, it scorched the plants; and they dried up because they had no roots. ⁷Other seed fell among thorny plants. The thorny plants grew and choked the seeds, and they produced nothing. ⁸Other seed fell into good soil and bore fruit. Upon growing and increasing, the seed produced in one case a yield of thirty to one, in another case a yield of sixty to one, and in another case a yield of one hundred to one." ⁹He said, "Whoever has ears to listen should pay attention!"

Jesus explains his parable

¹⁰When they were alone, the people around Jesus, along with the Twelve, asked him about the parables. ¹¹He said to them, "The secret of God's kingdom has been given to you, but to those who are outside everything comes in parables. ¹²This is so that they can look and see but have no insight, and they can hear but not understand. Otherwise, they might turn their lives around and be forgiven.

¹³"Don't you understand this parable? Then how will you understand all the parables? ¹⁴The farmer scatters the word. ¹⁵This is the meaning of the seed that fell on the path: When the word is scattered and people hear it, right away Satan comes and steals the word that was planted in them. ¹⁶Here's the meaning of the seed that fell on rocky ground: When people hear the word, they immediately receive it joyfully. ¹⁷Because they have no roots, they last for only a little while. When they experience distress or abuse because of the word, they immediately fall away. ¹⁸Others are like the seed scattered among the thorny plants. These are the ones who have heard the word; ¹⁹but the worries of this life, the false appeal of wealth, and the desire for more things break in and choke the word, and it bears no fruit. ²⁰The seed scattered on good soil are those who hear the word and embrace it. They bear fruit, in one case a yield of thirty to one, in another case sixty to one, and in another case one hundred to one."

Parables about lamps and measures

²¹Jesus said to them, "Does anyone bring in a lamp in order to put it under a basket or a bed? Shouldn't it be placed on a lampstand? ²²Everything hidden will be revealed, and everything secret will come out into the open. ²³Whoever has ears to listen should pay attention!"

²⁴He said to them, "Listen carefully! God will evaluate you with the same standard you use to evaluate others. Indeed, you will receive even more. ²⁵Those who have will receive more, but as for those who don't have, even what they don't have will be taken away from them."

More parables about God's kingdom

²⁶Then Jesus said, "This is what God's kingdom is like. It's as though someone scatters seed on the ground, ²⁷then sleeps and wakes night and day. The seed sprouts and grows, but the farmer doesn't know how. ²⁸The earth produces crops all by itself, first the stalk, then the head, then the full head of grain. ²⁹Whenever the crop is ready, the farmer goes out to cut the grain because it's harvesttime."

³⁰He continued, "What's a good image for God's kingdom? What parable can I use to

explain it? ³¹Consider a mustard seed. When scattered on the ground, it's the smallest of all the seeds on the earth; ³²but when it's planted, it grows and becomes the largest of all vegetable plants. It produces such large branches that the birds in the sky are able to nest in its shade."

LIGHTHOUSE

God's Kingdom

Small Beginnings *Mark 4:30-32*

Jesus helped people understand God's kingdom. He did this by comparing it to simple, everyday things that they knew and understood. They had experienced the hopeful moments of placing a tiny seed in the ground. They had also experienced the joyful harvests that followed months later. These were things they understood. In order to make his point even more clear, Jesus compared God's kingdom to the tiniest of seeds—a mustard seed. Despite its small size, this seed grows into a bush big enough for birds to nest in. He wanted the people listening not to overlook small beginnings, which can lead to great things. ◊

³³With many such parables he continued to give them the word, as much as they were able to hear. ³⁴He spoke to them only in parables, then explained everything to his disciples when he was alone with them.

Jesus stops a storm

³⁵Later that day, when evening came, Jesus said to them, "Let's cross over to the other side of the lake." ³⁶They left the crowd and took him in the boat just as he was. Other boats followed along. ³⁷Gale-force winds arose, and waves crashed against the boat so that the boat was swamped. ³⁸But Jesus was in the rear of the boat, sleeping on a pillow. They woke him up and said, "Teacher, don't you care that we're drowning?"

³⁹He got up and gave orders to the wind, and he said to the lake, "Silence! Be still!" The wind settled down and there was a great calm. ⁴⁰Jesus asked them, "Why are you frightened? Don't you have faith yet?"

⁴¹Overcome with awe, they said to each other, "Who then is this? Even the wind and the sea obey him!"

Jesus frees a demon-possessed man

5 Jesus and his disciples came to the other side of the lake, to the region of the Gerasenes. ²As soon as Jesus got out of the boat, a man possessed by an evil spirit came out of the tombs. ³This man lived among the tombs, and no one was ever strong enough to restrain him, even with a chain. ⁴He had been secured many times with leg irons and chains, but he broke the chains and smashed the leg irons. No one was tough enough to control him. ⁵Night and day in the tombs and the hills, he would howl and cut himself with stones. ⁶When he saw Jesus from far away, he ran and knelt before him, ⁷shouting, "What have you to do with me, Jesus, Son of the Most High God? Swear to God that you won't torture me!"

⁸He said this because Jesus had already commanded him, "Unclean spirit, come out of the man!"

⁹Jesus asked him, "What is your name?"

He responded, "Legion is my name, because we are many." ¹⁰They pleaded with Jesus not to send them out of that region. ¹¹A large herd of pigs was feeding on the hillside. ¹²"Send us into the pigs!" they begged. "Let us go into the pigs!" ¹³Jesus gave them permission, so the unclean spirits left the man and went into the pigs. Then the herd of about two thousand pigs rushed down the cliff into the lake and drowned.

¹⁴Those who tended the pigs ran away and told the story in the city and in the countryside. People came to see what had happened. ¹⁵They came to Jesus and saw the man who used to be demon-possessed. They saw the very man who had been filled with many demons sitting there fully dressed and completely sane, and they were filled with awe. ¹⁶Those who had actually seen what had happened to the demon-possessed man told the others about the pigs. ¹⁷Then they pleaded with Jesus to leave their region.

¹⁸While he was climbing into the boat, the one who had been demon-possessed pleaded with Jesus to let him come along as one of his disciples. ¹⁹But Jesus wouldn't allow it. "Go home to your own people," Jesus said, "and tell them what the Lord has done for you and how he has shown you mercy." ²⁰The man went

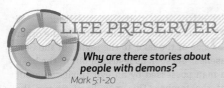

LIFE PRESERVER

Why are there stories about people with demons?
Mark 5:1-20

In some places people believe in demons or evil spirits. It is common for these people to believe that diseases are caused by evil spirits. Some also believe the only way for a person to be healed of demons is by throwing the demon out of the person's body, in a process called *exorcism*. Through prayer, they believe that the demon or evil spirit will be released from the sick person's body, and he or she will be healed.

Jesus healed people who were sick, or disabled, or said to be possessed by demons. Wise doctors today help us understand that people can act strangely if they are mentally or physically ill. It doesn't happen often, but sometimes a person can behave with so much cruelty that we use the word *demonic* to describe their evil deeds.

Jesus wants us to understand and help care for people and to pray for their healing just like he did. ◗

away and began to proclaim in the Ten Cities all that Jesus had done for him, and everyone was amazed.

Jesus heals two people

²¹Jesus crossed the lake again, and on the other side a large crowd gathered around him on the shore. ²²Jairus, one of the synagogue leaders, came forward. When he saw Jesus, he fell at his feet ²³and pleaded with him, "My daughter is about to die. Please, come and place your hands on her so that she can be healed and live." ²⁴So Jesus went with him.

A swarm of people were following Jesus, crowding in on him. ²⁵A woman was there who had been bleeding for twelve years. ²⁶She had suffered a lot under the care of many doctors, and had spent everything she had without getting any better. In fact, she had gotten worse. ²⁷Because she had heard about Jesus, she came up behind him in the crowd and touched his clothes. ²⁸She was thinking, If I can just touch his clothes, I'll be healed. ²⁹Her bleeding stopped immediately, and she sensed in her body that her illness had been healed.

³⁰At that very moment, Jesus recognized that power had gone out from him. He turned around in the crowd and said, "Who touched my clothes?"

³¹His disciples said to him, "Don't you see the crowd pressing against you? Yet you ask, 'Who touched me?'" ³²But Jesus looked around carefully to see who had done it.

³³The woman, full of fear and trembling, came forward. Knowing what had happened to her, she fell down in front of Jesus and told him the whole truth. ³⁴He responded, "Daughter, your faith has healed you; go in peace, healed from your disease."

³⁵While Jesus was still speaking with her, messengers came from the synagogue leader's house, saying to Jairus, "Your daughter has died. Why bother the teacher any longer?"

³⁶But Jesus overheard their report and said to the synagogue leader, "Don't be afraid; just keep trusting." ³⁷He didn't allow anyone to follow him except Peter, James, and John, James' brother. ³⁸They came to the synagogue leader's house, and he saw a commotion, with people crying and wailing loudly. ³⁹He went in and said to them, "What's all this commotion and crying about? The child isn't dead. She's only sleeping." ⁴⁰They laughed at him, but he threw them all out. Then, taking the child's parents and his disciples with him, he went to the room where the child was. ⁴¹Taking her hand, he said to her, "*Talitha koum*," which means, "Young woman, get up." ⁴²Suddenly the young woman got up and began to walk around. She was twelve years old. They were shocked! ⁴³He gave them strict orders that no one should know what had happened. Then he told them to give her something to eat.

Jesus in his hometown

6 Jesus left that place and came to his hometown. His disciples followed him. ²On the Sabbath, he began to teach in the synagogue. Many who heard him were surprised. "Where did this man get all this? What's this wisdom he's been given? What about the powerful acts accomplished through him? ³Isn't this the carpenter? Isn't he Mary's son and the brother of James, Joses, Judas, and Simon? Aren't his sisters here with us?" They were repulsed by him and fell into sin.

⁴Jesus said to them, "Prophets are honored everywhere except in their own hometowns,

among their relatives, and in their own households." [5]He was unable to do any miracles there, except that he placed his hands on a few sick people and healed them. [6]He was appalled by their disbelief.

Sending out the disciples

Then Jesus traveled through the surrounding villages teaching.

[7]He called for the Twelve and sent them out in pairs. He gave them authority over unclean spirits. [8]He instructed them to take nothing for the journey except a walking stick—no bread, no bags, and no money in their belts. [9]He told them to wear sandals but not to put on two shirts. [10]He said, "Whatever house you enter, remain there until you leave that place. [11]If a place doesn't welcome you or listen to you, as you leave, shake the dust off your feet as a witness against them." [12]So they went out and proclaimed that people should change their hearts and lives. [13]They cast out many demons, and they anointed many sick people with olive oil and healed them.

Death of John the Baptist

[14]Herod the king heard about these things, because the name of Jesus had become well-known. Some were saying, "John the Baptist has been raised from the dead, and this is why miraculous powers are at work through him." [15]Others were saying, "He is Elijah." Still others were saying, "He is a prophet like one of the ancient prophets." [16]But when Herod heard these rumors, he said, "John, whom I beheaded, has been raised to life."

[17]He said this because Herod himself had arranged to have John arrested and put in prison because of Herodias, the wife of Herod's brother Philip. Herod had married her, [18]but John told Herod, "It's against the law for you to marry your brother's wife!" [19]So Herodias had it in for John. She wanted to kill him, but she couldn't. [20]This was because Herod respected John. He regarded him as a righteous and holy person, so he protected him. John's words greatly confused Herod, yet he enjoyed listening to him.

[21]Finally, the time was right. It was on one of Herod's birthdays, when he had prepared a feast for his high-ranking officials and

military officers and Galilee's leading residents. [22]Herod's daughter Herodias[f] came in and danced, thrilling Herod and his dinner guests. The king said to the young woman, "Ask me whatever you wish, and I will give it to you." [23]Then he swore to her, "Whatever you ask I will give to you, even as much as half of my kingdom."

[24]She left the banquet hall and said to her mother, "What should I ask for?"

"John the Baptist's head," Herodias replied.

[25]Hurrying back to the ruler, she made her request: "I want you to give me John the Baptist's head on a plate, right this minute." [26]Although the king was upset, because of his solemn pledge and his guests, he didn't want to refuse her. [27]So he ordered a guard to bring John's head. The guard went to the prison, cut off John's head, [28]brought his head on a plate, and gave it to the young woman, and she gave it to her mother. [29]When John's disciples heard what had happened, they came and took his dead body and laid it in a tomb.

Jesus feeds five thousand people

[30]The apostles returned to Jesus and told him everything they had done and taught. [31]Many people were coming and going, so there was no time to eat. He said to the apostles, "Come by yourselves to a secluded place and rest for a while." [32]They departed in a boat by themselves for a deserted place.

[33]Many people saw them leaving and recognized them, so they ran ahead from all the cities and arrived before them. [34]When Jesus arrived and saw a large crowd, he had compassion on them because they were like sheep without a shepherd. Then he began to teach them many things.

[35]Late in the day, his disciples came to him and said, "This is an isolated place, and it's already late in the day. [36]Send them away so that they can go to the surrounding countryside and villages and buy something to eat for themselves."

[37]He replied, "You give them something to eat."

But they said to him, "Should we go off and buy bread worth almost eight months' pay[g] and give it to them to eat?"

---

[f]*Or the daughter of Herodias herself;* Gk uncertain [g]*Or two hundred denaria;* a denarion was a typical day's wage.

³⁸He said to them, "How much bread do you have? Take a look."

After checking, they said, "Five loaves of bread and two fish."

³⁹He directed the disciples to seat all the people in groups as though they were having a banquet on the green grass. ⁴⁰They sat down in groups of hundreds and fifties. ⁴¹He took the five loaves and the two fish, looked up to heaven, blessed them, broke the loaves into pieces, and gave them to his disciples to set before the people. He also divided the two fish among them all. ⁴²Everyone ate until they were full. ⁴³They filled twelve baskets with the leftover pieces of bread and fish. ⁴⁴About five thousand had eaten.

Jesus walks on water

⁴⁵Right then, Jesus made his disciples get into a boat and go ahead to the other side of the lake, toward Bethsaida, while he dismissed the crowd. ⁴⁶After saying good-bye to them, Jesus went up onto a mountain to pray. ⁴⁷Evening came and the boat was in the middle of the lake, but he was alone on the land. ⁴⁸He saw his disciples struggling. They were trying to row forward, but the wind was blowing against them. Very early in the morning, he came to them, walking on the lake. He intended to pass by them. ⁴⁹When they saw him walking on the lake, they thought he was a ghost and they screamed. ⁵⁰Seeing him was terrifying to all of them. Just then he spoke to them, "Be encouraged! It's me. Don't be afraid." ⁵¹He got into the boat, and the wind settled down. His disciples were so baffled they were beside themselves. ⁵²That's because they hadn't understood about the loaves. Their minds had been closed so that they resisted God's ways.

Healings at Gennesaret

⁵³When Jesus and his disciples had crossed the lake, they landed at Gennesaret, anchored the boat, ⁵⁴and came ashore. People immediately recognized Jesus ⁵⁵and ran around that whole region bringing sick people on their mats to wherever they heard he was. ⁵⁶Wherever he went—villages, cities, or farming communities—they would place the sick in the marketplaces and beg him to allow them to touch even the hem of his clothing. Everyone who touched him was healed.

LIFE PRESERVER

How did Jesus feed five thousand people?
Mark 6:30-44

Jesus feeding five thousand people is a well-known story. It is told in all four Gospels—Matthew, Mark, Luke, and John. This story is about Jesus and his ministry of caring for people. The people who came to hear Jesus teach were hungry. They had been there all day without food. But instead of sending the people away to eat, Jesus took one person's lunch and made it feed a whole crowd of people. In fact, there was so much food they had a lot left over.

In this miracle story, Jesus took five loaves and two fish, gave thanks, broke them apart, and gave them to his disciples to distribute. Jesus did the same thing at the Passover celebration with his disciples.

We hear these same words when we take Communion—*take, bless, break,* and *give.* This story teaches that when we share what we have no matter how small, it can grow. ◆

What contaminates a life?

7 The Pharisees and some legal experts from Jerusalem gathered around Jesus. ²They saw some of his disciples eating food with unclean hands. (They were eating without first ritually purifying their hands through washing. ³The Pharisees and all the Jews don't eat without first washing their hands carefully. This is a way of observing the rules handed down by the elders. ⁴Upon returning from the marketplace, they don't eat without first immersing themselves. They observe many other rules that have been handed down, such as the washing of cups, jugs, pans, and sleeping mats.) ⁵So the Pharisees and legal experts asked Jesus, "Why are your disciples not living according to the rules handed down by the elders but instead eat food with ritually unclean hands?"

⁶He replied, "Isaiah really knew what he was talking about when he prophesied about you hypocrites. He wrote,

This people honors me
* with their lips,*
* but their hearts are far away*
*   from me.*
⁷ *Their worship of me is empty*

since they teach instructions that are human words.[h]

[8]You ignore God's commandment while holding on to rules created by humans and handed down to you." [9]Jesus continued, "Clearly, you are experts at rejecting God's commandment in order to establish these rules. [10]Moses said, *Honor your father and your mother,*[i] and *The person who speaks against father or mother will certainly be put to death.*[j] [11]But you say, 'If you tell your father or mother, "Everything I'm expected to contribute to you is *corban* (that is, a gift I'm giving to God)," [12]then you are no longer required to care for your father or mother.' [13]In this way you do away with God's word in favor of the rules handed down to you, which you pass on to others. And you do a lot of other things just like that."

[14]Then Jesus called the crowd again and said, "Listen to me, all of you, and understand. [15]Nothing outside of a person can enter and

did you **know**? The Galilee Sea is really a lake. A sea has salt water, but the Galilee Sea has fresh water. It is the lowest lake in the world, at around 600 feet below sea level.

contaminate a person in God's sight; rather, the things that come out of a person contaminate the person."[k]

[17]After leaving the crowd, he entered a house where his disciples asked him about that riddle. [18]He said to them, "Don't you understand either? Don't you know that nothing from the outside that enters a person has the power to contaminate? [19]That's because it doesn't enter into the heart but into the stomach, and it goes out into the sewer." By saying this, Jesus declared that no food could contaminate a person in God's sight. [20]"It's what comes out of a person that contaminates someone in God's sight," he said. [21]"It's from the inside, from the human heart, that evil thoughts come: sexual sins, thefts, murders, [22]adultery, greed, evil actions, deceit, unrestrained immorality, envy, insults, arrogance, and foolishness. [23]All these evil things come

from the inside and contaminate a person in God's sight."

An immigrant's daughter is delivered

[24]Jesus left that place and went into the region of Tyre. He didn't want anyone to know that he had entered a house, but he couldn't hide. [25]In fact, a woman whose young daughter was possessed by an unclean spirit heard about him right away. She came and fell at his feet. [26]The woman was Greek, Syrophoenician by birth. She begged Jesus to throw the demon out of her daughter. [27]He responded, "The children have to be fed first. It isn't right to take the children's bread and toss it to the dogs."

[28]But she answered, "Lord, even the dogs under the table eat the children's crumbs."

[29]"Good answer!" he said. "Go on home. The demon has already left your daughter." [30]When she returned to her house, she found the child lying on the bed and the demon gone.

A deaf man is healed

[31]After leaving the region of Tyre, Jesus went through Sidon toward the Galilee Sea through the region of the Ten Cities. [32]Some people brought to him a man who was deaf and could hardly speak, and they begged him to place his hand on the man for healing. [33]Jesus took him away from the crowd by himself and put his fingers in the man's ears. Then he spit and touched the man's tongue. [34]Looking into heaven, Jesus sighed deeply and said, "*Ephphatha,*" which means, "Open up." [35]At once, his ears opened, his twisted tongue was released, and he began to speak clearly.

[36]Jesus gave the people strict orders not to tell anyone. But the more he tried to silence them, the more eagerly they shared the news. [37]People were overcome with wonder, saying, "He does everything well! He even makes the deaf to hear and gives speech to those who can't speak."

Jesus feeds four thousand people

8In those days there was another large crowd with nothing to eat. Jesus called his disciples and told them, [2]"I feel sorry for the crowd because they have been with me for

[h]Isa 29:13 [i]Exod 20:12; Deut 5:16 [j]Exod 21:17; Lev 20:9 [k]7:16 is omitted in most critical editions of the Gk New Testament *Whoever has ears to listen should pay attention!*

three days and have nothing to eat. ³If I send them away hungry to their homes, they won't have enough strength to travel, for some have come a long distance."

⁴His disciples responded, "How can anyone get enough food in this wilderness to satisfy these people?"

⁵Jesus asked, "How much bread do you have?"

They said, "Seven loaves."

⁶He told the crowd to sit on the ground. He took the seven loaves, gave thanks, broke them apart, and gave them to his disciples to distribute; and they gave the bread to the crowd. ⁷They also had a few fish. He said a blessing over them, then gave them to the disciples to hand out also. ⁸They ate until they were full. They collected seven baskets full of leftovers. ⁹This was a crowd of about four thousand people! Jesus sent them away, ¹⁰then got into a boat with his disciples and went over to the region of Dalmanutha.

Looking for proof

¹¹The Pharisees showed up and began to argue with Jesus. To test him, they asked for a sign from heaven. ¹²With an impatient sigh, Jesus said, "Why does this generation look for a sign? I assure you that no sign will be given to it." ¹³Leaving them, he got back in the boat and crossed to the other side of the lake.

Understanding about the bread

¹⁴Jesus' disciples had forgotten to bring any bread, so they had only one loaf with them in the boat. ¹⁵He gave them strict orders: "Watch out and be on your guard for the yeast of the Pharisees as well as the yeast of Herod."

did you know? The word *Messiah* comes from a Hebrew word. *Christ* comes from a Greek word. Both words mean "anointed one" or "chosen one." Peter said Jesus is the promised chosen one, sent from God.

¹⁶The disciples discussed this among themselves, "He said this because we have no bread."

¹⁷Jesus knew what they were discussing and said, "Why are you talking about the fact that you don't have any bread? Don't you grasp what has happened? Don't you understand? Are your hearts so resistant to what God is doing? ¹⁸Don't you have eyes? Why can't you see? Don't you have ears? Why can't you hear? Don't you remember? ¹⁹When I broke five loaves of bread for those five thousand people, how many baskets full of leftovers did you gather?"

They answered, "Twelve."

²⁰"And when I broke seven loaves of bread for those four thousand people, how many baskets full of leftovers did you gather?"

They answered, "Seven."

²¹Jesus said to them, "And you still don't understand?"

A blind man is healed

²²Jesus and his disciples came to Bethsaida. Some people brought a blind man to Jesus and begged him to touch and heal him. ²³Taking the blind man's hand, Jesus led him out of the village. After spitting on his eyes and laying his hands on the man, he asked him, "Do you see anything?"

²⁴The man looked up and said, "I see people. They look like trees, only they are walking around."

²⁵Then Jesus placed his hands on the man's eyes again. He looked with his eyes wide open, his sight was restored, and he could see everything clearly. ²⁶Then Jesus sent him home, saying, "Don't go into the village!"

Jesus predicts his death

²⁷Jesus and his disciples went into the villages near Caesarea Philippi. On the way he asked his disciples, "Who do people say that I am?"

²⁸They told him, "Some say John the Baptist, others Elijah, and still others one of the prophets."

²⁹He asked them, "And what about you? Who do you say that I am?"

Peter answered, "You are the Christ." ³⁰Jesus ordered them not to tell anyone about him.

³¹Then Jesus began to teach his disciples: "The Human One¹ must suffer many things and be rejected by the elders, chief priests, and the legal experts, and be killed, and

¹Or *Son of Man*

then, after three days, rise from the dead." ³²He said this plainly. But Peter took hold of Jesus and, scolding him, began to correct him. ³³Jesus turned and looked at his disciples, then sternly corrected Peter: "Get behind me, Satan. You are not thinking God's thoughts but human thoughts."

³⁴After calling the crowd together with his disciples, Jesus said to them, "All who want to come after me must say no to themselves, take up their cross, and follow me. ³⁵All who want to save their lives will lose them. But all who lose their lives because of me and because of the good news will save them. ³⁶Why would people gain the whole world but lose their lives? ³⁷What will people give in exchange for their lives? ³⁸Whoever is ashamed of me and my words in this unfaithful and sinful generation, the Human One^m will be ashamed of that person when he comes in the Father's glory with the holy angels."

9 ¹Jesus continued, "I assure you that some standing here won't die before they see God's kingdom arrive in power."

Jesus transformed

²Six days later Jesus took Peter, James, and John, and brought them to the top of a very high mountain where they were alone. He was transformed in front of them, ³and his clothes were amazingly bright, brighter than if they had been bleached white. ⁴Elijah and Moses appeared and were talking with Jesus. ⁵Peter reacted to all of this by saying to Jesus, "Rabbi, it's good that we're here. Let's make three shrines—one for you, one for Moses, and one for Elijah." ⁶He said this because he didn't know how to respond, for the three of them were terrified.

⁷Then a cloud overshadowed them, and a voice spoke from the cloud, "This is my Son, whom I dearly love. Listen to him!" ⁸Suddenly, looking around, they no longer saw anyone with them except Jesus.

⁹As they were coming down the mountain, he ordered them not to tell anyone what they had seen until after the Human One^n had risen from the dead. ¹⁰So they kept it to themselves, wondering, "What's this 'rising from

the dead'?" ¹¹They asked Jesus, "Why do the legal experts say that Elijah must come first?"

¹²He answered, "Elijah does come first to restore all things. Why was it written that the Human One^o would suffer many things and be rejected? ¹³In fact, I tell you that Elijah has come, but they did to him whatever they wanted, just as it was written about him."

A demon-possessed boy

¹⁴When Jesus, Peter, James, and John approached the other disciples, they saw a large crowd surrounding them and legal experts arguing with them. ¹⁵Suddenly the whole crowd caught sight of Jesus. They ran to greet him, overcome with excitement. ¹⁶Jesus asked them, "What are you arguing about?"

¹⁷Someone from the crowd responded, "Teacher, I brought my son to you, since he has a spirit that doesn't allow him to speak. ¹⁸Wherever it overpowers him, it throws him into a fit. He foams at the mouth, grinds his teeth, and stiffens up. So I spoke to your disciples to see if they could throw it out, but they couldn't."

¹⁹Jesus answered them, "You faithless generation, how long will I be with you? How long will I put up with you? Bring him to me."

²⁰They brought him. When the spirit saw Jesus, it immediately threw the boy into a fit. He fell on the ground and rolled around, foaming at the mouth. ²¹Jesus asked his father, "How long has this been going on?"

He said, "Since he was a child. ²²It has often thrown him into a fire or into water trying to

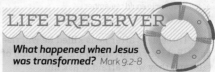

LIFE PRESERVER

What happened when Jesus was transformed? *Mark 9:2-8*

Jesus took on a divine appearance when he was transformed. It was like human and divine came together. This surprised the disciples who were with him. All of a sudden right before their eyes, Jesus got brighter and brighter. And then they heard a voice from the cloud telling them to listen to Jesus because he is God's Son. These words may sound familiar because they are similar to those the voice spoke at Jesus' baptism. ◖

---

^m Or *Son of Man* ^n Or *Son of Man* ^o Or *Son of Man*

kill him. If you can do anything, help us! Show us compassion!"

²³Jesus said to him, "'If you can do anything'? All things are possible for the one who has faith."

²⁴At that the boy's father cried out, "I have faith; help my lack of faith!"

²⁵Noticing that the crowd had surged together, Jesus spoke harshly to the unclean spirit, "Mute and deaf spirit, I command you to come out of him and never enter him again." ²⁶After screaming and shaking the boy horribly, the spirit came out. The boy seemed to be dead; in fact, several people said that he had died. ²⁷But Jesus took his hand, lifted him up, and he arose.

²⁸After Jesus went into a house, his disciples asked him privately, "Why couldn't we throw this spirit out?"

²⁹Jesus answered, "Throwing this kind of spirit out requires prayer."

Jesus predicts his death

³⁰From there Jesus and his followers went through Galilee, but he didn't want anyone to know it. ³¹This was because he was teaching his disciples, "The Human One*ᵖ will be delivered into human hands. They will kill

did you know? When Jesus described a place for truly evil people where "the fire never goes out" (Mark 9:48), he was probably thinking of a garbage dump called *Gehenna* (meaning "hell" in verse 47) in a ravine south of Jerusalem. Fires at the dump burned day and night and had burned there for as long as people could remember.

him. Three days after he is killed he will rise up." ³²But they didn't understand this kind of talk, and they were afraid to ask him.

³³They entered Capernaum. When they had come into a house, he asked them, "What were you arguing about during the journey?" ³⁴They didn't respond, since on the way they had been debating with each other about who was the greatest. ³⁵He sat down, called the Twelve, and said to them, "Whoever wants to

be first must be least of all and the servant of all." ³⁶Jesus reached for a little child, placed him among the Twelve, and embraced him. Then he said, ³⁷"Whoever welcomes one of these children in my name welcomes me; and whoever welcomes me isn't actually welcoming me but rather the one who sent me."

Recognize your allies

³⁸John said to Jesus, "Teacher, we saw someone throwing demons out in your name, and we tried to stop him because he wasn't following us."

³⁹Jesus replied, "Don't stop him. No one who does powerful acts in my name can quickly turn around and curse me. ⁴⁰Whoever isn't against us is for us. ⁴¹I assure you that whoever gives you a cup of water to drink because you belong to Christ will certainly be rewarded.

⁴²"As for whoever causes these little ones who believe in me to trip and fall into sin, it would be better for them to have a huge stone hung around their necks and to be thrown into the lake. ⁴³If your hand causes you to fall into sin, chop it off. It's better for you to enter into life crippled than to go away with two hands into the fire of hell, which can't be put out.�q ⁴⁵If your foot causes you to fall into sin, chop it off. It's better for you to enter life lame than to be thrown into hell with two feet.ʳ ⁴⁷If your eye causes you to fall into sin, tear it out. It's better for you to enter God's kingdom with one eye than to be thrown into hell with two. ⁴⁸That's a place *where worms don't die and the fire never goes out.*ˢ ⁴⁹Everyone will be salted with fire. ⁵⁰Salt is good; but if salt loses its saltiness, how will it become salty again? Maintain salt among yourselves and keep peace with each other."

Divorce and remarriage

10 Jesus left that place and went beyond the Jordan and into the region of Judea. Crowds gathered around him again and, as usual, he taught them. ²Some Pharisees came and, trying to test him, they asked, "Does the Law allow a man to divorce his wife?"

ᵖOr *Son of Man* q9:44 is omitted in most critical editions of the Gk New Testament *where worms don't die and the fire never goes out.* ʳ9:46 is omitted in most critical editions of the Gk New Testament *where worms don't die and the fire never goes out.* ˢIsa 66:24

³Jesus answered, "What did Moses command you?"

⁴They said, "Moses allowed a man to write a divorce certificate and to divorce his wife."

⁵Jesus said to them, "He wrote this commandment for you because of your unyielding hearts. ⁶At the beginning of creation, *God made them male and female.*ᵗ ⁷*Because of this, a man should leave his father and mother and be joined together with his wife,* ⁸*and the two will be one flesh.*ᵘ So they are no longer two but one flesh. ⁹Therefore, humans must not pull apart what God has put together."

¹⁰Inside the house, the disciples asked him again about this. ¹¹He said to them, "Whoever divorces his wife and marries another commits adultery against her; ¹²and if a wife divorces her husband and marries another, she commits adultery."

Jesus blesses children

¹³People were bringing children to Jesus so that he would bless them. But the disciples scolded them. ¹⁴When Jesus saw this, he grew angry and said to them, "Allow the children to come to me. Don't forbid them, because God's kingdom belongs to people like these children. ¹⁵I assure you that whoever doesn't welcome God's kingdom like a child will never enter it." ¹⁶Then he hugged the children and blessed them.

A rich man's question

¹⁷As Jesus continued down the road, a man ran up, knelt before him, and asked, "Good Teacher, what must I do to obtain eternal life?"

¹⁸Jesus replied, "Why do you call me good? No one is good except the one God. ¹⁹You know the commandments: *Don't commit murder. Don't commit adultery. Don't steal. Don't give false testimony. Don't cheat. Honor your father and mother.*ᵛ

²⁰"Teacher," he responded, "I've kept all of these things since I was a boy."

²¹Jesus looked at him carefully and loved him. He said, "You are lacking one thing. Go, sell what you own, and give the money to the poor. Then you will have treasure in heaven. And come, follow me." ²²But the man was dismayed at this statement and went away saddened, because he had many possessions.

²³Looking around, Jesus said to his disciples, "It will be very hard for the wealthy to

ᵗGen 1:27 ᵘGen 2:24 ᵛExod 12:16; Deut 16:20

Bless You! *Mark 10:13-16*

Sometimes being young feels really good. You don't have to pay your own bills or find a place to live. You get to play and have fun. But being young can also be hard, especially when it seems like no one listens to you.

Grown-ups sometimes forget that kids might have an idea that could solve a problem or that they might have something to teach adults. Jesus knew that. He welcomed kids, hugged them, and blessed them. Jesus' friends tried to send the kids away, because they didn't think Jesus should be bothered. But Jesus told his followers that kids can come to him any time they want. He said that unless people welcome God's kingdom like children, they will never enter it. No matter how old we are, Jesus wants us to come to him.

When have you felt like a grown-up really wanted to hear what you had to say?

How do you come to Jesus?

enter God's kingdom!" ²⁴His words startled the disciples, so Jesus told them again, "Children, it's difficult to enter God's kingdom! ²⁵It's easier for a camel to squeeze through the eye of a needle than for a rich person to enter God's kingdom."

²⁶They were shocked even more and said to each other, "Then who can be saved?"

²⁷Jesus looked at them carefully and said, "It's impossible with human beings, but not with God. All things are possible for God."

²⁸Peter said to him, "Look, we've left everything and followed you."

²⁹Jesus said, "I assure you that anyone who has left house, brothers, sisters, mother, father, children, or farms because of me and because of the good news ³⁰will receive one hundred times as much now in this life—houses, brothers, sisters, mothers, children, and farms (with harassment)—and in the coming age, eternal life. ³¹But many who are first will be last. And many who are last will be first."

Jesus predicts his death and resurrection

³²Jesus and his disciples were on the road, going up to Jerusalem, with Jesus in the lead. The disciples were amazed while the others following behind were afraid. Taking the Twelve aside again, he told them what was about to happen to him. ³³"Look!" he said. "We're going up to Jerusalem. The Human One^w will be handed over to the chief priests and the legal experts. They will condemn him to death and hand him over to the Gentiles. ³⁴They will ridicule him, spit on him, torture him, and kill him. After three days, he will rise up."

A request from James and John

³⁵James and John, Zebedee's sons, came to Jesus and said, "Teacher, we want you to do for us whatever we ask."

³⁶"What do you want me to do for you?" he asked.

LIFE PRESERVER

What was Jesus trying to teach the rich man?
Mark 10:17-22

Jesus taught that rich people can't buy their way into heaven. A rich man asked Jesus what he should do to live forever. He was a faithful Jew and observed all the commandments, but Jesus wanted something more. Jesus wanted the man to give away all his possessions in exchange for a treasure in heaven. The rich man was sad when he heard this because he owned many things.

Jesus knew that when people are attached to things they can buy with money, they often forget who they should really focus on. Getting rid of what he owned to focus on God wasn't easy for the rich man—and it's still hard today. ◢

---

³⁷They said, "Allow one of us to sit on your right and the other on your left when you enter your glory."

³⁸Jesus replied, "You don't know what you're asking! Can you drink the cup I drink or receive the baptism I receive?"

³⁹"We can," they answered.

Jesus said, "You will drink the cup I drink and receive the baptism I receive, ⁴⁰but to sit at my right or left hand isn't mine to give. It belongs to those for whom it has been prepared."

⁴¹Now when the other ten disciples heard about this, they became angry with James and John. ⁴²Jesus called them over and said, "You know that the ones who are considered the rulers by the Gentiles show off their authority over them and their high-ranking officials order them around. ⁴³But that's not the way it will be with you. Whoever wants to be great among you will be your servant. ⁴⁴Whoever wants to be first among you will be the slave of all, ⁴⁵for the Human One^x didn't come to be served but rather to serve and to give his life to liberate many people."

Healing of blind Bartimaeus

⁴⁶Jesus and his followers came into Jericho. As Jesus was leaving Jericho, together with his disciples and a sizable crowd, a blind beggar named Bartimaeus, Timaeus' son, was sitting beside the road. ⁴⁷When he heard

---

^w Or Son of Man ^x Or Son of Man

that Jesus of Nazareth was there, he began to shout, "Jesus, Son of David, show me mercy!" [48]Many scolded him, telling him to be quiet, but he shouted even louder, "Son of David, show me mercy!"

[49]Jesus stopped and said, "Call him forward."

They called the blind man, "Be encouraged! Get up! He's calling you."

[50]Throwing his coat to the side, he jumped up and came to Jesus.

[51]Jesus asked him, "What do you want me to do for you?"

The blind man said, "Teacher, I want to see."

[52]Jesus said, "Go, your faith has healed you." At once he was able to see, and he began to follow Jesus on the way.

Jesus enters Jerusalem

11 When Jesus and his followers approached Jerusalem, they came to Bethphage and Bethany at the Mount of Olives. Jesus gave two disciples a task, [2]saying to them, "Go into the village over there. As soon as you enter it, you will find tied up there a colt that no one has ridden. Untie it and bring it here. [3]If anyone says to you, 'Why are you doing this?' say, 'Its master needs it, and he will send it back right away.'"

[4]They went and found a colt tied to a gate outside on the street, and they untied it. [5]Some people standing around said to them, "What are you doing, untying the colt?" [6]They told them just what Jesus said, and they left them alone. [7]They brought the colt to Jesus and threw their clothes upon it, and he sat on it. [8]Many people spread out their clothes on the road while others spread branches cut from the fields. [9]Those in front of him and those following were shouting, "Hosanna! Blessings on the one who comes in the name of the Lord![y] [10]Blessings on the coming kingdom of our ancestor David! Hosanna in the highest!" [11]Jesus entered Jerusalem and went into the temple. After he looked around at everything, because it was already late in the evening, he returned to Bethany with the Twelve.

Bet you can read this in 3 minutes. Ready, set, go!

Fig tree and the temple

[12]The next day, after leaving Bethany, Jesus was hungry. [13]From far away, he noticed a fig tree in leaf, so he went to see if he could find anything on it. When he came to it, he found nothing except leaves, since it wasn't the season for figs. [14]So he said to it, "No one will ever again eat your fruit!" His disciples heard this.

[15]They came into Jerusalem. After entering the temple, he threw out those who were selling and buying there. He pushed over the tables used for currency exchange and the chairs of those who sold doves. [16]He didn't allow anyone to carry anything through the temple. [17]He taught them, "Hasn't it been written, *My house will be called a house of prayer for all nations?*[z] But you've turned it into a *hideout for crooks.*"[a] [18]The chief priests and legal experts heard this and tried to find a way to destroy him. They regarded him as dangerous because the whole crowd was enthralled at his teaching. [19]When it was evening, Jesus and his disciples went outside the city.

Power, prayer, and forgiveness

[20]Early in the morning, as Jesus and his disciples were walking along, they saw the fig tree withered from the root up. [21]Peter remembered and said to Jesus, "Rabbi, look how the fig tree you cursed has dried up."

[22]Jesus responded to them, "Have faith in God! [23]I assure you that whoever says to this mountain, 'Be lifted up and thrown into the sea'—and doesn't waver but believes that what is said will really happen—it will happen. [24]Therefore I say to you, whatever you pray and ask for, believe that you will receive it, and it will be so for you. [25]And whenever you stand up to pray, if you have something against anyone, forgive so that your Father in heaven may forgive you your wrongdoings."[b]

Controversy over authority

[27]Jesus and his disciples entered Jerusalem again. As Jesus was walking around the temple, the chief priests, legal experts, and elders came to him. [28]They asked, "What kind of authority do you have for doing these things? Who gave you this authority to do them?"

---

[y]Ps 118:26 [z]Isa 56:7 [a]Jer 7:11 [b]11:26 is omitted in most critical editions of the Gk New Testament *And if you don't forgive, neither will your Father in heaven forgive you your wrongdoings.*

²⁹Jesus said to them, "I have a question for you. Give me an answer, then I'll tell you what kind of authority I have to do these things. ³⁰Was John's baptism of heavenly or of human origin? Answer me."

³¹They argued among themselves, "If we say, 'It's of heavenly origin,' he'll say, 'Then why didn't you believe him?' ³²But we can't say, 'It's of earthly origin.'" They said this because they were afraid of the crowd, because they all thought John was a prophet. ³³They answered Jesus, "We don't know."

Jesus replied, "Neither will I tell you what kind of authority I have to do these things."

Parable of the tenant farmers

12 Jesus spoke to them in parables. "A man planted a vineyard, put a fence around it, dug a pit for the winepress, and built a tower. Then he rented it to tenant farmers and took a trip. ²When it was time, he sent a servant to collect from the tenants his share of the fruit of the vineyard. ³But they grabbed the servant, beat him, and sent him away empty-handed. ⁴Again the landowner sent another servant to them, but they struck him on the head and treated him disgracefully. ⁵He sent another one; that one they killed. The landlord sent many other servants, but the tenants beat some and killed others. ⁶Now the landowner had one son whom he loved dearly. He sent him last, thinking, They will respect my son. ⁷But those tenant farmers said to each other, 'This is the heir. Let's kill him, and the inheritance will be ours.' ⁸They grabbed him, killed him, and threw him out of the vineyard.

⁹"So what will the owner of the vineyard do? He will come and destroy those tenants and give the vineyard to others. ¹⁰Haven't you read this scripture, *The stone that the builders rejected has become the cornerstone.* ¹¹*The Lord has done this, and it's amazing in our eyes?"*ᶜ

¹²They wanted to arrest Jesus because they knew that he had told the parable against them. But they were afraid of the crowd, so they left him and went away.

A question about taxes

¹³They sent some of the Pharisees and supporters of Herod to trap him in his words. ¹⁴They came to him and said, "Teacher, we know that you're genuine and you don't worry about what people think. You don't show favoritism but teach God's way as it really is. Does the Law allow people to pay taxes to Caesar or not? Should we pay taxes or not?"

¹⁵Since Jesus recognized their deceit, he said to them, "Why are you testing me? Bring me a coin. Show it to me." ¹⁶And they brought one. He said to them, "Whose image and inscription is this?"

"Caesar's," they replied.

¹⁷Jesus said to them, "Give to Caesar what belongs to Caesar and to God what belongs to God." His reply left them overcome with wonder.

A question about the resurrection

¹⁸Sadducees, who deny that there is a resurrection, came to Jesus and asked, ¹⁹"Teacher, Moses wrote for us that *if a man's brother dies, leaving a widow but no children, the brother must marry the widow and raise up children for his brother.*ᵈ ²⁰Now there were seven brothers. The first one married a woman; when he died, he left no children. ²¹The second married her and died without leaving any children. The third did the same. ²²None of the seven left any children. Finally, the woman died. ²³At the resurrection, when

SAILBOAT

FORGIVENESS

The Circle of Forgiveness Mark 11:25

Jesus told the disciples to have faith when they prayed. Then he said they should always make sure they weren't upset with someone when they prayed. If they were, they must forgive that person first. Forgiveness is more than something God gives us for our sins. It's also something we must give others. God's forgiveness and our forgiveness are connected! It's like a circle. We must give the gift of forgiveness to others because we've received forgiveness from God. ◆

ᶜPs 118:22-23 ᵈDeut 25:5; Gen 38:8

they all rise up, whose wife will she be? All seven were married to her."

²⁴Jesus said to them, "Isn't this the reason you are wrong, because you don't know either the scriptures or God's power? ²⁵When people rise from the dead, they won't marry nor will they be given in marriage. Instead, they will be like God's angels. ²⁶As for the resurrection from the dead, haven't you read in the scroll from Moses, in the passage about the burning bush, how God said to Moses, *I am the God of Abraham, the God of Isaac, and the God of Jacob?*ᵉ ²⁷He isn't the God of the dead but of the living. You are seriously mistaken."

God's most important command

²⁸One of the legal experts heard their dispute and saw how well Jesus answered them. He came over and asked him, "Which commandment is the most important of all?"

²⁹Jesus replied, "The most important one is *Israel, listen! Our God is the one Lord,* ³⁰*and you must love the Lord your God with all your heart, with all your being, with all your mind, and with all your strength.*ᶠ ³¹The second is this, *You will love your neighbor as yourself.*ᵍ No other commandment is greater than these."

Memorize Mark 12:30-31

³²The legal expert said to him, "Well said, Teacher. You have truthfully said that God is one and there is no other besides him. ³³And to love God with all of the heart, a full understanding, and all of one's strength, and to love one's neighbor as oneself is much more important than all kinds of entirely burned offerings and sacrifices."

³⁴When Jesus saw that he had answered with wisdom, he said to him, "You aren't far from God's kingdom." After that, no one dared to ask him any more questions.

Jesus corrects the legal experts

³⁵While Jesus was teaching in the temple, he said, "Why do the legal experts say that the Christ is David's son? ³⁶David himself, inspired by the Holy Spirit, said, *The Lord said to my lord, 'Sit at my right side until I turn your enemies into your footstool.'*ʰ ³⁷David

himself calls him 'Lord,' so how can he be David's son?" The large crowd listened to him with delight.

³⁸As he was teaching, he said, "Watch out for the legal experts. They like to walk around in long robes. They want to be greeted with honor in the markets. ³⁹They long for places of honor in the synagogues and at banquets. ⁴⁰They are the ones who cheat widows out of their homes, and to show off they say long prayers. They will be judged most harshly."

A poor widow's contribution

⁴¹Jesus sat across from the collection box for the temple treasury and observed how the crowd gave their money. Many rich people were throwing in lots of money. ⁴²One poor widow came forward and put in two small copper coins worth a penny.ⁱ ⁴³Jesus called his disciples to him and said, "I assure you that this poor widow has put in more than everyone who's been putting money in the treasury. ⁴⁴All of them are giving out of their spare change. But she from her hopeless poverty has given everything she had, even what she needed to live on."

The temple's fate

13 As Jesus left the temple, one of his disciples said to him, "Teacher, look! What awesome stones and buildings!"

²Jesus responded, "Do you see these enormous buildings? Not even one stone will be left upon another. All will be demolished."

³Jesus was sitting on the Mount of Olives across from the temple. Peter, James, John, and Andrew asked him privately, ⁴"Tell us, when will these things happen? What sign will show that all these things are about to come to an end?"

Keep watch!

⁵Jesus said, "Watch out that no one deceives you. ⁶Many people will come in my name, saying, 'I'm the one!' They will deceive many people. ⁷When you hear of wars and reports of wars, don't be alarmed. These things must happen, but this isn't the end yet. ⁸Nations and kingdoms will fight against each

---

ᵉExod 3:6, 15-16 ᶠDeut 6:4-5 ᵍLev 19:18 ʰPs 110:1 ⁱOr two *lepta* (the smallest Greek copper coin, each worth 1/128 of a single day's pay), that is, a *kodrantes* (the smallest Roman coin, equal in value to two *lepta*)

other, and there will be earthquakes and famines in all sorts of places. These things are just the beginning of the sufferings associated with the end.

⁹"Watch out for yourselves. People will hand you over to the councils. You will be beaten in the synagogues. You will stand before governors and kings because of me so that you can testify before them. ¹⁰First, the good news must be proclaimed to all the nations. ¹¹When they haul you in and hand you over, don't worry ahead of time about what to answer or say. Instead, say whatever is given to you at that moment, for you aren't doing the speaking but the Holy Spirit is. ¹²Brothers and sisters will hand each other over to death. A father will turn in his children. Children will rise up against their parents and have them executed. ¹³Everyone will hate you because of my name. But whoever stands firm until the end will be saved.

¹⁴"When you see the disgusting and destructive thing standing where it shouldn't be (the reader should understand this), then those in Judea must escape to the mountains. ¹⁵Those on the roof shouldn't come down or enter their houses to grab anything. ¹⁶Those in the field shouldn't come back to grab their clothes. ¹⁷How terrible it will be at that time for women who are pregnant and for women who are nursing their children. ¹⁸Pray that it doesn't happen in winter. ¹⁹In those days there will be great suffering such as the world has never before seen and will never again see. ²⁰If the Lord hadn't shortened that time, no one would be rescued. But for the sake of the chosen ones, the ones whom God chose, he has cut short the time.

²¹"Then if someone says to you, 'Look, here's the Christ,' or 'There he is,' don't believe it. ²²False christs and false prophets will appear, and they will offer signs and wonders in order to deceive, if possible, those whom God has chosen. ²³But you, watch out! I've told you everything ahead of time.

²⁴"In those days, after the suffering of that time, the sun will become dark, and the moon won't give its light. ²⁵The stars will fall from the sky, and the planets and other heavenly bodies will be shaken. ²⁶Then they will see the Human One[j] coming in the clouds with great power and splendor. ²⁷Then he will send the angels and gather together his chosen people from the four corners of the earth, from the end of the earth to the end of heaven.

[j]Or Son of Man

It's Not the Amount That Matters Mark 12:41-44

Jesus told about a widow who was very poor. When she went to put in her offering, she gave two coins that were worth about one penny. Those coins were what she needed for food and survival. But she loved God and wanted to give. Jesus told his followers that the poor widow gave a lot more than the rich people who gave their extra money. The amount they gave was more, but the widow gave everything she had and trusted God with the outcome.

It doesn't matter how much we have. Jesus wants us to give everything that we have and everything that we are from our hearts. We can trust God to care for us and meet our needs. We can give our money, time, and talents to God and trust that we will always have what we need.

What do you have to give to Jesus?

How can you give more than just your spare change?

A lesson from the fig tree

²⁸"Learn this parable from the fig tree. After its branch becomes tender and it sprouts new leaves, you know that summer is near. ²⁹In the same way, when you see these things happening, you know that he's near, at the door. ³⁰I assure you that this generation won't pass away until all these things happen. ³¹Heaven and earth will pass away, but my words will certainly not pass away.

³²"But nobody knows when that day or hour will come, not the angels in heaven and not the Son. Only the Father knows. ³³Watch out! Stay alert! You don't know when the time is coming. ³⁴It is as if someone took a trip, left the household behind, and put the servants in charge, giving each one a job to do, and told the doorkeeper to stay alert. ³⁵Therefore, stay alert! You don't know when the head of the household will come, whether in the evening or at midnight, or when the rooster crows in the early morning or at daybreak. ³⁶Don't let him show up when you weren't expecting and find you sleeping. ³⁷What I say to you, I say to all: Stay alert!"

Preparation for burial

14 It was two days before Passover and the Festival of Unleavened Bread. The chief priests and legal experts through cunning tricks were searching for a way to arrest Jesus and kill him. ²But they agreed that it shouldn't happen during the festival; otherwise, there would be an uproar among the people.

³Jesus was at Bethany visiting the house of Simon, who had a skin disease. During dinner, a woman came in with a vase made of alabaster and containing very expensive perfume of pure nard. She broke open the vase and poured the perfume on his head. ⁴Some grew angry. They said to each other, "Why waste the perfume? ⁵This perfume could have been sold for almost a year's pay^k and the money given to the poor." And they scolded her. ⁶Jesus said, "Leave her alone. Why do you make trouble for her? She has done a good thing for me. ⁷You always have the poor with you; and whenever you want, you can do something good for them. But you won't always have me. ⁸She has done what she could. She has anointed my body ahead of time for burial. ⁹I tell you the truth that, wherever in the whole world the good news is announced, what she's done will also be told in memory of her."

Passover meal

¹⁰Judas Iscariot, one of the Twelve, went to the chief priests to give Jesus up to them. ¹¹When they heard it, they were delighted and promised to give him money. So he started looking for an opportunity to turn him in.

¹²On the first day of the Festival of Unleavened Bread, when the Passover lamb was sacrificed, the disciples said to Jesus, "Where do you want us to prepare for you to eat the Passover meal?"

¹³He sent two of his disciples and said to them, "Go into the city. A man carrying a water jar will meet you. Follow him. ¹⁴Wherever he enters, say to the owner of the house, 'The teacher asks, "Where is my guest room where I can eat the Passover meal with my disciples?" ' ¹⁵He will show you a large room upstairs already furnished. Prepare for us there." ¹⁶The disciples left, came into the city, found everything just as he had told them, and they prepared the Passover meal.

LIFE PRESERVER

Why did Jesus think the woman's gift was important?
Mark 14:1-9

The disciples knew it was important to take care of the poor. Jesus had taught on this subject many times. So they questioned the woman who poured very expensive perfume on Jesus. They believed she wasted money that could have been used to feed hungry people.

But Jesus was grateful for her generous act. Jesus knew he would soon die and be buried, so he received the woman's gift as preparation for what he faced. This story teaches that Jesus values both the feeding of the poor and individual acts of love and kindness. Both actions are important for people who follow Jesus. ◆

---

^kOr *three hundred denaria*; a denarion was equivalent to a day's pay.

[17]That evening, Jesus arrived with the Twelve. [18]During the meal, Jesus said, "I assure you that one of you will betray me—someone eating with me."

[19]Deeply saddened, they asked him, one by one, "It's not me, is it?"

[20]Jesus answered, "It's one of the Twelve, one who is dipping bread with me into this bowl. [21]The Human One[l] goes to his death just as it is written about him. But how terrible it is for that person who betrays the Human One![m] It would have been better for him if he had never been born."

[22]While they were eating, Jesus took bread, blessed it, broke it, and gave it to them, and said, "Take; this is my body." [23]He took a cup, gave thanks, and gave it to them, and they all drank from it. [24]He said to them, "This is my blood of the covenant, which is poured out for many. [25]I assure you that I won't drink wine again until that day when I drink it in a new way in God's kingdom." [26]After singing songs of praise, they went out to the Mount of Olives.

Predictions about disciples leaving Jesus

[27]Jesus said to them, "You will all falter in your faithfulness to me. It is written, *I will hit the shepherd, and the sheep will go off in all directions.*[n] [28]But after I'm raised up, I will go before you to Galilee."

[29]Peter said to him, "Even if everyone else stumbles, I won't."

[30]But Jesus said to him, "I assure you that on this very night, before the rooster crows twice, you will deny me three times."

[31]But Peter insisted, "If I must die alongside you, I won't deny you." And they all said the same thing.

Jesus in prayer

[32]Jesus and his disciples came to a place called Gethsemane. Jesus said to them, "Sit here while I pray." [33]He took Peter, James, and John along with him. He began to feel despair and was anxious. [34]He said to them, "I'm very sad. It's as if I'm dying. Stay here and keep alert." [35]Then he went a short distance

farther and fell to the ground. He prayed that, if possible, he might be spared the time of suffering. [36]He said, "Abba, Father, for you all things are possible. Take this cup of suffering away from me. However—not what I want but what you want."

[37]He came and found them sleeping. He said to Peter, "Simon, are you asleep? Couldn't you stay alert for one hour? [38]Stay alert and pray so that you won't give in to temptation. The spirit is eager, but the flesh is weak."

[39]Again, he left them and prayed, repeating the same words. [40]And, again, when he came back, he found them sleeping, for they couldn't keep their eyes open, and they didn't know how to respond to him. [41]He came a third time and said to them, "Will you sleep and rest all night? That's enough! The time has come for the Human One[o] to be betrayed into the hands of sinners. [42]Get up! Let's go! Look, here comes my betrayer."

Arrest

[43]Suddenly, while Jesus was still speaking, Judas, one of the Twelve, came with a mob carrying swords and clubs. They had been sent by the chief priests, legal experts, and elders. [44]His betrayer had given them a sign: "Arrest the man I kiss, and take him away under guard."

[45]As soon as he got there, Judas said to Jesus, "Rabbi!" Then he kissed him. [46]Then they came and grabbed Jesus and arrested him.

[47]One of the bystanders drew a sword and struck the high priest's slave and cut off his ear. [48]Jesus responded, "Have you come with swords and clubs to arrest me, like an outlaw? [49]Day after day, I was with you, teaching in the temple, but you didn't arrest me. But let the scriptures be fulfilled." [50]And all his disciples left him and ran away. [51]One young man, a disciple, was wearing nothing but a

did you know? The word *Gethsemane* means "oil press." An oil press was the machine used to juice the oil out of olives. No one knows for certain where Gethsemane was, but because of its name most people believe it was on the Mount of Olives.

---

[l]Or *Son of Man* [m]Or *Son of Man* [n]Zech 13:7 [o]Or *Son of Man*

linen cloth. They grabbed him, [52]but he left the linen cloth behind and ran away naked.

A hearing before the Sanhedrin

[53]They led Jesus away to the high priest, and all the chief priests, elders, and legal experts gathered. [54]Peter followed him from a distance, right into the high priest's courtyard. He was sitting with the guards, warming himself by the fire. [55]The chief priests and the whole Sanhedrin were looking for testimony against Jesus in order to put him to death, but they couldn't find any. [56]Many brought false testimony against him, but they contradicted each other. [57]Some stood to offer false witness against him, saying, [58]"We heard him saying, 'I will destroy this temple, constructed by humans, and within three days I will build another, one not made by humans.'" [59]But their testimonies didn't agree even on this point.

[60]Then the high priest stood up in the middle of the gathering and examined Jesus. "Aren't you going to respond to the testimony these people have brought against you?" [61]But Jesus was silent and didn't answer. Again, the high priest asked, "Are you the Christ, the Son of the blessed one?"

[62]Jesus said, "I am. And you will see the Human One[p] sitting on the right side of the Almighty[q] and coming on the heavenly clouds."

[63]Then the high priest tore his clothes and said, "Why do we need any more witnesses? [64]You've heard his insult against God. What do you think?"

They all condemned him. "He deserves to die!"

[65]Some began to spit on him. Some covered his face and hit him, saying, "Prophesy!" Then the guards took him and beat him.

Peter denies Jesus

[66]Meanwhile, Peter was below in the courtyard. A woman, one of the high priest's servants, approached [67]and saw Peter warming himself by the fire. She stared at him and said, "You were also with the Nazarene, Jesus."

[68]But he denied it, saying, "I don't know what you're talking about. I don't understand

what you're saying." And he went outside into the outer courtyard. A rooster crowed.

[69]The female servant saw him and began a second time to say to those standing around, "This man is one of them." [70]But he denied it again.

A short time later, those standing around again said to Peter, "You must be one of them, because you are also a Galilean."

[71]But he cursed and swore, "I don't know this man you're talking about." [72]At that very moment, a rooster crowed a second time. Peter remembered what Jesus told him, "Before a rooster crows twice, you will deny me three times." And he broke down, sobbing.

Trial before Pilate

15 At daybreak, the chief priests—with the elders, legal experts, and the whole Sanhedrin—formed a plan. They bound Jesus, led him away, and turned him over to Pilate. [2]Pilate questioned him, "Are you the king of the Jews?"

Jesus replied, "That's what you say." [3]The chief priests were accusing him of many things.

[4]Pilate asked him again, "Aren't you going to answer? What about all these accusations?" [5]But Jesus gave no more answers, so that Pilate marveled.

[6]During the festival, Pilate released one prisoner to them, whomever they requested. [7]A man named Barabbas was locked up with the rebels who had committed murder during an uprising. [8]The crowd pushed forward and asked Pilate to release someone, as he regularly did. [9]Pilate answered them, "Do you want me to release to you the king of the Jews?" [10]He knew that the chief priests had handed him over because of jealousy. [11]But the chief priests stirred up the crowd

to have him release Barabbas to them instead. [12]Pilate replied, "Then what do you want me to do with the one you call king of the Jews?"

[13]They shouted back, "Crucify him!"

[14]Pilate said to them, "Why? What wrong has he done?"

They shouted even louder, "Crucify him!"

[15]Pilate wanted to satisfy the crowd, so he released Barabbas to them. He had Jesus whipped, then handed him over to be crucified.

Jesus is tortured and killed

[16]The soldiers led Jesus away into the courtyard of the palace known as the governor's headquarters,[r] and they called together the whole company of soldiers.[s] [17]They dressed him up in a purple robe and twisted together a crown of thorns and put it on him. [18]They saluted him, "Hey! King of the Jews!" [19]Again and again, they struck his head with a stick. They spit on him and knelt before him to honor him. [20]When they finished mocking him, they stripped him of the purple robe and put his own clothes back on him. Then they led him out to crucify him.

[21]Simon, a man from Cyrene, Alexander and Rufus' father, was coming in from the countryside. They forced him to carry his cross. [22]They brought Jesus to the place called Golgotha, which means Skull Place. [23]They tried to give him wine mixed with myrrh, but he didn't take it. [24]They crucified him. They divided up his clothes, drawing lots for them to determine who would take what. [25]It was nine in the morning when they crucified him. [26]The notice of the formal charge against him was written, "The king of the Jews." [27]They crucified two outlaws with him, one on his right and one on his left.[t]

[r]Or *praetorium* [s]Or cohort (approximately six hundred soldiers) [t]15:28 is omitted in most critical editions of the Gk New Testament *The scripture was fulfilled, which says, He was numbered among criminals.*

God's THOUGHTS ◆ My THOUGHTS

Lying Is Never Good Mark 14:66-72

Getting caught in a lie is an awful, guilty feeling. Sometimes, we try to work our way out by making up more lies. But this is very hard to keep up! Lying is never a good way to go.

Peter found that out the hard way. He was one of Jesus' best friends. He was loyal and devoted. Even so, Jesus told Peter that Peter would deny being his friend (Mark 14:27-31). Peter didn't believe it. He loved Jesus and thought he would always claim Jesus as his friend, especially after everything they went through together.

But when Jesus was arrested, his followers got scared. They didn't know who they could trust. They didn't know what was going to happen to them. As Peter wandered around wondering what to do, three different people said they had seen him with Jesus. Peter lied each time and said he didn't know Jesus. The third time Peter remembered what Jesus said and started crying. His lies may have saved him from getting thrown into jail, but he betrayed his best friend. Peter probably wished he had been honest and brave. It is better to bravely tell the truth than to live with the guilt of lying.

When have you lied and felt terrible about it?

What do you think Peter felt after he had denied knowing Jesus three different times?

²⁹People walking by insulted him, shaking their heads and saying, "Ha! So you were going to destroy the temple and rebuild it in three days, were you? ³⁰Save yourself and come down from that cross!"

³¹In the same way, the chief priests were making fun of him among themselves, together with the legal experts. "He saved others," they said, "but he can't save himself. ³²Let the Christ, the king of Israel, come down from the cross. Then we'll see and believe." Even those who had been crucified with Jesus insulted him.

³³From noon until three in the afternoon the whole earth was dark. ³⁴At three, Jesus cried out with a loud shout, "*Eloi, eloi, lama sabachthani*," which means, "My God, my God, why have you left me?"

³⁵After hearing him, some standing there said, "Look! He's calling Elijah!" ³⁶Someone ran, filled a sponge with sour wine, and put it on a pole. He offered it to Jesus to drink, saying, "Let's see if Elijah will come to take him down." ³⁷But Jesus let out a loud cry and died.

³⁸The curtain of the sanctuary was torn in two from top to bottom. ³⁹When the centurion, who stood facing Jesus, saw how he died, he said, "This man was certainly God's Son."

⁴⁰Some women were watching from a distance, including Mary Magdalene and Mary the mother of James (the younger one) and Joses, and Salome. ⁴¹When Jesus was in Galilee, these women had followed and supported him, along with many other women who had come to Jerusalem with him.

Jesus' burial

⁴²Since it was late in the afternoon on Preparation Day, just before the Sabbath, ⁴³Joseph from Arimathea dared to approach Pilate and ask for Jesus' body. (Joseph was a prominent council member who also eagerly anticipated the coming of God's kingdom.) ⁴⁴Pilate wondered if Jesus was already dead. He called the centurion and asked him whether Jesus had already died. ⁴⁵When he learned from the centurion that Jesus was dead, Pilate gave the dead body to Joseph. ⁴⁶He bought a linen cloth, took Jesus down from the cross, wrapped him in the cloth, and laid him in a tomb that had been carved out of rock. He rolled a stone against the entrance to the tomb. ⁴⁷Mary Magdalene and Mary the mother of Joses saw where he was buried.

Empty tomb

16 When the Sabbath was over, Mary Magdalene, Mary the mother of James, and Salome bought spices so that they could go and anoint Jesus' dead body. ²Very early on the first day of the week, just after sunrise, they came to the tomb. ³They were saying to each other, "Who's going to roll the stone away from the entrance for us?" ⁴When they looked up, they saw that the stone had been rolled away. (And it was a very large stone!) ⁵Going into the tomb, they saw a young man in a white robe seated on the right side; and they were startled.

⁶But he said to them, "Don't be alarmed! You are looking for Jesus of Nazareth, who was crucified.ᵘ He has been raised. He isn't here. Look, here's the place where they laid him. ⁷Go, tell his disciples, especially Peter, that he is going ahead of you into Galilee. You will see him there, just as he told you." ⁸Overcome with terror and dread, they fled from the tomb. They said nothing to anyone, because they were afraid.ᵛ

Memorize Mark 16:6

SAILBOAT

COURAGE

Real Courage *Mark 15:43*

Joseph from Arimathea took a huge risk when he asked the Roman ruler for permission to take Jesus' body down from the cross and bury it. Pilate was so concerned with being popular that he allowed an innocent man to be killed in a cruel, painful manner. Pilate might have thought Joseph disagreed with his decision to kill Jesus and that could have cost Joseph his job or even his life. Joseph knew the risks before he made his request, but he did it anyway. That's real courage. ◆

ᵘOr *the Crucified One* ᵛIn most critical editions of the Gk New Testament, the Gospel of Mark ends at 16:8.

///

Endings Added Later

[⁹They promptly reported all of the young man's instructions to those who were with Peter. Afterward, through the work of his disciples, Jesus sent out, from the east to the west, the sacred and undying message of eternal salvation. Amen.]

[[⁹After Jesus rose up early on the first day of the week, he appeared first to Mary Magdalene, from whom he had cast out seven demons. ¹⁰She went and reported to the ones who had been with him, who were mourning and weeping. ¹¹But even after they heard the news, they didn't believe that Jesus was alive and that Mary had seen him.

¹²After that he appeared in a different form to two of them who were walking along in the countryside. ¹³When they returned, they reported it to the others, but they didn't believe them. ¹⁴Finally he appeared to the eleven while they were eating. Jesus criticized their unbelief and stubbornness because they didn't believe those who saw him after he was raised up. ¹⁵He said to them, "Go into the whole world and proclaim the good news to every creature. ¹⁶Whoever believes and is baptized will be saved, but whoever doesn't believe will be condemned. ¹⁷These signs will be associated with those who believe: they will throw out demons in my name. They will speak in new languages. ¹⁸They will pick up snakes with their hands. If they drink anything poisonous, it will not hurt them. They will place their hands on the sick, and they will get well."

¹⁹After the Lord Jesus spoke to them, he was lifted up into heaven and sat down on the right side of God. ²⁰But they went out and proclaimed the message everywhere. The Lord worked with them, confirming the word by the signs associated with them.]]

///

Luke

Luke begins with the Christmas story (Luke 1:26–2:38). It also tells what Jesus was like as a young boy (Luke 2:38-52) and goes on to tell about the rest of his life. The author of Luke said that he set out to write "a carefully ordered account" of the life of Jesus (Luke 1:3).

This book explains Jesus' mission in the world. Jesus said he came "to preach good news to the poor, to proclaim release to the prisoners and recovery of sight to the blind, to liberate the oppressed" (Luke 4:18).

Luke portrays Jesus searching for hurting people just like a shepherd goes looking for lost sheep (Luke 15:1-7). He cared for a child who wandered from home (Luke 15:11-32). He made friends with outcasts like Zacchaeus (Luke 19:1-10). Unlike other spiritual leaders of his day, Jesus invited women to learn from him (Luke 8:1-3). Jesus told a story about a good Samaritan to teach his followers to be kind to all people (Luke 10:25-37). Luke shows us God's compassion for everyone in the world! ⬦

things
YOU'LL DISCOVER

Luke brings the good news that Jesus is the Christ or Messiah who will save Israel, God's people. Luke also shows that Jesus will save people from all nations.

people
YOU'LL MEET

Herod—king of Judea (Luke 1; 3; 9)
John the Baptist—a prophet who prepared people to meet Jesus (Luke 1–9)
Mary and Joseph—the mother and father of Jesus (Luke 1–2)
Jesus—the Human One and God's Son (Luke 1–24)
The Twelve—Jesus' closest disciples, including Peter, James, and John (Luke 5–24)
Mary Magdalene, Joanna, Susanna—women who followed Jesus (Luke 8)

places
YOU'LL GO

Bethlehem (a town south of Jerusalem),
Nazareth (a town in northern Israel),
Jordan River,
Galilee (a lake and region in northern Israel),
Jerusalem,
Skull Place (the site outside Jerusalem where Jesus was crucified)

words
YOU'LL REMEMBER

"The Human One came to seek and save the lost" (Luke 19:10).

Luke's purpose

1 Many people have already applied themselves to the task of compiling an account of the events that have been fulfilled among us. ²They used what the original eyewitnesses and servants of the word handed down to us. ³Now, after having investigated everything carefully from the beginning, I have also decided to write a carefully ordered account for you, most honorable Theophilus. ⁴I want you to have confidence in the soundness of the instruction you have received.

John the Baptist's birth foretold

⁵During the rule of King Herod of Judea there was a priest named Zechariah who belonged to the priestly division of Abijah. His wife Elizabeth was a descendant of Aaron. ⁶They were both righteous before God, blameless in their observance of all the Lord's commandments and regulations. ⁷They had no children because Elizabeth was unable to become pregnant and they both were very old. ⁸One day Zechariah was serving as a priest before God because his priestly division was on duty. ⁹Following the customs of priestly service, he was chosen by lottery to go into the Lord's sanctuary and burn incense. ¹⁰All the people who gathered to worship were

did you know? In Bible times, women were sometimes engaged to be married at a very young age. Mary may have been as young as thirteen when she found out she was going to have a baby.

praying outside during this hour of incense offering. ¹¹An angel from the Lord appeared to him, standing to the right of the altar of incense. ¹²When Zechariah saw the angel, he was startled and overcome with fear. ¹³The angel said, "Don't be afraid, Zechariah. Your prayers have been heard. Your wife Elizabeth will give birth to your son and you must name him John. ¹⁴He will be a joy and delight to you, and many people will rejoice at his birth, ¹⁵for he will be great in the Lord's eyes. He must not drink wine and liquor. He will be filled with the Holy Spirit even before his birth. ¹⁶He will bring many Israelites back

to the Lord their God. ¹⁷He will go forth before the Lord, equipped with the spirit and power of Elijah. He will turn the hearts of fathersᵃ back to their children, and he will turn the disobedient to righteous patterns of thinking. He will make ready a people prepared for the Lord."

¹⁸Zechariah said to the angel, "How can I be sure of this? My wife and I are very old."

¹⁹The angel replied, "I am Gabriel. I stand in God's presence. I was sent to speak to you and to bring this good news to you. ²⁰Know this: What I have spoken will come true at the proper time. But because you didn't believe, you will remain silent, unable to speak until the day when these things happen."

²¹Meanwhile, the people were waiting for Zechariah, and they wondered why he was in the sanctuary for such a long time. ²²When he came out, he was unable to speak to them. They realized he had seen a vision in the temple, for he gestured to them and couldn't speak. ²³When he completed the days of his priestly service, he returned home. ²⁴Afterward, his wife Elizabeth became pregnant. She kept to herself for five months, saying, ²⁵"This is the Lord's doing. He has shown his favor to me by removing my disgrace among other people."

Jesus' birth foretold

²⁶When Elizabeth was six months pregnant, God sent the angel Gabriel to Nazareth, a city in Galilee, ²⁷to a virgin who was engaged to a man named Joseph, a descendant of David's house. The virgin's name was Mary. ²⁸When the angel came to her, he said, "Rejoice, favored one! The Lord is with you!" ²⁹She was confused by these words and wondered what kind of greeting this might be. ³⁰The angel said, "Don't be afraid, Mary. God is honoring you. ³¹Look! You will conceive and give birth to a son, and you will name him Jesus. ³²He will be great and he will be called the Son of the Most High. The Lord God will give him the throne of David his father. ³³He will rule over Jacob's house forever, and there will be no end to his kingdom."

³⁴Then Mary said to the angel, "How will this happen since I haven't had sexual relations with a man?"

ᵃOr *parents*

³⁵The angel replied, "The Holy Spirit will come over you and the power of the Most High will overshadow you. Therefore, the one who is to be born will be holy. He will be called God's Son. ³⁶Look, even in her old age, your relative Elizabeth has conceived a son. This woman who was labeled 'unable to conceive' is now six months pregnant. ³⁷Nothing is impossible for God."

³⁸Then Mary said, "I am the Lord's servant. Let it be with me just as you have said." Then the angel left her.

Mary visits Elizabeth

³⁹Mary got up and hurried to a city in the Judean highlands. ⁴⁰She entered Zechariah's home and greeted Elizabeth. ⁴¹When Elizabeth heard Mary's greeting, the child leaped in her womb, and Elizabeth was filled with the Holy Spirit. ⁴²With a loud voice she blurted out, "God has blessed you above all women, and he has blessed the child you carry. ⁴³Why do I have this honor, that the mother of my Lord should come to me? ⁴⁴As soon as I heard your greeting, the baby in my womb jumped for joy. ⁴⁵Happy is she who believed that the Lord would fulfill the promises he made to her."

Mary praises God

⁴⁶Mary said,
"With all my heart I glorify the Lord!
⁴⁷ In the depths of who I am
   I rejoice in God my savior.
⁴⁸ He has looked with favor
   on the low status of his servant.
   Look! From now on, everyone
   will consider me highly favored
⁴⁹ because the mighty one
   has done great things for me.
   Holy is his name.
⁵⁰ He shows mercy to everyone,
   from one generation to the next,
   who honors him as God.
⁵¹ He has shown strength with his arm.
   He has scattered those with arrogant
   thoughts and proud inclinations.
⁵² He has pulled the powerful
   down from their thrones
   and lifted up the lowly.
⁵³ He has filled the hungry with good things
   and sent the rich away empty-handed.

⁵⁴ He has come to the aid
   of his servant Israel,
   remembering his mercy,
⁵⁵ just as he promised to our ancestors,
   to Abraham and to Abraham's
   descendants forever."

SAILBOAT

Joy

Joy Despite the Circumstances
Luke 1:46-55
God chose Mary to be the mother of Jesus. This might seem like a great honor, but there were challenges. Mary was an unmarried, pregnant woman. Joseph, the man she was engaged to, wasn't the father of her baby. According to Jewish law, Joseph could have had her stoned for being unfaithful to him. While the people in her hometown watched and wondered, Mary went to visit her cousin Elizabeth, who was also miraculously pregnant. Instead of whining, Mary praised God. She praised God for what God was doing in her life, and for God's holiness, strength, and mercy. She trusted God and was filled with joy in spite of a hard situation. ♦

⁵⁶Mary stayed with Elizabeth about three months, and then returned to her home.

⁵⁷When the time came for Elizabeth to have her child, she gave birth to a boy. ⁵⁸Her neighbors and relatives celebrated with her because they had heard that the Lord had shown her great mercy. ⁵⁹On the eighth day, it came time to circumcise the child. They wanted to name him Zechariah because that was his father's name. ⁶⁰But his mother replied, "No, his name will be John."

⁶¹They said to her, "None of your relatives have that name." ⁶²Then they began gesturing to his father to see what he wanted to call him.

⁶³After asking for a tablet, he surprised everyone by writing, "His name is John." ⁶⁴At that moment, Zechariah was able to speak again, and he began praising God.

⁶⁵All their neighbors were filled with awe, and everyone throughout the Judean highlands talked about what had happened. ⁶⁶All who heard about this considered it carefully. They said, "What then will this child be?" Indeed, the Lord's power was with him.

Zechariah's prophecy

⁶⁷John's father Zechariah was filled with the Holy Spirit and prophesied,

⁶⁸"Bless the Lord God of Israel
 because he has come to help
 and has delivered his people.
⁶⁹ He has raised up a mighty savior for us
 in his servant David's house,

did you know? When Jesus was born, babies were wrapped snugly in cloth. This made the baby feel safe and warm.

⁷⁰ just as he said through the mouths
 of his holy prophets long ago.
⁷¹ He has brought salvation
 from our enemies
 and from the power
 of all those who hate us.
⁷² He has shown the mercy promised
 to our ancestors,
 and remembered his holy covenant,
⁷³ the solemn pledge he made
 to our ancestor Abraham.
He has granted ⁷⁴that we would be rescued
 from the power of our enemies
 so that we could serve him without fear,
⁷⁵ in holiness and righteousness
 in God's eyes,
 for as long as we live.
⁷⁶ You, child, will be called a prophet
 of the Most High,
 for you will go before the Lord
 to prepare his way.
⁷⁷ You will tell his people how to be saved
 through the forgiveness of their sins.
⁷⁸ Because of our God's deep compassion,
 the dawn from heaven
 will break upon us,
⁷⁹ to give light to those
 who are sitting in darkness
 and in the shadow of death,
 to guide us on the path of peace."

⁸⁰The child grew up, becoming strong in character. He was in the wilderness until he began his public ministry to Israel.

Jesus' birth

2In those days Caesar Augustus declared that everyone throughout the empire should be enrolled in the tax lists. ²This first enrollment occurred when Quirinius governed Syria. ³Everyone went to their own cities to be enrolled. ⁴Since Joseph belonged to David's house and family line, he went up from the city of Nazareth in Galilee to David's city, called Bethlehem, in Judea. ⁵He went to be enrolled together with Mary, who was promised to him in marriage and who was pregnant. ⁶While they were there, the time came for Mary to have her baby. ⁷She gave birth to her firstborn child, a son, wrapped him snugly, and laid him in a manger, because there was no place for them in the guestroom.

Announcement to shepherds

⁸Nearby shepherds were living in the fields, guarding their sheep at night. ⁹The Lord's angel stood before them, the Lord's glory shone around them, and they were terrified.

¹⁰The angel said, "Don't be afraid! Look! I bring good news to you—wonderful, joyous news for all people. ¹¹Your savior is born today in David's city. He is Christ the Lord. ¹²This is a sign for you: you will find a newborn baby wrapped snugly and lying in a manger." ¹³Suddenly a great assembly of the heavenly forces was with the angel praising God. They said, ¹⁴"Glory to God in heaven, and on earth peace among those whom he favors."

¹⁵When the angels returned to heaven, the shepherds said to each other, "Let's go right now to Bethlehem and see what's happened. Let's confirm what the Lord has revealed to us." ¹⁶They went quickly and found Mary and Joseph, and the baby lying in the manger. ¹⁷When they saw this, they reported what they had been told about this child. ¹⁸Everyone who heard it was amazed at what the shepherds told them. ¹⁹Mary committed these things to memory and considered them carefully. ²⁰The shepherds returned home, glorifying and praising God for all they had heard and seen. Everything happened just as they had been told.

Jesus' circumcision, naming, and temple presentation

²¹When eight days had passed, Jesus' parents circumcised him and gave him the name Jesus. This was the name given to him by the angel before he was conceived. ²²When the time came for their ritual cleansing, in

accordance with the Law from Moses, they brought Jesus up to Jerusalem to present him to the Lord. (²³It's written in the Law of the Lord, "Every firstborn male will be dedicated to the Lord.") ²⁴They offered a sacrifice in keeping with what's stated in the Law of the Lord, *A pair of turtledoves or two young pigeons.*ᵇ

Simeon's response to Jesus

²⁵A man named Simeon was in Jerusalem. He was righteous and devout. He eagerly anticipated the restoration of Israel, and the Holy Spirit rested on him. ²⁶The Holy Spirit revealed to him that he wouldn't die before he had seen the Lord's Christ. ²⁷Led by the Spirit, he went into the temple area. Meanwhile, Jesus' parents brought the child to the temple so that they could do what was customary under the Law. ²⁸Simeon took Jesus in his arms and praised God. He said,

²⁹"Now, master, let your servant go in peace
    according to your word,
³⁰ because my eyes have seen
    your salvation.
³¹ You prepared this salvation
    in the presence of all peoples.
³² It's a light for revelation to the Gentiles
    and a glory for your people Israel."

³³His father and mother were amazed by what was said about him. ³⁴Simeon blessed

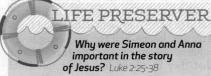

LIFE PRESERVER

Why were Simeon and Anna important in the story of Jesus? Luke 2:25-38

Mary and Joseph took Jesus to the temple in Jerusalem for his circumcision like all faithful Jewish parents. Simeon and Anna represent the blessing of the Jewish community. Simeon's words are borrowed from Isaiah and help connect what Jesus would do to heal Israel.

Anna, whom Luke describes as a prophet, saw what was going on and added her own words of praise for the work that Jesus would do. Mary and Joseph brought Jesus to the temple to "present him to the Lord" (Luke 2:22). Simeon and Anna were witnesses to this event and may have spoken about this experience with others. ◆

them and said to Mary his mother, "This boy is assigned to be the cause of the falling and rising of many in Israel and to be a sign that generates opposition ³⁵so that the inner thoughts of many will be revealed. And a sword will pierce your innermost being too."

Anna's response to Jesus

³⁶There was also a prophet, Anna the daughter of Phanuel, who belonged to the tribe of Asher. She was very old. After she married, she lived with her husband for seven years. ³⁷She was now an eighty-four-year-old widow. She never left the temple area but worshipped God with fasting and prayer night and day. ³⁸She approached at that very moment and began to praise God and to speak about Jesus to everyone who was looking forward to the redemption of Jerusalem.

Jesus as a child in Nazareth

³⁹When Mary and Joseph had completed everything required by the Law of the Lord, they returned to their hometown, Nazareth in Galilee. ⁴⁰The child grew up and became strong. He was filled with wisdom, and God's favor was on him.

Jesus in the temple at Passover

⁴¹Each year his parents went to Jerusalem for the Passover Festival. ⁴²When he was twelve years old, they went up to Jerusalem according to their custom. ⁴³After the festival was over, they were returning home, but the boy Jesus stayed behind in Jerusalem. His parents didn't know it. ⁴⁴Supposing that he was among their band of travelers, they journeyed on for a full day while looking for him among their family and friends. ⁴⁵When they didn't find Jesus, they returned to Jerusalem to look for him. ⁴⁶After three days they found him in the temple. He was sitting among the teachers, listening to them and putting questions to them. ⁴⁷Everyone who heard him was amazed by his understanding and his answers. ⁴⁸When his parents saw him, they were shocked.

His mother said, "Child, why have you treated us like this? Listen! Your father and I have been worried. We've been looking for you!"

ᵇLev 12:8; 5:11 LXX

⁴⁹Jesus replied, "Why were you looking for me? Didn't you know that it was necessary for me to be in my Father's house?" ⁵⁰But they didn't understand what he said to them.

⁵¹Jesus went down to Nazareth with them and was obedient to them. His mother cherished every word in her heart. ⁵²Jesus matured in wisdom and years, and in favor with God and with people.

John the Baptist's message

3 In the fifteenth year of the rule of the emperor Tiberius—when Pontius Pilate was governor over Judea and Herod was ruler[c] over Galilee, his brother Philip was ruler[d] over Ituraea and Trachonitis, and Lysanias was ruler[e] over Abilene, ²during the high priesthood of Annas and Caiaphas—God's word came to John son of Zechariah in the wilderness. ³John went throughout the region of the Jordan River, calling for people to be baptized to show that they were changing their hearts and lives and wanted God to forgive their sins. ⁴This is just as it was written in the scroll of the words of Isaiah the prophet,

A voice crying out in the wilderness:
  "Prepare the way for the Lord;
    make his paths straight.
⁵ *Every valley will be filled,*
  and every mountain and hill
    will be leveled.
The crooked will be made straight
  and the rough places made smooth.
⁶ *All humanity will see God's salvation."[f]*

⁷Then John said to the crowds who came to be baptized by him, "You children of snakes! Who warned you to escape from the angry judgment that is coming soon? ⁸Produce fruit that shows you have changed your hearts and lives. And don't even think about saying to yourselves, Abraham is our father. I tell you that God is able to raise up Abraham's children from these stones. ⁹The ax is already at the root of the trees. Therefore, every tree that doesn't produce good fruit will be chopped down and tossed into the fire."

¹⁰The crowds asked him, "What then should we do?"

¹¹He answered, "Whoever has two shirts

LIFE PRESERVER

Was it unusual for Jesus to sit with the teachers at the temple? *Luke 2:41-51*

Jesus' understanding of scripture was amazing. Evidently the questions he asked and the answers he gave to others' questions were really smart for someone who was 12 years old. Most likely Jesus was taught Hebrew scripture. We don't know what education he had outside the home. We also don't know what his parents taught him, but it's likely they knew and followed the Instruction to teach God's ways to their children (Deut 6:4-9).

Jewish teens still teach and read scripture in the synagogue when they celebrate their *Bar* or *Bat Mitzvah* on their thirteenth birthday. This story gives us one glimpse into the life of a young Jesus and the first group of people who listened to him. ◆

---

must share with the one who has none, and whoever has food must do the same."

¹²Even tax collectors came to be baptized. They said to him, "Teacher, what should we do?"

¹³He replied, "Collect no more than you are authorized to collect."

¹⁴Soldiers asked, "What about us? What should we do?"

He answered, "Don't cheat or harass anyone, and be satisfied with your pay."

Responses to John

¹⁵The people were filled with expectation, and everyone wondered whether John might be the Christ. ¹⁶John replied to them all, "I baptize you with water, but the one who is more powerful than me is coming. I'm not worthy to loosen the strap of his sandals. He will baptize you with the Holy Spirit and fire. ¹⁷The shovel he uses to sift the wheat from the husks is in his hands. He will clean out his threshing area and bring the wheat into his barn. But he will burn the husks with a fire that can't be put out." ¹⁸With many other words John appealed to them, proclaiming good news to the people.

¹⁹But Herod the ruler had been criticized harshly by John because of Herodias, Herod's brother's wife, and because of all the evil he

---

[c]Or *tetrarch* [d]Or *tetrarch* [e]Or *tetrarch* [f]Isa 40:3-5

had done. ²⁰He added this to the list of his evil deeds: he locked John up in prison.

Jesus' baptism

²¹When everyone was being baptized, Jesus also was baptized. While he was praying, heaven was opened ²²and the Holy Spirit came down on him in bodily form like a dove. And there was a voice from heaven: "You are my Son, whom I dearly love; in you I find happiness."

Jesus' genealogy

²³Jesus was about 30 years old when he began his ministry. People supposed that he was the son of Joseph son of Heli ²⁴son of Matthat son of Levi son of Melchi son of Jannai son of Joseph ²⁵son of Mattathias son of Amos son of Nahum son of Esli son of Naggai ²⁶son of Maath son of Mattathias son of Semein son of Josech son of Joda ²⁷son of Joanan son of Rhesa son of Zerubbabel son of Shealtiel son of Neri ²⁸son of Melchi son of Addi son of Cosam son of Elmadam son of Er ²⁹son of Joshua son of Eliezer son of Jorim son of Matthat son of Levi ³⁰son of Simeon son of Judah son of Joseph son of Jonam son of Eliakim ³¹son of Melea son of Menna son of Mattatha son of Nathan son of David ³²son of Jesse son of Obed son of Boaz son of Sala son of Nahshon ³³son of Amminadab son of Admin son of Arni son of Hezron son of Perez son of Judah ³⁴son of Jacob son of Isaac son of Abraham son of Terah son of Nahor ³⁵son of Serug son of Reu son of Peleg son of Eber son of Shelah ³⁶son of Cainan son of Arphaxad son of Shem son of Noah son of Lamech ³⁷son of Methuselah son of Enoch son of Jared son of Mahalalel son of Cainan ³⁸son of Enos son of Seth son of Adam son of God.

Jesus' temptation

4Jesus returned from the Jordan River full of the Holy Spirit, and was led by the Spirit into the wilderness. ²There he was tempted for forty days by the devil. He ate nothing during those days and afterward Jesus was starving. ³The devil said to him, "Since you are God's Son, command this stone to become a loaf of bread."

LIFE PRESERVER

What's important about Jesus' family tree in Luke?
Luke 3:23-38

There are two important things in Luke's list of Jesus' relatives. The list begins with a sentence about Jesus starting his ministry and ends with "son of Adam son of God" (Luke 3:28). Luke wanted readers to know that Jesus' ministry was connected with the history of God's people in the Old Testament. It's a continuing story. Luke knew this would be important for the Jews as they listened to Jesus talk about old and new things. Luke wanted readers to remember that Jesus was a part of Joseph's family, but he was also God's Son. 🌢

⁴Jesus replied, "It's written, *People won't live only by bread.*"ᵍ

⁵Next the devil led him to a high place and showed him in a single instant all the kingdoms of the world. ⁶The devil said, "I will give you this whole domain and the glory of all these kingdoms. It's been entrusted to me and I can give it to anyone I want. ⁷Therefore, if you will worship me, it will all be yours."

⁸Jesus answered, "It's written, *You will worship the Lord your God and serve only him.*"ʰ

⁹The devil brought him into Jerusalem and stood him at the highest point of the temple. He said to him, "Since you are God's Son, throw yourself down from here; ¹⁰for it's written: *He will command his angels concerning you, to protect you* ¹¹*and they will take you up in their hands so that you won't hit your foot on a stone.*"ⁱ

¹²Jesus answered, "It's been said, *Don't test the Lord your God.*"ʲ ¹³After finishing every temptation, the devil departed from him until the next opportunity.

Jesus announces good news to the poor

¹⁴Jesus returned in the power of the Spirit to Galilee, and news about him spread throughout the whole countryside. ¹⁵He taught in their synagogues and was praised by everyone.

¹⁶Jesus went to Nazareth, where he had been raised. On the Sabbath he went to the synagogue as he normally did and stood up to

ᵍDeut 8:3 ʰDeut 6:13 ⁱPs 91:11-12 ʲDeut 6:16

read. [17]The synagogue assistant gave him the scroll from the prophet Isaiah. He unrolled the scroll and found the place where it was written:

[18] *The Spirit of the Lord is upon me,*
> *because the Lord has anointed me.*
> *He has sent me to preach good news*
>> *to the poor,*
> *to proclaim release to the prisoners*
> *and recovery of sight to the blind,*
> *to liberate the oppressed,*

[19] *and to proclaim the year*
> *of the Lord's favor.*[k]

[20]He rolled up the scroll, gave it back to the synagogue assistant, and sat down. Every eye in the synagogue was fixed on him. [21]He began to explain to them, "Today, this scripture has been fulfilled just as you heard it."

[22]Everyone was raving about Jesus, so impressed were they by the gracious words flowing from his lips. They said, "This is Joseph's son, isn't it?"

[23]Then Jesus said to them, "Undoubtedly, you will quote this saying to me: 'Doctor, heal yourself. Do here in your hometown what we've heard you did in Capernaum.'" [24]He said, "I assure you that no prophet is welcome in the prophet's hometown. [25]And I can assure you that there were many widows in Israel during Elijah's time, when it didn't rain for three and a half years and there was a great food shortage in the land. [26]Yet Elijah was sent to none of them but only to a widow in the city of Zarephath in the region of Sidon. [27]There were also many persons with skin diseases in Israel during the time of the prophet Elisha, but none of them were cleansed. Instead, Naaman the Syrian was cleansed."

[28]When they heard this, everyone in the synagogue was filled with anger. [29]They rose up and ran him out of town. They led him to the crest of the hill on which their town had been built so that they could throw him off the cliff. [30]But he passed through the crowd and went on his way.

Jesus in Capernaum

[31]Jesus went down to the city of Capernaum in Galilee and taught the people each Sabbath. [32]They were amazed by his teaching because he delivered his message with authority.

[33]A man in the synagogue had the spirit of an unclean demon. He screamed, [34]"Hey! What have you to do with us, Jesus of Nazareth? Have you come to destroy us? I know who you are. You are the holy one from God."

[35]"Silence!" Jesus said, speaking harshly to the demon. "Come out of him!" The demon threw the man down before them, then came out of him without harming him.

[36]They were all shaken and said to each other, "What kind of word is this, that he can command unclean spirits with authority and power, and they leave?" [37]Reports about him spread everywhere in the surrounding region.

[38]After leaving the synagogue, Jesus went home with Simon. Simon's mother-in-law was sick with a high fever, and the family asked Jesus to help her. [39]He bent over her and spoke harshly to the fever, and it left her. She got up at once and served them.

[40]When the sun was setting, everyone brought to Jesus relatives and acquaintances with all kinds of diseases. Placing his hands

[k]Isa 61:1-2; 58:6

on each of them, he healed them. [41]Demons also came out of many people. They screamed, "You are God's Son." But he spoke harshly to them and wouldn't allow them to speak because they recognized that he was the Christ. [42]When daybreak arrived, Jesus went to a deserted place. The crowds were looking for him. When they found him, they tried to keep him from leaving them. [43]But he said to them, "I must preach the good news of God's kingdom in other cities too, for this is why I was sent." [44]So he continued preaching in the Judean synagogues.

Jesus calls disciples

5 One day Jesus was standing beside Lake Gennesaret when the crowd pressed in around him to hear God's word. [2]Jesus saw two boats sitting by the lake. The fishermen had gone ashore and were washing their nets. [3]Jesus boarded one of the boats, the one that belonged to Simon, then asked him to row out a little distance from the shore. Jesus sat down and taught the crowds from the boat. [4]When he finished speaking to the crowds, he said to Simon, "Row out farther, into the deep water, and drop your nets for a catch."

[5]Simon replied, "Master, we've worked hard all night and caught nothing. But because you say so, I'll drop the nets."

[6]So they dropped the nets and their catch was so huge that their nets were splitting.

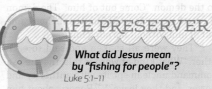

LIFE PRESERVER

What did Jesus mean by "fishing for people"?
Luke 5:1–11

When Jesus began his ministry, he invited fishermen to be his disciples. He knew he needed people to help him. Jesus saw Peter, James, John, and others working on the boats, casting their nets and bringing in the fish that would feed them and many others. Fishing was hard work.

Jesus invited these men to follow him and join him as he traveled. Like any good teacher, Jesus used language they would understand. He told them that instead of fishing for fish, they would fish for people (Luke 5:10). Their new job would be to help Jesus share his message of love and care for others. ◊

[7]They signaled for their partners in the other boat to come and help them. They filled both boats so full that they were about to sink. [8]When Simon Peter saw the catch, he fell at Jesus' knees and said, "Leave me, Lord, for I'm a sinner!" [9]Peter and those with him were overcome with amazement because of the number of fish they caught. [10]James and John, Zebedee's sons, were Simon's partners and they were amazed too.

Jesus said to Simon, "Don't be afraid. From now on, you will be fishing for people." [11]As soon as they brought the boats to the shore, they left everything and followed Jesus.

A man with a skin disease

[12]Jesus was in one of the towns where there was also a man covered with a skin disease. When he saw Jesus, he fell on his face and begged, "Lord, if you want, you can make me clean."

[13]Jesus reached out his hand, touched him, and said, "I do want to. Be clean." Instantly, the skin disease left him. [14]Jesus ordered him not to tell anyone. "Instead," Jesus said, "go and show yourself to the priest and make an offering for your cleansing, as Moses instructed. This will be a testimony to them." [15]News of him spread even more and huge crowds gathered to listen and to be healed from their illnesses. [16]But Jesus would withdraw to deserted places for prayer.

Jesus heals a paralyzed man

[17]One day when Jesus was teaching, Pharisees and legal experts were sitting nearby. They had come from every village in Galilee and Judea, and from Jerusalem. Now the power of the Lord was with Jesus to heal. [18]Some men were bringing a man who was paralyzed, lying on a cot. They wanted to carry him in and place him before Jesus, [19]but they couldn't reach him because of the crowd. So they took him up on the roof and lowered him—cot and all—through the roof tiles into the crowded room in front of Jesus. [20]When Jesus saw their faith, he said, "Friend, your sins are forgiven."

[21]The legal experts and Pharisees began to mutter among themselves, "Who is this who insults God? Only God can forgive sins!"

[22] Jesus recognized what they were discussing and responded, "Why do you fill your minds with these questions? [23] Which is easier—to say, 'Your sins are forgiven,' or to say, 'Get up and walk'? [24] But so that you will know that the Human One[1] has authority on the earth to forgive sins" —Jesus now spoke to the man who was paralyzed, "I say to you, get up, take your cot, and go home." [25] Right away, the man stood before them, picked up his cot, and went home, praising God.

[26] All the people were beside themselves with wonder. Filled with awe, they glorified God, saying, "We've seen unimaginable things today."

Jesus calls a tax collector

[27] Afterward, Jesus went out and saw a tax collector named Levi sitting at a kiosk for collecting taxes. Jesus said to him, "Follow me."

[28] Levi got up, left everything behind, and followed him. [29] Then Levi threw a great banquet for Jesus in his home. A large number of tax collectors and others sat down to eat with them. [30] The Pharisees and their legal experts grumbled against his disciples. They said, "Why do you eat and drink with tax collectors and sinners?"

[31] Jesus answered, "Healthy people don't need a doctor, but sick people do. [32] I didn't come to call righteous people but sinners to change their hearts and lives."

The old and the new

[33] Some people said to Jesus, "The disciples of John fast often and pray frequently. The disciples of the Pharisees do the same, but your disciples are always eating and drinking."

[34] Jesus replied, "You can't make the wedding guests fast while the groom is with them, can you? [35] The days will come when the groom will be taken from them, and then they will fast."

[36] Then he told them a parable. "No one tears a patch from a new garment to patch an old garment. Otherwise, the new garment would be ruined, and the new patch wouldn't match the old garment. [37] Nobody pours new wine into old wineskins. If they did, the new wine would burst the wineskins, the wine

would spill, and the wineskins would be ruined. [38] Instead, new wine must be put into new wineskins. [39] No one who drinks a well-aged wine wants new wine, but says, 'The well-aged wine is better.'"

Activities on the Sabbath

6 One Sabbath, as Jesus was going through the wheat fields, his disciples were picking the heads of wheat, rubbing them in their hands, and eating them. [2] Some Pharisees said, "Why are you breaking the Sabbath law?"

[3] Jesus replied, "Haven't you read what David and his companions did when they were hungry? [4] He broke the Law by going into God's house and eating the bread of the presence, which only the priests can eat. He also gave some of the bread to his companions." [5] Then he said to them, "The Human One[m] is Lord of the Sabbath."

[6] On another Sabbath, Jesus entered a synagogue to teach. A man was there whose right hand was withered. [7] The legal experts and the Pharisees were watching him closely to see if he would heal on the Sabbath. They were looking for a reason to bring charges against him. [8] Jesus knew their thoughts, so he said to the man with the withered hand, "Get up and stand in front of everyone." He got up and stood there. [9] Jesus said to the legal experts and Pharisees, "Here's a question for you: Is it legal on the Sabbath to do good or to do evil, to save life or to destroy it?" [10] Looking around at them all, he said to the man, "Stretch out your hand." So he did and his hand was made healthy. [11] They were furious and began talking with each other about what to do to Jesus.

Jesus chooses apostles

[12] During that time, Jesus went out to the mountain to pray, and he prayed to God all night long. [13] At daybreak, he called together his disciples. He chose twelve of them whom he called apostles: [14] Simon, whom he named Peter; his brother Andrew; James; John; Philip; Bartholomew; [15] Matthew; Thomas; James the son of Alphaeus; Simon, who was called a zealot; [16] Judas the son of James; and Judas Iscariot, who became a traitor.

[1] Or *Son of Man*   [m] Or *Son of Man*

Jesus' popularity increases

¹⁷Jesus came down from the mountain with them and stood on a large area of level ground. A great company of his disciples and a huge crowd of people from all around Judea and Jerusalem and the area around Tyre and Sidon joined him there. ¹⁸They came to hear him and to be healed from their diseases, and those bothered by unclean spirits were healed. ¹⁹The whole crowd wanted to touch him, because power was going out from him and he was healing everyone.

Happy people and doomed people

²⁰Jesus raised his eyes to his disciples and said:

"Happy are you who are poor,
because God's kingdom is yours.
²¹ Happy are you who hunger now,
because you will be satisfied.
Happy are you who weep now,
because you will laugh.
²²Happy are you when people hate you, reject you, insult you, and condemn your name as evil because of the Human One.ⁿ ²³Rejoice when that happens! Leap for joy because you have a great reward in heaven. Their ancestors did the same things to the prophets.
²⁴ But how terrible for you who are rich,
because you have already received
your comfort.
²⁵ How terrible for you who have plenty now,
because you will be hungry.
How terrible for you who laugh now,
because you will mourn and weep.
²⁶ How terrible for you when all speak well
of you.
Their ancestors did the same things to
the false prophets.

Behaving as God's children

²⁷"But I say to you who are willing to hear: Love your enemies. Do good to those who hate you. ²⁸Bless those who curse you. Pray for those who mistreat you. ²⁹If someone slaps you on the cheek, offer the other one as well. If someone takes your coat, don't withhold your shirt either. ³⁰Give to everyone who asks and don't demand your things

Bet you can *read this in 1 minute. Ready, set, go!*

back from those who take them. ³¹Treat people in the same way that you want them to treat you.

³²"If you love those who love you, why should you be commended? Even sinners love those who love them. ³³If you do good to those who do good to you, why should you be commended? Even sinners do that. ³⁴If you lend to those from whom you expect repayment, why should you be commended? Even sinners lend to sinners expecting to be paid back in full. ³⁵Instead, love your enemies, do good, and lend expecting nothing in return. If you do, you will have a great reward. You will be acting the way children of the Most High act, for he is kind to ungrateful and wicked people. ³⁶Be compassionate just as your Father is compassionate.

³⁷"Don't judge, and you won't be judged. Don't condemn, and you won't be condemned. Forgive, and you will be forgiven. ³⁸Give, and it will be given to you. A good portion—packed down, firmly shaken, and overflowing—will fall into your lap. The portion you give will determine the portion you receive in return."

Memorize
Luke 6:38

Avoiding self-deception

³⁹Jesus also told them a riddle. "A blind person can't lead another blind person, right? Won't they both fall into a ditch? ⁴⁰Disciples aren't greater than their teacher, but whoever is fully prepared will be like their teacher. ⁴¹Why do you see the splinter in your brother's or sister's eye but don't notice the log in your own eye? ⁴²How can you say to your brother or sister, 'Brother, Sister, let me take the splinter out of your eye,' when you don't see the log in your own eye? You deceive yourselves! First take the log out of your eye, and then you will see clearly to take the splinter out of your brother's or sister's eye.

⁴³"A good tree doesn't produce bad fruit, nor does a bad tree produce good fruit. ⁴⁴Each tree is known by its own fruit. People don't gather figs from thorny plants, nor do they pick grapes from prickly bushes. ⁴⁵A good person produces good from the good treasury of the inner self, while an evil person

ⁿOr Son of Man

produces evil from the evil treasury of the inner self. The inner self overflows with words that are spoken.

⁴⁶"Why do you call me 'Lord, Lord' and don't do what I say? ⁴⁷I'll show what it's like when someone comes to me, hears my words, and puts them into practice. ⁴⁸It's like a person building a house by digging deep and laying the foundation on bedrock. When the flood came, the rising water smashed against that house, but the water couldn't shake the house because it was well built. ⁴⁹But those who don't put into practice what they hear are like a person who built a house without a foundation. The floodwater smashed against it and it collapsed instantly. It was completely destroyed."

A servant is healed

7 After Jesus finished presenting all his words among the people, he entered Capernaum. ²A centurion had a servant who was very important to him, but the servant was ill and about to die. ³When the centurion heard about Jesus, he sent some Jewish elders to Jesus to ask him to come and heal his servant. ⁴When they came to Jesus, they earnestly pleaded with Jesus. "He deserves to have you do this for him," they said. ⁵"He loves our people and he built our synagogue for us."

⁶Jesus went with them. He had almost reached the house when the centurion sent friends to say to Jesus, "Lord, don't be bothered. I don't deserve to have you come under my roof. ⁷In fact, I didn't even consider myself worthy to come to you. Just say the word and my servant will be healed. ⁸I'm also a man appointed under authority, with soldiers under me. I say to one, 'Go,' and he goes, and to another, 'Come,' and he comes. I say to my servant, 'Do this,' and the servant does it."

⁹When Jesus heard these words, he was impressed with the centurion. He turned to the crowd following him and said, "I tell you, even in Israel I haven't found faith like this." ¹⁰When the centurion's friends returned to his house, they found the servant restored to health.

Jesus raises a widow's son

¹¹A little later Jesus went to a city called Nain. His disciples and a great crowd traveled with him. ¹²As he approached the city gate, a dead man was being carried out. He was his mother's only son, and she was a widow. A large crowd from the city was with her. ¹³When he saw her, the Lord had compassion for her and said, "Don't cry." ¹⁴He stepped forward and touched the stretcher on which the dead man was being carried. Those carrying him stood still. Jesus said, "Young man, I say to you, get up." ¹⁵The dead man sat up and began to speak, and Jesus gave him to his mother.

¹⁶Awestruck, everyone praised God. "A great prophet has appeared among us," they said. "God has come to help his people." ¹⁷This news about Jesus spread throughout Judea and the surrounding region.

did you know? In Jesus' time, Israel was ruled by the Roman Empire. Roman soldiers were sent to Israel to make sure the Jews obeyed and paid their taxes to Rome. A *centurion* was a Roman officer who commanded at least one hundred soldiers. Jewish people considered the centurion and his soldiers to be their enemies.

John the Baptist and Jesus

¹⁸John's disciples informed him about all these things. John called two of his disciples ¹⁹and sent them to the Lord. They were to ask him, "Are you the one who is coming, or should we look for someone else?"

²⁰When they reached Jesus, they said, "John the Baptist sent us to you. He asks, 'Are you the one who is coming, or should we look for someone else?'"

²¹Right then, Jesus healed many of their diseases, illnesses, and evil spirits, and he gave sight to a number of blind people. ²²Then he replied to John's disciples, "Go, report to John what you have seen and heard. *Those who were blind are able to see.* Those who were crippled now walk. People with skin diseases are cleansed. Those *who were deaf now hear. Those who were dead are raised up. And good news is preached to the poor.*ᵒ ²³Happy is anyone who doesn't stumble along the way because of me."

²⁴After John's messengers were gone, Jesus spoke to the crowds about John. "What did you go out into the wilderness to see? A stalk blowing in the wind? ²⁵What did you go out to see? A man dressed up in refined

ᵒIsa 35:5-6; 61:1

clothes? Look, those who dress in fashionable clothes and live in luxury are in royal palaces. [26]What did you go out to see? A prophet? Yes, I tell you, and more than a prophet. [27]He is the one of whom it's written: *Look, I'm sending my messenger before you, who will prepare your way before you.*[P] [28]I tell you that no greater human being has ever been born than John. Yet whoever is least in God's kingdom is greater than he." [29]Everyone who heard this, including the tax collectors, acknowledged God's justice because they had been baptized by John. [30]But the Pharisees and legal experts rejected God's will for themselves because they hadn't been baptized by John.

[31]"To what will I compare the people of this generation?" Jesus asked. "What are they like? [32]They are like children sitting in the marketplace calling out to each other, 'We played the flute for you and you didn't dance. We sang a funeral song and you didn't cry.' [33]John the Baptist came neither eating bread nor drinking wine, and you say, 'He has a demon.' [34]Yet the Human One[q] came eating and drinking, and you say, 'Look, a glutton and a drunk, a friend of tax collectors and sinners.' [35]But wisdom is proved to be right by all her descendants."

Forgiveness and gratitude

[36]One of the Pharisees invited Jesus to eat with him. After he entered the Pharisee's home, he took his place at the table. [37]Meanwhile, a woman from the city, a sinner, discovered that Jesus was dining in the Pharisee's house. She brought perfumed oil in a vase made of alabaster. [38]Standing behind him at his feet and crying, she began to wet his feet with her tears. She wiped them with her hair, kissed them, and poured the oil on them. [39]When the Pharisee who had invited Jesus saw what was happening, he said to himself, If this man were a prophet, he would know what kind of woman is touching him. He would know that she is a sinner.

[40]Jesus replied, "Simon, I have something to say to you."

"Teacher, speak," he said.

[41]"A certain lender had two debtors. One owed enough money to pay five hundred

people for a day's work.[r] The other owed enough money for fifty. [42]When they couldn't pay, the lender forgave the debts of them both. Which of them will love him more?"

[43]Simon replied, "I suppose the one who had the largest debt canceled."

Jesus said, "You have judged correctly."

[44]Jesus turned to the woman and said to Simon, "Do you see this woman? When I entered your home, you didn't give me water for my feet, but she wet my feet with tears and wiped them with her hair. [45]You didn't greet me with a kiss, but she hasn't stopped kissing my feet since I came in. [46]You didn't anoint my head with oil, but she has poured perfumed oil on my feet. [47]This is why I tell you that her many sins have been forgiven; so she has shown great love. The one who is forgiven little loves little."

[48]Then Jesus said to her, "Your sins are forgiven."

LIGHTHOUSE

CHANGED HEART AND LIFE

True Change *Luke 7:37-48*
Bible teachers think the perfumed oil mentioned in these verses may have cost one year's wages. We may wonder why the woman would have poured something that expensive over Jesus. Her actions bothered Simon but not Jesus. Jesus wasn't worried about what people thought. He didn't care about the woman's past. He knew her heart and forgave her sins. She was a living example of a changed heart and life. ◆

[49]The other table guests began to say among themselves, "Who is this person that even forgives sins?"

[50]Jesus said to the woman, "Your faith has saved you. Go in peace."

Women who followed Jesus

8 Soon afterward, Jesus traveled through the cities and villages, preaching and proclaiming the good news of God's kingdom. The Twelve were with him, [2]along with some women who had been healed of evil spirits and sicknesses. Among them were

LIFE PRESERVER

Were any women disciples?
Luke 8:1-3

Early in Jesus' ministry he traveled with the disciples and the women named in these verses. A *disciple* is someone who learns from a teacher. Though the twelve disciples that are named in the Bible were all men, these verses tell us that some women were disciples because they gave money to Jesus' ministry and traveled with him as he taught the good news. This meant that the women were able to share with Jesus and other followers. 💧

Mary Magdalene (from whom seven demons had been thrown out), ³Joanna (the wife of Herod's servant Chuza), Susanna, and many others who provided for them out of their resources.

Parable of the soils

⁴When a great crowd was gathering and people were coming to Jesus from one city after another, he spoke to them in a parable: ⁵"A farmer went out to scatter his seed. As he was scattering it, some fell on the path where it was crushed, and the birds in the sky came and ate it. ⁶Other seed fell on rock. As it grew, it dried up because it had no moisture. ⁷Other seed fell among thorny plants. The thorns grew with the plants and choked them. ⁸Still other seed landed on good soil. When it grew, it produced one hundred times more grain than was scattered." As he said this, he called out, "Everyone who has ears should pay attention."

⁹His disciples asked him what this parable meant. ¹⁰He said, "You have been given the mysteries of God's kingdom, but these mysteries come to everyone else in parables so that *when they see, they can't see, and when they hear, they can't understand.*⁵

¹¹"The parable means this: The seed is God's word. ¹²The seed on the path are those who hear, but then the devil comes and steals the word from their hearts so that they won't believe and be saved. ¹³The seed on the rock are those who receive the word joyfully when they hear it, but they have no

root. They believe for a while but fall away when they are tempted. ¹⁴As for the seed that fell among thorny plants, these are the ones who, as they go about their lives, are choked by the concerns, riches, and pleasures of life, and their fruit never matures. ¹⁵The seed that fell on good soil are those who hear the word and commit themselves to it with a good and upright heart. Through their resolve, they bear fruit.

Sharing the light

¹⁶"No one lights a lamp and then covers it with a bowl or puts it under a bed. Instead, they put it on top of a lampstand so that those who enter can see the light. ¹⁷Nothing is hidden that won't be exposed. Nor is anything concealed that won't be made known and brought to the light. ¹⁸Therefore, listen carefully. Those who have will receive more, but as for those who don't have, even what they seem to have will be taken away from them."

Jesus' family

¹⁹Jesus' mother and brothers came to him but were unable to reach him because of the crowd. ²⁰Someone told him, "Your mother and brothers are standing outside, wanting to see you."

²¹He replied, "My mother and brothers are those who listen to God's word and do it."

Jesus calms the sea

²²One day Jesus and his disciples boarded a boat. He said to them, "Let's cross over to the other side of the lake." So they set sail.

²³While they were sailing, he fell asleep. Gale-force winds swept down on the lake. The boat was filling up with water and they were in danger. ²⁴So they went and woke Jesus, shouting, "Master, Master, we're going to drown!" But he got up and gave orders to the wind and the violent waves. The storm died down and it was calm.

²⁵He said to his disciples, "Where is your faith?"

Filled with awe and wonder, they said to each other, "Who is this? He commands even the winds and the water, and they obey him!"

⁵Isa 6:9

Jesus frees a demon-possessed man

²⁶Jesus and his disciples sailed to the Gerasenes' land, which is across the lake from Galilee. ²⁷As soon as Jesus got out of the boat, a certain man met him. The man was from the city and was possessed by demons. For a long time, he had lived among the tombs, naked and homeless. ²⁸When he saw Jesus, he shrieked and fell down before him. Then he shouted, "What have you to do with me, Jesus, Son of the Most High God? I beg you, don't torture me!" ²⁹He said this because Jesus had already commanded the unclean spirit to come out of the man. Many times it had taken possession of him, so he would be bound with leg irons and chains and placed under guard. But he would break his restraints, and the demon would force him into the wilderness.

³⁰Jesus asked him, "What is your name?"

"Legion," he replied, because many demons had entered him. ³¹They pleaded with him not to order them to go back into the abyss.ᵗ ³²A large herd of pigs was feeding on the hillside. The demons begged Jesus to let them go into the pigs. Jesus gave them permission, ³³and the demons left the man and entered the pigs. The herd rushed down the cliff into the lake and drowned.

³⁴When those who tended the pigs saw what happened, they ran away and told the story in the city and in the countryside. ³⁵People came to see what had happened. They came to Jesus and found the man from whom the demons had gone. He was sitting at Jesus' feet, fully dressed and completely sane. They were filled with awe. ³⁶Those people who had actually seen what had happened told them how the demon-possessed man had been delivered. ³⁷Then everyone gathered from the region of the Gerasenes asked Jesus to leave their area because they were overcome with fear. So he got into the boat and returned across the lake. ³⁸The man from whom the demons had gone begged to come along with Jesus as one of his disciples. Jesus sent him away, saying, ³⁹"Return home and tell the story of what God has done for you." So he went throughout the city proclaiming what Jesus had done for him.

Jesus heals two women

⁴⁰When Jesus returned, the crowd welcomed him, for they had been waiting for him. ⁴¹A man named Jairus, who was a synagogue leader, came and fell at Jesus' feet. He pleaded with Jesus to come to his house ⁴²because his only daughter, a twelve-year-old, was dying.

As Jesus moved forward, he faced smothering crowds. ⁴³A woman was there who had been bleeding for twelve years. She had spent her entire livelihood on doctors, but no one could heal her. ⁴⁴She came up behind him and touched the hem of his clothes, and at once her bleeding stopped.

⁴⁵"Who touched me?" Jesus asked.

When everyone denied it, Peter said, "Master, the crowds are surrounding you and pressing in on you!"

⁴⁶But Jesus said, "Someone touched me. I know that power has gone out from me."

⁴⁷When the woman saw that she couldn't escape notice, she came trembling and fell before Jesus. In front of everyone, she explained why she had touched him and how she had been immediately healed.

⁴⁸"Daughter, your faith has healed you," Jesus said. "Go in peace."

⁴⁹While Jesus was still speaking, someone came from the synagogue leader's house, saying to Jairus, "Your daughter has died. Don't bother the teacher any longer."

⁵⁰When Jesus heard this, he responded, "Don't be afraid; just keep trusting, and she will be healed."

⁵¹When he came to the house, he didn't allow anyone to enter with him except Peter, John, and James, and the child's father and mother. ⁵²They were all crying and mourning for her, but Jesus said, "Don't cry. She isn't dead. She's only sleeping."

⁵³They laughed at him because they knew she was dead.

⁵⁴Taking her hand, Jesus called out, "Child, get up." ⁵⁵Her life returned and she got up at once. He directed them to give her something to eat. ⁵⁶Her parents were beside themselves with joy, but he ordered them to tell no one what had happened.

ᵗOr *underworld*

The Twelve sent out

9 Jesus called the Twelve together and he gave them power and authority over all demons and to heal sicknesses. [2] He sent them out to proclaim God's kingdom and to heal the sick. [3] He told them, "Take nothing for the journey—no walking stick, no bag, no bread, no money, not even an extra shirt. [4] Whatever house you enter, remain there until you leave that place. [5] Wherever they don't welcome you, as you leave that city, shake the dust off your feet as a witness against them." [6] They departed and went through the villages proclaiming the good news and healing people everywhere.

Herod's confusion

[7] Herod the ruler[u] heard about everything that was happening. He was confused because some people were saying that John had been raised from the dead, [8] others that Elijah had appeared, and still others that one of the ancient prophets had come back to life. [9] Herod said, "I beheaded John, so now who am I hearing about?" Herod wanted to see him.

Jesus feeds the five thousand

[10] When the apostles returned, they described for Jesus what they had done. Taking them with him, Jesus withdrew privately to a city called Bethsaida. [11] When the crowds figured it out, they followed him. He welcomed them, spoke to them about God's kingdom, and healed those who were sick.

[12] When the day was almost over, the Twelve came to him and said, "Send the crowd away so that they can go to the nearby villages and countryside and find lodging and food, because we are in a deserted place."

[13] He replied, "You give them something to eat."

But they said, "We have no more than five loaves of bread and two fish—unless we go and buy food for all these people." [14] (They said this because about five thousand men were present.)

Jesus said to his disciples, "Seat them in groups of about fifty." [15] They did so, and everyone was seated. [16] He took the five loaves and the two fish, looked up to heaven, blessed them, and broke them and gave them to the disciples to set before the crowd. [17] Everyone ate until they were full, and the disciples filled twelve baskets with the leftovers.

Following Christ

[18] Once when Jesus was praying by himself, the disciples joined him, and he asked them, "Who do the crowds say that I am?"

[19] They answered, "John the Baptist, others Elijah, and still others that one of the ancient prophets has come back to life."

[20] He asked them, "And what about you? Who do you say that I am?"

Peter answered, "The Christ sent from God."

[21] Jesus gave them strict orders not to tell this to anyone. [22] He said, "The Human One[v] must suffer many things and be rejected—by the elders, chief priests, and the legal experts—and be killed and be raised on the third day."

[23] Jesus said to everyone, "All who want to come after me must say no to themselves, take up their cross daily, and follow me. [24] All who want to save their lives will lose them. But all who lose their lives because of me will save them.

LIGHTHOUSE
LIFE

Upside Down Luke 9:24
Much of what Jesus taught seemed to be completely opposite of what the religious leaders taught. His teaching was fresh and different from anything people had heard. It seemed like he was turning things upside down, but he was just setting things right. Selfish people who focus completely on themselves are of little use to God. When people focus completely on God and give their lives to God, amazing things happen. ◊

[25] What advantage do people have if they gain the whole world for themselves yet perish or lose their lives? [26] Whoever is ashamed of me and my words, the Human One[w] will be ashamed of that person when he comes in his glory and in the glory of the Father and of the holy angels. [27] I assure you that

---

[u] Or tetrarch [v] Or Son of Man [w] Or Son of Man

some standing here won't die before they see God's kingdom."

Jesus transformed

28About eight days after Jesus said these things, he took Peter, John, and James, and went up on a mountain to pray. 29As he was praying, the appearance of his face changed and his clothes flashed white like lightning. 30Two men, Moses and Elijah, were talking with him. 31They were clothed with heavenly splendor and spoke about Jesus' departure, which he would achieve in Jerusalem. 32Peter and those with him were almost overcome by sleep, but they managed to stay awake and saw his glory as well as the two men with him. 33As the two men were about to leave Jesus, Peter said to him, "Master, it's good that we're here. We should construct three shrines: one for you, one for Moses, and one for Elijah"—but he didn't know what he was saying. 34Peter was still speaking when a cloud overshadowed them. As they entered the cloud, they were overcome with awe. 35Then a voice from the cloud said, "This is my Son, my chosen one. Listen to him!" 36Even as the voice spoke, Jesus was found alone. They were speechless and at the time told no one what they had seen.

Jesus heals a boy

37The next day, when Jesus, Peter, John, and James had come down from the mountain, a large crowd met Jesus. 38A man from the crowd shouted, "Teacher, I beg you to take a look at my son, my only child. 39Look, a spirit seizes him and, without any warning, he screams. It shakes him and causes him to foam at the mouth. It tortures him and rarely leaves him alone. 40I begged your disciples to throw it out, but they couldn't."

41Jesus answered, "You faithless and crooked generation, how long will I be with you and put up with you? Bring your son here." 42While he was coming, the demon threw him down and shook him violently. Jesus spoke harshly to the unclean spirit, healed the child, and gave him back to his father. 43Everyone was overwhelmed by God's greatness.

Jesus warns about his arrest

While everyone was marveling at everything he was doing, Jesus said to his disciples, 44"Take these words to heart: the Human One[x] is about to be delivered into human hands." 45They didn't understand this statement. Its meaning was hidden from them so they couldn't grasp it. And they were afraid to ask him about it.

Jesus corrects the disciples

46An argument arose among the disciples about which of them was the greatest. 47Aware of their deepest thoughts, Jesus took a little child and had the child stand beside him. 48Jesus said to his disciples, "Whoever welcomes this child in my name welcomes me. Whoever welcomes me, welcomes the one who sent me. Whoever is least among you all is the greatest."

49John replied, "Master, we saw someone throwing demons out in your name, and we tried to stop him because he isn't in our group of followers."

50But Jesus replied, "Don't stop him, because whoever isn't against you is for you."

Jesus sets out for Jerusalem

51As the time approached when Jesus was to be taken up into heaven, he determined to go to Jerusalem. 52He sent messengers on ahead of him. Along the way, they entered a Samaritan village to prepare for his arrival, 53but the Samaritan villagers refused to welcome him because he was determined to go to Jerusalem. 54When the disciples James and John saw this, they said, "Lord, do you want us to call fire down from heaven to consume them?" 55But Jesus turned and spoke sternly to them, 56and they went on to another village.

Following Jesus

57As Jesus and his disciples traveled along the road, someone said to him, "I will follow you wherever you go."

58Jesus replied, "Foxes have dens and the birds in the sky have nests, but the Human One[y] has no place to lay his head."

59Then Jesus said to someone else, "Follow me."

---

[x]Or Son of Man [y]Or Son of Man

He replied, "Lord, first let me go and bury my father."

⁶⁰Jesus said to him, "Let the dead bury their own dead. But you go and spread the news of God's kingdom."

⁶¹Someone else said to Jesus, "I will follow you, Lord, but first let me say good-bye to those in my house."

⁶²Jesus said to him, "No one who puts a hand on the plow and looks back is fit for God's kingdom."

Seventy-two sent out

10After these things, the Lord commissioned seventy-two others and sent them on ahead in pairs to every city and place he was about to go. ²He said to them, "The harvest is bigger than you can imagine, but there are few workers. Therefore, plead with the Lord of the harvest to send out workers for his harvest. ³Go! Be warned, though, that I'm sending you out as lambs among wolves. ⁴Carry no wallet, no bag, and no sandals. Don't even greet anyone along the way. ⁵Whenever you enter a house, first say, 'May peace be on this house.' ⁶If anyone there shares God's peace, then your peace will rest on that person. If not, your blessing will return to you. ⁷Remain in this house, eating and drinking whatever they set before you, for workers deserve their pay. Don't move from house to house. ⁸Whenever you enter a city and its people welcome you, eat what they set before you. ⁹Heal the sick who are there, and say to them, 'God's kingdom has come upon you.' ¹⁰Whenever you enter a city and the people don't welcome you, go out into the streets and say, ¹¹'As a complaint against you, we brush off the dust of your city that has collected on our feet. But know this: God's kingdom has come to you.' ¹²I assure you that Sodom will be better off on Judgment Day than that city.

Judgment against cities that reject Jesus

¹³"How terrible it will be for you, Chorazin. How terrible it will be for you, Bethsaida. If the miracles done among you had been done in Tyre and Sidon, they would have changed their hearts and lives long ago. They would have sat around in funeral clothes and ashes.

¹⁴But Tyre and Sidon will be better off at the judgment than you. ¹⁵And you, Capernaum, will you be honored by being raised up to heaven? No, you will be cast down to the place of the dead. ¹⁶Whoever listens to you listens to me. Whoever rejects you rejects me. Whoever rejects me rejects the one who sent me."

The seventy-two return

¹⁷The seventy-two returned joyously, saying, "Lord, even the demons submit themselves to us in your name."

¹⁸Jesus replied, "I saw Satan fall from heaven like lightning. ¹⁹Look, I have given you authority to crush snakes and scorpions underfoot. I have given you authority over all the power of the enemy. Nothing will harm you. ²⁰Nevertheless, don't rejoice because the spirits submit to you. Rejoice instead that your names are written in heaven."

²¹At that very moment, Jesus overflowed with joy from the Holy Spirit and said, "I praise you, Father, Lord of heaven and earth, because you've hidden these things from the wise and intelligent and shown them to babies. Indeed, Father, this brings you happiness. ²²My Father has handed all things over to me. No one knows who the Son is except the Father, or who the Father is except the Son and anyone to whom the Son wants to reveal him." ²³Turning to the disciples, he said privately, "Happy are the eyes that see what you see. ²⁴I assure you that many prophets and kings wanted to see what you see and hear what you hear, but they didn't."

Loving your neighbor

²⁵A legal expert stood up to test Jesus. "Teacher," he said, "what must I do to gain eternal life?"

²⁶Jesus replied, "What is written in the Law? How do you interpret it?"

²⁷He responded, "*You must love the Lord your God with all your heart, with all your being, with all your strength, and with all your mind, and love your neighbor as yourself.*"ᶻ

²⁸Jesus said to him, "You have answered correctly. Do this and you will live."

²⁹But the legal expert wanted to prove

ᶻDeut 6:5; Lev 19:18

that he was right, so he said to Jesus, "And who is my neighbor?"

³⁰Jesus replied, "A man went down from Jerusalem to Jericho. He encountered thieves, who stripped him naked, beat him up, and left him near death. ³¹Now it just so happened that a priest was also going down the same road. When he saw the injured man, he crossed over to the other side of the road and went on his way. ³²Likewise, a Levite came by that spot, saw the injured man, and crossed over to the other side of the road and went on his way. ³³A Samaritan, who was on a journey, came to where the man was. But when he saw him, he was moved with compassion. ³⁴The Samaritan went to him and bandaged his wounds, tending them with oil and wine. Then he placed the wounded man on his own donkey, took him to an inn, and took care of him. ³⁵The next day, he took two full days' worth of wages and gave them

did you know? Samaritans and Jews didn't get along. They shared some traditions and worshipped the same God, but they had different beliefs about where they were supposed to worship. Their differences led to fear, so the two groups didn't talk to each other.

to the innkeeper. He said, 'Take care of him, and when I return, I will pay you back for any additional costs.' ³⁶What do you think? Which one of these three was a neighbor to the man who encountered thieves?"

³⁷Then the legal expert said, "The one who demonstrated mercy toward him."

Jesus told him, "Go and do likewise."

Jesus visits Martha and Mary

³⁸While Jesus and his disciples were traveling, Jesus entered a village where a woman named Martha welcomed him as a guest. ³⁹She had a sister named Mary, who sat at

Love in Motion Luke 10:25-37

Children are all over some neighborhoods playing or riding their bikes. Sometimes neighborhood friends are so close that they run in and out of each other's houses like they live there too.

Jesus said that we should view everyone as our neighbors. To help us understand, he told a story about a man who was beaten and left on the side of the road. Three people walked by the wounded man. The first person was a priest who didn't want to get dirty, so he stepped over the man who had been attacked. The next person was a leader in the synagogue, which is a place for worship. He walked around the wounded man too.

Then a man from out of town came by. He was a Samaritan and wasn't supposed to talk with Jewish people. But this stranger knew he had to help the wounded man. The Samaritan took the Jewish man to a hotel to rest and to heal. Jesus said that the Samaritan acted like a neighbor.

When Jesus said to love God and love our neighbors as much as we love ourselves, he meant that we should love everybody. This includes our enemies and people who are different from us. We're called to show love because Jesus showed that kind of love to us.

How can you show love to a neighbor this week?

Who are some people in your town who are considered "different"? Talk to your parents about how you can be a neighbor to them.

the Lord's feet and listened to his message. [40]By contrast, Martha was preoccupied with getting everything ready for their meal. So Martha came to him and said, "Lord, don't you care that my sister has left me to prepare the table all by myself? Tell her to help me."

[41]The Lord answered, "Martha, Martha, you are worried and distracted by many things. [42]One thing is necessary. Mary has chosen the better part. It won't be taken away from her."

Teaching the disciples to pray

11 Jesus was praying in a certain place. When he finished, one of his disciples said, "Lord, teach us to pray, just as John taught his disciples."

[2]Jesus told them, "When you pray, say:

'Father, uphold the holiness of your name.
Bring in your kingdom.
[3] Give us the bread we need for today.
[4] Forgive us our sins,
    for we also forgive everyone
        who has wronged us.
And don't lead us
    into temptation.'"

LIGHTHOUSE

PRAYER

Jesus Teaches Us How to Pray *Luke 11:1-4*
When Jesus taught his followers how to pray, he gave us an example, which we call *The Lord's Prayer*. The prayer Jesus taught starts by reminding us that God is holy, or set apart. ◊

[5]He also said to them, "Imagine that one of you has a friend and you go to that friend in the middle of the night. Imagine saying, 'Friend, loan me three loaves of bread [6]because a friend of mine on a journey has arrived and I have nothing to set before him.' [7]Imagine further that he answers from within the house, 'Don't bother me. The door is already locked, and my children and I are in bed. I can't get up to give you anything.' [8]I assure you, even if he wouldn't get up and help because of his friendship, he will get up and give his friend whatever he needs because of his friend's brashness. [9]And I tell you: Ask and

you will receive. Seek and you will find. Knock and the door will be opened to you. [10]Everyone who asks, receives. Whoever seeks, finds. To everyone who knocks, the door is opened.

[11]"Which father among you would give a snake to your child if the child asked for a fish? [12]If a child asked for an egg, what father would give the child a scorpion? [13]If you who are evil know how to give good gifts to your children, how much more will the heavenly Father give the Holy Spirit to those who ask him?"

Controversy over Beelzebul

[14]Jesus was throwing out a demon that causes muteness. When the demon was gone, the man who couldn't speak began to talk. The crowds were amazed. [15]But some of them said, "He throws out demons with the authority of Beelzebul, the ruler of demons." [16]Others were testing him, seeking a sign from heaven.

[17]Because Jesus knew what they were thinking, he said to them, "Every kingdom involved in civil war becomes a wasteland, and a house torn apart by divisions will collapse. [18]If Satan is at war with himself, how will his kingdom endure? I ask this because you say that I throw out demons by the authority of Beelzebul. [19]If I throw out demons by the authority of Beelzebul, then by whose authority do your followers throw them out? Therefore, they will be your judges. [20]But if I throw out demons by the power[a] of God, then God's kingdom has already overtaken you. [21]When a strong man, fully armed, guards his own palace, his possessions are secure. [22]But as soon as a stronger one attacks and overpowers him, the stronger one takes away the armor he had trusted and divides the stolen goods.

[23]"Whoever isn't with me is against me, and whoever doesn't gather with me, scatters. [24]When an unclean spirit leaves a person, it wanders through dry places looking for a place to rest. But it doesn't find any. Then it says, 'I'll go back to the house I left.' [25]When it arrives, it finds the house cleaned up and decorated. [26]Then it goes and brings with it seven other spirits more evil than itself. They go in and make their home there. That person is worse off at the end than at the beginning."

[a]Or *finger*

On seeking signs

²⁷While Jesus was saying these things, a certain woman in the crowd spoke up: "Happy is the mother who gave birth to you and who nursed you."

²⁸But he said, "Happy rather are those who hear God's word and put it into practice."

²⁹When the crowds grew, Jesus said, "This generation is an evil generation. It looks for a sign, but no sign will be given to it except Jonah's sign. ³⁰Just as Jonah became a sign to the people of Nineveh, so the Human One^b will be a sign to this generation. ³¹The queen of the South will rise up at the judgment with the people of this generation and condemn them, because she came from a distant land to hear Solomon's wisdom. And look, someone greater than Solomon is here. ³²The people of Nineveh will rise up at the judgment with this generation and condemn it, because they changed their hearts and lives in response to Jonah's preaching—and one greater than Jonah is here.

³³"People don't light a lamp and then put it in a closet or under a basket. Rather, they place the lamp on a lampstand so that those who enter the house can see the light. ³⁴Your eye is the lamp of your body. When your eye is healthy, your whole body is full of light. But when your eye is bad, your whole body is full of darkness. ³⁵Therefore, see to it that the light in you isn't darkness. ³⁶If your whole body is full of light—with no part darkened—then it will be as full of light as when a lamp shines brightly on you."

Jesus condemns Pharisees and legal experts

³⁷While Jesus was speaking, a Pharisee invited him to share a meal with him, so Jesus went and took his place at the table. ³⁸When the Pharisee saw that Jesus didn't ritually purify his hands by washing before the meal, he was astonished.

³⁹The Lord said to him, "Now, you Pharisees clean the outside of the cup and platter, but your insides are stuffed with greed and wickedness. ⁴⁰Foolish people! Didn't the one who made the outside also make the inside? ⁴¹Therefore, give to those in need from the core of who you are and you will be clean all over.

⁴²"How terrible for you Pharisees! You give a tenth of your mint, rue, and garden herbs of all kinds, while neglecting justice and love for God. These you ought to have done without neglecting the others.

⁴³"How terrible for you Pharisees! You love the most prominent seats in the synagogues and respectful greetings in the marketplaces.

⁴⁴"How terrible for you! You are like unmarked graves, and people walk on them without recognizing it."

⁴⁵One of the legal experts responded, "Teacher, when you say these things, you are insulting us too."

⁴⁶Jesus said, "How terrible for you legal experts too! You load people down with impossible burdens and you refuse to lift a single finger to help them.

⁴⁷"How terrible for you! You built memorials to the prophets, whom your ancestors killed. ⁴⁸In this way, you testify that you approve of your ancestors' deeds. They killed the prophets, and you build memorials! ⁴⁹Therefore, God's wisdom has said, 'I will send prophets and apostles to them and they will harass and kill some of them.' ⁵⁰As a result, this generation will be charged with the murder of all the prophets since the beginning of time. ⁵¹This includes the murder of every prophet—from Abel to Zechariah—who was killed between the altar and the holy

LIFE PRESERVER

Why was Jesus so hard on the Pharisees? *Luke 11:37-52*

Jesus had an amazing ability to see people, listen to their words, and observe their behavior. He asked hard questions and had high expectations. He wasn't afraid to confront people who weren't living faithful lives. Here he confronted a group of religious leaders called Pharisees. These leaders were really good at interpreting the religious laws and following them exactly.

Jesus looked at the Pharisees and saw how well they followed the rules. But he also looked at their hearts and saw that they failed to take care of people in need. By not taking care of people who needed help, they failed to love God. ◆

^b Or *Son of Man*

place. Yes, I'm telling you, this generation will be charged with it.

[52] "How terrible for you legal experts! You snatched away the key of knowledge. You didn't enter yourselves, and you stood in the way of those who were entering."

[53] As he left there, the legal experts and Pharisees began to resent him deeply and to ask him pointed questions about many things. [54] They plotted against him, trying to trap him in his words.

Warnings to Jesus' friends

12 When a crowd of thousands upon thousands had gathered so that they were crushing each other, Jesus began to speak first to his disciples: "Watch out for the yeast of the Pharisees—I mean, the mismatch between their hearts and lives. [2] Nothing is hidden that won't be revealed, and nothing is secret that won't be brought out into the open. [3] Therefore, whatever you have said in the darkness will be heard in the light, and whatever you have whispered in the rooms deep inside the house will be announced from the rooftops.

[4] "I tell you, my friends, don't be terrified by those who can kill the body but after that can do nothing more. [5] I'll show you whom you should fear: fear the one who, after you have been killed, has the authority to throw you into hell. Indeed, I tell you, that's the one you should fear. [6] Aren't five sparrows sold for two small coins?[c] Yet not one of them is overlooked by God. [7] Even the hairs on your head are all counted. Don't be afraid. You are worth more than many sparrows.

Acknowledging the Human One

[8] "I tell you, everyone who acknowledges me before humans, the Human One[d] will acknowledge before God's angels. [9] But the one who rejects me before others will be rejected before God's angels. [10] Anyone who speaks a word against the Human One[e] will be forgiven, but whoever insults the Holy Spirit won't be forgiven. [11] When they bring you before the synagogues, rulers, and authorities, don't worry about how to defend yourself or what you should say. [12] The Holy Spirit will tell you at that very moment what you must say."

Warning against greed

[13] Someone from the crowd said to him, "Teacher, tell my brother to divide the inheritance with me."

[14] Jesus said to him, "Man, who appointed me as judge or referee between you and your brother?"

[15] Then Jesus said to them, "Watch out! Guard yourself against all kinds of greed. After all, one's life isn't determined by one's possessions, even when someone is very wealthy." [16] Then he told them a parable: "A certain rich man's land produced a bountiful crop. [17] He said to himself, What will I do? I have no place to store my harvest! [18] Then he thought, Here's what I'll do. I'll tear down my barns and build bigger ones. That's where I'll store all my grain and goods. [19] I'll say to myself, You have stored up plenty of goods, enough for several years. Take it easy! Eat, drink, and enjoy yourself. [20] But God said to him, 'Fool, tonight you will die. Now who will get the things you have prepared for yourself?' [21] This is the way it will be for those who hoard things for themselves and aren't rich toward God."

Warning about worry

[22] Then Jesus said to his disciples, "Therefore, I say to you, don't worry about your life, what you will eat, or about your body, what you will wear. [23] There is more to life than food and more to the body than clothing. [24] Consider the ravens: they neither plant nor harvest, they have no silo or barn, yet God feeds them. You are worth so much more than birds! [25] Who among you by worrying can add a single moment to your life?[f] [26] If you can't do such a small thing, why worry about the rest? [27] Notice how the lilies grow. They don't wear themselves out with work, and they don't spin cloth. But I say to you that even Solomon in all his splendor wasn't dressed like one of these. [28] If God dresses grass in the field so beautifully, even though it's alive today and tomorrow it's thrown into the furnace, how much more will God do for you, you people of weak faith! [29] Don't chase after what you will eat and what you will drink. Stop worrying.

[c] Or *two assaria—that is, 1/8 of a day's wage* [d] Or *Son of Man* [e] Or *Son of Man* [f] Or *eighteen inches to your height*

³⁰All the nations of the world long for these things. Your Father knows that you need them. ³¹Instead, desire his kingdom and these things will be given to you as well.

UMBRELLA
ANXIOUS

Worry-free and Focused Luke 12:22-31

Jesus told his followers not to worry. He reminded them that God takes care of plants and animals and makes them beautiful. If God takes care of the trees and the birds, God will take care of us as well. There are more important things to do than worry. Jesus wants his followers to focus on God. When we do, God will take care of the rest. God is in charge of the future and will give us what we need when we face it. ◖

³²"Don't be afraid, little flock, because your Father delights in giving you the kingdom. ³³Sell your possessions and give to those in need. Make for yourselves wallets that don't wear out—a treasure in heaven that never runs out. No thief comes near there, and no moth destroys. ³⁴Where your treasure is, there your heart will be too.

Warning about being prepared

³⁵"Be dressed for service and keep your lamps lit. ³⁶Be like people waiting for their master to come home from a wedding celebration, who can immediately open the door for him when he arrives and knocks on the door. ³⁷Happy are those servants whom the master finds waiting up when he arrives. I assure you that, when he arrives, he will dress himself to serve, seat them at the table as honored guests, and wait on them. ³⁸Happy are those whom he finds alert, even if he comes at midnight or just before dawn.ᵍ ³⁹But know this, if the homeowner had known what time the thief was coming, he wouldn't have allowed his home to be broken into. ⁴⁰You also must be ready, because the Human Oneʰ is coming at a time when you don't expect him."

⁴¹Peter said, "Lord, are you telling this parable for us or for everyone?"

⁴²The Lord replied, "Who are the faithful and wise managers whom the master will put in charge of his household servants, to give them their food at the proper time? ⁴³Happy are the servants whom the master finds fulfilling their responsibilities when he comes. ⁴⁴I assure you that the master will put them in charge of all his possessions.

⁴⁵"But suppose that these servants should say to themselves, My master is taking his time about coming. And suppose they began to beat the servants, both men and women, and to eat, drink, and get drunk. ⁴⁶The master of those servants would come on a day when they weren't expecting him, at a time they couldn't predict. The master will cut them into pieces and assign them a place with the unfaithful. ⁴⁷That servant who knew his master's will but didn't prepare for it or act on it will be beaten severely. ⁴⁸The one who didn't know the master's will but who did things deserving punishment will be beaten only a little. Much will be demanded from everyone who has been given much, and from the one who has been entrusted with much, even more will be asked.

Conflicts brought by Jesus

⁴⁹"I came to cast fire upon the earth. How I wish that it was already ablaze! ⁵⁰I have a baptism I must experience. How I am distressed until it's completed! ⁵¹Do you think that I have come to bring peace to the earth? No, I tell you, I have come instead to bring division. ⁵²From now on, a household of five will be divided—three against two and two against three. ⁵³Father will square off against son and son against father; mother against daughter and daughter against mother; and mother-in-law against daughter-in-law and daughter-in-law against mother-in-law."

Learning and practicing good judgment

⁵⁴Jesus also said to the crowds, "When you see a cloud forming in the west, you immediately say, 'It's going to rain.' And indeed it does. ⁵⁵And when a south wind blows, you say, 'A heat wave is coming.' And it does. ⁵⁶Hypocrites! You know how to interpret conditions on earth and in the sky. How is

ᵍOr in the second or third watch ʰOr Son of Man

it that you don't know how to interpret the present time? ⁵⁷And why don't you judge for yourselves what is right? ⁵⁸As you are going to court with your accuser, make your best effort to reach a settlement along the way. Otherwise, your accuser may bring you before the judge, and the judge hand you over to the officer, and the officer throw you into prison. ⁵⁹I tell you, you won't get out of there until you have paid the very last cent."ⁱ

Demand for genuine change

13 Some who were present on that occasion told Jesus about the Galileans whom Pilate had killed while they were offering sacrifices. ²He replied, "Do you think the suffering of these Galileans proves that they were more sinful than all the other Galileans? ³No, I tell you, but unless you change your hearts and lives, you will die just as they did. ⁴What about those eighteen people who were killed when the tower of Siloam fell on them? Do you think that they were more guilty of wrongdoing than everyone else who lives in Jerusalem? ⁵No, I tell you, but unless you change your hearts and lives, you will die just as they did."

⁶Jesus told this parable: "A man owned a fig tree planted in his vineyard. He came looking for fruit on it and found none. ⁷He said to his gardener, 'Look, I've come looking for fruit on this fig tree for the past three years, and I've never found any. Cut it down! Why should it continue depleting the soil's nutrients?' ⁸The gardener responded, 'Lord, give it one more year, and I will dig around it and give it fertilizer. ⁹Maybe it will produce fruit next year; if not, then you can cut it down.'"

Healing on a Sabbath

¹⁰Jesus was teaching in one of the synagogues on the Sabbath. ¹¹A woman was there who had been disabled by a spirit for eighteen years. She was bent over and couldn't stand up straight. ¹²When he saw her, Jesus called her to him and said, "Woman, you are set free from your sickness." ¹³He placed his hands on her and she straightened up at once and praised God.

¹⁴The synagogue leader, incensed that Jesus had healed on the Sabbath, responded, "There are six days during which work is permitted. Come and be healed on those days, not on the Sabbath day."

¹⁵The Lord replied, "Hypocrites! Don't each of you on the Sabbath untie your ox or donkey from its stall and lead it out to get a drink? ¹⁶Then isn't it necessary that this woman, a daughter of Abraham, bound by Satan for eighteen long years, be set free from her bondage on the Sabbath day?" ¹⁷When he said these things, all his opponents were put to shame, but all those in the crowd rejoiced at all the extraordinary things he was doing.

Growth of God's kingdom

¹⁸Jesus asked, "What is God's kingdom like? To what can I compare it? ¹⁹It's like a mustard seed that someone took and planted in a garden. It grew and developed into a tree and the birds in the sky nested in its branches."

²⁰Again he said, "To what can I compare God's kingdom? ²¹It's like yeast, which a woman took and hid in a bushel of wheat flour until the yeast had worked its way through the whole."

Who will be saved?

²²Jesus traveled through cities and villages, teaching and making his way to Jerusalem. ²³Someone said to him, "Lord, will only a few be saved?"

Jesus said to them, ²⁴"Make every effort to enter through the narrow gate. Many, I tell you, will try to enter and won't be able to. ²⁵Once the owner of the house gets up and shuts the door, then you will stand outside and knock on the door, saying, 'Lord, open the door for us.' He will reply, 'I don't know you or where you are from.' ²⁶Then you will begin to say, 'We ate and drank in your presence, and you taught in our streets.' ²⁷He will respond, 'I don't know you or where you are from. *Go away from me, all you evildoers!*'ʲ ²⁸There will be weeping and grinding of teeth when you see Abraham, Isaac, Jacob, and all the prophets in God's kingdom, but you yourselves will be thrown out. ²⁹People will come from east and west, north and south, and sit down to eat in God's kingdom. ³⁰Look! Those who are

---

ⁱOr *leptos* (1/128 of a day's wages)   ʲPs 6:9 LXX

last will be first and those who are first will be last."

Sorrow for Jerusalem

³¹At that time, some Pharisees approached Jesus and said, "Go! Get away from here, because Herod wants to kill you."

³²Jesus said to them, "Go, tell that fox, 'Look, I'm throwing out demons and healing people today and tomorrow, and on the third day I will complete my work. ³³However, it's necessary for me to travel today, tomorrow, and the next day because it's impossible for a prophet to be killed outside of Jerusalem.'

³⁴"Jerusalem, Jerusalem, you who kill the prophets and stone those who were sent to you! How often I have wanted to gather your people just as a hen gathers her chicks under her wings. But you didn't want that. ³⁵Look, your house is abandoned. I tell you, you won't see me until the time comes when you say, *Blessings on the one who comes in the Lord's name.*"ᵏ

Healing on the Sabbath

14 One Sabbath, when Jesus went to share a meal in the home of one of the leaders of the Pharisees, they were watching him closely. ²A man suffering from an abnormal swelling of the body was there. ³Jesus asked the lawyers and Pharisees, "Does the Law allow healing on the Sabbath or not?" ⁴But they said nothing. Jesus took hold of the sick man, cured him, and then let him go. ⁵He said to them, "Suppose your child or ox fell into a ditch on the Sabbath day. Wouldn't you immediately pull it out?" ⁶But they had no response.

Lessons on humility and generosity

⁷When Jesus noticed how the guests sought out the best seats at the table, he told them a parable. ⁸"When someone invites you to a wedding celebration, don't take your seat in the place of honor. Someone more highly regarded than you could have been invited by your host. ⁹The host who invited both of you will come and say to you, 'Give your seat to this other person.' Embarrassed, you will take your seat in the least important place. ¹⁰Instead, when you receive an invitation, go and sit in the least important place. When your host approaches you, he will say, 'Friend, move up here to a better seat.' Then you will be honored in the presence of all your fellow guests. ¹¹All who lift themselves up will be brought low, and those who make themselves low will be lifted up."

¹²Then Jesus said to the person who had invited him, "When you host a lunch or dinner, don't invite your friends, your brothers and sisters, your relatives, or rich neighbors. If you do, they will invite you in return and that will be your reward. ¹³Instead, when you give a banquet, invite the poor, crippled, lame, and blind. ¹⁴And you will be blessed because they can't repay you. Instead, you will be repaid when the just are resurrected."

¹⁵When one of the dinner guests heard Jesus' remarks, he said to Jesus, "Happy are those who will feast in God's kingdom."

¹⁶Jesus replied, "A certain man hosted a large dinner and invited many people. ¹⁷When it was time for the dinner to begin, he sent his servant to tell the invited guests, 'Come! The dinner is now ready.' ¹⁸One by one, they all began to make excuses. The first one told him, 'I bought a farm and must go and see it. Please excuse me.' ¹⁹Another said, 'I bought five teams of oxen, and I'm going to check on them. Please excuse me.' ²⁰Another said, 'I just got married, so I can't come.' ²¹When

LIFE PRESERVER

Why did Jesus talk so much about sharing food?
Luke 14:7-24

When someone is well known, people notice who they eat with. They notice where people sit. At dinner parties, important or wealthy people sit next to the host. You might even notice unwritten rules at school about where certain kids can sit at lunch. Most likely there is a table where some people are left out. Is there a table where everyone is welcome? Jesus wanted people to remember that it is important to include people who are alone, left out, or not on anyone's invitation list. ◆

ᵏPs 118:26

he returned, the servant reported these excuses to his master. The master of the house became angry and said to his servant, 'Go quickly to the city's streets, the busy ones and the side streets, and bring the poor, crippled, blind, and lame.' ²²The servant said, 'Master,

did you know? Sheep frequently got separated from the flock. A lost sheep was in danger of being attacked by a wolf. Sometimes, lost sheep fell off cliffs because they didn't pay attention to where they were going while they were eating grass.

your instructions have been followed and there is still room.' ²³The master said to the servant, 'Go to the highways and back alleys and urge people to come in so that my house will be filled. ²⁴I tell you, not one of those who were invited will taste my dinner.'"

Discipleship's demands

²⁵Large crowds were traveling with Jesus. Turning to them, he said, ²⁶"Whoever comes to me and doesn't hate father and mother, spouse and children, and brothers and sisters—yes, even one's own life—cannot be my disciple. ²⁷Whoever doesn't carry their own cross and follow me cannot be my disciple.

²⁸"If one of you wanted to build a tower, wouldn't you first sit down and calculate the cost, to determine whether you have enough money to complete it? ²⁹Otherwise, when you have laid the foundation but couldn't finish the tower, all who see it will begin to belittle you. ³⁰They will say, 'Here's the person who began construction and couldn't complete it!' ³¹Or what king would go to war against another king without first sitting down to consider whether his ten thousand soldiers could go up against the twenty thousand coming against him? ³²And if he didn't think he could win, he would send a representative to discuss terms of peace while his enemy was still a long way off. ³³In the same way, none of you who are unwilling to give up all your possessions can be my disciple.

³⁴"Salt is good. But if salt loses its flavor, how will it become salty again? ³⁵It has no value, neither for the soil nor for the manure pile. People throw it away. Whoever has ears to hear should pay attention."

Occasions for celebration

15All the tax collectors and sinners were gathering around Jesus to listen to him. ²The Pharisees and legal experts were grumbling, saying, "This man welcomes sinners and eats with them."

³Jesus told them this parable: ⁴"Suppose someone among you had one hundred sheep and lost one of them. Wouldn't he leave the other ninety-nine in the pasture and search for the lost one until he finds it? ⁵And when he finds it, he is thrilled and places it on his shoulders. ⁶When he arrives home, he calls together his friends and neighbors, saying to them, 'Celebrate with me because I've found my lost sheep.' ⁷In the same way, I tell you, there will be more joy in heaven over one sinner who changes both heart and life than over ninety-nine righteous people who have no need to change their hearts and lives.

⁸"Or what woman, if she owns ten silver coins and loses one of them, won't light a lamp and sweep the house, searching her home carefully until she finds it? ⁹When she finds it, she calls together her friends and neighbors, saying, 'Celebrate with me because I've found my lost coin.' ¹⁰In the same way, I tell you, joy breaks out in the presence of God's angels over one sinner who changes both heart and life."

¹¹Jesus said, "A certain man had two sons. ¹²The younger son said to his father, 'Father, give me my share of the inheritance.' Then the father divided his estate between them. ¹³Soon afterward, the younger son gathered everything together and took a trip to a land far away. There, he wasted his wealth through extravagant living.

¹⁴"When he had used up his resources, a severe food shortage arose in that country and he began to be in need. ¹⁵He hired himself out to one of the citizens of that country, who sent him into his fields to feed pigs. ¹⁶He longed to eat his fill from what the pigs ate, but no one gave him anything. ¹⁷When he came to his senses, he said, 'How many of my father's hired hands have more than enough food, but I'm starving to death! ¹⁸I will get up and go to my father, and say to him, "Father, I have sinned against heaven and against you. ¹⁹I no longer deserve to be called your son. Take me on as one of your hired hands." ' ²⁰So he got up and went to his father.

"While he was still a long way off, his father saw him and was moved with compassion. His father ran to him, hugged him, and kissed him. ²¹Then his son said, 'Father, I have sinned against heaven and against you. I no longer deserve to be called your son.' ²²But the father said to his servants, 'Quickly, bring out the best robe and put it on him! Put a ring on his finger and sandals on his feet! ²³Fetch the fattened calf and slaughter it. We must celebrate with feasting ²⁴because this son of mine was dead and has come back to life! He was lost and is found!' And they began to celebrate.

LIGHTHOUSE

CHANGED HEART AND LIFE

True Change Takes Action Luke 15:11-24

The young man in this story lost all his friends and had nothing to eat before he realized his mistakes. He treated his dad badly, and he sinned against God. He admitted his sins and accepted the consequences of his actions. The young man learned from his mistakes and grew into a different type of person. He truly changed his heart and life. ◊

²⁵"Now his older son was in the field. Coming in from the field, he approached the house and heard music and dancing. ²⁶He called one of the servants and asked what was going on. ²⁷The servant replied, 'Your brother has arrived, and your father has slaughtered the fattened calf because he received his son back safe and sound.' ²⁸Then the older son was furious and didn't want to enter in, but his father came out and begged him. ²⁹He answered his father, 'Look, I've served you all these years, and I never disobeyed your instruction. Yet you've never given me as much as a young goat so I could celebrate with my friends. ³⁰But when this son of yours returned, after gobbling up your estate on prostitutes, you slaughtered the fattened calf for him.' ³¹Then his father said, 'Son, you are always with me, and everything I have is yours. ³²But we had to celebrate and be glad because this brother of yours was dead and is alive. He was lost and is found.'"

Faithfulness with money

16 Jesus also said to the disciples, "A certain rich man heard that his household manager was wasting his estate. ²He called the manager in and said to him, 'What is this I hear about you? Give me a report of your administration because you can no longer serve as my manager.'

³"The household manager said to himself, What will I do now that my master is firing me as his manager? I'm not strong enough to dig and too proud to beg. ⁴I know what I'll do so that, when I am removed from my management position, people will welcome me into their houses.

⁵"One by one, the manager sent for each person who owed his master money. He said to the first, 'How much do you owe my master?' ⁶He said, 'Nine hundred gallons of olive oil.'ˡ The manager said to him, 'Take your contract, sit down quickly, and write four hundred fifty gallons.' ⁷Then the manager said to another, 'How much do you owe?' He said, 'One thousand bushels of wheat.'ᵐ He said, 'Take your contract and write eight hundred.'

⁸"The master commended the dishonest manager because he acted cleverly. People who belong to this world are more clever in dealing with their peers than are people who belong to the light. ⁹I tell you, use worldly wealth to make friends for yourselves so that when it's gone, you will be welcomed into the eternal homes.

¹⁰"Whoever is faithful with little is also faithful with much, and the one who is dishonest with little is also dishonest with much. ¹¹If you haven't been faithful with worldly wealth, who will trust you with true riches? ¹²If you haven't been faithful with someone else's property, who will give you your own? ¹³No household servant can serve two masters. Either you will hate the one and love the other, or you will be loyal to the one and have contempt for the other. You cannot serve God and wealth."

Memorize
Luke 16:10

Jesus responds to Pharisees

¹⁴The Pharisees, who were money-lovers, heard all this and sneered at Jesus. ¹⁵He said

---

ˡOr *one hundred jugs* (approximately nine gallons each) ᵐOr *eighty measures* (ten to twelve bushels each) to them, "You are the ones who justify your-selves before other people, but God knows your hearts. What is highly valued by people is deeply offensive to God. ¹⁶Until John, there was only the Law and the Prophets. Since then, the good news of God's kingdom is preached, and everyone is urged to enter it. ¹⁷It's easier for heaven and earth to pass away than for the smallest stroke of a pen in the Law to drop out. ¹⁸Any man who divorces his wife and marries another commits adultery, and a man who marries a woman divorced from her husband commits adultery.

¹⁹"There was a certain rich man who clothed himself in purple and fine linen, and who feasted luxuriously every day. ²⁰At his gate lay a certain poor man named Lazarus who was covered with sores. ²¹Lazarus longed to eat the crumbs that fell from the rich man's table. Instead, dogs would come and lick his sores.

²²"The poor man died and was carried by angels to Abraham's side. The rich man also died and was buried. ²³While being tormented in the place of the dead, he looked up and saw Abraham at a distance with Lazarus at his side. ²⁴He shouted, 'Father Abraham, have mercy on me. Send Lazarus to dip the tip of his finger in water and cool my tongue, because I'm suffering in this flame.' ²⁵But Abraham said, 'Child, remember that during your lifetime you received good things, whereas Lazarus received terrible things. Now Lazarus is being comforted and you are in great pain. ²⁶Moreover, a great crevasse has been fixed between us and you. Those who wish to cross over from here to you cannot. Neither can anyone cross from there to us.'

²⁷"The rich man said, 'Then I beg you, Father, send Lazarus to my father's house. ²⁸I have five brothers. He needs to warn them so that they don't come to this place of agony.' ²⁹Abraham replied, 'They have Moses and the Prophets. They must listen to them.' ³⁰The rich man said, 'No, Father Abraham! But if someone from the dead goes to them, they will change their hearts and lives.' ³¹Abraham said, 'If they don't listen to Moses and the Prophets, then neither will they be persuaded if someone rises from the dead.'"

Faithful service

17 Jesus said to his disciples, "Things that cause people to trip and fall into sin

must happen, but how terrible it is for the person through whom they happen. ²It would be better for them to be thrown into a lake with a large stone hung around their neck than to cause one of these little ones to trip and fall into sin. ³Watch yourselves! If your brother or sister sins, warn them to stop. If they change their hearts and lives, forgive them. ⁴Even if someone sins against you seven times in one day and returns to you seven times and says, 'I am changing my ways,' you must forgive that person."

⁵The apostles said to the Lord, "Increase our faith!"

⁶The Lord replied, "If you had faith the size of a mustard seed, you could say to this mulberry tree, 'Be uprooted and planted in the sea,' and it would obey you.

⁷"Would any of you say to your servant, who had just come in from the field after plowing or tending sheep, 'Come! Sit down for dinner'? ⁸Wouldn't you say instead, 'Fix my dinner. Put on the clothes of a table servant and wait on me while I eat and drink. After that, you can eat and drink'? ⁹You won't thank the servant because the servant did what you asked, will you? ¹⁰In the same way, when you have done everything required of you, you should say, 'We servants deserve no special praise. We have only done our duty.'"

Jesus heals a Samaritan

¹¹On the way to Jerusalem, Jesus traveled along the border between Samaria and Galilee. ¹²As he entered a village, ten men with skin diseases approached him. Keeping their distance

SAILBOAT

GIVING THANKS

Thanks to the Giver *Luke 17:11-19*
In Bible times having a skin disease was a bad thing, because infected people couldn't worship with other people. People with skin diseases were avoided by the rest of their community. When Jesus healed ten men with skin diseases, he didn't just make itchy, red patches disappear. Now those men could go about a normal way of life, including sabbath worship. The men received a miraculous gift, but only one remembered to thank Jesus, who gave him the gift! ◆

from him, [13]they raised their voices and said, "Jesus, Master, show us mercy!"

[14]When Jesus saw them, he said, "Go, show yourselves to the priests." As they left, they were cleansed. [15]One of them, when he saw that he had been healed, returned and praised God with a loud voice. [16]He fell on his face at Jesus' feet and thanked him. He was a Samaritan. [17]Jesus replied, "Weren't ten cleansed? Where are the other nine? [18]No one returned to praise God except this foreigner?" [19]Then Jesus said to him, "Get up and go. Your faith has healed you."

The kingdom is coming

[20]Pharisees asked Jesus when God's kingdom was coming. He replied, "God's kingdom isn't coming with signs that are easily noticed. [21]Nor will people say, 'Look, here it is!' or 'There it is!' Don't you see? God's kingdom is already among you."

[22]Then Jesus said to the disciples, "The time will come when you will long to see one of the days of the Human One,[n] and you won't see it. [23]People will say to you, 'Look there!' or 'Look here!' Don't leave or go chasing after them. [24]The Human One[o] will appear on his day in the same way that a flash of lightning lights up the sky from one end to the other. [25]However, first he must suffer many things and be rejected by this generation.

[26]"As it was in the days of Noah, so it will be during the days of the Human One.[p] [27]People were eating, drinking, marrying, and being given in marriage until the day Noah entered the ark and the flood came and destroyed them all. [28]Likewise in the days of Lot, people were eating, drinking, buying, selling, planting, and building. [29]But on the day Lot left Sodom, fire and sulfur rained down from heaven and destroyed them all. [30]That's the way it will be on the day the Human One[q] is revealed. [31]On that day, those on the roof, whose possessions are in the house, shouldn't come down to grab them. Likewise, those in the field shouldn't turn back. [32]Remember Lot's wife! [33]Whoever tries to preserve their life will lose it, but whoever loses their life will preserve it. [34]I tell you, on that night two

people will be in the same bed: one will be taken and the other left. [35]Two women will be grinding grain together: one will be taken and the other left."[r]

[37]The disciples asked, "Where, Lord?"

Jesus said, "The vultures gather wherever there's a dead body."

Justice for the faithful

18 Jesus was telling them a parable about their need to pray continuously and not to be discouraged. [2]He said, "In a certain city there was a judge who neither feared God nor respected people. [3]In that city there was a widow who kept coming to him, asking, 'Give me justice in this case against my adversary.' [4]For a while he refused but finally said to himself, I don't fear God or respect people, [5]but I will give this widow justice because she keeps bothering me. Otherwise, there will be no end to her coming here and embarrassing me." [6]The Lord said, "Listen to what the unjust judge says. [7]Won't God provide justice to his chosen people who cry out to him day and night? Will he be slow to help them? [8]I tell you, he will give them justice quickly. But when the Human One[s] comes, will he find faithfulness on earth?"

The Pharisee and the tax collector

[9]Jesus told this parable to certain people who had convinced themselves that they were righteous and who looked on everyone else with disgust: [10]"Two people went up to the temple to pray. One was a Pharisee and the other a tax collector. [11]The Pharisee stood and prayed about himself with these words, 'God, I thank you that I'm not like everyone else—crooks, evildoers, adulterers—or even like this tax collector. [12]I fast twice a week. I give a tenth of everything I receive.' [13]But the tax collector stood at a distance. He wouldn't even lift his eyes to look toward heaven. Rather, he struck his chest and said, 'God, show mercy to me, a sinner.' [14]I tell you, this person went down to his home justified rather than the Pharisee. All who lift themselves up will be brought low, and those who make themselves low will be lifted up."

---

[n]Or Son of Man [o]Or Son of Man [p]Or Son of Man [q]Or Son of Man [r]Critical editions of the Gk New Testament do not include 17:36 Two will be in a field: one will be taken and the other left. [s]Or Son of Man

Jesus blesses children

¹⁵People were bringing babies to Jesus so that he would bless them. When the disciples saw this, they scolded them. ¹⁶Then Jesus called them to him and said, "Allow the children to come to me. Don't forbid them, because God's kingdom belongs to people like these children. ¹⁷I assure you that whoever doesn't welcome God's kingdom like a child will never enter it."

LIGHTHOUSE

HEAVEN

Children Matter *Luke 18:15-17*
At a time when adults weren't expected even to acknowledge the presence of a child, Jesus invited a kid into the middle of his meeting. People thought kids should be quiet and learn from adults. But Jesus told the disciples that they needed to learn some things from kids. If they didn't, heaven would be off-limits to them. ◊

A rich man's question

¹⁸A certain ruler asked Jesus, "Good Teacher, what must I do to obtain eternal life?" ¹⁹Jesus replied, "Why do you call me good? No one is good except the one God. ²⁰You know the commandments: *Don't commit adultery. Don't murder. Don't steal. Don't give false testimony. Honor your father and mother.*"ᵗ ²¹Then the ruler said, "I've kept all of these things since I was a boy."

²²When Jesus heard this, he said, "There's one more thing. Sell everything you own and distribute the money to the poor. Then you will have treasure in heaven. And come, follow me." ²³When he heard these words, the man became sad because he was extremely rich.

²⁴When Jesus saw this, he said, "It's very hard for the wealthy to enter God's kingdom! ²⁵It's easier for a camel to squeeze through the eye of a needle than for a rich person to enter God's kingdom."

²⁶Those who heard this said, "Then who can be saved?"

²⁷Jesus replied, "What is impossible for humans is possible for God."

²⁸Peter said, "Look, we left everything we own and followed you."

²⁹Jesus said to them, "I assure you that anyone who has left house, husband, wife, brothers, sisters, parents, or children because of God's kingdom ³⁰will receive many times more in this age and eternal life in the coming age."

Jesus predicts his death and resurrection

³¹Jesus took the Twelve aside and said, "Look, we're going up to Jerusalem, and everything written about the Human Oneᵘ by the prophets will be accomplished. ³²He will be handed over to the Gentiles. He will be ridiculed, mistreated, and spit on. ³³After torturing him, they will kill him. On the third day, he will rise up." ³⁴But the Twelve understood none of these words. The meaning of this message was hidden from them and they didn't grasp what he was saying.

A blind man is healed

³⁵As Jesus came to Jericho, a certain blind man was sitting beside the road begging. ³⁶When the man heard the crowd passing by, he asked what was happening. ³⁷They told him, "Jesus the Nazarene is passing by."

³⁸The blind man shouted, "Jesus, Son of David, show me mercy." ³⁹Those leading the procession scolded him, telling him to be quiet, but he shouted even louder, "Son of David, show me mercy."

⁴⁰Jesus stopped and called for the man to be brought to him. When he was present Jesus asked, ⁴¹"What do you want me to do for you?"

He said, "Lord, I want to see."

⁴²Jesus said to him, "Receive your sight! Your faith has healed you." ⁴³At once he was able to see, and he began to follow Jesus, praising God. When all the people saw it, they praised God too.

A rich tax collector

19 Jesus entered Jericho and was passing through town. ²A man there named Zacchaeus, a ruler among tax collectors, was rich. ³He was trying to see who Jesus was, but, being a short man, he couldn't because of the crowd. ⁴So he ran ahead and climbed up a

ᵗDeut 5:16-20; Exod 20:12-16   ᵘOr *Son of Man*

sycamore tree so he could see Jesus, who was about to pass that way. [5]When Jesus came to that spot, he looked up and said, "Zacchaeus, come down at once. I must stay in your home today." [6]So Zacchaeus came down at once, happy to welcome Jesus.

[7]Everyone who saw this grumbled, saying, "He has gone to be the guest of a sinner."

[8]Zacchaeus stopped and said to the Lord, "Look, Lord, I give half of my possessions to the poor. And if I have cheated anyone, I repay them four times as much."

[9]Jesus said to him, "Today, salvation has come to this household because he too is a son of Abraham. [10]The Human One[v] came to seek and save the lost."

Memorize
Luke 19:10

Faithful service

[11]As they listened to this, Jesus told them another parable because he was near Jerusalem and they thought God's kingdom would appear right away. [12]He said, "A certain man who was born into royalty went to a distant land to receive his kingdom and then return. [13]He called together ten servants and gave each of them money worth four months' wages.[w] He said, 'Do business with this until I return.' [14]His citizens hated him, so they sent a representative after him who said, 'We don't want this man to be our king.' [15]After receiving his kingdom, he returned and called the servants to whom he had given the money to find out how much they had earned. [16]The first servant came forward and said, 'Your money has earned a return of one thousand percent.' [17]The king replied, 'Excellent! You are a good servant. Because you have been faithful in a small matter, you will have authority over ten cities.'

[18]"The second servant came and said, 'Master, your money has made a return of five hundred percent.' [19]To this one, the king said, 'You will have authority over five cities.'

[20]"Another servant came and said, 'Master, here is your money. I wrapped it up in a scarf for safekeeping. [21]I was afraid of you because you are a stern man. You withdraw what you haven't deposited and you harvest what you haven't planted.' [22]The king replied,

'I will judge you by the words of your own mouth, you worthless servant! You knew, did you, that I'm a stern man, withdrawing what I didn't deposit, and harvesting what I didn't plant? [23]Why then didn't you put my money in the bank? Then when I arrived, at least I could have gotten it back with interest.'

[24]"He said to his attendants, 'Take his money and give it to the one who has ten times as much.' [25]'But Master,' they said, 'he already has ten times as much!' [26]He replied, 'I say to you that everyone who has will be given more, but from those who have nothing, even what they have will be taken away. [27]As for my enemies who don't want me as their king, bring them here and slaughter them before me.'"

[28]After Jesus said this, he continued on ahead, going up to Jerusalem.

Procession into Jerusalem

[29]As Jesus came to Bethphage and Bethany on the Mount of Olives, he gave two disciples a task. [30]He said, "Go into the village over there. When you enter it, you will find tied up there a colt that no one has ever ridden. Untie it and bring it here. [31]If anyone asks, 'Why are you untying it?' just say, 'Its master needs it.'" [32]Those who had been sent found it exactly as he had said.

[33]As they were untying the colt, its owners said to them, "Why are you untying the colt?"

[34]They replied, "Its master needs it." [35]They brought it to Jesus, threw their clothes on the colt, and lifted Jesus onto it. [36]As Jesus rode along, they spread their clothes on the road.

[37]As Jesus approached the road leading down from the Mount of Olives, the whole throng of his disciples began rejoicing. They praised God with a loud voice because of all the mighty things they had seen. [38]They said,

"Blessings on the king who comes in the name of the Lord.
    Peace in heaven and glory in the
        highest heavens."

[39]Some of the Pharisees from the crowd said to Jesus, "Teacher, scold your disciples! Tell them to stop!"

[40]He answered, "I tell you, if they were silent, the stones would shout."

[v]Or Son of Man [w]Or he divided ten minas among them

Jesus predicts Jerusalem's destruction

⁴¹As Jesus came to the city and observed it, he wept over it. ⁴²He said, "If only you knew on this of all days the things that lead to peace. But now they are hidden from your eyes. ⁴³The time will come when your enemies will build fortifications around you, encircle you, and attack you from all sides. ⁴⁴They will crush you completely, you and the people within you. They won't leave one stone on top of another within you, because you didn't recognize the time of your gracious visit from God."

Jesus clears the temple

⁴⁵When Jesus entered the temple, he threw out those who were selling things there. ⁴⁶He said to them, "It's written, *My house will be a house of prayer, but you have made it a hide-out for crooks.*"ˣ

⁴⁷Jesus was teaching daily in the temple. The chief priests, the legal experts, and the foremost leaders among the people were seeking to kill him. ⁴⁸However, they couldn't find a way to do it because all the people were enthralled with what they heard.

UMBRELLA
GREED

Cheating in God's Temple *Luke 19:45-46*
Jesus felt angry when he saw sin, and he confronted it. Merchants sold animals and other things people needed to worship God inside the temple at high prices. They took advantage of people who wanted to connect with God. The temple in Jerusalem wasn't just another building. It was the place where people came to meet in the presence of God. The temple was where sacrifices were offered so that the sins of the people could be forgiven. It was meant to be a holy place, not a place where people were cheated. 💧

Controversy over authority

20On one of the days when Jesus was teaching the people in the temple and proclaiming the good news, the chief priests, legal experts, and elders approached him. ²They said, "Tell us: What kind of authority

do you have for doing these things? Who gave you this authority?"

³He replied, "I have a question for you. Tell me: ⁴Was John's baptism of heavenly or of human origin?"

⁵They discussed among themselves, "If we say, 'It's of heavenly origin,' he'll say, 'Why didn't you believe him?' ⁶But if we say, 'It's of human origin,' all the people will stone us to death because they are convinced that John was a prophet." ⁷They answered that they didn't know where it came from.

⁸Then Jesus replied, "Neither will I tell you what kind of authority I have to do these things."

Parable of the tenant farmers

⁹Jesus told the people this parable: "A certain man planted a vineyard, rented it to tenant farmers, and went on a trip for a long time. ¹⁰When it was time, he sent a servant to collect from the tenants his share of the fruit of the vineyard. But the tenants sent him away, beaten and empty-handed. ¹¹The man sent another servant. But they beat him, treated him disgracefully, and sent him away empty-handed as well. ¹²He sent a third servant. They wounded this servant and threw him out. ¹³The owner of the vineyard said, 'What should I do? I'll send my son, whom I love dearly. Perhaps they will respect him.' ¹⁴But when they saw him, they said to each other, 'This is the heir. Let's kill him so the inheritance will be ours.' ¹⁵They threw him out of the vineyard and killed him. What will the owner of the vineyard do to them? ¹⁶He will come and destroy those tenants and give the vineyard to others."

When the people heard this, they said, "May this never happen!"

¹⁷Staring at them, Jesus said, "Then what is the meaning of this text of scripture: *The stone that the builders rejected has become the cornerstone?*ʸ ¹⁸Everyone who falls on that stone will be crushed. And the stone will crush the person it falls on." ¹⁹The legal experts and chief priests wanted to arrest him right then because they knew he had told this parable against them. But they feared the people.

ˣIsa 56:7; Jer 7:11 ʸPs 118:22

An attempt to trap Jesus

Bet you can
read *this in 1 minute.* **Ready, set, go!**

²⁰The legal experts and chief priests were watching Jesus closely and sent spies who pretended to be sincere. They wanted to trap him in his words so they could hand him over to the jurisdiction and authority of the governor. ²¹They asked him, "Teacher, we know that you are correct in what you say and teach. You don't show favoritism but teach God's way as it really is. ²²Does the Law allow people to pay taxes to Caesar or not?"

²³Since Jesus recognized their deception, he said to them, ²⁴"Show me a coin.ᶻ Whose image and inscription does it have on it?"

"Caesar's," they replied.

²⁵He said to them, "Give to Caesar what belongs to Caesar and to God what belongs to God." ²⁶They couldn't trap him in his words in front of the people. Astonished by his answer, they were speechless.

Question about the resurrection

²⁷Some Sadducees, who deny that there's a resurrection, came to Jesus and asked, ²⁸"Teacher, Moses wrote for us that *if a man's brother dies* leaving a widow *but no children, the brother must marry the widow and raise up children for his brother.*ᵃ ²⁹Now there were seven brothers. The first man married a woman and then died childless. ³⁰The second ³¹and then the third brother married her. Eventually all seven married her, and they all died without leaving any children. ³²Finally, the woman died too. ³³In the resurrection, whose wife will she be? All seven were married to her."

³⁴Jesus said to them, "People who belong to this age marry and are given in marriage. ³⁵But those who are considered worthy to participate in that age, that is, in the age of the resurrection from the dead, won't marry nor will they be given in marriage. ³⁶They can no longer die, because they are like angels and are God's children since they share in the resurrection. ³⁷Even Moses demonstrated that the dead are raised—in the passage about the burning bush, when he speaks of the Lord as *the God of Abraham, the God of Isaac, and the God of Jacob.*ᵇ ³⁸He isn't the God of the dead but of the living. To him they are all alive."

³⁹Some of the legal experts responded, "Teacher, you have answered well." ⁴⁰No one dared to ask him anything else.

⁴¹Jesus said to them, "Why do they say that the Christ is David's son? ⁴²David himself says in the scroll of Psalms, *The Lord said to my lord, 'Sit at my right side ⁴³until I make your enemies a footstool for your feet.'*ᶜ ⁴⁴Since David calls him 'Lord,' how can he be David's son?"

Jesus condemns the legal experts

⁴⁵In the presence of all the people, Jesus said to his disciples, ⁴⁶"Watch out for the legal experts. They like to walk around in long robes. They love being greeted with honor in the markets. They long for the places of honor in the synagogues and at banquets. ⁴⁷They are the ones who cheat widows out of their homes, and to show off they say long prayers. They will be judged most harshly."

A poor widow's offering

21 Looking up, Jesus saw rich people throwing their gifts into the collection box for the temple treasury. ²He also saw a poor widow throw in two small copper coins worth a penny.ᵈ ³He said, "I assure you that this poor widow has put in more than them all. ⁴All of them are giving out of their spare change. But she from her hopeless poverty has given everything she had to live on."

The temple's fate

⁵Some people were talking about the temple, how it was decorated with beautiful stones and ornaments dedicated to God. Jesus said, ⁶"As for the things you are admiring, the time is coming when not even one stone will be left upon another. All will be demolished."

⁷They asked him, "Teacher, when will these things happen? What sign will show that these things are about to happen?"

⁸Jesus said, "Watch out that you aren't deceived. Many will come in my name, saying, 'I'm the one!' and 'It's time!' Don't follow them. ⁹When you hear of wars and rebellions, don't be alarmed. These things must happen first, but the end won't happen immediately."

ᶻOr *denarion* ᵃDeut 25:5; Gen 38:8 ᵇExod 3:6, 15-16 ᶜPs 110:1 ᵈOr *two lepta*

¹⁰Then Jesus said to them, "Nations and kingdoms will fight against each other. ¹¹There will be great earthquakes and wide-scale food shortages and epidemics. There will also be terrifying sights and great signs in the sky. ¹²But before all this occurs, they will take you into custody and harass you because of your faith. They will hand you over to synagogues and prisons, and you will be brought before kings and governors because of my name. ¹³This will provide you with an opportunity to testify. ¹⁴Make up your minds not to prepare your defense in advance. ¹⁵I'll give you words and wisdom that none of your opponents will be able to counter or contradict. ¹⁶You will be betrayed by your parents, brothers and sisters, relatives, and friends. They will execute some of you. ¹⁷Everyone will hate you because of my name. ¹⁸Still, not a hair on your heads will be lost. ¹⁹By holding fast, you will gain your lives.

²⁰"When you see Jerusalem surrounded by armies, then you will know that its destruction is close at hand. ²¹At that time, those in Judea must flee to the mountains, those in the city must escape, and those in the countryside must not enter the city. ²²These are the days of punishment, when everything written will find its fulfillment. ²³How terrible it will be at that time for women who are pregnant or for women who are nursing their children. There will be great agony on the earth and angry judgment on this people. ²⁴They will fall by the edge of the sword and be taken away as captives among all nations. Jerusalem will be plundered by Gentiles until the times of the Gentiles are concluded.

²⁵"There will be signs in the sun, moon, and stars. On the earth, there will be dismay among nations in their confusion over the roaring of the sea and surging waves. ²⁶The planets and other heavenly bodies will be shaken, causing people to faint from fear and foreboding of what is coming upon the world. ²⁷Then they will see the Human One[e] coming on a cloud with power and great splendor. ²⁸Now when these things begin to happen, stand up straight and raise your heads, because your redemption is near."

A lesson from the fig tree

²⁹Jesus told them a parable: "Look at the fig tree and all the trees. ³⁰When they sprout leaves, you can see for yourselves and know that summer is near. ³¹In the same way, when you see these things happening, you know that God's kingdom is near. ³²I assure you that this generation won't pass away until everything has happened. ³³Heaven and earth will pass away, but my words will certainly not pass away.

³⁴"Take care that your hearts aren't dulled by drinking parties, drunkenness, and the anxieties of day-to-day life. Don't let that day fall upon you unexpectedly, ³⁵like a trap. It will come upon everyone who lives on the face of the whole earth. ³⁶Stay alert at all times, praying that you are strong enough to escape everything that is about to happen and to stand before the Human One."[f]

³⁷Every day Jesus was teaching in the temple, but he spent each night on the Mount of Olives. ³⁸All the people rose early in the morning to hear him in the temple area.

Plot to kill Jesus

22The Festival of Unleavened Bread, which is called Passover, was approaching. ²The chief priests and the legal experts were looking for a way to kill Jesus, because they were afraid of the people. ³Then Satan entered Judas, called Iscariot, who was one of the Twelve. ⁴He went out and discussed with the chief priests and the officers of the temple guard how he could hand Jesus over to them. ⁵They were delighted and arranged payment for him. ⁶He agreed and began looking for an opportunity to hand Jesus over to them—a time when the crowds would be absent.

Disciples prepare for the Passover

⁷The Day of Unleavened Bread arrived, when the Passover had to be sacrificed. ⁸Jesus sent Peter and John with this task: "Go and prepare for us to eat the Passover meal."

⁹They said to him, "Where do you want us to prepare it?"

¹⁰Jesus replied, "When you go into the city,

---

[e]Or Son of Man [f]Or Son of Man

a man carrying a water jar will meet you. Follow him to the house he enters. ¹¹Say to the owner of the house, 'The teacher says to you, "Where is the guestroom where I can eat the Passover meal with my disciples?" ' ¹²He will show you a large upstairs room, already furnished. Make preparations there." ¹³They went and found everything just as he had told them, and they prepared the Passover meal.

The Passover meal

¹⁴When the time came, Jesus took his place at the table, and the apostles joined him. ¹⁵He said to them, "I have earnestly desired to eat this Passover with you before I suffer. ¹⁶I tell you, I won't eat it until it is fulfilled in God's kingdom." ¹⁷After taking a cup and giving thanks, he said, "Take this and share it among yourselves. ¹⁸I tell you that from now on I won't drink from the fruit of the vine until God's kingdom has come." ¹⁹After taking the bread and giving thanks, he broke it and gave it to them, saying, "This is my body, which is given for you. Do this in remembrance of me." ²⁰In the same way, he took the cup after the meal and said, "This cup is the new covenant by my blood, which is poured out for you.

²¹"But look! My betrayer is with me; his hand is on this table. ²²The Human One⁸ goes just as it has been determined. But how terrible it is for that person who betrays him." ²³They began to argue among themselves about which of them it could possibly be who would do this.

The disciples debate greatness

²⁴An argument broke out among the disciples over which one of them should be regarded as the greatest.

²⁵But Jesus said to them, "The kings of the Gentiles rule over their subjects, and those in authority over them are called 'friends of the people.' ²⁶But that's not the way it will be with you. Instead, the greatest among you must become like a person of lower status and the leader like a servant. ²⁷So which one is greater, the one who is seated at the table or the one who serves at the table? Isn't it the one who is seated at the table? But I am among you as one who serves.

²⁸"You are the ones who have continued with me in my trials. ²⁹And I confer royal power on you just as my Father granted royal power to me. ³⁰Thus you will eat and drink at my table in my kingdom, and you will sit on thrones overseeing the twelve tribes of Israel.

Peter's denial predicted

³¹"Simon, Simon, look! Satan has asserted the right to sift you all like wheat. ³²However, I have prayed for you that your faith won't fail. When you have returned, strengthen your brothers and sisters."

LIGHTHOUSE

PRAYER

Jesus Is on Our Side *Luke 22:31-32*

Jesus knew Peter was going to stumble in his faith, and he told Peter. That must have been difficult for Peter to hear, but Jesus didn't stop there. He told Peter he was praying for him, and that Peter would develop a faith that was stronger than ever. Jesus knew hard times were coming, so he prayed specifically for Peter. When we face hard times, we can remember we don't face them alone either. Jesus is praying for us too.

³³Peter responded, "Lord, I'm ready to go with you, both to prison and to death!"

³⁴Jesus replied, "I tell you, Peter, the rooster won't crow today before you have denied three times that you know me."

Call for preparedness

³⁵Jesus said to them, "When I sent you out without a wallet, bag, or sandals, you didn't lack anything, did you?"

They said, "Nothing."

³⁶Then he said to them, "But now, whoever has a wallet must take it, and likewise a bag.

⁸Or Son of Man

And those who don't own a sword must sell their clothes and buy one. ³⁷I tell you that this scripture must be fulfilled in relation to me: *And he was counted among criminals.*ʰ Indeed, what's written about me is nearing completion."

³⁸They said to him, "Lord, look, here are two swords."

He replied, "Enough of that!"

Jesus in prayer

³⁹Jesus left and made his way to the Mount of Olives, as was his custom, and the disciples followed him. ⁴⁰When he arrived, he said to them, "Pray that you won't give in to temptation." ⁴¹He withdrew from them about a stone's throw, knelt down, and prayed. ⁴²He said, "Father, if it's your will, take this cup of suffering away from me. However, not my will but your will must be done." ⁴³Then a heavenly angel appeared to him and strengthened him. ⁴⁴He was in anguish and prayed even more earnestly. His sweat became like drops of blood falling on the ground. ⁴⁵When he got up from praying, he went to the disciples. He found them asleep, overcome by grief. ⁴⁶He said to them, "Why are you sleeping? Get up and pray so that you won't give in to temptation."

Jesus' arrest

⁴⁷While Jesus was still speaking, a crowd appeared, and the one called Judas, one of the Twelve, was leading them. He approached Jesus to kiss him.

⁴⁸Jesus said to him, "Judas, would you betray the Human Oneⁱ with a kiss?"

⁴⁹When those around him recognized what was about to happen, they said, "Lord, should we fight with our swords?" ⁵⁰One of them struck the high priest's servant, cutting off his right ear.

⁵¹Jesus responded, "Stop! No more of this!" He touched the slave's ear and healed him.

⁵²Then Jesus said to the chief priests, the officers of the temple guard, and the elders who had come to get him, "Have you come with swords and clubs to arrest me, as though I were a thief? ⁵³Day after day I was with you in the temple, but you didn't arrest me. But this is your time, when darkness rules."

Peter denies knowing Jesus

⁵⁴After they arrested Jesus, they led him away and brought him to the high priest's house. Peter followed from a distance. ⁵⁵When they lit a fire in the middle of the courtyard and sat down together, Peter sat among them.

⁵⁶Then a servant woman saw him sitting in the firelight. She stared at him and said, "This man was with him too."

⁵⁷But Peter denied it, saying, "Woman, I don't know him!"

⁵⁸A little while later, someone else saw him and said, "You are one of them too."

But Peter said, "Man, I'm not!"

⁵⁹An hour or so later, someone else insisted, "This man must have been with him, because he is a Galilean too."

⁶⁰Peter responded, "Man, I don't know what you are talking about!" At that very moment, while he was still speaking, a rooster crowed. ⁶¹The Lord turned and looked straight at Peter, and Peter remembered the Lord's words: "Before a rooster crows today, you will deny me three times." ⁶²And Peter went out and cried uncontrollably.

Jesus taunted

⁶³The men who were holding Jesus in custody taunted him while they beat him. ⁶⁴They blindfolded him and asked him repeatedly, "Prophesy! Who hit you?" ⁶⁵Insulting him, they said many other horrible things against him.

Jesus before the Jerusalem leadership

⁶⁶As morning came, the elders of the people, both chief priests and legal experts, came together, and Jesus was brought before their council.

⁶⁷They said, "If you are the Christ, tell us!"

He answered, "If I tell you, you won't believe. ⁶⁸And if I ask you a question, you won't answer. ⁶⁹But from now on, *the Human One*ⁱ *will be seated on the right side of the power of God.*"ᵏ

⁷⁰They all said, "Are you God's Son, then?"

He replied, "You say that I am."

⁷¹Then they said, "Why do we need further testimony? We've heard it from his own lips."

ʰIsa 53:12 ⁱOr *Son of Man* ʲOr *Son of Man* ᵏPs 110:1

Jesus before Pilate

23 The whole assembly got up and led Jesus to Pilate and ²began to accuse him. They said, "We have found this man misleading our people, opposing the payment of taxes to Caesar, and claiming that he is the Christ, a king."

³Pilate asked him, "Are you the king of the Jews?"

Jesus replied, "That's what you say."

⁴Then Pilate said to the chief priests and the crowds, "I find no legal basis for action against this man."

⁵But they objected strenuously, saying, "He agitates the people with his teaching throughout Judea—starting from Galilee all the way here."

Jesus before Herod

⁶Hearing this, Pilate asked if the man was a Galilean. ⁷When he learned that Jesus was from Herod's district, Pilate sent him to Herod, who was also in Jerusalem at that time. ⁸Herod was very glad to see Jesus, for he had heard about Jesus and had wanted to see him for quite some time. He was hoping to see Jesus perform some sign. ⁹Herod questioned Jesus at length, but Jesus didn't respond to him. ¹⁰The chief priests and the legal experts were there, fiercely accusing Jesus. ¹¹Herod and his soldiers treated Jesus with contempt. Herod mocked him by dressing Jesus in elegant clothes and sent him back to Pilate. ¹²Pilate and Herod became friends with each other that day. Before this, they had been enemies.

Jesus and Barabbas

¹³Then Pilate called together the chief priests, the rulers, and the people. ¹⁴He said to them, "You brought this man before me as one who was misleading the people. I have questioned him in your presence and found nothing in this man's conduct that provides a legal basis for the charges you have brought against him. ¹⁵Neither did Herod, because Herod returned him to us. He's done nothing that deserves death. ¹⁶Therefore, I'll have him whipped, then let him go."¹

¹⁸But with one voice they shouted, "Away with this man! Release Barabbas to us." (¹⁹Barabbas had been thrown into prison because of a riot that had occurred in the city, and for murder.)

²⁰Pilate addressed them again because he wanted to release Jesus.

²¹They kept shouting out, "Crucify him! Crucify him!"

²²For the third time, Pilate said to them, "Why? What wrong has he done? I've found no legal basis for the death penalty in his case. Therefore, I will have him whipped, then let him go."

²³But they were adamant, shouting their demand that Jesus be crucified. Their voices won out. ²⁴Pilate issued his decision to grant their request. ²⁵He released the one they asked for, who had been thrown into prison because of a riot and murder. But he handed Jesus over to their will.

On the way to the cross

²⁶As they led Jesus away, they grabbed Simon, a man from Cyrene, who was coming in from the countryside. They put the cross on his back and made him carry it behind Jesus. ²⁷A huge crowd of people followed Jesus, including women, who were mourning and wailing for him. ²⁸Jesus turned to the women and said, "Daughters of Jerusalem, don't cry for me. Rather, cry for yourselves and your children. ²⁹The time will come when they will say, 'Happy are those who are unable to become pregnant, the wombs that never gave birth, and the breasts that never nursed a child.' ³⁰Then *they will say to the mountains, 'Fall on us,' and to the hills, 'Cover us.'*ᵐ ³¹If they do these things when the tree is green, what will happen when it is dry?"

Jesus on the cross

³²They also led two other criminals to be executed with Jesus. ³³When they arrived at the place called The Skull, they crucified him, along with the criminals, one on his right and the other on his left. ³⁴Jesus said, "Father, forgive them, for they don't know what they're doing." They drew lots as a way of dividing up his clothing.

---

¹Critical editions of the Gk New Testament do not include 23:17 *He had to release one prisoner for them because of the festival.*
ᵐHos 10:8

[35]The people were standing around watching, but the leaders sneered at him, saying, "He saved others. Let him save himself if he really is the Christ sent from God, the chosen one."

[36]The soldiers also mocked him. They came up to him, offering him sour wine [37]and saying, "If you really are the king of the Jews, save yourself." [38]Above his head was a notice of the formal charge against him. It read "This is the king of the Jews."

[39]One of the criminals hanging next to Jesus insulted him: "Aren't you the Christ? Save yourself and us!"

[40]Responding, the other criminal spoke harshly to him, "Don't you fear God, seeing that you've also been sentenced to die? [41]We are rightly condemned, for we are receiving the appropriate sentence for what we did. But this man has done nothing wrong." [42]Then he said, "Jesus, remember me when you come into your kingdom."

[43]Jesus replied, "I assure you that today you will be with me in paradise."

Jesus' death

[44]It was now about noon, and darkness covered the whole earth until about three o'clock, [45]while the sun stopped shining. Then the curtain in the sanctuary tore down the middle. [46]Crying out in a loud voice, Jesus said, "Father, *into your hands I entrust my life.*[n] After he said this, he breathed for the last time.

[47]When the centurion saw what happened, he praised God, saying, "It's really true: this man was righteous." [48]All the crowds who had come together to see this event returned to their homes beating their chests after seeing what had happened. [49]And everyone who knew him, including the women who had followed him from Galilee, stood at a distance observing these things.

Jesus' burial

[50]Now there was a man named Joseph who was a member of the council. He was a good and righteous man. [51]He hadn't agreed with the plan and actions of the council. He was from the Jewish city of Arimathea and eagerly anticipated God's kingdom. [52]This man went to Pilate and asked for Jesus' body. [53]Taking it down, he wrapped it in a linen cloth and laid it in a tomb carved out of the rock, in which no one had ever been buried. [54]It was the Preparation Day for the Sabbath, and the Sabbath was quickly approaching. [55]The women who had come with Jesus from

[n]Ps 31:5

Jesus' Sacrifice   Luke 23:44-56

So much had happened from the time Jesus was born until he hung on a cross. At his birth, angels sang to the shepherds. When Jesus grew older he taught, healed, and blessed people. His love changed people from the inside out so they knew who God is and how to really live out their relationship with God. Finally, Jesus became a sacrifice.

To *sacrifice* something means to give that thing up for someone or something else. Jesus' life was sacrificed so that people can know God. His death was a public event seen by many people who then told the story of what happened. Thousands of years later, we are still talking about it. The story of Jesus' sacrifice for us will be told forever.

Have you ever had to sacrifice something?

What does Jesus' sacrifice mean to you?

Galilee followed Joseph. They saw the tomb and how Jesus' body was laid in it, [56]then they went away and prepared fragrant spices and perfumed oils. They rested on the Sabbath, in keeping with the commandment.

The empty tomb

24 Very early in the morning on the first day of the week, the women went to the tomb, bringing the fragrant spices they had prepared. [2]They found the stone rolled away from the tomb, [3]but when they went in, they didn't find the body of the Lord Jesus. [4]They didn't know what to make of this. Suddenly, two men were standing beside them in gleaming bright clothing. [5]The women were frightened and bowed their faces toward the ground, but the men said to them, "Why do you look for the living among the dead? [6]He isn't here, but has been raised. Remember what he told you while he was still in Galilee, [7]that the Human One° must be handed

°Or *Son of Man*

over to sinners, be crucified, and on the third day rise again." [8]Then they remembered his words. [9]When they returned from the tomb, they reported all these things to the eleven and all the others. [10]It was Mary Magdalene, Joanna, Mary the mother of James, and the other women with them who told these

---

did you know? In Bible times, people who died were buried in excavated caves. Grooves were cut in the ground in front of the openings of these caves and then large flat, round stones were rolled into these grooves to keep out animals and thieves.

---

things to the apostles. [11]Their words struck the apostles as nonsense, and they didn't believe the women. [12]But Peter ran to the tomb. When he bent over to look inside, he saw only the linen cloth. Then he returned home, wondering what had happened.

God's THOUGHTS ◆ My THOUGHTS

Jesus' Resurrection Luke 24:1-12

Everything in the Bible leads up to Jesus' resurrection on the first Easter morning. In our time, Easter can seem to be about candy, bunnies, and baskets of eggs. However, we celebrate Easter because Jesus died, but the power of God brought him back to life! When you eat your candy, you know it's not coming back. You can stare at the empty wrappers and eggs and wish for more, but it's gone. It's not like that with Jesus. When Jesus' followers watched him die on the cross, they probably thought it was over. They might have wondered if everything Jesus had taught them was true. They probably wondered what they were supposed to do without him. They may have doubted their decision to follow him.

You can imagine Jesus' friends' surprise when they visited his tomb. The angel told the women not to look for the living among the dead. They went to visit a grave, but the angel told them Jesus wasn't there. Everything changed. He was alive again! Jesus died to bring us back to God's love. Then he told us to tell everyone that we can change our hearts and lives (Luke 24:47).

What is the best news about Easter?

How would you act if your heart and life is changed by Easter?

Encounter on the Emmaus road

¹³On that same day, two disciples were traveling to a village called Emmaus, about seven miles from Jerusalem. ¹⁴They were talking to each other about everything that had happened. ¹⁵While they were discussing these things, Jesus himself arrived and joined them on their journey. ¹⁶They were prevented from recognizing him.

¹⁷He said to them, "What are you talking about as you walk along?" They stopped, their faces downcast.

¹⁸The one named Cleopas replied, "Are you the only visitor to Jerusalem who is unaware of the things that have taken place there over the last few days?"

¹⁹He said to them, "What things?"

They said to him, "The things about Jesus of Nazareth. Because of his powerful deeds and words, he was recognized by God and all the people as a prophet. ²⁰But our chief priests and our leaders handed him over to be sentenced to death, and they crucified him. ²¹We had hoped he was the one who would redeem Israel. All these things happened three days ago. ²²But there's more: Some women from our group have left us stunned. They went to the tomb early this morning ²³and didn't find his body. They came to us saying that they had even seen a vision of angels who told them he is alive. ²⁴Some of those who were with us went to the tomb and found things just as the women said. They didn't see him."

²⁵Then Jesus said to them, "You foolish people! Your dull minds keep you from believing all that the prophets talked about. ²⁶Wasn't it necessary for the Christ to suffer these things and then enter into his glory?" ²⁷Then he interpreted for them the things written about himself in all the scriptures, starting with Moses and going through all the Prophets.

²⁸When they came to Emmaus, he acted as if he was going on ahead. ²⁹But they urged him, saying, "Stay with us. It's nearly evening, and the day is almost over." So he went in to stay with them. ³⁰After he took his seat at the table with them, he took the bread, blessed and broke it, and gave it to them. ³¹Their eyes were opened and they recognized him, but he disappeared from their sight. ³²They said to each other, "Weren't our hearts on fire when he spoke to us along the road and when he explained the scriptures for us?"

³³They got up right then and returned to Jerusalem. They found the eleven and their companions gathered together. ³⁴They were saying to each other, "The Lord really has risen! He appeared to Simon!" ³⁵Then the two disciples described what had happened along the road and how Jesus was made known to them as he broke the bread.

Jesus appears to the disciples

³⁶While they were saying these things, Jesus himself stood among them and said, "Peace be with you!" ³⁷They were terrified and afraid. They thought they were seeing a ghost.

³⁸He said to them, "Why are you startled? Why are doubts arising in your hearts? ³⁹Look at my hands and my feet. It's really me! Touch me and see, for a ghost doesn't have flesh and bones like you see I have." ⁴⁰As he said this, he showed them his hands and feet. ⁴¹Because they were wondering and questioning in the midst of their happiness, he said to them, "Do you have anything to eat?" ⁴²They gave him a piece of baked fish. ⁴³Taking it, he ate it in front of them.

⁴⁴Jesus said to them, "These are my words that I spoke to you while I was still with you—that everything written about me in the Law from Moses, the Prophets, and the Psalms must be fulfilled." ⁴⁵Then he opened their minds to understand the scriptures. ⁴⁶He said to them, "This is what is written: the Christ will suffer and rise from the dead on the third day, ⁴⁷and a change of heart and life for the forgiveness of sins must be preached in his name to all nations, beginning from Jerusalem. ⁴⁸You are witnesses of these things. ⁴⁹Look, I'm sending to you what my Father promised, but you are to stay in the city until you have been furnished with heavenly power."

Ascension of Jesus

⁵⁰He led them out as far as Bethany, where he lifted his hands and blessed them. ⁵¹As he blessed them, he left them and was taken up to heaven. ⁵²They worshipped him and returned to Jerusalem overwhelmed with joy. ⁵³And they were continuously in the temple praising God.

John

things
YOU'LL DISCOVER

John tells the story of Jesus with beautiful words and pictures. This book says that God loved the world so much that God sent Jesus to live with us on earth.

people
YOU'LL MEET

Jesus—called the Word, God's Son, and the Human One (John 1–21)

John the Baptist—a prophet who prepared people to meet Jesus (John 1–5; 10)

The Twelve—Jesus' closest disciples, including Peter, James, and John (John 1–21)

Pharisees—Jewish religious leaders (John 3–27)

Martha, Mary, and Lazarus—siblings who were good friends of Jesus (John 11)

Pilate—Roman governor of Judea (John 18–19)

places
YOU'LL GO

Nazareth (a town in northern Israel),

Jordan River,

Samaria (present-day northern West Bank),

Galilee (a lake and region in northern Israel),

Jerusalem,

Skull Place (the site outside Jerusalem where Jesus was crucified)

words
YOU'LL REMEMBER

"God so loved the world that he gave his only Son, so that everyone who believes in him won't perish but will have eternal life" (John 3:16).

The story of Jesus in the book of John is different from the story in any other New Testament book. It doesn't begin with Jesus' human birth. It starts before Jesus was born, before the world was created. The author wrote, "In the beginning was the Word and the Word was with God and the Word was God" (John 1:1). Jesus was "the Word" who was with God and who was God.

That's an amazing statement. Jesus is God who came to live on earth as a human being. He came so people can be sure of God's love and live with God forever (John 3:16).

This book gives many beautiful pictures of Jesus. He said, "I am the bread of life" (John 6:35). He feeds and satisfies us. He said, "I am the good shepherd" (John 10:11). He takes loving care of us. John tells the stories of Jesus turning water into wine (John 2:1-12), walking on water (John 6:15-21), and feeding thousands of people with a young boy's lunch (John 6:1-15). The author of John said that he wrote down all of these things so we can believe that Jesus is God's Son (John 20:31). John shows us who Jesus really is! ◆

Story of the Word

1 In the beginning was the Word
   and the Word was with God
   and the Word was God.
² The Word was with God
   in the beginning.
³ Everything came into being
   through the Word,
   and without the Word
   nothing came into being.
   What came into being
⁴ through the Word was life,ᵃ
   and the life was the light for all people.
⁵ The light shines in the darkness,
   and the darkness doesn't
      extinguish the light.

⁶A man named John was sent from God. ⁷He came as a witness to testify concerning the light, so that through him everyone would believe in the light. ⁸He himself wasn't the light, but his mission was to testify concerning the light.

⁹ The true light that shines on all people
   was coming into the world.

Bet you can read this in 30 seconds. **Ready, set, go!**

¹⁰ The light was in the world,
   and the world came into being
      through the light,
   but the world didn't recognize
      the light.
¹¹ The light came to his own people,
   and his own people didn't welcome him.
¹² But those who did welcome him,
   those who believed in his name,
   he authorized to become God's children,
¹³ born not from blood
   nor from human desire or passion,
   but born from God.
¹⁴ The Word became flesh
   and made his home among us.
   We have seen his glory,
      glory like that of a father's only son,
      full of grace and truth.

¹⁵John testified about him, crying out, "This is the one of whom I said, 'He who comes after me is greater than me because he existed before me.'"
¹⁶ From his fullness we have all received grace upon grace;
¹⁷ as the Law was given through Moses,

so grace and truth came into being
   through Jesus Christ.
¹⁸ No one has ever seen God.
   God the only Son,
   who is at the Father's side,
   has made God known.

John's witness

¹⁹This is John's testimony when the Jewish leaders in Jerusalem sent priests and Levites to ask him, "Who are you?"
²⁰John confessed (he didn't deny but confessed), "I'm not the Christ."
²¹They asked him, "Then who are you? Are you Elijah?"

John said, "I'm not."

"Are you the prophet?"

John answered, "No."

²²They asked, "Who are you? We need to give an answer to those who sent us. What do you say about yourself?"
²³John replied,

"I am a voice crying out in the wilderness,
   Make the Lord's path straight,ᵇ
   just as the prophet Isaiah said."

²⁴Those sent by the Pharisees ²⁵asked, "Why do you baptize if you aren't the Christ, nor Elijah, nor the prophet?"
²⁶John answered, "I baptize with water.

ᵃOr *Everything came into being through the Word,/and without the Word / nothing came into being that came into being. In the Word was life* ᵇIsa 40:3

Someone greater stands among you, whom you don't recognize. [27]He comes after me, but I'm not worthy to untie his sandal straps." [28]This encounter took place across the Jordan in Bethany where John was baptizing.

[29]The next day John saw Jesus coming toward him and said, "Look! The Lamb of God who takes away the sin of the world! [30]This is the one about whom I said, 'He who comes after me is really greater than me because he existed before me.' [31]Even I didn't recognize him, but I came baptizing with water so that he might be made known to Israel." [32]John testified, "I saw the Spirit coming down from heaven like a dove, and it rested on him. [33]Even I didn't recognize him, but the one who sent me to baptize with water said to me, 'The one on whom you see the Spirit coming down and resting is the one who baptizes with the Holy Spirit.' [34]I have seen and testified that this one is God's Son."

Jesus calls disciples

[35]The next day John was standing again with two of his disciples. [36]When he saw Jesus walking along he said, "Look! The Lamb of God!" [37]The two disciples heard what he said, and they followed Jesus.

[38]When Jesus turned and saw them following, he asked, "What are you looking for?"

They said, "Rabbi (which is translated *Teacher*), where are you staying?"

[39]He replied, "Come and see." So they went and saw where he was staying, and they remained with him that day. It was about four o'clock in the afternoon.

[40]One of the two disciples who heard what John said and followed Jesus was Andrew, the brother of Simon Peter. [41]He first found his own brother Simon and said to him, "We have found the Messiah" (which is translated *Christ*[c]). [42]He led him to Jesus.

Jesus looked at him and said, "You are Simon, son of John. You will be called Cephas" (which is translated *Peter*).

[43]The next day Jesus wanted to go into Galilee, and he found Philip. Jesus said to him, "Follow me." [44]Philip was from Bethsaida, the hometown of Andrew and Peter.

[45]Philip found Nathanael and said to him, "We have found the one Moses wrote about in the Law and the Prophets: Jesus, Joseph's son, from Nazareth."

[46]Nathanael responded, "Can anything from Nazareth be good?"

Philip said, "Come and see."

[47]Jesus saw Nathanael coming toward him and said about him, "Here is a genuine Israelite in whom there is no deceit."

SAILBOAT

HONEST AND TRUE

Genuine *John 1:47*

The Bible doesn't talk about Nathanael as much as it does some of the other disciples. What it does say is worth paying attention to. Jesus specifically talked about Nathanael's character. He said Nathanael didn't have any deceit in him. That meant Nathanael didn't lie or stretch the truth to make things easier for himself. Nathanael was known for being serious about his faith. He didn't make a show of being holy or religious. Jesus said Nathanael was a genuine Israelite. ◊

[48]Nathanael asked him, "How do you know me?"

Jesus answered, "Before Philip called you, I saw you under the fig tree."

[49]Nathanael replied, "Rabbi, you are God's Son. You are the king of Israel."

[50]Jesus answered, "Do you believe because I told you that I saw you under the fig tree? You will see greater things than these! [51]I assure you that you will see heaven open and God's angels going up to heaven and down to earth on the Human One."[d]

Wedding at Cana

2 On the third day there was a wedding in Cana of Galilee. Jesus' mother was there, and [2]Jesus and his disciples were also invited to the celebration. [3]When the wine ran out, Jesus' mother said to him, "They don't have any wine."

[4]Jesus replied, "Woman, what does that have to do with me? My time hasn't come yet." [5]His mother told the servants, "Do

[c]Or Anointed One [d]Or Son of Man

whatever he tells you." ⁶Nearby were six stone water jars used for the Jewish cleansing ritual, each able to hold about twenty or thirty gallons.

⁷Jesus said to the servants, "Fill the jars with water," and they filled them to the brim. ⁸Then he told them, "Now draw some from them and take it to the headwaiter," and they did. ⁹The headwaiter tasted the water that had become wine. He didn't know where it came from, though the servants who had drawn the water knew.

The headwaiter called the groom ¹⁰and said, "Everyone serves the good wine first. They bring out the second-rate wine only when the guests are drinking freely. You kept the good wine until now." ¹¹This was the first miraculous sign that Jesus did in Cana of Galilee. He revealed his glory, and his disciples believed in him.

¹²After this, Jesus and his mother, his brothers, and his disciples went down to Capernaum and stayed there for a few days.

Jesus in Jerusalem at Passover

¹³It was nearly time for the Jewish Passover, and Jesus went up to Jerusalem. ¹⁴He found in the temple those who were selling cattle, sheep, and doves, as well as those involved in exchanging currency sitting there. ¹⁵He made a whip from ropes and chased them all out of the temple, including the cattle and the sheep. He scattered the coins and overturned the tables of those who exchanged currency. ¹⁶He said to the dove sellers, "Get these things out of here! Don't make my Father's house a place of business." ¹⁷His disciples remembered that it is written, *Passion for your house consumes me.*ᵉ

¹⁸Then the Jewish leaders asked him, "By what authority are you doing these things? What miraculous sign will you show us?"

¹⁹Jesus answered, "Destroy this temple and in three days I'll raise it up."

²⁰The Jewish leaders replied, "It took forty-six years to build this temple, and you will raise it up in three days?" ²¹But the temple Jesus was talking about was his body. ²²After he was raised from the dead, his disciples remembered what he had said, and

did you know? The water Jesus turned into wine for the wedding party was the water the people used to wash their hands when they arrived.

they believed the scripture and the word that Jesus had spoken.

²³While Jesus was in Jerusalem for the Passover Festival, many believed in his name because they saw the miraculous signs that he did. ²⁴But Jesus didn't trust himself to them because he knew all people. ²⁵He didn't need anyone to tell him about human nature, for he knew what human nature was.

Jesus and Nicodemus

3There was a Pharisee named Nicodemus, a Jewish leader. ²He came to Jesus at night and said to him, "Rabbi, we know that you are a teacher who has come from God, for no one could do these miraculous signs that you do unless God is with him."

³Jesus answered, "I assure you, unless someone is born anew,ᶠ it's not possible to see God's kingdom."

⁴Nicodemus asked, "How is it possible for an adult to be born? It's impossible to enter the mother's womb for a second time and be born, isn't it?"

⁵Jesus answered, "I assure you, unless someone is born of water and the Spirit, it's not possible to enter God's kingdom. ⁶Whatever is born of the flesh is flesh, and whatever is born of the Spirit is spirit. ⁷Don't be surprised that I said to you, 'You must be born anew.' ⁸God's Spiritᵍ blows wherever it wishes. You hear its sound, but you don't know where it comes from or where it is going. It's the same with everyone who is born of the Spirit."

⁹Nicodemus said, "How are these things possible?"

¹⁰Jesus answered, "You are a teacher of Israel and you don't know these things? ¹¹I assure you that we speak about what we know and testify about what we have seen, but you don't receive our testimony. ¹²If I have told you about earthly things and you don't believe, how will you believe if I tell you

ᵉPs 69:9 ᶠOr *from above* ᵍOr *wind*

about heavenly things? [13]No one has gone up to heaven except the one who came down from heaven, the Human One.[h] [14]Just as Moses lifted up the snake in the wilderness, so must the Human One[i] be lifted up [15]so that everyone who believes in him will have eternal life. [16]God so loved the world that he gave his only Son, so that everyone who believes in him won't perish but will have eternal life. [17]God didn't send his Son into the world to judge the world, but that the world might be saved through him. [18]Whoever believes in him isn't judged; whoever doesn't believe in him is already judged, because they don't believe in the name of God's only Son.

[19]"This is the basis for judgment: The light came into the world, and people loved darkness more than the light, for their actions are evil. [20]All who do wicked things hate the light and don't come to the light for fear that their actions will be exposed to the light. [21]Whoever does the truth comes to the light so that it can be seen that their actions were done in God."

John's final witness

[22]After this Jesus and his disciples went into Judea, where he spent some time with them and was baptizing. [23]John was baptizing at Aenon near Salem because there was a lot of water there, and people were coming to him and being baptized. ([24]John hadn't yet been thrown into prison.)

[25]A debate started between John's disciples and a certain Jew about cleansing rituals. [26]They came to John and said, "Rabbi, look! The man who was with you across the Jordan, the one about whom you testified, is baptizing and everyone is flocking to him."

[27]John replied, "No one can receive anything unless it is given from heaven. [28]You yourselves can testify that I said that I'm not the Christ but that I'm the one sent before him. [29]The groom is the one who is getting married. The friend of the groom stands close by and, when he hears him, is overjoyed at the groom's voice. Therefore, my joy is now complete. [30]He must increase and I must decrease. [31]The one who comes from above is above all things. The one who is from the earth belongs to the earth and speaks as one from the earth. The one who comes from heaven is above all things. [32]He testifies to what he has seen and heard, but no one accepts his testimony. [33]Whoever accepts his testimony confirms that God is true. [34]The one whom God sent speaks God's words because God gives the

[h]Or *Son of Man* [i]Or *Son of Man*

God So Loved *John 3:16-21*

If you've ever wondered what it means to be a Christian, John 3:16 provides some answers. God loved us so much that God found a way to undo the sin in our lives so we can live with God forever. God sent Jesus Christ into the world to teach us about God, save us from our sins, and then send us to share the good news with others. Everyone who believes in Jesus has eternal life with God. Everyone. No matter where you come from. No matter who your family is. No matter what you've done. No matter what you think about yourself. God loved *you* so much that God gave his only Son Jesus so that *you* would believe and have eternal life with God.

Memorize John 3:16-17. Practice saying these verses to a friend or family member.

Write a letter to God about how these verses make you feel.

Spirit generously. ³⁵The Father loves the Son and gives everything into his hands. ³⁶Whoever believes in the Son has eternal life. Whoever doesn't believe in the Son won't see life, but the angry judgment of God remains on them."

Jesus leaves Judea

4 Jesus learned that the Pharisees had heard that he was making more disciples and baptizing more than John (²although Jesus' disciples were baptizing, not Jesus himself). ³Therefore, he left Judea and went back to Galilee.

Jesus in Samaria

⁴Jesus had to go through Samaria. ⁵He came to a Samaritan city called Sychar, which was near the land Jacob had given to his son Joseph. ⁶Jacob's well was there. Jesus was tired from his journey, so he sat down at the well. It was about noon.

⁷A Samaritan woman came to the well to draw water. Jesus said to her, "Give me some water to drink." ⁸His disciples had gone into the city to buy him some food.

⁹The Samaritan woman asked, "Why do you, a Jewish man, ask for something to drink from me, a Samaritan woman?" (Jews and Samaritans didn't associate with each other.)

¹⁰Jesus responded, "If you recognized God's gift and who is saying to you, 'Give me some water to drink,' you would be asking him and he would give you living water."

¹¹The woman said to him, "Sir, you don't have a bucket and the well is deep. Where would you get this living water? ¹²You aren't greater than our father Jacob, are you? He gave this well to us, and he drank from it himself, as did his sons and his livestock."

¹³Jesus answered, "Everyone who drinks this water will be thirsty again, ¹⁴but whoever drinks from the water that I will give will never be thirsty again. The water that I give will become in those who drink it a spring of water that bubbles up into eternal life."

¹⁵The woman said to him, "Sir, give me this water, so that I will never be thirsty and will never need to come here to draw water!"

¹⁶Jesus said to her, "Go, get your husband, and come back here."

¹⁷The woman replied, "I don't have a husband."

"You are right to say, 'I don't have a husband,'" Jesus answered. ¹⁸"You've had five husbands, and the man you are with now isn't your husband. You've spoken the truth."

¹⁹The woman said, "Sir, I see that you are a prophet. ²⁰Our ancestors worshipped on this mountain, but you and your people say that it is necessary to worship in Jerusalem."

²¹Jesus said to her, "Believe me, woman, the time is coming when you and your people will worship the Father neither on this mountain nor in Jerusalem. ²²You and your people worship what you don't know; we worship what we know because salvation is from the Jews. ²³But the time is coming—and is here!—when true worshippers will worship in spirit and truth. The Father looks for those who worship him this way. ²⁴God is spirit, and it is necessary to worship God in spirit and truth."

²⁵The woman said, "I know that the Messiah is coming, the one who is called the Christ. When he comes, he will teach everything to us."

²⁶Jesus said to her, "I Am—the one who speaks with you."ʲ

²⁷Just then, Jesus' disciples arrived and were shocked that he was talking with a woman. But no one asked, "What do you want?" or "Why are you talking with her?" ²⁸The woman put down her water jar and went into the city. She said to the people, ²⁹"Come and see a man who has told me everything I've done! Could this man be the Christ?" ³⁰They left the city and were on their way to see Jesus.

³¹In the meantime the disciples spoke to Jesus, saying, "Rabbi, eat."

³²Jesus said to them, "I have food to eat that you don't know about."

³³The disciples asked each other, "Has someone brought him food?"

³⁴Jesus said to them, "I am fed by doing the will of the one who sent me and by completing his work. ³⁵Don't you have a saying, 'Four more months and then it's time for harvest'? Look, I tell you: open your eyes and notice that

---

ʲOr It is I, the one who speaks with you.

the fields are already ripe for the harvest. ³⁶Those who harvest are receiving their pay and gathering fruit for eternal life so that those who sow and those who harvest can celebrate together. ³⁷This is a true saying, that one sows and another harvests. ³⁸I have sent you to harvest what you didn't work hard for; others worked hard, and you will share in their hard work."

³⁹Many Samaritans in that city believed in Jesus because of the woman's word when she testified, "He told me everything I've ever done." ⁴⁰So when the Samaritans came to Jesus, they asked him to stay with them, and he stayed there two days. ⁴¹Many more believed because of his word, ⁴²and they said to the woman, "We no longer believe because of what you said, for we have heard for ourselves and know that this one is truly the savior of the world."

LIFE PRESERVER

Why is the Samaritan woman important?

John 4:4-42

The story of Jesus and the Samaritan woman is very surprising. After Jesus chose his disciples, he appeared at a wedding, went to the temple at Passover, and met Nicodemus. Then he met the Samaritan woman at the well. Jesus did something very unusual when he spoke with this woman. Samaritans and Jews didn't get along with each other because of their religious differences. It was a big deal for a Jew to speak to a Samaritan. It was even more unusual for a man and a woman to speak to each other.

The Samaritan woman was at the well to get water. She was definitely interested when Jesus offered her "living water" so she would never be thirsty again (John 4:10). Their conversation continued, and Jesus let her know that he was the leader Israel was waiting for, the *Messiah* (in Hebrew) or the *Christ* (in Greek). Then the woman told other people what she experienced with Jesus, and they listened. This story shows how Jesus met and welcomed people of all kinds into God's love and presence. ◆

Jesus arrives in Galilee

⁴³After two days Jesus left for Galilee. (⁴⁴Jesus himself had testified that prophets have no honor in their own country.) ⁴⁵When he came to Galilee, the Galileans welcomed him because they had seen all the things he had done in Jerusalem during the festival, for they also had been at the festival.

Jesus' second miraculous sign in Galilee

⁴⁶He returned to Cana in Galilee where he had turned the water into wine. In Capernaum there was a certain royal official whose son was sick. ⁴⁷When he heard that Jesus was coming from Judea to Galilee, he went out to meet him and asked Jesus if he would come and heal his son, for his son was about to die. ⁴⁸Jesus said to him, "Unless you see miraculous signs and wonders, you won't believe."

⁴⁹The royal official said to him, "Lord, come before my son dies."

⁵⁰Jesus replied, "Go home. Your son lives." The man believed the word that Jesus spoke to him and set out for his home.

⁵¹While he was on his way, his servants were already coming to meet him. They said, "Your son lives!" ⁵²So he asked them at what time his son had started to get better. And they said, "The fever left him yesterday at about one o'clock in the afternoon." ⁵³Then the father realized that this was the hour when Jesus had said to him, "Your son lives." And he and his entire household believed in Jesus. ⁵⁴This was the second miraculous sign Jesus did while going from Judea to Galilee.

Sabbath healing

5After this there was a Jewish festival, and Jesus went up to Jerusalem. ²In Jerusalem near the Sheep Gate in the north city wall is a pool with the Aramaic name Bethsaida. It had five covered porches, ³and a crowd of people who were sick, blind, lame, and paralyzed sat there.ᵏ ⁵A certain man was there who had been sick for thirty-eight years. ⁶When Jesus saw him lying there, knowing that he had already been there a long time, he asked him, "Do you want to get well?"

ᵏCritical editions of the Gk New Testament do not include the following addition *waiting for the water to move.* ⁴*Sometimes an angel would come down to the pool and stir up the water. Then the first one going into the water after it had been stirred up was cured of any sickness.*

⁷The sick man answered him, "Sir,¹ I don't have anyone who can put me in the water when it is stirred up. When I'm trying to get to it, someone else has gotten in ahead of me."

⁸Jesus said to him, "Get up! Pick up your mat and walk." ⁹Immediately the man was well, and he picked up his mat and walked. Now that day was the Sabbath.

¹⁰The Jewish leaders said to the man who had been healed, "It's the Sabbath; you aren't allowed to carry your mat."

¹¹He answered, "The man who made me well said to me, 'Pick up your mat and walk.'"

¹²They inquired, "Who is this man who said to you, 'Pick it up and walk'?" ¹³The man who had been cured didn't know who it was, because Jesus had slipped away from the crowd gathered there.

¹⁴Later Jesus found him in the temple and said, "See! You have been made well. Don't sin anymore in case something worse happens to you." ¹⁵The man went and proclaimed to the Jewish leaders that Jesus was the man who had made him well.

¹⁶As a result, the Jewish leaders were harassing Jesus, since he had done these things on the Sabbath. ¹⁷Jesus replied, "My Father is still working, and I am working too." ¹⁸For this reason the Jewish leaders wanted even more to kill him—not only because he was doing away with the Sabbath but also because he called God his own Father, thereby making himself equal with God.

Work of the Father and the Son

¹⁹Jesus responded to the Jewish leaders, "I assure you that the Son can't do anything by himself except what he sees the Father doing. Whatever the Father does, the Son does likewise. ²⁰The Father loves the Son and shows him everything that he does. He will show him greater works than these so that you will marvel. ²¹As the Father raises the dead and gives life, so too does the Son give life to whomever he wishes. ²²The Father doesn't judge anyone, but he has given all judgment to the Son ²³so that everyone will honor the Son just as they honor the Father. Whoever

doesn't honor the Son doesn't honor the Father who sent him.

²⁴"I assure you that whoever hears my word and believes in the one who sent me has eternal life and won't come under judgment but has passed from death into life.

Memorize John 5:24

²⁵"I assure you that the time is coming—and is here!—when the dead will hear the voice of God's Son, and those who hear it will live. ²⁶Just as the Father has life in himself, so he has granted the Son to have life in himself. ²⁷He gives the Son authority to judge, because he is the Human One.ᵐ ²⁸Don't be surprised by this, because the time is coming when all who are in their graves will hear his voice. ²⁹Those who did good things will come out into the resurrection of life, and those who did wicked things into the resurrection of judgment. ³⁰I can't do anything by myself. Whatever I hear, I judge, and my judgment is just. I don't seek my own will but the will of the one who sent me.

Witnesses to Jesus

³¹"If I testify about myself, my testimony isn't true. ³²There is someone else who testifies about me, and I know his testimony about me is true. ³³You sent a delegation to John, and he testified to the truth. ³⁴Although I don't accept human testimony, I say these things so that you can be saved. ³⁵John was a burning and shining lamp, and, at least for a while, you were willing to celebrate in his light.

³⁶"I have a witness greater than John's testimony. The Father has given me works to do so that I might complete them. These works I do testify about me that the Father sent me. ³⁷And the Father who sent me testifies about

¹Or Lord ᵐOr Son of Man

me. You have never even heard his voice or seen his form, [38]and you don't have his word dwelling with you because you don't believe the one whom he has sent. [39]Examine the scriptures, since you think that in them you have eternal life. They also testify about me, [40]yet you don't want to come to me so that you can have life.

[41]"I don't accept praise from people, [42]but I know you, that you don't have God's love in you. [43]I have come in my Father's name, and you don't receive me. If others come in their own name, you receive them. [44]How can you believe when you receive praise from each other but don't seek the praise that comes from the only God?

[45]"Don't think that I will accuse you before the Father. Your accuser is Moses, the one in whom your hope rests. [46]If you believed Moses, you would believe me, because

[n]Or two hundred denaria

Moses wrote about me. [47]If you don't believe the writings of Moses, how will you believe my words?"

Feeding of the five thousand

6 After this Jesus went across the Galilee Sea (that is, the Tiberias Sea). [2]A large crowd followed him, because they had seen the miraculous signs he had done among the sick. [3]Jesus went up a mountain and sat there with his disciples. [4]It was nearly time for Passover, the Jewish festival.

[5]Jesus looked up and saw the large crowd coming toward him. He asked Philip, "Where will we buy food to feed these people?" [6]Jesus said this to test him, for he already knew what he was going to do.

[7]Philip replied, "More than a half year's salary[n] worth of food wouldn't be enough for each person to have even a little bit."

Nothing Is Impossible for God *John 6:5-13*

In the story of the boy and his lunch, Jesus made a little bit of food go a long way. Jesus taught the crowd all day and wanted a quiet evening with his friends. Instead, the people followed him because they wanted more instruction and time with him. By dinnertime, there were about five thousand hungry people. Jesus tested the disciples when he asked, "Where will we buy food to feed these people?" (John 6:5). Buying food wasn't an option because it was too late in the day, too far away, and too expensive.

Peter's brother found a boy who had some food—five loaves of bread and two fish. It seemed like an impossible situation, but Jesus knew exactly what to do. He took the boy's bread, gave thanks for it, and passed it around to the crowd. Then he gave thanks for the fish and passed it around too. Everyone ate as much as they wanted. When they were finished, there were twelve baskets of food left over!

We always have enough when we give what we have to God. No matter how little we think we have, it becomes more than we could have ever imagined when we put it in Jesus' hands.

When have you seen God make something out of nothing?

What do you have to offer for Jesus to help others?

⁸One of his disciples, Andrew, Simon Peter's brother, said, ⁹"A youth here has five barley loaves and two fish. But what good is that for a crowd like this?"

¹⁰Jesus said, "Have the people sit down." There was plenty of grass there. They sat down, about five thousand of them. ¹¹Then Jesus took the bread. When he had given thanks, he distributed it to those who were sitting there. He did the same with the fish, each getting as much as they wanted. ¹²When they had plenty to eat, he said to his disciples, "Gather up the leftover pieces, so that nothing will be wasted." ¹³So they gathered them and filled twelve baskets with the pieces of the five barley loaves that had been left over by those who had eaten.

¹⁴When the people saw that he had done a miraculous sign, they said, "This is truly the prophet who is coming into the world." ¹⁵Jesus understood that they were about to come and force him to be their king, so he took refuge again, alone on a mountain.

Jesus walks on water

¹⁶When evening came, Jesus' disciples went down to the lake. ¹⁷They got into a boat and were crossing the lake to Capernaum. It was already getting dark and Jesus hadn't come to them yet. ¹⁸The water was getting rough because a strong wind was blowing. ¹⁹When the wind had driven them out for about three or four miles, they saw Jesus walking on the water. He was approaching the boat and they were afraid. ²⁰He said to them, "I Am.ᵒ Don't be afraid." ²¹Then they wanted to take him into the boat, and just then the boat reached the land where they had been heading.

²²The next day the crowd that remained on the other side of the lake realized that only one boat had been there. They knew Jesus hadn't gone with his disciples, but that the disciples had gone alone. ²³Some boats came from Tiberias, near the place where they had eaten the bread over which the Lord had given thanks. ²⁴When the crowd saw that neither Jesus nor his disciples were there, they got into the boats and came to Capernaum looking for Jesus. ²⁵When they found him on the other side of the lake, they asked him, "Rabbi, when did you get here?"

Bread of life

²⁶Jesus replied, "I assure you that you are looking for me not because you saw miraculous signs but because you ate all the food you wanted. ²⁷Don't work for the food that doesn't last but for the food that endures for eternal life, which the Human Oneᵖ will give you. God the Father has confirmed him as his agent to give life."

²⁸They asked, "What must we do in order to accomplish what God requires?"

²⁹Jesus replied, "This is what God requires, that you believe in him whom God sent."

³⁰They asked, "What miraculous sign will you do, that we can see and believe you? What will you do? ³¹Our ancestors ate manna in the wilderness, just as it is written, *He gave them bread from heaven to eat.*"�q

³²Jesus told them, "I assure you, it wasn't Moses who gave the bread from heaven to you, but my Father gives you the true bread from heaven. ³³The bread of God is the one who comes down from heaven and gives life to the world."

³⁴They said, "Sir,ʳ give us this bread all the time!"

³⁵Jesus replied, "I am the bread of life. Whoever comes to me will never go hungry, and whoever believes in me will never be thirsty. ³⁶But I told you that you have seen me and still don't believe. ³⁷Everyone whom the Father gives to me will come to me, and I won't send away anyone who comes to me. ³⁸I have come down from heaven not to do my will, but the will of him who sent me. ³⁹This is

LIFE PRESERVER

What did Jesus mean when he said "I am the bread of life"? *John 6:26-40*

In John we read many statements Jesus made about himself that begin with the phrase "I am." In this passage Jesus wasn't talking simply about being physically hungry. The people were talking about physical hunger, but Jesus was talking about hunger for God. Jesus told them they wouldn't be spiritually hungry anymore if they followed him, because he is "the bread of life" (John 26:35). ◆

the will of the one who sent me, that I won't lose anything he has given me, but I will raise it up at the last day. ⁴⁰This is my Father's will: that all who see the Son and believe in him will have eternal life, and I will raise them up at the last day."

⁴¹The Jewish opposition grumbled about him because he said, "I am the bread that came down from heaven."

⁴²They asked, "Isn't this Jesus, Joseph's son, whose mother and father we know? How can he now say, 'I have come down from heaven'?"

⁴³Jesus responded, "Don't grumble among yourselves. ⁴⁴No one can come to me unless they are drawn to me by the Father who sent me, and I will raise them up at the last day. ⁴⁵It is written in the Prophets, And they will all be taught by God.ˢ Everyone who has listened to the Father and learned from him comes to me. ⁴⁶No one has seen the Father except the one who is from God. He has seen the Father. ⁴⁷I assure you, whoever believes has eternal life. ⁴⁸I am the bread of life. ⁴⁹Your ancestors ate manna in the wilderness and they died. ⁵⁰This is the bread that comes down from heaven so that whoever eats from it will never die. ⁵¹I am the living bread that came down from heaven. Whoever eats this bread will live forever, and the bread that I will give for the life of the world is my flesh."

⁵²Then the Jews debated among themselves, asking, "How can this man give us his flesh to eat?"

⁵³Jesus said to them, "I assure you, unless you eat the flesh of the Human Oneᵗ and drink his blood, you have no life in you. ⁵⁴Whoever eats my flesh and drinks my blood has eternal life, and I will raise them up at the last day. ⁵⁵My flesh is true food and my blood is true drink. ⁵⁶Whoever eats my flesh and drinks my blood remains in me and I in them. ⁵⁷As the living Father sent me, and I live because of the Father, so whoever eats me lives because of me. ⁵⁸This is the bread that came down from heaven. It isn't like the bread your ancestors ate, and then they died. Whoever eats this bread will live forever." ⁵⁹Jesus said these things while he was teaching in the synagogue in Capernaum.

⁶⁰Many of his disciples who heard this said, "This message is harsh. Who can hear it?"

⁶¹Jesus knew that the disciples were grumbling about this and he said to them, "Does this offend you? ⁶²What if you were to see the Human Oneᵘ going up where he was before? ⁶³The Spirit is the one who gives life and the flesh doesn't help at all. The words I have spoken to you are spirit and life. ⁶⁴Yet some of you don't believe." Jesus knew from the beginning who wouldn't believe and the one who would betray him. ⁶⁵He said, "For this reason I said to you that none can come to me unless the Father enables them to do so." ⁶⁶At this, many of his disciples turned away and no longer accompanied him.

⁶⁷Jesus asked the Twelve, "Do you also want to leave?"

⁶⁸Simon Peter answered, "Lord, where would we go? You have the words of eternal life. ⁶⁹We believe and know that you are God's holy one."

⁷⁰Jesus replied, "Didn't I choose you twelve? Yet one of you is a devil." ⁷¹He was speaking of Judas, Simon Iscariot's son, for he, one of the Twelve, was going to betray him.

Jesus goes to Jerusalem

7After this Jesus traveled throughout Galilee. He didn't want to travel in Judea, because the Jewish authorities wanted to kill him. ²When it was almost time for the Jewish Festival of Booths, ³Jesus' brothers said to him, "Leave Galilee. Go to Judea so that your disciples can see the amazing works that you do. ⁴Those who want to be known publicly don't do things secretly. Since you can do these things, show yourself to the world." ⁵His brothers said this because even they didn't believe in him.

⁶Jesus replied, "For you, anytime is fine. But my time hasn't come yet. ⁷The world can't hate you. It hates me, though, because I testify that its works are evil. ⁸You go up to the festival. I'm not going to this one because my time hasn't yet come." ⁹Having said this, he stayed in Galilee. ¹⁰However, after his brothers left for the festival, he went too—not openly but in secret.

¹¹The Jewish leaders were looking for Jesus at the festival. They kept asking, "Where is he?" ¹²The crowds were murmuring about

---

ˢIsa 54:13 ᵗOr Son of Man ᵘOr Son of Man

him. "He's a good man," some said, but others were saying, "No, he tricks the people." [13]No one spoke about him publicly, though, for fear of the Jewish authorities.

Jesus teaches in the temple

[14]Halfway through the festival, Jesus went up to the temple and started to teach. [15]Astonished, the Jewish leaders asked, "He's never been taught! How has he mastered the Law?"

[16]Jesus responded, "My teaching isn't mine but comes from the one who sent me. [17]Whoever wants to do God's will can tell whether my teaching is from God or whether I speak on my own. [18]Those who speak on their own seek glory for themselves. Those who seek the glory of him who sent me are people of truth; there's no falsehood in them. [19]Didn't Moses give you the Law? Yet none of you keep the Law. Why do you want to kill me?"

[20]The crowd answered, "You have a demon. Who wants to kill you?"

[21]Jesus replied, "I did one work, and you were all astonished. [22]Because Moses gave you the commandment about circumcision (although it wasn't Moses but the patriarchs), you circumcise a man on the Sabbath. [23]If a man can be circumcised on the Sabbath without breaking Moses' Law, why are you angry with me because I made an entire man well on the Sabbath? [24]Don't judge according to appearances. Judge with right judgment."

[25]Some people from Jerusalem said, "Isn't he the one they want to kill? [26]Here he is, speaking in public, yet they aren't saying anything to him. Could it be that our leaders actually think he is the Christ? [27]We know where he is from, but when the Christ comes, no one will know where he is from."

[28]While Jesus was teaching in the temple, he exclaimed, "You know me and where I am from. I haven't come on my own. The one who sent me is true, and you don't know him. [29]I know him because I am from him and he sent me." [30]So they wanted to seize Jesus, but they couldn't because his time hadn't yet come.

[31]Many from that crowd believed in Jesus. They said, "When the Christ comes, will he do more miraculous signs than this man does?"

[32]The Pharisees heard the crowd whispering such things about Jesus, and the chief priests and Pharisees sent guards to arrest him.

[33]Therefore, Jesus said, "I'm still with you for a little while before I go to the one who sent me. [34]You will look for me, but you won't find me, and where I am you can't come."

[35]The Jewish opposition asked each other, "Where does he intend to go that we can't find him? Surely he doesn't intend to go where our people have been scattered and are living among the Greeks! He isn't going to teach the Greeks, is he? [36]What does he mean when he says, 'You will look for me, but you won't find me, and where I am you can't come'?"

[37]On the last and most important day of the festival, Jesus stood up and shouted,

"All who are thirsty should come to me!
[38] All who believe in me should drink!
As the scriptures said concerning me,[v]
Rivers of living water will flow out from within him."

[39]Jesus said this concerning the Spirit. Those who believed in him would soon receive the Spirit, but they hadn't experienced the Spirit yet since Jesus hadn't yet been glorified.

[40]When some in the crowd heard these words, they said, "This man is truly the prophet." [41]Others said, "He's the Christ." But others said, "The Christ can't come from Galilee, can he? [42]Didn't the scripture say that the Christ comes from David's family and from Bethlehem, David's village?" [43]So the crowd was divided over Jesus. [44]Some wanted to arrest him, but no one grabbed him.

[45]The guards returned to the chief priests and Pharisees, who asked, "Why didn't you bring him?"

[46]The guards answered, "No one has ever spoken the way he does."

[47]The Pharisees replied, "Have you too been deceived? [48]Have any of the leaders believed in him? Has any Pharisee? [49]No, only this crowd, which doesn't know the Law. And they are under God's curse!"

[50]Nicodemus, who was one of them and had come to Jesus earlier, said, [51]"Our Law doesn't judge someone without first hearing him and learning what he is doing, does it?"

[v]Or *Whoever is thirsty should come to me and drink. Whoever believes in me, just as the scriptures said,* rivers of living water will flow out from within them.

⁵²They answered him, "You are not from Galilee too, are you? Look it up and you will see that the prophet doesn't come from Galilee."

///

Pharisees test Jesus

⁵³They each went to their own homes, **8** And Jesus went to the Mount of Olives. ²Early in the morning he returned to the temple. All the people gathered around him, and he sat down and taught them. ³The legal experts and Pharisees brought a woman caught in adultery. Placing her in the center of the group, ⁴they said to Jesus, "Teacher, this woman was caught in the act of committing adultery. ⁵In the Law, Moses commanded us to stone women like this. What do you say?" ⁶They said this to test him, because they wanted a reason to bring an accusation against him. Jesus bent down and wrote on the ground with his finger.

⁷They continued to question him, so he stood up and replied, "Whoever hasn't sinned should throw the first stone." ⁸Bending down again, he wrote on the ground. ⁹Those who heard him went away, one by one, beginning with the elders. Finally, only Jesus and the woman were left in the middle of the crowd. ¹⁰Jesus stood up and said to her, "Woman, where are they? Is there no one to condemn you?"

¹¹She said, "No one, sir."ʷ

Jesus said, "Neither do I condemn you. Go, and from now on, don't sin anymore."ˣ

///

Jesus continues to teach in the temple

¹²Jesus spoke to the people again, saying, "I am the light of the world. Whoever follows me won't walk in darkness but will have the light of life."

¹³Then the Pharisees said to him, "Because you are testifying about yourself, your testimony isn't valid."

¹⁴Jesus replied, "Even if I testify about myself, my testimony is true, since I know where I came from and where I'm going. You don't know where I come from or where I'm going. ¹⁵You judge according to human standards, but I judge no one. ¹⁶Even if I do judge, my judgment is truthful, because I'm not alone. My judgments come from me and from the Father who sent me. ¹⁷In your Law it is written that the witness of two people is true. ¹⁸I am one witness concerning myself, and the Father who sent me is the other."

¹⁹They asked him, "Where is your Father?"

Jesus answered, "You don't know me and you don't know my Father. If you knew me, you would also know my Father." ²⁰He spoke these words while he was teaching in the temple area known as the treasury. No one arrested him, because his time hadn't yet come.

²¹Jesus continued, "I'm going away. You will look for me, and you will die in your sin. Where I'm going, you can't come."

²²The Jewish leaders said, "He isn't going to kill himself, is he? Is that why he said, 'Where I'm going, you can't come'?"

²³He said to them, "You are from below; I'm from above. You are from this world; I'm not from this world. ²⁴This is why I told you that you would die in your sins. If you don't believe that I Am, you will die in your sins."

²⁵"Who are you?" they asked.

Jesus replied, "I'm exactly who I have claimed to be from the beginning. ²⁶I have many things to say in judgment concerning you. The one who sent me is true, and what I have heard from him I tell the world." ²⁷They didn't know he was speaking about his Father. ²⁸So Jesus said to them, "When the

LIFE PRESERVER

How is Jesus the "light of the world"? John 8:12

Light is a symbol that God is present with God's people. When God led the Israelites in the wilderness, God guided them during the day with a cloud and with lightning at night. There were lampstands in the temple to remind the people that God was present with them. Jesus wanted people to know that God was with them when they saw Jesus, because he was sent by God to be the "light of the world" (John 8:12). ◆

///

ʷOr Lord ˣCritical editions of the Gk New Testament do not contain 7:53–8:11.

Human One^y is lifted up,^z then you will know that I Am.^a Then you will know that I do nothing on my own, but I say just what the Father has taught me. ²⁹He who sent me is with me. He doesn't leave me by myself, because I always do what makes him happy." ³⁰While Jesus was saying these things, many people came to believe in him.

Children of Abraham

³¹Jesus said to the Jews who believed in him, "You are truly my disciples if you remain faithful to my teaching. ³²Then you will know

the truth, and the truth will set you free."

³³They responded, "We are Abraham's children; we've never been anyone's slaves. How can you say that we will be set free?"

³⁴Jesus answered, "I assure you that everyone who sins is a slave to sin. ³⁵A slave isn't a permanent member of the household, but a son is. ³⁶Therefore, if the Son makes you free, you really will be free. ³⁷I know that you are Abraham's children, yet you want to kill me because you don't welcome my teaching. ³⁸I'm telling you what I've seen when I am with the Father, but you are doing what you've heard from your father."

³⁹They replied, "Our father is Abraham."

Jesus responded, "If you were Abraham's children, you would do Abraham's works. ⁴⁰Instead, you want to kill me, though I am the one who has spoken the truth I heard from God. Abraham didn't do this. ⁴¹You are doing your father's works."

They said, "Our ancestry isn't in question! The only Father we have is God!"

⁴²Jesus replied, "If God were your Father, you would love me, for I came from God. Here I am. I haven't come on my own. God sent me. ⁴³Why don't you understand what I'm saying? It's because you can't really hear my words. ⁴⁴Your father is the devil. You are his children, and you want to do what your father wants. He was a murderer from the beginning. He has never stood for the truth, because there's no truth in him. Whenever that liar speaks, he speaks according to his own nature, because he's a liar and the father

of liars. ⁴⁵Because I speak the truth, you don't believe me. ⁴⁶Who among you can show I'm guilty of sin? Since I speak the truth, why don't you believe me? ⁴⁷God's children listen to God's words. You don't listen to me because you aren't God's children."

⁴⁸The Jewish opposition answered, "We were right to say that you are a Samaritan and have a demon, weren't we?"

⁴⁹"I don't have a demon," Jesus replied. "But I honor my Father and you dishonor me. ⁵⁰I'm not trying to bring glory to myself. There's one who is seeking to glorify me, and he's the judge. ⁵¹I assure you that whoever keeps my word will never die."

Abraham and Jesus

⁵²The Jewish opposition said to Jesus, "Now we know that you have a demon. Abraham and the prophets died, yet you say, 'Whoever keeps my word will never die.' ⁵³Are you greater than our father Abraham? He died and the prophets died, so who do you make yourself out to be?"

⁵⁴Jesus answered, "If I glorify myself, my glory is meaningless. My Father, who you say is your God, is the one who glorifies me. ⁵⁵You don't know him, but I do. If I said I didn't know him, I would be like you, a liar. But I do know him, and I keep his word. ⁵⁶Your father Abraham was overjoyed that he would see my day. He saw it and was happy."

⁵⁷"You aren't even 50 years old!" the Jewish opposition replied. "How can you say that you have seen Abraham?"

⁵⁸"I assure you," Jesus replied, "before Abraham was, I Am." ⁵⁹So they picked up stones to throw at him, but Jesus hid himself and left the temple.

Jesus heals a blind man

9As Jesus walked along, he saw a man who was blind from birth. ²Jesus' disciples asked, "Rabbi, who sinned so that he was born blind, this man or his parents?"

³Jesus answered, "Neither he nor his parents. This happened so that God's mighty works might be displayed in him. ⁴While it's daytime, we must do the works of him who

**Bet
you
can**
read
this in 1
minute.
Ready,
set, go!

---

^yOr Son of Man ^zOr exalted ^aOr that I am he

sent me. Night is coming when no one can work. [5]While I am in the world, I am the light of the world." [6]After he said this, he spit on the ground, made mud with the saliva, and smeared the mud on the man's eyes. [7]Jesus said to him, "Go, wash in the pool of Siloam" (this word means *sent*). So the man went away and washed. When he returned, he could see.

Disagreement about the healing

[8]The man's neighbors and those who used to see him when he was a beggar said, "Isn't this the man who used to sit and beg?"

[9]Some said, "It is," and others said, "No, it's someone who looks like him."

But the man said, "Yes, it's me!"

[10]So they asked him, "How are you now able to see?"

[11]He answered, "The man they call Jesus made mud, smeared it on my eyes, and said, 'Go to the pool of Siloam and wash.' So I went and washed, and then I could see."

[12]They asked, "Where is this man?"

He replied, "I don't know."

[13]Then they led the man who had been born blind to the Pharisees. [14]Now Jesus made the mud and smeared it on the man's eyes on a Sabbath day. [15]So Pharisees also asked him how he was able to see.

The man told them, "He put mud on my eyes, I washed, and now I see."

[16]Some Pharisees said, "This man isn't from God, because he breaks the Sabbath law." Others said, "How can a sinner do miraculous signs like these?" So they were divided. [17]Some of the Pharisees questioned the man who had been born blind again: "What do you have to say about him, since he healed your eyes?"

He replied, "He's a prophet."

Conflict over the healing

[18]The Jewish leaders didn't believe the man had been blind and received his sight until they called for his parents. [19]The Jewish leaders asked them, "Is this your son? Are you saying he was born blind? How can he now see?"

[20]His parents answered, "We know he is our son. We know he was born blind. [21]But we don't know how he now sees, and we don't know who healed his eyes. Ask him. He's old enough to speak for himself." [22]His parents said this because they feared the Jewish

authorities. This is because the Jewish authorities had already decided that whoever confessed Jesus to be the Christ would be expelled from the synagogue. [23]That's why his parents said, "He's old enough. Ask him."

UMBRELLA
FEAR

What God Thinks John 9:22

Some people love to argue, while others will do anything to avoid it, including telling a lie. When Jesus took away a man's blindness, the man's parents didn't want to be involved in an argument. They knew Jesus had healed their son. They also knew that if they told the truth the Jewish leaders would be unhappy with them and might even kick them out of the synagogue. That may have seemed like a good reason to stay quiet, but it wasn't. Jesus' actions toward their son should have been acknowledged, praised, and celebrated. It's always wise to be more concerned with what God thinks of us than what people think of us. ◊

[24]Therefore, they called a second time for the man who had been born blind and said to him, "Give glory to God. We know this man is a sinner."

[25]The man answered, "I don't know whether he's a sinner. Here's what I do know: I was blind and now I see."

[26]They questioned him: "What did he do to you? How did he heal your eyes?"

[27]He replied, "I already told you, and you didn't listen. Why do you want to hear it again? Do you want to become his disciples too?"

[28]They insulted him: "You are his disciple, but we are Moses' disciples. [29]We know that God spoke to Moses, but we don't know where this man is from."

[30]The man answered, "This is incredible! You don't know where he is from, yet he healed my eyes! [31]We know that God doesn't listen to sinners. God listens to anyone who is devout and does God's will. [32]No one has ever heard of a healing of the eyes of someone born blind. [33]If this man wasn't from God, he couldn't do this."

[34]They responded, "You were born completely in sin! How is it that you dare to teach us?" Then they expelled him.

Jesus finds the man born blind

[35]Jesus heard they had expelled the man born blind. Finding him, Jesus said, "Do you believe in the Human One?"[b]

[36]He answered, "Who is he, sir?[c] I want to believe in him."

[37]Jesus said, "You have seen him. In fact, he is the one speaking with you."

[38]The man said, "Lord,[d] I believe." And he worshipped Jesus.

Jesus teaches the Pharisees

[39]Jesus said, "I have come into the world to exercise judgment so that those who don't see can see and those who see will become blind."

[40]Some Pharisees who were with him heard what he said and asked, "Surely we aren't blind, are we?"

[41]Jesus said to them, "If you were blind, you wouldn't have any sin, but now that you

10 say, 'We see,' your sin remains. [1]I assure you that whoever doesn't enter into the sheep pen through the gate but climbs over the wall is a thief and an outlaw. [2]The one who enters through the gate is the shepherd of the sheep. [3]The guard at the gate opens the gate for him, and the sheep listen to his voice. He calls his own sheep by name and leads them out. [4]Whenever he has gathered all of his sheep, he goes before them and they follow him, because they know his voice. [5]They won't follow a stranger but will run away because they don't know the stranger's voice." [6]Those who heard Jesus use this analogy didn't understand what he was saying.

I am the gate

[7]So Jesus spoke again, "I assure you that I am the gate of the sheep. [8]All who came before me were thieves and outlaws, but the sheep didn't listen to them. [9]I am the gate. Whoever enters through me will be saved. They will come in and go out and find pasture. [10]The thief enters only to steal, kill, and destroy. I came so that they could have life—indeed, so that they could live life to the fullest.

I am the good shepherd

[11]"I am the good shepherd. The good shepherd lays down his life for the sheep. [12]When the hired hand sees the wolf coming, he leaves the sheep and runs away. That's because he isn't the shepherd; the sheep aren't really his. So the wolf attacks the sheep and scatters them. [13]He's only a hired hand and the sheep don't matter to him.

[14]"I am the good shepherd. I know my own sheep and they know me, [15]just as the Father knows me and I know the Father. I give up my life for the sheep. [16]I have other sheep that don't belong to this sheep pen. I must lead them too. They will listen to my voice and there will be one flock, with one shepherd.

[17]"This is why the Father loves me: I give up my life so that I can take it up again. [18]No one takes it from me, but I give it up because I want to. I have the right to give it up, and I have the right to take it up again. I received this commandment from my Father."

[19]There was another division among the Jews because of Jesus' words. [20]Many of them said, "He has a demon and has lost his mind. Why listen to him?" [21]Others said, "These aren't the words of someone who has a demon. Can a demon heal the eyes of people who are blind?"

Jesus at the Festival of Dedication

[22]The time came for the Festival of Dedication[e] in Jerusalem. It was winter, [23]and Jesus was in the temple, walking in the covered porch named for Solomon. [24]The Jewish opposition circled around him and asked, "How long will you test our patience? If you are the Christ, tell us plainly."

[25]Jesus answered, "I have told you, but you

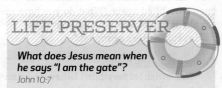

LIFE PRESERVER

What does Jesus mean when he says "I am the gate"?
John 10:7

Gates have a very practical purpose. They are an entry point to something important. Gates keep some things in and keep other things out. When Jesus told the people, "I am the gate" (John 10:7), he wanted them to know that he was the entry point to God. If people followed Jesus, they would be in the presence of God. ◊

[b]Or *Son of Man* [c]Or *Lord* [d]Or *Sir* [e]*Hanukkah*

don't believe. The works I do in my Father's name testify about me, ²⁶but you don't believe because you don't belong to my sheep. ²⁷My sheep listen to my voice. I know them and they follow me. ²⁸I give them eternal life. They will never die, and no one will snatch them from my hand. ²⁹My Father, who has given them to me, is greater than all, and no one is able to snatch them from my Father's hand. ³⁰I and the Father are one."

³¹Again the Jewish opposition picked up stones in order to stone him. ³²Jesus responded, "I have shown you many good works from the Father. For which of those works do you stone me?"

³³The Jewish opposition answered, "We don't stone you for a good work but for insulting God. You are human, yet you make yourself out to be God."

³⁴Jesus replied, "Isn't it written in your Law, *I have said, you are gods?*ᶠ ³⁵Scripture calls those to whom God's word came *gods,* and scripture can't be abolished. ³⁶So how can you say that the one whom the Father has made holy and sent into the world insults God because he said, 'I am God's Son'? ³⁷If I don't do the works of my Father, don't believe me. ³⁸But if I do them, and you don't believe me, believe the works so that you can know and recognize that the Father is in me and I am in the Father." ³⁹Again, they wanted to arrest him, but he escaped from them.

Jesus at the Jordan

⁴⁰Jesus went back across the Jordan to the place where John had baptized at first, and he stayed there. ⁴¹Many people came to him. "John didn't do any miraculous signs," they said, "but everything John said about this man was true." ⁴²Many believed in Jesus there.

Lazarus is ill

11A certain man, Lazarus, was ill. He was from Bethany, the village of Mary and her sister Martha. (²This was the Mary who anointed the Lord with fragrant oil and wiped his feet with her hair. Her brother Lazarus was ill.) ³So the sisters sent word to Jesus, saying, "Lord, the one whom you love is ill."

⁴When he heard this, Jesus said, "This illness isn't fatal. It's for the glory of God so that God's Son can be glorified through it." ⁵Jesus loved Martha, her sister, and Lazarus. ⁶When he heard that Lazarus was ill, he stayed where he was. After two days, ⁷he said to his disciples, "Let's return to Judea again."

⁸The disciples replied, "Rabbi, the Jewish opposition wants to stone you, but you want to go back?"

⁹Jesus answered, "Aren't there twelve hours in the day? Whoever walks in the day doesn't stumble because they see the light of the world. ¹⁰But whoever walks in the night does stumble because the light isn't in them."

¹¹He continued, "Our friend Lazarus is sleeping, but I am going in order to wake him up."

¹²The disciples said, "Lord, if he's sleeping, he will get well." ¹³They thought Jesus meant that Lazarus was in a deep sleep, but Jesus had spoken about Lazarus' death.

¹⁴Jesus told them plainly, "Lazarus has died. ¹⁵For your sakes, I'm glad I wasn't there so that you can believe. Let's go to him."

¹⁶Then Thomas (the one called Didymus) said to the other disciples, "Let us go too so that we may die with Jesus."

SAILBOAT

COURAGE

That's Courage *John 11:16*
The disciples didn't want Jesus to go to Bethany because it was near Jerusalem. Many of the religious leaders who opposed Jesus lived in Jerusalem. The disciples knew some people wanted Jesus stopped, so the disciples wanted Jesus to do the safe thing. Thomas was the exception. He knew Jesus had a dangerous mission, but Thomas was willing to go with him into a scary situation. Thomas had courage. ◆

Jesus with Martha and Mary

¹⁷When Jesus arrived, he found that Lazarus had already been in the tomb for four days. ¹⁸Bethany was a little less than two miles from Jerusalem. ¹⁹Many Jews had come to comfort Martha and Mary after their brother's death. ²⁰When Martha heard that Jesus was coming, she went to meet him,

while Mary remained in the house. ²¹Martha said to Jesus, "Lord, if you had been here, my brother wouldn't have died. ²²Even now I know that whatever you ask God, God will give you."

²³Jesus told her, "Your brother will rise again."

²⁴Martha replied, "I know that he will rise in the resurrection on the last day."

²⁵Jesus said to her, "I am the resurrection and the life. Whoever believes in me will live, even though they die. ²⁶Everyone who lives and believes in me will never die. Do you believe this?"

²⁷She replied, "Yes, Lord, I believe that you are the Christ, God's Son, the one who is coming into the world."

²⁸After she said this, she went and spoke privately to her sister Mary, "The teacher is here and he's calling for you." ²⁹When Mary heard this, she got up quickly and went to Jesus. ³⁰He hadn't entered the village but was still in the place where Martha had met him. ³¹When the Jews who were comforting Mary in the house saw her get up quickly and leave, they followed her. They assumed she was going to mourn at the tomb.

³²When Mary arrived where Jesus was and saw him, she fell at his feet and said, "Lord, if you had been here, my brother wouldn't have died."

³³When Jesus saw her crying and the Jews who had come with her crying also, he was deeply disturbed and troubled. ³⁴He asked, "Where have you laid him?"

They replied, "Lord, come and see."

³⁵Jesus began to cry. ³⁶The Jews said, "See how much he loved him!" ³⁷But some of them said, "He healed the eyes of the man born blind. Couldn't he have kept Lazarus from dying?"

Jesus at Lazarus' tomb

³⁸Jesus was deeply disturbed again when he came to the tomb. It was a cave, and a stone covered the entrance. ³⁹Jesus said, "Remove the stone."

Martha, the sister of the dead man, said, "Lord, the smell will be awful! He's been dead four days."

⁴⁰Jesus replied, "Didn't I tell you that if you believe, you will see God's glory?" ⁴¹So they removed the stone. Jesus looked up and said, "Father, thank you for hearing me. ⁴²I know you always hear me. I say this for the benefit of the crowd standing here so that they will believe that you sent me." ⁴³Having said this, Jesus shouted with a loud voice, "Lazarus, come out!" ⁴⁴The dead man came out, his feet bound and his hands tied, and his face covered with a cloth. Jesus said to them, "Untie him and let him go."

⁴⁵Therefore, many of the Jews who came with Mary and saw what Jesus did believed in him. ⁴⁶But some of them went to the Pharisees and told them what Jesus had done.

Caiaphas prophesies

⁴⁷Then the chief priests and Pharisees called together the council[g] and said, "What are we going to do? This man is doing many miraculous signs! ⁴⁸If we let him go on like this, everyone will believe in him. Then the Romans will come and take away both our temple and our people."

⁴⁹One of them, Caiaphas, who was high priest that year, told them, "You don't know anything! ⁵⁰You don't see that it is better for you that one man die for the people rather than the whole nation be destroyed." ⁵¹He didn't say this on his own. As high priest that year, he prophesied that Jesus would soon die for the nation—⁵²and not only for the nation. Jesus would also die so that God's children scattered everywhere would be gathered together as one. ⁵³From that day on they plotted to kill him.

The Passover draws near

⁵⁴Therefore, Jesus was no longer active in public ministry among the Jewish leaders. Instead, he left Jerusalem and went to a place near the wilderness, to a city called Ephraim, where he stayed with his disciples.

⁵⁵It was almost time for the Jewish Passover, and many people went from the countryside up to Jerusalem to purify themselves through ritual washing before the Passover. ⁵⁶They were looking for Jesus. As they spoke to each other in the temple, they said, "What do you think? He won't come to

the festival, will he?" ⁵⁷The chief priests and Pharisees had given orders that anyone who knew where he was should report it, so they could arrest him.

Mary anoints Jesus' feet

12 Six days before Passover, Jesus came to Bethany, home of Lazarus, whom Jesus had raised from the dead. ²Lazarus and his sisters hosted a dinner for him. Martha served and Lazarus was among those who joined him at the table. ³Then Mary took an extraordinary amount, almost three-quarters of a pound,ʰ of very expensive perfume made of pure nard. She anointed Jesus' feet with it, then wiped his feet dry with her hair. The house was filled with the aroma of the perfume. ⁴Judas Iscariot, one of his disciples (the one who was about to betray him), complained, ⁵"This perfume was worth a year's wages!ⁱ Why wasn't it sold and the money given to the poor?" (⁶He said this not because he cared about the poor but because he was a thief. He carried the money bag and would take what was in it.)

⁷Then Jesus said, "Leave her alone. This perfume was to be used in preparation for my burial, and this is how she has used it. ⁸You will always have the poor among you, but you won't always have me."

⁹Many Jews learned that he was there. They came not only because of Jesus but also to see Lazarus, whom he had raised from the dead. ¹⁰The chief priests decided that they would kill Lazarus too. ¹¹It was because of Lazarus that many of the Jews had deserted them and come to believe in Jesus.

Jesus enters Jerusalem

¹²The next day the great crowd that had come for the festival heard that Jesus was coming to Jerusalem. ¹³They took palm branches and went out to meet him. They shouted,

"Hosanna!
Blessings on the one who comes
*in the name of the Lord!*ʲ
Blessings on the king of Israel!"

¹⁴Jesus found a young donkey and sat on it, just as it is written,

¹⁵ *Don't be afraid, Daughter Zion.*
Look! Your king is coming,
*sitting on a donkey's colt.*ᵏ

¹⁶His disciples didn't understand these things at first. After he was glorified, they remembered that these things had been written about him and that they had done these things to him.

¹⁷The crowd who had been with him when he called Lazarus out of the tomb and raised him from the dead were testifying about him. ¹⁸That's why the crowd came to meet him, because they had heard about this miraculous sign that he had done. ¹⁹Therefore, the Pharisees said to each other, "See! You've accomplished nothing! Look! The whole world is following him!"

Jesus teaches about his death

²⁰Some Greeks were among those who had come up to worship at the festival. ²¹They came to Philip, who was from Bethsaida in Galilee, and made a request: "Sir, we want to see Jesus." ²²Philip told Andrew, and Andrew and Philip told Jesus.

did you know? Nard was a very expensive perfume made from a plant. The amount of nard Mary of Bethany used to anoint Jesus cost 300 *denarii*, which was as much money as most workers made in one year.

²³Jesus replied, "The time has come for the Human Oneˡ to be glorified. ²⁴I assure you that unless a grain of wheat falls into the earth and dies, it can only be a single seed. But if it dies, it bears much fruit. ²⁵Those who love their lives will lose them, and those who hate their lives in this world will keep them forever. ²⁶Whoever serves me must follow me. Wherever I am, there my servant will also be. My Father will honor whoever serves me.

²⁷"Now *I am deeply troubled.*ᵐ What should I say? 'Father, save me from this time'? No, for this is the reason I have come to this time. ²⁸Father, glorify your name!"

Then a voice came from heaven, "I have glorified it, and I will glorify it again."

ʰOr *a litra*, a Roman pound, approximately twelve ounces ⁱOr *three hundred denaria* ʲPs 118:26 ᵏZech 9:9 ˡOr *Son of Man* ᵐPs 6:2

²⁹The crowd standing there heard and said, "It's thunder." Others said, "An angel spoke to him."

³⁰Jesus replied, "This voice wasn't for my benefit but for yours. ³¹Now is the time for judgment of this world. Now this world's ruler will be thrown out. ³²When I am lifted up[n] from the earth, I will draw everyone to me." (³³He said this to show how he was going to die.)

LIGHTHOUSE

PRAYER

Prayer for Strength *John 12:27-28*

After Jesus told the disciples he would die soon, he talked to God about the situation. You might be surprised at *how* Jesus prayed. He didn't ask God to fix the problem. Instead, he asked God to be *glorified*, which means "made more visible," through the hard things that would happen to him. Jesus prayed for God to give him strength to do what he needed to do. ◊

³⁴The crowd responded, "We have heard from the Law that the Christ remains forever. How can you say that the Human One[o] must be lifted up? Who is this Human One?"[p]

³⁵Jesus replied, "The light is with you for only a little while. Walk while you have the light so that darkness doesn't overtake you. Those who walk in the darkness don't know where they are going. ³⁶As long as you have the light, believe in the light so that you might become people whose lives are determined by the light." After Jesus said these things, he went away and hid from them.

Fulfillment of prophecy

³⁷Jesus had done many miraculous signs before the people, but they didn't believe in him. ³⁸This was to fulfill the word of the prophet Isaiah:

Lord, who has believed
  through our message?
To whom is the arm of the Lord
  fully revealed?[q]

³⁹Isaiah explains why they couldn't believe:

⁴⁰ He made their eyes blind
  and closed their minds
  so that they might not see with their eyes,
  understand with their minds,
  and turn their lives around—
  and I would heal them.[r]

⁴¹Isaiah said these things because he saw Jesus' glory; he spoke about Jesus. ⁴²Even so, many leaders believed in him, but they wouldn't acknowledge their faith because they feared that the Pharisees would expel them from the synagogue. ⁴³They believed, but they loved human praise more than God's glory.

Summary of Jesus' teaching

⁴⁴Jesus shouted, "Whoever believes in me doesn't believe in me but in the one who sent me. ⁴⁵Whoever sees me sees the one who sent me. ⁴⁶I have come as a light into the world so that everyone who believes in me won't live in darkness. ⁴⁷If people hear my words and don't keep them, I don't judge them. I didn't come to judge the world but to save it. ⁴⁸Whoever rejects me and doesn't receive my words will be judged at the last day by the word I have spoken. ⁴⁹I don't speak on my own, but the Father who sent me commanded me regarding what I should speak and say. ⁵⁰I know that his commandment is eternal life. Therefore, whatever I say is just as the Father has said to me."

Foot washing

13 Before the Festival of Passover, Jesus knew that his time had come to leave this world and go to the Father. Having loved his own who were in the world, he loved them fully.

²Jesus and his disciples were sharing the evening meal. The devil had already provoked Judas, Simon Iscariot's son, to betray Jesus. ³Jesus knew the Father had given everything into his hands and that he had come from God and was returning to God. ⁴So he got up from the table and took off his robes. Picking up a linen towel, he tied it around his waist. ⁵Then he poured water into a washbasin and began to wash the disciples' feet, drying them with the towel he was wearing. ⁶When Jesus came to Simon Peter, Peter said to him, "Lord, are you going to wash my feet?"

---

[n]Or *exalted* [o]Or *Son of Man* [p]Or *Son of Man* [q]Isa 53:1 [r]Isa 6:10

[7]Jesus replied, "You don't understand what I'm doing now, but you will understand later."

[8]"No!" Peter said. "You will never wash my feet!"

Jesus replied, "Unless I wash you, you won't have a place with me."

[9]Simon Peter said, "Lord, not only my feet but also my hands and my head!"

[10]Jesus responded, "Those who have bathed need only to have their feet washed, because they are completely clean. You disciples are clean, but not every one of you." [11]He knew who would betray him. That's why he said, "Not every one of you is clean."

[12]After he washed the disciples' feet, he put on his robes and returned to his place at the table. He said to them, "Do you know what I've done for you? [13]You call me 'Teacher' and 'Lord,' and you speak correctly, because I am. [14]If I, your Lord and teacher, have washed your feet, you too must wash each other's feet. [15]I have given you an example: Just as I have done, you also must do. [16]I assure you, servants aren't greater than their master, nor are those who are sent greater than the one who sent them. [17]Since you know these things, you will be happy if you do them. [18]I'm not speaking about all of you. I know those whom I've chosen. But this is to fulfill the scripture, *The one who eats my bread has turned against me.*[s]

[19]"I'm telling you this now, before it happens, so that when it does happen you will believe that I Am. [20]I assure you that whoever receives someone I send receives me, and whoever receives me receives the one who sent me."

Announcement of the betrayal

[21]After he said these things, Jesus was deeply disturbed and testified, "I assure you, one of you will betray me."

[s]Ps 41:9

Washing Feet? Seriously? John 13:1-16

Imagine that you spend all day outside barefoot. You play games in the dirt. You walk down the street to see your friends and play with sidewalk chalk in the driveway. When you finally come home you aren't thinking about your feet, but your parents won't let you come inside until your dirty feet are clean!

When Jesus was on the earth, people wore sandals and walked on dirt roads everywhere they went. By the end of the day their feet were filthy. Jesus used dirty feet to teach his followers about serving each other. Before they shared a meal, Jesus tied a towel around his waist and washed his disciples' feet. This job was usually done by a servant with low status and little power. The disciples couldn't stand the thought of their leader stooping so low to clean their feet. Jesus told the disciples he wanted them to be leaders by serving people. Jesus didn't want the disciples to think they were too important to do what needed to be done. That included washing dirty feet.

We agree to serve other people when we choose to follow Jesus. Jesus says that if we can't serve people then we aren't really following him. The next time you have dirty feet, ask God to help you find ways to serve others.

What do you think of when you imagine yourself serving other people?

How can you look for ways to serve the people around you?

[22]His disciples looked at each other, confused about which of them he was talking about. [23]One of the disciples, the one whom Jesus loved, was at Jesus' side. [24]Simon Peter nodded at him to get him to ask Jesus who he was talking about. [25]Leaning back toward Jesus, this disciple asked, "Lord, who is it?"

[26]Jesus answered, "It's the one to whom I will give this piece of bread once I have dipped into the bowl." Then he dipped the piece of bread and gave it to Judas, Simon Iscariot's son. [27]After Judas took the bread, Satan entered into him. Jesus told him, "What you are about to do, do quickly." [28]No one sitting at the table understood why Jesus said this to him. [29]Some thought that, since Judas kept the money bag, Jesus told him, "Go, buy what we need for the feast," or that he should give something to the poor. [30]So when Judas took the bread, he left immediately. And it was night.

Love commandment

[31]When Judas was gone, Jesus said, "Now the Human One[t] has been glorified, and God has been glorified in him. [32]If God has been glorified in him, God will also glorify the Human One[u] in himself and will glorify him immediately. [33]Little children, I'm with you for a little while longer. You will look for me—but, just as I told the Jewish leaders, I also tell you now—'Where I'm going, you can't come.'

[34]"I give you a new commandment: Love each other. Just as I have loved you, so you also must love each other. [35]This is how everyone will know that you are my disciples, when you love each other."

Announcement of Peter's denial

[36]Simon Peter said to Jesus, "Lord, where are you going?"

Jesus answered, "Where I am going, you can't follow me now, but you will follow later."

[37]Peter asked, "Lord, why can't I follow you now? I'll give up my life for you."

[38]Jesus replied, "Will you give up your life for me? I assure you that you will deny me three times before the rooster crows.

The way, the truth, and the life

14 "Don't be troubled. Trust in God. Trust also in me. [2]My Father's house has room to spare. If that weren't the case, would I have told you that I'm going to prepare a place for you? [3]When I go to prepare a place for you, I will return and take you to be with me so that where I am you will be too. [4]You know the way to the place I'm going."

[5]Thomas asked, "Lord, we don't know where you are going. How can we know the way?"

[6]Jesus answered, "I am the way, the truth, and the life. No one comes to the Father except through me. [7]If you have really known me, you will also know the Father. From now on you know him and have seen him."

[8]Philip said, "Lord, show us the Father; that will be enough for us."

[9]Jesus replied, "Don't you know me, Philip, even after I have been with you all this time? Whoever has seen me has seen the Father. How can you say, 'Show us the Father'? [10]Don't you believe that I am in the Father and the Father is in me? The words I have spoken to you I don't speak on my own. The Father who dwells in me does his works. [11]Trust me when I say that I am in the Father and the Father is in me, or at least believe on account of the works themselves. [12]I assure you that whoever believes in me will do the works that I do. They will do even greater works than these because I am going to the Father. [13]I will do whatever you ask for in my name, so that the Father can be glorified in the Son. [14]When you ask me for anything in my name, I will do it.

I won't leave you as orphans

[15]"If you love me, you will keep my commandments. [16]I will ask the Father, and he will send another Companion,[v] who will be with you forever. [17]This Companion is the Spirit of Truth, whom the world can't receive because it neither sees him nor recognizes him. You know him, because he lives with you and will be with you.

[18]"I won't leave you as orphans. I will come to you. [19]Soon the world will no longer see me, but you will see me. Because I live, you will live too. [20]On that day you will know

Bet you can read this in 2 minutes. Ready, set, go!

that I am in my Father, you are in me, and I am in you. ²¹Whoever has my commandments and keeps them loves me. Whoever loves me will be loved by my Father, and I will love them and reveal myself to them."

²²Judas (not Judas Iscariot) asked, "Lord, why are you about to reveal yourself to us and not to the world?"

²³Jesus answered, "Whoever loves me will keep my word. My Father will love them, and we will come to them and make our home with them. ²⁴Whoever doesn't love me doesn't keep my words. The word that you hear isn't mine. It is the word of the Father who sent me.

²⁵"I have spoken these things to you while I am with you. ²⁶The Companion,ʷ the Holy Spirit, whom the Father will send in my name, will teach you everything and will remind you of everything I told you.

²⁷"Peace I leave with you. My peace I give you. I give to you not as the world gives. Don't be troubled or afraid. ²⁸You have heard me tell you, 'I'm going away and returning to you.' If you loved me, you would be happy that I am going to the Father, because the Father is greater than me. ²⁹I have told you before it happens so that when it happens you will believe. ³⁰I won't say much more to you because this world's ruler is coming. He has nothing on me. ³¹Rather, he comes so that the world will know that I love the Father and do just as

UMBRELLA
Fear

Free from Fear *John 14:27*
Right after Jesus promised his followers the Holy Spirit, he promised peace. Jesus knew the world is full of hard times and trouble, but he didn't want his followers to be worried and upset. Jesus made sure his followers didn't mistake the world's peace for God's peace. The peace Jesus gives isn't based on what happens in the world between nations or neighbors. Jesus' peace allows his followers to live without fear and anxiety. This peace comes from the presence of God in our hearts and lives. ◆

LIFE PRESERVER

What is "the true vine"?
John 15:1-8

A vineyard was a very familiar image for people when Jesus was on earth. Many people were farmers who tended plants and orchards. They understood what vines needed to grow and produce fruit. By using this image, Jesus told the disciples about his relationship with God. He told them about the importance of his love for them, his love for God, and their love for other people. When Jesus talked about fruit in the lives of his followers, he didn't mean apples, oranges, and bananas. He meant actions and attitudes that are filled with love, grace, honesty, and kindness. ◆

the Father has commanded me. Get up. We're leaving this place.

I am the true vine

15 "I am the true vine, and my Father is the vineyard keeper. ²He removes any of my branches that don't produce fruit, and he trims any branch that produces fruit so that it will produce even more fruit. ³You are already trimmed because of the word I have spoken to you. ⁴Remain in me, and I will remain in you. A branch can't produce fruit by itself, but must remain in the vine. Likewise, you can't produce fruit unless you remain in me. ⁵I am the vine; you are the branches. If you remain in me and I in you, then you will produce much fruit. Without me, you can't do anything. ⁶If you don't remain in me, you will be like a branch that is thrown out and dries up. Those branches are gathered up, thrown into a fire, and burned. ⁷If you remain in me and my words remain in you, ask for whatever you want and it will be done for you. ⁸My Father is glorified when you produce much fruit and in this way prove that you are my disciples.

Love each other

⁹"As the Father loved me, I too have loved you. Remain in my love. ¹⁰If you keep my commandments, you will remain in my love, just as I kept my Father's commandments and

remain in his love. [11]I have said these things to you so that my joy will be in you and your joy will be complete. [12]This is my commandment: love each other just as I have loved you. [13]No one has greater love than to give up one's life for one's friends. [14]You are my friends if you do what I command you. [15]I don't call you servants any longer, because servants don't know what their master is doing. Instead, I call you friends, because everything I heard from my Father I have made known to you. [16]You didn't choose me, but I chose you and appointed you so that you could go and produce fruit and so that your fruit could last. As a result, whatever you ask the Father in my name, he will give you. [17]I give you these commandments so that you can love each other.

Memorize
John 15:13-14

If the world hates you

[18]"If the world hates you, know that it hated me first. [19]If you belonged to the world, the world would love you as its own. However, I have chosen you out of the world, and you don't belong to the world. This is why the world hates you. [20]Remember what I told you, 'Servants aren't greater than their master.' If the world harassed me, it will harass you too. If it kept my word, it will also keep yours. [21]The world will do all these things to you on account of my name, because it doesn't know the one who sent me.

[22]"If I hadn't come and spoken to the people of this world, they wouldn't be sinners. But now they have no excuse for their sin. [23]Whoever hates me also hates the Father. [24]If I hadn't done works among them that no one else had done, they wouldn't be sinners. But now they have seen and hated both me and my Father. [25]This fulfills the word written in their Law, *They hated me without a reason.*[x]

[26]"When the Companion[y] comes, whom I will send from the Father—the Spirit of Truth who proceeds from the Father—he will testify about me. [27]You will testify too, because you have been with me from the beginning.

16 I have said these things to you so that you won't fall away. [2]They will expel

you from the synagogue. The time is coming when those who kill you will think that they are doing a service to God. [3]They will do these things because they don't know the Father or me. [4]But I have said these things to you so that when their time comes, you will remember that I told you about them.

I go away

"I didn't say these things to you from the beginning, because I was with you. [5]But now I go away to the one who sent me. None of you ask me, 'Where are you going?' [6]Yet because I have said these things to you, you are filled with sorrow. [7]I assure you that it is better for you that I go away. If I don't go away, the Companion[z] won't come to you. But if I go, I will send him to you. [8]When he comes, he will show the world it was wrong about sin, righteousness, and judgment. [9]He will show the world it was wrong about sin because they don't believe in me. [10]He will show the world it was wrong about righteousness because I'm going to the Father and you won't see me anymore. [11]He will show the world it was wrong about judgment because this world's ruler stands condemned.

I still have many things to say

[12]"I have much more to say to you, but you can't handle it now. [13]However, when the Spirit of Truth comes, he will guide you in all truth. He won't speak on his own, but will say whatever he hears and will proclaim to you what is to come. [14]He will glorify me, because he will take what is mine and proclaim it to you. [15]Everything that the Father has is mine. That's why I said that the Spirit takes what is mine and will proclaim it to you. [16]Soon you won't be able to see me; soon after that, you will see me."

I will see you again

[17]Some of Jesus' disciples said to each other, "What does he mean: 'Soon you won't see me, and soon after that you will see me' and 'Because I'm going to the Father'? [18]What does he mean by 'soon'? We don't understand what he's talking about."

[19]Jesus knew they wanted to ask him, so he

[x]Pss 35:19; 69:4 [y]Or Advocate [z]Or Advocate

UMBRELLA
STRESSED OUT

Peace in the Middle of Hard Times
John 16:33

Jesus said his followers would have peace. He told them to be encouraged because he had conquered the world. But in the midst of this good news, he also said they would feel stress. This isn't the I-can't-find-my-library-book-and-it's-due-today kind of stress, but real suffering. Following Jesus doesn't mean we get to skip all of life's challenges. Instead, it means Jesus is with us when we go through our share of challenges. The promise of God's presence brings peace. ◊

said, "Are you trying to find out from each other what I meant when I said, 'Soon you won't see me, and soon after that you will see me'? ²⁰I assure you that you will cry and lament, and the world will be happy. You will be sorrowful, but your sorrow will turn into joy. ²¹When a woman gives birth, she has pain because her time has come. But when the child is born, she no longer remembers her distress because of her joy that a child has been born into the world. ²²In the same way, you have sorrow now; but I will see you again, and you will be overjoyed. No one takes away your joy. ²³In that day, you won't ask me anything. I assure you that the Father will give you whatever you ask in my name. ²⁴Up to now, you have asked nothing in my name. Ask and you will receive so that your joy will be complete.

I have conquered the world

²⁵"I've been using figures of speech with you. The time is coming when I will no longer speak to you in such analogies. Instead, I will tell you plainly about the Father. ²⁶In that day you will ask in my name. I'm not saying that I will ask the Father on your behalf. ²⁷The Father himself loves you, because you have loved me and believed that I came from God. ²⁸I left the Father and came into the world. I tell you again: I am leaving the world and returning to the Father."

²⁹His disciples said, "See! Now you speak plainly; you aren't using figures of speech. ³⁰Now we know that you know everything and

you don't need anyone to ask you. Because of this we believe you have come from God."

³¹Jesus replied, "Now you believe? ³²Look! A time is coming—and is here!—when each of you will be scattered to your own homes and you will leave me alone. I'm not really alone, for the Father is with me. ³³I've said these things to you so that you will have peace in me. In the world you have distress. But be encouraged! I have conquered the world."

Jesus prays

17 When Jesus finished saying these things, he looked up to heaven and said, "Father, the time has come. Glorify your Son, so that the Son can glorify you. ²You gave him authority over everyone so that he could give eternal life to everyone you gave him. ³This is eternal life: to know you, the only true God, and Jesus Christ whom you sent. ⁴I have glorified you on earth by finishing the work you gave me to do.

LIGHTHOUSE
PRAISE GOD

Finish Well *John 17:4*
Jesus said one way to praise God is to complete the work God gives us to do. Starting the work is one thing, but finishing it is what really matters. That's what pleases God. ◊

⁵Now, Father, glorify me in your presence with the glory I shared with you before the world was created.

⁶"I have revealed your name to the people you gave me from this world. They were yours and you gave them to me, and they have kept your word. ⁷Now they know that everything you have given me comes from you. ⁸This is because I gave them the words that you gave me, and they received them. They truly understood that I came from you, and they believed that you sent me.

⁹"I'm praying for them. I'm not praying for the world but for those you gave me, because they are yours. ¹⁰Everything that is mine is yours and everything that is yours is mine; I have been glorified in them. ¹¹I'm no longer in the world, but they are in the world,

Bet you can
read this in 5 minutes. Ready, set, go!

even as I'm coming to you. Holy Father, watch over them in your name, the name you gave me, that they will be one just as we are one. [12] When I was with them, I watched over them in your name, the name you gave to me, and I kept them safe. None of them were lost, except the one who was destined for destruction, so that scripture would be fulfilled. [13] Now I'm coming to you and I say these things while I'm in the world so that they can share completely in my joy. [14] I gave your word to them and the world hated them, because they don't belong to this world, just as I don't belong to this world. [15] I'm not asking that you take them out of this world but that you keep them safe from the evil one. [16] They don't belong to this world, just as I don't belong to this world. [17] Make them holy in the truth; your word is truth. [18] As you sent me into the world, so I have sent them into the world. [19] I made myself holy on their behalf so that they also would be made holy in the truth.

[20] "I'm not praying only for them but also for those who believe in me because of their word. [21] I pray they will be one, Father, just as you are in me and I am in you. I pray that they also will be in us, so that the world will believe that you sent me. [22] I've given them the glory that you gave me so that they can be one just as we are one. [23] I'm in them and you are in me so that they will be made perfectly one. Then the world will know that you sent me and that you have loved them just as you loved me.

[24] "Father, I want those you gave me to be with me where I am. Then they can see my glory, which you gave me because you loved me before the creation of the world.

[25] "Righteous Father, even the world didn't know you, but I've known you, and these believers know that you sent me. [26] I've made your name known to them and will continue to make it known so that your love for me will be in them, and I myself will be in them."

Arrest in the garden

18 After he said these things, Jesus went out with his disciples and crossed over to the other side of the Kidron Valley. He and his disciples entered a garden there. [2] Judas, his betrayer, also knew the place because Jesus often gathered there with his disciples. [3] Judas brought a company of soldiers[a] and some guards from the chief priests and Pharisees. They came there carrying lanterns, torches, and weapons. [4] Jesus knew everything that was to happen to him, so he went out and asked, "Who are you looking for?"

[5] They answered, "Jesus the Nazarene."

He said to them, "I Am."[b] (Judas, his betrayer, was standing with them.) [6] When he said, "I Am," they shrank back and fell to the ground. [7] He asked them again, "Who are you looking for?"

They said, "Jesus the Nazarene."

[8] Jesus answered, "I told you, 'I Am.'[c] If you are looking for me, then let these people go." [9] This was so that the word he had spoken might be fulfilled: "I didn't lose anyone of those whom you gave me."

[10] Then Simon Peter, who had a sword, drew it and struck the high priest's servant, cutting off his right ear. (The servant's name was Malchus.) [11] Jesus told Peter, "Put your sword away! Am I not to drink the cup the Father has given me?" [12] Then the company of soldiers, the commander, and the guards from the Jewish leaders took Jesus into custody. They bound him [13] and led him first to Annas. He was the father-in-law of Caiaphas, the high priest that year. ([14] Caiaphas was the one who had advised the Jewish leaders that it was better for one person to die for the people.)

Peter denies Jesus

[15] Simon Peter and another disciple followed Jesus. Because this other disciple was known to the high priest, he went with Jesus into the high priest's courtyard. [16] However, Peter stood outside near the gate. Then the other disciple (the one known to the high priest) came out and spoke to the woman stationed at the gate, and she brought Peter in. [17] The servant woman stationed at the gate asked Peter, "Aren't you one of this man's disciples?"

"I'm not," he replied. [18] The servants and the guards had made a fire because it was cold. They were standing around it, warming

---

[a] Or *cohort* (approximately six hundred soldiers) [b] Or *It is* [c] Or *It is I*

themselves. Peter joined them there, standing by the fire and warming himself.

Jesus testifies

[19]Meanwhile, the chief priest questioned Jesus about his disciples and his teaching. [20]Jesus answered, "I've spoken openly to the world. I've always taught in synagogues and in the temple, where all the Jews gather. I've said nothing in private. [21]Why ask me? Ask those who heard what I told them. They know what I said."

[22]After Jesus spoke, one of the guards standing there slapped Jesus in the face. "Is that how you would answer the high priest?" he asked.

[23]Jesus replied, "If I speak wrongly, testify about what was wrong. But if I speak correctly, why do you strike me?" [24]Then Annas sent him, bound, to Caiaphas the high priest.

Peter denies Jesus again

[25]Meanwhile, Simon Peter was still standing with the guards, warming himself. They asked, "Aren't you one of his disciples?"

Peter denied it, saying, "I'm not."

[26]A servant of the high priest, a relative of the one whose ear Peter had cut off, said to him, "Didn't I see you in the garden with him?" [27]Peter denied it again, and immediately a rooster crowed.

Trial before Pilate

[28]The Jewish leaders led Jesus from Caiaphas to the Roman governor's palace.[d] It was early in the morning. So that they could eat the Passover, the Jewish leaders wouldn't enter the palace; entering the palace would have made them ritually impure.

[29]So Pilate went out to them and asked, "What charge do you bring against this man?"

[30]They answered, "If he had done nothing wrong, we wouldn't have handed him over to you."

[31]Pilate responded, "Take him yourselves and judge him according to your Law."

The Jewish leaders replied, "The Law doesn't allow us to kill anyone." ([32]This was so that Jesus' word might be fulfilled when he indicated how he was going to die.)

Pilate questions Jesus

[33]Pilate went back into the palace. He summoned Jesus and asked, "Are you the king of the Jews?"

[34]Jesus answered, "Do you say this on your own or have others spoken to you about me?"

[35]Pilate responded, "I'm not a Jew, am I? Your nation and its chief priests handed you over to me. What have you done?"

[36]Jesus replied, "My kingdom doesn't originate from this world. If it did, my guards would fight so that I wouldn't have been arrested by the Jewish leaders. My kingdom isn't from here."

[37]"So you are a king?" Pilate said.

Jesus answered, "You say that I am a king. I was born and came into the world for this reason: to testify to the truth. Whoever accepts the truth listens to my voice."

[38]"What is truth?" Pilate asked.

LIGHTHOUSE

GOD'S KINGDOM

Kingdom of Hearts *John 18:36*
Jesus made it clear that he didn't come to be the leader of the political world. He wasn't after Pilate's job or Herod's crown. Jesus came to earth to build God's kingdom in the hearts of people one person at a time. God's kingdom spans the nations of the world joining people of different races, gender, and political beliefs. ◊

Release of Barabbas

After Pilate said this, he returned to the Jewish leaders and said, "I find no grounds for any charge against him. [39]You have a custom that I release one prisoner for you at Passover. Do you want me to release for you the king of the Jews?"

[40]They shouted, "Not this man! Give us Barabbas!" (Barabbas was an outlaw.)

Jesus is whipped and mocked as king

19 Then Pilate had Jesus taken and whipped. [2]The soldiers twisted together a crown of thorns and put it on his head, and dressed him in a purple robe. [3]Over

[d]Or *praetorium*

and over they went up to him and said, "Greetings, king of the Jews!" And they slapped him in the face.

⁴Pilate came out of the palace again and said to the Jewish leaders, "Look! I'm bringing him out to you to let you know that I find no grounds for a charge against him." ⁵When Jesus came out, wearing the crown of thorns and the purple robe, Pilate said to them, "Here's the man."

did you know? Many paintings of Jesus on the cross show a sign above him that reads "INRI." These are the first letters of each of the four Latin words that mean "Jesus of Nazareth, King of the Jews." John said these same words were also written in Aramaic and Greek so everyone could read them.

⁶When the chief priests and their deputies saw him, they shouted out, "Crucify, crucify!"

Pilate told them, "You take him and crucify him. I don't find any grounds for a charge against him."

⁷The Jewish leaders replied, "We have a Law, and according to this Law he ought to die because he made himself out to be God's Son."

Pilate questions Jesus again

⁸When Pilate heard this word, he was even more afraid. ⁹He went back into the residence and spoke to Jesus, "Where are you from?" Jesus didn't answer. ¹⁰So Pilate said, "You won't speak to me? Don't you know that I have authority to release you and also to crucify you?"

¹¹Jesus replied, "You would have no authority over me if it had not been given to you from above. That's why the one who handed me over to you has the greater sin." ¹²From that moment on, Pilate wanted to release Jesus.

However, the Jewish leaders cried out, saying, "If you release this man, you aren't a friend of the emperor! Anyone who makes himself out to be a king opposes the emperor!"

¹³When Pilate heard these words, he led Jesus out and seated him on the judge's bench at the place called Stone Pavement (in Aramaic, *Gabbatha*). ¹⁴It was about noon on the Preparation Day for the Passover. Pilate said to the Jewish leaders, "Here's your king."

¹⁵The Jewish leaders cried out, "Take him away! Take him away! Crucify him!"

Pilate responded, "What? Do you want me to crucify your king?"

"We have no king except the emperor," the chief priests answered. ¹⁶Then Pilate handed Jesus over to be crucified.

Crucifixion

The soldiers took Jesus prisoner. ¹⁷Carrying his cross by himself, he went out to a place called Skull Place (in Aramaic, *Golgotha*). ¹⁸That's where they crucified him—and two others with him, one on each side and Jesus in the middle. ¹⁹Pilate had a public notice written and posted on the cross. It read "Jesus the Nazarene, the king of the Jews." ²⁰Many of the Jews read this sign, for the place where Jesus was crucified was near the city and it was written in Aramaic, Latin, and Greek. ²¹Therefore, the Jewish chief priests complained to Pilate, "Don't write, 'The king of the Jews' but 'This man said, "I am the king of the Jews."'"

²²Pilate answered, "What I've written, I've written."

²³When the soldiers crucified Jesus, they took his clothes and his sandals, and divided them into four shares, one for each soldier. His shirt was seamless, woven as one piece from the top to the bottom. ²⁴They said to each other, "Let's not tear it. Let's cast lots to see who will get it." This was to fulfill the scripture,

> They divided my clothes
> among themselves,
> and they cast lots for my clothing.ᵉ

That's what the soldiers did.

²⁵Jesus' mother and his mother's sister, Mary the wife of Clopas, and Mary Magdalene stood near the cross. ²⁶When Jesus saw his mother and the disciple whom he loved standing nearby, he said to his mother, "Woman, here is your son." ²⁷Then he said to the disciple, "Here is your mother." And from that time on, this disciple took her into his home.

²⁸After this, knowing that everything was already completed, in order to fulfill the scripture, Jesus said, "I am thirsty." ²⁹A jar full of sour wine was nearby, so the soldiers soaked a

ᵉPs 22:18

sponge in it, placed it on a hyssop branch, and held it up to his lips. ³⁰When he had received the sour wine, Jesus said, "It is completed." Bowing his head, he gave up his life.

Witness at the cross

³¹It was the Preparation Day and the Jewish leaders didn't want the bodies to remain on the cross on the Sabbath, especially since that Sabbath was an important day. So they asked Pilate to have the legs of those crucified broken and the bodies taken down. ³²Therefore, the soldiers came and broke the legs of the two men who were crucified with Jesus. ³³When they came to Jesus, they saw that he was already dead so they didn't break his legs. ³⁴However, one of the soldiers pierced his side with a spear, and immediately blood and water came out. ³⁵The one who saw this has testified, and his testimony is true. He knows that he speaks the truth, and he has testified so that you also can believe. ³⁶These things happened to fulfill the scripture, *They won't break any of his bones.*ᶠ ³⁷And another scripture says, *They will look at him whom they have pierced.*ᵍ

Jesus' body is buried

³⁸After this Joseph of Arimathea asked Pilate if he could take away the body of Jesus, but a secret one because he feared the Jewish authorities. Pilate gave him permission, so he came and took the body away. ³⁹Nicodemus, the one who at first had come to Jesus at night, was there too. He brought a mixture of myrrh and aloe, nearly seventy-five pounds in all.ʰ ⁴⁰Following Jewish burial customs, they took Jesus' body

and wrapped it, with the spices, in linen cloths. ⁴¹There was a garden in the place where Jesus was crucified, and in the garden was a new tomb in which no one had ever been laid. ⁴²Because it was the Jewish Preparation Day and the tomb was nearby, they laid Jesus in it.

Empty tomb

20 Early in the morning of the first day of the week, while it was still dark, Mary Magdalene came to the tomb and saw that the stone had been taken away from the tomb. ²She ran to Simon Peter and the other disciple, the one whom Jesus loved, and said, "They have taken the Lord from the tomb, and we don't know where they've put him." ³Peter and the other disciple left to go to the tomb. ⁴They were running together, but the other disciple ran faster than Peter and was the first to arrive at the tomb. ⁵Bending down to take a look, he saw the linen cloths lying there, but he didn't go in. ⁶Following him, Simon Peter entered the tomb and saw the linen cloths lying there. ⁷He also saw the face cloth that had been on Jesus' head. It wasn't with the other clothes but was folded up in its own place. ⁸Then the other disciple, the one who arrived at the tomb first, also went inside. He saw and believed. ⁹They didn't yet understand the scripture that Jesus must rise from the dead. ¹⁰Then the disciples returned to the place where they were staying.

Jesus appears to Mary

¹¹Mary stood outside near the tomb, crying. As she cried, she bent down to look into the tomb. ¹²She saw two angels dressed in white, seated where the body of Jesus had been, one at the head and one at the foot. ¹³The angels asked her, "Woman, why are you crying?"

She replied, "They have taken away my Lord, and I don't know where they've put him." ¹⁴As soon as she had said this, she turned around and saw Jesus standing there, but she didn't know it was Jesus.

¹⁵Jesus said to her, "Woman, why are you crying? Who are you looking for?"

SAILBOAT

FAMILY AND FRIENDS

Keeping a Promise Shows Love *John 19:27*
Promises are easy to make but difficult to keep. Jesus asked his disciple John to take care of his mother when he died. When John took Mary into his home, he showed his love for Jesus by keeping his promise. ◖

ᶠExod 12:46 ᵍZech 12:10 ʰOr *one hundred litra;* that is, one hundred Roman pounds

Thinking he was the gardener, she replied, "Sir, if you have carried him away, tell me where you have put him and I will get him."

¹⁶Jesus said to her, "Mary."

She turned and said to him in Aramaic, "Rabbouni" (which means *Teacher*).

¹⁷Jesus said to her, "Don't hold on to me, for I haven't yet gone up to my Father. Go to my brothers and sisters and tell them, 'I'm going up to my Father and your Father, to my God and your God.'"

¹⁸Mary Magdalene left and announced to the disciples, "I've seen the Lord." Then she told them what he said to her.

Jesus appears to the disciples

¹⁹It was still the first day of the week. That evening, while the disciples were behind closed doors because they were afraid of the Jewish authorities, Jesus came and stood among them. He said, "Peace be with you." ²⁰After he said this, he showed them his hands and his side. When the disciples saw the Lord, they were filled with joy. ²¹Jesus said to them again, "Peace be with you. As the Father sent me, so I am sending you." ²²Then he breathed on them and said, "Receive the Holy Spirit. ²³If you forgive anyone's sins, they are forgiven; if you don't forgive them, they aren't forgiven."

Jesus appears to Thomas and the disciples

²⁴Thomas, the one called Didymus,[i] one of the Twelve, wasn't with the disciples when Jesus came. ²⁵The other disciples told him, "We've seen the Lord!"

But he replied, "Unless I see the nail marks in his hands, put my finger in the wounds left by the nails, and put my hand into his side, I won't believe."

²⁶After eight days his disciples were again in a house and Thomas was with them. Even though the doors were locked, Jesus entered and stood among them. He said, "Peace be with you." ²⁷Then he said to Thomas, "Put your finger here. Look at my hands. Put your hand into my side. No more disbelief. Believe!"

²⁸Thomas responded to Jesus, "My Lord and my God!"

²⁹Jesus replied, "Do you believe because you see me? Happy are those who don't see and yet believe."

³⁰Then Jesus did many other miraculous signs in his disciples' presence, signs that aren't recorded in this scroll. ³¹But these things are written so that you will believe that Jesus is the Christ, God's Son, and that believing, you will have life in his name.

Jesus appears again to the disciples

21 Later, Jesus himself appeared again to his disciples at the Sea of Tiberias. This is how it happened: ²Simon Peter, Thomas (called Didymus[j]), Nathanael from Cana in Galilee, Zebedee's sons, and two other disciples were together. ³Simon Peter told them, "I'm going fishing."

They said, "We'll go with you." They set out in a boat, but throughout the night they caught nothing. ⁴Early in the morning, Jesus stood on the shore, but the disciples didn't realize it was Jesus.

⁵Jesus called to them, "Children, have you caught anything to eat?"

They answered him, "No."

⁶He said, "Cast your net on the right side of the boat and you will find some."

So they did, and there were so many fish that they couldn't haul in the net. ⁷Then the

UMBRELLA
DOUBTFUL

From Doubt to Belief   John 20:24-29

Thomas saw everything that happened to Jesus with his own eyes. He saw Jesus whipped and beaten. He knew Jesus was dead because he saw Jesus die. It's natural that Thomas doubted the claim that Jesus was alive. But he didn't ignore the possibility that Jesus was alive either. Thomas admitted that his faith was crushed. Jesus didn't leave Thomas out because he had doubt. Instead, Jesus met Thomas where he was and let Thomas see the scars on his hands and feet. Jesus' action breathed life into Thomas' fragile faith replacing Thomas' doubt with strong belief. ◆

---

[i]Or *the twin*   [j]Or *the twin*

disciple whom Jesus loved said to Peter, "It's the Lord!" When Simon Peter heard it was the Lord, he wrapped his coat around himself (for he was naked) and jumped into the water. [8]The other disciples followed in the boat, dragging the net full of fish, for they weren't far from shore, only about one hundred yards.

[9]When they landed, they saw a fire there, with fish on it, and some bread. [10]Jesus said to them, "Bring some of the fish that you've just caught." [11]Simon Peter got up and pulled the net to shore. It was full of large fish, one hundred fifty-three of them. Yet the net hadn't torn, even with so many fish. [12]Jesus said to them, "Come and have breakfast." None of the disciples could bring themselves to ask him, "Who are you?" They knew it was the Lord. [13]Jesus came, took the bread, and gave it to them. He did the same with the fish. [14]This was now the third time Jesus appeared to his disciples after he was raised from the dead.

Jesus and Peter

[15]When they finished eating, Jesus asked Simon Peter, "Simon son of John, do you love me more than these?"

Simon replied, "Yes, Lord, you know I love you."

Jesus said to him, "Feed my lambs." [16]Jesus asked a second time, "Simon son of John, do you love me?"

Simon replied, "Yes, Lord, you know I love you."

Jesus said to him, "Take care of my sheep." [17]He asked a third time, "Simon son of John, do you love me?"

Peter was sad that Jesus asked him a third time, "Do you love me?" He replied, "Lord, you know everything; you know I love you."

Jesus said to him, "Feed my sheep. [18]I assure you that when you were younger you tied your own belt and walked around wherever you wanted. When you grow old, you will

LIFE PRESERVER

Why did Jesus keep asking Peter the same question?
John 21:15-19

Peter must have wondered if Jesus believed him since Jesus asked him three times, "Do you love me?" When Jesus was on trial, Peter denied that he knew Jesus three times. Jesus wanted Peter to remember that an important way to show his love for Jesus was to love other people just as Jesus loved them. Jesus loves people like a good shepherd loves his sheep. He asked Peter to do the same thing. 🌢

stretch out your hands and another will tie your belt and lead you where you don't want to go." [19]He said this to show the kind of death by which Peter would glorify God. After saying this, Jesus said to Peter, "Follow me."

Jesus and the disciple whom he loved

[20]Peter turned around and saw the disciple whom Jesus loved following them. This was the one who had leaned against Jesus at the meal and asked him, "Lord, who is going to betray you?" [21]When Peter saw this disciple, he said to Jesus, "Lord, what about him?"

[22]Jesus replied, "If I want him to remain until I come, what difference does that make to you? You must follow me." [23]Therefore, the word spread among the brothers and sisters that this disciple wouldn't die. However, Jesus didn't say he wouldn't die, but only, "If I want him to remain until I come, what difference does that make to you?" [24]This is the disciple who testifies concerning these things and who wrote them down. We know that his testimony is true. [25]Jesus did many other things as well. If all of them were recorded, I imagine the world itself wouldn't have enough room for the scrolls that would be written.

Memorize
John 21:25

Acts

After Jesus rose from the dead, he told his closest followers to wait for the power of the Holy Spirit. Then they would tell the world about him, he said. They would start in their own city of Jerusalem and then travel to the whole world to share the good news (Acts 1:8).

Jesus' words soon came true. The Holy Spirit miraculously helped the disciples to speak in other languages that they hadn't learned. They boldly preached about Jesus. Thousands soon believed in Jesus, and many churches were born (Acts 2:1-42).

Acts tells the story of how these early Christians grew together in faith and spread the good news about Jesus. Leaders like Peter and John told about Jesus even when doing so landed them in prison (Acts 4:1-22). The apostles did miracles to prove God's power (Acts 5:12-16). Stephen was killed while telling the good news (Acts 6:8–8:2). A man named Saul hunted down Christians until he had a vision of Jesus. His name became Paul and he traveled to many places around the Mediterranean Sea telling people about Jesus (Acts 8:1–28:31). Acts shows us how to follow Jesus together! ◊

The risen Jesus with his disciples

1 Theophilus, the first scroll I wrote concerned everything Jesus did and taught from the beginning, [2]right up to the day when he was taken up into heaven. Before he was taken up, working in the power of the Holy Spirit, Jesus instructed the apostles he had chosen. [3]After his suffering, he showed them that he was alive with many convincing proofs. He appeared to them over a period of forty days, speaking to them about God's kingdom. [4]While they were eating together, he ordered them not to leave Jerusalem but to wait for what the Father had promised. He said, "This is what you heard from me: [5]John baptized with water, but in only a few days you will be baptized with the Holy Spirit."

[6]As a result, those who had gathered together asked Jesus, "Lord, are you going to restore the kingdom to Israel now?"

[7]Jesus replied, "It isn't for you to know the times or seasons that the Father has set by his own authority. [8]Rather, you will receive power when the Holy Spirit has come upon you, and you will be my witnesses in Jerusalem, in all Judea and Samaria, and to the end of the earth."

Memorize Acts 1:8

[9]After Jesus said these things, as they were watching, he was lifted up and a cloud took him out of their sight. [10]While he was going away and as they were staring toward heaven, suddenly two men in white robes stood next to them. [11]They said, "Galileans, why are you standing here, looking toward heaven? This Jesus, who was taken up from you into heaven, will come in the same way that you saw him go into heaven."

Jesus' followers in Jerusalem

[12]Then they returned to Jerusalem from the Mount of Olives, which is near Jerusalem—a sabbath day's journey away. [13]When they entered the city, they went to the upstairs room where they were staying. Peter, John, James, and Andrew; Philip and Thomas; Bartholomew and Matthew; James, Alphaeus' son; Simon the zealot; and Judas, James' son—[14]all were united in their devotion to prayer, along with some women, including Mary the mother of Jesus, and his brothers.

A replacement for Judas

[15]During this time, the family of believers was a company of about one hundred twenty persons. Peter stood among them and said, [16]"Brothers and sisters, the scripture that the Holy Spirit announced beforehand through David had to be fulfilled. This was the scripture concerning Judas, who became a guide for those who arrested Jesus. [17]This happened even though he was one of us and received a share of this ministry." ([18]In fact, he bought a field with the payment he received for his injustice. Falling headfirst, he burst open in the middle and all his intestines spilled out. [19]This became known to everyone living in Jerusalem, so they called that field in their own language Hakeldama, or "Field of Blood.")
[20]"It is written in the Psalms scroll,

Let his home become deserted
and let there be no one living in it;[a]
and

Give his position of leadership to another.[b]

[21]"Therefore, we must select one of those who have accompanied us during the whole time the Lord Jesus lived among us, [22]beginning from the baptism of John until the day when Jesus was taken from us. This person must become along with us a witness to his resurrection." [23]So they nominated two: Joseph called Barsabbas, who was also known as Justus, and Matthias.

[24]They prayed, "Lord, you know everyone's deepest thoughts and desires. Show us clearly which one you have chosen from among these two [25]to take the place of this ministry and apostleship, from which Judas turned

LIGHTHOUSE

PRAYER

Start with Prayer *Acts 1:13-14*
The remaining eleven disciples were without their leader. The last time this happened was when Jesus was crucified. When that happened the disciples scattered in different directions. This time they stayed together and prayed about what to do. When we don't know what to do, prayer is a good first step. ◆

[a]Ps 69:25 [b]Ps 109:8

away to go to his own place." [26]When they cast lots, the lot fell on Matthias. He was added to the eleven apostles.

Pentecost

2 When Pentecost Day arrived, they were all together in one place. [2]Suddenly a sound from heaven like the howling of a fierce wind filled the entire house where they were sitting. [3]They saw what seemed to be individual flames of fire alighting on each one of them. [4]They were all filled with the Holy Spirit and began to speak in other languages as the Spirit enabled them to speak.

[5]There were pious Jews from every nation under heaven living in Jerusalem. [6]When they heard this sound, a crowd gathered. They were mystified because everyone heard them speaking in their native languages. [7]They were surprised and amazed, saying, "Look, aren't all the people who are speaking Galileans, every one of them? [8]How then can each of us hear them speaking in our native language? [9]Parthians, Medes, and Elamites; as well as residents of Mesopotamia, Judea, and Cappadocia, Pontus and Asia, [10]Phrygia and Pamphylia, Egypt and the regions of Libya bordering Cyrene; and visitors from Rome (both Jews and converts to Judaism), [11]Cretans and Arabs—we hear them declaring the mighty works of God in our own languages!" [12]They were all surprised and bewildered. Some asked each other, "What does this mean?" [13]Others jeered at them, saying, "They're full of new wine!"

[14]Peter stood with the other eleven apostles. He raised his voice and declared, "Judeans and everyone living in Jerusalem! Know this! Listen carefully to my words! [15]These people aren't drunk, as you suspect; after all, it's only nine o'clock in the morning! [16]Rather, this is what was spoken through the prophet Joel:

[17] *In the last days, God says,*
   I will pour out my Spirit on all people.
   Your sons and daughters
     will prophesy.
   Your young will see visions.
   Your elders will dream dreams.

[18] *Even upon my servants,*
     men and women,
   I will pour out my Spirit in those days,
     and they will prophesy.
[19] *I will cause wonders to occur in the*
     heavens above
     and signs on the earth below,
     blood and fire and a cloud of smoke.
[20] *The sun will be changed into darkness,*
     and the moon will be changed into blood,
     before the great and spectacular day
     of the Lord comes.
[21] *And everyone who calls on the name*
     of the Lord will be saved.[c]

[22]"Fellow Israelites, listen to these words! Jesus the Nazarene was a man whose credentials God proved to you through miracles, wonders, and signs, which God performed through him among you. You yourselves know

The *Festival of Weeks* is a Jewish celebration that takes place fifty days after Passover. The Holy Spirit came to the first Christians during that festival, and it became known to them as *Pentecost Day*. *Pentecost* means "the fiftieth day." Christians today celebrate Pentecost seven weeks after Easter.

this. [23]In accordance with God's established plan and foreknowledge, he was betrayed. You, with the help of wicked men, had Jesus killed by nailing him to a cross. [24]God raised him up! God freed him from death's dreadful grip, since it was impossible for death to hang on to him. [25]David says about him,

   I foresaw that the Lord
     was always with me;
   because he is at my right hand
     I won't be shaken.
[26] *Therefore, my heart was glad*
     and my tongue rejoiced.
   Moreover, my body will live in hope,
[27] *because you won't abandon me*
     to the grave,
   nor permit your holy one
     to experience decay.
[28] *You have shown me the paths of life;*
   your presence will fill me
     with happiness.[d]

[c]Joel 2:28-32 [d]Ps 16:8-11

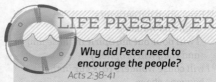

LIFE PRESERVER

Why did Peter need to encourage the people?
Acts 2:38-41

When Peter told the people to change their hearts and lives, he knew this was asking a lot. When a pastor preaches a sermon each week to all the people at church, the pastor is doing what Peter did. Peter reminded the people what Jesus did and what they must do in response. Baptism represents a change in life, and that change should be seen in a person's thoughts, words, and actions. This change may have sounded very difficult to people. Peter reminded them that they would receive the gift of the Holy Spirit when they asked God's forgiveness for their sins. ◊

²⁹"Brothers and sisters, I can speak confidently about the patriarch David. He died and was buried, and his tomb is with us to this very day. ³⁰Because he was a prophet, he knew that God promised him with a solemn pledge to seat one of his descendants on his throne. ³¹Having seen this beforehand, David spoke about the resurrection of Christ, that *he wasn't abandoned to the grave, nor did his body experience decay.*[e] ³²This Jesus God raised up. We are all witnesses to that fact. ³³He was exalted to God's right side and received from the Father the promised Holy Spirit. He poured out this Spirit, and you are seeing and hearing the results of his having done so. ³⁴David didn't ascend into heaven. Yet he says,

The Lord said to my Lord,
  'Sit at my right side,
³⁵ *until I make your enemies*
  a footstool for your feet.'[f]

³⁶"Therefore, let all Israel know beyond question that God has made this Jesus, whom you crucified, both Lord and Christ."

³⁷When the crowd heard this, they were deeply troubled. They said to Peter and the other apostles, "Brothers, what should we do?"

³⁸Peter replied, "Change your hearts and lives. Each of you must be baptized in the name of Jesus Christ for the forgiveness of your sins. Then you will receive the gift of

the Holy Spirit. ³⁹This promise is for you, your children, and for all who are far away—as many as the Lord our God invites." ⁴⁰With many other words he testified to them and encouraged them, saying, "Be saved from this perverse generation." ⁴¹Those who accepted Peter's message were baptized. God brought about three thousand people into the community on that day.

Community of believers

⁴²The believers devoted themselves to the apostles' teaching, to the community, to their shared meals, and to their prayers. ⁴³A sense of awe came over everyone. God performed many wonders and signs through the apostles. ⁴⁴All the believers were united and shared everything. ⁴⁵They would sell pieces of property and possessions and distribute the proceeds to everyone who needed them. ⁴⁶Every day, they met together in the temple and ate in their homes. They shared food with gladness and simplicity. ⁴⁷They praised God and demonstrated God's goodness to everyone. The Lord added daily to the community those who were being saved.

LIGHTHOUSE

CHANGED HEART

Time Together *Acts 2:46*
The first group of Christians set a great example for people who follow Jesus today. They met together in the temple (every day!) and went to each other's houses to eat meals. They spent time together and shared what they had with each other. Strong churches are built by people who love God and love each other. ◊

Healing of a crippled man

3 Peter and John were going up to the temple at three o'clock in the afternoon, the established prayer time. ²Meanwhile, a man crippled since birth was being carried in. Every day, people would place him at the temple gate known as the Beautiful Gate so he could ask for money from those entering

[e]Ps 16:10 [f]Ps 110:1

the temple. ³When he saw Peter and John about to enter, he began to ask them for a gift. ⁴Peter and John stared at him. Peter said, "Look at us!" ⁵So the man gazed at them, expecting to receive something from them. ⁶Peter said, "I don't have any money, but I will give you what I do have. In the name of Jesus Christ the Nazarene, rise up and walk!" ⁷Then he grasped the man's right hand and raised him up. At once his feet and ankles became strong. ⁸Jumping up, he began to walk around. He entered the temple with them, walking, leaping, and praising God. ⁹All the people saw him walking and praising God. ¹⁰They recognized him as the same one who used to sit at the temple's Beautiful Gate asking for money. They were filled with amazement and surprise at what had happened to him.

¹¹While the healed man clung to Peter and John, all the people rushed toward them at Solomon's Porch, completely amazed. ¹²Seeing this, Peter addressed the people: "You Israelites, why are you amazed at this? Why are you staring at us as if we made him walk by our own power or piety? ¹³The God of Abraham, Isaac, and Jacob—the God of our ancestors—has glorified his servant Jesus. This is the one you handed over and denied in Pilate's presence, even though he had already decided to release him. ¹⁴You rejected the holy and righteous one, and asked that a murderer be released to you instead. ¹⁵You killed the author of life, the very one whom God raised from the dead. We are witnesses of this. ¹⁶His name itself has made this man strong. That is, because of faith in Jesus' name, God has strengthened this man whom you see and know. The faith that comes through Jesus gave him complete health right before your eyes.

¹⁷"Brothers and sisters, I know you acted in ignorance. So did your rulers. ¹⁸But this is how God fulfilled what he foretold through all the prophets: that his Christ would suffer. ¹⁹Change your hearts and lives! Turn back to God so that your sins may be wiped away. ²⁰Then the Lord will provide a season of relief from the distress of this age and he will send Jesus, whom he handpicked to be your

did you know? Poor people who were unable to care for themselves would sit by the gate near the temple and ask for gifts from the people who passed by. In addition to money, people sometimes gave them food or clothes.

Christ. ²¹Jesus must remain in heaven until the restoration of all things, about which God spoke long ago through his holy prophets. ²²Moses said, *The Lord your God will raise up from your own people a prophet like me. Listen to whatever he tells you.* ²³*Whoever doesn't listen to that prophet will be totally cut off from the people.*⁸ ²⁴All the prophets who spoke—from Samuel forward—announced these days. ²⁵You are the heirs of the prophets and the covenant that God made with your ancestors when he told Abraham, *Through your descendants, all the families on earth will be blessed.*ʰ ²⁶After God raised his servant, he sent him to you first—to bless you by enabling each of you to turn from your evil ways."

Peter and John questioned

4 While Peter and John were speaking to the people, the priests, the captain of the temple guard, and the Sadducees confronted them. ²They were incensed that the apostles were teaching the people and announcing that the resurrection of the dead was happening because of Jesus. ³They seized Peter and John and put them in prison until the next day. (It was already evening.) ⁴Many who heard the word became believers, and their number grew to about five thousand.

⁵The next day the leaders, elders, and legal experts gathered in Jerusalem, ⁶along with Annas the high priest, Caiaphas, John, Alexander, and others from the high priest's family. ⁷They had Peter and John brought before them and asked, "By what power or in what name did you do this?"

⁸Then Peter, inspired by the Holy Spirit, answered, "Leaders of the people and elders, ⁹are we being examined today because something good was done for a sick person, a good deed that healed him? ¹⁰If so, then you and all

the people of Israel need to know that this man stands healthy before you because of the name of Jesus Christ the Nazarene—whom you crucified but whom God raised from the dead. [11]This Jesus is the stone you builders rejected; he has become the cornerstone! [12]Salvation can be found in no one else. Throughout the whole world, no other name has been given among humans through which we must be saved."

[13]The council was caught by surprise by the confidence with which Peter and John spoke. After all, they understood that these apostles were uneducated and inexperienced. They also recognized that they had been followers of Jesus. [14]However, since the healed man was standing with Peter and John before their own eyes, they had no rebuttal. [15]After ordering them to wait outside, the council members began to confer with each other. [16]"What should we do with these men? Everyone living in Jerusalem is aware of the sign performed through them. It's obvious to everyone and we can't deny it. [17]To keep it from spreading further among the people, we need to warn them not to speak to anyone in this name." [18]When they called Peter and John back, they demanded that they stop all speaking and teaching in the name of Jesus.

[19]Peter and John responded, "It's up to you to determine whether it's right before God to obey you rather than God. [20]As for us, we can't stop speaking about what we have seen and heard." [21]They threatened them further, then released them. Because of public support for Peter and John, they couldn't find a way to punish

SAILBOAT

COURAGE

Obey God, Not People Acts 4:1-22
Peter and John were in a tough position. The council ordered them to stop giving credit to Jesus for the miracles that were taking place when they prayed. The two didn't argue with the council, but they stood firm. They faced the challenge either to obey God or to obey people. John and Peter made the courageous choice to obey God. ◆

them. Everyone was praising God for what had happened, [22]because the man who had experienced this sign of healing was over 40 years old.

The believers pray

[23]After their release, Peter and John returned to the brothers and sisters and reported everything the chief priests and elders had said. [24]They listened, then lifted their voices in unison to God, "Master, you are the one who created the heaven, the earth, the sea, and everything in them. [25]You are the one who spoke by the Holy Spirit through our ancestor David, your servant:

Why did the Gentiles rage,
    and the peoples plot in vain?
[26] The kings of the earth took their stand
    and the rulers gathered together as one
        against the Lord and against his Christ.[i]

[27]Indeed, both Herod and Pontius Pilate, with Gentiles and Israelites, did gather in this city against your holy servant Jesus, whom you anointed. [28]They did what your power and plan had already determined would happen. [29]Now, Lord, take note of their threats and enable your servants to speak your word with complete confidence. [30]Stretch out your hand to bring healing and enable signs and wonders to be performed through the name of Jesus, your holy servant." [31]After they prayed, the place where they were gathered was shaken. They were all filled with the Holy Spirit and began speaking God's word with confidence.

Sharing among the believers

[32]The community of believers was one in heart and mind. None of them would say, "This is mine!" about any of their possessions, but held everything in common. [33]The apostles continued to bear powerful witness to the resurrection of the Lord Jesus, and an abundance of grace was at work among them all. [34]There were no needy persons among them. Those who owned properties or houses would sell them, bring the proceeds from the sales, [35]and place them in the care and under the authority of the apostles. Then it was distributed to anyone who was in need.

[i]Or anointed one; Ps 2:1-2

[36] Joseph, whom the apostles nicknamed Barnabas (that is, "one who encourages"), was a Levite from Cyprus. [37] He owned a field, sold it, brought the money, and placed it in the care and under the authority of the apostles.

Pretenders of sharing

However, a man named Ananias, along with his wife Sapphira, sold a piece of property. [2] With his wife's knowledge, he withheld some of the proceeds from the sale. He brought the rest and placed it in the care and under the authority of the apostles. [3] Peter asked, "Ananias, how is it that Satan has influenced you to lie to the Holy Spirit by withholding some of the proceeds from the sale of your land? [4] Wasn't that property yours to keep? After you sold it, wasn't the money yours to do with whatever you wanted? What made you think of such a thing? You haven't lied to other people but to God!" [5] When Ananias heard these words, he dropped dead. Everyone who heard this conversation was terrified. [6] Some young men stood up, wrapped up his body, carried him out, and buried him.

[7] About three hours later, his wife entered, but she didn't know what had happened to her husband. [8] Peter asked her, "Tell me, did you and your husband receive this price for the field?"

She responded, "Yes, that's the amount."

[9] He replied, "How could you scheme with each other to challenge the Lord's Spirit? Look! The feet of those who buried your husband are at the door. They will carry you out too." [10] At that very moment, she dropped

did you **know?** The name *Barnabas* means "one who encourages." Barnabas saw the good in people. Because of his encouraging spirit, many people came to believe in Jesus.

dead at his feet. When the young men entered and found her dead, they carried her out and buried her with her husband. [11] Trepidation and dread seized the whole church and all who heard what had happened.

Responses to the church

[12] The apostles performed many signs and wonders among the people. They would come together regularly at Solomon's Porch. [13] No one from outside the church dared to join them, even though the people spoke highly of them. [14] Indeed, more and more believers in the Lord, large numbers of both men and women, were added to the church. [15] As a result, they would even bring the sick out into the main streets and lay them on cots and mats so that at least Peter's shadow could fall on some of them as he passed by. [16] Even large numbers of persons from towns around Jerusalem would gather, bringing the sick and those harassed by unclean spirits. Everyone was healed.

The Jerusalem Council harasses the apostles

[17] The high priest, together with his allies, the Sadducees, was overcome with jealousy. [18] They seized the apostles and made a public show of putting them in prison. [19] An angel from the Lord opened the prison doors during the night and led them out. The angel told them, [20] "Go, take your place in the temple, and tell the people everything about this new life." [21] Early in the morning, they went into the temple as they had been told and began to teach.

When the high priest and his colleagues gathered, they convened the Jerusalem Council, that is, the full assembly of Israel's elders. They sent word to the prison to have the apostles brought before them. [22] However, the guards didn't find them in the prison. They returned and reported, [23] "We found the prison locked and well-secured, with guards

UMBRELLA
LYING

Tell the Truth, Not Lies *Acts 5:1-11*

We don't know how much money Ananias got when he sold his land. But we know the amount he gave to the apostles wasn't the whole amount. Ananias may have thought it was no big deal to stretch the truth. Peter made clear that Ananias' lie was actually a lie to the Holy Spirit. God wants people to tell the truth. ◆

standing at the doors, but when we opened the doors we found no one inside!" ²⁴When they received this news, the captain of the temple guard and the chief priests were baffled and wondered what might be happening. ²⁵Just then, someone arrived and announced, "Look! The people you put in prison are standing in the temple and teaching the people!" ²⁶Then the captain left with his guards and brought the apostles back. They didn't use force because they were afraid the people would stone them.

²⁷The apostles were brought before the council where the high priest confronted them: ²⁸"In no uncertain terms, we demanded that you not teach in this name. And look at you! You have filled Jerusalem with your teaching. And you are determined to hold us responsible for this man's death."

²⁹Peter and the apostles replied, "We must obey God rather than humans! ³⁰The God of our ancestors raised Jesus from the dead—whom you killed by hanging him on a tree. ³¹God has exalted Jesus to his right side as leader and savior so that he could enable Israel to change its heart and life and to find forgiveness for sins. ³²We are witnesses of such things, as is the Holy Spirit, whom God has given to those who obey him."

³³When the council members heard this, they became furious and wanted to kill the apostles. ³⁴One council member, a Pharisee and teacher of the Law named Gamaliel, well-respected by all the people, stood up and ordered that the men be taken outside for a few moments. ³⁵He said, "Fellow Israelites, consider carefully what you intend to do to these people. ³⁶Some time ago, Theudas appeared, claiming to be somebody, and some four hundred men joined him. After he was killed, all of his followers scattered, and nothing came of that. ³⁷Afterward, at the time of the census, Judas the Galilean appeared and got some people to follow him in a revolt. He was killed too, and all his followers scattered far and wide. ³⁸Here's my recommendation in this case: Distance yourselves from these men. Let them go! If their plan or activity is of human origin, it will end in ruin. ³⁹If it originates with God, you won't be able to stop them. Instead, you would actually find yourselves fighting God!" The council was convinced by

his reasoning. ⁴⁰After calling the apostles back, they had them beaten. They ordered them not to speak in the name of Jesus, then let them go. ⁴¹The apostles left the council rejoicing because they had been regarded as worthy to suffer disgrace for the sake of the name. ⁴²Every day they continued to teach and proclaim the good news that Jesus is the Christ, both in the temple and in houses.

Selection of seven to serve

6 About that time, while the number of disciples continued to increase, a complaint arose. Greek-speaking disciples accused the Aramaic-speaking disciples because their widows were being overlooked in the daily food service. ²The Twelve called a meeting of all the disciples and said, "It isn't right for us to set aside proclamation of God's word in order to serve tables. ³Brothers and sisters, carefully choose seven well-respected men from among you. They must be well-respected and endowed by the Spirit with exceptional wisdom. We will put them in charge of this concern. ⁴As for us, we will devote ourselves to prayer and the service of proclaiming the word." ⁵This proposal pleased the entire community. They selected Stephen, a man endowed by the Holy Spirit with exceptional faith, Philip, Prochorus, Nicanor, Timon, Parmenas, and Nicolaus from Antioch, a convert to Judaism. ⁶The community presented these seven to the apostles, who prayed and laid their hands on them. ⁷God's word continued to grow. The number of disciples in Jerusalem increased significantly. Even a large group of priests embraced the faith.

Arrest and murder of Stephen

⁸Stephen, who stood out among the believers for the way God's grace was at work in his life and for his exceptional endowment with divine power, was doing great wonders and signs among the people. ⁹Opposition arose from some who belonged to the so-called Synagogue of Former Slaves. Members from Cyrene, Alexandria, Cilicia, and Asia entered into debate with Stephen. ¹⁰However, they couldn't resist the wisdom the Spirit gave him as he spoke. ¹¹Then they secretly enticed some people to claim, "We heard him insult Moses and God." ¹²They stirred up the people,

the elders, and the legal experts. They caught Stephen, dragged him away, and brought him before the Jerusalem Council. ¹³Before the council, they presented false witnesses who testified, "This man never stops speaking against this holy place and the Law. ¹⁴In fact, we heard him say that this man Jesus of Nazareth will destroy this place and alter the customary practices Moses gave us." ¹⁵Everyone seated in the council stared at Stephen, and they saw that his face was radiant, just like an angel's.

7 The high priest asked, "Are these accusations true?"

²Stephen responded, "Brothers and fathers, listen to me. Our glorious God appeared to our ancestor Abraham while he was still in Mesopotamia, before he settled in Haran. ³God told him, 'Leave your homeland and kin, and go to the land that I will show you.'ʲ ⁴So Abraham left the land of the Chaldeans and settled in Haran. After Abraham's father died, God had him resettle in this land where you now live. ⁵God didn't give him an inheritance here, not even a square foot of land. However, God did promise to give the land as his possession to him and to his descendants, even though Abraham had no child. ⁶God put it this way: *His descendants will be strangers in a land that belongs to others, who will enslave them and abuse them for four hundred years.*ᵏ ⁷*And I will condemn the nation they serve as slaves,* God said, *and afterward they will leave*ˡ that land and serve me in this place. ⁸God gave him the covenant confirmed through circumcision. Accordingly, eight days after Isaac's birth, Abraham circumcised him. Isaac did the same with Jacob, and Jacob with the twelve patriarchs.

⁹"Because the patriarchs were jealous of Joseph, they sold him into slavery in Egypt. God was with him, however, ¹⁰and rescued him from all his troubles. The grace and wisdom he gave Joseph were recognized by Pharaoh, king of Egypt, who appointed him ruler over Egypt and over his whole palace. ¹¹A famine came upon all Egypt and Canaan, and great hardship came with it. Our ancestors had nothing to eat. ¹²When Jacob heard there was grain in Egypt, he sent our ancestors

there for the first time. ¹³During their second visit, Joseph told his brothers who he was, and Pharaoh learned about Joseph's family. ¹⁴Joseph sent for his father Jacob and all his relatives—seventy-five in all—and invited them to live with him. ¹⁵So Jacob went down to Egypt, where he and our ancestors died. ¹⁶Their bodies were brought back to Shechem and placed in the tomb that Abraham had purchased for a certain sum of money from Hamor's children, who lived in Shechem.

¹⁷"When it was time for God to keep the promise he made to Abraham, the number of our people in Egypt had greatly expanded. ¹⁸But then *another king rose to power over Egypt who didn't know anything about Joseph.*ᵐ ¹⁹He exploited our people and abused our ancestors. He even forced them to abandon their newly born babies so they would die. ²⁰That's when Moses was born. He was highly favored by God, and for three months his parents cared for him in their home. ²¹After he was abandoned, Pharaoh's daughter adopted and cared for him as though he were her own son. ²²Moses learned everything Egyptian wisdom had to offer, and he was a man of powerful words and deeds.

²³"When Moses was 40 years old, he decided to visit his family, the Israelites. ²⁴He saw one of them being wronged so he came to his rescue and evened the score by killing the Egyptian. ²⁵He expected his own kin to understand that God was using him to rescue them, but they didn't. ²⁶The next day he came upon some Israelites who were caught up in an argument. He tried to make peace between them by saying, 'You are brothers! Why are you harming each other?' ²⁷The one who started the fight against his neighbor pushed Moses aside and said, '*Who appointed you as our leader and judge?* ²⁸*Are you planning to kill me like you killed that Egyptian yesterday?*'ⁿ ²⁹When Moses heard this, he fled to Midian, where he lived as an immigrant and had two sons.

³⁰"Forty years later, an angel appeared to Moses in the flame of a burning bush in the wilderness near Mount Sinai. ³¹Enthralled by the sight, Moses approached to get a closer look and he heard the Lord's voice: ³²*I am*

ʲGen 12:1 ᵏGen 15:13 ˡGen 15:14 ᵐExod 1:8 ⁿExod 2:14

the God of your ancestors, the God of Abraham, Isaac, and Jacob.'° Trembling with fear, Moses didn't dare to investigate any further. 33The Lord continued, 'Remove the sandals from your feet, for the place where you are standing is holy ground. 34I have clearly seen the oppression my people have experienced in Egypt, and I have heard their groaning. I have come down to rescue them. Come! I am sending you to Egypt.'P

35"This is the same Moses whom they rejected when they asked, 'Who appointed you as our leader and judge?' This is the Moses whom God sent as leader and deliverer. God did this with the help of the angel who appeared before him in the bush. 36This man led them out after he performed wonders and signs in Egypt at the Red Sea and for forty years in the wilderness. 37This is the Moses who told the Israelites, 'God will raise up for you a prophet like me from your own people.'q 38This is the one who was in the assembly in the wilderness with our ancestors and with the angel who spoke to him on Mount Sinai. He is the one who received life-giving words to give to us. 39He's also the one whom our ancestors refused to obey. Instead, they pushed him aside and, in their thoughts and desires, returned to Egypt. 40They told Aaron, 'Make us gods that will lead us. As for this Moses who led us out of Egypt, we don't know what's happened to him!'r 41That's when they made an idol in the shape of a calf, offered a sacrifice to it, and began to celebrate what they had made with their own hands. 42So God turned away from them and handed them over to worship the stars in the sky, just as it is written in the scroll of the Prophets:

Did you bring sacrifices
    and offerings to me
    for forty years in the wilderness,
    house of Israel?
43 No! Instead, you took
    the tent of Moloch with you,
    and the star of your god Rephan,
    the images that you made
    in order to worship them.
    Therefore, I will send you far away,
    farther than Babylon.s

44"The tent of testimony was with our ancestors in the wilderness. Moses built it just as he had been instructed by the one who spoke to him and according to the pattern he had seen. 45In time, when they had received the tent, our ancestors carried it with them when, under Joshua's leadership, they took possession of the land from the nations whom God expelled. This tent remained in the land until the time of David. 46God approved of David, who asked that he might provide a dwelling place for the God of Jacob.t 47But it was Solomon who actually built a house for God. 48However, the Most High doesn't live in houses built by human hands. As the prophet says,

49 Heaven is my throne,
    and the earth is my footstool.
    'What kind of house will you build for me,'
    says the Lord,
    'or where is my resting place?
50 Didn't I make all these things
    with my own hand?'u

51"You stubborn people! In your thoughts and hearing, you are like those who have had no part in God's covenant! You continuously set yourself against the Holy Spirit, just like your ancestors did. 52Was there a single prophet your ancestors didn't harass? They even killed those who predicted the coming of the righteous one, and you've betrayed and murdered him! 53You received the Law given by angels, but you haven't kept it."

54Once the council members heard these words, they were enraged and began to grind their teeth at Stephen. 55But Stephen, enabled by the Holy Spirit, stared into heaven and saw God's majesty and Jesus standing at God's right side. 56He exclaimed, "Look! I can see heaven on display and the Human Onev standing at God's right side!" 57At this, they shrieked and covered their ears. Together, they charged at him, 58threw him out of the city, and began to stone him. The witnesses placed their coats in the care of a young man named Saul. 59As they battered him with stones, Stephen prayed, "Lord Jesus, accept my life!" 60Falling to his knees, he shouted, "Lord, don't hold this sin against them!" Then

---

°Exod 3:6 PExod 3:5, 7 qDeut 18:15 rExod 32:1 sAmos 5:25-27 tCritical editions of the Gk New Testament read *house of Jacob*. uIsa 66:1-2 vOr *Son of Man*

8 he died. [1]Saul was in full agreement with Stephen's murder.

The church scatters

At that time, the church in Jerusalem began to be subjected to vicious harassment. Everyone except the apostles was scattered throughout the regions of Judea and Samaria. [2]Some pious men buried Stephen and deeply grieved over him. [3]Saul began to wreak havoc against the church. Entering one house after another, he would drag off both men and women and throw them into prison.

Philip in Samaria

[4]Those who had been scattered moved on, preaching the good news along the way. [5]Philip went down to a city in Samaria[w] and began to preach Christ to them. [6]The crowds were united by what they heard Philip say and the signs they saw him perform, and they gave him their undivided attention. [7]With loud shrieks, unclean spirits came out of many people, and many who were paralyzed or crippled were healed. [8]There was great rejoicing in that city.

[9]Before Philip's arrival, a certain man named Simon had practiced sorcery in that city and baffled the people of Samaria. He claimed to be a great person. [10]Everyone, from the least to the greatest, gave him their undivided attention and referred to him as "the power of God called Great." [11]He had their attention because he had baffled them with sorcery for a long time. [12]After they came to believe Philip, who preached the good news about God's kingdom and the name of Jesus Christ, both men and women were baptized. [13]Even Simon himself came to believe and was baptized. Afterward, he became one of Philip's supporters. As he saw firsthand the signs and great miracles that were happening, he was astonished.

[14]When word reached the apostles in Jerusalem that Samaria had accepted God's word, they commissioned Peter and John to go to Samaria. [15]Peter and John went down to Samaria where they prayed that the new believers would receive the Holy Spirit. ([16]This was because the Holy Spirit had not yet fallen on any of them; they had only been baptized in the name of the Lord Jesus.) [17]So Peter and John laid their hands on them, and they received the Holy Spirit.

[18]When Simon perceived that the Spirit was given through the laying on of the apostles' hands, he offered them money. [19]He said, "Give me this authority too so that anyone on whom I lay my hands will receive the Holy Spirit."

[20]Peter responded, "May your money be condemned to hell along with you because you believed you could buy God's gift with money! [21]You can have no part or share in God's word because your heart isn't right with God. [22]Therefore, change your heart and life! Turn from your wickedness! Plead with the Lord in the hope that your wicked intent can be forgiven, [23]for I see that your bitterness has poisoned you and evil has you in chains."

[24]Simon replied, "All of you, please, plead to the Lord for me so that nothing of what you have said will happen to me!" [25]After the apostles had testified and proclaimed the Lord's word, they returned to Jerusalem, preaching the good news to many Samaritan villages along the way.

Philip and the Ethiopian eunuch

[26]An angel from the Lord spoke to Philip, "At noon, take[x] the road that leads from Jerusalem to Gaza." (This is a desert road.) [27]So he did. Meanwhile, an Ethiopian man was on his way home from Jerusalem, where he had come to worship. He was a eunuch and an official responsible for the entire treasury of Candace. (Candace is the title given to the Ethiopian queen.) [28]He was reading the prophet Isaiah while sitting in his carriage. [29]The Spirit told Philip, "Approach this carriage and stay with it."

[30]Running up to the carriage, Philip heard the man reading the prophet Isaiah. He asked, "Do you really understand what you are reading?"

[31]The man replied, "Without someone to guide me, how could I?" Then he invited Philip to climb up and sit with him. [32]This was the passage of scripture he was reading:

*Like a sheep he was led to the slaughter
  and like a lamb before its shearer is silent
  so he didn't open his mouth.*
³³ *In his humiliation
  justice was taken away from him.
  Who can tell the story of his descendants
  because his life was taken
  from the earth?*[y]

³⁴The eunuch asked Philip, "Tell me, about whom does the prophet say this? Is he talking about himself or someone else?" ³⁵Starting with that passage, Philip proclaimed the good news about Jesus to him. ³⁶As they went down the road, they came to some water.

The eunuch said, "Look! Water! What would keep me from being baptized?"[z] ³⁸He ordered that the carriage halt. Both Philip and the eunuch went down to the water, where Philip baptized him. ³⁹When they came up out of the water, the Lord's Spirit suddenly took Philip away. The eunuch never saw him again but went on his way rejoicing. ⁴⁰Philip found himself in Azotus. He traveled through that area, preaching the good news in all the cities until he reached Caesarea.

Saul encounters the risen Jesus

9Meanwhile, Saul was still spewing out murderous threats against the Lord's disciples. He went to the high priest, ²seeking letters to the synagogues in Damascus. If he found persons who belonged to the Way, whether men or women, these letters would authorize him to take them as prisoners to Jerusalem. ³During the journey, as he approached Damascus, suddenly a light from heaven encircled him. ⁴He fell to the ground and heard a voice asking him, "Saul, Saul, why are you harassing me?"

⁵Saul asked, "Who are you, Lord?"

"I am Jesus, whom you are harassing," came the reply. ⁶"Now get up and enter the city. You will be told what you must do."

⁷Those traveling with him stood there speechless; they heard the voice but saw no one. ⁸After they picked Saul up from the

ground, he opened his eyes but he couldn't see. So they led him by the hand into Damascus. ⁹For three days he was blind and neither ate nor drank anything.

¹⁰In Damascus there was a certain disciple named Ananias. The Lord spoke to him in a vision, "Ananias!"

He answered, "Yes, Lord."

¹¹The Lord instructed him, "Go to Judas' house on Straight Street and ask for a man from Tarsus named Saul. He is praying. ¹²In a vision he has seen a man named Ananias enter and put his hands on him to restore his sight."

¹³Ananias countered, "Lord, I have heard many reports about this man. People say he has done horrible things to your holy people in Jerusalem. ¹⁴He's here with authority from the chief priests to arrest everyone who calls on your name."

¹⁵The Lord replied, "Go! This man is the agent I have chosen to carry my name before Gentiles, kings, and Israelites. ¹⁶I will show him how much he must suffer for the sake of my name."

¹⁷Ananias went to the house. He placed his hands on Saul and said, "Brother Saul, the Lord sent me—Jesus, who appeared to

did you know? The Way referred to following the teachings of Jesus. Luke used this phrase often in the books of Luke and Acts. When John the Baptist preached, he quoted from Isaiah 40 and said a voice in the wilderness would cry out, "Prepare the way for the Lord" (Luke 3:4). Jesus was considered to be the way to God, the way of love and justice, the one who showed his people how to live. People who follow Jesus today are called Christians.

you on the way as you were coming here. He sent me so that you could see again and be filled with the Holy Spirit." ¹⁸Instantly, flakes fell from Saul's eyes and he could see again. He got up and was baptized. ¹⁹After eating, he regained his strength.

He stayed with the disciples in Damascus for several days. ²⁰Right away, he began to preach about Jesus in the synagogues. "He is God's Son," he declared.

---

[y] Isa 53:7-8   [z] Critical editions of the Gk New Testament do not include 8:37 *Philip said to him, "If you believe with all your heart, you can be." The eunuch answered, "I believe that Jesus Christ is God's Son."*

²¹Everyone who heard him was baffled. They questioned each other, "Isn't he the one who was wreaking havoc among those in Jerusalem who called on this name? Hadn't he come here to take those same people as prisoners to the chief priests?" ²²But Saul grew stronger and stronger. He confused the Jews who lived in Damascus by proving that Jesus is the Christ.

²³After this had gone on for some time, the Jews hatched a plot to kill Saul. ²⁴However, he found out about their scheme. They were keeping watch at the city gates around the clock so they could assassinate him. ²⁵But his disciples took him by night and lowered him in a basket through an opening in the city wall.

²⁶When Saul arrived in Jerusalem, he tried to join the disciples, but they were all afraid of him. They didn't believe he was really a disciple. ²⁷Then Barnabas brought Saul to the apostles and told them the story about how Saul saw the Lord on the way and that the Lord had spoken to Saul. He also told them about the confidence with which Saul had preached in the name of Jesus in Damascus. ²⁸After this, Saul moved freely among the disciples in Jerusalem and was speaking with confidence in the name of the Lord. ²⁹He got into debates with the Greek-speaking Jews as well, but they tried to kill him. ³⁰When the family of believers learned about this, they escorted him down to Caesarea and sent him off to Tarsus.

³¹Then the church throughout Judea, Galilee, and Samaria enjoyed a time of peace. God strengthened the church, and its life was marked by reverence for the Lord. Encouraged by the Holy Spirit, the church continued to grow in numbers.

Peter heals and raises the dead

³²As Peter toured the whole region, he went to visit God's holy people in Lydda. ³³There he found a man named Aeneas who was paralyzed and had been confined to his bed for eight years. ³⁴Peter said to him, "Aeneas, Jesus Christ heals you! Get up and make your bed." At once he got up. ³⁵Everyone who lived in Lydda and Sharon saw him and turned to the Lord.

³⁶In Joppa there was a disciple named Tabitha (in Greek her name is Dorcas). Her life overflowed with good works and compassionate acts on behalf of those in need. ³⁷About that time, though, she became so ill that she died. After they washed her body, they laid her in an upstairs room. ³⁸Since Lydda was near Joppa, when the disciples heard that Peter was there, they sent two people to Peter. They urged, "Please come right away!" ³⁹Peter went with them. Upon his arrival, he was taken to the upstairs room. All the widows stood beside him, crying as they showed the tunics and other clothing Dorcas made when she was alive.

⁴⁰Peter sent everyone out of the room, then knelt and prayed. He turned to the body and said, "Tabitha, get up!" She opened her eyes, saw Peter, and sat up. ⁴¹He gave her his hand and raised her up. Then he called God's holy people, including the widows, and presented her alive to them. ⁴²The news spread throughout Joppa, and many put their faith in the Lord. ⁴³Peter stayed for some time in Joppa with a certain tanner named Simon.

Peter, Cornelius, and the Gentiles

10 There was a man in Caesarea named Cornelius, a centurion in the Italian Company.ᵃ ²He and his whole household were pious, Gentile God-worshippers. He gave generously to those in need among the Jewish people and prayed to God constantly. ³One day at nearly three o'clock in the afternoon, he clearly saw an angel from God in a vision. The angel came to him and said, "Cornelius!"

⁴Startled, he stared at the angel and replied, "What is it, Lord?"

The angel said, "Your prayers and your compassionate acts are like a memorial offering to God. ⁵Send messengers to Joppa at once and summon a certain Simon, the one known as Peter. ⁶He is a guest of Simon the tanner, whose house is near the seacoast." ⁷When the angel who was speaking to him had gone, Cornelius summoned two of his household servants along with a pious soldier from his personal staff. ⁸He explained everything to them, then sent them to Joppa.

⁹At noon on the following day, as their

ᵃOr cohort (approximately six hundred soldiers)

journey brought them close to the city, Peter went up on the roof to pray. ¹⁰He became hungry and wanted to eat. While others were preparing the meal, he had a visionary experience. ¹¹He saw heaven opened up and something like a large linen sheet being lowered to the earth by its four corners. ¹²Inside the sheet were all kinds of four-legged animals, reptiles, and wild birds.ᵇ ¹³A voice told him, "Get up, Peter! Kill and eat!"

¹⁴Peter exclaimed, "Absolutely not, Lord! I have never eaten anything impure or unclean."

¹⁵The voice spoke a second time, "Never consider unclean what God has made pure." ¹⁶This happened three times, then the object was suddenly pulled back into heaven.

¹⁷Peter was bewildered about the meaning of the vision. Just then, the messengers sent by Cornelius discovered the whereabouts of Simon's house and arrived at the gate. ¹⁸Calling out, they inquired whether the Simon known as Peter was a guest there.

¹⁹While Peter was brooding over the vision, the Spirit interrupted him, "Look! Three people are looking for you. ²⁰Go downstairs. Don't ask questions; just go with them because I have sent them."

²¹So Peter went downstairs and told them, "I'm the one you are looking for. Why have you come?"

²²They replied, "We've come on behalf of Cornelius, a centurion and righteous man, a God-worshipper who is well-respected by all Jewish people. A holy angel directed him to summon you to his house and to hear what you have to say." ²³Peter invited them into the house as his guests.

The next day he got up and went with them, together with some of the believers from Joppa. ²⁴They arrived in Caesarea the following day. Anticipating their arrival, Cornelius had gathered his relatives and close friends. ²⁵As Peter entered the house, Cornelius met him and fell at his feet in order to honor him. ²⁶But Peter lifted him up, saying, "Get up! Like you, I'm just a human." ²⁷As they continued to talk, Peter went inside and found a large gathering of people. ²⁸He said to them, "You all realize that it is forbidden for a Jew to associate or visit with outsiders.

However, God has shown me that I should never call a person impure or unclean. ²⁹For this reason, when you sent for me, I came without objection. I want to know, then, why you sent for me."

³⁰Cornelius answered, "Four days ago at this same time, three o'clock in the afternoon, I was praying at home. Suddenly a man in radiant clothing stood before me. ³¹He said, 'Cornelius, God has heard your prayers, and your compassionate acts are like a memorial offering to him. ³²Therefore, send someone to Joppa and summon Simon, who is known as Peter. He is a guest in the home of Simon the tanner, located near the seacoast.' ³³I sent for you right away, and you were kind enough to come. Now, here we are, gathered in the presence of God to listen to everything the Lord has directed you to say."

³⁴Peter said, "I really am learning that God doesn't show partiality to one group of people over another. ³⁵Rather, in every nation, whoever worships him and does what is right is acceptable to him. ³⁶This is the message of peace he sent to the Israelites by proclaiming the good news through Jesus Christ: He is Lord of all! ³⁷You know what happened throughout Judea, beginning in Galilee after the baptism John preached. ³⁸You know about Jesus of Nazareth, whom God anointed with the Holy Spirit and endowed with power. Jesus traveled around doing good and healing everyone oppressed by the devil because God was with him. ³⁹We are witnesses of everything he did, both in Judea and in Jerusalem. They killed him by hanging him on a tree,

LIFE PRESERVER

What did Peter want people to remember?
Acts 10:34-43

Cornelius was the first person who wasn't Jewish, called a *Gentile*, to become a Christian. The good news about Jesus was meant for all people, both Jews and Gentiles. Peter wanted to help Christians understand that God loves every person. Peter told all people that God would forgive their sins if they changed their hearts and lives. ♦

ᵇOr *birds in the sky*

⁴⁰but God raised him up on the third day and allowed him to be seen, ⁴¹not by everyone but by us. We are witnesses whom God chose beforehand, who ate and drank with him after God raised him from the dead. ⁴²He commanded us to preach to the people and to testify that he is the one whom God appointed as judge of the living and the dead. ⁴³All the prophets testify about him that everyone who believes in him receives forgiveness of sins through his name."

⁴⁴While Peter was still speaking, the Holy Spirit fell on everyone who heard the word. ⁴⁵The circumcised believers who had come with Peter were astonished that the gift of the Holy Spirit had been poured out even on the Gentiles. ⁴⁶They heard them speaking in other languages and praising God. Peter asked, ⁴⁷"These people have received the Holy Spirit just as we have. Surely no one can stop them from being baptized with water, can they?" ⁴⁸He directed that they be baptized in the name of Jesus Christ. Then they invited Peter to stay for several days.

Jerusalem church questions Peter

11 The apostles and the brothers and sisters throughout Judea heard that even the Gentiles had welcomed God's word. ²When Peter went up to Jerusalem, the circumcised believers criticized him. ³They accused him, "You went into the home of the uncircumcised and ate with them!"

⁴Step-by-step, Peter explained what had happened. ⁵"I was in the city of Joppa praying when I had a visionary experience. In my vision, I saw something like a large linen sheet being lowered from heaven by its four corners. It came all the way down to me. ⁶As I stared at it, wondering what it was, I saw four-legged animals—including wild beasts—as well as reptiles and wild birds.ᶜ ⁷I heard a voice say, 'Get up, Peter! Kill and eat!' ⁸I responded, 'Absolutely not, Lord! Nothing impure or unclean has ever entered my mouth.' ⁹The voice from heaven spoke a second time, 'Never consider unclean what God has made pure.' ¹⁰This happened three times, then everything was pulled back into heaven. ¹¹At that moment three men who had been sent to

me from Caesarea arrived at the house where we were staying. ¹²The Spirit told me to go with them even though they were Gentiles. These six brothers also went with me, and we entered that man's house. ¹³He reported to us how he had seen an angel standing in his house and saying, 'Send to Joppa and summon Simon, who is known as Peter. ¹⁴He will tell you how you and your entire household can be saved.' ¹⁵When I began to speak, the Holy Spirit fell on them, just as the Spirit fell on us in the beginning. ¹⁶I remembered the Lord's words: 'John will baptize with water, but you will be baptized with the Holy Spirit.' ¹⁷If God gave them the same gift he gave us who believed in the Lord Jesus Christ, then who am I? Could I stand in God's way?"

¹⁸Once the apostles and other believers heard this, they calmed down. They praised God and concluded, "So then God has enabled Gentiles to change their hearts and lives so that they might have new life."

The Antioch church

¹⁹Now those who were scattered as a result of the trouble that occurred because of Stephen traveled as far as Phoenicia, Cyprus, and Antioch. They proclaimed the word only to Jews. ²⁰Among them were some people from Cyprus and Cyrene. They entered Antioch and began to proclaim the good news about the Lord Jesus also to Gentiles. ²¹The Lord's power was with them, and a large number came to believe and turned to the Lord.

²²When the church in Jerusalem heard about this, they sent Barnabas to Antioch. ²³When he arrived and saw evidence of God's grace, he was overjoyed and encouraged everyone to remain fully committed to the Lord. ²⁴Barnabas responded in this way because he was a good man, whom the Holy Spirit had endowed with exceptional faith. A considerable number of people were added to the Lord. ²⁵Barnabas went to Tarsus in search of Saul. ²⁶When he found him, he brought him to Antioch. They were there for a whole year, meeting with the church and teaching large numbers of people. It was in Antioch where the disciples were first labeled "Christians."

ᶜOr birds in the sky

²⁷About that time, some prophets came down from Jerusalem to Antioch. ²⁸One of them, Agabus, stood up and, inspired by the Spirit, predicted that a severe famine would overtake the entire Roman world. (This occurred during Claudius' rule.) ²⁹The disciples decided they would send support to the brothers and sisters in Judea, with everyone contributing to this ministry according to each person's abundance. ³⁰They sent Barnabas and Saul to take this gift to the elders.

Herod imprisons Peter

12 About that time King Herod began to harass some who belonged to the church. ²He had James, John's brother, killed with a sword. ³When he saw that this pleased the Jews, he arrested Peter as well. This happened during the Festival of Unleavened Bread. ⁴He put Peter in prison, handing him over to four squads of soldiers, sixteen in all, who guarded him. He planned to charge him publicly after the Passover. ⁵While Peter was held in prison, the church offered earnest prayer to God for him.

⁶The night before Herod was going to bring Peter's case forward, Peter was asleep between two soldiers and bound with two chains, with soldiers guarding the prison entrance. ⁷Suddenly an angel from the Lord appeared and a light shone in the prison cell. After nudging Peter on his side to awaken him, the angel raised him up and said, "Quick! Get up!" The chains fell from his wrists. ⁸The angel continued, "Get dressed. Put on your sandals." Peter did as he was told. The angel said, "Put on your coat and follow me." ⁹Following the angel, Peter left the prison. However, he didn't realize the angel had actually done all this. He thought he was seeing a vision. ¹⁰They passed the first and second guards and came to the iron gate leading to the city. It opened for them by itself. After leaving the prison, they proceeded the length of one street, when abruptly the angel was gone.

did you know? The man referred to here was not James the disciple, who was killed by King Herod (Acts 12:2). This James was the brother of Jesus and the leader of the church in Jerusalem.

¹¹At that, Peter came to his senses and remarked, "Now I'm certain that the Lord sent his angel and rescued me from Herod and from everything the Jewish people expected." ¹²Realizing this, he made his way to Mary's house. (Mary was John's mother; he was also known as Mark.) Many believers had gathered there and were praying. ¹³When Peter knocked at the outer gate, a female servant named Rhoda went to answer. ¹⁴She was so overcome with joy when she recognized Peter's voice that she didn't open the gate. Instead, she ran back in and announced that Peter was standing at the gate.

SAILBOAT

Joy

Real Prayer, Real Joy Acts 12:1-14
Rhoda, a servant in a house full of Christians who were praying, answered the door when Peter came to the house after he had been miraculously released from prison. She was so excited to hear Peter's voice and eager to share the good news with the people who were there that she forgot to open the gate and let him in! Receiving a direct, specific answer to prayer is exciting and sometimes takes us by surprise. ◆

¹⁵"You've lost your mind!" they responded. She stuck by her story with such determination that they began to say, "It must be his guardian angel." ¹⁶Meanwhile, Peter remained outside, knocking at the gate. They finally opened the gate and saw him there, and they were astounded.

¹⁷He gestured with his hand to quiet them down, then recounted how the Lord led him out of prison. He said, "Tell this to James and the brothers and sisters." Then he left for another place.

¹⁸The next morning the soldiers were flustered about what had happened to Peter. ¹⁹Herod called for a thorough search. When Peter didn't turn up, Herod interrogated the guards and had them executed. Afterward, Herod left Judea in order to spend some time in Caesarea.

²⁰Herod had been furious with the people of Tyre and Sidon for some time. They made a pact to approach him together, since their

region depended on the king's realm for its food supply. They persuaded Blastus, the king's personal attendant, to join their cause, then appealed for an end to hostilities. ²¹On the scheduled day Herod dressed himself in royal attire, seated himself on the throne, and gave a speech to the people. ²²Those assembled kept shouting, over and over, "This is a god's voice, not the voice of a mere human!" ²³Immediately an angel from the Lord struck Herod down, because he didn't give the honor to God. He was eaten by worms and died.

²⁴God's word continued to grow and increase. ²⁵Barnabas and Saul returned to Antioch from Jerusalem^d after completing their mission, bringing with them John, who was also known as Mark.

Barnabas and Saul sent to minister

13 The church at Antioch included prophets and teachers: Barnabas, Simeon (nicknamed Niger), Lucius from Cyrene, Manaen (a childhood friend of Herod the ruler), and Saul. ²As they were worshipping the Lord and fasting, the Holy Spirit said, "Appoint Barnabas and Saul to the work I have called them to undertake." ³After they fasted and prayed, they laid their hands on these two and sent them off.

Serving in Cyprus

⁴After the Holy Spirit sent them on their way, they went down to Seleucia. From there they sailed to Cyprus. ⁵In Salamis they proclaimed God's word in the Jewish synagogues. John was with them as their assistant. ⁶They traveled throughout the island until they arrived at Paphos. There they found a certain man named Bar-Jesus, a Jew who was a false prophet and practiced sorcery. ⁷He kept company with the governor of that province, an intelligent man named Sergius Paulus. The governor sent for Barnabas and Saul since he wanted to hear God's word. ⁸But Elymas the sorcerer^e (for that's what people understood his name meant) opposed them, trying to steer the governor away from the faith. ⁹Empowered by the Holy Spirit, Saul, also known as Paul, glared at Bar-Jesus and ¹⁰said, "You are a deceiver and trickster! You devil!

You attack anything that is right! Will you never stop twisting the straight ways of the Lord into crooked paths? ¹¹Listen! The Lord's power is set against you. You will be blind for a while, unable even to see the daylight." At once, Bar-Jesus' eyes were darkened, and he began to grope about for someone to lead him around by the hand. ¹²When the governor saw what had taken place, he came to believe, for he was astonished by the teaching about the Lord.

Paul and Barnabas in Pisidian Antioch

¹³Paul and his companions sailed from Paphos to Perga in Pamphylia. John deserted them there and returned to Jerusalem. ¹⁴They went on from Perga and arrived at Antioch in Pisidia. On the Sabbath, they entered and found seats in the synagogue there. ¹⁵After the reading of the Law and the Prophets, the synagogue leaders invited them, "Brothers, if one of you has a sermon for the people, please speak."

¹⁶Standing up, Paul gestured with his hand and said, "Fellow Israelites and Gentile God-worshippers, please listen to me. ¹⁷The God of this people Israel chose our ancestors. God made them a great people while they lived as strangers in the land of Egypt. With his great power, he led them out of that country. ¹⁸For about forty years, God put up with them in the wilderness. ¹⁹God conquered seven nations in the land of Canaan and gave the Israelites their land as an inheritance. ²⁰This happened over a period of about four hundred fifty years.

"After this, he gave them judges until the time of the prophet Samuel. ²¹The Israelites requested a king, so God gave them Saul, Kish's son, from the tribe of Benjamin, and he served as their king for forty years. ²²After God removed him, he raised up David to be their king. God testified concerning him, '*I have found David, Jesse's son, a man who shares my desires.*^f Whatever my will is, he will do.' ²³From this man's descendants, God brought to Israel a savior, Jesus, just as he promised. ²⁴Before Jesus' appearance, John proclaimed to all the Israelites a baptism to show they were changing their hearts and

---

^dCritical editions of the Gk New Testament read *returned to Jerusalem*. ^eOr *magician* (Gk *magos*) ^fTg 1 Sam 13:14

lives. ²⁵As John was completing his mission, he said, 'Who do you think I am? I'm not the one you think I am, but he is coming after me. I'm not worthy to loosen his sandals.'

²⁶"Brothers, children of Abraham's family, and you Gentile God-worshippers, the message about this salvation has been sent to us. ²⁷The people in Jerusalem and their leaders didn't recognize Jesus. By condemning him they fulfilled the words of the prophets that are read every Sabbath. ²⁸Even though they didn't find a single legal basis for the death penalty, they asked Pilate to have him executed. ²⁹When they finished doing everything that had been written about him, they took him down from the cross[g] and laid him in a tomb. ³⁰But God raised him from the dead! ³¹He appeared over many days to those who had traveled with him from Galilee to Jerusalem. They are now his witnesses to the people.

³²"We proclaim to you the good news. What God promised to our ancestors, ³³he has fulfilled for us, their children, by raising up Jesus. As it was written in the second psalm, *You are my son; today I have become your father.*[h]

³⁴"God raised Jesus from the dead, never again to be subjected to death's decay. Therefore, God said, *I will give to you the holy and firm promises I made to David.*[i] ³⁵In another place it is said, *You will not let your holy one experience death's decay.*[j] ³⁶David served God's purpose in his own generation, then he died and was buried with his ancestors. He experienced death's decay, ³⁷but the one whom God has raised up didn't experience death's decay.

³⁸"Therefore, brothers and sisters, know this: Through Jesus we proclaim forgiveness of sins to you. From all those sins from which you couldn't be put in right relationship with God through Moses' Law, ³⁹through Jesus everyone who believes is put in right relationship with God. ⁴⁰Take care that the prophets' words don't apply to you:

⁴¹*Look, you scoffers,*
    marvel and die.
I'm going to do work in your day —

a work you won't believe
    even if someone told you."[k]

⁴²As Paul and Barnabas were leaving the synagogue, the people urged them to speak about these things again on the next Sabbath. ⁴³When the people in the synagogue were dismissed, many Jews and devout converts to Judaism accompanied Paul and Barnabas, who urged them to remain faithful to the message of God's grace.

⁴⁴On the next Sabbath, almost everyone in the city gathered to hear the Lord's word. ⁴⁵When the Jews saw the crowds, they were overcome with jealousy. They argued against what Paul was saying by slandering him. ⁴⁶Speaking courageously, Paul and Barnabas said, "We had to speak God's word to you first. Since you reject it and show that you are unworthy to receive eternal life, we will turn to the Gentiles. ⁴⁷This is what the Lord commanded us:

I have made you a light for the Gentiles,
    so that you could bring salvation to the
end of the earth."[l]

⁴⁸When the Gentiles heard this, they rejoiced and honored the Lord's word. Everyone who was appointed for eternal life believed, ⁴⁹and the Lord's word was broadcast throughout the entire region. ⁵⁰However, the Jews provoked the prominent women among the Gentile God-worshippers, as well as the city's leaders. They instigated others to harass Paul and Barnabas, and threw them out of their district. ⁵¹Paul and Barnabas shook the dust from their feet and went to Iconium. ⁵²Because of the abundant presence of the Holy Spirit in their lives, the disciples were overflowing with happiness.

Paul and Barnabas in Iconium

14 The same thing happened in Iconium. Paul and Barnabas entered the Jewish synagogue and spoke as they had before. As a result, a huge number of Jews and Greeks believed. ²However, the Jews who rejected the faith stirred up the Gentiles, poisoning their minds against the brothers. ³Nevertheless, Paul and Barnabas stayed there for quite some time, confidently speaking about the Lord. And the Lord confirmed the word

---

[g]Or *tree* [h]Ps 2:7 [i]Isa 55:3 [j]Ps 16:10 [k]Hab 1:5 [l]Isa 49:6

Memorize
Acts 13:38-39

about his grace by the signs and wonders he enabled them to perform. [4]The people of the city were divided—some siding with the Jews, others with the Lord's messengers. [5]Then some Gentiles and Jews, including their leaders, hatched a plot to mistreat and stone Paul and Barnabas. [6]When they learned of it, these two messengers fled to the Lycaonian cities of Lystra and Derbe and the surrounding area, [7]where they continued to proclaim the good news.

Healing a crippled man in Lystra

[8]In Lystra there was a certain man who lacked strength in his legs. He had been crippled since birth and had never walked. Sitting there, he [9]heard Paul speaking. Paul stared at him and saw that he believed he could be healed.

[10]Raising his voice, Paul said, "Stand up straight on your feet!" He jumped up and began to walk.

[11]Seeing what Paul had done, the crowd shouted in the Lycaonian language, "The gods have taken human form and come down to visit us!" [12]They referred to Barnabas as Zeus and to Paul as Hermes, since Paul was the main speaker. [13]The priest of Zeus, whose temple was located just outside the city, brought bulls and wreaths to the city gates. Along with the crowds, he wanted to offer sacrifices to them.

[14]When the Lord's messengers Barnabas and Paul found out about this, they tore their clothes in protest and rushed out into the crowd. They shouted, [15]"People, what are you doing? We are

SAILBOAT

HONEST AND TRUE

Paul and Barnabas Had Good Character
Acts 14:12-15

The people of Lystra thought Paul and Barnabas were gods. They brought gifts and wanted to worship the men. Paul and Barnabas could have lived like kings, but being rich and famous wasn't worth changing the good news about Jesus. Paul and Barnabas were honest and true. ◆

humans too, just like you! We are proclaiming the good news to you: turn to the living God and away from such worthless things. He *made the heaven, the earth, the sea, and everything in them.*[m] [16]In the past, he permitted every nation to go its own way. [17]Nevertheless, he hasn't left himself without a witness. He has blessed you by giving you rain from above as well as seasonal harvests, and satisfying you with food and happiness." [18]Even with these words, they barely kept the crowds from sacrificing to them.

[19]Jews from Antioch and Iconium arrived and won the crowds over. They stoned Paul and dragged him out of the city, supposing he was dead. [20]When the disciples surrounded him, he got up and entered the city again. The following day he left with Barnabas for Derbe.

Returning to Antioch

[21]Paul and Barnabas proclaimed the good news to the people in Derbe and made many disciples. Then they returned to Lystra, Iconium, and Antioch, where [22]they strengthened the disciples and urged them to remain firm in the faith. They told them, "If we are to enter God's kingdom, we must pass through many troubles." [23]They appointed elders for each church. With prayer and fasting, they committed these elders to the Lord, in whom they had placed their trust.

[24]After Paul and Barnabas traveled through Pisidia, they came to Pamphylia. [25]They proclaimed the word in Perga, then went down to Attalia. [26]From there they sailed to Antioch, where they had been entrusted by God's grace to the work they had now completed. [27]On their arrival, they gathered the church together and reported everything that God had accomplished through their activity, and how God had opened a door of faith for the Gentiles. [28]They stayed with the disciples a long time.

The Jerusalem Council

15 Some people came down from Judea teaching the family of believers, "Unless you are circumcised according to the custom we've received from Moses, you can't be saved." [2]Paul and Barnabas took sides against these Judeans and argued strongly against their position.

The church at Antioch appointed Paul, Barnabas, and several others from Antioch to go up to Jerusalem to set this question before the apostles and the elders. ³The church sent this delegation on their way. They traveled through Phoenicia and Samaria, telling stories about the conversion of the Gentiles to everyone. Their reports thrilled the brothers and sisters. ⁴When they arrived in Jerusalem, the church, the apostles, and the elders all welcomed them. They gave a full report of what God had accomplished through their activity. ⁵Some believers from among the Pharisees stood up and claimed, "The Gentiles must be circumcised. They must be required to keep the Law from Moses."

⁶The apostles and the elders gathered to consider this matter. ⁷After much debate, Peter stood and addressed them, "Fellow believers, you know that, early on, God chose me from among you as the one through whom the Gentiles would hear the word of the gospel and come to believe. ⁸God, who knows people's deepest thoughts and desires, confirmed this by giving them the Holy Spirit, just as he did to us. ⁹He made no distinction between us and them, but purified their deepest thoughts and desires through faith. ¹⁰Why then are you now challenging God by placing a burden on the shoulders of these disciples that neither we nor our ancestors could bear? ¹¹On the contrary, we believe that we and they are saved in the same way, by the grace of the Lord Jesus."

¹²The entire assembly fell quiet as they listened to Barnabas and Paul describe all the signs and wonders God did among the Gentiles through their activity. ¹³When Barnabas and Paul also fell silent, James responded, "Fellow believers, listen to me. ¹⁴Simon reported how, in his kindness, God came to the Gentiles in the first place, to raise up from them a people of God. ¹⁵The prophets' words agree with this; as it is written,

¹⁶ After this I will return,
    and I will rebuild David's fallen tent;
    I will rebuild what has been torn down.
    I will restore it

¹⁷ so that the rest of humanity
    will seek the Lord,
    even all the Gentiles
    who belong to me.
The Lord says this,
    the one who does these things[n]
¹⁸ known from earliest times.

¹⁹"Therefore, I conclude that we shouldn't create problems for Gentiles who turn to God. ²⁰Instead, we should write a letter, telling them to avoid the pollution associated with idols, sexual immorality, eating meat from strangled animals, and consuming blood. ²¹After all, Moses has been proclaimed in every city for a long time, and is read aloud every Sabbath in every synagogue."

Letter to the Gentile believers

²²The apostles and the elders, along with the entire church, agreed to send some delegates chosen from among themselves to Antioch, together with Paul and Barnabas. They selected Judas Barsabbas and Silas, who were leaders among the brothers and sisters. ²³They were to carry this letter:

The apostles and the elders, to the Gentile brothers and sisters in Antioch, Syria, and Cilicia. Greetings! ²⁴We've heard that some of our number have disturbed you with unsettling words we didn't authorize. ²⁵We reached a united decision to select some delegates and send them to you along with our dear friends Barnabas and Paul. ²⁶These people have devoted their lives to the name of our Lord Jesus Christ. ²⁷Therefore, we are sending Judas and Silas. They will confirm what we have written. ²⁸The Holy Spirit has led us to the decision that no burden should be placed on you other than these essentials: ²⁹refuse food offered to idols, blood, the meat from strangled animals, and sexual immorality. You will do well to avoid such things. Farewell.

³⁰When Barnabas, Paul, and the delegates were sent on their way, they went down to Antioch. They gathered the believers and delivered the letter. ³¹The people read it, delighted with its encouraging message. ³²Judas and Silas were prophets, and they said many

---

[n]Amos 9:11-12

things that encouraged and strengthened the brothers and sisters. ³³Judas and Silas stayed there awhile, then were sent back with a blessing of peace from the brothers and sisters to those who first sent them.° ³⁵Paul and Barnabas stayed in Antioch, where, together with many others, they taught and proclaimed the good news of the Lord's word.

Paul and Barnabas part company

³⁶Some time later, Paul said to Barnabas, "Let's go back and visit all the brothers and sisters in every city where we preached the Lord's word. Let's see how they are doing." ³⁷Barnabas wanted to take John Mark with them. ³⁸Paul insisted that they shouldn't

did you know? People traveled on the sea in ships powered by ten to fifty oarsmen. Most ships were used to move cargo. When people traveled by ship, they often had to bring enough food of their own for the entire journey.

take him along, since he had deserted them in Pamphylia and hadn't continued with them in their work. ³⁹Their argument became so intense that they went their separate ways. Barnabas took Mark and sailed to Cyprus. ⁴⁰Paul chose Silas and left, entrusted by the brothers and sisters to the Lord's grace. ⁴¹He traveled through Syria and Cilicia, strengthening the churches.

Paul adds Timothy

16Paul reached Derbe, and then Lystra, where there was a disciple named Timothy. He was the son of a believing Jewish woman and a Greek father. ²The brothers and sisters in Lystra and Iconium spoke well of him. ³Paul wanted to take Timothy with him, so he circumcised him. This was because of the Jews who lived in those areas, for they all knew Timothy's father was Greek. ⁴As Paul and his companions traveled through the cities, they instructed Gentile believers to keep the regulations put in place by the apostles and elders in Jerusalem. ⁵So the churches were strengthened in the faith and every day their numbers flourished.

Vision of the Macedonian

⁶Paul and his companions traveled throughout the regions of Phrygia and Galatia because the Holy Spirit kept them from speaking the word in the province of Asia. ⁷When they approached the province of Mysia, they tried to enter the province of Bithynia, but the Spirit of Jesus wouldn't let them. ⁸Passing by Mysia, they went down to Troas instead. ⁹A vision of a man from Macedonia came to Paul during the night. He stood urging Paul, "Come over to Macedonia and help us!" ¹⁰Immediately after he saw the vision, we prepared to leave for the province of Macedonia, concluding that God had called us to proclaim the good news to them.

Lydia's conversion

¹¹We sailed from Troas straight for Samothrace and came to Neapolis the following day. ¹²From there we went to Philippi, a city of Macedonia's first district and a Roman colony. We stayed in that city several days. ¹³On the Sabbath we went outside the city gate to the riverbank, where we thought there might be a place for prayer. We sat down and began to talk with the women who had gathered. ¹⁴One of those women was Lydia, a Gentile God-worshipper from the city of Thyatira, a dealer in purple cloth. As she listened, the Lord enabled her to embrace Paul's message. ¹⁵Once she and her household were baptized, she urged, "Now that you have decided that I am a believer in the Lord, come and stay in my house." And she persuaded us.

Paul and Silas in prison

¹⁶One day, when we were on the way to the place for prayer, we met a slave woman. She had a spirit that enabled her to predict the future. She made a lot of money for her owners through fortune-telling. ¹⁷She began following Paul and us, shouting, "These people are servants of the Most High God! They are proclaiming a way of salvation to you!" ¹⁸She did this for many days.

This annoyed Paul so much that he finally turned and said to the spirit, "In the name of Jesus Christ, I command you to leave her!" It left her at that very moment.

°Critical editions of the Gk New Testament do not include 15:34 *Silas decided to remain there.*

¹⁹Her owners realized that their hope for making money was gone. They grabbed Paul and Silas and dragged them before the officials in the city center. ²⁰When her owners approached the legal authorities, they said, "These people are causing an uproar in our city. They are Jews ²¹who promote customs that we Romans can't accept or practice." ²²The crowd joined in the attacks against Paul and Silas, so the authorities ordered that they be stripped of their clothes and beaten with a rod. ²³When Paul and Silas had been severely beaten, the authorities threw them into prison and ordered the jailer to secure them with great care. ²⁴When he received these instructions, he threw them into the innermost cell and secured their feet in stocks.

UMBRELLA
GREED

The Fortunate Fortune-teller *Acts 16:16-24*
Paul freed a slave woman from a spirit that made her able to predict the future. Her owners were angry because they didn't care about her well-being and used her to make money for themselves. Running into Paul was very good fortune for the woman who used to be a fortune-teller and was now free to follow Jesus. ◊

²⁵Around midnight Paul and Silas were praying and singing hymns to God, and the other prisoners were listening to them. ²⁶All at once there was such a violent earthquake that it shook the prison's foundations. The doors flew open and everyone's chains came loose. ²⁷When the jailer awoke and saw the open doors of the prison, he thought the prisoners had escaped, so he drew his sword and was about to kill himself. ²⁸But Paul shouted loudly, "Don't harm yourself! We're all here!"

²⁹The jailer called for some lights, rushed in, and fell trembling before Paul and Silas. ³⁰He led them outside and asked, "Honorable masters, what must I do to be rescued?"

³¹They replied, "Believe in the Lord Jesus, and you will be saved—you and your entire household." ³²They spoke the Lord's word to him and everyone else in his house. ³³Right then, in the middle of the night, the jailer welcomed them and washed their wounds. He and everyone in his household were immediately baptized. ³⁴He brought them into his home and gave them a meal. He was overjoyed because he and everyone in his household had come to believe in God.

³⁵The next morning the legal authorities sent the police to the jailer with the order "Release those people."

³⁶So the jailer reported this to Paul, informing him, "The authorities sent word that you both are to be released. You can leave now. Go in peace."

³⁷Paul told the police, "Even though we are Roman citizens, they beat us publicly without first finding us guilty of a crime, and they threw us into prison. And now they want to send us away secretly? No way! They themselves will have to come and escort us out." ³⁸The police reported this to the legal authorities, who were alarmed to learn that Paul and Silas were Roman citizens. ³⁹They came and consoled Paul and Silas, escorting them out of prison and begging them to leave the city.

⁴⁰Paul and Silas left the prison and made their way to Lydia's house where they encouraged the brothers and sisters. Then they left Philippi.

More troubles for Paul

17 Paul and Silas journeyed through Amphipolis and Apollonia, then came to Thessalonica, where there was a Jewish synagogue. ²As was Paul's custom, he entered the synagogue and for three Sabbaths interacted with them on the basis of the scriptures. ³Through his interpretation of the scriptures, he demonstrated that the Christ had to suffer and rise from the dead. He declared, "This Jesus whom I proclaim to you is the Christ." ⁴Some were convinced and joined Paul and Silas, including a larger number of Greek God-worshippers and quite a few prominent women.

⁵But the Jews became jealous and brought along some thugs who were hanging out in the marketplace. They formed a mob and started a riot in the city. They attacked Jason's house, intending to bring Paul and Silas before the people. ⁶When they didn't find them, they dragged Jason and some believers

before the city officials. They were shouting, "These people who have been disturbing the peace throughout the empire have also come here. [7] What is more, Jason has welcomed them into his home. Every one of them does what is contrary to Caesar's decrees by naming someone else as king: Jesus." [8] This provoked the crowd and the city officials even more. [9] After Jason and the others posted bail, they released them.

[10] As soon as it was dark, the brothers and sisters sent Paul and Silas on to Beroea. When they arrived, they went to the Jewish synagogue. [11] The Beroean Jews were more honorable than those in Thessalonica. This was evident in the great eagerness with which they accepted the word and examined the scriptures each day to see whether Paul and Silas' teaching was true. [12] Many came to believe, including a number of reputable Greek women and many Greek men.

[13] The Jews from Thessalonica learned that Paul also proclaimed God's word in Beroea, so they went there too and were upsetting and disturbing the crowds. [14] The brothers and sisters sent Paul away to the seacoast at once, but Silas and Timothy remained at Beroea. [15] Those who escorted Paul led him as far as Athens, then returned with instructions for Silas and Timothy to come to him as quickly as possible.

[16] While Paul waited for them in Athens, he was deeply distressed to find that the city was flooded with idols. [17] He began to interact with the Jews and Gentile God-worshippers in the synagogue. He also addressed whoever happened to be in the marketplace each day. [18] Certain Epicurean and Stoic philosophers engaged him in discussion too. Some said, "What an amateur! What's he trying to say?" Others remarked, "He seems to be a proclaimer of foreign gods." (They said this because he was preaching the good news about Jesus and the resurrection.) [19] They took him into custody and brought him to the council on Mars Hill. "What is this new teaching? Can we learn what you are talking about? [20] You've told us some strange things and we want to know what they mean." ([21] They said this because all Athenians as well as the foreigners who live in Athens used to spend their time doing nothing but talking about or listening to the newest thing.)

[22] Paul stood up in the middle of the council on Mars Hill and said, "People of Athens, I see that you are very religious in every way. [23] As I was walking through town and carefully observing your objects of worship, I even found an altar with this inscription: 'To an unknown God.' What you worship as unknown, I now proclaim to you. [24] God, who made the world and everything in it, is Lord of heaven and earth. He doesn't live in temples made with human hands. [25] Nor is God served by human hands, as though he needed something, since he is the one who gives life, breath, and everything else. [26] From one person God created every human nation to live on the whole earth, having determined their appointed times and the boundaries of their lands. [27] God made the nations so they would seek him, perhaps even reach out to him and find him. In fact, God isn't far away from any of us. [28] In God we live, move, and exist. As some of your own poets said, 'We are his offspring.'

[29] "Therefore, as God's offspring, we have no need to imagine that the divine being is like a gold, silver, or stone image made by human skill and thought. [30] God overlooks ignorance of these things in times past, but now directs everyone everywhere to change their hearts and lives. [31] This is because God has set a day when he intends to judge the world justly by a man he has appointed. God has given proof of this to everyone by raising him from the dead."

[32] When they heard about the resurrection from the dead, some began to ridicule Paul. However, others said, "We'll hear from you about this again." [33] At that, Paul left the council. [34] Some people joined him and came to believe, including Dionysius, a member

LIFE PRESERVER

What was Paul trying to get people to understand about God? Acts 17:22-31

In the city of Athens some people worshipped a god who didn't have a name, a god who was unknown. When some religious leaders in Athens argued with Paul about Jesus, God's Son, Paul told them that Jesus is the true name of the god that was unknown. ◊

of the council on Mars Hill, a woman named Damaris, and several others.

Paul in Corinth

18 After this, Paul left Athens and went to Corinth. ²There he found a Jew named Aquila, a native of Pontus. He had recently come from Italy with his wife Priscilla because Claudius had ordered all Jews to leave Rome. Paul visited with them. ³Because they practiced the same trade, he stayed and worked with them. They all worked with leather. ⁴Every Sabbath he interacted with people in the synagogue, trying to convince both Jews and Greeks. ⁵Once Silas and Timothy arrived from Macedonia, Paul devoted himself fully to the word, testifying to the Jews that Jesus was the Christ. ⁶When they opposed and slandered him, he shook the dust from his clothes in protest and said to them, "You are responsible for your own fates! I'm innocent! From now on I'll go to the Gentiles!" ⁷He left the synagogue and went next door to the home of Titius Justus, a Gentile God-worshipper. ⁸Crispus, the synagogue leader, and his entire household came to believe in the Lord. Many Corinthians believed and were baptized after listening to Paul.

⁹One night the Lord said to Paul in a vision, "Don't be afraid. Continue speaking. Don't be silent. ¹⁰I'm with you and no one who attacks you will harm you, for I have many people in this city." ¹¹So he stayed there for eighteen months, teaching God's word among them.

¹²Now when Gallio was the governor of the province of Achaia, the Jews united in their opposition against Paul and brought him before the court. ¹³"This man is persuading others to worship God unlawfully," they declared.

¹⁴Just as Paul was about to speak, Gallio said to the Jews, "If there had been some sort of injury or criminal behavior, I would have reason to accept your complaint. ¹⁵However, since these are squabbles about a message, names, and your own Law, deal with them yourselves. I have no desire to sit in judgment over such things." ¹⁶He expelled them from the court, ¹⁷but everyone seized Sosthenes, the synagogue leader, and gave him a beating in the presence of the governor. None of this mattered to Gallio.

¹⁸After Paul stayed in Corinth for some

God's THOUGHTS ◆ My THOUGHTS

The Community of Believers Grows   Acts 18:18-23

Sometimes vacations mean spending lots of time in the car, traveling the country and stopping at various points along the way. To take a road trip, the person driving must plan how to get there, where to stay, and what sights to see along the way.

Churches spread throughout the world because faithful followers of Jesus traveled and started churches everywhere they could. Paul went to Corinth and started a church there. Then he went to Ephesus and Caesarea. Everywhere he went he was greeted by friends. Together they told people the good news about Jesus and started churches where people could follow Jesus and worship the Lord.

Do you know who started your church? Every church has its own story, but we are all connected to the apostles, such as Paul and Peter, who planted early churches that spread the good news of Jesus all over the world.

Ask your parents to help you find out more about the history of your church.

What role do you have in your church?

time, he said good-bye to the brothers and sisters. At the Corinthian seaport of Cenchreae he had his head shaved, since he had made a solemn promise. Then, accompanied by Priscilla and Aquila, he sailed away to Syria. ¹⁹After they arrived in Ephesus, he left Priscilla and Aquila and entered the synagogue and interacted with the Jews. ²⁰They asked him to stay longer, but he declined. ²¹As he said farewell to them, though, he added, "God willing, I will return." Then he sailed off from Ephesus. ²²He arrived in Caesarea, went up to Jerusalem and greeted the church, and then went down to Antioch.

²³After some time there he left and traveled from place to place in the region of Galatia and the district of Phrygia, strengthening all the disciples.

Apollos and his ministry

²⁴Meanwhile, a certain Jew named Apollos arrived in Ephesus. He was a native of Alexandria and was well-educated and effective in his use of the scriptures. ²⁵He had been instructed in the way of the Lord and spoke as one stirred up by the Spirit. He taught accurately the things about Jesus, even though he was aware only of the baptism John proclaimed and practiced. ²⁶He began speaking with confidence in the synagogue. When Priscilla and Aquila heard him, they received him into their circle of friends and explained to him God's way more accurately. ²⁷When he wanted to travel to Achaia, the brothers and sisters encouraged him and wrote to the disciples so they would open their homes to him. Once he arrived, he was of great help to those who had come to believe through grace. ²⁸He would vigorously defeat Jewish arguments in public debate, using the scriptures to prove that Jesus was the Christ.

Paul in Ephesus

19 While Apollos was in Corinth, Paul took a route through the interior and came to Ephesus, where he found some disciples. ²He asked them, "Did you receive the Holy Spirit when you came to believe?"

They replied, "We've not even heard that there is a Holy Spirit."

³Then he said, "What baptism did you receive, then?"

They answered, "John's baptism."

⁴Paul explained, "John baptized with a baptism by which people showed they were changing their hearts and lives. It was a baptism that told people about the one who was coming after him. This is the one in whom they were to believe. This one is Jesus." ⁵After they listened to Paul, they were baptized in the name of the Lord Jesus. ⁶When Paul placed his hands on them, the Holy Spirit came on them, and they began speaking in other languages and prophesying. ⁷Altogether, there were about twelve people.

LIGHTHOUSE

CHANGED HEART AND LIFE

Believe, Receive Acts 19:1-6

While Paul was traveling, he encountered some people who believed Jesus is God's Son. They had been baptized in water, like John the Baptist taught, to show that they were changing their hearts and lives. Paul explained about Jesus, so they were baptized to become followers of Jesus. Then Paul prayed for them, and the Holy Spirit caused them to praise God in other languages. First they were taught, then they believed, and finally they received. ◆

⁸Paul went to the synagogue and spoke confidently for the next three months. He interacted with those present and offered convincing arguments concerning the nature of God's kingdom. ⁹Some people had closed their minds, though. They refused to believe and publicly slandered the Way. As a result, Paul left them, took the disciples with him, and continued his daily interactions in Tyrannus' lecture hall. ¹⁰This went on for two years, so that everyone living in the province of Asia—both Jews and Greeks—heard the Lord's word.

¹¹God was doing unusual miracles through Paul. ¹²Even the small towels and aprons that had touched his skin were taken to the sick, and their diseases were cured and the evil spirits left them.

¹³There were some Jews who traveled around throwing out evil spirits. They tried to use the power of the name of the Lord Jesus against some people with evil spirits. They said, "In the name of the Jesus whom Paul

preaches, I command you!" ¹⁴The seven sons of Sceva, a Jewish chief priest, were doing this.

¹⁵The evil spirit replied, "I know Jesus and I'm familiar with Paul, but who are you?" ¹⁶The person who had an evil spirit jumped on them and overpowered them all with such force that they ran out of that house naked and wounded. ¹⁷This became known to the Jews and Greeks living in Ephesus. Everyone was seized with fear and they held the name of the Lord Jesus in the highest regard.

¹⁸Many of those who had come to believe came, confessing their past practices. ¹⁹This included a number of people who practiced sorcery. They collected their sorcery texts and burned them publicly. The value of those materials was calculated at more than someone might make if they worked for one hundred sixty-five years.ᵖ ²⁰In this way the Lord's word grew abundantly and strengthened powerfully.

²¹Once these things had come to an end, Paul, guided by the Spirit, decided to return to Jerusalem, taking a route that would carry him through the provinces of Macedonia and Achaia. He said, "After I have been there, I must visit Rome as well." ²²He sent two of his assistants, Timothy and Erastus, to Macedonia, while he remained awhile in the province of Asia.

²³At that time a great disturbance erupted about the Way. ²⁴There was a silversmith named Demetrius. He made silver models of Artemis' temple, and his business generated a lot of profit for the craftspeople. ²⁵He called a meeting with these craftspeople and others working in related trades and said, "Friends, you know that we make an easy living from this business. ²⁶And you can see and hear that this Paul has convinced and misled a lot of people, not only in Ephesus but also throughout most of the province of Asia. He says that gods made by human hands aren't really gods. ²⁷This poses a danger not only by discrediting our trade but also by completely dishonoring the great goddess Artemis. The whole province of Asia—indeed, the entire civilized world—worships her, but her splendor will soon be extinguished."

²⁸Once they heard this, they were beside

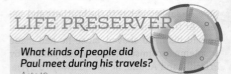

LIFE PRESERVER

What kinds of people did Paul meet during his travels?
Acts 19

Paul traveled many places teaching people about Jesus and how to live as Christians. When he got to Ephesus, he met people who had "closed their minds" (Acts 19:9). He met people who practiced sorcery, which is a form of magic. Paul's preaching threatened the silversmith's business of making silver idols. Paul caused quite a disturbance among the people. This chapter gives us an idea of the kinds of people Paul met and what ministry was like for him. He didn't let anything stop him from sharing the good news with the people. ◆

themselves with anger and began to shout, "Great is Artemis of the Ephesians!"

²⁹The city was thrown into turmoil. They rushed as one into the theater. They seized Gaius and Aristarchus, Paul's traveling companions from the province of Macedonia. ³⁰Paul wanted to appear before the assembly, but the disciples wouldn't allow him. ³¹Even some officials of the province of Asia, who were Paul's friends, sent word to him, urging him not to risk going into the theater. ³²Meanwhile, the assembly was in a state of confusion. Some shouted one thing, others shouted something else, and most of the crowd didn't know why they had gathered. ³³The Jews sent Alexander to the front, and some of the crowd directed their words toward him. He gestured that he wanted to offer a defense before the assembly, ³⁴but when they realized he was a Jew, they all shouted in unison, "Great is Artemis of the Ephesians!" This continued for about two hours.

³⁵The city manager brought order to the crowd and said, "People of Ephesus, doesn't everyone know that the city of Ephesus is guardian of the temple of the great Artemis and of her image, which fell from heaven? ³⁶Therefore, since these facts are undeniable, you must calm down. Don't be reckless. ³⁷The men you brought here have neither robbed the temple nor slandered our goddess. ³⁸Therefore, if Demetrius and the craftspeople with him have a charge against anyone,

ᵖOr *fifty thousand silver drachmen* (a drachme is equivalent in value to a denarion, a typical day's wage) the courts are in session and governors are available. They can press charges against each other there. ³⁹Additional disputes can be resolved in a legal assembly. ⁴⁰As for us, we are in danger of being charged with rioting today, since we can't justify this unruly gathering." ⁴¹After he said this, he dismissed the assembly.

Paul visits Macedonia and Greece

20When the riot was over, Paul sent for the disciples, encouraged them, said good-bye, and left for the province of Macedonia. ²He traveled through that region with a message of encouragement. When he came to Greece, ³he stayed for three months. Because the Jews hatched a plot against Paul as he was about to sail for Syria, he decided instead to return through Macedonia. ⁴He was accompanied by Sopater, Pyrrhus' son from Beroea, Aristarchus and Secundus from Thessalonica, Gaius from Derbe, Timothy, and Tychicus and Trophimus from the province of Asia. ⁵They went on ahead and waited for us in Troas. ⁶We sailed from Philippi after the Festival of Unleavened Bread and met them five days later in Troas, where we stayed for a week.

Meeting with believers in Troas

⁷On the first day of the week, as we gathered together for a meal, Paul was holding a discussion with them. Since he was leaving the next day, he continued talking until midnight. ⁸There were many lamps in the upstairs room where we had gathered. ⁹A young man named Eutychus was sitting in the window. He was sinking into a deep sleep as Paul talked on and on. When he was sound asleep, he fell from the third floor and died. ¹⁰Paul went down, fell on him and embraced him, then said, "Don't be alarmed. He's alive!" ¹¹Then Paul went back upstairs and ate. He talked for a long time—right up until daybreak—then he left. ¹²They took the young man away alive, and they were greatly comforted.

Farewell to the Ephesian leaders

¹³We went on to the ship and sailed for Assos, where we intended to take Paul on board. Paul had arranged this, since he intended to make his way there by land. ¹⁴When he met us at Assos, we took him aboard and went on to Mitylene. ¹⁵The next day we sailed from there and arrived opposite Chios. On the day after, we sailed to Samos, and on the following day we came to Miletus. ¹⁶Paul had decided to sail past Ephesus so that he wouldn't need to spend too much time in the province of Asia. He was hurrying to reach Jerusalem, if possible, by Pentecost Day.

¹⁷From Miletus he sent a message to Ephesus calling for the church's elders to meet him. ¹⁸When they arrived, he said to them, "You know how I lived among you the whole time I was with you, beginning with the first day I arrived in the province of Asia. ¹⁹I served the Lord with great humility and with tears in the midst of trials that came upon me because of the Jews' schemes. ²⁰You know I held back nothing that would be helpful so that I could proclaim to you and teach you both publicly and privately in your homes. ²¹You know I have testified to both Jews and Greeks that they must change their hearts and lives as they turn to God and have faith in our Lord Jesus. ²²Now, compelled by the Spirit, I'm going to Jerusalem. I don't know what will happen to me there. ²³What I do know is that the Holy Spirit testifies to me from city to city that prisons and troubles await me. ²⁴But nothing, not even my life, is more important than my completing my mission. This is nothing other than the ministry I received from the Lord Jesus: to testify about the good news of God's grace.

LIGHTHOUSE

GOOD NEWS

Paul's Life, God's Mission Acts 20:24
Paul said that it was more important to tell people about the good news of God's grace than do anything else in life. Jesus gave Paul this mission, and Paul was determined to fulfill it. Knowing that Jesus changed Paul's heart and life, Paul knew that other people needed to experience the power of God's love and grace in their lives. He spent the rest of his life telling others about Jesus. ◗

²⁵"I know that none of you will see me again—you among whom I traveled and proclaimed the kingdom. ²⁶Therefore, today I testify to you that I'm not responsible for

anyone's fate. ²⁷I haven't avoided proclaiming the entire plan of God to you. ²⁸Watch yourselves and the whole flock, in which the Holy Spirit has placed you as supervisors, to shepherd God's church, which he obtained with the death of his own Son.⁹ ²⁹I know that, after my departure, savage wolves will come in among you and won't spare the flock. ³⁰Some of your own people will distort the word in order to lure followers after them. ³¹Stay alert! Remember that for three years I constantly and tearfully warned each one of you. I never stopped warning you! ³²Now I entrust you to God and the message of his grace, which is able to build you up and give you an inheritance among all whom God has made holy. ³³I haven't craved anyone's silver, gold, or clothing. ³⁴You yourselves know that I have provided for my own needs and for those of my companions with my own hands. ³⁵In everything I have shown you that, by working hard, we must help the weak. In this way we remember the Lord Jesus' words: 'It is more blessed to give than to receive.'"

³⁶After he said these things, he knelt down with all of them to pray. ³⁷They cried uncontrollably as everyone embraced and kissed Paul. ³⁸They were especially grieved by his statement that they would never see him again. Then they accompanied him to the ship.

Paul travels to Jerusalem

21 After we tore ourselves away from them, we set sail on a straight course to Cos, reaching Rhodes the next day, and then Patara. ²We found a ship crossing over to Phoenicia, boarded, and put out to sea. ³We spotted Cyprus, but passed by it on our left. We sailed on to the province of Syria and landed in Tyre, where the ship was to unload its cargo. ⁴We found the disciples there and stayed with them for a week. Compelled by the Spirit, they kept telling Paul not to go to Jerusalem. ⁵When our time had come to an end, we departed. All of them, including women and children, accompanied us out of town where we knelt on the beach and prayed. ⁶We said good-bye to each other, then we boarded the ship and they returned to their homes.

⁷Continuing our voyage, we sailed from Tyre and arrived in Ptolemais. We greeted the brothers and sisters there and spent a day with them. ⁸The next day we left and came to Caesarea. We went to the house of Philip the evangelist, one of the Seven, and stayed with him. ⁹He had four unmarried daughters who were involved in the work of prophecy. ¹⁰After staying there for several days, a prophet named Agabus came down from Judea. ¹¹He came to us, took Paul's belt, tied his own feet and hands, and said, "This is what the Holy Spirit says: 'In Jerusalem the Jews will bind the man who owns this belt, and they will hand him over to the Gentiles.'" ¹²When we heard this, we and the local believers urged Paul not to go up to Jerusalem.

¹³Paul replied, "Why are you doing this? Why are you weeping and breaking my heart? I'm ready not only to be arrested but even to die in Jerusalem for the sake of the name of the Lord Jesus."

¹⁴Since we couldn't talk him out of it, the only thing we could say was, "The Lord's will be done."

¹⁵After this, we got ready and made our way up to Jerusalem. ¹⁶Some of the disciples from Caesarea accompanied us and led us to Mnason's home, where we were guests. He was from Cyprus and had been a disciple a long time. ¹⁷When we arrived in Jerusalem, the brothers and sisters welcomed us warmly.

Meeting the Jerusalem church leaders

¹⁸On the next day Paul and the rest of us went to see James. All of the elders were present. ¹⁹After greeting them, he gave them a detailed report of what God had done among the Gentiles through his ministry. ²⁰Those who heard this praised God. Then they said to him, "Brother, you see how many thousands of Jews have become believers, and all of them keep the Law passionately. ²¹They have been informed that you teach all the Jews who live among the Gentiles to reject Moses, telling them not to circumcise their children nor to live according to our customs. ²²What about this? Without a doubt, they will hear that you have arrived. ²³You must therefore do what we tell you. Four men among us have made

⁹Or *with the death of his own, or with his own death*

a solemn promise. ²⁴Take them with you, go through the purification ritual with them, and pay the cost of having their heads shaved. Everyone will know there is nothing to those reports about you but that you too live a life in keeping with the Law. ²⁵As for the Gentile believers, we wrote a letter about what we decided, that they avoid food offered to idols, blood, the meat from strangled animals, and sexual immorality." ²⁶The following day Paul took the men with him and went through the purification ritual with them. He entered the temple and publicly announced the completion of the days of purification, when the offering would be presented for each one of them.

Paul seized by the people

²⁷When the seven days of purification were almost over, the Jews from the province of Asia saw Paul in the temple. Grabbing him, they threw the whole crowd into confusion by shouting, ²⁸"Fellow Israelites! Help! This is the man who teaches everyone everywhere against our people, the Law, and this place. Not only that, he has even brought Greeks into the temple and defiled this holy place."

^{did you} **know?** Gamaliel was a Pharisee who encouraged tolerance toward the followers of Jesus. The word *Pharisee* means "interpreter." As a religious leader, a Pharisee's job was to interpret the Law (called *the Instruction* in the Old Testament) for the Jewish people.

(²⁹They said this because they had seen Trophimus the Ephesian in the city with him earlier, and they assumed Paul had brought him into the temple.) ³⁰The entire city was stirred up. The people came rushing, seized Paul, and dragged him out of the temple. Immediately the gates were closed. ³¹While they were trying to kill him, a report reached the commander of a company of soldiers that all Jerusalem was in a state of confusion. ³²Without a moment's hesitation, he took some soldiers and officers and ran down to the mob. When the mob saw the commander and his soldiers, they stopped beating Paul. ³³When the commander arrived, he arrested Paul and ordered him to be bound with two chains. Only then

did he begin to ask who Paul was and what he had done.

³⁴Some in the crowd shouted one thing, others shouted something else. Because of the commotion, he couldn't learn the truth, so he ordered that Paul be taken to the military headquarters. ³⁵When Paul reached the steps, he had to be carried by the soldiers in order to protect him from the violence of the crowd. ³⁶The mob that followed kept screaming, "Away with him!"

³⁷As Paul was about to be taken into the military headquarters, he asked the commander, "May I speak with you?"

He answered, "Do you know Greek? ³⁸Aren't you the Egyptian who started a revolt and led four thousand terrorists into the desert some time ago?"

³⁹Paul replied, "I'm a Jew from Tarsus in Cilicia, a citizen of an important city. Please, let me speak to the people." ⁴⁰With the commander's permission, Paul stood on the steps and gestured to the people. When they were quiet, he addressed them in Aramaic.

Paul's defense before his accusers

22 "Brothers and fathers, listen now to my defense." ²When they heard him address them in Aramaic, they became even more quiet. ³Paul continued, "I'm a Jew, born in Tarsus in Cilicia but raised in this city. Under Gamaliel's instruction, I was trained in the strict interpretation of our ancestral Law. I am passionately loyal to God, just like you who are gathered here today. ⁴I harassed those who followed this Way to their death, arresting and delivering both men and women into prison. ⁵The high priest and the whole Jerusalem Council can testify about me. I received letters from them, addressed to our associates in Damascus, then went there to bring those who were arrested to Jerusalem so they could be punished.

⁶"During that journey, about noon, as I approached Damascus, suddenly a bright light from heaven encircled me. ⁷I fell to the ground and heard a voice asking me, 'Saul, Saul, why are you harassing me?' ⁸I answered, 'Who are you, Lord?' 'I am Jesus the Nazarene, whom you are harassing,' he replied. ⁹My traveling companions saw the light, but they didn't hear the voice of the one who spoke to

me. [10]I asked, 'What should I do, Lord?' 'Get up,' the Lord replied, 'and go into Damascus. There you will be told everything you have been appointed to do.' [11]I couldn't see because of the brightness of that light, so my companions led me by the hand into Damascus.

[12]"There was a certain man named Ananias. According to the standards of the Law, he was a pious man who enjoyed the respect of all the Jews living there. [13]He came and stood beside me. 'Brother Saul, receive your sight!' he said. Instantly, I regained my sight and I could see him. [14]He said, 'The God of our ancestors has selected you to know his will, to see the righteous one, and to hear his voice. [15]You will be his witness to everyone concerning what you have seen and heard. [16]What are you waiting for? Get up, be baptized, and wash away your sins as you call on his name.'

[17]"When I returned to Jerusalem and was praying in the temple, I had a visionary experience. [18]I saw the Lord speaking to me. 'Hurry!' he said. 'Leave Jerusalem at once because they won't accept your testimony about me.' [19]I responded, 'Lord, these people know I used to go from one synagogue to the next, beating those who believe in you and throwing them into prison. [20]When Stephen your witness was being killed, I stood there giving my approval, even watching the clothes that belonged to those who were killing him.' [21]Then the Lord said to me, 'Go! I will send you far away to the Gentiles.'"

[22]The crowd listened to Paul until he said this. Then they shouted, "Away with this man! He's not fit to live!" [23]As they were screaming, throwing off their garments, and flinging dust into the air, [24]the commander directed that Paul be taken into the military headquarters. He ordered that Paul be questioned under the whip so that he could find out why they were shouting at him like this.

[25]As they were stretching him out and tying him down with straps, Paul said to the centurion standing there, "Can you legally whip a Roman citizen who hasn't been found guilty in court?"

[26]When the centurion heard this, he went to the commander and reported it. He asked,

"What are you about to do? This man is a Roman citizen!"

[27]The commander went to Paul and demanded, "Tell me! Are you a Roman citizen?" He said, "Yes."

[28]The commander replied, "It cost me a lot of money to buy my citizenship."

Paul said, "I'm a citizen by birth." [29]At once those who were about to examine him stepped away. The commander was alarmed when he realized he had bound a Roman citizen.

Paul appears before the Jewish council

[30]The commander still wanted to know the truth about why Paul was being accused by the Jews. Therefore, the next day he ordered the chief priests and the entire Jerusalem Council to assemble. Then he took Paul out of prison and had him stand before them.

23 Paul stared at the council and said, "Brothers, I have lived my life with an altogether clear conscience right up to this very day." [2]The high priest Ananias ordered those standing beside Paul to strike him in the mouth. [3]Then Paul said to him, "God is about to strike you, you whitewashed wall! You sit and judge me according to the Law, yet disobey the Law by ordering that I be struck."

[4]Those standing near him asked, "You dare to insult God's high priest?"

[5]Paul replied, "Brothers, I wasn't aware that he was the high priest. It is written, *You will not speak evil about a ruler of your people.*[r]

[6]Knowing that some of them were Sadducees and the others Pharisees, Paul exclaimed in the council, "Brothers, I'm a Pharisee and a descendant of Pharisees. I am on trial because of my hope in the resurrection of the dead!"

[7]These words aroused a dispute between the Pharisees and Sadducees, and the assembly was divided. [8]This is because Sadducees say that there's no resurrection, angel, or spirit, but Pharisees affirm them all. [9]Council members were shouting loudly. Some Pharisees who were legal experts stood up and insisted forcefully,

[r]Exod 22:28

"We find nothing wrong with this man! What if a spirit or angel has spoken to him?" [10]The dispute became so heated that the commander feared they might tear Paul to pieces. He ordered soldiers to go down and remove him by force from their midst. Then they took him back to the military headquarters.

[11]The following night the Lord stood near Paul and said, "Be encouraged! Just as you have testified about me in Jerusalem, so too you must testify in Rome."

A murder plot discovered

[12]The next morning some Jewish leaders formulated a plot and solemnly promised that they wouldn't eat or drink until they had killed Paul. [13]More than forty people were involved in the conspiracy. [14]They went to the chief priests and elders and said, "We have solemnly promised to eat nothing until we have killed Paul. [15]You and the council must explain to the commander that you need Paul brought down to you. Pretend that you want to examine his case more closely. We're prepared to kill him before he arrives."

[16]Paul's sister had a son who heard about the ambush and he came to the military headquarters and reported it to Paul. [17]Paul called for one of the centurions and said, "Take this young man to the commander because he has something to report to him."

[18]He took him to the commander and said, "The prisoner Paul asked me to bring this young man to you. He has something to tell you."

[19]The commander took him by the hand and withdrew to a place where they could speak privately. He asked, "What do you have to report to me?"

[20]He replied, "The Jewish leaders have conspired to ask that you bring Paul down to the council tomorrow. They will pretend that they want to investigate his case more closely. [21]Don't fall for it! More than forty of them are waiting to ambush him. They have solemnly promised not to eat or drink until they have killed him. They are ready now, awaiting your consent."

[22]The commander dismissed the young man, ordering him, "Don't tell anyone that you brought this to my attention."

[23]The commander called two centurions and said, "Prepare two hundred soldiers, seventy horsemen, and two hundred spearmen to leave for Caesarea at nine o'clock tonight. [24]Have horses ready for Paul to ride, so they may take him safely to Governor Felix." [25]He wrote the following letter:

[26]Claudius Lysias, to the most honorable Governor Felix: Greetings. [27]This man was seized by the Jews and was almost killed by them. I was nearby with a unit of soldiers, and I rescued him when I discovered that he was a Roman citizen. [28]I wanted to find out why they were accusing him, so I brought him to their council. [29]I discovered that they were accusing him about questions related to their Law. I found no charge deserving of death or imprisonment. [30]When I was informed of a conspiracy against his life, I sent him to you at once and ordered his accusers to bring their case against him before you.

[31]Following their orders, the soldiers took Paul during the night and brought him to Antipatris. [32]The following day they let the horsemen continue on with Paul while they returned to the military headquarters in Jerusalem. [33]The horsemen entered Caesarea, delivered the letter to the governor, and brought Paul before him. [34]After he read the letter, he asked Paul about his home province. When he learned that he was from Cilicia, [35]the governor said, "I will hear your case when your accusers arrive." Then he ordered that Paul be kept in custody in Herod's palace.

Paul's trial before Felix

24 Five days later the high priest Ananias came down with some elders and a lawyer named Tertullus. They pressed charges against Paul before the governor. [2]After the governor summoned Paul, Tertullus began to make his case against him. He declared, "Under your leadership, we have experienced substantial peace, and your administration has brought reforms to our nation. [3]Always and everywhere, most honorable Felix, we acknowledge this with deep gratitude. [4]I don't want to take too much of your time, so I ask that you listen with your usual courtesy to our brief statement of the facts. [5]We have found this man to be a troublemaker who stirs up riots among all the Jews throughout the empire. He's a ringleader of the Nazarene faction [6]and even tried to defile the temple. That's when we arrested him.[8] [8]By examining him yourself, you will be able to verify the allegations we are bringing against him." [9]The Jews reinforced the action against Paul, affirming the truth of these accusations.

[10]The governor nodded at Paul, giving him permission to speak.

He responded, "I know that you have been judge over this nation for many years, so I gladly offer my own defense. [11]You can verify that I went up to worship in Jerusalem no more than twelve days ago. [12]They didn't find me arguing with anyone in the temple or stirring up a crowd, whether in the synagogue or anywhere else in the city. [13]Nor can they prove to you the allegations they are now bringing against me. [14]I do admit this to you, that I am a follower of the Way, which they call a faction. Accordingly, I worship the God of our ancestors and believe everything set out in the Law and written in the Prophets. [15]The hope I have in God I also share with my accusers, that there will be a resurrection of both the righteous and the unrighteous. [16]On account of this, I have committed myself to maintaining a clear conscience before God and with all people. [17]After an absence of several years, I came to Jerusalem to bring gifts for the poor of my nation and to offer sacrifices. [18]When they found me in the temple, I was ritually pure. There was no crowd and no disturbance. [19]But there were some Jews from the province of Asia. They should be here making their accusations, if indeed they have something against me. [20]In their absence, have these people who are here declare what crime they found when I stood before the Jerusalem Council. [21]Perhaps it concerns this one statement that I blurted out when I was with them: 'I am on trial before you today because of the resurrection of the dead.'"

[22]Felix, who had an accurate understanding of the Way, adjourned the meeting. He said, "When Lysias the commander arrives from Jerusalem, I will decide this case." [23]He arranged for a centurion to guard Paul. He was to give Paul some freedom, and his friends were not to be hindered in their efforts to provide for him.

Paul in custody

[24]After several days, Felix came with his wife Drusilla, who was Jewish, and summoned Paul. He listened to him talk about faith in Christ Jesus. [25]When he spoke about upright behavior, self-control, and the coming judgment, Felix became fearful and said, "Go away for now! When I have time, I'll send for you." [26]At the same time, he was hoping that Paul would offer him some money, so he often sent for him and talked with him.

[27]When two years had passed, Felix was succeeded by Porcius Festus. Since Felix wanted to grant a favor to the Jews, he left Paul in prison.

Paul appeals to Caesar

25 Three days after arriving in the province, Festus went up to Jerusalem from Caesarea. [2]The chief priests and Jewish leaders presented their case against Paul. Appealing to him, [3]they asked as a favor from Festus that he summon Paul to Jerusalem. They were planning to ambush and kill him along the way. [4]But Festus responded by keeping Paul in Caesarea, since he was to return there very soon himself. [5]"Some of your leaders can come down with me," he said. "If he's done anything wrong, they can bring charges against him."

[6]He stayed with them for no more than eight or ten days, then went down to Caesarea. The following day he took his seat in the court and ordered that Paul be brought in. [7]When he arrived, many Jews who had come down from Jerusalem surrounded him. They brought serious charges against him, but they couldn't prove them. [8]In his own defense, Paul said, "I've done nothing wrong against the Jewish Law, against the temple, or against Caesar."

[9]Festus, wanting to put the Jews in his debt, asked Paul, "Are you willing to go up to Jerusalem to stand trial before me concerning these things?"

[10]Paul replied, "I'm standing before Caesar's court. I ought to be tried here. I have

---

[8]Critical editions of the Gk New Testament do not include *We wanted to put him on trial according to our Law,* [7] *but Lysias the commander arrived and took him from our hands with great force.* [8] *Then he ordered his accusers to appear before you.*

done nothing wrong to the Jews, as you well know. ¹¹If I'm guilty and have done something that deserves death, then I won't try to avoid death. But if there is nothing to their accusations against me, no one has the authority to hand me over to them. I appeal to Caesar!"

¹²After Festus conferred with his advisors, he responded, "You have appealed to Caesar. To Caesar you will go."

King Agrippa informed about Paul

¹³After several days had passed, King Agrippa and Bernice arrived in Caesarea to welcome Festus. ¹⁴Since they were staying there for many days, Festus discussed the case against Paul with the king. He said, "There is a man whom Felix left in prison. ¹⁵When I was in Jerusalem, the Jewish chief priests and elders brought charges against him and requested a guilty verdict in his case. ¹⁶I told them it is contrary to Roman practice to hand someone over before they have faced their accusers and had opportunity to offer a defense against the charges. ¹⁷When they came here, I didn't put them off. The very next day I took my seat in the court and ordered that the man be brought before me. ¹⁸When the accusers took the floor, they didn't charge him with any of the crimes I had expected. ¹⁹Instead, they quibbled with him about their own religion and about some dead man named Jesus, who Paul claimed was alive. ²⁰Since I had no idea how to investigate these matters, I asked if he would be willing to go to Jerusalem to stand trial there on these issues. ²¹However, Paul appealed that he be held in custody pending a decision from His Majesty the emperor, so I ordered that he be held until I could send him to Caesar."

²²Agrippa said to Festus, "I want to hear the man myself."

"Tomorrow," Festus replied, "you will hear him."

²³The next day Agrippa and Bernice came with great fanfare. They entered the auditorium with the military commanders and the city's most prominent men. Festus then ordered that Paul be brought in. ²⁴Festus said, "King Agrippa and everyone present with us: You see this man! The entire Jewish community, both here and in Jerusalem, has appealed to me concerning him. They've been calling for

his immediate death. ²⁵I've found that he has done nothing deserving death. When he appealed to His Majesty, I decided to send him to Rome. ²⁶I have nothing definite to write to our lord emperor. Therefore, I've brought him before all of you, and especially before you, King Agrippa, so that after this investigation, I might have something to write. ²⁷After all, it would be foolish to send a prisoner without specifying the charges against him."

Paul's defense before Agrippa

26 Agrippa said to Paul, "You may speak for yourself."

So Paul gestured with his hand and began his defense. ²"King Agrippa, I consider myself especially fortunate that I stand before you today as I offer my defense concerning all the accusations the Jews have brought against me. ³This is because you understand well all the Jewish customs and controversies. Therefore, I ask you to listen to me patiently. ⁴Every Jew knows the way of life I have followed since my youth because, from the beginning, I was among my people and in Jerusalem. ⁵They have known me for a long time. If they wanted to, they could testify that I followed the way of life set out by the most exacting group of our religion. I am a Pharisee. ⁶Today I am standing trial because of the hope in the promise God gave our ancestors. ⁷This is the promise our twelve tribes hope to receive as they earnestly worship night and day. The Jews are accusing me, King Agrippa, because of this hope! ⁸Why is it inconceivable to you that God raises the dead?

⁹"I really thought that I ought to oppose the name of Jesus the Nazarene in every way possible. ¹⁰And that's exactly what I did in Jerusalem. I locked up many of God's holy people

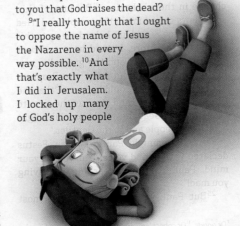

in prison under the authority of the chief priests. When they were condemned to death, I voted against them. [11]In one synagogue after another—indeed, in all the synagogues—I would often torture them, compelling them to slander God. My rage bordered on the hysterical as I pursued them, even to foreign cities.

[12]"On one such journey, I was going to Damascus with the full authority of the chief priests. [13]While on the road at midday, King Agrippa, I saw a light from heaven shining around me and my traveling companions. That light was brighter than the sun. [14]We all fell to the ground, and I heard a voice that said to me in Aramaic, 'Saul, Saul, why are you harassing me? It's hard for you to kick against a spear.'[t] [15]Then I said, 'Who are you, Lord?' The Lord replied, 'I am Jesus, whom you are harassing. [16]Get up! Stand on your feet! I have appeared to you for this purpose: to appoint you as my servant and witness of what you have seen and what I will show you. [17]I will rescue you from your own people and from the Gentiles. I am sending you [18]to open their eyes. Then they can turn from darkness to light and from the power of Satan to God, and receive forgiveness of sins and a place among those who are made holy by faith in me.'

[19]"So, King Agrippa, I wasn't disobedient to that heavenly vision. [20]Instead, I proclaimed first to those in Damascus and Jerusalem, then to the whole region of Judea and to the Gentiles. My message was that they should change their hearts and lives and turn to God, and that they should demonstrate this change in their behavior. [21]Because of this, some Jews seized me in the temple and tried to murder me. [22]God has helped me up to this very day. Therefore, I stand here and bear witness to the lowly and the great. I'm saying nothing more than what the Prophets and Moses declared would happen: [23]that the Christ would suffer and that, as the first to rise from the dead, he would proclaim light both to my people and to the Gentiles."

[24]At this point in Paul's defense, Festus declared with a loud voice, "You've lost your mind, Paul! Too much learning is driving you mad!"

[25]But Paul replied, "I'm not mad, most honorable Festus! I'm speaking what is sound and true. [26]King Agrippa knows about these things, and I have been speaking openly to him. I'm certain that none of these things have escaped his attention. This didn't happen secretly or in some out-of-the-way place. [27]King Agrippa, do you believe the prophets? I know you do."

[28]Agrippa said to Paul, "Are you trying to convince me that, in such a short time, you've made me a Christian?"

[29]Paul responded, "Whether it is a short or a long time, I pray to God that not only you but also all who are listening to me today will become like me, except for these chains."

[30]The king stood up, as did the governor, Bernice, and those sitting with them. [31]As they left, they were saying to each other, "This man is doing nothing that deserves death or imprisonment."

[32]Agrippa said to Festus, "This man could have been released if he hadn't appealed to Caesar."

Paul's voyage to Rome

27When it was determined that we were to sail to Italy, Paul and some other prisoners were placed in the custody of a centurion named Julius of the Imperial Company.[u] [2]We boarded a ship from Adramyttium that was about to sail for ports along the coast of the province of Asia. So we put out to sea. Aristarchus, a Macedonian from Thessalonica, came with us. [3]The next day we landed in Sidon. Julius treated Paul kindly and permitted him to go to some friends so they could take care of him. [4]From there we sailed off. We passed

SAILBOAT

KINDNESS

Kindness Remembered Acts 27:3

Julius was a Roman soldier who treated Paul kindly. Before they boarded the ship, he allowed Paul to spend time with his friends. Julius the centurion, who led a group of one hundred soldiers, is remembered for his kindness to Paul. ◆

[t]Or goads [u]Or cohort (approximately six hundred soldiers)

Cyprus, using the island to shelter us from the headwinds. [5]We sailed across the open sea off the coast of Cilicia and Pamphylia, and landed in Myra in Lycia. [6]There the centurion found an Alexandrian ship headed for Italy and put us on board. [7]After many days of slow and difficult sailing, we arrived off the coast of Cnidus. The wind wouldn't allow us to go farther, so we sailed under the shelter of Crete off Salmone. [8]We sailed along the coast only with difficulty until we came to a place called Good Harbors,[v] near the city of Lasea.

[9]Much time had been lost, and the voyage was now dangerous since the Day of Reconciliation had already passed. Paul warned them, [10]"Men, I see that our voyage will suffer damage and great loss, not only for the cargo and ship but also for our lives." [11]But the centurion was persuaded more by the ship's pilot and captain than by Paul's advice. [12]Since the harbor was unsuitable for spending the winter, the majority supported a plan to put out to sea from there. They thought they might reach Phoenix in Crete and spend the winter in its harbor, which faced southwest and northwest.

[13]When a gentle south wind began to blow, they thought they could carry out their plan. They pulled up anchor and sailed closely along the coast of Crete. [14]Before long, a hurricane-strength wind known as a northeaster swept down from Crete. [15]The ship was caught in the storm and couldn't be turned into the wind. So we gave in to it, and it carried us along. [16]After sailing under the shelter of an island called Cauda, we were able to control the lifeboat only with difficulty. [17]They brought the lifeboat aboard, then began to wrap the ship with cables to hold it together. Fearing they might run aground on the sandbars of the Gulf of Syrtis, they lowered the anchor and let the ship be carried along. [18]We were so battered by the violent storm that the next day the men began throwing cargo overboard. [19]On the third day, they picked up the ship's gear and hurled it into the sea. [20]When neither the sun nor the moon appeared for many days and the raging storm continued

to pound us, all hope of our being saved from this peril faded.

[21]For a long time no one had eaten. Paul stood up among them and said, "Men, you should have complied with my instructions not to sail from Crete. Then we would have avoided this damage and loss. [22]Now I urge you to be encouraged. Not one of your lives will be lost, though we will lose the ship. [23]Last night an angel from the God to whom I belong and whom I worship stood beside me. [24]The angel said, 'Don't be afraid, Paul! You must stand before Caesar! Indeed, God has also graciously given you everyone sailing with you.' [25]Be encouraged, men! I have faith in God that it will be exactly as he told me. [26]However, we must run aground on some island."

[27]On the fourteenth night, we were being carried across the Adriatic Sea. Around midnight the sailors began to suspect that land was near. [28]They dropped a weighted line to take soundings and found the water to be about one hundred twenty feet deep. After proceeding a little farther, we took soundings again and found the water to be about ninety feet deep. [29]Afraid that we might run aground somewhere on the rocks, they hurled out four anchors from the stern and began to pray for daylight. [30]The sailors tried to abandon the ship by lowering the lifeboat into the sea, pretending they were going to lower anchors from the bow. [31]Paul said to the centurion and his soldiers, "Unless they stay in the ship, you can't be saved from peril." [32]The soldiers then cut the ropes to the lifeboat and let it drift away.

[33]Just before daybreak, Paul urged everyone to eat. He said, "This is the fourteenth day you've lived in suspense, and you've not had even a bite to eat. [34]I urge you to take some food. Your health depends on it. None of you will lose a single hair from his head." [35]After he said these things, he took bread, gave thanks to God in front of them all, then broke it and began to eat. [36]Everyone was encouraged and took some food. ([37]In all, there were two hundred seventy-six of us on the ship.) [38]When they had eaten as much as they

[v]Or Fair Havens

wanted, they lightened the ship by throwing the grain into the sea.

[39] In the morning light they saw a bay with a sandy beach. They didn't know what land it was, but they thought they might possibly be able to run the ship aground. [40] They cut the anchors loose and left them in the sea. At the same time, they untied the ropes that ran back to the rudders. They raised the foresail to catch the wind and made for the beach. [41] But they struck a sandbar and the ship ran aground. The bow was stuck and wouldn't move, and the stern was broken into pieces by the force of the waves. [42] The soldiers decided to kill the prisoners to keep them from swimming to shore and escaping. [43] However, the centurion wanted to save Paul, so he stopped them from carrying out their plan. He ordered those who could swim to jump overboard first and head for land. [44] He ordered the rest to grab hold of planks or debris from the ship. In this way, everyone reached land safely.

On the Island of Malta

28 After reaching land safely, we learned that the island was called Malta. [2] The islanders showed us extraordinary kindness. Because it was rainy and cold, they built a fire and welcomed all of us. [3] Paul gathered a bunch of dry sticks and put them on the fire. As he did, a poisonous snake, driven out by the heat, latched on to his hand. [4] When the islanders saw the snake hanging from his hand, they said to each other, "This man must be a murderer! He was rescued from the sea, but the goddess Justice hasn't let him live!" [5] Paul shook the snake into the fire and suffered no harm. [6] They expected him to swell up with fever or suddenly drop dead. After waiting a long time and seeing nothing unusual happen to him, they changed their minds and began to claim that he was a god.

[7] Publius, the island's most prominent person, owned a large estate in that area. He welcomed us warmly into his home as his guests for three days. [8] Publius' father was

God's THOUGHTS ◆ My THOUGHTS

Paul Trusts God   Acts 28:1-10

Paul and his shipmates had a crazy journey on a boat across the Mediterranean Sea (Acts 27). The trip took much longer than planned, and then they were caught in a storm that almost drowned them. Eventually they found land. They were confused and didn't know where they were. When the sun finally came up, they were on an island called Malta. When Paul built a fire, a poisonous snake bit his hand, but he threw it off. When the people realized that he was unharmed, they thought Paul was a god. Paul stayed on the island for three months and healed many sick people.

Being shipwrecked wasn't in Paul's original plan. The crew didn't mean to land on Malta. But washing up on the island was an answer to prayer, even though Paul didn't know at first what was in store for him there. Ultimately, Paul was able to show the power of God by healing sick people. No matter what happens—even if things don't follow our plans—God will use us to do God's work wherever we find ourselves.

When have you been frustrated by hard times in your life?

Have you ever seen God take a bad situation and turn it into something good?

bedridden, sick with a fever and dysentery. Paul went to see him and prayed. He placed his hand on him and healed him. ⁹Once this happened, the rest of the sick on the island came to him and were healed. ¹⁰They honored us in many ways. When we were getting ready to sail again, they supplied us with what we needed.

Paul makes it to Rome

¹¹After three months we put out to sea in a ship that had spent the winter at the island. It was an Alexandrian ship with carvings of the twin gods Castor and Pollux as its figurehead. ¹²We landed in Syracuse where we stayed three days. ¹³From there we sailed to Rhegium. After one day a south wind came up, and we arrived on the second day in Puteoli. ¹⁴There we found brothers and sisters who urged us to stay with them for a week. In this way we came to Rome. ¹⁵When the brothers and sisters there heard about us, they came as far as the Forum of Appius and the Three Taverns to meet us. When Paul saw them, he gave thanks to God and was encouraged. ¹⁶When we entered Rome, Paul was permitted to live by himself, with a soldier guarding him.

Paul meets Jewish leaders in Rome

¹⁷Three days later, Paul called the Jewish leaders together. When they gathered, he said, "Brothers, although I have done nothing against our people or the customs of our ancestors, I'm a prisoner from Jerusalem. They handed me over to the Romans, ¹⁸who intended to release me after they examined me, because they couldn't find any reason for putting me to death. ¹⁹When the Jews objected, I was forced to appeal to Caesar. Don't think I appealed to Caesar because I had any reason to bring charges against my nation. ²⁰This is

why I asked to see you and speak with you: it's because of the hope of Israel that I am bound with this chain."

²¹They responded, "We haven't received any letters about you from Judea, nor have any of our brothers come and reported or said anything bad about you. ²²But we think it's important to hear what you think, for we know that people everywhere are speaking against this faction."

²³On the day scheduled for this purpose, many people came to the place where he was staying. From morning until evening, he explained and testified concerning God's kingdom and tried to convince them about Jesus through appealing to the Law from Moses and the Prophets. ²⁴Some were persuaded by what he said, but others refused to believe. ²⁵They disagreed with each other and were starting to leave when Paul made one more statement: "The Holy Spirit spoke correctly when he said to your ancestors through Isaiah the prophet,

²⁶ *Go to this people and say:*
    You will hear, to be sure,
      but never understand;
    and you will certainly see but never
      recognize what you are seeing.
²⁷ *This people's senses*
    have become calloused,
    and they've become hard of hearing,
    and they've shut their eyes
      so that they won't see with their eyes
      or hear with their ears
      or understand with their minds,
        and change their hearts and lives
        *that I may heal them.*ʷ
²⁸"Therefore, be certain of this: God's salvation has been sent to the Gentiles. They will listen!"ˣ

Paul's ministry in Rome

³⁰Paul lived in his own rented quarters for two full years and welcomed everyone who came to see him. ³¹Unhindered and with complete confidence, he continued to preach God's kingdom and to teach about the Lord Jesus Christ.

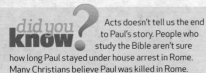

did you know? Acts doesn't tell us the end to Paul's story. People who study the Bible aren't sure how long Paul stayed under house arrest in Rome. Many Christians believe Paul was killed in Rome.

ʷIsa 6:9-10 ˣCritical editions of the Gk New Testament do not include 28:29 *After he said this, the Jews left, debating among themselves.*

Romans

Romans tells how we can know God's love and live the way God wants us to live. The letter begins with the apostle Paul saying that all people sin. Sometimes we do bad things and sometimes we fail to do good things. We don't do what God wants us to do. Paul lists the things people do wrong. Some wrongs are large, and some are small. Some are easy to see. Some are hidden. All sin hurts our relationship with God.

But God forgives our sins because of God's grace (Rom 3:21–6:23). *Grace* is kindness from God that we don't deserve. On our own, we can never fix our broken relationship with God, but God can fix it! God can forgive us and make things right.

Paul also explains how God's Spirit helps us act as Christians should (Rom 12–16).

Greeting

1 From Paul, a slave of Christ Jesus, called to be an apostle and set apart for God's good news. ²⁻³God promised this good news about his Son ahead of time through his prophets in the holy scriptures. His Son was descended from David. ⁴He was publicly identified as God's Son with power through his resurrection from the dead, which was based on the Spirit of holiness. This Son is Jesus Christ our Lord. ⁵Through him we have received God's grace and our appointment to be apostles. This was to bring all Gentiles to faithful obedience for his name's sake. ⁶You who are called by Jesus Christ are also included among these Gentiles.

⁷To those in Rome who are dearly loved by God and called to be God's people.

Grace to you and peace from God our Father and the Lord Jesus Christ.

Thanksgiving and Paul's plans to visit

⁸First of all, I thank my God through Jesus Christ for all of you, because the news about your faithfulness is being spread throughout the whole world. ⁹I serve God in my spirit by preaching the good news about God's Son, and God is my witness that I continually mention you ¹⁰in all my prayers. I'm always asking that somehow, by God's will, I might succeed in visiting you at last. ¹¹I really want to see you to pass along some spiritual gift to you so that you can be strengthened. ¹²What I mean is that we can mutually encourage each other while I am with you. We can be encouraged by the faithfulness we find in each other, both your faithfulness and mine.

¹³I want you to know, brothers and sisters, that I planned to visit you many times, although I have been prevented from coming until now. I want to harvest some fruit among you, just as I have done among the other Gentiles. ¹⁴I have a responsibility both to Greeks and to those who don't speak Greek, both to the wise and to the foolish.

God's righteousness is revealed

¹⁵That's why I'm ready to preach the gospel also to you who are in Rome. ¹⁶I'm not ashamed of the gospel: it is God's own power

for salvation to all who have faith in God, to the Jew first and also to the Greek. ¹⁷God's righteousness is being revealed in the gospel, from faithfulnessª for faith,ᵇ as it is written, *The righteous person will live by faith.*ᶜ

Gentiles are without excuse

¹⁸God's wrath is being revealed from heaven against all the ungodly behavior and the injustice of human beings who silence the truth with injustice. ¹⁹This is because what is known about God should be plain to them

did you know? Paul wrote many letters to different churches. At the beginning of his letters, Paul always offered the grace and peace of Jesus to the people he was writing. When Paul heard that the Roman believers had helped many people, he wrote to tell them how valuable they were to God's kingdom. Even though Paul couldn't meet with them, he still thanked God for the Christians in Rome.

because God made it plain to them. ²⁰Ever since the creation of the world, God's invisible qualities—God's eternal power and divine nature—have been clearly seen, because they are understood through the things God has made. So humans are without excuse. ²¹Although they knew God, they didn't honor God as God or thank him. Instead, their reasoning became pointless, and their foolish hearts were darkened. ²²While they were claiming to be wise, they made fools of themselves. ²³They exchanged the glory of the immortal God for images that look like mortal humans: birds, animals, and reptiles. ²⁴So God abandoned them to their hearts' desires, which led to the moral corruption of degrading their own bodies with each other. ²⁵They traded God's truth for a lie, and they worshipped and served the creation instead of the creator, who is blessed forever. Amen.

²⁶That's why God abandoned them to degrading lust. Their females traded natural sexual relations for unnatural sexual relations. ²⁷Also, in the same way, the males traded natural sexual relations with females, and burned with lust for each other. Males performed shameful actions with males, and

they were paid back with the penalty they deserved for their mistake in their own bodies. ²⁸Since they didn't think it was worthwhile to acknowledge God, God abandoned them to a defective mind to do inappropriate things. ²⁹So they were filled with all injustice, wicked behavior, greed, and evil behavior. They are full of jealousy, murder, fighting, deception, and malice. They are gossips, ³⁰they slander people, and they hate God. They are rude and proud, and they brag. They invent ways to be evil, and they are disobedient to their parents. ³¹They are without understanding, disloyal, without affection, and without mercy. ³²Though they know God's decision that those who persist in such practices deserve death, they not only keep doing these things but also approve others who practice them.

UMBRELLA
LYING

People Who Don't Follow God   *Romans 1:29*
Some people know about God, but still choose not to follow God. Some people spend their whole lives enjoying God's creation but don't think to worship God who made all these things. Paul taught that people believe in a lie when they think they don't need God. God wants us to follow the truth and not lie to ourselves by thinking that we are just fine when we do things our own way. Paul knew there were a lot of people in Rome who didn't follow God's ways. He wanted to remind the Christians there to follow God no matter what other people did. ◊

Jews are without excuse

2 So every single one of you who judge others is without any excuse. You condemn yourself when you judge another person because the one who is judging is doing the same things. ²We know that God's judgment agrees with the truth, and his judgment is against those who do these kinds of things. ³If you judge those who do these kinds of things while you do the same things yourself, think about this: Do you believe that you will escape God's judgment?

Bet you can read this in 5 minutes. **Ready, set, go!**

⁴Or do you have contempt for the riches of God's generosity, tolerance, and patience? Don't you realize that God's kindness is supposed to lead you to change your heart and life? ⁵You are storing up wrath for yourself because of your stubbornness and your heart that refuses to change. God's just judgment will be revealed on the day of wrath. ⁶*God will repay everyone based on their works.*ᵈ ⁷On the one hand, he will give eternal life to those who look for glory, honor, and immortality based on their patient good work. ⁸But on the other hand, there will be wrath and anger for those who obey wickedness instead of the truth because they are acting out of selfishness and disobedience. ⁹There will be trouble and distress for every human being who does evil, for the Jew first and also for the Greek. ¹⁰But there will be glory, honor, and peace for everyone who does what is good, for the Jew first and also for the Greek. ¹¹God does not have favorites.

¹²Those who have sinned outside the Law will also die outside the Law, and those who have sinned under the Law will be judged by the Law. ¹³It isn't the ones who hear the Law who are righteous in God's eyes. It is the ones who do what the Law says who will be treated as righteous. ¹⁴Gentiles don't have the Law. But when they instinctively do what the Law requires they are a Law in themselves, though they don't have the Law. ¹⁵They show the proof of the Law written on their hearts, and their consciences affirm it. Their conflicting thoughts will accuse them, or even make a defense for them, ¹⁶on the day when, according to my gospel, God will judge the hidden truth about human beings through Christ Jesus.

Jews will be judged as well

¹⁷But,
if you call yourself a Jew;
if you rely on the Law;
if you brag about your relationship to God;
¹⁸ if you know the will of God;
if you are taught by the Law
so that you can figure out
the things that really matter;
¹⁹ if you have persuaded yourself that
you are:

ᵈPs 62:12; Prov 24:12

a guide for the blind;
a light to those who are in darkness;
20 an educator of the foolish;
a teacher of infants (since you have
the full content of knowledge and
truth in the Law);
21 then why don't you who are teaching
others teach yourself?
If you preach, "No stealing," do you steal?
22 If you say, "No adultery," do you commit
adultery?
If you hate idols, do you rob temples?
23 If you brag about the Law, do you shame God by breaking the Law? 24 As it is written: *The name of God is discredited by the Gentiles because of you.*[e]

25 Circumcision is an advantage if you do what the Law says. But if you are a person who breaks the Law, your status of being circumcised has changed into not being circumcised. 26 So if the person who isn't circumcised keeps the Law, won't his status of not being circumcised be counted as if he were circumcised? 27 The one who isn't physically circumcised but keeps the Law will judge you. You became a lawbreaker after you had the written Law and circumcision. 28 It isn't the Jew who maintains outward appearances who will receive praise from God, and it isn't people who are outwardly circumcised on their bodies. 29 Instead, it is the person who is a Jew inside, who is circumcised in spirit, not literally. That person's praise doesn't come from people but from God.

God's faithfulness and justice

3 So what's the advantage of being a Jew? Or what's the benefit of circumcision? 2 Plenty in every way. First of all, the Jews were trusted with God's revelations. 3 What does it matter, then, if some weren't faithful? Their lack of faith won't cancel God's faithfulness, will it? 4 Absolutely not! God must be true, even if every human being is a liar, as it is written:
*So that it can show
that you are right in your words;
and you will triumph
when you are judged.*[f]
5 But if our lack of righteousness confirms God's justice, what will we say? That God, who

brings wrath upon us, isn't just (I'm speaking rhetorically)? 6 Absolutely not! If God weren't just, how could he judge the world? 7 But if God's truth is demonstrated by my lie and it increases his glory, why am I still judged as a sinner? 8 Why not say, "Let's do evil things so that good things will come out of it"? (Some people who slander us accuse us of saying that, but these people deserve criticism.)

All are under the power of sin

9 So what are we saying? Are we better off? Not at all. We have already stated the charge: both Jews and Greeks are all under the power of sin. 10 As it is written,
*There is no righteous person,
    not even one.*
11 *There is no one who understands.
    There is no one who looks for God.*
12 *They all turned away.
    They have become worthless together.
    There is no one who shows kindness.
    There is not even one.*[g]
13 *Their throat is a grave
    that has been opened.
    They are deceitful with their tongues,
        and the poison of vipers
        is under their lips.*[h]
14 *Their mouths are full of cursing
        and bitterness.*[i]
15 *Their feet are quick to shed blood;*
16 *destruction and misery
    are in their ways;*
17 *and they don't know the way of peace.*[j]
18 *There is no fear of God
    in their view of the world.*[k]
19 Now we know that whatever the Law says, it speaks to those who are under the Law, in order to shut every mouth and make it so the whole world has to answer to God. 20 It follows that no human being will be treated as righteous in his presence by doing what the Law says, because the knowledge of sin comes through the Law.

God's righteousness
through faithfulness of Christ

21 But now God's righteousness has been revealed apart from the Law, which is confirmed by the Law and the Prophets. 22 God's

---

[e] Isa 52:5 LXX [f] Ps 51:4 [g] Ps 14:1-3 [h] Ps 5:9 [i] Ps 10:7 [j] Isa 59:7-8 [k] Ps 36:1

righteousness comes through the faithfulness of Jesus Christ for all who have faith in him. There's no distinction. ²³All have sinned and fall short of God's glory, ²⁴but all are treated as righteous freely by his grace because of a ransom that was paid by Christ Jesus. ²⁵Through his faithfulness, God displayed Jesus as the place of sacrifice where mercy is found by means of his blood. He did this to demonstrate his righteousness in passing over sins that happened before, ²⁶during the time of God's patient tolerance. He also did this to demonstrate that he is righteous in the present time, and to treat the one who has faith in Jesus as righteous.

Memorize
Rom 3:23-24

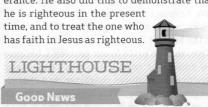

LIGHTHOUSE

GOOD NEWS

Jesus Was Faithful on the Cross
Romans 3:23-26

Paul said that everyone sins (Rom 3:23). This means we all are selfish and do things that keep us from God. When we trust in Jesus who was faithful by dying on the cross, we are forgiven and have a relationship with God. Our sin is forgiven when we trust in Jesus. That is good news! ◊

²⁷What happens to our bragging? It's thrown out. With which law? With what we have accomplished under the Law? ²⁸No, not at all, but through the law of faith. We consider that a person is treated as righteous by faith, apart from what is accomplished under the Law. ²⁹Or is God the God of Jews only? Isn't God the God of Gentiles also? Yes, God is also the God of Gentiles. ³⁰Since God is one, then the one who makes the circumcised righteous by faith will also make the one who isn't circumcised righteous through faith. ³¹Do we then cancel the Law through this faith? Absolutely not! Instead, we confirm the Law.

Abraham's faith was credited as righteousness

4 So what are we going to say? Are we going to find that Abraham is our ancestor on the basis of genealogy? ²Because if Abraham was made righteous because of his actions, he would have had a reason to brag, but not in front of God. ³What does the scripture say? *Abraham had faith in God, and it was credited to him as righteousness.*[1] ⁴Workers' salaries aren't credited to them on the basis of an employer's grace but rather on the basis of what they deserve. ⁵But faith is credited as righteousness to those who don't work, because they have faith in God who makes the ungodly righteous. ⁶In the same way, David also pronounces a blessing on the person to whom God credits righteousness apart from actions:

⁷ *Happy are those whose actions*
outside the Law are forgiven,
and whose sins are covered.
⁸ *Happy are those whose sin isn't counted*
against them by the Lord.[m]

⁹Is this state of happiness only for the circumcised or is it also for those who aren't circumcised? We say, "Faith was credited to Abraham as righteousness." ¹⁰So how was it credited? When he was circumcised, or when he wasn't circumcised? In fact, it was credited while he still wasn't circumcised, not after he was circumcised. ¹¹He received the sign of circumcision as a seal of the righteousness that comes from the faith he had while he still wasn't circumcised. It happened this way so that Abraham could be the ancestor of all those people who aren't circumcised, who have faith in God, and so are counted as righteous. ¹²He could also be the ancestor of those circumcised people, who aren't only circumcised but who also walk in the path of faith, like our ancestor Abraham did while he wasn't circumcised.

Abraham's promise is received through faith

¹³The promise to Abraham and to his descendants, that he would inherit the world, didn't come through the Law but through the righteousness that comes from faith. ¹⁴If they inherit because of the Law, then faith has no effect and the promise has been canceled. ¹⁵The Law brings about wrath. But when there isn't any law, there isn't any violation of

[1]Gen 15:6   [m]Ps 32:1-2

the law. [16]That's why the inheritance comes
through faith, so that it will be on the basis
of God's grace. In that way, the promise is
secure for all of Abraham's descendants, not
just for those who are related by Law but also
for those who are related by the faith of Abraham, who is the father of all of us. [17]As it is
written: *I have appointed you to be the father
of many nations.*[n] So Abraham is our father
in the eyes of God in whom he had faith, the
God who gives life to the dead and calls things
that don't exist into existence. [18]When it was
beyond hope, he had faith in the hope that he
would become the father of many nations,
in keeping with the promise God spoke to
him: *That's how many descendants you will
have.*[o] [19]Without losing faith, Abraham, who
was nearly 100 years old, took into account
his own body, which was as good as dead, and
Sarah's womb, which was dead. [20]He didn't
hesitate with a lack of faith in God's promise,
but he grew strong in faith and gave glory to
God. [21]He was fully convinced that God was
able to do what he promised. [22]Therefore, it
was credited to him as righteousness.
[23]But the scripture that says *it was credited to him*[p] wasn't written only for Abraham's sake. [24]It was written also for our sake,
because it is going to be credited to us too. It
will be credited to those of us who have faith
in the one who raised Jesus our Lord from the
dead. [25]He was handed over because of our
mistakes, and he was raised to meet the requirements of righteousness for us.

Therefore, we have peace with God

5 Therefore, since we have been made righteous through his faithfulness,[q] we have
peace with God through our Lord Jesus Christ.
[2]We have access by faith into this grace in
which we stand through him, and we boast
in the hope of God's glory. [3]But not only that!
We even take pride in our problems, because
we know that trouble produces endurance,
[4]endurance produces character, and character produces hope. [5]This hope doesn't put us
to shame, because the love of God has been
poured out in our hearts through the Holy
Spirit, who has been given to us.
[6]While we were still weak, at the right

[n]Gen 17:5 [o]Gen 15:5 [p]Gen 15:6 [q]Or *faith*

God's Thoughts / My Thoughts

Standing in Grace *Romans 5:1-11*

Think of the last time a parent, teacher, sibling, or friend gave you a second chance or something you didn't deserve. That's grace. *Grace* is favor we don't deserve. It's a do-over that frees us from guilty feelings and embarrassment. It's a chance to start a friendship over, retake a test, or ask again for something you want in a nicer way.

Grace is also the reason we can have a relationship with God. Sin keeps us from being friends with God. But Paul said that because of God's faithfulness and our trust in God, we can have "peace with God" (Rom 5:1). Peace means that everything is okay between God and us. The great thing about God's grace toward us is that we get to show grace toward other people. When we think about how much we need God's grace in our lives, we want to share grace with other people even more!

What is the greatest way someone has shown you grace?

If a friend hurts you, how can you show grace to your friend?

moment, Christ died for ungodly people. [7]It isn't often that someone will die for a righteous person, though maybe someone might dare to die for a good person. [8]But God shows his love for us, because while we were still sinners Christ died for us. [9]So, now that we have been made righteous by his blood, we can be even more certain that we will be saved from God's wrath through him. [10]If we were reconciled to God through the death of his Son while we were still enemies, now that we have been reconciled, how much more certain is it that we will be saved by his life? [11]And not only that: we even take pride in God through our Lord Jesus Christ, the one through whom we now have a restored relationship with God.

Grace now rules

[12]Just as through one human being sin came into the world, and death came through sin, so death has come to everyone, since everyone has sinned. [13]Although sin was in the world, since there was no Law, it wasn't taken into account until the Law came. [14]But death ruled from Adam until Moses, even over those who didn't sin in the same way Adam did—Adam was a type of the one who was coming.

[15]But the free gift of Christ isn't like Adam's failure. If many people died through what one person did wrong, God's grace is multiplied even more for many people with the gift—of the one person Jesus Christ—that comes through grace. [16]The gift isn't like the consequences of one person's sin. The judgment that came from one person's sin led to punishment, but the free gift that came out of many failures led to the verdict of acquittal. [17]If death ruled because of one person's failure, those who receive the multiplied grace and the gift of righteousness will even more certainly rule in life through the one person Jesus Christ.

[18]So now the righteous requirements necessary for life are met for everyone through the righteous act of one person, just as judgment fell on everyone through the failure of one person. [19]Many people were made righteous through the obedience of one person, just as many people were made sinners through the disobedience of one person.

[20]The Law stepped in to amplify the failure, but where sin increased, grace multiplied even more. [21]The result is that grace will rule through God's righteousness, leading to eternal life through Jesus Christ our Lord, just as sin ruled in death.

Our new life in Christ

6 So what are we going to say? Should we continue sinning so grace will multiply? [2]Absolutely not! All of us died to sin. How can we still live in it? [3]Or don't you know that all who were baptized into Christ Jesus were baptized into his death? [4]Therefore, we were buried together with him through baptism into his death, so that just as Christ was raised from the dead through the glory of the Father, we too can walk in newness of life. [5]If we were united together in a death like his, we will also be united together in a resurrection like his. [6]This is what we know: the person that we used to be was crucified with him in order to get rid of the corpse that had been controlled by sin. That way we wouldn't be slaves to sin anymore, [7]because a person who has died has been freed from sin's power. [8]But if we died with Christ, we have faith that we will also live with him. [9]We know that Christ has been raised from the dead and he will never die again. Death no longer has power over him. [10]He died to sin once and for all with his death, but he lives for God with his life. [11]In the same way, you also should consider yourselves dead to sin but alive for God in Christ Jesus.

[12]So then, don't let sin rule your body, so that you do what it wants. [13]Don't offer parts of your body to sin, to be used as weapons to do wrong. Instead, present yourselves to God as people who have been brought back to life from the dead, and offer all the parts of your body to God to be used as weapons to do right. [14]Sin will have no power over you, because you aren't under Law but under grace.

Freedom from sin

[15]So what? Should we sin because we aren't under Law but under grace? Absolutely not! [16]Don't you know that if you offer yourselves to someone as obedient slaves, that

Bet you can *read this in 2 minutes. Ready, set, go!*

you are slaves of the one whom you obey? That's true whether you serve as slaves of sin, which leads to death, or as slaves of the kind of obedience that leads to righteousness. [17]But thank God that although you used to be slaves of sin, you gave wholehearted obedience to the teaching that was handed down to you, which provides a pattern. [18]Now that you have been set free from sin, you have become slaves of righteousness. [19](I'm speaking with ordinary metaphors because of your limitations.) Once, you offered the parts of your body to be used as slaves to impurity and to lawless behavior that leads to still more lawless behavior. Now, you should present the parts of your body as slaves to righteousness, which makes your lives holy. [20]When you were slaves of sin, you were free from the control of righteousness. [21]What consequences did you get from doing things that you are now ashamed of? The outcome of those things is death. [22]But now that you have been set free from sin and become slaves to God, you have the consequence of a holy life, and the outcome is eternal life. [23]The wages that sin pays are death, but God's gift is eternal life in Christ Jesus our Lord.

Memorize
Rom 6:23

Freedom from the Law

7Brothers and sisters, I'm talking to you as people who know the Law. Don't you know that the Law has power over someone only as long as he or she lives? [2]A married woman is united with her husband under the Law while he is alive. But if her husband dies, she is released from the Law concerning her husband. [3]So then, if she lives with another man while her husband is alive, she's committing adultery. But if her husband dies, she's free from the Law, so she won't be committing adultery if she marries someone else. [4]Therefore, my brothers and sisters, you also died with respect to the Law through the body of Christ, so that you could be united with someone else. You are united with the one who was raised from the dead so that we can bear fruit for God. [5]When we were self-centered,

the sinful passions aroused through the Law were at work in all the parts of our body, so that we bore fruit for death. [6]But now we have been released from the Law. We have died with respect to the thing that controlled us, so that we can be slaves in the new life under the Spirit, not in the old life under the written Law.

The function of the Law

[7]So what are we going to say? That the Law is sin? Absolutely not! But I wouldn't have known sin except through the Law. I wouldn't have known the desire for what others have if the Law had not said, *Don't desire to take what others have.*[r] [8]But sin seized the opportunity and used this commandment to produce all kinds of desires in me. Sin is dead without the Law. [9]I used to be alive without the Law, but when the commandment came, sin sprang to life, [10]and I died. So the commandment that was intended to give life brought death. [11]Sin seized the opportunity through the commandment, deceived me, and killed me. [12]So the Law itself is holy, and the commandment is holy, righteous, and good.

Living under the Law

[13]So did something good bring death to me? Absolutely not! But sin caused my death

did you **know?** The leaders of the church in Rome were Jewish. They had been raised with the Instruction from Moses and knew its teachings.

through something good so that sin would be exposed as sin. That way sin would become even more thoroughly sinful through the commandment. [14]We know that the Law is spiritual, but I'm made of flesh and blood, and I'm sold as a slave to sin. [15]I don't know what I'm doing, because I don't do what I want to do. Instead, I do the thing that I hate. [16]But if I'm doing the thing that I don't want to do, I'm agreeing that the Law is right. [17]But now I'm not the one doing it anymore. Instead, it's sin that lives in me. [18]I know that good doesn't live in me—that is, in my body. The desire to

[r]Exod 20:17; Deut 5:21

do good is inside of me, but I can't do it. ¹⁹I don't do the good that I want to do, but I do the evil that I don't want to do. ²⁰But if I do the very thing that I don't want to do, then I'm not the one doing it anymore. Instead, it is sin that lives in me that is doing it.

²¹So I find that, as a rule, when I want to do what is good, evil is right there with me. ²²I gladly agree with the Law on the inside, ²³but I see a different law at work in my body. It wages a war against the law of my mind and takes me prisoner with the law of sin that is in my body. ²⁴I'm a miserable human being. Who will deliver me from this dead corpse? ²⁵Thank God through Jesus Christ our Lord! So then I'm a slave to God's Law in my mind, but I'm a slave to sin's law in my body.

Set free by the Spirit

8 So now there isn't any condemnation for those who are in Christ Jesus. ²The law of the Spirit of life in Christ Jesus has set you free from the law of sin and death. ³God has done what was impossible for the Law, since it was weak because of selfishness. God condemned sin in the body by sending his own Son to deal with sin in the same body as humans, who are controlled by sin. ⁴He did this so that the righteous requirement of the Law might be fulfilled in us. Now the way we live is based on the Spirit, not based on selfishness. ⁵People whose lives are based on selfishness think about selfish things, but people whose lives are based on the Spirit think about things that are related to the Spirit. ⁶The attitude that comes from selfishness leads to death, but the attitude that comes from the Spirit leads to life and peace. ⁷So the attitude that comes from selfishness is hostile to God. It doesn't submit to God's Law, because it can't. ⁸People who are self-centered aren't able to please God.

⁹But you aren't self-centered. Instead you are in the Spirit, if in fact God's Spirit lives in you. If anyone doesn't have the Spirit of Christ, they don't belong to him. ¹⁰If Christ is in you, the Spirit is your life because of God's righteousness, but the body is dead because of sin. ¹¹If the Spirit of the one who raised Jesus from the dead lives in you, the one who raised Christ from the dead will give life to

your human bodies also, through his Spirit that lives in you.

¹²So then, brothers and sisters, we have an obligation, but it isn't an obligation to ourselves to live our lives on the basis of selfishness. ¹³If you live on the basis of selfishness, you are going to die. But if by the Spirit you put to death the actions of the body, you will live. ¹⁴All who are led by God's Spirit are God's sons and daughters. ¹⁵You didn't receive a spirit of slavery to lead you back again into fear, but you received a Spirit that shows you are adopted as his children. With this Spirit, we cry, "Abba, Father." ¹⁶The same Spirit agrees with our spirit, that we are God's children. ¹⁷But if we are children, we are also heirs. We are God's heirs and fellow heirs with Christ, if we really suffer with him so that we can also be glorified with him.

Our suffering and our hope

¹⁸I believe that the present suffering is nothing compared to the coming glory that is going to be revealed to us. ¹⁹The whole creation waits breathless with anticipation for the revelation of God's sons and daughters. ²⁰Creation was subjected to frustration, not by its own choice—it was the choice of the one who subjected it—but in the hope ²¹that the creation itself will be set free from slavery to decay and brought into the glorious freedom of God's children. ²²We know that the whole creation is groaning together and suffering labor pains up until now. ²³And it's not only the creation. We ourselves who have the Spirit as the first crop of the harvest also groan inside as we wait to be adopted and for our bodies to be set free. ²⁴We were saved in hope. If we see what we hope for, that isn't hope. Who hopes for what they already see? ²⁵But if we hope for what we don't see, we wait for it with patience.

²⁶In the same way, the Spirit comes to help our weakness. We don't know what we should pray, but the Spirit himself pleads our case with unexpressed groans. ²⁷The one who searches hearts knows how the Spirit thinks, because he pleads for the saints, consistent with God's will. ²⁸We know that God works all things together for good for the ones who love God, for those who are called according to his

purpose. ²⁹We know this because God knew them in advance, and he decided in advance that they would be conformed to the image of his Son. That way his Son would be the first of many brothers and sisters. ³⁰Those who God decided in advance would be conformed to his Son, he also called. Those whom he called, he also made righteous. Those whom he made righteous, he also glorified.

³¹So what are we going to say about these things? If God is for us, who is against us? ³²He didn't spare his own Son but gave him up for us all. Won't he also freely give us all things with him?

³³Who will bring a charge against God's elect people? It is God who acquits them. ³⁴Who is going to convict them? It is Christ Jesus who died, even more, who was raised, and who also is at God's right side. It is Christ Jesus who also pleads our case for us.

³⁵Who will separate us from Christ's love? Will we be separated by trouble, or distress, or harassment, or famine, or nakedness, or danger, or sword? ³⁶As it is written,

^sPs 44:22

We are being put to death all day long for your sake.

We are treated like sheep for slaughter.^s

³⁷But in all these things we win a sweeping victory through the one who loved us. ³⁸I'm convinced that nothing can separate us from God's love in Christ Jesus our Lord: not death or life, not angels or rulers, not present things or future things, not powers ³⁹or height or depth, or any other thing that is created.

Memorize
Rom 8:38-39

did you know? Paul became an apostle for Jesus after he was confronted in a vision by the risen Christ. Before that, Paul was a Pharisee who brought charges against the followers of Jesus.

The tragedy of Israel's unbelief

9 I'm speaking the truth in Christ—I'm not lying, as my conscience assures me with the Holy Spirit: ²I have great sadness and

God's THOUGHTS ▸ My THOUGHTS

All Things Work Together Romans 8:28

Sometimes it seems like bad things keep happening. It may be something small, like not being able to find one sock in the morning and then feeling thrown off for the whole day. Or it can be something more serious, like your parents fighting and everything feels weird. We can start to lose hope in our lives when bad things happen.

God even uses hard times to bring us closer to God. Paul wrote that "God works all things together for good for the ones who love God" (Rom 8:28). Good, bad, happy, sad—God takes all our circumstances and brings good from them.

Sometimes life may be so hard and we may feel so frustrated that we won't know how to pray. Paul said when that happens the Spirit will pray for us. God is on our side when we're stuck in a tough spot. We can trust God's promise to work all things for good!

Take some old magazines and other discarded items from around the house and use them to make a poster with Romans 8:28 on it. Remember that God brings good things out of "junk."

When have you seen God work all things together for good?

constant pain in my heart. ³I wish I could be cursed, cut off from Christ if it helped my brothers and sisters, who are my flesh-and-blood relatives. ⁴They are Israelites. The adoption as God's children, the glory, the covenants, the giving of the Law, the worship, and the promises belong to them. ⁵The Jewish ancestors are theirs, and the Christ descended from those ancestors. He is the one who rules over all things, who is God, and who is blessed forever. Amen.

Israel and God's choice

⁶But it's not as though God's word has failed. Not all who are descended from Israel are part of Israel. ⁷Not all of Abraham's children are called Abraham's descendants, but instead *your descendants will be named through Isaac.*ᵗ ⁸That means it isn't the natural children who are God's children, but it is the children from the promise who are counted as descendants. ⁹The words in the promise were: *A year from now I will return, and Sarah will have a son.*ᵘ

¹⁰Not only that, but also Rebecca conceived children with one man, our ancestor Isaac. ¹¹When they hadn't been born yet and when they hadn't yet done anything good or bad, it was shown that God's purpose would continue because it was based on his choice. ¹²It wasn't because of what was done but because of God's call. This was said to her: *The older child will be a slave to the younger one.*ᵛ ¹³As it is written, *I loved Jacob, but I hated Esau.*ʷ

¹⁴So what are we going to say? Isn't this unfair on God's part? Absolutely not! ¹⁵He says to Moses, *I'll have mercy on whomever I choose to have mercy, and I'll show compassion to whomever I choose to show compassion.*ˣ ¹⁶So then, it doesn't depend on a person's desire or effort. It depends entirely on God, who shows mercy. ¹⁷Scripture says to Pharaoh, *I have put you in this position for this very thing: so I can show my power in you and so that my name can be spread through the entire earth.*ʸ ¹⁸So then, God has mercy on whomever he wants to, but he makes resistant whomever he wants to.

¹⁹So you are going to say to me, "Then why does he still blame people? Who has ever resisted his will?" ²⁰You are only a human being. Who do you think you are to talk back to God? *Does the clay say to the potter, "Why did you make me like this?"*ᶻ ²¹Doesn't the potter have the power over the clay to make one pot for special purposes and another for garbage from the same lump of clay? ²²What if God very patiently puts up with pots made for wrath that were designed for destruction, because he wanted to show his wrath and to make his power known? ²³What if he did this to make the wealth of his glory known toward pots made for mercy, which he prepared in advance for glory? ²⁴We are the ones God has called. We don't come only from the Jews but we also come from the Gentiles.

²⁵As it says also in Hosea,
*I will call "my people" those
   who aren't my people,
   the one who isn't well loved,
   I will call "loved one."*ᵃ
²⁶And in the place where it was said to them,
*"You aren't my people,"
   there they will be called
   "the living God's children."*ᵇ
²⁷But Isaiah cries out for Israel,
*Though the number of Israel's children
   will be like the sand of the sea,
   only a remaining part will be saved,*
²⁸*because the Lord does what he says
   completely and quickly.*ᶜ
²⁹As Isaiah prophesied,
*If the Lord of the heavenly forces
   had not left descendants for us,
   we would have been like Sodom,
   and we would have become
   like Gomorrah.*ᵈ

Israel and God's righteousness

³⁰So what are we going to say? Gentiles who weren't striving for righteousness achieved righteousness, the righteousness that comes from faith. ³¹But though Israel was striving for a Law of righteousness, they didn't arrive. ³²Why? It's because they didn't go for it by faith but they went for it as if it could be reached by doing something. They have tripped over a stumbling block. ³³As it is written:

ᵗGen 21:12 ᵘGen 18:10, 14 ᵛGen 25:23 ʷMal 1:2-3 ˣExod 33:19 ʸExod 9:16 ᶻIsa 29:16; 45:9 ᵃHos 2:23 ᵇHos 1:10 ᶜIsa 10:22-23 LXX ᵈIsa 1:9

Look! I'm putting a stumbling block
in Zion,
which is a rock that offends people.
And the one who has faith in him
will not be put to shame.[e]

10 Brothers and sisters, my heart's desire is for Israel's salvation. That's my prayer to God for them. [2]I can vouch for them: they are enthusiastic about God. However, it isn't informed by knowledge. [3]They don't submit to God's righteousness because they don't understand his righteousness, and they try to establish their own righteousness. [4]Christ is the goal of the Law, which leads to righteousness for all who have faith in God.

[5]Moses writes about the righteousness that comes from the Law: *The person who does these things will live by them.*[f] [6]But the righteousness that comes from faith talks like this: *Don't say in your heart, "Who will go up into heaven?"*[g] (that is, to bring Christ down) [7]or *"Who will go down into the region below?"*[h] (that is, to bring Christ up from the dead). [8]But what does it say? *The word is near you, in your mouth and in your heart*[i] (that is, the message of faith that we preach). [9]Because if you confess with your mouth "Jesus is Lord" and in your heart you have faith that God raised him from the dead, you will be saved. [10]Trusting with the heart leads to righteousness, and confessing with the mouth leads to salvation. [11]The scripture says, *All who have faith in him won't be put to shame.*[j] [12]There is no distinction between Jew and Greek, because the same Lord is Lord of all, who gives richly to all who call on him. [13]*All who call on the Lord's name will be saved.*[k]

[14]So how can they call on someone they don't have faith in? And how can they have faith in someone they haven't heard of? And how can they hear without a preacher? [15]And how can they preach unless they are sent? As it is written, *How beautiful are the feet of those who announce the good news.*[l] [16]But everyone hasn't obeyed the good news. As Isaiah says, *Lord, who has had faith in our message?*[m] [17]So, faith comes

Bet you can read this in 2 minutes. Ready, set, go!

from listening, but it's listening by means of Christ's message. [18]But I ask you, didn't they hear it? Definitely! *Their voice has gone out into the entire earth, and their message has gone out to the corners of the inhabited world.*[n] [19]But I ask you again, didn't Israel understand? First, Moses says, *I will make you jealous of those who aren't a people, of a people without understanding.*[o] [20]And Isaiah even dares to say, *I was found by those who didn't look for me; I revealed myself to those who didn't ask for me.*[p] [21]But he says about Israel, *All day long I stretched out my hands to a disobedient and contrary people.*[q]

Israel and God's faithfulness

11 So I ask you, has God rejected his people? Absolutely not! I'm an Israelite, a descendant of Abraham, from the tribe of Benjamin. [2]God hasn't rejected his people, whom he knew in advance. Or don't you know what the scripture says in the case of Elijah, when he pleads with God against Israel? [3]*Lord, they have killed your prophets, and they have torn down your altars. I'm the only one left, and they are trying to take my life.*[r] [4]But what is God's reply to him? *I have kept for myself seven thousand people who haven't bowed their knees to Baal.*[s] [5]So also in the present time there is a remaining group by the choice of God's grace. [6]But if it is by grace, it isn't by what's done anymore. If it were, God's grace wouldn't be grace.

[7]So what? Israel didn't find what it was looking for. Those who were chosen found it, but the others were resistant. [8]As it is written, *God gave them a dull spirit, so that their eyes would not see and their ears not hear, right up until the present day.*[t] [9]And David says,

Their table should become a pitfall
and a trap,
a stumbling block and payback to them
for what they have done.
[10]Their eyes should be darkened
so they can't see,
and their backs always bent.[u]

[11]So I'm asking you: They haven't stumbled so that they've fallen permanently, have they? Absolutely not! But salvation has come to the

[e]Isa 28:16; 8:14 [f]Lev 18:5 [g]Deut 9:4; 30:12 [h]Deut 30:13 [i]Deut 30:14 [j]Isa 28:16 [k]Joel 2:32 [l]Isa 52:7; Nah 1:15 [m]Isa 53:1 [n]Ps 19:4 [o]Deut 32:21 [p]Isa 65:1 [q]Isa 65:2 [r]1 Kgs 19:10, 14 [s]1 Kgs 19:18 [t]Deut 29:4; Isa 29:10 [u]Ps 69:22-23

Gentiles by their failure, in order to make Israel jealous. ¹²But if their failure brings riches to the world, and their defeat brings riches to the Gentiles, how much more will come from the completion of their number! ¹³I'm speaking to you Gentiles. Considering that I'm an apostle to the Gentiles, I publicize my own ministry ¹⁴in the hope that somehow I might make my own people jealous and save some of them. ¹⁵If their rejection has brought about a close relationship between God and the world, how can their acceptance mean anything less than life from the dead?

UMBRELLA
JEALOUSY

God's Love for Israel *Romans 11:1-15*
The Jewish people of Israel were chosen by God and tried to follow God's Law to stay pure and faithful to God. Many *Gentiles* (non-Jewish people) started following Jesus and became God's children too. Paul said this would make Israel jealous. Paul used the word *jealous* to show how excited he wanted the Jewish people to get about following Jesus. ◉

¹⁶But if part of a batch of dough is offered to God as holy, the whole batch of dough is holy too. If a root is holy, the branches will be holy too. ¹⁷If some of the branches were broken off, and you were a wild olive branch, and you were grafted in among the other branches and shared the root that produces the rich oil of the olive tree, ¹⁸then don't brag like you're better than the other branches. If you do brag, be careful: it's not you that sustains the root, but it's the root that sustains you. ¹⁹You will say then, "Branches were broken off so that I could be grafted in." ²⁰Fine. They were broken off because they weren't faithful, but you stand only by your faithfulness.^v So don't think in a proud way; instead be afraid. ²¹If God didn't spare the natural branches, he won't spare you either. ²²So look at God's kindness and harshness. It's harshness toward those who fell, but it's God's kindness for you, provided you continue in his kindness;

otherwise, you could be cut off too. ²³And even those who were cut off will be grafted back in if they don't continue to be unfaithful, because God is able to graft them in again. ²⁴If you were naturally part of a wild olive tree and you were cut off from it, and then, contrary to nature, you were grafted into the cultivated olive tree, won't these natural branches stand an even better chance of being grafted back onto their own olive tree?

All Israel will be saved

²⁵I don't want you to be unaware of this secret,^w brothers and sisters. That way you won't think too highly of yourselves. A part of Israel has become resistant until the full number of the Gentiles comes in. ²⁶In this way, all Israel will be saved, as it is written:

> The deliverer will come from Zion.
> He will remove ungodly behavior
>   from Jacob.
> ²⁷This is my covenant with them,
>   when I take away their sins.^x

²⁸According to the gospel, they are enemies for your sake, but according to God's choice, they are loved for the sake of their ancestors. ²⁹God's gifts and calling can't be taken back. ³⁰Once you were disobedient to God, but now you have mercy because they were disobedient. ³¹In the same way, they have also been disobedient because of the mercy that you received, so now they can receive mercy too. ³²God has locked up all people in disobedience, in order to have mercy on all of them.

³³God's riches, wisdom, and knowledge are so deep! They are as mysterious as his judgments, and they are as hard to track as his paths!

> ³⁴Who has known the Lord's mind?
>   Or who has been his mentor?^y
> ³⁵Or who has given him a gift
>   and has been paid back by him?^z
> ³⁶All things are from him and through him
>   and for him.
> May the glory be to him forever. Amen.

Living sacrifice and transformed lives

12So, brothers and sisters, because of God's mercies, I encourage you to present your bodies as a living sacrifice that is

LIFE PRESERVER

What did Paul mean by being "transformed"?
Romans 12:1-2

Paul wanted the Roman Christians to know that following Jesus wouldn't be easy. He wanted them to know it would require them to live differently, to be transformed. To be *transformed* means a person is changed.

Paul said, "Don't be conformed to the patterns of this world" (Rom 12:2). Paul knew that people would offer Roman Christians other ideas about how to live. The Bible teaches that we should live simply and share what we have. Our world still encourages us to buy things we don't need and look out mostly for ourselves. When we are selfish, we are conforming instead of being transformed. ♦

holy and pleasing to God. This is your appropriate priestly service. ²Don't be conformed to the patterns of this world, but be transformed by the renewing of your minds so that you can figure out what God's will is—what is good and pleasing and mature.

Transformed relationships

³Because of the grace that God gave me, I can say to each one of you: don't think of yourself more highly than you ought to think. Instead, be reasonable since God has measured out a portion of faith to each one of you. ⁴We have many parts in one body, but the parts don't all have the same function. ⁵In the same way, though there are many of us, we are one body in Christ, and individually we belong to each other. ⁶We have different gifts that are consistent with God's grace that has been given to us. If your gift is prophecy, you should prophesy in proportion to your faith. ⁷If your gift is service, devote yourself to serving. If your gift is teaching, devote yourself to teaching. ⁸If your gift is encouragement, devote yourself to encouraging. The one giving should do it with no strings attached. The leader should lead with passion. The one showing mercy should be cheerful.

⁹Love should be shown without pretending. Hate evil, and hold on to what is good. ¹⁰Love each other like the members of your family. Be the best at showing honor to each other. ¹¹Don't hesitate to be enthusiastic—be on fire in the Spirit as you serve the Lord! ¹²Be happy in your hope, stand your ground when you're in trouble, and devote yourselves to prayer. ¹³Contribute to the needs of God's people, and welcome strangers into your home. ¹⁴Bless people who harass you—bless and don't curse them. ¹⁵Be happy with those who are happy, and cry with those who are crying. ¹⁶Consider everyone as equal, and don't think that you're better than anyone else. Instead, associate with people who have no status. Don't think that you're so smart. ¹⁷Don't pay back anyone for their evil actions with evil actions, but show respect for what everyone else believes is good.

¹⁸If possible, to the best of your ability, live at peace with all people. ¹⁹Don't try to get revenge for yourselves, my dear friends, but leave room for God's wrath. It is written, *Revenge belongs to me; I will pay it back, says the Lord.*[a] ²⁰Instead, *If your enemy is hungry, feed him; if he is thirsty, give him a drink. By doing this, you will pile burning coals of fire upon his head.*[b] ²¹Don't be defeated by evil, but defeat evil with good.

13 Every person should place themselves under the authority of the government. There isn't any authority unless it comes from God, and the authorities that are there have been put in place by God. ²So anyone who opposes the authority is standing against what God has established. People who take this kind of stand will get punished. ³The authorities don't frighten people who are doing the right thing. Rather, they frighten people who are doing wrong. Would you rather not be afraid of authority? Do what's right, and you will receive its approval. ⁴It is God's servant given for your benefit. But if you do what's wrong, be afraid because it doesn't have weapons to enforce the law for nothing. It is God's servant put in place to carry out his punishment on those who do what is wrong. ⁵That is why it is necessary to place yourself under the government's authority, not only to avoid God's punishment but also for the sake of your conscience. ⁶You should also pay taxes for the same reason, because the authorities

---

[a]Deut 32:35 [b]Prov 25:21-22

are God's assistants, concerned with this very thing. [7]So pay everyone what you owe them. Pay the taxes you owe, pay the duties you are charged, give respect to those you should respect, and honor those you should honor.

[8]Don't be in debt to anyone, except for the obligation to love each other. Whoever loves another person has fulfilled the Law. [9]The commandments, *Don't commit adultery, don't murder, don't steal, don't desire what others have,*[c] and any other commandments, are all summed up in one word: *You must love your neighbor as yourself.*[d] [10]Love doesn't do anything wrong to a neighbor; therefore, love is what fulfills the Law.

The day is near

[11]As you do all this, you know what time it is. The hour has already come for you to wake up from your sleep. Now our salvation is nearer than when we first had faith. [12]The night is almost over, and the day is near. So let's get rid of the actions that belong to the darkness and put on the weapons of light. [13]Let's behave appropriately as people who live in the day, not in partying and getting drunk, not in sleeping around and obscene behavior, not in fighting and obsession. [14]Instead, dress yourself with the Lord Jesus Christ, and don't plan to indulge your selfish desires.

Welcoming each other like Christ

14 Welcome the person who is weak in faith—but not in order to argue about differences of opinion. [2]One person believes in eating everything, while the weak person eats only vegetables. [3]Those who eat must not look down on the ones who don't, and the ones

[c]Exod 20:13-15, 17; Deut 5:17-19, 21   [d]Lev 19:18

Be on Fire in the Spirit! *Romans 12:9-18*

On cold autumn nights it's nice to gather with friends around a bonfire, roast marshmallows, and drink hot cocoa. When it's completely dark outside and the air is cold, the fire gives enough warmth for the whole gathering. You might even start to get hot if you get too close. Fire is powerful and gives warmth to everyone near it.

Paul said people who follow Christ should be "on fire in the Spirit" (Rom 12:11). This means we should be a force God can use to spread God's love everywhere we go. Other people should know that they can come to us for love, kindness, peace, forgiveness, and the warmth of friendship.

Paul told us to love without pretending. That means we should do more than just say hi and pretend to be interested in the people we say we love. The challenge is to love people like real family. This passage teaches us to hate evil, hold on to good, be the best at honoring each other, be happy in hope, stand our ground in trouble, devote ourselves to prayer, be giving, be welcoming, be a blessing, be compassionate, be comforting, be humble, be forgiving, and be at peace with everyone. When we do these things, everyone around us will want to warm up in the glow of the Spirit within us.

When have you pretended to love someone?

Pray for the fire of the Spirit to help you live out what Paul teaches about loving people.

who don't eat must not judge the ones who do, because God has accepted them. [4]Who are you to judge someone else's servants? They stand or fall before their own Lord (and they will stand, because the Lord has the power to make them stand). [5]One person considers some days to be more sacred than others, while another person considers all days to be the same. Each person must have their own convictions. [6]Someone who thinks that a day is sacred, thinks that way for the Lord. Those who eat, eat for the Lord, because they thank God. And those who don't eat, don't eat for the Lord, and they thank the Lord too. [7]We don't live for ourselves and we don't die for ourselves. [8]If we live, we live for the Lord, and if we die, we die for the Lord. Therefore, whether we live or die, we belong to God. [9]This is why Christ died and lived: so that he might be Lord of both the dead and the living. [10]But why do you judge your brother or sister? Or why do you look down on your brother or sister? We all will stand in front of the judgment seat of God. [11]Because it is written,

As I live, says the Lord,
  every knee will bow to me,
  and every tongue will give praise
    to God.[e]

[12]So then, each of us will give an account of ourselves to God.

[13]So stop judging each other. Instead, this is what you should decide: never put a stumbling block or obstacle in the way of your brother or sister. [14]I know and I'm convinced in the Lord Jesus that nothing is wrong to eat in itself. But if someone thinks something is wrong to eat, it becomes wrong for that person. [15]If your brother or sister is upset by your food, you are no longer walking in love. Don't let your food destroy someone for whom Christ died. [16]And don't let something you consider to be good be criticized as wrong. [17]God's kingdom isn't about eating food and drinking but about righteousness, peace, and joy in the Holy Spirit. [18]Whoever serves Christ this way pleases God and gets human approval.

[19]So let's strive for the things that bring peace and the things that build each other up. [20]Don't destroy what God has done because of

food. All food is acceptable, but it's a bad thing if it trips someone else. [21]It's a good thing not to eat meat or drink wine or to do anything that trips your brother or sister. [22]Keep the belief that you have to yourself—it's between you and God. People are blessed who don't convict themselves by the things they approve. [23]But those who have doubts are convicted if they go ahead and eat, because they aren't acting on the basis of faith. Everything that isn't based on faith is sin.

15 We who are powerful need to be patient with the weakness of those who don't have power, and not please ourselves. [2]Each of us should please our neighbors for their good in order to build them up. [3]Christ didn't please himself, but, as it is written, *The insults of those who insulted you fell on me.*[f] [4]Whatever was written in the past was written for our instruction so that we could have hope through endurance and through the encouragement of the scriptures. [5]May the God of endurance and encouragement give you the same attitude toward each other, similar to Christ Jesus' attitude. [6]That way you can glorify the God and Father of our Lord Jesus Christ together with one voice.

[7]So welcome each other, in the same way that Christ also welcomed you, for God's glory. [8]I'm saying that Christ became a servant of those who are circumcised for the sake of God's truth, in order to confirm the promises given to the ancestors, [9]and so that

LIFE PRESERVER

What are "stumbling blocks"? Romans 14:13

Stumbling blocks are things that get in our way and trip us up. When kids are little and just starting to walk, parents make their homes safe. They cover electrical outlets so little ones don't put their fingers in them and get shocked. They make sure toys are kept out of the way so unsteady toddlers don't trip and fall over them.

Paul talked about things Christians do that might be obstacles or stumbling blocks that could trip up other people and make it hard for those people to follow Jesus. Paul asked the early Christians to think about other people before they took action. ◆

[e]Isa 45:23 [f]Ps 69:9

the Gentiles could glorify God for his mercy. As it is written,

> Because of this I will confess you
> among the Gentiles,
> and I will sing praises to your name.[g]

[10]And again, it says,

> Rejoice, Gentiles, with his people.[h]

[11]And again,

> Praise the Lord, all you Gentiles,
> and all the people should sing
> his praises.[i]

[12]And again, Isaiah says,

> There will be a root of Jesse,
> who will also rise to rule the Gentiles.
> The Gentiles will place their hope
> in him.[j]

> **Memorize**
> **Rom 15:13**

[13]May the God of hope fill you with all joy and peace in faith so that you overflow with hope by the power of the Holy Spirit.

Paul's ministry to the Gentiles

[14]My brothers and sisters, I myself am convinced that you yourselves are full of goodness, filled with all knowledge, and are able to teach each other. [15]But I've written to you in a sort of daring way, partly to remind you of what you already know. I'm writing to you in this way because of the grace that was given to me by God. [16]It helps me to be a minister of Christ Jesus to the Gentiles. I'm working as a priest of God's gospel so that the offering of the Gentiles can be acceptable and made holy by the Holy Spirit. [17]So in Christ Jesus I brag about things that have to do with God. [18]I don't dare speak about anything except what Christ has done through me to bring about the obedience of the Gentiles. He did it by what I've said and what I've done, [19]by the power of signs and wonders, and by the power of God's Spirit. So I've completed the circuit of preaching Christ's gospel from Jerusalem all the way around to Illyricum. [20]In this way, I have a goal to preach the gospel where they haven't heard of Christ yet, so that I won't be building on someone else's foundation. [21]Instead, as it's written, Those who hadn't been told about him will see, and those who hadn't heard will understand.[k]

Travel plans to visit Rome

[22]That's why I've been stopped so many times from coming to see you. [23]But now, since I don't have any place to work in these regions anymore, and since I've wanted to come to see you for many years, [24]I'll visit you when I go to Spain. I hope to see you while I'm passing through. And I hope you will send me on my way there, after I have first been reenergized by some time in your company.

[25]But now I'm going to Jerusalem, to serve God's people. [26]Macedonia and Achaia have been happy to make a contribution for the poor among God's people in Jerusalem. [27]They were happy to do this, and they are actually in debt to God's people in Jerusalem. If the Gentiles got a share of the Jewish people's spiritual resources, they ought to minister to them with material resources. [28]So then after I have finished this job and have safely delivered the final amount of the Gentiles' offering to them, I will leave for Spain, visiting you on the way. [29]And I know that when I come to you I will come with the fullest blessing of Christ.

[30]Brothers and sisters, I urge you, through our Lord Jesus Christ and through the love of the Spirit, to join me in my struggles in your prayers to God for me. [31]Pray that I will be rescued from the people in Judea who don't believe. Also, pray that my service for Jerusalem will be acceptable to God's people there [32]so that I can come to you with joy by God's will and be reenergized with your company. [33]May the God of peace be with you all. Amen.

Introduction to Phoebe

16 I'm introducing our sister Phoebe to you, who is a servant[l] of the church in Cenchreae. [2]Welcome her in the Lord in a way that is worthy of God's people, and give her whatever she needs from you, because she

did you know? Paul couldn't travel to Rome himself to take his letter to the Romans. So he chose Phoebe, a church leader he trusted very much, to take the letter in his place. She did, and then she read the letter to the church in Rome. She preached and taught about Jesus on Paul's behalf.

[g]Ps 18:49 [h]Deut 32:43 [i]Ps 117:1 [j]Isa 11:10 [k]Isa 52:15 [l]Or deacon

herself has been a sponsor of many people, myself included.

Greetings to Roman Christians

[3]Say hello to Prisca and Aquila, my coworkers in Christ Jesus, [4]who risked their own necks for my life. I'm not the only one who thanks God for them, but all the churches of the Gentiles do the same. [5]Also say hello to the church that meets in their house. Say hello to Epaenetus, my dear friend, who was the first convert[m] in Asia for Christ. [6]Say hello to Mary, who has worked very hard for you. [7]Say hello to Andronicus and Junia, my relatives and my fellow prisoners. They are prominent among the apostles, and they were in Christ before me. [8]Say hello to Ampliatus, my dear friend in the Lord. [9]Say hello to Urbanus, our coworker in Christ, and my dear friend Stachys. [10]Say hello to Apelles, who is tried and true in Christ. Say hello to the members of the household of Aristobulus. [11]Say hello to my relative Herodion. Say hello to the members of the household of Narcissus who are in the Lord. [12]Say hello to Tryphaena and Tryphosa, who are workers for the Lord. Say hello to my dear friend Persis, who has worked hard in the Lord. [13]Say hello to Rufus, who is an outstanding believer, along with his mother and mine. [14]Say hello to Asyncritus, Phlegon, Hermes, Patrobas, Hermas, and the brothers and sisters who are with them. [15]Say hello to Philologus and Julia, Nereus and his sister, and Olympas, and all the saints who are with them. [16]Say hello to each other with a holy kiss. All the churches of Christ say hello to you.

Warning against divisions

[17]Brothers and sisters, I urge you to watch out for people who create divisions and problems against the teaching that you learned. Keep away from them. [18]People like that aren't serving the Lord. They are serving their own feelings. They deceive the hearts of innocent people with smooth talk and flattery. [19]The news of your obedience has reached everybody, so I'm happy for you. But I want you to be wise about what's good, and innocent about what's evil. [20]The God of peace will soon crush Satan[n] under your feet. The grace of our Lord Jesus Christ be with you.

Greetings from Paul's coworkers

[21]Timothy my coworker says hello to you, and Lucius, Jason, and Sosipater, my relatives. [22]I'm Tertius, and I'm writing this letter to you in the Lord—hello! [23]Gaius, who is host to me and to the whole church, says hello to you. Erastus the city treasurer says hello to you, along with our brother Quartus.[o]

Final prayer

[25]May the glory be to God who can strengthen you with my good news and the message that I preach about Jesus Christ. He can strengthen you with the announcement of the secret[p] that was kept quiet for a long time. [26]Now that secret is revealed through what the prophets wrote. It is made known to the Gentiles[q] in order to lead to their faithful obedience based on the command of the eternal God. [27]May the glory be to God, who alone is wise! May the glory be to him through Jesus Christ forever! Amen.

LIFE PRESERVER

What's unusual about this list of people? *Romans 16:1-16*

Romans is a letter written to the Christians in Rome. But Paul ended his letter by sending greetings to twenty-nine people. What's unusual is that nine of the people named are women. It's also a diverse group of people. Some of these people were family while others were leaders in the church. Some were slaves while others had been freed from slavery. In the early Roman church, Jesus' followers included anyone (man or woman, Jew or Gentile) who trusted in Jesus and his teachings.

[m]*Or is the firstfruits* [n]*Or the Adversary* [o]Critical editions of the Gk New Testament do not include 16:24 *The grace of our Lord Jesus Christ be with you.* [p]*Or mystery* [q]*Or all the Gentiles*

1 Corinthians

things YOU'LL DISCOVER

This letter from the apostle Paul to Christians living in the city of Corinth tells how people can grow spiritually, learning to love and help each other.

people YOU'LL MEET

Paul—a missionary for the church (1 Cor 1–15)
Apollos and Cephas (Peter)—other well-known Christian leaders (1 Cor 3)

places YOU'LL GO

Corinth (present-day Greece)

words YOU'LL REMEMBER

"Love is patient, love is kind, it isn't jealous, it doesn't brag, it isn't arrogant, it isn't rude, it doesn't seek its own advantage, it isn't irritable, it doesn't keep a record of complaints, it isn't happy with injustice, but it is happy with the truth" (1 Cor 13:4-6).

Corinth was an important city in Greece. Its harbor for ships made it an excellent place for doing business. It was home to a sports competition called the *Isthmian Games*, which was like the ancient Olympics. Military leaders liked to retire in this city of wealthy and smart people. But Corinth was also known for having temples to many gods and for widespread sin.

Acts 18:1-18 tells how Paul started the church in Corinth and taught the new Christians there for a year and a half. After he left, those Christians began to fight. They quarreled over who was most important. They argued about the right way to worship God.

Paul wrote this letter to correct his friends in Corinth. He reminded them that God is wiser than all of them. He told them to quit taking sides in unimportant arguments (1 Cor 1:10–3:23). He wrote about several kinds of serious sins (1 Cor 5–8). He also explained how God's Spirit gives spiritual gifts to help Christians grow (1 Cor 12; 14).

But Paul's most important message was *love*. First Corinthians contains well-known words you may hear in many different settings, including weddings. This frequently quoted passage begins, "Love is patient, love is kind" (1 Cor 13:4). Paul wrote these words to teach people about true love. This letter shows us how to get along and grow up together! ◊

Greeting

1 From Paul, called by God's will to be an apostle of Jesus Christ, and from Sosthenes our brother.

²To God's church that is in Corinth:

To those who have been made holy to God in Christ Jesus, who are called to be God's people.

Together with all those who call upon the name of our Lord Jesus Christ in every place—he's their Lord and ours!

³Grace to you and peace from God our Father and the Lord Jesus Christ.

Thanksgiving for the Corinthians

⁴I thank my God always for you, because of God's grace that was given to you in Christ Jesus. ⁵That is, you were made rich through him in everything: in all your communication and every kind of knowledge, ⁶in the same way that the testimony about Christ was confirmed with you. ⁷The result is that you aren't missing any spiritual gift while you wait for our Lord Jesus Christ to be revealed. ⁸He will also confirm your testimony about Christ until the end so that you will be blameless on the day of our Lord Jesus Christ. ⁹God is faithful, and you were called by him to partnership with his Son, Jesus Christ our Lord.

Rival groups in Corinth

¹⁰Now I encourage you, brothers and sisters, in the name of our Lord Jesus Christ: Agree with each other and don't be divided into rival groups. Instead, be restored with the same mind and the same purpose. ¹¹My brothers and sisters, Chloe's people gave me some information about you, that you're fighting with each other. ¹²What I mean is this: that each one of you says, "I belong to Paul," "I belong to Apollos," "I belong to Cephas," "I belong to Christ." ¹³Has Christ been divided? Was Paul crucified for you, or were you baptized in Paul's name? ¹⁴Thank God that I didn't baptize any of you, except Crispus and Gaius, ¹⁵so that nobody can say that you were baptized in my name! ¹⁶Oh, I baptized the house of Stephanas too. Otherwise, I don't know if I baptized anyone else. ¹⁷Christ didn't send me to baptize but to preach the good

news. And Christ didn't send me to preach the good news with clever words so that Christ's cross won't be emptied of its meaning.

did you **know?** Corinth was a port city that had a reputation for being wild. Traders from all over the world went through Corinth. And people from many different cultures and traditions lived in Corinth.

Human wisdom versus the cross

¹⁸The message of the cross is foolishness to those who are being destroyed. But it is the power of God for those of us who are being saved. ¹⁹It is written in scripture: *I will destroy the wisdom of the wise, and I will reject the intelligence of the intelligent.*[a] ²⁰Where are the wise? Where are the legal experts? Where are today's debaters? Hasn't God made the wisdom of the world foolish? ²¹In God's wisdom, he determined that the world wouldn't come to know him through its wisdom. Instead, God was pleased to save those who believe through the foolishness of preaching. ²²Jews ask for signs, and Greeks look for wisdom, ²³but we preach Christ crucified, which is a scandal to Jews and foolishness to Gentiles. ²⁴But to those who are called—both Jews and Greeks—Christ is God's power and God's wisdom. ²⁵This is because the foolishness of God is wiser than human wisdom, and the weakness of God is stronger than human strength.

²⁶Look at your situation when you were called, brothers and sisters! By ordinary human standards not many were wise, not many were powerful, not many were from the upper class. ²⁷But God chose what the world considers foolish to shame the wise. God chose what the world considers weak to shame the strong. ²⁸And God chose what the world considers low-class and low-life—what is considered to be nothing—to reduce what is considered to be something to nothing. ²⁹So no human being can brag in God's presence. ³⁰It is because of God that you are in Christ Jesus. He became wisdom from God for us. This means that he made us righteous and holy, and he delivered us.

Bet you can read this in 2 minutes. Ready, set, go!

[a]Isa 29:14

[31]This is consistent with what was written: *The one who brags should brag in the Lord!*[b]

2 When I came to you, brothers and sisters, I didn't come preaching God's secrets to you like I was an expert in speech or wisdom. [2]I had made up my mind not to think about anything while I was with you except Jesus Christ, and to preach him as crucified. [3]I stood in front of you with weakness, fear, and a lot of shaking. [4]My message and my preaching weren't presented with convincing wise words but with a demonstration of the Spirit and of power. [5]I did this so that your faith might not depend on the wisdom of people but on the power of God.

Definition of wisdom

[6]What we say is wisdom to people who are mature. It isn't a wisdom that comes from the present day or from today's leaders who are being reduced to nothing. [7]We talk about God's wisdom, which has been hidden as a secret. God determined this wisdom in advance, before time began, for our glory. [8]It is a wisdom that none of the present-day rulers have understood, because if they did understand it, they would never have crucified the Lord of glory! [9]But this is precisely

Memorize
1 Cor 2:9

what is written: *God has prepared things for those who love him that no eye has seen, or ear has heard, or that haven't crossed the mind of any human being.*[c] [10]God has revealed these things to us through the Spirit. The Spirit searches everything, including the depths of God. [11]Who knows a person's depths except their own spirit that lives in them? In the same way, no one has known the depths of God except God's Spirit. [12]We haven't received the world's spirit but God's Spirit so that we can know the things given to us by God. [13]These are the things we are talking about—not with words taught by human wisdom but with words taught by the Spirit—we are interpreting spiritual things to spiritual people. [14]But people who are unspiritual don't accept the things from God's Spirit. They are foolishness to them and can't be understood, because they can only be comprehended in a spiritual

way. [15]Spiritual people comprehend everything, but they themselves aren't understood by anyone. [16]*Who has known the mind of the Lord, who will advise him?*[d] But we have the mind of Christ.

Wisdom applied to divisions in the church

3 Brothers and sisters, I couldn't talk to you like spiritual people but like unspiritual people, like babies in Christ. [2]I gave you milk to drink instead of solid food, because you weren't up to it yet. [3]Now you are still not up to it because you are still unspiritual. When jealousy and fighting exist between you, aren't you unspiritual and living by human standards? [4]When someone says, "I belong to Paul," and someone else says, "I belong to Apollos," aren't you acting like people without the Spirit? [5]After all, what is Apollos? What is Paul? They are servants who helped you to believe. Each one had a role given to them by the Lord: [6]I planted, Apollos watered, but God made it grow. [7]Because of this, neither the one who plants nor the one who waters is anything, but the only one who is anything is God who makes it grow. [8]The one who plants and the one who waters work together, but each one will receive their own reward for their own labor. [9]We are God's coworkers, and you are God's field, God's building.

[10]I laid a foundation like a wise master builder according to God's grace that was

LIFE PRESERVER

What are "divisions in the church"? *1 Corinthians 3:1-9*

At times people in church face problems because they just don't get along with each other. They argue and refuse to listen or say "I'm sorry" to each other. Sometimes people follow different leaders. These actions cause people to take sides against each other, which creates a division. That was happening in the church at Corinth. Paul wanted people to know that he and Apollos were both God's servants. There was no competition between them. They worked together. Paul didn't want the Corinthian church to be divided for any reason. ◆

given to me, but someone else is building on top of it. Each person needs to pay attention to the way they build on it. [11]No one can lay any other foundation besides the one that is already laid, which is Jesus Christ. [12]So, whether someone builds on top of the foundation with gold, silver, precious stones, wood, grass, or hay, [13]each one's work will be clearly shown. The day will make it clear, because it will be revealed with fire—the fire will test the quality of each one's work. [14]If anyone's work survives, they'll get a reward. [15]But if anyone's work goes up in flames, they'll lose it. However, they themselves will be saved as if they had gone through a fire. [16]Don't you know that you are God's temple and God's Spirit lives in you? [17]If someone destroys God's temple, God will destroy that person, because God's temple is holy, which is what you are.

[18]Don't fool yourself. If some of you think they are worldly-wise, then they should become foolish so that they can become wise. [19]This world's wisdom is foolishness to God. As it is written, *He catches the wise in their cleverness.*[e] [20]And also, *The Lord knows that the thoughts of the wise are silly.*[f] [21]So then, no one should brag about human beings. Everything belongs to you—[22]Paul, Apollos, Cephas, the world, life, death, things in the present, things in the future—everything belongs to you, [23]but you belong to Christ, and Christ belongs to God.

Paul's role as an apostle

4 So a person should think about us this way—as servants of Christ and managers of God's secrets. [2]In this kind of situation, what is expected of a manager is that they prove to be faithful. [3]I couldn't care less if I'm judged by you or by any human court; I don't even judge myself. [4]I'm not aware of anything against me, but that doesn't make me innocent, because the Lord is the one who judges me. [5]So don't judge anything before the right time—wait until the Lord comes. He will bring things that are hidden in the dark to light, and he will make people's motivations public. Then there will be recognition for each person from God.

[6]Brothers and sisters, I have applied these things to myself and Apollos for your benefit. I've done this so that you can learn what it means not to go beyond what has been written and so none of you will become arrogant by supporting one of us against the other. [7]Who says that you are better than anyone else? What do you have that you didn't receive? And if you received it, then why are you bragging as if you didn't receive it? [8]You've been filled already! You've become rich already! You rule like kings without us! I wish you did rule so that we could be kings with you! [9]I suppose that God has shown that we apostles are at the end of the line. We are like prisoners sentenced to death, because we have become a spectacle in the world, both to angels and to humans. [10]We are fools for Christ, but you are wise through Christ! We are weak, but you are strong! You are honored, but we are dishonored! [11]Up to this very moment we are hungry, thirsty, wearing rags, abused, and homeless. [12]We work hard with our own hands. When we are insulted, we respond with a blessing; when we are harassed, we put up with it; [13]when our reputation is attacked, we are encouraging. We have become the scum of the earth, the waste that runs off everything, up to the present time.

[14]I'm not writing these things to make you ashamed but to

SAILBOAT

KINDNESS

How to Respond to Meanness

1 Corinthians 4:12

Christians are supposed to love each other and avoid arguments, even when it isn't easy to do. But how are we supposed to treat people who aren't Christians? Paul said Christians should have a kind attitude toward everyone. When people were unkind to the Christians in Corinth, Paul told them to say something good in response. When people tried to hurt them or their church, he said church members should ignore the mean things that were said and not fight back. Paul forgave people who didn't follow Jesus when they were unkind, because they didn't understand God's love. But he expected Christians to be kind and show love to all people. ♦

[e]Job 5:13 [f]Ps 94:11

warn you, since you are my loved children.
[15] You may have ten thousand mentors in Christ, but you don't have many fathers. I gave birth to you in Christ Jesus through the gospel, [16] so I encourage you to follow my example. [17] This is why I've sent Timothy to you; he's my loved and trusted child in the Lord; he'll remind you about my way of life in Christ Jesus. He'll teach the same way as I teach everywhere in every church. [18] Some have become arrogant as if I'm not coming to see you. [19] But, if the Lord is willing, I'll come to you soon. Then I won't focus on what these arrogant people say, but I'll find out what power they possess. [20] God's kingdom isn't about words but about power. [21] Which do you want? Should I come to you with a big stick to punish you, or with love and a gentle spirit?

Confronting sexual immorality in the church

5 Everyone has heard that there is sexual immorality among you. This is a type of immorality that isn't even heard of among the Gentiles—a man is having sex with his father's wife! [2] And you're proud of yourselves instead of being so upset that the one who did this thing is expelled from your community. [3] Though I'm absent physically, I'm present in the spirit and I've already judged the man who did this as if I were present. [4] When you meet together in the name of our Lord Jesus, I'll be present in spirit with the power of our Lord Jesus. [5] At that time we need to hand this man over to Satan to destroy his human weakness so that his spirit might be saved on the day of the Lord.

[6] Your bragging isn't good! Don't you know that a tiny grain of yeast makes a whole batch of dough rise? [7] Clean out the old yeast so you can be a new batch of dough, given that you're supposed to be unleavened bread. Christ our Passover lamb has been sacrificed, [8] so let's celebrate the feast with the unleavened bread of honesty and truth, not with old yeast or with the yeast of evil and wickedness.

[9] I wrote to you in my earlier letter not to associate with sexually immoral people. [10] But I wasn't talking about the sexually immoral people in the outside world by any means—or

the greedy, or the swindlers, or people who worship false gods—otherwise, you would have to leave the world entirely! [11] But now I'm writing to you not to associate with anyone who calls themselves "brother" or "sister" who is sexually immoral, greedy, someone who worships false gods, an abusive person, a drunk, or a swindler. Don't even eat with anyone like this. [12] What do I care about judging outsiders? Isn't it your job to judge insiders? [13] God will judge outsiders. *Expel the evil one from among you!*[g]

Confronting lawsuits in the church

6 When someone in your assembly has a legal case against another member, do they dare to take it to court to be judged by people who aren't just, instead of by God's people? [2] Or don't you know that God's people will judge the world? If the world is to be judged by you, are you incompetent to judge trivial cases? [3] Don't you know that we will judge angels? Why not ordinary things? [4] So then if you have ordinary lawsuits, do you appoint people as judges who aren't respected by the church? [5] I'm saying this because you should be ashamed of yourselves! Isn't there one person among you who is wise enough to pass judgment between believers? [6] But instead, does a brother or sister have a lawsuit against another brother or sister, and do they do this in front of unbelievers? [7] The fact that you have lawsuits against each other means that you've already lost your case. Why not be wronged instead? Why not be cheated? [8] But instead you are doing wrong and cheating—and you're doing it to your own brothers and sisters.

[9] Don't you know that people who are unjust won't inherit God's kingdom? Don't be deceived. Those who are sexually immoral, those who worship false gods, adulterers, both participants in same-sex intercourse,[h] [10] thieves, the greedy, drunks, abusive people, and swindlers won't inherit God's kingdom. [11] That is what some of you used to be! But you were washed clean, you were made holy to God, and you were made right with God in the name of the Lord Jesus Christ and in the Spirit of our God.

[g] Deut 17:7; 19:19; 22:21, 24; 24:7   [h] Or *submissive and dominant male sexual partners*

Avoid sexual immorality

¹²I have the freedom to do anything, but not everything is helpful. I have the freedom to do anything, but I won't be controlled by anything. ¹³Food is for the stomach and the stomach is for food, and yet God will do away with both. The body isn't for sexual immorality but for the Lord, and the Lord is for

Paul believed it was okay for people to be married or to be single. Most people in that culture were married. However, when Paul wrote this letter, Christians were picked on, hurt, and sometimes killed for believing in Jesus. Paul knew it was easier to stand up for Jesus if a Christian was risking only his or her own life and not the life of a spouse.

the body. ¹⁴God has raised the Lord and will raise us through his power. ¹⁵Don't you know that your bodies are parts of Christ? So then, should I take parts of Christ and make them a part of someone who is sleeping around?ⁱ No way! ¹⁶Don't you know that anyone who is joined to someone who is sleeping around is one body with that person? The scripture says, *The two will become one flesh.*ʲ ¹⁷The one who is joined to the Lord is one spirit with him. ¹⁸Avoid sexual immorality! Every sin that a person can do is committed outside the body, except those who engage in sexual immorality commit sin against their own bodies. ¹⁹Or don't you know that your body is a temple of the Holy Spirit who is in you? Don't you know that you have the Holy Spirit from God, and you don't belong to yourselves? ²⁰You have been bought and paid for, so honor God with your body.

Memorize
1 Cor 6:19-20

Marriage and celibacy

7Now, about what you wrote: "It's good for a man not to have sex with a woman." ²Each man should have his own wife, and each woman should have her own husband because of sexual immorality. ³The husband should meet his wife's sexual needs, and the wife should do the same for her husband. ⁴The wife doesn't have authority over her

own body, but the husband does. Likewise, the husband doesn't have authority over his own body, but the wife does. ⁵Don't refuse to meet each other's needs unless you both agree for a short period of time to devote yourselves to prayer. Then come back together again so that Satan might not tempt you because of your lack of self-control. ⁶I'm saying this to give you permission; it's not a command. ⁷I wish all people were like me, but each has a particular gift from God: one has this gift, and another has that one.

⁸I'm telling those who are single and widows that it's good for them to stay single like me. ⁹But if they can't control themselves, they should get married, because it's better to marry than to burn with passion. ¹⁰I'm passing on the Lord's command to those who are married: A wife shouldn't leave her husband, ¹¹but if she does leave him, then she should stay single or be reconciled to her husband. And a man shouldn't divorce his wife.

¹²I'm telling everyone else (the Lord didn't say this specifically): If a believer has a wife who doesn't believe, and she agrees to live with him, then he shouldn't divorce her. ¹³If a woman has a husband who doesn't believe and he agrees to live with her, then she shouldn't divorce him. ¹⁴The husband who doesn't believe belongs to God because of his wife, and the wife who doesn't believe belongs to God because of her husband. Otherwise, your children would be contaminated by the world, but now they are spiritually set apart. ¹⁵But if a spouse who doesn't believe chooses to leave, then let them leave. The brother or sister isn't tied down in these circumstances. God has called you to peace. ¹⁶How do you know as a wife if you will save your husband? Or how do you know as a husband if you will save your wife?

¹⁷Nevertheless, each person should live the kind of life that the Lord assigned when he called each one. This is what I teach in all the churches. ¹⁸If someone was circumcised when called, he shouldn't try to reverse it. If someone wasn't circumcised when he was called, he shouldn't be circumcised. ¹⁹Circumcision is nothing; not being circumcised

---

ⁱOr *a prostitute;* commonly, women who sell their bodies to multiple sex partners but includes those who are sexually immoral
ʲGen 2:24

is nothing. What matters is keeping God's commandments. [20]Each person should stay in the situation they were in when they were called. [21]If you were a slave when you were called, don't let it bother you. But if you are actually able to be free, take advantage of the opportunity. [22]Anyone who was a slave when they were called by the Lord has the status of being the Lord's free person. In the same way, anyone who was a free person when they were called is Christ's slave. [23]You were bought and paid for. Don't become slaves of people. [24]So then, brothers and sisters, each of you should stay with God in the situation you were in when you were called.

[25]I don't have a command from the Lord about people who have never been married,[k] but I'll give you my opinion as someone you can trust because of the Lord's mercy. [26]So I think this advice is good because of the present crisis: Stay as you are. [27]If you are married, don't get a divorce. If you are divorced, don't try to find a spouse. [28]But if you do marry, you haven't sinned; and if someone who hasn't been married gets married, they haven't sinned. But married people will have a hard time, and I'm trying to spare you that. [29]This is what I'm saying, brothers and sisters: The time has drawn short. From now on, those who have wives should be like people who don't have them. [30]Those who are sad should be like people who aren't crying. Those who are happy should be like people who aren't happy. Those who buy something should be like people who don't have possessions. [31]Those who use the world should be like people who aren't preoccupied with it, because this world in its present form is passing away.

[32]I want you to be free from concerns. A man who isn't married is concerned about the Lord's concerns—how he can please the Lord. [33]But a married man is concerned about the world's concerns—how he can please his wife. [34]His attention is divided. A woman who isn't married or who is a virgin is concerned about the Lord's concerns so that she can be dedicated to God in both body and spirit. But a married woman is concerned about the world's concerns—how she can please her

husband. [35]I'm saying this for your own advantage. It's not to restrict you but rather to promote effective and consistent service to the Lord without distraction.

[36]If someone thinks he is acting inappropriately toward an unmarried woman whom he knows, and if he has strong feelings and it seems like the right thing to do, he should do what he wants—he's not sinning—they should get married. [37]But if a man stands firm in his decision, and doesn't feel the pressure, but has his own will under control, he does right if he decides in his own heart not to marry the woman. [38]Therefore, the one who marries the unmarried woman does right, and the one who doesn't get married will do even better. [39]A woman is obligated to stay in her marriage as long as her husband is alive. But if her husband dies, she is free to marry whomever she wants, only it should be a believer in the Lord. [40]But in my opinion, she will be happier if she stays the way she is. And I think that I have God's Spirit too.

Meat sacrificed to false gods

8 Now concerning meat that has been sacrificed to a false god: We know that we all have knowledge. Knowledge makes people arrogant, but love builds people up. [2]If anyone thinks they know something, they don't yet know as much as they should know. [3]But if someone loves God, then they are known by God.

[4]So concerning the actual food involved in these sacrifices to false gods, we know that a false god isn't anything in this world, and that there is no God except for the one God. [5]Granted, there are so-called "gods," in heaven and on the earth, as there are many gods and many lords. [6]However, for us believers,

There is one God the Father.
All things come from him,
and we belong to him.
And there is one Lord Jesus Christ.
All things exist through him,
and we live through him.

[7]But not everybody knows this. Some are eating this food as though it really is food sacrificed to a real idol, because they were used to idol worship until now. Their conscience

[k]Or virgins

is weak because it has been damaged. [8]Food won't bring us close to God. We're not missing out if we don't eat, and we don't have any advantage if we do eat. [9]But watch out or else this freedom of yours might be a problem for those who are weak. [10]Suppose someone sees you (the person who has knowledge) eating in an idol's temple. Won't the person with a weak conscience be encouraged to eat the meat sacrificed to false gods? [11]The weak brother or sister for whom Christ died is destroyed by your knowledge. [12]You sin against Christ if you sin against your brothers and sisters and hurt their weak consciences this way. [13]This is why, if food causes the downfall of my brother or sister, I won't eat meat ever again, or else I may cause my brother or sister to fall.

Waiving rights for the gospel

9 Am I not free? Am I not an apostle? Haven't I seen Jesus our Lord? Aren't you my work in the Lord? [2]If I'm not an apostle to others, at least I am to you! You are the seal that shows I'm an apostle. [3]This is my defense against those who criticize me. [4]Don't we have the right to eat and drink? [5]Don't we have the right to travel with a wife who believes like the rest of the apostles, the Lord's brothers, and Cephas? [6]Or is it only I and Barnabas who don't have the right to not work for our living? [7]Who joins the army and pays their own way? Who plants a vineyard and doesn't eat its fruit? Who shepherds a flock and doesn't drink its milk? [8]I'm not saying these things just based on common sense, am I? Doesn't the Law itself say these things? [9]In Moses' Law it's written: *You will not muzzle the ox when it is threshing.*[1] Is God worried about oxen, [10]or did he say this entirely for our sake? It was written for our sake because the one who plows and the one who threshes should each do so with the hope of sharing the produce. [11]If we sowed spiritual things in you, is it so much to ask to harvest some material things from you?

[12]If others have these rights over you, don't we deserve them all the more? However, we haven't made use of this right, but we put up

with everything so we don't put any obstacle in the way of the gospel of Christ. [13]Don't you know that those who serve in the temple get to eat food from the temple, and those who serve at the altar share part of what is sacrificed on the altar? [14]In the same way, the Lord commanded that those who preach the gospel should get their living from the gospel. [15]But I haven't taken advantage of this. And I'm not writing this so that it will be done for me. It's better for me to die than to lose my right to brag about this! [16]If I preach the gospel, I have no reason to brag, since I'm obligated to do it. I'm in trouble if I don't preach the gospel. [17]If I do this voluntarily, I get rewarded for it. But if I'm forced to do it, then I've been charged with a responsibility. [18]What reward do I get? That when I preach, I offer the good news free of charge. That's why I don't use the rights to which I'm entitled through the gospel.

[19]Although I'm free from all people, I make myself a slave to all people, to recruit more of them. [20]I act like a Jew to the Jews, so I can recruit Jews. I act like I'm under the Law to those under the Law, so I can recruit those who are under the Law (though I myself am not under the Law). [21]I act like I'm outside the Law to those who are outside the Law, so I can recruit those outside the Law (though I'm not outside the law of God but rather under the law of Christ). [22]I act weak to the weak, so I can recruit the weak. I have become all things to all people, so I could save some by all possible means. [23]All the things I do are for the sake of the gospel, so I can be a partner with it.

[24]Don't you know that all the runners in the stadium run, but only one gets the prize? So run to win. [25]Everyone who competes practices self-discipline in everything. The runners do this to get a crown of leaves that shrivel up and die, but we do it to receive a crown that never dies. [26]So now this is how I run—not without a clear goal in sight. I fight like a boxer in the ring, not like someone who is shadowboxing. [27]Rather, I'm landing punches on my own body and subduing it like a slave. I do this to be sure that I myself won't be disqualified after preaching to others.

[1]Deut 25:4

Warning from the wilderness generation

10 Brothers and sisters, I want you to be sure of the fact that our ancestors were all under the cloud and they all went through the sea. ²All were baptized into Moses in the cloud and in the sea. ³All ate the same spiritual food, ⁴and all drank the same spiritual drink. They drank from a spiritual rock that followed them, and the rock was Christ. ⁵However, God was unhappy with most of them, and they were struck down in the wilderness. ⁶These things were examples for us, so we won't crave evil things like they did. ⁷Don't worship false gods like some of them did, as it is written, *The people sat down to eat and drink and they got up to play.*ᵐ ⁸Let's not practice sexual immorality, like some of them did, and twenty-three thousand died in one day. ⁹Let's not test Christ, like some of them did, and were killed by the snakes. ¹⁰Let's not grumble, like some of them did, and were killed by the destroyer. ¹¹These things happened to them as an example and were written as a warning for us to whom the end of time has come. ¹²So those who think they are standing need to watch out or else they may fall. ¹³No temptation has seized you that isn't common for people. But God is faithful. He won't allow you to be tempted beyond your abilities. Instead, with the temptation,

UMBRELLA
TEMPTED

We Can Do the Right Thing
1 Corinthians 10:13

Temptation is that feeling you get when you really want to do something you know is the wrong thing to do. Some people are tempted to eat certain foods that aren't good for them. Other people want to do things that might hurt themselves or others. Being tempted to do something isn't wrong. But giving in to it leads to wrong actions. Paul said that God will keep us from doing the wrong thing when we're tempted if we let God help us with the temptation. Just because we think about doing something, we don't have to do it. Paul also said that no matter what temptation we face, it's nothing new. God is cheering for us to pass every challenge we face. ◊

God will also supply a way out so that you will be able to endure it.

Avoid false gods to glorify God

¹⁴So then, my dear friends, run away from the worship of false gods! ¹⁵I'm talking to you like you are sensible people. Think about what I'm saying. ¹⁶Isn't the cup of blessing that we bless a sharing in the blood of Christ? Isn't the loaf of bread that we break a sharing in the body of Christ? ¹⁷Since there is one loaf of bread, we who are many are one body, because we all share the one loaf of bread. ¹⁸Look at the people of Israel. Don't those who eat the sacrifices share from the altar? ¹⁹What am I saying then? That food sacrificed to a false god is anything, or that a false god is anything? ²⁰No, but this kind of sacrifice is sacrificed to demons and not to God. I don't want you to be sharing in demons. ²¹You can't drink the cup of the Lord and the cup of demons; you can't participate in the table of the Lord and the table of demons. ²²Or should we make the Lord jealous? We aren't stronger than he is, are we?

²³Everything is permitted, but everything isn't beneficial. Everything is permitted, but everything doesn't build others up. ²⁴No one should look out for their own advantage, but

UMBRELLA
STRESSED OUT

Run to Win *1 Corinthians 9:24-25*

Many people enjoy watching sporting events to see which team or athlete wins. Sports were popular even when Paul lived. He compared being a Christian to an athlete who runs in a race. Only one runner can get first place, and it takes hard work to win. An athlete becomes a winner by not giving up. The same kind of determination can help us choose to do things God's way. Wanting to do the right thing for God shows how much we love God. We keep trying hard, even when we're tired or stressed out. Just like an athlete practices every day, we can read the Bible, pray, talk to others who are trying to follow Jesus, and be ready to work hard in every situation. ◊

ᵐExod 32:6

they should look out for each other. ²⁵Eat everything that is sold in the marketplace, without asking questions about it because of your conscience. ²⁶*The earth and all that is in it belong to the Lord.*ⁿ ²⁷If an unbeliever invites you to eat with them and you want to go, eat whatever is served, without asking questions because of your conscience. ²⁸But if someone says to you, "This meat was sacrificed in a temple," then don't eat it for the sake of the one who told you and for the sake of conscience. ²⁹Now when I say "conscience" I don't mean yours but the other person's. Why should my freedom be judged by someone else's conscience? ³⁰If I participate with gratitude, why should I be blamed for food I thank God for? ³¹So, whether you eat or drink or whatever you do, you should do it all for God's glory. ³²Don't offend either Jews or Greeks, or God's church. ³³This is the same thing that I do. I please everyone in everything I do. I don't look out for my own advantage, but I look out for many people so that they can be saved. ¹Follow my example, just like I follow Christ's.

Appropriate dress in worship

²I praise you because you remember all my instructions, and you hold on to the traditions exactly as I handed them on to you. ³Now I want you to know that the head of every man is Christ, and the head of the woman is the man, and the head of Christ is God. ⁴Every man who prays or prophesies with his head covered shames his head. ⁵Every woman who prays or prophesies with her head uncovered disgraces her head. It is the same thing as having her head shaved. ⁶If a woman doesn't cover her head, then she should have her hair cut off. If it is disgraceful for a woman to have short hair or to be shaved, then she should keep her head covered. ⁷A man shouldn't have his head covered, because he is the image and glory of God; but the woman is man's glory. ⁸Man didn't have his origin from woman, but woman from man; ⁹and man wasn't created for the sake of the woman, but the woman for the sake of the man. ¹⁰Because of this a woman should have authority over her head, because of the angels. ¹¹However, woman isn't independent from man, and man isn't independent from woman in the Lord. ¹²As woman came from man so also man comes from woman. But everything comes from God. ¹³Judge for yourselves: Is it appropriate for a woman to pray to God with her head uncovered? ¹⁴Doesn't nature itself teach you that if a man has long hair, it is a disgrace to him; ¹⁵but if a woman has long hair, it is her glory? This is because her long hair is given to her for a covering. ¹⁶But if someone wants to argue about this, we don't have such a custom, nor do God's churches.

The community meal

¹⁷Now I don't praise you as I give the following instruction because when you meet together, it does more harm than good. ¹⁸First of all, when you meet together as a church, I hear that there are divisions among you, and I partly believe it. ¹⁹It's necessary that there are groups among you, to make it clear who is genuine. ²⁰So when you get together in one place, it isn't to eat the Lord's meal. ²¹Each of you goes ahead and eats a private meal. One person goes hungry while another is drunk. ²²Don't you have houses to eat and drink in? Or do you look down on God's churches and humiliate those who have nothing? What can I say to you? Will I praise you? No, I don't praise you in this.

²³I received a tradition from the Lord, which I also handed on to you: on the night on which he was betrayed, the Lord Jesus took bread. ²⁴After giving thanks, he broke

LIFE PRESERVER

Why does the Bible talk about what to wear in worship? *1 Corinthians 11:2-16*

This is a hard passage to understand because it talks about customs that are very different from how we live today. Christians in Corinth were concerned about what women wore to worship. In that culture it was a custom for women to cover their heads in worship. Paul reminded the Corinthian Christians of this custom. When you look around in church today, you know most Christians don't follow this custom. However, people of other cultures still cover their heads as part of their faith. ◖

it and said, "This is my body, which is for you; do this to remember me." ²⁵He did the same thing with the cup, after they had eaten, saying, "This cup is the new covenant in my blood. Every time you drink it, do this to remember me." ²⁶Every time you eat this bread and drink this cup, you broadcast the death of the Lord until he comes.

²⁷This is why those who eat the bread or drink the cup of the Lord inappropriately will be guilty of the Lord's body and blood. ²⁸Each individual should test himself or herself, and eat from the bread and drink from the cup in that way. ²⁹Those who eat and drink without correctly understanding the body are eating and drinking their own judgment. ³⁰Because of this, many of you are weak and sick, and quite a few have died. ³¹But if we had judged ourselves, we wouldn't be judged. ³²However, we are disciplined by the Lord when we are judged so that we won't be judged and condemned along with the whole world. ³³For these reasons, my brothers and sisters, when you get together to eat, wait for each other. ³⁴If some of you are hungry, they should eat at home so that getting together doesn't lead to judgment. I will give directions about the other things when I come.

Spiritual gifts

12Brothers and sisters, I don't want you to be ignorant about spiritual gifts. ²You know that when you were Gentiles you were often misled by false gods that can't even speak. ³So I want to make it clear to you that no one says, "Jesus is cursed!" when speaking by God's Spirit, and no one can say, "Jesus is Lord," except by the Holy Spirit. ⁴There are different spiritual gifts but the same Spirit; ⁵and there are different ministries and the same Lord; ⁶and there are different activities but the same God who produces all of them in everyone. ⁷A demonstration of the Spirit is given to each person for the common good. ⁸A word of wisdom is given by the Spirit to one person, a word of knowledge to another according to the same Spirit, ⁹faith to still another by the same Spirit, gifts of healing to another in the one Spirit, ¹⁰performance

did you know? The practice of eating a piece of bread and drinking juice at church is called *Communion* or the *Lord's Supper*. A minister often says these words from 1 Corinthians when Communion is offered at church. The word *communion* means "the act of sharing." We celebrate our relationship with God through this act of sharing food together.

of miracles to another, prophecy to another, the ability to tell spirits apart to another, different kinds of tongues° to another, and the interpretation of the tongues to another. ¹¹All these things are produced by the one and same Spirit who gives what he wants to each person.

¹²Christ is just like the human body—a body is a unit and has many parts; and all the parts of the body are one body, even though there are many. ¹³We were all baptized by one Spirit into one body, whether Jew or Greek, or slave or free, and we all were given one Spirit to drink. ¹⁴Certainly the body isn't one part but many. ¹⁵If the foot says, "I'm not part of the body because I'm not a hand," does that mean it's not part of the body? ¹⁶If the ear says, "I'm not part of the body because I'm not an eye," does that mean it's not part of the body? ¹⁷If the whole body were an eye, what would happen to the hearing? And if the whole body were an ear, what would happen to the sense of smell? ¹⁸But as it is, God has placed each one of the parts in the body just like he wanted. ¹⁹If all were one and the same body part, what would happen to the body? ²⁰But as it is, there are many parts but one body. ²¹So the eye can't say to the hand, "I don't need you," or in turn, the head can't say to the feet, "I don't need you." ²²Instead, the parts of the body that people think are the weakest are the most necessary. ²³The parts of the body that we think are less honorable are the ones we honor the most. The private parts of our body that aren't presentable are the ones that are given the most dignity. ²⁴The parts of our body that are presentable don't need this. But God has put the body together, giving greater honor to the part with less honor

°Or *ecstatic speech* or *languages* could be used for *tongues* or *tongue* throughout chaps 12–14.

LIFE PRESERVER

What are "spiritual gifts"?
1 Corinthians 12

Every part of our body helps the rest of our body in some way. Big toes help us to have balance. Thumbs help us grasp things. Spleens help keep our blood clean. Earlobes help catch sound waves and direct the noises to our eardrums. Paul wrote that this is similar to being a Christian. There are many kinds of people in a church, and each person has different talents or gifts. Paul wanted to make it clear that no one person or gift is better than another. We need each other!

Today we're thankful that some people teach and other people play music in church. We're glad to have people who can cook and people who like to visit anyone who is sick. Together we are "the body of Christ" (1 Cor 12:27). ◆

25so that there won't be division in the body and so the parts might have mutual concern for each other. 26If one part suffers, all the parts suffer with it; if one part gets the glory, all the parts celebrate with it. 27You are the body of Christ and parts of each other. 28In the church, God has appointed first apostles, second prophets, third teachers, then miracles, then gifts of healing, the ability to help others, leadership skills, different kinds of tongues. 29All aren't apostles, are they? All aren't prophets, are they? All aren't teachers, are they? All don't perform miracles, do they? 30All don't have gifts of healing, do they? All don't speak in different tongues, do they? All don't interpret, do they? 31Use your ambition to try to get the greater gifts. And I'm going to show you an even better way.

Love: the universal spiritual gift

13 If I speak in tongues of human beings and of angels but I don't have love, I'm a clanging gong or a clashing cymbal. 2If I have the gift of prophecy and I know all the mysteries and everything else, and if I have such complete faith that I can move mountains but I don't have love, I'm nothing. 3If I give away everything that I have and hand over my own body to feel good about what I've done but I don't have love, I receive no benefit whatsoever.

Bet you can read this in 5 minutes. **Ready, set, go!**

4Love is patient, love is kind, it isn't jealous, it doesn't brag, it isn't arrogant, 5it isn't rude, it doesn't seek its own advantage, it isn't irritable, it doesn't keep a record of complaints, 6it isn't happy with injustice, but it is happy with the truth. 7Love puts up with all things, trusts in all things, hopes for all things, endures all things.

Memorize 1 Cor 13:4-6

8Love never fails. As for prophecies, they will be brought to an end. As for tongues, they will stop. As for knowledge, it will be brought to an end. 9We know in part and we prophesy in part; 10but when the perfect comes, what is partial will be brought to an end. 11When I was a child, I used to speak like a child, reason like a child, think like a child. But now that I have become a man, I've put an end to childish things. 12Now we see a reflection in a mirror; then we will see face-to-face. Now I know partially, but then I will know completely in the same way that I have been completely known. 13Now faith, hope, and love remain—these three things—and the greatest of these is love.

Spiritual gifts and church order

14 Pursue love, and use your ambition to try to get spiritual gifts but especially so that you might prophesy. 2This is because those who speak in a tongue don't speak to people but to God; no one understands it—they speak mysteries by the Spirit. 3Those who prophesy speak to people, building them up, and giving them encouragement and comfort. 4People who speak in a tongue build up themselves; those who prophesy build up the church. 5I wish that all of you spoke in tongues, but I'd rather you could prophesy. Those who prophesy are more important than those who speak in tongues, unless they are able to interpret them so that the church might be built up. 6After all, brothers and sisters, if I come to you speaking in tongues, how will I help you unless I speak to you with a revelation, some knowledge, a prophecy, or a teaching? 7Likewise, things that aren't alive like a harp or a lyre can make a sound, but if there aren't different notes in the sounds they make, how will the tune from the harp or the lyre be recognized? 8And if a trumpet call is unrecognizable, then who will prepare for battle? [9]It's the same way with you: If you don't use language that is easy to understand when you speak in a tongue, then how will anyone understand what is said? [10]It will be as if you are speaking into the air! There are probably many language families in the world, and none of them are without meaning. [11]So if I don't know the meaning of the language, then I will be like a foreigner to those who speak it, and they will be like foreigners to me. [12]The same holds true for you: since you are ambitious for spiritual gifts, use your ambition to try to work toward being the best at building up the church.

[13]Therefore, those who speak in a tongue should pray to be able to interpret. [14]If I pray in a tongue, my spirit prays but my mind isn't productive. [15]What should I do? I'll pray in the Spirit, but I'll pray with my mind too; I'll sing a psalm in the Spirit, but I'll sing the psalm with my mind too. [16]After all, if you praise God in the Spirit, how will the people who aren't trained in that language say "Amen!" to your

thanksgiving, when they don't know what you are saying? [17]You may offer a beautiful prayer of thanksgiving, but the other person is not being built up. [18]I thank God that I speak in tongues more than all of you. [19]But in the church I'd rather speak five words in my right mind than speak thousands of words in a tongue so that I can teach others.

[20]Brothers and sisters, don't be like children in the way you think. Well, be babies when it comes to evil, but be adults in your thinking. [21]In the Law it is written: *I will speak to this people with foreign languages and foreigners' lips, but they will not even listen to me this way,*[p] says the Lord. [22]So then, tongues are a sign for those who don't believe, not for those who believe. But prophecy is a sign for believers, not for those who don't believe. [23]So suppose that the whole church is meeting and everyone is speaking in tongues. If people come in who are outsiders or unbelievers, won't they say that you are out of your minds? [24]But if everyone is

[p]Isa 28:11-12

Love Is the Main Thing *1 Corinthians 13*

Sometimes in life we get focused on the good things we're doing and forget why we're doing them. We work really hard to get an A. We practice every night to shoot better baskets, strum better chords, or run a little bit faster. We work on a mission project at church and go to Bible studies. Before we know it, we're busy doing a lot of good things. But Paul wrote that if we do all those things but don't love people, then all of those things mean absolutely nothing. If we don't love each other above everything else, then the way we use our gifts and talents is not important.

Love is the main thing. When we get confused about what we're supposed to do or who we're supposed to be, love is the main thing. When we forget what our gifts are or how we're supposed to use them, love is the main thing. Every single thing we do is supposed to come from a heart of love that we have for each other. Love is the main thing for people who follow Jesus.

Why do you think love is the greatest thing?

How can you love others more this week?

prophesying when an unbeliever or outsider comes in, they are tested by all and called to account by all. ²⁵The secrets of their hearts are brought to light. When that happens, they will fall on their faces and worship God, proclaiming out loud that truly God is among you!

²⁶What is the outcome of this, brothers and sisters? When you meet together, each one has a psalm, a teaching, a revelation, a tongue, or an interpretation. All these things must be done to build up the church. ²⁷If some speak in a tongue, then let two or at most three speak, one at a time, and someone must interpret. ²⁸However, if there is no interpreter, then they should keep quiet in the meeting. They should speak privately to themselves and to God. ²⁹In the case of prophets, let two or three speak and have the rest evaluate what is said. ³⁰And if some revelation comes to someone else who is sitting down, the first one should be quiet. ³¹You can all prophesy one at a time so that everyone can learn and be encouraged. ³²The spirits of prophets are under the control of the prophets. ³³God isn't a God of disorder but of peace. Like in all the churches of God's people, ³⁴the women should be quiet during the meeting. They are not allowed to talk. Instead, they need to get under control, just as the Law says. ³⁵If they want to learn something, they should ask their husbands at home. It is disgraceful for a woman to talk during the meeting.

³⁶Did the word of God originate with you? Has it come only to you? ³⁷If anyone thinks that they are prophets or "spiritual people," then let them recognize that what I'm writing to you is the Lord's command. ³⁸If someone doesn't recognize this, they aren't recognized. ³⁹So then, brothers and sisters, use your ambition to try to get the gift of prophecy, but don't prevent speaking in tongues. ⁴⁰Everything should be done with dignity and in proper order.

The resurrection

15 Brothers and sisters, I want to call your attention to the good news that I preached to you, which you also received and in which you stand. ²You are being saved through it if you hold on to the message I preached to you, unless somehow you believed it for nothing. ³I passed on to you as most important what I also received: Christ died for our sins in line with the scriptures, ⁴he was buried, and he rose on the third day in line with the scriptures. ⁵He appeared to Cephas, then to the Twelve, ⁶and then he appeared to more than five hundred brothers and sisters at once—most of them are still alive to this day, though some have died. ⁷Then he appeared to James, then to all the apostles, ⁸and last of all he appeared to me, as if I were born at the wrong time. ⁹I'm the least important of the apostles. I don't deserve to be called an apostle, because I harassed God's church. ¹⁰I am what I am by God's grace, and God's grace hasn't been for nothing. In fact, I have worked harder than all the others—that is, it wasn't me but the grace of God that is with me. ¹¹So then, whether you heard the message from me or them, this is what we preach and this is what you have believed.

¹²So if the message that is preached says that Christ has been raised from the dead, then how can some of you say, "There's no resurrection of the dead"? ¹³If there's no resurrection of the dead, then Christ hasn't been raised either. ¹⁴If Christ hasn't been raised, then our preaching is useless and your faith is useless. ¹⁵We are found to be false witnesses about God, because we testified against God that he raised Christ, when he didn't raise him if it's the case that the dead aren't raised. ¹⁶If the dead aren't raised, then Christ hasn't been raised either. ¹⁷If Christ hasn't been raised, then your faith is worthless; you are still in your sins, ¹⁸and what's more, those who have died in Christ are gone forever. ¹⁹If we have a hope in Christ only in this life, then we deserve to be pitied more than anyone else.

²⁰But in fact Christ has been raised from the dead. He's the first crop of the harvest⁹ of those who have died. ²¹Since death came through a human being, the resurrection of the dead came through one too. ²²In the same way that everyone dies in Adam, so also everyone will be given life in Christ. ²³Each event will happen in the right order: Christ, the first crop of the harvest,ʳ then those who belong to Christ at his coming, ²⁴and then the

---

⁹Or *firstfruits* ʳOr *firstfruits*

end, when Christ hands over the kingdom to God the Father, when he brings every form of rule, every authority and power to an end. [25]It is necessary for him to rule until *he puts all enemies under his feet.*[s] [26]Death is the last enemy to be brought to an end, [27]since he has brought everything under control under his feet. When it says that everything has been brought under his control, this clearly means everything except for the one who placed everything under his control. [28]But when all things have been brought under his control, then the Son himself will also be under the control of the one who gave him control over everything so that God may be all in all.

[29]Otherwise, what are those who are getting baptized for the dead doing? If the dead aren't raised, then why are they being baptized for them? [30]And what about us? Why are we in danger all day every day? [31]Brothers and sisters, I swear by the pride I have in you in Christ Jesus our Lord, I'm facing death every day. [32]From a human point of view, what good does it do me if I fought wild animals in Ephesus? If the dead aren't raised, *let's eat and drink because tomorrow we'll die.*[t] [33]Don't be deceived, bad company corrupts good character. [34]Sober up by acting like you should and don't sin. Some of you are ignorant about God—I say this because you should be ashamed of yourselves!

[35]But someone will say, "How are the dead raised? What kind of body will they have when they come back?" [36]Look, fool! When you put a seed into the ground, it doesn't come back to life unless it dies. [37]What you put in the ground doesn't have the shape that it will have, but it's a bare grain of wheat or some other seed. [38]God gives it the sort of shape that he chooses, and he gives each of the seeds its own shape. [39]All flesh isn't alike. Humans have one kind of flesh, animals have another kind of flesh, birds have another kind of flesh, and fish have another kind. [40]There are heavenly bodies and earthly bodies. The heavenly bodies have one kind of glory, and the earthly bodies have another kind of glory. [41]The sun has one kind of glory, the moon has another kind of glory, and the stars have another kind of glory (but one star is different from another star in its glory). [42]It's the same with the resurrection of the dead: a rotting body is put into the ground, but what is raised won't ever decay. [43]It's degraded when it's put into the ground, but it's raised in glory. It's weak when it's put into the ground, but it's raised in power. [44]It's a physical body when it's put into the ground, but it's raised as a spiritual body.

If there's a physical body, there's also a spiritual body. [45]So it is also written, *The first human, Adam, became a living person,*[u] and the last Adam became a spirit that gives life. [46]But the physical body comes first, not the spiritual one—the spiritual body comes afterward. [47]The first human was from the earth made from dust; the second human is from heaven. [48]The nature of the person made of dust is shared by people who are made of dust, and the nature of the heavenly person is shared by heavenly people. [49]We will look like[v] the heavenly person in the same way as we have looked like the person made from dust.

[50]This is what I'm saying, brothers and sisters: Flesh and blood can't inherit God's kingdom. Something that rots can't inherit something that doesn't decay. [51]Listen, I'm telling you a secret: All of us won't die, but we will all be changed—[52]in an instant, in the blink of an eye, at the final trumpet. The trumpet will blast, and the dead will be raised with bodies that won't decay, and we will be changed. [53]It's necessary for this rotting body to be clothed with what can't decay, and for the body that is dying to be clothed in what can't die. [54]And when the rotting body has been clothed in what can't decay, and the dying body has been clothed in what can't die, then this statement in scripture will happen:

Death has been swallowed up
  by a victory.[w]
[55] *Where is your victory, Death?*
  Where is your sting, Death?[x]

([56]Death's sting is sin, and the power of sin is the Law.) [57]Thanks be to God, who gives us this victory through our Lord Jesus Christ! [58]As a result of all this, my loved brothers and sisters, you must stand firm, unshakable, excelling in the work of the Lord as always, because you know that your labor isn't going to be for nothing in the Lord.

---

[s]Ps 110:1 [t]Isa 22:13 [u]Gen 2:7 [v]Or *bear the image of* [w]Isa 25:8 [x]Hos 13:14

Collection for Jerusalem

16 Concerning the collection of money for God's people: You should do what I have directed the churches in Galatia to do. ²On the first day of the week, each of you should set aside whatever you can afford from what you earn so that the collection won't be delayed until I come. ³Then when I get there, I'll send whomever you approve to Jerusalem with letters of recommendation to bring your gift. ⁴If it seems right for me to go too, they'll travel with me.

Plans to visit

⁵I'll come to you after I go through Macedonia, and because I'm going through Macedonia, ⁶I may stay with you or even spend the winter there in Corinth so that you can send me on my way to wherever I'm off to next. ⁷I don't want to make a quick visit to you, since I hope to spend some time with you if the Lord lets it happen. ⁸I'll stay here in Ephesus until the Festival of Pentecost. ⁹In spite of the fact that there are many opponents, a big and productive opportunity has opened up for my mission here.

¹⁰If Timothy comes to you, be sure that he has no reason to be afraid while he's with you, because he does the work of the Lord just like I do. ¹¹So don't let anyone disrespect him, but send him on in peace so he can join me. I'm waiting for him along with the brothers and sisters. ¹²Concerning Apollos our brother: I strongly encouraged him to visit you with the brothers and sisters, but he didn't want to go now. He'll come when he has an opportunity.

Final greeting

¹³Stay awake, stand firm in your faith, be brave, be strong. ¹⁴Everything should be done in love.

¹⁵Brothers and sisters, I encourage you to do something else. You know that the people

in Stephanas' household were the first crop of the harvest to come from the mission to Achaia. They have dedicated themselves to the service of God's people. ¹⁶So accept the authority of people like them and of anyone who cooperates and works hard. ¹⁷I'm so happy that Stephanas, Fortunatus, and Achaicus have arrived; they've made up for my missing you. ¹⁸Indeed they've provided my spirit and yours with a much-needed rest. Therefore, give them proper recognition.

¹⁹The churches in the province of Asia greet you. Aquila and Prisca greet you warmly in the Lord, together with the church that meets in their house. ²⁰All the brothers and sisters greet you. You in turn should greet each other with a holy kiss. ²¹Here is my greeting in my own handwriting—Paul.

²²A curse on anyone who doesn't love the Lord. Come, Lord! ²³The grace of the Lord Jesus be with you. ²⁴My love is with all of you in Christ Jesus.

SAILBOAT

COURAGE

Staying Strong in Faith *1 Corinthians 16:13*
Paul concluded his first letter to the Corinthians with several words of encouragement. Paul told them to stay awake and stand firm in their faith. Paul wanted them to pay attention to what was going on around them and to their own thoughts and actions. He wanted them to be faithful to God, not changing their faith every time a different idea or difficult circumstance happened. God wants the same from us too. Paul also told the people to be brave and strong. Being brave and strong doesn't mean that we're never afraid. It means that we do the right thing even when it's difficult or costs us something. It takes courage to keep going when we feel weak, but God will give us all the strength we need. ◊

2 Corinthians

1302

things
YOU'LL DISCOVER

This second letter to Christians in the city of Corinth continues the message Paul started in 1 Corinthians. Paul told people to quit being self-centered and get along. He also gave reasons why the Corinthians should listen to his message.

people
YOU'LL MEET

Paul—a missionary of the church (2 Cor 1–13)
False apostles—people who fought Paul for leadership of the church in Corinth (2 Cor 11–12)

places
YOU'LL GO

Corinth (present-day Greece),
Macedonia (present-day northern Greece),
Judea (present-day Israel)

words
YOU'LL REMEMBER

"He said to me, 'My grace is enough for you, because power is made perfect in weakness.' So I'll gladly spend my time bragging about my weaknesses so that Christ's power can rest on me.... When I'm weak, then I'm strong" (2 Cor 12:9-10).

Paul started the church in Corinth and taught the Christians there for more than a year and a half. After Paul left, those Christians began fighting. So he wrote them a letter telling them to get along.

As time passed, their quarrels and problems grew worse. Other teachers came to Corinth and claimed they knew more about following God than Paul did. They said Paul was undependable. They said he bragged a lot. They claimed he was a liar. They even wondered if he was keeping the money he collected for poor people in Jerusalem.

Paul wasn't happy. So he wrote again to the Christians in Corinth. He defended himself and his way of working for God. He explained how God had called him to tell others about Jesus. He listed the troubles he faced as a leader of churches. Paul wanted these Christians to know that he was serious about following God. He wanted everyone to hear and live by the truth about Jesus. This letter shows us we need to listen to leaders who know God!

Greeting

1 From Paul, an apostle of Christ Jesus by God's will, and Timothy our brother.

To God's church that is in Corinth, along with all of God's people throughout Achaia.

²Grace to you and peace from God our Father and from our Lord Jesus Christ.

God's comfort in trouble

³May the God and Father of our Lord Jesus Christ be blessed! He is the compassionate Father and God of all comfort. ⁴He's the one who comforts us in all our trouble so that we can comfort other people who are in every kind of trouble. We offer the same comfort that we ourselves received from God. ⁵That is because we receive so much comfort through Christ in the same way that we share so many of Christ's sufferings. ⁶So if we have trouble, it is to bring you comfort and salvation. If we are comforted, it is to bring you comfort from the experience of endurance while you go through the same sufferings that we also suffer. ⁷Our hope for you is certain, because we know that as you are partners in suffering, so also you are partners in comfort.

SAILBOAT

Thankful for God's Comfort

2 Corinthians 1:4

Paul said that God comforts us like a good father comforts his children. This comfort makes us feel loved and protected. God's comfort doesn't stop with us. Because we're thankful and feel secure in God's comfort, we can give that same comfort to people around us. We please God by passing on God's comfort and encouraging other people to keep helping each other. ◆

///

⁸Brothers and sisters, we don't want you to be unaware of the troubles that we went through in Asia. We were weighed down with a load of suffering that was so far beyond our strength that we were afraid we might not survive. ⁹It certainly seemed to us as if we had gotten the death penalty. This was so that we would have confidence in God, who raises the dead, instead of ourselves. ¹⁰God rescued us from a terrible death, and he will rescue us. We have set our hope on him that he will rescue us again, ¹¹since you are helping with your prayer for us. Then many people can thank God on our behalf for the gift that was given to us through the prayers of many people.

Paul explains his change of plans

¹²We have conducted ourselves with godly sincerity and pure motives in the world, and especially toward you. This is why we are confident, and our conscience confirms this. We didn't act with human wisdom but we relied on the grace of God. ¹³We don't write anything to you except what you can read and also understand. I hope that you will understand totally ¹⁴since you have already understood us partly. Understand that in the day of our Lord Jesus, we will make you proud as you will also make us proud.

¹⁵Because I was sure of this, I wanted to visit you first so that you could have a second opportunity to see me. ¹⁶I wanted to visit you on my way to Macedonia, and then come to you again on my way back from Macedonia, at which point I was hoping you would help me on my way to Judea.

¹⁷So I wasn't unreliable when I planned to do this, was I? Or do I make decisions with a substandard human process so that I say "Yes, yes" and "No, no" at the same time? ¹⁸But as God is faithful, our message to you isn't both yes and no. ¹⁹God's Son, Jesus Christ, is the one who was preached among you by us—through me, Silvanus, and Timothy—he wasn't yes and no. In him it is always yes. ²⁰All of God's promises have their yes in him. That is why we say Amen through him to the glory of God.

²¹God is the one who establishes us with you in Christ and who anointed us. ²²God also sealed us and gave the Spirit as a down payment in our hearts. ²³I call on God as my witness—I didn't come again to Corinth because I wanted to spare you. ²⁴It isn't that we are trying to control your faith, but we are working with you for your happiness, because you stand firm in your faith. **2** ¹So I decided that, for my own sake, I wouldn't visit you again while I was upset. ²If I make you sad, who will be there to make me glad when you are sad because of me?

Paul's former letter

³That's why I wrote this very thing to you, so that when I came I wouldn't be made sad by the ones who ought to make me happy. I have confidence in you, that my happiness means your happiness. ⁴I wrote to you in tears, with a very troubled and anxious heart. I didn't write to make you sad but so you would know the overwhelming love that I have for you.

⁵But if someone has made anyone sad, that person hasn't hurt me but all of you to some degree (not to exaggerate). ⁶The punishment handed out by the majority is enough for this person. ⁷This is why you should try your best to forgive and to comfort this person now instead, so that this person isn't overwhelmed by too much sorrow. ⁸So I encourage you to show your love for this person.

> **did you know?** Before Paul became an apostle for Jesus, he was training to be a religious leader called a *Pharisee*. During that time in his life, he tried to impress other Pharisees and God by arresting the followers of Jesus. Paul did this because he thought followers of Jesus were breaking the Law from Moses.

⁹This is another reason why I wrote you. I wanted to test you and see if you are obedient in everything. ¹⁰If you forgive anyone for anything, I do too. And whatever I've forgiven (if I've forgiven anything), I did it for you in the presence of Christ. ¹¹This is so that we won't be taken advantage of by Satan, because we are well aware of his schemes.

SAILBOAT

FORGIVENESS

Forgive Each Other *2 Corinthians 2:7-11*

Forgiveness doesn't come naturally. We must decide to forgive other people and then trust God to help us feel the peace that comes with forgiveness. Paul wanted the people in the Corinthian church to forgive a person who had sinned. He wanted to make sure everyone understood how important it was to forgive people just like God forgave and showed love to them. This is still true today. Christians aren't perfect. Sometimes we do things that need to be forgiven. God gives us strength to forgive each other. ◖

Paul's ministry

¹²When I came to Troas to preach Christ's gospel, the Lord gave me an opportunity to preach. ¹³But I was worried because I couldn't find my brother Titus there. So I said good-bye to them and went on to Macedonia.

¹⁴But thank God, who is always leading us around through Christ as if we were in a parade. He releases the fragrance of the knowledge of him everywhere through us. ¹⁵We smell like the aroma of Christ's offering to God, both to those who are being saved and to those who are on the road to destruction. ¹⁶We smell like a contagious dead person to those who are dying, but we smell like the fountain of life to those who are being saved.

Who is qualified for this kind of ministry? ¹⁷We aren't like so many people who hustle the word of God to make a profit. We are speaking through Christ in the presence of God, as those who are sincere and as those who are sent from God.

3 Are we starting to commend ourselves again? We don't need letters of introduction to you or from you like other people, do we? ²You are our letter, written on our hearts, known and read by everyone. ³You show that you are Christ's letter, delivered by us. You weren't written with ink but with the Spirit of the living God. You weren't written on tablets of stone but on tablets of human hearts.

⁴This is the confidence that we have through Christ in the presence of God. ⁵It isn't that we ourselves are qualified to claim that anything came from us. No, our qualification is from God. ⁶He has qualified us as ministers of a new covenant, not based on what is written but on the Spirit, because what is written kills, but the Spirit gives life.

Ministers of the new covenant

⁷The ministry that brought death was carved in letters on stone tablets. It came with such glory that the Israelites couldn't look for long at Moses' face because his face was shining with glory, even though it was a fading glory. ⁸Won't the ministry of the Spirit be much more glorious? ⁹If the ministry that brought condemnation has glory, how much more glorious is the ministry that brings righteousness? ¹⁰In fact, what was glorious

isn't glorious now, because of the glory that is brighter. [11]If the glory that fades away was glorious, how much more glorious is the one that lasts!

---

did you know?

Clay pots were used to store many different things in Bible times. People kept everyday items such as food and water in these pots. They also used clay pots to hold precious treasures, such as expensive spices or sacred scrolls. The pots were valuable because of what was inside them.

---

[12]So, since we have such a hope, we act with great confidence. [13]We aren't like Moses, who used to put a veil over his face so that the Israelites couldn't watch the end of what was fading away. [14]But their minds were closed. Right up to the present day the same veil remains when the old covenant is read. The veil is not removed because it is taken away by Christ. [15]Even today, whenever Moses is read, a veil lies over their hearts. [16]But whenever someone turns back to the Lord, the veil is removed. [17]The Lord is the Spirit, and where the Lord's Spirit is, there is freedom. [18]All of us are looking with unveiled faces at the glory of the Lord as if we were looking in a mirror. We are being transformed into that same image from one degree of glory to the next degree of glory. This comes from the Lord, who is the Spirit.

4 This is why we don't get discouraged, given that we received this ministry in the same way that we received God's mercy. [2]Instead, we reject secrecy and shameful actions. We don't use deception, and we don't tamper with God's word. Instead, we commend ourselves to everyone's conscience in the sight of God by the public announcement of the truth. [3]And even if our gospel is veiled, it is veiled to those who are on the road to destruction. [4]The god of this age has blinded the minds of those who don't have faith so they couldn't see the light of the gospel that reveals Christ's glory. Christ is the image of God.

[5]We don't preach about ourselves. Instead, we preach about Jesus Christ as Lord, and we describe ourselves as your slaves for Jesus' sake. [6]God said that light should shine out of the darkness. He is the same one who shone in our hearts to give us the light of the knowledge of God's glory in the face of Jesus Christ.

Physical bodies and eternal glory

[7]But we have this treasure in clay pots so that the awesome power belongs to God and doesn't come from us. [8]We are experiencing all kinds of trouble,

Memorize 2 Cor 4:8-9

but we aren't crushed. We are confused, but we aren't depressed. [9]We are harassed, but we aren't abandoned. We are knocked down, but we aren't knocked out.

[10]We always carry Jesus' death around in our bodies so that Jesus' life can also be seen in our bodies. [11]We who are alive are always being handed over to death for Jesus' sake so that Jesus' life can also be seen in our bodies that are dying. [12]So death is at work in us, but life is at work in you.

[13]We have the same faithful spirit as what is written in scripture: *I had faith, and so I spoke.*[a] We also have faith, and so we also speak. [14]We do this because we know that the one who raised the Lord Jesus will also raise us with Jesus, and he will bring us into his presence along with you. [15]All these things are for your benefit. As grace increases to benefit more and more people, it will cause gratitude to increase, which results in God's glory.

[16]So we aren't depressed. But even if our bodies are breaking down on the outside, the person that we are on the inside is being renewed every day. [17]Our temporary minor problems are producing an eternal stockpile of glory for us that is beyond all comparison. [18]We don't focus on the things that can be seen but on the things that can't be seen. The things that can be seen don't last, but the things that can't be seen are eternal.

5 We know that if the tent that we live in on earth is torn down, we have a building from God. It's a house that isn't handmade, which is eternal and located in heaven. [2]We groan while we live in this residence. We really want to dress ourselves with our building from heaven—[3]since we assume that

---

[a]Ps 116:10 (115:1 LXX)

when we take off this tent, we won't find out that we are naked. ⁴Yes, while we are in this tent we groan, because we are weighed down. We want to be dressed not undressed, so that what is dying can be swallowed up by life. ⁵Now the one who prepared us for this very thing is God, and God gave us the Spirit as a down payment for our home.

⁶So we are always confident, because we know that while we are living in the body, we are away from our home with the Lord. ⁷We live by faith and not by sight. ⁸We are confident, and we would prefer to leave the body and to be at home with the Lord. ⁹So our goal is to be acceptable to him, whether we are at home or away from home. ¹⁰We all must

LIFE PRESERVER

What does it mean to "live by faith and not by sight"? *2 Corinthians 5:7*

One way to understand what it means to live by faith is to think about a person who is blind. She is able to live safely in her home because she knows where everything is. She has faith that everything will stay in its place so that she will be able to get around.

Paul reminded Christians that faith is important. When we want answers to difficult questions or to know for sure what's going to happen, we can remember to have faith in God. ◗

God's THOUGHTS ◆ My THOUGHTS

Knocked Down, but We Get Up Again   2 Corinthians 4:7-18

Sometimes it may seem like the whole world is against you, and all you want to do is stay in bed. Paul and the people who traveled with him had days like that while they spread the good news of Jesus Christ around the world. People chased Paul out of town. He would visit a church he had started only to find the people angry with each other and taking sides. He spent weeks sailing from place to place only to end up shipwrecked. But Paul loved God so much that he put his discomfort aside and stayed focused on telling people about Jesus everywhere he went.

Paul told the Christians in Corinth about some of his difficult experiences. But he went on to share a promise: "We are experiencing all kinds of trouble, but we aren't crushed. We are confused, but we aren't depressed. We are harassed, but we aren't abandoned. We are knocked down, but we aren't knocked out" (2 Cor 4:8-9). No matter what came his way or how hard things got, Paul knew for sure that Jesus was working in and through him to share the good news.

This promise is true for us today. No matter how hard things get or what troubles we face, God will always take care of us. We may get knocked down, but we won't be knocked out. We can always get up by the power of the Spirit.

When have you felt "knocked down"?

How have you experienced the Spirit helping you get up again?

appear before Christ in court so that each person can be paid back for the things that were done while in the body, whether they were good or bad.

Ministry of reconciliation

[11]So we try to persuade people, since we know what it means to fear the Lord. We are well known by God, and I hope that in your heart we are well known by you as well. [12]We aren't trying to commend ourselves to you again. Instead, we are giving you an opportunity to be proud of us so that you could answer those who take pride in superficial appearance, and not in what is in the heart. [13]If we are crazy, it's for God's sake. If we are rational, it's for your sake. [14]The love of Christ controls us, because we have concluded this: one died for the sake of all; therefore, all died. [15]He died for the sake of all so that those who are alive should live not for themselves but for the one who died for them and was raised.

[16]So then, from this point on we won't recognize people by human standards. Even though we used to know Christ by human standards, that isn't how we know him now. [17]So then, if anyone is in Christ, that person is part of the new creation. The old things have gone away, and look, new things have arrived!

Memorize 2 Cor 5:17

[18]All of these new things are from God, who reconciled us to himself through Christ and who gave us the ministry of reconciliation. [19]In other words, God was reconciling the world to himself through Christ, by not counting people's sins against them. He has trusted us with this message of reconciliation. [20]So we are ambassadors who represent Christ. God is negotiating with you through us. We beg you as Christ's representatives, "Be reconciled to God!" [21]God caused the one who didn't know sin to be sin for our sake so that through him we could become the righteousness of God. [1]Since we work together with him, we are also begging you not to receive the grace of God in vain. [2]He says, *I listened to you at the right time, and I helped you on the day of salvation.*[b] Look,

now is the right time! Look, now is the day of salvation!

[3]We don't give anyone any reason to be offended about anything so that our ministry won't be criticized. [4]Instead, we commend ourselves as ministers of God in every way. We did this with our great endurance through problems, disasters, and stressful situations. [5]We went through beatings, imprisonments, and riots. We experienced hard work, sleepless nights, and hunger. [6]We displayed purity, knowledge, patience, and generosity. We served with the Holy Spirit, genuine love, [7]telling the truth, and God's power. We carried the weapons of righteousness in our right hand and our left hand. [8]We were treated with honor and dishonor and with verbal abuse and good evaluation. We were seen as both fake and real, [9]as unknown and well known, as dying—and look, we are alive! We were seen as punished but not killed, [10]as going through pain but always happy, as poor but making many rich, and as having nothing but owning everything.

LIGHTHOUSE

GOOD NEWS

Paul Shares the Good News

2 Corinthians 6:3-10

Paul faced many different reactions when he shared the good news. Sometimes people decided to follow Jesus. Other times people tried to hurt Paul because they were so angry about God's truth. Paul said he always told the truth about God's amazing plan. Not only did Paul share the good news, he was careful to live like God wanted. Other people notice when we follow God's will. God's power gives us the strength to do what God wants us to do even when it's hard. ♦

Call to relationship and holiness

[11]Corinthians, we have spoken openly to you, and our hearts are wide open. [12]There are no limits to the affection that we feel for you. You are the ones who placed boundaries on your affection for us. [13]But as a fair trade—I'm talking to you like you are children—open your hearts wide too.

[b]Isa 49:8

¹⁴Don't be tied up as equal partners with people who don't believe. What does righteousness share with that which is outside the Law? What relationship does light have with darkness? ¹⁵What harmony does Christ have with Satan?ᶜ What does a believer have in common with someone who doesn't believe? ¹⁶What agreement can there be between God's temple and idols? Because we are the temple of the living God. Just as God said, *I live with them, and I will move among them. I will be their God, and they will be my people.*ᵈ ¹⁷Therefore, *come out from among them and be separated, says the Lord. Don't touch what is unclean. Then I will welcome you.*ᵉ ¹⁸*I will be a father to you, and you will be my sons and daughters, says the Lord Almighty.*ᶠ 7 ¹My dear friends, since we have these promises, let's cleanse ourselves from anything that contaminates our body or spirit so that we make our holiness complete in the fear of God.

²Make room in your hearts for us. We didn't do anything wrong to anyone. We didn't ruin anyone. We didn't take advantage of anyone. ³I'm not saying this to make you feel guilty. I've already said that you are in our hearts so that we die and live together with you. ⁴I have every confidence in you. I'm terribly proud of you. I'm filled with encouragement. I'm overwhelmed with happiness while in the middle of our problems.

Titus' good report

⁵Even after we arrived in Macedonia, we couldn't rest physically. We were surrounded by problems. There was external conflict, and there were internal fears. ⁶However, God comforts people who are discouraged, and he comforted us by Titus' arrival. ⁷We weren't comforted only by his arrival but also by the comfort he had received from you. He told us about your desire to see me, how you were sorry, and about your concern for me, so that I was even happier.

⁸Even though my letter hurt you, I don't regret it. Well—I did regret it just a bit because I see that that letter made you sad, though only for a short time. ⁹Now I'm glad—not because you were sad but because you were made sad

enough to change your hearts and lives. You felt godly sadness so that no one was harmed by us in any way. ¹⁰Godly sadness produces a changed heart and life that leads to salvation and leaves no regrets, but sorrow under the influence of the world produces death. ¹¹Look at what this very experience of godly sadness has produced in you: such enthusiasm, what a desire to clear yourselves of blame, such indignation, what fear, what purpose, such concern, what justice! In everything you have shown yourselves to be innocent in the matter.

¹²So although I wrote to you, it wasn't for the sake of the one who did wrong, or for the sake of the one who was wronged, but to show you your own enthusiasm for us in the sight of God. ¹³Because of this we have been encouraged. And in addition to our own encouragement, we were even more pleased at how happy Titus was. His mind has been put at rest by all of you. ¹⁴If I've bragged about you to him in any way, I haven't been embarrassed. Instead, our bragging to Titus has also been proven to be true, just like everything we said to you was true. ¹⁵His devotion to you is growing even more as he remembers how all of you were obedient when you welcomed him with fear and trembling. ¹⁶I'm happy, because I can completely depend on you.

Encouragement to give generously

8 Brothers and sisters, we want to let you know about the grace of God that was given to the churches of Macedonia. ²While they were being tested by many problems, their extra amount of happiness and their extreme poverty resulted in a surplus of rich generosity. ³I assure you that they gave what they could afford and even more than they could afford, and they did it voluntarily. ⁴They urgently begged us for the privilegeᵍ of sharing in this service for the saints. ⁵They even exceeded our expectations, because they gave themselves to the Lord first and to us, consistent with God's will. ⁶As a result, we challenged Titus to finish this work of grace with you the way he had started it.

Bet you can read this in 3 minutes. Ready, set, go!

ᶜOr *Beliah* ᵈLev 26:11-12 ᵉIsa 52:11; Ezek 20:34, 41 ᶠ2 Sam 7:14 ᵍOr *grace*

[7]Be the best in this work of grace in the same way that you are the best in everything, such as faith, speech, knowledge, total commitment, and the love we inspired in you. [8]I'm not giving an order, but by mentioning the commitment of others, I'm trying to prove the authenticity of your love also. [9]You know the grace of our Lord Jesus Christ. Although he was rich, he became poor for your sakes, so that you could become rich through his poverty.

[10]I'm giving you my opinion about this. It's to your advantage to do this, since you not only started to do it last year but you wanted to do it too. [11]Now finish the job as well so that you finish it with as much enthusiasm as you started, given what you can afford. [12]A gift is appreciated because of what a person can afford, not because of what that person can't afford, if it's apparent that it's done willingly. [13]It isn't that we want others to have financial ease and you financial difficulties, but it's a matter of equality. [14]At the present moment, your surplus can fill their deficit so that in the future their surplus can fill your deficit. In this way there is equality. [15]As it is written, *The one who gathered more didn't have too much, and the one who gathered less didn't have too little.*[h]

Plans for the Collection

[16]But thank God, who put the same commitment that I have for you in Titus' heart. [17]Not only has he accepted our challenge but he's on his way to see you voluntarily, and he's excited. [18]We are sending the brother who is famous in all the churches because of his work for the gospel along with him.

[19]In addition to this, he is chosen by the churches to be our traveling companion in this work of grace, which we are taking care of for the sake of the glory of the Lord himself, and to show our desire to help. [20]We are trying to avoid being blamed by anyone for the way we take care of this large amount of money. [21]We care about doing the right thing, not only in the Lord's eyes but also in the eyes of other people.

[22]We are sending our brother with them. We have tested his commitment in many ways and many times. Now he's even more

committed, because he has so much confidence in you. [23]If there is any question about Titus, he is my partner and coworker among you. If there is any question about our brothers, they are the churches' apostles and an honor to Christ. [24]So show them the proof of your love and the reason we are so proud of you, in such a way that the churches can see it.

9 It's unnecessary for me to write to you about this service for God's people. [2]I know about your willingness to help. I brag about you to the Macedonians, saying, "Greece has been ready since last year," and your enthusiasm has motivated most of them.

[3]But I'm sending the brothers so that our bragging about you in this case won't be empty words, and so that you can be prepared, just as I keep telling them you will be. [4]If some Macedonians should come with me and find out that you aren't ready, we (not to mention you) would be embarrassed as far as this project goes.

[5]This is why I thought it was necessary to encourage the brothers to go to you ahead of time and arrange in advance the generous gift you have already promised. I want it to be a real gift from you. I don't want you to feel like you are being forced to give anything. [6]What I mean is this: the one who sows a small number of seeds will also reap a small crop, and the one who sows a generous amount of seeds will also reap a generous crop.

[7]Everyone should give whatever they have decided in their heart. They shouldn't give with hesitation or because of pressure. God loves a cheerful giver. [8]God has the power to provide you with more than enough of every kind of grace. That way, you will have everything you need always and in everything to provide more than enough for every kind of good work. [9]As it is written, *He scattered everywhere; he gave to the needy; his righteousness remains forever.*[i]

[10]The one who supplies seed for planting and bread for eating will supply and multiply your seed and will increase your crop, which is righteousness. [11]You will be made rich in every way so that you can be generous in every way. Such generosity produces thanksgiving to God through us. [12]Your ministry of this service to God's people isn't only fully meeting their

[h]Exod 16:18 [i]Ps 112:9

needs but it is also multiplying in many expressions of thanksgiving to God. ¹³They will give honor to God for your obedience to your confession of Christ's gospel. They will do this because this service provides evidence of your obedience, and because of your generosity in sharing with them and with everyone. ¹⁴They will also pray for you, and they will care deeply for you because of the outstanding grace that God has given to you. ¹⁵Thank God for his gift that words can't describe!

Paul's personal request for obedience

10I, Paul, make a personal request to you with the gentleness and kindness of Christ. I'm shy when I'm with you, but I'm bossy when I'm away from you! ²I beg you that when I'm with you in person, I won't have to boss you around. I'm afraid that I may have to use that kind of behavior with those people who think we live by human standards. ³Although we live in the world, we don't fight our battles with human methods. ⁴Our weapons that we fight with aren't human, but instead they are powered by God for the destruction of fortresses. They destroy arguments, ⁵and every defense that is raised up to oppose the knowledge of God. They capture every thought to make it obedient to Christ. ⁶Once your obedience is complete, we are ready to punish any disobedience.

⁷Look at what is right in front of you! If anyone is sure about belonging to Christ, that person should think again. We belong to

did you **know?** Paul was close to the Christians in Corinth. As far as we know, he wrote and visited them more than other churches. According to the Bible, Paul wrote at least four letters to the Corinthians and visited at least three times.

Christ just like that person. ⁸Even if I went on to brag about our authority, I wouldn't be ashamed of it. The Lord gave us that authority to build you up and not to destroy you.

⁹I don't want it to seem like I'm trying to intimidate you with my letters. ¹⁰I know what

Give Cheerfully   *2 Corinthians 9:7-8*

Sometimes we have to give away something we really don't want to give up. Maybe there was a time when your mom made you sell some toys at a garage sale. Perhaps your dad told you to give some of your allowance in the church offering. Or maybe a kid begged for half of your cupcake at lunch, and you really didn't want to give it to him. It can be hard to give away things that belong to us.

When the apostles planted new churches, they relied on other churches to help them by giving money. Some people really wanted to help, but others didn't. Usually people gave generously to help the apostles spread the good news everywhere they went.

Paul told people that they shouldn't give unless they really wanted to give out of cheerful generosity. The phrase "God loves a cheerful giver" comes from this passage. When you have a choice to either give or not give, remember Paul's instruction for how people should give. Do you feel good about giving? Is your heart happy to help someone?

Memorize the last sentence of 2 Corinthians 9:7:
"God loves a cheerful giver."

Pray for God to give you a generous heart.

some people are saying: "His letters are severe and powerful, but in person he is weak and his speech is worth nothing." ¹¹These people need to think about this—that when we are with you, our actions will show that we are the same as the words we wrote when we were away from you. ¹²We won't dare to place ourselves in the same league or to compare ourselves with some of those who are promoting themselves. When they measure themselves by themselves, and compare themselves with themselves, they have no understanding.

¹³We won't take pride in anything more than what is appropriate. Let's look at the boundaries of our work area that God has assigned to us. It's an area that includes you. ¹⁴We aren't going out of bounds, as if our work area doesn't extend as far as you. We were the first ones to travel as far as Corinth with the gospel of Christ. ¹⁵We don't take pride in what other people do outside of our boundaries. We hope that our work will be extended even more by you as your faith grows, until it expands fully (within the boundaries, of course). ¹⁶We hope that our work grows even to the point of the gospel being preached in places beyond Corinth, without bragging about what has already been done in another person's work area. ¹⁷But, *the one who brags should brag in the Lord.*ʲ ¹⁸It isn't the person who promotes himself or herself who is approved but the person whom the Lord commends.

Confrontation of the super-apostles

11 I hope that you will put up with me while I act like a fool. Well, in fact, you are putting up with me! ²I'm deeply concerned about you with the same concern that God has. As your father, I promised you in marriage to one husband. I promised to present you as an innocent virgin to Christ himself. ³But I'm afraid that your minds might be seduced in the same way as the snake deceived Eve with his devious tricks. You might be unable to focus completely on a genuine and innocent commitment to Christ.

⁴If a person comes and preaches some other Jesus than the one we preached, or if you receive a different Spirit than the one you had received, or a different gospel than the one you embraced, you put up with it so

easily! ⁵I don't consider myself as second-rate in any way compared to the "super-apostles." ⁶But even if I'm uneducated in public speaking, I'm not uneducated in knowledge. We have shown this to you in every way and in everything we have done. ⁷Did I commit a sin by humbling myself to give you an advantage because I preached the gospel of God to you free of charge? ⁸I robbed other churches by taking a salary from them in order to serve you! ⁹While I was with you, I didn't burden any of you even though I needed things. The believers who came from Macedonia gave me everything I needed. I kept myself from being a financial drain on you in any way, and I will continue to keep myself from being a burden.

¹⁰Since Christ's truth is in me, I won't stop telling the entire area of Greece that I'm proud of what I did. ¹¹Why? Is it because I don't love you? God knows that I do! ¹²But I'm going to continue to do what I'm doing. I want to contradict the claims of the people who want to be treated like they are the same as us because of what they brag about. ¹³Such people are false apostles and dishonest workers who disguise themselves as apostles of Christ. ¹⁴And no wonder! Even Satan disguises himself as an angel of light. ¹⁵It is no great surprise then that his servants also disguise themselves as servants of righteousness. Their end will be what their actions deserve.

LIFE PRESERVER

What are "false apostles"?
2 Corinthians 11:13

When Paul wrote this letter, there were teachers who didn't really talk about Jesus or teach the same things Paul taught. Paul called them *super-apostles*. He was upset because he knew these people wanted the Corinthians to think they were very important. But Paul said these pretenders were bragging about being servants of Christ in order to get attention. He wanted the Christians in Corinth to be aware of them so they would know that they should continue to follow Paul's preaching and teaching. Paul loved all the churches that he ministered to and didn't want them to get hurt by selfish people who might take their money or teach things that weren't true. ◊

Paul defends himself

¹⁶I repeat, no one should take me for a fool. But if you do, then allow me to be a fool so that I can brag like a fool for a bit. ¹⁷I'm not saying what I'm saying because the Lord tells me to. I'm saying it like I'm a fool. I'm putting my confidence in this business of bragging. ¹⁸Since so many people are bragging based on human standards, that is how I'm going to brag too. ¹⁹Because you, who are so wise, are happy to put up with fools. ²⁰You put up with it if someone enslaves you, if someone exploits you, if someone takes advantage of you, if someone places themselves over you, or if someone hits you in the face. ²¹I'm ashamed to say that we have been weak in comparison! But in whatever they challenge me, I challenge them (I'm speaking foolishly).

²²Are they Hebrews? So am I. Are they Israelites? So am I. Are they descendants of Abraham? So am I. ²³Are they ministers of Christ? I'm speaking like a crazy person. What I've done goes well beyond what they've done. I've worked much harder. I've been imprisoned much more often. I've been beaten more times than I can count. I've faced death many times. ²⁴I received the "forty lashes minus one" from the Jews five times. ²⁵I was beaten with rods three times. I was stoned once. I was shipwrecked three times. I spent a day and a night on the open sea. ²⁶I've been on many journeys. I faced dangers from rivers, robbers, my people, and Gentiles. I faced dangers in the city, in the desert, on the sea, and from false brothers and sisters. ²⁷I faced these dangers with hard work and heavy labor, many sleepless nights, hunger and thirst, often without food, and in the cold without enough clothes.

²⁸Besides all the other things I could mention, there's my daily stress because I'm concerned about all the churches. ²⁹Who is weak without me being weak? Who is led astray without me being furious about it? ³⁰If it's necessary to brag, I'll brag about my weaknesses. ³¹The God and Father of the Lord Jesus, the one who is blessed forever, knows that I'm not lying. ³²At Damascus the governor under King Aretas was guarding the city of Damascus in order to capture me, ³³but I got away from him by being lowered in a basket through a window in the city wall.

Paul's visions and revelations from the Lord

12It is necessary to brag, not that it does any good. I'll move on to visions and revelations from the Lord. ²I know a man in Christ who was caught up into the third heaven fourteen years ago. I don't know whether it was in the body or out of the body. God knows. ³⁻⁴I know that this man was caught up into paradise and that he heard unspeakable words that were things no one is allowed to repeat. I don't know whether it was in the body or apart from the body. God knows. ⁵I'll brag about this man, but I won't brag about myself, except to brag about my weaknesses.

⁶If I did want to brag, I wouldn't make a fool of myself because I'd tell the truth. I'm holding back from bragging so that no one will give me any more credit than what anyone sees or hears about me. ⁷I was given a thorn in my body because of the outstanding revelations I've received so that I wouldn't be conceited. It's a messenger from Satan sent to torment me so that I wouldn't be conceited.

⁸I pleaded with the Lord three times for it to leave me alone. ⁹He said to me, "My grace is enough for you, because power is made perfect in weakness." So I'll gladly spend my time bragging about my weaknesses so that Christ's power can rest on me. ¹⁰Therefore, I'm all right with weaknesses, insults, disasters,

Memorize
2 Cor 12:9-10

SAILBOAT

Joy

God Is Strong when We're Weak

2 Corinthians 12:10

Paul learned something very interesting about living as a follower of Christ. He found that it wasn't up to him to make sure everything was successful. Sometimes Paul couldn't keep from going through bad situations. He learned that God faithfully finished the work that needed to be done. All Paul had to do was trust God. Even when Paul probably thought things were a disaster that he couldn't fix, God had no difficulty making everything go according to God's will. We can praise God because we know that things would turn out differently without God's strength and involvement. ♦

harassments, and stressful situations for the sake of Christ, because when I'm weak, then I'm strong.

[11]I've become a fool! You made me do it. Actually, I should have been commended by you. I'm not inferior to the super-apostles in any way, even though I'm a nonentity. [12]The signs of an apostle were performed among you with continuous endurance through signs, wonders, and miracles. [13]How were you treated worse than the other churches, except that I myself wasn't a financial burden on you? Forgive me for this wrong!

Paul's plans to visit and a warning

[14]Look, I'm ready to visit you a third time, and I won't be a burden on you. I don't want your things; I want you. It isn't the children's responsibility to save up for their parents but parents for children. [15]I will very gladly spend and be spent for your sake. If I love you more, will you love me less?

[16]We all know that I didn't place a burden on you, but in spite of that you think I'm a con artist who fooled you with a trick. [17]I haven't taken advantage of you through any of the people I sent to you, have I? [18]I strongly encouraged Titus to go to you and sent the brother with him. Titus didn't take advantage of you, did he? Didn't we live by the same Spirit? Didn't we walk in the same footsteps?

[19]Have you been thinking up to now that we are defending ourselves to you? Actually, we are speaking in the sight of God and in Christ. Dear friends, everything is meant to build you up. [20]I'm afraid that maybe when I come you will be different from the way I want you to be, and that I'll be different from the way you want me to be. I'm afraid that there might be fighting, obsession, losing your temper, competitive opposition, backstabbing, gossip, conceit, and disorderly conduct. [21]I'm afraid that when I come again, my God may embarrass me in front of you. I might have to go into mourning over all the people who have sinned before and haven't changed their hearts and lives from what they used to practice: moral corruption, sexual immorality, and doing whatever feels good.

13This is the third time that I'm coming to visit you. Every matter is settled on the evidence of two or three witnesses. [2]When I was with you on my second visit, I already warned those who continued to sin. Now I'm repeating that warning to all the rest of you while I'm at a safe distance: if I come again, I won't spare anyone. [3]Since you are demanding proof that Christ speaks through me, Christ isn't weak in dealing with you but shows his power among you. [4]Certainly he was crucified because of weakness, but he lives by the power of God. Certainly we also are weak in him, but we will live together with him, because of God's power that is directed toward you.

[5]Examine yourselves to see if you are in the faith. Test yourselves. Don't you understand that Jesus Christ is in you? Unless, of course, you fail the test. [6]But I hope that you will realize that we don't fail the test. [7]We pray to God that you don't do anything wrong, not because we want to appear to pass the test but so that you might do the right thing, even if we appear to fail.

[8]We can't do anything against the truth but only to help the truth. [9]We are happy when we are weak but you are strong. We pray for this: that you will be made complete. [10]This is why I'm writing these things while I'm away. I'm writing so that I won't need to act harshly when I'm with you by using the authority that the Lord gave me. He gave it to me so that I could build you up, not tear you down.

Final greeting

[11]Finally, brothers and sisters, good-bye. Put things in order, respond to my encouragement, be in harmony with each other, and live in peace—and the God of love and peace will be with you.

[12]Say hello to each other with a holy kiss.[k] All of God's people say hello to you.

[13]The grace of the Lord Jesus Christ, the love of God, and the fellowship of the Holy Spirit be with you all.

---

[k]2 Cor 13:12-13 is in some versions equivalent to 13:12-14.

Galatians

The young Christians in Galatia got off to a good start. They understood that Jesus died on the cross to make them right with God. They learned that forgiveness couldn't be earned by being good but was a gift of God's grace. It was an undeserved kindness from God.

But now the Galatians were all mixed up. Paul accused them of following "another gospel" (Gal 1:6), which could never make them right with God. Paul taught that people are made right with God by the faithfulness of Jesus Christ, not through the good things they do. Paul reminded the Galatians that God's gift of forgiveness is freely given to people who believe in Jesus.

Paul was sad because the Galatians had forgotten the real Jesus. He told them that they would grow as Christians by relying on God's Spirit (Gal 5:16-26). Jesus not only makes us right with God, but God's Spirit works inside us so we want to follow God's ways. God changes us into people who are loving, joyful, and kind. Galatians shows us the real way to become more like Jesus! ◊

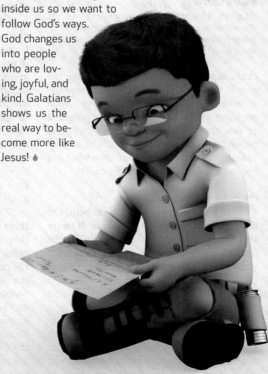

Greeting

1 From Paul, an apostle who is not sent from human authority or commissioned through human agency, but sent through Jesus Christ and God the Father who raised him from the dead; ²and from all the brothers and sisters with me.

To the churches in Galatia.

³Grace and peace to you from God the Father and the Lord Jesus Christ. ⁴He gave himself for our sins, so he could deliver us from this present evil age, according to the will of our God and Father. ⁵To God be the glory forever and always! Amen.

The gospel challenged in Galatia

⁶I'm amazed that you are so quickly deserting the one who called you by the grace of Christ to follow another gospel. ⁷It's not really another gospel, but certain people are

did you know? Barnabas was Jewish, from the tribe of Levi. Titus was Greek and worked with Paul in Corinth. By taking these two men with him, Paul showed the leaders in Jerusalem how Jewish and non-Jewish followers of Jesus could spread the message about Jesus together.

confusing you and they want to change the gospel of Christ. ⁸However, even if we ourselves or a heavenly angel should ever preach anything different from what we preached to you, they should be under a curse. ⁹I'm repeating what we've said before: if anyone preaches something different from what you received, they should be under a curse!

Paul's leadership

¹⁰Am I trying to win over human beings or God? Or am I trying to please people? If I were still trying to please people, I wouldn't be Christ's slave. ¹¹Brothers and sisters, I want you to know that the gospel I preached isn't human in origin. ¹²I didn't receive it or learn it from a human. It came through a revelation from Jesus Christ.

¹³You heard about my previous life in Judaism, how severely I harassed God's church and tried to destroy it. ¹⁴I advanced in Judaism beyond many of my peers, because I was much more militant about the traditions of

my ancestors. ¹⁵But God had set me apart from birth and called me through his grace. He was pleased ¹⁶to reveal his Son to me, so that I might preach about him to the Gentiles. I didn't immediately consult with any human being. ¹⁷I didn't go up to Jerusalem to see the men who were apostles before me either, but I went away into Arabia and I returned again to Damascus. ¹⁸Then after three years I went up to Jerusalem to visit Cephas and stayed with him fifteen days. ¹⁹But I didn't see any other of the apostles except James the brother of the Lord. ²⁰Before God, I'm not lying about the things that I'm writing to you! ²¹Then I went into the regions of Syria and Cilicia, ²²but I wasn't known personally by the Christian churches in Judea. ²³They only heard a report about me: "The man who used to harass us now preaches the faith that he once tried to destroy." ²⁴So they were glorifying God because of me.

Confirmation of Paul's leadership

2 Then after fourteen years I went up to Jerusalem again with Barnabas, and I took Titus along also. ²I went there because of a revelation, and I laid out the gospel that I preach to the Gentiles for them. But I did it privately with the influential leaders to make sure that I wouldn't be working or that I hadn't worked for nothing. ³However, not even Titus, who was with me and who was a Greek, was required to be circumcised. ⁴But false brothers and sisters, who were brought in secretly, slipped in to spy on our freedom, which we have in Christ Jesus, and to make us slaves. ⁵We didn't give in and submit to them for a single moment, so that the truth of the gospel would continue to be with you.

⁶The influential leaders didn't add anything to what I was preaching—and whatever they were makes no difference to me, because God doesn't show favoritism. ⁷But on the contrary, they saw that I had been given the responsibility to preach the gospel to the people who aren't circumcised, just as Peter had been to the circumcised. ⁸The one who empowered Peter to become an apostle to the circumcised empowered me also to be one to the Gentiles. ⁹James, Cephas, and John, who are considered to be key leaders, shook hands with me and Barnabas as equals when they

recognized the grace that was given to me. So it was agreed that we would go to the Gentiles, while they continue to go to the people who were circumcised. ¹⁰They asked only that we would remember the poor, which was certainly something I was willing to do.

The Jewish-Gentile controversy

¹¹But when Cephas came to Antioch, I opposed him to his face, because he was wrong. ¹²He had been eating with the Gentiles before certain people came from James. But when they came, he began to back out and separate himself, because he was afraid of the people who promoted circumcision. ¹³And the rest of the Jews also joined him in this hypocrisy so that even Barnabas got carried away with them in their hypocrisy. ¹⁴But when I saw that they weren't acting consistently with the truth of the gospel, I said to Cephas in front of everyone, "If you, though you're a Jew, live like a Gentile and not like a Jew, how can you require the Gentiles to live like Jews?"

UMBRELLA
FEAR

Don't Be Afraid of What People Think
Galatians 2:11-14

Before Jesus, Jewish people lived separate from non-Jewish people. After many different kinds of people became Christians, including Jews, they began to learn how to accept each other's differences. Paul found out that Cephas was ignoring non-Jewish believers called *Gentiles* when the Jews were around. It still wasn't popular to have friends outside the Jewish community, and Cephas was afraid of what Jews would say if they saw him with Gentiles. Paul said this behavior was wrong, and Cephas shouldn't worry about being seen with either Jews or Gentiles. ◖

¹⁵We are born Jews—we're not Gentile sinners. ¹⁶However, we know that a person isn't made righteous by the works of the Law but rather through the faithfulness of Jesus Christ. We ourselves believed in Christ Jesus so that we could be made righteous by the faithfulness of Christ and not by the works of the Law—because no one will be made righteous by the works of the Law. ¹⁷But if it is discovered that we ourselves are sinners while we are trying to be made righteous in Christ, then is Christ a servant of sin? Absolutely not! ¹⁸If I rebuild the very things that I tore down, I show that I myself am breaking the Law. ¹⁹I died to the Law through the Law, so that I could live for God. ²⁰I have been crucified with Christ and I no longer live, but Christ lives in me. And the life that I now live in my body, I live by faith, indeed, by the faithfulness of God's Son, who loved me and gave himself for me. ²¹I don't ignore the grace of God, because if we become righteous through the Law, then Christ died for no purpose.

Works versus the Spirit

3 You irrational Galatians! Who put a spell on you? Jesus Christ was put on display as crucified before your eyes! ²I just want to know this from you: Did you receive the Spirit by doing the works of the Law or by believing what you heard? ³Are you so irrational? After you started with the Spirit, are you now finishing up with your own human effort? ⁴Did you experience so much for nothing? I wonder if it really was for nothing. ⁵So does the one providing you with the Spirit and working miracles among you do this by you doing the works of the Law or by you believing what you heard?

Abraham: an example of righteousness

⁶Understand that in the same way that Abraham *believed God and it was credited to him as righteousness,*[a] ⁷those who believe are the children of Abraham. ⁸But when it saw ahead of time that God would make the Gentiles righteous on the basis of faith, scripture preached the gospel in advance to Abraham: *All the Gentiles will be blessed in you.*[b] ⁹Therefore, those who believe are blessed together with Abraham who believed.

¹⁰All those who rely on the works of the Law are under a curse, because it is written, *Everyone is cursed who does not keep on doing all the things that have been written in the Law scroll.*[c] ¹¹But since no one is

^aGen 15:6 ^bGen 12:3 ^cDeut 27:26

made righteous by the Law as far as God is concerned, it is clear that *the righteous one will live on the basis of faith*.[d] [12]The Law isn't based on faith; rather, *the one doing these things will live by them*.[e] [13]Christ redeemed us from the curse of the Law by becoming a curse for us—because it is written, *Everyone who is hung on a tree is cursed*.[f] [14]He redeemed us so that the blessing of Abraham would come to the Gentiles through Christ Jesus, and that we would receive the promise of the Spirit through faith.

[15]Brothers and sisters, I'll use an example from human experience. No one ignores or makes additions to a validated will. [16]The promises were made to Abraham and to his descendant. It doesn't say, "and to the descendants," as if referring to many rather than just one. It says, "and to your descendant," who is Christ. [17]I'm saying this: the Law, which came four hundred thirty years later, doesn't invalidate the agreement that was previously validated by God so that it cancels the promise. [18]If the inheritance were based upon the Law, it would no longer be from the promise. But God has given it graciously to Abraham through a promise.

did you know?

When people were baptized, they received new clothes to wear as a sign of their new life. This tradition continued for centuries. Many years later baptisms happened only at Easter. This is how the tradition of new clothes for Easter started.

The Law's origin and purpose

[19]So why was the Law given? It was added because of offenses, until the descendant would come to whom the promise had been made. It was put in place through angels by the hand of a mediator. [20]Now the mediator does not take one side; but God is one. [21]So, is the Law against the promises of God? Absolutely not! If a Law had been given that was able to give life, then righteousness would in fact have come from the Law. [22]But scripture locked up all things under sin, so that the promise based on the faithfulness of Jesus Christ might be given to those who have faith.

LIFE PRESERVER

Who are God's children?
Galatians 3:26-29

Some things never change. The world of the early Christians was just as filled with differences as our world today. For many years God's chosen people were the Jews. God set the people of Israel apart from other people to follow God's Instruction. When Jesus died and rose again so that everyone could have salvation, Gentiles were able to join God's people. This was difficult for Jewish Christians to understand after so many years of separation from Gentiles. Paul's letter was meant to teach these Christians that their differences didn't matter. It didn't matter if someone was Greek or Jewish, a slave or a free person, a woman or a man. Paul said that everyone who has been baptized is equal in Christ. ◊

[23]Before faith came, we were guarded under the Law, locked up until faith that was coming would be revealed, [24]so that the Law became our custodian until Christ so that we might be made righteous by faith.

God's children are heirs in Christ

[25]But now that faith has come, we are no longer under a custodian.

[26]You are all God's children through faith in Christ Jesus. [27]All of you who were baptized into Christ have clothed yourselves with Christ. [28]There is neither Jew nor Greek; there is neither slave nor free; nor is there male and female, for you are all one in Christ Jesus. [29]Now if you belong to Christ, then indeed you are Abraham's descendants, heirs according to the promise.

4 I'm saying that as long as the heirs are minors, they are no different from slaves, though they really are the owners of everything. [2]However, they are placed under trustees and guardians until the date set by the parents. [3]In the same way, when we were minors, we were also enslaved by this world's system. [4]But when the fulfillment of the time came, God sent his Son, born through a woman, and born under the Law. [5]This was so he could redeem those under the Law so that we could be adopted. [6]Because you are

---

[d]Hab 2:4 [e]Lev 18:5 [f]Deut 21:23

sons and daughters, God sent the Spirit of his Son into our hearts, crying, "Abba, Father!" [7]Therefore, you are no longer a slave but a son or daughter, and if you are his child, then you are also an heir through God.

Paul's concern for the Galatians

[8]At the time, when you didn't know God, you were enslaved by things that aren't gods by nature. [9]But now, after knowing God (or rather, being known by God), how can you turn back again to the weak and worthless world system? Do you want to be slaves to it again? [10]You observe religious days and months and seasons and years. [11]I'm afraid for you! Perhaps my hard work for you has been for nothing.

LIGHTHOUSE

FORGETTING GOD

Put God First *Galatians 4:8-9*
Paul was worried about the church in Galatia because the people wasted a lot of time on activities that kept them from spending time with God. The Galatians had become so focused on these other things that they didn't realize they were forgetting to worship God and put God first in their lives. ◊

[12]I beg you to be like me, brothers and sisters, because I have become like you! You haven't wronged me. [13]You know that I first preached the gospel to you because of an illness. [14]Though my poor health burdened you, you didn't look down on me or reject me, but you welcomed me as if I were an angel from God, or as if I were Christ Jesus! [15]Where then is the great attitude that you had? I swear that, if possible, you would have dug out your eyes and given them to me. [16]So then, have I become your enemy by telling you the truth? [17]They are so concerned about you, though not with good intentions. Rather, they want to shut you out so that you would run after them. [18]However, it's always good to have people concerned about you with good intentions, and not just when I'm there with you. [19]My little children, I'm going through labor pains again until Christ is formed in

you. [20]But I wish I could be with you now and change how I sound, because I'm at a loss about you.

Slave versus free

[21]Tell me—those of you who want to be under the Law—don't you listen to the Law? [22]It's written that Abraham had two sons, one by the slave woman and one by the free woman. [23]The son by the slave woman was conceived the normal way, but the son by the free woman was conceived through a promise. [24]These things are an allegory: the women are two covenants. One is from Mount Sinai, which gives birth to slave children; this is Hagar. [25]Hagar is Mount Sinai in Arabia, and she corresponds to the present-day Jerusalem, because the city is in slavery with her children. [26]But the Jerusalem that is above is free, and she is our mother. [27]It's written:

Rejoice, barren woman, you who
    have not given birth.
Break out with a shout, you who
    have not suffered labor pains;
because the woman who has been
deserted will have many more children
    than the woman who has a husband.[g]

[28]Brothers and sisters, you are children of the promise like Isaac. [29]But just as it was then, so it is now also: the one who was conceived the normal way harassed the one who was conceived by the Spirit. [30]But what does the scripture say? *Throw out the slave woman and her son, because the slave woman's son won't share the inheritance with the free woman's son.*[h] [31]Therefore, brothers and sisters, we aren't the slave woman's children, but we are the free woman's children.

5 Christ has set us free for freedom. Therefore, stand firm and don't submit to the bondage of slavery again.

Arguments against being circumcised

[2]Look, I, Paul, am telling you that if you have yourselves circumcised, having Christ won't help you. [3]Again I swear to every man who has himself circumcised that he is required to do the whole Law. [4]You people who are trying to be made righteous by the Law have been estranged from Christ. You have

[g]Isa 54:1   [h]Gen 21:10

fallen away from grace! [5]We eagerly wait for the hope of righteousness through the Spirit by faith. [6]Being circumcised or not being circumcised doesn't matter in Christ Jesus, but faith working through love does matter.

[7]You were running well—who stopped you from obeying the truth? [8]This line of reasoning doesn't come from the one who calls you. [9]A little yeast works through the whole lump of dough. [10]I'm convinced about you in the Lord that you won't think any other way. But the one who is confusing you will pay the penalty, whoever that may be. [11]Brothers and sisters, if I'm still preaching circumcision, why am I still being harassed? In that case, the offense of the cross would be canceled. [12]I wish that the ones who are upsetting you would castrate themselves!

[13]You were called to freedom, brothers and sisters; only don't let this freedom be an opportunity to indulge your selfish impulses, but serve each other through love. [14]All the Law has been fulfilled in a single statement: *Love your neighbor as yourself.*[i] [15]But if you bite and devour each other, be careful that you don't get eaten up by each other!

Two different ways of living

[16]I say be guided by the Spirit and you won't carry out your selfish desires. [17]A person's selfish desires are set against the Spirit, and the Spirit is set against one's selfish desires. They are opposed to each other, so you shouldn't do whatever you want to do. [18]But if you are being led by the Spirit, you aren't under the Law. [19]The actions that are produced by selfish motives are obvious, since they include sexual immorality, moral corruption, doing whatever feels good, [20]idolatry, drug use and casting spells, hate, fighting,

[i]Lev 19:18

God's THOUGHTS ◆ My THOUGHTS

Christians Who Bear Fruit Galatians 5:22-26

If you planted an apple tree in your backyard, you would water the tree and watch it grow, patiently waiting for the day when it grew fruit. If one season went by with no apples, you might think the tree simply needed to grow a little bit more. If a second season went by and still there were no apples, you might begin to think there was a problem. If this continued season after season even though the tree got bigger, you would know something was wrong. Fruit trees are supposed to grow fruit!

Fruit is also a word we use to talk about proof that we follow Jesus. When we choose to follow Jesus, study the Bible, and join a community of believers, beautiful things start to grow in us—things like love, joy, peace, patience, kindness, goodness, faithfulness, gentleness, and self-control. The Bible calls these things "the fruit of the Spirit" (Gal 5:22-23).

Think about your journey with Jesus. Are you like the apple tree that never grows an apple, or are you bursting with fruit? Can others look at you and see love and joy, peace and patience? Do people know you as kind, good, faithful, gentle, and in control? As you grow in faith, pray for more and more fruit. Take a look at your life and see if you're growing the fruit of the Spirit. Ask people you trust to help you see how this fruit is growing because you want to follow Jesus.

Looking at the list of qualities called the fruit of the Spirit, which ones are easy to see in your life right now?

Which ones do you need to pray to grow in your life?

obsession, losing your temper, competitive opposition, conflict, selfishness, group rivalry, [21]jealousy, drunkenness, partying, and other things like that. I warn you as I have already warned you, that those who do these kinds of things won't inherit God's kingdom.

Memorize
Gal 5:22-23

[22]But the fruit of the Spirit is love, joy, peace, patience, kindness, goodness, faithfulness, [23]gentleness, and self-control. There is no law against things like this. [24]Those who belong to Christ Jesus have crucified the self with its passions and its desires.

[25]If we live by the Spirit, let's follow the Spirit. [26]Let's not become arrogant, make each other angry, or be jealous of each other.

Caring and sharing

6 Brothers and sisters, if a person is caught doing something wrong, you who are spiritual should restore someone like this with a spirit of gentleness. Watch out for yourselves so you won't be tempted too. [2]Carry each other's burdens and so you will fulfill the law

Bet you can read this in 1 minute. **Ready, set, go!**

did you know? Many people who study the Bible believe Paul had problems with his eyesight. Whenever Paul wrote something himself instead of having a scribe write it, he pointed out how big he had to write.

of Christ. [3]If anyone thinks they are important when they aren't, they're fooling themselves. [4]Each person should test their own work and be happy with doing a good job and not compare themselves with others. [5]Each person will have to carry their own load.

[6]Those who are taught the word should share all good things with their teacher. [7]Make no mistake, God is not mocked. A person will harvest what they plant. [8]Those who plant only for their own benefit will harvest

devastation from their selfishness, but those who plant for the benefit of the Spirit will harvest eternal life from the Spirit. [9]Let's not get tired of doing good, because in time we'll have a harvest if we don't give up. [10]So then, let's work for the good of all whenever we have an opportunity, and especially for those in the household of faith.

SAILBOAT

LOVE

Don't Give Up! *Galatians 6:9*
When we feel bored or tired, we may have trouble finding the energy to think about other people. But good things happen when we act without selfishness. Paul asked the Galatians not to get tired of doing good things for people. He said that working for the good of other people would produce good results. Loving people keeps us from becoming selfish. ◆

Final greeting

[11]Look at the large letters I'm making with my own handwriting! [12]Whoever wants to look good by human standards will try to get you to be circumcised, but only so they won't be harassed for the cross of Christ. [13]Those who are circumcised don't observe the Law themselves, but they want you to be circumcised, so they can boast about your physical body.[j]

[14]But as for me, God forbid that I should boast about anything except for the cross of our Lord Jesus Christ. The world has been crucified to me through him, and I have been crucified to the world. [15]Being circumcised or not being circumcised doesn't mean anything. What matters is a new creation. [16]May peace and mercy be on whoever follows this rule and on God's Israel.

[17]From now on, no one should bother me because I bear the marks of Jesus on my body.

[18]Brothers and sisters, may the grace of our Lord Jesus Christ be with your spirit. Amen.

---

[j]In Gk the word traditionally rendered as *flesh* is rendered here as *physical body*, but it has a wide range of meaning. Gal 5:13-25; 6:8, 12 contain nine close occurrences of the same word in Gk, but it is rendered as *selfish* in regard to impulses, desires, motives, or benefit, and *human standards* in 6:12.

Ephesians

Right from the start, this letter is all about the wonderful things God has done. It begins by saying that God has blessed us (Eph 1:3). This letter explains how we can understand and enjoy these spiritual blessings.

The letter tells the Christians in Ephesus that their sin made them spiritually dead (Eph 2:1). Because they were human, they broke God's teaching and rebelled against God. But God reached out to them. When they were dead, God gave them new life in Christ. God raised them up and made them right with God. This was a gift they didn't deserve. God did all of this because of God's love (Eph 2:4-10)! The same is true for us. Although we have sinned against God, God reaches out to us. God offers us the gift of new life in Christ.

New life from God changes us. We begin to think and act more like God wants us to act. It's as if we put on fresh clothes every day (Eph 4:20-24). This new life changes how we talk (Eph 4:29-32), how we love people (Eph 5:1-20), and how we get along with our families (Eph 6:1-4). Ephesians shows us how to enjoy new life in Jesus! ◊

Greeting

1 From Paul, an apostle of Christ Jesus by God's will.

To the holy and faithful people in Christ Jesus in Ephesus.[a]

[2] Grace and peace to you from God our Father and our Lord Jesus Christ.

The believers' blessings

[3] Bless the God and Father of our Lord Jesus Christ! He has blessed us in Christ with every spiritual blessing that comes from heaven. [4] God chose us in Christ to be holy and blameless in God's presence before the creation of the world. [5] God destined us to be his adopted children through Jesus Christ because of his love. This was according to his goodwill and plan [6] and to honor his glorious grace that he has given to us freely through the Son whom he loves. [7] We have been ransomed through his Son's blood, and we have forgiveness for our failures based on his overflowing grace, [8] which he poured over us with wisdom and understanding. [9] God revealed his hidden design[b] to us, which is according to his goodwill and the plan that he intended to accomplish through his Son. [10] This is what God planned for the climax of all times:[c] to bring all things together in Christ, the things in heaven along with the things on earth. [11] We have also received an inheritance in Christ. We were destined by the plan of God, who accomplishes everything according to his design. [12] We are called to be an honor to God's glory because we were the first to hope in Christ. [13] You too heard the word of truth in Christ, which is the good news of your salvation. You were sealed with the promised Holy Spirit because you believed in Christ. [14] The Holy Spirit is the down payment on our inheritance, which is applied toward our redemption as God's own people, resulting in the honor of God's glory.

Paul's prayer for the Ephesians

[15] Since I heard about your faith in the Lord Jesus and your love for all God's people, this is the reason that [16] I don't stop giving thanks to God for you when I remember you in my prayers. [17] I pray that the God of our Lord Jesus Christ, the Father of glory, will give you a spirit of wisdom and revelation that makes

[a] The location of Ephesus was added in some later manuscripts, probably to make the opening of this letter similar to the others in the collection of Paul's letters. [b] Or *mystery* [c] Or *the fullness of times*

God's Thoughts ◆ My Thoughts

Open the Eyes of Your Heart Ephesians 1:15-19

This letter to the Christians in Ephesus was written to encourage a young church in their ministry. Paul wrote that he never stopped thanking God for this church and for the ways the people had supported him. He prayed that the eyes of their hearts would have enough light to see the amazing things God had done, was doing, and would do in and through them.

When you go to church the next time, look around and thank God for everyone you see. Pray for your friends and family, that God will show them what God wants them to do. Be like the church in this passage who loved all of God's people.

Who has prayed for you and encouraged you?

How can you "open the eyes of your heart" to the things God is doing in you?

God known to you. [18]I pray that the eyes of your heart will have enough light to see what is the hope of God's call, what is the richness of God's glorious inheritance among believers, [19]and what is the overwhelming greatness of God's power that is working among us believers. This power is conferred by the energy of God's powerful strength. [20]God's power was at work in Christ when God raised him from the dead and sat him at God's right side in the heavens, [21]far above every ruler and authority and power and angelic power, any power that might be named not only now but in the future. [22]God put everything under Christ's feet and made him head of everything in the church, [23]which is his body. His body, the church, is the fullness of Christ, who fills everything in every way.

SAILBOAT

GIVING THANKS

Give Thanks to God *Ephesians 1:16*
Paul heard that the Ephesian Christians were living faithfully and was happy they were doing so well. Every time Paul prayed for the Ephesians, he remembered to thank God for the wonderful things they said to all believers. Thanking God is an important part of prayer. When we're thankful, we're able to remember all the good things God has done for us. ◊

Saved from sin to life

2 At one time you were like a dead person because of the things you did wrong and your offenses against God. [2]You used to live like people of this world. You followed the rule of a destructive spiritual power. This is the spirit of disobedience to God's will that is now at work in persons whose lives are characterized by disobedience. [3]At one time you were like those persons. All of you used to do whatever felt good and whatever you thought you wanted so that you were children headed for punishment just like everyone else.

[4-5]However, God is rich in mercy. He brought us to life with Christ while we

Memorize Eph 2:4-5

were dead as a result of those things that we did wrong. He did this because of the great love that he has for us. You are saved by God's grace! [6]And God raised us up and seated us in the heavens with Christ Jesus. [7]God did this to show future generations the greatness of his grace by the goodness that God has shown us in Christ Jesus.

[8]You are saved by God's grace because of your faith.[d] This salvation is God's gift. It's not something you possessed. [9]It's not something you did that you can be proud of. [10]Instead, we are God's accomplishment, created in Christ Jesus to do good things. God planned for these good things to be the way that we live our lives.

Bet you can read this in 30 seconds. Ready, set, go!

The reconciliation of God's people

[11]So remember that once you were Gentiles by physical descent, who were called "uncircumcised" by Jews who are physically circumcised. [12]At that time you were without Christ. You were aliens rather than citizens of Israel, and strangers to the covenants of God's promise. In this world you had no hope and no God. [13]But now, thanks to Christ Jesus, you who once were so far away have been brought near by the blood of Christ.

[14]Christ is our peace. He made both Jews and Gentiles into one

SAILBOAT

FORGIVENESS

God Forgives Disobedience
Ephesians 2:1-10
It's normal to feel guilty after being disobedient and doing something against God's will. But disobedience is also selfish, and being selfish causes harm to us or other people. Think about it like this: Kids depend on parents and other people to take care of them and help them grow up. If those parents act selfishly, children might not get the food and love they need to survive and thrive. Sometimes it's hard not to do selfish things, but God will help. God is merciful. *Mercy* is an act of kindness that we don't deserve. Because God loves us, God forgives our disobedience and allows us to start over. ◊

[d]*Or through his faithfulness*

group. With his body, he broke down the barrier of hatred that divided us. ¹⁵He canceled the detailed rules of the Law so that he could create one new person out of the two groups, making peace. ¹⁶He reconciled them both as one body to God by the cross, which ended the hostility to God.

¹⁷When he came, he announced the good news of peace to you who were far away from God and to those who were near. ¹⁸We both have access to the Father through Christ by the one Spirit. ¹⁹So now you are no longer strangers and aliens. Rather, you are fellow citizens with God's people, and you belong to God's household. ²⁰As God's household, you are built on the foundation of the apostles and prophets with Christ Jesus himself as the cornerstone. ²¹The whole building is joined together in him, and it grows up into a temple that is dedicated to the Lord. ²²Christ is building you into a place where God lives through the Spirit.

Paul, apostle to the Gentiles

3 This is why I, Paul, am a prisoner of Christ for you Gentiles.

²You've heard, of course, about the responsibility to distribute God's grace, which God gave to me for you, right? ³God showed me his secret plan^e in a revelation, as I mentioned briefly before (⁴when you read this, you'll understand my insight into the secret plan^f about Christ). ⁵Earlier generations didn't know this hidden plan that God has now revealed to his holy apostles and prophets

LIGHTHOUSE

It's Up to Us *Ephesians 3:2-7*
Paul told the Ephesians that he had a special message about God for them from Christ Jesus. We can share this good news too. Some people are like Paul and become missionaries. *Missionaries* travel to faraway countries and places to help others who suffer and to tell people about Jesus. God gives all followers of Jesus opportunities to share the good news about Jesus. ◆

through the Spirit. ⁶This plan is that the Gentiles would be coheirs and parts of the same body, and that they would share with the Jews in the promises of God in Christ Jesus through the gospel. ⁷I became a servant of the gospel because of the grace that God showed me through the exercise of his power.

⁸God gave his grace to me, the least of all God's people, to preach the good news about the immeasurable riches of Christ to the Gentiles. ⁹God sent me to reveal the secret plan^g that had been hidden since the beginning of time by God, who created everything. ¹⁰God's purpose is now to show the rulers and powers in the heavens the many different varieties of his wisdom through the church. ¹¹This was consistent with the plan he had from the beginning of time that he accomplished through Christ Jesus our Lord. ¹²In Christ we have bold and confident access to God through faith in him.^h ¹³So then, I ask you not to become discouraged by what I'm suffering for you, which is your glory.

Paul's prayer for the Ephesians

¹⁴This is why I kneel before the Father. ¹⁵Every ethnic group in heaven or on earth is recognized by him. ¹⁶I ask that he will strengthen you in your inner selves from the riches of his glory through the Spirit. ¹⁷I ask that Christ will live in your hearts through faith. As a result of having strong roots in love, ¹⁸I ask that you'll have the power to grasp love's width and length, height and depth, together with all believers. ¹⁹I ask that you'll know the love of Christ that is beyond knowledge so that you will be filled entirely with the fullness of God.

²⁰Glory to God, who is able to do far beyond all that we could ask or imagine by his power at work within us; ²¹glory to him in the church and in Christ Jesus for all generations, forever and always. Amen.

Unity of the body of Christ

4 Therefore, as a prisoner for the Lord, I encourage you to live as people worthy of the call you received from God. ²Conduct yourselves with all humility, gentleness, and patience. Accept each other with love,

---

^e Or *mystery* ^f Or *mystery* ^g Or *mystery* ^h Or *through his faithfulness*

LIFE PRESERVER

Why was unity so important? *Ephesians 4:1-6*

Unity is the main theme of Ephesians. *Unity* means to get along and live in harmony with other people. Paul wanted Jews and Gentiles to know how important it is for all human beings to live in peace together. This letter teaches that part of God's plan for the world is for people to live in unity. Ephesians 4:4-6 lists seven reasons why church unity is important. There is one body, one spirit, one hope in a calling, one Lord, one faith, one baptism, and one God of all. Seven was the perfect number. ◊

³and make an effort to preserve the unity of the Spirit with the peace that ties you together. ⁴You are one body and one spirit, just as God also called you in one hope. ⁵There is one Lord, one faith, one baptism, ⁶and one God and Father of all, who is over all, through all, and in all.

⁷God has given his grace to each one of us measured out by the gift that is given by Christ. ⁸That's why scripture says, *When he climbed up to the heights, he captured prisoners, and he gave gifts to people.*ⁱ

⁹What does the phrase "he climbed up" mean if it doesn't mean that he had first gone down into the lower regions, the earth? ¹⁰The one who went down is the same one who climbed up above all the heavens so that he might fill everything.

¹¹He gave some apostles, some prophets, some evangelists, and some pastors and teachers. ¹²His purpose was to equip God's people for the work of serving and building up the body of Christ ¹³until we all reach the unity of faith and knowledge of God's Son. God's goal is for us to become mature adults—to be fully grown, measured by the standard of the fullness of Christ. ¹⁴As a result, we aren't supposed to be infants any longer who can be tossed and blown around by every wind that comes from teaching with deceitful scheming and the tricks people play to deliberately mislead others. ¹⁵Instead, by speaking the truth with love, let's grow in every way into Christ, ¹⁶who is the head. The whole body grows from him, as it is joined and held together by all the supporting ligaments. The body makes itself grow in that it builds itself up with love as each one does its part.

The old and new life

¹⁷So I'm telling you this, and I insist on it in the Lord: you shouldn't live your life like the Gentiles anymore. They base their lives on pointless thinking, ¹⁸and they are in the dark in their reasoning. They are disconnected from God's life because of their ignorance and their closed hearts. ¹⁹They are people who lack all sense of right and wrong, and who have turned themselves over to doing whatever feels good and to practicing every sort of corruption along with greed.

²⁰But you didn't learn that sort of thing from Christ. ²¹Since you really listened to him and you were taught how the truth is in Jesus, ²²change the former way of life that was part of the person you once were, corrupted by deceitful desires. ²³Instead, renew the thinking in your mind by the Spirit ²⁴and clothe yourself with the new person created according to God's image in justice and true holiness.

²⁵Therefore, after you have gotten rid of lying, *Each of you must tell the truth to your neighbor*ʲ because we are parts of each other in the same body. ²⁶*Be angry without sinning.*ᵏ Don't let the sun set on your anger. ²⁷Don't provide an opportunity for the devil. ²⁸Thieves should no longer steal. Instead, they should go to work, using their hands to do good so that they will have something to share with whoever is in need.

²⁹Don't let any foul words come out of your mouth. Only say what is helpful when it is needed for building up the community so that it benefits those who hear what you say. ³⁰Don't make the Holy Spirit of God unhappy—you were sealed by him for the day of redemption. ³¹Put aside all bitterness, losing your temper, anger, shouting, and slander, along with every other evil. ³²Be kind, compassionate, and forgiving to each other, in the same way God forgave you in Christ.

Memorize
Eph 4:32

ⁱPs 68:18 ʲZech 8:16 ᵏPs 4:4

5 Therefore, imitate God like dearly loved children. [2]Live your life with love, following the example of Christ, who loved us and gave himself for us. He was a sacrificial offering that smelled sweet to God.

[3]Sexual immorality, and any kind of impurity or greed, shouldn't even be mentioned among you, which is right for holy persons. [4]Obscene language, silly talk, or vulgar jokes aren't acceptable for believers. Instead, there should be thanksgiving. [5]Because you know for sure that persons who are sexually immoral, impure, or greedy—which happens when things become gods—those persons won't inherit the kingdom of Christ and God.

Be children of light

[6]Nobody should deceive you with stupid ideas. God's anger comes down on those who are disobedient because of this kind of thing. [7]So you shouldn't have anything to do with them. [8]You were once darkness, but now you are light in the Lord, so live your life as children of light. [9]Light produces fruit that consists of every sort of goodness, justice, and truth. [10]Therefore, test everything to see what's pleasing to the Lord, [11]and don't participate in the unfruitful actions of darkness. Instead, you should reveal the truth about them. [12]It's embarrassing to even talk about what certain persons do in secret. [13]But everything exposed to the light is revealed by the light. [14]Everything that is revealed by the light is light. Therefore, it says, *Wake up, sleeper!*[l] *Get up from the dead,*[m] *and Christ will shine on you.*[n]

Be filled with the Spirit

[15]So be careful to live your life wisely, not foolishly. [16]Take advantage of every opportunity because these are evil times. [17]Because of this, don't be ignorant, but understand the Lord's will. [18]Don't get drunk on wine, which produces depravity. Instead, be filled with the Spirit in the following ways: [19]speak to each other with psalms, hymns, and spiritual songs; sing and make music to the Lord in your hearts; [20]always give thanks to God the Father for everything in the name of our Lord Jesus Christ; [21]and submit to each other out of respect for Christ. [22]For example, wives should submit to their husbands as if to the Lord. [23]A husband is the head of his wife like Christ is head of the church, that is, the savior of the body. [24]So wives submit to their husbands in everything like the church submits to Christ. [25]As for husbands, love your wives just like Christ loved the church and gave himself for her. [26]He did this to make her holy by washing her in a bath of water with the word. [27]He did this to present himself with a splendid church, one without any sort of stain or wrinkle on her clothes, but rather one that is holy and blameless. [28]That's how husbands ought to love their wives—in the same way as they do their own bodies. Anyone who loves his wife loves himself. [29]No one ever hates his own body, but feeds it and takes care of it just like Christ does for the church [30]because we are parts of his body. [31]*This is why a man will leave his father and mother and be united with his wife, and the two of them will be one body.*[o] [32]Marriage is a significant allegory,[p] and I'm applying it to Christ and the church. [33]In any case, as for you individually, each one of you should love his wife as himself, and wives should respect[q] their husbands.

6 As for children, obey your parents in the Lord, because it is right. [2]The commandment *Honor your father and mother* is the first one with a promise attached: [3]*so that things will go well for you, and you will live for a long time in the land.*[r] [4]As for parents, don't provoke your children to anger, but raise them with discipline and instruction about the Lord.

[5]As for slaves, obey your human masters with fear and trembling and with sincere devotion to Christ. [6]Don't work to make yourself look good and try to flatter people, but act like slaves of Christ carrying out God's will from the heart. [7]Serve your owners enthusiastically, as though you were serving the Lord and not human beings. [8]You know that the Lord will reward every person who does what is right, whether that person is a slave or a free person. [9]As for masters, treat your slaves in the same way. Stop threatening them, because you know that both you

---

[l]Isa 26:19; 51:17; 52:1; 60:1 [m]Isa 26:19 [n]Isa 60:1 [o]Gen 2:24 [p]Or *mystery* [q]Or *fear* [r]Exod 20:12; Deut 5:16

and your slaves have a master in heaven. He doesn't distinguish between people on the basis of status.

Put on the armor of God

[10]Finally, be strengthened by the Lord and his powerful strength. [11]Put on God's armor so that you can make a stand against the tricks of the devil. [12]We aren't fighting against human enemies but against rulers, authorities, forces of cosmic darkness, and spiritual powers of evil in the heavens. [13]Therefore, pick up the full armor of God so that you can stand your ground on the evil day and after you have done everything possible to still stand. [14]So stand with the belt of truth around your waist, justice as your breastplate, [15]and put shoes on your feet so that you are ready to spread the good news of peace. [16]Above all, carry the shield of faith so that you can extinguish the flaming arrows of the evil one. [17]Take the helmet of salvation and the sword of the Spirit, which is God's word.

[18]Offer prayers and petitions in the Spirit all the time. Stay alert by hanging in there and praying for all believers. [19]As for me, pray that when I open my mouth, I'll get a message that confidently makes this secret plan[s] of the gospel known. [20]I'm an ambassador in chains for the sake of the gospel. Pray so that the Lord will give me the confidence to say what I have to say.

Final greeting

[21]Tychicus, my loved brother and faithful servant of the Lord, can inform you about my situation and what I'm doing. [22]I've sent him for this reason—so that you will know about us. He can reassure you.

[23]May there be peace with the brothers and sisters as well as love with the faith that comes from God the Father and the Lord Jesus Christ. [24]May grace be with all those who love our Lord Jesus Christ forever.

[s]Or mystery

Armor of God   *Ephesians 6:10-18*

Soccer players wear shin guards and long socks to protect them from being injured when they are kicked. They wear cleats that dig into the ground so they don't slip and fall all over the field. Football players wear shoulder pads, thigh pads, cleats, and a helmet with a face guard to protect their bodies against the weight and force of the tackles. People in the military put on heavy-duty pants and coats, and a helmet to protect them in the event of a battle. This real-life armor helps keep people safe.

The Bible talks about another kind of armor: spiritual armor. Paul reminds us that there is evil in the world, and we can protect ourselves from it by putting on the full armor of God. This armor includes the belt of truth, the breastplate of justice, shoes that make us run to spread the good news of peace, the shield of faith, the helmet of salvation, and the sword of the Spirit. These things are like our spiritual uniform as we live our lives as Christians in this world. The next time you get dressed, think about putting on the armor of God over your clothes and be brave as you follow Jesus.

Draw a picture of each of the pieces of spiritual armor. Imagine that you are putting them on over your clothes every day.

How do you think the full armor of God can protect you?

Philippians

The apostle Paul was a prisoner in Rome, locked in chains for his faith in Jesus. He was suffering and knew he might die soon. But his words in this letter may surprise you. From his prison cell, Paul wrote a hopeful and joyful letter to his friends in the city of Philippi.

Paul began this letter by remembering that the Philippians were his trusted partners in spreading the word about Jesus (Phil 1:3-8). Their friendship went back to the time Paul started their church (Acts 16:11-40).

Then Paul wrote important lessons about living with joy that were true for his friends at Philippi and for us today. He taught that we find joy when we serve each other like Jesus served us (Phil 2:1-11). He taught that knowing Jesus is the most valuable part of life (Phil 3:7-11). Paul said that God gives us peace when we pray (Phil 4:6-8). Paul taught that we can be happy whether we are hungry or well-fed, well-off or poor (Phil 4:12), and that we can face anything because God makes us strong (Phil 4:13). God will meet our every need (Phil 4:19). This letter shows us that Jesus can make us joyful no matter what we face in life! ◊

Greeting

1 From Paul and Timothy, slaves of Christ Jesus.

To all those in Philippi who are God's people in Christ Jesus, along with your supervisors^a and servants.^b [a][b] ²May the grace and peace from God our Father and the Lord Jesus Christ be with you.

Thanksgiving and prayer

³I thank my God every time I mention you in my prayers. ⁴I'm thankful for all of you every time I pray, and it's always a prayer full of joy. ⁵I'm glad because of the way you have been my partners in the ministry of the gospel from the time you first believed it until now. ⁶I'm sure about this: the one who started a good work in you will stay with you to complete the job by the day of Christ Jesus. ⁷I have good reason to think this way about all of you because I keep you in my heart. You are all my partners in God's grace, both during my time in prison and in the defense and support of the gospel. ⁸God is my witness that I feel affection for all of you with the compassion of Christ Jesus.

⁹This is my prayer: that your love might become even more and more rich with knowledge and all kinds of insight. ¹⁰I pray this so that you will be able to decide what really matters and so you will be sincere and blameless

on the day of Christ. ¹¹I pray that you will then be filled with the fruit of righteousness, which comes from Jesus Christ, in order to give glory and praise to God.

Priority of the gospel

¹²Brothers and sisters, I want you to know that the things that have happened to me have actually advanced the gospel. ¹³The whole Praetorian Guard and everyone else knows that I'm in prison for Christ. ¹⁴Most of the brothers and sisters have had more confidence through the Lord to speak the word boldly and bravely because of my jail time. ¹⁵Some certainly preach Christ with jealous and competitive motives, but others preach with good motives. ¹⁶They are motivated by love, because they know that I'm put here to give a defense of the gospel; ¹⁷the others preach Christ because of their selfish ambition. They are insincere, hoping to cause me more pain while I'm in prison.

¹⁸What do I think about this? Just this: since Christ is proclaimed in every possible way, whether from dishonest or true motives, I'm glad and I'll continue to be glad. ¹⁹I'm glad because I know that this will result in my release through your prayers and the help of the Spirit of Jesus Christ. ²⁰It is my expectation and hope that I won't be put to shame in anything. Rather, I hope with daring courage that Christ's greatness will be seen in my body, now as always, whether I live or die. ²¹Because for me, living serves Christ and dying is even better. ²²If I continue to live in this world, I get results from my work. ²³But I don't know what I prefer. I'm torn between the two because I want to leave this life and be with Christ, which is far better. ²⁴However, it's more important for me to stay in this world for your sake. ²⁵I'm sure of this: I will stay alive and remain with all of you to help

LIGHTHOUSE

WISDOM

Start with What Really Matters
Philippians 1:1-11

How we start something makes a big difference in where we end up. From the start of his letter to the church in Philippi, Paul pointed out what matters most. He gave thanks to God for the faithfulness of the people, and then prayed they would grow deeper in love with God and each other. Paul said that love would help them know what was important and stay close to Jesus. The things that really matter are the things that last: love, faith, hope, and peace. These things will help us believe in Jesus, follow Jesus, and grow more in love with God. ◆

^aOr overseers, bishops ^bOr deacons

your progress and the joy of your faith, ²⁶and to increase your pride in Christ Jesus through my presence when I visit you again.

Live worthy of the gospel

²⁷Most important, live together in a manner worthy of Christ's gospel. Do this, whether I come and see you or I'm absent and hear about you. Do this so that you stand firm, united in one spirit and mind as you struggle together to remain faithful to the gospel. ²⁸That way, you won't be afraid of anything your enemies do. Your faithfulness and courage are a sign of their coming destruction and your salvation, which is from God. ²⁹God has generously granted you the privilege, not only of believing in Christ but also of suffering for Christ's sake. ³⁰You are having the same struggle that you saw me face and now hear that I'm still facing.

Imitate Christ

2 Therefore, if there is any encouragement in Christ, any comfort in love, any sharing in the Spirit, any sympathy, ²complete my joy by thinking the same way, having the same love, being united, and agreeing with each other. ³Don't do anything for selfish purposes, but with humility think of others as better than yourselves. ⁴Instead of each person watching out for their own good, watch out for what is better for others. ⁵Adopt the attitude that was in Christ Jesus:

⁶ Though he was in the form of God,
 he did not consider being equal
 with God something to exploit.
⁷ But he emptied himself
 by taking the form of a slave
 and by becoming like human beings.
When he found himself
 in the form of a human,
⁸ he humbled himself by becoming
 obedient to the point of death,

even death on a cross.
⁹ Therefore, God highly honored him
 and gave him a name above all names,
¹⁰ so that at the name of Jesus everyone
 in heaven, on earth,
 and under the earth might bow
¹¹ and every tongue confess
 that Jesus Christ is Lord,
 to the glory of God the Father.

Carry out your salvation

¹²Therefore, my loved ones, just as you always obey me, not just when I am present but now even more while I am away, carry out your own salvation with fear and trembling. ¹³God is the one who enables **Memorize Phil 2:13** you both to want and to actually live out his good purposes. ¹⁴Do everything without grumbling and arguing ¹⁵so that you may be blameless and pure, innocent children of God surrounded by people who are crooked and corrupt. Among these people you shine like stars in the world ¹⁶because you hold on to the word of life. This will allow me to say on the day of Christ that I haven't run for nothing or worked for nothing. ¹⁷But even if I am poured out like a drink offering upon the altar of service for your faith, I am glad. I'm glad with all of you. ¹⁸You should be glad about this in the same way. Be glad with me!

Sending Timothy and Epaphroditus

¹⁹I hope in the Lord Jesus to send Timothy to see you soon so that I may be encouraged by hearing about you. ²⁰I have no one like him. He is a person who genuinely cares about your well-being. ²¹All the others put their own business ahead of Jesus Christ's business. ²²You know his character, how he labors with me for the gospel like a son works with his father. ²³So he is the one that I hope to send as soon as I find out how things turn out here for me. ²⁴I trust in the Lord that I also will visit you soon.

²⁵I think it is also necessary to send Epaphroditus to you. He is my brother, co-worker, and fellow soldier; and he is your representative who serves my needs. ²⁶He misses you all, and he was upset because you heard he was sick. ²⁷In fact, he was so sick that he nearly died. But God had mercy on

him—and not just on him but also on me, because his death would have caused me great sorrow. ²⁸Therefore, I am sending him immediately so that when you see him again you can be glad and I won't worry. ²⁹So welcome him in the Lord with great joy and show great respect for people like him. ³⁰He risked his life and almost died for the work of Christ, and he did this to make up for the help you couldn't give me.

Values and priorities

3 So then, my brothers and sisters, be glad in the Lord. It's no trouble for me to repeat the same things to you because they will help keep you on track. ²Watch out for the "dogs." Watch out for people who do evil things. Watch out for those who insist on circumcision, which is really mutilation. ³We are the circumcision. We are the ones who serve by God's Spirit and who boast in Christ Jesus. We don't put our confidence in rituals performed on the body, ⁴though I have good reason to have this kind of confidence. If anyone else

has reason to put their confidence in physical advantages, I have even more:

⁵I was circumcised on the eighth day.

I am from the people of Israel and the tribe of Benjamin.

I am a Hebrew of the Hebrews.

With respect to observing the Law, I'm a Pharisee.

⁶With respect to devotion to the faith, I harassed the church.

With respect to righteousness under the Law, I'm blameless.

⁷These things were my assets, but I wrote them off as a loss for the sake of Christ. ⁸But even beyond that, I consider everything a loss in comparison with the superior value of knowing Christ Jesus my Lord. I have lost everything for him, but what I lost I think of as sewer trash, so that I might gain Christ ⁹and be found in him. In Christ I have a righteousness that is not my own and that does not come from the Law but rather from the faithfulness of Christ. It is the righteousness of God that is based on faith.

God's THOUGHTS ◆ My THOUGHTS

You Can Do It! *Philippians 3:12-16*

When you feel like you're never going to finish a task or a project you're working on, someone might say to you, "You can do it!" They might encourage you and tell you they believe in you. Knowing someone believes we can do something helps us to feel good—even when we're not sure we'll ever get to the end of our work.

Paul wrote these verses to encourage the followers of Jesus at Philippi to keep doing the work of spreading the good news. He compared the life of a believer with someone running a race and working toward a goal.

When we feel frustrated or even just lazy in our faith, we can hear these words of encouragement telling us that we can do it. When we think we have sinned too much or made too many bad decisions, we're reminded to forget the past and keep moving forward. This letter teaches us to pursue God like a prize. We do this by running after and searching for God, growing in our faith, and being changed along the way.

How can you pursue God?

How can you grow a little more in faith every day?

¹⁰The righteousness that I have comes from knowing Christ, the power of his resurrection, and the participation in his sufferings. It includes being conformed to his death ¹¹so that I may perhaps reach the goal of the resurrection of the dead.

¹²It's not that I have already reached this goal or have already been perfected, but I pursue it, so that I may grab hold of it because Christ grabbed hold of me for just this purpose. ¹³Brothers and sisters, I myself don't think I've reached it, but I do this one thing: I forget about the things behind me and reach out for the things ahead of me. ¹⁴The goal I pursue is the prize of God's upward call in Christ Jesus. ¹⁵So all of us who are spiritually mature should think this way, and if anyone thinks differently, God will reveal it to him or her. ¹⁶Only let's live in a way that is consistent with whatever level we have reached.

Imitate Paul

¹⁷Brothers and sisters, become imitators of me and watch those who live this way—you can use us as models. ¹⁸As I have told you many times and now say with deep sadness, many people live as enemies of the cross. ¹⁹Their lives end with destruction. Their god is their stomach, and they take pride in their disgrace because their thoughts focus on earthly things. ²⁰Our citizenship is in heaven. We look forward to a savior that comes from there—the Lord Jesus Christ. ²¹He will transform our humble bodies so that they are like his glorious body, by the power that also makes him able to subject all things to himself.

Stand firm in the Lord

4 Therefore, my brothers and sisters whom I love and miss, who are my joy and crown, stand firm in the Lord.

Loved ones, ²I urge Euodia and I urge Syntyche to come to an agreement in the Lord. ³Yes, and I'm also asking you, loyal friend, to help these women who have struggled together with me in the ministry of the gospel, along with Clement and the rest of my coworkers whose names are in the scroll of life.

Memorize
Phil 4:4

⁴Be glad in the Lord always! Again I say, be glad! ⁵Let your gentleness show in your

treatment of all people. The Lord is near. ⁶Don't be anxious about anything; rather, bring up all of your requests to God in your prayers and petitions, along with giving thanks. ⁷Then the peace of God that exceeds all understanding will keep your hearts and minds safe in Christ Jesus.

UMBRELLA
ANXIOUS

Let God Take Care of Worries
Philippians 4:6-7
Many things are difficult to deal with in life, and at times we may feel anxious. Sometimes we worry about friendships, school, money, the weather, and more. Worry sometimes takes over, making it hard to feel safe. Paul said not to worry about anything but to pray to God. Ask God for help and then give God thanks. It may seem strange to think about thanking God when we're worried, but God deserves our thanks. Giving thanks will bring us peace when we remember how God loves and blesses us! ♦

⁸From now on, brothers and sisters, if anything is excellent and if anything is admirable, focus your thoughts on these things: all that is true, all that is holy, all that is just, all that is pure, all that is lovely, and all that is worthy of praise. ⁹Practice these things: whatever you learned, received, heard, or saw in us. The God of peace will be with you.

Paul's thanks for gifts

¹⁰I was very glad in the Lord because now at last you have shown concern for me again.

LIFE PRESERVER

How can God's peace be in our hearts? *Philippians 4:4-7*

In four short verses, Paul explains what he wanted the Christians in the church at Philippi to remember. He told them to be glad and treat everyone with kindness. He reminded them not to worry about tomorrow. And he told them to pray, telling God about worries and thanking God for joys. Living like this, Paul said, would put God's peace in their hearts—and ours as well! ♦

(Of course you were always concerned but had no way to show it.) [11]I'm not saying this because I need anything, for I have learned how to be content in any circumstance. [12]I know the experience of being in need and of having more than enough; I have learned the secret to being content in any and every circumstance, whether full or hungry or whether having plenty or being poor. [13]I can endure all these things through the power of the one who gives me strength. [14]Still, you have done well to share my distress.

[15]You Philippians know from the time of my first mission work in Macedonia how no church shared in supporting my ministry except you. [16]You sent contributions repeatedly to take care of my needs even while I was in Thessalonica. [17]I'm not hoping for a gift, but I am hoping for a profit that accumulates in your account. [18]I now have plenty and it is more than enough. I am full to overflowing because I received the gifts that you sent from Epaphroditus. Those gifts give off a fragrant aroma, an acceptable sacrifice that pleases God. [19]My God will meet your every need out of his riches in the glory that is found in Christ Jesus. [20]Let glory be given to God our Father forever and always. Amen.

Final greeting

[21]Greet all God's people in Christ Jesus. The brothers and sisters with me send you their greeting. [22]All God's people here, especially those in Caesar's household, send you their greeting. [23]The grace of the Lord Jesus Christ be with your spirits.

Colossians

things YOU'LL DISCOVER

Colossians is a letter written to Christians who were beginning to forget who Jesus really is. This letter was meant to remind them of the truth about Jesus and to encourage them to be faithful.

people YOU'LL MEET

Paul—a missionary of the church (Col 1–4)
Epaphras—founder of the church in Colossae (Col 1; 4)
Tychicus, Onesimus, Aristarchus, Mark, Justus, Luke, Demas, Nympha, Archippuss—some of Paul's friends and helpers (Col 4)

places YOU'LL GO

Colossae (present-day Turkey), **Laodicea** (present-day Turkey)

words YOU'LL REMEMBER

"Think about the things above and not things on earth" (Col 3:2).

A man named **Epaphras** was the first to tell the people in Colossae about Jesus (Col 1:7). Yet Paul loved and admired this young church. He had prayed for them and asked God to fill them with wisdom and understanding (Col 1:3-14).

This group of Christians needed a clear understanding of Jesus, and this letter helped correct some of their wrong ideas. Some of the Colossians tried to earn God's favor by following Jewish Law, which included teaching about food, religious holidays, and the Sabbath. Others worshiped angels and spiritual powers.

These wrong ideas led people away from the simple truth about Jesus. So Paul worked hard to explain Jesus to them. His letter teaches that Jesus is more important than any other being. Jesus created all things. Jesus shows us who God is, and his death made peace between God and people (Col 1:16-20). Jesus is God in a human body (Col 2:9).

Paul said that staying close to Jesus was the most important thing the Colossians could do. They should live as if they were headed for heaven. He wanted them to get rid of all sin, work hard, and remember that God is the one who gives new life.

The same is true for us today. Because Christ Jesus is God, we should live for him (Col 2:6). This letter reminds us who Jesus really is! ◆

Greeting

1 From Paul, an apostle of Christ Jesus by God's will, and Timothy our brother. ²To the holy and faithful brothers and sisters in Christ in Colossae.

Grace and peace to you from God our Father.

Thanksgiving and prayer for the Colossians

³We always give thanks to God, the Father of our Lord Jesus Christ, when we pray for you. ⁴We've done this since we heard of your faith in Christ Jesus and your love for all God's people. ⁵You have this faith and love because of the hope reserved for you in heaven. You previously heard about this hope through the true message, the good news, ⁶which has come to you. This message has been bearing fruit and growing among you since the day you heard and truly understood God's grace, in the same way that it is bearing fruit and growing in the whole world. ⁷You learned it from Epaphras, who is the fellow slave we love and Christ's faithful minister for your sake. ⁸He informed us of your love in the Spirit.

⁹Because of this, since the day we heard about you, we haven't stopped praying for you and asking for you to be filled with the knowledge of God's will, with all wisdom and spiritual understanding. ¹⁰We're praying this so that you can live lives that are worthy of the Lord and pleasing to him in every way: by producing fruit in every good work and growing in the knowledge of God; ¹¹by being strengthened through his glorious might so that you endure everything and have patience; ¹²and by giving thanks with joy to the Father. He made it so you could take part in the inheritance, in light granted to God's holy people. ¹³He rescued us from the control of darkness and transferred us into the kingdom of the Son he loves. ¹⁴He set us free through the Son and forgave our sins.

Hymn about Christ's work

¹⁵The Son is the image
of the invisible God,
the one who is first over all creation,ᵃ

¹⁶ Because all things were created
by him:
both in the heavens
and on the earth,

the things that are visible
and the things that are invisible.
Whether they are thrones or powers,
or rulers or authorities,
all things were created
through him and for him.

¹⁷ He existed before all things,
and all things are held together in him.

¹⁸ He is the head of the body, the church,
who is the beginning,
the one who is firstborn
from among the deadᵇ
so that he might occupy
the first place in everything.

did you know? Paul never visited Colossae. This is the only letter we have where Paul wrote to a church he never visited or planned to visit. There may have been other letters like this, but if they existed, they were lost. Paul probably wrote many more letters than the ones that are included in the Bible.

¹⁹ Because all the fullness of God
was pleased to live in him,
²⁰ and he reconciled all things to himself
through him—
whether things on earth
or in the heavens.
He brought peace
through the blood of his cross.

²¹Once you were alienated from God and you were enemies with him in your minds, which was shown by your evil actions. ²²But now he has reconciled you by his physical body through death, to present you before God as a people who are holy, faultless, and without blame. ²³But you need to remain well established and rooted in faith and not shift away from the hope given in the good news that you heard. This message has been preached throughout all creation under heaven. And I, Paul, became a servant of this good news.

Paul's service for the church

²⁴Now I'm happy to be suffering for you. I'm completing what is missing from Christ's

Bet you can read this in 2 minutes. Ready, set, go!

ᵃOr *firstborn of all creation* ᵇOr *first over the dead*

sufferings with my own body. I'm doing this for the sake of his body, which is the church. ²⁵I became a servant of the church by God's commission, which was given to me for you, in order to complete God's word. ²⁶I'm completing it with a secret plan^c that has been hidden for ages and generations but which has now been revealed to his holy people. ²⁷God wanted to make the glorious riches of this secret plan^d known among the Gentiles, which is Christ living in you, the hope of glory. ²⁸This is what we preach as we warn and teach every person with all wisdom so that we might present each one mature in Christ. ²⁹I work hard and struggle for this goal with his energy, which works in me powerfully.

2 I want you to know how much I struggle for you, for those in Laodicea, and for all who haven't known me personally. ²My goal is that their hearts would be encouraged and united together in love so that they might have all the riches of assurance that come with understanding, so that they might have the knowledge of the secret plan^e of God, namely Christ. ³All the treasures of wisdom and knowledge are hidden in him. ⁴I'm telling you this so that no one deceives you with convincing arguments, ⁵because even though I am absent physically, I'm with you in spirit. I'm happy to see the discipline and stability of your faith in Christ.

Error threatening the church

⁶So live in Christ Jesus the Lord in the same way as you received him. ⁷Be rooted and built up in him, be established in faith, and overflow with thanksgiving just as you were taught. ⁸See to it that nobody enslaves you with philosophy and foolish deception, which conform to human traditions and the way the world thinks and acts rather than Christ. ⁹All the fullness of deity lives in Christ's body. ¹⁰And you have been filled by him, who is the head of every ruler and authority. ¹¹You were also circumcised by him. This wasn't performed by human hands—the whole body was removed through this circumcision by Christ. ¹²You were buried with him through baptism and raised with him through faith in the power of God, who raised him from the dead.

¹³When you were dead because of the things you had done wrong and because your body wasn't circumcised, God made you alive with Christ and forgave all the things you had done wrong. ¹⁴He destroyed the record of the debt we owed, with its requirements that worked against us. He canceled it by nailing it to the cross. ¹⁵When he disarmed the rulers and authorities, he exposed them to public disgrace by leading them in a triumphal parade.

¹⁶So don't let anyone judge you about eating or drinking or about a festival, a new moon observance, or sabbaths. ¹⁷These religious practices are only a shadow of what was coming—the body that cast the shadow is Christ. ¹⁸Don't let anyone who wants to practice harsh self-denial and worship angels rob you of the prize. They go into detail about what they have seen in visions and have become unjustifiably arrogant by their selfish way of thinking. ¹⁹They don't stay connected to the head. The head nourishes and supports the whole body through the joints and ligaments, so the body grows with a growth that is from God.

²⁰If you died with Christ to the way the world thinks and acts, why do you submit to rules and regulations as though you were living in the world? ²¹"Don't handle!" "Don't taste!" "Don't touch!" ²²All these things cease to exist when they are used. Such rules are human commandments and teachings.

LIGHTHOUSE

WISDOM

Knowing the Truth from a Lie
Colossians 2:8
There have always been ideas that are not true. These wrong ideas can appear to be true and mislead people. One example of a wrong idea is that we are happier the more things we own. This idea has been around for a long time but is simply not true. When Paul wrote to the Colossians, he was concerned for them. He didn't want these Christians to believe the wrong ideas of their time. Paul instructed the Colossians to check the ideas and teachings they heard against the true teaching of Christ. ◗

^cOr *mystery* ^dOr *mystery* ^eOr *mystery*

²³They look like they are wise with this self-made religion and their self-denial by the harsh treatment of the body, but they are no help against indulging in selfish immoral behavior.

Your life hidden in Christ

3 Therefore, if you were raised with Christ, look for the things that are above where Christ is sitting at God's right side. ²Think about the things above and not things on earth. ³You died, and your life is hidden with Christ in God. ⁴When Christ, who is your life, is revealed, then you also will be revealed with him in glory.

Memorize Col 3:2

⁵So put to death the parts of your life that belong to the earth, such as sexual immorality, moral corruption, lust, evil desire, and greed (which is idolatry). ⁶The wrath of God is coming upon disobedient people because of these things. ⁷You used to live this way, when you were alive to these things. ⁸But now set aside these things, such as anger, rage, malice, slander, and obscene language. ⁹Don't lie to each other. Take off the old human nature with its practices ¹⁰and put on the new nature, which is renewed in knowledge by conforming to the image of the one who created it. ¹¹In this image there is neither Greek nor Jew, circumcised nor uncircumcised, barbarian, Scythian, slave nor free, but Christ is all things and in all people.

¹²Therefore, as God's choice, holy and loved, put on compassion, kindness, humility, gentleness, and patience. ¹³Be tolerant with each other and, if someone has a complaint against anyone, forgive each other. As the Lord forgave you, so also forgive each other. ¹⁴And over all these things put on love, which is the perfect bond of unity. ¹⁵The peace of Christ must control your hearts—a peace into which you were called in one body. And be thankful people. ¹⁶The word of Christ must live in you richly. Teach and warn each other with all wisdom by singing psalms, hymns, and spiritual songs. Sing to God with gratitude in your hearts. ¹⁷Whatever you do, whether in speech or action, do it all in the name of the Lord Jesus and give thanks to God the Father through him.

¹⁸Wives, submit to your husbands in a way that is appropriate in the Lord. ¹⁹Husbands, love your wives and don't be harsh with them.

God's THOUGHTS ♦ My THOUGHTS

Try to Get Along Colossians 3:12-17

People are different in many ways. We all have wonderful differences, such as hair color, skin color, height, weight, background, culture, and family traditions. Sadly, the differences that make people so amazing can be the very things that turn us against each other. Sometimes people act out against anyone who is different.

Christians know that Jesus makes us all one. We're called to put away the differences that can separate us. To be *unified* means to live in harmony with each other. We have to do some hard work to become unified. Paul said we have to put on compassion, kindness, humility, gentleness, and patience. We also have to accept people's differences, be quick to forgive each other, and truly love people. Paul's letter teaches that love is the bond—or glue—that brings unity.

Think about the people in your church. How can you love each other more? • *Pray for your church to have unity in Christ and love each other.*

²⁰Children, obey your parents in everything, because this pleases the Lord. ²¹Parents, don't provoke your children in a way that ends up discouraging them.

²²Slaves, obey your masters on earth in everything. Don't just obey like people pleasers when they are watching. Instead, obey with the single motivation of fearing the Lord. ²³Whatever you do, do it from the heart for the Lord and not for people. ²⁴You know that you will receive an inheritance as a reward. You serve the Lord Christ. ²⁵But evildoers will receive their reward for their evil actions. There is no discrimination.

4 Masters, be just and fair to your slaves, knowing that you yourselves have a master in heaven.

²Keep on praying and guard your prayers with thanksgiving. ³At the same time, pray for us also. Pray that God would open a door for the word so we can preach the secret plan^f of Christ—which is why I'm in chains. ⁴Pray that I might be able to make it as clear as I ought to when I preach. ⁵Act wisely toward outsiders, making the most of the opportunity. ⁶Your speech should always be gracious and sprinkled with insight so that you may know how to respond to every person.

Final greeting

⁷Tychicus, our dearly loved brother, faithful minister, and fellow slave in the Lord, will inform you about everything that has happened to me. ⁸This is why I sent him to you, so that you'll know all about us and so he can encourage your hearts. ⁹I sent him with Onesimus, our faithful and dearly loved brother, who is one of you. They will let you know about everything here.

¹⁰Aristarchus, my fellow prisoner, says hello to you. So does Mark, Barnabas' cousin (you received instructions about him; if he comes to you, welcome him). ¹¹Jesus, called Justus, also says hello. These are my only fellow workers for God's kingdom who are Jewish converts. They have been an encouragement to me. ¹²Epaphras, who is one of you, says hello. He's a slave of Christ Jesus who always wrestles for you in prayers so that you will stand firm and be fully mature and complete in the entire will of God. ¹³I can vouch for him that he has worked hard for you and for those in Laodicea and Hierapolis. ¹⁴Luke, the dearly loved physician, and Demas say hello.

¹⁵Say hello to the brothers and sisters in Laodicea, along with Nympha and the church that meets in her house. ¹⁶After this letter has been read to you publicly, make sure that the church in Laodicea reads it and that you read the one from Laodicea. ¹⁷And tell Archippus, "See to it that you complete the ministry that you received in the Lord."

¹⁸I, Paul, am writing this greeting personally. Remember that I'm in prison. Grace be with you.

SAILBOAT

COURAGE

God's Strength Is Greater Colossians 4:2-6
Following Jesus was difficult for early Christians because it was against the rules of the Roman Empire to be a Christian. During this time people were often punished if it was discovered that they followed Jesus. The punishment might be mean words, physical harm, prison, or even death. The threat of these punishments could be scary. Paul encouraged the Christians in Colossae to continue praying and to be thankful. He knew God's strength is greater than the scary things that faced him and the Colossians. Paul cared deeply about the people of Colossae and wanted them to have courage as they followed God. ◊

^fOr mystery

1Thessalonians

things
YOU'LL DISCOVER

This letter tells the story of a young church formed by the apostle Paul in the city of Thessalonica. Even after Paul left them and moved on to other places, the people continued to grow in love for Jesus.

people
YOU'LL MEET

Paul—a missionary of the church (1 Thess 1–5)
Silvanus and Timothy—Paul's missionary partners (1 Thess 1; 3)

places
YOU'LL GO

Thessalonica
(present-day Greece),
Macedonia
(present day northern Greece),
Achaia (present-day Greece)

words
YOU'LL REMEMBER

"Rejoice always. Pray continually" (1 Thess 5:16-17).

The apostle Paul preached and taught in Thessalonica until some rough people ran him out of the city (Acts 17:1-10). But Paul's short visit made a lasting impact. The story of how the Thessalonians followed Jesus spread far and wide. Everyone heard how the believers in Thessalonica turned from idols to serve the living God (1 Thess 1:9).

This letter shows that Paul was excited about the faith of these young Christians. But he still worried about them. They had to struggle on their own, trying to live for God in a city known for sin, greed, and spiritual lies.

Paul wanted to know how they were doing, so he sent his friend and helper Timothy to meet with them. Timothy strengthened and encouraged them, and he brought back to Paul good news about the Thessalonians' faithfulness and love (1 Thess 3:1-6). They were still growing in their faith.

This letter is full of good news about following Jesus. It tells us to be faithful even when life is hard. It tells us to pursue good, rejoice always, pray continually, and give thanks in every situation! ◊

Greeting

1 From Paul, Silvanus, and Timothy.
To the Thessalonians' church that is in God the Father and the Lord Jesus Christ. Grace and peace to all of you.

Thanksgiving to God

[2] We always thank God for all of you when we mention you constantly in our prayers. [3] This is because we remember your work that comes from faith,[a] your effort that comes from love, and your perseverance that comes from hope in our Lord Jesus Christ in the presence of our God and Father. [4] Brothers and sisters, you are loved by God, and we know that he has chosen you. [5] We know this because our good news didn't come to you just in speech but also with power and the Holy Spirit and with deep conviction. You know as well as we do what kind of people we were when we were with you, which was for your sake. [6] You became imitators of us and of the Lord when you accepted the message that came from the Holy Spirit with joy in spite of great suffering. [7] As a result you became an example to all the believers in Macedonia and Achaia. [8] The message about the Lord rang out from you, not only in Macedonia and Achaia but in every place. The news about your faithfulness to God has spread so that we don't even need to mention it. [9] People tell us about what sort of welcome we had from you and how you turned to God from idols. As a result, you are serving[b] the living and true God, [10] and you are waiting for his Son from heaven. His Son is Jesus, who is the one he raised from the dead and who is the one who will rescue us from the coming wrath.

During his first visit to Thessalonica, Paul was only able to speak in the Jewish synagogues on three Sabbath days. In those three days he shared the good news of Jesus with many people whose lives changed because of what they heard. Sadly there were people who didn't like the attention Paul received, and they planned to attack him. When Paul heard of this plan, he quickly left Thessalonica.

Paul's ministry in Thessalonica

2 As you yourselves know, brothers and sisters, our visit with you wasn't a waste of time. [2] On the contrary, we had the courage through God to speak God's good news in spite of a lot of opposition, although we had already suffered and were publicly insulted in Philippi, as you know. [3] Our appeal isn't based on false information, the wrong motives, or deception. [4] Rather, we have been examined and approved by God to be trusted with the good news, and that's exactly how we speak. We aren't trying to please people, but we are trying to please God, who continues to examine our hearts. [5] As you know, we never used flattery, and God is our witness that we didn't have greedy motives. [6] We didn't ask for special treatment from people—not from you or from others—[7] although we could have thrown our weight around as Christ's apostles. Instead, we were gentle with you

Thessalonica had two hundred thousand people. It was a port city and a stop on a Roman road called the *Egnatian Way*. Thessalonica was an important city for business by land and by sea. Many people heard the message about Jesus while they were there and then spread the message as they traveled to other places.

like a nursing mother caring for her own children. [8] We were glad to share not only God's good news with you but also our very lives because we cared for you so much. [9] You remember, brothers and sisters, our efforts and hard work. We preached God's good news to you, while we worked night and day so we wouldn't be a burden on any of you. [10] You and God are witnesses of how holy, just, and blameless we were toward you believers. [11] Likewise, you know how we treated each of you like a father treats his own children. [12] We appealed to you, encouraged you, and pleaded with you to live lives worthy of the God who is calling you into his own kingdom and glory.

How the Thessalonians received God's message

[13] We also thank God constantly for this: when you accepted God's word that you heard

from us, you welcomed it for what it truly is. Instead of accepting it as a human message, you accepted it as God's message, and it continues to work in you who are believers. [14]Brothers and sisters, you became imitators of the churches of God in Judea, which are in Christ Jesus. This was because you also suffered the same things from your own people as they did from the Jews. [15]They killed both the Lord Jesus and the prophets and drove us out. They don't please God, and they are hostile to the entire human race [16]when they try to stop us from speaking to the Gentiles so they can be saved. Their sins are constantly pushing the limit.[c] God's wrath has caught up with them in the end.

Paul's desire to visit

[17]Brothers and sisters, we were separated from you for a while physically but not in our hearts. We made every effort in our desire to see you again face-to-face. [18]We wanted to come to you—I, Paul, tried over and over again—and Satan stopped us. [19]What is our hope, joy, or crown that we can brag about in front of our Lord Jesus when he comes? Isn't it all of you? [20]You are our glory and joy!

[3]So when we couldn't stand it any longer, we thought it was a good idea to stay on in Athens by ourselves, [2]and we sent you Timothy, who is our brother and God's coworker in the good news about Christ. We sent him to strengthen and encourage you in your faithfulness. [3]We didn't want any of you to be shaken by these problems. You know very well that we were meant to go through this. [4]In fact, when we were with you, we kept on predicting that we were going to face problems exactly like what happened, as you know. [5]That's why I sent Timothy to find out about your faithfulness when I couldn't stand it anymore. I was worried that the tempter might have tempted you so that our work would have been a waste of time.

Paul's prayer for the Thessalonians

[6]Now Timothy has returned to us from you and has given us good news about your faithfulness and love! He says that you always have good memories about us and that

you want to see us as much as we want to see you. [7]Because of this, brothers and sisters, we were encouraged in all our distress and trouble through your faithfulness. [8]For now we are alive if you are standing your ground in the Lord. [9]How can we thank God enough for you, given all the joy we have because of you before our God? [10]Night and day, we pray more than ever to see all of you in person and to complete whatever you still need for your faith. [11]Now may our God and Father himself and our Lord Jesus guide us on our way back to you. [12]May the Lord cause you to increase and enrich your love for each other and for everyone in the same way as we also love you. [13]May the love cause your hearts to be strengthened, to be blameless in holiness before our God and Father when our Lord Jesus comes with all his people. Amen.

Living that pleases God

[4]So then, brothers and sisters, we ask and encourage you in the Lord Jesus to keep living the way you already are and even do better in how you live and please God—just as you learned from us. [2]You know the instructions we gave you through the Lord Jesus. [3]God's will is that your lives are dedicated to him.[d] This means that you stay away from sexual immorality [4]and learn how to control

UMBRELLA
HARD TIMES

Continue in Faithfulness
1 Thessalonians 3:1-5
It must have been difficult for the early Christians in Thessalonica. Paul shared with them the message of Jesus and then had to leave their city quickly because he was in danger. The new Christians were probably afraid of the danger not only for Paul but for themselves. So Paul sent Timothy to Thessalonica to encourage the new believers and strengthen their faith. Paul reminded the Thessalonians that hard times will happen for people who follow Jesus. He reminded them to endure the challenges and continue to be faithful. ♦

[c]Or They constantly fill up the measure of their sin. [d]Or holy, sanctified

your own body in a pure[e] and respectable way. [5]Don't be controlled by your sexual urges like the Gentiles who don't know God. [6]No one should mistreat or take advantage of their brother or sister in this issue. The Lord punishes people for all these things, as we told you before and sternly warned you. [7]God didn't call us to be immoral but to be dedicated to him.[f] [8]Therefore, whoever rejects these instructions isn't rejecting a human authority. They are rejecting God, who gives his Holy Spirit to you.

[9]You don't need us to write about loving your brothers and sisters because God has already taught you to love each other. [10]In fact, you are doing loving deeds for all the brothers and sisters throughout Macedonia. Now we encourage you, brothers and sisters, to do so even more. [11]Aim to live quietly, mind your own business, and earn your own living, just as I told you. [12]That way you'll behave appropriately toward outsiders, and you won't be in need.

Believers who have died

[13]Brothers and sisters, we want you to know about people who have died[g] so that you won't mourn like others who don't have any hope. [14]Since we believe that Jesus died

and rose, so we also believe that God will bring with him those who have died in Jesus. [15]What we are saying is a message from the Lord: we who are alive and still around at the Lord's coming definitely won't go ahead of those who have died. [16]This is because the Lord himself will come down from heaven with the signal of a shout by the head angel and a blast on God's trumpet. First, those who are dead in Christ will rise. [17]Then, we who are living and still around will be taken up together with them in the clouds to meet with the Lord in the air. That way we will always be with the Lord. [18]So encourage each other with these words.

The Lord's coming

5 We don't need to write to you about the timing and dates, brothers and sisters. [2]You know very well that the day of the Lord is going to come like a thief in the night. [3]When they are saying, "There is peace and security," at that time sudden destruction will attack them, like labor pains start with a pregnant woman, and they definitely won't escape. [4]But you aren't in darkness, brothers and sisters, so the day won't catch you by surprise like a thief. [5]All of you are children of light and children of the day. We don't belong

[e]Or *holy, sanctified* [f]Or *holy, sanctified* [g]Or *fallen asleep*

Meeting in the Air   *1 Thessalonians 4:13–5:2*

This letter contains an amazing promise. Paul described what will happen when Jesus comes back to earth for his followers. Paul said that people who have already died will be raised, followers who are still alive will rise up, and the two groups will meet together in the sky.

Because of Jesus we can have hope even when we're sad about people who have died. We may cry because we aren't with those friends or family members now, but we can also hold on to the hope that followers of Jesus will have everlasting life.

What do you imagine when you read these verses?

Draw a picture of what you think a meeting with Jesus in the air would look like.

to night or darkness. [6]So then, let's not sleep like the others, but let's stay awake and stay sober. [7]People who sleep sleep at night, and people who get drunk get drunk at night. [8]Since we belong to the day, let's stay sober, wearing faithfulness and love as a piece of armor that protects our body[h] and the hope of salvation as a helmet. [9]God didn't intend for us to suffer his wrath but rather to possess salvation through our Lord Jesus Christ. [10]Jesus died for us so that, whether we are awake or asleep, we will live together with him. [11]So continue encouraging each other and building each other up, just like you are doing already.

Final instructions and blessing

[12]Brothers and sisters, we ask you to respect those who are working with you, leading you, and instructing you. [13]Think of them highly with love because of their work. Live in peace with each other. [14]Brothers and sisters, we urge you to warn those who are disorderly. Comfort the discouraged. Help the weak. Be patient with everyone. [15]Make sure no one repays a wrong with a wrong, but always pursue the good for each other and everyone else. [16]Rejoice always. [17]Pray continually. [18]Give thanks in every situation because this is God's will for you in Christ Jesus.

Memorize
1 Thess 5:16-18

[h]Or *breastplate*

LIFE PRESERVER

Would this letter really have been read out loud?
1 Thessalonians 5:27

This letter was written about twenty years after Jesus died when Christians gathered in each other's homes to worship and be together. It's very likely it would have been read out loud in these homes. Probably no more than thirty or forty people would have been present to hear what Paul wrote. It's a fairly short letter, so it wouldn't have taken long to read out loud. ◆

[19]Don't suppress the Spirit. [20]Don't brush off Spirit-inspired messages, [21]but examine everything carefully and hang on to what is good. [22]Avoid every kind of evil. [23]Now, may the God of peace himself cause you to be completely dedicated to him; and may your spirit, soul, and body be kept intact and blameless at our Lord Jesus Christ's coming. [24]The one who is calling you is faithful and will do this.

Final greeting

[25]Brothers and sisters, pray for us. [26]Greet all the brothers and sisters with a holy kiss. [27]By the Lord's authority, I order all of you to have this letter read aloud to all the brothers and sisters. [28]The grace of our Lord Jesus Christ be with all of you.

2 Thessalonians

The apostle Paul's first letter to these young Christians was full of happy news. This second letter to the Thessalonians addresses a new problem. Paul taught that one day the world would end with the return of Jesus to earth. Paul said Jesus would come suddenly, "like a thief in the night" (1 Thess 5:2).

False teachers twisted Paul's words. They said that Jesus had already come back. Some of the Thessalonians quit their jobs because they expected Jesus to return immediately. Paul encouraged the Christians in Thessalonica to stay loyal to the truth he taught. He wanted them to follow Jesus faithfully, work hard, and serve God while they waited for Jesus to return.

This letter proves that even the most faithful Christians can follow wrong ideas. Second Thessalonians reminds us to hold tightly to truth and work hard to serve God in everything we do! ◊

things
YOU'LL DISCOVER

This second letter to the Christians in the city of Thessalonica corrects their wrong ideas about the end of the world and the return of Jesus to earth. It tells Christians to work hard while they wait for Jesus.

people
YOU'LL MEET

Paul—a missionary of the church (2 Thess 1–3)
Silvanus and Timothy—Paul's missionary partners (2 Thess 1; 3)

places
YOU'LL GO

Thessalonica
(present-day Greece)

words
YOU'LL REMEMBER

"May [God] encourage your hearts and give you strength in every good thing you do or say" (2 Thess 2:17).

Greeting

1 From Paul, Silvanus, and Timothy:
To the church of the Thessalonians, which is in God our Father, and in the Lord Jesus Christ. ²Grace and peace to all of you from God our Father and the Lord Jesus Christ.

Thanksgiving and encouragement

³Brothers and sisters, we must always thank God for you. This is only right because your faithfulness is growing by leaps and bounds, and the love that all of you have for each other is increasing. ⁴That's why we ourselves are bragging about you in God's churches. We tell about your endurance and faithfulness in all the harassments and trouble that you have put up with. ⁵This shows that God's judgment is right, and that you will be considered worthy of God's kingdom for which you are suffering. ⁶After all, it's right for God to pay back the ones making trouble for you with trouble ⁷and to pay back you who are having trouble with relief along with us. This payback will come when the Lord Jesus is revealed from heaven with his powerful angels. ⁸He will give justice with blazing fire to those who don't recognize God and don't obey the good news of our Lord Jesus. ⁹They will pay the penalty of eternal destruction away from the Lord's presence and away from his mighty glory. ¹⁰This will happen when he comes on that day to receive honor from his holy people and to be admired by everyone who has believed—and our testimony to you was believed.

¹¹We are constantly praying for you for this: that our God will make you worthy of his calling and accomplish every good desire and faithful work by his power. ¹²Then the name of our Lord Jesus will be honored by you, and you will be honored by him, consistent with the grace of our God and the Lord Jesus Christ.

Day of the Lord

2 Brothers and sisters, we have a request for you concerning our Lord Jesus Christ's coming and when we are gathered together to be with him. ²We don't want you to be easily confused in your mind or upset if you hear that the day of the Lord is already here, whether you hear it through some spirit, a

UMBRELLA
ANGRY

Don't Seek Revenge *2 Thessalonians 1:6-8*

When the early Christians in the city of Thessalonica read this letter from Paul, they were being treated unfairly because of their beliefs. As followers of Jesus they were subject to punishment, such as being beaten, put in jail, or even killed. The early Christians probably felt not only afraid but also angry. Some of them might have wanted to take revenge on the people in charge. But Paul said it wasn't their job to seek revenge. He said God would eventually pay back the people who made trouble for these Christians when Jesus is revealed from heaven. ◊

message, or a letter supposedly from us. ³Don't let anyone deceive you in any way. That day won't come unless the rebellion comes first and the person who is lawless is revealed, who is headed for destruction. ⁴He is the opponent of every so-called god or object of worship and promotes himself over them. So he sits in God's temple, displaying himself to show that he is God. ⁵You remember that I used to tell you these things while I was with you, don't you? ⁶Now you know what holds him back so that he can be revealed when his time comes. ⁷The hidden plan to live without any law is at work now, but it will be secret only until the one who is holding it

LIGHTHOUSE
WISDOM

Love the Truth *2 Thessalonians 2:10*

In Paul's time, when people wanted to communicate with someone who lived far away, they wrote a letter, which was then delivered by hand. This process took much longer than it takes today, so people waited a long time to hear from each other. In the time between Paul's first and second letters to the Christians in the city of Thessalonica, confusion about the good news arose. People who rejected the good news of Jesus used this confusion to teach wrong ideas to these early Christians. Paul said that people who chose not to love truth were headed for destruction. ◊

back is out of the way. [8]Then the person who is lawless will be revealed. The Lord Jesus will destroy him with the breath from his mouth. When the Lord comes, his appearance will put an end to him. [9]When the person who is lawless comes, it will happen through Satan's effort, with all kinds of fake power, signs, and wonders. [10]It will happen with every sort of wicked deception of those who are heading toward destruction because they have refused to love the truth that would allow them to be saved. [11]This is why God will send them an influence that will mislead them so that they will believe the lie. [12]The result will be that everyone will be judged who is not convinced by the truth but is happy with injustice.

Prayer of thanks and encouragement

[13]But we always must thank God for you, brothers and sisters who are loved by God. This is because he chose you from the beginning to be the first crop of the harvest. This brought salvation, through your dedication to God by the Spirit and through your belief in the truth. [14]God called all of you through our good news so you could possess the honor of our Lord Jesus Christ. [15]So then, brothers and sisters, stand firm and hold on to the traditions we taught you, whether we taught you in person or through our letter. [16]Our Lord Jesus Christ himself and God our Father loved us and through grace gave us eternal comfort and a good hope. [17]May he encourage your hearts and give you strength in every good thing you do or say.

Memorize
2 Thess 2:17

Prayer request

3 Finally, brothers and sisters, pray for us so that the Lord's message will spread quickly and be honored, just like it happened with you. [2]Pray too that we will be rescued from inappropriate and evil people since everyone that we meet won't respond with faith. [3]But the Lord is faithful and will give you

strength and protect you from the evil one. [4]We are confident about you in the Lord—that you are doing and will keep doing what we tell you to do. [5]May the Lord lead your hearts to express God's love and Christ's endurance.

Discipline for the undisciplined

[6]Brothers and sisters, we command you in the name of our Lord Jesus Christ to stay away from every brother or sister who lives an undisciplined life that is not in line with the traditions that you received from us. [7]You yourselves know how you need to imitate us because we were not undisciplined when we were with you. [8]We didn't eat anyone's food without paying for it. Instead, we worked night and day with effort and hard work so that we would not impose on you. [9]We did this to give you an example to imitate, not because we didn't have a right to insist on financial support. [10]Even when we were with you we were giving you this command: "If anyone doesn't want to work, they shouldn't eat." [11]We hear that some of you are living an undisciplined life. They aren't working, but they are meddling in other people's business. [12]By the Lord Jesus Christ, we command and encourage such people to work quietly and put their own food on the table. [13]Brothers and sisters, don't get discouraged in doing what is right. [14]Take note of anyone who doesn't obey what we have said in this letter. Don't associate with them so they will be ashamed of themselves. [15]Don't treat them like enemies, but warn them like you would do for a brother or sister.

Final greeting

[16]May the Lord of peace himself give you peace always in every way. The Lord be with all of you. [17]I, Paul, am writing this greeting with my own hand. This verifies that the letter is from me, as in every letter of mine. This is how I write. [18]The grace of our Lord Jesus Christ be with all of you.

1 Timothy

First Timothy is the first of three letters addressed to people in charge of leading God's people in local churches. Sometimes these books are called *pastoral letters*. These letters help church leaders know how to lead and organize churches, what to teach people, and how to stay faithful to God. But these letters aren't just for pastors. They have a message for all Christians.

This letter is addressed to Timothy, the most well-known of Paul's partners. Timothy's grandmother and mother taught him the scriptures (2 Tim 3:14-15), and Paul called Timothy his "true child in the faith" (1 Tim 1:2). While still a young man, Timothy traveled with Paul as he spread the good news about Jesus to Asia (present-day Turkey), Greece, and Italy.

Timothy was involved in the leadership of the church in Ephesus (1 Tim 1:3). Paul told Timothy not to let anyone look down on him because of his young age, but to set an example for other believers instead. He said Timothy should use the gifts God gave him to lead the church. Paul told Timothy to focus not only on his own growth but also on teaching well (1 Tim 4:12-16).

First Timothy gives a picture of how God expects groups of Christians to grow up. This letter shows us how a church should work! ◆

things YOU'LL DISCOVER

First Timothy is a letter addressed from the apostle Paul to Timothy, his younger missionary partner. Timothy had the job of leading the church in Ephesus, and this letter told him how to do his job well.

people YOU'LL MEET

Paul—a missionary of the church (1 Tim 1–6)
Timothy—Paul's missionary partner and pastor of the church in Ephesus (1 Tim 1–6)
Hymenaeus and Alexander—two false teachers (1 Tim 1)

places YOU'LL GO

Ephesus (present-day Turkey)

words YOU'LL REMEMBER

"There is one God and one mediator between God and humanity, the human Christ Jesus" (1 Tim 2:5).

Greeting

1 From Paul, who is an apostle of Jesus Christ by the command of God our savior and of Christ Jesus our hope.

[2] To Timothy, my true child in the faith.

Grace, mercy, and peace from God the Father and from Christ Jesus our Lord.

Timothy's purpose in Ephesus

[3] When I left for Macedonia, I asked you to stay behind in Ephesus so that you could instruct certain individuals not to spread wrong teaching. [4] They shouldn't pay attention to myths and endless genealogies. Their teaching only causes useless guessing games instead of faithfulness to God's way of doing things. [5] The goal of instruction is love from a pure heart, a good conscience, and a sincere faith. [6] Because they missed this goal, some people have been distracted by talk that doesn't mean anything. [7] They want to be teachers of Law without understanding either what they are saying or what they are talking about with such confidence. [8] Now we know that the Law is good if used appropriately. [9] We understand this: the Law isn't established for a righteous person but for people who live without laws and without obeying any authority. They are the ungodly and the sinners. They are people who are not spiritual, and nothing is sacred to them. They kill their fathers and mothers, and murder others. [10] They are people who are sexually unfaithful, and people who have intercourse with the same sex. They are kidnappers,[a] liars, individuals who give false testimonies in court, and those who do anything else that is opposed to sound teaching. [11] Sound teaching agrees with the glorious gospel of the blessed God that has been trusted to me.

Thanksgiving

[12] I thank Christ Jesus our Lord, who has given me strength because he considered me faithful. So he appointed me to ministry [13] even though I used to speak against him, attack his people, and I was proud. But I was shown mercy because I acted in ignorance and without faith. [14] Our Lord's favor poured all over me along with the faithfulness and love that are in Christ Jesus. [15] This saying is reliable and deserves full acceptance: "Christ Jesus came into the world to save sinners"—and I'm the biggest sinner of all. [16] But this is why I was shown mercy, so that Christ Jesus could show his endless patience to me first of all. So I'm an example for those who are going to believe in him for eternal life. [17] Now to the king of the ages, to the immortal, invisible, and only God, may honor and glory be given to him forever and always! Amen.

Importance of faith and a good conscience

[18] Timothy, my child, I'm giving you these instructions based on the prophecies that were once made about you. So if you follow them, you can wage a good war [19] because you have faith and a good conscience. Some people have ruined their faith because they refused to listen to their conscience, [20] such as Hymenaeus and Alexander. I've handed them over to Satan so that they can be taught not to speak against God.

Prayer for everyone

2 First of all, then, I ask that requests, prayers, petitions, and thanksgiving be made for all people. [2] Pray for kings and everyone who is in authority so that we can live a quiet and peaceful life in complete godliness

Bet you can read this in 2 minutes. Ready, set, go!

LIGHTHOUSE
PRAYER

Pray for All People 1 Timothy 2:1-6
One of Paul's first instructions to Timothy was to pray for all people, including people who were in positions of authority. Paul wanted Timothy to pray this way because God wants everyone to know the truth about Jesus. These instructions on prayer to the early church are still great guidelines for prayer today.

[a] Or slave dealers

and dignity. [3]This is right and it pleases God our savior, [4]who wants all people to be saved and to come to a knowledge of the truth. [5]There is one God and one mediator between God and humanity, the human Christ Jesus, [6]who gave himself as a payment to set all people free. This was a testimony that was given at the right time. [7]I was appointed to be a preacher and apostle of this testimony— I'm telling the truth and I'm not lying! I'm a teacher of the Gentiles in faith and truth.

Instructions for men and women

[8]Therefore, I want men to pray everywhere by lifting up hands that are holy, without anger or argument. [9]In the same way, I want women to enhance their appearance with clothing that is modest and sensible, not with elaborate hairstyles, gold, pearls, or expensive clothes. [10]They should make themselves attractive by doing good, which is appropriate for women who claim to honor God. [11]A wife[b] should learn quietly with complete submission. [12]I don't allow a wife[c] to teach or to control her husband.[d] Instead, she should be a quiet listener. [13]Adam was formed first, and then Eve. [14]Adam wasn't deceived, but rather his wife[e] became the one who stepped over the line because she was completely deceived. [15]But a wife[f] will be brought safely through childbirth,[g] if they both continue in faith, love, and holiness, together with self-control.

Supervisors in God's household

3This saying is reliable: if anyone has a goal to be a supervisor[h] in the church, they want a good thing. [2]So the church's supervisor must be without fault. They should be faithful to their spouse, sober, modest, and honest. They should show hospitality and be skilled at teaching. [3]They shouldn't be addicted to alcohol or be a bully. Instead, they should be gentle, peaceable, and not greedy. [4]They should manage their own household well—they should see that their children are obedient with complete respect, [5]because if they don't know how to manage their own

household, how can they take care of God's church? [6]They shouldn't be new believers so that they won't become proud and fall under the devil's spell. [7]They should also have a good reputation with those outside the church so that they won't be embarrassed and fall into the devil's trap.

Servants in God's household

[8]In the same way, servants[i] in the church should be dignified, not two-faced, heavy drinkers, or greedy for money. [9]They should hold on to the faith that has been revealed with a clear conscience. [10]They should also be tested and then serve if they are without fault. [11]In the same way, women who are servants[j] in the church should be dignified and not gossip. They should be sober and faithful in everything they do. [12]Servants[k] must be faithful to their spouse and manage their children and their own households well. [13]Those who have served well gain a good standing and considerable confidence in the faith that is in Christ Jesus.

Leading God's household

[14]I hope to come to you quickly. But I'm writing these things to you so that [15]if I'm delayed, you'll know how you should behave in God's household. It is the church of the living God and the backbone and support of the truth. [16]Without question, the mystery of godliness is great: he was revealed as a human, declared righteous by the Spirit, seen by angels, preached throughout the nations, believed in around the world, and taken up in glory.

4The Spirit clearly says that in latter times some people will turn away from the faith. They will pay attention to spirits that deceive and to the teaching of demons. [2]They will be controlled by the pretense of lying, and their own consciences will be seared. [3]They will prohibit marriage and eating foods that God created—and he intended them to be accepted with thanksgiving by those who are faithful and have come to know the truth. [4]Everything that has been created

[b]Or a woman [c]Or a woman [d]Or a man [e]Or the woman [f]Or a woman [g]Or saved through childbearing [h]Or bishop, overseer [i]Or deacons [j]Or wives, omit who are servants [k]Or deacons

by God is good, and nothing that is received with thanksgiving should be rejected. ⁵These things are made holy by God's word and prayer. ⁶If you point these things out to the believers, you will be a good servant of Christ Jesus who has been trained by the words of faith and the good teaching that you've carefully followed. ⁷But stay away from the godless myths that are passed down from the older women.

> **did you know?** Timothy became a follower of Jesus as a young child. His mother Eunice and his grandmother Lois first taught him about Jesus. They were both Jewish women who became followers of Jesus. Timothy was probably a young teen when he began traveling with Paul to teach about Jesus.

Practices of spiritual leadership

Train yourself for a holy life! ⁸While physical training has some value, training in holy living is useful for everything. It has promise for this life now and the life to come. ⁹This saying is reliable and deserves complete acceptance. ¹⁰We work and struggle for this: "Our hope is set on the living God, who is the savior of all people, especially those who believe." ¹¹Command these things. Teach them. ¹²Don't let anyone look down on you because you are young. Instead, set an example for the believers through your speech, behavior, love, faith, and by being sexually pure. ¹³Until I arrive, pay attention to public reading, preaching, and teaching. ¹⁴Don't neglect the spiritual gift in you that was given through prophecy when the elders laid hands on you. ¹⁵Practice

God's THOUGHTS ▸ My THOUGHTS

Age Doesn't Matter in Faith *1 Timothy 4:7-12*

You might think you have to be a certain age in order to be a leader in church. But God doesn't ask people to lead only when they have grown up and are fully mature. In fact, Timothy was young when he led a church in the early days of spreading the good news.

Some people thought Timothy was too young to know what he was talking about, so they didn't listen to him. But Paul, who mentored Timothy, encouraged Timothy to keep going. He believed that Timothy was old enough and also faithful enough to lead. Paul's advice to Timothy was to set an example to the believers by speaking positive words, behaving in a godly way, loving at all costs, having faith, and insisting on purity. Paul instructed Timothy to be an example of what a true follower of Jesus looked like.

Age doesn't matter to God. You can be 10 years old or 100 years old, and God may ask you to be a leader. How will you be an example for your community?

What young people do you know who make a difference for Jesus?

How can you set an example for other Christians through your speech, behavior, love, faith, and purity?

these things, and live by them so that your progress will be visible to all. [16]Focus on working on your own development and on what you teach. If you do this, you will save yourself and those who hear you.

Caring for God's family

5 Don't correct an older man, but encourage him like he's your father; treat younger men like your brothers, [2]treat older women like your mother, and treat younger women like your sisters with appropriate respect.

[3]Take care of widows who are truly needy. [4]But if a particular widow has children or grandchildren, they should first learn to respect their own family and repay their parents, because this pleases God. [5]A widow who is truly needy and all alone puts her hope in God and keeps on going with requests and prayers, night and day. [6]But a widow who tries to live a life of luxury is dead even while she is alive. [7]Teach these things so that the families[l] will be without fault. [8]But if someone doesn't provide for their own family, and especially for a member of their household, they have denied the faith. They are worse than those who have no faith.

[9]Put a widow on the list who is older than 60 years old and who was faithful to her husband. [10]She should have a reputation for doing good: raising children, providing hospitality to strangers, washing the feet of the saints, helping those in distress, and dedicating herself to every kind of good thing. [11]But don't accept younger widows for the list. When their physical desires distract them from Christ, they will want to get married. [12]Then they will be judged for setting aside their earlier commitment. [13]Also, they learn to be lazy by going from house to house. They are not only lazy, but they also become gossips and busybodies, talking about things they shouldn't. [14]So I want younger widows to marry, have children, and manage their homes so that they won't give the enemy any reason to slander us. ([15]Some have already turned away to follow Satan.) [16]If any woman who is a believer has widows in her family, she should take care of them and not burden the church, so that it can help other widows who are truly needy.

Instructions for elders

[17]Elders who lead well should be paid double, especially those who work with public speaking and teaching. [18]The scripture says, *Don't put a muzzle on an ox while it treads grain*,[m] and *Workers deserve their pay*.[n] [19]Don't accept an accusation made against an elder unless it is confirmed by two or three witnesses. [20]Discipline those who are sinning in front of everyone so that all the others will be afraid. [21]I charge you before God and Christ Jesus and the elect angels to follow these practices without bias, and without playing favorites. [22]Don't rush to commission anyone to leadership, and don't participate in the sins of others. Keep yourself morally pure.

[23]Don't drink water anymore, but use a little wine because of your stomach problems and your frequent illnesses. [24]The sins of some people are obvious, and the sins are judged before the people must face judgment, but the sins of other people show up later. [25]In the same way, the good that people do is also obvious and can't be hidden.

Conduct of Christian slaves

6 Those who are under the bondage of slavery should consider their own masters as worthy of full respect so that God's name and our teaching won't get a bad reputation. [2]And those who have masters who are believers shouldn't look down on them because they are brothers. Instead, they should serve them more faithfully, because the people who benefit from your good service are believers who are loved. Teach and encourage these things.

Warning about false teachers

[3]If anyone teaches anything different and doesn't agree with sound teaching about our Lord Jesus Christ and teaching that is consistent with godliness, [4]that person is conceited. They don't understand anything but have a sick obsession with debates and arguments. This creates jealousy, conflict, verbal abuse, and evil suspicions. [5]There is constant bickering between people whose minds are ruined and who have been robbed of the truth. They think that godliness is a way to make money! [6]Actually, godliness is a great source

[l]Or they [m]Deut 25:4 [n]Luke 10:7

of profit when it is combined with being happy with what you already have. ⁷We didn't bring anything into the world and so we can't take anything out of it: ⁸we'll be happy with food and clothing. ⁹But people who are trying to get rich fall into temptation. They are trapped by many stupid and harmful passions that plunge people into ruin and destruction. ¹⁰The love of money is the root of all kinds of evil. Some have wandered away from the faith and have impaled themselves with a lot of pain because they made money their goal.

Memorize 1 Tim 6:11

¹¹But as for you, man of God, run away from all these things. Instead, pursue righteousness, holy living, faithfulness, love, endurance, and gentleness. ¹²Compete in the good fight of faith. Grab hold of eternal life—you were called to it, and you made a good confession of it in the presence of many witnesses. ¹³I command you in the presence of God, who gives life to all things, and Christ Jesus, who made the good confession when testifying before Pontius Pilate. ¹⁴Obey this order without fault or failure until the appearance of our Lord Jesus Christ. ¹⁵The timing of this appearance is revealed by God alone, who is the blessed and only master, the King of kings and Lord of lords. ¹⁶He alone has immortality and lives in light that no one can come near. No human being has ever seen or is able to see him. Honor and eternal power belong to him. Amen.

LIFE PRESERVER

How should wealthy people live? *1 Timothy 6:17-19*

In the New Testament we read about how hard it is for a rich person to get into heaven (Matt 19:16-24). Paul said Christians shouldn't put their hope in money but should put their hope in God. Paul encouraged people who were rich to do good, be generous, and share with others. His letter reminds us all that God will provide for God's children. ◊

Wealth of good works

¹⁷Tell people who are rich at this time not to become egotistical and not to place their hope on their finances, which are uncertain. Instead, they need to hope in God, who richly provides everything for our enjoyment. ¹⁸Tell them to do good, to be rich in the good things they do, to be generous, and to share with others. ¹⁹When they do these things, they will save a treasure for themselves that is a good foundation for the future. That way they can take hold of what is truly life.

Protect the tradition

²⁰Timothy, protect what has been given to you in trust. Avoid godless and pointless discussions and the contradictory claims of so-called "knowledge." ²¹When some people adopted this false knowledge, they missed the goal of faith.

May grace be with you all.

2 Timothy

Second Timothy was apparently written by the apostle Paul in prison. This letter might be Paul's last words to his friend and ministry partner Timothy during a difficult time.

As in his first letter to Timothy, Paul told his younger friend how to be a good leader. He reminded Timothy to run away from sin and instead "pursue righteousness, faith, love, and peace" together with other followers of Christ (2 Tim 2:22). Paul said Timothy should follow Paul's example and correct people whose wrong teachings led other people away from Jesus. Paul encouraged Timothy to study the scriptures, which would give him everything he needed to do good (2 Tim 3:14-17).

In this short letter Paul explained how he served God and spread the good news about Jesus. He was in prison, but he wasn't afraid to suffer for Jesus. He trusted God to take care of him (2 Tim 1:8-14). This letter reminds us to serve God well and to always be faithful! ◊

things
YOU'LL DISCOVER

Paul's second letter to Timothy tells him to keep working hard at growing in faith and leading other Christians. It also tells us about Paul's days in prison where he wrote this letter.

people
YOU'LL MEET

Paul—a missionary of the church (2 Tim 1–4)

Timothy—Paul's missionary partner and pastor of the church in Ephesus (2 Tim 1–4)

Demas—a friend who left Paul (2 Tim 4)

Alexander—a false teacher (2 Tim 4)

Crescens, Titus, Mark, Tychicus, Carpus, Prisca, Aquila, Onesiphorus, Linus, Claudia—a few of Paul's friends and helpers (2 Tim 4)

places
YOU'LL GO

Galatia, Troas, Miletus (present-day Turkey), **Dalmatia** (present-day Serbia, Bosnia, and Herzegovina), **Corinth** (present-day Greece)

words
YOU'LL REMEMBER

"Every scripture is inspired by God and is useful for teaching, for showing mistakes, for correcting, and for training character, so that the person who belongs to God can be equipped to do everything that is good" (2 Tim 3:16-17).

Greeting

1 From Paul, an apostle of Christ Jesus by God's will, to promote the promise of life that is in Christ Jesus. ²To Timothy, my dear child.

Grace, mercy, and peace from God the Father and Christ Jesus our Lord.

Thanksgiving and prayer

³I'm grateful to God, whom I serve with a good conscience as my ancestors did. I constantly remember you in my prayers day and night. ⁴When I remember your tears, I long to see you so that I can be filled with happiness. ⁵I'm reminded of your authentic faith, which first lived in your grandmother Lois and your mother Eunice. I'm sure that this faith is also inside you. ⁶Because of this, I'm reminding you to revive God's gift that is in you through the laying on of my hands. ⁷God didn't give us a spirit that is timid but one that is powerful, loving, and self-controlled.

Memorize 2 Tim 1:7

UMBRELLA

FEAR

Power, Love, and Self-control *2 Timothy 1:7*
At the time this letter was written, Paul was in jail for preaching about Jesus. In spite of how afraid he may have felt, Paul encouraged his friend Timothy. He knew Timothy would face similar trials as he preached and taught about Jesus. To encourage him, Paul reminded Timothy that God gives Christians power, love, and self-control. ◗

//

Don't be ashamed of the testimony

⁸So don't be ashamed of the testimony about the Lord or of me, his prisoner. Instead, share the suffering for the good news, depending on God's power. ⁹God is the one who saved and called us with a holy calling. This wasn't based on what we have done, but it was based on his own purpose and grace that he gave us in Christ Jesus before time began. ¹⁰Now his grace is revealed through the appearance of our savior, Christ Jesus. He destroyed death and brought life and immortality into clear focus through the good news. ¹¹I was appointed a messenger, apostle, and teacher of this good news. ¹²This is also why I'm suffering the way I do, but I'm not ashamed. I know the one in whom I've placed my trust. I'm convinced that God is powerful enough to protect what he has placed in my trust until that day. ¹³Hold on to the pattern of sound teaching that you heard from me with the faith and love that are in Christ Jesus. ¹⁴Protect this good thing that has been placed in your trust through the Holy Spirit who lives in us.

¹⁵You know that everyone in Asia has turned away from me, including Phygelus and Hermogenes. ¹⁶May the Lord show mercy to Onesiphorus' household, because he supported me many times and he wasn't ashamed of my imprisonment. ¹⁷After I arrived in Rome, he quickly looked for me and found me. ¹⁸May the Lord allow him to find his mercy on that day (and you know very well how much he served me in Ephesus).

Pass on the message and share suffering

2 So, my child, draw your strength from the grace that is in Christ Jesus. ²Take the things you heard me say in front of many other witnesses and pass them on to faithful people who are also capable of teaching others.

³Accept your share of suffering like a good soldier of Christ Jesus. ⁴Nobody who serves in the military gets tied up with civilian matters, so that they can please the one who recruited them. ⁵Also in the same way, athletes don't win unless they follow the rules. ⁶A hardworking farmer should get the first share of the crop. ⁷Think about what I'm saying; the Lord will give you understanding about everything.

⁸Remember Jesus Christ, who was raised from the dead and descended from David. This is my good news. ⁹This is the reason I'm suffering to the point that I'm in prison like a common criminal. But God's word cannot be imprisoned. ¹⁰This is why I endure everything for the sake of those who are chosen by God so that they too may experience salvation in Christ Jesus with eternal glory. ¹¹This saying is reliable:

"If we have died together,
we will also live together.

[12] If we endure, we will also rule together.
If we deny him, he will also deny us.
[13] If we are disloyal, he stays faithful"
because he can't be anything else
than what he is.

Speak, instruct, and act correctly

[14] Remind them of these things and warn them in the sight of God not to engage in battles over words that aren't helpful and only destroy those who hear them. [15] Make an effort to present yourself to God as a tried-and-true worker, who doesn't need to be ashamed but is one who interprets the message of truth correctly. [16] Avoid their godless discussions, because they will lead many people into ungodly behavior, [17] and their ideas will spread like an infection. This includes Hymenaeus and Philetus, [18] who have deviated from the truth by claiming that the resurrection has already happened. This has undermined some people's faith.

[19] God's solid foundation is still standing with this sign: *The Lord knows the people who belong to him,*[a] and *Everyone who confesses the Lord's name must avoid wickedness.*[b] [20] In a mansion, there aren't just gold and silver bowls but also some bowls that are made of wood and clay. Some are meant for special uses, some for garbage.[c] [21] So if anyone washes filth off themselves, they will be set apart as a "special bowl." They will be useful to the owner of the mansion for every sort of good work.

Avoid conflict with opponents

[22] Run away from adolescent cravings. Instead, pursue righteousness, faith, love, and peace together with those who confess the Lord with a clean heart. [23] Avoid foolish and thoughtless discussions, since you know that they produce conflicts. [24] God's slave shouldn't be argumentative but should be kind toward all people, able to teach, patient, [25] and should correct opponents with gentleness. Perhaps God will change their mind and give them a knowledge of the truth. [26] They may come to their senses and escape from the devil's trap that holds them captive to do his will.

Avoid people like this

3 Understand that the last days will be dangerous times. [2] People will be selfish and love money. They will be the kind of people who brag and who are proud. They will slander others, and they will be disobedient to their parents. They will be ungrateful, unholy, [3] unloving, contrary, and critical. They will be without self-control and brutal, and they won't love what is good. [4] They will be people who are disloyal, reckless, and conceited. They will love pleasure instead of loving God. [5] They will look like they are religious but deny God's power. Avoid people like this. [6] Some will slither into households and control immature women who are burdened with sins and driven by all kinds of desires. [7] These women are always learning, but they can never arrive at an understanding of the truth. [8] These people oppose the truth in the same way that Jannes and Jambres opposed Moses. Their minds are corrupt and their faith is counterfeit. [9] But they won't get very far. Their foolishness will become obvious to everyone like those others.

Take Paul as your model

[10] But you have paid attention to my teaching, conduct, purpose, faithfulness, patience, love, and endurance. [11] You have seen me experience physical abuse and ordeals in places such as Antioch, Iconium, and Lystra. I put up with all sorts of abuse, and the Lord rescued me from it all! [12] In fact, anyone who wants to live a holy life in Christ Jesus will be harassed. [13] But evil people and swindlers will grow even worse, as they deceive others while being deceived themselves.

[14] But you must continue with the things you have learned and found convincing. You know who taught you. [15] Since childhood you have known the holy scriptures that help you to be wise in a way that leads to salvation

[a] Num 16:5 LXX   [b] Possibly modeled on Isa 26:13   [c] Or *dishonorable purposes*

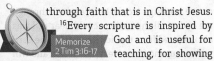
through faith that is in Christ Jesus. [16]Every scripture is inspired by God and is useful for teaching, for showing mistakes, for correcting, and for training character, [17]so that the person who belongs to God can be equipped to do everything that is good.

Timothy's commission and Paul's departure

4 I'm giving you this commission in the presence of God and of Christ Jesus, who is coming to judge the living and the dead, and by his appearance and his kingdom. [2]Preach the word. Be ready to do it whether it is convenient or inconvenient. Correct, confront, and encourage with patience and instruction. [3]There will come a time when people will not tolerate sound teaching. They will collect teachers who say what they want

to hear because they are self-centered. [4]They will turn their back on the truth and turn to myths. [5]But you must keep control of yourself in all circumstances. Endure suffering, do the work of a preacher of the good news, and carry out your service fully.

[6]I'm already being poured out like a sacrifice to God, and the time of my death is near. [7]I have fought the good fight, finished the race, and kept the faith. [8]At last the champion's wreath that is awarded for righteousness[d] is waiting for me. The Lord, who is the righteous[e] judge, is going to give it to me on that day. He's giving it not only to me but also to all those who have set their heart on waiting for his appearance.

Final instructions

[9]Do your best to come to me quickly. [10]Demas has fallen in love with the present world and has deserted me and has gone to

[d]Or *justice* [e]Or *just*

God's Word Is a Guide for Life *2 Timothy 3:16-17*

Textbooks teach skills and information we need for school. Music books teach us how to play our instruments and master songs. Rule books teach us the rules of games so we can play fairly and enjoy the fullness of a game. These books give us the information we need to succeed at the task set before us.

The Bible is like a guidebook for the Christian life. It contains instructions, stories, poems, and prayers that help us understand who God is and who we are to God. The Bible tells us our story and gives us a glimpse of our future.

Paul said that "every scripture is inspired by God and is useful for teaching, for showing mistakes, for correcting, and for training character" (2 Tim 3:16). The Bible as our scripture shows us what we need to do to grow as followers of Jesus. This helps us get ready to do the good things that God has for us to do. The next time you pick up your Bible, imagine that you are picking up the guidebook for life and look for what God might be showing you within its pages.

What is your favorite Bible verse? Why?

How has reading the Bible helped you to grow?

Thessalonica. Crescens has gone to Galatia, and Titus has gone to Dalmatia. [11]Only Luke is with me. Get Mark, and bring him with you. He has been a big help to me in the ministry. [12]I sent Tychicus to Ephesus. [13]When you come, bring along the coat I left with Carpus in Troas. Also bring the scrolls and especially the parchments. [14]Alexander, the craftsman who works with metal, has really hurt me. The Lord will pay him back for what he has done. [15]But watch out for him, because he opposes our teaching.

[16]No one took my side at my first court hearing. Everyone deserted me. I hope that God doesn't hold it against them! [17]But the Lord stood by me and gave me strength, so that the entire message would be preached through me and so all the nations could hear it. I was also rescued from the lion's mouth! [18]The Lord will rescue me from every evil action and will save me for his heavenly kingdom. To him be the glory forever and always. Amen.

Final greetings

[19]Say hello to Prisca and Aquila and the household of Onesiphorus. [20]Erastus stayed in Corinth, and I left Trophimus in Miletus because of his illness. [21]Try hard to come to me before winter. Eubulus, Pudens, Linus, Claudia, and all the brothers and sisters say hello.

[22]The Lord be with your spirit. Grace be with you all.

Titus

Titus traveled widely with the apostle Paul, helping spread the news about Jesus across the Mediterranean Sea. Then Paul left Titus on the island of Crete to lead the church. The people of Crete were known throughout the region as pirates and slave traders. One of their own poets even said, "People from Crete are always liars, wild animals, and lazy gluttons" (Titus 1:12). Titus' job was to help the Christians living in Crete grow strong in their faith and follow Jesus.

This letter, apparently written by Paul, encouraged Titus and gave him helpful tips on many topics. It told Titus to go to each city and appoint leaders, called *elders*, and described what a good elder is like. The letter also told Titus to teach people in the church how to act according to God's way.

The Christians on Crete lived in a place where following Jesus wasn't popular or easy. But God loved them and wanted them to do what was right. Titus chose to do the hard work of helping these new Christians grow up spiritually. This letter shows us that God wants all people to live for God! ◊

Greeting

1 From Paul, a slave of God and an apostle of Jesus Christ. I'm sent to bring about the faith of God's chosen people and a knowledge of the truth that agrees with godliness. [2]Their faith and this knowledge are based on the hope of eternal life that God, who doesn't lie, promised before time began. [3]God revealed his message at the appropriate time through preaching, and I was trusted with preaching this message by the command of God our savior. [4]To Titus, my true child in a common faith.

Grace and peace from God the Father and Christ Jesus our savior.

Appointing elders

[5]The reason I left you behind in Crete was to organize whatever needs to be done and to appoint elders in each city, as I told you. [6]Elders should be without fault. They should be faithful to their spouse,[a] and have faithful children who can't be accused of self-indulgence or rebelliousness. [7]This is because supervisors[b] should be without fault as God's managers: they shouldn't be stubborn, irritable, addicted to alcohol, a bully, or greedy. [8]Instead, they should show hospitality, love what is good, and be reasonable, ethical, godly, and self-controlled. [9]They must pay attention to the reliable message as it has been taught to them so that they can encourage people with healthy instruction and refute those who speak against it.

Correcting rebellious people

[10]In fact, there are many who are rebellious people, loudmouths,

SAILBOAT

HONEST AND TRUE

Characteristics of Leaders Titus 1:7-9
Paul told Titus that the people who would make good leaders were people who were welcoming, reasonable, godly, and self-controlled. They should be ethical, love what is good, and be solid in their faith so they could stand up to people who had different ideas. ◖

and deceivers, especially some of those who are Jewish believers.[c] [11]They must be silenced because they upset entire households. They teach what they shouldn't to make money dishonestly. [12]Someone who is one of their own prophets said, "People from Crete are always liars, wild animals, and lazy gluttons." [13]This statement is true. Because of this, correct them firmly, so that they can be healthy in their faith. [14]They shouldn't pay attention to Jewish myths and commands from people who reject the truth. [15]Everything is clean to those who are clean, but nothing is clean to those who are corrupt and without faith. Instead, their mind and conscience are corrupted. [16]They claim to know God, but they deny God by the things that they do. They are detestable, disobedient, and disqualified to do anything good.

Teaching all people how to be godly

2 But you should talk in a way that is consistent with sound teaching. [2]Tell the older men to be sober, dignified, sensible, and healthy in respect to their faith, love, and patience.

[3]Likewise, tell the older women to be reverent in their behavior, teaching what is good, rather than being gossips or addicted to heavy drinking. [4]That way they can mentor young women to love their husbands and children, [5]and to be sensible, morally pure, working at home, kind and submissive to their own husbands, so that God's word won't be ridiculed. [6]Likewise, encourage the younger men to be sensible [7]in every way. Offer yourself as a role model of good actions. Show integrity, seriousness, [8]and a sound message that is above criticism when you teach, so that any opponent will be ashamed because they won't find anything bad to say about us.

[9]Tell slaves to submit to their own masters and please them in everything they do. They shouldn't talk back [10]or steal. Instead, they should show that they are completely reliable in everything so that they might make the teaching about God our savior attractive in every way.

[11]The grace of God has appeared, bringing salvation to all people. [12]It educates us so that we can live sensible, ethical, and godly

---

[a]Or they should be a one-woman man. [b]Or overseers, bishops [c]Or from the circumcision

lives right now by rejecting ungodly lives and the desires of this world. ¹³At the same time we wait for the blessed hope and the glorious appearance of our great God and savior Jesus Christ. ¹⁴He gave himself for us in order to rescue us from every kind of lawless behavior, and cleanse a special people for himself who are eager to do good actions.

¹⁵Talk about these things. Encourage and correct with complete authority. Don't let anyone disrespect you. **3** ¹Remind them to submit to rulers and authorities. They should be obedient and ready to do every good thing. ²They shouldn't speak disrespectfully about anyone, but they should be peaceful, kind, and show complete courtesy toward everyone. ³We were once foolish, disobedient, deceived, and slaves to our desires and various pleasures too. We were spending our lives in evil behavior and jealousy. We were disgusting, and we hated other people. ⁴But "when God our savior's kindness and love appeared, ⁵he saved us because of his mercy, not because of righteous things we had done. He did it through the washing of new birth and the renewing by the Holy Spirit, ⁶which God poured out upon us generously through Jesus Christ our savior.

⁷So, since we have been made righteous by his grace, we can inherit the hope for eternal life." ⁸This saying is reliable. And I want you to insist on these things, so that those who have come to believe in God might give careful attention to doing good. These things are good and useful for everyone.

Memorize Titus 3:7

Final instructions and greetings

⁹Avoid stupid controversies, genealogies, and fights about the Law, because they are useless and worthless. ¹⁰After a first and second warning, have nothing more to do with a person who causes conflict, ¹¹because you know that someone like this is twisted and sinful—so they condemn themselves.

¹²When I send Artemas or Tychicus to you, try to come to me in Nicopolis, because I've decided to spend the winter there. ¹³Help Zenas the lawyer and Apollos on their journey with enthusiasm so that they won't need anything. ¹⁴But our people should also learn to devote themselves to doing good in order to meet pressing needs so they aren't unproductive.

¹⁵Everyone with me greets you; greet those who love us faithfully.

Grace be with all of you.

Do the Right Thing   Titus 3:9-14

A *do-gooder* is someone who always wants to do the right thing. She wouldn't dare break a rule or talk back to her parents. He would never want to make a bad impression by acting out at a bad moment. Do-gooders are made fun of sometimes because most of us can't make ourselves do the right thing every single time.

As Christians we're all called to be do-gooders. We are supposed to do the right thing all the time, whether someone is looking or not! Doing what is right and good helps us to meet other people's needs by showing God's love.

Doing the right thing can be a challenge when doing what is right isn't always the easiest or most popular decision. But God promised to be with us. Go about your day looking for opportunities to do the right thing, and then pray for the courage to act!

How can you do the right thing? • Say a prayer to God, asking for the courage to do what is right even when times are tough.

Philemon

Philemon is the shortest of the apostle Paul's letters. Because it is only one chapter long, there aren't any chapter numbers—only verse numbers.

This letter tells the story of Onesimus, a slave who ran or may have been sent away from his master Philemon. Onesimus met Paul while Paul was in prison, and he chose to follow Jesus. After a while, Paul sent Onesimus back to Philemon.

Slavery was common during New Testament times. Many people sold themselves as slaves to pay back money they owed. Returning to a master after being away would be a hard thing for a slave to do. Onesimus faced trouble when he went back to Philemon.

Paul wrote to Philemon and asked him to welcome Onesimus as a "dearly loved brother" (Phlm 16). Paul pointed out that Onesimus was more than a slave; he was a fellow believer. Paul urged Philemon to receive Onesimus into his home and church. Paul even said he would pay back anything Onesimus owed.

This short letter is a beautiful story of welcome and freedom. It reminds us to show love and kindness to all people, regardless of their circumstances! ◊

Greeting

¹From Paul, who is a prisoner for the cause of Christ Jesus, and our brother Timothy.

To Philemon our dearly loved co-worker, ²Apphia our sister, Archippus our fellow soldier, and the church that meets in your house.

³May the grace and peace from God our Father and the Lord Jesus Christ be with you.

Bet you can

read this in 10 minutes. Ready, set, go!

Paul's prayer for Philemon

⁴Philemon, I thank my God every time I mention you in my prayers ⁵because I've heard of your love and faith-

Memorize
Phlm 4-5

fulness, which you have both for the Lord Jesus and for all God's people. ⁶I pray that your partnership in the faith might become effective by an understanding of all that is good among us in Christ. ⁷I have great joy and encouragement because of your love, since the hearts of God's people are refreshed by your actions, my brother.

Paul's appeal for Onesimus

⁸Therefore, though I have enough confidence in Christ to command you to do the right thing, ⁹I would rather appeal to you through love. I, Paul—an old man, and now also a prisoner for Christ Jesus—¹⁰appeal to you for my child Onesimus. I became his father in the faith during my time in prison. ¹¹He was useless to you before, but now he is useful to both of us. ¹²I'm sending him back to you, which is like sending you my own heart. ¹³I considered keeping him with me so that he might serve me in your place during my time in prison because of the gospel. ¹⁴However, I didn't want to do anything without your consent so that your act of kindness would occur willingly and not under pressure. ¹⁵Maybe this is the reason that Onesimus was separated from you for a while so that you might have him back forever—¹⁶no longer as a slave but more than a slave—that is, as a dearly loved brother. He is especially a dearly loved brother to me. How much more can he become a

LIFE PRESERVER

Why does the Bible talk about Christians owning slaves? Philemon 16

When Paul wrote this letter to Philemon, slavery was legal in the Roman Empire. Not only was slavery legal, it was a common practice. As a wealthy man it's likely that Philemon owned slaves before he chose to follow Jesus.

Other books of the Bible include instructions to slaves about how they should live and obey their masters. If you were an African girl or boy living as a slave in the early history of the United States or in many other parts of the world, those passages would have been read to tell you about your lowly place in society.

We know it is wrong to own another human being. Paul questioned the practice of owning slaves because he asked Philemon to treat Onesimus as if the runaway slave were Paul himself. In other letters Paul said that all people are the same in Christ (Gal 3:26-28; Col 3:11), and he reminded people who owned slaves that they also had a master in heaven (Eph 6:9; Col 4:1). ◆

brother to you, personally and spiritually in the Lord!

¹⁷So, if you really consider me a partner, welcome Onesimus as if you were welcoming me. ¹⁸If he has harmed you in any way or owes you money, charge it to my account. ¹⁹I, Paul, will pay it back to you (I'm writing this with my own hand). Of course, I won't mention that you owe me your life.

²⁰Yes, brother, I want this favor from you in the Lord! Refresh my heart in Christ. ²¹I'm writing to you, confident of your obedience and knowing that you will do more than what I ask. ²²Also, one more thing—prepare a guest room for me. I hope that I will be released from prison to be with you because of your prayers.

Final greeting

²³Epaphras, who is in prison with me for the cause of Christ Jesus, greets you, ²⁴as well as my coworkers Mark, Aristarchus, Demas, and Luke.

²⁵May the grace of the Lord Jesus Christ be with your spirit.

Hebrews

Hebrews is unlike any other New Testament book. It reads more like a sermon, which is a message that a pastor preaches, than the letters that come before and after it. This book gives many unique details about Jesus' role in the plan God began in the Old Testament.

This book tells us that God once spoke to people through prophets. But now God speaks through God's Son Jesus. God gave us teaching through Jewish Law, which is recorded in the Old Testament. But that Instruction in the Old Testament now points us to Jesus.

Commandments and sacrifices were meant to bring people and God back together when people sinned. But Jesus came as the great high priest and final sacrifice for our sins. From now on, Jesus opens the way for us to get close to God (Heb 10:19-23)!

Hebrews 11 contains what is sometimes called the Bible's *Hall of Faith*. It reminds us about the stories of Old Testament people who trusted God and did amazing things with God's help. Hebrews explains what Jesus did for us and encourages us to trust God! ◊

The Son is God's ultimate messenger

1 In the past, God spoke through the prophets to our ancestors in many times and many ways. ²In these final days, though, he spoke to us through a Son. God made his Son the heir of everything and created the world through him. ³The Son is the light of God's glory and the imprint of God's being. He maintains everything with his powerful message. After he carried out the cleansing of people from their sins, he sat down at the right side of the highest majesty. ⁴And the Son became so much greater than the other messengers, such as angels, that he received a more important title than theirs.

Speaking to the Son and angels

⁵After all, when did God ever say to any of the angels:

You are my Son.
  Today I have become your Father?ᵃ

Or, even,

I will be his Father,
  and he will be my Son?ᵇ

⁶But then, when he brought his firstborn into the world, he said,

All of God's angels must worship him.ᶜ

⁷He talks about the angels:

He's the one who uses the spirits
  for his messengers
  and who uses flames of fire
    as ministers.ᵈ

⁸But he says to his Son,

God, your throne is forever
  and your kingdom's scepter
    is a rod of justice.

⁹ You loved righteousness
  and hated lawless behavior.
    That is why God, your God,
    has anointed you with oil
      instead of your companions.ᵉ

¹⁰And he says,

You, Lord, laid the earth's foundations
  in the beginning,

and the heavens are made
  by your hands.
¹¹ They will pass away,
  but you remain.
They will all wear out like old clothes.
¹² You will fold them up like a coat.
They will be changed
  like a person changes clothes,
    but you stay the same,
    and the years of your life
      won't come to an end.ᶠ

¹³When has he ever said to any of the angels,

Sit at my right side
  until I put your enemies
    under your feet like a footstool?ᵍ

¹⁴Aren't all the angels ministering spirits who are sent to serve those who are going to inherit salvation?

Listen to the Son's message

2 This is why it's necessary for us to pay more attention to what we have heard, or else we may drift away from it. ²If the message that was spoken by angels was reliable, and every offense and act of disobedience received an appropriate consequence, ³how will we escape if we ignore such a great salvation? It was first announced through the Lord, and then it was confirmed by those who heard him. ⁴God also vouched for their message with signs, amazing things, various miracles, and gifts from the Holy Spirit, which were handed out the way he wanted.

did you **know?** The message that was spoken by angels refers to the Instruction from Moses, which is called *the Law* in the New Testament.

ᵃPs 2:7 ᵇ2 Sam 7:14; 1 Chron 17:13 ᶜDeut 32:43 and Ps 97:7 LXX ᵈPs 104:4 ᵉPs 45:6-7 ᶠPs 102:25-27 ᵍPs 110:1

Jesus is the enthroned human being

⁵God didn't put the world that is coming (the world we are talking about) under the angels' control. ⁶Instead, someone declared somewhere,

What is humanity
that you think about them?
Or what are the human beings
that you care about them?
⁷ For a while you made them lower
than angels.
You crowned the human beings
with glory and honor.
⁸ You put everything
under their control.ʰ

When he puts everything under their control, he doesn't leave anything out of control. But right now, we don't see everything under their control yet. ⁹However, we do see the one who was made lower in order than the angels for a little while—it's Jesus! He's the one who is now crowned with glory and honor because of the suffering of his death. He suffered death so that he could taste death for everyone through God's grace.

Qualified to be a high priest

¹⁰It was appropriate for God, for whom and through whom everything exists, to use experiences of suffering to make perfect the pioneer of salvation. This salvation belongs to many sons and daughters whom he's leading to glory. ¹¹This is because the one who makes people holy and the people who are being made holy all come from one source. That is why Jesus isn't ashamed to call them brothers and sisters when he says,

¹² I will publicly announce your name
to my brothers and sisters.
I will praise you in the middle
of the assembly.ⁱ
¹³He also says,
I will rely on him.ʲ
And also,
Here I am with the children
whom God has given to me.ᵏ

¹⁴Therefore, since the children share in flesh and blood, he also shared the same things in the same way. He did this to destroy

the one who holds the power over death—the devil—by dying. ¹⁵He set free those who were held in slavery their entire lives by their fear of death. ¹⁶Of course, he isn't trying to help angels, but rather he's helping Abraham's descendants. ¹⁷Therefore, he had to be made like his brothers and sisters in every way. This was so that he could become a merciful and faithful high priest in things relating to God, in order to wipe away the sins of the people. ¹⁸He's able to help those who are being tempted, since he himself experienced suffering when he was tempted.

UMBRELLA
TEMPTED

Overcoming Temptation *Hebrews 2:18*
Most early Christians were Jewish. As their Christian beliefs became clear, they shared their trust in Jesus by thinking about their Jewish faith. These early Christians were also concerned about being bullied, or even killed, if they followed Jesus. When bullied, some Christians thought about not following Jesus. But Jesus was tempted too. He faced suffering and death. So Jesus can help us stay close to God when bullies or even friends don't want us to follow Jesus. 🖌

We are Jesus' house

3 Therefore, brothers and sisters who are partners in the heavenly calling, think about Jesus, the apostle and high priest of our confession. ²Jesus was faithful to the one who appointed him just like Moses was faithful in God's house. ³But he deserves greater glory than Moses in the same way that the builder of the house deserves more honor than the house itself. ⁴Every house is built by someone, but God is the builder of everything. ⁵Moses was faithful in all God's house as a servant in order to affirm the things that would be spoken later. ⁶But Jesus was faithful over God's house as a Son. We are his house if we hold on to the confidence and the pride that our hope gives us.

ʰPs 8:4-6 ⁱPs 22:22 ʲIsa 8:17 LXX ᵏIsa 8:18

Respond to Jesus' voice now
[7]So, as the Holy Spirit says,

Today, if you hear his voice,
[8] *don't have stubborn hearts*
as they did in the rebellion,
on the day when they tested me
in the desert.
[9] *That is where your ancestors*
challenged and tested me,
though they had seen my work
for forty years.
[10] *So I was angry with them.*
I said, "Their hearts always go off course,
and they don't know my ways."
[11] *Because of my anger I swore:*
"They will never enter my rest!"[l]

[12]Watch out, brothers and sisters, so that none of you have an evil, unfaithful heart that abandons the living God. [13]Instead, encourage each other every day, as long as it's called "today," so that none of you become insensitive to God because of sin's deception. [14]We are partners with Christ, but only if we hold on to the confidence we had in the beginning until the end.

[15]When it says,

Today, if you hear his voice,
don't have stubborn hearts
as they did in the rebellion.[m]

[16]Who was it who rebelled when they heard his voice? Wasn't it all of those who were brought out of Egypt by Moses? [17]And with whom was God angry for forty years? Wasn't it with the ones who sinned, whose bodies fell in the desert?

SAILBOAT

OBEDIENCE

Faithfulness of Jesus *Hebrews 3:2-6*
Being *faithful* means trusting God. You have faith when you respond to God's love and care. The writer of Hebrews compared the faithfulness of Jesus with the faithfulness of Moses. Moses was a faithful prophet and an important person who made it possible for us to understand Jesus. The writer used the idea of a house to illustrate the point. Moses was faithful because he helped build the house, and Jesus is the Son who lives in God's house. ◆

[18]And against whom did he swear that they would never enter his rest, if not against the ones who were disobedient? [19]We see that they couldn't enter because of their lack of faith.

Enter the rest

4 Therefore, since the promise that we can enter into rest is still open, let's be careful so that none of you will appear to miss it. [2]We also had the good news preached to us, just as the Israelites did. However, the message they heard didn't help them because they weren't united in faith with the ones who listened to it. [3]We who have faith are entering the rest. As God said,

And because of my anger I swore:
"They will never enter into my rest!"[m]

And yet God's works were completed at the foundation of the world. [4]Then somewhere he said this about the seventh day of creation: *God rested on the seventh day from all his works.*[o] [5]But again, in the passage above, God said, *They will never enter my rest!*[p] [6]Therefore, it's left open for some to enter it, and the ones who had the good news preached to them before didn't enter because of disobedience. [7]Just as it says in the passage above, God designates a certain day as "today," when he says through David much later,

Today, if you hear his voice,
don't have stubborn hearts.[q]

[8]If Joshua gave the Israelites rest, God wouldn't have spoken about another day later on. [9]So you see that a sabbath rest is left open for God's people. [10]The one who entered God's rest also rested from his works, just as God rested from his own.

First summary of the message

[11]Therefore, let's make every effort to enter that rest so that no one will fall by following the same example of disobedience, [12]because God's word is living, active, and sharper than any two-edged sword. It penetrates to the point that it separates the soul from the spirit and the joints from the marrow. It's able to judge the heart's thoughts and intentions. [13]No creature is

Bet you can read this in 2 minutes. Ready, set, go!

[l]Ps 95:7-11 [m]Ps 95:7-8 [n]Ps 95:11 [o]Gen 2:2 [p]Ps 95:11 [q]Ps 95:7-8

hidden from it, but rather everything is naked and exposed to the eyes of the one to whom we have to give an answer.

¹⁴Also, let's hold on to the confession since we have a great high priest who passed through the heavens, who is Jesus, God's Son; ¹⁵because we don't have a high priest who can't sympathize with our weaknesses but instead one who was tempted in every way that we are, except without sin.

¹⁶Finally, let's draw near to the throne of favor with confidence so that we can receive mercy and find grace when we need help.

Introduction to a deeper teaching

5 Every high priest is taken from the people and put in charge of things that relate to God for their sake, in order to offer gifts and sacrifices for sins. ²The high priest is able to deal gently with the ignorant and those who are misled since he himself is prone to weakness. ³Because of his weakness, he must offer sacrifices for his own sins as well as for the people. ⁴No one takes this honor for themselves but takes it only when they are called by God, just like Aaron.

⁵In the same way Christ also didn't promote himself to become high priest. Instead, it was the one who said to him,

You are my Son.

Today I have become your Father,

⁶as he also says in another place,

You are a priest forever,

*according to the order of Melchizedek.*ᵀ

⁷During his days on earth, Christ offered prayers and requests with loud cries and tears as his sacrifices to the one who was able to save him from death. He was heard because of his godly devotion. ⁸Although he was a Son, he learned obedience from what he suffered. ⁹After he had been made perfect, he became the source of eternal salvation for everyone who obeys him. ¹⁰He was appointed by God to be a high priest according to the order of Melchizedek.

¹¹We have a lot to say about this topic, and it's difficult to explain, because you have been lazy and you haven't been listening. ¹²Although you should have been teachers by now, you need someone to teach you an introduction to the basics about God's message. You have come to the place where you need milk instead of solid food. ¹³Everyone who lives on milk is not used to the word of righteousness, because they are babies. ¹⁴But solid food is for the mature, whose senses are trained by practice to distinguish between good and evil.

LIGHTHOUSE

Good News

Becoming a Spiritual Grown-up

Hebrews 5:11-14

The good news was presented to the people, and they accepted it. Unfortunately, they didn't follow what they were taught. The author of Hebrews was frustrated. If these early Christians practiced what they learned, they would grow up and become teachers of the good news. Instead, they were more like babies who could only drink milk and not eat solid food. People become spiritual grown-ups by obediently following Jesus. ◊

Let's press on to maturity

6 So let's press on to maturity, by moving on from the basics about Christ's word. Let's not lay a foundation of turning away from dead works, of faith in God, ²of teaching about ritual ways to wash with water, laying on of hands, the resurrection from the dead, and eternal judgment—all over again. ³We're going to press on, if God allows it.

⁴Because it's impossible to restore people to changed hearts and lives who turn away once they have seen the light, tasted the heavenly gift, become partners with the Holy Spirit, ⁵and tasted God's good word and the powers of the coming age. ⁶They are crucifying God's Son all over again and exposing him to public shame. ⁷The ground receives a blessing from God when it drinks up the rain that regularly comes and falls on it and yields a useful crop for those people for whom it is being farmed. ⁸But if it produces thorns and

did you know? No other plants could grow in places where thornbushes grew. People in ancient times burned fields where thornbushes grew.

thistles, it's useless and close to being cursed. It ends up being burned.

Make your hope sure

⁹But we are convinced of better things in your case, brothers and sisters, even though we are talking this way—things that go together with salvation. ¹⁰God isn't unjust so that he forgets your efforts and the love you have shown for his name's sake when you served and continue to serve God's holy people. ¹¹But we desperately want each of you to show the same effort to make your hope sure until the end. ¹²This is so you won't be lazy but follow the example of the ones who inherit the promises through faith and patience.

Our hope in Jesus' priesthood

¹³When God gave Abraham his promise, he swore by himself since he couldn't swear by anyone greater. ¹⁴He said, *I will certainly bless you and multiply your descendants.*ˢ ¹⁵So Abraham obtained the promise by showing patience. ¹⁶People pledge by something greater than themselves. A solemn pledge

ˢGen 22:17

guarantees what they say and shuts down any argument. ¹⁷When God wanted to further demonstrate to the heirs of the promise that his purpose doesn't change, he guaranteed it with a solemn pledge. ¹⁸So these are two things that don't change, because it's impossible for God to lie. He did this so that we, who have taken refuge in him, can be encouraged to grasp the hope that is lying in front of us. ¹⁹This hope, which is a safe and secure anchor for our whole being, enters the sanctuary behind the curtain. ²⁰That's where Jesus went in advance and entered for us, since he became a high priest according to the order of Melchizedek. ¹This Melchizedek, who was king of Salem and priest of the Most High God, met Abraham as he returned from the defeat of the kings, and Melchizedek blessed him. ²Abraham gave a tenth of everything to him. His name means first "king of righteousness," and then "king of Salem," that is, "king of peace." ³He is without father or mother or any family. He has no beginning or end of life, but he's like God's Son and remains a priest for all time.

God Is Our Anchor   Hebrews 6

If you were in a ship on the ocean, you would probably see an anchor attached to the side of it. If a storm came and the water got rough, a captain would drop the anchor to steady the boat. The anchor is a safety tool the crew uses to keep the ship safe and prevent it from being carried away by rough water or strong currents.

Hebrews teaches that God is our anchor when life feels like a wavy ocean. Sometimes problems come up, and we get knocked around. Sometimes we make bad choices, and the consequences feel like rough waters. Or sometimes we just forget about God, and we lose the ground beneath our feet. But God promised to hold us and bless us. That promise is something we can hope in. We can expect God to hold us steady—like an anchor—when life gets crazy.

Draw an anchor and think about the ways that God keeps you safe and secure.

What do you think it means to grasp the hope that is right in front of you?

A priest like Melchizedek

[4]See how great Melchizedek was! Abraham, the father of the people, gave him a tenth of everything he captured. [5]The descendants of Levi who receive the office of priest have a commandment under the Law to collect a tenth of everything from the people who are their brothers and sisters, though they also are descended from Abraham. [6]But Melchizedek, who isn't related to them, received a tenth of everything from Abraham and blessed the one who had received the promises. [7]Without question, the less important person is blessed by the more important person. [8]In addition, in one case a tenth is received by people who die, and in the other case, the tenth is received by someone who continues to live, according to the record. [9]It could be said that Levi, who received a tenth, paid a tenth through Abraham [10]because he was still in his ancestor's body when Abraham paid the tenth to Melchizedek.

[11]So if perfection came through the levitical office of priest (for the people received the Law under the priests), why was there still a need to speak about raising up another priest according to the order of Melchizedek rather than one according to the order of Aaron? [12]When the order of the priest changes, there has to be a change in the Law as well. [13]The person we are talking about belongs to another tribe, and no one ever served at the altar from that tribe. [14]It's clear that our Lord came from the tribe of Judah, but Moses never said anything about priests from that tribe. [15]And it's even clearer if another priest appears who is like Melchizedek. [16]He has become a priest by the power of a life that can't be destroyed, rather than a legal requirement about physical descent. [17]This is confirmed:

You are a priest forever,
according to the order of Melchizedek.[t]

Able to save completely

[18]On the one hand, an earlier command is set aside because it was weak and useless [19](because the Law made nothing perfect). On the other hand, a better hope is introduced, through which we draw near to God. [20]And this was not done without a solemn pledge!

The others have become priests without a solemn pledge, [21]but this priest was affirmed with a solemn pledge by the one who said,

The Lord has made a solemn pledge
and will not change his mind:
You are a priest forever.[u]

[22]As a result, Jesus has become the guarantee of a better covenant. [23]The others who became priests are numerous because death prevented them from continuing to serve. [24]In contrast, he holds the office of priest permanently because he continues to serve forever. [25]This is why he can completely save those who are approaching God through him, because he always lives to speak with God for them.

[26]It's appropriate for us to have this kind of high priest: holy, innocent, incorrupt, separate from sinners, and raised high above the heavens. [27]He doesn't need to offer sacrifices every day like the other high priests, first for their own sins and then for the sins of the people. He did this once for all when he offered himself. [28]The Law appoints people who are prone to weakness as high priests, but the content of the solemn pledge, which came after the Law, appointed a Son who has been made perfect forever.

Meeting tents, sacrifices, and covenants

8 Now the main point of what we are saying is this: We have this kind of high priest. He sat down at the right side of the throne of the majesty in the heavens. [2]He's serving as a priest in the holy place, which is the true meeting tent that God, not any human being, set up. [3]Every high priest is appointed to offer gifts and sacrifices. So it's necessary for this high priest also to have something to offer. [4]If he was located on earth, he wouldn't be a priest because there are already others who offer gifts based on the Law. [5]They serve in a place that is a copy and shadow of the heavenly meeting tent. This is indicated when Moses was warned by God when he was about to set up the meeting tent: *See that you follow the pattern that I showed you on the mountain in every detail.*[v] [6]But now, Jesus has received a superior priestly service just as he arranged a better covenant that is enacted with better promises.

[t]Ps 110:4 [u]Ps 110:4 [v]Exod 25:40

⁷If the first covenant had been without fault, it wouldn't have made sense to expect a second. ⁸But God did find fault with them, since he says,

Look, the days are coming, says the Lord,
  when I will make a covenant
  with the house of Israel,
  and I will make a new covenant
  with the house of Judah.
⁹ It will not be like the covenant
  that I made with their ancestors
  on the day I took them by the hand
  to lead them out of the land of Egypt,
  because they did not continue
  to keep my covenant,
  and I lost interest in them,
  says the Lord.
¹⁰ This is the covenant that I will make
  with the house of Israel
  after those days, says the Lord.
I will place my laws in their minds,
  and write them on their hearts.
I will be their God,
  and they will be my people.
¹¹ and each person
  won't ever teach a neighbor
  or their brother or sister, saying,
  "Know the Lord,"
  because they will all know me,
  from the least important of them
  to the most important;
¹² because I will be lenient
  toward their unjust actions,
  and I won't remember
  their sins anymore.^w

¹³When it says new, it makes the first obsolete. And if something is old and outdated, it's close to disappearing.

Christ's service
in the heavenly meeting tent

9 So then the first covenant had regulations for the priests' service and the holy place on earth. ²They pitched the first tent called the holy place. It contained the lampstand, the table, and the loaves of bread presented to God. ³There was a tent behind the second curtain called the holy of holies. ⁴It had the gold altar for incense and the chest containing the covenant, which was covered with gold on all sides. In the chest there was a gold jar containing manna, Aaron's rod that budded, and the stone tablets of the covenant. ⁵Above the chest there were magnificent winged creatures^x casting their shadow over the seat of the chest, where sin is taken care of. Right now we can't talk about these things in detail. ⁶When these things have been prepared in this way, priests enter the first tent all the time as they perform their service. ⁷But only the high priest enters the second tent once a year. He never does this without blood, which he offers for himself and for the sins the people committed in ignorance. ⁸With this, the Holy Spirit is showing that the way into the holy place hadn't been revealed yet while the first tent was standing. ⁹This is a symbol for the present time. It shows that the gifts and sacrifices that are being offered can't perfect the conscience of the one who is serving. ¹⁰These are superficial regulations that are only about food, drink, and various ritual ways to wash with water. They are regulations that have been imposed until the time of the new order.

¹¹But Christ has appeared as the high priest of the good things that have happened.

LIGHTHOUSE

GOOD NEWS

A New Covenant Hebrews 9:8-15

Making bad choices hurts a relationship with God. Sometimes those choices are an accident. Other times the bad choice is made on purpose. Either way, those choices are sin. Sin is anything that separates people from God. Before Jesus came to earth, God's people followed the Instruction from Moses. This Instruction included very specific guidelines on sacrifices and offerings to make after specific types of sin. The writer of Hebrews referred to these practices for dealing with sin as the first covenant. When Jesus came to earth, he established a new covenant. He gave up his life as a sacrifice for sin so that people can have a restored relationship with God. Jesus overcame the separation between people and God once and for all by his death on the cross. Through Jesus people have the opportunity to be in relationship with God. ◢

^wJer 31:31-34 ^xHeb cherubim

He passed through the greater and more perfect meeting tent, which isn't made by human hands (that is, it's not a part of this world). [12]He entered the holy of holies once for all by his own blood, not by the blood of goats or calves, securing our deliverance for all time. [13]If the blood of goats and bulls and the sprinkled ashes of cows made spiritually contaminated people holy and clean, [14]how much more will the blood of Jesus wash our consciences clean from dead works in order to serve the living God? He offered himself to God through the eternal Spirit as a sacrifice without any flaw.

Christ's death and the new covenant

[15]This is why he's the mediator of a new covenant (which is a will): so that those who are called might receive the promise of the eternal inheritance on the basis of his death. His death occurred to set them free from the offenses committed under the first covenant. [16]When there is a will, you need to confirm the death of the one who made the will. [17]This is because a will takes effect only after a death, since it's not in force while the one who made the will is alive. [18]So not even the first covenant was put into effect without blood. [19]Moses took the blood of calves and goats, along with water, scarlet wool, and hyssop, and sprinkled both the Law scroll itself and all the people after he had proclaimed every command of the Law to all the people. [20]While he did it, he said, *This is the blood of the covenant that God established for you.*[y] [21]And in the same way he sprinkled the meeting tent and also all the equipment that would be used in the priests' service with blood. [22]Almost everything is cleansed by blood, according to the Law's regulations, and there is no forgiveness without blood being shed.

[23]So it was necessary for the copies of the heavenly things to be cleansed with these sacrifices, but the heavenly things had to be cleansed with better sacrifices than these. [24]Christ didn't enter the holy place (which is a copy of the true holy place) made by human hands, but into heaven itself, so that he now appears in God's presence for us. [25]He didn't enter to offer himself over and over again,

like the high priest enters the earthly holy place every year with blood that isn't his. [26]If that were so, then Jesus would have to suffer many times since the foundation of the world. Instead, he has now appeared once at the end of the ages to get rid of sin by sacrificing himself. [27]People are destined to die once and then face judgment. [28]In the same way, Christ was also offered once to take on himself the sins of many people. He will appear a second time, not to take away sin but to save those who are eagerly waiting for him.

Christ's once-for-all sacrifice

10The Law is a shadow of the good things that are coming, not the real things themselves. It never can perfect the ones who are trying to draw near to God through the same sacrifices that are offered continually every year. [2]Otherwise, wouldn't they have stopped being offered? If the people carrying out their religious duties had been completely cleansed once, no one would have been aware of sin anymore. [3]Instead, these sacrifices are a reminder of sin every year, [4]because it's impossible for the blood of bulls and goats to take away sins.

[5]Therefore, when he comes into the world he says,

> You didn't want a sacrifice or an offering,
> but you prepared a body for me;
> [6] you weren't pleased with entirely burned
> offerings or a sin offering.
> [7] So then I said,
> "Look, I've come to do your will, God.
> This has been written about me
> in the scroll."[z]

[8]He says above, *You didn't want* and *you weren't pleased with a sacrifice or an offering* or *with entirely burned offerings or a purification offering,*[a] which are offered because the Law requires them. [9]Then he said, *Look, I've come to do your will.*[b] He puts an end to the first to establish the second. [10]We have been made holy by God's will through the offering of Jesus Christ's body once for all.

Memorize
Heb 10:10

[11]Every priest stands every day serving and offering the same sacrifices over and

over, sacrifices that can never take away sins. [12]But when this priest offered one sacrifice for sins for all time, he sat down at the right side of God. [13]Since then, he's waiting until his enemies are made into a footstool for his feet, [14]because he perfected the people who are being made holy with one offering for all time.

[15]The Holy Spirit affirms this when saying,

[16] *This is the covenant*
 that I will make with them.
 After these days, says the Lord,
 I will place my laws in their hearts
 and write them on their minds.
[17] *And I won't remember their sins*
 and their lawless behavior anymore.[c]

[18]When there is forgiveness for these things, there is no longer an offering for sin.

Second summary of the message

[19]Brothers and sisters, we have confidence that we can enter the holy of holies by means of Jesus' blood, [20]through a new and living way that he opened up for us through the curtain, which is his body, [21]and we have a great high priest over God's house.

[22]Therefore, let's draw near with a genuine heart with the certainty that our faith gives us, since our hearts are sprinkled clean from an evil conscience and our bodies are washed with pure water.

[23]Let's hold on to the confession of our hope without wavering, because the one who made the promises is reliable.

[24]And let us consider each other carefully for the purpose of sparking love and good deeds. [25]Don't stop meeting together with other believers, which some people have gotten into the habit of doing. Instead, encourage each other, especially as you see the day drawing near.

Judgment for intentional sin

[26]If we make the decision to sin after we receive the knowledge of the truth, there isn't a sacrifice for sins left any longer. [27]There's only a scary expectation of judgment and of a burning fire that's going to devour God's opponents. [28]When someone rejected the Law from Moses, they were put to death without mercy on the basis of the testimony of two or three witnesses. [29]How much worse punishment do you think is deserved by the person who walks all over God's Son, who acts as if the blood of the covenant that made us holy is just ordinary blood, and who insults the Spirit of grace? [30]We know the one who said,

 Judgment is mine; I will pay people back.[d]

And he also said,

 The Lord will judge his people.[e]

[31]It's scary to fall into the hands of the living God!

Confidence and faith to endure

[32]But remember the earlier days, after you saw the light. You stood your ground while you were suffering from an enormous amount of pressure. [33]Sometimes you were exposed to insults and abuse in public. Other times you became partners with those who were treated that way. [34]You even showed sympathy toward people in prison and accepted the confiscation of your possessions with joy, since you knew that you had better and lasting possessions. [35]So don't throw away your confidence—it brings a great reward. [36]You need to endure so that you can receive the promises after you do God's will.

[37] *In a little while longer,*
 the one who is coming will come
 and won't delay;
[38] *but my righteous one will live by faith,*
 and my whole being won't be pleased
 with anyone who shrinks back.[f]

[39]But we aren't the sort of people who timidly draw back and end up being destroyed. We're the sort of people who have faith so that our whole beings are preserved.

Description of faith

11 Faith is the reality of what we hope for, the proof of what we don't see. [2]The elders in the past were approved because they showed faith.

Memorize Heb 11:1

Acts of faith by God's people

[3]By faith we understand that the universe has been created by a word from God so that the visible came into existence from the invisible.

[c]Jer 31:33-34 [d]Deut 32:35 [e]Deut 32:36; Ps 135:14 [f]Hab 2:3-4

⁴By faith Abel offered a better sacrifice to God than Cain, which showed that he was righteous, since God gave approval to him for his gift. Though he died, he's still speaking through faith.

⁵By faith Enoch was taken up so that he didn't see death, and *he wasn't found because God took him up.*⁸ He was given approval for having pleased God before he was taken up. ⁶It's impossible to please God without faith because the one who draws near to God must believe that he exists and that he rewards people who try to find him.

⁷By faith Noah responded with godly fear when he was warned about events he hadn't seen yet. He built an ark to deliver his household. With his faith, he criticized the world

and became an heir of the righteousness that comes from faith.

⁸By faith Abraham obeyed when he was called to go out to a place that he was going to receive as an inheritance. He went out without knowing where he was going.

⁹By faith he lived in the land he had been promised as a stranger. He lived in tents along with Isaac and Jacob, who were coheirs of the same promise. ¹⁰He was looking forward to a city that has foundations, whose architect and builder is God.

¹¹By faith even Sarah received the ability to have a child, though she herself was barren and past the age for having children, because she believed that the one who promised was faithful. ¹²So descendants were born

⁸Gen 5:24

What Does Faith Mean? Hebrews 11

When you walk into a room and flip the light switch, you don't wonder whether or not there will be light. You just expect it to come on. When you get out of bed in the morning, you don't worry that your feet won't hit the ground. You count on the floor being firm under your toes.

Although we can't see God—much like we can't see electricity or gravity—we count on God to be there. Hebrews says, "Faith is the reality of what we hope for, the proof of what we don't see" (Heb 11:1). We trust God even though we can't see God. We trust that we will live forever with God, which we hope for even though we can't see it right now. We believe God is real and active in our lives. Even though we can't see God face-to-face, we see evidence of God's work in our lives and in our world.

It's easy to stop trusting sometimes, especially when we don't see God. That's why it's important to remember the stories of the great heroes of faith in the Bible. The writer of Hebrews reminds us of how Abraham, Sarah, Moses, and Joseph had faith to trust the promises of God, even when they couldn't see or understand God's work. Their stories help us keep faith when times get hard. The next time you wonder about faith, read Hebrews 11 and be encouraged by the stories of the people listed there. Ask God to give you more faith every day.

Memorize Hebrews 11:1. Remember that even when you can't see or understand, you can trust that God is faithful to you.

Who is your favorite person of faith? Why? Look in Hebrews 11 for examples if you need help.

from one man (and he was as good as dead). They were as many as the number of the stars in the sky and as countless as the grains of sand on the seashore. ¹³All these people died in faith without receiving the promises, but they saw the promises from a distance and welcomed them. They confessed that they were strangers and immigrants on earth. ¹⁴People who say this kind of thing make it clear that they are looking for a homeland. ¹⁵If they had been thinking about the country that they had left, they would have had the opportunity to return to it. ¹⁶But at this point in time, they are longing for a better country, that is, a heavenly one. Therefore, God isn't ashamed to be called their God—he has prepared a city for them.

¹⁷By faith Abraham offered Isaac when he was tested. The one who received the promises was offering his only son. ¹⁸He had been told concerning him, *Your legitimate descendants will come from Isaac.*ʰ ¹⁹He figured that God could even raise him from the dead. So in a way he did receive him back from the dead.

²⁰By faith Isaac also blessed Jacob and Esau concerning their future.

²¹By faith Jacob blessed each of Joseph's sons as he was dying and *bowed in worship over the head of his staff.*ⁱ

²²By faith Joseph recalled the exodus of the Israelites at the end of his life, and gave instructions about burying his bones.

²³By faith Moses was hidden by his parents for three months when he was born, because they saw that the child was beautiful and they weren't afraid of the king's orders.

²⁴By faith Moses refused to be called the son of Pharaoh's daughter when he was grown up. ²⁵He chose to be mistreated with God's people instead of having the temporary pleasures of sin. ²⁶He thought that the abuses he suffered for Christ were more valuable than the treasures of Egypt, since he was looking forward to the reward.

²⁷By faith he left Egypt without being afraid of the king's anger. He kept on going as if he could see what is invisible.

²⁸By faith he kept the Passover and the sprinkling of blood, in order that the destroyer could not touch their firstborn children.

²⁹By faith they crossed the Red Sea as if they were on dry land, but when the Egyptians tried it, they were drowned.

³⁰By faith Jericho's walls fell after the people marched around them for seven days.

³¹By faith Rahab the prostitute wasn't killed with the disobedient because she welcomed the spies in peace.

³²What more can I say? I would run out of time if I told you about Gideon, Barak, Samson, Jephthah, David, Samuel, and the prophets. ³³Through faith they conquered kingdoms, brought about justice, realized promises, shut the mouths of lions, ³⁴put out raging fires, escaped from the edge of the sword, found strength in weakness, were mighty in war, and routed foreign armies. ³⁵Women received back their dead by resurrection. Others were tortured and refused to be released so they could gain a better resurrection.

³⁶But others experienced public shame by being taunted and whipped; they were even put in chains and in prison. ³⁷They were stoned to death, they were cut in two, and they died by being murdered with swords. They went around wearing the skins of sheep and goats, needy, oppressed, and mistreated. ³⁸The world didn't deserve them. They wandered around in deserts, mountains, caves, and holes in the ground.

³⁹All these people didn't receive what was promised, though they were given approval for their faith. ⁴⁰God provided something better for us so they wouldn't be made perfect without us.

Let's also run the race

12 So then, with endurance, let's also run the race that is laid out in front of us, since we have such a great cloud of witnesses surrounding us. Let's throw off any extra baggage, get rid of the sin that trips us up, ²and fix our eyes on Jesus, faith's pioneer and perfecter. He endured the cross, ignoring the shame, for the sake of the joy that was laid out in front of him, and sat down at the right side of God's throne.

Run the race with discipline

³Think about the one who endured such opposition from sinners so that you won't be

LIFE PRESERVER

What race are we invited to run? *Hebrews 12:1-2*

The race we're invited to join is the Christian life. All the people who believed the truth about God's love and forgiveness even before Jesus, including the people listed in Hebrews 11, surround us like a "great cloud of witnesses" (Heb 12:1). If you've ever watched a marathon or other race, you probably saw a lot of people along the sidelines cheering for the runners. That's what the great cloud of witnesses does for us as we follow Jesus. ◊

discouraged and you won't give up. [4]In your struggle against sin, you haven't resisted yet to the point of shedding blood, [5]and you have forgotten the encouragement that addresses you as sons and daughters:

My child, don't make light
  of the Lord's discipline
  or give up when you are corrected
  by him,
[6] because the Lord disciplines
  whomever he loves,
  and he punishes every son or daughter
  whom he accepts.[j]

[7]Bear hardship for the sake of discipline. God is treating you like sons and daughters! What child isn't disciplined by his or her father? [8]But if you don't experience discipline, which happens to all children, then you are illegitimate and not real sons and daughters. [9]What's more, we had human parents who disciplined us, and we respected them for it. How much more should we submit to the Father of spirits and live? [10]Our human parents disciplined us for a little while, as it seemed best to them, but God does it for our benefit so that we can share his holiness. [11]No discipline is fun while it lasts, but it seems painful at the time. Later, however, it yields the peaceful fruit of righteousness for those who have been trained by it.

[12]So strengthen your drooping hands and weak knees! [13]Make straight paths for your feet so that if any part is lame, it will be healed rather than injured more seriously. [14]Pursue the goal of peace along with everyone—and

holiness as well, because no one will see the Lord without it. [15]Make sure that no one misses out on God's grace. Make sure that no root of bitterness grows up that might cause trouble and pollute many people. [16]Make sure that no one becomes sexually immoral or ungodly like Esau. He sold his inheritance as the oldest son for one meal. [17]You know that afterward, when he wanted to inherit the blessing, he was rejected because he couldn't find a way to change his heart and life, though he looked for it with tears.

Priestly service in heavenly Jerusalem

[18]You haven't drawn near to something that can be touched: a burning fire, darkness, shadow, a whirlwind, [19]a blast of a trumpet, and a sound of words that made the ones who heard it beg that there wouldn't be one more word. [20]They couldn't stand the command, *If even a wild animal touches the mountain, it must be stoned.*[k] [21]The sight was so frightening that Moses said, "I'm terrified and shaking!"

[22]But you have drawn near to Mount Zion, the city of the living God, heavenly Jerusalem, to countless angels in a festival gathering, [23]to the assembly of God's firstborn children who are registered in heaven, to God the judge of all, to the spirits of the righteous who have been made perfect, [24]to Jesus the mediator of the new covenant, and to the sprinkled blood that speaks better than Abel's blood.

[25]See to it that you don't resist the one who is speaking. If the people didn't escape when they refused to listen to the one who warned them on earth, how will we escape if we reject the one who is warning from heaven? [26]His voice shook the earth then, but now he has made a promise: *Still once more I will shake not only the earth but heaven also.*[l] [27]The words "still once more" reveal the removal of what is shaken—the things that are part of this creation—so that what isn't shaken will remain. [28]Therefore, since we are receiving a kingdom that can't be shaken, let's continue to express our gratitude.[m] With this gratitude, let's serve[n] in a way that is pleasing to God with respect and awe, [29]because our God really is a consuming fire.

[j]Prov 3:11-12 [k]Exod 19:12-13 [l]Exod 19:18 [m]Or hold on to grace [n]Or offer priestly service

Our acts of service and sacrifice

13 Keep loving each other like family. [2]Don't neglect to open up your homes to guests, because by doing this some have been hosts to angels without knowing it. [3]Remember prisoners as if you were in prison with them, and people who are mistreated as if you were in their place. [4]Marriage must be honored in every respect, with no cheating on the relationship, because God will judge the sexually immoral person and the person who commits adultery. [5]Your way of life should be free from the love of money, and you should be content with what you have. After all, he has said, *I will never leave you or abandon you.*[o] [6]This is why we can confidently say,

The Lord is my helper,
and I won't be afraid.
What can people do to me?[p]

[7]Remember your leaders who spoke God's word to you. Imitate their faith as you consider the way their lives turned out. [8]Jesus Christ is the same yesterday, today, and forever!

[9]Don't be misled by the many strange teachings out there. It's a good thing for the heart to be strengthened by grace rather than by food. Food doesn't help those who live in this context. [10]We have an altar, and those who serve as priests in the meeting tent don't have the right to eat from it. [11]The blood of the animals is carried into the holy of holies by the high priest as an offering for sin, and their bodies are burned outside the camp. [12]And so Jesus also suffered outside the city gate to make the people holy with his own blood. [13]So now, let's go to him outside the camp, bearing his shame. [14]We don't have a permanent city here, but rather we are looking for the city that is still to come.

[15]So let's continually offer up a sacrifice of praise through him, which is the fruit from our lips that confess his name. [16]Don't forget to do good and to share what you have because God is pleased with these kinds of sacrifices.

Closing greeting and blessing

[17]Rely on your leaders and defer to them, because they watch over your whole being as people who are going to be held responsible for you. They need to be able to do this with pleasure and not with complaints about you, because that wouldn't help you. [18]Pray for us. We're sure that we have a good conscience, and we want to do the right thing in every way. [19]I'm particularly asking you to do this so that I can be returned to you quickly.

[20]May the God of peace,
　　who brought back
　　　the great shepherd of the sheep,
　　our Lord Jesus,
　　from the dead by the blood
　　　of the eternal covenant,
[21]equip you with every good thing
　　to do his will,
　　by developing in us what pleases him
　　　through Jesus Christ.
　　To him be the glory forever and always.
　　Amen.

[22]I urge you, brothers and sisters, to put up with this message of encouragement, since I've only written a short letter to you! [23]You should know that our brother Timothy has been set free. If he comes soon, we will travel together to see you.

[24]Greet your leaders and all of God's holy people. The group from Italy greets you. [25]May grace be with all of you.

[o]Deut 31:6; Gen 28:15 [p]Ps 118:6

James

Many New Testament books highlight the truth that we are made right with God through trusting Jesus' faithfulness, not by doing good things. For example, the letter to the Ephesians says, "You are saved by God's grace because of your faith. This salvation is God's gift. It's not something you possessed. It's not something you did that you can be proud of" (Eph 2:8-9). But James made a different point. He wrote that good deeds are always a part of real faith.

James didn't say that we can get God to love us by doing lots of good things. James wrote that those who live by faith and trust in Jesus will show God's goodness with their words and actions. If we claim we trust God but always treat people badly, that's a problem! If we believe that God loves us even when we don't deserve it, we will show love to other people. This letter teaches that trusting Jesus should change how we act. We should use our words to speak kindly. We shouldn't favor rich and popular people over people who are poor and unknown. We should pray for the sick. We should care for orphans and people who have no home.

James says that we're fooling ourselves if we hear God's commands and don't follow them (Jas 1:22). This letter shows us what real faith looks like! ◊

Greeting

1 From James, a slave of God and of the Lord Jesus Christ.

To the twelve tribes who are scattered outside the land of Israel.

Greetings!

Stand firm

[2] My brothers and sisters, think of the various tests you encounter as occasions for joy. [3] After all, you know that the testing of your faith produces endurance. [4] Let this endurance complete its work so that you may be fully mature, complete, and lacking in nothing. [5] But anyone who needs wisdom should ask God, whose very nature is to give to everyone without a second thought, without keeping score. Wisdom will certainly be given to those who ask. [6] Whoever asks shouldn't hesitate. They should ask in faith, without doubting. Whoever doubts is like the surf of the sea, tossed and turned by the wind. [7] People like that should never imagine that they will receive anything from the Lord. [8] They are double-minded, unstable in all their ways.

[9] Brothers and sisters who are poor should find satisfaction in their high status. [10] Those who are wealthy should find satisfaction in their low status, because they will die off like wildflowers. [11] The sun rises with its scorching heat and dries up the grass so that its flowers fall and its beauty is lost. Just like that, in the midst of their daily lives, the wealthy will waste away. [12] Those who stand firm during testing are blessed. They are tried and true. They will receive the life God has promised to those who love him as their reward.

Our cravings versus God's gifts

[13] No one who is tested should say, "God is tempting me!" This is because God is not tempted by any form of evil, nor does he tempt anyone. [14] Everyone is tempted by their own cravings; they are lured away and enticed by them. [15] Once those cravings conceive, they give birth to sin; and when sin grows up, it gives birth to death.

[16] Don't be misled, my dear brothers and sisters. [17] Every good gift, every perfect gift, comes from above. These gifts come down from the Father, the creator of the heavenly lights, in whose character there is no change

at all. [18] He chose to give us birth by his true word, and here is the result: we are like the first crop from the harvest of everything he created.

Welcoming and doing the word

[19] Know this, my dear brothers and sisters: everyone should be quick to listen, slow to speak, and slow to grow angry. [20] This is because an angry person doesn't produce God's righteousness. [21] Therefore, with humility, set aside all moral filth and the growth of wickedness, and welcome the word planted deep inside you—the very word that is able to save you.

[22] You must be doers of the word and not only hearers who mislead themselves. [23] Those who hear but don't do the word are like those who look at their faces in a mirror. [24] They look at themselves, walk away, and immediately forget what they were like. [25] But there are those who study the perfect law, the law of freedom, and continue to do it. They don't listen and then forget, but they put it into practice in their lives. They will be blessed in whatever they do.

Memorize
James 1:22

[26] If those who claim devotion to God don't control what they say, they mislead themselves. Their devotion is worthless. [27] True devotion, the kind that is pure and faultless before God the Father, is this: to care for orphans and widows in their difficulties and to keep the world from contaminating us.

Don't show favoritism

2 My brothers and sisters, when you show favoritism you deny the faithfulness of our Lord Jesus Christ, who has been resurrected in glory. [2] Imagine two people coming into your meeting. One has a gold ring and fine clothes, while the other is poor, dressed in filthy rags. [3] Then suppose that you were to take special notice of the one wearing fine clothes, saying, "Here's an excellent place.

Sit here." But to the poor person you say, "Stand over there"; or, "Here, sit at my feet." [4]Wouldn't you have shown favoritism among yourselves and become evil-minded judges?

[5]My dear brothers and sisters, listen! Hasn't God chosen those who are poor by worldly standards to be rich in terms of faith? Hasn't God chosen the poor as heirs of the kingdom he has promised to those who love him? [6]But you have dishonored the poor. Don't the wealthy make life difficult for you? Aren't they the ones who drag you into court? [7]Aren't they the ones who insult the good name spoken over you at your baptism?

[8]You do well when you really fulfill the royal law found in scripture, *Love your neighbor as yourself.*[a] [9]But when you show favoritism, you are committing a sin, and by that same law you are exposed as a lawbreaker. [10]Anyone who tries to keep all of the Law but fails at one point is guilty of failing to keep all of it. [11]The one who said, *Don't commit adultery*, also said, *Don't commit murder.*[b] So if you don't commit adultery but do commit murder, you are a lawbreaker. [12]In every way, then, speak and act as people who will be judged by the law of freedom. [13]There will be no mercy in judgment for anyone who hasn't shown mercy. Mercy overrules judgment.

Showing faith

[14]My brothers and sisters, what good is it if people say they have faith but do nothing to show it? Claiming to have faith can't save anyone, can it? [15]Imagine a brother or sister who is naked and never has enough food to eat. [16]What if one of you said, "Go in peace! Stay warm! Have a nice meal!"? What good is it if you don't actually give them what their body needs? [17]In the same way, faith is dead when it doesn't result in faithful activity.

[18]Someone might claim, "You have faith and I have action." But how can I see your faith apart from your actions? Instead, I'll show you my faith by putting it into practice in faithful action. [19]It's good that you believe that God is one. Ha! Even the demons believe this, and they tremble with fear. [20]Are you so slow? Do you need to be shown that faith without actions has no value at all? [21]What about Abraham, our father? Wasn't he shown to be righteous through his actions when he offered his son Isaac on the altar? [22]See, his faith was at work along with his actions. In fact, his faith was made complete by his faithful actions. [23]So the scripture was fulfilled that says, *Abraham believed God, and God regarded him as righteous.*[c] What is more, Abraham was called God's friend. [24]So you see that a person is shown to be righteous through faithful actions and not through faith alone. [25]In the same way, wasn't Rahab the prostitute shown to be righteous when she received the messengers as her guests and then sent them on by another road? [26]As the lifeless body is dead, so faith without actions is dead.

Taming the tongue

3My brothers and sisters, not many of you should become teachers, because we know that we teachers will be judged more strictly. [2]We all make mistakes often, but those who don't make mistakes with their words have reached full maturity. Like a bridled horse, they can control themselves entirely. [3]When we bridle horses and put bits in their mouths to lead them wherever we want, we can control their whole bodies.

[4]Consider ships: They are so large that strong winds are needed to drive them. But pilots direct their ships wherever they want with a little rudder. [5]In the same way, even though the tongue is a small part of the body, it boasts wildly.

Think about this: A small flame can set a whole forest on fire. [6]The tongue is a small flame of fire, a world of evil at work in us. It contaminates our entire lives. Because of it, the circle of life is set on fire. The tongue itself is set on fire by the flames of hell.

[7]People can tame and already have tamed every kind of animal, bird, reptile, and fish. [8]No one can tame the tongue, though. It is a restless evil, full of deadly poison. [9]With it we both bless the Lord and Father and curse human beings made in God's likeness. [10]Blessing and cursing come from the same mouth. My brothers and sisters, it just shouldn't be this way!

[a]Lev 19:18 [b]Exod 20:13, 15 LXX (English: 20:13-14); Deut 5:17-18 [c]Gen 15:6

[11]Both fresh water and salt water don't come from the same spring, do they? [12]My brothers and sisters, can a fig tree produce olives? Can a grapevine produce figs? Of course not, and fresh water doesn't flow from a salt-water spring either.

Wisdom from above

[13]Are any of you wise and understanding? Show that your actions are good with a humble lifestyle that comes from wisdom. [14]However, if you have bitter jealousy and selfish ambition in your heart, then stop bragging and living in ways that deny the truth. [15]This is not the wisdom that comes down from above. Instead, it is from the earth, natural and demonic. [16]Wherever there is jealousy and selfish ambition, there is disorder and everything that is evil. [17]What of the wisdom from above? First, it is pure, and then peaceful, gentle, obedient, filled with mercy and good actions, fair, and genuine. [18]Those who make peace sow the seeds of justice by their peaceful acts.

Conflict with people and God

4 What is the source of conflict among you? What is the source of your disputes? Don't they come from your cravings that are at war in your own lives? [2]You long for something you don't have, so you commit murder. You are jealous for something you can't get,

Use Your Words Well   James 3:1-10

What is the most powerful muscle in your whole body? You might think it's your biceps because they lift heavy objects. It could be your thighs and hamstrings because they hold your body upright. But the most powerful muscle in your body is actually your tongue.

Your tongue is stronger than any other muscle because it helps you make words. And words can cause hurt, conflict, destruction, and pain. Or they can bring blessing, love, forgiveness, kindness, and unity.

People often say that sticks and stones can break our bones, but words will never hurt us. But this isn't true. Words can hurt badly. In fact, James said that we need to bridle our tongues like a horse so that we can tell them what to say. He wrote that huge ships are controlled by small rudders that tell them which way to go. Even though the tongue is small, it can lead us into dangerous places, so we need to tame it. We need to train our tongues to say words that build up instead of tear down. We need to use our words to speak kindness, encouragement, hope, and forgiveness.

The next time you open your mouth to speak, think about what you're going to say. Is it kind? Does it encourage? Does it forgive? Does it build up? Tell your tongue what to say, and choose your words well.

How have you seen words tear people down?

How can you use your words to build people up today?

so you struggle and fight. You don't have because you don't ask. ³You ask and don't have because you ask with evil intentions, to waste it on your own cravings.

⁴You unfaithful people! Don't you know that friendship with the world means hostility toward God? So whoever wants to be the world's friend becomes God's enemy. ⁵Or do you suppose that scripture is meaningless? Doesn't God long for our faithfulness in[d] the life he has given to us?[e] ⁶But he gives us more grace. This is why it says, *God stands against the proud, but favors the humble.*[f] ⁷Therefore, submit to God. Resist the devil, and he will run away from you. ⁸Come near to God, and he will come near to you. Wash your hands, you sinners. Purify your hearts, you double-minded. ⁹Cry out in sorrow, mourn, and weep! Let your laughter become mourning and your joy become sadness. ¹⁰Humble yourselves before the Lord, and he will lift you up.

SAILBOAT

HUMILITY

God Will Lift You Up James 4:10

Picture yourself reaching for a book, toy, or game on a shelf that is too high for you. Imagine that you really want to get that item down. If you simply think you're big enough to reach it, you won't be able to do so. You'll feel frustrated. Thinking about yourself in an unrealistic way isn't helpful. But if you accept that you're too small to reach the item by yourself and ask for help, you'll probably be able to get it. Someone who is taller can lift you up and help you reach it. This is the same idea we find in this passage from James. When we're realistic about who we are in the presence of God, God lifts us up!

¹¹Brothers and sisters, don't say evil things about each other. Whoever insults or criticizes a brother or sister insults and criticizes the Law. If you find fault with the Law, you are not a doer of the Law but a judge over it. ¹²There is only one lawgiver and judge, and he is able to save and to destroy. But you who judge your neighbor, who are you?

¹³Pay attention, you who say, "Today or tomorrow we will go to such-and-such a town. We will stay there a year, buying and selling, and making a profit." ¹⁴You don't really know about tomorrow. What is your life? You are a mist that appears for only a short while before it vanishes. ¹⁵Here's what you ought to say: "If the Lord wills, we will live and do this or that." ¹⁶But now you boast and brag, and all such boasting is evil. ¹⁷It is a sin when someone knows the right thing to do and doesn't do it.

5 Pay attention, you wealthy people! Weep and moan over the miseries coming upon you. ²Your riches have rotted. Moths have destroyed your clothes. ³Your gold and silver have rusted, and their rust will be evidence against you. It will eat your flesh like fire. Consider the treasure you have hoarded in the last days. ⁴Listen! Hear the cries of the wages of your field hands. These are the wages you stole from those who harvested your fields. The cries of the harvesters have reached the ears of the Lord of heavenly forces. ⁵You have lived a self-satisfying life on this earth, a life of luxury. You have stuffed your hearts in preparation for the day of slaughter. ⁶You have condemned and murdered the righteous one, who doesn't oppose you.

Courageous patience

⁷Therefore, brothers and sisters, you must be patient as

LIGHTHOUSE

FOREVER

Wait with Patience James 5:7

James told his readers to wait patiently for Jesus' return to earth. Followers of Jesus look forward to this day because he is coming back to fully unite us with God forever. This is exciting because only goodness exists in the full presence of God. When we spend forever with God, we will no longer suffer like we do on earth. Things like hunger, sadness, violence, and even death will no longer exist. Sometimes waiting for Jesus' return can be difficult. We'll continue to face difficult times while we wait, but we're called to be patient because we know the best is yet to come!

---

[d] Or *jealously longs for* [e] Or *Doesn't the spirit that God placed in us have jealous desires?* [f] Prov 3:34

you wait for the coming of the Lord. Consider the farmer who waits patiently for the coming of rain in the fall and spring, looking forward

to the precious fruit of the earth. [8]You also must wait patiently, strengthening your resolve, because the coming of the Lord is near. [9]Don't complain about each other, brothers and sisters, so that you won't be judged. Look! The judge is standing at the door!

[10]Brothers and sisters, take the prophets who spoke in the name of the Lord as an example of patient resolve and steadfastness. [11]Look at how we honor those who have practiced endurance. You have heard of the endurance of Job. And you have seen what the Lord has accomplished, for the Lord is full of compassion and mercy.

Final instructions

[12]Most important, my brothers and sisters, never make a solemn pledge—neither by heaven nor earth, nor by anything else. Instead, speak with a simple "Yes" or "No," or else you may fall under judgment.

[13]If any of you are suffering, they should pray. If any of you are happy, they should sing. [14]If any of you are sick, they should call for the elders of the church, and the elders should pray over them, anointing them with oil in the name of the Lord. [15]Prayer that comes from faith will heal the sick, for the Lord will restore them to health. And if they have sinned, they will be forgiven.

[16]For this reason, confess your sins to each other and pray for each other so that you may be healed. The prayer of the righteous person is powerful in what it can achieve. [17]Elijah was a person just like us. When he earnestly prayed that it wouldn't rain, no rain fell for three and a half years. [18]He prayed again, God sent rain, and the earth produced its fruit.

[19]My brothers and sisters, if any of you wander from the truth and someone turns back the wanderer, [20]recognize that whoever brings a sinner back from the wrong path will save them from death and will bring about the forgiveness of many sins.

1 Peter

First Peter is a letter written to people who suffered because they believed in Jesus. The author wrote that they were "distressed for a short time by various trials" (1 Pet 1:6). Their faith was being "tested by fire" (1 Pet 1:7). They lived as "immigrants and strangers" among their neighbors (1 Pet 2:11). They were being "mocked because of Christ's name" (1 Pet 4:14).

Those are tough challenges to face. But this letter encouraged its readers to hold tightly to Jesus, especially when suffering. It teaches that God loves us and cares for us even when other people attack or make fun of us. The author called Christians "a chosen race, a royal priesthood, a holy nation, a people who are God's own possession" (1 Pet 2:9). For this reason, we can tell everyone about God's wonderful acts.

Peter was arrested more than once and even faced death for preaching about Jesus (Acts 4:1-22; 12:1-17). Yet he told the people who threatened him, "We must obey God rather than humans!" (Acts 5:29). Peter no longer let people scare him into disobeying God. First Peter reminds us that we are called to follow God even when our faith is tested. This book encourages us to be strong, knowing that God will always take care of us. ◊

things
YOU'LL DISCOVER

First Peter encourages Christians to keep trusting Jesus even when they experience all kinds of suffering or pain.

people
YOU'LL MEET

Peter—one of Jesus' closest followers (1 Pet 1–5)
Diaspora—a name for Christians scattered in many places (1 Pet 1)
Silvanus, Mark—two of Peter's friends and helpers (1 Pet 5)

places
YOU'LL GO

Pontus, Galatia, Cappadocia, Asia, and **Bithynia** (present-day Turkey)

words
YOU'LL REMEMBER

"Throw all your anxiety onto [God], because [God] cares for you" (1 Pet 5:7).

Greeting

1 Peter, an apostle of Jesus Christ,
To God's chosen strangers in the world of the diaspora, who live in Pontus, Galatia, Cappadocia, Asia, and Bithynia. ²God the Father chose you because of what he knew beforehand. He chose you through the Holy Spirit's work of making you holy and because of the faithful obedience and sacrifice of Jesus Christ. May God's grace and peace be multiplied to you.

Thanksgiving

³May the God and Father of our Lord Jesus Christ be blessed! On account of his vast mercy, he has given us new birth. You have been born anew into a living hope through the resurrection of Jesus Christ from the dead. ⁴You have a pure and enduring inheritance that cannot perish—an inheritance that is presently kept safe in heaven for you. ⁵Through his faithfulness, you are guarded by God's power so that you can receive the salvation he is ready to reveal in the last time.

⁶You now rejoice in this hope, even if it's necessary for you to be distressed for a short time by various trials. ⁷This is necessary so that your faith may be found genuine. (Your faith is more valuable than gold, which will be destroyed even though it is itself tested by fire.) Your genuine faith will result in praise, glory, and honor for you when Jesus Christ is revealed. ⁸Although you've never seen him, you love him. Even though you don't see him now, you trust him and so rejoice with a glorious joy that is too much for words. ⁹You are receiving the goal of your faith: your salvation.

¹⁰The prophets, who long ago foretold the grace that you've received, searched and explored, inquiring carefully about this salvation. ¹¹They wondered what the Spirit of Christ within them was saying when he bore witness beforehand about the suffering that would happen to Christ and the glory that would follow. They wondered what sort of person or what sort of time they were speaking about. ¹²It was revealed to them that in their search they were not serving themselves but you. These things, which

even angels long to examine, have now been proclaimed to you by those who brought you the good news. They did this in the power of the Holy Spirit, who was sent from heaven.

SAILBOAT

JOY

Joy Beyond Words *1 Peter 1:8-9*
The early Christians who first read this letter hadn't met Jesus. They lived after Jesus was no longer physically on earth. These Christians learned about Jesus and his teachings from other believers and through writings such as this letter. Over time they came to believe and trust in Jesus. As they got to know Jesus better, they grew to love him even though they never physically met him. This knowledge of Jesus and his salvation brought them joy that was too great for words!

Response of obedience

¹³Therefore, once you have your minds ready for action and you are thinking clearly, place your hope completely on the grace that will be brought to you when Jesus Christ is revealed. ¹⁴Don't be conformed to your former desires, those that shaped you when you were ignorant. But, as obedient children, ¹⁵you must be holy in every aspect of your lives, just as the one who called you is holy. ¹⁶It is written, *You will be holy, because I am holy.*[a] ¹⁷Since you call upon a Father who judges all people according to their actions without favoritism, you should conduct yourselves with reverence during the time of your dwelling in a strange land. ¹⁸Live in this way, knowing that you were not liberated by perishable things like silver or gold from the empty lifestyle you inherited from your ancestors. ¹⁹Instead, you were liberated by the precious blood of Christ, like that of a flawless, spotless lamb. ²⁰Christ was chosen before the

did you know? The English word *angel* comes from the Greek word *angelos*, which means "messenger." The angels brought messages from God to God's people.

[a]Lev 19:2

creation of the world, but was only revealed at the end of time. This was done for you, [21]who through Christ are faithful to the God who raised him from the dead and gave him glory. So now, your faith and hope should rest in God.

[22]As you set yourselves apart by your obedience to the truth so that you might have genuine affection for your fellow believers, love each other deeply and earnestly. [23]Do this because you have been given new birth—not from the type of seed that decays but from seed that doesn't. This seed is God's life-giving and enduring word.

[24]Thus,

All human life on the earth is like grass,
and all human glory
  is like a flower in a field.
The grass dries up and its flower falls off,
[25] *but the Lord's word endures forever.*[b]

This is the word that was proclaimed to you as good news.

Your identity as believers

2 Therefore, get rid of all ill will and all deceit, pretense, envy, and slander. [2]Instead, like a newborn baby, desire the pure milk of the word. Nourished by it, you will grow into salvation, [3]since you have tasted that the Lord is good.

[4]Now you are coming to him as to a living stone. Even though this stone was rejected by humans, from God's perspective it is chosen, valuable. [5]You yourselves are being built like living stones into a spiritual temple. You are being made into a holy priesthood to offer up spiritual sacrifices that are acceptable to God through Jesus Christ. [6]Thus it is written in scripture, *Look! I am laying a cornerstone in Zion, chosen, valuable. The person who believes in him will never be shamed.*[c] [7]So God honors you who believe. For those who refuse to believe, though, the stone the builders tossed aside has become the capstone. [8]This is a stone that makes people stumble and a rock that makes them fall. Because they refuse to believe in the word, they stumble. Indeed, this is the end to which they were appointed. [9]But you are a chosen race, a royal priesthood, a holy nation, a people who are God's

own possession. You have become this people so that you may speak of the wonderful acts of the one who called you out of darkness into his amazing light. [10]Once you weren't a people, but now you are God's people. Once you hadn't received mercy, but now you have received mercy.

Life as strangers in the world

[11]Dear friends, since you are immigrants and strangers in the world, I urge that you avoid worldly desires that wage war against your lives. [12]Live honorably among the unbelievers. Today, they defame you, as if you were doing evil. But in the day when God visits to judge they will glorify him, because they have observed your honorable deeds.

[13]For the sake of the Lord submit to every human institution. Do this whether it means submitting to the emperor as supreme ruler, [14]or to governors as those sent by the emperor. They are sent to punish those doing evil and to praise those doing good. [15]Submit to them because it's God's will that by doing good you will silence the ignorant talk of foolish people. [16]Do this as God's slaves, and yet also as free people, not using your freedom as a cover-up for evil. [17]Honor everyone. Love the family of believers. Have respectful fear of God. Honor the emperor.

[18]Household slaves, submit by accepting the authority of your masters with all respect. Do this not only to good and kind masters but also to those who are harsh. [19]Now, it is commendable if, because of one's

---

---

understanding of God, someone should endure pain through suffering unjustly. [20]But what praise comes from enduring patiently when you have sinned and are beaten for it? But if you endure steadfastly when you've done good and suffer for it, this is commendable before God.

[21]You were called to this kind of endurance, because Christ suffered on your behalf. He left you an example so that you might follow in his footsteps. [22]He committed no sin, nor did he ever speak in ways meant to deceive. [23]When he was insulted, he did not reply with insults. When he suffered, he did not threaten revenge. Instead, he entrusted himself to the one who judges justly. [24]He carried in his own body on the cross the sins we committed. He did this so that we might live in righteousness, having nothing to do with sin. By his wounds you were healed. [25]Though you were like straying sheep, you have now returned to the shepherd and guardian of your lives.

3 Wives, likewise, submit to your own husbands. Do this so that even if some of them refuse to believe the word, they may be won without a word by their wives' way of life. [2]After all, they will have observed the reverent and holy manner of your lives. [3]Don't try to make yourselves beautiful on the outside, with stylish hair or by wearing gold jewelry or fine clothes. [4]Instead, make yourselves beautiful on the inside, in your hearts, with the enduring quality of a gentle, peaceful spirit. This type of beauty is very precious in God's eyes. [5]For it was in this way that holy women who trusted in God used to make themselves beautiful, accepting the authority of their own husbands. [6]For example, Sarah accepted Abraham's authority when she called him *master*. You have become her children when you do good and don't respond to threats with fear.

[7]Husbands, likewise, submit by living with your wife in ways that honor her, knowing that she is the weaker partner. Honor her all the more, as she is also a coheir of the gracious care of life. Do this so that your prayers won't be hindered.

[8]Finally, all of you be of one mind, sympathetic, lovers of your fellow believers, compassionate, and modest in your opinion of yourselves. [9]Don't pay back evil for evil or insult for insult. Instead, give blessing in return. You were called to do this so that you might inherit a blessing. [10]For

> *those who want to love life*
> *and see good days*
> *should keep their tongue*
> *from evil speaking*
> *and their lips from speaking lies.*
> [11] *They should shun evil and do good;*
> *seek peace and chase after it.*
> [12] *The Lord's eyes are on the righteous*
> *and his ears are open to their prayers.*
> *But the Lord cannot tolerate*
> *those who do evil.*[d]

[13]Who will harm you if you are zealous for good? [14]But happy are you, even if you suffer because of righteousness! Don't be terrified or upset by them. [15]Instead, regard Christ as holy in your hearts. Whenever anyone asks you to speak of your hope, be ready to defend it. [16]Yet do this with respectful humility, maintaining a good conscience. Act in this way so that those who malign your good lifestyle in Christ may be ashamed when they slander you. [17]It is better to suffer for doing good (if this could possibly be God's will) than for doing evil.

[18]Christ himself suffered on account of sins, once for all, the righteous one on behalf of the unrighteous. He did this in order to bring you into the presence of God. Christ was put to death as a human, but made alive by the Spirit. [19]And it was by the Spirit that he went to preach to the spirits in prison. [20]In the past, these spirits were disobedient—when God patiently waited during the time of Noah. Noah built an ark in which a few (that is, eight) lives were rescued through water. [21]Baptism is like that. It saves you now—not because it removes dirt from your body but because it is the mark of a good conscience toward God. Your salvation comes through the resurrection of Jesus Christ, [22]who is at God's right side. Now that he has gone into heaven, he rules over all angels, authorities, and powers.

4 Therefore, since Christ suffered as a human, you should also arm yourselves

---

[d]Ps 34:12-16

with his way of thinking. This is because whoever suffers is finished with sin. ²As a result, they don't live the rest of their human lives in ways determined by human desires but in ways determined by God's will. ³You have wasted enough time doing what unbelievers desire—living in their unrestrained immorality and lust, their drunkenness and excessive feasting and wild parties, and their forbidden worship of idols. ⁴They think it's strange that you don't join in these activities with the same flood of unrestrained wickedness. So they slander you. ⁵They will have to reckon with the one who is ready to judge the living and the dead. ⁶Indeed, this is the reason the good news was also preached to the dead. This happened so that, although they were judged as humans according to human standards,

they could live by the Spirit according to divine standards.

⁷The end of everything has come. Therefore, be self-controlled and clearheaded so you can pray. ⁸Above all, show sincere love to each other, because love brings about the forgiveness of many sins. ⁹Open your homes to each other without complaining. ¹⁰And serve each other according to the gift each person has received, as good managers of God's diverse gifts. ¹¹Whoever speaks should do so as those who speak God's word. Whoever serves should do so from the strength that God furnishes. Do this so that in everything God may be honored through Jesus Christ. To him be honor and power forever and always. Amen.

Bet you can read this in 1 minute. Ready, set, go!

Be Encouraged! Keep on Keeping on!   1 Peter 4:12–5:11

Life can be really hard sometimes, and following Jesus can be a real challenge. Sometimes we're tempted to do things we know we shouldn't do. We face tests of faith and strength. We are sometimes teased because of what we believe. The early church experienced these same challenges.

First Peter is a letter that was meant to encourage people who followed Jesus to keep going, keep working, keep believing, and keep looking for Jesus to come back again. It also taught that the suffering they were going through was a blessing.   The people had given their lives, their reputations, and their families to Jesus. This letter reminded them to stand strong in that commitment and not to waver even in hard times.

Imagine that every difficult situation you ever faced was tied up in a bag for you to carry around on your back. That would be a heavy load to carry around! This letter says we should throw all of our worries on Jesus because Jesus knows how to take care of us. He will take our tough times and put them on his back. This is the kind of God we serve—the kind who takes our burdens away.

When life is hard and you feel tempted to give up, remember the early church and stand strong. Believe the promises of God, and give your anxiety to Jesus. He cares about you.

What does it mean to "keep on keeping on" in faith?

Memorize 1 Peter 5:7 and remember it when you feel worried.

Stand firm in the last times

[12]Dear friends, don't be surprised about the fiery trials that have come among you to test you. These are not strange happenings. [13]Instead, rejoice as you share Christ's suffering. You share his suffering now so that you may also have overwhelming joy when his glory is revealed. [14]If you are mocked because of Christ's name, you are blessed, for the Spirit of glory—indeed, the Spirit of God—rests on you.

[15]Now none of you should suffer as a murderer or thief or evildoer or rebel. [16]But don't be ashamed if you suffer as one who belongs to Christ. Rather, honor God as you bear Christ's name. Give honor to God, [17]because it's time for judgment to begin with God's own household. But if judgment starts with us, what will happen to those who refuse to believe God's good news? [18]If the righteous are barely rescued, what will happen to the godless and sinful? [19]So then, those who suffer because they follow God's will should commit their lives to a trustworthy creator by doing what is right.

5 Therefore, I have a request for the elders among you. (I ask this as a fellow elder and a witness of Christ's sufferings, and as one who shares in the glory that is about to be revealed.) I urge the elders: [2]Like shepherds, tend the flock of God among you. Watch over it. Don't shepherd because you must, but do it voluntarily for God. Don't shepherd greedily, but do it eagerly. [3]Don't shepherd by ruling over those entrusted to your care, but become examples to the flock. [4]And when the chief shepherd appears, you will receive an unfading crown of glory.

[5]In the same way, I urge you who are younger: accept the authority of the elders. And everyone, clothe yourselves with humility toward each other. God stands against the proud, but he gives favor to the humble.

[6]Therefore, humble yourselves under God's power so that he may raise you up in the last day. [7]Throw all your anxiety onto him, because he cares about you. **Memorize 1 Pet 5:7** [8]Be clearheaded. Keep alert. Your accuser, the devil, is on the prowl like a roaring lion, seeking someone to devour. [9]Resist him, standing firm in the faith. Do so in the knowledge that your fellow believers are enduring the same suffering throughout the world. [10]After you have suffered for a little while, the God of all grace, the one who called you into his eternal glory in Christ Jesus, will himself restore, empower, strengthen, and establish you. [11]To him be power forever and always. Amen.

Final greeting

[12]I have written and sent these few lines to you by Silvanus. I consider him to be a faithful brother. In these lines I have urged and affirmed that this is the genuine grace of God. Stand firm in it. [13]The fellow-elect church in Babylon greets you, and so does my son Mark. [14]Greet each other with the kiss of love. Peace to you all who are in Christ.

2 Peter

Second Peter was an encouraging letter sent to Christians who heard confusing messages about their faith. Some false teachers were spreading wrong ideas about Jesus. Those false teachers put followers of Christ in a bad spot. Christians were in danger of believing untruths that could lead them away from Jesus.

The people who received this letter were doing their best to stand firm on the truth (2 Pet 1:12). This letter reminded them that God already told them what they needed to know. They knew God spoke big promises. They knew God called them to stop sinning and follow God's ways. They knew about Jesus. Those things were a great start. But this letter encouraged Christians to keep growing in their faith (2 Pet 1:3-11).

Second Peter also referred to Jesus coming back to earth, reminding readers that Jesus wants all people to change their hearts and lives. This letter said that Christians should keep doing good things until he comes (2 Pet 3:9, 14) and to be on guard so they aren't led off course (2 Pet 3:17). This letter reminds us to do our best to follow Jesus and to hold firm to what we know to be true. ◊

things YOU'LL DISCOVER

Second Peter tells Christians to remember the truth about Jesus even when other people are telling lies. It encourages Christians to rely on God's power and truth to grow.

people YOU'LL MEET

Peter—one of Jesus' closest followers (2 Pet 1–3)
False teachers—people spreading lies about Jesus (2 Pet 2)

places YOU'LL GO

Pontus, Galatia, Cappadocia, Asia, and **Bithynia** (present-day Turkey)

words YOU'LL REMEMBER

"Grow in the grace and knowledge of our Lord and savior Jesus Christ. To him belongs glory now and forever" (2 Pet 3:18).

Greeting

1 From Simon Peter, a slave and apostle of Jesus Christ.

To those who received a faith equal to ours through the justice of our God and savior Jesus Christ.

[2] May you have more and more grace and peace through the knowledge of God and Jesus our Lord.

Christian life in outline

[3] By his divine power the Lord has given us everything we need for life and godliness through the knowledge of the one who called us by his own honor and glory. [4] Through his honor and glory he has given us his precious and wonderful promises, that you may share the divine nature and escape from the world's immorality that sinful craving produces.

Bet you can read this in 3 minutes. *Ready, set, go!*

[5] This is why you must make every effort to add moral excellence to your faith; and to moral excellence, knowledge; [6] and to knowledge, self-control; and to self-control, endurance; and to endurance, godliness; [7] and to godliness, affection for others; and to affection for others, love. [8] If all these are yours and they are growing in you, they'll keep you from becoming inactive and unfruitful in the knowledge of our Lord Jesus Christ. [9] Whoever lacks these things is shortsighted and blind, forgetting that they were cleansed from their past sins.

[10] Therefore, brothers and sisters, be eager to confirm your call and election. Do this and you will never ever be lost. [11] In this way you will receive a rich welcome into the everlasting kingdom of our Lord and savior Jesus Christ.

Reminder of the Christian life

[12] So I'll keep reminding you about these things, although you already know them and stand secure in the truth you have. [13] I think it's right that I keep stirring up your memory, as long as I'm alive. [14] After all, our Lord Jesus Christ has shown me that I am about to depart from this life. [15] I'm eager for you always to remember these things after my death.

Christ's return is true

[16] We didn't repeat crafty myths when we told you about the powerful coming of our Lord Jesus Christ. Quite the contrary, we witnessed his majesty with our own eyes. [17] He received honor and glory from God the Father when a voice came to him from the magnificent glory, saying, "This is my dearly loved Son, with whom I am well-pleased." [18] We ourselves heard this voice from heaven while we were with him on the holy mountain. [19] In addition, we have a most reliable prophetic word, and you would do well to pay attention to it, just as you would to a lamp shining in a dark place, until the day dawns and the morning star rises in your hearts. [20] Most important, you must know that no prophecy of scripture represents the prophet's own understanding of things, [21] because no prophecy ever came by human will. Instead, men and women led by the Holy Spirit spoke from God.

LIGHTHOUSE

GOOD NEWS

The Truth of the Good News *2 Peter 1:16*

The early Christians believed in Jesus and were following his teachings. But some people who weren't Christians told them Jesus was only a character in a story. This caused a lot of doubt for the early Christians. They didn't want to be fools and follow a teacher who wasn't real. To help them combat those false teachings, Peter reminded them that he knew Jesus, had witnessed Jesus' miracles, and was a student of Jesus. Peter assured the early Christians with his own testimony that Jesus was a real person who walked on the earth. ◊

Appearance of false teachers

2 But false prophets also arose among the people. In the same way, false teachers will come among you. They will introduce destructive opinions and deny the master who bought them, bringing quick destruction on themselves. [2] Many will follow them in their unrestrained immorality, and because of these false teachers the way of truth will be slandered. [3] In their greed they will take advantage of you with lies. The judgment pronounced against them long ago hasn't fallen idle, nor is their destruction sleeping.

Active judgment of God

[4]God didn't spare the angels when they sinned but cast them into the lowest level of the underworld and committed them to chains of darkness, keeping them there until the judgment. [5]And he didn't spare the ancient world when he brought a flood on the world of ungodly people, even though he protected Noah, a preacher of righteousness, along with seven others. [6]God condemned the cities of Sodom and Gomorrah to total destruction, reducing them to ashes as a warning to ungodly people. [7]And he rescued righteous Lot, who was made miserable by the unrestrained immorality of unruly people. ([8]While that righteous man lived among them he felt deep distress every day on account of the immoral actions he saw and heard.) [9]These things show that the Lord knows how to rescue the godly from their trials, and how to keep the unrighteous for punishment on the Judgment Day. [10]This is especially true for those who follow after the corrupt cravings of the sinful nature and defy the Lord's authority.

Evil character of the false teachers

These reckless, brash people aren't afraid to insult the glorious ones, [11]yet angels, who are stronger and more powerful, don't use insults when pronouncing the Lord's judgment on them. [12]These false teachers are like irrational animals, mere creatures of instinct, born to be captured and destroyed. They slander what they don't understand and, like animals, they will be destroyed. [13]In this way, they will receive payment for their wrongdoing.

They even enjoy unruly parties in broad daylight. They are blots and blemishes, taking delight in their seductive pleasures while feasting with you. [14]They are always looking for someone with whom to commit adultery. They are always on the lookout for opportunities to sin. They ensnare people whose faith is weak. They have hearts trained in greed. They are under God's curse. [15]Leaving the straight path, they have gone off course, following the way of Balaam son of Bosor, who loved the payment of doing wrong. [16]But Balaam was rebuked for his wrongdoing. A donkey, which has no voice, spoke with a human voice and put a stop to the prophet's madness.

[17]These false teachers are springs without water, mists driven by the wind. The underworld has been reserved for them. [18]With empty, self-important speech, they use sinful cravings and unrestrained immorality to ensnare people who have only just escaped life with those who have wandered from the truth. [19]These false teachers promise freedom, but they themselves are slaves of immorality; whatever overpowers you, enslaves you. [20]If people escape the moral filth of this world through the knowledge of our Lord and savior Jesus Christ, then get tangled up in it again and are overcome by it, they are worse off than they were before. [21]It would be better for them never to have known the way of righteousness than, having come to know it, to turn back from the holy commandment entrusted to them. [22]They demonstrate the truth of the proverb: "A dog returns to its own vomit, and a washed sow wallows in the mud."

Delay of Christ's coming in judgment

3 My dear friends, this is now my second letter to you. I have written both letters to stir up your sincere understanding with a reminder. [2]I want you to recall what the holy prophets foretold as well as what the Lord and savior commanded through your apostles. [3]Most important, know this: in the last days scoffers will come, jeering, living by their own cravings, [4]and saying, "Where is the promise of his coming? After all, nothing has changed—not since the beginning of creation, nor even since the ancestors died."

[5]But they fail to notice that, by God's word, heaven and earth were formed long ago out of water and by means of water. [6]And it was through these that the world of that time was flooded and destroyed. [7]But by the same word, heaven and earth are now held in reserve for fire, kept for the Judgment Day and destruction of ungodly people.

[8]Don't let it escape your notice, dear friends, that with the Lord a single day is like a thousand years and a thousand years are like a single day. [9]The Lord isn't slow to keep

his promise, as some think of slowness, but he is patient toward you, not wanting anyone to perish but all to change their hearts and lives. ¹⁰But the day of the Lord will come like a thief. On that day the heavens will pass away with a dreadful noise, the elements will be consumed by fire, and the earth and all the works done on it will be exposed.

¹¹Since everything will be destroyed in this way, what sort of people ought you to be? You must live holy and godly lives, ¹²waiting for and hastening the coming day of God. Because of that day, the heavens will be destroyed by fire and the elements will melt away in the flames. ¹³But according to his promise we are waiting for a new heaven and a new earth, where righteousness is at home.

Preparing for Christ's coming in judgment

¹⁴Therefore, dear friends, while you are waiting for these things to happen, make every effort to be found by him in peace—pure and faultless. ¹⁵Consider the patience of our Lord to be salvation, just as our dear friend and brother Paul wrote to you according to the wisdom given to him, ¹⁶speaking of these things in all his letters. Some of his remarks are hard to understand, and people who are ignorant and whose faith is weak twist them to their own destruction, just as they do the other scriptures.

Final instruction

¹⁷Therefore, dear friends, since you have been warned in advance, be on guard so that you aren't led off course into the error of sinful people, and lose your own safe position. ¹⁸Instead, grow in the grace and knowledge of our Lord and savior Jesus Christ. To him belongs glory now and forever. Amen.

Memorize
2 Pet 3:18

When Is Jesus Coming Back? *2 Peter 3:1-13*

Have you ever waited for something to come in the mail? Maybe around the time of your birthday, you run to the mailbox every day to see if anything has come. When you wake up you wonder first thing, *Is my present here yet?* The excitement and anticipation can feel unbearable!

The early Christians thought Jesus was coming back soon. They watched and waited every day, expecting to see Jesus. But years went by and Jesus didn't return. People who didn't believe in God made fun of them because they clung to Jesus' promise that he would return for his followers and lead them to heaven.

We still wait for Jesus to return for us. This letter to the early Christians reminds us that God's timing is not the same as ours. God doesn't rely on clocks and calendars. God sees all the way into the past and all the way into the future. The author wrote that "with the Lord a single day is like a thousand years and a thousand years are like a single day" (2 Pet 3:8).

God's time may be different from ours, but God has perfect timing. Even when it feels like we've been waiting forever, we can stay excited—like we're waiting for that package to arrive.

When have you waited for something?

How is God's time different from ours?

1 John

Some early Christians thought this letter was written by John, the good friend of Jesus, but the letter itself doesn't say. It might have come from another John who was a leader among the first Christians, maybe the person called "the elder" in 2 John and 3 John.

Even if we aren't sure who wrote 1 John, the message of this short book sounds like the Gospel of John. It's all about love and cautions against sin.

This letter uses many kind and tender words. But it's also firm about truth. It says that if we claim to believe in Jesus, we should love like Jesus loves. That doesn't mean we always do things right. In fact, this letter says that if we think we haven't sinned, we're fooling ourselves. But we can admit our sins, and God will forgive us (1 John 1:8-9). Then we can get back to doing our best to love other people.

Love isn't simply something we feel. It's something we do. This letter says, "Let's not love with words or speech but with action and truth" (1 John 3:18). Because Jesus gave his life for us, we should give our best for other people (1 John 3:16). If we really love God, then our lives should be full of love for people (1 John 4:7-8). This letter reminds us that God loves us—so we can love others! ♦

Announcement about the word of life

1 We announce to you what existed from the beginning, what we have heard, what we have seen with our eyes, what we have seen and our hands handled, about the word of life. ²The life was revealed, and we have seen, and we testify and announce to you the eternal life that was with the Father and was revealed to us. ³What we have seen and heard, we also announce it to you so that you can have fellowship with us. Our fellowship is with the Father and with his Son, Jesus Christ. ⁴We are writing these things so that our joy can be complete.

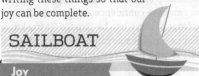

SAILBOAT

Joy

Complete Joy 1 John 1:3-4

Jesus' disciples spent a lot of time with him. They learned his teachings firsthand, were there when he was crucified, and saw him after he rose from the dead. When Jesus left earth and went back to heaven, he gave the first disciples the job of spreading the good news that Jesus made a way for people to have a relationship with God. The disciples knew from their own experience how wonderful that was, and they wanted others to experience that same joy. ◆

The message: God is light

⁵This is the message that we have heard from him and announce to you: "God is light and there is no darkness in him at all." ⁶If we claim, "We have fellowship with him," and live in the darkness, we are lying and do not act truthfully. ⁷But if we live in the light in the same way as he is in the light, we have fellowship with each other, and the blood of Jesus, his Son, cleanses us from every sin. ⁸If we claim, "We don't have any sin," we deceive ourselves and the truth is not in us. ⁹But if we confess our sins, he is faithful and just to forgive us our sins and cleanse us from everything we've done wrong. ¹⁰If we claim, "We have never sinned," we make him a liar and his word is not in us.

Living in the light

2 My little children, I'm writing these things to you so that you don't sin. But if you do sin, we have an advocate with the Father, Jesus Christ the righteous one. ²He is God's way of dealing with our sins, not only ours but the sins of the whole world. ³This is how we know that we know him: if we keep his commandments. ⁴The one who claims, "I

did you know? Christ is a Greek word meaning "chosen one." It can be placed before or after Jesus' name to read as either *Christ Jesus*, meaning "the chosen one Jesus"; or *Jesus Christ*, meaning "Jesus the chosen one."

know him," while not keeping his commandments, is a liar, and the truth is not in this person. ⁵But the love of God is truly perfected in whoever keeps his word. This is how we know we are in him. ⁶The one who claims to remain in him ought to live in the same way as he lived.

⁷Dear friends, I'm not writing a new commandment to you, but an old commandment that you had from the beginning. The old commandment is the message you heard. ⁸On the other hand, I am writing a new commandment to you, which is true in him and in you, because the darkness is passing away and the true light already shines. ⁹The one who claims to be in the light while hating a brother or sister is in the darkness even now. ¹⁰The person loving a brother and sister stays in the light, and there is nothing in the light that causes a person to stumble. ¹¹But the person who hates a brother or sister is in the darkness and lives in the darkness, and doesn't know where to go because the darkness blinds the eyes.

Motivations for writing

¹²Little children, I'm writing to you because your sins have been forgiven through Jesus' name. ¹³Parents, I'm writing to you because you have known the one who has existed from the beginning. Young people, I'm writing to you because you have conquered the evil one. ¹⁴Little children, I write to you because you know the Father. Parents, I write to you because you have known the one who has existed from the beginning. Young people, I write to you because you are strong, the word of God remains in you, and you have conquered the evil one.

Warning about the world

[15]Don't love the world or the things in the world. If anyone loves the world, the love of the Father is not in them. [16]Everything that is in the world—the craving for whatever the body feels, the craving for whatever the eyes see and the arrogant pride in one's possessions—is not of the Father but is of the world. [17]And the world and its cravings are passing away, but the person who does the will of God remains forever.

LIGHTHOUSE

FOREVER

Doing God's Will *1 John 2:16-17*
The author of this letter told readers that everything in this world will one day pass away, along with the cravings for whatever our eyes see and our bodies feel. These cravings aren't part of God's plan for us. Being prideful about the things we own isn't God's plan either. These temptations will pass away. What matters most is doing God's will—following the way Jesus made for us. This is the path that leads to forever with God.

Remaining in the truth

[18]Little children, it is the last hour. Just as you have heard that the antichrist is coming, so now many antichrists have appeared. This is how we know it is the last hour. [19]They went out from us, but they were not really part of us. If they had been part of us, they would have stayed with us. But by going out from us, they showed they all are not part of us. [20]But you have an anointing from the holy one, and all of you know the truth. [21]I don't write to you because you don't know the truth but because you know it. You know that no lie comes from the truth. [22]Who is the liar? Isn't it the person who denies that Jesus is the Christ? This person is the antichrist: the one who denies the Father and the Son. [23]Everyone who denies the Son does not have the Father, but the one who confesses the Son has the Father also.

[24]As for you, what you heard from the beginning must remain in you. If what you heard from the beginning remains in you, you will also remain in relationship to the Son and in the Father. [25]This is the promise that he himself gave us: eternal life. [26]I write these things to you about those who are attempting to deceive you. [27]As for you, the anointing that you received from him remains on you, and you don't need anyone to teach you the truth. But since his anointing teaches you about all things (it's true and not a lie), remain in relationship to him just as he taught you.

Remaining until Jesus appears

[28]And now, little children, remain in relationship to Jesus, so that when he appears we can have confidence and not be ashamed in front of him when he comes. [29]If you know that he is righteous, you also know that every person who practices righteousness is born from him.

3 See what kind of love the Father has given to us in that we should be called God's children, and that is what we are! Because the world didn't recognize him, it doesn't recognize us.

[2]Dear friends, now we are God's children, and it hasn't yet appeared what we will be. We know that when he appears we will be like him because we'll see him as he is. [3]And all who have this hope in him purify themselves even as he is pure. [4]Every person who practices sin commits an act of rebellion, and sin is rebellion. [5]You know that he appeared to take away sins, and there is no sin in him. [6]Every person who remains in relationship to him does not sin. Any person who sins has not seen him or known him.

Practicing sin or righteousness

[7]Little children, make sure no one deceives you. The person who practices righteousness is righteous, in the same way that Jesus is righteous. [8]The person who practices sin belongs to the devil, because the devil has been sinning since the beginning. God's Son appeared for this purpose: to destroy the works of the devil. [9]Those born from God don't practice sin because God's DNA[a] remains in them. They can't sin because they are born from God. [10]This is how God's children and the devil's children are apparent: everyone who doesn't practice righteousness is not

---

[a]Or *genetic character*

from God, including the person who doesn't love a brother or sister. ¹¹This is the message that you heard from the beginning: love each other. ¹²Don't behave like Cain, who belonged to the evil one and murdered his brother. And why did he kill him? He killed him because his own works were evil, but the works of his brother were righteous.

Loving each other

¹³Don't be surprised, brothers and sisters, if the world hates you. ¹⁴We know that we have transferred from death to life, because we love the brothers and sisters. The person who does not love remains in death. ¹⁵Everyone who hates a brother or sister is a murderer, and you know that murderers don't have eternal life residing in them. ¹⁶This is how we know love: Jesus laid down his life for us, and we ought to lay down our lives for our brothers and sisters. ¹⁷But if someone has material possessions and sees a brother or sister in need but refuses to help—how can the love of God dwell in a person like that?

¹⁸Little children, let's not love with words or speech but with action and truth. ¹⁹This is how we will know that we belong to the truth and reassure our hearts in God's presence. ²⁰Even if our hearts condemn us, God is greater than our hearts and knows all things. ²¹Dear friends, if our hearts don't condemn us, we have confidence in relationship to God. ²²We receive whatever we ask from him because we keep his commandments and do what pleases him. ²³This is his commandment, that we

SAILBOAT

LOVE

Show Love Through Action *1 John 3:18*
It can be difficult to be consistent with our words and actions. This letter tells readers that their words should match their actions. When Christians say they love someone, their behavior should show that this is true. It's easier to say we love someone than show them that we love them. The next time you think about how much you love someone, show them! ⬦

believe in the name of his Son, Jesus Christ, and love each other as he commanded us. ²⁴Those who keep his commandments dwell in God and God dwells in them. This is how we know that he dwells in us, because of the Spirit he has given us.

Testing the spirits

4 Dear friends, don't believe every spirit. Test the spirits to see if they are from God because many false prophets have gone into the world. ²This is how you know if a spirit comes from God: every spirit that confesses that Jesus Christ has come as a human[b] is from God, ³and every spirit that doesn't confess Jesus is not from God. This is the spirit of the antichrist, which you have heard is coming and is now already in the world. ⁴You are from God, little children, and you have defeated these people because the one who is in you is greater than the one who is in the world. ⁵They are from the world. So they speak from the world's point of view and the world listens to them. ⁶We are from God. The person who knows God listens to us. Whoever is not from God doesn't listen to us. This is how we recognize the Spirit of truth and the spirit of error.

Love and God

⁷Dear friends, let's love each other, because love is from God, and everyone who loves is born from God and knows God. ⁸The person who doesn't love does not know God, because God is love. ⁹This is how the love of God is revealed to us: God has sent his only Son into the world so that we can live through him. ¹⁰This is love: it is not that we loved God but that he loved us and sent his Son as the sacrifice that deals with our sins. ¹¹Dear friends, if God loved us this way, we also ought to love each other. ¹²No one has ever seen God. If we love each other, God remains in us and his love is made perfect in us. ¹³This is how we know we remain in him and he remains in us, because he has given us a measure of his Spirit. ¹⁴We have seen

Memorize
1 John 4:7-8

and testify that the Father has sent the Son to be the savior of the world. [15]If any of us confess that Jesus is God's Son, God remains in us and we remain in God. [16]We have known and have believed the love that God has for us.

God is love, and those who remain in love remain in God and God remains in them. [17]This is how love has been perfected in us, so that we can have confidence on the Judgment Day, because we are exactly the same as God is in this world. [18]There is no fear in love, but perfect love drives out fear, because fear expects punishment. The person who is afraid has not been made perfect in love. [19]We love because God first loved us. [20]Those who say, "I love God" and hate their brothers or sisters are liars. After all, those who don't love their brothers or sisters whom they have seen can hardly love God whom they have not seen! [21]This commandment we have from him: Those who claim to love God ought to love their brother and sister also.

[5]Everyone who believes that Jesus is the Christ has been born from God. Whoever loves someone who is a parent loves the child born to the parent. [2]This is how we know that we love the children of God: when we love God and keep God's commandments. [3]This is the love of God: we keep God's commandments. God's commandments are not difficult, [4]because everyone who is born from God defeats the world. And this is the victory that has defeated the world: our faith. [5]Who defeats the world? Isn't it the one who believes that Jesus is God's Son?

Bet you can!
read this in 1 minute. Ready, set, go!

Testimony about Jesus

[6]This is the one who came by water and blood: Jesus Christ. Not by water only but by water and blood. And the Spirit is the one who testifies, because the Spirit is the truth. [7]The three are testifying—[8]the Spirit, the water, and the blood—and the three are united in agreement. [9]If we receive human testimony,

Love Each Other! 1 John 4:7-8

Being a Christian is all about love: loving God and loving each other. Love is the most important thing when we follow Jesus. In fact, this letter says that if we don't love each other, we can't say that we love God.

Do you see how important love is? We obey our parents out of love. We treat people with kindness because of love. We serve people because of love. We give our gifts and talents because of love. We share our belongings because of love. Love is how we live our faith and show that we are followers of Jesus.

Make a list of all the ways you can show love to others. Pick a few to do today. Decide that love is so important that everything you do is an act of love. When you and a friend have a fight, find a way to show love. When you're upset with your parents, find a way to show love. When you see someone in need, find a way to show love. Love requires action—so act with love for each other!

How can you show love today?

What does it mean that God is love?

God's testimony is greater, because this is what God testified: he has testified about his Son. [10]The one who believes in God's Son has the testimony within; the one who doesn't believe God has made God a liar, because that one has not believed the testimony that God gave about his Son. [11]And this is the testimony: God gave eternal life to us, and this life is in his Son. [12]The one who has the Son has life. The one who doesn't have God's Son does not have life.

Confidence in prayer

[13]I write these things to you who believe in the name of God's Son so that you can know that you have eternal life. [14]This is the confidence that we have in our relationship with God: If we ask for anything in agreement with his will, he listens to us. [15]If we know that he listens to whatever we ask, we know that we have received what we asked from him. [16]If anyone sees a brother or sister committing a sin that does not result in death, they should pray, and God will give life to them—that is, to those who commit sins that don't result in death. There is a sin that results in death—I'm not saying that you should pray about that. [17]Every unrighteous action is sin, but there is a sin that does not result in death.

Be on guard

[18]We know that everyone born from God does not sin, but the ones born from God guard themselves,[c] and the evil one cannot touch them. [19]We know we are from God, and the whole world lies in the power of the evil one. [20]We know that God's Son has come and has given us understanding to know the one who is true. We are in the one who is true by being in his Son, Jesus Christ. This is the true God and eternal life. [21]Little children, guard yourselves from idols!

---

[c]Or but the one who is born from God guards him from sin

2 John

Second John is the shortest book in the Bible. Because it is only one chapter long, there aren't any chapter numbers—only verse numbers. This book is a letter written by someone called "the elder" to "the chosen gentlewoman and her children" (2 John 1). *Elder* was a common title for a Christian leader at the time the letter was written. The "gentlewoman and her children" might have been actual people, or they may have been a church and its members. Many women in the early church opened their homes to local Christians and served as leaders in those small house churches.

Whoever these people were, the letter makes clear that they had plenty of love for each other. They lived the truth they had been taught. They understood God's command to love. And they knew that the duty to love was nothing new. They knew love was the most important command they could follow.

But readers of this letter may have been confused about other things. There were people spreading the lie that Jesus didn't come to earth as an actual human being but was just a spirit. Some of the early Christians helped this lie spread further by welcoming people who taught these wrong ideas into their homes. The elder said that giving these teachers food and shelter was like supporting their evil actions, and he taught that Christians shouldn't help these fakes.

The elder encouraged the gentlewoman and her children to live in love, and also to stand firm in the truth. That message remains for us today! ◆

Greeting

[1] From the elder.

To the chosen gentlewoman and her children, whom I truly love (and I am not the only one, but also all who know the truth), [2] because of the truth that remains with us and will be with us forever. [3] Grace, mercy, and peace from God the Father and from Jesus Christ, the Son of the Father, will be ours who live in truth and love.

Love each other

[4] I was overjoyed to find some of your children living in the truth, just as we had been commanded by the Father. [5] Now, dear friends, I am requesting that we love each other. It's not as though I'm writing a new command to you, but it's one we have had from the beginning. [6] This is love: that we live according to his commands. This is the command that you heard from the beginning: live in love.

> **Memorize**
> 2 John 6

Reject false teachers

[7] Many deceivers have gone into the world who do not confess that Jesus Christ came as a human being. This kind of person is the deceiver and the antichrist. [8] Watch yourselves so that you don't lose what we've worked for but instead receive a full reward. [9] Anyone who goes too far and does not continue in the teaching about Christ does not have God. Whoever continues in this teaching has both the Father and the Son. [10] Whoever comes to

did you know? With only 304 words, 2 John is the shortest book in the Bible. Other short books are Obadiah, Titus, Philemon, 3 John, and Jude.

you who does not affirm this teaching should neither be received nor welcomed into your home, [11] because welcoming people like that is the same thing as sharing in their evil actions.

Plans to visit

[12] I have a lot to tell you. I don't want to use paper and ink, but I hope to visit you and talk with you face-to-face, so that our joy can be complete.

Final greeting

[13] Your chosen sister's children greet you.

LIGHTHOUSE

WISDOM

Avoid Wrong Ideas About Jesus 2 John 7
At the time this letter was written, there were groups of people teaching untrue things about Jesus. One group taught the belief that Jesus wasn't fully human and that his suffering and death on the cross were an illusion. These wrong ideas must have been upsetting to people who followed Jesus. This letter was written to teach and warn those followers about these wrong ideas. The elder called the people who taught these wrong ideas *deceivers* (or *liars*) and the *antichrist*. Antichrist means to be against Christ. ◆

3 John

Third John is one of the shortest books in the Bible. Because it is only one chapter long, there aren't any chapter numbers—only verse numbers. Third John is a letter written by "the elder" to a man named Gaius (3 John 1).

The elder encouraged Gaius for his faith, praising him for standing strong in truth and showing love through his actions. But the elder criticized a man named Diotrephes who took the warning too far against people who taught wrong ideas about Jesus. Christians were taught to shut their doors and not give food or housing to people who spread lies about Jesus. But Diotrephes refused to welcome genuine believers who visited. He even kicked out of the church anyone who welcomed these true Christians. The elder said he planned to come and correct Diotrephes face-to-face. In the meantime, he was glad he had friends like Gaius who lived according to the truth.

This letter shows us that we should be on guard against wrong ideas but always welcome real believers. It reminds us to be faithful, stand strong in truth, and show love through our actions! ◑

things
YOU'LL DISCOVER

This book encourages Christians to welcome real believers and show them hospitality.

people
YOU'LL MEET

The elder—the author of this letter (3 John 1)

Gaius—the man who received this letter (3 John 1)

Diotrephes—a man who rejected the elder and other believers (3 John 9-10)

Demetrius—a man loved by many people (3 John 12)

words
YOU'LL REMEMBER

"I have no greater joy than this: to hear that my children are living according to the truth" (3 John 4).

Greeting

[1] From the elder.

To my dear friend Gaius, whom I truly love. [2] Dear friend, I'm praying that all is well with you and that you enjoy good health in the same way that you prosper spiritually.

Bet you can read this in 3 minutes. Ready, set, go!

Encouragement for Gaius

[3] I was overjoyed when the brothers and sisters arrived and spoke highly of your faithfulness to the truth, shown by how you live according to the truth. [4] I have no greater joy than this: to hear that my children are living according to the truth. [5] Dear friend, you act faithfully in whatever you do for our brothers and sisters, even though they are strangers. [6] They spoke highly of your love in front of the church. You all would do well to provide for their journey in a way that honors God, [7] because they left on their journey for the sake of Jesus Christ without accepting any support from the Gentiles. [8] Therefore, we ought to help people like this so that we can be coworkers with the truth.

Memorize 3 John 4

Criticism of Diotrephes

[9] I wrote something to the church, but Diotrephes, who likes to put himself first, doesn't welcome us. [10] Because of this, if I come, I will bring up what he has done—making unjustified and wicked accusations against us. And as if that were not enough, he not only refuses to welcome the brothers and sisters but stops those who want to do so and even throws them out of the church! [11] Dear friend, don't imitate what is bad but what is good. Whoever practices what is good belongs to God. Whoever practices what is bad has not seen God.

Approval of Demetrius

[12] Everyone speaks highly of Demetrius, even the truth itself. We also speak highly of him, and you know that what we say is true.

Final greeting

[13] I have a lot to say to you, but I don't want to use pen and ink. [14] I hope to see you soon, and we will speak face-to-face.

[15] Peace be with you. Your friends here greet you. Greet our friends there by name.

God's THOUGHTS ◆ My THOUGHTS

Loving People Who Do Mean Things 3 John

Sometimes people's actions are mean. Some people simply want to be in charge and care only about their own plans. Other people think they know better and make sure they get their way. When we feel like people are being mean to us, we can remember that we are still called to love and keep on doing good things.

This letter teaches that whoever does good things in this world belongs to God. We shouldn't give up doing good things when we face people who are selfish. Instead, we should keep on sharing God's love, spreading the good news of Jesus Christ, and helping the church to grow.

There will always be people who try to keep us from doing good things. But God knows our hearts and will help us love them. Pray for people who frustrate you, and make sure you act with kindness even when other people act mean.

When have you experienced someone standing in the way of your act of kindness?

How can you love people who are mean to you?

Jude

Jude is only one chapter long so there aren't any chapter numbers—only verse numbers. This book is a letter that warns of danger. The people who received this letter were told to "fight for the faith delivered once and for all to God's holy people" (Jude 3). They were to make sure they believed the facts about Jesus, and to teach other people those same important truths.

Not long after Jesus lived and taught, some people began to change the true story of Jesus into something they liked better. Those people twisted the truth. They thought that because God had forgiven their sins, they could do whatever they wanted and God would continue to forgive them. But living that way didn't follow what Jesus taught. It wasn't the new life that God planned for everyone who believes in Jesus.

Jude tells its readers to guard themselves from false beliefs and to confront people who spread lies. It relies on several examples from the Old Testament and other Jewish books to make its point. This letter reminds us that we're called to follow God and stand strong in our faith even when people around us aren't doing the same. ◊

things YOU'LL DISCOVER

This short letter tells Christians to defend the truth against people who spread lies about Jesus. Its sharp words were written to address a problem that needed immediate action.

people YOU'LL MEET

Jude—a brother of Jesus (Jude 1-25)
Michael—an angel of high position (Jude 9)
Cain—the oldest son of Adam and Eve (Jude 11)
Balaam—an evil magician paid to curse the Israelites (Jude 11)
Enoch—a man who lived for God (Jude 14)

places YOU'LL GO

Sodom and Gomorrah (present-day Israel), **Egypt**

words YOU'LL REMEMBER

"Keep each other in the love of God, wait for the mercy of our Lord Jesus Christ, who will give you eternal life" (Jude 21).

Greeting

¹Jude, a slave of Jesus Christ and brother of James.

To those who are called, loved by God the Father and kept safe by Jesus Christ.

²May you have more and more mercy, peace, and love.

Certain judgment of the false teachers

³Dear friends, I wanted very much to write to you concerning the salvation we share. Instead, I must write to urge you to fight for the faith delivered once and for all to God's holy people. ⁴Godless people have slipped in among you. They turn the grace of our God into unrestrained immorality and deny our only master and Lord, Jesus Christ. Judgment was passed against them a long time ago.

⁵I want to remind you of something you already know very well. The Lord, who once saved a people out of Egypt, later destroyed those who didn't maintain their faith. ⁶I remind you too of the angels who didn't keep their position of authority but deserted their own home. The Lord has kept them in eternal chains in the underworld until the judgment of the great day. ⁷In the same way, Sodom and Gomorrah and neighboring towns practiced immoral sexual relations and pursued other sexual urges. By undergoing the punishment of eternal fire, they serve as a warning.

⁸Yet, even knowing this, these dreamers in the same way pollute themselves, reject authority, and slander the angels. ⁹The archangel Michael, when he argued with the devil about Moses' body, did not dare charge him with slander. Instead, he said, "The Lord

did you know? The name *Jude* in Hebrew is short for *Judah*, which was a very common name in Bible times. The Greek version of the name is *Judas*.

God's THOUGHTS / My THOUGHTS

Don't Get Confused   Jude 5, 17-25

Have you ever noticed that commercials can make you think the product being advertised is something you need and can't live without? Sometimes two different companies are selling the same thing, and they both want you to buy it from them. They tell you they will offer you the best deal, give you something extra, or put the item on sale so you will choose to buy it. It can be confusing, especially since we don't really need most of what commercials sell.

We can get different messages about God as well. We can get confused about what we believe and why we believe it. Some people believe one thing, while other people believe something else. But Jude reminds us not to lose our way. When we get confused about following Jesus, we should talk to our parents, teachers, or pastors, and look to the Bible. We should think about how we've grown as followers of Jesus and remember all that God has done in us.

When you hear confusing messages about what you should believe, remember to pray. Pray for God to give you understanding and help you avoid the things that take your mind off God. Pray for understanding so you know the difference between God's truth and something you don't need.

When have you been confused about Jesus or your faith?

How can you hold on to God's truth and not lose your way?

rebuke you!" [10]But these people slander whatever they don't understand. They are destroyed by what they know instinctively, as though they were irrational animals.

Prophecies about the false teachers

[11]They are damned, for they follow in the footsteps of Cain. For profit they give themselves over to Balaam's error. They are destroyed in the uprising of Korah. [12]These people are like jagged rocks just below the surface of the water waiting to snag you when they join your love feasts. They feast with you without reverence. They care only for themselves. They are waterless clouds carried along by the winds; fruitless autumn trees, twice dead, uprooted; [13]wild waves of the sea foaming up their own shame; wandering stars for whom the darkness of the underworld is reserved forever.

[14]Enoch, who lived seven generations after Adam, prophesied about these people when he said, "See, the Lord comes with his countless holy ones, [15]to execute judgment on everyone and to convict everyone about every ungodly deed they have committed in their ungodliness as well as all the harsh things that sinful ungodly people have said against him." [16]These are faultfinding grumblers, living according to their own desires. They speak arrogant words and they show partiality to people when they want a favor in return.

[17]But you, dear friends, remember the words spoken beforehand by the apostles of our Lord Jesus Christ. [18]They said to you, "In the end time scoffers will come living according to their own ungodly desires." [19]These people create divisions. Since they don't have the Spirit, they are worldly.

A strategy for the faithful

[20]But you, dear friends: build each other up on the foundation of your most holy faith,

pray in the Holy Spirit, [21]keep each other in the love of God, wait for the mercy of our Lord Jesus Christ, who will give you eternal life. [22]Have mercy on those who doubt. [23]Save some by snatching them from the fire. Fearing God, have mercy on some, hating even the clothing contaminated by their sinful urges.

Memorize Jude 21

UMBRELLA
DOUBTFUL

Show Kindness *Jude 22*

There are many times in life when we doubt. Doubt is when we lack confidence that something is true or that we can do something. Just as Christians today have doubts about their faith, some followers of Jesus in the early church struggled with doubt. There is an instruction here for fellow believers to have mercy on people who doubt. To have mercy means to show kindness to a Christian who is experiencing doubt instead of judging them. Through kindness and encouragement, we can help people work through their doubt to have an awesome experience following Jesus! ◑

Blessing

[24]To the one who is able
  to protect you from falling,
    and to present you blameless
    and rejoicing
    before his glorious presence,
[25]to the only God our savior,
  through Jesus Christ our Lord,
    belong glory, majesty, power,
    and authority,
    before all time, now and forever.
    Amen.

Revelation

Revelation begins with the author, named as John, describing a vision of Jesus. John was a prisoner on Patmos, a rocky island off the coast of present-day Turkey. John said that he came under the Holy Spirit's power and heard a loud voice telling him to write down everything he was about to see. John's vision of Jesus starts with messages Jesus gave to churches in seven different cities (Rev 1–3). These messages offered encouragement to people who were living faithfully and warning to people who were not.

The book goes on to describe John's visions of heaven. There are many images—such as seals, trumpets, and bowls—that were used to create a picture of the troubles Christians faced at the time the book was written. These images also encouraged early Christians that good would win over evil in the days to come. These symbols are often hard for us to understand, but they may have been clearer to ancient readers.

The visions in Revelation can sometimes be confusing or even scary. But the end of the book says that Jesus will make all things new (Rev 21:5). It tells us that God will create a new heaven and earth where God will live among God's people. And it says that God's presence is a place where "there will be no mourning, crying, or pain anymore, for the former things have passed away" (Rev 21:4). Revelation shows us that God reigns now and forever! ♦

things YOU'LL DISCOVER

This book comforted early Christians who were put into prison or killed because of their faith in Jesus. Revelation encourages all Christians to be faithful even during difficult times.

people YOU'LL MEET

John—the author of this book (Rev 1–22)

Living creatures and elders—beings that worship God (Rev 4–7; 11; 14)

The Lamb—a name for Jesus, who paid the price for humanity's sin (Rev 5–7; 12–22)

The dragon and the beast—creatures who oppose God (Rev 13–20)

places YOU'LL GO

Ephesus, Smyrna, Pergamum, Thyatira, Sardis, Philadelphia, Laodicea (present-day Turkey)

words YOU'LL REMEMBER

"All is done. I am the Alpha and Omega, the beginning and the end. To the thirsty I will freely give water from the life-giving spring" (Rev 21:6).

Greetings

1 A revelation of Jesus Christ, which God gave him to show his servants what must soon take place. Christ made it known by sending it through his angel to his servant John, ²who bore witness to the word of God and to the witness of Jesus Christ, including all that John saw. ³Favored is the one who reads the words of this prophecy out loud, and favored are those who listen to it being read, and keep what is written in it, for the time is near.

⁴John, to the seven churches that are in Asia:

Grace and peace to you from the one who is and was and is coming, and from the seven spirits that are before God's throne, ⁵and from Jesus Christ—the faithful witness, the firstborn from among the dead, and the ruler of the kings of the earth.

To the one who loves us and freed us from our sins by his blood, ⁶who made us a kingdom, priests to his God and Father— to him be glory and power forever and always. Amen.

⁷Look, he is coming with the clouds! Every eye will see him, including those who pierced him, and all the tribes of the earth will mourn because of him. This is so. Amen. ⁸"I am the Alpha and the Omega," says the Lord God, "the one who is and was and is coming, the Almighty."

Christ appears to John

⁹I, John, your brother who shares with you in the hardship, kingdom, and endurance that we have in Jesus, was on the island called Patmos because of the word of God and my witness about Jesus. ¹⁰I was in a Spirit-inspired trance on the Lord's day, and I heard behind me a loud voice that sounded like a trumpet. ¹¹It said, "Write down on a scroll whatever you see, and send it to the seven churches: to Ephesus, Smyrna, Pergamum, Thyatira, Sardis, Philadelphia, and Laodicea."

¹²I turned to see who was speaking to me, and when I turned, I saw seven oil lamps burning on top of seven gold stands. ¹³In the middle of the lampstands I saw someone who

LIFE PRESERVER

What is a "revelation"?
Revelation 1:1

A *revelation* is something that is revealed that wasn't known before. The last book in the New Testament begins and ends by telling readers that Jesus will soon return and that God will rule the earth. That is the revelation. This book reads like a letter about the end of this world, but a new world is coming where good beats evil forever. ◆

looked like the Human One.ᵃ He wore a robe that stretched down to his feet, and he had a gold sash around his chest. ¹⁴His head and hair were white as white wool—like snow— and his eyes were like a fiery flame. ¹⁵His feet were like fine brass that has been purified in a furnace, and his voice sounded like rushing water. ¹⁶He held seven stars in his right hand, and from his mouth came a sharp, two-edged sword. His appearance was like the sun shining with all its power.

¹⁷When I saw him, I fell at his feet like a dead man. But he put his right hand on me

Alpha is the first letter of the Greek alphabet. *Omega* is the last letter of the Greek alphabet. Using the English alphabet, God might have said, "I am A to Z and everything in between."

and said, "Don't be afraid. I'm the first and the last, ¹⁸and the living one. I was dead, but look! Now I'm alive forever and always. I have the keys of Death and the Grave. ¹⁹So write down what you have seen, both the scene now before you and the things that are about to unfold after this. ²⁰As for the mystery of the seven stars that you saw in my right hand and the seven gold lampstands, here is what they mean: the seven stars are the angels of the seven churches, and the seven lampstands are the seven churches.

Message to Ephesus

2 "Write this to the angel of the church in Ephesus:

ᵃOr Son of Man

These are the words of the one who holds the seven stars in his right hand and walks among the seven gold lampstands: ²I know your works, your labor, and your endurance. I also know that you don't put up with those who are evil. You have tested those who say they are apostles but are not, and you have found them to be liars. ³You have shown endurance and put up with a lot for my name's sake, and you haven't gotten tired. ⁴But I have this against you: you have let go of the love you had at first. ⁵So remember the high point from which you have fallen. Change your hearts and lives and do the things you did at first. If you don't, I'm coming to you. I will move your lampstand from its place if you don't change your hearts and lives. ⁶But you have this in your favor: you hate what the Nicolaitans are doing, which I also hate. ⁷If you can hear, listen to what the Spirit is saying to the churches. I will allow those who emerge victorious to eat from the tree of life, which is in God's paradise.

LIGHTHOUSE
Life

God's Tree of Life *Revelation 2:1-7*
The people of the church in Ephesus needed to remember what they had forgotten. God encouraged them to keep doing right and reminded them about God's reward for them—a juicy fruit from the tree of life. Long ago the tree of life appeared at the beginning of God's story (Gen 2:9). Adam and Eve could eat the tree's life-giving fruit forever, but the serpent convinced them to choose the death-dealing fruit from the tree of the knowledge of good and evil. All the way on the other side of the story, the tree of life appears again. In the new world the tree of life is planted in God's city where people who follow God can always take and eat from it (Rev 22:1-2). ◆

Message to Smyrna

⁸"Write this to the angel of the church in Smyrna:
These are the words of the one who is the first and the last, who died and came back to life: ⁹I know your hardship and poverty (though you are actually rich). I also know the hurtful things that have been spoken about you by those who say they are Jews (though they

are not, but are really Satan's synagogue). ¹⁰Don't be afraid of what you are going to suffer. Look! The devil is going to throw some of you into prison in order to test you. You will suffer hardship for ten days. Be faithful even to the point of death, and I will give you the crown of life. ¹¹If you can hear, listen to what the Spirit is saying to the churches. Those who emerge victorious won't be hurt by the second death.

Message to Pergamum

¹²"Write this to the angel of the church in Pergamum:
These are the words of the one who has the sharp, two-edged sword: ¹³I know that you are living right where Satan's throne is. You are holding on to my name, and you didn't break faith with me even at the time that Antipas, my faithful witness, was killed among you, where Satan lives. ¹⁴But I have a few things against you, because you have some there who follow Balaam's teaching. Balaam had taught Balak to trip up the Israelites so that they would eat food sacrificed to idols and commit sexual immorality. ¹⁵In the same way, you have some who follow the Nicolaitans' teaching. ¹⁶So change your hearts and lives. If you don't, I am coming to you soon, and I will make war on them with the sword that comes from my mouth. ¹⁷If you can hear, listen to what the Spirit is saying to the churches. I will give those who emerge victorious some of the hidden manna to eat. I will also give to each of them a white stone with a new name written on it, which no one knows except the one who receives it.

Message to Thyatira

¹⁸"Write this to the angel of the church in Thyatira:
These are the words of God's Son, whose eyes are like a fiery flame, and whose feet are like fine brass. ¹⁹I know your works, your love and faithfulness, your service and endurance. I also know that the works you have done most recently are even greater than those you did at first. ²⁰But I have this against you: you put up with that woman, Jezebel, who calls herself a prophet. You allow her to teach and to mislead my servants into committing sexual

immorality and eating food sacrificed to idols. ²¹I gave her time to change her heart and life, but she refuses to change her life of prostitution. ²²Look! I'm throwing her onto a sickbed. I am casting those who have committed adultery with her into terrible hardship—if they don't change their hearts from following her practices—²³and I will even put her children to death with disease. Then all the churches will know that I'm the one who examines minds and hearts, and that I will give to each of you what your actions deserve. ²⁴As for the rest of you in Thyatira—those of you who don't follow this teaching and haven't learned the so-called "deep secrets" of Satan—I won't burden you with anything else. ²⁵Just hold on to what you have until I come. ²⁶To those who emerge victorious, keeping my practices until the end, I will give authority over the nations—²⁷to rule the nations with an iron rod and smash them like pottery—²⁸just as I received authority from my Father. I will also give them the morning star. ²⁹If you can hear, listen to what the Spirit is saying to the churches.

Message to Sardis

3 "Write this to the angel of the church in Sardis:

These are the words of the one who holds God's seven spirits and the seven stars: I know your works. You have the reputation of being alive, and you are in fact dead. ²Wake up and strengthen whatever you have left, teetering on the brink of death, for I've found that your works are far from complete in the eyes of my God. ³So remember what you received and heard. Hold on to it and change your hearts and lives. If you don't wake up, I will come like a thief, and you won't know what time I will come upon you. ⁴But you do have a few people in Sardis who haven't stained their clothing. They will walk with me clothed in white because they are worthy. ⁵Those who emerge victorious will wear white clothing like this. I won't scratch out their names from the scroll of life, but will declare their names in the presence of my Father and his angels. ⁶If you can hear, listen to what the Spirit is saying to the churches.

Message to Philadelphia

⁷"Write this to the angel of the church in Philadelphia:

These are the words of the one who is holy and true, who has the key of David. Whatever he opens, no one will shut; and whatever he shuts, no one opens. ⁸I know your works. Look! I have set in front of you an open door that no one can shut. You have so little power, and yet you have kept my word and haven't denied my name. ⁹Because of this I will make the people from Satan's synagogue (who say they are Jews and really aren't, but are lying)—I will make them come and bow down at your feet and realize that I have loved you. ¹⁰Because you kept my command to endure, I will keep you safe through the time of testing that is about to come over the whole world, to test those who live on earth. ¹¹I'm coming soon. Hold on to what you have so that no one takes your crown. ¹²As for those who emerge victorious, I will make them pillars in the temple of my God, and they will never leave it. I will write on them the name of my God and the name of the city of my God, the New Jerusalem that comes down out of heaven from my God. I will also write on them my own new name. ¹³If you can hear, listen to what the Spirit is saying to the churches.

Message to Laodicea

¹⁴"Write this to the angel of the church in Laodicea:

These are the words of the Amen, the faithful and true witness, the ruler[b] of God's creation. ¹⁵I know your works. You are neither cold nor hot. I wish that you were either cold or hot. ¹⁶So because you are lukewarm, and neither hot nor cold, I'm about to spit you out of my mouth. ¹⁷After all, you say, 'I'm rich, and I've grown wealthy, and I don't need a thing.' You don't realize that you are miserable, pathetic, poor, blind, and naked. ¹⁸My advice is that you buy gold from me that has been purified by fire so that you may be rich, and white clothing to wear so that your nakedness won't be shamefully exposed, and ointment to put on your eyes so that you may see. ¹⁹I correct and discipline those whom I love. So be earnest and change your hearts and lives. ²⁰Look!

[b] Or beginning

I'm standing at the door and knocking. If any hear my voice and open the door, I will come in to be with them, and will have dinner with them, and they will have dinner with me. ²¹As for those who emerge victorious, I will allow them to sit with me on my throne, just as I emerged victorious and sat down with my Father on his throne. ²²If you can hear, listen to what the Spirit is saying to the churches."

John sees God's heavenly throne

4 After this I looked and there was a door that had been opened in heaven. The first voice that I had heard, which sounded like a trumpet, said to me, "Come up here, and I will show you what must take place after this." ²At once I was in a Spirit-inspired trance and I saw a throne in heaven,

Bet you can read this in 4 minutes. Ready, set, go!

and someone was seated on the throne. ³The one seated there looked like jasper and carnelian, and surrounding the throne was a rainbow that looked like an emerald. ⁴Twenty-four thrones, with twenty-four elders seated upon them, surrounded the throne. The elders were dressed in white clothing and had gold crowns on their heads. ⁵From the throne came lightning, voices, and thunder. In front of the throne were seven flaming torches, which are the seven spirits of God. ⁶Something like a glass sea, like crystal, was in front of the throne.

In the center, by the throne, were four living creatures encircling the throne. These creatures were covered with eyes on the front and on the back. ⁷The first living creature was like a lion. The second living creature was like an ox. The third living creature

God's THOUGHTS ◆ My THOUGHTS

Seeing Clearly   *Revelation 3:14-22*

Sometimes when life is good, we think we can rely on ourselves to keep it that way. Think of it like this: Perhaps spelling is easy for you so you never study for a spelling test. Why would you? You're smart and a good student. But you aren't seeing the situation clearly. When the spelling words get harder, you start making bad grades on your tests. Suddenly your teacher realizes you only looked like a good student.

The church in Laodicea had a similar attitude. Laodicea was a city in modern-day Turkey with a medical school famous for making medicine for eyes. According to John's vision, the Christians in that city thought they were doing fine and didn't need anything. They were wealthy, had nice clothes, and had doctors. The problem was that they relied on themselves instead of God for everything. Their attitude caused them to be *lukewarm*, which means they only went through the motions of being a good church.

These Christians thought they could see clearly, but they needed God's ointment so that they weren't blind to what God wanted them to do. Jesus said that the Christians in Laodicea needed to change their hearts and lives and follow God. Simply looking like a good church wasn't enough.

Can you think of a food that doesn't taste good when it's lukewarm?

Pray to God for clear thinking about your need to rely on God.

had a face like a human being. And the fourth living creature was like an eagle in flight. [8]Each of the four living creatures had six wings, and each was covered all around and on the inside with eyes. They never rest day or night, but keep on saying,

"Holy, holy, holy is the Lord God Almighty,
who was and is and is coming."

[9]Whenever the living creatures give glory, honor, and thanks to the one seated on the throne, who lives forever and always, [10]the twenty-four elders fall before the one seated on the throne. They worship the one who lives forever and always. They throw down their crowns before the throne and say,

[11] "You are worthy, our Lord and God,
to receive glory and honor and power,
because you created all things.
It is by your will that they existed
and were created."

The Lamb takes the scroll

5 Then I saw a scroll in the right hand of the one seated on the throne. It had writing on the front and the back, and it was sealed with seven seals. [2]I saw a powerful angel, who proclaimed in a loud voice, "Who is worthy to open the scroll and break its seals?" [3]But no one in heaven or on earth or under the earth could open the scroll or look inside it. [4]So I began to weep and weep, because no one was found worthy to open the scroll or to look inside it. [5]Then one of the elders said to me, "Don't weep. Look! The Lion of the tribe of Judah, the Root of David, has emerged victorious so that he can open the scroll and its seven seals."

[6]Then, in between the throne and the four living creatures and among the elders, I saw a Lamb, standing as if it had been slain. It had seven horns and seven eyes, which are God's seven spirits, sent out into the whole earth. [7]He came forward and took the scroll from the right hand of the one seated on the throne. [8]When he took the scroll, the four living creatures and the twenty-four elders fell down before the Lamb. Each held a harp and gold bowls full of incense, which are the prayers of the saints. [9]They took up a new song, saying,

"You are worthy to take the scroll
and open its seals,

because you were slain,
and by your blood
you purchased for God
persons from every tribe, language,
people, and nation.

[10] You made them a kingdom and priests
to our God,
and they will rule on earth."

[11]Then I looked, and I heard the sound of many angels surrounding the throne, the living creatures, and the elders. They numbered in the millions—thousands upon thousands. [12]They said in a loud voice,

"Worthy is the slaughtered Lamb
to receive power, wealth, wisdom,
and might,
and honor, glory,
and blessing."

[13]And I heard every creature in heaven and on earth and under the earth and in the sea—I heard everything everywhere say,

"Blessing, honor, glory, and power
belong to the one seated on the throne
and to the Lamb
forever and always."

[14]Then the four living creatures said, "Amen," and the elders fell down and worshipped.

LIGHTHOUSE

PRAISE GOD

All God's Creation Will Praise God
Revelation 5:13

Everything made by God will praise God sooner or later. When Jesus entered Jerusalem, he said that if his disciples stopped praising God, the stones would shout (Luke 19:37-40). The book of Revelation shows that all creation will recognize and admit that God is Lord of all. Nothing will be able to hold back its praise. No one will be silent. All creation will praise God.

Opening the first six seals

6 Then I looked on as the Lamb opened one of the seven seals. I heard one of the four living creatures say in a voice like thunder, "Come!" [2]So I looked, and there was a white horse. Its rider held a bow and was given a crown. And he went forth from victory to victory.

³When the Lamb opened the second seal, I heard the second living creature say, "Come!" ⁴Out came another horse, fiery red. Its rider was allowed to take peace from the earth so that people would kill each other. He was given a large sword.

⁵When he opened the third seal, I heard the third living creature say, "Come!" So I looked, and there was a black horse. Its rider held a balance for weighing in his hand. ⁶I heard what sounded like a voice from among the four living creatures. It said, "A quart of wheat for a denarion,ᶜ and three quarts of barley for a denarion, but don't damage the olive oil and the wine."

⁷When he opened the fourth seal, I heard the voice of the fourth living creature say, "Come!" ⁸So I looked, and there was a pale green horse. Its rider's name was Death, and the Grave was following right behind. They were given authority over a fourth of the earth, to kill by sword, famine, disease, and the wild animals of the earth.

⁹When he opened the fifth seal, I saw under the altar those who had been slaughtered on account of the word of God and the witness they had given. ¹⁰They cried out with a loud voice, "Holy and true Master, how long will you wait before you pass judgment? How long before you require justice for our blood, which was shed by those who live on earth?" ¹¹Each of them was given a white robe, and they were told to rest a little longer, until their fellow servants and brothers and sisters—who were about to be killed as they were—were finished.

¹²I looked on as he opened the sixth seal, and there was a great earthquake. The sun became black as funeral clothing, and the entire moon turned red as blood. ¹³The stars of the sky fell to the earth as a fig tree drops its fruit when shaken by a strong wind. ¹⁴The sky disappeared like a scroll being rolled up, and every mountain and island was moved from its place. ¹⁵Then the kings of the earth, the officials and the generals, the rich and the powerful, and everyone, slave and free, hid themselves in caves and in the rocks of the mountains. ¹⁶They called to the mountains and the rocks, "Fall on us and hide us from the

ᶜA denarion was a day's pay for a laborer.

face of the one seated on the throne and from the Lamb's wrath! ¹⁷The great day of their wrath has come, and who is able to stand?"

One hundred forty-four thousand sealed

7 After this I saw four angels standing at the four corners of the earth. They held back the earth's four winds so that no wind would blow against the earth, the sea, or any tree. ²I saw another angel coming up from the east, holding the seal of the living God. He cried out with a loud voice to the four angels who had been given the power to damage the earth and sea. ³He said, "Don't damage the earth, the sea, or the trees until we have put a seal on the foreheads of those who serve our God."

SAILBOAT

OBEDIENCE

God Protects People Who Obey
Revelation 7:2-3
Things were bad for people on earth in this part of John's vision, but they were about to get a lot worse. War was loose in the world. Along with war came sickness, famine, and finally death. The sun had turned black, and the moon had turned red. And everyone—no matter how important they thought they were—ran to hide from all the terrible things happening. But some people found relief. Before the next terrible event started, God put a special mark on the people who still obeyed God. God's mark protected them from the locusts that tormented everyone else (Rev 9:2-4).◗

⁴Then I heard the number of those who were sealed: one hundred forty-four thousand, sealed from every tribe of the Israelites:
⁵From the tribe of Judah,
    twelve thousand were sealed;
from the tribe of Reuben,
    twelve thousand;
from the tribe of Gad, twelve thousand;
⁶from the tribe of Asher, twelve thousand;
from the tribe of Naphtali,
    twelve thousand;
from the tribe of Manasseh,
    twelve thousand;
⁷from the tribe of Simeon,
    twelve thousand;

from the tribe of Levi, twelve thousand;
from the tribe of Issachar,
 twelve thousand;
⁸from the tribe of Zebulun,
 twelve thousand;
from the tribe of Joseph,
 twelve thousand;
from the tribe of Benjamin,
 twelve thousand were sealed.

The great crowd and seventh seal

⁹After this I looked, and there was a great crowd that no one could number. They were from every nation, tribe, people, and language. They were standing before the throne and before the Lamb. They wore white robes and held palm branches in their hands. ¹⁰They cried out with a loud voice:

> "Victory belongs to our God
> who sits on the throne,
> and to the Lamb."

Memorize Rev 7:10

¹¹All the angels stood in a circle around the throne, and around the elders and the four living creatures. They fell facedown before the throne and worshipped God, ¹²saying,

> "Amen! Blessing and glory
> and wisdom and thanksgiving
> and honor and power and might
> be to our God forever and always.
> Amen."

¹³Then one of the elders said to me, "Who are these people wearing white robes, and where did they come from?"

¹⁴I said to him, "Sir, you know."

Then he said to me, "These people have come out of great hardship. They have washed their robes and made them white in the Lamb's blood. ¹⁵This is the reason they are before God's throne. They worship him day and night in his temple, and the one seated on the throne will shelter them. ¹⁶They won't hunger or thirst anymore. No sun or scorching heat will beat down on them, ¹⁷because the Lamb who is in the midst of the throne will shepherd them. He will lead them to the springs of life-giving water,ᵈ and God will wipe away every tear from their eyes."

8 Then, when the Lamb opened the seventh seal, there was silence in heaven for about half an hour.

The first four trumpet plagues

²Then I saw the seven angels who stand before God, and seven trumpets were given to them. ³Another angel came and stood at the altar, and he held a gold bowl for burning incense. He was given a large amount of incense, in order to offer it on behalf of the prayers of all the saints on the gold altar in front of the throne. ⁴The smoke of the incense offered for the prayers of the saints rose up before God from the angel's hand. ⁵Then the angel took the incense container and filled it with fire from the altar. He threw it down to the earth, and there were thunder, voices, lightning, and an earthquake.

⁶Then the seven angels who held the seven trumpets got ready to blow them. ⁷The first angel blew his trumpet, and hail and fire mixed with blood appeared, and was thrown down to the earth. A third of the earth was burned up. A third of the trees were burned up. All the green grass was burned up. ⁸Then the second angel blew his trumpet, and something like a huge mountain burning with fire was thrown down into the sea. A third of the sea became blood, ⁹a third of the creatures living in the sea died, and a third of the ships were destroyed. ¹⁰Then the third angel blew his trumpet, and a great star, burning like a torch, fell from heaven. It fell on a third of the rivers and springs of water. ¹¹The star's name is Wormwood, and a third of the waters became wormwood, and many people died from the water, because it became so bitter. ¹²Then the fourth angel blew his trumpet, and a third of the sun was struck, and a third of the moon, and a third of the stars so that a third of them became dark. The day lost a third of its light, and the night lost a third of its light too.

¹³Then I looked and I heard an eagle flying high overhead. It said with a loud voice, "Horror, horror, oh! The horror for those who live on earth because of the blasts of the remaining trumpets that the three angels are about to blow!"

The fifth and sixth trumpet plagues

9 Then the fifth angel blew his trumpet, and I saw a star that had fallen from heaven to earth, and he was given the key to the shaft

ᵈOr *the water of life*

of the abyss. [2]He opened the shaft of the abyss; and smoke rose up from the shaft, like smoke from a huge furnace. The sun and air were darkened by the smoke from the shaft. [3]Then locusts came forth from the smoke and onto the earth. They were given power like the power that scorpions have on the earth. [4]They were told not to hurt the grass of the earth or any green plant or any tree. They could only hurt the people who didn't have the seal of God on their foreheads. [5]The locusts weren't allowed to kill them, but only to make them suffer for five months—and the suffering they inflict is like that of a scorpion when it strikes a person. [6]In those days people will seek death, but they won't find it. They will want to die, but death will run away from them.

[7]The locusts looked like horses ready for battle. On their heads were what seemed to be gold crowns. Their faces were like human faces, [8]their hair was like women's hair, and their teeth were like lions' teeth. [9]In front they had what seemed to be iron armor upon their chests, and the sound of their wings was like the sound of many chariots and horses racing into battle. [10]They also have tails with stingers, just like scorpions; and in their tails is their power to hurt people for five months. [11]Their king is an angel from the abyss, whose Hebrew name is Abaddon,[e] and whose Greek name is Apollyon.[f]

[12]The first horror has passed. Look! Two horrors are still coming after this.

[13]Then the sixth angel blew his trumpet, and I heard a voice from the four horns of the gold altar that is before God. [14]It said to the sixth angel, who had the trumpet, "Release the four angels who are bound at the great river Euphrates." [15]Then the four angels who had been made ready for that hour, day, month, and year were released to kill a third of humankind. [16]The number of cavalry troops was two hundred million. I heard their number. [17]And this is the way I saw the horses and their riders in the vision: they had breastplates that were fiery red, dark blue, and yellow as sulfur. The horses' heads were like lions' heads, and out of their mouths came fire, smoke, and sulfur. [18]By these three

---

---

plagues a third of humankind was killed: by the fire, smoke, and sulfur coming out of their mouths. [19]The horses' power is in their mouths and their tails, for their tails are like snakes with heads that inflict injuries.

[20]The rest of humankind, who weren't killed by these plagues, didn't change their hearts and lives and turn from their handiwork. They didn't stop worshipping demons and idols made of gold, silver, bronze, stone, and wood—idols that can't see or hear or walk. [21]They didn't turn away from their murders, their spells and drugs, their sexual immorality, or their stealing.

John receives the open scroll

10Then I saw another powerful angel coming down from heaven. He was robed with a cloud, with a rainbow over his head. His face was like the sun, and his feet were like fiery pillars. [2]He held an open scroll in his hand. He put his right foot on the sea and his left foot on the land. [3]He called out with a loud voice like a lion roaring, and when he called out, the seven thunders raised their voices. [4]When the seven thunders spoke, I was about to write, but I heard a voice from heaven say, "Seal up what the seven thunders have said, and don't write it down."

[5]Then the angel I saw standing on the sea and on the land raised his right hand to

---

[e]Destruction [f]Destroyer

heaven. ⁶He swore by the one who lives forever and always, who created heaven and what is in it, the earth and what is in it, and the sea and what is in it, and said, "The time is up. ⁷In the days when the seventh angel blows his trumpet, God's mysterious purpose will be accomplished, fulfilling the good news he gave to his servants the prophets."

⁸Then the voice I heard from heaven spoke to me again and said, "Go, take the opened scroll from the hand of the angel who stands on the sea and on the land." ⁹So I went to the angel and told him to give me the scroll. He said to me, "Take it and eat it. It will make you sick to your stomach, but sweet as honey in your mouth." ¹⁰So I took the scroll from the angel's hand and ate it. And it was sweet as honey in my mouth, but when I swallowed it, it made my stomach churn. ¹¹I was told, "You must prophesy again about many peoples, nations, languages, and kings."

Two witnesses

11 Then I was given a measuring rod, which was like a pole. And I was told, "Get up and measure God's temple, the altar, and those who worship there. ²But don't measure the court outside the temple. Leave that out, because it has been given to the nations, and they will trample the holy city underfoot for forty-two months.

did you know? These Bible verses were the inspiration for some of the lyrics in the "Hallelujah Chorus" from George Frideric Handel's *Messiah*. This chorus is sung every year in many churches around the world at Easter or Christmas.

³"And I will allow my two witnesses to prophesy for one thousand two hundred sixty days, wearing mourning clothes. ⁴These are the two olive trees and the two lampstands that stand before the Lord of the earth. ⁵If anyone wants to hurt them, fire comes out of their mouth and burns up their enemies. So if anyone wants to hurt them, they have to be killed in this way. ⁶They have the power to close up the sky so that no rain will fall for as long as they prophesy. They also have power over the waters, to turn them into blood, and to strike the earth with any plague, as often as they wish.

⁷"When they have finished their witnessing, the beast that comes up from the abyss will make war on them, gain victory over them, and kill them. ⁸Their dead bodies will lie on the street of the great city that is spiritually called Sodom and Egypt, where also their Lord was crucified. ⁹And for three and a half days, members of the peoples, tribes, languages, and nations will look at their dead bodies, but they won't let their dead bodies be put in a tomb. ¹⁰Those who live on earth will rejoice over them. They will celebrate and give each other gifts, because these two prophets had brought such pain to those who live on earth.

¹¹"But after three and a half days, the breath of life from God entered them, and they stood on their feet. Great fear came over those who saw them. ¹²Then they heard a loud voice from heaven say to them, 'Come up here.' And they went up to heaven in a cloud, while their enemies watched them. ¹³At that hour there was a great earthquake, and a tenth of the city fell. Seven thousand people were killed by the earthquake, and the rest were afraid and gave glory to the God of heaven."

¹⁴The second horror is over. The third horror is coming soon.

Seventh trumpet

¹⁵Then the seventh angel blew his trumpet, and there were loud voices in heaven saying,

"The kingdom of the world has become
the kingdom of our Lord and his Christ,
and he will rule forever and always."

¹⁶Then the twenty-four elders, who were seated on their thrones before God, fell on their faces and worshipped God. ¹⁷They said,

"We give thanks to you,
Lord God Almighty,
who is and was,
for you have taken your great power
and enforced your rule.
¹⁸The nations were enraged,
but your wrath came.
The time came for the dead to be judged.
The time came to reward your servants,
the prophets and saints,
and those who fear your name,
both small and great,
and to destroy those
who destroy the earth."

¹⁹Then God's temple in heaven was opened, and the chest containing his covenant appeared in his temple. There were lightning, voices, thunder, an earthquake, and large hail.

A woman, her child, and the dragon

12Then a great sign appeared in heaven: a woman clothed with the sun, with the moon under her feet and a crown of twelve stars on her head. ²She was pregnant, and she cried out because she was in labor, in pain from giving birth. ³Then another sign appeared in heaven: it was a great fiery red dragon, with seven heads and ten horns, and seven royal crowns on his heads. ⁴His tail swept down a third of heaven's stars and threw them to the earth. The dragon stood in front of the woman who was about to give birth so that when she gave birth, he might devour her child. ⁵She gave birth to a son, a male child who is to rule all the nations with an iron rod. Her child was snatched up to God and his throne. ⁶Then the woman fled into the desert, where God has prepared a place for her. There she will be taken care of for one thousand two hundred sixty days.

Michael and the dragon

⁷Then there was war in heaven: Michael and his angels fought the dragon. The dragon and his angels fought back, ⁸but they did not prevail, and there

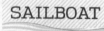

SAILBOAT

GIVING THANKS

Be Thankful God Keeps God's Promises
Revelation 11:17-18

In John's vision, the elders gave thanks for the end of the old world before the beginning of the new world (Rev 21:1–22:5). The elders had plenty for which to thank God. This was the time when all the promises God had made were going to be fulfilled. Justice would be done, and everyone would get what they deserved. People who had served God would be rewarded with never-ending life with God in the new Jerusalem (Rev 21:1-7). People who had disobeyed and insisted on doing their own thing would be punished for rejecting God's plan (Rev 20:11-15). The elders weren't grateful that people were being punished. They were thankful that God's final plan of justice and mercy was unfolding. ◊

was no longer any place for them in heaven. ⁹So the great dragon was thrown down. The old snake, who is called the devil and Satan, the deceiver of the whole world, was thrown down to the earth; and his angels were thrown down with him. ¹⁰Then I heard a loud voice in heaven say,

> "Now the salvation and power
> and kingdom of our God,
> and the authority of his Christ
> have come.
> The accuser of our brothers and sisters,
> who accuses them day and night
> before our God,
> has been thrown down.
> ¹¹They gained the victory over him
> on account of the blood of the Lamb
> and the word of their witness.
> Love for their own lives
> didn't make them afraid to die.
> ¹²Therefore, rejoice, you heavens
> and you who dwell in them.
> But oh! The horror for the earth and sea!

did you know? Michael was the head angel. One of his jobs was to lead all the other angels in battle. God promised that when the final battle came, Michael would lead the rest of the angels in protecting God's children (Dan 12:1).

> The devil has come down to you
> with great rage,
> for he knows that he only has
> a short time."

The dragon pursues the woman

¹³When the dragon saw that he had been thrown down to the earth, he chased the woman who had given birth to the male child. ¹⁴But the woman was given the two wings of the great eagle so that she could fly to her place in the desert. There she would be taken care of—out of the snake's reach—for a time and times and half a time. ¹⁵Then from his mouth the snake poured a river of water after the woman so that the river would sweep her away. ¹⁶But the earth helped the woman. The earth opened its mouth and swallowed the river that the dragon poured out of his mouth. ¹⁷So the dragon was furious with the woman, and he went off to make war on the rest of her

children, on those who keep God's commandments and hold firmly to the witness of Jesus.

The beast from the sea

13 [18]Then the dragon stood on the seashore, and I saw a beast coming up out of the sea. It had ten horns and seven heads. Each of its horns was decorated with a royal crown, and on its heads were blasphemous names. [2]The beast I saw was like a leopard. Its feet were like a bear's, and its mouth was like a lion's mouth. The dragon gave it his power, throne, and great authority. [3]One of its heads appeared to have been slain and killed, but its deadly wound was healed. So the whole earth was amazed and followed the beast. [4]They worshipped the dragon because it had given the beast its authority. They worshipped the beast and said, "Who is like the beast, and who can fight against it?"

[5]The beast was given a mouth that spoke boastful and blasphemous things, and it was given authority to act for forty-two months. [6]It opened its mouth to speak blasphemies against God. It blasphemed God's name and his dwelling place (that is, those who dwell in heaven).

[7]It was also allowed to make war on the saints and to gain victory over them. It was given authority over every tribe, people, language, and nation. [8]All who live on earth worshipped it, all whose names hadn't been written—from the time the earth was made—in the scroll of life of the Lamb who was slain. [9]Whoever has ears must listen: [10]If any are to be taken captive, then into captivity they will go. If any are to be killed by the sword, then by the sword they will be killed. This calls for endurance and faithfulness on the part of the saints.

The beast from the land

[11]Then I saw another beast coming up from the earth. It had two horns like a lamb, but it was speaking like a dragon. [12]It exercises all the authority of the first beast in its presence. It also makes the earth and those who live in it worship the first beast, whose fatal wound was healed. [13]It does great signs so that it even makes fire come down from heaven to earth in the presence of the people. [14]It deceives those who live on earth by the signs that it was allowed to do in the presence of the beast. It told those who live on earth to make an image for the beast who had been wounded by the sword and yet came to life again. [15]It was allowed to give breath to the beast's image so that the beast's image would even speak and cause anyone who didn't worship the beast's image to be put to death. [16]It forces everyone—the small and great, the rich and poor, the free and slaves—to have a mark put on their right hand or on their forehead. [17]It will not allow anyone to make a purchase or sell anything unless the person has the mark with the beast's name or the number of its name. [18]This calls for wisdom. Let the one who understands calculate the beast's number, for it's a human being's number. Its number is six hundred sixty-six.

LIGHTHOUSE
WISDOM

Don't Be Fooled by a Copycat
Revelation 13:11-15

In John's vision, people were tricked into worshipping the evil beast. Paul warned the Corinthian church that evil can disguise itself "as an angel of light" (2 Cor 11:14). This means that evil can act as a copycat and appear to be good. And that's how the people in John's vision were fooled: evil copied the miracles of God. Just as Jesus came back to life, the fatally hurt beast seemed to be brought back from the dead. The beast also made fire come down from heaven just like Elijah called down God's fire (1 Kgs 18:22-39). None of these "miracles" meant the beast was as strong as God. They only meant the beast was good at copying God in order to fool people. Even Pharaoh's magicians copied some of God's wonders in Egypt, but God proved to be stronger (Exod 7:10-12; 8:18-19). If the people in John's vision really knew God, they wouldn't have fallen for the beast's tricks, because God would never tell people to worship an idol (Deut 4:15-19).

The Lamb and the one hundred forty-four thousand

14 Then I looked, and there was the Lamb, standing on Mount Zion. With him were one hundred forty-four thousand who had his name and his Father's name written on their foreheads. [2]I heard a sound from heaven that was like the sound of rushing water and loud thunder. The sound I heard was like that of harpists playing their harps. [3]They sing a new song in front of the throne, the four living creatures, and the elders. And no one could learn the song except the one hundred forty-four thousand who had been purchased from the earth. [4]They weren't defiled with women, for these people who follow the Lamb wherever he goes are virgins. They were purchased from among humankind as early produce for God and the Lamb. [5]No lie came from their mouths; they are blameless.

Messages of three angels

[6]Then I saw another angel flying high overhead with eternal good news to proclaim to those who live on earth, and to every nation, tribe, language, and people. [7]He said in a loud voice, "Fear God and give him glory, for the hour of his judgment has come. Worship the one who made heaven and earth, the sea and springs of water."

[8]Another angel, a second one, followed and said, "Fallen, fallen is Babylon the great! She made all the nations drink the wine of her lustful passion."

[9]Then another angel, a third one, followed them and said in a loud voice, "If any worship the beast and

SAILBOAT

COURAGE

Courage that Lasts Forever
Revelation 14:6-13
It might seem that the followers of Jesus were in a terrible spot. On one side, the beast would kill everyone who didn't worship its image or take its number. On the other side, God would punish everyone who worshipped the beast and took its number. Each way led to suffering! But God gives courage to God's followers in frightening times—just like God gave courage to God's followers in the past. God gave Moses courage to stand up to Pharaoh (Exod 4:1-17). God gave David the courage to stand up to Goliath (1 Sam 17:33-51). God gave courage to Shadrach, Meshach, and Abednego to keep them from bowing to Nebuchadnezzar's gold statue (Dan 3:8-27). Being brave can be costly, but God will honor courageous people forever (Rev 6:9-11; 7:14-17; 14:12-13). ◆

its image, and receive a mark on their foreheads or their hands, [10]they themselves will also drink the wine of God's passionate anger, poured full strength into the cup of his wrath. They will suffer the pain of fire and sulfur in the presence of the holy angels and the Lamb. [11]The smoke of their painful suffering goes up forever and always. There is no rest day or night for those who worship the beast and its image, and those who receive the mark of its name."

[12]This calls for the endurance of the saints, who keep God's commandments and keep faith with Jesus.

[13]And I heard a voice from heaven say, "Write this: Favored are the dead who die in the Lord from now on."

"Yes," says the Spirit, "so they can rest from their labors, because their deeds follow them."

Two harvests of the earth

[14]Then I looked, and there was a white cloud. On the cloud was seated someone who looked like the Human One.[g] He had a gold crown on his head and a sharp sickle in his hand. [15]Another angel came out of the temple, calling in a loud voice to the one seated on the cloud: "Use your sickle to reap the harvest, for the time to harvest has come, and the harvest of the earth is ripe." [16]So the one seated on the cloud swung his sickle over the earth, and the earth was harvested.

[17]Then another angel came out of the temple in heaven, and he also had a sharp sickle. [18]Still another angel, who has power over fire, came out from the altar. He said in a loud voice to the one who had the sharp sickle, "Use your sharp sickle to cut the clusters in the vineyard of the earth, because its grapes are ripe." [19]So the angel swung his sickle into the earth, and cut the vineyard of the earth, and he put what he reaped into the great winepress of God's passionate anger. [20]Then the winepress was trampled outside the city, and the blood came out of the winepress as high as the horses' bridles for almost two hundred miles.[h]

Song of Moses and the Lamb

15Then I saw another great and awe-inspiring sign in heaven. There were

[g]Or Son of Man [h]Or one thousand six hundred stades

seven angels with seven plagues—and these are the last, for with them God's anger is brought to an end. [2] Then I saw what appeared to be a sea of glass mixed with fire. Those who gained victory over the beast, its image, and the number of its name were standing by the glass sea, holding harps from God. [3] They sing the song of Moses, God's servant, and the song of the Lamb, saying,

"Great and awe-inspiring are your works,
　　Lord God Almighty.
Just and true are your ways,
　　king of the nations.
[4] Who won't fear you, Lord,
　　and glorify your name?
　　You alone are holy.
All nations will come and fall down
　　in worship before you,
　　for your acts of justice
　　have been revealed."

Seven bowl plagues

[5] After this I looked, and the temple in heaven—that is, the tent of witness—was opened. [6] The seven angels, who have the seven plagues, came out of the temple. They were clothed in pure bright linen and had gold sashes around their waists. [7] Then one of the four living creatures gave the seven angels seven gold bowls full of the anger of the God who lives forever and always. [8] The temple was filled with smoke from God's glory and power, and no one could go into the temple until the seven plagues of the seven last angels were brought to an end.

16 Then I heard a loud voice from the temple say to the seven angels, "Go and pour out the seven bowls of God's anger on the earth." [2] So the first angel poured his bowl on the earth, and a nasty and terrible sore appeared on the people who had the beast's mark and worshipped its image. [3] The second angel poured his bowl into the sea, and the sea turned into blood, like the blood of a corpse, and every living thing in the sea died. [4] The third angel poured his bowl into the rivers and springs of water, and they turned into blood. [5] Then I heard the angel of the waters say,

"You are just, holy one, who is and was,
　　because you have given these judgments.
[6] They poured out the blood
　　of saints and prophets,
　　and you have given them blood
　　to drink. They deserve it!"
[7] And I heard the altar say,
　　"Yes, Lord God Almighty,
　　your judgments are true and just."

[8] The fourth angel poured his bowl on the sun, and it was allowed to burn people with fire. [9] The people were burned by intense heat, and they cursed the name of the God who had power over these plagues. But they didn't change their hearts and lives and give him glory. [10] The fifth angel poured his bowl over the beast's throne, and darkness covered its kingdom. People bit their tongues because of their pain, [11] and they cursed the God of heaven because of their pains and sores; but they didn't turn away from what they had done.

[12] Then the sixth angel poured his bowl on the great river Euphrates. Its water was dried up so that the way was ready for the kings from the east. [13] Then I saw three unclean spirits, like frogs, come from the dragon's mouth, the beast's mouth, and the mouth of the false prophet. [14] These are demonic spirits that do signs. They go out to the kings of the whole world, to gather them for battle on the great day of God the Almighty. ([15] Look! I'm coming like a thief! Favored are those who stay awake and clothed so that they don't go around naked and exposed to shame.) [16] The spirits gathered them at the place that is called in Hebrew, Harmagedon.[i]

[17] Then the seventh angel poured his bowl into the air, and a loud voice came out from the temple, from the throne, saying, "It is done!" [18] There were lightning strikes, voices, and thunder, and a great earthquake occurred. The earthquake was greater than any that have occurred since there have been people on earth. [19] The great city split into three parts, and the cities of the nations fell. God remembered Babylon the great so that he gave her the wine cup of his furious anger. [20] Every island fled, and the mountains disappeared. [21] Huge hailstones weighing about one hundred pounds came down from heaven on the people. They cursed God for the plague of hail, because the plague was so terrible.

Babylon and the beast

17 Then one of the seven angels who had the seven bowls spoke with me. "Come," he said, "I will show you the judgment upon the great prostitute, who is seated on deep waters. ²The kings of the earth have committed sexual immorality with her, and those who live on earth have become drunk with the wine of her whoring."

³Then he brought me in a Spirit-inspired trance to a desert. There I saw a woman seated on a scarlet beast that was covered with blasphemous names. It had seven heads and ten horns. ⁴The woman wore purple and scarlet clothing, and she glittered with gold and jewels and pearls. In her hand she held a gold cup full of the vile and impure things that came from her activity as a prostitute. ⁵A name—a mystery—was written on her forehead: "Babylon the great, the mother of prostitutes and the vile things of the earth." ⁶I saw that the woman was drunk on the blood of the saints and the blood of Jesus' witnesses. I was completely stunned when I saw her.

⁷Then the angel said to me, "Why are you amazed? I will tell you the mystery of the woman and the seven-headed, ten-horned beast that carries her. ⁸The beast that you saw was and is not, and is about to come up out of the abyss and go to destruction. Those who live on earth, whose names haven't been written in the scroll of life from the time the earth was made, will be amazed when they see the beast, because it was and is not and will again be present. ⁹This calls for an understanding mind. The seven heads are seven mountains on which the woman is seated. They are also seven kings. ¹⁰Five kings have fallen, the one is, and the other hasn't yet come. When that king comes, he must remain for only a short time. ¹¹As for the beast that was and is not, it is itself an eighth king that belongs to the seven, and it is going to destruction. ¹²The ten horns that you saw are ten kings, who haven't

God's THOUGHTS ▶ My THOUGHTS

Pain Can Be Useful? *Revelation 16:10*

At times pain is the result of disobedience. But pain can also show us that something is wrong. Think of it like this: Sometimes we hurt because we do something risky and get injured. If you jump off the roof while pretending to be a superhero and break your arm, you hurt because you did something risky. You may also experience pain as punishment for disobeying your parents' instruction to stay off the roof. But other times we get sick and our bodies hurt even though we didn't do anything risky or wrong. Pain from a fever tells us that we have an infection that needs attention.

The pain in this part of Revelation was intended to get people's attention. God was looking for people to return to God before it was too late. God doesn't enjoy seeing people in pain. God wanted these people to change their hearts and lives because of their pain. God gave them miraculous signs to show God's love and power, but the people turned instead to God's enemy. That's like having a fever and choosing not to rest, drink plenty of water, visit the doctor, and take medicine to get well.

When have you experienced pain that was useful?

Why do you think the people in this passage didn't listen to their pain and turned away from God instead?

yet received royal power. But they will receive royal authority for an hour, along with the beast. [13]These kings will be of one mind, and they will give their power and authority to the beast. [14]They will make war on the Lamb, but the Lamb will emerge victorious, for he is Lord of lords and King of kings. Those with him are called, chosen, and faithful."

[15]Then he said to me, "The waters that you saw, where the prostitute is seated, are peoples, crowds, nations, and languages. [16]As for the ten horns that you saw, they and the beast will hate the prostitute. They will destroy her and strip her bare. They will devour her flesh and burn her with fire [17]because God moved them to carry out his purposes. That is why they will be of one mind and give their royal power to the beast, until God's words have been accomplished. [18]The woman whom you saw is the great city that rules over the kings of the earth."

Babylon's fall

18 After this I saw another angel coming down from heaven. He had great authority, and the earth was filled with light because of his glory. [2]He called out with a loud voice, saying, "Fallen, fallen is Babylon the great! She has become a home for demons and a lair for every unclean spirit. She is a lair for every unclean bird, and a lair for every unclean and disgusting beast [3]because all the nations have fallen[j] due to the wine of her lustful passion. The kings of the earth committed sexual immorality with her, and the merchants of the earth became rich from the power of her loose and extravagant ways."

[4]Then I heard another voice from heaven say, "Come out of her, my people, so that you don't take part in her sins and don't receive any of her plagues. [5]Her sins have piled up as high as heaven, and God remembered her unjust acts. [6]Give her what she has given to others. Give her back twice as much for what she has done. In the cup that she has poured, pour her twice as much. [7]To the extent that she glorified herself and indulged her loose and extravagant ways, give her pain and grief. In her heart she says, 'I sit like a queen! I'm not a widow. I'll never see grief.' [8]This is why her

plagues will come in a single day—deadly disease, grief, and hunger. She will be consumed by fire because the Lord God who judges her is powerful.

[9]"The kings of the earth, who committed sexual immorality with her and shared her loose and extravagant ways, will weep and mourn over her when they see the smoke from her burning. [10]They will stand a long way off because they are afraid of the pain she suffers, and they will say, 'Oh, the horror! Babylon, you great city, you powerful city! In a single hour your judgment has come.'

[11]"The merchants of the earth will weep and mourn over her, for no one buys their cargoes anymore—[12]cargoes of gold, silver, jewels, and pearls; fine linen, purple, silk, and scarlet; all those things made of scented wood, ivory, fine wood, bronze, iron, and marble; [13]cinnamon, incense, fragrant ointment, and frankincense; wine, oil, fine flour, and wheat; cattle, sheep, horses, and carriages; and slaves, even human lives. [14]The fruit your whole being craved has gone from you. All

UMBRELLA
PRIDE

God Will Bring Down the Proud
Revelation 18:7

Throughout God's story, the city of Babylon served as an image for different things. It symbolized God's judgment and punishment on the Israelites for their constant disobedience (2 Kgs 25:1-21). It symbolized human-made strength and wealth in the mind of King Nebuchadnezzar (Dan 4:28-30). In Revelation Babylon is a mixture of all these things: wealth, power, and trouble for God's people. In John's vision, the people of Babylon didn't think they needed God at all. They had power, riches, and the attention of all the rulers of the world. They thought they could do whatever they wanted to whomever they wanted to do it, and nothing would upset their powerful position. But just as Nebuchadnezzar learned that only God gives and takes power (Dan 4:28-37), the people of Babylon learned that God brings down people who are proud and lifts up people who are humble. ◆

your glitter and glamour are lost to you, never ever to be found again.'

15"The merchants who sold these things, and got so rich by her, will stand a long way off because they fear the pain she suffers. They will weep and mourn, and say, 16'Oh, the horror! The great city that wore fine linen, purple, and scarlet, who glittered with gold, jewels, and pearls—17in just one hour such great wealth was destroyed.'

"Every sea captain, every seafarer, sailors, and all who make their living on the sea stood a long way off. 18They cried out as they saw the smoke from her burning and said, 'What city was ever like the great city?' 19They threw dust on their heads, and they cried out, weeping and mourning. They said, 'Oh, the horror! The great city, where all who have ships at sea became so rich by her prosperity—in just one hour she was destroyed. 20Rejoice over her, heaven—you saints, apostles, and prophets—because God has condemned her as she condemned you.'"

21Then a powerful angel picked up a stone that was like a huge millstone and threw it into the sea, saying, "With such violent force the great city of Babylon will be thrown down, and it won't be found anymore. 22The sound of harpists and musicians, of pipers and trumpeters, will never be heard among you again. No craftsman of any kind will ever be found among you again. The sound of the hand mill will never be heard among you again. 23The light of a lamp will never shine among you again. The sound of a bridegroom and bride will never be heard among you again because your merchants ran the world, because all the nations were deceived by the spell you cast, and because 24the blood of prophets, of saints, and of all who have been slaughtered on the earth was found among you.k"

Celebration in heaven

19 After this I heard what sounded like a huge crowd in heaven. They said, "Hallelujah! The salvation and glory and power of our God!

2 His judgments are true and just, because he judged the great prostitute, who ruined the earth by her whoring,

and he exacted the penalty for the blood of his servants from her hand."

3Then they said a second time, "Hallelujah! Smoke goes up from her forever and always."

4The twenty-four elders and the four living creatures fell down and worshipped God, who is seated on the throne, and they said, "Amen. Hallelujah!"

5Then a voice went out from the throne and said,

"Praise our God, all you his servants, and you who fear him, both small and great."

6And I heard something that sounded like a huge crowd, like rushing water and powerful thunder. They said,

"Hallelujah! The Lord our God, the Almighty, exercised his royal power!

7 Let us rejoice and celebrate, and give him the glory, for the wedding day of the Lamb has come, and his bride has made herself ready.

8 She was given fine, pure white linen to wear, for the fine linen is the saints' acts of justice."

9Then the angel said to me, "Write this: Favored are those who have been invited to the wedding banquet of the Lamb." He said to me, "These are the true words of God." 10Then I fell at his feet to worship him. But he said, "Don't do that! I'm a servant just like you and your brothers and sisters who hold firmly to the witness of Jesus. Worship God! The witness of Jesus is the spirit of prophecy!"

Christ defeats the beast

11Then I saw heaven opened, and there was a white horse. Its rider was called Faithful and True, and he judges and makes war justly. 12His eyes were like a fiery flame, and on his head were many royal crowns. He has a name written on him that no one knows but himself. 13He wore a robe dyedl with blood, and his name was called the Word of God. 14Heaven's armies, wearing fine linen that was white and

kOr her lCritical editions of the Gk New Testament read dipped or covered with.

pure, were following him on white horses. [15]From his mouth comes a sharp sword that he will use to strike down the nations. He is the one who will rule them with an iron rod. And he is the one who will trample the winepress of the Almighty God's passionate anger. [16]He has a name written on his robe and on his thigh: King of kings and Lord of lords.

[17]Then I saw an angel standing in the sun, and he called out with a loud voice and said to all the birds flying high overhead, "Come and gather for God's great supper. [18]Come and eat the flesh of kings, the flesh of generals, the flesh of the powerful, and the flesh of horses and their riders. Come and eat the flesh of all, both free and slave, both small and great." [19]Then I saw that the beast and the kings of the earth and their armies had gathered to make war against the rider on the horse and his army. [20]But the beast was seized, along with the false prophet who had done signs in the beast's presence. (He had used the signs to deceive people into receiving the beast's mark and into worshipping the beast's image.) The two of them were thrown alive into the fiery lake that burns with sulfur. [21]The rest were killed by the sword that comes from the mouth of the rider on the horse, and all the birds ate their fill of their flesh.

Satan confined

20Then I saw an angel coming down from heaven, holding in his hand the key to the abyss and a huge chain. [2]He seized the dragon, the old snake, who is the devil and Satan, and bound him for a thousand years. [3]He threw him into the abyss, then locked and sealed it over him. This was to keep him from continuing to deceive the nations until the thousand years were over. After this he must be released for a little while.

The saints rule with Christ

[4]Then I saw thrones, and people took their seats on them, and judgment was given in their favor.[m] They were the ones who had been beheaded for their witness to Jesus and God's word, and those who hadn't worshipped the beast or its image, who hadn't received the mark on their forehead or hand. They

came to life and ruled with Christ for one thousand years. [5]The rest of the dead didn't come to life until the thousand years were over. This is the first resurrection. [6]Favored and holy are those who have a share in the first resurrection. The second death has no power over them, but they will be priests of God and of Christ, and will rule with him for one thousand years.

Satan's defeat

[7]When the thousand years are over, Satan will be released from his prison. [8]He will go out to deceive the nations that are at the four corners of the earth—Gog and Magog. He will gather them for battle. Their number is like the sand of the sea. [9]They came up across the whole earth and surrounded the saints' camp, the city that God loves. But fire came down from heaven and consumed them. [10]Then the devil, who had deceived them, was thrown into the lake of fire and sulfur, where the beast and the false prophet also were. There painful suffering will be inflicted upon them day and night, forever and always.

Final judgment

[11]Then I saw a great white throne and the one who is seated on it. Before his face both earth and heaven fled away, and no place was found for them. [12]I saw the dead, the great and the small, standing before the throne, and scrolls were opened. Another scroll was opened too; this is the scroll of life. And the dead were judged on the basis of what was written in the scrolls about what they had done. [13]The sea gave up the dead that were in it, and Death and the Grave gave up the dead that were in them, and people were judged by what they had done. [14]Then Death and the Grave were thrown into the fiery lake. This, the fiery lake, is the second death. [15]Then anyone whose name wasn't found written in the scroll of life was thrown into the fiery lake.

New heaven and new earth

21Then I saw a new heaven and a new earth, for the former heaven and the former earth had passed away, and the sea

---

[m]Or to them

was no more. ²I saw the holy city, New Jerusalem, coming down out of heaven from God, made ready as a bride beautifully dressed for her husband. ³I heard a loud voice from the throne say, "Look! God's dwelling is here with humankind. He will dwell with them, and they will be his peoples. God himself will be with them as their God. ⁴He will wipe away every tear from their eyes. Death will be no more. There will be no mourning, crying, or pain anymore, for the former things have passed away." ⁵Then the one seated on the throne said, "Look! I'm making all things new." He also said, "Write this down, for these words are trustworthy and true." ⁶Then he said to me, "All is done. I am the Alpha and the Omega, the beginning and the end. To the thirsty I will freely give water from the life-giving spring. ⁷Those who emerge victorious will inherit these things. I will be their God, and they will be my sons and daughters. ⁸But for the cowardly, the faithless, the vile, the murderers, those who commit sexual immorality, those who use drugs and cast spells, the idolaters and all liars—their share will be in the lake that burns with fire and sulfur. This is the second death."

Memorize Rev 21:6

UMBRELLA
GRIEF

No More Tears *Revelation 21:3-4*

People cry for many different reasons. There are tears for breaking an arm, for hurtful words, and for saying good-bye to friends or family. Some of the most painful tears come when people we love die. But God takes away all reasons for tears in John's vision of a new world. Anything that might have caused sadness is gone from the city where God lives with God's people forever. Death and the grave have been thrown into the lake of fire (Rev 20:14). In this new Jerusalem there are no more good-byes. There are no more accidents or evil deeds. Even rainy days are gone! God will fill God's city and people with joy and light. ◊

New Jerusalem

⁹Then one of the seven angels who had the seven bowls full of the seven last plagues spoke with me. "Come," he said, "I will show you the bride, the Lamb's wife." ¹⁰He took me in a Spirit-inspired trance to a great, high mountain, and he showed me the holy city, Jerusalem, coming down out of heaven from God. ¹¹The city had God's glory. Its brilliance was like a priceless jewel, like jasper that was as clear as crystal. ¹²It had a great high wall with twelve gates. By the gates were twelve angels, and on the gates were written the names of the twelve tribes of Israel's sons. ¹³There were three gates on the east, three gates on the north, three gates on the south, and three gates on the west. ¹⁴The city wall had twelve foundations, and on them were the twelve names of the Lamb's twelve apostles.

¹⁵The angel who spoke to me had a gold measuring rod with which to measure the city, its gates, and its wall. ¹⁶Now the city was laid out as a square. Its length was the same as its width. He measured the city with the rod, and it was fifteen hundred miles.ⁿ Its length and width and height were equal. ¹⁷He also measured the thickness of its wall. It was two hundred sixteen feetᵒ thick, as a person—or rather, an angel—measures things. ¹⁸The wall was built of jasper, and the city was pure gold, like pure glass. ¹⁹The city wall's foundations were decorated with every kind of jewel. The first foundation was jasper, the second was sapphire, the third was chalcedony, and the fourth was emerald. ²⁰The fifth was sardonyx, the sixth was carnelian, the seventh was chrysolite, and the eighth was beryl. The ninth was topaz, the tenth was chrysoprase, the eleventh was jacinth, and the twelfth was amethyst. ²¹The twelve gates were twelve pearls; each one of the gates was made from a single pearl. And the city's main street was pure gold, as transparent as glass.

²²I didn't see a temple in the city, because its temple is the Lord God Almighty and the Lamb. ²³The city doesn't need the sun or the moon to shine on it, because God's glory is its light, and its lamp is the Lamb.

Bet you can
read this in 6 minutes. Ready, set, go!

ⁿ*Or twelve thousand stades* ᵒ*Or one hundred forty-four pechon (cubits)*

[24] The nations will walk by its light, and the kings of the earth will bring their glory into it. [25] Its gates will never be shut by day, and there will be no night there. [26] They will bring the glory and honor of the nations into it. [27] Nothing unclean will ever enter it, nor anyone who does what is vile and deceitful, but only those who are registered in the Lamb's scroll of life.

22 Then the angel showed me the river of life-giving water,[p] shining like crystal, flowing from the throne of God and the Lamb [2] through the middle of the city's main street. On each side of the river is the tree of life, which produces twelve crops of fruit, bearing its fruit each month. The tree's leaves are for the healing of the nations. [3] There will no longer be any curse. The throne of God and the Lamb will be in it, and his servants will worship him. [4] They will see his face, and his name will be on their foreheads. [5] Night will be no more. They won't need the light of a lamp or the light of the sun, for the Lord God will shine on them, and they will rule forever and always.

LIGHTHOUSE

HEAVEN

It Starts and Ends with a Garden
Revelation 22:1-5

When God created the world, God planted a perfect garden where people could live with God in peace and beauty. Among all the trees in the garden, God planted the tree of life. Its fruit could give the first humans, Adam and Eve, eternal life if they ate it. But Adam and Eve chose to eat fruit from the tree of the knowledge of good and evil (Gen 3). Human beings lost the garden—only to find it again at the end of time. In John's vision, this garden sits in the middle of a perfect city. A stream flows from God's throne, and a tree rests along either side of the cool, clear water. Anyone can come and eat the fruit of this life-giving tree anytime they want. God returned the lost garden through God's Son Jesus (John 3:16)! It's here in a new world, where God's story doesn't end but continues on forever. ◊

Jesus is coming soon

[6] Then he said to me, "These words are trustworthy and true. The Lord, the God of the spirits of the prophets, sent his angel to show his servants what must soon take place.

[7] "Look! I'm coming soon. Favored is the one who keeps the words of the prophecy contained in this scroll."

[8] I, John, am the one who heard and saw these things. When I heard and saw them, I fell down to worship at the feet of the angel who had shown them to me. [9] But he said to me, "Don't do that! I'm a servant just like you and your brothers and sisters, the prophets, and those who keep the words of this scroll. Worship God!" [10] Then he said to me, "Don't seal up the words of the prophecy contained in this scroll, because the time is near. [11] Let those who do wrong keep doing what is wrong. Let the filthy still be filthy. Let those who are righteous keep doing what is right. Let those who are holy still be holy.

[12] "Look! I'm coming soon. My reward is with me, to repay all people as their actions deserve. [13] I am the alpha and the omega, the first and the last, the beginning and the end. [14] Favored are those who wash their robes so that they may have the right of access to the tree of life and may enter the city by the gates. [15] Outside are the dogs, the drug users and spell-casters, those who commit sexual immorality, the murderers, the idolaters, and all who love and practice deception.

[16] "I, Jesus, have sent my angel to bear witness to all of you about these things for the churches. I'm the root and descendant of David, the bright morning star. [17] The Spirit and the bride say, 'Come!' Let the one who hears say, 'Come!' And let the one who is thirsty come! Let the one who wishes receive life-giving water[q] as a gift."

[18] Now I bear witness to everyone who hears the words of the prophecy contained in this scroll: If anyone adds to them, God will add to that person the plagues that are written in this scroll. [19] If anyone takes away from the words of this scroll of prophecy, God will take away that person's share in the tree of life and the holy city, which are described in this scroll.

[20] The one who bears witness to these things says, "Yes, I'm coming soon." Amen. Come, Lord Jesus!

[21] The grace of the Lord Jesus be with all.

P Or *the water of life* q Or *the water of life*

CEB

DEEP BLUE

EXPLORATION TOOLS

Discovery CENTRAL DICTIONARY

A

Abba—An Aramaic word meaning *the father*, *my father*, or *our father*. Jesus used this word as a familiar name for God, the Father.

adultery—Intimate and sinful physical relations between a married man and a woman who is not his wife, or between a married woman and a man who is not her husband.

Adversary—A name in the Old Testament for a prosecutor in the heavenly council of divine beings. Later called *Satan*, an evil being, in the New Testament.

alabaster—A soft stone, light and creamy in color and often having a striped appearance. In Bible times, people used alabaster for vases and flasks or for boxes to hold perfume and precious ointments.

allotment—In early Old Testament times, the portion of land given to each of the tribes occupying Canaan.

Almighty—Having all power. A name used to describe God's greatness, power, and might.

Alpha and Omega—The first and last letters of the Greek alphabet. In the New Testament, the letters are used together as symbols for God and Jesus Christ.

altar—A stone or pile of stones on which sacrifices were offered to God.

ambush—Waiting in a hiding place in order to attack an enemy by surprise.

Amen—A Hebrew word meaning *we agree*. This word is often used at the end of songs or prayers.

angel—In the New Testament, a spiritual being or messenger from God sometimes said to appear in human form. Called a *messenger* in the Old Testament.

anoint—To pour oil on the head or body of a person or on an object. In biblical times, anointing was often part of a religious ceremony showing that a person had been set apart for the service of the Lord.

antichrist—An enemy of Christ.

apostle—A title meaning *messenger* or *someone who is sent*. The title given to the twelve disciples sent out by Jesus. Also refers to Paul and to other leaders in the early church. See also ***disciple***.

Arabah—See ***desert slopes***.

Aramaic—A language closely related to

Hebrew. During the time of Jesus, Aramaic was the everyday language of the Jewish people.

arid southern plain—Or *Negeb*, a dry desert region in the southern region of Israel.

ark of Noah—A floating vessel like a very large houseboat bigger than a football field in which Noah, his family, and at least one pair each of all living creatures took refuge during the flood that covered the earth.

armor—Protective equipment given to soldiers to protect them during battle. The phrase *armor of God* is a way of speaking of the protection God gives people to stand against evil.

ascend—To go up. Forty days after Jesus' resurrection, he ascended into heaven.

B

Baal—The name of the chief god of the Canaanites.

Babylon—An ancient city of Mesopotamia that was the capital city of the great Babylonian Empire under King Nebuchadnezzar. When Nebuchadnezzar captured Judah, the Hebrew people were taken as captives to Babylon.

balances—A type of scale made by hanging one pan from each end of a beam balanced on a cord or from a shaft. To weigh metal or grain, blocks or stones of a given size were put in one pan, and the material to be weighed was put in the other. Material or weights were added until the pans hung evenly.

banner—A sign or symbol held high on a pole as the emblem of a tribe. Soldiers used banners like flags to rally the troops. They sounded trumpets when the banners were raised.

banquet—A large meal with many rich foods.

baptism—A ceremonial act using water to symbolize washing or making pure in the sight of God.

barley—An important grain that was cheaper and ripened earlier than wheat. Barley

was used as food for animals and humans and was especially important to the poor.

barren—Not able to have children; not able to grow crops.

basin—A bowl-like container of any size.

battering ram—A large pole with a heavy head supported in a framework set on wheels so it could be rammed against the gates and walls of a city to break them down. See also *siege*.

Bethlehem—A town in Judah about six miles north of Jerusalem. It is best known as the birthplace of Jesus.

birthright—The special rights and privileges of the oldest son. In Old Testament times, the oldest son inherited more of his father's wealth than did his younger brothers and became head of the family after his father's death. See also **heritage** and **inheritance**.

blessed—See **happy**.

blind—Without sight. Not able to see.

body—In the Old Testament, *body* refers to the whole physical makeup of a person. In the New Testament, the word has added meanings. Jesus used bread as a symbol of his body. The church is often called *the body of Christ*.

bread—An important food made from wheat or barley flour, mixed with water, kneaded, and baked.

bread of the presence—Twelve loaves of bread made of fine flour, arranged in two stacks on a table in the temple or sanctuary as an offering to God.

breastplate—A piece of armor made of solid metal, attached to, or worn over a tunic to protect the chest, shoulders, and back of a soldier.

C

calf, gold—In the Old Testament, an image of a bull made of wood and covered with gold.

Canaan—The land God promised to the people of Israel. Canaan is also called the *promised land*.

captivity—Being taken and kept imprisoned

or enslaved by force, especially being taken from one's own country and made to live in another land. During the Babylonian captivity, the people of Judah were conquered by Nebuchadnezzar and carried off to Babylon.

caravan—A group of people, especially merchants with pack animals, traveling together, often through dangerous areas.

carpenter—A person who repairs or makes things out of wood.

census—A count of all people in a land.

centurion—The commanding officer of one hundred foot soldiers, part of a division in the Roman army.

chaff—The useless dry husks of grain that were blown away from the good seed in the process of winnowing. See also **winnow**.

chariot—A two-wheeled, horse-drawn vehicle used in war and for travel, especially by kings and officials.

chest containing the covenant—A wooden box covered with gold that held the stone tablets containing the Ten Commandments. The Israelites carried the chest with them during their wanderings in the wilderness, and they later placed the chest in the temple.

chest piece—A decorated piece of material attached by golden rings to the priestly vest (*ephod*), a garment worn by the high priest in the sanctuary.

children, God's—God's spiritual family.

change your heart and mind—Turning away from sin and back to God. (Older Bible versions use the term *repent*.)

Christ—Greek word meaning *the anointed one* or *the Messiah*. A title given to the king expected by the Jews. It became a name or surname for Jesus.

Christian—A person who follows Jesus.

church—A fellowship of believers in Jesus Christ gathered together for the purpose of worship, prayer, instruction, and fellowship. *Church* also refers to the whole group of believers in Jesus Christ from every land and continent.

circumcision—The act of cutting off the foreskin of a baby boy. This act dedicated

the child and was a sign of the covenant between God and the Israelites.

cistern—A lined pit dug in the earth for the storage of water.

city—In Old Testament times, a walled town.

cloak—An outer garment worn over a coat.

coat—A long tunic-like shirt with long sleeves worn as an undergarment.

colt—A young horse or donkey.

commandment—A law or order from someone in authority.

communion—The act of sharing. It is important in the covenant relationship between God and humanity. This relationship is remembered in the sacrament of the *Lord's Supper*, which is also called *Communion*. See also **covenant**.

confession—An act in the worship of God in which a person humbly admits sins and asks for God's forgiveness.

congregation—A gathering or assembly. A term used for all the Israelites living in the wilderness. The term is also used for the assembly of people before God for worship or judgment.

cornerstone—A stone at the corner of a building that holds two walls together. New Testament writers referred to Jesus as the cornerstone of the Christian life.

council—An assembly made up of people with authority.

covenant—An agreement or solemn promise binding people together in a firm relationship. *Covenant* was the word used for the special relationship between God and Israel. God was to be their God, and they were to be God's people. The early Christians in the New Testament thought of their relationships to each other and to Jesus as a covenant binding them together.

cross—A large beam set in the ground as a way to kill criminals. Often, a crossbar was attached to the beam, which by the fourth century after Christ was pictured as a "T." Jesus was put to death on a cross, and this event is described in all four Gospels.

crown—A headdress often made of rich

material and decorated with designs or jewels. There were also simple metal headbands that served as crowns.

crown of thorns—A circle of thorny briers made by Roman soldiers and pushed down on Jesus' head as part of their torture and mockery of him. They insulted Jesus with this make-believe crown.

crucifixion—Nailing or tying a person to a cross or sometimes to a tree as a means of death.

D

Day, Judgment—See *Day of the Lord*.

David's City—See *Jerusalem*.

Day of the Lord—The day when God will be fully revealed and will judge all the people. This day is also called *Judgment Day, day of God*, and *the day*.

Dead Sea—A lake fed by the Jordan River. This lake is over 1,200 feet below sea level and has the highest percentage of salt in any water in the world.

debt—Something owed by one person to another.

decree—Something a king would declare or proclaim. A decree was usually written down and then read aloud to the people to let them know what they were supposed to do.

dedicate—To set apart an offering, a building, or a person for some sacred purpose.

defile—To make people, foods, places, or objects unclean in a religious sense. Priests in the Old Testament gave instructions on how to clean whatever had been defiled. Jesus used the word *defile* in a deeper sense to mean that people's words, thoughts, and actions might be unclean and might defile them in the sight of God.

demon—In the Old Testament, a nameless god or spirit that might be friendly or unfriendly. In the New Testament, *demon* refers only to evil spirits who are the cause of all kinds of misfortunes.

denarion—An ancient Roman silver coin, about the size of a dime. A person would

usually receive one denarius for one day of work.

desert slopes—Or *Arabah*, the region that slopes down to the Dead Sea.

devil—A term used when speaking of evil as if it were a person. One who leads people to sin and disturbs their relationship with God. In the New Testament, it often refers to Satan. See also **Adversary** and **Satan**.

devoted—Things forbidden for common use. Set apart for God.

devout—Being free from wrong or sin. Devoted to God.

disciple—A student or learner. One who accepts and follows a certain teaching or teacher. In the Bible, the term most often means those who follow Jesus. See also **apostle**.

discipline—In the Bible this word refers to training and instruction. It also means correction and punishment.

door, doorkeeper—An entrance and one who watches or guards it.

dwelling—A portable sanctuary for the worship of God, carried by the Israelites during their wilderness journey from Egypt to Canaan. The *chest containing the covenant* was kept in it, and for the Israelites it was a symbol of the presence of God. The dwelling was also called the *meeting tent* (or *tabernacle* in older Bible versions). See also **chest containing the covenant**, **Canaan**, **Egypt**, **Exile**, and **Israel**.

E

earth—In Bible times, dry land.

early produce—The sacrificial offering of giving the first and best from the yearly crop of vegetables, grain, and animals to God.

Eden—The name given for the garden where Adam and Eve lived.

edict—See *decree*.

Egypt—A land on the southern coast of the Mediterranean Sea in northeast Africa. Egyptians had many contacts with the Israelites, sometimes friendly and sometimes not. It was from Egypt that Moses led the Israelites into the land of Canaan.

elder—The leader of a family, tribe, synagogue, or community.

elevated fortress—A fortified building or stronghold within a city for the purpose of defense.

epistle—A letter, especially the letters included the New Testament. See also **letter**.

Equipment, temple—The utensils and containers used in the temple for offerings and sacrifices.

eternal life—Life with God that isn't destroyed by death. Eternal life can begin here and now.

evangelist—A person who announces good news. A title of early Christian missionaries and preachers of the gospel. Also indicates the authors of the New Testament gospels.

evil—Sinful. Wicked. Something that causes harm, including suffering.

exile, the—The time in biblical history when the Babylonians conquered the city of Jerusalem and carried many of the Jews away to live in Babylon.

exodus, the—A going out. Refers to the people *going out* from Egypt under the leadership of Moses. The deliverance of the people from slavery and the journey to the land of Canaan.

F

faith—Trusting in God. Faith is the confident response people make to God's love and care.

family—A group of people related to each other by kinship or marriage.

famine—A time when there is not enough food.

fast, fasting—To go without food and water for a period of time for a religious reason.

fear—Panic, worry, or dread. *Fear of God* and *fear of the Lord* mean having awe, respect, love, trust, and faith.

fellowship—Friendship. Communion. See also **communion**.

festival—A religious celebration to remember an event from the past and/or to thank and honor God. Jewish festivals include the Festival of Booths, Hanukkah, Festival of Pentecost, Passover, and Festival of Unleavened Bread.

fig—A sweet fruit that grows on trees. An important food in Bible times.

footstool—The footrest for a king's throne or steps leading to the throne.

forgiveness—The pardoning of an offender, the giving up of a claim to a debt, or the release from an obligation. Forgiveness is God's gracious taking away of the barriers that separate people from God.

fortress—A place for defense against military attacks. See also **refuge**.

foundation—The base on which a structure is built.

fountain—A spring of water flowing from an opening in a hillside or valley. An important source of water in Bible times.

fragrant—Having a sweet or pleasant odor. See also **odor**.

frankincense—A fragrant gum taken from tree bark that was an important ingredient in incense. One of the gifts the magi brought to baby Jesus in the manger. See also **incense** and **magi**.

G

Galilee—A small region east of the Mediterranean Sea. Almost all of Jesus' life took place within the borders of this tiny region.

Galilee, Sea of—A lake that empties into the Jordan River. Many people and places associated with Jesus came from this area.

gate—An opening in the wall of a city. There were usually an outer gate and an inner gate built at angles to the wall, with a lookout tower. Near the gate was the center of interest in the town, and most business was carried on there. Just inside the gate was the busy marketplace.

genealogy—A list of names that tells the family history of a person. A family tree. A genealogy can also show the relationships of families, clans, tribes, or nations.

Gentile—In the New Testament, a word for a person who was not a Jew. In the plural it meant *nations* in general. See also **Jew**.

gleaning—The practice of picking up what had been left behind in the fields after harvesting. The law said that the poor must be allowed to glean.

glory—Honor and praise. The word describes the presence of God. People glorify or magnify God by praising and honoring God.

God (names of)—Other ways of referring to God are: Lord, rock, Father, savior, king, judge, shepherd, creator, and almighty as well as descriptive expressions like *the living God*, *the everlasting God*, *the Alpha and Omega* (first and the last).

God (nature of)—To the Israelites, God is the living God who was the Lord, the ruler of their lives. The Old Testament reports the historical events of the Israelites as the acts of God. The Israelites live out their special history as the people with whom God made a covenant. In the New Testament, God is revealed in Jesus Christ, and humanity's relationship with God is made richer because it could be experienced in a very personal way. It can be compared to a relationship with an earthly parent or friend.

goldsmith—A person who works with and makes things out of gold.

gospel—The good news about Jesus Christ: that his birth, life, death, and resurrection have accomplished salvation. *Gospel* is also the name given to each of the first four books of the New Testament.

governor—A ruler appointed by a king to govern a specific territory or province.

grace—God's faithful love for humanity that cannot be earned but is offered as a free gift.

H

Happy—Favored with spiritual happiness. (Older Bible versions use the term *blessed*.) When *blessed* is applied to God, it is an exclamation of worship.

harass—To cause someone to suffer because of his or her beliefs, especially religious beliefs.

harp—A stringed musical instrument small enough to be carried.

harvest—The gathering of ripe crops.

heaven—The place where God lives.

Hebrew—The ancient language of the Jewish people. Most of the Old Testament books were written in Hebrew. *Hebrew* also refers to the people descended from Abraham and Sarah.

hell—The New Testament name for the place under the world for the punishment of the dead.

heritage—Possessions passed down from one generation to another. See also **birthright** and **inheritance**.

high priest—Chief of the priests in the temple at Jerusalem. He acted as the representative of the people before God.

highway—A road built up higher than the land on either side.

holiness—More than any other word, *holiness* suggests the nature of God. Includes a sense of tremendous and mysterious energy that is above and beyond humanity.

holy—Sacred. Set apart for God. See also **sacred**.

holy one—In the Old Testament, a name for God that emphasizes that God is the source of holiness in all other things. In the New Testament, *holy one* refers to the Messiah. See also **holy** and **Messiah**.

Holy Spirit—The mysterious power of God. Sometimes called the *Spirit* or the *Spirit of the Lord*.

hosanna—A term meaning *save us, we ask you*. At Jesus' triumphal entry into Jerusalem, the people waved palm branches and sang, "Hosanna!"

hospitality—Welcoming strangers or guests

as if they were family members, giving them food, shelter, protection, and much more.

heavenly forces, Lord of —A divine name frequently used in the Bible that puts the Lord in charge of the heavenly beings who perform God's command and carry out God's purpose for the world.

human one — In the Old Testament, a reference to a human being. In the New Testament, Human One is a title for Jesus.

hymn—A song of praise.

hypocrite—A Greek word that means *playing or acting out a part*. A person who pretends to be something he or she is not.

I

idol, idolatry—An image of a god made of wood, stone, or metal. It may also be any other symbol of the supernatural that is an object of worship. Idolatry is worshipping an idol.

immigrant—A person who moves from one country or land to live in another place among strangers. In the Old Testament the Israelites are usually instructed to treat immigrants the same as their family and friends.

incense—A mixture of gums and spices made into a powder and burned so that the smell of the smoke would rise in the air as an offering to God or to *the gods*.

inheritance—A possession handed down from the past. The word refers to possessions such as land or wealth. In the New Testament *inheritance* more often refers to spiritual gifts from God, such as eternal life or the kingdom of God. See also **birthright** and **heritage**.

iniquity—Another word for *sin*. Any action that separates people from God or destroys a person's relationship with another person.

Instruction, the—In the Old Testament, the behaviors, rules, and commandments for living together in community. The Old Testament Instruction was based on a covenant, or agreement, between God and the Israelites. The first five books of the Old Testament contain the Instruction, including the Ten Commandments.

iron—A type of very strong metal. Iron is used in the Bible as a symbol for hardness, strength, and harshness.

Israel, Israelites—A name given to Jacob after his vision of God. The descendants of Jacob are called *Israelites*. Israel was the name of the kingdom under Saul, David, and Solomon. When the kingdom split into two parts, the northern part continued to be called Israel. It came to an end in 722 BCE. The name Israel is used not only for the land but also for the people as a whole in their exodus from Egypt, their desert wanderings, and their entrance into Canaan. See also **Judah**.

ivory—A white bone-like substance that makes up the tusks of elephants and walruses. In Bible times, people carved ivory to make decorations for thrones and houses. Ivory was a sign of great wealth.

J

jealousy—Strong hatred and suspicion that grows out of envy and greed.

Jerusalem—The capital city under King David, who brought the chest of the covenant to the city and made it the religious center of the Israelites. David's son Solomon built the temple there, and Jerusalem became a holy city. When the kingdom was divided, Jerusalem was the capital of the southern kingdom, Judah. The city was finally conquered and burned by Nebuchadnezzar, and its important leaders were taken to Babylon. The city of Jerusalem is also called Salem, Zion, David's City, and Jebus.

Jesus Christ—The central person in the New Testament. Jesus was the personal name of the person whose title is *the Christ*, from which the Christian religion gets its name. In Hebrew Jesus is a form of the name Joshua and means *God saves*. See also **Christ**.

Jew—A word that refers to members of the

southern kingdom of Judah who were in Babylon during the time of exile. Later, it was used to refer to people who were not Gentiles and who lived in the province of Judah. Any person who worships God and follows Judaism. See also **Gentile**.

Jewish leaders—In John's gospel some of the officials who put Jesus on trial.

Jubilee year—The year of liberty. Every fiftieth year was set by law as the time when all slaves were to be released and all property was to be returned to its original owners.

Judah—The fourth son of Jacob and leader of the tribe descended from him that took his name. The tribes and territory of Judah became the southern kingdom of Judah after the death of King Solomon. The kingdom of Judah came to an end in 586 BCE.

Judge—A title for God, who is the judge of all the earth, and for Jesus, who set a new standard of judgment.

Judaism—The religious practices, or way of life, for the Jewish community.

justice—Fairness, righteousness. See also **righteousness**.

K

king—A male ruler who has power over a nation.

kingdom of heaven (Matthew), God's kingdom—A kingdom that is not only in the world that we know, but includes all places and all times. A kingdom designed to carry out the purposes of God.

knead—To pound or press dough with the hands until it forms a well-mixed mass.

L

lamb—A young sheep. In Old Testament times, the lamb was used for food and for sacrifices in the temple. In the New Testament, Jesus is called the *lamb of God*.

lamentation—An expression of sorrow or grief. See also **mourn**.

lamp—A pottery saucer filled with olive oil that had a wick of twisted threads resting on the edge or held in a spout.

lampstand—A device used for raising a lamp high so that its light will cover a large area.

landmark—A mark showing the boundaries of an area of land. In Bible times, stones were piled to mark the boundaries between the fields of two neighbors. They also marked districts and nations.

Last Supper—The final meal Jesus ate with his disciples on the night before his death.

Law—The New Testament word for *the Instruction* found in the first five books of the Old Testament. Jesus taught that the most important instruction is the law that we love each other. See **Instruction**.

legal expert—In New Testament times, one who knew and interpreted the Instruction from Moses. See **Instruction**.

leather—Animal skins prepared for use as clothes, shoes, tent coverings, bottles for water or wine, and writing materials.

leaven—Any substance, such as yeast, that was added to bread dough to make it rise. During the Passover Festival each year, Jews eat bread that has been made without leaven to remind them of the exodus from Egypt. See also **Exodus** and **Passover**.

letter—A written message sent to a person or people at a distance. Many of the books in the New Testament were written in the form of letters.

Leviathan—In the Old Testament, the name of a dragon, a symbol of disorder and evil, subdued by God at the time of creation. The name is also used to refer to any sea monster.

liberty—Freedom from bondage, slavery, or the control of another.

lily—A general term for a variety of springtime flowers that grew in Bible lands.

locust—A flying, grasshopper-like insect. Locusts travel in large groups and can destroy crops.

Lord—Lord is a title of honor and majesty for God and also for Jesus.

Lord's prayer—The title given to the prayer Jesus taught his disciples. This prayer is recorded in Matthew 6:9-13 and Luke 11:2-4.

Lord's supper—A sacrament, or sacred observance, that continues the fellowship Jesus began with his disciples at the Last Supper. Also called *Holy Communion* or *Eucharist*. This meal is a time when Christians remember Jesus Christ. See also **Communion** and **Last Supper**.

lots—Small stones or cubes used to make choices. *Casting lots* (throwing them on the ground) is similar to how we throw dice today.

love—The deep personal attachment that includes loyalty, goodwill, devotion, and responsibility. People are the object of God's love; humanity's love for God is the response people make to God's love.

lute—A stringed instrument made of gut strings on a wooden frame.

lyre—A stringed instrument similar to a harp.

M

Magi—Magicians and interpreters of the stars. Matthew's gospel reports that magi came from the East to worship the baby Jesus. These magi or *astrologers* studied the stars to learn of Jesus' birth and also how to find him.

magic, magician—In ancient times, power that was believed to be supernatural.

magnify—See **glory**.

manger—A box made of stones or hollowed out of rock, used for feeding cattle. The first bed of the baby Jesus was a manger.

manna—The bread-like substance the Israelites gathered and ate for part of their food during the long journey through the wilderness. This Hebrew word means *What is it?*

Messiah—Anointed one. The Israelites looked forward to the coming of an ideal king who they believed God would send to restore a kingdom to Israel. Some who recognized Jesus as the long-awaited king gave him the title of Messiah.

midwife—A woman skilled in helping during childbirth.

mill, millstones—Hard, rough stones used to grind grain to make flour. People would hold one stone in their hand and push it back and forth against another, crushing the grain between them. Because they were heavy and strong, millstones could also be used as weapons.

minister—As a noun it means *one who serves*. In the Old Testament, the word was used most often as a verb meaning *to serve*, especially to serve God in worship and carrying out sacrifices. In the New Testament, Jesus showed by his own life the importance of humble service.

miracle—Any event in which a person sees the supernatural power of God at work. Other words used in the Bible to mean miracle are *signs, wonders,* and *mighty acts.*

money—Something accepted as payment for goods or labor.

mortar—A building material, usually clay mixed with straw, used while damp and soft to bind bricks or stones together. Also, a bowl in which grain, herbs, spices, and dyes were crushed with a tool called a pestle.

mourning—An expression of grief or sadness.

mourning clothes, funeral clothes—Dark clothing worn as an expression of grief over death.

mustard seed—The seed from a mustard plant. This seed is known for being tiny in size.

myrrh—A sweet-smelling, gum-like substance made from certain plants and trees. An important ingredient in the sacred anointing oil and in perfumes. Myrrh mixed with wine was given to relieve pain.

mystery—A hidden or secret truth. In the New Testament, the word is a *secret plan* that refers to God's purpose, which is hidden from all, except those who see it revealed in the life and ministry of Jesus.

myth—A story told to explain an event or happening that is not understood or to explain the beginning of a custom or practice that has been forgotten.

N

nard—An expensive, fragrant ointment prepared from the roots and stems of the spikenard plant. The ointment was used to anoint the head. See also **anoint**.

nations—The whole of humanity divided into kinship groups, not into countries or states as we know them today. The nation of Israel made a covenant with God to be God's people. See also **covenant** and *Israel*.

Nazareth—The village where Jesus lived as a child and where he grew to adulthood.

nazirite—A person who made a special solemn promise to serve God. Nazirites promised not to cut their hair, drink wine, or have anything to do with dead bodies. Samson, Samuel, and John the Baptist were all nazirites.

nettle—A fast-growing wild plant with thorns that sting when touched. Nettles grow quickly in fields that are not taken care of.

nets—Mesh traps woven of twine or cord and used for catching fish, birds, and animals.

new moon—The beginning of the month. It was observed as a holy day of rejoicing, special feasting, and sacrifices.

O

odor—A scent or fragrance. During worship in Old Testament times, the sacrifices and offerings were completely burned so that nothing but smoke was left to rise in God's presence. In the New Testament, one's acts of love are spoken of as a fragrant offering to God in the name of Christ.

offering—A gift given to God as an act of worship.

officer—In Bible times, a servant or minister of the king, the army, or the temple.

oil—A liquid substance for cooking and also used during anointing. People often made

oil by pressing olives, the fruit of the olive tree. See also **anoint** and **olive tree**.

olive tree—An evergreen tree with fruit good for eating and rich in oil. The olive branch is a symbol of peace and well-being.

oracle—A speech or pronouncement given by an inspired prophet, king, or priest as a message from God. The prophets often used the phrases *The Lord proclaims* or *This is what the Lord says*.

ordinance—An instruction or rule for governing social and religious customs. See also **commandment**.

oven—In biblical times, an outdoor baking device. It was a large round jar of burned clay with the fire built on pebbles at the bottom. Flat cakes of dough were stuck against the hot inner wall or laid on the pebbles after the fire was down. The fuel was usually dried grass or bushes.

P

Palestine—According to the Roman Empire, the name for the land occupied by the twelve tribes of Israel during Old Testament times. The common Hebrew name for the land was Canaan. See also **Canaan**.

palm—A tall, thin tree with a group of branches at the top. People ate its fruit, called dates, and they wove mats from its leaves. They often used the palm tree as a symbol for righteousness.

parable—A short story that teaches an important lesson. Jesus used parables to teach about God and God's kingdom in ways that his listeners could understand.

paradise—The New Testament name for the place of the righteous after death.

parchment—A writing material made from the skins of sheep or goats. Parchment replaced papyrus because it could last longer.

passion, the—A term used for the suffering and death of Jesus. It refers to the last days of Jesus' life and includes such events as the Last Supper, the agony in

Gethsemane, the arrest, trial, crucifixion, death, and burial.

Passover, the—The first of three great religious festivals in the Jewish year. The Passover and Festival of Unleavened Bread were celebrated in the spring to mark the deliverance of the Israelites from Egyptian slavery. See also **festival** and **unleavened**.

Pentecost—The Greek term for the Jewish Festival of Weeks held fifty days after Passover. It marked the beginning of the offering of early produce from the harvest. It was on the Pentecost day that the Holy Spirit came upon Jesus' disciples gathered in Jerusalem after he ascended. See also **ascension**, **festival**, and **Passover**.

people, God's—One of the many Old Testament expressions that refer to the special covenant relationship between God and the Israelite people. The New Testament meaning identifies *God's people* with the church grounded upon faith in Jesus Christ. See also **covenant** and **Israel**.

perfume—Sweet-smelling substances used in cosmetics, in preparing the dead for burial, in scenting furniture and clothing, and in incense for worship.

Pharaoh—A title given to the king of Egypt.

Pharisees—Jewish religious leaders committed to following the Instruction set down in the *Torah*—the first five books of the Old Testament.

pillar—Rough, uncut stone with a round top set up as a monument to help people remember an important event or as an object of worship. A pillar is also a support column for a roof.

pit—An unmeasured, deep, bottomless hole.

plague—A destructive event, such as a disease, that spreads quickly, causes great suffering, and kills many people.

plow, plowshare—A tool used for breaking up the ground.

potter—A person who makes things out of clay. A potter often uses a wheel to shape clay into bowls, jars, and plates.

prayer—Any attempt to communicate with God. Prayer may be spoken or silent. It may include praise, confession, thanksgiving, repentance, or meditation on behalf of oneself or another person.

priest—A person who took care of the temple, taught the Instruction, and took part in the sacrifices. See also **high priest**, **temple**, and **Instruction**.

priestly vest—The upper garment of plain linen worn by a priest. The high priest wore a more elaborate vest (*ephod*) embroidered in colors of gold, blue, crimson, and purple.

prince—A ruler, such as a king.

prophecy—A message from God (pronounced *prof-uh-see*).

prophesy—To give a message from God (pronounced *prof-uh-sigh*).

prophet—A spokesperson for God. One who was inspired to speak God's message of purpose and judgment to the people. See also **prophecy** and **prophesy**.

province—A division of an empire ruled by an appointed official.

pruning tool—A blade attached to a handle, used for removing surplus twigs and trimming vines.

psalms—Poems, prayers, and hymns for use in public and private worship. Psalms tell of joy and sorrow, sin and suffering, evil and righteousness.

purify—To make clean.

Purim—A two-day Jewish festival, selected by throwing dice (*pur*) for celebrating the deliverance of the Jews in Persia from Haman's plot to kill them. The story is told in the book of Esther.

Q

quail—A reddish-brown bird used in Bible times for food. The Israelites ate quail on their journey from Egypt to Canaan.

quiver—A container for carrying arrows.

R

Rabbi, Rabboni—Hebrew word meaning *master*. A respectful title for a teacher.

rampart—The outer defense around a city that consists of a broad, sloping embankment usually made of earth.

raven—A large, crow-like bird that travels in flocks and scavenges for food.

reap—To harvest grain. See also **sow**.

reconcile, reconciliation—The achievement of a state of harmony, or the overcoming of conflict or separation. People are separated from God due to their sin, and reconciliation (called *atonement* in other Bible versions) brings agreement and restoration between people and God.

Reconciliation, Day of—A Jewish holy day of fasting and repentance. Called *Yom Kippur* in Hebrew.

redeem, redeemer, redemption—*Redeem* means to reclaim, to get back, or to buy back. *A redeemer* is the person who performs these acts. *Redemption* is the act of liberating or getting back.

reed—The flowering stem of several tall grasses that grow in marshy places. Reeds are sometimes called *rushes*. People in Bible times used reeds to make many things, including measuring rods, writing pens, baskets, and mats.

refine, refining—To strain or filter out impurities from metals by melting them in large containers in a hot furnace. The act of purifying. *Refine* is used as a figure of speech to describe the way God cleanses or purifies God's people. See also **purify**.

refuge—A place of escape, a stronghold. The word is used to describe God's protection. See also **stronghold**.

renewal—The act of reforming completely, being made new spiritually.

resurrection—Coming back to life after being dead. Resurrection is the central truth of the Christian gospel. It is the reality that Jesus was alive after he died on a cross. This was the event the disciples preached to the world to show that Jesus was the Christ, God's son.

revelation—Making known the nature and will of God. In the Bible, God is represented as becoming known by God's actions in history and especially in Jesus Christ. The Bible is a record of this revelation and also one of the ways in which God becomes known to humans.

righteous, righteousness—Being free from sin and doing what is right. Having a right relationship with God.

rod—A staff. A stick cut from a branch of a tree. Shepherds and travelers who traveled on foot used staffs. Rods were also used as measuring sticks and as poles for carrying things.

Rome—The capital city of the Roman Empire, the most powerful empire in New Testament times.

S

sabbath—From a word meaning *to rest* or *to be at an end*. The Ten Commandments provided that the last day of the seven-day week be a day set aside to rest and worship God.

sacrifice—Something presented as a gift or offering to God. In the Old Testament, a sacrifice involved the killing, burning, and sometimes eating of an animal at the altar. A person could make an offering of grain, flour, fruit, or vegetables. Such items were presented with symbolic gestures such as waving, lifting, or burning. See also **offering**.

sacred—Holy. Set apart for God. See also **holy**.

Sadducees—Jewish religious leaders who didn't believe in the resurrection of the dead.

saint—A person who is holy or set apart for God's use. In the New Testament, the word is used for members of the Christian church. *Saint* was particularly associated with the love Christians showed to one another.

salvation—The saving, redeeming, or delivering of something. *Salvation* is a major theme in the Bible. See also **savior**.

sanctuary—The holy place set apart for the worship of God by the people.

Sanhedrin—The supreme Jewish council in Jerusalem following the Exile. It consisted of seventy-one members chosen from the priests, scribes, Sadducees, and Pharisees. The Sanhedrin made laws for the Jews and judged those who broke the laws. See also **Exile**, **Pharisees**, **priest**, **Sadducees**, and **legal expert**.

sandals—Flat soles of leather or wood tied to the feet with strips of leather. Sandals were the usual shoes of Bible times.

Satan—See **Adversary**.

savior—A person who saves. *Savior* is a name for Jesus. See also **salvation**.

scepter—A rod or staff carried by a king or queen as a sign of authority and power. The word is also used as a figure of speech to mean *rule* or *ruler*.

scripture—In the New Testament, *scripture* refers to the sacred writings of the Jews, the Hebrew Bible or Old Testament. The present-day Christian Bible, which contains the Old Testament and the New Testament, is often called *the Scriptures*. *Scripture* is sometimes used to refer to a verse or passage from the Bible.

scroll—A roll of papyrus paper or parchment made by fastening the sheets together and rolling them around a rod. Writing was done in columns, and the scroll was rolled from right to left as it was read. Many years after the New Testament was completed, the Christian Bible was bound into books with pages.

seal—Bone, metal, stone, or precious gems that had been carved with a design. This design was pressed into clay or wax to serve as a person's signature. Seals were used to close letters or official documents.

seer—One who sees. In the Old Testament, a *seer* was usually a person who had visions and could predict the future. *Prophets* were sometimes called seers in everyday language.

selah—A word of uncertain meaning. Probably a musical direction to choirs or musicians.

servant, the Lord's—A person who serves God like a devoted slave or servant works for a master. Israel, the nation, was often called *the Lord's servant*. The Isaiah scroll tells of a *suffering servant* whose labor costs him pain and humiliation. The servant willingly accepts the suffering and through it accomplishes salvation. Christians have recognized in this description the likeness of Jesus Christ.

sheath—The case or covering for a sword or bow.

shepherd—One who takes care of sheep. The shepherd's care of sheep is often used as a metaphor to show God's love, mercy, and compassion for God's people.

shrine—A religious place of sacrifice, worship, and festival.

sickle—A tool for reaping grain. See also **reap**.

siege—A military blockade in which attackers tried to cut off a city's water and food supply and weaken the city walls by tunneling under them or smashing them with battering rams. A method of warfare used to capture cities or land. See also **battering ram**.

signs and wonders—Refers to the acts of God throughout history. In the Old Testament, the phrase is mostly connected to the events surrounding the exodus from Egypt. In the New Testament, the phrase refers to the miracles of Jesus Christ and the works of the apostles, which revealed God's will and purpose. See also **apostle**, **Exodus**, and **miracle**.

sin—Any action that separates people from God or destroys relationships between people. Sin is also called an *iniquity* or *transgression*.

skin disease—In Bible times, people who had skin disease were thought to be unclean and had to live apart from others. In some Bible versions this is called *leprosy*, but that disease was not known in Bible times.

slavery—The ownership of one person by another. In Bible times, slavery was a common practice.

sling—A weapon for hurling small stones or clay pellets. A sling was made of two pieces of leather or cloth joined to a pouch-shaped piece of leather that held a stone. One end was tied to the wrist and the other end was held with the hand. The stone was swung over the head in a circle and then let go.

slothful—Lazy.

snare—A device used to catch birds and animals.

solemn promise—A commitment made to God. (A *vow* in older Bible versions.)

solemn pledge—A promise made and often accompanied by formal words and actions. People often called upon God as a witness to a solemn pledge. Breaking a solemn pledge was a serious matter. (An *oath* in older Bible versions.)

Son, God's—In the Old Testament, *God's son* is a phrase used to refer to divine beings, messengers, or godlike persons. Israel was called God's son because God had chosen the nation to be God's people. In the New Testament, the term refers to Jesus as God's special or unique Son. The plural phrase *children of God* refers to followers of Jesus.

Son of Man—See **Human One**.

sorcery—The use of power that was supposedly gained through the use of charms, magic, or divination. The Israelites were not supposed to practice sorcery.

sow—To plant seeds. See also **reap**.

sparrow—A perching, seed-eating bird that did not have much value in Bible times.

spice—The sweet-smelling leaves, roots, and gums of certain vegetables and herbs that were used in cosmetics, oil, incense, perfume, and preparing a body for burial. In Bible times spices were not generally used for cooking as they are today.

spirit—A term applied to God, gods, bodiless beings, and to the divine element in humans. It was sometimes used to indicate God's power in humans. The phrase *God's spirit* refers to God's activity and God's power in the world.

staff—A long pole used by shepherds and travelers for climbing and defense. See **rod**.

stone—To kill someone by throwing rocks.

supervisor—One who directs a work gang, a household, or a group performing some special task.

synagogue—A place of assembly for worship used by Jewish communities.

T

tablet—A writing surface made from stone, wood, metal, wax, or clay.

tanner, tanning—A person who prepares leather from the skins of animals. *Tanning* is the process of conditioning and softening skins.

tax—Payment that people make to support the government. The tax in Bible times was paid in money, treasure, farm products, or hours of labor.

tax collector—An official who collects and keeps accounts of taxes.

teacher—Anyone who instructs.

temple—The great sacred building in Jerusalem where the Jewish people gathered to worship God. It was also called *the house of the Lord* or *the house of God*.

Ten Commandments—Instructions that summarize the covenant between God and God's people making clear the people's duty to God and to others. The Ten Commandments are found in Exodus 20:1-17.

meeting tent—Another name for God's dwelling. See **dwelling**.

testimony—Evidence given by a witness to the action and demands of God.

thistles, thorns—Wild plants with sharp spines on their stems and leaves.

threshing, threshing floor—The process of separating the kernels of grain from the straw. The stalks of grain were beaten with a stick or trampled by oxen on the threshing floor.

throne—The ceremonial chair or seat of someone in authority.

Thummim—See **Urim**.

tenth-part gift—In Bible times people acknowledged God's ownership of the land by giving one-tenth of the produce to God. (Older Bible versions call this a *tithe*.) The prophets and Jesus criticized people who gave only material possessions but didn't practice justice or show love to others.

tomb—A cave cut into the rock of a hillside and used as a burial place for the dead.

tongues, gift of—Also referred to as *speaking in tongues*. An experience in which a person praying through the Holy Spirit utters words or sounds in a language that wasn't previously learned.

tower—A high, narrow structure generally higher than things around it. Built of brick or stone, towers served as places of refuge or defense against military attack.

transgression—See **sin**.

trap—A device used to catch birds and animals.

tribe—A group of clans or families held together by bonds of blood and kinship. The people of Israel consisted of twelve tribes who were the descendants of Jacob. The names of the tribes were also given to the land the people lived on.

tribute—Another word for tax. A payment one nation made to another for protection or after defeat.

trumpet—A musical instrument.

tunic—A kind of coat. A long, shirt-like undergarment draped over one shoulder.

turban—A head covering. A cloth wrapped around the head.

turtledove—A small type of pigeon used in sacrificial offerings.

U

uncircumcised—All people who did not keep the law of circumcision. In the Old Testament, it usually referred to the Philistines. In the New Testament, it referred to all Gentiles. See also **circumcision**.

unclean—Not pure according to religious instructions. Old Testament instructions declared that certain animals, foods, places, objects, and persons were unclean. To come in contact with any of these things made a person unclean. To be clean, one had to go through a cleansing ritual.

unleavened bread—Bread or cakes baked without yeast. See also **leaven**.

upper room—A room in the upper floor of a house or a room on the roof, usually for guests. In the New Testament, an upper room was the place chosen by Jesus for his last meal with his disciples.

Urim and Thummim—Objects used to determine the will of God. These objects may have been stones or pieces of metal. The priests would shake them in a container and throw them on the ground like dice. How the Urim and the Thummim landed would tell the priests what to do.

V

veil—A head covering worn usually by women. Also a covering between two holy spaces in God's house.

vests—Special clothes worn by the priests conducting religious ceremonies.

village—A small grouping of houses and other buildings.

vineyard—A planting of grapevines.

vision—An experience similar to a dream in which God reveals the presence of God or the will of God to someone.

W

walls—Enclosure of bricks, wood, stone, or other materials for privacy or protection. Stone walls were built around cities for defense against enemy attack. They were usually tall and thick, with watchtowers and a gate.

watchman—A sentry or guard. A watchman was placed in the fields and vineyards during the time of the ripening and harvesting of crops to frighten away thieves, birds, and animals. The watchman of a city patrolled the walls of the city at night and was especially helpful during times of attack.

way—A path, road, or street along which a person passes to get from one place to another.

well—A source or storage place for water.

western foothills—Or *Shephelah*, a region in Israel not far from Jerusalem.

wheat—A grain crop that produced some of the most important foods in Bible times. Wheat was made into flour for bread or was roasted and eaten as parched grain.

whirlwind—Several kinds of winds: a high, destructive wind, a tornado, or spinning clouds of dust.

widow, widower—A woman whose husband has died; or a man whose wife has died.

wilderness—A word that refers to sandy deserts, rocky plateaus, barren pasturelands, and desolate mountain regions.

winepress—A vat in which the juice was pressed from grapes. The vat was usually hollowed-out rock on a hill near the vineyard. Grapes were spread over the floor. Then barefoot people walked and jumped on the grapes to press out the juice. A hole in the rock allowed the juice to trickle down to a lower vat where it was left to become vine. The wine was then put into jars and wineskins.

winged heavenly creatures—Are not *messengers* or *angels*. (Older Bibles called them *cherubim*.) See **chest containing the covenant**, which had images of two such creatures on top of it.

winnow—The process of separating the kernel of grain from the chaff by throwing the cut stalks of grain into the air with a long-handled fork. The grain seeds would fall back into a pile, and the light straw chaff would be carried away by the wind. See also **chaff**.

wither—To shrivel or dry up.

witness—A person who has firsthand knowledge of a fact or an event. In the New Testament, those who testified to the truth of God and those who testified to what they had seen or heard about Jesus were called witnesses.

word, the Lord's—In the Old Testament, God's declaration of God's will and purpose. God's word and God's act were the same. In some places in the New Testament, *the word* still has this meaning. In other places, it becomes *the Word of Christ*

meaning the gospel that he first preached. In the Gospel of John and in Revelation, *Word* or *Word of God* is used to mean Jesus Christ himself as God's clearest word to humanity.

world—In the Old Testament, *world* most often referred to the lands around the Mediterranean Sea. By New Testament times, the known world was as large as the Roman Empire. *World* was also used to mean not so much lands and nations but the concerns and actions of humans. The *world* in this sense shows the difference between the concerns and actions of humans from God's Kingdom.

worship—An acknowledgment of worthiness, respect, and reverence. In the Bible, *worship* is an act or attitude intended to recognize the worth of God, to honor God.

Y

Yahweh (YHWH)—An English-language version of the probable name by which the ancient Israelites thought of God. It is believed that the name would have been pronounced *Yahweh*, but it was seldom spoken. It is translated as Lord in English Bibles.

yeast—See **leaven**.

yoke—A wooden frame placed over the necks of two oxen to harness them together. A single shaft was connected to the middle of the yoke bar, which pulled a plow, sled, or cart.

youth—The time between a person's birth and his or her years of greatest vigor and opportunity, but not years of greatest maturity and judgment. The prophets called the early years of Israel the nation's youth.

Z

Zion—Another name for the city of Jerusalem, where the temple was built.

I WONDER
what to do when I'm...

Afraid

Genesis 21:17-18
Genesis 26:24
Deuteronomy 31:6-8
Psalm 4:8
Psalm 23:4
Psalm 37:1, 3
Psalm 46:1-2
Psalm 56:4, 11
Psalm 91:1-6
Isaiah 35:4
Isaiah 41:10
Isaiah 43:5
Mark 5:36
Acts 18:9-10
Romans 8:37-39
2 Corinthians 1:10
2 Timothy 1:7
Hebrews 13:6

Angry

Psalm 4:4
Psalm 37:8
Proverbs 15:1, 18
Proverbs 16:32
Proverbs 19:11
Proverbs 22:8
Ecclesiastes 7:9
Ephesians 4:26-27, 29-32
Colossians 3:8
2 Thessalonians 1:6-8
James 1:19-20

Anxious

Deuteronomy 31:8
Psalm 32:6-7
Psalm 55:22
Proverbs 12:25
Ecclesiastes 2:22-23
Ecclesiastes 11:1-10
Isaiah 41:13
Matthew 6:25-34
Matthew 11:28-29
Luke 12:22-31
John 14:27
Philippians 4:6-7
2 Thessalonians 3:16
1 Peter 5:7

Curious about Church

Matthew 16:16-19
Romans 12:4-8
Ephesians 3:7-13
Colossians 1:15-20
1 Timothy 3:14-16

Depressed

Psalm 31:24
Psalm 34:18
Psalm 42
Psalm 62:5
Psalm 91
Proverbs 23:18
Isaiah 49:13-15
Isaiah 40:31
Isaiah 57:15
Isaiah 61:1-3
Lamentations 3:19-24
Romans 5:5
1 Peter 5:7
Revelation 21:4

Disappointed

Joshua 1:9
Psalm 22:4-5
Psalm 46
Psalm 62:5
Isaiah 49:23
Matthew 19:25-26
Mark 9:21-24
John 15:7
Romans 5:5
Romans 8:28
Romans 8:37-39

Disappointed (cont)
1 Corinthians 16:13-14
2 Corinthians 4:7-9
Ephesians 3:20
Colossians 1:9-12

Discouraged
Deuteronomy 31:8
Psalm 25:3
Psalm 27:13-14
Psalm 62:5
Psalm 130:5, 7
Isaiah 40:31
Isaiah 65:24
Jeremiah 29:11
Lamentations 3:19-24
Matthew 11:28-30
Romans 8:26-28
Ephesians 3:13
James 4:8, 10

Doubting
Matthew 21:21-22
Mark 9:24
Mark 11:23
John 20:24-29
James 1:6-7
Jude 22

Feeling Guilty
Psalm 32
Psalm 38
Psalm 103:11
Psalm 119:132-136
Psalm 130:3-4
Romans 8:1-2
2 Corinthians 12:9
Ephesians 2:1-10
Hebrews 4:14-16
Hebrews 10:22-23
James 4:7-8

Feeling Unloved
Psalm 139
Matthew 10:30-31
John 3:16
John 15:9-11
Romans 5:8
Romans 8:35-39
2 Thessalonians 2:13-17
1 John 3:1
1 John 4:9

Grieving
Psalm 23:4
Psalm 31:9
Psalm 119:76-77
Isaiah 25:8
Isaiah 61:1-2
Jeremiah 31:13
Lamentations 3:22-33
Matthew 5:4
John 16:20-22
1 Corinthians 15:20-28
1 Thessalonians 4:13-14
1 Peter 1:1-9
Revelation 21:3-4

Harassed
Genesis 50:20
Psalm 37:1-7
Lamentations 3:19-24
Matthew 5:10-12
1 Corinthians 4:12
2 Corinthians 4:8-12
2 Corinthians 12:10
2 Timothy 1:11-12
2 Timothy 3:11-12
Hebrews 11:37
1 Peter 2:20-24
1 Peter 3:13-14

Hopeless
Psalm 25:3
Psalm 33:17-22
Psalm 42:5
Psalm 62:5
Psalm 119:116
Psalm 130
Psalm 146:5
Psalm 147:11
Proverbs 23:18
Isaiah 40:31
Isaiah 57:15
Jeremiah 29:11
Jeremiah 32:17
Lamentations 3:19-24
Romans 5:3-5
Romans 12:12
Romans 15:4, 13
1 Thessalonians 1:3
Hebrews 10:35

Impatient
Psalm 37:1-9
Psalm 40:1-3
Romans 2:7
Colossians 1:11
Colossians 3:12-17
1 Timothy 1:16
Hebrews 6:12
James 5:7
2 Peter 3:9

In Need
Psalm 18:35-36
Psalm 72:12-13
Psalm 142
Matthew 6:8
John 6:35
Ephesians 3:20-21
Philippians 4:19

Needing Direction
Psalm 25:4-5
Psalm 143:8
Proverbs 2:1-6
Proverbs 3:5-6
Isaiah 58:11
Romans 12:2
Colossians 1:9-10
2 Timothy 3:16-17
James 1:5-8

Needing to Forgive
Matthew 6:12, 14-15
Matthew 18:21-22
Mark 11:25
Luke 6:37
Luke 17:3-4
2 Corinthians 2:7-11
Ephesians 4:32
Colossians 3:12-14
James 2:12-13

Sick
Psalm 23:4
Psalm 41:3
Psalm 73:26
Isaiah 40:31
Isaiah 57:18
Malachi 4:2
Matthew 8:16-17
Matthew 11:28

Sick (cont)
Matthew 25:36
Hebrews 12:12-13
James 5:14-15

Suffering
Psalm 34:19
Psalm 119:50, 76-77
Lamentations 3:19-24
Nahum 1:7
John 16:33
Romans 5:3-5
Romans 8:16-17, 28
Romans 12:12
2 Corinthians 1:6-7
1 Peter 3:13-17
1 Peter 4:12-13
1 Peter 5:10-11

Tempted
Matthew 6:13
Matthew 26:41
Mark 14:38
Luke 11:4

Luke 22:40
1 Corinthians 10:13
Hebrews 2:18
Hebrews 4:15-16
James 1:12-16
1 Peter 5:8-10

Thankful
1 Chronicles 16:8
Psalm 7:17
Psalm 30:12
Psalm 100
Psalm 107:1
Psalm 136:1
1 Corinthians 15:57
2 Corinthians 2:14
Philippians 4:4
Colossians 3:15
1 Thessalonians 5:18

Weak/Weary
1 Chronicles 16:11
Psalm 6:2
Psalm 18:2, 32

Psalm 22:15, 19
Psalm 28:7
Psalm 29:11
Psalm 73:26
Psalm 86:16
Psalm 118:14
Isaiah 30:15
Isaiah 35:3
Isaiah 40:29-31
Isaiah 41:10
Matthew 11:28
Matthew 26:41
1 Corinthians 9:24-25
2 Corinthians 12:9-10
Galatians 6:9

Wanting to Pray
Psalm 6:9
Psalm 17:1
Psalm 86:6-7
Matthew 6:5-13
Luke 11:1-4
Romans 12:12
Colossians 4:2

DEEP BLUE
Notes
BY TOPIC

LIGHTHOUSE NOTES

SAILBOAT NOTES

UMBRELLA NOTES

Life Preserver
Notes
BY BOOK
OF THE BIBLE

God's Thoughts My Thoughts

DEVOTIONS

Bet you can

READING CHALLENGES

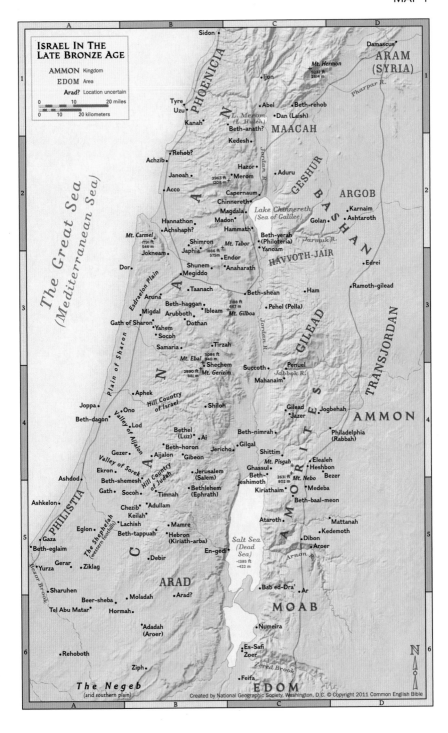

MAP 1

ISRAEL IN THE
LATE BRONZE AGE

AMMON Kingdom
EDOM   Area
Arad? Location uncertain

0   10   20 miles
0   10   20 kilometers

D Sidon

Damascus
ARAM
(SYRIA)

Mt. Hermon
9232 ft
2814 m

Pharpar R.

PHOENICIA

Tyre
Uzu
Kanah

Ijon
Abel
Beth-rehob
Dan (Laish)

L. Merom
(L. Huleh)

MAACAH

Beth-anath?
Kedesh

Achzib
Rehob?

Janoah

Hazor
Merom
3963 ft
1208 m

Aduru

GESHUR

Acco
Capernaum
Chinnereth

Karnaim
Ashtaroth

ARGOB

Hannathon
Achshaph
Magdala
Madon

Lake Chinnereth
(Sea of Galilee)

Golan

BASHAN

Mt. Carmel
1791 ft
546 m
Jokneam
Shimron
Japhia
1886 ft
575m

Hammath

Beth-yerah
(Philoteria)
Yanoam

Jarmuk R.

Mt. Tabor
Endor
Anaharath

HAVVOTH-JAIR

Edrei

Dor
Shunem
Megiddo

Taanach

Beth-shean
Ham

Ramoth-gilead

Esdraelon Plain

Aruna
Beth-haggan
Arubboth
Ibleam
2188 ft
667 m
Mt. Gilboa

Pehel (Pella)

Migdal
Gath of Sharon
Dothan

Plain of Sharon

Yahem
Socoh

Samaria
Tirzah

GILEAD

Mt. Ebal
3084 ft
940 m
Shechem
2890 ft
881 m
Mt. Gerizim

Succoth
Mahanaim

Penuel
Jabbok R.

TRANSJORDAN

Aphek
Hill Country
of Israel

Shiloh

Gilead
Jazer

Jogbehah

Joppa
Ono
Beth-dagon
Lod

Bethel
(Luz)
Ai

Beth-nimrah
Gilgal

AMMON

Gezer
Beth-horon
Aijalon
Gibeon

Jericho

Shittim
Mt. Pisgah

Philadelphia
(Rabbah)

Ashdod
Ekron
Beth-shemesh
Gath
Socoh

Valley of Sorek
Hill Country
of Judah
Jerusalem
(Salem)
Timnah

Ghassul
Beth-
jeshimoth
Kiriathaim

Elealeh
Heshbon
2631 ft
802 m
Mt. Nebo
Bezer
Medeba

Ashkelon
Bethlehem
(Ephrath)

Beth-baal-meon

PHILISTIA

Chezib
Keilah

Mamre

Ataroth

Mattanah
Kedemoth

Gaza
Eglon
Lachish
Beth-tappuah

Hebron
(Kiriath-arba)

Dibon
Aroer

Beth-eglaim
Gerar
Ziklag

Debir

En-gedi

Arnon

Besor Brook
Yurza

Salt Sea
(Dead
Sea)
-1385 ft
-422 m

MOAB

Sharuhen
Beer-sheba
Moladah
Arad?

Bab ed-Dra'
Ar

Tel Abu Matar
Hormah

Adadah
(Aroer)

Numeira

ARAD

Es-Safi
Zoer

Rehoboth

Ziph

Zered Brook

Feifa

EDOM

The Negeb
(arid southern plain)

N

The Great Sea
(Mediterranean Sea)

Jordan R.

Valley of Aijalon

The Shephelah
(western foothills)

AMORITES

CANAAN

Created by National Geographic Society, Washington, D.C. © Copyright 2011 Common English Bible

MAP 2

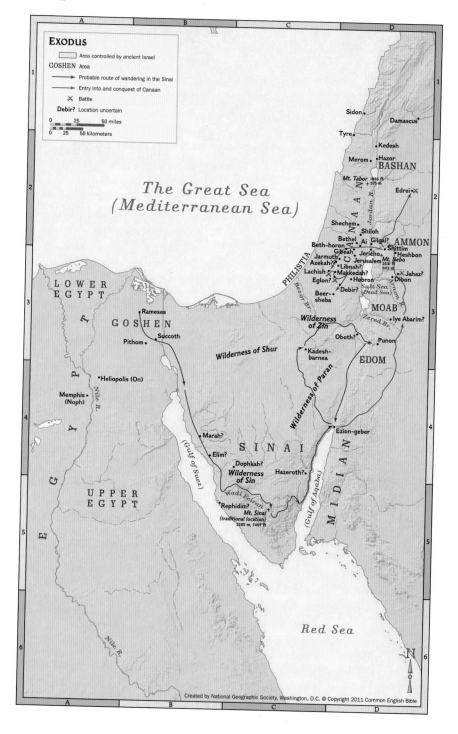

Exodus

- Area controlled by ancient Israel
- GOSHEN Area
- → Probable route of wandering in the Sinai
- → Entry into and conquest of Canaan
- ✕ Battle
- Debir? Location uncertain

0   25   50 miles
0   25   50 kilometers

The Great Sea
(Mediterranean Sea)

Sidon

Damascus

Tyre
Kedesh

Merom   Hazor
BASHAN

Mt. Tabor 1886 ft
+575 m
Edrei ✕

Shechem
Shiloh
Bethel
Beth-horon   Ai   Gilgal?   AMMON
Gibeah   Shittim
Jarmuth   Jericho   Heshbon
Azekah?   Jerusalem   *Mt. Nebo* 2631 ft 802 m
Lachish   Libnah?   Jahaz ✕
Makkedah?   Dibon
Eglon?   Hebron
Debir?   *Salt Sea (Dead Sea)*
Beer-
sheba   MOAB

Wilderness of Zin   Iye Abarim?
Zered Br.
Oboth?   Punon

LOWER
EGYPT

GOSHEN

Rameses

Pithom

Succoth

Wilderness of Shur

Kadesh-
barnea

EDOM

Heliopolis (On)

Memphis
(Noph)

Wilderness of Paran

Marah?
Ezion-geber

Elim?
S I N A I

Dophkah?
*Wilderness
of Sin*
Hazeroth?

M I D I A N

UPPER
EGYPT

Wadi Feiran

Rephidim?   *Mt. Sinai
(traditional location)*
2285 m, 7497 ft

(*Gulf of Suez*)

(*Gulf of Aqaba*)

PHILISTIA

Rd. or Br.

Jordan R.

CANAAN

Red Sea

N

Created by National Geographic Society, Washington, D.C. © Copyright 2011 Common English Bible

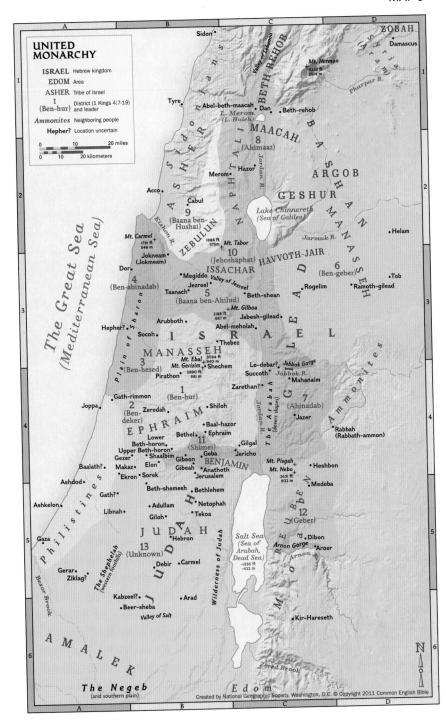

MAP 3

UNITED MONARCHY

ISRAEL Hebrew kingdom
EDOM Area
ASHER Tribe of Israel
1
(Ben-hur) District (1 Kings 4:7-19) and leader
Ammonites Neighboring people
Hepher? Location uncertain

0   10   20 miles
0   10   20 kilometers

ZOBAH
• Damascus
Sidon •
+Mt. Hermon
9232 ft
2814 m
Valley of Lebanon
BETH-REHOB
Pharpar R.
Tyre •
• Abel-beth-maacah
L. Merom
(L. Huleh)
Dan • • Beth-rehob
MAACAH
8
(Ahimaaz)
ARGOB
Merom •   Hazor •
GESHUR
Acco •
Cabul •
9
(Baana ben-Hushai)
ZEBULUN
Lake Chinnereth
(Sea of Galilee)
• Helam
Mt. Carmel
1791 ft
546 m
Jokneam
(Jokmeam)
+Mt. Tabor
1886 ft
575 m
10
(Jehoshaphat)
HAVVOTH-JAIR
Jarmuk R.
Dor •
ISSACHAR
Megiddo •   Valley of Jezreel
• Jezreel
6
(Ben-geber)
• Tob
4
(Ben-abinadab)
Taanach •   **5**
(Baana ben-Ahilud)
• Beth-shean
Rogelim •
• Ramoth-gilead
+Mt. Gilboa
2188 ft
667 m
• Jabesh-gilead
Hepher? •
Arubboth •
Abel-meholah •
I S R A   E   L
Socoh •
• Thebez
MANASSEH
3
(Ben-hesed)
Mt. Ebal 3084 ft
940 m
• Shechem
Mt. Gerizim
2890 ft
881 m
Pirathon •
Lo-debar•
Jabbok Gorge
Succoth •   *Jabbok R.*
• Mahanaim
Zarethan •
Gath-rimmon •
1
(Ben-hur)
2
(Ben-deker)
Zeredah • Shiloh •
Joppa •
• Baal-hazor
EPHRAIM
Lower
Beth-horon • Bethel • • Ephraim
11
(Shimei)
Gilgal •
7
(Ahinadab)
• Jazer
Upper Beth-horon •   Geba •
Gezer • Shaalbim • Gibeon • • Jericho
Makaz • Elon •   Gibeah • BENJAMIN
Baalath? •   Anathoth •
Ashdod • Ekron • Sorek • Jerusalem •
Gath? •
Mt. Pisgah+
Mt. Nebo+
2631 ft
802 m
• Heshbon
• Rabbah
(Rabbath-ammon)
Ashkelon •   • Beth-shemesh • Bethlehem
• Medeba
Libnah • • Adullam • Netophah
Gaza •   Giloh •   • Tekoa
12
(Geber)
Salt Sea
(Sea of
Arabah,
Dead Sea)
-1385 ft
-422 m
• Dibon
Gerar • J U D A H
Hebron •
13
(Unknown)
Arnon Gorge
• Aroer
Ziklag? • The Shephelah
(western foothills)
Debir • • Carmel
Wilderness of Judah
Arnon
Kabzeel? •
• Arad
Beer-sheba •
Valley of Salt
• Kir-Hareseth
A M A L E K
Besor Brook
The Negeb
(arid southern plain)
Zered Brook
E d o m

The Great Sea
(Mediterranean Sea)
Plain of Sharon
SIDONIANS
ASHER
NAPHTALI
Jordan R.
BASHAN
MANASSEH
GILEAD
Ammonites
The Arabah
(desert slopes)
Jordan R.
REUBEN
MOAB
Philistines
Kishon R.

N

Created by National Geographic Society, Washington, D.C. © Copyright 2011 Common English Bible

MAP 4

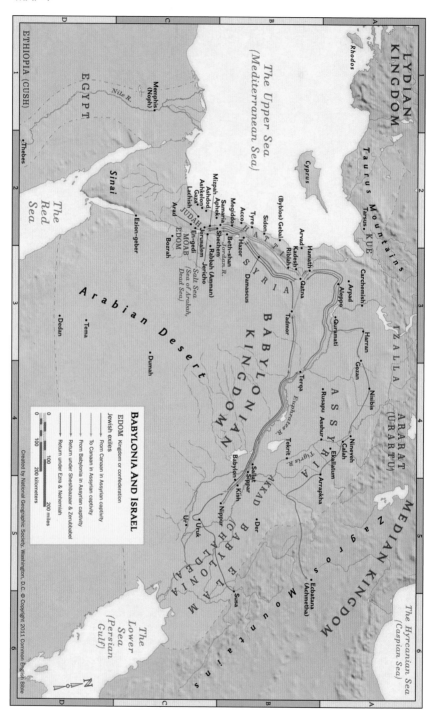

BABYLONIA AND ISRAEL

EDOM   Kingdom or confederation

Jewish exiles

→ From Canaan in Assyrian captivity

→ To Canaan in Assyrian captivity

→ From Babylonia in Assyrian captivity

→ Return under Sheshbazzar & Zerubbabel

→ Return under Ezra & Nehemiah

0   100   200 kilometers

0   100   200 miles

Created by National Geographic Society, Washington, D.C. © Copyright 2011 Common English Bible

LYDIAN KINGDOM

Rhodos

The Upper Sea
(Mediterranean Sea)

Cyprus

Taurus Mountains

KUE

IZALLA

ARARAT
(URARTU)

MEDIAN KINGDOM

Zagros Mountains

The Hyrcanian Sea
(Caspian Sea)

ETHIOPIA (CUSH)

EGYPT

Memphis
(Noph)

Nile R.

Thebes

Sinai

The Red Sea

Ezion-geber

Arabian Desert

Dedan

Tema

Dumah

(Byblos) Gebal

Arvad
Kadesh

Qatna
Hamath

Riblah

Tadmor

Acco
Tyre
Sidon

Megiddo
Samaria
Aphek
Mizpah
Ashdod
Ashkelon
Gaza
Lachish
Arad

JUDAH
Jerusalem
En-gedi
Jericho
Rabbah (Amman)
Shechem
Beth-shan
Hazor

Jordan R.

Salt Sea
(Sea of Arabah,
Dead Sea)

EDOM
MOAB
Bozrah

Damascus

SYRIA

HATTI

BABYLONIAN KINGDOM

Euphrates R.

Carchemish
Arpad
Aleppo
Qurnati

Harran
Gozan
Nisibis

Terqa
Rusapu
Asshur
Ekallatum
Nineveh
Calah
Arrapkha

ASSYRIA

Tigris R.

Tekrit

Babylon
Sallat
Sippar
Kish

AKKAD

Der

Nippur
Uruk
Ur

BABYLONIA
(CHALDEA)

ELAM

Susa

Echatana
(Achmetha)

The Lower Sea
(Persian Gulf)

N

MAP 5

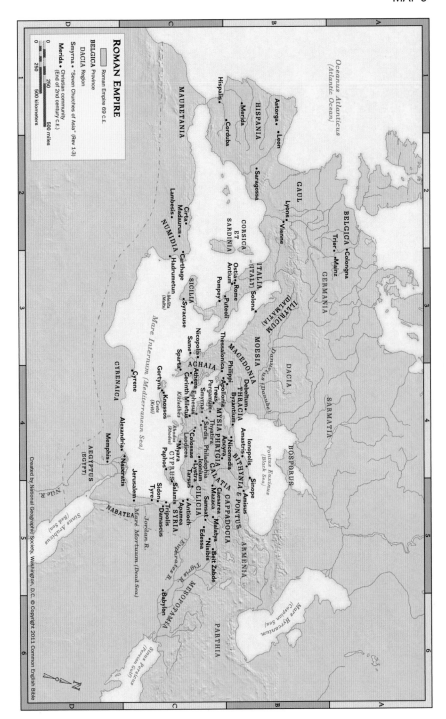

ROMAN EMPIRE

☐ Roman Empire 69 C.E.

BELGICA Province

DACIA Region

Smyrna • "Seven Churches of Asia" (Rev 13)
(End of 2nd century C.E.)

Merida • Christian community

0   250   500 kilometers

0   250   500 miles

MAP 6

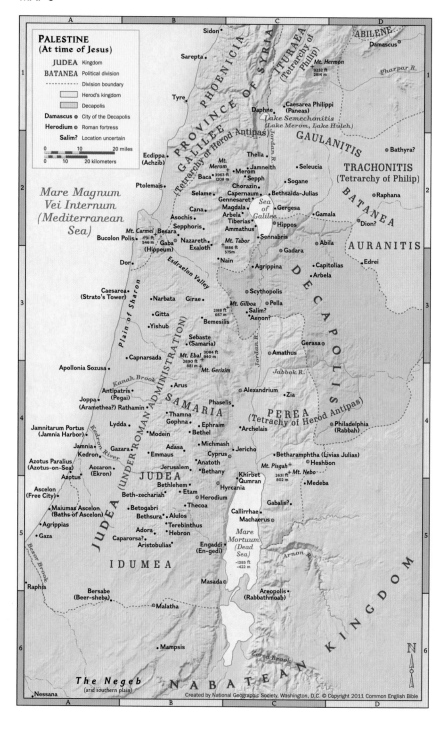

PALESTINE
(At time of Jesus)

JUDEA — Kingdom
BATANEA — Political division
- - - - — Division boundary
▢ — Herod's kingdom
▢ — Decapolis
Damascus ◉ — City of the Decapolis
Herodium ▪ — Roman fortress
Salim? — Location uncertain

0 — 10 — 20 miles
0 — 10 — 20 kilometers

Mare Magnum
Vei Internum
(Mediterranean Sea)

ABILENE

Sidon

Sarepta

Damascus

Pharpar R.

PHOENICIA

Tyre

Daphne

Caesarea Philippi (Paneas)

Mt. Hermon
9232 ft
2814 m

ITURAEA
(Tetrarchy of Philip)

Lake Semechonitis
(Lake Merom, Lake Huleh)

GAULANITIS

Bathyra?

Ecdippa (Achzib)

Thella

Jamneith

Seleucia

TRACHONITIS
(Tetrarchy of Philip)

Ptolemais

Mt. Merom
Baca 3963 ft
1208 m

Merom

Sepph

Sogane

Raphana

Chorazin

Bethsaida-Julias

BATANEA

Selame

Capernaum

Cana

Gennesaret

Sea of Galilee

Gergesa

Gamala

Dion?

AURANITIS

Asochis

Magdala

Arbela

Tiberias

Hippos

Sepphoris

Ammathus

Mt. Carmel
1791 ft
546 m

Besara

Nazareth

Sennabris

Abila

Bucolon Polis

Gaba (Hippeum)

Exaloth

Mt. Tabor
1886 ft
575m

Gadara

Capitolias

Dor

Nain

Agrippina

Arbela

Edrei

Esdraelon Valley

Scythopolis

Pella

DECAPOLIS

Caesarea (Strato's Tower)

Narbata

Girae

Mt. Gilboa
2188 ft
667 m

Salim?

Gitta

Bemesilis

Aenon?

Gerasa

Yishub

Sebaste (Samaria)

Mt. Ebal
3084 ft
940 m

Amathus

Jabbok R.

Apollonia Sozusa

Capnarsada

Mt. Gerizim
2890 ft
881 m

Kanah Brook

Arus

Alexandrium

Zia

Antipatris (Pegai)

Phaselis

PEREA
(Tetrarchy of Herod Antipas)

Joppa (Aramethea?)

Rathamin

Thamna

Ephraim

Archelais

Philadelphia (Rabbah)

Jamnitarum Portus (Jamnia Harbor)

Lydda

Gophna

Bethel

Michmash

Modein

Adasa

Cyprus

Jericho

Betharamphtha (Livias Julias)

Jamnia

Gazara

Emmaus

Anatoth

Mt. Pisgah
2631 ft
802 m

Mt. Nebo

Heshbon

Azotus Paralius (Azotus-on-Sea)

Kedron

Accaron (Ekron)

Jerusalem

Bethany

Medeba

Azotus

JUDEA

Bethlehem

Khirbet Qumran

Ascelon (Free City)

Beth-zechariah

Etam

Herodium

Hyrcania

Maiumas Ascelon (Baths of Ascelon)

Betogabri

Thecoa

Gabalis?

Agrippias

Bethsura?

Alulos

Callirrhae

Machaerus

Gaza

Adora

Terebinthus

Hebron

Mare Mortuum (Dead Sea)
-1385 ft
-422 m

Caparorsa?

Aristobulias?

Engaddi (En-gedi)

IDUMEA

Raphia

Masada

Areopolis (Rabbathmoab)

Besor Brook

Bersabe (Beer-sheba)

Malatha

Arnon R.

Mampsis

NABATEAN KINGDOM

Zered Brook

The Negeb
(arid southern plain)

Nessana

N

Created by National Geographic Society, Washington, D.C. © Copyright 2011 Common English Bible

Mare Magnum Vei Internum (Mediterranean Sea)

JUDEA (UNDER ROMAN ADMINISTRATION)

SAMARIA

GALILEE
(Tetrarchy of Herod Antipas)

PROVINCE OF SYRIA

Plain of Sharon

Kedron River

Jordan R.

MAP 7

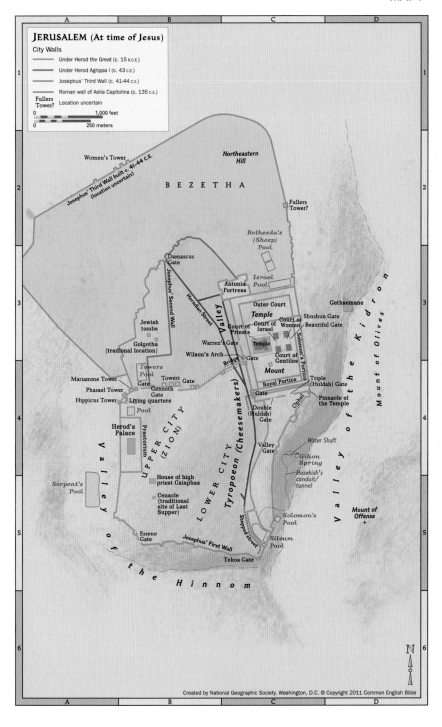

JERUSALEM (At time of Jesus)

City Walls

Under Herod the Great (c. 15 B.C.E.)
Under Herod Agrippa I (c. 43 C.E.)
Josephus' Third Wall (c. 41-44 C.E.)
Roman wall of Aelia Capitolina (c. 135 C.E.)

Fullers Tower? Location uncertain

0   1,000 feet
0   250 meters

Women's Tower

Northeastern Hill

Josephus' Third Wall built c. 41-44 C.E. (location uncertain)

B E Z E T H A

Fullers Tower?

Bethesda's (Sheep) Pool

Damascus Gate

Josephus' Second Wall

Herodian Street

Valley

Antonia Fortress

Israel Pool

Jewish tombs

Golgotha (tradional location)

Outer Court

Temple

Court of Israel

Court of Women

Shushun Gate

Beautiful Gate

Gethsemane

Court of Priests

Temple

Solomon's Portico

Warren's Gate

Wilson's Arch

Bridge

Gate

Court of Gentiles

Towers Pool

Gate

Towers Gate

Mount

Mariamme Tower

Gate

Royal Portico

Phasael Tower

Genneth Gate

Hippicus Tower

Living quarters

Gate

Triple (Huldah) Gate

Ophel

Pinnacle of the Temple

Pool

Double (Huldah) Gate

U P P E R   C I T Y   (Z I O N)

Herod's Palace

Praetorium

Valley Gate

Valley of the Kidron

Mount of Olives

Water Shaft

Gihon Spring

Hezekiah's conduit/ tunnel

House of high priest Caiaphas

Cenacle (traditional site of Last Supper)

Serpent's Pool

L O W E R   C I T Y

Tyropoeon (Cheesemakers)

Stepped Street

Solomon's Pool

Mount of Offense +

Essene Gate

Josephus' First Wall

Siloam Pool

V a l l e y   o f   t h e   H i n n o m

Tekoa Gate

N

Created by National Geographic Society, Washington, D.C. © Copyright 2011 Common English Bible

MAP 8

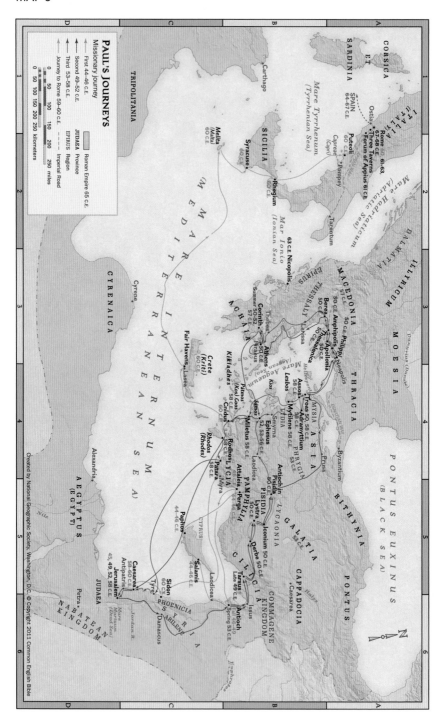

PAUL'S JOURNEYS
Missionary journey
First 44–46 C.E.
Second 49–52 C.E.
Third 53–58 C.E.
Journey to Rome 59–60 C.E.

Roman Empire 65 C.E.
JUDEA Province
EPIRUS Region
Imperial Road

0   50   100 150 200 250 kilometers
0   50   100   150   200   250 miles

Created by National Geographic Society, Washington, D.C. © Copyright 2011 Common English Bible